EQUITABLE REMEDIES, RESTITUTION AND DAMAGES

CASES AND MATERIALS

Eighth Edition

■ ■ ■

By

Candace S. Kovacic–Fleischer

Professor of Law
Washington College of Law
The American University

Jean C. Love

John A. & Elizabeth H. Sutro Professor of Law
Santa Clara University School of Law
Martha–Ellen Tye Professor of Law Emerita
University of Iowa

Grant S. Nelson

William H. Rehnquist Professor of Law
Pepperdine University
Professor of Law Emeritus
University of California, Los Angeles

AMERICAN CASEBOOK SERIES®

WEST®

A Thomson Reuters business

Mat #40755058

American Casebook Series is a trademark registered in the U.S. Patent and Trademark Office.

COPYRIGHT © 1959, 1973, 1980, 1986, 1994 WEST PUBLISHING CO.
© West, a Thomson business, 2000, 2005
© 2011 Thomson Reuters
    610 Opperman Drive
    St. Paul, MN 55123
    1-800-313-9378
Printed in the United States of America

ISBN: 978-0-314-19493-0

*To Bob—Whose dedication to this book
continues to inspire us.*

C.S.K–F., J.C.L., G.S.N.

* * * * * * * * * * * * * * * * *

To Walter and Ilona.

C.S.K–F.

To Pat.

J.C.L.

To Judy.

G.S.N.

Preface to Eighth Edition

The Eighth Edition of Cases and Materials on Equitable Remedies, Restitution and Damages is a casebook designed for a modern Remedies course. It provides comprehensive coverage of legal and equitable remedies in actions for both public and private wrongs. At the same time, it is also suitable for courses that focus on more discrete topics, such as Equity, Injunctions, Restitution, or Damages.

The Eighth Edition retains the overall organization of the Seventh Edition. The first half of the casebook introduces injunctive relief, damages, restitution, and declaratory relief. The second half of the book creates opportunities to consider these four remedies in the context of tort and contract actions for various types of harm.

While preserving most of the classic cases from the Seventh Edition, the Eighth Edition contains many new lead cases and completely updated note materials as well. We continue to feature highly teachable cases that students will find intuitively interesting and engaging.

The updates to the first half of the casebook include references to recent United States Supreme Court cases on such topics as injunctive relief, punitive damages, and attorneys' fees. The sections on restitution incorporate important material from the Restatement (Third) of Restitution and Unjust Enrichment, which resolves many of the confusions that have arisen since the publication of the prior 1938 Restatement. The second half of the casebook contains new cases on current topics, including public nuisance actions against lead paint manufacturers, school desegregation, arbitration, injunctions against defamatory statements, and no contact orders obtained by parents of a minor against her boyfriend based on allegations of harassment.

As in prior editions, we have edited our cases carefully, retaining each court's description of the relevant facts and the competing legal principles that govern the remedial issues under consideration. We have deleted string citations, footnotes, and irrelevant textual material. Our deletions are marked by three asterisks; the court's deletions are marked by ellipses. We have retained the numbering of the footnotes as they appear in the original works; our footnotes are marked by an asterisk. Our manuscript went to press in June 2010, and we will be supplementing the Eighth Edition in the future to keep it up to date on recent developments.

For their support and encouragement of this casebook, we thank our respective law schools. In addition, we would like to thank our lead secretary, Frankie Winchester, and our research assistants, Erik Kaeding, Courtney

Ketchersid, and Megan McKinney. Finally, as always, we want to express special gratitude to our families and friends for their support, encouragement, and understanding during the preparation of this text.

CANDACE S. KOVACIC-FLEISCHER
JEAN C. LOVE
GRANT S. NELSON

October, 2010

PREFACE TO SEVENTH EDITION

The Seventh Edition of Cases and Materials on Equitable Remedies, Restitution and Damages builds upon the organization and the classic cases of the Sixth Edition, continuing to provide comprehensive coverage of the legal and equitable remedies that are available in actions for both public and private wrongs. At the same time, the Seventh Edition contains over 90 new cases and completely updated note materials. This casebook continues to feature discussion-provoking cases, and offers innumerable opportunities to debate competing remedial policies in the classroom.

Although this casebook is designed for a Remedies course (of any length), it is also suitable for a separate course in Equity, Injunctions, Restitution, or Damages. In fact, the first edition of this casebook was designed exclusively for a course in Equity, and only gradually did it evolve into a comprehensive Remedies text, as detailed in the Preface to the Sixth Edition. The first half of the Seventh Edition introduces the "basic principles" of injunctive relief, damages, restitution, and declaratory relief, in that order. The second half of the Seventh Edition provides an opportunity to consider these four types of relief as remedies for various types of harms in actions for tortious misconduct, breach of contract, and unjust enrichment.

The Seventh Edition contains extensive revisions to the early chapters on "basic principles." The chapter on injunctive relief now features federal cases so that the reader can focus on a single set of procedures for seeking to obtain injunctive relief. Also, the cases in that chapter are now evenly balanced between actions for public and private wrongs. The chapter on damages has been greatly expanded, so that it is now equal in length to the chapter on injunctive relief. The chapter on damages focuses on a close comparison of the damages recoverable in actions for tortious misconduct and for breach of contract, and then ends with a section on damages for harm to the person which facilitates consideration of the many remedial issues posed by contemporary tort reform. The chapter on restitution has been reorganized to emphasize the distinctions between legal and equitable restitutionary remedies, and it now gives greater emphasis to the importance of proving a "benefit to the defendant" as a predicate to the recovery of restitutionary relief. The chapter on declaratory judgments now devotes more space to the history of the development of this modern statutory remedy, and the cases in that chapter are now evenly balanced between actions for public and private wrongs.

The second half of the casebook is filled with cases of current interest, such as the line of cases seeking injunctive relief that culminated in Bush v. Gore. In Chapter 6 (on tort remedies), the reader will consider such topics as whether there should be a cause of action for loss of consortium of a companion animal, whether right to farm statutes are unconstitutional, whether presumed general damages should be available for violations of constitutional rights, and whether defamatory statements may be enjoined. In Chapter 7 (on contractual remedies), the reader will consider the distinction between the remedies for affirming and for disaffirming a contract, as well as the distinction between the remedies for breach of contract and for fraud. At the end of Chapter 7, the reader will have an opportunity to consider the explosive expansion in the use of arbitration, with a special focus on the questions of when an arbitration agreement is unconscionable and when an arbitration award may be vacated. In Chapter 8 (on the right to jury trial), the reader will study the distinction between the federal approach and the various state approaches to the right to jury trial.

While new cases have been added to the Seventh Edition, this casebook continues to feature cases on such topics as the legal and equitable remedies available to the victims of discrimination; emotional distress damages for the breach of a contract to provide child care or to construct a house; remedies for the breach of a surrogate mother contract; remedies for the breach of a promise to provide services during marriage or cohabitation; injunctions against nude dancing, gang activities, or activities related to prostitution; injunctions against abortion protests; and restitution to governments for the costs of tobacco-related illnesses. It also continues to feature cases involving environmental interests, commercial interests, and intellectual property law.

As in prior editions, we have edited our cases carefully, retaining each court's description of the relevant facts and of the competing legal principles that govern the remedial issues at hand, while deleting string cites, footnotes, and irrelevant textual material. Our deletions are marked by three asterisks; the court's deletions are marked by ellipses. We have retained the numbering of the footnotes as they appear in the original works; our footnotes are marked by an asterisk. Our manuscript went to press in December 2004, and we will be supplementing the Seventh Edition in the future to keep it up to date on recent developments.

We are very sad to report that our lead co-author, Bob Leavell, passed away in July of 2004. Bob was a brilliant contributor to this book and an important mentor for the three of us who remain responsible for this new edition. His influence endures.

For their support and encouragement of this casebook, we thank our respective law schools. In addition, we owe particular gratitude to our wonderful lead secretary, Melanie Stutzman, University of Iowa, and to our primary research assistant, Bill Fritz, for the endless hours that it took them to produce the Seventh Edition in its sleek new format. We are similarly grateful to Frankie Winchester, American University, who was the talented lead secretary on the Sixth Edition, and who has contributed substantially to the production of the Seventh Edition. We are also grateful to Christopher Clinton, Phil Lerch, Ebony Robinson, Kathleen Tam, and Josh Weidemann for their research assistance, and to Elizabeth Craig and Michelle Roddy for their painstaking proofreading. Finally, as always, we want to express special gratitude to our families and friends for their support, encouragement, and understanding during the preparation of this text.

JEAN C. LOVE
GRANT S. NELSON
CANDACE S. KOVACIC-FLEISCHER

April, 2005

PREFACE TO SIXTH EDITION

In the Preface to the First Edition of this book in 1958, Professor M. T. Van Hecke noted that since 1948 the course in Equity had been modified so that it received fewer credit hours, was dispersed among other courses, or was limited to a course entitled Equitable Remedies. He noted that at the same time courts and legislatures were improving equitable remedies "to be used more effectively in times of changing conditions and needs." Fifteen years later, in the Preface to the Second Edition of this book, Professors Robert N. Leavell and Grant S. Nelson noted that "the trend to which Professor Van Hecke alluded in his Preface has continued unabated." Professors Leavell and Nelson also noted that courses in Remedies and Restitution fared better than a course in Equity, but that even those courses "are still rather grudgingly given the hours in the single quarter or semester allotted to them". In the Preface to the Third Edition, Professors Leavell, Nelson and Jean Love optimistically believed that the result of developments in public law would "certainly" lead to "curriculum adjustment in many law schools, with increased emphasis upon the study of courses such as 'Remedies'." The Fourth Edition was expanded for use in a variety of Remedies or Equity courses, and the Fifth Edition emphasized a "full purpose text."

Despite all of the developments described in earlier Prefaces, the trend identified by Professor Van Hecke and confirmed by Professors Leavell and Nelson, seems for the most part to continue still. Although areas of substantive law have increased enormously since 1958, both through the statutes and common law, the remedial aspects of those developments have not been given as great an emphasis in law schools as they deserve. Except in jurisdictions where Remedies is a category on the Bar Examination, the course is generally not required and its popularity varies. Few schools seem to have multiple offerings in Remedies, such as separate courses in Equity, Restitution, or Damages, each of which would contain enough substance to warrant an entire course.

Nonetheless, the Sixth Edition continues to be a full purpose text, which can be used for a variety of Remedies courses. In most schools, however, the Remedies professors will use the book for one course. The Sixth Edition contains cases from a variety of subject areas from which professors can choose to teach remedial principles. The Sixth Edition uses the same organizational structure as the Fifth although Chapter 8, "Restitution as the Only Remedy" has been folded into Chapter 4, "Restitution". More explanatory material has also been added to that Chapter because Restitution continues to be underutilized and not well understood.

While new cases have been added to the Sixth Edition to reflect new developments in the substantive law in many areas, the Sixth Edition has retained many of the cases from the Fifth Edition. To make room for the new cases, the remaining cases have been tightly edited, and some of the older cases and older string cites of authorities have been removed. As with the prior editions we have omitted from all of the cases string cites, footnotes and discussion not material to the remedial issues at hand. Those deletions have been marked with ellipses. We have retained the original footnote numbering of the cases and use asterisks for the footnotes we have supplied.

We want to thank our respective law schools for their generous encouragement and support. We would like to thank the talented and dedicated students who worked with us, as well as the talented and dedicated administrative assistants, without whose technical expertise we could not have completed this text in the era of computers. We would also like to thank the talented staff at West Group who moved the production along efficiently, but with tact, and whose production abilities we admire. Finally, as always, we want to express special gratitude to our families and friends for their support, encouragement and understanding during the preparation of this text.

ROBERT N. LEAVELL
JEAN C. LOVE
GRANT S. NELSON
CANDACE S. KOVACIC-FLEISCHER

April, 2000

PREFACE TO FIFTH EDITION

In this edition we added three new chapters or subchapters—one on Basic Principles of Damages, the others on equitable defenses and personal injury—in order to make the book a full purpose remedies text. At the same time we retained the book's basic organization, its traditional emphasis and its examination of contemporary issues. We kept many of the discussion-provoking, classic cases, and also added many current cases that we expect will be good teaching vehicles.

We made one organizational change, rearranging the restitution materials. Those materials retain the same comprehensive coverage. There is an introductory chapter that contains cases and materials which explore the fundamentals of all restitutionary remedies, both legal and equitable. The remainder of restitution is dispersed throughout the book to integrate that material with other remedial concepts and to illustrate the uses of the various remedies in a wide variety of factual contexts. Any teacher wishing to teach restitution as a separate unit can still do so by assigning the units titled Restitution in order.

Despite these changes we believe that we have sufficiently preserved the approach and content of the earlier Edition so that the book will seem quite familiar to those teachers now using it. As in prior editions, we have omitted strings of citations, footnotes and dissenting opinions not useful for teaching purposes. We have marked citation and textual deletions with ellipses. We have retained the numbering of footnotes in the original works, and have used asterisks to indicate our footnotes.

We are grateful to our respective law schools and administrations for their substantial encouragement and assistance. We would like to thank the talented students who worked with us on the manuscript, galleys and page-proofs. Finally, we express special gratitude to our families for their support and understanding during the period that we were preparing this edition of the casebook.

ROBERT N. LEAVELL
JEAN C. LOVE
GRANT S. NELSON
CANDACE S. KOVACIC-FLEISCHER

June, 1994

Preface to Fourth Edition

The change in the title of the Fourth Edition (from "Equitable Remedies and Restitution" to "Equitable Remedies, Restitution and Damages") reflects the expanded scope of the new edition. Extensive coverage is now given to damages, in addition to the remedies that were previously covered—injunctions, specific performance, declaratory judgments, rescission, reformation and the restitutionary remedies. As a result, the casebook is now suitable for courses in Remedies, Equitable Remedies, Equity, Injunctions, Damages, or Restitution. The new edition is designed for a 3 or 4 hour course in Remedies, but the materials can be used selectively for shorter courses.

The organization of the Fourth Edition is primarily by types of equitable remedies, starting with an expanded chapter on injunctive relief. We believe that this is the preferable organization for a course that focuses on remedies (as opposed to substantive bases for imposing liability). Within each chapter, we frequently cluster the cases by subject matter. At the same time, we often sequence the cases so that the student focuses first on the plaintiffs case for equitable relief, then on the defenses to the remedy, and finally on the nature of the equitable decree. As part of the discussion of the plaintiff's case for equitable relief, we consider the plaintiff's legal remedies (emphasizing damages) because traditionally a plaintiff may obtain equitable relief only upon proof that the legal remedy is inadequate. Tort damages are covered in the chapter on injunctions; breach of contract damages are discussed in the chapter on specific performance; and fraud damages are examined in the chapter on rescission.

The Fourth Edition also develops a theoretical perspective by which remedies may be evaluated. It presents contrasting perspectives on the economic efficiency of damages and equitable remedies. These materials offer an opportunity to discuss important social policy issues raised by the law of remedies.

This edition has been thoroughly updated and it examines such contemporary social issues as the use of contempt to enforce child support decrees, the measure of restitutionary recovery in *Marvin*-type cases, the use of injunctive and legal relief to enforce surrogate mother contracts, and the development of common law remedies for retaliatory discharge and sexual harassment. In addition, it contains completely revised sections on the private enforcement of public nuisance law and the remedial discretion exercised by federal courts in environmental litigation. Finally, remedies for violations of constitutional and civil rights receive expanded coverage in this edition, although the coverage is pervasive throughout the book, rather than concentrated in one chapter (as in the prior edition).

While the casebook has been revised and updated, users of the earlier edition should feel comfortable with the Fourth Edition because it evolved quite naturally from the Third Edition. Neither the fundamental style nor organization of the book has been changed. The book is longer, but that is due primarily to our decision to publish the text in a single-column format. We expect that readers of the Fourth Edition will welcome this modification.

As in prior editions, we have omitted strings of citations, footnotes and dissenting opinions not useful for teaching purposes. We have marked textual deletions with ellipses. Footnotes are ours unless otherwise indicated.

We are grateful to our respective law schools and administrations for their substantial encouragement and assistance. We would like to thank the talented students who worked with us on the manuscript, galleys and page-proofs. Finally, we express special gratitude to our families for their support and understanding during the period that we were preparing this edition of the casebook.

ROBERT N. LEAVELL
JEAN C. LOVE
GRANT S. NELSON

June, 1986

PREFACE TO THIRD EDITION

At the time of the publication of the last Edition the equity and restitution areas were drawing special attention because of developments in the public law area, especially where civil rights are involved. This interest has increased as the courts continue to experiment with such remedies as the injunction, receivers and masters. Recent expressions of a need to return to a focus upon basics in law teaching and in lawyer preparation have added to a "renaissance" in the remedies area. Such statements have come from, among others, Chief Justice Warren Burger; the American Bar Association in its recently published report, "Lawyer Competence: The Role of Law Schools"; the supreme courts of several states, and; the federal courts of appeal in their revisions of standards for both admission and the privilege of continuing in the federal court practice.

One result of these developments is certain to be curriculum adjustment in many law schools, with increased emphasis upon the study of courses such as "Remedies." Especially attractive will be those courses which consider current remedies developments in the public law area and which offer a general examination of traditional legal and equitable remedies in a variety of contexts.

This Edition is organized with those objectives in mind. It retains the coverage of basic remedies materials to be found in the earlier Edition, together with greatly expanded material on damages. The Third Edition contains a substantial amount of new material, including over 100 new cases and dozens of textual notes. Also, a significant new chapter has been added, entitled "Traditional Relief in a Modern Context: Selected Civil Rights Remedies."

Despite these additions we feel we have sufficiently preserved the approach and content of the earlier Edition so that the book will seem quite familiar to those teachers using it now. For example, substantial attention continues to be given to the history of equity, specific performance, injunctions, practicability concerns, reformation, rescission, restitution, enforcement of decrees and law-equity merger problems. Moreover, this expansion in coverage has been accomplished without adding to the length of the book.

We are grateful to our respective law schools and administrations for their substantial encouragement and assistance. We also wish to thank those students who assisted us in the preparation of this Edition.

ROBERT N. LEAVELL
JEAN C. LOVE
GRANT S. NELSON

April, 1980

Preface to Second Edition

In the fifteen years since the First Edition the trend to which Professor Van Hecke alluded in his Preface has continued unabated. As a course, Equity finds it difficult to compete at all. Courses in Remedies and Restitution fair somewhat better; however, they are still rather grudgingly given the hours in the single quarter or semester allotted to them.

How this has come about is not easy to understand. Practitioners—and bar examiners—do not appear to have followed the academicians' tendency, and continue to indicate their feeling about the importance of this material in the education of a lawyer. It is due in part to the increasing complexity of several areas of public law, and the need to give more time and classroom hours to them. Recently, courses in environmental law, consumer protection, special problems of the poor, civil rights, and the like, have added to the brisk competition for classroom hours. This latter development, however, should stimulate a renewed interest in the basic course in equitable remedies and restitution.

Indeed, it is when new social demands make special demands upon the growth capacity of the law that the value of an understanding of equity and remedies is most apparent. Teachers with interests in such fields as those just mentioned will recognize the need for a grounding in equitable remedies and related legal remedies such as quasi-contract, and an appreciation of the origin and the creative spirit which infuses them.

Although we generally have followed Professor Van Hecke's organization, we also have found it necessary to add a substantial amount of new material to reflect recent developments. New material is especially evident in Chapter 6, reflecting the increasing use of the injunctive remedy in new and varied contexts. In a few areas we have made important changes in coverage and arrangement. Recent developments with respect to the right to trial by jury in situations involving mixed questions of law and equity require more attention than could be given to them if developed in relation to part of the content of one or more chapters. For this reason we have devoted a short chapter to this and related problems. Secondly, in the interests of keeping the book lean and readily adaptable to use in those courses where the teacher feels the hours allocated to the course are relatively small, we have reduced to very brief note status the material which deals with "Lack of Power and Mistaken Exercise of Power." However, we have sought to emphasize throughout the book the modifications which are taking place in the election of remedies situations, and the general impact upon this area of the merger of law and equity and the modern procedural systems. Finally, we have reduced substantially materials on Bills of Peace and Quieting Title in order to provide for consideration of Receiverships, Masters, Monitors and Sequestration.

We have added to the title the term "Restitution", to make it more descriptive of the book as conceived by Professor Van Hecke. The extensive treatment given by him to quasi-contract, placed alongside the restitutionary material from equity, is continued in the current edition.

The cases and materials have been closely edited. Save in special situations, strings of citations, footnotes and dissenting opinions not useful for teaching purposes have been omitted. Footnotes are ours unless otherwise specified.

We express our appreciation for the permission granted by the publishers and authors of the selections from books and articles reproduced herein. We are also grateful for the assistance and encouragement of our law school administrations and for the valuable contributions of student research.

Finally, to our wives and families we express special gratitude for their patience and understanding during the period we worked on the Second Edition.

ROBERT N. LEAVELL
GRANT S. NELSON

May, 1973

PREFACE TO FIRST EDITION

There have been two significant developments in Equity since the publication in 1948 of the Fourth Edition of Cook's Cases and Materials. (1) The status of the course in Equity in the law schools has been increasingly modified to conform to other changes in the curriculum. The modifications have taken these forms: dropping the separate course and distributing parts of the subject matter to other courses, including new courses in Equitable Remedies; retaining the separate course and considerably reducing the number of class-room hours available. (2) Meanwhile, uninhibited by these considerations, the courts and legislatures have continued to improve the equitable and related statutory remedies, so that the flexibility, discretionary concern for the individual situation and capacity for growth of these remedies might enable them to be used more effectively in times of changing conditions and needs. This casebook on Equitable Remedies is an effort to meet these developments.

It is substantially a new book, both in content and arrangement. The areas of substantive equity taught elsewhere in today's curriculum have been largely omitted. The cases and materials here presented, most of them the products of the last fifteen years, hew closely to the equitable and statutory remedies and to their operation, especially in courts where law and equity have been at least administratively merged.

The declaratory judgment cases are distributed for immediate contrast with the handling of comparable problems by the other remedies; the section on Declaratory Judgments is therefore largely a point of reference for the basic literature and statutes. Because the chapter on Jurisdiction seems to become more meaningful after the class has seen the various remedies in operation, it is placed last. However, those who prefer to take Jurisdiction first and to make other changes in the arrangement and order of chapters and sections will incur no appreciable loss.

The cases and materials have been closely edited. Save in special situations, strings of citations, footnotes and dissenting opinions not useful for teaching purposes have been omitted.

I want to thank the teachers of Equity in some forty schools who helpfully responded to my requests for advice and suggestions as to inclusion and exclusion, order and arrangement. I also want record my indebtedness to Mr. W. E. Bondurant, Jr., of the Roswell, New Mexico, Bar, to Mr. John P. Frank, of the Phoenix, Arizona, Bar, to Chief Judge Charles E. Clark, of the U.S. Court of Appeals for the Second Circuit, to Professor J. Francis Paschal, of Duke University, and to the late Professor Edgar N. Durfee, of the University of Michigan, for guidance and counsel.

And, I want to dedicate this book to Mrs. Van Hecke for her encouraging, companionable assistance.

M. T. VAN HECKE

Chapel Hill, North Carolina
December, 1958

SUMMARY OF CONTENTS

———

TABLE OF CONTENTS

―――――――

TABLE OF CASES

The principal cases are in bold type. Cases cited or discussed in the text are in roman type. References are to pages. Cases cited in principal cases and within other quoted materials are not included.

EQUITABLE REMEDIES, RESTITUTION AND DAMAGES

CASES AND MATERIALS

Eighth Edition

CHAPTER 1

INTRODUCTION TO REMEDIES

■ ■ ■

SECTION 1. SPECIFIC, SUBSTITUTIONARY, AND DECLARATORY REMEDIES

Why study remedies? The remedies in litigation are the bottom line for a plaintiff, who might be your client, and you will want to be prepared to advise your client about his or her remedial options. Also, the rules of remedies often reflect our society's values. When will the court order someone to do something and when will the court instead substitute money for the defendant's performance? Sometimes the answer will be a practical one—the court will find that it is impossible to order performance. But, in other cases, the decision will reflect social, political, and economic values.

The law of remedies is subdivided into a number of categories. One subdivision is the difference between specific, substitutionary, and declaratory relief. Specific relief remedies the wrong by requiring the defendant to perform a legal duty, such as returning stolen property or performing the terms of a contract. Substitutionary relief substitutes money for the specific relief. Declaratory relief tells people what their rights are, but orders no other remedy.

Another subdivision, which is largely historical in nature, is the difference between equitable and legal relief (*see infra* Chapter 1.3). Equitable relief is often specific, but can be substitutionary, as in the case of back pay in some discrimination cases. Legal relief is usually substitutionary, but can be specific, as in the case of legal replevin and ejectment. Equitable relief ordinarily takes the form of a court order directing the defendant to do or not to do something. Since it is a court order, if the defendant does not comply, the defendant can be held in contempt. There is normally no jury trial in a proceeding for equitable relief. Legal relief ordinarily takes the form of a judgment stating that the plaintiff is entitled to some type of substitutionary remedy, such as damages. If the defendant does not satisfy the judgment, the defendant cannot be held in contempt. Rather, the plaintiff can only levy execution on the judgment. A jury trial typically is available in an action for legal relief.

1

SECTION 2.   REMEDIES FOR TORTIOUS WRONGS, BREACH OF CONTRACT, AND UNJUST ENRICHMENT

This book will focus on remedies for tortious conduct, breach of contract, and unjust enrichment. The law of torts determines the type of conduct society wants to deter. The law of contracts determines those types of promises upon which society can rely. The law of unjust enrichment determines when someone's gain is unjust and restitution is appropriate. The remedial rules in tort serve to make the plaintiff whole, as if there had not been a tort. At times, those rules will also punish. In contract, the remedial rules serve to compensate people for breaches of contract without deterring commerce. In unjust enrichment, the remedial rules focus on defining a gain and determining whether it should be disgorged.

SECTION 3.   HISTORICAL INTRODUCTION TO LAW AND EQUITY

The fact that we continue today to recognize certain substantive and remedial concepts as "equitable" and others as "legal" is largely the product of historical accident rather than design. As a result, an inquiry into the historical development and evolution of equity, as a substantive and procedural companion to the common law, is essential to a proper understanding of the role of equity in our contemporary legal system.

Development of Equity from the Common Law

For our purposes, the historical development of law and equity necessary for an understanding of our Anglo–American legal system begins in England about the year 1150. Until that time, justice for most people was provided by the Saxon courts of the hundred and the shire, and later, by the Norman manorial and other local courts. These courts were administered by people who were usually uneducated and unsophisticated in the law. Consequently, justice was often crude and unwritten. Because it tended to follow local custom, it varied substantially from community to community. *See* William F. Walsh, Equity 2 (1930). While this system was extremely rudimentary, it seems to have met society's needs at the time. On the other hand, as one scholar has noted, "another and superior kind of justice was administered where the king * * * or lords were involved, by the king and witan before the [Norman] conquest, by the king and his court thereafter." *Id*.

During the twelfth century, Henry II created a national system of courts to administer legal matters. Gradually the local customary courts were eliminated and the national system of courts was expanded. Access to the king's courts was obtained through the issuance of writs by the king's secretary, the chancellor, who was often a religious leader and an expert in canon law. Writs were issued freely to meet new factual situations whenever justice would be served. In the early development of the king's courts, there was no distinction between law and equity. As one scholar pointed out, law and equity "originated in one and the same procedure and existed for a long time, not only side by side, but quite undifferentiated from each other. * * * There was no equity as a separate body of law; for the king's justices felt themselves able to dispense such equity as justice required." Willard T. Barbour, *Some Aspects of Fifteenth-Century Chancery*, 31 Harv. L. Rev. 834 (1918).

The newly-established system flourished. The justices of the courts granted relief freely, whether of a legal or equitable type, as part of the common law. For example, a thirteenth-century common law court could be found enforcing specific performance of lease covenants or enjoining waste by life tenants. *See* William F. Walsh, Equity 5–7 (1930).

Development of Equity as an Independent Court

Gradually, however, during the thirteenth and fourteenth centuries, the law courts became less flexible and less open to new forms of writs. If petitioners' cases did not fit within the confines of existing writs, relief was unavailable. The law courts also became less willing to grant specific performance, injunctions, or other types of specific relief. Damages became the pervasive, and often the only, remedy.

There were other reasons for disenchantment with the law courts. For one thing, the King's courts often were unable to command obedience from powerful defendants. This was especially the case where the prevailing parties were poor or uninfluential. Additionally, the law courts often used juries as factfinders. Since most jurors were uneducated and unsophisticated, cases involving complex facts or numerous parties proved problematic for the jury system, as did controversies involving complicated financial accounting.

In response to these problems, a competing court system arose called the Court of Chancery. The chancellor, who had traditionally been regarded as the government's leading moral authority, had by this time become the chief law member of the King's Council and, after the King, the most powerful governmental officer. Frustrated law petitioners began taking their cases directly to the King, who, in turn, referred them to the chancellor. Consequently, by the middle of the fourteenth century, Chancery or "Equity" had "come to be recognized as a separate judicial tribunal or court." Walter W. Cook, 5 Encyclopedia of the Social Sciences 584 (1931).

The procedures utilized by the two competing systems differed markedly. In the law courts, after the plaintiff had obtained the appropriate writ, the judge usually heard the case sitting with a jury. If the plaintiff prevailed, the judgment did not order the defendant to do anything—rather, it was an adjudication of the defendant's liability. The defendant's failure or refusal to satisfy the judgment could not be punished by contempt. Typically, the plaintiff would have the sheriff conduct an execution sale of any property that the plaintiff could locate. The sale, to be sure, passed good title to this property to the execution sale purchaser. But the judgment operated *in rem*, and not *in personam*. In Chancery, after the plaintiff had filed a petition, the Chancellor heard the case sitting without a jury (or sitting with an advisory jury). When the plaintiff prevailed, the defendant was ordered to perform. Refusal or recalcitrance triggered a contempt proceeding. Prison awaited such a defendant. Thus, while Chancery did not then act *in rem,* it clearly acted *in personam.*

Equity expanded in a variety of ways. First, it was willing, unlike its law counterpart, to grant injunctions and specific performance. It enforced contracts that were not under seal (a seal was required for the law court's writ of covenant) and granted specific performance of contracts where the remedy at law was inadequate. For example, because land was deemed to be unique, contracts for the sale of land were routinely enforced by specific performance, which meant that the defendant was ordered to execute and deliver a deed to the prevailing plaintiff. Similarly, in the tort context, equity issued injunctions against recurring or continuing trespasses. Second, by the fifteenth century, the Court of Chancery had developed two new substantive bodies of law. The first was the concept of the *use,* a forerunner to the modern trust. The other was the law of mortgages, a topic that is still thought of as equitable to this day.

The doctrine of uses allowed the separation of the legal title to land from the equitable title, transferring the title of the land to a trustee for the "use" of the beneficiary, the *cestui que trust.* The use of the property, with its rents and privileges, would go to the *cestui,* the holder of the equitable title, while the feudal incidents of wardship, marriage, and military tenure would be avoided by the use of the trustees. Further, the use was utilized to avoid the common law prohibitions against gifts of land by will and *inter vivos* transfers except by livery of seisin, transfer of possession, or its equivalent. Prior to the time such uses could be enforced in Chancery, the *cestui* was often powerless against a dishonest trustee because the law courts refused to recognize the use. In the view of a law court, the trustee, after all, had legal title and that was enough to allow him to proceed as if he were the "real" owner of the land. Chancery focused on the fact that the *cestui* retained equitable title and was thus the land's beneficial owner. As one commentator noted, Chancery "was especially well qualified to act, not only because it was developing a system of law outside of the common law, * * * but also because its procedure *in personam* was exactly adapted to compel specific performance with the terms of the use on the part of the trustee." William F. Walsh, Equity 20 (1930).

In addition, law courts proved inadequate to deal with the law of mortgages. As it developed in the fourteenth and fifteenth centuries, the common law mortgage was a fee simple conveyance subject to a condition subsequent. Suppose a lender loaned $5,000 to a landowner-borrower. As security, the landowner would deliver the foregoing deed to the lender. The lender would go into possession of the land, because the law of usury then prohibited the collection of *any* interest. If the borrower paid the debt on the due date ("law day"), the borrower would have the right to reenter and terminate the lender's estate. If the borrower failed to pay on time, however, the land belonged forever to the lender. Law courts found no reason to create exceptions to this harsh process. Indeed it was virtually an absolute rule—it applied if the borrower was a day late and even if the borrower was unable to find the lender to make payment. Law courts, being both literalists and inflexible, offered no relief to borrowers. In essence, "a deal was a deal." Equity, on the other hand, provided relief to these tardy borrowers:

> Tardy mortgagors began seeking redress from Chancery. Initially, Chancery authorized the [borrower] to "pay late" or "redeem tardily" only if the borrower was able to establish a significant excuse for the default, such as fraud, accident, misrepresentation, or duress. However, by the end of the 17th century, the [borrower] routinely was permitted, as a matter of right, to redeem the land by payment of the mortgage debt, so long as the [borrower] tendered the principal and interest (by now the collection of interest was permitted) within a reasonable time after the law day. Specific grounds for equitable relief were no longer required. * * * The foregoing right to pay late became known as the [borrower's] equity of redemption or, less frequently, the equity of tardy redemption. Eventually, this concept evolved * * * to connote the [borrower's] ownership interest in the land prior to the satisfaction of the mortgage. The term "equity" became and is today the pervasively used term to describe this interest.

Restatement (Third) of Prop.: Mortgages § 3.1, cmt. a (1997).* Later, Chancery created the remedy of foreclosure on behalf of the lender, which counter-balanced the tardy borrower's equity of redemption.

Conflict Between Law and Equity Resolved

Inevitably, a period of serious conflict developed between the two court systems. With growing frequency, the courts of equity were encroaching on the traditional powers of the courts of the common law. Cases involving similar fact situations often were resolved in opposite fashions, depending upon whether the case had been brought in law or equity. Consider, for example, the following illustration of the conflict between the two court systems:

> A typical situation in this struggle involved an action at law on a specialty (that is, bond under seal) that had been obtained from the defendant by "fraud in the inducement," such as misrepresentation concerning the value or quality of something sold by plaintiff to defendant on credit where the bond in a large penal sum was given to

* Copyright 1997 by the American Law Institute. Reprinted with the permission of the American Law Institute.

secure payment of the purchase price. If the defendant had indeed executed the bond, knowing it was a bond, then the kind of fraud by which the defendant was induced to execute it was not recognized in the law courts as a defense to an action on the bond. Equity, however, did recognize this kind of fraud and would entertain a suit by the debtor against the creditor (obligee on the bond) for a rescission of the bond. If the debtor succeeded in showing the fraud the chancellor would order the obligee to deliver the bond up for cancellation or to give a release of it under seal, on condition that the debtor restore to the creditor whatever benefit was received in the course of the transaction. Equity would, in short, try to put the parties back into the position they occupied before the fraudulent transaction took place.

If the debtor discovered the fraud and brought a bill in equity before the creditor obtained a judgment at law, then the chancellor would enjoin the creditor from pursuing an action at law pending determination of the issue of fraud. If the chancellor found fraud, he would make this temporary injunction a permanent one as part of his final decree. If he found no fraud, he would dissolve the temporary injunction and the creditor would be free to continue prosecuting the action at law. If a judgment at law had already been obtained, effective equitable relief would necessarily involve interference with the law court's judgment.

Fleming James, Jr., Geoffrey C. Hazard & John Leubsdorf Civil Procedure § 1.6 (5th ed. 2001).*

The conflict came to a head in the early 1600s. A dispute arose between Chief Justice Coke of the Court of King's Bench and Lord Chancellor Ellesmere of the Court of Chancery. The question focused on whether equity could prevent the enforcement of a law court's judgment by issuing an injunction restraining the law plaintiff from enforcing the law court's judgment. The Chancellor had granted injunctive relief because the law defendant had an equitable defense to the action at law which the law court refused to consider, given its precedents. The law judges insisted that the Statute of Praemunire, which prohibited any attack on a judgment of a law court, nullified any action by Chancery that interfered with the enforcement of a judgment of a law court. The question cut to the very existence of equity as a credible force in the English legal system. The dispute was referred by the King to an advisory body. On the recommendation of this body (and of the attorney general), the King decided in favor of the Chancellor. Conceptually, it was said there was no conflict. Since equity was said to act *in personam* and not *in rem*, the injunction issued by the court of equity left the law judgment intact. Any enforcement of the law judgment would be valid and an execution sale thereon would result in a proper transfer of title. However, the executing judgment-holder would face the consequences of being held

_____

* Reprinted with permission of Little, Brown and Company.

in contempt of court by the Chancellor. Thus, Chancery scored a practical, if not a completely theoretical, victory. Even though the legal judgment was technically unaffected by the injunction, the threat of contempt of court was quite likely to stop the legal proceedings. Since the resolution of the Coke–Ellesmere dispute, the existence and effectiveness of equitable jurisdiction has never been seriously challenged by the common law.

Procedural Unification of Law and Equity

Chancery's victory probably represented its high water mark for at least two reasons. First, equity, as a magnanimous victor, voluntarily restricted its jurisdiction by placing increased emphasis on the necessity of an inadequate legal remedy as a condition precedent to its relief. Second, legislation reforming the law courts' jurisdiction often made resort to equity unnecessary. For example, with the enactment of the Statute of Uses, common law recognition was given to uses and jurisdiction over them was placed in the common law courts. As a result, while equity retained jurisdiction over "active" trusts, it no longer was needed to execute inactive uses.

The separate system of law and equity courts was, of course, transplanted to this continent during the British colonial period. However, by the latter part of the eighteenth century, some momentum had developed in both England and the United States to accomplish a procedural merger of law and equity. The principal reasons for this movement are not difficult to understand. The separate development of law and equity courts had resulted in two judicial systems, each with different substantive rules, and each having a significantly different system of pleading and procedure. *See* William F. Walsh, Equity 36 (1930). Consequently, a party who selected the wrong court was forced to begin again in the correct court, assuming that the incorrect selection had not foreclosed this option. Moreover, equitable defenses could not be set up in law actions; the defendant could establish an equitable defense only by suit in equity to restrain the plaintiff from prosecuting the action at law. All this involved "delay, expense, duplication of actions, and the scandal of different results in the same case if brought in one court instead of in the other." *Id.*

In England, the Supreme Court of Judicature Act of 1873 ultimately was the merger vehicle. *See* Supreme Court of Judicature Act, 1873, 36 & 37 Vict., c. 66 (Eng.); *see also* Constitutional Reform Act, 2005, c. 4 (Eng.) (enacting the most recent constitutional reforms to the justice system of the United Kingdom). The 1873 Act fused the Court of Chancery together with the law courts. Thus, the modern English system has a court of general jurisdiction called the High Court with three divisions: the Chancery Division, Queen's Bench Division, and Family Division. Procedurally, equity and law are merged within the High Court such that:

> Each High Court judge is attached to one of the divisions, but they
> may be transferred to one of the others.... Different classes of
> business are allocated for administrative convenience to each division

by rules of court, although technically all the jurisdiction of the High Court belongs to all of the divisions alike.

S.H. Bailey, J.P.L. Ching & N.W. Taylor, Smith, Bailey, and Gunn on the Modern English Legal System 107 (5th ed. 2007).

Although the Judicature Act accomplished the *"procedural* fusion of law and equity," a substantive division between these bodies of law remains in the English system. *Id.* at 8. Accordingly:

> Matters of both law and equity can now be determined in the course of one set of proceedings: if there is any conflict between rules of law and rules of equity, the latter are to prevail. In most instances there are differences between the operation of law and equity rather than conflict. For example, different remedies may be available in respect of what both systems acknowledge to be a wrong (*e.g.* damages (common law) and an injunction (equity) in respect of a nuisance). Equity may impose additional obligations on a person while recognising his or her rights at common law (*e.g.* by accepting that a trustee is the legal owner of property while requiring him or her to hold it for the benefit of another).

Id.

In the United States, the merger process was both gradual and complex, although it was largely achieved before 1873. The United States Constitution as adopted in 1789, together with early amendments, differentiated between law and equity in a variety of contexts. Article III, the Judicial Article, refers to "all cases, in law and equity"; the Eleventh Amendment to any "suit in law or equity"; and the Seventh Amendment to "suits at common law."

At the time the Constitution was adopted, equity jurisdiction was recognized in some of the original states. As of 1787, chancery courts existed

> in New York, South Carolina, Maryland, Virginia, and, to an extent, in New Jersey; in Pennsylvania, Delaware and North Carolina, there were no such courts though the common law courts had certain equity powers; in Connecticut and Rhode Island, the Legislature exercised some powers of a Court of Chancery; in Massachusetts and New Hampshire, there were common law courts only having a very few limited powers; Georgia had only common law courts.

Charles Warren, *New Light on the History of the Federal Judiciary Act of 1789*, 37 Harv. L. Rev. 49, 96 (1923). This early American antipathy to equity jurisdiction was due, in part, to the lack of jury trial in equity cases, to abuses by colonial governors while serving as chancellors, and to resentment over the discretionary powers and royalist associations of the English Court of Chancery. *See* Austin W. Scott & Sidney P. Simpson, Cases and Materials on Civil Procedure 162–63 (1950).

At the federal level, "Congress did not, as no doubt it might have done, create separate national courts of equity and law, but organized only one system of courts in which might be tried cases at law, and cases in equity, according as the same judge happened to be playing the role of common law judge, or of chancellor." Charles T. McCormick, *The Fusion of Law and Equity*, 6 N.C. L. Rev. 283, 284 (1928). But the declaration at law and the bill in equity "retained their distinct names and characteristics, and the case had to be one in law or in equity." *Id.* Moreover, the "law-equity" differentiation in the Constitution resulted in "some expressions in opinions of the courts and in the writings of commentators which might lend color to the view that the Constitution has indelibly impressed the separation of law and equity upon national judicial procedure." *Id.* at 286.

Because of the diversity in the status of equity in the several states, Congress in 1792 provided in effect that the procedure in equity cases in the federal courts should conform to that of the English Court of Chancery, as modified by rules of the United States Supreme Court. This was in sharp contrast to the provision that, in common-law cases, the procedure in the federal courts was to conform to that of the state in which the federal court was sitting. The latter was justified by the relative uniformity of common-law procedure in the state courts. Accordingly, the Supreme Court in 1822 prescribed rules to govern equity procedure in the federal courts. These were revised in 1842 and again in 1912. With respect to the substantive law of equity, the Court ruled in 1851[1] that equity cases were to be governed by federal common law under the doctrine of Swift v. Tyson, 41 U.S. (16 Pet.) 1, 10 L.Ed. 865 (1842). From that time until 1938,[2] the federal courts enunciated their own views of principles of equity jurisprudence, without restriction by the decisions of state courts. Thus, "federal equity" attempted uniformity throughout the United States in its substantive as well as its procedural aspects.

The first major state effort at merging law and equity appeared in New York in 1848 with the adoption of the Field Code, which classified law and equity as one procedural category of civil suits. The substantive rights available under equity were retained; the Field Code was aimed at improving the procedures and mechanics of the legal process. Within twenty-five years, at least two dozen states had enacted statutes or rules similar to the Field Code. *See* Charles E. Clark, Code Pleading 21–31 (2d ed. 1947). In 1938, with the adoption of the Federal Rules of Civil Procedure, the procedural merger of law and equity was largely complete. Rule 2 of the Federal Rules of Civil Procedure states: "There shall be one form of action to be known as 'civil action.'" Today, forty-seven of the fifty states and the District of Columbia have accomplished such a procedural merger, either through the Field Code approach or through adoption of the Federal Rules.

---

1. Russell v. Southard, 53 U.S. (12 How.) 139, 13 L.Ed. 927 (1851).

2. Erie R.R. Co. v. Tompkins, 304 U.S. 64, 58 S.Ct. 817, 82 L.Ed. 1188 (1938); *see* Ruhlin v. New York Life Insurance Co., 304 U.S. 202, 58 S.Ct. 860, 82 L.Ed. 1290 (1938) (*Erie* principle extended to equity cases).

The three states which have not joined law and equity are Delaware, Mississippi, and Tennessee. For example, the Tennessee Code Annotated (1994) provides:

§ 16–10–101. The circuit court is a court of general jurisdiction, and the judge thereof shall administer right and justice according to law, in all cases where the jurisdiction is not conferred upon another tribunal.

§ 16–11–101. The chancery court has all the powers, privileges, and jurisdiction properly and rightfully incident to a court of equity.

See also Del. Code Ann. tit. 10, § 341 *et seq.* (1999); Miss. Const. art. 6, § 159.[3]

In New Jersey, a procedural dichotomy between law and equity persists notwithstanding merger. Even though the Superior Court has both equitable and legal jurisdiction, it continues to be divided into "law" and "chancery" divisions. Consequently, "actions in which the plaintiff's primary right or the principal relief sought is equitable * * * shall be brought in the Chancery Division* * *." N.J. Civ. Prac. R. 4:3–1(a)(1).

Law and Equity After Procedural Merger

As a result of the merger process, certain procedures associated with equity have lost much of their uniquely equitable identification. Interpleader is a good example of this phenomenon. Ironically, like many of the early equitable doctrines, interpleader has its roots in the common law. In the 1300s, interpleader was in common usage in the conflicts arising at law under writs of wardship and actions of detinue. The death of a man frequently prompted litigation as to the wardship of any surviving infant children and their inherited properties. The person with custody of the children would be the focus of several claims to the wardship by relatives of the deceased, in response to which the custodian would deliver the children to the court for a determination of the rightful guardian. In actions of detinue, goods or money were often delivered to third-party stakeholders upon the completion of a contracted duty. If the stakeholder could not determine whether the duty had been properly discharged, the stakes could be delivered up to the court for proper adjudication. Ralph V. Rogers, *Historical Origins of Interpleader*, 51 Yale L.J. 924 (1942).

The common-law usage of interpleader died with the disuse of wardship and detinue between 1500 and 1800. Chancery stepped in to rescue

---

3. Although Tennessee adopted procedural rules in 1970 substantially the same as the Federal Rules, separate courts of law and equity remain. *See* Donald F. Paine, *Recent Developments in Tennessee Procedure: The New Tennessee Rules of Civil Procedure*, 37 Tenn.L.Rev. 501 (1970). *See also* Frederic S. LeClercq, *The Tennessee Court System*, 8 Memphis St.L.Rev. 185, 281 (1978).

In Mississippi, as in Tennessee, the law court is a court of general jurisdiction, and the chancery court is a court of limited jurisdiction. Derr Plantation, Inc. v. Swarek, 14 So.3d 711, 715 (Miss. 2009). In determining whether a claim is legal or equitable, the Mississippi Supreme Court has held that "[t]he reviewing court must look to the substance, not the form, of a claim." *Id.* at 716–17 (chancery court has jurisdiction over an action for specific performance of a land sale contract, even though the plaintiff-buyer also is seeking damages, because real estate is unique).

the discarded common-law doctrine. Beginning about 1700, courts of equity adopted the form and name of the common-law interpleader procedure. Since equity could effectively enjoin the claiming parties from pursuing their several actions at law, they were forced to interplead among themselves and resolve the issue as to which of the claiming parties had the valid claim to the stakes in question.

Interpleader was codified by the 1938 Federal Rules of Civil Procedure and the 1958 Federal Interpleader Act. These rules and statutes relaxed the traditional equitable requirements and returned interpleader to the courts of law for wide usage in those cases which expose a defendant to multiple claims for the same debt or property. Charles A. Wright & Mary Kay Kane, Law of Federal Courts 534–42 (6th ed. 2002).

Despite the merger process, many substantive doctrines that were developed in equity, such as subrogation, the mortgagor's equity of redemption, and promissory estoppel, continue to retain their equitable identification. Certain remedies, such as specific performance, injunctions, mortgage foreclosure by judicial suit, and constructive trust, continue to be categorized as "equitable." And vestiges of the separate systems of law and equity survive in modern enforcement procedures. *See* Dan B. Dobbs, Handbook on the Law of Remedies §§ 1.2, 2.1 (2d ed. 1993). Decrees of specific performance and injunctions, for example, are characteristically *in personam* orders embodied in a decree signed by the judge who hands it down. The enforcement of such an order is often closely monitored and supervised by the judge who issued it. The contempt power will be used to fine or jail a recalcitrant defendant. By way of contrast, a judge's role in enforcing legal judgments for damages is substantially more limited. Most money judgments are not personal orders to pay and thus not enforceable by the contempt power. Rather, the usual practice is simply to state in the record of the clerk that judgment is entered in favor of the plaintiff for a specified sum. It then remains for the counsel of the judgment creditor to utilize execution to enforce it. Levying execution typically entails finding the assets of the defendant, perfecting a judgment lien thereon, and then having the sheriff sell the assets and apply the proceeds of the sale to satisfy the judgment. Finally, the distinction between law and equity continues to be of vital importance in determining the right of the parties to a trial by jury. The Seventh Amendment of the Constitution and similar state provisions provide for the right to a jury in actions at law, but not in equity.

Equitable doctrines also have continuing vitality insofar as they inspire judges to consider themselves as being bound by a higher obligation. Judges often say that they are sitting "as chancellors" or "wearing the hat of the chancellor," especially when dealing with such traditionally equitable defenses or remedies as unclean hands or specific performance. They also continue to express a greater willingness to experiment with innovative remedies when exercising "equitable jurisdiction." These characteristics of modern equity judges are in some measure the result of the conduct on the bench of the great chancellors who trained for the church before becoming judges. These men had been students of the Canon Law and were aware of the influence of Roman law and equity upon the growth of the civil law system that prevailed in most of Europe. As judges, they were inclined to deal with the cases before them as the equities required, rather than being bound by stare decisis. Modern judges who are exercising "equitable jurisdiction," like the early chancellors, feel less constricted in their application of precedents than do their counterparts who are exercising jurisdiction over claims for legal relief.

NOTE

There are a number of remedies, both legal and equitable, which we mention only incidentally, or not at all. Legal remedies which may play a role in aid of both jurisdiction and satisfaction, such as attachment and garnishment, are left to procedure and other courses. Similarly, we do not discuss the "creditor's bill" in equity, which is used to marshal assets and impose equitable liens when garnishment is not adequate.

We do not cover the great "prerogative writs" developed by the law courts. These include "quo warranto," to call into question the charter or grant of privilege under which one purports to act; "prohibition," to restrain an official from acts not legally appropriate; "certiorari," to remove a matter from a lower court to a higher; and "habeas corpus." These writs often afford the only adequate remedy for controlling the improper conduct of public officials. *See* Charles A. Wright & Arthur R. Miller, Federal Practice and Procedure: Civil § 1021 (3d ed. 2002); Charles A. Wright, Arthur R. Miller, Edward Cooper & Richard Freer, Federal Practice and Procedure: Jurisdiction § 3507 (3d ed. 2008); Charles A. Wright, Arthur R. Miller & Edward Cooper, Federal Practice and Procedure: Jurisdiction §§ 3932, 3507 (2d ed. 1996).

Another writ that we do not cover is the writ of sequestration, which was developed as a remedy that sought to coerce the defendant to obey an outstanding equity decree. When a defendant refused to carry out such an *in personam* order, the court, on the request of the plaintiff, appointed sequestrators to take possession of the defendant's chattels and real estate and to obtain the rents and profits. Sequestration remains a part of the heritage of remedies to which a court of equity may resort in proper circumstances, and, in some states, it is expressly provided for by statute. *See, e.g.,* Mo. Rev. Stat. § 511.340 (2000). Moreover, Rule 70 of the Federal Rules of Civil Procedure specifically provides that "[i]f a judgment requires a party to convey land, to deliver a deed or other document, or to perform any other specific act and the party fails to comply within the time specified," the court may order the act to be done—at the disobedient party's expense—by another person appointed by the court.

Other remedies of lesser significance today are a bill in equity to remove a cloud on a title to land (which has been replaced in many jurisdictions by a statutory quiet title action), a bill quia timet (to obtain cancellation of an instrument), a bill to preserve evidence, and a writ of assistance (to put the plaintiff in possession after a decree recognizing such a right). It is important to have in mind that any court of general jurisdiction has the power to permit the use of these writs and remedies as part of its inherent equity jurisdiction.

CHAPTER 2

BASIC PRINCIPLES OF SPECIFIC EQUITABLE REMEDIES

■ ■ ■

SECTION 1. OVERVIEW OF PROCEDURES AND STANDARDS FOR ISSUING INJUNCTIVE RELIEF

A. INTRODUCTION TO BASIC TERMS

DAN B. DOBBS, LAW OF REMEDIES
162–64 (2d ed. 1993).*

Injunction as a Coercive Order

An injunction is a remedy in the form of an in personam order, usually issued by a trial court of general jurisdiction. It directs the defendant to act, or to refrain from acting in a specified way, and it is enforceable by the contempt power. The injunction must be obeyed until it is stayed, dissolved, or reversed, even if it is erroneously issued.

Any in personam order that is enforceable by contempt power is an injunctive order, although more specific names are sometimes used to indicate the factual context to which the injunction belongs. For instance, specific performance is a remedy by which the defendant is ordered to perform a contract and the specific performance order is thus a form of injunction. Reinstatement in a job is a remedy for job discrimination in some cases and the reinstatement order is a form of injunction. Preliminary injunctions and temporary restraining orders are likewise injunctive forms. Even the automatic stay in bankruptcy operates like an injunction.

An injunction may form the only remedy in a case, or it may be one part of more complex remedies. As the only remedy, the injunction might simply enjoin the defendant's repeated trespass on the plaintiff's land or prohibit infringement of a trademark. * * * Injunctions that forbid future misconduct are also frequently coupled with an award of damages for harms already done.

---

* Reprinted with permission of West Publishing Co.

Mandatory vs. Prohibitory Injunctions

Classification. Injunctions are sometimes classified as being either mandatory or prohibitory. The prohibitory injunction forbids an act. "The defendant is hereby enjoined from trespassing upon Blackacre," is a prohibitory injunction. The mandatory injunction orders an affirmative act or course of conduct. "The defendant is hereby ordered to remove all boulders he has previously deposited upon Blackacre," is a mandatory injunction.

Formal but not substantive differences. In both of the examples given above, the defendant's trespass on Blackacre might have been the result of identical acts—deposit of boulders on the plaintiff's land. One of the injunctions, however, addresses the trespass as a continuing trespass or frames the order prohibitively; the other frames the order as a mandatory injunction. In many situations the two kinds of injunctions are different in form, but not in purpose or effect. Courts say that they will ignore the prohibitory locutions and classify the injunction as mandatory if it is "really" mandatory. This practice calls on standards even less certain than the formal language of the injunction, however. For instance, one court held that an injunction against working for the plaintiff's competitors was mandatory.

Reluctance to use mandatory injunctions. Although the difference between mandatory and prohibitory injunctions is often formal, simply a way of phrasing the order, courts sometimes attach significance to that difference. Sometimes the distinction has a procedural effect [(as when a mandatory injunction is stayed "automatically" as soon as the defendant perfects an appeal)]. At other times, courts may be reluctant to award a mandatory injunction because it may be especially intrusive, or more difficult to supervise and enforce. Such intrusions or difficulties, however, usually result, if at all, only because of the injunction's content rather than its mandatory form. Courts are right to weigh intrusion carefully in injunction cases, but the mandatory form of the injunction is not often a good measure of that intrusion and in any event the intrusion effected must be weighed against the intrusion required to provide a suitable remedy.

Preventive, Reparative and Structural Injunctions

Reparative and preventive injunctions. A second set of classifications for injunctions may be more meaningful. The second set describes injunctions as reparative, preventive, or structural. The reparative injunction requires the defendant to restore the plaintiff to a preexisting entitlement. The mandatory injunction requiring a trespasser to remove the boulders he deposited is in this category. A preventive injunction attempts to prevent the loss of an entitlement in the future. It might be prohibitory, as where the defendant is enjoined not to obstruct ingress into the plaintiff's premises. Of course some injunctive orders both repair and prevent harm.

The difference between reparative and preventive injunctions is important in presenting evidence and formulating decrees. The reparative injunction goes when the evidence shows that an existing right has been violated but can be repaired or restored effectively. The preventive injunction, on the other hand, is not proper unless the defendant is threatening to commit a wrong in the future. The defendant's past trespass upon the plaintiff's land by dumping boulders on it is not by that act alone threatening to wrong the plaintiff in the future. So a reparative injunction might go to require removal of the boulders, but not a preventive injunction to forbid future trespasses. On the other hand, when demonstrators show intransigent determination to continue trespassing indefinitely, a preventive injunction may be appropriate.

Structural injunctions. Professor Owen Fiss has argued that there is a third type of injunction that belongs in this set. The structural or restructuring injunction attempts to remodel an existing social or political institution to bring it into conformity with constitutional demands. Examples are the injunction that restructures a school system to facilitate equality of educational opportunity, or restructures a prison to eliminate cruel and inhuman punishments. Such injunctions would be simple reparative or preventive injunctions if they merely ordered authorities to carry out or to cease some specific act. However, restructuring injunctions are typically complex and invasive. They are likely to involve the judge in tasks traditionally considered to be non-judicial, that is, less about rights and duties and more about management. For this reason, structural injunctions are likely to be used, as they are now, only as public law remedies for serious and pervasive rights violations.

B. INTRODUCTION TO FEDERAL RULE OF CIVIL PROCEDURE 65

Throughout Chapter 2, we will focus primarily on federal cases. The federal rules governing injunctive relief are set forth below. Temporary restraining orders and preliminary injunctions are issued prior to a trial on the merits of a case; permanent injunctions are issued after such a trial has taken place. Temporary restraining orders may be issued immediately with or without notice to the defendant (although Rule 65(b) focuses exclusively on temporary restraining orders that are issued without notice). The term of a temporary restraining order is not to exceed fourteen days unless it is extended by the court. Preliminary injunctions may be granted under Rule 65(a) only after notice to the defendant, and only after an adversary hearing, which is usually held within fourteen to twenty-eight days after the filing of the complaint. The preliminary injunction remains in effect until the trial court rules on the plaintiff's request for a permanent injunction. Both types of pre-trial injunctions usually will not be issued until the plaintiff has posted a bond or given some other type of security pursuant to Rule 65(c). Once a pre-trial injunction has been granted, the defendant who violates it may be held in contempt of court. The people who are bound by an injunction are identified in Rule 65(d)(2).

Rule 65 addresses procedural issues only, and does not discuss the substantive standards for determining whether to grant injunctive relief. Therefore, the federal judiciary has had to articulate the substantive standards by means of case law. In Chapter 2, Section 1.C, we introduce you to the substantive standards. We then discuss the application of those standards in Chapter 2, Sections 2 and 4.

Federal Rules of Civil Procedure

Rule 65. Injunctions and Restraining Orders

(a) Preliminary Injunction.

(1) *Notice.* The court may issue a preliminary injunction only on notice to the adverse party.

(2) *Consolidating the Hearing with the Trial on the Merits.* Before or after beginning the hearing on a motion for a preliminary injunction, the court may advance the trial on the merits and consolidate it with the hearing. Even when consolidation is not ordered, evidence that is received on the motion and that would be admissible at trial becomes a part of the trial record and need not be repeated at trial. But the court must preserve any party's right to a jury trial.

(b) Temporary Restraining Order.

(1) *Issuing Without Notice.* The court may issue a temporary restraining order without written or oral notice to the adverse party or its attorney only if:

(A) specific facts in an affidavit or a verified complaint clearly show that immediate and irreparable injury, loss, or damage will result to the movant before the adverse party can be heard in opposition; and

(B) the movant's attorney certifies in writing any efforts made to give notice and the reasons why it should not be required.

(2) *Contents; Expiration.* Every temporary restraining order issued without notice must state the date and hour it was issued; describe the injury and state why it is irreparable; state why the order was issued without notice; and be promptly filed in the clerk's office and entered in the record. The order expires at the time after entry—not to exceed 14 days—that the court sets, unless before that time the court, for good cause, extends it for a like period or the adverse party consents to a longer extension. The reasons for an extension must be entered in the record.

(3) *Expediting the Preliminary-Injunction Hearing.* If the order is issued without notice, the motion for a preliminary injunction must be set for hearing at the earliest possible time, taking precedence over all other matters except hearings on older matters of the same character. At the hearing, the party who obtained the order must

proceed with the motion; if the party does not, the court must dissolve the order.

(4) *Motion to Dissolve.* On 2 days' notice to the party who obtained the order without notice—or on shorter notice set by the court—the adverse party may appear and move to dissolve or modify the order. The court must then hear and decide the motion as promptly as justice requires.

(c) Security. The court may issue a preliminary injunction or a temporary restraining order only if the movant gives security in an amount that the court considers proper to pay the costs and damages sustained by any party found to have been wrongfully enjoined or restrained. The United States, its officers, and its agencies are not required to give security.

(d) Contents and Scope of Every Injunction and Restraining Order.

(1) *Contents.* Every order granting an injunction and every restraining order must:

(A) state the reasons why it issued;

(B) state its terms specifically; and

(C) describe in reasonable detail—and not by referring to the complaint or other document—the act or acts restrained or required.

(2) *Persons Bound.* The order binds only the following who receive actual notice of it by personal service or otherwise:

(A) the parties;

(B) the parties' officers, agents, servants, employees, and attorneys; and

(C) other persons who are in active concert or participation with anyone described in Rule 65(d) (2) (A) or (B).

* * *

NOTE

Stylistic changes were made to the Federal Rules of Civil Procedure in 2007, and one substantive change was made to Rule 65 in 2009. Rule 65 used to say that a temporary restraining order expired at the end of ten business days unless, prior to that time, it was extended for a like period. Rule 65(b)(2) was revised (effective December 1, 2009) to say that a temporary restraining order expires at the end of fourteen calendar days unless, prior to that time, it is extended for a like period. Throughout the Eighth Edition, you will see references to the old rule in cases that were decided prior to December 1, 2009.

* * *

C. INTRODUCTION TO STANDARDS FOR ISSUING INJUNCTIVE RELIEF

The next three cases will compare and contrast the standards for issuing temporary restraining orders, preliminary injunctions, and permanent injunctions. In order to demonstrate the relationship between these three types of injunctive relief, we will focus on a single question: Is it a denial of equal protection to bar a girl or a young woman from participating in a contact sport solely on the basis of her gender? Because the cases below span three decades, they provide a brief overview of the development of the law of equal protection in the context of sex-based classifications.

1. Temporary Restraining Orders

CLINTON v. NAGY

United States District Court, Northern District of Ohio, 1974.
411 F.Supp. 1396.

LAMBROS, DISTRICT JUDGE.

Plaintiff, Brenda Clinton, brought this action, through her mother and next friend, Johnnie Clinton, seeking the issuance of a temporary restraining order and a preliminary and permanent injunction against defendants John S. Nagy, Commissioner of the Division of Recreation of the City of Cleveland; Robert Maver, Director of the Cleveland Browns Muny Football Association; Charles Hall, Director of Class "F" Muny League teams; and Ralph J. Perk, Mayor of the City of Cleveland. Plaintiff filed the action pursuant to 42 U.S.C.A. § 1983 and seeks to enjoin defendants from depriving her of equal recreational opportunities because of her sex and a declaratory judgment that the policies, customs, and practices of the defendants are in violation of the Constitution and laws of the United States. Notice of a hearing on the motion for temporary relief was afforded defendants, and this matter was heard on Friday, November 1, 1974. The Court granted plaintiff's motion for the temporary restraining order. The Court's ruling therein is set forth with more particularity below.

Plaintiff's claim is that she is a twelve year old female who expressed her interest to her mother and to Mr. William Thomas, coach of the 97th Street Bulldogs football team, in September 1974, of her desire to play football with Mr. Thomas' team.

The 97th Street Bulldogs football team is licensed by the City as part of the Cleveland Browns Muny Football Association. Plaintiff alleges that neither her mother nor Coach Thomas have any objections to plaintiff's participation on the team. * * * [O]n September 28, 1974, plaintiff was suited and prepared to play with the 97th Street Bulldogs. On that date, and on several subsequent Saturday afternoons, plaintiff was suited and ready to play but was informed by defendant Charles Hall that she would not be permitted to play because she was a female. * * *

Plaintiff, therefore, instituted this suit seeking an order to restrain the defendants from denying her an opportunity to qualify to participate as a member of the 97th Street Bulldogs in the last games of the season, on Saturday, November 2, 1974, and Saturday, November 9, 1974, solely on the basis of her sex. At the hearing on the temporary restraining order, the defendants, through counsel, did not dispute that the reason that plaintiff was not permitted to play with the Bulldogs was because of her sex. The defendants argued, however, that the City's rules and regulations which govern the playing of sports specifically exclude females from participating in contact sports and that such exclusion is lawful because it bears a rational relationship to a legitimate state purpose of providing for the safety and welfare of females.

Accordingly, the sole issue before this Court at the hearing on the motion for a temporary restraining order was whether plaintiff had shown a substantial likelihood of success on the merits of her claim that the defendants should be enjoined from enforcing the City's regulations which exclude females from the opportunity to qualify for participation in Muny league football, a contact sport, because such regulations do not bear a reasonable relationship to any legitimate state purpose. Morris v. Michigan State Board of Education, 472 F.2d 1207 (6th Cir.1973). In this regard, defendants urged that the exclusion of females from contact sports was necessary for their safety and welfare and asserted that the testimony of its medical experts at the hearing on the merits would establish that the rule adopted by the Cleveland Division of Recreation is rationally related to that purpose. Defendants contended that their experts would testify that even at age ten, eleven, or twelve, boys are beginning to develop speed and greater physical stamina at a faster pace than are girls of those ages. * * *

Although the defendants stated, moreover, that the testimony of two medical experts would show that based upon a statistical analysis of variable strengths, males were generally stronger than females, the present action was not brought as a class action seeking to enjoin defendants from refusing to allow females to play football. This action was brought by one named-plaintiff who alleges that she has a right to pursue the opportunity to *qualify* to play football with the Muny leagues. * * *

The plaintiff has cited several recent cases in which courts have struck down school regulations which bar females from participating in school athletics solely on the basis of their sex. Defendants argued, however, that all of those cases have involved the question of whether the school or athletic board had a legitimate state purpose in denying women an equal opportunity to qualify for *non-contact* sports * * *.

* * *

In evaluating the plaintiff's motion for the issuance of a temporary restraining order herein the Court concludes that plaintiff has shown a substantial likelihood of success on the merits of her claim that defendants have precluded her from participating in the Muny League football games because she is a female, and solely because she is a female. Defendants have offered no evidence, nor did defendants indicate that they would present evidence to this Court that Miss Clinton does not possess the qualifications and physical ability required of male members to participate in the league's games. The defendants offered no argument nor did they put forward a factual basis on which this Court could conclude that Miss Brenda Clinton is more susceptible to injury than are the other "Bulldogs." * * *

Defendants argued, however, that even if Brenda were qualified to play as a "Bulldog" the temporary restraining order should not issue because she had made no showing that she would suffer irreparable harm if she were not permitted to play with that team. The Court is unable to concur in defendants' assertion.

Of course, females have not engaged in traditionally male sports, and as a result, in many instances females lack the requisite training to qualify for membership on all-male teams, particularly those teams established for the playing of "contact" sports. Perhaps those who find merit in the more traditional male-female roles may have great difficulty in understanding how a young girl will suffer irreparable harm if she is precluded from engaging in the rough and sometimes even brutal contest of football. Many adults, no doubt, may feel that young girls will in fact suffer great harm, both physically and socially, if they are permitted to participate in "boys' " games. However, football is by its very nature a physically dangerous game, and the threat of injuries to young boys has alarmed many parents in the community for years.

Nevertheless, organized contact sports such as football continue to be played, and those individuals who encourage young men to participate in these sports seem to do so with a sincere belief that although the game is potentially dangerous, the rewards which will be reaped from participation in the game offset the potential dangers. Organized contact sports have generally been thought of as an opportunity and means for a young boy to develop strength of character, leadership qualities and to provide competitive situations through which he will better learn to cope with the demands of the future. Yet, although these are presumably qualities to which we desire all of the young to aspire, the opportunity to qualify to engage in sports activities through which such qualities may be developed has been granted to one class of the young and summarily denied to the other.

It is necessary that we begin to focus on the individual rather than thinking in broad generalities, which have oftentimes resulted in the imposition of irrational barriers, against one class or another. The issue before this Court is whether one young person, Brenda Clinton, who apparently qualifies to play with the 97th Street Bulldogs in every respect except for her sex, should be given the opportunity to participate in the game of football and to develop strength and character in that way in which she, with her mother's approval, believes will be the most valuable to her. The Court concludes that to deprive a qualified twelve year old girl of an opportunity to engage in that activity would cause her to suffer irreparable harm, particularly in light of the fact that there are only two remaining games this season, on November 2, 1974, and November 9, 1974.

The motion for the temporary restraining order is granted. Accordingly, the defendants, their agents, employees, and all persons having actual knowledge of this order are hereby enjoined from prohibiting plaintiff Brenda Clinton from participating as a member of the 97th Street Bulldogs in its football games solely because of her sex. As this Court has already cautioned plaintiff, nothing in this order should be construed as requiring Coach Thomas to put Brenda Clinton into a game, should he determine that she does not qualify on the day of a game or should he deem another member of the team to be better suited to play in the position for which Miss Clinton has qualified.

This matter is set down for a hearing on plaintiff's motion for a preliminary injunction, to be consolidated with a hearing on the merits of her claim for permanent injunctive and declaratory relief on November 26, 1974, at 1:30.

NOTES

1. Did the *Clinton* court enter a prohibitory or a mandatory injunction? Was the temporary restraining order a reparative, a preventive, or a structural injunction?

2. To qualify for the temporary restraining order, the plaintiff in *Clinton* had to show a "substantial likelihood of success" on her equal protection claim. In 1973, the Sixth Circuit had decided two sex discrimination cases, each of which interpreted Reed v. Reed, 404 U.S. 71, 92 S.Ct. 251, 30 L.Ed.2d 225 (1971), as saying that sex-based classifications were to be subjected to low-level, rational-basis scrutiny. Robinson v. Board of Regents of Eastern Kentucky University, 475 F.2d 707, 711 (6th Cir.1973), *cert. denied*, 416 U.S. 982, 94 S.Ct. 2382, 40 L.Ed.2d 758 (1974) (upholding dormitory curfew restrictions that applied only to women students under "rational relationship or traditional standard of equal protection review" because "the goal of safety is a legitimate concern of the Board of Regents"); Morris v. Michigan State Board of Education, 472 F.2d 1207, 1209 (6th Cir.1973) (striking down the Michigan High School Athletic Association's regulation which prohibited girls from engaging in interscholastic athletic contests insofar as it governed noncontact sports, but upholding the regulation insofar as it covered contact sports). Are you satisfied that Brenda Clinton established a "substantial likelihood of success" on the merits of her equal protection claim under *Reed* as interpreted by the Sixth Circuit?

3. The trial court judge in *Clinton* concentrated on the two most important criteria for determining whether to grant a temporary restraining order: 1) whether the plaintiff has shown a substantial likelihood of success on the merits; and 2) whether the plaintiff has proven irreparable harm. The other two criteria are whether the balance of hardships tips in the plaintiff's favor, and whether the issuance of the injunction would be harmful to the public interest. For a discussion of all four criteria in an opinion granting a temporary restraining order to a girl who was a sophomore in high school, and who wanted to try out for the boys' wrestling team, see Saint v. Nebraska School Activities Association, 684 F.Supp. 626 (D.Neb.1988).

2. Preliminary Injunctions

ADAMS v. BAKER

United States District Court, District of Kansas, 1996.
919 F.Supp. 1496.

THEIS, DISTRICT JUDGE.

[Plaintiff, Tiffany Adams, filed this action under 42 U.S.C. § 1983, alleging that the defendant school district had violated her right to equal protection by refusing to allow her to try out for the Valley Center High School wrestling team because of her gender.] * * * Plaintiff seeks injunctive relief and money damages. The court held a hearing on December 5–6, 1995, at which evidence was presented concerning the school's decision to prohibit girls from participating on the high school wrestling team. At the close of the hearing, the court issued a temporary restraining order requiring the defendants either to permit the plaintiff to try out for the wrestling team or to discontinue its wrestling program for male students.* The order has been extended three times by consent of the parties[1] and is set to expire on February 2, 1996.

FINDINGS OF FACT

1. Plaintiff, Tiffany Adams, is a fifteen-year-old female. She is a freshman at Valley Center High School * * * . The defendants in this case are the school district, members of the Valley Center school board and the superintendent of the district, Bob Neel. * * * Witnesses at the hearing included Valley Center High School's * * * wrestling coach, Carl Konecny.

2. Valley Center High School offers fifteen sports for student participation. Boys may participate in football, soccer, basketball, wrestling, tennis, and baseball. Volleyball, soccer, tennis, basketball, softball, and cheerleading are available for girls. There are also coed track, cross country and golf teams. * * * The percentage of girls participating in

---

* A third option would have been to form a girl's wrestling team, but that option was not feasible at the time the temporary restraining order was issued. 919 F.Supp. at 1502 n.3.

1. The temporary restraining order was extended because it appeared the matter would be resolved without further court proceedings, but it now appears a settlement is not imminent. Nevertheless, the case seems to be appropriate for settlement as the claim for injunctive relief is the meat of the case, and the economic damages are limited to attorney fees, which, the court notes, a delay would only serve to increase.

sports at Valley Center High School over the last eight years has been roughly proportionate to the percentage of female students at the school. * * *

3. Last school year, while in the eighth grade, plaintiff was a member of the Valley Center Junior High School wrestling team. Plaintiff compiled a record of five wins and three losses. Three of the wins came by forfeit because some boys refused to compete against a girl in wrestling. Plaintiff lost one match to another female wrestler. * * *

4. This school year plaintiff sought to try out for the high school wrestling team, but was prohibited from doing so. The only reason given for refusing to allow plaintiff's participation is her gender. * * *

5. Carl Konecny was plaintiff's coach last year and is her coach again this season. * * *

* * *

9. Konecny testified to problems that a male coach has with coaching a female wrestler. Konecny testified that sometimes there are enough boys at a wrestling meet that the boys must use both the boys' and girls' locker rooms. Konecny testified that treating injuries may involve touching the arms or chest area. Nevertheless, Konecny coached plaintiff last season and testified that he would be able to do so this season. * * *

10. Konecny testified that he was concerned for plaintiff's safety because of a difference in lifting ability. On average, a high school boy who weighs 145 pounds can bench press over 200 pounds. Last year during the off-season, plaintiff could bench press only 120 pounds. However, there was no evidence regarding what weight plaintiff can lift now or what she would be able to do after conditioning. Furthermore, there was testimony that some boys are not as strong as others, and there was no evidence that boys are required to demonstrate the ability to lift over 200 pounds in order to try out for the wrestling team. * * *

11. Konecny testified that the sport of wrestling involves a risk of injury. He related that at a recent varsity meet, one boy bled from a cut above his eye. Another landed on his head and was knocked unconscious. Konecny did not believe, however, that such injuries are more serious to girls than to boys. * * *

* * *

14. Evidence was presented that there are over 800 girls competing in wrestling in the United States. * * * Konecny testified that his team has this season competed against other teams with female participants. * * *

* * *

20. Neel testified that he became aware of Tiffany Adams' desire to participate in wrestling at the beginning of the school year. At a school

board meeting, parents commented on the situation and requested that the board restrict participation in wrestling to boys. * * *

21.   On November 16, 1995, the matter was taken up by the school board, but a motion to have only single-sex wrestling resulted in a tie vote. One board member was absent. * * *

22.   After the meeting, Neel talked to parents and the district's attorneys * * *. Neel made the final decision not to allow plaintiff to wrestle after determining that Title IX does not require coed participation in contact sports. * * *

23.   Neel testified that in deciding to prohibit plaintiff from trying out, he considered several factors: parents' moral objections; the possibility of sexual harassment lawsuits; plaintiff's safety; that state law and Title IX do not require coed wrestling; and disruption of the school setting. * * *

* * *

27.   There is no evidence that plaintiff suffered more than minor injuries last season. There was testimony that because plaintiff could be competing against eighteen-year-old boys this season, she may be at greater risk of injury. However, because wrestling matches are based on weight class, plaintiff would not be wrestling boys who are significantly larger than her. Plaintiff could potentially face an opponent who, as a senior, would be more experienced, but there is no reason to believe this would be more likely or more dangerous for a freshman girl than for a freshman boy. * * *

* * *

33.   Plaintiff testified that she wants to wrestle because she likes the sport and she appreciates the self-discipline it teaches and that she only wished for the chance to try out for the team on an equal basis. * * * By the time of the hearing on this matter, the plaintiff had already missed a number of practices and one wrestling meet. * * * The plaintiff testified that there is no way to make up for the lost practice time and lost opportunity to compete that has already been caused by the district's prohibition. * * *

CONCLUSIONS OF LAW

* * *

2.   A party seeking a preliminary injunction must establish (1) a substantial likelihood that it will prevail on the merits; (2) that it will suffer irreparable injury unless the injunction issues; (3) that the threatened injury to the moving party outweighs whatever damage the proposed injunction will cause the opposing party; and (4) that the injunction would not be adverse to the public interest. * * *

3. The function of a preliminary injunction is to preserve the status quo pending trial on the merits. * * *

* * *

I. Likelihood of Success on the Merits

* * *

9. Plaintiff bases her § 1983 claim on an allegation of deprivation of equal protection as guaranteed by the fourteenth amendment to the United States Constitution. It is undisputed that the defendants seek to deny the plaintiff the opportunity to participate in wrestling on the basis of gender. A party seeking to uphold a classification based on gender carries the burden of showing an "exceedingly persuasive justification" for the classification. Mississippi Univ. for Women v. Hogan, 458 U.S. 718, 723, 102 S.Ct. 3331, 3336, 73 L.Ed.2d 1090 (1982). Gender based discrimination is permissible only where the discrimination is "substantially related" to the achievement of "important governmental objectives." Id. In this case, the defendants identified several rationales behind the decision to prohibit girls from wrestling at Valley Center High School. The reasons given were safety, fear of sexual harassment litigation, potential disruption of the school setting, student and parent objections based on moral beliefs, and a variety of inconveniences.

10. The court concludes that the last two rationales do not constitute "important governmental objectives" in this case. The school district certainly does not consider itself subject to every parental complaint or whim. Furthermore, it is not the duty of the school to shield students from every situation which they may find objectionable or embarrassing due to their own prejudices. The defendants also identified potential problems with coaching techniques, availability of locker room facilities and other inconveniences. However, the district's interest in avoiding such trivial problems is hardly an important governmental objective. At any rate, according to the testimony of the defense witnesses, these problems could be overcome with minimal effort.

11. The court agrees that student safety is an important governmental objective. * * * Force v. Pierce City R–VI Sch. Dist., 570 F.Supp. 1020, 1022 (W.D.Mo.1983). However, the district's policy of prohibiting females from wrestling is not substantially related to that objective. The defendants' only evidence that plaintiff's safety is at greater risk because of her gender is based on generalized assumptions about the differences between males and females regarding physical strength. * * * The evidence shows that some females are stronger than some males. The school can take into account differences of size, strength, and experience without assuming those qualities based on gender. Furthermore, there was evidence presented of injuries boys have sustained while wrestling, and it is certainly improper to subject boys to greater danger than girls. As the court stated in Force, the defendants' safety arguments "suggest the very sort of well-

meaning but overly 'paternalistic' attitude about females which the Supreme Court has viewed with such concern." *Id.* at 1029.

12. Likewise, a school district has an interest in avoiding sexual harassment litigation. However, prohibiting female participation in activities is not substantially related to that goal. The evidence before the court stated the obvious, that wrestling is an athletic activity and not a sexual activity. There is no reason to suspect that girls who seek to join the wrestling team would be likely to mistake the contact which is inherent in the sport for sexual misconduct. A school district best avoids sexual harassment litigation by acting to prevent sexual harassment rather than excluding females from participating in activities.

13. Finally, the court concludes that the defendants' actions are not substantially related to the goal of avoiding disruption of the school setting. According to the defense witnesses' testimony, there was no such disruption when plaintiff wrestled last year. Furthermore, the only evidence of potential disruption this year is the suggestion that some boys may quit the wrestling team if plaintiff is allowed to participate, which the court concludes does not really constitute disruption of the school setting at all. A gender-based classification simply is not necessary to keep Valley Center High School running smoothly.

14. In sum, the plaintiff has shown that she is likely to succeed on the merits of her § 1983 claim based on equal protection. * * *

II.   *Irreparable Injury*

15. Although plaintiff seeks money damages as well as injunctive relief, the court rejects the defendant's contention that this is dispositive on the issue of irreparable harm.

16. Without temporary injunctive relief, plaintiff would miss more opportunities to compete, practice, and learn the sport of wrestling. Such missed opportunities would cause her to fall behind in her development as an athlete and would quite probably, as a practical matter, prevent her from being able to compete in the future. The defense witnesses testified at the hearing that plaintiff, as a freshman, is inexperienced compared to some of the boys on the Valley Center team and other teams, some of whom are seniors. If not allowed to participate this season, the boys in her own class will gain experience relative to the plaintiff.

17. Furthermore, the plaintiff has alleged deprivation of her constitutional rights. Where such allegations are made, no further showing of irreparable harm is required. * * * A deprivation of a constitutional right is, itself, irreparable harm.

III.   *Balance of the Hardships*

18. Again, the only hardship defendants have alleged relate to accommodating a female wrestler's need for a place to change, differences in coaching techniques, and the like. These problems were overcome last year without major difficulties, and the court is confident that the same

coach can find solutions to problems as they arise this year. The court concludes, therefore, that a preliminary injunction would pose minimal hardship to the defendants and that any such hardship is outweighed by the irreparable injury that plaintiff would suffer if not allowed to participate.

IV.   Public Interest

19.   The defendant has not argued that granting the plaintiff's motion for preliminary injunction would be harmful to the public interest.

20.   The public interest would best be served by enjoining the defendants from infringing on the plaintiff's right to equal protection. * * *

CONCLUSION

The court finds that all factors to be considered in determining whether a preliminary injunction should be issued have been met by the plaintiff. Plaintiff has established a substantial likelihood of success on the merits by showing that prohibiting her from participating in wrestling on the basis of gender does not significantly advance a substantial government interest. To deny a preliminary injunction would cause plaintiff irreparable injury in lost practice time and competitive opportunities, as well as the injury inherent in a denial of constitutional rights. It is highly unlikely that the defendant will suffer any damage because of the injunction, and any such damage is outweighed by the potential harm to the plaintiff. The public interest also favors granting the injunction as the public as a whole has an interest in protecting constitutional rights.

* * *

It is by this court therefore ordered that plaintiff's motion for preliminary injunction * * * is hereby granted. The defendants are hereby preliminarily enjoined from denying the plaintiff, on the basis of gender, the opportunity to participate in wrestling at Valley Center High School.

NOTES

1.   The *Adams* court subjected the sex-based classification to "intermediate" scrutiny under *Hogan*, rather than to "low-level" scrutiny under *Reed*. Was it therefore easier for Tiffany Adams than for Brenda Clinton to establish a "substantial likelihood of success on the merits"? For an interesting discussion of equal protection analysis regarding gender-based classifications post-*Hogan*, see Candace S. Kovacic–Fleischer, United States v. Virginia's *New Gender Equal Protection Analysis with Ramifications for Pregnancy, Parenting and Title VII*, 50 Vand. L. Rev. 845 (1997).

2.   The *Adams* court correctly identified the two component parts of the "irreparable harm" requirement. First, the plaintiff must prove the inadequacy of the legal remedy. Second, the plaintiff must prove the urgency of the plaintiff's need for injunctive relief.

3.   There is no reported opinion in either *Clinton* or *Adams* regarding the issuance of a permanent injunction. The standard for determining wheth-

er to issue a permanent injunction is similar to the standard for determining whether to grant a pre-trial injunction, but it is different in two important respects. First, because the permanent injunction may only be issued after a trial on the merits, the movant must show "actual success on the merits." Fogie v. THORN Americas, Inc., 95 F.3d 645, 654 (8th Cir.1996). Second, because the permanent injunction is not issued under emergency circumstances, it does not require proof of "irreparable harm." Rather, it simply requires proof of an "inadequate legal remedy." Walgreen Co. v. Sara Creek Property Co., 966 F.2d 273 (7th Cir.1992). As you read the following case, in which the plaintiff requested a permanent injunction, notice that the court's opinion focuses exclusively on the question of whether the movant has shown "actual success on the merits." A more complete opinion (like the opinion in *Adams*) also would have discussed the questions of whether there was an inadequate remedy at law, whether the balance of hardships tipped in the plaintiff's favor, and whether the issuance of the injunction would have been harmful to the public interest.

3. Permanent Injunctions

FORCE v. PIERCE CITY R–VI SCHOOL DISTRICT

United States District Court, Western District of Missouri, 1983.
570 F.Supp. 1020.

ROSS T. ROBERTS, DISTRICT JUDGE.

Nichole Force, a thirteen year old female student enrolled in the eighth grade at the Pierce City, Missouri, Junior High School, seeks an injunction which would allow her to compete for a place on the school's eighth grade football team. Her claims are relatively simple and straightforward: that defendants' refusal to accord her that opportunity is based—and based solely—upon the fact that she is a female rather than a male, and that a sex-based determination of that sort violates her right to the equal protection of the laws under the Fourteenth Amendment, and in turn 42 U.S.C. § 1983.

Named as defendants are the Pierce City R–VI School District, which operates and administers the Pierce City Junior High School facility, the Superintendent of the School District (John A. Williams), and the Principal of the School (Raymond Dykens). * * *

The matter was tried to the Court, in a full plenary hearing,[1] on August 1, 2 and 3, 1983. * * *

I. BACKGROUND

Pierce City Junior High School is a public school facility made up of the seventh, eighth and ninth grades. It is operated as a component part of the defendant Pierce City R–VI School District ("the District"). The District itself is an entity established under state law, *see generally*

---

1. The parties have agreed that the trial of this action on the merits should be advanced and consolidated with the hearing on plaintiff's motion for a preliminary injunction. *See* Rule 65(a)(2), Fed.R.Civ.P.

ORDERED that defendant John A. Williams, as Superintendent of Schools of the Pierce City R–VI School District, and defendant Raymond Dykens, as Principal of the Pierce City Junior High School, and defendant Pierce City R–VI School District, and each of them shall be and are hereby permanently restrained and enjoined from refusing to allow Nichole Force to compete for membership on the Pierce City Junior High School eighth grade interscholastic football team on the same basis that males are allowed to compete, during the time that she shall be enrolled in or eligible for enrollment in the eighth grade at such school facility * * *.

NOTES

1. In the decades since *Force* was handed down, the federal courts have continued to grant injunctive relief requiring that junior and senior high school girls be afforded the opportunity to try out for boys' teams in contact sports. *See, e.g.,* Lantz v. Ambach, 620 F.Supp. 663 (S.D.N.Y.1985) (football). They also have held that it is a denial of equal protection to fail to provide adequate protective equipment, such as shoulder pads, on the basis of sex. *See, e.g.,* Elborough v. Evansville Community School Dist., 636 F.Supp.2d 812, 823–25 (W.D. Wis. 2009)(football). At the end of the twentieth century, approximately 800 girls played high school football, with most of them playing the position of placekicker. B. Glenn George, *Fifty/Fifty: Ending Sex Segregation in School Sports*, 63 Ohio St. L.J. 1107, 1146 (2002). During the early part of the twenty-first century, that number doubled with over 1,600 girls playing on high school football teams nationwide in 2003. Adam S. Darowski, Note, *For Kenny, Who Wanted to Play Women's Field Hockey*, 12 Duke J. Gender L. & Policy 153, 153 n.3 (2005). The federal courts also have continued to deny injunctions to boys who have petitioned to join girls' teams. *See, e.g.,* Clark v. Arizona Interscholastic Ass'n, 886 F.2d 1191 (9th Cir.1989) (volleyball); Kleczek v. Rhode Island Interscholastic League, Inc., 768 F.Supp. 951 (D.R.I.1991) (field hockey). At the same time, in cases where junior or senior high schools have created separate teams for boys and girls in the same sport, the federal courts often have refused to enjoin prohibitions on girls joining boys' teams. *See* Karen Tokarz, Women, Sports and the Law: A Comprehensive Research Guide to Sex Discrimination in Sports (1986); Jane C. Avery, Annotation, *Validity, Under Federal Law, of Sex Discrimination in Athletics*, 23 A.L.R. Fed. 664 (1975). For a discussion of the relationship between the Fourteenth Amendment and Title IX, see Dana Robinson, Comment, *A League of Their Own: Do Women Want Sex–Segregated Sports?*, 9 J. Contemp. Legal Issues 321 (1998).

2. The Equal Protection Clause also has been invoked successfully by plaintiffs who were seeking to obtain the issuance of permanent injunctions prohibiting junior and senior high schools from requiring girls to play half-court basketball when boys were permitted to play full-court basketball. *See, e.g.,* Dodson v. Arkansas Activities Ass'n, 468 F.Supp. 394 (E.D.Ark.1979). *See generally* Patricia A. Cain, *Women, Race, and Sports: Life Before Title IX*, 4 J. Gender Race & Just. 337 (2001); Polly J. Price, *Lessons from "Small Cases:" Reflections on* Dodson v. Arkansas Activities Association, 27 U. Ark. Little Rock L. Rev. 367 (2005)(a tribute to United States Circuit Judge Richard

Sheppard Arnold, written by one of his clerks who first learned to play basketball under half-court rules, and who would not have had the opportunity to play full-court basketball in both high school and college but for *Dodson*).

3. The plaintiff in *Force* requested a preliminary injunction in October of 1982. How might she have benefited from requesting provisional injunctive relief in July or August of 1982?

SECTION 2.   PROVISIONAL INJUNCTIONS

A.   PROCEDURES AND STANDARDS FOR ISSUING TEMPORARY RESTRAINING ORDERS

The first four cases in this section focus on the procedures for issuing an ex parte temporary restraining order. The last case illustrates the traditional standard that the federal courts have developed for determining whether to issue provisional injunctive relief.

MARQUETTE v. MARQUETTE

Court of Appeals of Oklahoma, 1984.
686 P.2d 990.

REYNOLDS, JUDGE:

Jeff L. Marquette appeals trial court's orders of October 13, 1982, and November 19, 1982, restraining him from abusing, injuring, threatening or harassing his ex-wife, Julie M. Marquette. Trial court entered both orders under the Protection from Domestic Abuse Act, 22 O.S.Supp.1983 § 60 *et seq.* [The statute provides that a victim of domestic abuse, stalking, or harassment may file a petition for a protective order with the district court in the county in which the victim resides.]

Appellant and Appellee were divorced on September 10, 1982. Appellee was given custody of the parties' two young sons. On October 13, 1982, Appellee filed a petition for [a] protective order.[2] She gave the following reasons for requesting the protective order:

> continued harassment & assault following the divorce granted Sept. 10, 1982. Throws children's clothes, shoes, toys, & children at me. Verbal threats are made to me in front of the children. I am afraid of being harmed as I have in the past. And afraid of emotional damage these scenes are doing to my children.

Appellee requested the court to enter an emergency ex parte order.[3] The court granted her request, and set a show cause hearing on November 1,

---

2. 22 O.S.Supp.1983 § 60.2 provides a sample petition. Tulsa County used this sample and provided it to Appellee. This form simplified the petitioning process since, for the most part, Appellee was able to check the appropriate box.

3. 22 O.S.Supp.1983 § 60.2(B) (Petition for Protective Order):

  5. (Check A or B)

1982. The ex parte order prohibited Appellant from abusing, injuring, visiting, communicating with, or threatening Appellee. It also instructed Appellant not to abuse or injure the minor children.

Appellant filed a demurrer and motion to dismiss on October 26, 1982. The hearing was passed by agreement from November 1 to November 3, 1982. On November 3, 1982, trial court modified the ex parte order to provide Appellant with specific visitation hours. Full hearing was again continued until November 19, 1982. * * * Following trial on November 19, 1982, trial court entered a mutual protective order.[5]

[Although the temporary restraining order was no longer in effect, the appellate court held that the case was not moot because "[d]omestic violence has wide-ranging ramification[9]" and therefore the appeal presented a question of "broad public interest."]

* * *

Appellant contends [the] trial court erred by overruling his demurrer to Appellee's petition for protective order. He alleges the language of the petition does not rise to the level of domestic abuse as defined by statute. The Act defines domestic abuse as: "a. causing or attempting to cause serious physical harm, or b. threatening another with imminent serious physical harm * * *." 22 O.S.Supp.1983 § 60.1. * * * Appellee's petition alleged harassment, assault, throwing children, verbal threats, and fear of harm. "Serious bodily injury" has been defined as that which would "give rise to apprehension of danger to life, to health or limbs." Hall v. State, 309 P.2d 1096 (Okl.Crim.App.1957). We will not give a "blood and guts" interpretation to the requirement of "serious physical harm". We find the language of the petition was sufficient to withstand a general demurrer.

* * *

Appellant's final assertion of error alleges denial of due process under the October 13 ex parte order. The due process guarantee is intended to protect an individual against arbitrary acts of the government. Appellant was effectively denied his right to visit his children from October 13 until

---

(A) ☐ The victim is in immediate and present danger of abuse from the defendant and an emergency ex parte order is necessary to protect the victim from serious harm. The plaintiff requests the following relief in the emergency ex parte order: (check one or more)

☐ order the defendant not to abuse or injure the victim.

☐ order the defendant not to visit, assault, molest, harass or otherwise interfere with the victim.

☐ order the defendant not to threaten the victim.

☐ order the defendant to leave the residence located at _____ on or before _____.

☐ _____(describe other relief that plaintiff requests).

(B) ☐ The plaintiff does not request an emergency ex parte order.

5. The Act does not specifically provide for such an order, nor was it requested by Appellant at trial. However, since Appellee does not raise the question of its validity as to her, we will not consider it on appeal.

9. Taub, *Ex Parte Proceedings in Domestic Violence Situations: Alternative Frameworks for Constitutional Scrutiny*, 9 Hofstra L. Rev. 95 (1980) * * *.

November 3. This occurred because he could not communicate with his ex-wife, the custodial parent.

This interference with Appellant's visitation rights is significant. Appellant alleges this right has been violated without procedural due process. We do not take the interference with parental visitation lightly, but we note that such interference can only occur for a total of ten days prior to the deprived parent receiving a full hearing. This infringement must be balanced against the government's interest in issuing the order and the risk of erroneous deprivation under existing procedures.[23]

The State's interest in providing this protection to the victims of domestic abuse is apparent. The legislation promotes the health, safety and general welfare of its citizens. Domestic violence has become a problem of considerable magnitude.

The consequences of allowing battering to continue can be serious. Experts believe that domestic violence is likely to escalate in cyclical fashion, at times resulting in the woman's death. Women caught in the cycle of abuse may, in the process of defending themselves, kill their assailant. Children exposed to such patterns of violence not only may suffer immediate emotional distress, but also may reproduce their parents' behavior patterns as adults.[24]

Temporary restraining orders issued without notice have survived constitutional attack. *See, e.g.*, United States v. Spilotro, 680 F.2d 612 (9th Cir.1982); State v. B Bar Enterprises, Inc., 133 Ariz. 99, 649 P.2d 978 (Ariz.1982). The Act provides the following procedures prior to issuance of the ex parte order. An ex parte order is not issued unless good cause is shown by petitioner at a hearing held by the court. Only then may the court issue such order as is necessary to protect the victim from immediate and present danger of domestic abuse. Under the 1983 version of the Act, a hearing must be held within ten days after the petition is filed regardless of whether an ex parte order has been issued. Although there is always some chance of erroneous deprivation, the trial court will have opportunity to judge the credibility of the petitioner prior to issuing the order. The court may be able to see first hand the evidence of domestic violence.

Carefully considering all the above factors, we find the procedural safeguards employed under the Act prior to the issuance of an ex parte order, coupled with the state's interest in securing immediate protection for abused victims, of sufficient weight to meet Appellant's due process challenge.

* * *

---

23. Mathews v. Eldridge, 424 U.S. 319, 96 S.Ct. 893, 47 L.Ed.2d 18 (1976); State *ex rel.* Williams v. Marsh, 626 S.W.2d 223 (Mo.1982) (en banc) [(issuance of ex parte protective order was not denial of due process)]; *see also* Taub, *supra* note 9, at 107.

24. Taub, *supra* note 9, p. 96 (footnotes omitted) * * *.

We hold the trial court properly exercised its authority under the Act. Affirmed.

NOTES

1. State family law courts traditionally have issued injunctions against acts of domestic violence, harassment and molestation, but usually only in connection with divorce and related proceedings. *See, e.g.,* Keller v. Keller, 158 N.W.2d 694 (N.D.1968). The Oklahoma statute in *Marquette,* by contrast, authorizes a court of general jurisdiction to protect a broader class of victims under a wider range of circumstances.

2. In response to a nationwide concern about domestic violence, every state has enacted legislation similar to the Oklahoma statute authorizing ex parte and permanent protective orders. *See* Catherine F. Klein & Leslie Orloff, *Providing Legal Protection for Battered Women: An Analysis of State Statutes and Case Law,* 21 Hofstra L. Rev. 801 (1993). For an analysis of the effectiveness of this legislation, see Kim Kinports & Karla Fischer, *Orders of Protection in Domestic Violence Cases: An Empirical Assessment of the Reform Statutes,* 2 Tex. J. Women & L. 163 (1993). *See generally* Frederica L. Lehrman, Domestic Violence Practice and Procedure (1996). For a discussion of the interstate enforcement of protection orders, see Emily J. Sack, *Domestic Violence Across State Lines: The Full Faith and Credit Clause, Congressional Power, and Interstate Enforcement of Protection Orders,* 98 Nw. U. L. Rev. 827 (2004). For a recommendation that "domestic violence" be defined broadly to encompass not only serious physical harm, but also serious psychological, emotional, and economic abuse, see Margaret E. Johnson, *Redefining Harm, Reimagining Remedies, and Reclaiming Domestic Violence Law,* 42 U.C. Davis L. Rev. 1107 (2009).

3. Although there have been relatively few procedural due process challenges to statutes authorizing the issuance of ex parte protective orders, all of the reported cases have upheld the facial constitutionality of such statutes. *See, e.g.,* Baker v. Baker, 494 N.W.2d 282 (Minn.1992); Schramek v. Bohren, 145 Wis.2d 695, 429 N.W.2d 501 (Wis.App.1988). Some courts, including the *Marquette* court, have applied the *Mathews* balancing test when considering the procedural due process question. Other courts have applied the more specific test set forth in Mitchell v. W.T. Grant Co., 416 U.S. 600, 94 S.Ct. 1895, 40 L.Ed.2d 406 (1974), which requires "either a pre-deprivation hearing or at least four minimum procedural safeguards: participation by a judicial officer; a prompt post-deprivation hearing; verified petitions or affidavits containing detailed allegations based on personal knowledge; and risk of immediate and irreparable harm." Blazel v. Bradley, 698 F.Supp. 756, 764 (W.D.Wis.1988) (upholding the facial constitutionality of Wisconsin's domestic abuse statute, but ruling that the statute was unconstitutional "as applied" to the facts of the case because the plaintiff, who had alleged that the defendant had hit her two weeks earlier, had not alleged a risk of "immediate" or "imminent" physical harm).

IN RE VUITTON ET FILS S.A.

United States Court of Appeals, Second Circuit, 1979.
606 F.2d 1.

Before MOORE, FRIENDLY and MESKILL, CIRCUIT JUDGES.

PER CURIAM:

This is a petition by Vuitton et Fils S.A. ("Vuitton") for a writ of mandamus directed to the United States District Court for the Southern District of New York, Charles L. Brieant, Jr., Judge, instructing the court to issue [an] ex parte temporary restraining order in an action entitled Vuitton et Fils S.A. v. Dame Belt & Bag Co., Inc., and Morty Edelstein, 79 Civ. 0262. In our judgment, we are justified in asserting mandamus jurisdiction in this peculiar case * * *.

Vuitton is a French company * * * engaged in the sale and distribution of expensive leather goods, including a wide variety of luggage, handbags, wallets and jewelry cases, all under a trademark registered with the United States Patent Office in 1932. This trademark, a distinctive arrangement of initials and designs, has been extensively advertised over the years. Recently, Vuitton has had the misfortune of having to compete with New York area retailers who have been able to obtain counterfeit Vuitton merchandise from various sources and who sell that merchandise at prices considerably below those charged by Vuitton for the authentic items. This, of course, has not pleased Vuitton and, in response, it has commenced 84 actions nationwide and 53 actions in this Circuit charging trademark infringement and unfair competition. * * *

On January 16, 1979, Vuitton filed a complaint in the district court seeking preliminary and permanent injunctions against the defendants * * * and requesting damages. The gist of the complaint was that the defendants had infringed Vuitton's trademark and engaged in unfair competition by offering for sale luggage and handbags identical in appearance to those merchandised by Vuitton. Accompanying the complaint was an affidavit by Vuitton's attorney explaining why service of process had not been effected and requesting that an ex parte temporary restraining order be issued against the defendants under Fed.R.Civ.P. 65(b). Vuitton explains its need for an ex parte order in the following terms:

> Vuitton's experience, based upon the 84 actions it has brought and the hundreds of other investigations it has made ... has led to the conclusion that there exist various closely-knit distribution networks for counterfeit Vuitton products. * * *

> Vuitton's experience in several of the earliest filed cases also taught it that once one member of this community of counterfeiters learned that he had been identified by Vuitton and was about to be enjoined from continuing his illegal enterprise, he would immediately transfer his inventory to another counterfeit seller, whose identity would be unknown to Vuitton.

... [I]n most Vuitton cases defendants maintain few, if any, records. The now too familiar refrain from a "caught counterfeiter" is "I bought only a few pieces from a man I never saw before and whom I have never seen again. All my business was in cash. I do not know how to locate the man from whom I bought and I cannot remember the identity of the persons to whom I sold."

... If after Vuitton has identified a counterfeiter with an inventory of fake merchandise, that counterfeiter is permitted to dispose of that merchandise with relative impunity *after* he learns of the imminence of litigation but *before* he is enjoined from doing so, Vuitton's trademark enforcement program will be stymied and the community of counterfeiters will be permitted to continue to play its "shell game" at great expense and damage to Vuitton.

A hearing on this application was held the next day, January 17, 1979, before Judge Brieant. Counsel for Vuitton explained: "All we seek this Court to do but for a few hours is to maintain the status quo, namely the defendants' inventory of counterfeit Vuitton merchandise." Vuitton also explained that, if notice of the pending litigation was required, "by the time this Court entered an order, most if not all of the merchandise would have been removed from the premises." Because Vuitton was capable of giving the defendants in this action notice, however, a matter readily conceded by Vuitton, the district court declined to grant the request. * * *

Rule 65(b) provides in relevant part as follows:

A temporary restraining order may be granted without written or oral notice to the adverse party or his attorney only if (1) it clearly appears from specific facts shown by affidavit or by the verified complaint that immediate and irreparable injury, loss, or damage will result to the applicant before the adverse party or his attorney can be heard in opposition, and (2) the applicant's attorney certifies to the court in writing the efforts, if any, which have been made to give the notice and the reasons supporting his claim that notice should not be required.

As explained by the Supreme Court in Granny Goose Foods, Inc. v. Teamsters, 415 U.S. 423, 438–39, 94 S.Ct. 1113, 39 L.Ed.2d 435 (1974), "[t]he stringent restrictions imposed ... on the availability of ex parte temporary restraining orders reflect the fact that our entire jurisprudence runs counter to the notion of court action taken before reasonable notice and an opportunity to be heard has been granted both sides of a dispute. Ex parte temporary restraining orders are no doubt necessary in certain circumstances, ... but under federal law they should be restricted to serving their underlying purpose of preserving the status quo and preventing irreparable harm just so long as is necessary to hold a hearing, and no longer." * * * *See generally Developments in the Law—Injunctions*, 78 Harv.L.Rev. 994, 1060 (1965) (footnote omitted):

The ex parte temporary restraining order is indispensable to the commencement of an action when it is the sole method of preserving a state of affairs in which the court can provide effective final relief. Immediate action is vital when imminent destruction of the disputed property, its removal beyond the confines of the state, or its sale to an innocent third party is threatened. In these situations, giving the defendant notice of the application for an injunction could result in an inability to provide any relief at all.

[A]lthough this Court has "frowned upon temporary restraining orders issued without even telephoned notice," * * * there are occasions when such orders are to be countenanced. In our judgment, this case is just such an occasion.

* * * In a trademark infringement case such as this, a substantial likelihood of confusion constitutes, in and of itself, irreparable injury sufficient to satisfy the requirements of Rule 65(b) (1). *See* P. Daussa Corp. v. Sutton Cosmetics (P.R.) Inc., 462 F.2d 134, 136 (2d Cir. 1972) * * *. Here, we believe that such a likelihood of product confusion exists. The allegedly counterfeit Vuitton merchandise is virtually identical to the genuine items. Indeed, the very purpose of the individuals marketing the cheaper items is to confuse the buying public into believing it is buying the true article.

We also believe that Vuitton has demonstrated sufficiently why notice should not be required in a case such as this one. If notice is required, that notice all too often appears to serve only to render fruitless further prosecution of the action. This is precisely contrary to the normal and intended role of "notice," and it is surely not what the authors of the rule either anticipated or intended.

Accordingly, we hold that, when a proper showing is made, such as was made in this case, and when the rule is otherwise complied with, a plaintiff is entitled to have issued an ex parte temporary restraining order. Such an order should be narrow in scope and brief in its duration. The petition is granted.

RENO AIR RACING ASSOCIATION, INC. v. McCORD

United States Court of Appeals, Ninth Circuit, 2006.
452 F.3d 1126.

McKEOWN, CIRCUIT JUDGE.

* * *

This appeal highlights the sometimes routine fashion in which TROs are issued to unsuspecting parties, who, lacking fair notice of the prohibited conduct, may unwittingly invite a contempt citation. * * *

BACKGROUND

Since 1964, Reno Air has operated the National Championship Air Races, an annual air show at the Reno/Stead Airport in Nevada. The show features airplanes that race around pylons [1]for cash prizes and stunt aircraft that perform acrobatic maneuvers. Each year, approximately 80,000 to 90,000 people attend the event, which generates millions of dollars of revenue. Reno Air extensively advertises and promotes the event through a variety of print and electronic media, referring to it both as "Reno Air Races" and "National Championship Air Races."

Since commencement of the races in 1964, Reno Air has used a logo featuring a checkered pylon with two airplanes circling it ("pylon logo") to identify the event and merchandise promoting the event. Reno Air is the registered owner of two federal trademarks, numbers 1,322,146 and 1,371,797, for the "pylon logo;" the marks are identical, although one is a trademark and the other a service mark. The marks have been registered with the United States Patent and Trademark Office since 1985 * * * . The trademark registrations are in four classes that include entertainment services, printed materials, cloth patches, caps and t-shirts. Through special licensing agreements, Reno Air permits vendors situated inside the gates of the show to sell merchandise bearing the trademarks.

McCord owns Western Sales Distributing Company, a sole proprietorship. Between 1999 and 2002, McCord sold merchandise, including t-shirts, caps and mugs, depicting the term "Reno Air Races" and artwork containing images of at least one airplane and a pylon, from booths located just outside of the gates of the air races. In 1999, McCord sold approximately $4,433 worth of such merchandise; in 2000, he sold $10,152; in 2001, $3,174; and in 2002, $9,152.

Sometime in 2000, McCord received a letter and telephone call from Reno Air's attorney, who objected to McCord's sale of merchandise at the air races. The following year, a representative from Reno Air advised McCord that his sale of such merchandise violated Reno Air's rights. * * *

On September 13, 2002, Reno Air filed a complaint in the District of Nevada, alleging McCord's infringement of the federally registered "pylon logo" mark in violation of 15 U.S.C. § 1114(1)(a) and infringement of the unregistered "Reno Air Races" mark in violation of 15 U.S.C. § 1125(a). That same day, Reno Air also filed an ex parte application for a TRO pursuant to Rule 65(b) and a motion for a preliminary injunction. Reno Air's TRO application stated that notice to McCord was unnecessary because "of the immediate and irreparable harm that will occur if the restraining order is not immediately issued ... and because of the significant risk that [McCord] may leave the Reno/Stead Airport area and destroy or conceal [his] infringing merchandise once [he] receive[s] notice of the lawsuit."

The district court granted the application after a telephonic hearing, and issued an ex parte TRO that prohibited McCord from engaging in the following activities:

---

1. A "pylon" is defined as a "post or tower marking a prescribed course of flight for an airplane." * * *

(1) making, manufacturing, [or] distributing * * * any goods, packaging or any other items which bear the trademarks set forth in Exhibit F to Mr. Houghton's declaration, or any confusingly similar variations thereof;

(2) disposing of, destroying, moving, relocating or transferring any and all goods and other items ... bearing the trademarks set forth in Exhibit F to Mr. Houghton's declaration, or any confusingly similar variations thereof * * *.

"Exhibit F," to which the TRO referred extensively, contained a picture of a t-shirt design sold by McCord that depicted a stylized image of two airplanes and a checkered pylon, with the words "Reno Air Races" underneath.

Reno Air served McCord with the TRO late in the afternoon on September 13, 2002, the Friday of the air races weekend. McCord was— outside the gates of the show when he was served and was packing up for the day. He did not read the TRO until later that evening and over the weekend had difficulty locating an attorney with whom he could consult about the meaning of the injunction. Even after the weekend, finding an attorney in the Reno area who did had not have a conflict of interest as a result of a prior relationship with Reno Air was not easy. McCord finally located an attorney in Carson City, Nevada.

As of Saturday, September 14, 2002, McCord stopped selling t-shirts containing the exact design pictured in Exhibit F. McCord continued to sell merchandise containing the term "Reno Air Races" and depicting a pylon and airplanes until the end of the air show on Sunday, September 15, 2002.

In April 2003, more than six months after the show closed, Reno Air filed a motion for contempt and claimed that McCord violated the TRO. The district court denied this application without prejudice to its renewal at trial. A two-day bench trial was held in February 2004. The district court entered a final judgment in April 2004.

The district court found that McCord infringed "Reno Air Races" and the "pylon logo," which were protectable marks under the Lanham Act. The district court awarded Reno Air $6,727 in damages arising from the sale of infringing merchandise and permanently enjoined McCord from "making, manufacturing, [or] distributing ... any goods, packaging or any other items which bear the Marks, or any confusingly similar variations thereof."[4] The district court also found McCord in civil contempt for continuing to sell infringing merchandise after being served with the TRO on September 13, 2002. The district court imposed contempt sanctions in

---

4. The district court declined to award attorneys' fees under 15 U.S.C. § 1117(a), which provides that "[t]he court in exceptional cases may award reasonable attorney fees to the prevailing party." The district court reasoned that the evidence did not justify a finding that this was an "exceptional case" under § 1117(a)—i.e., a case in which the infringement was "willful, deliberate, knowing or malicious." Earthquake Sound Corp. v. Bumper Indus., 352 F.3d 1210, 1217 (9th Cir.2003).

an amount equal to Reno Air's reasonable attorneys' fees and costs in connection with the TRO and contempt motion.

ANALYSIS

I. Contempt

* * *

"Civil contempt in this context consists of a party's disobedience to a specific and definite court order by failure to take all reasonable steps within the party's power to comply." In re Dual–Deck Video Cassette Recorder Antitrust Litig., 10 F.3d 693, 695 (9th Cir.1993).[5] The contempt " 'need not be willful,' " *id.* * * *; however, a person should not be held in contempt if his action "appears to be based on a good faith and reasonable interpretation of the court's order." *Id.* * * *

A. Ex Parte Proceeding

We consider first whether the TRO was properly granted ex parte without notice. Rule 65(b) provides, in relevant part:

> A [TRO] may be granted without written or oral notice to the adverse party ... *only if* (1) it clearly appears ... that immediate and irreparable injury, loss, or damage will result to the applicant before the adverse party or that party's attorney can be heard in opposition, and (2) the applicant's attorney certifies to the court in writing the efforts, if any, which have been made to give the notice and the reasons supporting the claim that notice should not be required. * * *

Fed.R.Civ.P. 65(b) (emphasis added). * * *

* * *[C]ourts have recognized very few circumstances justifying the issuance of an ex parte TRO. For example, an ex parte TRO may be appropriate "where notice to the adverse party is impossible * * * because a known party cannot be located in time for a hearing." Am. Can Co. v. Mansukhani, 742 F.2d 314, 322 (7th Cir.1984). Obviously, this exception is inapplicable as Reno Air knew exactly where McCord was—outside of the air show gates—and thus, never suggested that McCord could not be found or that notice would have been, in any way, "impossible."

In cases where notice could have been given to the adverse party, courts have recognized "a very narrow band of cases in which ex parte orders are proper because notice to the defendant would render fruitless the further prosecution of the action." *Am. Can Co.,* 742 F.2d at 322. In the trademark arena, such cases include situations where an alleged infringer is likely to dispose of the infringing goods before the hearing. *See* In the Matter of Vuitton et Fils S.A., 606 F.2d 1, 5 (2d Cir.1979)

---

5. McCord's contention that the district court wrongly characterized the contempt as "civil" rather than "criminal" is without merit. [The purpose of criminal contempt is to punish, and the sanction is a fixed fine or a fixed jail term.] Where the purpose of contempt is "remedial, i.e. to compensate for the costs of the contemptuous conduct or to coerce future compliance with the court's order, the contempt order is civil." Portland Feminist Women's Health Ctr. v. Advocates for Life, Inc., 877 F.2d 787, 790 (9th Cir.1989). * * *

(*"Vuitton "*). To justify an ex parte proceeding on this latter ground, "the applicant must do more than assert that the adverse party would dispose of evidence if given notice." First Tech. Safety Sys., Inc. v. Depinet, 11 F.3d 641, 650 (6th Cir.1993). "[P]laintiffs must show that defendants would have disregarded a direct court order and disposed of the goods within the time it would take for a hearing ... [and] must support such assertions by showing that the adverse party has a history of disposing of evidence or violating court orders or that persons similar to the adverse party have such a history." *Id.* at 650–51; *see also Vuitton,* 606 F.2d at 4–5.

* * *

Reno Air's TRO application and supporting evidence can be described as thin and barebones at best. The application stated that the TRO "must issue without notice ... because of the significant risk that Defendant may leave the Reno/Stead Airport area and destroy or conceal [his] infringing merchandise once [he] receive[s] notice of the lawsuit." The only "evidence" offered to support this assertion was a declaration from Reno Air's counsel that "[i]n [his] experience, this is a common occurrence when dealing with infringers at one time famous events such as the 'Reno Air Races' and it is well-recognized in the case law." This conclusory statement from counsel hardly qualified as evidence and certainly did not link the TRO application to McCord. * * * Reno Air offered no support that there was a "significant risk" that McCord, who had been working in the Reno area for many years, "may leave the Reno/Stead Airport area." Were a single conclusory statement by counsel about infringers sufficient to meet the dictates of Rule 65, then ex parte orders without notice would be the norm and this practice would essentially gut Rule 65's notice requirements.

B.   Specificity Requirement

The TRO was also deficient for lack of specificity. Rule 65(d) requires that any injunction or restraining order be "specific in terms" and describe "in reasonable detail, and not by reference to the complaint or other document, the act or acts sought to be restrained." Fed.R.Civ.P. 65(d). "If an injunction does not clearly describe prohibited or required conduct, it is not enforceable by contempt." Gates v. Shinn, 98 F.3d 463, 468 (9th Cir.1996). As the Supreme Court explained in Int'l Longshoremen's Ass'n. v. Philadelphia Marine Trade Ass'n, 389 U.S. 64, 88 S.Ct. 201, 19 L.Ed.2d 236 (1967):

> The judicial contempt power is a potent weapon. When it is founded upon a decree too vague to be understood, it can be a deadly one. Congress responded to that danger by requiring that a federal court frame its orders so that those who must obey them will know what the court intends to require and what it means to forbid.

Id. at 76, 88 S.Ct. 201 * * *. Thus, we look to the language of the TRO to determine if it provided McCord with fair and well-defined notice of the prohibited conduct. * * *

The TRO enjoined McCord from making, distributing or disposing of "items which bear the trademarks set forth in Exhibit F to Mr. Houghton's declaration, or any confusingly similar variations thereof." McCord suggests that the TRO's reference to an outside document—Exhibit F— automatically violated Rule 65(d). Although a number of our sister circuits read the "no reference" requirement strictly,[6] we have permitted incorporation by reference in certain limited scenarios, for example, where the referenced document is "physically attached to the [order] itself." State of California v. Campbell, 138 F.3d 772, 783 (9th Cir.1998) * * *.

Here, the district court noted that Exhibit F was "made a part of the [TRO] and provided to McCord at the time that the order was served on him." Thus, while ordinarily the TRO should not incorporate by reference another document, * * * the reference to the attached Exhibit F does not, in and of itself, invalidate the contempt finding. We emphasize, however, that incorporation by reference should be the rare exception rather than the rule, and district courts should be particularly cautious where the injunctive order is issued at the outset of litigation, before the receiving party has acquired a context for understanding the referenced document and the subject matter of the dispute. The language of Rule 65 is exacting and we underscore that the narrow exceptions do not merit expansion, and certainly not in this case.

More problematic in this case is the fact that neither the TRO nor Exhibit F clearly identified and described the "trademarks" at issue. The operative language of the TRO did not reference the trademark registrations and curiously did not describe the marks themselves. The referenced attachment, Exhibit F, simply contained a copy of a t-shirt design sold by McCord. * * * Nothing in Exhibit F identified what trademarks were contained in Exhibit F. Looking at this t-shirt design, one is hard pressed to know what trademarks are referenced in the order, whether the "trademarks" invoked in the TRO referred to the t-shirt, the design as a whole, the phrase "Reno Air Races," * * * the checkered pylon, one or more airplanes, the pylon plus one or more airplanes, or some other combination.

In addition to the unexplained "trademarks," McCord points to the ambiguity of the phrase "confusingly similar variations thereof." If a reader of the TRO were left in the dark about what trademarks were covered, then surely bootstrapping the order to include "confusingly similar variations thereof" would leave the reader's head spinning with more confusion. "Variations of what?" one might ask. Because the under-

---

6. *See e.g.,* H.K. Porter Co. v. Nat'l Friction Prods. Corp., 568 F.2d 24, 27 (7th Cir.1977) (holding that incorporation by reference was a "serious and decisive" error that precluded a finding of contempt) * * *.

lying order failed to identify the trademarks with sufficient specificity, the order was hardly enforceable as to the "variations thereof" language.

* * * The recipient of a TRO, which usually takes effect immediately, should not be left guessing as to what conduct is enjoined. The benchmark for clarity and fair notice is not lawyers and judges, who are schooled in the nuances of trademark law. The "specific terms" and "reasonable detail" mandated by Rule 65(d) should be understood by the lay person, who is the target of the injunction. This is a circumstance, among many in the legal field, that cries out for "plain English."

Here, the TRO was issued the same day the action commenced, and the parties had no prior litigation history. Although they had engaged in limited communications, Reno Air could not even find the letter it purportedly sent to McCord. Given this backdrop and the failure of the TRO (and Exhibit F) to clearly identify the trademarks at issue, the TRO's prohibition—i.e. enjoining infringement of "the trademarks set forth in Exhibit F ... or any confusingly similar variations thereof"—would certainly have left a lay person scratching his head in confusion. The TRO failed to meet even the most minimal fair notice requirement.

As the TRO was improperly issued ex parte and failed to describe the prohibited conduct with specificity, the order cannot serve as the foundation for a finding of civil contempt. * * *

II.   Trademark Infringement

A claim of trademark infringement under § 1114(1)(a) of the Lanham Act requires a trademark holder to demonstrate: (1) ownership of a valid mark (i.e., a protectable interest), and (2) that the alleged infringer's use of the mark " 'is likely to cause confusion, or to cause mistake, or to deceive' " consumers. * * *

* * *

B.   LIKELIHOOD OF CONFUSION

The core element of trademark infringement is whether customers are likely to be confused about the source or sponsorship of the products. * * *

* * *

McCord * * * argues that the district court erred because the airplane/ pylon motif used in his merchandise does not resemble Reno Air's "pylon logo." In his brief, McCord summarizes this argument as follows: "Now Appellate court, please compare these two. They don't look anything alike, do they?"

When viewed in isolation, it is true that there is no identical resemblance between the airplane/pylon motif in McCord's designs and Reno Air's registered "pylon logo." For example, the airplanes in McCord's design contain greater detail than the plane silhouettes in the "pylon logo," and unlike the "pylon logo," the pylon in McCord's design has a flag above it and is not centered between the planes. However, * * * McCord sold merchandise featuring the airplane/pylon motif alongside the terms "Reno Air Races," outside the gates of the air show, in close proximity to the sale of official merchandise. Considering the airplane/pylon depictions in the context in which they appeared to ordinary consumers in the market-place, * * * the district court did not clearly err in finding substantial similarity. * * *

* * *

CONCLUSION

The TRO cannot support a finding of civil contempt because it was improperly issued ex parte and failed to describe the prohibited conduct with specificity. We vacate and reverse [the part of the district court's order] finding McCord in contempt for violating the TRO and imposing contempt sanctions. We affirm the judgment in all other respects.

GIL PHARMACEUTICAL CORP. v. ADVANCED GENERIC CORP.

United States District Court, Puerto Rico, 2010.
692 F. Supp.2d 212.

Besosa, District Judge.

Procedural History

The plaintiff, Gil Pharmaceutical Corporation ("Gil" or "plaintiff"), first filed this case in the Court of First Instance of the Commonwealth of Puerto Rico, Caguas Superior Division * * * . Gil alleged, *inter alia,* that defendants Advanced Generic Corporation and others ("Generic" or "defendants") violated Puerto Rico's Trademark Law * * * by selling pharmaceutical products under marks or labels confusingly similar to the markings registered by trademark to Gil. * * * Gil requested *ex parte* injunctive relief. The Puerto Rico Trademark Act provides, in pertinent part:

> When the registered owner of the mark * * * files a complaint * * * alleging that the defendant is violating his property rights on said registered mark, through * * * adoption of a mark that is so similar to that of the registered owner that it creates the probability of confusion, the court shall issue an ex parte temporary order directed to the defendant party requiring him/her to immediately paralyze, cease or desist, under admonition of contempt of court the use of the mark to which the suit refers * * * .

> * * *

> The provisional order shall provide for the holding of [an adversary] hearing within ten (10) days * * * .

P.R. Laws Ann. Tit. 10, §§ 171–171y.

On January 26, 2010, Caguas Superior Court Judge Julio A. Diaz–
Valdes granted a hearing for the following day, January 27, 2010, to
address issues related to Gil's request for provisional injunctive relief
pursuant to the Puerto Rico Trademark Act. * * * Judge Valdes * * *
notified Gil of its responsibility to serve the January 26, 2010, order on
defendants, together with the complaint and the summons, no later than
that same day at 5:00 p.m. * * *

At the January 27, 2010, hearing, Gil informed Judge Valdes that it
was unable to serve the defendants through Generic's resident agent.
* * * With only the plaintiff present, Judge Valdes held the hearing. * * *
Judge Valdes issued an *ex parte* temporary restraining order requiring
Generic (and all named defendants) "to immediately stop, cease and desist
of using in their products the name or trademark of 'Biogil' and 'Biotect
Plus'." * * * Judge Valdes also scheduled a hearing for February 4, 2010,
for defendants to show cause as to why the provisional injunctive relief
order should be vacated and why a preliminary injunction should not
issue.

On February 2, 2010, Generic filed a notice of removal to the United
States District Court for the District of Puerto Rico. * * * On February
26, 2010, Generic filed an emergency motion to set aside or dissolve the *ex
parte* temporary restraining order issued by the Caguas Superior Court.
* * * That same day, this Court issued an order requiring Gil to show
cause, no later than March 1, 2010 at 9.00 a.m., as to why the TRO should
not be dissolved or set aside. * * *

At the March 1, 2010, hearing this Court ordered: (1) the dissolution
of the January 27, 2010 TRO pursuant to Federal Rule of Civil Procedure
65; * * * (3) [and] the referral of the case to a magistrate judge for a
preliminary injunction hearing at the earliest possible date * * * .

* * *

DISCUSSION
* * *

I. *Temporal Limitations on* Ex Parte *TROs*

Although Judge Valdes set forth no explicit temporal limitation for
the *ex parte* TRO against the defendants, the Puerto Rico Trademark Act
* * * makes clear that a temporary restraining order is exactly that—
temporary—and that it is not meant to last indefinitely; rather, it is
intended to keep the status quo intact until both parties can be heard and
present information to the deciding court for a more informed and more
permanent solution. Judge Valdes, in keeping with this implied statutory
limitation, scheduled a hearing for February 4, 2010, seven days after the
TRO's enactment on January 27, 2010. The only reason the hearing did
not occur is because the case was removed to federal court on February 2,
2010.

Regardless of what may have occurred at a hearing before the Commonwealth court, once this case was removed to the Federal Court, federal law, not Commonwealth law, governed the proceedings, including management of the orders and rulings made prior to removal. *See* Granny Goose Foods, Inc. v. Bhd. of Teamsters, Local 70, 415 U.S. 423, 437, 94 S.Ct. 1113, 39 L.Ed.2d 435 (1974) * * * . According to 28 U.S.C. § 1450, whenever a case is removed to federal court "[a]ll injunctions, orders, and other proceedings had in such action prior to its removal shall remain in full force and effect until dissolved or modified by the district court." * * * Thus, even had the TRO issued by Judge Valdes remained active at the time this Court acted—more than thirty days from the TRO's enactment (a highly dubious assumption)—that order "would still have had no binding effect" on this Court's discretion. *See Granny Goose Foods,* 415 U.S. at 437.

"The Supreme Court has made clear" that "when a case is removed to federal district court, that court *must* dissolve an ex parte state court injunction or temporary restraining order—once the maximum time limits that Federal Rule of Civil Procedure 65(b) authorizes for an ex parte order have expired." Biomedical Instrument and Equip. Corp. v. Cordis Corp., 797 F.2d 16, 18 (1st Cir.1986) (citing,—*inter alia, Granny Goose Foods,* 415 U.S. at 439–40). According to Rule 65(b), an *ex parte* TRO expires "at the time after entry—not to exceed 14 days—that the court sets, unless before that time the court, for good cause, extends it for a like period or the adverse party consents to a longer extension." Fed.R.Civ.P. 65(b)(2). Further, "the reasons for an extension must be entered in the record." *Id.* The court must hear and decide an adverse party's motion to dissolve the *ex parte* TRO when that party gives two days notice to the party who obtained the order. *Id.*

II. *Affirmative Duties of Parties Seeking Injunctive Relief*

A court granting *ex parte* temporary injunctive relief is generally required by Rule 65(b) to hold a hearing on a preliminary injunction * * * . Likewise, the party requesting injunctive relief also has certain duties it must abide: "The party who obtained the restraining order must proceed with the application for a preliminary injunction when the motion therefor comes on for a hearing; if the party does not, the court must dissolve the order." * * *

During the approximately thirty days between the enactment of Gil's TRO against Generic and this Court's dissolution of that TRO pursuant to Rule 65(b), Gil failed * * * [to] take any affirmative steps to make a showing of good cause for the TRO's extension or to apply for a preliminary injunction. * * *

* * *

[O]n April 6, 2010, the magistrate judge has scheduled a preliminary injunction hearing, during which time perhaps Gil will act more aggressively in protecting its interests than it has shown thus far.

MORGAN STANLEY DW, INC. v. FRISBY

United States District Court, Northern District of Georgia, 2001.
163 F.Supp.2d 1371.

THRASH, DISTRICT JUDGE.

This is a diversity action in which the Plaintiff seeks a temporary restraining order against former employees for allegedly violating a non-solicitation agreement. * * *

I. BACKGROUND

Plaintiff Morgan Stanley[1] hired Defendants Spencer Frisby and Patrick Lovell as brokers in one of its Atlanta, Georgia offices. They were responsible for selling Morgan Stanley's financial products such as securities, commodities, financial futures, insurance, tax advantaged investments, and mutual funds. The Defendants signed employment agreements at the time they were hired by Plaintiff. The agreements included a non-solicitation covenant providing that the Defendants would not, for one year after their termination or resignation from Morgan Stanley, solicit those clients within a 100–mile radius of their north Atlanta office whom they serviced or learned about while employed by Morgan Stanley.

On Friday, August 3, 2001, both Defendants resigned from Morgan Stanley to accept a position with PaineWebber, a competing brokerage firm. Their identical letters of resignation instructed Morgan Stanley to provide their new contact information at PaineWebber to the customers with whom they had worked at Morgan Stanley. Defendants also informed Morgan Stanley that they had retained the same attorneys to represent them in any potential lawsuit brought by Morgan Stanley as a result of their resignation.

In its request for a temporary restraining order, Morgan Stanley alleged that in the few days following Defendants' resignation, Morgan Stanley discovered that: (1) the phone numbers of many of the Morgan Stanley clients whom Defendants had serviced during their employment were now incorrect in Morgan Stanley's computer database; (2) immediately after leaving Morgan Stanley, the Defendants began a swift and methodical effort to solicit, by overnight mailings, the customers with whom they did business while at Morgan Stanley; (3) over 30 Morgan Stanley customers with whom Defendants had dealings while employed by Morgan Stanley have contacted Morgan Stanley to terminate their brokerage relationship and transfer their accounts to the Defendants at Paine-Webber; and (4) Defendants' efforts at solicitation have included financial incentives to Morgan Stanley clients such as Paine Webber's agreement to pay all costs of transfer and/or reduced commissions.

Morgan Stanley viewed these actions as unlawful efforts to solicit clients in violation of a binding and legally enforceable non-solicitation

---

1. Morgan Stanley was formerly known as Dean Witter Reynolds, Inc.

agreement signed by Defendants. Plaintiff Morgan Stanley has initiated arbitration proceedings available to it under the NASD Code, and it requests that this Court restrain Defendants from continuing their unlawful conduct in the meantime. Defendants oppose the motion on the merits. They do not contest the Court's jurisdiction to issue a temporary restraining order pending arbitration.

II. INJUNCTIVE RELIEF STANDARD

"A preliminary injunction is an extraordinary and drastic remedy not to be granted until the movant clearly carries the burden of persuasion as to the four prerequisites." * * * In order to obtain a preliminary injunction, a movant must demonstrate "(1) a substantial likelihood that he will ultimately prevail on the merits; (2) that he will suffer irreparable injury unless the injunction issues; (3) that the threatened injury to the movant outweighs whatever damage the proposed injunction may cause the opposing party; and (4) that the injunction, if issued, would not be adverse to the public interest." * * * Gold Coast Publications, Inc. v. Corrigan, 42 F.3d 1336, 1343 (11th Cir.1994). The same standard applies to a request for a temporary restraining order. Ingram v. Ault, 50 F.3d 898, 900 (11th Cir.1995).

III. DISCUSSION

Plaintiff seeks a temporary restraining order pending a decision on the enforceability of a restrictive covenant signed by Defendants when they accepted employment with Morgan Stanley. * * *

* * *

A. *Irreparable Harm*

Morgan Stanley argues it is entitled to a temporary restraining order because the injury to its business caused by Defendants' solicitation of Morgan Stanley's customers is imminent and irreparable. * * * Plaintiff asserts that the loss of valuable customer relationships and good-will, which is on-going and cannot be adequately addressed by monetary damages, is sufficient to show irreparable harm to their company. * * *

Although there is some authority to support Plaintiff's position, the Court agrees with the Defendants that Morgan Stanley will not suffer irreparable harm if the request for a temporary restraining order is denied. * * *

* * *

* * * Morgan Stanley cannot demonstrate irreparable harm because any injury it may suffer due to actions allegedly taken by Defendants is compensable by the award of money damages. The United States Supreme Court has stated that the mere loss of income, no matter how great, does not constitute irreparable harm:

[I]t seems clear that the temporary loss of income, ultimately to be recovered, does not usually constitute irreparable injury ... The key word in this consideration is *irreparable*. Mere injuries, however substantial, in terms of money, time and energy necessarily expended in the absence of a stay are not enough.

Sampson v. Murray, 415 U.S. 61, 90, 94 S.Ct. 937, 39 L.Ed.2d 166 (1974) (citation omitted) (emphasis in original) [(provisional injunction reversed in an action by a probationary employee to enjoin the termination of her employment)]. Moreover, Judge Shoob of this Court denied a similar motion on these grounds. Judge Shoob, in Merrill Lynch, Pierce, Fenner & Smith, Inc. v. de Liniere, 572 F.Supp. 246 (N.D.Ga.1983), expressly rejected the argument that a brokerage firm suffers anything other than economic loss when a departing broker seeks to solicit and service his clients:

[T]he Court finds that any loss of business to Merrill Lynch may be adequately redressed with money damages for breach of contract. The only possible irreparable result would be some vaguely defined loss of business momentum but the Court finds that to be unrealistic in the securities field. The real loss is in commission revenue generated by [the departing broker] from former ... customers, and that can be readily calculated from the commissions he and his new firm derived from [those customers].

Id. at 249. The cognizable injury to brokerage firms such as Plaintiff is lost commissions. Money damages easily compensate Plaintiffs for this type of loss.

The securities industry is highly regulated. Each individual transaction is monitored electronically. Every customer transfer from Morgan Stanley is documented. Every executed trade is recorded. Every dollar earned in fees by Defendants Frisby and Lovell doing business with those customers that Morgan Stanley considers its own can be traced precisely. Any loss Morgan Stanley might suffer as a result of Defendants' departure is calculable. * * * Plaintiff has failed to demonstrate irreparable harm if a temporary restraining order is not issued.[2]

B. *Likelihood of Success on the Merits*

Morgan Stanley contends that the non-solicitation covenant Defendants signed is a legally enforceable agreement not to solicit certain of Morgan Stanley's clients. Specifically, Plaintiff argues the covenant is narrowly tailored to protect Morgan Stanley's legitimate business inter-

---

2. The Court respectfully disagrees with others who have reached a different conclusion in similar cases. *See* Merrill Lynch, Pierce, Fenner & Smith, Inc. v. Bradley, 756 F.2d 1048 (4th Cir.1985) [(holding that the balance of hardships favored the plaintiff because Merrill Lynch faced "irreparable, noncompensable harm in the loss of its customers" and the defendant "did not establish that the provisional injunction pending expedited arbitration would cause him harm")] * * *.

ests in the training it gives to its brokers and their exposure to its product lines, marketing strategies, client relationships and good will. * * *

* * *

Plaintiff is not likely to succeed on the merits because the non-solicitation clause contained in its employment contract is overbroad and unenforceable under Georgia law. Restrictive covenants against competition in employment agreements are in partial restraint of trade and, therefore, are enforced only where the restrictions are "strictly limited, both in time and geographical effect, and when the restrictions are otherwise reasonable, considering the business interests of the employer needing protection and the effect of the restrictions on the employee." Sanford v. RDA Consultants, Ltd., 244 Ga.App. 308, 310, 535 S.E.2d 321 (2000). * * * Under Georgia law, a single unreasonable provision in a restrictive covenant [in an employment contract] will void the entire contract, and courts will not "blue line" the covenant to salvage any non-offending parts. de Liniere, 572 F.Supp. at 248 n.1 * * *.

In this case, the restrictive covenant is overbroad because it prohibits Defendants from contacting not only clients that they have serviced, but anyone whose names became known to Defendants during their employment with Plaintiff. The clause does not specify any particular manner in which such names may have become known to Defendants. For example, the restrictive covenant would prohibit the Defendants from soliciting the business of clients of other Morgan Stanley brokers whose names became known to them through casual conversation at the office. Morgan Stanley has no legitimate interest in prohibiting this type of competition. Such a prohibition is an unduly strict restraint on trade, and would not pass the strict scrutiny standard enforced by the Georgia courts. * * * If the restrictive covenant is unenforceable in Georgia, Plaintiff is unlikely to succeed on the merits of its claim.

* * *

Furthermore, Morgan Stanley is estopped * * * by its unclean hands from seeking equitable relief from this Court. Equity does not permit Morgan Stanley to enforce restrictive covenants against Defendants Frisby and Lovell when it actively recruits brokers from competitors and encourages them to retain and use copies of client records to solicit the transfer of client accounts from those competitors without regard to any agreements between the brokers and the competitor.

Finally, it appears that Morgan Stanley is unlikely to succeed before the NASD arbitration panel. As long as the departing broker obeys the unwritten rules against taking original records or soliciting clients before resigning, the brokerage firms have a long record of losing arbitration proceedings. * * * Frequently, when brokerage firms do obtain court-ordered injunctive relief, the NASD panels dissolve that relief. * * *

* * *

* * * For the reasons stated above, the Court holds that Plaintiff has failed to demonstrate sufficient likelihood of success on the merits to justify issuance of a temporary restraining order.

C. Balance of the Equities

In its brief in support of its request for a temporary restraining order, Morgan Stanley does not discuss whether and how the harm to it outweighs the damage to the Defendants of the relief requested. As have others, this Court holds that the balance of the equities clearly tips in favor of Defendants and their customers. Brokerage firms can survive the denial of an injunction far more readily than their departing employees can survive its issuance. In *de Liniere,* Judge Shoob noted that if an injunction issued, the broker would be prevented from servicing the customers for whom he had worked for over two years. *de Liniere,* 572 F.Supp. at 249. Defendants in this case would similarly suffer. Prior to beginning employment with Morgan Stanley, Defendant Frisby was not licensed to sell securities. Defendant Lovell had been registered to sell securities for less than a year and, therefore, had limited experience or training. The only client base Defendants possess is that gained during their employment with Plaintiff. To deprive them of contact with their customers would "leave [them] with no client base in a business that thrives on commissions from regular clients." *Id.* The damage to Defendants Frisby and Lovell of a temporary restraining order would equal almost a complete loss of income. According to Plaintiff's website, on the other hand, Morgan Stanley operates over 700 offices in 28 countries. This year, Morgan Stanley employs over 60,000 people. * * * While this number includes both brokers and other staff, the Court is hesitant to believe that the departure of two brokers will so damage Plaintiff's business as to tip the equities into its favor. The Court holds that balance of the equities clearly favors the denial of Plaintiff's requested temporary restraining order.

D. Public Interest

Again, Plaintiff Morgan Stanley does not discuss whether issuing a temporary restraining order in this situation would further the public interest. The Court agrees with Defendants that the entry of injunctive relief is not in the public interest. The court in Prudential Securities v. Plunkett, 8 F.Supp.2d 514, 520 (E.D.Va.1998) noted that the broker-client relationship was similar to that of attorney-client or doctor-patient. Personal trust and confidence pervades each of these relationships, and "[c]lients should be free to deal with the broker of their choosing and not subjected to the turnover of their accounts to brokers associated with the firm but unfamiliar to the client, unless the client gives informed consent to the turnover." *Id.* * * * "The public has little interest in having its choice restricted to brokers *other* than the one who has served them, pending the resolution of this dispute." *de Liniere,* 572 F.Supp. at 249 (emphasis in original). In a time of market volatility, the inability of a client to consult a trusted advisor for even a single day could result in enormous financial losses to the client. This danger outweighs any injury to the Plaintiff that may occur due to the disloyalty of its former employees. Issuance of a temporary restraining order in this case is not in the public interest.

IV. CONCLUSION

For the reasons set forth above, the Motion for Temporary Restraining Order * * * is DENIED.

NOTES

1. For a case with facts that are virtually identical to those in *Frisby*, but with a totally different outcome, see Morgan Stanley DW Inc. v. Rothe, 150 F.Supp.2d 67 (D.D.C.2001) (granting plaintiff's motion for a temporary restraining order). The court held that the contract was "fully enforceable" because it contained "only modest restrictions"; that the plaintiff would suffer "irreparable harm" if the temporary restraining order were not granted because the plaintiff would lose "customer trust and goodwill"; that the balance of hardships tipped in favor of the plaintiff because "nothing in the record suggests that the defendant's 'right to earn a living' is substantially put at risk"; and that issuing an injunction would not harm the public interest because the public "has no interest in destroying contracts * * * and encouraging unethical business behavior." *Id.* at 74, 77, 78, 79.

The disparate outcomes in *Frisby* and *Rothe* may be attributable to the varying degrees of judicial hostility toward covenants not to compete in employment contracts. The history of the varying judicial attitudes regarding the enforcement of such covenants is discussed below by Judge Richard Posner:

> The English common law called such covenants "restraints of trade" and refused to enforce them unless they were adjudged "reasonable" in time and geographical scope. * * * The original rationale had nothing to do with restraint of trade in its modern, antitrust sense. It was paternalism in a culture of poverty, restricted employment, and an exiguous social safety net. The fear behind it was that workers would be tricked into agreeing to covenants that would, if enforced, propel them into destitution. * * *
>
> Later, however, the focus of concern shifted to whether a covenant not to compete might have anticompetitive consequences, since the covenant would eliminate the covenantor as a potential competitor of the covenantee within the area covered by, and during the term of, the covenant. * * *
>
> At the same time that the concerns behind judicial hostility to covenants not to compete have waned, recognition of their social value has grown. The clearest case for such a covenant is where the employee's work gives him access to the employer's trade secrets. * * *

A related function of such a covenant is to protect the employer's investment in the employee's "human capital," or earning capacity. * * * The employer may give the employee training that the employee could use to compete against the employer.

Outsource International, Inc. v. Barton, 192 F.3d 662, 669–70 (7th Cir.1999) (Posner, J., dissenting).

2. The question of whether an award of damages is an adequate legal remedy for breach of contract is discussed in Ocean Spray Cranberries, Inc. v. PepsiCo, Inc., 160 F.3d 58 (1st Cir.1998) (denying preliminary injunction to enforce exclusive distribution agreement):

> Historically, equity would not supply relief where legal remedies sufficed, and damages at law usually do provide remedies for breach of contract. * * * Modern theorists have explained why it is often "efficient" to limit the remedy to damages and exclude injunctive relief. *E.g.*, Patton v. Mid–Continent Sys., Inc., 841 F.2d 742, 750 (7th Cir.1988) (Posner, J.).
>
> Still, injunctive relief requiring performance of a contract may ordinarily be granted (if other prerequisites are met) where monetary damages will not afford complete relief. A common example is agreements involving the sale of real property; specific performance is often granted because property is considered unique. *See, e.g.*, Walgreen Co. v. Sara Creek Property Co., 966 F.2d 273, 278 (7th Cir.1992). The same principle applies where harm caused by a breach, although economic in nature, is impossible to measure accurately. *See* Ross–Simons of Warwick, Inc. v. Baccarat, Inc., 102 F.3d 12, 19 (1st Cir.1996) [(preliminary injunction granted because lost profits and goodwill were "immeasurable")].

Id. at 61. The "inadequacy of legal remedy" requirement favors legal remedies over equitable remedies. For a scholarly critique of this "hierarchy of remedies," see Douglas Laycock, The Death of the Irreparable Injury Rule (1991); Doug Rendleman, *Irreparability, Irreparably Damaged*, 90 Mich. L. Rev. 1642 (1992).

3. The Eleventh Circuit has adopted the "traditional" standard for determining whether to grant a provisional injunction, and therefore the traditional standard was applied by the trial court judge in *Frisby*. Many of the other federal circuits, however, have recognized an "alternative" standard, as illustrated by the next case.

B. PROCEDURES AND STANDARDS FOR ISSUING PRELIMINARY INJUNCTIONS

Although temporary restraining orders sometimes may be issued through the use of an ex parte procedure, preliminary injunctions may only be granted after the trial court has conducted an adversary proceeding. Federal courts have "consistently treated Rule 65 (a)(1) as mandatory and have not hesitated to dissolve preliminary injunctions issued without notice or the opportunity for a hearing on disputed questions of fact and law." Phillips v. Chas. Schreiner Bank, 894 F.2d 127, 130 (5th Cir.1990).

SAVE OUR SONORAN, INC. v. FLOWERS

United States Court of Appeals, Ninth Circuit, 2005.
408 F.3d 1113.

THOMAS, CIRCUIT JUDGE.

In this appeal, we consider the management of the waterways in Arizona's Sonoran desert. This case, of course, inevitably brings to mind the exchange between Claude Rains and Humphrey Bogart in *Casablanca* (Warner Bros.1942), which aptly distills this dispute to its essence:

Captain Renault: What in heaven's name brought you to Casablanca?

Rick: My health. I came to Casablanca for the waters.

Captain Renault: The waters? What waters? We're in the desert.

Rick: I was misinformed.

In our case, it was not Rick Blaine, but the United States Army Corps of Engineers that came to the desert for the waters. An aspiring desert developer, 56th & Lone Mountain, L.L.C. ("Lone Mountain"), sought and obtained a Clean Water Act ("CWA") dredge and fill permit from the Corps for the construction of a gated community near Phoenix. The permit was required, and the Corps' jurisdiction invoked, because water courses through the washes and arroyos of the arid development site during periods of heavy rain. The desert washes are considered navigable waters and therefore fall under the jurisdiction of the federal government. *See* 33 C.F.R. § 328.3(a)(3). [The CWA prohibits the discharge of any pollutant into navigable waters unless authorized by a CWA permit.]

At some point, a non-profit environmental organization, Save Our Sonoran ("SOS"), [whose members lived in close proximity to the proposed development,] became aware of the project. It was not, shall we say, the beginning of a beautiful friendship. SOS eventually filed this action against the Corps and Lone Mountain, alleging violations of the National Environmental Policy Act ("NEPA") and the CWA. The district court issued a preliminary injunction suspending development during the pendency of the litigation. Save Our Sonoran, Inc. v. Flowers, 227 F.Supp.2d 1111 (D.Ariz.2002). Lone Mountain appealed. * * *

[The parties did not contest the Corps' determination that the washes were navigable waters. The issue on appeal was whether the Corps' Environmental Assessment [EA] was too narrow in scope.]

I

At the center of this controversy is a 608–acre parcel of undeveloped land ("the property"), an alluvial fan containing a significant number of braided washes. The washes constitute approximately 31.3 acres—about 5% of the site. However, as the District Court found, the washes affect the entire property. Though surrounded on all four sides by other development, the property is essentially unimproved and remains undeveloped desert, albeit not in pristine condition. * * * The property was purchased from the State at a public auction by Lone Mountain's predecessor for $38.5 million.

Lone Mountain developed a plan to construct an upscale gated residential community consisting of 794 single-family homes. According to the plan, over half of the property would be maintained permanently as open space, including "the bulk of the larger washes."

Pursuant to the CWA, 33 U.S.C. § 1344, Lone Mountain applied for a Section 404 permit from the Corps to fill in 7.5 acres of natural waterways that flow through the property. The permit requested allowance of sixty-six projects in the form of combined road and utility crossings, pad fill, as well as utility, remediation, drainage, and flood control measures.

In response to the application, the Corps issued its environmental assessment [(EA)] and a finding of no significant impact. In reaching this conclusion, the Corps examined only the washes rather than the entire project. Within this limited area, the Corps concluded that the sixty-six dredge and fill projects would not significantly affect the environment, nor would they disturb the habitats of any endangered species. The Corps determined that no environmental impact statement [(EIS)] was necessary, and stated its intent to authorize Lone Mountain to build the sixty-six projects.

The Corps invited public comment on the permit * * *. The United States Environmental Protection Agency ("EPA") and the United States Fish and Wildlife Service ("FWS") opposed the issuance of the permit and disagreed with the Corps' findings with respect to whether the site was a potentially suitable habitat for the cactus ferruginous pygmy owl, which is listed as an endangered species. * * *

The Corps * * * reiterated its preliminary findings, and issued the permit to Lone Mountain * * *.

The district court granted a temporary restraining order to SOS and, after a hearing, the district court ordered preliminary injunctive relief. * * *

After SOS was informed that Lone Mountain was continuing construction on the site, * * * the district court made clear that * * * the status quo could be preserved only if Lone Mountain ceased any and all development on the site until a hearing on the merits could be held.

* * *

III

A

As we observed in Clear Channel Outdoor, Inc. v. City of Los Angeles, "[t]he standard for granting a preliminary injunction balances the plaintiff's likelihood of success against the relative hardship to the parties." 340 F.3d 810, 813 (9th Cir.2003). We have described two sets of criteria for preliminary injunctive relief. Under the "traditional" criteria, a plaintiff must show "(1) a strong likelihood of success on the merits, (2) the possibility of irreparable injury to plaintiff if preliminary relief is not granted, (3) a balance of hardships favoring the plaintiff, and (4) advancement of the public interest (in certain cases)." Johnson v. Cal. State Bd. of Accountancy, 72 F.3d 1427, 1430 (9th Cir.1995). Alternatively, a court may grant the injunction if the plaintiff "demonstrates *either* a combination of probable success on the merits and the possibility of irreparable injury *or* that serious questions are raised and the balance of hardships tips sharply in his favor." *Id.* * * *

As we have said many times regarding the two alternative formulations of the preliminary injunction test: "These two formulations represent two points on a sliding scale in which the required degree of irreparable harm increases as the probability of success decreases. They are not separate tests but rather outer reaches of a single continuum." Baby Tam & Co. v. City of Las Vegas, 154 F.3d 1097, 1100 (9th Cir.1998) * * *.

* * *

B

The district court correctly held that the Corps had improperly constrained its NEPA analysis to the washes, rather than considering the development's effect on the environment as a whole. NEPA requires federal agencies to prepare an environment impact statement for all "major Federal actions significantly affecting the quality of the human environment." 42 U.S.C. § 4332(2)(C). A section 404 permit issued by the Corps is a "Federal action" to which NEPA applies. * * *

Although the Corps' permitting authority is limited to those aspects of a development that directly affect jurisdictional waters, it has responsibility under NEPA to analyze all of the environmental consequences of a project. Put another way, while it is the development's impact on jurisdictional waters that determines the scope of the Corps' permitting authority, it is the impact of the permit on the environment at large that determines the Corps' NEPA responsibility. The Corps' responsibility under NEPA to consider the environmental consequences of a permit extends even to environmental effects with no impact on jurisdictional waters at all.

An examination of the record leads us to conclude that the district court did not abuse its discretion in determining there were serious questions as to whether the Corps had correctly confined its analysis. * * * It is significant at the onset to recall that two federal agencies, the EPA and the FWS—not the usual suspects in opposing the action of a federal agency—disagreed with the acreage limitations set forth in the permit applications and thus with the Corps' interpretation of its NEPA responsibility. It is also of importance to our conclusion regarding the

Corps' NEPA responsibility that the Corps concluded that the "no action" alternative—denying the permit—would have the effect of halting the project.

* * * Because the jurisdictional waters run throughout the property like capillaries through tissue, any development the Corps permits would have an effect on the whole property. The NEPA analysis should have included the entire property.

* * *

C
* * *

* * * [B]ecause the uplands are inseparable from the washes, the district court was correct to conclude that the Corps' permitting authority, and likewise the court's authority to enjoin development, extended to the entire project. Lone Mountain cannot begin developing any portion of the land in the absence of an appropriately broad NEPA analysis by the Corps. Given all of this, it is clear that the district court did not abuse its discretion in concluding that SOS has raised serious issues that go to the merits of the case. * * *

D

Nor did the district court err in its hardship analysis. The Supreme Court has recognized that "[e]nvironmental injury, by its nature, can seldom be adequately remedied by money damages and is often permanent or at least of long duration, *i.e.,* irreparable." Amoco Prod. Co. v. Village of Gambell, 480 U.S. 531, 545, 107 S.Ct. 1396, 94 L.Ed.2d 542 (1987). Here, the district court properly observed that once the desert is disturbed, it can never be restored. Thus, the court concluded, the plaintiffs had adequately demonstrated the possibility of irreparable harm. * * *

Lone Mountain argues that there is no presumption of irreparable harm in procedural violations of environmental statutes. This is doubtless an accurate observation, * * * but it is irrelevant here, because the district court did not apply such a presumption. Rather, the district court carefully concluded that an expanded assessment of the project by the Corps would have a dramatic effect on the nature of the development and, thus, on the surrounding environment. Therefore, the court concluded, proceeding with immediate development of the property without a proper environmental assessment could result in unauthorized development and environmental injury to the jurisdictional waters.* * *

* * *

The district court did not abuse its discretion in balancing the hardships. The district court determined that the balance of hardships tipped in SOS's favor because, if wrongfully restrained, Lone Mountain "may suffer financial harm," but if an injunction does not issue, unlawful disruption to the desert is likely irreparable. The district court's analysis is a classic, and quite proper, examination of the relative hardships in an environmental case. Indeed, we have long held that "when environmental injury is 'sufficiently likely, the balance of harms will usually favor the issuance of an injunction to protect the environment.'" Sierra Club v. U.S. Forest Serv., 843 F.2d 1190, 1195 (9th Cir.1988) (quoting *Amoco,* 480 U.S. at 545, 107 S.Ct. 1396).

Lone Mountain argues that the district court erred because the financial hardship it faces from the injunction is concrete and supported by evidence whereas SOS's claims of harm are not. * * * Contrary to Lone Mountain's assertions, the district court did consider the financial evidence presented by Lone Mountain, and it did not abuse its discretion in balancing the hardships.

E

In sum, the district court did not abuse its discretion in its traditional preliminary injunction analysis. Given the factual findings of the court, the Corps improperly limited the scope of its NEPA analysis.

However, we emphasize that our review at this juncture is limited. The grant of a preliminary injunction does not make the grant of permanent injunctive relief inevitable. * * *

IV

The district court required SOS to provide a $50,000 security pursuant to Fed.R.Civ.P. 65(c). * * *

* * *

V

[W]e conclude that the district court did not abuse its discretion either in granting the preliminary injunction or in setting the bond amount. We affirm the orders of the district court and remand for the remaining proceedings in the case. * * *

NOTES

1. Each federal circuit that has adopted an alternative test for determining whether to grant provisional injunctive relief has formulated its test somewhat differently. For example, the Seventh Circuit sought to improve upon the Ninth Circuit's sliding scale test in Roland Machinery Co. v. Dresser Industries, Inc., 749 F.2d 380 (7th Cir. 1984)(Posner, J): 7th Cir

The first bone of contention between the parties is the proper standard for granting a preliminary injunction * * *.

* * * Beneath the welter of apparently conflicting precedents we sense agreement on the following principles:

1. In every case in which the plaintiff wants a preliminary injunction he must show that he has "no adequate remedy at law," and * * * that he will suffer "irreparable harm" if the preliminary injunction is not granted. The absence of an adequate remedy at law is a precondition to any form of equitable relief. The requirement of irreparable harm is needed to take care of the case where although the ultimate relief that the plaintiff is seeking is equitable, implying that he has no adequate

remedy at law, he can easily wait till the end of trial to get that relief. (On the distinction between "no adequate remedy at law" and "irreparable harm" see Fiss & Rendleman, Injunctions 59 (2d ed.1984).) Only if he will suffer irreparable harm in the interim—that is, harm that cannot be prevented or fully rectified by the final judgment after trial—can he get a preliminary injunction. * * *

2. In saying that the plaintiff must show that an award of damages at the end of trial will be inadequate, we do not mean wholly ineffectual; we mean seriously deficient as a remedy for the harm suffered. *See* Semmes Motors, Inc. v. Ford Motor Co., 429 F.2d 1197, 1205 (2d Cir.1970) (Friendly, J.) * * *.

3. In deciding whether to grant a preliminary injunction, the court must also consider any irreparable harm that the defendant might suffer from the injunction—harm that would not be either cured by the defendant's ultimately prevailing in the trial on the merits or fully compensated by the injunction bond that Rule 65(c) of the Federal Rules of Civil Procedure requires the district court to make the plaintiff post. The cases do not usually speak of the defendant's *irreparable* harm, but the qualification is implicit; if the defendant will not be irreversibly injured by the injunction because a final judgment in his favor would make him whole, the injunction will not really harm him. But since the defendant may suffer irreparable harm from the entry of a preliminary injunction, the court must not only determine that the plaintiff will suffer irreparable harm if the preliminary injunction is denied—a threshold requirement for granting a preliminary injunction—but also weigh that harm against any irreparable harm that the defendant can show he will suffer if the injunction is granted.

4. Besides showing that he has no adequate remedy at law and that he will suffer irreparable harm unless the preliminary injunction is granted, the plaintiff has another threshold to cross: that of showing some likelihood of succeeding on the merits. It is not enough that the failure to get the injunction will be a disaster for him whereas the injunction would be only a minor inconvenience to the defendant. Equity jurisdiction exists only to remedy legal wrongs * * *. But * * * the threshold is low. It is enough that "the plaintiff's chances are better than negligible. . . ." Omega Satellite Products Co. v. City of Indianapolis, 694 F.2d 119, 123 (7th Cir.1982). * * *

5. If the plaintiff does show some likelihood of success, the court must then determine how likely that success is, because this affects the balance of relative harms (point 3 above). The more likely the plaintiff is to win, the less heavily need the balance of harms weigh in his favor; the less likely he is to win, the more need it weigh in his favor. This is a most important principle, and one well supported by cases in this and other circuits, and by scholarly commentary. * * *

A variant of this "sliding scale" approach is illustrated by Charlie's Girls, Inc. v. Revlon, Inc., 483 F.2d 953, 954 (2d Cir.1973) (per curiam): "One moving for a preliminary injunction assumes the burden of demonstrating either a combination of probable success and the possibility of irreparable injury or that serious questions are raised and the balance of hardships tips sharply in his favor." *See also* William Inglis & Sons Baking Co. v. ITT Continental Baking Co., 526 F.2d 86, 88 (9th Cir.1975). * * *

The idea underlying these equivalent approaches is that the task for the district judge in deciding whether to grant or deny a motion for preliminary injunction is to minimize errors: the error of denying an injunction to one who will in fact (though no one can know this for sure) go on to win the case on the merits, and the error of granting an injunction to one who will go on to lose. The judge must try to avoid the error that is more costly in the circumstances. That cost is a function of the gravity of the error if it occurs and the probability that it will occur. The error of denying an injunction to someone whose legal rights have in fact been infringed is thus more costly the greater the magnitude of the harm that the plaintiff will incur from the denial and the greater the probability that his legal rights really have been infringed. And similarly the error of granting an injunction to someone whose legal rights will turn out not to have been infringed is more costly the greater the magnitude of the harm to the defendant from the injunction and the smaller the likelihood that the plaintiff's rights really have been infringed.

6. Sometimes an order granting or denying a preliminary injunction will have consequences beyond the immediate parties. If so, those interests—the "public interest" if you will—must be reckoned into the weighing process just described. *See* Yakus v. United States, 321 U.S. 414, 440–41, 64 S.Ct. 660, 674–75, 88 L.Ed. 834 (1944) * * *.

Id. at 385–88.

2. For scholarly commentary on the standards for issuing preliminary injunctions, see Thomas R. Lee, *Preliminary Injunctions and the Status Quo*, 58 Wash. & Lee L. Rev. 109 (2001); Douglas Lichtman, *Uncertainty and the Standard for Preliminary Relief*, 70 U. Chi. L. Rev. 197 (2003).

3. The next case was decided by the Eighth Circuit, which at first applied the following "traditional standard" in considering requests for provisional relief: 1) whether there is a substantial probability that the movant will succeed at trial; 2) whether the moving party will suffer irreparable injury absent the injunction; 3) the harm to other interested parties if the relief is granted; and 4) the effect on the public interest. Minnesota Bearing Co. v. White Motor Corp., 470 F.2d 1323 (8th Cir. 1973). Later, in Fennell v. Butler, 570 F.2d 263 (8th Cir. 1976), the Eighth Circuit suggested that it was willing to apply the "alternative test" that had been adopted in the early 1970s by both the Second Circuit and the Ninth Circuit. Under this "alternative test," a provisional injunction would issue upon a demonstration of "a combination of probable success and the possibility of irreparable injury" or upon proof that "serious questions are raised and the balance of hardships tips sharply in [the moving party's] favor." Charlie's Girls, Inc. v. Revlon, Inc., 483 F.2d 953 (2d Cir. 1973); *see also* William Inglis & Sons Baking Co. v. ITT Continental Baking Co., 526 F.2d 86 (9th Cir. 1975)(adopting the *Charlie's Girls* test).

Three years after *Fennell*, the Second Circuit modified the *Charlie's Girls* test in Jackson Dairy, Inc. v. H.P. Hood & Sons, Inc., 596 F.2d 70, 72 (2d Cir. 1979)(per curiam): "The standard in the Second Circuit for injunctive relief * * * calls for a showing of (a) irreparable harm and (b) either (1) likelihood of success on the merits or (2) sufficiently serious questions going to the merits to make them fair ground for litigation and a balance of hardships tipping decidedly toward the party requesting the preliminary relief." (The Ninth Circuit continued to apply the *Charlie's Girls* test.)

Five years after *Fennell*, the Eighth Circuit merged its traditional test and the Second Circuit's alternative test into a single, flexible, alternative standard that called for a balancing of the following four "relevant factors" in determining whether to grant a provisional injunction: 1) the likelihood of success on the merits; 2) the threat of irreparable harm to the moving party; 3) the balance of the hardships; and 4) the public interest. Dataphase Systems, Inc. v. CL Systems, Inc., 640 F.2d 109, 113 (8th Cir. 1981).

The Eighth Circuit offered the following observations about the advantages of its new alternative standard over its traditional standard:

> The major difficulty with application of the traditional test has arisen from the phrase "probability of success on the merits." Some have read this element of the test to require in every case that the party seeking [provisional] relief prove a greater than fifty per cent likelihood that he will prevail on the merits. Under this view, even if the balance of the other three factors strongly favored the moving party, [provisional] relief would be denied if the movant could not prove a mathematical probability of success at trial. Although this construction of the "probability of success" requirement is technically possible, we reject it.

> The very nature of the inquiry on petition for [provisional] relief militates against a wooden application of the probability test. At base, the question is whether the balance of equities so favors the movant that justice requires the court to intervene to preserve the status quo until the merits are determined. The equitable nature of the proceeding mandates that the court's approach be flexible enough to encompass the particular circumstances of each case. Thus, an effort to apply the probability language to all cases with mathematical precision is misplaced.

> In balancing the equities no single factor is determinative. The likelihood that plaintiff ultimately will prevail is meaningless in isolation. In every case, it must be examined in the context of the relative injuries to the parties and the public. If the chance of irreparable injury to the movant should relief be denied is outweighed by the likely injury to other parties litigant should the injunction be granted, the moving party faces a heavy burden of demonstrating that he is likely to prevail on the merits. Conversely, where the movant has raised a substantial question and the equities are otherwise strongly in his favor, the showing of success on the merits can be less.

It follows that the court ordinarily is not required at an early stage to draw the fine line between a mathematical probability and a substantial possibility of success. This endeavor may, of course, be necessary in some circumstances when the balance of equities may come to require a more careful evaluation of the merits. But where the balance of other factors tips decidedly toward plaintiff a [provisional] injunction may issue if the movant has raised questions so serious and difficult as to call for more deliberate investigation.

Id.

CDI ENERGY SERVICES, INC. v. WEST RIVER PUMPS, INC.

United States Court of Appeals, Eighth Circuit, 2009.
567 F.3d 398.

MELLOY, CIRCUIT JUDGE.

CDI Energy Services, Inc. ("CDI"), sells and services equipment for use in the oilfield industry. CDI maintained a field office in Dickinson, North Dakota, with three employees, John Martinson, Dale Roller, and Kent Heinle. CDI alleges that these men started a competing company, West River Pumps, Inc. ("West River"), stole proprietary information, and solicited business from CDI's clients while still employed by CDI. Upon discovering its employees' actions, CDI filed the present diversity action asserting * * * state-law claims of breach of loyalty [and] trade-secret misappropriation * * * . CDI obtained an initial, ex parte temporary restraining order and moved for preliminary injunctive relief. After the parties briefed the matter and submitted affidavits, the district court denied the motion for a preliminary injunction and dissolved the temporary restraining order. * * *

I. BACKGROUND

In February 2000, CDI entered the market for selling and servicing oilfield equipment in Dickinson, North Dakota, by hiring Martinson and Roller to open a CDI field office. At that time, Martinson and Roller were experienced in the industry, had client contacts in the area, and were working for one of CDI's competitors. While the men still were working for their previous employer, CDI encouraged them to solicit business from the competitor's clients and bring those clients with them to CDI. Roller and Martinson did so. One of the clients Roller brought with him to CDI subsequently accounted for approximately half of CDI's business.

At CDI, Martinson served as the district manager in North Dakota, and Roller served as the sales and service representative. Martinson hired defendant Kent Heinle in 2007 to work for CDI as a service technician.

In 2007, while employed by CDI, the three men formed West River and contacted CDI's clients. They informed CDI's clients of their plan to commence operations as a separate business and asked those clients to do business with West River. They also secured permission from several clients to move the clients' equipment from CDI's shop to West River's new location. On October 16, 2007, the three men resigned from CDI.

Martinson, Roller and Heinle were CDI's only employees in the area, and when they left CDI, CDI no longer had a presence in the local market. CDI's nearest field office was over 140 miles away in eastern Montana.

CDI argues that it made substantial investments to train Martinson, Roller, and Heinle, develop business in the Dickinson area, and develop trade-secret information. CDI argues that these investments and efforts support its breach of loyalty and trade-secret claims because the investments demonstrate the value that the defendants took from CDI. * * * The defendants argue that CDI provided no education or formal training but that CDI hired them specifically because they already had experience in the industry and, in fact, had customers they could bring to CDI.

CDI argues that it took efforts reasonable under the circumstances to protect certain information as trade secrets. CDI identifies customer lists, customer contact information, business strategies, customer repair and purchase histories, and CDI pricing information as trade secrets. * * * The defendants assert that CDI's Dickinson office was open * * * and CDI made no substantial efforts to ensure that the materials were kept confidential.

The defendants admit that Martinson, Roller, and Heinle took limited records with them when they left CDI. * * * They assert none of the materials are trade secrets.

In assessing the propriety of preliminary injunctive relief, the district court applied the factors from Dataphase Systems, Inc. v. C.L. Systems, Inc., 640 F.2d 109, 114 (8th Cir.1981) (en banc). The court found CDI had not made a showing sufficient to demonstrate that any of the materials the defendants took constituted trade secrets under North Dakota law. Accordingly, the court found CDI had not established a likelihood of success on the merits of the trade-secret claim. Regarding the men's solicitation of CDI's customers while still employed by CDI, the court found CDI was likely to succeed on the merits of a statutory claim for breach of loyalty. *See* N.D. Cent.Code. § 34–02–14. Proceeding with the *Dataphase* analysis, the court examined the threat of irreparable harm and the balance of the harms of granting or not granting injunctive relief. Finally, the court examined the public's interest and held that injunctive relief was not warranted.

II. DISCUSSION

"A district court has broad discretion when ruling on preliminary injunction requests, and we will reverse only for clearly erroneous factual determinations, an error of law, or an abuse of discretion." Coca–Cola Co. v. Purdy, 382 F.3d 774, 782 (8th Cir.2004). In *Dataphase,* we held that the relevant factors to consider when assessing the propriety of preliminary injunctive relief include: (1) the likelihood of success on the merits; (2) the presence or risk of irreparable harm; (3) the balancing of the harms of granting or denying an injunction; and (4) the public's interest. * * *

a. *Likelihood of Success on the Merits*

We find no error in the district court's conclusion that CDI failed to meet its burden to prove that the defendants had taken trade-secret information or that CDI itself had taken reasonable steps to protect any purported trade secrets. The information at issue was of the type that may, in some industries, be treated as trade-secret information * * * . CDI, however, failed to show that any of the information in this case actually was a trade secret, i.e., information that has economic value by virtue of having been kept secret and that cannot be "ascertain[ed] by proper means." *See* N.D. Cent.Code § 47–25.1–01(4) * * * .

It appears undisputed that the potential customers for CDI and West River in the area surrounding Dickinson are a small collection of easily identifiable, locally operating oilfield companies. Information about these companies would be easily obtainable, if not already known, by relevant actors in the local oilfield service and equipment industry. Also, the record shows little effort by CDI to conceal data as trade secrets * * * .

With no likelihood of success on the merits, there is little justification for granting a preliminary injunction regarding the trade-secret claim. *See* Oglala Sioux Tribe v. C & W Enters., Inc., 542 F.3d 224, 233 (8th Cir.2008) (ceasing a *Dataphase* analysis after finding no likelihood of success on the merits). Regardless, because the district court determined CDI was likely to succeed on the merits of its other claims, we address the remaining factors below.

Regarding a likelihood of success on the statutory breach-of-loyalty claim under North Dakota Century Code § 34–02–14, the defendants do not seriously contest the district court's finding that CDI is likely to prevail. North Dakota law is clear in setting forth a duty of loyalty that precludes employees from soliciting their employer's customers while still working for the employer. *Id.* CDI argues that this finding alone mandates a grant of equitable relief in the form of a preliminary injunction. In so arguing, CDI misconstrues Eighth Circuit law. While the absence of a likelihood of success on the merits strongly suggests that preliminary injunctive relief should be denied, a finding of a likelihood of success on the merits only justifies preliminary relief if there is a risk of irreparable harm and the balance of the factors support an injunction. *See, e.g.,* Gelco Corp. v. Coniston Partners, 811 F.2d 414, 420 (8th Cir.1987) ("The failure to show irreparable harm is, by itself, a sufficient ground upon which to deny a preliminary injunction, for the basis of injunctive relief in the federal courts has always been irreparable harm and inadequacy of legal remedies.") (internal quotation and alteration omitted). Accordingly, it is necessary to balance the likelihood of success on the non-trade-secret claims against the remaining factors.

b.   Irreparable Harm

The district court determined that any harm in the present case can be addressed through an award of damages because the harm to CDI, to a large extent, has already occurred. The non-trade-secret claims rest on the possibly wrongful appropriation of CDI's clients, an act the defendants have already carried out. As such, it is not entirely clear how injunctive relief would actually assist CDI in any manner. This clearly was the district court's view of the case, and the court noted further that it did not want to order (and lacked the authority to order) the customers to cease doing business with defendants and return to CDI.

Also, the record strongly suggests that, without the individual defendants as employees, CDI had no local personnel in place to service the customers. * * *

Given this state of affairs, it was appropriate for the district court to view the irreparable-harm factor as weighing against the issuance of a preliminary injunction. The harm that had already occurred could be remedied through damages. * * * Also, CDI failed to show that an injunction would actually serve to lessen any possible ongoing damages by causing customers to return to CDI.

c.   Balance of Harms

The district court viewed any potential harm to the defendants in granting preliminary relief as substantial and any additional harm to CDI in denying the order as minor. The defendants are a small local business and its three owners. The record shows the individual defendants are substantially invested in West River. The customers that West River took from CDI comprise the majority of the defendants' business, and it appears undisputed that an injunction would put the defendants out of business. Because CDI asserts that it has already lost almost its entire business in North Dakota, it is difficult to appreciate what additional harm to CDI an injunction might prevent. Moreover, because former CDI customers might turn to a third party for service, the issuance of an injunction, if anything, would seem likely to harm both parties. As the district court stated, "It would be detrimental to the customers/clients, and not particularly helpful to CDI, if the Court were to enjoin West River . . . from servicing those customers without forcing them to return to CDI."

d.   Public Interest

Finally, public interest does not factor strongly into the final balance in this case because North Dakota has enacted legislation that favors both parties. The need to preserve the public's access to services, however, pushes this factor slightly in favor of denying a preliminary injunction. This was the view of the district court, and we agree.

North Dakota generally prohibits contractual restrictions on an employee's ability to practice his "profession, trade, or business." N.D.

Cent.Code § 9–08–06; *see also* Warner and Co. v. Solberg, 634 N.W.2d 65, 70 (N.D.2001). Describing this prohibition, the North Dakota Supreme Court has stated, "It is the right of the public's access to the services offered by the employee that is more significant than the employee's interests." *Warner,* 634 N.W.2d at 70. As relevant to this *Dataphase* factor, then, North Dakota deems the public's access to services to be a more pressing policy concern than the details of the relationship between a particular employee and employer.

North Dakota also considers employee loyalty to be in the public interest and prohibits employees from soliciting their employers' customers while still working for the employer. *See* N.D. Cent.Code § 34–02–14. This second public policy, however, is rather limited in that North Dakota cabins the restriction on solicitation to the duration of the employment relationship. *Warner,* 634 N.W.2d at 73 ("Our decisions ... prohibit restraints on solicitation after the employment ceases."). Given the limited nature of the restriction on solicitation, the policy precluding contractual restrictions on practicing a trade, and the clear public interest in preserving access to services, the district court acted well within its discretion when it held the public policy factor was a "close call" that weighed "more against the issuance of a preliminary injunction."

Finding no error in the district court's assessment of the record or abuse of its considerable discretion in the application of the *Dataphase* factors, we affirm the judgment of the district court.

WINTER v. NATURAL RESOURCES DEFENSE COUNCIL, INC.

Supreme Court of the United States, 2008.
129 S. Ct. 365, 172 L.Ed.2d 249.

CHIEF JUSTICE ROBERTS delivered the opinion of the Court.

"To be prepared for war is one of the most effectual means of preserving peace." * * * So said George Washington in his first Annual Address to Congress, 218 years ago. One of the most important ways the Navy prepares for war is through integrated training exercises at sea. * * *

I

The Navy deploys its forces in "strike groups," which are groups of surface ships, submarines, and aircraft centered around either an aircraft carrier or an amphibious assault ship. * * * Before deploying a strike group, the Navy requires extensive integrated training * * * .

Antisubmarine warfare is currently the Pacific Fleet's top war-fighting priority. * * * Modern diesel-electric submarines pose a significant threat to Navy vessels because they can operate almost silently, making them extremely difficult to detect and track. * * *

The most effective technology for identifying submerged diesel-electric submarines within their torpedo range is active sonar, which involves emitting pulses of sound underwater and then receiving the acoustic waves that echo off the target. * * * This case concerns the Navy's use of "mid-frequency active" (MFA) sonar * * * .

* * *

The waters off the coast of southern California (SOCAL) are an ideal location for conducting integrated training exercises, as this is the only area on the west coast that is relatively close to land, air, and sea bases, as well as amphibious landing areas. * * * A strike group cannot be certified for deployment until it has successfully completed the integrated training exercises * * * . The use of MFA sonar during these exercises is "mission-critical," given that MFA sonar is the only proven method of identifying submerged diesel-electric submarines operating on battery power. * * *

Sharing the waters in the SOCAL operating area are at least 37 species of marine mammals, including dolphins, whales, and sea lions. The parties strongly dispute the extent to which the Navy's training activities will harm those animals or disrupt their behavioral patterns. The Navy emphasizes that it has used MFA sonar during training exercises in SOCAL for 40 years, without a single documented sonar-related injury to any marine mammal. The Navy asserts that, at most, MFA sonar may cause temporary hearing loss or brief disruptions of marine mammals' behavioral patterns.

The plaintiffs are the Natural Resources Defense Council, Jean–Michael Cousteau (an environmental enthusiast and filmmaker), and several other groups devoted to the protection of marine mammals and ocean habitats. They contend that MFA sonar can cause much more serious injuries to marine mammals than the Navy acknowledges, including permanent hearing loss, decompression sickness, and major behavioral disruptions. According to the plaintiffs, several mass strandings of marine mammals (outside of SOCAL) have been "associated" with the use of active sonar. They argue that certain species of marine mammals—such as beaked whales—are uniquely susceptible to injury from active sonar; these injuries would not necessarily be detected by the Navy, given that beaked whales are "very deep divers" that spend little time at the surface.

II

The procedural history of this case is rather complicated. The Marine Mammal Protection Act of 1972 (MMPA), 86 Stat. 1027, generally prohibits any individual from "taking" a marine mammal * * * . The Secretary of Defense may "exempt any action or category of actions" from the MMPA if such actions are "necessary for national defense." § 1371(f)(1). In January 2007, [the Secretary] granted the Navy a 2–year exemption from the MMPA for the training exercises at issue in this case. * * * The exemption was conditioned on the Navy adopting several mitigation procedures, including: * * * (4) requiring reduction of active sonar transmission levels by 6 dB if a marine mammal is detected within 1,000 yards of the bow of the vessel, or by 10 dB if detected within 500 yards; [and] (5)

requiring complete shutdown of active sonar transmission if a marine mammal is detected within 200 yards of the vessel * * * .

The National Environmental Policy Act of 1969 (NEPA), 83 Stat. 852, requires federal agencies "to the fullest extent possible" to prepare an environmental impact statement (EIS) for "every ... major Federal actio[n] significantly affecting the quality of the human environment." 42 U.S.C. § 4332(2)(C) (2000 ed.). An agency is not required to prepare a full EIS if it determines—based on a shorter environmental assessment (EA)—that the proposed action will not have a significant impact on the environment. 40 CFR §§ 1508.9(a), 1508.13 (2007).

In February 2007, the Navy issued an EA concluding that the 14 SOCAL training exercises scheduled through January 2009 would not have a significant impact on the environment. * * * The EA divided potential injury to marine mammals into two categories: Level A harassment, defined as the potential destruction or loss of biological tissue (*i.e.,* physical injury), and Level B harassment, defined as temporary injury or disruption of behavioral patterns such as migration, feeding, surfacing, and breeding. * * *

The Navy's computer models predicted that the SOCAL training exercises would cause only eight Level A harassments of common dolphins each year, and that even these injuries could be avoided * * *, given that dolphins travel in large pods easily located by Navy lookouts. * * * The EA also predicted 274 Level B harassments of beaked whales per year, none of which would result in permanent injury. * * * Beaked whales spend little time at the surface, so the precise effect of active sonar on these mammals is unclear. Erring on the side of caution, the Navy classified all projected harassments of beaked whales as Level A. * * * In light of its conclusion that the SOCAL training exercises would not have a significant impact on the environment, the Navy determined that it was unnecessary to prepare a full EIS. * * *

Shortly after the Navy released its EA, the plaintiffs sued the Navy, seeking declaratory and injunctive relief on the grounds that the Navy's SOCAL training exercises violated NEPA * * *. The District Court granted plaintiffs' motion for a preliminary injunction and prohibited the Navy from using MFA sonar during its remaining training exercises. The court held that plaintiffs had "demonstrated a probability of success" on their claims under NEPA * * * . The court also determined that equitable relief was appropriate because, under Ninth Circuit precedent, plaintiffs had established at least a " 'possibility' "of irreparable harm to the environment. * * * Based on scientific studies, declarations from experts, and other evidence in the record, the District Court concluded that there was in fact a "near certainty" of irreparable injury to the environment, and that this injury outweighed any possible harm to the Navy. * * *

The Navy filed an emergency appeal, and the Ninth Circuit stayed the injunction pending appeal. 502 F.3d 859, 865 (2007). After hearing oral argument, the Court of Appeals agreed with the District Court that preliminary injunctive relief was appropriate. The appellate court concluded, however, that a blanket injunction prohibiting the Navy from using MFA sonar in SOCAL was overbroad, and remanded the case to the District Court "to narrow its injunction * * *." 508 F.3d 885, 887 (2007).

On remand, the District Court entered a new preliminary injunction allowing the Navy to use MFA sonar only as long as it implemented the following mitigation measures (in addition to the measures the Navy had adopted pursuant to its MMPA exemption): (1) imposing a 12–mile "exclusion zone" from the coastline; (2) using lookouts to conduct additional monitoring for marine mammals; (3) restricting the use of "helicopter-dipping" sonar; (4) limiting the use of MFA sonar in geographic "choke points"; (5) shutting down MFA sonar when a marine mammal is spotted within 2,200 yards of a vessel; and (6) powering down MFA sonar by 6 dB during significant surface ducting conditions, in which sound travels further than it otherwise would due to temperature differences in adjacent layers of water. 530 F.Supp.2d 1110, 1118–1121 (C.D.Cal.2008). The Navy filed a notice of appeal, challenging only the last two restrictions.

The Navy then sought relief from the Executive Branch. * * *

* * * [T]he Council on Environmental Quality (CEQ) authorized the Navy to implement "alternative arrangements" to NEPA compliance in light of "emergency circumstances." See 40 CFR § 1506.11. The CEQ determined that alternative arrangements were appropriate because the District Court's injunction "create[s] a significant and unreasonable risk that Strike Groups will not be able to train and be certified as fully mission capable." * * * Under the alternative arrangements, the Navy would be permitted to conduct its training exercises under the mitigation procedures adopted in conjunction with the exemption from the MMPA. * * *

In light of these actions, the Navy then moved to vacate the District Court's injunction with respect to the 2,200–yard shutdown zone and the restrictions on training in surface ducting conditions. The District Court refused to do so, 527 F.Supp.2d 1216 (2008), and the Court of Appeals affirmed. The Ninth Circuit held that there was a serious question regarding whether the CEQ's interpretation of the "emergency circumstances" regulation was lawful. Specifically, the court questioned whether there was a true "emergency" in this case, given that the Navy has been on notice of its obligation to comply with NEPA from the moment it first planned the SOCAL training exercises. 518 F.3d at 681. * * * The court also held that plaintiffs had established a likelihood of success on their claim that the Navy was required to prepare a full EIS for the SOCAL training exercises. * * * The Ninth Circuit agreed with the District Court's holding that the Navy's—EA which resulted in a finding of no significant environmental impact—was "cursory, unsupported by cited evidence, or unconvincing." *Ibid.*

The Court of Appeals further determined that plaintiffs had carried their burden of establishing a "possibility" of irreparable injury. Even under the Navy's own figures, the court concluded, the training exercises would cause 564 physical injuries to marine mammals, as well as 170,000 disturbances of marine mammals' behavior. * * * Lastly, the Court of Appeals held that the balance of hardships and consideration of the public interest weighed in favor of the plaintiffs. The court emphasized that the negative impact on the Navy's training exercises was "speculative," since the Navy has never before operated under the procedures required by the District Court. * * * The Ninth Circuit concluded that the District Court's preliminary injunction struck a proper balance between the competing interests at stake.

III

A

A plaintiff seeking a preliminary injunction must establish that he is likely to succeed on the merits, that he is likely to suffer irreparable harm in the absence of preliminary relief, that the balance of equities tips in his favor, and that an injunction is in the public interest. See *Munaf v. Geren,* 553 U.S. 674, 689–690, 128 S.Ct. 2207, 2218–2219, 171 L.Ed.2d 1 (2008)[(requiring proof of a "likelihood of success on the merits")]; *Amoco Production Co. v. Gambell,* 480 U.S. 531, 542, 107 S.Ct. 1396, 94 L.Ed.2d 542 (1987)[(requiring proof of "irreparable injury" and "inadequacy of legal remedies")]; *Weinberger v. Romero–Barcelo,* 456 U.S. 305, 311–312, 102 S.Ct. 1798, 72 L.Ed.2d 91 (1982)[(same)(also requiring a balancing of "the parties' competing interests" and a consideration of "the public interest")].

The District Court and the Ninth Circuit concluded that plaintiffs have shown a likelihood of success on the merits of their NEPA claim. The Navy strongly disputes this determination, arguing that plaintiffs' likelihood of success is low because the CEQ reasonably concluded that "emergency circumstances" justified alternative arrangements to NEPA compliance. * * *

The District Court and the Ninth Circuit also held that when a plaintiff demonstrates a strong likelihood of prevailing on the merits, a preliminary injunction may be entered based only on a "possibility" of irreparable harm. * * * The lower courts held that plaintiffs had met this standard because the scientific studies, declarations, and other evidence in the record established to "a near certainty" that the Navy's training exercises would cause irreparable harm to the environment. * * *

The Navy challenges these holdings, arguing that plaintiffs must demonstrate a likelihood of irreparable injury—not just a possibility—in order to obtain preliminary relief. On the facts of this case, the Navy contends that plaintiffs' alleged injuries are too speculative to give rise to irreparable injury, given that ever since the Navy's training program began 40 years ago, there has been no documented case of sonar-related injury to marine mammals in SOCAL. * * * For their part, plaintiffs assert that they would prevail under any formulation of the irreparable injury standard, because the District Court found that they had established a "near certainty" of irreparable harm.

We agree with the Navy that the Ninth Circuit's "possibility" standard is too lenient. Our frequently reiterated standard requires plaintiffs seeking preliminary relief to demonstrate that irreparable injury is *likely* in the absence of an injunction. *Los Angeles v. Lyons,* 461 U.S. 95, 103, 103 S.Ct. 1660, 75 L.Ed.2d 675 (1983); * * * see also 11A C. Wright, A. Miller, & M. Kane, Federal Practice and Procedure § 2948.1, p. 139 (2d ed.1995) (hereinafter Wright & Miller) (applicant must demonstrate that in the absence of a preliminary injunction, "the applicant is likely to suffer irreparable harm before a decision on the merits can be rendered"); *id.,* at 155 * * * ("a preliminary injunction will not be issued simply to prevent the possibility of some remote future injury"). Issuing a preliminary injunction based only on a possibility of irreparable harm is inconsistent with our characterization of injunctive relief as an extraordinary remedy that may only be awarded upon a clear showing that the plaintiff is entitled to such relief. * * *.

It is not clear that articulating the incorrect standard affected the Ninth Circuit's analysis of irreparable harm. Although the court referred to the "possibility" standard, and cited Circuit precedent along the same lines, it affirmed the District Court's conclusion that plaintiffs had established a " 'near certainty' "of irreparable harm. * * * At the same time, however, the nature of the District Court's conclusion is itself unclear. The District Court originally found irreparable harm from sonar-training exercises generally. But by the time of the District Court's final decision, the Navy challenged only two of six restrictions imposed by the court. * * * The District Court did not reconsider the likelihood of irreparable harm in light of the four restrictions not challenged by the Navy. This failure is significant in light of the District Court's own statement that the 12-mile exclusion zone from the coastline—one of the unchallenged mitigation restrictions—"would bar the use of MFA sonar in a significant portion of important marine mammal habitat." * * *

We also find it pertinent that this is not a case in which the defendant is conducting a new type of activity with completely unknown effects on the environment. * * * Part of the harm NEPA attempts to prevent in requiring an EIS is that, without one, there may be little if any information about prospective environmental harms and potential mitigating measures. Here, in contrast, the plaintiffs are seeking to enjoin—or substantially restrict—training exercises that have been taking place in SOCAL for the last 40 years. * * *

As explained in the next section, even if plaintiffs have shown irreparable injury from the Navy's training exercises, any such injury is outweighed by the public interest and the Navy's interest in effective, realistic training of its sailors. A proper consideration of these factors alone requires denial of the requested injunctive relief. For the same reason, we do not address the lower courts' holding that plaintiffs have also established a likelihood of success on the merits.

B

A preliminary injunction is an extraordinary remedy never awarded as of right. * * * In each case, courts "must balance the competing claims of injury and must consider the effect on each party of the granting or withholding of the requested relief." *Amoco Production Co.,* 480 U.S., at 542, 107 S.Ct. 1396. "In exercising their sound discretion, courts of equity should pay particular regard for the public consequences in employing the extraordinary remedy of injunction." *Romero-Barcelo,* 456 U.S., at 312, 102 S.Ct. 1798 * * *. In this case, the District Court and the Ninth Circuit significantly understated the burden the preliminary injunction would impose on the Navy's ability to conduct realistic training exercises, and the injunction's consequent adverse impact on the public interest in national defense.

* * *

Here, the record contains declarations from some of the Navy's most senior officers, all of whom underscored the threat posed by enemy submarines and the need for extensive sonar training to counter this threat. * * *

* * *

These interests must be weighed against the possible harm to the ecological, scientific, and recreational interests that are legitimately before this Court. * * * Plaintiffs contend that the Navy's use of MFA sonar will injure marine mammals or alter their behavioral patterns, impairing plaintiffs' ability to study and observe the animals.

While we do not question the seriousness of these interests, we conclude that the balance of equities and consideration of the overall public interest in this case tip strongly in favor of the Navy. For the plaintiffs, the most serious possible injury would be harm to an unknown number of the marine mammals that they study and observe. In contrast, forcing the Navy to deploy an inadequately trained antisubmarine force jeopardizes the safety of the fleet. * * *

The public interest in conducting training exercises with active sonar under realistic conditions plainly outweighs the interests advanced by the plaintiffs. Of course, military interests do not always trump other considerations, and we have not held that they do. In this case, however, the proper determination of where the public interest lies does not strike us as a close question.

* * *

IV

As noted above, we do not address the underlying merits of plaintiffs' claims. While we have authority to proceed to such a decision at this point, * * * doing so is not necessary here. * * *

* * *

The factors examined above—the balance of equities and consideration of the public interest—are pertinent in assessing the propriety of any injunctive relief, preliminary or permanent. * * * Given that the ultimate legal claim is that the Navy must prepare an EIS, not that it must cease sonar training, there is no basis for enjoining such training in a manner credibly alleged to pose a serious threat to national security. * * * A court concluding that the Navy is required to prepare an EIS has many remedial tools at its disposal, including declaratory relief or an injunction tailored to the preparation of an EIS rather than the Navy's training in the interim. * * * In the meantime, we see no basis for jeopardizing national security, as the present injunction does. * * * [O]ur analysis of the propriety of preliminary relief is applicable to any permanent injunction as well.

* * * The District Court abused its discretion by imposing a 2,200–yard shutdown zone and by requiring the Navy to power down its MFA sonar during significant surface ducting conditions. The judgment of the Court of Appeals is reversed, and the preliminary injunction is vacated to the extent it has been challenged by the Navy.

JUSTICE BREYER, with whom JUSTICE STEVENS joins as to Part I, concurring in part and dissenting in part. [Opinion omitted.]

JUSTICE GINSBURG, with whom JUSTICE SOUTER joins, dissenting.

The central question in this action under the National Environmental Policy Act of 1969 (NEPA) was whether the Navy must prepare an environmental impact statement (EIS). * * * If the Navy had completed the EIS before taking action, as NEPA instructs, the parties and the public could have benefited from the environmental analysis—and the Navy's training could have proceeded without interruption. Instead, the Navy acted first, and thus thwarted the very purpose an EIS is intended to serve. * * * I would hold that, in imposing manageable measures to mitigate harm until completion of the EIS, the District Court conscientiously balanced the equities * * * .

* * *

III

A

Flexibility is a hallmark of equity jurisdiction. "The essence of equity jurisdiction has been the power of the Chancellor to do equity and to mould each decree to the necessities of the particular case. Flexibility rather than rigidity has distinguished it." *Weinberger v. Romero–Barcelo,* 456 U.S. 305, 312, 102 S.Ct. 1798, 72 L.Ed.2d 91 (1982) (quoting *Hecht Co. v. Bowles,* 321 U.S. 321, 329, 64 S.Ct. 587, 88 L.Ed. 754 (1944)). Consistent with equity's character, courts do not insist that litigants uniformly show a particular, predetermined quantum of probable success or injury before awarding equitable relief. Instead, courts have evaluated claims for equitable relief on a "sliding scale," sometimes awarding relief based on a lower likelihood of harm when the likelihood of success is very high. 11A C. Wright, A. Miller, & M. Kane, Federal Practice and Procedure § 2948.3, p. 195 (2d ed.1995). This Court has never rejected that formulation, and I do not believe it does so today.

Equity's flexibility is important in the NEPA context. Because an EIS is the tool for *uncovering* environmental harm, environmental plaintiffs may often rely more heavily on their probability of success than the likelihood of harm. The Court is correct that relief is not warranted "simply to prevent the possibility of some remote future injury." *Ante,* at 375 (quoting Wright & Miller, *supra,* § 2948.1, at 155). "However, the injury need not have been inflicted when application is made or be certain to occur; a strong threat of irreparable injury before trial is an adequate basis." Wright & Miller, *supra,* § 2948.1, at 155–156 (footnote omitted). I agree with the District Court that NRDC made the required showing here.

B

The Navy's own EA predicted substantial and irreparable harm to marine mammals. Sonar is linked to mass strandings of marine mammals, hemorrhaging around the brain and ears, acute spongiotic changes in the central nervous system, and lesions in vital organs. * * *[4]

In my view, this likely harm * * * cannot be lightly dismissed, even in the face of an alleged risk to the effectiveness of the Navy's 14 training exercises. * * *

In light of the likely, substantial harm to the environment, NRDC's almost inevitable success on the merits of its claim that NEPA required the Navy to prepare an EIS, the history of this litigation, and the public interest, I cannot agree that the mitigation measures the District Court imposed signal an abuse of discretion. Cf. *Amoco Production Co. v. Gambell,* 480 U.S. 531, 545, 107 S.Ct. 1396, 94 L.Ed.2d 542 (1987) ("Environmental injury, by its nature, can seldom be adequately remedied by money damages and is often permanent or at least of long duration, *i.e.,* irreparable. If such injury is sufficiently likely, therefore, the balance of harms will usually favor the issuance of an injunction to protect the environment.").

For the reasons stated, I would affirm the judgment of the Ninth Circuit.

---

4. The majority reasons that the environmental harm deserves less weight because the training exercises "have been taking place in SOCAL for the last 40 years," such that "this is not a case in which the defendant is conducting a new type of activity with completely unknown effects on the environment." * * * But the EA explains that the proposed action is not a continuation of the "status quo training." * * * Instead, the EA is based on the Navy's proposal to employ a "surge" training strategy, * * * in which the commander "would have the option to conduct two concurrent major range events" * * * .

NOTES

1. *Winter* sets forth a 4–prong test for preliminary injunctive relief. Did the Court actually decide the case on the basis of whether the plaintiff was "likely to suffer irreparable harm in the absence of preliminary relief"?

2. The Ninth Circuit has adopted the 4–prong test for preliminary injunctive relief that was set forth in *Winter*, and it has stated "[t]o the extent that our cases have suggested a lesser standard, they are no longer controlling, or even viable." American Trucking Association, Inc. v. City of Los Angeles, 559 F.3d 1046, 1052 (9th Cir. 2009). How would *Save Our Sonoran* be decided today under *American Trucking*?

3. Does *Winter* reject the "sliding scale" test for injunctive relief in the federal court system? Consider the next case.

CITIGROUP GLOBAL MARKETS, INC. v. VCG SPECIAL OPPORTUNITIES MASTER FUND LIMITED

United States Court of Appeals, Second Circuit, 2010.
598 F.3d 30.

Before FEINBERG, WALKER, KATZMAN, CIRCUIT JUDGES.

JOHN M. WALKER, JR., CIRCUIT JUDGE:

VCG Special Opportunities Master Fund Limited ("VCG") appeals from the November 12, 2008 order of the United States District Court for the Southern District of New York * * * granting the plaintiff-appellee Citigroup Global Markets, Inc.'s ("CGMI") motion for a preliminary injunction and enjoining VCG from proceeding with an arbitration initiated against CGMI before the Financial Industry Regulatory Authority ("FINRA"). * * * [The issue in this case is whether] the "serious questions" standard for assessing a movant's likelihood of success on the merits remains valid in the wake of recent Supreme Court cases * * * .

BACKGROUND

On July 17, 2006, VCG, a hedge fund based on the Isle of Jersey, entered into a brokerage services agreement with CGMI. Under the agreement, CGMI was obligated to provide prime brokerage services by clearing and settling trades in fixed income securities for VCG. VCG then entered into a credit default swap agreement with Citibank, N.A. (Citibank) (a sister-affiliate of appellee CGMI under the corporate umbrella of Citigroup, Inc.). VCG alleges that it was a "customer" of CGMI, which allegedly acted as the middleman with respect to the series of transactions culminating in the credit default swap agreement with Citibank. After entering into the swap, Citibank eventually declared a writedown of the assets covered in its credit default swap agreement with VCG, triggering VCG's obligation to pay Citibank a total of $10,000,000.

VCG sued Citibank, seeking a declaration that, by declaring the writedown, Citibank had violated the terms of the parties' credit default swap agreement. The district court found in Citibank's favor and also found that VCG was in breach of the agreement by failing to fulfill its payment obligation. *VCG Special Opportunities Master Fund Ltd. v. Citibank, N.A.,* 594 F.Supp.2d 334 (S.D.N.Y.2008), *aff'd,* No. 08–5707, 2009 WL 4576542 (2d Cir. Dec. 8, 2009).

In addition to litigating its claims against Citibank, VCG began arbitration proceedings against CGMI before the FINRA pursuant to FINRA Rule 12200. In response, CGMI filed a complaint in the district court to permanently enjoin the arbitration and for a declaration that CGMI had no obligation to arbitrate with VCG regarding the claims submitted to the FINRA arbitrators. On June 20, 2008, CGMI moved for a temporary restraining order and preliminary injunction against the FIN-RA arbitration pending a final resolution of CGMI's claims. CGMI assert-ed that it was not a party to, and did not broker, the VCG–Citibank credit default swap. * * * Specifically, CGMI argued that VCG was not a "customer" of CGMI for purposes of those transactions and, therefore, CGMI was under no obligation to arbitrate VCG's claims under the FINRA rules.

In opposition to the preliminary injunction motion, VCG submitted a declaration stating that "CGMI recommended and set the terms for" the credit default swap and that VCG's employees had "dealt with several CGMI representatives in connection with the transaction, but most often with Jeff Gapusan, Donald Qu[i]ntin, and Jaime Aldama." Wong Decl. ¶ 7.[2] * * *

In arguing that it had not acted as a middleman for the VCG–Citibank credit default swap and that VCG was not its "customer," CGMI contended that the people identified by VCG as its CGMI contacts were acting as agents of Citibank rather than CGMI, though they were formally employed by CGMI at the time of the VCG–Citibank negotiations. * * *

On November 12, 2008, the district court granted CGMI's motion for a preliminary injunction. In granting the injunction, the district court applied this circuit's long-established standard for the entry of a prelimi-nary injunction, under which the movant is required to show " 'irrepara-ble harm absent injunctive relief, and either a likelihood of success on the merits, or a serious question going to the merits to make them a fair ground for trial, with a balance of hardships tipping decidedly in plaintiff's favor.' " *Citigroup Global Mkts. Inc. v. VCG Special Opportunities Master Fund Ltd.,* No. 08–cv–5520, 2008 WL 4891229, at *2 (S.D.N.Y. Nov. 12, 2008) (quoting *Almontaser v. N.Y. City Dep't of Educ.,* 519 F.3d 505, 508 (2d Cir.2008)). The district court held that CGMI had demonstrated a likelihood of irreparable harm, but had failed to make a showing of "probable success" on the merits based on its claim that there was no customer relationship between CGMI and VCG with respect to the credit default swap transactions. * * * The district court found, however, that CGMI had provided evidence that raised "serious questions" as to wheth-

---

2. * * * As each of the documents underlying the swap agreement demonstrates, and contrary to the statements in Wong's declaration, Citibank, *not* CGMI, was the party with whom VCG contracted, and VCG, *not* CGMI, was to be paid 5.5% per annum [on an underlying debt obligation of $10,000,000, which was secured by the referenced mortgages.] * * *

er VCG was in fact a customer of CGMI with respect to the swap transaction and granted the preliminary injunction on that basis. * * *

* * * Finally, the district court found that the balance of hardships tipped decidedly in CGMI's favor given that an injunction would simply freeze the arbitration without destroying VCG's ability to continue that arbitration in the event that the district court determined that the dispute fell within the scope of the FINRA rules. * * *

On May 29, 2009, the district court denied VCG's motion for reconsideration, rejecting VCG's argument that *Winter v. Natural Resources Defense Council, Inc.,* — U.S. —, 129 S.Ct. 365, 172 L.Ed.2d 249 (2008), had eliminated the "serious questions" prong of this circuit's preliminary injunction standard. * * *

DISCUSSION

* * *

VCG first contends that the district court abused its discretion by applying the wrong legal standard to CGMI's request for a preliminary injunction. VCG argues that three recent decisions of the Supreme Court—*Munaf v. Geren,* 553 U.S. 674, 128 S.Ct. 2207, 171 L.Ed.2d 1 (2008); *Winter,* — U.S. —, 129 S.Ct. 365, 172 L.Ed.2d 249; and *Nken v. Holder,* — U.S. —, 129 S.Ct. 1749, 173 L.Ed.2d 550 (2009)—have eliminated this circuit's "serious questions" standard for the entry of a preliminary injunction, and that, in light of the district court's finding that CGMI failed to demonstrate its likelihood of success on the merits, the entry of a preliminary injunction in this case must be reversed. In the alternative, VCG argues that even if this circuit's standard for a preliminary injunction remains intact, the district court committed several legal errors in determining that CGMI had presented "serious questions" as to the arbitrability of VCG's claims.

Winter articulates the following standard for issuing a preliminary injunction:

> A plaintiff seeking a preliminary injunction must establish that he is likely to succeed on the merits, that he is likely to suffer irreparable harm in the absence of preliminary relief, that the balance of equities tips in his favor, and that an injunction is in the public interest.

Winter, 129 S.Ct. at 374 * * *. Although not stated explicitly in its briefs, we take VCG's position to be that the standard articulated by these three Supreme Court cases requires a preliminary injunction movant to demonstrate that it is more likely than not to succeed on its underlying claims, or in other words, that a movant must show a greater than fifty percent probability of success on the merits. Thus, according to VCG, a showing of "serious questions" that are a fair ground for litigation will not suffice. *See* VCG Br. 23–25 (describing the required showing as a "probability" of success, as opposed to a "possibility").

I. The Continued Viability of the "Serious Questions" Standard

For the last five decades, this circuit has required a party seeking a preliminary injunction to show "(a) irreparable harm and (b) either (1) likelihood of success on the merits or (2) sufficiently serious questions going to the merits to make them a fair ground for litigation and a balance of hardships tipping decidedly toward the party requesting the preliminary relief." *Jackson Dairy, Inc. v. H.P. Hood & Sons, Inc.,* 596 F.2d 70, 72 (2d Cir.1979) * * * . The "serious questions" standard permits a district court to grant a preliminary injunction in situations where it cannot determine with certainty that the moving party is more likely than not to prevail on the merits of the underlying claims, but where the costs outweigh the benefits of not granting the injunction. * * * Because the moving party must not only show that there are "serious questions" going to the merits, but must additionally establish that "the balance of hardships tips *decidedly*" in its favor, *Jackson Dairy,* 596 F.2d at 72 (emphasis added), its overall burden is no lighter than the one it bears under the "likelihood of success" standard.

The value of this circuit's approach to assessing the merits of a claim at the preliminary injunction stage lies in its flexibility in the face of varying factual scenarios and the greater uncertainties inherent at the outset of particularly complex litigation. Preliminary injunctions should not be mechanically confined to cases that are simple or easy. Requiring in every case a showing that ultimate success on the merits is more likely than not "is unacceptable as a general rule. The very purpose of an injunction . . . is to give temporary relief based on a preliminary estimate of the strength of plaintiff's suit, prior to the resolution at trial of the factual disputes and difficulties presented by the case. Limiting the preliminary injunction to cases that do not present significant difficulties would deprive the remedy of much of its utility." 11A Charles Alan Wright, Arthur R. Miller & Mary Kay Kane, *Federal Practice and Procedure* § 2948.3 (2d ed.2009); *see also Dataphase Sys., Inc. v. CL Sys., Inc.,* 640 F.2d 109, 113 (8th Cir.1981) (en banc) ("The very nature of the inquiry on petition for preliminary relief militates against a wooden application of the probability test. . . . The equitable nature of the proceeding mandates that the court's approach be flexible enough to encompass the particular circumstances of each case. Thus, an effort to apply the probability language to all cases with mathematical precision is misplaced.").[5]

---

5. We note that, prior to *Winter,* seven of the twelve regional Courts of Appeals, including this circuit and the Eighth Circuit in *Dataphase,* applied a preliminary injunction standard that permitted flexibility when confronting some probability of success on the merits that falls short of a strict fifty-one percent. *See Lands Council v. Martin,* 479 F.3d 636, 639 (9th Cir.2007), *overruled in part by Am. Trucking Ass'ns v. City of Los Angeles,* 559 F.3d 1046, 1052 & n. 10 (9th Cir.2009) (recognizing that the Ninth Circuit's previous standard as articulated in *Lands Council* was overruled at least with respect to the formerly permissible showing of a "possibility" of irreparable harm); *Oklahoma ex rel. Okla. Tax Comm'n v. Int'l Registration Plan, Inc.,* 455 F.3d 1107, 1112–13 (10th Cir.2006); *Mich. Bell Tel. Co. v. Engler,* 257 F.3d 587, 592 (6th Cir.2001); *Davenport v. Int'l Broth. of Teamsters, AFL–CIO,* 166 F.3d 356, 361 (D.C.Cir.1999); *Duct-O-Wire Co. v. U.S. Crane, Inc.,* 31 F.3d 506, 509 (7th Cir.1994); *Gen. Mills, Inc. v. Kellogg Co.,* 824 F.2d

Indeed, the Supreme Court, prior to the trilogy of cases cited by VCG, has counseled in favor of a preliminary injunction standard that permits the entry of an injunction in cases where a factual dispute renders a fully reliable assessment of the merits impossible. In *Ohio Oil Co. v. Conway*, 279 U.S. 813, 49 S.Ct. 256, 73 L.Ed. 972 (1929), the Court dealt with a factual dispute, relating to the effect on the plaintiff of a state tax on oil revenues, which had to "be resolved before the constitutional validity of [a] statute [could] be determined." * * * Faced with this situation, the Court instructed that "[w]here the questions presented by an application for an interlocutory injunction are grave, and the injury to the moving party [in the absence of such an injunction] will be certain and irreparable . . . the injunction usually will be granted." *Id.*

The Supreme Court's recent opinions in *Munaf, Winter,* and *Nken* have not undermined its approval of the more flexible approach signaled in *Ohio Oil.* None of the three cases comments at all, much less negatively, upon the application of a preliminary injunction standard that softens a strict "likelihood" requirement in cases that warrant it. *Munaf* involved a preliminary injunction barring the transfer to Iraqi custody of an individual captured in Iraq by the Multinational Force–Iraq. *Munaf,* 128 S.Ct. at 2214–15. That injunction was premised on "jurisdictional issues . . . so serious, substantial, difficult and doubtful, as to make them fair ground for litigation and thus for more deliberative investigation." * * * The Supreme Court vacated that injunction on the grounds that a "likelihood of jurisdiction" was irrelevant to the preliminary injunction consideration and could not substitute for a consideration of the merits. The Court in *Munaf* * * * provided nothing in the way of a definition of the phrase "a likelihood of success." * * *

Nor does *Winter* address the requisite probability of success of the movant's underlying claims. While *Winter* rejected the Ninth Circuit's conceptually separate "possibility of irreparable harm" standard, 129 S.Ct. at 375–76, it expressly withheld any consideration of the merits of

---

622, 624–25 (8th Cir.1987); *Blackwelder Furniture Co. of Statesville v. Seilig Mfg. Co.,* 550 F.2d 189, 195 (4th Cir.1977), *overruled by Real Truth About Obama, Inc. v. Fed. Election Comm'n,* 575 F.3d 342, 346–47 (4th Cir.2009).

On the other hand, three of our sister circuits have traditionally limited their preliminary injunction standards to the four factors cited in *Winter,* without reference to the possibility of obtaining an injunction based on a showing of serious questions going to the merits. *See Snook v. Trust Co. of Ga. Bank of Savannah, N.A.,* 909 F.2d 480, 483 n. 3 (11th Cir.1990) (noting that the "serious questions" standard had not been recognized in the Eleventh Circuit); *Concerned Women for Am., Inc. v. Lafayette County,* 883 F.2d 32, 34 (5th Cir.1989); *In re Arthur Treacher's Franchisee Litig.,* 689 F.2d 1137, 1147 n. 14 (3d Cir.1982) (rejecting the Second Circuit's "serious questions" standard * * *). The First Circuit does not generally provide for the possibility of a flexible showing as to the merits, *see Weaver v. Henderson,* 984 F.2d 11, 12 (1st Cir.1993) ("In the ordinary course, plaintiffs who are unable to convince the trial court that they will probably succeed on the merits will not obtain interim injunctive relief."), but has in the past recognized a potentially more flexible approach, *see Tuxworth v. Froehlke,* 449 F.2d 763, 764 (1st Cir.1971) ("No preliminary injunction should be granted in any case unless there appears to be a reasonable possibility of success on the merits. Granted that the necessary degree of likelihood of success depends upon various considerations, we must perceive at least some substantial possibility." * * *).

the parties' underlying claims * * *. Rather, the Court decided the case upon the balance of the equities and the public interest. * * * [6]

Finally, *Nken* likewise did not address the issue of a moving party's likelihood of success on the merits. *Nken* provides a four factor standard for granting a stay pending appeal, which the Court recognized as over-lapping substantially with the preliminary injunction standard. 129 S.Ct. at 1761. Although the Court repeated the "likely to succeed on the merits" phrasing, it did not suggest that this factor requires a showing that the movant is "more likely than not" to succeed on the merits.[7]

If the Supreme Court had meant for *Munaf, Winter*, or *Nken* to abrogate the more flexible standard for a preliminary injunction, one would expect some reference to the considerable history of the flexible standards applied in this circuit, seven of our sister circuits, and in the Supreme Court itself.[8] * * * We have found no command from the Supreme Court that would foreclose the application of our established "serious questions" standard as a means of assessing a movant's likeli-hood of success on the merits. Our standard accommodates the needs of the district courts in confronting motions for preliminary injunctions in factual situations that vary widely in difficulty and complexity. Thus, we hold that our venerable standard for assessing a movant's probability of success on the merits remains valid and that the district court did not err in applying the "serious questions" standard to CGMI's motion.[9]

---

6. To this extent, *Winter* reiterates the majority position of the circuits, including this one, that a showing of irreparable harm is fundamental to any grant of injunctive relief. *See, e.g., Almontaser,* 519 F.3d at 508 ("A party seeking a preliminary injunction *must* show irreparable harm absent injunctive relief...." (internal quotation marks omitted and emphasis added)); * * * *Dataphase Sys., Inc.,* 640 F.2d at 114 n. 9 ("This court previously noted that under any test the movant is required to show the threat of irreparable harm.") * * *.

7. The Supreme Court implies just the opposite in *Nken,* which contrasts a showing of a likelihood of success with a chance of success that is only "better than negligible." 129 S.Ct. at 1761. Because a "serious questions" showing necessarily requires more than that the chances for success are only "better than negligible," this circuit's "serious questions" standard does not conflict with the Supreme Court's decision in *Nken.*

8. As the Supreme Court noted in *Nken,* "[t]here is substantial overlap between [the factors governing a motion to stay] and the factors governing preliminary injunctions; not because the two are one and the same, but because similar concerns arise whenever a court order may allow or disallow anticipated action before the legality of that action has been conclusively determined." 129 S.Ct. at 1761 (internal citation omitted). In that light, we note that the Supreme Court followed a flexible approach when, in recently addressing the standard for issuing a stay pending the disposition of a petition for a writ of certiorari, it stated that the grant of such a motion required a likelihood of irreparable harm, but required only a "reasonable probability that four Justices will consider the issue sufficiently meritorious to grant certiorari" and a "fair prospect that a majority of the Court will vote to reverse the judgment below." *Hollingsworth v. Perry,* —— U.S. ——, 130 S.Ct. 705, 710, —— L.Ed.2d —— (2010) (per curiam). Acknowledging the use of a sliding scale in certain situations, the Court further stated that "[i]n close cases the Circuit Justice or the Court will balance the equities and weigh the relative harms to the applicant and to the respondent." *Id.*

9. We note that two of our sister circuits have retreated from a flexible approach in assessing the merits of a movant's case in light of *Winter. See Real Truth About Obama,* 575 F.3d at 346–47; *Am. Trucking Ass'ns,* 559 F.3d at 1052. We think the Fourth and Ninth Circuits have misread *Winter's* import.

II. THE DISTRICT COURT'S ANALYSIS

Having determined that the district court did not err by applying the "serious questions" standard to CGMI's motion for a preliminary injunction, we turn to VCG's contentions that the district court misapplied that standard. VCG argues that the district court erred in assessing the issue of arbitrability when it * * * (2) failed to recognize that VCG was a "customer" of CGMI as a matter of law; * * * and (4) inappropriately weighed the balance of hardships.

* * *

* * * Because the relevant question, in light of the contradictions in the record, is whether VCG was a "customer" of CGMI in even the broadest sense of the word, and because this issue is in sharp dispute, the district court committed no error of law or fact in holding that this uncertainty poses a serious question going to the merits of CGMI's claims.

* * *

VCG next argues that the district court failed to consider that VCG would be "deprived of its right to a speedy resolution of its grievance with a broker-dealer" and would have "to incur the cost and expend the energy involved in litigating the threshold arbitrability question." * * * The district court did not neglect these concerns: it expressly considered the impact of delay on VCG and weighed that hardship against those that would be imposed on CGMI in the absence of a preliminary injunction. The district court's balancing of those hardships did not constitute an abuse of discretion.

CONCLUSION

For the foregoing reasons, we affirm the district court's orders granting CGMI's motion for a preliminary injunction and denying VCG's motion for reconsideration.

SECTION 3. BONDS AND OTHER FORMS OF SECURITY

Rule 65(c) of the Federal Rules of Civil Procedure conditions the issuance of a provisional injunction upon the following requirements:

> The court may issue a preliminary injunction or a temporary restraining order only if the movant gives security in an amount that the court considers proper to pay the costs and damages sustained by any party found to have been wrongfully enjoined or restrained. The United States, its officers, and its agencies are not required to give security.

Usually the "security" given by a plaintiff pursuant to Rule 65(c) is a bond, but other forms of security, such as posting the equity in one's home, also are acceptable. *See* Hill v. Xyquad, Inc., 939 F.2d 627, 632 (8th

Cir.1991). Almost all states have a similar statute or rule providing for the giving of security prior to the issuance of provisional injunctive relief. The purposes of the security requirement are discussed in Dan B. Dobbs, *Should Security Be Required as a Pre–Condition to Provisional Injunctive Relief?*, 52 N.C. L. Rev. 1091 (1974):*

> [O]ne purpose in requiring a security as a condition to provisional relief is the fear that provisional relief, necessarily given after an attenuated hearing or none at all, is especially prone to error. * * * Perhaps one purpose of the injunction bond, then, is simply to recompense the defendant who has been subjected to a process of law that does not meet the kind of standards ordinarily adopted.
>
> A second policy or purpose of the injunction bond may be more direct: it may be required as a means of guaranteeing that the provisional relief is sought only by those in genuine need of such relief and reasonably confident of the outcome. In other words, its purpose may be more or less frankly to discourage too easy an access to the judicial process in those cases where that process does not involve a full trial of the issues. Not only does access to provisional relief risk harm to the defendant, it also risks enormous pressures that often are not generated when a full trial and hearing are held. The defendant enjoined on a few hours' notice to cease a nuisance may be subjected to enormous losses that could readily be avoided if he were merely subjected to the normal suit for injunction with the usual notice and a full opportunity to defend. By the same token, the plaintiff with even color of a complaint is likely to be well aware of the pressure he can generate by a claim for preliminary injunction. He may be tempted by tactics if not by need, to pursue such a remedy unless he is discouraged. The bond, if required in a substantial sum, may operate to deter frivolous claims for provisional relief.

Id. at 1093–94.

A. IS THE GIVING OF SECURITY UNDER RULE 65(c) MANDATORY OR DISCRETIONARY?

The text of Rule 65(c) appears to impose a mandatory security requirement upon the issuance of any form of provisional injunctive relief, with only one statutory exception. However, because the rule is administered by judges who are sitting in equity, and because equitable remedies are inherently discretionary in nature, the federal courts have adopted various techniques for softening the apparent mandate of Rule 65(c). One technique is to say: "[T]he rule makes security mandatory, *see* American Hospital Supply Corp. v. Hospital Products Ltd., 780 F.2d 589, 597 (7th Cir.1986), but also anticipates the exercise of discretion in determining the amount of the bond to be posted * * *." Gateway Eastern Railway Co. v.

Terminal Railroad Ass'n, 35 F.3d 1134, 1141 (7th Cir.1994). *See also* Habitat Education Center v. United States Forest Service, 607 F.3d 453 (7th Cir. 2010). A second technique is to state: "While we recognize that the language of Rule 65(c) appears to be mandatory, and that many circuits have so interpreted it, the rule in our circuit has long been that the district court possesses discretion over whether to require the posting of security." Moltan Co. v. Eagle–Picher Industries, Inc., 55 F.3d 1171, 1176 (6th Cir.1995). A third technique is to say: "Although the amount of the bond is left to the discretion of the court, the posting requirement is much less discretionary. While there are exceptions, the instances in which a bond may not be required are so rare that the requirement is almost mandatory." Frank's GMC Truck Center, Inc. v. General Motors Corp., 847 F.2d 100, 103 (3d Cir.1988).

BOROUGH OF PALMYRA BOARD OF EDUCATION v. F.C.

United States District Court, District of New Jersey, 1998.
2 F.Supp.2d 637.

SIMANDLE, DISTRICT JUDGE.

Plaintiff Borough of Palmyra Board of Education ("Board") brought this action appealing the November 13, 1997, decision of Administrative Law Judge Joseph Fidler ("ALJ") of the New Jersey Office of Administrative Law. In that decision, the ALJ determined that under Section 504 of the Rehabilitation Act, 29 U.S.C. § 794, and the implementing regulations at 34 C.F.R. § 104.33, the Board is responsible for the tuition and transportation costs of defendant F.C.'s attendance at a private school. Defendant F.C., a minor through his parents R.C. and M.C. (collectively, "the Cs"), counterclaimed seeking temporary and permanent injunctive relief compelling the Board to comply with the ALJ's decision. Presently before the court is F.C.'s motion, upon order to show cause, seeking a preliminary injunction to compel the Board to comply with the ALJ's decision by paying for F.C.'s tuition in the private program pending final review of the ALJ's decision and the Board's cross-motion for a stay of that decision.

* * *

I. BACKGROUND

F.C. is a 15-year-old student who resides within the Palmyra Board of Education District. He has been diagnosed with a severe case of Attention Deficit Hyperactivity Disorder ("ADHD"). The counterclaim alleges that F.C.'s disorder causes him to be easily distracted, disorganized, and impulsive and has negatively affected his performance in school. * * * The Cs suspected that F.C. suffered from ADHD as early as November 1992, and informed the Board of their suspicions at that time. * * * In April 1993, the Board confirmed that F.C. did suffer from ADHD, but informed the Cs that F.C. was not eligible for special educational services under the

Individuals with Disabilities Education Act ("IDEA"). * * * The Board allegedly did not inform the Cs that F.C. might be eligible for special services under Section 504 of the Rehabilitation Act of 1973 ("Section 504"), 29 U.S.C. § 794, until June 1994. * * *

In April 1995, the Board produced a written Section 504 plan for F.C. The Cs allege that the plan failed to address F.C.'s unique academic and affective disorders and was never fully implemented by the Board. * * * Dissatisfied with the Board's efforts to accommodate F.C.'s disability, the Cs sought an administrative hearing before the New Jersey Department of Education in October 1996, and placed him at the Hill Top Preparatory School, a private school for educationally handicapped students, in February 1997. * * * The matter was transferred to the New Jersey Office of Administrative Law, which is responsible for conducting hearings for contested issues under Section 504. * * *

* * * The ALJ issued a 43–page opinion on November 13, 1997, concluding that the Board had indeed failed to provide F.C. with a free appropriate education as required by Section 504 and 34 C.F.R. § 104.33. * * * The ALJ further found that because the Board's Section 504 plan for F.C. was "seriously deficient," the Cs were entitled under 34 C.F.R. § 104.33 to enroll F.C. in the Hill Top School. * * * Pursuant to his findings, the ALJ ordered the Board to reimburse the Cs for the costs of F.C.'s private placement from the time of his enrollment until the Board offers F.C. a free appropriate education, consistent with the requirements of Section 504 and 34 C.F.R. § 104.33. * * * The Board has yet to comply with the ALJ's decision.

* * *

II.   DISCUSSION
* * *

[The court concluded that the Cs had established both a likelihood of success on the merits and the probability of irreparable harm to F.C. if the preliminary injunction did not issue. Furthermore, the court concluded that it would be in the public interest to grant the preliminary injunction.]

5.   Security Bond

In the event the court denies the Board's motion for a stay and issues a preliminary injunction in favor of the Cs, the Board asks the court to order the Cs to post a bond in the full amount of the cost of F.C.'s tuition and transportation expenses. The Board argues that the posting of a bond in the full amount will protect the Board in the event it is successful on this appeal. The Cs respond that they have inquired into the possibility of posting a bond, but are simply financially incapable of doing so. * * * The court accepts their certification.

Under Fed.R.Civ.P. 65(c), a court generally may not issue a preliminary injunction unless the party seeking the injunction provides a security bond in the event the injunction is later found improper, as the rule on its face admits no exceptions. Hoxworth v. Blinder, Robinson & Co., 903 F.2d 186, 210 (3d Cir.1990). There are situations, however, where the bond requirement may be waived. Temple Univ. v. White, 941 F.2d 201, 219 (3d Cir.1991), *cert. denied sub nom.* Snider v. Temple Univ., 502 U.S. 1032, 112 S.Ct. 873, 116 L.Ed.2d 778 (1992). The Third Circuit has held that in determining whether to waive the bond requirement, the district court should consider the possible loss to the enjoined party together with the hardship that a bond requirement would impose on the applicant. *Id.* The court should also consider whether the applicant seeks to enforce a federal right and, if so, whether imposing the bond requirement would unduly interfere with that right. *Id.* at 220. Thus, a narrow exception to the Rule 65(c) bond requirement may be recognized in non-commercial and public interest cases. *See* Instant Air Freight Co. v. C.F. Air Freight, Inc., 882 F.2d 797, 803 n.8 (3d Cir.1989). In this case, the Cs are seeking to enforce F.C.'s rights under a federal statute, the Rehabilitation Act. The Cs have also demonstrated that they cannot afford to post a bond in the amount of F.C.'s remaining unpaid tuition and transportation costs, which the Board currently owes under the ALJ's order. It would be especially ironic if the prevailing party's financial inability to post a security bond deprived it of the very benefits of preliminary injunctive relief to which it has demonstrated entitlement under the Rehabilitation Act. Finally, the Board has not shown that it will suffer substantial losses if a decision compelling it to comply with the ALJ's order is ultimately reversed, since presumably the Board could seek reimbursement from the Cs in the rather unlikely event the ALJ's decision is reversed. Therefore, the court concludes that the security bond requirement of Fed.R.Civ.P. 65(c) should be waived in this case due to extraordinary circumstances.

III.   CONCLUSION

The Board's motion for a stay of the Decision of the Administrative Law Judge dated November 13, 1997, will be denied. The motion of the parents of F.C. for a preliminary injunction enforcing the ALJ's Decision requiring the Board to reimburse the Cs for their past tuition payments to Hill Top Preparatory School and to make payment pending final determination of the appeal is granted in part, and the Board shall be ordered to make payment to Hill Top of tuition on behalf of F.C. in the amount of $11,115.00 within fifteen (15) days hereof, and to make payment to the parents of F.C. for remaining transportation expenses in the amount of $1,000.00 within fifteen (15) days hereof. The requirement for the Cs to post a preliminary injunction security bond under Fed.R.Civ.P. 65(c) is waived, as explained above. * * *

NOTES

1.   As illustrated by *Borough of Palmyra*, those federal courts that have adopted either the quasi-mandatory or the discretionary interpretation of Rule 65(c) routinely recognize an exception to Rule 65(c) for "indigent plaintiffs." *Accord* Heather K. v. City of Mallard, 887 F.Supp. 1249, 1268

(N.D. Iowa 1995) (bond waived for indigent, asthmatic plaintiff who sought provisionally to require the unconditional enforcement of defendant's general ban on open burning). Some federal courts have extended the exception for "indigent plaintiffs" to selected corporate plaintiffs that are still solvent, but that are requesting provisional relief "to provide some cash flow." *E.g.*, Kamine/Besicorp Allegany L.P. v. Rochester Gas & Electric Corp. 908 F.Supp. 1180 (W.D.N.Y.1995) (temporary restraining order granted requiring specific performance of contract whereby defendant agreed to purchase electric power from plaintiff for twenty-five years; no bond required). It has been suggested that the imposition of a mandatory security requirement without an exception for "indigent plaintiffs" would violate constitutional principles of due process. Dan B. Dobbs, *Should Security Be Required as a Pre–Condition to Provisional Injunctive Relief?*, 52 N.C. L. Rev. 1092, 1114–17 (1974). On the other hand, who qualifies as an "indigent plaintiff"? And is the issuance of a provisional injunction without a bond a violation of the defendant's constitutional due process rights?

2. Those federal courts that have adopted a mandatory interpretation of Rule 65(c) require that a bond be posted by an indigent plaintiff, but in no more than a nominal amount. *See, e.g.*, Wilson v. Office of Civilian Health & Medical Program of the Uniformed Services (CHAMPUS), 866 F.Supp. 903 (E.D.Va.1994) (action by breast cancer patient for preliminary injunction requiring defendant to pay for high-dose chemotherapy with peripheral stem cell rescue), *aff'd*, 65 F.3d 361 (4th Cir.1995):

> In this case, the Court finds that the Plaintiff is without adequate resources to post a bond in any meaningful amount. * * * Furthermore, this Court notes the extreme urgency with which this injunction must be issued, the dire circumstances surrounding plaintiff's health, and the substantial likelihood that the Plaintiff will prevail on the merits of her claim.

> It is apparent that to require a bond would not only defeat Plaintiff's otherwise meritorious claim, it may also cost the Plaintiff her life. However, while no Fourth Circuit case is directly on point, the Court believes that the permissive language of Rule 65(c) provides it with the discretion necessary to avoid this unspeakably harsh result. Accordingly, * * * the Court finds that the Plaintiff shall be required to post a bond of zero dollars. *See* Warner v. Ryobi Motor Products Corp., 818 F.Supp. 907, 909 (D.S.C.1992) (requiring bond of only $250 where Plaintiff had limited financial resources); Kulakowski v. Rochester Hosp. Serv. Corp., 779 F.Supp. 710, 717 (W.D.N.Y.1991) (requiring no bond amount where Plaintiff showed inability to pay).

Id. at 910; *accord* Smith v. Newport News Shipbuilding Health Plan, Inc., 148 F.Supp.2d 637 (E.D.Va.2001) (same).

3. "Public interest plaintiffs" also are routinely exempted from Rule 65(c), either through the creation of an exception or by requiring the posting of only a nominal security. A good illustration of this type of case is a suit brought by a public interest plaintiff under the National Environmental Policy Act (NEPA). *See, e.g.*, Davis v. Mineta, 302 F.3d 1104 (10th Cir.2002) (large bond reversed and remanded for entry of minimal bond); Friends of the

Earth, Inc. v. Brinegar, 518 F.2d 322 (9th Cir.1975) ($4,500,000 bond reduced to $1,000); Colorado Wild, Inc. v. U.S. Forest Service, 523 F.Supp.2d 1213, 1230–31 (D. Colo. 2007)(no bond required where NEPA plaintiffs, who were non-profit groups, submitted declarations by their executive directors that they would not be able to proceed with their case if a bond were required). *But see* Habitat Education Center v. United States Forest Service, 607 F.3d 453 (7th Cir. 2010)($10,000 bond required where NEPA plaintiff, a nonprofit enterprise, admitted that posting the bond would cause it no hardship). For an excellent discussion of why public interest plaintiffs should get injunctions based on nominal bonds, see Alexander T. Henson & Kenneth F. Gray, *Injunction Bonding in Environmental Litigation*, 19 Santa Clara L. Rev. 541 (1979). *See generally* Daniel R. Mandelker, NEPA Law and Litigation § 4.53 (2003) (preliminary injunction bonds).

4. The Third Circuit interprets Rule 65(c) as "almost mandatory" with limited exceptions. One commentator has recommended that Rule 65(c) be revised so as to codify the Third Circuit's interpretation. Erin Connors Morton, Note, *Security for Interlocutory Injunctions Under Rule 65(c): Exceptions to the Rule Gone Awry*, 46 Hastings L.J. 1863 (1995).

5. Some states have adopted the language of Rule 65(c) and, like the federal judiciary, the courts in these states have had difficulty in construing it. *See, e.g.*, Anders v. Fowler, 423 So.2d 838 (Ala.1982) (mandatory requirement); Keith v. Day, 60 N.C.App. 559, 299 S.E.2d 296 (1983) (mandatory requirement with a few, limited exceptions). Other states have departed from the federal model, as described in Dan B. Dobbs, *Should Security be Required as a Pre-Condition to Provisional Relief?*, 52 N.C. L. Rev. 1091, 1097–98 (1974).

6. In a few states, the security requirement is truly imperative in that the failure to post security is jurisdictional. In those states, a provisional injunction issued without a bond is void, and a person cannot be held in contempt for violating the order. *See, e.g.*, Bruce v. Maurais, 69 Or.App. 267, 684 P.2d 1243 (1984); William G. Reeves, Comment, *Damages Recoverable on Injunction Bonds in Missouri*, 44 Mo. L. Rev. 269, 270 (1979). In the federal system and in most states, by contrast, the failure to post security is not jurisdictional, and the person against whom a provisional injunction is issued without security must comply with the injunction unless and until it is dissolved, stayed, or reversed on appeal. *See, e.g.*, Popular Bank of Florida v. Banco Popular de Puerto Rico, 180 F.R.D. 461 (S.D.Fla.1998).

B. INJUNCTION BOND RULE

In a frequently-cited footnote, the United States Supreme Court adopted the "injunction bond rule": "A party injured by the issuance of an injunction later determined to be erroneous has no action for damages in the absence of a bond." W.R. Grace & Co. v. Local Union 759, 461 U.S. 757, 770 n.14, 103 S.Ct. 2177, 2185–86 n.14, 76 L.Ed.2d 298 (1983). This passage has been interpreted by the lower federal courts to mean that, when there is a bond, the face value of the bond imposes a ceiling on the amount of damages that the defendant can recover for the wrongful issuance of provisional equitable relief. *See generally* Jay M. Zitter, Annotation, *Recovery of Damages Resulting from Wrongful Issuance of Injunction as Limited to Amount of Bond*, 30 A.L.R. 4th 273 (1981). When combined with the understanding that Rule 65(c) generally is mandatory, the injunction bond rule "assures the enjoined party that it may readily collect damages * * * in the event that it was wrongfully enjoined, without further litigation and without regard to the possible insolvency" of the applicant, and "it provides the plaintiff with notice of the maximum extent of its potential liability * * *." Phillips v. Charles Schreiner Bank, 894 F.2d 127, 131 (5th Cir.1990).

SPRINT COMMUNICATIONS CO. v. CAT COMMUNICATIONS INTERNATIONAL, INC.

United States Court of Appeals, Third Circuit, 2003.
335 F.3d 235.

SCIRICA, CHIEF JUDGE.

The principal issue on appeal is whether the District Court erred by retroactively increasing the amount of an injunction bond upon dissolution of a preliminary injunction.

I.

A.

Sprint Communications Company L.P. is a provider of long distance telephone service. CAT Communications International, Inc. is a reseller of local telephone service. The underlying dispute here arises from the allegedly improper use of Sprint's services by CAT Communications's customers.

Telephone users typically receive their local telephone service from a Local Exchange Carrier, which operates in a geographically defined exchange area. CAT Communications is a Competitive Local Exchange Carrier that leases lines from other Local Exchange Carriers and sells local telephone service available on these lines to the public on a prepaid basis. CAT Communications has no telephone facilities of its own.

As a long distance carrier, Sprint carries long distance calls forwarded to it by Local Exchange Carriers. In order to bill the long distance callers using its services, Sprint usually receives billing name and address information from the Local Exchange Carriers. As an alternative, the Local Exchange Carriers may provide billing and collecting services on behalf of Sprint.

Sprint contends that its network received unauthorized long distance telephone calls from CAT Communications's local service customers. The calls originated from several states, the largest number coming from New Jersey. None of these calls were paid for.

B.

Sprint asked CAT Communications to prevent its customers from gaining access to Sprint's network and also to provide a billing mechanism or billing information to facilitate Sprint's collection efforts. When CAT Communications did not respond, Sprint filed suit in federal court alleging trespass [and] conversion * * *.

In May 2000, the District Court heard arguments on Sprint's request for a preliminary injunction to prevent the unauthorized and unpaid use of its network. Sprint wanted CAT Communications to restrict its customers' access to Sprint's long distance network. CAT Communications argued that the expense of instituting the restriction should foreclose issuing a preliminary injunction. Because CAT Communications provided "[n]o affidavits or similar proofs" supporting its argument, the District Court found that the cost to CAT Communications of such restriction was at that point "mere conjecture." * * * Moreover, the District Court held the possible cost of the restriction would not be "significant when compared to the harm sustained by Sprint." *Id.* At the time, Sprint had shown "a total of $178,000 in unpaid long distance phone bills" attributed to the unauthorized use of its network by CAT Communications's customers.
* * *

The District Court issued an order [on May 15, 2000] preliminarily restraining CAT Communications "from permitting [its] customers to access or place calls on ... Sprint's ... long distance network" and directing it to "take such measures as are necessary to block all [its] customers' " access. * * * The injunction order required Sprint to post a $250,000 bond "for payment of such costs and damages as may be incurred or suffered by ... CAT Communications if found to have been wrongfully enjoined." * * *

Soon after the order was issued, CAT Communications moved to modify the preliminary injunction. But it withdrew the motion after the District Court amended the injunction order.[1] CAT Communications appealed the preliminary injunction but then withdrew its appeal.

C.

CAT Communications complied with the preliminary injunction by ordering blocks on its customers' access to Sprint's network. The blocks were actually instituted by the Local Exchange Carriers that own the local lines, not by CAT Communications, a reseller of local service that does not have its own telephone facilities. In some areas, the Local Exchange Carriers charged fees to CAT Communications in order to institute and maintain the blocks. Particularly, in New Jersey, Verizon charged a nonrecurring $10.55 fee to impose a block on each CAT Communications customer and a $12.41 per line monthly charge to maintain the block.

---

1. The original order required CAT Communications to prevent all its customers [from obtaining] access to Sprint's network. The order was amended [on June 16, 2000] to require CAT Communications to prevent access by "persons who become CAT Communications' customers after May 15, 2000," the date the preliminary injunction was granted. * * *

With these charges, CAT Communications began to accrue significant costs under the preliminary injunction.

But CAT Communications took no action until November 2001, when it sought to terminate the preliminary injunction and increase the amount of the injunction bond. At that time, CAT Communications asserted that the blocking charges stood at over $2.7 million and were projected to rise. In January 2002, Sprint and CAT Communications filed motions for summary judgment. The original District Judge had by then retired and a hearing on these motions was set for April 2002 before a new District Judge.

The District Court * * * denied summary judgment [to both Sprint and CAT] on the trespass and conversion claims. * * * It also dissolved the preliminary injunction and, at the same time, increased the injunction bond to $4.95 million. The increase in the bond amount was based on the "accrued" blocking fees charged to CAT Communications.

Sprint appeals the dissolution of the preliminary injunction and the simultaneous increase in the amount of the injunction bond. Because our focus is on the latter issue, we address the bond increase first.

II.

We normally review district court judgments fixing the amount of an injunction bond for abuse of discretion. * * * But here it is a question of law whether a district court may retroactively increase a bond amount, after the bond has been posted, in order to cover the asserted costs and damages incurred by the enjoined party. On this matter, we exercise plenary review. * * *

Generally, a bond is a condition of preliminary injunctive relief. Fed.R.Civ.P. 65(c) requires a successful applicant for a preliminary injunction to post a bond, "in such sum as the [district] court deems proper, for the payment of such costs and damages as may be incurred or suffered by any party who is found to have been wrongfully enjoined."[4] Thus, the injunction bond "provides a fund to use to compensate incorrectly enjoined defendants." Instant Air Freight Co. v. C.F. Air Freight, Inc., 882 F.2d 797, 804 (3d Cir.1989) (quotations omitted).

The injunction bond also serves other functions. "It is generally settled that, with rare exceptions, a [party] wrongfully enjoined has recourse only against the bond." Id.; see also Hoxworth v. Blinder, Robinson & Co., Inc., 903 F.2d 186, 210 n.31 (3d Cir.1990) (Applicants "derive some protection from the bond requirement, for [enjoined parties] injured by wrongfully issued preliminary injunctions can recover only against the bond itself."). Thus, the bond generally limits the liability of the applicant and informs the applicant of "the price [it] can expect to pay if the injunction was wrongfully issued." Instant Air Freight, 882 F.2d at

---

4. We have held that, under limited circumstances, a district court need not require a bond as a condition of preliminary injunctive relief. See Temple Univ. v. White, 941 F.2d 201 (3d Cir.1991). * * *

805; *see also id.* at 805 n.9 ("The bond can thus be seen as a contract in which the court and [the applicant] 'agree' to the bond amount as the 'price' of a wrongful injunction.") (quotations omitted).

The functions of the bond are illustrated in the course of litigation involving preliminary injunctive relief. When a court grants an applicant's request for a preliminary injunction, it will generally condition this grant on the applicant's posting a bond. The applicant then decides whether to accept the preliminary relief by posting the bond or to withdraw its request. The applicant may base its decision on whether it wants to expose itself to liability up to the bond amount. If the preliminary injunction takes effect and it is later determined a party was wrongfully enjoined, that party may then seek recovery against the posted bond. The recovery generally cannot exceed the amount posted.

If a retroactive increase is permissible, the injunction bond is no longer cabined; the bond no longer fixes exposure nor caps liability. A retroactive increase subjects the successful applicant to an unexpected and unanticipated liability.

Here, Sprint went forward with the preliminary injunction believing its liability was capped at $250,000 if CAT Communications were wrongfully enjoined. But the retroactive bond increase subjects Sprint to the possibility that CAT Communications may recover $4.95 million in costs and damages. Because the bond limits liability at the amount posted when the applicant accepted the preliminary injunction, the District Court erred in ordering a retroactive increase.

Rejecting a retroactive increase in the bond amount upon dissolution of a preliminary injunction accords with a recent decision by the United States Court of Appeals for the Seventh Circuit. *See* Mead Johnson & Co. v. Abbott Labs., 209 F.3d 1032 (7th Cir.2000). After appellate reversal of a preliminary injunction, the defendant on a petition for rehearing asked for a remand so that the district court might increase the amount of the injunction bond. In addressing the petition for rehearing, the court of appeals held that "there is neither logical nor legal room for a[n] ... increase in an injunction bond" after the preliminary injunction has been reversed. *Id.* at 1034 * * *.

A retroactive increase in the amount of an injunction bond on dissolution or reversal is generally improper. The injunction bond should maintain the limit on the applicant's liability and allow the applicant to "know just what [its] exposure is when the bond is set by the district court." *Id.* (quotations omitted).[6]

6. In rejecting the bond increase and maintaining the limit on Sprint's potential liability, our holding caps the amount of CAT Communications' possible recovery at a level which may be below the costs it has incurred. But CAT Communications had ample opportunity to address its potential damages from a wrongful injunction before the preliminary injunction was issued. Furthermore, while CAT Communications moved for modification and filed an appeal soon after the order was issued, it voluntarily withdrew these challenges to the preliminary injunction. It was not until almost eighteen months after the preliminary injunction was granted, after it had allegedly accrued over $2.7 million in blocking fees, that CAT Communications initiated a sustained challenge to the amount of the injunction bond.

III.

* * * [W]e review the decision to dissolve the preliminary injunction for abuse of discretion.

* * *

Sprint contends there are no changed circumstances to justify the dissolution of the preliminary injunction. Although not entirely clear, it appears from its oral opinion that, almost two years after the preliminary injunction was issued, the District Court came to a different conclusion from the original judge on the likelihood of success on the merits and the proper weighing of competing interests and harms. On this record, it appears that the "changed circumstances" here consisted mainly of the increase in costs of compliance asserted by CAT Communications. * * *

* * * The District Court apparently found that over the course of time the circumstances were such that the preliminary injunction proved unwarranted. In so doing, the District Court did not abuse its discretion.

* * *

We recognize that matters addressed by preliminary injunctive relief change over time. If at the present time Sprint believes it needs a preliminary injunction, it may seek such equitable relief before the District Court, subject to its willingness to post a bond in the appropriate amount. The District Court can decide whether a preliminary injunction should issue and, if so, the proper amount of an injunction bond to cover the costs and damages of such an injunction going forward.

IV.

For these reasons, we will reverse the increase in the amount of the injunction bond and order that the amount of the bond be maintained at $250,000. We will also affirm the dissolution of the preliminary injunction.

NOTES

1. Both the federal judiciary and the vast majority of the states adhere to the rule that the plaintiff's liability is limited by the amount of the injunction bond. Jay M. Zitter, Annotation, *Recovery of Damages Resulting from Wrongful Issuance of Injunction as Limited to Amount of Bond*, 30 A.L.R. 4th 273 (1981). The minority view holds that, since the amount of the bond is often based upon conjecture, liability should not be limited to the amount of the bond. *Id.* The majority rule often is justified by referring to the historical development of the bond:

> While we hesitate to resurrect ancient law, common law history is instructive. The practice of giving tangible items as security, called

---

9. In affirming the dissolution of the preliminary injunction, we do not mean to suggest that the injunction was improvidently granted by the original judge. * * * In fact, it appears that, given the record before him, the original judge did not abuse his discretion in granting the preliminary relief.

"gage," in order to acquire credit arose before any consensual theory of contract obligation emerged. The creditor took possession of the gage and retained it until he was repaid. But there was no underlying duty on the part of the debtor—if he failed to pay, the creditor held the security, but had no action on the debt. A surety was referred to as a "pledge," and was at first literally "an animated gage ... delivered over to slavery but subject to redemption." 2 F. Pollock & F. Maitland, The History of English Law, 185–86 (2d ed. 1899).

Although these devices were used for a number of purposes, they also served a role very similar to that of the Rule 65 injunction bond involved in this case. For example, at early common law the plaintiff in a replevin action against a distrainor was required to give "gage and pledge"—*i.e.*, a surety's bond. *Id.* at 577 * * *.

At later common law, a bond was a sealed and delivered instrument binding the obligor to pay a sum of money. 1A A. Corbin, Contracts, § 258, at 455 (1963). It did not need to be supported by consideration. 12 Halsbury's Laws of England § 1400 (4th ed. 1975). While common law bonds may be used for many purposes, including security for the performance of independent obligations, *see id.* § 1387, the term "bond" does not refer to the duty whose performance is secured, but only to the security itself. *See id.* § 1385.

Thus even if a duty independent of the security posted under Rule 65 can be implied, the district court's theory that a suit to enforce that duty is an action "on the bond" finds no justification in common law bond history. * * *

But more importantly, no underlying duty to recompense the victim of wrongful provisional relief independent of the security instrument may be implied. It is a well-settled rule that there can be no recovery for damages sustained by a wrongful issuance of a preliminary injunction in the absence of a bond * * *, unless the defendant sues for malicious prosecution or on a theory of unjust enrichment, Northern Oil Co. v. Socony Mobil Oil Co., 347 F.2d 81, 83 (2d Cir.1965); 11 C. Wright & A. Miller, Federal Practice and Procedure § 2973, at 652 (1973) * * *. If a bond is posted, liability is limited by the terms of the bond or the order of the court that required the posting. *See* 11 Wright & Miller, *supra*, § 2973, at 652 * * *.

Buddy Systems, Inc. v. Exer–Genie, Inc., 545 F.2d 1164, 1167–68 (9th Cir. 1976) (holding that the defendant was not entitled to recover any damages after the bond had been exonerated), *cert. denied*, 431 U.S. 903, 97 S.Ct. 1694, 52 L.Ed.2d 387 (1977).

2. In Dickey v. Rosso, 23 Cal.App.3d 493, 100 Cal.Rptr. 358 (1972), the defendant challenged the constitutionality of the majority rule:

The Rossos contend that the limitation of damages for the improper issuance of * * * [a preliminary] injunction to the amount of the undertaking violates due process of law. They argue that the legal procedures for the use of injunctive remedies fail to make them whole for all losses the use of these remedies may have caused them and that no effective means were given them to challenge the trial court's determination of the amount of the undertaking.

We find no merit in this argument. In creating legal procedures for use of the provisional remedy of injunctive relief the state has two conflicting interests to balance—that of defendants, who should be compensated for damage caused by legal procedures whose use is later shown to have been unjustified; and that of honest plaintiffs, who should not be deterred from using the courts by fear of incurring unlimited liability from their use of the court's process. The state has established an entirely reasonable scheme for the use of injunctive relief, in that plaintiff is told in advance what his maximum summary liability will be for making use of the court's injunctive powers pending a determination of the merits of his cause, and defendant is provided an opportunity to make a showing what the amount of his damages is likely to be as a consequence of plaintiff's use of the remedy of injunctive relief. Thereafter the court fixes the amount of the undertaking in connection with the use of injunctive relief. If at a later time defendant discovers further possibilities of damages arising during the pendency of the litigation and makes a proper showing of the possibility of such damages, the court may require plaintiff to increase the amount of his undertaking as a condition of the continuance of injunctive relief. * * * The possibility that damages might be inestimable, a possibility not apparent here, is outweighed by the need to provide honest plaintiffs with recourse to the courts.

Twice the Rossos requested the trial court to increase the amount of the undertaking on the preliminary injunction. Twice the trial court in its sound discretion rejected their request. The Rossos did not seek to challenge the trial court's exercise of its discretion by writ or by appeal, and consequently the cause of their present discontent lies not in lack of effective process but in lack of effective use of existing process.

Id. at 497–98, 100 Cal. Rptr. at 361–62.

3. After conducting an injunction bond hearing in a case brought by an "indigent plaintiff" or a "public interest plaintiff," a federal trial court judge may of course decide not to require the posting of security. In such cases, the plaintiff will be immune from liability for a wrongfully issued injunction or the plaintiff's liability will be limited to the amount of the bond.

At the other end of the spectrum, a plaintiff with substantial assets may ask a federal trial court judge to waive the bond requirement (or not to increase the amount of a posted bond) in exchange for a promise by the plaintiff to pay all of the defendant's damages in the event that the provisional injunction is wrongfully issued. Some federal circuits have held that it is not an abuse of discretion for a trial court judge to grant such a request, even over the defendant's objections. Continuum Co. v. Incepts, Inc., 873 F.2d 801 (5th Cir.1989) (refusing to replace a $200,000 bond with $2,000,000 bond because "providing a bond in the amount of $2,000,000 would impose a great hardship" on the plaintiff, and the plaintiff's annual profit of $2.5 million "indicated that it would be able to satisfy any judgment for damages that might be obtained against it as a result of a wrongful issuance of an injunction"); Continental Oil Co. v. Frontier Refining Co., 338 F.2d 780 (10th

Cir.1964) (refusing to require an injunction bond because the evidence showed that the plaintiff was a corporation with "substantial assets"). By contrast, the Second Circuit has been willing to forego the posting of security by a plaintiff with substantial assets only upon the written agreement of the parties. Pharmaceutical Society of the State of New York, Inc. v. New York State Department of Social Services, 50 F.3d 1168, 1175 (2d Cir.1995) (no agreement); Helene Curtis v. National Wholesale Liquidators, Inc., 890 F.Supp. 152, 160 (E.D.N.Y.1995) (agreement).

C. IS A FAILURE TO CONDUCT A RULE 65(c) HEARING AN ABUSE OF DISCRETION?

The burden is on the defendant to file a motion requesting the trial court judge to conduct an injunction bond hearing, and a failure to do so constitutes a waiver of the bond requirement by the defendant on appeal. *See, e.g.*, Connecticut General Life Insurance Co. v. New Images of Beverly Hills, 321 F.3d 878, 882–83 (9th Cir.2003) (citing to other cases). The next case considers the question of whether a failure to conduct a Rule 65(c) hearing constitutes an abuse of discretion.

RATHMANN GROUP v. TANENBAUM

United States Court of Appeals, Eighth Circuit, 1989.
889 F.2d 787.

Before McMillian and Wollman, Circuit Judges, and Heaney, Senior Circuit Judge.

Heaney, Senior Circuit Judge.

Joel Tanenbaum appeals an order of the district court entering a preliminary injunction restraining him from competing with his former employer, The Rathmann Group, Inc. (Rathmann), for a period of one year from the date of Tanenbaum's resignation. * * *

Background

Rathmann operates a beauty and barbershop supply business. It purchased its business from Fred F. Foster in 1988. Tanenbaum had worked as a sales agent for Foster since 1979. At the time he went to work for Foster, Tanenbaum signed an agreement stipulating that if his employment with Foster were to terminate for any reason, he would not work as a sales agent for manufacturers of beauty and barbershop supplies in a twelve-state area of the midwest for a period of one year. All other terms of the employment contract between Foster and Tanenbaum were oral. Following Foster's sale of his business to Rathmann, Tanenbaum sought to clarify the terms of his employment under the company's new management. Rathmann and Tanenbaum executed a written contract describing Tanenbaum's sales territory and commission arrangement on January 6, 1989. The contract contained no noncompete agreement and made no mention of the agreement Tanenbaum previously had entered into with Foster. Rathmann previously had rejected an integration clause proposed by Tanenbaum, however, which stated that the contract represented the sole and complete agreement between the parties.

Tanenbaum submitted his resignation to Rathmann on May 9, 1989. He then organized his own beauty and barbershop supply business and began soliciting trade from customers of Rathmann in his former territory. Rathmann subsequently sought injunctive relief against Tanenbaum to enforce the noncompete agreement Tanenbaum had signed with Foster in 1979. After hearing arguments from both parties, the district court entered a temporary restraining order (TRO), conditioned on Rathmann's posting a $5000.00 bond, granting the relief Rathmann sought for the period from May 24, 1989 to May 30, 1989.

The district court held an evidentiary hearing on May 30, 1989 to consider Rathmann's motion for a preliminary injunction. Thereafter, the court continued the TRO until June 6, 1989, conditioned on Rathmann's posting an additional $5000 bond. On June 22, 1989, the district court issued an order granting the motion for a preliminary injunction. The injunction restrained Tanenbaum and his affiliates from competing with Rathmann in a twelve-state area of the midwest until May 9, 1990, one year from the date on which Tanenbaum had resigned. The court did not indicate that it intended the injunction to be permanent in nature; and the preliminary injunction was not conditioned on the posting of any additional bond by Rathmann.

DISCUSSION

Tanenbaum raises two issues on appeal. First, he claims that the district court erred in failing to condition its preliminary injunction on the posting of further security by Rathmann. Second, Tanenbaum contends that because the preliminary injunction grants Rathmann all the equitable relief to which it would be entitled if the noncompete agreement between Tanenbaum and Foster were found to be valid and enforceable by Rathmann after trial on the merits, the injunction is in effect a permanent one. As such, according to Tanenbaum, the injunction should not have been ordered without notice to the parties that the court was considering permanent relief. We address these arguments in turn.

I.

* * *

Rathmann argues that the two $5,000 bonds it posted on the issuance and extension of the TRO constitute sufficient security for the preliminary injunction. We disagree. Although the amount of the bond required by Rule 65(c) rests within the discretion of the trial court, * * * we believe that the district court abused its discretion because it neglected to consider the question of requiring a bond in addition to the $10,000 already posted on the issuance and continuation of the TRO. *See* Roth v. Bank of the Commonwealth, 583 F.2d 527, 539 (6th Cir.1978) (finding error, not because trial court failed to require a bond in any particular amount, but because court failed to exercise discretion required by Rule 65(c) by expressly considering question of requiring bond).

The district court apparently considered the need for plaintiff to post a bond twice during the proceedings of this case; when it issued the TRO and required a $5,000 bond, and when it continued the TRO and required an additional $5,000 bond. That the district court required an additional $5,000 bond merely to extend the duration of the TRO by one week suggests that the court recognized the potential loss to defendant which an improperly granted injunction could cause. Anomalously, however, the district court's order of the preliminary injunction restricting Tanenbaum from competing with Rathmann for an entire year makes no mention of the need for additional security from Rathmann to protect Tanenbaum from an erroneously granted preliminary injunction. Evidence in the record indicates that Tanenbaum may lose gross income of $13,000 per month as a result of the injunction. The $10,000 that Rathmann posted pursuant to the TRO thus is inadequate to protect Tanenbaum in the event that a trial on the merits results in a decision in his favor. Consequently, we believe that the district court improperly failed to consider whether Rathmann should post an additional bond as a condition of the court's issuing its preliminary injunction.

II.

Tanenbaum's second contention, that the district court improperly issued what effectively was a permanent injunction preventing Tanenbaum from competing with Rathmann for a period of one year, also has merit. * * * In deciding whether to grant the preliminary injunction, the district court applied the standard set forth in Dataphase Systems, Inc. v. C L Systems, Inc., 640 F.2d 109, 114 (8th Cir.1981) (en banc). The court found that Rathmann could suffer irreparable harm absent the injunction, that such harm would outweigh the potential injury to Tanenbaum that granting the injunction would cause, that Rathmann was likely to succeed on the merits, and that the injunction would not harm the public interest. While we express no opinion on the ultimate merits of the case, we believe that the district court properly applied the *Dataphase* standard. The district court's preliminary injunction, however, extends until May 9, 1990, one year from the date on which Tanenbaum resigned from Rathmann's employ. Because the noncompete agreement that Tanenbaum entered into with Foster mandated no competition between the parties for the same one-year period, Rathmann's success at trial on the merits would give Rathmann precisely the same injunctive relief that the preliminary injunction provides.

An order that grants the plaintiff all the relief it ultimately may be entitled to and that makes no provision for further hearings is a permanent injunction. * * *

* * * Although we acknowledge the district court's discretion to issue a preliminary injunction, we believe that the scope of the injunction issued

exceeds the limits necessary to protect Rathmann until the matter can be decided on the merits. Additionally, we believe that the district court erred in failing to notify the parties in advance of the relief its order contemplated. *Cf.* Ecolab, Inc. v. Morisette, 879 F.2d 325, 327 (8th Cir.1989) (per curiam) ("A district court normally should not consolidate a hearing on a preliminary injunction with a trial on the merits unless the court gives the parties clear notice of its intent to do so.") (citations omitted). Tanenbaum received no indication from the court that it would order anything other than preliminary relief following the May 30, 1989 evidentiary hearing. Consequently, we believe that the court's issuance of a preliminary injunction coextensive with the temporal duration of the noncompete agreement at issue was improper.

We remand the case to the district court for a prompt trial on the merits and for an increase in the bond posted as security by Rathmann. The bond should be of an amount adequate to protect Tanenbaum's business until such time as the district court enters its final decision.

Note

Federal trial court rulings regarding the security for provisional injunctions are reviewed by appellate courts pursuant to an "abuse of discretion" standard. If the trial court judge refuses to hold a hearing on the security issue (over the defendant's objection), the appellate court will find an abuse of discretion, regardless of whether the appellate court construes Rule 65(c) as "mandatory," or as "almost mandatory with a few exceptions," or as "discretionary." *See, e.g.,* Roth v. Bank of the Commonwealth, 583 F.2d 527, 539 (6th Cir.1978) (affirming a provisional injunction in part, but remanding with instructions to conduct a hearing on the security issue); *see also* System Operations Inc. v. Scientific Games Development Corp., 555 F.2d 1131, 1145 (3d Cir.1977). Also, if the trial court judge conducts a hearing on the security requirement, but fails to provide an explanation for its decision to set the amount of the security at the chosen figure, the appellate court will find an abuse of discretion, regardless of how the appellate court construes Rule 65(c). *See, e.g.,* Gateway Eastern Railway Co. v. Terminal Railroad Ass'n, 35 F.3d 1134, 1142 (7th Cir.1994) (affirming a preliminary injunction, but remanding for more definite findings with regard to the bond).

D.   RECOVERY OF DAMAGES

NINTENDO OF AMERICA, INC. v. LEWIS GALOOB TOYS, INC.

United States Court of Appeals, Ninth Circuit, 1994.
16 F.3d 1032.

Before LAY,[1] HALL and THOMPSON, CIRCUIT JUDGES.

DAVID R. THOMPSON, CIRCUIT JUDGE:

Nintendo of America, Inc. appeals the execution of a $15 million bond in favor of Lewis Galoob Toys, Inc. Nintendo posted the bond as security

---

1. Hon. Donald P. Lay, Senior Circuit Judge for the Eighth Circuit, sitting by designation.

for a preliminary injunction against Galoob in a copyright infringement action Nintendo later lost. The district court awarded Galoob the entire amount of the bond after finding the injunction caused Galoob at least $15 million in damages.

Nintendo argues the district court erred in three ways: First, by not weighing equitable considerations before deciding to execute the bond; second, by improperly finding the injunction harmed Galoob; and third, by improperly calculating the amount of Galoob's damages.

FACTS

The Nintendo Entertainment System ("NES") was the most popular home video game system in the United States from the late 1980s until the early 1990s. Its manufacturer, Nintendo of America, Inc., began selling the NES in 1986. By 1991, Nintendo had sold over thirty million units in the United States.

Several years after Nintendo introduced the NES, Lewis Galoob Toys, Inc. announced its intention to begin selling the Game Genie, an electronic device allowing NES owners to change aspects of NES video games. For example, the Game Genie would permit a video game character to run faster, jump higher, or become immortal.

At the time of Galoob's announcement of the Game Genie, in May 1990, NES product sales were at or near their peak. Nintendo sold nearly fifteen million NES video games that year, exceeding any other year's sales. Consumer interest in the Game Genie was similarly intense. Immediately after the product announcement, Galoob received orders for over 550,000 Game Genies, and expected to sell well over a million units in 1990. Expert witnesses later testified Galoob could have sold as many as 6.5 million units over the product's lifetime.

Only one month after Galoob's announcement, however, Nintendo obtained a preliminary injunction against the sale of the Game Genie. Nintendo's lawsuit and request for a preliminary injunction responded to an earlier lawsuit filed by Galoob in which Galoob sought a declaratory judgment that its Game Genie did not violate any of Nintendo's intellectual property rights.

At the hearing for the preliminary injunction, Galoob asserted that the Game Genie fell under an exception to rights provided to a copyright owner by the Copyright Act. Specifically, Galoob contended that the Game Genie allowed an "adaptation . . . created as an essential step in the utilization of [a] computer program," which 17 U.S.C. § 117 states is a permissible use of a copyrighted work. The district court granted the injunction, believing at the time it was likely "Nintendo will prevail on its claims that Galoob [has infringed] Nintendo's copyright rights; [and] that Nintendo will suffer immediate and irreparable harm as well as the loss of profits." The district court required Nintendo to post a $100,000 bond as security for the injunction. This amount was later raised to $5 million and then to $15 million. Nintendo resisted these increases, but nevertheless posted bond in the increased amounts.

At the copyright infringement trial, Galoob asserted additional legal theories it had not asserted at the preliminary injunction hearing. It contended that the Game Genie was a fair use of Nintendo's copyrights under 17 U.S.C. § 107 and that the game did not create infringing derivative works. Galoob prevailed at trial and in July 1991, the district court vacated the injunction. The injunction had been in effect approximately one year.

In August 1991, Galoob began selling the Game Genie. It sold about one million units in the United States that year and expected to sell as many as 800,000 in 1992. In September 1991, the district court ordered the execution of the bond in favor of Galoob "in an amount to be determined by the Court."

In December 1991, the court held a "lost sales" hearing to determine the number of Game Genie sales Galoob lost because of the injunction. To establish the number of lost sales, Galoob presented evidence comparing the Game Genie to another NES accessory called the "Nintendo Advantage." The Advantage is a joystick, manufactured and sold by Nintendo. * * *

* * *

The district court determined Galoob lost at least 1.6 million Game Genie sales. * * *

* * *

By multiplying the 1.6 million unit sales lost by the net wholesale price of $34.28, times the 27.6 percent profit margin, the district court found Galoob suffered at least $15,138,048 in lost profits due to the injunction. The court also calculated Galoob lost $315,569 in interest it would have earned on its lost profits and $480,000 in costs it incurred "when [Galoob] ceased production and distribution and thereafter recommenced those activities upon dissolution of the injunction." Because the total of these amounts exceeded the $15 million bond Nintendo posted, the district court awarded Galoob the entire amount of the bond, plus costs, under Federal Rule of Civil Procedure 65.1.* * *

STANDARD OF REVIEW

We review de novo a district court's decision to execute a bond. * * * A district court's computation of damages is a finding we review under the clearly erroneous standard. * * *

DISCUSSION

The first issue we consider is whether Galoob was wrongfully enjoined. We conclude it was. We then consider what standard we should apply to ascertain whether the district court erred in determining that

Galoob was entitled to damages. Finally, we consider whether the district court erred in computing the amount of damages.

* * *

Under Rule 65(c), before a court may execute a bond, it must find the enjoined or restrained party was "wrongfully enjoined or restrained." This circuit has yet to define wrongful enjoinment. We hold today that a party has been wrongfully enjoined within the meaning of Rule 65(c) when it turns out the party enjoined had the right all along to do what it was enjoined from doing.[4] *See* Blumenthal v. Merrill Lynch, Pierce, Fenner & Smith, Inc., 910 F.2d 1049, 1054 (2d Cir.1990) ("A party has been 'wrongfully enjoined' under Fed.R.Civ.P. 65(c) if it is ultimately found that the enjoined party had at all times the right to do the enjoined act.").

Here, Nintendo obtained a preliminary injunction enjoining Galoob from selling the Game Genie. As it turned out, Galoob prevailed in the underlying litigation. The district court held Galoob could sell the Game Genie and vacated the preliminary injunction. We affirmed on appeal. * * * Thus, Galoob was wrongfully enjoined.

This brings us to the next question: Is Galoob entitled to have the bond executed in its favor? Although there seems to be some variance in how other circuits respond to this question, we join what appears to be the majority and hold there is a rebuttable presumption that a wrongfully enjoined party is entitled to have the bond executed and recover provable damages up to the amount of the bond. *See, e.g.*, National Kidney Patients Ass'n v. Sullivan, 958 F.2d 1127, 1134 (D.C.Cir.1992) (a "defendant injured by a wrongfully issued preliminary injunction is presumptively entitled to recovery on the injunction bond"), *cert. denied*, 506 U.S. 1049, 113 S.Ct. 966, 122 L.Ed.2d 122 (1993).

We believe this rule is sound. By adhering to this standard, the party enjoined will usually recover damages, thus discouraging parties from requesting injunctions based on tenuous legal grounds. *See* Coyne–Delany Co. v. Capital Dev. Bd., 717 F.2d 385, 392 (7th Cir.1983) (" . . . [this test] discourages the seeking of preliminary injunctions on flimsy (though not necessarily frivolous) grounds."). Furthermore, a presumption that damages will be awarded from the bond assures district court judges that defendants will receive compensation for their damages in cases where it is later determined a party was wrongfully enjoined. * * * Moreover, demands on judicial resources may be relieved to some extent, because a defendant who can recover damages against a preliminary injunction bond will be less likely to file a separate malicious prosecution action. * * * Finally, this standard provides an equitable means by which courts can decline to impose damages on the rare party who has lost a case on the

---

4. We prefer the wording of Rule 65(c), which speaks in terms of a party who has been "wrongfully enjoined," rather than the wording in some cases in other circuits which refers to an injunction as having been "wrongfully issued." Fed.R.Civ.P. 65(c). A court that complies with the applicable law in issuing a preliminary injunction does not "wrongfully" issue it. Indeed, in an earlier appeal in this case we upheld the district court's issuance of the preliminary injunction. * * *

merits but nevertheless should not suffer the execution of the preliminary injunction bond.

Nintendo argues it rebutted this presumption. Nintendo points out it acted in good faith in bringing its copyright infringement lawsuit, Galoob failed to assert defenses to the preliminary injunction it could have asserted at the preliminary injunction hearing, public policy favors the issuance of injunctions in intellectual property infringement suits, and to award Galoob $15 million imposes a punitive sanction against Nintendo. We consider each of these arguments in turn.

We reject Nintendo's good faith argument. Good faith in the maintenance of litigation is the standard expected of all litigants. That a party lives up to this standard simply means the party did what it ought to have done. On the other hand, if a party obtains a preliminary injunction in bad faith, that party "flunks [the good faith test and] the presumption in favor of enforcement [of the bond] congeals virtually into a rock." * * *

Nintendo's argument that Galoob failed to assert all of its defenses at the time Nintendo sought the preliminary injunction raises the specter of bad faith on the part of Galoob. The essence of this argument is that Galoob took advantage of Nintendo by initially making its case appear to be worse than it really was, thus lulling Nintendo into obtaining the preliminary injunction. The implication of the argument is that Galoob cunningly got the court to raise the amount of the bond on two successive occasions, finally pushing it up to $15 million, while concealing the hole cards it intended to play at the time of trial. Nintendo argues it would be inequitable to permit Galoob to recover damages when it pursued such wily litigation tactics. In support of this argument, Nintendo relies on *Page Communications Eng'rs, Inc. v. Froehlke*, 475 F.2d 994 (D.C.Cir. 1973).

Page Communications is inapposite. There, the court declined to award damages to an enjoined defendant in a contract action. The defendant earlier agreed to produce "all 'records relating to the evaluation of proposals submitted' by the various offerors, and all 'documents setting forth the basis for award.' " *Page Communications*, 475 F.2d at 996. Although this language described a particular report the defendant possessed, the defendant intentionally declined to produce the report. In granting the injunction for the plaintiff, the district court believed erroneously it had examined all the relevant evidence. Because the defendant was responsible for the missing evidence, and because the district court would probably not have granted the [preliminary] injunction had it seen the report, the court concluded that in light of these circumstances, it would be inequitable to assess damages against the plaintiff. *Id.* at 997.

Here, Galoob did not fail to produce evidence. It did not deceive the court. There is no indication in the record that Galoob sandbagged Nintendo into prevailing on its application for the preliminary injunction, knowing all the while that it could have defeated that application. Those facts simply are not in this case. All that appears is that Galoob had additional defenses it asserted at the time of trial, defenses it had not asserted at the preliminary injunction hearing. And while it is true Galoob persuaded the court on two successive occasions to increase the amount of the bond, thus raising the stakes of the game, it is also true that Nintendo called these raises by putting up additional amounts of the bond. We conclude Galoob's litigation conduct does not preclude it from recovering on the bond.

Nintendo's public policy argument is premised on its assertion that public policy favors the issuance of injunctions in intellectual property infringement lawsuits. This assertion is correct only when a permanent injunction is sought once infringement has been established. * * * Public policy does not advocate the liberal issuance of preliminary injunctions in copyright infringement actions.

* * *

We next consider whether the district court erred in determining that Galoob suffered at least $15 million in damages by reason of the issuance of the injunction. * * *

* * * According to Nintendo, Galoob was not damaged by the injunction because the injunction only delayed Game Genie sales, it did not prevent them permanently. * * *

We reject this argument. It is premised largely on speculation, and as the district court stated, it "defies common sense." * * *

The next question is: Did the district court err in computing the amount of damages Galoob suffered? * * *

* * * [I]n determining the number of lost sales, the district court repeatedly used the most conservative ends of available ranges. While it is true that Galoob did not likely lose exactly 1.6 million sales of the Game Genie, it is reasonably certain it lost at least that amount. * * *

With regard to the court's finding that Galoob's profit margin for the Game Genie was 27.6 percent, the court began with the "rational and reliable" estimate of Galoob's economist that the profit margin was 42.74 percent, considered the evidence and contentions of the parties and reduced that figure to 27.6 percent. It did not clearly err in making this finding.

CONCLUSION

Galoob was wrongfully enjoined from selling the Game Genie. As a result, it was presumptively entitled to recover damages. Nintendo did not rebut this presumption. Galoob proved with reasonable certainty it was damaged by the injunction. The district court did not err in finding Galoob's damages exceeded the $15 million amount of the bond. Galoob was entitled to have the full amount of the bond executed in its favor.

NOTES

1. A defendant can collect damages against a bond under Rule 65(c) only if the defendant is "found to have been wrongfully enjoined or restrained." The *Nintendo* court adopted the "final judgment" construction of Rule 65(c). *See generally* Note, *Recovery for Wrongful Interlocutory Injunctions under Rule 65(c)*, 99 Harv. L. Rev. 828, 836 (1986). A court that has adopted the "final judgment" rule takes the position that a defendant who has prevailed at the time of the final judgment is a party who has been wrongfully enjoined because the defendant "had a right all along to do what [the defendant] was enjoined from doing." Global Naps, Inc. v. Verizon New England, Inc., 489 F.3d 13, 22 (1st Cir. 2007). Plaintiffs occasionally make the counterargument that "an injunction cannot be wrongful unless it is shown that issuance of the injunction was an abuse of discretion at the time it was issued." *Id.* Almost every circuit that has considered this argument has rejected it. *Id.*; *but see* H & R Block, Inc. v. McCaslin, 541 F.2d 1098, 1099–1100 (5th Cir. 1976)(per curiam).

2. When is a wrongfully enjoined party entitled to have the bond executed in its favor? Should damages be automatically recoverable against the bond? For a discussion of this option, see Alabama *ex rel.* Siegelman v. United States Environmental Protection Agency, 925 F.2d 385, 389 (11th Cir.1991). Or should the trial court have open-ended discretion to award or deny damages on an injunction bond, unless the plaintiff acted in bad faith in seeking a provisional injunction? For a discussion of this option, see Page Communications Engineers, Inc. v. Froehlke, 475 F.2d 994, 997 (D.C.Cir. 1973). Or should there be a rebuttable presumption that a wrongfully enjoined party is entitled to have the bond executed in its favor? For a discussion of this option, see Coyne–Delany Co. v. Capital Development Board, 717 F.2d 385, 390 (7th Cir.1983).

The Ninth Circuit in *Nintendo* adopted the rebuttable presumption approach, and therefore gave Nintendo an opportunity to show that it would be inequitable to allow Galoob to recover damages against the bond. Nintendo's primary argument, relying on *Page*, was that Galoob had acted in "bad faith." Another type of misconduct which may rebut the presumption that the defendant is entitled to recover damages against the bond is a "failure to mitigate damages." *See Coyne–Delany Co.*, 717 F.2d at 392. And at least one federal court has refused to allow the enjoined defendant to have the bond executed in its favor when the provisional injunction had to be dissolved due to a subsequently enacted statute. Kansas *ex rel.* Stephan v. Adams, 705 F.2d 1267 (10th Cir.1983).

3. What damages are recoverable against a security posted under Rule 65(c)? As illustrated by *Nintendo*, an enjoined defendant may recover compensatory damages for the harm actually caused by the provisional injunction. *Accord* Chambron v. Lost Colony Homeowners Ass'n, 317 S.C. 43, 451 S.E.2d 410 (1994) (damages recoverable only for the duration of a wrongfully issued preliminary injunction, and not for the duration of a subsequent wrongfully issued permanent injunction). The damages are measured by the principles governing the assessment of common law damages. *See, e.g.*, Carr v. Citizens

Bank & Trust Co., 228 Va. 644, 325 S.E.2d 86 (1985). *See generally* Dan B. Dobbs, *Should Security Be Required as a Pre–Condition to Provisional Injunctive Relief?*, 52 N.C. L. Rev. 1091, 1125–27, 1131–32 (1974). Many state courts, but not the federal courts, also allow an award of attorney's fees. *Id.* at 1133–36. As a general rule, only those fees incurred in defending against the provisional relief may be recovered against the bond. *Id.*

4. As the foregoing materials illustrate, numerous significant substantive and policy problems concerning injunction bonds remain largely unresolved and continue to perplex courts. Consider, in this regard, Professor Dobbs's thoughtful commentary:

> Injunction bond cases raise many problems, not the least of which is the fact that judges often underestimate the potential harm to a defendant. This comment, however, only addresses two structural problems that suggest the need for a more comprehensive statutory scheme.

> A bond requirement usually adds to the plaintiff's cost of litigating. Usually the plaintiff pays a premium (annually) for a commercial bond. Alternatives may be cheaper. The court may permit some other form of security; the plaintiff might be permitted to file a certificate of deposit with the clerk, so that if the plaintiff wins, all interest payable on the certificate will accrue to the plaintiff. Or the plaintiff might obtain a non-commercial bond, persuading friends to stand as surety.

> Even these cheaper forms of providing security, however, cost something. Time to make such special arrangements may not be available to one who seeks a preliminary injunction. Those who do not have the funds to risk and those who do not have even the premium funds, may be excluded from access to courts by the bond requirement. Even those who have funds may be deterred from resort to court. So the decision to preserve the defendant's fair-trial/due process rights by a bond requirement has at least a degree of cost attached.

> In addition, some of the potential plaintiffs who are short on funds are likely to be sympathetic; even more, they may at times represent important public interests, suing to enforce rights which, if vindicated, will aid many people or protect the environment from irreparable harm.

> When costs threaten to prevent litigation in the public interest, some courts have thought that the bond requirements should be ameliorated. But we do not know before trial that the plaintiff will vindicate the public interest; the defendant might be innocent and victimized. Even if we think provisionally that the plaintiff is acting in the public interest to resolve an issue by litigation, it does not follow that the private defendant should pay for the public's chance. The public interest should be paid for by the public treasury, until we can determine that the defendant really was rightfully enjoined. So a more just solution to the defendants who prove in the end to be victims rather than wrongdoers is to invest public funds in a bond or other security, then to demand that those funds be repaid by defendants who are proven to be wrongdoers.

> Public interest comes into bonding rules in another way, too. Public entities are often exempted from the bond requirement. Perhaps the

exemption resulted because legislatures assumed that the public entity would be solvent and would pay damages it did to an innocent citizen by obtaining unjustified preliminary relief. But this is not the law in the federal system or in most states. Instead, recovery is allowed only against any security that is filed. Public entities, which are forbidden to take property without payment, should not be permitted to take other rights without a trial.

Dan B. Dobbs, Law of Remedies 205 (2d ed. 1993).[1]

SECTION 4. PERMANENT INJUNCTIONS

The four cases in this section illustrate the application of the standard for determining whether to issue a permanent injunction in the context of contract, property and tort actions.

WALGREEN CO. v. SARA CREEK PROPERTY CO.

United States Court of Appeals, Seventh Circuit, 1992.
966 F.2d 273.

Before POSNER and KANNE, CIRCUIT JUDGES, and WOOD, JR., SENIOR CIRCUIT JUDGE.

POSNER, CIRCUIT JUDGE.

This appeal from the grant of a permanent injunction raises fundamental issues concerning the propriety of injunctive relief. 775 F.Supp. 1192 (E.D.Wis.1991). The essential facts are simple. Walgreen has operated a pharmacy in the Southgate Mall in Milwaukee since its opening in 1951. Its current lease, signed in 1971 and carrying a 30–year, 6–month term, contains, as had the only previous lease, a clause in which the landlord, Sara Creek, promises not to lease space in the mall to anyone else who wants to operate a pharmacy or a store containing a pharmacy. Such an exclusivity clause, common in shopping-center leases, is occasionally challenged on antitrust grounds * * *—implausibly enough, given the competition among malls; but that is an issue for another day, since in this appeal Sara Creek does not press the objection it made below to the clause on antitrust grounds.

In 1990, fearful that its largest tenant—what in real estate parlance is called the "anchor tenant"—having gone broke was about to close its store, Sara Creek informed Walgreen that it intended to buy out the anchor tenant and install in its place a discount store operated by Phar–Mor Corporation, a "deep discount" chain, rather than, like Walgreen, just a "discount" chain. Phar–Mor's store would occupy 100,000 square feet, of which 12,000 would be occupied by a pharmacy the same size as Walgreen's. The entrances to the two stores would be within a couple of hundred feet of each other.

Walgreen filed this diversity suit for breach of contract against Sara Creek and Phar–Mor and asked for an injunction against Sara Creek's letting the anchor premises to Phar–Mor. After an evidentiary hearing, the judge found a breach of Walgreen's lease and entered a permanent injunction against Sara Creek's letting the anchor tenant premises to Phar–Mor until the expiration of Walgreen's lease. He did this over the defendants' objection that Walgreen had failed to show that its remedy at law—damages—for the breach of the exclusivity clause was inadequate. Sara Creek had put on an expert witness who testified that Walgreen's damages could be readily estimated, and Walgreen had countered with evidence from its employees that its damages would be very difficult to compute, among other reasons because they included intangibles such as loss of goodwill.

Sara Creek reminds us that damages are the norm in breach of contract as in other cases. Many breaches, it points out, are "efficient" in the sense that they allow resources to be moved into a more valuable use. * * * Perhaps this is one—the value of Phar–Mor's occupancy of the anchor premises may exceed the cost to Walgreen of facing increased competition. If so, society will be better off if Walgreen is paid its damages, equal to that cost, and Phar–Mor is allowed to move in rather than being kept out by an injunction. That is why injunctions are not granted as a matter of course, but only when the plaintiff's damages remedy is inadequate. * * * Walgreen's is not, Sara Creek argues; the projection of business losses due to increased competition is a routine exercise in calculation. Damages representing either the present value of lost future profits or (what should be the equivalent * * *) the diminution in the value of the leasehold have either been awarded or deemed the proper remedy in a number of reported cases for breach of an exclusivity clause in a shopping-center lease. * * * Why, Sara Creek asks, should they not be adequate here?

Sara Creek makes a beguiling argument that contains much truth, but we do not think it should carry the day. For if, as just noted, damages have been awarded in some cases of breach of an exclusivity clause in a shopping-center lease, injunctions have been issued in others. * * * The choice between remedies requires a balancing of the costs and benefits of the alternatives. Hecht Co. v. Bowles, 321 U.S. 321, 329, 64 S.Ct. 587, 591, 88 L.Ed. 754 (1944); Yakus v. United States, 321 U.S. 414, 440, 64 S.Ct. 660, 674, 88 L.Ed. 834 (1944). The task of striking the balance is for the trial judge, subject to deferential appellate review in recognition of its particularistic, judgmental, fact-bound character. * * * As we said in an appeal from a grant of a preliminary injunction—but the point is applicable to review of a permanent injunction as well—"The question for us [appellate judges] is whether the [district] judge exceeded the bounds of permissible choice in the circumstances, not what we would have done if we had been in his shoes." Roland Machinery Co. v. Dresser Industries, Inc., 749 F.2d 380, 390 (7th Cir.1984).

The plaintiff who seeks an injunction has the burden of persuasion—damages are the norm, so the plaintiff must show why his case is abnormal. But when, as in this case, the issue is whether to grant a permanent injunction, not whether to grant a temporary one, the burden is to show that damages are inadequate, not that the denial of the injunction will work irreparable harm. "Irreparable" in the injunction context means not rectifiable by the entry of a final judgment. * * * It has nothing to do with whether to grant a permanent injunction, which, in the usual case anyway, *is* the final judgment. The use of "irreparable harm" or "irreparable injury" as synonyms for inadequate remedy at law is a confusing usage. It should be avoided. * * *

The benefits of substituting an injunction for damages are twofold. First, it shifts the burden of determining the cost of the defendant's conduct from the court to the parties. If it is true that Walgreen's damages are smaller than the gain to Sara Creek from allowing a second pharmacy into the shopping mall, then there must be a price for dissolving the injunction that will make both parties better off. Thus, the effect of upholding the injunction would be to substitute for the costly processes of forensic fact determination the less costly processes of private negotiation. Second, a premise of our free-market system, and the lesson of experience here and abroad as well, is that prices and costs are more accurately determined by the market than by government. A battle of experts is a less reliable method of determining the actual cost to Walgreen of facing new competition than negotiations between Walgreen and Sara Creek over the price at which Walgreen would feel adequately compensated for having to face that competition.

That is the benefit side of injunctive relief but there is a cost side as well. Many injunctions require continuing supervision by the court, and that is costly. Roland Machinery Co. v. Dresser Industries, Inc., *supra,* 749 F.2d at 391–92; Rodriguez v. VIA Metropolitan Transit System, 802 F.2d 126, 132 (5th Cir.1986); Bethlehem Engineering Export Co. v. Christie, 105 F.2d 933, 935 (2d Cir.1939) (L. Hand, J.). A request for specific performance (a form of mandatory injunction) of a franchise agreement was refused on this ground in North American Financial Group, Ltd. v. S.M.R. Enterprises, Inc., 583 F.Supp. 691, 699 (N.D.Ill.1984); *see* Edward Yorio, Contract Enforcement: Specific Performance and Injunctions § 3.3.2 (1989). This ground was also stressed in Rental Development Corp. v. Lavery, 304 F.2d 839, 841–42 (9th Cir.1962), a case involving a lease. Some injunctions are problematic because they impose costs on third parties. * * * A more subtle cost of injunctive relief arises from the situation that economists call "bilateral monopoly," in which two parties can deal only with each other: the situation that an injunction creates. * * * The sole seller of widgets selling to the sole buyer of that product would be an example. But so will be the situation confronting Walgreen and Sara Creek if the injunction is upheld. Walgreen can "sell" its injunctive right only to Sara Creek, and Sara Creek can "buy" Walgreen's surrender of its right to enjoin the leasing of the anchor tenant's space to

Phar–Mor only from Walgreen. The lack of alternatives in bilateral monopoly creates a bargaining range, and the costs of negotiating to a point within that range may be high. Suppose the cost to Walgreen of facing the competition of Phar–Mor at the Southgate Mall would be $1 million, and the benefit to Sara Creek of leasing to Phar–Mor would be $2 million. Then at any price between those figures for a waiver of Walgreen's injunctive right both parties would be better off, and we expect parties to bargain around a judicial assignment of legal rights if the assignment is inefficient. R.H. Coase, *"The Problem of Social Cost,"* 3 J. Law & Econ. 1 (1960). But each of the parties would like to engross as much of the bargaining range as possible—Walgreen to press the price toward $2 million, Sara Creek to depress it toward $1 million. With so much at stake, both parties will have an incentive to devote substantial resources of time and money to the negotiation process. The process may even break down, if one or both parties want to create for future use a reputation as a hard bargainer; and if it does break down, the injunction will have brought about an inefficient result. All these are in one form or another costs of the injunctive process that can be avoided by substituting damages.

The costs and benefits of the damages remedy are the mirror of those of the injunctive remedy. The damages remedy avoids the cost of continuing supervision and third-party effects, and the cost of bilateral monopoly as well. It imposes costs of its own, however, in the form of diminished accuracy in the determination of value, on the one hand, and of the parties' expenditures on preparing and presenting evidence of damages, and the time of the court in evaluating the evidence, on the other.

The weighing up of all these costs and benefits is the analytical procedure that is or at least should be employed by a judge asked to enter a permanent injunction, with the understanding that if the balance is even the injunction should be withheld. The judge is not required to explicate every detail of the analysis and he did not do so here, but as long we are satisfied that his approach is broadly consistent with a proper analysis we shall affirm; and we are satisfied here. The determination of Walgreen's damages would have been costly in forensic resources and inescapably inaccurate. * * * The lease had ten years to run. So Walgreen would have had to project its sales revenues and costs over the next ten years, and then project the impact on those figures of Phar–Mor's competition, and then discount that impact to present value. All but the last step would have been fraught with uncertainty.

* * * Of course one can hire an expert to make such predictions, Glen A. Stankee, *"Econometric Forecasting of Lost Profits: Using High Technology to Compute Commercial Damages,"* 61 Fla. B.J. 83 (1987), and if injunctive relief is infeasible the expert's testimony may provide a tolerable basis for an award of damages. We cited cases in which damages have been awarded for the breach of an exclusivity clause in a shopping-center lease. But they are awarded in such circumstances not because anyone thinks them a clairvoyant forecast but because it is better to give a

wronged person a crude remedy than none at all. It is the same theory on which damages are awarded for a disfiguring injury. No one thinks such injuries readily monetizable, City of Panama, 101 U.S. 453, 464, 25 L.Ed. 1061 (1880); McCarty v. Pheasant Run, Inc., 826 F.2d 1554, 1557 (7th Cir.1987); Marcus L. Plant, *"Damages for Pain and Suffering,"* 19 Ohio St. L.J. 200, 205–06 (1958), but a crude estimate is better than letting the wrongdoer get off scot-free (which, not incidentally, would encourage more such injuries). Randall R. Bovbjerg et al., *"Valuing Life and Limb in Tort: Scheduling 'Pain and Suffering,' "* 83 Nw. U.L. Rev. 908 (1989). Sara Creek presented evidence of what happened (very little) to Walgreen when Phar–Mor moved into other shopping malls in which Walgreen has a pharmacy, and it was on the right track in putting in comparative evidence. But there was a serious question whether the other malls were actually comparable to the Southgate Mall, so we cannot conclude, in the face of the district judge's contrary conclusion, that the existence of comparative evidence dissolved the difficulties of computing damages in this case. Sara Creek complains that the judge refused to compel Walgreen to produce all the data that Sara Creek needed to demonstrate the feasibility of forecasting Walgreen's damages. Walgreen resisted, on grounds of the confidentiality of the data and the cost of producing the massive data that Sara Creek sought. Those are legitimate grounds; and the cost (broadly conceived) they expose of pretrial discovery, in turn presaging complexity at trial, is itself a cost of the damages remedy that injunctive relief saves.

Damages are not always costly to compute, or difficult to compute accurately. In the standard case of a seller's breach of a contract for the sale of goods where the buyer covers by purchasing the same product in the market, damages are readily calculable by subtracting the contract price from the market price and multiplying by the quantity specified in the contract. But this is not such a case and here damages would be a costly and inaccurate remedy; and on the other side of the balance some of the costs of an injunction are absent and the cost that is present seems low. The injunction here, like one enforcing a covenant not to compete (standardly enforced by injunction, Yorio, *supra,* 401–08), is a simple negative injunction—Sara Creek is not to lease space in the Southgate Mall to Phar–Mor during the term of Walgreen's lease—and the costs of judicial supervision and enforcement should be negligible. There is no contention that the injunction will harm an unrepresented third party. It may harm Phar–Mor, but that harm will be reflected in Sara Creek's offer to Walgreen to dissolve the injunction. (Anyway, Phar–Mor is a party.) The injunction may also, it is true, harm potential customers of Phar–Mor—people who would prefer to shop at a deep-discount store than an ordinary discount store—but their preferences, too, are registered indirectly. The more business Phar–Mor would have, the more rent it will be willing to pay Sara Creek, and therefore the more Sara Creek will be willing to pay Walgreen to dissolve the injunction.

The only substantial cost of the injunction in this case is that it may set off a round of negotiations between the parties. In some cases, illustrated by Boomer v. Atlantic Cement Co., 26 N.Y.2d 219, 309 N.Y.S.2d 312, 257 N.E.2d 870 (1970), this consideration alone would be enough to warrant the denial of injunctive relief. The defendant's factory was emitting cement dust that caused the plaintiffs harm monetized at less than $200,000, and the only way to abate the harm would have been to close down the factory, which had cost $45 million to build. An injunction against the nuisance could therefore have created a huge bargaining range (could, not would, because it is unclear what the current value of the factory was), and the costs of negotiating to a point within it might have been immense. If the market value of the factory was actually $45 million, the plaintiffs would be tempted to hold out for a price to dissolve the injunction in the tens of millions and the factory would be tempted to refuse to pay anything more than a few hundred thousand dollars. Negotiations would be unlikely to break down completely, given such a bargaining range, but they might well be protracted and costly. There is nothing so dramatic here. Sara Creek does not argue that it will have to close the mall if enjoined from leasing to Phar–Mor. Phar–Mor is not the only potential anchor tenant. Liza Danielle, Inc. v. Jamko, Inc., 408 So.2d 735, 740 (Fla.App.1982), on which Sara Creek relies, presented the converse case where the grant of the injunction would have forced an existing tenant to close its store. The size of the bargaining range was also a factor in the denial of injunctive relief in Gitlitz v. Plankinton Building Properties, Inc., 228 Wis. 334, 339–40, 280 N.W. 415, 418 (1938).

To summarize, the judge did not exceed the bounds of reasonable judgment in concluding that the costs (including forgone benefits) of the damages remedy would exceed the costs (including forgone benefits) of an injunction. We need not consider whether, as intimated by Walgreen, exclusivity clauses in shopping-center leases should be considered presumptively enforceable by injunctions. Although we have described the choice between legal and equitable remedies as one for case-by-case determination, the courts have sometimes picked out categories of cases in which injunctive relief is made the norm. The best-known example is specific performance of contracts for the sale of real property. * * * The rule that specific performance will be ordered in such cases as a matter of course is a generalization of the considerations discussed above. Because of the absence of a fully liquid market in real property and the frequent presence of subjective values (many a homeowner, for example, would not sell his house for its market value), the calculation of damages is difficult; and since an order of specific performance to convey a piece of property does not create a continuing relation between the parties, the costs of supervision and enforcement if specific performance is ordered are slight. The exclusivity clause in Walgreen's lease relates to real estate, but we hesitate to suggest that every contract involving real estate should be enforceable as a matter of course by injunctions. Suppose Sara Creek had covenanted to keep the entrance to Walgreen's store free of ice and snow, and breached the covenant. An injunction would require continuing supervision, and it would be easy enough if the injunction were denied for Walgreen to hire its own ice and snow remover and charge the cost to Sara Creek. *Cf.* City of Michigan City v. Lake Air Corp., 459 N.E.2d 760 (Ind.App.1984). On the other hand, injunctions to enforce exclusivity clauses are quite likely to be justifiable by just the considerations present here—damages are difficult to estimate with any accuracy and the injunction is a one-shot remedy requiring no continuing judicial involvement. So there is an argument for making injunctive relief presumptively appropriate in such cases, but we need not decide in this case how strong an argument.

Affirmed.

HARLINGTON WOOD, JR., SENIOR CIRCUIT JUDGE, concurring.

I gladly join in the affirmance reached in Judge Posner's expert analysis.

eBAY INC. v. MERCEXCHANGE, L.L.C.

Supreme Court of the United States, 2006.
547 U.S. 388, 126 S. Ct. 1837, 164 L.Ed.2d 641.

JUSTICE THOMAS delivered the opinion of the Court.

Ordinarily, a federal court considering whether to award permanent injunctive relief to a prevailing plaintiff applies the four-factor test historically employed by courts of equity. Petitioners eBay Inc. and Half.com, Inc., argue that this traditional test applies to disputes arising under the Patent Act. * * *

I

Petitioner eBay operates a popular Internet Web site that allows private sellers to list goods they wish to sell, either through an auction or at a fixed price. Petitioner Half.com, now a wholly owned subsidiary of eBay, operates a similar Web site. Respondent MercExchange, L.L.C., holds a number of patents, including a business method patent for an electronic market designed to facilitate the sale of goods between private individuals by establishing a central authority to promote trust among participants. * * * MercExchange sought to license its patent to eBay and Half.com, as it had previously done with other companies, but the parties failed to reach an agreement. MercExchange subsequently filed a patent infringement suit against eBay and Half.com in the United States District Court for the Eastern District of Virginia. A jury found that MercExchange's patent was valid, that eBay and Half.com had infringed that patent, and that an award of damages was appropriate.

Following the jury verdict, the District Court denied MercExchange's motion for permanent injunctive relief. 275 F.Supp.2d 695 (2003). The Court of Appeals for the Federal Circuit reversed, applying its "general rule that courts will issue permanent injunctions against patent infringement absent exceptional circumstances." 401 F.3d 1323, 1339 (2005). We granted certiorari to determine the appropriateness of this general rule.

II

According to well-established principles of equity, a plaintiff seeking a permanent injunction must satisfy a four-factor test before a court may grant such relief. A plaintiff must demonstrate: (1) that it has suffered an irreparable injury; (2) that remedies available at law, such as monetary damages, are inadequate to compensate for that injury; (3) that, considering the balance of hardships between the plaintiff and defendant, a remedy in equity is warranted; and (4) that the public interest would not be disserved by a permanent injunction. *See, e.g.,*Weinberger v. Romero–Barcelo, 456 U.S. 305, 311–313, 102 S.Ct. 1798, 72 L.Ed.2d 91 (1982); Amoco Production Co. v. Gambell, 480 U.S. 531, 542, 107 S.Ct. 1396, 94 L.Ed.2d 542 (1987). The decision to grant or deny permanent injunctive relief is an act of equitable discretion by the district court, reviewable on appeal for abuse of discretion. *See, e.g., Romero–Barcelo,* 456 U.S., at 320, 102 S.Ct. 1798.

These familiar principles apply with equal force to disputes arising under the Patent Act. As this Court has long recognized, "a major departure from the long tradition of equity practice should not be lightly implied." *Ibid.; see also Amoco, supra,* at 542, 107 S.Ct. 1396. Nothing in the Patent Act indicates that Congress intended such a departure. To the contrary, the Patent Act expressly provides that injunctions "may" issue "in accordance with the principles of equity." 35 U.S.C. § 283.[2]

To be sure, the Patent Act also declares that "patents shall have the attributes of personal property," § 261, including "the right to exclude others from making, using, offering for sale, or selling the invention," § 154(a)(1). According to the Court of Appeals, this statutory right to exclude alone justifies its general rule in favor of permanent injunctive relief. * * * But the creation of a right is distinct from the provision of remedies for violations of that right. Indeed, the Patent Act itself indicates that patents shall have the attributes of personal property "[s]ubject to the provisions of this title," 35 U.S.C. § 261, including, presumably, the provision that injunctive relief "may" issue only "in accordance with the principles of equity," § 283.

This approach is consistent with our treatment of injunctions under the Copyright Act. Like a patent owner, a copyright holder possesses "the right to exclude others from using his property." Fox Film Corp. v. Doyal, 286 U.S. 123, 127, 52 S.Ct. 546, 76 L.Ed. 1010 (1932); *see also id.,* at 127–128, 52 S.Ct. 546 ("A copyright, like a patent, is at once the equivalent given by the public for benefits bestowed by the genius and meditations and skill of individuals and the incentive to further efforts for the same important objects" (internal quotation marks omitted)). Like the Patent

---

2. Section 283 provides that "[t]he several courts having jurisdiction of cases under this title may grant injunctions in accordance with the principles of equity to prevent the violation of any right secured by patent, on such terms as the court deems reasonable."

PERMANENT INJUNCTIONS

Act, the Copyright Act provides that courts "may" grant injunctive relief "on such terms as it may deem reasonable to prevent or restrain infringement of a copyright." 17 U.S.C. § 502(a). And as in our decision today, this Court has consistently rejected invitations to replace traditional equitable considerations with a rule that an injunction automatically follows a determination that a copyright has been infringed. *See, e.g.,* New York Times Co. v. Tasini, 533 U.S. 483, 505, 121 S.Ct. 2381, 150 L.Ed.2d 500 (2001) * * *; Dun v. Lumbermen's Credit Assn., 209 U.S. 20, 23–24, 28 S.Ct. 335, 52 L.Ed. 663 (1908).

Neither the District Court nor the Court of Appeals below fairly applied these traditional equitable principles in deciding respondent's motion for a permanent injunction. Although the District Court recited the traditional four-factor test, * * * it appeared to adopt certain expansive principles suggesting that injunctive relief could not issue in a broad swath of cases. Most notably, it concluded that a "plaintiff's willingness to license its patents" and "its lack of commercial activity in practicing the patents" would be sufficient to establish that the patent holder would not suffer irreparable harm if an injunction did not issue. * * * But traditional equitable principles do not permit such broad classifications. For example, some patent holders, such as university researchers or self-made inventors, might reasonably prefer to license their patents, rather than undertake efforts to secure the financing necessary to bring their works to market themselves. Such patent holders may be able to satisfy the traditional four-factor test, and we see no basis for categorically denying them the opportunity to do so. To the extent that the District Court adopted such a categorical rule, then, its analysis cannot be squared with the principles of equity adopted by Congress. The court's categorical rule is also in tension with Continental Paper Bag Co. v. Eastern Paper Bag Co., 210 U.S. 405, 422–430, 28 S.Ct. 748, 52 L.Ed. 1122 (1908), which rejected the contention that a court of equity has no jurisdiction to grant injunctive relief to a patent holder who has unreasonably declined to use the patent [because the patent holder has a right to exclude others from using the invention].

In reversing the District Court, the Court of Appeals departed in the opposite direction from the four-factor test. The court articulated a "general rule," unique to patent disputes, "that a permanent injunction will issue once infringement and validity have been adjudged." * * * The court further indicated that injunctions should be denied only in the "unusual" case, under "exceptional circumstances" and " 'in rare instances ... to protect the public interest.' " * * * Just as the District Court erred in its categorical denial of injunctive relief, the Court of Appeals erred in its categorical grant of such relief. * * *

Because we conclude that neither court below correctly applied the traditional four-factor framework that governs the award of injunctive relief, we vacate the judgment of the Court of Appeals, so that the District Court may apply that framework in the first instance. In doing so, we take no position on whether permanent injunctive relief should or should not issue in this particular case, or indeed in any number of other disputes arising under the Patent Act. We hold only that the decision whether to grant or deny injunctive relief rests within the equitable discretion of the district courts, and that such discretion must be exercised consistent with traditional principles of equity, in patent disputes no less than in other cases governed by such standards.

Accordingly, we vacate the judgment of the Court of Appeals and remand the case for further proceedings consistent with this opinion.

CHIEF JUSTICE ROBERTS, with whom JUSTICE SCALIA and JUSTICE GINSBURG join, concurring.

I agree with the Court's holding that "the decision whether to grant or deny injunctive relief rests within the equitable discretion of the district courts, and that such discretion must be exercised consistent with traditional principles of equity, in patent disputes no less than in other cases governed by such standards," * * * and I join the opinion of the Court. That opinion rightly rests on the proposition that "a major departure from the long tradition of equity practice should not be lightly implied." Weinberger v. Romero–Barcelo, 456 U.S. 305, 320, 102 S.Ct. 1798, 72 L.Ed.2d 91 (1982) * * *.

From at least the early 19th century, courts have granted injunctive relief upon a finding of infringement in the vast majority of patent cases. This "long tradition of equity practice" is not surprising, given the difficulty of protecting a right to *exclude* through monetary remedies that allow an infringer to *use* an invention against the patentee's wishes—a difficulty that often implicates the first two factors of the traditional four-factor test. This historical practice, as the Court holds, does not *entitle* a patentee to a permanent injunction or justify a *general rule* that such injunctions should issue. * * * At the same time, there is a difference between exercising equitable discretion pursuant to the established four-factor test and writing on an entirely clean slate. "Discretion is not whim, and limiting discretion according to legal standards helps promote the basic principle of justice that like cases should be decided alike." Martin v. Franklin Capital Corp., 546 U.S. 132, 139, 126 S.Ct. 704, 710, 163 L.Ed.2d 547 (2005). When it comes to discerning and applying those standards, in this area as others, "a page of history is worth a volume of logic." New York Trust Co. v. Eisner, 256 U.S. 345, 349, 41 S.Ct. 506, 65 L.Ed. 963 (1921) (opinion for the Court by Holmes, J.).

JUSTICE KENNEDY, with whom JUSTICE STEVENS, JUSTICE SOUTER, and JUSTICE BREYER join, concurring.

The Court is correct, in my view, to hold that courts should apply the well-established, four-factor test—without resort to categorical rules—in deciding whether to grant injunctive relief in patent cases. The Chief Justice is also correct that history may be instructive in applying this test. * * * The traditional practice of issuing injunctions against patent infringers, however, does not seem to rest on "the difficulty of protecting a right to *exclude* through monetary remedies that allow an infringer to *use* an invention against the patentee's wishes." * * * Both the terms of the Patent Act and the traditional view of injunctive relief accept that the existence of a right to exclude does not dictate the remedy for a violation of that right. * * * To the extent earlier cases establish a pattern of granting an injunction against patent infringers almost as a matter of course, this pattern simply illustrates the result of the four-factor test in the contexts then prevalent. The lesson of the historical practice, therefore, is most helpful and instructive when the circumstances of a case bear substantial parallels to litigation the courts have confronted before.

In cases now arising trial courts should bear in mind that in many instances the nature of the patent being enforced and the economic function of the patent holder present considerations quite unlike earlier cases. An industry has developed in which firms use patents not as a basis for producing and selling goods but, instead, primarily for obtaining licensing fees. See FTC, To Promote Innovation: The Proper Balance of Competition and Patent Law and Policy, ch. 3, pp. 38–39 (Oct.2003), available at http://www.ftc.gov/os/2003/10/innovationrpt.pdf (as visited May 11, 2006, and available in Clerk of Court's case file). For these firms, an injunction, and the potentially serious sanctions arising from its violation, can be employed as a bargaining tool to charge exorbitant fees to companies that seek to buy licenses to practice the patent. See *ibid*. When the patented invention is but a small component of the product the companies seek to produce and the threat of an injunction is employed simply for undue leverage in negotiations, legal damages may well be sufficient to compensate for the infringement and an injunction may not serve the public interest. In addition injunctive relief may have different consequences for the burgeoning number of patents over business methods, which were not of much economic and legal significance in earlier times. The potential vagueness and suspect validity of some of these patents may affect the calculus under the four-factor test.

The equitable discretion over injunctions, granted by the Patent Act, is well suited to allow courts to adapt to the rapid technological and legal developments in the patent system. For these reasons it should be recognized that district courts must determine whether past practice fits the circumstances of the cases before them. With these observations, I join the opinion of the Court.

NOTES

1. What are the differences between the articulation of the standard for determining whether to issue a permanent injunction in *Walgreen* and in *eBay*? What is the difference between the first and second prong of the *eBay* test? Professor Rendleman has observed that, prior to reading *eBay*, "[r]emedies specialists had never heard of the four-point test." Doug Rendelman, *The Trial Judge's Equitable Discretion Following* eBay v. MercExchange, 27 Rev. Litig. 63, 76 n.71 (2007).

2. In Monsanto Co. v. Geerston Seed Farms, 130 S.Ct. 2743 (2010), the Court applied the *eBay* test to a request for permanent injunctive relief that

had been granted by the lower courts to enforce the National Environmental Protection Act (NEPA). The Court reversed and remanded the case on the ground that the injunction had been worded too broadly. In the course of its opinion, the court emphasized the fact that an injunction should issue only if the traditional four-factor test is satisfied, and that it is erroneous to make an assumption that an injunction is generally an appropriate remedy for a NEPA violation.

SMITH v. WESTERN ELECTRIC CO.

Missouri Court of Appeals, 1982.
643 S.W.2d 10.

DOWD, PRESIDING JUDGE.

* * *

The petition seeks an injunction to prevent plaintiff's employer from exposing him to tobacco smoke in the workplace and from affecting his pay or employment conditions because of his medical reaction to tobacco smoke. The petition alleges that by allowing smoking in the work area, defendant permits its employees to be exposed to a health hazard and thereby breaches its duty to provide a safe place in which to work.

Plaintiff contends the trial court erred in dismissing his petition in that it invokes legal principles entitling him to relief and shows that injunctive relief is appropriate. Plaintiff further contends that federal law does not preempt state common law in this case.

* * *

The petition includes the following allegations. Plaintiff has been employed by defendant since 1950 and has worked in defendant's Missouri branch since 1967. He is a nonsmoker sharing an open office area with other employees, many of whom smoke tobacco products as they work. In 1975 plaintiff began to experience serious respiratory tract discomfort as a result of inhaling tobacco smoke in the workplace. A subsequent medical evaluation determined that plaintiff suffers a severe adverse reaction to tobacco smoke. His symptoms include sore throat, nausea, dizziness, headache, blackouts, loss of memory, difficulty in concentration, aches and pains in joints, sensitivity to noise and light, cold sweat, gagging, choking sensations, and lightheadedness. After a sufficient period of non-exposure to smoke, plaintiff's symptoms abate somewhat. The symptoms have become increasingly severe over the years, however. Doctors evaluating and treating plaintiff have advised him to avoid contact with tobacco smoke whenever possible.

The petition further alleges that plaintiff first complained to defendant about the tobacco smoke in the workplace in 1975. Defendant thereafter moved plaintiff to different locations within the plant, but no improvement resulted because each location contained significant amounts of tobacco smoke. In 1978 plaintiff was informed that he should no longer submit complaints about the smoke through defendant's anonymous complaint procedure since defendant would not process them. In response to recommendations of the National Institute for Occupational Safety and Health, defendant adopted a smoking policy in April 1980. The declared policy was to protect the rights of both smokers and nonsmokers by providing accommodations for both groups and by making a reasonable effort to separate the groups in work areas. Because defendant has failed to implement its policy by making such a reasonable effort, improvement of the air in the workplace has not resulted.

According to the petition, in August 1980, plaintiff filed with defendant a Handicapped Declaration Statement that he was handicapped by his susceptibility to tobacco smoke. Refusing to segregate smokers or to limit smoking to non-work areas, defendant informed plaintiff he could either continue to work in the same location and wear a respirator or apply for a job in the computer room (where smoking is prohibited). The latter option would entail a pay decrease of about $500 per month. Defendant thereafter provided plaintiff with a respirator that has proven ineffective in protecting plaintiff from tobacco smoke.

The petition states that plaintiff has exhausted all avenues of relief through defendant; he has no adequate remedy at law; he is suffering and will continue to suffer irreparable physical injuries and financial losses unless defendant improves working conditions. * * *

* * *

The allegations of the instant case, taken as true, show that the tobacco smoke of co-workers smoking in the work area is hazardous to the health of employees in general and plaintiff in particular. The allegations also show that defendant knows the tobacco smoke is harmful to plaintiff's health and that defendant has the authority, ability, and reasonable means to control smoking in areas requiring a smoke-free environment. Therefore, by failing to exercise its control and assume its responsibility to eliminate the hazardous condition caused by tobacco smoke, defendant has breached and is breaching its duty to provide a reasonably safe workplace. *See* Shimp v. New Jersey Bell Telephone Co., 145 N.J.Super. 516, 368 A.2d 408 (1976). * * *

* * *

If plaintiff's petition establishes defendant's failure to provide a safe place for plaintiff to work, we must next consider whether injunctive relief would be an appropriate remedy. An injunction may issue "to prevent the doing of any legal wrong whatever, whenever in the opinion of the court an adequate remedy cannot be afforded by an action for damages." § 526.030 RSMo 1978. * * *

The petition alleges that plaintiff's continuing exposure to smoke in the workplace is increasingly deleterious to his health and is causing irreparable harm. Assuming the allegations and reasonable inferences therefrom to be true, we think it is fair to characterize deterioration of plaintiff's health as "irreparable" and as a harm for which money damages cannot adequately compensate. This is particularly true where the harm has not yet resulted in full-blown disease or injury. Money damages, even though inadequate, are the best possible remedy once physical damage is done, but they are certainly inadequate to compensate permanent injury which could have been prevented. Plaintiff should not be required to await the harm's fruition before he is entitled to seek an inadequate remedy. Moreover, the nature of plaintiff's unsafe work environment represents a recurrent risk of harm that would necessitate a multiplicity of lawsuits. Finally, the petition states that plaintiff has no adequate remedy at law and alleges facts indicating that prior to this action plaintiff unsuccessfully pursued relief, both through his employer's in-house channels and through administrative agencies. Viewing the petition favorably, as we must to determine its sufficiency, we find that [an] injunction would be an appropriate remedy.

The judgment is reversed and the cause remanded.

NOTE

The future threat of physical injury is a justification for granting equitable relief, regardless of whether the plaintiff who is seeking the injunction is the person who is directly at risk of harm or a governmental agency whose job it is to protect the general public against the threatened risk of harm. For example, in Metzler v. Lykes Pasco, Inc., 972 F.Supp. 1438 (S.D.Fla.1997), the Secretary of Labor obtained a permanent injunction ordering the defendant (a fruit grower who hired "farm labor contractors" to transport migrant workers) to ensure that the contractors transported the workers only in safe, authorized vehicles. The court explained its ruling as follows:

> To show that it is entitled to a permanent injunction, the Secretary must demonstrate (1) success on the merits of its claim; (2) that it will suffer irreparable harm in the absence of an injunction and has no adequate remedy at law; (3) the threatened injury to the plaintiff outweighs any injury the defendant will suffer if the Court grants an injunction; and (4) an injunction will not harm the public interest. * * * Fogie v. THORN Americas, Inc., 95 F.3d 645, 654 (8th Cir.1996). * * *

* * *

> An award of damages cannot adequately compensate the Secretary for the injuries that migrant and seasonal workers suffer by riding in unsafe vehicles each day to and from work. Furthermore, damages are impossible to calculate. How does one award damages for the risk that workers will be injured because they are riding on unsecured benches in a van that must suddenly screech to a halt? What is the appropriate amount of damages to award for the potential that a worker cannot recover any money for his injuries because a van has no insurance? Because the Secretary has no adequate remedy at law for the daily transportation of workers in unsafe and underinsured vans, she has shown irreparable harm.

The threatened injury to the Secretary outweighs any injury that Lykes Pasco will suffer from the injunction * * * [requiring Pasco's guards to check certificates of registration as vehicles pass through the entrances to the company's groves]. The Secretary is charged with enforcing the Migrant and Seasonal Agricultural Worker Protection Act * * *. If the Court does not grant an injunction * * *, the risk to migrant workers of disabling injuries and death will continue unabated * * *. On the other hand, Lykes Pasco will suffer minimal inconvenience. * * *

Finally, it will not harm the public interest to grant an injunction. In contrast, it greatly serves the public interest to insure compliance with a law designed to protect those at the bottom economic rung of society from decades of exploitation.

Id. at 1445.

MATLOCK v. WEETS

Supreme Court of Iowa, 1995.
531 N.W.2d 118.

Considered by LARSON, P.J., and CARTER, LAVORATO, NEUMAN and AN-DREASEN, JJ.

ANDREASEN, JUSTICE.

This appeal involves the issuance of a temporary and permanent injunction * * * .

I. BACKGROUND.

Robin Matlock and Jon Weets began dating in October 1991. The relationship lasted only four to five weeks before Robin broke it off. On March 30, 1993, approximately seventeen months after she terminated the relationship, Robin petitioned for an injunction to enjoin Jon from following her, being in the vicinity of her home or her place of employment, or from contacting her in any manner. * * *

A. Shortly after Robin ended the relationship with Jon, he began to noticeably approach, follow, and watch her. He continued to call her and leave presents for her on the back step of her house. She asked him to stop. He then began sending her cards and letters. In January 1992 he also began jogging by her house.

In February 1992 Jon brought some Valentine's Day gifts to Robin's house. He entered the house uninvited, walked over to the kitchen table and laid the gifts down. Robin's mother, who lived with Robin, was at home alone at the time. She was startled and frightened by his entering the house.

In February or March of 1992 Jon began frequently showing up at various places on Robin's way to work, her way home for lunch, her way back to work, and her way home from work. This was especially unusual because Robin's route varied each day of the week. Robin's mother cleaned house in the mornings for different families in the area, and she relied on Robin to drive her to work to a different house each morning. Robin picked her mother up and took her home during the lunch hour. * * *

During the weekends Jon would pass Robin's house often. He would begin passing her house at 6:30 a.m., passing her house at least four or six times before noon. This caused Robin to fear for her own and her mother's safety. * * *

In August of 1992 Jon sent her some birthday cards, another letter, and a tape. * * *

* * * Robin began feeling greater anxiety and fear for her safety. She spoke with a police officer about the situation. The officer spoke with Jon, and Jon said he would stop following Robin and sending her letters. Shortly thereafter, Jon sent her two more letters. * * * The officer talked to Jon again and told him to leave Robin alone, but Jon continued to show up in Robin's presence.

* * *

Robin then contacted the Scott County Attorney. The county attorney spoke with Jon, who was a former client, and told him to stop; but he was concerned that Jon knew just how far he could go and would not stop. He also told Robin he was concerned that Jon would show up at her doorstep and try to commit suicide in front of her because he had attempted a similar act in the past.

B.   The court granted a temporary injunction * * * . After a hearing, the court issued a permanent injunction. The court also found Jon guilty of contempt for violating the terms of the temporary injunction on four separate occasions and sentenced him to fifteen consecutive days of incarceration.

* * *

III.   ISSUANCE OF INJUNCTIONS.
* * *

An injunction "should be granted with caution and only when clearly required to avoid irreparable damage." * * * An injunction is appropriate only when the party seeking it has no adequate remedy at law. * * *

A.   The court granted the temporary injunction based on the affidavit Robin submitted with her petition. * * * The injunction stated:

> It is therefore ordered that a writ of temporary injunction shall issue immediately without bond enjoining and restraining the Respondent from approaching within 100 feet of the Petitioner, her place of residence, or her place of employment, and further enjoining and restraining the Respondent from sitting or standing within sight of Petitioner's residence, from passing Petitioner's residence on foot or by vehicle, from following the Petitioner to and from her residence, or from awaiting the Petitioner at any location in the vicinity of her

residence, her mother's places of employment, the Petitioner's places of employment, or the Petitioner's usual places of doing business, including Eagle Foods on Locust Street. The Respondent is further enjoined and restrained from taking any action to contact, in person, by telephone, or by mail, the Petitioner or her family, or from taking any other action to harass the Petitioner.

Jon asserts the issuance of the temporary injunction was improper because he claims the affidavit Robin filed in support of her petition does not establish she was under any threat of irreparable or substantial harm by Jon, the affidavit does not allege any confrontation which placed Robin in fear of her physical safety, and the order granting the temporary injunction does not make specific findings relating to the hardship that would be imposed on Jon as a result of the issuance of a temporary injunction.

* * * In her affidavit, Robin states she fears for her own safety and the safety of her mother, that she has sought the assistance of a mental health counselor, and that her constant fear for her personal safety has been a detriment to her mental health. Jon's actions have interfered with many aspects of Robin's life.

* * * Under the circumstances of this case, we find the temporary injunction issued by the court was warranted.

B.   After a hearing, the court granted a permanent injunction. The permanent injunction is substantially similar to the temporary injunction. * * *

Jon claims he does not intentionally follow Robin, but rather their meetings are coincidental. The district court, however, specifically found Jon's claim not to be credible. The court found his actions are psychologically harassing to Robin and determined that his obsessive behaviors appear dangerous to a reasonable person. Based on our de novo review, we agree with the court's findings and conclusions.

* * * An actual assault or verbal physical threat is not necessary before behavior reasonably seen to be dangerous may be enjoined. Although courts generally do not issue an injunction for an act which is subject to a penal law, * * * if the criminal act is connected with the violation of a private right, an injunction may issue * * *. The party seeking the injunction must show the inadequacy of the legal remedy. * * *

Apparently law enforcement had not been persuaded that Jon's behavior constituted a criminal offense. As a result, Robin is unable to invoke protection from the criminal justice system. Money damages will not relieve her of the fear and psychological terror she feels because of Jon's behavior. Her earlier efforts to get him to stop his behavior all failed. Also, Jon has repeatedly promised to leave Robin alone and then failed to follow through on his promise. This shows Jon's inability to change his own behavior without external intervention. Therefore, Robin lacks an adequate legal remedy and is entitled to a permanent injunction.

SECTION 5. DEFENSES TO REQUESTS FOR EQUITABLE RELIEF

A. UNCLEAN HANDS

"Unclean hands" is an equitable affirmative defense. The contours of the defense were described by the United States Supreme Court in Precision Instrument Manufacturing Co. v. Automotive Maintenance Machinery Co., 324 U.S. 806, 65 S.Ct. 993, 89 L.Ed. 1381 (1945):

The * * * equitable maxim that "he who comes into equity must come with clean hands" * * * is far more than a banality. It is a self-imposed ordinance that closes the doors of a court of equity to one tainted with inequitableness or bad faith relative to the matter in which he seeks relief, however improper may have been the behavior of the defendant. That doctrine is rooted in the historical concept of equity as a vehicle for affirmatively enforcing the requirements of conscience and good faith. * * * Thus while "equity does not demand that its suitors shall have led blameless lives" * * * as to other matters, it does require that they shall have acted fairly and without fraud or deceit as to the controversy in issue. * * *

This maxim necessarily gives wide range to the equity court's discretion in refusing to aid the unclean litigant. * * * Accordingly, one's conduct need not necessarily have been of such a nature as to be punishable as a crime or as to justify legal proceedings of any character. Any willful act concerning the cause of action which rightfully can be said to transgress equitable standards of conduct is sufficient cause for the invocation of the maxim by the chancellor.

Id. at 814–15, 65 S.Ct. at 997–98, 89 L.Ed. 1381.

SALOMON SMITH BARNEY, INC. v. VOCKEL

United States District Court, Eastern District of Pennsylvania, 2000.
137 F.Supp.2d 599.

BARTLE, DISTRICT JUDGE.

Before the court is the motion of plaintiff Salomon Smith Barney Inc. ("Smith Barney") for a preliminary injunction against one of its former financial consultants, Stewart M. Vockel, III ("Vockel"), who resigned from Smith Barney on April 28, 2000. * * *

* * * Until the dispute between the parties can be arbitrated on the merits, Smith Barney asks this court to restrain Vockel from using, disclosing, or misappropriating Smith Barney's customer information, to compel Vockel to undo account transfers for any former Smith Barney accounts he successfully caused to be transferred to his new employer, and

to require Vockel to return all documents containing Smith Barney client information. The complaint does not seek a permanent injunction or other relief.

We denied the request for a temporary restraining order on May 1, 2000. On May 3, 2000, we held a preliminary injunction hearing.

* * *

I.

* * *

Stewart Vockel has worked as a bond trader or financial consultant for a number of years. Merrill Lynch, Pierce, Fenner & Smith, Inc. ("Merrill Lynch") hired him as a financial consultant in 1991. He left Merrill Lynch and started with the Philadelphia branch of Smith Barney in November, 1994.

In late January, 2000, Vockel approached his long-time acquaintance Elliott Goodfriend, who is the Philadelphia Branch Manager for Paine Webber Inc. ("Paine Webber"), about the possibility of moving from Smith Barney to Paine Webber. On approximately March 28, 2000 Paine Webber made Vockel an offer of employment, which included a sizeable signing bonus. Vockel accepted.

In early April, approximately one week after Vockel received the offer, the administrative manager in Paine Webber's Philadelphia office * * * told Vockel that Paine Webber needed his Smith Barney client account statements. On or about April 19, 2000, while still employed by Smith Barney and without asking for permission from it or any of his clients, Vockel provided to Paine Webber the account statements for 254 of the 470 accounts he was servicing at Smith Barney. Paine Webber forwarded this material to an outside firm which, at Paine Webber's expense, prepared solicitation packages and then mailed them to the account holders. The solicitation package contained a cover letter drafted and signed by Vockel, an account transfer form with each client's Smith Barney account number(s) preprinted on it, and a Paine Webber "new account" form.

The solicitation packages were mailed, via overnight delivery, on Friday, April 28, 2000. That same day, in the late afternoon, Vockel submitted his letter of resignation to Smith Barney. * * * Vockel spent the weekend calling his clients. He told them about his move to Paine Webber and explained that they soon would be receiving solicitation packages that would enable them to transfer their accounts to his new employer.

This was not the first time Vockel had solicited his clients to transfer their accounts to his new place of employment. As noted above, from 1991 through October, 1994, Vockel worked at Merrill Lynch before moving to Smith Barney. At the time he left Merrill Lynch, he had been managing accounts worth approximately $23 million. Sometime between August and

October, 1994, after initial discussions with John Adamiak, the Branch Manager of Smith Barney's Philadelphia office, Vockel received a job offer. The Smith Barney offer, like his recent Paine Webber offer, included a substantial signing bonus. Adamiak told Vockel that Smith Barney wanted his Merrill Lynch client account statements, which Vockel provided to Smith Barney while still a financial consultant at Merrill Lynch. Adamiak told Vockel to resign from Merrill Lynch late in the day on a Friday afternoon. He did so on October 28, 1994. That same day a solicitation package, arranged and paid for by Smith Barney, was mailed to each of the clients Vockel had advised while at Merrill Lynch. The package contained an account transfer form and a letter signed by Vockel, which had been jointly drafted by Vockel and Adamiak, that informed Vockel's Merrill Lynch clients of his move to Smith Barney. The letter also urged them to transfer their accounts. Vockel used the October, 1994 solicitation letter as a model when he drafted his April, 2000 cover letter. In fact, the two letters are nearly identical.

When Vockel resigned from Merrill Lynch in 1994, the firm either instituted or threatened suit. Smith Barney participated in the settlement of the matter.

As a result of the joint solicitation efforts of Vockel and Smith Barney in 1994, nearly all of Vockel's Merrill Lynch clients transferred their accounts. Approximately 60% of the accounts he oversaw at Smith Barney followed him from Merrill Lynch, and another 30% of his accounts resulted from referrals from those clients who had followed him from Merrill Lynch to Smith Barney. When he left Smith Barney on April 28, 2000, he was managing approximately 470 accounts worth a total of approximately $70 million, and annually these accounts generated over $500,000 in commissions.

* * *

At about the time he joined Smith Barney, Adamiak told Vockel that Merrill Lynch differed from Smith Barney in that Merrill Lynch considered clients *"theirs"* while Smith Barney knew clients were the *"broker's"* and was there to help the broker service his or her clients' accounts. Nonetheless, in November, 1994, Vockel signed a "Principles Of Employment" agreement with Smith Barney that provided:

> [Y]ou must never use (except when necessary in your employment with us) nor disclose with anyone not affiliated with [Smith Barney] . . . any confidential or unpublished information you obtain as a result of your employment with us. This applies both while you are employed with us and after that employment ends. If you leave our employ, you may not retain or take with you any writing or other record which relates to the above.

* * * Significantly, however, Vockel never signed a non-compete agreement.

II.

Even assuming that Smith Barney would otherwise be entitled to a preliminary injunction, Vockel contends that it should be denied because Smith Barney does not come into the court with clean hands. The Supreme Court has declared, "It is one of the fundamental principles upon which equity jurisprudence is founded, that before a complainant can have a standing in court he must first show that not only has he a good and meritorious cause of action, but he must come into court with clean hands." Keystone Driller Co. v. General Excavator Co., 290 U.S. 240, 244, 54 S.Ct. 146, 78 L.Ed. 293 (1933) * * *.

In further explaining the application of the equitable maxim of clean hands, the Supreme Court stated, "The governing principle is that whenever a party who, as actor, seeks to set the judicial machinery in motion and obtain some remedy, has violated conscience, or good faith, or other equitable principle, in his prior conduct, then the doors of the court will be shut against him in limine." Id. at 244–45, 54 S.Ct. 146 * * *. The rule is not without its limitations. We are not to consider misconduct that has no connection to the case at hand. Rather, any "unconscionable act" of the plaintiff must have "immediate and necessary relation to the equity that he seeks in respect of the matter in litigation." Id. at 245, 54 S.Ct. 146 * * *.

Plaintiff has painted a picture of Vockel making off with valuable client information in order to woo them surreptitiously and expeditiously to his new employer, one of Smith Barney's arch competitors, and doing so in a manner that made it nearly impossible for Smith Barney to prevent the loss of valuable business. If it does not obtain preliminary relief in this case, argued Smith Barney, clients will be hoodwinked into transferring accounts without realizing what they are doing. According to Smith Barney, competing brokerage firms might be encouraged to lure its brokers away and deprive it of business in which it had invested so many resources to develop.

Unfortunately for Smith Barney, in determining the issue of clean hands, we look solely at the conduct of the plaintiff—the one who seeks the aid of the chancellor—and not the conduct of the defendant. * * *

* * *

Smith Barney seeks the help of a court of equity to prevent the same conduct by Vockel which it had previously abetted and from which it has handsomely profited. Now it wants the court to prevent the loss of that profit. If what Vockel is doing in 2000 is wrong, it is hard to see why Vockel's and Smith Barney's conduct in 1994 was not wrong. At the very least, Smith Barney is "tainted with inequitableness or bad faith relative to the matter in which [it] . . . seeks relief." * * * The misdeeds of Smith Barney have an "immediate and necessary relation to the equity that [it] . . . seeks" in this case. Keystone Driller, 290 U.S. at 245, 54 S.Ct. 146. * * *

While we do not condone the behavior of Vockel, it is the behavior of Smith Barney on which we must focus here. * * * Simply put, Smith Barney has not shown that it has come into this court with clean hands. In fact, the opposite has been established. Accordingly, as a court sitting in equity, we will not aid a wrongdoer. We will leave the parties to their monetary and other remedies before the National Association of Securities Dealers.

III.

The motion of Salomon Smith Barney Inc. for a preliminary injunction will be denied.

NOTES

1. In what types of situations should a court of equity decline to recognize the unclean hands defense? Consider Murray v. Lawson, 264 N.J.Super. 17, 624 A.2d 3 (1993), *aff'd as modified by* 138 N.J. 206, 649 A.2d 1253 (1994), *cert. denied*, 515 U.S. 1110, 115 S.Ct. 2264, 132 L.Ed.2d 269 (1995) (doctor who had assaulted anti-abortion protestor sought injunction to restrict picketing by protestors in front of doctor's home in an effort to protect his "residential privacy"):

> The doctrine of unclean hands expresses the principle that a court should not grant equitable relief to one who is a wrongdoer with respect to the subject matter of the suit. * * * However, the doctrine "does not repel all sinners from courts of equity, nor does it apply to every unconscientious act or inequitable conduct" of a complainant. * * * The doctrine may be relaxed in the interest of fairness. * * *
>
> * * * Dr. Murray's assault was punished [by the imposition of a $100 fine] in the appropriate forum, municipal court.
>
> A judge's discretionary decision not to invoke the unclean hands doctrine is justified where the conduct was "not the kind of conduct which a court must punish in order to vindicate its authority." * * * Judge Boyle ruled that Dr. Murray's admitted "swing" at Lawson reflected the emotionally charged issues involved and that he would focus on balancing the rights of the parties, not on the misguided assault. In our view he did not abuse his discretion or misapply the law in so deciding.

Id. at 37, 624 A.2d at 14.

2. When is a court justified in awarding equitable relief, even if the plaintiff's hands are unclean, in order to protect the "public interest"? Consider EEOC v. Recruit U.S.A., Inc., 939 F.2d 746 (9th Cir.1991):

> We need not decide whether the EEOC violated one or both of Title VII's confidentiality provisions. Even assuming it did, we nevertheless hold that the district court did not abuse its discretion in granting the preliminary injunction [prohibiting the defendants from destroying business records pertaining to allegedly discriminatory business practices]. Under traditional equitable principles, the substantial public interest

permeating this case warrants a departure from the "clean hands" doctrine.

* * * [T]he clean hands doctrine should not be strictly enforced when to do so would frustrate a substantial public interest. In such cases, equity's lodestar that "justice be done" prevails. The Supreme Court has instructed that the clean hands doctrine

> does not mean that courts must always permit a defendant wrongdoer to retain the profits of his wrongdoing merely because the plaintiff himself is possibly guilty of transgressing the law in the transactions involved. The maxim that he who comes into equity must come with clean hands is not applied by way of punishment for an unclean litigant but "upon considerations that make for the advancement of right and justice * * *." It is not a rigid formula which "trammels the free and just exercise of discretion."

Yellow Cab, 321 U.S. at 387, 64 S.Ct. at 624 (quoting Keystone Driller Co. v. General Excavator Co., 290 U.S. 240, 245–46, 54 S.Ct. 146, 147–48, 78 L.Ed. 293 (1933)) * * *.

In investigating race, sex, and age discrimination complaints, the EEOC is effectuating a compelling governmental and public interest in eradicating unlawful employment discrimination and in vindicating the rights of victims of such illegal practices.

A court's equitable powers should be used, as they were here, to effectuate the policy goals underlying legislation.

Id. at 753.

3. Most jurisdictions confine the unclean hands defense to requests for equitable relief, although they may recognize the companion principle of *in pari delicto* (barring a plaintiff who is equally at fault) in actions at law. *E.g.*, McKinley v. Weidner, 73 Or.App. 396, 698 P.2d 983 (1985) (refusing to recognize the unclean hands defense in a legal malpractice action). A few jurisdictions have extended the unclean hands defense to actions at law. *E.g.*, Unilogic, Inc. v. Burroughs Corp., 10 Cal.App.4th 612, 12 Cal.Rptr.2d 741 (1992) (recognizing the unclean hands defense in an action for conversion; citing cases from California and two other jurisdictions that had recognized the unclean hands defense in legal malpractice actions). The California courts have provided the following rationale for extending the unclean hands doctrine to actions at law: "A defendant may set up as many defenses as he may have, regardless of the question as to whether they are of a legal or equitable nature, because the distinction which exists under the common law between actions at law and suits in equity * * * [has] been abolished." Fibreboard Paper Products Corp. v. East Bay Union of Machinists, 227 Cal.App.2d 675, 728, 39 Cal.Rptr. 64, 97 (1964). Professor Dobbs, however, cautions against the extension of the unclean hands defense to actions at law:

> If judges had the power to deny damages and other legal remedies because a plaintiff came into court with unclean hands, citizens would not have rights, only privileges. Discretion to deny legal relief would mean that the judge might refuse to permit recovery of personal injury damages to a pedestrian struck down in a crosswalk on the ground that she was on

her way to an illicit rendezvous and would not have been injured had she stayed home with her family. The merger of law and equity suggests that substantive defenses, based on identifiable legal rules or policy, should apply in both law and equity, as in fact is the case with estoppel. But the merger does not suggest that a judge has discretion to bar rights as well as to limit remedies.

Dan B. Dobbs, The Law of Remedies § 2.4(2) (2d ed. 1993).*

B. LACHES

JARROW FORMULAS, INC. v. NUTRITION NOW, INC.

United States Court of Appeals, Ninth Circuit, 2002.
304 F.3d 829.

Before ARCHER,** O'SCANNLAIN, and SILVERMAN, CIRCUIT JUDGES.

O'SCANNLAIN, CIRCUIT JUDGE.

We must decide whether laches bars a manufacturer of nutritional supplements from suing its competitor for false advertising under the Lanham Act when the analogous state statute of limitations period has expired.

I

Nutrition Now, Inc. ("Nutrition Now") distributes PB8, a popular probiotic nutritional supplement designed to aid digestion. Since initial distribution in 1985, Nutrition Now has made three central claims. First, PB8 contains fourteen billion "good" bacteria per capsule. Second, PB8 contains eight different types of bacteria. Third, PB8 does not require refrigeration. Nutrition Now has always prominently displayed these claims on PB8's product label. The claims also have played a central role in Nutrition Now's marketing campaign, which totals "hundreds of thousands" of dollars per year and includes the use of national magazine advertisements.

Jarrow Formulas, Inc. ("Jarrow") offers a competing probiotic supplement. In 1993, Nutrition Now and Jarrow participated in an industry trade show. Jarrow Rogovin, the president of Jarrow, approached Martin Rifkin, the president of Nutrition Now, at the show. Rogovin vigorously complained to Rifkin that Nutrition Now's claims regarding PB8 were false and misleading.

A few months later, Jarrow filed a complaint with the Grievance Committee of the National Nutritional Foods Association. Jarrow alleged that Nutrition Now's claims were "false, unfair, misleading, and illegal" and amounted to "consumer fraud." Jarrow claimed that Institut Rosell ("Rosell"), the manufacturer of its competing product, had tested PB8 and

---

* Reprinted with permission of West Publishing Co.

** The Honorable Glenn L. Archer, Senior Circuit Judge of the United States Court of Appeals for the Federal Circuit, sitting by designation.

verified that the claims were false. Jarrow urged the Committee to take appropriate action, including releasing a statement declaring the claims false and misleading.*

* * *

* * * [A few days later,] Rogovin sent a letter expressly threatening litigation. The letter stated, "I could be suing you for unfair competition already. I could also have just turned Nutrition Now in to the Federal Trade Commission (FTC) for consumer fraud."

Undeterred, Nutrition Now continued to make its claims about PB8. Indeed, Nutrition Now kept the product label unchanged and continued to use the claims as a central part of its marketing campaign. Jarrow, despite its threat of litigation in 1993, waited until August 2000 to file suit. In its suit, Jarrow asserts that Nutrition Now's claims are false and misleading in violation of § 43(a)(1)(B) of the Lanham Act, 15 U.S.C. § 1125(a)(1)(B). * * * [Jarrow sought a permanent injunction ordering Nutrition Now to abandon its presentation of PB8.]

Nutrition Now moved for summary judgment on the grounds that the statute of limitations and laches bar Jarrow's claims. The district court held that Jarrow's action was barred by laches, and dismissed the suit. The court declined to address the statute of limitations question.

* * *

III

* * *

A

"Laches is an equitable time limitation on a party's right to bring suit," Boone v. Mech. Specialties Co., 609 F.2d 956, 958 (9th Cir.1979), resting on the maxim that "one who seeks the help of a court of equity must not sleep on his rights." Piper Aircraft Corp. v. Wag–Aero, Inc., 741 F.2d 925, 939 (7th Cir.1984) (Posner, J., concurring). It is well established that laches is a valid defense to Lanham Act claims, including those for false advertising. E.g., * * * Conopco, Inc. v. Campbell Soup Co., 95 F.3d 187, 191 (2d Cir.1996); see also GoTo.com, Inc. v. Walt Disney Co., 202 F.3d 1199, 1209 (9th Cir.2000) (considering laches defense to a trademark infringement suit under § 43(a)(1)(A)). A party asserting laches must show that it suffered prejudice as a result of the plaintiff's unreasonable delay in filing suit. * * *

Laches, an equitable defense, is distinct from the statute of limitations, a creature of law. * * * Statutes of limitations generally are limited to actions at law and therefore inapplicable to equitable causes of action. E.g., Patton v. Bearden, 8 F.3d 343, 347 (6th Cir.1993). Laches serves as

---

* Ultimately, the Committee took no action.

the counterpart to the statute of limitations, barring untimely equitable causes of action. * * *

While laches and the statute of limitations are distinct defenses, a laches determination is made with reference to the limitations period for the analogous action at law. If the plaintiff filed suit within the analogous limitations period, the strong presumption is that laches is inapplicable. *E.g.*, Shouse v. Pierce County, 559 F.2d 1142, 1147 (9th Cir.1977) ("It is extremely rare for laches to be effectively invoked when a plaintiff has filed his action before limitations in an analogous action at law has run."). However, if suit is filed outside of the analogous limitations period, courts often have presumed that laches is applicable. Brown v. Kayler, 273 F.2d 588, 592 (9th Cir.1959) * * *.

The proper interplay between laches and the statute of limitations for Lanham Act claims is somewhat elusive. *See, e.g.,* Restatement (Third) of Unfair Competition § 31 cmt. a (discussing the uncertain role of the statute of limitations for Lanham Act claims). The Lanham Act contains no explicit statute of limitations. * * * When a federal statute lacks a specific statute of limitations, we generally presume that Congress intended to "borrow" the limitations period from the most closely analogous action under state law.*

* * *

* * * We have stated in contexts outside of the Lanham Act that the presumptive applicability of laches turns on whether the limitations period for the analogous action at law has expired. *E.g., Shouse,* 559 F.2d at 1147; *Brown,* 273 F.2d at 592 * * *. Therefore, consistent with the views of our sister circuits, we hold that if a § 43(a) claim is filed within the analogous state limitations period, the strong presumption is that laches is inapplicable; if the claim is filed after the analogous limitations period has expired, the presumption is that laches is a bar to suit. *See* Lyons Partnership, L.P. v. Morris Costumes, Inc., 243 F.3d 789, 799 (4th Cir.2001); Kason Indus., Inc. v. Component Hardware Group, Inc., 120 F.3d 1199, 1203 (11th Cir.1997) * * *.

We must next determine *when* the analogous statute of limitations has expired for the purpose of fixing the presumption for laches. For many Lanham Act claims, the alleged violations are ongoing, *i.e.,* the wrongful acts occurred both within and without the limitations period. * * * As such, the statute of limitations is conceivably only a bar to monetary relief for the period outside the statute of limitations; the plaintiff is free to pursue monetary and equitable relief for the time within the limitations period. *E.g.,* * * * 4 J. Thomas McCarthy, McCarthy on Trademarks and Unfair Competition § 31.33 (4th ed. 2001) ("Usually, infringement is a continuing wrong, and the statute of limitations is no bar except as to damages beyond the statutory period.").

---

* The California statute of limitations for fraud is three years. *See* Cal. Civ. Proc. Code § 338(d).

We hold that the presumption of laches is triggered if any part of the claimed wrongful conduct occurred beyond the limitations period. To hold otherwise would "effectively swallow the rule of laches, and render it a spineless defense." * * * The plaintiff should not be entitled to the strong presumption against laches simply because some of the defendant's wrongful conduct occurred within the limitations period. Laches penalizes dilatory conduct; as such, the presumption is that a § 43(a) plaintiff is barred if he fails to file suit promptly when the defendant commences the wrongful conduct.

We further hold, consistent with our precedent, that in determining the presumption for laches, the limitations period runs from the time the plaintiff knew or should have known about his § 43(a) cause of action. * * * This principle is grounded in the fact that laches penalizes inexcusable dilatory behavior; if the plaintiff legitimately was unaware of the defendant's conduct, laches is no bar to suit. *See* Halstead v. Grinnan, 152 U.S. 412, 417, 14 S.Ct. 641, 38 L.Ed. 495 (1894) ("There must, of course, have been knowledge on the part of the plaintiff of the existence of the rights, for there can be no laches in failing to assert rights of which a party is wholly ignorant, and whose existence he had no reason to apprehend."); City of Davis v. Coleman, 521 F.2d 661, 677 (9th Cir.1975) ("An indispensable element of lack of diligence is knowledge, or reason to know, of the legal right, assertion of which is 'delayed.' ").

In sum, we presume that laches is not a bar to suit if the plaintiff files within the limitations period for the analogous state action; the presumption is reversed if the plaintiff files suit after the analogous limitations period has expired. For purposes of laches, the limitations period may expire even though part of the defendant's conduct occurred within the limitations period. Further, the state limitations period runs from the time the plaintiff knew or should have known about his § 43(a) cause of action.

Jarrow and Nutrition Now agree that the analogous limitations period is California's period for fraud, which is three years. * * * It is undisputed that Jarrow knew of its cause of action in 1993, which is well beyond the three-year limitations period. Therefore, we presume that laches is applicable.

B

As the party asserting laches, Nutrition Now must show that (1) Jarrow's delay in filing suit was unreasonable, and (2) Nutrition Now would suffer prejudice caused by the delay if the suit were to continue. * * *

A determination of whether a party exercised unreasonable delay in filing suit consists of two steps. * * * First, we assess the length of delay, which is measured from the time the plaintiff knew or should have known about its potential cause of action. * * * Second, we decide whether the plaintiff's delay was reasonable. * * * The reasonableness of the plaintiff's delay is considered in light of the time allotted by the analogous limitations period. * * * We also consider whether the plaintiff has proffered a legitimate excuse for its delay. * * *

The district court did not err in concluding that Jarrow exercised unreasonable delay in filing suit. Jarrow knew of its potential cause of action in 1993, but waited until 2000 to file suit.[6] Jarrow's seven-year delay is more than double the time available to file suit under the analogous limitations period. * * *

Further, Jarrow does not offer a legitimate excuse for its lengthy delay. Jarrow attributes its delay to a problem with its supplier, Rosell. Jarrow avers that it did not wish to file suit without laboratory analysis from Rosell proving Nutrition Now's claims false. Rosell, however, had a policy of not providing laboratory analysis to be used in litigation. Jarrow promptly filed suit after Rosell changed its policy.

As the district court correctly noted, Rosell's litigation policy did not excuse Jarrow's delay in filing suit. Jarrow could have sought laboratory testing from another source. While Jarrow stresses that Rosell possessed unique expertise regarding probiotic nutritional supplements, it made no attempt to solicit an alternative tester. * * *

Laches will not apply unless Nutrition Now will suffer prejudice from Jarrow's delay if the suit were to proceed. * * * The district court concluded that Nutrition Now would suffer prejudice because it used the challenged claims as a significant part of PB8's marketing to the public.

* * *

At bottom, Nutrition Now has invested enormous resources in tying PB8's identity to the challenged claims. After waiting for several years, Jarrow now seeks to compel Nutrition Now to abandon its presentation of PB8, forcing it to adopt a materially different characterization of its product. If Jarrow had filed suit sooner, Nutrition Now could have invested its resources in shaping an alternative identity for PB8 in the minds of the public. *See, e.g.,* * * * *Conopco, Inc.,* 95 F.3d at 192–93 (finding prejudice because defendant may have chosen an alternative marketing position if the plaintiff had filed suit earlier). In light of the presumption of prejudice and our deferential standard of review, we must conclude that Nutrition Now would be prejudiced if Jarrow's suit were to proceed.

* * *

D

Jarrow argues that regardless of whether Nutrition Now can show unreasonable delay and prejudice, the public's interest defeats application

---

6. Jarrow arguably should have known about its potential cause of action in 1985, when Nutrition first made the challenged claims about PB8. Ultimately, the result does not depend upon whether 1985 or 1993 is the appropriate date. Accordingly, we need not decide whether Jarrow should have known about its cause of action in 1985. * * *

of laches. Because laches is an equitable remedy, laches will not apply if the public has a strong interest in having the suit proceed. *See, e.g.,* Maryland–National Capital Park & Planning Comm'n v. United States Postal Serv., 487 F.2d 1029, 1042 (D.C.Cir.1973) ("Equitable remedies depend not only on a determination of legal rights and wrongs, but on such matters as laches, good (or bad) faith, and most important an appraisal of the public interest."); *cf.* Portland Audubon Soc'y. v. Lujan, 884 F.2d 1233, 1241 (9th Cir.1989) ("We have repeatedly cautioned against application of the equitable doctrine of laches to public interest environmental litigation."). The public's interest is of overriding importance, and as such, should be considered apart from any presumption of laches. *Cf. Conopco, Inc.,* 95 F.3d at 187 ("[T]he public good is of *paramount* importance when considering the equitable defense of laches." (emphasis added)).

Jarrow contends that Nutrition Now is duping the public into buying a worthless product. Because consumers are allegedly taking PB8 under the false impression that it will improve their health, Jarrow argues that the public has a strong interest in allowing the suit to proceed.

Jarrow correctly notes that the public has *some* interest in its suit. * * * However, if a plaintiff could defeat laches simply by asserting the public's interest in accurate advertising, laches would in effect not be a defense to Lanham Act false advertising claims. * * *

Of course, the public has a particularly strong interest in an accurate description of health and medical products. * * * Nevertheless, in order to ensure that laches remains a viable defense to Lanham Act claims, the public's interest will trump laches only when the suit concerns allegations that the product is harmful or otherwise a threat to public safety and well being. * * *

Jarrow vigorously asserts that PB8 lacks the potency and effectiveness of competing probiotic supplements. However, the critical question is whether consumer health will be materially affected as a *consequence* of taking PB8. * * * Consumer health may be *benefitted* by taking probiotic nutritional supplements. But, we cannot conclude that the failure to take an effective probiotic supplement puts consumer health in jeopardy. For example, Jarrow has not shown that probiotic supplements are akin to drugs such as heart medicine, which if ineffective, would lead to severe consequences.

Further, Nutrition Now does not promote PB8 in a manner that implicates public health concerns. Nutrition Now is not misleading consumers into departing from established medical care. For example, Nutrition Now does not urge consumers to take PB8 in lieu of prescribed medication. Nutrition Now markets PB8 as a *supplement* to, not a panacea for, better health.

Apart from alleging that PB8 is generally ineffective, Jarrow also claims that PB8 contains a dangerous strain of bacteria, S. faecium. However, Jarrow's allegations regarding the effect of this strain are conclusory, and at best, merely suggest that the strain is controversial. On this record, we cannot conclude that the district court erred.

E

Alternatively, Jarrow argues that Nutrition Now is precluded from asserting laches because of unclean hands. A party with unclean hands may not assert laches. *E.g.,* * * * *GoTo.com, Inc.,* 202 F.3d at 1209 (applying unclean hands doctrine to Lanham Act trademark infringement action). The unclean hands doctrine "closes the doors of a court of equity to one tainted with inequitableness or bad faith relative to the matter in which he seeks relief." Precision Instr. Mfg. Co. v. Auto. Maint. Mach. Co., 324 U.S. 806, 814, 65 S.Ct. 993, 89 L.Ed. 1381 (1945). * * *

* * *

Jarrow * * * claims that Nutrition Now is barred by unclean hands because of its conduct in defending Jarrow's accusations in 1993. When Jarrow initially leveled its accusations about PB8, Nutrition Now retained Alpha Omega ("Alpha"), a microbiology laboratory. Alpha tested samples of PB8 and transmitted its findings to Nutrition Now. Unbeknownst to Alpha, Nutrition Now prepared a report based on the findings. Nutrition Now also created a graphic letterhead for Alpha for use on the report, without Alpha's knowledge or permission. Nutrition Now transmitted the report to a "small number of health stores," along with a cover letter disparaging Jarrow's accusations.

Alpha promptly complained to Nutrition Now. Alpha charged that the report contained information that it did not verify and would not stand by. Alpha also resented the fact that Nutrition Now put Alpha's letterhead on a report that it did not prepare. Nutrition Now promptly ceased using the report after receiving Alpha's complaint.

Nutrition Now's actions, while troubling, do not amount to unclean hands. The report was distributed to only a "small number" of stores. Nutrition Now promptly ceased using the report after Alpha complained. It is also significant that Jarrow was not misled by the report. Perhaps, Nutrition Now's hands are not as "clean as snow." *GoTo.com, Inc.,* 202 F.3d at 1210. However, we cannot conclude that its actions rise to the level of unclean hands.

* * *

Affirmed.

DAINGERFIELD ISLAND PROTECTIVE SOCIETY v. LUJAN

United States Court of Appeals, District of Columbia Circuit, 1990.
920 F.2d 32.

Before WALD, MIKVA, and RUTH BADER GINSBURG, CIRCUIT JUDGES.

RUTH BADER GINSBURG, CIRCUIT JUDGE:

The origin of this case is a 1970 agreement ("Exchange Agreement") by which the National Park Service ("NPS," "the Service") completed its acquisition of Dyke Marsh, an environmentally sensitive wetland on the Potomac River between Alexandria and Mount Vernon, Virginia. In exchange for the wetland property it acquired, NPS granted developer Charles Fairchild & Co. an easement to build an interchange on the George Washington Memorial Parkway ("Parkway"). Fairchild hoped that this interchange would one day channel traffic to Potomac Greens, a mammoth office, hotel and residential complex he planned to build on land he leased from intervenor-appellee Richmond, Fredericksburg & Potomac Railroad Co. ("RF & P"). Twenty years later, Fairchild's hopes remain unrealized: no construction has begun on either the interchange or the Potomac Greens complex.

Daingerfield Island Protective Society and its coappellants (collectively, "the Society") commenced this action in 1986 to set aside the 1970 Exchange Agreement * * * [on the ground that the Secretary of the Department of Interior had failed to comply with several statutory requirements prior to approving the land exchange] and to void the approval of the interchange design * * *. The court rejected * * * the attack on the 1970 Exchange Agreement on the ground of laches. * * *

* * *

I.

In the years before the 1970 Exchange Agreement, Fairchild unsuccessfully pursued various development strategies on his Dyke Marsh property. * * * Because the marsh is a vital habitat to wading and water birds and various other small animals, environmental groups joined area residents, who feared the effects of new development, to oppose Fairchild's plans. These groups pressed the government to acquire the entire Dyke Marsh area. By 1966, NPS owned most of the acreage. * * * Facing dimming prospects of development on his 28.8–acre Dyke Marsh tract, Fairchild turned his attention to the 38–acre property across the Parkway that he leased from RF & P.

The 1970 Exchange Agreement provided that Fairchild would be entitled to Parkway access as soon as he deeded his Dyke Marsh property to the government. After delaying for more than a year, Fairchild conveyed a deed to the property in June 1971 and signed the Exchange Agreement on July 6, 1971. * * * The Agreement provided that Fairchild's construction could not commence until NPS * * * approved the design of the Parkway interchange * * *.

Fairchild did not submit construction plans for the interchange until 1975. * * * His relations with NPS grew acrimonious, as the Service opposed Fairchild's complicated "reverse-flow" design. * * * In 1976, * * * the National Capital Region of NPS * * * recommended repurchasing Fairchild's access rights. NPS did not adopt this recommendation, probably because it doubted that funds would be available for the repurchase.

In May 1978, the Society sought to enjoin the Department of Interior and NPS from approving any interchange design. In its prayer for relief, the Society did not demand that the Agreement be set aside, nor, except for a hint in Paragraph 22 of its 52 paragraph complaint, did it even allege that the 1970 Exchange Agreement was unlawful. Rather, the Society's attention trained on NPS's consideration of the interchange design. * * * Because NPS had not yet acted on any proposed design, the district court dismissed the Society's challenge, without prejudice, as premature. * * *

In April 1981, after Fairchild at last gave up on his "reverse-flow" plan, NPS approved the interchange design, reserving its right to make changes when Fairchild submitted more detailed plans. * * * NPS's October 1983 Environmental Assessment concluded that the design was satisfactory, noting that because of the terms of the 1970 Exchange Agreement, the Service could not recommend a "no build" alternative. * * * NPS issued a deed for the easement in August 1984. Prior to these approvals, in early 1982, RF & P had responded to Fairchild's delays by terminating his lease. The deed therefore went to RF & P as successor to Fairchild. * * *

In 1986, RF & P entered a joint venture with developer Savage/Fogarty Companies, Inc.; in late summer, Savage/Fogarty announced the joint venture's plans to build a somewhat smaller Potomac Greens complex. * * * The Society then commenced this action. The Society's complaint, filed in August 1986, alleged that when NPS approved the 1970 land exchange, the Service violated NEPA (Count I), the Land and Water Conservation Fund Act (Count II), the Mount Vernon Highway Act and the Capper–Cramton Act (Count III), the National Park Service Organic Act (Count IV), the National Capital Planning Act (Count V), the Administrative Procedure Act ("APA") (Count VI), and the National Historic Preservation Act (Count IX). * * *

The federal defendants and * * * [RF & P], raising threshold defenses, moved for dismissal or summary judgment. * * *

* * *

III.

We turn next to the district court's dismissal, for untimeliness, of the attack on the 1970 Exchange Agreement. Laches, an affirmative defense under Rule 8(c) of the Federal Rules of Civil Procedure, requires a showing of inexcusable delay and undue prejudice; Both must be shown; a finding of laches cannot rest simply on the length of delay. See, e.g., Gull Airborne Instruments, Inc. v. Weinberger, 694 F.2d 838, 843 (D.C.Cir. 1982). As the district court acknowledged, * * * laches is a disfavored defense in environmental suits. * * * "Nearly every circuit ... and numerous district courts have recognized the salutary principle that '[l]aches must be invoked sparingly in environmental cases because ordinarily the plaintiff will not be the only victim of alleged environmental damage. A less grudging application of the doctrine might defeat Congress's environmental policy.'" Park County Resource Council, Inc. v. United States Dep't of Agriculture, 817 F.2d 609, 617 (10th Cir.1987) (quoting Preservation Coalition, Inc. v. Pierce, 667 F.2d 851, 854 (9th Cir.1982), and collecting cases from the First, Second, Fourth, Fifth, Sixth, Eighth, and Ninth Circuits).

Because laches is an equitable doctrine, courts have generally held that it "is primarily addressed to the discretion of the trial court." * * * However, the district court's discretion is "confined by established standards." Park County Resource Council, 817 F.2d at 617; see also Ecology Center of Louisiana, Inc. v. Coleman, 515 F.2d 860, 867 n.8 (5th Cir.1975). A district court's ruling on laches does not qualify for deference if the court applied the wrong legal standard. Several appellate decisions, reversing district court judgments, are illustrative. See, e.g., * * * Coalition for Canyon Preservation v. Bowers, 632 F.2d 774 (9th Cir.1980) * * *.

We have no cause to disturb the district court's finding that the Society's delay in bringing suit was inexcusable.[6] We reverse the court's laches ruling, nevertheless, on the ground that federal appellees and RF & P failed to demonstrate sufficient prejudice from the delay.

* * * The documented expenditures of the three appellees, so far as we can tell, add up to less than $692,000. This figure is quite modest, compared to other cases in which no dispositive prejudice was found. See, e.g., Environmental Defense Fund v. Tennessee Valley Auth., 468 F.2d 1164 (6th Cir.1972) ($29 million expended in reliance); Park County Resource Council, 817 F.2d at 609 ($1 million); Coalition for Canyon Preservation, 632 F.2d at 774 ($1 million); Ecology Center of Louisiana, 515 F.2d at 860 ($1 million).

Moreover, in environmental suits, the amount of money spent in reliance has not been considered the prime factor in the prejudice inquiry. Two factors have been accorded heavier weight. The first is the percentage of estimated total expenditures disbursed at the time of suit. See, e.g., Park County Resource Council, 817 F.2d at 618. Here, the estimated total expenditures are about $500 million, hence the amount disbursed so far is relatively insignificant. Second, courts have examined whether the relief plaintiffs seek is still practicable. This consideration—the crucial one in the prior cases—has turned on the degree to which construction is complete. See Preservation Coalition, 667 F.2d at 855 ("Delay may be

---

6. The Society argues that its delay in opposing the exchange agreement should be measured from 1984, when NPS conveyed the easement deed to RF & P, or 1986, when RF & P formed its joint venture with Savage/Fogarty to develop the property. Appellants, particularly appellant Northeast Citizens Association, further argue that their vigor in opposing the Potomac Greens development as early as 1971 demonstrates that they did not sleep on their rights. We find decisive, however, the fact that the Society filed suit in 1978 to challenge the tentative interchange plans without (contrary to its current claim) challenging the Exchange Agreement. If, as the Society claims, the talk during 1976–84 of repurchasing Fairchild's access rights led it to believe that no challenge to the Exchange Agreement was necessary, why did it file suit in 1978 to challenge the interchange design plans, which presupposed the Agreement's validity?

prejudicial if substantial work has been completed before the suit was brought, but even substantial completion is sometimes insufficient to bar suit.") (emphasis deleted). *Compare, e.g., Coalition for Canyon Preservation*, 632 F.2d at 774 (no significant prejudice where right of way cleared, but road not built) *and* Watershed Assocs. Rescue v. Alexander, 586 F.Supp. 978 (D.Neb.1982) (no significant prejudice; right of way cleared, but construction of levee not begun), *with* Citizens & Landowners Against the Miles City/New Underwood Powerline v. Secretary, United States Dep't of Energy, 683 F.2d 1171 (8th Cir.1982) (prejudice found, since challenged power line nearly complete) *and* National Parks & Conservation Ass'n v. Hodel, 679 F.Supp. 49 (D.D.C.1987) (prejudice found, since challenged restaurant on Daingerfield Island completed before suit filed). Here, not only has construction not begun, but a construction permit has not issued * * *.

No Pryderi

* * *

* * * In both of the briefs that the Society filed in this court, it contended that in every environmental case where a court grounded summary judgment on the defense of laches, the harm-generating activity plaintiffs sought to prevent had already begun to occur, typically because construction of the project plaintiffs sought to block was underway. Since appellees had cited no contrary decision, nor had we discovered one in our own research, we asked federal appellees at oral argument whether one existed. They were unable to identify such a case. Here, no construction has begun on the interchange or on the Potomac Greens complex; the damage that plaintiffs sought to prevent thus has not begun to occur. The defense of laches, we hold, must be rejected under the circumstances this case presents.

CONCLUSION

We * * * reverse * * * [the district court's] ruling that the Society's challenges to the 1970 Exchange Agreement were barred by laches, and remand for further proceedings consistent with this opinion.

* * *

NOTES

1.   The defense of laches is discussed in Gull Airborne Instruments, Inc. v. Weinberger, 694 F.2d 838 (D.C.Cir.1982):

> The laches doctrine, of course, reflects the principle that "equity aids the vigilant, not those who slumber on their rights," and is designed to promote diligence and prevent enforcement of stale claims. * * * 2 J. Pomeroy, Equity Jurisprudence § 418 (5th ed. 1941). To establish a successful laches defense, the defendant must show that the plaintiff was guilty of unreasonable delay prejudicial to the defendant. * * *

There are, therefore, two factors to be considered in determining whether laches applies: lack of diligence by the plaintiff and injurious reliance thereon by the defendant. * * * If only a short period of time elapses between accrual of the claim and suit, the magnitude of prejudice required before suit would be barred is great; if the delay is lengthy, a lesser showing of prejudice is required. * * *

* * *

Two kinds of prejudice support a laches defense. Plaintiff's delay in filing suit may have resulted in a loss of evidence or witnesses supporting defendant's position or the defendant may have changed its position in a manner that would not have occurred but for plaintiff's delay.

Id. at 843–45.

2. A particular period of delay may be long enough to preclude a plaintiff from obtaining provisional injunctive relief (based on a failure to prove "irreparable harm"), but not long enough to rise to the level of laches in a subsequent permanent injunction proceeding. *E.g.*, Citibank, N.A. v. Citytrust, 756 F.2d 273 (2d Cir.1985) (the plaintiff in a trademark infringement action was not entitled to a preliminary injunction where the plaintiff delayed in seeking the injunction by nine months from the date of notice in the press and by ten weeks from the date of actual notice); Citibank, N.A. v. Citytrust, 644 F.Supp. 1011 (E.D.N.Y.1986) (the defendant in the same case was not entitled to a summary judgment based on the defense of laches). *See generally* Sandra Edelman, *Delay in Filing Preliminary Injunction Motions: Update 2002*, 92 Trademark Rep. 647 (2002) (analyzing trademark and unfair competition cases; stating that, in most federal courts, a delay of a year or longer usually bars a preliminary injunction, but, in the Second Circuit, a delay of six months or longer creates a significant risk that a preliminary injunction will be denied).

SECTION 6.   APPEALS FROM INJUNCTION RULINGS

A.   JURISDICTION OVER APPEALS FROM PERMANENT AND PRELIMINARY INJUNCTION RULINGS

Permanent injunction rulings are "final decisions," and therefore the federal appellate courts routinely exercise jurisdiction over appeals from such rulings. Preliminary injunction rulings, by contrast, are "interlocutory orders," and ordinarily interlocutory orders are not subject to appeal because Congress wants to avoid piecemeal litigation. However, Congress has explicitly authorized the exercise of jurisdiction over appeals from preliminary injunction rulings because such injunctions often have "serious and perhaps irreparable consequences." Carson v. American Brands, Inc., 450 U.S. 79, 84, 101 S.Ct. 993, 997, 67 L.Ed.2d 59 (1981). The federal statutes governing jurisdiction over appeals from permanent and preliminary injunction rulings, 28 U.S.C. §§ 1291–1292, are set forth below:

§ 1291. Final decisions of district courts

The courts of appeals * * * shall have jurisdiction of appeals from all final decisions of the district courts of the United States, * * * except where a direct review may be had in the Supreme Court. * * *

§ 1292. Interlocutory decisions

(a) [T]he courts of appeals shall have jurisdiction of appeals from:

(1) Interlocutory orders of the district courts of the United States * * * or of the judges thereof, granting, continuing, modifying, refusing or dissolving injunctions, or refusing to dissolve or modify injunctions, except where a direct review may be had in the Supreme Court * * *.

Whenever an intermediate federal court takes jurisdiction over an appeal from an injunction ruling, the case is heard by a 3–judge "merits panel." The merits panel reviews the trial court judge's decision for an "abuse of discretion." For examples of federal appellate court opinions applying the abuse of discretion standard, see *supra* Chapter 2, Sections 1–5. Occasionally when an intermediate federal appellate court takes jurisdiction over an appeal from an injunction ruling, the appellant needs immediate "pre-appeal injunctive relief." In such circumstances, a 3–judge "motions panel" is convened expeditiously and is asked either to stay an injunction that the trial court has granted, or to grant an injunction that the trial court has refused to issue. Pre-appeal injunctive relief remains in effect until such time as the merits panel announces its decision in the case. The purpose of pre-appeal injunctive relief is to preserve the case for a subsequent hearing by the merits panel. Sometimes the same three judges will sit on both the motions panel and the merits panel, but, more often, the two panels will be composed of different judges. *E.g.*, Federal Trade Commission v. Weyerhaeuser Co., 648 F.2d 739 (D.C.Cir.1981) (motions panel); Federal Trade Commission v. Weyerhaeuser Co., 665 F.2d 1072 (D.C.Cir.1981) (merits panel). For a discussion of pre-appeal injunctive relief, see *infra* Chapter 2, Section 6.C.

NOTES

1. Although Congress has authorized the exercise of appellate jurisdiction over all preliminary injunction rulings, some states have authorized appellate jurisdiction over such rulings only in extraordinary circumstances:

> The purpose of a preliminary injunction is ordinarily to preserve the *status quo* pending trial on the merits. Its issuance is a matter of discretion to be exercised by the hearing judge after a careful balancing of the equities. Its impact is temporary and lasts no longer than the pendency of the action. Its decree bears no precedent to guide the final determination of the rights of the parties. In form, purpose, and effect, it is purely interlocutory. Thus, the threshold question presented by a purported appeal from an order granting a preliminary injunction is whether the appellant has been deprived of any substantial right which might be lost should the order escape appellate review before final

judgment. If no such right is endangered, the appeal cannot be maintained. * * *

* * *

Our refusal to allow defendants' appeal is not a surrender to technical requirements of finality. The statutes and rules governing appellate review are more than procedural niceties. They are designed to streamline the judicial process, to forestall delay rather than engender it. "There is no more effective way to procrastinate the administration of justice than that of bringing cases to an appellate court piecemeal through the medium of successive appeals from intermediate orders." * * *

State v. Fayetteville St. Christian School, 299 N.C. 351, 357–58, 261 S.E.2d 908, 913 (N.C.1980) (refusing to exercise appellate jurisdiction over an order restraining defendants from operating day-care centers without complying with licensing requirements, since defendants had all held valid licenses in the past, and could renew them pending a trial on the merits of their constitutional challenge to the licensing requirements). By contrast, a few states permit a wider scope of interlocutory review than that authorized by the federal statutes and rules of civil procedure. *See, e.g.,* Winslow Christian, *Interlocutory Review in California—Practical Justice Unguided by Standards,* 47 Law & Contemp. Probs. 111 (1984).

2. In response to concerns about piecemeal appellate review, federal appellate courts increasingly are willing to address the merits of a case when considering an interlocutory appeal from a district court's preliminary injunction ruling, as illustrated by Doe v. Sundquist, 106 F.3d 702 (6th Cir.1997), *cert. denied,* 522 U.S. 810, 118 S.Ct. 51, 139 L.Ed.2d 16 (1997) (affirming district court's denial of preliminary injunction to adoptive parents and birth mothers who were challenging the constitutionality of a Tennessee statute that allowed the disclosure of previously confidential adoption records):

We generally decline comment on the merits of the case [when reviewing a district court's preliminary injunction ruling because] * * * we do not consider issues not passed upon by the district court. Pinney Dock & Transport Co. v. Penn Cent. Corp., 838 F.2d 1445, 1461 (6th Cir.1988). The axiom is not jurisdictional, however. If an issue unaddressed by the district court "is presented with sufficient clarity and completeness and its resolution will materially advance the progress" of the litigation, *id.,* we have often chosen to consider that issue * * *. The sort of judicial restraint that is normally warranted on interlocutory appeals does not prevent us from reaching clearly defined issues in the interest of judicial economy. * * *

We have never applied the *Pinney Dock* exception precisely to an appeal from the grant or denial of a preliminary injunction, but we find that the principle applies squarely to such a case when the legal issues have been briefed and the factual record does not need expansion. Other appeals courts have readily addressed the merits of cases on interlocutory appeal from the denial of a preliminary injunction. *E.g.,* Illinois Council on Long Term Care v. Bradley, 957 F.2d 305, 310 (7th Cir.1992) * * *. Indeed, the U.S. Supreme Court has noted that one purpose of interlocutory appeals is "to save parties the expense of further litigation." Thornburgh v. American College of Obstetricians & Gynecologists, 476 U.S. 747, 756, 106 S.Ct. 2169, 2176, 90 L.Ed.2d 779 (1986) * * *. We remand to the district court to dismiss plaintiff's complaint with prejudice with respect to the federal constitutional issues * * *.

Id. at 707–08.

B. JURISDICTION OVER APPEALS FROM TEMPORARY RESTRAINING ORDER RULINGS

Because § 1292(a)(1), the federal statute that authorizes the exercise of appellate jurisdiction over a preliminary injunction ruling, refers to "injunctions," and not to "restraining orders," the federal courts have adopted the general rule that an interlocutory order granting, continuing, modifying, refusing, or dissolving a temporary restraining order is not appealable. *See, e.g.,* Connell v. Dulien Steel Products, Inc., 240 F.2d 414, 417 (5th Cir.1957) [(temporary restraining order was not appealable where the restraint was to last "until the final decision of the court on the plaintiff's motion for a preliminary injunction")]. The *Connell* court gave three "practical reasons" for generally disallowing appeals from temporary restraining orders: (1) they are "usually effective for only brief periods of time, far less than the time required for appeal"; (2) they are "[sometimes] issued without notice to the adverse party, and thus the trial judge has had opportunity to hear only one side of the case"; and (3) the trial court "should have ample opportunity to have a full presentation of the facts and law before entering an order that is appealable * * *." *Id.* at 418. At the same time, the federal courts also have recognized exceptions to the general rule. For example, they have taken the position that, "if the temporary restraining order is continued for a substantial length of time past the period permitted by Rule 65(b), without consent of the party against whom it is directed," then it will be treated as if it were a preliminary injunction subject to appeal under § 1292(a)(1). *Id.* And they have held that, when a temporary restraining order ruling has "the effect" of a "final decision," then it will be treated as if it were a permanent injunction subject to appeal under § 1291. Kimball v. Commandant Twelfth Naval District, 423 F.2d 88 (9th Cir.1970). The following cases illustrate both the general rule and the exceptions to it. *See generally* Robert C. Dorr & Mark Traphagen, *Federal Ex Parte Temporary Relief,* 6 Den. L.J. 767 (1984); Note, *Duration of Temporary Restraining Orders in Federal Court,* 12 U. Balt. L. Rev. 276 (1983).

CHICAGO UNITED INDUSTRIES, LTD. v. CITY OF CHICAGO

United States Court of Appeals, Seventh Circuit, 2006.
445 F.3d 940.

POSNER, CIRCUIT JUDGE.

This appeal presents jurisdictional issues, specifically regarding temporary restraining orders and preliminary injunctions, arising from a dispute between the City of Chicago and one of its contractors, Chicago United Industries. * * * Believing that CUI had billed the City for goods that the contractor knew it had not delivered, the City, after months of wrangling, notified CUI that it proposed to cancel all CUI's contracts with the City and bar it ("debarment," the parties call this) from further contracts with the City. The company was given 30 days to respond to the proposal; it responded; and the City then terminated the contracts and instituted a three-year bar, whereupon CUI filed this suit in the federal district court in Chicago. The suit sought injunctive relief on the ground that the City had violated the due process clause of the Fourteenth Amendment by failing to give CUI a predeprivation hearing. CUI moved for a preliminary injunction, and (until it was granted) a temporary restraining order, to prevent the cancellation and debarment.

The court issued the TRO on August 31, 2005, the day after CUI had moved for it, saying that "plaintiffs have no adequate remedy at law as there is no appeal provision of the debarment at the City level, and any further administrative appeal would be an inadequate opportunity to present the constitutional matters at issue in this litigation." The court added that the plaintiffs would "suffer irreparable harm if the temporary restraining order is not granted since continuation of the debarment, even for a short period of time, will materially impair their business and their ability to do business." The TRO stated that the defendants were "temporarily restrained and enjoined from 1) enforcing the debarment of [CUI] 2) from canceling any existing contracts that CUI has with the City of Chicago and 3) from conducting any further decertification or administrative hearing regarding, related to or based upon the issue of debarment pending further action of this Court."

The order was to remain in force for 10 [business] days, but at the end of that period the court renewed it for another 10 [business] days. During the extension period, the City notified CUI that it was withdrawing its cancellation of CUI's contracts with the City and rescinding the debarment order, though without prejudice to seeking both cancellation and debarment in the future based on the same alleged fraudulent billing. On the basis of these representations, the City moved to dismiss CUI's lawsuit as moot. The district court, troubled by the "without prejudice" qualification, denied the motion. [On September 22,] [t]he temporary restraining order was then extended by agreement of the parties * * * to October 31.

During this further extension period, CUI asked the district court to modify the order to prevent the City from circumventing it. Also on the table was the need to set a date for the hearing on CUI's motion for a preliminary injunction. Because a temporary restraining order cannot remain in force for more than 20 days without the consent of the parties, Fed.R.Civ.P. 65(b), the district court offered to hold the hearing on November 7. The City asked for an extension. The district court offered to extend the date to November 21, provided the City agreed to an extension of the restraining order for another month, to November 28. The City agreed. But before either date arrived, the court modified the TRO, essentially as requested by CUI, by adding to its previous terms that the City was also restrained "from [1] awarding any of the following contracts [ten are listed] to any company other than Chicago United if it is the lowest responsive bidder, or using its emergency purchasing power to circumvent the award to Chicago United and pay a higher price to some other company, unless and until the City provides this Court with a showing that awarding the contract to or purchasing such goods from such other company is in accordance with the *status quo ante* * * * ... and ... [2] imposing any restrictions on communications between Chicago United and employees of the City with the exception that Chicago United and its attorneys may not speak directly with any employees of the City regarding matters directly related to this action." [The City objected to the modification of the temporary restraining order, and it filed a notice of appeal on October 24.]

A temporary restraining order is not appealable, despite its close resemblance to a preliminary injunction, which is appealable. 28 U.S.C. § 1292(a)(1). But if kept in force by the district court for more than 20 days without the consent of the parties, the order is deemed a preliminary injunction and so is appealable, since otherwise a district court could by the simple expedient of extending the TRO circumvent * * * the right of appeal granted by section 1292(a)(1). Sampson v. Murray, 415 U.S. 61, 86–88, 94 S.Ct. 937, 39 L.Ed.2d 166 (1974) * * * . CUI argues that the City consented to the * * * extension [of the TRO] and therefore cannot appeal. [The City argued that it did not consent to the *modification* of the TRO and therefore it could appeal.]

The City could have elided the issue of consent by waiting until November 29, the day after the expiration of the period of extension that the parties had agreed upon, to appeal. For at that point there would have been no doubt that the temporary restraining order was appealable. Instead the City filed its notice of appeal during the extension period. The preliminary-injunction hearing had been set for November 21, and evidently the City didn't want to participate in such a hearing. Had it done so, and a preliminary injunction been issued, the City could, again uncontroversially, have appealed. * * *

In any event it is apparent that the City * * * consented to the extension of the *existing* TRO, not to the entry of a modified order the text of which it had not seen because the district judge had not yet drafted it. The judge had told the City that he would accept a modified order if the parties could agree to one, and if not he would review competing draft orders submitted by the parties and decide which one to adopt. But he entered the modified order right after CUI submitted its draft order and *before* the City submitted its draft order.

CUI ripostes that there was no "modification," that all that the new provisions that we quoted did was to particularize the original order, which had forbidden cancellation and debarment, so that in consenting to the extension of the original order the City should be taken to have consented to the additional provisions. That argument is frivolous. The additional provisions are vague, open-ended, and onerous, enjoining as they do conduct that goes far beyond cancellation and debarment. The City cannot be deemed to have consented to them.

* * *

CUI further argues that the 20–day rule applies only when a TRO is issued without notice. This is a plausible reading of Rule 65(b), but would not make any sense, and is generally and we think correctly rejected. Nutrasweet Co. v. Vit–Mar Enterprises, Inc., 112 F.3d 689, 693–94 (3d Cir.1997), and cases cited there; Connell v. Dulien Steel Products, Inc., 240 F.2d 414, 417–18 (5th Cir.1957); see also Sampson v. Murray, *supra,* 415 U.S. at 85–88, 94 S.Ct. 937; Granny Goose Foods, Inc. v. Brotherhood of Teamsters & Auto Truck Drivers Local No. 70 of Alameda County, 415 U.S. 423, 442–45, 94 S.Ct. 1113, 39 L.Ed.2d 435 (1974) * * * . For it would enable a district court to issue a preliminary injunction of indefinite duration without any possibility of the defendant's appealing, simply by calling the injunction a temporary restraining order and being careful to notify the defendant in advance of issuing it. Moreover, a TRO issued after notice, especially if there is a hearing, is procedurally as well as functionally even more like a preliminary injunction than a TRO issued without notice and hearing, so it would be a considerable paradox if only the latter type of TRO were appealable after 20 days. * * * The proper interpretation of the "without notice" language in Rule 65(b) is that the rule imposes *additional* restrictions on temporary restraining orders issued without notice, but imposes the 20–day limit on *all* TROs.

To summarize our discussion to this point, the temporary restraining order in this case was modified without party consent and so, the 20 days having expired, was appealable. * * * But although we thus have jurisdiction of the appeal, we must decide whether the measures taken by the City after the suit was filed have rendered the case moot. [The Court found that the request for injunctive relief was moot because the City had reinstated all of the cancelled contracts, rescinded the debarment, and adopted a new rule that authorized a hearing prior to debarment if there were genuine issues of fact.]

* * *

All this said, the suit is saved from complete mootness, though only barely, by CUI's claim to have lost $500,000 in profits as a result of the termination and debarment proceedings. * * * [I]t is at least plausible that CUI lost profits, even though the contracts were terminated, and the debarment order effective, for only one week, until the first of the TROs was entered. * * *

* * *

So while the request for injunctive relief is moot, the case as a whole is not. The temporary restraining order is vacated; and [the case is remanded for] further proceedings * * * in the district court.

NOTES

1.   In *Connell*, the Fifth Circuit was willing to be somewhat flexible in its administration of Rule 65's time limits regarding the duration of temporary restraining orders. The goal was to give the trial court an opportunity to conduct a hearing in which there was a "full presentation of both sides" prior to any exercise of appellate jurisdiction over an interlocutory order. Other federal circuits have been less flexible because their goal has been to protect the defendant's right to appeal an interlocutory order that may have serious, and perhaps irreparable, consequences. For example, the Eighth Circuit has held that a 20-day temporary restraining order, which suspended the defendant's tender offer, was "in substance a preliminary injunction" and "therefore appealable." Edudata Corp. v. Scientific Computers, Inc., 746 F.2d 429 (8th Cir.1984). The court emphasized the fact that the order "on its face" was "to last more than the ten days to which temporary restraining orders are initially limited" by Rule 65(b). *Id.* The court acknowledged that a temporary restraining order may be extended to last 20 days, but only "for good cause shown," and there had been no such showing in this case. *Id.* Similarly, the Ninth Circuit has exercised appellate jurisdiction over a 30-day temporary restraining order that precluded the defendant from enforcing a non-competition agreement against the plaintiffs. Bennett v. Medtronic, Inc., 285 F.3d 801, 804 (9th Cir.2002). The court first emphasized the fact that there had been "an opportunity to file extensive written materials and present oral argument," but then the court said: "The duration of the order also compels us to treat it as a preliminary injunction, considering that the district court granted relief for three times the period contemplated by Rule 65." *Id.*

2.   One way to extend the duration of a temporary restraining order is to obtain the consent of the opposing party. A few cases have held that a temporary restraining order is nonappealable if the defendant has consented to an extension of an indefinite duration. Fernandez–Roque v. Smith, 671 F.2d 426, 430 (11th Cir.1982); Ross v. Evans, 325 F.2d 160 (5th Cir.1963). More recent cases, however, have expressed a willingness to exercise appellate jurisdiction over a stipulated temporary restraining order as if it were an appealable preliminary injunction, particularly if the defendant has been held in contempt. United States v. Bayshore Associates, Inc., 934 F.2d 1391, 1397 (6th Cir.1991) (citing to cases from the Second, Third, and Eighth circuits).

3.   On occasion, an appeal is allowed from the issuance of a mandatory temporary restraining order that complies with the time constraints set forth in Rule 65. *See, e.g.*, Adams v. Vance, 570 F.2d 950 (D.C.Cir.1978). In *Adams*, the Inupiat Eskimos obtained a temporary restraining order from the district court directing the Secretary of State to object immediately to the Interna-

tional Whaling Commission's proposed ban on hunting bowhead whales, an endangered species. (The Secretary of State, with the approval of the President, had decided that it would be diplomatic to request reconsideration of the ban rather than to file a formal objection.) The court of appeals took jurisdiction over the case for the following reasons:

> The grant of a temporary restraining order under Rule 65(b), Fed. R. Civ. P., is generally not appealable. However, "[t]he label attached to an order by the trial court is not decisive with regard to whether it falls under Rule 65(a) or Rule 65(b) and the appellate court will look to other factors to determine whether an appeal should be allowed." Wright & Miller, Federal Practice and Procedure § 2962, at 619 (1973). Here the order was in purpose and effect a mandatory injunction appealable under 28 U.S.C.A. § 1292(a)(1). It did not merely preserve the status quo pending further proceedings, but commanded an unprecedented action irreversibly altering the delicate diplomatic balance in the environmental arena. When an order directs action so potent with consequences so irretrievable, we provide an immediate appeal to protect the rights of the parties.

570 F.2d at 953 (The court of appeals vacated the temporary restraining order and, as a result, the United States did not formally object to the ban, but the government was successful in persuading the International Whaling Commission to permit Alaskan natives to engage in subsistence hunting of a limited number of bowhead whales.). *Accord* Belknap v. Leary, 427 F.2d 496, 498 (2d Cir.1970) (Friendly, J.) ("We regard * * * [Justice Constance Baker Motley's temporary restraining order requiring the police to provide 'adequate' protection against physical harm at any public demonstration over Memorial Day weekend, based on the failure of the police to provide such protection at a previous anti-war demonstration,] as a mandatory injunction, appealable under 28 U.S.C. § 1292(a)(1), even though it is of short duration.") (The court of appeals vacated the temporary restraining order on the ground that it was not necessary due to the corrective measures that had been taken by the Mayor and the Police Commissioner.).

4. Sometimes, instead of treating a temporary restraining order as if it were a preliminary injunction, the federal courts exercise appellate jurisdiction on the theory that a grant of a temporary restraining order is a "final decree," akin to a permanent injunction, and therefore appealable under 28 U.S.C. § 1291. The next case illustrates the "final decree" theory.

ROMER v. GREEN POINT SAVINGS BANK

United States Court of Appeals, Second Circuit, 1994.
27 F.3d 12.

Before: PRATT, WALKER and LEVAL, CIRCUIT JUDGES.

LEVAL, CIRCUIT JUDGE:

This motion and appeal concerns a temporary restraining order issued by the district court barring the consummation of a conversion plan, converting a mutual savings bank into a public stock company. The Green Point Savings Bank ("Green Point") is a mutual savings bank chartered under the laws of New York. Early in 1993 Green Point's board of trustees began considering alternate forms of corporate structure. In April the board retained the services of various consultants, including Adams Cohen Securities, Inc., to assist it in formulating and executing a conversion plan. On May 13, 1993, the board adopted a plan to convert to a capital stock bank (the "Plan"). The board then retained R.P. Financial, Inc., an appraisal firm, to determine the market value of the bank.

The crucial component of the conversion plan was a stock offering. As part of the plan, eligible Green Point depositors—those with $100 or more on deposit in accounts at Green Point as of February 28, 1993—would receive subscription rights to purchase shares of common stock at the initial offering price.

Under New York's banking laws, such conversions must be approved by the Superintendent of Banks of the State of New York ("Superintendent"). *See* N.Y.Comp.Codes R. & Regs. tit. 3, § 86.4(a)(1). Green Point submitted its conversion plan to the Superintendent on September 13, 1993. The Superintendent approved the plan on November 4, 1993, whereupon Green Point began mailing proxy materials for a December 10 depositors' meeting at which approval for the Plan would be sought.

Republic New York Corporation ("Republic"), a bank holding company, in the meantime had proposed to acquire Green Point and was rejected by Green Point's board of trustees. On November 4, Republic publicly issued a merger proposal, which Green Point again rejected. The maneuverings between the two drew public attention to the details of Green Point's conversion plan.

On November 12, 1993, a group of Green Point depositors ("Plaintiffs") filed a class action in the Eastern District of New York against Green Point, members of Green Point's board of trustees, Adams Cohen Securities, and R.P. Financial (collectively the "Defendants"), alleging that the Defendants had conspired to deter them from exercising their subscription rights, asserting violations of § 10(b) of the Securities Exchange Act of 1934, *see* 15 U.S.C. § 78j(b), and Securities and Exchange Commission Rule 10b–5, *see* 17 C.F.R. § 240.10b–5. The complaint alleged that Green Point had made materially false and misleading statements in order "to induce depositors to vote for the Proposed Conversion but to forego their right to purchase shares of [Green Point] common stock." The complaint claimed further that the Defendants had breached their fiduciary duties.

Central to the complaint was the allegation that the officers and trustees of Green Point had structured the conversion, not for the benefit of the depositors, but to enrich themselves by providing for their acquisition of undervalued Green Point shares not purchased by the depositors. The complaint alleged that the proxy materials failed to disclose the enormous value to these insiders of their stock acquisition rights.

The Superintendent meanwhile directed that Green Point supplement its proxy materials to include disclosures of the stock benefits to be received by insiders in the conversion and information about the Republic offer. In compliance, Green Point mailed supplementary materials on November 26, 1993.

On December 6, 1993, the Superintendent launched a special investigation of the plan. * * * As stated by the Superintendent, the purposes of the special investigation were "to ensure that the Trustees of Green Point properly valued the Bank in its sale to the public, that the depositors obtained adequate disclosure with respect to the conversion and that the solicitation process was conducted in a manner that was fair to the depositors." * * *

* * *

* * * [The conversion plan was approved] at the December 10 meeting. By the end of the depositors' subscription period on December 15, about 10,700 of the 246,000 depositors had subscribed to purchase approximately $835 million worth of stock.

* * * Under applicable New York law, however, Green Point was required to complete these sales within 45 days from the end of the subscription period unless the deadline was extended by the Superintendent. * * * The sale-deadline date was thus January 29, 1994. After that date, even if an extension had been granted, subscribers would be free to retract or amend their subscriptions. * * * Accordingly, if the sales were not concluded by January 29, Green Point would be required to issue a new prospectus, and depositors would be entitled to decide anew whether to subscribe and for how much stock.

The Superintendent concluded his investigation on January 23, 1994, and required modification of the conversion plan in several respects; the most significant change eliminated the compensation packages that had been arranged for Green Point executives and trustees and precluded the insiders from acquiring Green Point shares in the conversion and for a substantial time thereafter. This order, together with the supplementary mailing earlier ordered by the Superintendent, cured the principal defects attacked by Plaintiffs in the federal complaint. The Superintendent found that Green Point's plan of conversion, as modified, was in the "best interests" of the bank and its depositors and therefore approved the consummation of the modified plan. * * *

The day after the Superintendent issued his opinion, the Plaintiffs sought a temporary restraining order ("TRO") in the New York Supreme Court to prevent the Superintendent from filing Green Point's restated organization certificate. In a decision dated January 25, 1994, the state court rejected their claims and refused to grant the temporary restraining order. * * *

Plaintiffs then sought a TRO in this action barring the conversion. On January 26, 1994, the district court granted the motion and issued an order barring Green Point from taking further action to accomplish the conversion, pending a preliminary-injunction hearing scheduled for February 3, 1994.

The next day, January 27, 1994, Defendants appealed and moved in this court to stay the district court's restraining order and to expedite the appeal. On January 28 we heard the matter as an emergency. We * * * [announced our decision in an order dated January 28], noting that a formal opinion would follow. This is that opinion.

DISCUSSION

As a preliminary matter we note that the district court's order, although in the form of a TRO, had the effect of a final permanent injunction. By restraining all activity on the conversion until at least February 3, 1994, making it impossible for Green Point to meet the 45-day sale-date, the district court's order would have prevented Green Point's conversion plan from taking effect within the time allowed by law. After the January 29 sale-date, depositors who had subscribed to buy shares in the conversion would be released from their commitments, and any conversion would need to begin with a resolicitation. Thus the district court's order had a far more drastic effect than is normal for a TRO. It effectively granted the Plaintiffs final victory in the litigation.

As a general matter, appeal lies only from final judgments of the district court, 28 U.S.C. § 1291, or interlocutory orders that grant or refuse injunctions. 28 U.S.C. § 1292(a)(1). As a TRO is interlocutory and is not technically an injunction, it is ordinarily not appealable. * * * However, when a grant or denial of a TRO "might have a 'serious, perhaps irreparable, consequence,' and ... can be 'effectually challenged' only by immediate appeal," we may exercise appellate jurisdiction. Carson v. American Brands, Inc., 450 U.S. 79, 84, 101 S.Ct. 993, 996–97, 67 L.Ed.2d 59 (1981) (citation omitted) * * *. Because the district court's order met this standard, this court had jurisdiction to entertain Green Point's appeal, as well as the motion for a stay that accompanied it.

Although the application before us was for a stay and an expedited appeal, it was recognized by all the participants that, just as the district court's order would grant victory to the Plaintiffs, a stay of that order would grant victory to the Defendants. If we stayed the district court's TRO, the conversion plan would take effect the next day, mooting Plaintiffs' efforts to block it. A stay ordinarily seeks to preserve the status quo pending further litigation. Because far more turned on our ruling, we determined to expedite the appeal and confront directly the issues it raised.

Although interim orders ordinarily are reviewed with considerable deference, greater scrutiny is required when the order will effectively award victory in the litigation. When a district court's order, albeit in the form of a TRO or preliminary injunction, will finally dispose of the matter in dispute, it is not sufficient for the order to be based on a likelihood of success or balance of hardships * * *; the district court's decision must be correct (insofar as possible on what may be an incomplete record), and appellate review should be plenary. * * * Because the district court's order had the effect of a permanent injunction finally resolving the issue before the court, we review it in the same manner as we would review such a final injunctive order.

We find it was error for the district court to issue the TRO. In our view, virtually all of the pertinent considerations disfavored granting such an order. The dispute involved a State chartered bank regulated by the State Superintendent; the Superintendent, after making modifications, had approved the Plan as being in the interest of the bank and its depositors. The New York State court had refused Plaintiffs' application to enjoin the conversion. The State Superintendent, furthermore, had cured the problems that were the focus of Plaintiffs' complaint. Finally, Plaintiffs pointed to no irreparable harm or violation of law justifying the issuance of a temporary restraint, much less a conclusive bar to the closing of the conversion.

In contrast, the harm inflicted by the TRO was great. It would prevent Green Point from closing its conversion sales within 45 days, with the consequence either of terminating the offer, or, if extended by the Superintendent, freeing subscribers to rescind or amend their subscriptions. * * * To inform the subscribers of their new rights, acquired as the result of the expiration of the 45–day period, Green Point would have been required to issue a supplemental prospectus, implicating a new round of SEC clearances, and considerable attendant delay and expense. Because financial markets are in constant flux, furthermore, the substantial delays that would necessarily have resulted would have required potential investors to make a new investment decision. The delay might easily have upset the expectations of both the bank and the depositor/offerees under the Plan.

We find that Plaintiffs demonstrated no violation of their rights, no irreparable harm, no likelihood of success, perhaps not even a fair question for litigation, certainly no balance of hardships tipping in their direction, and no entitlement to injunctive relief.

* * *

The district court's order contained no findings of fact or substantive conclusions of law, beyond stating that the Plaintiffs were "likely to suffer irreparable harm" and "have a likelihood of success on the merits." * * * We recognize that the district court's order was in form a TRO, and that Rule 52(a)'s requirement of findings of fact and conclusions of law upon the issuance of interlocutory injunctions does not apply to a TRO. Fed. R.Civ.P. 52(a). TROs are exempted from the requirement of express findings presumably because they are characteristically issued in haste, in emergency circumstances, to forestall irreparable harm, are of quite limited duration, and are exempt from appellate review. Nonetheless, courts should not be excessively tied to labels. In the rare instance like this one, where the TRO will dispose of all that is at stake in the litigation, it is highly useful for the district court to make findings to explain its ruling. Such an order is appealable under the principles of *Carson,* 450 U.S. at 84, 101 S.Ct. at 996–97; without findings to explain the district court's action, the court of appeals will have difficulty understanding the basis of the ruling and determining whether the district court applied the law correctly.

CONCLUSION

For the reasons stated above * * * we have granted the motion to expedite the appeal and have vacated the TRO issued by the district court.

NOTE

When a federal district court denies a temporary restraining order (as opposed to granting such an order), the federal appellate courts generally are less apt to exercise their jurisdiction. *E.g.,* First Eagle SoGen Funds, Inc. v. Bank for International Settlements, 252 F.3d 604, 607 (2d Cir.2001) (declining to exercise appellate jurisdiction over the district court's denial of a temporary restraining order that would have stopped the buyback of the publicly-held shares of the Bank for International Settlements on the ground that the plaintiff had an adequate legal remedy in the form of damages). Nevertheless, some federal courts, such as the First Circuit, make no distinction between temporary restraining orders that have been denied and those that have been granted, exercising appellate jurisdiction whenever there has been a "full presentation of both sides" or when the order "effectively forecloses further interlocutory relief." *E.g.,* Coalition for Basic Human Needs v. King, 654 F.2d 838 (1st Cir.1981) (exercising appellate jurisdiction over the denial of a temporary restraining order that would have required the defendant to continue to pay welfare benefits to the plaintiffs because there were "no factual issues" that "rationally demanded development"; granting the motion for a pre-appeal injunction that ordered the payment of welfare benefits pending appeal); Levesque v. Maine, 587 F.2d 78 (1st Cir.1978) (exercising appellate jurisdiction over the denial of a temporary restraining order that would have reinstated the plaintiff as the Commissioner of the Department of Manpower because the denial of the order "effectively foreclosed further interlocutory relief"; affirming the denial of the temporary restraining order). Moreover, all federal courts will exercise appellate jurisdiction over the denial of a temporary restraining order when the district court's order effectively disposes of the litigation, and "might have a 'serious, perhaps irreparable consequence' that ... can be 'effectually challenged' only by immediate appeal." *First Eagle SoGen Funds, Inc.,* 252 F.3d at 607.

C. PROCEDURES AND STANDARDS FOR ISSUING PRE–APPEAL INJUNCTIVE RELIEF

There are two basic types of pre-appeal injunctive relief: (1) a stay of a grant of a provisional or permanent injunction; and (2) an injunction that is issued pending an appeal from a denial of a request for provisional or permanent injunctive relief. The function of pre-appeal injunctive relief is to preserve the case for a hearing on the merits, just as the function of provisional injunctive relief is to preserve the case for a trial on the merits. Therefore, the procedures and standards for issuing pre-appeal injunctive relief are very similar to those for issuing provisional injunctive relief, although they are not identical.

Under Federal Rule of Civil Procedure 62(a), there are no "automatic stays" of "an interlocutory or final judgment in an action for an injunction * * *." Consequently, the appellant must move to obtain pre-appeal injunctive relief in order to prevent the immediate effectiveness of the trial court's injunction ruling. Such a motion is usually submitted first to the trial court judge under Federal Rule of Civil Procedure 62(c), which provides that, when an appeal is taken from an interlocutory or final judgment granting, dissolving, or denying an injunction, "the court may suspend, modify, restore, or grant an injunction on terms for bond or other terms that secure the opposing party's rights." If the trial court denies the motion, the appellant may renew the request before a motions panel pursuant to Federal Rule of Appellate Procedure 8(a)(2)(A)(ii). Only when the appellant shows that "moving first in the district court would be impracticable" does Rule 8(a)(2)(A)(i) permit the appellant to submit a request for pre-appeal injunctive relief directly to the court of appeals or to one of its judges. Rule 8(a)(2)(C) specifies that the moving party must give reasonable notice of the motion to all parties, and Rule 8(a)(2)(E) provides that the court "may condition relief on the party's filing a bond or other appropriate security * * *."

NOTES

1. Although federal law provides for no automatic stay of an interlocutory or final judgment in an injunction proceeding, several states have adopted different rules, as discussed in *Developments in the Law—Injunctions*, 78 Harv. L. Rev. 996 (1965)*:

> Today, a great variety of rules involving combinations of automatic stays and supersedeas [which "supersedes" the judgment of the lower court pending appeal] have developed in American jurisdictions * * *: (1) automatic stays of all injunctions by filing of appeal; (2) the California rule: automatic stay of mandatory injunctions; stay of prohibitory injunctions on a showing of hardship; (3) automatic stays of mandatory injunctions; no stay or supersedeas available for prohibitory injunctions; (4) the federal rule: no automatic stays; supersedeas in all cases in which a proper showing can be made; (5) supersedeas, available on showing of necessity for mandatory but not for prohibitory injunctions.
>
> Of these rules, only the federal (4) has sufficient flexibility; under all the others, once an injunction is shown to be mandatory or prohibitory, certain consequences—stay or no stay—automatically flow. * * * The mandatory-prohibitory distinction bears no necessary relation to the

---

* Copyright © 1965 by The Harvard Law Review Association. Reprinted with permission.

hardships resulting from an injunction. If D has been enjoined from seeding clouds over his ranch because the seeding results in diverting rainfall from P's land, the injunction should be stayed if at the moment D has a crop that might die from lack of water while P's land is fallow, notwithstanding the fact that the injunction would likely be considered prohibitory. Conversely, if D has been removing large quantities of water from a stream and is ordered to furnish some to P, the injunction should not be stayed pending appeal if D's supply is in excess of his needs and P's is insufficient, despite the fact that the injunction would generally be termed mandatory. In actuality, it is frequently impossible to tell whether action or nonaction is required: when a school board is ordered to stop discriminating * * *, is an act or nonact called for? Many jurisdictions retaining the mandatory-prohibitory distinction recognize its limitations and provide that a stay may be granted or denied contrary to the rule by the exercise of special power when necessity requires; these courts may, however, be unduly reluctant to exercise a power regarded as extraordinary.

Id. at 1073–74.

Consider the impact of the California rule. If the plaintiff succeeds in obtaining a preliminary injunction that orders the defendant to remove a fence obstructing access to the plaintiff's property, what will happen when the defendant appeals the issuance of the preliminary injunction? *See* Kettenhofen v. Superior Court, 55 Cal.2d 189, 10 Cal.Rptr. 356, 358 P.2d 684 (1961).

2. The next case considers the standards for determining whether a federal court should grant a motion for pre-appeal injunctive relief. *See generally* John Y. Gotanda, *The Emerging Standards for Issuing Appellate Stays*, 45 Baylor L. Rev. 809 (1993).

MICHIGAN COALITION OF RADIOACTIVE MATERIAL USERS, INC. v. GRIEPENTROG

United States Court of Appeals, Sixth Circuit, 1991.
945 F.2d 150.

Before MARTIN and NELSON, CIRCUIT JUDGES and JARVIS,* DISTRICT JUDGE.

BOYCE F. MARTIN, JR., CIRCUIT JUDGE.

The defendants in this action have filed a motion pursuant to Fed. R.App.P. 8(a) seeking a stay of the judgment * * * pending their appeal of the district court's grant of summary judgment in favor of the plaintiff. 769 F.Supp. 999. * * * This opinion will clarify the standards we apply in reviewing an application for a stay of judgment pursuant to Fed.R.App.P. 8(a).

The defendants are heads of agencies delegated by the states of Nevada, Washington, and South Carolina, to administer the operation of low-level radioactive waste disposal sites located in these states. There are

* The Honorable James H. Jarvis, United States District Court for the Eastern District of Tennessee, sitting by designation.

only three such sites in the United States: the Beatty site in Nevada, the Richland site in Washington, and the Barnwell site in South Carolina. These "sited states," as they are called, objected to the handling of low-level nuclear waste generated by other states and attempted to restrict access to their disposal systems. Congress responded by passing the Low-Level Radioactive Waste Policy Act in 1980 in an effort to motivate other states to assume some of the burden for disposal of such waste. Because progress was not as rapid as hoped, Congress amended the Act in 1985, adding specific incentives and penalties to encourage other states to develop disposal capacities by December 31, 1992. 42 U.S.C. § 2021b *et seq.* Pursuant to the scheme established by the amended Act, * * * the sited states are required to make their disposal capacity available for low-level radioactive waste from non-sited states for the period between January 1, 1986, through December 31, 1992.

In 1990, the defendants concluded that Michigan was not in compliance with the Act and effective November 10, 1990, denied waste generators in Michigan access to their disposal facilities. The plaintiff, the Michigan Coalition of Radioactive Material Users, Inc., is an association whose members engage in the use of radioactive materials and who generate low-level radioactive waste. MICHRAD, as the Coalition calls itself, filed suit seeking declaratory and injunctive relief prohibiting the defendants from denying MICHRAD access to the waste disposal facilities located in the defendants' states. The parties filed cross motions for summary judgment. The district court granted judgment in favor of MICHRAD, finding that Michigan had complied with the requirements of the Act and that the defendants had no authority to deny waste generators in Michigan access to the sited states' facilities prior to January 1, 1993. The district court permanently enjoined the defendants from denying access to disposal facilities in their respective states for disposal of low-level radioactive waste generated in Michigan prior to January 1, 1993. An appropriate appeal has followed.

Pursuant to Rule 8(a) of the Federal Rules of Appellate Procedure, 28 U.S.C. Rules, the defendants now request us to issue an order staying the district court's judgment and granting them a permanent injunction. Ordinarily, Rule 8(a) requires that such a motion be made in the first instance in the district court. However,

> [a] motion for such relief may be made to the court of appeals or to a judge thereof, but the motion shall show that the application to the district court for the relief sought is not practicable, or that the district court has denied an application, or has failed to afford the relief which the applicant requested.

Fed.R.App.P. 8(a). In this case, the defendants did file a motion for stay of judgment and permanent injunction pending appeal in the district court. The district court denied both of defendants' motions, concluding that the potential harm to defendants in the absence of a stay is outweighed by public safety concerns in the state of Michigan.

4 factors

In determining whether a stay should be granted under Fed.R.Civ.P. 8(a), we consider the same four factors that are traditionally considered in evaluating the granting of a preliminary injunction. * * * These well-known factors are: (1) the likelihood that the party seeking the stay will prevail on the merits of the appeal; (2) the likelihood that the moving party will be irreparably harmed absent a stay; (3) the prospect that others will be harmed if the court grants the stay; and (4) the public interest in granting the stay. * * * These factors are not prerequisites that must be met, but are interrelated considerations that must be balanced together. * * *

Although the factors to be considered are the same for both a preliminary injunction and a stay pending appeal, the balancing process is not identical due to the different procedural posture in which each judicial determination arises. Upon a motion for a preliminary injunction, the court must make a decision based upon "incomplete factual findings and legal research." * * *

Conversely, a motion for a stay pending appeal is generally made after the district court has considered fully the merits of the underlying action and issued judgment, usually following completion of discovery. As a result, a movant seeking a stay pending review on the merits of a district court's judgment will have greater difficulty in demonstrating a likelihood of success on the merits. In essence, a party seeking a stay must ordinarily demonstrate to a reviewing court that there is a likelihood of reversal. Presumably, there is a reduced probability of error, at least with respect to a court's findings of fact, because the district court had the benefit of a complete record that can be reviewed by this court when considering the motion for a stay.

To justify the granting of a stay, however, a movant need not always establish a high probability of success on the merits. * * * The probability of success that must be demonstrated is inversely proportional to the amount of irreparable injury plaintiffs will suffer absent the stay. * * * Simply stated, more of one excuses less of the other. This relationship, however, is not without its limits; the movant is always required to demonstrate more than the mere "possibility" of success on the merits. * * * For example, even if a movant demonstrates irreparable harm that decidedly outweighs any potential harm to the defendant if a stay is granted, he is still required to show, at a minimum, "serious questions going to the merits." * * *

In evaluating the harm that will occur depending upon whether or not the stay is granted, we generally look to three factors: (1) the substantiality of the injury alleged; (2) the likelihood of its occurrence; and (3) the adequacy of the proof provided. * * * In evaluating the degree of injury, it is important to remember that

[t]he key word in this consideration is irreparable. Mere injuries, however substantial, in terms of money, time and energy necessarily expended in the absence of a stay, are not enough. The possibility that

adequate compensatory or other corrective relief will be available at a later date, in the ordinary course of litigation, weighs heavily against a claim of irreparable harm.

Sampson v. Murray, 415 U.S. 61, 90, 94 S.Ct. 937, 953, 39 L.Ed.2d 166 (1974) (quoting Virginia Petroleum Jobbers Ass'n v. Federal Power Comm'n, 259 F.2d 921, 925 (D.C.Cir.1958)). In addition, the harm alleged must be both certain and immediate, rather than speculative or theoretical. * * * In order to substantiate a claim that irreparable injury is likely to occur, a movant must provide some evidence that the harm has occurred in the past and is likely to occur again. * * *

* * * With these standards in mind, we turn to the facts of this case.

EVALUATION OF THE FOUR FACTORS

A. Likelihood of Success

Based upon the record before us, we find that the defendants have demonstrated a sufficient probability of success on the merits. Specifically, we believe the defendants present a compelling argument that the district court erred in finding that it had personal jurisdiction over the various sited state representatives. In its decision concerning the jurisdictional question, the district court concluded that the long-standing business relationship between the plaintiffs and defendants, coupled with the fact that the defendants' actions were felt in Michigan, provided sufficient grounds for jurisdiction. * * *

* * *

→ Technical

* * * Based upon the record before us, we feel it a close question as to whether the defendants' contacts to Michigan were sufficient "such that [they] should reasonably anticipate being haled into court there." World–Wide Volkswagen Corp. v. Woodson, 444 U.S. 286, 297, 100 S.Ct. 559, 567, 62 L.Ed.2d 490 (1980).

B. Irreparable Injury

As we stated earlier, the harm alleged should be evaluated in terms of its substantiality, the likelihood of its occurrence, and the proof provided by the movant. * * * Furthermore, the harm alleged is considered in light of our earlier discussion concerning the defendants' jurisdictional argument. Ohio *ex rel.* Celebrezze, 812 F.2d at 290 (a stay may be granted with a high probability of success and some injury). The harm identified by the defendants is that the low-level radioactive waste, once received, must be buried in perpetuity and defendants will be burdened therefore with the responsibility of ensuring perpetual care for the waste. The defendants point out that this harm is also certain to occur because the defendants do not possess adequate short-term storage facilities to store the waste generated by Michigan until the final resolution of their appeal. The amount of waste produced by the plaintiff's members makes up a significant percentage of the waste currently being accepted by the sited states.

Thus, we find that this factor weighs in favor of the defendants because of the great likelihood that this storage problem will continue to occur.

C.   Harm to Others

We find that the harm to the plaintiff if the stay is issued is relatively slight. Currently, the plaintiff's members are storing their low-level radioactive waste in on-site temporary storage facilities. The plaintiff has not alleged that its members cannot provide the required storage capacity, but merely that they find it inconvenient. In fact, plaintiff admits that some of its members have the storage capacity for some years to come. Plaintiff argues strenuously that having its members house the low-level waste in temporary storage facilities is detrimental to public safety concerns. The fact that the plaintiff's members routinely use these facilities in order to store their waste pending shipment belies this argument. To be sure, public safety concerns would be implicated if, by granting the stay, the plaintiff's members would be forced to use these temporary storage facilities as permanent facilities; here the plaintiff's members will only be required to use these facilities on a temporary basis until the state of Michigan complies with the amendments to the Act. * * *

D.   The Public Interest

In the most general sense, the public interest in this case lies heavily in providing safe and environmentally sound management, storage, and disposal of radioactive waste. Indeed, this was the underlying purpose behind the passage of the Low–Level Radioactive Waste Policy Act. In deciding whether or not the stay should be granted, however, our immediate concern is with the current public safety aspects. * * * The plaintiff argues that the public is put at risk if its members are required to store low-level radiation at temporary facilities until the resolution of defendants' appeal. We find no reason to believe that the storage of waste at the plaintiff's members' temporary storage facilities puts the public at a greater risk than it would otherwise face when the waste is stored at these locations pending transport to the defendants' facilities. Undoubtedly, as we noted, the public safety would be implicated if the plaintiff's members were required to store permanently the waste in these temporary facilities. Such, however, is simply not the case. The public safety is not adversely affected by the granting of the stay and, therefore, we conclude that the public interest in the development of long-term disposal sites is controlling.

CONCLUSION

Thus, applying the above standards to the facts of this case, it is our belief that the defendants have adequately demonstrated the need for a stay. We grant the defendants' motion that the judgment of the district court requiring the sited states to accept low-level radioactive waste be stayed pending a decision on the merits. The panel of this Court hearing the merits of the appeal will consider the defendants' motion for a permanent injunction.

NOTES

1.   The "merits panel" in *MICHRAD* reversed the trial court's summary judgment in favor of the plaintiff on the ground that the defendants were not subject to personal jurisdiction in Michigan. 954 F.2d 1174 (6th Cir.1992).

2.   Regardless of whether the appeal is from a permanent injunction (*e.g., MICHRAD*) or from a provisional injunction ruling (*e.g.*, Federal Trade Commission v. Weyerhaeuser Co., 648 F.2d 739 (D.C.Cir.1981) (granting pre-appeal injunctive relief after trial court had denied provisional injunction)), a federal court will apply the same criteria in determining whether to grant pre-appeal injunctive relief.

3.   Because there is substantial overlap between the factors governing provisional injunctive relief and the factors governing stays, the Court's opinion in Winter v. Natural Resources Defense Council, Inc., 129 S.Ct. 365 (2008) will be highly relevant to the development of the law governing stays. Similarly, the law governing stays may have a significant impact on the law governing provisional injunctions as well. For example, in Nken v. Holder, 129 S.Ct. 1749 (2009)(action by an immigrant to stay an order removing him from the United States; lower court had denied stay under a restrictive statutory standard), the Court announced that Nken's motion for a stay ought to be governed not by a restrictive statutory standard, but rather by a more flexible equitable standard:

> (1) whether the stay applicant has made a strong showing that he is likely to succeed on the merits, (2) whether they applicant will be irreparably injured absent a stay; (3) whether issuance of the stay will substantially injure the other parties interested in the proceeding: and (4) where the public interest lies.

Hilton v. Braunskill, 481 U.S. 770, 776 (1987). The Court noted that "the first two factors * * * are most critical," and then observed:

> It is not enough that the chance of success on the merits be "better than negligible." * * * By the same token, simply showing some "possibility of irreparable injury" fails to satisfy the second factor. As the Court pointed out earlier this Term, the " 'possibility' standard is too lenient." *Winter, supra*, 129 S.Ct. at 375.

Nken v. Holder, 129 S.Ct. 1749, 1761 (2009)(Chief Justice Roberts wrote the opinion of the Court, joined by Justices Breyer, Ginsburg, Souter, and Stevens. The Court remanded the case to the Fourth Circuit for consideration of Nken's motion for a stay under the equitable standard set forth in the Court's opinion. The Government rendered moot the question of whether the equitable standard entitled Nken to a stay by promising that it would not remove Nken from the country until his case had been resolved. The Fourth Circuit then held that the Board of Immigration Appeals (BIA) had abused its discretion when it issued its removal order. Therefore, the Fourth Circuit remanded the case to the BIA for further proceedings.)

4. Federal Rule of Appellate Procedure 8(a)(2)(A)(i) permits one appellate judge to stay a trial court's preliminary injunction when it would be "impracticable" to convene a motions panel. Federal Rule of Appellate Procedure 27(c) provides that a court of appeals "may review the action of a single judge." The speed at which injunctive litigation can move is illustrated by Planned Parenthood of the Blue Ridge v. Camblos, 116 F.3d 707 (4th Cir.1997). *Planned Parenthood* involved a claim that the Parental Notification Act, passed by the Virginia General Assembly "after 18 years of debate" and "by a substantial margin," was "facially unconstitutional." *Id.* at 708–09. The Act prohibited "a physician from performing an abortion on an unemancipated minor unless one parent has been notified twenty-four hours in advance of the procedure." *Id.* at 708. The Act included a judicial bypass procedure. *Id.* at 708–09. A federal district court, after conducting a hearing one month before its ruling, preliminarily enjoined Virginia from implementing the Act on June 30, 1997. The district judge's ruling was handed down approximately eight hours before the Act was scheduled to take effect on July 1, 1997. In discussing the timing of the proceedings on appeal, Circuit Judge Luttig said:

At 4:00 p.m. on Monday afternoon, following issuance of the district court's order and the district court's subsequent denial of the Commonwealth's motion for stay of its decision, the Commonwealth filed with me, as a single Circuit Judge, a motion to stay the district court's injunction. At 7:45 p.m. that night, following a review of the parties' submissions before the district court, the district court's opinion, and the applicable Supreme Court precedents, I stayed the judgment of the district court pending appeal.

Id. at 709.

In discussing his reasons for granting the stay, Circuit Judge Luttig said:

The district court conclusorily determined * * * that the balance of harms in this case favored the plaintiffs. This determination rested seemingly exclusively on the court's conclusion that the Act was likely unconstitutional. That is, because the court decided that the statute was unconstitutional, it reasoned that the Commonwealth had no legitimate interest in its enforcement, and that therefore the plaintiffs' interest in the right to abortion was necessarily paramount. Enjoining the Act, the district court reasoned, would only "maintain the status quo." * * * Once it is apparent that plaintiffs cannot show a substantial likelihood of prevailing on the merits of their claims, however, it is apparent that the particular balancing of harms undertaken by the court was necessarily in error. In fact, if anything, the balance tips in favor of the Commonwealth, notwithstanding the fundamental right at issue for the state's minor women. The state not only has an interest in ensuring that the laws enacted by the General Assembly and signed into law by the Governor are implemented, but the state also has a special interest in legislation requiring parental notification of a minor's intention to obtain an abortion, as the Supreme Court has repeatedly recognized. At the very least, these interests must prevail where, as here, its legislation is under facial challenge only and the likelihood that that legislation will ultimately be held unconstitutional is remote.

Because the district court precipitately interposed itself into the democratic processes of the Commonwealth of Virginia, and it did so on the basis of a palpable misunderstanding of the applicable Supreme Court authorities, an immediate stay of that court's injunction against enforcement of the Commonwealth's newly-enacted Parental Notification Act was warranted, and for these reasons did it issue. In this context, the status quo is that which the People have wrought, not that which unaccountable federal judges impose upon them. In the end, if the necessary, but awesome, power of the federal judiciary is to be respected, it must respect the People and their institutions of government—even in the matters most profound.

Id. at 721.

The en banc court, reviewing "the action of a single judge" pursuant to Rule 27(c), denied plaintiffs' motion to vacate Judge Luttig's stay. Planned Parenthood v. Camblos, 125 F.3d 884 (4th Cir.1997). The en banc court later reversed the district court. 155 F.3d 352 (4th Cir.1998) (resolving the merits of the dispute because the facts were undisputed and the case posed a pure question of law; vacating the preliminary injunction and remanding the case for entry of a final judgment in favor of the Commonwealth of Virginia because the Act included a judicial bypass procedure).

Can you think of a number of reasons why a party might want to apply to one appellate judge to seek a stay? What are the requirements for obtaining such a stay? Do you agree with Judge Luttig's analysis of the status quo?

SECTION 7. FIRST AMENDMENT CONSIDERATIONS

When a court issues an injunction that allegedly interferes with a defendant's free speech rights, the injunction can be characterized as a "prior restraint." The Supreme Court has declared that "prior restraints on speech and publication are the most serious and least tolerable infringement on First Amendment rights." Nebraska Press Ass'n v. Stuart, 427 U.S. 539, 559, 96 S.Ct. 2791, 2803, 49 L.Ed.2d 683 (1976) (holding a "gag order" unconstitutional). A prior restraint comes to the court "bearing a heavy presumption against its constitutional validity." New York Times v. United States, 403 U.S. 713, 714, 91 S.Ct. 2140, 2141, 29 L.Ed.2d 822 (1971). The prohibition on prior restraints embedded in the First Amendment was in part a reaction against the licensing requirements for publication that had existed in England. 4 William Blackstone, Commentaries 151–52.

It is not easy to define a "prior restraint." One commentator has suggested that the "clearest definition" of prior restraint is "an administrative system or a judicial order that prevents speech from occurring." Erwin Chemerinsky, Constitutional Law 918 (2d ed. 2002). The Supreme Court has held that licensing systems constitute a prior restraint if they serve no important purpose or if they leave too much discretion in the hands of the administrators of the system. The Court has also required procedural safeguards. To pass constitutional muster, a licensing system must provide for a prompt decision to issue or deny the license and for a prompt and final judicial determination of the validity of any preclusion of speech. *Id*. at 932. The following cases apply these criteria to the issuance of provisional injunctions.

CARROLL v. PRESIDENT AND COMMISSIONERS OF PRINCESS ANNE

Supreme Court of the United States, 1968.
393 U.S. 175, 89 S.Ct. 347, 21 L.Ed.2d 325.

JUSTICE FORTAS delivered the opinion of the Court.

Petitioners are identified with a "white supremacist" organization called the National States Rights Party. They held a public assembly or rally near the courthouse steps in the town of Princess Anne, the county seat of Somerset County, Maryland, in the evening of August 6, 1966. The authorities did not attempt to interfere with the rally. Because of the tense atmosphere which developed as the meeting progressed, about 60 state policemen were brought in, including some from a nearby county. They were held in readiness, but for tactical reasons only a few were in evidence at the scene of the rally.

Petitioners' speeches, amplified by a public address system so that they could be heard for several blocks, were aggressively and militantly racist. Their target was primarily Negroes and, secondarily, Jews. It is sufficient to observe, with the court below, that the speakers engaged in deliberately derogatory, insulting, and threatening language, scarcely disguised by protestations of peaceful purposes; and that listeners might well have construed their words as both a provocation to the Negroes in the crowd and an incitement to the whites. The rally continued for something more than an hour, concluding at about 8:25 p.m. The crowd listening to the speeches increased from about 50 at the beginning to about 150, of whom 25% were Negroes.

In the course of the proceedings it was announced that the rally would be resumed the following night, August 7.

On that day, the respondents, officials of Princess Anne and of Somerset County, applied for and obtained a restraining order from the Circuit Court for Somerset County. The proceedings were ex parte, no notice being given to petitioners and, so far as appears, no effort being made informally to communicate with them, although this is expressly contemplated under Maryland procedure. The order restrained petitioners for 10 days from holding rallies or meetings in the county "which will tend to disturb and endanger the citizens of the County." As a result, the rally scheduled for August 7 was not held. After the trial which took place 10 days later, an injunction was issued by the Circuit Court on August 31, in effect extending the restraint for 10 additional months. The court had before it, in addition to the testimony of witnesses, tape recordings made by the police of the August 6 rally.

* * *

On appeal, the Maryland Court of Appeals affirmed the 10–day order, but reversed the 10–month order * * *.

Petitioners sought review by this Court, * * * asserting that the case is not moot and that the decision of the Maryland Court of Appeals continues to have an adverse effect upon petitioners' rights. * * *

We agree with petitioners that the case is not moot. Since 1966, petitioners have sought to continue their activities, including the holding of rallies in Princess Anne and Somerset County, and it appears that the decision of the Maryland Court of Appeals continues to play a substantial role in the response of officials to their activities. * * *

* * * We turn to the constitutional problems raised by the 10–day injunctive order. * * *

We need not decide the thorny problem of whether, on the facts of this case, an injunction against the announced rally could be justified. The 10–day order here must be set aside because of a basic infirmity in the procedure by which it was obtained. It was issued ex parte, without notice to petitioners and without any effort, however informal, to invite or permit their participation in the proceedings. There is a place in our jurisprudence for ex parte issuance, without notice, of temporary restraining orders of short duration; but there is no place within the area of basic freedoms guaranteed by the First Amendment for such orders where no showing is made that it is impossible to serve or to notify the opposing parties and to give them an opportunity to participate.

We do not here challenge the principle that there are special, limited circumstances in which speech is so interlaced with burgeoning violence that it is not protected by the broad guarantee of the First Amendment. * * * Ordinarily, the State's constitutionally permissible interests are adequately served by criminal penalties imposed after freedom to speak has been so grossly abused that its immunity is breached. The impact and consequences of subsequent punishment for such abuse are materially different from those of prior restraint. Prior restraint upon speech suppresses the precise freedom which the First Amendment sought to protect against abridgment.

The Court has emphasized that "(a) system of prior restraints of expression comes to this Court bearing a heavy presumption against its constitutional validity." * * * Freedman v. State of Maryland, 380 U.S. 51, 57, 85 S.Ct. 734, 738, 13 L.Ed.2d 649 (1965). And even where this presumption might otherwise be overcome, the Court has insisted upon careful procedural provisions, designed to assure the fullest presentation and consideration of the matter which the circumstances permit. * * *

Measured against these standards, it is clear that the 10–day restraining order in the present case, issued ex parte, without formal or informal notice to the petitioners or any effort to advise them of the proceeding, cannot be sustained. * * *

In the present case, the record discloses no reason why petitioners were not notified of the application for injunction. They were apparently present in Princess Anne. They had held a rally there on the night preceding the application for and issuance of the injunction. They were scheduled to have another rally on the very evening of the day when the injunction was issued. And some of them were actually served with the writ of injunction at 6:10 that evening. In these circumstances, there is no justification for the ex parte character of the proceedings in the sensitive area of First Amendment rights.

* * * The facts in any case involving a public demonstration are difficult to ascertain and even more difficult to evaluate. Judgment as to whether the facts justify the use of the drastic power of injunction necessarily turns on subtle and controversial considerations and upon a delicate assessment of the particular situation in light of legal standards which are inescapably imprecise. In the absence of evidence and argument offered by both sides and of their participation in the formulation of value judgments, there is insufficient assurance of the balanced analysis and careful conclusions which are essential in the area of First Amendment adjudication.

The same is true of the fashioning of the order. An order issued in the area of First Amendment rights must be couched in the narrowest terms that will accomplish the pin-pointed objective permitted by constitutional mandate and the essential needs of the public order. * * * The participation of both sides is necessary for this purpose.[11] Certainly, the failure to invite participation by the party seeking to exercise First Amendment rights reduces the possibility of a narrowly drawn order, and substantially imperils the protection which the Amendment seeks to ensure.

Finally, respondents urge that the failure to give notice and an opportunity for hearing should not be considered to invalidate the order because, under Maryland procedure, petitioners might have obtained a hearing on not more than two days' notice. * * * But this procedural right does not overcome the infirmity in the absence of a showing of justification for the ex parte nature of the proceedings. The issuance of an injunction which aborts a scheduled rally or public meeting, even if the restraint is of short duration, is a matter of importance and consequence in view of the First Amendment's imperative. The denial of a basic procedural right in these circumstances is not excused by the availability of post-issuance procedure which could not possibly serve to rescue the

---

11. *Cf.* Williams v. Wallace, 240 F.Supp. 100 (D.C.M.D.Ala.1965). There District Judge Johnson initially refused to issue an injunction ex parte against the absent state officials. Then, after a hearing at which the plaintiffs submitted a detailed plan for their proposed Selma–Montgomery march, he enjoined the State from interfering with the march as proposed in the plan.

August 7 meeting, but, at best, could have shortened the period in which petitioners were prevented from holding a rally.

We need not here decide that it is impossible for circumstances to arise in which the issuance of an ex parte restraining order for a minimum period could be justified because of the unavailability of the adverse parties or their counsel, or perhaps for other reasons. In the present case, it is clear that the failure to give notice, formal or informal, and to provide an opportunity for an adversary proceeding before the holding of the rally was restrained, is incompatible with the First Amendment. Because we reverse the judgment below on this basis, we need not and do not decide whether the facts in this case provided a constitutionally permissible basis for temporarily enjoining the holding of the August 7 rally.

Reversed.

[JUSTICES BLACK and DOUGLAS concurred.]

NOTE

Many states have now amended their procedural rules governing the issuance of temporary restraining orders so as to incorporate the Court's holding in *Carroll*. *See, e.g.*, United Farm Workers v. Quincy Corp., 681 So.2d 773 (Fla.Dist.Ct.App.1996) (quashing an ex parte temporary restraining order that would have interfered with union organizing efforts.).

NATIONAL SOCIALIST PARTY OF AMERICA v. VILLAGE OF SKOKIE

Supreme Court of the United States, 1977.
432 U.S. 43, 97 S.Ct. 2205, 53 L.Ed.2d 96.

PER CURIAM.

On April 29, 1977, the Circuit Court of Cook County entered an injunction against petitioners. Petitioners planned to hold a "peaceable public assembly" in the village on May 1, 1977. The village had a population of 70,000, of which 40,500 were Jewish. Roughly 5,000 to 7,000 were survivors of German concentration camps. The injunction prohibited them from performing any of the following actions within the village of Skokie, Ill.: "[m]arching, walking or parading in the uniform of the National Socialist Party of America; [m]arching, walking or parading or otherwise displaying the swastika on or off their person; [d]istributing pamphlets or displaying any materials which incite or promote hatred against persons of Jewish faith or ancestry or hatred against persons of any faith or ancestry, race or religion." The Illinois Appellate Court denied an application for stay pending appeal. Applicants then filed a petition for a stay in the Illinois Supreme Court, together with a request for a direct expedited appeal to that court. The Illinois Supreme Court denied both the stay and leave for an expedited appeal. Applicants then filed an application for a stay with Mr. Justice Stevens, as Circuit Justice, who referred the matter to the Court.

Treating the application as a petition for certiorari from the order of the Illinois Supreme Court, we grant certiorari and reverse the Illinois Supreme Court's denial of a stay. That order is a final judgment for purposes of our jurisdiction, since it involved a right "separable from, and collateral to" the merits. Cohen v. Beneficial Loan Corp., 337 U.S. 541, 546, 69 S.Ct. 1221, 1225, 93 L.Ed. 1528 (1949). * * * It finally determined the merits of petitioners' claim that the outstanding injunction will deprive them of rights protected by the First Amendment during the period of appellate review which, in the normal course, may take a year or more to complete. If a State seeks to impose a restraint of this kind, it must provide strict procedural safeguards, Freedman v. Maryland, 380 U.S. 51, 85 S.Ct. 734, 13 L.Ed.2d 649 (1965), including immediate appellate review, see Nebraska Press Assn. v. Stuart, 423 U.S. 1319, 1327, 96 S.Ct. 237, 251, 46 L.Ed.2d 199, 237 (1975) (Blackmun, J., in chambers). Absent such review, the State must instead allow a stay. The order of the Illinois Supreme Court constituted a denial of that right.

Reversed and remanded for further proceedings not inconsistent with this opinion.

MR. JUSTICE WHITE would deny the stay.

MR. JUSTICE REHNQUIST, with whom the CHIEF JUSTICE and MR. JUSTICE STEWART join, dissenting. [JUSTICE REHNQUIST objected to the Court's exercise of appellate jurisdiction because no Illinois court had yet heard or decided the case on the merits.]

SECTION 8. MODIFICATION AND DISSOLUTION OF PERMANENT INJUNCTIONS

A permanent injunction is an "ambulatory" decree of indefinite duration that "marches along with time." Ladner v. Siegel, 298 Pa. 487, 148 A. 699 (1930). Therefore, it may become necessary for the court that issued the injunction to modify it or to dissolve it at the request of either party. Federal Rule of Civil Procedure 60(b) states: "On motion and just terms, the court may relieve a party * * * from a final judgment * * * for the following reasons: * * * (5) * * * applying it prospectively is no longer equitable; or (6) any other reason that justifies relief." The Rule "encompasses the traditional power of a court of equity to modify its decree in light of changed circumstances." Frew ex rel. Frew v. Hawkins, 540 U.S. 431, 441, 124 S.Ct. 899, 906, 157 L.Ed.2d 855 (2004).

The meaning of Rule 60(b) was explored by the Supreme Court in the 1990s in the context of institutional reform litigation. Rufo v. Inmates of Suffolk County Jail, 502 U.S. 367, 112 S.Ct. 748, 116 L.Ed.2d 867 (1992). The plaintiffs in Rufo were inmates who had proven that they were being held under unconstitutional conditions and who had obtained a federal court order permanently enjoining the government defendants from housing two inmates in a single jail cell. The defendants refused to comply with the injunction, which led to a new round of litigation that culminated in the entrance of a consent decree. The consent decree provided that the defendants would build a larger jail that would be designed for single-cell occupancy. While the new jail was under construction, the sheriff moved to modify the consent decree to allow for double-bunking. The sheriff argued that the modification was required by a change in the law (a recent Supreme Court decision holding that double-celling was sometimes constitutional) and by a change in the facts (an upsurge in the inmate population). The plaintiffs objected that the recent Supreme Court decision had not cast doubt on the legality of single-celling, and that there had been no change in the facts because the defendants had anticipated the upsurge in the inmate population. The federal district court refused to grant the requested modification, and the court of appeals affirmed. The lower courts applied the very restrictive *Swift* standard for the modification of injunctions, which had been articulated by the Supreme Court in the 1930s, one decade prior to the enactment of Rule 60(b): "Nothing less than a clear showing of grievous wrong evoked by new and unforeseen conditions should lead us to change what was decreed after years of litigation with the consent of all concerned." United States v. Swift & Co., 286 U.S. 106, 119, 52 S.Ct. 460, 464, 76 L.Ed. 999 (1932).

The Supreme Court granted certiorari in *Rufo* to determine whether Rule 60(b) implicitly codified the *Swift* standard. The Court first addressed the question of whether a consent decree is subject to Rule 60(b), and then considered the *Swift* standard:

> [A] consent decree is * * * subject to Rule 60(b). A consent decree no doubt embodies an agreement of the parties and thus in some respects is contractual in nature. But it is an agreement that the parties desire and expect will be reflected in and be enforceable as a judicial decree and that is subject to the rules generally applicable to other judgments and decrees. Railway Employees v. Wright, 364 U.S. 642, 650–51, 81 S.Ct. 368, 372–73, 5 L.Ed.2d 349 (1961). The District Court recognized as much but held that Rule 60(b)(5) codified the "grievous wrong" standard of United States v. Swift, *supra*, that a case for modification under this standard had not been made, and that resort to Rule 60(b)(6) was also unavailing. This construction of Rule 60(b) was error.

> *Swift* was the product of a prolonged antitrust battle between the Government and the meat-packing industry. In 1920, the defendants agreed to a consent decree that enjoined them from manipulating the meat-packing industry and banned them from engaging in the manufacture, sale, or transportation of other foodstuffs. * * * In 1930, several meat-packers petitioned for modification of the decree, arguing that conditions in the meat-packing and grocery industries had changed. * * * The Court rejected their claim, finding that the meat-packers were positioned to manipulate transportation costs and fix grocery prices in 1930, just as they had been in 1920. * * * It was in

this context that Justice Cardozo, for the Court, set forth the much-quoted *Swift* standard, requiring "[n]othing less than a clear showing of grievous wrong evoked by new and unforeseen conditions" ... as a predicate to modification of the meat-packers' consent decree. * * *

Read out of context, this language suggests a "hardening" of the traditional flexible standard for modification of consent decrees. * * * But that conclusion does not follow when the standard is read in context. See United States v. United Shoe Machinery Corp., 391 U.S. 244, 248, 88 S.Ct. 1496, 1499, 20 L.Ed.2d 562 (1968) [(modifying an injunction at the plaintiff's request on the basis of changed conditions)]. The *Swift* opinion pointedly distinguished the facts of that case from one in which genuine changes required modification of a consent decree, stating:

> The distinction is between restraints that give protection to rights fully accrued upon facts so nearly permanent as to be substantially impervious to change, and those that involve the supervision of changing conduct or conditions and are thus provisional and tentative.... The consent is to be read as directed toward events as they then were. It was not an abandonment of the right to exact revision in the future, if revision should become necessary in adaptation to events to be.

286 U.S., at 114–115, 52 S.Ct., at 462.

Our decisions since *Swift* reinforce the conclusion that the "grievous wrong" language of *Swift* was not intended to take on a talismanic quality, warding off virtually all efforts to modify consent decrees. *Railway Employes* emphasized the need for flexibility in administering consent decrees, stating: "There is ... no dispute but that a sound judicial discretion may call for the modification of the terms of an injunctive decree if the circumstances, whether of law or fact, obtaining at the time of its issuance have changed, or new ones have since arisen." 364 U.S., at 647, 81 S.Ct., at 371–372.

The same theme was repeated in our decision last Term in Board of Ed. of Oklahoma City Public Schools v. Dowell, 498 U.S. 237, 246–248, 111 S.Ct. 630, 636–637, 112 L.Ed.2d 715 (1991), in which we rejected the rigid use of the *Swift* "grievous wrong" language as a barrier to a motion to dissolve a desegregation decree.

There is thus little basis for concluding that Rule 60(b) misread the *Swift* opinion and intended that modifications of consent decrees in all cases were to be governed by the standard actually applied in *Swift*. That Rule, in providing that, on such terms as are just, a party may be relieved from a final judgment or decree where it is no longer equitable that the judgment have prospective application, permits a less stringent, more flexible standard.

The upsurge in institutional reform litigation since Brown v. Board of Education, 347 U.S. 483, 74 S.Ct. 686, 98 L.Ed. 873 (1954), has made the ability of a district court to modify a decree in response to changed circumstances all the more important. Because such decrees often remain in place for extended periods of time, the likelihood of significant changes occurring during the life of the decree is increased.

502 U.S. at 378–80, 112 S.Ct. at 757–58 (vacating the decision below and remanding for application of the "changed conditions" standard).

The Supreme Court reiterated its commitment to modifying or dissolving consent decrees that have been entered against state governmental officials when there has been a "significant change in facts or law" in Frew *ex rel.* Frew v. Hawkins, 540 U.S. 431, 441, 124 S.Ct. 899, 906, 157 L.Ed.2d 855 (2004) (action to enforce federal Medicaid statute against state public officials by means of injunctive relief). The court refused to hold that the Eleventh Amendment precluded the enforcement of such a consent decree because the case came within the *Ex parte Young* doctrine, which permits prospective injunctive relief to be granted against state public officials in order to enforce federal law, but the Court cautioned:

> When a suit under *Ex parte Young* requires a detailed order to ensure compliance with a decree for prospective relief, * * * [t]he federal court must exercise its equitable jurisdiction to ensure that when the objects of the decree have been attained, responsibility for discharging the State's obligations is returned promptly to the State and its officials. * * * If the State establishes reason to modify the decree, the court should make the necessary changes; where it has not done so, however, the decree should be enforced according to its terms.

Id. (reversing and remanding for further proceedings consistent with the opinion). *See also* Horne v. Flores, 129 S.Ct. 2579 (2009).

NOTES

1. In *Rufo*, on remand, the district court held that the county sheriff was not entitled to a modification of the consent decree. 148 F.R.D. 14 (D.Mass.1993), *aff'd*, 12 F.3d 286 (1st Cir.1993). Later, the district court yielded to the sheriff's request for a modification. 844 F.Supp. 31 (D.Mass. 1994). Finally, in 1997, the county sheriff moved to terminate the consent decree pursuant to the Prison Litigation Reform Act (PLRA), and that request was honored by the First Circuit. 129 F.3d 649 (1st Cir.1997) (agreeing to "terminate," but not to "vacate" the consent decree). For an interesting discussion of *Rufo*, see David I. Levine, *The Modification of Equitable Decrees in Institutional Reform Litigation: A Commentary on the Supreme Court's Adoption of the Second Circuit's Flexible Test*, 58 Brook. L. Rev. 1239 (1993).

2. Most lower federal courts have interpreted *Rufo* broadly to mean that the "changed conditions" standard applies to all requests for the modification or dissolution of a permanent injunction, regardless of whether the original equitable decree was issued in the context of institutional reform litigation or

in some other context, such as commercial or antitrust litigation. *See, e.g.,* Bellevue Manor Associates v. United States, 165 F.3d 1249, 1255 n.5 (9th Cir.1999) (commercial contract case; citing to cases from other federal circuits "confirming the applicability of the flexible *Rufo* standard beyond the institutional reform context"); Gismondi, Paglia, Sherling, M.D., P.C. v. Franco, 206 F.Supp.2d 597 (S.D.N.Y. 2002) (applying the *Rufo* "changed conditions" test to vacate a covenant not to compete after the plaintiff had gone out of business); *see also* Agostini v. Felton, 521 U.S. 203, 117 S.Ct. 1997, 138 L.Ed.2d 391 (1997) (applying the *Rufo* "changed conditions" test in the context of an Establishment Clause case).

3. Note that, when modifying a provisional injunction, a court exercises the same discretion that it exercised in granting or denying the injunctive relief in the first place. Sierra Club v. United States Army Corps of Engineers, 732 F.2d 253, 256 (2d Cir.1984). It is only when modifying a final or permanent injunction that the court must consider whether there has been a significant change in the law or the facts. *Id.*

4. Some states refuse to allow the modification of a consent decree on the ground that it constitutes a binding contract between the parties to the litigation. *See, e.g.,* Cecil Township v. Klements, 821 A.2d 670 (Pa. Commw.Ct.2003).

BOARD OF EDUCATION OF OKLAHOMA CITY PUBLIC SCHOOLS v. DOWELL

Supreme Court of the United States, 1991.
498 U.S. 237, 111 S.Ct. 630, 112 L.Ed.2d 715.

CHIEF JUSTICE REHNQUIST delivered the opinion of the Court.

Petitioner Board of Education of Oklahoma City sought dissolution of a decree entered by the District Court imposing a school desegregation plan. The District Court granted relief over the objection of respondents Robert L. Dowell *et al.*, black students and their parents. The Court of Appeals for the Tenth Circuit reversed, holding that the Board would be entitled to such relief only upon " '[n]othing less than a clear showing of grievous wrong evoked by new and unforeseen conditions....' " 890 F.2d 1483, 1490 (1989) (citation omitted). * * *

I

This school desegregation litigation began almost 30 years ago. In 1961, respondents, black students and their parents, sued petitioners, the Board of Education of Oklahoma City (Board), to end *de jure* segregation in the public schools. In 1963, the District Court found that Oklahoma City had intentionally segregated both schools and housing in the past, and that Oklahoma City was operating a "dual" school system—one that was intentionally segregated by race. * * * In 1965, the District Court found that the School Board's attempt to desegregate by using neighborhood zoning failed to remedy past segregation because residential segregation resulted in one-race schools. * * * Residential segregation had once been state imposed, and it lingered due to discrimination by some realtors and financial institutions. * * * The District Court found that school segregation had caused some housing segregation. * * * In 1972, finding that previous efforts had not been successful at eliminating state imposed segregation, the District Court ordered the Board to adopt the "Finger Plan," Dowell v. Board of Education of Oklahoma City Public Schools, 338 F.Supp. 1256, *aff'd*, 465 F.2d 1012 (CA10), *cert. denied*, 409 U.S. 1041, 93 S.Ct. 526, 34 L.Ed.2d 490 (1972), under which kindergarteners would be assigned to neighborhood schools unless their parents opted otherwise; children in grades 1–4 would attend formerly all white schools, and thus black children would be bused to those schools; children in grade 5 would attend formerly all black schools, and thus white children would be bused to those schools; students in the upper grades would be bused to various areas in order to maintain integrated schools; and in integrated neighborhoods there would be stand-alone schools for all grades.

In 1977, after complying with the desegregation decree for five years, the Board made a "Motion to Close Case." The District Court held in its "Order Terminating Case":

> The Court has concluded that [the Finger Plan] worked and that substantial compliance with the constitutional requirements has been achieved. * * *

This unpublished order was not appealed.

In 1984, the School Board faced demographic changes that led to greater burdens on young black children. As more and more neighborhoods became integrated, more stand-alone schools were established, and young black students had to be bused farther from their inner-city homes to outlying white areas. In an effort to alleviate this burden and to increase parental involvement, the Board adopted the Student Reassignment Plan (SRP), which relied on neighborhood assignments for students in grades K–4 beginning in the 1985–1986 school year. Busing continued for students in grades 5–12. Any student could transfer from a school where he or she was in the majority to a school where he or she would be in the minority. Faculty and staff integration was retained, and an "equity officer" was appointed.

In 1985, respondents filed a "Motion to Reopen the Case," contending that the School District had not achieved "unitary" status and that the SRP was a return to segregation. Under the SRP, 11 of 64 elementary schools would be greater than 90% black, 22 would be greater than 90% white plus other minorities, and 31 would be racially mixed. The District Court refused to reopen the case * * *. Because unitariness had been achieved, the District Court concluded that court-ordered desegregation must end.

The Court of Appeals for the Tenth Circuit reversed * * *. It held that * * * nothing in [the 1977] order indicated that the 1972 injunction itself was terminated. The court reasoned that the finding that the system was unitary merely ended the District Court's active supervision of the case, and because the school district was still subject to the desegregation decree, respondents could challenge the SRP. The case was remanded to determine whether the decree should be lifted or modified.

On remand, the District Court found that demographic changes made the Finger Plan unworkable * * *. The District Court found that present residential segregation was the result of private decisionmaking and economics, and that it was too attenuated to be a vestige of former school segregation. It also found that the district had maintained its unitary status, and that the neighborhood assignment plan was not designed with discriminatory intent. The court concluded that the previous injunctive decree should be vacated and the school district returned to local control.

The Court of Appeals again reversed, 890 F.2d 1483 (1989) * * *. Relying on United States v. Swift & Co., 286 U.S. 106, 52 S.Ct. 460, 76 L.Ed. 999 (1932), it held that a desegregation decree remains in effect until a school district can show "grievous wrong evoked by new and unforeseen conditions," 286 U.S., at 119, 52 S.Ct., at 464, and "dramatic changes in conditions unforeseen at the time of the decree that ... impose extreme and unexpectedly oppressive hardships on the obligor." 890 F.2d, at 1490 (quoting T. Jost, *From Swift to Stotts and Beyond: Modification of Injunctions in the Federal Courts*, 64 Tex.L.Rev. 1101, 1110 (1986)). Given that a number of schools would return to being primarily one-race schools under the SRP, circumstances in Oklahoma City had not changed enough to justify modification of the decree. * * *

* * *

II

We must first consider whether respondents may contest the District Court's 1987 order dissolving the injunction which had imposed the desegregation decree. Respondents did not appeal from the District Court's 1977 order finding that the school system had achieved unitary status, and petitioner contends that the 1977 order bars respondents from contesting the 1987 order. We disagree, for the 1977 order did not dissolve the desegregation decree, and the District Court's unitariness finding was too ambiguous to bar respondents from challenging later action by the Board.

* * *

III

The Court of Appeals relied upon language from this Court's decision in United States v. Swift & Co., *supra*, for the proposition that a desegregation decree could not be lifted or modified absent a showing of "grievous wrong evoked by new and unforeseen conditions." * * * It also held that "compliance alone cannot become the basis for modifying or dissolving an injunction." * * *

In *Swift*, several large meat-packing companies entered into a consent decree whereby they agreed to refrain forever from entering into the grocery business. The decree was by its terms effective in perpetuity. The defendant meatpackers and their allies had over a period of a decade attempted, often with success in the lower courts, to frustrate operation of the decree. It was in this context that the language relied upon by the Court of Appeals in this case was used.

United States v. United Shoe Machinery Corp., 391 U.S. 244, 88 S.Ct. 1496, 20 L.Ed.2d 562 (1968), explained that the language used in *Swift* must be read in the context of the continuing danger of unlawful restraints on trade which the Court had found still existed. * * * In the present case, a finding by the District Court that the Oklahoma City School District was being operated in compliance with the commands of the Equal Protection Clause of the Fourteenth Amendment, and that it was unlikely that the school board would return to its former ways, would be a finding that the purposes of the desegregation litigation had been fully achieved. No additional showing of "grievous wrong evoked by new and unforeseen conditions" is required of the school board.

In Milliken v. Bradley, 433 U.S. 267, 97 S.Ct. 2749, 53 L.Ed.2d 745 (1977) (*Milliken II*), we said:

> [F]ederal-court decrees must directly address and relate to the constitutional violation itself. Because of this inherent limitation upon federal judicial authority, federal-court decrees exceed appropriate limits if they are aimed at eliminating a condition that does not violate the Constitution or does not flow from such a violation....

Id., at 282, 97 S.Ct., at 2758. From the very first, federal supervision of local school systems was intended as a temporary measure to remedy past discrimination. *Brown* considered the "complexities arising from the *transition* to a system of public education freed of racial discrimination" in holding that the implementation of desegregation was to proceed "with all deliberate speed." 349 U.S., at 299–301, 75 S.Ct., at 755–57 (emphasis added). * * *

Considerations based on the allocation of powers within our federal system, we think, support our view that the quoted language from *Swift* does not provide the proper standard to apply to injunctions entered in school desegregation cases. Such decrees, unlike the one in *Swift,* are not intended to operate in perpetuity. Local control over the education of children allows citizens to participate in decisionmaking, and allows innovation so that school programs can fit local needs. * * * The legal justification for displacement of local authority by an injunctive decree in a school desegregation case is a violation of the Constitution by the local authorities. Dissolving a desegregation decree after the local authorities have operated in compliance with it for a reasonable period of time properly recognizes that "necessary concern for the important values of local control of public school systems dictates that a federal court's regulatory control of such systems not extend beyond the time required to remedy the effects of past intentional discrimination." * * *

* * *

A district court need not accept at face value the profession of a school board which has intentionally discriminated that it will cease to do so in the future. But in deciding whether to modify or dissolve a desegregation decree, a school board's compliance with previous court orders is obviously relevant. In this case the original finding of de jure segregation was entered in 1961, the injunctive decree from which the Board seeks relief was entered in 1972, and the Board complied with the decree in good faith until 1985. Not only do the personnel of school boards change over time, but the same passage of time enables the District Court to observe the good faith of the school board in complying with the decree. The test espoused by the Court of Appeals would condemn a school district, once governed by a board which intentionally discriminated, to judicial tutelage for the indefinite future. Neither the principles governing the entry and dissolution of injunctive decrees, nor the commands of the Equal Protection Clause of the Fourteenth Amendment, require any such Draconian result.

Petitioner urges that we reinstate the decision of the District Court terminating the injunction, but we think that the preferable course is to remand the case to that court so that it may decide, in accordance with this opinion, whether the Board made a sufficient showing of constitutional compliance as of 1985, when the SRP was adopted, to allow the injunction to be dissolved. * * *

In considering whether the vestiges of de jure segregation [have] been eliminated as far as practicable, the District Court should look not only at student assignments, but "to every facet of school operations—faculty, staff, transportation, extra-curricular activities and facilities." * * *

After the District Court decides whether the Board was entitled to have the decree terminated, it should proceed to decide respondent's challenge to the SRP. A school district which has been released from an injunction imposing a desegregation plan no longer requires court authorization for the promulgation of policies and rules regulating matters such as assignment of students and the like, but it of course remains subject to the mandate of the Equal Protection Clause of the Fourteenth Amendment. If the Board was entitled to have the decree terminated as of 1985, the District Court should then evaluate the Board's decision to implement the SRP under appropriate equal protection principles. * * *

The judgment of the Court of Appeals is reversed, and the case is remanded to the District Court for further proceedings consistent with this opinion.

JUSTICE SOUTER took no part in the consideration or decision of this case.

JUSTICE MARSHALL, with whom JUSTICE BLACKMUN and JUSTICE STEVENS join, dissenting.

Oklahoma gained statehood in 1907. For the next 65 years, the Oklahoma City School Board maintained segregated schools—initially relying on laws requiring dual school systems; thereafter, by exploiting residential segregation that had been created by legally enforced restrictive covenants. In 1972—18 years after this Court first found segregated schools unconstitutional—a federal court finally interrupted this cycle, enjoining the Oklahoma City School Board to implement a specific plan for achieving actual desegregation of its schools.

The practical question now before us is whether, 13 years after that injunction was imposed, the same School Board should have been allowed to return many of its elementary schools to their former one-race status. The majority today suggests that 13 years of desegregation was enough. The Court remands the case for further evaluation of whether the purposes of the injunctive decree were achieved sufficient to justify the decree's dissolution. However, the inquiry it commends to the District Court fails to recognize explicitly the threatened reemergence of one-race schools as a relevant "vestige" of de jure segregation.

In my view, the standard for dissolution of a school desegregation decree must reflect the central aim of our school desegregation precedents. In Brown v. Board of Education, 347 U.S. 483, 74 S.Ct. 686, 98 L.Ed. 873 (1954) (*Brown I*), a unanimous Court declared that racially "[s]eparate educational facilities are inherently unequal." *Id.,* at 495, 74 S.Ct., at 692. This holding rested on the Court's recognition that state-sponsored segregation conveys a message of "inferiority as to th[e] status [of Afro-American school children] in the community that may affect their hearts and minds in a way unlikely ever to be undone." *Id.,* at 494, 74 S.Ct., at 691. Remedying this evil and preventing its recurrence were the motivations animating our requirement that formerly de jure segregated school districts take all feasible steps to *eliminate* racially identifiable schools. * * *

I believe a desegregation decree cannot be lifted so long as conditions likely to inflict the stigmatic injury condemned in *Brown I* persist and there remain feasible methods of eliminating such conditions. Because the record here shows, and the Court of Appeals found, that feasible steps could be taken to avoid one-race schools, it is clear that the purposes of the decree have not yet been achieved and the Court of Appeals' reinstatement of the decree should be affirmed. * * *[1]

* * *

Consistent with the mandate of *Brown I,* our cases have imposed on school districts an unconditional duty to eliminate *any* condition that perpetuates the message of racial inferiority inherent in the policy of state-sponsored segregation. The racial identifiability of a district's schools is such a condition. Whether this "vestige" of state-sponsored segregation will persist cannot simply be ignored at the point where a district court is

---

1. The issue of decree *modification* is not before us. However, I would not rule out the possibility of petitioner demonstrating that the purpose of the decree at issue could be realized by less burdensome means. Under such circumstances a modification affording petitioner more flexibility in redressing the lingering effects of past segregation would be warranted. * * *

contemplating the dissolution of a desegregation decree. In a district with a history of state-sponsored school segregation, racial separation, in my view, *remains* inherently unequal.

I dissent.

NOTES

1. On remand, the injunction in *Dowell* was dissolved. 778 F.Supp. 1144 (W.D.Okla.1991), *aff'd*, 8 F.3d 1501 (10th Cir.1993).

2. For an analysis of all federal district court opinions concerning school desegregation from June 1, 1992 to June 1, 2002, see Wendy Parker, *The Decline of Judicial Decisionmaking: School Desegregation and District Court Judges*, 81 N.C. L. Rev. 1623 (2003); *see also* Wendy Parker, *Connecting the Dots: Grutter, School Desegregation, and Federalism*, 45 Wm. & Mary L. Rev. 1691 (2004).

SECTION 9. CONTEMPT

A. THE NATURE OF CONTEMPT

DAN B. DOBBS, HANDBOOK ON THE LAW OF REMEDIES

93–94 (1973).*

A person may find himself in contempt of court for one of two basically different reasons. One reason is that he has in some manner interfered with the trial of a case. This includes disruptive conduct in court, or obstruction of the court's process, as by intimidating jurors, for example. * * * In cases of contempt like this that affect the trial adversely, there is no difference between law and equity; either kind of court may punish such contempts. The problems of such punishment are serious ones, but they are not necessarily remedial.

A rather different kind of contempt occurs when one disobeys a court order. The final judgment at law is not an *order* to the defendant; it is an *adjudication* of his rights or liabilities. No one may be held in contempt for failing to pay some debt as adjudicated by the law court. On the other hand, many equity decrees are personal orders, directing the defendant to act or refrain from acting. Disobedience of such a decree, if done knowingly and with the power to obey it, will constitute contempt, for which sanctions such as fine and imprisonment are appropriate. * * *

NOTES

1. The contempt power can be traced back to English common law and the notion that the King could do no wrong. Since the courts acted for the King, judges had the inherent power to maintain order in the court by

---

* Reprinted with permission of West Publishing Co.

conducting summary contempt proceedings. *See generally* Ronald L. Goldfarb, The Contempt Power (1963).

2. Both of the two types of contempt identified by Professor Dobbs will be considered in Chapter 2, Section 9. Cases in which the contemnor interfered with the trial of the case will be considered first because those are the cases in which the Supreme Court of the United States has most frequently discussed the constitutional constraints on the exercise of the judiciary's inherent power of contempt.

3. When the federal courts were established in 1789, they were given statutory authority to punish "all contempts of authority" by "fine or imprisonment." Judiciary Act of 1789, 1 Stat. 83. Congress curtailed this open-ended authority to deal with contempt in the Act of 1831, 4 Stat. 487, and the contempt power continues to be restricted by 18 U.S.C. § 401, enacted in 1948, which provides:

> A court of the United States shall have the power to punish by fine or imprisonment, at its discretion, such contempt of its authority, and none other, as
>
> (1) Misbehavior of any person in its presence or so near thereto as to obstruct the administration of justice;
>
> (2) Misbehavior of any of its officers in their official transactions;
>
> (3) Disobedience or resistance to its lawful writ, process, order, rule, decree, or command.

For a discussion of the federal judiciary's contempt power, see Joel M. Androphy & Keith A. Byers, *Federal Contempt of Court*, 61 Tex. B.J. 16 (1998).

4. For a discussion of the distinctions between summary and nonsummary proceedings, and between criminal and civil contempt, see Timothy L. Bertschy & Nathaniel E. Strickler, *The Power Behind the Robe: A Primer on Contempt Law*, 97 Ill. B.J. 246 (2009).

B. VIOLATIONS OF JUDICIAL RULES AND ORDERS RELATING TO THE ADMINISTRATION OF JUSTICE

1. Summary vs. Nonsummary Proceedings and Procedural Due Process

HARRIS v. UNITED STATES
Supreme Court of the United States, 1965.
382 U.S. 162, 86 S.Ct. 352, 15 L.Ed.2d 240.

MR. JUSTICE DOUGLAS delivered the opinion of the Court.

This case brings back to us a question resolved by a closely divided Court in Brown v. United States, 359 U.S. 41, 79 S.Ct. 539, 3 L.Ed.2d 609 [(1959)], concerning the respective scope of Rule 42(a) and of Rule 42(b) of the Federal Rules of Criminal Procedure. Petitioner was a witness before a grand jury and refused to answer certain questions on the ground of self-incrimination. He and the grand jury were brought before the District Court which directed him to answer the questions propounded before the grand jury, stating that petitioner would receive immunity from prosecution. He refused again to give any answers to the grand jury. He was thereupon brought before the District Court and sworn. The District Court repeated the questions and directed petitioner to answer, but he refused on the ground of privilege. The prosecution at once requested that petitioner be found in contempt of court "under Rule 42(a)." Counsel for petitioner protested and requested an adjournment and a public hearing where he would be permitted to call witnesses. The District Court denied the motion and thereupon adjudged petitioner guilty of criminal contempt, imposing a sentence of one year's imprisonment. The Court of Appeals affirmed, 334 F.2d 460. * * * Rule 42(a) is entitled "Summary Disposition" and reads as follows:

> A criminal contempt may be punished summarily if the judge certifies that he saw or heard the conduct constituting the contempt and that it was committed in the actual presence of the court. The order of contempt shall recite the facts and shall be signed by the judge and entered of record.

Rule 42(a) was reserved "for exceptional circumstances," Brown v. United States, 359 U.S. 41, 54, 79 S.Ct. 539, 548 (dissenting opinion), such as acts threatening the judge or disrupting a hearing or obstructing court proceedings. *Ibid.* We reach that conclusion in light of "the concern long demonstrated by both Congress and this Court over the possible abuse of the contempt power," *ibid.*, and in light of the wording of the Rule. Summary contempt is for "misbehavior" (*Ex parte* Terry, 128 U.S. 289, 314, 9 S.Ct. 77, 83, 32 L.Ed. 405 [(1888) (contemnor assaulted a United States marshall)]) in the actual presence of the Court. Then speedy punishment may be necessary in order to achieve "summary vindication of the court's dignity and authority," Cooke v. United States, 267 U.S. 517, 534, 45 S.Ct. 390, 394, 69 L.Ed. 767 [(1925)]. But swiftness was not a prerequisite of justice here. Delay necessary for a hearing would not imperil the grand jury proceedings.

Cases of the kind involved here are foreign to Rule 42(a). The real contempt, if such there was, was contempt before the grand jury—the refusal to answer to it when directed by the court. Swearing the witness and repeating the questions before the judge was an effort to have the refusal to testify "committed in the actual presence of the court" for the purposes of Rule 42(a). It served no other purpose, for the witness had been adamant and had made his position known. The appearance before the District Court was not a new and different proceeding, unrelated to the other. It was ancillary to the grand jury hearing and designed as an aid to it. Even though we assume arguendo that Rule 42(a) may at times reach testimonial episodes, nothing in this case indicates that petitioner's refusal was such an open, serious threat to orderly procedure that instant and summary punishment, as distinguished from due and deliberate procedures * * *, was necessary. Summary procedure * * * was designed to fill "the need for immediate penal vindication of the dignity of the court." *Ibid*. We start from the premise long ago stated in Anderson v. Dunn, 6 Wheat. 204, 231, 5 L.Ed. 242 [(1821)], that the limits of the power to punish for contempt are "[t]he least possible power adequate to the end proposed." In the instant case, the dignity of the court was not being affronted: no disturbance had to be quelled; no insolent tactics had to be stopped. The contempt here committed was far outside the narrow category envisioned by Rule 42(a).

Rule 42(b) provides the normal procedure. It reads:

> A criminal contempt except as provided in subdivision (a) of this rule shall be prosecuted on notice. The notice shall state the time and place of hearing, allowing a reasonable time for the preparation of the defense, and shall state the essential facts constituting the criminal contempt charged and describe it as such. The notice shall be given orally by the judge in open court in the presence of the defendant or, on application of the United States attorney or of an attorney appointed by the court for that purpose, by an order to show cause or an order of arrest. The defendant is entitled to a trial by jury in any case in which an act of Congress so provides. He is entitled to admission to bail as provided in these rules. If the contempt charged involves disrespect to or criticism of a judge, that judge is disqualified from presiding at the trial or hearing except with the defendant's consent. Upon a verdict or finding of guilt the court shall enter an order fixing the punishment.

Such notice and hearing serve important ends. What appears to be a brazen refusal to cooperate with the grand jury may indeed be a case of frightened silence. Refusal to answer may be due to fear—fear of reprisals on the witness or his family. Other extenuating circumstances may be present.[4] We do not suggest that there were circumstances of that nature here. We are wholly ignorant of the episode except for what the record shows and it reveals only the barebones of demand and refusal. If justice is to be done, a sentencing judge should know all the facts. We can imagine situations where the questions are so inconsequential to the grand jury but the fear of reprisal so great that only nominal punishment, if any, is indicated. Our point is that a hearing and only a hearing will elucidate all the facts and assure a fair administration of justice. Then courts will not act on surmise or suspicion but will come to the sentencing stage of the proceeding with insight and understanding.

---

4. Chief Justice Taft said in Cooke v. United States, *supra*, 267 U.S. at 537, 45 S.Ct. at 395:

"Due process of law, therefore, in the prosecution of contempt, except of that committed in open court, requires that the accused should be advised of the charges and have a reasonable opportunity to meet them by way of defense or explanation. We think this includes the assistance of counsel, if requested, and the right to call witnesses to give testimony, relevant either to the issue of complete exculpation or in extenuation of the offense and in mitigation of the penalty to be imposed."

We are concerned solely with "procedural regularity" which, as Mr. Justice Brandeis said in Burdeau v. McDowell, 256 U.S. 465, 477, 41 S.Ct. 574, 576, 65 L.Ed. 1048 [(1921)] (dissenting), has been "a large factor" in the development of our liberty. Rule 42(b) prescribes the "procedural regularity" for all contempts in the federal regime[5] except those unusual situations envisioned by Rule 42(a) where instant action is necessary to protect the judicial institution itself.

We overrule Brown v. United States, *supra*, and reverse and remand this case for proceedings under Rule 42(b).

MR. JUSTICE STEWART, with whom MR. JUSTICE CLARK, MR. JUSTICE HARLAN, and MR. JUSTICE WHITE join, dissenting.

The issue in this case is the procedure to be followed when a witness has refused to answer questions before a grand jury after he has been ordered to do so by a district court. This issue, involving Rule 42(a) and Rule 42(b) of the Federal Rules of Criminal Procedure, was, as the Court says, resolved in Brown v. United States, 359 U.S. 41, 79 S.Ct. 539, 3 L.Ed.2d 609 [(1959)]. That was six years ago. Since then this Court has made no changes in Rule 42(a) or 42(b). But today *Brown* is overturned, and the question it "resolved" is now answered in the opposite way.*

The particular question at issue here is of limited importance. But in this area the Court's duty is important, involving as it does the responsibility for clear and consistent guidance to the federal judiciary in the application of ground rules of our own making. We are not faithful to that duty, I think, when we overturn a settled construction of those rules for no better reasons than those the Court has offered in this case.

* * *

The procedure followed by the District Court in this case was in precise conformity with Rule 42(a) and with longsettled and consistently followed practice. It is a procedure which, in this context, is at least as fair as a Rule 42(b) proceeding. The petitioner, represented by counsel, was accorded an additional chance to purge himself of contempt; he and his counsel were accorded full opportunity to offer any explanation they might have had in extenuation of the contempt—to inform the "sentencing judge of all the facts." And finally, there is no reason to assume that a sentence imposed for obduracy before a grand jury is likely to be more severe in a Rule 42(a) proceeding than one imposed after a proceeding under Rule 42(b). * * * A sentence for contempt is reviewable on appeal in either case, and there is nothing to suggest that in the exercise of this reviewing

---

5. In more than one instance in the Southern District of New York, from which this case comes, witnesses cited for testimonial contempt before the grand jury were given hearings under Rule 42(b). * * *

* The majority opinion in *Brown* was written by Justice Stewart, and Justices Warren, Black, Douglas, and Brennan dissented. The composition of the Court changed between 1959 and 1965. Justices Frankfurter and Whittaker, who had voted with the majority in *Brown*, were replaced by Justices White and Goldberg.

power an appellate court will have any more information to go on in the one case than in the other.

For these reasons I would affirm the judgment of the Court of Appeals.

NOTES

1. *Harris* was a case in which a witness before a *grand jury* who had received immunity from prosecution refused to testify, and the Court held that the witness could only be held in contempt by means of a *nonsummary* proceeding. In United States v. Wilson, 421 U.S. 309, 95 S.Ct. 1802, 44 L.Ed.2d 186 (1975), by contrast, a witness for the prosecution who had received immunity refused to testify during a *criminal trial*, and the Court held that the witness could be held in contempt by means of a *summary* proceeding. *Wilson* emphasized the fact that the trial court judge had witnessed the contemptuous conduct and therefore a summary proceeding was appropriate. *Wilson* also explained that the refusal to testify was contemptuous of judicial authority because it literally disrupted the progress of the trial.

2. The distinction between summary and nonsummary proceedings depends in part on geographical considerations. In Nye v. United States, 313 U.S. 33, 61 S.Ct. 810, 85 L. Ed. 1172 (1941), the Court held that summary contempt proceedings are limited to acts of misbehavior that do not simply obstruct justice, but that occur in the physical presence of the judge (or that take place close enough to the judge as to be disruptive to the orderly conduct of judicial proceedings). Consider the facts in United States v. Rangolan, 464 F.3d 321 (2d Cir. 2006). On the third day of a trial, one of the jurors informed the court that the plaintiff had approached him before the court was in session in a cafeteria that was located ten floors below the courtroom to hand him a stack of papers (which he had rejected). This event delayed the start of deliberations by about thirty minutes. The court held that this was an indirect contempt of court that required a nonsummary proceeding.

2. Criminal vs. Civil Contempt Sanctions and the Right to Jury Trial

BLOOM v. ILLINOIS

Supreme Court of the United States, 1968.
391 U.S. 194, 88 S.Ct. 1477, 20 L.Ed.2d 522.

MR. JUSTICE WHITE delivered the opinion of the Court.

Petitioner was convicted in an Illinois state court of criminal contempt and sentenced to imprisonment for 24 months for willfully petitioning to admit to probate a will falsely prepared and executed after the death of the putative testator. Petitioner made a timely demand for jury trial which was refused. Since in Duncan v. State of Louisiana, 391 U.S. 145, 88 S.Ct. 1444, 20 L.Ed.2d 491 [(1968)], the Constitution was held to guarantee the right to jury trial in serious criminal cases in state courts, we must now decide whether it also guarantees the right to jury trial for a criminal contempt punished by a two-year prison term.

I.

Whether federal and state courts may try criminal contempt cases without a jury has been a recurring question in this Court. Article III, § 2, of the Constitution provides that "[t]he Trial of all Crimes, except in Cases of Impeachment, shall be by Jury * * *." The Sixth Amendment states that "[i]n all criminal prosecutions, the accused shall enjoy the right to a speedy and public trial, by an impartial jury * * *." The Fifth and Fourteenth Amendments forbid both the Federal Government and the States from depriving any person of "life, liberty, or property, without due process of law." Notwithstanding these provisions, * * * the Court consistently [has] upheld the constitutional power of the state and federal courts to punish any criminal contempt without a jury trial * * * because at common law contempt was tried without a jury and because the power of courts to punish for contempt without the intervention of any other agency was considered essential to the proper and effective functioning of the courts and to the administration of justice.

* * *

* * * [I]n Cheff v. Schnackenberg, 384 U.S. 373, 86 S.Ct. 1523, 16 L.Ed.2d 629 (1966), which involved a prison term of six months for contempt of a federal court, the Court rejected the claim that the Constitution guaranteed a right to jury trial in all criminal contempt cases. Contempt did not "of itself" warrant treatment as other than a petty offense; the six months' punishment imposed permitted dealing with the case as a prosecution for "a petty offense, which under our decisions does not require a jury trial." 384 U.S. 373, 379–380, 86 S.Ct. 1523, 1525 (1966). * * * It was not necessary in *Cheff* to consider whether the constitutional guarantees of the right to jury trial applied to a prosecution for a serious contempt. Now, however, because of our holding in Duncan v. State of Louisiana, *supra*, that the right to jury trial extends to the States, and because of Bloom's demand for a jury in this case, we must once again confront the broad rule that all criminal contempts can be constitutionally tried without a jury. * * *

In proceeding with this task, we are acutely aware of the responsibility we assume in entertaining challenges to a constitutional principle which is firmly entrenched and which has behind it weighty and ancient authority. Our deliberations have convinced us, however, that serious contempts are so nearly like other serious crimes that they are subject to the jury trial provisions of the Constitution, now binding on the States, and that the traditional rule is constitutionally infirm insofar as it permits other than petty contempts to be tried without honoring a demand for a jury trial. We accept the judgment of * * * *Cheff* that criminal contempt is a petty offense unless the punishment makes it a serious one; but, in our view, dispensing with the jury in the trial of contempts subjected to severe punishment represents an unacceptable construction of the Constitution * * *. The rule of our prior cases has strong, though sharply challenged, historical support; but neither this circumstance nor the considerations of necessity and efficiency normally offered in defense of the established rule, justify denying a jury trial in serious criminal contempt cases. The Constitution guarantees the right to jury trial in state court prosecutions for contempt just as it does for other crimes.

II.

Criminal contempt is a crime in the ordinary sense; it is a violation of the law, a public wrong which is punishable by fine or imprisonment or both. * * * Criminally contemptuous conduct may violate other provisions of the criminal law; but even when this is not the case convictions for criminal contempt are indistinguishable from ordinary criminal convictions, for their impact on the individual defendant is the same. Indeed, the role of criminal contempt and that of many ordinary criminal laws seem identical—protection of the institutions of our government and enforcement of their mandates.

Given that criminal contempt is a crime in every fundamental respect, the question is whether it is a crime to which the jury trial provisions of the Constitution apply. We hold that it is, primarily because in terms of those considerations which make the right to jury trial fundamental in criminal cases, there is no substantial difference between serious contempts and other serious crimes. Indeed, in contempt cases an even more compelling argument can be made for providing a right to jury trial as a protection against the arbitrary exercise of official power. Contemptuous conduct, though a public wrong, often strikes at the most vulnerable and human qualities of a judge's temperament. Even when the contempt is not a direct insult to the court or the judge, it frequently represents a rejection of judicial authority, or an interference with the judicial process or with the duties of officers of the court.

The court has long recognized the potential for abuse in exercising the summary power to imprison for contempt—it is an "arbitrary" power which is "liable to abuse." *Ex parte* Terry, 128 U.S. 289, 313, 9 S.Ct. 77, 82, 32 L.Ed. 405 (1888). "[I]ts exercise is a delicate one, and care is needed to avoid arbitrary or oppressive conclusions." Cooke v. United States, 267 U.S. 517, 539, 45 S.Ct. 390, 396, 69 L.Ed. 767 (1925).

* * *

* * * Before the 19th century was out, a distinction had been carefully drawn between contempts occurring within the view of the court, for which a hearing and formal presentation of evidence were dispensed with, and all other contempts where more normal adversary procedures were required. *Ex parte* Terry, 128 U.S. 289, 9 S.Ct. 77, 32 L.Ed. 405 (1888) * * *. Later, the Court could say "it is certain that in proceedings for criminal contempt the defendant is presumed to be innocent, he must be proved to be guilty beyond a reasonable doubt, and cannot be compelled to testify against himself." Gompers v. Buck's Stove & Range Co., 221 U.S. 418, 444, 31 S.Ct. 492, 499, 55 L.Ed. 797 (1911). * * * Chief Justice Taft

speaking for a unanimous Court in Cooke v. United States, 267 U.S. 517, 537, 45 S.Ct. 390, 395, 69 L.Ed. 767 (1925), said:

> Due process of law, therefore, in the prosecution of contempt, except of that committed in open court, requires that the accused should be advised of the charges and have a reasonable opportunity to meet them by way of defense or explanation. We think this includes the assistance of counsel, if requested, and the right to call witnesses to give testimony, relevant either to the issue of complete exculpation or in extenuation of the offense and in mitigation of the penalty to be imposed.

Cf. Blackmer v. United States, 284 U.S. 421, 440, 52 S.Ct. 252, 255, 76 L.Ed. 375 (1932). It has also been recognized that the defendant in criminal contempt proceedings is entitled to a public trial before an unbiased judge. *In re* Oliver, 333 U.S. 257, 68 S.Ct. 499, 92 L.Ed. 682 (1948) * * *.[7] In the federal system many of the procedural protections available to criminal contemnors are set forth in Fed.Rule Crim.Proc. 42.

Judicial concern has not been limited to procedure. * * * [O]ver the years in the federal system, there has been a recurring necessity to set aside punishments for criminal contempt as either unauthorized by statute or too harsh. *E.g.*, *Ex parte* Robinson, 19 Wall. 505, 22 L.Ed. 205 (1874) [(holding that disbarring an attorney is not authorized by federal statute as a punishment for criminal contempt)]; * * *; Yates v. United States, 355 U.S. 66, 78 S.Ct. 128, 2 L.Ed.2d 95 (1957) [(holding that eleven refusals to answer questions at trial should have been sanctioned as only one criminal contempt, and not as eleven criminal contempts)].[8]

This course of events demonstrates the unwisdom of vesting the judiciary with completely untrammeled power to punish contempt, and makes clear the need for effective safeguards against that power's abuse. Prosecutions for contempt play a significant role in the proper functioning of our judicial system; but despite the important values which the contempt power protects, courts and legislatures have gradually eroded the power of judges to try contempts of their own authority. In modern times,

---

7. It has also been held that a defendant in criminal contempt proceedings is eligible for executive pardon, *Ex parte* Grossman, 267 U.S. 87, 45 S.Ct. 332, 69 L.Ed. 527 (1925), and entitled to the protection of the statute of limitations, Gompers v. United States, 233 U.S. 604, 611–613, 34 S.Ct. 693, 695–696, 58 L.Ed. 1115 (1914) * * *.

8. Limitations on the maximum penalties for criminal contempt are common in the States. According to Note, *Constitutional Law: The Supreme Court Constructs a Limited Right to Trial by Jury for Federal Criminal Contemnors*, 1967 Duke L.J. 632, 654, n.84, in 26 States the maximum penalty that can be imposed in the absence of a jury trial is six months or less, in three States a jury trial must be provided upon demand of the defendant, in three other States the maximum penalty cannot exceed one year (this group of States includes Illinois, however, which, as the present case demonstrates, has no such limitation), in 15 States there is either no limitation upon the maximum penalty which may be imposed, or else that maximum exceeds one year, and finally, in three States, while there are statutes relating to particular kinds of contempt, there are no general contempt provisions. Independent examination suggests that the available materials concerning the law of contempt in some States are such that precise computation is difficult. It is clear, however, that punishment for contempt is limited to one year or less in over half the States.

Most other Western countries seem to be highly restrictive of the latitude given judges to try their own contempts without a jury. * * *

procedures in criminal contempt cases have come to mirror those used in ordinary criminal cases. Our experience teaches that convictions for criminal contempt, not infrequently resulting in extremely serious penalties, * * * are indistinguishable from those obtained under ordinary criminal laws. If the right to jury trial is a fundamental matter in other criminal cases, which we think it is, it must also be extended to criminal contempt cases.

III.

Nor are there compelling reasons for a contrary result. * * *

We cannot say that the need to further respect for judges and courts is entitled to more consideration than the interest of the individual not to be subjected to serious criminal punishment without the benefit of all the procedural protections worked out carefully over the years and deemed fundamental to our system of justice. Genuine respect, which alone can lend true dignity to our judicial establishment, will be engendered, not by the fear of unlimited authority, but by the firm administration of the law through those institutionalized procedures which have been worked out over the centuries.

We place little credence in the notion that the independence of the judiciary hangs on the power to try contempts summarily and are not persuaded that the additional time and expense possibly involved in submitting serious contempts to juries will seriously handicap the effective functioning of the courts. We do not deny that serious punishment must sometimes be imposed for contempt, but we reject the contention that such punishment must be imposed without the right to jury trial. The goals of dispatch, economy, and efficiency are important, but they are amply served by preserving the power to commit for civil contempt and by recognizing that many contempts are not serious crimes but petty offenses not within the jury trial provisions of the Constitution. When a serious contempt is at issue, considerations of efficiency must give way to the more fundamental interest of ensuring the even-handed exercise of judicial power. In isolated instances recalcitrant or irrational juries may acquit rather than apply the law to the case before them. Our system has wrestled with this problem for hundreds of years, however, and important safeguards have been devised to minimize miscarriages of justice through the malfunctioning of the jury system. Perhaps to some extent we sacrifice efficiency, expedition, and economy, but the choice in favor of jury trial has been made, and retained, in the Constitution. We see no sound reason in logic or policy not to apply it in the area of criminal contempt.

Some special mention of contempts in the presence of the judge is warranted. Rule 42(a) of the Federal Rules of Criminal Procedure provides that "[a] criminal contempt may be punished summarily if the judge certifies that he saw or heard the conduct constituting the contempt and that it was committed in the actual presence of the court." This rule reflects the common-law rule which is widely if not uniformly followed in the States. Although Rule 42(a) is based in part on the premise that it is not necessary specially to present the facts of a contempt which occurred in the very presence of the judge, it also rests on the need to maintain order and a deliberative atmosphere in the courtroom. The power of a judge to quell disturbance cannot attend upon the impaneling of a jury. There is, therefore, a strong temptation to make exception to the rule we establish today for disorders in the courtroom. We are convinced, however, that no special rule is needed. It is old law that the guarantees of jury trial found in Article III and the Sixth Amendment do not apply to petty offenses. Only today we have reaffirmed that position. Duncan v. State of Louisiana, *supra*, 391 U.S., at 159–162, 88 S.Ct., at 1452–1454, 20 L.Ed.2d 491. By deciding to treat criminal contempt like other crimes insofar as the right to jury trial is concerned, we similarly place it under the rule that petty crimes need not be tried to a jury.

IV.

Petitioner Bloom was held in contempt of court for filing a spurious will for probate. At his trial it was established that the putative testator died on July 6, 1964, and that after that date Pauline Owens, a practical nurse for the decedent, engaged Bloom to draw and execute a will in the decedent's name. The will was dated June 21, 1964. Bloom knew the will was false when he presented it for admission in the Probate Division of the Circuit Court of Cook County. The State's Attorney of that county filed a complaint charging Bloom with contempt of court. At trial petitioner's timely motion for a jury trial was denied. Petitioner was found guilty of criminal contempt and sentenced to imprisonment for 24 months. On direct appeal to the Illinois Supreme Court, his conviction was affirmed. That court held that neither state law nor the Federal Constitution provided a right to jury trial in criminal contempt proceedings. 35 Ill.2d 255, 220 N.E.2d 475 (1966). * * *

Petitioner Bloom contends that the conduct for which he was convicted of criminal contempt constituted the crime of forgery under Ill.Rev. Stat. c. 38, § 17–3. Defendants tried under that statute enjoy a right to jury trial and face a possible sentence of one to 14 years, a fine not to exceed $1,000, or both. Petitioner was not tried under this statute, but rather was convicted of criminal contempt. Under Illinois law no maximum punishment is provided for convictions for criminal contempt. People v. Stollar, 31 Ill.2d 154, 201 N.E.2d 97 (1964). In *Duncan* we have said that we need not settle "the exact location of the line between petty offenses and serious crimes" but that "a crime punishable by two years in prison is * * * a serious crime and not a petty offense." 391 U.S., at 161, 162, 88 S.Ct., at 1454. Bloom was sentenced to imprisonment for two years. * * * [C]riminal contempt is not a crime of the sort that requires the right to jury trial regardless of the penalty involved. Under the rule in *Cheff*, when the legislature has not expressed a judgment as to the seriousness of an offense by fixing a maximum penalty which may be imposed, we are to look to the penalty actually imposed as the best evidence of the seriousness of the offense. * * * Under this rule it is clear that Bloom was entitled to the right to trial by jury, and it was constitutional error to deny him that right. Accordingly, we reverse and remand for proceedings not inconsistent with this opinion.

For concurring opinion of MR. JUSTICE FORTAS, see 88 S.Ct. 1459. [Opinion omitted.]

MR. JUSTICE HARLAN, whom MR. JUSTICE STEWART joins, dissenting.

NOTE

The Supreme Court eventually did establish a fixed dividing line between petty and serious offenses: "those crimes carrying a sentence of more than six months are serious crimes and those carrying a sentence of six months or less are petty crimes." Codispoti v. Pennsylvania, 418 U.S. 506, 512, 94 S.Ct. 2687, 2691, 41 L.Ed.2d 912 (1974). The Court has not yet specified what magnitude of a contempt fine will constitute a serious criminal contempt sanction. *See* Muniz v. Hoffman, 422 U.S. 454, 477, 95 S.Ct. 2178, 2190, 45 L.Ed.2d 319 (1975) (holding that a fine of $10,000 imposed on a union was insufficient to trigger the Sixth Amendment right to a jury trial). *See generally* Eric Fleisig-Greene, Note, *Why Contempt is Different: Agency Costs and "Petty Crime" in Summary Contempt Proceedings*, 112 Yale L.J. 1223 (2003). Congress has defined a "petty offense" to include fines up to $5,000 for an individual and up to $10,000 for an organization such as a union or a corporation, but lower federal court judges are in disagreement about whether the statute controls the constitutional right to jury trial. *See, e.g.,* United States v. Soderna, 82 F.3d 1370 (7th Cir.1996), *cert. denied,* 519 U.S. 1006, 117 S.Ct. 507, 136 L.Ed.2d 398 (1996) (majority held that $10,000 fine imposed on an individual was a "petty sanction"); *see also* United States v. Twentieth Century Fox Film Corp., 882 F.2d 656 (2d Cir.1989) (adopting a "bright line" rule that "the jury right is available for a criminal contempt whenever the fine imposed on an organization exceeds $100,000").

SHILLITANI v. UNITED STATES

Supreme Court of the United States, 1966.
384 U.S. 364, 86 S.Ct. 1531, 16 L.Ed.2d 622.

MR. JUSTICE CLARK delivered the opinion of the Court.

These consolidated cases again present the difficult question whether a charge of contempt against a witness for refusal to answer questions before a grand jury requires an indictment and jury trial. In both cases, contempt proceedings were instituted after petitioners had refused to testify under immunity granted by the respective District Courts. Neither petitioner was indicted or given a jury trial. Both were found guilty and sentenced to two years' imprisonment, with the proviso that if either answered the questions before his sentence ended, he would be released.
* * *

I.

Shillitani appeared under subpoena before a grand jury investigating possible violations of the federal narcotics laws. On three occasions he refused to answer questions, invoking his privilege against self-incrimination. At the Government's request, the District Judge then granted him immunity * * * and ordered him to answer certain questions. When called before the grand jury again, Shillitani persisted in his refusal. Thereafter, in a proceeding under Rule 42(b) of the Federal Rules of Criminal Procedure, the District Court found him guilty of criminal contempt. * * * Shillitani was sentenced to prison for two years "or until the further order of this Court. Should * * * Mr. Shillitani answer those questions before the expiration of said sentence, or the discharge of the said grand jury, whichever may first occur, the further order of this Court may be made terminating the sentence of imprisonment." The Court of Appeals affirmed, rejecting Shillitani's constitutional objection to the imposition of a two-year sentence without indictment or trial by jury on the basis that "the contempt proceedings preceded any compliance" and the "sentence contained a purge clause." It further construed the sentence as giving Shillitani an unqualified right to be released if and when he obeyed the order to testify. 345 F.2d, at 294.

* * *

II.

We believe that the character and purpose of these actions clearly render them civil rather than criminal contempt proceedings. * * * [T]he judgments imposed conditional imprisonment for the obvious purpose of compelling the witnesses to obey the orders to testify. When the petitioners carry "the keys of their prison in their own pockets," * * * the action "is essentially a civil remedy designed for the benefit of other parties and has quite properly been exercised for centuries to secure compliance with judicial decrees." * * * In short, if the petitioners had chosen to obey the order they would not have faced jail. This is evident from the statement of the District Judge at the time he sentenced Shillitani:

> I want to make it clear that the sentence of the Court is not intended so much by way of punishment as it is intended solely to secure for the grand jury answers to the questions that have been asked of you.

* * * While all of the parties before this Court briefed the issues with reference to criminal contempt, counsel for petitioners and the Government conceded at argument that the contempt orders were remedial, and therefore might well be deemed civil in nature rather than criminal.

The fact that both the District Court and the Court of Appeals called petitioners' conduct "criminal contempt" does not disturb our conclusion. * * * Despite the fact that Shillitani and Pappadio were ordered imprisoned for a definite period, their sentences were clearly intended to operate in a prospective manner—to coerce, rather than punish. As such, they relate to civil contempt. While any imprisonment, of course, has punitive and deterrent effects, it must be viewed as remedial if the court conditions release upon the contemnor's willingness to testify. * * * The test may be stated as: what does the court primarily seek to accomplish by imposing sentence? Here the purpose was to obtain answers to the questions for the grand jury.[5]

III.

There can be no question that courts have inherent power to enforce compliance with their lawful orders through civil contempt. * * * And it is essential that courts be able to compel the appearance and testimony of witnesses. * * * A grand jury subpoena must command the same respect. * * * Where contempt consists of a refusal to obey a court order to testify at any stage in judicial proceedings, the witness may be confined until compliance. * * *[6] The conditional nature of the imprisonment—based entirely upon the contemnor's continued defiance—justifies holding civil contempt proceedings absent the safeguards of indictment and jury, * * * provided that the usual due process requirements are met. However, the justification for coercive imprisonment as applied to civil contempt depends upon the ability of the contemnor to comply with the court's order. Maggio v. Zeitz, 333 U.S. 56, 76, 68 S.Ct. 401, 411, 92 L.Ed. 476 (1948). Where the grand jury has been finally discharged, a contumacious witness can no longer be confined since he then has no further opportunity to purge himself of contempt. Accordingly, the contempt orders entered against Shillitani and Pappadio were improper insofar as they imposed sentences that extended beyond the cessation of the grand jury's inquiry into petitioners' activities. Having sought to deal only with civil contempt, the District Courts lacked authority to imprison petitioners for a period longer than the term of the grand jury. This limitation accords with the doctrine that a court must exercise "[t]he least possible power adequate to the end proposed." Anderson v. Dunn, 6 Wheat. 204, 231, 5 L.Ed. 242 (1821) * * *.[9] Since the term of the grand jury in these cases expired in March 1965, the judgments here for review are vacated, and the cases remanded with directions that they be dismissed. * * *

MR. JUSTICE BLACK concurs in the result.

MR. JUSTICE HARLAN dissented and MR. JUSTICE STEWART dissented in part, *see* 86 S.Ct. 1537.

MR. JUSTICE WHITE took no part in the decisions of these cases.

NOTES

1. In comparing the criminal contempt sanctions imposed in *Bloom* with the civil contempt sanctions imposed in *Shillitani*, note that the civil contempt sanctions are "coercive" and operate prospectively, while the criminal

---

5. On the contrary, a criminal contempt proceeding would be characterized by the imposition of an unconditional sentence for punishment or deterrence. *See* Cheff v. Schnackenberg, 384 U.S. at 377, 86 S.Ct. at 1524.

6. The court may also impose a determinate sentence which includes a purge clause. This type of sentence would benefit an incorrigible witness. * * *

9. This doctrine further requires that the trial judge first consider the feasibility of coercing testimony through the imposition of civil contempt. The judge should resort to criminal sanctions only after he determines, for good reason, that the civil remedy would be inappropriate.

contempt sanctions are "punitive" and operate retroactively. *See generally* Gompers v. Buck's Stove & Range Co., 221 U.S. 418, 31 S.Ct. 492, 55 L.Ed. 797 (1911). In the context of a case in which a witness refuses to testify before a grand jury, a judge may attempt to coerce a witness' testimony by jailing the witness or by imposing a per diem fine payable to the state until such time as the witness agrees to testify. *See, e.g., In re* Grand Jury Proceedings, 280 F.3d 1103 (7th Cir.2002) (imposing a jail term of up to six months and a fine of $1,500 per day until such time as the contemnor agreed to provide information to the grand jury). Coercive civil contempt sanctions are indeterminate; the witness is said to have the keys to the jail in his or her pocket. The order may be lifted at any time, but it must be lifted when the term of the grand jury expires. 28 U.S.C. § 1826(a). If the civil contempt sanction fails to coerce the desired testimony, then the judge may punish the recalcitrant witness by imposing a determinate criminal contempt sanction of a fixed jail term or a fixed fine payable to the state. 18 U.S.C. § 401. *See, e.g.,* United States v. Marquardo, 149 F.3d 36 (1st Cir.1998).

2. Since the purpose of civil contempt is remedial, "it matters not with what intent the defendant did the prohibited act." McComb v. Jacksonville Paper Co., 336 U.S. 187, 191, 69 S.Ct. 497, 499, 93 L.Ed. 599 (1949). By contrast, criminal contempt is punishable only where it is "willful."

SIMKIN v. UNITED STATES

United States Court of Appeals, Second Circuit, 1983.
715 F.2d 34.

Before Newman and Winter, Circuit Judges, and Maletz, Senior Judge.*

Newman, Circuit Judge:

This appeal concerns the recurring and troublesome problem of determining at what point, if ever, during the maximum eighteen-month period in which a recalcitrant grand jury witness may be incarcerated for civil contempt, 28 U.S.C. § 1826 (1976), the witness should be released because the contempt sanction has lost all coercive effect. Morris Simkin appeals from the June 29, 1983, order of the District Court for the Eastern District of New York (Mark A. Costantino, Judge) denying his motion for release from commitment for civil contempt. * * *

I.

Simkin's present predicament is an outgrowth of criminal drug charges brought against him in 1981. On July 8, 1981, he pled guilty to one count of possessing with intent to distribute one-eighth of a kilogram of cocaine. 21 U.S.C. § 841(a)(1) (1976). Prior to sentencing, prosecutors urged him to disclose his sources of supply and his customers, and assured him that his cooperation would be brought to the attention of the sentencing judge and might well avoid the risk of the maximum fifteen-

---

* The Honorable Herbert N. Maletz of the United States Court of International Trade, sitting by designation.

year sentence he faced. Asserting fear for his own safety and that of his mother and uncle, Simkin resolutely refused to furnish any information. On May 4, 1982, he was sentenced by Judge Nickerson to a term of three years, suspended after six months, probation for five years, and a special parole term of three years. He began serving the six-month committed portion of the sentence on July 6, 1982.

A few weeks prior to his scheduled release, Simkin was subpoenaed before a grand jury in the Eastern District of New York. In connection with that appearance he was granted use immunity. 18 U.S.C. § 6002 (1976). Continuing to assert fear of reprisal upon himself and family members if he divulged his drug suppliers and customers, Simkin refused to answer questions before the grand jury. On November 3, 1982, Judge Costantino adjudged Simkin in civil contempt and ordered him confined until he testified, but in no event longer than the eighteen-month term of the grand jury, which had been empanelled on September 22, 1982. Judge Costantino also specified that the civil contempt sanction would interrupt the criminal sentence Simkin was then serving. *See* United States v. Dien, 598 F.2d 743, 744–45 & n.1 (2d Cir.1979).

Simkin applied to Judge Costantino for termination of the civil contempt sanction on December 19, 1982, and February 8, May 4, and June 29, 1983. On each occasion his lawyer contended that Simkin was irrevocably committed not to answer the grand jury's questions and that continued incarceration was no longer coercive but instead had become punitive. Counsel contended that Simkin's refusal was based not only on fear for himself and his family, but also on religious grounds. This latter concern was said to arise from "Jewish law and liturgy," not further identified, which was alleged to cast disdain upon an informant. Judge Costantino declined counsel's request to hear from Simkin in person and denied all four requests for release. This appeal is taken from the denial of the June 29 motion.

II.

It is familiar ground that a civil contempt sanction is a coercive device, imposed to secure compliance with a court order, Shillitani v. United States, 384 U.S. 364, 86 S.Ct. 1531, 16 L.Ed.2d 622 (1966); Maggio v. Zeitz, 333 U.S. 56, 68 S.Ct. 401, 92 L.Ed. 476 (1948), and that "[w]hen it becomes obvious that sanctions are not going to compel compliance, they lose their remedial characteristics and take on more of the nature of punishment." Soobzokov v. CBS, Inc., 642 F.2d 28, 31 (2d Cir.1981). When a recalcitrant witness is jailed for refusing to furnish unprivileged information in state court proceedings, it has been held that at some point in what otherwise would be an indefinite period of confinement due process considerations oblige a court to release a contemnor from civil contempt if the contemnor has then shown that there is no substantial likelihood that continued confinement will accomplish its coercive purpose. *See, e.g.,* Lambert v. Montana, 545 F.2d 87 (9th Cir.1976) [(contemnor refused to disclose the identity of a person who had discharged a weapon in the direction of two persons, although he knew who did it; contemnor had been in jail for sixteen months)]; *In re* Farr, 36 Cal.App.3d 577, 111 Cal.Rptr. 649 (1974) [(contemnor was a newspaper reporter who refused to disclose his sources; contemnor had been in jail for 45 days)]; Catena v. Seidl, 65 N.J. 257, 321 A.2d 225 (1974) [(contemnor refused to answer questions regarding organized crime activities; contemnor had been in jail for five years, he was 73 years old, and his health was deteriorating)].

With respect to recalcitrant witnesses before federal grand juries, Congress has determined that eighteen months is the maximum period of confinement for civil contempt. 28 U.S.C. § 1826. We agree with the views of the Third Circuit, expressed by Judge Adams, that in the absence of unusual circumstances, a reviewing court should be reluctant to conclude, as a matter of due process, that a civil contempt sanction has lost its coercive impact at some point prior to the eighteen-month period prescribed as a maximum by Congress. *In re* Grand Jury Investigation (Braun), 600 F.2d 420, 427 (3d Cir.1979).

There remains, nevertheless, a broad discretion in the district courts to determine that a civil contempt sanction has lost its coercive effect upon a particular contemnor at some point short of eighteen months. *In re* Grand Jury Investigation (Braun), *supra*, 600 F.2d at 428 * * *. The exercise of that discretion confronts a district judge with a perplexing task. The judge need not, of course, accept as conclusive a contemnor's avowed intention never to testify. United States v. Dien, *supra*, 598 F.2d at 745. Even if the judge concludes that it is the contemnor's present intention never to testify, that conclusion does not preclude the possibility that continued confinement will cause the witness to change his mind. *Id.* What is required of the judge is a conscientious effort to determine whether there remains a realistic possibility that continued confinement might cause the contemnor to testify. The burden is properly placed on the contemnor to demonstrate that no such realistic possibility exists. As long as the judge is satisfied that the coercive sanction might yet produce its intended result, the confinement may continue. But if the judge is persuaded, after a conscientious consideration of the circumstances pertinent to the individual contemnor, that the contempt power has ceased to have a coercive effect, the civil contempt remedy should be ended. The contemnor will not have avoided all sanction by his irrevocable opposition to the court's order. Once it is determined that the civil contempt remedy is unavailing, the criminal contempt sanction is available, *see* Shillitani v. United States, *supra*, 384 U.S. at 371 n.9, 86 S.Ct. at 1536 n.9, and can fully vindicate the court's authority, *see, e.g.,* United States v. Patrick, 542 F.2d 381, 384, 392–93 (7th Cir.1976) (four-year criminal contempt sentence imposed upon recalcitrant grand jury witness previously confined for civil contempt), *cert. denied,* 430 U.S. 931, 97 S.Ct. 1551, 51 L.Ed.2d 775 (1977).

In this case, appellant acknowledges that his fear of reprisal does not provide a legal basis for declining to answer the grand jury's questions, *see* Piemonte v. United States, 367 U.S. 556, 559 n.2, 81 S.Ct. 1720, 1722 n.2,

6 L.Ed.2d 1028 (1961) * * *. Instead, he urges that this fear provides a circumstance that should demonstrate to the District Court that the contempt sanction will not be effective. *Cf.* Harris v. United States, 382 U.S. 162, 166–67, 86 S.Ct. 352, 355–56, 15 L.Ed.2d 240 (1965) (fear may warrant lenient sentence of criminal contempt); United States v. Gomez, *supra*, 553 F.2d at 959 (same). Having remained in confinement for nearly eight months since the imposition of the civil contempt sanction, Simkin asserts that he should have been released by the District Court on June 29, or that at the least he should have been permitted to testify before the Court to persuade Judge Costantino that further confinement would be futile.

A district judge's determination whether a civil contempt sanction has lost any realistic possibility of having a coercive effect is inevitably far more speculative than his resolution of traditional factual issues. Since a prediction is involved and since that prediction concerns such uncertain matters as the likely effect of continued confinement upon a particular individual, we think a district judge has virtually unreviewable discretion both as to the procedure he will use to reach his conclusion, and as to the merits of his conclusion. *See* Soobzokov v. CBS, Inc., *supra*, 642 F.2d at 31 ("Ordinarily, it is for the district judge to determine when and if the borderline between coercion and punishment has been reached."); *see also In re* Grand Jury Investigation (Braun), *supra*. We have located no decision of a court of appeals requiring a district court to take testimony from a contemnor on the issue of the utility of continued confinement, or rejecting a district court's conclusion that such confinement is warranted.

However, we can extend such deference to the decision of a district judge only if it appears that the judge has assessed the likelihood of a coercive effect upon the particular contemnor. There must be an individualized decision, rather than application of a policy that the maximum eighteen-month term must be served by all recalcitrant witnesses. If a judge orders continued confinement without regard to its coercive effect upon the contemnor or as a warning to others who might be tempted to violate their testimonial obligations, he has converted the civil remedy into a criminal penalty.

There are ambiguities in the record before us concerning Judge Costantino's purpose in ordering continued confinement. Some of his statements in colloquy with Simkin's counsel suggest a legitimate view that continued confinement might yet prove effective in this case. For example, at the May 4 hearing, the Judge noted counsel's opportunity to make a subsequent application, which suggests his willingness to be persuaded that the coercive sanction has become ineffective sometime during the eighteen months. In this vein, he told counsel on June 29, "You say give it a second look. I am always doing that."

Other statements could refer either to Simkin's circumstances or the general use of the civil contempt sanction. On February 8, Judge Costantino told counsel that confinement "might become persuasive at some point." On June 29, he likened the sanction to "a tourniquet, the tighter you make the tourniquet, the more unhappy the individual might be."

Still other statements strongly suggest that an individualized decision was not made. The June 29 hearing included the following statement:

> I ... can't in good conscience just say, well, since he is not going to talk I have to let him out. Suppose everyone came before me and said the same thing. It is not his case that I am worried about. He is only one case. It is another hundred cases I may get on civil contempt, all of whom can [by their testimony] root out some type of evil.

When counsel inquired at what point the "tourniquet" might lose its effectiveness, the Judge replied, "I assume Congress answered that one when they said that you can be held for the life of the Grand Jury." Later, when counsel urged the Judge to hear testimony by Simkin, which might be persuasive of his determination never to answer questions, the Judge responded:

> No, I would never be persuaded by that because that is not what civil contempt is all about.... Civil contempt says that if he is never going to talk then he has to suffer the consequences....

That last comment nicely illustrates our concern. If the contemnor is "never" going to talk, then suffering the consequences is punishment. If he may yet decide to talk, then the consequences of not doing so continue to be a coercive sanction and a proper application of the civil contempt power.

We do not minimize the difficulty a district judge faces in determining whether in a particular case continued confinement of a recalcitrant witness retains any realistic possibility of achieving its intended purpose. Nevertheless, an individualized decision must be made in each case, and we are left in considerable doubt as to whether such a decision was made in this case. We therefore remand the matter to the District Court for determination whether under all the circumstances the contemnor has shown that there is no realistic possibility that *his* continued confinement will have a coercive effect upon *him*.

Remanded.

NOTE

The Second Circuit's holding in the *Simkin* case has been followed by several other circuits, including the First Circuit, the Seventh Circuit, and the Eleventh Circuit. *See, e.g., In re* Crededio, 759 F.2d 589 (7th Cir.1985). Nevertheless, in most cases, the trial court judge has refused to release the recalcitrant witness, and the appellate court has concluded that the district court did not abuse its discretion. *Id.* (affirming the district court's decision not to release the contemnor, a man who refused to testify before the grand jury for a variety of personal reasons, including fear for his own safety; the contemnor had been in jail for seven months); *see also In re* Grand Jury Proceedings of Special April 2002 Grand Jury, 347 F.3d 197 (7th Cir.2003).

Judge Posner dissented in the *In re* Crededio case, noting that 18 months (the maximum period of time that a recalcitrant grand jury witness can be held in jail under 28 U.S.C. § 1826) is "almost as much time as the average federal criminal defendant serves who is sentenced to 5 years in prison," and taking the position that: "As soon as it is clear that inducement won't work, the purpose of civil contempt lapses, and the continued imprisonment of the man becomes penal, and requires a criminal proceeding." 759 F.2d at 594.

How should *Simkin* be applied to a case in which a corporate officer has been charged with securities fraud and has been incarcerated for seven years for civil contempt because he refuses to comply with an order requiring him to produce corporate assets and records concerning property (including rare coins and antiquities) worth approximately $16 million? In Armstrong v. Guccione, 470 F.3d 89 (2d Cir. 2006), the majority of the court took the position that a contemnor may be jailed indefinitely. Nevertheless, the majority did schedule a hearing before a new trial court judge to determine whether Armstrong was in possession of the property. Judge Sotomayor, who concurred, was of the opinion that, for purposes of drawing the line between coercive and punitive sanctions, "inability to perform and resolute unwillingness to perform must, at some point, be treated similarly." *Id.* at 116. The majority disagreed with her on the theory that eliminating the distinction would encourage resistance to a court's lawful order.

C. VIOLATIONS OF EQUITABLE REMEDIAL DECREES

Contempt proceedings for the enforcement of equitable decrees are always nonsummary proceedings and are commonly regarded as either civil or criminal, depending on whether the dominant purpose is to coerce the defendant into affording the plaintiff the relief awarded in the original case, or to punish the defendant for offending against the authority of the court. The classification, which is sometimes confusing for courts and practitioners alike, can have numerous practical consequences. This is because "civil contempt must conform to civil procedures and criminal contempt is administered within the framework of criminal procedures." Doug Rendleman, *Compensatory Contempt: Plaintiff's Remedy When a Defendant Violates an Injunction*, 1980 U. Ill. L.F. 971. Thus, this distinction is important in determining parties, pleading and practice, particularity of the charge, burden and quantum of proof, availability of the privilege against self-incrimination, jury trial, terms of the order, and scope of appellate review. *See* Dan B. Dobbs, *Contempt of Court*, 56 Cornell L. Rev. 183 (1971); Earl C. Dudley, Jr., *Getting Beyond the Civil/Criminal Distinction: A New Approach to Regulation of Indirect Contempts*, 79 Va. L. Rev. 1025 (1993); Margit Livingston, *Disobedience and Contempt*, 75 Wash. L. Rev. 345 (2000); Robert J. Martineau, *Contempt of Court: Eliminating the Confusion Between Civil and Criminal Contempt*, 50 U. Cinn. L. Rev. 677 (1981).

1. Criminal Contempt Sanctions

YOUNG v. UNITED STATES EX REL. VUITTON ET FILS S.A.

Supreme Court of the United States, 1987.
481 U.S. 787, 107 S.Ct. 2124, 95 L.Ed.2d 740.

JUSTICE BRENNAN delivered the opinion of the Court with respect to Parts I, II, III–A, and IV, and an opinion with respect to Part III–B, in which JUSTICE MARSHALL, JUSTICE BLACKMUN, and JUSTICE STEVENS join.

Petitioners in these cases were found guilty of criminal contempt by a jury, pursuant to 18 U.S.C. § 401(3), for their violation of the District Court's injunction prohibiting infringement of respondent's trademark. They received sentences ranging from six months to five years. [Sol Klayminc, one of the petitioners, received the five year sentence.]

I

The injunction that petitioners violated in these cases is a result of the settlement of a lawsuit brought in December 1978, in the District Court for the Southern District of New York, by Louis Vuitton, S.A., a French leather goods manufacturer, against Sol Klayminc, his wife Sylvia, * * * and their family-owned businesses * * *. Vuitton alleged in its suit that the Klaymincs were manufacturing imitation Vuitton goods for sale and distribution. Vuitton's trademark was found valid in Vuitton et Fils S.A. v. J. Young Enterprises, Inc., 644 F.2d 769 (CA9 1981), and Vuitton and the Klaymincs then entered into a settlement agreement in July 1982. Under this agreement, the Klaymincs agreed to pay Vuitton $100,000 in damages, and consented to the entry of a permanent injunction prohibiting them from, *inter alia,* "manufacturing * * * [or] selling * * * any product bearing any * * * colorable imitation" of Vuitton's registered trademark. * * *

In early 1983, Vuitton and other companies concerned with possible trademark infringement were contacted by a Florida investigation firm with a proposal to conduct an undercover "sting" operation. The firm was retained * * *.

[O]n March 31, 1983, Vuitton attorney J. Joseph Bainton requested that the District Court appoint him and his colleague Robert P. Devlin as special counsel to prosecute a criminal contempt action for violation of the injunction against infringing Vuitton's trademark. * * * Bainton * * * indicated that the next step of the "sting" was to be a meeting * * * at which Sol was to deliver 25 counterfeit Vuitton handbags. * * *

The court * * * found probable cause to believe that petitioners were engaged in conduct contumacious of the court's injunctive order, and appointed Bainton and Devlin to represent the United States in the investigation and prosecution of such activity * * *. A week after Bainton's appointment, * * * the court suggested that Bainton inform the

United States Attorney's Office of his appointment and the impending investigation. Bainton did so, offering to make available any tape recordings or other evidence, but the Chief of the Criminal Division of that Office expressed no interest beyond wishing Bainton good luck.

* * * On the basis of [the] evidence [obtained during the sting], * * * the District Court signed an order on April 26 directing petitioners to show cause why they * * * should not be cited for contempt for either violating or aiding and abetting the violation of the court's July 1982 permanent injunction. * * * Petitioners' pretrial motions opposing the order to show cause and the appointment of Bainton and Devlin as special prosecutors were denied, United States ex rel. Vuitton et Fils S.A. v. Karen Bags, Inc., 592 F.Supp. 734 (SDNY 1984), and two of the defendants subsequently entered guilty pleas. Sol Klayminc ultimately was convicted, following a jury trial, of criminal contempt under 18 U.S.C. § 401(3),[2] and the other petitioners were convicted of aiding and abetting that contempt. * * *

On appeal to the Court of Appeals for the Second Circuit petitioners argued, *inter alia,* that the appointment of Bainton and Devlin as special prosecutors violated their right to be prosecuted only by an impartial prosecutor. The court rejected their contention, 780 F.2d 179 (1985) * * *. It suggested that an interested attorney will often be the only source of information about contempts occurring outside the court's presence * * * and stated that the supervision of contempt prosecutions by the judge is generally sufficient to prevent the "danger that the special prosecutor will use the threat of prosecution as a bargaining chip in civil negotiations.... " * * *

II

A

Petitioners first contend that the District Court lacked authority to appoint *any* private attorney to prosecute the contempt action against them, and that, as a result, only the United States Attorney's Office could have permissibly brought such a prosecution. We disagree. * * * [I]t is long settled that courts possess inherent authority to initiate contempt proceedings for disobedience to their orders, authority which necessarily encompasses the ability to appoint a private attorney to prosecute the contempt.

By its terms, Rule 42(b) speaks only to the procedure for *providing notice* of criminal contempt.[4] * * * The Rule's reference to the appoint-

---

2. That provision states: "A court of the United States shall have power to punish by fine or imprisonment * * * such contempt of its authority, and none other, as ... (3) Disobedience or resistance to its lawful writ, * * * decree, or command."

4. The Rule provides in relevant part:

"(b) Disposition Upon Notice and Hearing. A criminal contempt except as provided in subdivision (a) of this rule shall be prosecuted on notice. * * * The notice shall be given orally by the judge in open court in the presence of the defendant or, on application of the United States

ment of a private attorney to * * * submit a show cause order assumes a *pre-existing practice* of private prosecution of contempts * * *.

* * *

The ability to punish disobedience to judicial orders is regarded as essential to ensuring that the Judiciary has a means to vindicate its own authority without complete dependence on other Branches. * * * The ability to appoint a private attorney to prosecute a contempt action satisfies the need for an independent means of self-protection, without which courts would be "mere boards of arbitration whose judgments and decrees would be only advisory." * * *8

* * *

B

Petitioners contend that the ability of courts to initiate contempt prosecutions is limited to the summary punishment of in-court contempts that interfere with the judicial process. They argue that out-of-court contempts, which require prosecution by a party other than the court, are essentially conventional crimes, prosecution of which may be initiated only by the Executive Branch.

The underlying concern that gave rise to the contempt power was not, however, merely the disruption of court proceedings. Rather, it was disobedience to the orders of the Judiciary, regardless of whether such disobedience interfered with the conduct of trial. * * *

The distinction between in-court and out-of-court contempts has been drawn not to define when a court has or has not the authority to initiate prosecution for contempt, but for the purpose of prescribing what procedures must attend the exercise of that authority. As we said in Bloom v. Illinois, 391 U.S. 194, 204, 88 S.Ct. 1477, 1483, 20 L.Ed.2d 522 (1968), "[b]efore the 19th century was out, a distinction had been carefully drawn between contempts occurring within the view of the court, for which a hearing and formal presentation of evidence were dispensed with, and all other contempts where more normal adversary procedures were required." * * *

---

attorney or of an attorney appointed by the court for that purpose, by an order to show cause or an order of arrest."

8. Justice Scalia's concurrence suggests that our precedents regarding a court's inherent contempt authority have lost their force because of our decision in Bloom v. Illinois, 391 U.S. 194, 88 S.Ct. 1477, 20 L.Ed.2d 522 (1968). * * * The argument is that since *Bloom* rejected the holding in *In re* Debs, 158 U.S. 564, 15 S.Ct. 900, 39 L.Ed. 1092 (1895), that courts have inherent power summarily to punish serious contempts, and since the cases between *Bloom* and *Debs* assumed the existence of this summary power, these precedents cannot provide guidance for a court's authority with respect to contempts of court. These precedents, however, both acknowledge the inherent power of a court to institute contempt proceedings, and assume that in such proceedings the court may summarily determine guilt with respect to serious criminal contempts. *Bloom* held that the second assumption was incorrect, but did nothing to undermine the first. * * * That case therefore cannot justify ignoring our consistent pronouncements on the inherent authority of a court to institute contempt proceedings.

The manner in which the court's prosecution of contempt is exercised * * * may be regulated by Congress * * *, and by this Court through constitutional review, *Bloom, supra,* * * * or supervisory power, Cheff v. Schnackenberg, 384 U.S. 373, 384, 86 S.Ct. 1523, 1526, 16 L.Ed.2d 629 (1966). * * * [W]hile the exercise of the contempt power is subject to reasonable regulation, "the attributes which inhere in that power * * * can neither be abrogated nor rendered practically inoperative." * * * Thus, while the prosecution of in-court and out-of-court contempts must proceed in a different manner, they both proceed at the instigation of the court.

The fact that we have come to regard criminal contempt as "a crime in the ordinary sense," *Bloom, supra,* 391 U.S., at 201, 88 S.Ct., at 1481, does not mean that any prosecution of contempt must now be considered an execution of the criminal law in which only the Executive Branch may engage. Our insistence on the criminal character of contempt prosecutions has been intended to rebut earlier characterizations of such actions as undeserving of the protections normally provided in criminal proceedings. * * * That criminal procedure protections are now required in such prosecutions should not obscure the fact that these proceedings are not intended to punish conduct proscribed as harmful by the general criminal laws. Rather, they are designed to serve the limited purpose of vindicating the authority of the court. In punishing contempt, the Judiciary is sanctioning conduct that violates specific duties imposed by the court itself, arising directly from the parties' participation in judicial proceedings.

Petitioners' assertion that the District Court lacked authority to appoint a private attorney to prosecute the contempt action in these cases is thus without merit. While contempt proceedings are sufficiently criminal in nature to warrant the imposition of many procedural protections, their fundamental purpose is to preserve respect for the judicial system itself. As a result, courts have long had, and must continue to have, the authority to appoint private attorneys to initiate such proceedings when the need arises.

C

While a court has the authority to initiate a prosecution for criminal contempt, its exercise of that authority must be restrained by the principle that "only '[t]he least possible power adequate to the end proposed' should be used in contempt cases." * * * We have suggested, for instance, that, when confronted with a witness who refuses to testify, a trial judge should first consider the feasibility of prompting testimony through the imposition of civil contempt, utilizing criminal sanctions only if the civil remedy is deemed inadequate. Shillitani v. United States, 384 U.S. 364, 371, n. 9, 86 S.Ct. 1531, 1536, n. 9, 16 L.Ed.2d 622 (1966).

This principle of restraint in contempt counsels caution in the exercise of the power to appoint a private prosecutor. We repeat that the rationale for the appointment authority is necessity. * * * The logic of this rationale is that a court ordinarily should first request the appropriate prosecuting authority to prosecute contempt actions, and should appoint a private prosecutor only if that request is denied. Such a procedure ensures that the court will exercise its inherent power of self-protection only as a last resort.

* * *

In this case, the District Court did not first refer the case to the United States Attorney's Office before the appointment of Bainton and Devlin as special prosecutors. We need not address the ramifications of that failure, however. Even if a referral had been made, we hold, in the exercise of our supervisory power, that the court erred in appointing as prosecutors counsel for an interested party in the underlying civil litigation.

III

A

* * *

* * * [The] distinctive role of the prosecutor is expressed in Ethical Consideration (EC) 7–13 of Canon 7 of the American Bar Association (ABA) Model Code of Professional Responsibility (1982): "The responsibility of a public prosecutor differs from that of the usual advocate; his duty is to seek justice, not merely to convict."

Because of this unique responsibility, federal prosecutors are prohibited from representing the Government in any matter in which they, their family, or their business associates have any interest. 18 U.S.C. § 208(a). * * * The concern that representation of other clients may compromise the prosecutor's pursuit of the Government's interest rests on recognition that a prosecutor would owe an ethical duty to those other clients. * * *

Private attorneys appointed to prosecute a criminal contempt action represent the United States, not the party that is the beneficiary of the court order allegedly violated. * * * The prosecutor is appointed solely to pursue the public interest in vindication of the court's authority. A private attorney appointed to prosecute a criminal contempt therefore certainly should be as disinterested as a public prosecutor who undertakes such a prosecution.

* * *

Regardless of whether the appointment of private counsel in this case resulted in any prosecutorial impropriety (an issue on which we express no opinion), that appointment illustrates the *potential* for private interest to influence the discharge of public duty. * * * Vuitton had various civil claims pending against some of the petitioners. These claims theoretically could have created temptation to use the criminal investigation to gather information of use in those suits, and could have served as bargaining leverage in obtaining pleas in the criminal prosecution. In short, as will generally be the case, the appointment of counsel for an interested party to bring the contempt prosecution in this case at a minimum created *opportunities* for conflicts to arise, and created at least the *appearance* of impropriety. [17]

* * *

The use of this Court's supervisory authority has played a prominent role in ensuring that contempt proceedings are conducted in a manner consistent with basic notions of fairness. See, *e.g., Cheff,* 384 U.S., at 380, 86 S.Ct., at 1526 (requiring jury trial for imposition of contempt sentences greater than six months) * * * . We rely today on that authority to hold that counsel for a party that is the beneficiary of a court order may not be appointed as prosecutor in a contempt action alleging a violation of that order.

* * *

IV

Between the private life of the citizen and the public glare of criminal accusation stands the prosecutor. That state official has the power to employ the full machinery of the state in scrutinizing any given individual. Even if a defendant is ultimately acquitted, forced immersion in criminal investigation and adjudication is a wrenching disruption of everyday life. For this reason, we must have assurance that those who would wield this power will be guided solely by their sense of public responsibility for the attainment of justice. A prosecutor of a contempt action who represents the private beneficiary of the court order allegedly violated cannot provide such assurance, for such an attorney is required by the very standards of the profession to serve two masters. The appointment of counsel for Vuitton to conduct the contempt prosecution in these cases therefore was improper. Accordingly, the judgment of the Court of Appeals is reversed.

JUSTICE BLACKMUN, concurring.

I join Justice Brennan's opinion. I would go further, however, and hold that the practice—federal or state—of appointing an interested party's counsel to prosecute for criminal contempt is a violation of due process. This constitutional concept, in my view, requires a disinterested prosecutor with the unique responsibility to serve the public, rather than

---

17. The potential for misconduct that is created by the appointment of an interested prosecutor is not outweighed by the fact that counsel for the beneficiary of the court order may often be most familiar with the allegedly contumacious conduct. That familiarity may be put to use in *assisting* a disinterested prosecutor in pursuing the contempt action, but cannot justify permitting counsel for the private party to be in control of the prosecution. Nor does a concern for reimbursement of the prosecutor support such an appointment * * *. The Solicitor General has represented to the Court that * * * the statutes appropriating funds for the operation of the federal courts [have been construed] to permit reimbursement of legal fees to attorneys appointed as special prosecutors in contempt actions, * * * and that such payments have been approved in the past at the hourly rate at which Justice Department attorneys are compensated. * * * Furthermore, the normal practice of first referring the matter to the United States Attorney's Office should minimize the number of instances in which such reimbursement is necessary.

a private client, and to seek justice that is unfettered. See *Brotherhood of Locomotive Firemen & Enginemen v. United States*, 411 F.2d 312, 319 (CA5 1969); see generally Note, *Private Prosecutors in Criminal Contempt Actions under Rule 42(b) of the Federal Rules of Criminal Procedure*, 54 Ford.L.Rev. 1141, 1146–1166 (1986).

JUSTICE SCALIA, concurring in the judgment.

I agree with the Court that the District Court's appointment of J. Joseph Bainton and Robert P. Devlin as special counsel to prosecute petitioners for contempt of an injunction earlier issued by that court was invalid * * *. In my view, however, those appointments were defective because of a failing more fundamental than that relied upon by the Court. Prosecution of individuals who disregard court orders (except orders necessary to protect the courts' ability to function) is not an exercise of "[t]he judicial power of the United States," U.S. Const., Art. III, §§ 1, 2. * * *

I

* * *

The judicial power is the power to decide, in accordance with law, who should prevail in a case or controversy. * * * That includes the power to serve as a neutral adjudicator in a criminal case, but does not include the power to seek out law violators in order to punish them—which would be quite incompatible with the task of neutral adjudication. It is accordingly well established that the judicial power does not generally include the power to prosecute crimes. * * * Rather, since the prosecution of law violators is part of the implementation of the laws, it is—at least to the extent that it is publicly exercised—executive power, vested by the Constitution in the President. Art. II, § 2, cl. 1. * * *

* * * The Court asserts, however, that there is a special exception for prosecutions of criminal contempt, which are the means of securing compliance with court orders. Unless these can be prosecuted by the courts themselves, the argument goes, efficaciousness of judicial judgments will be at the mercy of the Executive, an arrangement presumably too absurd to contemplate. * * *

Far from being absurd, however, it is a carefully designed and critical element of our system of Government [i.e., checks and balances]. * * *

* * *

II

The Court appeals to a "longstanding acknowledgment that the initiation of contempt proceedings to punish disobedience to court orders is a part of the judicial function." * * *

* * *

* * * But that principle [of necessity] would at most require that courts be empowered to prosecute for contempt those who interfere with the orderly conduct of their business or disobey orders necessary to the conduct of that business (such as subpoenas). It would not require that they be able to prosecute and punish, not merely disruption of their functioning, but disregard of the *product* of their functioning, their judgments. * * *

III

* * *

* * * [I]t seems to me that *Bloom* is * * * highly relevant to the present cases. [*Bloom*] * * * makes clear that the argument from necessity to the existence of an inherent power must be restrained by the totality of the Constitution, lest it swallow up the carefully crafted guarantees of liberty. * * * While this principle may have varying application to the jury-trial and separation-of-powers guarantees, it is inconceivable to me that it would not prevent so flagrant a violation of the latter as permitting a judge to promulgate a rule of behavior, prosecute its violation, and adjudicate whether the violation took place. That arrangement is no less fundamental a threat to liberty than is deprivation of a jury trial * * *.

* * *

I would therefore hold that the federal courts have no power to prosecute contemners for disobedience of court judgments, and no derivative power to appoint an attorney to conduct contempt prosecutions. That is not to say, of course, that the federal courts may not impose criminal sentences for such contempts. But they derive that power from the same source they derive the power to pass on other crimes which it has never been contended they may prosecute: a statute enacted by Congress criminalizing the conduct which has been on the books in one form or another since the Judiciary Act of 1789, *supra,* at 2131. See 18 U.S.C. § 401.

IV

I agree with the Court that the District Judge's error in appointing Bainton and Devlin to prosecute these contempts requires reversal of the convictions. * * *

JUSTICE POWELL, with whom THE CHIEF JUSTICE and JUSTICE O'CONNOR join, concurring in part and dissenting in part. [Opinion omitted.]

JUSTICE WHITE, dissenting.

* * * [A]s I understand Rule 42, it was intended to embrace the prior practice and to authorize, but not to require, the appointment of attorneys for interested parties. I would leave amendment of the Rule to the rulemaking process. * * * I would affirm the Court of Appeals.

NOTES

1. *Young* was decided under the Court's supervisory power (as opposed to its power of constitutional review). Therefore, *Young* does not apply to state court judges and some states continue the traditional practice of allowing private attorneys who represent the beneficiaries of equitable decrees to prosecute criminal contempt proceedings for the following reasons:

> [T]remendous fiscal and administrative burdens would result from a substitute procedural requirement. Contempt proceedings often arise in domestic relations cases in state courts. However, unlike the federal system, there is no fund in Tennessee from which to compensate private counsel appointed to prosecute criminal contempt actions. It is unrealistic to expect district attorneys to prosecute contempt actions arising from alleged violations of civil court orders. District attorneys already have a heavy caseload prosecuting violations of the general criminal laws. Were we to hold that due process precludes a litigant's private attorney from prosecuting contempt proceedings, many citizens would be deprived of the benefits to which they have already been adjudged entitled by state courts and many state court orders would remain unenforced. The minimal risk that a defendant will be erroneously deprived of his or her liberty interest if a litigant's private attorney prosecutes a contempt proceeding is far outweighed by the very real fiscal and administrative burdens certain to accompany the adoption of a substitute procedure.

Wilson v. Wilson, 984 S.W.2d 898, 903 (Tenn.1998). Other states, however, have opted to follow *Young*:

> We agree with the Court in *Young* that criminal contempt should, in the first instance, be referred to the executive branch for prosecution. * * * We are confident that in most cases the executive branch will act to preserve respect for judicial authority. In the unusual case in which a court believes that prosecution is necessary, even after the executive branch has declined to act, a court may appoint a private prosecutor.

Rogowicz v. O'Connell, 147 N.H. 270, 273, 786 A.2d 841, 844 (2001) (holding that the lawyer for a woman who had obtained a protective order against a man with whom she had been in a romantic relationship for several years "should have been disqualified" from representing the woman in a criminal contempt proceeding to enforce the order; reversing the criminal contempt sanction). *See generally* Michael Edmund O'Neill, *Private Vengeance and the Public Good*, 12 U. Pa. J. Const. L. 659 (2010)(Alabama, Georgia, Indiana, New Jersey, New York, Ohio, Pennsylvania, Tennessee, Vermont , Virginia, West Virginia, and Wisconsin allow private counsel to participate in criminal prosecutions in some way).

2. The United States Supreme Court granted a writ of certiorari in Robertson v. U.S. *ex rel.* Watson, 130 S.Ct. 1011 (2009)(a domestic violence action) limited to the question of whether "an action for criminal contempt in a congressionally created court may constitutionally be brought in the name and pursuant to the power of a private person, rather than in the name and pursuant to the power of the United States." After oral argument, a majority

of the Court dismissed the writ of certiorari as improvidently granted. The four dissenters would have held: "The answer to that question is no." 130 S.Ct. 2184 (2010) (Roberts, C.J.) (Chief Justice Roberts was joined by Justices Scalia, Kennedy, and Sotomayor). Justice Sotomayor, joined by Justice Kennedy, wrote separately to explain:

> The Chief Justice would hold that criminal prosecutions, including criminal contempt proceedings, must be brought on behalf of the government. I join his opinion with the understanding that the narrow holding it proposes does not address civil contempt proceedings or consider more generally the legitimacy of the existing regimes for the enforcement of restraining orders.

Id. at 2191.

3. In *Young*, the district court imposed criminal contempt sanctions, which were definite, retroactive sanctions designed to punish the contemnors. In the next case, what type of contempt sanction does the district court impose, and why?

3. Civil Compensatory Contempt Sanctions

CANCER RESEARCH INSTITUTE, INC. v. CANCER RESEARCH SOCIETY, INC.

United States District Court, Southern District of New York, 1990.
744 F.Supp. 526.

KEENAN, DISTRICT JUDGE.

BACKGROUND

This action in which plaintiff sought to protect the exclusivity of its tradename was the subject of a prior decision where this Court permanently enjoined defendant from using the name Cancer Research Society or any other name confusingly similar to plaintiff's name. *See* Cancer Research Institute v. Cancer Research Society, 694 F.Supp. 1051 (S.D.N.Y. 1988). * * * Plaintiff now seeks an order adjudging defendant in civil contempt for violating the terms of the Judgment and Permanent Injunction of April 29, 1988, which embodied the decree of this Court's decision. Plaintiff also requests attorney's fees because it contends the alleged contumacy was willful. * * *

FACTS

The Judgment and Permanent Injunction entered by this Court on April 29, 1988 permanently enjoined defendant "from listing or advertising itself in any telephone directory in the United States under the name Cancer Research Society...." * * * The Court instructed defendant to notify before June 1, 1988 the publishers of all directories in which the offending listing had already appeared, or in which it was about to appear and could not be halted, that the listing must be deleted from all future directories. * * * Paragraph 3 of the injunction required the defendant to "take immediate steps to attempt to secure the withdrawal of any such listings which were placed prior to April 29, 1988," and were slated to appear in directories which had "not yet reached their closing dates."

When plaintiff initially brought this motion, it adduced evidence of 10 instances of purported violations of the April 29 injunction. This figure swelled to 178 violations in plaintiff's estimation by the time the extensive submissions were entirely before the Court.

The Purported Violations

Plaintiff claims that defendant's failure to secure the timely deletion of prohibited listings from numerous directories published between late 1988 and late 1989 warrants a finding of contempt. * * *

To bolster its assertions of non-compliance, plaintiff surveyed 15 directory companies, responsible for the publication of 39 directories containing the prohibited listing, to determine whether they received cancellation orders from defendant and, if so, whether the cancellation orders were received in time to delete defendant's listings from directories that were still open when the Court issued its injunction. The results of this survey * * * reveal "that no record of formal cancellation order [prior to late 1989] . . . could be found for 33 directories." * * *

Defendant's Compliance Efforts

Defendant concedes, as it must, that listings have appeared which violate the terms of the injunction. Defendant seeks, however, to lay the entire blame at the feet of its advertising agency, American Ad Management ("AAM") or the individual directories it maintains published the prohibited listing despite cancellation orders. Indeed, defendant claims it was unaware that any of its cancellation orders were ineffectual until it received plaintiff's contempt motion papers. * * *

* * *

Judy Leverich, AAM's former coordinator responsible for canceling telephone directory listings, sent a "Form 3235," the acknowledged form for canceling telephone directory listings, to various directory publishers to cancel approximately 150 listings for the name Cancer Research Society. She believes that the "vast majority" of the cancellations were effective, and assumes that error on the publishers' part caused the instances where the cancellations were not honored. * * *

DISCUSSION

A party may be held in civil contempt "only if there is a clear and unambiguous order, noncompliance is proved clearly and convincingly, and 'the defendant has not been reasonably diligent and energetic in attempting to accomplish what was ordered.' " * * * The sanction imposed on a civil contemnor should be calculated to advance either (or both) of two ends: to coerce future compliance with the court's order or to compensate the complainant for losses stemming from the contemnor's past noncompliance. *See* Perfect Fit Industries, Inc. v. Acme Quilting Co.,

673 F.2d 53, 56–57 (2d Cir.), *cert. denied*, 459 U.S. 832, 103 S.Ct. 73, 74 L.Ed.2d 71 (1982) * * *. Punishment of the contemnor is not a proper purpose of a civil contempt sanction. *See* Manhattan Industries v. Sweater Bee by Banff, Ltd., 885 F.2d 1, 5 (2d Cir.1989), *cert. denied*, 494 U.S. 1029, 110 S.Ct. 1477, 108 L.Ed.2d 614 (1990).

Sanctions can be imposed "without a finding of wilfulness." * * * The contemnor's intent, however, may be considered in fashioning an appropriate remedy. * * * Guided by these principles, the Court turns to plaintiff's application.

* * *

Plaintiff identifies no fewer than 66 instances where the prohibited listing appeared in editions of directories which were published at a time when the deletion would have been effected had defendant acted to ensure compliance with the injunction. * * * Paragraph 4 of the injunction required defendant to delete its old telephone listings by sending out notices to directories "on or before June 1, 1988." It cannot be seriously urged that defendant complied with this instruction. AAM, defendant's advertising agency, mailed the majority of the cancellation notices at the end of August 1988, and some as late as September 1989. * * * Moreover, it appears that AAM's practice was to wait until about five days before the deadline for accomplishing directory changes, creating the risk that the cancellation would not arrive in time to achieve deletion.

* * *

* * * Defendant points out that it engaged an advertising agency which it reasonably believed would carry out the requirements of the injunction. * * * The record reveals, however, that defendant failed " 'to energetically police compliance' with the" injunction. * * *

* * * Having found clear and convincing proof of numerous violations of the Court's injunction occasioned by defendant's lack of diligence, the Court finds that defendant is in contempt.

* * * The record does not reveal that defendant continues to violate the injunction. Although its compliance was late, its exhibits display current compliance. Coercion is not called for here.

Sanctions must be imposed, however, "once the plaintiff has proved that he has suffered harm because of a violation of the terms of the injunction." * * * Proof of actual damages, of course, is a precise guide in determining the appropriate award for complainant. *See* Powell v. Ward, 643 F.2d 924, 934 (2d Cir.), *cert. denied*, 454 U.S. 832, 102 S.Ct. 131, 70 L.Ed.2d 111 (1981). Plaintiff adduces no evidence of actual damages resulting from defendant's continued use of the prohibited listing after the injunction issued. Defendant asserts that plaintiff's inability to demonstrate actual loss forecloses more than nominal recovery. The Court disagrees.

"[A] civil contempt fine is not always dependent on a demonstration of 'actual pecuniary loss.'" *Manhattan Industries*, 885 F.2d at 5 (citation omitted). In circumstances where "'it seems obvious that there must have been some economic injury to [plaintiff]'...., under a theory of unjust enrichment, a contempt plaintiff is entitled to defendant's profits without submitting proof of direct injury." *Id.* at 6 (citations omitted). Here, the Court has already found that the prohibited listing caused a substantial diminution in plaintiff's contributions in 1987 and 1988. *See Cancer Research, supra,* 694 F.Supp. at 1054. No principled reason appears in the record to not extend this finding to revenue generated from listings in 1988–1989 directories.

In plaintiff's earlier submissions, it requested $2,400 per violation. Without a factual predicate, plaintiff characterized this figure as a) an approximation of plaintiff's losses per prohibited listing; or b) defendant's unjust enrichment per listing. As the number of documented instances of violations grew to 178 in plaintiff's estimation, plaintiff submitted the appropriate sanction to the Court's discretion. The Court, however, knows of no authority for plaintiff's suggestion when the contempt sanction is calculated to compensate the plaintiff's loss. The law is clear that the Court possesses broad discretion to fashion a monetary remedy only where the purpose of the sanction is coercive. *See Perfect Fit Industries, supra,* 673 F.2d at 57.

When actual loss cannot be demonstrated, plaintiff is entitled to compensatory damages under an unjust enrichment theory. There, plaintiff may recover defendant's net profits derived from the continued use of the prohibited listing after the injunction issued. *See Manhattan Industries,* 885 F.2d at 7. The Court presently is unable to compute what profits defendant derived from the presence of the prohibited listing in directories after the injunction issued. Plaintiff must conduct discovery on this issue. Accordingly, plaintiff shall complete discovery on the question of what portion of defendant's net profits it is entitled to for the period after the injunction's issuance through the last date a then-current directory carried the prohibited listing.

Plaintiff seeks to recover attorney's fees and its costs in prosecuting this motion. A complainant may not be awarded attorney's fees and costs absent a showing the contumacy was willful. *See Manhattan Industries,* 885 F.2d at 8. The record does not disclose any deliberateness on defendant's part in the continued appearance of the prohibited listing. The Court declines to award attorney's fees.

CONCLUSION

For the reasons developed above, the Court finds defendant in contempt. Plaintiff is to complete discovery on the damages issue within 60 days of this decision. The Court declines to award attorney's fees and costs. * * *

NOTES

1. Compensatory civil contempt is like criminal contempt in that both types of sanctions operate "retroactively." Criminal contempt sanctions, however, are "punitive" in nature: fixed jail terms or fixed fines payable to the government. Civil compensatory contempt sanctions are "compensatory" monetary judgments assessed in accord with the financial losses caused by the contemnor's misconduct and payable to the people who suffered those losses. The "central irony" underlying compensatory contempt sanctions is that the injunction was awarded because the plaintiff's legal remedy was considered to be inadequate, yet once the defendant has violated the injunction, the only relief that the judge is able to award the plaintiff is the monetary remedy that the judge previously had deemed to be inadequate. Doug Rendleman, *Compensatory Contempt: Plaintiff's Remedy When a Defendant Violates an Injunction*, 1980 U. Ill. L.F. 971, 974. The irony is heightened by the fact that there is a right to jury trial when a court awards a legal remedy, but not when a judge imposes a compensatory contempt sanction. *Id.* at 982–83. Despite this "central irony," the federal courts and the majority of state courts permit the imposition of compensatory contempt sanctions. *See generally* Annotation, *Right of Injured Party to Award of Compensatory Damages or Fine in Contempt Proceedings*, 85 A.L.R. 3d 895 (1978). *But see* Dodson v. Dodson, 380 Md. 438, 845 A.2d 1194 (2004) (refusing to recognize a compensatory contempt sanction where the contemnor had negligently violated an injunction because compensatory contempt proceedings are essentially tort actions, and yet there is no right to a jury trial).

2. "Willfulness" is not an element of civil (as opposed to criminal) contempt. That is why, for example, the court in *Cancer Research* was able to impose a compensatory contempt sanction based upon the complainant's proof of nothing more than negligence. *See generally* Doug Rendleman, *Compensatory Contempt: Plaintiff's Remedy When a Defendant Violates an Injunction*, 1980 U. Ill. L.F. 971, 979.

3. There is a difference of opinion as to whether "willfulness" must be proven in order to recover attorney's fees and other costs in compensatory contempt proceedings. Some federal circuits do require proof of willfulness, *see, e.g.*, Omega World Travel, Inc. v. Omega Travel, Inc., 710 F.Supp. 169, 173 (E.D.Va.1989), *aff'd*, 905 F.2d 1530 (4th Cir.1990), although the Second Circuit may no longer be one of them. *See* Weitzman v. Stein, 98 F.3d 717, 719 (2d Cir.1996) ("[W]hile willfulness may not necessarily be a prerequisite to an award of fees and costs, a finding of willfulness strongly supports granting them."). Most federal courts today do not impose a willfulness requirement. *See, e.g.*, John Zink Co. v. Zink, 241 F.3d 1256, 1261 (10th Cir.2001) (citing to cases from the Third, Fifth, Sixth, Seventh, Ninth, Eleventh, and District of Columbia Circuits). The rationale for awarding attorney's fees without proof of willfulness is that, especially in a case where contumacious conduct was quickly detected and ended, a failure to compensate the expenses of enforcing the order, where the defendants' behavior was genuinely, if not willfully, worthy of a contempt sanction, "would not only permit the offender to violate the court's order with impunity, but would

leave the party that obtained the order worse off for its efforts to secure compliance with * * * the court's command." Shady Records, Inc. v. Source Enterprises, Inc., 351 F.Supp.2d 64 (S.D.N.Y.2004) (action to enforce temporary restraining order in a copyright infringement action).

4. Compensatory contempt sanctions may be measured in accord with the law of compensatory damages or in accord with the principles of restitution. When a judge uses the "compensatory damages" measure, the focus usually is on the plaintiff's "actual" or "pecuniary" losses. *E.g.*, Lyon v. Bloomfield, 355 Mass. 738, 247 N.E.2d 555 (1969) ("pecuniary injury," including loss of rental value, is the appropriate measure of harm for the violation of an injunction prohibiting trespass to land). *But see* Sebastian v. Texas Department of Corrections, 558 F.Supp. 507 (S.D.Tex.1983) (emotional distress and harm to reputation are losses for which monetary relief is recoverable in a civil compensatory contempt proceeding). When a judge uses the "restitutionary" measure, as in the *Cancer Research* case, the focus shifts to the contemnor's gains (*see infra* Chapter 4). For a case holding that a patentee who had sought a second contempt sanction against its competitor could obtain a compensatory contempt sanction in the amount of the competitor's gross profits (rather than its net profits) because an award of gross profits would provide a "natural means of imposing a penalty that is proportionate to the severity of the contempt," see Brine, Inc. v. STX, L.L.C., 367 F. Supp.2d 61 (D. Mass. 2005). The amounts awarded in compensatory contempt proceedings vary widely. Annotation, *Right of Injured Party to Award of Compensatory Damages or Fine in Contempt Proceedings*, 85 A.L.R. 3d 895, § 6 (1978).

5. Note that the plaintiff in *Cancer Research* requested a compensatory contempt sanction of $2,400 per violation. Although a per diem fine payable to the state is an appropriate coercive contempt sanction, a per diem fine payable to the complainant is not usually considered to be an appropriate compensatory contempt sanction. Getka v. Lader, 71 Wis.2d 237, 238 N.W.2d 87 (1976).

6. Punitive damages are not recoverable in compensatory contempt proceedings, but one commentator has suggested that they ought to be. Doug Rendleman, *Compensatory Contempt: Plaintiff's Remedy When A Defendant Violates an Injunction*, 1980 U. Ill. L.F. 971, 986. Do you agree?

7. Criminal contempt sanctions are comparable to criminal penalties. Compensatory contempt sanctions are comparable to tort damages. Therefore, the truly unique contempt sanction is the civil coercive contempt sanction. *See generally* Jennifer Fleischer, *In Defense of Civil Contempt Sanctions*, 36 Colum. L.J. & Soc. Probs. 35 (2002).

3. Civil Coercive Contempt Sanctions

WRONKE v. MADIGAN

United States District Court, Central District of Illinois, 1998.
26 F.Supp.2d 1102.

McCUSKEY, DISTRICT JUDGE.

On July 8, 1996, Petitioner, Kenneth L. Wronke, filed his petition under 28 U.S.C. § 2254 for a writ of habeas corpus. Wronke challenges an order entered on October 5, 1995, in the circuit court of Champaign County. The court found Wronke in indirect civil contempt of court and ordered him to be transported to the Champaign County Correctional Center until he purged himself of the contempt. * * *

FACTS

On July 12, 1990, Elinor Wronke n/k/a Elinor Canady filed a petition for dissolution of marriage in the circuit court of Champaign County. The case was originally assigned to Judge Harold L. Jensen. A judgment dissolving the marriage of the parties was entered on August 30, 1990. On July 15, 1991, a memorandum order was entered which resolved all remaining issues, including the amount of child support to be paid by Wronke for the two minor children of the parties. * * *

On October 5, 1995, Judge Ford found Wronke in indirect civil contempt of court and ordered that he was to be transported to the Champaign County Correctional Center until he purged himself of the contempt order. Judge Ford stated that Wronke could purge the contempt by "removing or causing to be removed, the names of his children from the sign along State Route 49 within 14 days of this order" and by "paying the child support arrearage of $44,226.20."

* * *

After the appellate court affirmed the circuit court's contempt order, Wronke filed a petition for leave to appeal with the Illinois Supreme Court. Leave to appeal was denied on October 2, 1996. * * * Wronke then filed a petition for certiorari to the United States Supreme Court. This petition was denied on January 21, 1997 * * *.

ANALYSIS

"Normally, the federal courts do not become involved in child support disputes, as this is one of the matters most clearly allocated to the state courts in our federal system." Puchner v. Kruziki, 111 F.3d 541, 542 (7th Cir.), *cert. denied*, 522 U.S. 862, 118 S.Ct. 166, 139 L.Ed.2d 109 (1997). In this case, as in *Puchner,* Wronke's failure to pay child support became a federal case when he sought a writ of habeas corpus under 28 U.S.C. § 2254 "challenging his incarceration pursuant to a contempt order entered by the state court judge." * * *

* * *

Wronke first argues that he is entitled to habeas corpus relief because he was denied his request for a jury trial and has, in fact, spent much more than six months in custody. Wronke also argues that his "incarceration for civil contempt interminably was contrary and repugnant to existing law constitutionally." * * *

It is true that a criminal contemnor cannot be imprisoned more than a total of six months without a jury trial. Cheff v. Schnackenberg, 384 U.S. 373, 380, 86 S.Ct. 1523, 16 L.Ed.2d 629 (1966). However, a jury trial is not required in civil contempt proceedings. Cheff, 384 U.S. at 377, 86 S.Ct. 1523; see also Hicks v. Feiock, 485 U.S. 624, 637, 108 S.Ct. 1423, 99 L.Ed.2d 721 (1988) (it is only when the punishment is criminal in nature that federal constitutional protections must be applied in the contempt proceeding).

Civil and criminal contempt differ in important respects. * * * " 'If it is for civil contempt the punishment is remedial, and for the benefit of the complainant. But if it is for criminal contempt the sentence is punitive, to vindicate the authority of the court.' " *Hicks*, 485 U.S. at 631, 108 S.Ct. 1423, 99 L.Ed.2d 721 (1988) (quoting Gompers v. Buck's Stove & Range Co., 221 U.S. 418, 441, 31 S.Ct. 492, 55 L.Ed. 797 (1911)). "[C]ivil contempt is a tool used by courts to compel compliance with their orders. The contemnor 'holds the keys to the jailhouse' in his own hands, and compliance produces an immediate release." *Puchner*, 111 F.3d at 543. In other words, imprisonment for civil contempt is "wholly avoidable." *Puchner*, 111 F.3d at 544. A civil or remedial contempt order is always dischargeable upon full compliance with the court's order. * * *

In this case, the court determined that Wronke was in indirect civil contempt of court because he violated a court order when he put his children's names on a sign and because he failed to pay $44,226.20 in court ordered child support, which the court found he had the ability to pay. Wronke could have avoided the contempt finding by complying with the terms of the circuit court's orders. In addition, Wronke could purge himself of the contempt, and secure his release from the Champaign County Correctional Center, by removing the names from the sign and by paying the overdue child support. Accordingly, Wronke's sanction is clearly civil in nature. * * * Therefore, Wronke had no right to a jury trial before being incarcerated for civil contempt.

Wronke's challenge to the indefinite length of his incarceration also fails on the merits. Incarceration for civil contempt may continue indefinitely. United States ex rel. Thom v. Jenkins, 760 F.2d 736, 740 (7th Cir.1985) * * *. This is because the contemnor has the ability to secure his release by complying with the court's orders. Accordingly, a civil contemnor may be incarcerated until he either complies with the court's order or adduces evidence as to his present inability to comply with that order. * * *

It is therefore ordered that the petition for writ of habeas corpus is denied.

NOTES

1.   The primary problem with the civil coercive contempt sanction is that the contemnor may stubbornly refuse to take advantage of the opportunity to

purge the contempt. *See generally* Doug Rendleman, *Disobedience and Coercive Contempt Confinement: The Terminally Stubborn Contemnor*, 48 Wash. & Lee L. Rev. 185 (1991). For example, in Sanders v. Shephard, 163 Ill.2d 534, 645 N.E.2d 900, 206 Ill.Dec. 648 (1994), a father was found in civil contempt for his failure to comply with an order directing him to produce his daughter, whom he had previously taken from the child's mother. The abduction had occurred in 1984, and the father had been sentenced to three years in prison for the criminal offense. Shortly before his scheduled release, the mother had obtained an ex parte temporary restraining order under the Illinois Domestic Violence Act. When the father failed to produce the child immediately upon his release from prison, the judge sentenced him to six months in jail, provided that he could purge the contempt at any time. The father did not produce the child. The judge then renewed the order every six months. In 1990, after the father had been in jail for three years, he filed a motion seeking to vacate the contempt on the grounds that the contempt sanction no longer had a coercive effect, and that his continued incarceration was therefore a denial of due process, citing to *In re* Crededio, 759 F.2d 589 (7th Cir.1985) (*see supra* Chapter 2.9.B.2). The trial court judge denied the motion to vacate, concluding that the sanction remained coercive, and the Supreme Court of Illinois affirmed:

> Although the passage of time is one consideration in determining whether a sanction for civil contempt remains coercive, time alone is not necessarily determinative. For obvious reasons, courts are reluctant to set precise limits on the length of time a civil contemnor may be obliged to stay in jail. The judge in the proceedings below carefully considered the record before him * * *. The present case involves a missing child; according to the evidence, the respondent was the last person seen with the child and, following the abduction, he made a number of threats against her. As we have noted, a judge's determination of this question is entitled to great deference. * * * There was sufficient evidence from which the [trial court] judge could find that the sanction continued to have a coercive effect.

163 Ill.2d at 544–45, 645 N.E.2d at 905–06, 206 Ill. Dec. at 653–54.

One suggested solution to the problem of the "stubborn contemnor" is the imposition of a single, fixed jail term with a purge clause. *See* Linda S. Beres, *Games Civil Contemnors Play*, 18 Harv. J.L. & Pub. Pol'y 795 (1995). Another suggested solution to the problem is the imposition of a statutory cap on civil coercive contempt sanctions for violations of equitable decrees, analogous to the statutory cap imposed on civil coercive contempt sanctions by the Federal Recalcitrant Witness Act, 28 U.S.C. § 1826(a) (placing an 18–month cap on the maximum period of confinement for civil coercive contempt when the contemnor is a recalcitrant witness in a proceeding before a federal court or grand jury). *See* Doug Rendleman, *Disobedience and Coercive Contempt Confinement: The Terminally Stubborn Contemnor*, 48 Wash. & Lee L. Rev. 185 (1991). In 1989, Congress enacted such a statutory cap in response to the case of Morgan v. Foretich, 564 A.2d 1 (D.C.App.1989) (*reh'g granted; opinion vacated*). Dr. Elizabeth Morgan divorced her husband, Dr. Eric Foretich, in 1983. In 1984, the trial court awarded Dr. Morgan custody of their daughter, Hillary, with visitation rights for Dr. Foretich. In 1985, Dr. Morgan alleged that her ex-husband was sexually abusing the child. In 1986, the trial court concluded that Dr. Morgan had failed to prove by a preponderance of the evidence that Dr. Foretich was sexually abusing the child. On August 19, 1987, the court ordered a two-week, unsupervised visitation of the child with Dr. Foretich, beginning three days later. Dr. Morgan, who remained convinced that her ex-husband was sexually abusing the child, had her parents smuggle Hillary out of the United States, and refused to make Hillary available for visitation. Deborah Zimmerman, *Civil Contemnors, Due Process, and the Right to Jury Trial*, 3 Wyo. L. Rev. 205, 206 (2003). The judge held Dr. Morgan in civil contempt of court, and ordered that she be jailed unless and until she delivered Hillary to Dr. Foretich. Dr. Morgan refused to purge herself of the contempt. She sat in jail for two years, until she was released by an act of Congress. D.C. Code Ann. § 11–741 (placing an 18–month cap on civil coercive contempt sanctions imposed in child custody proceedings by the judges of the District of Columbia).

A third technique for dealing with the problem of the "stubborn contemnor" is to impose a mixed civil and criminal contempt sanction. For example, in Ervin v. Iowa District Court, 495 N.W.2d 742 (Iowa 1993), the trial court judge found that Ervin's failure to comply with the court-imposed duty to construct fire lanes by moving tires at his tire reclamation plant was willful, and Ervin was sentenced to "six months in jail, with the provision that he be released after twenty days and given an opportunity to purge himself of contempt. Failure to begin construction of the fire lanes within two days following release would result in incarceration for the remainder of the six-month term." *Id.* at 744. The Iowa Supreme Court affirmed the imposition of the mixed civil and criminal contempt sanction because the trial court judge had conducted the contempt proceeding in accord with the rules of criminal procedure.

2. As illustrated by *Wronke*, the civil coercive contempt sanction is an effective means of enforcing an injunction that orders a defendant to perform an identifiable, affirmative act, provided the defendant is not a "stubborn contemnor," because the act of purging the contempt brings the defendant into compliance with the terms of the equitable decree. However, it is a less effective means of enforcing an injunction that prohibits the defendant from engaging in a certain type of conduct, such as trespassing on the plaintiff's land, particularly if the injunction is a general prohibition for the future. In the latter type of case, the court orders the defendant to go to jail or to pay a fine until the defendant agrees to comply with the terms of the prohibitory injunction, and the defendant may then purge the contempt by promising to comply with the terms of the decree, but there is no guarantee that the defendant will in fact continue to abide by the terms of the injunction in the future. To deal with this situation, trial court judges began to experiment with the imposition of "prospective coercive fines" in the 1980s and 1990s. For example, several state and federal courts imposed prospective fines on Operation Rescue in an effort to coerce compliance with injunctions that prohibited Operation Rescue from blocking the entrances to abortion clinics. *See, e.g.,* Roe v. Operation Rescue, 919 F.2d 857 (3d Cir.1990); New York State National Organization for Women v. Terry, 886 F.2d 1339 (2d Cir.1989); Vermont Women's Health Center v. Operation Rescue, 159 Vt. 141, 617 A.2d

411 (1992). In *Vermont Women's Health Center*, the Vermont Supreme Court explained why the imposition of prospective coercive fines against Operation Rescue participants was appropriate:

> [D]efendants argue that the [trial] court erred in imposing prospective coercive fines of $10,000 per day for the first violation of the order and $20,000 per day for further violations. Although purely prospective fines are not favored in Vermont, State v. Pownal Tanning Co., 142 Vt. 601, 606, 459 A.2d 989, 992 (1983), civil contempt fines may be imposed in an appropriate circumstance * * *. When imposed as a coercive sanction, the fine must be purgeable—that is, capable of being avoided by defendants through adherence to the court's order. *Pownal Tanning Co.*, 142 Vt. at 604, 459 A.2d at 991. Further, the situation must be such that "it is easy to gauge the compliance or noncompliance with an order." *Id.* at 606, 459 A.2d at 992.

> Both requirements imposed by *Pownal Tanning Co.* are met here. The fine will be due only upon a further violation of the injunction by one of the class of persons to which it is directed, with service or actual notice of its provisions. * * * [T]he injunction prohibits clearly defined conduct, participation in which can be readily ascertained.

> Further, the circumstances present here are extreme and extraordinary. In concluding that prospective fines were needed, the [trial] court emphasized the "violent tendencies" of defendants and the magnitude of the harm. It found that defendants' acts were "willful, outrageous, and presented a clear and present danger to the public health and safety." It also found that defendants claimed to act under "higher law" and did not feel bound by the injunction. This latter finding supports the conclusion that some coercive sanction is necessary in this case to deter repetition. We conclude that the imposition of a prospective coercive fine is reasonable in this case. *See* New York State National Organization for Women v. Terry, 886 F.2d 1339, 1353–54 (2d Cir.1989). Our disfavor of the use of prospective coercive fines must give way in this narrow and exceptional set of circumstances. No abuse of discretion is shown.

Id. at 151–52, 617 A.2d at 417. The Supreme Court of the United States considered the constitutionality of "prospective fines" in the next case.

4. Criminal vs. Civil Contempt Sanctions

INTERNATIONAL UNION, UNITED MINE WORKERS v. BAGWELL

Supreme Court of the United States, 1994.
512 U.S. 821, 114 S.Ct. 2552, 129 L.Ed.2d 642.

JUSTICE BLACKMUN delivered the opinion of the Court.

We are called upon once again to consider the distinction between civil and criminal contempt. Specifically, we address whether contempt fines levied against a union for violations of a labor injunction are coercive civil fines, or are criminal fines that constitutionally could be imposed only through a jury trial. * * *

I

Petitioners * * * engaged in a protracted labor dispute with the Clinchfield Coal Company and Sea "B" Mining Company (collectively, the companies) over alleged unfair labor practices. In April 1989, the companies filed suit in the Circuit Court of Russell County, Virginia, to enjoin the union from conducting unlawful strike-related activities. The trial court entered an injunction which * * * prohibited the union and its members from, among other things, obstructing ingress and egress to company facilities, throwing objects at and physically threatening company employees, placing tire-damaging "jackrocks" on roads used by company vehicles, and picketing with more than a specified number of people at designated sites. The court additionally ordered the union * * * to place supervisors at picket sites * * *.

On May 18, 1989, the trial court held a contempt hearing and found that petitioners had committed 72 violations of the injunction. After fining the union $642,000 for its disobedience, the court announced that it would fine the union $100,000 for any future violent breach of the injunction and $20,000 for any future nonviolent infraction, "such as exceeding picket numbers, [or] blocking entrances or exits." * * * [The court later vacated the $642,000 fine because it was "criminal in nature," and therefore it violated the Constitution of the United States because it had been imposed through civil proceedings.]

In seven subsequent contempt hearings held between June and December 1989, the court found the union in contempt for more than 400 separate violations of the injunction, many of them violent. Based on the court's stated "intention that these fines are civil and coercive," * * * each contempt hearing was conducted as a civil proceeding before the trial judge, in which the parties conducted discovery, introduced evidence, and called and cross-examined witnesses. The trial court required that contumacious acts be proved beyond a reasonable doubt, but did not afford the union a right to jury trial.

As a result of these contempt proceedings, the court levied over $64 million in fines against the union, approximately $12 million of which was ordered payable to the companies. Because the union objected to payment of any fines to the companies and in light of the law enforcement burdens posed by the strike, the court ordered that the remaining roughly $52 million in fines be paid to the Commonwealth of Virginia and Russell and Dickenson Counties, "the two counties most heavily affected by the unlawful activity." * * *

While appeals from the contempt orders were pending, the union and the companies settled the underlying labor dispute, agreed to vacate the contempt fines, and jointly moved to dismiss the case. A special mediator representing the Secretary of Labor * * * and the governments of Russell and Dickenson Counties * * * supported the parties' motion to vacate the outstanding fines. The trial court granted the motion to dismiss, dissolved the injunction, and vacated the $12 million in fines payable to the companies. After reiterating its belief that the remaining $52 million owed to the counties and the Commonwealth were coercive, civil fines, the trial court refused to vacate these fines, concluding they were "payable in effect to the public." * * *

The companies withdrew as parties in light of the settlement and declined to seek further enforcement of the outstanding contempt fines. Because the Commonwealth Attorneys of Russell and Dickenson Counties also had asked to be disqualified from the case, the court appointed respondent John L. Bagwell to act as Special Commissioner to collect the unpaid contempt fines on behalf of the counties and the Commonwealth. * * *

The Court of Appeals of Virginia reversed and ordered that the contempt fines be vacated pursuant to the settlement agreement. Assuming for the purposes of argument that the fines were civil, the court concluded that "civil contempt fines imposed during or as a part of a civil proceeding between private parties are settled when the underlying litigation is settled by the parties and the court is without discretion to refuse to vacate such fines." * * *

On consolidated appeals, the Supreme Court of Virginia reversed. The court held that whether coercive, civil contempt sanctions could be settled by private parties was a question of state law, and that Virginia public policy disfavored such a rule, "if the dignity of the law and public respect for the judiciary are to be maintained." * * * The court also rejected petitioners' contention that the outstanding fines were criminal and could not be imposed absent a criminal trial. Because the trial court's prospective fine schedule was intended to coerce compliance with the injunction and the union could avoid the fines through obedience, the court reasoned, the fines were civil and coercive and properly imposed in civil proceedings. * * *

[The Union in *Bagwell* had argued before the Virginia Supreme Court that coercive civil contempt sanctions were only appropriate to enforce a mandatory injunction, and not to enforce a prohibitory injunction. The Virginia Supreme Court responded as follows:

We reject this contention because we think it presents a distinction without a difference.

When a court orders a defendant to perform an affirmative act and provides that the defendant shall be fined a fixed amount for each day he refuses to comply, the defendant has control of his destiny. The same is true with respect to the court's orders in the present case. A prospective fine schedule was established solely for the purpose of coercing the Union to refrain from engaging in certain conduct. Consequently, the Union controlled its own fate.

* * * Furthermore, other courts share our view respecting the validity of employing a prospective, civil fine schedule to coerce defendants into future compliance with a court's *prohibitory* injunc-

tion. *See, e.g.,* New York State National Organization for Women v. Terry, 886 F.2d 1339, 1351 (2d Cir.1989), *cert. denied,* 495 U.S. 947, 110 S.Ct. 2206, 109 L.Ed.2d 532 (1990); Aradia Women's Health Center v. Operation Rescue, 929 F.2d 530, 532–33 (9th Cir.1991) * * *.

244 Va. 463, 478, 423 S.E.2d 349, 357–58 (1992).]

II

A

"Criminal contempt is a crime in the ordinary sense," Bloom v. Illinois, 391 U.S. 194, 201, 88 S.Ct. 1477, 1481, 20 L.Ed.2d 522 (1968), and "criminal penalties may not be imposed on someone who has not been afforded the protections that the Constitution requires of such criminal proceedings," Hicks v. Feiock, 485 U.S. 624, 632, 108 S.Ct. 1423, 1429–1430, 99 L.Ed.2d 721 (1988). *See* Gompers v. Bucks Stove & Range Co., 221 U.S. 418, 444, 31 S.Ct. 492, 499, 55 L.Ed. 797 (1911) (privilege against self-incrimination, right to proof beyond a reasonable doubt). For "serious" criminal contempts involving imprisonment of more than six months, these protections include the right to jury trial. * * * In contrast, civil contempt sanctions, or those penalties designed to compel future compliance with a court order, are considered to be coercive and avoidable through obedience, and thus may be imposed in an ordinary civil proceeding upon notice and an opportunity to be heard. Neither a jury trial nor proof beyond a reasonable doubt is required.[2]

Although the procedural contours of the two forms of contempt are well established, the distinguishing characteristics of civil versus criminal contempts are somewhat less clear.[3] In the leading early case addressing this issue in the context of imprisonment, Gompers v. Bucks Stove & Range Co., 221 U.S., at 441, 31 S.Ct., at 498, the Court emphasized that whether a contempt is civil or criminal turns on the "character and purpose" of the sanction involved. Thus, a contempt sanction is considered civil if it "is remedial, and for the benefit of the complainant. But if it is for criminal contempt the sentence is punitive, to vindicate the authority of the court." * * *

As *Gompers* recognized, however, the stated purposes of a contempt sanction alone cannot be determinative. * * * Most contempt sanctions, like most criminal punishments, to some extent punish a prior offense as well as coerce an offender's future obedience. The *Hicks* Court accordingly held that conclusions about the civil or criminal nature of a contempt

---

2. We address only the procedures required for adjudication of indirect contempts, i.e., those occurring out of court. Direct contempts that occur in the court's presence may be immediately adjudged and sanctioned summarily, * * * and, except for serious criminal contempts in which a jury trial is required, * * * the traditional distinction between civil and criminal contempt proceedings does not pertain * * *.

3. Numerous scholars have criticized as unworkable the traditional distinction between civil and criminal contempt. *See, e.g.,* Dudley, *Getting Beyond the Civil/Criminal Distinction: A New Approach to the Regulation of Indirect Contempts,* 79 Va. L. Rev. 1025, 1033 (1993) [(suggesting that there should be a right to jury trial for all indirect contempt sanctions)] * * *.

sanction are properly drawn, not from "the subjective intent of a State's laws and its courts," * * * but "from an examination of the character of the relief itself" * * *.

The paradigmatic coercive, civil contempt sanction * * * involves confining a contemnor indefinitely until he complies with an affirmative command such as an order "to pay alimony, or to surrender property ordered to be turned over to a receiver, or to make a conveyance." * * * Imprisonment for a fixed term similarly is coercive when the contemnor is given the option of earlier release if he complies. Shillitani v. United States, 384 U.S. 364, 370, n.6, 86 S.Ct., 1531, 1536, n.6, 16 L.Ed.2d 622 (1966) (upholding as civil "a determinate [2–year] sentence which includes a purge clause"). In these circumstances, the contemnor is able to purge the contempt and obtain his release by committing an affirmative act, and thus " 'carries the keys of his prison in his own pocket.' " * * *

By contrast, a fixed sentence of imprisonment is punitive and criminal if it is imposed retrospectively for a "completed act of disobedience," * * * such that the contemnor cannot avoid or abbreviate the confinement through later compliance. Thus, the *Gompers* Court concluded that a 12–month sentence imposed on Samuel Gompers for violating an anti-boycott injunction was criminal. When a contempt involves the prior conduct of an isolated, prohibited act, the resulting sanction has no coercive effect. "[T]he defendant is furnished no key, and he cannot shorten the term by promising not to repeat the offense." *Id.*, at 442, 31 S.Ct., at 498.

This dichotomy between coercive and punitive imprisonment has been extended to the fine context. A contempt fine accordingly is considered civil and remedial if it either "coerce[s] the defendant into compliance with the court's order, [or] . . . compensate[s] the complainant for losses sustained." United States v. Mine Workers, 330 U.S. 258, 303–304, 67 S.Ct. 677, 701, 91 L.Ed. 884 (1947). Where a fine is not compensatory, it is civil only if the contemnor is afforded an opportunity to purge. *See* Penfield Co. of Cal. v. SEC, 330 U.S. 585, 590, 67 S.Ct. 918, 921, 91 L.Ed. 1117 (1947). Thus, a "flat, unconditional fine" totaling even as little as $50 announced after a finding of contempt is criminal if the contemnor has no subsequent opportunity to reduce or avoid the fine through compliance. *Id.*, at 588, 67 S.Ct., at 920.

A close analogy to coercive imprisonment is a per diem fine imposed for each day a contemnor fails to comply with an affirmative court order. Like civil imprisonment, such fines exert a constant coercive pressure, and once the jural command is obeyed, the future, indefinite, daily fines are purged. Less comfortable is the analogy between coercive imprisonment and suspended, determinate fines. In this Court's sole prior decision squarely addressing the judicial power to impose coercive civil contempt fines, *Mine Workers, supra,* it held that fixed fines also may be considered purgeable and civil when imposed and suspended pending future compliance. * * * *Mine Workers* involved a $3,500,000 fine imposed against the union for nationwide post-World War II strike activities. Finding that the determinate fine was both criminal and excessive, the Court reduced the sanction to a flat criminal fine of $700,000. The Court then imposed and suspended the remaining $2,800,000 as a coercive civil fine, conditioned on the union's ability to purge the fine through full, timely compliance with the trial court's order.[4] The Court concluded, in light of this purge clause, that the civil fine operated as "a coercive imposition upon the defendant union to compel obedience with the court's outstanding order." 330 U.S., at 307, 67 S.Ct., at 703.

This Court has not revisited the issue of coercive civil contempt fines addressed in *Mine Workers*. Since that decision, the Court has erected substantial procedural protections in other areas of contempt law, such as criminal contempts, *e.g.*, Bloom v. Illinois, 391 U.S. 194, 88 S.Ct. 1477, 20 L.Ed.2d 522 (1968), and summary contempts, *e.g.*, * * * Codispoti v. Pennsylvania, 418 U.S. 506, 513, 94 S.Ct. 2687, 2691, 41 L.Ed.2d 912 (1974) * * *. Lower federal courts and state courts such as the trial court here nevertheless have relied on *Mine Workers* to authorize a relatively unlimited judicial power to impose noncompensatory civil contempt fines.

B

Underlying the somewhat elusive distinction between civil and criminal contempt fines, and the ultimate question posed in this case, is what procedural protections are due before any particular contempt penalty may be imposed. Because civil contempt sanctions are viewed as nonpunitive and avoidable, fewer procedural protections for such sanctions have been required. To the extent that such contempts take on a punitive character, however, and are not justified by other considerations central to the contempt power, criminal procedural protections may be in order.

The traditional justification for the relative breadth of the contempt power has been necessity: Courts independently must be vested with "power to impose silence, respect, and decorum, in their presence, and submission to their lawful mandates, and ... to preserve themselves and their officers from the approach and insults of pollution." Anderson v. Dunn, 6 Wheat. 204, 227, 5 L.Ed. 242 (1821). * * *

But the contempt power also uniquely is "liable to abuse." * * * Unlike most areas of law, where a legislature defines both the sanctionable conduct and the penalty to be imposed, civil contempt proceedings leave the offended judge solely responsible for identifying, prosecuting, adjudicating, and sanctioning the contumacious conduct. * * * Young v. United States *ex rel*. Vuitton et Fils S.A., 481 U.S. 787, 822, 107 S.Ct. 2124, 2145, 95 L.Ed.2d 740 (1987) (Scalia, J., concurring in judgment) * * *. Accordingly, "in [criminal] contempt cases an even more compelling

---

4. Although the size of the fine was substantial, the conduct required of the union to purge the suspended fine was relatively discrete. According to the Court, purgation consisted of (1) withdrawal of the union's notice terminating the Krug–Lewis labor agreement; (2) notifying the union members of this withdrawal; and (3) withdrawing and notifying the union members of the withdrawal of any other notice questioning the ongoing effectiveness of the Krug–Lewis agreement. United States v. Mine Workers, 330 U.S. 258, 305, 67 S.Ct. 677, 702, 91 L.Ed. 884 (1947).

argument can be made [than in ordinary criminal cases] for providing a right to jury trial as a protection against the arbitrary exercise of official power." *Bloom*, 391 U.S., at 202, 88 S.Ct., at 1482.

Our jurisprudence in the contempt area has attempted to balance the competing concerns of necessity and potential arbitrariness by allowing a relatively unencumbered contempt power when its exercise is most essential, and requiring progressively greater procedural protections when other considerations come into play. The necessity justification for the contempt authority is at its pinnacle, of course, where contumacious conduct threatens a court's immediate ability to conduct its proceedings, such as where a witness refuses to testify, or a party disrupts the court. * * * In light of the court's substantial interest in rapidly coercing compliance and restoring order, and because the contempt's occurrence before the court reduces the need for extensive fact-finding and the likelihood of an erroneous deprivation, summary proceedings have been tolerated.

Summary adjudication becomes less justifiable once a court leaves the realm of immediately sanctioned, petty direct contempts. If a court delays punishing a direct contempt until the completion of trial, for example, due process requires that the contemnor's rights to notice and a hearing be respected. * * * Direct contempts also cannot be punished with serious criminal penalties absent the full protections of a criminal jury trial. *Bloom*, 391 U.S., at 210, 88 S.Ct., at 1486.

Still further procedural protections are afforded for contempts occurring out of court, where the considerations justifying expedited procedures do not pertain. Summary adjudication of indirect contempts is prohibited, * * * and criminal contempt sanctions are entitled to full criminal process * * *. Certain indirect contempts nevertheless are appropriate for imposition through civil proceedings. Contempts such as failure to comply with document discovery, for example, while occurring outside the court's presence, impede the court's ability to adjudicate the proceedings before it and thus touch upon the core justification for the contempt power. Courts traditionally have broad authority through means other than contempt— such as by striking pleadings, assessing costs, excluding evidence, and entering default judgment—to penalize a party's failure to comply with the rules of conduct governing the litigation process. * * * Such judicial sanctions never have been considered criminal, and the imposition of civil, coercive fines to police the litigation process appears consistent with this authority. Similarly, indirect contempts involving discrete, readily ascertainable acts, such as turning over a key or payment of a judgment, properly may be adjudicated through civil proceedings since the need for extensive, impartial fact-finding is less pressing.

For a discrete category of indirect contempts, however, civil procedural protections may be insufficient. Contempts involving out-of-court disobedience to complex injunctions often require elaborate and reliable fact-finding. * * * Such contempts do not obstruct the court's ability to adjudicate the proceedings before it, and the risk of erroneous deprivation from the lack of a neutral factfinder may be substantial. * * * Under these circumstances, criminal procedural protections such as the rights to counsel and proof beyond a reasonable doubt are both necessary and appropriate to protect the due process rights of parties and prevent the arbitrary exercise of judicial power.

C

In the instant case, neither any party nor any court of the Commonwealth has suggested that the challenged fines are compensatory. At no point did the trial court attempt to calibrate the fines to damages caused by the union's contumacious activities or indicate that the fines were "to compensate the complainant for losses sustained." *Mine Workers*, 330 U.S., at 303–04, 67 S.Ct., at 701. The nonparty governments, in turn, never requested any compensation or presented any evidence regarding their injuries, never moved to intervene in the suit, and never actively defended the fines imposed. The issue before us accordingly is limited to whether these fines, despite their noncompensatory character, are coercive civil or criminal sanctions.

The parties propose two independent tests for determining whether the fines are civil or criminal. Petitioners argue that because the injunction primarily prohibited certain conduct rather than mandated affirmative acts, the sanctions are criminal. Respondents in turn urge that because the trial court established a prospective fine schedule that the union could avoid through compliance, the fines are civil in character.

Neither theory satisfactorily identifies those contempt fines that are criminal and thus must be imposed through the criminal process. Petitioners correctly note that *Gompers* suggests a possible dichotomy "between refusing to do an act commanded,—remedied by imprisonment until the party performs the required act; and doing an act forbidden,—punished by imprisonment for a definite term." 221 U.S., at 443, 31 S.Ct., at 498. The distinction between mandatory and prohibitory orders is easily applied in the classic contempt scenario, where contempt sanctions are used to enforce orders compelling or forbidding a single, discrete act. In such cases, orders commanding an affirmative act simply designate those actions that are capable of being coerced.

But the distinction between coercion of affirmative acts and punishment of prohibited conduct is difficult to apply when conduct that can recur is involved, or when an injunction contains both mandatory and prohibitory provisions. Moreover, in borderline cases injunctive provisions containing essentially the same command can be phrased either in mandatory or prohibitory terms. Under a literal application of petitioners' theory, an injunction ordering the union: "Do not strike," would appear to be prohibitory and criminal, while an injunction ordering the union: "Continue working," would be mandatory and civil. *See* * * * Dobbs, *Contempt of Court: A Survey*, 56 Cornell L. Rev. 183, 239 (1971). In enforcing the present injunction, the trial court imposed fines without regard to the mandatory or prohibitory nature of the clause violated. Accordingly, even though a parsing of the injunction's various provisions might support the classification of contempts such as rock throwing and placing tire-damaging "jackrocks" on roads as criminal and the refusal to place supervisors at picket sites as civil, the parties have not asked us to review the order in that manner. In a case like this involving an injunction that prescribes a detailed code of conduct, it is more appropriate to identify the character of the entire decree. *Cf. Hicks*, 485 U.S., at 638, n.10, 108 S.Ct., at 1433, n.10 (internal quotation marks omitted) (Where both civil and criminal relief is imposed "the criminal feature of the order is dominant and fixes its character for purposes of review").

Despite respondents' urging, we also are not persuaded that dispositive significance should be accorded to the fact that the trial court prospectively announced the sanctions it would impose. Had the trial court simply levied the fines after finding the union guilty of contempt, the resulting "determinate and unconditional" fines would be considered "solely and exclusively punitive." * * * Respondents nevertheless contend that the trial court's announcement of a prospective fine schedule allowed the union to "avoid paying the fine[s] simply by performing the ... act required by the court's order," *Hicks*, 485 U.S., at 632, 108 S.Ct., at 1429, and thus transformed these fines into coercive, civil ones. Respondents maintain here, as the Virginia Supreme Court held below, that the trial court could have imposed a daily civil fine to coerce the union into compliance, and that a prospective fine schedule is indistinguishable from such a sanction.

Respondents' argument highlights the difficulties encountered in parsing coercive civil and criminal contempt fines. The fines imposed here concededly are difficult to distinguish either from determinate, punitive fines or from initially suspended, civil fines. Ultimately, however, the fact that the trial court announced the fines before the contumacy, rather than after the fact, does not in itself justify respondents' conclusion that the fines are civil or meaningfully distinguish these penalties from the ordinary criminal law. Due process traditionally requires that criminal laws provide prior notice both of the conduct to be prohibited and of the sanction to be imposed. The trial court here simply announced the penalty—determinate fines of $20,000 or $100,000 per violation—that would be imposed for future contempts. The union's ability to avoid the contempt fines was indistinguishable from the ability of any ordinary citizen to avoid a criminal sanction by conforming his behavior to the law. The fines are not coercive day fines, or even suspended fines, but are more closely analogous to fixed, determinate, retrospective criminal fines which petitioners had no opportunity to purge once imposed. We therefore decline to conclude that the mere fact that the sanctions were announced in advance rendered them coercive and civil as a matter of constitutional law.

Other considerations convince us that the fines challenged here are criminal. The union's sanctionable conduct did not occur in the court's presence or otherwise implicate the court's ability to maintain order and adjudicate the proceedings before it. Nor did the union's contumacy involve simple, affirmative acts, such as the paradigmatic civil contempts examined in *Gompers*. Instead, the Virginia trial court levied contempt fines for widespread, ongoing, out-of-court violations of a complex injunction. In so doing, the court effectively policed petitioners' compliance with an entire code of conduct that the court itself had imposed. The union's contumacy lasted many months and spanned a substantial portion of the State. The fines assessed were serious, totaling over $52 million.[5] Under such circumstances, disinterested fact-finding and evenhanded adjudication were essential, and petitioners were entitled to a criminal jury trial.

* * * [T]his Court has recognized that * * * the label affixed to a contempt ultimately "will not be allowed to defeat the applicable protections of federal constitutional law." Hicks v. Feiock, 485 U.S., at 631, 108 S.Ct., at 1429. We conclude that the serious contempt fines imposed here were criminal and constitutionally could not be imposed absent a jury trial.

III

Our decision concededly imposes some procedural burdens on courts' ability to sanction widespread, indirect contempts of complex injunctions through noncompensatory fines. Our holding, however, leaves unaltered the longstanding authority of judges to adjudicate direct contempts summarily, and to enter broad compensatory awards for all contempts through civil proceedings. *See, e.g.*, Sheet Metal Workers v. EEOC, 478 U.S. 421, 106 S.Ct. 3019, 92 L.Ed.2d 344 (1986). Because the right to trial by jury applies only to serious criminal sanctions, courts still may impose noncompensatory, petty fines for contempts such as the present ones without conducting a jury trial. We also do not disturb a court's ability to levy, albeit through the criminal contempt process, serious fines like those in this case.

Ultimately, whatever slight burden our holding may impose on the judicial contempt power cannot be controlling. * * * *Bloom*, 391 U.S., at 208, 88 S.Ct., at 1485. Where, as here, "a contempt is at issue, considerations of efficiency must give way to the more fundamental interest of ensuring the even-handed exercise of judicial power." *Id.* at 209, 88 S.Ct., at 1486.

---

5. "[P]etty contempt like other petty criminal offenses may be tried without a jury," Taylor v. Hayes, 418 U.S. 488, 495, 94 S.Ct. 2697, 2701, 41 L.Ed.2d 897 (1974), and the imposition only of serious criminal contempt fines triggers the right to jury trial. *Bloom*, 391 U.S., at 210, 88 S.Ct., at 1486. The Court to date has not specified what magnitude of contempt fine may constitute a serious criminal sanction, although it has held that a fine of $10,000 imposed on a union was insufficient to trigger the Sixth Amendment right to jury trial. *See* Muniz v. Hoffman, 422 U.S. 454, 477, 95 S.Ct. 2178, 2190, 45 L.Ed.2d 319 (1975); *see also* 18 U.S.C. § 1(3) (1982 ed., Supp. V) (defining petty offenses as crimes "the penalty for which ... does not exceed imprisonment for a period of six months or a fine of not more than $5,000 for an individual and $10,000 for a person other than an individual, or both") (repealed 1984). We need not answer today the difficult question where the line between petty and serious contempt fines should be drawn, since a $52 million fine unquestionably is a serious contempt sanction.

The judgment of the Supreme Court of Virginia is reversed.

JUSTICE SCALIA, concurring.

I join the Court's opinion classifying the $52 million in contempt fines levied against petitioners as criminal. As the Court's opinion demonstrates, our cases have employed a variety of not easily reconcilable tests for differentiating between civil and criminal contempts. Since all of those tests would yield the same result here, there is no need to decide which is the correct one—and a case so extreme on its facts is not the best case in which to make that decision. I wish to suggest, however, that when we come to making it, a careful examination of historical practice will ultimately yield the answer.

That one and the same person should be able to make the rule, to adjudicate its violation, and to assess its penalty is out of accord with our usual notions of fairness and separation of powers. * * * And it is worse still for that person to conduct the adjudication without affording the protections usually given in criminal trials. Only the clearest of historical practice could establish that such a departure from the procedures that the Constitution normally requires is not a denial of due process of law. * * *

At common law, contempts were divided into criminal contempts, in which a litigant was punished for an affront to the court by a fixed fine or period of incarceration; and civil contempts, in which an uncooperative litigant was incarcerated (and, in later cases, fined[1]) until he complied with a specific order of the court. * * * Incarceration until compliance was a distinctive sanction, and sheds light upon the nature of the decrees enforced by civil contempt. That sanction makes sense only if the order requires performance of an identifiable act (or perhaps cessation of continuing performance of an identifiable act). A general prohibition for the future does not lend itself to enforcement through conditional incarceration, since no single act (or the cessation of no single act) can demonstrate compliance and justify release. * * *

As one would expect from this, the orders that underlay civil contempt fines or incarceration were usually mandatory rather than prohibitory, * * * directing litigants to perform acts that would further the litigation (for example, turning over a document), or give effect to the court's judgment (for example, executing a deed of conveyance). * * * The mandatory injunctions issued upon termination of litigation usually required "a single simple act." H. McClintock, Principles of Equity § 15, pp. 32–33 (2d ed.1948). Indeed, there was a "historical prejudice of the court of chancery against rendering decrees which called for more than a single affirmative act." Id., § 61, at 160. And where specific performance of contracts was sought, it was the categorical rule that no decree would

---

1. The per diem fines that came to be used to coerce compliance with decrees were in most relevant respects like conditional prison terms. With them, as with incarceration, the penalty continued until the contemnor complied, and compliance stopped any further punishment but of course did not eliminate or restore any punishment already endured.

issue that required ongoing supervision. * * * Compliance with these "single act" mandates could, in addition to being simple, be quick; and once it was achieved the contemnor's relationship with the court came to an end * * *.

Even equitable decrees that were prohibitory rather than mandatory were, in earlier times, much less sweeping than their modern counterparts. Prior to the labor injunctions of the late 1800's, injunctions were issued primarily in relatively narrow disputes over property. * * *

Contemporary courts have abandoned these earlier limitations upon the scope of their mandatory and injunctive decrees. * * * They routinely issue complex decrees which involve them in extended disputes and place them in continuing supervisory roles over parties and institutions. *See, e.g.*, Missouri v. Jenkins, 495 U.S. 33, 56–58, 110 S.Ct. 1651, 1665–1666, 109 L.Ed.2d 31 (1990); Swann v. Charlotte–Mecklenburg Bd. of Ed., 402 U.S. 1, 16, 91 S.Ct. 1267, 1276, 28 L.Ed.2d 554 (1971). Professor Chayes has described the extent of the transformation:

> "[The modern decree] differs in almost every relevant characteristic from relief in the traditional model of adjudication, not the least in that it is the centerpiece.... It provides for a complex, on-going regime of performance rather than a simple, one-shot, one-way transfer. Finally, it prolongs and deepens, rather than terminates, the court's involvement with the dispute." Chayes, *The Role of the Judge in Public Law Litigation*, 89 Harv. L. Rev. 1281, 1298 (1976).

The consequences of this change for the point under discussion here are obvious: When an order governs many aspects of a litigant's activities, rather than just a discrete act, determining compliance becomes much more difficult. Credibility issues arise, for which the fact-finding protections of the criminal law (including jury trial) become much more important. And when continuing prohibitions or obligations are imposed, the order cannot be complied with (and the contempt "purged") in a single act; it continues to govern the party's behavior, on pain of punishment— not unlike the criminal law.

The order at issue here provides a relatively tame example of the modern, complex decree. The amended injunction prohibited, inter alia, rock throwing, the puncturing of tires, threatening, following or interfering with respondents' employees, placing pickets in other than specified locations, and roving picketing; and it required, inter alia, that petitioners provide a list of names of designated supervisors. * * * Although it would seem quite in accord with historical practice to enforce, by conditional incarceration or per diem fines, compliance with the last provision—a discrete command, observance of which is readily ascertained—using that same means to enforce the remainder of the order would be a novelty.

* * * As the scope of injunctions has expanded, they have lost some of the distinctive features that made enforcement through civil process acceptable. It is not that the times, or our perceptions of fairness, have changed (that is in my view no basis for either tightening or relaxing the

traditional demands of due process); but rather that the modern judicial order is in its relevant essentials not the same device that in former times could always be enforced by civil contempt. So adjustments will have to be made. We will have to decide at some point which modern injunctions sufficiently resemble their historical namesakes to warrant the same extraordinary means of enforcement. We need not draw that line in the present case, and so I am content to join the opinion of the Court.

JUSTICE GINSBURG, with whom the CHIEF JUSTICE joins, concurring in part and concurring in the judgment.

The issue in this case is whether the contempt proceedings brought against the petitioner unions are to be classified as "civil" or "criminal." As the Court explains, if those proceedings were "criminal," then the unions were entitled under our precedents to a jury trial, and the disputed fines, imposed in bench proceedings, could not stand. * * *

I

Gompers v. Bucks Stove & Range Co., 221 U.S. 418, 31 S.Ct. 492, 55 L.Ed. 797 (1911), as the Court notes, * * * is a pathmarking case in this area. The civil contempt sanction, *Gompers* instructs, is designed "to coerce the defendant to do the thing required by the order for the benefit of the complainant * * *."

The criminal contempt sanction, by contrast, * * * operates not to coerce a future act from the defendant for the benefit of the complainant, but to uphold the dignity of the law, by punishing the contemnor's disobedience. * * *

Even as it outlined these civil and criminal contempt prototypes, however, the Court in *Gompers* acknowledged that the categories, when filled by actual cases, are not altogether neat and tidy. Civil contempt proceedings, although primarily remedial, also "vindicat[e] ... the court's authority"; and criminal contempt proceedings, although designed "to vindicate the authority of the law," may bestow "some incidental benefit" upon the complainant, because "such punishment tends to prevent a repetition of the disobedience." * * *

II

* * *

Two considerations persuade me that the contempt proceedings in this case should be classified as "criminal" rather than "civil." First, were we to accept the logic of Bagwell's argument that the fines here were civil, because "conditional" and "coercive," no fine would elude that categorization. The fines in this case were "conditional," Bagwell says, because they would not have been imposed if the unions had complied with the injunction. The fines would have been "conditional" in this sense, however, even if the court had not supplemented the injunction with its fines schedule; indeed, any fine is "conditional" upon compliance or noncompliance before its imposition. *Cf. ante* at 2562 (the unions' ability to avoid imposition of the fines was "indistinguishable from the ability of any ordinary citizen to avoid a criminal sanction by conforming his behavior to the law"). Furthermore, while the fines were "coercive," in the sense that one of their purposes was to encourage union compliance with the injunction, criminal contempt sanctions may also "coerce" in the same sense, for they, too, "ten[d] to prevent a repetition of the disobedience." * * * Bagwell's thesis that the fines were civil, because "conditional" and "coercive," would so broaden the compass of those terms that their line-drawing function would be lost.[1]

Second, the Virginia courts' refusal to vacate the fines, despite the parties' settlement and joint motion, * * * is characteristic of criminal, not civil, proceedings. In explaining why the fines outlived the underlying civil dispute, the Supreme Court of Virginia stated: "Courts of the Commonwealth must have the authority to enforce their orders by employing coercive, civil sanctions if the dignity of the law and public respect for the judiciary are to be maintained." 244 Va. 463, 478, 423 S.E.2d 349, 358 (1992). The Virginia court's references to upholding public authority and maintaining "the dignity of the law" reflect the very purposes *Gompers* ranked on the criminal contempt side. * * * Moreover, with the private complainant gone from the scene, and an official appointed by the Commonwealth to collect the fines for the Commonwealth's coffers, it is implausible to invoke the justification of benefitting the civil complainant. The Commonwealth here pursues the fines on its own account, not as the agent of a private party, and without tying the exactions exclusively to a claim for compensation. If, as the trial court declared, the proceedings were indeed civil from the outset, then the court should have granted the parties' motions to vacate the fines.

Concluding that the fines at issue "are more closely analogous to ... criminal fines" than to civil fines, * * * I join the Court's judgment and all but Part II–B of its opinion.

NOTES

1. What is the holding of *Bagwell*? Some courts have said that *Bagwell* requires criminal procedures, including the right to jury trial for the imposition of a "serious sanction," whenever a court imposes a civil coercive contempt sanction to enforce a "complex injunction." *See, e.g.*, National Organization for Women v. Operation Rescue, 37 F.3d 646 (D.C.Cir.1994) (reversing a prospective civil coercive contempt fine imposed in accordance with a previously-announced schedule of sanctions to enforce a "complex injunction" prohibiting the obstruction of access to abortion clinics). Often,

---

1. Bagwell further likens the prospective fines schedule to the civil contempt fine imposed in United States v. Mine Workers, 330 U.S. 258, 67 S.Ct. 677, 91 L.Ed. 884 (1947). In that case, however, the contemnor union was given an opportunity, after the fine was imposed, to avoid the fine by "effect[ing] full compliance" with the injunction. As the Court explains, *see ante*, at 2558, n.4, for purposes of allowing the union to avoid the fine, "full compliance" with the broad no-strike injunction, * * * was reduced to the performance of three affirmative acts. This opportunity to purge, consistent with the civil contempt scenario described in *Gompers*, * * * was unavailable to the unions in this case.

however, these same courts have found that the injunction at issue was a "simple," rather than a "complex" injunction. *See, e.g.,* United States v. Santee Sioux Tribe, 254 F.3d 728, 736 (8th Cir.2001). *But see* Jake's, Ltd. v. City of Coates, 356 F.3d 896 (8th Cir.2004). Other courts have said that *Bagwell's* discussion of "complex injunctions" is "dicta": "We read *Bagwell* to leave in place just two traditional types of contempt: civil contempt and criminal contempt." Federal Trade Commission v. Kuykendall, 371 F.3d 745 (10th Cir.2004) (en banc). *Accord* Federal Trade Commission v. Trudeau, 579 F.3d 754 (7th Cir.2009). These courts are willing to uphold prospective civil coercive contempt fines, provided there is a "purge clause" which gives the defendants "an opportunity to purge * * * [the fines] once imposed." New York State National Organization for Women v. Terry, 159 F.3d 86, 94 (2d Cir.1998), *cert. denied,* 527 U.S. 1003, 119 S.Ct. 2336, 144 L.Ed.2d 234 (1999) (defendants were given an opportunity to purge prospective civil coercive fines by publishing, within sixty days from the date of the hearing when the court had assessed the fines, an affirmation of their intent to abide by the permanent injunction prohibiting the obstruction of access to abortion clinics). *See also* Jessica Kornberg, *Rethinking Civil Contempt Incarceration,* 44 No.1 Crim. L. Bull. Art. 4 (2008)(observing that, since *Bagwell,* the ability to purge has emerged as the dominant approach to defining the distinction between civil and criminal contempt).

2. Note that all of the justices in *Bagwell* distinguished civil coercive contempt sanctions from civil compensatory contempt sanctions, thereby suggesting that civil procedures continue to be appropriate for the imposition of compensatory contempt sanctions. *See, e.g.,* Federal Trade Commission v. Kuykendall, 371 F.3d 745 (10th Cir.2004) (en banc) (affirming the imposition of a civil compensatory contempt sanction through civil proceedings to enforce an injunction that banned telemarketers from the magazine sales business).

3. According to the Supreme Court's opinion in *Bagwell,* what types of contempt sanctions could the trial court judge in *Bagwell* have imposed sitting without a jury? For a discussion of the Court's holding in *Bagwell,* see Philip A. Hostak, *International Union, United Mineworkers v. Bagwell: A Paradigm Shift in the Distinction Between Civil and Criminal Contempt,* 81 Cornell L. Rev. 162 (1995); Margit Livingston, *Disobedience and Contempt,* 75 Wash. L. Rev. 345 (2000).

4. *Bagwell* left open the question of where to draw the line between a "petty" and a "serious" criminal contempt fine against a union or corporation. For lower federal court cases discussing this issue, see United States v. Twentieth Century Fox Film Corp., 882 F.2d 656, 664–65 (2d Cir.1989), *cert. denied,* 493 U.S. 1021, 110 S.Ct. 722, 107 L.Ed.2d 741 (1990) (a corporation has a right to jury trial if a criminal contempt fine exceeds $100,000; if a fine is below that amount, "it will remain appropriate to consider whether the fine has such a significant financial impact upon a particular organization as to indicate that the punishment is for a serious offense"); United States v. Troxler Hosiery Co., 681 F.2d 934 (4th Cir.1982) ($80,000 criminal contempt fine imposed without a jury trial on a corporation with a net worth of $540,000); United States v. NYNEX Corp., 781 F.Supp. 19 (D.D.C.1991) ($1,000,000 criminal contempt fine imposed without a jury trial on a corporation with an annual net income of over $1 billion) (court concluded that it was

better "to weigh a fine against a firm's ability to pay in ascertaining whether a fine is so serious as to warrant a trial by jury"). For commentary on the issue, see F. Joseph Warin & Michael D. Bopp, *Corporations, Criminal Contempt and the Constitution: Do Corporations Have a Sixth Amendment Right to Trial by Jury in Criminal Contempt Actions and, if so, Under What Circumstances?*, 1997 Colum. Bus. L. Rev. 1; Melissa Hartigan, Comment, *Creatures of the Common Law: The Petty Offense Doctrine and 18 U.S.C. § 19*, 59 Mont. L. Rev. 343 (1998). *See also* Margaret Meriwether Cordray, *Contempt Sanctions and the Excessive Fines Clause*, 76 N.C. L. Rev. 407 (1998) (arguing that both criminal and civil contempt fines ought to be subject to review under the Eighth Amendment's Excessive Fines Clause).

5. *Bagwell* did not discuss the question of how to draft a purge clause when imposing a civil coercive fine. In the case of a mandatory injunction (or an injunction prohibiting the performance of an identifiable act), it is relatively simple: the court imposes the coercive fine unless and until the defendant performs (or agrees to perform) the act required by the equitable decree. In the case of a prohibitory injunction requiring the cessation of continuing misconduct, such as a continuing trespass, it is more complicated: the court imposes the coercive fine unless and until the defendant publicly announces its intent to abide by the terms of the decree. *See, e.g.*, New York State National Organization for Women v. Terry, 159 F.3d 86 (2d Cir.1998).

6. *Bagwell* also did not discuss how to administer a purge clause. When a court imposes a civil coercive jail sanction, it is administered by a two-step process: First the injunction is issued, and then the defendant is held in contempt and sent to jail until the purgation conditions are fulfilled. In NLRB v. Ironworkers Local 433, 169 F.3d 1217, 1221 (9th Cir.1999), the court concluded that *Bagwell* did not alter the standard three-step process for administering civil coercive contempt fines:

1) a court issues an equitable decree;

2) a court finds that the defendant has violated the decree and issues a conditional order threatening to impose a specified penalty unless the defendant purges the contempt; and

3) a court exacts the threatened penalty if the purgation conditions are not fulfilled by imposing a "non-compliance" fine in a fixed amount pursuant to civil (as opposed to criminal) procedures.

For a discussion of this three-step process, see NLRB v. Blevins Popcorn Co., 659 F.2d 1173, 1184–85 (D.C.Cir.1981); Hoffman v. Beer Drivers & Salesmen's Local Union No. 888, 536 F.2d 1268, 1273 (9th Cir.1976) ("Always the final order requiring payment will follow the act or omission which constitutes the failure to purge.")

7. In *Bagwell*, the Court identified the "paradigmatic coercive, civil contempt sanction" as involving the confinement of a contemnor "indefinitely" until he complies with an affirmative command. A few courts have interpreted this passage as a repudiation of the *Simkin* doctrine (*see supra* Chapter 2.9.B.2), which permits the release of a stubborn contemnor from jail when the coercive contempt sanction has lost its coercive impact. *See, e.g.*, Chadwick v. Janecka, 312 F.3d 597, 608 (3d Cir.2002) (refusing to release a

"stubborn" contemnor on the ground that a civil coercive contempt sanction may be imposed indefinitely; contemnor had been in jail for five years).

8. The following case, which was decided after *Bagwell*, involves the enforcement of a structural injunction. Recall that, in *Bagwell*, Justice Scalia identified structural injunctions as "complex" injunctions. *See also* Evans v. Williams, 206 F.3d 1292 (D.C.Cir.2000) (reversing a $5,096,340 prospective civil coercive contempt sanction imposed in a civil proceeding to enforce a structural injunction which the appellate court described as "complex"). Did *Bagwell* influence the trial court's enforcement of the structural injunction in the next case?

UNITED STATES v. TENNESSEE

United States District Court, Western District of Tennessee, 1995.
925 F.Supp. 1292.

McCalla, District Judge.

This case is before the Court for a determination regarding compliance by the State of Tennessee, Governor Sundquist, Commissioner Cardwell, and Superintendent Jackson with the provisions of the Emergency Order of June 30, 1995 (hereinafter "Emergency Order"), and the Preliminary Injunction of July 10, 1995 (hereinafter "Preliminary Injunction") (also hereinafter "Orders"). The question of compliance arises in the context of a contempt finding by the Court at a hearing on August 9, 1995 * * *. [The court imposed civil contempt sanctions.] Since that finding, defendants have filed two motions for a determination of partial or complete compliance as to four provisions of the Orders.

Because the context in which the Orders and the contempt finding arose is important for determining whether or not the defendants are now in compliance (i.e. have purged themselves of contempt), and because a discussion of the factual background of the contempt finding and a thorough discussion of the proof presented at a hearing on October 10–11, 1995, may be beneficial to all the parties in framing their future responses and to the defendants in conforming their conduct to achieve compliance, the matters before the Court will be discussed in some detail. * * *

I. Background—How the Case and This Issue Arose

The Arlington Developmental Center is a state operated, residential mental retardation facility housing 383 developmentally disabled persons located in Arlington, Tennessee. ADC's population consists primarily of individuals currently assessed as severely or profoundly retarded or developmentally disabled, some of whom have associated physical handicaps, and mental or behavioral problems. ADC is an Intermediate Care Facility for the Mentally Retarded ("ICFMR"). [The total budget for ADC for 1995 is approximately $39 million.] The federal government pays sixty-six per cent of the costs of operation of this facility, with the State of Tennessee paying the remaining thirty-four per cent. * * *

The United States and the State of Tennessee have been in dispute regarding conditions at ADC since 1990. In 1991, the United States Department of Justice ("DOJ"), as part of an investigation of possible statutory and constitutional violations concerning the resident population at ADC, issued a findings letter citing deficiencies to the State of Tennessee. The State of Tennessee refused to correct the deficiencies cited in the DOJ findings letter. On January 21, 1992, the United States filed this action against the State of Tennessee and Arlington Developmental Center, pursuant to the Civil Rights of Institutionalized Persons Act ("CRIPA"), 42 U.S.C. §§ 1997–1997j (1988).

The trial of this case took place over a two month period beginning on August 30, 1993. On November 22, 1993, the Court issued an oral opinion and, on February 18, 1994, filed Supplemental Findings of Fact. * * * [T]he Court held that conditions at ADC were in violation of the rights of its residents under the United States Constitution. *See* Youngberg v. Romeo, 457 U.S. 307, 102 S.Ct. 2452, 73 L.Ed.2d 28 (1982).

Concurrent with the oral ruling of November 22, 1993, the Court entered a preliminary injunction and established a schedule for submittal of a remedial plan by the State of Tennessee. As a result of that procedure, the United States and the State of Tennessee negotiated a plan to remedy the unconstitutional conditions at ADC. On September 2, 1994, the parties submitted a Stipulated Remedial Order to settle the case. As part of the settlement, the United States and the State of Tennessee agreed to the appointment of a Monitor to assist and oversee the State's compliance with the agreed-upon remedial plan. The Court, with the concurrence of both parties, appointed Linda R. O'Neall, Ph.D., to perform that function.

II. History of Noncompliance

The Remedial Plan negotiated by the State of Tennessee contains a "schedule of implementation" setting out the time frames in which each of the remedial actions agreed to by the State was to be completed.[5] A large number of items were to be commenced within the first ninety days of implementation of the plan. Accordingly, the Monitor conducted the First Semi–Annual Compliance Review at ADC from November 28, 1994, through December 2, 1994. Based on this review, the Monitor issued a

---

5. The implementation schedule contains approximately 103 deadlines for more than 150 requirements. The deadlines vary from actions to be taken "immediately" (i.e., beginning as of September 1, 1994) to some actions to be completed 36 months from the plan commencement date. For example, nurse staffing pursuant to paragraph "II.A." was to be completed within three months (i.e., by December 1, 1994). Similarly, a chief psychologist (paragraph "II.B.") and staff psychologists (paragraph "II.C.") were to be retained within three months (i.e., by December 1, 1994). A psychiatrist (paragraph "II.E.") was to be retained within thirty days (i.e., by October 1, 1994). A Developmental Medicine Physician (paragraph "VI.A.") was to be retained within six months (i.e., by March 1, 1995). The effectiveness of certain provisions was dependent on timely completion of other provisions. For example, various committees were to begin to function within specified periods of time and the functioning of those committees was dependent upon the professionals being retained within the timeline set out in the agreed-upon implementation schedule. *See, e.g.,* paragraph III.L. (Behavior Management Committee, beginning at six months; i.e., March 1, 1995).

compliance report to the parties on March 9, 1995. The report then went through a comment and response period and was ultimately the subject of a compliance hearing on April 10, 1995.

At the April 10, 1995, hearing, the Court determined that the State had achieved full compliance with only five of the sixty-five self-imposed deadlines within the first ninety day period. In anticipation of this finding of noncompliance, the State, after negotiation with the United States, proposed a "Plan of Correction" that was submitted to the Court as Exhibit 6 to the hearing of April 10, 1995. * * *

The Plan of Correction supplements the Stipulated Remedial Order and, like the Remedial Plan, also contains a schedule for completion of specific actions. For example, under the individual case management section relating to seizure management, nurses were to be assigned individual resident caseloads by no later than April 20, 1995. Additionally, under paragraph II.C. of the Plan of Correction, the State of Tennessee was to have 136 nursing positions "on staff" by July 1, 1995. * * *

However, the record supports the conclusion that, between April 10, 1995, and June 30, 1995, the State abandoned its goal of achieving compliance with its own Stipulated Remedial Order and its own Plan of Correction. The State effectively ceased its efforts to obtain a developmental physician and recruit nurses [(only 106 nurses were working at ADC)], the number of primary care physicians (including Medical Director) decreased to two (well below the minimum requirement and the number previously anticipated by the State), and conditions at ADC deteriorated even further. * * *

Several patient deaths and the second compliance inspection by the Monitor and her Developmental Medicine Expert on June 27–30, 1995, led the United States and the Monitor to request an Emergency Order on June 30, 1995. The United States and the Monitor requested that the order require the State to rectify certain fundamental services which it had allowed to deteriorate between April 10, 1995, and June 30, 1995, and require the State to employ within the near future certain professional staff, mandated by the Remedial Order and the Plan of Correction. The State acknowledged that the facts constituting an emergency existed, and agreed to the Emergency Order requirements. * * *

A hearing to determine whether the emergency continued to exist * * * was scheduled for July 10, 1995. At that hearing it was established that the State was not in compliance with the Emergency Order. * * *

At the end of the July 10, 1995, hearing, additional time to achieve compliance with the Emergency Order and Preliminary Injunction provisions was granted, and a compliance hearing was scheduled for August 9, 1995. * * *

Based on the evidence presented on August 9, 1995, it was incontrovertible that the State was not in compliance and had failed to perform as it had agreed. Moreover, the State admitted that it did not even have a current plan to implement the various remedial provisions to which it had agreed. * * * The Court, therefore, found the State in contempt and ordered minimal coercive and remedial sanctions to assure that the State would accomplish the five emergency provisions which were agreed to on June 30, 1995, but which had not been achieved by the State. * * *

The financial sanction imposed was, to some degree, symbolic[10] (one thousand dollars ($1,000.00) per day per violation) since the ADC budget is relatively large and sixty-six (66) percent of that budget is federally funded. * * * To directly address emergency matters, a coercive sanction, therefore, was imposed on the Tennessee Commissioner of Mental Health and Mental Retardation. Specifically, the Commissioner was required to spend every fourth weekend at ADC until the State was in full compliance with the five emergency remedial provisions to which it had agreed on June 30, 1995, but which, as of August 9, 1995, it had not done.

On August 9, 1995, the Court found the State had failed to comply with the following five paragraphs: paragraph 1 (retention of a developmental physician), paragraph 2 (performance of duties of a developmental physician), paragraph 5 (retention of a full-time psychiatrist), paragraph 7 (entry by Arlington Developmental Center into contracts with two developmental nurse consultants), and paragraph 8 (hiring of 136 nurses as set out in the April 10, 1995, Plan of Correction).

III. APPLICABLE LAW

A. Civil Contempt

Federal courts have inherent powers to assure the administration of justice. * * * The most prominent among these inherent powers is the contempt sanction, "which a judge must have and exercise in protecting the authority and dignity of the court...." * * * Civil contempt is the power of the court to impose sanctions to coerce compliance with its orders. * * * Both imprisonment and fines, when coercive or conditional, are legitimate civil contempt sanctions. See, e.g., Shillitani, 384 U.S. at 370, 86 S.Ct. at 1535 (imprisonment); United States v. Bayshore Associates, Inc., 934 F.2d 1391, 1400 (6th Cir.1991) (fines).

---

10. Achieving accountability and responsiveness by governmental entities and officials poses special problems for courts in fashioning civil coercive and remedial sanctions for failure of those officials and entities to comply with Court orders. While private individuals and corporations may be highly motivated by the prospect of significant financial losses since the financial fates of individuals and their businesses are closely tied, public officials are, in many respects, essentially independent from the effect of financial losses imposed on the governmental entity by whom they are employed.

Moreover, in dealing with publicly funded entities, fines are often an indiscriminate and potentially counterproductive means of enforcing compliance. Thus the value of fines in forcing a governmental entity to comply with either an agreed upon or imposed court order is often largely symbolic and generally must be narrowly crafted in order to avoid impairing the ability of the governmental entity to perform the tasks required by the order. Moreover, public policy concerns regarding the possible impairment of delivery of important social services dictate that special attention be given to craft remedies that in fact require the public official and governmental entity to perform his or her or its function as opposed to penalizing innocent taxpayers and individuals in need of critical public services.

B. Purging Contempt

Once subject to contempt for failure to comply with a court order, the contemnor must be afforded an opportunity to purge itself of the contempt. International Union, United Mine Workers of Am. v. Bagwell, 512 U.S. 821, 828, 114 S.Ct. 2552, 2558, 129 L.Ed.2d 642 (1994); *Shillitani*, 384 U.S. at 371, 86 S.Ct. at 1536. Compliance with that court order will purge the contempt and free the contemnor from coercive sanctions.[14] *See Bayshore Associates*, 934 F.2d 1391, 1400 (6th Cir.1991) ("[O]nce the defendant performs the act required by the court, he must be released"). * * * In making its determinations on compliance and the appropriateness of continued contempt sanctions, a court should be guided by the remedial purpose of contempt. * * *

The Sixth Circuit test for judging compliance is whether the contemnors "took all reasonable steps within their power to comply with the court's order." Glover v. Johnson, 934 F.2d 703, 708 (6th Cir.1991) (quoting *Peppers*, 873 F.2d at 969). Precisely what "all reasonable steps within [the contemnor's] power" are varies from case to case according to the requirements of the order and the particular circumstances of the case. In every case, however, a contemnor must have the ability to comply with the order before failure to comply can form the basis of contempt.[15] * * * Other than a showing of the impossibility of compliance, nothing short of substantial compliance, as measured under the *Peppers* test, will suffice to purge contempt for noncompliance with a court order. The Sixth Circuit has explicitly rejected the contention that a good faith effort is sufficient, *Peppers*, 873 F.2d at 968, * * * and has not adopted the less demanding diligent efforts test favored in other circuits.[16]

Courts have been particularly unsympathetic to purported excuses for less-than-substantial compliance where the contemnor has participated in drafting the order against which compliance is measured. *See, e.g., Glover*, 934 F.2d at 708–09 (finding state prison officials in contempt for failing to abide by order consisting of negotiated settlement between the parties); *see also* Spallone v. United States, 493 U.S. 265, 276, 110 S.Ct. 625, 632–

---

14. Whether a contemnor has complied with the court order for which it was held in contempt is a distinct inquiry from a finding of contempt. In a civil contempt proceeding, a finding of contempt must be based on clear and convincing proof that the alleged contemnor violated a prior order of the court. Glover v. Johnson, 934 F.2d 703, 707 (6th Cir.1991) * * *.

15. In a contempt proceeding for failure to comply with a court order, the contemnor has a defense if it is factually impossible to comply with the order. United States v. Rylander, 460 U.S. 752, 757, 103 S.Ct. 1548, 1552–53, 75 L.Ed.2d 521 (1983); Maggio v. Zeitz, 333 U.S. 56, 75–76, 68 S.Ct. 401, 411–12, 92 L.Ed. 476 (1948). The contemnor, however, has the burden of production with respect to this defense. * * * Failure to comply with a court order will not be excused for "mere financial hardship." United States v. Work Wear Corp., 602 F.2d 110, 116 (6th Cir.1979). Further, a present inability to comply that results from the contemnor's own actions will not be a defense to contempt. United States v. Lay, 779 F.2d 319, 320 (6th Cir.1985) (holding no defense for "self-induced inability to comply" where "the defendant consciously and willfully placed himself in a financial status in order to avoid responsibility for complying with the court orders") * * *.

16. For the diligent efforts test rejected by this Circuit, *see, e.g.*, Newman v. Graddick, 740 F.2d 1513, 1525 (11th Cir.1984) (holding that "a person who attempts with reasonable diligence to comply with a court order should not be held in contempt").

33, 107 L.Ed.2d 644 (1990) (upholding finding of contempt against city that had failed to take action required by consent decree). A party participating in drafting an order does so with an understanding of what it reasonably can accomplish. When that party subsequently fails to live up to the particulars of the order, it is more difficult for a court to excuse that failure than if the order had been court imposed.

C. Contempt Sanctions for Noncompliance With a Court Order

Once a contemnor has been found in noncompliance, such that contempt is not purged, the court has the option of continuing the sanctions already in place or imposing new sanctions determined to be more effective in carrying out the underlying remedial purpose. * * * The range of sanctions available to courts include fine, imprisonment, receivership, and a broader category of creative, non-traditional sanctions. *See* 42 U.S.C. § 401 (1988) (authorizing "fine or imprisonment"); *Hicks*, 485 U.S. at 632, 108 S.Ct. at 1429–30 (fines and imprisonment); *Shillitani*, 384 U.S. at 370–71, 86 S.Ct. at 1535–36 (imprisonment); *Gompers*, 221 U.S. at 441, 31 S.Ct. at 498 (fines and imprisonment); Reed v. Rhodes, 642 F.2d 186 (6th Cir.1981) (receivership and appointment of judicial administrator); Glover v. Johnson, 934 F.2d 703, 707–15 (appointment of a special administrator, which was not among the "traditional civil contempt sanctions"). The choice of a sanction also necessitates a decision on how severe that particular sanction should be.

There are two guiding principles for the selection of civil contempt sanctions. First, the sanction must be coercive or remedial rather than punitive. * * * The contemnor is not simply being punished for past behavior, but rather encouraged to shape its behavior to comply with the order based on the undesirability of suffering the sanction. The goal of sanctions, then, is to coerce the contemnor to act in such a way that the remedial purposes of the order are furthered. When using civil contempt in such a way, the court "must then consider the character and magnitude of the harm threatened by the continued contumacy, and the probable effectiveness of any suggested sanction in bringing about the result desired." United States v. United Mine Workers of Am., 330 U.S. 258, 304, 67 S.Ct. 677, 701, 91 L.Ed. 884 (1947). Second, particularly when imposing sanctions against state officials, the court should select the least intrusive sanction that the court determines will coerce the contemnor to comply. Spallone v. United States, 493 U.S. 265, 276, 110 S.Ct. 625, 632–33, 107 L.Ed.2d 644 (1990) * * *. In any given case, there may be many sanctions that will coerce compliance and further the remedial purpose of the order, but a court does not automatically impose the most severe and intrusive. There are two competing concerns in this determination: intrusiveness and effectiveness. Determining the relative intrusiveness of different possible sanctions in a particular case is a common sense inquiry. *See, e.g.,* Hutto v. Finney, 437 U.S. 678, 691, 98 S.Ct. 2565, 2573–74, 57 L.Ed.2d 522 (1978) (noting that a fine is a less intrusive sanction than imprisonment); Glover v. Johnson, 855 F.2d 277, 287 (6th Cir.1988) (suggesting that, while the court's appointment of a judicial administrator in the instant case was too intrusive, using a court monitor to enforce its orders would be permissible); Reed v. Rhodes, 642 F.2d 186 (6th Cir.1981) (approving the appointment of an administrator to oversee compliance with court order but disapproving receivership as too intrusive in the instant case). Determining what sanctions will be effective to coerce compliance involves a court's discretion and judgment based on an understanding of the case and the contemnor, particularly with respect to the nature of prior noncompliance.

Given that contempt sanctions are within a court's discretion and that there is no simple formula for assigning a particular sanction to a given case, a court clearly can consider a contemnor's history of compliance or noncompliance in shaping an appropriate contempt sanction. *Compare* Glover v. Johnson, 934 F.2d 703, 715 (6th Cir.1991) (noting that a "persistent pattern of obfuscation, hyper-technical objections, delay, and litigation by exhaustion on the part of the defendants to avoid compliance with the letter and spirit of the district court's orders" made the sanction of appointing an administrator justified where it had been found too intrusive three years earlier) *with* Glover v. Johnson, 855 F.2d 277, 287 (6th Cir.1988). While there is no intent requirement for civil contempt, the issue of the contemnor's willfulness in not complying with court orders may be taken into consideration in determining the extent of the contempt sanction. * * * The contemnor's relative intent clearly is relevant in gauging how severe a sanction is necessary in a given case. * * * When a contemnor's noncompliance has been based in part on conscious decisions to take less than "all reasonable steps within their power to comply," a court clearly would be entitled to take such into consideration in shaping contempt sanctions.

IV. THE OCTOBER 10–11, 1995, HEARING

On October 10–11, 1995, the Court held a hearing on defendants' compliance with the remedial provisions of the June 30, 1995, Emergency Order and July 10, 1995, Preliminary Injunction. * * *

V.

A. Findings Regarding Purgation of Contempt and Compliance/Noncompliance With Remedial Decree

There is no dispute that the defendants have now fully complied with two of the five provisions which were the subject of the Contempt Order * * *. Dr. Askins was employed as a full-time psychiatrist at ADC; thus, paragraph 5 of the Emergency Order and Preliminary Injunction has been satisfied. * * * Similarly, contracts have been executed with two developmental nurse consultants, Karen McGowan and Carolyn Smith[; thus,] * * * the defendants complied with paragraph 7.

Conversely, the State of Tennessee concedes that it has not complied with paragraph 2 * * *. Thus, the only two paragraphs as to which there is a dispute regarding compliance are paragraphs 1 (retention of a full-time developmental physician) and 8 (hiring of 136 nurses).

* * *

B.   What Are the Best and Least Intrusive Remedial Sanctions Available?

The $1,000.00 a day fines as to the paragraphs as to the which the State is not in compliance are not seriously contested. The State does not argue that those sanctions are inappropriate but only argues that as to two (2) of the paragraphs they are in "partial compliance" and that the sanctions are no longer necessary. As previously noted, however, Courts are particularly unsympathetic to excuses for less than substantial compliance where the contemnor has participated in drafting the order against which compliance is measured. * * * The fines imposed as to paragraphs 1, 2, and 8 should, therefore, remain in effect until the State of Tennessee achieves compliance.

The more troubling question is whether or not the requirement that Commissioner Cardwell spend every fourth weekend at Arlington Developmental Center until compliance is achieved should remain in effect. * * *

Commissioner Cardwell has testified that she is "the chief executive officer with the State responsible for complying with the [Remedial Order]." * * * When specifically asked against whom sanctions should be imposed for failure to comply, Commissioner Cardwell has insisted that she is the responsible party. * * * Based on her insistence, the Court has directed remedial sanctions against her. * * *

It is unclear, however, whether the Commissioner, despite her assertion that she is the chief executive officer for the State of Tennessee for Arlington Developmental Center, is involved in the day-to-day operations at ADC.[39] From her testimony, it appears that she is far more familiar with other institutions run by the State of Tennessee and that, in fact, her visits to Arlington Developmental Center have served as an orientation for her to that facility. * * * A substantial question exists regarding the identity of the person or persons against whom creative sanctions would be most effective in achieving the remedial purpose of the orders in this case. Neither the United States nor the State of Tennessee * * * have briefed all of the creative alternatives[40] which may be available to the

---

39. It should be noted that the Superintendent at Arlington Developmental Center, Max Jackson, has yet to testify at any proceedings in this case. Mr. Jackson is charged with the day-to-day management of ADC and plays an important role in implementation of key provisions of the remedial plan.

40. For example, creative alternatives might include a requirement of an administrator's off-hours schedule (to cover weekends, second and third shifts), imposition of an administrator to more closely monitor the day-to-day progress at Arlington Developmental Center, imposition of a direct administrative penalty or bonus system dependent on the percentage of compliance obtained with the overall Remedial Plan or Plan of Correction or Preliminary Injunction. Such

Court in lieu of the relatively simple, though highly effective sanction imposed.

The United States strongly argues that the Court should continue the only sanction which has been effective in achieving efforts towards compliance by the State of Tennessee. Undoubtedly, the requirement that the Commissioner spend every fourth weekend at Arlington Developmental Center initially was a very effective remedial sanction. It is equally clear, however, that since it appears the State may have made a deliberate decision to change its course and not comply with the Remedial Order, Plan of Correction, and Preliminary Injunction, a more comprehensive sanction scheme, tailored to assure compliance in this complex environment would be useful.

The United States shall, therefore, submit within thirty (30) days of the entry of this order a comprehensive legal analysis of the remedies available for use in this case, including a proposed remedial sanction scheme. The State of Tennessee likewise may, but is not required to, submit its own proposed remedial sanctions scheme and the authorities supporting it. * * *

The Court will then consider whether or not it should adopt, as part of the remedies available in the context of contempt as to the Preliminary Injunction (and the Contempt Order of August 24, 1995) any or all of the proposed remedial sanctions. * * * The parties should focus on the problems enunciated in note 10 regarding how to require government administrators to be responsive and the degree to which individual government administrators may be personally sanctioned.

As an interim step, in lieu of the requirement that Commissioner Cardwell spend every fourth weekend at Arlington Developmental Center, four (4) key administrators, Medical Director Akers, Superintendent Jackson, Director of Nursing Lester, and Remedial Order Facilitator Hansen, are required to be available one day a month at Arlington Developmental Center for transcribed group and/or individual question and answer sessions. * * *

The sessions will focus on implementation not only of the Preliminary Injunction but also of the Remedial Order and Plan of Correction. The first question and answer session shall be scheduled within three (3) weeks of the date of entry of this order. If satisfactory with the Monitor, the parties may schedule the session for a weekend date if they conclude that such a schedule would least interfere with operations of the institution.

NOTES

1. The preliminary injunction at issue in *United States v. Tennessee* is an excellent example of a "structural injunction" which seeks to reform an

types of alternatives should be considered not only in the context of defendants' contempt concerning the preliminary injunction but also at any later proceeding should the defendants be found in contempt concerning implementation of the Remedial Order or Plan of Correction.

entire institution, such as a school or a prison. *See generally* Owen M. Fiss, The Civil Rights Injunction 86–93 (1978). Judges who grant such injunctions find themselves acting in a somewhat controversial managerial role.

2. When a court issues a structural injunction, it is common for it to appoint a monitor, as was done in *United States v. Tennessee*. In more extreme situations, the court may appoint a temporary receiver to run the institution until it can be brought into compliance with the court's decree. *See, e.g.,* Shaw v. Allen, 771 F.Supp. 760 (S.D.W.Va.1990) (receiver appointed to take over and manage a state jail); Morgan v. McDonough, 540 F.2d 527 (1st Cir.1976) (receiver appointed to implement a school desegregation plan at a public high school).

D. VIOLATIONS OF JUDICIAL RULES AND ORDERS RELATING TO THE ADMINISTRATION OF JUSTICE REVISITED

JONES v. CLINTON

United States District Court, Eastern District of Arkansas, 1999.
36 F.Supp.2d 1118.

SUSAN WEBBER WRIGHT, CHIEF JUDGE.

What began as a civil lawsuit against the President of the United States for alleged sexual harassment eventually resulted in an impeachment trial of the President in the United States Senate on two Articles of Impeachment for his actions during the course of this lawsuit and a related criminal investigation being conducted by the Office of the Independent Counsel ("OIC"). * * *

* * *

Plaintiff's complaint was filed on May 6, 1994. * * * [T]he Supreme Court handed down an opinion holding that there is no constitutional impediment to allowing plaintiff's case to proceed while the President is in office. *See* Clinton v. Jones, 520 U.S. 681, 117 S.Ct. 1636, 137 L.Ed.2d 945 (1997).

* * *

At his deposition, the President was questioned extensively about his relationship with Ms. Lewinsky. * * * [T]he President testified in response to questioning from plaintiff's counsel and his own attorney that he had no recollection of having ever been alone with Ms. Lewinsky and he denied that he had engaged in an "extramarital sexual affair," in "sexual relations," or in a "sexual relationship" with Ms. Lewinsky. * * *

* * *

On August 17, 1998, the President appeared before a grand jury in Washington, D.C., as part of OIC's criminal investigation and testified about his relationship with Ms. Lewinsky and his actions during this civil lawsuit. That evening, the President discussed the matter in a televised address to the Nation. In his address, the President stated that although his answers at his January 17th deposition were "legally accurate," he did not volunteer information and that he did indeed have a relationship with Ms. Lewinsky that was inappropriate and wrong. * * * The President acknowledged misleading people, in part because the questions posed to him "were being asked in a politically inspired lawsuit which has since been dismissed," and because he "had real and serious concerns about an Independent Counsel investigation that began with private business dealings 20 years ago...." * * * It was during the President's televised address that the Court first learned the President may be in contempt.* * *

On September 9, 1998, the Independent Counsel * * * submitted his findings from his investigation of the Lewinsky matter to the United States House of Representatives pursuant to 28 U.S.C. § 595(c). The House of Representatives thereupon commenced impeachment proceedings, ultimately passing two Articles of Impeachment against the President, one alleging perjury in his August 17th testimony before the grand jury and the other alleging obstruction of justice in this civil case. The matter then proceeded to trial in the United States Senate.

On November 13, 1998, while the impeachment proceedings were taking place in the House of Representatives, the plaintiff reached an out-of court settlement for $850,000.00 and withdrew her appeal of this Court's April 1st decision granting summary judgment to defendants. * * * Thereafter, on February 12, 1999, the Senate acquitted the President of both Articles of Impeachment.

Following the acquittal of the President, this Court held a telephone conference on February 16, 1999, to address * * * the issue of whether the President should be subject to contempt proceedings. * * *

* * *

The threshold question in this matter is whether a President of the United States can be held in civil contempt of court and thereby sanctioned. * * * [T]his Court has considered the matter and finds no constitutional barrier * * *.

* * *

[A] federal district court has two principal sources of authority for finding a party in civil contempt of its discovery orders: Fed.R.Civ.P. 37(b)(2) and the court's inherent power. * * * Pursuant to Rule 37(b)(2), a court may hold a party in contempt of court for failing to obey an order to provide discovery. * * * However, when rules alone do not provide courts with sufficient authority to protect their integrity and prevent abuses of the judicial process, the inherent power fills the gap.* * * In this regard, a court has the "inherent power to protect [its] integrity and prevent abuses of the judicial process" by holding a party in contempt and imposing sanctions for violations of the court's orders. * * * When the source of the civil contempt is a failure to comply with a discovery order, the analysis and available remedies under Fed.R.Civ.P. 37 and the court's inherent power are essentially the same. * * * Two requirements must be met before a party may be held in civil contempt: the court must have fashioned an Order that is clear and reasonably specific, and the party must have violated that Order. * * * Generally, these two requirements must be shown by clear and convincing evidence. * * * [T]his Court addresses the President's contumacious conduct under Fed.R.Civ.P. 37(b)(2), finding that rule sufficient in its scope to redress the abuse of the judicial process that occurred in this case.

* * *

Fed.R.Civ.P. 37(b)(2) sets forth a broad range of sanctions that a district court may impose upon parties for their failure to comply with the court's discovery orders. The Rule provides that if a party fails to obey an order to provide or permit discovery, the court "may make such orders in regard to the failure as are just" and, among others, impose the following sanctions: (1) the court may order that the matters regarding which the order was made or any other designated facts be taken as established for the purposes of the action in accordance with the claim of the party obtaining the order; (2) the court may refuse to allow the disobedient party to support or oppose designated claims or defenses, or prohibit that party from introducing designated matters in evidence; (3) the court may strike any pleadings or parts thereof, stay further proceedings until the order is obeyed, dismiss the action or proceeding or any part thereof, or render a judgment of default against the disobedient party; and (4) the court may, in lieu of any of the foregoing sanctions or in addition thereto, enter an order treating as a contempt of court the failure of the party to obey the court's orders. Fed.R.Civ.P. 37(b)(2). In addition to those sanctions, the Rule provides:

> In lieu of any of the foregoing orders or in addition thereto, the court shall require the party failing to obey the order ... to pay the reasonable expenses, including attorney's fees, caused by the failure, unless the court finds that the failure was substantially justified or that other circumstances make an award of expenses unjust.

Fed.R.Civ.P. 37(b)(2).

* * *

* * * [T]he record leaves no doubt that the President violated this Court's discovery Orders regarding disclosure of information deemed by this Court to be relevant to plaintiff's lawsuit. The Court therefore adjudges the President to be in civil contempt of court pursuant to Fed.R.Civ.P. 37(b)(2).

* * *

The Court now turns to the issue of appropriate sanctions. Several of the sanctions contemplated by Fed.R.Civ.P. 37(b)(2) are unavailable to this Court as the underlying lawsuit has been terminated. The Court cannot, for example, order that the matters upon which the President gave false statements be taken as established, nor can the Court render a default judgment against the President, both of which the Court would have considered had this Court's grant of summary judgment to defendants been reversed and remanded. Moreover, as the Court earlier noted, the determination of appropriate sanctions must take into account that this case was dismissed on summary judgment as lacking in merit—a decision that would not have changed even had the President been truthful with respect to his relationship with Ms. Lewinsky—and that plaintiff was made whole, having settled this case for an amount in excess of that prayed for in her complaint. Nevertheless, the President's contumacious conduct in this case, coming as it did from a member of the bar and the chief law enforcement officer of this Nation, was without justification and undermined the integrity of the judicial system. * * * Accordingly, the Court imposes the following sanctions:

First, the President shall pay plaintiff any reasonable expenses, including attorney's fees, caused by his willful failure to obey this Court's discovery Orders. Plaintiff's former counsel are directed to submit to this Court a detailed statement of any expenses and attorney's fees incurred in connection with this matter within twenty (20) days of the date of entry of this Memorandum Opinion and Order.

Second, the President shall reimburse this Court its expenses in traveling to Washington, D.C. at his request to preside over his tainted deposition. The Court therefore will direct that the President deposit into the registry of this Court the sum of $1,202.00, the total expenses incurred by this Court in traveling to Washington, D.C.

In addition, the Court will refer this matter to the Arkansas Supreme Court's Committee on Professional Conduct for review and any disciplinary action it deems appropriate for the President's possible violation of the Model Rules of Professional Conduct. Relevant to this case, Rule 8.4 of the Model Rules provides that it is professional misconduct for a lawyer to, among other things, "engage in conduct involving dishonesty, fraud, deceit or misrepresentation," or to "engage in conduct that is prejudicial to the administration of justice." * * *

* * *

In addressing only the President's sworn statements concerning his relationship with Ms. Lewinsky, this Court is fully aware that the President may have engaged in other contumacious conduct warranting the imposition of sanctions. * * * The Court determines, however, that this matter can be summarily addressed by focusing on those specific instances of the President's misconduct with which there is no factual dispute and which primarily occurred directly before the Court.* * *

This is not to say that the Court considers other instances of possible Presidential misconduct in this case unworthy of the Court's attention. In fact, the Court fully considered addressing all of the President's possible misconduct pursuant to the criminal contempt provisions set forth in Fed.R.Crim.P. 42, but determined that such action is not necessary at this time for two primary reasons.

First, the summary adjudication procedures delineated in Rule 42(a) are most likely inapplicable in this case since the power summarily to convict and punish for contempt of court under that rule generally "rests on the proposition that a hearing to determine guilt of contempt is not necessary when contumacious conduct occurs in the actual presence of a judge who observes it, and when immediate action is required to preserve order in the proceedings and appropriate respect for the tribunal." * * * Here, the Court was not aware of any of the instances of the President's possible misconduct until well after this case had been dismissed on summary judgment, and immediate action was not required to preserve order in the proceedings. *See* International Union, United Mine Workers of Am. v. Bagwell, 512 U.S. 821, 832–33, 114 S.Ct. 2552, 129 L.Ed.2d 642 (1994) (noting that "[s]ummary adjudication becomes less justifiable once a court leaves the realm of immediately sanctioned, petty direct contempts," and that "[if] a court delays punishing a direct contempt until the completion of trial, for example, due process requires that the contemnor's rights to notice and a hearing be respected").

Second, resolving the matter expeditiously and without hearings pursuant to Rule 42(b) is in the best interests of both the President and this Court. * * * Because much of the President's conduct has been or is being investigated by OIC, and in order to prevent any potential double jeopardy issues from arising,* * * this Court will forego proceeding under Fed.R.Crim.P. 42 and address the President's contempt by focusing on those undisputed matters that are capable of being summarily addressed pursuant to Fed.R.Civ.P. 37(b)(2). *See Bagwell*, 512 U.S. at 833, 114 S.Ct. 2552 (noting that certain indirect contempts are appropriate for imposition through civil proceedings, including contempts impeding the courts ability to adjudicate the proceedings before it and those contempts involving discrete, readily ascertainable acts).

Nevertheless, the Court will convene a hearing at the request of the President should he desire an opportunity in which to demonstrate why he is not in civil contempt of court * * *.

* * *

The Court takes no pleasure whatsoever in holding this Nation's President in contempt of court * * *. As noted earlier, however, this Court has attempted throughout this case to apply the law to the President in the same manner as it would apply the law to any other litigant, keeping in mind the duties and status of the Presidency and the "high respect" that is to be accorded his office. *See* Clinton v. Jones, 520 U.S. at 707, 117 S.Ct. 1636. In that regard, there simply is no escaping the fact that the President deliberately violated this Court's discovery Orders and thereby undermined the integrity of the judicial system. Sanctions must be imposed, not only to redress the President's misconduct, but to deter others who might themselves consider emulating the President of the United States by engaging in misconduct that undermines the integrity of the judicial system. * * *

NOTE

The President subsequently notified Judge Wright that while he "dispute[d] allegations that he knowingly and intentionally gave false testimony under oath," he would not request a hearing or file a notice of appeal. 57 F.Supp.2d 719, 720 (D.Ark.1999). Plaintiff's lawyers claimed attorney's fees and expenses in a total amount of $446,358.03. They contended that the breadth of the fees and expenses was justified because "sanctions may be imposed to punish the President's misconduct." *Id.* at 724. Judge Wright rejected their argument, emphasizing that sanctions for compensatory contempt "must be based upon evidence of actual loss." *Id.* She then ordered the President to pay: 1) $1,202.00 into the registry of the court to cover her travel expenses; and 2) $89,484.05 to the plaintiff to cover the portion of her attorney's fees that were directly attributable to the President's contempt of court. *Id.* at 729.

E. PERSONS BOUND BY AN EQUITABLE REMEDIAL DECREE

Courts have not been consistent in answering the question of who may be bound by an equitable remedial decree. In the eighteenth and nineteenth centuries, courts held that "only parties to the injunction suit could be bound." Richard A. Bales & Ryan A. Allison, *Enjoining Nonparties*, 26 Am. J. Trial Advoc. 79, 80 (2002). But this rule proved to be too narrow "because defendants could disobey the court simply by acting through nonparties." *Id.* Eventually, courts established six categories of nonparties that could be held in contempt for the violation of an equitable decree:

(1) agents of the enjoined party, (2) aiders and abettors of the enjoined party, (3) persons cognizant of the decree, (4) successors in interest of the enjoined party, (5) those coming into contact with a particular res, and (6) members of the same class in a class action suit.

Id.; *see also* Note, *Binding Nonparties to Injunction Decrees*, 49 Minn. L. Rev. 719 (1965).

Rule 65(d)(2) of the Federal Rules of Civil Procedure provides:

[An injunction or restraining order] binds only the following who receive actual notice of it by personal service or otherwise:

(A) the parties;

(B) the parties' officers, agents, servants, employees, and attorneys; and

> (C) other persons who are in active concert or participation with anyone described in Rule 65(d) (2) (A) or (B).

Rule 65(d) (2) does not refer to each of the six categories identified above, but it has been interpreted expansively because it has been deemed to codify, and not to limit, the federal judiciary's inherent common law power. *See*, *e.g.*, United States v. Hall, 472 F.2d 261 (5th Cir. 1972) (holding nonparty in criminal contempt for interfering with the enforcement of a desegregation decree).

Holding nonparties in contempt for violating equitable decrees raises obvious procedural due process questions. The courts have determined that "due process is not at risk," however, for the following reasons:

> Contempt proceedings operate to ensure that nonparties have had their day in court. In order to hold a nonparty in contempt, a court first must determine that she was in active concert or participation with the party specifically enjoined (typically, the named defendant). * * * This means, of course, that the nonparty must be legally identified with that defendant, or, at least, deemed to have aided and abetted that defendant in the enjoined conduct. * * * The existence of such a linkage makes it fair to bind the nonparty, even if she has not had a separate opportunity to contest the original injunction, because her close alliance with the enjoined defendant adequately assures that her interests were sufficiently represented. * * *

> The coin, however, has a flip side. A nonparty who has acted independently of the enjoined defendant will not be bound by the injunction, and, if she has had no opportunity to contest its validity, cannot be found in contempt without a separate adjudication. * * * This tried and true dichotomy safeguards the rights of those who truly are strangers to an injunctive decree. It does not offend due process.

Microsystems Software, Inc. v. Scandinavia Online AB, 226 F.3d 35, 43 (1st Cir.2000).

NOTES

1. In recognition of procedural due process constraints, the federal courts have held that "[t]he reference in Rule 65(d) to 'officers' means only *current* officers." Saga International, Inc. v. John D. Brush & Co., 984 F.Supp. 1283, 1286 (C.D.Cal.1997). They also have taken the position that injunctions can bind "only a party to the action, those who aid and abet a party, and those in privity with a party." *Id.* In the famous words of Judge Learned Hand:

> [N]o court can make a decree which will bind anyone but a party; a court of equity is as much limited as a court of law; it cannot lawfully enjoin the world at large, no matter how broadly it words its decree. If it assumes to do so, * * * the persons enjoined are free to ignore it. [A court] is not vested with sovereign powers to declare conduct unlawful; its

jurisdiction is limited to those over whom it gets personal service, and who therefore can have their day in court. * * * This means that the respondent must either abet the defendant, or must be legally identified with him.

Alemite Manufacturing Corp. v. Staff, 42 F.2d 832, 832–33 (2d Cir.1930). Therefore, if a corporation is enjoined from infringing a patent, the injunction cannot be enforced through civil contempt proceedings brought against a former officer, even if the former officer has started a new business that sells the same infringing goods, provided the former officer is not acting in concert with the defendant corporation. Saga International, Inc. v. John D. Brush & Co., 984 F.Supp. 1283 (C.D.Cal.1997). The concept of "acting in concert" has been defined as follows:

> There are two elements to proving the "acting in concert" theory: The first is a state of mind: a nonparty must know of the judicial decree, and nonetheless act in defiance of it. The second is legal identification: the challenged action must be taken for the benefit of, or to assist, a party subject to the decree.

Goya Foods, Inc. v. Wallack Management Co., 290 F.3d 63, 75 (1st Cir.2002) (imposing civil compensatory sanctions on nonparties who had "aided and abetted" the defendants).

2. Although Rule 65(d)(2) makes no reference to binding "successors," the United States Supreme Court has ruled that a bona fide successor corporation can be held in contempt for a violation of an order issued against its predecessor. Golden State Bottling Co. v. NLRB, 414 U.S. 168, 94 S.Ct. 414, 38 L.Ed.2d 388 (1973). For an analysis of the *Golden State* case, see Doug Rendleman, *Beyond Contempt: Obligors to Injunctions*, 53 Tex. L. Rev. 873, 891–92 (1975).

3. Similarly, although Rule 65(d)(2) makes no reference to in rem injunctions, and does not authorize the enforcement of an injunction against a nonparty who is interfering with the implementation of a court order establishing public rights, the Supreme Court has expressed its support of lower federal court cases that have enforced such injunctions:

> In our view, the commercial fishing associations and their members [(who were citizens of Washington and who had violated the terms of an injunction against the state requiring the state to respect several treaties that gave Indian tribes a right to a 45%–50% share of the harvestable fish passing through recognized tribal fishing grounds)] are probably subject to injunction under either the rule that nonparties who interfere with the implementation of court orders establishing public rights may be enjoined, *e.g.*, United States v. Hall, 472 F.2d 261 (CA 5 1972) * * *, or the rule that a court possessed of the res in a proceeding in rem, such as one to apportion a fishery, may enjoin those who would interfere with that custody.

Washington v. Washington State Commercial Passenger Fishing Vessel Ass'n, 443 U.S. 658, 692 n.32, 99 S.Ct. 3055, 3078 n.32, 61 L.Ed.2d 823, 850 n.32 (1979) (holding that the injunction against the state was binding on its citizens). *See generally* Doug Rendleman, *Beyond Contempt: Obligors to Injunctions*, 53 Tex. L. Rev. 873, 911–16 (1975).

4. Before nonparties may be held in criminal contempt, it must be proven that they had actual knowledge of the terms of the injunction and that they willfully violated it. For example, in Washington v. Washington State Commercial Passenger Fishing Vessel Ass'n, 443 U.S. 658, 99 S.Ct. 3055, 61 L.Ed.2d 823 (1979), the prosecutor failed to prove beyond a reasonable doubt that three of the nonparties had actual knowledge of the order, and therefore, they could not be held in contempt. Actual knowledge may be proven by direct or circumstantial evidence. State v. Linsky, 117 N.H. 866, 379 A.2d 813 (1977) (the prosecutor demonstrated that nonparty protestors had actual knowledge of an injunction, which prohibited trespassing at a nuclear construction site, by proving that the injunction had been read over a loud speaker and that copies of the injunction had been posted at various places; criminal contempt sanction affirmed).

ROE v. OPERATION RESCUE

United States Court of Appeals, Third Circuit, 1995.
54 F.3d 133.

ROTH, CIRCUIT JUDGE.

This is an action brought for declaratory and injunctive relief to stop blockades of abortion clinics. Aspects of this dispute have been before the courts for almost seven years. In the latest episode, the District Court for the Eastern District of Pennsylvania denied appellants' motion to hold Operation Rescue, Randall A. Terry, Robert Lewis, and Joseph Roach in [civil] contempt for violating a Revised Permanent Injunction, issued on July 17, 1989. Plaintiffs, National Abortion Rights Action League of Pennsylvania ("NARAL–PA") * * * [and several abortion and family planning clinics] appeal that order. * * *

I.

The underlying action was originally brought on June 29, 1988, by eleven plaintiffs, consisting of NARAL–PA, seven abortion and family planning clinics, two pregnant women, and a physician who regularly performed abortions. It was brought in response to Operation Rescue's "publicly announced plans to close down clinics that offer abortions in the Philadelphia area by staging massive demonstrations and blockades at . . . [those] facilities." Roe v. Operation Rescue, 919 F.2d 857, 861 (3d Cir. 1990) ("Roe IV"). * * * Operation Rescue and Randall Terry were among the named defendants. [The plaintiffs were granted a temporary restraining order after an adversary hearing on June 30, 1988. ("Roe I")].

* * *

In March 1989, the district court permanently enjoined the defendants from "trespassing on, blocking, obstructing ingress or egress from any facility at which abortions are performed in the City of Philadelphia or metropolitan area" and from "physically abusing or tortuously harassing persons entering, leaving, working at, or using any services at any facility at which abortions are performed in the City of Philadelphia and metropolitan area." Roe v. Operation Rescue, 710 F.Supp. 577, 589 (E.D.Pa.1989) ("Roe II") * * *. Subsequently, on plaintiffs' motion to modify the permanent injunction to provide for the United States Marshal for the Eastern District of Pennsylvania to read the injunction at protest sites, the district court granted the Revised Permanent Injunction at issue here. * * *

The present appeal arose out of the third civil contempt motion to be filed in this on-going case. On September 7, 1993, plaintiffs sought civil contempt sanctions against Operation Rescue, Randall Terry, and non-party respondents Joseph Roach, [and] Robert Lewis * * * for alleged violations on July 9, 1993, of the district court's Revised Permanent Injunction. * * *

At the hearing, the plaintiffs presented evidence that during the summer of 1993 Operation Rescue National organized, publicized, and raised money for a nationwide campaign to protest abortion rights in seven cities, designated "Cities of Refuge."[1] The campaign was to take place from July 8 through 18, 1993. Philadelphia was named as one of the "Cities of Refuge." Evidence established that Operation Rescue National, Randall Terry, and the Executive Director of Operation Rescue National, Keith Tucci, advertised and promoted the campaign in anti-abortion magazines.

* * *

Testimony at the December 1 hearing established that from July 9th through the 18th several blockades and numerous anti-abortion demonstrations and protests occurred in the Philadelphia area. On the morning of July 9th, over 100 anti-abortion protestors assembled on the grounds of the Crozer–Chester Medical Center, in front of the Reproductive Health and Counseling Center ("RHCC"). The demonstrators, many of whom wore "Operation Rescue"/"Cities of Refuge" badges and "Rescue" arm bands, effectively blocked the clinic's three doors from approximately 10:30 a.m. until 3:30–3:45 p.m.

Witnesses testified that appellees Joseph Roach and Robert Lewis directed the protesters, moving those needing rest into the shade and interacting with the police. There was, however, no evidence that Roach or Lewis physically blocked a door. At about 12:45 p.m., a United States Marshal read the Revised Permanent Injunction over a bull horn to the protestors. Witnesses stated that Roach and Lewis, who conceded that they had actual knowledge of the injunction at the time of the blockade, did nothing to disperse the blockade after the injunction was read.

An individual who attended the Cities of Refuge events at the Valley Forge Hilton on July 14, 1993, testified that appellee Lewis acted as

---

1. As discussed below, we hold that the two groups, Operation Rescue and Operation Rescue National, are interchangeable.

Master of Ceremonies and introduced Keith Tucci as the Operation Rescue National leader. Tucci in turn thanked individuals including "Bob" and "Joe," presumably referring to Robert Lewis and Joseph Roach, for their local leadership. The witness testified that Roach and Lewis wore red arm bands, designating their marshal status, and that at the close of the evening they directed the group where "to meet for tomorrow's events."

After the hearing, the district court denied plaintiffs' motion. Finding that Roach and Lewis had actual knowledge of the court's order and "were present and active at certain events occurring from July 8, 1993, through July 18, 1993," the district court nonetheless held that the plaintiffs failed to establish that either Roach or Lewis violated the Revised Permanent Injunction. Roe v. Operation Rescue, No. 88–5157, slip op. at 1 (E.D.Pa. Dec. 10, 1993) ("Roe V"). The court concluded that "Roach and Lewis wore red arm bands, but it was not established by clear and convincing evidence that the bands were associated with one particular group, namely Operation Rescue." Id. * * * He then found that the plaintiffs had failed to establish that Terry's activities violated the Revised Permanent Injunction. * * * [The district court judge found that Terry was not physically present at the July 9th blockade.]

* * *

II.

Our review of the denial of a contempt motion is for abuse of discretion by the district court. Reversal is appropriate "only where the denial is based on an error of law or a finding of fact that is clearly erroneous." Harley–Davidson, Inc. v. Morris, 19 F.3d 142, 145 (3d Cir. 1994) * * *.

III.

* * *

A. Operation Rescue

A plaintiff must prove three elements by clear and convincing evidence to establish that a party is liable for civil contempt: "(1) that a valid order of the court existed; (2) that the defendants had knowledge of the order; and (3) that the defendants disobeyed the order." * * * Although the district court made no specific findings regarding Operation Rescue's role in the July 9th RHCC blockade, the court's conclusion that "it was not established by clear and convincing evidence that the red arm bands [that Roach and Lewis had worn] were associated with Terry or Operation Rescue," * * * suggests that the court implicitly concluded that Operation Rescue had no involvement in the July 9th blockade and therefore did not disobey the order.

* * * By focusing on the arm bands, the court appears to have ignored the vast documentary evidence that plaintiffs presented at the hearing, linking Operation Rescue to the blockade.

Included in the documentary evidence establishing the connection between Operation Rescue, Operation Rescue National, and the RHCC campaign are the literature, fund-raising letters, and organizing materials put out by Operation Rescue, Operation Rescue National, Randall Terry, and Keith Tucci to promote the Cities of Refuge Campaign. These include the materials publicizing and raising funds for the Cities of Refuge campaign, some of which urged "non-violent direct action" in the Philadelphia area during the period from July 8–17, 1993. * * *

We find the Appellees' argument that Operation Rescue National is a separate and distinct organization from Operation Rescue to be disingenuous. Indeed, the record supports the conclusion that there is a similarity of membership and an interchangeable use of names between the two groups. Even if the record does not establish that Operation Rescue and Operation Rescue National are identical, it indicates that Operation Rescue National and Operation Rescue acted in concert to conduct the Cities of Refuge Campaign.

* * *

In light of the overwhelming record evidence of Operation Rescue involvement, we believe that the trial court abused its discretion by basing its decision solely on its finding that the red arm bands were not proven by clear and convincing evidence to be associated with Operation Rescue and thereby concluding that Operation Rescue was not implicated in the July 9th blockade.

B. Randall Terry

* * *

We have previously held that an instigator of contemptuous conduct may not "absolve himself of contempt liability by leaving the physical performance of the forbidden conduct to others." Roe IV at 871. In upholding the district court's finding that defendant Michael McMonagle violated the TRO in a 1989 blockade, this court found that actual trespass was not "a necessary precondition for holding McMonagle in civil contempt" where he had instructed protestors during the blockade and spoken with police officials at the scene. Id. When a party to the Revised Permanent Injunction urges others to participate in conduct violative of the Injunction, such encouragement may itself suffice to support a finding of contempt.

Although Terry was not physically present at the July 9th RHCC blockade, uncontroverted evidence establishes Terry's involvement in at least two activities related to the blockade in violation of the Revised Permanent Injunction. First, prior to the blockade, Terry * * * [helped] to organize, publicize, and raise money for the Cities of Refuge campaign

that, as discussed above, instigated the July 9th blockade of the RHCC
* * *.

Second, Terry was a featured speaker at a nationally-publicized rally
in the Philadelphia area on the night of the blockade.* * * Testimony
revealed that his presence was meant to attract people to the Philadelphia
area events, thus facilitating the July 9th blockade. * * *

Given these facts, the trial court's conclusion that "[p]laintiffs failed
to establish that defendant Terry was present or active in any of the
events in question" suggests that the court relied on the erroneous legal
conclusion that a contemnor must participate on the scene in order to
violate the Revised Permanent Injunction. * * * We reverse the trial
court's decision because it is based on a clear error of law. * * *

C.   Roach and Lewis

The district court refused to hold Roach and Lewis in contempt on the
grounds that the plaintiffs failed to prove that the two men violated the
Revised Permanent Injunction. * * *

Case law establishes, and the trial court acknowledged, that individuals, who are neither parties to a proceeding nor named in the court order
at issue, may nonetheless be subject to the court's contempt powers if they
have "knowledge of a valid court order and abet others in violating it."
Roe IV at 857 * * *. Moreover, the Revised Permanent Injunction, by its
terms, prohibits non-parties with actual knowledge of the Injunction from
"acting in concert" with the named parties to frustrate the injunction or
avoid compliance with it. * * *

The district court found that Roach and Lewis had knowledge of the
Revised Permanent Injunction. * * * Roach and Lewis have not challenged that finding. There is, moreover, clear and convincing evidence in
the record to show that Roach and Lewis acted in concert with Operation
Rescue and Randall Terry to violate the Revised Permanent Injunction by
organizing the Cities of Refuge campaign in the Philadelphia area in
general and by leading the July 9th blockade of RHCC in particular.
Undisputed testimony established that Roach and Lewis attended the
RHCC blockade. * * *

* * *

The trial court thus appears to have misread the Revised Permanent
Injunction's "acting in concert" clause by failing to hold these two nonparties in contempt where undisputed evidence established their coordi-
nated activities with Operation Rescue and Terry to organize and run the
July 9th blockade. * * *

IV.

For the reasons stated above, we will reverse the judgment of the
district court and remand this case to the district court with instructions
to enter an order granting plaintiffs' motion to hold Operation Rescue,

Randall Terry, Robert Lewis, and Joseph Roach in civil contempt of the Permanent Revised Injunction, issued July 17, 1989, and for further proceedings consistent with this opinion.

PEOPLE v. CONRAD

Court of Appeal, First District, California, 1997.
55 Cal.App.4th 896, 64 Cal.Rptr.2d 248.

WALKER, ASSOCIATE JUSTICE.

Cheryl Conrad, Sandra Evans, Bryan Kemper, Ruben Obregon, Michael Ross, Johnny Schwab, Joanne Holden, Alice Gambino, and Jeffrey White appeal their misdemeanor convictions for disobedience of a lawful court order. (Pen.Code, § 166, subd. (a)(4).) Appellants are abortion protesters who were arrested for picketing in front of the Planned Parenthood clinic in Vallejo. The clinic has a valid court order enjoining the similar activity of Christine Williams, Solano Citizens for Life, "and their agents, representatives, employees and members, and each of them, and each and every person acting at the direction of or in combination or in concert with defendants." Appellants claim, first, that the trial judge applied the wrong legal standard to find that they acted "in concert" with the enjoined parties so as to make them liable for violating the injunction and, second, that, measured by the correct standard, the evidence was insufficient to sustain their convictions. * * *

FACTS

The Planned Parenthood clinic in Vallejo is situated at 990 Broadway, a "busy avenue, with light commercial establishments on either side of" the clinic. A parking lot surrounds the premises, and two driveways cross the public sidewalk that borders the lot, providing access from Broadway to the clinic and other businesses. The injunction we construe here was issued on August 1, 1991, after the enjoined parties had repeatedly obstructed the clinic entrances, interfered with traffic on the driveways, and harassed and intimidated clinic patients and staff. The injunction forbids specific harassing conduct and banishes the enjoined parties' "picketing, demonstrating [and] counseling" activity to the sidewalk opposite the clinic on the other side of Broadway.

Uncontradicted evidence adduced at a bench trial showed that on June 10, 1994, appellants White and Schwab, among others, picketed the clinic from the sidewalk that borders the parking lot. The clinic director, Lynde Ann Rouche, tried to hand them copies of the injunction, but they refused to take them, insisting that "it didn't apply to them." Rouche spoke to White, who she knew from photographs, had an "important role with Operation Rescue of California." White told her the protesters were there to "test the injunction" by "getting arrested." Eventually, White and Schwab "chose to be arrested." After they were cited and released, everyone left. Norman Reece, an enjoined party who pickets the Vallejo clinic "between one [and] five times a week," observed the demonstration from his van, which was parked across the street.

On July 11, 1994, appellants again picketed Planned Parenthood on the clinic side of Broadway. Again, Rouche tried to hand them copies of the injunction, and, again, they insisted it did not apply to them. Again, Reece drove up in his van, but when he slowed down, appellant Ross waved him away. Rouche testified, "Mr. Ross was frantically motioning [Reece] to continue on, indicating ... 'Go away.'" When Ross gestured, Reece drove away. Eventually, the Vallejo police arrested the protesters who refused to cross Broadway in accordance with the injunction.

Kathleen Nolan, the executive associate for Planned Parenthood, testified that the clinic had a written policy, devised with legal counsel, outlining, among other things, the scope of the injunction. According to Nolan, "It stated that anybody who was doing the same things that those specific people had been enjoined against were acting in concert with those people." In other words, she said, "the injunction covered anybody committing the same acts as the specific [enjoined] people made." Rouche testified that she had the same understanding, and that she had served the injunction on pro-choice demonstrators as well as on appellants.

After the prosecution rested, appellants made a motion for acquittal, which the court denied. Appellants' testimony was all to the same effect: they were not members of Solano Citizens for Life, and did not know any of the enjoined parties. Most had traveled from other parts of California with a pro-life caravan of sorts, Operation Rescue's "Summer of Missions," a four-week camping trip and anti-abortion campaign with planned stops throughout the state. They had stopped in Vallejo expressly to test the limits of the injunction, which the California Supreme Court had recently upheld for the first time.[3] A flyer distributed by Operation Rescue of California, advertising the Summer of Missions, mentioned the Vallejo injunction specifically.

* * *

When he took the stand, Ross explained why he had motioned for Reece to leave: "[White] mentioned to me that there was another pro-lifer across the street that was named in the injunction and he, [White], ... asked me to wave him off." Ross denied knowing Reece, but he conceded that it was probably White's intention to minimize contact with any enjoined party because "if that person was named on the injunction, it wouldn't look good for us to have that person there."

The prosecutor made her closing argument, incorporating the statements she had made against appellants' motion for acquittal: "[A] group

---

3. *See* Planned Parenthood Shasta–Diablo, Inc. v. Williams (1994) 7 Cal.4th 860, 30 Cal. Rptr.2d 629, 873 P.2d 1224 (*Williams I*). The United States Supreme Court later vacated the judgment in *Williams I* and remanded the matter for reconsideration in light of Madsen v. Women's Health Center, Inc. (1994) 512 U.S. 753, 114 S.Ct. 2516, 129 L.Ed.2d 593 (*Madsen*). (*See* Williams v. Planned Parenthood Shasta–Diablo, Inc. (1994) 513 U.S. 956, 115 S.Ct. 413, 130 L.Ed.2d 329.) On remand, in *Williams II*, our Supreme Court reaffirmed the judgment of the Court of Appeal, upholding the injunction.

of anti-abortion protesters doing the very things that are enjoined in the permanent injunction with knowledge of the injunction are in a sense standing in the shoes of the named litigants." "[Appellants say they are acting independently.] That's playing games; that is the shell game. That is just semantics. It's clearly an intentional ploy to challenge the order and that's exactly what they did and that's why we're here."

The trial judge found the appellants guilty, presumably on the legal theory he articulated before he denied their motion for acquittal: "First of all, I don't think the concept of acting 'in concert' is so narrowly interpreted that it would allow a group to escape the restrictions of an injunction [ ]or injunctive order by the expediency of simply saying they belong to an organization with a different name, despite the fact that they share a mutuality of purpose and that they are participating in the same prohibit[ed] activity."

The Injunction's Scope

Appellants argue that acting "in concert" with enjoined parties requires more than simply knowing of the injunction and acting in ways the parties are enjoined from acting. We agree.

"Injunctions ... are remedies imposed for violations (or threatened violations) of a legislative or judicial decree." * * * They may work to deprive the enjoined parties of rights others enjoy precisely because the enjoined parties have abused those rights in the past. * * *

Injunctions are not effective against the world at large. * * * This is * * * because injunctions are fashioned and enforced without the safeguards that attend the passage and govern the enforcement of more general prohibitions. * * *

On the other hand, as the trial court recognized, enjoined parties may not play jurisdictional "shell games." They may not nullify an injunctive decree by carrying out prohibited acts with or through nonparties to the original proceeding. * * * Roe v. Operation Rescue (3rd Cir.1995) 54 F.3d 133, 139 * * *. Any such nonparty who knowingly violates the terms of an injunction is subject to the contempt powers of the court. * * *

It is clear from this language that, in addition to knowledge of the injunction, some actual relationship with an enjoined party is required to bring a nonparty actor within the injunction's scope. An enjoined party, in other words, has to be demonstrably implicated in the nonparty's activity. Mere "mutuality of purpose" is not enough. Here, it must be appellants' actual relationship to an enjoined party, and not their convictions about abortion, that make them contemnors.[6] In sum, we conclude that a nonparty to an injunction is subject to the contempt power of the court when, with knowledge of the injunction, the nonparty violates its terms with or for those who are restrained.

---

6. Otherwise, our Supreme Court could not have declared the injunction content-neutral, as it did in *Williams II*. (*See id., supra,* 10 Cal.4th at p. 1019, 43 Cal.Rptr.2d 88, 898 P.2d 402.)

Here, the prosecutor argued, and the trial court appeared to accept, that knowing of the injunction and doing what it forbade, without more, placed appellants "in concert" with the enjoined parties and, therefore, in contempt of the injunction. As we have explained, while knowledge is required, it is not alone enough to make a contemner of an independent actor. (*Cf.* Fed. Rules Civ.Proc., rule 65(d), 28 U.S.C.) We must determine, therefore, whether the evidence linking the enjoined parties to the appellants was sufficient to prove that appellants acted with or for them.

Sufficiency of the Evidence

* * * [T]he relevant question is whether, after viewing the evidence in the light most favorable to the prosecution, any rational trier of fact could have found the essential elements of the crime beyond a reasonable doubt. (Jackson v. Virginia (1979) 443 U.S. 307, 318–319, 99 S.Ct. 2781, 2789, 61 L.Ed.2d 560.) * * *

Here, the evidence showed that appellants knew the provisions of the injunction, and had come to Vallejo specifically to do what the enjoined parties could not. It did not show, however, appellants' membership in, or affiliation with, any enjoined organization or person; it did not show a connection between Operation Rescue, or any of the groups that sponsored appellants' journey to Vallejo, and any enjoined organization or person; and it did not show that appellants were playing the "shell games" with which the court was properly concerned. (*Compare* Roe v. Operation Rescue, *supra*, 54 F.3d at pp. 139–140.) Instead, it showed a single interaction between appellants and an enjoined party, Ross's motioning to Reece to leave the vicinity of the demonstration. This, we conclude, is too insubstantial, in the light of the whole record, to support the conclusion that appellants acted "in concert" with Reece. We, therefore, reverse appellants' convictions.

Phelan, P.J., and Corrigan, J., concur.

F.　BARRING COLLATERAL ATTACKS ON INJUNCTIONS

If an injunction has been issued erroneously, must the defendant either obey the court's order or appeal the ruling? Or may the defendant disobey the court's order and mount a collateral attack on the court's decree during the hearing in which the defendant is ordered to show cause why the defendant should not be held in contempt of court? The answer to this question varies from one jurisdiction to another. Also, the answer to this question varies, depending upon the nature of the court's error in issuing the injunction. The cases described in the Note below consider the most serious type of error: the wrongful exercise of subject matter jurisdiction. The lead cases which follow the Note discuss a more problematic type of error: the issuance of an injunction that violates the First Amendment's prior restraint doctrine.

NOTE

In United States v. United Mine Workers of America, 330 U.S. 258, 67 S.Ct. 677, 91 L.Ed. 884 (1947), a case in which the trial court had granted an anti-strike temporary restraining order, the United States Supreme Court upheld the defendants' criminal contempt convictions in a federal district court against a collateral attack on the ground that a court of equity has jurisdiction to determine whether it has subject matter jurisdiction when issuing a temporary restraining order. In that case, there was a substantial question of whether Congress had deprived federal district courts of jurisdiction to issue anti-strike injunctions. *Compare In re* Green, 369 U.S. 689, 82 S.Ct. 1114, 8 L.Ed.2d 198 (1962) (allowing a collateral attack on the ground of federal preemption and reversing a criminal contempt conviction for the violation of a temporary restraining order that had been entered by a state court without subject matter jurisdiction).

WALKER v. CITY OF BIRMINGHAM

Supreme Court of the United States, 1967.
388 U.S. 307, 87 S.Ct. 1824, 18 L.Ed.2d 1210.

MR. JUSTICE STEWART delivered the opinion of the Court.

On Wednesday, April 10, 1963, officials of Birmingham, Alabama, filed a bill of complaint in a state circuit court asking for injunctive relief against 139 individuals and two organizations. The bill and accompanying affidavits stated that during the preceding seven days:

> [R]espondents [had] sponsored and/or participated in and/or conspired to commit and/or to encourage and/or to participate in certain movements, plans or projects commonly called "sit-in" demonstrations, "kneel-in" demonstrations, mass street parades, trespasses on private property after being warned to leave the premises by the owners of said property, congregating in mobs upon the public streets and other public places, unlawfully picketing private places of business in the City of Birmingham, Alabama; violation of numerous ordinances and statutes of the City of Birmingham and State of Alabama. * * *

It was alleged that this conduct was "calculated to provoke breaches of the peace," "threaten[ed] the safety, peace and tranquility of the City," and placed "an undue burden and strain upon the manpower of the Police Department."

The bill stated that these infractions of the law were expected to continue and would "lead to further imminent danger to the lives, safety, peace, tranquility and general welfare of the people of the City of Birmingham," and that the "remedy by law [was] inadequate." The circuit judge granted a temporary injunction as prayed in the bill, enjoining the petitioners from among other things, participating in or encouraging mass street parades or mass processions without a permit as required by a Birmingham ordinance.

Five of the eight petitioners were served with copies of the writ early the next morning. Several hours later four of them held a press conference. There a statement was distributed, declaring their intention to disobey the injunction because it was "raw tyranny under the guise of maintaining law and order." At this press conference one of the petitioners stated: "That they had respect for the Federal Courts, or Federal Injunctions, but in the past the State Courts had favored local law enforcement, and if the police couldn't handle it, the mob would."

That night a meeting took place at which one of the petitioners announced that "[i]njunction or no injunction we are going to march tomorrow." The next afternoon, Good Friday, a large crowd gathered in the vicinity of Sixteenth Street and Sixth Avenue North in Birmingham. A group of about 50 or 60 proceeded to parade along the sidewalk while a crowd of 1,000 to 1,500 onlookers stood by, "clapping, and hollering, and [w]hooping." Some of the crowd followed the marchers and spilled out into the street. At least three of the petitioners participated in this march.

Meetings sponsored by some of the petitioners were held that night and the following night, where calls for volunteers to "walk" and go to jail were made. On Easter Sunday, April 14, a crowd of between 1,500 and 2,000 people congregated in the midafternoon in the vicinity of Seventh Avenue and Eleventh Street North in Birmingham. One of the petitioners was seen organizing members of the crowd in formation. A group of about 50, headed by three other petitioners, started down the sidewalk two abreast. At least one other petitioner was among the marchers. Some 300 or 400 people from among the onlookers followed in a crowd that occupied the entire width of the street and overflowed onto the sidewalks. Violence occurred. Members of the crowd threw rocks that injured a newspaperman and damaged a police motorcycle.

The next day the city officials who had requested the injunction applied to the state circuit court for an order to show cause why the petitioners should not be held in contempt for violating it. At the ensuing hearing the petitioners sought to attack the constitutionality of the injunction on the ground that it was vague and overbroad and restrained free speech. They also sought to attack the Birmingham parade ordinance upon similar grounds, and upon the further ground that the ordinance had previously been administered in an arbitrary and discriminatory manner.

The circuit judge refused to consider any of these contentions, pointing out that there had been neither a motion to dissolve the injunction, nor an effort to comply with it by applying for a permit from the city commission before engaging in the Good Friday and Easter Sunday parades. Consequently, the court held that the only issues before it were whether it had jurisdiction to issue the temporary injunction, and whether thereafter the petitioners had knowingly violated it. Upon these issues the court found against the petitioners, and imposed upon each of them a sentence of five days in jail and a $50 fine, in accord with an Alabama statute.

The Supreme Court of Alabama affirmed. That court, too, declined to consider the petitioners' constitutional attacks upon the injunction and the underlying Birmingham parade ordinance.

* * *

Howat v. State of Kansas, 258 U.S. 181, 42 S.Ct. 277, 66 L.Ed. 550 (1922), was decided by this Court almost 50 years ago. That was a case in which people had been punished by a Kansas trial court for refusing to obey an antistrike injunction issued under the state industrial relations act. They had claimed a right to disobey the court's order upon the ground that the state statute and the injunction based upon it were invalid under the Federal Constitution. The Supreme Court of Kansas had affirmed the judgment, holding that the trial court "had general power to issue injunctions in equity, and that even if its exercise of the power was erroneous, the injunction was not void, and the defendants were precluded from attacking it in this collateral proceeding * * *, that, if the injunction was erroneous, jurisdiction was not thereby forfeited, that the error was subject to correction only by the ordinary method of appeal, and disobedience to the order constituted contempt." 258 U.S., at 189, 42 S.Ct., at 280.

This Court, in dismissing the writ of error, not only unanimously accepted but fully approved the validity of the rule of state law upon which the judgment of the Kansas court was grounded:

An injunction duly issuing out of a court of general jurisdiction with equity powers, upon pleadings properly invoking its action, and served upon persons made parties therein and within the jurisdiction, must be obeyed by them, however erroneous the action of the court may be, even if the error be in the assumption of the validity of a seeming, but void law going to the merits of the case. It is for the court of first instance to determine the question of the validity of the law, and until its decision is reversed for error by orderly review, either by itself or by a higher court, its orders based on its decision are to be respected, and disobedience of them is contempt of its lawful authority, to be punished. 258 U.S., at 189–90, 42 S.Ct., at 280.

The rule of state law accepted and approved in Howat v. State of Kansas is consistent with the rule of law followed by the federal courts.

In the present case, however, we are asked to hold that this rule of law, upon which the Alabama courts relied, was constitutionally impermissible. We are asked to say that the Constitution compelled Alabama to allow the petitioners to violate this injunction, to organize and engage in these mass street parades and demonstrations, without any previous effort on their part to have the injunction dissolved or modified, or any attempt to secure a parade permit in accordance with its terms. Whatever the limits of Howat v. State of Kansas, we cannot accept the petitioners' contentions in the circumstances of this case.

Without question the state court that issued the injunction had, as a court of equity, jurisdiction over the petitioners and over the subject matter of the controversy. And this is not a case where the injunction was transparently invalid or had only a frivolous pretense to validity. We have consistently recognized the strong interest of state and local governments in regulating the use of their streets and other public places. When protest takes the form of mass demonstrations, parades, or picketing on public streets and sidewalks, the free passage of traffic and the prevention of public disorder and violence become important objects of legitimate state concern.

* * *

The generality of the language contained in the Birmingham parade ordinance upon which the injunction was based would unquestionably raise substantial constitutional issues concerning some of its provisions. The petitioners, however, did not even attempt to apply to the Alabama courts for an authoritative construction of the ordinance. Had they done so, those courts might have given the licensing authority granted in the ordinance a narrow and precise scope * * *. [I]t could not be assumed that this ordinance was void on its face.

The breadth and vagueness of the injunction itself would also unquestionably be subject to substantial constitutional question. But the way to raise that question was to apply to the Alabama courts to have the injunction modified or dissolved. The injunction in all events clearly prohibited mass parading without a permit, and the evidence shows that the petitioners fully understood that prohibition when they violated it.

The petitioners also claim that they were free to disobey the injunction because the parade ordinance on which it was based had been administered in the past in an arbitrary and discriminatory fashion. In support of this claim they sought to introduce evidence that, a few days before the injunction issued, requests for permits to picket had been made to a member of the city commission. One request had been rudely rebuffed, and this same official had later made clear that he was without power to grant the permit alone, since the issuance of such permits was the responsibility of the entire city commission. Assuming the truth of this proffered evidence, it does not follow that the parade ordinance was void on its face. The petitioners, moreover, did not apply for a permit either to the commission itself or to any commissioner after the injunction issued. Had they done so, and had the permit been refused, it is clear that their claim of arbitrary or discriminatory administration of the ordinance would have been considered by the state circuit court upon a motion to dissolve the injunction.

This case would arise in quite a different constitutional posture if the petitioners, before disobeying the injunction, had challenged it in the Alabama courts, and had been met with delay or frustration of their constitutional claims. But there is no showing that such would have been the fate of a timely motion to modify or dissolve the injunction. There was an interim of two days between the issuance of the injunction and the Good Friday march. The petitioners give absolutely no explanation of why they did not make some application to the state court during that period. The injunction had issued ex parte; if the court had been presented with the petitioners' contentions, it might well have dissolved or at least modified its order in some respects. If it had not done so, Alabama procedure would have provided for an expedited process of appellate review. It cannot be presumed that the Alabama courts would have ignored the petitioners' constitutional claims. Indeed, these contentions were accepted in another case by an Alabama appellate court that struck down on direct review the conviction under this very ordinance of one of these same petitioners. Shuttlesworth v. City of Birmingham, 180 So.2d 114 (Ala.App.1965), further appeal pending.

* * *

The Alabama Supreme Court has apparently never in any criminal contempt case entertained a claim of nonjurisdictional error. In Fields v. City of Fairfield, 273 Ala. 588, 143 So.2d 177, decided just three years before the present case, the defendants, members of a "White Supremacy" organization who had disobeyed an injunction, sought to challenge the constitutional validity of a permit ordinance upon which the injunction was based. The Supreme Court of Alabama, finding that the trial court had jurisdiction, applied the same rule of law which was followed here:

> As a general rule, an unconstitutional statute is an absolute nullity and may not form the basis of any legal right or legal proceedings, yet until its unconstitutionality has been judicially declared in appropriate proceedings, no person charged with its observance under an order or decree may disregard or violate the order or the decree with immunity from a charge of contempt of court; and he may not raise the question of its unconstitutionality in collateral proceedings on appeal from a judgment of conviction for contempt of the order or decree * * *. 273 Ala., at 590, 143 So.2d, at 180.

These precedents clearly put the petitioners on notice that they could not bypass orderly judicial review of the injunction before disobeying it. Any claim that they were entrapped or misled is wholly unfounded, a conclusion confirmed by evidence in the record showing that when the petitioners deliberately violated the injunction they expected to go to jail.

The rule of law that Alabama followed in this case reflects a belief that in the fair administration of justice no man can be judge in his own case, however exalted his station, however righteous his motives, and irrespective of his race, color, politics, or religion. This Court cannot hold that the petitioners were constitutionally free to ignore all the procedures of the law and carry their battle to the streets. One may sympathize with the petitioners' impatient commitment to their cause. But respect for judicial process is a small price to pay for the civilizing hand of law, which alone can give abiding meaning to constitutional freedom.

Affirmed.

MR. CHIEF JUSTICE WARREN, whom MR. JUSTICE BRENNAN and MR. JUSTICE FORTAS join, dissenting.

Petitioners in this case contend that they were convicted under an ordinance that is unconstitutional on its face because it submits their First and Fourteenth Amendment rights to free speech and peaceful assembly to the unfettered discretion of local officials. They further contend that the ordinance was unconstitutionally applied to them because the local officials used their discretion to prohibit peaceful demonstrations by a group whose political viewpoint the officials opposed. The Court does not dispute these contentions, but holds that petitioners may nonetheless be convicted and sent to jail because the patently unconstitutional ordinance was copied into an injunction—issued ex parte without prior notice or hearing on the request of the Commissioner of Public Safety—forbidding all persons having notice of the injunction to violate the ordinance without any limitation of time. I dissent because I do not believe that the fundamental protections of the Constitution were meant to be so easily evaded, or that "the civilizing hand of law" would be hampered in the slightest by enforcing the First Amendment in this case.

* * *

I do not believe that giving this Court's seal of approval to such a gross misuse of the judicial process is likely to lead to greater respect for the law any more than it is likely to lead to greater protection for First Amendment freedoms. The ex parte temporary injunction has a long and odious history in this country, and its susceptibility to misuse is all too apparent from the facts of the case. As a weapon against strikes, it proved so effective in the hands of judges friendly to employers that Congress was forced to take the drastic step of removing from federal district courts the jurisdiction to issue injunctions in labor disputes. The labor injunction fell into disrepute largely because it was abused in precisely the same way that the injunctive power was abused in this case. Judges who were not sympathetic to the union cause commonly issued, without notice or hearing, broad restraining orders addressed to large numbers of persons and forbidding them to engage in acts that were either legally permissible or, if illegal, that could better have been left to the regular course of criminal prosecution. The injunctions might later be dissolved, but in the meantime strikes would be crippled because the occasion on which concerted activity might have been effective had passed. Such injunctions, so long discredited as weapons against concerted labor activities, have now been given new life by this Court as weapons against the exercise of First Amendment freedoms. Respect for the courts and for judicial process was not increased by the history of the labor injunction.

Nothing in our prior decisions, or in the doctrine that a party subject to a temporary injunction issued by a court of competent jurisdiction with power to decide a dispute properly before it must normally challenge the injunction in the courts rather than by violating it, requires that we affirm the convictions in this case. The majority opinion in this case rests essentially on a single precedent, and that a case the authority of which has clearly been undermined by subsequent decisions. Howat v. State of Kansas, 258 U.S. 181, 42 S.Ct. 277, 66 L.Ed. 550 (1922), was decided in the days when the labor injunction was in fashion. Kansas had adopted an Industrial Relations Act, the purpose of which in effect was to provide for compulsory arbitration of labor disputes by a neutral administrative tribunal, the "Court of Industrial Relations." Pursuant to its jurisdiction to investigate and perhaps improve labor conditions in the coal mining industry, the "Court" subpoenaed union leaders to appear and testify. In addition, the State obtained an injunction to prevent a strike while the matter was before the "Court." The union leaders disobeyed both the subpoena and the injunction, and sought to challenge the constitutionality of the Industrial Relations Act in the ensuing contempt proceeding. The Kansas Supreme Court held that the constitutionality of the Act could not be challenged in a contempt proceeding, and this Court upheld that determination.

Insofar as Howat v. State of Kansas might be interpreted to approve an absolute rule that any violation of a void court order is punishable as contempt, it has been greatly modified by later decisions. In *In re* Green, 369 U.S. 689, 82 S.Ct. 1114, 8 L.Ed.2d 198 (1962), we reversed a conviction for contempt of a state injunction forbidding labor picketing because the petitioner was not allowed to present evidence that the labor dispute was arguably subject to the jurisdiction of the National Labor Relations Board and hence not subject to state regulation. If an injunction can be challenged on the ground that it deals with a matter arguably subject to the jurisdiction of the National Labor Relations Board, then a fortiori it can be challenged on First Amendment grounds.

It is not necessary to question the continuing validity of the holding in Howat v. State of Kansas, however, to demonstrate that neither it nor the *Mine Workers*[10] case supports the holding of the majority in this case. In *Howat* the subpoena and injunction were issued to enable the Kansas Court of Industrial Relations to determine an underlying labor dispute. In the *Mine Workers* case, the District Court issued a temporary antistrike injunction to preserve existing conditions during the time it took to decide whether it had authority to grant the Government relief in a complex and difficult action of enormous importance to the national economy. In both cases the orders were of questionable legality, but in both cases they were reasonably necessary to enable the court or administrative tribunal to decide an underlying controversy of considerable importance before it at the time. This case involves an entirely different situation. The Alabama Circuit Court did not issue this temporary injunction to preserve existing conditions while it proceeded to decide some underlying dispute. There was no underlying dispute before it, and the court in practical effect merely added a judicial signature to a preexisting criminal ordinance. Just as the court had no need to issue the injunction to preserve its ability to

---

10. United States v. United Mine Workers, 330 U.S. 258, 67 S.Ct. 677, 91 L.Ed. 884 (1947).

decide some underlying dispute, the city had no need of an injunction to impose a criminal penalty for demonstrating on the streets without a permit. The ordinance already accomplished that. In point of fact, there is only one apparent reason why the city sought this injunction and why the court issued it: to make it possible to punish petitioners for contempt rather than for violating the ordinance, and thus to immunize the unconstitutional statute and its unconstitutional application from any attack. I regret that this strategy has been so successful.

It is not necessary in this case to decide precisely what limits should be set to the *Mine Workers* doctrine in cases involving violations of the First Amendment. Whatever the scope of that doctrine, it plainly was not intended to give a State the power to nullify the United States Constitution by the simple process of incorporating its unconstitutional criminal statutes into judicial decrees. I respectfully dissent.

MR. JUSTICE DOUGLAS, with whom THE CHIEF JUSTICE, MR. JUSTICE BRENNAN, and MR. JUSTICE FORTAS concur, dissenting.

The right to defy an unconstitutional statute is basic in our scheme. Even when an ordinance requires a permit to make a speech, to deliver a sermon, to picket, to parade, or to assemble, it need not be honored when it is invalid on its face. * * *

By like reason, where a permit has been arbitrarily denied one need not pursue the long and expensive route to this Court to obtain a remedy. The reason is the same in both cases. For if a person must pursue his judicial remedy before he may speak, parade, or assemble, the occasion when protest is desired or needed will have become history and any later speech, parade, or assembly will be futile or pointless.

* * *

MR. JUSTICE BRENNAN, with whom THE CHIEF JUSTICE, MR. JUSTICE DOUGLAS, and MR. JUSTICE FORTAS join, dissenting.

Under cover of exhortation that the Negro exercise "respect for judicial process," the Court empties the Supremacy Clause of its primacy by elevating a state rule of judicial administration above the right of free expression guaranteed by the Federal Constitution. And the Court does so by letting loose a devastatingly destructive weapon for suppression of cherished freedoms heretofore believed indispensable to maintenance of our free society. * * *

I.

Petitioners are eight Negro Ministers. They were convicted of criminal contempt for violation of an ex parte injunction issued by the Circuit Court of Jefferson County, Alabama, by engaging in street parades without a municipal permit on Good Friday and Easter Sunday 1963. These were the days when Birmingham was a world symbol of implacable official hostility to Negro efforts to gain civil rights, however peacefully sought. The purpose of these demonstrations was peaceably to publicize and dramatize the civil rights grievances of the Negro people. The underlying permit ordinance made it unlawful "to organize or hold * * * or to take part or participate in, any parade or procession or other public demonstration on the streets * * * " without a permit. A permit was issuable by the City Commission "unless in its judgment the public welfare, peace, safety, health, decency, good order, morals or convenience require that it be refused."

Attempts by petitioners at the contempt hearing to show that they tried to obtain a permit but were rudely rebuffed by city officials were aborted when the trial court sustained objections to the testimony. It did appear, however, that on April 3, a member of the Alabama Christian Movement for Human Rights (ACMHR) was sent by one of the petitioners, the Reverend Mr. Shuttlesworth, to Birmingham city hall to inquire about permits for future demonstrations. The member stated at trial:

> I asked (Police) Commissioner Connor for the permit, and asked if he could issue the permit, or other persons who would refer me to, persons who would issue a permit. He said, "No, you will not get a permit in Birmingham, Alabama to picket. I will picket you over to the City Jail," and he repeated that twice.

Two days later the Reverend Mr. Shuttlesworth sent a telegram to Police Commissioner Connor requesting a permit on behalf of ACMHR to picket on given dates "against the injustices of segregation and discrimination." Connor replied that the permit could be granted only by the full Commission and stated, "I insist that you and your people do not start any picketing on the streets in Birmingham, Alabama." Petitioners were also frustrated in their attempts at the contempt hearing to show that permits were granted, not by the Commission, but by the city clerk at the request of the traffic department, and that they were issued in a discriminatory manner.

On April 6–7 and April 9–10, Negroes were arrested for parading without a permit. Late in the night of April 10, the city requested and immediately obtained an ex parte injunction without prior notice to petitioners. Notice of the issuance was given to five of the petitioners on April 11. The decree tracked the wording of the permit ordinance, except that it was still broader and more pervasive. It enjoined:

> * * * engaging in, sponsoring, inciting or encouraging mass street parades or mass processions or like demonstrations without a permit, trespass on private property after being warned to leave the premises by the owner or person in possession of said private property, congregating on the street or public places into mobs, and unlawfully picketing business establishments or public buildings in the City of Birmingham, Jefferson County, State of Alabama or performing acts calculated to cause breaches of the peace in the City of Birmingham, Jefferson County, in the State of Alabama or from conspiring to engage in unlawful street parades, unlawful processions, unlawful demonstrations, unlawful boycotts, unlawful trespasses, and unlawful

picketing or other like unlawful conduct or from violating the ordinances of the City of Birmingham and the Statutes of the State of Alabama or from doing any acts designed to consummate conspiracies to engage in said unlawful acts of parading, demonstrating, boycotting, trespassing and picketing or other unlawful acts, or from engaging in acts and conduct customarily known as "kneel-ins" in churches in violation of the wishes and desires of said churches. * * *

Several of the Negro ministers issued statements that they would refuse to comply with what they believed to be, and is indeed, a blatantly unconstitutional restraining order.

On April 12, Good Friday, a planned march took place, beginning at a church in the Negro section of the city and continuing to city hall. The police, who were notified in advance by one of the petitioners of the time and route of the march, blocked the streets to traffic in the area of the church and excluded white persons from the Negro area. Approximately 50 persons marched, led by three petitioners, Martin Luther King, Ralph Abernathy, and Shuttlesworth. A large crowd of Negro onlookers which had gathered outside the church remained separate from the procession. A few blocks from the church the police stopped the procession and arrested, and jailed, most of the marchers, including the three leaders.

On Easter Sunday another planned demonstration was conducted. The police again were given advance notice, and again blocked the streets to traffic and white persons in the vicinity of the church. Several hundred persons were assembled at the church. Approximately 50 persons who emerged from the church began walking peaceably. Several blocks from the church the procession was stopped, as on Good Friday, and about 20 persons, including five petitioners, were arrested. The participants in both parades were in every way orderly; the only episode of violence, according to a police inspector, was rock throwing by three onlookers on Easter Sunday, after petitioners were arrested; the three rock throwers were immediately taken into custody by the police.

On Monday, April 15, petitioners moved to dissolve the injunction, and the city initiated criminal contempt proceedings against petitioners. At the hearing, held a week later, the Jefferson County Court considered the contempt charge first. Petitioners urged that the injunction and underlying permit ordinance were impermissibly vague prior restraints on exercise of First Amendment rights and that the ordinance had been discriminatorily applied. The court, however, limited evidence primarily to two questions: notice of and violation of the injunction. The court stated that "the validity of its injunction order stands upon its prima facie authority to execute the same." Petitioners were found guilty of criminal contempt and sentenced to five days in jail and a $50 fine. The Alabama Supreme Court, adopting the reasoning of United States v. United Mine Workers, 330 U.S. 258, 67 S.Ct. 677, 91 L.Ed. 884, applicable to federal court orders, affirmed, holding that the validity of the injunction and underlying permit ordinance could not be challenged in a contempt proceeding. 279 Ala. 53, 181 So.2d 493.

II.

The holding of the Alabama Supreme Court, and the affirmance of its decision by this Court, rest on the assumption that petitioners may be criminally punished although the parade ordinance and the injunction be unconstitutional on their faces as in violation of the First Amendment, and even if the parade ordinance was discriminatorily applied. It must therefore be assumed, for purposes of review of the Alabama Supreme Court's decision, and in assessing the Court's affirmance, that petitioners could successfully sustain the contentions (into which the Alabama courts refused to inquire) that the ordinance and injunction are in fact facially unconstitutional as excessively vague prior restraints on First Amendment rights and that the ordinance had been discriminatorily applied. * * *

* * *

Like the Court, I start with the premise that States are free to adopt rules of judicial administration designed to require respect for their courts' orders. *See* Howat v. State of Kansas, 258 U.S. 181, 42 S.Ct. 277, 66 L.Ed. 550. But this does not mean that this valid state interest does not admit of collision with other and more vital interests. Surely the proposition requires no citation that a valid state interest must give way when it infringes on rights guaranteed by the Federal Constitution. The plain meaning of the Supremacy Clause requires no less.

In the present case we are confronted with a collision between Alabama's interest in requiring adherence to orders of its courts and the constitutional prohibition against abridgment of freedom of speech, more particularly "the right of the people peaceably to assemble," and the right "to petition the Government for a redress of grievances." * * * Special considerations have time and again been deemed by us to attend protection of these freedoms in the face of state interests the vindication of which results in prior restraints upon their exercise, or their regulation in a vague or overbroad manner, or in a way which gives unbridled discretion to limit their exercise to an individual or group of individuals. To give these freedoms the necessary "breathing space to survive," * * * the Court has modified traditional rules of standing and prematurity. * * * We have molded both substantive rights and procedural remedies in the face of varied conflicting interests to conform to our overriding duty to insulate all individuals from the "chilling effect" upon exercise of First Amendment freedoms generated by vagueness, overbreadth and unbridled discretion to limit their exercise.

The vitality of First Amendment protections has, as a result, been deemed to rest in large measure upon the ability of the individual to take his chances and express himself in the face of such restraints, armed with the ability to challenge those restraints if the State seeks to penalize that expression. * * *

Yet by some inscrutable legerdemain these constitutionally secured rights to challenge prior restraints invalid on their face are lost if the State takes the precaution to have some judge append his signature to an ex parte order which recites the words of the invalid statute. * * *

* * *

The suggestion that petitioners be muffled pending outcome of dissolution proceedings without any measurable time limits is particularly inappropriate in the setting of this case. Critical to the plain exercise of the right of protest was the timing of that exercise. First, the marches were part of a program to arouse community support for petitioners' assault on segregation there. A cessation of these activities, even for a short period, might deal a crippling blow to petitioners' efforts. Second, in dramatization of their cause, petitioners, all ministers, chose April 12, Good Friday, and April 14, Easter Sunday, for their protests hoping to gain the attention to their cause which such timing might attract. Petitioners received notice of the order April 11. The ability to exercise protected protest at a time when such exercise would be effective must be as protected as the beliefs themselves. * * *

* * * Convictions for contempt of court orders which invalidly abridge First Amendment freedoms must be condemned equally with convictions for violation of statutes which do the same thing. I respectfully dissent.

NOTES

1. The *Walker* case has been analyzed extensively. *See* Vince Blasi, *Prior Restraints on Demonstrations*, 68 Mich. L. Rev. 1481, 1560–63 (1970); Martin Edelman, *The Absurd Remnant: Walker v. Birmingham Two Years Later*, 34 Albany L. Rev. 523 (1970); Note, 56 Calif. L. Rev. 517 (1968); Note, 81 Harv. L. Rev. 141 (1967).

2. In Shuttlesworth v. City of Birmingham, 394 U.S. 147, 89 S.Ct. 935, 22 L.Ed.2d 162 (1969), the Court struck down the City of Birmingham's ordinance which made it "unlawful to organize * * * or to participate in any parade or procession or other public demonstration on the streets * * * unless a permit therefore has been secured from the commission * * *." Justice Stewart wrote the opinion for the Court:

> The petitioner was convicted for violation of [the ordinance] and was sentenced to 90 days' imprisonment at hard labor and an additional 48 days at hard labor in default of payment of a $75 fine and $24 costs. * * *

> There can be no doubt that the Birmingham ordinance, as it was written, conferred upon the City Commission virtually unbridled and absolute power to prohibit [a parade] * * *. The ordinance as it was written, therefore, fell squarely within the ambit of the many decisions of this Court over the last 30 years, holding that a law subjecting the exercise of First Amendment freedoms to the prior restraint of a license, without narrow, objective and definite standards to guide the licensing

authority, is unconstitutional. * * * And our decisions have made clear that a person faced with such an unconstitutional licensing law may ignore it and engage with impunity in the exercise of the right of free expression for which the law purports to require a license. * * *

It is argued, however, that what was involved here was not "pure speech" * * *.

But our decisions have also made clear that picketing and parading may * * * constitute methods of expression, entitled to First Amendment protection. * * *

Id. at 148–59, 89 S.Ct. at 937–43. For a discussion of the circumstances surrounding the Court's opinion in *Shuttlesworth*, see Taylor Branch, Parting the Waters: America in the King Years 1954–63 (Simon & Schuster 1988); David Luban, *Difference Made Legal: The Court and Dr. King*, 87 Mich. L. Rev. 2152 (1989); Martin Luther King, Jr., *Letter from the Birmingham Jail*, 26 U.C. Davis L. Rev. 835 (1993).

3. What if a federal district court issues an adversary temporary restraining order against Operation Rescue and its participants, prohibiting the defendants from "engaging in illegal activities designed to disrupt access to abortion facilities," and then extends the duration of the temporary restraining order beyond the time limits set forth in Rule 65(b) in order to conduct a lengthy preliminary injunction proceeding? If the defendants violate the injunction on the 28th day, and if they are charged with criminal contempt, can they mount a successful collateral attack on the ground that the temporary restraining order is void, or are they bound by the terms of the order? The Second Circuit held that the defendants were bound by the terms of the order extending the time limits because they had notice of the order and an opportunity to present their opposition to it, and then the court applied the collateral bar doctrine: "The bottom line is that appellants could have appealed the extension of the TRO. They could have asked the district court to issue an order vacating the TRO. What they could not do, however, is disobey the Order without consequences." *In re* Criminal Contempt Proceedings Against Crawford, 329 F.3d 131, 139 (2d Cir.2003), *cert. denied*, 540 U.S. 881, 124 S.Ct. 339, 157 L.Ed.2d 147 (2003).

4. The collateral bar doctrine is relevant only in criminal contempt proceedings. It does not apply to a civil contempt proceeding because, when a defendant attacks a court order imposing a coercive or a compensatory contempt sanction, and the order is overturned, there is no basis for any continuing coercion, and the plaintiff is no longer entitled to compensation. Such an attack is more in the nature of a direct attack than a collateral attack. If one interprets the *Bagwell* case (*see supra* Chapter 2.9.C.4) as redrawing the line between civil and criminal contempt, then *Bagwell* could have the unintended consequence of extending the applicability of the collateral bar rule to cases involving the enforcement of "complex injunctions." *See* John R.B. Palmer, Note, *Collateral Bar and Contempt: Challenging a Court Order after Disobeying It*, 88 Cornell L. Rev. 215 (2002). Since that would be inconsistent with the coercive and compensatory functions of civil contempt sanctions, the better way to read *Bagwell* is to assume that it provides for the

imposition of civil contempt sanctions through criminal procedures, but has no impact whatsoever on the collateral bar doctrine. *Id.*

5. The California Supreme Court, in *In re* Berry, 68 Cal.2d 137, 436 P.2d 273, 65 Cal.Rptr. 273 (1968) and in People v. Gonzalez, 12 Cal.4th 804, 910 P.2d 1366, 50 Cal.Rptr.2d 74 (1996), declined to follow *Walker. In re Berry* was an action involving a petition for a writ of habeas corpus which alleged that the petitioners had been wrongfully imprisoned for contempt of a temporary restraining order issued to enjoin certain conduct in connection with a threatened strike by employees of Sacramento, California. The Court held that the collateral attack upon the injunction in question was not barred because the order was "void in its entirety": "the order which petitioners are charged with disobeying is unconstitutionally overbroad in that it unnecessarily restricts the exercise of First Amendment rights; the order is too vague and uncertain to satisfy the requirements of notice and fair trial inherent in the due process clause of the Fourteenth Amendment * * *." 68 Cal.2d at 157, 436 P.2d at 286, 65 Cal.Rptr. at 286. Accordingly, the writ was granted and release of the petitioners was ordered. For a discussion of the California rule, which has been adopted by a few other states, including Texas and Washington, see Richard Labunski, *The "Collateral Bar" Rule and the First Amendment: The Constitutionality of Enforcing Unconstitutional Orders*, 37 Amer. U. L. Rev. 323 (1988); Richard Labunski, *A First Amendment Exception to the "Collateral Bar" Rule: Protecting Freedom of Expression and the Legitimacy of Courts*, 22 Pepp. L. Rev. 405 (1995).

6. The *Carroll* case (*see supra* Chapter 2.7), decided by the United States Supreme Court one year after *Walker*, generally prohibits the issuance of ex parte orders that impinge on the exercise of first amendment rights unless it is impossible to serve or notify the opposing parties and give them an opportunity for a hearing. Should the fact that an order is issued in violation of the *Carroll* rationale be recognized as a defense to a contempt prosecution? The *Carroll* case itself involved a direct appeal from the granting of an ex parte order and thus did not specifically deal with the question. In Board of Education v. Kankakee Federation of Teachers Local No. 886, 46 Ill.2d 439, 264 N.E.2d 18 (1970), *cert. denied*, 403 U.S. 904, 91 S.Ct. 2203, 29 L.Ed.2d 679 (1971), an ex parte temporary restraining order was issued against striking teachers who disobeyed it. The Illinois Supreme Court upheld a contempt judgment and stated:

> Here, the unlawful strike of the teachers was already in progress when the temporary order was sought, and the picketing the Board was seeking to restrain was being carried on for the purpose of fostering and supporting such unlawful strike. Accordingly, the first amendment considerations which controlled in *Carroll* were not present in this case. * * *

> More in keeping with the circumstances of this case are the teachings of Howat v. Kansas, 258 U.S. 181, 42 S.Ct. 277, 66 L.Ed. 550 (1922) and its progeny, one of the latest of which is *Walker v. City of Birmingham* * * *. The simple and logical rationale of these decisions is that where a court of equity issues an injunction, with jurisdiction of the subject matter and the persons and upon pleadings properly invoking its action, the injunction must be obeyed however erroneous the action of the court

may be, until it is reversed for error by orderly review, either by the court itself or a higher court. Disobedience of such an injunction is contempt of the lawful authority of the court, and punishable as such. (*See:* 388 U.S., at 314, 87 S.Ct., at 1828, 18 L.Ed.2d, at 1216 (1967)). We agree with the trial court that the principle of these cases is controlling here, and while we do not believe the temporary restraining order was erroneous, that issue is not before us.

Id. at 444, 264 N.E.2d at 21. *Compare* Commonwealth *ex rel.* Costa v. Boley, 441 Pa. 495, 272 A.2d 905 (1971) (order issued ex parte in violation of the *Carroll* case termed "void on its face" in the context of an appeal). In United Mine Workers of America Union Hospital v. United Mine Workers of America District No. 50, 52 Ill.2d 496, 502, 288 N.E.2d 455, 458 (1972), the Illinois Supreme Court explained *Kankakee* by emphasizing that "picketing has not been accorded the same unlimited protection by the first and fourteenth amendments as other forms of speech and communication," and therefore the TRO was not "transparently invalid."

IN RE PROVIDENCE JOURNAL CO.

United States Court of Appeals, First Circuit, 1986.
820 F.2d 1342.

WISDOM, CIRCUIT JUDGE.

This appeal presents an apparent conflict between two fundamental legal principles: the hallowed First Amendment principle that the press shall not be subjected to prior restraints; the other, the sine qua non of orderly government, that, until modified or vacated, a court order must be obeyed. The district court adjudged the defendants/appellants, the Providence Journal Company and its executive editor, Charles M. Hauser, (collectively referred to as the "Journal") guilty of criminal contempt. The Journal admits that it violated the order but argues that the order was a prior restraint and that the unconstitutionality of the order is a defense in the contempt proceeding. * * *

FACTS

[For three years, the FBI conducted warrantless electronic surveillance of Raymond L.S. Patriarca, reputedly a prominent figure in organized crime. Later, the FBI destroyed the tape recordings, but not the memoranda compiled from the recordings. The Journal sued to obtain the memoranda from the FBI under the Freedom of Information act. The First Circuit ruled that it was within the FBI's discretion to refuse the Journal's request. After Patriarca died, the Journal renewed its request, and the FBI granted it. Patriarca's son then filed a complaint against the Journal, alleging that the FBI had wrongfully released the memoranda, thereby violating the son's privacy rights. The son sought a temporary restraining order. One day later, after an adversary hearing, a temporary restraining order was issued that enjoined the Journal from disseminating or publishing the memoranda. The next day, the Journal violated the decree by publishing an article on the deceased Patriarca that included information taken from the memoranda. The son filed a motion to hold the Journal in contempt. When the son later declined to prosecute the criminal contempt motion, the district court appointed a special prosecutor. The court imposed an 18–month jail term on Hauser, which was suspended, ordered him to perform 200 hours of public service, and fined the Journal $100,000. The Journal appealed and the contempt sanctions were stayed pending appeal.]

DISCUSSION

This appeal propounds a question that admits of no easy answer. Each party stands on what each regards as an unassailable legal principle. The special prosecutor relies on the bedrock principle that court orders, even those that are later ruled unconstitutional, must be complied with until amended or vacated. This principle is often referred to as the "collateral bar" rule. The Journal relies on the bedrock principle that prior restraints against speech are prohibited by the First Amendment. In this opinion we endeavor to avoid deciding which principle should take precedence by reaching a result consistent with both principles.

Of all the constitutional imperatives protecting a free press under the First Amendment, the most significant is the restriction against prior restraint upon publication. "[T]he chief purpose of [the First Amendment's free press] guaranty [is] to prevent previous restraints upon publication." Indeed, "prior restraints upon speech and publication are the most serious and least tolerable infringement on First Amendment rights." * * *

* * *

At first glance, *Walker* would appear to control the instant case. * * * The *Walker* Court was, however, careful to point out that the order [in that case] was not "transparently invalid." * * *

Court orders are accorded a special status in American jurisprudence. While one may violate a statute and raise as a defense the statute's unconstitutionality, such is not generally the case with a court order. Nonetheless, court orders are not sacrosanct. An order entered by a court clearly without jurisdiction over the contemnors or the subject matter is not protected by the collateral bar rule. Were this not the case, a court could wield power over parties or matters obviously not within its authority—a concept inconsistent with the notion that the judiciary may exercise only those powers entrusted to it by law.

The same principle supports an exception to the collateral bar rule for transparently invalid orders. * * * The key to both exceptions is the notion that although a court order—even an arguably incorrect court order—demands respect, so does the right of the citizen to be free of clearly improper exercises of judicial authority.

Although an exception to the collateral bar rule is appropriate for transparently void orders, it is inappropriate for arguably proper orders.

This distinction is necessary both to protect the authority of the courts when they address close questions and to create a strong incentive for parties to follow the orderly process of law. No such protection or incentive is needed when the order is transparently invalid because in that instance the court is acting so far in excess of its authority that it has no right to expect compliance and no interest is protected by requiring compliance.

The line between a transparently invalid order and one that is merely invalid is, of course, not always distinct. As a general rule, if the court reviewing the order finds the order to have had any pretense to validity at the time it was issued, the reviewing court should enforce the collateral bar rule. * * *

* * *

In its nearly two centuries of existence, the Supreme Court has never upheld a prior restraint on pure speech. In New York Times Co. v. United States, the Pentagon Papers case, the Court held that the New York Times and other newspapers could not be restrained even during wartime from publishing documents that had been classified top secret and obtained without authorization. Notwithstanding that the source who had provided the documents had obtained them possibly as a result of criminal conduct and notwithstanding the government's contention that publication would gravely and irreparably jeopardize national security, the Court refused to uphold the restraint. * * * We now turn to consider whether the order issued by the district court on November 13, 1985, was * * * transparently invalid. * * *

The distinction between pure speech and speech involving conduct clearly distinguishes the order at issue in *Walker* from the order at issue in the instant case. * * *

Although the Supreme Court has never upheld a prior restraint on publication of news, the Court has implied that such a restraint might be appropriate in a very narrow range of cases, when either national security or an individual's right to a fair trial is at stake. An individual's right to protect his privacy from damage by private parties, although meriting great protection, is simply not of the same magnitude. * * *

An additional point to note is that the prior restraint was issued prior to a full and fair hearing with all the attendant procedural protections. * * * [T]he transparent unconstitutionality of the order is made even more patent by the absence of such a hearing. * * *

Although the Journal arguably had avenues of appellate relief immediately available to it, we decline to invoke the collateral bar rule because of the Journal's failure to avail itself of these opportunities. When, as here, the court order is a transparently invalid prior restraint on pure speech, the delay and expense of an appeal is unnecessary. Indeed, the delay caused by an appellate review requirement could, in the case of a prior restraint involving news concerning an imminent event, cause the restrained information to lose its value. The absence of such a requirement will not, however, lead to wide-spread disregard of court orders. Rarely will a party be subject to a transparently invalid court order. Prior restraints on pure speech represent an unusual class of orders because they are presumptively unconstitutional. And even when a party believes it is subject to a transparently invalid order, seeking review in an appellate court is a far safer means of testing the order. For if the party chooses to violate the order and the order turns out not to be transparently invalid, the party must suffer the consequences of a contempt citation.

* * *

Because the order was transparently invalid, the appellants should have been allowed to challenge its constitutionality at the contempt proceedings. A fortiori, the order cannot serve as the basis for a contempt citation. The order of the district court finding the Providence Journal Company and its executive editor, Charles M. Hauser, in criminal contempt is therefore reversed.

IN RE PROVIDENCE JOURNAL CO.

United States Court of Appeals, First Circuit, 1987.
820 F.2d 1354.*

ORDER

We hereby grant petitioner's suggestion for rehearing en banc. We do not, however, vacate the panel's opinion and order dated December 31, 1986, 820 F.2d 1342. Rather, we issue the attached en banc opinion as an addendum to, and modification of, said panel opinion; and as so modified said panel opinion and order may stand as reflecting the opinion of the en banc court.

JUDGE SELYA does not concur in the above order and attached en banc opinion. Rather, he believes the court should hold a hearing and decide the case anew after full briefing and argument.

OPINION ON REHEARING

PER CURIAM.

In reflecting en banc upon the conflicting principles of "collateral bar" and "no prior restraint against pure speech," the court recognizes, with the panel, the difficulties of imposing upon a publisher the requirement of pursuing the normal appeal process. Not only would such entail time and expense, but the right sought to be vindicated could be forfeited or the value of the embargoed information considerably cheapened. Never-

---

* *Appeal dismissed*, 485 U.S. 693, 108 S.Ct. 1502, 99 L.Ed.2d 785 (1988). The United States Supreme Court had granted certiorari, but after the case was briefed and argued, the Court dismissed the writ upon learning that the special counsel appointed to prosecute the contempt charges had failed to secure the proper authorization from the Solicitor General to allow him to represent the Federal government before the Supreme Court as required by 28 U.S.C. § 518(a). *Id.* at 699–700, 108 S.Ct. at 1506–07.

theless, it seems to us that some finer tuning is available to minimize the disharmony between respect for court orders and respect for free speech.

It is not asking much, beyond some additional expense and time, to require a publisher, even when it thinks it is the subject of a transparently unconstitutional order of prior restraint, to make a good faith effort to seek emergency relief from the appellate court. If timely access to the appellate court is not available or if timely decision is not forthcoming, the publisher may then proceed to publish and challenge the constitutionality of the order in the contempt proceedings.[1] In such event whatever added expense and time are involved, such a price does not seem disproportionate to the respect owing court processes; and there is no prolongation of any prior restraint. On the other hand, should the appellate court grant the requested relief, the conflict between principles has been resolved and the expense and time involved have vastly been offset by aborting any contempt proceedings.

We realize that our ruling means that a publisher seeking to challenge an order it deems transparently unconstitutional must concern itself with establishing a record of its good faith effort. But that is a price we should pay for the preference of court over party determination of invalidity. In the instant case, assertions have been made that some eight-and-one-half hours elapsed between the issuance of the order by the district court and the deadline for publication. Not only are we left without a clear conviction that timely emergency relief was available within the restraints governing the publisher's decision making, but we would deem it unfair to subject the publisher to the very substantial sanctions imposed by the district court because of its failure to follow the procedure we have just announced. We recognize that our announcement is technically dictum, but are confident that its stature as a deliberate position taken by us in this en banc consideration will serve its purpose.

1. *See* Goodale, *The Press Ungagged: The Practical Effect on Gag Order Litigation of Nebraska Press Association v. Stuart,* 29 Stan.L.Rev. 497, 509–10 (1977) (arguing that Walker v. City of Birmingham "may require no more than an attempt to appeal a void restraining order up to the time the constitutionally protected action is planned to take place.").

CHAPTER 3

BASIC PRINCIPLES OF DAMAGES

■ ■ ■

SECTION 1. LEGAL RELIEF DEFINED

As stated in Chapter 2, equitable relief is an order to the defendant to do or not do something that will give the plaintiff specific relief. Prior to ordering equitable relief, a court typically requires that legal relief be inadequate. Thus, legal relief must be different from equitable relief.

What is legal relief? Is it specific relief or is it substitutionary relief? One might think that it is substitutionary relief, in that legal damages give a plaintiff money to substitute for a remedy that would specifically undo the wrong. For example, if the wrong is a tort of taking an original oil painting, the specific remedy would be getting the painting back, while substitutionary relief would be money as a substitute for the painting in order to compensate for the loss of the painting. However, one cannot simply say that legal relief is substitutionary, while equitable relief is specific. Sometimes, by the quirk of historic rules, legal relief is specific. As will be seen in later chapters, replevin, which is a remedy that enables a plaintiff to get back personal property, can be either legal or equitable. Ejectment is a legal remedy that enables a plaintiff to get possession of real property, although in the proper circumstances a court may issue an equitable order that the defendant return real property to the plaintiff. But, as a general matter, legal relief is substitutionary and involves money damages.

Since the distinction between legal and equitable relief is not always a distinction between monetary and specific relief, there must be other distinctions. Originally the distinction was historic, as described in Chapter 1. However, since 1938, when the Federal Rules of Civil Procedure merged law and equity, the distinction between law and equity in the federal courts has not been jurisdictional. Only in a few states does a plaintiff now need to choose between bringing an action in a court of equity or a court of law. But a plaintiff needs to know whether relief is legal or equitable for other purposes. For example, as will be explained in Chapter 8, parties are entitled to a jury trial if the relief is legal, but not if it is equitable. Also, as was explained in Chapter 2, if the relief is equitable, it is enforced with contempt; but if legal, by attachment of assets pursuant to a judgment lien, usually executed by a sheriff or similar official. *See generally* Restatement (Second) of Judgments (1982).

SECTION 2. GOALS OF DAMAGES

What are the goals of damages? Professor Dobbs describes the primary goal of damages as follows:

> The stated goal of the damages remedy is compensation of the plaintiff for legally recognized losses. This means that the plaintiff should be fully indemnified for his loss, but that he should not recover any windfall. Stated in this way, damages is an instrument of corrective justice, an effort to put the plaintiff in his or her rightful position.

Dan B. Dobbs, Law of Remedies § 3.1, at 210 (2d ed. 1993). Additional goals of damages may include vindication, deterrence, and punishment.

What is the plaintiff's rightful position? In tort law, the remedial goal is to put the plaintiff in a position as if the tort had not occurred. This is done by compensating the plaintiff to "make the plaintiff whole."

In contract law, the remedial goal is to put the plaintiff in a position as if the contract had been performed, and thus to give the plaintiff the benefit of the bargain. This compensates the plaintiff on the basis of the plaintiff's expectancy interest, what plaintiff was expecting from the contract. Where this cannot be done, the court may award the plaintiff damages that seek to compensate the plaintiff for those expenses incurred in seeking to perform the contract. This compensates the plaintiff's reliance interest.

Restitutionary relief, does not focus upon the plaintiff's losses, rather; it seeks to return to the plaintiff any benefit conferred by the plaintiff upon the defendant that would be unjust for the defendant to retain. Restitution will be discussed in Chapter 4. That Chapter also will address the dual nature of restitution, as a source of liability and as a remedy.

SECTION 3. TERMINOLOGY
AND LIMITATIONS

A. IMPORTANCE OF TERMINOLOGY

The law of remedies is full of terminology. Unfortunately that terminology is confusing in at least three ways: (1) there can be multiple terms for the same concept, (2) there can be multiple meanings for one term, or (3) there can be multiple views among lawyers and judges as to the meaning of a term.

MOLZOF v. UNITED STATES

Supreme Court of the United States, 1992.
502 U.S. 301, 112 S.Ct. 711, 116 L.Ed.2d 731.

JUSTICE THOMAS delivered the opinion of the Court.

* * *

I

Petitioner Shirley Molzof is the personal representative of the estate of Robert Molzof, her late husband. On October 31, 1986, Mr. Molzof, a veteran, underwent lung surgery at a Veterans' Administration hospital in Madison, Wisconsin. After surgery, he was placed on a ventilator. For some undisclosed reason, the ventilator tube that was providing oxygen to him became disconnected. The ventilator's alarm system also was disconnected. As a result of this combination of events, Mr. Molzof was deprived of oxygen for approximately eight minutes before his predicament was discovered. Because of this unfortunate series of events, triggered by the hospital employees' conceded negligence, Mr. Molzof suffered irreversible brain damage, leaving him permanently comatose.

Mr. Molzof's guardian ad litem filed suit in District Court under the Federal Tort Claims Act (FTCA or Act) seeking damages for supplemental medical care, future medical expenses, and loss of enjoyment of life. Respondent (the Government) admitted liability, and the case proceeded to a bench trial on the issue of damages. The District Court determined that the free medical care being provided to Mr. Molzof by the veterans' hospital was reasonable and adequate, that Mrs. Molzof was satisfied with those services and had no intention of transferring Mr. Molzof to a private hospital, and that it was in Mr. Molzof's best interests to remain at the veterans' hospital because neighboring hospitals could not provide a comparable level of care. In addition to ordering the veterans' hospital to continue the same level of care, the court awarded Mr. Molzof damages for supplemental care—physical therapy, respiratory therapy, and weekly doctor's visits—not provided by the veterans' hospital.

The District Court refused, however, to award damages for medical care that would duplicate the free medical services already being provided by the veterans' hospital. Similarly, the court declined to award Mr. Molzof damages for loss of enjoyment of life. Mr. Molzof died after final judgment had been entered, and Mrs. Molzof was substituted as plaintiff in her capacity as personal representative of her late husband's estate.

The United States Court of Appeals for the Seventh Circuit affirmed the District Court's judgment. * * * The Court of Appeals agreed with the District Court that, given the Government's provision of free medical care to Mr. Molzof and Mrs. Molzof's apparent satisfaction with that care, any award for future medical expenses would be punitive in effect and was therefore barred by the FTCA prohibition on "punitive damages." * * *

With respect to the claim for Mr. Molzof's loss of enjoyment of life, the Court of Appeals stated that Wisconsin law was unclear on the question whether a comatose plaintiff could recover such damages. * * *. The court decided, however, that "even if Wisconsin courts recognized the claim for loss of enjoyment of life, in this case it would be barred as punitive under the Federal Tort Claims Act," * * * because "an award of damages for loss of enjoyment of life can in no way recompense, reimburse or otherwise redress a comatose patient's uncognizable loss" * * *. We granted certiorari to consider the meaning of the term "punitive damages" as used in the FTCA. * * *

II

Prior to 1946, the sovereign immunity of the United States prevented those injured by the negligent acts of federal employees from obtaining redress through lawsuits; compensation could be had only by passage of a private bill in Congress. * * * The FTCA replaced that "notoriously clumsy" system of compensation with a limited waiver of the United States' sovereign immunity. * * * In this case, we must determine the scope of that waiver as it relates to awards of "punitive damages" against the United States. The FTCA provides in pertinent part as follows:

> The United States shall be liable, respecting the provisions of this title relating to tort claims, in the same manner and to the same extent as a private individual under like circumstances, *but shall not be liable* for interest prior to judgment or *for punitive damages.* 28 U.S.C. § 2674 (emphasis added).

As this provision makes clear, in conjunction with the jurisdictional grant over FTCA cases in 28 U.S.C. § 1346(b), the extent of the United States' liability under the FTCA is generally determined by reference to state law. * * *

Nevertheless, the meaning of the term "punitive damages" as used in § 2674, a federal statute, is by definition a federal question. * * * Petitioner argues that "§ 2674 must be interpreted so as to permit awards against the United States of those state-law damages which are intended by state law to act as compensation for injuries sustained as a result of the tort, and to preclude awards of damages which are intended to act as punishment for egregious conduct." * * * The Government, on the other hand, suggests that we define "punitive damages" as "damages that are in excess of, or bear no relation to, compensation." * * * Thus, the Government contends that any damages other than those awarded for a plaintiff's *actual* loss—which the Government narrowly construes to exclude damages that are excessive, duplicative, or for an inherently noncompensable loss * * *—are "punitive damages" because they are punitive *in effect*.

We agree with petitioner's interpretation of the term "punitive damages," and conclude that the Government's reading of § 2674 is contrary to the statutory language. § 2674 prohibits awards of "punitive damages," not "damage awards that may have a punitive effect." "Punitive damages" is a legal term of art that has a widely accepted common-law meaning; "[p]unitive damages have long been a part of traditional state tort law." Silkwood v. Kerr–McGee Corp., 464 U.S. 238, 255, 104 S.Ct. 615, 625, 78 L.Ed.2d 443 (1984). Although the precise nature and use of punitive damages may have evolved over time, and the size and frequency of such awards may have increased, this Court's decisions make clear that the concept of "punitive damages" has a long pedigree in the law. "It is a well-established principle of the common law, that in actions of trespass and all actions on the case for torts, a jury may inflict what are called exemplary, punitive, or vindictive damages upon a defendant, having in view the enormity of his offense rather than the measure of compensation to the plaintiff." * * *

Legal dictionaries in existence when the FTCA was drafted and enacted indicate that "punitive damages" were commonly understood to be damages awarded to punish defendants for torts committed with fraud, actual malice, violence, or oppression. *See, e.g.,* Black's Law Dictionary 501 (3d ed. 1933); The Cyclopedic Law Dictionary 292 (3d ed. 1940). * * * The common law definition of "punitive damages" focuses on the nature of the defendant's conduct. As a general rule, the common law recognizes that damages intended to compensate the plaintiff are different in kind from "punitive damages."

A cardinal rule of statutory construction holds that:

> [W]here Congress borrows terms of art in which are accumulated the legal tradition and meaning of centuries of practice, it presumably knows and adopts the cluster of ideas that were attached to each borrowed word in the body of learning from which it was taken and the meaning its use will convey to the judicial mind unless otherwise instructed. In such case, absence of contrary direction may be taken as satisfaction with widely accepted definitions, not as a departure from them. Morissette v. United States, 342 U.S. 246, 263, 72 S.Ct. 240, 250, 96 L.Ed. 288 (1952).

* * *

The Government's interpretation of § 2674 appears to be premised on the assumption that the statute provides that the United States "shall be liable only for compensatory damages." But the first clause of § 2674, the provision we are interpreting, does not say that. What it clearly states is that the United States "shall not be liable ... for punitive damages." The difference is important. The statutory language suggests that to the extent a plaintiff may be entitled to damages that are not legally considered "punitive damages," but which are for some reason above and beyond ordinary notions of compensation, the United States is liable for them "in the same manner and to the same extent as a private individual." These damages in the "gray" zone are not by definition "punitive damages" barred under the Act. In the ordinary case in which an award of compensatory damages is subsequently reduced on appeal, one does not say that the jury or the lower court mistakenly awarded "punitive damages" above and beyond the actual compensatory damages. It is simply a matter of excessive or erroneous compensation. Excessiveness principles affect only the amount, and not the nature, of the damages that may be recovered. The term "punitive damages," on the other hand, embodies an element of the defendant's conduct that must be proved before such damages are awarded.

* * *

The Government's interpretation of "punitive damages" would be difficult and impractical to apply. Under the Government's reading, an argument could be made that Mr. Molzof's damages for future medical expenses would have to be reduced by the amount he saved on rent, meals, clothing, and other daily living expenses that he did not incur while hospitalized. Otherwise, these duplicative damages would be "punitive damages" because they have the effect of making the United States pay twice. The difficulties inherent in attempting to prove such offsets would be enormous. That the Government has refused to acknowledge the practical implications of its theory is evidenced by its representations at oral argument that, as a general matter, it is willing to accept state-law definitions of compensatory awards for purposes of the FTCA, * * * and that "there are very few circumstances" in which States have authorized damages awards that the Government would challenge as punitive. * * *

* * * At oral argument, however, the Government * * * asserted that its position was that state compensatory awards are recoverable under the Act so long as they are a "reasonable" approximation of the plaintiff's actual damages. * * * But the Government's restrictive reading of the statute would involve the federal courts in the impractical business of determining the actual loss suffered in each case, and whether the damages awarded are a "reasonable" approximation of that loss.

* * *

We conclude that § 2674 bars the recovery only of what are *legally* considered "punitive damages" under traditional common-law principles. * * * Our interpretation of the term "punitive damages" requires us to reverse the Court of Appeals' decision that Mrs. Molzof is not permitted to recover damages for her husband's future medical expenses and his loss of enjoyment of life. It is undisputed that the claims in this case are based solely on a simple negligence theory of liability. Thus, the damages Mrs. Molzof seeks to recover are not punitive damages under the common law or the FTCA because their recoverability does not depend upon any proof that the defendant has engaged in intentional or egregious misconduct and their purpose is not to punish. We must remand, however, because we are in no position to evaluate the recoverability of those damages under Wisconsin law. * * * It may be that under Wisconsin law the damages sought in this case are not recoverable as compensatory damages. This might be true because Wisconsin law does not recognize such damages, or because it requires a setoff when a defendant already has paid (or agreed to pay) expenses incurred by the plaintiff, or for some other reason. These questions were not resolved by the lower courts.

III

The judgment of the Court of Appeals is reversed, and the case is remanded for further proceedings consistent with this opinion.

NOTES

1. Compensatory or actual damages are to be contrasted with nominal damages in that compensatory or actual damages measure a loss while nominal damages indicate that the plaintiff was wronged, but either had no loss or could not prove it. For examples of nominal damages, see Jacque v. Steenberg Homes, Inc., *infra* Chapter 3, Section 5.A, and Freund v. Washington Square Press, Inc., *infra* Chapter 7, Section 1.A. In most cases, the terms compensatory damages and actual damages are used interchangeably. As *Molzof* indicates, that is not always the case.

2. For a contract case involving whether damages should be labeled compensatory or punitive see Bi–Economy Market, Inc. v. Harleysville Insurance Co., 10 N.Y.3d 187, 193, 886 N.E.2d 127, 131, 856 N.Y.S.2d 505 (2008) (stating, "[t]he dissent also blurs the significant distinction between consequential and punitive damages. The two types of damages serve different purposes and are evidenced by different facts.") For more about consequential damages, see the next Section of this Chapter.

3. *Molzof* raises several other issues that will be addressed later in this Chapter. For a discussion of the collateral source rule see Section 4.C; punitive damages, Section 5.A; damages in personal injury and wrongful death suits, Section 7.

B. GENERAL AND SPECIAL DAMAGES

Except as in cases such as *Molzoff*, which involved whether a comatose plaintiff could "actually" suffer loss of enjoyment, the terms "actual damages" and "compensatory damages" are synonyms. The two components that make up compensatory (or actual) damages are "general" and "special" damages. General damages are usually defined as those that provide compensation for the harm that is "generally" sustained in the normal course of things, while special damages provide compensation for harm that is "special" to the individual plaintiff. These definitions are not necessarily any more helpful than are their labels in identifying types of damages. The cases below put the definitions in context. The cases also illustrate how the rules governing recovery differ significantly between contract and tort actions even though the terminology used in both is the same.

The distinction between general and special damages in both contract and tort actions is also important for pleading purposes. Rule 9(g) of the

Federal Rules of Civil Procedure provides, "If an item of special damage is claimed, it must be specifically stated." *See generally*, Jeffrey R. Cagle, Craig D. Cherry and Melanie I. Kemp, *The Classification of General and Special Damages for Pleading Purposes in Texas*, 51 Baylor L. Rev. 629 (1999).

American List, below, identifies the distinction between general and special damages in a contract cause of action. These two types of damage are also referred to as "direct" and "consequential" damages. *See* Wartsila NSD North America, Inc. v. Hill International, Inc., 530 F.3d 269, 273–280 (3d Cir. 2008). As you read *American List*, pay particular attention to the difference in how direct and consequential damages must be proved. *Wheeler*, which follows, identifies the distinction between general and special damages in a tort cause of action. Notice how damages that are either general or special in tort are different from damages with those labels in contract. As you read both cases, consider how the differences between general and special damages in contract and tort reflect the different policies underlying those actions.

AMERICAN LIST CORP. v. U.S. NEWS & WORLD REPORT, INC.

Court of Appeals of New York, 1989.
75 N.Y.2d 38, 550 N.Y.S.2d 590, 549 N.E.2d 1161.

ALEXANDER, JUDGE.

* * *

I

Defendant publishes a national weekly news magazine which, in 1983, had the third largest circulation for such magazines in the Nation. In an attempt to expand its circulation by entering the college student market, defendant negotiated an agreement with plaintiff whereby, for a 10–year period, plaintiff would compile and rent to defendant mailing lists of college student names. Plaintiff had previously produced such mailing lists for high school, but not college, students. Consequently defendant agreed to finance plaintiff's start-up costs by paying a larger fee per name in the first five years of the arrangement. A schedule of the estimated number of names to be provided and the fees to be paid by defendant as well as the estimated losses and profits of plaintiff in each of the 10 years contemplated by the agreement was appended to the agreement. In addition, the agreement, which was drafted by defendant, provided that "[U.S. News & World Report has] agreed to take as much as 25% more names than the estimated compilation at the cost pername [*sic*] shown in years one through five." The agreement further provided for an annual review of the estimated figures for the purpose of adjusting the cost per name to be charged to defendant.

The agreement was signed by the parties on January 25 and 26, 1984. Martin Lerner, plaintiff's president, signed on behalf of plaintiff and

Joseph Acerno, the vice-president of circulation, signed on behalf of defendant. One year after the contract was signed, defendant was purchased by a new owner and Acerno was replaced by Jacob Weintraub. Weintraub canceled the contract in September 1985 although prior to that cancellation, defendant had accepted and paid for names provided by plaintiff for three mailings conducted over a one and one-half-year period.

Plaintiff commenced this action for breach of contract. After a bench trial, Supreme Court found defendant liable and awarded damages of $1,449,344 for the breach, which sum constituted the balance due plaintiff on the contract for the years 1985 to 1994, as reduced to present value. * * *

Defendant argues that the damages awarded to plaintiff are actually "lost future profits" which are special damages and not compensable absent a showing that they were foreseeable and contemplated by the parties at the time the contract was made (see, Kenford Co. v. County of Erie, 67 N.Y.2d 257, 502 N.Y.S.2d 131, 493 N.E.2d 234) (Kenford I), a showing plaintiff failed to make because the lost future profits it seeks, like the lost future profits sought in Kenford I, are too speculative for calculation. Plaintiff counters that it seeks general rather than special damages and that it has sufficiently proven that its damages are the natural and direct consequence of defendant's breach of their agreement.

* * *

II

We reject at the outset defendant's contention that the courts below improperly awarded plaintiff "lost future profits" which are special damages not sufficiently proven at the trial.

The distinction between general and special contract damages is well defined but its application to specific contracts and controversies is usually more elusive. General damages are those which are the natural and probable consequence of the breach * * * while special damages are extraordinary in that they do not so directly flow from the breach. These extraordinary damages are recoverable only upon a showing that they were foreseeable and within the contemplation of the parties at the time the contract was made (* * * Hadley v. Baxendale, 9 Exch. 341, 156 Eng.Rep. 145). Thus in Kenford I, 67 N.Y.2d 257, 502 N.Y.S.2d 131, 493 N.E.2d 234, supra, the nonbreaching party to a contract for the management of a domed sports stadium claimed special damages in the form of the lost future profits which that party would have received from its operation of the stadium. We concluded that the claimed lost future profits could not be recovered because it could not be demonstrated that such damages were caused by the breach, the alleged loss was not capable of proof with reasonable certainty, and it had not been proven that those damages were within the contemplation of the parties at the time the contract was made (id., at 261–263, 502 N.Y.S.2d 131, 493 N.E.2d 234; see also, Hadley v. Baxendale, 9 Exch. 341, 156 Eng.Rep. 145, supra [(plaintiff failed to prove foreseeability of claimed damages for lost profits of mill operation resulting from common carrier's breach of contract to timely deliver broken mill shaft for repairs)]).

Here, by contrast, it is clear that plaintiff has sought only to recover moneys which defendant undertook to pay under the contract, thereby assuming a definite obligation. By the express terms of the agreement drafted by defendant, its appended schedule reflected the "cost of this joint venture" to defendant and set forth the fees to be paid to plaintiff for a specific number of names to be provided by plaintiff in each of the 10 years contemplated by the arrangement. That schedule also contemplated that plaintiff would suffer losses during the first five years because of its additional start-up costs, and defendant agreed to pay a larger fee per name for names provided during that period. These contemplated losses, however, do not alter the fact that defendant agreed to pay a specific amount over a period of 10 years—a sum explicitly stated in the contract schedule to be $3,027,500 and thus unquestionably within the contemplation of the parties. Moreover, contrary to defendant's contention, the fact that plaintiff did not incur costs as great as anticipated during part of the time in which the parties had contemplated that plaintiff would suffer losses is irrelevant to defendant's obligation under the agreement. Thus, as the trial proof establishes, plaintiff has sufficiently demonstrated that the moneys it seeks—the present value of the balance owed by defendant under the contract less the costs reasonably saved by plaintiff as a result of the breach—are general damages flowing as a natural and probable consequence of the breach.

* * *

[A]ffirmed.

NOTES

1. How did the court in *American List* distinguish between general and special damages in contract law? *See* Tractebel Energy Marketing, Inc. v. AEP Power Marketing, Inc., 487 F.3d 89, 109–10 (2d Cir. 2007) (measuring damages for buyer's breach at the start of a long term contract to purchase electricity):

> Lost profits are consequential damages when, as a result of the breach, the non-breaching party suffers loss of profits on collateral business arrangements. In the typical case, the ability of the non-breaching party to operate his business, and thereby generate profits on collateral transactions, is contingent on the performance of the primary contract. When the breaching party does not perform, the non-breaching party's business is in some way hindered, and the profits from potential collateral exchanges are "lost." Every lawyer will recall from his or her first-year contracts class the paradigmatic example of *Hadley v. Baxendale*, where Baxendale's failure to deliver a crank shaft on time caused Hadley to lose profits from the operation of his mill. 9 Ex. 341, 156 Eng. Rep. 145 (1854). In New York, a party is entitled to recover this form of

lost profits only if (1) it is demonstrated with certainty that the damages have been caused by the breach, (2) the extent of the loss is capable of proof with reasonable certainty, and (3) it is established that the damages were fairly within the contemplation of the parties. * * *

> By contrast, when the non-breaching party seeks only to recover money that the breaching party agreed to pay under the contract, the damages sought are general damages. *See* Am. List Corp. v. U.S. News & World Report, Inc., 75 N.Y.2d 38, 44, 549 N.E.2d 1161, 550 N.Y.S.2d 590 (1989). The damages may still be characterized as lost profits since, had the contract been performed, the non-breaching party would have profited to the extent that his cost of performance was less than the total value of the breaching party's promised payments. But, in this case, the lost profits are the direct and probable consequence of the breach.[20] *See id.* The profits are precisely what the non-breaching party bargained for, and only an award of damages equal to lost profits will put the non-breaching party in the same position he would have occupied had the contract been performed.[21] *See id.*

Tractebel, at 109–10. *See also* Aristocrat Leisure Ltd. v. Deutsche Bank Trust Co. Americas, 618 F.Supp. 2d 280, 292 (S.D.N.Y. 2009) (measuring damages for breach of indenture agreement to convert bonds into shares):

> There are two categories of damages available in a breach of contract case, (1) general or market damages, and (2) special or consequential damages. * * * The Second Circuit explains that "[a] plaintiff is seeking general damages when he tries to recover the value of the very performance promised[,]" whereas consequential damages "seek to compensate a plaintiff for additional losses (other than the value of the promised performance) that are incurred as a result of the defendant's breach." Schonfeld v. Hilliard, 218 F.3d 164, 175–176 (2d Cir. 2000) (citations and quotations omitted). Once the fact of damages is established, a plaintiff is entitled to the general damages that are the natural and probable consequence of the breach. * * * To collect consequential damages, however, a plaintiff must demonstrate that the parties contemplated those special damages as the probable result of the breach at the time of or prior to contracting.

For further discussion of consequential damages and other damages for breach of contract, see Chapter 7.

---

20. New York long ago clarified the distinction between profits as general or consequential damages in Masterton & Smith v. Mayor of Brooklyn, 7 Hill 61, 68–69 (N.Y. Sup. Ct. 1845):

When the books and cases speak of the profits anticipated from a good bargain as matters too remote and uncertain to be taken into [ ] account in ascertaining the true measure of damages, they usually have reference to dependant and collateral engagements entered into on the faith and in expectation of the performance of the principal contract.... But profits or advantages which are the direct and immediate fruits of the contract entered into between the parties stand upon a different footing.... [I]t is difficult to comprehend why, in case one party has deprived the other of the gains or profits of the contract by refusing to perform it, this loss should not constitute a proper item in estimating the damages.

21. The non-breaching party is, of course, under a duty to mitigate damages to the extent practicable, *see* Losei Realty Corp. v. City of New York, 254 N.Y. 41, 47, 171 N.E. 899 (1930), and any proceeds generated from mitigation should be accounted for in the ultimate award of damages.

2. Why is it easier for a plaintiff to prove general than special (consequential) damages in a contract action?

3. *Hadley*, cited in *American List* and *Tractebel Energy Marketing*, is the longstanding English case which first articulated the contract rule that special damages must be contemplated by the parties at the time of contracting. What policies underlie that rule?

4. Incidental damages are costs incurred in mitigation. In *American List*, the plaintiff did not try to mitigate. Why not?

WHEELER v. HUSTON

Supreme Court of Oregon, 1980.
288 Or. 467, 605 P.2d 1339.

PETERSON, J.

* * *

The plaintiff, a milkman, fell while making a delivery to the defendants, and sued for damages. The defendants denied responsibility for the fall, denied that the plaintiff sustained injury, and claimed that the plaintiff was also at fault.

The plaintiff prayed for general damages and for special damages of $9,120.25 (lost wages of $6,000 and medical expenses of $3,120.25). The defendants also disputed the correctness of the amount of lost wages claimed to have been sustained.

The jury returned a special verdict * * *. They found * * * that the plaintiff's "total money damages" were $9,120.25, the exact amount of the claimed special damages. The verdict form made no apportionment between special damages and general damages.

The trial court asked the foreman of the jury if the verdict of $9,120.25 was intended to award only the special damages pertaining to medical care and lost wages and nothing for general damages, or if the jury intended to include some amount for general damages in the award. The foreman of the jury responded that the jury intended to award medical expenses and lost wages. Over defendants' objections that the first verdict should be received, the court then reinstructed the jury that under the law of the state of Oregon the jury could not award special damages without an award of general damages, and sent out the jury for further deliberations.[4]

After further deliberations, the jury returned with a verdict which assessed plaintiff's "total money damages" in the sum of $20,000. Judgment was entered on this verdict.

The defendants appealed to the Court of Appeals, which affirmed per curiam. * * *

---

4. The defendants also [claim] * * * that the trial judge, under * * * the Oregon Constitution, was prohibited from making such inquiry. We need not and do not decide this issue.

In Eisele v. Rood, 275 Or. 461, 551 P.2d 441 (1976), we held that a verdict for only special damages was valid if the "plaintiff's evidence of injury is merely subjective in nature" or if there is evidence that the plaintiff's injury "was not caused by the accident." 275 Or. at 467, 551 P.2d at 444. We granted review to reconsider the *Eisele* rule.

The Development of the Rule in Oregon

The issue presented in this case has been before this court at least 20 times in the past 27 years, and continues to create confusion within the appellate courts, the trial courts, and among trial lawyers. A brief overview of the cases is in order.

Hall v. Cornett, 193 Or. 634, 240 P.2d 231 (1952), was a personal injury action resulting from an automobile collision. The total special damages claimed were $1,006.40. The jury returned a verdict in favor of the plaintiff for "One Dollar as General Damages, and the further sum of $1,006.40 Special Damages." The trial court refused to receive the verdict and instructed the jury that if it found for the plaintiff, it must award an amount which would reasonably compensate her for the damages sustained. After further deliberation the jury returned a verdict for "$300 as general damages and the further sum of $707.40 special damages." The trial court * * * set the judgment aside and granted a new trial. We affirmed, stating that the jury

> stubbornly adhered to what was apparently a compromise verdict between some who found liability and others who found none. Our statute provides that a judgment may be set aside and a new trial granted on the motion of the party aggrieved in the event of irregularity in the proceedings of the jury by which such party was prevented from having a fair trial, or for misconduct of the jury. * * *

Mullins v. Rowe, 222 Or. 519, 353 P.2d 861 is a 1960 case involving a claim for general and special damages on a cause of action arising out of an automobile accident. There was evidence that the plaintiff had incurred $332 for medical services, but there was evidence that all the bills were not chargeable to the accident. The verdict was for the plaintiff in the sum of $332 general damages and "special damages in the sum of $None." The trial court * * * granted a new trial. This court reversed.

> It may well be true, as contended in the plaintiff's brief and argument, that the jury simply compromised the question of liability and entered a verdict for the doctor bills, but to speculate concerning the mental processes of juries is forbidden the courts under Oregon Constitution, Art. VII, § 3. * * *

> * * *

Flansberg v. Paulson, 239 Or. 610, 399 P.2d 356 (1965), also involved a claim for personal injuries allegedly sustained in a rear-end automobile collision. The plaintiff sought general damages of $10,000 and special damages of $315.65. The jury first returned a verdict for the plaintiff and assessed no general damages and special damages of $315.65. Following reinstruction, the jury retired again and returned a verdict assessing general damages of $315.65, with no special damages. The trial court * * * declared a mistrial. The defendant appealed. We affirmed in an opinion written by Chief Justice McAllister, who stated:

> The line between the rule enunciated in Hall v. Cornett, *supra*, and the later rule of Mullins v. Rowe, *supra*, may be narrow, but it is discernible. * * *

Justice O'Connell dissented, saying:

* * *

> If a verdict for general damages (in the exact amount of the claimed special damages) is good * * *, a verdict for special damages without general damages should also be good * * *.

* * *

Finally, in Eisele v. Rood, 275 Or. 461, 551 P.2d 441 (1976), we clearly enunciated a rule to the effect that whether a verdict in the amount of the claimed special damages was proper would be determined by the sufficiency of the evidence to prove, as a matter of law, that general damage resulted from the accident. *Eisele* was also an action for personal injuries allegedly received in a rear-end automobile accident. The verdict was for no general damages and $1200 special damages. * * *

There was evidence that the plaintiff's symptoms were primarily subjective or non-existent. Justice Howell * * * wrote the opinion for the majority, and he stated the rule to be as follows:

> * * * As a general rule, a verdict for special damages without an allowance for general damages is improper. However, when the issue of general damages is controverted in the pleadings and the evidence on that point is in conflict, the jury may conclude that plaintiff did not actually suffer any general damages but did reasonably incur special damages for medical expenses and/or loss of wages. * * * However, if there is uncontroverted, objective evidence that plaintiff sustained general damages as a result of the defendant's conduct, an award of special damages alone is improper. (Footnotes omitted.) 275 Or. at 467, 551 P.2d at 444.

DISCUSSION

The rulings of this court have not gone without criticism. Justice O'Connell dissented in *Flansberg*, *supra*, and in other cases. Professor Frank R. Lacy has also urged that this court adopt a rule validating specials-only verdicts. Lacy, *Chief Justice O'Connell's Contributions to the Law of Civil Procedure*, 56 Or.L.Rev. 191, 213 (1977). * * * The solution proposed by Justice O'Connell and Professor Lacy has the virtues of ease of administration, certainty, and to some extent recognizes the power of a jury to afford "rough justice,"[5] but no court has gone so far as to validate all jury verdicts for only the specials.

We confess that this "verdict for the claimed specials" issue raises thorny problems, and our protracted labors for a satisfactory solution have not entirely solved the problem. * * * Perhaps nothing short of a capitulation to judicial expediency and carte blanche approval of verdicts in the amount of the claimed specials will end the repeated appeals in this area. We have considered such a solution and reject it.

We are persuaded that the *Eisele* rule (as restated below) should be retained. However, in *Eisele* we did not consider the situation in which the amount of special damages incurred was in dispute. An unsegregated verdict in such a case for the exact amount of the claimed specials might well include general damages. We therefore restate the rule applicable to verdicts for only the amount of the claimed specials as follows:

1. If there is a question whether any general damages were sustained, the jury may conclude that the plaintiff suffered no general damages but did reasonably incur wage loss and/or medical expense. Such verdicts are valid and include cases in which (a) the plaintiff's evidence of injury is subjective, (b) there is evidence that the plaintiff's injuries for which general damages are claimed were not caused by the accident, and (c) the objective evidence of a substantial injury sustained by plaintiff * * * could be disbelieved by the trier of fact.

2. Even in the case where the jury must award some general damages, if there is a substantial dispute as to the amount of the special damages to which the plaintiff is entitled, an unsegregated verdict in the exact amount of the claimed specials will be upheld. * * *

* * *

We hold, therefore, that if the plaintiff claims that the right to recover general damages has been established as a matter of law, and that the jury must therefore award some general damages if they find defendant liable, the plaintiff should request that an appropriate instruction be given to that effect. * * *

Or if the plaintiff claims that the right to recover special damages in a certain amount has been established as a matter of law, an appropriate request for an instruction should be made. * * *

If the plaintiff's attorney * * * fails to bring these matters to the attention of the trial judge * * *, any objection to a verdict in the amount of only the claimed specials will be deemed waived.

Whether the plaintiff in the instant case sustained any general damages as a result of the fall was disputed, as was the amount of the claimed special damages.

* * *

---

5. According to Roscoe Pound (as quoted in L. Moore, The Jury, at v (1973)) " * * * jury lawlessness is the great corrective of law in its actual administration."

* * * We therefore reverse with instructions to the trial court, to enter judgment in accordance with the first verdict returned.

NOTES

1. In Fatehi v. Johnson, 207 Or. App. 719, 143 P.3d 561 (2006), Oregon's Court of Appeals held that the jury could award "economic damages" without "noneconomic damages" because the plaintiff had testified in his deposition that he had only one prior accident, but evidence at trial showed that he had six, which raised a question about which accident had caused his pain and suffering. In quoting the test that *Wheeler* had articulated, the Court of Appeals replaced the term "general damages" with "noneconomic damages." What term must it have substituted for "special damages"? If you go back and reread the test in *Wheeler*, but with these substitutions, is the case more easily understood? Why would those substitutions not be appropriate in contract cases?

2. *Wheeler's* is not the only resolution of the issue of special and general damages in personal injury cases. Snover v. McGraw, 172 Ill.2d 438, 217 Ill.Dec. 734, 667 N.E.2d 1310, 1314 (1996) reviewed cases throughout the United States and observed that some courts hold that an award of special damages without general damages "requires reversal *per se*." *Snover* followed *Wheeler's* "flexible approach based on an examination of the evidence" to allow juries to deny damages for pain and suffering if, but only if, the evidence did not support them. Justice Harrison dissented in *Snover* and was quoted approvingly in Grant v. Stoyer, 10 P.3d 594, 599, n.34 (Alas. 2000) ("we agree with Justice Harrison's dissent in [*Snover*]: 'Any pain severe enough to justify medical care is severe enough to warrant compensation.' *Id.* at 1316 (Harrison, J., dissenting).")

3. The suggestion in *Wheeler* that the objection to "special only" damages is waived unless the plaintiff has requested a jury instruction stating that the plaintiff is entitled to general damages as a matter of law has not been adopted by all jurisdictions. *See, e.g.*, Symon v. Burger, 528 N.E.2d 850 (Ind.Ct.App.1988) (holding that award in amount of specials only could stand because evidence of specials was controverted; no special verdict was requested); Smith v. Sheehy, 45 A.D.3d 670, 846 N.Y.S.2d 232 (App. Div. 2007) (ordering new trial on amount of future pain and suffering damages despite plaintiff's failure to object to the verdict before jury was discharged).

4. What are "nominal" damages? In Mays v. Vejo, 224 Or. App. 426, 198 P.3d 943 (2008), the judge instructed the jury in an auto accident case that the jury "must award 'some' noneconomic damages if it chose to award economic damages." It awarded the plaintiff approximately $3000 in economic damages and $1.00 in noneconomic damages. The Appellate Court of Oregon said, "plaintiff asserts that the trial court erred in accepting the jury's verdict awarding economic damages with only nominal noneconomic damages. Defendant responds by arguing that the $1.00 in noneconomic damages complied with the instruction to award 'some' noneconomic damages if awarding economic damages." The court ruled for the plaintiff and ordered a new trial

because the exceptions articulated in *Wheeler* for allowing special damages to be awarded without pain and suffering damages were not applicable.

5. What would have happened if the jury in *Mays,* above in note 4, had awarded the plaintiff only $1.00 and no other damages. *See* Cowan v. Flannery, 461 N.W.2d 155, 158–59 (Iowa 1990):

> [b]ecause damages are an element of a negligence or comparative fault action, nominal damages should not be awarded. If a party has suffered personal injury as a result of another's negligence or fault, the injured party is entitled to actual or substantial damages, not nominal damages.

This contrasts with contract actions in which nominal damages are permitted as a statement that the defendant breached the contract, even if damages were not proven. *See* Freund v. Washington Square Press, Inc., *infra* Chapter 7, Section 1.

6. One difficulty with the terms "special" and "general" damages is that they are not always consistently defined. *Compare* Nunsuch v. United States, 221 F.Supp.2d 1027, 1035 (D.Ariz.2001) ("Impairment of earning capacity * * * is an item of general damage * * *," *quoting* Mandelbaum v. Knutson, 11 Ariz.App. 148, 149, 462 P.2d 841, 842 (1969)), *with* Norfleet v. Southern Baptist Hospital, 623 So. 2d 891, 896 (La. App. 4th Cir. 1993) ("A plaintiff is not entitled to special damages for impairment of earning capacity where her physical ability to continue prior work is not diminished * * *)," *quoting* Adams v. Phillips, 506 So. 2d 651, 654 (La. App. 4th Cir. 1987)). To add to the confusion, the terms "consequential damages" and "foreseeability" also have different meanings, depending upon whether they are used in a tort or a contract action.

7. Why are there different limitations on the types of damages recoverable in tort and contract law? Consider the next cases.

C. THE INTERSECTION OF, AND BOUNDARIES BETWEEN, NEGLIGENCE AND CONTRACT LAW

1. Contract and Tort as Alternative Actions

The previous sections of this chapter demonstrated that contract and tort causes of action are governed by different rules for recovery of damages. The same situation, however, may be viewed as an action in either contract or tort; for example, an action involving fraudulently induced contracts may be brought as either. For further discussion about the intersection of tort and contract law in fraud actions see Chapter 7, Sections A and B. Although two or more causes of action can arise from the same situation, the elements of proof will be different. For example, in tort a plaintiff will need to prove intent or negligence of the wrongdoer and its breach, while in contract the plaintiff will need to prove the enforceability of a promise but not the motivation of the breaching party.

When different causes of actions arise from the same situation, a plaintiff will want to recover under the action that provides the most favorable outcome. In choosing among actions, some of the factors a plaintiff will consider include the strength of the types of proof, the applicability of statutes of limitations and the availability of favorable recovery rules, including the availability of punitive damages. Because a plaintiff may not be able to assess the strength of different elements of proof prior to discovery or trial, Federal Rule of Civil Procedure 8(d)(2) provides "[a] party may set out two or more statements of a claim or defense alternatively or hypothetically," but a party may not knowingly plead inconsistent facts. If a plaintiff should succeed under all alternatively pleaded actions, the plaintiff must choose one theory for recovery so as not to receive a windfall.

Some actions may be brought in either breach of contract or the tort of negligence, as the next case involving legal malpractice demonstrates; however, there are limits to combining tort and contract actions, as Subsections 2 and 3 of this Section will demonstrate. Unfortunately, as will also be discussed in these subsections, jurisdictions do not agree on the limits of the limitations.

GENERAL NUTRITION CORPORATION v. GARDERE WYNNE SEWELL, LLP.

United States District Court for the Western District of Pennsylvania, 2008.
2008 WL 3982914.

TERRENCE F. McVERRY, UNITED STATES DISTRICT COURT JUDGE.

Pending now before the Court is the MOTION TO DISMISS * * *.

* * *

The gravamen of this case is a claim that Gardere provided improper legal advice to Plaintiff General Nutrition Corporation ("GNC") as to the consequences of terminating contracts with Franklin Publications, Inc. for the production, purchase and sale of two magazines. Acting on Gardere's allegedly faulty advice, GNC terminated the contracts in the expectation that Franklin's damages, if any, would be limited under the Uniform Commercial Code (UCC) to $1–3 million and that Franklin would be precluded from recovering its lost profits estimated at approximately $34.5 million. Franklin filed suit in the United States District Court for the Southern District of Ohio (the "Ohio court") and Gardere defended the litigation by contending that the contract involved a sale of goods which was governed by the UCC, which did not permit recovery of consequential damages. On July 13, 2007, the Ohio court ruled on summary judgment that the contract predominantly involved the sale of services, such that the UCC did not apply to limit Franklin's damages. After this adverse development, GNC fired Gardere, hired replacement counsel, and paid a substantial sum to Franklin to settle the case.

Plaintiff asserts claims against Gardere for negligence, breach of contract, and breach of fiduciary duty. * * *

Initially, Gardere contends that GNC's claims are barred by what it calls the "judgment rule." In essence, the "judgment rule" provides that lawyers are not required to be infallible in their predictions of how a court will decide a matter. However, as explained in *Collas v. Garnick*, 425 Pa. Super. 8, 624 A.2d 117, 120 (Pa. Super. 1993) (citations omitted):

> Although a lawyer is not expected to be infallible, he or she is expected to conduct that measure of research sufficient to allow the client to make an informed decision. In order for a lawyer to advise a client adequately, he or she is obligated to scrutinize any contract which the client is to execute, and thereafter must disclose to the client the full import of the instrument and any possible consequences which might arise therefrom. The lawyer, moreover, must be familiar with well settled principles of law and the rules of practice which are of frequent application in the ordinary business of the profession.

> Thus, in order to assert the "judgment rule," Defendant must establish that it enabled GNC to make an informed judgment. * * * These issues are fact-intensive and the discovery process must be engaged to fully develop the record evidence before the application of the "judgment rule" may be determined, possibly at the summary judgment stage.

* * *

Gardere argues that the negligence claim is barred by the applicable two-year statute of limitations. Gardere cites several cases for the proposition that the limitations period commences upon the occurrence of the alleged breach of duty. *See, e.g., Wachovia Bank, N.A. v. Ferretti*, 2007 PA Super 320, 935 A.2d 565, 572 (Pa. Super. 2007). However, *Wachovia Bank* also holds that the limitations period is tolled "when the client, despite the exercise of due diligence, cannot discover the injury or its cause." *Id.* at 573. GNC contends that it did not reasonably discover that Gardere's alleged improper advice was the cause of its injury until it received the adverse summary judgment ruling from the Ohio court during the litigation. For example, the amended complaint alleges that even after Franklin provided an expert report from a law professor, Gardere continued to assure GNC that its analysis of GNC's potential liability was correct. * * *

Gardere argues that GNC's claims are barred because it settled the lawsuit with Franklin. The Court cannot agree. * * * [T]he settlement of the underlying case by GNC—the defendant—resulted in its alleged damages being made actual and concrete. Indeed, GNC arguably had a duty to mitigate its damages by entering into a reasonable compromise and settlement of the claim.

Gardere contends that the breach of contract claim should be dismissed because it merely repackages the negligence claim. * * * Pennsylvania law permits a plaintiff to assert legal malpractice claims under both tort and contract theories. * * * The tort theory is based on a failure to exercise the requisite standard of care while a contract theory is based on an attorney's failure to follow instructions contained in the parties' agreement. * * *

In this case * * * the complaint alleges that GNC and Gardere entered into a contract specifically to provide legal advice about the termination of the Franklin contracts and that Gardere represented that such advice fell within its professional competence. Thus, the complaint contains sufficient allegations to support a contract-based legal malpractice claim, although the tort and contract theories may ultimately be duplicative. Further, the assertion of a contract theory does not appear to be a transparent attempt to avoid the statute of limitations. The complaint provides adequate notice for Gardere to develop its defenses and Gardere will have an ample opportunity to renew its arguments, if applicable, upon a more fully-developed record. * * *

Finally, Gardere argues that the breach of fiduciary duty claim should be dismissed because the complaint fails to plead how the duty was breached or how the breach caused actual loss. Again, the Court cannot agree. The complaint clearly avers that Gardere knew or should have known that its pre-litigation advice was faulty and that it should have timely disclosed its error to GNC. The complaint also alleges that Gardere's subsequent litigation strategy was motivated by self-interest (i.e., to hide its earlier error) rather than the best interests of GNC and thereby breached the duty of loyalty. * * *

Accordingly, the MOTION TO DISMISS is **DENIED.**

NOTES

1. What was the malpractice in *General Nutrition*? Note how the consequence of the malpractice involved remedial theory.

2. *See also* Insurance Company of North America v. Cease Electric Inc., 276 Wis.2d 361, 380, 688 N.W.2d 462, 471 (2004) (noting that in Wisconsin professional malpractice claims, including those for architects, attorneys and engineers "lie both in tort and contract."); Kilpatrick v. Wiley, Rein & Fielding, 909 P.2d 1283, 1289 (Utah App.1996) ("Clients wronged by their lawyers may sue for damages based on breach of contract, breach of fiduciary duty, or negligence.") For further discussion of jurisdictional differences see subsection 2.b.ii. of this Section.

2. Limitations on Negligence Recovery in Contract Actions Without Harm to Body or Property

a. *Emotional Distress and Pain and Suffering*

ERLICH v. MENEZES

Supreme Court of California, 1999.
21 Cal.4th 543, 87 Cal.Rptr.2d 886, 981 P.2d 978.

BROWN, J.

* * *

I. FACTUAL AND PROCEDURAL BACKGROUND

* * * Barry and Sandra Erlich contracted with John Menezes, a licensed general contractor, to build a "dreamhouse" on their ocean-view lot. The Erlichs moved into their house in December 1990. In February 1991, the rains came. [T]he house leaked from every conceivable location. Walls were saturated in [an upstairs bedroom], two bedrooms downstairs, and the pool room. Nearly every window in the house leaked. The living room filled with three inches of standing water. In several locations water "poured in streams" from the ceilings and walls. The ceiling in the garage became so saturated ... the plaster liquefied and fell in chunks to the floor.

* * *

The Erlichs eventually had their home inspected by another general contractor and a structural engineer. In addition to confirming defects in the roof, exterior stucco, windows and waterproofing, the inspection revealed serious errors in the construction of the home's structural components. * * *

* * *

Both of the Erlichs testified that they suffered emotional distress as a result of the defective condition of the house and Menezes' invasive and unsuccessful repair attempts. Barry Erlich testified he felt "absolutely sick" and had to be "carted away in an ambulance" when he learned the full extent of the structural problems. He has a permanent heart condition, known as superventricular tachyarrhythmia, attributable, in part, to excessive stress. Although the condition can be controlled with medication, it has forced him to resign his positions as athletic director, department head and track coach.

Sandra Erlich feared the house would collapse in an earthquake and feared for her daughter's safety. Stickers were placed on her bedroom windows, and alarms and emergency lights installed so rescue crews would find her room first in an emergency.

Plaintiffs sought recovery on several theories, including breach of contract, fraud, negligent misrepresentation, and negligent construction. Both the breach of contract claim and the negligence claim alleged numerous construction defects.

Menezes prevailed on the fraud and negligent misrepresentation claims. The jury found he breached his contract with the Erlichs by negligently constructing their home and awarded $406,700 as the cost of repairs. Each spouse was awarded $50,000 for emotional distress, and Barry Erlich received an additional $50,000 for physical pain and suffering and $15,000 for lost earnings.

By a two-to-one majority, the Court of Appeal affirmed the judgment, including the emotional distress award. The majority noted the breach of a contractual duty may support an action in tort. The jury found Menezes was negligent. Since his negligence exposed the Erlichs to "intolerable living conditions and a constant, justifiable fear about the safety of their home," the majority decided the Erlichs were properly compensated for their emotional distress.

The dissent pointed out that no reported California case has upheld an award of emotional distress damages based upon simple breach of a contract to build a house. Since Menezes' negligence directly caused only economic injury and property damage, the Erlichs were not entitled to recover damages for their emotional distress.

We granted review to resolved the question.

* * *

II. DISCUSSION

A.

In an action for breach of contract, the measure of damages is "the amount which will compensate the party aggrieved for all the detriment proximately caused thereby, or which, in the ordinary course of things, would be likely to result therefrom" (Civ.Code, § 3300), provided the damages are "clearly ascertainable in both their nature and origin" (Civ.Code, § 3301). In an action not arising from contract, the measure of damages is "the amount which will compensate for all the detriment proximately caused thereby, whether it could have been anticipated or not" (Civ.Code, § 3333).

"Contract damages are generally limited to those within the contemplation of the parties when the contract was entered into or at least reasonably foreseeable by them at that time; consequential damages beyond the expectation of the parties are not recoverable. * * * This limitation on available damages serves to encourage contractual relations and commercial activity by enabling parties to estimate in advance the financial risks of their enterprise." * * * "In contrast, tort damages are awarded to [fully] compensate the victim for [all] injury suffered. * * * "

" '[T]he distinction between tort and contract is well grounded in common law, and divergent objectives underlie the remedies created in the two areas. Whereas contract actions are created to enforce the intentions of the parties to the agreement, tort law is primarily designed to vindicate "social policy." * * * ' " While the purposes behind contract and tort law are distinct, the boundary line between them is not * * * and the distinction between the remedies for each are not " 'found ready made.' " (quoting Holmes, The Common Law (1881) p. 13.) These uncertain boundaries and the apparent breadth of the recovery available for tort actions creates pressure to obliterate the distinction between contracts and torts—an expansion of tort law at the expense of contract principles which Grant Gilmore aptly dubbed "contorts." In this case we consider whether a negligent breach of a contract will support an award of damages for emotional distress—either as tort damages for negligence or as consequential or special contract damages.

B.

In concluding emotional distress damages were properly awarded, the Court of Appeal correctly observed that "the same wrongful act may constitute both a breach of contract and an invasion of an interest protected by the law of torts." This is true; however, conduct amounting to a breach of contract becomes tortious only when it also violates a duty independent of the contract arising from principles of tort law.

* * *

Plaintiff's theory of tort recovery is that mental distress is a foreseeable consequence of negligent breaches of standard commercial contracts. However, foreseeability alone is not sufficient to create an independent tort duty. "Whether a defendant owes a duty of care is a question of law. Its existence depends upon the foreseeability of the risk and a weighing of policy considerations for and against imposition of liability." * * * Because the consequences of a negligent act must be limited to avoid an intolerable burden on society * * *, the determination of duty "recognizes that policy considerations may dictate a cause of action should not be sanctioned no matter how foreseeable the risk." * * * In short, foreseeability is not synonymous with duty; nor is it a substitute.

The question remains: is the mere negligent breach of a contract sufficient? The answer is no. It may admittedly be difficult to categorize the cases, but to state the rule succinctly: "[C]ourts will generally enforce the breach of a contractual promise through contract law, except when the actions that constitute the breach violate a social policy that merits the imposition of tort remedies." * * * The familiar paradigm of tortious breach of contract in this state is the insurance contract. There we relied on the covenant of good faith and fair dealing, implied in every contract, to justify tort liability. * * * In holding that a tort action is available for breach of the covenant in an insurance contract, we have "emphasized the 'special relationship' between insurer and insured, characterized by elements of public interest, adhesion, and fiduciary responsibility." * * *

* * *

Our previous decisions detail the reasons for denying tort recovery in contract breach cases: the different objectives underlying tort and contract breach; the importance of predictability in assuring commercial stability in contractual dealings; the potential for converting every contract breach into a tort, with accompanying punitive damage recovery, and the preference for legislative action in affording appropriate remedies. * * * The same concerns support a cautious approach here. Restrictions on contract remedies serve to protect the "freedom to bargain over special risks and [to] promote contract formation by limiting liability to the value of the promise." * * *

Generally, outside the insurance context, "a tortious breach of contract ... may be found when (1) the breach is accompanied by a traditional common law tort, such as fraud or conversion; (2) the means used to breach the contract are tortious, involving deceit or undue coercion or; (3) one party intentionally breaches the contract intending or knowing that such a breach will cause severe, unmitigable harm in the form of mental anguish, personal hardship, or substantial consequential damages." * * * Focusing on intentional conduct gives substance to the proposition that a breach of contract is tortious only when some independent duty arising from tort law is violated. * * * If every negligent breach of a contract gives rise to tort damages the limitation would be meaningless, as would the statutory distinction between tort and contract remedies.

In this case, the jury concluded Menezes did not act intentionally; nor was he guilty of fraud or misrepresentation. This is a claim for negligent breach of a contract, which is not sufficient to support tortious damages for violation of an independent tort duty.

* * *

* * * [A] preexisting contractual relationship, without more, will not support a recovery for mental suffering where the defendant's tortious conduct has resulted only in economic injury to the plaintiff. * * *

* * *

In *Camenisch* [*v. Superior Court* (1996)], 44 Cal.App.4th 1689, 52 Cal.Rptr.2d 450, the plaintiff sought emotional distress damages because the lawyer's negligent estate planning advice thwarted his tax avoidance goals. * * * The Court of Appeal rejected the claim for emotional distress damages. * * * The prospect of paying taxes is generally considered distressing, and the prospect of paying a greater levy than necessary is even more disquieting. However, the emotional upset derives from an inherently economic concern. * * *

* * *

Here, the breach—the negligent construction of the Erlichs' house— did not cause physical injury. No one was hit by a falling beam. Although the Erlichs state they feared the house was structurally unsafe and might collapse in an earthquake, they lived in it for five years. The only physical injury alleged is Barry Erlich's heart disease, which flowed from the emotional distress and not directly from the negligent construction.

The Erlichs may have hoped to build their dream home and live happily ever after, but there is a reason that tag line belongs only in fairy tales. Building a house may turn out to be a stress-free project; it is much more likely to be the stuff of urban legends—the cause of bankruptcy, marital dissolution, hypertension and fleeting fantasies ranging from homicide to suicide. As Justice Yegan noted below, "No reasonable homeowner can embark on a building project with certainty that the project will be completed to perfection. Indeed, errors are so likely to occur that few if any homeowners would be justified in resting their peace of mind on [its] timely or correct completion...." * * *

D.

Having concluded tort damages are not available, we finally consider whether damages for emotional distress should be included as consequential or special damages in a contract claim. "Contract damages are generally limited to those within the contemplation of the parties when the contract was entered into or at least reasonably foreseeable by them at the time; consequential damages beyond the expectations of the parties are not recoverable. This limitation on available damages serves to encourage contractual relations and commercial activity by enabling parties to estimate in advance the financial risks of their enterprise." * * *

" '[W]hen two parties make a contract, they agree upon the rules and regulations which will govern their relationship; the risks inherent in the agreement and the likelihood of its breach. The parties to the contract in essence create a mini-universe for themselves, in which each voluntarily chooses his contracting partner, each trusts the other's willingness to keep his word and honor his commitments, and in which they define their respective obligations, rewards and risks. Under such a scenario, it is appropriate to enforce only such obligations as each party voluntarily assumed, and to give him only such benefits as he expected to receive; this is the function of contract law.' " * * *

* * *

Accordingly, damages for mental suffering and emotional distress are generally not recoverable in an action for breach of an ordinary commercial contract in California. * * * "Recovery for emotional disturbance will be excluded unless the breach also caused bodily harm or the contract or the breach is of such a kind that serious emotional disturbance was a particularly likely result." (Rest.2d Contracts, § 353.) The Restatement specifically notes the breach of a contract to build a home is not "particularly likely" to result in "serious emotional disturbance." (*Ibid.*)

Cases permitting recovery for emotional distress typically involve mental anguish stemming from more personal undertakings the traumatic results of which were unavoidable. *See, e.g.,* Burgess v. Superior Court, *supra,* 2 Cal.4th 1064, 9 Cal.Rptr.2d 615, 831 P.2d 1197 (infant injured during childbirth); Molien v. Kaiser Foundation Hospitals (1980) 27 Cal.3d 916, 167 Cal.Rptr. 831, 616 P.2d 813 (misdiagnosed venereal disease and subsequent failure of marriage); * * * Chelini v. Nieri (1948) 32 Cal.2d 480, 196 P.2d 915 (failure to adequately preserve a corpse). Thus, when the express object of the contract is the mental and emotional well-being of one of the contracting parties, the breach of the contract may give rise to damages for mental suffering or emotional distress. *See* Wynn v. Monterey Club (1980) 111 Cal.App.3d 789, 799–801, 168 Cal.Rptr. 878 (agreement of two gambling clubs to exclude husband's gambling-addicted wife from clubs and not to cash her checks); Ross v. Forest Lawn

Memorial Park (1984) 153 Cal.App.3d 988, 992–996, 203 Cal.Rptr. 468 (cemetery's agreement to keep burial service private and to protect grave from vandalism); Windeler v. Scheers Jewelers (1970) 8 Cal.App.3d 844, 851–852, 88 Cal.Rptr. 39 (bailment for heirloom jewelry where jewelry's great sentimental value was made known to bailee).

* * *

Plaintiffs argue strenuously that a broader notion of damages is appropriate when the contract is for the construction of a home. Amici curiae urge us to permit emotional distress damages in cases of negligent construction of a personal residence when the negligent construction causes gross interference with the normal use and habitability of the residence.

Such a rule would make the financial risks of construction agreements difficult to predict. Contract damages must be clearly ascertainable in both nature and origin. * * * A contracting party cannot be required to assume limitless responsibility for all consequences of a breach and must be advised of any special harm that might result in order to determine whether or not to accept the risk of contracting. * * *

Moreover, adding an emotional distress component to recovery for construction defects could increase the already prohibitively high cost of housing in California, affect the availability of insurance for builders, and greatly diminish the supply of affordable housing. The potential for such broad-ranging economic consequences—costs likely to be paid by the public generally—means the task of fashioning appropriate limits on the availability of emotional distress claims should be left to the Legislature. (See Tex. Prop.Code Ann. § 27.001 et seq. (1999); Hawaii Rev. Stat. § 663–8.9 (1998).)

Permitting damages for emotional distress on the theory that certain contracts carry a lot of emotional freight provides no useful guidance. Courts have carved out a narrow range of exceptions to the general rule of exclusion where emotional tranquillity is the contract's essence. Refusal to broaden the bases for recovery reflects a fundamental policy choice. A rule which focuses not on the risks contracting parties voluntarily assume but on one party's reaction to inadequate performance, cannot provide any principled limit on liability.

* * *

* * * The available damages for defective construction are limited to the cost of repairing the home, including lost use or relocation expenses, or the diminution in value. * * * The Erlichs received more than $400,000 in traditional contract damages to correct the defects in their home. While their distress was undoubtedly real and serious, we conclude the balance of policy considerations—the potential for significant increases in liability in amounts disproportionate to culpability, the court's inability to formulate appropriate limits on the availability of claims, and the magnitude of the impact on stability and predictability in commercial affairs—counsel against expanding contract damages to include mental claims in negligent construction cases.

DISPOSITION

The judgment of the Court of Appeal is reversed and the matter is remanded for further proceedings consistent with this opinion.

GEORGE, C.J., KENNARD, J., BAXTER, J., and CHIN, J., concur.

Concurring and Dissenting Opinion by WERDEGAR, J.

I concur in the majority opinion insofar as it holds that a plaintiff may not recover damages for emotional distress based on a defendant's negligent breach of a contract to build a house when the defendant has breached no duty independent of the contract. * * * I read the record differently as to whether these plaintiffs did, in fact, present an independent claim for negligence * * *. I * * * express no opinion on the circumstances under which a tort plaintiff may recover damages for emotional distress.

MOSK, J., concurs.

NOTES

1. For a discussion "challeng[ing] the general rule against recovery for mental distress damages, arguing that the current patchwork of exceptions is unworkable" see Ronnie Cohen and Shannon O'Byrne, *Cry Me a River: Recovery of Mental Distress Damages in a Breach of Contract Action—A North American Perspective*, 42 Am. Bus. L.J. 97 (2005).

2. Most jurisdictions have refused to permit the recovery of emotional distress damages for the breach of a contract to construct a house. *See, e.g.,* Hancock v. Northcutt, 808 P.2d 251 (Alaska 1991); Kleinke v. Farmers Cooperative Supply & Shipping, 202 Wis.2d 138, 549 N.W.2d 714 (1996); *see also* Rathgeber v. James Hemenway, Inc., 335 Or. 404, 69 P.3d 710 (2003) (emotional distress damages not recoverable for breach of real estate agent's contract); Francis v. Lee Enterprises, Inc., 89 Haw. 234, 971 P.2d 707 (1999) (emotional distress damages not recoverable for breach of employment contract). A case from Louisiana did allow the recovery of emotional distress damages in such cases. *See,* Heath v. Brandon Homes, Inc., 825 So.2d 1262 (La.Ct.App.2002). *See generally* James Acret, 1 Construction Law Digests § 11.36 (2004). For a discussion of the general rule that punitive damages are not recoverable for breach of contract, see *infra* Chapter 3.5.B.

3. Toward the end of its opinion, the court in *Erlich* mentioned an additional reason for disallowing tort damages for a "negligent" breach of contract. The court said, "a preexisting contractual relationship, without more, will not support a recovery for mental suffering where the defendant's tortious conduct has resulted only in economic injury to the plaintiff." The court was referring to what has become known as the "economic loss" rule. Note the phrase "without more". As the court in *Erlich* noted, a breach of contract accompanied by an intentional tort, including fraud, or physical

injury (except to a product that could be warranted in the contract) would allow a court to award tort damages to a plaintiff.

b. *Economic Loss Rule*

Besides the general rule that, except in rare circumstances, emotional distress damages are not available in breach of contract actions, another rule, the "economic loss rule," substantially restricts when a plaintiff who suffered no bodily or "other" property harm may bring an action in negligence. As seen in *General Nutrition* above, the economic loss rule is not applied to all negligence cases without bodily or property damage. For an excellent discussion of the contours of the economic loss rule see Dan B. Dobbs, Symposium: *Dan B. Dobbs Conference on Economic Tort Law: An Introduction to Non–Statutory Economic Loss Claims*, 48 Ariz. L. Rev. 713 (2006).

Unfortunately, application of the economic loss rule varies substantially from jurisdiction to jurisdiction. *See* Susan M. Glenn and Paula M. Burlison, *The Economic Loss Rule Survives* Colleton Prep, 20 S. Carolina Lawyer 32, 33 (2009) ("The economic loss rule is a confusing doctrine, the subject of numerous articles attempting to sort through the possible rationales for the rule and the various ways in which it can be applied," *citing* Anita Bernstein, *Keep It Simple: An Explanation of the Rule of No Recovery for Pure Economic Loss*, 48 Ariz. L. Rev. 773 (2006); and R. Joseph Barton, Note, *Drowning in a Sea of Contract: Application of the Economic Loss Rule to Fraud and Misrepresentation Claims*, 41 Wm. & Mary L. Rev. 1789 (2000)). *See also* Christopher W. Arledge, *When Does a Contract Breach also Give Rise to a Tort Claim? A Primer for Practitioners*, 8 Orange County Lawyer 42 (2006); Andrew Gray, Note, *Drowning in a Sea of Confusion: Applying the Economic Loss Doctrine to Component Parts, Service Contracts and Fraud*, 84 Wash. U. L. Rev. 1513 (2006); Reeder R. Fox & Patrick J. Loftus, *Riding the Choppy Waters of* East River: *Economic Loss Doctrine Ten Years Later*, 64 Def. Couns. J. 260 (1997); Frank Nussbaum, *The Economic Loss Rule and Intentional Torts: A Shield or a Sword*, 8 St. Thomas L. Rev. 473 (1996).

As you read the following cases, keep track of the differing situations in which tort damages for negligence may not be allowed. Also keep track of the differing exceptions to the economic loss rule. Which of the alternatives presented make sense to you?

i. *Defective Products*

LINCOLN GENERAL INSURANCE COMPANY v. DETROIT DIESEL CORPORATION ET AL.

Supreme Court of Tennessee, 2009.
293 S.W.3d 487.

JANICE M. HOLDER, CHIEF JUSTICE.

* * *

Senators Rental, Inc. ("Senators Rental"), an insured of Lincoln General Insurance Company ("Lincoln General"), purchased a bus manufactured by Prevost Car (US) Inc. ("Prevost"). The engine in the bus was produced by Detroit Diesel Corporation ("Detroit Diesel"). On May 8, 2006, the bus was traveling south on Interstate 65 near Goodlettsville, Tennessee, when it caught fire due to an alleged engine defect. The fire did not cause personal injury or damage to any property other than the bus itself. Lincoln General paid Senators Rental $405,250 for the fire damage pursuant to its insurance policy.

Lincoln General filed a complaint against Prevost and Detroit Diesel. The complaint included counts of breach of express and implied warranties, negligence, and strict products liability. Prevost and Detroit Diesel removed the case to the United States District Court for the Middle District of Tennessee. Prevost filed a motion to dismiss for failure to state a claim pursuant to Federal Rule of Civil Procedure 12(b)(6), arguing that Lincoln General's tort claims are barred by the economic loss doctrine.

On July 1, 2008, the United States District Court certified one question of law to this Court, which we accepted pursuant to Tennessee Supreme Court Rule 23.

* * *

The economic loss doctrine is implicated in products liability cases when a defective product damages itself without causing personal injury or damage to other property. In this context, "economic loss" is defined generally as "the diminution in the value of the product because it is inferior in quality and does not work for the general purposes for which it was manufactured and sold." Comment, *Manufacturers' Liability to Remote Purchasers for "Economic Loss" Damages—Tort or Contract?*, 114 U. Pa. L. Rev. 539, 541 (1966). Two types of economic loss, direct and consequential, occur when a defective product is damaged. *See, e.g.*, Restatement (Third) of Torts: Products Liability § 21, cmt. d (1998). Direct economic loss may be measured by the defective product's cost of repair or replacement. *Id.* Consequential economic losses, such as lost profits, result from the product owner's inability to use the product. *Id.*

The question certified presents us with our first opportunity to examine the proper application of the economic loss doctrine when only the defective product is damaged. In the seminal case of *East River Steamship Corp. v. Transamerica Delaval, Inc.*, 476 U.S. 858, 868–71, 106 S. Ct. 2295, 90 L. Ed. 2d 865 (1986), the United States Supreme Court examined three approaches to the economic loss doctrine used by various state and federal courts, which it described as the "majority," "minority," and "intermediate" positions, and adopted the majority approach. In *East River*, a shipbuilder contracted with a manufacturer for the production of turbines to propel four oil-transporting super tankers. While at sea, the turbines malfunctioned due to design and manufacturing defects. Only the turbines themselves were damaged. In a unanimous decision, the Supreme

Court held that the economic loss doctrine barred the shipbuilder's products liability suit in admiralty against the manufacturer.

In adopting the "majority approach" to the economic loss doctrine, the Supreme Court chose a bright-line rule that precludes recovery in tort when a product damages itself without causing personal injury or damage to other property. In reaching this conclusion, the Supreme Court observed that "[w]hen a product injures only itself the reasons for imposing a tort duty are weak and those for leaving the party to its contractual remedies are strong." *Id.* at 871. Specifically, the Supreme Court reasoned that damage to a defective product is merely a failure of the product to meet the purchaser's expectations, a risk that the parties had the opportunity to allocate by negotiating contract terms and acquiring insurance. *Id.* at 871–72. In contrast, the " 'cost of an injury and the loss of time or health may be an overwhelming misfortune,' and one the person is not prepared to meet." *Id.* at 871 * * *. Finally, the Supreme Court expressed concern that permitting recovery in tort for purely economic loss could subject the manufacturer to an indefinite amount of damages. *Id.* at 874. A warranty action, on the other hand, has a "built-in limitation on liability." *Id.*

In contrast, the "minority approach" to the economic loss doctrine permits tort recovery for purely economic loss.[4] The Supreme Court explained that jurisdictions following the minority approach do not distinguish between economic loss and personal injury or property damage because in either circumstance, the damage was caused by the defendant's conduct. *Id.* at 869 * * *. In the minority view, the manufacturer's duty to produce non-defective products and tort law's corresponding concern with safety apply equally when the harm is purely economic. * * * Ultimately, the Supreme Court rejected the minority approach because it "fails to account for the need to keep products liability and contract law in separate spheres and to maintain a realistic limitation on damages." *E. River S.S. Corp.*, 476 U.S. at 870–71.

Lincoln General urges us to recognize a variation of the third approach to the economic loss doctrine, the "intermediate approach." States that follow the intermediate approach permit tort recovery for damage to the defective product alone under limited exceptions that "turn on the nature of the defect, the type of risk, and the manner in which the injury arose." *Id.* at 870. The exception advanced by Lincoln General would permit recovery for unreasonably dangerous products that cause damage to themselves during sudden, calamitous events.[5] This exception would require courts to distinguish between those products that expose a product owner to an unreasonable risk of injury during an abrupt and disastrous occurrence and those products that merely disappoint a product owner's expectations. *See id.* at 869–70.

4. Our research indicates that tort recovery for purely economic loss is permissible in at least three states. [citations omitted]

5. A number of cases express agreement with a form of the intermediate approach based on unreasonably dangerous products; sudden, calamitous events; or both. [citations omitted]

The *East River* Court rejected the dichotomy between disappointed and endangered product owners as "too indeterminate to enable manufacturers easily to structure their business behavior." *Id.* at 870. * * *

We agree with the United States Supreme Court that the owner of a defective product that creates a risk of injury and was damaged during a fire, a crash, or other similar occurrence is in the same position as the owner of a defective product that malfunctions and simply does not work. It follows that the remedies available to these similarly situated product owners should derive from the parties' agreements, not from the law of torts, lest we disrupt the parties' allocation of risk. *See Prosser & Keeton on the Law of Torts* § 101(3), at 709 (5th ed. 1984) ("[R]isk of harm to the product itself due to the condition of the product would seem to be a type of risk that the parties to a purchase and sale contract should be allowed to allocate pursuant to the terms of the contract."). To hold otherwise would make it more difficult for parties to predict the consequences of their business transactions, the cost of which ultimately falls on consumers in the form of increased prices. * * *

It is difficult, moreover, for parties and courts to apply a rule that focuses on the degree of risk and the manner in which the product was damaged as opposed to a rule that hinges on harm the plaintiff actually sustains. Lincoln General suggests, nonetheless, that adopting the bright-line rule espoused in *East River* would come at too great a price—the decreased safety of Tennessee citizens. We believe, however, that deterrence is adequately promoted by existing law that permits tort recovery for personal injury and damage to property other than the product itself. As explained by the Illinois Supreme Court, "[b]ecause no manufacturer can predict with any certainty that the damage his unsafe product causes will be confined to the product itself, tort liability will continue to loom as a possibility." *Trans States Airlines v. Pratt & Whitney Can., Inc.*, 177 Ill. 2d 21, 682 N.E.2d 45, 53, 224 Ill. Dec. 484 (Ill. 1997).

* * *

In our view, the *East River* approach fairly balances the competing policy interests and clearly delineates between the law of contract and the law of tort. We therefore hold that Tennessee law does not recognize an exception to the economic loss doctrine under which recovery in tort is possible for damage to the defective product itself when the defect renders the product unreasonably dangerous and causes damage by means of a sudden, calamitous event.

In so holding, we join the majority of state appellate courts that have considered the adoption of an exception to the economic loss doctrine based on unreasonably dangerous products; sudden, calamitous events; or both. [citations omitted].

Finally, our holding is consistent with the Restatement (Third) of Torts: Products Liability (1998). Section 21 specifically excludes harm to "the defective product itself" from the definition of "harm to persons or property" for which economic loss is recoverable.[7]

CONCLUSION

In addressing the United States District Court's certified question, we are persuaded that the rationale proffered by the United States Supreme Court in *East River* is sound. We therefore hold that Tennessee does not recognize an exception to the economic loss doctrine under which recovery in tort is possible for damage to the defective product itself when the defect renders the product unreasonably dangerous and causes the damage by means of a sudden, calamitous event. * * *

NOTES

1. The Tennessee Supreme Court in *Lincoln General* followed East River Steamship Corp. v. Transamerica Delaval, Inc., 476 U.S. 858, 106 S.Ct. 2295, 90 L.Ed.2d 865 (1986). *East River* was an action in negligence and strict liability brought by charterers of ships against turbine manufacturers for the cost of repairing the defective turbines and for income lost while the ships were out of service. The ships' owners had contracted with the turbine manufacturers to build turbines, but the manufacturers claimed that the statute of limitations had run on any warranty claims. The charterers had chartered the ships "as is" from the ships' owners for 20 or 22 years, and had assumed responsibility for maintenance and repairs and for obtaining certain forms of insurance. The charterers and the turbine manufacturers had not contracted with one another. The court held that admiralty law recognized products liability actions, including negligence and strict liability claims. However, the Court ruled that the plaintiffs were barred from recovery in strict liability because the defective turbine component parts had caused damage only to the turbines themselves, and not to persons or "other" property. The Court also ruled that the plaintiffs owed no duty based on negligence to avoid causing purely economic loss. For a discussion about the development of the economic loss rule and its variations, see Gennady A. Gorel, Note, *The Economic Loss Doctrine: Arguing for the Intermediate Rule and Taming the Tort–Eating Monster*, 37 Rutgers L. J. 517, 518 (2006) ("the economic loss doctrine was expanded to save 'contract law from drowning in a sea of tort' * * *. Today, it is tort law that needs protection from 'the tort-eating monster.'")

2. What is "Other Property"? Assume the following: (1) that instead of an insurance company seeking reimbursement from the manufacturer of the bus and the "producer" of the engine, the plaintiff was the purchaser of the

---

7. Restatement (Third) of Torts: Products Liability § 21 provides, in its entirety:

"For purposes of this Restatement, harm to persons or property includes economic loss if caused by harm to:

(a) the plaintiff's person; or

(b) the person of another when harm to the other interferes with an interest of the plaintiff protected by tort law; or

(c) the plaintiff's property *other than the defective product itself.*"

(emphasis added).

bus, (2) the plaintiff did not have insurance on the bus and (3) the plaintiff sued the manufacturer of the engine for damage to the bus. How would the hypothetical plaintiff's case be resolved under each of the three variations of the economic loss rule? Which variation would you argue should be applied if you were a justice on a state supreme court? Just as jurisdictions do not agree about the scope of the economic loss rule, they also do not agree about its subsidiary issue, what is meant by "other property." For example, in Staton Hills Winery Co. v. Collons, 96 Wash. App. 590, 595–602, 980 P.2d 784, 787–90 (1999), the Washington Court of Appeals applied Washington's "intermediate" economic loss rule and held that the winery, which had purchased storage tanks to hold wine, could not sue the seller of the tanks in products liability for the value of the spoiled wine caused by a defect in the storage tank. To reach that decision, the court reviewed a variety of approaches used to determine what is meant by "other property" for purposes of allowing a plaintiff to recover for that property's destruction. The court concluded:

> Holding a manufacturer or distributor of products liable in tort for an unsafe product that creates an unreasonable risk of harm to persons or property furthers the safety-insurance policy of tort law, which has traditionally redressed injuries classified as physical harm or property damage. * * * But tort law policies are not applicable where a product's defect is merely its failure to meet the purchaser's expectation. In that case, the purchaser has the ability to self-protect during the bargaining process; it would violate contract law to allow the purchaser to recover more in tort litigation than it could obtain in the contract bargaining process. * * *

* * *

> * * * [W]e consider the extent to which the risk was foreseeable and whether the product purchaser had the bargaining capacity to limit its exposure to the risk. Where the risk was foreseeable and the parties were bargaining at arms length, contract policies are implicated. But tort policies come into play where it would have been difficult to anticipate the harm or where the parties had disparate bargaining positions. Finally, we consider whether the risk that the defective product would harm other property included a further risk to persons or additional other property.

> Here, there was no unreasonable risk of harm to people or property. The risk posed by the negligent application of the epoxy was that the epoxy would not properly adhere to the metal tank, thereby failing to protect the wine from contact with the metal. * * * [T]he peeling epoxy did not pose a risk of harm to any person or property, other than the wine inside. Further, the Winery contemplated the risk of spoiled wine when it prepared a purchase order for tanks that were to be sandblasted and then coated with two layers of a food-grade epoxy material. Finally, the spoiled wine did not pose a further risk to persons or other property as the hydrocarbon contamination was not toxic and was readily apparent when the Winery opened the tank. * * *

* * *

* * * [W]e conclude that Collons' alleged failure to meet contract requirements was the type of product performance claim that is properly
remediable only under breach of warranty law. * * *

* * *

* * * [T]he price of a bright-line rule would be high. To allow automatic
recovery in tort for damages a defective product causes to other property,
regardless of the particular circumstances, would in some cases defeat the
expectations created by agreement where the product was not unreasonably unsafe. * * *

Id. But see Comptech Int'l, Inc. v. Milam Commerce Park, Ltd., 753 So.2d
1219, 1226–27 (Fla.1999) (holding that plaintiff-tenant, who had contracted
with defendant-lessor to repair plaintiff's warehouse that at all times held
computers, was not barred by the economic loss rule from recovering, in
negligence, the value of the computers destroyed in the fire caused by the
repairs because the repairs were a service, not a good, but also because "to
the extent the warehouse is the object of the contract, the computers in the
warehouse are indeed other property.") *See also* Jacob Kreutzer, *Somebody
Has to Pay: Products Liability for Spyware*, 45 Am. Bus. L.J. 61 (2008)
(arguing that damage done by spyware is "other property" for purposes of
products liability); Charles E. Cantu, *A Continuing Whimsical Search for the
True Meaning of the Term "Product" in Products Liability Litigation*, 35 St.
Mary's L.J. 341 (2004); John W. Reis, Column, Trial Lawyers Forum, *Economic Loss Rule: The "Integral Part" Approach to the "Other Property"
Exception*, 76 Fla. Bar J. 42 (2002).

    ii.   Defective Services

TERRACON CONSULTANTS WESTERN, INC.
v. MANDALAY RESORT GROUP

Supreme Court of Nevada, 2009.
206 P.3d 81.

GIBBONS, J. HARDESTY, C.J., PARRAGUIRRE, DOUGLAS, CHERRY, SAITTA and
PICKERING, JJ., concur.

* * *

Respondents Mandalay Resort Group, Mandalay Development, and
Mandalay Corporation (collectively, Mandalay) managed the construction
of the approximately $1 billion Mandalay Resort and Casino (the resort) in
Las Vegas. To complete the resort, Mandalay hired various subcontractors, including appellants Terracon Consultants Western, Inc., Terracon,
Inc. (collectively, Terracon) * * *. The parties do not dispute that Terracon's work was limited to providing professional engineering advice and
that Terracon was not involved in physically constructing the property.
* * *

In accordance with the written contract's terms, Terracon prepared a
geotechnical report with its foundation design recommendations, which
Mandalay implemented as it began erecting the resort. Based upon Terra-

con's soil analysis and the anticipated weight of the building, Terracon predicted a certain amount of settling underneath the foundation. According to Mandalay's complaint, however, the ultimate amount of settling exceeded Terracon's projections. Because Clark County believed that the settling presented a potential danger to the resort's structural integrity, the county required Mandalay to repair and reinforce the foundation before proceeding with the construction. Consequently, Mandalay sued Terracon for damages in state court, alleging that the deficient engineering advice caused the resort's foundation problems. Mandalay's theories of recovery included breach of contract, breach of the covenant of good faith and fair dealing, and professional negligence.

Terracon removed the matter to the United States District Court for the District of Nevada and, thereafter, moved for partial summary judgment on Mandalay's professional negligence claim * * *

* * *

* * * [A]fter determining that Nevada law was unclear * * *. The federal court thus asked this court to address the scope of Nevada's economic loss doctrine * * *.

* * * [W]e permitted certain professional organizations to file a brief as amici curiae.[4]

* * *

The economic loss doctrine is a judicially created rule that primarily emanates from products liability jurisprudence. * * * This court has explained that " '[t]he economic loss doctrine marks the fundamental boundary between contract law, which is designed to enforce the expectancy interests of the parties, and tort law, which imposes a duty of reasonable care and thereby [generally] encourages citizens to avoid causing physical harm to others.' " * * * Applying the economic loss doctrine to accomplish its general purpose, this court has concluded that the doctrine bars unintentional tort actions when the plaintiff seeks to recover "purely economic losses." * * *

DISCUSSION

The economic loss doctrine's purpose

The seminal Nevada decision concerning the economic loss doctrine is *Stern*, 98 Nev. 409, 651 P.2d 637. In *Stern*, we considered an action brought by MGM Grand Hotel employees against those involved in the hotel's design and construction to recover lost wages and employment benefits after a fire damaged the hotel. The plaintiffs in *Stern* sued under negligent interference with contractual relations and prospective economic

---

4. The amici curiae brief was submitted on behalf of the American Institute of Architects (AIA), AIA Nevada; AIA Las Vegas; the American Council of Engineering Companies; the American Council of Engineering Companies of Nevada; the Design Professionals Coalition of the American Council of Engineering Companies; the National Society of Professional Engineers; the Nevada Society of Professional Engineers; ASFE/The Best People on Earth; the American Society of Civil Engineers; and the Nevada Section of the American Society of Civil Engineers.

advantage theories, among others. In *Stern,* we began our analysis by pointing out that purely economic losses are recoverable in actions for tortious interference with contractual relations or prospective economic advantage when the alleged interference is *intentional.* * * *

* * * [W]e reasoned that allowing the plaintiffs to sue under a negligence theory for purely economic losses, without accompanying personal injury or property damage, would have defeated the primary purpose of the economic loss doctrine: "to shield a defendant from unlimited liability for all of the economic consequences of a negligent act, particularly in a commercial or professional setting, and thus to keep the risk of liability reasonably calculable." * * * [W]e determined that, although the plaintiffs suffered financial injury, namely, lost wages, benefits, and union dues, they had no possessory or proprietary interest in the hotel property and they suffered no accompanying personal injuries as a result of the fire that would permit them to recover in tort. *Id.; see also Robins Dry Dock & Repair Co. v. Flint,* 275 U.S. 303, 309, 48 S. Ct. 134, 72 L. Ed. 290 (1927) (explaining the general rule that a party cannot recover in tort for its economic losses unless that party suffers an accompanying physical injury or damage to its property). * * *

While the doctrine generally provides that purely economic losses are not recoverable in tort absent personal injury or property damage, courts have made exceptions to allow such recovery in certain categories of cases, such as negligent misrepresentation and professional negligence actions against attorneys, accountants, real estate professionals, and insurance brokers. * * * In determining whether an exception to the economic loss doctrine should be made to allow negligence-based claims against professionals who provide design-related services in the commercial property development or improvement process, we first examine the policy considerations. * * *

Policy considerations underlying the economic loss doctrine

The economic loss doctrine draws a legal line between contract and tort liability. * * * The doctrine expresses the policy that the need for useful commercial economic activity and the desire to make injured plaintiffs whole is best balanced by allowing tort recovery only to those plaintiffs who have suffered personal injury or property damage.* * * [W]hen economic loss occurs as a result of negligence in the context of commercial activity, contract law can be invoked to enforce the quality expectations derived from the parties' agreement. * * *

In addition * * * the doctrine works to reduce the cost of tort actions, but still provides tort victims with a remedy because less expensive alternative forms of compensation, such as insurance, generally are available to a financially injured party. * * *

Another consideration behind the economic loss doctrine is balancing the disproportion between liability and fault. * * * [I]mposing unbounded tort liability for pure financial harm could result in "incentives that are perverse," such as insurance premiums that are too expensive for the average economic actor to afford. * * *

Exceptions to the economic loss doctrine

Nevertheless, as pointed out above, exceptions to the economic loss doctrine exist in broad categories of cases * * *. For example, negligent misrepresentation is a special financial harm claim for which tort recovery is permitted because without such liability the law would not exert significant financial pressures to avoid such negligence.* * * An exception also has been created for commercial fishermen, who generally are permitted to sue for economic losses as "favorites of admiralty" law. * * *

With regard to the particular type of claim at issue here, those jurisdictions that * * * permit tort-based claims against design professionals when only economic loss is at issue, reason that the economic loss doctrine does not apply to bar tort claims grounded on negligently rendered services. *See, e.g., McCarthy Well Co. v. St. Peter Creamery,* 410 N.W.2d 312 (Minn. 1987) (concluding that under Minnesota law, the economic loss doctrine barred tort actions only in cases governed by the Uniform Commercial Code and was thus not applicable in cases where the alleged negligence involved the performance of services rather than the sale of goods). Other courts have reasoned that tort claims against design professionals where only economic losses occurred are permissible when design professionals owe duties beyond the terms of the contract. * * * Still other courts allow recovery on the basis that such claims are foreseeable. * * *

The economic loss doctrine applies to preclude Mandalay's professional negligence claim

Guided by the doctrine's purpose * * * and, after contemplating the competing policy reasons set forth above, we conclude that the economic loss doctrine should apply to bar the professional negligence claim at issue here.

* * *

Based on the same policy considerations that guide our decision here, other jurisdictions have reached the same conclusion. * * *

We perceive no significant policy distinction that would drive us to permit tort-based claims to recover economic losses against design professionals, such as architects and engineers, who provided their professional services in the commercial property development and improvement process, when we have concluded that such claims are barred under the economic loss doctrine if brought against contractors and subcontractors involved in physically constructing improvements to real property. *See Calloway v. City of Reno,* 116 Nev. 250, 993 P.2d 1259 (2000). The work provided by construction contractors or the services rendered by design professionals in the commercial building process are both integral to the building process and impact the quality of building projects. Therefore, when the quality is deemed defective, resulting in economic loss, remedies are properly addressed through contract law. * * *

* * *

CONCLUSION

We conclude that, in a commercial property construction defect action in which the plaintiffs seek to recover purely economic losses through negligence-based claims, the economic loss doctrine applies to bar such claims against design professionals who have provided professional services in the commercial property development or improvement process. Accordingly, we answer the U.S. District Court's certified question in the affirmative.

NOTES

1.   The Supreme Court of Nevada in *Terracon* cited Calloway v. City of Reno, 116 Nev. 250, 993 P.2d 1259 (2000), as support for holding that the economic loss rule applied to actions against design professionals. In *Calloway* the Court had held that the economic loss rule barred homeowners who did not suffer bodily injury or property injury except to their homes from suing subcontractors in negligence for construction defects, limiting the homeowners to contractual remedies. Prior to the decision in *Calloway*, but after the events at issue, the Nevada legislature passed a prospective statute that permits homeowners to bring a negligence claim "in a construction defects cause of action initiated under [the statute]," Olson v. Richard, 120 Nev. 240, 244, 89 P.3d 31, 33 (2004). For a discussion of the Nevada statute, see Gary Ashman, Note, *The Long and Winding Road of Economic Loss Doctrine in* Calloway v. City of Reno, 3 Nev. L.J. 167 (2002). The court in *Terracon* was able to rely on the reasoning of *Calloway* despite the action of the Nevada legislature because *Terracon* involved commercial construction. Do you agree that the economic loss rule can be applied in a commercial, but not in a residential context?

2.   The reasoning of *McCarthy Well Co.*, from Minnesota, cited in *Terracon*, was adopted in Wisconsin in Insurance Co. of North America v. Cease Electric Inc., 276 Wis. 2d 361, 372–81, 688 N.W.2d 462, 467–72 (2004):

There is a split among the jurisdictions as to whether the economic loss doctrine applies to contracts for services. As one treatise noted, "the judiciary remains hopelessly divided on whether the doctrine should be extended to services. . . ." Philip L. Brunner and Patrick J. O'Connor, Jr., Construction Law § 19:10, at n. 14 (May 2004). This court has not yet addressed whether the doctrine covers such claims. * * *

* * *

* * * Unlike contracts for products or goods, which enjoy the benefit of well-developed law under the U.C.C., no such benefit exists for contracts for services. This is because the U.C.C. does not apply to service con-

tracts. * * * As a result, the built-in warranty provisions that the U.C.C. may provide in a contract for the sale of products or goods would not apply to a contract for services.

* * *

Often the circumstances surrounding service contracts are simple and informal (e.g., electricians, plumbers, lawn care providers, etc.). * * *

* * * Certainly, parties to service contracts, oral or written, can by means of contractual provisions allocate risk and limit remedies. Yet given the informality of such agreements, few parties actually address the allocation of risk or the limitation of remedies. They neither discuss it themselves nor hire attorneys to draft written agreements.

* * *

* * * Wisconsin courts have previously held that claims for professional malpractice lie both in tort and contract. * * * Because actions against professionals often involve purely economic loss without personal injury or property damage, the economic loss doctrine could be used to effectively extinguish such causes of action in tort.

Inevitably, this court would find itself on a slippery slope of having to decide whether an exception should be made for some or all professional groups. For an illustration of this problem, we need look no further than what is occurring in Illinois, where the state supreme court has exempted some professions from the economic loss doctrine, [accountants and attorneys], but not others, [engineers and architects]. * * *

* * *

Today, we choose to avoid those ends by avoiding this beginning. Accordingly, we determine that the economic loss doctrine is inapplicable to claims for the negligent provision of services. This bright line rule will limit the uncertainty and increased litigation that would accompany any other decision.

3. For a discussion of the varying approaches to the economic loss rule in a case involving a gravel supplier who delivered defective gravel, see Plourde Sand & Gravel Co. v. JGI Eastern, Inc., 154 N.H. 791, 917 A.2d 1250 (2007).

4. For a discussion of contract drafting for design professionals, see Carl J. Circo, *Contract Theory and Contract Practice: Allocating Design Responsibility in the Construction Industry*, 58 Fla. L. Rev. 561 (2006). For a discussion about the history of the development of a "professional services" exception to the economic loss rule and the conflicting applications of the rule, see Charles R. Walker, Casenote, *Moransais v. Heathman and the Florida Economic Loss Rule: Attempting to Leash the Tort–Eating Monster*, 52 Fla. L. Rev. 769 (2000).

3. **Negligence Actions Precluded by Economic Loss Rule Without Harm to Body or Property Despite Unavailability of Alternative Contract Action**

AIKENS v. BALTIMORE & OHIO RAILROAD CO.

Superior Court of Pennsylvania, 1985.
348 Pa.Super. 17, 501 A.2d 277.

Before OLSZEWSKI, POLOVICH, and MONTGOMERY, J.J.

OLSZEWSKI, JUDGE:

* * * Appellants, employees of the Motor Coils Manufacturing Company, Inc., brought suit seeking damages for lost wages, alleging that appellees' negligence caused a train derailment which damaged the Motor Coils plant. As a result of the derailment, production at the plant was curtailed and appellants suffered loss of work and wages. Appellants did not suffer personal injury or property damage from the derailment.

On appeal, the appellants raise two issues. First, appellants argue that Pennsylvania should recognize a cause of action to compensate a party suffering purely economic loss, absent any direct physical injury or property damage, as a result of the negligence of another party. We find this argument to be without merit.

The general rule is stated in the Restatement (Second) of Torts Sec. 766C:

> **Negligent Interference with Contract or Prospective Contractual Relation.** One is not liable to another for pecuniary harm not deriving from physical harm to the other, if that harm results from the actor's negligently
>
> (a) causing a third person not to perform a contract with the other, or
>
> (b) interfering with the other's performance of his contract or making the performance more expensive or burdensome, or
>
> (c) interfering with the other's acquiring a contractual relation with a third person.

Thus, recovery for purely economic loss occasioned by tortious interference with contract or economic advantage is not available under a negligence theory. * * * A cause of action exists in this situation only if the tortious interference was intentional or involved parties in a special relationship to one another. See * * * W. Prosser, Handbook of the Law of Torts Sec. 130 (4th Ed.1971).

The roots of this well-established rule reach back to the United States Supreme Court decision of Robins Dry Dock and Repair Company v. Flint, 275 U.S. 303, 48 S.Ct. 134, 72 L.Ed. 290 (1927). Writing for the Court, Mr. Justice Holmes stated:

> [A]s a general rule, at least, a tort to the person or property of one man does not make the tort-feasor liable to another merely because

the injured person was under a contract with that other unknown to the doer of the wrong. The law does not spread its protection so far.

275 U.S. at 309, 48 S.Ct. at 135, 72 L.Ed. at 292. Therefore, negligent harm to economic advantage alone is too remote for recovery under a negligence theory. The reason a plaintiff cannot recover stems from the fact that the negligent actor has no knowledge of the contract or prospective relation and thus has no reason to foresee any harm to the plaintiff's interest. * * *

Recently, the Georgia Court of Appeals was faced with a factual setting quite similar to the case at bar. In Willis v. Georgia Northern Railway Company, 169 Ga.App. 743, 314 S.E.2d 919 (1984), the appellants were employees of a plant which was damaged when eight loaded railcars owned by the appellee railroad broke free and rolled into the plant. The plant employees sued the railroad for lost wages. The Georgia Court held that the employees' right to wages existed by virtue of their relationship with the plant and not the railroad. Thus, loss of wages was not a probable consequence of the railroad's negligence and the damages claimed were too remote. *Id.* We find this reasoning persuasive.

Finally, we note that allowance of a cause of action for negligent interference with economic advantage would create an undue burden upon industrial freedom of action, and would create a disproportion between the large amount of damages that might be recovered and the extent of the defendant's fault. *See* Restatement (Second) of Torts § 766C, comment a (1979). To allow a cause of action for a negligent cause of purely economic loss would be to open the door to every person in the economic chain of the negligent person or business to bring a cause of action. Such an outstanding burden is clearly inappropriate and a danger to our economic system.

Accordingly, we decline appellants' invitation to adopt the reasoning of the California Supreme Court in J'Aire Corp. v. Gregory, 24 Cal.3d 799, 157 Cal.Rptr. 407, 598 P.2d 60 (1979), and to extend negligence liability to embrace purely economic loss. Such an extension would clearly lead to problems in consistency and foreseeablility and could be harmful in scope. Instead, we adopt the majority rule of the Restatement (Second) of Torts § 766C, and hold that no cause of action exists for negligence that causes only economic loss.

* * *

Order Affirmed.

NOTES

1. In *J'aire*, cited in *Aikens*, the California Supreme Court held that a defendant who was not in privity of contract with the plaintiff could recover damages for economic loss in a negligence cause of action, "where a special relationship exists between the parties," based on examination of six factors. Greystone Homes, Inc. v. Midtec, Inc., 168 Cal. App. 4th 1194, 1229, 86 Cal. Rptr. 3d 196, 222 (2008) (quoting *J'aire*).

2. If the plaintiffs in the *Aikens* case had suffered personal injury, they would have been entitled to recover compensatory damages for their economic losses in the form of a claim for lost earning capacity. Therefore, the economic loss doctrine only precludes a plaintiff from recovering damages in a negligence cause of action for pure economic loss.

IN RE TAIRA LYNN MARINE LTD. NO. 5, LLC v. JAYS SEAFOOD, INC.

United States Court of Appeals for the Fifth Circuit, 2006.
444 F.3d 371.

BENAVIDES, STEWART, and OWEN, CIRCUIT JUDGES.

CARL E. STEWART, CIRCUIT JUDGE:

* * *

I. FACTUAL AND PROCEDURAL BACKGROUND

On June 19, 2001, the M/V MR. BARRY and its tow, the T/B KIRBY 31801, allided with the Louisa Bridge in St. Mary Parish, Louisiana. Kirby Inland Marine, L.P. ("Kirby Inland") owned the barge; Taira Lynn Marine, Inc. ("Taira Lynn") owned and operated the tug; and the Louisiana Department of Transportation and Development ("the State") owns the bridge. The cargo on the barge, a gaseous mixture of propylene/propane, discharged into the air as a result of the allision. Consequently, the Louisiana State Police ordered a mandatory evacuation of all businesses and residences within a certain radius of the Louisa Bridge.

Taira Lynn initiated the underlying litigation under the Limitation of Liability Act, 46 U.S.C. app. § 183 (2000), in which several hundred claims were filed.* * * Fourteen businesses and business owners (collectively, "Claimants") that are parties to this appeal filed claims in the limitation action seeking to recover damages under the general maritime law, OPA [the Oil Pollution Act of 1990, 33 U.S.C. §§ 2701–2761 (2000)], CERCLA [the Comprehensive Environmental Response, Compensation, and Liability Act, 42 U.S.C. §§ 9601–9675 (2000)], and state law.

* * * Taira Lynn, Kirby Inland and the State then filed motions for partial summary judgment on the grounds that Claimants' recovery for economic losses unaccompanied by damage to a proprietary interest is barred * * *.

* * * [T]he court denied the motions for partial summary judgment* * * The district court certified the judgment as appealable pursuant to 28 U.S.C. § 1292(b) and this court granted permission to appeal.

Before we address the claims at issue, we find it necessary to emphasize what is *not* before us. Appellants' motion for summary judgment did not include claims involving personal injury, physical damage, or the claims of commercial fishermen. Thus, the only claims before this court are claims for purely economic losses.

* * *

III. Claims Pursuant to General Maritime Law

A. Applicable Law

It is unmistakable that the law of this circuit does not allow recovery of purely economic claims absent physical injury to a proprietary interest in a maritime negligence suit. In *Robins Dry Dock & Repair v. Flint*, 275 U.S. 303, 309, 48 S. Ct. 134, 72 L. Ed. 290 (1927), the Supreme Court held that a tortfeasor is not liable for negligence to a third person based on his contract with the injured party. In *Louisiana ex. rel. Guste v. M/V TESTBANK*, 752 F.2d 1019, 1023 (5th Cir. 1985) (en banc), this court concluded that *Robins* is a pragmatic limitation on the doctrine of foreseeability. We reasoned that "[i]f a plaintiff connected to the damaged chattels by contract cannot recover, others more remotely situated are foreclosed *a fortiori*." 752 F.2d at 1024. Accordingly, we reaffirmed the rule that there can be no recovery for economic loss absent physical injury to a proprietary interest. *Id.*

B. Summary of the Claims

Because of the number of parties involved in this appeal, we find it helpful to briefly summarize the underlying claims. Cajun Wireline, Inc. ("Cajun"), a full service slick wireline provider, claims that three of its jack up boats could not perform their duties due to the allision and subsequent evacuation. Coastline Marine, Inc. ("Coastline"), a pile driving business, claims it was unable to perform work on its contracts as a result of the evacuations. Pam Dore, doing business as Cove Marina ("Cove Marina"), claims loss of revenues and sales from a convenience store as a result of the evacuation. Legnon Enterprises ("Legnon") claims lost charter revenues and lost sales and revenues due to the evacuation. Coy Reeks, doing business as Riverfront Seawalls and Bulkheads ("Riverfront"), claims he had to leave his equipment on the island during the evacuation and as a result could not work for one week. Twin Brothers Marine ("Twin Brothers"), a fabrication and dock facility, claims it was forced to halt work in progress for two construction projects. Marine Turbine Technologies ("MTT") claims that it suffered physical damage in the form of toxic gas permeation on its property. North American Salt Company/Carey Salt Company ("North American") claims it had to suspend operations due to the discharge of the gas into the air. Morton International ("Morton") claims it began to shut down operations before the evacuation order was issued and that its wholly owned subsidiary, CVD Incorporated d/b/a Rohm & Haas Advanced Materials ("Advanced Materials"), suffered physical damage. Advanced Materials is a chemical vapor deposition facility that manufactures material used to make specialty lenses for military equipment and other purposes. It claims that two of its manufacturing runs had to be prematurely terminated and the company lost the materials in those runs and could not sell the products. Big D's Seafood ("Big D's"), Blue Gulf Seafood, Inc. ("Blue Gulf"), and Bagala's Quality Oysters ("Bagala's") claim lost revenues from their wholesale fishing operations. Mason Seafood ("Mason") claims it lost eighty-eight boxes of dressed crabs that spoiled in a freezer when law enforcement officials shut off the electricity during the evacuation.

C. Analysis

1. *Claimants alleging no physical damage*

The district court concluded that [six claimants] suffered no physical damage; however, the court endorsed a geographic exception to the *TESTBANK* rule and concluded that the claimants should have the opportunity to prove that their damages were foreseeable and proximately caused by the allision. The court concluded that [two claimants] suffered physical damage * * * and denied summary judgment as to those claims as well. The district court concluded that [two claimants'] claims of physical damage in the forms of the presence of gas on their properties satisfied *TESTBANK*; accordingly, it denied summary judgment. * * *

Appellants' argue that the district court erred in denying their motions for partial summary judgment * * *

Contrary to the district court's conclusion, twelve of the fourteen businesses that are parties to this appeal suffered no physical damage attributable to the allision and thus, their claims are barred by *TESTBANK*. There is no geographic exception to the *TESTBANK* rule and there is no exception based on the number of claimants. * * *

Likewise, the district court erred in concluding that * * * the physical presence of the gas on their property satisfies *TESTBANK*'s physical damage requirement are unpersuasive. * * * [C]laimants have not raised an issue of fact as to whether the gas physically damaged their property nor caused any personal injury; * * *

* * *

Finally, we note that Claimants may not recover under state law. * * * ("Maritime law specifically denies recovery to non proprietors for economic damages * * *"). * * *

2. *Claimants alleging physical damage*

As noted above, Mason and Advanced Materials claim to have suffered physical damage. Mason claims it lost eighty-eight boxes of dressed crabs that spoiled in a freezer when law enforcement officials shut off the electricity during the evacuation. Advanced Materials claims that two manufacturing runs had to be prematurely terminated and the company lost the materials in those runs and could not sell the products. * * *

Contrary to the district court's conclusion, neither of these claimants suffered physical damage as a result of the allision. Mason's crabs spoiled because the electricity was turned off during the evacuation, not because of contact with the barge, the bridge, or the gaseous cargo. Likewise, Advanced Materials claims losses from its inability to sell products that were in the process of being manufactured; it is not claiming that its property was damaged as a direct result of the allision. * * *

Moreover, even if we were to conclude that Mason's and Advanced Materials's inability to sell their products qualified as physical damage for purposes of *TESTBANK*, they would not be entitled to recover because their damages were not foreseeable. * * * Here, the barge allided with a bridge, causing the release of gas, which resulted in a mandatory evacuation during which the law enforcement officials turned off the electricity. The spoiling of Mason's crabs and the premature shut down of Advanced Materials's manufacturing run due to the evacuation and loss of electricity were simply not foreseeable results of the release of the gaseous cargo. * * *

IV. Claims Pursuant to CERCLA

CERCLA provides a remedy to a claimant seeking to recover response costs for removal and remediation of hazardous substances released into the environment. * * *

* * *

* * * [N]one of the claimants has even alleged that it incurred costs in acting to contain the gaseous cargo; therefore, none of the claimants is entitled to recover under CERCLA. * * *

V. Claims Pursuant to OPA

OPA provides that "[n]otwithstanding any other provision of law ... each responsible party for a vessel or a facility from which oil is discharged ... into or upon the navigable waters or adjoining shorelines ... is liable for the removal costs and damages specified in subsection (b) of this section that result from such incident." 33 U.S.C. § 2702(a). Section 2702(b)(2)(B) allows recovery of "damages for injury to, or economic losses resulting from destruction of real or personal property, which shall be recoverable by a claimant who owns or leases that property." Section 2702(b)(2)(E) provides recovery of "[d]amages equal to the loss of profits or impairment of earning capacity due to the injury, destruction, or loss of real property, personal property or natural resources, which shall be recoverable by any claimant."

* * *

* * * Any property damage upon which Claimants must rely to recover under § 2702(b)(2)(E) did not result from the discharge or threatened discharge of oil. Claimants have not raised an issue of fact as to whether their economic losses are due to damage to property resulting from the discharge of the gas. Therefore, Claimants cannot recover under OPA and the district court erred in denying Appellants' motions for partial summary judgment.

VI. Conclusion

For the foregoing reasons we reverse the district court's denial of Appellants' motions for partial summary judgment.

NOTES

1. Section § 183(a) and (b) of the Limitation of Liability Act, which Taira Lynn used, provides that the liability of an owner of a vessel should not exceed the value of the vessel. If the damages did exceed that value they would be paid pro rata. How does the Limitation of Liability Act compare with the economic loss doctrine?

2. How does the Oil Pollution Act [OPA], quoted in *In Re Taira Lynn Marine,* compare with the common law economic loss rule? For a discussion of OPA, which was enacted after the Exxon Valdez oil spill, and OPA's relationship to the Limitation of Liability Act, see Blair N.C. Wood, Note & Comment, *The Oil Pollution Act of 1990: Improper Expenses to Include in Reaching the Limit on Liability,* 8 Appalachian J. L. 179 (2009).

3. In *Terracon Consultants,* from Subsection 2.b.ii. above, the Supreme Court of Nevada said, "the [economic loss] doctrine works to reduce the cost of tort actions, but still provides tort victims with a remedy because less expensive alternative forms of compensation, such as insurance, generally are available to a financially injured party." *See* Bi–Economy Market, Inc. v Harleysville Insurance Co., 10 N.Y.3d 187, 886 N.E.2d 127, 856 N.Y.S.2d 505 (2008) (case involving business interruption insurance). What about the workers in *Aikens* or the workers in *Stern,* the "seminal Nevada decision concerning the economic loss doctrine" relied upon in *Terracon Consultants?*

SECTION 4.   PRINCIPLES OF MEASUREMENT

A.   SPECULATION, CERTAINTY AND DIFFICULTY IN MEASUREMENT

JOHNSON v. BAKER

Court of Appeals of Kansas, 1986.
11 Kan.App.2d 274, 719 P.2d 752.

RICHARD A. MEDLEY, DISTRICT JUDGE, Assigned:

This is a legal malpractice case. Plaintiffs sought the recovery of damages for both a breach of contract and negligence. They appeal the amount of the damages awarded on the negligence claim and the denial of any recovery for breach of contract.

On February 13, 1981, Joyce Johnson retained the defendant, Lyle Baker, a practicing attorney in Wichita, to represent her in a divorce from her husband, Richard Lee Johnson. Joyce Johnson's primary concern was that defendant secure an agreement from her husband to pay the expenses and cost of college for the parties' daughter, plaintiff Kelly Ann Johnson. Defendant negotiated a property settlement agreement between the Johnsons and incorporated it into the decree of divorce and the journal entry of judgment. Defendant made no attempt, nor did he advise Joyce Johnson to attempt, to secure the signature of Richard Johnson on the journal entry. Baker also did not attempt to reduce the parties' agreement to writing in any instrument other than the journal entry of judgment. He stated that he did not think it was necessary for the parties to sign the journal entry and decree of divorce, although he admitted he was familiar with the provisions of K.S.A. 1980 Supp. 60–1610(a) (repealed L.1982, ch. 152, § 30) with respect to agreements for support of children who have reached the age of majority.

Thereafter, defendant Baker learned that Richard Johnson refused to pay college expenses for his daughter. Baker informed Mrs. Johnson that she should retain another lawyer to represent her in enforcing the provisions of the journal entry because he would undoubtedly be needed as a witness on her behalf in any court hearing. Plaintiff Joyce Johnson hired attorney Keith Richey to represent her and Richey filed a motion to compel Mr. Johnson to perform the obligation stated in the journal entry. Judge Beasley of the Sedgwick County District Court denied the motion concluding that the court lacked jurisdiction to enforce the provision in question because there was no prior written agreement pursuant to K.S.A. 1980 Supp. 60–1610(a). Mrs. Johnson did not appeal from this ruling although she was aware that she had the right to do so.

In February 1983, the plaintiffs filed this action against Baker for breach of contract and negligent failure to obtain an enforceable agreement against Richard Johnson for Kelly's college expenses. * * * [T]he court held that defendant was liable for negligence because his failure to obtain a separate signed agreement did not meet the standard of care normally exercised in the community and resulted in the unfavorable ruling by Judge Beasley.

The trial court assessed Joyce Johnson's damages at $559.40 and fixed Kelly's damages as equivalent to the cost of tuition ($5,380) plus room and board ($3,600) for the two years she has attended college, reduced by the $6,042 received in grants and scholarships, for a net recovery of $2,938. Plaintiffs appeal the amount of damages awarded * * *.

* * *

Plaintiffs contend that the trial court erred in calculating the damages of Kelly Johnson because it failed to award damages equivalent to the cost of tuition, room and board for her remaining two years of education. Defendant contends that the evidence of future damage was too speculative to justify a greater award.

Damages cannot be awarded when they are too conjectural and speculative to form a sound basis for measurement. * * * It has also been held, however, that absolute certainty is not required in establishing damages * * *.

From the record we have before us, it is clear that Kelly Johnson had enrolled at Kansas Newman College for at least twelve hours a semester during her first two years and had made passing grades. All contingencies of the parties' agreement were met during the first two years of Kelly's college education and it does not appear to us to be too speculative or uncertain to conclude that those contingencies would have been met for the next two years. However, the record reveals that Kelly was enrolled in a two-year program at Kansas Newman and her testimony was unclear with respect to the amount of additional time she would need to complete her education. We conclude that the trial court's refusal to assess damages for tuition, room and board for future educational endeavors by Kelly is supported by the evidence.

Plaintiffs also contend that the court should have included in its award the cost of Kelly's books for a four-year education. However, the testimony offered to prove the amount of this expense was vague and indefinite. In addition, the exhibit which plaintiffs assert estimates the cost of books was not included in the record on appeal. The burden is upon the appellant to designate a record sufficient to present its points to the appellate court and to establish the claimed error. * * *

* * *

The judgment of the trial court is affirmed in all respects except insofar as the award of damages was reduced in contradiction of the collateral source rule. * * *

NOTES

1. What evidence might have enabled Kelly Johnson to recover for two more years of college, even if at the time of trial she was not sure that she would attend? If Kelly had chosen to attend two more years of college, could she have sought to protect her right to college payments by bringing an action for a declaratory judgment? For a discussion of the declaratory judgment remedy, see *infra* Chapter 5.

2. Was the court correct in subtracting from the judgment the amount of the grants and scholarships Kelly Johnson received? The collateral source rule is discussed *infra* in Section 4.C of this Chapter.

3. Did the father in the litigation preceding the decision in *Johnson* save two years of tuition but lose a daughter?

LEWIS RIVER GOLF, INC. v. O.M. SCOTT & SONS

Supreme Court of Washington, 1993.
120 Wash.2d 712, 845 P.2d 987.

BRACHTENBACH, JUSTICE.

The main issue is narrow and essentially factual, i.e., should the testimony of plaintiff's damage expert have been stricken because it was speculative or not supported in the record?

* * *

* * * Plaintiff, Lewis River Golf, Inc., grew sod or turf. It bought seed from defendant, O.M. Scott & Sons, under an express warranty. The sod grown from the seed had weeds. Plaintiff claimed that the express warranty was breached. Plaintiff lost most of its commercial customers and had been sued by two of its buyers dissatisfied with the sod. Defendant's proposed remedies were unsuccessful in resolving the weed problem. Plaintiff cut production from 275 acres to 45 acres and destroyed all of the turf raised from defendant's seed.

Plaintiff sued defendant for losses, including lost profits. In 1985, a jury awarded plaintiff $1,327,000. The verdict was unsegregated as to the elements of the damages found. In an unpublished 1987 opinion the Court of Appeals affirmed the verdict on liability, but held that the testimony of plaintiff's expert included two improper calculations, that is, inclusion of lost profits on unplanted acreage and certain interest costs. * * *

Thus, in 1989, when the case was again tried to a jury, there was no question of liability. The trial was limited to determination of damages. However, between the first and second trials, the facts about damages had changed. Plaintiff had sold its sod business. Plaintiff contended that, along with specific damages, it suffered a loss on the sale of its sod business because of damage to its reputation or goodwill from the sale of "bad" sod resulting from defendant's defective seed. * * * The jury * * * awarded * * * $1,026,800 * * * for the loss plaintiff "suffered on the sale of its sod division."

Defendant again appealed to the Court of Appeals. * * * [T]hat court * * * reversed the verdict as to the loss on sale of the business. * * * We reverse the Court of Appeals to the extent that it reversed the verdict; thus, the judgment below is affirmed in its entirety.

* * *

Recovery of consequential damages is expressly authorized by the Uniform Commercial Code, which governs this action. RCW 62A.2–715(2)(a). The question then is whether the damage to plaintiff's reputation or goodwill is the type of consequential damage allowed under the statute. There is no doubt that such a damage claim is recognized. * * *

* * *

It is true that damages must be proved with reasonable certainty. * * * However, this reasonable certainty requirement must be considered in light of several underlying principles. First, RCW 62A.1–106 provides:

> The remedies provided by this Title shall be liberally administered to the end that the aggrieved party may be put in as good a position as if the other party had fully performed. . . .

Second, the official comment to RCWA 62A.2–715 states:

> The burden of proving the extent of loss incurred by way of consequential damage is on the buyer, but the section of liberal administration of remedies *rejects any doctrine of certainty which requires almost mathematical precision in the proof of loss. Loss may*

be determined in any manner which is reasonable under the circumstances.

(Italics ours.) RCWA 62A.2–715, official comment 4. Third is the established principle that "the doctrine respecting the matter of certainty, properly applied, is concerned more with the *fact of damage than with the extent or amount of damage.*" * * *

* * *

Further, it is well recognized that the type of damages here involved are not subject to proof of mathematical certainty. * * *

With respect to loss of goodwill, proving damages with reasonable certainty should track the generally expansive recent history of lost profits. However, unlike lost profits, *goodwill relates to the future* and, thus, no actual profit base will exist for use at trial. Accordingly, the expert testimony of accountants and economists will prove invaluable to the aggrieved buyer in presenting his claim for loss of goodwill. *Such testimony will generally be accepted by the courts in assessing goodwill claims.* * * *

Anderson, *Incidental and Consequential Damages*, 7 J.L. & Com. 327, 422 (1987).

It is important to note that defendant *concedes* the *fact* of damage. * * *

We now turn to defendant's challenge to the expert's testimony. At several points during the trial, defendant made the following motions to strike the testimony of plaintiff's expert:

[I]t is not supported by credible facts in the record. It is based on opinions or assumptions that are contrary to facts in this record. * * *

My point is it is just so far out that it should be stricken. * * *

[W]e moved to strike Jolivet's [expert] testimony for the reason he is not supported, and it is outside the total overall perimeter, and the jury would have to speculate. * * *

At the end of the case, defendant moved, in part, as follows:

I will separately move, Your Honor, then for a directed verdict or to strike out the testimony that's been offered claimed to be in support of a loss business value pursuant to that element of their case, again being far too speculative to submit to a jury and as being unsupported by credible evidence * * *.

Several of the grounds advanced in support of its motions are without merit. First, defendant asserts that the expert's opinion is not supported by *credible* evidence. If the evidence was properly admitted, credibility is for the jury. Second, the assertion that the evidence is "just so far out" is a meaningless phrase. This leaves the claim that the expert's testimony was too speculative and based on unsupported assumptions.

* * *

We first note that defendant does not contend that the witness was not qualified as an expert. * * * Defendant does not contend that the methodology used by the expert was invalid. Defendant's expert used the same methodology. * * *

* * *

Plaintiff's expert was a Harvard educated economist and a former professor of finance at the University of Washington. He examined and relied upon plaintiff's financial records and facts furnished him prior to trial by the owner of plaintiff corporation, as authorized by ER 703.

The ultimate opinion which defendant attacks is the expert's estimate of the loss plaintiff allegedly sustained when it sold its sod business. To calculate that loss, the expert assumed a sod farm of 195 acres, a certain marketable amount of sod per acre, the ability to sell that sod, and a certain profit margin. He then calculated the net earnings, after taxes, and applied a price earnings ratio to arrive at his opinion of the value of the business. From that value he deducted the price realized when the business was sold, resulting in his opinion of the loss sustained upon sale of the business. The jury awarded $181,917 less than his estimate of loss.

Defendant first attacks the size of the farm, assumed by the expert to be 195 acres. * * * To eliminate any doubt on this critical point, the trial court included in the verdict form a question: "Do you find that the seeding rate for VBB seed as actually planted by Stading was the seeding rate Dr. Jolivet [the expert] used in his testimony? ANSWER: Yes." * * * The record supports the expert's use of a farm of 195 acres as a base of production.

Defendant next challenges the expert's assumption that the sod farm would produce 40,000 marketable square feet of sod per acre. Two items of testimony clearly support this fact. * * *

Next defendant questions the expert's conclusion that plaintiff would have been able to sell the sod it produced at market price. Plaintiff was selling such quantities that he purchased additional sod from a competitor who testified that plaintiff was probably selling all the sod he could produce. * * * That same competitor went out of business, removing a large supplier. * * * One landscaper who was installing 1 to 1½ million square feet of sod a year testified that he quit buying sod from defendant's seed because of devastating problems with VBB turf. * * * The expert calculated plaintiff's expected market share at 5.8 percent of total market, and estimated that plaintiff would maintain that share with acceptable sod. All in all, there was support for that opinion.

Defendant challenges the level of profit which he assumed plaintiff would earn. While defendant questions the validity of the figures used, the expert started with actual profit for one year, analyzed a 6–year period, and then used an average price for a 3–year period. * * * It was for the jury to determine whether the average profit level would be maintained. There were facts to which the expert applied his expertise. * * *

* * *

The trial court properly admitted the expert testimony and properly denied defendant's motions to strike.

NOTES

1.   Why were damages awarded in *Lewis River* and not in *Johnson?*

2.   The case frequently cited to describe certainty is Story Parchment Co. v. Paterson Parchment Paper Co., 282 U.S. 555, 51 S.Ct. 248, 75 L.Ed. 544 (1931), in which the plaintiff sought damages under the Sherman Anti–Trust Act for defendant's monopolization of the vegetable parchment trade. Justice Sutherland said:

> Nor can we accept the view of that court that the verdict of the jury, insofar as it included damages for * * * [the difference between the amounts actually realized by petitioner and what would have been realized by it from sales at reasonable prices except for the unlawful acts of the respondents] cannot stand because it was based upon mere speculation and conjecture. This characterization of the basis for the verdict is unwarranted. It is true that there was uncertainty as to the extent of the damage, but there was none as to the fact of damage; and there is a clear distinction between the measure of proof necessary to establish the fact that petitioner had sustained some damage, and the measure of proof necessary to enable the jury to fix the amount. * * *

> Where the tort itself is of such a nature as to preclude the ascertainment of the amount of damages with certainty, it would be a perversion of fundamental principles of justice to deny all relief to the injured person, and thereby relieve the wrongdoer from making any amend for his acts. In such case, while the damages may not be determined by mere speculation or guess, it will be enough if the evidence shows the extent of the damages as a matter of just and reasonable inference, although the result be only approximate. The wrongdoer is not entitled to complain that they cannot be measured with the exactness and precision that would be possible if the case, which he alone is responsible for making, were otherwise.

Id. at 562–63, 51 S.Ct. at 250–51.

3.   Tractebel Energy Marketing, Inc. v. AEP Power Marketing, Inc. 487 F.3d 89 (2d Cir. 2007) involved a 20–year contract to buy and sell electricity that began in 2000. The buyer breached its requirement to purchase a minimum amount of electricity over 20 years because "[t]he collapse of the energy market in 2001–02 significantly diminished the value of the [contract] to it." *Id.* at 93. The trial court refused to award the seller anything for that breach because, among other things, it held that the damages were not proved

with "sufficient certainty." Citing *Story*, the Court of Appeals for the Second Circuit reversed, saying:

> It has long been established in New York that a breaching party is liable for all direct and proximate damages which result from the breach. * * * The damages, however, "must be not merely speculative, possible, and imaginary, but they must be *reasonably certain* and such only as actually follow or may follow from the breach of the contract." * * * "Certainty," as it pertains to general damages, refers to the *fact* of damage, not the amount. For "when it is certain that damages have been caused by a breach of contract, and the only uncertainty is as to their amount, there can rarely be good reason for refusing, on account of such uncertainty, any damages whatever for the breach. A person violating his contract should not be permitted entirely to escape liability because the amount of the damage which he has caused is uncertain."[22] * * * "[T]he burden of uncertainty as to the amount of damage is upon the wrongdoer...." * * * "The plaintiff need only show a 'stable foundation for a reasonable estimate'" of the damage incurred as a result of the breach. * * * "Such an estimate necessarily requires some improvisation, and the party who has caused the loss may not insist on theoretical perfection." * * *

Id. at 110–11.

4. Professor Robert M. Lloyd instructs judges and lawyers how to assess the validity of financial experts' opinions in *Proving Lost Profits after Daubert: Five Questions Every Court Should Ask Before Admitting Expert Testimony*, 41 U. Rich. L. Rev. 379 (2007). For a discussion of *Tractebel* and the issues it raises with respect to measuring damages, see Matthew Milikowsky, *A Not Intractable Problem: Reasonable Certainty,* Tractebel, *and the Problem of Damages for Anticipatory Breach of a Long–Term Contract in a Thin Market*, 108 Colum. L. Rev. 452 (2008). For a discussion of recovering damages despite uncertainty, see Dan B. Dobbs, Law of Remedies § 3.4, at 321–24 (2d ed. 1993).

5. For a case which held that the plaintiffs' trial testimony about their lost profits was insufficient, see Holt Atherton Industries, Inc. v. Heine, 835 S.W.2d 80 (Tex.1992). There the defendant had delayed repairing the Heine's bulldozer because of a warranty dispute. The Heines brought suit; the defendant defaulted; and after a hearing, the trial court awarded the Heines $120,000 in lost profits for the nine months during which the defendant had

---

22. In Story Parchment Company v. Paterson Parchment Paper Company, the United States Supreme Court quoted the following discussion with approval:

> It is sometimes said that speculative damages cannot be recovered, because the amount is uncertain; but such remarks will generally be found applicable to such damages as it is uncertain whether sustained at all from the breach.... The general rule is, that all damages resulting necessarily and immediately and directly from the breach are recoverable, and not those that are contingent and uncertain. The latter description embraces, as I think, such only as are not the certain result of the breach, and does not embrace such as are the certain result, but uncertain in amount.

282 U.S. 555, 562–63, 51 S. Ct. 248, 75 L. Ed. 544 (1931) (internal quotation marks and citation omitted). *Accord* New York Trust Co. v. Island Oil & Transp. Corp., 34 F.2d 653, 654 (2d Cir. 1929) (Hand, J.) ("It is, indeed, one of the consequences of the doctrine of anticipatory breach that, if damages are assessed before the time of performance has expired, the court must take the chance of forecasting the future as best it can.") * * *

the bulldozer. A majority of the Texas Supreme Court reversed, holding that the damages testimony was insufficient. The dissent disagreed. As you read the opinions below, consider which one you would have joined. Also, consider what the Heine's lawyer could have done to avoid this outcome. The majority, holding that plaintiff had not proved his damages, said:

When Mr. Heine was examined by his counsel, only one question was asked which touched on lost profits. The relevant question and answer are:

Q. Now as a result of the defendant keeping the [bull]dozer for eight months, did you lose out on $200,200 in lost income during that time period?

A. Yes, sir, I did.

Even if this testimony were otherwise sufficient, lost income is not the correct measure of damages. * * *

* * * [T]he trial judge asked additional questions to determine what the Heines' lost profits were and how the Heines concluded that their lost income was $200,200. * * * Mr. Heine could not provide answers to the judge's questions but suggested that Mrs. Heine could be more helpful because she kept the books for the Heines. Mrs. Heine testified that she could not say what their lost profits were without looking at their books. When the judge asked what the Heines showed as profits on their income tax returns for 1985 or 1986, the years preceding the year that Holt Atherton kept their bulldozer, Mrs. Heine did not know. However, Mr. Heine responded that their income tax return showed profits of about $120,000. * * *

* * *

In response to further questions by the trial judge, Mr. Heine testified that the Heines lost several contracts because they did not have their bulldozer available. Mr. Heine was not able to specify which contracts they lost, how many they lost, how much profit they would have had from the contracts, or who would have awarded them contracts. * * *

Id. at 84–85. The dissent said:

Denial of relief in this case has ramifications that extend to all commercial litigation in which profits are an issue. The majority begins by eroding the distinction we have long recognized between uncertainty as to the occurrence of lost profits and uncertainty merely as to their exact amount. The former, but not the latter, is fatal to recovery. * * *

* * *

The majority's professed lack of "any basis for determining whether the damages were established with reasonable certainty or were based on pure speculation," * * * discounts the Heines' response to the trial court's inquiry about how they "calculate[d]" their damages. They referenced hourly charges, lost contracts, cost factors, and down-time adjustments. Estimations, when "given in terms of calculations, [constitute] more than conjecture, speculation or guesswork" and must be evaluated by the finder of fact. * * *

Though criticized by the majority for failing to explain "that they had lost out on *specific* contracts," * * * the Heines were not necessarily required to identify specific, measurable, lost contracts because they were an existing business with a history of profitability. Such an operation ordinarily encounters lesser evidentiary hurdles to show lost profits already sustained than would a business with little record of past earnings that seeks to show future lost profits. * * * Among the methods a party may use to calculate its lost profits is *either* a history of profitability *or* the actual existence of lost contracts. * * *

There is undoubtedly some legal evidence to support the Heines' lost profits damages. Since there is no factual insufficiency point of error requiring further review by the court of appeals, its judgment should be affirmed.

Id. at 87–88.

6. Courts used to apply a "new business rule" to deny new businesses recovery of lost profits because they would be too speculative; however, "the trend in recent cases has been to award lost profits for a new business when they can be proved with reasonable certainty." RSB Laboratory Services, Inc. v. BSI, Corp., 368 N.J.Super. 540, 557, 847 A.2d 599, 610 (App.Div.2004). *See* MindGames, Inc. v. Western Publishing Co., 218 F.3d 652, 654–55 (7th Cir.2000); Hiller v. Manufacturers Product Research Group of North America, Inc., 59 F.3d 1514, 1518 (5th Cir.1995); Hog Slat, Inc. v. Ebert, 104 F.Supp.2d 1112, 1120 (N.D.Iowa 2000); *see also* Dan B. Dobbs, Law of Remedies § 3.4, at 320–21 (2d ed. 1993) (explaining modern rule allowing new businesses more latitude in proving lost expected profits); Roger I. Abrams, Donald Welsch & Bruce Jonas, *Stillborn Enterprises: Calculating Expectation Damages Using Forensic Economics*, 57 Ohio St. L.J. 809 (1996) (demonstrating how sophisticated econometric tools can project future losses in new business cases).

B. ADJUSTMENTS FOR TIME

1. Prejudgment Interest

The topic addressed in this section might appear to be technical and trivial. It is indeed technical, but far from trivial. Prejudgment interest, as the case and the notes below demonstrate, can involve a great amount of money; therefore, whether it is allowed and how it is to be calculated are both significant aspects of any legal monetary judgment and a frequent subject of litigation.

KANSAS v. COLORADO

Supreme Court of the United States, 2001.
533 U.S. 1, 121 S.Ct. 2023, 150 L. Ed. 2d 72.

JUSTICE STEVENS delivered the opinion of the Court.

The Arkansas River rises in the mountains of Colorado just east of the Continental Divide, descends for about 280 miles to the Kansas border, then flows through that State, Oklahoma, and Arkansas and empties into the Mississippi River. On May 20, 1901, Kansas first invoked this Court's original jurisdiction to seek a remedy for Colorado's diversion of water from the Arkansas River * * *. In opinions written during the past century, * * * we have described the history and the importance of the river. For present purposes it suffices to note that two of those cases * * * led to the negotiation of the Arkansas River Compact (Compact), an agreement between Kansas and Colorado that in turn was approved by Congress in 1949. * * * The case before us today involves a claim by Kansas for damages based on Colorado's violations of that Compact.

* * *

In 1986, we granted Kansas leave to file a complaint alleging three violations of the Compact by Colorado. * * * After taking evidence in the liability phase of the proceeding, [the] Special Master * * * recommended * * * that the Court find that post-Compact increases in groundwater well pumping in Colorado had materially depleted the waters of the river in violation of Article IV–D [of the Compact]. * * * We remanded the case to the Special Master to determine an appropriate remedy for the violations of Article IV–D.

* * *

* * * [T]he Special Master recommends that damages be measured by Kansas' losses, rather than Colorado's profits, attributable to Compact violations after 1950; that the damages be paid in money rather than water; and that the damages should include prejudgment interest from 1969 to the date of judgment. Colorado * * * [first] contends that the recommended award of damages would violate the Eleventh Amendment to the United States Constitution * * *.

We have decided that a State may recover monetary damages from another State in an original action, without running afoul of the Eleventh Amendment. * * *

* * *

Colorado next excepts to the Special Master's conclusion that the damages award should include prejudgment interest despite the fact that Kansas' claim is unliquidated.[2] At one point in time, the fact that the claim was unliquidated would have been of substantial importance. As a general matter, early common-law cases drew a distinction between liquidated and unliquidated claims and refused to allow interest on the latter. *See, e.g.,* Comment, *Prejudgment Interest: Survey and Suggestion*, 77 Nw.

---

2. Though final damages have not yet been calculated, the importance of this issue is illustrated by breaking down the damages claimed by Kansas. Of $62,369,173 in damages so claimed, $9,218,305 represents direct and indirect losses in actual dollars when the damage occurred. Of the remaining $53,150,868, about $12 million constitutes an adjustment for inflation (a type of interest that Colorado concedes is appropriate) while the remaining amount (approximately $41 million) represents additional interest intended to compensate for lost investment opportunities. * * * The magnitude of prejudgment interest ultimately awarded in this case will, of course, turn on the date from which interest accrues. * * *

U.L.Rev. 192, 196, and n. 26 (1982) (discussing history and collecting sources). This rule seems to have rested upon a belief that there was something inherently unfair about requiring debtors to pay interest when they were unable to halt its accrual by handing over to their creditors a fixed and unassailable amount. * * *

This common-law distinction has long since lost its hold on the legal imagination. Beginning in the early part of the last century, numerous courts and commentators have rejected the distinction for failing to acknowledge the compensatory nature of interest awards.[3] This Court allied itself with the evolving consensus in 1933, when we expressed the opinion that the distinction between cases of liquidated and unliquidated damages "is not a sound one." Funkhouser v. J.B. Preston Co., 290 U.S. 163, 168, 54 S.Ct. 134, 78 L.Ed. 243 (1933). The analysis supporting that conclusion gave no doubt as to our reasoning: "Whether the case is of the one class or the other, the injured party has suffered a loss which may be regarded as not fully compensated if he is confined to the amount found to be recoverable as of the time of breach and nothing is added for the delay in obtaining the award of damages." Ibid. Our cases since 1933 have consistently acknowledged that a monetary award does not fully compensate for an injury unless it includes an interest component. * * *

* * *

* * * [T]he Special Master was correct in determining that the unliquidated nature of the damages does not preclude an award of prejudgment interest.[4]

* * *

Colorado's third exception takes issue with both the rate of interest adopted by the Special Master and the date from which he recommended that interest begin to accrue. As to the second of these two concerns, Colorado submits that, if any prejudgment interest is to be awarded, it should begin to accrue in 1985 (when Kansas filed its complaint in this action), rather than in 1969 (when, the Special Master concluded, Colorado knew or should have known that it was violating the Compact). On the other hand, Kansas has entered an exception, arguing that the accrual of interest should begin in 1950. * * *

---

3. For sources from the early part of the century criticizing, qualifying, or rejecting the distinction, see, e.g., Faber v. New York, 222 N.Y. 255, 262, 118 N.E. 609, 610–611 (1918); Bernhard v. Rochester German Ins. Co., 79 Conn. 388, 398, 65 A. 134, 138 (1906); Restatement of Contracts § 337, p. 542 (1932); C. McCormick, Law of Damages § 51, p. 210 (1935); 1 T. Sedgwick, Measure of Damages § 315 (9th ed.1912); cf. 3 S. Williston, Law of Contracts § 1413, p. 2508 (1920) ("The disinclination to allow interest on claims of uncertain amount seems based on practice rather than theoretical grounds"). For a thorough modern treatment of the issue, see 1 D. Dobbs, Law of Remedies § 3.6(3) (2d ed.1993).

4. Justice O'Connor argues that the state of the law was insufficiently evolved by 1949 for Colorado to have had notice that the courts might award prejudgment interest if it violated its obligations under the Compact. * * * Though the law was indeed in flux at that time, this Court had already made it clear that it put no stock in the traditional common-law prohibition * * *. The contemporary Restatement of Contracts was in accord. See Restatement of Contracts § 337(b), at 542. * * *

The Special Master credited the testimony of Kansas' three experts who calculated the interest rates that they thought necessary to provide full compensation for the damages caused by Colorado's violations of the Compact in the years since 1950. As a result of inflation and changing market conditions those rates varied from year to year. In their calculation of the damages suffered by Kansas farmers, the experts used the interest rates that were applicable to individuals in the relevant years rather than the (lower) rates available to States.

* * * [I]f, as we have already decided, * * * it is permissible for the State to measure a portion of its damages by losses suffered by individual farmers, it necessarily follows that the courts are free to utilize whatever interest rate will most accurately measure those losses. The money in question in this portion of the damages award is revenue that would—but for Colorado's actions—have been earned by individual farmers. Thus, the Special Master correctly concluded that the economic consequences of Colorado's breach could best be remedied by an interest award that mirrors the cost of any additional borrowing the farmers may have been forced to undertake in order to compensate for lost revenue.

Although the Special Master rejected Colorado's submission that there is a categorical bar to the award of prejudgment interest on unliquidated claims, he concluded that such interest should not "be awarded according to [any] rigid theory of compensation for money withheld," but rather should respond to " 'considerations of fairness.' " * * *

* * * [W]e cannot say that by 1949 our case law had developed sufficiently to put Colorado on notice that, upon a violation of the Compact, we would automatically award prejudgment interest from the time of injury. * * * We, therefore, believe that the Special Master acted properly in carefully analyzing the facts of the case and in only awarding as much prejudgment interest as was required by a balancing of the equities.

We also agree with the Special Master that the equities in this case do not support an award of prejudgment interest from the date of the first violation of the Compact, but rather favor an award beginning on a later date. * * * [The Special Master] relied on the fact that in the early years after the Compact was signed, no one had any thought that the pact was being violated. * * * In addition, he considered the long interval that passed between the original injuries and these proceedings, as well as the dramatic impact of compounding interest over many years. * * *

* * * Kansas argues that the Special Master's reasoning would be appropriate if damages were being awarded as a form of punishment, but does not justify a refusal to provide full compensation to an injured party. * * * Kansas' argument is consistent with a "rigid theory of compensation for money withheld," but, for the reasons discussed above, we are persuaded that the Special Master correctly declined to adopt such a theory. * * *

In its third exception, Colorado argues that, if prejudgment interest is to be awarded at all, the equities are best balanced by limiting such interest to the time after the complaint was filed [in 1985] * * *.

* * *

Once it became obvious that a violation of the Compact had occurred, it was * * * clear that the proceedings necessary to evaluate the significance of the violations would be complex and protracted. * * * Colorado's request that we deny prejudgment interest for [the 1969–1985] period is reasonable.

* * *

Colorado's final objection challenges the Special Master's determination of the value of the crop losses attributable to the Compact violations, the largest component of Kansas' damages claim. * * * [The Court overruled Colorado's fourth exception.]

We remand the case to the Special Master for preparation of a final judgment consistent with this opinion.

JUSTICE O'CONNOR, with whom JUSTICE SCALIA and JUSTICE THOMAS join, concurring in part and dissenting in part.

I agree with the Court's disposition of this case as to Colorado's first and fourth exceptions to the Special Master's Third Report, concerning the award and determination of damages * * *, [but] I believe that the award of prejudgment interest to Kansas, coming over half a century after the Arkansas River Compact's (hereinafter Compact) negotiation and approval, is clearly improper under our precedents.

We are dealing with an interstate compact apportioning the flow of a river between two States. A compact is a contract. * * * It is a fundamental tenet of contract law that parties to a contract are deemed to have contracted with reference to principles of law existing at the time the contract was made. * * * Specifically, the question is whether, at the time the Compact was negotiated and approved, Colorado and Kansas could fairly be said to have intended, or at least to have expected or assumed, that Colorado might be exposing itself to liability for prejudgment interest in the event of the Compact's breach. * * *

I fail to see how Colorado and Kansas could have contemplated that prejudgment interest would be awarded. * * * [In the 1940s], the state of the law * * * was uncertain at best * * *.

There is nothing fair about awarding prejudgment interest as a remedy for the Compact's breach when all available evidence suggests that the signatories to the Compact neither intended nor contemplated such an unconventional remedy. * * * Had Kansas and Colorado anticipated or even suspected what the Court today effects, they almost certainly would have negotiated a provision in the Compact to address the situation. States in the future very likely will do so in the wake of the Court's decision, which creates a very different backdrop from the one against

which Kansas and Colorado operated. In the absence of such a provision, however, "the loss [as to interest] should remain where it has fallen."
* * *

For the foregoing reasons, I respectfully dissent from the Court's award of prejudgment interest.

NOTES

1. Although in Kansas v. Colorado, the Supreme Court discredited the "liquidated v. unliquidated" distinction for prejudgment interest awards, some courts continue to deny an award of prejudgment interest on the ground that the underlying obligation was "unliquidated." *See, e.g.* Tupelo Redevelopment Agency v. Abernathy, 913 So.2d 278, 290 (Miss. 2005) (holding, in eminent domain case, that prejudgment interest "is available only if the money due was liquidated and there was no legitimate dispute that the money was owed"); TVI, Inc. v. Infosoft Technologies, Inc., 2008 WL 239784, 64 U.C.C. Rep. Serv. 2d 1040 (E.D. Mo. 2008) (holding in breach of sales of goods contract, "Missouri does not allow prejudgment interest when a claim is unliquidated because 'where the person liable does not know the amount he owes he should not be considered in default because of failure to pay.' "). For a partial solution to that problem, see Spreader Specialists, Inc. v. Monroc, Inc., 114 Idaho 15, 21–22, 752 P.2d 617, 623–24 (Idaho Ct.App.1987):

> But here Spreader does not seek money it could have earned on investment if Monroc had timely paid compensation. Rather, Spreader seeks to recover a sum *actually expended* by it as a result of Monroc's tortious conduct. The interest on the loan for repairs was an expense occasioned by Spreader's effort to mitigate its losses. Accordingly, we hold that interest charges incurred on a loan obtained in good faith, as part of a reasonable course of action to mitigate losses, may be recovered as an item of consequential damages.

2. There is not consensus among states about which damages are considered unliquidated. Compare the statements in the following cases. In Historic Charleston Holdings, LLC v. Mallon, 381 S.C. 417, 435–436, 673 S.E.2d 448, 457–458 (2009) the Supreme Court of South Carolina said,

> * * * Generally, prejudgment interest may not be recovered on an unliquidated claim in the absence of agreement or statute. * * * The fact that the amount due is disputed does not render the claim unliquidated for purposes of awarding prejudgment interest. Rather, the proper test is "whether or not the measure of recovery, not necessarily the amount of damages, is fixed by conditions existing at the time the claim arose."
> * * *

* * *

The record reveals that the disagreement between Mallon and [Historic Charleston Holdings [HCH]] over [HCH's] method of accounting led to the escrow of the 15 Felix proceeds at issue in the instant case. Prior to the sale of 15 Felix, the net proceeds from the sales of Dixie's property had been divided fifty-fifty. The logical conclusion to be drawn from this pattern of events is that the members of Dixie were contemplating a future distribution of the escrowed funds that, depending on the outcome of a complete accounting, may not have been the standard fifty-fifty split. Under these circumstances, we find that the measure of recovery for prejudgment interest was unliquidated at the time the parties' claims to the proceeds arose * * *.

In Hysten v. Burlington Northern Santa Fe Railway Co., 530 F.3d 1260, 1280–81 (10th Cir. 2008), the Tenth Circuit, applying Kansas law, said:

> At the outset, we reject Burlington Northern's suggestion that a dispute as to liability on the underlying substantive claim prevents the amount of damages from becoming liquidated. * * *
>
>   * * *
>
> We recognize that Mr. Hysten sought $64,588.40 in back pay, but the jury awarded only $30,000. This suggests some uncertainty as to how long Mr. Hysten was owed backpay, or how much he was owed, or both. However, this uncertainty does not mean that the entirety of the requested backpay award was unliquidated.

In Trinity Products, Inc. v. Burgess Steel, L.L.C., 486 F.3d 325, 336 (8th Cir. 2007), the Eighth Circuit, applying Missouri law, said:

> Trinity also argues that it should be awarded prejudgment interest on the jury's *quantum meruit* award for extra work. * * *
>
> * * * Missouri law denies prejudgment interest when a claim is unliquidated because "where the person liable does not know the amount he owes he should not be considered in default because of failure to pay." * * * A claim is liquidated for this purpose if it is fixed or readily determinable, that is, "ascertainable by computation." * * * A quantum meruit claim for commercial services is liquidated if the reasonable value of those services can be objectively determined, because the defendant was under a duty to liquidate and pay that amount. * * * Here, Trinity's Count IV claims for additional stub outs ($3,300), for providing additional transportation services ($8,000), and for shipping the first north tower from the project site ($4,000), were readily ascertainable. * * *

For a discussion of "the historical distinction between liquidated and unliquidated claims" see Aric Jarrett, Comment, *Full Compensation, Not Overcompensation: Rethinking Prejudgment Interest Offsets in Washington*, 30 Seattle U. L. Rev. 703, 711 (2007).

    3. At least one jurisdiction takes the position that " 'if the claim is liquidated, interest follows as a matter of right, but if it is unliquidated, the allowance of interest is in the discretion of the trial court'." Poundstone v. Patriot Coal Co., Ltd., 485 F.3d 891, 901 (6th Cir. 2007) (applying Kentucky law).

    4. The following case describes when prejudgment interest is appropriate, without referring to the unliquidated or liquidated categorization of the damages.

ENCON UTAH, LLC v. FLUOR AMES KRAEMER, LLC

Supreme Court of Utah, 2009.
210 P.3d 263.

DURRANT, ASSOCIATE CHIEF JUSTICE. CHIEF JUSTICE DURHAM, JUSTICE WILKINS, JUSTICE PARRISH, and JUSTICE NEHRING concur in ASSOCIATE CHIEF JUSTICE DURRANT's opinion.

DURRANT, ASSOCIATE CHIEF JUSTICE:

* * *

In December 2000, UDOT entered into a Design–Build Contract ("prime contract") with FAK to construct the Legacy Parkway. * * *

In May 2002, FAK entered into a subcontract with Encon, under which Encon would manufacture, furnish, and install concrete bridge girders. The total amount Encon was to be paid under the subcontract was $6,842,342.

In April 2003, UDOT partially terminated the prime contract with FAK due to an injunction obtained by an environmental organization enjoining the project's construction. In May 2003, FAK sent Encon a notice of partial termination of the subcontract.

* * *

* * * After a four-day bench trial, the court entered judgment in favor of Encon and jointly against the FAK parties, awarding Encon termination damages, prejudgment interest, and attorney fees. The total amount awarded to Encon was $1,699,563.50.

* * *

On appeal, the FAK parties challenge each of these components * * *.

* * *

III. THE TRIAL COURT DID NOT ERROR IN AWARDING PREJUDGMENT INTEREST TO ENCON

The FAK parties next argue that the trial court erred in awarding prejudgment interest to Encon.[20] * * *

"Prejudgment interest may be recovered where the damage is complete, the amount of the loss is fixed as of a particular time, and the loss is measurable by facts and figures." Prejudgment interest is appropriate when "the loss ha[s] been fixed as of a definite time and the amount of the loss can be calculated with mathematical accuracy in accordance with well-established rules of damages." The trial court adopted a semblance of

---

20. The trial court determined that prejudgment interest was appropriate under Utah Code section 15–1–1 "and that interest accrues at 10% per annum from September 15, 2004 ... through March 15, 2007" with "a per diem rate of $345.42" for a total award of $314,676.

this language, ruling that prejudgment interest was appropriate because Encon's damages were "subject to mathematical calculation."

Each of these iterations of the standard for recovering prejudgment interest is correct. None suggests or requires, as the FAK parties claim, that at the time the damages accrued, all of the damage figures must be known and remain static throughout the litigation. Rather, the standard focuses on the measurability and calculability of the damages.

The court of appeals has explained that "losses that cannot be calculated with mathematical accuracy are *those in which damage amounts are to be determined by the broad discretion of the trier of fact*, such as in cases of personal injury, wrongful death, defamation of character, and false imprisonment."[23] Thus, prejudgment interest is inappropriate in cases where the trier of fact is left to assess damages based on "a mere description of the wrongs done or injuries inflicted."

We have held that prejudgment interest is appropriate in cases where the "amount due under [a] contract was ascertainable by calculation and it was only the method to be used in making the calculation that was uncertain."

* * *

The FAK parties next present two related arguments: Encon's damages were not subject to mathematical calculation because (a) the trial court "was required to use its best judgment in choosing between conflicting expert testimony" on the issue of damages, and (b) the trial court "was required to determine [the] reasonableness of overhead and profit."

The FAK parties contend that because the trial court had to determine each of several cost categories based on conflicting expert testimony, the court "necessarily used its best judgment to decide between competing expert testimony."

* * *

In this case, the court was not left to its best judgment to ascertain damages. Rather, the court reviewed the terms of Encon's fixed price contract, the percentage of work Encon completed, and noted that the parties agreed that 10% profit on that work was reasonable. Thus, the court based its final decision on measurable facts and figures.

* * *

---

23. *Bennett v. Huish*, 2007 UT App 19, P 45, 155 P.3d 917 (emphasis added); *see also Fell v. Union Pac. Ry. Co.*, 32 Utah 101, 88 P. 1003, 1006 (Utah 1907) (Establishing the standard for prejudgment interest by explaining that it should not be awarded in cases where the fact finder must determine damages by exercising its broad discretion. We listed, for example, "all personal injury cases, cases of death by wrongful act, libel, slander, false imprisonment, malicious prosecution, assault and battery, and all cases where the damages are incomplete and are peculiarly within the province of the jury to assess at the time of the trial."); *Shoreline Dev. v. Utah County*, 835 P.2d 207, 211 (Utah Ct. App. 1992) ("If the jury must determine the loss by using its best judgment as to valuation rather than fixed standards of valuation, prejudgment interest is inappropriate.").

Additionally, we note that the purpose of awarding prejudgment interest is "to compensate a party for the depreciating value of the amount owed over time and, as a corollary, to deter parties from intentionally withholding an amount that is liquidated and owing." A party can only be properly compensated for the "value of the amount owed over time" if the amount owed is subject to mathematical calculation. This does not require, however, that a party must demonstrate that its damage figures are known and static from the date the claim is filed through the final judgment.

Were we to hold that the damage figures could never change, we would foreclose the possibility of awarding prejudgment interest in nearly every case. As Encon points out, a prevailing party could only recover under the FAK parties' standard if a prevailing party never changed its claimed damages, no aspect of the damages calculation was disputed at trial, and the court awarded the entire claim without reduction or adjustment. This result does not serve the policy underlying the availability of prejudgment interest nor is it consistent with our standard that damages be measurable by facts and figures.

* * *

We affirm each of the trial court's decisions * * *.

NOTES

1. The court in *Encon* noted that "prejudgment interest is inappropriate" " 'in cases of personal injury, wrongful death, defamation of character, and false imprisonment.' " *See also*, Jackson v. Tullar, 285 S.W. 3d 290, 299 (Ky. Ct. App. 2007) (holding, in personal injury case, "damages that were established by proof offered during the trial are unliquidated and not subject to prejudgment interest."); City of Atlanta v. Landmark Environmental Industries, Inc., 272 Ga. App. 732, 740–741, 613 S.E.2d 131, 140 (2005) (affirming, in ground contamination case, that damages "not ascertained at the time of the loss" were unliquidated and that "Georgia law does not allow prejudgment interest on unliquidated damages.") Is it possible that some elements of the damages in cases of personal injury or ground contamination could have arisen at a fixed time with a fixed amount? *Cf.* Donatelli v. Beaumont, 204 P.3d 201 (Utah Ct.App.2009) (discussing statutory right to recover prejudgment interest on special damages in personal injury cases) (applying New Jersey law).

2. The award of prejudgment interest can be appropriate in both tort and breach of contract actions. *See* Olcott v. Delaware Flood Co., 327 F.3d 1115, 1126 (10th Cir.2003). The Restatement of Contracts and the Restatement of Torts both provide for the recovery of prejudgment interest. Restatement (Second) of Contracts § 354 (1981); Restatement (Second) of Torts § 913 (1979).

3. "Tort reform" packages sometimes include provisions restricting prejudgment interest. For example, a Missouri statute, Mo. Rev. Stat. § 538.300 (Supp.1991), exempts medical malpractice cases from prejudgment

interest provisions. For a discussion of the Missouri interest statutes, see Vincent v. Johnson, 833 S.W.2d 859, 866 (Mo.1992) (*en banc*).

2. Calculating Prejudgment and Postjudgment Interest

In calculating interest, you may remember from high school mathematics that the plaintiff will need to identify a principal amount, a time period, and an interest rate, $P \times t \times r$. In the case below, consider the variety of ways in which those factors can be chosen.

GATTI v. COMMUNITY ACTION AGENCY OF GREENE COUNTY, INC.

United States District Court, Northern District of New York, 2003.
263 F.Supp.2d 496.

TREECE, MAGISTRATE JUDGE

Plaintiff, Adrienne Gatti ("Gatti"), brought this action pursuant to the Federal Age Discrimination in Employment Act ("ADEA"), 29 U.S.C. § 621 *et seq.*, and New York State Human Rights Law ("NYHRL") N.Y. EXEC. LAW § 296, alleging that the Defendants, Community Action Agency of Greene County, Inc. ("Community Action") and Edward Daly ("Daly"), Executive Director, unlawfully terminated her and subjected her to a hostile working environment because of her age. * * *

* * *

A jury trial commenced on October 25, 2002. Approximately a week later, on November 1, 2002, the jury returned a verdict in favor of Gatti in the amount of $181,761.00. The jury found against both Defendants on all of her causes of action and awarded her back and front pay in the amounts of $57,453.00 and $44,308.00 respectively, and further awarded her for past emotional distress and mental anguish in the amount of $80,000.00. * * *

* * *

Plaintiff seeks * * * an award of pre-judgment interest on her back pay award, pursuant to 29 U.S.C. § 626(b), in the amount of $8,873.45. [Plaintiff asserted that there was no federal law on the rate of pre-judgment interest, and therefore the New York statutory interest rate of nine percent should be applied. The court disagreed.] "In an ADEA case, pre-judgment interest is designed to compensate the plaintiff for loss of the use of money wrongfully withheld through an unlawful discharge." * * * The decision to award pre-judgment interest is "[o]rdinarily left to the discretion of the district court." * * * The Second Circuit has held that, "[t]o the extent ... that the damages awarded to the plaintiff represent compensation for lost [back] wages, 'it is ordinarily an abuse of discretion not to include pre-judgment interest.' " * * *

The Supreme Court has determined that "discretionary awards of prejudgment interest ... should be a function of (i) the need to fully compensate the wronged party for actual damages suffered, (ii) consider-ations of fairness and the relative equities of the award, (iii) the remedial purpose of the statute involved, and/or (iv) such other general principles as are deemed relevant by the court." Wickham Contracting Co. v. Local Union No. 3, 955 F.2d 831, 833–34 (2d Cir.1992) (citing Loeffler v. Frank, 486 U.S. 549, 557–58, 108 S.Ct. 1965, 100 L.Ed.2d 549 (1988)).

Similarly, determining the rate to apply for pre-judgment interest is within the discretion of the district court. Courts in the Second Circuit often apply the rate of interest set forth in 28 U.S.C. § 1961. Section 1961 provides in pertinent part:

> Interest shall be allowed on any money judgment in a civil case recovered in a district court.... Such interest shall be calculated from the date of the entry of the judgment, at a rate equal to the weekly average 1–year constant maturity Treasury yield, as published by the Board of Governors of the Federal Reserve System, for the calendar week preceding the date of the judgment.

The appropriate methodology employed in calculating the amount of pre-judgment interest involves three steps. * * * First, the award should be divided pro rata over the appropriate time period. * * * Second, once the award is divided, the average annual United States treasury bill rate of interest referred to in § 1961 will be applied. * * * Finally, in order to guarantee complete compensation to the plaintiff, the interest will be compounded annually. * * * ("Given that the purpose of back pay is to make the plaintiff whole, it can only be achieved if interest is compound-ed.").

In light of the above calculation, Gatti's back pay award of $57,453 should be divided over fifty-one months (July 1998 to November 2002). This results in $1,126.53 per month or $13,518.35 per year in back pay. The rate of interest according to the most recent publication by the Board of Governors of the Federal Reserve System is 1.27 percent.[13] * * *

Applying this rate and compounding the interest annually results in an award of $2,275.31 in prejudgment interest. Additionally, the judgment shall reflect a post-judgment interest rate of 1.27 percent, pursuant to § 1961.

* * *

NOTES

1. Contrast the prejudgment interest rate used in *Gatti* with that used in Alfano v. CIGNA Life Insurance Co., 2009 WL 890626 (S.D.N.Y. 2009) (holding that the defendant's termination of plaintiff's long-term disability benefits violated ERISA and that "while there is no applicable federal statute

---

13. Even though 28 U.S.C. § 1961 is considered a post-judgment interest statute, the statute's established rate calculation is applied retroactively as prejudgment interest. Furthermore, this is the appropriate rate to be applied, notwithstanding there are pendent state actions (i.e. ADEA and NYHRL). * * *

establishing a prejudgment interest rate, New York has adopted a statutory prejudgment interest rate of 9% * * *. Although CIGNA argues that the Treasury rate constitutes a more appropriate rate * * *, there is no reason to think that that rate more accurately captures the time value of money in New York, or the true loss to plaintiff, particularly given the New York State Legislature's determination otherwise").

2. Besides the method used in *Gatti*, there are other methods that courts use to determine the prejudgment interest rate. *See, e.g.,* Ohio River Co. v. Peavey Co., 556 F.Supp. 87, 93 (E.D.Mo.1982) (In admiralty cases "prejudgment interest is not tied to the forum state's statutory limit. Instead, the rate of interest should be fixed at a rate in keeping with interest rates prevailing at the time repairs were completed."), *rev'd in part and remanded*, 731 F.2d 547 (8th Cir.1984) (instructing district court to increase rate, since evidence showed that average borrowing rate from time of accident to trial was 15.45%, and district court had awarded only 10%). *But see* Macal v. Stinson, 468 N.W.2d 34, 36 (Iowa 1991) ("There was no showing the Stinsons knew it would be necessary for the Macals to borrow money at a higher rate [than the statutory rate of five percent] if they breached the contract.").

3. A number of states have set prejudgment interest rates by statute. *See, e.g.,* General Electric Capital Corp. v. House Manufacturing Co., Inc. 2009 WL 2254966 (E.D. Ark. 2009) (diversity case applying Connecticut law, 10%); O'Daniel v. Roosa, 2009 WL 3055428 (D.S.D. 2009) (applying South Dakota law, 10%); Stevens v. Brink's Home Security, Inc., 162 Wash.2d 42, 169 P.3d 473 (2007) (affirming application of Washington's 12% pre- and post-judgment interest rates in a state minimum wage case, instead of the 2% over six-month treasury bill rate applicable to tort cases).

4. For a discussion of one effect that the rate of prejudgment interest can have, see Jay M. Feinman, *Incentives for Litigation or Settlement in Large Tort Cases: Responding to Insurance Company Intransigence*, 13 Roger Williams U. L. Rev. 189 (2008). Professor Feinman theorizes that as states cap nonpecuniary and punitive damage awards, defendants have less incentive to settle because they no longer risk receiving large judgments based on those categories. Defendants thus gain by delay unless the prejudgment interest rate is high. But for a litigator's view that encouraging settlements is not an appropriate goal of prejudgment interest rates, see Thomas R. Bender, *Does the Right to Trial by Jury Place Constitutional Limits on Prejudgment Interest?* 39 Suffolk U. L. Rev. 935 (2006) (discussing Rhode Island's 12% prejudgment interest rate).

5. As noted in *Gatti*, post-judgment interest is payable at a rate set by statute from the date of judgment until payment. *See also* Condus v. Howard Savings Bank, 999 F.Supp. 594, 597–598 (D.N.J.1998) (discussing both New Jersey and federal post-judgment interest statutes). What incentives or disincentives for the defendant are created by the rate set for post-judgment interest?

3. Present Value and Inflation

Some monetary judgments are equitable and can be paid over time, such as child support. For a discussion of equity see Chapter 2. Because courts do not retain jurisdiction over cases with legal judgments once they are final, a plaintiff who recovers will receive a lump-sum judgment, unless a statute or a settlement agreement provides otherwise. Consequently, money to compensate future losses is paid before it is needed, and the plaintiff may have the opportunity to invest it and earn extra money. On the other hand, the value of money may decrease in the future because of inflation so that a present award of future money may be inadequate. The following case illustrates some of the approaches courts take to try to ensure that the plaintiff gets neither too much nor too little to take care of future needs.

STRINGHAM v. UNITED PARCEL SERVICE, INC.

Appellate Court of Illinois, Second District, 1989.
181 Ill.App.3d 312, 130 Ill.Dec. 81, 536 N.E.2d 1292.

JUSTICE REINHARD delivered the opinion of the court:

Defendant, United Parcel Service, Inc. (UPS), appeals from a judgment of the circuit court of Winnebago County entered on a jury verdict for $252,631.08 ($505,262.16 reduced 50% by the negligence of plaintiff's decedent) in favor of plaintiff, Valerie R. Stringham, as administrator of the estate of David E. Stringham, deceased, and for the use and benefit of her two children, Tracy and Tina Stringham, in this wrongful death action [from an automobile accident].

* * *

Defendant next argues that the circuit court erred in allowing the testimony of plaintiff's witness, Jack Skeels, an economist, as to the value of decedent's projected future earnings because Skeels, in calculating the present value of future earnings, had incorporated a factor accounting for inflation. Defendant maintains that, under Illinois law, the effects of inflation are not to be considered in determining the present value of future earnings. Defendant contends that Skeels' testimony resulted in an excessive verdict unsupported by any proper evidence.

While Skeels' testimony describing the method he followed in computing decedent's future earnings is somewhat lacking in clarity, from examination of this testimony and the written income loss analysis prepared by Skeels and entered into evidence, we understand the method employed by Skeels to be as follows. Skeels first projected how long decedent would have been expected to work, had he lived, based upon actuarial data. Skeels then determined the amount decedent would be expected to earn during his working life based upon decedent's income and certain personal characteristics. In doing so, rather than assuming decedent's income level would remain constant, Skeels generated an age income profile predicting, based upon statistical data, how decedent's income would change over time due to factors such as increased experience. The income age profile data does not account for the effect of inflation on wage levels, as it is apparently based upon data comparing income levels of workers of different ages at the same point in time.

Skeels next discounted decedent's future earnings to present value. In doing so, Skeels used a base discount rate of 7.3% from which he subtracted 6%, representing "growth of earnings," giving a net discount rate of 1.3% used in the present value calculation. Skeels stated during cross-examination that growth of earnings is essentially inflation and that subtracting it from the discount rate "squeezed out" the effect of inflation from the calculation.

Defendant argues that the use of inflation or growth of earnings factors in calculating present value is improper. * * *

It is well established that, in weighing the amount of damages to be assessed against a tort-feasor, the jury must discount the amount of future damages to their present value. * * * There is, however, little authority in Illinois governing whether inflation may be taken into account in computing future awards, and if so, how it is to be taken into account.

In Jones & Laughlin Steel Corp. v. Pfeifer (1983), 462 U.S. 523, 103 S.Ct. 2541, 76 L.Ed.2d 768, the United States Supreme Court noted that at one time, many American courts did not allow consideration of the effects of inflation in computing awards of lost earnings. (*Pfeifer*, 462 U.S. at 539–40, 103 S.Ct. at 2552, 76 L.Ed.2d at 785; *see also* Comment, *Inflation, Productivity, and the Total Offset Method of Calculating Damages for Lost Future Earnings*, 49 U.Chi.L.Rev. 1003, 1011 (1982) (hereinafter *Damages for Lost Future Earnings*).) These courts accepted evidence of both individual and societal factors that would lead to wage increases even in an inflation-free economy but required proof that those factors were not influenced by predictions of future price inflation, reasoning that such estimates were unreliably speculative. (*Pfeifer*, 462 U.S. at 540, 103 S.Ct. at 2552, 76 L.Ed.2d at 785.) However, in discounting to present value, these courts applied a market interest rate. As market interest rates increase in response to inflation, the Court stated:

> The effect of [this method] was to deny the plaintiff the benefit of the impact of inflation on his future earnings, while giving the defendant the benefit of inflation's impact on the interest rate that is used to discount those earnings to present value. Although the plaintiff in such a situation could invest the proceeds of the litigation at an "inflated" rate of interest, the stream of income that he received provided him with only enough dollars to maintain his existing *nominal* income; it did not provide him with a stream comparable to what his lost wages would have been in an inflationary economy. (Emphasis in original.) (462 U.S. at 540, 103 S.Ct. at 2552, 76 L.Ed.2d at 785.)

In other words, predicting future earnings without considering the effects of inflation on wage levels produces an unrealistically low estimate of the plaintiff's total future earnings. When this estimate is discounted by the market interest rate, the plaintiff will receive an award which, even if invested at that rate, would yield fewer dollars than if the plaintiff had continued earnings which kept pace with inflation. * * *

Because of this problem, today, in a majority of jurisdictions, courts attempt to account for the effects of inflation in some way. * * * Courts have developed several approaches. One approach incorporates inflation into the computation of future earnings and then discounts that amount using the market interest rate as the discount rate. Another approach does not consider inflation in estimating total earnings but uses a discount rate equal to the market interest rate minus the inflation rate. * * * Both these approaches yield identical results. * * *

Still other courts employ two other methods. One, the "partial offset" or "real interest" method, assumes that market interest rates exceed inflation by an essentially constant amount over time. This amount, generally believed to be 1.5% to 2%, is known as the "real" interest rate. * * * A court employing the partial offset method does not allow consideration of inflation in estimating total future earnings, but, in discounting to present value, uses the real interest rate rather than the market rate.

The final method, the "total offset" method, assumes that inflation and other factors affecting growth of wages will equal the ideal discount rate. Hence, in predicting total future earnings inflation is not considered, nor is any discounting to present value performed as the two steps would cancel each other out. * * *

In the instant case, plaintiff's economist appears to have employed a method accounting for inflation by subtracting the inflation rate from the appropriate market interest rate in discounting to present value, which is equivalent to first increasing future earnings by the inflation rate and then discounting by the market interest rate. * * *

* * *

Illinois Pattern Jury Instructions, Civil, No. 34.05 (2d ed. 1971) (IPI Civil 2d) defines present value as follows:

"Present cash value" means the sum of money needed now, which, together with what that sum will earn in the future, will equal the amounts of the pecuniary benefits at the times in the future when they would have been received.

* * * [T]wo steps are involved in determining a proper award based on loss of future earnings, and IPI Civil 2d No. 34.05 only pertains to the second step in the process. Before the amount of future earnings can be discounted to present value, it must be determined what that amount is. We agree that once the amount of future earnings to be discounted is known, the inflation rate plays no role in the discount process. However, inflation is relevant to the initial step of determining the total amount of future earnings. In the instant case, plaintiff's economist subtracted inflation from the interest rate during the discount stage. However, as previously noted, this method is mathematically equivalent to inflating earnings and discounting by an unadjusted market interest rate. Thus, we

do not find the result of this method inconsistent with the definition of present value in IPI Civil 2d, No. 34.05.

We * * * believe it is illogical and indefensible to build inflation into the discount rate and yet ignore it in calculating the lost future wages that are to be discounted. * * * We further find that the method employed by plaintiff's economist is an appropriate method of accounting for the impact of inflation. We do not hold that it is the only proper method. * * *

* * *

Affirmed.

NOTE

As one might have gathered from reading *Stringham*, the computations are complex. An attorney without sufficient mathematical expertise would be wise to hire an expert. To understand the conclusions of the expert, however, every lawyer, and even every judge, should read Professor Robert M. Lloyd's article, *Discounting Lost Profits in Business Litigation: What Every Lawyer and Judge Needs to Know*, 9 Transactions 9, 11–12 (2007). Professor Lloyd demystifies the field and writes for lawyers and judges who might not have sophisticated mathematical or financial backgrounds. He says confusion about present value creates an "inconsistent, and unfair body of law." Throughout his article Professor Lloyd analyzes a number of opinions that make up this "inconsistent and unfair body of law". He cautions:

> Any reader who has difficulty understanding the concepts discussed below should note that in many of the cases discussed later in this article, a court dismissed a challenge to an expert's choice of a discount rate with an assertion that the jury could determine for itself whether the discount rate was appropriate. Implicit in this is the assumption that the average juror, a person with much less education and intelligence than the average reader of this article, will understand these concepts. Moreover, the reader of this article has advantages unavailable to the juror. The reader can move through the material at his own pace and refer back to prior material, whereas the juror must depend on an oral presentation in question and answer format by a witness who may be trying to obfuscate in order to conceal the weaknesses in his client's case.

One of the concepts Professor Lloyd explains is the formula used to compute present value:

> Discounting is simply the process of determining the appropriate interest rate and then calculating the amount that would have to be invested today at that rate to produce the cash flow in question. * * *

* * *

* * * [T]he future value of any sum is the present value (i.e., the value today) multiplied by one plus the interest rate per compounding

period, multiplied by the number of compounding periods. This may be expressed mathematically as: $FV = PV(1 + i)n$ * * *.

* * *

By solving this formula for the present value, we can determine the amount that must be invested today to have a specified amount at a specified time in the future. This formula is: $PV = FV/(1+i)n$ * * *.

The table below shows the present value of the $100,000 in damages discounted for periods of one to five years at 10% with annual compounding.

Year	Amount	Present Value at 10%
1	$100,000.00	$90,909.09
2	$100,000.00	$82,644.63
3	$100,000.00	$75,131.48
4	$100,000.00	$68,301.35
5	$100,000.00	$62,092.13

Id. at 13-15. He goes on to say that this is the easy part:

> Even though many lawyers and judges do not understand the mechanics of discounting to present value, it is not the mechanics that cause the problems. The mechanics are almost invariably done right. The problem comes with the choice of the discount rate. * * *

Id. at 20. One can see that the choice of the rate makes an enormous difference in the amount of the recovery. The higher the rate, the lower plaintiff's recovery on the theory that the plaintiff can invest the money well to have the correct amount at the correct time in the future.

As a result of Professor Lloyd's explanation, can you see which computation discussed in *Stringham* would benefit the plaintiff and which would benefit the defendant? (Those with math anxiety can skip this question and make a note to hire an expert.)

PRESENT VALUE OF LOST EARNINGS OF $25,000 A YEAR,
FOR VARIOUS PERIODS AND DISCOUNT RATES

	Discount Rate		
Period	**2%**	**5%**	**10%**
10 Years	$224,565	$193,043	$153,615
20 Years	$408,785	$311,555	$212,840
30 Years	$501,603	$384,313	$235,673

Richard A. Posner, Economic Analysis of Law § 6.11, at 212 (5th ed. 1998).

C. COLLATERAL SOURCE RULE

HELFEND v. SOUTHERN RAPID TRANSIT DISTRICT

Supreme Court of California, 1970.
2 Cal.3d 1, 84 Cal.Rptr. 173, 465 P.2d 61.

In Bank. Opinion by TOBRINER, ACTING C.J., expressing the unanimous view of the court. McCOMB, J., PETERS, J., MOSK, J., BURKE, J., and SULLIVAN, J., concurred.

* * *

1. THE FACTS.

Shortly before noon on July 19, 1965, plaintiff drove his car in central Los Angeles east on Third Street approaching Grandview. * * * While traveling in the second lane from the curb, plaintiff observed an automobile * * * stopping in his lane and preparing to back into a parking space. Plaintiff put out his left arm to signal the traffic behind him that he intended to stop; he then brought his vehicle to a halt so that the other driver could park.

* * * [A] bus driver for the Southern California Rapid Transit District, pulled out of a bus stop at the curb of Third Street and headed in the same direction as plaintiff. [The bus] pulled out into the lane closest to the center of the street in order to pass. The right rear of the bus sideswiped plaintiff's vehicle, knocking off the rear-view mirror and crushing plaintiff's arm * * *.

An ambulance took plaintiff to Central Receiving Hospital for emergency first aid treatment. Upon release from the hospital plaintiff proceeded to consult Dr. Saxon, an orthopedic specialist, who sent plaintiff immediately to the Sherman Oaks Community Hospital where he received treatment for about a week. Plaintiff underwent physical therapy for about six months in order to regain normal use of his left arm and hand. He acquired some permanent discomfort but no permanent disability from the injuries sustained in the accident. * * *

Plaintiff filed a tort action against the Southern California Rapid Transit District, a public entity, and Mitchell, an employee of the transit district. At trial plaintiff claimed slightly more than $2,700 in special damages, including $921 in doctor's bills, a $336.99 hospital bill, and about $45 for medicines. Defendant requested permission to show that about 80 percent of the plaintiff's hospital bill had been paid by plaintiff's Blue Cross insurance carrier and that some of his other medical expenses may have been paid by other insurance. * * * The court ruled that defendants should not be permitted to show that plaintiff had received medical coverage from any collateral source.

After the jury verdict in favor of plaintiff in the sum of $16,400, defendants appealed * * *.

2. THE COLLATERAL SOURCE RULE.

The Supreme Court of California has long adhered to the doctrine that if an injured party receives some compensation for his injuries from a source wholly independent of the tortfeasor, such payment should not be deducted from the damages which the plaintiff would otherwise collect from the tortfeasor. * * * As recently as August 1968 we unanimously reaffirmed our adherence to this doctrine, which is known as the "collateral source rule." * * *

Although the collateral source rule remains generally accepted in the United States,[3] nevertheless many other jurisdictions[4] have restricted[5] or repealed it. * * *

* * *

* * * [P]laintiff received benefits from his medical insurance coverage only because he had long paid premiums to obtain them. Such an origin does constitute a completely independent source.* * *

The collateral source rule as applied here embodies the venerable concept that a person who has invested years of insurance premiums to assure his medical care should receive the benefits of his thrift.[14]

The tortfeasor should not garner the benefits of his victim's providence.

The collateral source rule expresses a policy judgment in favor of encouraging citizens to purchase and maintain insurance for personal injuries and for other eventualities. Courts consider insurance a form of

---

3. See * * * Fleming, *The Collateral Source Rule and Loss Allocation in Tort Law* (1966) 54 Cal.L.Rev. 1478, 1482–1483 and fn. 10; 2 Harper & James, The Law of Torts (1968 Supp.) § 25.22, at p. 152. * * *

4. * * * [T]he House of Lords * * * has recently reaffirmed the rule and applied it to a case of a tort victim who, following the automobile accident in which he was disabled, received a pension. * * * Most other western European nations have repudiated the rule. * * *

5. The New York Court of Appeals has, for example, quite reasonably held that an injured physician may not recover from a tortfeasor for the value of medical and nursing care rendered gratuitously as a matter of professional courtesy. (See *Coyne* v. *Campbell* (1962) 11 N.Y.2d 372 [230 N.Y.S.2d 1, 183 N.E.2d 891].) The doctor owed at least a moral obligation to render gratuitous services in return, if ever required; but he had neither paid premiums for the services under some form of insurance coverage nor manifested any indication that he would endeavor to repay those who had given him assistance. Thus this situation differs from that in which friends and relatives render assistance to the injured plaintiff with the expectation of repayment out of any tort recovery; in that case, the rule has been applied. * * * On the other hand, New York has joined most states in holding that a tortfeasor may not mitigate damages by showing that an injured plaintiff would receive a disability pension. * * * In these cases the plaintiff had actually or constructively paid for the pension by having received lower wages or by having contributed directly to the pension plan.

14. See *Thompson* v. *Mattucci* (1963) 223 Cal.App.2d 208, 209–210 [35 Cal.Rptr. 741] (Blue Cross payment for hospital bills does not reduce plaintiff's recovery); *Gersick* v. *Shilling* (1950) 97 Cal.App.2d 641, 649–650 [218 P.2d 583] (error to have admitted testimony that plaintiff's medical bills had been paid by Blue Cross or that plaintiff had received United States Employment Service disability payments). In *Lewis* v. *County of Contra Costa* (1955) 130 Cal.App.2d 176 [278 P.2d 756], the court held that the collateral source rule prohibited the trial court from admitting evidence that at the time of the accident plaintiff had accumulated sufficient sick leave to cover the period of his disablement. The court reasoned that "In a very real sense of the term it is as if he had drawn upon his savings account in an amount equal to his salary during the period of his disablement." * * *

investment, the benefits of which become payable without respect to any other possible source of funds. If we were to permit a tortfeasor to mitigate damages with payments from plaintiff's insurance, plaintiff would be in a position inferior to that of having bought no insurance, because his payment of premiums would have earned no benefit. Defendant should not be able to avoid payment of full compensation for the injury inflicted merely because the victim has had the foresight to provide himself with insurance.

Some commentators object that the above approach to the collateral source rule provides plaintiff with a "double recovery," rewards him for the injury, and defeats the principle that damages should compensate the victim but not punish the tortfeasor. We agree with Professor Fleming's observation, however, that "double recovery is justified only in the face of some exceptional, supervening reason, as in the case of accident or life insurance, where it is felt unjust that the tortfeasor should take advantage of the thrift and prescience of the victim in having paid the premium." * * *

[I]nsurance policies increasingly provide for either subrogation or refund of benefits upon a tort recovery, and such refund is indeed called for in the present case. * * * Hence, the plaintiff receives no double recovery;[15] the collateral source rule simply serves as a means of by-passing the antiquated doctrine of non-assignment of tortious actions and permits a proper transfer of risk from the plaintiff's insurer to the tortfeasor by way of the victim's tort recovery. The double shift from the tortfeasor to the victim and then from the victim to his insurance carrier can normally occur with little cost in that the insurance carrier is often intimately involved in the initial litigation and quite automatically receives its part of the tort settlement or verdict.

Even in cases in which the contract or the law precludes subrogation or refund of benefits,[17] or in situations in which the collateral source waives such subrogation or refund, the rule performs entirely necessary functions in the computation of damages. For example, the cost of medical care often provides both attorneys and juries in tort cases with an important measure for assessing the plaintiff's general damages. (Cf., e.g., *Rose v. Melody Lane* (1952) 39 Cal.2d 481, 489 [247 P.2d 335].) To permit the defendant to tell the jury that the plaintiff has been recompensed by a collateral source for his medical costs might irretrievably upset the complex, delicate, and somewhat indefinable calculations which result in the normal jury verdict. (See *Hoffman v. Brandt* (1966) 65 Cal.2d 549, 554–

---

15. In reaffirming our adherence to the collateral source rule in this tort case involving a plaintiff with collateral payments from his insurance coverage, we do not suggest that the tortfeasor be required to pay doubly for his wrong * * *.

17. "Certain insurance benefits are regarded as the proceeds of an investment rather than as an indemnity for damages. Thus it has been held that the proceeds of a life insurance contract made for a fixed sum rather than for the damages caused by the death of the insured are proceeds of an investment and can be received independently of the claim for damages against the person who caused the death of the insured. * * *"

555 [55 Cal.Rptr. 417, 421 P.2d 425]; *Garfield v. Russell* (1967) 251 Cal.App.2d 275, 279 [59 Cal.Rptr. 379].)

We also note that generally the jury is not informed that plaintiff's attorney will receive a large portion of the plaintiff's recovery in contingent fees * * *. Hence, the plaintiff rarely actually receives full compensation for his injuries as computed by the jury. The collateral source rule partially serves to compensate for the attorney's share and does not actually render "double recovery" for the plaintiff. Indeed, many jurisdictions that have abolished or limited the collateral source rule have also established a means for assessing the plaintiff's costs for counsel directly against the defendant rather than imposing the contingent fee system. In sum, the plaintiff's recovery for his medical expenses from both the tortfeasor and his medical insurance program will not usually give him "double recovery," but partially provides a somewhat closer approximation to full compensation for his injuries.[20]

If we consider the collateral source rule as applied here in the context of the entire American approach to the law of torts and damages, we find that the rule presently performs a number of legitimate and even indispensable functions. Without a thorough revolution in the American approach to torts and the consequent damages, the rule at least with respect to medical insurance benefits has become so integrated within our present system that its precipitous judicial nullification would work hardship. In this case the collateral source rule lies between two systems for the compensation of accident victims: the traditional tort recovery based on fault and the increasingly prevalent coverage based on non-fault insurance. Neither system possesses such universality of coverage or completeness of compensation that we can easily dispense with the collateral source rule's approach to meshing the two systems. * * * The reforms which many academicians propose cannot easily be achieved through piecemeal common law development; the proposed changes, if desirable, would be more effectively accomplished through legislative reform. * * *

* * * [W]e have pointed out the several legitimate and fully justified compensatory functions of the rule. In fact, if the collateral source rule were * * * punitive, it could apply only in cases of oppression, fraud, or malice and would be inapplicable to most tort, and almost all negligence, cases regardless of whether a governmental entity were involved. (See Civ. Code, § 3294; Note (1967) 55 Cal.L.Rev. 1059, 1165.) We therefore reaffirm our adherence to the collateral source rule in tort cases in which the plaintiff has been compensated by an independent collateral source—such as insurance, pension, continued wages, or disability payments—for which he had actually or constructively * * * paid or in cases in which the collateral source would be recompensed from the tort recovery through

---

20. Of course, only in cases in which the tort victim has received payments or services from a collateral source will he be able to mitigate attorney's fees by means of the collateral source rule. Thus the rule provides at best only an incomplete and haphazard solution to providing all tort victims with full compensation. Depriving some tort victims of the salutary protections of the collateral source rule will, short of a thorough reform of our tort system, only decrease the available compensation for injuries. * * *

subrogation, refund of benefits, or some other arrangement. Hence, we conclude that in a case in which a tort victim has received partial compensation from medical insurance coverage entirely independent of the tortfeasor the trial court properly followed the collateral source rule and foreclosed defendant from mitigating damages by means of the collateral payments.

3. THE COLLATERAL SOURCE RULE, PUBLIC ENTITIES, AND PUBLIC EMPLOYEES.

Having concluded that the collateral source rule is not simply punitive in nature, we hold, for the reasons set out infra, that the rule as delineated here applies to governmental entities as well as to all other tortfeasors. We must therefore disapprove of any indications to the contrary in City of Salinas v. Souza & McCue Constr. Co., supra, 66 Cal.2d 217, 226–228.

Defendants would have this court create a special form of sovereign immunity as a novel exception to the collateral source rule for tortfeasors who are public entities or public employees. * * * We see no justification for such special treatment. * * *

* * *

4. THE TRIAL COURT PROPERLY REFUSED TO PERMIT THE DEFENDANT TO INQUIRE WHETHER PLAINTIFF HAD BEEN COMPENSATED BY A COLLATERAL SOURCE IN THE ABSENCE OF SOME ALLEGATION THAT SUCH INFORMATION BEARS A PROPER RELATIONSHIP TO THE ISSUES IN THE CASE.

Defendant attempted to inquire before the jury as to whether plaintiff had been compensated by a collateral source. * * * Apparently, defendant also sought to inquire about the collateral source payments for the limited purpose of questioning the reasonableness and necessity of medical treatment costs or for showing that plaintiff was a malingerer. (See *Hoffman* v. *Brandt, supra,* 65 Cal.2d 549, 554–555; *Garfield* v. *Russell, supra,* 251 Cal.App.2d 275, 278–279.)[22]

Hoffman, Garfield, and Evidence Code section 352 require the trial court to assess the prejudicial effect of telling the jury about insurance coverage, even with appropriate cautionary instructions, against the probability that the party who seeks to present evidence of insurance coverage can show a proper relationship between the coverage and an issue in the case. * * * In the present case it would have been nearly impossible for defense counsel to show that plaintiff was a malingerer merely because he might have possessed multiple insurance coverage. Plaintiff sustained extremely severe injuries when defendant's bus crushed his arm.

* * * Furthermore, if the Blue Cross policy required the refund of nearly all the benefits from any tort recovery that plaintiff might receive, defendant could hardly show malingering.[23]

---

22. * * * During the argument the defense counsel admitted that he did not have the facts upon which he could posit the claim of malingering * * *

23. We are persuaded by the reasoning of the United States Supreme Court as to whether evidence of plaintiff's insurance coverage would ever be admissible to show the extent and

* * * [W] must conclude that the trial court correctly refused to permit defendant to inquire within the hearing of the jury as to the nature and extent of plaintiff's insurance coverage.

The judgment is affirmed.

NOTES

1.   As *Helfend* notes, the collateral source rule is both a rule of damages and an evidentiary rule. As a rule of damages, it forces the defendant to pay for the entire loss to the plaintiff, even if the plaintiff has received compensation for some or all of the loss from an independent, collateral source. As a rule of evidence, it precludes the introduction of evidence that could be prejudicial to the plaintiff regarding compensation for the loss that the plaintiff has received from a collateral source. For an argument that the inadmissibility of collateral source payments prejudices the defendant see Steve B. Hantler, Victor E. Schwartz, Cary Silverman, and Emily J. Laird, *Moving Toward the Fully Informed Jury*, 3 Geo.J.L. & Pub. Pol'y 21 (2005); Jamie L. Wershbale, *Tort Reform in America: Abrogating the Collateral Source Rule Across the States*, 75 Def. Couns. J. 346 (2008).

2.   Many states have passed legislation to do away with or modify the collateral source rule in all or some types of cases. States modify the rule in a variety of ways. Some will allow evidence of collateral source payments to be admitted at trial, but will also allow introduction of evidence of the amount of premiums the plaintiff paid. Some states will exclude both types of evidence if the plaintiff could face a subrogation action by the payor. Another modification is to prohibit admission of any collateral source evidence in a jury trial, but to allow a judge to reduce the award by the amount of the collateral source payments. For a discussion of these and other statutory adjustments to the collateral source rule as well as judicial decisions invalidating or upholding the statutes *see* Christian D. Shaine, Note, *Preserving the Collateral Source Rule: Modern Theories of Tort Law and a Proposal for Practical Application*, 47 Case W. Res. L. Rev. 1075 (1997) (recommending retention of collateral source rule coupled with greater use of subrogation). Jamie L. Wershbale, *Tort Reform in America: Abrogating the Collateral Source Rule Across the States*, 75 Def. Couns. 346 (2008).

ARAMBULA v. WELLS

Court of Appeal, Fourth District, California, 1999.
72 Cal.App.4th 1006, 85 Cal.Rptr.2d 584.

CROSBY, J.

Charity begins at home. And there it should stay, assuming the donor so intended. To promote the charitable impulse, we apply the collateral

---

duration of his disability or to indicate that he might be a malingerer: "In our view the likelihood of misuse by the jury clearly outweighs the value of this evidence. Insofar as the evidence bears on the issue of malingering, there will generally be other evidence having more probative value and involving less likelihood of prejudice than the receipt of a disability pension. Moreover, it would violate the spirit of the federal statutes if the receipt of disability benefits under the Railroad Retirement Act of 1937, 50 Stat. 309, as amended, 45 U.S.C. § 228b(a)4, were considered as evidence of malingering by an employee asserting a claim under the Federal Employers' Liability Act. We have recently had occasion to be reminded that evidence of collateral benefits is readily subject to misuse by a jury. Tipton v. Socony Mobil Oil Co., Inc., 375 U.S. 34, 11 L.Ed.2d 4, 84 S.Ct. 1. * * * *"

source rule to gratuitous payments (including moneys to cover lost wages) by family or friends to assist tort victims through difficult times.

I

In June 1996, Michael Arambula was injured in a rearend automobile accident caused by Phyllis Wells. Arambula was employed as a field supervisor in a family-owned company. * * * Despite missing work because of his injuries, he continued to receive his $2,800 weekly salary. He testified his brother "wished" to be reimbursed, but he had not promised to do so.

Arambula sued Wells for negligence. His claim for damages included loss of earnings during his period of disability. * * *

* * *

At the start of trial, Wells moved in limine to exclude all evidence and testimony regarding Arambula's lost wages claim of approximately $50,000. Her attorney, relying on dicta in a footnote in Helfend v. Southern Cal. Rapid Transit Dist. (1970) 2 Cal.3d 1, 6, fn. 5, 84 Cal.Rptr. 173, 465 P.2d 61, argued, "Plaintiff is not receiving payment by means of disability insurance, pension or from utilizing ... sick time or vacation time. Further, plaintiff has failed to provide any documentation or demand that the monies received from his employer will be required to be reimbursed."

The judge agreed. Based on *Helfend*, he instructed the jury not to award damages for lost earnings "because his employer paid for the time he was off without any requirement to do so and there was no agreement by plaintiff to refund same."

The jury awarded $54,334 to Arambula * * *.

II

Under the collateral source rule, plaintiffs in personal injury actions can still recover full damages even though they already have received compensation for their injuries from such "collateral sources" as medical insurance. * * * The idea is that tortfeasors should not recover a windfall from the thrift and foresight of persons who have actually or constructively secured insurance, pension or disability benefits to provide for themselves and their families. A contrary rule, it is feared, would misallocate liability for tort-caused losses and discourage people from obtaining benefits from independent collateral sources. * * *

Several post-*Helfend* decisions have allowed plaintiffs to recover the costs of gratuitous medical care as an element of their damages even without any contractual right to reimbursement * * *. [A] majority of jurisdictions and many commentators are in accord. (*See* 4 Harper, James & Gray, The Law of Torts (2d ed.1986) § 25.22, p. 661.) * * *

* * *

* * * [P]ublic policy concerns weigh heavily in favor of application of the collateral source rule to gratuitous payments and services. Just as the Supreme Court in *Helfend* found the rule "expresses a policy judgment in favor of encouraging citizens to purchase and maintain insurance for personal injuries and for other eventualities," * * * so too we adhere to the rule to promote policy concerns favoring private charitable assistance. Indeed, until recent times, family assistance has been the primary means of coping with a tragedy in this country. Were we to permit a tortfeasor to mitigate damages because of a third party's charitable gift, the plaintiff would be in a worse position than had nothing been done. Why would a family member (or a stranger) freely give of his or her money or time if the wrongdoer would ultimately reap the benefits of such generosity?

The concept of charity is embedded in basic notions of civic virtue * * *. When called upon to construe private humanitarianism, "courts do not now adopt an antagonistic spirit toward [a donor's] charitable intent for it is the rule that where doubt exists, a gift must be interpreted in favor of a charity." * * *

* * *

This is more than "do-gooderism"; the state's own self-interest is involved as well. To the extent that private generosity steps to the fore, the impact on the state is lightened * * *.

Charitable contributions are primarily motivated by the intended use to which donations are put. Under these circumstances, we logically turn to the intent of the donors. Who did they intend to help when they gratuitously agreed to cover lost wages? The person who caused the accident? Or the victim? We doubt such gifts would continue if, notwithstanding a donor's desire to aid the injured, the person who caused the injury ultimately stood to gain a windfall. Donors should not have to consult with a lawyer to make sure their largesse is not hijacked by the tortfeasor.

* * *

Even without an ironclad requirement of reimbursement, the plaintiff may be motivated to repay the donor from any tort recovery, or, inspired by example, to similar acts of generosity on the notion that one good act leads to another. Such reimbursement would avoid any prospects of a double recovery, as if there ever could be a double recovery where pain and suffering is concerned.

The rationale of the collateral source rule thus favors sheltering gratuitous gifts of money or services intended to benefit the victims, just as it favors insurance payments from coverage they had arranged. * * *

III

A

While a gift is presumptively intended for the benefit of the donee, the presumption should be a rebuttable one. * * *

We also do not decide whether the collateral source rule extends to payments from a public source.[4] The question of gratuitous *public* benefits is not at issue here and invokes a host of other concerns, which must be considered in light of their specific factual contexts. * * *

B

The collateral source rule operates both as a substantive rule of damages and as a rule of evidence. As a rule of evidence, it precludes the introduction of evidence of the plaintiff being compensated by a collateral source unless there is a "persuasive showing" that such evidence is of "substantial probative value" for purposes other than reducing damages. * * *[5]

We do not resolve such issues of admissibility here, but leave them to the sound discretion of the trial judge on remand. * * * We note, however, our decision does not automatically bar evidence that Arambula's wages were paid by his brother during his period of disability. For example, such evidence may be admissible, in the court's reasonable discretion and subject to a limiting instruction, to impeach his claimed inability to work. Evidence of actual wage payments may be persuasive to show that no time was lost, the employee actually performed substantial services during the period of disability, or had a motive to malinger. * * *

* * *

* * * [T]he cause * * * is remanded to the trial court for a limited new trial to determine the amount of damages for lost wages (if any) legally caused by defendant's negligence. The judgment for damages in his favor is otherwise affirmed.

Notes

1. What if Arambula's family had provided home health-care services gratuitously? Should Arambula have been permitted to introduce evidence on the reasonable value of his family's care? This issue was discussed in Bandel v. Friedrich, 122 N.J. 235, 238–39, 584 A.2d 800, 802 (1991), where the adult plaintiff's mother had provided twenty-four-hour care for three years prior to the trial, and where the trial court judge had refused to permit the plaintiff to

---

4. *See e.g.*, Washington by Washington v. Barnes Hospital (Mo.1995) 897 S.W.2d 611 (collateral source rule does not apply to free governmental benefits previously received by plaintiff); 4 Harper, James & Gray, The Law of Torts, supra, § 25.22 at pp. 663–664 ("[u]nless such [a contrary legislative] intent is made fairly clear, however, it seems reasonable to suppose that statutory benefits and free services furnished by government to needy classes of people are meant simply to make sure certain of their needs will be fulfilled and not to confer an additional bounty on the recipient"); *but see* Ensor v. Wilson (Ala.1987) 519 So.2d 1244 (collateral source rule applies to future special education benefits by governmental entity because of uncertainty of their continued existence).

5. The Legislature, as part of the Medical Injury Compensation Reform Act of 1975 (MICRA), has abrogated the collateral source rule as a rule of evidence in medical malpractice cases. MICRA allows defendants to introduce evidence the plaintiffs had received collateral source benefits, and it prohibits "collateral sources" from obtaining reimbursement from malpractice defendants. (Civ.Code, § 3333.1.)

offer expert testimony as to the reasonable value of his mother's care, "although it did allow the plaintiff to introduce proof of the reasonable value of future services to be provided, presumably because Mrs. Bandel could not forever nurse her son." The Supreme Court of New Jersey said:

> We acknowledge ourselves as latecomers to the issue of an injured plaintiff's entitlement to recover the value of gratuitously provided health care as an element of compensatory damages. The majority of jurisdictions that have considered the issue recognize that a plaintiff may recover the value of those services. *See generally* 22 Am.Jur.2d Damages §§ 209, 570–71 (1988) (stating majority rule and listing jurisdictions following it). Some have expressed the view that a failure to account for the value of such services amounts to an undeserved windfall or benefit to the tortfeasor. Thus, Oddo v. Cardi, 100 R.I. 578, 218 A.2d 373 (1966), citing Coyne v. Campbell, 11 N.Y.2d 372, 377, 183 N.E.2d 891, 894, 230 N.Y.S.2d 1, 5 (1962) (Fuld, J., dissenting), reasoned that the "fortuitous circumstance" of free assistance should not reduce recovery. Judge Fuld's dissent further noted that barring compensation for gratuitously rendered services could discriminate against the poor, who presumably would be affected more than the rich, who could afford nursing services. *Coyne, supra,* 11 N.Y.2d at 378 n.2, 183 N.E.2d at 894 n.2, 230 N.Y.S.2d at 6 n.2.
> * * *
>
>   * * *
>
> We * * * find no distinction that can be extrapolated from the common-law collateral source rule between the gratuitous payment for a third party's services and free provision of such home health-care services. In both situations, the payor/provider ensures that the tort victim receives the necessary assistance to overcome his or her incapacity and indirectly compensates for a part of the victim's loss attributable to the injuries.

Id. at 239–42, 584 A.2d at 802–04. *See generally* Joseph M. Engl, Comment, *Gratuitous Nursing Services Rendered By Extended Family Members and Other Parties: Can Injured Parties Receive Reimbursement Under Wisconsin's Collateral Source Rule?* 85 Marq. L. Rev. 1003 (2002). For a suggestion that the goal of compensatory damages should be rehabilitation, and that the plaintiff should therefore have a choice between home-health care and institutional care, see Hall *ex rel.* Hall v. Rodricks, 340 N.J.Super. 264, 774 A.2d 551 (App.Div.2001); *see generally* Ellen S. Pryor, *Rehabilitating Tort Compensation,* 91 Geo. L.J. 659 (2003).

    2. In Johnson v. Baker, *supra* Chapter 3, Section 4.A, Kelly Johnson received grants and scholarships, and the trial court judge deducted their value from the damages awarded to the plaintiff. Does *Arambula* suggest that the trial court judge should have applied the collateral source rule? The appellate court in *Johnson* reversed the trial court judge: "[W]e hold that the collateral source doctrine applies to payments or services received gratuitously as well as those received as the result of some obligation." 11 Kan.App.2d at 278, 719 P.2d at 756. Did Kelly Johnson receive a windfall? As between a tortfeasor and an innocent party, should any windfall go to the innocent

party? *See generally* Robert A. Katz, *Too Much of a Good Thing: When Charitable Gifts Augment Victim Compensation*, 53 DePaul L. Rev. 547 (2003).

3. In Molzof v. United States, *supra* Chapter 3, Section 3.A, the Supreme Court remanded Mr. Molzof's FTCA case to the lower courts to evaluate whether plaintiff's future medical expenses were recoverable under Wisconsin law. Because the evidence indicated that the plaintiff would remain at the Veteran's Administration hospital and receive free medical care, the district court granted the defendant's motion for summary judgment. The Seventh Circuit reversed and remanded with instructions to award the plaintiff's future medical expenses in the amount of $1,280,529. 6 F.3d 461 (7th Cir.1993). The Seventh Circuit ruled that Wisconsin had "long been committed to the collateral source rule," and the fact that the medical services would be rendered gratuitously did not preclude the plaintiff from recovering the value of those services. *Id.* at 464. In response to the government's argument that the free medical care would be coming from the defendant, and not from a "collateral source," the Seventh Circuit said: "Application of the collateral source rule depends less upon the source of funds than upon the character of the benefits received." *Id.* at 465. The court then observed that state collateral source rules had been applied against the government in FTCA cases "(1) if payment to the plaintiff comes from a specially funded source distinct from the unsegregated general revenues of the Federal Treasury * * *, or (2) if the plaintiff contributed to the government payments and, thus, was entitled to the payments irrespective of the damages award * * *." *Id.* at 466. Thus the collateral source rule applied to exclude admissibility at trial of government payments in the form of civil service sick leave payments, Medicare payments, and social security benefits. *See generally* John F. Wagner, Jr., Annotation, *Application of the Collateral Source Rule in Actions Under the Federal Tort Claims Act (28 U.S.C. § 2674)*, 104 A.L.R. Fed. 492 (1991). In Mr. Molzof's case, the Seventh Circuit concluded that veteran's health care benefits were analogous to traditional employee health care benefits, whereby an employee secures health care by contributing part of the employee's salary to sustain the program. In the case of veterans like Mr. Molzof, the contribution was their service to the country.

4. *See, also*, Haughton v. Blackships, Inc., 462 F.2d 788 (5th Cir.1972) (private employer's pension funds could not be set off against the plaintiff's damages). In such cases, there is a heightened concern about the prejudicial effect of erroneously admitting collateral source evidence because the jury may factor in such evidence when determining the issue of liability. *See* Phillips v. Western Co. of North America, 953 F.2d 923 (5th Cir.1992) (reversing a jury verdict for the defendant because the trial court's decision to admit evidence that, after the accident, the defendant had begun to pay long-term disability benefits to the plaintiff "was not harmless error").

5. The next case is from Louisiana and refers to "patrimony," with which students of civil law are familiar. The following will help students who concentrate on common law:

> Patrimonial rights generally attach to things (here, "things" are broadly defined as material objects or intangibles that generally are subject to appropriation) and, consequently, are subject to pecuniary evaluation and

form part of a person's patrimony. Also, patrimonial rights ordinarily are transferable and heritable. * * *

Extrapatrimonial rights, by contrast, form a residual category of rights incapable of pecuniary valuation or appropriation by another.

Patrick N. Broyles, Comment, *Intercontinental Identity: The Right to the Identity in the Louisiana Civil Code*, 65 La. L. Rev. 823, 834 (2005).

METOYER v. AUTO CLUB FAMILY INSURANCE CO.

United States District Court for the Eastern District of Louisiana, 2008.
536 F. Supp. 2d 664.

Carl Barbier, District Judge.

Before the Court is Plaintiff's Motion in Limine to Exclude Evidence of Louisiana Recovery Authority Proceeds as a Collateral Source * * *.

* * *

1. Procedural History and Background Facts

Plaintiff Carlos Metoyer sustained damage to his New Orleans home as a result of Hurricane Katrina and filed suit on March 1, 2007 to recover sums alleged due under his insurance contract with Defendant. * * * Plaintiff was awarded a $150,000 grant from the Louisiana Recovery Authority ("LRA") to rebuild his home and a $10,000 grant from the U.S. Small Business Association.

2. Parties' Arguments

Plaintiff argues that the LRA funds constitute a collateral source, and therefore he seeks to have any evidence of LRA funds excluded from evidence so as not to taint the jury. Moreover, Plaintiff asserts that [Auto Club Family Insurance Company] ACFIC should not be allowed to introduce evidence of LRA proceeds as a credit to absolve itself of liability under the insurance contract.

Given the lack of case law regarding the application of the collateral source rule to LRA proceeds, Plaintiff seeks to apply the framework employed by the United States District Court of the Virgin Islands in *Antilles Ins., Inc. v. James.* 30 V.I. 230, 1994 WL 371405 (D.V.I. 1994).[1] In *Antilles,* plaintiffs suffered losses to their home in St. Croix caused by Hurricane Hugo. * * * While seeking the proceeds from their insurance policy, Plaintiffs received payment from the Virgin Islands Hurricane Hugo Insurance Claims Fund Program ("Hugo Fund"). * * * Uncompensated for their insured losses, Plaintiffs brought suit against their insurer for negligence in failing to disclose information about its affiliation with another insurance company. * * *. After a jury trial, plaintiffs were

---

1. The District Court of the Virgin Islands is not a Court of the United States as that term is usually thought of. * * * [I]ts powers are broader as a court of the territory than a United States District Court. * * * In essence, the District Court of the Virgin Islands functions as a District Court of the United States would, and also as an appellate court for the territorial court of the Virgin Islands. * * *

awarded damages for their property damage claim and loss of use. * * * On appeal, defendant insurer argued that the application of the collateral source rule was inappropriate. * * *

In the *Antilles* case cited by the Plaintiff, the court was sitting as an appellate court for the territory of the Virgin Islands, and not as a federal district court would. Because the court is not sitting as a federal court, it must apply the law of the Virgin Islands. * * * Therefore, any holding the *Antilles* court must be persuasive in nature, and only insofar as a state supreme court would be.

The court upheld the application of the collateral source rule, largely focusing on the purpose of the Hugo Fund payments. * * *. The court reasoned that the Hugo Fund was designed to benefit the Virgin Islands rather than "to discharge any liability or obligation of a tortfeasor such as Antilles." * * * Likening the LRA to the Hugo Fund, Plaintiff here argues that LRA proceeds should not result in a credit against ACFIC's liability. Furthermore, in being forced to recover from outside sources, that is, the LRA, Plaintiff claims the diminution of his patrimony was an additional damage which justifies the additional proceeds.

Defendant counters that the collateral source rule only applies to situations involving actions in tort, not breach of contract. Additionally, Defendant rebuts Plaintiff's claim that his patrimony was diminished because he provided no consideration for the LRA benefit. Defendant then goes on to distinguish the instant matter from *Antilles:* this case is based on breach of contract, whereas *Antilles* involved a tort action; * * *.

3. DISCUSSION
* * *

a. Does the Collateral Source Rule Apply to Actions in Contract?

Commentators have noted that courts have rarely considered whether the collateral source rule applies in contract actions. *See e.g.* John G. Fleming, *The Collateral Source Rule and Contract Damages,* 71 CAL. L. REV. 56, 56 & n.1 (1983) * * *.

The Louisiana Supreme Court recently explored the history and application of the rule in Louisiana courts. *See Bozeman v. State,* 879 So. 2d 692 (La. 2004). The Court noted that the collateral source rule is "a rule of evidence and damages that is of common law origin, yet embraced and applied by Louisiana courts." * * * The supreme court cited and adopted the rule to be used in Louisiana from the Restatement (Second) of Torts § 920A (1979).[2] Under the rule, as applied in Louisiana, the court held the a "tortfeasor may not benefit . . . because of monies received by

---

2. That section provides as follows: "(1) A payment made by a tortfeasor or by a person acting for him to a person whom he has injured is credited against his tort liability, as are payments made by another who is, or believes he is, subject to the same tort liability. (2) Payments made to or benefits conferred on the injured party from other sources are not credited against the tortfeasor's liability, although they cover all or a part of the harm from which the tortfeasor is liable." Restatement (Second) of Torts § 920A (1979).

the plaintiff from sources independent of the tortfeasor's procuration or contribution." * * * The court further noted that the rule has been applied to a variety of situations "although it typically applies to tort cases." * * *.[3]

In the tort context, courts have cited many reasons for the existence of the collateral source rule. As stated above, the most common reason for the rule is that a defendant should not be allowed to benefit from the outside benefits provided for the plaintiff. * * * The *Kansas City Southern Railway* court recognized that the classic example of the collateral source rule occurred in insurance cases. The classic formulation of the rule is that a tortfeasor's liability should be the same, regardless of whether the plaintiff had the foresight to buy insurance. *Kan. City So. Ry.*, 846 So. 2d at 740.

Louisiana courts have held that this "double recovery" is not a windfall for a plaintiff at all. * * * In terms of insurance, the *Bryant* court determined that the plaintiff has paid premiums which are a diminution of his patrimony as that cash would otherwise have been available to him. * * *

If these were the only reasons given for the collateral source rule, it would be easy to declare that its application should be applied in this case. However, the *Bozeman* court continued that a "major policy reason for applying the collateral source rule to damages has been, and continues to be, tort deterrence." *Bozeman*, 879 So. 2d at 700. Therefore there is an element [of] punitive damages to a collateral source award. In general, Louisiana law prohibits punitive or exemplary damages in contract actions. * * *[4] However, Professor Fleming, disposes of this argument. He argues that * * * even though the law often recognizes the concept of efficient breach, it is questionable what effect the application of the collateral source rule would have on the doctrine. It seems especially questionable whether the possibility of a third party benefit inuring to the aggrieved party would enter into the calculations of an efficient breacher. *Id.* Therefore, Professor Fleming concludes that "the policies underlying the law of contract do not dictate an application of the collateral source rule different from that in tort." *Id.*[5]

* * *

---

3. The court noted that the rule was applied to a worker's compensation case involving services rendered by the United States Department of Veterans Affairs * * *.

4. It is worth noting that insurance companies have been considered to be companies that provide a vital public service, and therefore unjustifiable breach by such a company of its contract of insurance can sometimes lead to punitive damages.

5. *But see Pan Pac. Retail Props v. Gulf Ins. Co.*, 471 F.3d 961, 973 (9th Cir. 2006). In *Pan Pacific*, the Ninth Circuit, applying California law, concluded that a plaintiff in a breach of an insurance contract cannot benefit from the collateral source rule because to do so would violate the "contractual damage rule that no one shall profit more from the breach of an obligation than from its full performance." *Id.* In other words, the *Pan Pacific* court was concerned that the plaintiff would end up with a double recovery. That fear is unfounded in the case at bar because of the subrogation of the LRA to the insured.

Defendant is correct that in this case, Plaintiff's petition alleges a breach of contract and not a tort. Plaintiff has not pointed to a single case where the collateral source rule was applied to actions for breach of contract. While the Court could not find any Louisiana case which held such, several cases from other jurisdictions have addressed the issue. A recent California case seems to encompass the rule well. In *El Escorial Owners' Assn. v. DLC Plastering, Inc.*, 154 Cal. App. 4th 1337, 65 Cal. Rptr. 3d 524, 542 (Cal. Ct. App. 2007), the California Court of Appeal considered an action by a condominium owners' association against multiple contractors and subcontractors relating to construction defects.

The court noted that the collateral source rule is generally not used in breach of contract claims. However, the court continued that "where a person suffers property damage, the amount of damages shall not be reduced by the receipt by him of payment for his loss from a source wholly independent of the person who caused the injury." * * * The Court essentially held that even though the action was termed a breach of contract, the action had elements of tort because the plaintiff had to prove that the construction was substandard or negligently performed.[7]

Therefore, it seems that there cannot be a blanket prohibition of the application of the collateral source rule to contract claims as the defendant suggests. Even if such a claim could be sustained, it is not clear that there is not an element of tort in Plaintiff's claim, despite its title as a "Breach of Contract". * * *

b. Should the Collateral Source Rule Apply in this Situation?

Defendant claims that the collateral source rule should not apply because the Plaintiff's patrimony was not diminished in accepting the LRA money. * * * While the *Bryant* court explained that this diminution of patrimony is what prevented a double recovery, the court did not hold that a reduction in a person's patrimony is *required* in order to prevent double recovery.

Even assuming that Defendant is correct, and that Plaintiff's patrimony is not diminished, this conclusion does not prevent the application of the collateral source rule. In *Bonnet ex rel. Bonnet v. Slaughter*, 422 So. 2d 499, 503 (La. App. 4 Cir. 1982), the court considered a tort claim wherein a woman claimed lost wages for the time she had to spend with her injured son. The defendant claimed that the woman collected welfare during this time, and therefore defendant should be entitled to a credit against the lost wages claim for the amount that welfare paid. The court held that welfare payments were a collateral source, and therefore defen-

---

7. To be sure, there are cases which have held that the collateral source rule cannot be used in breach of contract actions. In *Four Seasons Mfg. v. 1001 Coliseum, LLC*, 870 N.E. 2d 494, 507 (Ind. Ct. App. 2007), the court held that in a breach of contract claim, a non-breaching party is not entitled to be put in a better situation than he would have been had the contract not been breached. Therefore, the court held that a non-breaching party is required to mitigate his damages, and the breaching party is entitled to set off the amount of the damages mitigated. *Id.* Neither party seems to be suggesting that the LRA or Road Home is a form of mitigation of damages. * * *

dant is not entitled to such an offset. *Id.* Without delving too deeply into the facts of how the welfare program was run in 1982, the *Slaughter* court does not mention whether the plaintiff's patrimony was diminished in any way by accepting welfare payments.

In *Bozeman,* the Louisiana Supreme Court held that a tort victim who received medical care through Medicaid cannot recover the write-off amount above what Medicaid paid for the medical care. *Bozeman,* 879 So. 2d at 705. The court based its reasoning partly on the fact that Medicaid is a completely free service to the nation's poor, and is not funded through contributions by the patient, or the patient's employer. Therefore there is not a reduction in the victim's patrimony. In *Bozeman,* there is a danger of double recovery, because the victim would have received the medical care, and an amount above what the medical care cost the public. For public policy reasons, the court held that the plaintiff was not entitled to the higher amount.

In the case at bar, there is no danger of a double recovery or windfall. The LRA is a program whose intent is to compensate Louisiana home-owners affected by Hurricane Katrina. *See* http://www.road2la.org/about-us/default.htm. The program is provided free of cost to eligible home-owners and is funded by a grant through the United States Department of Housing and Urban Development. *Id.* The LRA required that, when it awards a grant, it will be subrogated to the rights of the homeowner with regards to insurance payments. *Id.* Therefore the Plaintiffs should not be put in the position greater than they were before a breach of contract.

This subrogation right negates the negative effects of the collateral source rule in a contract claim. * * * Further, it could not have been the intention of the Federal Government grant writers, or the Louisiana Legislature that insurance companies should benefit from the provisions of the LRA. * * *

Finally the Court notes that if the Defendant's position is adopted, it will amount to a windfall, not for plaintiffs, but for insurers. Accordingly, Plaintiff's Motion in Limine to Exclude Evidence of Louisiana Recovery Authority Proceeds as a Collateral Source will be granted.

* * *

NOTES

1. *Metoyer* was subsequently settled although a dispute arose as to the settlement. *Metoyer v. Auto Club Family Ins. Co.,* 2008 U.S. Dist. LEXIS 43932 (E.D. La. May 27, 2008).

2. *Metoyer* discussed *Bozeman* which affirmed "the lower courts' deter-minations that Medicaid recipients are unable to recover the 'write-off' amounts as damages." *Bozeman v. State,* 879 So.2d 692, 693 (La. 2004). *Bozeman* explained "write-offs":

When an injured plaintiff is a Medicaid recipient, federal and state law require that the healthcare providers accept as full payment, an amount set by the Medicaid fee schedule, which, invariably, is lower than the amount charged by the healthcare provider. The difference between what is charged by the healthcare providers and what is paid by Medicaid is referred to as the "write-off" amount.

For a contrary holding *see* Wills v. Foster, 229 Ill. 2d 393, 418–419, 892 N.E.2d 1018, 1033, 323 Ill. Dec. 26, 41 (2008) (citing Restatement (Second) of Torts § 920A in case involving Medicare and Medicaid write-offs to hold "All plaintiffs are entitled to seek to recover the full reasonable value of their medical expenses."). *See generally* Brandon R. Keel, Note, *Profiting Under the Veil of Compensation:* Wills v. Foster *and the Application of the Collateral Source Rule to Medicare and Medicaid*, 58 DePaul L. Rev. 789 (2009); Stephen L. Olson & Pat Wasson, *Is the Collateral Source Rule Applicable to Medicare and Medicaid Write–Offs?* 71 Def. Couns. J. 172 (2004).

3. The court in *Metoyer* refers to the "concept of efficient breach." How does the doctrine of efficient breach relate to whether punitive damages are allowed in contract actions. For further discussion of the efficient breach doctrine see Section 5.B of this Chapter.

4. Does the fact that the collateral source rule has a deterrent purpose make it punitive? *See Molzoff*, in Section 3 of this Chapter.

5. *Metoyer* holds that the collateral source rule applies to contract actions. *See also* Ventura Associates, Inc. v. International Outsourcing Services, Inc., 2009 WL 691066 (S.D.N.Y. 2009) (applying collateral source rule to business loss insurance payments plaintiff received that reimbursed losses caused by defendant who breached contract with plaintiff by not distributing promised promotional debit cards). *But see* Plut v. Fireman's Insurance Co., 85 Cal.App.4th 98, 108, 102 Cal.Rptr.2d 36, 43 (2000) (the rationale for the collateral source rule is "less compelling" in the case of breach of contract); Rest. 2d Contracts, § 347, com. e, p. 116.

D. DEFENSES

1. Offset the Benefits Rule

CHAFFEE v. SESLAR
Supreme Court of Indiana, 2003.
786 N.E.2d 705.

DICKSON, JUSTICE.

In this interlocutory appeal, the defendant, Dr. Kenneth Chaffee ("Dr. Chaffee"), challenges the trial court's order permitting the plaintiff, Heather Seslar ("Seslar"), to seek damages including the expenses of raising and educating her child born following an unsuccessful sterilization procedure. * * *

The facts in this case are relatively uncomplicated. On March 26, 1998, Dr. Chaffee performed a partial salpingectomy on Seslar. * * * The purpose of the procedure was to sterilize Seslar, who had already borne four children, so that she could not become pregnant again. After undergoing the surgery, however, Seslar conceived, and on August 5, 1999, she delivered a healthy baby.

On March 15, 2000, pursuant to Indiana's medical malpractice statutes, Seslar filed a proposed complaint with the Indiana Department of Insurance alleging that Dr. Chaffee's performance of the procedure had been negligent and seeking damages for the future expenses of raising the child through college, including all medical and educational expenses. Dr. Chaffee filed a motion for preliminary determination, requesting an order limiting the amount of recoverable damages and a determination that the costs of raising a healthy child born after a sterilization procedure are not recoverable as a matter of law. The trial court denied Dr. Chaffee's motion but certified its order for interlocutory appeal.

In this appeal from the trial court ruling, the parties identify and disagree regarding two issues: (1) whether the cost of rearing a normal, healthy child born after an unsuccessful sterilization procedure are cognizable, and (2) whether our recent decision in Bader v. Johnson, 732 N.E.2d 1212 (Ind.2000) compels the recognition of such damages.

In *Bader,* the plaintiffs alleged that, because of the prior birth of a child with congenital defects, they had consulted the defendants, health-care providers offering genetic counseling services, during a subsequent pregnancy. The plaintiffs contended that the defendants' failure to communicate adverse test results deprived them of the opportunity to terminate the pregnancy and resulted in the birth of a child whose multiple birth defects led to her death four months after birth. The plaintiffs' claim was not that the defendant caused the resulting abnormalities in their child, but that the defendant's negligence "caused them to lose the ability to terminate the pregnancy and thereby avoid the costs associated with carrying and giving birth to a child with severe defects." * * * The plaintiffs in *Bader* sought various damages including medical costs attributable to the birth defects during the child's minority,* * * but they did not seek the general costs of rearing the child. We permitted the plaintiffs to seek the damages they sought, noting that their claims "should be treated no differently than any other medical malpractice case." * * * We were not confronted with, nor did we address, a challenge to the anticipated ordinary costs of rearing and raising the child.

* * *

This issue has been receiving considerable attention in other jurisdictions. There are three principal lines of authority regarding resolution of actions for medical negligence resulting in an unwanted pregnancy. In the first, followed by a small group of jurisdictions, the parents of a child born after a negligently performed sterilization procedure are entitled to recover all costs incurred in rearing the child without any offset for the benefits conferred by the presence of the child. This approach has been followed in California, New Mexico, Oregon, and Wisconsin. *See* Custodio v. Bauer, 251 Cal.App.2d 303, 59 Cal.Rptr. 463 (Cal.Ct.App.1967); Lovelace Med. Ctr. v. Mendez, 111 N.M. 336, 805 P.2d 603 (N.M.1991); Zehr v. Haugen,

318 Or. 647, 871 P.2d 1006 (1994); Marciniak v. Lundborg, 153 Wis.2d 59, 450 N.W.2d 243 (1990). Generally, these courts find that damages are recoverable using the standard analysis in negligence cases, and refuse to alter that analysis because of public policy considerations or to permit reduction for the benefits conferred by a child.

Under the second approach, the plaintiff may recover all damages that flow from the wrongful act, but the calculation of damages includes a consideration of the offset of the benefits conferred on the parents by the child's birth. This is consistent with the Restatement (Second) of Torts § 920 (1977), which requires that in situations where the defendant's conduct has harmed the plaintiff or the plaintiff's property but "in so doing has conferred a special benefit to the interest of the plaintiff that was harmed, the value of the benefit conferred is considered in mitigation of damages, to the extent that this is equitable." *Id.* The trier of fact is permitted to determine and award all past and future expenses and damages incurred by the parent, including the cost of rearing the child, but is also instructed that it should make a deduction for the benefits, including, for example, the services, love, joy, and affection that the parents will receive by virtue of having and raising the child. *See* Univ. of Arizona Health Sciences Ctr. v. Superior Court, 136 Ariz. 579, 667 P.2d 1294, 1299 (1983); Ochs v. Borrelli, 187 Conn. 253, 445 A.2d 883, 886 (1982); Sherlock v. Stillwater Clinic, 260 N.W.2d 169, 175–76 (Minn.1977). As between the first and second approaches, we find the latter preferable.

A third view holds that parents of healthy children born after an unsuccessful sterilization procedure involving medical negligence are entitled to pregnancy and childbearing expenses, but not child-rearing expenses. This is the view of the vast majority of jurisdictions * * *.[2] Courts that follow this approach have identified a variety of policy reasons in support of their decisions, including the speculative nature of the damages, the disproportionate nature of the injury to the defendant's culpability, and a refusal to consider the birth of a child to be a compensable "damage." * * *

Although raising an unplanned child, or any child for that matter, is costly, we nevertheless believe that all human life is presumptively invaluable. * * * A child, regardless of the circumstances of birth, does not constitute a "harm" to the parents so as to permit recovery for the costs associated with raising and educating the child. We reach the same outcome as the majority of jurisdictions, and hold that the value of a child's life to the parents outweighs the associated pecuniary burdens as a matter of law. Recoverable damages may include pregnancy and childbearing expenses, but not the ordinary costs of raising and educating a normal, healthy child conceived following an allegedly negligent sterilization procedure.

---

2. Those other jurisdictions include: * * * the District of Columbia (Flowers v. District of Columbia, 478 A.2d 1073 (D.C.1984)); * * * Georgia (Atlanta Obstetrics & Gynecology Group v. Abelson, 260 Ga. 711, 398 S.E.2d 557 (1990)); * * * Iowa (Nanke v. Napier, 346 N.W.2d 520 (Iowa 1984)); * * * Missouri (Girdley v. Coats, 825 S.W.2d 295 (Mo.1992)) * * *.

In its resolution of this difficult issue, the Illinois Supreme Court wrote that a parent cannot be said to have been "damaged" by the birth and rearing of a normal, healthy child, and that "it is a matter of universally-shared emotion and sentiment that the intangible ... 'benefits' of parenthood far outweigh any of the mere monetary burdens involved." Cockrum v. Baumgartner, 95 Ill.2d 193, 199, 69 Ill.Dec. 168, 447 N.E.2d 385, 388 (1983) (quoting Pub. Health Trust v. Brown, 388 So.2d 1084, 1085–86 (Fla.App.1980)). We agree.

* * *

We hold that the costs involved in raising and educating a normal, healthy child conceived subsequent to an allegedly negligent sterilization procedure are not cognizable as damages in an action for medical negligence. The order of the trial court denying the defendant's motion for preliminary determination is reversed, and this cause is remanded for further proceedings consistent with this opinion.

SHEPARD, C.J., and BOEHM, JJ., concur.

SULLIVAN, J., dissenting, would adopt and apply Restatement (Second) of Torts § 920 in this case.

RUCKER, JUSTICE, dissenting.

In *Bader*, * * * this court * * * decided to treat a so-called wrongful birth cause of action the same as any other claim for medical negligence. In doing so, we determined that existing law controlled the nature and extent of available damages.

At the time *Bader* was decided, at least twenty-two states and the District of Columbia had recognized a claim of wrongful birth, while at least eight states had barred such claims either by statute or judicial decision. * * * As one might expect, those jurisdictions recognizing a tort of wrongful birth differed not only on the elements of the tort but also on the recoverable damages. For example, some courts allowed recovery for extraordinary medical and related expenses associated with a child's disability, while others did not. * * * At least one state that permitted such recovery, applied a benefits rule, which offset the recovery of expenses by the value of the benefit that parents receive as parents. *Id.* (citing Eisbrenner v. Stanley, 106 Mich.App. 357, 308 N.W.2d 209 (1981), *abrogated by* Taylor v. Kurapati, 236 Mich.App. 315, 600 N.W.2d 670, 673 (1999)) * * *. Too, several states recognizing the tort of wrongful birth differed over whether to allow recovery for emotional distress damages.

By treating the plaintiffs' claim no differently than any other claim of medical negligence, this court declined to engage in the foregoing debate. Today's decision changes course, enters the debate, and retreats from the principle we announced in *Bader*.

* * *

Although the claim in this case alleges a "wrongful pregnancy" as opposed to a "wrongful birth" the rationale the majority uses to limit the recoverable damages is equally applicable to both. * * *

* * * Because I see no reason to depart from *Bader,* I would apply here the same analysis used for other medical malpractice cases. If Seslar proves negligence, then she is "entitled to damages proximately caused by the tortfeasor's breach of duty." * * * The expense of raising and educating a child falls in this category. Therefore I dissent and would affirm the judgment of the trial court.

NOTES

1. The Restatement (Second) of Torts § 920 (1979), which was cited in *Chaffee*, provides as follows:

§ 920. Benefit to Plaintiff Resulting from Defendant's Tort

When the defendant's tortious conduct has caused harm to the plaintiff or to his property and in so doing has conferred a special benefit to the interest of the plaintiff that was harmed, the value of the benefit conferred is considered in mitigation of damages, to the extent that this is equitable.

The Restatement (Second) of Contracts § 347(c) (1978) has a provision requiring the nonbreaching party to subtract from the damage award any costs or losses that the nonbreaching party avoided by being excused from the performance of the contract.

2. Judge Paul H. Mitrovich thoughtfully critiques the denial of recovery for "wrongful parentage" damages in *Ohio Wrongful Pregnancy, Wrongful Birth, and Wrongful Life Law Needs to Be Revisited to Obtain a More Equitable Result and Consistency of Law*, 33 Ohio N.U.L. Rev. 623 (2007). *See also* Kathryn C. Vikingstad, Note, *The Use and Abuse of the Tort Benefit Rule in Wrongful Parentage Cases*, 82 Chi–Kent L. Rev. 1063 (2007). For an interesting approach to measuring damages in such cases see, Michael T. Murtaugh, *Wrongful Birth: The Courts' Dilemma in Determining a Remedy for a "Blessed Event"*, 27 Pace L. Rev. 241 (2007) (suggesting damages should compensate a mother based on her reason for not wanting to get pregnant).

2. Avoidable Consequences or Mitigation

ALBERT v. MONARCH FEDERAL SAVINGS & LOAN ASS'N

Superior Court of New Jersey, Appellate Division, 2000.
327 N.J.Super. 462, 743 A.2d 890.

SKILLMAN, P.J.A.D.

Plaintiff Tere Albert suffered personal injuries when she tripped and fell over a raised portion of the sidewalk in front of the commercial premises owned by defendant Monarch Federal Savings and Loan Association (Monarch). Plaintiff's most serious injury was carpal tunnel syndrome in her right wrist.

Plaintiff subsequently brought this personal injury action against * * * Monarch. * * * A jury found both parties negligent, attributing thirty percent fault to plaintiff, and awarded plaintiff $50,000 for her injuries. The court molded the jury verdict and entered judgment in favor of plaintiff for $35,000 plus prejudgment interest. The trial court denied plaintiff's motion for a new trial on damages only.

On appeal, plaintiff does not challenge the jury's liability verdict. Plaintiff's only arguments are that the trial court erred by instructing the jury with respect to her duty to mitigate damages by undergoing surgical treatment and that the jury's damages verdict was against the weight of the credible evidence.

The obligation of the plaintiff in a personal injury action to obtain surgical treatment to minimize his or her damages is governed by well-established principles:

> [A] person injured by another's wrong is obliged to exercise ordinary care to seek medical or surgical treatment so as to effect a cure and minimize damages. Failure or refusal to do so bars recovery for consequences which could have been averted by the exercise of such care. However, in this state the injured person is regarded as having the right to avoid "if he chooses, peril to life, however slight, and undue risks to health, and anguish that goes beyond the bounds of reason." And a refusal to accept an operation is not unreasonable and "therefore unjustifiable in the legal sense, unless it is free from danger to life and health and extraordinary suffering, and, according to the best medical or surgical opinion, offers a reasonable prospect of restoration or relief from the disability."

Budden v. Goldstein, 43 N.J.Super. 340, 350, 128 A.2d 730 (App.Div.1957) (citations omitted) (quoting Robinson v. Jackson, 116 N.J.L. 476, 478, 184 A. 811 (E. & A.1936)) * * *; see generally W.E. Shipley, Annotation, Duty of Injured Person to Submit to Surgery to Minimize Tort Damages, 62 A.L.R.3d 9, 17 (1975); Fowler v. Harper, et al., The Law of Torts, (2d ed.1986) § 25.4 at 515–16; Restatement (Second) of Torts § 918(1) (1979).

There was no evidence presented at trial that the surgical procedure for carpal tunnel syndrome would involve an "undue risk to health" or even a slight "peril to life." There also was no evidence that the surgery would involve "extraordinary suffering." Consequently, the only question is whether the evidence was sufficient to support a finding by the jury that the surgery would offer "a reasonable prospect of restoration or relief from the disability." Budden, supra, 43 N.J.Super. at 350, 128 A.2d 730. If such a finding could be made, defendant was entitled to a jury instruction concerning plaintiff's duty to mitigate damages by undergoing surgical treatment.

Plaintiff's own medical expert, Dr. Richard F. Caponetti, testified that he had performed numerous surgical procedures to relieve carpal tunnel syndrome and that this surgery has "a good track record." Dr. Caponetti also testified that plaintiff's treating physician had recommended that she have surgery, and that he agreed "[plaintiff] was in need of surgery for a carpal tunnel." This testimony would have supported a jury finding that a person in plaintiff's position exercising ordinary and reasonable care for her own health and comfort would have agreed to undergo the surgical procedure for carpal tunnel syndrome.

Plaintiff relies upon Dr. Caponetti's further testimony that the surgery for carpal tunnel syndrome does not have a "guaranteed" successful outcome and that "some [patients] might even get worse following the surgery." However, the same comment could be made about any surgical procedure because, as the court observed in Cline v. United States, 270 F.Supp. 247, 251 (S.D.Fla.1967), "[t]here is ... some element of doubt and risk attendant upon each surgical operation." Consequently, if a trial court's obligation to instruct the jury concerning the plaintiff's duty to mitigate damages by undergoing surgery were contingent upon a medical expert's opinion that a surgical procedure was guaranteed to be successful, there never would be a case in which such an instruction would be appropriate. However, unless a surgical procedure poses a "peril to life," "undue risk to health," or "anguish that goes beyond the bounds of reason," a mitigation instruction is appropriate if evidence is presented that surgery "offers a reasonable prospect of restoration or relief from the disability." *Budden, supra,* 43 N.J.Super. at 350, 128 A.2d 730. Dr. Caponetti's testimony provided an adequate foundation for the jury to make such a finding.

In view of our conclusion that the trial court properly submitted to the jury the issue of plaintiff's duty to mitigate her damages by undergoing surgery for carpal tunnel syndrome, we are also satisfied that the $50,000 jury verdict in plaintiff's favor was not against the weight of the evidence and did not represent a miscarriage of justice.

Affirmed.

SNEAD v. HOLLOMAN
Court of Appeals of North Carolina, 1991.
101 N.C.App. 462, 400 S.E.2d 91.

* * *

WYNN, JUDGE.

[The plaintiff was injured in an automobile accident.]

* * *

The defendants * * * assign as error the trial judge's failure to instruct the jury on the plaintiff's duty to mitigate personal injury damages. The defendants contend that the plaintiff failed to keep up the exercise regimen prescribed by his orthopedic surgeon, and that such failure justified a jury instruction on the duty to mitigate personal injury damages.

To support their contention, the defendants rely upon the doctrine of unavoidable consequences which was defined by the North Carolina Supreme Court as follows:

> The rule in North Carolina is that an injured plaintiff, whether his case be in tort or contract, must exercise reasonable care and diligence to avoid or lessen the consequences of the defendant's wrong. If he fails to do so, for any part of the loss incident to such failure, no recovery can be had. This rule is known as the doctrine of unavoidable consequences or the duty to minimize damages. Failure to minimize damages does not bar the remedy; it goes only to the amount of damages recoverable.

Miller v. Miller, 273 N.C. 228, 239, 160 S.E.2d 65, 73–74 (1968) (citations omitted).

This court has also addressed this issue by stating that "[d]amages will not be reduced merely because the injured party fails to follow the medical advice given. All he must do is to act reasonably concerning the advice which he receives. Since the test is one of reasonableness, * * * it is a jury question except in the clearest of cases." Radford v. Norris, 63 N.C.App. 501, 502–03, 305 S.E.2d 64, 65 (1983), *disc. review denied*, 314 N.C. 117, 332 S.E.2d 483 (1985) * * *.

In *Radford,* the issue was whether the trial judge erred in failing to instruct the jury on the plaintiff's duty to minimize damages. There, the plaintiff, who was injured in a collision with the defendant, consulted an orthopedic surgeon who prescribed a program of back exercises as part of the treatment for plaintiff's back injury. The plaintiff testified that he attempted to do the exercises in the beginning, but stopped doing them because they were too painful. The orthopedic surgeon testified that the back exercises were routine and were designed to work out stiffness and pain in the plaintiff's back. When the plaintiff advised the doctor that he had discontinued the exercises, the doctor repeatedly advised the plaintiff to resume the exercises. The doctor further testified that although he could not say with a reasonable degree of medical certainty that the exercises would have cured the plaintiff's back pain had they been performed regularly, he knew the exercises would make the pain better. Nonetheless, the plaintiff did not resume the regimen.

The *Radford* court held that the above evidence tended to show that the plaintiff's regular and continued performance of the exercises would have alleviated the pain and, thus, the pain was a consequence that may have been avoided. * * * Since the defendant in *Radford* properly requested an instruction on avoidable consequences which was improperly denied, the *Radford* court remanded the case for a jury determination of the reasonableness of plaintiff's failure to follow his doctor's advice.

We are unable to make a meaningful distinction between the facts in *Radford* and those present here. In the instant case, the plaintiff's orthopedic surgeon, Dr. Tejpal Singh Dhillon, prescribed a certain exercise regimen which the plaintiff, for some unexplained reason, discontinued performing after one month. * * *

* * * Since the defendants properly requested that the jury be instructed on the plaintiff's duty to minimize damages, we conclude that the trial judge's failure to so instruct the jury was reversible error under the holding in *Radford.* Accordingly, we remand this case for a new trial on the issue of damages.

NOTES

1. Must a plaintiff endure short-term pain in order to possibly alleviate future pain?

2. Is the refusal to lose weight a failure to avoid the consequences of the defendant's action? Consider Aisole v. Dean, 574 So.2d 1248 (La.1991):

> In their reply brief, the defendants request a reduction in damages based on the plaintiff's failure to mitigate. Specifically, the defendants contend that because Mrs. Aisole is overweight[9] and did not attempt to lose weight at the suggestion of her doctors, she breached her duty to mitigate damages. The defendants maintain the plaintiff's pre-existing condition did not exacerbate her injuries but rather prevented her prompt recovery.
>
> It is a well-established principle of law that a tortfeasor takes his victim as he finds him and although the damages caused are greater because of the victims' prior condition which is aggravated by the tort, the tortfeasor is nevertheless responsible for the consequences of his tort. * * * Our jurisprudence has also recognized that an injured plaintiff has a duty to take reasonable steps to mitigate damages. * * * Reading these two doctrines together, we conclude that although a tortfeasor takes his victim as he finds him at the time of the injury, after that time, the victim has an affirmative responsibility to make every reasonable effort to mitigate damages.

Id. at 1253–54. *Compare* Tanberg v. Ackerman Investment Co., 473 N.W.2d 193, 196 (Iowa 1991) (plaintiff does not need to actually lose weight, but must reasonably attempt to do so to mitigate damages).

3. Should a person's religious belief be an exception to the avoidable consequences rule if the person refuses to mitigate damages by accepting medical treatment for that reason? *See* Anne C. Loomis, Casenote and Comment: *Thou Shalt Take Thy Victim as Thou Findest Him: Religious Conviction as a Pre–Existing State Not Subject to the Avoidable Consequences Doctrine*, 14 Geo. Mason L. Rev. 473 (2007).

4. What policies are served by the avoidable consequences rule?

SECTION 5. PUNITIVE DAMAGES AND LIQUIDATED DAMAGES

A. TORT

JACQUE v. STEENBERG HOMES, INC.

Supreme Court of Wisconsin, 1997.
209 Wis.2d 605, 563 N.W.2d 154.

WILLIAM A. BABLITCH, JUSTICE.

Steenberg Homes had a mobile home to deliver. Unfortunately for Harvey and Lois Jacque (the Jacques), the easiest route of delivery was

---

9. At the time of the accident, the plaintiff was 5'1" tall and weighed 245 pounds. At trial, the plaintiff weighed 250 pounds.

across their land. * * * At trial, Steenberg Homes conceded the intentional trespass, but argued that no compensatory damages had been proved, and that punitive damages could not be awarded without compensatory damages. * * *

I.

The relevant facts follow. Plaintiffs, Lois and Harvey Jacques, are an elderly couple, now retired from farming, who own roughly 170 acres * * *. The defendant, Steenberg Homes, Inc. (Steenberg), is in the business of selling mobile homes. In the fall of 1993, a neighbor of the Jacques purchased a mobile home from Steenberg. Delivery of the mobile home was included in the sales price.

Steenberg determined that the easiest route to deliver the mobile home was across the Jacques' land. Steenberg preferred transporting the home across the Jacques' land because the only alternative was a private road which was covered in up to seven feet of snow and contained a sharp curve which would require sets of "rollers" to be used when maneuvering the home around the curve. Steenberg asked the Jacques on several separate occasions whether it could move the home across the Jacques' farm field. The Jacques refused. * * *

On the morning of delivery, * * * the Jacques showed the [defendant's] assistant manager an aerial map and plat book of the township to prove their ownership of the land, and reiterated their demand that the home not be moved across their land.

At that point, the assistant manager asked Mr. Jacque how much money it would take to get permission. Mr. Jacque responded that it was not a question of money; the Jacques just did not want Steenberg to cross their land. Mr. Jacque testified that he told Steenberg to "[F]ollow the road, that is what the road is for." * * *

* * *

The [defendant's] employees, after beginning down the private road, ultimately used a "bobcat" to cut a path through the Jacques' snow-covered field and hauled the home across the Jacques' land to the neighbor's lot. One employee testified that upon returning to the office and informing the assistant manager that they had gone across the field, the assistant manager reacted by giggling and laughing. * * *

When a neighbor informed the Jacques that Steenberg had, in fact, moved the mobile home across the Jacques' land, Mr. Jacque called the Manitowoc County Sheriff's Department. After interviewing the parties and observing the scene, an officer from the sheriff's department issued a $30 citation to Steenberg's assistant manager.

The Jacques commenced an intentional tort action * * * seeking compensatory and punitive damages from Steenberg. The case was tried before a jury on December 1, 1994. * * * The jury awarded the Jacques $1 nominal damages and $100,000 punitive damages. Steenberg filed post-verdict motions claiming that the punitive damage award must be set aside because Wisconsin law did not allow a punitive damage award unless the jury also awarded compensatory damages. Alternatively, Steenberg asked the circuit court to remit the punitive damage award. The circuit court granted Steenberg's motion to set aside the award. * * *

* * *

II.

* * *

Steenberg argues that, as a matter of law, punitive damages could not be awarded by the jury because punitive damages must be supported by an award of compensatory damages and here the jury awarded only nominal and punitive damages. The Jacques contend that the rationale supporting the compensatory damage award requirement is inapposite when the wrongful act is an intentional trespass to land. * * *

* * *

The general rule was stated in Barnard v. Cohen, 165 Wis. 417, 162 N.W. 480 (1917), where the question presented was: "In an action for libel, can there be a recovery of punitory damages if only nominal compensatory damages are found?" With the bare assertion that authority and better reason supported its conclusion, the Barnard court said no. * * * Barnard continues to state the general rule of punitive damages in Wisconsin. * * * The rationale for the compensatory damage requirement is that if the individual cannot show actual harm, he or she has but a nominal interest, hence, society has little interest in having the unlawful, but otherwise harmless, conduct deterred, therefore, punitive damages are inappropriate. * * *

However, whether nominal damages can support a punitive damage award in the case of an intentional trespass to land has never been squarely addressed by this court. Nonetheless, Wisconsin law is not without reference to this situation. In 1854 the court established punitive damages, allowing the assessment of "damages as a punishment to the defendant for the purpose of making an example." McWilliams v. Bragg, 3 Wis. 424, 425 (1854) [(action for assault and battery)]. The McWilliams court related the facts and an illustrative tale from the English case of Merest v. Harvey, 128 Eng.Rep. 761 (C.P.1814), to explain the rationale underlying punitive damages.

In Merest, a landowner was shooting birds in his field when he was approached by the local magistrate who wanted to hunt with him. Although the landowner refused, the magistrate proceeded to hunt. When the landowner continued to object, the magistrate threatened to have him jailed and dared him to file suit. Although little actual harm had been caused, the English court upheld damages of 500 pounds, explaining "in a case where a man disregards every principle which actuates the conduct of gentlemen, what is to restrain him except large damages?" * * *

To explain the need for punitive damages, even where actual harm is slight, *McWilliams* related the hypothetical tale from *Merest* of an intentional trespasser:

> Suppose a gentleman has a paved walk in his paddock, before his window, and that a man intrudes and walks up and down before the window of his house, and looks in while the owner is at dinner, is the trespasser permitted to say "here is a halfpenny for you which is the full extent of the mischief I have done." Would that be a compensation? I cannot say that it would be. . . .

McWilliams, 3 Wis. at 428. Thus, in the case establishing punitive damages in this state, this court recognized that in certain situations of trespass, the actual harm is not in the damage done to the land, which may be minimal, but in the loss of the individual's right to exclude others from his or her property, and the court implied that this right may be punished by a large damage award despite the lack of measurable harm.

* * *

* * * This court has long recognized "[e]very person ['s] constitutional right to the exclusive enjoyment of his own property for any purpose which does not invade the rights of another person." Diana Shooting Club v. Lamoreux, 114 Wis. 44, 59, 89 N.W. 880 (1902) (holding that the victim of an intentional trespass should have been allowed to take judgment for nominal damages and costs). * * *

Yet a right is hollow if the legal system provides insufficient means to protect it. * * * Harvey and Lois Jacque have the right to tell Steenberg Homes and any other trespasser, "No, you cannot cross our land." But that right has no practical meaning unless protected by the State. And, as this court recognized as early as 1854, a "halfpenny" award does not constitute state protection.

* * *

Society has an interest in punishing and deterring intentional trespassers beyond that of protecting the interests of the individual landowner. Society has an interest in preserving the integrity of the legal system. Private landowners should feel confident that wrongdoers who trespass upon their land will be appropriately punished. When landowners have confidence in the legal system, they are less likely to resort to "self-help" remedies. In *McWilliams,* the court recognized the importance of " 'prevent[ing] the practice of dueling, [by permitting] juries to *punish* insult by exemplary damages.' " *McWilliams,* 3 Wis. at 428. Although dueling is rarely a modern form of self-help, one can easily imagine a frustrated landowner taking the law into his or her own hands when faced with a brazen trespasser, like Steenberg, who refuses to heed no trespass warnings.

People expect wrongdoers to be appropriately punished. Punitive damages have the effect of bringing to punishment types of conduct that, though oppressive and hurtful to the individual, almost invariably go unpunished by the public prosecutor. * * * The $30 forfeiture was certainly not an appropriate punishment for Steenberg's egregious trespass in the eyes of the Jacques. It was more akin to *Merest*'s "halfpenny." If punitive damages are not allowed in a situation like this, what punishment will prohibit the intentional trespass to land? Moreover, what is to stop Steenberg Homes from concluding, in the future, that delivering its mobile homes via an intentional trespass and paying the resulting Class B forfeiture, is not more profitable than obeying the law? Steenberg Homes plowed a path across the Jacques' land and dragged the mobile home across that path, in the face of the Jacques' adamant refusal. A $30 forfeiture and a $1 nominal damage award are unlikely to restrain Steenberg Homes from similar conduct in the future. An appropriate punitive damage award probably will.

* * * We conclude that both the private landowner and society have much more than a nominal interest in excluding others from private land. * * * Consequently, the *Barnard* rationale will not support a refusal to allow punitive damages when the tort involved is an intentional trespass to land. * * *

* * *

IV.

* * * Because we conclude that the nominal damages awarded to the Jacques support the jury's punitive damage award, * * * we review the $100,000 award to determine whether it is clearly excessive. * * *

The award of punitive damages in a particular case is entirely within the discretion of the jury. Notwithstanding the jury's broad discretion, the circuit court has the power to reduce the amount of punitive damages to an amount that it determines is fair and reasonable. * * *

The Due Process Clause prohibits the court from imposing a " 'grossly excessive' " punishment on a tortfeasor. BMW of North America, Inc. v. Gore, 517 U.S. 559, 560, 116 S.Ct. 1589, 1592, 134 L.Ed.2d 809 (1996) (quoting TXO Production Corp. v. Alliance Resources Corp., 509 U.S. 443, 454, 113 S.Ct. 2711, 2718, 125 L.Ed.2d 366 (1993)). * * * Only when a punitive damage award can be fairly categorized as grossly excessive in relation to the State's legitimate interests in punishment and deterrence does it enter the zone of arbitrariness that violates the Due Process Clause. * * *

The Supreme Court has recently clarified the three factors a court must consider when determining whether a punitive damage award violates the Due Process Clause: (1) the degree of reprehensibility of the conduct; (2) the disparity between the harm or potential harm suffered by the plaintiff and the punitive damage award; and (3) the difference between this remedy and the civil or criminal penalties authorized or imposed in comparable cases. *Gore,* 517 U.S. at 574–75, 584–85, 116 S.Ct. at 1598–99, 1603.

We turn first to the reprehensibility factor. The most important indicium of the reasonableness of a punitive damage award is the degree of reprehensibility of the defendant's conduct. Punitive damages should reflect the egregiousness of the offense. * * * In other words, some wrongs are more blameworthy than others and the punishment should fit the crime. In this case, the "crime" was Steenberg's brazen, intentional trespass on the Jacques' land.

* * *

We now turn to the next factor in the *Gore* analysis: the disparity between the harm or potential harm suffered by the Jacques and the punitive damage award. * * *

* * *

When compensatory damages are awarded, we consider the ratio of compensatory to punitive damages. This is so because compensatory damages represent the actual harm inflicted on the plaintiff. However, when nominal damages support a punitive damage award, use of a multiplier is of dubious assistance because the nominal damage award may not reflect the actual harm caused. If it did, the breathtaking 100,000 to 1 ratio of this case could not be upheld. However, in the proper case, a $1 nominal damage award may properly support a $100,000 punitive damage award where a much larger compensatory award might not. This could include situations where egregious acts result in injuries that are hard to detect or noneconomic harm that is difficult to measure. In these instances, as in the case before us, a mathematical bright line between the constitutional and the unconstitutional would turn the concept of punitive damages on its head.

Finally, we turn to the third factor in the *Gore* analysis: we compare the punitive damage award and the civil or criminal penalties that could be imposed for comparable misconduct. * * * Since punitive damages are assessed for punishment, it is relevant to compare the punitive damage award to the maximum fine in the section of the Wisconsin Criminal Code that contains a similar offense. * * *

We consider this factor largely irrelevant in the present case because the "conduct at issue" here was scarcely that contemplated * * * by the legislature when it enacted this statute which provides a [maximum] penalty [of $1,000] for simply "entering or remaining" on the land of another. Here, not only did Steenberg Homes illegally enter and remain on the Jacques' land, first they plowed a path across the Jacques' field, then they transported a mobile home over the path. * * *

* * *

Punitive damages, by removing the profit from illegal activity, can help to deter such conduct. In order to effectively do this, punitive damages must be in excess of the profit created by the misconduct so that the defendant recognizes a loss. It can hardly be said that the $30 forfeiture paid by Steenberg significantly affected its profit for delivery of the mobile home. One hundred thousand dollars will.

Finally, a substantial punitive damage award serves to assure that tort claims involving egregious conduct will be prosecuted. * * * A $100,000 punitive damage award will not only give potential trespassers reason to pause before trespassing, it will also give aggrieved landowners reason to pursue a trespass action.

In sum, although actual harm and criminal penalties have some relevance to the amount of punitive damages and may be factors in determining the reasonableness of the punitive damage award, we have not been willing in the past, and are not willing in this case, to adopt a mathematical formula for awarding such damages. * * * The punitive award neither shocks our conscience, nor takes our breath away. On the contrary, it is the brazen conduct of Steenberg Homes that we find shocking * * *.

In conclusion, we hold that when nominal damages are awarded for an intentional trespass to land, punitive damages may, in the discretion of the jury, be awarded. * * * [And] we hold that the $100,000 punitive damages awarded by the jury is not excessive. Accordingly, we reverse and remand to the circuit court for reinstatement of the punitive damage award.

NOTE

The majority of jurisdictions in the United States take the position that a plaintiff may recover nominal plus punitive damages in actions where nominal damages are recoverable, such as claims for the commission of an intentional tort. John J. Kircher & Christine Wiseman, Punitive Damages: Law and Practice § 5:21 (2d ed. 2004). The remaining jurisdictions condition the recovery of punitive damages on the recovery of compensatory damages. *Id.*

STATE FARM MUTUAL AUTO. INS. CO. v. CAMPBELL

Supreme Court of the United States, 2003.
538 U.S. 408, 123 S.Ct. 1513, 155 L.Ed.2d 585.

JUSTICE KENNEDY delivered the opinion of the Court.

We address once again the measure of punishment, by means of punitive damages, a State may impose upon a defendant in a civil case. The question is whether, in the circumstances we shall recount, an award of $145 million in punitive damages, where full compensatory damages are $1 million, is excessive and in violation of the Due Process Clause of the Fourteenth Amendment to the Constitution of the United States.

I

In 1981, Curtis Campbell (Campbell) was driving with his wife, Inez Preece Campbell, in Cache County, Utah. He decided to pass six vans traveling ahead of them on a two-lane highway. Todd Ospital was driving a small car approaching from the opposite direction. To avoid a head-on collision with Campbell, who by then was driving on the wrong side of the highway and toward oncoming traffic, Ospital swerved onto the shoulder, lost control of his automobile, and collided with a vehicle driven by Robert G. Slusher. Ospital was killed, and Slusher was rendered permanently disabled. The Campbells escaped unscathed.

In the ensuing wrongful death and tort action, Campbell insisted he was not at fault. Early investigations did support differing conclusions as to who caused the accident, but "a consensus was reached early on by the investigators and witnesses that Mr. Campbell's unsafe pass had indeed caused the crash." 65 P.3d at 1141 (Utah 2001). Campbell's insurance company, petitioner State Farm Mutual Automobile Insurance Company (State Farm), nonetheless decided to contest liability and declined offers by Slusher and Ospital's estate (Ospital) to settle the claims for the policy limit of $50,000 ($25,000 per claimant). State Farm also ignored the advice of one of its own investigators and took the case to trial, assuring the Campbells that "their assets were safe, that they had no liability for the accident, that [State Farm] would represent their interests, and that they did not need to procure separate counsel." * * * To the contrary, a jury determined that Campbell was 100 percent at fault, and a judgment was returned for $185,849, far more than the amount offered in settlement.

At first State Farm refused to cover the $135,849 in excess liability. Its counsel made this clear to the Campbells: " 'You may want to put for sale signs on your property to get things moving.' " * * * Nor was State Farm willing to post a supersedeas bond to allow Campbell to appeal the judgment against him. Campbell obtained his own counsel to appeal the verdict. During the pendency of the appeal, in late 1984, Slusher, Ospital, and the Campbells reached an agreement whereby Slusher and Ospital agreed not to seek satisfaction of their claims against the Campbells. In exchange the Campbells agreed to pursue a bad faith action against State Farm and to be represented by Slusher's and Ospital's attorneys. * * * No settlement could be concluded without Slusher's and Ospital's approval, and Slusher and Ospital would receive 90 percent of any verdict against State Farm.

In 1989, the Utah Supreme Court denied Campbell's appeal in the wrongful death and tort actions. Slusher v. Ospital, 777 P.2d 437 (Utah 1989). State Farm then paid the entire judgment, including the amounts in excess of the policy limits. The Campbells nonetheless filed a complaint against State Farm alleging bad faith, fraud, and intentional infliction of emotional distress. * * * At State Farm's request the trial court bifurcated the trial into two phases conducted before different juries [on issues of liability and issues of damages]. In the first phase the jury determined that State Farm's decision not to settle was unreasonable because there was a substantial likelihood of an excess verdict.

Before the second phase of the action against State Farm we decided BMW of North America, Inc. v. Gore, 517 U.S. 559, 116 S.Ct. 1589, 134 L.Ed.2d 809 (1996) [(action for fraud causing economic loss to plaintiff)], and refused to sustain a $2 million punitive damages award which accompanied a verdict of only $4,000 in compensatory damages. * * *

* * * The Utah Supreme Court aptly characterized [the second] phase of the trial:

> State Farm argued during phase II that its decision to take the case to trial was an "honest mistake" that did not warrant punitive damages. In contrast, the Campbells introduced evidence that State Farm's decision to take the case to trial was a result of a national scheme to meet corporate fiscal goals by capping payouts on claims company wide. This scheme was referred to as State Farm's "Performance, Planning and Review," or PP & R, policy. * * * 65 P.3d at 1143.

Evidence pertaining to the PP & R policy concerned State Farm's business practices for over 20 years in numerous States. Most of these practices bore no relation to third-party automobile insurance claims, the type of claim underlying the Campbells' complaint against the company. The jury awarded the Campbells $2.6 million in compensatory damages and $145 million in punitive damages, which the trial court reduced to $1 million and $25 million respectively. * * *

The Utah Supreme Court sought to apply the three guideposts we identified in Gore, supra, at 574–575, 116 S.Ct. 1589, and it reinstated the $145 million punitive damages award. Relying in large part on the extensive evidence concerning the PP & R policy, the court concluded State Farm's conduct was reprehensible. The court also relied upon State Farm's "massive wealth" and on testimony indicating that "State Farm's actions, because of their clandestine nature, will be punished at most in one out of every 50,000 cases as a matter of statistical probability," * * * and concluded that the ratio between punitive and compensatory damages was not unwarranted. Finally, the court noted that the punitive damages award was not excessive when compared to various civil and criminal penalties State Farm could have faced, including $10,000 for each act of fraud, the suspension of its license to conduct business in Utah, the disgorgement of profits, and imprisonment. * * *

II

We recognized in Cooper Industries, Inc. v. Leatherman Tool Group, Inc., 532 U.S. 424, 121 S.Ct. 1678, 149 L.Ed.2d 674 (2001), that in our judicial system compensatory and punitive damages, although usually awarded at the same time by the same decisionmaker, serve different purposes. * * * Compensatory damages "are intended to redress the concrete loss that the plaintiff has suffered by reason of the defendant's wrongful conduct." * * * By contrast, punitive damages serve a broader function; they are aimed at deterrence and retribution. *Cooper Industries, supra,* at 432, 121 S.Ct. 1678 * * *.

While States possess discretion over the imposition of punitive damages, it is well established that there are procedural and substantive constitutional limitations on these awards. * * * TXO Production Corp. v. Alliance Resources Corp., 509 U.S. 443, 113 S.Ct. 2711, 125 L.Ed.2d 366 (1993) * * *. The Due Process Clause of the Fourteenth Amendment prohibits the imposition of grossly excessive or arbitrary punishments on a tortfeasor. * * * *Gore,* 517 U.S., at 562, 116 S.Ct. 1589 * * *. The reason is that "[e]lementary notions of fairness enshrined in our constitutional jurisprudence dictate that a person receive fair notice not only of the conduct that will subject him to punishment, but also of the severity of the penalty that a State may impose." *Id.,* at 574, 116 S.Ct. 1589 * * *. To the extent an award is grossly excessive, it furthers no legitimate purpose and constitutes an arbitrary deprivation of property. * * *

Although these awards serve the same purposes as criminal penalties, defendants subjected to punitive damages in civil cases have not been accorded the protections applicable in a criminal proceeding. This increases our concerns over the imprecise manner in which punitive damages systems are administered. We have admonished that "[p]unitive damages pose an acute danger of arbitrary deprivation of property. Jury instructions typically leave the jury with wide discretion in choosing amounts, and the presentation of evidence of a defendant's net worth creates the potential that juries will use their verdicts to express biases against big businesses, particularly those without strong local presences." *Honda Motor, supra,* at 432, 114 S.Ct. 2331 * * *.

In light of these concerns, in *Gore, supra,* we instructed courts reviewing punitive damages to consider three guideposts: (1) the degree of reprehensibility of the defendant's misconduct; (2) the disparity between the actual or potential harm suffered by the plaintiff and the punitive damages award; and (3) the difference between the punitive damages awarded by the jury and the civil penalties authorized or imposed in comparable cases. * * * We reiterated the importance of these three guideposts in *Cooper Industries* and mandated appellate courts to conduct *de novo* review of a trial court's application of them to the jury's award. * * *

III

Under the principles outlined in BMW of North America, Inc. v. Gore, this case is neither close nor difficult. It was error to reinstate the jury's $145 million punitive damages award. We address each guidepost of *Gore* in some detail.

A

"[T]he most important indicium of the reasonableness of a punitive damages award is the degree of reprehensibility of the defendant's conduct." * * * We have instructed courts to determine the reprehensibility of a defendant by considering whether: the harm caused was physical as opposed to economic; the tortious conduct evinced an indifference to or a reckless disregard of the health or safety of others; the target of the conduct had financial vulnerability; the conduct involved repeated actions or was an isolated incident; and the harm was the result of intentional malice, trickery, or deceit, or mere accident. * * * The existence of any one of these factors weighing in favor of a plaintiff may not be sufficient to sustain a punitive damages award; and the absence of all of them renders any award suspect. It should be presumed a plaintiff has been made whole for his injuries by compensatory damages, so punitive damages should only be awarded if the defendant's culpability, after having paid compensatory damages, is so reprehensible as to warrant the imposition of further sanctions to achieve punishment or deterrence. * * *

Applying these factors in the instant case, we must acknowledge that State Farm's handling of the claims against the Campbells merits no praise. The trial court found that State Farm's employees altered the company's records to make Campbell appear less culpable. State Farm disregarded the overwhelming likelihood of liability and the near-certain probability that, by taking the case to trial, a judgment in excess of the policy limits would be awarded. State Farm amplified the harm by at first assuring the Campbells their assets would be safe from any verdict and by later telling them, postjudgment, to put a for-sale sign on their house. While we do not suggest there was error in awarding punitive damages based upon State Farm's conduct toward the Campbells, a more modest punishment for this reprehensible conduct could have satisfied the State's legitimate objectives, and the Utah courts should have gone no further.

This case, instead, was used as a platform to expose, and punish, the perceived deficiencies of State Farm's operations throughout the country. The Utah Supreme Court's opinion makes explicit that State Farm was being condemned for its nationwide policies rather than for the conduct direct toward the Campbells. * * *

* * *

A State cannot punish a defendant for conduct that may have been lawful where it occurred. * * * Nor, as a general rule, does a State have a legitimate concern in imposing punitive damages to punish a defendant for unlawful acts committed outside of the State's jurisdiction. * * *

* * * Lawful out-of-state conduct may be probative when it demonstrates the deliberateness and culpability of the defendant's action in the State where it is tortious, but that conduct must have a nexus to the specific harm suffered by the plaintiff. A jury must be instructed, furthermore, that it may not use evidence of out-of-state conduct to punish a defendant for action that was lawful in the jurisdiction where it occurred. * * *

For a more fundamental reason, however, the Utah courts erred in relying upon this and other evidence: The courts awarded punitive damages to punish and deter conduct that bore no relation to the Campbells' harm. A defendant's dissimilar acts, independent from the acts upon which liability was premised, may not serve as the basis for punitive damages. A defendant should be punished for the conduct that harmed the plaintiff, not for being an unsavory individual or business. * * *

* * *

* * * Although evidence of other acts need not be identical to have relevance in the calculation of punitive damages, the Utah court erred here because evidence pertaining to [first party] claims that had nothing to do with a third-party lawsuit was introduced at length. * * * The Campbells attempt to justify the courts' reliance upon this unrelated testimony on the theory that each dollar of profit made by underpaying a third-party claimant is the same as a dollar made by underpaying a first-party one. * * * For the reasons already stated, this argument is unconvincing. The reprehensibility guidepost does not permit courts to expand the scope of the case so that a defendant may be punished for any malfeasance, which in this case extended for a 20–year period. In this case, because the Campbells have shown no conduct by State Farm similar to that which harmed them, the conduct that harmed them is the only conduct relevant to the reprehensibility analysis.

B

Turning to the second *Gore* guidepost, we have been reluctant to identify concrete constitutional limits on the ratio between harm, or potential harm, to the plaintiff and the punitive damages award. * * * We decline again to impose a bright-line ratio which a punitive damages award cannot exceed. Our jurisprudence and the principles it has now established demonstrate, however, that, in practice, few awards exceeding a single-digit ratio between punitive and compensatory damages, to a significant degree, will satisfy due process. In *Haslip,* in upholding a punitive damages award, we concluded that an award of more than four times the amount of compensatory damages might be close to the line of constitutional impropriety. * * * We cited that 4–to–1 ratio again in *Gore.* 517 U.S., at 581, 116 S.Ct. 1589. The Court further referenced a long legislative history, dating back over 700 years and going forward to today, providing for sanctions of double, treble, or quadruple damages to deter and punish. * * * While these ratios are not binding, they are instructive. They demonstrate what should be obvious: Single-digit multipliers are more likely to comport with due process, while still achieving the State's goals of deterrence and retribution, than awards with ratios in the range of 500 to 1, *id.,* at 582, 116 S.Ct. 1589, or, in this case, of 145 to 1.

Nonetheless, because there are no rigid benchmarks that a punitive damages award may not surpass, ratios greater than those we have previously upheld may comport with due process where "a particularly

egregious act has resulted in only a small amount of economic damages."
Ibid.; *see also ibid.* (positing that a higher ratio *might* be necessary where
"the injury is hard to detect or the monetary value of noneconomic harm
might have been difficult to determine"). The converse is also true,
however. When compensatory damages are substantial, then a lesser ratio,
perhaps only equal to compensatory damages, can reach the outermost
limit of the due process guarantee. The precise award in any case, of
course, must be based upon the facts and circumstances of the defendant's
conduct and the harm to the plaintiff.

In sum, courts must ensure that the measure of punishment is both
reasonable and proportionate to the amount of harm to the plaintiff and
to the general damages recovered. In the context of this case, we have no
doubt that there is a presumption against an award that has a 145–to–1
ratio. The compensatory award in this case was substantial; the Campbells
were awarded $1 million for a year and a half of emotional distress. This
was complete compensation. The harm arose from a transaction in the
economic realm, not from some physical assault or trauma; there were no
physical injuries; and State Farm paid the excess verdict before the
complaint was filed, so the Campbells suffered only minor economic
injuries for the 18–month period in which State Farm refused to resolve
the claim against them. * * *

The Utah Supreme Court sought to justify the massive award by
pointing to * * * the fact that State Farm's policies have affected numerous Utah consumers; the fact that State Farm will only be punished in one
out of every 50,000 cases as a matter of statistical probability; and State
Farm's enormous wealth. * * * [T]he Campbells' inability to direct us to
testimony demonstrating harm to the people of Utah (other than those
directly involved in this case) indicates that the adverse effect on the
State's general population was in fact minor.

The remaining premises for the Utah Supreme Court's decision bear
no relation to the award's reasonableness or proportionality to the harm.
They are, rather, arguments that seek to defend a departure from well-
established constraints on punitive damages. * * * Here the argument
that State Farm will be punished in only the rare case, coupled with
reference to its assets (which, of course, are what other insured parties in
Utah and other States must rely upon for payment of claims) had little to
do with the actual harm sustained by the Campbells. The wealth of a
defendant cannot justify an otherwise unconstitutional punitive damages
award. * * *

C

The third guidepost in *Gore* is the disparity between the punitive
damages award and the "civil penalties authorized or imposed in comparable cases." * * * We note that, in the past, we have also looked to criminal
penalties that could be imposed. * * * The existence of a criminal penalty
does have bearing on the seriousness with which a State views the

wrongful action. When used to determine the dollar amount of the award, however, the criminal penalty has less utility. * * *

Here, we need not dwell long on this guidepost. The most relevant civil sanction under Utah state law for the wrong done to the Campbells appears to be a $10,000 fine for an act of fraud, * * * an amount dwarfed by the $145 million punitive damages award. The Supreme Court of Utah speculated about the loss of State Farm's business license, the disgorgement of profits, and possible imprisonment, but here again its references were to the broad fraudulent scheme drawn from evidence of out-of-state and dissimilar conduct. This analysis was insufficient to justify the award.

IV

An application of the *Gore* guideposts to the facts of this case, especially in light of the substantial compensatory damages awarded (a portion of which contained a punitive element), likely would justify a punitive damages award at or near the amount of compensatory damages. The punitive award of $145 million, therefore, was neither reasonable nor proportionate to the wrong committed, and it was an irrational and arbitrary deprivation of the property of the defendant. The proper calculation of punitive damages under the principles we have discussed should be resolved, in the first instance, by the Utah courts.

The judgment of the Utah Supreme Court is reversed, and the case is remanded for proceedings not inconsistent with this opinion.

JUSTICE SCALIA, dissenting.

I adhere to the view expressed in my dissenting opinion in BMW of North America, Inc. v. Gore, 517 U.S. 559, 598–99, 116 S.Ct. 1589, 134 L.Ed.2d 809 (1996), that the Due Process Clause provides no substantive protections against "excessive" or " 'unreasonable' " awards of punitive damages. * * * I would affirm the judgment of the Utah Supreme Court.

JUSTICE THOMAS, dissenting.

I would affirm the judgment below because "I continue to believe that the Constitution does not constrain the size of punitive damages awards." Cooper Industries, Inc. v. Leatherman Tool Group, Inc., 532 U.S. 424, 443, 121 S.Ct. 1678, 149 L.Ed.2d 674 (2001) (THOMAS, J., concurring) * * *.

JUSTICE GINSBURG, dissenting.

* * *

* * * Neither the amount of the award nor the trial record * * * justifies this Court's substitution of its judgment for that of Utah's competent decisionmakers. In this regard, I count it significant that, on the key criterion "reprehensibility," there is a good deal more to the story than the Court's abbreviated account tells.

Ample evidence allowed the jury to find that State Farm's treatment of the Campbells typified its "Performance, Planning and Review" (PP & R) program; implemented by top management in 1979, the program had "the explicit objective of using the claims-adjustment process as a profit center." * * * "[T]he Campbells presented considerable evidence," the trial court noted, documenting "that the PP & R program ... has functioned, and continues to function, as an unlawful scheme ... to deny benefits owed consumers by paying out less than fair value in order to meet preset, arbitrary payout targets designed to enhance corporate profits." * * * That policy, the trial court observed, was encompassing in scope; it "applied equally to the handling of both third-party and first-party claims." * * *

Evidence the jury could credit demonstrated that the PP & R program regularly and adversely affected Utah residents. Ray Summers, "the adjuster who handled the Campbell case and who was a State Farm employee in Utah for almost twenty years," described several methods used by State Farm to deny claimants fair benefits, for example, "falsifying or withholding of evidence in claim files." * * * A common tactic, Summers recounted, was to "unjustly attac[k] the character, reputation and credibility of a claimant and mak[e] notations to that effect in the claim file to create prejudice in the event the claim ever came before a jury." * * * State Farm manager Bob Noxon, Summers testified, resorted to a tactic of this order in the Campbell case when he "instruct[ed] Summers to write in the file that Todd Ospital (who was killed in the accident) was speeding because he was on his way to see a pregnant girlfriend." * * * In truth, "[t]here was no pregnant girlfriend." * * * Expert testimony noted by the trial court described these tactics as "completely improper." * * *

* * *

I remain of the view that this Court has no warrant to reform state law governing awards of punitive damages. *Gore,* 517 U.S., at 607, 116 S.Ct. 1589 (GINSBURG, J., dissenting). Even if I were prepared to accept the flexible guides prescribed in *Gore,* I would not join the Court's swift conversion of those guides into instructions that begin to resemble marching orders. For the reasons stated, I would leave the judgment of the Utah Supreme Court undisturbed.

NOTES

1. On remand, the Supreme Court of Utah "recalculated" the punitive damages award and "reduced the jury's award to $9,018,780.75 in punitive damages, a figure nine times the amount of compensatory and special damages awarded to the Campbells." 98 P.3d 409 (Utah 2004), *cert. denied,* 125 S.Ct. 114 (2004).

2. Several states have enacted "tort reform" legislation capping the amount of punitive damages recoverable or dividing a punitive damages award between the plaintiff and the state. Victor Schwartz, Mark A. Behrens, Cary Silverman, *I'll Take That: Legal and Public Policy Problems Raised by Statutes that Require Punitive Damages Awards to be Shared with the State,*

68 Mo. L. Rev. 525 (2003); Nitin Sud, *Punitive Damages: Achieving Fairness and Consistency After* State Farm v. Campbell, 72 Def. Couns. J. 67 (2005) (summarizing punitive damages legislation in twenty-five states). Judges also have begun to reform the law of punitive damages. For example, in Dardinger v. Anthem Blue Cross & Blue Shield, 98 Ohio St.3d 77, 781 N.E.2d 121 (2002), the jury found in a wrongful death action that the defendant had denied health care benefits "in bad faith" to the wife of the plaintiff after she had been diagnosed with brain cancer. The jury awarded compensatory damages in the amounts of $1,350 on the breach of contract claim and $2.5 million on the bad-faith claim. It awarded $49 million in punitive damages on the bad-faith claim. The appellate court imposed a remittitur of $19 million so that the final punitive damages award was $30 million. The court said:

> [A] punitive damages award is about the defendant's actions. "The purpose of punitive damages is not to compensate a plaintiff but to punish the guilty, deter future misconduct, and to demonstrate society's disapproval." Davis v. Wal–Mart Stores, Inc. (2001), 93 Ohio St.3d 488, 493, 756 N.E.2d 657 (Sweeney, J., concurring in part and dissenting in part). At the punitive-damages level, it is the societal element that is most important. The plaintiff remains a party, but the de facto party is our society, and the jury is determining whether and to what extent we as a society should punish the defendant.
>
> There is a philosophical void between the reasons we award punitive damages and how the damages are distributed. The community makes the statement, while the plaintiff reaps the monetary award. Numerous states have formalized through legislation a mechanical means to divide a punitive damages award between the plaintiff and the state. In some states, the state's portion goes to a special fund, in others, to the general fund. Annotation (1993) 16 ALR 5th 129. In Ohio, punitive damages are an outgrowth of the common law. * * * Therefore, Ohio's courts have a central role to play in the distribution of punitive damages. Punitive damages awards should not be subject to bright-line division, but instead should be considered on a case-by-case basis, with those awards making the most significant societal statements being the most likely candidates for alternative distribution.
>
> Clearly, we do not want to dissuade plaintiffs from moving forward with important societal undertakings. The distribution of the jury's award must recognize the effort the plaintiff undertook in bringing about the award and the important role a plaintiff plays in bringing about necessary changes that society agrees need to be made. Plaintiffs themselves might get involved in how the award is distributed. * * *
>
> In this case, should Dardinger accept this court's remittitur, the jury's punitive damages award would be reduced to $30 million. To that $30 million would be added statutory postjudgment interest. See R.C. 1343.03(A). From that corpus, $10 million should go to Dardinger. From the remainder should be drawn an amount for the payment of litigation fees, including attorney fees. The amount of attorney fees should be determined by the contract between Dardinger and his attorney, and should be based upon the amount originally in the corpus, $30 million

plus statutory interest. The final net amount remaining after the prescribed payments should go to a place that will achieve a societal good, a good that can rationally offset the harm done by the defendants in this case. Due to the societal stake in the punitive damages award, we find it most appropriate that it go to a state institution. In this case we order that the corpus of the punitive damages award go to a cancer research fund, to be called the Esther Dardinger Fund, at the James Cancer Hospital and Solove Research Institute at the Ohio State University.

Id. at 103–06, 781 N.E.2d at 145–46. *See generally* Catherine M. Sharkey, *Punitive Damages as Societal Damages*, 113 Yale L.J. 347 (2003).

3. For scholarly commentary on *State Farm*, see Steven L. Chaneson & John Y. Gotanda, *The Foggy Road for Evaluating Punitive Damages: Lifting the Haze from the BMW/State Farm Guideposts*, 37 U. Mich. J.L. Reform 441 (2004); Erwin Chemerinsky, *The Constitution and Punishment*, 56 Stan. L. Rev. 1049 (2004); Anthony J. Franze & Sheila B. Scheurman, *Instructing Juries on Punitive Damages: Due Proces Revisited after State Farm*, 6 U. Pa. J. Const. L. 423 (2004); John C.P. Goldberg, *Tort Law for Federalists (and the Rest of Us): Private Law in Disguise*, 28 Harv. J.L. & Pub. Pol'y 3 (2004); Laura J. Hines, *Due Process Limitations on Punitive Damages: Why State Farm Won't Be the Last Word*, 37 Akron L. Rev. 779 (2004); Pamela S. Karlen, *"Pricking the Lines": The Due Process Clause, Punitive Damages, and Criminal Punishment*, 88 Minn. L. Rev. 880 (2004); Dan Markel, *Retributive Damages: A Theory of Punitive Damages as Intermediate Sanction*, 94 Cornell L. Rev. 239 (2009); Dan Markel, *How Should Punitive Damages Work?*, 157 U. Pa. L. Rev. 1383 (2009); Caprice L. Roberts, *Ratios, (Ir)rationality, & Civil Rights Punitive Awards*, 39 Akron L. Rev. 1019 (2006); Anthony J. Sebok, *Punitive Damages: From Myth to Theory*, 92 Iowa L. Rev. 957 (2007); Benjamin C. Zipursky, *A Theory of Punitive Damages*, 84 Tex. L. Rev. 105 (2005). For an excellent overview of both the common law and the constitutional law of punitive damages, see Doug Rendleman, *Common Law Punitive Damages: Something for Everyone?*, 7 U. St. Thomas L. Rev. 1 (2010).

4. Of the more than 80 cases applying *State Farm* in the first year after that case was handed down, more than 80% of the cases limited the punitive-to-compensatory ratio to 9–to–1 or less, and 45% of the cases approved ratios of 3–to–1 or less. Samuel A. Thumma, *Post–'Campbell' Cases*, Nat'l L.J., June 7, 2004, at 13.

5. In *TXO*, the Supreme Court, in dictum, discussed the question of whether it is constitutionally permissible to award substantial punitive damages when only a small amount of actual damages has been awarded:

> For instance, a man wildly fires a gun into a crowd. By sheer chance, no one is injured and the only damage is to a $10 pair of glasses. A jury could reasonably find only $10 in compensatory damages, but thousands of dollars in punitive damages to teach a duty of care. We would allow a jury to impose substantial punitive damages in order to deter future bad acts.

TXO Production Corp. v. Alliance Resources Corp., 509 U.S. 443, 459–60, 113 S.Ct. 2711, 2721, 125 L.Ed.2d 366 (1993). After *State Farm*, how do you think the Supreme Court will rule on such a case?

MATHIAS v. ACCOR ECONOMY LODGING, INC.

United States Court of Appeals, Seventh Circuit, 2003.
347 F.3d 672.

Before POSNER, KANNE, and EVANS, CIRCUIT JUDGES.

POSNER, CIRCUIT JUDGE.

The plaintiffs brought this diversity suit governed by Illinois law against affiliated entities (which the parties treat as a single entity, as shall we) that own and operate the "Motel 6" chain of hotels and motels. One of these hotels (now a "Red Roof Inn," though still owned by the defendant) is in downtown Chicago. The plaintiffs, a brother and sister, were guests there and were bitten by bedbugs, which are making a comeback in the U.S. as a consequence of more conservative use of pesticides. * * * The plaintiffs claim that in allowing guests to be attacked by bedbugs in a motel that charges upwards of $100 a day for a room and would not like to be mistaken for a flophouse, the defendant was guilty of "willful and wanton conduct" and thus under Illinois law is liable for punitive as well as compensatory damages. * * * The jury agreed and awarded each plaintiff $186,000 in punitive damages though only $5,000 in compensatory damages. * * *

The defendant argues that at worst it is guilty of simple negligence, and if this is right the plaintiffs were not entitled by Illinois law to any award of punitive damages. It also complains that the award was excessive—indeed that any award in excess of $20,000 to each plaintiff would deprive the defendant of its property without due process of law. The first complaint has no possible merit, as the evidence of gross negligence, indeed of recklessness in the strong sense of an unjustifiable failure to avoid a *known* risk, * * * was amply shown. In 1998, EcoLab, the extermination service that the motel used, discovered bedbugs in several rooms in the motel and recommended that it be hired to spray every room, for which it would charge the motel only $500; the motel refused. The next year, bedbugs were again discovered in a room but EcoLab was asked to spray just that room. The motel tried to negotiate "a building sweep [by EcoLab] free of charge," but, not surprisingly, the negotiation failed. By the spring of 2000, the motel's manager "started noticing that there were refunds being given by my desk clerks and reports coming back from the guests that there were ticks in the rooms and bugs in the rooms that were biting." She looked in some of the rooms and discovered bedbugs. The defendant asks us to disregard her testimony as that of a disgruntled ex-employee, but of course her credibility was for the jury, not the defendant, to determine.

Further incidents of guests being bitten by insects and demanding and receiving refunds led the manager to recommend to her superior in the company that the motel be closed while every room was sprayed, but this was refused. This superior, a district manager, was a management-level employee of the defendant, and his knowledge of the risk and failure to take effective steps either to eliminate it or to warn the motel's guests are imputed to his employer for purposes of determining whether the employer should be liable for punitive damages. * * * The employer's liability for compensatory damages is of course automatic on the basis of the principle of respondeat superior, since the district manager was acting within the scope of his employment.

The infestation continued and began to reach farcical proportions, as when a guest, after complaining of having been bitten repeatedly by insects while asleep in his room in the hotel, was moved to another room only to discover insects there; and within 18 minutes of being moved to a third room he discovered insects in that room as well and had to be moved still again. (Odd that at that point he didn't flee the motel.) By July, the motel's management was acknowledging to EcoLab that there was a "major problem with bed bugs" and that all that was being done about it was "chasing them from room to room." Desk clerks were instructed to call the "bedbugs" "ticks," apparently on the theory that customers would be less alarmed, though in fact ticks are more dangerous than bedbugs because they spread Lyme Disease and Rocky Mountain Spotted Fever. Rooms that the motel had placed on "Do not rent, bugs in room" status nevertheless were rented.

It was in November that the plaintiffs checked into the motel. They were given Room 504, even though the motel had classified the room as "DO NOT RENT UNTIL TREATED," and it had not been treated. Indeed, that night 190 of the hotel's 191 rooms were occupied, even though a number of them had been placed on the same don't-rent status as Room 504. * * *

Although bedbug bites are not as serious as the bites of some other insects, they are painful and unsightly. Motel 6 could not have rented any rooms at the prices it charged had it informed guests that the risk of being bitten by bedbugs was appreciable. Its failure either to warn guests or to take effective measures to eliminate the bedbugs amounted to fraud * * *. There was, in short, sufficient evidence of "willful and wanton conduct" within the meaning that the Illinois courts assign to the term to permit an award of punitive damages in this case.

But in what amount? In arguing that $20,000 was the maximum amount of punitive damages that a jury could constitutionally have awarded each plaintiff, the defendant points to the U.S. Supreme Court's recent statement that "few awards [of punitive damages] exceeding a single-digit ratio between punitive and compensatory damages, to a significant degree, will satisfy due process." State Farm Mutual Automobile Ins. Co. v. Campbell, 538 U.S. 408, 123 S.Ct. 1513, 1524, 155 L.Ed.2d 585 (2003). The Court went on to suggest that "four times the amount of compensatory damages might be close to the line of constitutional impropriety." *Id.* * * * Hence the defendant's proposed ceiling in this case of $20,000, four times the compensatory damages awarded to each plaintiff.

The ratio of punitive to compensatory damages determined by the jury was, in contrast, 37.2 to 1.

The Supreme Court did not, however, lay down a 4–to–1 or single-digit-ratio rule—it said merely that "there is a presumption against an award that has a 145–to–1 ratio * * *." We must consider why punitive damages are awarded and why the Court has decided that due process requires that such awards be limited. The second question is easier to answer than the first. The term "punitive damages" implies punishment, and a standard principle of penal theory is that "the punishment should fit the crime" in the sense of being proportional to the wrongfulness of the defendant's action, though the principle is modified when the probability of detection is very low (a familiar example is the heavy fines for littering) or the crime is potentially lucrative (as in the case of trafficking in illegal drugs). Hence, with these qualifications, which in fact will figure in our analysis of this case, punitive damages should be proportional to the wrongfulness of the defendant's actions.

* * *

England's common law courts first confirmed their authority to award punitive damages in the eighteenth century, *see* Dorsey D. Ellis, Jr., *"Fairness and Efficiency in the Law of Punitive Damages,"* 56 S. Cal. L.Rev. 1, 12–20 (1982), at a time when the institutional structure of criminal law enforcement was primitive and it made sense to leave certain minor crimes to be dealt with by the civil law. And still today one function of punitive-damages awards is to relieve the pressures on an overloaded system of criminal justice by providing a civil alternative to criminal prosecution of minor crimes. An example is deliberately spitting in a person's face, a criminal assault but because minor readily deterrable by the levying of what amounts to a civil fine through a suit for damages for the tort of battery. Compensatory damages would not do the trick in such a case, and this for three reasons: because they are difficult to determine in the case of acts that inflict largely dignitary harms; because in the spitting case they would be too slight to give the victim an incentive to sue, and he might decide instead to respond with violence—and an age-old purpose of the law of torts is to provide a substitute for violent retaliation against wrongful injury—and because to limit the plaintiff to compensatory damages would enable the defendant to commit the offensive act with impunity provided that he was willing to pay, and again there would be a danger that his act would incite a breach of the peace by his victim.

When punitive damages are sought for billion-dollar oil spills and other huge economic injuries, the considerations that we have just canvassed fade. As the Court emphasized in *Campbell*, the fact that the plaintiffs in that case had been awarded very substantial compensatory damages—$1 million for a dispute over insurance coverage—greatly reduced the need for giving them a huge award of punitive damages ($145 million) as well in order to provide an effective remedy. Our case is closer to the spitting case. The defendant's behavior was outrageous but the compensable harm done was slight and at the same time difficult to quantify because a large element of it was emotional. And the defendant may well have profited from its misconduct because by concealing the infestation it was able to keep renting rooms. * * * The award of punitive damages in this case thus serves the additional purpose of limiting the defendant's ability to profit from its fraud by escaping detection and (private) prosecution. If a tortfeasor is "caught" only half the time he commits torts, then when he is caught he should be punished twice as heavily in order to make up for the times he gets away.

Finally, if the total stakes in the case were capped at $50,000 (2 x [$5,000 + $20,000]), the plaintiffs might well have had difficulty financing this lawsuit. It is here that the defendant's aggregate net worth of $1.6 billion becomes relevant. A defendant's wealth is not a sufficient basis for awarding punitive damages. State Farm Mutual Automobile Ins. Co. v. Campbell, *supra*, 123 S.Ct. at 1525 * * *. That would be discriminatory and would violate the rule of law * * * by making punishment depend on status rather than conduct. Where wealth in the sense of resources enters is in enabling the defendant to mount an extremely aggressive defense against suits such as this and by doing so to make litigating against it very costly, which in turn may make it difficult for the plaintiffs to find a lawyer willing to handle their case, involving as it does only modest stakes, for the usual 33–40 percent contingent fee.

All things considered, we cannot say that the award of punitive damages was excessive, albeit the precise number chosen by the jury was arbitrary. It is probably not a coincidence that $5,000 + $186,000 = $191,000/191 = $1,000: i.e., $1,000 per room in the hotel. * * * We can take judicial notice that deliberate exposure of hotel guests to the health risks created by insect infestations exposes the hotel's owner to sanctions under Illinois and Chicago law that in the aggregate are comparable in severity to the punitive damage award in this case.

* * *

Affirmed.

PHILIP MORRIS USA v. WILLIAMS

Supreme Court of the United States, 2007.
549 U.S. 346, 127 S. Ct. 1057, 166 L.Ed.2d 940.

JUSTICE BREYER delivered the opinion of the Court.

The question we address today concerns a large state-court punitive damages award. We are asked whether the Constitution's Due Process Clause permits a jury to base that award in part upon its desire to *punish* the defendant for harming persons who are not before the court (*e.g.,* victims whom the parties do not represent). We hold that such an award would amount to a taking of "property" from the defendant without due process.

I

This lawsuit arises out of the death of Jesse Williams, a heavy cigarette smoker. Respondent, Williams' widow, represents his estate in this state lawsuit for negligence and deceit against Philip Morris, the manufacturer of Marlboro, the brand that Williams favored. A jury found that Williams' death was caused by smoking; that Williams smoked in significant part because he thought it was safe to do so; and that Philip Morris knowingly and falsely led him to believe that this was so. The jury ultimately found that Philip Morris was negligent (as was Williams) and that Philip Morris had engaged in deceit. In respect to deceit, the claim at issue here, it awarded compensatory damages of about $821,000 (about $21,000 economic and $800,000 noneconomic) along with $79.5 million in punitive damages.

The trial judge subsequently found the $79.5 million punitive damages award "excessive," * * * and reduced it to $32 million. Both sides appealed. The Oregon Court of Appeals rejected Philip Morris' arguments and restored the $79.5 million jury award. Subsequently, Philip Morris sought review in the Oregon Supreme Court (which denied review) and then here. We remanded the case in light of State Farm Mut. Automobile Ins. Co. v. Campbell, 538 U.S. 408, 123 S.Ct. 1513, 155 L.Ed.2d 585 (2003). 540 U.S. 801, 124 S.Ct. 56, 157 L.Ed.2d 12 (2003). The Oregon Court of Appeals adhered to its original views. And Philip Morris sought, and this time obtained, review in the Oregon Supreme Court.

Philip Morris then made two arguments relevant here. First, it said that the trial court should have accepted, but did not accept, a proposed "punitive damages" instruction that specified the jury could not seek to punish Philip Morris for injury to other persons not before the court. In particular, Philip Morris pointed out that the plaintiff's attorney had told the jury to "think about how many other Jesse Williams in the last 40 years in the State of Oregon there have been.... In Oregon, how many people do we see outside, driving home ... smoking cigarettes? ... [C]igarettes ... are going to kill ten [of every hundred]. [And] the market share of Marlboros [i.e., Philip Morris] is one-third [i.e., one of every three killed]." * * * In light of this argument, Philip Morris asked the trial court to tell the jury that "you may consider the extent of harm suffered by others in determining what [the] reasonable relationship is" between any punitive award and "the harm caused to Jesse Williams" by Philip Morris' misconduct, "[but] you are not to punish the defendant for the impact of its alleged misconduct on other persons, who may bring lawsuits of their own in which other juries can resolve their claims...." * * * The judge rejected this proposal and instead told the jury that "[p]unitive damages are awarded against a defendant to punish misconduct and to deter misconduct," and "are not intended to compensate the plaintiff or anyone else for damages caused by the defendant's conduct." * * * In Philip Morris' view, the result was a significant likelihood that a portion of the $79.5 million award represented punishment for its having harmed others, a punishment that the Due Process Clause would here forbid.

Second, Philip Morris pointed to the roughly 100–to–1 ratio the $79.5 million punitive damages award bears to $821,000 in compensatory damages. * * * Philip Morris claimed that, in light of [*State Farm*], the punitive award was "grossly excessive." * * *

The Oregon Supreme Court rejected these and other Philip Morris arguments. In particular, it rejected Philip Morris' claim that the Constitution prohibits a state jury "from using punitive damages to punish a defendant for harm to nonparties." 340 Or. 35, 51–52, 127 P.3d 1165, 1175 (2006). And in light of Philip Morris' reprehensible conduct, it found that the $79.5 million award was not "grossly excessive."

Philip Morris then sought certiorari. It asked us to consider, among other things, (1) its claim that Oregon had unconstitutionally permitted it to be punished for harming nonparty victims; and (2) whether Oregon had in effect disregarded "the constitutional requirement that punitive damages be reasonably related to the plaintiff's harm." * * * We granted certiorari limited to these two questions.

For reasons we shall set forth, we consider only the first of these questions. * * *

II

This Court has long made clear that "[p]unitive damages may properly be imposed to further a State's legitimate interests in punishing unlawful conduct and deterring its repetition." * * * At the same time, we have emphasized the need to avoid an arbitrary determination of an award's amount. * * *

For these and similar reasons, this Court has found that the Constitution imposes certain limits, in respect both to procedures for awarding punitive damages and to amounts forbidden as "grossly excessive." * * * Because we shall not decide whether the award here at issue is "grossly excessive," we need now only consider the Constitution's procedural limitations.

III

In our view, the Constitution's Due Process Clause forbids a State to use a punitive damages award to punish a defendant for injury that it inflicts upon nonparties or those whom they directly represent, *i.e.,* injury that it inflicts upon those who are, essentially, strangers to the litigation. For one thing, the Due Process Clause prohibits a State from punishing an individual without first providing that individual with "an opportunity to present every available defense." * * * Yet a defendant threatened with punishment for injuring a nonparty victim has no opportunity to defend against the charge, by showing, for example in a case such as this, that the other victim was not entitled to damages because he or she knew that smoking was dangerous or did not rely upon the defendant's statements to the contrary.

For another, to permit punishment for injuring a nonparty victim would add a near standardless dimension to the punitive damages equation. How many such victims are there? How seriously were they injured? Under what circumstances did injury occur? The trial will not likely answer such questions as to nonparty victims. The jury will be left to speculate. * * *

Finally, we can find no authority supporting the use of punitive damages awards for the purpose of punishing a defendant for harming others. We have said that it may be appropriate to consider the reasonableness of a punitive damages award in light of the *potential* harm the defendant's conduct could have caused. But we have made clear that the potential harm at issue was harm potentially caused *the plaintiff.* * * *

Respondent argues that she is free to show harm to other victims because it is relevant to a different part of the punitive damages constitutional equation, namely, reprehensibility. That is to say, harm to others shows more reprehensible conduct. Philip Morris, in turn, does not deny that a plaintiff may show harm to others in order to demonstrate reprehensibility. Nor do we. Evidence of actual harm to nonparties can help to show that the conduct that harmed the plaintiff also posed a substantial risk of harm to the general public, and so was particularly reprehensible * * *. Yet for the reasons given above, a jury may not go further than this and use a punitive damages verdict to punish a defendant directly on account of harms it is alleged to have visited on nonparties.

Given the risks of unfairness that we have mentioned, it is constitutionally important for a court to provide assurance that the jury will ask the right question, not the wrong one. * * * We therefore conclude that the Due Process Clause requires States to provide assurance that juries are not asking the wrong question, *i.e.,* seeking, not simply to determine reprehensibility, but also to punish for harm caused strangers.

IV

* * *

The instruction that Philip Morris said the trial court should have given distinguishes between using harm to others as part of the "reasonable relationship" equation (which it would allow) and using it directly as a basis for punishment. The instruction asked the trial court to tell the jury that "you *may* consider the extent of harm suffered by others *in determining what [the] reasonable relationship is*" between Philip Morris' punishable misconduct and harm caused to Jesse Williams, *"[but] you are not to punish the defendant for the impact of its alleged misconduct on other persons, who may bring lawsuits of their own* in which other juries can resolve their claims...." (emphasis added). And as the Oregon Supreme Court explicitly recognized, Philip Morris argued that the Constitution "prohibits the state, acting through a civil jury, from using punitive damages to punish a defendant for harm to nonparties." * * *

The court rejected that claim. In doing so, it pointed out (1) that this Court in *State Farm* had held only that a jury could not base its award upon "dissimilar" acts of a defendant. * * * It added (2) that "[i]f a jury cannot punish for the conduct, then it is difficult to see why it may consider it at all." * * * And it stated (3) that "[i]t is unclear to us how a jury could 'consider' harm to others, yet withhold that consideration from the punishment calculus." * * *

The Oregon court's first statement is correct. We did not previously hold explicitly that a jury may not punish for the harm caused others. But we do so hold now. We do not agree with the Oregon court's second statement. We have explained why we believe the Due Process Clause prohibits a State's inflicting punishment for harm caused strangers to the litigation. At the same time we recognize that conduct that risks harm to many is likely more reprehensible than conduct that risks harm to only a few. * * *

The Oregon court's third statement raises a practical problem. How can we know whether a jury, in taking account of harm caused others under the rubric of reprehensibility, also seeks to *punish* the defendant for having caused injury to others? Our answer is that state courts cannot authorize procedures that create an unreasonable and unnecessary risk of any such confusion occurring. In particular, we believe that where the risk of that misunderstanding is a significant one—because, for instance, of the sort of evidence that was introduced at trial or the kinds of argument the plaintiff made to the jury—a court, upon request, must protect against that risk. Although the States have some flexibility to determine what *kind* of procedures they will implement, federal constitutional law obligates them to provide *some* form of protection in appropriate cases.

V

As the preceding discussion makes clear, we believe that the Oregon Supreme Court applied the wrong constitutional standard when considering Philip Morris' appeal. We remand this case so that the Oregon Supreme Court can apply the standard we have set forth. Because the application of this standard may lead to the need for a new trial, or a change in the level of the punitive damages award, we shall not consider whether the award is constitutionally "grossly excessive." We vacate the Oregon Supreme Court's judgment and remand the case for further proceedings not inconsistent with this opinion.

JUSTICE STEVENS, dissenting.

The Due Process Clause of the Fourteenth Amendment imposes both substantive and procedural constraints on the power of the States to impose punitive damages on tortfeasors. * * * I remain firmly convinced that the cases announcing those constraints were correctly decided. In my view the Oregon Supreme Court faithfully applied the reasoning in those opinions to the egregious facts disclosed by this record. I agree with

Justice Ginsburg's explanation of why no procedural error even arguably justifying reversal occurred at the trial in this case. * * *

Of greater importance to me, however, is the Court's imposition of a novel limit on the State's power to impose punishment in civil litigation. Unlike the Court, I see no reason why an interest in punishing a wrongdoer "for harming persons who are not before the court" * * * should not be taken into consideration when assessing the appropriate sanction for reprehensible conduct.

Whereas compensatory damages are measured by the harm the defendant has caused the plaintiff, punitive damages are a sanction for the public harm the defendant's conduct has caused or threatened. * * *

In the case before us, evidence attesting to the possible harm the defendant's extensive deceitful conduct caused other Oregonians was properly presented to the jury. No evidence was offered to establish an appropriate measure of damages to compensate such third parties for their injuries, and no one argued that the punitive damages award would serve any such purpose. To award compensatory damages to remedy such third-party harm might well constitute a taking of property from the defendant without due process * * *. But a punitive damages award, instead of serving a compensatory purpose, serves the entirely different purposes of retribution and deterrence that underlie every criminal sanction. * * * This justification for punitive damages has even greater salience when, as in this case, see Ore.Rev.Stat. § 31.735(1) (2003), the award is payable in whole or in part to the State rather than to the private litigant.

While apparently recognizing the novelty of its holding, * * * the majority relies on a distinction between taking third-party harm into account in order to assess the reprehensibility of the defendant's conduct—which is permitted—and doing so in order to punish the defendant "directly"—which is forbidden. * * * This nuance eludes me. When a jury increases a punitive damages award because injuries to third parties enhanced the reprehensibility of the defendant's conduct, the jury is by definition punishing the defendant—directly—for third-party harm. A murderer who kills his victim by throwing a bomb that injures dozens of bystanders should be punished more severely than one who harms no one other than his intended victim. Similarly, there is no reason why the measure of the appropriate punishment for engaging in a campaign of deceit in distributing a poisonous and addictive substance to thousands of cigarette smokers statewide should not include consideration of the harm to those "bystanders" as well as the harm to the individual plaintiff. The Court endorses a contrary conclusion without providing us with any reasoned justification.

* * *

Essentially for the reasons stated in the opinion of the Supreme Court of Oregon, I would affirm its judgment.

JUSTICE THOMAS, dissenting.

I join Justice Ginsburg's dissent in full. I write separately to reiterate my view that " 'the Constitution does not constrain the size of punitive damages awards.' " * * *

JUSTICE GINSBURG, with whom JUSTICE SCALIA and JUSTICE THOMAS join, dissenting.

The purpose of punitive damages, it can hardly be denied, is not to compensate, but to punish. Punish for what? Not for harm actually caused "strangers to the litigation," * * * the Court states, but for the *reprehensibility* of defendant's conduct * * *.

The right question regarding reprehensibility, the Court acknowledges, * * * would train on "the harm that Philip Morris was prepared to inflict on the smoking public at large." * * * The Court identifies no evidence introduced and no charge delivered inconsistent with that inquiry.

The Court's order vacating the Oregon Supreme Court's judgment is all the more inexplicable considering that Philip Morris did not preserve any objection to the charges in fact delivered to the jury, to the evidence introduced at trial, or to opposing counsel's argument. The sole objection Philip Morris preserved was to the trial court's refusal to give defendant's requested charge number 34. * * * The proposed instruction [No. 34] read in pertinent part:

> If you determine that some amount of punitive damages should be imposed on the defendant, it will then be your task to set an amount that is appropriate. This should be such amount as you believe is necessary to achieve the objectives of deterrence and punishment. While there is no set formula to be applied in reaching an appropriate amount, I will now advise you of some of the factors that you may wish to consider in this connection.

> (1) The size of any punishment should bear a reasonable relationship to the harm caused to Jesse Williams by the defendant's punishable misconduct. Although you may consider the extent of harm suffered by others in determining what that reasonable relationship is, you are not to punish the defendant for the impact of its alleged misconduct on other persons, who may bring lawsuits of their own in which other juries can resolve their claims and award punitive damages for those harms, as such other juries see fit.

> . . . .

> (2) The size of the punishment may appropriately reflect the degree of reprehensibility of the defendant's conduct—that is, how far the defendant has departed from accepted societal norms of conduct. * * *

Under that charge, just what use could the jury properly make of "the extent of harm suffered by others"? The answer slips from my grasp. A judge seeking to enlighten rather than confuse surely would resist delivering the requested charge.

* * *

For the reasons stated, and in light of the abundant evidence of "the potential harm [Philip Morris'] conduct could have caused," * * * I would affirm the decision of the Oregon Supreme Court.

NOTES

1.   On remand, the Oregon Supreme Court ruled that there was an "independent and adequate state ground" for affirming the trial court judge's refusal to give the proposed jury instruction. 344 Or. 45, 176 P.3d 1255 (2008). More specifically, the Oregon Supreme Court found two errors in parts of the 3–page proposed jury instruction No. 34 that had not been considered by the United States Supreme Court. Under Oregon law, an appellate court will not reverse a trial court's refusal to give a proposed jury instruction unless the instruction is "clear and correct in all respects." *Id.* at 56, 176 P.3d at 1261. Therefore the Oregon Supreme Court affirmed the decision of the Court of Appeals (awarding $79.5 million in punitive damages to the plaintiff) without reaching the federal question. The United States Supreme Court granted certiorari to consider the question of whether the punitive damages judgment was "unconstitutionally excessive," 128 S.Ct. 2904 (2008), but after the oral argument (during which Philip Morris conceded that the Oregon Supreme Court had acted in "good faith"), the Court ruled that certiorari had been improvidently granted. 129 S.Ct. 1436 (2009).

2.   In *Philip Morris v. Williams*, did the Court make a turn towards procedural due process and away from substantive due process?

3.   For scholarly commentary on *Philip Morris v. Williams*, see Thomas B. Colby, *Clearing the Smoke from* Phillip Morris v. Williams: *The Past, Present, and Future of Punitive Damages*, 118 Yale L.J. 392 (2008); Mark A. Geistfeld, *Punitive Damages, Retribution, and Due Process*, 81 S. Cal. L. Rev. 263 (2008); Sheila B. Scheuerman & Anthony J. Franze, *Instructing Juries on Punitive Damages: Due Process After* Philip Morris v. Williams, 10 U. Pa. J. Const. L. 1147 (2008); Catherine M. Sharkey, *Federal Incursions and State Defiance: Punitive Damages in the Wake of* Philip Morris v. Williams, 46 Willamette L. Rev. 449 (2010).

4.   For scholarly commentary on punitive damages and class actions, see Elizabeth J. Cabraser & Robert J. Nelson, *Class Action Treatment of Punitive Damages Issues After* Philip Morris v. Williams: *We Can Get There From Here*, 2 Charleston L. Rev. 407 (2008); Francis E. McGovern, *Punitive Damages and Class Actions*, 70 La. L. Rev. 435 (2010); Sheila B. Scheuerman, *Two Worlds Collide: How the Supreme Court's Recent Punitive Damages Decisions Affect Class Actions*, 60 Baylor L. Rev. 880 (2008).

EXXON SHIPPING COMPANY v. BAKER

Supreme Court of the United States, 2008.
128 S. Ct. 2605.

JUSTICE SOUTER delivered the opinion of the Court:

* * *

I

On March 24, 1989, the supertanker *Exxon Valdez* grounded on Bligh Reef off the Alaskan coast, fracturing its hull and spilling millions of gallons of crude oil into Prince William Sound. The owner, petitioner Exxon Shipping Co. * * * and its owner, petitioner Exxon Mobil Corp. (collectively, Exxon), have settled state and federal claims for environmental damage, with payments exceeding $1 billion, and this action by respondent Baker and others * * * was brought for economic losses to individuals dependent on Prince William Sound for their livelihoods.

A

The tanker was over 900 feet long and was used by Exxon to carry crude oil from the end of the Trans–Alaska Pipeline in Valdez, Alaska, to the lower 48 States. On the night of the spill it was carrying 53 million gallons of crude oil, or over a million barrels. Its captain was one Joseph Hazelwood, who had completed a 28–day alcohol treatment program while employed by Exxon, as his superiors knew, but dropped out of a prescribed follow-up program and stopped going to Alcoholics Anonymous meetings. According to the District Court, "[t]here was evidence presented to the jury that after Hazelwood was released from [residential treatment], he drank in bars, parking lots, apartments, airports, airplanes, restaurants, hotels, at various ports, and aboard Exxon tankers." * * * The jury also heard contested testimony that Hazelwood drank with Exxon officials and that members of the Exxon management knew of his relapse. * * * Although Exxon had a clear policy prohibiting employees from serving onboard within four hours of consuming alcohol, * * * Exxon presented no evidence that it monitored Hazelwood after his return to duty or considered giving him a shoreside assignment * * *. Witnesses testified that before the *Valdez* left port on the night of the disaster, Hazelwood downed at least five double vodkas in the waterfront bars of Valdez, an intake of about 15 ounces of 80–proof alcohol, enough "that a non-alcoholic would have passed out." * * *

The ship sailed at 9:12 p.m. on March 23, 1989, guided by a state-licensed pilot for the first leg out * * *. At 11:20 p.m., Hazelwood took active control and, owing to poor conditions in the outbound shipping lane, * * * [moved the Valdez] east across the inbound lane to a less icy path. * * * The * * * move put it in the path of an underwater reef off Bligh Island, thus requiring a turn back west into the shipping lane around Busby Light, north of the reef.

Two minutes before the required turn, however, Hazelwood left the bridge and went down to his cabin in order, he said, to do paperwork. This decision was inexplicable. There was expert testimony that, even if their presence is not strictly necessary, captains simply do not quit the bridge during maneuvers like this, and no paperwork could have justified it. And in fact the evidence was that Hazelwood's presence was required, both because there should have been two officers on the bridge at all times and his departure left only one, and because he was the only person on the entire ship licensed to navigate this part of Prince William Sound. To make matters worse, before going below Hazelwood put the tanker on autopilot, speeding it up, making the turn trickier, and any mistake harder to correct.

As Hazelwood left, he instructed the remaining officer, third mate Joseph Cousins, to move the tanker back into the shipping lane once it came abeam of Busby Light. Cousins, unlicensed to navigate in those waters, was left alone with helmsman Robert Kagan, a nonofficer. For reasons that remain a mystery, they failed to make the turn at Busby Light, and a later emergency maneuver attempted by Cousins came too late. The tanker ran aground on Bligh Reef, tearing the hull open and spilling 11 million gallons of crude oil into Prince William Sound.

After Hazelwood returned to the bridge and reported the grounding to the Coast Guard, he tried but failed to rock the *Valdez* off the reef, a maneuver which could have spilled more oil and caused the ship to founder. The Coast Guard's nearly immediate response included a blood test of Hazelwood (the validity of which Exxon disputes) showing a blood-alcohol level of .061 eleven hours after the spill. * * * Experts testified that to have this much alcohol in his bloodstream so long after the accident, Hazelwood at the time of the spill must have had a blood-alcohol level of around .241, * * * three times the legal limit for driving in most States.

In the aftermath of the disaster, Exxon spent around $2.1 billion in cleanup efforts. * * * Exxon pleaded guilty to violations of the Clean Water Act, the Refuse Act, and the Migratory Bird Treaty Act and agreed to pay a $150 million fine, later reduced to $25 million plus restitution of $100 million. A civil action by the United States and the State of Alaska for environmental harms ended with a consent decree for Exxon to pay at least $900 million toward restoring natural resources, and it paid another $303 million in voluntary settlements with fishermen, property owners, and other private parties.

B

The remaining civil cases were consolidated into this one against Exxon, Hazelwood, and others. The District Court for the District of Alaska divided the plaintiffs seeking compensatory damages into three classes: commercial fishermen, Native Alaskans, and landowners. At Exxon's behest, the court also certified a mandatory class of all plaintiffs seeking punitive damages, whose number topped 32,000. Respondents * * * are members of that class.

For the purposes of the case, Exxon stipulated to its negligence in the *Valdez* disaster and its ensuing liability for compensatory damages. The court designed the trial accordingly: Phase I considered Exxon and Hazelwood's recklessness and thus their potential for punitive liability; Phase II set compensatory damages for commercial fishermen and Native Alaskans [(the landowners settled their compensatory damages claims)]; and Phase III determined the amount of punitive damages for which Hazelwood and Exxon were each liable. * * *

In Phase I, the jury heard extensive testimony about Hazelwood's alcoholism and his conduct on the night of the spill, as well as conflicting testimony about Exxon officials' knowledge of Hazelwood's backslide. At the close of Phase I, the Court instructed the jury in part that

> [a] corporation is responsible for the reckless acts of those employees who are employed in a managerial capacity while acting in the scope of their employment. The reckless act or omission of a managerial officer or employee of a corporation, in the course and scope of the performance of his duties, is held in law to be the reckless act or omission of the corporation. * * *

* * * Exxon did not dispute that Hazelwood was a managerial employee * * * and the jury found both Hazelwood and Exxon reckless and thus potentially liable for punitive damages * * *.

In Phase II the jury awarded $287 million in compensatory damages to the commercial fishermen. After the Court deducted released claims, settlements, and other payments, the balance outstanding was $19,590,257. Meanwhile, most of the Native Alaskan class had settled their compensatory claims for $20 million, and those who opted out of that settlement ultimately settled for a total of around $2.6 million.

In Phase III, the jury heard about Exxon's management's acts and omissions arguably relevant to the spill. * * * At the close of evidence, the court instructed the jurors on the purposes of punitive damages, emphasizing that they were designed not to provide compensatory relief but to punish and deter the defendants. * * * The court charged the jury to consider the reprehensibility of the defendants' conduct, their financial condition, the magnitude of the harm, and any mitigating facts. * * * The jury awarded $5,000 in punitive damages against Hazelwood and $5 billion against Exxon.

On appeal, the Court of Appeals for the Ninth Circuit upheld the Phase I jury instruction on corporate liability for acts of managerial agents under Circuit precedent. See In re Exxon Valdez, 270 F.3d, at 1236 (citing Protectus Alpha Nav. Co. v. North Pacific Grain Growers, Inc., 767 F.2d 1379 (C.A.9 1985)). With respect to the size of the punitive damages award, however, the Circuit remanded twice for adjustments in light of this Court's due process cases before ultimately itself remitting the award to $2.5 billion. See 270 F.3d, at 1246–1247, 472 F.3d 600, 601, 625 (2006) *(per curiam),* and 490 F.3d 1066, 1068 (2007).

We granted certiorari to consider whether maritime law allows corporate liability for punitive damages on the basis of the acts of managerial agents, whether the Clean Water Act (CWA), 86 Stat. 816, 33 U.S.C. § 1251 *et seq.* (2000 ed. and Supp. V), forecloses the award of punitive damages in maritime spill cases, and whether the punitive damages awarded against Exxon in this case were excessive as a matter of maritime common law. * * *

II

On the first question, Exxon says that it was error to instruct the jury [under maritime law] that a corporation "is responsible for the reckless acts of . . . employees . . . in a managerial capacity while acting in the scope of their employment." * * * The Courts of Appeals have split on this issue * * *. [Justice Souter observed that some courts have held that a corporation may never be vicariously liable for punitive damages, while other courts have recognized corporate liability in punitive damages for reckless acts of managerial employees, which is consistent with land-based common law.]

* * *

The Court is equally divided on this question * * *. We therefore leave the Ninth Circuit's opinion undisturbed in this respect, though it should go without saying that the disposition here is not precedential on the derivative liability question. * * *

III

* * *

[The Court held that the Clean Water Act's penalties for water pollution do not preempt a claim for punitive damages under maritime common law.]

IV

Finally, Exxon raises an issue of first impression about punitive damages in maritime law, which falls within a federal court's jurisdiction to decide in the manner of a common law court, subject to the authority of Congress to legislate otherwise if it disagrees with the judicial result. * * * Exxon challenges the size of the remaining $2.5 billion punitive damages award. * * * [It argues] that this award exceeds the bounds justified by the punitive damages goal of deterring reckless (or worse) behavior and the consequently heightened threat of harm. The claim goes to our understanding of the place of punishment in modern civil law and reasonable standards of process in administering punitive law, subjects that call for starting with a brief account of the history behind today's punitive damages.

A

The modern Anglo–American doctrine of punitive damages dates back at least to 1763, when a pair of decisions by the Court of Common Pleas recognized the availability of damages "for more than the injury received." Wilkes v. Wood, Lofft 1, 18, 98 Eng. Rep. 489, 498 (1763) (Lord Chief Justice Pratt). In Wilkes v. Wood, one of the foundations of the Fourth Amendment, exemplary damages awarded against the Secretary of State, responsible for an unlawful search of John Wilkes's papers, were a spectacular £4,000. * * * And in Huckle v. Money, 2 Wils. 205, 206–207, 95 Eng. Rep. 768, 768–769 (K.B.1763), the same judge * * * [upheld] a jury's award of £300 (against a government officer again) although "if the jury had been confined by their oath to consider the mere personal injury only, perhaps [£20] damages would have been thought damages sufficient."

Awarding damages beyond the compensatory was not, however, a wholly novel idea even then, legal codes from ancient times through the Middle Ages having called for multiple damages for certain especially harmful acts. * * * But punitive damages were a common law innovation untethered to strict numerical multipliers, and the doctrine promptly crossed the Atlantic * * * to become widely accepted in American courts by the middle of the 19th century * * *.

B

* * *

Regardless of the alternative rationales over the years, the consensus today is that punitives are aimed not at compensation but principally at retribution and deterring harmful conduct. * * * The prevailing rule in American courts also limits punitive damages to cases of what the Court in [Day v. Woodworth, 13 How. 363, 371, 14 L. Ed. 181 (1852)], spoke of as "enormity," where a defendant's conduct is "outrageous," 4 Restatement [(Second) of Torts] § 908(2), owing to * * * "willful, wanton, and reckless indifference for the rights of others," or behavior even more deplorable * * *.

* * *

C

State regulation of punitive damages varies. A few States award them rarely, or not at all. Nebraska bars punitive damages entirely, on state constitutional grounds. * * * Four others permit punitive damages only when authorized by statute: Louisiana, Massachusetts, and Washington as a matter of common law, and New Hampshire by statute codifying common law tradition. * * * Michigan courts recognize only exemplary damages supportable as compensatory, rather than truly punitive, * * * while Connecticut courts have limited what they call punitive recovery to the "expenses of bringing the legal action, including attorney's fees, less taxable costs" * * *.

As for procedure, in most American jurisdictions the amount of the punitive award is generally determined by a jury in the first instance, and that "determination is then reviewed by trial and appellate courts to ensure that it is reasonable." * * * Many States have gone further by imposing statutory limits on punitive awards, in the form of absolute monetary caps, see, *e.g.,* Va.Code Ann. § 8.01–38.1 (Lexis 2007) ($350,000 cap), a maximum ratio of punitive to compensatory damages, see, *e.g.,* Ohio Rev.Code Ann. § 2315.21(D)(2)(a) (Lexis 2001) (2:1 ratio in most tort cases), or, frequently, some combination of the two, see, *e.g.,* Alaska Stat. § 09.17.020(f) (2006) (greater of 3:1 ratio or $500,000 in most actions). The States that rely on a multiplier have adopted a variety of ratios, ranging from 5:1 to 1:1.

Despite these limitations, punitive damages overall are higher and more frequent in the United States than they are anywhere else. * * * In England and Wales, punitive, or exemplary, damages are available only for oppressive, arbitrary, or unconstitutional action by government servants; injuries designed by the defendant to yield a larger profit than the likely cost of compensatory damages; and conduct for which punitive damages are expressly authorized by statute. Rookes v. Barnard, [1964] 1 All E.R. 367, 410–411 (H.L.). Even in the circumstances where punitive damages are allowed, they are subject to strict, judicially imposed guidelines. The Court of Appeal in Thompson v. Commissioner of Police of Metropolis, [1998] Q.B. 498, 518, said that a ratio of more than three times the amount of compensatory damages will rarely be appropriate; awards of less than £5,000 are likely unnecessary; awards of £25,000 should be exceptional; and £50,000 should be considered the top.

* * *

D

American punitive damages have been the target of audible criticism in recent decades, * * * but the most recent studies tend to undercut much of it * * *. A survey of the literature reveals that discretion to award punitive damages has not mass-produced runaway awards, and although some studies show the dollar amounts of punitive-damages awards growing over time, even in real terms, by most accounts the median ratio of punitive to compensatory awards has remained less than 1:1. Nor do the data substantiate a marked increase in the percentage of cases with punitive awards over the past several decades. The figures thus show an overall restraint and suggest that in many instances a high ratio of punitive to compensatory damages is substantially greater than necessary to punish or deter.

The real problem, it seems, is the stark unpredictability of punitive awards. Courts of law are concerned with fairness as consistency, and evidence that the median ratio of punitive to compensatory awards falls within a reasonable zone, or that punitive awards are infrequent, fails to tell us whether the spread between high and low individual awards is acceptable. The available data suggest it is not. * * *

* * *

E

The Court's response to outlier punitive damages awards has thus far been confined by claims at the constitutional level, and our cases have announced due process standards that every award must pass. * * *

Today's enquiry differs from due process review because the case arises under federal maritime jurisdiction, and we are reviewing a jury award for conformity with maritime law, rather than the outer limit allowed by due process; we are examining the verdict in the exercise of federal maritime common law authority, which precedes and should obviate any application of the constitutional standard. * * *

Our review of punitive damages today, then, considers not their intersection with the Constitution, but the desirability of regulating them as a common law remedy for which responsibility lies with this Court as a source of judge-made law in the absence of statute. Whatever may be the constitutional significance of the unpredictability of high punitive awards, this feature of happenstance is in tension with the function of the awards as punitive, just because of the implication of unfairness that an eccentrically high punitive verdict carries in a system whose commonly held notion of law rests on a sense of fairness in dealing with one another. Thus, a penalty should be reasonably predictable in its severity, so that even Justice Holmes's "bad man" can look ahead with some ability to know what the stakes are in choosing one course of action or another. See The Path of the Law, 10 Harv. L.Rev. 457, 459 (1897). And when the bad man's counterparts turn up from time to time, the penalty scheme they face ought to threaten them with a fair probability of suffering in like degree when they wreak like damage. * * * The common sense of justice would surely bar penalties that reasonable people would think excessive for the harm caused in the circumstances.

F

1

With that aim ourselves, we have three basic approaches to consider, one verbal and two quantitative. As mentioned before, a number of state courts have settled on criteria for judicial review of punitive-damages awards that go well beyond traditional "shock the conscience" or "passion and prejudice" tests. Maryland, for example, has set forth a nonexclusive list of nine review factors under state common law that include "degree of heinousness," "the deterrence value of [the award]," and "[w]hether [the punitive award] bears a reasonable relationship to the compensatory damages awarded." Bowden v. Caldor, Inc., 350 Md. 4, 25–39, 710 A.2d 267, 277–284 (1998). * * *

These judicial review criteria are brought to bear after juries render verdicts under instructions offering, at best, guidance no more specific for reaching an appropriate penalty. In Maryland, for example, which allows punitive damages for intentional torts and conduct characterized by "actual malice," U.S. Gypsum Co. v. Mayor and City Council of Baltimore, 336 Md. 145, 185, 647 A.2d 405, 424–425 (1994), juries may be instructed that

An award for punitive damages should be:

(1) In an amount that will deter the defendant and others from similar conduct.

(2) Proportionate to the wrongfulness of the defendant's conduct and the defendant's ability to pay.

(3) But not designed to bankrupt or financially destroy a defendant.

Md. Pattern Jury Instr., Civil, No. 10:13 (4th ed.2007).

* * *

* * * Instructions can go just so far in promoting systemic consistency when awards are not tied to specifically proven items of damage (the cost of medical treatment, say), and although judges in the States that take this approach may well produce just results by dint of valiant effort, our experience with attempts to produce consistency in the analogous business of criminal sentencing leaves us doubtful that anything but a quantified approach will work. * * *

* * *

2

This is why our better judgment is that eliminating unpredictable outlying punitive awards by more rigorous standards than the constitutional limit will probably have to take the form adopted in those States that have looked to the criminal-law pattern of quantified limits. One option would be to follow the States that set a hard dollar cap on punitive damages, * * * a course that arguably would come closest to the criminal law, rather like setting a maximum term of years. The trouble is, though, that there is no "standard" tort or contract injury, making it difficult to settle upon a particular dollar figure as appropriate across the board. And of course a judicial selection of a dollar cap would carry a serious drawback; a legislature can pick a figure, index it for inflation, and revisit its provision whenever there seems to be a need for further tinkering, but a court cannot say when an issue will show up on the docket again. * * *

The more promising alternative is to leave the effects of inflation to the jury or judge who assesses the value of actual loss, by pegging punitive to compensatory damages using a ratio or maximum multiple. * * * As the earlier canvass of state experience showed, this is the model many States have adopted, * * * and Congress has passed analogous legislation from time to time, as for example in providing treble damages in antitrust, racketeering, patent, and trademark actions, see 15 U.S.C. §§ 15, 1117 (2000 ed. and Supp. V); 18 U.S.C. § 1964(c); 35 U.S.C. § 284. And of course the potential relevance of the ratio between compensatory and punitive damages is indisputable, being a central feature in our due process analysis. * * *

Still, some will murmur that this smacks too much of policy and too little of principle. * * * But the answer rests on the fact that we are acting here in the position of a common law court of last review, faced with a perceived defect in a common law remedy. Traditionally, courts have accepted primary responsibility for reviewing punitive damages and thus for their evolution, and if, in the absence of legislation, judicially derived standards leave the door open to outlier punitive-damages awards, it is hard to see how the judiciary can wash its hands of a problem it created, simply by calling quantified standards legislative. * * *

* * *

Although the legal landscape is well populated with examples of ratios and multipliers expressing policies of retribution and deterrence, most of them suffer from features that stand in the way of borrowing them as paradigms of reasonable limitations suited for application to this case. While a slim majority of the States with a ratio have adopted 3:1, others see fit to apply a lower one, see, *e.g.*, Colo.Rev.Stat. Ann. § 13–21–102(1)(a) (2007) (1:1); Ohio Rev.Code Ann. § 2315.21(D)(2)(a) (Lexis 2005) (2:1), and a few have gone higher, see, *e.g.*, Mo. Ann. Stat. § 510.265(1) (Supp.2008) (5:1). Judgments may differ about the weight to be given to the slight majority of 3:1 States, but one feature of the 3:1 schemes dissuades us from selecting it here. With a few statutory exceptions, generally for intentional infliction of physical injury or other harm, * * * the States with 3:1 ratios apply them across the board (as do other States using different fixed multipliers). That is, the upper limit is not directed to cases like this one, where the tortious action was worse than negligent but less than malicious, exposing the tortfeasor to certain regulatory sanctions and inevitable damage actions; the 3:1 ratio in these States also applies to awards in quite different cases involving some of the most egregious conduct, including malicious behavior and dangerous activity carried on for the purpose of increasing a tortfeasor's financial gain. We confront, instead, a case of reckless action, profitless to the tortfeasor, resulting in substantial recovery for substantial injury. Thus, a legislative judgment that 3:1 is a reasonable limit overall is not a judgment that 3:1 is a reasonable limit in this particular type of case.

* * *

3

There is better evidence of an accepted limit of reasonable civil penalty, however, in several studies mentioned before, showing the median ratio of punitive to compensatory verdicts, reflecting what juries and judges have considered reasonable across many hundreds of punitive awards. * * * We think it is fair to assume that the greater share of the verdicts studied in these comprehensive collections reflect reasonable judgments about the economic penalties appropriate in their particular cases.

These studies cover cases of the most as well as the least blameworthy conduct triggering punitive liability, from malice and avarice, down to recklessness * * *. The data put the median ratio for the entire gamut of circumstances at less than 1:1, * * * meaning that the compensatory award exceeds the punitive award in most cases. In a well-functioning system, we would expect that awards at the median or lower would roughly express jurors' sense of reasonable penalties in cases with no earmarks of exceptional blameworthiness within the punishable spectrum (cases like this one, without intentional or malicious conduct, and without behavior driven primarily by desire for gain, for example) and cases (again like this one) without the modest economic harm or odds of detection that have opened the door to higher awards. * * * On these assumptions, a median ratio of punitive to compensatory damages of about 0.65:1 probably marks the line near which cases like this one largely should be grouped. Accordingly, given the need to protect against the possibility (and the disruptive cost to the legal system) of awards that are unpredictable and unnecessary, either for deterrence or for measured retribution, we consider that a 1:1 ratio, which is above the median award, is a fair upper limit in such maritime cases.

* * * [O]ur explanation of the constitutional upper limit confirms that the 1:1 ratio is not too low. In *State Farm,* we said that a single-digit maximum is appropriate in all but the most exceptional of cases, and "[w]hen compensatory damages are substantial, then a lesser ratio, perhaps only equal to compensatory damages, can reach the outermost limit of the due process guarantee." 538 U.S., at 425, 123 S.Ct. 1513.

V

Applying this standard to the present case, we take for granted the District Court's calculation of the total relevant compensatory damages at $507.5 million. See *In re Exxon Valdez,* 236 F.Supp.2d 1043, 1063 (D.Alaska 2002). A punitive-to-compensatory ratio of 1:1 thus yields maximum punitive damages in that amount.

We therefore vacate the judgment and remand the case for the Court of Appeals to remit the punitive damages award accordingly.

JUSTICE ALITO took no part in the consideration or decision of this case.

JUSTICE SCALIA, with whom JUSTICE THOMAS joins, concurring.

I join the opinion of the Court, including the portions that refer to constitutional limits that prior opinions have imposed upon punitive damages. While I agree with the argumentation based upon those prior holdings, I continue to believe the holdings were in error. * * *

JUSTICE STEVENS, concurring in part and dissenting in part.

While I join Parts I, II, and III of the Court's opinion, I believe that Congress, rather than this Court, should make the empirical judgments expressed in Part IV. While maritime law " 'is judge-made law to a great extent,' " * * * it is also statutory law to a great extent; indeed, "[m]aritime tort law is now dominated by federal statute." Miles v. Apex Marine Corp., 498 U.S. 19, 36, 111 S.Ct. 317, 112 L.Ed.2d 275 (1990). For that reason, when we are faced with a choice between performing the traditional task of appellate judges reviewing the acceptability of an award of punitive damages, on the one hand, and embarking on a new lawmaking venture, on the other, we "should carefully consider whether [we], or a legislative body, are better equipped to perform the task at hand." * * *

Evidence that Congress has affirmatively chosen *not* to restrict the availability of a particular remedy favors adherence to a policy of judicial restraint in the absence of some special justification. * * * Applying the traditional abuse-of-discretion standard that is well grounded in the common law, I would affirm the judgment of the Court of Appeals.

* * *

JUSTICE GINSBURG, concurring in part and dissenting in part.

I join Parts I, II, and III of the Court's opinion, and dissent from Parts IV and V.

This case is unlike the Court's recent forays into the domain of state tort law under the banner of substantive due process.* * * The controversy here presented "arises under federal maritime jurisdiction," * * * and, beyond question, "the Court possesses the power to craft the rule it announces today" * * * . The issue, therefore, is whether the Court, though competent to act, should nevertheless leave the matter to Congress. The Court has explained, in its well stated and comprehensive opinion, why it has taken the lead. While recognizing that the question is close, I share Justice Stevens' view that Congress is the better equipped decisionmaker.

First, I question whether there is an urgent need in maritime law to break away from the "traditional common-law approach" * * *.

Second, assuming a problem in need of solution, the Court's lawmaking prompts many questions. The 1:1 ratio is good for this case, the Court believes, because Exxon's conduct ranked on the low end of the blameworthiness scale: Exxon was not seeking "to augment profit," nor did it act "with a purpose to injure" * * *. What ratio will the Court set for defendants who acted maliciously or in pursuit of financial gain? * * * Should the magnitude of the risk increase the ratio and, if so, by how much? Horrendous as the spill from the *Valdez* was, millions of gallons more might have spilled as a result of Captain Hazelwood's attempt to rock the boat off the reef. * * * In the end, is the Court holding only that 1:1 is the maritime-law ceiling, or is it also signaling that any ratio higher than 1:1 will be held to exceed "the constitutional outer limit"? * * * On next opportunity, will the Court rule, definitively, that 1:1 is the ceiling due process requires in all of the States, and for all federal claims?

* * *

For the reasons stated, I agree with Justice Stevens that the new law made by the Court should have been left to Congress. I would therefore affirm the judgment of the Court of Appeals.

JUSTICE BREYER, concurring in part and dissenting in part.

I join Parts I, II, and III of the Court's opinion. But I disagree with its conclusion in Parts IV and V that the punitive damages award in this case must be reduced.

Like the Court, I believe there is a need, grounded in the rule of law itself, to assure that punitive damages are awarded according to meaningful standards that will provide notice of how harshly certain acts will be punished and that will help to assure the uniform treatment of similarly situated persons. * * * Legal standards, however, can secure these objectives without the rigidity that an absolute fixed numerical ratio demands. * * *

In my view, a limited exception to the Court's 1:1 ratio is warranted here. As the facts set forth in Part I of the Court's opinion make clear, this was no mine-run case of reckless behavior. The jury could reasonably have believed that Exxon knowingly allowed a relapsed alcoholic repeatedly to pilot a vessel filled with millions of gallons of oil through waters that provided the livelihood for the many plaintiffs in this case. Given that conduct, it was only a matter of time before a crash and spill like this occurred. And as Justice Ginsburg points out, the damage easily could have been much worse. * * *

* * *

NOTES

1.   *Exxon* was decided as a matter of maritime law, which is one area of federal common law. It is not clear to what extent *Exxon* may apply to other areas of federal law. *See, e.g.*, Kunz v. DeFelice, 538 F.3d 667 (7th Cir. 2008)(*Exxon* does not apply beyond the maritime context to § 1983 actions). But, without a doubt, *Exxon* will be cited as persuasive authority when state courts are resolving punitive damages cases as a matter of state common law. *See, e.g.*, Amerigraphics, Inc. v. Mercury Cas. Co., 182 Cal. App. 4th 1538, 107 Cal. Rptr.3d 307 (2010). And *Exxon* may also be invoked by way of analogy when a state or federal court is determining the constitutionality of a punitive damages award under the Due Process Clause. *See, e.g.*, Southern Union Co. v. Irvin, 563 F.3d 788, 792 (9th Cir. 2009)("[T]he constitution permits a three to one ratio of punitive to compensatory damages in this case, but not more.")

2.   Note that Justices Scalia and Thomas, who have routinely dissented in the Due Process Clause cases regarding punitive damages, were able to join Justice Souter in *Exxon* because it was a federal common law case.

3.   For scholarly commentary on *Exxon*, see Jeffrey L. Fisher, *The Exxon Valdez Case and Regularizing Punishment*, 26 Alaska L. Rev. 1 (2009); Victor E. Schwartz, Cary Silverman, Christopher E. Appel, *The Supreme Court's Common Law Approach to Excessive Punitive Damage Awards: A Guide for the Development of State Law*, 60 S.C. L. Rev. 881 (2009); Catherine M. Sharkey, *The Exxon Valdez Litigation Marathon: A Window on Punitive Damages*, 7 U. St. Thomas L.J. 25 (2009).

B.   CONTRACT

1.   Rule of No Punitive Damages for Breach of Contract

As we saw in *Erlich* in Section 3.C of this Chapter, emotional distress damages are unavailable for a breach of contract unless the breach is accompanied by a tort. The case that follows adopts that rule and also explains why punitive damages cannot be recovered for a breach of contract.

FRANCIS v. LEE ENTERPRISES, INC.

Supreme Court of Hawai'i, 1999.
89 Haw. 234, 971 P.2d 707.

MOON, C.J., KLEIN, LEVINSON, NAKAYAMA, and RAMIL, JJ.

Opinion of the Court by MOON, C.J.

* * *

The federal district court * * * certified the following question to this court: Does Hawai'i law recognize a tortious breach of contract cause of action in the employment context?

Although, in the past, this court has recognized a cause of action for tortious breach of contract in certain circumstances, we believe that such a rule unnecessarily blurs the distinction between—and undermines the discrete theories of recovery relevant to—tort and contract law. Based on our reexamination of the rule announced in Dold v. Outrigger Hotel, 54 Haw. 18, 501 P.2d 368 (1972), we now hold that Hawai'i law will not allow tort recovery in the absence of conduct that (1) violates a duty that is independently recognized by principles of tort law and (2) transcends the breach of the contract. Consistent with this rule, emotional distress damages will only be recoverable where the parties specifically provide for them in the contract or where the nature of the contract clearly indicates that such damages were within the contemplation or expectation of the parties. Therefore, in answer to the certified question, Hawai'i does *not* recognize tortious breach of contract actions in the employment context.

I.   BACKGROUND

* * * KGMB is the local affiliate of the CBS television network. Francis, a well-known local sports figure, played football for fourteen years in the National Football League. On January 18, 1996, Francis and

KGMB entered into a written employment contract under which Francis worked for KGMB as its sports director until he was terminated on January 20, 1997.

After he was terminated, Francis filed suit in the first circuit court. [KGMB removed the case to the federal district court.] Francis's complaint contained five claims for relief, including: breach of contract (Count I); tortious breach of contract (Count II); promissory estoppel (Count III); wrongful termination in violation of public policy (Count IV); and punitive damages (Count V). In connection with Count II, the tortious breach of contract claim, Francis alleged that KGMB acted "wilfully, wantonly, recklessly and/or in bad faith" in breaching the written employment contract.

* * *

III. DISCUSSION

Francis argues that the "well-settled rule that a wanton or reckless breach of contract is actionable in tort" applies, without exception, to written employment contracts. Francis makes this argument because he seeks traditional tort damages due to KGMB's alleged breach of the employment contract at issue. Although Francis correctly states the rule relating to tortious breach of contract announced in Dold v. Outrigger Hotel, 54 Haw. 18, 501 P.2d 368 (1972), we believe * * * that the rule was improvidently created, and today we abolish it.

* * *

* * * [W]e note that our decision today does not affect this court's prior decisions recognizing the tort of bad faith in the first-party insurance context. * * *

* * *

* * * [W]e grounded our [prior decisions] on the "atypical" relationship existing between the insured and the insurer. * * * Moreover, we recognized that the adhesionary aspects of an insurance contract further justify the availability of a tort recovery. * * * Without the threat of a tort action, insurance companies have little incentive to promptly pay proceeds rightfully due to their insureds, as they stand to lose very little by delaying payment.

* * *

An employment contract will indeed often have a personal element. Employment is an important aspect of most persons' lives, and the breach of an employment contract may result in emotional distress. The primary purpose in forming such contracts, however, is economic and not to secure the protection of personal interests. The psychic satisfaction of the employment is secondary.

* * *

With respect to punitive damages, we agree with those courts that have refused to allow such damages in contract actions "unless the conduct constituting the breach is also a tort for which punitive damages are recoverable." * * * Traditionally, damages for breach of contract have been awarded "to compensate the aggrieved party rather than to punish the breaching party." * * * Restatement (Second) of Contracts § 355 comment a (1979) ("The purpose of awarding contract damages is to compensate the injured party . . . [and not] to punish the party in breach or to serve as an example to others unless the conduct constituting the breach is also a tort[.]").

* * * [T]his court is not aware of any Hawai'i decision, outside of the insurance context,[3] where a court has allowed or upheld the award of punitive damages for breach of a purely contractual obligation.

Based on our analysis above, * * * punitive damages will *never* be recoverable, absent conduct that violates a duty that is independently recognized by principles of tort law. Of course, the existence of a contract will not defeat otherwise valid claims for relief sounding in tort, such as fraud, where punitive damages are allowed in order to vindicate social policy.

* * *

Presently, contract law allows—and at times even encourages—intentional breaches of contract. *See* R. Posner, Economic Analysis of Law § 3.8 (1972) (explaining fundamental principles of contract damages). Whereas society views intentional torts as reprehensible, many people have argued that intentional breaches of contract are morally neutral. Proponents of this amoral view forcefully argue that "efficient" breaches of contract, i.e., breaches where the gain to the breaching party exceeds the loss to the party suffering breach, actually result in a net benefit to society because such breaches allow resources to move to their more optimal use. *See* Posner, § 3.8 at 55–57; see *also Hickman,* 665 S.W.2d at 280 ("The law has long recognized the view that a contracting party has the option to breach a contract and pay damages if it is more efficient to do so.") Even Justice Holmes recognized, over 100 years ago, that breaching a contract constitutes a morally neutral act, stating that "the duty to keep a contract at common law means a prediction that you must pay damages if you do not keep it—*and nothing else.*" O. Holmes, *The Path of the Law*, 10 Harv. L.Rev. 457, 462 (1897) (emphasis added). Based on these policy considerations and the compensatory objectives of contract law, many courts—including the courts of this jurisdiction—focus on the loss to the nonbreaching party rather than whether the breach was intentional. * * *

* * *

_____

3. [O]ur decision today in no way affects our prior decisions * * * recognizing the tort of bad faith within the insurance context. * * * [T]he fact that an insured might conceivably recover punitive damages, where an insurer commits the tort of bad faith, does not imply that such damages are recoverable for breach of an employment contract.

Moreover, Francis does not offer a principled way for courts to distinguish non-tortious, though intentional, breaches of contract from "wilful" or "wanton" breaches that justify the award of tort damages. The attempt to draw such a line would necessarily drain judicial resources as litigants invite courts to make such distinctions in every action for breach of an employment contract. * * *

* * *

IV. CONCLUSION

For the foregoing reasons, we answer the certified question in the negative, hold that Hawai'i law does not recognize tortious breach of contract actions in the employment context, and return this case for further proceedings in the United States District Court for the District of Hawai'i.

NOTES

1. The *Francis* court referred to the concept of "efficient breach." Justice Brown of the California Supreme Court also has discussed this topic:

> [P]unitive damage awards should not be a routine cost of doing business that an industry can simply pass on to its customers through price increases, while continuing the conduct the law proscribes. In contract law, we recognize "efficient breach" as being socially beneficial * * *, but in the law of punitive damages there is no such thing as "efficient" oppression, fraud or malice. The purpose of punitive damages is to *prevent* oppression, fraud and malice, not merely to force defendants to internalize the social costs of that conduct.

Lane v. Hughes Aircraft Co., 22 Cal.4th 405, 427, 993 P.2d 388, 402, 93 Cal.Rptr. 60, 75 (2000) (concurring opinion).

2. When he was a law professor, Judge Posner of the Seventh Circuit wrote The Economic Analysis of the Law, the 1972 edition of which was cited in *Francis*. On the bench, Judge Posner has explained the concept of "efficient breach," but he also has noted that it cannot justify all breaches:

> Even if the breach is deliberate, it is not necessarily blameworthy. The promisor may simply have discovered that his performance is worth more to someone else. If so, efficiency is promoted by allowing him to break his promise, provided he makes good the promisee's actual losses. If he is forced to pay more than that, an efficient breach may be deterred, and the law doesn't want to bring about such a result. * * *
>
> Not all breaches of contract are involuntary or otherwise efficient. Some are opportunistic; the promisor wants the benefit of the bargain without bearing the agreed-upon cost, and exploits the inadequacies of purely compensatory remedies (the major inadequacies being that pre-and post-judgment interest rates are frequently below market levels when the risk of nonpayment is taken into account and that the winning party cannot recover his attorney's fees). * * *

Patton v. Mid–Continent Systems, Inc., 841 F.2d 742, 750–51 (7th Cir.1988).

Can you think of other reasons, besides the inadequacy of interest rates, that might defeat the ability of the promisor to "make good the promisees' actual losses"? *See supra* Chapter 3, Section 3.B; *see also* Dan B. Dobbs, Law of Remedies § 12.5(2) (2d ed. 1993).

3. Judge Friendly, in Thyssen, Inc. v. S.S. Fortune Star, 777 F.2d 57 (2d Cir.1985), summarized a variety of justifications for the rule that punitive damages are not available in a contract action:

> Appellee must * * * overcome the principle, succinctly stated in Restatement (Second) of Contracts § 355 (1979):

> > Punitive damages are not recoverable for a breach of contract unless the conduct constituting the breach is also a tort for which punitive damages are recoverable.

> *See also* 11 Williston on Contracts § 1340, at 209–11 (W. Jaeger 3d ed.1968); 5 Corbin on Contracts § 1077, at 438–39 (1964); Sullivan, *Punitive Damages in the Law of Contract*, 61 Minn. L. Rev. 207, 207 (1977). This rule applies although the breach is intentional or even when it has been effected with malicious intent. Simpson, *Punitive Damages for Breach of Contract*, 20 Ohio St. L.J. 284, 284 (1959); Farnsworth, Contracts § 12.8, at 842 (1982). Under Holmes' theory that a contract is simply a set of alternative promises either to perform or to pay damages for nonperformance, Holmes, The Common Law 235–36 (M. Howe ed.1963), the rule would require no other explanation. Nevertheless, a good many have been offered. One is that the law of contracts governs primarily commercial relationships, where the amount required to compensate for loss is easily fixed, in contrast to the law of torts, which compensates for injury to personal interests that are more difficult to value, thus justifying noncompensatory recoveries. Sullivan, *supra*, at 222. Another, given by Corbin, *supra*, § 1077, at 438, is that breaches of contract do not cause the kind of "resentment or other mental and physical discomfort as do the wrongs called torts and crimes," and no retributive purpose would be served by punitive damages in contract cases. A third explanation, offered by economists, is the notion that breaches of contract that are in fact efficient and wealth-enhancing should be encouraged, and that such "efficient breaches" occur when the breaching party will still profit after compensating the other party for its "expectation interest." The addition of punitive damages to traditional contract remedies would prevent many such beneficial actions from being taken. *See* Farnsworth, *supra*, § 12.3 at 817–18 * * *. In any event the general rule is well established, although certain exceptions have been adopted.

> The most common exception * * * is where the breach constitutes an independent, wilful tort in addition to being a breach of contract. 5 Corbin, *supra*, § 1077, at 445; Farnsworth, *supra*, § 12.8, at 843.

Id. at 63; Robinson Helicopter Co. v. Dana Corp., 34 Cal.4th 979, 22 Cal. Rptr.3d 352, 102 P.3d 268 (2004) involved such an "independent, wilful tort." There the court upheld a $6 million punitive damages award to a helicopter manufacturer against a supplier of defective helicopter parts because the defendant had committed the "independent tort" of fraud.

4. Since punitive damages may not be awarded in breach of contract actions, what happens when the parties to a contract agree as to the damages that should be recoverable in the event of a breach of contract? *See* the next sub-section.

2. Liquidated Damages

NPS, LLC v. MINIHANE

Supreme Judicial Court of Massachusetts, 2008.
886 N.E.2d 670.

MARSHALL, C.J., GREANEY, IRELAND, SPINA, COWIN, CORDY, & BOTSFORD, JJ.

COWIN, J.

In this case we decide whether an acceleration clause in a ten-year license agreement for luxury seats for New England Patriots professional football games at Gillette Stadium is enforceable. The agreement requires the purchaser of the license to pay, upon default, the amounts due for all years remaining on the license. The plaintiff contends that the clause is a lawful liquidated damages provision; the defendant, who defaulted in the first year of the agreement, argues that it is an unlawful penalty. * * *

Background.

* * * The plaintiff, NPS, LLC (NPS), is the developer of Gillette Stadium (stadium), the home field of the New England Patriots professional football team (Patriots). In 2002, while the stadium was still under construction, NPS entered into an agreement with the defendant, Paul Minihane, for the purchase of a ten-year license for two luxury seats in the Club Level III section. The agreement called for the defendant to pay $3,750 per seat annually for each of the ten seasons from 2002 to 2011. The agreement included a liquidated damages provision, set forth in the margin,[2] which provides that in the event of a default, including failure to pay any amount due under the license agreement, the payments would be accelerated so that the defendant would be required to pay the balance for all the years remaining on the contract.[3]

Upon executing the agreement, the defendant paid a $7,500 security deposit; he later made a payment of $2,000 toward the license fee for the 2002 season. Although he or his guests attended all but one of the 2002 preseason and regular season Patriots games at the stadium using the tickets for the Club Seats, he made no further payments.

---

2. "15. *Default.* * * * In the event that Licensee shall not have cured the default or breach specified in said notice by the date specified in said notice, Owner may terminate the right of Licensee to the use and possession of the Club Seats and all other rights and privileges of Licensee under the Agreement and declare the entire unpaid balance of the License Fee (which for the purposes hereof shall include the total aggregate unpaid balance of the annual License Fees for the remainder of the Term) immediately due and payable, whereupon Owner shall have no further obligation of any kind to Licensee. Owner shall have no duty to mitigate any damages incurred by it as a result of a default by Licensee hereunder...."

3. The defendant is a licensed real estate broker and has experience as a general contractor and real estate developer.* * *

After giving notice to the defendant, NPS accelerated the payments and filed a complaint in the Superior Court seeking the full amount due under the contract. After a bench trial, the judge ruled that the liquidated damages provision was unenforceable * * *. After taking further evidence on the issue of actual damages, the judge issued a memorandum of decision and order in which he awarded damages to NPS in the amount of $6,000. This appeal followed * * *.

Discussion.

* * * Whether a liquidated damages provision in a contract is an unenforceable penalty is a question of law. * * *

It is well settled that "a contract provision that clearly and reasonably establishes liquidated damages should be enforced, so long as it is not so disproportionate to anticipated damages as to constitute a penalty." * * * A liquidated damages provision will usually be enforced provided two criteria are satisfied: first, that at the time of contracting the actual damages flowing from a breach were difficult to ascertain; and second, that the sum agreed on as liquidated damages represents a "reasonable forecast of damages expected to occur in the event of a breach." * * * Where damages are easily ascertainable, and the amount provided for is grossly disproportionate to actual damages, or unconscionably excessive, the court will award the aggrieved party no more than its actual damages. * * * [T]he reasonableness of the measure of anticipated damages depends on the circumstances of each case. * * * In assessing reasonableness, * * * we do not take a "second look" at the actual damages after the contract has been breached. * * *

In this case, the trial judge found that, at the time the parties entered into the license agreement, the harm resulting from a possible breach was difficult to ascertain. That finding was supported by the evidence, which indicated that the damages sustained by NPS would vary depending on the demand for tickets at the time of breach. Although the Patriots had won their first Super Bowl championship in 2002, shortly before the parties entered into their agreement, the demand for luxury stadium seats was then and remains variable and depends, according to the evidence, on the current performance of the team, as well as other factors, such as the popularity of the players and the relative popularity of other sports, that are unpredictable at the time of contract. Therefore, to predict at the time of contract how long it would take NPS to resell the defendant's seat license would be extremely difficult, if not impossible.

The judge went on to find, however, that the sum provided for in the agreement—acceleration of all payments for the remaining term of the contract—was "grossly disproportionate to a reasonable estimate of actual damages made at the time of contract formation." That finding was not supported by the evidence. It is the defendant's burden to show that the amount of liquidated damages is "unreasonably and grossly disproportionate to the real damages from a breach" or "unconscionably excessive." * * * Having presented little evidence beyond his assertion that the contract as a whole was unconscionable, the defendant in this case has not sustained that burden.

The liquidated damages provision here is similar to one we upheld in Cummings Props., LLC v. National Communications Corp., 449 Mass. 490, 869 N.E.2d 617 (2007). In that case, a tenant who defaulted on a commercial lease was required by the terms of the agreement to pay the entire amount of rent remaining under the lease. * * * The judge here did not have the benefit of our decision in *Cummings*, which was issued more than a year after the trial in this case; however, for present purposes, we see no meaningful distinction between the two provisions. In upholding the liquidated damages provision in *Cummings*, we noted that "to the extent that the liquidated damages amount represented the agreed rental value of the property over the remaining life of the lease, decreasing in amount as the lease term came closer to expiration, it appears to be a reasonable anticipation of damages that might accrue from the nonpayment of rent." *Id.* at 496–497. The same is true here. This, like *Cummings*, is a case where the damages were difficult to estimate at the outset, and the defendant is required to pay no more than the total amount he would have paid had he performed his obligations under the agreement. The sum provided for therefore bears a reasonable relationship to the anticipated actual damages resulting from a breach. It anticipates a worst-case scenario, that is, NPS's inability to resell the seat for the remaining term of the license.[7] However, the defendant has not shown that this outcome is sufficiently unlikely that it renders the amount grossly disproportionate to a reasonable estimate of actual damages.

The defendant stood to receive a substantial benefit from this agreement: guaranteed luxury seating for all Patriots home games, as well as a hedge against future price increases over ten years. He was not deprived of an opportunity to learn and consider the terms of the agreement. Those terms may be harsh, especially when, as here, the breach occurred early in the life of the agreement. But the defendant has not shown that in the circumstances they are "unreasonably and grossly disproportionate to the real damages from a breach." * * *

On appeal, the parties have not raised the issue whether, if the liquidated damages provision is enforced, mitigation should be considered. However, because mitigation was raised (albeit obliquely) in the defendant's amended answer to the complaint,[8] and because we hold that the liquidated damages provision is enforceable, we consider the issue, which appears to be one of first impression in Massachusetts.

We will follow the rule in many other jurisdictions and hold that, in the case of an enforceable liquidated damages provision, mitigation is

---

7. We note in passing that there was evidence at trial that NPS in fact had not been able to resell the defendant's seat, some four years after the defendant committed a breach of the agreement. * * *

8. The defendant's amended answer states as an affirmative defense that the agreement was unconscionable because it provided that NPS had no duty to mitigate its damages in the event of a breach.

irrelevant and should not be considered in assessing damages. When parties agree in advance to a sum certain that represents a reasonable estimate of potential damages, they exchange the opportunity to determine actual damages after a breach, including possible mitigation, for the "peace of mind and certainty of result" afforded by a liquidated damages clause. * * * In such circumstances, to consider whether a plaintiff has mitigated its damages not only is illogical, but also defeats the purpose of liquidated damages provisions. See Barrie School v. Patch, 401 Md. 497, 513–514, 933 A.2d 382 (2007) (sum that stipulates damages in advance "replaces any determination of actual loss," so that if liquidated damages provision is enforceable, court need not consider mitigation). Since the liquidated damages provision at issue here is enforceable, the question is irrelevant.

Conclusion.

The ruling of the Superior Court that the liquidated damages provision of the license agreement is unenforceable is set aside, and the judgment is modified to award NPS the total amount of unpaid license fees due under the agreement, $65,500, plus interest. As so modified, the judgment is affirmed.

So ordered.

NOTES

1. The court in *NPS, LLC v. Minihane* does not discuss why Paul Minihane did not pay for his seats after the first year. Would the reason matter? Why, in note 3, did the court discuss his background? Should that be relevant to the law of liquidated damages? On September 3, 2009, James V. Grimaldi wrote for the Washington Post about people the Redskins' management was suing for failing to pay for their long term season tickets. According to the article, one was a 72–year-old real estate agent who had had season tickets since the 1960s. Her business was hurt by the "housing market crash" and she asked the Redskins' management to "waive" her "$5,300-a-year contract for two loge seats. The management declined and sued to enforce her ten-year contract. She could not afford a lawyer. The management recovered $66,3654 in a default judgment. She cannot afford to pay it and may lose her home." James V. Grimaldi, *Hard Luck Runs Into Team's Hard Line*, Washington Post, September 3, 2009, at A1. On November 12, 2009, the Washington Post reported that within a few days of the September article, the Redskins' management "dropped their efforts to collect a payment from her." Washington Post, Style, at C1.

2. *Minihane* articulates the long standing rule regarding liquidated damages clauses. The rule has often been questioned, however. Judge Posner, in XCO International, Inc. v. Pacific Scientific Co., 369 F.3d 998 (7th Cir. 2004), which involved an action for breach of a patent assignment contract, identified several concerns with the rule:

When damages for breach of contract would be difficult for a court to determine after the breach occurs, it makes sense for the parties to specify in the contract itself what the damages for a breach shall be; this reduces uncertainty and litigation costs and economizes on judicial resources as well. Indeed, even if damages wouldn't be difficult to determine after the fact, it is hard to see why the parties shouldn't be allowed to substitute their own *ex ante* determination for the *ex post* determination of a court. Damages would be just another contract provision that parties would be permitted to negotiate under the general rubric of freedom of contract. One could even think of a liquidated damages clause as a partial settlement, as in cases in which damages are stipulated and trial confined to liability issues. And of course settlements are favored.

Yet it is a rule of the common law of contracts, in Illinois as elsewhere, that unless the parties' *ex ante* estimate of damages is reasonable, their liquidated damages provision is unenforceable, as constituting a penalty intended to "force" performance. * * * The reason for the rule is mysterious; it is one of the abiding mysteries of the common law. At least in a case such as this, where both parties are substantial commercial enterprises (ironically, it is the larger firm [in this case] that is crying "penalty clause"), and where damages are liquidated for breach by either party, making an inference of fraud or duress implausible, it is difficult to see why the law should take an interest in whether the estimate of harm underlying the liquidation of damages is reasonable. Courts don't review the other provisions of contracts for reasonableness; why this one?

It is true that if there is a very stiff penalty for breach, parties will be discouraged from committing "efficient" breaches, that is, breaches that confer a greater benefit on the contract breaker than on the victim of the breach, in which event breach plus compensation for the victim produces a net gain with no losers and should be encouraged. (This is a reason why injunctions are not routinely granted in contract cases—why, in other words, the party who breaks his contract is usually allowed to walk away from it, provided only that he compensates the other party for the cost of the breach to that party.) But against this consideration must be set the worthwhile effect of a penalty as a signal that the party subject to it is likely to perform his contract promise. This makes him a more attractive contract partner, since if he doesn't perform he will be punished severely. His willingness to assume that risk signals his confidence that he will be able to perform and thus avoid the penalty. It makes him a credible person to do business with, and thus promotes commerce.

Granted, the case for a contractual specification of damages is stronger the more difficult it is to estimate damages and so the greater the expense to the parties and the judiciary, and hence to society, of determining the plaintiff's damages by the clumsy and costly methods of litigation. That presumably is why the enforceability of liquidated damages clauses depends on the difficulty of estimating, when the contract is signed, what the damages will be if the contract is broken. Yet in such cases the plaintiff will often be able to obtain injunctive relief instead of damages, on the ground that his damages remedy is inadequate, that being the standard criterion for injunctive relief; and an injunction often has a punitive effect because the cost to the defendant of complying with it will often exceed the harm to the plaintiff from the enjoined conduct.

The fact that injunctions are sometimes granted in contract cases shows, therefore, that "punishment" is not wholly alien to contractual remedies. At a minimum one might suppose penalty clauses tolerable to the extent that the penalty portion approximated the costs in attorneys' fees and other expenses of proving damages for breach of contract.

The explanation for the rule against penalty clauses may be purely historical—and "it is revolting to have no better reason for a rule of law than that so it was laid down in the time of Henry IV." O.W. Holmes, *The Path of the Law*, 10 Harv. L. Rev. 457, 469 (1897). The slow pace at which the common law changes makes it inevitable that some common law rules will be vestigial, even fossilized. When a person comes into court seeking relief, the court naturally is inclined to ask why it should get involved in the matter. The court is busy, its resources limited. It wants to see some potential benefit from judicial intervention before it will lift a finger. The rules of contract law have remote origins, predating the era of freedom of contract and the ideology of free markets. * * *

* * *

The element common to most liquidated damages clauses that get struck down as penalty clauses is that they specify the same damages regardless of the severity of the breach. * * * One can see the problem: if a contract provides that breaches of different gravity shall be sanctioned with equal severity, it is highly likely that the sanction specified for the mildest breach is a penalty (that, or the sanctions for all the other possible breaches must be inadequate). That would have been the case here if instead of fixing the damages at $100,000 per year [from the date of the termination of the contract until the date that the last patent expired, which in this case was from 1998 to 2003], the damages clause had recited for example that in the event of breach PacSci must pay XCO $500,000, period. * * *

* * *

Yet the proportionality of the damages specification highlights by way of contrast the only halfway decent argument that PacSci has against the validity of the liquidated damages clause. This is that the clause fails to differentiate between different *kinds* of breach, some more serious than others, as distinct from different degrees of seriousness within a given kind. * * * [B]ut it is an argument not for invalidating the clause but for interpreting it reasonably. * * *

Id. at 1001–04.

3.   In *XCO*, Judge Posner implies that courts should not interfere with liquidated damages clauses, but notes that clauses that make no differentiation for the types of breach should be interpreted reasonably. How does he resolve the apparent contradiction? Consider the Seventh Circuit's opinion in the next case.

ENERGY PLUS CONSULTING v. ILLINOIS FUEL CO.

United States Court of Appeals, Seventh Circuit, 2004.
371 F.3d 907.

Before BAUER, POSNER, and WILLIAMS, CIRCUIT JUDGES.

WILLIAMS, CIRCUIT JUDGE.

* * *

The contract at issue arose from Washington County, Illinois' (the "County") efforts to lease a coal reserve given to it by Exxon Corporation. In April 2001, the County entered into a contract with [Energy Plus Consulting] EPC (the "Standstill Agreement") granting EPC the exclusive right, for eighteen months, to contract with third parties to develop the reserve. The County, however, reserved its right to reject third-party proposals submitted by EPC.

* * * EPC solicited several companies potentially interested in exploring the reserve, including the defendants, Illinois Fuel Company, LLC and Appalachian Fuels, LLC (referenced jointly as "Fuels"). On August 13, 2001, Fuels and EPC signed an agreement (the "Agreement") which provided that EPC would present Fuels to the County as a potential candidate interested in exploring the reserve. In turn, upon entering into an option contract with the County providing Fuels an exclusive right to explore the reserve, Fuels would pay EPC $100,000. The Agreement also included the following clause:

Fuels shall pay to Energy Plus Seven–Hundred Twenty–Thousand Dollars ($720,000) upon whichever shall occur first:

(A.) the expiration of ninety days from the date of execution of the Option, unless Fuels has released the Option, or

(B.) the execution of a Mining Lease.

The Agreement further specified that if Fuels executed a mining lease with the County, Fuels would also pay EPC $720,000 on the date of execution for the next four years.

On August 13, 2001, following the execution of the Agreement between Fuels and EPC, Fuels and the County executed an option contract granting Fuels the exclusive right to explore and lease the reserve. The option expired the sooner of February 13, 2002 or the date upon which Fuels completed its due diligence. After executing the option contract, Fuels paid EPC $100,000, as required under the Agreement.

On November 15, 2001, four days after the expiration of the ninety-day deadline in the Agreement, EPC and Fuels amended the Agreement (the "Amendment"), extending the ninety-day deadline for Fuels to either pay $720,000 or release the option until December 31, 2001. Fuels paid $50,000 for the extension. The Amendment also stipulated that Fuels could extend the deadline to February 13, 2002 if Fuels paid EPC another $50,000 by no later than December 31, 2001.

On January 4, 2002, four days after the deadline to release the option agreement expired, Fuels notified the County by letter that it would not exercise the option and also informed EPC of its decision * * *. In response, EPC demanded that Fuels pay it $720,000 pursuant to the Amendment's provision which required the payment if Fuels did not release the option on or before December 31, 2001. When Fuels refused to pay, EPC filed this lawsuit * * * alleging breach of contract. * * * The district court * * * granted summary judgment in favor of Fuels, finding that the clause calling for the $720,000 payment was an unenforceable penalty. * * *

* * *

* * * In Illinois, a liquidated damages clause is valid and enforceable when: "(1) the actual damages from a breach are difficult to measure at the time the contract was made; and (2) the specified amount of damages is reasonable in light of the anticipated or actual loss caused by the breach."[2] Checkers Eight LP v. Hawkins, 241 F.3d 558, 562 (7th Cir. 2001); see also Lake River Corp. v. Carborundum Co., 769 F.2d 1284, 1289 (7th Cir.1985). Although this test is instructive, we are mindful that there is no fixed rule applicable to all liquidated damages provisions, as each must be evaluated on its own facts and circumstances. * * * Further, while "the distinction between a penalty and liquidated damages is not an easy one to draw," close cases will be resolved in favor of finding the disputed clause a penalty. * * *

The provision of the contract requiring Fuels to pay the $720,000 that EPC demands is a penalty under Illinois law because the clause mandating the payment was not reasonable at the time of contracting. * * * Here, Fuels was required to pay EPC $720,000 no matter when notice of the breach occurred. In other words, whether Fuels notified EPC on January 1, January 31, or any other future date that it would not exercise the option, the sum in damages, $720,000, would remain the same. In the alternative, if EPC received notice that Fuels released the option anytime before the ninety days expired, EPC would receive no money. *Lake River* made clear that this type of single sum payment, one that bears no relation to the gravity of the breach, is unreasonable. * * *

The November 15 Amendment is additional evidence of this single sum's unreasonableness. It gave Fuels the option of purchasing a forty-five day extension beyond December 31 for $50,000. This suggests that, at least as of November 15, the cost of keeping the reserves off the market beyond December 31 was closer to $50,000. Thus, EPC's requirement of a $720,000 payment, even for notifying EPC one day after the specified

2. Some Illinois courts also include a third prong: "[whether] the parties intended to agree in advance to the settlement of damages that might arise from the breach...." * * * The third prong does not materially alter the analysis here.

deadline that Fuels would not exercise the option, is an unenforceable penalty under Illinois law.

* * *

For the foregoing reasons, we affirm the district court's order granting summary judgment in favor of the defendants.

NOTES

1.   If you had been counsel for EPC, how would you have drafted the contract between it and Fuels? *See, e.g.*, Henry F. Luepke III, *How to Draft and Enforce A Liquidated Damages Clause*, 61 Journal of the Missouri Bar 324 (2005) (discussing the law of Missouri).

2.   The transaction in *Minihane* was a contract for the sale of football seats, and in *Energy Plus Consulting* the contract involved options on coal reserves. When a contract is for the sale of goods, § 2–718(1) of the Uniform Commercial Code governs:

> (1) Damages for breach by either party may be liquidated in the agreement but only at an amount which is reasonable in the light of the anticipated or actual harm caused by the breach, the difficulties of proof of loss, and the inconvenience or nonfeasibility of otherwise obtaining an adequate remedy. A term fixing unreasonably large liquidated damages is void as a penalty.

What effect, if any, would the Uniform Commercial Code have in either *Minihane* or *Energy Plus* (if it were deemed to be applicable)?

3.   How should a judge who believes strictly in freedom of contract have decided *Energy Plus*? For a critique of the rules governing enforceability of liquidated damages clauses, see Larry A. DiMatteo, *Penalties as Rational Response to Bargaining Irrationality*, 2006 Mich. St. L. Rev. 883, 884–890 (2006); Frederic L. Kirgis, *Fuzzy Logic and the Sliding Scale Theorem*, 53 Ala. L. Rev. 421 (2002). The history of liquidated damages clauses and the relationship between § 2–718(1) of the Uniform Commercial Code and § 356(1) of the Restatement (Second) of Contracts are discussed in Note, Susan V. Ferris, *Liquidated Damages Recovery Under the Restatement (Second) of Contracts*, 67 Cornell L. Rev. 862 (1982); *see also* Samuel A. Rea, Jr., *Efficiency Implications of Penalties and Liquidated Damages*, 13 J. Legal Stud. 147 (1984).

4.   The law of liquidated damages varies among jurisdictions and even within jurisdictions. Can you think why? *See* Daniel Browder, Comment, *Liquidated Damages in Montana*, 67 Mont. L. Rev. 361 (2006) (describing unsettled law of liquidated damages in Montana).

5.   What happens if a liquidated damages clause is invalidated as a penalty? *See* Coffman v. Olson & Co., P.C., 906 N.E.2d 201 (Ind. Ct. App. 2009) (determining damages after invalidating liquidated damages clause as a penalty).

6.   Can a liquidated damages clause ever provide for an amount of damages that is too small? *See* Varner v. B.L. Lanier Fruit Co., 370 So.2d 61

(Fla.Dist.Ct.App.1979) (finding a liquidated damages clause unreasonably low and holding it unconscionable); *see also* U.C.C. § 2–718, cmt. ("An unreasonably small amount * * * might be stricken under the section on unconscionable contracts.")

SECTION 6.   ATTORNEY'S FEES

ALYESKA PIPELINE SERVICE CO.
v. WILDERNESS SOCIETY

Supreme Court of the United States, 1975.
421 U.S. 240, 95 S.Ct. 1612, 44 L.Ed.2d 141.

Mr. Justice White delivered the opinion of the Court.

This litigation was initiated by respondents Wilderness Society, Environmental Defense Fund, Inc., and Friends of the Earth in an attempt to prevent the issuance of permits by the Secretary of the Interior which were required for the construction of the trans-Alaska oil pipeline. The Court of Appeals awarded attorneys' fees to respondents against petitioner Alyeska Pipeline Service Co. based upon the court's equitable powers and the theory that respondents were entitled to fees because they were performing the services of a "private attorney general." * * *

I

A major oil field was discovered in the North Slope of Alaska in 1968. In June 1969, the oil companies constituting the consortium owning Alyeska submitted an application to the Department of the Interior for rights-of-way for a pipeline that would transport oil from the North Slope across land in Alaska owned by the United States * * *.

Respondents brought this suit in March 1970, and sought declaratory and injunctive relief against the Secretary of the Interior on the grounds that he intended to issue the right-of-way and special land-use permits in violation of § 28 of the Mineral Leasing Act of 1920, * * * and without compliance with the National Environmental Policy Act of 1969 (NEPA) * * *. The District Court granted a preliminary injunction against issuance of the right-of-way and permits. [Alaska and Alyeska intervened. In 1972, the Interior Department released a six-volume Environmental Impact Statement and a three-volume Economic and Security Analysis. After time for public comment, the Secretary granted the permits to Alyeska. The District Court dissolved the preliminary injunction, denied the permanent injunction, and dismissed the complaint. The Court of Appeals for the District of Columbia Circuit reversed. Congress then enacted legislation to allow the the permits sought by Alyeska to be granted.]

With the merits of the litigation effectively terminated by this legislation, the Court of Appeals turned to the questions involved in respondents' request for an award of attorneys' fees. * * * Since there was no applicable statutory authorization for such an award, the court proceeded to consider whether the requested fee award fell within any of the exceptions to the general "American rule" that the prevailing party may not recover attorneys' fees as costs or otherwise. The exception for an award against a party who had acted in bad faith was inapposite, since the position taken by the federal and state parties and Alyeska "was manifestly reasonable and assumed in good faith...." * * * Application of the "common benefit" exception which spreads the cost of litigation to those persons benefiting from it would "stretch it totally outside its basic rationale...." *Ibid.*[14] The Court of Appeals nevertheless held that respondents had acted to vindicate "important statutory rights of all citizens ..." * * *; had ensured that the governmental system functioned properly; and were entitled to attorneys' fees lest the great cost of litigation of this kind, particularly against well-financed defendants such as Alyeska, deter private parties desiring to see the laws protecting the environment properly enforced. Title 28 U.S.C. § 2412 was thought to bar taxing any attorneys' fees against the United States, and it was also deemed inappropriate to burden the State of Alaska with any part of the award. But Alyeska, the Court of Appeals held, could fairly be required to pay one-half of the full award to which respondents were entitled for having performed the functions of a private attorney general. * * *[17]

II

In the United States, the prevailing litigant is ordinarily not entitled to collect a reasonable attorneys' fee from the loser. We are asked to fashion a far-reaching exception to this "American Rule"; but having considered its origin and development, we are convinced that it would be inappropriate for the Judiciary, without legislative guidance, to reallocate the burdens of litigation in the manner and to the extent urged by respondents and approved by the Court of Appeals.

At common law, costs were not allowed; but for centuries in England there has been statutory authorization to award costs, including attorneys' fees. Although the matter is in the discretion of the court, counsel fees are regularly allowed to the prevailing party.[18] [A detailed discussion of the history of attorneys' fees in the United States is omitted.]

* * *

14. "[T]his litigation may well have provided substantial benefits to particular individuals and, indeed, to every citizen's interest in the proper functioning of our system of government. But imposing attorneys' fees on Alyeska will not operate to spread the costs of litigation proportionately among these beneficiaries...." 161 U.S.App.D.C., at 449, 495 F.2d, at 1029.

17. The Court of Appeals also directed that "[t]he fee award need not be limited ... to the amount actually paid or owed by (respondents). It may well be that counsel serve organizations like (respondents) for compensation below that obtainable in the market because they believe the organizations further a public interest. Litigation of this sort should not have to rely on the charity of counsel any more than it should rely on the charity of parties volunteering to serve as private attorneys general. The attorneys who worked on this case should be reimbursed the reasonable value of their services, despite the absence of any obligation on the part of (respondents) to pay attorneys' fees." *Id.*, at 457, 495 F.2d, at 1037.

18. * * * "It is now customary in England, after litigation of substantive claims has terminated, to conduct separate hearing before special 'taxing Masters' in order to determine the appropriateness and the size of an award of counsel fees. To prevent the ancillary proceedings from becoming unduly protracted and burdensome, fees which may be included in an award are

* * * [S]tatutory allowances are now available [in the United States] in a variety of circumstances, but they also differ considerably among themselves. Under the antitrust laws, for instance, allowance of attorneys' fees to a plaintiff awarded treble damages is mandatory. In patent litigation, in contrast, "[t]he court in exceptional cases may award reasonable attorney fees to the prevailing party." * * * Under Title II of the Civil Rights Act of 1964, * * * the prevailing party is entitled to attorneys' fees, at the discretion of the court, but we have held that Congress intended that the award should be made to the successful plaintiff absent exceptional circumstances. * * *

It is true that under some, if not most, of the statutes providing for the allowance of reasonable fees, Congress has opted to rely heavily on private enforcement to implement public policy and to allow counsel fees so as to encourage private litigation. * * * But congressional utilization of the private-attorney-general concept can in no sense be construed as a grant of authority to the Judiciary to jettison the traditional rule against nonstatutory allowances to the prevailing party and to award attorneys' fees whenever the courts deem the public policy furthered by a particular statute important enough to warrant the award.

Congress itself presumably has the power and judgment to pick and choose among its statutes and to allow attorneys' fees under some, but not others. But it would be difficult, indeed, for the courts, without legislative guidance, to consider some statutes important and others unimportant and to allow attorneys' fees only in connection with the former. * * *

* * *

We do not purport to assess the merits or demerits of the "American Rule" with respect to the allowance of attorneys' fees. It has been criticized in recent years,[45] and courts have been urged to find exceptions to it. It is also apparent from our national experience that the encouragement of private action to implement public policy has been viewed as desirable in a variety of circumstances. But the rule followed in our courts with respect to attorneys' fees has survived. It is deeply rooted in our history and in congressional policy; and it is not for us to invade the legislature's province by redistributing litigation costs in the manner suggested by respondents and followed by the Court of Appeals.

usually prescribed, even including the amounts that may be recovered for letters drafted on behalf of a client." Fleischmann Distilling Corp. v. Maier Brewing Co., 386 U.S. 714, 717, 87 S.Ct. 1404, 1406, 18 L.Ed.2d 475 (1967) (footnotes omitted). *See generally* Goodhart, *Costs*, 38 Yale L.J. 849 (1929); C. McCormick, Law of Damages 234–236 (1935).

45. *See, e.g.,* McLaughlin, *The Recovery of Attorney's Fees: A New Method of Financing Legal Services*, 40 Ford.L.Rev. 761 (1972); Ehrenzweig, *Reimbursement of Counsel Fees and the Great Society*, 54 Calif.L.Rev. 792 (1966); Stoebuck, *Counsel Fees Included in Costs: A Logical Development*, 38 U.Colo.L.Rev. 202 (1966); Kuenzel, *The Attorney's Fee: Why Not a Cost of Litigation?*, 49 Iowa L.Rev. 75 (1963); McCormick, *Counsel Fees and Other Expenses of Litigation as an Element of Damages*, 15 Minn.L.Rev. 619 (1931); Comment, *Court Awarded Attorney's Fees and Equal Access to the Courts*, 122 U.Pa.L.Rev. 636, 648–655 (1974); Note, *Attorney's Fees: Where Shall the Ultimate Burden Lie?*, 20 Vand.L.Rev. 1216 (1967). *See also* 1 Speiser § 12.8; Posner, *An Economic Approach to Legal Procedure and Judicial Administration*, 2 J.Legal Studies, 399, 437–438 (1973).

The decision below must therefore be reversed.

MR. JUSTICE DOUGLAS and MR. JUSTICE POWELL took no part in the consideration or decision of this case.

MR. JUSTICE BRENNAN, dissenting. [Opinion omitted.]

MR. JUSTICE MARSHALL, dissenting.

In reversing the award of attorneys' fees to the respondent environmentalist groups, the Court today disavows the well-established power of federal equity courts to award attorneys' fees when the interests of justice so require. While under the traditional American Rule the courts ordinarily refrain from allowing attorneys' fees, we have recognized several judicial exceptions to that rule for classes of cases in which equity seemed to favor fee shifting. * * *

* * *

* * * [W]hile as a general rule attorneys' fees are not to be awarded to the successful litigant, the courts as well as the Legislature may create exceptions to that rule. * * * Under the judge-made exceptions, attorneys' fees have been assessed, without statutory authorization, for willful violation of a court order, Toledo Scale Co. v. Computing Scale Co., 261 U.S. 399, 426–428, 43 S.Ct. 458, 465–466, 67 L.Ed. 719 (1923); for bad faith or oppressive litigation practices, Vaughan v. Atkinson, 369 U.S. 527, 530–531, 82 S.Ct. 997, 999, 8 L.Ed.2d 88 (1962); and where the successful litigants have created a common fund for recovery or extended a substantial benefit to a class, Central Railroad & Banking Co. v. Pettus, 113 U.S. 116, 5 S.Ct. 387, 28 L.Ed. 915 (1885) * * *. While the Court today acknowledges the continued vitality of these exceptions, it turns its back on the theory underlying them, and on the generous construction given to the common-benefit exception in our recent cases. * * *

* * *

* * * Since the Court of Appeals held Alyeska accountable for a fair share of the fees to ease the burden on the public-minded citizen litigators, I would affirm the judgment below.

NOTES

1. *Alyeska* noted that attorney's fees can be allocated by statute and other exceptions to the American rule, but did not mention another exception, presumably because it was inapplicable: that attorney's fees may be provided for by contract. What happens if a contract provides that, in the case of litigation, one party will recover fees if that party prevails, but is silent as to the other party's right to recover? *See* Ribbens International, S.A. v. Transport International Pool, Inc., 47 F.Supp.2d 1117, 1119 (C.D.Cal.1999) (Even though Pennsylvania law governed the issues of liability and damages, California law governed the right to recover attorney's fees so that California Civil Code § 1717(a) applied: "Section 1717(a) imposes an obligation of mutuality on such one-way attorney's fees provisions, requiring California courts to

award reasonable attorney's fees to any prevailing party in an action involving a contract that specifically provides that only one or the other party could receive attorney's fees in an action relating to that contract.").

2. Congress responded to *Alyeska* by passing the Civil Rights Attorney's Fees Awards Act of 1976, 42 U.S.C.A. § 1988, which provides that "the court in its discretion, may allow the prevailing party * * * a reasonable attorney's fee" in a number of specified civil rights actions, including those filed under 42 U.S.C.A. § 1983. *See* Evans v. Jeff D., 475 U.S. 717, 106 S.Ct. 1531, 89 L.Ed.2d 747 (1986) (Brennan, J., dissenting) ("Congress found that *Alyeska* had a 'devastating' impact on civil rights litigation, and it concluded that the need for corrective legislation was 'compelling.' ").

3. Some states still have the "private attorney general" or "common benefit" rule. *See* Bell v. Birmingham News Co., 576 So.2d 669 (Ala.Civ.App. 1991) ("Alabama follows the 'American Rule' * * * that fees may be recovered only where authorized by statute, when provided in a contract, or by special equity, such as in a proceeding where the efforts of an attorney create a fund out of which fees may be paid. * * * In addition to the exception concerning a benefit, such fees may be awarded when the interests of justice so require.").

4. *Alyeska* noted the criticism of the "American Rule." Earlier, in Fleischmann Distilling Corp. v. Maier Brewing Co., 386 U.S. 714, 718, 87 S.Ct. 1404, 1407, 18 L.Ed.2d 475 (1967), the Court had catalogued several justifications for the American rule: e.g., "since litigation is at best uncertain, one should not be penalized for merely defending or prosecuting a lawsuit * * * "; and "the poor might be unjustly discouraged from instituting actions to vindicate their rights if the penalty for losing included the fees of their opponents' counsel."

5. Is there a justification for shifting attorney's fees only to losing defendants, but not to losing plaintiffs? Is the justification any less persuasive in cases solely between private parties, to which the government is not a party? Is the justification related to the presumed resources of the parties? In this regard, the Equal Access to Justice Act generally allows fee awards against the United States, or its agencies or officials, but only to individuals whose net worth does not exceed $2,000,000, and to businesses or other entities with a net worth not exceeding $7,000,000, which do not employ more than 500 employees. 28 U.S.C.A. § 2412(d)(2)(B) (2004). Would it be feasible, and fair, to turn the statute on its head, and allow the Government to recover fees against losing plaintiffs whose resources exceed those limits? Would it be desirable, in cases solely between private parties, to provide for fee-shifting to allow the recovery of attorney's fees against any party with resources over a pre-established amount?

6. In Swedish Hospital Corp. v. Shalala, 1 F.3d 1261 (D.C.Cir.1993), the court upheld an award of 20% of the common fund for attorneys' fees. The court thoroughly reviewed the issues involved in making such an award:

A. Lodestar Versus Percentage of the Fund

    1. General Principles Governing Fee Awards

* * * Over time, courts have fashioned several equitable exceptions to this "American rule." One of the earliest, and still most common, exceptions is the "common fund" doctrine typically applied in class actions like the present one. * * * That doctrine allows a party who creates, preserves, or increases the value of a fund in which others have an ownership interest to be reimbursed from that fund for litigation expenses incurred, including counsel fees. It is by now well established that "a litigant or lawyer who recovers a common fund for the benefit of persons other than himself or his client is entitled to a reasonable attorney's fee from the fund as a whole." * * * The underlying justification for attorney reimbursement from a common fund, as explained by the Supreme Court in three early cases, is that unless the costs of litigation were spread to the beneficiaries of the fund they would be unjustly enriched by the attorney's efforts. * * *

When awarding attorneys' fees, federal courts have a duty to ensure that claims for attorneys' fees are reasonable. *See* Hensley v. Eckerhart, 461 U.S. 424, 433 (1983) * * *. Special problems exist in assessing the reasonableness of fees in a class action suit since class members with low individual stakes in the outcome often do not file objections, and the defendant who contributed the fund will usually have no interest in how the fund is divided between the plaintiffs and class counsel.

2. *The Percentage-of-the-Fund Method for Calculating Fees*

Historically, courts have exercised considerable discretion and applied a reasonableness standard, focusing upon the particular circumstances of a case, in determining the amount of a common fund fee award. The percentage-of-the-fund method of calculating attorneys' fees in common fund cases was most common. * * * *See also* Court Awarded Attorney Fees, Report of the Third Circuit Task Force, 108 F.R.D. 237, 242 (1986) ("*Third Circuit Task Force Report*").

3. *The Lodestar and Twelve–Factor Tests*

The application of a percentage-of-the-fund approach sometimes resulted in large fee awards, and in the 1970s several courts began a movement to alternative methods of calculating attorneys' fees. In 1973, the Third Circuit led the way in Lindy Bros. Builders, Inc. of Philadelphia v. American Radiator & Standard Sanitary Corp., 487 F.2d 161 (3d Cir.1973), instructing judges in that circuit to first compute the product of the reasonable hours expended and the reasonable hourly rate to arrive at the "lodestar." That amount could then be adjusted upward or downward, based upon additional factors such as the contingent nature of the case and the quality of the attorneys' work. This so-called "lodestar/multiplier" approach thus shifted the emphasis from a fair percentage of recovery to the value of the time expended by counsel.

A year later in a case involving a fee-shifting statute rather than a common fund, the Fifth Circuit identified twelve factors as relevant to determining a reasonable fee award * * *. Johnson v. Georgia Highway Express, Inc., 488 F.2d 714 (5th Cir.1974), *abrogated in part on other grounds,* Blanchard v. Bergeron, 489 U.S. 87 (1989).

After the emergence of *Lindy* and *Johnson*, the federal courts experimented with combinations of the *Lindy* lodestar and *Johnson* twelve-factor approaches in both common fund and fee-shifting contexts. In the context of the fee-shifting statutes, the lodestar approach but without enhancement for the *Johnson* factors has emerged as the prevailing method of fee calculation. *See, e.g.,* City of Burlington v. Dague, 112 S.Ct. 2638 (1992) * * *. However, at the same time, many courts and commentators have noted differences between the fee-shifting and common fund cases, raising questions as to whether the same methodology should apply. A Third Circuit task force appointed to compare the respective merits of the lodestar and percentage-of-the-fund approaches concluded that the lodestar technique, at least as encumbered with the *Johnson* factors, is a "cumbersome, enervating, and often surrealistic process of preparing and evaluating fee petitions that now plagues the Bench and Bar." *Third Circuit Task Force Report,* 108 F.R.D. at 255.

The task force enumerated nine deficiencies in the lodestar process: 1) it "increases the workload of an already overtaxed judicial system"; 2) the elements of the process "are insufficiently objective and produce results that are far from homogeneous"; 3) the process "creates a sense of mathematical precision that is unwarranted in terms of the realities of the practice of law"; 4) the process "is subject to manipulation by judges who prefer to calibrate fees in terms of percentages * * *"; 5) the process, although designed to curb abuses, has led to other abuses, such as encouraging lawyers to expend excessive hours engaging in duplicative and unjustified work, inflating their "normal billing rates, and including fictitious hours"; 6) it "creates a disincentive for the early settlement of cases"; 7) it "does not provide the district court with enough flexibility to reward or deter lawyers so that desirable objectives, such as early settlement, will be fostered"; 8) the process "works to the particular disadvantage of the public interest bar" because, for example, the "lodestar" is set lower in civil rights cases than in securities and antitrust cases; and 9) despite the apparent simplicity of the lodestar approach, "considerable confusion and lack of predictability remain in its administration." *Id.* at 246–49.

The task force, though recommending the retention of a lodestar approach in statutory fee cases, concluded that in common fund cases the best determinant of the reasonable value of services rendered to the class by counsel is a percentage of the fund. *Id.* at 255.

Id. at 1265–72.

BUCKHANNON BOARD AND CARE HOME v. WEST VIRGINIA DEPARTMENT OF HEALTH AND HUMAN RESOURCES

Supreme Court of the United States, 2001.
532 U.S. 598, 121 S.Ct. 1835, 149 L.Ed.2d 855.

CHIEF JUSTICE REHNQUIST delivered the opinion of the Court

Numerous federal statutes allow courts to award attorney's fees and costs to the "prevailing party." The question presented here is whether this term includes a party that has failed to secure a judgment on the merits or a court-ordered consent decree, but has nonetheless achieved the desired result because the lawsuit brought about a voluntary change in the defendant's conduct. * * *

Buckhannon Board and Care Home, Inc., which operates care homes that provide assisted living to their residents, failed an inspection by the West Virginia Office of the State Fire Marshal because some of the residents were incapable of "self-preservation" as defined under state law. * * * On October 28, 1997, after receiving cease and desist orders requiring the closure of its residential care facilities within 30 days, Buckhannon Board and Care Home, Inc., on behalf of itself and other similarly situated homes and residents (hereinafter petitioners), brought suit in the United States District Court for the Northern District of West Virginia against the State of West Virginia, two of its agencies, and 18 individuals (hereinafter respondents), seeking declaratory and injunctive relief [1] that the "self-preservation" requirement violated the Fair Housing Amendments Act of 1988 (FHAA), * * * 42 U.S.C. § 3601 et seq., and the Americans with Disabilities Act of 1990 (ADA), * * * 42 U.S.C. § 12101 et seq.

Respondents agreed to stay enforcement of the cease-and-desist orders pending resolution of the case and the parties began discovery. In 1998, the West Virginia Legislature enacted two bills eliminating the "self-preservation" requirement, * * * and respondents moved to dismiss the case as moot. The District Court granted the motion, finding that the 1998 legislation had eliminated the allegedly offensive provisions * * *.

Petitioners requested attorney's fees as the "prevailing party" under the FHAA, 42 U.S.C. § 3613(c)(2) ("[T]he court, in its discretion, may allow the prevailing party . . . a reasonable attorney's fee and costs"), and ADA, 42 U.S.C. § 12205 ("[T]he court . . ., in its discretion, may allow the prevailing party . . . a reasonable attorney's fee, including litigation expenses, and costs"). Petitioners argued that they were entitled to attorney's fees under the "catalyst theory," which posits that a plaintiff is a "prevailing party" if it achieves the desired result because the lawsuit brought about a voluntary change in the defendant's conduct. * * *

* * *

In the United States, parties are ordinarily required to bear their own attorney's fees—the prevailing party is not entitled to collect from the loser. See Alyeska Pipeline Service Co. v. Wilderness Society, 421 U.S. 240, 247, 95 S.Ct. 1612, 44 L.Ed.2d 141 (1975). * * * Congress, however, has authorized the award of attorney's fees to the "prevailing party" in numerous statutes in addition to those at issue here, such as the Civil Rights Act of 1964, * * * 42 U.S.C. § 2000e–5(k), the Voting Rights Act Amendments of 1975, * * * 42 U.S.C. § 1973l(e), and the Civil Rights Attorney's Fees Awards Act of 1976, * * * 42 U.S.C. § 1988. See generally

---

1. The original complaint also sought money damages, but petitioners relinquished this claim on January 2, 1998.

Marek v. Chesny, 473 U.S. 1, 105 S.Ct. 3012, 87 L.Ed.2d 1 (1985) (Appendix to opinion of BRENNAN, J., dissenting).

In designating those parties eligible for an award of litigation costs, Congress employed the term "prevailing party," a legal term of art. Black's Law Dictionary 1145 (7th ed.1999) defines "prevailing party" as "[a] party in whose favor a judgment is rendered, regardless of the amount of damages awarded <in certain cases, the court will award attorney's fees to the prevailing party>.—Also termed *successful party.*" This view that a "prevailing party" is one who has been awarded some relief by the court can be distilled from our prior cases.

In Hanrahan v. Hampton, 446 U.S. 754, 758, 100 S.Ct. 1987, 64 L.Ed.2d 670 (1980) (per curiam), we reviewed the legislative history of § 1988 and found that "Congress intended to permit the interim award of counsel fees only when a party has prevailed on the merits of at least some of his claims." * * * We have held that even an award of nominal damages suffices under this test. *See* Farrar v. Hobby, 506 U.S. 103, 113 S.Ct. 566, 121 L.Ed.2d 494 (1992).[6]

In addition to judgments on the merits, we have held that settlement agreements enforced through a consent decree may serve as the basis for an award of attorney's fees. *See* Maher v. Gagne, 448 U.S. 122, 100 S.Ct. 2570, 65 L.Ed.2d 653 (1980). Although a consent decree does not always include an admission of liability, * * * it nonetheless is a court-ordered "chang[e] [in] the legal relationship between [the plaintiff] and the defendant." Texas State Teacher's Ass'n v. Garland Independent School District, 489 U.S. 782, 792, 109 S.Ct. 1486, 103 L.Ed.2d 866 (1989) * * *.[7] These decisions, taken together, establish that enforceable judgments on the merits and court-ordered consent decrees create the "material alteration of the legal relationship of the parties" necessary to permit an award of attorney's fees. * * *

We think, however, the "catalyst theory" falls on the other side of the line from these examples. It allows an award where there is no judicially sanctioned change in the legal relationship of the parties. Even under a limited form of the "catalyst theory," a plaintiff could recover attorney's fees if it established that the "complaint had sufficient merit to withstand a motion to dismiss for lack of jurisdiction or failure to state a claim on which relief may be granted." Brief for United States as *Amicus Curiae* 27. This is not the type of legal merit that our prior decisions, based upon plain language and congressional intent, have found necessary. * * * A defendant's voluntary change in conduct, although perhaps accomplishing what the plaintiff sought to achieve by the lawsuit, lacks the necessary judicial *imprimatur* on the change. * * *

---

6. However, in some circumstances such a "prevailing party" should still not receive an award of attorney's fees. *See* Farrar v. Hobby, *supra*, at 115–116, 113 S.Ct. 566.

7. * * * Private settlements do not entail the judicial approval and oversight involved in consent decrees. * * *

* * * We cannot agree that the term "prevailing party" authorizes federal courts to award attorney's fees to a plaintiff who, by simply filing a nonfrivolous but nonetheless potentially meritless lawsuit (it will never be determined), has reached the "sought-after destination" without obtaining any judicial relief. * * *

* * *

Petitioners * * * assert that the "catalyst theory" is necessary to prevent defendants from unilaterally mooting an action before judgment in an effort to avoid an award of attorney's fees. They also claim that the rejection of the "catalyst theory" will deter plaintiffs with meritorious but expensive cases from bringing suit. We are skeptical of these assertions, which are entirely speculative and unsupported by any empirical evidence * * *.

Petitioners discount the disincentive that the "catalyst theory" may have upon a defendant's decision to voluntarily change its conduct, conduct that may not be illegal. "The defendants' potential liability for fees in this kind of litigation can be as significant as, and sometimes even more significant than, their potential liability on the merits," Evans v. Jeff D., 475 U.S. 717, 734, 106 S.Ct. 1531, 89 L.Ed.2d 747 (1986), and the possibility of being assessed attorney's fees may well deter a defendant from altering its conduct.

And petitioners' fear of mischievous defendants only materializes in claims for equitable relief, for so long as the plaintiff has a cause of action for damages, a defendant's change in conduct will not moot the case. Even then, it is not clear how often courts will find a case mooted: "It is well settled that a defendant's voluntary cessation of a challenged practice does not deprive a federal court of its power to determine the legality of the practice" unless it is "absolutely clear that the allegedly wrongful behavior could not reasonably be expected to recur." Friends of Earth, Inc. v. Laidlaw Environmental Services (TOC), Inc., 528 U.S. 167, 189, 120 S.Ct. 693, 145 L.Ed.2d 610 (2000) * * *. If a case is not found to be moot, and the plaintiff later procures an enforceable judgment, the court may of course award attorney's fees. Given this possibility, a defendant has a strong incentive to enter a settlement agreement, where it can negotiate attorney's fees and costs. * * *

We have also stated that "[a] request for attorney's fees should not result in a second major litigation," Hensley v. Eckerhart, 461 U.S. 424, 437, 103 S.Ct. 1933, 76 L.Ed.2d 40 (1983). * * * Among other things, a "catalyst theory" hearing would require analysis of the defendant's subjective motivations in changing its conduct, an analysis that "will likely depend on a highly factbound inquiry and may turn on reasonable inferences from the nature and timing of the defendant's change in conduct." * * *

* * * For the reasons stated above, we hold that the "catalyst theory" is not a permissible basis for the award of attorney's fees under the FHAA, 42 U.S.C. § 3613(c)(2), and ADA, 42 U.S.C. § 12205.

The judgment of the Court of Appeals is

Affirmed.

JUSTICE SCALIA, with whom JUSTICE THOMAS joins, concurring. [Opinion omitted.]

JUSTICE GINSBURG, with whom JUSTICE STEVENS, JUSTICE SOUTER, and JUSTICE BREYER join, dissenting.

The Court today holds that a plaintiff whose suit prompts the precise relief she seeks does not "prevail," and hence cannot obtain an award of attorney's fees, unless she also secures a court entry memorializing her victory. The entry need not be a judgment on the merits. Nor need there be any finding of wrongdoing. A court-approved settlement will do.

* * * The decision allows a defendant to escape a statutory obligation to pay a plaintiff's counsel fees, even though the suit's merit led the defendant to abandon the fray, to switch rather than fight on, to accord plaintiff sooner rather than later the principal redress sought in the complaint. Concomitantly, the Court's constricted definition of "prevailing party," and consequent rejection of the "catalyst theory," impede access to court for the less well heeled, and shrink the incentive Congress created for the enforcement of federal law by private attorneys general.

In my view, the "catalyst rule," as applied by the clear majority of Federal Circuits, is a key component of the fee-shifting statutes Congress adopted to advance enforcement of civil rights. Nothing in history, precedent, or plain English warrants the anemic construction of the term "prevailing party" the Court today imposes.

* * *

* * * [P]laintiffs were denied fees not because they failed to achieve the relief they sought. On the contrary, they gained the very change they sought through their lawsuit when West Virginia repealed the self-preservation rule that would have stopped Buckhannon from caring for people like Dorsey Pierce.

* * *

One can entirely agree with Black's Law Dictionary that a party "in whose favor a judgment is rendered" prevails, and at the same time resist, as most Courts of Appeals have, any implication that *only* such a party may prevail. * * * Notably, this Court did not refer to Black's Law Dictionary in Maher v. Gagne, 448 U.S. 122, 100 S.Ct. 2570, 65 L.Ed.2d 653 (1980), which held that a consent decree could qualify a plaintiff as "prevailing." * * *

* * *

A lawsuit's ultimate purpose is to achieve actual relief from an opponent. Favorable judgment may be instrumental in gaining that relief. Generally, however, "the judicial decree is not the end but the means. At the end of the rainbow lies not a judgment, but some action (or cessation of action) by the defendant...." Hewitt v. Helms, 482 U.S. 755, 761, 107 S.Ct. 2672, 96 L.Ed.2d 654 (1987). * * *

* * *

In opposition to the argument that defendants will resist change in order to stave off an award of fees, one could urge that the catalyst rule may lead defendants promptly to comply with the law's requirements: the longer the litigation, the larger the fees. * * * [W]hy should this court's fee-shifting rulings drive a plaintiff prepared to accept adequate relief, though out-of-court and unrecorded, to litigate on? And if the catalyst rule leads defendants to negotiate not only settlement terms but also allied counsel fees, is that not a consummation to applaud, not deplore?

* * *

* * * Congress prescribed fee-shifting provisions like those included in the FHAA and ADA to encourage private enforcement of laws designed to advance civil rights. Fidelity to that purpose calls for court-awarded fees when a private party's lawsuit, whether or not its settlement is registered in court, vindicates rights Congress sought to secure. I would so hold and therefore dissent from the judgment and opinion of the Court.

NOTES

1. The "lodestar" method, and not the percentage of recovery method, is used to determine the fees payable by a defendant under a fee-shifting statute. Also, in that context, no enhancement of the lodestar amount is permitted to reflect that counsel took the risk of representing the plaintiffs on a contingent basis. City of Burlington v. Dague, 505 U.S. 557, 112 S.Ct. 2638, 120 L.Ed.2d 449 (1992). The Supreme Court reasoned in *Dague* that the contingency already was being considered in the hourly rates charged by the attorneys, and therefore no enhancement for risk was proper in determining what was a "reasonable fee," and also that a proceeding to determine such an enhancement would add complexity and arbitrariness to the process of determining fees.

In Perdue v. Kenny A., ___ U.S. ___, 130 S.Ct. 1662, 176 L.Ed.2d 494 (2010), however, the Court unanimously held that a lodestar award could be increased to recognize superior quality of the attorneys' services and the results achieved, but only in "rare" and "exceptional" circumstances. Despite that holding, five justices agreed to vacate the enhancement to the lodestar granted by the District Court and affirmed by the Court of Appeals for the Fifth Circuit, in a protracted litigation of considerable public importance concerning the foster care system of the State of Georgia. The majority held that the District Court had not sufficiently articulated objective reasons for the enhancement, such as the inability to attract counsel to take the case at lodestar rates, or that such rates failed to reflect the market value of such services. The majority added that enhancements to the lodestar for the superiority of the attorneys' work and of the results they achieved could not be justified on an "impressionistic basis". *Id.* at 1676.

"The bar against risk multipliers in statutory fee cases does not apply to common fund cases" when the fee is payable by the class, and the court can award either a percentage of the recovery, or a fee that adds a multiplier to the lodestar amount. Vizcaino v. Microsoft Corporation, 290 F.3d 1043, 1051 (9th Cir.), *cert. denied*, 537 U.S. 1018, 123 S.Ct. 536, 154 L.Ed.2d 425 (2002). Further, except in a class action in which the court determines all fees, an attorney's recovery from a client with whom he has a retainer contract can exceed the statutory award. Venegas v. Mitchell, 495 U.S. 82, 110 S.Ct. 1679, 109 L.Ed.2d 74 (1990).

Are these distinctions valid in light of the fact that the court is professing in all cases to be awarding a "reasonable" fee? Stated otherwise, why should the fee that is "reasonable" differ in a fee-shifting case and a common fund case, particularly if the plaintiffs' recovery is the same?

2.   In applying the lodestar method, only time spent on the portions of the case in which plaintiffs were successful is compensated. Hensley v. Eckerhart, 461 U.S. 424, 103 S.Ct. 1933, 76 L.Ed.2d 40 (1980). *See, e.g.*, Diaz–Rivera v. Rivera–Rodriguez, 377 F.3d 119 (1st Cir.2004) (District Court properly reduced the claimed attorney's fee by one-third to reflect the fact that plaintiffs did not prevail on one of their major claims, but, when plaintiffs established a constitutional violation which "represented a significant legal conclusion serving an important public purpose, the court also properly awarded fees as to matters on which plaintiffs' victory did not gain them substantial monetary relief.").

3.   As *Buckhannon* shows, to recover under typical fee shifting statutes, a plaintiff must be the "prevailing party." *E.g.*, Equal Access to Justice Act, 28 U.S.C.A. § 2412(d); Civil Rights Attorneys' Fees Awards Act, 42 U.S.C.A. § 1988. Although this standard may sometimes be met without the party having obtained a "favorable 'final judgment following a full trial on the merits,'" the party "must have established his entitlement to some relief on the merits of his claims," Hanrahan v. Hampton, 446 U.S. 754, 757, 100 S.Ct. 1987, 1989, 64 L.Ed.2d 670 (1980), and "be able to point to a resolution of the dispute which changes the legal relationship between itself and the defendant." Texas State Teachers Ass'n v. Garland Independent School District, 489 U.S. 782, 792, 109 S.Ct. 1486, 1493, 103 L.Ed.2d 866 (1989). This test is not met by the plaintiff merely being able to obtain a ruling that the complaint should not be dismissed for failure to state a claim on which relief can be granted. Hewitt v. Helms, 482 U.S. 755, 760, 107 S.Ct. 2672, 2676, 96 L.Ed.2d 654 (1987). Nor can a plaintiff recover attorney's fees when the recovery is only nominal damages on a $17 million compensatory damages claim. Farrar v. Hobby, 506 U.S. 103, 113 S.Ct. 566, 121 L.Ed.2d 494 (1992). What does *Buckhannon* add to these prior holdings?

4.   After *Buckhannon*, the Supreme Court has held, in Sole v. Wyner, 551 U.S. 74, 127 S.Ct. 2188, 167 L.Ed.2d 1069 (2007), that a party which obtains short-lived and tentative relief by the granting of a preliminary injunction, but later loses on the merits, is not a "prevailing party," for "fleeting success" is not enough. However, several Court of Appeals decisions hold, post–*Buckhannon*, that in at least some circumstances obtaining a preliminary injunction may suffice. See, *e.g.*, Select Milk Producers, Inc. v.

Johanns, 400 F.3d 939, 945–48 (D.C.Cir. 2005) (where preliminary injunction results in some permanent savings for plaintiffs, and is based on considered scrutiny of merits by court, plaintiffs were "prevailing parties"); People Against Police Violence v. City of Pittsburgh, 520 F.3d 226 (3d Cir. 2008) (plaintiffs prevailed where statute changed, in their favor, after preliminary injunction granted). Congress has amended the Freedom of Information Act to make *Buckhannon* inapplicable to proceedings under that Act. See 5 U.S.C. § 552(a)(4)(E)(ii) (2007).

5. In Evans v. Jeff D., 475 U.S. 717, 732, 106 S.Ct. 1531, 89 L.Ed.2d 747 (1986), an attorney from the Idaho Legal Aid Society was appointed to represent a class of children suffering from emotional and physical handicaps in the care of the state. The suit alleged deficiencies in both the educational programs and the health care services provided. One week before trial, the state offered to settle the case with greater injunctive relief than the court had indicated it was willing to grant, conditioned on the plaintiffs' attorney waiving attorney's fees. The attorney felt ethically bound to recommend that the plaintiffs accept a settlement, but conditioned the waiver of fees on the court's approval. The majority held that Congress did not intend to ban fee waivers, saying "we believe that a general proscription against negotiated waiver of attorney's fees in exchange for a settlement on the merits would itself impede vindication of civil rights, at least in some cases, by reducing the attractiveness of settlement." *Id.* at 732, 106 S.Ct. at 1540. Justice Brennan, for the dissent, said that "the *proper* question is whether permitting negotiated fee waivers is consistent with Congress' goal of attracting competent counsel," but noted that the decision did not affect the ability of bar associations to deem it "unethical for defense counsel to seek fee waivers" as some had already done. *Id.* at 765, 106 S.Ct. at 1557.

6. A number of federal and state governmental bodies have sued tobacco companies for reimbursement of the cost of medical treatment for illnesses caused by tobacco. *See, e.g.,* City of St. Louis v. American Tobacco Co., *infra* Chapter 6, Section 2.C.2. Some states have settled with the companies for billions of dollars. These settlements have raised a number of interesting attorney's fees issues. For a panel discussion of some of the issues, see Daniel J. Capra, et al., *The Tobacco Litigation and Attorneys' Fees*, 67 Ford. L. Rev. 2827 (1999).

SECTION 7. APPLYING THE BASIC PRINCIPLES: DAMAGES FOR TORTIOUS INTERFERENCE WITH THE PERSON

A. COMPENSATORY DAMAGES FOR HARM TO THE PERSON

1. **Compensatory Damages for Physical Injury**

a. *Basic Categories of Recovery*

DAN B. DOBBS, THE LAW OF REMEDIES
647–648 (2d ed. 1993).*

§ 8.1 Damages for Personal Injury

§ 8.1(1) Elements of Damages for Personal Injury

Compensation Elements Generally

Compensatory, lump-sum awards. The traditional theory is that, except for punitive damages imposed as punishment for more serious wrongdoings, awards for personal injury are aimed at compensating the victim or making good the losses proximately resulting from the injury. Personal injury awards are lump-sum awards; unlike workers' compensation awards, they are not paid out in weekly or monthly sums. For this reason all damages for personal injury, including damages expected to accrue in the future, traditionally must be proved and calculated at the trial.[2]

Elements. Plaintiffs prove three basic elements of recovery in personal injury actions. (1) Time losses. The plaintiff can recover loss [of] wages or the value of any lost time or earning capacity where injuries prevent work. (2) Expenses incurred by reason of the injury. These are usually medical expenses and kindred items. (3) Pain and suffering in its various forms, including emotional distress and consciousness of loss.

Permanent or future harm. One characteristic or attribute of each element of damage is that it may be permanent, or if not permanent, may continue to cause harm for some period in the future. Permanency and continuation of harm in the future are not logically elements of harm in themselves. They are not losses but they are characteristics that reflect the degree of loss which the plaintiff suffers. If an injury is permanent or will continue in the future, the plaintiff may lose time from her job, may have additional medical expense, or may suffer pain long after the trial is over. The plaintiff is entitled to recover for such future losses with respect

---

* Reprinted with permission of West Publishing Co.

2. Periodic payment statutes and structured settlements may provide for payment of damages over a period of time, but nevertheless rely primarily on an up-front determination of the amount of damages. See § 8.5(5) below.

to each of the elements. Proof of future loss may be especially difficult or uncertain in many cases, however. In addition, adjustments must be made when future losses are estimated to account for inflation and the effects of prepayment.

Elements apply in injury claims generally. Although details may differ in particular jurisdictions, the basic elements just listed are always recognized as recoverable items in some form, not only in the various states, but also under federal tort systems such as the FELA[7] and Jones Act.[8] The same elements are recognized as recoverable in any kind of tort claim for personal injury. Pain and suffering, for example, is equally recoverable in a strict products liability claim, in an ordinary negligence case, and in a civil rights action. * * * The identity of the elements in all tort cases flows from the compensatory theory of recovery. That is, since the law attempts to measure compensation for losses, differences in losses require a different recovery but differences in the tort that leads to those losses do not.

McDONALD v. UNITED STATES

United States District Court, Middle District of Pennsylvania, 1983.
555 F.Supp. 935.

CONABOY, DISTRICT JUDGE.

Plaintiff Lucy McDonald instituted this action pursuant to the Federal Tort Claims Act, 28 U.S.C. §§ 1346(b), 2671 et seq. (1976), and the National Swine Flu Immunization Program of 1976 (Swine Flu Act), formerly codified at 42 U.S.C. § 247b(j)-(*l*) (1976), seeking to recover compensatory damages for injuries allegedly suffered as a result of her inoculation with the swine influenza vaccine.[2] * * * A non-jury trial was held * * *.

I. SUMMARY OF CONTENTIONS AND HOLDING

The central issue involved here is the diagnosis of the Plaintiff's neurological disorder. The Plaintiff's primary contention is that she is suffering from Guillain–Barre Syndrome (GBS) caused by the swine flu inoculation she received on November 14, 1976. The Defendant's position is that the Plaintiff's illness is not GBS, but Transverse Myelitis (TM), a disease of the spinal cord, which the Defendant contends has no causal relationship to the swine flu vaccine.

* * *

---

7. 45 U.S.C.A. § 51. *See*, reflecting damage elements, Chesapeake & O.R. Co. v. Carnahan, 241 U.S. 241, 243, 36 S.Ct. 594, 594, 60 L.Ed. 979 (1916) (FELA damages include pain and mental anguish, bodily injury, pecuniary loss including "loss of power and capacity for work" and its effect upon plaintiff's future).

8. 46 U.S.C.A. § 688. *See*, reflecting damage elements, Allen v. Seacoast Products, Inc., 623 F.2d 355 (5th Cir.1980) (pain, earning power, medical).

2. Francis McDonald's claim was dismissed before trial by the multidistrict court for failure to file an appropriate administrative claim, a jurisdictional prerequisite under the Federal Tort Claims Act. 28 U.S.C. § 2675(a) * * *.

* * * [T]he Court finds that the Plaintiff developed GBS as a proximate result of her swine flu inoculation; and is entitled to recover from the Defendant for the damages she has suffered.

* * *

II. INTRODUCTION

The National Swine Flu Immunization Program of 1976 was an attempt by the federal government to inoculate the entire adult population of the United States against the perceived threat of a swine flu epidemic. From its commencement on October 1, 1976 until its suspension on December 16, 1976, over forty-five million Americans were vaccinated, resulting in the largest immunization program ever in this country's history. * * *

* * *

With respect to liability for personal injuries and deaths arising from the program, the Swine Flu Act contained the following relevant procedural provisions:

1) The Act created a cause of action against the United States for any personal injury or wrongful death sustained as a result of the swine flu inoculation resulting from the act or omission of the program participant upon any theory of liability that would govern in an action against such program participant including negligence, strict liability in tort, and breach of warranty. 42 U.S.C. § 247b(k)(2)(A).

2) The Swine Flu Act made the above cause of action the exclusive remedy and abolished any causes of action against the vaccine manufacturer by individual claimants. 42 U.S.C. § 247b(k)(3).

3) It made the procedures of the Federal Tort Claims Act applicable to suits brought pursuant to the Swine Flu Act. 42 U.S.C. § 247b(k)(4).

* * * [U]nder the terms of the final pretrial order * * *, a plaintiff must establish by the fair weight or preponderance of the evidence * * * [only] causation and damages * * *.

* * *

III. PLAINTIFF'S PERSONAL AND MEDICAL HISTORY

Lucy McDonald, presently 39 years old, was born on May 3, 1943 in Pittston, Pennsylvania. She is a high school graduate and was awarded an academic scholarship to College Misericordia in Dallas, Pennsylvania. Her intention of becoming a teacher was interrupted when she was forced to withdraw after one academic year to care for her parents, who were both in ill health. * * *

Lucy married Francis McDonald, now 43, on August 12, 1972. They have no children. Francis, a carpenter and construction worker until he sustained a fall in June of 1977, is permanently disabled for social security purposes, and suffers from a progressive congenital hearing deficit which makes communication with his wife difficult.

In 1971 the Plaintiff began work in the garment industry in the shipping department of the Lee Manufacturing Company. She soon was promoted to a presser's position (the highest paid in the facility) and was described as an excellent worker and employee. She would have remained in her employment were it not for her illness.

* * *

IV. THE SWINE FLU INOCULATION AND THE ONSET OF PLAINTIFF'S MALADIES
* * *

* * * A reasonable reading of the evidence and the testimony in this case reveals * * * beyond question * * * that * * * [the plaintiff] is entitled to recover damages for her condition.

* * *

VIII. DAMAGES

A. *Amendment of the Administrative Claim*

* * *

In view of the foregoing discussion, the Court concludes that the Plaintiff has adduced sufficient proof of "newly discovered evidence" and/or "intervening facts" to satisfy the dictates of § 2675(b) and, therefore, her motion to amend the *ad damnum* clause of her complaint to reflect damages in excess of the monetary amount requested at the administrative level will be granted.

B. *Applicable Law and Measure of Recovery*

In an action brought under the Federal Tort Claims Act, it is "the law of the state where the act or omission occurred" which provides the applicable standards of substantive liability. 28 U.S.C. § 1346(b) * * *. Since the Swine Flu Act incorporates by reference the liability provisions of the Federal Tort Claims Act, state law standards also apply to claims brought pursuant to the Swine Flu Act. * * * Lucy McDonald received her swine flu vaccination in Pittston, Pennsylvania and, therefore, the Pennsylvania law of damages for personal injuries governs the extent of the Defendant's liability in this action. * * *

In Pennsylvania, the courts have consistently held that "damages are to be compensatory to the full extent of the injury sustained." * * * Under this state's law, a plaintiff is entitled to be compensated for all past medical expenses reasonably and necessarily incurred and all future medical expenses reasonably likely to be incurred for the treatment and care of his injuries; past lost earnings and lost future earning capacity; and past, present and future pain and suffering. * * * A plaintiff in

Pennsylvania must only prove these elements of damage with reasonable certainty. * * * *See also* Story Parchment Co. v. Paterson Parchment Paper Co., 282 U.S. 555, 562, 51 S.Ct. 248, 250, 75 L.Ed. 544 (1931) (reasonable certainty rule bars only those damages which "are not the certain result of the wrong, not * * * those damages which are definitely attributable to the wrong and only uncertain in respect of their amount.").

1. Past Medical Expenses

The parties have stipulated that the reasonable and necessarily incurred past medical expenses related to Lucy McDonald's present illness total $56,645.18.

2. Future Medical Expenses

It was unequivocally confirmed by every physician testifying in this case that Lucy McDonald's primary medical deficits of lower extremity paraplegia and bowel and bladder dysfunction are now permanent. As a result of this debilitating condition, she will require, among other things, the constant care and treatment of professionally trained medical personnel in order to prevent the serious complications sometimes associated with her present illness, such as prolonged hospitalization, surgical intervention, and inordinately expensive therapy. At trial and in an earlier report, Dr. Rhamy outlined the essential treatment, its cost, and some of the prophylactic measures which should be taken in an effort to care for and rehabilitate the Plaintiff over the remaining years of her life. In this regard, the Court finds that based on the United States Life Expectancy Tables, Lucy McDonald's present life expectancy is approximately 40 years. Dr. Rhamy expressly indicated that with the appropriate medical attention he has recommended, Lucy McDonald can expect to attain this normal life expectancy. In calculating an award for the future medical expenses to which the Plaintiff is entitled in this case, we have divided this element of damages into four areas: medical treatment, nursing care, miscellaneous equipment and devices, and architectural changes in the Plaintiff's house. We will address these items *seriatim*.

a. Medical Treatment

The Plaintiff does and must continue to take numerous medications for problems related to her present neurological and urological condition. The total lifetime costs of these medications is $33,499.00.

In an effort to prevent osteoporosis of the bones, a common phenomenon in paraplegics, regular orthopedic evaluations must be undertaken at a cost of $100.00 per year and $4,000.00 over the Plaintiff's lifetime. As an additional orthopedic measure, an award of $7,200.00 will be made for the reasonable likelihood of future surgery to correct para-articular calcification of the hip joints, which occurs in one-half of all paraplegics.

With respect to the Plaintiff's skin condition, Dr. Rhamy testified that it is very likely, a 68% chance, that the Plaintiff will develop additional decubiti over the sacral part of her body. He estimated the cost of treatment, including possible surgery, to range from $16,500.00 to $68,000.00. The Court will award $16,500.00 for such future care.

Lucy McDonald's urological condition will require the closest monitoring and the most frequent treatment because of her permanent bowel and bladder dysfunction. * * * [T]he Court will approve most of the urological treatment recommendations and award $135,550.00 as damages for such requirements. The total amount of the medical treatment expenses is therefore $197,749.00.

b. Nursing Care

As previously noted, the testimony at trial was, in the Court's view, persuasive in demonstrating that the Plaintiff will require continual nursing care throughout her lifetime to prevent and treat the potential serious complications of her disease. The issue that arises, however, for the Court's determination in awarding damages is the degree or type of nursing care which is reasonably necessary for the Plaintiff. Several options were referred to at trial.

At the outset, the Court rejects the government's proposal regarding institutionalized care or apartment-type community living for the handicapped for Lucy McDonald. These options were suggested by the Defendant's expert economist, Dr. George Reavy, solely from an economic standpoint and were unsupported by any medical evidence establishing them as feasible alternatives for this particular Plaintiff. On the other hand, Plaintiff herself testified that it is very important for her to stay in her present home; she describes it as being the "family homestead" and the gathering place for her brothers and sisters and their families. Dr. Turchetti, a psychiatrist, opined that such alternatives as proffered by the government would be markedly detrimental to the Plaintiff's emotional condition. He stated that to Lucy McDonald her present home represents security and to strip her away from this would be "cruel." * * * Dr. Rhamy also testified that, in his opinion, an extended care treatment center would not be conducive to the normal interpersonal relationship of a husband and wife. Based on this uncontradicted medical testimony and in a compassionate sense of fairness to the plight of the Plaintiff, the Court concludes that the Defendant's proposals are not a reasonable solution to this Plaintiff's present and future nursing care needs.

Dr. Rhamy testified as to two alternatives, a "low" and "high" nursing care plan for the Plaintiff. The "low" plan consisted of a licensed practical nurse (LPN) for one eight-hour shift and a helper or nurse's aid for the other 16 hours of the day, seven days of the week. The "high" alternative would be an LPN on an around the clock basis, seven days of the week.

* * *

Nurse Harring presented a schedule of nursing care for the Plaintiff which, considering all the medical testimony presented regarding the

Plaintiff's present physical status and her future medical needs, the Court finds to be the most feasible option in this case. This plan consists of: (1) the services of a RN for one eight-hour shift per day for five days of the week (40 hours per week); (2) the services of an LPN for one eight-hour shift for seven days of the week (56 hours per week); and (3) the services of a nurse's aide or helper for the remaining shift during the week and the extra shift on the weekends (72 hours per week). Nurse Harring also testified that the reasonable and average eight-hour shift rate in this geographical area for an RN is $75.00 and for an LPN is $65.00. It was earlier established by Dr. Rhamy that the nurse's aide or helper would be a minimum wage worker at a present rate of $3.35 per hour. Computing these hourly figures over the life expectancy of the Plaintiff, the Court will award $2,228,096.00 as damages for the reasonable future cost of necessary nursing care for the Plaintiff.[56]

c. Miscellaneous Equipment and Devices

As previously referred to, the Plaintiff's present life expectancy is approximately 40 years. The uncontroverted testimony of several of Plaintiff's expert medical witnesses, specifically Drs. Rhamy, Lichtenfeld and Poser and Nurse Harring, established that at present and over the course of her entire lifetime Lucy McDonald will require numerous items of paraplegic equipment to assist her in maintaining a state of optimum physical health. * * *

The final item listed, the van, deserves brief comment. Dr. Rhamy and Nurse Harring testified specifically as to the necessity of this mode of transportation for a paraplegic, especially one with a bowel and bladder disorder. Plaintiff is unable to move independently, or even easily with assistance, from her wheelchair into a regular automobile. As a result, at times the ordeal of the transfer process not only physically tires her but it also causes undue pressure upon her bladder and involuntary urination. Dr. Rhamy as well as Dr. Turchetti noted that a van would be important for Lucy McDonald's emotional well-being also, in that it would greatly facilitate her access to numerous social activities and thereby assist her in regaining some of the self-esteem and respect she now so obviously lacks. Dr. Rhamy poignantly described the Plaintiff's present status as a "prisoner in her own house." * * * The Plaintiff herself testified that a van would be most useful for these daily activities and would also enable * * * [Lucy] and Francis to resume taking weekend trips to visit friends and relatives as they did prior to her disability.

Under these circumstances, we believe that the necessary cost for a hydraulic-lift van, as established by Dr. Rhamy and unchallenged by the Defendant, is a proper element of damages in the instant case.

---

56. The weekly cost under this nursing plan is $1,071.20; thus, the yearly figure would be $55,702.40 and, accordingly, calculating this yearly rate over the 40 year life expectancy of the Plaintiff produces the sum of $2,228,096.00. We believe this to be a conservative amount since no doubt the cost of nursing care will greatly escalate over the next forty years.

d.   Necessary Architectural Changes in Plaintiff's House

The Court received into evidence at trial a report prepared by Richard Hardy, an architect, in the firm of Pyros & Sanderson, Wilkes–Barre, Pennsylvania, outlining proposed alterations to the McDonald home to suitably accommodate Lucy in her present condition. The total estimated cost of this project is $77,000.00. The propriety of the architectural changes is consistent with the testimony of Drs. Rhamy and Lichtenfeld and Nurse Harring, and was not contradicted by the testimony of any defense witnesses. After examining the specifics of this plan, the Court finds that the recommendations and estimates contained therein are both reasonable and necessary to enable the Plaintiff to adjust as conveniently as possible to her paraplegic lifestyle.[59]

3.   Lost Earnings

The testimony on this issue was presented by Dr. Andrew Verzilli, Professor of Economics, Drexel University, on behalf of the Plaintiff, and by Dr. George C. Reavy, Economic Consultant, University of Scranton, for the Defendant.

a.   Wages

There was no dispute in this case that the amount of the past lost wages sustained by the Plaintiff from December, 1976 until the date of trial was $44,800.00.

Under Pennsylvania law, "[w]hen an injury is a permanent one, one which will cause a loss or lessening of future earning power, a recovery may be had for the probable loss of future earnings." Kaczkowski v. Bolubasz, 491 Pa. 561, 566 n.7, 421 A.2d 1027 (1980), quoting McCormick, Damages, at 299 (20th reprint 1975). * * *

On this issue of Lucy McDonald's lost future earnings, there was disagreement between the expert economists on the initial factor of the Plaintiff's work-life expectancy. Dr. Verzilli's calculations were based on an assumed retirement age of 65, an approximately 26 year future work life period. Dr. Reavy's projection of a 15.19 year work life expectancy for the Plaintiff, on the other hand, was founded upon the U.S. Department of Labor, Tables for Working Life for Men and Women (1977).

The Plaintiff argues that the utilization of these tables in this case would be inappropriate because they unjustly interdict a consideration of her particular economic condition. At trial, Dr. Reavy, upon cross-examination, indicated that one of the principal contributing factors to the shortened work life expectancy of a female, as reflected in these tables, is the prospect of child-bearing and the concomitant departure from the work force by a woman. In this case, however, the McDonalds did not have any children at the time Lucy, then 33, contracted GBS and, as a result of

---

59.   Mr. Hardy also outlined and estimated the cost of constructing a new one-story custom home as an alternative to remodeling the McDonald's present home. Such a project would cost approximately $135,665.00; however, as noted previously, the Plaintiff has no desire to nor is it psychologically advisable for her to vacate the present family residence.

this illness, it is exceedingly unlikely they ever will. Moreover, as noted, shortly after the onset of her disease, the Plaintiff's husband, Francis, was seriously injured and remains physically disabled for social security purposes. The Plaintiff also testified that she enjoyed her work at Lee Manufacturing and would have continued there if not for her illness. On this latter point, Leo Gutstein, the owner of Lee Manufacturing, testified that Lucy was a valued employee and a presser position would have remained available to her if she did not become disabled.

In determining the Plaintiff's "probable" loss of future earnings in light of these circumstances, particularly her husband's inability to provide an income for the household, the Court concludes that the Plaintiff would have remained in the work force until age 65. Thus, her present work life expectancy is 26 years.

With respect to the Plaintiff's future earnings figure, both economic experts, relying upon the testimony of Mr. Gutstein, used an average annual figure of $13,650.00. Specifically, Mr. Gutstein testified that if Lucy was presently employed as a presser in his facility, she would be earning $7.50 per hour and working an estimated 35 hours per week. Computed over a 52 week period, these wages translate into an annual salary of $13,650.00. The Court accepts this as a reasonable method of arriving at the Plaintiff's annual earnings figure.

The Plaintiff also seeks an upward adjustment of this yearly amount by a 2% productivity factor in accordance with the standards set forth by the Supreme Court of Pennsylvania in *Kaczkowski v. Bolubasz, supra.*
* * *

In this case, Dr. Verzilli, the Plaintiff's economist, testified that based on the Plaintiff's actual earning history at Lee Manufacturing and the testimony of Leo Gutstein, the owner of Lee Manufacturing, a 2% productivity factor for the Plaintiff would be appropriate. Mr. Gutstein testified that despite some industry declines, his business has grown substantially from the time period of 1976 to the present. He attributes this to diversification of his business through the addition of more product lines. In terms of productivity of his employees, he stated that Lee Manufacturing has made substantial capital expenditures for automated equipment, which has resulted in: (1) production being greater with a consistent work force, and (2) his shops and its employees earning substantially above the industry standards. Finally, in his role as financial planner for the company, he estimated that the future growth of Lee Manufacturing, exclusive of inflation, would be 3 to 5 percent annually. Additionally, Dr. Verzilli stated that this two percent figure is actually lower than the Plaintiff's past growth rate from 1970 to 1976. He further noted that it would be unrealistic to assume no growth in the Plaintiff's future earnings.

Dr. Reavy, the Defendant's economist, was of the opinion that no productivity factor increase was warranted in this case. In determining this, he measured the percentage change in the Plaintiff's hourly wage rate in 1973 of $4.43 per hour, to the present estimated rate of $7.50 per hour. He determined that although this indicated a 69.3% increase in the Plaintiff's hourly wage rate, when compared to the rise in the consumer price index of 120.4% for the same time period, he concluded that there had been no real growth in the Plaintiff's wages. The Court is of the view, however, that this method of comparison does not accurately reflect the *Kaczkowski* Court's concept of productivity or "merit" increases. *See id.* at 565 n. 5, 421 A.2d 1027. It should be borne in mind that the consumer price index is the government's measure of inflation, the impact of which has already been taken into account with future interest rates under the total offset approach of *Kaczkowski*.[63] The inflation figure, therefore, should not be the sole factor considered in the computation of a productivity component, a "separate and distinct phenomena" which is "controlled by different variables than the inflationary factor." *Id.* at 570, 565 n.5, 421 A.2d 1027. As noted above, a consideration of future wage or productivity increases should be based on such factors as the age, experience, skill, and education of the individual as well as, we believe, the future economic condition of the particular industry or company with which the individual would have been employed if not for the permanent injuries sustained. *See* 54 Temp.L.Q. 576, 586–87 n.81. Such an analysis entails, by necessity, an *ad hoc* case-by-case determination.

In view of the testimony adduced by the Plaintiff's expert economist and by her former employer, the Court finds that a proper foundation has been laid in this case to justify the requested 2% productivity factor adjustment in the amount of Plaintiff's lost future earnings. While we recognize, as did the court in *Kaczkowski,* that such an award "may be subject to a degree of speculation," nonetheless, we also share that tribunal's view that "it is exceedingly more accurate to assume that the future will not remain stagnant with the past." *Id.* at 580, 421 A.2d 1027.[64] The Plaintiff's future lost earning capacity in this case is therefore $437,209.00.

With respect to fringe benefits, both economists agreed that this item constitutes a significant portion of the financial package for a worker and has traditionally been considered as part of compensation. In this case, Dr. Verzilli opined that a 20% adjustment to earnings should be made to account for such benefits. He reached this conclusion by examining the union (ILGWU) contract relative to Lee Manufacturing Company for the years 1979 through 1982, which establishes and identifies the contributions based on the worker's payroll that would be provided by the employer, on behalf of its employees, for three types of benefits: (1) a

---

63. See footnote 43, *supra.* [Footnote 43 states: "The theoretical premise of this decision is that future inflation and future interest rates are presumed to be equal and cancel one another. The application of the 'total offset' rule has been held to be appropriate in an action brought under the Swine Flu Act. Barnes v. United States, 685 F.2d 66, 70 (3d Cir.1982)."]

64. In Posner, Economic Analysis of Law (2d ed. 1977), the author comments that in general a 3% productivity factor would be the appropriate figure to utilize in computing lost future earnings. He further notes that such average annual increases are "felt even in industries where productivity is not increasing secularly: employe[r]s in such industries must raise wages to levels competitive with those in other industries or lose their work force." *Id.* at 147, n.5.

health and welfare fund; (2) a retirement fund; and (3) a health services plan. Dr. Reavy, however, examined these documents and concluded that an appropriate value for these benefits would be approximately 5% of earnings. After careful consideration of the testimony of both the economic experts and after reviewing the relevant sections of the union contract and other documents submitted, the Court finds that a reasonable estimate of the value of fringe benefits in this case is 15 percent of past and future lost earnings, or $72,301.35.

b. Household Services

The Plaintiff also seeks compensation for the past and future value of the daily household services she is unable to perform because of her illness. * * * Considering the particular factual circumstances of this case, however, the Court finds that such an award would not be appropriate.

The Plaintiff did testify that presently she is able to do some cooking, cleaning and laundry, albeit in a limited capacity. Apparently the remainder of these household tasks has previously been undertaken by her husband, Francis, who has been required to stay at home at all times to care for Lucy. There was no indication from the testimony that the McDonalds have incurred any additional expenses for such services from the onset of the Plaintiff's disabilities until trial and, thus, we believe there is no basis for a monetary award for this time period.

Several factors persuade the Court that an award for the future value of household services would also be inappropriate in this case. These include: (1) the Plaintiff's husband's ability to perform these chores, especially since he will not be working and moreover, will no longer be required to provide "nursing care" for the Plaintiff; (2) Lucy's increased ability to undertake these tasks in view of the proposed architectural changes in the McDonald home for which compensation has been granted by the Court; and (3) the capability of a minimum wage-worker, for which sufficient damages have also been awarded to employ under the nursing care category heretofore discussed, to render some assistance with these services. With these considerations in mind, the Court concludes that the value of the Plaintiff's household services is not a compensable element of damages in this case.

The total lost earnings of the Plaintiff are as follows:

Past Earnings	$ 44,800.00
Future Earning Capacity	437,209.00
Fringe Benefits	72,301.35
TOTAL	$554,310.35

4. Pain and Suffering

The final element of damages to be awarded is compensation for the past, present and future pain and suffering of the Plaintiff as a result of her affliction with GBS. * * * Under Pennsylvania law, such an award should include compensation for a Plaintiff's physical pain and suffering, as well as for any mental anguish, inconvenience, disfigurement, humiliation and the loss of enjoyment of life. * * * The nature of pain and suffering is such that there is no legal yardstick by which to measure accurately reasonable compensation for it * * *; thus, we are confronted with the unenviable task of dispassionately translating "such catastrophic human loss as [the Plaintiff] suffered into money damages. In this process systematic logic is not helpful and precision is not achievable." Frankel v. Heym, 466 F.2d 1226, 1228 (3d Cir.1972).

In view of the Court's previous discussion, there is no need to set forth in detail the devastation that has beset Lucy McDonald as a result of the swine flu vaccine. She presently is and will permanently continue to be totally dependent on others for virtually every intimate aspect of her everyday life. She will require extensive future medical care but, even with this, she is highly susceptible to infection and illness. She will never again be able to walk or engage in any activity requiring the use of her lower extremities; her legs are simply useless. She has been unable in the past six years to attend church or any social activities for fear of becoming incontinent. She has become, in Dr. Lichtenfeld's words, a "prisoner to her physical condition, humiliation and embarrassment." Additionally, the job she enjoyed and the career she looked forward to are gone. More importantly, the joys of motherhood, a prospect she so fondly embraced, will never be known to her. Even a normal marital relationship with her husband is now impossible. Quite naturally, there has been an extreme transformation in Lucy McDonald's emotional well-being—from an affable, happy-go-lucky active person to an invalid, greatly disturbed by acute depression and a severe loss of self-esteem and dignity. Reflecting her religious background, Lucy ascribes the present torment to her "penance on earth."

Under these circumstances, we believe that a substantial award as compensation for Lucy McDonald's pain and suffering is warranted. In so doing, we share the sentiments of the Court in Barnes v. United States, 685 F.2d 66 (3d Cir.1982) that "[m]oney is not a substitute for what she and her family have lost, but nevertheless Congress provided for such an eventuality in the legislation creating the National Swine Flu Immunization Program of 1976 * * *." 516 F.Supp. at 1390. The sum of $600,000.00 is awarded as just and reasonable compensation for pain and suffering.

A summary of the damages (rounded off to dollars) to be awarded the Plaintiff is as follows:

Past Medical Expenses	$ 56,645.00
Future Medical Expenses	
a. Medical Treatment	197,749.00
b. Nursing Care	2,228,096.00
c. Miscellaneous Equipment	257,670.00
d. Architectural Changes	77,000.00
Lost Earnings	554,310.00
Pain and Suffering	600,000.00
TOTAL	$3,971,470.00

5. Delay Damages

As an additional element of compensation, the Plaintiff requests an award of delay damages pursuant to Pennsylvania Rule of Civil Procedure 238 [(setting the rate of prejudgment interest at ten percent)]. Section 2674 of the Federal Tort Claims Act (FTCA) provides, in pertinent part, that:

> The United States shall be liable, respecting the provisions of this title relating to tort claims, in the same manner and to the same extent as a private individual under like circumstances, *but shall not be liable for interest prior to judgment or for punitive damages.* (emphasis added).

As previously noted, the Swine Flu Act provides that a claim for any injury sustained from the swine flu program must be brought directly against the United States under the procedures of the Federal Tort Claims Act. * * *

* * *

With respect to the question in this case, the "plain language" of the Swine Flu Act, as noted above, similarly requires that the liability of the United States be limited to the "same extent" as in any other action under the FTCA. *See* 42 U.S.C. § 247b(k)(2)(A). Such explicit statutory direction compels this Court to conclude that encompassed within this congressional limitation is the prohibition against prejudgment interest, as set forth in section 2674 of the FTCA. It is well settled that interest prior to judgment is not recoverable in other actions brought pursuant to the Federal Tort Claims Act. * * *

* * *

For the foregoing reasons, the Plaintiff's request for delay damages pursuant to Pennsylvania Rule of Civil Procedure 238 will be denied.

IX. CONCLUSION

The Court is not unaware of the unusual length of this Opinion. We are mindful too of the exceptional size of the award of damages. But we are equally cognizant of, and deeply impressed with, the enormous impact of the Plaintiff's extensive injuries. No smaller award could adequately compensate her since her total life, as well as her body, has been drastically and permanently crippled. We have tried, then, in fairness to both parties, to be thorough and complete in laying out our reasoning and analysis of the testimony and the evidence presented in this case.

* * * The Plaintiff * * * is entitled to an award of $3,971,470.00.
* * *

NOTES

1. Should different actuarial tables be used for women and men to measure future work-life expectancy? *See* Dan B. Dobbs, Law of Remedies § 8.5(2) (2d ed. 1993); Martha Chamallas, *Questioning the Use of Race–Specific and Gender–Specific Economic Data in Tort Litigation: A Constitutional Argument*, 63 Fordham L. Rev. 73 (1994); Martha Chamallas, *The Architecture of Bias: Deep Structures in Tort Law*, 146 U. Pa. L. Rev. 463, 480–89 (1998); Martha Chamallas, *Civil Rights in Ordinary Torts Cases: Race, Gender, and the Calculation of Economic Loss*, 38 Loy. L.A. L. Rev. 1435 (2005). *See generally* Martha Chamallas & Jennifer B. Wriggins, The Measure of Injury: Race, Gender and Tort Law (2010).

2. For a suggestion that rehabilitation ought to be a primary goal of tort law, see Ellen S. Pryor, *Rehabilitating Tort Compensation*, 91 Geo. L.J. 659 (2003). *See also* Samuel R. Bagenstos & Margo Schlanger, *Hedonic Damages, Hedonic Adaptation, and Disability*, 60 Vand. L. Rev. 745 (2007).

3. Should the inability to have children be a compensable loss? If so, how should it be measured?

b. General Damages for Physical Injury

DEBUS v. GRAND UNION STORES OF VERMONT

Supreme Court of Vermont, 1993.
159 Vt. 537, 621 A.2d 1288.

Before ALLEN, C.J, and GIBSON, DOOLEY, MORSE and JOHNSON, JJ.

JOHNSON, JUSTICE.

Defendant Grand Union appeals from a jury verdict and award of personal injury damages made to plaintiff on her premises-liability claim. Defendant contends the trial court erred by allowing plaintiff to make a per diem damage argument to the jury, and claims that such arguments are overly prejudicial and should not be allowed. * * *

Plaintiff was injured while shopping at defendant's store on August 23, 1985, when a pallet of boxes, piled high and imbalanced, toppled over and fell upon her. * * * Plaintiff suffered injuries resulting in a 20% permanent disability. The jury awarded plaintiff damages of $346,276.23.

I.

During closing argument, plaintiff suggested that the jury think about plaintiff's injury in terms of daily pain and suffering, and then determine what amount of damages would be appropriate compensation for each day of suffering. An average daily figure was suggested to the jury, which it could then multiply by the number of days plaintiff would live, counting from the day of the accident until the end of her life expectancy, some thirty-five years. The jury was told to consider the figure only if it found the calculations useful in quantifying plaintiff's damages. Defendant contends that such per diem arguments are unduly prejudicial and should have been disallowed by the trial court. Defendant further contends that if per diem arguments are permissible, the court should give cautionary instructions.

A per diem argument is a tool of persuasion used by counsel to suggest to the jury how it can quantify damages based on the evidence of pain and suffering presented. * * * Other jurisdictions are divided as to whether to allow such arguments. *Compare* Paducah Area Public Library v. Terry, 655 S.W.2d 19, 25 (Ky.Ct.App.1983) (allowing per diem argument), and Cafferty v. Monson, 360 N.W.2d 414, 417 (Minn.Ct.App.1985) (same); *with* Ferry v. Checker Taxi Co., 165 Ill.App.3d 744, 117 Ill.Dec. 382, 387, 520 N.E.2d 733, 738 (1987) (noting impropriety of per diem arguments), *and* Botta v. Brunner, 26 N.J. 82, 138 A.2d 713, 723–25 (1958) (same). The principal reason advanced against per diem arguments is that a jury's verdict must be based on the evidence before it, and a per diem figure, which is not in evidence, allows the jury to calculate damages based solely on the argument of counsel. * * * Further, courts have reasoned that a per diem argument unfairly assumes that pain is constant, uniform, and continuous, and that the pain will prevail for the rest of plaintiff's life. Therefore, it creates an "illusion of certainty" in a disability that is more likely to be subject to great variation. * * * Finally, some courts conclude that the jury will be too easily misled by the plaintiff's argument. * * *

On the other hand, jurisdictions that have allowed per diem arguments counter that sufficient safeguards exist in the adversarial system to overcome the objections to its use. They point out that a plaintiff's hypothesis on damages, even if presented on a per diem basis, must be reasonable or suffer serious and possibly fatal attack by opposing counsel; further, the notion that pain is constant and uniform may be easily rebutted by reference to the evidence or the jury's own experience. * * * Most importantly, they note that juries are entitled to draw inferences from the evidence before them and that the extent of damages attributable to pain and suffering is a permissible inference. * * *

After review of the arguments and authorities, we are persuaded that there is nothing inherently improper or prejudicial about per diem arguments if they are made under the ordinary supervision and control of the trial court. In cases where claims for pain and suffering are made, juries are forced to equate pain with damages. The jury can benefit by guidance offered by counsel in closing argument as to how they can construct that equation. * * * We permit counsel reasonable latitude in this phase of the trial to summarize the evidence, to persuade the jury to accept or reject a plaintiff's claim, and to award a specific lump sum. If a lump sum is to be suggested to the jury*, it cannot be impermissible to explain how the lump sum was determined. * * *

---

* Counsel's request that the jury award a lump sum amount is not error per se. * * * Although the lump sum may be more consistent with counsel's hope than with the reality of the evidence,

Nor do we agree with defendant that per diem arguments must be accompanied by specific instructions. Juries are routinely instructed that arguments and suggestions by counsel are not evidence, whether or not a party makes a per diem argument. It may well be that other instructions may be required when per diem arguments are used, but we leave to the trial courts the fashioning of instructions and controls appropriate to the cases before them.

Our holding should not be taken to grant the plaintiff carte blanche to depart from any reasonable view of the evidence. Rather, it reflects our confidence that the defendant's opportunity to refute the plaintiff's closing argument will ensure that an absurd hypothesis will be rejected. Even if it is not, and a verdict is excessive, the trial court has adequate mechanisms, such as remittitur, to deal with it.

The question remains as to whether the per diem argument in the present case was improper. In closing argument, plaintiff's counsel told the jury the per diem figure was only a suggestion for its consideration, and that determining a fair amount would be entirely up to the jury. He did not argue that plaintiff's pain was constant, uniform, and easy to quantify on a daily basis. In fact, counsel told the jury that pain fluctuates and that he was only suggesting an average figure for their consideration, and told them to "[d]isregard it if it is not helpful." Defendant had a full opportunity to rebut the per diem argument and did so. We cannot conclude that this argument invaded the province of the jury.

The case was submitted to the jury with appropriate instructions. The trial court cautioned the jury that "the arguments of the attorneys and any statements which they made in their arguments or in their summation is not evidence and will not be considered by you as evidence," and that "it is your recollection of the witness's testimony and not the attorney's statements which shall control you in reaching your decision."

The court made it clear to the jury that the final determination of damages was to be made on the evidence alone and not on persuasive arguments for any particular formulas. That the jury was able to make this distinction between presented evidence and suggested formulas is demonstrated by their arriving at a total damages award $166,194 below the figure suggested by plaintiff's counsel, which figure counsel calculated in part by using the per diem formula. There was no error.

* * *

Affirmed.

ALLEN, CHIEF JUSTICE, dissenting.

* * *

It is unnecessary here to set forth the various arguments in favor of or against per diem arguments as they have been thoroughly and exhaus-

---

use of a lump sum, like a per diem damages argument, is not reversible error unless shown to be prejudicial.

tively discussed in opinions from virtually every other jurisdiction over the past thirty years. See cases cited in Annotation, *Per Diem or Similar Mathematical Basis for Fixing Damages for Pain and Suffering,* 3 A.L.R.4th 940 (1981). I believe the better answer is to permit counsel to argue to the trier of fact the appropriateness of employing a time-unit calculation technique for fixing damages for pain and suffering, but to prohibit any suggestion by counsel of specific monetary amounts either on a lump sum or time-unit basis. * * *

* * *

I further disagree with the majority in its reluctance to require a specific cautionary instruction, beyond the general language offered that "the arguments of the attorneys and any statements which they made in their arguments or in their summation [are] not in evidence and will not be considered by you as evidence." The instruction approved by the majority may be adequate to deal with remarks of an attorney that are plainly argumentative. The difficulty is that remarks regarding numbers or dollar amounts may not appear to be argument, but rather evidence itself. Hence, an instruction not to consider argument as evidence does not cure the problem.

* * *

The majority relies on the proposition that "[i]n closing argument, plaintiff's counsel told the jury the per diem figure was only a suggestion for its consideration, and that determining a fair amount would be entirely up to the jury." The majority is overly generous. Counsel's remarks are at best ambiguous and come at the beginning of a lengthy and detailed mathematical presentation. That presentation, stated in part, follows:

> What award will it take to tell Grand Union what accountability means and that this is what the people in Bennington County think a human life and human suffering is worth[?]

> Now, let's just take one element. We have talked about pain and suffering. What would be fair compensation for pain and suffering? *Entirely up to you.* I have a suggestion. If you think about what it is like for Susanne to go through one day with the pain that she has and think about what would be fair compensation for that one day, what do you think it would be? Would it be $100 to go through that in a day? Would it be $75? Would it be $50, $40?

> Ladies and gentlemen, we want to be scrupulously fair about our request to you. So I am going to suggest to you that you award Susanne $30 a day for the loss of those three elements: pain and suffering, mental anguish, and loss of enjoyment of life. That is $10 a day for each one. *I put it to you for your consideration to follow that through.*

You would do it this way, there are 365 days a year. I am just going to put here pain and suffering, mental anguish, loss of enjoyment of life. Now there are 365 days in a year. And Susanne's six years she has already suffered in these ways and 29 more, that is 35 years total that she should be compensated for. And if you multiply 35 times 365, there are 12,775 days. And if you multiply that figure by the $30 per day I just suggested, it comes out to $383,250—sorry. $383,250.

Now, another way of thinking of that is if you divide 35 years into this figure of $383,250 it comes out to slightly under $11,000 a year. Maybe that would be a help to think for you $11,000 a year to live the way she lives, to lose what she has lost. *Perhaps that would be a help for you; I don't know.* (Emphasis added.)

The caveats in this argument are nearly invisible, and an additional statement in rebuttal is no better. The residue is a set of specific numbers that are, by the majority's holding, proper, but which at least deserve a specific cautionary instruction. Yet the majority would substitute counsel's at best ambiguous message for a clear instruction from the bench about the use of the numbers.

I would not, and I dissent.

BOAN v. BLACKWELL

Supreme Court of South Carolina, 2001.
343 S.C. 498, 541 S.E.2d 242.

PLEICONES, JUSTICE.

* * *

Petitioners admitted liability [in this automobile negligence case], and the only issue for the jury was the amount of damages to be awarded to respondent. In the course of charging the jury on damages, the trial judge stated:

In determining the amount of compensation for personal injuries, it is proper to take into consideration past and present aspects of that injury. This would include, as I have told you, *physical and mental pain and suffering endured,* expenses incurred for necessary medical treatment, loss of time and income which resulted from the impairment of the ability to work, *the loss of enjoyment of life suffered as a result of the injury,* and any other losses which are reflected by the character of the injury. Now in this connection, I charge you that mental pain and suffering, sometimes called mental distress, is a proper element of actual damages where it is the natural and proximate consequence of a negligent act committed by another.

Now an injured party may also recover for such future damages as it is reasonably certain will of necessity result from the injury received. The principal underlying compensation for future damages is that only one action can be brought, and, therefore, only one recovery had. It is proper to include in the estimate of future damages compensation for pain and suffering which will with reasonable certainty result. (Emphasis added.)

Petitioners objected to the charge, stating, "[Y]ou charged on both lost enjoyment of life and pain and suffering. Our courts have indicated that that is basically the same element of damages, and we don't believe they should be able to recover for it twice." The trial judge declined to act on petitioners' objection.

On appeal, the Court of Appeals held the single reference to "loss of enjoyment of life" in the damages charge "simply indicated to the jury what it could consider when assessing damages for pain and suffering." * * * The court acknowledged its holding in Stroud v. Stroud, 299 S.C. 394, 385 S.E.2d 205 (Ct.App.1989), that loss of enjoyment of life is merely a component of pain and suffering and not a separately compensable element of damages. After reviewing the entire charge in this case, however, the court found no violation of *Stroud* and consequently held there was no reversible error. * * *

* * *

In Stroud v. Stroud, *supra*, the Court of Appeals held, "[l]oss of enjoyment of life is not a separate species of damage deserving a distinct award, but instead is only an element of general damages for pain and suffering." * * * We disagree, and find more persuasive the decisions of the United States District Court for the district of South Carolina which permit a separate recovery for loss of enjoyment of life. *See* McNeill v. United States, 519 F.Supp. 283 (D.S.C.1981) * * *.

An award for pain and suffering compensates the injured person for the physical discomfort and the emotional response to the sensation of pain caused by the injury itself. Separate damages are given for mental anguish where the evidence shows, for example, that the injured person suffered shock, fright, emotional upset, and/or humiliation as the result of the defendant's negligence. * * *

On the other hand, damages for "loss of enjoyment of life" compensate for the limitations, resulting from the defendant's negligence, on the injured person's ability to participate in and derive pleasure from the normal activities of daily life, or for the individual's inability to pursue his talents, recreational interests, hobbies, or avocations.[1] *See* Overstreet v. Shoney's, Inc., 4 S.W.3d 694 (Tenn.Ct.App.1999); Sawyer v. Midelfort, 227 Wis.2d 124, 595 N.W.2d 423 (1999) * * *. For example, an award for the diminishment of pleasure resulting from the loss of use of one of the senses, or for a paraplegic's loss of the ability to participate in certain physical activities, falls under the rubric of hedonic damages. In our view,

---

1. It is for this reason that "loss of enjoyment of life" damages are sometimes referred to as "hedonic damages." *See, e.g.,* Crowe, *The Semantical Bifurcation of Noneconomic Loss: Should Hedonic Damages Be Recognized Independently of Pain and Suffering Damage?* 74 Iowa L.Rev. 1275 (1990).

"loss of enjoyment of life" damages compensate the individual not only for the subjective knowledge that one can no longer enjoy all of life's pursuits, but also for the objective loss of the ability to engage in these activities.

We hold that, where supported by the evidence, the jury shall be charged that the injured person is entitled to recover damages for loss of enjoyment of life. In our view, a separate charge on hedonic damages will minimize the risk that a jury will under- or over-compensate an injured person for her noneconomic losses. While there are cases in which it is difficult to segregate the various components of these types of damages, we conclude that a separate charge will clarify for the jurors the issues they should consider in awarding money for injuries which are not readily reducible to specific amounts. In situations where the differences may be difficult to discern, defendants may request the submission of a special interrogatory. * * *

We agree with the Court of Appeals that there was no error in the charge given in this trial. Accordingly, the decision of the Court of Appeals is affirmed as modified.

TOAL, C.J., MOORE, WALLER and BURNETT, JJ., concur.

NOTES

1. Most jurisdictions recognize damages for the loss of enjoyment of life, either as a separate element of general damages or as a part of pain and suffering. *See generally* Dan B. Dobbs, Law of Remedies § 8.1(4) (2d ed. 1993); Annotation, *Loss of Enjoyment of Life as a Distinct Element or Factor in Awarding Damages for Bodily Injury*, 34 A.L.R. 4th 293 (1984). The majority of jurisdictions regard this loss as an objective loss, which means that they permit the recovery of hedonic damages by a plaintiff who is permanently comatose, such as the plaintiff in *Molzof, supra*, Chapter 3, Section 3.A. *See, e.g.*, Flannery v. United States, 171 W.Va. 27, 297 S.E.2d 433 (1982). *But see* McDougald v. Garber, 73 N.Y.2d 246, 538 N.Y.S.2d 937, 536 N.E.2d 372 (1989) (stating the minority position that loss of enjoyment of life is purely subjective; denying the recovery of such damages to a permanently comatose plaintiff).

2. Many jurisdictions permit per diem arguments regarding pain and suffering, while others do not. *See generally* Annotation, *Per Diem or Similar Mathematical Basis for Fixing Damages for Pain and Suffering*, 3 A.L.R. 4th 940 (1981). For a critique of per diem arguments, see Joseph H. King, Jr., *Counting Angels and Weighing Anchors: Per Diem Arguments for Noneconomic Personal Injury Tort Damages*, 71 Tenn. L. Rev. 1, 11 (2003); Martin V. Totaro, Note, *Modernizing the Critique of Per Diem Pain and Suffering Damages*, 92 Va. L. Rev. 289 (2006) (taking into account the impact of modern methods of pain management). *See also* Lars Noah, *Comfortably Numb: Medicalizing (and Mitigating) Pain-and-Suffering Damages*, 42 U. Mich. J.L. Reform 431 (2009).

3. Should damages for future nonpecuniary losses be reduced to present value? Most federal and state courts have said "no." *See, e.g.*, Flanigan v.

Burlington Northern Inc., 632 F.2d 880, 886 (8th Cir.1980) ("Requiring the reduction of an award for pain and suffering to its present value would improperly allow a jury to infer that pain and suffering can be reduced to a precise arithmetic calculation."); Lamke v. Louden, 269 N.W.2d 53, 56 (Minn. 1978) ("The purpose of giving damages for pain and suffering is to compensate the injured party for his future expenses."); Friedman v. C & S Car Service, 108 N.J. 72, 79, 527 A.2d 871, 875 (1987) ("[A]lthough there is merit in requiring a discount to present value with regard to damages encompassing future pecuniary losses, this position loses cogency in a case * * * involving a damages award for non-economic losses, given the inherently speculative nature of damages for pain and suffering * * *.").

On the other hand, Judge Posner of the Seventh Circuit has suggested that, if a jurisdiction permits per diem arguments regarding pain and suffering, then it ought to reduce future pain and suffering to present value. Abernathy v. Superior Hardwoods, Inc., 704 F.2d 963 (7th Cir.1983) (Posner, J.) (applying a "real" discount rate of 2% to an award of damages for future pain and suffering; the plaintiff's lawyer had made a per diem argument in "real" (that is inflation-free) terms, suggesting that the jury award $10 per day for a period of 40 years). *See also* Oliveri v. Delta S.S. Lines, Inc., 849 F.2d 742 (2d Cir. 1988) (recognizing that the majority of the federal courts refuse to reduce pain and suffering to present value, but adopting the minority rule that the time value of money be taken into account; instructing trial court judges to use a "generalized approach" to discounting future nonpecuniary losses in an effort to "minimize the significance of our difference with other circuits on this issue"). *But see* United States v. Harue Hayashi, 282 F.2d 599, 605 (9th Cir.1960) ("[T]he use of the [per diem argument] did not ... convert the award [for pain and suffering] into one for pecuniary loss, thereby necessitating a reduction to present value."); *accord* Friedman v. C & S Car Service, 108 N.J. 72, 77–79, 527 A.2d 871, 874–75 (1987).

4. Tort reform legislation often caps general damages for noneconomic losses, either comprehensively or in a particular type of tort action, such as a medical malpractice action. For example, the Idaho legislature has enacted the following comprehensive tort reform statute:

§ 6–1603. Limitations on noneconomic damages.

(1) In no action seeking damages for personal injury, including death, shall a judgment for noneconomic damages be entered for a claimant exceeding the maximum amount of two hundred fifty thousand dollars ($250,000); provided, however, that beginning on July 1, 2004, and each July 1 thereafter, the cap on noneconomic damages established in this section shall increase or decrease in accordance with the percentage amount of increase or decrease by which the Idaho industrial commission adjusts the average annual wage as computed pursuant to section 72–409(2), Idaho Code.

(2) The limitation contained in this section applies to the sum of: (a) noneconomic damages sustained by a claimant who incurred personal injury or who is asserting a wrongful death; (b) noneconomic damages

sustained by a claimant, regardless of the number of persons responsible for the damages or the number of actions filed.

(3) If a case is tried to a jury, the jury shall not be informed of the limitation contained in subsection (1) of this section.

(4) The limitation of awards of noneconomic damages shall not apply to:

(a) Causes of action arising out of willful or reckless misconduct.

(b) Causes of action arising out of an act or acts which the trier of fact finds beyond a reasonable doubt would constitute a felony under state or federal law.

Idaho Code § 6–1603 (Michie 2004); *see also* Kirkland v. Blaine County Medical Center, 134 Idaho 464, 4 P.3d 1115 (2000) (the statutory cap did not violate the state constitution); *see generally* Victor E. Schwartz & Cary Silverman, *Hedonic Damages: The Rapidly Bubbling Cauldron*, 6 Brook. L. Rev. 1037 (2004) (advocating the enactment of comprehensive statutory caps on noneconomic damages).

Although the Idaho statute has a "floating cap," many medical malpractice tort reform statutes have a "fixed cap." *See, e.g.*, Cal. Civ. Code § 3333.2 (West 2004) (capping noneconomic damages at $250,000); *see also* Fein v. Permanente Medical Group, 38 Cal.3d 137, 211 Cal.Rptr. 368, 695 P.2d 665 (1985) (the statutory cap did not violate the state constitution); *see generally* Catherine M. Sharkey, *Unintended Consequences of Medical Malpractice Damage Caps*, 80 N.Y.U. L. Rev. 391 (2005). *But see* Lebron v. Gottlieb Memorial Hosp., 237 Ill.2d 217, ___ N.E.2d ___ (Ill. 2010) (statutory cap on noneconomic damages in medical malpractice tort reform statute violated state constitution).

For a discussion of the constitutionality of statutory caps on noneconomic damages under state constitutions, see Matthew W. Light, Note, *Who's the Boss?: Statutory Damages Caps, Courts, and State Constitutional Law*, 58 Wash. & Lee L. Rev. 315 (2001); *see also* Thomas R. Phillips, *The Constitutional Right to a Remedy*, 78 N.Y.U. L. Rev. 1309 (2003) (discussing the state constitutional "right to a remedy" that is guaranteed through "open access to the courts" by many state constitutions).

5. Some commentators have suggested that the United States Supreme Court should strike down excessive awards of damages for pain and suffering under the Due Process Clause of the United States Constitution, just as the Court currently strikes down excessive punitive damages judgments. *See, e.g.*, Paul De Camp, *Beyond State Farm: Due Process Constraints on Noneconomic Compensatory Damages*, 27 Harv. J.L. & Pub. Pol'y 231 (2003); Paul V. Niemeyer, *Awards for Pain and Suffering: The Irrational Centerpiece of our Tort System*, 90 Va. L. Rev. 1401 (2004); Victor E. Schwartz & Leah Lorber, *Twisting the Purpose of Pain and Suffering Awards: Turning Compensation into "Punishment,"* 54 S.C. L. Rev. 47 (2002). Other commentators have recommended that both trial and appellate courts engage in a "comparability" review of pain and suffering damage awards. *See, e.g.*, David Baldus, John C. McQueen, & George Woodworth, *Improving Judicial Oversight of Jury Damages Assessments: A Proposal for the Comparative Additur/Remittitur Review of Awards for Nonpecuniary Harms and Punitive Damages*, 80 Iowa L.

Rev. 1109 (1995). And, in 1986, the New York legislature mandated a "comparability" review of noneconomic damages awards in lieu of imposing statutory caps on such damages. *See, e.g.*, Donlon v. City of New York, 284 App.Div.2d 13, 727 N.Y.S.2d 94 (2001) (discussing the legislative history). *But see* Jo Ellen Lind, *The End of Trial on Damages? Intangible Losses and Comparability Review*, 51 Buff. L. Rev. 251 (2003). Finally, a few commentators have recommended the "scheduling" of amounts to be awarded for pain and suffering by (1) awarding fixed damage amounts according to the severity of the injury and the age of the injured party; or by (2) replacing a single arbitrary cap on all nonpecuniary awards with a system of flexible floors and ceilings that vary with the severity of the injury and the age of the victim. *See, e.g.*, Randall R. Bovbjerg, Frank A. Sloan & James F. Blumstein, *Valuing Life and Limb in Tort: Scheduling "Pain and Suffering,"* 83 Nw. U. L. Rev. 908, 938–39 (1989).

6. Several commentators have warned that the imposition of statutory caps on noneconomic damages will have a disparate impact upon women, particularly in medical malpractice and products liability cases where women have suffered reproductive injuries. Martha Chamallas, *The Architecture of Bias: Deep Structures in Tort Law*, 146 U. Pa. L. Rev. 463, 503–04, 519–21 (1998); Lucinda M. Finley, *Female Trouble: The Implications of Tort Reform for Women*, 64 Tenn. L. Rev. 847 (1997); Thomas Koenig & Michael Rustad, *His and Her Tort Reform: Gender Injustice in Disguise*, 70 Wash. L. Rev. 1 (1995).

7. Professor King advocates the abolition of all damages for noneconomic harm in personal injury actions, but he simultaneously proposes the recognition of comprehensive damages for medical and rehabilitative expenses plus an award of reasonable attorney's fees to prevailing plaintiffs. Joseph H. King, Jr., *Pain and Suffering, Noneconomic Damages, and the Goals of Tort Law*, 57 SMU L. Rev. 163 (2004).

c. Special Damages for Physical Injury

EARL v. BOUCHARD TRANSPORTATION COMPANY, INC.

United States District Court, Eastern District of New York, 1990.
735 F.Supp. 1167.

WEINSTEIN, DISTRICT JUDGE.

Plaintiff James Earl, a 66–year-old former tugboat deck hand, brings an action against his employer under the Jones Act, 46 U.S.C.App. § 688, and general maritime law for injuries suffered as a result of two separate accidents in 1984. As a consequence of his injuries he claims he was forced to retire on May 16, 1985, approximately a month before turning 62. He claims damages for, *inter alia,* loss of future earnings on the grounds that, absent injury, he would have continued to work at least an additional three years and five weeks—that is, until his 65th birthday, if not longer.

After a three day trial, the jury found for plaintiff and awarded him a total of $855,000 in damages, of which $425,000 was attributed to lost earnings suffered as a result of the second accident. Defendant moves for a new trial or remittitur.

There exists at least some evidence to support a finding that Earl, absent the accident, would have been able to work past the age of 62 and that he would have done so. Regardless of his pre-accident intentions, it is apparent that plaintiff's earning capacity—or work-capital—was permanently impaired or depleted as a result of his injuries.

Theoretically the human working machine can last (with some decreases in effectiveness through illness and decrepitude)—and thus has economic value—almost to the point of death. As a matter of law, then, an award taking into account any loss of value due to injury or death caused by a tortfeasor, can take into account even this residual and declining loss of value up to the time of predicted death. There is a considerable effort in a shrinking labor market to keep older people employed beyond the usual date of retirement. *See* Lewin, *Too Much Retirement Time? A Move is Afoot to Change It,* N.Y. Times, Apr. 22, 1990, § 1, at 1, col. 1. In fact, realities of the labor market in an industrial-commercial world make it unlikely that the last possible moment of a worker's time would be purchased by an employer. Moreover, as age increases, the probability that the worker may claim total disability, using the injury as justification for not pushing himself or herself to work probably increases.

These subtle nuances between loss of full work-capital value at one end of the spectrum and malingering at the other are generally best left to the judgment of the community as reflected in the jury's verdict. In computing the full value of a tort victim's depleted work-capital the jury may consider a variety of factors that differ from plaintiff to plaintiff, such as past earnings, the marketplace value of an individual's skills, the availability of suitable employment, and average work-life expectancy as projected by government statistical tables. This value may be affected as a result of particularized evidence bearing on a plaintiff's pre-accident intentions and proclivities. For example, if the jury credited evidence that before being injured a plaintiff had intended to retire early, a reduction of the full value of an award would be justified under the doctrine of mitigation of damages, which requires tort victims to find alternative employment whenever possible. The award may be increased to the full or close to full value if, on the other hand, the jurors believed that a plaintiff was likely to work beyond that age at which the statistical tables or their common sense experiences would normally predict retirement.

Where a jury verdict seems lopsidedly to favor one side or the other, the court has the obligation to require some equalization. This is such a case. Defendant's contention that there was no loss of earning capacity is unfounded. Nevertheless, for the reasons discussed below, defendants' motion for remittitur as to the award for future loss of earnings must be granted since an excessive award was made. Other adjustments are referred to below.

I. BACKGROUND

* * *

Earl claimed that he injured his right elbow in an August 29, 1984 accident and that he injured his ankle and reinjured his elbow in a second accident on December 13, 1984. Both accidents occurred while he was working on the [defendant's tugboat].

* * * He * * * claimed that his injuries eventually forced him to retire on May 16, 1985—three years and five weeks before his planned retirement at age 65.

Evidence adduced by defendants at trial indicated that plaintiff's intention prior to the accidents had been to retire in June of 1985 when he turned 62 years of age. * * *

Plaintiff testified that he "would probably have retired ... at 65." * * * In his closing argument, plaintiff's counsel presented the jury with two possible scenarios: retirement at age 65 as plaintiff testified was his intention, or retirement at age 67, based on the average work-life expectancy of a then 62-year-old man. In its charge to the jury the court presented the issue of retirement age as one of disputed fact.

* * *

II. APPLICABLE LAW

* * *

In a recent Jones Act case the trial court observed that "[d]amages in tort cases are designed to provide reparation for the injury caused [because] the 'cardinal principle of damages in Anglo–American law is that of *compensation* for the injury caused to plaintiff by defendant's breach of duty.' " * * *

* * *

III. DEPLETION OF WORK-CAPITAL

"An injury that reduces the period of work-life expectancy deprives the worker of the value of work-capital." * * * [T]he life-expectancy of the plaintiff in the case at bar was not shortened. His work expectancy was, the jury found, reduced. While fortunately not terminal, James Earl's injuries were nonetheless permanently and fully disabling and, according to the jury, prevented him from working.

Regardless of whether or not a plaintiff would have exercised the choice to work as long as he could have, he or she is entitled to damages "measured by the extent to which [the plaintiff's] capacity for earnings has been reduced." Restatement (Second) of Torts § 924 comment c. *See also* 2 S. Speiser, C. Krause & A. Gans, The American Law of Torts § 8:27, at 630. In effect, the " 'economic horizon of the [plaintiff] has been shortened because of the injuries.' "

There is no requirement that an injured plaintiff even be employed at the time of the accident in order to recover for impairment of earning capacity. * * * Gault v. Monongahela Power Co., 159 W.Va. 318, 223 S.E.2d 421, 426–27 (1976) (although plaintiff had ostensibly retired, he had intended to return to work as pipefitter and was therefore entitled to damages for impairment of earning capacity).

Earning capacity is determined by what a plaintiff "*could* have earned even if he or she never worked to that capacity in the past." 2 M. Minzer, J. Nates, C. Kimball, D. Axelrod & R. Goldstein, Damages in Tort Actions § 10.22[3][a] (citations omitted). As a California appellate court has observed, "[i]mpairment of the capacity or power to work is an injury separate from the actual loss of earnings." Hilliard v. A.H. Robins Co., 196 Cal.Rptr. 117, 143, 148 Cal.App.3d 374 (1983) * * *.

This principle is most clearly illustrated by cases involving injured students, homemakers, and infants. *See, e.g.,* Feldman v. Allegheny Airlines, Inc., 524 F.2d 384, 388 (2d Cir.1975) (in determining future earnings of college-educated 25 year old woman who was unemployed when killed in plane crash, fact finder properly considered fact that she had been capable of working full-time for forty years until she was 65, had planned to attend law school and would have continued to work part-time for an estimated eight years while raising children); Pucino v. Crete, No. 89–644, 1990 WL 21303 (N.D.N.Y. Feb.28, 1990) (LEXIS, Genfed library, Dist. file) (future earnings of aviation student killed while in last year of college are to be determined by wages he could have been expected to make as pilot over course of his pre-accident work-life expectancy); Kavanaugh v. Nussbaum, 129 A.D.2d 559, 514 N.Y.S.2d 55 (2d Dep't 1987) (injured infant's future earning capacity calculated using work-life expectancy of person having normal statistical life and work-life expectancies), *aff'd as modified on other grounds,* 71 N.Y.2d 535, 528 N.Y.S.2d 8, 523 N.E.2d 284 (1988); Ward v. La. & Ark. Railway, 451 So.2d 597, 608 (La.App. 2d Cir.1984) (injured high school student entitled to recover for loss of earning capacity even though she had not as yet entered work force); Grimes v. Haslett, 641 P.2d 813, 818 n.3 (Alaska 1982) ("The right of an injured homemaker to recover for impaired earning capacity regardless of whether she was employed before the injury exemplifies the distinction between an award for lost earnings and an award for lost earning capacity.").

At most, some courts have required that the plaintiff have been *employable* or *potentially* employable, rather than actually employed at the time of the accident. For example, in Espana v. United States, 616 F.2d 41 (2d Cir.1980), the court of appeals observed that tort victims such as housewives or students who, prior to injury, have not earned as much as they could in the marketplace, are entitled to recover damages for loss of full-time earning capacity. * * * In contrast, the court found that a plaintiff who had attempted and was unable before his accident to find full-time employment was not entitled to full-time compensation. * * *

The conceptual difference between the loss of earning capacity and the loss of actual wages is also illustrated by cases holding that the injured party is not barred from recovering for loss of earning capacity even if he or she earns as much as or more than before the injury. * * * The rationale behind this seemingly paradoxical result is consistent with the concept of lost earning capacity, for "by having one less trade at his disposal the injured Plaintiff has a reduction in future employability." * * *

Nor does the ability to recover for impaired earning capacity even where there is no actual wage loss necessarily undermine the doctrine of mitigation of damages. Under this doctrine, a Jones Act claimant, like other tort victims, has an obligation to mitigate damages where possible by finding other employment. * * * Nonetheless, the plaintiff who does so may still recover a reduced award provided the diminution of his or her work-capital is reflected in the smaller number of employment options available to that person as a result of injury. *But see* Alferoff v. Casagrande, 122 A.D.2d 183, 504 N.Y.S.2d 719, 721 (2d Dept. 1986) (student may not recover for diminution of earning capacity in intended profession as cosmetologist since post-injury job as receptionist paid higher salary).

In the case at bar, plaintiff's announced plan, as testified to by defense witnesses, to retire at age 62, if it had been credited, would have been strong evidence of malingering. It could have shown that in fact he had not lost any of his work capital—*e.g.,* the ability to earn money in the marketplace—and that he had refused or otherwise failed to mitigate his damages. It is clear, however, that the jury believed plaintiff to be completely disabled as a result of his accident, and thus exempt from the obligation to mitigate damages by continuing to work as a deck hand or by seeking other employment.

IV.   DETERMINING WORK-LIFE EXPECTANCY

Courts have varied in their approaches to calculating work-life expectancy. The Supreme Court, discussing the calculation of future loss of income in the Longshore and Harbor Workers' Compensation Act, 33 U.S.C. § 901 *et seq.,* observed that:

> [t]he lost stream [of income's] length cannot be known with certainty.... Given the complexity of trying to make an exact calculation, litigants frequently follow the relatively simple course of assuming that the worker would have continued to work up until a specific date certain.

Jones & Laughlin Steel Corp. v. Pfeifer, 462 U.S. 523, 533–54, 103 S.Ct. 2541, 2548–49, 76 L.Ed.2d 768 (1983). *See, e.g.,* Andrulonis v. United States, 724 F.Supp. 1421, 1517 & n.604 (N.D.N.Y. 1989) (court assumes, for convenience and in absence of statistical basis for either plaintiff's or defendant's proffer, that plaintiff would have worked to age 65).

In general "[t]he admissibility of evidence regarding future earning capacity is within the wide discretion of the trial judge." * * * For example, trial courts have considered the likelihood that economic down-turns in a particular industry would have resulted in lower wages in future years, as well as the likelihood that a given plaintiff would have been impervious to such economic vicissitudes. *See, e.g.,* Pretre v. United States, 531 F.Supp. 931, 935 (E.D.Mo.1981) (although defendant established that plaintiff would have been laid off due to his seniority ranking four years after being injured, court found he would have sought similar work and ordered him compensated for loss of earning capacity, "not merely for the loss of income from any particular job"). *Compare, e.g.,* Masinter v. Tenneco Oil Co., 867 F.2d 892, 899 (5th Cir.1989) (based on evidence of subsequent reduction in work force and in absence of evidence showing that longshoreman plaintiff would have been retained, it was not clearly erroneous for trial court to decide that plaintiff in future would have earned only 75% of his past earnings) *with* Connecticut National Bank v. OMI Corp., 733 F.Supp. 14 (S.D.N.Y.1990) (awarding full compensation for future loss of earnings despite showing that there was a general loss of seamen's jobs after seaman's death where widow claimed that she and decedent would have moved to area where shipping industry was healthiest).

In the absence of a mandatory retirement policy, a wide range of evidence bearing on retirement is admissible. Evidence regarding the pre-accident intentions of the plaintiff is highly probative. * * * Statistical charts, such as the mortality tables and work-life expectancy tables prepared by the United States Department of Labor, compile averages and are often deemed authoritative, particularly in the absence of contradictory particularized evidence. *See, e.g.,* Madore v. Ingram Tank Ships, Inc., 732 F.2d 475, 478 (5th Cir.1984) (district court was incorrect in basing work-life expectancy on assumption that Jones Act plaintiff, absent injury, would have worked until age 65 where no particularized evidence existed to contradict United States Department of Labor statistical averages assigning him a work-life expectancy of fewer years); Freeman v. Harold Dickey Transport, Inc., 467 So.2d 194, 197 (La.Ct.App. 3d Cir.1985) (plaintiff failed to prove that, absent injury, he would have been physically able to work beyond actuarial work-life expectancy).

These tables are not binding on the fact finder. *See* Espana v. United States, 616 F.2d 41, 44 (2d Cir.1980) (mortality tables do not constitute absolute guides, but are data to be taken into account in calculating basis for damages award in light of all the evidence; court was not clearly erroneous in concluding that, absent accident, plaintiff's work life would have ended early at age 60 due to preexisting degenerative back condition) * * *; McDonald v. United States, 555 F.Supp. 935, 968 (M.D.Pa.1983) (where female plaintiff did not have children and, as result of illness probably could not have any, shortened work-life expectancy projected by U.S. Dept. of Labor table and based on assumption that women leave workforce to bear children, is not applicable) * * *. Moreover, the statistical charts are updated on average every 10 years and therefore exhibit a lag in reflecting changing work and mortality patterns.

In the instant case the issue of plaintiff's retirement intentions was fully litigated. The jury obviously credited Earl's testimony. Unfortunately, it went far beyond that which could reasonably be inferred from the evidence. Even when viewed in the light most favorable to the plaintiff, the record does not support an award based upon a projected pre-accident work-life expectancy of 70 or more years—an assumption required by the jury award. Plaintiff's own testimony contradicts his claim that a statistical work-life expectancy of a 62 year old man—that is, a work-life expectancy of age 67—should be accepted. A retirement age of 65, on the other hand, has some support in the record and appears to be fair in view of all of the circumstances. It stretches the record as far as possible to favor the plaintiff and the jury's award.

V. Calculating Damages

Once the injured victim proves that he or she could have been gainfully employed, it is necessary to show with sufficient certainty the amount of damages. More is involved in computing the value of the diminution of work-capital " 'than comparing the amount earned before and after the injury.' " * * * It has long been the practice in New York, for example, to allow juries to consider the possibility that an injured victim would have advanced through promotions and thus be entitled to a recovery higher than that indicated by an average of his past earnings. * * * The Supreme Court has observed, "[a]s in all damages awards for tortious injury, '[i]nsistence on mathematical precision would be illusory and the judge or juror must be allowed a fair latitude to make reasonable approximations guided by judgment and practical experience.' " Sea–Land Services, Inc. v. Gaudet, 414 U.S. 573, 590, 94 S.Ct. 806, 817, 39 L.Ed.2d 9 (1974) (citation omitted). Nonetheless, the trier of fact must not be left to speculate and to unreasonably inflate an award.

In determining damages for the diminution in the plaintiff's earning capacity, courts have normally utilized an "oversimplified formula ... which seeks to determine what the [plaintiff's] earnings would have been had he survived in good health, multiplied by [plaintiff's] work life expectancy with the resultant dollar figure arrived at, then discounted to the present value." Connecticut National Bank v. OMI Corp., 733 F.Supp. 14 (S.D.N.Y.1990) (Carter, J.) * * *. In cases such as that at bar, past earnings—in the absence of unusual proven circumstances—serve as a dependable and adequate guide to future loss.

Earl was employed full-time before the accidents and there was no indication that he would or could have "retooled" at the age of 62 to go into a higher paying field. Any speculation that he might have been the beneficiary of an increase in wages is in effect cancelled out by the not-insubstantial possibility that he had never intended to work past age 62.

A. Computations

The reduced award was computed as follows, giving plaintiff every benefit of the doubt:

1) $105,000 was allowed for lost wages, based upon an average of $37,468.72 for five previous years, with a 25% agreed upon tax rate, making net loss of earnings $87,006.15. Fringe benefits were agreed on as $5,784.00 per year, or $17,908.15 for the three years and five weeks. The total is $104,914.30, rounded off to $105,000.00. There was no proof of increases in future wage rates. No allowance for discount was made because the judgment was entered after the probable date of retirement. No interest was sought for delayed payment, except as indicated in 3), below.

2) Pain and suffering and lost pleasure awards were exaggerated. An award of $100,000 for five years past is allowed. Assuming a possible additional life expectancy of 14 years an additional amount of $280,000 is permitted. The total is $380,000.

3) Maintenance and cure and interest factors were computed without objection at a rate most favorable to plaintiff in the sum of $40,000. This amount included past and future medical expenses. * * *

The total award that could possibly be justified is $525,000.00. This sum seems excessive, but it allows maximum effect to the jury's exceptionally sympathetic verdict for the plaintiff.

CONCLUSION

Unless plaintiff agrees to a remittitur to $525,000.00, a new trial is granted.

NOTES

1. The court in *Earl* refers to students, homemakers and infants as plaintiffs who need to recover for lost earning capacity and notes that mathematical precision is not required. How much proof is needed? In Bernard v. Royal Insurance Co., 586 So.2d 607, 615 (La.Ct.App.1991), the plaintiff testified that "she planned to work at the Lead Prevention Center for a year or two and obtain a master's and doctorate degree in public health * * * [and go] to medical school." There was testimony that she spoke of going to medical school, was qualified to be a graduate student and was saving money for graduate school. The court said:

> [Ms. Bernard's lost earning capacity based on becoming a doctor is] premised on the highly speculative assumption that Ms. Bernard would eventually obtain a doctorate in tropical medicine. She graduated in May, 1983 from Xavier University with a B.S. degree. At the time of the accident (1985) Ms. Bernard had taken no steps to begin a graduate program. She did not work in her specialty or at a full-time job from May, 1983 until July, 1985. Ms. Bernard's only employment after college was as a substitute teacher for two years and she did not remember whether she earned enough money to file a tax return. In her 1987 deposition she stated (as an aside) that she considered going to medical school "some time in the future." In her 1989 deposition she mentioned that she intended to seek a graduate degree in public health. * * *

* * * [T]he calculation of $1,630,415 was based on very unrealistic assumptions. We must lower the award to the highest reasonable award under the circumstances.

Dr. Wolfson's alternative calculations are based on the plausible assumption that Ms. Bernard would work in a laboratory, a position she accepted just prior to her accident. Her salary would have been $12,600, [and] she would receive promotions over the years * * *.

We amend the loss of future earning capacity from $1,850,000 to $867,833.

Id. at 616–17.

For other cases discussing the future lost earning capacity of students and infants, see Athridge v. Iglesias, 950 F.Supp. 1187, 1193 (D.D.C.1996) (plaintiff, who had suffered permanent brain damage due to an automobile accident at the age of 15, was awarded $1,400,000 for future lost earning capacity because his siblings were all enrolled in professional schools and, prior to the accident, "he had expressed an interest in becoming a lawyer"); Rappold v. Snorac, Inc., 289 App.Div.2d 1044, 735 N.Y.S.2d 687 (2001) (plaintiff, who had just completed his first year of law school before he suffered severe brain injury in an auto accident, was permitted to recover $4,000,000 for future lost earning capacity); Brueckner v. Norwich University, 169 Vt. 118, 128, 730 A.2d 1086, 1094 (1999) (plaintiff, who had withdrawn from a military college due to hazing by upperclassmen, was permitted to recover $300,000 for past and future lost earning capacity where his expert witness, using U.S. Census Bureau data, and discounting the figures to present value, testified that, "if plaintiff were a college graduate he would earn between $600,000 and $932,593 more over the course of his working life than he would as a high school graduate"); *see also* Altman v. Alpha Obstetrics and Gynecology P.C., 255 App.Div.2d 276, 278, 679 N.Y.S.2d 642, 644 (1998) (plaintiff, an infant who suffered permanent brain damage at birth due to the defendant's medical malpractice, was permitted to recover $3,000,000 in future lost earning capacity because "the record reveals that education, as well as scholastic performance, is of considerable importance to the plaintiff's family"); *see generally* William H. Danne, Jr., Annotation, *Admissibility and Sufficiency in Personal Injury or Wrongful Death Action of Evidence as to Earnings or Earning Capacity from Position or Field for Which Person Has Not Fulfilled Education, Training, or Like Eligibility Requirement*, 2002 A.L.R. 5th 25.

2. In Sheppard v. Crow–Barker–Paul No. 1 Limited Partnership, 192 Ariz. 539, 968 P.2d 612 (Ariz.Ct.App.1998), the plaintiff was a star basketball player in the Riverside Church program in New York City whose friends sometimes called him "NBA" or "Franchise." He was playing in a basketball tournament in Scottsdale, Arizona, when a teammate closed a sliding glass door in the defendant's hotel that shattered, cutting through the plaintiff's left arm and causing permanent damage. The plaintiff chose not to request special damages for the loss of his future earning capacity as a professional basketball player, nor for the loss of his chance to become a professional basketball player. Instead, he confined himself to a general damages claim for loss of enjoyment of life, and he was awarded a $445,000 verdict, which was

affirmed on appeal. Arizona follows *Boan, supra* Chapter 3, Section 7.A.1.b., and defines loss of enjoyment of life as a separate item of general damages. Ogden v. J.M. Steel Erecting, Inc., 201 Ariz. 32, 31 P.3d 806 (Ariz.Ct.App. 2001) (review denied).

3. What is the scope of the duty to mitigate? *Compare* Walmsley v. Brady, 793 F.Supp. 393, 394–95 (D.R.I.1992) ("While it may be true that Dr. Walmsley's career as a veterinarian of some sort is not ended, it may be just as true that she no longer can practice the variety of veterinary medicine [(equine medicine, with a focus on surgery)] for which she has been trained. It would not be unreasonable for a jury to decide that a physician has a right to practice in the particular field of medicine he or she has chosen, as opposed to practicing in *any* field of medicine.") *and* Hale v. Aetna Life & Casualty Insurance Co., 580 So.2d 1053, 1056 (La.Ct.App.1991) ("We have been cited no case and have been unable to find one, that says that an individual fails to mitigate his damages if he does not go to college or otherwise retrain himself, and thereby acquire the capability of earning the same income he enjoyed before suffering an accident which rendered him incapable of returning to his former employment."), *with* Burke v. Safeway Stores, Inc., 554 So.2d 184, 190 (La.Ct.App.1989). In *Burke*, the plaintiff no longer had the manual dexterity in her left index finger necessary to be a legal secretary, and her therapist recommended that she return to school to become teacher. The trial court awarded Ms. Burke $67,191 for future lost earning capacity over a 5–year period in which she would be a full-time student. The appellate court affirmed. As to past lost earnings, however, the appellate court imposed a duty to mitigate. The court noted that the plaintiff could either have obtained employment or begun her studies before the date of the trial. In fact, she "began to pursue her education at one point but dropped out due to her child's illness." The court did not limit mitigation to finding a comparable job, saying: "[W]e will reduce her past economic losses by a sum that she could have earned had she obtained employment in a minimum wage job."

Is *Burke* inconsistent with *Walmsley* and *Hale*? In *Burke,* should the plaintiff's leaving school to take care of a sick child have negated damages for that period? Had she been working, might she have been able to claim accrued sick leave? Is *Burke* incorrect? Should mitigation be more onerous for a plaintiff in a tort action than in a contract action? *See* Parker v. Twentieth Century–Fox Film Corp., *supra* Chapter 7, Section 4.A (Actress Shirley Maclaine Parker was not required to deduct the salary she would have earned had she made the film that defendant offered to substitute for the contractual one because making the substitute film was not required to mitigate her damages: the offered film was a western, not a musical, and was to be filmed in Australia, not the United States.).

4. The Internal Revenue Code provides that damages "for personal injury" are not taxable income. 26 U.S.C.A. § 104(a). The United States Supreme Court has announced a federal common law rule that evidence regarding the tax savings must be admitted, and the Court has approved an instruction telling the jury that the amount of damages which it awards will not be subject to income taxes. Norfolk & Western Railway Co. v. Liepelt, 444 U.S. 490, 100 S.Ct. 755, 62 L.Ed.2d 689 (1980) (FELA case). The *Liepelt* rule was applied by the *Earl* court. By contrast with the federal rule, most state

courts do not admit evidence of tax savings and take the position that "refusal to give a nontaxability instruction is not reversible error" because "allowing the instruction would invite numerous cautionary instructions on such topics as attorney's fees, insurance coverage, and court costs." Rego Co. v. McKown-Katy, 801 P.2d 536, 538 (Colo.1990). See *generally* Dan B. Dobbs, Law of Remedies § 8.6(4) (2d ed. 1993).

2. Compensatory Damages for Emotional Distress

LARSEN v. BANNER HEALTH SYSTEM

Supreme Court of Wyoming, 2003.
81 P.3d 196.

Before HILL, C.J., and GOLDEN, LEHMAN, and VOIGT, JJ., and PRICE, D.J.
LEHMAN, JUSTICE.

* * *

ISSUE

The issue presented by the certified question is:

Whether a mother and daughter, who were separated for forty-three years because a hospital switched two newborn babies at birth, can maintain a negligence action in which the only alleged damages are great emotional pain, humiliation, anxiety, grief, and expenses for psychological counseling?

FACTS

The certification order from the United States District Court [for the District of Wyoming] sets forth a brief statement of facts relevant to the certified question. Those facts are as follows:

At 3:07 a.m. on April 8, 1958, Jean Morgan gave birth to a baby girl, Debra, at Campbell County Memorial hospital. Shortly thereafter, Polly Leyva gave birth to a baby girl named Shirley. The hospital staff switched Shirley and Debra in those early morning hours when the respective mothers were unconscious. When the mothers regained consciousness, Debra went home with Polly Leyva and Shirley went home with Jean Morgan.

The members of the hospital staff who switched the newborns and then failed to correct the mistake were acting within the scope of their employment for Banner Health System. * * *

Shirley "Morgan" grew up in the Morgan home, however, she did not look like the other Morgan children due to a darker skin coloration. Because Shirley had a darker complexion, James Morgan, the "father," openly and frequently asserted that Shirley was not his child. The complaint alleges that due to James' mistrust, Shirley was ostracized and "terribly mistreated" by James Morgan and the Morgan siblings.

negligence alleging only mental injury had been recognized in Wyoming."
Id. * * *

Our most recent in-depth discussion of the availability of emotional
distress damages in negligence actions is found in Long–Russell v. Hampe,
2002 WY 16, 39 P.3d 1015 (Wyo.2002). The plaintiff in *Hampe* claimed
that her attorney was negligent when handling her divorce, which involved child custody issues. We were called upon to answer certified
questions that required us to decide whether damages for emotional
suffering could be awarded in a legal malpractice action where the basis
for the claim was the attorney's negligence. We answered those questions
in the negative. * * *

* * *

* * * [T]he parties in *Hampe* * * * had an attorney client relationship. A similar type of relationship exists between a patient and her doctor
and hospital. Both types of claims arise from a relationship based on
breach of contract and breach of a fiduciary duty. * * * *Hampe* similarly
contained elements of damage that resulted from a disturbance in the
parent-child relationship. Therefore, *Hampe* appears at first glance to be
controlling.

However, an important distinction must be made between *Hampe* and
the instant case. Factoring into our decision in *Hampe* was our concern for
the issues surrounding child custody. In *Hampe,* we cited to a Colorado
case for its discussion of the child custody issues. We stated, "[w]ith
specific regard to the claim relating to child custody, we view with favor
the case McGee v. Hyatt Legal Services, Inc., 813 P.2d 754, 758–59
(Colo.App.1990), for the additional guidance it provides." *Hampe,* ¶ 13. We
noted that court's concerns about

> the impossibility of quantifying intangible injuries to the parent-child
> relationship, the effect recognition of damages would have on the
> district court's authority to regulate and supervise custody decisions
> which must turn on the best interests of the child, the certainty of
> some significant level of emotional disturbance in the dissolution of a
> marriage which includes a child custody component (especially one
> burdened with a high level of animosity), as well as the certainty that
> neither parent can reasonably expect full-time custody of the children
> because of the statutorily required liberal visitation with the non-
> custodial parent.

Hampe, ¶ 13. Therein lies the difference.

* * *

As mentioned previously, many jurisdictions have in at least some
fashion modified the traditional rule requiring actual or threatened physical impact. However, most jurisdictions still require proof of a physical
manifestation of emotional distress. Boyles v. Kerr, 855 S.W.2d 593, 598–
99 (Tex.1993) (collecting cases). Several jurisdictions have recognized a

general right to recover for negligently inflicted emotional distress. * * * Some jurisdictions allow recovery where the claimant establishes the breach of some independent duty. *Boyles,* at 598–99 (citing Burgess v. Superior Court, 2 Cal.4th 1064, 9 Cal.Rptr.2d 615, 831 P.2d 1197 (1992) * * *; Oswald v. LeGrand, 453 N.W.2d 634 (Iowa 1990) * * *). It is the independent duty exception to the general rule prohibiting recovery for strictly emotional damages that [plaintiffs] urge us to apply.

The Iowa Supreme Court has set forth a good description of this exception. "An exception exists 'where the nature of the relationship between the parties is such that there arises a duty to exercise ordinary care to avoid causing emotional harm.'" Lawrence v. Grinde, 534 N.W.2d 414, 421 (Iowa 1995) (quoting Oswald v. LeGrand, 453 N.W.2d at 639). This exception is applied in circumstances involving contractual relationships for services that carry with them deeply emotional responses in the event of breach. *Lawrence,* at 421. Iowa has thus recognized the propriety of recovery of emotional distress in actions involving: 1) medical malpractice from negligent examination and treatment of a pregnant woman and her premature fetus; 2) a son when he saw the negligence of another cause injury to his mother; 3) negligent delivery of a telegram announcing the death of a loved one; and 4) negligent performance of a contract to provide funeral services. *Lawrence,* 534 N.W.2d at 421.

* * *

We * * * [adopt] Iowa's application of the independent duty exception because this expression is narrowly tailored and well reasoned. Under this exception recovery exists only in circumstances involving contractual services that carry with them deeply emotional responses in the event of breach. There must be a close nexus between the negligent action at issue and extremely emotional circumstances. *Lawrence,* 534 N.W.2d at 421. Whether this exception should be applied in Wyoming requires that we determine whether to extend a limited duty of care to those who suffer mental distress in the above-mentioned limited circumstances. In making this determination we seek to balance the view that a negligent act should have some end to its legal consequences against the view that the injured party has the right to recover for all harm caused. *Gates,* 719 P.2d at 196. Key policy factors to be considered are:

> (1) the foreseeability of harm to the plaintiff, (2) the closeness of the connection between the defendant's conduct and the injury suffered, (3) the degree of certainty that the plaintiff suffered injury, (4) the moral blame attached to the defendant's conduct, (5) the policy of preventing future harm, (6) the extent of the burden upon the defendant, (7) the consequences to the community and the court system, and (8) the availability, cost and prevalence of insurance for the risk involved.

Gates, 719 P.2d at 196 (citing Tarasoff v. Regents of University of California, 17 Cal.3d 425, 131 Cal.Rptr. 14, 551 P.2d 334, 342 (1976)).

First, we consider the foreseeability of harm to the plaintiff. As noted in *Gates,* this is a vague test that essentially results in the court setting a legal duty and then outlining the policy principles that urge us to recognize such a duty. However, it is clear that the independent duty exception is based on the principle of foreseeability. * * * We can easily conclude that it is foreseeable that when two babies are switched at birth the parties involved will experience emotional distress when the error is discovered. * * *

Second, we consider the closeness between the defendant's conduct and the injury suffered. In instances where the independent duty exception is applied there is a closeness between the defendant's conduct and the injury because the exception is limited to instances where the parties had some sort of relationship. The very nature of the exception requires that the defendant's conduct be sufficiently close to the injury suffered. In such cases, there is a direct link between the injured party and the defendant. Although the holding in *Daily* was limited to automobile collisions, in that decision we recognized that a difference exists between a claim asserted by a "bystander" and a claim asserted by a direct victim of a traditional completed tort. * * * Cases involving babies that have been switched at the hospital present the direct victims of a tort. The concerns related to the closeness of "bystanders" are thus not present. * * *

Third, we must be concerned with whether there is some certainty that the plaintiff suffered an injury. * * * In this particular case, a mother and daughter learned after forty-three years that they had been separated because two babies had been switched at birth. Little doubt remains that the parties involved in such an occurrence will suffer emotional distress. Indeed, the parties have lost the affection and close companionship that attends the parent-child relationship. The parties have bonded with other persons and recognized those persons as their own family only to shockingly discover that they are not related by blood, as they had once believed.

Fourth, we consider the moral blame attached to the defendant's conduct. This factor is used to determine whether the defendant is morally culpable before imposing liability. Moral blame generally results from situations in which the defendant had direct control over establishing and ensuring proper procedures to avoid the harm caused or where the defendant is the party best in the position to prevent the injury. * * * Traditionally, the reason for denying recovery for purely mental disturbances relied upon the judgment that a defendant who is merely negligent is not so blameworthy that he should be required to compensate for mental disturbances. However, we think moral blame does attach to the defendant's conduct when babies are switched at the hospital. The hospital has sole control over the babies and its identification procedures, and it is the hospital that is in the best position to prevent such an injury. We, therefore, think that moral blame must attach to such conduct.

The fifth and sixth factors, the policy in preventing future harm and the burden on the defendant in this instance, can be discussed together. We find it imperative that hospitals have procedures to ensure that newborn children are given to the proper parent. * * * Furthermore, the burden placed upon the defendant to avoid such harm in the future would not be so great. Procedures for the identification and safety of newborn babies are available and can easily be used.

Seventh, we must determine the consequence to the community and the court system. This factor has generally been thought of as weighing the negative aspects of creating a new cause of action. As noted previously, we are concerned that additional liability may impose a great burden on our court system. However, we think the independent duty exception, as described by the Iowa Supreme Court, is sufficiently limited in scope so as to avoid an overwhelming burden. * * *

An additional limitation on the independent duty exception as recognized by Iowa is the requirement that the distress inflicted be "so severe that no reasonable man could be expected to endure it." *Lawrence,* 534 N.W.2d at 421 (citing Restatement, Second, Torts). This same limitation exists on intentional infliction of emotional distress (IIED) as recognized in Wyoming, which comes from Restatement, Second, Torts § 46. *Leithead,* 721 P.2d at 1065 * * *.

* * *

Under this seventh factor, we additionally recognize that the parent-child relationship is intangible and it will likely be hard to value. However, such a valuation would be no harder than valuing the loss of society, care, and attention in a wrongful death action.[3] "Recovery of damages for mental injury is not novel to Wyoming jurisprudence." *Daily,* 906 P.2d at 1044. Similarly intangible and inherently difficult to measure are pain and suffering damages, but they are sought and awarded in nearly all tort actions. We also acknowledge that tort damages are compensatory in nature and seek to put the plaintiff in the same position he would have been in but for the defendant's negligence. While a monetary award will not restore intangible relationships, it is currently the best solution our system offers. * * *

The procedures by which courts can control juries combined with the limited nature of the exception and the requirement of severe emotional distress convinces us that the negative aspects of recognizing the independent duty exception are reasonably limited. Therefore, under the seventh factor we determine that our courts will not be unduly burdened by this exception to the general rules limiting emotional damages.

The eighth and final factor is the availability, cost, and prevalence of insurance for the risk involved. Aside from the current issues surrounding

---

3. We seek to clarify that this statement is in no way intended to indicate a retreat from the holding that mental suffering is not a compensable damage under the wrongful death statute. *See* Knowles v. Corkill, 2002 WY 119, 51 P.3d 859 (Wyo.2002).

the cost of medical malpractice insurance, we note that insurance is quite prevalent. Hospitals are insured for all types of losses related to the birth of a child. Although we have said this previously, because of the current issues surrounding medical malpractice insurance it bears repeating: this exception is extremely limited. The exception only applies when there is a contract for services that carries deeply emotional responses in the event of breach. Although some level of emotion attends every situation involving one's health, we do not anticipate that every area of healthcare will carry the deeply emotional responses sufficient to sustain this exception.

After applying the balancing of factors test "it is difficult for the court, on the basis of natural justice, to reach the conclusion that this type of action will not lie. Human tendencies and sympathies suggest otherwise." * * * Accordingly, we hold that in Wyoming, in the limited circumstances where a contractual relationship exists for services that carry with them deeply emotional responses in the event of breach, there arises a duty to exercise ordinary care to avoid causing emotional harm. * * *

* * *

For the reasons fully explained above we answer the certified question in the affirmative. A mother and daughter, who were separated for forty-three years because the hospital switched two newborn babies at birth, can maintain a negligence action in which the only alleged damages are great emotional pain, humiliation, anxiety, grief, and expenses for psychological counseling.

PRICE, DISTRICT JUDGE, dissenting.

I respectfully dissent.

The majority again expands the traditional rule disallowing recovery for mental or emotional injury only when such injury is linked to an actual or threatened physical impact. Although the majority says one thing, it clearly does the other. * * *

* * *

This certainly opens the door for a number of cases to be considered by the trial courts. As one commentator has stated:

> It is difficult to imagine how a set of rules could be developed and applied on a case-by-case basis to distinguish severe from nonsevere emotional harm. Severity is not an either/or proposition; it is rather a matter of degree. Thus, any attempt to formulate a general rule would almost inevitably result in a threshold requirement of severity so high that only a handful would meet it, or so low that it would be an ineffective screen. A middle-ground rule would be doomed, for it would call upon courts to distinguish between large numbers of cases factually too similar to warrant different treatment. Such a rule would, of course, be arbitrary in its application.

Richard N. Pearson, *Liability to Bystanders for Negligently Inflicted Emotional Harm—A Comment on the Nature of Arbitrary Rules*, 34 U. Fla. L. Rev. 477, 511 (1982) * * *.

It is the expansion of this holding to many medical malpractice cases that concerns me. In the current times of medical malpractice issues, insurance and possible resulting loss of doctors in Wyoming, I predict this case will add fuel to the fire. After all, legal malpractice does not give rise to a claim for emotional distress but medical malpractice will. * * * Even though the majority tries to limit this expansion, I predict it will not * * *.

* * * I dissent and would answer the certified question in the negative.

NOTE

For scholarly commentary supporting the outcome in *Larsen*, see Dan B. Dobbs, *Undertakings and Special Relationships in Claims for Negligent Infliction of Emotional Distress*, 50 Ariz. L. Rev. 49 (2008); *see also* John Kircher, *The Four Faces of Tort Law: Liability for Emotional Harm*, 90 Marq. L. Rev. 789 (2007). Wyoming continues to regard *Larsen* as an exception to its general rule that damages for emotional distress are only recoverable "when they are accompanied by physical injury, exposure to physical harm or willful, wanton or malicious conduct." Hendricks v. Hurley, 184 P.3d 680 (Wyo. 2008).

3. Loss of Consortium

DuPONT v. UNITED STATES

United States District Court, Southern District, West Virginia 1997.
980 F.Supp. 192.

GOODWIN, DISTRICT JUDGE.

* * *

BACKGROUND

This action arises out of Jean D. DuPont's claim that she slipped and fell on a defective floor in a Charleston, West Virginia, United States Post Office. As a result of the January 8, 1995 fall, Mrs. DuPont suffered knee and hip injuries. Pursuant to the Federal Tort Claims Act (FTCA), 28 U.S.C. §§ 2671–2680, Mrs. DuPont sued the United States Postal Service under a negligence theory and submitted her claim for administrative determination. The Postal Service denied her claim on November 8, 1996. On May 2, 1997, Mrs. DuPont and her husband, Philip DuPont, filed the instant action. The complaint re-alleged Mrs. DuPont's negligence claims and also included a claim by Mr. DuPont for loss of consortium. The DuPonts asserted that, "Plaintiffs' claims have first been presented to the United States Postal Service and ... have been finally denied," and that the FTCA therefore allowed this Court subject matter jurisdiction over the action. * * *

In its motion to dismiss, the Government contends that the Court lacks subject matter jurisdiction over Mr. DuPont's claim because he failed to submit the claim for administrative determination as required by FTCA § 2675(a). * * *

* * *

HISTORICAL BACKGROUND

The action for loss of spousal consortium originates with the Roman notion of *paterfamilias,* the male head of household. Roman law did not recognize women and children as independent persons with the ability to bring their own causes of action. Therefore, only the *paterfamilias* could vindicate wrongs done to household members. English courts subsequently adopted the action and applied it in the employment context, allowing masters to recover for the diminished value of injured servants. English courts also applied the *paterfamilias* action to the family and analogized the master with the husband/father and the servant with the wife/children. *See* Susan G. Ridgeway, Comment, *Loss of Consortium and Loss of Services Actions: A Legacy of Separate Spheres,* 50 Mont. L.Rev. 349, 349–64 (1989) (providing extensive historical overview of loss of consortium claim). By the eighteenth century, English courts recognized the husband's actionable right for loss of a wife's consortium, a chattel action protecting the husband's legal interest in his wife's services, society, and sexual relations. *See* Seagraves v. Legg, 147 W.Va. 331, 337, 127 S.E.2d 605 (1962) (noting that common-law loss of consortium action "was based on the theory that the wife was a chattel, or property of the husband"), *overruled by* W. Va.Code § 48–3–19a. Because the law deemed husband and wife one person, with all rights vested in the husband, a wife did not have an action for loss of consortium. *See* Jo–Anne M. Baio, Note, *Loss of Consortium: A Derivative Injury Giving Rise to a Separate Cause of Action,* 50 Fordham L.Rev. 1344, 1346–47 & nn.16–18 (1982).

American courts adopted the English action for loss of consortium and established consortium as a contractual right vesting on marriage. When legislatures began to recognize women as legal individuals with concomitant rights to own property, make contracts, and sue, courts extended to women a limited right of consortium. Although courts recognized a husband's right to recover for loss of his wife's services, as well as for loss of the "emotional" or "sentimental" aspects of consortium (i.e., companionship, affection, fidelity, and sexual relations), wives were limited to loss of consortium actions based solely on material loss (e.g., loss of support). It was not until the seminal case of Hitaffer v. Argonne Co., 183 F.2d 811 (D.C.Cir.), *cert. denied,* 340 U.S. 852, 71 S.Ct. 80, 95 L.Ed. 624 (1950), that the law began to recognize that "[i]nvasion of the consortium is an independent wrong directly to the spouse so injured." *Id.* at 815. Since *Hitaffer,* courts and legislatures have allowed that each spouse has a separate and actionable right for loss of the material support and services of the other, as well as for loss of "companionship, love, felicity, and sexual relations." *Id.* at 819; *see Baio, supra,* at 1345 & n.9 ("It is also now generally recognized that loss of consortium is a separate injury of the loss of consortium spouse."); *Ridgeway, supra,* at 349–64.

Federal Tort Claims Act

As noted in Henderson v. United States, 785 F.2d 121 (4th Cir.1986), plaintiffs must satisfy certain prerequisites before filing a civil action under the FTCA. * * * "The FTCA clearly provides that, prior to bringing an action against the United States in federal court, a claimant 'shall have first presented the claim to the appropriate Federal agency and his claim shall have been finally denied by the agency.'" *Id.* (quoting 28 U.S.C. § 2675(a)) * * *. Multiple plaintiffs must satisfy the jurisdictional requirements individually. * * * Further, "[i]t is well-settled that the requirement of filing an administrative claim is jurisdictional and may not be waived." *Henderson,* 785 F.2d at 123 * * *.

FTCA § 1346(b)(1) requires federal courts to determine the Government's liability in accordance with the law of the state in which the alleged acts of negligence occurred. In this case, the Government argues that West Virginia treats an action for loss of consortium as the separate and independent claim of the uninjured spouse. A significant number of courts have found that when loss of consortium is a separate and independent claim under applicable state law, it must be expressly raised in an administrative claim to satisfy the FTCA's jurisdictional requirements. * * *

Loss of Consortium Actions in West Virginia

West Virginia recognizes that a loss of consortium action is distinct from the injured spouse's underlying tort claim. The West Virginia Supreme Court of Appeals has determined that consortium is a legally protected right. *See* Poling v. Motorists Mutual Insurance Co., 192 W.Va. 46, 49, 450 S.E.2d 635 (1994) (each spouse has a right to consortium); * * * Shreve v. Faris, 144 W.Va. 819, 824, 111 S.E.2d 169 (1959) ("Loss of consortium by a husband resulting from injuries sustained by his wife is a right which gives rise to damages."). The right to consortium is "peculiar and exclusive" to each spouse and may not be asserted by the other. *Shreve,* 144 W.Va. at 824, 111 S.E.2d 169 * * *. Because the loss of consortium action compensates a spouse for loss of his or her individual rights in the marriage relationship, the action is independent of the injured spouse's tort claim. *See, e.g., Poling,* 192 W.Va. at 49, 450 S.E.2d 635 (wife has separate cause of action for loss of consortium arising out of alleged bad faith insurance practices) * * *; Restatement (Second) of Torts § 693 cmt. g (1976) (noting that "[t]he invasion of the deprived spouse's interests in the marriage is a separate tort against that spouse"). A loss of consortium claim is derivative only in the sense that the claim depends on an injury to another. Clearly, the claim asserts a spouse's independent rights in the marriage relationship. *See* Baio, *supra,* at 1351–54.

Although the loss of consortium claim is a separate cause of action, plaintiffs commonly join loss of consortium and tort actions. *See* King v. Bittinger, 160 W.Va. 129, 231 S.E.2d 239 (1976) * * *; *see also* Belcher v. Goins, 184 W.Va. 395, 403, 407, 400 S.E.2d 830 (1990) (noting in analogous context of loss of parental consortium actions that "[a] claim for parental consortium ordinarily must be joined with the injured parent's action against the alleged tortfeasor"); *cf.* Weaver v. Union Carbide Corp., 180 W.Va. 556, 558, 378 S.E.2d 105 (1989) (determining that loss of consortium claim may be brought without tort claim under certain circumstances). Indeed, the success of a loss of consortium claim may hinge on the underlying tort action. That the two claims are interrelated and may be joined, however, does not detract from the notion that the claims are distinct. "The invasion of the deprived spouse's interests in the marriage is a separate tort against that spouse, although it is conditioned upon factors that also constitute a tort against the impaired spouse." Restatement (Second) of Torts § 693 cmt. g (1976).

This Court is of the opinion that the West Virginia Supreme Court of Appeals recognizes a loss of consortium claim as an independent cause of action. Therefore, the FTCA required Mr. DuPont to submit his claim for administrative determination before bringing it in federal court. * * * The Court finds that Mr. DuPont's failure to submit his loss of consortium claim for the Postal Service's administrative review renders this Court without subject matter jurisdiction over the claim. Accordingly, the Court grants the Government's motion to dismiss Philip DuPont's claim for lack of subject matter jurisdiction and orders his loss of consortium claim dismissed.

BELCHER v. GOINS

Supreme Court of Appeals of West Virginia, 1990.
184 W.Va. 395, 400 S.E.2d 830.

McHUGH, JUSTICE.

The primary issue presented in this case is whether this jurisdiction recognizes a child's claim for loss or impairment of parental consortium against a tortfeasor for nonfatal, negligently inflicted injuries sustained by the parent. * * * While this Court herein recognizes such a claim by a minor child, or by a handicapped child of any age who is dependent upon the injured parent, the plaintiff here was not a minor or handicapped child at the time the cause of action accrued. * * *

I

Phyllis Belcher, mother of the plaintiff, Stephanie L. Belcher, was injured when the car she was driving was negligently struck head-on by a car driven by the defendant, Sherry L. Goins. Phyllis Belcher's claim against the defendant has been settled and dismissed with prejudice.

At the time of the collision the plaintiff was over eighteen years of age but resided in her mother's home with her mother. The plaintiff was not in or near her mother's car at the time of the collision.

As a count in her amended complaint, the plaintiff sought recovery from the defendant for "loss of love, companionship, and consortium of and from her mother," for mental anguish and for nursing and household services provided by the plaintiff to her mother after her mother was injured.

* * *

II.

A.

Traditionally, at common law "consortium" was defined as consisting of the alliterative trio of (1) services, (2) society and (3) sexual relations, and the husband was entitled to recover damages from a tort-feasor when *one or more* of these elements of the relationship with his wife were lost or impaired due to an injury to her. * * *

Similarly, "parental consortium" refers to the relationship between parent and child and is the right of the child to the intangible benefits of the companionship, comfort, guidance, affection and aid of the parent. Gail v. Clark, 410 N.W.2d 662, 668 (Iowa 1987) (recognizing parental consortium claim under state dramshop statute). As a leading text writer has stated, it is useful to refer to the parent-child relationship, as well as the husband-wife relationship, as constituting consortium; the important aspects of the parent-child relationship, apart from the parent's duty of pecuniary support, are the intangibles which follow from living together as a family, including the affection, society, companionship, the mutual learning and the moral support given and received. 1 H. Clark, The Law of Domestic Relations in the United States, § 12.1, at 651 (2d ed. 1987).

The legislature of this state has recognized the validity of a claim by family members, including minor children, for damages for loss of consortium, including mental anguish, in cases involving the wrongful death of a family member.[4] * * *

B.

There is a split of authorities as to whether a minor child has a legally cognizable claim for loss or impairment of parental consortium, against a tortfeasor who negligently injures, but does not kill, the minor child's parent. Adhering to the early common-law rule, most state courts have refused to recognize such a claim. * * * The initial rationale for this rule was that, for purposes of tortious interference with domestic relations, a child was viewed as being analogous to a servant of the father without any legal right to the care and assistance of the father as master. * * *

---

4. In the wrongful death context, compensatory damages awarded for loss of these intangibles are often referred to as "solatium."

Two of the more prominent, modern reasons for the majority rule are (1) judicial inertia, that is, as with wrongful death consortium claims, courts should defer to the legislature for recognition of a claim for loss or impairment of parental consortium resulting from nonfatal physical injury to the parent; and, alternatively, (2) judicial policy or "line drawing," that is, although they need not defer to the legislature, courts should refuse to recognize such a claim because it involves a type of tort claim, specifically, one for indirect, emotional injury, which traditionally has been disfavored at common law due to the potentially broad scope or reach of the duty. Stated another way, should the tortfeasor inflicting nonfatal physical injury be liable also for consortium impairment claims of siblings, grandchildren or others who could demonstrate emotional injuries similar to those of minor children?

* * *

Dean Roscoe Pound, the eminent jurisprudential scholar, as early as the year 1916, lamented the early common-law rule denying a claim for loss or impairment of parental consortium in cases involving nonfatal physical injury to the parent. Pound, *Individual Interests in the Domestic Relations,* 14 Mich. L.Rev. 177, 185–86 (1916). Since 1980, nine state courts of last resort [in Alaska, Arizona, Massachusetts, Michigan, Texas, Vermont, Washington, Wisconsin, and Wyoming] have recognized such a claim. These courts analogize a parental consortium claim in a nonfatal injury case to a parental consortium claim in a wrongful death case and to a spousal consortium claim in a wrongful death case or in a nonfatal injury case; in these analogous situations recovery of nonpecuniary damages is allowed, and, therefore, the claim in question should also be allowed. These courts also emphasize that the concept of *a claim for spousal consortium was judicially created* and that courts have the inherent power, and should exercise that power, to *evolve the common law* by recognizing new claims under changed societal conditions, in this context, the modern view that minor children have many of the same rights as adults, rather than being mere chattels. Furthermore, these courts recognizing the parental consortium claim respond to the fear of an ever-widening circle of liability by limiting the scope of the tortfeasor's duty to the immediate or nuclear family of the physically injured plaintiff, and then only so far as the parent/minor child (or parent/minor or handicapped child) relationship, in addition to the husband-wife relationship. Of course, the legislature subsequently may agree completely or disagree completely with the judicial recognition of a new claim; or the legislature subsequently may delineate somewhat different contours to the new claim.[6]

---

6. * * * Minor children or, in some instances, minor and adult children *are* entitled under *statutes* in some states to recover for lost or impaired parental consortium in cases involving nonfatal injuries suffered by the parent. *See, e.g.,* Fla.Stat.Ann. § 768.0415 (West 1988) * * *. Most of the commentators strongly favor recognition of a parental consortium claim in a nonfatal injury case. *See, e.g.,* 1 H. Clark, The Law of Domestic Relations in the United States § 12.6, at 689–92 (2d ed.1987); Prosser and Keeton on the Law of Torts § 125, at 935–36 (W. Keeton gen. ed. 5th ed.1984); Love, *Tortious Inference with the Parent–Child Relationship: Loss of an Injured*

C.

Several reasons typically have been offered to deny recognition of a parental consortium claim in a nonfatal injury case: (1) the weight of precedent refuses to recognize such a claim; (2) courts should defer to the legislature in this area; (3) double recovery; (4) multiplicity of actions; (5) difficulty of assessing the amount of damages; (6) increased liability insurance costs; (7) adverse effect on family relations; and (8) exposure to potentially unlimited liability. Virtually all of the courts recognizing a parental consortium claim in a nonfatal injury case address these matters. This Court believes each of these reasons are unpersuasive. We address each of these points in order.

First, this Court is more concerned with the persuasiveness of precedent than with the weight of precedent. While thirteen of the twenty-two state courts of last resort which have decided this issue since 1980 have denied a claim for parental consortium in a nonfatal injury case, we are not bound by the mere weight of judicial precedent but rather by the rule which embodies the more persuasive reasoning. * * *

Second, with respect to deferral to the legislature, in addition to observing that *the analogous claim for spousal consortium was judicially created,* we echo the sentiments of the Vermont court in *Hay:*

> The argument that this Court should prohibit the present claim for parental consortium from going to a jury because the issue is more appropriate for legislative resolution is wholly unpersuasive; such an argument ignores our responsibility to face a difficult legal question and accept judicial responsibility for a needed change in the common law. This Court has often met changing times and new social demands by expanding outmoded common law concepts. * * *

Hay v. Medical Center Hospital, 145 Vt. 533, 543–44, 496 A.2d 939, 945 * * *. Virtually all of the other courts recognizing the claim at issue also *expressly* refused to defer to the legislature for substantially the same reasons.

Related to deferral to the legislature are two subsidiary arguments: lack of legal entitlement to parental consortium and the distinction between spousal and parental consortium. As to the former, we, like almost all of the courts recognizing the claim in question, believe the legislature has implicitly recognized legal entitlement to parental consortium in nonfatal injury cases by explicitly recognizing entitlement to parental consortium in wrongful death cases. * * *

Another basis for recognizing legal entitlement to parental consortium is the similarity of such consortium to spousal consortium, which is already judicially recognized. While the element of sexual relations is present in spousal, but not in parental, consortium, we are not persuaded that this single distinction is significant enough to deny the minor child's

---

Person's Society and Companionship, 51 Ind. L.J. 590 (1976); Petrilli, *A Child's Right to Collect for Parental Consortium Where Parent Is Seriously Injured,* 26 J. Fam. L. 317 (1988) * * *.

claim. "Sexual relations are but one element of the spouse's consortium action. The other elements—love, companionship, affection, society, comfort, services and solace—are similar in both relationships and in each are deserving of protection." Berger v. Weber, 411 Mich. 1, 14, 303 N.W.2d 424, 426 (1981).

* * *

We also reject the third major reason for denying a claim of parental consortium in a nonfatal injury case, specifically, double recovery. The argument is that, as a practical matter, juries already award damages for loss or impairment of parental consortium in a nonfatal injury case as an undisclosed part of the *parent's* recovery of noneconomic damages. This argument, however, actually is support for open recognition of the minor child's action. The double recovery problem is easily eliminated by limiting the injured *parent's* recovery in this area to the loss or impairment of the parent's *pecuniary* ability to support the child; similarly, the *child's* cause of action would be limited to the loss of the parent's *society,* companionship and the like. * * *

Moreover, this same argument as to double recovery would apply also to spousal consortium (the physically injured spouse's award might include an undisclosed amount for the other spouse's consortium loss or impairment). As in a parental consortium case, in a spousal consortium case the jury should be instructed as to the distinctive types of damages of the parties. We will assume that juries follow the court's instructions, including these instructions.

The fourth major reason for denying a parental consortium claim in a nonfatal injury case, namely, multiplicity of actions, is likewise unsound as a reason for totally denying such a claim. Virtually all of the courts recognizing this type of claim address this argument by requiring joinder of the minor children's parental consortium claims with the injured parent's claim, unless that is not feasible. We adopt this approach, too.

* * *

Fifth, we find unpersuasive the argument that the claim at issue should not be recognized because of the difficulty in assessing the amount of damages. A factfinder's calculation of damages for a minor child's loss of parental consortium is not any more difficult than the calculation necessary for indeterminate damages in other actions, such as for spousal consortium in a nonfatal injury case, spousal or parental consortium in a wrongful death case or for pain and suffering in a nonfatal injury case. As an adjunct to this argument, it has been contended that monetary compensation will not enable the minor child to regain what was lost (the society, companionship and the like) when the parent was seriously injured. This Court agrees with the following response to that contention:

Although a monetary award may be a poor substitute for the loss of a parent's society and companionship, it is the only workable way that our legal system has found to ease the injured party's tragic loss. We recognize this as a shortcoming of our society, yet we believe that allowing such an award is clearly preferable to completely denying recovery.

Theama v. City of Kenosha, 117 Wis.2d 508, 523, 344 N.W.2d 513, 520 (1984).

Another reason advanced for denying recognition of a parental consortium claim in a nonfatal injury case is that recognition of such a claim would increase the liability insurance costs to society. We are unswayed by this assertion and concur with these comments:

> [P]roperly, the provision and cost of such [liability] insurance varies with potential liability under the law, not the law with the cost of insurance. * * *

Norwest v. Presbyterian Intercommunity Hospital, 293 Or. 543, 552, 652 P.2d 318, 323 (1982) * * *.

* * *

A seventh reason offered for opposing recognition of the claim in question is that each of the minor children likely would attempt to magnify the quality of his or her relationship with the parent *vis-a-vis* the other minor children in order to enhance his or her own damage award. The same situation is present, however, in wrongful death actions. * * *

Finally, there is the fear of exposure to liability to a potentially unlimited number of people who could claim and prove a loss or impairment of consortium because of the close relationship with the physically injured person. This fear is unfounded * * *.

The "new class of plaintiffs" which we recognize here is *limited* to minor children, as well as physically or mentally handicapped children of any age who are dependent upon the injured parent physically, emotionally and financially. Because of the *crucial* role of the parent in these *vitally important* relationships, damages are almost certain to be inflicted when a tortfeasor interferes with these relationships by seriously injuring the parent physically.

We note that two state courts of last resort, namely, those in Arizona and Washington, * * * have allowed recovery of parental consortium damages by any adult child, as well as by a minor child, in a case involving nonfatal injury to the parent. There is some logic to that approach, in that adult children, too, may suffer a real loss when the parent-child relationship is disturbed by the tortious infliction of physical injuries upon the parent. We note also that the West Virginia wrongful death statute allows recovery of parental consortium damages by adult, as well as by minor, children. Nevertheless, due to the very broad impact of extending this new common-law claim to all adult children, this Court at this time declines to follow the Arizona and Washington opinions in this regard.

In summary, this Court concludes that each of the above reasons offered for not recognizing a parental consortium claim in a nonfatal injury case is without merit. We particularly believe that the procedural concerns (double recovery, multiplicity of actions, etc.) should not bar recognition of this claim, for "[i]f existing procedures make it difficult to consolidate different claims for trial or to avoid overlapping recoveries for the same loss, the obvious answer is not to deny that there is a claim but to reform the procedures. Shortfalls in procedural reform do not justify shortchanging otherwise valid claims." *Norwest*, 293 Or. at 552–53, 652 P.2d at 323. We have outlined above the procedures to be utilized in this new type of action.

* * *

E.

* * *

We wish to point out that a minor or handicapped child's claim for loss or impairment of parental consortium is different from a claim for negligent infliction of emotional distress. Negligent infliction of emotional distress usually requires that the plaintiff witness a physical injury to a closely related person, suffer mental anguish that manifests itself as a physical injury and the plaintiff must be within the zone of danger so as to be subject to an unreasonable risk of bodily harm created by the defendant. *See* Harless v. First National Bank, 169 W.Va. 673, 689, 289 S.E.2d 692, 702 (1982). In contrast, a minor or handicapped child's claim for loss or impairment of parental consortium does not require that such child be within the zone of danger. Consortium claims are *sui generis.*

III.

* * * [This case] raises the issue of whether parental consortium includes the value of nursing, domestic or household services provided by a child to the injured parent. We hold that this item is not an element of parental consortium.

The courts recognizing a parental consortium claim in a nonfatal injury case do not include as an element of such consortium the value of these or any other services provided by a child to the injured parent. Instead, the injured *parent* would be entitled to claim recovery of the value of such services provided by a child or by anyone else providing such services with or without charge. Thus, "parental consortium" does not include the value of nursing, domestic or household services provided by a minor or handicapped child to the injured parent.

IV.

The plaintiff here was not a minor or handicapped child at the time the cause of action accrued. Accordingly, having answered the certified questions, we remand this case with directions for the trial court to enter judgment for the defendant on this claim.

NOTE

For another point of view, see Butz v. World Wide, Inc., 492 N.W.2d 88 (N.D.1992):

On June 15, 1984, Charles Butz, Jr., husband of Rose and father of the Butz children, was severely injured in a boating accident. He was riding on a "Super Tube" that was being pulled behind a boat on a lake. While on the "Super Tube," he collided with another boat parked along the shore, causing his injuries. The "Super Tube" was manufactured by World Wide, Inc., and sold by Cass Oil Co.

On January 15, 1985, Charles Butz, Jr., commenced an action in district court against World Wide, Inc., and Cass Oil Co. (World Wide) for the personal injuries sustained in the accident. On June 2, 1987, the jury returned a verdict for Charles Butz, Jr., in excess of $500,000. * * *

On May 2, 1990, Rose and the Butz children brought their loss of consortium claims against World Wide, nearly three years subsequent to the entry of the jury verdict. World Wide moved for summary judgment * * *. World Wide contended that North Dakota does not recognize a cause of action for loss of parental consortium; further, any claim for loss of consortium must mandatorily be joined with the original personal injury action, or thereafter be barred. * * *

* * *

* * * [T]he district court awarded Rose the stipulated $30,000 in damages for her loss of spousal consortium. The district court dismissed the Butz children's claim for loss of parental consortium.

* * *

* * * [Three of our earlier decisions] permitted parents recovery for loss of their children's society, comfort, and companionship. Parents were an already-existing class of plaintiffs in wrongful death and personal injury actions for children * * *. [Our decisions in those three cases] did not expand the class of plaintiffs, [they] merely expanded the damages which could be recovered in wrongful death or personal injury cases. Thus, the argument that [those three cases] allow children to bring an action for loss of parental consortium is overbroad and unpersuasive.

We continue to believe the ten reasons for denying children a cause of action for loss of parental consortium, set out in the annotation found at 69 A.L.R.3d 528,[4] quoted with approval in Hastings v. James River

---

4. 69 A.L.R.3d 528, has currently been superseded by 11 A.L.R.4th 549. The new Annotation enumerates the very same ten reasons for denying children a cause of action for loss of parental consortium. They are:

(1) the absence of any enforceable claim on the child's part to the parent's services, (2) the absence of precedents, (3) the uncertainty and remoteness of the damages involved, (4) the possible overlap with the parent's recovery, (5) the multiplication of litigation, (6) the possibility of upsetting settlements made with parents, (7) the danger of fabricated actions, (8) the increase in insurance costs, (9) the public policy expressed in some jurisdictions in the

Aerie No. 2337, Etc., 246 N.W.2d 747 (N.D.1976), are still valid. Further-more, we believe our rationale in *Morgel* remains a sound interpretation of the law.

> We agree with the California Court which, in Borer v. American Airlines, Inc., 19 Cal.3d 441, 138 Cal.Rptr. 302, 563 P.2d 858, 862 (1977), said that the question of a child's right to recover for loss of parental consortium is one of policy. Because we believe that the question is one of policy, *we conclude that the birth of the child's cause of action for loss of parental consortium should be attended to by the Legislature as its obstetrician.*

Morgel v. Winger, 290 N.W.2d 266, 267 (N.D.1980) (emphasis added).

Id. at 88–89, 93–94.

B. SURVIVAL AND WRONGFUL DEATH STATUTES
DAN B. DOBBS, LAW OF REMEDIES
§ 8.3(1), at 670 (2d ed. 1993).*

Three distinct and basic common law rules bore on recovery of damages in death cases. These rules remain important today as the reasons for modern statutory changes. These rules were: (1) If the tortfeasor died after committing a tort against his victim, the victim's claim died as well. (2) If the tort *victim* died, his cause of action was at an end, "drowned," in the larger matter of a crime against the Crown. (3) The victim's survivors had no independent claim of their own against the tortfeasor for the loss of their support or for their grief and sorrow. There has never been any good explanation for all these rules.

NOTES

1. If you were a legislator who wanted to overturn the three common law rules identified by Professor Dobbs, what type of legislation would you pass? With regard to the death of the tortfeasor, would you allow the claim to proceed against the tortfeasor's estate? With regard to the death of the tort victim, would you allow the estate of the victim to sue the tortfeasor? If so, what would be the measure of damages? Would you measure the estate's claim by reference to what the victim would have recovered if the victim had lived? Would you then reduce that amount by what the estate will "save" in the future because it will not have to support the deceased? To whom would the proceeds of the claim be paid—first to the creditors, and then to the people named in the decedent's will? Would you also allow the victim's immediate family members to sue for loss of consortium and for loss of society and companionship?

---

enactment of "heart balm" statutes, and (10) family problems arising from segregated awards to children.

11 A.L.R.4th at 553–54.

* Reprinted with permission of West Publishing Co.

2. For a discussion of the history of wrongful death actions, see John Fabian Witt, *From Loss of Services to Loss of Support: The Wrongful Death Statutes, The Origins of Modern Tort Law, and the Making of the Nineteenth–Century Family*, 25 Law & Soc. Inquiry 717 (2000).

3. The wrongful death statutes which actually have been enacted in every state and by Congress do not authorize the recovery of all of the damages identified in Note 1, above. The reasons are probably more historical than theoretical. In any event, the statutes take one of three general forms:

(1) "survivor statutes" which provide that the claim of the deceased victim survives death and may be pursued by the victim's estate. (2) "wrongful death statutes" which create a cause of action in a specified class of persons to compensate them for loss resulting from the victim's death, and (3) hybrid statutes which in some fashion permit claims on the basis of both survival and wrongful death.

Dan B. Dobbs, The Law of Remedies, pp. 671–72 (2d ed. 1993). California has enacted a set of statutes that define a survival cause of action and a wrongful death cause of action independently of each other. Compare the California statutes, below, with the "hybrid statute" from Tennessee that is discussed in *Jordan*, below.

CALIFORNIA'S SURVIVAL AND WRONGFUL DEATH STATUTES
CALIFORNIA CODE OF CIVIL PROCEDURE

§ 377.20 Cause of action survives; limitations; loss or damage simultaneous with death

(a) Except as otherwise provided by statute, a cause of action for or against a person is not lost by reason of the person's death, but survives subject to the applicable limitations period.

* * *

§ 377.30 Surviving cause of action; person to whom passes; commencement of action

A cause of action that survives the death of the person entitled to commence an action or proceeding passes to the decedent's successor in interest * * * and an action may be commenced by the decedent's personal representative or, if none, by the decedent's successor in interest.

§ 377.34 Damages recoverable

In an action or proceeding by a decedent's personal representative or successor in interest on the decedent's cause of action, the damages recoverable are limited to the loss or damage that the decedent sustained or incurred before death, including any penalties or punitive or exemplary damages that the decedent would have been entitled to recover had the decedent lived, and do not include damages for pain, suffering, or disfigurement.

§ 377.60   Persons with standing

A cause of action for the death of a person caused by the wrongful act or neglect of another may be asserted by any of the following persons or by the decedent's personal representative on their behalf:

(a) The decedent's surviving spouse, domestic partner, children, and issue of deceased children, or, if there is no surviving issue of the decedent, the persons, including the surviving spouse or domestic partner, who would be entitled to the property of the decedent by intestate succession.

* * *

§ 377.61   Damages Recoverable

In an action under this article, damages may be awarded that, under all the circumstances of the case, may be just, but may not include damages recoverable under Section 377.34. The court shall determine the respective rights in an award of the persons entitled to assert the cause of action.

QUIROZ v. SEVENTH AVENUE CENTER

Court of Appeal, Sixth District, California, 2006.
140 Cal.App.4th 1256, 45 Cal.Rptr.3d 222.

DUFFY, J.

[Gilbert Quiroz, a dependent adult, resided at Seventh Avenue Center, a skilled nursing facility located in Santa Cruz. After his untimely death, his mother, Maria Quiroz, brought a wrongful death cause of action. Thirteen months after his death, she filed an amended complaint that added to the wrongful death claim a survivor claim that requested enhanced damages for pain and suffering experienced by the decedent before death. While such damages are not available under California Code of Civil Procedure § 377.34, they are specifically made recoverable in cases involving elder abuse under California Welfare and Institutions Code § 15600 et seq. See California Civil Code § 3333.2, providing:

> (a) In any action for injury against a health care provider based on professional negligence, the injured plaintiff shall be entitled to recover noneconomic losses to compensate for pain, suffering, inconvenience, physical impairment, disfigurement and other nonpecuniary damage.

> (b) In no action shall the amount of damages for noneconomic losses exceed two hundred fifty thousand dollars ($250,000).

Defendant claimed that the survivorship claim was barred by the one-year statute of limitations applicable to such claims. Plaintiff argued that the two claims, wrongful death and survivorship, were sufficiently related to justify applying the "relation back" doctrine, in which case the survivorship claim would be viewed as timely filed at the time of the original filing of the wrongful death claim. In determining whether to apply this "relation back" doctrine, the court analyzed the two types of claims.]

* * *

LEGAL OVERVIEW OF CLAIMS
* * *

I. *Wrongful Death*

"At common law, personal tort claims expired when either the victim or the tortfeasor died. * * * Today, a cause of action for wrongful death exists only by virtue of legislative grace. * * * The statutorily created 'wrongful death cause of action does not effect a survival of the decedent's cause of action[. Instead,] it "gives to the representative a totally new right of action, on different principles." * * *' * * *'" The cause of action "for wrongful death belongs 'not to the decedent [or prospective decedent], but to the persons specified' [by statute].* * *'" It is a new cause of action that arises on the death of the decedent and it is vested in the decedent's heirs. * * *

A cause of action for wrongful death is thus a statutory claim. (Code Civ. Proc., §§ 377.60–377.62.) Its purpose is to compensate specified persons—heirs—for the loss of companionship and for other losses suffered as a result of a decedent's death. * * * Persons with standing to bring a wrongful death claim are enumerated at Code of Civil Procedure section 377.60, which provides in pertinent part: "A cause of action for the death of a person caused by the wrongful act or neglect of another may be asserted by any of the following persons or by the decedent's personal representative on their behalf: (a) The decedent's surviving spouse, domestic partner, children, and issue of deceased children, or, if there is no surviving issue of the decedent, the persons, including the surviving spouse or domestic partner, who would be entitled to the property of the decedent by intestate succession."

The elements of the cause of action for wrongful death are the tort (negligence or other wrongful act), the resulting death, and the damages, consisting of the *pecuniary loss* suffered by the *heirs.* * * * The wrongful death statute "limits the right of recovery to a class of persons who, because of their relation to the deceased, are presumed to be injured by his [or her] death * * * and bars claims by persons who are not in the chain of intestate succession." * * *

Damages awarded to an heir in a wrongful death action are in the nature of compensation for personal injury to the heir. * * * "A plaintiff in a wrongful death action is entitled to recover damages for his own pecuniary loss, which may include (1) the loss of the decedent's financial support, services, training and advice, and (2) the pecuniary value of the decedent's society and companionship—but he may *not* recover for such things as the grief or sorrow attendant upon the death of a loved one, or for his sad emotions, or for the sentimental value of the loss." * * * "The damages recoverable in [wrongful death] are expressly limited to those *not* recoverable in a survival action under Code of Civil Procedure section 377.34." * * * (* * * Code Civ. Proc., § 377.61.)

II. *Survivor Claims*

Unlike a cause of action for wrongful death, a survivor cause of action is not a new cause of action that vests in the heirs on the death of the decedent. It is instead a separate and distinct cause of action which belonged to the decedent before death but, by statute, survives that event. * * * The survival statutes do not create a cause of action. Rather, "[t]hey merely prevent the abatement of the cause of action of the injured person, and provide for its enforcement by or against the personal representative of the deceased." * * *

A cause of action that survives the death of a person passes to the decedent's successor in interest and is enforceable by the "decedent's personal representative or, if none, by the decedent's successor in interest." (Code Civ. Proc., § 377.30.) In the typical survivor action, the damages recoverable by a personal representative or successor in interest on a decedent's cause of action are limited by statute to "the loss or damage that the decedent sustained or incurred before death, including any penalties or punitive or exemplary damages that the decedent would have been entitled to recover had the decedent lived, and *do not* include damages for pain, suffering, or disfigurement." (Code Civ. Proc., § 377.34, italics added.)

But there is at least one exception to the rule that damages for the decedent's predeath pain and suffering are not recoverable in a survivor action. Such damages are expressly recoverable in a survivor action under the Elder Abuse Act if certain conditions are met. Specifically, Welfare and Institutions Code section 15657 provides for heightened remedies, including recovery for the decedent's predeath pain, suffering, and disfigurement, to a successor in interest to a decedent's cause of action "[w]here it is proven by clear and convincing evidence that a defendant is liable for physical abuse as defined in Section 15610.63, or neglect as defined in Section 15610.57, and that the defendant has been guilty of recklessness, oppression, fraud, or malice in the commission of this abuse ... in addition to all other remedies provided by law." (See Welf. & Inst.Code., § 15657, subds. (a) & (b).)

The ability of the decedent's successor in interest to recover damages for the decedent's predeath pain, suffering, or disfigurement under this section specifically trumps the general prohibition on such recovery provided at Code of Civil Procedure section 377.34. (Welf. & Inst.Code, § 15657, subd. (b).) But it is also expressly subject to the dollar amount limitation of Civil Code section 3333.2—a maximum of $250,000 for noneconomic losses in an action for injury against a health care provider based on professional negligence. (*Ibid.*)

Thus, under the Elder Abuse Act, where neglect or abuse of an elder or dependent adult is reckless or done with oppression, fraud, or malice such that the statutory prerequisites are satisfied, damages for the victim's predeath pain, suffering, or disfigurement are recoverable *in a survivor action* pursued by the victim's personal representative or successor in interest, notwithstanding the usual prohibition on such recovery under Code of Civil Procedure section 377.34. (Welf. & Inst.Code, § 15657.) * * *

* * *

DISCUSSION

I. *Issues on Appeal*

Fundamentally, at issue in this appeal is whether the survivor action first brought by plaintiff on behalf of the decedent, Gilbert Quiroz, after the running of the statute of limitations, is time-barred. This issue turns on whether the cause of action relates back to the timely filed wrongful death cause of action filed by plaintiff on her own behalf.

Appellant further contends that she, on her own behalf, is entitled to heightened remedies under the Elder Abuse Act in connection with her wrongful death claim * * *.

II. *The Survivor Action is Barred by the Statute of Limitations*

* * *

It is not disputed here that the original complaint, which contained one cause of action for wrongful death, was timely filed within one year from the decedent's date of death.[26] It is likewise not disputed that the first amended complaint, which first asserted a survivor cause of action— whether sounding in negligence or elder abuse—was filed after the then-applicable one-year limitations period. It follows that the survivor action is consequently barred by the statute of limitations, as a matter of law, unless the claim "relates back" to the original complaint's filing date.

* * *

The relation-back doctrine deems a later-filed pleading to have been filed at the time of an earlier complaint which met the applicable limitations period, thus avoiding the bar. In order for the relation-back doctrine to apply, "the amended complaint must (1) rest on the *same general set of facts,* (2) involve the *same injury,* and (3) refer to the *same instrumentality,* as the original one." * * * In addition, "a new plaintiff *cannot* be joined after the statute of limitations has run where he or she seeks to enforce an *independent right* or to impose greater liability upon the defendant." * * *

---

26. * * * As a usual matter, the accrual of a cause of action for wrongful death is the date of death. * * *

Here, we readily conclude, as did the court below, that the survivor cause of action pleaded a *different injury* than the initial complaint. We also conclude that the two claims in the amended pleading were asserted by different plaintiffs, Maria G. Quiroz acting in two separate capacities with respect to each, and that the addition of fresh allegations concerning her representative capacity in pursuit of the new survivor claim was not just the mere technical substitution of the proper party plaintiff on a previously existing claim. This survivor claim, which plaintiff pursued as the decedent's successor in interest, pleaded injury to the decedent, Gilbert Quiroz. In contrast, the earlier-filed wrongful death claim pleaded only injury to plaintiff, acting for herself, as the decedent's heir. As a matter of law, these distinct claims are technically asserted by different plaintiffs and they seek compensation for different injuries. *Bartalo v. Superior Court* (1975) 51 Cal.App.3d 526, 533, 124 Cal.Rptr. 370 [husband's claim for loss of consortium was wholly different legal liability or obligation from wife's personal injury claim and therefore it did not relate back]; *Dominguez v. City of Alhambra* (1981) 118 Cal.App.3d 237, 243, 173 Cal.Rptr. 345 [plaintiff could not amend her complaint for wrongful death after the statute of limitations had passed to state wholly distinct survivor cause of action for decedent's injuries]; * * * Accordingly, the doctrine of relation back does not apply and the entire survivor claim is barred by the statute of limitations.

On the same reasoning, courts have reached the opposite result—permitting the relation-back doctrine to save a cause of action from the bar of the statute of limitations—in cases in which the converse scenario is presented. A claim that is first asserted by amendment after the limitations period has passed will not be barred so long as the amendment is based on the same general set of facts and involves the *same injury.* This holds true even where the amendment names or substitutes a new party plaintiff, as long as the new plaintiff is not seeking to enforce an independent right or to impose a greater liability on the defendant. * * * (*Pasadena Hospital Assn. Ltd. v. Superior Court* (1988) 204 Cal.App.3d 1031, 1034–1037, 251 Cal.Rptr. 686 [relation-back doctrine will apply where plaintiff timely filed complaint and later sought amendment to add his professional corporation as a plaintiff because both plaintiffs were asserting the *same injury and damages* and the substantive basis of the cause of action had not changed] * * *.)

The trial court here correctly viewed the untimely survivor cause of action as pleading a different injury than the original cause of action for wrongful death. The survivor cause of action was asserted by a technically different plaintiff asserting an independent and greater liability against the defendants. This new claim was first asserted after the running of the statute of limitations, and because the injuries to be compensated by the two claims are different, the relation-back doctrine does not apply. The survivor cause of action, whether construed as a claim for negligence or for statutory dependent-adult abuse, is therefore barred.

* * *

III.   *Plaintiff Has no Claim, in Her Own*
Right, Under the Elder Abuse Act

As best as we can decipher it, appellant's other major contention is that the trial court erred by striking the Elder Abuse Act allegations and prayer from the complaint because, she argues, these matters related to her timely filed wrongful death claim. This contention is premised on the notion that the Elder Abuse Act is so broad as to afford appellant a claim under it such that she is entitled to the Act's heightened remedies, including attorney fees, on her own wrongful death claim. * * *

* * *

Appellant's contention that the breadth of the Elder Abuse Act provides her with her own independent claim through which she may recover heightened remedies rests on an erroneous reading of the Act and its legislative history. She urges us to construe the Act to afford her such a claim with accompanying remedies. Yet she cites no section of the Act that actually provides for this. * * * Nor can appellant point to any part of the Act's legislative history that suggests that this construction was intended. Indeed, the legislative history of the 1991 amendments to the Elder Abuse Act, of which we have taken judicial notice, demonstrates that the enhanced remedies provided under the Act were intended to apply to actions by or on behalf of *victims* of elder or dependent care abuse. The legislative history does not reveal any intent to apply the Act to a wrongful death action brought by a decedent's heir on his or her own behalf.

* * *

The legislative purpose in allowing for heightened remedies in a survivor action under the Elder Abuse Act was to "enable interested persons to engage attorneys to take up the cause of abused elderly persons and dependent adults." * * * The Legislature amended the Elder Abuse Act in 1991 to provide for these heightened remedies in order to shift "the focus in protecting vulnerable and dependent adults from reporting abuse and using law enforcement to combat it, 'to private, civil enforcement of laws against elder abuse and neglect.' " "[T]he Legislature declared that 'infirm elderly persons and dependent adults are a disadvantaged class, that cases of abuse of these persons are seldom prosecuted as criminal matters, and few civil cases are brought in connection with this abuse due to problems of proof, court delays, and the lack of incentives to prosecute these suits.' * * *" As was stated in the Senate Rules Committee's analysis of Senate Bill 679, "in practice, the death of the victim and the difficulty in finding an attorney to handle an abuse case where attorneys fees may not be awarded, impedes many victims from suing successfully. * * * This bill would address the problem by: ... authorizing the court to award attorney's fees in specified cases; [and by] allowing pain and suffering damages to be awarded when a verdict of intentional and reckless abuse was handed down after the abused elder dies." * * * In other words, when attorney fees are available and the amount of the potential recovery is higher because of the availability of damages for the victim's predeath pain and suffering, more attorneys will have incentive to take and pursue a victim's case, even if the victim has died or might die during the course of litigation.

But, contrary to appellant's entreaties, none of these indicators of the Act's expansive scope or character means that a relative or an heir of an elder or dependent adult has an independent claim under the Act or that such a person may recover statutory heightened remedies in his or her own wrongful death claim. Under the Act, these claims and remedies are afforded only to *victims* of elder or dependent adult abuse. In the event of the victim's death, the cause of action survives, in which case it is or becomes a survivor action pursued by the personal representative of the estate or the decedent's successor in interest *on the decedent's behalf.* Accordingly, appellant has not demonstrated here that the court abused its discretion in striking the elder abuse allegations and prayer from the complaint vis-à-vis her own wrongful death cause of action.

* * *

The judgment is affirmed.

JORDAN v. BAPTIST THREE RIVERS HOSP.

Supreme Court of Tennessee, 1999.
984 S.W.2d 593.

HOLDER, J.

* * *

BACKGROUND

This cause of action arises out of the death of Mary Sue Douglas ("decedent"). The plaintiff, Martha P. Jordan, is a surviving child of the decedent and the administratrix of the decedent's estate. The plaintiff, on behalf of the decedent's estate, filed a medical malpractice action against the defendants, Baptist Three Rivers Hospital, Mark W. Anderson, M.D., Noel Dominguez, M.D., and Patrick Murphy, M.D. The plaintiff has alleged that the defendants' negligence caused the decedent's death.

The plaintiff's complaint sought damages for loss of consortium and for the decedent's loss of enjoyment of life or hedonic damages. The defendants filed a motion to strike * * * asserting that Tennessee law does not permit recovery for loss of parental consortium and for hedonic damages.

The trial court granted the defendants' motion to strike and granted the plaintiff permission to file an interlocutory appeal. * * * We granted appeal to determine whether claims for loss of spousal and parental consortium in wrongful death cases are viable in Tennessee under Tenn. Code Ann. § 20–5–113.[20] We express no opinion as to whether the loss of

---

20. This Court has previously held that claims for hedonic damages are not viable in Tennessee in wrongful death cases. *See* Spencer v. A–1 Crane Serv., Inc., 880 S.W.2d 938, 943

parental consortium may be recovered in personal injury actions in which the parent or parents survive. That issue will be addressed in an appropriate case.

DEVELOPMENT OF WRONGFUL DEATH STATUTE

A wrongful death cause of action did not exist at common law. *See* Annotation, *Modern Status of Rule Denying a Common–Law Recovery for Wrongful Death,* 61 A.L.R.3d 906 (1975). Pursuant to the common law, actions for personal injuries that resulted in death terminated at the victim's death because "in a civil court the death of a human being could not be complained of as an injury." W. Page Keeton et al., Prosser and Keeton on the Law of Torts § 127, at 945 (5th ed. 1984) (*"Prosser"*). "The [legal] result was that it was cheaper for the defendant to kill the plaintiff than to injure him, and that the most grievous of all injuries left the bereaved family of the victim ... without a remedy." *Id.* This rule of non-liability for wrongful death was previously the prevailing view in both England and in the United States. * * *

In 1846, the British Parliament enacted a wrongful death statute designed to abrogate the common law rule's harsh effect of denying recovery for personal injuries resulting in death. The English statute was referred to as "Lord Campbell's Act" and created a cause of action for designated survivors that accrued upon the tort victim's death. *See* Malone, *The Genesis of Wrongful Death,* 17 Stan. L.Rev. 1043, 1051 (1965); *Prosser,* § 127, at 945.

Jurisdictions in the United States were quick to follow England's lead. * * * In 1847, New York became the first American jurisdiction to enact a wrongful death statute. * * * Presently, every jurisdiction in the United States has a wrongful death statute. * * * These statutes, including that of Tennessee, embody the substantive provisions of Lord Campbell's Act and permit designated beneficiaries to recover losses sustained as a result of the tort victim's death. * * *

Tennessee was one of the earliest states to abrogate judicially "[t]he artificial rule of the common law that every right of action for personal injury died with the person injured." * * * As early as 1836, the Tennessee legislature enacted a statute providing for the survival of all civil actions for which suit had been commenced prior to the victim's death. In 1850, our legislature made its initial attempt to permit recovery in wrongful death cases. * * *

* * *

Specifically, Tenn.Code Ann. § 20–5–102, the direct descendent of the 1836 statute, provides that

(Tenn.1994). [In *Spencer,* the Court observed that hedonic damages had been recognized in survival/wrongful death actions in only one state and by the federal courts only in constitutional tort actions. The court expressed concern that this item of damages was "too speculative."]

> [n]o civil action commenced, whether founded on wrongs or contracts,
> shall abate by the death of either party ...; nor shall any right of
> action arising hereafter based on the wrongful act or omission of
> another be abated by the death of the party wronged; but the right of
> action shall pass in like manner as [described in Tenn.Code Ann.
> § 20–5–106].

Moreover, Tenn.Code Ann. § 20–5–106, the modern version of the 1877
statute, provides in part:

> The right of action which a person, who dies from injuries received
> from another, or whose death is caused by the wrongful act, omission,
> or killing by another, would have had against the wrongdoer, in case
> death had not been ensued, shall not abate or be extinguished by the
> person's death but shall pass to the person's surviving spouse and, in
> case there is no surviving spouse, to the person's children or next of
> kin; or to the person's personal representative, for the benefit of the
> person's surviving spouse or next of kin.

Tenn.Code Ann. § 20–5–106(a). Thus, an examination of the development
of Tennessee's wrongful death law * * * establishes that the right of
recovery in a wrongful death case is strictly a creation of statute. * * *

Because a cause of action for wrongful death is a creation of statute,
recoverable damages must be determined by reference to the particular
statute involved. Although all states have abolished the rule of non-
liability when personal injury results in death, the statutory methods of
doing so fall into two distinct categories—wrongful death statutes and
survival statutes. *See* Sea–Land Servs., Inc. v. Gaudet, 414 U.S. 573, 575
n.2, 94 S.Ct. 806, 39 L.Ed.2d 9 (1974).

The majority of states have enacted "survival statutes." These statutes permit the victim's cause of action to survive the death, so that the
victim, through the victim's estate, recovers damages that would have
been recovered *by the victim* had the victim survived. * * * *Prosser*, § 126,
at 942–43. Survival statutes do not create a new cause of action; rather,
the cause of action vested in the victim at the time of death is transferred
to the person designated in the statutory scheme to pursue it, and the
action is enlarged to include damages for the death itself. *Prosser*, § 126,
at 942–43. "[T]he recovery is the same one the decedent would have been
entitled to at death, and thus includes such items as wages lost after
injury and before death, medical expenses incurred, and pain and suffering," and other appropriate compensatory damages suffered by the victim
from the time of injury to the time of death. *Id.* at 943.

In contrast to survival statutes, "pure wrongful death statutes"
create a *new* cause of action in favor of the survivors of the victim for *their*
loss occasioned by the death. * * * These statutes proceed "on the theory
of compensating the individual beneficiaries for the loss of the economic
benefit which they might reasonably have expected to receive from the
decedent in the form of support, services or contributions during the
remainder of [the decedent's] lifetime if [the decedent] had not been

killed." *Prosser,* § 127, at 949. Hence, most wrongful death jurisdictions have adopted a "pecuniary loss" standard of recovery, allowing damages for economic contributions the deceased would have made to the survivors had death not occurred and for the economic value of the services the deceased would have rendered to the survivors but for the death. * * *

Tennessee's approach to providing a remedy for death resulting from personal injury is a hybrid between survival and wrongful death statutes, resulting in a statutory scheme with a "split personality." 27 Tenn. L.Rev. at 454. The pertinent damages statute, Tenn.Code Ann. § 20–5–113, has been in existence in one form or another since 1883. It provides:

> Where a person's death is caused by the wrongful act, fault, or omission of another, and suit is brought for damages ... the party suing shall, if entitled to damages, have the right to recover the mental and physical suffering, loss of time, and necessary expenses resulting to the deceased from the personal injuries, *and also the damages resulting to the parties for whose use and benefit the right of action survives from the death consequent upon the injuries received.*

Tenn.Code Ann. § 20–5–113 (emphasis added).

The plain language of Tenn.Code Ann. § 20–5–113 reveals that it may be classified as a survival statute because it preserves whatever cause of action was vested in the victim at the time of death. Jones v. Black, 539 S.W.2d 123 (Tenn.1976) * * *. The survival character of the statute is evidenced by the language "the party suing shall have the right to recover [damages] *resulting to the deceased from the personal injuries.*" Thrailkill v. Patterson, 879 S.W.2d 836, 841 (Tenn.1994) (emphasis added). * * *

Notwithstanding the accurate, technical characterization of Tenn. Code Ann. § 20–5–113 as survival legislation, the statute also creates a cause of action that compensates survivors for their losses. The statute provides that damages may be recovered *"resulting to the parties for whose use and benefit the right of action survives from the death."* Id. (emphasis added). Hence, survivors of the deceased may recover damages for *their* losses suffered as a result of the death as well as damages sustained by the deceased from the time of injury to the time of death. *Jones,* 539 S.W.2d at 124 (Tennessee's wrongful death legislation provides "for elements of damages consistent with a theory of survival of the right of action of the deceased but also allows damages consistent ... with the creation of a new cause of action in the beneficiaries."). Our inquiry shall focus on whether survivors should be permitted to recover consortium losses.

LOSS OF SPOUSAL CONSORTIUM

In 1903, this Court held in Davidson Benedict Co. v. Severson, 109 Tenn. 572, 72 S.W. 967 (Tenn.1903), that consortium damages were not available under Tennessee's wrongful death statute. The plaintiff urges this Court to revisit and reverse the holding in *Davidson* based on the following assertions: (1) that the *Davidson* holding was contrary to the plain language of the wrongful death statute; (2) that permitting consortium damages in personal injury but not in wrongful death cases is illogical; (3) that the majority of jurisdictions now permit loss of consortium damages in wrongful death cases; and (4) that the doctrine of stare decisis should not commit this Court "to the sanctification of ancient fallacy." Upon careful review, we agree with the plaintiff.

STARE DECISIS AND STATUTORY CONSTRUCTION

* * *

The defendant asserts that any "change to the meaning of Tenn.Code Ann. § 20–5–113 should be left to the legislature." The issue before us, however, involves a matter of statutory interpretation and not the implementation of public policy.

Next, the defendant argues that the wrongful death statute is in derogation of the common law and, therefore, should be strictly construed. The defendant maintains that interpreting the wrongful death statute to permit recovery of "parental consortium claims . . . would be to afford the statute a liberal construction."

* * * Statutes in derogation of the common law are generally strictly construed. The rule requiring strict construction amounts to a recognition of a presumption against the legislature's intention to change existing law. * * * Remedial statutes, however, generally reflect a legislative intent to amend an area of the common law and shall be construed liberally. * * *

This Court's role in statutory interpretation is to ascertain and to effectuate the legislature's intent. * * * Generally, legislative intent shall be derived from the plain and ordinary meaning of the statutory language when a statute's language is unambiguous. * * * When a statute's language is ambiguous and the parties legitimately derive different interpretations, we must look to the entire statutory scheme to ascertain the legislative intent. * * *

The defendant argues that this Court has previously held that Tenn. Code Ann. § 20–5–113 is a survival statute and that survival statutes generally do not permit recovery under consortium theories. While this Court in Jones v. Black, 539 S.W.2d 123 (Tenn.1976), previously classified Tennessee's wrongful death statute as a survival statute for purposes of limitations of action[1], we are not confined to interpret the statute according to the strictures of a judicially imposed classification when such an interpretation would ignore unambiguous statutory language. Accordingly, our analysis of Tenn.Code Ann. § 20–5–113 shall focus on the statute's language and not on what damages "survival" statutes in other states generally permit. It must be remembered that, notwithstanding the accurate, technical characterization of Tenn.Code Ann. § 20–5–113 as survival

---

1. In *Jones v. Black*, the court observed that the Tennessee statutes "preserve the right of action which the deceased himself would have had," and therefore the statute of limitations should be determined by reference to the deceased, rather than by reference to the beneficiaries. As a result, the court was unwilling to toll the statute of limitations due to the beneficiary's minority.

legislation, the statute also provides for a cause of action that compensates survivors for *their* losses.

Damages under our wrongful death statute can be delineated into two distinct classifications. Thrailkill v. Patterson, 879 S.W.2d 836 (Tenn. 1994); Davidson Benedict Co. v. Severson, 109 Tenn. 572, 72 S.W. 967 (Tenn.1903). The first classification permits recovery for injuries sustained by the deceased from the time of injury to the time of death. Damages under the first classification include medical expenses, physical and mental pain and suffering, funeral expenses, lost wages, and loss of earning capacity. * * *

The second classification of damages permits recovery of incidental damages suffered by the decedent's next of kin. * * * Incidental damages have been judicially defined to *include* the pecuniary value of the decedent's life. Spencer v. A–1 Crane Serv., Inc., 880 S.W.2d 938, 943 (Tenn. 1994). Pecuniary value has been judicially defined to include "the expectancy of life, the age, condition of health and strength, capacity for labor and earning money through skill, any art, trade, profession and occupation or business, and personal habits as to sobriety and industry." *Id.* Pecuniary value also takes into account the decedent's probable living expenses had the decedent lived. Wallace v. Couch, 642 S.W.2d 141 (Tenn.1982) * * *.

The wrongful death statute neither explicitly precludes consortium damages nor reflects an intention to preclude consortium damages. The statute's language does not limit recovery to purely economic losses. To the contrary, the statute's plain language appears to encompass consortium damages.

Indeed, this Court has recognized that pecuniary value cannot be defined to a mathematical certainty as such a definition "would overlook the value of the [spouse's] personal interest in the affairs of the home and the economy incident to [the spouse's] services." *Thrailkill,* 879 S.W.2d at 841. We further believe that the pecuniary value of a human life is a compound of many elements. An individual family member has value to others as part of a functioning social and economic unit. This value necessarily includes the value of mutual society and protection, *i.e,* human companionship. Human companionship has a definite, substantial and ascertainable pecuniary value, and its loss forms a part of the value of the life we seek to ascertain. While uncertainties may arise in proof when defining the value of human companionship, the one committing the wrongful act causing the death of a human being should not be permitted to seek protection behind the uncertainties inherent in the very situation his wrongful act has created. Moreover, it seems illogical and absurd to believe that the legislature would intend the anomaly of permitting recovery of consortium losses when a spouse is injured and survives but not when the very same act causes a spouse's death.

* * * Accordingly, we reverse Davidson Benedict v. Severson, 109 Tenn. 572, 72 S.W. 967 (Tenn.1903), to the extent that *Davidson Benedict*

prohibits consideration of spousal consortium losses when calculating the pecuniary value of a deceased's life under the wrongful death statute.

LOSS OF PARENTAL CONSORTIUM

The wrongful death statute precludes neither a minor child nor an adult child from seeking compensation for the child's consortium losses. Moreover, Tenn.Code Ann. § 20–5–110 provides that "a suit for the wrongful killing of the spouse may be brought in the name of the surviving spouse for the benefit of the surviving spouse and the children of the deceased." This provision when read in pari materia with Tenn. Code Ann. § 20–5–113 seemingly permits consideration of parental consortium damages. * * *

A review of case law in other jurisdictions indicates a trend to expand consortium claims to include the impairment of a child's relationship with a parent. Comment, *Belcher v. Goins: West Virginia Joins the Distinct Minority of Jurisdictions in Recognizing a Claim for Loss of Parental Consortium,* 94 W. Va. L.Rev. 261, 262 (1991). In cases involving a parent's death, "[t]he general rule ... followed is that a child's loss of nurture, education and moral training which it probably would have received from a parent wrongfully killed is a pecuniary loss to be considered as an element of the damages suffered by the child." *Recovery for Wrongful Death* at § 3:47 (listing thirty-four jurisdictions so holding). * * *

A basis for placing an economic value on parental consortium is that the education and training which a child may reasonably expect to receive from a parent are of actual and commercial value to the child. Accordingly, a child sustains a pecuniary injury for the loss of parental education and training when a defendant tortiously causes the death of the child's parent. * * *

* * *

Adult children may be too attenuated from their parents in some cases to proffer sufficient evidence of consortium losses. Similarly, if the deceased did not have a close relationship with any of the statutory beneficiaries, the statutory beneficiaries will not likely sustain compensable consortium losses or their consortium losses will be nominal. The age of the child does not, in and of itself, preclude consideration of parental consortium damages. The adult child inquiry shall take into consideration factors such as closeness of the relationship and dependence (*i.e.,* of a handicapped adult child, assistance with day care, etc.).

CONCLUSION

We hold that consortium-type damages may be considered when calculating the pecuniary value of a deceased's life. This holding does not create a new cause of action but merely refines the term "pecuniary value." Consortium losses are not limited to spousal claims but also necessarily encompass a child's loss, whether minor or adult. Loss of consortium consists of several elements, encompassing not only tangible services provided by a family member, but also intangible benefits each family member receives from the continued existence of other family members. Such benefits include attention, guidance, care, protection, training, companionship, cooperation, affection, love, and in the case of a spouse, sexual relations. Our holding conforms with the plain language of the wrongful death statutes, the trend of modern authority, and the social and economic reality of modern society.

The decision of the of the trial court granting the defendants' motion to strike is reversed. * * *

ANDERSON, C.J., DROWOTA, and BIRCH, JJ., and RUSSELL, SPECIAL JUSTICE, concurring.

NOTES

1.   The Supreme Court of Tennessee took up the question of whether a parent may recover "filial consortium losses" for the death of a minor child in Hancock v. Chattanooga–Hamilton County Hosp. Authority, 54 S.W.3d 234 (Tenn. 2001):

> In *Jordan,* an adult child was allowed to recover damages for the loss of parental consortium. * * * Our decision in *Jordan* did not reach the issue of whether Tenn.Code Ann. § 20–5–113 allows recovery for the loss of consortium of one's child. With that issue now squarely before us, we extend our holding in *Jordan* to allow recovery of filial consortium damages. The loss of a child may result in the same loss of consortium as is caused by the loss of a parent. Nothing in the language of Tenn.Code Ann. § 20–5–113 or in our holding in *Jordan* provides a valid distinction between recovery for parental consortium damages and recovery for filial consortium damages. Instead, our holding in *Jordan* was founded on the basic premise that the pecuniary value of a person's life includes loss of consortium.
>
> Interpreting Tenn.Code Ann. § 20–5–113 to include filial consortium damages is also consistent with the trend of modern authority. Consortium damages historically have been available to the spouse of an injured person to compensate for the loss of the injured spouse's service and society. In recent years, however, numerous jurisdictions have broadened consortium damages to include loss of comfort, companionship, and support in the parent-child relationship. Filial consortium damages are available to parents in wrongful death actions in a majority of jurisdictions through explicit statutory language or judicial interpretation of wrongful death statutes that are similar to Tennessee's statutes. Our interpretation of Tenn.Code Ann. § 20–5–113 is therefore supported by modern society's understanding of the role of a child in the family unit.

Id. at 236–37.

2.   The next case discusses the damages recoverable in a "survival" action.

DURHAM v. MARBERRY

Supreme Court of Arkansas, 2004.
356 Ark. 481, 156 S.W.3d 242.

ANNABELLE CLINTON IMBER, JUSTICE.

This case arises out of a lawsuit that includes both wrongful death and survival claims. The appellants, co-administrators of the estate of Amanda Lynn Durham, sued appellees Harold D. Marberry and Advantage Mobile Homes, Inc., for damages incurred when a mobile home transport vehicle collided with the vehicle driven by Miss Durham. It is undisputed that Miss Durham was killed instantly in the accident. The trial court granted partial summary judgment to the appellees with regard to claimed "loss of life" damages, finding that at least some period of life between injury and death is a condition for recovery of loss-of-life damages by a decedent's estate. Pursuant to Arkansas Rule of Civil Procedure 54(b), the trial court then certified its order regarding the loss-of-life damages claim as final for purposes of appeal. The appellants contend on appeal that no period of life between injury and death is required to recover loss-of-life damages. * * *

As a point of order, we note that both the appellants and the appellees have provided notice to this court that they have arrived at a contingent high-low settlement agreement. The settlement amount is contingent upon our decision in this appeal; therefore, we agree with both parties that the contingent agreement does not moot this appeal. Because this appeal involves the construction of a statute and is an issue of first impression before this court, we have jurisdiction pursuant to Ark. Sup.Ct. R. 1–2(b)(1) and (6).

* * *

INTERPRETATION OF ARK.CODE ANN. § 16–62–101(b)

The Arkansas survival statute provides for the recovery of loss-of-life damages and reads as follows:

16–62–101 Survival of actions—Wrongs to person or property.

(a)(1) For wrongs done to the person or property of another, an action may be maintained against a wrongdoer, and the action may be brought by the person injured or, after his or her death, by his or her executor or administrator against the wrongdoer or, after the death of the wrongdoer, against the executor or administrator of the wrongdoer, in the same manner and with like effect in all respects as actions founded on contracts.

(2) Nothing in subdivision (a)(1) of this section shall be so construed as to extend its provisions to actions of slander or libel.

(b) *In addition to all other elements of damages provided by law, a decedent's estate may recover for the decedent's loss of life as an independent element of damages.*

Ark.Code Ann. § 16–62–101 (Supp.2003) (emphasis added). The issue in this appeal is the interpretation of subsection (b), which was added by the Arkansas General Assembly in Act 1516 of 2001. As we stated in City of Maumelle v. Jeffrey Sand Co., 353 Ark. 686, 120 S.W.3d 55 (2003):

> We review issues of statutory interpretation *de novo* because it is for this court to decide what a statute means. * * * The purpose of statutory construction is to give effect to the intent of the General Assembly. * * * In doing so, we give the words of the statute their ordinary and usually accepted meaning in common language. * * * If the language of a statute is clear and unambiguous and conveys a clear and definite meaning, it is unnecessary to resort to the rules of statutory interpretation. * * *

City of Maumelle v. Jeffrey Sand Co., 353 Ark. at 691, 120 S.W.3d at 57.

Prior to the passage of Act 1516 of 2001, Arkansas had no statutory provision for loss-of-life damages, nor was there any such provision in our case law. Historically, damages recovered by a decedent's estate under the survival statute, with the exception of funeral expenses, compensated the decedent and were incurred pre-death. These include damages for medical expenses due to the injury, lost wages between injury and death, pain and suffering, etc. *See, e.g.*, Advocat, Inc. v. Sauer, 353 Ark. 29, 111 S.W.3d 346 (2003); New Prospect Drilling Co. v. First Commercial Trust, N.A., 332 Ark. 466, 966 S.W.2d 233 (1998). The appellees argued below that the General Assembly's amendment did not add a new element of damages, and that loss-of-life damages are merely a type of pain and suffering. However, subsection (b) states that loss-of-life damages are "in addition to all other elements of damages provided by law." Therefore, logically, they must be new, because the phrase "all other elements of damages provided by law" would encompass every element of damages—including pain and suffering—that was already recoverable under both statutory and case law. Indeed, the Arkansas Model Jury Instructions—Civil were re-written to include loss of life as a separate element of damages recoverable by an estate in a wrongful death action. *See* AMI Civ. 4th 2216 (2004).

On appeal, the appellees concede that loss-of-life damages are a new element of damages, but they now argue that damages for loss of life are the equivalent of, and synonymous with, damages for the loss of enjoyment of life, and these types of damages are incurred pre-death and require a period of conscious life between injury and death.

There is some confusion amongst both case law and legal scholarship as to the definition of "loss of enjoyment of life" damages. Some cases and scholars have used the term "loss of enjoyment of life" to describe damages that compensate a pre-death loss of the ability to enjoy life's activities while still living.[2] Still others have used this term to mean the loss of the enjoyment of being alive that is incurred at the point of death

---

2. *See, e.g.,* Kirk v. Washington State Univ., 109 Wash.2d 448, 746 P.2d 285 (1987); Virginia Smith Gautier, *Hedonic Damages: A Variation in Paths, the Questionable Expert and a Recommendation for Clarity in Mississippi,* 65 Miss. L.J. 735 (1996).

forward.[3] So the term "loss of enjoyment of life" is confusing and, at times, has been used in a way that is equivalent to "loss of life."

* * *

* * * [O]ur review of case law from other jurisdictions shows that some jurisdictions award damages for loss of the enjoyment of life that are pre-death, while others award damages for loss of life that begin at death and run forward until the end of life expectancy. This distinction between damages for "loss of life" and those for "loss of enjoyment of life" is borne out by the legal scholarship written over the last quarter-century. Contrary to the appellees' assertion, although damages for "loss of life," and "loss of enjoyment of life" are both hedonic, "loss of life" damages are not the equivalent of those for "loss of enjoyment of life." *See* * * * Maurice B. Graham & Michael D. Murphy, *Hedonic Damages—Where Are We?*, 51 J. Mo. B. 265 (1995) (Graham and Murphy point out that damage awards for loss of enjoyment of life are much less controversial than loss-of-life damages).

This history is important, because it is with this backdrop that our legislature amended the Arkansas survival statute in 2001. Interestingly, the appellees cite Evans v. United States, 504 U.S. 255 (1992) for the proposition, "It is a familiar 'maxim that a statutory term is generally presumed to have its common-law meaning.'" *Id.* at 259 (quoting Taylor v. United States, 495 U.S. 575, 592 (1990)). The General Assembly presumably understood the difference between "loss of life" damages and "loss of enjoyment of life" damages, and they chose to allow for the recovery of loss-of-life damages in the Arkansas survival statute.

The appellees contend that *only* those damages suffered by a decedent between injury and death are compensable under the Arkansas survival statute. Thus, their argument is that Miss Durham's estate is not entitled to loss-of-life damages, since she was killed instantly in the accident and there was no period of time between her injury and death. In short, her injury *was* her death.

In Ark.Code Ann. § 16–62–101(b), the Arkansas General Assembly chose to use the term "loss of life damages" in its amendment to the survival statute. Thus, the appellees' arguments regarding the meaning and inception of the term "loss of enjoyment of life damages" is irrelevant. Relevant to our inquiry instead is the plain language of the statute as amended. If the statute's language is clear and unambiguous and conveys a clear and definite meaning, we do not resort to rules of statutory interpretation. * * * By its ordinary meaning in common parlance, "loss of life" cannot occur prior to death because it necessarily

---

3. *See, e.g.,* Katsetos v. Nolan, 368 A.2d 172 (Conn.1976) (a plaintiff is entitled to "just damages" which include "compensation for the destruction of her capacity to carry on and *enjoy life's activities* in a way she would have done *had she lived*" (emphasis added)); Jennifer L. Jones, *Hedonic Damages: Above and Beyond Section 1983*, 31 Santa Clara L.Rev. 809 (1991) (using the phrases "loss of the pleasure of being alive" and "lost value of life" interchangeably to describe post-death damages).

presupposes death has occurred. One cannot both live and experience loss of life simultaneously.

Loss-of-life damages seek to compensate a decedent for the loss of the value that the decedent would have placed on his or her own life. "Survival" actions have traditionally included those damages suffered by the decedent between injury and death. Nonetheless, Ark.Code Ann. § 16–62–101 makes no distinction between "personal injury" or "death" when it speaks of the term "injury." In other words, when a person is killed instantaneously, as was Miss Durham, her injury *is* her death, which is compensated by loss-of-life damages.

In sum, because the legislature chose to amend the survival statute to add loss-of-life damages as a separate and independent element in addition to all other elements of damage already allowed by law, the appellants are correct that loss-of-life damages are a new element of damages. Moreover, because the phrase "loss of life damages" as used by the legislature in § 16–62–101(b) is clear and unambiguous, and, since loss-of-life damages can only begin accruing at the point when life is lost, at death, there is no reason to believe the legislature intended to require the decedent to live for a period of time between injury and death. Therefore, we hold that it is not necessary for a decedent to live for a period of time between injury and death in order to recover loss-of-life damages under Ark.Code Ann. § 16–62–101(b). Accordingly, we hold that the trial court erred in granting partial summary judgment to the appellees on the loss-of-life damages claim, and we reverse and remand.

* * *

Reversed and remanded.

NOTES

1.   In One National Bank v. Pope, 272 S.W.3d 98 (Ark. 2008), the court for the first time considered the question of what evidence is required to submit the loss-of-life element of damage to a jury. The estate of the deceased took the position that section 16–62–101(b) only requires proof that a living person died from the wrongful acts of another. The defendant responded that "without some evidence of how a particular decedent saw his or her life, a jury is left to conjecture and speculation" and that it is "the quality of life, not the fact of life, that paves the way to recovery" of loss-of-life damages. *Id.* at 101. The court held that an estate seeking loss-of-life damages pursuant to section 16–62–101(b) "must present *some* evidence, that the decedent valued his or her life, from which a jury could infer and derive that value and on which it could base an award of damages." *Id.* at 102. The court then examined the evidence in the case and held:

> Here, the testimony clearly demonstrated that Ms. Kaz was a mother of four, as well as a grandmother, that she was close to her oldest daughter, that she had worked as a waitress, that she lived with a man for whom she had come to Arkansas, and that, at the time of the accident, she was

on her way to a family get-together. While not direct evidence with
respect to the value Ms. Kaz would have placed on her life, we hold that
this circumstantial evidence was substantial evidence from which the jury
could have inferred the value she would have placed on her life and on
which the jury could have awarded the Estate loss-of-life damages.
Accordingly, because there was substantial evidence from which a jury
could have determined that the Estate was entitled to loss-of-life damages, we hold that the circuit court erred in granting [the defendant's]
motion for directed verdict.

Id. at 103.

The motor-vehicle accident that took the life of the deceased in *One
National Bank* also caused the deaths of two of her daughters. The trial court
judge in *One National Bank* permitted the estates of the daughters to recover
loss-of-life damages. Each estate was awarded $1,101,585 for loss of life and
funeral expenses.

2. Jurisdictions vary as to whether punitive damages can be assessed
against a deceased defendant. For example, the California survival statute
expressly authorizes the recovery of punitive damages, while Tennessee's
"hybrid statute" does not.

3. In the next case, the United States Supreme Court construes the
federal Death on the High Seas Act (DOSHA). The statute clearly creates a
wrongful death cause action. The question presented to the Court was
whether DOHSA also creates a maritime survival action.

DOOLEY v. KOREAN AIR LINES CO.

Supreme Court of the United States, 1998.
524 U.S. 116, 118 S.Ct. 1890, 141 L.Ed.2d 102.

Thomas, J., delivered the opinion for a unanimous Court.

* * *

I

On September 1, 1983, Korean Air Lines Flight KE007, en route from
Anchorage, Alaska, to Seoul, South Korea, strayed into the airspace of the
former Soviet Union and was shot down over the Sea of Japan. All 269
people on board were killed.

Petitioners, the personal representatives of three of the passengers,
brought lawsuits against respondent Korean Air Lines Co., Ltd. (KAL), in
the United States District Court for the District of Columbia. These cases
were consolidated in that court, along with the other federal actions
arising out of the crash. After trial, a jury found that KAL had committed
"willful misconduct," thus removing the Warsaw Convention's $75,000
cap on damages, and in a subsequent verdict awarded $50 million in
punitive damages. The Court of Appeals for the District of Columbia
Circuit upheld the finding of willful misconduct, but vacated the punitive
damages award on the ground that the Warsaw Convention does not
permit the recovery of punitive damages. * * *

The Judicial Panel on Multidistrict Litigation thereafter remanded, for damages trials, all of the individual cases to the District Courts in which they had been filed. In petitioners' cases, KAL moved for a pretrial determination that the Death on the High Seas Act (DOHSA), 46 U.S.C.App. § 761 *et seq.*, provides the exclusive source of recoverable damages. DOHSA provides, in relevant part:

> Whenever the death of a person shall be caused by wrongful act, neglect, or default occurring on the high seas beyond a marine league from the shore of any State, or the District of Columbia, or the Territories or dependencies of the United States, the personal representative of the decedent may maintain a suit for damages in the district courts of the United States, in admiralty, for the exclusive benefit of the decedent's wife, husband, parent, child or dependent relative . . . § 761.

> The recovery in such suit shall be a fair and just compensation for the pecuniary loss sustained by the persons for whose benefit the suit is brought . . . § 762.

KAL argued that, in a case of death on the high seas, DOHSA provides the exclusive cause of action and does not permit damages for loss of society, survivors' grief, and decedents' pre-death pain and suffering. The District Court for the District of Columbia disagreed, holding that because petitioners' claims were brought pursuant to the Warsaw Convention, DOHSA could not limit the recoverable damages. The Court determined that Article 17 of the Warsaw Convention "allows for the recovery of all 'damages sustained,' " meaning any "actual harm" that any party "experienced" as a result of the crash. * * *

While petitioners' cases were awaiting damages trials, we reached a different conclusion in Zicherman v. Korean Air Lines Co., 516 U.S. 217, 116 S.Ct. 629, 133 L.Ed.2d 596 (1996), another case arising out of the downing of Flight KE007. In *Zicherman*, we held that the Warsaw Convention "permit[s] compensation only for legally cognizable harm, but leave[s] the specification of what harm is legally cognizable to the domestic law applicable under the forum's choice-of-law rules," and that where "an airplane crash occurs on the high seas, DOHSA supplies the substantive United States law." * * * Accordingly, the petitioners could not recover damages for loss of society: "[W]here DOHSA applies, neither state law, * * * nor general maritime law, * * * can provide a basis for recovery of loss-of-society damages." We did not decide, however, whether the petitioners in Zicherman could recover for their decedents' pre-death pain and suffering * * *.

After the *Zicherman* decision, KAL again moved to dismiss all of petitioners' claims for nonpecuniary damages. The District Court granted this motion, holding that United States law (not South Korean law) governed these cases; that DOHSA provides the applicable United States law; and that DOHSA does not permit the recovery of nonpecuniary damages—including petitioners' claims for their decedents' pre-death pain and suffering.

On appeal, petitioners argued that although DOHSA does not itself permit recovery for a decedent's pre-death pain and suffering, general maritime law provides a survival action that allows a decedent's estate to recover for injuries (including pre-death pain and suffering) suffered by the decedent. The Court of Appeals rejected this argument and affirmed. * * * Assuming arguendo that there is a survival cause of action under general maritime law, the court held that such an action is unavailable when the death is on the high seas:

> For deaths on the high seas, Congress decided who may sue and for what. Judge-made general maritime law may not override such congressional judgments, however ancient those judgments may happen to be. Congress made the law and it is up to Congress to change it. * * *

We granted certiorari * * * to resolve a Circuit split concerning the availability of a general maritime survival action in cases of death on the high seas. * * *

II

Before Congress enacted DOHSA in 1920, the general law of admiralty permitted a person injured by tortious conduct to sue for damages, but did not permit an action to be brought when the person was killed by that conduct. * * * This rule stemmed from the theory that a right of action was personal to the victim and thus expired when the victim died. Accordingly, in the absence of an act of Congress or state statute providing a right of action, a suit in admiralty could not be maintained in the courts of the United States to recover damages for a person's death. * * *

Congress passed such a statute, and thus authorized recovery for deaths on the high seas, with its enactment of DOHSA. DOHSA provides a cause of action for "the death of a person ... caused by wrongful act, neglect, or default occurring on the high seas," § 761; this action must be brought by the decedent's personal representative "for the exclusive benefit of the decedent's wife, husband, parent, child, or dependent relative" * * *. The Act limits recovery in such a suit to "a fair and just compensation for the pecuniary loss sustained by the persons for whose benefit the suit is sought." § 762. DOHSA also includes a limited survival provision: In situations in which a person injured on the high seas sues for his injuries and then dies prior to completion of the suit, "the personal representative of the decedent may be substituted as a party and the suit may proceed as a suit under this chapter for the recovery of the compensation provided in section 762." § 765. [Another section* establishes] a limitations period. § 763a. * * * DOHSA does not authorize recovery for

---

* Section 763a says: "Unless otherwise specified by law, a suit for recovery of damages for personal injury, or death, or both, arising out of a maritime tort, shall not be maintained unless commenced within three years from the date the cause of action accrued."

the decedent's own losses, nor does it allow damages for non-pecuniary losses.

In Mobil Oil Corp. v. Higginbotham, 436 U.S. 618, 98 S.Ct. 2010, 56 L.Ed.2d 581 (1978) [(holding that widows could not recover damages for "loss of society" under either DOHSA or general maritime law)], we * * * noted that while we could "fil[l] a gap left by Congress' silence," we were not free to "rewrit[e] rules that Congress has affirmatively and specifically enacted." * * * Because "Congress ha[d] struck the balance for us" in DOHSA by limiting the available recovery to pecuniary losses suffered by surviving relatives, * * * we had "no authority to substitute our views for those expressed by Congress." * * * Higginbotham, however, involved only the scope of the remedies available in a wrongful death action, and thus did not address the availability of other causes of action.

Conceding that DOHSA does not authorize recovery for a decedent's pre-death pain and suffering, petitioners seek to recover such damages through a general maritime survival action. Petitioners argue that general maritime law recognizes a survival action, which permits a decedent's estate to recover damages that the decedent would have been able to recover but for his death, including pre-death pain and suffering. And, they contend, because DOHSA is a wrongful death statute—giving surviving relatives a cause of action for losses they suffered as a result of the decedent's death—it has no bearing on the availability of a survival action.

We disagree. DOHSA expresses Congress' judgment that there should be no such cause of action in cases of death on the high seas. By authorizing only certain surviving relatives to recover damages, and by limiting damages to the pecuniary losses sustained by those relatives, Congress provided the exclusive recovery for deaths that occur on the high seas. Petitioners concede that their proposed survival action would necessarily expand the class of beneficiaries in cases of death on the high seas by permitting decedents' estates (and their various beneficiaries) to recover compensation. They further concede that their cause of action would expand the recoverable damages for deaths on the high seas by permitting the recovery of non-pecuniary losses, such as pre-death pain and suffering. Because Congress has already decided these issues, it has precluded the judiciary from enlarging either the class of beneficiaries or the recoverable damages. As we noted in Higginbotham, "Congress did not limit DOHSA beneficiaries to recovery of their pecuniary losses in order to encourage the creation of nonpecuniary supplements." * * *

The comprehensive scope of DOHSA is confirmed by its survival provision, * * * which limits the recovery in such cases to the pecuniary losses suffered by surviving relatives. The Act thus expresses Congress' "considered judgment" * * * on the availability and contours of a survival action in cases of death on the high seas. For this reason, it cannot be contended that DOHSA has no bearing on survival actions; rather, Congress has simply chosen to adopt a more limited survival provision. * * * Even in the exercise of our admiralty jurisdiction, we will not upset the balance struck by Congress by authorizing a cause of action with which Congress was certainly familiar but nonetheless declined to adopt.

In sum, Congress has spoken on the availability of a survival action, the losses to be recovered, and the beneficiaries, in cases of death on the high seas. Because Congress has chosen not to authorize a survival action for a decedent's pre-death pain and suffering, there can be no general maritime survival action for such damages. The judgment of the Court of Appeals is

Affirmed.

NOTE

Congress reacted to *Mobil Oil* by passing the following amendment to DOHSA. The Amendment creates a new cause of action for nonpecuniary damages under certain circumstances:

> If the death resulted from a commercial aviation accident occurring on the high seas beyond 12 nautical miles from the shore of any State, or the District of Columbia, or the Territories or dependencies of the United States, additional compensation for nonpecuniary damages for wrongful death of a decedent is recoverable. Punitive damages are not recoverable.

46 App. U.S.C.A. § 762(b)(1). Nonpecuniary damages are defined as damages for loss of care, comfort, and companionship. 46 App. U.S.C.A. § 762(b)(2). The Amendment is retroactive and applicable to any death occurring after July 16, 1996. Pub. L. 106–181, Title IV, § 404(c) (Apr. 5, 2000). July 16, 1996, was the day before TWA Flight 800 crashed into the ocean as it was taking off from New York City.

CHAPTER 4

BASIC PRINCIPLES OF RESTITUTION AND UNJUST ENRICHMENT

■ ■ ■

SECTION 1. OVERVIEW

Much of this chapter is unlike the rest of this text. The previous two chapters discuss equitable and legal remedies. Although restitution is at times referred to as an alternative remedy in contract and tort law, it is more than a remedy. Just as torts and contracts are areas of substantive law, so too is restitution. *See* Restatement (Third) of Restitution and Unjust Enrichment, Section 1, comment *a*. (Council Draft, 2009).

Restitution was recognized as a substantive field in large part because of the American Law Institute's publication in 1937 of the Restatement of the Law of Restitution, which combined disparately classified rules with a common purpose under one heading. *See* Andrew Kull, *James Barr Ames and the Early Modern History of Unjust Enrichment*, 25 Oxford Journal of Legal Studies 297 (2005) *citing* Douglas Laycock, *The Scope & Significance of Restitution*, 67 Tex. L. Rev. 1277 (1989). From 1939 to 1958 legal textbooks on restitution were published and separate courses taught, but by the 1970's restitution was "folded into" remedies and became part of those courses, as it is here. *See* Douglas Laycock, *How Remedies Became a Field: A History*, 27 Rev. Litig. 161, 255 (2008). The subsuming of restitution into the field of remedies may have diminished its significance as a source of liability, with the result that it became unfamiliar to lawyers and judges, as evidenced by many contradictory statements about what it is and when it applies. (A warning to the student, reading cases in restitution can be a difficult task).

Although there are Restatements (Second) in Contracts and even (Third) in Torts, until recently the only Restatement in Restitution was the one written in 1937. Lack of a later Restatement may have contributed to the confusion. A second Restatement of Restitution was begun in the 1980's, but not completed. In 2000 the first partial discussion draft appeared for the ALI's ten-year project for a Restatement (Third) of Restitution and Unjust Enrichment finalized in 2010.* This Restatement (Third) should be a welcome addition to the field. As Professor Andrew

---

* Citations here will be to Tentative Drafts of the Restatement (Third) of Restitution and Unjust Enrichment, which was approved at the May, 2010, meeting of the ALI. The final version may contain changes from the finalized tentative draft, but no changes in meaning. Cases in this text may cite to earlier drafts of the Restatement (Third). For a discussion of how a Restatement

Kull, Reporter for the Restatement (Third) said, "the word 'restitution' is a term of art that has frequently proved confusing." Restatement (Third) of Restitution and Unjust Enrichment, Section 1, comment *c*, Tentative Draft No. 7 (2010). He said further that despite the confusion the term restitution invites, "it remains the word most commonly employed throughout the common-law world to refer to this set of legal obligations and their associated remedies, some but not all of which involve a literal restitution in the sense of restoration or giving back." *Id*. Thus, Professor Kull retained the term, but added "Unjust Enrichment" to the title because "the substantive part of the law of restitution is concerned with identifying those forms of enrichment that the law treats as 'unjust' for purposes of imposing liability." *Id*., comment *b*. He said the terms will "generally be treated as synonymous" with "more particular meaning that the words may carry * * * clear from the context." *Id*., comment *c*.

While the Restatement (Third) of Restitution and Unjust Enrichment should bring clarity to the field, students cannot abandon the current precedents in favor of the Restatement (Third). The ALI is neither a legislature nor a judiciary; therefore, its Restatements are not precedential. Many, but not all, courts adopt provisions of Restatements as the law of their jurisdiction. Since courts today still cite the Restatement (First) and are citing drafts of the Restatement (Third), it is anticipated that lawyers and judges will seek guidance from the Third. Courts may also continue, however, to refer to their own precedents, particularly in the near future. Thus, this Chapter will not only cover both the substance and remedies of restitution and unjust enrichment, but will also point out some of the variations and, at times, confusions in court precedents. *See, e.g.,* Thompson v. Bayer Corporation, 2009 WL 362982 (E.D. Ark. 2009) (itemizing differences among states in their unjust enrichment laws as reason for denying national class action certification). These variations do not appear to be the result of conflicting policy decisions among jurisdictions, but rather appear to be the result of a lack of modern treatises to clarify the subject, which can be remedied by the Restatement (Third).

SECTION 2. TERMINOLOGY

CANDACE KOVACIC–FLEISCHER, APPLYING RESTITUTION TO REMEDY A DISCRIMINATORY DENIAL OF PARTNERSHIP

34 Syracuse L. Rev. 743 (1983).*

Restitution or "liability based in unjust enrichment" is a "generally accepted and widely applied" source of liability * * *. Restitution pre-

is created see Douglas Rendleman, *Restating Restitution: The Restatement Process and Its Critics*, 65 Wash & Lee L. Rev. 933 (2008).

* Reprinted with permission of Syracuse Law Review and the author.

vents a defendant's unjust enrichment by enabling a plaintiff to seek recovery, in law or equity, of a benefit that the defendant unjustly gained or retained at the plaintiff's expense. If the benefit to be recovered is money, the action is at law and is often referred to as quasi-contract. If the benefit to be recovered is specific property or money that has been traced, the action is in equity and is often referred to as a constructive trust.

* * *

Despite "imprecision," the many definitions of restitution articulated throughout the years consistently contain the following three elements: "(1) the defendant has been enriched by the receipt of a benefit; (2) the defendant's enrichment is at the plaintiff's expense; and (3) it would be unjust to allow the defendant to retain the benefit." Because it is unjust for the defendant to retain the gain, plaintiff's recovery is generally measured by the amount of the defendant's gain, not by the amount of the plaintiff's loss.

* * *

[R]estitution "has been slow to emerge as a general theory"[89] and is not well understood. As Professor Dawson said in 1951, "it is doubtful even now whether most lawyers have an adequate conception of the range and resources of the remedy." It is doubtful whether the situation has much improved * * *.[90]

One reason restitution is not well understood may be that there is a great deal of confusion in terminology. The word "restitution" is used to refer both to a cause of action and a remedy. At times restitution is used synonymously with "unjust enrichment" and "quasi-contract." Quasi-contract, in turn, is used synonymously with contract-implied-in-law and both are at times confused with contract-implied-in-fact. In addition, restitution "sometimes refer[s] to the disgorging of something which has been taken and other times refer[s] to compensation for injury done."

The confusion has a historic base. Much of the common law developed and evolved through the expansion of forms of action or the substitution

89. J. Dawson, Unjust Enrichment 22 (1951). Professor Dawson also said: "[M]any lawyers still approach the restitution remedies with uncertainty and wonder." Dawson, *Restitution or Damages!*, 20 Ohio St. L.J. 175 (1959) * * *. "[Restitution's] outlines have been dimly perceived and little discussed." *Id.*

90. For example, Professor Douthwaite stated: "When considering the measure of compensation for a wrong, the practitioner typically thinks in terms of proven damages * * *. But if he so restricts his thinking he may be depriving his client of a considerable sum of money." Douthwaite, *The Tortfeasor's Profits—A Brief Survey*, 19 Hastings L.J. 1071, 1071 (1968). Professor Douthwaite said, over ten years later, that "[i]t simply isn't true to say that restitutionary problems don't often come up on the practitioner's desk. The trouble is that usually he hasn't thought about the restitutionary implications or potential of the problem before him." G. Douthwaite [, Attorney's Guide to Restitution] § 1.1, at 2 [(1977)].

of a procedurally preferable form for an older form. Fictions were frequently used to facilitate the expansion or substitution. * * *

* * *

The continued use of the old terms that evolved from the old fictions has not only made application of the terms difficult, but has also obscured the fact that restitution, or liability in unjust enrichment, is an important source of liability. Restitution can provide a plaintiff with a remedy that is measured by the amount of the defendant's gain in situations that could alternatively be remedied with typical tort damages, which compensate for a plaintiff's loss, or with contract damages, which put a plaintiff in the position she would have been in if the contract had been performed. Restitution can also provide that the defendant disgorge his benefit in situations in which neither contract nor tort actions will provide relief.

NOTE

The next two cases illustrate confusions caused by the terminology in the field of restitution. As you read them, look for inconsistencies and contradictions between them. Then determine which of those courts' definitions appear to be correct and why.

KOSSIAN v. AMERICAN NATIONAL INSURANCE CO.

Court of Appeal of California, Fifth District, 1967.
254 Cal.App.2d 647, 62 Cal.Rptr. 225.

STONE, ASSOCIATE JUSTICE.

On February 19, 1964, fire destroyed a portion of the Bakersfield Inn, owned by one Reichert. At the time, the property was subject to a first deed of trust in which defendant was the beneficiary. Pursuant to the requirements of the deed of trust, defendant's interest in the property was protected by policies of fire insurance. On March 16, 1964, Reichert, as owner in possession, entered into a written contract with plaintiff whereby plaintiff agreed to clean up and remove the debris from the fire damaged portion of the Inn for the sum of $18,900. Defendant had no knowledge of the execution of the agreement between plaintiff and Reichert.

Plaintiff commenced work in the middle of March 1964, and completed it in early April. During the entire time work was in progress Reichert was in possession of the premises as owner, although defendant caused a notice of Reichert's default under the deed of trust to be filed four days after the contract for demolition was entered into between plaintiff and Reichert. The record does not reflect that plaintiff had actual knowledge of the notice of default until after the work was completed.

Some time after plaintiff had fully performed the contract, Reichert filed a petition in bankruptcy. The trustee in bankruptcy abandoned the premises comprising the Bakersfield Inn, together with any interest in the four fire insurance policies up to the amount of $424,000. Each policy contained a provision insuring against the cost of cleaning up and removing debris caused by fire damage.

Following abandonment of the policies by the trustee in bankruptcy, Reichert and his wife assigned their interest in them to defendant in accordance with the terms of the deed of trust. Defendant submitted proofs of loss, claiming a total of $160,000, including the sum of $18,000 as the estimated cost for removing and cleaning up debris. These claims were rejected by the carriers; negotiations followed; the compromise figure of $135,620 was agreed upon and this amount paid to defendant. We do not have an itemization of the adjusted claims of loss upon which the compromised loss settlement was made, so that the record is not clear as to what part of the $18,900 cost of debris removal defendant received. It is clear, however, that the insurance payment included at least a part of the cost of debris removal and demolition.

Defendant demonstrates, by a careful analysis of the facts, that there was no direct relationship between plaintiff and defendant in regard to either the work performed on the property after the fire or in relation to the fire insurance policies. The contract for debris removal was between plaintiff and Reichert, and defendant did not induce plaintiff, directly or indirectly, to enter into that contract. Plaintiff had no lien against the property resulting from his work, and * * * [any such lien] would have been wiped out by defendant's foreclosure of its first deed of trust.

Had the circumstances been simply that defendant, by foreclosure, took the property improved by plaintiff's debris removal, there would be a benefit conferred upon defendant by plaintiff, but no unjust enrichment. * * * It is the additional fact that defendant made a claim to the insurance carriers for the value of work done by plaintiff that is the nub of the case.

Defendant argues that plaintiff was not a party to the insurance contracts, while defendant had a contract right to collect indemnity for losses resulting from the fire, including the debris removal cost. This contract right was embodied in the insurance policies. * * *

Defendant says it made no agreement, express or implied, with plaintiff that it would pay for the debris removal or that any part of the insurance proceeds would be applied for that purpose. Therefore, concludes defendant, there being no privity of relationship between it and plaintiff, and no fraud or deceit alleged or proved, defendant has the right to the property benefited by plaintiff's work and labor expended in removing the debris and to the insurance payments as well.

Plaintiff makes no claim to the insurance "fund" upon the ground he relied thereon similar to the reliance of a mechanic or materialman that forms the basis of an equitable claim to a building fund. * * * He relies upon the basic premise that defendant should not be allowed to have the fruits of plaintiff's labor and also the money value of that labor. This, of course, is a simplified pronouncement of the doctrine of unjust enrichment, a theory which can, in some instances, have validity without privity of relationship. The most prevalent implied-in-fact contract recognized under the doctrine of unjust enrichment is predicated upon a relationship between the parties from which the court infers an intent. However, the doctrine also recognizes an obligation *imposed* by law regardless of the intent of the parties. In these instances there need be no relationship that gives substance to an implied intent basic to the "contract" concept, rather the obligation is imposed because good conscience dictates that under the circumstances the person benefitted should make reimbursement. * * *

Plaintiff's claim does not rest upon a quasi contract implied in fact, but upon an equitable obligation imposed by law. It is true that defendant's right to the insurance payment was a contract right embodied in the policies of insurance, nevertheless the indemnity payment was based in part upon a claim of loss that did not exist because plaintiff had already remedied the loss by his work for which he was not paid.

We are cited no California cases that are close aboard, and independent research reveals none. Lack of precedent applicable to the facts peculiar to this case is not surprising, however, as the authors of the Restatement recognize that the essential nature of equity cases concerned with problems of restitution makes definitive precedent unlikely. We are guided by the "Underlying Principles" delineated in the Restatement on Restitution: "The rules stated in the Restatement of this Subject depend for their validity upon certain basic assumptions in regard to what is required by justice in the various situations. In this Topic, these are stated in the form of principles. They cannot be stated as rules since either they are too indefinite to be of value in a specific case or, for historical or other reasons, they are not universally applied. They are distinguished from rules in that they are intended only as general guides for the conduct of the courts...." (P. 11.)

The governing principle is expressed in the opening sentence of the Restatement on Restitution, as follows: "The Restatement of this Subject deals with situations in which one person is accountable to another on the ground that otherwise he would unjustly benefit or the other would unjustly suffer loss." (P. 1.)

The question, simply stated, is whether in a jurisdiction that recognizes the equitable doctrine of unjust enrichment one party should be indemnified twice for the same loss, once in labor and materials and again in money, to the detriment (forfeiture) of the party who furnished the labor and materials. We conclude that the doctrine of unjust enrichment is applicable to the facts of this case, and that plaintiff is entitled to reimbursement out of the insurance proceeds paid defendant for work done by plaintiff.

The facts concerning the amount of insurance recovered by defendant and the percentage of the total proof of loss attributable to plaintiff's work are not altogether clear, probably because this is a proceeding for summary judgment before trial of the action. In any event, it is clear that defendant, in addition to taking over the property which plaintiff cleared of debris, also received indemnity insurance payments covering at least part of the cost for clearing that property of debris. The amount can be made certain by a trial on the merits, and if it develops that defendant recovered only a part of the cost for debris removal, this fact does not preclude a partial recovery by plaintiff. We learn from the Restatement, page 611: "Where a person is entitled to restitution from another because the other, without tortious conduct, has received a benefit, the measure of recovery for the benefit thus received is the value of what was received...."

Thus, to the extent defendant received insurance for debris removal performed by plaintiff, plaintiff should recover. If defendant received less than the value of plaintiff's work, as defendant seems to contend, then plaintiff should recover *pro tanto*.

The judgment is reversed.

BASTIAN v. GAFFORD

Supreme Court of Idaho, 1977.
98 Idaho 324, 563 P.2d 48.

DONALDSON, JUSTICE.

On appeal, plaintiff-appellant contends that because the trial court in its decision failed to distinguish between contracts implied in fact and quasi-contracts, the court did not decide this case on the theory alleged in appellant's complaint. We agree and therefore reverse the judgment and remand this case for a new trial.

During March, 1972, the defendant-respondent V.H. Gafford asked plaintiff-appellant Leo Bastian if he would be interested in constructing an office building upon a parcel of respondent's real property located in Twin Falls, Idaho. After several discussions between the parties, appellant orally agreed to construct the building and began drafting the plans therefor. After the plans were substantially completed, respondent contacted First Federal Savings and Loan Association of Twin Falls to seek financing for the building. He was informed that First Federal required a firm bid by a contractor and would not finance the project on a cost-plus basis. Respondent told appellant of the need for a firm bid, but appellant refused to submit one stating that he would only construct the building on a cost-plus basis. Respondent thereafter hired an architect to prepare a second set of plans, and employed another contractor to construct the building using those plans. On June 29, 1972, appellant filed a materialmen's lien upon respondent's real property in the amount of $3,250 for goods and services rendered in preparing the plans. He then commenced this action to foreclose that lien, alleging an implied-in-fact contract to compensate him for his services. After a trial on the merits, however, the court entered judgment for respondent on the ground that respondent had not been unjustly enriched. Since he did not use appellant's plans in constructing the office building, respondent received no benefit from them and was therefore not required to compensate appellant for drafting them.

In basing its decision on unjust enrichment, the trial court failed to distinguish between a quasi-contract and a contract implied in fact. Although unjust enrichment is necessary for recovery based upon quasi-contract, it is irrelevant to a contract implied in fact. * * * For appellant to recover under the latter theory, it is not necessary that respondent either use the plans or derive any benefit from them. * * * It is enough that he requested and received them under circumstances which imply an agreement that he pay for appellant's services.

It is apparent from the record that the requested performance may not have been limited to the drafting of the building plans. We express no opinion on what performance was requested, on whether the requested performance was tendered, and on whether the circumstances imply an agreement to compensate appellant.

The judgment is reversed and the cause is remanded for a new trial. Costs to appellants.

NOTE

As you have seen, *Kossian* and *Bastian* used the terms "unjust enrichment", "contract implied in fact" and "quasi-contract." The next case adds the terms "contract implied in law" and "*quantum meruit*" as synonyms for quasi-contract. Unfortunately, the term *quantum meruit* is used to refer to both a contract implied in fact and restitution/unjust enrichment even though those are distinct topics. *Quantum meruit* means "as much as he deserves" and is usually applied when services have not been paid for. *See* Candace S. Kovacic[-Fleischer], *A Proposal to Simplify* Quantum Meruit *Litigation*, 35 Am. U.L. Rev. 547 (1986). As the Restatement (Third) of Restitution and Unjust Enrichment observes,

> Judicial opinions abound in contradictory statements about the nature and function of a recovery in quantum meruit. Most of these statements may be readily harmonized if the dual function of the pleading is recalled—sometimes implied contract, sometimes unjust enrichment—and if the different strands are simply sorted out.

Restatement (Third) of Restitution and Unjust Enrichment, § 31, comment *e*, Tentative Draft No. 7 (2010). For further discussion of *quantum meruit*, see Chapter 7, Section 5.

CRAWFORD'S AUTO CENTER, INC. v. PENNSYLVANIA
Commonwealth Court of Pennsylvania, 1995.
655 A.2d 1064.

FRIEDMAN, JUDGE.

* * *

Beginning on or about June 1, 1982, as part of an ongoing criminal investigation of chop shops[2] in southeastern Pennsylvania, PSP [Pennsyl-

---

2. The term "chop shop" refers to an illicit operation involving the dismantling of stolen or fraudulently obtained vehicles. * * *

vania State Police] troopers directed Crawford's to tow, pick-up, recover, impound and store allegedly stolen vehicles and vehicle parts. These vehicles and vehicle parts included four forty-foot trailers, a Peterbilt Tractor/Sleeper Cab and various truck parts, including a Marmon Detroit diesel engine, a Marmon rear axle tandem assembly, a Mack transmission and Mack carrier axles. According to Crawford's President, Stephen Behrndt, the PSP directed Crawford's to impound the items and, despite repeated inquiries from Crawford's, the PSP did not release the items for return to owners or for sale. * * *

* * * [I]n July of 1985, Crawford's sent a statement to the PSP seeking $67,204 as reimbursement for their towing and storage. * * * For several months thereafter, Crawford's sent statements to the PSP each month, adding $2,250 for monthly storage charges to the past due balance. * * * By the time Crawford's filed its complaint against the PSP in December of 1985, the total charges on the items remaining at Crawford's amounted to $78,454. * * *

In 1986, as a result of the PSP's efforts, * * * two sheriff's sales were held. * * * From these sales, Crawford's received $14,500, of the over $78,000 it claimed. * * *

In June of 1993, after a hearing, the Board found that the PSP had no liability for payment of the remaining towing and storage fees because no contractual relationship existed between Crawford's and the PSP.

On appeal, Crawford's contends that the PSP is liable for the towing and storage charges on theories of implied-in-fact contract or of quasi-contract. The PSP disagrees and, in addition, claims that Crawford's action was not brought within six months of when it accrued and, thus, is time barred.

I. IMPLIED CONTRACT CLAIM

Contracts may be express or implied. An express contract is one where the parties specifically express the terms of the agreement, either orally or in writing. * * * An implied contract is one where the parties assent to formation of a contract, but instead of being expressed in words, the intention to incur an obligation is inferred from the conduct of the parties in light of the surrounding circumstances, including the course of dealing. * * * Here, Crawford's and the PSP had no express written or oral contract. However, Crawford's asserts that an implied-in-fact contract arose because the PSP, knowing that Crawford's was in the business of towing and storing vehicles, requested Crawford's services, and Crawford's responded by performance. The PSP disagrees with Crawford's, arguing that * * * no exchange of legal consideration occurred. We agree with Crawford's.

The Restatement of Contracts provides: "A promise may be stated in words either oral or written *or may be inferred wholly or partly from conduct.*"[5] Restatement (Second) of Contracts § 4 (1981) (emphasis added). The legal effect of a contract inferred from conduct, called an implied or implied-in-fact contract, is the same as that of an express one. The distinction between an express and an implied contract lies "merely in the mode of manifesting assent.... [I]ntention to make a promise may be manifested in language or by implication from other circumstances, including course of dealing or usage of trade or course of performance." Restatement (Second) of Contracts § 4 cmt. a (1981).

* * *

Having concluded that an implied-in-fact contract arose here when the PSP asked Crawford's to perform a service for it and Crawford's responded with performance, we must still determine the terms of the contract. The terms of such a contract may be inferred from the conduct of the parties, as "understood in light of the circumstances, including course of dealing or usage of trade or course of performance." Restatement (Second) of Contracts § 5 cmt. a (1981). Here, the previous course of dealing included a request for services by the PSP with Crawford's usually receiving payment for its services through a variety of sources, including portions of the proceeds of the sale of the vehicle or vehicle parts * * * or from the owner or insurance company seeking release of the vehicle. * * * Thus, we can infer a promise that Crawford's would be paid for its services from the previous course of dealings. The question presented here is how and if payment is to be made when the usual sources of payment have been exhausted and have not covered the costs of the services.

The testimony of both the PSP troopers involved and Crawford's indicates that the towing and storage related to this criminal investigation was not comparable to any previous course of dealings between the parties because of the number and size of the vehicles and vehicle parts, the need to keep them secured, the length of time that they remained stored, and the difficulty identifying owners. * * * Meanwhile, the vehicles and vehicle parts depreciated while storage costs increased. Thus, when the sheriff's sales finally occurred, they yielded only 18.5% of Crawford's charges. * * *

Under these circumstances, the previous course of dealings does not establish the exclusive basis for determining how Crawford's is to be paid for its services, and we simply cannot accept the Board's conclusion that, as a matter of law, the PSP had no liability for payment of the towing and storage costs. Rather, we believe that an implied contract was formed but that an essential term was omitted, perhaps because the parties failed to foresee the situation which arose. Although the rule has not yet been

---

5. An illustration of an implied-in-fact contract, remarkably similar to the situation here, follows the rule set forth above: A telephones to his grocer, "Send me a ten-pound bag of flour." The grocer sends it. A has thereby promised to pay the grocer's current price therefor. Restatement (Second) of Contracts § 4 illus. 1 (1981).

specifically adopted in Pennsylvania, we are guided by section 204 of the Restatement (Second) of Contracts:

§ 204.   Supplying an Omitted Essential Term

When the parties to a bargain sufficiently defined to be a contract have not agreed with respect to a term which is essential to a determination of their rights and duties, a term which is reasonable in the circumstances is supplied by the court.

Comment d to section 204 discusses the process of supplying a missing term:

Sometimes it is said that the search is for the term the parties would have agreed to if the question had been brought to their attention. Both the meaning of the words used and the probability that a particular term would have been used if the question had been raised may be factors in determining what term is reasonable in the circumstances. But where there is in fact no agreement, the court should supply a term which comports with community standards of fairness and policy rather than analyze a hypothetical model of the bargaining process.... [W]here there is a contract for the sale of goods but nothing is said as to price the price is a reasonable price at the time for delivery.

Restatement (Second) of Contracts § 204 cmt. d (1981). The reporter's note to this section of the Restatement states that the section is new and cites to treatises on the law of contracts by Corbin and by Williston. In discussing similar situations, Corbin states:

In innumerable cases, courts have been required to determine whether one who has received services rendered by another ever made a promise to pay for them....

When an express request for services has been made by the party who receives them and who is benefitted by them, this fact alone may be sufficient to justify the inference of a promise to pay reasonable value * * *.

3 Arthur L. Corbin, Corbin on Contracts § 566 (1960).

Applying the inference of a promise to pay a reasonable value, we conclude that the PSP is liable to Crawford's for the reasonable value of its services and that the $14,500 received from the sale of vehicles and vehicle parts under the Vehicle Code does not adequately compensate Crawford's for its efforts. We, thus, reject the notion that the amounts received from sheriff's sales, insurance companies, restitution, etcetera are the exclusive source of payment in a situation such as this where Crawford's provided its services at the request of the PSP. However, we do not necessarily accept Crawford's contention that the amount billed, based upon the posted amounts and later increases in the posted amounts, reflects the reasonable value of Crawford's services. For example, Crawford's and similarly situated salvors may ordinarily give volume discounts or negotiate reduced rates. Therefore, we will remand to the Board to supply the omitted essential term and for computation of a reasonable payment to Crawford's in light of the circumstances.

II. QUASI CONTRACT CLAIM

We could end our analysis at this point; however, we recognize that the line between implied-in-fact contracts and quasi or implied-in-law contracts is sometimes indistinct. * * * Moreover, we acknowledge that we base our conclusion that an implied in fact contract arose between the PSP and Crawford's on section 204 of the Restatement of Contracts, a new section which has not been discussed and adopted by the Pennsylvania Supreme Court. Accordingly, we also analyze this case under the concept of quasi contract.

A quasi contract is not really a contract at all, but a fictional contract which is a form of the remedy of restitution. * * * "A quasi contract arises where the law imposes a duty upon a person, not because of any express or implied promise on his part to perform it, but even in spite of any intention he might have to the contrary." * * * A quasi contract requires that a party unjustly enriched by the services of another pay a reasonable amount for those services. * * * The PSP argues that it was not unjustly enriched but that, even if it was, public policy precludes requiring payment for Crawford's services. We disagree.

The doctrine of unjust enrichment expresses the general principle that a party unjustly enriched at the expense of another should be required to make restitution for the benefits received where it is just and equitable to do so, and "where such action involves no violation or frustration of law or opposition to public policy, either directly or indirectly." Black's Law Dictionary 1377 (5th ed. 1979) * * *. Here, the PSP had a duty to pursue its criminal investigations and Crawford's services enabled them to do so. Thus, the PSP benefited from Crawford's services and Crawford's suffered a detriment by towing and picking up vehicles and vehicle parts and storing them securely in their yard for approximately four years without payment. For the PSP to retain this benefit without compensating Crawford's for its services constitutes unjust enrichment.[13] In such a situation, restitution under the *quantum meruit* theory[14] is appropriate, unless public policy precludes payment.

The PSP contends that the Board lacks authority to direct the PSP to pay Crawford's charges because such direction would have a chilling effect on the PSP's willingness and enthusiasm for enforcing the laws of the Commonwealth and would, therefore, be against public policy. We fail to see how imposing liability on the PSP as an agency would chill the PSP's

---

13. The Board determined that the PSP had not been unjustly enriched, but rather had aided Crawford's in fostering and advancing its business. * * * The Board is undoubtedly correct that Crawford's business is aided by good relations with the PSP; however, that does not negate the PSP's responsibility to treat Crawford's justly and equitably. In this situation, given the magnitude of the towing and storage, the complications which arose and the duration of the storage, the PSP received benefits far in excess of any aid to Crawford's business.

14. *Quantum merit* describes the extent of the PSP's liability on a contract implied-in-law and actually means "as much as he deserves." Black's Law Dictionary (5th ed. 1979).

performance of its mandatory duties. Rather, we agree with Crawford's that imposing liability on the PSP in this instance would encourage the PSP to take timely action to dispose of items such as those involved here and not unfairly burden salvors with unwarranted storage. Indeed, we believe that non-payment would be more likely to have a chilling effect on performance of the PSP's duties because salvors and others might be less inclined to aid the PSP if the PSP could refuse payment under these circumstances. Requiring the PSP to pay for these services simply means that the PSP must have an adequate budget to perform its statutorily mandated duties; this should present no public policy difficulty. Therefore, had we not determined that an implied-in-fact contract existed, the PSP would have been liable to Crawford's under a quasi contract theory, and Crawford's would be entitled to recover in *quantum meruit*.

III.   Accrual of Crawford's Cause of Action

Finally, we address the PSP's contention that Crawford's action is untimely. Section 6 of the Act of May 20, 1937, P.L. 728, as amended, 72 P.S. § 4651–6, provides that claims against the Commonwealth must be presented to the Board within six months after the claim accrues. According to the PSP because the towing involved a flat fee and the storage a daily flat fee, Crawford's could have detailed the charges immediately. Thus, the PSP argues that Crawford's cause of action accrued at the time Crawford's initially towed or stored the items. Crawford's counters, asserting that the statute of limitations does not begin to run until the claimant is affirmatively notified that the invoices will not be honored. We agree.

* * *

Order

* * * [T]he order of the Board of Claims * * * is reversed and this case is remanded to the Board of Claims to hold a hearing, if necessary, and to issue a decision supplying the omitted essential term of the implied contract between the Pennsylvania State Police and Crawford's Auto Center, Inc. by computing a reasonable payment to Crawford's Auto Center, Inc. in light of the circumstances.

SECTION 3.   REQUIREMENTS

Just as courts use a variety of terms for claims in restitution and unjust enrichment, so too do they use a variety of "elements" to define the claims. Some are problematic. For example, courts often say that a defendant must "appreciate" or "accept" a benefit in situations when the defendant is unaware of having received the benefit. *See, e.g.*, Massachusetts Eye and Ear Infirmary v. QLT Photo–Therapeutics, Inc., 552 F.3d 47 (1st Cir. 2009); Hill v. Cross Country Settlements, LLC., 402 Md. 281, 936 A.2d 343, 351 (Md. 2007). In one such case the Wisconsin Court of Appeals did some mental gymnastics to allow a plaintiff to bring suit for unjust enrichment for a mistaken payment, a claim which the court noted was a classic unjust enrichment cause of action. In Buckett v. Jante, 2009 WI App. 55, 316 Wis. 2d 804, 767 N.W.2d 376 (Wis.Ct.App. 2009), the Bucketts claimed that they had paid property taxes on a portion of the Jante's land, thinking it was theirs. An eminent domain survey showed that it was not. In analyzing the Buckett's unjust enrichment claim to be repaid, which the trial court had dismissed, the Court of Appeals of Wisconsin said:

> We begin with an examination of the pleadings to determine whether Buckett stated a claim for relief. To establish a claim for unjust enrichment, the plaintiff must prove three elements: (1) the plaintiff conferred a benefit upon the defendant; (2) the defendant had an appreciation or knowledge of the benefit; and (3) the defendant accepted or retained the benefit under circumstances making it inequitable for the defendant to retain the benefit without payment of its value. * * * The circuit court ruled that Buckett could not prove * * * that the Jantes had knowledge of the tax payments sufficient to satisfy element two. * * *

* * *

2. ELEMENT TWO (APPRECIATION AND KNOWLEDGE OF THE BENEFIT)

The circuit court * * * granted summary judgment because Buckett could not prove that the Jantes appreciated or knew about Buckett's tax payments contemporaneous with Buckett's actual payment. The Jantes and the circuit court believed that element two comes with a bright-line rule that when the benefited party receives a benefit but is "unaware of that benefit until after it had been done, [it] was not unjust for [the benefited party] to keep the [benefit]." Since the Jantes did not have knowledge of the benefit at the precise time that Buckett conferred the benefit, the circuit court held that Buckett could not prove element two.

We agree that Buckett cannot prove the Jantes had knowledge or appreciation of Buckett's tax payments at the precise time he made them. But, element two does not state that the benefit must be contemporaneous with the knowledge or appreciation. Instead, element two of an unjust enrichment claim is "an appreciation or knowledge by the defendant of the benefit." * * * We have found no Wisconsin law creating a bright-line rule requiring contemporaneous knowledge or appreciation, and the plain meaning of knowledge or appreciation provides little guidance. Therefore, we look to the case law to see if we can divine the meaning.

Our review of Wisconsin case law reveals that *Nelson v. Preston*, 262 Wis. 547, 55 N.W.2d 918 (1952), is the first case which explicitly stated that knowledge or appreciation is an element of unjust enrichment. * * *

Nelson cited *Dunnebacke Co. v. Pittman*, 216 Wis. 305, 257 N.W. 30 (1934), for these three requirements. But, *Dunnebacke* listed only the first and third elements, not the second. * * *. It stated that the elements the plaintiff must prove are "(1) that the defendant has received a benefit from the plaintiff, [and] (2) that the retention of the benefit by the defendant is inequitable." *Id.* (citation omitted). However, *Dunnebacke* denied recovery because the plaintiff improved the defendants' property without their knowledge, the defendants wanted the improvement removed, and they never showed any intent to retain the improvement. *Id.* at 312. The *Dunnebacke* court explained that "[h]ad the [defendants] been present during the time that the construction work was going on, and had they made no protest, we should have a different situation with which to deal." *Id.* Thus the essence of the knowledge or appreciation requirement is to provide the defendant an opportunity to protest or reject the benefit.

The *Dunnebacke* court also explained that the choice need not happen contemporaneously with the conferral of the benefit. If the benefited party does not have contemporaneous knowledge, the plaintiff may still be able to establish a factual basis for recovery if subsequent conduct evinces an attempt to accept the benefits. *Id.* Appreciation or knowledge of the benefit * * * does not require that the timing of the choice coincide with the precise time the benefit is conferred if the nature of the benefit is such that it can subsequently be returned.

Id. at 812–16, 767 N.W.2d at 380–82.

The Restatement (Third) of Restitution and Unjust Enrichment provides restitution's basic principles in its first section:

RESTATEMENT (THIRD) OF RESTITUTION AND UNJUST ENRICHMENT*
Tentative Draft No. 7 (2010).

§ 1. Restitution and Unjust Enrichment

A person who is unjustly enriched at the expense of another is subject to liability in restitution.

NOTE

The Restatement (Third) addresses the issue of "appreciation" in Comment d to § 1. The Reporter's Note to it says that "it is both mysterious and potentially mischievous", and that the "attempt" to "limit the far reaching notion of unjust enrichment within the confines of a checklist . . . usually leads to trouble." As an example, it cites DCB Construction Co. v. Central City Development Co., 965 P.2d 115, 118–20 (Colo. 1998). In *DCB* the Supreme Court of Colorado said,

Because experience has demonstrated some flaws in the old test, we now clarify and restate the test for recovery under a theory of unjust enrich-

---

* Reprinted with permission from the American Law Institute.

ment as: (1) at plaintiff's expense (2) defendant received a benefit (3) under circumstances that would make it unjust for defendant to retain the benefit without paying.

Id. at 119–20, *citing* Candace S. Kovacic, *A Proposal to Simplify* Quantum Meruit *Litigation*, 35 Am. U.L. Rev. 547, 554–560 (1986).

SECTION 4.   RELATIONSHIP BETWEEN RESTITUTION AND CONTRACT

A.   EXPRESS CONTRACT PRECLUDING RESTITUTION

As was seen in the previous sections, the law of restitution and unjust enrichment has many terms referring to contracts, and yet it is not a contractual theory. The use of this terminology goes back to at least 1760 when Lord Mansfield decided Moses v. Macferlan, 97 Eng. Rep. 676 (K.B. 1760). There, for "value received" Jacob had signed four notes promising to repay Moses. Moses endorsed the promissory notes to Macferlan so that he could collect the money from Jacob, and Macferlan signed an agreement indemnifying Moses should Jacob not pay. When that happened, despite the indemnity agreement, Macferlan sued Moses for the amount of the notes. The "Court of Conscience," a local court, thought they did not have the authority to consider the indemnity agreement and awarded the money to Macferlan. Moses then brought suit in the King's Bench "upon the case for money had and received to the plaintiff's use" to recover the money from Macferlan. "Money had and received" was a "common count" under the writ of *indebitatus assumpsit. Assumpsit* was an action that came to replace the actions of covenant, which would enforce a contract only if it were under seal, and debt, which would enforce a promise to pay but used the procedure of wager of law. *See* James Oldham, Reinterpretations of 18th-Century English Contract Theory: The View from Lord Mansfield's Trial Notes, 76 Geo. L.J. 1949 (1988). The wager of law allowed "the defendant to 'wage his law' by bringing to court a specified number of 'oath helpers,' or compurgators, who, under oath, affirmed defendant's position that no debt was owed. This 'wager of law' automatically entitled the defendant to prevail." *Id.* at 1953, n. 24.

One of Macferlan's defenses was that Moses' claim did not fit the requirements of *assumpsit* because he, Macferlan, never promised to pay Moses the money he had recovered in his suit against Moses. As Lord Mansfield wrote, Macferlan argued "an action of debt would not lie here; and no *assumpsit* will lie, where an action of debt may not be brought" and "no *assumpsit* lies, except upon an express or implied contract: but here it is impossible to presume any contract to refund money, which the defendant recovered by an adverse suit." Lord Mansfield held, "If the defendant be under an obligation, from the ties of natural justice, or refund, the law implies a debt, and gives this action, founded in the equity of the plaintiff's case, as it were upon a contract ('*quasi ex contractu*,' as the Roman law expresses it)."

From this opinion come the terms *quasi* contract (*quasi ex contractu*) and implied in law ("the law implies a debt"). As a result, today the term *assumpsit* retains its original meaning of enforcing contracts, but it acquired an additional meaning in *Moses v. Macferlan,* "to recover back money, which ought not in justice to be kept." Thus, *assumpsit* and its related contractual terms are used in two fields, contracts and restitution/unjust enrichment. *Moses* is still cited for its role in the development of this field. *See, e.g.*, Dastgheib v. Genentech, Inc., 457 F. Supp. 2d 536 (E.D. Pa. 2006) (the most renowned eighteenth-century case of a plaintiff bringing an action in *assumpit* and seeking a refund of unjustly obtained funds from a defendant is *Moses v. Macferlan*, 97 Eng. Rep. 676 (K.B. 1760)); Chiofalo v. Ridgewood Savings Bank, 11 Misc. 3d 899; 816 N.Y.S.2d 324 (Civ. Ct. 2006) (" '[T]he gist of this kind of action is that the defendant, upon the circumstances of the case, is obliged by the ties of natural justice and equity to refund the money,' " *quoting Moses v Macferlan*).

Modern procedure no longer restricts law suits to narrow facts specified in old writs or arcane procedures that make evidence of express promises inadmissible. Express contracts are not irrelevant to the law of restitution, however. *Moses* did not involve Moses' seeking to avoid a bad bargain. Consider the next case.

COUNTY COMMISSIONERS v. J. ROLAND DASHIELL & SONS, INC.

Court of Appeals of Maryland, 2000.
358 Md. 83, 747 A.2d 600.

Argued before BELL, C.J., and ELDRIDGE, RODOWSKY, RAKER, WILNER, CATHELL and ROBERT L. KARWACKI (retired, specially assigned), JJ.

CATHELL, JUDGE.

On July 10, 1997, J. Roland Dashiell & Sons, Inc. (Dashiell), respondent, filed a complaint in the Circuit Court for Caroline County against the County Commissioners of Caroline County (County), petitioner, * * * claiming damages in excess of $2,000,000.00 for the alleged extra cost of work and delays and seeking the payment of $326,621.00 withheld by the County as liquidated damages pursuant to the Standard Form of Agreement Between Owner and Contractor dated February 22, 1994 (Dashiell Contract).

* * * On August 26, 1997, petitioner filed a Motion to Dismiss. * * * [T]he Circuit Court entered judgment in favor of the County * * *.

* * * [T]he intermediate appellate court affirmed the circuit court's decision as to the contract claims, holding that respondent's failure to comply with the Dashiell Contract's claim provisions barred its claims for breach of contract. That court also affirmed the circuit court's decision

that respondent's quasi-contractual claim for *quantum meruit* was barred because there was an express contract between the parties. * * *

The Court of Special Appeals, however, did reverse the circuit court's decision to grant summary judgment on Dashiell's quasi-contractual claim for unjust enrichment.[2] * * *

* * *

I. FACTS

* * *

On February 22, 1994, the County entered into the Dashiell Contract with respondent for construction of the proposed renovation [of the County's correctional facility]. For a total sum of $3,075,383.00, respondent agreed to furnish all labor, equipment, materials, and services, and perform all of the work necessary to renovate and expand the detention center by a date no later than 425 calendar days after the date of commencement. Section 3.2 * * * specifically provides that liquidated damages of $500 per calendar day would be assessed if Dashiell failed to complete the project within the 425 calendar-day period.

* * *

* * * Almost immediately thereafter, respondent began to encounter construction delays for which it requested an extension. By letter dated November 15, 1994, a sixty-day extension of time was granted respondent. * * *

* * * By letter dated February 23, 1995, Steven P. Dashiell, respondent's executive vice-president, informed [the architectural firm] that respondent "[was] currently working to develop a claim for lost time due to weather." By letter dated February 16, 1996, Stephen P. Dashiell again contacted [the architectural firm] stating that "the purpose of this letter is to tender formal notice that J. Roland Dashiell & Sons, Inc. *will be* preparing a claim against Caroline County * * *. * * * Neither" of these letters constituted a proper claim in compliance with section 4.3 of the General Conditions of the Contract for Construction. Instead these letters merely indicated that respondent intended to file claims in the future.

* * *

By letter dated July 15, 1996, Dashiell finally submitted a claim * * *. Dashiell sought a change order extending the contract completion date by 522 days and increasing the contract price by $1,061,038.00 for delays incurred up to and including June 20, 1996, allegedly due to architectural and engineer design deficiencies, weather delays, and concealed or un-

---

2. Neither the opinion of the Court of Special Appeals nor the written and oral presentations by the respondent in this Court make clear, either factually or from the standpoint of the measure of recovery, exactly what the perceived difference is in this case between the *quantum meruit* claim and the "unjust enrichment" claim. Nevertheless, we shall use the purportedly distinguishing terminology that has been employed in this case. The distinction, if any, makes no difference in the result.

known conditions. * * * The County has occupied the renovated detention center since June 6, 1996.

* * *

II. Discussion & Analysis
* * *

Before we begin our analysis of the law of contracts, a review of the basic definitions of different contract forms is helpful. An express contract has been defined as "an actual agreement of the parties, the terms of which are openly uttered or declared at the time of making it, being stated in distinct and explicit language, either orally or in writing." * * * "An implied contract is an agreement which legitimately can be inferred from intention of the parties as evidenced by the circumstances and 'the ordinary course of dealing and the common understanding of men.'" * * * Finally, significant to our analysis is the definition of a quasi-contract. * * * [T]he Restatement (Second) of Contracts 4 (1981) describes quasi-contracts in the following manner:

> Quasi-contracts have often been called implied contracts or contracts implied in law; but, unlike true contracts, quasi-contracts are not based on the apparent intention of the parties to undertake the performances in question, nor are they promises.[6] They are obligations created by law for reasons of justice.

While the relationship of express contracts with the doctrine of unjust enrichment appears to be an issue of first impression in this Court, the Court of Special Appeals has interpreted these legal concepts on several occasions. As the Court of Special Appeals has noted:

> The general rule is that no quasi-contractual claim can arise when a contract exists between the parties concerning the same subject matter on which the quasi-contractual claim rests. (Citations omitted.) The reason for this rule is not difficult to discern. When parties enter into a contract they assume certain risks with an expectation of a return. Sometimes, their expectations are not realized, but they discover that under the contract they have assumed the risk of having those expectations defeated. As a result, they have no remedy under the contract for restoring their expectations. In desperation, they turn to quasi-contract for recovery. This the law will not allow.

Mass Transit Admin. v. Granite Constr. Co., 57 Md.App. 766, 776, 471 A.2d 1121, 1126 (1984) (quoting Industrial Lift Truck Serv. Corp. v.

---

6. Historically, there were two types of implied contracts: contract implied by fact and contract implied by law. They have distinct meanings. An implied by fact contract is "inferred from conduct of parties and arises where plaintiff, without being requested to do so, renders services under circumstances indicating that he expects to be paid therefor, and defendant, knowing such circumstances, avails himself of benefit of those services." *Black's Law Dictionary, supra,* at 323. A contract implied by law is now what commonly is called quasi-contract, *id.* at 324 ("Quasi contract"), which we have defined, *supra.* For clarity, we will refer to a contract implied by fact as an implied contract and a contract implied by law as a quasi-contract.

Mitsubushi Int'l Corp., 104 Ill.App.3d 357, 360–61, 60 Ill.Dec. 100, 432 N.E.2d 999, 1002 (1982)) * * *.

As the federal district court said in Dunnaville v. McCormick & Co., 21 F.Supp.2d 527, 535 (1998), "[u]njust enrichment and *quantum meruit*, both 'quasi-contract' causes of action, are remedies to provide relief for a plaintiff when an enforceable contract does not exist but fairness dictates that the plaintiff receive compensation for services provided."

This rationale has been followed universally in both federal and state courts. * * *

* * *

Generally, courts are hesitant to deviate from the principle of the rule and allow unjust enrichment claims only when there is evidence of fraud or bad faith, there has been a breach of contract or a mutual rescission of the contract, when rescission is warranted, or when the express contract does not fully address a subject matter. None of these exceptions that have been recognized elsewhere apply in the case *sub judice*.

In the case *sub judice* there was an express contract between the County and respondent for the renovation of the Caroline County Detention Center. * * * The subject matter of respondent's claim—recovery of money for work performed on the Detention Center—is covered specifically by several valid and enforceable provisions of the written contract between the parties. As well as covering the basic guidelines for construction of the building addition, the contract clearly addressed the process for submitting claims, for liquidated damages, and for the waiver of rights and duties. Respondent's claim that the County has been unjustly enriched because of its use of the detention center is clearly without merit. Even if the County was enriched, such enrichment was not unjust because it was in strict compliance with the terms of their contract. To hold otherwise would turn the basic foundation of contract law on its ear. "This rule holds the contract parties to their agreement and prevents a party who made a bad business decision from asking the court to restore his expectations." * * * Both the County and respondent got what they bargained for by the terms of the contract.

The contract defined the relationship of the parties with respect to its general subject matter. Respondent is now attempting, via a theory of unjust enrichment, to get over $2,000,000.00 in damages and a return of $326,621.00 that the County withheld as liquidated damages for delay, even though its contract with the County specifically covers this subject matter. Respondent's attempt to recover under a theory of quasi-contract is nothing more than a unilateral attempt to amend the agreement in a manner that the law does not allow. * * * We hold that, generally, quasi-contract claims such as *quantum meruit* and unjust enrichment cannot be asserted when an express contract defining the rights and remedies of the parties exists.

* * *

We hold that the circuit court properly ruled that the express, written contract between the County and respondent barred respondent's quasi-contractual claims.

Judgment of the Court of Special Appeals Reversed in Part; Case Remanded to That Court with Instructions to Affirm the Judgment of the Circuit Court for Caroline County * * *.

NOTES

1. *Crawford's Auto Center*, in Section 2 of this Chapter, involved a two count complaint: Count 1 Implied Contract and Count 2 Quasi Contract. That translates to a claim in contract and a second one in restitution. Why is that not inconsistent with *County Commissioners*, above? *See* 3Com Corp. v. Electronic Recovery Specialists, Inc., 104 F. Supp.2d 932, 940 (N.D. Ill. 2000), which says:

> Breach of contract and restitution are inherently incompatible causes of action. * * * However, plaintiff is entitled to plead in the alternative in its complaint. *See* Fed.R.Civ.P. 8(e)(2). Therefore, at this preliminary stage of the litigation plaintiff may proceed under both theories. That is, plaintiff may allege the existence of a governing contract in count I and alternatively seek restitution in count VII without defaulting the latter claim on a motion to dismiss. Courts in this circuit repeatedly have held that such alternative pleading is sufficient to withstand a challenge on the pleadings. * * *

For further discussion of alternative pleading see Chapter 3, Section C.1.

2. If the express contract does not cover the subject matter of the claim an action in restitution is appropriate. *See, e.g.*, Porter v. Hu, 116 Haw. 42, 169 P.3d 994 (Haw. Ct. of App. 2007) ("While it is stated that an action for unjust enrichment cannot lie in the face of an express contract, a contract does not preclude restitution if it does not address the specific benefit at issue."); *cf.* Ken Hood Construction Co. v. Pacific Coast Construction, Inc., 203 Or. App. 768, 126 P.3d 1254 (Ct. App. 2006) ("The trial court, having concluded that there was no contract, proceeded to the second step of the sequential analysis and addressed * * * damages under a *quantum meruit* theory * * *. In light of our conclusion that the parties had a contract, that was error.") In Mid–Hudson Catskill Rural Migrant Ministry, Inc. v. Fine Host Corp., 418 F. 3d 168, 175–176 (2d Cir. 2005), then Judge Sonia Sotomayor explained,

> * * * New York law does not permit recovery in *quantum meruit* * * * if the parties have a valid, enforceable contract that governs the same subject matter as the *quantum meruit* claim. * * * *See Clark–Fitzpatrick, Inc.*, 70 N.Y.2d at 389 ("It is impermissible ... to seek damages in an action sounding in quasi contract where the suing party has fully performed on a valid written agreement, the existence of which is undisputed, and the scope of which clearly covers the dispute between the parties.").

3. As you read the next case, consider whether the majority or dissent correctly describes the concept of an express contract precluding an action in restitution.

IN RE ESTATE OF BUNDE

Court of Appeals of Michigan, 2002.
2002 WL 737781. Unpublished Opinion.

Before GRIFFIN, P.J., and HOLBROOK, JR., and HOEKSTRA, JJ.
PER CURIAM.

* * *

Plaintiff's complaint alleged that Kurt E. Bunde made three promises to her during his lifetime, which induced plaintiff to move in with Bunde and work with him in his bakery:

(1) We will be partners and work together in the bakery.

(2) You will never have to worry about having enough money to take care of yourself.

(3) I am going to live forever. But, if I die first, you will have this home (at 370 Blue Star Highway) forever.

Plaintiff lived with Bunde until his death in January 1999 and worked in the bakery with him until 1996, when it was sold. Plaintiff argues that these promises formed an enforceable contract to which Bunde's estate should be held. [The trial court granted defendant's motion for summary disposition.]

First, this Court must address the terms of the agreement. Plaintiff has stated that the agreement is comprised of three promises Bunde made. However, this Court finds that plaintiff has abandoned enforcement of the first promise * * *. Additionally, plaintiff testified that at no time did she expect to be paid for her work in the bakery. When the bakery was sold in 1996, plaintiff was present at the closing sale. Plaintiff made no claim to the proceeds and did not expect to receive any portion. Therefore, we conclude that only the second and third promises are part of the alleged contract and accordingly limit our analysis.

Plaintiff argues that the agreement between plaintiff and Bunde was not a contract to make a will, but rather an enforceable, express oral contract or, alternatively, a contract implied in fact. We disagree.

* * *

Plaintiff also appears to argue an agreement should be implied in law. With an implied-in-law contract the court conclusively implies an intent to pay for services in order to prevent unjust enrichment. * * * A contract implied in law is "an obligation imposed by law to do justice even though it is clear that *no promise was made or ever intended.*" * * *

In the instant case, plaintiff consistently contends that Bunde made promises and even testified as such in her deposition. * * * [P]laintiff contended in her complaint that "Bunde requested the services [plaintiff's work in the bakery], and knew, or reasonably should have known that [*plaintiff*] *expected to be paid by Bunde for her work.*" However, plaintiff testified that she never expected compensation for this work. * * *

Plaintiff argues that, in light of the trial court's own findings, the court should have granted partial summary disposition in favor of plaintiff. Plaintiff contends that these findings confirm that Bunde made certain promises to plaintiff, and thus, plaintiff is entitled to their enforcement. Defendant does not contest, for summary disposition purposes, the fact that certain promises were made by Bunde.

This Court has already determined that in order for plaintiff to be successful on appeal based on either an express or implied-in-fact theory, she would need to show that evidence of a writing regarding the alleged agreement existed. However, none of the court's findings indicate the existence of such a written agreement. * * * Regarding plaintiff's implied-in-law theory, findings by the court that support the existence of express oral promises by Bunde undermine this theory, not sustain it. Therefore, the trial court's findings were not inconsistent with granting summary disposition in favor of defendant.

* * *

Affirmed.

HOLBROOK, JR., J. (dissenting).

[E]ven if the agreement is properly characterized as a contract to make a will, I do not believe summary disposition was properly granted. Accordingly, I dissent.

* * * A close examination of plaintiff's deposition testimony shows that while plaintiff indicated that she did not believe she was entitled to a percentage of the proceeds from the 1996 sale of the bakery, she nonetheless wanted to have the promise of support enforced. * * *

The majority finds it significant that plaintiff repeatedly averred that she did not expect to be paid a salary or receive a paycheck in return for her promise to move to South Haven and work side-by-side with decedent in his bakery. However, plaintiff did not bargain for a paycheck or a salary for her work in the bakery. Rather, she bargained for decedent's monetary obligation of support as well as a place to live. It is not dispositive that plaintiff did not expect a fixed regular compensation to be satisfied through the issuance of a check.

* * *

Given the special relationship that later developed between plaintiff and decedent, a presumption arises that the benefits conferred by plaintiff, including the personal services rendered in caring for decedent and the Blue Star home, were rendered gratuitously. * * * This presumption, however, is rebuttable. I do not believe it can be conclusively said that no evidence existed showing that plaintiff expected to be compensated for her actions. * * * Certainly, decedent's expressions of an intent to compensate plaintiff serve as strong evidence rebutting the presumption. Further, the commercial nature of the services rendered in the bakery, the hours spent working in the bakery, the fact that plaintiff had worked for the decedent before in a similar capacity for which she received payment, and plaintiff's claim that decedent expressly indicated that she would be compensated for her work, "was more than sufficient ... to present a question of fact as to the parties' expectations." Roznowski v. Bozyk, 73 Mich.App 405, 409, 251 NW2d 606 (1977). * * * While it is a close question, I also do not believe that recovery under either an implied-in-law, or *quantum meruit*, theory of restitution is precluded. * * *

* * *

I am not judging the merits of plaintiff's claims for an implied-in-law contract and *quantum meruit*, but merely indicating that I believe that she should be given her day in court to prove her case. Both these equitable theories of recovery are based on the principle against unjust enrichment. In the case at hand, I believe an argument can be made that, under the circumstances, * * * restitution for the benefit conferred on decedent is just. I disagree with the majority that such equitable relief is not available because plaintiff consistently argues that promises were made to her by decedent. Plaintiff should not be asked to undermine one of her claims in order to maintain another. Assuming the evidence fails to show either an express contract on a contract implied-in-fact, or that some legal principle precludes enforcement of a contract despite the mutual assent of the parties, plaintiff has every right to plead these equitable theories as an alternative basis for relief. There is nothing in the nature of either remedy that precludes their imposition when a plaintiff pleads an express contract. Again, both theories of recovery are not based on the lack of exchanged promises, but on the notion that services have been rendered, and in the absence of an enforceable contract, justice requires that the plaintiff be compensated for the value of the services. The absence of an enforceable contract does not presume the absence of an exchange of promises. *See generally* Dobbs, The Law of Remedies (2d ed) § 4.2(3), pp. 384–88.

* * *

Accordingly, I would reverse the grant of summary disposition to defendant.

B. RESTITUTIONARY RECOVERY FOR BREACH OF CONTRACT

There is considerable confusion about what, if anything, a restitutionary remedy for breach of contract should be. According to one view, when a breaching party materially breaches a contract before only money is due, the contract price does not limit the amount of restitutionary relief for the nonbreaching party. See Dan B. Dobbs, Law of Remedies § 12.20(2)(1993); 1 George E. Palmer, Law of Restitution § 4.4 (1978). For example, when a contractor materially breaches a construction contract so as to justify a builder stopping performance before the completion date, some courts have awarded the builder, under the theory of unjust enrichment, the value of its labor and materials even when that amount would have been more than if the builder had completed the contract. *Cf.* Ducolon Mechanical, Inc. v. Shinstine/Forness, Inc., 77 Wash. App. 707, 713, 893 P.2d 1127, 1130 (1995) ("While many jurisdictions permit a non-defaulting contractor to recover in excess of the contract, few, if any, permit a defaulting contractor to recover in excess of the contract price.")

The Restatement (Third) of Restitution and Unjust Enrichment takes issue with the idea that one should be able to recover more than an agreed price without some wrongdoing because contract law is not fault based. Restatement (Third) of Restitution and Unjust Enrichment, § 39, comment *a*, Tentative Draft No. 7 (2010). The Restatement (Third) has a chapter entitled Restitution and Contract that has two subtopics: Restitution to a Performing Party with No Claim on the Contract and Alternative Remedies for Breach of an Enforceable Contract. The first deals with cases such as *Kossian v. Bastion* in Section 2 of this Chapter. The second has three subsections, two of which it characterizes as "contract remedies that are independent of unjust enrichment" but are often referred to in terms of restitution. *Id. See also* §§ 37, 38. Those two contract remedy sections are Rescission as a Remedy for Breach of Contract (§ 37) and Performance–Based Damages for Breach of Contract (§ 38). The latter is explained as the same as reliance damages. Section 38 explicitly limits those damages to "not leave the plaintiff in a better position as contractual performance would have done," and is explained in Comment *a* as "modif[ying] the prior treatment of those few cases—prominent in theory, but rare in practice—in which a plaintiff seeks 'restitution' to escape the consequences of an unfavorable bargain."

Section 39, however, introduces a restitutionary remedy for breach of contract that is not found in either the first or second Restatements of Contracts, *id.* § 39, Reporter's Note *a*, for "exceptional cases." *Id.* at comment *a*. Section 39 states:

§ 39. Profit Derived from Opportunistic Breach

(1) If a deliberate breach of contract results in profit to the defaulting promisor and the available damage remedy affords inadequate protection to the promisee's contractual entitlement, the promisee has a claim to restitution of the profit realized by the promisor as a result of the breach. Restitution by the rule of this Section is an alternative to a remedy in damages.

Section 39 is elaborated in comment *b* as involving cases "in which the promisee's contractual position is vulnerable to abuse." Restatement (Third) of Restitution and Unjust Enrichment, § 39, Tentative Draft No. 7 (2010).

Section 39 contains a number of examples where damages would not provide an adequate remedy, but the situation would be too late for specific performance. For example, Illustration 9, based on Coca Cola Bottling Co. of Elizabethtown v. Coca Cola Co., 988 F.2d 386 (3d Cir. 1993), involves a license agreement between an owner of a soft-drink trademark and a bottler. The agreement required use of cane sugar as the sweetener. The bottler had substituted a cheaper sweetener for the cane sugar and had saved $5,000,000 when the facts come to light. The products were practically indistinguishable. The bottler would be required to disgorge the $5,000,000, and the owner would not have to prove damages.

SECTION 5. LAW AND EQUITY

A. RESTITUTIONARY CLAIM CAN BE EITHER LEGAL OR EQUITABLE

Because a restitutionary claim is often referred to as "an equitable obligation imposed by law," *see Kossian* from Section 1 of this Chapter, a number of courts have applied the technical requirements of "Equity" to the claim, while ignoring the phrase "imposed by law." Because procedural "Equitable Remedies" are awarded without juries and when the legal remedy is supposed to be inadequate, *see* Chapters 2 and 8, a number of jurisdictions have applied those procedures to actions in which plaintiffs seek to recover money judgments in unjust enrichment. *See, e.g.*, American Honda Motor Co., Inc. v. Motorcycle Information Network, Inc., 390 F. Supp. 2d 1170 (M.D. Fla. 2005) ("It is well settled in Florida that unjust enrichment is an equitable remedy and is, therefore, not available where there is an adequate legal remedy."); *In Re* Lupron Marketing and Sales Practices Litigation, 295 F. Supp. 2d 148 (D. Mass. 2003) ("Unjust enrichment is regarded by most (but not all) states as an equitable claim. * * * As I have concluded that plaintiffs have an adequate remedy at law under their RICO claims, Count XVII will be dismissed."); Porter v. Hu, 116 Haw. 42, 169 P.3d 994 (Ct.App. 2007) ("[T]he circuit court did not * * * convert a contract case into an equity case, thereby depriving Defendants of a jury trial. Rather, the circuit court conducted a jury trial on the matters triable to a jury and also imposed an equitable remedy upon determining that the contract remedies available did not adequately address Defendants' unjust enrichment."). *But see* Realmark Developments, Inc. v. Ranson, 214 W. Va. 161, 588 S.E.2d 150 (2003) (reversing trial court's denial of jury trial, saying, "Clearly, the right to recover for unjust enrichment is based on the principles of equity. However, the remedy sought in this case is a money judgment and, thus, is governed by law, * * * and therefore, can be tried before a jury."); Dastgheib v. Genentech, Inc. 457 F. Supp. 2d 536 (E.D. Pa. 2006) ("[T]he Court holds that Dastgheib's claim for unjust enrichment under North Carolina is legal rather than equitable in nature and that, therefore, Dastgheib is entitled to a jury trial.").

Restitution is not limited to equity, as many other courts have recognized. The Restatement (Third) of the Law of Restitution and Unjust Enrichment makes this clear:

§ 4.   Restitution May be Legal or Equitable or Both.

(1) Liabilities and remedies within the law of restitution and unjust enrichment may have originated in law, in equity, or in a combination of the two.

(2) A claimant otherwise entitled to a remedy for unjust enrichment, including a remedy originating in equity, need not demonstrate the inadequacy of available remedies at law.

Restatement (Third) of the Law of Restitution and Unjust Enrichment, § 4, Tentative Draft No. 7 (2010).

Professor Andrew Kull, the Reporter of the Restitution (Third), reviewed the development of restitution and concluded that "[a] statement to the effect that 'restitution is equitable' is a harmless platitude so long as 'equity' means only 'fairness.' The same statement becomes mischievous when it is offered as the basis for defining the jurisdiction of courts or agencies, or the kinds of relief they are authorized to administer." *Id.* at § 4, Reporter's Note c.

B. TYPES OF EQUITABLE REMEDIES

The cases in the preceding sections of this Chapter, and many in later sections, involve legal remedies in restitution. Like other legal remedies, they result in judgments that state that the plaintiff is entitled to a recovery. They are not court orders telling a defendant to do or not do something. Those are equitable and would be enforced by contempt. A plaintiff enforces a legal judgment by having it enforced by a sheriff or other official attaching the defendant's assets, or by other means prescribed by statute.

The following cases describe equitable remedies in restitution. These remedies involve a concept known as "tracing". These remedies are characterized as constructive trusts, equitable liens or subrogation, depending in large part upon the extent of the tracing. As you will see, their primary value is in giving the plaintiff priority over nonsecured creditors. As you read these cases, look for *in personam* orders and the language of conveyance that are some of the hallmarks of equity.

RESTATEMENT (THIRD) OF RESTITUTION AND UNJUST ENRICHMENT*
Tentative Draft No. 6 (2008).

§ 55. Constructive Trust

(1) If a recipient is unjustly enriched by the acquisition of legal title to specifically identifiable property at the expense of the claimant or in

---

* Reprinted with permission of the American Law Institute.

violation of the claimant's rights, the recipient may be declared a constructive trustee, for the benefit of the claimant, of the property in question and its traceable product.

HUNTER v. SHELL OIL CO.

United States Court of Appeals, Fifth Circuit, 1952.
198 F.2d 485.

STRUM, CIRCUIT JUDGE.

This appeal presents for review a judgment for the plaintiff in two consolidated suits instituted by Shell Oil Company against Paul B. Hunter, and others, to impress constructive trusts upon certain royalty interests, mineral interests and leasehold estates in oil, gas and other minerals, acquired by them in the circumstances hereinafter mentioned.

From 1930 to 1941, when he was discharged, the defendant-Hunter was employed by Shell Oil Company as senior geologist in its Houston office, where he was in direct charge of Shell's extensive exploration activities in a large area along the Gulf coast of Texas and Louisiana. Hunter's principal duties were to collect geological and geophysical information for use by Shell and to advise the company where to purchase oil and gas interests, where to drill test wells, and the like, for which purpose he was employed and paid full time. This information was highly confidential. Hunter's relationship with Shell was of a fiduciary nature, in which the utmost good faith is mandatory. At all times during Hunter's employment, Shell had a rule prohibiting its employees from acquiring royalty and other mineral interests. This rule applied to Hunter, and he was aware of it.

Early in 1941, Shell discovered that Hunter had been unauthorizedly divulging confidential information to one A.M. Joncas, one R.J. St. Germain, and to Southland Royalty Company, based upon which, and acting in numerous instances through the hereinafter mentioned corporations for concealment, they bought up royalty and other interests in oil lands discovered by Hunter in Texas, Louisiana and Arkansas, for which Hunter received, as his compensation for furnishing said information, fractional participations in their purchases. * * * The company immediately discharged Hunter, and soon thereafter instituted these suits against him and some of those acting in concert with him in buying up mineral interests based upon Hunter's information. * * *

Shell asserts that by disclosing such confidential information, which was its exclusive property, and in aiding his associates to acquire the above mentioned mineral interests, Hunter breached his fiduciary duty to his employer; placed himself in a position where his personal interests conflicted with those of his employer; and that in consequence Hunter and the persons and corporations who acquired mineral interests through his unauthorized disclosures, hold such interests as constructive trustees for Shell.

After a trial with an advisory jury, extending over a period of five months, the trial court found for the plaintiff as to 59 of the areas involved, and for the defendants as to 15 other areas, holding that mineral interests in the 59 areas had been purchased by Hunter's associates through unauthorized information furnished by Hunter in breach of his fiduciary duty to his employer, Shell Oil Company. * * *

Judgment was thereafter entered impressing trusts upon the interests acquired by the defendants in the 59 areas * * *. The defendants were also required to convey to Shell all such interests as were still held by them, and which Shell elects to recover in kind, conditioned upon Shell reimbursing defendants for the original cost of such interests. The judgment further authorized the pursuit and recapture by Shell, on the same terms, of such interests as may have been conveyed by defendants to *non* bona fide purchasers, or at its election to have a judgment against the seller-defendant for the sale price, or for the reasonable market value thereof, and to recover the purchase price or market value of interests sold to bona fide purchasers.

Following a lengthy period of accounting, money judgments were also entered against certain of the defendants in the aggregate sum of $130,378.92, representing income and other money accruals from their ostensible ownership of the interests upon which trusts were impressed, some of which had been sold by defendants to bona fide purchasers.

* * *

An agent may trade for his own benefit outside the scope of his principal's business without being accountable for the profits realized. But he is forbidden to deal with a subject matter of the agency, or to use for his own advantage information acquired while acting within the scope of the agency. Nor may an agent put himself in a position in which his personal interests may come into conflict with his duty to his principal, or which may afford him an opportunity to subordinate the interests of his employer to his own individual benefit while discharging his duties. Such conduct is not only morally wrong, it is contrary to public policy. When property has thus been wrongfully acquired, equity converts the holder into a trustee, and compels him to account for all gains from such conduct. * * *

* * *

We are in accord with the trial court's findings and judgment. Generally speaking, the breach by Hunter of his fiduciary duty to Shell, and the advantage he and his associates knowingly reaped therefrom is abundantly established. Appellants contend, however, that as to certain of the areas upon which trusts were impressed, e.g. areas not under Hunter's supervision as a geologist for Shell; areas which were proven or otherwise generally known to be favorable areas when Joncas purchased; areas in which Joncas could have secured the necessary geological data from others and was not beholden to Hunter for it; areas in which it had been previously announced that a test drill would be made; and areas in which Shell's information was only of the type known as "reconnaissance shooting" and therefore without substantial value, the proof is insufficient to establish a trust in favor of Shell.

The trial judge found the evidence "clear [and] convincing" as to the 59 areas upon which he imposed a trust in favor of the plaintiff. We agree * * *.

The trial judge also found that the conveyance to Hunter by his associates of mineral interests in areas where plaintiff had no confidential information was a consideration and an incentive to Hunter to disclose confidential information belonging to plaintiff as to other areas in which plaintiff, through Hunter, was possessed of such information. The evidence fully supports this conclusion.

* * *

Viewing the evidence as a whole, the trial judge is well supported in his findings and judgment.

Affirmed.

NOTES

1. Do you think that the result in *Hunter* would have been different if Hunter had not been labeled a fiduciary? *See* Blank v. Baronowski, 959 F.Supp. 172, 177–78 (S.D.N.Y.1997):

> [U]nder New York law, a party claiming entitlement to a constructive trust must ordinarily establish four elements: (1) a confidential or fiduciary relationship; (2) an express or implied promise; (3) a transfer made in reliance on that promise; and (4) unjust enrichment. * * * These elements are not always required, however, and the constructive trust doctrine has been interpreted in a flexible manner to prevent unjust enrichment [and] may be imposed notwithstanding the lack of fiduciary relationship.

See also Allred v. Fairchild, 785 So.2d 1064, 1067 (Miss.2001) ("A constructive trust is one that arises by operation of law against one who, by fraud, actual or constructive, by duress or abuse of confidence, by commission of wrong, or by any form of unconscionable conduct, artifice, concealment, or questionable means, or who in any way against equity and good conscience, either has obtained or holds the legal right to property which he ought not, in equity and good conscience, to hold and enjoy."); Hettinga v. Sybrandy, 126 Idaho 467, 470, 886 P.2d 772, 775 (1994) (stating that while a constructive trust can be based on a fiduciary relationship, such a relationship is not the only justification for it). For other cases involving disloyal agents see *infra* Chapter 7.B.3.

2. In *Hunter*, besides affirming the constructive trusts ordered by the district court, the appellate court also upheld "money judgments * * * of $130,378.92, representing income and other money accruals from [the defendants'] ostensible ownership of the interests upon which trusts were impressed, some of which had been sold by defendants to bona fide purchasers."

Thus, *Hunter* demonstrates that the plaintiff may consider separately each transaction that violated the defendant's duty of loyalty and choose the remedies considered to be most advantageous.

3.   A constructive trust is distinguished from a resulting trust because a constructive trust is a remedy for an action in unjust enrichment, while a resulting trust arises from the express or implied intent of the parties. *See* Sheldon Petroleum Co. v. Peirce, 546 S.W. 2d 954 (Tex. Civ. App. 1977). That distinction corresponds with the distinction between a contract implied-in-law and a contract implied-in-fact: the first does not require that the parties intend to agree, while the latter does.

4.   The next cases provide examples of tracing.

G & M MOTOR CO. v. THOMPSON

Supreme Court of Oklahoma, 1977.
567 P.2d 80.

BERRY, JUSTICE.

The question to be decided has not heretofore been decided in Oklahoma. Specifically, may a trial court impress a constructive trust upon proceeds of life insurance policies where a portion of the premiums were paid with wrongfully obtained funds? We hold sound reason and interest of justice require an affirmative answer.

The facts, for the purpose of deciding this question, are simple. A. Wayne Thompson was an accountant for G & M Motor Company [Motor Company] from January 1, 1968, until his death on August 2, 1970. During this period decedent embezzled $78,856.45 from Motor Company; a portion of which was used to pay premiums on various insurance policies insuring the life of decedent. The trial court impressed a constructive trust upon various items of real and personal property and a portion of the insurance proceeds in possession of decedent's surviving wife, Shirley Thompson, and child.

Court of Appeals, Division 1, upon wife's appeal, affirmed trial court's impressment of a constructive trust on the real and personal property, but modified the trust on insurance proceeds. The court, relying on American National Bank of Okmulgee v. King, 158 Okl. 278, 13 P.2d 164, said "only that part of the funds that the trial court found was used to pay for the payments of the policies while deceased was employed for appellee ... together with interest at the rate of 10% per annum from date of judgment ... until paid" are subject to a constructive trust in favor of Motor Company.

Motor Company, after motion for rehearing was denied, sought certiorari.

* * *

The proper basis for impressing a constructive trust is to prevent unjust enrichment. Restatement of Restitution § 160, Comment c

[(1937)]. The Restatement of Restitution foresaw that a wrongdoer may exchange misappropriated property for other property; thus, § 202 provides:

> Where a person wrongfully disposes of property of another knowing that the disposition is wrongful and acquires in exchange other property, the other is entitled ... to enforce ... a constructive trust of the property so acquired.

The drafters explained § 202 as follows:

> Where a person by the consciously wrongful disposition of the property of another acquires other property, the person whose property is so used is ... entitled ... to the property so acquired. If the property so acquired is or becomes more valuable than the property used in acquiring it, the profit thus made by the wrongdoer cannot be retained by him; the person whose property was used in making the profit is entitled to it. The result, it is true, is that the claimant obtains more than the amount of which he was deprived, more than restitution for his loss; he is put in a better position than that in which he would have been if no wrong had been done to him. Nevertheless, since the profit is made from his property, it is just that he should have the profit rather than that the wrongdoer should keep it. It is true that if there had been a loss instead of a profit, the wrongdoer would have had to bear the loss, since the wrongdoer would be personally liable to the claimant for the value of the claimant's property wrongfully used by the wrongdoer. If, however, the wrongdoer were permitted to keep the profit, there would be an incentive to wrongdoing, which is removed if he is compelled to surrender the profit. The rule which compels the wrongdoer to bear any losses and to surrender any profits operates as a deterrent upon the wrongful disposition of the property of others. Accordingly, the person whose property is wrongfully used in acquiring other property can by a proceeding in equity reach the other property and compel the wrongdoer to convey it to him. The wrongdoer holds the property so acquired upon a constructive trust for the claimant.

Thus, it is not necessary for a plaintiff to have suffered any loss or suffer a loss as great as the benefit of defendant. *See id.* § 160, Comment d.

Where the wrongdoer mingles wrongfully and rightfully acquired funds, [the] owner of [the] wrongfully acquired funds is entitled to share proportionately in acquired property to the extent of his involuntary contribution. *Id.* § 210(2). This principle is specifically applicable to life insurance proceeds where a portion of the premiums were paid with wrongfully acquired money. *Id.* § 210, Comment a. The drafters said:

> Just as the claimant is entitled to enforce a constructive trust upon property which is wholly the product of his property, so he is entitled to enforce a constructive trust upon property which is the product in part of his own property and in part of the property of the wrongdoer. The difference is that where the property is the product of his

property only in part, he is not entitled by enforcing a constructive trust to recover the whole of the property, but only a share in such proportion as the value of his property bore to the value of the mingled fund.

More particularly, § 210, Comment d, Illustration 5 addressed the instant matter. Illustration 5 provides:

> A insures his life for $10,000 and pays the premiums half with money wrongfully taken from B and half with money of his own. A dies. B is entitled to half of the proceeds of the policy. . . .

The record indicates trial court determined extent of premiums paid with wrongfully acquired funds and impressed a constructive trust upon proceeds consistent with Illustration 5.

Having carefully considered the matter, we adopt the Restatement view. However, Motor Company has sought no more than the embezzled monies, interest and costs. Further, the surviving wife is an innocent beneficiary. Therefore, we cannot say trial court's judgment is against the clear weight of evidence. We hold Motor Company is entitled to a pro rata share of insurance proceeds, but not to exceed the total amount of embezzled monies, interest and costs.

* * * Judgment of trial court affirmed.

NOTES

1. Because of outcomes in cases such as *G & M Motor Co.*, where a claimant does not seek to recover the appreciated insurance proceeds above the amount of the claimant's loss, the Restatement (Third) added Section 61(b), which limits claimants of insurance proceeds to the amount of their loss if the claim is "from assets that would otherwise go to innocent dependents of a deceased recipient" who paid the insurance premiums with wrongfully obtained money. Restatement (Third) of the Law of Restitution and Unjust Enrichment, § 61(b), Tentative Draft No. 7 (2010). *See also id.* at comment *c.*

2. *In re Foster*, below, involves a "Ponzi" scheme. Wiand v. Waxenberg, 611 F. Supp. 2d 1299, 1312 (M.D. Fla. 2009) explains:

> A Ponzi scheme is a "phony investment plan in which monies paid by later investors are used to pay artificially high returns to the initial investors, with the goal of attracting more investors." United States v. Silvestri, 409 F.3d 1311, 1317 n.6 (11th Cir. 2005). In order to prove the existence of a Ponzi scheme, the Receiver must establish that: (1) deposits were made by investors; (2) the Receivership Entities conducted little or no legitimate business operations as represented to investors; (3) the purported business operations of the Receivership Entities produced little or no profits or earnings; and (4) the source of payments to investors was from cash infused by new investors.

In Cunningham v. Brown, 265 U.S. 1, 44 S. Ct. 424, 68 L. Ed. 873 (1924), cited in *Foster*, the Supreme Court heard the original "Ponzi scheme" case. The bankrupt swindler was named Charles Ponzi.

IN RE FOSTER

United States Court of Appeals, Tenth Circuit, 2001.
275 F.3d 924.

Before MURPHY and BALDOCK, CIRCUIT JUDGES, and VAN BEBBER, DISTRICT JUDGE.

BALDOCK, CIRCUIT JUDGE.

* * *

The Debtor, Bryan K. Foster ("Foster"), operated several "Ponzi" investment schemes whereby returns to investors were paid not from profits derived from an underlying business venture, but with funds received from new investors. The business venture in which investors believed they were investing did not exist. Defendant Dale Kinzler ("Kinzler") was one of several individuals Foster fraudulently induced to invest funds in the scheme. Foster commingled in general bank accounts the funds from his fraudulent activities.

On August 15, 1996, several investors filed an involuntary petition against Foster under Chapter 7 of the Bankruptcy Code in the District of Colorado. *See* 11 U.S.C. 303. On September 18, 1996, Foster consented to entry of an order for relief. *See id.* Between the filing of the petition and the entry of the order for relief (the "Gap Period"), Foster initiated a series of transfers to Kinzler. The Trustee sought to avoid these transfers pursuant to 549 of the Bankruptcy Code.

* * * The parties do not dispute that the transfers occurred without court approval and after commencement of the case; the parties dispute whether the transferred funds were property of the estate. Kinzler argued before both the bankruptcy court and district court that the funds were subject to a constructive trust and thus not property of the estate. The bankruptcy court agreed and dismissed the Trustee's 549 complaint. The district court affirmed the bankruptcy court order.

Property subject to a trust is not property of the bankruptcy estate. *See* Cunningham v. Brown, 265 U.S. 1, 11, 68 L. Ed. 873, 44 S.Ct. 424 (1924) * * *.

Under Colorado law, a constructive trust is a judicially created equitable remedy applied to prevent unjust enrichment. * * * To warrant imposition of a constructive trust over the property of a debtor, a claimant must (1) show fraud or mistake in the debtor's acquisition of the property; and (2) be able to trace the wrongfully held property. * * * The parties agree Foster acquired the funds through fraud. The bankruptcy court applied a judicial tracing fiction known as the lowest intermediate balance rule to conclude Kinzler met the tracing requirement.

The lowest intermediate balance rule permits a claimant to trace trust funds deposited into a general account. Under this rule, any funds removed from the account are presumed to be the debtor's personal funds to the extent these funds exceed the beneficiary's equitable interest. * * * Although new deposits are not subject to the equitable claim of the trust beneficiary, subsequent withdrawals are presumed to draw first upon the new funds. * * * Applying the rule, the constructive trust beneficiary may retrieve the lowest balance recorded after the funds were commingled.[1] The bankruptcy court applied this rule to determine the amount of funds subject to Kinzler's constructive trust.

On appeal, the Trustee contends that the bankruptcy court should not have applied an equitable tracing fiction to elevate the claim of one defrauded creditor over the claims of other similarly situated creditors.[2] * * *

The bankruptcy court failed to consider whether its use of a tracing fiction was equitable in this case. The lowest intermediate balance rule is an equitable fiction that should not be employed where equity does not warrant the result. * * * Courts refuse to employ the lowest intermediate balance fiction where the commingled account is comprised largely of funds acquired from other fraud victims. *See Cunningham*, 265 U.S. at 13, 44 S.Ct. 424 ("The rule is useful to work out equity between a wrongdoer and a victim; but when the fund with which the wrongdoer is dealing is made up of the fruits of frauds perpetrated against a myriad of victims, the case is different.") * * *.

Kinzler cannot directly trace the funds received in the post-petition transfer to the funds he invested and must rely on the judicial tracing fiction to meet the tracing requirement. We recognize that Kinzler transferred funds to Foster immediately prior to the bankruptcy filing and that these funds comprised a significant portion of the balance in Foster's account on the date the bankruptcy petition was filed. Foster, however, deposited the funds into a general account in which he commingled funds received from other investors. All transfers from this account, including the transfer to Kinzler, were comprised of funds received from victims of Foster's fraud.

---

1. An example may illustrate the rule's application: Assume a fiduciary commingles $10,000 of trust money with $10,000 of personal money in his personal account. The fiduciary then withdraws $10,000 from the account. Applying the rule, the fiduciary draws first upon his own funds. Thus, the $10,000 remaining in the account is the trust money. Assume the fiduciary later withdraws an additional $5,000. Only $5,000 remains in the account and the trust balance is thus reduced to $5,000. Assume the fiduciary then deposits $5,000 of personal funds in the account, bringing the account balance back up to $10,000. Because new deposits are not subject to the trust, the trust balance remains at $5,000. Although any later withdrawals will draw first upon the new funds, the trustee cannot recover more than $5,000. Thus, the trustee can recover the lowest balance recorded after the fiduciary commingled funds. *See In re* Mahan, 817 F.2d at 685 (citing 76 Am.Jur. Trusts 2d. 307 (1992)).

2. The Trustee also contends that the bankruptcy court erred in failing to consider the equities of the case before imposing the equitable remedy of a constructive trust. Alternatively, the Trustee urges this Court to adopt recent Sixth Circuit Court of Appeals precedent which holds that a bankruptcy court's imposition of a constructive trust is an impermissible circumvention of the Bankruptcy Code's system of ratable distribution and per se reversible error. In re Omegas Group, Inc., 16 F.3d 1443, 1453 (6th Cir.1994). Because we conclude the district court erred in applying a tracing fiction without first determining whether other creditors were similarly situated, we need not address these arguments.

The Trustee asserts that Foster's creditors are almost exclusively similarly-situated fraud victims. A tracing fiction should not be employed to elevate Kinzler's claim over the claims of other creditors if those creditors are similarly situated. The court did not determine if the other creditors are similarly situated and thus erred in employing the tracing fiction.

In a bankruptcy proceeding, the bankruptcy court must weigh the claims of the remaining creditors before employing an equitable fiction such as the lowest intermediate balance rule. The court did not determine if the equities support use of the tracing fiction. Accordingly, this matter must be reversed and remanded.

NOTES

1. In *In re Foster* the bankruptcy court, which was reversed by the Tenth Circuit, had found that Kinzler, defrauded by Foster, was entitled to a constructive trust "to elevate his claim" over claims of other defrauded creditors. If the competing claimants to the fund had been business creditors rather than similarly situated defrauded creditors, the bankruptcy court's conclusion would have been correct. The rationale for the rule that would enable a defrauded creditor to obtain a constructive trust from the wrongdoer's bank account was stated by Judge Swan of the Second Circuit, sitting with Judges Learned Hand and Chase, in 1935:

> The usual formula is to say that, where a fund is composed partly of the defrauded claimant's money and partly of the fiduciary's own money, the fiduciary is presumed to intend to draw out the money he can legally use rather than that of the claimant. * * * But, when courts speak of "presumed intent," they mean that a rule of law is announced which takes no account at all of the actor's real intent. Equity marshals the withdrawals against the fiduciary's own funds so long as it can because that result is deemed fairer. There is good reason for this because the fiduciary's creditors have accepted the risk of his solvency, while his cestuis have accepted only the risk of his honesty. * * * The credit which the bankrupts were privileged to use without defrauding any one they should be deemed to have drawn against, rather than against funds held in trust for persons who relied upon their honesty.

In re Kountze Bros., 79 F.2d 98, 101–102 (2d Cir. 1935). As *Foster* demonstrates, however, priority over creditors based on tracing rules is not automatic.

2. For a case in which use of tracing fictions was deemed inequitable, see SEC v. Byers, 637 F. Supp. 2d 166, 175–177 (S.D. N.Y. 2009). There the SEC had filed a complaint that alleged "that Byers and Shereshevsky operated a massive Ponzi scheme that defrauded more than 1,000 investors of approximately $255 million." The court appointed a receiver who recommended a *pro rata* distribution of the remaining assets among the defrauded creditors. Over many objections the court approved the receiver's plan based on the investors' being similarly situated as to the fraud. The court explained:

The Receiver's recommendation is supported by the case law, which is quite clear that *pro rata* distributions are the most fair and most favored in receivership cases. Indeed, the Second Circuit has explicitly held that "the use of a *pro rata* distribution has been deemed especially appropriate for fraud victims of a Ponzi scheme, in which earlier investors' returns are generated by the influx of fresh capital from unwitting newcomers rather than through legitimate investment activity." [*SEC v. Credit Bancorp., Ltd.*, 290 F.3d 80, 89 (2d. Cir. 2002)] * * *.

The alternatives to *pro rata* distribution that have been proposed would create unfair results by rewarding certain investors over others based on arbitrary factors. *Cf. Credit Bancorp*, 290 F.3d at 89 (noting that, in Ponzi schemes, "whether at any given moment a particular customer's assets are traceable is 'a result of the merely fortuitous fact that the defrauders spent the money of the other victims first' ") (quoting *United States v. Durham*, 86 F.3d 70, 72 (5th Cir. 1996)). * * *

See also United States v. Ramunno, 588 F. Supp. 2d 1360, 1361–1362 (N.D. Ga. 2008) (stating "Mr. Martin is one of approximately 100 victims who suffered a combined loss in excess of $20 million. * * * The only difference between Mr. Martin and the other victims is that he was defrauded last. This distinction should not dictate that he receive more of the forfeited assets than the other victims of the fraud."). This result is supported by Section 59(4) of the Restatement (Third) of Restitution and Unjust Enrichment, Tentative Draft No. 7 (2010).

3.   In Bender v. CenTrust Mortgage Corp., 51 F.3d 1027, 1030 (11th Cir. 1995), Bender, the former president of CenTrust Mortgage, had been fired by the Resolution Trust Corporation (RTC) after it became the receiver of CenTrust. Bender was suing the RTC and CenTrust for wrongful termination. He asked the court to impose a constructive trust on the proceeds from RTC's sale of CenTrust because of the lawsuit. The court denied his request and explained:

> A constructive trust cannot be imposed on general assets. * * * "[I]t is well settled that Florida courts will impress property with a constructive trust only if the trust res is specific, identifiable property or if it can be clearly traced in assets of the defendant which are claimed by the party seeking such relief." * * * This specific property must be the subject of the inequitable transaction. * * *

> Bender argues that * * * here the assets are related to the lawsuit or are traceable to such assets, rather than unrelated general assets. We find Bender's argument to be unpersuasive where Bender cannot trace his benefits and compensation to a designated fund * * *.

> It is axiomatic that a constructive trust is inappropriate relief for the mere failure to pay a debt. * * * "Cases in which the remedy sought is the recovery of money (whether as collection on a debt or as damages) do not fall within the jurisdiction of equity ... and the imposition of a constructive trust will generally not be the appropriate remedy." Additionally, there is no showing of irreparable injury. * * * Bender's concern for the ultimate collectibility of a judgment against * * * CenTrust

Mortgage does not support his asserted right to set aside a fund for "losses and/or damages and costs" while such claims are being resolved. *Id.* at 1030.

4. In its footnote 1, the court in *In re* Foster described one method of tracing funds. There are actually a number of methods to choose from, *see* 1 Dan B. Dobbs, Law of Remedies § 6.1(4) (2d ed. 1993). So that no tracing rule is used to disadvantage a wronged claimant, Section 59 (2)(a) of the Restatement (Third) says, "If property of the claimant has been commingled by a recipient who is a conscious wrongdoer * * * (a) withdrawals that yield a traceable product and withdrawals that are dissipated are marshaled so far as possible in favor of the claimant." Restatement (Third) of the Law of Restitution and Unjust Enrichment, § 59(2)(a), Tentative Draft No. 7 (2010). In all of the methods, the "lowest intermediate balance rule" discussed in *In re Foster* sets the bottom limit for funds that can be traced. What is the rationale for that limit?

5. St. Paul Fire & Marine Insurance Co. v. Seafare Corp., 831 F.2d 57 (4th Cir.1987), provides an example of tracing, or "trust pursuit," saying:

> Under the doctrine of trust pursuit, the beneficiary of a constructive trust may assert his rights in the proceeds from the disposition of trust property. These proceeds must be capable of being traced through any intermediate transfers, but even property which has been converted from one form to another (e.g., from a restaurant [claimed to have been fraudulently acquired], to the charred remains of the restaurant, to the insurance proceeds, as here) may be so pursued.

Id. at 58. *See also* Wilde v. Wilde, 576 F.Supp.2d 595 (S.D.N.Y. 2008) (tracing in detail how funds embezzled by stepson had been spent.)

6. For a discussion of the relationship between the state law of constructive trusts and the bankruptcy code, see *In re* Corzo, 406 B.R. 154 (Bankr.S.D. Fla. 2008) and cases cited therein. *See also* Andrew Kull, *Restitution in Bankruptcy: Reclamation and Constructive Trust*, 72 Am. Bank. L.J. 265 (1998); Emily L. Sherwin, *Constructive Trusts in Bankruptcy*, 1989 U. Ill. L. Rev. 297.

RESTATEMENT (THIRD) OF RESTITUTION AND UNJUST ENRICHMENT*

Tentative Draft No. 6 (2008).

§ 56. Equitable Lien

(1) If a recipient is unjustly enriched by a transaction in which

    (a) the claimant's assets or services are applied to enhance or preserve the value of particular property to which the recipient has legal title * * *

* * *

the claimant may be granted an equitable lien on the property in question.

---

(2) An equitable lien secures the obligation of the recipient to pay the claimant the amount of the recipient's unjust enrichment * * *.

VERITY v. VERITY

Supreme Court, Special Term, Nassau County, Part II, 1959.
21 Misc.2d 385, 191 N.Y.S.2d 204.

EDWARD ROBINSON, JR., JUSTICE.

In this action the plaintiff [wife] prayed for judgment impressing a trust upon several parcels of real property set forth in the complaint; upon the proceeds of the sale of one parcel of property which had been sold prior to the action; declaring that the defendant [husband] held said properties in trust for himself and the plaintiff as tenants by the entirety and directing the defendant to convey the legal title to the premises to himself and plaintiff as tenants by the entirety. She further asks that the defendant be directed to account for the rents from the properties and that he be declared to hold them in trust to the extent of plaintiff's interest therein. The plaintiff alleges in the complaint that the properties were purchased beginning in the year 1922 "jointly and with funds mutually earned, procured and contributed." She further alleges that the defendant Charles H. Verity, Jr., her husband, had promised on diverse occasions to transfer the properties to both names as tenants by entirety. * * *

From the evidence adduced upon the trial, I find the following facts: The plaintiff and the defendant intermarried at Baldwin, New York on May 8, 1915 and have since been and now are husband and wife. As husband and wife they moved into and occupied as their home a small building on property owned by the father of the defendant. The plaintiff had no money at the time she was married. Neither did the defendant. At that time the defendant was farming. He had some horses and did some contracting work. The plaintiff helped the defendant, her husband, in his farming work, picking and crating tomatoes and doing anything else that she could do to help him. The first piece of property which they purchased was acquired with money from the farming and contracting work. This property was eventually sold and still using the money from the farming, contracting and later house moving work, they eventually acquired the properties in question upon this trial. As the premises were acquired the plaintiff worked with the defendant in finishing the houses.

* * *

In the year 1924 the plaintiff spoke to the defendant inquiring as to why the deeds to the various properties purchased to that time were not in both names and he answered, "What difference is it whose name it is in? It belongs to the both of us." The plaintiff believed from this statement that she was a joint owner of the properties with her husband. She was doing all of the bookkeeping work in connection with the properties including the collecting and recording of the rents and the paying of taxes as the defendant Verity could not read or write except for the signing of his name. The parties moved to New Jersey in 1933 where they lived on a farm owned by the defendant's father. Unhappy differences later arose as a result of which the defendant Verity was on October 11, 1951 committed to an insane asylum from which he was discharged about March 12, 1952. He then went to live with his brother on Long Island. Plaintiff continued to manage the Baldwin properties until May, 1953 when the defendant Verity took over the collecting. He continued the collections and management until plaintiff was appointed Receiver in this action. During the years from 1952 to 1957, the plaintiff in good faith and believing that the property was jointly owned by her and her husband paid from her own funds for taxes, insurance and liens on the various parcels * * * a total of $1,401.47.

* * *

Where a relation of confidence has been abused, and a person has never had title to the property but has expended money in the improvement of the property on the basis of an oral promise to convey, which money does not constitute the entire consideration for the purchase or the interest claimed, that person is entitled, not to a conveyance of the property, but only to an equitable lien thereon for the amount expended. * * *

In this case the only moneys alleged or proved to have been used in the purchase of the property were moneys derived from the husband's business in which the plaintiff helped. She had no funds of her own at that time and made no contribution from her own holdings.

The Married Women's Property acts do not relieve a wife of the duty of rendering services to her husband. While they give her the benefit of what she earns, under her own contracts, by labor performed for anyone except her husband, her common-law duty to him remained, and if he promises to pay her for working for him, it is a promise to pay for that which legally belongs to him. The fact that he cannot require her to perform services for him outside of the household does not affect the question, for he could not require it at common law. Such services as she does render him whether within or without the strict line of her duties belong to him. If he pays for them it is a gift. If he promises to pay her a certain sum for them, it is a promise to make her a gift of that sum. She cannot enforce such a promise by a suit against him. * * *

On the facts established in this case, the plaintiff has failed to establish a cause of action for the relief demanded in the complaint. In equity, however, she is entitled to an equitable lien upon the parcels for the moneys expended from her own funds for the protection of the property. Plaintiff will be adjudged to have an equitable lien upon the premises [for a total of $1,401.47].

* * *

This constitutes the decision of the court * * *.

NOTES

1. What did Mrs. Verity get when the court issued an equitable lien, and how did that differ from what she was seeking through a constructive trust? *See* Wilde v. Wilde, 576 F. Supp. 2d 595 (D.N.Y. 2008) in which the court describes the difference:

> When misappropriated funds are commingled with other funds, either in an account or through purchase of property, the constructive trust extends only to the portion traceable to the misappropriated funds. * * * Restatement (First) of Restitution § 210 (1937). When a constructive trust extends only to a portion of the property, it is generally known as an equitable lien. Restatement (First) of Restitution §§ 210, 161 cmt. a; Restatement (Third) of Restitution § 56; 1 Dobbs, *Law of Remedies* § 4.3(1) & (3).

2. In *Verity* the court said that if Mr. Verity "pays for [Mrs. Verity's services] it is a gift. If he promises to pay her a certain sum for them, it is a promise to make her a gift of that sum. She cannot enforce such a promise by a suit against him." Why not? If you do not know, review your Contracts notes on consideration.

3. The court said that Mrs. Verity "had no funds of her own" at the time the property was purchased. It also said that neither she nor her husband had money "at the time she was married." Why do you think her economic status was treated differently than his for her constructive trust claim? Do you agree?

4. Although some of the language in *Verity* may seem outdated, presumptions about familial relationships in more modern times often produce similar results. *See* Kuder v. Schroeder in Section 7.B of this Chapter. There a majority of the Court of Appeals of North Carolina held:

> Under the law of this State, there is a personal duty of each spouse to support the other, a duty arising from the marital relationship, and carrying with it the corollary right to support from the other spouse. * * * So long as the coverture endures, this duty of support may not be abrogated or modified by the agreement of the parties to a marriage. * * *

110 N.C.App. 355, 358, 430 S.E.2d 271, 273 (1993). For cases discussing cohabitants seeking to recover on the basis of unjust enrichment after separation, see Section 5 in Chapter 7.

Even as there must be tracing for a constructive trust, there must be tracing for an equitable lien. *See In re* Marriage of Marshall, 86 Wash.App. 878, 940 P.2d 283 (1997), in which the court said:

> Ms. Marshall is seeking reimbursement against the community assets in toto for the general use of her separate property. Washington law does not support such a claim. "Equitable liens do not apply to property generally. They must attach to a specific property on a specifically documented theory.... The claim for an equitable lien must be sup-

ported by direct evidence of a contribution to the property on which the lien is asserted." * * *

> Because Ms. Marshall sought to impose the lien on community property generally, and failed to provide direct evidence of contributions to specific items of community property on which she asserted her lien, we conclude that the trial court did not abuse its discretion in refusing to impose the equitable lien.

Id. at 882–83, 940 P.2d at 285.

RESTATEMENT (THIRD) OF RESTITUTION AND UNJUST ENRICHMENT*

Tentative Draft No. 6 (2008).

§ 57. Subrogation as a Remedy

(1) If a recipient is unjustly enriched by a transaction in which property of the claimant is used to discharge an obligation of the recipient or a lien on the recipient's property, the claimant may obtain restitution

> (a) by succeeding to the rights of the obligee or lienor against the recipient or the recipients property, as though such discharge had not occurred, and

> (b) by succeeding to the rights of the recipient in the transaction concerned.

NOTES

1. For those unfamiliar with the language of commercial lenders, it might be easier generally to refer to obligees as lenders or creditors and obligors as borrowers or debtors. Lienors are lenders whose loan is secured. A secured loan is secured by property held by the debtor. If the borrower defaults, the lender can claim the property on which the lender has a security interest to pay off the loan, assuming that the lender has complied with the relevant secured creditor statutes. This part of the debtor's assets cannot be used to satisfy another creditor's debt unless that creditor has a lien that takes priority by statute. If the borrower is insolvent, creditors without security interests (unsecured creditors) will divide the remaining assets, if any, *pro rata*. Thus under § 57, if a recipient of wrongfully acquired money uses the money to pay off all or part of a secured debt (a lien), then the claimant "succeed[s] to the rights" of the lender whose debt was paid off. If the lender had a security interest in the property, then the claimant becomes the secured creditor. For more details, including the distinction between obligors and debtors, see Article 9 of the Uniform Commercial Code.

2. In the case below, an embezzler (recipient) used the embezzled funds to buy some commercial real estate. The seller of the property accepted some of the embezzled money, not knowing it was embezzled, as a down payment on the property and took back a mortgage on the property. Thus the seller

---

* Reprinted with permission of the American Law Institute.

became a lender—a secured creditor—a lien holder (lienor). With these definitions in mind, see how the claimant's situation fits the terms of § 57, and how, if the embezzler had used lawfully acquired money to buy the property, he would have had an equitable lien under § 56, after having defaulted.

CEDAR LANE INVESTMENTS v. AMERICAN ROOFING SUPPLY OF COLORADO SPRINGS, INC.

Colorado Court of Appeals, Div. IV, 1996.
919 P.2d 879.

BRIGGS, JUDGE.

Allan Capps, a stockholder and employee of American Roofing, embezzled more than $200,000 from the company. Approximately $50,000 of this amount was used as a down payment on commercial real estate that he and his wife purchased from Cedar Lane pursuant to an installment land contract. * * *

After the Cappses entered into possession, they made 30 payments totalling $22,300 and constructed improvements on the real estate costing in excess of $16,000. The cost of the improvements was also funded with money Allan Capps stole from American Roofing.

The Cappses defaulted on the installment land contract * * *. Cedar Lane then commenced a forcible entry and detainer (F.E.D.) action against them. At that time, American Roofing had filed a *lis pendens* and a judgment lien against the real estate. However, while its counsel attended the F.E.D. hearing, American Roofing did not formally intervene.

One of the issues the Cappses raised at the hearing was whether they were entitled to any equitable relief from their default on the installment land contract. * * * Cedar Lane's counsel argued, among other things, that the Cappses had no equitable interest in the property because the money they expended for the down payment and improvements belonged not to the Cappses but to American Roofing.

After the hearing, the trial court indicated it was satisfied with the statement of Cedar Lane's counsel that American Roofing would be allowed to claim whatever interest it believed it had in the property. The court therefore concluded that the Cappses had no right, title, or interest in the property, terminated the installment land contract, and granted Cedar Lane immediate possession.

Cedar Lane then commenced this quiet title action. American Roofing filed a counterclaim seeking recovery of the money taken from it by Allan Capps and paid to Cedar Lane. It set forth a claim for relief based on * * * a claim of unjust enrichment.

Both parties filed motions for summary judgment. Cedar Lane, relying in part on its asserted status as a bona fide purchaser without knowledge that Capps had stolen the money invested in the property, argued that American Roofing had no right, title, or interest in the property and requested that title be quieted in it. American Roofing * * * requested that the court impose a constructive trust or equitable lien on the real estate.

The trial court * * * ruled that American Roofing was not entitled to equitable relief because Cedar Lane had received the funds from the Cappses without knowledge of any claim by American Roofing. * * *

* * *

To recover under a theory of unjust enrichment or quantum meruit, American Roofing must establish that: (1) a benefit was conferred on Cedar Lane; (2) the benefit was appreciated by Cedar Lane; and (3) the benefit was accepted by Cedar Lane under circumstances that would make it inequitable for Cedar Lane to retain the benefit without payment of its value. * * *

A constructive trust is a remedy for unjust enrichment. *See* 1 D. Dobbs, Law of Remedies § 4.3(2) at 597 (2d ed. 1993). It is an equitable device used to compel a person who unfairly holds property of another to convey that property to one to whom it justly belongs. Its purpose is to prevent the unjust enrichment of the person holding the property at the expense of the rightful owner. * * *

An equitable lien is a special and limited form of a constructive trust. It provides a security interest in the property which can be used to satisfy the claim of a person who may have only a partial interest in the property. * * *

Cedar Lane relies on the supreme court's conclusion in *In re* Marriage of Allen, *supra*, that neither a constructive trust nor an equitable lien may be used to defeat the interests of a bona fide purchaser for value. * * *

* * *

By accepting the obligations of the installment land contract and transferring possession of the real estate to the Cappses, Cedar Lane initially gave sufficient consideration to defeat a claim of unjust enrichment. However, after the forfeiture and successful prosecution of the F.E.D. action, Cedar Lane again had possession of the real estate and all the rights of ownership, including the right to sell the property. It also had the $50,000 paid as a down payment and the $22,500 in interest payments, as well as the $16,000 in improvements to the real estate.

By reacquiring the improved real estate without payment of additional consideration or other obligation, Cedar Lane recaptured the "value" it gave. Thus, for purposes of considering whether to impose a constructive trust or an equitable lien, Cedar Lane's status as a bona fide purchaser for value protects it only to the extent it was not unjustly enriched as the result of the installment land contract forfeiture. American Roofing is therefore entitled to equitable relief to the extent that Cedar Lane was unjustly enriched. * * *

* * *

To ignore that Cedar Lane has regained possession of the property, with improvements, without repaying any of the funds received from the Cappses is to ignore the equitable realities. The result would be that a vendor unjustly enriched by receiving stolen funds, unlike other vendors, would have immunity from a claim for equitable relief upon the purchaser's default under an installment land contract.

American Roofing should * * * have no better equitable claim than would the Cappses if they had invested their own funds as purchasers of the property. * * * Whether an equitable remedy will be provided depends on a number of factors, including the amount of the purchaser's equity in the property, * * * the value of the improvements to the property, and the adequacy of the property's maintenance.

Even if we were to treat * * * Cedar Lane * * * as a bona fide purchaser, * * * [a] second [theory] * * * of unjust enrichment * * * leads to the same result.

* * * [A] purchaser defaulting on an installment land contract may have a claim for equitable relief from the strict terms of the contract. Here, the Cappses' claim for equitable relief was dismissed because the money invested in the property belonged not to them but to American Roofing. But for the fortuity that the funds Cedar Lane received had been stolen, it would have been subject to claim of unjust enrichment by the Cappses. Accordingly, to the extent that the circumstances would establish that Cedar Lane has been unjustly enriched, American Roofing is entitled to be subrogated to the position of defaulting purchasers in order to avoid the unjust enrichment at its expense. *See generally* 1 D. Dobbs, Law of Remedies, *supra*, § 4.3(4), at 604, 606 ("Subrogation may also arise because it is imposed by courts to prevent unjust enrichment.... So the plaintiff is permitted to stand in the shoes of [the party holding the right] and enforce the claim which [that party] had.") * * *.

We recognize that equitable relief, including subrogation, ordinarily does not run against a bona fide purchaser. *See generally* 1 D. Dobbs, Law of Remedies, *supra*, § 4.71. However, the ordinary claim for equitable relief against a person who receives stolen funds is based solely on the fact that the funds were stolen.

In contrast, the claim for unjust enrichment by American Roofing does not arise *solely* because the funds were stolen. Rather, the claim arises out of the default of the installment land contract, which raises separate equitable concerns. The equitable subrogation merely transferred the separately existing claim for unjust enrichment from the Cappses to American Roofing. In effect, the claim for unjust enrichment survives *despite* the fact the funds were stolen. Otherwise, * * * a vendor under an installment land contract receiving stolen funds could always defeat a claim for unjust enrichment, no matter how unjust the enrichment, while other vendors could not.

* * *

Under the circumstances here, an equitable lien in favor of American Roofing may be appropriate to the extent that Cedar Lane was unjustly enriched by the investment of American Roofing's money in the real estate. Accordingly, further proceedings are required so that the trial court can make the necessary factual findings and if appropriate, fashion a suitable remedy.

JUDGE KAPELKE * * * dissenting * * *.

Because I disagree with the conclusion reached by the majority * * *, I respectfully dissent * * *.

The trial court determines that American Roofing was not entitled to relief on its claim of unjust enrichment because Cedar Lane was a bona fide purchaser for value. In my view, the trial court's conclusion is supported by the record and the applicable law. * * *

* * *

NOTES

1. Cedar Lane claimed the defense of a "bona fide purchaser without knowledge that Capps had stolen the money invested in the property." Section 67(1) of the Restatement (Third) of Restitution and Unjust Enrichment says: "A payee without notice takes payment free of a restitution claim to which it would otherwise be subject * * * ". The court in *Cedar Lane* notes that there were two transactions between Cedar Lane and the Cappses, first the sale of the land to the Cappses and second the repossession of the land. Do you see why in the first transaction Cedar Lane was a bona fide purchaser without knowledge of the embezzlement, but in the second, according to the majority, it was not?

2. You may have noticed that equitable restitution cases generally do not discuss the usual equitable prerequisite that a legal remedy be inadequate. Restatement (Third) § 4, quoted in Section 5.A of this Chapter, says that a claimant does not need to prove that a legal remedy is inadequate to obtain relief in restitution, even if the claim arises in equity. The Restatement is following the cases, which for the most part do not discuss the adequacy of the legal remedy. The Restatement (Third) explains that it is often clear that the legal remedy is inadequate, such as in the case of a claimant seeking priority over creditors when the debtor is insolvent and in the case of rescission. *See* Restatement (Third) of Restitution and Unjust Enrichment, Tentative Draft No. 7 (2010), comment *e. See also* George P. Roach, *How Restitution and Unjust Enrichment Can Improve Your Corporate Claim*, 26 Rev. Litig. 265 (2007) (discussing Section 4 of the Restatement). For further discussion of rescission, see *infra* Chapter 7, Section 2.A.

C. DISTINGUISHING LEGAL AND EQUITABLE REMEDIES

Prior to the publication of Restatement (Third) § 4, the issue whether restitution is legal or equitable reached the U.S. Supreme Court. In

Great–West Life & Annuity Insurance Co. v. Knudson, 534 U.S. 204, 122 S.Ct. 708, 151 L.Ed. 2d 635 (2002), the Court was asked to interpret Section 502(a)(3) of the Employee Retirement Income Security Act of 1974 (ERISA), which authorizes "a participant, beneficiary, or fiduciary" to seek an injunction or "obtain other appropriate equitable relief," Section 29 U.S.C. 1132(a)(3). In *Great-West*, Mrs. Knudson, who had been injured in a car accident, was covered by her husband's Health and Welfare Plan for Employees and Dependents, administered by Great–West. Great–West paid approximately $340,000 of her expenses. After she recovered damages from the car manufacturer, most of which were put in a trust fund for her future medical expenses, Great–West, pursuant to the reimbursement provisions of the Plan, sought to recover what it had paid. Noting that the proceeds of the suit were not in Mrs. Knudson's possession, the Court explained:

> Here, petitioners seek, in essence, to impose personal liability on respondents for a contractual obligation to pay money—relief that was not typically available in equity. * * *
>
>   * * *
>
> * * * [P]etitioners argue that their suit is authorized by § 502(a)(3)(B) because they seek restitution, which they characterize as a form of equitable relief. However, not all relief falling under the rubric of restitution is available in equity. In the days of the divided bench, restitution was available in certain cases at law, and in certain others in equity. See, *e.g.*, 1 Dobbs § 1.2, at 11; *id.*, § 4.1(1), at 556; *id.*, § 4.1(3), at 564–565; *id.*, §§ 4.2–4.3, at 570–624; 5 Corbin § 1102, at 550; Muir, *ERISA Remedies: Chimera or Congressional Compromise?*, 81 Iowa L. Rev. 1, 36–37 (1995); Redish, *Seventh Amendment Right to Jury Trial: A Study in the Irrationality of Rational Decision Making*, 70 Nw. U. L. Rev. 486, 528 (1975). Thus, "restitution is a legal remedy when ordered in a case at law and an equitable remedy . . . when ordered in an equity case," and whether it is legal or equitable depends on "the basis for [the plaintiff's] claim" and the nature of the underlying remedies sought. Reich v. Continental Casualty Co., 33 F.3d 754, 756 (CA7 1994) (Posner, J.).
>
> In cases in which the plaintiff "could not assert title or right to possession of particular property, but in which nevertheless he might be able to show just grounds for recovering money to pay for some benefit the defendant had received from him," the plaintiff had a right to restitution at law through an action derived from the common law writ of assumpsit. 1 Dobbs § 4.2(1), at 571. * * * In such cases, the plaintiff's claim was considered legal because he sought "to obtain a judgment imposing a merely personal liability upon the defendant to pay a sum of money." Restatement of Restitution § 160, Comment a, pp. 641–642 (1936). Such claims were viewed essentially as actions at law for breach of contract (whether the contract was actual or implied).

In contrast, a plaintiff could seek restitution in equity, ordinarily in the form of a constructive trust or an equitable lien, where money or property identified as belonging in good conscience to the plaintiff could clearly be traced to particular funds or property in the defendant's possession. See 1 Dobbs § 4.3(1), at 587–588; Restatement of Restitution, *supra*, § 160, Comment a, at 641–642; 1 G. Palmer, Law of Restitution § 1.4, p. 17; § 3.7, p. 262 (1978). A court of equity could then order a defendant to transfer title (in the case of the constructive trust) or to give a security interest (in the case of the equitable lien) to a plaintiff who was, in the eyes of equity, the true owner. But where "the property [sought to be recovered] or its proceeds have been dissipated so that no product remains, [the plaintiff's] claim is only that of a general creditor," and the plaintiff "cannot enforce a constructive trust of or an equitable lien upon other property of the [defendant]." Restatement of Restitution, supra, § 215, Comment a, at 867. Thus, for restitution to lie in equity, the action generally must seek not to impose personal liability on the defendant, but to restore to the plaintiff particular funds or property in the defendant's possession.

Id. at 210–14, 122 S.Ct. at 712–15.

Four years after deciding *Knudson*, the Supreme Court decided an ERISA case with similar facts, except that the $750,000 recovery that the injured husband and wife received from the tortfeasor was in their possession rather than in a trust. Since none of the $750,000 had ever been in the possession of the insurance company, which was seeking reimbursement, the money could not be traced from the insurance company to the bank account of the insured. Therefore, an equitable restitutionary remedy of constructive trust could not be imposed upon the $750,000. The insurance company used another theory.

SEREBOFF v. MID ATLANTIC MEDICAL SERVICES, INC.

Supreme Court of the United States, 2006.
547 U.S. 356, 126 S. Ct. 1869, 164 L. Ed. 2d 612.

ROBERTS, C. J., delivered the opinion for a unanimous Court.

In this case we consider again the circumstances in which a fiduciary under the Employee Retirement Income Security Act of 1974 (ERISA) may sue a beneficiary for reimbursement of medical expenses paid by the ERISA plan, when the beneficiary has recovered for its injuries from a third party.

I

Marlene Sereboff's employer sponsors a health insurance plan administered by respondent Mid Atlantic Medical Services, Inc., and covered by ERISA, 88 Stat. 829, as amended, 29 U.S.C. § 1001 et seq. (2000 ed. and Supp. III). Marlene Sereboff and her husband Joel are beneficiaries under the plan. The plan provides for payment of certain covered medical expenses and contains an "Acts of Third Parties" provision. This provision "applies when [a beneficiary is] sick or injured as a result of the act or omission of another person or party," and requires a beneficiary who "receives benefits" under the plan for such injuries to "reimburse [Mid Atlantic]" for those benefits from "[a]ll recoveries from a third party (whether by lawsuit, settlement, or otherwise)." App. to Pet. for Cert. 38a. The provision states that "[Mid Atlantic's] share of the recovery will not be reduced because [the beneficiary] has not received the full damages claimed, unless [Mid Atlantic] agrees in writing to a reduction." *Ibid.*

The Sereboffs were involved in an automobile accident in California and suffered injuries. Pursuant to the plan's coverage provisions, the plan paid the couple's medical expenses. The Sereboffs filed a tort action in state court against several third parties, seeking compensatory damages for injuries suffered as a result of the accident. Soon after the suit was commenced, Mid Atlantic sent the Sereboffs' attorney a letter asserting a lien on the anticipated proceeds from the suit, for the medical expenses Mid Atlantic paid on the Sereboffs' behalf. * * *

The Sereboffs' tort suit eventually settled for $750,000. Neither the Sereboffs nor their attorney sent any money to Mid Atlantic in satisfaction of its claimed lien which, after Mid Atlantic completed its payments on the Sereboffs' behalf, totaled $74,869.37.

Mid Atlantic filed suit in District Court under § 502(a)(3) of ERISA, 29 U.S.C. § 1132(a)(3), seeking to collect from the Sereboffs the medical expenses it had paid on their behalf. * * *

On the merits, the District Court found in Mid Atlantic's favor * * * and the Fourth Circuit affirmed in relevant part. 407 F.3d 212 (2005). The Fourth Circuit observed that the Courts of Appeals are divided on the question whether § 502(a)(3) authorizes recovery in these circumstances. * * * We granted certiorari to resolve the disagreement. * * *

II

A

A fiduciary may bring a civil action under § 502(a)(3) of ERISA "(A) to enjoin any act or practice which violates any provision of this subchapter or the terms of the plan, or (B) to obtain other appropriate equitable relief (i) to redress such violations or (ii) to enforce any provisions of this subchapter or the terms of the plan." 29 U.S.C. § 1132(a)(3). There is no dispute that Mid Atlantic is a fiduciary under ERISA and that its suit in District Court was to "enforce ... the terms of" the "Acts of Third Parties" provision in the Sereboffs' plan. The only question is whether the relief Mid Atlantic requested from the District Court was "equitable" under § 502(a)(3)(B).

This is not the first time we have had occasion to clarify the scope of the remedial power conferred on district courts by § 502(a)(3)(B). In Mertens v. Hewitt Associates, 508 U.S. 248, 113 S. Ct. 2063, 124 L. Ed. 2d

161 (1993), we construed the provision to authorize only "those categories of relief that were typically available in equity," and thus rejected a claim that we found sought "nothing other than compensatory damages." * * *. We elaborated on this construction of § 502(a)(3)(B) in Great–West Life & Annuity Ins. Co. v. Knudson, 534 U.S. 204, 122 S. Ct. 708, 151 L. Ed. 2d 635 (2002), which involved facts similar to those in this case. Much like the "Acts of Third Parties" provision in the Sereboffs' plan, the plan in *Knudson* reserved " 'a first lien upon any recovery, whether by settlement, judgment or otherwise,' that the beneficiary receives from [a] third party." * * *

In response to the argument that Great–West's claim in *Knudson* was for "restitution" and thus equitable under § 502(a)(3)(B) and *Mertens*, we noted that "not all relief falling under the rubric of restitution [was] available in equity." * * * We explained that one feature of equitable restitution was that it sought to impose a constructive trust or equitable lien on "particular funds or property in the defendant's possession." * * * That requirement was not met in Knudson, because "the funds to which petitioners claim[ed] an entitlement" were not in Knudson's possession, but had instead been placed in a "Special Needs Trust" under California law. * * * The kind of relief Great–West sought, therefore, was "not equitable—the imposition of a constructive trust or equitable lien on particular property—but legal—the imposition of personal liability for the benefits that [Great–West] conferred upon [Knudson]." * * *

That impediment to characterizing the relief in *Knudson* as equitable is not present here. As the Fourth Circuit explained below, in this case Mid Atlantic sought "specifically identifiable" funds that were "within the possession and control of the Sereboffs"—that portion of the tort settlement due Mid Atlantic under the terms of the ERISA plan, set aside and "preserved [in the Sereboffs'] investment accounts." * * * Unlike Great–West, Mid Atlantic did not simply seek "to impose personal liability ... for a contractual obligation to pay money." * * *. It alleged breach of contract and sought money, to be sure, but it sought its recovery through a constructive trust or equitable lien on a specifically identified fund, not from the Sereboffs' assets generally, as would be the case with a contract action at law. ERISA provides for equitable remedies to enforce plan terms, so the fact that the action involves a breach of contract can hardly be enough to prove relief is not equitable; that would make § 502(a)(3)(B)(ii) an empty promise. * * *

B

* * * Our case law from the days of the divided bench confirms that Mid Atlantic's claim is equitable. In Barnes v. Alexander, 232 U.S. 117, 34 S. Ct. 276, 58 L. Ed. 530 (1914), for instance, attorneys Street and Alexander performed work for Barnes, another attorney, who promised them "one-third of the contingent fee" he expected in the case. * * * In upholding their equitable claim to this portion of the fee, Justice Holmes recited "the familiar rul[e] of equity that a contract to convey a specific

object even before it is acquired will make the contractor a trustee as soon as he gets a title to the thing." * * * On the basis of this rule, he concluded that Barnes' undertaking "create[d] a lien" upon the portion of the monetary recovery due Barnes from the client,* * * which Street and Alexander could "follow ... into the hands of ... Barnes," "as soon as [the fund] was identified" * * *.

Much like Barnes' promise to Street and Alexander, the "Acts of Third Parties" provision in the Sereboffs' plan specifically identified a particular fund, distinct from the Sereboffs' general assets—"[a]ll recoveries from a third party (whether by lawsuit, settlement, or otherwise)"— and a particular share of that fund to which Mid Atlantic was entitled— "that portion of the total recovery which is due [Mid Atlantic] for benefits paid." App. to Pet. for Cert. 38a. Like Street and Alexander in *Barnes*, therefore, Mid Atlantic could rely on a "familiar rul[e] of equity" to collect for the medical bills it had paid on the Sereboffs' behalf. * * * This rule allowed them to "follow" a portion of the recovery "into the [Sereboffs'] hands" "as soon as [the settlement fund] was identified," and impose on that portion a constructive trust or equitable lien. * * *

The Sereboffs object that Mid Atlantic's suit would not have satisfied the conditions for "equitable restitution" at common law, particularly the "strict tracing rules" that allegedly accompanied this form of relief. * * * When an equitable lien was imposed as restitutionary relief, it was often the case that an asset belonging to the plaintiff had been improperly acquired by the defendant and exchanged by him for other property. A central requirement of equitable relief in these circumstances, the Sereboffs argue, was the plaintiff 's ability to " 'trac[e]' the asset into its products or substitutes," or "trace his money or property to some particular funds or assets." 1 D. Dobbs, Law of Remedies § 4.3(2), pp 591, n 10, 592 (2d ed. 1993).

But * * * an equitable lien sought as a matter of restitution, and an equitable lien "by agreement," of the sort at issue in *Barnes*, were different species of relief. * * * [S]ee also 1 Dobbs, *supra*, § 4.3(3), at 601; 1 G. Palmer, Law of Restitution § 1.5, p 20 (1978). *Barnes* confirms that no tracing requirement of the sort asserted by the Sereboffs applies to equitable liens by agreement or assignment: The plaintiffs in *Barnes* could not identify an asset they originally possessed, which was improperly acquired and converted into property the defendant held, yet that did not preclude them from securing an equitable lien. To the extent Mid Atlantic's action is proper under *Barnes*, therefore, its asserted inability to satisfy the "strict tracing rules" for "equitable restitution" is of no consequence. * * *

* * *

Under the teaching of *Barnes* and similar cases, Mid Atlantic's action in the District Court properly sought "equitable relief" under § 502(a)(3); the judgment of the Fourth Circuit is affirmed in relevant part.

It is so ordered.

NOTE

In VRG Corp. v. GKN Realty Corp., 135 N.J. 539, 641 A.2d 519 (1994), a real estate broker sought an equitable lien "by agreement." There a real estate broker, VRG Corporation, obtained tenants for a developer, Golden Reef Corporation, with the agreement that commissions would be paid from the rental income. Golden Reef sold the shopping center to GKN Realty Corporation. The sales contract between them contained an indemnification agreement "which stated that Golden Reef was to be responsible for payment of the broker's commissions." *Id.* at 544–45, 641 A.2d at 521. After VRG brought suit against both the Golden Reef and GKN seeking an equitable lien on the rental payments for the amount of the commissions, Golden Reef filed a Chapter 11 bankruptcy petition. A majority of the New Jersey Supreme Court affirmed the trial court's denial of the lien, which had been reversed by the appellate division. The majority said:

> Although VRG presents its claim in the contemporary setting of brokerage services rendered in connection with the development, completion and management of a modern-day shopping center, the remedy that it seeks—the equitable lien—has its roots in the traditions of equity. The equitable principles that gave rise to the remedy continue to shape it.

> An equitable lien is "a right of special nature in a fund and constitutes a charge or encumbrance upon the fund." * * * Generally, "[t]he theory of equitable liens has its ultimate foundation ... in contracts, express or implied, which either deal with or in some manner relate to specific property, such as a tract of land, particular chattels or securities, a certain fund, and the like." 4 John N. Pomeroy, *A Treatise on Equity Jurisprudence* § 1234, at 695 (Spencer W. Symons ed., 5th ed. 1941) * * *. An equitable lien "may be created by express executory contracts relating to specific property then existing, or property to be afterward acquired." * * * "The whole doctrine of equitable liens or mortgages is founded upon that cardinal maxim of equity which regards as done that which has been agreed to be, and ought to have been, done." * * *

> * * * Our courts today * * * recognize that a contract to pay for services out of a designated fund gives the party performing the services an equitable lien on that fund when it comes into existence. * * * Nevertheless, the language purporting to express such an understanding must itself be clear. * * *

> * * *

> Additionally, unjust enrichment may constitute a ground for imposing an equitable lien. * * * An equitable lien may be created "[w]here property of one person can by a proceeding in equity be reached by another as security for a claim on the ground that otherwise the former would be unjustly enriched." *Restatement of Restitution* § 161 (1937) * * *

* * *

III

A.

We consider initially whether under the circumstances an equitable lien arises based on the express or implied intention of the parties. * * *

The trial court held that "there is no equitable lien enforceable against GKN" and entered final judgment dismissing VRG's claim. The court concluded:

> The law is clear; [in order to create an equitable lien] there must be some manifestation of intention to have some particular property subjected to the payment of a debt. However, in this case, I find no intention by GKN or Golden Reef that the rental payments serve as security for the payment of VRG's rental commissions.

The Appellate Division disagreed * * *:

> It is uncontroverted that VRG desired full payment upon the opening of the shopping center but that [Golden Reef] wished to pay part in advance with the remainder coming from the "stream" of rental income. Given these circumstances there can be no question but that it was the rental monies that both parties intended to be the source of payment once the advance was exhausted.

* * *

The contract itself does not express the intent found by the Appellate Division. VRG and GKN did not explicitly agree that the broker's commission would be paid out of the rental income generated by tenants of the shopping mall. * * *

* * *

B.

We also conclude that there is no basis for this Court to impose an equitable lien on the rental incomes grounded in the doctrine of unjust enrichment. Unjust enrichment may sometimes be a factor in creating an equitable lien. * * * *Restatement of Restitution* § 161 (1937) * * *.

There is no dispute that the leases were the fruits of VRG's labor. * * * The difficulty, however, is that VRG seeks to impose an equitable lien not on the property of Golden Reef, *i.e.,* the proceeds from the sale of the shopping center, but the property of GKN, *i.e.,* its rental income from the shopping center. GKN, in paying fair market value for the shopping center, did not receive an unexpected benefit or undeserved windfall because Golden Reef later broke its promise to pay VRG's commissions. * * *

The dissenting judge said:

> * * * After identifying the established grounds for imposition of an equitable lien * * * the Court ignores the equitable roots of the doctrine and declines to recognize a lien in favor of VRG, primarily because the commission agreement does not specifically pledge the rental payments as collateral for VRG's commissions. In my view, the Court disregards the

underlying equities among the parties and diminishes the equitable considerations that prompted chancery courts to create and apply the doctrine of equitable liens.

* * *

The equitable-lien doctrine traces its origins to the difference between remedies in contract actions traditionally provided at common law, which were typically pecuniary and personal, and equitable remedies, which generally were directed against some specific property or fund as contrasted with the right to recover a sum of money out of the defendant's general assets. * * *

The law is well settled that an equitable lien "may be created by an express contract which shows an intention to charge some particular property with a debt or obligation," * * * or it may be created without agreement based on general considerations of right and justice arising from the conduct and relations between the parties. * * *

* * *

* * * Thus, by linking its obligation to pay VRG's brokerage commission with the collection of each installment of monthly rent under each of the leases procured by VRG, Golden Reef effectively acknowledged its intention to pay VRG from the monthly rent collections, although no express pledge of the rents as collateral is set forth in the commission agreement. * * *

* * *

* * * Imposition of an equitable lien against the rental payments due under the shopping-center leases would result in no injustice to GKN. It acquired the shopping center with full notice of VRG's claim and contract rights, and it structured the transaction in a manner that exposed it to the very risk that has transpired: that Golden Reef would fail to pay the balance of commissions and VRG would assert its claim against GKN. That VRG has no express security interest in the rents because its commission agreement did not provide "that the rents were to be pledged or dedicated as security for payment of commissions" * * * is no bar to recognition of an equitable lien. To the contrary, "[e]quitable liens become necessary on account of the absence of similar remedies at law." * * * VRG's claim, in the context of GKN's indefensible failure to assure that Golden Reef paid VRG's commissions as a condition of closing, presents a classic example of the equitable lien doctrine's capacity to provide relief that would not otherwise be available in a suit for money damages.

Id. at 545–70, 641 A.2d at 522–35.

SECTION 6. DEFENDANT'S GAIN MEASURES RECOVERY

The Restatement (Third) of Restitution and Unjust Enrichment compares and contrasts restitution with tort and contract causes of action:

> Restitution is the law of nonconsensual and nonbargained benefits in the same way that torts is the law of nonconsensual and nonlicensed harms. Both subjects deal with the consequences of transactions in which the parties have not specified for themselves what the consequences of their interaction should be. The law of torts identifies those circumstances in which a person is liable for injury inflicted, measuring liability by the extent of the harm; the law of restitution identifies those circumstances in which a person is liable for benefits received, measuring liability by the extent of the benefit.
>
> Restitution is concerned with the receipt of benefits that yield a measurable increase in the recipient's wealth. Subject to that limitation, the benefit that is the basis of a restitution claim may take any form, direct or indirect. It may consist of services as well as property. A saved expenditure or a discharged obligation is no less beneficial to the recipient than a direct transfer.*

Restatement (Third) of Restitution and Unjust Enrichment, § 1, comment *d*, Tentative Draft No. 7 (2010).

Professor Dobbs describes the difference between recovery in tort and restitution:

> Sometimes a restitutionary recovery is more desirable for the plaintiff than a recovery of damages. Suppose the defendant steals the plaintiff's watch, the value of which was admittedly only $10. The defendant is able to sell the watch for more than its value, say $20. The plaintiff's *loss* is a watch valued at $10 and his *damages* recovery measured by loss is $10. But the defendant's *gain* is $20 and the plaintiff's *restitutionary* recovery measured by that gain is $20. In this example, the plaintiff is entitled to restitution. Not all restitution is in money as it is in the watch example. The watch example shows, however, that when restitution is made in money, the restitution remedy can yield results quite different from the money remedy called damages.

Dan B. Dobbs, Law of Remedies (2d ed. 1993); *see also* Daniel Friedmann, *Restitution for Wrongs: The Measure of Recovery*, 79 Tex. L. Rev. 1879 (2001) (reviewing various measurements of recovery and suggesting factors for consideration).

Professor Dobbs describes a thief who is the recipient of the $20. The amount of a recipient's gain that is considered unjust varies with the degree of the recipient's fault, ranging from no fault, as in the case of a recipient who is the beneficiary of a claimant's mistaken payment, to conscious wrongdoing, as in the case of Professor Dobbs' thief. While one goal of restitution is to deprive wrongdoers of their ill-gotten gains, that goal is not appropriate when the recipient is innocent. Thus the Restatement (Third) would limit the claimant's recovery against an innocent recipient to the amount of the claimant's loss. Restatement (Third) of

---

* Reprinted with permission of the American Law Institute.

Restitution and Unjust Enrichment at § 49 (3) and comment *b*, Tentative Draft No. 5 (2007).

OLWELL v. NYE & NISSEN CO.

Supreme Court of Washington, 1946.
26 Wash.2d 282, 173 P.2d 652.

MALLERY, JUSTICE.

On May 6, 1940, plaintiff, E.L. Olwell, sold and transferred to the defendant corporation his one-half interest in Puget Sound Egg Packers, a Washington corporation having its principal place of business in Tacoma. By the terms of the agreement, the plaintiff was to retain full ownership in an "Eggsact" egg-washing machine, formerly used by Puget Sound Egg Packers. The defendant promised to make it available for delivery to the plaintiff on or before June 15, 1940. It appears that the plaintiff arranged for and had the machine stored in a space adjacent to the premises occupied by the defendant but not covered by its lease. Due to the scarcity of labor immediately after the outbreak of the war, defendant's treasurer, without the knowledge or consent of the plaintiff, ordered the egg washer taken out of storage. The machine was put into operation by defendant on May 31, 1941, and thereafter for a period of three years was used approximately one day a week in the regular course of the defendant's business. Plaintiff first discovered this use in January or February of 1945 when he happened to be at the plant on business and heard the machine operating. Thereupon plaintiff offered to sell the machine to defendant for $600 or half of its original cost in 1929. A counter offer of $50 was refused and approximately one month later this action was commenced to recover the reasonable value of defendant's use of the machine, and praying for $25 per month from the commencement of the unauthorized use until the time of trial. * * * The court entered judgment for plaintiff in the amount of $10 per week for the period of 156 weeks covered by the statute of limitations, or $1,560, and gave the plaintiff his costs.

Defendant has appealed to this court assigning error upon the judgment, upon the trial of the cause on the theory of unjust enrichment, upon the amount of damages, and upon the court's refusal to make a finding as to the value of the machine and in refusing to consider such value in measuring damages. The theory of the respondent was that the tort of conversion could be "waived" and suit brought in quasi-contract, upon a contract implied in law, to recover, as restitution, the profits which inured to appellant as a result of its wrongful use of the machine. With this the trial court agreed and in its findings of facts found that the use of the machine "resulted in a benefit to the users, in that said use saves the users approximately $1.43 per hour of use as against the expense which would be incurred were eggs to be washed by hand; that said machine was used by Puget Sound Egg Packers and defendant, on an average of one day per week from May of 1941, until February of 1945 at an average saving of $10.00 per each day of use."

In substance, the argument presented by the assignments of error is that the principle of unjust enrichment, or quasi-contract, is not of universal application, but is imposed only in exceptional cases because of special facts and circumstances and in favor of particular persons; that respondent had an adequate remedy in an action at law for replevin or claim and delivery; that any damages awarded to the plaintiff should be based upon the use or rental value of the machine and should bear some reasonable relation to its market value. Appellant therefore contends that the amount of the judgment is excessive.

It is uniformly held that in cases where the defendant *tortfeasor* has benefited by his wrong, the plaintiff may elect to "waive the tort" and bring an action in assumpsit for restitution. Such an action arises out of a duty imposed by law devolving upon the defendant to repay an unjust and unmerited enrichment. Woodward, The Law of Quasi–Contracts, § 272(2), p. 439; Keener on Quasi–Contracts, p. 160. *See also* Professor Corbin's articles, *Waiver of Tort and Suit in Assumpsit*, 19 Yale Law Journal, p. 221, and *Quasi-Contractual Obligations*, 21 Yale Law Journal, p. 533.

It is clear that the saving in labor cost which appellant derived from its use of respondent's machine constituted a benefit.

According to the Restatement of Restitution, § 1(b), p. 12,

> A person confers a benefit upon another if he gives to the other possession of or some other interest in money, land, chattels, or choses in action, performs services beneficial to or at the request of the other, satisfies a debt or a duty of the other, or in any way adds to the other's security or advantage. *He confers a benefit not only where he adds to the property of another, but also where he* saves the other from expense or loss. The word "benefit", therefore denotes any form of advantage. (Italics ours.)

It is also necessary to show that while appellant benefited from its use of the egg-washing machine, respondent thereby incurred a loss. It is argued by appellant that since the machine was put into storage by respondent, who had no present use for it, and for a period of almost three years did not know that appellant was operating it and since it was not injured by its operation and the appellant never adversely claimed any title to it, nor contested respondent's right of repossession upon the latter's discovery of the wrongful operation, that the respondent was not damaged because he is as well off as if the machine had not been used by appellant.

The very essence of the nature of property is the right to its exclusive use. Without it, no beneficial right remains. However plausible, the appellant cannot be heard to say that his wrongful invasion of the respondent's property right to exclusive use is not a loss compensable in law. To hold otherwise would be subversive of all property rights since his use was admittedly wrongful and without claim of right. The theory of unjust enrichment is applicable in such a case.

We agree with appellant that respondent could have elected a "common garden variety of action," as he calls it, for the recovery of damages. It is also true that except where provided for by statute, punitive damages are not allowed, the basic measure for the recovery of damages in this state being compensation. If, then, respondent had been *limited* to redress *in tort* for damages, as appellant contends, the court below would be in error in refusing to make a finding as to the value of the machine. In such case the award of damages must bear a reasonable relation to the value of the property. * * *

But respondent here had an election. He chose rather to waive his right of action *in tort* and to sue *in assumpsit* on the implied contract. Having so elected, he is entitled to the measure of restoration which accompanies the remedy.

> Actions for restitution have for their primary purpose taking from the defendant and restoring to the plaintiff something to which the plaintiff is entitled, or if this is not done, causing the defendant to pay the plaintiff an amount which will restore the plaintiff to the position in which he was before the defendant received the benefit. If the value of what was received and what was lost were always equal, there would be no substantial problem as to the amount of recovery, since actions of restitution are not punitive. In fact, however, the plaintiff frequently has lost more than the defendant has gained, and sometimes the defendant has gained more than the plaintiff has lost.

> In such cases the measure of restitution is determined with reference to the tortiousness of the defendant's conduct or the negligence or other fault of one or both of the parties in creating the situation giving rise to the right to restitution. If the defendant was tortious in his acquisition of the benefit, he is required to pay for what the other has lost, although that is more than the recipient benefited. *If he was consciously tortious in acquiring the benefit, he is also deprived of any profit derived from his subsequent dealing with it.* If he was no more at fault than the claimant, he is not required to pay for losses in excess of benefit received by him and he is permitted to retain gains which result from his dealing with the property. (Italics ours.)

Restatement of Restitution, pp. 595, 596. Respondent may recover the profit derived by the appellant from the use of the machine.

Respondent has prayed "on his first cause of action for the sum of $25.00 per month from the time defendant first commenced to use said machine subsequent to May 1940 (1941) until present time." In computing judgment, the court below computed recovery on the basis of $10 per week [for a period of 156 weeks, or $1,560]. This makes the judgment excessive since it cannot exceed the amount prayed for.

* * *

We therefore direct the trial court to reduce the judgment, based upon the prayer of the complaint, to $25 per month for thirty-six months, or $900.

The judgment as modified is affirmed. * * *

SCRUSHY v. TUCKER

Supreme Court of Alabama, 2006.
955 So. 2d 988.

LYONS, JUSTICE.

Richard M. Scrushy, the defendant in this case, appealed from a partial summary judgment entered in favor of the plaintiff, Wade Tucker, concerning bonuses paid by HealthSouth Corporation to Scrushy during the years 1997 through 2002. * * *

I. FACTUAL BACKGROUND AND PROCEDURAL HISTORY

We detailed the factual background and procedural history of this case in *Scrushy I*:

"Wade Tucker, a shareholder of HealthSouth Corporation, filed a shareholder's derivative lawsuit on behalf of HealthSouth against Scrushy, the former chief executive officer for HealthSouth, and numerous other defendants. This case is one of three civil actions filed as a result of alleged fraudulent accounting practices at HealthSouth. * * * In addition, criminal charges were brought against Scrushy in the same federal court. * * * After a lengthy trial, Scrushy was acquitted of the criminal charges against him.

"Tucker's complaint alleges that Scrushy and others perpetrated an accounting fraud against HealthSouth, resulting in massive financial losses by HealthSouth and ultimately its shareholders. Tucker's complaint alleges claims of insider open-market trading, fraud, breach of fiduciary duty by corporate directors, professional negligence by auditors, aiding and abetting or civil conspiracy by an investment banking firm, and breach of contract. Tucker's complaint also alleges that Scrushy was unjustly enriched when he accepted bonuses as a result of overvalued financial statements that misstated Health-South's net income, which, Tucker alleges, was in violation of a contract between HealthSouth and Scrushy. As to the claim of unjust enrichment, Tucker's complaint alleges, in pertinent part, as follows:

" '34. Beginning in or about January 1997, and continuing into March 2003, defendants Scrushy [and others] knowingly and willfully conspired and agreed with each other, to commit the wrongdoing alleged herein, specifically, to misrepresent and false-ly inflate earnings and HealthSouth's true financial condition. Scrushy [and other defendants] engaged in this fraud, misrepre-sentation and manipulation of income and earnings of Health-South to enrich themselves by artificially inflating HealthSouth's publicly reported earnings and earnings per share an[d] by fraudulently enhancing its reported financial condition.

" '35.   Since 1999, Scrushy [and other defendants] overstated HealthSouth's earnings by at least $1.4 Billion. * * * When HealthSouth's earnings fell short of estimates, Scrushy directed HealthSouth's accounting personnel ... to "fix it" by artificially inflating the company's earnings to match Wall Street expectations.

" '36.   Scrushy [and other defendants] also created false journal entries to HealthSouth's income statement and balance sheet accounts....

* * *

" '120.   What is more, incentive compensation to Scrushy [and other defendants] in executive management, is based on HealthSouth's reported financial results. As these results are and were false, Scrushy [and the others] ... benefitted improperly and were unjustly enriched to the extent they received incentive compensation based on exaggerated revenues and profits.

" ' ....

" 'COUNT VII

" 'Unjust Enrichment

" '188.   Plaintiff realleges and incorporates by reference the allegations in the preceding paragraphs 1 through 187 as though fully set out herein.

" '189.   As a result of the transactions set out herein, all Individual Defendants [and other defendants] held money which, in equity and good conscience and under law, belongs to HealthSouth. Defendants have unjustly enriched themselves by breaches of the duty not to engage in self-dealing and interested transactions as pled herein. All such monies in the hands of defendants are due to be repaid to and for the benefit of HealthSouth.'

"* * * After Scrushy was acquitted of the criminal charges, Tucker moved for a partial summary judgment in this case, seeking only restitution from Scrushy of bonuses he received from 1996 to 2002. * * *

* * *

"With regard to the bonuses paid to Scrushy in 1996, the trial court held that because HealthSouth earned positive net income in 1996 issues of material fact precluded a summary judgment as to the 1996 bonuses. With regard to the bonuses paid to Scrushy in 1997–2002, however, the trial court concluded as follows:

" 'As to all bonuses paid to Defendant Scrushy for the years 1997 through 2002 inclusive, HealthSouth incurred actual losses and no bonus pool existed out of which the bonuses for these years could properly have been paid to Scrushy. Scrushy was unjustly enriched by these payments to the detriment of Health-South and to allow Scrushy to retain the benefit of these payments would be unconscionable. These payments must be returned and Plaintiff Tucker is entitled to summary judgment for the bonuses paid to Scrushy for the years 1997 through 2002 inclusive.'

"The trial court entered a total judgment against Scrushy in the amount of $47,828,106, representing the bonuses paid for the years 1997–2002, plus prejudgment interest. * * * Scrushy appealed * * *."

955 So.2d at 991–95.

* * *

III.   ANALYSIS
* * *

D.   Unjust Enrichment

Scrushy next argues that Tucker did not establish the necessary elements to prove unjust enrichment. Specifically, he argues that Tucker did not prove that it would be unconscionable for Scrushy to keep the bonuses he earned from 1997 through 2002 * * * because, Scrushy says, the judgment did not "balance the equities," did not consider Scrushy's "detrimental reliance," and did not account for the absence of any evidence indicating unconscionability. Scrushy contends that he relied to his detriment on the finality of the bonus compensation when he paid taxes on that income, when he made substantial charitable contributions based on that income, and when he otherwise incurred expenses that he cannot now retrieve. In effect, he says, the trial court has ordered him to forfeit those bonuses, and he cites cases from both Alabama and Delaware holding that equity "abhors a forfeiture."[2]

* * *

The Supreme Court of Delaware discussed the theory of unjust enrichment as follows:

"For a court to order restitution it must first find the defendant was unjustly enriched at the expense of the plaintiff. 'Unjust enrichment is defined as "the unjust retention of a benefit to the loss of another, or the retention of money or property of another against the

---

2. Scrushy relies on the affidavit of Dr. Wayne Guay, whom he describes in his brief as "a leading expert on executive compensation." Dr. Guay offered in his affidavit his opinion that many public corporations award bonus compensation even when the corporation's net income is negative. Dr. Guay's opinion, however, does not take into consideration HealthSouth's unequivocal statement in its Form 14A disclosure that "[n]o bonuses are payable unless annual net income exceeds budgeted net income." Other corporations may award bonuses in the face of negative net income, but that was clearly not HealthSouth's practice.

fundamental principles of justice or equity and good conscience." '
* * * To obtain restitution, the plaintiffs were required to show that
the defendants were unjustly enriched, that the defendants secured a
benefit, and that it would be unconscionable to allow them to retain
that benefit. Restitution is permitted even when the defendant retaining the benefit is not a wrongdoer. * * *

" 'Restitution serves to "deprive the defendant of benefits that in
equity and good conscience he ought not to keep, even though he may
have received those benefits honestly in the first instance, and even
though the plaintiff may have suffered no demonstrable losses." '
* * *"

Schock v. Nash, 732 A.2d 217, 232–33 (Del. 1999) (footnotes omitted;
bracketed cites added).

The law in Alabama concerning unjust enrichment is substantially
the same:

"To prevail on a claim of unjust enrichment, the plaintiff must show
that the 'defendant holds money which, *in equity and good conscience*,
belongs to the plaintiff or holds money which was improperly paid to
defendant because of *mistake or fraud*.' * * * 'The doctrine of unjust
enrichment is an old *equitable* remedy permitting the court in equity
and good conscience to disallow one to be unjustly enriched at the
expense of another.' * * *"

* * *

Avis Rent A Car Sys., Inc. v. Heilman, 876 So. 2d 1111, 1122–23 (Ala.
2003).

We conclude that, under the law of either Delaware or Alabama,
Scrushy was unjustly enriched by the payment of the bonuses, which were
the result of the vast accounting fraud perpetrated upon HealthSouth and
its shareholders, and that equity and good conscience require restitution
in the form of repayment of those bonuses. Even though for purposes of
the judgment the parties stipulated that Scrushy did not participate in
and is not responsible for any of the criminal activities that resulted in the
falsification of the financial statements, the trial court noted in its
judgment that Scrushy does not dispute that the financial information
originally filed by HealthSouth was inaccurate and unreliable. As between
Scrushy and HealthSouth, it would be unconscionable to allow Scrushy to
retain millions of dollars awarded to him in the form of bonuses at the
expense of the corporation he served as chief executive officer and its
shareholders.

E.   Equity

Finally, Scrushy argues that the trial court erred in entering what he
describes as an "inequitable order" requiring him to repay funds he never
received. He argues that it was inequitable for the trial court to order him
to repay the gross amount of the bonuses awarded rather than the net

after-tax amount he received. Equitable principles of unjust enrichment, he argues, can require him to repay only the amount he "unjustly" received, and because he never "received" the portion of the bonuses allocated to taxes, he should not be compelled to return that portion of the bonuses.

We find no merit to this argument. Scrushy was credited with the gross amount, and HealthSouth was concomitantly deprived of the amount paid to Scrushy in bonuses, regardless of whether Scrushy paid a certain percentage of those funds in taxes. Whether Scrushy can obtain a refund of the taxes paid upon his restitution of the bonuses is a matter between Scrushy and the taxing authorities.

IV. Conclusion

We conclude that the trial court properly entered the partial summary judgment as to the bonuses awarded to Scrushy for the years 1997–2002. We therefore affirm that judgment.

Note

The recovery of benefits can be sought in contexts other than common law. For an interesting article that discusses "clawbacks," which the authors define as "a theory for recovering benefits that have been conferred under a claim of right," in the context of the Madoff hedge fund fraud and compensation contracts for executives of companies in financial crisis, see Miriam A. Cherry and Jarrod Wong, *Clawbacks: Prospective Contract Measures in an Era of Excessive Executive Compensation and Ponzi Schemes*, 94 Minn. L. Rev. 368 (2009). The authors propose that clawback provisions be included in contracts and amendments to securities laws.

MASSACHUSETTS EYE AND EAR INFIRMARY v. QLT PHOTOTHERAPEUTICS, INC.

United States Court of Appeals for the First Circuit, 2009.
552 F.3d 47.

Before HOWARD, BALDOCK and SELYA, CIRCUIT JUDGES.

HOWARD, CIRCUIT JUDGE. These appeals require us to grapple with the metes and bounds of Massachusetts unjust enrichment and restitution law. Like many such cases, the present case involves one party's conferral of a valuable benefit during ongoing contract negotiations, followed by an irreparable breach in the bargaining process. What makes this case unusual is that its subject matter—the development of a blockbuster pharmaceutical—poses challenges in valuing the benefit conferred, and potentially implicates federal patent law. Defendant QLT Phototherapeutics, Inc. ("QLT") appeals a jury finding that it was unjustly enriched because plaintiff Massachusetts Eye and Ear Infirmary ("MEEI") conferred on QLT several benefits during the course of the development of Visudyne, a successful (and highly profitable) treatment for age-related macular degeneration ("AMD"), a leading cause of adult blindness.

* * * The jury awarded MEEI a running royalty of 3.01% of global net Visudyne sales as damages. QLT prosecutes its ensuing appeal with great vigor. * * *

* * *

Visudyne traces its ancestry to a field of cow parsley located on a remote island north of Vancouver, Canada. Dr. Julia Levy,[3] an immunologist at the University of British Columbia, learned by happenstance that her children's burn-like lesions resulted from contact with a photosensitizer chemical found in cow parsley that, when activated by light, literally burned them. This led Dr. Levy to orient her research to photodynamic therapy ("PDT"), which uses light to activate photosensitizer compounds. Photodynamic therapy works by shining light on the photosensitizer, which energizes the photosensitizer and transforms it into a toxic chemical.

Successful exploitation of this light-induced toxicity for therapeutic purposes requires "targeting" the photosensitizer so that it kills only unwanted cells. Dr. Levy eventually helped develop a proprietary photosensitizer called benzoporphyrin derivative monoacid ("BPD"), which had a unique ability to deliver itself to new blood vessels immediately upon injection. * * * QLT eventually acquired the sole right to license BPD from the University of British Columbia. In exchange for this patent right, QLT agreed to pay a royalty of 2% of net sales.

Although BPD held promise, it was, for a time, a drug in search of a disease. Dr. Levy initially hoped to develop the drug as a cancer treatment. This was the state of affairs when Dr. Levy first made contact with researchers at Massachusetts General Hospital ("MGH"), and later, MEEI.

Dr. Levy's contacts at MGH, Drs. Tayyaba Hassan, Reginald Birngruber and Ursula Schmidt–Erfurth, collaborated on using photodynamic therapy to close blood vessels initially in chick embryos, and later, in rabbit eyes. In due course, this group experimented with a variety of compounds for this purpose, including BPD, which was obtained from QLT.

Eventually, Dr. Schmidt–Erfurth brought the BPD compound to the attention of MEEI. Dr. Schmidt–Erfurth proposed studying the use of BPD to treat intraocular tumors and, at the suggestion of Dr. Evangelos Gragoudas, to close normal choroidal blood vessels without damaging the retina.

Independently, Dr. Gragoudas hired Dr. Joan Miller, a former MEEI fellow, to investigate whether BPD could be used to treat AMD * * *. The condition takes two forms: "dry" and "wet." Although the wet form accounts for only 10% of all occurrences of AMD, it leads to the condition known as either choroidal neovasculature ("CNV") or neovasculature, which causes 90% of AMD-related vision loss. CNV is the result of the

---

3. Dr. Julia Levy was a founder of QLT * * *.

proliferation of unwanted blood vessels in the choroid. Thus, closing such vessels would effectively palliate AMD.

Dr. Miller conducted her experiments using primate eyes, which, like human eyes, have retinas and retinal vessels. The rabbit eyes that Dr. Schmidt–Erfurth used to conduct her experiments lacked retinal vessels. This was a consequential distinction: in the early 1990s, the prevailing view held that the most cogent way to prove that PDT could be used to treat AMD was to show that PDT could close the abnormal choroidal vessels that cause CNV without damaging the underlying, healthy retinal vessels. This demonstration was important because damage to normal retinal vessels would lead to a loss of vision. Consequently, Dr. Schmidt–Erfurth's experiments on rabbit eyes, which lack such normal vessels, could not predict PDT's suitability for use in treating AMD.

* * * QLT did not provide any funding for Dr. Miller's initial research. Dr. Miller's BPD-based experiments proved successful. * * * As a result of these experiments, a QLT representative observed that BPD had finally found its disease: it could be used to treat age-related macular degeneration.

Energized by Dr. Miller's findings, QLT executed a preclinical agreement, in which it agreed to fund Dr. Miller's further investigations of BPD. In addition, QLT and Dr. Miller signed confidential disclosure agreements.

Dr. Miller's additional experiments were successful * * *. In the year 2000, after several years of clinical trials in relation to which Dr. Miller drafted the clinical protocols and served as principal investigator, the FDA approved the BPD-based process for treating age-related macular degeneration. This treatment is marketed as Visudyne.

* * *

Long before final FDA approval, the parties recognized the potential for Visudyne's commercial exploitation. In November 1993, Dr. Ed Levy approached CIBA Vision (sometimes "CIBA")[5], a Swiss company, about a partnership for manufacturing and distributing what became Visudyne. To entice CIBA Vision, Dr. Ed Levy provided it with some of Dr. Miller's confidential research.[6] This disclosure violated * * * confidentiality agreements between Dr. Miller and QLT, which permitted QLT access to Dr. Miller's research results but explicitly prohibited QLT from disclosing those results to third parties.[7] Dr. Ed Levy made several other unauthorized disclosures. For example, in a January 1994 meeting with CIBA,

---

5. CIBA Vision is now known as Novartis Opthalmics, Inc., but for the sake of simplicity we continue to refer to CIBA Vision as a separate entity.

6. Dr. Ed Levy, the husband of Dr. Julia Levy, was another senior officer of QLT. * * *

7. As part of the Confidential Disclosure Agreement, QLT promised "not to use the Confidential Information for any purpose other than the evaluation of Products under the terms of the Agreement" and "to maintain Confidential Information in confidence." The parties further agreed that "misuse or improper disclosure of Confidential Information would irreparably harm the business of the disclosing party or that party's affiliates." * * *

QLT disclosed additional treatment parameters gleaned from Dr. Miller's work. Such disclosures served their intended purpose: they whetted CIBA's appetite.

QLT further determined that it would be advantageous to have Dr. Miller present her research to CIBA Vision. Consequently, QLT approached Dr. Miller and requested that she make such a presentation. Dr. Miller was reticent about disclosing her results because QLT and MEEI had not yet negotiated a licensing arrangement for her treatment, but Dr. Ed Levy promised Dr. Miller that QLT would enter into a licensing agreement with MEEI. In early March of 1994, QLT confirmed in writing its promise to license Dr. Miller's treatment from MEEI. Armed with these assurances, Dr. Miller agreed to make a presentation of her confidential work to CIBA Vision. * * *

Pleased with Dr. Miller's presentation, CIBA Vision expressed a desire to enter into a partnership with QLT. * * *

* * *

* * * [I]n February 1995, QLT signed a definitive agreement with CIBA Vision.

* * *

* * * In Massachusetts, a claim for unjust enrichment does not require consideration, but there must be "unjust enrichment of one party and unjust detriment to another party." * * * [S]ee also 26 Samuel Williston & Richard A. Lord, *A Treatise on the Law of Contracts* § 68:5 (4th ed. 1993) (establishing that unjust enrichment requires: (1) a benefit conferred upon the defendant by the plaintiff; (2) an appreciation or knowledge by the defendant of the benefit; and (3) acceptance or retention by the defendant of the benefit under the circumstances would be inequitable without payment for its value) * * *.

Furthermore, Massachusetts courts have recognized that misuse of confidential information may lead to unjust enrichment. Under Massachusetts law, "a constructive trust is ... imposed to avoid unjust enrichment of one party at the expense of the other where information confidentially given or acquired was used to the advantage of the recipient at the expense of the one who disclosed the information." * * * In short, we previously have found that in order for MEEI to show unjust enrichment based on unauthorized disclosure of confidential information, MEEI had to prove that QLT used MEEI's confidential information at MEEI's expense.

* * *

The evidence was sufficient for the jury to find that each element of unjust enrichment was satisfied. * * * This evidence supported the jury's finding that Dr. Miller's efforts constituted a benefit to QLT (which QLT sought and appreciated). The jury could rationally infer that, if QLT did not value either the ability to disclose Dr. Miller's confidential research results or the credibility that Dr. Miller (and MEEI) gave QLT in its overtures to CIBA Vision, QLT would not have made so many promises to pay fair compensation to MEEI. Accordingly, the jury concluded that QLT obtained a significant benefit from the early disclosure of Dr. Miller's confidential information and from Dr. Miller's active involvement in the courtship of CIBA Vision, without which QLT's collaboration with CIBA Vision may not have borne fruit. Finally, the evidence permitted a finding that the benefit and detriment were incurred in a context in which MEEI expected compensation.

Despite QLT's arguments to the contrary, we find no legal impediment to this conclusion. *See* 41 C.J.S. *Implied Contracts* § 9 ("A 'benefit' for purposes of an unjust enrichment claim is any form of advantage that has a measurable value, including the advantage of being saved from an expense or loss."); *Anisgard v. Bray*, 11 Mass. App. Ct. 726, 419 N.E.2d 315, 318 (Mass. App. Ct. 1981) (finding the conferral of a benefit (and ultimately unjust enrichment) where plaintiff contributed substantially to a venture and, after inconclusive contract negotiations, defendants used plaintiff's contributions without compensation) * * *

QLT argues that the evidence adduced at trial was legally insufficient to permit the jury to find any causal relationship between the disclosure of confidential information and QLT's eventual Visudyne sales. To support this proposition, QLT primarily relies on *Demoulas v. Demoulas Super Mkts.*, 677 N.E.2d 159, 196, 424 Mass. 501 (Mass. 1997). That case is inapposite. * * * The court held as a matter of law that one who is unjustly enriched due to the diversion of corporate opportunities and/or the breach of a fiduciary duty is entitled to a credit for amounts that she personally invests. * * * Thus, the most that *Demoulas* can stand for here is that QLT should have had the opportunity to prove that its Visudyne profits did not derive entirely or even partially from the disclosure of MEEI's confidential information. * * * [T]he jury awarded MEEI only a portion of the damages that it sought, properly leaving the remainder of the profits for QLT. *Demoulas* does not require a contrary result.

* * *

The parties agree that a royalty rate based on the net sales of Visudyne is the appropriate measure of QLT's unjust enrichment. * * * Unfortunately, the parties agree on little else. Consequently, we return to the basics of unjust enrichment.

In this case, the appropriate measure of damages should be an approximation of the value of the benefit MEEI conferred on QLT. * * *. When a defendant has received a benefit that is significantly greater than the plaintiff's loss and justice so requires, "the defendant may be under a duty to give the plaintiff the amount by which he has been enriched." Restatement of Restitution § 1 cmt. e. The passage of time has not dulled this conception; the tentative draft of the Restatement (Third) of Restitution advocates the same result: a party's recovery based on an indefinite agreement is "measured solely by the value of the claimant's performance to the defendant." Restatement (Third) of Restitution and Unjust Enrichment § 31 cmt. h (T.D. No. 3, 2004).

* * *

Courts that have considered the issue have permitted disgorgement of the malefactor's profits as a remedy for unjust enrichment in patent disputes. *See, e.g., Univ. of Colo. Found., Inc. v. Am. Cyanamid Co.*, 342 F.3d 1298, 1311–13 (Fed. Cir. 2003) (applying Colorado law).[23] Although Massachusetts courts have not squarely considered the availability of profit disgorgement in an unjust enrichment action, we think it likely that they would approve of a disgorgement remedy in the present unjust enrichment context. *See Demoulas*, 677 N.E.2d at 196 (noting that disgorgement is necessary to prevent unjust enrichment in breach of fiduciary duty context).

With this case law in mind, we evaluate the jury's damage award. The jury heard all of the evidence supporting the conferral of both the confidential information and the patent application benefits. In addition, each side presented damages experts to help the jury understand how to express the benefits conferred as an ongoing royalty. * * *

MEEI's expert provided important background evidence showing reasonable royalties in the pharmaceutical industry, and further described other QLT and Novartis licenses to give the jury a background as to the outer limits of a license that MEEI could have negotiated from QLT. In addition, MEEI's damages expert testified that a reasonable royalty could be as high as 13.5%, which would constitute approximately 50% of QLT's net profits from the sale of Visudyne. * * *

QLT also presented evidence from its own damages expert. QLT's expert attempted to discredit the surveys upon which MEEI's expert relied. Similarly, QLT's expert opined that a fair royalty to MEEI could not exceed the royalty paid for the use of BPD, which was 2%. Furthermore, QLT's expert posited that the jury should consider the fact that Dr. Julia Levy was a co-inventor and had the right to practice the invention independently. QLT's expert therefore believed that QLT did not have to pay any royalties, and [that a 0.5% royalty negotiated with another entity] was not only fair, but munificent.

From this competing testimony, the jury had enough information to establish an approximate valuation of the benefit MEEI conferred on QLT. The damages experts ensured that the jury engaged in an effort to determine a reasonable approximation of the value of the benefits MEEI conferred on QLT. It is true that MEEI's expert referred to QLT's profits from the sale of Visudyne, but this was in no way inconsistent with our holding in Incase[, Inc. v. Timex Corp., 488 F.3d 46 (1st Cir. 2007)]. After all, QLT's profits served as a reasonable approximation of the value of the

---

23. Professor Laycock * * * has identified a trend among courts to permit disgorgement of profits in unjust enrichment cases. See Douglas Laycock, The Scope and Significance of Restitution, 67 Tex. L. Rev. 1277, 1288–89 (1989).

benefit conferred at a particularly critical time in the life cycle of a nascent biotechnology company with a product (BPD) in search of an application. We further note—as the parties agreed at trial—that royalty rates based on sales are the preferred method to express the value conferred in the pharmaceutical context. Given these considerations, we cannot conclude that the damages evidence was insufficient as a matter of law to permit a reasonable approximation of the value of the benefit conferred on QLT.

Nor do we fault the amount of the award. The jury grappled with highly complex, voluminous evidence and reached a reasonable conclusion. It rejected MEEI's out-sized valuation of its own contributions to Visudyne, while simultaneously rejecting QLT's cramped view. The trial court agreed, noting that it would have awarded a slightly higher royalty rate, but also noting its belief that the jury's rate was within the realm of reasonability * * * We see no reason to disturb the jury's findings.

* * *

For the reasons described above, the district court judgment as to liability and damages is **affirmed** in all respects. * * *

SECTION 7. DEFENSES TO CLAIMS IN UNJUST ENRICHMENT

A. VOLUNTEERS OR OFFICIOUS INTERMEDDLERS

There are a number of defenses in restitution. Some are identified in Chapter 8 of the Restatement (Third) of Restitution and Unjust Enrichment, Tentative Draft No. 7 (2010). Some exist as limitations to what is unjust. *See id.*, Section 62, comment *a*. The defense of a "bona fide purchaser for value" was discussed in *Cedar Lane Investments* in Section 5.B of this Chapter. Both Scrushy and QLT in the two previous cases tried, unsuccessfully, to raise some standard defenses. Scrushy argued that he relied on his bonuses "when he paid taxes on that income, when he made substantial charitable contributions based on that income, and when he otherwise incurred expenses that he cannot now retrieve." His "change of position" defense was unsuccessful. QLT argued that it should have an opportunity to prove that its "profits did not derive entirely or even partially from its wrongdoing." Since the jury awarded less than MEEI had sought, QLT did not lose all of the "fruit of its labors." This section discusses a few of the defenses in more detail.

HI–LAND APARTMENTS, INC. v. CITY OF HILLSBORO

Court of Appeals of Ohio, Fourth District, 1994.
95 Ohio App.3d 305, 642 N.E.2d 421.

PETER B. ABELE, JUDGE.

This is an appeal from a judgment entered by the Highland County Court of Common Pleas finding the city of Hillsboro, defendant below and appellant herein, responsible for $4,072.15 voluntarily expended by Hi-Land Apartments, Inc., Jack A. Bennington, and Charlene Bennington, plaintiffs below and appellees herein, for stone and surfacing material used on the alley known as "North Glenn Street" in the city of Hillsboro, and finding appellant responsible for $3,280.86 voluntarily expended by appellees for snow removal, grading, gravel surfacing, and pothole repair in the alley.

* * *

The trial court found [that the city of Hillsboro] accepted "North Glenn Street" as an alley and thereby assumed the duty of maintaining it as an alley. The trial court further found that because [the city of Hillsboro] failed to maintain the alley in a reasonable manner, [Hi-Land Apartments and the Benningtons] should be reimbursed for their efforts to maintain the alley in a reasonable manner. The trial court held as follows:

> It is therefore the decision of the Court that the city of Hillsboro had an obligation to maintain said North Glenn Street but had failed to do so in a reasonable manner and had failed to provide stone and surface material, grading, pothole repair and snow removal and being under an obligation therefore, it is further the decision of the Court that the materials and services provided by the plaintiff as stated aforesaid in the sum of $7353.01 are a fair and reasonable amount and were reasonably necessary and that the plaintiff should recover said sum from the city of Hillsboro.

* * *

We find the trial court erred by permitting appellees to recover funds they voluntarily expended to maintain the alley. Appellees cite no statute, court decision, or other authority permitting a volunteer to recover sums expended performing a city's duty to maintain an alley without the city's consent. We note there is no contract between the parties. We find no tort basis for requiring appellant to reimburse appellees for their voluntary efforts. We find no equitable basis upon which to permit appellees to recover sums they voluntarily expended to maintain the alley.

Courts have traditionally declined to aid volunteers. In Farm Bureau Mutual Automobile Insurance Co. v. Buckeye Union Casualty Co. (1946), 147 Ohio St. 79, 33 O.Op. 259, 67 N.E.2d 906, * * * the court held:

5. The doctrine of contribution rests upon principles of equity.

6. One who, with knowledge of the facts and without legal liability, makes a payment of money, thereby becomes a volunteer.

7. Equity will not aid a volunteer. * * * "[O]ne who officiously confers a benefit upon another is not entitled to restitution."

In the case sub judice, the parties agree that appellees acted as volunteers. Appellee Jack A. Bennington testified he acted out of concern for the families and other residents who depended on the alley for ingress and egress. Although appellees' concern and actions may be admirable, neither the law nor equity permits recovery for voluntary acts.[1]

Judgment reversed * * *.

NOTES

1. What policy underlies the theory that "volunteers" should not get paid? Does it matter whether the "volunteer" is reacting to an emergency or a hazard? In the cases involving preservation of another's property (outside the area of maritime law) there generally can be no restitutionary relief unless the plaintiff has some relationship to the property or its owner. *See* 2 George E. Palmer, Law of Restitution § 10.3 (1978). Restitutionary relief may be available for services rendered voluntarily under emergency conditions to protect the well-being of the person or property of another, however. Where the plaintiff's intervention protected another from serious bodily harm or pain (such as intervention by a physician in an attempt to preserve the life or health of the defendant), quasi-contract relief has been granted. *See* Restatement of Restitution § 116 (1937); *see also* 2 George E. Palmer, Law of Restitution § 10 (1978). Quasi-contractual recovery for conferring non-emergency benefits, such as hospital treatment and care, funeral expenses and "necessaries" supplied to a spouse, child or other relative are discussed by Professor Palmer. *Id.* For cases involving compensation under Restatement of Restitution § 115 to parties who repaired damage from hazardous conditions caused by others, see *infra* Chapter 6, Section 2.C.2.

2. Somewhat different are those cases where the plaintiff "voluntarily" sustains a physical injury in order to prevent what he or she reasonably, and spontaneously, concludes is a risk of more serious injury to the defendant. Here, "enrichment" in the usual sense is not present, but rather the physical well-being of the party whose hurt was prevented, and who, as a consequence, will enjoy greater ability to increase his or her estate. In these cases, the courts deny recovery from the benefitted party in the absence of a subsequent promise to compensate the injured plaintiff. *See* Webb v. McGowin, 232 Ala. 374, 168 So. 199 (1936), *discussed in* 1 Arthur L. Corbin, Contracts § 231 (1963), *but see* Harrington v. Taylor, 225 N.C. 690, 36 S.E.2d 227 (1945). *See also* John P. Dawson, *Rewards for the Rescue of Human Life?*, *in* 20th Century Comparative and Conflicts Law—Legal Essays in Honor of Hessell E. Yntema 142 (1961); Mark Moller, Note, *Sympathy, Community and Promising: Adam Smith's Case for Reviving Moral Consideration*, 66 U. Chi. L. Rev. 213 (1999); Michael Swygert and Katherine Earl Yanes, *Unified Theory of Justice: The Integration of Fairness into Efficiency*, 73 Wash. L. Rev. 249 (1998).

---

1. If a political subdivision is statutorily obligated to repair and maintain roadways, courts have generally been called upon to issue a writ of mandamus to compel the performance of those mandatory duties. * * *

B. SERVICES RENDERED WITHOUT AN EXPECTATION OF COMPENSATION

VORTT EXPLORATION v. CHEVRON U.S.A.

Supreme Court of Texas, 1990.
787 S.W.2d 942.

HIGHTOWER, JUSTICE.

* * *

The subject of this dispute is a 160 acre tract of land located in Young County. Both Chevron and Vortt acquired mineral rights to various portions of the tract. In 1978 Vortt contacted Chevron requesting that they enter a farm-out agreement concerning a particular portion of the tract owned by Chevron. Chevron rejected the request to enter a farm-out agreement. Soon thereafter Vortt proposed that the two companies enter a joint operating agreement. Chevron informed Vortt that it might be interested in such an arrangement and requested that Vortt submit a proposal. Chevron and Vortt negotiated the specifics of the arrangement until 1983 without reaching an agreement. During this time, they corresponded frequently in an attempt to come to an agreement.

During the negotiations, Vortt provided Chevron with confidential seismic services, graphics, and maps in an attempt to reach a joint operating agreement. After receiving the information, Chevron drilled a producing well at the location identified in the information. Chevron then brought suit to invalidate certain leases held by Vortt. Vortt counter-claimed asserting the validity of the leases, or alternatively to recover under *quantum meruit* for the seismic services which were provided to Chevron. The trial court rendered judgment in favor of Vortt on its *quantum meruit* claim [in the amount of $178,750]. The court of appeals reversed the trial court's judgment and rendered judgment in favor of Chevron. In rendering judgment, the court of appeals held that there was not a factual finding that Vortt furnished this information under such circumstances as to "reasonably notify Chevron that Vortt expected to be paid for the services and assistance" which were provided. * * *

* * *

* * * The trial court made several findings of fact. Those pertinent to the court of appeals' holding are as follows:

9) Vortt provided the aforesaid services and assistance to Chevron in the belief that Chevron and Vortt would jointly develop the subject 160 acres for the production of oil and gas, and but for such belief [Vortt] would not have provided such services and assistance to Chevron, which were undertaken for both Chevron and Vortt.

13) Chevron was reasonably notified that Vortt in performing such services and assistance for Chevron, expected to join with Chevron in

a mutually satisfactory agreement for their joint production of oil and gas from the subject 160 acres.

Findings nine and thirteen reflect, as stated by the court of appeals, that "Chevron was on notice that Vortt, in performing the services and assistance, expected to join with Chevron in a mutually satisfactory agreement for production of the well and would not have provided such services and assistance except for such belief." The court of appeals stated that this notification did not rise to the level of notification * * * that would reasonably notify Chevron that Vortt expected to be *paid* for the seismic information. * * *

The expected payment does not have to be monetary; it may be any form of compensation. [Q]*uantum meruit* recovery has been allowed when the original payment sought was an interest in land. * * *

Chevron knew that Vortt furnished the information with the expectation that a joint operating agreement would be reached. The parties had negotiated for over four years trying to achieve this end. At trial, Vortt's president testified that he shared the confidential seismic services, graphics, maps and other seismic information in the spirit of cooperation and that he would not have done so if he had not believed that a joint operating agreement would be reached. We hold that the trial court's findings of fact reflect that Chevron was reasonably notified that Vortt expected to be paid for the services and assistance which were rendered.

For the reasons stated, we reverse the judgment of the court of appeals and remand the cause to that court to consider the points of error which it did not reach.

HECHT, J., files a dissenting opinion in which PHILLIPS, C.J., and GONZALEZ, J., join.

I dissent. I agree with the Court that the only issue presented to us in this *quantum meruit* case is whether there is any evidence that Vortt Exploration Company, Inc. gave Chevron U.S.A., Inc. seismic information under circumstances as reasonably notified Chevron that Vortt expected to be paid for the information. * * *

* * *

Was ever fainter hope more richly rewarded? For not refusing to look at Vortt's information, Chevron must pay ten times its cost. The Court's ruling today should be a tremendous encouragement to benefaction. A frustrated negotiator should never overlook this tactic in attempting to induce agreement. The recipient of such charity, however, should beware.

I would hold that Chevron could not reasonably have expected to pay when Vortt did not expect to be paid. Accordingly, I would affirm the judgment of the court of appeals.

NOTES

1. The court in *Vortt* uses the term *quantum meruit,* which can refer to either a contract implied-in-fact or a contract implied-in-law (quasi contract).

For further discussion of *quantum meruit* see Chapter 7, Section 5. Plaintiff's lack of expectation of payment may defeat recovery in either action. Lack of expectation of payment is closely related, if not synonymous with, giving a gift or being a volunteer.

2. Do you agree with the majority or the dissent in *Vortt*? Similar to *Vortt* are Professional Recruiters, Inc. v. Oliver, 235 Neb. 508, 456 N.W.2d 103, 109 (1990) ("Both parties knew or should have known that Professional Recruiters expected a fee if McMaster was hired.") and Ticor Title Insurance Co. v. Mundelius, 887 S.W.2d 726, 728 (Mo.Ct.App.1994) ("In this case, Ticor's relationship [as escrow agent] with the defendant gave Ticor reason to believe it would be reimbursed."). *But see* Lirtzman v. Fuqua Industries, Inc., 677 F.2d 548 (7th Cir.1982) (services rendered gratuitously in hopes of more future business endeavors; thus no quasi-contract or expectation of payment); Bloomgarden v. Coyer, 479 F.2d 201, 212 (D.C.Cir.1973) ("There simply was no basis on which a jury could rationally find that when he brought the parties together he entertained any thought of a finder's fee for himself, or that those with whom he dealt held the payment of such a fee in prospect.").

DUSENKA v. DUSENKA

Supreme Court of Minnesota, 1946.
221 Minn. 234, 21 N.W.2d 528.

MATSON, JUSTICE. Appeal from an order denying plaintiff's motion for a new trial.

* * *

For several years prior to 1937, the defendant, Frank Dusenka, Jr., in partnership with his father, Frank Dusenka, Sr., operated an on-sale liquor tavern in Minneapolis. In 1937, the elder Dusenka transferred his one-half interest in the business to his son, the defendant, in consideration of the son's promise to support and maintain his father during his lifetime, subject, however, to the understanding that the father would continue to assist in the operation of the business. Plaintiff, wife of the senior Dusenka and stepmother of defendant, was not informed of the transfer and did not learn thereof until after the death of her husband. Practically every day, before and after 1937, inclusive of the period covered by this suit, namely, from September 1, 1938, to February 3, 1943, plaintiff accompanied her husband to the place of business around eight or nine in the morning, remained there until about one in the afternoon, and returned later in the evening. Plaintiff prepared breakfast for her husband after arriving at the tavern and also prepared certain other meals at the tavern for him and defendant as well. She at times also performed such services as cleaning up and scrubbing, tending bar, and furnishing some meals for guests or patrons that might come to the place. Plaintiff testified that her husband first became ill in 1938; that in 1939 he required hospitalization; and that thereafter "he feel badly and I help him." About February 3, 1943, her husband became seriously ill and died about February 9. Plaintiff received no pay from defendant for services performed between September 1938 and February 3, 1943, but for services performed subsequently to the death of her husband, at plaintiff's request, she was paid by defendant.

Plaintiff's suit is for remuneration for services rendered to defendant between September 1, 1938, and February 3, 1943. There was no contract, either express or implied, between plaintiff and defendant, for the performance of these services. We have no evidence that defendant ever expected to be required to pay for them. Plaintiff, by her brief, concedes that at no time before or during the performance of these services was there any intention or expectation of payment on her part, and she alleges that she rendered these services in the belief that "the place she was helping to run belonged to her 'mister' instead of the defendant." Furthermore, there is no evidence that plaintiff, either before or during the period when she rendered the services, ever requested, or intended, that defendant should pay for even a part of the services to correspond to what she thought was his share in the business as distinguished from that of her husband. Plaintiff does contend, however, that she always believed she was rendering these services for her husband and not for her stepson, the defendant. Clearly, plaintiff assumed at all times prior to her husband's death that he and defendant operated the business as partners. In fact, not until after her husband's death, when she discovered that he had in 1937 transferred his entire interest in the business to defendant, did she conceive a desire to be paid.

From the time the elder Dusenka in 1937 transferred his interest to his son until the time of his death, he received no regular wages or pay for his services, but at all times he enjoyed, and exercised, the unrestricted right or privilege of taking from the cash register whatever money he needed for living expenses, for the maintenance of his home and family, and for the payment of medical and hospital bills.

At the close of plaintiff's case, defendant rested provisionally and moved for a directed verdict on the ground that plaintiff had failed to show an employment or agreement for hire.

1. In determining the principles to be applied, significant is the admitted fact that neither plaintiff nor defendant had, prior to or during the performance of plaintiff's services, any intention or expectation that plaintiff should be paid. Plaintiff's intention or desire to be paid was not conceived until after the services had been fully performed. Obviously, there was no actual contract to pay, either express or implied in fact. A contract may be implied in fact, but not contrary to the common and undisputed intention of both parties. 1 Williston, Contracts, Rev. Ed., § 21, note 1. * * *

2. Where services are admittedly rendered or benefits conferred voluntarily, without intention of receiving compensation on the part of the one rendering the services, and the person for whom they were rendered

accepted them in reliance upon such intention, no actual contract to pay is *implied in fact*.

* * *

3.   If plaintiff is to recover at all, it must be on the theory of a quasi contract, which is sometimes called a contract implied in law. Unfortunately, much confusion has resulted from a careless use of terminology and failure to observe a clear distinction between actual contracts and quasi contracts. * * * The quasi-contractual obligation is raised or imposed by law and is independent of any real or expressed intent of the parties. The obligation is called quasi-contractual because as a matter of legal history the remedy took the contract form just as if based on an actual contract or agreement. * * * Under the theory of a quasi contract, the obligation is defined in equity and good conscience and is imposed by law to prevent unjust enrichment at the expense of another. *See* Restatement, Restitution, § 1.

In applying the principles of quasi contract to the instant case, the question is whether defendant wrongfully and knowingly permitted plaintiff, through her mistake as to the ownership of the business, to confer upon him, without compensation, the benefit of her services to his unjust enrichment. Restatement, Restitution, § 40, comment c. Neither her husband, the elder Dusenka, nor defendant informed plaintiff of the sale and transfer by her husband of his one-half share in the business to defendant. If there was a duty by the stepson to tell his stepmother that which her husband, for some unknown reason, had not told her, does it reasonably follow that, if she had been so informed, she would have ceased to perform the services without compensation? The evidence indicates that plaintiff's services were rendered for the primary purpose of easing the daily tasks of her sick and ailing husband, whose health she wished to protect. She accompanied him in the morning and at the tavern prepared his and her own breakfast, as well as the other meals of the day. It is apparent that the other tasks she performed were comparatively light and, for the most part, designed to relieve her husband. She came voluntarily and apparently enjoyed the atmosphere. Plaintiff's motive is apparent from the fact that, although she always assumed that defendant owned a half interest in the business, she never at any time asked or expected to be paid by defendant in proportion to such interest. She also knew that her husband had children by his first marriage and that, in case of his death, these children would normally inherit a two-thirds interest in the half share that she supposed he still owned. If plaintiff had been informed of the transfer of her husband's interest, there is no reason to suppose, under all the circumstances of this case, that she would have altered her course of conduct or her expectations, in the slightest degree, and for this reason we can attach no significance to, nor imply any breach of good faith in, defendant's failure to disclose his purchase of the father's interest. Defendant was in a difficult position. If he had asked plaintiff to stay away from the tavern, he would have offended and embarrassed his own father, who was in need of assistance. We find no unjust enrichment for defendant. He had obligated himself to maintain his father for life, and, in fulfillment of that obligation, he permitted his father, plaintiff's husband, to have unrestricted access to the cash register to take whatever money he desired or needed for the payment of his personal and family expenses, inclusive of clothes, groceries, and all medical and hospital bills. We find no evidence of fraud * * *. Construing the evidence in the light most favorable to plaintiff, we hold that the court properly directed a verdict for defendant.

Affirmed.

KUDER v. SCHROEDER

Court of Appeals of North Carolina, 1993.
110 N.C.App. 355, 430 S.E.2d 271.

WELLS, JUDGE.

* * *

Plaintiff and defendant were married in March of 1978. One child was born to their marriage in June of 1984. After plaintiff and defendant were married, they entered into an oral agreement that plaintiff would forego her career as a veterinarian and would work as a teacher in a local community college to support their family in order that defendant might pursue his undergraduate education * * *. Defendant agreed that upon the completion of his undergraduate studies, he would provide the family's total support, so that plaintiff could then give up her employment and devote her full time to being a wife and mother. Pursuant to this agreement, plaintiff did work and provide the sole support for their family. Plaintiff and defendant subsequently amended or extended their agreement to allow defendant to obtain a master's degree and a law degree. Following his graduation from law school, defendant was unable to earn sufficient income to fully support the family, but in December of 1989, defendant obtained a position with a law firm which provided him with sufficient income to fully support the family. Three months later, in April of 1990, defendant told plaintiff he no longer loved her and that there was no hope for their marriage; whereupon, the parties separated.

Plaintiff contends that the oral agreement asserted by her in her complaint is a valid and binding contract, entitling her to damages for its breach. Taking plaintiff's allegations as true, we are sympathetic to her apparent dilemma, and certainly would not condone defendant's apparent knavish ingratitude, but we do not find support in the law of this State for such a claim and therefore hold that the trial court correctly dismissed plaintiff's claims.

Under the law of this State, there is a personal duty of each spouse to support the other, a duty arising from the marital relationship, and carrying with it the corollary right to support from the other spouse. So long as the coverture endures, this duty of support may not be abrogated or modified by the agreement of the parties to a marriage. * * *

For the reasons stated, the trial court's order must be and is

Affirmed.

GREENE, JUDGE, dissenting.

I agree with the majority * * * that the trial court correctly dismissed plaintiff's breach of contract action. I, however, would reverse the trial court's dismissal of plaintiff's claim for unjust enrichment.

I reiterate the allegations of plaintiff's complaint in order to provide a fuller appreciation of the facts at issue. * * * Plaintiff also agreed that she would have only one child while defendant was in school. * * *

* * *

Upon graduation from law school, defendant told plaintiff that, instead of entering the private practice of law, he wanted to start his own legal research business. The parties, plaintiff reluctantly, once more extended their original agreement * * *. Plaintiff, who by this time had reached the age of forty, also agreed to forego having more children.

* * *

* * * [O]ur courts recognize the validity of an agreement of the type at issue provided that the parties to such agreement are unmarried cohabiting partners. *See* Suggs v. Norris, 88 N.C.App. 539, 364 S.E.2d 159, *cert. denied*, 322 N.C. 486, 370 S.E.2d 236 (1988) (citing Marvin v. Marvin, 18 Cal.3d 660, 557 P.2d 106 (1976)). I find it incongruous that, given a cohabiting partner on the one hand and a spouse on the other hand, both of whom pursuant to an agreement provide total financial support for their partner in order for that partner to obtain a degree, an advanced degree, or a professional license with the expectation that both parties would benefit therefrom, upon the dissolution of the relationship, the cohabiting partner is entitled to compensation for such contribution to the educational achievements of his partner, but a spouse who made the same contribution is not. I am at a loss to understand the "public policy" supporting such a rule.

* * *

* * * In order to state a claim for unjust enrichment, the plaintiff's allegations must reveal that she rendered to the defendant services or support which conferred on the defendant a measurable benefit, that defendant accepted the services or support, and that "the services [or support] were rendered and accepted between the two parties with the mutual understanding that plaintiff was to be compensated for her efforts." * * * In other words, the beneficial services or support must not have been conferred officiously or gratuitously. In North Carolina, it is presumed that services or support provided by one spouse for the other are rendered gratuitously; however, this presumption may be rebutted "by

proof of an agreement to [compensate], or of facts and circumstances permitting the inference that [compensation] was intended on the one hand and expected on the other." * * *

Courts in other jurisdictions when faced with situations such as the one presented by the facts of this case have allowed plaintiff spouses to go forward with their claims for restitution on the theory of unjust enrichment. *See, e.g.*, Pyeatte [v. Pyeatte, 661 P.2d 196, 207 (Ariz.App. 1982)]. * * * Allowing such claims is eminently reasonable when one considers that, in North Carolina, the alternative leaves the non-student supporting spouse with virtually no remedy. This is so because the non-student supporting spouse has no right to alimony because he is not a "dependent" spouse. * * * Indeed, he has demonstrated the capability of supporting not only himself, but his spouse, and, often, children as well. And although North Carolina recognizes as distributional factors for purposes of equitable distribution of marital property contributions made by one spouse to help educate or develop the career potential of the other spouse, or which increase the value of the other spouse's professional license, this remedy is of little value in cases where the student spouse leaves the supporting spouse immediately or soon after obtaining his professional license. * * *

* * *

* * * [T]he allegations in plaintiff's complaint are sufficient to rebut the presumption that her services were rendered gratuitously. * * * I conclude that plaintiff has stated a claim for unjust enrichment, and would hold that the trial court erred in dismissing it. * * *

WYNN, JUDGE, concurring.

I concur fully in the majority opinion and write separately to point out that the law provides different protection for married couples and unmarried cohabitants, and to address the issue of unjust enrichment, on which the dissenting opinion invites comment.

* * *

I note that the law has not abandoned spouses who find themselves in the situation of the plaintiff. The legislature has enacted the equitable distribution statute, pursuant to which support such as the plaintiff has rendered in the present case is a distributional factor supporting an unequal distribution of the marital property. * * * It is unfortunate that the circumstances of the present case are such that the marital estate consists of little property. To make up for this by reaching the result that the dissenting opinion urges, however, would result in unwarranted litigation in those situations where a supporting spouse claims recovery under a theory of unjust enrichment in an amount in excess of the value of the marital property. The ramifications of the dissent's view cannot be ignored, as they would clearly result in an alteration of the laws relating to divorce, alimony, and property division that is best left to the legislature.

NOTES

1. The dissent in *Kuder* implies that a cohabitant might be better off than a wife when the relationship disintegrates. For a discussion of recovery in actions of unjust enrichment or of contract implied in fact in cases involving cohabitants, see Section 5.B of this Chapter and Chapter 7, Section 5.

2. In Borelli v. Brusseau, 12 Cal.App.4th 647, 652, 16 Cal.Rptr.2d 16, 19 (1993), a widow sought specific performance of her husband's promise to convey to her certain nonmarital property if she would nurse him herself at home so that he could avoid a nursing home. The majority, citing two cases, one from 1937 and one from 1941, held: "[A] wife is obligated by the marriage contract to provide nursing type care to an ill husband. Therefore, contracts whereby the wife is to receive compensation for providing such services are void as against public policy and there is no consideration for the husband's promise." The dissent said:

> Statements in * * * cases to the effect that a husband has an entitlement to his wife's "services" * * * smack of the common law doctrine of coverture which treated a wife as scarcely more than an appendage to her husband. * * *

> No one doubts that spouses owe each other a duty of support or that this encompasses "the obligation to provide medical care." * * * There is nothing * * * which requires that this obligation be *personally* discharged by a spouse except the [1937 and 1941] decisions themselves. However, at the time [they] were decided—before World War II—it made sense for those courts to say that a wife could perform her duty of care only by doing so personally. That was an accurate reflection of the real world for women years before the exigency of war produced substantial employment opportunities for them. For most women at that time there was no other way to take care of a sick husband except personally. * * *

> The majority's rule leaves married people with contracting powers which are more limited than those enjoyed by unmarried persons or than is justified by legitimate public policy. In this context public policy should not be equated with coerced altruism. Mr. Borelli was a grown man who, having amassed a sizeable amount of property, should be treated—at least on demurrer—as competent to make the agreement alleged by plaintiff. The public policy of California will not be outraged by affording plaintiff the opportunity to try to enforce that agreement.

Id. at 656–62, 16 Cal.Rptr.2d at 21–25. For a discussion of using contracts to protect the nonwage earning spouse, see Martha M. Ertman, *Commercializing Marriage: A Proposal for Valuing Women's Work Through Premarital Security Agreements*, 77 Tex. L. Rev. 17 (1998). *But see* Brian Bix, *Bargaining in the Shadow of Love: The Enforcement of Premarital Agreements and How We Think About Marriage*, 40 Wm. & Mary L. Rev. 145 (1998) (enumerating the values in enforcing premarital agreements despite arguments that they may at times undercompensate women). For suggestions for restructuring how assets and income are distributed after divorce, see Gaytri Kachroo, *Mapping*

Alimony: From Status to Contract and Beyond, 5 Pierce L. Rev. 163 (2007); Shari Motro, *Labor, Luck, and Love: Reconsidering the Sanctity of Separate Property*, 102 Nw. U.L. Rev. 1623 (2008).

3. Contrast *Dusenka, Kuder* and *Borelli* with Pyeatte v. Pyeatte, 135 Ariz. 346, 661 P.2d 196 (1982) (awarding "restitution" to divorced wife in the amount of the financial contribution made by plaintiff to defendant's living expenses and direct educational expenses while he was in law school):

> * * * Where both spouses perform the usual and incidental activities of the marital relationship, upon dissolution there can be no restitution for performance of these activities. Where, however, the facts demonstrate an agreement [that is, "expectation of compensation" in the form of reciprocal help with education costs] between the spouses and an extraordinary or unilateral effort by one spouse which inures solely to the benefit of the other by the time of dissolution, the remedy of restitution is appropriate.

> Arizona courts have traditionally utilized the equitable restitutionary device of the constructive trust to prevent unjust enrichment between spouses upon dissolution when there is property to which such a trust may attach. * * * We see no reason in law or equity why restitution should not be available in an appropriate circumstance to prevent the unjust enrichment of a spouse when a constructive trust is not available, as here, when no property exists. We analogize the two restitutionary devices solely to the extent of illustrating their common essence—prevention of the unjust enrichment of one spouse at the expense of the other.

> * * *

> The record shows that the appellee conferred benefits on appellant—financial subsidization of appellant's legal education—with the agreement and expectation that she would be compensated therefor by his reciprocal efforts after his graduation and admission to the Bar. Appellant has left the marriage with the only valuable asset acquired during the marriage—his legal education and qualification to practice law. It would be inequitable to allow appellant to retain this benefit without making restitution to appellee. However, we need not decide what limits or standards would apply in the absence of an agreement. Commentators have discerned in various statutory enactments and the developing case law a renewed and expanded recognition of marriage's economic underpinnings. *See* Comment, *The Interest of the Community in a Professional Education*, 10 Calif.W.L.Rev. 590 (1974); Erickson, *Spousal Support Toward the Realization of Educational Goals: How the Law Can Ensure Reciprocity*, 1978 Wis.L.Rev. 947. By our decision herein, we reject the view that the economic element necessarily inherent in the marital institution (and particularly apparent in its dissolution) requires us to treat marriage as a strictly financial undertaking upon the dissolution of which each party will be fully compensated for the investment of his various contributions. When the parties have been married for a number of years, the courts cannot and will not strike a balance regarding the contributions of each to the marriage and then translate that into a monetary award. To do so would diminish the individual personalities of the husband and wife to

economic entities and reduce the institution of marriage to that of a closely held corporation.

Id. at 353–57, 661 P.2d at 203–07. *See also* Holterman v. Holterman, 3 N.Y.3d 1, 814 N.E.2d 765, 781 N.Y.S.2d 458 (2004), where the New York Court of Appeals upheld a divorce decree that awarded to the wife "$214,200 as her equitable share of husband's enhanced earnings premised on his medical license":

> Here, the Supreme Court issued a careful, comprehensive decision addressing all relevant factors, including the parties' 19–year marriage, wife's employment and monetary contributions during husband's final two years of medical school, the parties' mutual decision that wife would forgo her career to take care of the children and home, the gross disparity in the parties' current and probable future incomes, the fact that husband was 44 years of age and wife was 46 years of age at the time of trial and husband's good health in contrast to wife's chronic health difficulties. In light of these considerations, particularly wife's economic and noneconomic contributions to husband's acquisition of his medical license and subsequent career, the termination of wife's career to raise the parties' two children and maintain the marital household, wife's absence from the job market for more than 17 years, the length of the marriage and wife's long-term health problems, we cannot conclude that Supreme Court abused its discretion in awarding wife 35% as her marital portion of husband's enhanced earning capacity as a physician practicing medicine in New York.

Id. at 8–9, 814 N.E.2d at 769, 781 N.Y.S.2d at 462.

For a discussion of the jurisdictions that do or do not take one spouse's degree into account in allocating assets and support at the dissolution of a marriage, see D. Kelly Weisberg & Susan Frelich Appleton, *Investments in a Spouse's Future Success: Degrees, Earning Capacity, and Goodwill, in* Modern Family Law: Cases and Materials at 714–29 (1998). *Compare, e.g.,* Postema v. Postema, 189 Mich.App. 89, 105, 471 N.W.2d 912, 917 (1991) ("Where a degree is the end product of a concerted family effort, fairness and equity will not permit the degree holder to reap the benefits of the degree without compensating the other spouse for unrewarded sacrifices, efforts and contributions toward attainment of the degree."), *and* Dugan v. Dugan, 92 N.J. 423, 434, 457 A.2d 1, 6 (1983) ("Much of the economic value produced during an attorney's marriage will inhere in the goodwill of the law practice. It would be inequitable to ignore the contribution of the non-attorney spouse to the development of that economic resource."), *with* Prahinski v. Prahinski, 321 Md. 227, 234, 582 A.2d 784, 787 (1990) (holding that the value of the wife's "time and effort which made the practice successful" was not part of attorney husband's professional goodwill). For a discussion of spousal interest in professional degrees, see Carol S. Gailor & Meredith J. McGill, *The Equitable Distribution of Professional Degrees Upon Divorce in North Carolina,* 10 Campbell L. Rev. 69 (1987); Alicia Brokars Kelly, *The Marital Partnership Pretense and Career Assets: The Ascendancy of Self*

Over the Marital Community, 81 B.U. L. Rev. 59 (2001). *See generally,* Pamela Laufer–Ukeles, *Selective Recognition of Gender Difference in the Law: Revaluing the Caretaker Role*, 31 Harv.J.L. & Gender 1 (2008); Cynthia Lee Starnes, *Mothers as Suckers: Pity, Partnership and Divorce Discourse*, 90 Iowa L. Rev. 1513 (2005).

4.   Why do you think the courts found expectation of payment in *Vortt,* but not in *Dusenka* and *Kuder?* Notice that *Vortt* says that "expectation of payment need not be monetary." Under that test, do you think Mrs. Dusenka, for example, was not expecting payment?

C. CHANGE OF POSITION

MESSERSMITH v. G.T. MURRAY & CO.

Supreme Court of Wyoming, 1983.
667 P.2d 655.

Before ROONEY, C.J., and THOMAS, ROSE, BROWN and CARDINE, JJ.

BROWN, JUSTICE.

* * *

At about 9:00 a.m. on July 28, 1982, Frances Messersmith called the offices of G.T. Murray and Company. She talked with James King, a stockbroker, about the possibility of selling some stock. She stated she had no idea what it was worth but wanted to find out. When asked the name of the stock, she read off what appeared on the stock certificate, "Western Preferred." King looked up the name and discovered that Western Preferred was selling for approximately $46 per share. Frances Messersmith expressed some surprise but indicated she had 200 shares and would like to sell them. King told her he would take care of the sale and asked her to bring the stock certificate to his office. By the time she arrived at 10:00 a.m., the sale was completed; the stock had been sold for $47 per share.

After the necessary paperwork was completed and some ten days had passed, the Messersmiths received a check in the amount of $9,260.70. This represented the net proceeds from the sale of 200 shares of Western Preferred at $47 per share.

On October 1, 1982, King received a phone call from appellee's parent company, Bache. He was informed that an error had been made in the sale of the Messersmiths' stock. It turned out that that stock had been subject to a reverse stock split two years before. At that time holders of the stock had been directed to return their stock certificates in order to receive new stock issued as a result of a merger with another company. One share of the new stock had been issued for every 40 shares turned in. Though the Messersmiths never responded to the notification, their 200 shares of the old stock actually equalled five shares of the new stock valued at $47 per share, and had a gross value of $235.

After being informed of the problem, King called the Messersmiths. He told them that they had been overpaid by about $9,000. He was advised that $8,000 had been used as a down payment on a house and the rest had been spent.

On October 8, 1982, appellee initiated this lawsuit in order to recover the overpayment. The trial court found in its favor and ordered the appellants to pay appellee $8,810.70.

* * *

* * * [A]ppellants claim that since appellee was in a better position to discover the mistake, it should suffer the loss. * * *

* * *

Lack of due care will not serve to bar an action for restitution of funds mistakenly paid where no damage to the payee has resulted.

* * * [A]ppellants contend that they changed their position as a result of the overpayment and that it would be unjust to force them to return the money. Normally, payees will not be required to return the overpayment where they have changed their position such that demanding a refund would be unfair. * * * To constitute such a change, the burden is on the payee to establish that the change has been detrimental to the payee and that it was material and irrevocable such that the payee cannot be returned to the status quo. * * * However, a mere change in the form of the proceeds does not qualify when the payee has retained the value. * * * In other words, the payor can recover the proceeds only to the extent that the payee will not be damaged.

Here, appellants spent approximately $1,200 on bills. In Ohio Co. v. Rosemeier, *supra*, 288 N.E.2d at 329, the payee used the money to pay off a mortgage. The court there said: "Since the value of the original payment was retained by the defendant, she has not detrimentally changed her position by liquidating her mortgage." Accordingly, to the extent the Messersmiths paid off debts there was no loss of value.

Appellants applied the remaining $8,000 of the overpayment towards the purchase of a house. Though the briefs both make reference to the fact that the money was placed in escrow and subject to forfeiture, no evidence of such was produced at trial. The only competent evidence in the record is Frances Messersmith's statement that she had put $8,000 on a home. Such evidence is insufficient to establish that appellants did not retain the value. Merely putting money down on a house is just a change of form. Since the burden of proof was upon appellants to establish a loss of value and they failed to introduce any evidence to prove that they have not retained the value of the overpayment, we must affirm the trial court's finding. No change of circumstances was established.

Affirmed.

NOTES

1.   Do you agree that there is no detriment to the defendant from the change of form of the $8,000 in *Messersmith*? *See* Monroe Financial Corp. v. DiSilvestro, 529 N.E.2d 379 (Ind.Ct.App.1988). In *Monroe Financial Corp.*, DiSilvestro had received payment for stocks she did not own from a stock broker because there was confusion with the name of the stock. The defendant claimed her use of the money to redecorate part of her home was a change of circumstance defense. The majority said:

> The rule permitting a party to recover money paid under a unilateral mistake of fact is subject to a limitation. That is that the party receiving the money must not have so changed his position so as to make it inequitable to require him to make repayment. * * *

> * * * If we were to hold that DiSilvestro has successfully circumvented the duty to repay the amount mistakenly paid by MFC [Monroe Financial Corp.] due to her purchases and expenditures, we would be encouraging payees to hastily convert such receipts into tangible personal property in order to avoid a clear equitable duty. We should not adopt a principle of law which encourages a race to furniture and appliance stores.

Id. at 385. The dissent disagreed, saying:

> Indiana courts have not considered whether the application of money paid under a mistake of fact to purchase tangible property constitutes a detrimental change of position. * * *

> * * *

> * * * In each of the cases relied upon by MFC the courts held that the expenditure of money paid under a mistake of fact to discharge a debt did not constitute detrimental reliance. The underlying rationale of these cases is that an individual who receives money under a mistake of fact is not excused from repayment where he has expended the money in a way which he was otherwise required to. In each of the cases discussed above the defendant had applied the money received to the payment of an existing mortgage or to pay off other pre-existing debts.

> In this case the evidence reveals that MFC is a professional stockbroker with connections of some sort in New York. In reliance upon MFC's professed expertise in stock matters, DiSilvestro sold her stock through MFC, upon MFC's terms, and upon MFC's dictated price. Without any knowledge of MFC's self-induced negligence she spent the money and it is gone. Under the majority's unfortunate ruling, DiSilvestro will now have a judgment lien upon her residence, and if she is unable to pay it she will lose her home upon an execution sale. Absent MFC's negligence, there would have been no sale, no purchase of improvements, and no judgment lien. It is to be emphasized that this is not the payment of an old debt, but the incurrence of new obligations in reliance upon a misplaced trust in MFC. If the facts of this case do not show a detrimental change of position, I am at a loss to know what facts would so qualify.

Id. at 385–86. *Cf.* CSX Transportation, Inc. v. Appalachian Railcar Services, Inc., 509 F.3d 384 (7th Cir. 2007) (equating change of circumstances with laches). *See also* Hanoch Dagan, *Mistakes*, 79 Tex. L. Rev. 1795, 1814–17 (2001)(suggesting that the change of position defense might have a variety of fault-based analyses).

2.   For a case accepting the defense of changed position, see Association Life Insurance Co. v. Jenkins, 793 F.Supp. 161 (M.D.Tenn.1992). In *Association Life Insurance Co.*, an insurance company mistakenly paid claims to defendants. The court said:

> [T]he defendants would suffer great injury or injustice if the Court allowed Association Life to recover the money it paid under mistake of fact. The defendants relied on the benefit payments in undergoing the medical treatment. [One plaintiff] changed his position by undergoing medical treatment that he may not have had if he could not have relied on the benefits. Also, since those payments have been paid to the physicians and medical suppliers and are not in the hands of the defendant, the nature of the benefits received by the defendants is not a windfall. * * *

Id. at 165.

D.   INNOCENT THIRD PARTY CREDITOR

ST. MARY'S MEDICAL CENTER, INC. v. UNITED FARM BUREAU FAMILY LIFE INSURANCE CO.

Court of Appeals of Indiana, First District, 1993.
624 N.E.2d 939.

NAJAM, JUDGE.

* * *

* * * The facts disclose that on January 23, 1991, Munford was admitted to St. Mary's as an outpatient. She listed Farm Bureau as her insurance carrier and assigned her insurance benefits directly to St. Mary's. While a patient of St. Mary's, Munford incurred medical expenses in the amount of $3,836.47. On February 5, 1991, St. Mary's submitted a claim to Farm Bureau for Munford's medical expenses. Thereafter, Farm Bureau made partial payment to St. Mary's in the amount of $3,685.87, which St. Mary's applied to Munford's bill, leaving a small unpaid balance.

After making payment to St. Mary's, Farm Bureau discovered that Munford's insurance coverage had lapsed on December 1, 1990, nearly two months prior to her admission. Farm Bureau then notified St. Mary's of the mistaken payment and requested a refund. St. Mary's had no knowledge of the lapse in Munford's coverage until notified by Farm Bureau. * * *

* * * Farm Bureau requested that St. Mary's refund the $3,685.87 payment. St. Mary's refused, advising Farm Bureau that it was not St. Mary's policy to refund payment for medical services rendered. Farm

Bureau filed a complaint against St. Mary's * * *. The complaint alleged a mistake of fact as to Munford's insurance coverage and prayed for restitution of the amount paid to St. Mary's. The trial court granted restitution, and St. Mary's appeals.

DISCUSSION AND DECISION

St. Mary's asserts it is an innocent third party creditor and, thus, Farm Bureau is not entitled to restitution because (1) the payment was made solely due to Farm Bureau's mistake, (2) St. Mary's made no misrepresentations to induce the payment, and (3) St. Mary's acted in good faith without prior knowledge of Farm Bureau's mistake. Our research has failed to disclose any Indiana authority on innocent third party creditors in this context. While this is a case of first impression in Indiana, other jurisdictions have addressed the issue. * * *

GENERAL RULE OF RESTITUTION

It is generally recognized in the law of restitution that if one party pays money to another party under a mistake of fact that a contract or other obligation required such payment, the payor is entitled to restitution. *See* Restatement of Restitution § 18 (1937). Restitution in such cases is grounded in the equitable principle that one who has paid money to another who is not entitled to have it should not suffer unconscionable loss nor unjustly enrich the other. See *id.* at § 1. Unjust enrichment is typically regarded as a prerequisite to restitution. *Id.* * * *.

* * *

St. Mary's appeals based upon the innocent third party creditor exception to the general rule of restitution for payment made under mistake of fact. This exception, not previously recognized in Indiana, derives from the fact that there has been no unjust enrichment of the innocent third party creditor. Federated Mutual Ins. Co. v. Good Samaritan Hospital (1974), 191 Neb. 212, 214–15, 214 N.W.2d 493, 495. * * * The creditor is not unjustly enriched because the creditor is actually owed the money it receives and has exchanged value for the right to receive the money. * * * On this theory, St. Mary's contends that it gave value to Munford in the form of medical services, that it was entitled to receive payment for such services and, therefore, was not unjustly enriched. In addition, St. Mary's contends that it made no misrepresentations and acted in good faith without knowledge of Farm Bureau's mistake. Thus, St. Mary's asserts that it is an innocent third party creditor of Munford and should not be required to make restitution to Farm Bureau.

* * *

INNOCENT THIRD PARTY CREDITOR EXCEPTION

St. Mary's cites a number of cases from other jurisdictions to support its argument, including *Good Samaritan Hospital* * * *.

The decision in *Good Samaritan Hospital* was based on the rationale of Section 14(1) of the Restatement of Restitution, which provides that:

A creditor of another or one having a lien on another's property who has received from a third person any benefit in discharge of the debt or lien, is under no duty to make restitution therefor, although the discharge was given by mistake of the transferor as to his interests or duties, if the transferee made no misrepresentations and did not have notice of the transferor's mistake.

* * *

Further, the [*Good Samaritan*] court noted the health insurance industry's "widespread use of assignments of policy benefits to hospitals by patients," stating that:

To subject a hospital to possible refund liability if the insurer later discovers a mistaken overpayment, lasting until all such claims are barred by the statute of limitations, would be to place an undue burden of contingent liability on such institutions. * * * By this ruling, we place the burden for determining the limits of policy liability squarely upon the only party (as between the insurer and the assignee hospital) in a position to know the policy provisions and its liability under that contract of insurance. Someone must suffer the loss, and as between plaintiff insurer and defendant hospital, the party making the mistake should bear that loss.[4]

* * *

APPLICATION OF THE INNOCENT THIRD PARTY CREDITOR EXCEPTION

The equitable principles of restitution make a distinction between insurance payments made to the insured under mistake of fact, which entitle the insurer to restitution absent a change of position on the part of the insured, and those payments made under mistake of fact to an innocent third party creditor of the insured. * * * There is no unjust enrichment in the latter situation because the payee provided valuable services and was paid without knowledge of any misrepresentation or mistake. * * *

Farm Bureau contends that if we adopt this exception it will result in disparate treatment of insurance companies, place insurers under a substantial burden and exclude them from the protection of the doctrine of restitution. Farm Bureau also asserts that requiring the hospital to make restitution would not place an under burden upon it.

We agree with St. Mary's that requiring an innocent provider to refund an insurer's payment made by mistake would place an undue burden of contingent liability upon the provider * * *. Further, the adoption of this exception places no additional burden upon insurance

---

4. While the court in *Good Samaritan Hospital* discussed the issue of the hospital's liability to the insurer, it was not presented with and did not reach the question of the insurer's right to recover its mistaken payment from the insured.

companies. It merely requires that an insurer verify coverage before paying a claim, which is what an insurer must do in every case. If a mistake is made, as occurred here, then an insurer can maintain an action for restitution against the insured who was unjustly enriched by payment for medical services.

Finally, St. Mary's correctly observes that this exception to the general rule of restitution would apply to any innocent third party who receives payment of a debt due to a mistaken fact and has exchanged value for the right to receive the payment. As Justice Holmes wrote, "[T]he standards of the law are standards of general application." Oliver Wendell Holmes, Jr., The Common Law 108 (1881). We adopt the innocent third party creditor exception not only for insurance companies and medical providers but as a general rule which may apply to all persons similarly situated.

* * *

Reversed with instructions.

Notes

1.   Despite its footnote 4, did the court in *St. Mary's* imply that plaintiff could recover from the patient? How would such a suit fare under *Association Life*, which is described in the Note immediately preceding *St. Mary's*?

2.   For a discussion of the restitutionary principles of the third party creditor defense and the compromise of policies implicit in that defense, see Andrew Kull, *Defenses to Restitution: The Bona Fide Creditor*, 81 B.U. L. Rev. 919 (2001).

SECTION 8.   RESTITUTION AS THE ONLY CAUSE OF ACTION

Ever since Moses v. Macferlan in 1760, in Section 2 of this Chapter, lawyers have used common law actions in restitution to avoid the legal impediments of other actions, or to bring actions where none existed. Thus, Professor Graham Douthwaite regretted that lawyers do not have a better understanding of restitution because "[r]estitutionary problems arise in a bedazzling variety of situations." Graham Douthwaite, Attorney's Guide to Restitution § 1.1 (1977). In many of the cases in earlier Sections of this Chapter, restitution was just one of the plaintiff's options. For example, in *Crawford's Auto Center, Inc.*, in Section 2 of this Chapter, Crawford's could have recovered in contract implied in fact or contract implied in law (restitution) and in Olwell v. Nye & Nissen Co., *supra* Chapter 4, Section 4, Mr. Olwell could have recovered in tort, but instead "waived the tort and sued in *assumpsit*" (*i.e.*, the restitutionary version of *assumpsit*). In other cases in this Chapter, restitution was the plaintiff's only action, as in *Kossian*, where Mr. Kossian did not have a contract with the defendant, nor was he the victim of a tort.

The cases in this Section represent situations in which restitution might "save the day" because another action was barred. As you read later Chapters in this text, you will find other cases in which restitution is an important cause of action.

BAILEY–ALLEN CO. v. KURZET

Court of Appeals of Utah, 1994.
876 P.2d 421.

BILLINGS, PRESIDING JUDGE.

* * *

In July 1990, Stanley Kurzet and Bailey–Allen Company, Inc. entered into a contract for the construction of the Kurzets' home. * * *

* * * In October 1990, Mr. Kurzet terminated Bailey–Allen's services, based on its failure to provide proof of insurance and Mr. Kurzet's dissatisfaction with Bailey–Allen's attention to the project. At the time of the termination, the work under the contract was approximately 10% complete, with the house framed and the roof partially finished.

Bailey–Allen filed a complaint against the Kurzets in December 1990, alleging breach of contract, mechanics' lien, unjust enrichment, and failure to obtain a construction bond. * * *

After hearing the evidence, the court determined * * * that Bailey–Allen's failure to provide evidence of insurance and its lack of supervision of the project were material breaches of the contract that justified the termination. The court determined the Kurzets had not breached the contract.

The trial court then concluded that Bailey–Allen was entitled to recover under its unjust enrichment theory and went on to consider the amount of damages due, concluding that "the most logical basis [was] the percentage of defendants' residence that was completed during the period plaintiff was on the job." Accordingly, the court awarded Bailey–Allen $15,500 "in *quantum meruit*/unjust enrichment, based on the contract between plaintiff and defendants, $10,000 representing 1/10 of the contract price for services in completing 1/10 of the construction, and $5,500 for services involving negotiations for the purchase of lumber." Bailey–Allen was held liable to the Kurzets for $1800 in costs for repairing Bailey–Allen's faulty construction of a retaining wall, for $2000 for repairing its faulty construction of concrete steps, and for $559 in costs for unnecessary materials.

The court entered judgment for Bailey–Allen in the amount of $11,141, representing its damages offset by the amounts owed to the Kurzets. The court awarded Bailey–Allen prejudgment interest and post-judgment interest. * * *

I. DAMAGE AWARD

A. *Recovery Under the Contract*

* * *

* * * Because Bailey–Allen failed to substantially perform as by the contract, it cannot recover under the contract.

B. *Recovery in Quantum Meruit*

The Kurzets argue that the existence of a written contract bars an action in *quantum meruit*. They are correct that recovery in *quantum meruit* typically presupposes that no enforceable written or oral contract exists. * * * However, as explained above, there is no enforceable contract between Bailey–Allen and the Kurzets. Thus, recovery under *quantum meruit* may be appropriate.

* * * [A] non-breaching party is discharged from its contract duties but may have a quasi-contractual duty to pay the value of the benefit conferred in excess of the damage caused by the contractor's breach. Corbin §§ 700, at 309–10, 707, at 329. * * *

Quantum meruit has two branches, both rooted in justice. * * * The branch applicable to this case is a contract implied in law, also known as quasi-contract or unjust enrichment, which is a legal action in restitution. * * * To prove a contract implied in law or unjust enrichment, the following must be shown: "(1) the defendant received a benefit; (2) an appreciation or knowledge by the defendant of the benefit; (3) under circumstances that would make it unjust for the defendant to retain the benefit without paying for it." * * * The benefit conferred on the defendant, and not the plaintiff's detriment or the reasonable value of its services, is the measure of recovery. * * *

The trial court's findings of fact and conclusions of law do not specifically address the three requirements for recovery under unjust enrichment, nor do the undisputed underlying facts make clear that a quasi-contract award is appropriate. Instead the court's findings are internally inconsistent. For example, the trial court concluded that Bailey–Allen conferred a $10,000 benefit "regardless of whether plaintiff performed its duties under the contract." The Kurzets argue persuasively that Bailey–Allen * * * conferred no benefit upon them. The trial court seemed to agree, at least in theory, in finding that the 10% of the work completed during Bailey–Allen's tenure was not necessarily due to its presence or performance.

* * * Mr. Kurzet's testimony suggests he failed to realize any benefit conferred directly by Bailey–Allen. In fact, the core of the Kurzets' defense is that Bailey–Allen failed to perform any of the material terms of the contract and that any portion of the project completed was accomplished by other parties. * * * [T]he trial court did not find explicitly that it would be unjust to allow the Kurzets to retain, without payment, the construction completed before Bailey–Allen was terminated.

We are simply unable to determine whether the trial court's award of $10,000 "in *quantum meruit*/unjust enrichment" was predicated on the proper legal standard. We therefore reverse the award and remand for analysis and findings. * * *

C. Measure of Damages

If the trial court determines on remand that an award is warranted, we offer the following guidance for assessing the measure of damages. The Restatement (Second) of Contracts suggests a measure of damages referred to as "restitution in favor of party in breach." Restatement (Second) of Contracts § 374 (1981). Section 374 states that the breaching party is liable for the loss caused by the breach, but may recover the benefit conferred if it exceeds that loss. *Id.* The party seeking restitution must prove the measure of that benefit. *Id.*

Therefore, if on remand the trial court determines that recovery under *quantum meruit* is appropriate, it must make findings on the damages caused by Bailey–Allen's breach. The court should also make particularized findings on any benefit conferred on the Kurzets by Bailey–Allen. * * * Bailey–Allen should ultimately recover only the benefit conferred in excess of the damage it caused. We also note that the percentage of the work completed, if it resulted from Bailey–Allen's efforts, is not an unreasonable measure of the benefit conferred. * * * [S]ee also Restatement (Second) of Contracts § 374 (1981) (deeming contract price inconclusive evidence of benefit conferred and stating "in no case will the party in breach be allowed to recover more than a ratable portion of the total contract price where such a portion can be determined").

* * *

Bailey–Allen was not entitled to recover damages under the contract. However, it may be entitled to recover in *quantum meruit*. Accordingly, we reverse and remand for the entry of findings consistent with this opinion and, if those findings support an award in *quantum meruit*, for the entry of a judgment. We reverse the award of prejudgment interest, and we direct the trial court to award postjudgment interest, if a judgment is awarded, only from the date the new judgment on remand is entered. * * *

NOTE

In *Bailey–Allen*, the building company could not recover damages for breach of contract because it was the breaching party. *See also* Ben Lomond, Inc. v. Allen, 758 P.2d 92 (Alaska 1988) (buyer, who defaulted on contract to purchase home after conveying a lot valued at $12,000 to seller as a down payment, was entitled to legal restitution measured by $12,000 minus nonbreaching defendant's consequential damages, which included some part of the finance charges incurred from the date of the breach until the date of the resale of the house). Early cases did not allow a breaching party to recover, but some courts started to acknowledge the potential unjust enrichment of the nonbreaching party. In Britton v. Turner, 6 N.H. 481 (1834), an employer hired someone to thresh grain for one year for $120, to be paid at the end of the year. The employee quit after working nine and one-half months, and the employer refused to pay him because of his breach. The court, rejecting the harsh majority rule at that time, allowed the employee to recover the value of his work minus the defendant's damages.

HARRISON v. PRITCHETT

District Court of Appeal of Florida, First District, 1996.
682 So.2d 650.

VAN NORTWICK, JUDGE.

Brenda Joy Harrison appeals a final judgment on the pleadings in her action which sought damages for breach of an oral contract and in *quantum meruit* arising out of Harrison's alleged provision of certain services to appellee, Marvin Pritchett. * * *

The pleadings reflect that Harrison and Pritchett were involved in a "long-standing personal relationship" which ended in 1994. In July 1994, Harrison filed a two-count complaint seeking damages for certain services that she provided Pritchett, "his family and employees including cleaning, cooking, shopping, catering, hair cutting, laundry, driving and other personal services, over the period of 1984 to 1994." In her count for breach of an oral agreement, Harrison alleges that in 1984 Pritchett agreed to establish a $250,000 trust fund for the benefit of Harrison and that, in consideration of Pritchett's promise, Harrison provided the above services. She further alleges that Pritchett failed and refused to perform this oral agreement, in that either a trust fund in the amount of $250,000 was not established or that the trust fund was established and subsequently liquidated, and that as the result of Pritchett's breach Harrison has sustained damages in the amount of $250,000. In her *quantum meruit* count, Harrison alleges that from 1976 through 1994 she provided the above services to Pritchett, his family and employees; that Harrison expected to be paid for such services; that Pritchett accepted and received benefit from the services provided by Harrison; and that Pritchett failed to pay Harrison the reasonable value of $250,000 for the services.

* * * [T]he trial court granted Pritchett a judgment on the pleadings as to both counts based solely upon the application of the statute of frauds. * * *

* * * The alleged agreement in the instant case was not in writing and, as alleged, contemplated performance for longer than one year. Harrison argues that, because she has performed her obligations under the oral agreement, the instant agreement is removed from the statute by the doctrine of part performance. We cannot agree. * * * [T]his court has limited "the application of the narrow doctrine of 'part performance' to ... action[s] which ... involve an agreement to convey land * * *."

Accordingly, we affirm the trial court's ruling with respect to the count based on the alleged oral agreement.

* * *

The application of the statute of frauds to the count for *quantum meruit*, however, requires a different analysis. * * *

* * *

The question of whether the statute of frauds applies in *quantum meruit* actions does not appear to have been directly addressed by a Florida appellate court holding. Nevertheless, the conceptual basis on which an action for *quantum meruit* is based compels our holding that the statute is inapplicable. An action founded on *quantum meruit* is "a common law variety of restitution," * * * otherwise referred to as a "quasi-contract" or a contract implied in law. * * * The Restatement of Contracts distinguishes an action on a contract from a *quantum meruit* or restitution action for the purposes of the statute of frauds, informing us that "[a]n action for restitution . . . is not regarded as an action 'upon' the contract within the meaning or purpose of the Statute of Frauds, and the remedy is not in general affected by the Statute." Restatement (Second) of Contracts 141, cmt. a (1981). Thus,

> [w]hen a plaintiff uses *quantum meruit* to obtain recovery when the statute of frauds otherwise would deny recovery, modern courts with one exception allow recovery and are consistent in measuring recovery when the plaintiff has performed services for the defendant. The one exception is for the more modern requirement that agreements to pay brokerage or finder's fees be in writing.

Candace S. Kovacic, *A Proposal to Simplify Quantum Meruit Litigation,* 35 Am.U.L.Rev. 547, 595–96 (1986) * * *. Although not directly ruling upon the issue before us in the instant case, Florida courts have recognized that a party can bring an action in *quantum meruit* when an action on an oral contract is excluded by the operation of the statute of frauds. *See* Miller v. Greene, 104 So.2d 457, 462 (Fla.1958); Collier v. Brooks, 632 So.2d at 158 n.20; Neveils v. Thagard, 145 So.2d 495, 497 (Fla.1st DCA1962); *see also* Rohrback v. Dauer, 469 So.2d 833, 834 n.1 (Fla.3d DCA1985); and Hiatt v. Vaughn, 430 So.2d 597, 598 n.2 (Fla. 4th DCA1983). Accordingly, because the trial court erroneously applied the statute of frauds to the *quantum meruit* count, we reverse as to that count.

Affirmed in part, reversed in part, and remanded for proceedings consistent with this opinion.

WOLF and PADOVANO, JJ., concur.

NOTE

The cases in this section are using the term *quantum meruit* with its restitutionary, contract implied in law meaning as an alternative action to breach of contract. In these cases the term cannot be used with its contract implied in fact meaning because a contract implied in fact is a contract. The article by Professor Kovacic–Fleischer, cited in *Harrison*, discusses the confusion created by the dual use of the term *quantum meruit* and reviews a variety of types of cases in which *quantum meruit* in the restitutionary sense is an alternative to a barred contract action. Candace Kovacic–Fleischer, *A Proposal to Simplify Quantum Meruit Litigation,* 35 Am. U. L. Rev. 547 (1986). Professor Kovacic–Fleischer explored the use of restitution as an alternative action when a U.S. district court, affirmed by a circuit court, held that Title VII of the Civil Rights Act of 1964 did not apply to partnerships in *Applying Restitution to Remedy a Discriminatory Denial of Partnership,* 34 Syracuse L. Rev. 743 (1983). That holding was reversed by the Supreme Court in Hishon v. King & Spalding, 467 U.S. 69, 104 S.Ct. 2229, 81 L.Ed.2d 59 (1984), but a restitutionary theory could still provide an alternative cause of action.

CHAPTER 5

DECLARATORY JUDGMENTS

■ ■ ■

The declaratory judgment derives from Roman law, and it was "received" into the civil law of Europe during the Middle Ages. Edwin M. Borchard, *The Declaratory Judgment—A Needed Procedural Reform*, 28 Yale L.J. 1, 105 (1918). At that time, the remedy was used primarily to determine questions of status, of property rights, and of the validity or invalidity of wills and other legal instruments. *Id.*

During the late 1800s, the declaratory judgment remedy was recognized in England. Itzhak Zamir, The Declaratory Judgment (2d ed. 1993). During the 1900s, it was introduced into the United States. The pioneer discussions of the declaratory judgment remedy in this country are Edson R. Sunderland, *A Modern Evolution in Remedial Rights—The Declaratory Judgment*, 16 Mich. L. Rev. 69 (1917), and Edwin M. Borchard, *The Declaratory Judgment—A Needed Procedural Reform*, 28 Yale L.J. 1, 105 (1918). The principal treatises are Edwin M. Borchard, Declaratory Judgments (2d ed. 1941), and Walter Anderson, Actions for Declaratory Judgments (2d ed. 1951).

The Uniform Declaratory Judgments Act was approved by the Commissioners on Uniform Laws in 1922, and the Federal Declaratory Judgment Act was enacted by Congress in 1934. Today, approximately 40 states have adopted the Uniform Act (sometimes with modifications), and the remaining states have enacted various types of statutes or rules of court that authorize the remedy.

The primary purpose of the declaratory judgment remedy is to determine rights, obligations, and status. Thus, it is a "preventive," rather than a "coercive," remedy (such as injunctive relief or damages). It "permits one who is walking in the dark to ascertain where he is and where he is going, to turn on the light before he steps rather than after he has stepped in a hole." Loyd v. City of Irwinton, 142 Ga.App. 626, 236 S.E.2d 889 (1977).

Uniform Declaratory Judgments Act (1922)

§ 1. *Scope.* Courts of record within their respective jurisdictions shall have power to declare rights, status, and other legal relations whether or not further relief is or could be claimed. No action or proceeding shall be open to objection on the ground that a declaratory judgment or decree is prayed for. The declaration may be either affirmative or negative in form and effect; and such declarations shall have the force and effect of a final judgment or decree.

§ 2. *Power to Construe, etc.* Any person interested under a deed, will, written contract or other writings constituting a contract, or whose rights, status or other legal relations are affected by a statute, municipal ordinance, contract or franchise, may have determined any question of construction or validity arising under the instrument, statute, ordinance, contract, or franchise and obtain a declaration of rights, status or other legal relations thereunder.

§ 3. *Before Breach.* A contract may be construed either before or after there has been a breach thereof.

§ 4. *Executor, etc.* Any person interested as or through an executor, administrator, trustee, guardian or other fiduciary, creditor, devisee, legatee, heir, next of kin, or cestui que trust, in the administration of a trust, or of the estate of a decedent, an infant, lunatic, or insolvent, may have a declaration of rights or legal relations in respect thereto: (a) To ascertain any class of creditors, devisees, legatees, heirs, next of kin or others; or (b) To direct the executors, administrators, or trustees to do or abstain from doing any particular act in their fiduciary capacity; or (c) To determine any question arising in the administration of the estate or trust, including questions of construction of wills and other writings.

§ 5. *Enumeration Not Exclusive.* The enumeration in sections 2, 3, and 4 does not limit or restrict the exercise of the general powers conferred in section 1, in any proceeding where declaratory relief is sought, in which a judgment or decree will terminate the controversy or remove an uncertainty.

§ 6. *Discretionary.* The court may refuse to render or enter a declaratory judgment or decree where such judgment or decree, if rendered or entered, would not terminate the uncertainty or controversy giving rise to the proceeding.

§ 7. *Review.* All orders, judgments and decrees under this Act may be reviewed as other orders, judgments and decrees.

§ 8. *Supplemental Relief.* Further relief based on a declaratory judgment or decree may be granted whenever necessary or proper. The application therefor shall be by petition to a court having jurisdiction to grant the relief. * * *

§ 9. *Jury Trial.* When a proceeding under this Act involves the determination of an issue of fact, such issue may be tried and determined in the same manner as issues of fact are tried and determined in other civil actions in the court in which the proceeding is pending.

* * *

§ 11. *Parties*. When declaratory relief is sought, all persons shall be made parties who have or claim any interest which would be affected by the declaration, and no declaration shall prejudice the rights of persons not parties to the proceeding. * * *

§ 12. *Construction*. This act is declared to be remedial; its purpose is to settle and to afford relief from uncertainty and insecurity with respect to rights, status and other legal relations; and is to be liberally construed and administered.

* * *

FEDERAL DECLARATORY JUDGMENT ACT

28 U.S.C.A. §§ 2201–02.

§ 2201. Creation of remedy.

(a) In a case of actual controversy within its jurisdiction, except with respect to federal taxes * * *, a proceeding under section 505 or 1146 of title 11, or in any civil action involving an antidumping or countervailing duty proceeding regarding a class or kind of merchandise of a free trade area country (as defined in section 516 (f)(10) of the Tariff Act of 1930), as determined by the administering authority, any court of the United States, upon the filing of an appropriate pleading, may declare the rights and other legal relations of any interested party seeking such declaration, whether or not further relief is or could be sought. Any such declaration shall have the force and effect of a final judgment or decree and shall be reviewable as such.

* * *

§ 2202. Further relief.

Further necessary or proper relief based on a declaratory judgment or decree may be granted after reasonable notice and hearing, against any adversary party whose rights have been determined by such judgment.

FEDERAL RULES OF CIVIL PROCEDURE

Rule 57: Declaratory Judgments

These rules govern the procedure for obtaining a declaratory judgment under 28 U.S.C. § 2201. Rules 38 and 39 govern a demand for a jury trial. The existence of another adequate remedy does not preclude a declaratory judgment that is otherwise appropriate. The court may order a speedy hearing of a declaratory-judgment action.

NOTES

1. Congress' reasons for enacting the Federal Declaratory Judgment Act are explained in S. Rep. 73–1005, at 2–3, 5 (1934):

> The declaratory judgment differs in no respect from any other judgment except that it is not followed by a decree for damages, injunction, specific performance, or other immediately coercive decree. It declares conclusively and finally the rights of parties in litigation over a contested issue, a form of relief which often suffices to settle controversies and fully administer justice. It enables parties in disputes over their rights over a contract, deed, lease, will or any other written instrument to sue for a declaration of rights, without breach of the contract, etc., citing as defendants those who oppose their claims of right. It has been employed in State courts mainly for the construction of instruments of all kinds, for the determination of status in marital or domestic relations, for the determination of the rights contested under a statute or municipal ordinance, where it was not possible or necessary to obtain an injunction.

> The procedure has been especially useful in avoiding the necessity, now so often present, of having to act at one's peril or to act on one's own interpretation of his rights, or abandon one's rights because of a fear of incurring damages. * * * In jurisdictions having the declaratory judgment procedure, it is not necessary to bring about such social and economic waste and destruction in order to obtain a determination of one's rights.

* * *

> The fact is that the declaratory judgment has often proved so necessary that it has been employed under other names for years, and that in many cases the injunction procedure is abused in order to render what is in effect a declaratory judgment. For example, in the case of Pierce v. Society of Sisters (268 U.S. 510, 525, 45 S.Ct. 571, 1925), the court issued an injunction against the enforcement of an Oregon statute which was not to come into force until 2 years later; in rendering a judgment declaring the statute void, the court in effect issued a declaratory judgment by what was, in effect, apparently, an abuse of the injunction. *See also* Village of Euclid v. Ambler Realty Co. (272 U.S. 365, 47 S.Ct. 114, 1926). Much of the hostility to the extensive use of the injunction power by the Federal courts will be obviated by enabling the courts to render declaratory judgments.

> An important practical advantage of the declaratory judgment lies in the fact that it enables litigants to narrow the issue, speed the decision, and settle the controversy before an accumulation of differences and hostility has engendered a wide and general conflict, involving numerous collateral issues. * * *

For commentary on the federal statute at the time of its enactment, see Edwin Borchard, *The Federal Declaratory Judgments Act*, 21 Va. L. Rev. 35 (1934).

2. The declaratory judgment is a modern, statutory remedy that "can be either legal or equitable." Thus, for example, in Maryland "prior to the 1984 procedural merger of law and equity, * * * a declaratory judgment proceeding could be brought on the law or equity side of a circuit court." Kann v. Kann, 344 Md. 689, 700, 690 A.2d 509, 514 (1997).

3. Because the declaratory judgment remedy is a modern remedy, rather than an old English equitable remedy (such as injunctive relief), there is no need for the plaintiff to prove the inadequacy of the plaintiff's legal remedy in order to qualify for declaratory relief. See Fed.R.Civ.Pro. 57.

4. In both the federal and state court systems, the right to jury trial in a declaratory judgment proceeding "depends on whether the action is the counterpart to one in equity or in law." In re Environmental Insurance Declaratory Judgment Actions, 149 N.J. 278, 292, 693 A.2d 844, 850 (1997); see generally Jean E. Maess, Annotation, Right to Jury Trial in Action for Declaratory Relief in State Court, 33 A.L.R. 4th 146 (1984). For a more complete consideration of this issue, see infra Chapter 8.

5. The statute of limitations is a defense to a declaratory judgment action. The federal circuits that have considered the question agree that "an action for declaratory relief will be barred to the same extent the applicable statute of limitations bars the concurrent legal remedy." Algrant v. Evergreen Valley Nurseries Ltd. Partnership, 126 F.3d 178, 181 (3d Cir.1997). Otherwise, litigants could circumvent the statute of limitations merely be "draping their claim in the raiment of the Declaratory Judgment Act." Id. at 185 (quoting Gilbert v. City of Cambridge, 932 F.2d 51, 58 (1st Cir.1991)).

6. Laches is also a defense to a declaratory judgment action. E.g., Hutchinson v. Pfeil, 105 F.3d 562 (10th Cir.1997). See generally Developments in the Law: Declaratory Judgments—1941–1949, 62 Harv. L. Rev. 787, 830–33 (1949). Laches is discussed supra, Chapter 2, Section 5.B.

7. Because Article III of the Constitution limits the jurisdiction of the federal courts, "there were reasonable expressions of doubt that constitutional limitations on federal judicial power would permit any federal declaratory judgment procedure." Public Service Commission v. Wycoff Co., 344 U.S. 237, 241, 73 S.Ct. 236, 239, 97 L.Ed. 291 (1952). But, after the Uniform Declaratory Judgments Act had been adopted by several state legislatures, the United States Supreme Court held that it could exercise appellate jurisdiction over a high state court's ruling which had been entered pursuant to that state's declaratory judgments statute. Nashville, C. & St. L. Ry. v. Wallace, 288 U.S. 249, 53 S.Ct. 345, 77 L.Ed. 730 (1933) (action to secure a judicial declaration under Tennessee's Declaratory Judgments Act that a state excise tax was invalid "as applied" under the Commerce Clause; statute held constitutional). The next year, Congress passed the Federal Declaratory Judgment Act.

AETNA LIFE INSURANCE CO. v. HAWORTH

Supreme Court of the United States, 1937.
300 U.S. 227, 57 S.Ct. 461, 81 L.Ed. 617.

MR. CHIEF JUSTICE HUGHES delivered the opinion of the Court.

The question presented is whether the District Court had jurisdiction of this suit under the Federal Declaratory Judgment Act. * * *

* * *

The question arises upon the plaintiff's complaint which was dismissed by the District Court upon the ground that it did not set forth a "controversy" in the constitutional sense and hence did not come within the legitimate scope of the statute. 11 F.Supp. 1016. The decree of dismissal was affirmed by the Circuit Court of Appeals. 84 F.2d 695. We granted certiorari. * * *

From the complaint it appears that plaintiff is an insurance company which had issued to the defendant Edwin P. Haworth five policies of insurance upon his life, the defendant Cora M. Haworth being named as beneficiary. The complaint set forth the terms of the policies. They contained various provisions which for the present purpose it is unnecessary fully to particularize. It is sufficient to observe that they all provided for certain benefits in the event that the insured became totally and permanently disabled. * * *

The complaint alleges that * * * the insured ceased to pay premiums * * * and claimed the disability benefits as stipulated. * * * These claims, which were repeatedly renewed, were presented in the form of affidavits accompanied by certificates of physicians. * * *

* * *

Plaintiff * * * contends that there is an actual controversy with defendants as to the existence of the total and permanent disability of the insured and as to the continuance of the obligations asserted despite the nonpayment of premiums. Defendants have not instituted any action wherein the plaintiff would have an opportunity to prove the absence of the alleged disability and plaintiff points to the danger that it may lose the benefit of evidence through disappearance, illness, or death of witnesses; and meanwhile, in the absence of a judicial decision with respect to the alleged disability, the plaintiff in relation to these policies will be compelled to maintain reserves in excess of $20,000.

The complaint asks for a decree that the four policies be declared to be null and void by reason of lapse for nonpayment of premiums and that the obligation upon the remaining policy be held to consist solely in the duty to pay the sum of $45 upon the death of the insured, and for such further relief as the exigencies of the case may require.

The Constitution * * * limits the exercise of the judicial power to "cases" and "controversies." "The term 'controversies,' if distinguishable at all from 'cases,' is so in that it is less comprehensive than the latter, and includes only suits of a civil nature." * * * The Declaratory Judgment Act of 1934, in its limitation to "cases of actual controversy," manifestly has regard to the constitutional provision and is operative only in respect to controversies which are such in the constitutional sense. The word "actual" is one of emphasis rather than of definition. Thus the operation of the Declaratory Judgment Act is procedural only. In providing remedies and defining procedure in relation to cases and controversies in the constitutional sense the Congress is acting within its delegated power over the jurisdiction of the federal courts which the Congress is authorized to establish. * * * Exercising this control of practice and procedure the Congress is not confined to traditional forms or traditional remedies. * * * In dealing with methods within its sphere of remedial action the Congress may create and improve as well as abolish or restrict. The Declaratory Judgment Act must be deemed to fall within this ambit of congressional power, so far as it authorizes relief which is consonant with the exercise of the judicial function in the determination of controversies to which under the Constitution the judicial power extends.

A "controversy" in this sense must be one that is appropriate for judicial determination. * * * A justiciable controversy is thus distinguished from a difference or dispute of a hypothetical or abstract character; from one that is academic or moot. * * * The controversy must be definite and concrete, touching the legal relations of parties having adverse legal interests. * * * It must be a real and substantial controversy admitting of specific relief through a decree of a conclusive character, as distinguished from an opinion advising what the law would be upon a hypothetical state of facts. * * * Where there is such a concrete case admitting of an immediate and definitive determination of the legal rights of the parties in an adversary proceeding upon the facts alleged, the judicial function may be appropriately exercised although the adjudication of the rights of the litigants may not require the award of process or the payment of damages. * * * And as it is not essential to the exercise of the judicial power that an injunction be sought, allegations that irreparable injury is threatened are not required. * * *

With these principles governing the application of the Declaratory Judgment Act, we turn to the nature of the controversy, the relation and interests of the parties, and the relief sought in the instant case.

There is here a dispute between parties who face each other in an adversary proceeding. The dispute relates to legal rights and obligations arising from the contracts of insurance. The dispute is definite and concrete, not hypothetical or abstract. Prior to this suit, the parties had taken adverse positions with respect to their existing obligations. Their contentions concerned the disability benefits which were to be payable upon prescribed conditions. On the one side, the insured claimed that he had become totally and permanently disabled and hence was relieved of the obligation to continue the payment of premiums and was entitled to the stipulated disability benefits and to the continuance of the policies in force. The insured presented this claim formally, as required by the policies. It was a claim of a present, specific right. On the other side, the company made an equally definite claim that the alleged basic fact did not exist, that the insured was not totally and permanently disabled and had not been relieved of the duty to continue the payment of premiums, that in consequence the policies had lapsed, and that the company was thus freed from its obligation either to pay disability benefits or to continue the insurance in force. Such a dispute is manifestly susceptible of judicial determination. It calls, not for an advisory opinion upon a hypothetical basis, but for an adjudication of present right upon established facts.

That the dispute turns upon questions of fact does not withdraw it, as the respondent seems to contend, from judicial cognizance. The legal consequences flow from the facts and it is the province of the courts to ascertain and find the facts in order to determine the legal consequences. That is everyday practice. * * *

If the insured had brought suit [pursuant to diversity jurisdiction] to recover the disability benefits currently payable under two of the policies there would have been no question that the controversy was of a justiciable nature, whether or not the amount involved would have permitted its determination in a federal court. * * * [T]he character of the controversy and of the issue to be determined is essentially the same whether it is presented by the insured or by the insurer. * * *

* * *

Our conclusion is that the complaint presented a controversy to which the judicial power extends and that authority to hear and determine it has been conferred upon the District Court by the Declaratory Judgment Act. The decree is reversed and the cause is remanded for further proceedings in conformity with this opinion.

NOTES

1. The Restatement (Second) of Judgments § 76 (1980) provides:

> A judgment in an action brought to declare rights or other legal relations of the parties is conclusive in a subsequent action between them as to the matters declared, and, in accordance with the rules of issue preclusion, as to any issues actually litigated by them and determined in the action.

The comments to section 76 explain that a declaratory judgment is preclusive as to matters actually declared, but does not bar claims that were not adjudicated, even though they could have been asserted in the complaint. *Id.* cmts. b, c, e.

2. The United States Supreme Court has decided several cases in which it has interpreted the Federal Declaratory Judgment Act so as not to expand federal question jurisdiction. *E.g.*, Skelly Oil Co. v. Phillips Petroleum Co., 339 U.S. 667, 70 S.Ct. 876, 94 L.Ed. 1194 (1950). It has been clear for decades that a declaratory judgment plaintiff may not anticipate a declaratory judgment defendant's federal affirmative defense. *Id.* On the other hand, a declaratory judgment plaintiff has been allowed to anticipate a declaratory judgment defendant's federal cause of action. Franchise Tax Board v. Construction Laborers Vacation Trust, 463 U.S. 1, 19 n.19, 103 S.Ct. 2841, 2851 n.19, 77 L.Ed.2d 420 (1983). However, the Court in dictum recently ques-

tioned whether a declaratory judgment plaintiff ought to be allowed to anticipate a declaratory judgment defendant's federal cause of action when the declaratory judgment plaintiff plans to assert a nonfederal affirmative defense. Textron Lycoming Reciprocating Engine Division, Avco Corp. v. UAW, 523 U.S. 653, 118 S.Ct. 1626, 140 L.Ed.2d 863 (1998) (Justice Breyer wrote a concurring opinion to emphasize that he disagreed with the Court's dictum.). *See generally* Donald L. Doernberg & Michael B. Mushlin, *The Trojan Horse: How the Declaratory Judgment Act Created a Cause of Action and Expanded Federal Jurisdiction While the Supreme Court Wasn't Looking*, 36 UCLA L. Rev. 529 (1989).

MARYLAND CASUALTY CO. v. PACIFIC COAL & OIL CO.

Supreme Court of the United States, 1941.
312 U.S. 270, 61 S.Ct. 510, 85 L.Ed. 826.

MR. JUSTICE MURPHY delivered the opinion of the Court.

Petitioner issued a conventional liability policy to the insured, the Pacific Coal & Oil Co., in which it agreed to indemnify the insured for any sums the latter might be required to pay to third parties for injuries to person and property caused by automobiles hired by the insured. Petitioner also agreed that it would defend any action covered by the policy which was brought against the insured to recover damages for such injuries.

While the policy was in force, a collision occurred between an automobile driven by respondent Orteca and a truck driven by an employee of the insured. Orteca brought an action in an Ohio state court against the insured to recover damages resulting from injuries sustained in this collision. Apparently this action has not proceeded to judgment.

Petitioner then brought this action against the insured and Orteca. Its complaint set forth the facts detailed above and further alleged that at the time of the collision the employee of the insured was driving a truck sold to him by the insured on a conditional sales contract. Petitioner claimed that this truck was not one "hired by the insured," and hence that it was not liable to defend the action by Orteca against the insured or to indemnify the latter if Orteca prevailed. It sought a declaratory judgment to this effect against the insured and Orteca, and a temporary injunction restraining the proceedings in the state court pending final judgment in this suit.

Orteca demurred to the complaint on the ground that it did not state a cause of action against him. The District Court sustained his demurrer and the Circuit Court of Appeals affirmed. Maryland Casualty Co. v. Pacific Coal & Oil Co., 6 Cir., 111 F.2d 214. * * *

The question is whether petitioner's allegations are sufficient to entitle it to the declaratory relief prayed in its complaint. This raises the question whether there is an "actual controversy" within the meaning of the Declaratory Judgment Act * * *.

* * *

That the complaint in the instant case presents such a controversy is plain. Orteca is now seeking a judgment against the insured in an action which the latter claims is covered by the policy, and sections 9510–3 and 9510–4 of the Ohio Code (Page's Ohio General Code, Vol. 6, §§ 9510–3, 9510–4) give Orteca a statutory right to proceed against petitioner by supplemental process and action if he obtains a final judgment against the insured which the latter does not satisfy within thirty days after its rendition. * * *

It is clear that there is an actual controversy between petitioner and the insured. *Compare* Aetna Life Ins. Co. v. Haworth, *supra.* If we held contrariwise as to Orteca because, as to him, the controversy were yet too remote, it is possible that opposite interpretations of the policy might be announced by the federal and state courts. For the federal court, in a judgment not binding on Orteca, might determine that petitioner was not obligated under the policy, while the state court, in a supplemental proceeding by Orteca against petitioner, might conclude otherwise. * * *

Thus we hold that there is an actual controversy between petitioner and Orteca, and hence, that petitioner's complaint states a cause of action against the latter. However, our decision does not authorize issuance of the injunction prayed by petitioner. Judicial Code § 265, 28 U.S.C. § 379, 28 U.S.C.A. § 379 [(prohibiting a federal court from enjoining a pending state court proceeding)]; *see* Central Surety & Insurance Corp. v. Norris, 103 F.2d 116, 117 (5th Cir. 1939) [(refusing to enjoin a pending state court proceeding; observing that both the state tort action and the federal declaratory judgment action could proceed until one had been decided, and then "it would be used in a proper manner in disposing of the other")] * * *.

The judgment of the Circuit Court of Appeals is reversed and the cause is remanded for further proceedings in conformity with this opinion.

MR. JUSTICE BLACK did not participate in the consideration or decision of this case.

WILTON v. SEVEN FALLS CO.

Supreme Court of the United States, 1995.
515 U.S. 277, 115 S.Ct. 2137, 132 L.Ed.2d 214.

JUSTICE O'CONNOR delivered the opinion of the Court.

This case asks whether the discretionary standard set forth in Brillhart v. Excess Ins. Co. of America, 316 U.S. 491, 62 S.Ct. 1173, 86 L.Ed. 1620 (1942), or the "exceptional circumstances" test developed in Colorado River Water Conservation Dist. v. United States, 424 U.S. 800, 96 S.Ct. 1236, 47 L.Ed.2d 483 (1976), and Moses H. Cone Memorial Hospital v. Mercury Constr. Corp., 460 U.S. 1, 103 S.Ct. 927, 74 L.Ed.2d 765 (1983), governs a district court's decision to stay a declaratory judgment action during the pendency of parallel state court proceedings, and under what standard of review a court of appeals should evaluate the district court's decision to do so.

I

In early 1992, a dispute between respondents (the Hill Group) and other parties over the ownership and operation of oil and gas properties in Winkler County, Texas, appeared likely to culminate in litigation. The Hill Group asked petitioners (London Underwriters) to provide them with coverage under several commercial liability insurance policies. London Underwriters refused to defend or indemnify the Hill Group in a letter dated July 31, 1992. In September 1992, after a 3-week trial, a Winkler County jury entered a verdict in excess of $100 million against the Hill Group on various state law claims.

The Hill Group gave London Underwriters notice of the verdict in late November 1992. On December 9, 1992, London Underwriters filed suit in the United States District Court for the Southern District of Texas, basing jurisdiction upon diversity of citizenship under 28 U.S.C. § 1332. London Underwriters sought a declaration under the Declaratory Judgment Act, 28 U.S.C. § 2201(a) (1988 ed., Supp. V), that their policies did not cover the Hill Group's liability for the Winkler County judgment. After negotiations with the Hill Group's counsel, London Underwriters voluntarily dismissed the action on January 22, 1993. London Underwriters did so, however, upon the express condition that the Hill Group give London Underwriters two weeks' notice if they decided to bring suit on the policy.

On February 23, 1993, the Hill Group notified London Underwriters of their intention to file such a suit in Travis County, Texas. London Underwriters refiled their declaratory judgment action in the Southern District of Texas on February 24, 1993. As promised, the Hill Group initiated an action against London Underwriters on March 26, 1993, in state court in Travis County. The Hill Group's codefendants in the Winkler County litigation joined in this suit and asserted claims against certain Texas insurers, thus rendering the parties nondiverse and the suit nonremovable.

On the same day that the Hill Group filed their Travis County action, they moved to dismiss or, in the alternative, to stay London Underwriters' federal declaratory judgment action. After receiving submissions from the parties on the issue, the District Court entered a stay on June 30, 1993. The District Court observed that the state lawsuit pending in Travis County encompassed the same coverage issues raised in the declaratory judgment action and determined that a stay was warranted in order to avoid piecemeal litigation and to bar London Underwriters' attempts at forum shopping. London Underwriters filed a timely appeal. * * *

The United States Court of Appeals for the Fifth Circuit affirmed. 41 F.3d 934 (1994). Noting that under Circuit precedent, "[a] district court has broad discretion to grant (or decline to grant) a declaratory judgment," * * * the Court of Appeals did not require application of the test articulated in *Colorado River, supra,* and *Moses H. Cone, supra,* under which district courts must point to "exceptional circumstances" to justify staying or dismissing federal proceedings. Citing the interests in avoiding duplicative proceedings and forum shopping, the Court of Appeals reviewed the District Court's decision for abuse of discretion, and found none. * * *

We granted certiorari * * *. We now affirm.

II

Over 50 years ago, in Brillhart v. Excess Ins. Co. of America, 316 U.S. 491, 62 S.Ct. 1173, 86 L.Ed. 1620 (1942), this Court addressed circumstances virtually identical to those present in the case before us today. An insurer, anticipating a coercive suit, sought a declaration in federal court of nonliability on an insurance policy. The District Court dismissed the action in favor of pending state garnishment proceedings, to which the insurer had been added as a defendant. * * * [T]his Court held that, "[a]lthough the District Court had jurisdiction of the suit under the Federal Declaratory Judgments Act, it was under no compulsion to exercise that jurisdiction." * * * The Court explained that "[o]rdinarily it would be uneconomical as well as vexatious for a federal court to proceed in a declaratory judgment suit where another suit is pending in a state court presenting the same issues, not governed by federal law, between the same parties." * * * The question for a district court presented with a suit under the Declaratory Judgment Act, the Court found, is "whether the questions in controversy between the parties to the federal suit, and which are not foreclosed under the applicable substantive law, can better be settled in the proceeding pending in the state court." * * *

Brillhart makes clear that district courts possess discretion in determining whether and when to entertain an action under the Declaratory Judgment Act, even when the suit otherwise satisfies subject matter jurisdictional prerequisites. Although *Brillhart* did not set out an exclusive list of factors governing the district court's exercise of this discretion, it did provide some useful guidance in that regard. The Court indicated, for example, that in deciding whether to enter a stay, a district court should examine "the scope of the pending state court proceeding and the nature of defenses open there." * * * This inquiry, in turn, entails consideration of "whether the claims of all parties in interest can satisfactorily be adjudicated in that proceeding, whether necessary parties have been joined, whether such parties are amenable to process in that proceeding, etc." * * * *Brillhart* indicated that, at least where another suit involving the same parties and presenting opportunity for ventilation of the same state law issues is pending in state court, a district court might be indulging in "[g]ratuitous interference" * * * if it permitted the federal declaratory action to proceed.

Brillhart, without more, clearly supports the District Court's decision in this case. (That the court here stayed, rather than dismissed, the action is of little moment in this regard, because the state court's decision will bind the parties under principles of res judicata.) Nonetheless, London Underwriters argue, and several Courts of Appeals have agreed, that intervening case law has supplanted *Brillhart*'s notions of broad discretion with a test under which district courts may stay or dismiss actions properly within their jurisdiction only in "exceptional circumstances." In London Underwriters' view, recent cases have established that a district court must point to a compelling reason—which, they say, is lacking here—in order to stay a declaratory judgment action in favor of pending state proceedings. * * *

In Colorado River Water Conservation Dist. v. United States, 424 U.S. 800, 96 S.Ct. 1236, 47 L.Ed.2d 483 (1976), the Government brought an action in Federal District Court under 28 U.S.C. § 1345 seeking a declaration of its water rights, the appointment of a water master, and an order enjoining all uses and diversions of water by other parties. * * * Without discussing *Brillhart*, the Court began with the premise that federal courts have a "virtually unflagging obligation" to exercise the jurisdiction conferred on them by Congress. * * * The Court determined, however, that a district court could nonetheless abstain from the assumption of jurisdiction over a suit in "exceptional" circumstances, and it found such exceptional circumstances on the facts of the case. * * * Specifically, the Court deemed dispositive a clear federal policy against piecemeal adjudication of water rights; the existence of an elaborate state scheme for resolution of such claims; the absence of any proceedings in the District Court, other than the filing of the complaint, prior to the motion to dismiss; * * * and the prior participation of the Federal Government in related state proceedings.

* * *

Relying on these post-*Brillhart* developments, London Underwriters contend that the *Brillhart* regime, under which district courts have substantial latitude in deciding whether to stay or to dismiss a declaratory judgment suit in light of pending state proceedings (and need not point to "exceptional circumstances" to justify their actions), is an outmoded relic of another era. We disagree. * * * Distinct features of the Declaratory Judgment Act, we believe, justify a standard vesting district courts with greater discretion in declaratory judgment actions than that permitted under the "exceptional circumstances" test of *Colorado River* * * *. No subsequent case, in our view, has called into question the application of the *Brillhart* standard to the *Brillhart* facts.

Since its inception, the Declaratory Judgment Act has been understood to confer on federal courts unique and substantial discretion in deciding whether to declare the rights of litigants. On its face, the statute provides that a court "*may* declare the rights and other legal relations of any interested party seeking such declaration," 28 U.S.C. § 2201(a) (1988 ed., Supp. V) (emphasis added). *See generally* E. Borchard, Declaratory Judgments 312–314 (2d ed. 1941) * * *. When all is said and done, we have concluded, "the propriety of declaratory relief in a particular case will depend upon a circumspect sense of its fitness informed by the teachings and experience concerning the functions and extent of federal judicial power." * * *

* * *

We agree, for all practical purposes, with Professor Borchard, who observed half a century ago that "[t]here is ... nothing automatic or obligatory about the assumption of 'jurisdiction' by a federal court" to hear a declaratory judgment action. Borchard, Declaratory Judgments, at 313. By the Declaratory Judgment Act, Congress sought to place a remedial arrow in the district court's quiver; it created an opportunity, rather than a duty, to grant a new form of relief to qualifying litigants. Consistent with the nonobligatory nature of the remedy, a district court is authorized, in the sound exercise of its discretion, to stay or to dismiss an action seeking a declaratory judgment before trial or after all arguments have drawn to a close.[1] In the declaratory judgment context, the normal principle that federal courts should adjudicate claims within their jurisdiction yields to considerations of practicality and wise judicial administration.

III

* * * The Court of Appeals reviewed the District Court's decision to stay London Underwriters' action for abuse of discretion, and found none. London Underwriters urge us to follow those other Courts of Appeals that review decisions to grant (or to refrain from granting) declaratory relief de novo. * * * We decline this invitation. We believe it more consistent with the statute to vest district courts with discretion in the first instance, because facts bearing on the usefulness of the declaratory judgment remedy, and the fitness of the case for resolution, are peculiarly within their grasp. * * *

IV

In sum, we conclude that Brillhart v. Excess Ins. Co. of America, 316 U.S. 491, 62 S.Ct. 1173, 86 L.Ed. 1620 (1942), governs this declaratory judgment action and that district courts' decisions about the propriety of hearing declaratory judgment actions, which are necessarily bound up with their decisions about the propriety of granting declaratory relief, should be reviewed for abuse of discretion. We do not attempt at this time to delineate the outer boundaries of that discretion in other cases, for example, cases raising issues of federal law or cases in which there are no parallel state proceedings. Like the Court of Appeals, we conclude only that the District Court acted within its bounds in staying this action for declaratory relief where parallel proceedings, presenting opportunity for

---

1. We note that where the basis for declining to proceed is the pendency of a state proceeding, a stay will often be the preferable course, because it assures that the federal action can proceed without risk of a time bar if the state case, for any reason, fails to resolve the matter in controversy. *See, e.g.,* P. Bator, D. Meltzer, P. Mishkin, & D. Shapiro, Hart and Wechsler's The Federal Courts and the Federal System 1451, n. 9 (3d ed. 1988).

ventilation of the same state law issues, were underway in state court. The judgment of the Court of Appeals for the Fifth Circuit is

Affirmed.

JUSTICE BREYER took no part in the consideration or decision of this case.

NOTES

1. Section 6 of the Uniform Declaratory Judgments Act is even more explicit than the Federal Declaratory Judgment Act about the discretionary nature of the procedure: "The court may refuse to render or enter a declaratory judgment or decree where such judgment or decree, if rendered or entered, would not terminate the uncertainty or controversy giving rise to the proceeding." For a discussion of the implications of *Wilton*, see Grace M. Giesel, *The Expanded Discretion of Lower Courts to Regulate Access to the Federal Courts After* Wilton v. Seven Falls Co.: *Declaratory Judgment Actions and Implications Far Beyond*, 33 Hous. L. Rev. 393 (1996); Steven Plitt & Joshua D. Rogers, *Charting a Course for Federal Removal Through the Abstention Doctrine: A Titanic Experience in the Sargasso Sea of Jurisdictional Manipulation*, 56 DePaul L. Rev. 107 (2006).

2. As a general rule, declaratory relief is not appropriate in the case of a completed tort. *E.g.*, Bird v. Rozier, 948 P.2d 888 (Wyo.1997) (plaintiff who alleges that the defendant acted negligently, but who fails to allege that the plaintiff sustained the type of actual harm for which compensatory damages would be awarded, is not entitled to declaratory judgment). *See generally* George B. Fraser, *A Survey of Declaratory Judgment Actions in the United States*, 39 Iowa L. Rev. 639, 649–50 (1954).

3. In breach of contract cases, the courts are more willing than in tort cases to allow either party to the contract to sue for declaratory relief. For example, in Warren v. Kaiser Foundation Health Plan, Inc., 47 Cal.App.3d 678, 121 Cal.Rptr. 19 (1975), the plaintiff sought a declaration that the expenses of hospitalizing his severely burned wife in a non-Kaiser facility were covered under the emergency clause of his Kaiser health insurance coverage. Kaiser demurred to the complaint on the ground that the claim was not covered by the Kaiser plan and that declaratory relief was an inappropriate remedy because the plaintiff could sue for breach of contract:

> Any doubt should be resolved in favor of granting declaratory relief. * * * While the court may refuse to entertain the action where "the rights of the complaining party have crystallized into a cause of action for past wrongs, [and] all relationship between the parties has ceased to exist * * * " (Travers v. Louden, 254 Cal.App.2d 926, 929, 62 Cal.Rptr. 654, 656), it may not exclude the action where the alternative remedy of suing upon the matured breach is not as "speedy and adequate or as well suited to the plaintiff's needs as declaratory relief." (Maguire v. Hibernia S. & L. Soc., 23 Cal.2d 719, 732, 146 P.2d 673, 680; 3 Witkin, Cal. Procedure (2d ed.), Pleading, § 724.) A lawsuit for breach of contract is neither as speedy and adequate nor as well suited as declaratory relief to the plaintiff's needs where, despite the breach, a relationship between the

parties continues so that a declaration may guide their future conduct * * *, or where the use of declaratory relief will avoid a multiplicity of suits that may ensue if a different remedy is pursued * * *.

Here, although the complaint claims that Kaiser breached its contract, it also shows on its face that the relationship between appellant and Kaiser is a continuing one since appellant continued to be a member of the plan after the claimed breach. A declaration of the right of a member of the plan for reimbursement of medical expense incurred in an emergency so grave as to preclude access to Kaiser contract hospitals and physicians will guide the future conduct of the parties. If nothing else, a declaration in Kaiser's favor will be the warning that the plan may not be adequate to the needs of its members, including appellant. Here, also, the remedy of declaratory relief will avoid multiplicity of litigation. Appellant has incurred substantial obligations for the care of his late wife. If those obligations must be reimbursed by Kaiser, threatened lawsuits by those who provided the medical and hospital care will be avoided.

Id. at 683–84, 121 Cal.Rptr. at 22.

4. One year after deciding *Wilton*, the Supreme Court distinguished a claim for damages from a claim for declaratory relief. Quackenbush v. Allstate Insurance Co., 517 U.S. 706, 116 S.Ct. 1712, 135 L.Ed.2d 1 (1996). The Court ruled that a federal district court may not dismiss, but may only stay, an action for damages, and emphasized that such stays should be granted sparingly. *Id.* Reading *Wilton* and *Quackenbush* together, lower federal courts have concluded that, when a federal court plaintiff seeks both damages and a declaratory judgment, *Quackenbush* prevails and the trial court is not free to dismiss the case under *Wilton*. *E.g.*, Snodgrass v. Provident Life & Accident Insurance Co., 147 F.3d 1163 (9th Cir.1998) (state court action that had been filed by surgeon who had suffered serious injury to his dominant hand against disability insurer was removed to federal court; surgeon sought a declaration of total disability and also sought damages for both breach of contract and the infliction of emotional distress; federal district court on its own motion remanded to state court; federal appellate court reversed for abuse of discretion with instructions that the district court retain jurisdiction). Similarly, when a federal court plaintiff sues for both restitutionary and declaratory relief, the trial court "must * * * hear the *quantum meruit* claim properly before it." TIG Insurance Co. v. Deaton, Inc., 932 F.Supp. 132, 138 (W.D.N.C. 1996).

5. When an immunity doctrine bars a claim for damages or restitution against a defendant who has engaged in past unconstitutional misconduct, the courts hold that the plaintiff may not go forward on the same substantive theory with a request for declaratory relief. *E.g.*, Ashcroft v. Mattis, 431 U.S. 171, 97 S.Ct. 1739, 52 L.Ed.2d 219 (1977) (father of 18–year-old son who had been killed by police officers while attempting to escape arrest could not go forward with declaratory judgment suit after claim for damages had been dismissed due to the defendants' successful assertion of qualified, public official immunity); Lister v. Board of Regents, 72 Wis.2d 282, 240 N.W.2d 610 (1976) (law graduates not allowed to seek declaratory judgment against regents who allegedly had charged the students erroneously for out-of-state

tuition; defendants successfully asserted both sovereign and public official immunity). For a discussion of the availability of both injunctive and declaratory relief against governmental entities and public officials who are threatening to engage in future, unconstitutional misconduct, see *infra* Chapter 6, Section 4.B.

STEFFEL v. THOMPSON

Supreme Court of the United States, 1974.
415 U.S. 452, 94 S.Ct. 1209, 39 L.Ed.2d 505.

MR. JUSTICE BRENNAN delivered the opinion of the Court.

When a state criminal proceeding under a disputed state criminal statute is pending against a federal plaintiff at the time his federal complaint is filed, Younger v. Harris, 401 U.S. 37, 91 S.Ct. 746, 27 L.Ed.2d 669 (1971), and Samuels v. Mackell, 401 U.S. 66, 91 S.Ct. 764, 27 L.Ed.2d 688 (1971), held, respectively, that, unless bad-faith enforcement or other special circumstances are demonstrated, principles of equity, comity, and federalism preclude issuance of a federal injunction restraining enforcement of the criminal statute and, in all but unusual circumstances, a declaratory judgment upon the constitutionality of the statute. This case presents the important question reserved in Samuels v. Mackell, *id.*, at 73–74, 91 S.Ct., at 768–769, whether declaratory relief is precluded when a state prosecution has been threatened, but is not pending, and a showing of bad-faith enforcement or other special circumstances has not been made.

Petitioner, and others, filed a complaint in the District Court for the Northern District of Georgia, invoking the Civil Rights Act of 1871, 42 U.S.C.A. § 1983 * * *. The complaint requested a declaratory judgment * * * that [Georgia's criminal trespass statute] was being applied in violation of petitioner's First and Fourteenth Amendment rights, and an injunction restraining respondents—the Solicitor of the Civil and Criminal Court of DeKalb County, the chief of the DeKalb County Police, the owner of the North DeKalb Shopping Center, and the manager of that shopping center—from enforcing the statute so as to interfere with petitioner's constitutionally protected activities.

The parties stipulated to the relevant facts: On October 8, 1970, while petitioner and other individuals were distributing handbills protesting American involvement in Vietnam on an exterior sidewalk of the North DeKalb Shopping Center, shopping center employees asked them to stop handbilling and leave. They declined to do so, and police officers were summoned. The officers told them that they would be arrested if they did not stop handbilling. The group then left to avoid arrest. Two days later petitioner and a companion returned to the shopping center and again began handbilling. The manager of the center called the police, and petitioner and his companion were once again told that failure to stop their handbilling would result in their arrests. Petitioner left to avoid arrest. His companion stayed, however, continued handbilling, and was

arrested and subsequently arraigned on a charge of criminal trespass
* * *. Petitioner alleged in his complaint that, although he desired to
return to the shopping center to distribute handbills, he had not done so
because of his concern that he, too, would be arrested * * *; the parties
stipulated that, if petitioner returned and refused upon request to stop
handbilling, a warrant would be sworn out and he might be arrested and
charged with a violation of the Georgia statute.

After hearing, the District Court denied all relief and dismissed the
action * * *.

* * *

* * * At the threshold we must consider whether petitioner presents
an "actual controversy," a requirement imposed by Art. III of the Constitution and the express terms of the Federal Declaratory Judgment Act
* * *.

* * * [P]etitioner has alleged threats of prosecution that cannot be
characterized as "imaginary or speculative." * * * He has been twice
warned to stop handbilling that he claims is constitutionally protected and
has been told by the police that if he again handbills at the shopping
center and disobeys a warning to stop he will likely be prosecuted. The
prosecution of petitioner's handbilling companion is ample demonstration
that petitioner's concern with arrest has not been "chimerical." In these
circumstances, it is not necessary that petitioner first expose himself to
actual arrest or prosecution to be entitled to challenge a statute that he
claims deters the exercise of his constitutional rights. * * *

Nonetheless, there remains a question as to the continuing existence
of a live and acute controversy that must be resolved on the remand we
order today * * *. Since we cannot ignore the recent developments
reducing the Nation's involvement in that part of the world, it will be for
the District Court on remand to determine if subsequent events have so
altered petitioner's desire to engage in handbilling at the shopping center
that it can no longer be said that this case presents "a substantial
controversy, between parties having adverse legal interests, of sufficient
immediacy and reality to warrant the issuance of a declaratory judgment."
Maryland Casualty Co. v. Pacific Coal & Oil Co., 312 U.S. 270, 273, 61
S.Ct. 510, 512, 85 L.Ed. 826 (1941). * * *

We now turn to the question of whether the District Court and the
Court of Appeals correctly found petitioner's request for declaratory relief
inappropriate.

When no state criminal proceeding is pending at the time the federal
complaint is filed, federal intervention does not result in duplicative legal
proceedings or disruption of the state criminal justice system; nor can
federal intervention, in that circumstance, be interpreted as reflecting
negatively upon the state court's ability to enforce constitutional principles. In addition, while a pending state prosecution provides the federal
plaintiff with a concrete opportunity to vindicate his constitutional rights,

a refusal on the part of the federal courts to intervene when no state proceeding is pending may place the hapless plaintiff between the Scylla of intentionally flouting state law and the Charybdis of forgoing what he believes to be constitutionally protected activity in order to avoid becoming enmeshed in a criminal proceeding. *Cf.* Dombrowski v. Pfister, 380 U.S. 479, 490, 85 S.Ct. 1116, 1123, 14 L.Ed.2d 22 (1965).

When no state proceeding is pending and thus considerations of equity, comity, and federalism have little vitality, the propriety of granting federal declaratory relief may properly be considered independently of a request for injunctive relief. Here, the Court of Appeals held that, because injunctive relief would not be appropriate since petitioner failed to demonstrate irreparable injury—a traditional prerequisite to injunctive relief * * *—it followed that declaratory relief was also inappropriate. Even if the Court of Appeals correctly viewed injunctive relief as inappropriate—a question we need not reach today since petitioner has abandoned his request for that remedy, * * * the court erred in treating the requests for injunctive and declaratory relief as a single issue. "When no state prosecution is pending and the only question is whether declaratory relief is appropriate * * * the congressional scheme that makes the federal courts the primary guardians of constitutional rights, and the express congressional authorization of declaratory relief, afforded because it is a less harsh and abrasive remedy than the injunction, become the factors of primary significance." Perez v. Ledesma, 401 U.S. 82, 104, 91 S.Ct. 674, 686, 27 L.Ed.2d 701 (1971) (separate opinion of Brennan, J.).

The subject matter jurisdiction of the lower federal courts was greatly expanded in the wake of the Civil War. A pervasive sense of nationalism led to enactment of the Civil Rights Act of 1871, * * * empowering the lower federal courts to determine the constitutionality of actions, taken by persons under color of state law, allegedly depriving other individuals of rights guaranteed by the Constitution and federal law, see 42 U.S.C.A § 1983, 28 U.S.C.A. § 1343(3). Four years later, in the Judiciary Act of March 3, 1875, * * * Congress conferred upon the lower federal courts, for but the second time in their nearly century-old history, general federal-question jurisdiction subject only to a jurisdictional-amount requirement, see 28 U.S.C.A. § 1331. * * * These two statutes, together with the Court's decision in *Ex parte* Young, 209 U.S. 123, 28 S.Ct. 441, 52 L.Ed. 714 (1908)—holding that state officials who threaten to enforce an unconstitutional state statute may be enjoined by a federal court of equity and that a federal court may, in appropriate circumstances, enjoin future state criminal prosecutions under the unconstitutional Act—have "established the modern framework for federal protection of constitutional rights from state interference." Perez v. Ledesma, *supra*, 401 U.S., at 107, 91 S.Ct., at 688 (separate opinion of Brennan, J.).

* * *

* * * Congress in 1934 enacted the Declaratory Judgment Act, 28 U.S.C.A. §§ 2201–2202. That Congress plainly intended declaratory relief

to act as an alternative to the strong medicine of the injunction and to be utilized to test the constitutionality of state criminal statutes in cases where injunctive relief would be unavailable is amply evidenced by the legislative history of the Act, traced in full detail in Perez v. Ledesma, *supra*, 401 U.S., at 111–115, 91 S.Ct., at 690–692 (separate opinion of Brennan, J.).

* * *

The "different considerations" entering into a decision whether to grant declaratory relief have their origins in the preceding historical summary. First, as Congress recognized in 1934, a declaratory judgment will have a less intrusive effect on the administration of state criminal laws. As was observed in Perez v. Ledesma, 401 U.S., at 124–126, 91 S.Ct., at 696–697 (separate opinion of Brennan, J.):

> Of course, a favorable declaratory judgment may nevertheless be valuable to the plaintiff though it cannot make even an unconstitutional statute disappear. A state statute may be declared unconstitutional in toto—that is, incapable of having constitutional applications; or it may be declared unconstitutionally vague or overbroad—that is, incapable of being constitutionally applied to the full extent of its purport. In either case, a federal declaration of unconstitutionality reflects the opinion of the federal court that the statute cannot be fully enforced. If a declaration of total unconstitutionality is affirmed by this Court, it follows that this Court stands ready to reverse any conviction under the statute. If a declaration of partial unconstitutionality is affirmed by this Court, the implication is that this Court will overturn particular applications of the statute, but that if the statute is narrowly construed by the state courts it will not be incapable of constitutional applications. Accordingly, the declaration does not necessarily bar prosecutions under the statute, as a broad injunction would. Thus, where the highest court of a State has had an opportunity to give a statute regulating expression a narrowing or clarifying construction but has failed to do so, and later a federal court declares the statute unconstitutionally vague or overbroad, it may well be open to a state prosecutor, after the federal court decision, to bring a prosecution under the statute if he reasonably believes that the defendant's conduct is not constitutionally protected and that the state courts may give the statute a construction so as to yield a constitutionally valid conviction. Even where a declaration of unconstitutionality is not reviewed by this Court, the declaration may still be able to cut down the deterrent effect of an unconstitutional state statute. The persuasive force of the court's opinion and judgment may lead state prosecutors, courts, and legislators to reconsider their respective responsibilities toward the statute. Enforcement policies or judicial construction may be changed, or the legislature may repeal the statute and start anew. Finally, the federal court judgment may have some res judicata effect, though this point is not free from

difficulty and the governing rules remain to be developed with a view to the proper workings of a federal system. What is clear, however, is that even though a declaratory judgment has "the force and effect of a final judgment," 28 U.S.C.A. § 2201, it is a much milder form of relief than an injunction. Though it may be persuasive, it is not ultimately coercive; noncompliance with it may be inappropriate, but is not contempt.

Second, engrafting upon the Declaratory Judgment Act a requirement that all of the traditional equitable prerequisites to the issuance of an injunction be satisfied before the issuance of a declaratory judgment is considered would defy Congress' intent to make declaratory relief available in cases where an injunction would be inappropriate. * * * Thus, the Court of Appeals was in error when it ruled that a failure to demonstrate irreparable injury * * * precluded the granting of declaratory relief.

The only occasions where this Court has disregarded these "different considerations" and found that a preclusion of injunctive relief inevitably led to a denial of declaratory relief have been cases in which principles of federalism militated altogether against federal intervention in a class of adjudications. See Great Lakes Dredge & Dock Co. v. Huffman, 319 U.S. 293, 63 S.Ct. 1070, 87 L.Ed. 1407 (1943) (federal policy against interfering with the enforcement of state tax laws). In the instant case, principles of federalism not only do not preclude federal intervention, they compel it. Requiring the federal courts totally to step aside when no state criminal prosecution is pending against the federal plaintiff would turn federalism on its head. * * *

We therefore hold that, regardless of whether injunctive relief may be appropriate, federal declaratory relief is not precluded when no state prosecution is pending and a federal plaintiff demonstrates a genuine threat of enforcement of a disputed state criminal statute, whether an attack is made on the constitutionality of the statute on its face or as applied. The judgment of the Court of Appeals is reversed, and the case is remanded for further proceedings consistent with this opinion.

MR. JUSTICE STEWART, with whom THE CHIEF JUSTICE joins, concurring.

While joining the opinion of the Court, I add a word by way of emphasis.

Our decision today must not be understood as authorizing the invocation of federal declaratory judgment jurisdiction by a person who thinks a state criminal law is unconstitutional, even if he genuinely feels "chilled" in his freedom of action by the law's existence, and even if he honestly entertains the subjective belief that he may now or in the future be prosecuted under it.

The petitioner in this case has succeeded in objectively showing that the threat of imminent arrest, corroborated by the actual arrest of his companion, has created an actual concrete controversy between himself and the agents of the State. He has, therefore, demonstrated "a genuine threat of enforcement of a disputed state criminal statute * * *." Cases where such a "genuine threat" can be demonstrated will, I think, be exceedingly rare.

[The concurring opinions of Justice Rehnquist and Justice White have been deleted.]

NOTES

1. Federal court cases continue to adhere to *Steffel's* ruling that "a threat of prosecution is not enough to confer standing" although a declaratory judgment may be appropriate if there is a "specific warning of an intent to prosecute." San Diego County Gun Rights Committee v. Reno, 98 F.3d 1121, 1127 (9th Cir.1996) (declaratory judgment denied where there was "no threat of arrest, prosecution or incarceration"); *see generally* W.E. Shipley, Annotation, *Validity, Construction, and Application of Criminal Statutes or Ordinances as Proper Subject for Declaratory Judgment*, 10 A.L.R. 3d 727 (1966).

2. State courts have followed *Steffel's* lead in holding that a plaintiff who is not entitled to an injunction may nevertheless be entitled to a declaratory judgment. Carroll County Ethics Comm'n v. Lennon, 119 Md.App. 49, 703 A.2d 1338 (1998).

3. When a prosecution is pending, both state and federal courts are generally unwilling to grant declaratory relief for purposes of testing the validity of a criminal statute. *See* Norcisa v. Board of Selectmen of Provincetown, 368 Mass. 161, 171–72, 330 N.E.2d 830, 836 (1975) (see *supra* Chapter 6.4.B) ("The fundamental jurisprudential considerations underlying the general prohibition against enjoining a pending criminal prosecution apply with full force to support a prohibition against issuing declaratory decrees concerning a pending criminal prosecution. To conclude otherwise would encourage fragmentation and proliferation of litigation and disrupt the orderly administration of the criminal law.").

4. *Steffel* has now been extended beyond the realm of threatened prosecutions by government to the realm of threatened enforcement actions by private parties. MedImmune, Inc. v. Genentech, Inc., 549 U.S. 118 (2007)(patent licensee was not required by Article III to break or terminate the license agreement before seeking a declaratory judgment in federal court that the underlying patent was invalid, unenforceable, or not infringed; rejecting the Federal Circuit's "reasonable apprehension of imminent suit" test for establishing the existence of a case or controversy; reaffirming the Court's holding in *Maryland Casualty* that the declaratory-judgment plaintiff-insurer in that case could prove a case or controversy under Article III even though the insured had not threatened to file suit against the insurer). For scholarly commentary on *MedImmune*, see Ronald A. Bleeker & Michael V. O'Shaughnessy, *One Year After MedImmune—The Impact of Patent Licensing and Negotiation*, 17 Fed. Circuit B.J. 401 (2008); Jennifer R. Saionz, *Declaratory Judgment Actions in Patent Cases: The Federal Circuit's Response to* MedImmune v. Genentech, 23 Berkeley Tech. L.J. 161 (2008).

CHAPTER 6

===

REMEDIES FOR SELECTED
TORTIOUS WRONGS

■ ■ ■

SECTION 1. INTERFERENCE WITH
PERSONAL PROPERTY
INTERESTS

A. CHOOSING THE CAUSE OF ACTION
AND THE REMEDIES

When a plaintiff sues for interference with an interest in personal property, the plaintiff may bring a cause of action for strict liability, negligence, recklessness, or for the commission of an intentional tort. The next two cases discuss the differences between a cause of action for conversion and a cause of action for trespass to chattels.

BARAM v. FARUGIA

United States Court of Appeals, Third Circuit, 1979.
606 F.2d 42.

Before ALDISERT, and WEIS, CIRCUIT JUDGES, and DIAMOND,* DISTRICT JUDGE.

ALDISERT, CIRCUIT JUDGE.

In this age of space travel and computer technology, a horse named Foxey Toni requires us to return to a more tranquil era and examine elements of trover and conversion under Pennsylvania common law. We must decide in this diversity case whether payment of the horse's full value to the owner by one converter precludes recovery by the original owner in a conversion action against persons who received possession from the original converter. * * *

Dr. Joseph Baram, appellee, acquired legal title to Foxey Toni, a bay filly race horse, for $3,000 [on September 22, 1975] in a claiming race at

---

* Honorable Gustave Diamond, of the United States District Court for the Western District of Pennsylvania, sitting by designation.

639

the Keystone Race Track, Bucks County, Pennsylvania. Dennis Fredella became the trainer for Foxey Toni and was given authority to enter her in races in Dr. Baram's name. Foxey Toni raced under Dr. Baram's name on October 11, October 17, and November 8, 1975. Thereafter, a Certificate of Foal Registration for the horse, issued by the Jockey Club of America, came into Fredella's possession at a time when he was indebted to appellant Robert Farugia. Without the knowledge or consent of Dr. Baram, Farugia obtained possession of the horse from Fredella and was given the foal certificate bearing the forged signature of Dr. Baram. The district court found that both Fredella and Farugia knew or should have known that the signature on the foal certificate had been forged and that Fredella had no authority to transfer Foxey Toni. * * *

Farugia first dated the certificate, transferring the horse to himself, and then transferred her to appellant Glenn Hackett and himself. Foxey Toni was subsequently raced in Canada by the putative new owners without the knowledge or consent of Dr. Baram. After Dr. Baram learned of these events, he met with Farugia and demanded the return of Foxey Toni. Farugia refused to return the horse or pay her value of $3,000, but offered instead a modest cash settlement. Dr. Baram rejected the settlement offer and initiated litigation.

Dr. Baram filed a complaint sounding in "Trespass for Conversion" in the district court against Farugia, Hackett, and Fredella. A default judgment for failure to appear was entered against Fredella. Dr. Baram acknowledged at trial that, as a result of previous criminal proceedings against Fredella in state court, he had been paid $3,000 by Fredella covering Dr. Baram's claim "for the value of the horse, Foxey Toni," and that he "agreed to accept that." * * * This case then proceeded as a bench trial for compensatory and punitive damages for conversion against Farugia and Hackett. The court awarded compensatory damages of $3,000 against both defendants for the value of Foxey Toni and assessed punitive damages of $5,000 against Farugia. The court dismissed the complaint against Fredella with prejudice. This appeal by Farugia and Hackett followed.

Appellants argue that the judgment must be reversed because the $3,000 payment by the converter Fredella for the value of the horse extinguished any further claim in conversion by Dr. Baram. We agree with appellants' argument and are satisfied that conversion under the common law of Pennsylvania may be conceptualized as follows. Conversion is an act of willful interference with the dominion or control over a chattel, done without lawful justification, by which any person entitled to the chattel is deprived of its use and possession. The tort is predicated on interference with dominion or control over the chattel incident to some general or special ownership rather than on damage to the physical condition of the chattel. A person not in lawful possession of a chattel may commit conversion by intentionally dispossessing the lawful possessor of the chattel, by intentionally using a chattel in his possession without authority so to use it, by receiving a chattel pursuant to an unauthorized sale with intent to acquire for himself or for another a proprietary interest in it, by disposing of a chattel by an unauthorized sale with intent to transfer a proprietary interest in it, or by refusing to surrender a chattel on demand to a person entitled to lawful possession.

The modern law remedy for conversion has emerged from the common law action of trover, which was premised on the theory that the defendant had appropriated the plaintiff's chattel, for which he must pay. * * * A plaintiff who proved conversion in a common law trover action was entitled to damages equal to the full value of the chattel at the time and place of conversion. * * * According to Professor Prosser,

> [w]hen the defendant satisfied the judgment in trover, the title to the chattel passed to him, and the plaintiff had nothing more to do with it. The effect was that the defendant was compelled, because of his wrongful appropriation, to buy the chattel at a forced sale, of which the action of trover was the judicial instrument.

* * * The title-passing and forced-sale concepts distinguished trover from the common law action of trespass, which was premised on the theory that the plaintiff remained the owner of the chattel and was entitled only to the damages he had sustained through loss of possession, and from the action of replevin, which also left title in the plaintiff and returned the chattel to his possession. * * * The modern day tort of conversion retains the conceptual underpinnings of trover and is generally applicable only to cases such as this one in which there has been a major or serious interference with a chattel or with the plaintiff's right in it. It is the seriousness of the interference that justifies the forced judicial sale to the defendant, described by Prosser as "the distinguishing feature of the action." The Restatement (Second) of Torts preserves this conceptual basis:

> When the defendant satisfies the judgment in the action for conversion, title to the chattel passes to him, so that he is in effect required to buy it at a forced judicial sale. Conversion is therefore properly limited, and has been limited by the courts, to those serious, major, and important interferences with the right to control the chattel which justify requiring the defendant to pay its full value.

§ 222A, Comment c. (1965). Although Pennsylvania law is unclear about whether title passes on entry of judgment against the converter or only when the converter satisfies the judgment, the rule recognized in most states is that title to the chattel passes only when the judgment against the converter is satisfied. We need not venture our opinion on how the Pennsylvania courts would resolve this question, however, because in this case both the judicial order that Fredella pay the value as a condition of his probation and actual payment of $3,000 to Dr. Baram, events related to the first conversion, preceded judgment on the second claim. This sequence indicates that title passed to Fredella at some point prior to judgment in the second action. We now apply these precepts to the uncontroverted facts presented at the trial below or as specifically found by the fact finder.

Conversion as recognized under Pennsylvania common law occurred on November 29, 1975, when Fredella transferred Foxey Toni's foal certificate and delivered possession of her to Farugia. This was a classic example of intentionally dispossessing another of his chattel, using a chattel in a bailee's possession without authority so to use it, and disposing of a chattel by sale without authority and intending to transfer a proprietary interest in it. * * *

Had there been no payment by the converter Fredella or acceptance by the owner, Dr. Baram, at least two subsequent and separate acts of conversion would have been committed by Farugia: receiving a chattel pursuant to an unauthorized sale on November 29, 1975, with intent to acquire for himself or for another a proprietary interest in it, and refusing to surrender the chattel on demand when requested by Dr. Baram on May 27, 1976. At a minimum, Hackett would have committed conversion when, with Farugia, he refused Dr. Baram's demand to surrender possession. * * *

But before the analysis can proceed further, we must consider the effect of the acceptance by Dr. Baram of the payment of $3,000 by Fredella prior to his obtaining judgment against Farugia and Hackett. * * *

On receipt by Dr. Baram of the $3,000 from Fredella, and acknowledgment that this sum reflected the true value of the horse, a common law forced sale was effected, passing title from the legal owner to the converter at the time and place of the original conversion. Had the converter made no offer of an amount reflecting the horse's value, and had Dr. Baram not received full value, he could have made out a conversion action against Farugia and Hackett. But the acceptance by Dr. Baram of the horse's true market value with the resultant passage of title in the nature of "a forced judicial sale" had the effect of vesting title in Fredella retroactively from November 29, 1975, the date of the conversion. * * * With title so vested, Fredella therefore had the right to transfer Foxey Toni on November 29, 1975, and Farugia, by the same reasoning, then took possession of the horse from a person legally entitled to possess and transfer. Dr. Baram retroactively lost his right to possession of Foxey Toni, and without a right of possession at the time of the alleged conversion could not maintain an action for conversion against Farugia and Hackett. * * * Thus, although successive and independent actionable conversions of the same chattel are possible, satisfaction of the earlier conversion by payment in full of the value of the chattel acts as a complete bar to subsequent recoveries. * * * We hold therefore that after receiving total satisfaction for the value of the chattel, Dr. Baram no longer possessed a common law cause of action in conversion * * * against Farugia and Hackett. * * *

Accordingly, the judgment of the district court will be reversed and the proceedings remanded with a direction to enter judgment in favor of the appellants.

NOTES

1. If the restitutionary measure of relief is greater than the measure of recovery in conversion, the plaintiff may "waive the tort" and sue for unjust enrichment. Varel Manufacturing Co. v. Acetylene Oxygen Co., 990 S.W.2d 486, 498 (Tex.App.1999). For a discussion of the restitutionary remedy, see *supra* Chapter 4, Section 6.

2. Under Pennsylvania's law, as interpreted by the Third Circuit, a plaintiff who sues for conversion may recover nominal damages. Sprague, Levinson & Thall v. Advest, Inc., 623 F.Supp. 11 (E.D.Pa.1985) (where plaintiff proved no nominal damages and no pecuniary loss in a conversion action, punitive damages verdict set aside).

3. The next case discusses the cause of action for trespass to chattels, which is an alternative cause of action for interference with personal property that is sometimes called "the little brother of conversion." The Restatement of Torts would allow the recovery of nominal damages where the trespass to the chattel is "dispossession," but not for "harmless intermeddlings with the chattel." Restatement of Torts (Second) § 218, cmt. d. (1965). By contrast, a plaintiff who sues for trespass to land may recover nominal damages and then claim punitive damages for any type of interference with real property without proof of actual harm. *Id.* cmt. e.; *see also supra* Chapter 3, Section 5.A.

COMPUSERVE INC. v. CYBER PROMOTIONS, INC.

United States District Court, Southern District of Ohio, 1997.
962 F.Supp. 1015.

GRAHAM, DISTRICT JUDGE.

This case presents novel issues regarding the commercial use of the Internet, specifically the right of an online computer service to prevent a commercial enterprise from sending unsolicited electronic mail advertising to its subscribers.

Plaintiff CompuServe Incorporated ("CompuServe") is one of the major national commercial online computer services. It operates a computer communication service through a proprietary nationwide computer network. In addition to allowing access to the extensive content available within its own proprietary network, CompuServe also provides its subscribers with a link to the much larger resources of the Internet. This allows its subscribers to send and receive electronic messages, known as "e-mail," by the Internet. Defendants Cyber Promotions, Inc. and its president Sanford Wallace are in the business of sending unsolicited e-mail advertisements on behalf of themselves and their clients to hundreds of thousands of Internet users, many of whom are CompuServe subscribers. CompuServe has notified defendants that they are prohibited from using its computer equipment to process and store the unsolicited e-mail and has requested that they terminate the practice. Instead, defendants have sent an increasing volume of e-mail solicitations to CompuServe subscribers. CompuServe has attempted to employ technological means to block the flow of defendants' e-mail transmissions to its computer equipment, but to no avail.

This matter is before the Court on the application of CompuServe for a preliminary injunction which would extend the duration of the temporary restraining order issued by this Court on October 24, 1996 and which would in addition prevent defendants from sending unsolicited advertisements to CompuServe subscribers.

* * *

I.

The Court will begin its analysis of the issues by acknowledging, for the purpose of providing a background, certain findings of fact recently made by another district court in a case involving the Internet:

    1. The Internet is not a physical or tangible entity, but rather a giant network which interconnects innumerable smaller groups of linked computer networks. It is thus a network of networks....

* * *

    4. Some of the computers and computer networks that make up the network are owned by governmental and public institutions, some are owned by non-profit organizations, and some are privately owned. The resulting whole is a decentralized, global medium of communications—or "cyberspace"—that links people, institutions, corporations, and governments around the world....

    11. No single entity—academic, corporate, governmental, or non-profit—administers the Internet. It exists and functions as a result of the fact that hundreds of thousands of separate operators of computers and computer networks independently decided to use common data transfer protocols to exchange communications and information with other computers (which in turn exchange communications and information with still other computers). There is no centralized storage location, control point, or communications channel for the Internet, and it would not be technically feasible for a single entity to control all of the information conveyed on the Internet.

American Civil Liberties Union v. Reno, 929 F.Supp. 824, 830–832 (E.D.Pa.1996). * * *

Internet users often pay a fee for Internet access. However, there is no per-message charge to send electronic messages over the Internet and such messages usually reach their destination within minutes. Thus electronic mail provides an opportunity to reach a wide audience quickly and at almost no cost to the sender. It is not surprising therefore that some companies, like defendant Cyber Promotions, Inc., have begun using the Internet to distribute advertisements by sending the same unsolicited commercial message to hundreds of thousands of Internet users at once. Defendants refer to this as "bulk e-mail," while plaintiff refers to it as "junk e-mail." In the vernacular of the Internet, unsolicited e-mail advertising is sometimes referred to pejoratively as "spam."

CompuServe subscribers use CompuServe's domain name "CompuServe.com" together with their own unique alpha-numeric identifier to form a distinctive e-mail mailing address. That address may be used by the subscriber to exchange electronic mail with any one of tens of millions of other Internet users who have electronic mail capability. E-mail sent to CompuServe subscribers is processed and stored on CompuServe's proprietary computer equipment. Thereafter, it becomes accessible to CompuServe's subscribers, who can access CompuServe's equipment and electronically retrieve those messages.

Over the past several months, CompuServe has received many complaints from subscribers threatening to discontinue their subscription unless CompuServe prohibits electronic mass mailers from using its equipment to send unsolicited advertisements. CompuServe asserts that the volume of messages generated by such mass mailings places a significant burden on its equipment which has finite processing and storage capacity. CompuServe receives no payment from the mass mailers for processing their unsolicited advertising. However, CompuServe's subscribers pay for their access to CompuServe's services in increments of time and thus the process of accessing, reviewing and discarding unsolicited e-mail costs them money, which is one of the reasons for their complaints. CompuServe has notified defendants that they are prohibited from using its proprietary computer equipment to process and store unsolicited e-mail and has requested them to cease and desist from sending unsolicited e-mail to its subscribers. Nonetheless, defendants have sent an increasing volume of e-mail solicitations to CompuServe subscribers.

In an effort to shield its equipment from defendants' bulk e-mail, CompuServe has implemented software programs designed to screen out the messages and block their receipt. In response, defendants have modified their equipment and the messages they send in such a fashion as to circumvent CompuServe's screening software. * * *

III.

This Court shall first address plaintiff's motion as it relates to perpetuating the temporary restraining order filed on October 24, 1996. That order enjoins defendants from:

(i) Using CompuServe accounts or CompuServe's equipment or support services to send or receive electronic mail or messages or in connection with the sending or receiving of electronic mail or messages * * *.

[The court decided to grant a preliminary injunction perpetuating the temporary restraining order.]

IV.

This Court will now address the second aspect of plaintiff's motion in which it seeks to enjoin defendants Cyber Promotions, Inc. and its president Sanford Wallace from sending any unsolicited advertisements to any electronic mail address maintained by CompuServe.

CompuServe predicates this aspect of its motion for a preliminary injunction on the common law theory of trespass to personal property or to chattels, asserting that defendants' continued transmission of electronic messages to its computer equipment constitutes an actionable tort.

Trespass to chattels has evolved from its original common law application, concerning primarily the asportation of another's tangible property, to include the unauthorized use of personal property:

> Its chief importance now, is that there may be recovery ... for interferences with the possession of chattels which are not sufficiently important to be classed as conversion, and so to compel the defendant to pay the full value of the thing with which he has interfered. Trespass to chattels survives today, in other words, largely as a little brother of conversion.

Prosser & Keeton, Prosser and Keeton on Torts, § 14, 85–86 (1984).

* * *

Both plaintiff and defendants cite the Restatement (Second) of Torts to support their respective positions. In determining a question unanswered by state law, it is appropriate for this Court to consider such sources as the restatement of the law and decisions of other jurisdictions. * * *

The Restatement § 217(b) states that a trespass to chattel may be committed by intentionally using or intermeddling with the chattel in possession of another. Restatement § 217, Comment e defines physical "intermeddling" as follows:

> ... intentionally bringing about a physical contact with the chattel. The actor may commit a trespass by an act which brings him into an intended physical contact with a chattel in the possession of another[.]

Electronic signals generated and sent by computer have been held to be sufficiently physically tangible to support a trespass cause of action. Thrifty–Tel, Inc. v. Bezenek, 46 Cal.App.4th 1559, 1567, 54 Cal.Rptr.2d 468 (1996); State v. McGraw, 480 N.E.2d 552, 554 (Ind.1985) (Indiana Supreme Court recognizing in dicta that a hacker's unauthorized access to a computer was more in the nature of trespass than criminal conversion); and State v. Riley, 121 Wash.2d 22, 846 P.2d 1365 (1993) (computer hacking as the criminal offense of "computer trespass" under Washington law). It is undisputed that plaintiff has a possessory interest in its computer systems. Further, defendants' contact with plaintiff's computers is clearly intentional. Although electronic messages may travel through the Internet over various routes, the messages are affirmatively directed to their destination.

Defendants * * * argue that they did not, in this case, physically dispossess plaintiff of its equipment or substantially interfere with it. However, the Restatement (Second) of Torts § 218 defines the circumstances under which a trespass to chattels may be actionable:

> One who commits a trespass to a chattel is subject to liability to the possessor of the chattel if, but only if,
>
> (a) he dispossesses the other of the chattel, or
>
> (b) the chattel is impaired as to its condition, quality, or value, or
>
> (c) the possessor is deprived of the use of the chattel for a substantial time, or
>
> (d) bodily harm is caused to the possessor, or harm is caused to some person or thing in which the possessor has a legally protected interest.

Therefore, an interference resulting in physical dispossession is just one circumstance under which a defendant can be found liable. Defendants * * * cite only two cases which make any reference to the Restatement. In Glidden v. Szybiak, 95 N.H. 318, 63 A.2d 233 (1949), the court simply indicated that an action for trespass to chattels could not be maintained in the absence of some form of damage. The court held that where plaintiff did not contend that defendant's pulling on her pet dog's ears caused any injury, an action in tort could not be maintained. * * * In contrast, plaintiff in the present action has alleged that it has suffered several types of injury as a result of defendants' conduct. * * *

A plaintiff can sustain an action for trespass to chattels, as opposed to an action for conversion, without showing a substantial interference with its right to possession of that chattel. * * * Harm to the personal property or diminution of its quality, condition, or value as a result of defendants' use can also be the predicate for liability. Restatement § 218(b).

> An unprivileged use or other intermeddling with a chattel which results in actual impairment of its physical condition, quality or value to the possessor makes the actor liable for the loss thus caused. In the great majority of cases, the actor's intermeddling with the chattel impairs the value of it to the possessor, as distinguished from the mere affront to his dignity as possessor, only by some impairment of the physical condition of the chattel. There may, however, be situations in which the value to the owner of a particular type of chattel may be impaired by dealing with it in a manner that does not affect its physical condition.... In such a case, the intermeddling is actionable even though the physical condition of the chattel is not impaired.

The Restatement (Second) of Torts § 218, comment h. In the present case, any value CompuServe realizes from its computer equipment is wholly derived from the extent to which that equipment can serve its subscriber base. * * * Therefore, the value of that equipment to CompuServe is diminished even though it is not physically damaged by defendants' conduct.

Next, plaintiff asserts that it has suffered injury aside from the physical impact of defendants' messages on its equipment. Restatement § 218(d) also indicates that recovery may be had for a trespass that causes harm to something in which the possessor has a legally protected interest.
* * *

Many subscribers have terminated their accounts specifically because of the unwanted receipt of bulk e-mail messages. * * * Defendants' intrusions into CompuServe's computer systems, insofar as they harm plaintiff's business reputation and goodwill with its customers, are actionable under Restatement § 218(d).

The reason that the tort of trespass to chattels requires some actual damage as a prima facie element, whereas damage is assumed where there is a trespass to real property, can be explained as follows:

> The interest of a possessor of a chattel in its inviolability, unlike the similar interest of a possessor of land, is not given legal protection by an action for nominal damages for harmless intermeddlings with the chattel. In order that an actor who interferes with another's chattel may be liable, his conduct must affect some other and more important interest of the possessor. Therefore, one who intentionally intermeddles with another's chattel is subject to liability only if his intermeddling is harmful to the possessor's materially valuable interest in the physical condition, quality, or value of the chattel, or if the possessor is deprived of the use of the chattel for a substantial time, or some other legally protected interest of the possessor is affected as stated in Clause (c). Sufficient legal protection of the possessor's interest in the mere inviolability of his chattel is afforded by his privilege to use reasonable force to protect his possession against even harmless interference.

Restatement (Second) of Torts § 218, Comment e. Plaintiff CompuServe has attempted to exercise this privilege to protect its computer systems. However, defendants' persistent affirmative efforts to evade plaintiff's security measures have circumvented any protection those self-help measures might have provided. In this case CompuServe has alleged and supported by affidavit that it has suffered several types of injury as a result of defendants' conduct. The foregoing discussion simply underscores that the damage sustained by plaintiff is sufficient to sustain an action for trespass to chattels. However, this Court also notes that the implementation of technological means of self-help, to the extent that reasonable measures are effective, is particularly appropriate in this type of situation and should be exhausted before legal action is proper.

* * *

Defendants' intentional use of plaintiff's proprietary computer equipment exceeds plaintiff's consent and, indeed, continued after repeated demands that defendants cease. Such use is an actionable trespass to plaintiff's chattel. The First Amendment to the United States Constitution provides no defense for such conduct.

Plaintiff has demonstrated a likelihood of success on the merits which is sufficient to warrant the issuance of the preliminary injunction it has requested.

As already discussed at some length, plaintiff has submitted affidavits supporting its contention that it will suffer irreparable harm without the grant of the preliminary injunction. * * *

Normally, a preliminary injunction is not appropriate where an ultimate award of monetary damages will suffice. * * * However, money damages are only adequate if they can be reasonably computed and collected. Plaintiff has demonstrated that defendants' intrusions into their computer systems harm plaintiff's business reputation and goodwill. This is the sort of injury that warrants the issuance of a preliminary injunction because the actual loss is impossible to compute. * * *

Plaintiff has shown that it will suffer irreparable harm without the grant of the preliminary injunction.

It is improbable that granting the injunction will cause substantial harm to defendant. Even with the grant of this injunction, defendants are free to disseminate their advertisements in other ways not constituting trespass to plaintiff's computer equipment. Further, defendants may continue to send electronic mail messages to the tens of millions of Internet users who are not connected through CompuServe's computer systems.

Finally, the public interest is advanced by the Court's protection of the common law rights of individuals and entities to their personal property. * * * High volumes of junk e-mail devour computer processing and storage capacity, slow down data transfer between computers over the Internet by congesting the electronic paths through which the messages travel, and cause recipients to spend time and money wading through messages that they do not want. * * * Further, those subscribing to CompuServe are not injured by the issuance of this injunction. Plaintiff has made a business decision to forbid Cyber Promotions and Mr. Wallace from using its computers to transmit messages to CompuServe subscribers. If CompuServe subscribers are unhappy with that decision, then they may make that known, perhaps by terminating their accounts and transferring to an Internet service provider which accepts unsolicited e-mail advertisements. That is a business risk which plaintiff has assumed.

* * *

V.

Based on the foregoing, plaintiff's motion for a preliminary injunction is granted. * * * Cyber Promotions, Inc. and its president Sanford Wallace are enjoined from sending any unsolicited advertisements to any electronic mail address maintained by plaintiff CompuServe during the pendency of this action.

NOTE

Numerous cases have recognized a cause of action for trespass to chattels in the context of electronic communications where there is proof that the defendant has caused actual harm. *See* Marjorie A. Shields, Annotation, *Applicability of Common Law Trespass Actions to Electronic Communications*, 107 A.L.R. 5th 549 (2003); *see also* Intel Corp. v. Hamidi, 30 Cal.4th 1342, 1 Cal.Rptr.3d 32, 71 P.3d 296 (2003) (distinguishing *CompuServe* on the ground that the plaintiff in *Hamidi* had failed to prove actual harm). For a suggestion that unsolicited commercial e-mail is a "nuisance," see Adam Mossoff, *Spam—Oy, What a Nuisance!*, 19 Berkeley Tech. L.J. 625 (2004) (Nuisance doctrine is superior to trespass to chattels action because it does not require courts to find that spam has "dispossessed" a plaintiff from the plaintiff's computer network.). For articles by commentators who are critical of the concept of "cyberproperty," see Michael A. Carrier & Greg Lastowka, *Against Cyberproperty*, 22 Berkeley Tech. L.J. 1485 (2007); Greg Lastowka, *Decoding Cyberproperty*, 40 Ind. L. Rev. 23 (2007).

B. DAMAGES

When a plaintiff sues for interference with personal property rights, the court typically measures general compensatory damages by reference to the "fair market value" of the property. In addition, the plaintiff may seek to recover special or consequential damages. The following cases discuss the application of the "fair market value" test to various types of fact situations and then trace the development of the modern rules of law regarding damages for loss of use and emotional distress.

TERRELL v. TSCHIRN

Supreme Court of Mississippi, 1995.
656 So.2d 1150.

JAMES L. ROBERTS, JR., JUSTICE, For the Court:

* * *

STATEMENT OF FACTS AND PROCEDURAL HISTORY

In March of 1988, Darryl Tschirn, Jr. of Metairie, Louisiana, received a 1988 Chevrolet Camaro IROC as a high school graduation present, and title to the car was put in his name. Tschirn maintained only liability insurance on the vehicle. He installed a stereo unit in the car himself at a cost of six hundred dollars. He also put a different set of tires on the car. The sales receipt for the car was put into evidence and reflected a total cash price including tax and license of $22,489.99.

On July 24, 1989, Tschirn was attending a meeting in New Orleans, Louisiana. After leaving the meeting he discovered his car was missing. Tschirn called the police and filed a report. Tschirn was contacted in August of 1990 and was informed that the police had located his stolen vehicle. The car, which had been partially dismantled, was found in Terrell's possession.

Carl Jack Terrell owned a used car and auto salvage business in Magnolia, Pike County, Mississippi. At the time of trial he had been in the salvage business for approximately eighteen years. Terrell also rebuilt automobiles himself and did most of the work at his place of business. He stated that he liked to rebuild pickups and Camaros.

Terrell testified that it was his practice to require proof of title only when he bought an automobile for resale. He did not require or even ask for a title or proof of ownership when he was buying a car for salvage. He described a salvage vehicle as "[a] vehicle that is being sold for parts" which he sold to the public, other dealers or other salvage yards. When asked how he knew whether the cars he bought for parts were not stolen Terrell replied, "I don't know that."

Terrell testified as to how he acquired possession of Tschirn's vehicle. A man whose name Terrell could not recall but which he remembered sounded Cajun, came by his place of business. The man indicated that he was in the towing business and that once he held a car for a certain length of time he was allowed to dispose of it. He asked Terrell if he would be willing to do business. Terrell told the man he would be interested in some parts for pickups or Camaros because those were the types of vehicles he liked to rebuild.

Terrell bought salvage vehicles from this man on approximately six occasions and paid cash for those vehicles. Terrell stated that he never asked for title to these vehicles because they usually just amounted to parts, no more than "half a car was there." He stated that the man knew he was rebuilding a Camaro and on one occasion brought him what turned out to be Tschirn's stolen car. Terrell described the condition of the car when he bought as follows: "There were no mechanical parts to the car, the motor/transmission was all gone. The doors were gone. The hood was there but it was damaged, and the fender and grill was primarily what I needed for the car I was working on...."

[The car was identified by the police when Terrell pulled it on a flat bed trailer from his place of business to a car crusher.]

DISCUSSION

[Plaintiff was represented by his father, a Louisiana lawyer.]

* * * This case was submitted to the jury on the basis of negligence and/or gross negligence and/or intentional tort and/or negligent conversion. The jury found for the plaintiff.

Terrell argues that although he may have been negligent in not requiring title when he bought vehicles for salvage and in telling the unidentified man that he would be interested in parts for Camaros and pickups and then paying cash for Tschirn's Camaro, there was no causal connection between this negligence and Tschirn's injury, the loss of his car. Tschirn argues that but for Terrell providing an outlet for stolen vehicles and but for Terrell paying cash for stolen vehicles and but for Terrell and others like him not requiring paperwork, the car thieves would have no place to dispose of stolen goods and therefore would have no motive to steal.

Although remote, there does seem to be some causal connection between Terrell's negligence and Tschirn's injury. The unidentified man knew Terrell did not require title when he bought cars for parts and Terrell told the man he would be interested in Camaro parts. It is conceivable that this knowledge sent the unidentified man on a search for a Camaro which could be stolen and then sold to Terrell. * * *

It is not necessary to rely on the negligence theory. When Terrell bought the stolen car he was guilty of conversion. "Conversion requires an intent to exercise dominion or control over goods which is inconsistent with the true owner's right." Walker v. Brown, 501 So.2d 358, 361 (Miss.1987) * * *.

Prosser and Keeton also point out that good faith is not necessarily an excuse.

> The intent required is not necessarily a matter of conscious wrongdoing. It is rather an intent to exercise a dominion or control over the goods which is in fact inconsistent with the plaintiff's rights. * * *

Prosser and Keeton on the Law of Torts 92–93 (W. Page Keeton 5th ed. 1984). * * * When Terrell took possession of Tschirn's Camaro with the intent to exercise proprietary control and to put it to his own use he was guilty of conversion and therefore liable to Tschirn for damages.

Terrell contends that the jury was presented insufficient evidence on which to assess damages and that the evidence that was presented was uncertain and speculative. The jury found for Tschirn and awarded him damages in the amount of $14,500.

The plaintiff bears the burden of proof as to the amount of damages. * * * In a suit for conversion, the value of the personal property at the time and place of conversion must be shown to prove the extent of damages.

In his case in chief, Tschirn put on no evidence of the value of his car when it was stolen. The sales receipt for the car was put into evidence. It showed the car plus tax and license cost $22,489.99 when it was bought in March of 1988. The car was stolen some 16 months later in July of 1989.

Tschirn testified that he had put on different tires, but the cost of the new tires was not given. He also stated he had installed a $600.00 stereo. There was no evidence as to the mileage on the car or the car's condition at the time it was stolen. Tschirn did state he "took good care" of the car and that there was a cigarette burn on the passenger seat. There was absolutely no testimony or other evidence introduced as to any expenses incurred because of the loss of the car.

At the close of Tschirn's case in chief, Terrell moved for a directed verdict because there had been no proof as to the value of the car or other damages. The Court reserved his ruling until the defendant put on his case in order to see if any evidence as to the value of the car would be presented.

Tschirn tried to establish the worth of the stolen car through Terrell's testimony on cross-examination. The evidence presented to the jury from which to assess damages was speculative at best. Tschirn put on no evidence as to damages in his case in chief and so on cross-examination he badgered Terrell into stating that a fourteen month old car, fully loaded and in mint condition might be worth about half of its value new. Tschirn also tried to get Terrell to say that such a Camaro would cost around $24,000 new, making half around $12,000. Terrell repeatedly stated that he could not give an answer without seeing the car.

* * *

This is not a case were the amount of damages would be extremely difficult to prove. Tschirn had available to him sources and means whereby damages could have been ascertained with a fair degree of certainty. Norman Sandifer, one of the Tschirn's witnesses, was a salvage dealer and could have been asked about the value of the car. Tschirn could have further testified about the mileage and condition of his car at the time it was stolen and to the expenses he incurred because of its loss. For example, Tschirn could have presented receipts for rental cars if any. The price listed in the National Automobile Dealers Association's Blue Book could have been introduced. No doubt there were other ways to better determine the extent of damages than badgering the defendant into making a less than definite guess.

This is an occasion where the trial judge probably should have directed a verdict for Terrell. However, Terrell chose to put on further evidence and did not raise in this appeal the issue of the trial court's denial of directed verdict. Because of the speculative nature of the damages in this case, we find the jury's verdict was against the overwhelming weight of the evidence and this case should be reversed and remanded for a new trial.

CONCLUSION

* * * The evidence was sufficient at the very least to show Terrell was guilty of conversion by purchasing Tschirn's stolen vehicle. However, the evidence was insufficient for the jury to reasonably and competently assess damages. For that reason, this case is reversed and remanded for a new trial.

NOTES

1. If the plaintiff in *Terrell* proves compensatory damages upon remand, he will also be entitled to prejudgment interest. Phillips Distributors, Inc. v. Texaco, Inc., 190 So.2d 840 (Miss.1966). He will not be entitled to punitive damages, however, both because he did not request them and because the defendant was a "good faith" converter. *Id.*

2. Some courts state that a plaintiff may testify as to the fair market value of the personal property at issue in an action for trespass to chattels or conversion, provided the plaintiff is familiar with the fair market value of the property at the time of the tort (as compared with either the purchase price of the property or its replacement cost). Blackmon v. Mixson, 755 S.W.2d 179, 181 (Tex.App.1988). In *Blackmon*, the plaintiff failed to meet the above criteria when the plaintiff testified as follows on direct examination:

> [BLACKMON'S ATTORNEY]: Do you feel like you are aware, Mr. Mixson, excuse me, Mr. Blackmon, of the market value of the trailer that burned at the time, based on your survey of trailers at that time?
>
> [BLACKMON]: Oh I would think it was probably comparable with what we got the replacement for [*i.e.*, $16,000].
>
> [BLACKMON'S ATTORNEY]: And that was a similar trailer to the one that burned?
>
> [BLACKMON]: Similar, yes.

The court upheld the jury's special verdict that the fair market value of Blackmon's trailer was "$0.00" because the jury's finding "simply reflect[ed] what the jury [had] heard about market value—nothing."

3. The fair market value of property varies with the context in which the standard is applied. Charles McCormick, Damages §§ 43, 44 (1925). If the plaintiff is a merchant, the wholesale price may be the fair market value, but if the plaintiff is a consumer, the retail price may be the fair market value. *See, e.g.*, Merchant v. Peterson, 38 Wash. App. 855, 690 P.2d 1192 (1984).

FAWCETT v. HEIMBACH

Court of Appeals of Minnesota, 1999.
591 N.W.2d 516.

HALBROOKS, JUDGE.

* * *

FACTS

In the summer of 1980, Heimbach had the opportunity to purchase shares of common stock in Medical Graphics Corporation (MGC). The stock was "legend stock," and it could not be sold, traded or pledged for a period of two years. The minimum block of shares that could be purchased was 8,000.

Heimbach was not financially able to purchase the minimum increment and asked Fawcett to join him in the purchase of the stock. Heimbach and Fawcett agreed they would contribute equally to the purchase of 8,000 shares * * *.

[Heimbach sold approximately half of the shares without Fawcett's permission or knowledge and then he put the rest in a margin account in his own name. He borrowed funds against the shares in the margin account, and when the indebtedness of the margin account exceeded the value of the shares, the stock was sold as part of a margin call. The stock was worth $1.90 per share at the time of purchase; it rose to about $11.50 per share in 1983 when Heimbach sold half of it; and it was worth about $14.50 per share at the time of the margin call in 1986. In 1994, when the stock was worth $6.75 per share, Fawcett discovered for the first time that Heimbach had converted the stock.]

On September 11, 1996, Fawcett filed an action for conversion, fraud, breach of contract, and breach of fiduciary duty against Heimbach. The case was tried to the court.

The court found Heimbach converted Fawcett's shares on three occasions. It concluded the damages for each instance of conversion would be the value of the stock at the time of the conversion. The court also held Heimbach violated Minn.Stat. § 80A.01 and Fawcett was entitled to recover attorney fees under Minn.Stat. § 80A.23, subd. 2.

On appeal, Heimbach contends the court erred by (1) fixing damages for conversion of stock at the time of conversion rather than the time Fawcett became aware of the conversion and (2) awarding attorney fees to Fawcett under the Minnesota Securities Act.

* * *

ANALYSIS

Heimbach contends the trial court erred as a matter of law in its determination of damages for the conversion of the MGC stock. Heimbach argues Minnesota has adopted the New York rule for determining the damages in cases involving the conversion of securities, and that rule states the recoverable damages for commodities of fluctuating value is the highest replacement value of the converted shares within a reasonable period of time following the discovery of the conversion. Hornblower & Weeks–Hemphill Noyes v. Lazere, 301 Minn. 462, 222 N.W.2d 799 (1974).

The trial court agreed that Minnesota has adopted the New York rule, but found the *Hornblower* case did not fully explain the New York rule. The trial court held the New York rule gives the injured party the option of claiming: (1) the market value at the time of conversion to afford him the basic remedy in a falling market; or (2) the highest replacement value between the discovery of the conversion and a reasonable period for replacement, when the basic measure of damages for conversion does not provide fair compensation.

Our resolution of this issue requires an examination of the history and reasoning behind the New York rule. Conversion is an act of willful interference with the personal property of another that is without justification or that is inconsistent with the rights of the person entitled to the use, possession, or ownership of the property. * * * The general measure of damages for wrongful conversion of property is the market value of the property at the time of conversion. Gallagher v. Jones, 129 U.S. 193, 9 S.Ct. 335, 337, 32 L.Ed. 658 (1889) (stating ordinarily goods have a fixed or relatively stable market value at which they can be replaced, so the measure of damages when they are converted is their value at the time of conversion) * * *.

However, when converted goods have a fluctuating value, such as stock, courts have supplemented the general rule to provide a more equitable remedy to the injured party. C.B. Higgins, Annotation, *Measure of Damages for Conversion of Corporate Stock or Certificate*, 31 A.L.R.3d 1286, 1305, 1314–32 (1970). In *Gallagher*, the United States Supreme Court annunciated the rule to be applied in calculating damages when stock is converted. It stated the measure of damages is

> the highest intermediate value reached by the stock between the time of the wrongful act complained of and a reasonable time thereafter, to be allowed to the party injured to place himself in the position he would have been in had not his rights been violated.

Gallagher, 129 U.S. at 200, 9 S.Ct. at 337. The Court explained that when dealing with goods whose market value is volatile, allowing the injured party only the value of the stock at the time of conversion would provide an inadequate and unjust remedy, because "[t]he real injury sustained by the principal consists * * * in the sale of [the stock] at an unfavorable time, and for an unfavorable price." *Id.*

In selecting an appropriate measure for damages, the court rejected the "English" rule, which permitted the plaintiff the highest value of the stock between the time of conversion and the time of trial. *Id.* at 201, 9 S.Ct. at 337. Instead, it used the New York modification of the rule. *Id.* at 202, 9 S.Ct. at 338; *see also* Schultz v. Commodity Futures Trading Commission, 716 F.2d 136, 140 (2d Cir.1983) (discussing *Gallagher*). This rule awarded the plaintiff

> the highest intermediate value of the stock between the time of its conversion and a reasonable time after the owner has received notice of it to enable him to replace the stock.

Gallagher, 129 U.S. at 202, 9 S.Ct. at 337.

The Second Circuit Court of Appeals has refined the New York rule as set forth in *Gallagher* in order to prevent inappropriate windfalls to plaintiffs which may occur when wrongfully converted stock reaches a higher price in the period between its conversion and the notice of conversion than in the period between notice of conversion and a reasonable time after notice. *Schultz*, 716 F.2d at 140 * * *. In these cases, the injured party should not receive the windfall of the higher price reached during the period before he receives notice of the conversion because "if he had desired to dispose of [his property] in that interval, he would have learned of the conversion." *Schultz*, 716 F.2d at 141 * * *. Thus, the measure of damages for wrongful conversion under the New York rule is either

> (1) its value at the time of conversion or (2) its highest intermediate value between notice of the conversion and a reasonable time thereafter during which the stock could have been replaced had that been desired, whichever of (1) or (2) is higher.

* * *

In *Hornblower*, the court considered whether damages should be assessed at: (1) the highest market value the stock achieves between the date of conversion and the date of its return, or (2) the highest market value the stock reaches within a reasonable time after the owner of the stock has knowledge of the conversion. *Hornblower*, 301 Minn. at 473, 222 N.W.2d at 806. It did not address the situation where there is a falling market and the owner of the stock seeks to recover the value of the stock at the time of conversion rather than within a reasonable time after the owner had knowledge of the conversion.

Faced with this situation now, we conclude when the market value of the stock is lower within a reasonable time after the owner learns of the conversion than at the time of the conversion, the owner has the option of claiming the market value at the time of conversion. Thus, where there is a rising market, it is most equitable to both the perpetrator and the injured party to determine damages within a reasonable time after the injured party should have known of the conversion. But where there is a falling market, it would be inequitable to provide the injured party with less than the value of the stock at the time of the conversion. * * *

DECISION

The trial court properly determined the damages for the conversion of Fawcett's stock at the time the stock was converted rather than within a reasonable time after Fawcett discovered the stock had been converted. * * *

Affirmed in part and reversed in part.

DeSPIRITO v. BRISTOL COUNTY WATER CO.

Supreme Court of Rhode Island, 1967.
102 R.I. 50, 227 A.2d 782.

JOSLIN, JUSTICE.

This action of trespass on the case for negligence was tried to a justice of the superior court sitting without a jury and resulted in a judgment of $576.50 plus costs for the plaintiff. It is here on the defendant's appeal.

The facts are that plaintiff's cellar was flooded with water to a depth of about eighteen inches following a break in the drainpipe which ran from the foundation of his residence to the street and which, until damaged, drew off any ground or surface water which might have accumulated in the surrounding area. Immediately following the break and continuing until the drainpipe was repaired ten days thereafter, water seeped into the cellar, damaging the residence as well as certain of plaintiff's household goods and personal effects. It was to recover for the costs and expenses incurred in remedying those damages that plaintiff brought this action.

* * *

While defendant challenges the decision of the trial justice on the question of liability, its principle objection goes to his rulings on the admissibility of certain evidence on the question of damages. * * * [Defendant] argues that the full measure of damages for the destruction of or injury to personal property is the difference between its fair market value just before destruction or injury and its fair market value immediately thereafter.

The general rule is, of course, as defendant suggests, and in proving his damages for an injury to or loss of items of personal property a party usually is restricted to testimony which evidences the difference between the before and after fair market values. * * * There is, however, a distinctive rule for proving damages for the loss of or the injury to more or less worn wearing apparel in use and to household goods and effects owned and kept for personal use. That exception is predicated upon the principle that the law is always concerned that an injured party shall be fully compensated for whatever injury he may have sustained. Working from that premise the courts have long recognized that property of these kinds cannot in any real sense be said to goods are sold. And in such a market it must, of course, be conceded that full and fair market value cannot generally be obtained and that sales are usually at a sacrifice. Accordingly in such cases, instead of adhering to the before and after market values as the rule of damages, the courts, giving due consideration to the attendant circumstances and conditions, permit recovery of the actual value to the owner of the thing lost or damaged, excluding, of course, any fanciful or sentimental value that might be placed upon it. * * * Annotation, *Valuation of Wearing Apparel or Household Goods Kept by Owner for Personal Use, in Action for Loss or Conversion of, or Injury to, Property*, 34 A.L.R. 3d 816 (1970).

In determining the recoverable actual value a trial justice has a wide latitude and, depending on the particular conditions and circumstances, he may admit evidence of the cost of an article when new, the length of time it has been in use, its condition at the time of the loss or injury, the expense to the owner of replacing it with another item of a like kind and in a similar condition, and any other facts which will assist in determining the worth of that article to its owner at the time of the injury. Under this rule, evidence of the necessary expenditures made by plaintiff in repairing or replacing a washing machine, a sump pump, a heating unit, while not controlling on the extent of his actual loss, was clearly admissible for such weight as it might receive from the trier of the facts. * * *

The defendant further contends that plaintiff, by reason of a lack of expertise, was not competent to testify to the cost of repairing and replacing his damaged household effects. Once again defendant invokes a rule of general application and asks us to apply to an unique situation the broad principle that the fair value of personal property may only be testified to by a person whose "knowledge of the matter in issue is so far superior to that of men in general that his opinion will probably aid in reaching a just conclusion." McGovern v. Michael, 62 R.I. 485, 489, 6 A.2d 709, 712. * * *

Here, however, just as in the instance of the true measure of damages for the loss of or injury to wearing apparel in use and household goods and effects owned or kept for personal use, the general rule of *McGovern* * * * does not obtain, and it is customarily held that the mere fact of ownership of these particular kinds of property is usually sufficient to qualify the owner to give his estimate of what his actual loss has been. It was for the trier of the facts to evaluate that testimony and to adjudge the credit to be attached to plaintiff as a witness. * * *

* * *

The defendant's appeal is denied and dismissed, and the judgment appealed from is affirmed.

CAMPINS v. CAPELS

Court of Appeals of Indiana, 1984.
461 N.E.2d 712.

MILLER, JUDGE.

Julio Campins, Jr. brings his appeal to this court after John Capels and his wife, Dana, recovered $11,100* in their suit against him, individually, and as his two business entities, Hollywood Gold and Silver and Zebone Gallery, Jewelry & Coin. The Capelses sued under IND.CODE 34–4–30–1, which authorized them to sue for treble damages because they were victims of a criminal offense against property—they suffered a burglary and consequent theft of their jewelry. The trial court ruled Campins liable for the value of some of their jewelry because he had purchased and had then destroyed some pieces when he knew or should have known they were stolen. This being the offense of criminal mischief, the trial court awarded the Capelses treble damages. * * *

---

* The trial court computed damages as follows:

3 USAC award rings at $1,000 each	=	$ 3,000
1 Free design wedding band at $700	=	700
TOTAL	=	$ 3,700
Application of treble damages		x3
TOTAL	=	$11,100

FACTS [AND CONCLUSIONS OF LAW]

Sometime between January 11 and January 13, 1981, one Earl Hall, eighteen years old, stole various items of jewelry from the Capelses' home (for which he was later convicted). * * * On January 15 or 16, in the course of the search, Mrs. Capels spoke with Campins, sole proprietor of two gold and silver dealerships. She claims he admitted purchasing some of the Capelses' jewelry but told her he had already melted it down with the exception of a sterling silver ring which he returned to her. Upon Campins's refusal to make restitution for the destruction of the jewelry, the Capelses brought suit against him. * * *

* * *

At trial, the nucleus of the action revolved around the jewelry allegedly melted down at Zebone Gallery, particularly three national racing championship rings awarded by United States Auto Club (USAC) and a free-form wedding band with twelve diamonds. * * *

After presenting evidence of Campins's liability, the Capelses presented evidence of the value of their rings. Mrs. Capels's wedding band, having been recently appraised at $700, was easily valuated. The USAC rings * * * proved a different matter.

The three USAC rings at issue here had been awarded to Capels in 1972, 1977, and 1978. (He had won five in all.) Each ring signified a national championship earned in a particular automobile category and given to the car's owner and the driver. In 1972, Parnelli Jones gave Capels his owner's ring in appreciation for his work as chief mechanic of Jones's Indy car. Capels later won his 1977 and 1978 rings as the actual owner of championship dirt division cars, driven by Bill Vukovich and Pancho Carter. The 1972 ring signified Capels's work as supervisor of what the media labelled a "super team" after having been instrumental in winning three straight Indy car championships (1970, 1971, 1972). As for his own owner's rings, they represented the large financial investment as well as time required to excel in any division of USAC competition. Sentimentally, Capels described these rings as being enduring symbols of his accomplishments and USAC's recognition thereof. * * *

Each heavy, gold ring bore a synthetic stone and had been molded to display the USAC emblem, the name of the recipient, the specific achievement being rewarded, and the year of that achievement. They were custom-made annually by Josten's with a different design each year. Capels specifically testified there was no market for these rings: "You can't buy these rings from any gift shop or jewelry store or anything." Record, p. 26. Capels admitted that in 1977, he purchased a duplicate of his 1977 ring for a business associate for $349, and Campins himself testified the price of gold at the time of the theft was double that of at least 1979, from $300 to $580–$600. Capels went on to testify he would not have sold the rings, even for $1,500 or $2,000 apiece. He then estimated their worth as between $700 and $1000, finally settling on $750 when asked to be specific.

In his assessment of the case, the trial judge concluded the following: * * *

> 3. Defendant is liable to Plaintiffs for the value of the three USAC award rings and one free-design wedding band, such value being as of the time of the destruction of the rings, and under provisions of Indiana Code 34–4–30–1 Defendant is liable to Plaintiffs for treble damages. * * *

DECISION

Campins realized or should have realized he was destroying property to which he had no rightful claim. The trial court did not err in establishing Campins's liability for criminal mischief. * * *

The remaining issue, now that liability has been established, is the size of the actual damages which Campins asserts are excessive. * * *

When personal property is the subject of an award, damages are measured by its fair market value at the time of the loss, fair market value being the price a willing seller will accept from a willing buyer. * * * Such appears to be the measure of worth for the twelve-diamond wedding band, appraised at $700. This assessment has never really been contested by Campins; he mainly questions the value placed on the USAC rings. And to our knowledge, the problems raised in valuating them have never been addressed in Indiana.

Both parties have argued this issue in terms of the methods of valuating used household goods and wearing apparel. Such system would appear appropriate because used household goods and clothing have a greater actual value to their owners than they do on the secondhand market, similar to the problem here, where Capels's feelings about the rings as mementoes outstrips his feelings for them as jewelry. Instead of allowing only the fair market value of secondhand goods, the court determines "the owner may recover the value of the goods to him, based on his actual money loss resulting from his being deprived of the property, or the difference in actual value caused by the injury *excluding any fanciful or sentimental values which he might place on them.*" Anchor Stove & Furniture Co. v. Blackwood (1941) 109 Ind.App. 357, 363, 35 N.E.2d 117, 119 (emphasis added) * * *. And, indeed, this standard is prevalent throughout the diverse jurisdictions. * * * We believe that standard is useful but not altogether appropriate to the problem here.

First of all, jewelry is neither a household good * * * nor wearing apparel * * *. Thus, ordinarily, jewelry is valuated at its fair market value. * * * However, these USAC rings were not ordinary jewelry and could not be bought and sold in a readily available market. Rather, they were coveted awards and symbols of certain achievements accomplished by very few, such awards not having many willing sellers and therefore no real market. These rings should be valued differently than other jewelry.

* * * This, therefore, is our starting point—how do we find jewelry's actual value to its owner when it has a high value for its extrinsic content but also has a primary function and a consequently raised value based on pure sentimentality?

We find a basis for proceeding in the fundamental reasoning behind awarding higher actual values to owners of used household goods and wearing apparel:

> The underlying principle of universal application is that of fair and just compensation for the loss or damage sustained.... Where subordinate rules for the measure of damages [fair market value for personal property] run counter to the paramount rule of fair and just compensation, the former must yield to the principle underlying all such rules.

Aufderheide v. Fulk, 112 N.E. at 400. * * *

The emphasis in the cases where the actual value of the goods exceeded the market value or where there was no market value at all is upon looking at all the circumstances and the available elements of loss in a rational, reasonable fashion. * * * We believe the best method to ensure fairness to both parties is to receive a wide range of elements for consideration in the actual value. * * * Such elements that have been introduced and relied upon are often such typical factors as cost of replacement, original cost, and cost to reproduce. * * * But our courts and juries have also examined elements of a less prosaic nature, such as the proposed use of woodland for a forestry course (Alfred Atmore Pope Foundation Inc. v. New York, New Haven & Hartford Railroad Co., *supra*), uniqueness (Lack v. Anderson (1946) La.App., 27 So.2d 653), the feelings of the owner (Harvey v. Wheeler Transfer & Storage Co., (1938) 227 Wis. 36, 277 N.W. 627), and the cost to build and decorate a room to match a single painting (Cherry v. McCutchen, (1942) 68 Ga.App. 682, 23 S.E.2d 587). We believe that sentimental value, in limited circumstances, is also such a consideration.

When we refer to sentimental value, we do not mean mawkishly emotional or unreasonable attachments to personal property. *See* Mieske v. Bartell Drug Co., (1979) 92 Wash.2d 40, 593 P.2d 1308. Rather, we are referring to the feelings generated by items of almost purely sentimental value, such as heirlooms (Brown v. Frontier Theatres, Inc., (1963) Tex., 369 S.W.2d 299), family papers and photographs (Bond v. A.H. Belo Corp., (1980) Tex.Civ.App., 602 S.W.2d 105), handicrafts (Monahan v. Scott Cleaning Co., (1922) Mo.App., 241 S.W. 956), and trophies (Shaffer v. Honeywell, Inc., (1976) S.D., 249 N.W.2d 251). What we are referring to basically are those items generally capable of generating sentimental feelings, not just emotions peculiar to the owner. In other words, any owner of these USAC rings would have similar feelings. The most apt analogy to our situation is that of the trophies. In two cases, courts have awarded damages based on the consideration of the "blood, sweat and tears" expended to win these objects. Mosely v. Sears, Roebuck & Co.,

(1964) La.App., 167 So.2d 408 (tennis trophies); Shaffer v. Honeywell, Inc., *supra* (horse trophies); *see also* Monahan v. Scott Cleaning Co., *supra* (hand-crocheted bedspread valued by work, labor and time spent). We see no difference in giving special consideration to items such as these and to the three USAC rings, awarded for three years of "blood, sweat and tears" and thus having special sentimental meaning for Capels. The question remains whether Capels's evidence supported the $3000 award.

Capels testified not only to the actual worth of the rings as mere pieces of custom-embossed gold but also to his emotional attachment to each. He described the pride and gratification he felt upon their ownership and elaborated on the effort required to win them. Actual estimates of their worth—to him—ranged from $700 to $1000 each; however, he himself settled upon the $750 figure. Campins alternatively argues each ring was worth $67 (wholesale gold), $135–200 (retail gold), or $349 (replacement in 1977). We believe the evidence justified an award of $750.

* * *

In light of the substantial evidence of the replacement value of the rings, the increase in the price of gold, and Capels's justifiable sentimental feelings, we would see no error in finding damages in the amount of $750 apiece.[2] * * *

However, while we ultimately conclude the court did not act erroneously in allowing an award in excess of the replacement value of the rings (based on the unique circumstances here and special attachment to this property), we can hardly deem it appropriate to fix a value higher than that asserted by the owner. Capels finally settled upon a figure of $750 per ring; the court's award of $1000 apiece could only have been improperly based on speculation. To decide otherwise would be to open a Pandora's box of problems in the computation and proof of actual value. By our decision here, we simply conclude that certain property, by its very nature, has an element of sentiment essential to its existence. In this case, we refer to symbols for achievements of national stature and recognition and the calculation of their actual value. But we must also add the proviso that even for significant awards or mementos we do not intend to permit fanciful speculation as to their worth. We must fashion our remedy within the realm of sensibility, as here, where $750 is only slightly above the established range of replacement values. Such would naturally also be our standard in valuating similar significant awards, such as an Oscar, the Heisman Trophy, or an Olympic medal, where the recipient retains the honor despite the loss of the trophy, such trophy being merely the symbol of the achievement and perhaps replaceable by a surrogate. A certain amount of sentiment is inherent in the value of these objects to the owner, and each case must be based on its own facts. But we must refrain from

---

2. It is improper to consider evidence of what a person would not sell an item for. In other words, Capels's statement that he "wouldn't have sold those rings for Fifteen Hundred to Two Thousand Dollars to anybody" could not have been used for purposes of estimating damages. *See* Cherry v. McCutchen, (1941) 65 Ga.App. 301, 16 S.E.2d 167; Young's Bus Lines, Inc. v. Redmon, (1931) Tex.Civ.App., 43 S.W.2d 266. Thus, Capels cannot so argue this statement as part of the evidence.

considering all but reasonable estimates of that element of sentiment. We believe in this case, Capels's $750 figure was just such a reasonable value of each ring with the sentiment included therein. We therefore affirm the judgment but modify the award.*

NOTES

1. *Campins* states the "minority view" insofar as it permits the recovery of compensatory damages for the "sentimental value" of personal property. *See, e.g.*, Landers v. Municipality of Anchorage, 915 P.2d 614 (Alaska 1996) (declining to adopt the "minority view").

2. Looking back over the cases in this section on general compensatory damages, note that the basic yardstick for measuring such damages is fair market value. Plaintiffs whose personal property has been taken or destroyed are allowed to recover the fair market value of the property at the time of the tort, and plaintiffs whose property has been damaged are permitted to receive the sum by which the fair market value has been diminished. Usually the application of these formulas to the facts is straightforward, but sometimes interesting questions arise as to "what time" and "which market." When the property has a depressed fair market value, as in the case of household goods, or no fair market value, as in the case of heirlooms, the courts have modified the basic rules in an effort to ensure that the victim of the tort receives adequate compensation.

3. Once the proper formula for measuring general compensatory damages has been selected, the plaintiff's lawyer must introduce sufficient proof of value so that the formula can be applied to the facts of the case by the judge or jury. Under the standard formula, the plaintiff's lawyer must introduce objective proof, such as expert witness testimony, of fair market value. Under the modified formulas, the plaintiff's lawyer may put the owner of the property on the stand to testify as to the property's value to the owner.

4. The next case deals with the difficult issues that arise when property is damaged, and the owner chooses to repair it.

FARMERS INSURANCE CO. v. R.B.L. INVESTMENT CO.

Court of Appeals of Arizona, Division 2, 1983.
138 Ariz. 562, 675 P.2d 1381.

HATHAWAY, JUDGE.

Whether the owner of a negligently damaged motor vehicle may be compensated for damages for loss in the fair market value above and

---

* The appellate court computed damages as follows:

3 USAC award rings at $750 each	=	$2,250
1 Free design wedding band at $700	=	700
TOTAL	=	$2,950
Application of treble damages		x3
TOTAL	=	$8,850

beyond the cost of repair, and whether he may be compensated for loss of use of the motor vehicle during the period in which it is being repaired, are questions raised on this appeal. * * *

On October 30, 1980, a new, unsold, 1980 Audi, available for sale from appellant's new car dealership, while being taken for a test drive, was involved in a collision with a vehicle insured by Farmers. Farmers admitted that the accident was the fault of its insured.

Repairs to the new Audi at the retail cost of $3,495.70, were required. Farmers offered to pay the repair costs, but appellant refused the offer on the basis that it would not fully compensate the loss. Farmers thereafter erroneously issued its draft to appellant for the sum of $9,460, which appellant accepted and cashed. Farmers asked for a refund of all funds in excess of its original $3,495.70 offer, and appellant counteroffered to return the amount in excess of the loss it claimed. Farmers refused and this suit ensued for return of the funds. This accounts for the unusual posture wherein Farmers, in seeking recovery of the overpayment, is litigating the damage and losses of the "defendant"/appellant.

The issue of the proper measure of appellant's damages was tried to the trial court on stipulated facts. The trial court's findings of facts include:

... 9.   That the dealer's wholesale factory cost of the car is $15,526.00.

10.   That the amount of $3,122.63 was spent to fix the car after it was damaged in the accident.

11.   That the dealership spent $1,971.91 in interest to the Valley National Bank paid on this particular car during the time it was in the shop being repaired.

12.   That also, added to these numbers are normal, average gross profit in the sum of $889.00, and from that total they are deducting the amount of money for which the car was sold, $13,500.00, leaving a difference of $8,009.54 due from plaintiff.

The trial court held that the compensable damages were limited to the cost of repair. It is from this ruling that the appeal is taken. The judgment appealed from was based upon the trial court's minute entry of November 24, 1982, wherein the trial court stated:

... 2.   Present Arizona law provides for no award for decrease in value where the property can be repaired.

3.   Present Arizona law makes no provision for collection of interest for floor-planning or delay in sale.

Appellant begins its loss-to-fair-market-value argument with a submission that an automobile that has been in a major accident is worth less than an identical automobile that has not been in an accident, suggesting that one need only examine their own biases as a consumer to acknowledge a disparity in the price they would be willing to pay for either vehicle. They further argue that where the choice is between an automobile that is "new" versus one that was new but was in an accident and is now repaired, the disparity is magnified.

The issue of the proper measure of damages for injury to personalty was discussed in Anderson v. Alabam Freight Lines, 64 Ariz. 313, 169 P.2d 865 (1946), where the Arizona Supreme Court stated:

> "The measure of damages for injuries to personal property less than its destruction is the difference in the value of the property immediately before and immediately after the injuries." [quoting from Mesa City v. Lesueur, 21 Ariz. 532, 540, 190 P. 573, 576.]

> In addition to the costs of repairs and value of loss of use, the evidence in this case shows that the value of appellee's truck immediately before the accident was approximately $10,000, and immediately following the accident, in its damaged condition, was approximately $6,500, or a difference of $3,500. The judgment of the trial court was for the latter amount. There was, therefore, ample evidence to justify the judgment independently of the costs of repairs, loss of time, and similar items. The court also found that the cost of repairs would exceed $2,500, *and that when made, the truck would have a value of $1,000 less than it had immediately preceding the accident.* (Emphasis added) 64 Ariz. at 319, 169 P.2d at 869.

We find that Anderson v. Alabam Freight Lines, *supra*, deals with a factual situation where damages in the form of a loss of market value existed over and above the cost of repairs and is therefore controlling in the instant case. We find inapposite Reckart v. Avra Valley Air, Inc., 19 Ariz.App. 538, 509 P.2d 231 (1973); Downs v. Shouse, 18 Ariz.App. 225, 501 P.2d 401 (1972); Melvin v. Stephens, 10 Ariz.App. 357, 458 P.2d 977 (1969), all cited by appellee in support of its position. Those cases do not involve facts such as presented in the instant situation where the damaged party had actual, provable losses for market value and loss of use over and above the cost of repairs. We believe that the rule is clearly enunciated in the Restatement (Second) of Torts, § 928 (1977):

> § 928. Harm to Chattels. When one is entitled to a judgment for harm to chattels not amounting to a total destruction in value, the damages include compensation for

> > (a) the difference between the value of the chattel before the harm and the value after the harm or, at his election in an appropriate case, the reasonable cost of repair or restoration, *with due allowance for any difference between the original value and the value after repairs,* and

> > (b) the loss of use. (Emphasis added)

Other authority supporting damages for depreciation beyond the cost of repair includes Professor Dobbs, who writes:

> There seems no warrant at all for insisting that the owner content himself with the repair costs if they are less than the depreciation,

provided depreciation can be and is adequately proven. However satisfactory the repairs may be in, say, the operation of a car, the owner may quite possibly find that the trade-in value of his car is less when he seeks to purchase a new automobile, or that its cash sale value is less throughout the immediate life of the car. If this sort of depreciation is real, and can be established, there seems no reason at all to deny full compensation by limiting recovery to cost of repairs. D. Dobbs, Remedies, § 5.10, at 380 (1973).

Jurisdictions that have addressed the issue seem to have generally held that the measure of compensation to the owner of a negligently damaged motor vehicle may include the cost of repair and proven residual diminution in fair market value. *See, e.g.,* Perma Ad Ideas of America, Inc. v. Mayville, 158 Ga.App. 707, 282 S.E.2d 128, 130 (1981); Trailmobile Division of Pullman, Inc. v. Higgs, 12 Ill.App.3d 323, 297 N.E.2d 598 (1973); Gary v. Allstate Insurance Company, 250 So.2d 168 (La.App.1971). We believe this is the appropriate standard.

Appellant contends that the trial court erred by denying as a matter of law the claim for interest paid during the period of repair on the loan it had taken out to purchase and "floor" the damaged vehicle. It is argued that having the vehicle available for show and sale is the "use" to which the vehicle would have been put but for the negligence of Farmers' insured. The interest expense paid during the period of time between the accident and the vehicle's repair is stipulated to be $1,971.91, and is the interest paid by appellant to the Valley National Bank for the car while being repaired only. The repairs took many months due to parts shipping. Loss of use is an appropriate item of damages. Restatement (Second) of Torts, § 928(b); *see also,* Fred Frederick Motors, Inc. v. Krause, 12 Md.App. 62, 277 A.2d 464 (1971); Trailmobile Division of Pullman, Inc. v. Higgs, *supra.* Professor Dobbs, in his treatise on remedies, states, at p. 168–9:

> * * * In cases where the plaintiff's claim is one for the loss of use of his property, the rental value of the property during the period in which the plaintiff was deprived of it is often one element of damages he is allowed to recover. If his automobile is damaged and he loses the use of it for a month, he may be entitled to its rental value or the rental value of some substitute transportation, as well as to some recovery for the physical damage itself. *But it would be possible, if the occasion arose, to mentally convert the car into cash. Instead of talking of renting the car, it would then be possible to talk of 'renting' the cash—that is, to talk of paying interest for the use of money in a sum equal to the value of the car.* The amount of interest on the cash value of the car is not necessarily the same as the amount of rental value of the car itself. Nevertheless, rental value of the car and interest on the cash value of the car can be seen as two measurements of the same underlying value, since it is almost always acceptable to express the value of property in terms of money.... If for any reason he is willing to base his loss of use claim on interest rather than rental values of

the tangible form of his property, there is no reason to deny it, and sometimes this is convenient to both parties. [footnotes omitted] (Emphasis added).

We deem the out-of-pocket interest expense paid by appellant to be includable as a fair measure of compensation for the loss of use of the vehicle during the period of repairs. The time in the shop for repairs was occasioned through negligent conduct and the interest expense incurred when the vehicle was not available for sale by appellant would not have been incurred but for the negligence of the plaintiff's insured. It is a direct and proximate result of the plaintiff's insured's negligence and should be compensable. *Cf.* Higgins v. Guerin, 74 Ariz. 187, 245 P.2d 956 (1952). It is the policy of the law to award those damages which will fairly and adequately compensate the injured party. Higgins v. Guerin, *supra.*

The parties stipulated that the vehicle cost the dealership $15,526 wholesale and the average gross profit on such a car is $889,[2] making its pre-collision value total $16,415. After the repairs were performed, the automobile sold for $13,500, leaving appellant out of pocket $2,915 after repairs. The judgment is modified to include this amount plus $1,971.91 for loss of use.

As modified, the judgment is affirmed.

HOWARD, C.J., and BIRDSALL, J., concur.

NOTES

1. With regard to general damages for harm to personal property, when a court gives the plaintiff the option of recovering the cost of repair, rather than the diminution in fair market value, a question arises as to whether either the pre-tort fair market value of the property or the diminution in fair market value ought to place a ceiling on the recovery of repair costs. A number of courts impose such a limit, and "in most cases, such a rule is appropriate; to permit the plaintiff to charge $5,000 for repairing a car when the car itself is worth only $4,000, or to permit the plaintiff to spend $10,000 to repair a car when its market value has been reduced only $1,000 is certainly to permit either a windfall or waste if such repairs are actually made; and to permit an unduly subjective valuation by the plaintiff if the repairs are not actually made." Dan B. Dobbs, Law of Remedies § 5.14(1) (2d ed. 1993). However, there are special cases when it is "inappropriate" to impose such a ceiling. *Id.* For example, when the damaged property is being used to produce income, the plaintiff ought to be allowed to repair the property to protect the flow of income. *Id.* And, when the plaintiff's general compensatory damages are measured by the value of the property to the owner, the plaintiff ought to be allowed to repair the property at whatever price it takes to restore it in order to ensure "full compensation for the

---

2. "In addition to the cost of repairs and loss of use of a motor vehicle damaged in an accident, the loss of sale value arising from the mere fact of the injury is an element of damages to be considered, where the vehicle cannot be made entirely good by repairs." 15 Blashfield Automobile Law & Practice, § 480.11, at 42–3 (3rd ed. 1969).

plaintiff's idiosyncratic attachment" to the property. *Id.*; *see also* Alaska Const. Equip., Inc. v. Star Trucking, Inc., 128 P.3d 164 (Alaska 2006) (no cap on loss of use damages in a case of the total destruction of property).

2.   Special or consequential damages are recoverable for harm to personal property when they do not overlap with the measure of general damages, are reasonably foreseeable, and can be proven with reasonable certainty. Dan B. Dobbs, Law of Remedies § 5.15(1) (2d ed. 1993). There is a duty to mitigate special damages, but there is no ceiling on the amount recoverable. *Id.* § 5.15(2). Such damages usually fall into one of two categories: (1) loss of use, including lost profits; and (2) emotional harm resulting from interference with personal property rights. *Id.* § 5.15(1).

3.   Loss of use damages may be measured in one of four ways: (1) lost profits; (2) cost of renting substitute property; (3) the fair rental value of the plaintiff's property; or (4) interest. *Id.* For an excellent discussion of the various measures of loss of use damages, see Alan Brownstein, *What's The Use? A Doctrinal and Policy Critique of the Measurement of Loss of Use Damages*, 37 Rutgers L. Rev. 433, 436–75 (1985). *See also* PurCo Fleet Services, Inc. v. Koenig, 2010 WL 185415 (Colo. App. 2010)(adopting Professor Brownstein's recommendation that, in the commercial context, loss of use damages should be measured by the *net* rental value of the plaintiff's chattel).

4.   When the plaintiff uses the property to make a profit, the plaintiff may recover the loss of profits attributable to the defendant's wrongdoing, provided the plaintiff makes an effort to mitigate damages. Usually the best way to mitigate damages is to rent substitute property. Consequently, plaintiffs who use property for commercial purposes will more frequently ask the court to measure loss of use damages by reference to the cost of renting a substitute than by reference to the amount of lost profits. Dan B. Dobbs, Law of Remedies § 5.15(2) (2d ed. 1993).

5.   Although special damages usually are awarded only for "actual losses," in the case of harm to personal property, many courts allow recovery for loss of use even when the plaintiff has not rented a substitute vehicle (perhaps in part because courts ordinarily deny special damages for inconvenience). One court has described the loss for which the plaintiff in such a case is being allowed to recover as an "opportunity cost." Kuwait Airways Corp. v. Ogden Allied Aviation Services, 726 F.Supp. 1389 (E.D.N.Y.1989). One commentator has recommended that loss of use damages be measured by "awarding interest on the fair market value of the chattel where no substitute is hired." Alan Brownstein, *What's The Use? A Doctrinal and Policy Critique of the Measurement of Loss of Use Damages*, 37 Rutgers L. Rev. 433, 498–507 (1985). The issue is one that arises in the reported cases most often when the plaintiff owns commercial property (such as an airplane) that has been damaged. *See* J.H. Cooper, Annotation, *Measure of Damages for Destruction of or Injury to Airplane*, 73 A.L.R. 2d 719 (1960). For a more complete discussion of the matter, see Dan B. Dobbs, The Law of Remedies § 5.15(2) (2d ed. 1993).

6.   In some cases, the courts have allowed a plaintiff to recover loss of use damages for a longer period of time than that necessary to make repairs. For example, when the plaintiff does not have sufficient funds to pay the

repair bill and thus is unable to retrieve the property from the repair shop, some courts will allow the plaintiff to recover loss of use damages beyond the repair period, particularly when the defendant engages in "unreasonably dilatory settlement tactics." Urico v. Parnell Oil Co., 708 F.2d 852, 855–56 (1st Cir.1983) (liability was uncontested and insurer had agreed to pay for repairs, but then refused to make payments unless plaintiff waived all other claims); McPherson v. Kerr, 195 Mont. 454, 636 P.2d 852, 856 (1981) ("No reasonable man could be expected to expend $1,100 which he doesn't have to mitigate an injury for which he is not responsible."). *But see* Badillo v. Hill, 570 So.2d 1067, 1069 (Fla.Dist.Ct.App.1990) ("A breakdown in settlement negotiations with the defendant or his insurer, regardless of who is at fault, is not relevant to expand the time frame * * * [because] once the courts start to consider subjective peculiar circumstances beyond the fact of injury, it would make the rule of law difficult to apply and could open the door to the possibility of considerable abuse.").

7. All of the rules regarding "loss of use" damages described in Notes 1–6 above have been developed in the context of negligence actions. What if the plaintiff is suing for the commission of an intentional tort? The traditional common law rules distinguish between an action for trespass to chattels (in which damages for loss of use are recoverable because the plaintiff retains or regains possession of the property) and an action for conversion (in which damages for loss of use are not recoverable because the plaintiff has "forced a sale" of the property on the defendant and is instead entitled to recover prejudgment interest on the fair market value of the property from the date of the conversion). *E.g.*, Ehman v. Libralter Plastics, Inc., 207 Mich.App. 43, 523 N.W.2d 639 (1994) (refusing to award "lost profits" to a commercial plaintiff whose unique property was converted, but awarding prejudgment interest from the date of the conversion at a statutory rate). For a suggestion that modern courts may be willing to allow the recovery of "lost profits" in conversion actions under appropriate circumstances, see Dan B. Dobbs, The Law of Remedies 561 (2d ed. 1993).

8. The traditional common law rule that loss of use damages may not be recovered in a conversion action was erroneously applied to negligence claims in which personal property had been severely damaged or destroyed. *E.g.*, Langham v. Chicago, R.I. & P.Ry. Co., 201 Iowa 897, 901, 208 N.W. 356, 358 (1925) (loss of use damages recoverable only if general damages are measured by cost of repair), *overruled by* Long v. McAllister, 319 N.W.2d 256 (Iowa 1982). *See generally* Dan B. Dobbs, Law of Remedies § 5.11, at 384–85 (1973). The courts have corrected the error, however, and the majority of states now take the position that loss of use damages are recoverable in negligence actions, even in cases of total destruction, because it may take the plaintiff a certain amount of time to replace property that has been destroyed. *See, e.g.*, Chlopek v. Schmall, 224 Neb. 78, 396 N.W.2d 103 (1986). *See generally* Dan B. Dobbs, The Law of Remedies 561 (2d ed. 1993).

9. Emotional distress is the second type of harm for which plaintiffs may seek special compensatory damages in claims for harm to personal property. As with loss of use damages, the availability of special damages for this type of harm varies, depending upon the cause of action that the plaintiff brings. The point can best be illustrated by looking at cases involving harm to pets.

Domestic animals are treated as personal property, and general compensatory damages are usually fixed by reference to the pet's fair market value, *see, e.g.,* Lachenman v. Stice, 838 N.E.2d 451 (Ind. App. 2005)(refusing to permit plaintiff to recover for the "sentimental value" of a dog), although some jurisdictions allow the owner of a pet to recover the pet's value to the owner. *E.g.,* Robin Miller, Annotation, *Damages for Killing or Injuring Dog,* 61 A.L.R.5th 635 (1998); Jay M. Zitter, Annotation, *Measure, Elements, and Amount of Damages for Killing or Injuring Cat,* 8 A.L.R. 4th 1287 (1981). Because the measure of general compensatory damages will not compensate the owner for what often feels like the loss of a member of the family, plaintiffs may ask for emotional distress damages in addition to general compensatory damages. The courts respond to such requests in various ways, depending upon the alleged state of the defendant's mind. Emotional distress damages are generally denied in negligence actions, but an increasing number of courts are allowing the recovery of emotional distress damages when the plaintiff sues for intentional or reckless misconduct. Steven M. Wise, *Recovery of Common Law Damages for Emotional Distress, Loss of Society, and Loss of Companionship for the Wrongful Death of a Companion Animal,* 4 Animal L. 33 (1998). For example, in Fackler v. Genetzky, 257 Neb. 130, 595 N.W.2d 884 (1999), the plaintiffs sued their veterinarian for professional malpractice (alleging the use of improper procedures to administer injections, thereby causing the death of two racehorses). The trial court entered a partial summary judgment in favor of the defendant based upon its determination that emotional distress damages are not recoverable for the death of an animal. The appellate court affirmed, drawing the following distinction between actions for negligence and actions for intentional or reckless misconduct:

> In other jurisdictions, the general rule is that an animal, regardless of sentimental attachment, is personal property, and recovery cannot be had for emotional damages resulting from the negligent destruction of that property. *See, e.g.,* Nichols v. Sukaro Kennels, 555 N.W.2d 689 (Iowa 1996); Julian v. De Vincent, 155 W.Va. 320, 184 S.E.2d 535 (1971) * * *. *But see,* Campbell v. Animal Quarantine Station, 63 Haw. 557, 632 P.2d 1066 (1981); Fredeen v. Stride, 269 Or. 369, 525 P.2d 166 (1974); La Porte v. Associated Independents, Inc., 163 So.2d 267 (Fla.1964).

> Some courts have recognized a cause of action for intentional infliction of emotional distress where the intentional killing of an animal was concerned. *See,* Richardson v. Fairbanks North Star Borough, 705 P.2d 454 (Alaska 1985); Gill v. Brown, 107 Idaho 1137, 695 P.2d 1276 (Idaho App.1985).

> In considering the cases involving negligent injury or destruction of animals, however, we determine that the majority approach is well reasoned and consistent with settled principles of Nebraska law. This court has clearly held that animals are personal property and that emotional damages cannot be had for the negligent destruction of personal property. People may develop an emotional attachment to personal property, whether animals or inanimate objects with sentimental value, but the law does not recognize a right to money damages for emotional distress resulting from the negligent destruction of such property.

Id. at 139–40, 595 N.W.2d at 891–92. In *Gill* and *Richardson*, where the plaintiffs had been the victims of egregious misconduct, they sued for intentional or reckless infliction of emotional distress, and thus the claims were for personal injury, not property damage. *See also* Brown v. Muhlenberg Township, 269 F.3d 205, 217–19 (3d Cir.2001). In the next case, by contrast, the court explicitly allows a plaintiff who has sued for conversion to recover special compensatory damages for emotional distress.

10. Legislatures are beginning to enact statutes that authorize the recovery of noneconomic damages for the intentional or negligent killing or injuring of a pet, and that also authorize the recovery of punitive damages for the malicious killing or injuring of a pet. *See, e.g.,* 510 Ill. Comp. Stat. Ann. 70/16.3 (Supp. 2008); Tenn. Code Ann. § 44–17–403 (2004). Such legislation usually places a "cap" on the amount of damages recoverable. For a discussion of these statutes and a proposal that courts should, as a matter of common law, authorize compensatory damages for the loss of society and companionship of a pet in addition to damages for emotional distress caused by the death of a pet, see Margit Livingston, *The Calculus of Animal Valuation: Crafting a Viable Remedy,* 82 Neb. L. Rev. 783 (2004).

GONZALES v. PERSONAL STORAGE, INC.

Court of Appeal, Fourth District, California, 1997.
56 Cal.App.4th 464, 65 Cal.Rptr.2d 473.

BENKE, ACTING PRESIDING JUSTICE.

In this case we consider the question of whether a self-storage facility which converted approximately $60,000 of a tenant's personal property is liable for the severe emotional distress the tenant suffered when the tenant learned about the conversion. * * *

FACTUAL BACKGROUND

Plaintiff and respondent Lucy R. Gonzales is a native of the Philippines and was married for many years to an officer in the United States Navy. As a result of her husband's travels during the course of his naval career, Gonzales had collected a number of rare and valuable pieces of furniture and personal belongings. Gonzales was also an active member of the local Filipino community and in 1968 she founded the Maria Clara de Pilipinas Sorority. Under her direction the sorority works with high school girls in the Filipino community preparing them for the annual spring debutante ball. * * *

In 1989 Gonzales's marriage was dissolved and she was required to sell her family home and move into her daughter's home. Because of the large quantity of her personal belongings, she decided to rent storage space at a facility operated by defendant and appellant Personal Storage, Inc. (Personal Storage). At the time she entered into a lease with Personal Storage, Gonzales explained to the person showing her the facility that she had a large amount of rare furniture, keepsakes, heirlooms and other personal belongings which she needed to store because of her divorce. After executing the lease, Gonzales stored her personal belongings at

Personal Storage's facility. As contemplated by her lease, Gonzales put a lock on her storage space.

According to both Gonzales and one of the experts retained by Personal Storage, the replacement value of the items Gonzales stored was approximately $196,000. A second expert called by Personal Storage stated the items would probably have a fair market value of 25 to 35 percent of their replacement value.[1]

[In 1990–91, Gonzales fell into a pattern of falling behind on her rent and then paying up when she received a notice from Personal Storage. In January of 1992, after she had fallen behind again on her rent payments, Personal Storage placed an advertisement for an auction of Gonzales' personal goods without notifying her of the action. The advertisement provided a detailed description of the items in Gonzales' unit. On February 4, a thin woman and an elderly man came to the storage facility and the woman falsely claimed to be Gonzales. The imposter tendered the amount of the rent then due in the amount of $336 and was allowed to remove all of Gonzales' belongings from the unit and into a U–Haul truck.]

On February 6, 1992, Personal Storage received a cashier's check from Gonzales in the amount of $526. On February 7, 1992, Gonzales called Personal Storage to verify receipt of her payment. A Personal Storage employee told her there had been "a mix-up." The employee then told Gonzales that someone had come to Personal Storage on February 4, paid the outstanding rent and emptied the storage unit.

Gonzales was emotionally devastated by the loss of her belongings. She did not leave her room for a week after hearing the news. * * * She eventually filed for bankruptcy.

Gonzales stopped participating in community events, and the 1992 debutante ball for the Maria Clara de Pilipinas Sorority was canceled because Gonzales could not function. Gonzales was treated by a therapist from February 1992 to August 1992. The therapist diagnosed Gonzales as suffering from depression which was unresolved when Gonzales stopped treatment in August 1992.

The therapist saw Gonzales again in 1994 and again diagnosed her as suffering from depression. The therapist noted Gonzales continued to

---

1. The following is a partial inventory of the items Gonzales stored: All her family photographs, including the only photograph of a child she lost at the age of five months, a written family history, acacia wood furniture which had been made for her in the Philippines, Persian and Chinese rugs, marble breakfast tables, gold breakfast chairs, a jade centerpiece, oil paintings, Nortitake 12–place China set, Rose 12–place China set, Leonor 12–piece silver set, gold goblets, silver goblets, a silver punch set, Oneida serving trays, Oneida chafing dishes, a Korean cabinet with ivory and jade inlay, Korean frames with ivory and jade inlay, an Italian chandelier, multiple framed silks from Thailand and Vietnam, a tea cart and set with pearl inlay, collectible elephants, reindeers, German pilsners, Hataka dolls, a Korean stove, stereos, 24 formal Philippine gowns, 12 evening gowns, shoes, handbags, suits, multiple bedding sets, bamboo serving trays, Hawaiian costumes and Hawaiian record collection, Gonzales's assorted awards and mementos, her daughter's wedding and debutante gowns, serving and entertaining sets, 24 jade eggs from Taiwan, a Chinese abacus, a Chinese wine set, an antique Chinese teapot, a tea set made in occupied Japan, and original Hawaiian doll collector items.

experience weight gain, withdrawal from friends, family and activities, sleep disruption, uncontrollable crying and difficulty leaving home.

PROCEDURAL HISTORY

Gonzales filed a complaint against Personal Storage in which she alleged claims for breach of contract, breach of warranty, breach of the implied covenant of good faith and fair dealing, negligence and conversion. * * *

At the close of evidence in the trial of Gonzales's claims, the trial court directed a verdict in her favor as to Personal Storage's liability for negligence, violation of the California Self–Storage Facility Act and conversion. The court found that as a matter of law Personal Storage had no right in January 1992 to take possession of or attempt to sell Gonzales's property without again providing her the preliminary lien and notice of lien sale required by the California Self–Storage Facility Act.

The jury returned a verdict finding that Personal Storage had breached its contract with Gonzales, causing her $59,559 in damage; the jury found that she had suffered $59,559 in property damage as a result of Personal Storage's negligence and $232,582 in emotional distress damages. The jury also awarded Gonzales $87,466 in damages for conversion; unlike the damages for negligence the conversion damages included interest and time expended in attempting to recover the lost goods.

ISSUES ON APPEAL

On appeal the only issue Personal Storage raises is its contention the jury should not have been permitted to award Gonzales damages for her emotional distress.

* * *

DISCUSSION

A. *Emotional Distress Damages*

* * *

[W]ere Gonzales's claims solely for negligence, we would be inclined to agree with Personal Storage that she cannot recover damages for her emotional distress. However, the limits imposed with respect to recovery for emotional distress caused by a defendant's negligence do not apply when distress is the result of a defendant's commission of the distinct torts of trespass, nuisance or conversion. Indeed, with respect to trespass, the law is clear that "damages may be recovered for annoyance and distress, including mental anguish, proximately caused by a trespass." (Armitage v. Decker (1990) 218 Cal.App.3d 887, 905, 267 Cal.Rptr. 399.) Thus the plaintiffs in Armitage v. Decker were allowed to recover for distress they suffered "as a result of having their property line buried under large amounts of dirt, making it appear that one side of their property abuts a quarry, after having spent a long time looking for the best piece of property they could afford. The evidence also supported a conclusion that the [plaintiffs] suffered distress due to the spillage of dirt onto their property and the threat of interference with drainage on their property, as well as concern over appellant's operation of the bulldozer on the berm." (*Id.* at pp. 905–906, 267 Cal.Rptr. 399.)

* * *

* * * [W]e note the Restatement of Torts Second section 927, comment m, states that where property has been converted: "If the deprivation is the legal cause of harm to the feelings, damages may be allowable for the harm, as when the defendant intentionally deprives the plaintiff of essential household furniture, which humiliates the plaintiff, a result that the defendant should have realized would follow." (*See also* Fredeen v. Stride (1974) 269 Or. 369, 525 P.2d 166, 168 [veterinarian's conversion of plaintiff's dog supports emotional distress damages].)

* * *

In this regard it is also important to recognize that negligent damage to personal property, for which the law generally will not permit recovery of emotional distress damages (*see* Cooper v. Superior Court, *supra*, 153 Cal.App.3d at pp. 1012–1013, 200 Cal.Rptr. 746), is distinct from the conversion of personal property. * * *

The act of dominion over the property of another which is necessary for conversion is important to consider here because it will invariably provide the converter with very direct knowledge of the likely consequences of such interference. For instance, where a converter takes possession and disposes of household goods or family heirlooms on the basis of a reasonable but erroneous belief as to title, the converter may legitimately contend that he acted without knowledge as to rightful ownership. However, the converter cannot claim he was unaware of the potential emotional harm his interference would cause. In contrast, the negligent destroyer of personal property—the defendant who fails to properly secure the bulldozer or the warehouseman who leaves paint rags next to a gas burner—has considerably less direct knowledge of the emotional consequences of his conduct. * * * Thus, in the context of a conversion claim, there is far less likelihood that allowing recovery for emotional distress damages will create liability which is out of proportion to the nature of the defendant's act. It follows that when a defendant is guilty of conversion, there is considerably less justification for imposing the limits on emotional distress damages which exist in negligence cases, such as Cooper.

In sum then, we conclude that notwithstanding further developments in the law of negligence, damages for emotional distress growing out of a defendant's conversion of personal property are recoverable.

B. Trial Court's Instruction

The only difficulty we have in affirming the jury's award of emotional distress damages is that no instruction was given which permitted the jury to award emotional distress damages as an element of Gonzales's conversion claim. In instructing the jury, the trial court permitted an award of emotional distress damages only as an element of Gonzales's negligence claim. As our previous discussion suggests, this was an error. * * *

However, in the particular context of this case, the trial court's error in including emotional distress damages as an element of the negligence case and failing to allow them on the conversion claim was not prejudicial. * * * Thus the emotional distress portion of the judgment cannot be disturbed.

C.   SPECIFIC RELIEF

1.   Legal Replevin

FUENTES v. SHEVIN

Supreme Court of the United States, 1972.
407 U.S. 67, 92 S.Ct. 1983, 32 L.Ed.2d 556.

MR. JUSTICE STEWART delivered the opinion of the Court.

We here review the decisions of two three-judge federal District Courts that upheld the constitutionality of Florida and Pennsylvania laws authorizing the summary seizure of goods or chattels in a person's possession under a writ of replevin. Both statutes provide for the issuance of writs ordering state agents to seize a person's possessions, simply upon the ex parte application of any other person who claims a right to them and posts a security bond. Neither statute provides for notice to be given to the possessor of the property, and neither statute gives the possessor an opportunity to challenge the seizure at any kind of prior hearing. The question is whether these statutory procedures violate the Fourteenth Amendment's guarantee that no State shall deprive any person of property without due process of law.

* * *

Under the Florida statute challenged here, "[a]ny person whose goods or chattels are wrongfully detained by any other person ... may have a writ of replevin to recover them...." Fla.Stat.Ann. § 78.01 (Supp.1972–1973). There is no requirement that the applicant make a convincing showing before the seizure that the goods are, in fact, "wrongfully detained." Rather, Florida law automatically relies on the bare assertion of the party seeking the writ that he is entitled to one and allows a court clerk to issue the writ summarily. It requires only that the applicant file a complaint, initiating a court action for repossession and reciting in conclusory fashion that he is "lawfully entitled to the possession" of the property, and that he file a security bond "in at least double the value of the property to be replevied conditioned that plaintiff will prosecute his action to effect and without delay and that if defendant recovers judgment against him in the action, he will return the property, if return thereof is adjudged, and will pay defendant all sums of money recovered against plaintiff by defendant in the action." Fla.Stat.Ann. § 78.07 (Supp.1972–1973).

On the sole basis of the complaint and bond, a writ is issued "command[ing] the officer to whom it may be directed to replevy the goods and chattels in possession of defendant ... and to summon the defendant to answer the complaint." Fla.Stat.Ann. § 78.08 (Supp.1972–1973). If the goods are "in any dwelling house or other building or enclosure," the officer is required to demand their delivery; but if they are not delivered, "he shall cause such house, building or enclosure to be broken open and shall make replevin according to the writ...." Fla.Stat. Ann. § 78.10 (Supp.1972–1973).

Thus, at the same moment that the defendant receives the complaint seeking repossession of property through court action, the property is seized from him. He is provided no prior notice and allowed no opportunity whatever to challenge the issuance of the writ. After the property has been seized, he will eventually have an opportunity for a hearing, as the defendant in the trial of the court action for repossession, which the plaintiff is required to pursue. And he is also not wholly without recourse in the meantime. For under the Florida statute, the officer who seizes the property must keep it for three days, and during that period the defendant may reclaim possession of the property by posting his own security bond in double its value. But if he does not post such a bond, the property is transferred to the party who sought the writ, pending a final judgment in the underlying action for repossession. Fla.Stat.Ann. § 78.13 (Supp.1972–1973).

* * *

Although these prejudgment replevin statutes are descended from the common-law replevin action of six centuries ago, they bear very little resemblance to it. Replevin at common law was an action for the return of specific goods wrongfully taken or "distrained." Typically, it was used after a landlord (the "distrainor") had seized possessions from a tenant (the "distrainee") to satisfy a debt allegedly owed. If the tenant then instituted a replevin action and posted security, the landlord could be ordered to return the property at once, pending a final judgment in the underlying action. However, this prejudgment replevin of goods at common law did not follow from an entirely ex parte process of pleading by the distrainee. For "[t]he distrainor could always stop the action of replevin by claiming to be the owner of the goods; and as this claim was often made merely to delay the proceedings, the writ de proprietate probanda was devised early in the fourteenth century, which enabled the sheriff to determine summarily the question of ownership. If the question of ownership was determined against the distrainor the goods were delivered back to the distrainee (pending final judgment)." 3 W. Holdsworth, History of English Law 284 (1927).

Prejudgment replevin statutes like those of Florida * * * are derived from this ancient possessory action in that they authorize the seizure of property before a final judgment. But the similarity ends there. As in the present cases, such statutes are most commonly used by creditors to seize goods allegedly wrongfully detained—not wrongfully taken—by debtors. At common law, if a creditor wished to invoke state power to recover goods wrongfully detained, he had to proceed through the action of debt or detinue. These actions, however, did not provide for a return of property before final judgment. And, more importantly, on the occasions when the common law did allow prejudgment seizure by state power, it provided some kind of notice and opportunity to be heard to the party then in possession of the property, and a state official made at least a summary determination of the relative rights of the disputing parties before stepping into the dispute and taking goods from one of them.

For more than a century the central meaning of procedural due process has been clear: "Parties whose rights are to be affected are entitled to be heard; and in order that they may enjoy that right they must first be notified." Baldwin v. Hale, 1 Wall. 223, 233, 17 L.Ed. 531. * * * The issue is whether procedural due process in the context of these cases requires an opportunity for a hearing before the State authorizes its agents to seize property in the possession of a person upon the application of another.

* * *

The requirement of notice and an opportunity to be heard raises no impenetrable barrier to the taking of a person's possessions. But the fair process of decision making that it guarantees works, by itself, to protect against arbitrary deprivation of property. For when a person has an opportunity to speak up in his own defense, and when the State must listen to what he has to say, substantively unfair and simply mistaken deprivations of property interests can be prevented. * * *

If the right to notice and a hearing is to serve its full purpose, then, it is clear that it must be granted at a time when the deprivation can still be prevented. At a later hearing, an individual's possessions can be returned to him if they were unfairly or mistakenly taken in the first place. Damages may even be awarded to him for the wrongful deprivation. But no later hearing and no damage award can undo the fact that the arbitrary taking that was subject to the right of procedural due process has already occurred. "This Court has not ... embraced the general proposition that a wrong may be done if it can be undone." Stanley v. Illinois, 405 U.S. 645, 647, 92 S.Ct. 1208, 1210, 31 L.Ed.2d 551.

* * *

There are "extraordinary situations" that justify postponing notice and opportunity for a hearing. Boddie v. Connecticut, 401 U.S., at 379, 91 S.Ct., at 786. These situations, however, must be truly unusual. * * * There may be cases in which a creditor could make a showing of immediate danger that a debtor will destroy or conceal disputed goods. But the statutes before us are not "narrowly drawn to meet any such unusual condition." Sniadach v. Family Finance Corp., *supra*, 395 U.S. at 339, 89 S.Ct. at 1821. And no such unusual situation is presented by the facts of these cases.

* * *

We hold that the Florida and Pennsylvania prejudgment replevin provisions work a deprivation of property without due process of law insofar as they deny the right to a prior opportunity to be heard before chattels are taken from their possessor. Our holding, however, is a narrow one. We do not question the power of a State to seize goods before a final judgment in order to protect the security interests of creditors so long as those creditors have tested their claim to the goods through the process of a fair prior hearing. The nature and form of such prior hearings, moreover, are legitimately open to many potential variations and are a subject, at this point, for legislation—not adjudication. * * *

For the foregoing reasons, the judgments of the District Courts are vacated and these cases are remanded for further proceedings consistent with this opinion.

NOTES

1. In Mitchell v. W.T. Grant Co., 416 U.S. 600, 94 S.Ct. 1895, 40 L.Ed.2d 406 (1974), the United States Supreme Court retreated from its holding in *Fuentes* and upheld the constitutionality of Louisiana's sequestration statute (the equivalent of a replevin statute), even though the statute did not provide for a preseizure notice and hearing. Rather, Louisiana's statute provided for a prompt post-seizure hearing akin to the type of hearing that a court of equity conducts when a defendant moves to dissolve an ex parte temporary restraining order. The Court in *Mitchell* identified the following procedural safeguards as being necessary to satisfy minimal constitutional due process requirements in the context of replevin:

   a. The complaint must contain nonconclusory allegations of ownership or possessory rights;

   b. The request for replevin must be presented to a judge who decides whether to authorize the seizure;

   c. The plaintiff must post a bond that will protect the defendant against damages caused by an improper seizure;

   d. The defendant must be entitled immediately to seek dissolution of the order authorizing the seizure during an adversary hearing in which the plaintiff bears the burden of proving the existence of the facts that entitle the plaintiff to claim an interest in the property; and

   e. The defendant must have an opportunity to counterbond in order to regain possession of the property pending a full trial on the merits.

2. When a plaintiff is granted replevin of personal property, the plaintiff is allowed to recover compensatory damages for any diminution in the fair market value of the property plus loss of use damages. Foresight Enterprises, Inc. v. Leisure Time Properties, Inc., 466 So.2d 283 (Fla.Dist.Ct.App.1985).

TEXTRON FINANCIAL CORP. v. UNIQUE MARINE, INC.

United States District Court, Southern District of Florida, 2008.
2008 WL 4716965.

ANDREA M. SIMONTON, UNITED STATES MAGISTRATE JUDGE.

Presently pending before the Court are Plaintiff's Motions filed on October 20, 2008, seeking a Temporary Restraining Order (DE #3), Emergency Break Orders (DE #4) and Emergency Pre-Judgment Writs of Replevin (DE #5). These motions requested *ex parte* relief and are referred to the undersigned Magistrate Judge (DE #7). A hearing was held on October 22, 2008 * * *.

I. BACKGROUND

According to the Verified Complaint and the exhibits attached thereto, Plaintiff, Textron Financial Corporation, is a company that has a long-standing contractual agreement with Defendant, Unique Marine, Inc., wherein Textron provides financing for boats and boating equipment that are sold by Unique Marine (DE #1). Todd Ebelin is the President of Unique Marine and signed a personal guaranty for Unique Marine's debts to Textron (DE #1, Exs. A, B).

Stacey Huerth is the corporate representative for Textron who verified the Complaint and testified at the October 22, 2008 hearing. She explained that Unique Marine orders new inventory by placing an order with a manufacturer. The manufacturer, after receiving financing approval from Textron, delivers the new inventory to Unique Marine and sends the invoice to Textron. As Ms. Huerth testified at the hearing, Unique Marine must pay down the invoice price * * * by paying Textron a monthly fee * * *. Once Unique Marine sells an item of inventory financed by Textron, Unique Marine is obligated, under the terms of the Credit Agreement, to pay the remaining unpaid balance of the invoice price. The Credit Agreement expressly requires Unique Marine to hold the proceeds of the sale in trust for Textron and immediately remit to Textron the amount necessary to cover the invoice price of that item (DE #1, Ex. A at P 8).

* * * On a recent inspection, Textron discovered that Unique Marine sold six items of inventory financed by Textron, which Unique Marine had neither reported nor paid for as required by the parties' Credit Agreement. * * * The total value of these Sold And Unpaid ("SAU") items of inventory is $270,731.50.

* * *

Textron alleges that Unique Marine breached the parties' Credit Agreement * * *. [I]n the event of Unique Marine's default, Textron is entitled to accelerate the payment of all sums due to it and, therefore, Textron demanded $3,540,163.65, representing the unpaid principal balance due ($3,513,460.42) plus interest and fees as of September 30, 2008 ($26,703.23) (DE #1 at 3–4). Because Unique Marine has failed to satisfy its debt, Textron asserts that it is entitled to collect the Collateral set forth in the Credit Agreement * * *.

* * *

II. THE INSTANT MOTIONS

According to Textron, it has an immediate possessory right to the Inventory and Collateral based on Unique Marine's default under the Credit Agreement and it fears that Unique Marine will wrongfully dissipate its assets over the course of these proceedings. Thus, it filed the three presently pending motions on an *ex parte* basis. First, it seeks Emergency Pre–Judgement Writs of Replevin (DE #5) and the issuance of Emergency Break Orders (DE #4) pursuant to Florida Law, which will permit it to recover the Inventory and Collateral from Unique Marine, and physically enter Unique Marine's property if it is necessary to do so in order to execute the writs. Textron also seeks an Emergency Temporary Restraining Order (DE #3) because it claims that there is a risk that Unique Marine will continue to wrongfully sell and transfer the Inventory and Collateral that belongs to Textron during the time that it takes to effectuate the physical seizure of the property.

III. LEGAL FRAMEWORK FOR ANALYSIS

A. Prejudgment Writs of Replevin and Break Orders

Federal Rule of Civil Procedure 64 governs the seizure of property in connection with a civil action. It provides:

> At the commencement of and throughout an action, every remedy is available that, under the law of the state where the court is located, provides for seizing a person or property to secure satisfaction of the potential judgment. But a federal statute governs to the extent it applies.

Fed. R. Civ. P. 64(a). Replevin is a remedy that is expressly available under this Rule. Fed. R. Civ. P. 64(b).

Replevin is a statutory remedy under Florida law that permits "[a]ny person whose personal property is wrongfully detained by any other person [to] recover said personal property and any damages sustained by reason of the wrongful taking or detention...." Fla. Stat. § 78.01. In order to obtain the

> issuance of a writ of replevin prior to final judgment, the plaintiff shall first file with the clerk of the court a complaint reciting and showing the following information:

(1) A description of the claimed property that is sufficient to make possible its identification. * * *

(2) A statement that the plaintiff is the owner of the claimed property or is entitled to possession of it, describing the source of such title or right. * * *

(3) A statement that the property is wrongfully detained by the defendant, the means by which the defendant came into possession thereof, and the cause of such detention according to the best knowledge, information, and belief of the plaintiff.

* * *

Fla. Stat. § 78.055. * * *

Although due process requires providing the defendant advance notice and an opportunity to be heard prior to the issuance of an ordinary writ of replevin, Florida law allows a plaintiff to secure an *ex parte* prejudgment writ of replevin if

(1) ... the grounds relied upon for the issuance of the writ clearly appear from specific facts show by the verified petition ... [and]

(2) ... if the court finds   that the defendant is engaging in, or is about to engage in, conduct that may place the claimed property in danger of destruction, concealment, waste, removal from the state, removal from the jurisdiction of the court, or transfer to an innocent purchaser during the pendency of the action or that the defendant has failed to make payment as agreed.

Fla. Stat. § 78.068. * * *

Moreover, a plaintiff seeking to obtain a prejudgment writ of replevin "must post bond in the amount of twice the value of the goods subject to the writ or twice the balance remaining due and owing, whichever is lesser as determined by the court, as security for the payment of damages the defendant may sustain when the writ is obtained wrongfully." Fla. Stat. § 78.068(3).

Finally, "the plaintiff may petition the court for a 'break order' directing the sheriff to enter physically any dwelling house or other building or enclosure. Upon a showing of probable cause by the plaintiff, the court shall enter such 'break order.'" Fla. Stat. § 78.10.

"The law in Florida is clear that a writ of replevin may only issue against specific property as to which a claimant has a possessory right." * * * It is not designed "for the purpose of recovering the amount which might be found to be due from the defendant to the plaintiff on account, but to recover the property in dispute.'" * * * Nor can a writ of replevin reach intangible property in the form of checking accounts. * * *

B.   Temporary Restraining Order

Pursuant to the Federal Rules,

[t]he court may issue a temporary restraining order without written or oral notice to the adverse party or its attorney only if:

> (A) specific facts in an affidavit or a verified complaint clearly show that immediate and irreparable injury, loss, or damage will result to the movant before the adverse party can be heard in opposition; and
>
> (B) the movant's attorney certifies in writing any efforts made to give notice and the reasons why it should not be required.

Fed. R. Civ. P. 65(b).

As recognized by the Eleventh Circuit Court of Appeals in *Schiavo v. Schiavo,* 403 F.3d 1223, 1225–26 (11th Cir. 2005), the same four factors apply to the determination of whether to grant a temporary restraining order or preliminary injunction: "(1) a substantial likelihood of success on the merits; (2) that irreparable injury will be suffered if the relief is not granted; (3) that the threatened injury outweighs the harm the relief would inflict on the non-movant; and (4) that entry of the relief would serve the public interest." The primary difference between the entry of a temporary restraining order and a preliminary injunction is that a temporary restraining order may be entered before the defendant has an adequate opportunity to respond, even if notice has been provided.

A District Court can order an asset freeze as part of preliminary injunctive relief only with respect to assets in which an equitable interest is claimed and established. *Grupo Mexicano de Desarrollo, S.A. v. Alliance Bond Fund, Inc.,* 527 U.S. 308, 318–33, 119 S. Ct. 1961, 144 L. Ed. 2d 319 (1999) * * *.

IV.   ANALYSIS

* * *

A.   Prejudgment Writs of Replevin and Break Orders

Textron requests writs of replevin authorizing federal and state agents to enter Unique Marine's business * * * for the purpose of securing the Collateral listed in Exhibit C to the Verified Complaint and placing those items within Textron's possession pending the disposition of this case or further Order of this Court. All of the elements necessary in order to issue Prejudgment Writs of Replevin and Break Orders are present in this case.

The undersigned notes that Textron stated that it was unable to identify with specificity items in Unique Marine's possession which it obtained by trading items purchased with proceeds provided by Textron; and, therefore, Textron requested the issuance of a writ that would permit it to replevy such items without the need for a further Order of this Court. Based on the fact that the a temporary restraining order will prevent the disposition or transfer of any such items, the undersigned recommends that writs of replevin be issued only as to those items of inventory specifically listed in Exhibit C to Plaintiff's Verified Complaint, and that Plaintiff be permitted file a motion requesting writs of replevin as to any additional items that it identifies during the course of carrying out the seizures of Collateral. This determination was reinforced at the hearing by the testimony that Unique Marine also receives financing from another source, and therefore it is likely that other vessels will be present which are not collateral subject to replevin and which Plaintiff acknowledged that it does not seek to possess.

Basic Statutory Requirements—Fla. Stat. § 78.055

There is a sufficient description of the Collateral to be replevied set forth in the Monthly Billing Summaries identified as Exhibit C to Textron's Complaint. Fla. Stat. § 78.055(1). The Complaint and the attached Credit Agreement demonstrate that Textron is entitled to a security interest in the Collateral upon Unique Marine's default under the terms of the Agreement. Fla. Stat. §§ 78.055(2)-(3). * * * Simply stated, upon Unique Marine's breach of the Credit Agreement—by failing to timely make monthly curtailment payments and by selling inventory financed by Textron without holding the proceeds in trust and immediately remitting payments to Textron—allowed Textron to immediately demand accelerated payment of its unpaid debts and established Textron's superior right to possess the Collateral held by Unique Marine (DE #1, Ex. A at ¶ 11) * * *.

2. *Requirements for Issuing an Ex Parte Writ—Fla. Stat. § 78.068*

It is appropriate to issue a prejudgment writ of replevin on a *ex parte* basis, without providing Unique Marine notice or an opportunity to be heard.

First, the facts supporting replevin clearly appear in the record, Fla. Stat. § 78.068(1). * * *

Second, * * * there is a well-founded risk that Unique Marine will conceal, remove or transfer the Collateral, Fla. Stat. § 78.068(2); and, that Unique Marine has "failed to make payment as agreed." *Id.*

At the outset, the undersigned finds that the property at issue consists of boating and marine equipment that is transitory by nature, which presents a *prima facie* inference that it is capable of being removed from this jurisdiction. * * *

Unique Marine has also promised payments to Textron that it failed to provide. * * *

3. *Bond—Fla. Stat. § 78.068*

In order to obtain a prejudgment writ of replevin, Textron "must post bond in the amount of twice the value of the goods subject to the writ or twice the balance remaining due and owing, whichever is lesser as determined by the court". Fla. Stat. § 78.068(3).

The undersigned finds that the value of the goods subject to the writ is $3,134,345.92 (DE #1 at P 42), and that the balance remaining due and owing is $3,540,163.65 (DE #4 at P 15). Although the amount of bond based on these findings is $6,268,691.84, Textron has agreed to post a $6,300,000 bond. * * *

4. Break Orders—Fla. Stat. § 78.10

Florida law expressly requires the Court, upon a showing of probable cause, to enter a break order, "directing the sheriff to enter physically any dwelling house or other building or enclosure" for the purpose of executing a writ of replevin. There is probable cause to believe that, during the time that the writs are executed, Unique Marine's business premises will be inaccessible due to locks or other impediments to entry and that it will be necessary for the United States Marshals Service and/or the Florida Sheriff to hire a locksmith to remove any such impediments. Textron has agreed to bear the costs associated with carrying out any break order; and, Textron has agreed that the property should be re-secured immediately after the writs are executed by replacing any locks or barriers that were removed to gain entry. The facts alleged in the Verified Complaint, combined with the testimony of Ms. Huerth at the hearing, including the testimony regarding Textron's monthly inspections of inventory, establish probable cause to believe that the inventory is located at these premises.

B. Temporary Restraining Order

* * * Textron seeks a temporary restraining order which, in essence, enjoins Defendant from disposing of any inventory which was financed by Plaintiff ("the collateral") * * *.

* * *

1. Likelihood of Success

The undersigned finds that Textron is substantially likely to succeed on the merits of its claims for a preliminary injunction; for breach of contract; to enforce Todd Ebelin's personal guarantee; and for replevin.

The facts of this case are straightforward. Textron financed inventory for Unique Marine to sell from its dealership; in exchange, Unique Marine was obligated to pay monthly curtailments; and, if any item financed by Textron was sold, Unique Marine was obligated to hold the proceeds in trust and immediately remit a payment to Textron to cover the unpaid invoice price of that item. Based on Textron's allegations, Unique Marine failed to do this, which constituted a breach of the Credit Agreement and vested Textron's security interest in the Collateral as defined in the Credit Agreement. * * * Though the undersigned recognizes that Unique Marine has not had the opportunity to respond to these allegations, there are no viable defenses available to Unique Marine that are apparent in the record as it currently stands. Therefore, there is a substantial likelihood that Textron will obtain a preliminary injunction; prevail on its breach of contract claim; * * * and secure writs of replevin over the Collateral.

2. Irreparable and Immediate Injury

In the absence of a temporary restraining order, the undersigned finds that Textron will suffer irreparable and immediate injury.

* * * In light of the fact that Unique Marine allegedly ignored the terms of the Credit Agreement by surreptitiously selling items that Textron had financed without reimbursing Textron, it follows that Unique Marine will be inclined to disregard Textron's security interest in other items of collateral and there is no reason to believe that Unique Marine will refrain from transferring, selling or concealing those items if it is not subject to the terms of a temporary restraining order. * * * There is a significant risk that Unique Marine will continue to liquidate the assets that constitute the Collateral owed to Textron and, for all practical purposes, frustrate Textron's rights to collect the Collateral under the terms of the Credit Agreement. * * *

3. Balancing the Harm

The undersigned finds that the potential hardship that a temporary restraining order will impose on Unique Marine outweighs the risk to Textron if a temporary restraining order is not granted. Although the amount of money that Unique Marine owes to Textron is substantial, Textron acknowledged that its solvency was not dependent on collecting this debt. Unique Marine appears to be a smaller corporation, and the harm associated with granting the relief sought in the temporary restraining order poses a greater risk of affecting its business. Nevertheless, the undersigned concludes that the likelihood that Textron will succeed on the merits of its claims and the likelihood that Unique Marine will frustrate its efforts to enforce the default provisions of the Credit Agreement in the absence of a temporary restraining order are so significant that they overcome the increased risk of potential hardship to Unique Marine if a temporary restraining order is improvidently granted.

4. Public Interest

The undersigned finds that the public interest in the outcome of this matter is limited because it involves a private commercial contract. To the extent that the public interest must be weighed at all, this factor tips in Textron's favor because the public is well served when courts enforce the terms of individuals' binding agreements. * * * In addition, innocent purchasers will be protected from buying boats which Unique Marine does not have the right to sell.

5. Certification of Reasons to Withhold Notice

There is good cause for issuing a temporary restraining order without providing notice to Unique Marine based on Textron's assertions that

Unique Marine has already breached the parties' Credit Agreement by selling two boats * * * . This conduct suggests that Unique Marine will similarly attempt to prevent Textron from collecting a judgment by secreting away the Collateral if it is provided advanced notice of the temporary restraining order.

6. Bond

In light of the fact that Textron is required to post a substantial bond ($6,300,000) in connection with its writs of replevin, the undersigned finds that a nominal bond in the amount of $100,000 constitutes sufficient security for the purposes of entering a temporary restraining order.

V. CONCLUSION

For the reasons stated above, which are based upon a review of the record as a whole, the undersigned

RECOMMENDS the immediate entry of the Order to Issue Pre–Judgment Writs of Replevin [as] well as the Break Orders * * *. The undersigned further

RECOMMENDS the immediate entry of the Temporary Restraining Order * * *.

* * *

2. Equitable Replevin

Prof. Van Hecke, the author of the first edition of this casebook, coined the phrase "equitable replevin" to describe the equitable remedy that parallels the legal remedy of replevin. The essence of the equitable replevin remedy is "compulsion upon the defendant to deliver the chattel in specie when it has been demonstrated that the plaintiff has a special need therefor." M.T. Van Hecke, *Equitable Replevin*, 33 N.C. L. Rev. 57, 79 (1954). The primary difference between legal and equitable replevin is that equitable replevin operates in personam and is enforceable through the court's use of its contempt power, whereas the writ of legal replevin is targeted at the disputed property and is executed by the sheriff, who removes the property from the defendant's possession and delivers it to the plaintiff unless the defendant files a counterbond. *Id*. Legal replevin might appear to be an "adequate legal remedy" that would preclude access to equitable replevin, but there are two reasons that might make it an inferior remedy. First, the defendant can regain possession of the property pending a trial on the merits by counterbonding. Second, legal replevin orders are not enforceable by contempt, and therefore a defendant may be free to secrete, alienate, damage or destroy the chattel and ultimately be answerable only in damages. In some states, the distinction between the two types of replevin has become blurred because the legislature has blended them together, creating a modern statutory replevin procedure. Dan B. Dobbs, Law of Remedies § 5.17(3) (2d ed. 1993).

MODERN DUST BAG CO. v. COMMERCIAL TRUST CO.

Court of Chancery of Delaware, 1952.
33 Del.Ch. 208, 91 A.2d 469.

BRAMHALL, VICE CHANCELLOR.

Upon petition to this court by plaintiff a rule was issued upon the defendant to show cause why this court should not issue an order upon defendant to deliver to plaintiff certain warehouse receipts held by defendant upon payment into court by the plaintiff of such sum as the court might fix as security for the payment of defendant's claim against the plaintiff, in the event that the defendant should prevail in this action.

The warehouse receipts represent certain paper belonging to plaintiff, of a special kind and quality required by the plaintiff in the conduct of its business that is not available for purchase by reason of the fact that the concern from whom plaintiff originally purchased the paper is now in bankruptcy and the particular kind and quality of paper represented by the warehouse receipts cannot be purchased elsewhere. The plaintiff has been using this particular type of paper in the manufacture of certain articles, in which a continuity of product is required. Since it will be necessary for plaintiff shortly to begin to use another kind of paper in the manufacture of its products, plaintiff cannot the use the paper represented by the warehouse receipts, in which event it will be of no value to plaintiff and have little or no market value.

* * *

Plaintiff does not have an adequate remedy at law. An action for the value of the paper would not give plaintiff complete relief since plaintiff is not in a position to purchase the paper in question on the market or elsewhere. Plaintiff's damage, therefore, cannot be definitely determined. Under the practice in this state in an action in replevin defendant would be entitled to retain possession of the paper by posting the required bond. I know of no adequate remedy at law under which the plaintiff might proceed. Plaintiff is therefore entitled to equitable relief.

* * *

In the case of Price v. Gordon, 129 Fla. 715, 177 So. 276, 279, complainants after leasing a house and taking possession thereof found it [infested with vermin] unfit for habitation and notified defendant that they would not be bound by the terms of the lease. Upon subsequently returning to the house for their personal belongings they were refused permission to remove them. In an action for a mandatory preliminary injunction to compel defendants to return the personal property to complainants, the Chancellor directed the delivery of the personal belongings to the defendant forthwith upon posting of a bond by complainants in a sufficient amount to protect defendants. In affirming upon appeal the supreme court of Florida said:

Under the facts alleged in the bill of complaint and shown by affidavits in support thereof, the showing was adequate that the complainants could not have full, complete and adequate relief in a court of law and that a more ample and appropriate remedy would be afforded by resort to equity. A sick person's medicines and a person's entire supply of wearing apparel, except that which they may have on their person at the time the other is taken from their possession, are not things that may be taken from one without authority of law and he, or she, be required to await the slow process of replevin or other law procedure, to regain possession of same. The necessity for the use of such articles is immediate and continuing. It is not a sufficient answer that such persons so deprived of the possession of such articles may go into the marts of trade and buy more and resupply themselves with the same class of articles which have been wrongfully taken from their possession. Although by doing so and awaiting process of a court of law, such person might have ultimate and complete remedy, that remedy would not be full and adequate as would be the remedy which he may have by proceeding in equity, as was done in this case.

Defendant does not of course claim title to the paper. It is merely trying to impress thereon its lien for an unpaid balance which may or may not hereafter be determined to be due it by plaintiff. Defendant will suffer no injury by the substitution of cash for the security of the warehouse receipts. In fact, it would seem that defendant's position relative to the security offered for the payment of defendant's claim would be definitely improved. In view of the fact that the paper will shortly be of no value at all to the plaintiff, to permit the defendant to retain the warehouse receipts as security for the disputed claim of defendant, pending the determination of this dispute, would cause the plaintiff to sustain irreparable injury and would be of little or no benefit to defendant. I conclude that equity has jurisdiction and that the prayer of the petition should be granted.

3. Merger of Law and Equity

VINEBERG v. BISSONNETTE

United States District Court, District of Rhode Island, 2007.
529 F. Supp. 2d 300, *aff'd* 548 F.3d 50.

MARY M. LISI, CHIEF JUDGE.

This is an action to recover personal property, for declaratory and injunctive relief, and for money damages. Plaintiffs, Robert S. Vineberg, Michael D. Vineberg, and Sydney Feldhammer, as Trustees of the Dr. and Mrs. Stern Foundation ("Plaintiffs" or "Stern Estate"), have moved for summary judgment on the replevin and conversion claims against Defendant Maria–Louise Bissonnette ("Defendant").

* * *

II. BACKGROUND

The majority of the salient facts are undisputed. In or about 1913, Dr. Max Stern's ("Dr. Stern") father, Julius Stern, opened an art gallery in Dusseldorf, Germany. Julius Stern died in 1934, leaving the art gallery and its inventory to Dr. Stern. Dr. Stern was of Jewish descent and, under the Nuremberg laws,[2] was subject to official persecution by the German government. In 1935, the Reich Chamber for the Fine Arts ("Reich Chamber"), an organization of the Nazi government, sent letters to Dr. Stern demanding that he liquidate his inventory and gallery. On or about September 13, 1937, Dr. Stern received a final order to sell his inventory immediately through a dealer approved by the Reich Chamber.[3] Dr. Stern consigned most of his inventory and private collection, constituting hundreds of works, to the Lempertz Auction House ("LAH"), in Cologne, Germany. On or about November 13, 1937, LAH auctioned the items consigned to it by Dr. Stern, including the property that is the subject of the dispute in this matter, a nineteenth century painting by Franz Xaver Winterhalter entitled "Madchen aus den Sabiner Bergen" ("Girl from the Sabiner Mountains") ("the Painting"). The items consigned to LAH by Dr. Stern were sold at well below market value.

Dr. Stern fled Germany for Paris in December 1937. Upon discovering that Dr. Stern left Germany, the German government issued an order freezing his assets. Dr. Stern never received the proceeds of the LAH sale. Dr. Stern eventually left Paris to join his sister in London prior to the outbreak of World War II. Dr. Stern later emigrated to Canada and became a preeminent art collector and dealer there. [Dr. Stern died in 1987 and bequeathed his interest in the Painting to the Stern Estate.]

LAH was heavily damaged in 1943 by wartime bombing and its Nazi-era records were destroyed. Post-war efforts to locate paintings from the LAH auction were hindered by the near-total destruction of LAH records. In spite of this, after the end of World War II, Dr. Stern made numerous attempts to locate his art collection. * * *

---

2. The Nuremberg laws "were aimed at the Jewish people" and "among other things, deprived Jews of their German citizenship ... [and] of the right to work as doctors, dentists, lawyers, and journalists; and deprived Jews of any right to own property." Arthur S. Gold and William R. Coulson, *The Nuremberg War Crimes Trials: 60 Years Later*, CBA [Chicago Bar Association] Record, Feb./March 2006 at 40.

3. Adolf Hitler's "Nazi regime engaged in a systematic effort to confiscate thousands of works of art throughout Europe." Orkin v. Taylor, 487 F.3d 734, 736 (9th Cir.), *cert. denied*, 552 U.S. 990, 128 S. Ct. 491, 169 L. Ed. 2d 340 (2007). At the end of World War II, it was estimated that 150,000 pieces of art had been looted in Western Europe and nearly 500,000 in Eastern Europe. Benjamin E. Pollock, *Out of the Night and Fog: Permitting Litigation to Prompt An International Resolution to Nazi–Looted Art Claims*, 43 Hous. L. Rev. 193 (2006). "Being associated with great works of art became another characteristic defining the Aryan conception of moral, intellectual and genetic superiority, and looted artworks were considered trophies." Kelly Diane Walton, *Leave No Stone Unturned: The Search for Art Stolen by the Nazis and the Legal Rules Governing Restitution of Stolen Art*, 9 Fordham Intell. Prop. Media and Ent. L.J. 549, 553 (1999). Many individuals of Jewish descent exchanged artwork for exit visas and in some rare circumstances individuals were released from concentration camps in exchange for artwork held by their families.

Dr. Karl Wilharm ("Wilharm") acquired the Painting through the LAH auction. Wilharm was Defendant's stepfather. Wilharm kept the Painting in his private collection except for one occasion, in 1954, when it was exhibited at a museum in Kassel, Germany. Defendant has had the Painting in her possession since 1959. Defendant inherited the Painting, from her mother's estate, in 1991. Defendant has resided in the United States since at least 1956 and in Rhode Island since at least 1991.

In April 2003, Estates Unlimited, Inc. received the Painting on consignment from Defendant. In April 2004, on behalf of the Stern Estate, the Art Loss Register ("ALR") agreed to list the lost inventory of Dr. Stern's gallery auctioned by LAH on its Holocaust related database. The Stern Estate also listed the Painting with Germany's Lost Art Internet Database. The Painting was to be auctioned by Estates Unlimited at a public auction scheduled for January 6, 2005. Just prior to the scheduled auction, however, the Stern Estate learned from ALR that the Painting was on consignment at Estates Unlimited. ALR contacted Estates Unlimited and informed Estates Unlimited of the Stern Estate's claimed ownership of the Painting. As a result, Estates Unlimited agreed to withdraw the Painting from the auction. Estates Unlimited then informed Defendant of the Stern Estate's claim of ownership.

In January 2005, the Stern Estate made a claim for restitution of the Painting with the Holocaust Claims Processing Office of the state of New York Banking Department ("HCPO"). In February 2005, HCPO sent a demand letter to Defendant through Estates Unlimited seeking restitution of the Painting. Defendant refused to return the Painting to the Stern Estate. From February 2005 through April 2006, HCPO and Defendant attempted to resolve the matter. On or about April 19, 2006, Defendant's former counsel notified the Stern Estate's counsel that the Painting had been sent to Germany "due to the institution of an action in German Courts to definitely determine title to the [P]ainting."[8] * * * After the Painting arrived in Germany, Defendant obtained an appraisal of the Painting in the range of 50,000 to 70,000 Euros (approximately $67,000 to $94,000). The instant action was instituted by the Stern Estate on May 8, 2006. The Stern Estate has moved for summary judgment against Defendant on its claims for replevin and conversion.

* * *

V. REPLEVIN

The Court acknowledges the highly unusual posture of this matter. Over 70 years ago, the Nazi party took art from Jewish citizens as part of a systematic plan to rob Jewish citizens of their property, their identity and, ultimately, their lives. See generally Kelly Diane Walton, 9 Fordham Intell. Prop. Media and Ent. L.J. 549. Only ten Holocaust-related suits

---

8. In the German action, Defendant informed the court that other "auction houses have also refused to accept the [P]ainting for auction in view of the recovery claims asserted. [Defendant] wishes to sell the [P]ainting by way of auction...." * * * On June 12, 2007, this Court issued an order restraining Defendant from moving the Painting without prior permission from this Court.

were filed in "American courts from 1945–1995, and less than a handful of cases concerning looted art have been brought since World War II." Benjamin E. Pollock, 43 Hous. L. Rev. at 208 * * *. Plaintiffs request that this Court return to the Stern Estate artwork taken from Dr. Stern pursuant to the infamous Nuremberg laws of Nazi Germany.

A.   Statute of Limitations

In her answer, Defendant raised the affirmative defense of statute of limitations. * * * The extent of Defendant's statute of limitations argument is contained in one sentence in her opposition memorandum: "[i]n defense, [Defendant] argues the equitable doctrine of laches and the legal defense of statute of limitations." * * * A defendant can waive the affirmative defense of statute of limitations. * * * Where a party fails to adequately develop an argument, the "district court is free to disregard" it. * * * This Court finds that * * * the statute of limitations defense is waived.

B.   The Merits of the Replevin Action

* * * Pursuant to Rule 64, replevin is available "under the circumstances and in the manner provided by the law of the state in which the district court is held, existing at the time the remedy is sought...." Fed. R. Civ. P. 64 * * *. The Rhode Island Superior Court Rules of Civil Procedure provide that a motion for a writ of replevin shall be granted upon a showing that there is (1) a probability of a judgment being rendered in favor of the plaintiff and (2) a "substantial need for transfer of possession of the" property pending adjudication of the claim. R.I. Super. R. Civ. P. 64(a).

Replevin is an "action for the repossession of personal property wrongfully taken or detained by the defendant...." * * * R. I. Gen. Laws § 34–21–1 provides, in part, that "[w]henever any goods or chattels of more than [$5,000] value shall be unlawfully taken or unlawfully detained from the owner or from the person entitled to possession thereof ... the owner or the other person may cause the same to be replevied by writ of replevin issuing from the superior court." R.I. Gen. Laws § 34–21–1. Replevin is "available to persons claiming possession of goods or chattels either wrongfully taken or wrongfully detained. Nothing more than the right of present possession, founded upon a general or special ownership of the goods or chattels, is necessary to enable a plaintiff to maintain the action." * * * "An action in replevin merely adjudicates who has the superior right to possession of goods." * * * The parties agree that to recover the Painting in a replevin action the Stern Estate must show that (1) it is the lawful owner of the Painting, (2) the Painting was taken from Dr. Stern, unlawfully, that is, without his permission, and (3) Defendant is in wrongful possession of the Painting.

1.   Ownership of the Painting

* * * The Court concludes that the Stern Estate is the lawful owner of the Painting.

2. *Unlawful Taking of the Painting*

In her opposition memorandum Defendant does not dispute the fact that the Nazi government forced Dr. Stern to liquidate inventory in his art gallery and controlled the manner of the forced sale. Dr. Stern fled the country before he realized any proceeds from the forced sale. * * * The Nazi party's actions in this instance are therefore properly classified as looting or stealing. * * *

3. *Wrongful Possession of the Painting*

The Court acknowledges that Defendant acquired the Painting through no wrongdoing on her part. Defendant's predecessor-in-interest, Wilharm, however, as a result of the acquisition of the Painting through the forced sale, did not acquire good title to the Painting. "Where pillage has taken place, the title of the original owner is not extinguished." * * * O'Keeffe v. Snyder, 83 N.J. 478, 416 A.2d 862, 867 (N.J. 1980) ("generally speaking, if the paintings were stolen, the thief acquired no title and could not transfer good title to others regardless of their good faith and ignorance of the theft") * * *. Legal title to the Painting remained in Dr. Stern and was transferred to the Stern Estate upon Dr. Stern's death. Because Defendant's predecessor-in-interest did not have title to the Painting, Defendant cannot lay valid claim to ownership of the Painting. * * *[15]

VI. LACHES

Defendant argues that the doctrine of laches prevents entry of summary judgment in this matter.[16] * * * A court applying the defense of laches applies a two part test: (1) there must be negligence on the part of the plaintiff that leads to a delay in the prosecution of the case, and (2) the delay must prejudice the defendant. * * * The prejudice may come from "loss of evidence, change of title, intervention of equities and other causes * * *."

Defendant argues that Dr. Stern was not diligent in pursuing the Painting. * * *

* * *

---

15. The Court is aware that replevin is a "provisional remedy that applies prior to trial on the merits. Stated differently, the replevin statute applies only when the plaintiff seeks pretrial seizure of personal property pending a trial to determine ownership." * * * However, because the Court has concluded that, as a matter of law, the Stern Estate is the owner of the Painting, a trial on the merits to determine ownership is not necessary.

16. "The defense of laches is peculiar to courts of equity and does not apply to actions at law." * * * Replevin is an action at law. Battalion Westerly Rifles v. Swan, 22 R.I. 333, 47 A. 1090, 1090 (1901) * * *. The Rhode Island Supreme Court, however, has acknowledged that although "the concept of laches originated in the courts of chancery, it is today often employed in situations in which the relief sought is not readily classifiable as equitable in nature." * * * Although the Court notes that a question exists whether the doctrine of laches applies to this matter, for the purposes of this decision, the Court assumes without deciding that the doctrine of laches applies to a replevin action.

* * * [T]he Court concludes that Dr. Stern and the Stern Estate exercised reasonably due diligence in searching for the Painting.

Defendant's claim of laches also fails because she cannot show prejudice. * * * "The only prejudice alleged by [Defendant] is [her] inability to sell [the property] due to the pending lawsuit. This allegation simply does not rise to the level of material prejudice [in order to invoke the defense of laches]." * * * This Court concludes that Defendant's laches argument, even if applicable, is unavailing.

* * *

For the foregoing reasons, the Stern Estate's motion for summary judgment on the replevin claim is granted. This Court therefore issues a writ of replevin. Defendant is ordered forthwith to turn over the Painting to the Stern Estate.[17]

NOTE

The court refers to this replevin action as one in law and is therefore uncertain that laches should apply. As seen in *Modern Dust Bag Co.*, replevin can also be equitable, with all of the requirements found in equitable actions. *See supra* Chapter 2. Could *Vineberg* be in equity? Does it matter whether the painting is still in Germany?

NUTRASWEET CO. v. VIT–MAR ENTERPRISES, INC.

United States Court of Appeals, Third Circuit, 1999.
176 F.3d 151.

Before SLOVITER, GARTH, and MAGILL, CIRCUIT JUDGES.

MAGILL, SENIOR CIRCUIT JUDGE.

The NutraSweet Company (NutraSweet) obtained a preliminary injunction and writ of replevin granting NutraSweet possession of goods that were allegedly acquired by fraud. Tekstilschik (Tek), an intervener and the purported owner of the goods, challenges both the preliminary injunction and writ of replevin. * * *

I.

* * *

NutraSweet produces a sugar substitute called "Equal Sweetener with NutraSweet" (Equal). In 1995, Vit–Mar Enterprises (Vitmar) and The Shiba Group (Shiba) proposed to distribute Equal to the Ukraine and Russia. NutraSweet agreed and sold several containers of Equal to Vitmar and Shiba for approximately $1.5 million.

NutraSweet shipped the Equal with bills of lading that specifically restricted distribution to Russia and the Ukraine. Despite NutraSweet's

---

17. As noted, the Stern Estate's complaint also includes a claim, in the alternative, for conversion. Because the Court has granted summary judgment on the replevin claim, it need not reach the Stern Estate's conversion claim.

attempts to restrict distribution of the Equal to Russia and the Ukraine, several containers were allegedly imported back into the United States. In May 1996 NutraSweet learned that U.S. Customs was prepared to release a shipment of the Equal into the U.S. market. NutraSweet filed a complaint and an Order to Show Cause in federal district court, seeking a writ of replevin and temporary restraining order (TRO). NutraSweet argued that the goods were obtained by fraud and that it was likely to succeed in recovering title to the goods. The District Court granted NutraSweet's request for a TRO and writ of replevin. After NutraSweet posted a $329,000 bond, the U.S. Marshals seized the Equal.

When Tek learned that the goods had been seized, it intervened in this case to challenge the TRO. Initially the District Court refused to lift the TRO. After considering Tek's appeal, we instructed the District Court to vacate the TRO as to Tek because it had the effect of a preliminary injunction but had been entered without development of a preliminary injunction record and findings of fact. * * * However, we left the door open for the District Court to enter a preliminary injunction after it developed a proper record and made the requisite findings of fact.

On remand, the District Court vacated the TRO, but entertained argument concerning the propriety of a preliminary injunction. After a hearing, the District Court entered a preliminary injunction, prohibiting Tek, its agents, and those acting in concert with Tek from "taking possession, control, or custody and/or marketing, selling, or otherwise distributing the shipments of Equal." In addition to opposing the preliminary injunction, Tek sought to vacate the writ of replevin, but the District Court denied its motion. The District Court later modified the writ of replevin to allow NutraSweet to take possession of the Equal, and NutraSweet increased its bond to $658,000. [The trial court did not permit Tek to file a counterbond.]

II.

Tek first argues that the District Court erred in granting the preliminary injunction. We agree.

We have appellate jurisdiction to review a district court's interlocutory order granting a preliminary injunction under 28 U.S.C. § 1292(a)(1). * * *

A preliminary injunction is an extraordinary remedy that should be granted only if "(1) the plaintiff is likely to succeed on the merits; (2) denial will result in irreparable harm to the plaintiff; (3) granting the injunction will not result in irreparable harm to the defendant; and (4) granting the injunction is in the public interest." * * * A plaintiff's failure to establish any element in its favor renders a preliminary injunction inappropriate. * * *

We had serious concern about the District Court's finding that NutraSweet's relationships with its domestic customers and distributors would be irreparably harmed in the absence of a preliminary injunction. * * * Nevertheless, whether or not there was a possibility of irreparable harm to NutraSweet at the time NutraSweet applied for a preliminary injunction, it now appears that NutraSweet can suffer no harm because, as explained above, NutraSweet has obtained possession of the Equal by the District Court's order modifying the writ of replevin.

Because the writ of replevin now adequately protects NutraSweet's interest in preventing distribution of the goods in the United States during the pendency of this suit, the preliminary injunction entered by the District Court now becomes an unnecessary remedy that must be vacated. * * *

III.

Tek also contends that the District Court erred in issuing the writ of replevin. We decline to rule on Tek's challenge to the writ of replevin because we lack appellate jurisdiction.[4]

Congress has conferred jurisdiction on the courts of appeal over interlocutory orders in limited situations. * * * Section 1292(a) allows courts of appeal to hear challenges to "[i]nterlocutory orders of the district court of the United States ... granting, continuing, modifying, refusing, or dissolving injunctions, or refusing to dissolve or modify injunctions...." 28 U.S.C. § 1292(a)(1). * * *

We lack jurisdiction to hear Tek's challenge to the writ of replevin because it does not fall within the definition of "injunction." Unlike an injunction, the writ of replevin in this case was directed to the U.S. Marshals, not to a party to the suit against whom the order could be enforced by threat of contempt. * * * Furthermore, the writ, as modified, does accord NutraSweet some of the relief it ultimately desires (possession of the Equal), but it is only a provisional remedy, and the District Court reserved the right to order NutraSweet to return the Equal to Tek if NutraSweet does not ultimately prevail. * * * Because the writ of replevin is not an injunction for purposes of section 1292(a)(1), we hold that it is not an appealable interlocutory order. *See, e.g.,* HBE Leasing Corp. v. Frank, 48 F.3d 623, 632 (2d Cir.1995) ("the provisional remedies of attachment and replevin ... do not constitute injunctions for the purposes of section 1292 (a)(1)"); FDIC v. Elio, 39 F.3d 1239, 1249 (1st Cir.1994) ("attachments are not among the interlocutory orders appealable under 28 U.S.C. § 1292(a)") * * *; *accord* 16 Charles A. Wright, Arthur R. Miller & Edward H. Cooper, Federal Practice & Procedure § 3922.3, at 116 (1996) ("Enforcement of such traditional security devices as attachment and replevin ordinarily is thought not to involve an injunction within the meaning of § 1292(a)(1).").

IV.

For the foregoing reasons, we will reverse and remand with instructions to vacate the preliminary injunction. We dismiss Tek's appeal of the writ of replevin for lack of jurisdiction.

---

4. Although the parties did not raise this Court's jurisdiction to consider the validity of the writ of replevin, this Court, as a court of limited jurisdiction, must *sua sponte* raise the issue of appellate jurisdiction. * * *

D. RESTITUTION: PERSONAL AND INTANGIBLE PROPERTY INTERESTS

Olwell v. Nye & Nissen Co., *supra* Chapter 4, Section 6, illustrates the use of restitution where a tortious interference with personal property has enriched the wrongdoer. In *Olwell* the plaintiff "waived the tort and sued in *assumpsit*." Why can't the plaintiff in the next case waive the tort?

JOHN A. ARTUKOVICH & SONS, INC. v. RELIANCE TRUCK CO.

Supreme Court of Arizona, 1980.
126 Ariz. 246, 614 P.2d 327.

HOLOHAN, VICE CHIEF JUSTICE.

After trial to the court plaintiff, John A. Artukovich & Sons, Inc., was granted judgment for compensatory damages of $6,956.59 and punitive damages of $6,000.00 against defendant, Reliance Truck Company, for conversion of plaintiff's crane. The Court of Appeals set aside the trial court's judgment for conversion, and ordered plaintiff's recovery to be reduced to compensatory damages of $1,456.59, which represented the out-of-pocket expenses actually incurred by plaintiff as a result of defendant's unauthorized use of the crane. * * *

The facts necessary for determination of this matter are as follows: Plaintiff in an agreement dated July 1, 1975, leased its crane to the Ashton Company for use in Tucson, Arizona, in the construction of the addition to the University Stadium. The lease was for a nine-month term commencing on September 1, 1975, or the first day the crane was actually used, whichever came first, for a stated rental and provided for delivery to Ashton "F.O.B., Tempe, Arizona" on or about July 26, 1975.

Ashton hired the defendant to transport the crane from Tempe to Tucson by August 1, 1975. On Wednesday, July 23, 1975, Reliance dismantled and loaded the crane on its trucks in Tempe for the trip to Tucson. Meantime, Reliance was notified of the arrival in West Phoenix of a 246,000 lb. transformer that Reliance had previously contracted to put into place at a West Phoenix Arizona Public Service sub-station. Reliance's operation manager, Sam Curl, called Ashton's equipment manager to request permission to use the crane to unload the transformer prior to the trip to Tucson. The Ashton employee told Curl that he would have to talk to Harold Ashton but he would get back to Curl. The crane was moved to the West Phoenix jobsite on Thursday and reassembled on Friday before Curl called Ashton Company again and was told, "That the deal would have to be made with John Artukovich." Reliance already owed another Artukovich Company some money.

Curl testified he tried unsuccessfully to obtain permission from Artukovich by telephoning on Friday afternoon and left a message. Nevertheless, on Saturday Reliance used the crane without ever having received permission from Artukovich. The crane was then delivered to Tucson where after replacement of the cable and a safety inspection it was used by Ashton pursuant to the lease.

There was no evidence that Reliance made any further efforts to seek out Artukovich and pay a rental fee for the use of the crane. Artukovich found out about the unauthorized use from Ashton and sued Reliance on three counts: Counts I and III sounding in tort for the act of conversion and Count II on an implied contract theory. The trial judge's minute entry, dated November 3, 1978, awarded plaintiff judgment as follows:

1. For use of the crane (one month minimum rental) $5,500.00.

2. Crane inspection fee, $493.05.

3. Replaced cable, $963.54.

4. Attorney's fees in the amount of $3,500.00.

5. Punitive damages in the amount of $2,500.00.

6. Plaintiff's costs.

After defendant's motion for a new trial questioned the correctness of awarding attorney's fees and punitive damages in the same action, plaintiff's judgment for the lump sum of $12,956.59 was vacated and plaintiff was given judgment in the amount of $6,956.59 for actual damages and $6,000.00 punitive damages plus costs. Defendant filed a timely appeal which resulted in the above described action by the Court of Appeals.

The issues presented are (1) can plaintiff, Artukovich, recover on a theory of conversion from the defendant, Reliance, and (2) if not, is plaintiff entitled to judgment based on an implied contract theory.

Before plaintiff can recover in an action for the wrongful detention of its property it must show that it had a legal right to use the property and was in a position to use it and was prevented from such use only by the defendant's wrongful detention. * * *

Plaintiff's lease to Ashton, provided for delivery of a crane F.O.B. Tempe. Since Ashton had taken possession of the crane by authorizing its agent, Reliance, to transport the crane to Tucson, plaintiff, Artukovich, no longer had any right to use nor was it in a position to use the crane at the time of Reliance's unauthorized use. Plaintiff, therefore, cannot recover damages for its loss of use of the crane on a theory of conversion.

Although plaintiff may not recover on its tort theory, Count II of the complaint set forth a claim based on implied contract. * * * [T]he trial judge found sufficient evidence to support plaintiff's claim based on an implied contract. Our review of the evidence leads us to the same conclusion.

Contracts implied-in-law or quasi-contracts, also called constructive contracts, are inferred by the law as a matter of reason and justice from the acts and conduct of the parties and circumstances surrounding the transactions, * * * and are imposed for the purpose of bringing about justice without reference to the intentions of the parties. * * *

Restatement of Restitution, § 1 provides, "A person who has been unjustly enriched at the expense of another is required to make restitution to the other." Comment (a) to that section notes that a person is enriched if he received a benefit and is unjustly enriched if retention of that benefit would be unjust. Comment (b) defines a benefit as being any form of advantage. The facts in this case show that the defendant did receive a benefit or advantage through the use of plaintiff's crane. Defendant received $6,000.00 for putting the transformer in place pursuant to a contract with Arizona Public Service. The defendant has acknowledged throughout the litigation that it recognized and intended to pay someone a reasonable rental value for the crane's use.

Thus, the only issue remaining is what should plaintiff recover for the defendant's unauthorized use of its crane.

Unjust enrichment does not depend upon the existence of a valid contract, * * * nor is it necessary that plaintiff suffer a loss corresponding to the defendant's gain for there to be a valid claim for an unjust enrichment. * * * Thus, even though plaintiff had no right to use the crane at the time of defendant's unauthorized use, the defendant is liable to plaintiff because the defendant received a benefit by using plaintiff's crane to perform the contract with Arizona Public Service. To allow the defendant to use plaintiff's crane without compensating plaintiff for its use would unjustly enrich the defendant and would be inequitable. * * * *See also* Restatement of Restitution, § 1, Comment (e) * * *.

The judgment of the trial court is reversed, and the cause is remanded to Superior Court with direction to enter judgment for the plaintiff on Count II of the Complaint, and proceed to re-try only the issue of damages. * * *

STRUCKMEYER, C.J., and HAYS, CAMERON and GORDON, JJ., concur.

CABLEVISION OF BRECKENRIDGE, INC. v. TANNHAUSER CONDOMINIUM ASS'N

Supreme Court of Colorado, 1982.
649 P.2d 1093.

LOHR, JUSTICE.

* * *

This case was tried to the district court under a stipulated set of facts which included those that follow. Cablevision is a corporation engaged in providing cable television and FM radio to its subscribers in areas where the television signals are weak or nonexistent. This is a frequently encountered problem in the vicinity of Breckenridge, Colorado, because the topography of the community and its distance from the originating broadcast stations generally result in an inability to receive a useful broadcast signal when using only the traditional antennas normally employed by individual households.

In order to provide its service, Cablevision constructed several antennas on a mountain peak near Breckenridge, by which it receives six television stations as well as FM radio. At the point of reception, the television signals are strong enough to reproduce a black and white picture, but are too weak to allow color reproduction. Consequently, the signals are fed into a "pre-amp," which magnifies their strength. The signals are then transmitted to a "head-end" building, located near the receiving antennas, where they are passed through a channel processor and mixer for the purpose of improving the clarity of the picture produced by the transmission. From this building, the signals are sent by coaxial cable to the "hub" facility in Breckenridge, and thence through distribution lines to the individual subscribers. * * * Cablevision's capital investment in the transmission system is approximately $450,000.

[I]n October 1972 Cablevision entered into an oral agreement for the provision of subscription cable services with Judy Keller, who was acting on behalf of the owners of the condominium units comprising the Tannhauser I development in Breckenridge. The Tannhauser I building consisted of 33 condominium units, and each was to receive the Cablevision service. Pursuant to this agreement Cablevision installed the equipment necessary to provide its service to each of the units. * * * From January 1, 1972, through March 1974, Tannhauser I paid for the service to these 33 units at a specified rate per unit.

Effective May 1974, Cablevision ceased billing for service to 33 units and began billing for service to only three units. This was done at the request of Jerry White, * * * who apparently acted as a representative for the Tannhauser I owners. * * * [I]t is undisputed that the Cablevision amplifier inside Tannhauser I was removed; that White then substituted his own amplifier and connected it to the Cablevision line; and that, following May 1, television and FM radio service was still provided to all 33 units of Tannhauser I despite the payment to Cablevision for service to only three of those units. This state of affairs continued from May 1, 1974, to approximately December 1, 1976.

In the fall of 1974 a second building, known as Tannhauser II * * * was constructed * * *. White supervised and assisted in the installation of a cable between Tannhauser I and Tannhauser II enabling extension of the Cablevision service to each of the 25 units in Tannhauser II. Tannhauser II began receiving the Cablevision transmission approximately November 30, 1974. Cablevision subsequently discovered the unauthorized use of its transmission by Tannhauser I and II and terminated all service to the condominiums about December 1, 1976.

Thereafter, Cablevision brought the present action. * * *

* * * [A]s part of the pre-trial stipulation of facts summarized above, the parties submitted for judicial resolution the following single stipulated issue:

Have the Defendants, or any of them, breached any contract with Plaintiff, written or oral, in fact or implied, for which Plaintiff is entitled for damages, actual or punitive?

* * * The court * * * adopted the stipulation of the parties as its findings of fact and concluded:

[T]he plaintiff's property and services in the furnishing of cable television is a legally protected interest for which it is entitled to charge an appropriate and lawful rate to its subscribers. The defendants, through the actions stated in the Stipulation, have converted those protected interests without fully paying for them.

Based upon the damages hearing, the court entered judgment for actual damages of $11,597.50 plus statutory interest and court costs, and denied the prayer for punitive damages. * * *

The court of appeals reversed. It held that the trial court erred in ruling that the defendants were liable on the basis that they converted Cablevision's property interests because, pursuant to the parties' stipulation, "the only issue before the trial court was whether any defendant breached any contract with [Cablevision]." It further held that, because the stipulation did not establish the essential elements of a contract, Cablevision had not proved its breach of contract claim. Therefore, it directed the trial court to enter judgment for the defendants.

* * *

As stipulated by the parties, the issue for decision was whether "the Defendants, or any of them, breached any contract with Plaintiff, written or oral, in fact or *implied*." (Emphasis added.) We read the mention of "implied" contracts as a reference to the doctrine of quasi-contract or unjust enrichment, under which courts imply a contract as a matter of law where necessary to avoid unjust enrichment. This interpretation is based in part upon the apparent intent of parties in distinguishing "implied contracts" and contracts "in fact," and draws further support from the inclusion of unjust enrichment claims in the complaint.

In addressing only the issue of whether the stipulated evidence established a contract in fact, the court of appeals did not consider this alternative basis of liability. We conclude that the facts of this case present an appropriate basis for application of the doctrine of unjust enrichment, and reverse the decision of the court of appeals for that reason.

To recover under a theory of quasi-contract or unjust enrichment, a plaintiff must show (1) that a benefit was conferred on the defendant by the plaintiff, (2) that the benefit was appreciated by the defendant, and (3) that the benefit was accepted by the defendant under such circumstances that it would be inequitable for it to be retained without payment of its value. * * * Application of the doctrine does not depend upon the existence of a contract, express or implied in fact, but on the need to avoid unjust enrichment of the defendant notwithstanding the absence of an actual agreement to pay for the benefit conferred. * * * [S]ee generally 1 G. Palmer, The Law of Restitution § 1.2 (1978). * * * The scope of this remedy is broad, cutting across both contract and tort law, with its application guided by the underlying principle of avoiding the unjust enrichment of one party at the expense of another. 1 G. Palmer, The Law of Restitution § 1.1 (1978) * * *.

In the present case, we conclude that a benefit was conferred upon the defendants by Cablevision and that the defendants appreciated this benefit. The defendants' initial payment for this service in connection with the 33 Tannhauser I condominium units and their continued payment for service to three of those units amply demonstrate both the beneficial service provided by Cablevision and the appreciation of that service by the defendants. Instructive in this regard is the broad definition of benefit contained in the Restatement of Restitution § 1, comment b (1937):

> A person confers a benefit upon another if he gives to the other possession of or some other interest in money, land, chattels, or choses in action, performs services beneficial to or at the request of the other, satisfies a debt or a duty of the other, or in any way adds to the other's security or advantage. He confers a benefit not only where he adds to the property of another, but also where he saves the other from expense or loss. The word "benefit," therefore, denotes any form of advantage.

We also conclude that the defendants have retained this service under such circumstances that it would be inequitable to allow its use without payment for its value. The stipulated facts demonstrate that Cablevision never intended to provide its service to all of Tannhausers I and II in exchange for payment in connection with only three units. Indeed, upon discovery of the unauthorized use of its signals, Cablevision terminated all service to the defendants. Further, the defendants were not innocent or unwilling recipients of this benefit, but actively facilitated its provision.

The defendants contend that Cablevision was not harmed by the use made of its signal because it received compensation for the three signals delivered to the three Tannhauser I units pursuant to oral agreement; additional signals were not appropriated by the defendants; and the amplification and use of these signals within Tannhausers I and II did not impair Cablevision's ability to serve its other subscribers. However, this argument ignores the substance and effect of the defendants' conduct and the nature of the harm suffered by Cablevision. The ability of Cablevision to charge for its service is necessary to its economic viability. " * * * By retransmission of the signals purchased in connection with three Tannhauser I units to non-subscribers, the defendants have undercut Cablevision's ability to sell its signal to these other potential customers. These business realities highlight the inequity of permitting the defendants to retain the benefits of Cablevision's service without payment of its value."

* * *

The defendants have accepted a service from Cablevision that is customarily paid for and, in fact, was initially paid for by these defendants. The defendants were active participants in obtaining this benefit from Cablevision, and, based on the initial agreement to serve Tannhauser I, their representatives must have acted with the knowledge that Cablevision expected compensation for each Tannhauser unit receiving the Cablevision transmission. Under these facts, restitution is appropriate to avoid unjust enrichment to the defendants. * * *

The damages awarded were based upon the rate prescribed in Cablevision's franchise from Breckenridge, which correspond to the rate paid for the three Tannhauser I units during the period of unauthorized use of the Cablevision signals. This was an appropriate measure of the benefit conferred upon the defendants and the amount of restitution due. *See* * * * Restatement of Restitution, *supra*, § 157.

Although we do not reach the correctness of the grounds relied upon by the trial court in support of its decision, we conclude that the judgment was proper based upon a theory of quasi-contract or unjust enrichment, and that the court of appeals therefore erred in reversing that judgment. * * *

We reverse the decision of the court of appeals and return the case to that court for remand to the trial court with directions to enter judgment in accordance with the views expressed in this opinion.

Lee, J., does not participate.

UNIVERSITY OF COLORADO FOUNDATION, INC. v. AMERICAN CYANAMID CO.

United States Court of Appeals, Federal Circuit, 2003.
342 F.3d 1298.

Before Rader, Bryson, and Gajarsa, Circuit Judges.

Gajarsa, Circuit Judge.

Drs. Robert H. Allen and Paul A. Seligman (collectively, "the Doctors") developed an idea to reformulate a prenatal multivitamin/mineral supplement. The Doctors described their idea in a confidential manuscript to American Cyanamid Company ("Cyanamid's") Chief of Nutritional Science, Dr. Leon Ellenbogen, who copied parts of that manuscript to obtain U.S. Patent No. 4,431,634 ("the '634 patent"). The United States District Court for the District of Colorado held, *inter alia*, Cyanamid liable for fraudulent nondisclosure and unjust enrichment. * * * In addition to compensatory damages, the district court awarded exemplary damages of $500,000 to each of the Doctors. Because the district court did not err in its determination of unjust enrichment and calculation of damages, we affirm.

* * *

Prenatal supplements containing 60–65 mg of iron are widely used to ensure that pregnant women absorb the approximately 3.5 mg of supplemental iron per day they require because iron deficiency is a serious concern for pregnant and lactating women. Cyanamid's Lederle Laboratories manufactures and markets Materna 1.60 ("Materna"), a prenatal multivitamin/mineral supplement containing 60 mg of iron.

In 1979, Stuart Pharmaceutical, the manufacturer of a competing prenatal supplement Stuartnatal 1 + 1 ("Stuartnatal"), began advertising that its product provided superior iron absorption to that of Materna. To refute these claims and protect Cyanamid's market share, Dr. Ellenbogen asked his friend and long-time professional colleague, Dr. Allen, a professor of medicine, professor of biochemistry, and Director of Hematology at the University of Colorado Health Sciences Center, if he would be interested in performing a study to compare the iron absorption in women of Stuartnatal to that of Materna. Dr. Allen together with his colleague Dr. Seligman, a hematologist and professor of medicine at the University of Colorado Health Sciences Center, conducted the comparison study * * *.

* * *

The Doctors wrote up the results of their studies in an article entitled, "Inadequate Iron Absorption from Many Prenatal Multivitamin–Mineral Supplements." * * * The Doctors submitted a manuscript of the article to the New England Journal of Medicine for consideration in July of 1981, and sent a confidential copy to Dr. Ellenbogen. In the manuscript, the Doctors claimed credit for the design and conduct of the studies, and the discovery and testing of a range of reformulations to increase iron absorption from prenatal multivitamin/mineral supplements. Dr. Ellenbogen voiced no complaint or objection to this, nor to the fact that he was never mentioned or credited in the manuscript with any of the studies' designs or results. Nevertheless, and within days of receiving the confidential manuscript, Dr. Ellenbogen filled out a Cyanamid form claiming inventorship of the reformulated Materna, and Cyanamid began the first steps toward patenting it.

Cyanamid began selling a reformulated Materna in the fall of 1981. Reformulated Materna improved iron absorption over the previous version of the product. Shortly before announcing the reformulation, and without informing the Doctors or the University, Cyanamid filed a patent application in December of 1981, claiming exclusive rights to the reformulation and naming Dr. Ellenbogen as its sole inventor. Cyanamid copied significant portions of the confidential manuscript, * * * into a patent application. The '634 patent issued from this application in 1984.

* * *

* * * When the Doctors finally obtained a copy of the '634 patent and saw the copied data table and the content based almost entirely on their confidential manuscript, they and the University filed an action against Cyanamid asserting claims for fraudulent nondisclosure, unjust enrichment, and equitable remedy under the federal patent laws.

* * *

* * * [T]he district court * * * found Cyanamid liable for fraud and unjust enrichment. * * *

Applying federal patent law, the district court * * * concluded that the Doctors were the inventors and that Ellenbogen had no role in conceiving the invention. The court * * * separately addressed the Doctors' alternative claims for fraudulent nondisclosure, unjust enrichment, and equitable remedy under federal patent law.

First, on the fraudulent nondisclosure claim, the district court based its compensatory damages award on the "payment that Cyanamid would have made to secure the Doctors' cooperation in filing the required documents with the PTO [Patent and Trademark Office], an assignment of ownership rights and/or an exclusive license from the University." The district court found Cyanamid liable to the plaintiffs for $22,546,000 in fraud damages (royalties at 6% from issuance of the '634 patent in 1984 until Cyanamid ceased enforcing the '634 patent due to this pending litigation in 1994).

Second, to determine the equitable remedy for unjust enrichment, the district court calculated the "incremental profits" from the sale of Materna attributable to the right to exclude generic competition that Cyanamid gained from the '634 patent. The district court found that Cyanamid was unjustly enriched by $23,243,228 at the plaintiffs' expense. Finding that the plaintiffs are not entitled to double recovery for their fraud and unjust enrichment claims, the district court only awarded an equitable remedy for unjust enrichment and struck the award of fraud damages.

Third, as to the federal equitable remedy, the district court found that the Doctors' status as equitable titleholders of the '634 patent constituted a separate and independent ground mandating that Cyanamid disgorge its incremental profits.

Last, the district court awarded $500,000 in exemplary damages to each of the Doctors because Cyanamid's conduct was attended by circumstances of fraud, malice, and willful and wanton conduct. Cyanamid timely appealed the liability judgments on the claims for fraudulent nondisclosure, unjust enrichment, equitable remedy under federal patent law, the associated monetary awards, and the district court's award of exemplary damages. * * *

* * *

The district court determined that the work, studies and ideas ultimately patented by Cyanamid were discovered by the Doctors, "[e]ntirely independent of Cyanamid." * * * The district court also found that Cyanamid had no co-inventorship interest in the reformulations and had no right to patent the reformulations by copying the Doctors' confidential manuscripts. * * * [T]he district court applied principles of unjust enrichment to determine the parties' rights with respect to each other and declined to assess the parties' rights to exclude as against the rest of the world pursuant to federal patent principles.

Cyanamid, citing Waner v. Ford Motor Co., 331 F.3d 851 (Fed.Cir. 2003), argues that federal patent law precludes any state law unjust enrichment award, because the Doctors did not protect their ideas either as trade secrets or patents. Further, Cyanamid alleges the district court's findings regarding unjust enrichment essentially create state patent rights—a result the Supreme Court prohibited in Bonito Boats, Inc. v. Thunder Craft Boats, Inc., 489 U.S. 141, 109 S.Ct. 971, 103 L.Ed.2d 118 (1989). * * *

* * *

* * * The Supreme Court has summarized its preemption approach as follows: "States may not offer *patent-like* protection to intellectual creations which would otherwise remain unprotected as a matter of federal law." Bonito Boats, 489 U.S. at 156 (emphasis added) * * *. In that case, the Supreme Court struck down a state statute that prohibited copying boat hull designs, because "the Florida statute allows petitioner to [ ]assert a substantial property right in the idea, thereby constricting the spectrum of useful public knowledge." Bonito Boats, 489 U.S. at 159 (emphasis added).

The right involved here and compensated for under a theory of unjust enrichment, however, is not "patent-like" at all. * * * [T]he unjust enrichment claim springs not from an attempt to enforce intellectual property rights, but instead from Cyanamid's alleged wrongful use of the Doctors' research results. * * * [A] claim for unjust enrichment is "not simply an attempt to enforce property rights" * * *; rather, under Colorado law,* * * the Doctors' claim of unjust enrichment is a legal claim to remedy the breach of a contract implied in law for disclosure of their confidential manuscript in exchange for a promise not to disseminate the idea without the Doctors' consent. * * * The fact that Cyanamid improperly secured the '634 patent and used this patent to obtain incremental profits only pertains to restitution for the unjust enrichment claim.

* * *

Cyanamid argues that the judgment on the claim for unjust enrichment should be reversed because the plaintiffs failed to prove a material element of that claim. Specifically, Cyanamid asserts that the Doctors have no basis for a claim of unjust enrichment because the benefits that the Doctors admittedly derived through their collaboration with Cyanamid, together with the fact that they never sought to patent or practice the invention at issue, establish that the '634 patent was not obtained at the plaintiffs' expense, as is required under Colorado law. We reject this argument.

Under Colorado law, the elements of the claim of unjust enrichment are stated as: (1) at plaintiff's expense (2) defendant received a benefit (3) under circumstances that would make it unjust for defendant to retain the benefit without paying for it. * * * The Restatement of Restitution states "[a] person who has been unjustly enriched at the expense of another is required to make restitution to the other." Restatement of Restitution § 1 (1937). The comment to this section explains that "[a] person is enriched if he has received a benefit. A person is unjustly enriched if the retention of the benefit would be unjust."

The Doctors' claim of unjust enrichment is a legal claim in quasi-contract for money damages based upon principles of restitution. *See* 1 George E. Palmer, The Law of Restitution §§ 1.1, 1.2 (1978). When restitution is the primary basis of a claim, as opposed to a remedy for bargains gone awry, it invokes what has been characterized in Colorado as a "contract implied in law." * * *

The unjust enrichment claim in the context of a contract implied in law does not depend in any way upon a promise or privity between the parties. * * * "[A] 'contract implied in law' is not really a contract at all, and may even be imposed in the face of a clearly expressed contrary intent if justice requires." * * *

Considering the first prong of the test, in this case there is no question that any benefit Cyanamid received came at the Doctors' expense. * * * The Doctors therefore performed critical Studies IA, II, and IIA on their own initiative and at their own expense.

The second prong examines whether Cyanamid was benefited or enriched. The district court found that Cyanamid was unjustly enriched by its conduct in taking for itself exclusivity rights in the Doctors' reformulation technology and then secretly patenting that technology without the Doctors' or University's knowledge or consent. This taking not only deprived the University of the financial gain it could have realized had Cyanamid paid for an exclusive license or assignment of rights and filed its patent application, but also betrayed the Doctors and deprived both them and the University of their prerogative not to patent the Doctors' invention or to exclude others from benefiting from it.

Finally, the third prong of the test requires consideration of whether it would be unjust to allow Cyanamid to retain the benefit conferred without paying for its value. The incremental profits Cyanamid earned by virtue of its possession and enforcement of the wrongfully secured '634 patent are the direct result of misconduct. * * *

* * *

We must next determine the appropriate measure of Cyanamid's unjust enrichment. Cyanamid argues that the proper measure of damages is the value that Cyanamid would have paid in 1981 to acquire the research results and for any cooperation needed to apply for the '634 patent, not disgorgement of Cyanamid's profits as the district court found. * * *

* * *

We conclude that under Colorado law, the district court did not abuse its discretion by ordering Cyanamid to disgorge the incremental profits directly attributable to its misconduct. Colorado law supports the benefits-based approach used by the district court to effect equitable relief in appropriate cases. *See* EarthInfo, Inc. v. Hydrosphere Res. Consultants, Inc., 900 P.2d 113, 118 (Colo.1995) (*en banc*) (adopting a case by case approach to determining whether profits may be awarded as restitution in a claim for unjust enrichment). This is true even if it results in plaintiff receiving a greater reward than if simply awarded damages for the defendant's misconduct:

> Restitution, which seeks to prevent unjust enrichment of the defendant, differs in principle from damages, which measure the remedy by the plaintiff's loss and seek to provide compensation for that loss. As a consequence, *"in some cases the defendant gains more than the plaintiff loses,* so that the two remedies may differ in practice as well as in principle."

Id. (quoting 1 Dan B. Dobbs, Law of Remedies § 4.1(1), at 555, 557 (2d ed.1993)) (emphasis added).

No wooden formulas exist for determining when restitution of profits realized by a party is permissible. *Id.* at 119. Because it is an equitable remedy, "whether profits are awarded to a nonbreaching party shall be determined within the discretion of the trial court on a case by case basis." *Id.* at 118. As the Colorado Supreme Court envisioned it, in determining whether restitution of profits or disgorgement in a given case is appropriate:

> [C]ourts must resort to general considerations of fairness, taking into account the nature of the defendant's wrong, the relative extent of his or her contribution, and the feasibility of separating this from the contribution traceable to the plaintiff's interest. 1 George E. Palmer, The Law of Restitution § 2.12 at 161 (1978) [hereinafter "Palmer"]. Thus, the more culpable the defendant's behavior, and the more direct the connection between the profits and the wrongdoing, the more likely that plaintiff can recover all defendant's profits. *See, e.g.,* Douglas Laycock, *The Scope and Significance of Restitution,* 67 Tex. L. Rev. 1277, 1289 (1989). The trial court must ultimately decide whether the whole circumstances of a case point to the conclusion that the defendant's retention of any profit is unjust.

Id. at 119.

Applying these principles of Colorado law to this case, we conclude that the district court properly limited the equitable remedy by calculating the incremental profits from the sale of Materna *attributable to the right to exclude* generic competition that Cyanamid gained from the '634 patent—not the total profits Cyanamid made by selling a product incorporating the Doctors' invention. The district court found Cyanamid liable in the amount of $53,106,066, which included $22,243,228 for unjust enrichment, 8% statutory prejudgment interest through January 1, 2002, and the additional prejudgment interest that had accrued from January 1, 2002, to the date of judgment. * * *

* * *

Cyanamid argues that the award of exemplary damages was erroneous because the trial evidence provides no basis for an award of exemplary damages. We reject this argument.

Under § 13–12–102(1) of the Colorado Revised Statutes, a factfinder may award exemplary damages in an amount not to exceed the amount of actual damages if it determines that the defendant's tortious conduct "is attended by circumstances of fraud, malice or willful and wanton conduct." The district court cited this express language when it awarded exemplary damages of $500,000 to each of the Doctors. As discussed above, the district court detailed Cyanamid's misconduct in numerous factual findings. Accordingly, we affirm the district court's award of exemplary damages to each of the Doctors.

* * *

In light of our conclusion that the district court properly awarded damages for unjust enrichment, we need not review the district court's alternative grounds for damages based on fraudulent nondisclosure and equitable remedy under the federal patent laws.

* * *

NOTES

1.   Much of the law of remedies in the intangible property area involves claims to a right in a patent, copyright, trademark or trade name. As one can see in *University of Colorado Foundation,* federal law may preempt the common law of remedies for the infringement of intangible property rights in the areas of patent and copyright protection. Patent law provides for restitutionary recovery: should other similar statutes as well? *Compare* Dane S. Ciolino, *Reconsidering Restitution in Copyright,* 48 Emory L.J. 1 (1999) (suggesting that restitutionary remedies would contribute little or nothing to copyright's economic and creative incentives), *with* Mohamed Yusuf M. Mohamed, *Unjust Enrichment for Patent Infringement: A Novel Idea?* 4 J. Intell. Prop. L. 123 (1996) (suggesting that restitutionary recovery is necessary if a patentee is to be adequately compensated for an infringement). *See generally* 1 George Palmer, Law of Restitution § 2.7 (1978); Dan B. Dobbs, Law of Remedies § 10.5(3) (2d ed. 1993); Ralph S. Brown, *Civil Remedies for Intellectual Property Invasions: Themes and Variations,* 55 Law & Contemp. Probs. 45 (1992) (discussing remedies which are available for violating the Copyright Act of 1976, the Patent Act of 1952, and the Trademark Act of 1946 (the Lanham Act)); Kenneth H. York, *Extension of Restitutional Remedies in the Tort Field,* 4 UCLA L. Rev. 499 (1957). *Cf.* Chau Vo, *Finding A Workable Exception to the Work Made For Hire Presumption of Ownership,* 32 Loy. L.A. L. Rev. 611 (1999) (suggesting that an employee should have the right to

rescind a contract with an employer and recapture the copyright in works made for hire).

2. Illustrative of the cases in which restitution was found to be an appropriate remedy for misuse of trade secrets and similar interests are: Massachusetts Eye and Ear Infirmary v. QLT Phototherapeutics, 552 F.3d 47 (1st Cir. 2009) in Section 6 of Chapter 4; G.S. Rasmussen & Associates v. Kalitta Flying Service, Inc., 958 F.2d 896 (9th Cir.1992) (quasi-contract action for unauthorized use of plaintiff's "Certificate" from the Federal Aviation Authority allowing modification of cargo planes to increase cargo carrying capacity; the procedure and protection in question were not pre-empted by federal copyright or patent law); Skinner v. Shirley of Hollywood, 723 F.Supp. 50 (N.D.Ill.1989) (quasi-contract action for alleged appropriation of plaintiff's customer list and good will); Ocor Products Corp. v. Walt Disney Productions, Inc., 682 F.Supp. 90 (D.N.H.1988) (quasi-contract action for misuse of unregistered bag design).

SECTION 2. INTERFERENCE WITH REAL PROPERTY AND ENVIRONMENTAL INTERESTS

A. DAMAGES

1. Trespass

MYERS v. ARNOLD

Appellate Court of Illinois, 1980.
83 Ill.App.3d 1, 38 Ill.Dec. 228, 403 N.E.2d 316.

MILLS, PRESIDING JUSTICE:

This case involves 60–80 truckloads of concrete—all dumped on plaintiffs' property. A jury found such dumping wrongful and gave plaintiffs a verdict of $12,000. Defendant appeals, claiming: (1) The trial court erred when it allowed plaintiffs to recover the cost of repair rather than the diminution in market value * * *.

* * *

In 1972 or 1973, the plaintiffs purchased a 20–acre tract of land near Leroy, Illinois. In July of 1974, they began constructing a residence on the western portion of this land and at the time of trial they were residing at this location. The land is divided diagonally by a creek and when the land was originally purchased, the plaintiffs intended to construct their present residence, sell it, and then build another residence on the eastern portion of the property.

The creek which ran through the plaintiffs' property created an erosion problem and it was thought that broken concrete could be used to correct this problem. In the fall of 1974, the plaintiffs discovered that the defendant was engaged in a road repair and construction project on U.S.

Route 16 near Leroy. Plaintiff, Mrs. Anna Myers, contacted Howard Arnold, president of the defendant, about getting some concrete fill * * *. According to Mrs. Myers' testimony, she told the supervisor that she wanted a couple of loads of concrete and that she preferred that it not include rubble or dirt. * * * [T]he amount of concrete delivered far exceeded the amount desired. The concrete contained reinforcing rods, was stacked 8 feet high in some places, and covered an area approximately 50–150 feet. It had been placed where the plaintiffs intended to build the second house. Mrs. Myers immediately contacted Howard Arnold but he would not agree to remove the concrete.

On the issue of damages, the plaintiffs presented the testimony of John Nord who is self-employed in the refuse removal and demolition business. He detailed the various costs for removing the concrete and estimated that the total expense would be $18,200. However, he admitted that if he were able to find area farmers who wanted the material for erosion control, the costs would be decreased because the material would not have to be hauled as far as he had planned when estimating the cost of removal.

* * *

By way of an offer of proof, the defendant presented the testimony of a real estate appraiser who had examined plaintiffs' property four days before trial. The appraiser testified that on the date of trial the fair market value of the plaintiffs' property was $750 per acre. This value, however, was based only on the land and did not include plaintiffs' house. In 1974, plaintiffs' property would have been worth $650 per acre. The appraiser also testified that the fact that one-half acre of plaintiffs' property was covered with concrete would have no great effect on its value for resale purposes.

At the conference on instructions, the court—over the defendant's objection—ruled that it would give the plaintiffs' instruction concerning the measure of damages. This instruction measures damages by the reasonable expense of removing the concrete. The court therefore rejected defendant's tendered instruction which stated that the measure of damages was "the lesser of the reasonable expense of necessary repairs to the property which was damaged or the difference between the fair market value of the property immediately before the occurrence plus [sic] its fair market value immediately after the occurrence."

I

The defendant argues that the trial court erred in failing to give its tendered instruction on the issue of damages. Defendant therefore claims that this case must be remanded because the verdict of $12,000 (which represents the cost of repair) far exceeds the diminution in the market value of the plaintiffs' property.

Initially, we note that defendant's tendered instruction did not state the rule on which the defendant relies. The tendered instruction would have informed the jury that the measure of damages was the lesser of the reasonable expense of repair or the difference in the fair market value of the property before the occurrence "plus" its fair market value after the occurrence. The word "plus" should not appear in this instruction. Illinois Pattern Jury Instruction, Civil, Number 30.11, uses the word "and" where defendant submitted the word "plus." We are confident defendant would not have the jury fix damages in the manner provided by the tendered instruction.

* * *

Defendant relies on the rule generally stated that tort damages for an injury to real property are to be measured by the difference between the market value of the property before the injury and its value after the injury.

* * *

We believe that the criticisms which have been directed at an automatic application of the diminution rule are well founded. (*See generally* Dobbs, Handbook on the Law of Remedies, § 5.1 (1973).) The law of torts attempts primarily to restore the injured party to as good a position as he held prior to the tort. (Restatement of Torts 2d, § 901 (1979).) In accomplishing that result, courts must be mindful of the fact that rules governing the proper measure of damages in a particular case are guides only and should not be applied in an arbitrary, formulaic, or inflexible manner, particularly where to do so would not do substantial justice. * * *

When a land owner has shown that he has suffered a compensable injury, we believe it is necessary to examine the exact interest harmed before answering the question of what amount is necessary to fully compensate for that harm. Allowing a plaintiff to recover the lesser of the cost of repair or the diminution in market value may be appropriate where the interest which has been harmed is purely financial, as where the land was purchased as a business investment with an eye towards speculation or where it is held solely for the production of income. However, the same measure of damages may be painfully inadequate when the land is held for a personal use such as a family residence and the harm may be corrected with a reasonable expenditure even though the expenditure exceeds the amount the land has diminished in value. In the latter case, the full repair cost will come much closer to restoring what was actually lost and will not require the injured party to correct the harm with funds from his own pocket. Automatic application of the rule advocated by the defendant could, in many cases, force plaintiffs to sell their property to a defendant and, in effect, grant a private right of eminent domain. To grant such a right in cases such as the one at bench would inadequately protect plaintiffs' legitimate interest in the use and enjoyment of their property. The courts of this state have recently begun to recognize this fact as they have rejected application of the diminution rule in similar cases.

In Arras v. Columbia Quarry Co. (1977), 52 Ill.App.3d 560, 10 Ill.Dec. 192, 367 N.E.2d 580, the defendant's blasting activities destroyed a well located on land where plaintiffs had lived for almost 30 years. At the trial of that case, the only evidence which was presented on the issue of damages was expert testimony concerning the cost of drilling a new well. On appeal, the defendant strenuously argued that the only relevant measure of damages was the diminution in the fair market value of the property. Our sister court disagreed and felt that the permanent/nonpermanent dichotomy * * * was a logical and well reasoned approach. The rule which the court adopted requires a determination of whether the injury is permanent or nonpermanent. If permanent, the measure of damages is the market value of the realty before the injury less its market value after the injury. When the injury is nonpermanent, the measure of damages is the cost of restoring the property to its original condition. Similarly, in Zosky v. Couri (1979), 77 Ill.App.3d 1033, 33 Ill.Dec. 837, 397 N.E.2d 170, the permanent/nonpermanent approach was applied where the injury consisted of tire ruts on the plaintiff's lawn.

We agree with the approach adopted in *Arras* and *Zosky* and conclude that the plaintiffs in this case were entitled to recover the cost of repairing the damages. Here, as in those cases, the damage was to realty held for personal rather than a business use, the injury was capable of repair, and this repair could be accomplished without expending amounts wholly disproportionate to the value of the land. The trial court, accordingly, did not err in refusing defendant's tendered instruction.

NOTES

1. Illinois continues to recognize the "permanent/nonpermanent dichotomy." *See, e.g.*, First Baptist Church of Lombard v. Toll Highway Authority, 301 Ill.App.3d 533, 703 N.E.2d 978, 234 Ill.Dec. 878 (1998). The following analysis by the Louisiana Supreme Court aptly summarizes the current approaches to measuring damages for torts to real estate:

> [A]lthough expressed in differing ways, many * * * courts essentially limit the owner's damage to the lesser of cost to repair and diminution in market value caused by the damage. * * * Other courts, although applying cost to restore as the appropriate measure of damages in all cases of reparable injury to property, use the fair market value of the property before the injury, rather than the diminution in value, as a ceiling on the damage award. * * *
>
> Recently, courts and commentators have criticized these types of simplistic tests * * *. "Such ceilings on recovery not only seem unduly mechanical but also seem wrong from the point of view of reasonable compensation. If the plaintiff wishes to use the damaged property, not sell it, repair or restoration at the expense of the defendant is the only remedy that affords full compensation. To limit repair costs to diminution in value is to either force a landowner to sell the property he wishes to keep or to make repairs partly out of his own pocket." D. Dobbs, Handbook on the Law of Remedies 317 (1973). * * *

In recognition of the need for a more flexible approach, * * * the Restatement (Second) of Torts provides, in pertinent part, that whenever there is injury to land, damages should include "the difference between the value of the land before the harm, and the value after the harm, or at [the owner's] election in an appropriate case, the cost of restoration that has been or may be reasonably incurred ...." Restatement (Second) of Torts § 929 (1977). The official comment on this section indicates that (i) costs of restoration are ordinarily allowable as the measure of damages (ii) but that courts will use diminution in value when the cost of restoring the land to its original position is "disproportionate" to the diminution in value—(iii) "unless there is a reason personal to the owner for restoring the original condition." *Id.* § 929, comment b. In the latter case, the damages will ordinarily include the amount necessary for repairs, even though this amount might be greater than the total value of the property.

Roman Catholic Church of the Archdiocese of New Orleans v. Louisiana Gas Service Co., 618 So.2d 874, 876–78 (La.1993). For a recent example of the traditional "lesser of diminution and cost of repair" approach, see Poffenbarger v. Merit Energy Co., 972 So. 2d 792 (Ala. 2007). For further analysis, see Carol C. Chomsky, *Of Spoil Pits and Swimming Pools: Reconsidering the Measure of Damages for Construction Contracts*, 75 Minn. L. Rev. 1445, 1481–82 (1991).

2. Should a plaintiff be entitled to recover loss of use damages during the period of repair? *See* Nisbet v. Yelnick, 124 Ill.App.3d 466, 79 Ill.Dec. 877, 464 N.E.2d 781 (1984) (plaintiff awarded damages for loss of use of home in addition to cost of repairing defects).

3. In Rovetti v. City & County of San Francisco, 131 Cal.App.3d 973, 183 Cal.Rptr. 1 (1982), the court awarded $58,479 to repair the plaintiff's home; $18,000 of this sum represented compensation for the effects of inflation between the time of the damage and the time of the trial seven years later. The court explained that increasing an award to compensate for the effects of inflation insures that a plaintiff will not receive less than the amount to which the plaintiff is entitled.

4. Is it fair to draw a distinction between commercial and residential property for purposes of determining when restoration damages are available in trespass cases? Suppose, for example, that a trespasser dumps 60 loads of concrete on land that is used in a sod growing business. If the trespass did not cause the land to decline in value because it is suitable for other commercial uses, should restoration damages be denied? Should the owner have to relocate her business? *See* Wujcik v. Gallagher & Henry Contractors, 232 Ill.App.3d 323, 172 Ill.Dec. 920, 596 N.E.2d 199 (1992) ("[W]e agree with the reasoning that the diminution in value may be an inadequate measure of damages when land is damaged, even with commercial property."). Consider the following analysis of the "commercial-residential" distinction in the context of trespass damages to a golf course:

We conclude that "personal reason" damages are available for trespass to commercial property. The aesthetic considerations found worthy of compensation in *Heninger* do not appear to us any less applicable in the setting of a golf course, where trees contribute measurably to the property's value and the customers' enjoyment of the facility.

Gandy v. Asplundh Tree Expert Co., 2005 WL 2680067 (Cal.App.2005).

5.   In addition to general compensatory damages, other types of damages are available in trespass actions. For example, consequential compensatory damages may be recovered for "physical harm to the possessor of the land at the time of the trespass, * * * or to his [or her] things, or to members of the household or to their things." Baker v. Shymkiv, 6 Ohio St.3d 151, 451 N.E.2d 811, 814 (1983). Moreover, although damages for emotional distress are often disallowed in trespass actions, some jurisdictions recognize mental anguish as a compensable harm if it is "the direct and natural result of a specific trespass." See, e.g., Senn v. Bunick, 40 Or.App. 33, 594 P.2d 837, 841 (1979) (plaintiff awarded damages for mental distress caused by destruction of fence and dumping of dirt on his land); accord McGregor v. Barton Sand & Gravel, Inc., 62 Or.App. 24, 660 P.2d 175 (1983). Others allow recovery for emotional distress when the trespass was committed "under circumstances of insult or contumely or wilfully." See, e.g., Rushing v. Hooper–McDonald, 293 Ala. 56, 300 So.2d 94, 98 (1974) (plaintiff stated cause of action for emotional distress where defendant dumped asphalt on plaintiff's land seven times).

HENINGER v. DUNN

California Court of Appeal, 1980.
101 Cal.App.3d 858, 162 Cal.Rptr. 104.

CHRISTIAN, ASSOCIATE JUSTICE.

Appellants David and Eliza Heninger sued respondents Bernard and Elise Dunn for an injunction and damages for trespass. After a nonjury trial the court granted injunctive relief as prayed, but denied any award of damages. The appeal challenges the judgment insofar as it denied damages.

In April 1971 respondents, who owned mountain land adjoining land owned by appellants, bulldozed a rough road, approximately seven-tenths of a mile long, on appellants' land. Respondents acted despite appellants' objections, relying on the advice of an attorney who had erroneously told respondents that they held a valid easement permitting the cutting of the road. The bulldozing killed or damaged 225 trees, and destroyed much vegetative undergrowth, but the road provided additional access to appellants' property, thereby increasing its market value $5,000—from $179,000 just before the trespass to $184,000 immediately following the trespass.

The trial court found that it was technically possible to replace the dead or dying trees, at a cost of $221,647, and that the vegetative undergrowth could be restored at a cost of $19,610. But the court denied damages because there was no depreciation in the value of appellants' property, concluding that "[i]t is the rule in California that if the cost of repair or restoration of damaged property amounts to more than its depreciation in value because of the damage, the plaintiff cannot obtain a greater sum than the amount of the depreciation." Appellants contend that the court's understanding of the rule of damages was incorrect, and that the proper measure of their damages was the lesser of costs of restoration or the pretrespass value of their property, i.e., $179,000.

The measure of damages in California for tortious injury to property is "the amount which will compensate for all the detriment proximately caused thereby.…" (Civ.Code, § 3333.) Such damages are generally determined as the difference between the value of the property before and after the injury. * * *

One alternative measure of damages is the cost of restoring the property to its condition prior to the injury.

* * *

The rule precluding recovery of restoration costs in excess of diminution in value is, however, not of invariable application. Restoration costs may be awarded even though they exceed the decrease in market value if "there is a reason personal to the owner for restoring the original condition" (Rest.2d Torts, § 929, com. b, at pp. 545–546), or "where there is reason to believe that the plaintiff will, in fact, make the repairs" (22 Am.Jur.2d, Damages, § 132, at p. 192). * * *

* * *

The "personal reason" exception has been invoked in many jurisdictions in cases involving destruction of shade or ornamental trees that were of personal value to the owner. In recent years, "courts throughout the country have placed a greater emphasis on the rights of a property owner to enjoy the aesthetic value of trees and shrubbery, notwithstanding the fact they may have little commercial value or that their destruction may, indeed, even enhance the market value of the property." (Rector, etc. v. C.S. McCrossan (1975) 306 Minn. 143, 146, 235 N.W.2d 609, 610.) Where such trees or shrubbery are destroyed by a trespasser, "[s]ound principle and persuasive authority support the allowance to an aggrieved landowner of the fair cost of restoring his land to a reasonable approximation of its former condition, without necessary limitation to the diminution in the market value of the land * * *." (Huber v. Serpico (1962) 71 N.J.Super. 329, 345, 176 A.2d 805, 813.) * * * If restoration of the land to a reasonable approximation of its former condition is impossible or impracticable, the landowner may recover the value of the trees or shrubbery, either as timber or for their aesthetic qualities, again without regard to the diminution in the value of the land.

* * *

The common law principles guiding the assessment of damages for destruction of trees with personal value to their owner are controlling in the present case. * * *

There was substantial evidence that appellants had personal reasons for restoring the land to its original condition. David Heninger testified, "I think the land is beautiful, the natural forest beautiful, and I would like to see it remain that way." He and his family lived on the land, and, aside from the portion of the property on which they resided, they intended to leave it unimproved. The cost of a substantially identical restoration, however, including the transplanting of a large number of mature trees and the restoration of the vegetative undergrowth is, at $241,257, a manifestly unreasonable expense in relation to the value of the land prior to the trespass.

A plant ecologist estimated the cost to restore the vegetative undergrowth at $19,610. This estimate included the costs of planting 230 sapling trees as well as numerous shrubs and ground cover. The plant ecologist testified that a restoration of small trees and shrubs "would leave a scar, but it would not be unsightly," and that it would prevent erosion. On retrial, the court's determination whether a reasonable restoration is possible should focus on the question whether an award of the cost of restoring the vegetative undergrowth (or some other method of covering the scar on the land and preventing further erosion) would achieve compensation within the overall limits of what the court determines to be just and reasonable.

Appellants contend that they are entitled to recover double damages pursuant to Civil Code section 3346, which provides for recovery of "twice the sum as would compensate for the actual detriment" for wrongful injury to timber, trees, or underwood as a result of a trespass that was "casual or involuntary" or committed by a defendant with "probable cause to believe that the land on which the trespass was committed was his own."[3] * * *

Statutes providing for recovery of double or treble damages for injuries to trees are intended to make timber appropriation unprofitable. * * *

Whatever the original policy behind Civil Code section 3346 and the context within which it is normally used, the language of the statute is broad-sweeping, applying to "timber, trees, or underwood." Its application in a case involving damage to fruit trees has been upheld. (Paul A. Mosesian & Sons v. Danielian (1942) 52 Cal.App.2d 387, 388–389, 126 P.2d 363.) The term "underwood" commonly includes seedlings, saplings, shrubs, bushes, and small trees. * * * Neither the language of the statute

---

3. Civil Code section 3346:

"(a) For wrongful injuries to timber, trees, or underwood upon the land of another, or removal thereof, the measure of damages is three times such sum as would compensate for the actual detriment, except that where the trespass was casual or involuntary, or that the defendant in any action brought under this section had probable cause to believe that the land on which the trespass was committed was his own or the land of the person in whose service or by whose direction the act was done, the measure of damages shall be twice the sum as would compensate for the actual detriment. * * * *"

For a discussion of the relationship between such statutory penalties and punitive damages, see D. Dobbs, Handbook on the Law of Remedies 210 (1973) [(plaintiff may choose between the recovery of treble damages or punitive damages)].

nor past judicial constructions supports respondents' contention that it is applicable only to injuries to trees that are valuable as timber.

[W]e conclude that the damages to be doubled or trebled pursuant to Civil Code section 3346 are those determined by the trier of fact to constitute just compensation within the overall limits of reasonableness, regardless of what specific measure of damages is used. (*See* Roche v. Casissa, *supra*, 154 Cal.App.2d 785, 788, 316 P.2d 776 [(upholding trebling of damages measured by the diminution in the value of land on which trees stood)].)

NOTES

1. Courts increasingly allow recovery of replacement costs in excess of the diminution measure where a trespass destroys trees and other vegetation that are ornamental or have other personal value to the owner. *See, e.g.,* Wujcik v. Gallagher & Henry Contractors, 232 Ill.App.3d 323, 172 Ill.Dec. 920, 596 N.E.2d 199 (1992); Rodrian v. Seiber, 194 Ill.App.3d 504, 141 Ill.Dec. 585, 551 N.E.2d 772 (1990); Hornsby v. Bayou Jack Logging, 872 So.2d 1244 (La.Ct.App.2004); Szymanski v. Brown, 221 Mich.App. 423, 562 N.W.2d 212 (1997); Keitges v. VanDermeulen, 240 Neb. 580, 483 N.W.2d 137 (1992); Hill v. Cox, 110 Wash.App.394, 41 P.3d 495 (2002). Moreover, some courts hold that timber trespass damages may even exceed the pre-tort value of the land. *See, e.g.,* Hornsby v. Bayou Jack Logging, 872 So.2d 1244 (La.Ct.App.2004) (upholding damages award for replacement cost that defendant alleged represented twelve times the pre-tort value of the land). *But see* Allyn v. Boe, 87 Wash.App. 722, 943 P.2d 364 (1997) (replacement cost damages in an amount that exceeded two times the pre-tort value of the land deemed unreasonable). On the other hand, courts continue to limit damages to diminution value where the trees are not ornamental, rare or unique. *See, e.g.,* Linebarger v. Owenby, 83 S.W.3d 435 (Ark.App.2002); Kebschull v. Nott, 220 Mont. 64, 714 P.2d 993 (1986). Is the award of restoration damages in excess of the diminution amount in timber cases economically efficient? *See* Robert F. Copple, *The New Economic Efficiency in Natural Resources Damage Assessments*, 66 U. Colo. L. Rev. 675, 709 (1995).

2. The trial court's decision in *Heninger* illustrates the operation of a general principle of damages known as the "benefits rule." Professor Dobbs describes the rule as follows:

> Where the defendant's tortious conduct causes damages, but also operates directly to confer some benefit upon the plaintiff, the plaintiff's claim for damages may be diminished by the amount of the benefit received. In the language of the Restatement of Torts, this is to be done, however, only where it is "equitable."

Dan B. Dobbs, Handbook on the Law of Remedies § 3.6, at 181 (1973). For a discussion of the "offset the benefits rule," see Chapter 3, Section 4.D.1.

3. When real property has no buildings or trees on it, the courts are reluctant to allow recovery in excess of the diminution in fair market value. For example, in Whitaker Acres, Inc. v. Schrenk, 170 Ga.App. 238, 316 S.E.2d 537 (1984), the plaintiff sought to recover the costs of restoring a lot

"uniquely suited" to his house building needs, but the court applied the traditional measure of damages on the ground that the property's uniqueness resulted only from the plaintiff's "subjective evaluation."

4. Often trespass to land results in a judgment for nominal damages, but not for compensatory damages. When should the knowing trespasser in such circumstances be held liable for punitive damages? This issue is explored in Jacque v. Steenberg Homes, Inc., *supra* Chapter 3.5.A.

2. Nuisance

WILLIAMS v. MONSANTO CO.

Missouri Court of Appeals, Eastern District, 1993.
856 S.W.2d 338.

SMITH, JUDGE.

Plaintiff appeals from the judgment of the trial court based in part on a jury verdict [for the defendant] on plaintiff's claim of nuisance and in part from the court's direction of a defendant's verdict on plaintiff's trespass count. * * *

Plaintiff owned and operated an automobile repair business on land abutting property owned by Monsanto upon which it operates a chemical plant. Beginning in the spring of 1984 and continuing for several months, particulate from the Monsanto plant fell on occasion on the premises used by plaintiff "dusting" his and his customers' vehicles. Monsanto admitted that particulate did fall on several occasions on the plaintiff's premises although it disputed that the severity of the fall-out was as plaintiff contended. Plaintiff also contended that the particulate, sodium tripoly-phosphate (STP), caused pitting of the paint of customers' cars and resulted in loss of business. Monsanto's evidence was that STP is a food additive used in a variety of products such as pasta and canned hams and does not cause pitting of automobile paint. Only plaintiff professed to have found such pitting. Monsanto would provide for having cars dusted by the particulate to be cleaned by a neighborhood car wash.

Monsanto expended approximately $500,000 attempting to identify the source of the particulate leak and to remedy it. Testimony from governmental employees involved with pollution control indicated that Monsanto was extremely cooperative and involved in attempting to correct the problem. Some of the complaints made against Monsanto turned out to involve emissions from a neighboring plant, Carondolet Coke Plant. Two witnesses with business in close proximity to plaintiff testified that they had no problems in operating their businesses in the area and had never observed or had complaints by customers of damage to their automobiles caused by white dust from Monsanto.

Plaintiff contended that the loss of customers caused him to have to close his business with a resulting loss of income. There was considerable evidence that plaintiff's business was a losing proposition before any complaint of emissions occurred, that he was seriously overextended before the emissions, and that none of his major customers reduced their business during the period in question, although he had lost the customer providing about 50% of his revenue in the year before the emissions began for reasons unrelated to the emissions.

Plaintiff's amended petition was in fourteen counts including among others trespass, nuisance, negligence, intentional infliction of emotional distress, and consortium claims by plaintiff's wife. The court limited the trial to trespass and nuisance and at the close of the evidence, refused to instruct on the trespass issue thereby effectively directing a verdict on that claim. The jury unanimously found for defendant on the nuisance claim. On appeal plaintiff challenges the court's action in directing a verdict on the trespass claim [and] in failing to grant a judgment notwithstanding the verdict to plaintiff on the nuisance claim * * *.

The availability and relationship between nuisance actions and trespass actions in suits involving pollutants was discussed thoroughly by Judge Simon in Maryland Heights Leasing, Inc. v. Mallinckrodt, 706 S.W.2d 218 (Mo.App.1985). For trespass to lie the pollution must be at a level so as to constitute an actual interference with the possession of the land, not merely interference with its use and enjoyment. Id. at [14–15]. Quoting from Borland v. Sanders Lead Co., 369 So.2d 523 (Ala.1979) [8, 11–14] the court stated that "if, as a result of the defendant's operation, the polluting substance is deposited upon the plaintiff's property, thus interfering with his exclusive possessory interest by causing substantial damage to the res, then the plaintiff may seek his remedy in trespass...."[1] Maryland Heights, supra at [13]. Nuisance, on the other hand, requires an interference with the use and possession of the land. As stated in Maryland Heights, again quoting from Borland, "For example, if the smoke or polluting substance emitting from a defendant's operation causes discomfort and annoyance to the plaintiff in his use and enjoyment of the property, then the plaintiff's remedy is for nuisance."

The evidence presented here all dealt with the effect of the STP on the operation of the defendant's business. None of the evidence dealt with the damage which the STP did to the property itself. The evidence established that whatever injury plaintiff suffered it was to the use and enjoyment of his property and was not substantial damage to the res itself. The trial court did not err in directing a verdict on the trespass claim.

Plaintiff next contends that the evidence established as a matter of law that he was entitled to a verdict on the nuisance claim. Nuisance requires that one unreasonably use his property such that it substantially impairs the rights of another to peacefully use his property. Racine v. Glendale Shooting Club, Inc., 755 S.W.2d 369 (Mo.App.1988) [1–3]; Davis v. J.C. Nichols Company, 714 S.W.2d 679 (Mo.App.1986) [6–9]. Whether a

---

1. Several cases have indicated that trespass occurs upon unauthorized entry, regardless of the amount of force used or the damage done. See Vecchiotti v. Tegethoff, 745 S.W.2d 741 (Mo.App.1987) [10–12]; Crook v. Sheehan Enterprises, Inc., 740 S.W.2d 333 (Mo.App.1987) [1, 2]; Weldon v. Town Properties, Inc., 633 S.W.2d 196 (Mo.App.1982) [7, 8]. Each of those cases involved actual physical entry by a person, not entry by airborne pollutants.

use is unreasonable to the point of a nuisance depends upon factors such as the locality, character of the neighborhood, nature of use, extent of injury, and effect upon enjoyment of life.

Here no other neighbors complained during the period in question. The area was largely industrial, with a coke plant and a cement plant nearby. Monsanto made substantial, expensive efforts to diagnose and correct the problem. It provided car cleaning at its expense when requested for vehicles which were dusted by STP. There was considerable evidence that plaintiff exaggerated his claims and that his business difficulties arose from causes other than Monsanto. The questions of whether a use is "unreasonable" and whether it impairs "substantially" the rights of another to use his property are particularly fact intensive and are particularly suited for jury resolution. *Davis, supra*, at [10, 11]. The trial court did not err in denying plaintiff's motion for judgment notwithstanding the verdict and for new trial premised on the absence of evidence to support the verdict.

* * *

Judgment affirmed.

GARY M. GAERTNER, P.J., and STEPHAN, J., concur.

NOTE

Consider the following analysis by a commentator on real property law about the relationship between trespass and nuisance actions:

> Trespass is defined as an intrusion or invasion of tangible property, either real or personal, which interferes with the possessor's interest in the right of *exclusive possession* of the property. An intrusion can, and often does, constitute both trespass and nuisance because it interferes with both the right of possession and the use and enjoyment of the possessor's property. However, a person who intentionally interferes with another's exclusive right of possession of the res, without privilege to do so, is liable to the other for trespass without proof of actual damages, while intentional nuisance requires proof of actual damages.

> Because trespass protects a possessor's right to exclusive possession of the property, trespass requires proof of an entry on the plaintiff's land, either by the defendant, or by some physical or observable object which the defendant caused to enter onto the property. The modern action for trespass to land evolved from the common-law action which required proof that the intrusion actually interfered with the right of exclusive possession of the property. Nuisance applied in cases in which the injuries were indirect and less substantial. The distinction between injuries which were direct and substantial and those which were considered indirect and less substantial eventually evolved into a fictitious "dimensional" test: "[I]f the intruding agent could be seen by the naked eye, the intrusion was considered a trespass. If the agent could not be seen, it was considered indirect and less substantial, hence, a nuisance."

The traditional rule limiting trespass to invasion of things that can be seen with the naked eye is an arbitrary one that has been discarded in some modern airborne pollution cases. However, the traditional distinction serves a useful function. By limiting actions for trespass to physical intrusion, the law affirms the nature of the interest protected—the right of plaintiff's exclusive possession of the res. By limiting liability for injury to the res that results from intrusion of an observable object onto the property, the rule also limits the scope of a defendant's liability for trespass.

Historically, a plaintiff could maintain an action for trespass even though a defendant was not at fault in causing the invasion of plaintiff's property. With the development of negligence law, however, the strict liability rule of trespass became difficult to justify. As one writer pointed out, "There is no great triumph of reason in a rule which makes a street railway, whose car jumps the track, liable only for negligence to a pedestrian on the sidewalk, but absolutely liable to the owner of the plate glass window behind him."

Today, the "strict liability" rule in trespass has been repudiated both in England and in the United States, and under the law of trespass, like nuisance, a defendant is only liable for an intentional, reckless, or negligent intrusion onto the plaintiff's property, unless the defendant is engaged in an "ultra-hazardous" activity for which strict liability is imposed.

A historical distinction between trespass and trespass on the case has occasionally created a problem for modern courts in cases in which the invasion is "indirect" rather than "direct." Under traditional common law, trespass required proof of direct, rather than indirect invasion by the defendant, and any "indirect" invasion constituted trespass on the case requiring proof of substantial damages. This distinction has been discarded by most courts today. Under the modern view, the defendant may be liable for trespass even though a substance was not placed directly on plaintiff's land so long as the force causing the deposit, such as natural flow to the land, was direct. Thus, if a defendant places a pile of sand and gravel onto her own property, and rain causes the sand and gravel to flow onto the property of a neighbor, an action for trespass is appropriate. The defendant is liable even though the entry of the "thing" was indirect, rather than direct, so long as the defendant acted with knowledge that an invasion was "substantially certain" to follow as a result of defendant's actions.

Holding a defendant liable in trespass for indirectly as well as directly causing matter to be deposited on the plaintiff's land is consistent with the rule that a defendant is liable for the direct and indirect consequences of her intentional tort. Imposing liability for indirect trespass only in cases in which a defendant has "knowledge" that such actions are "substantially certain" to cause a trespass is also consistent with the modern rule requiring proof of defendant's intent, recklessness, or negligence in order to recover damages for trespass unless the defendant is engaged in an ultra hazardous activity.

Nuisance law protects the plaintiff's right to use and enjoy his property. Unlike trespass, nuisance does not require a physical invasion of the property but occurs if a condition is maintained on the defendant's land that interferes with the plaintiff's use and enjoyment of the plaintiff's property. A nuisance is a state of affairs, and may be merely a right thing in the wrong place, like a pig in the parlor instead of the barnyard.

In order to recover damages for private nuisance, a plaintiff must prove that the defendant engaged in an "unreasonable" activity on the defendant's land that "substantially" interfered with the plaintiff's enjoyment of his property. In order to determine whether a defendant's use of his own land is "unreasonable" and to determine whether the defendant's interference with plaintiff's use and enjoyment was substantial, nuisance law requires a court to engage in a balancing test and to weigh the particular facts in each case. Because the facts of each case are unique and the outcome of each dispute depends on balancing of equitable factors, the law of nuisance has been called a "quintessential judgment-entitlement" rule in contrast to the more "mechanical" rule of trespass. It has also been frequently criticized for its doctrinal confusion, "ad hocery" and question-begging Latin phrases.

Frona M. Powell, *Trespass, Nuisance, and the Evolution of Common Law in Modern Pollution Cases*, 21 Real Estate L.J. 182, 185–89 (1992);* *see also* Adams v. Cleveland–Cliffs Iron Co., 237 Mich.App. 51, 602 N.W.2d 215 (1999) (airborne particulate, noise, and vibrations did not constitute a trespass; discussing the distinction between trespass and nuisance actions). Do odors from a sewage treatment plant constitute a trespass? *See* Brown v. County Commissioner of Scioto County, 87 Ohio App.3d 704, 622 N.E.2d 1153 (1993).

DAN B. DOBBS, LAW OF REMEDIES
513–17 (2d ed. 1993).**

§ 5.6   Harms to Interests in Use and Enjoyment: Damages for Nuisance

§ 5.6(1)   Substantive Background: Nuisance and Trespass

The use and enjoyment interest in land might be invaded both by trespass and by nuisance. The balancing of hardships in injunction cases may at times differ according to whether the theory of the plaintiff's claim is trespass or nuisance, but the measurement of harm to the landowner's enjoyment interest is much the same in either case, once it is established that the owner's legal right has been violated. Even so, the most common way in which use and enjoyment interests are violated is through a private nuisance.

As a matter of substantive law, a nuisance is in fact defined as an unreasonable interference with the use and enjoyment of land as distinct from an interference with possession, which has traditionally been allocated to the trespass action. Pollution of the air or water, or excessive noise or lights, if extreme enough, can count as nuisances. So may certain invasions, like the backup of water or sewage, which may be considered

---

* Reprinted with permission of Warren, Gorham & Lamont, Inc.

** Reprinted with Permission of West Publishing Co.

too indirect to qualify as trespasses. Even dangerous conditions outside the land, or unpleasant ones, might at times qualify. The distinction between nuisance and trespass may be less significant than it once was, and today it may be possible for a plaintiff to claim a trespass when pollution of the land occurs—a micro-trespass.

Damages for nuisance vary with the facts. If the effects of the nuisance are more or less permanent, the diminution in land value due to the nuisance will be recoverable; if temporary, the diminished rental value during the period of harm. Cost of repair and personal discomfort or inconvenience may also form bases for recovery. Where the nuisance causes harm besides that claimed by the plaintiff personally, damages awards can be structured to provide incentives to cease pollution.

§ 5.6(2)   Nuisance Damages Generally

Objective or Market Measures

Diminished market value. Apart from special and punitive damages, the measures most commonly invoked when the plaintiff has lost use and enjoyment of land are the diminished land value, the diminished rental value and the cost of repairing the condition in question. These measures are appropriate when the nuisance or trespass actually involves physical harm to the land. The same measures of damages are invoked when the nuisance does no physical harm at all, but affects use and enjoyment directly. Noise, air pollution and sight nuisances are in this category. Interference with easements is treated in the same way as nuisances. If the nuisance is significant and the effects more or less permanent, the diminished use and enjoyment will be reflected in diminished market value and the plaintiff may recover an award based on that diminution.

Diminished rental value. If the effects of the nuisance are transitory, as in the case of a pollution which has now been stopped at its source and the effects of which will abate with time, then the damages are not measured by depreciation in market value but by depreciation in rental value of the property for the period in which the nuisance has been or will be in existence. This is a market measure, but it is one based on the rental rather than the sales market; it reflects the fact that the harm will last only a limited period of time.

Costs of repair or abatement. In some cases it will be appropriate for the plaintiff to recover costs reasonably incurred in abating the nuisance or in preventing future injury. For example, the plaintiff who has sewer lines relaid after a sewage backup may avoid future damage and, if the expense was reasonably incurred to that end, it is a recoverable element in the nuisance action. In the case of hazardous substances controlled by federal law under CERCLA[7] liability is for the cost of removal or remedial

---

7. The Comprehensive Environmental Response, Compensation and Liability Act (CERCLA), 42 U.S.C.A. § 9601 *et seq.* (also known as the Superfund Act). References here include the amendments known as SARA. See § 5.2(5) for further explication of CERCLA.

action, but remedial action is site clean-up, not necessarily full compensation for consequential damages. On the other hand, CERCLA also authorizes recovery by the state or other governmental entity for damage to natural resources themselves. To the extent the nuisance is abated, permanent damages are not to be assessed.

Ceilings on recovery of repair or abatement costs. There are limits to damages recovered to remove the nuisance or minimize future harm. The expense incurred for such purposes must be reasonable. In addition, some cases have said that the recovery of damages based on the cost of repair or the like may not exceed the sum by which the property value has been diminished. There are no doubt cases for which this rule is correct, as suggested by the rules concerning physical harms of land. But if the expenditure is reasonably made to forestall future damages, that expenditure should qualify as an item recoverable under the affirmative version of the avoidable consequences rule; this in turn seems to imply that the plaintiff could recover for the expenditures reasonably made even if hindsight shows that the attempt to minimize damages cost more than it saved.

Damages Not Based on Property Value or Repair

Personal discomfort, illness and anguish. Plaintiffs often emphasize personal discomfort, illness or mental anguish resulting from the nuisance. These are recoverable elements of damages, as is simple inconvenience caused by the nuisance. In contrast, courts usually compensate only for pecuniary losses when the tort physically harms the property or dispossess the plaintiff. In those cases, as distinct from nuisance cases, the plaintiff might recover the diminished value of the property or the cost or repair, or (in dispossession cases) the use value of the property, but no damages for emotional distress. Where serious personal injury results from a nuisance, as in some toxic torts cases, the damages emphasis tends to become an emphasis on personal injury rather than property damage.

Combining claims for discomfort and claims for diminished value. In many cases plaintiffs claim both discomfort damages and diminished value damages. But since the diminished value award is itself a reflection of the discount that potential buyers would require to be willing to live with the discomforts of the nuisance in question, it may be quite inappropriate to award both a sum for diminished value and an additional sum for [the] discomfort the plaintiff will suffer from a continuance of the nuisance in the future. Many writers wish to see the law expand liability for the plaintiff's subjective sense of loss in addition to liability for market diminution, so perhaps plaintiffs should have a choice of either measure, but not both.

Most decisions, however, seem to have gone further by routinely allowing the plaintiff to recover both depreciated value *and* discomfort or illness, with a little authority to the contrary. The recovery of both seems right enough where the sums are trivial or where the plaintiff's illness is idiosyncratic and unlikely to be reflected in diminished value, where the illness is likely to continue even if the plaintiff were to correct the nuisance or leave it, and where the recovery for illness or discomfort is limited to that which occurs before judgment. Otherwise a recovery of both diminished value and future discomfort seems duplicative.

NOTE

The distinction between damages for loss of use and damages for annoyance and discomfort is discussed in Miller v. Carnation Co., 39 Colo.App. 1, 564 P.2d 127 (1977) (trespass and nuisance action brought by husband and wife against adjoining egg ranch for harm caused by flies and rodents) (affirming the trial court's judgment):

> In its special verdict, the jury apportioned the damages, awarding $28,000 for deprivation of use and enjoyment of the property, evenly divided between Mr. and Mrs. Miller, and $72,000 for "annoyance, discomfort, inconvenience, and loss of ability to enjoy their lives," attributing $18,000 to Mr. Miller and $54,000 to Mrs. Miller. [The jury also awarded $300,000 in punitive damages.]

> Contrary to Carnation's contention, damages for loss of use and enjoyment of property, on the one hand, and for annoyance and discomfort, on the other hand, are not duplicative. The use and enjoyment of land is a proprietary interest, while annoyance and discomfort are personal, not proprietary, interests. In its remittitur [of the $28,000 for loss of use and enjoyment to $13,000], the trial court correctly limited recovery for loss of use and enjoyment to the loss of rental value occasioned by the invasion. This distinction between the elements of damage leads to the rule that the owner of land who is not an occupant may recover only for the impaired value of his property, while an occupant-owner may recover both his proprietary and personal loss. Restatement of Torts, § 929, Comment g; Restatement, Second, Torts, § 929, Comment e (Tentative Draft No. 19).

Id. at 4–5, 564 P.2d at 130; *see also* Tracy A. Bateman, Annotation, *Nuisance as Entitling Owner or Occupant of Real Estate to Recover Damages for Personal Inconvenience, Discomfort, Annoyance, Anguish, or Sickness, Distinct from or in Addition to, Damages for Depreciation in Value of Property or its Use*, 25 A.L.R. 5th 568 (1994).

3. Permanent vs. Temporary Trespasses and Nuisances

The distinction between permanent and temporary harm arises in both trespass and nuisance actions. The distinction is relevant to the accrual date for the statute of limitations in actions for damages, and it is also relevant to the measure of compensatory damages, as illustrated by the following case.

COOK v. DeSOTO FUELS, INC.

Missouri Court of Appeals, Eastern District, 2005.
169 S.W.3d 94.

GLENN A. NORTON, JUDGE.

* * *

I. BACKGROUND

DeSoto owned and operated an Amoco gas station located near property owned by Claude and Mary Jeanne Cook. At some point, a leak allegedly developed in at least one of the three underground storage tanks ("USTs") that supplied the station with gasoline, resulting in the contamination of the Cooks' property.

The Cooks had two wells on their property. One well provided water for the Cooks' own residence and the other supplied water to a residence that the Cooks rented out to tenants. One of the Cooks' tenants noticed a strong odor of gasoline and a rainbow sheen in the water and reported this to the Missouri Department of Natural Resources. In July of 1993, the Department tested the well supplying the rental property for contamination. At some point during that year, Claude Cook also noticed that the water had an odor and he became aware that the Department's tests showed the presence of contaminants.

The Department tested the water in both of the wells in December of 1993. The Department's Preliminary Report, issued on March 25, 1994, indicated that the water from both of the Cooks' wells was contaminated with constituents of gasoline. The report identified four nearby gas station sites, including DeSoto's gas station, as possible sources of the pollution. The Department concluded that additional work was needed to determine which of those four sites was the source of the contamination. Also in March of 1994, the Cooks drilled a new well on the property "as a precaution." This new well became contaminated within a month, so the Cooks had their residence connected to the city water supply.

On March 8, 1996, the Department issued its Final Report. It described the existence of contamination and again identified the same four potentially responsible parties, including DeSoto, which by then had ceased operating its gas station. The following year, the Department installed two groundwater monitoring wells in an effort to identify the cause and source of the contamination. In September of 1997, the Department issued an addendum to its Final Report, this time identifying DeSoto's former Amoco station as the sole source of the contamination.

The record does not reveal when the Cooks had actual notice of any of the Department's reports. But in August of 2000, the Cooks entered into a contract to sell their property, and the prospective buyer's investigation revealed an unacceptable level of contamination. After the contract was cancelled, the Cooks hired counsel, who discovered and reviewed the Department's files.

The Cooks filed their petition against DeSoto and two other defendants on March 30, 2001, claiming * * * trespass and private nuisance. * * * The Cooks claimed that the defendants' conduct resulted in the continuing entry, trespass, or intrusion onto their property and that the defendants continued to unreasonably interfere with the Cooks' use and enjoyment of their property by releasing chemicals onto their property.

Amoco, one of the original defendants, moved for summary judgment based on the statute of limitations. DeSoto filed a separate motion, stating that it "affirmatively adopts as its own and joins in" Amoco's motion for summary judgment. While Amoco's motion was pending and before it was noticed for hearing, Amoco was dismissed from the lawsuit and withdrew its motion for summary judgment. Subsequently, DeSoto withdrew its motion for summary judgment, but later filed another motion seeking to "readopt and reassert" Amoco's motion for summary judgment as DeSoto's own, including the arguments and assertions in Amoco's supporting memorandum and exhibits. The Cooks filed a motion to strike DeSoto's motion based on a failure to comply with Rule 74.04, which the trial court denied. The court granted summary judgment in favor of DeSoto based on the five-year statute of limitations in section 516.120 RSMo 2000. The Cooks appeal.

II. DISCUSSION

* * *

B. Statute of Limitations

Whether the statute of limitations bars a lawsuit depends on the nature of the cause of action and when the action accrued. *Schwartz v. Mills*, 685 S.W.2d 956, 958 (Mo.App. E.D.1985). Here, the parties disagree about both. DeSoto argues that the five-year statute of limitations in section 516.120 governs this action and that the Cooks' alleged damages were capable of ascertainment more than five years before the lawsuit was filed. While the Cooks do not challenge whether that five-year period of limitation applies, they do claim that the record is insufficient to prove that the damage to their property was capable of ascertainment more than five years prior to the filing of their petition. They claim that there was no evidence of when the Department's reports were received by the Cooks or made available to the public and that they filed their petition less than five years after the Department released the document identifying DeSoto as the responsible party. Further, the Cooks argue that their claims are separable as to each accrued injury because the contamination of their property constitutes a continuing trespass or a temporary nuisance. DeSoto responds that the facts of this case do not support either a continuing trespass or a temporary nuisance theory because there was only "one leak of gasoline, which has remained in the ground."

We conclude that the Cooks' causes of action initially accrued more than five years before they filed this lawsuit because the damage to their property and its cause were capable of ascertainment more than five years prior to this lawsuit. Nevertheless, DeSoto has not established that the Cooks' claims are totally time-barred because they have asserted claims for a continuing trespass and a temporary nuisance and therefore can recover for those damages that accrued within the statutory period preceding this lawsuit-namely, five years for the trespass claim and ten years for the nuisance claim.

We begin our discussion by noting that, while there are differences between a trespass and a nuisance cause of action, the two are neither mutually exclusive nor inconsistent. Restatement (Second) of Torts section 821D cmt. e (1979). Thus, where the elements of both actions are fully present, plaintiffs may choose to proceed upon one or both theories. *Id.* While trespass involves interference with the plaintiffs' possessory rights and requires an intentional act that results in a physical invasion of the plaintiffs' property, nuisance involves an unreasonable land use that interferes with the plaintiffs' right of enjoyment and does not require an intentional act. See *Frank v. Environmental Sanitation Management, Inc.,* 687 S.W.2d 876, 879–80 (Mo. banc 1985); *Looney v. Hindman,* 649 S.W.2d 207, 212–14 (Mo. banc 1983); *Thomas v. City of Kansas City,* 92 S.W.3d 92, 97–98 (Mo.App. W.D.2002); *Maryland Heights Leasing, Inc. v. Mallinckrodt, Inc.,* 706 S.W.2d 218, 221, 224–26 (Mo.App. E.D.1985). A nuisance can be based on the defendant's negligence or on the existence of a "continuing known invasion" that the defendant failed to remedy despite the plaintiffs' complaints. *Frank,* 687 S.W.2d at 881–82. Certain types of physical invasions can constitute both a trespass and a nuisance. *See Maryland Heights,* 706 S.W.2d at 221, 224–26 (use of radioactive materials resulting in emission of radiation can constitute both trespass and nuisance); *Rosenfeld v. Thoele,* 28 S.W.3d 446, 449–50 (Mo.App. E.D.2000) (placement of debris on neighbor's property can constitute both trespass and nuisance). The Cooks' allegations that DeSoto caused gasoline to enter their property can constitute a claim for both trespass and nuisance because that contamination involves a direct physical invasion that interferes with both the right to possession and the use and enjoyment of property. We now consider whether these claims are time-barred.

1. *Trespass*

The Cooks' trespass claim is governed by the five-year statute of limitations in section 516.120. * * * This type of action does not accrue "when the wrong is done," but rather "when the damage resulting therefrom is sustained and is capable of ascertainment, and, if more than one item of damage, then the last item, so that all resulting damage may be recovered, and full and complete relief obtained." Section 516.100. "In common parlance, 'capable of ascertainment' may be construed to mean capable of being ascertained by a reasonable person using reasonable diligence." *Lockett v. Owens–Corning Fiberglas,* 808 S.W.2d 902, 907

(Mo.App. E.D.1991)Whether damages are capable of ascertainment is an objective test, ordinarily decided as a matter of law. *Carr v. Anding,* 793 S.W.2d 148, 150 (Mo.App. E.D.1990). It is met when the plaintiffs' right to sue arises and they could have first maintained the action successfully. *Id.* This occurs when the damage is substantially complete and the fact of damage can be discovered or made known, even if the exact amount of damage is not yet ascertainable, even if some additional damage may occur in the future and even if the plaintiffs have not actually discovered the injury. *See Lockett,* 808 S.W.2d at 907; *Modern Tractor and Supply Co. v. Leo Journagan Construction Co., Inc.,* 863 S.W.2d 949, 952 (Mo.App. S.D.1993); *Jordan v. Willens,* 937 S.W.2d 291, 294 (Mo.App. W.D.1996). It has been said that knowledge of a trespass is sufficient to begin the running of the statute of limitations. *Jordan,* 937 S.W.2d at 295 n. 6.

Here, the Cooks had actual knowledge of the fact that their property had been damaged by April of 1994 when their new well became contaminated, if not sooner. But, when viewing the record in a light most favorable to the plaintiffs, it appears that the plaintiffs were not kept informed about the status of the Department's investigations and were not immediately made aware that the Department's reports identified DeSoto as one of four parties potentially responsible for causing the contamination. Although it is not clear from the record when the plaintiffs had actual notice of those reports, actual notice is not required under the "capable of ascertainment" test.

We find that the Cooks were capable of ascertaining DeSoto's identity as one of four possible tortfeasors by early March in 1996, if not sooner, since by then the Department had finished its second report suggesting that DeSoto may be the source of the contamination, and almost two years had elapsed since the Cooks began using the municipal water supply instead of their own well. Even if the Department failed to keep the Cooks informed about who might have been responsible for the contamination, a reasonable person would have inquired about the status of the investigation by that time.

We note that there is some authority for the proposition that a cause of action does not accrue until both the damages and the cause of those damages are reasonably ascertainable. *See, e.g., Elmore v. Owens–Illinois, Inc.,* 673 S.W.2d 434, 436 (Mo. banc 1984); *Shade v. Missouri Highway and Transportation Commission,* 69 S.W.3d 503, 514 (Mo.App. W.D.2001); *but see, e.g., King v. Nashua Corp.,* 763 F.2d 332, 333 (8th Cir.1985) (stating that "Missouri courts have made it clear that [section 516.100] focuses on the damage and not the discovery of its cause"). But even if an action does not accrue until the cause of the damage is capable of ascertainment, in this case the Cooks certainly should have known about both the damage (groundwater contamination) and its cause (gasoline from nearby USTs) more than five years prior to this lawsuit.

The Cooks suggest that the action did not accrue until after the Department released its addendum in 1997 that identified DeSoto as the sole source of the contamination. We disagree. While neither party cites any case where the plaintiffs knew what caused their injuries but were temporarily unable to ascertain precisely who was responsible for the damage, at least one Missouri case has rejected the argument that the plaintiff's inability to discover the identity of the tort-feasor should delay the accrual of the cause of action. *See Frazee v. Partney,* 314 S.W.2d 915, 916–17, 920–21 (Mo.1958) (wrongful death action resulting from an automobile accident where the defendant, who caused the accident but then drove away, was not identified within the limitations period). Given the small number of reasonably ascertainable potentially responsible parties identified by the Department in this case, we find that the accrual of this action should not be delayed by the Cooks' failure or inability to ascertain precisely which of the four potentially responsible parties actually caused their damages.

Therefore, with respect to the initial invasion of contaminants, the Cooks' cause of action accrued before March 30, 1996, more than five years before this lawsuit was filed. Thus, unless the Cooks have also alleged a continuing trespass, their trespass claim would be totally barred by the statute of limitations.

2. *Continuing Trespass*

In the "peculiar and particular circumstances" where a "continuing or repeated wrong" is involved, an additional layer of analysis is required to determine when the cause of action accrued with respect to each successive trespass under section 516.100:

> if the wrong done is of such a character that it may be said that all of the damages, past and future, are capable of ascertainment in a single action so that the entire damage accrues in the first instance, [then] the statute of limitation begins to run from that time. If, on the other hand, the wrong may be said to continue from day to day, and to create a fresh injury from day to day, and the wrong is capable of being terminated, [then] a right of action exists for the damages suffered within the statutory period immediately preceding suit.

Davis v. Laclede Gas Co., 603 S.W.2d 554, 556 (Mo. banc 1980) (construing section 516.100 RSMo 1969). In order for this analysis to apply, "the wrong must be continuing or repeating." *D'Arcy and Associates, Inc. v. K.P.M.G. Peat Marwick, L.L.P.,* 129 S.W.3d 25, 30 (Mo.App. W.D.2004). As this Court has stated, when there is only one wrong that results in continuing damage, the cause of action accrues once that wrong has been committed and the resulting damage becomes capable of ascertainment. *Arst v. Max Barken, Inc.,* 655 S.W.2d 845, 847 (Mo.App. E.D.1983). But when there are continuing or repeated wrongs that are capable of being terminated, successive causes of action accrue every day the wrong continues or each time it gets repeated, the end result being that the plaintiff is only barred from recovering those damages that were ascertainable prior to the statutory period immediately preceding the lawsuit. *See Davis,* 603 S.W.2d at 556; *Cacioppo v. Southwestern Bell Telephone Co.,* 550 S.W.2d

919, 925 (Mo.App.1977). The continuing wrong doctrine has been applied in both nuisance and trespass cases. * * *

In this case, the Cooks have alleged that DeSoto's negligence has caused an underground flow or migration of contaminants onto their property. But DeSoto's negligence is not the relevant wrong for purposes of analyzing whether the Cooks have alleged a continuing trespass. Rather, the wrong is the actual physical invasion of the Cooks' property. Thus, the relevant question is whether the Cooks have alleged a continuous or repeated invasion of their property. The Cooks claim that DeSoto's conduct resulted in the "continuing entry, trespass, and intrusion onto Plaintiffs' property by the petroleum products from the Station without Plaintiffs' permission." The petition also refers to "the releases" in the plural form. Although the petition is not very specific, we find that the Cooks have adequately alleged the existence of a continuous, ongoing, intermittent, or repeated flow or migration of contaminants from DeSoto's property onto their property. In this way, the Cooks have alleged the type of "fresh injury from day to day" described in *Davis*. *See* 603 S.W.2d at 556. They seek damages for the cleanup and restoration of their property, and there is nothing in the record to suggest that this is the type of wrong that is not capable of being terminated.

In its brief, DeSoto asserts that this case involves only a single leak of gasoline. We agree that the existence of a single leak or migration of contaminants would not constitute a continuing wrong, even if the contaminants remained present in the ground. * * * The mere presence of contaminants does not reveal whether there was one wrong resulting in continuing damage, or whether there were continuous or repeated wrongs that created fresh injuries from day to day and were capable of being terminated. *See Davis*, 603 S.W.2d at 556. But as explained above, the Cooks have alleged the existence of a continuous or repeated migration of contaminants onto their property. And we find nothing in DeSoto's motion for summary judgment or elsewhere in the record that supports its factual assertion about the nature of the leak.

Therefore, the Cooks have adequately presented a continuing trespass claim, which, if proven, would permit them to recover for those damages that accrued within the five-year period preceding this lawsuit. But under their trespass theory, they are barred from recovering any damages that were capable of ascertainment more than five years before the lawsuit; that is, before March 30, 1996.

3. *Temporary Nuisance*

The parties disagree about how to characterize the Cooks' nuisance claim. A nuisance can be either permanent or temporary. * * * This distinction has important consequences, yet determining "[w]hether a particular nuisance is 'permanent' or 'temporary, continuing or abatable' is one of the most baffling areas of the law." *Spain v. City of Cape Girardeau*, 484 S.W.2d 498, 503–504 (Mo.App.1972). A nuisance is temporary if it is abatable; it is permanent if abatement is impracticable or impossible. * * * It need not be shown that the entire nuisance can be eliminated in order for the nuisance to be characterized as temporary; rather, it is only necessary that the nuisance can be reduced or lessened to the point that it no longer constitutes a "substantial" interference. * * *

In determining whether a nuisance is permanent or temporary, the character of the source of the injury—not the character of the injury itself—is determinative. * * * The fact that an injury stems from a permanent structure, however, does not necessarily mean that the resulting nuisance is a permanent one. If the source of the injury is a permanent construction that is necessarily injurious as installed, such that the inherent character of the structure will cause injury even in its usual and lawful operation, then the nuisance is characterized as permanent. * * * But if the source of the injury is a structure that is not inherently injurious but only becomes harmful through its use—such as, through negligence or failure to maintain the structure—then the nuisance is characterized as temporary. * * *

Nuisance claims involving environmental contamination have sometimes been characterized as permanent and other times as temporary. *See, e.g., Frank,* 687 S.W.2d at 883 (finding that an award of permanent damages was appropriate where leachate had escaped from defendant's landfill and caused permanent damage to the plaintiff's property despite expensive and sophisticated leachate control plans); *but see, e.g., Hanes,* 58 S.W.3d at 3–4 (finding that odors and contamination from the defendant's hog farms constituted a temporary and abatable nuisance); *Shelley,* 37 S.W.2d at 520 (leak in oil pipeline caused by the defendant's negligence was deemed a temporary nuisance). Although the cases distinguishing between temporary and permanent nuisances are not always consistent, there appears to be at least one constant: "a nuisance created by negligence is a temporary one." *Spain,* 484 S.W.2d at 504. And where the nature of the cause of action is doubtful as between a temporary or permanent nuisance, courts should treat it as temporary. *Thomas,* 92 S.W.3d. at 101; *Schwartz,* 685 S.W.2d at 958.

The effect of characterizing a nuisance as permanent is to "give the defendant, because of his wrongful act, the right to continue the wrong; a right equivalent to an easement." *Schwartz,* 685 S.W.2d at 958. But if a nuisance is characterized as temporary, then the defendant is under the legal obligation to terminate the injury. *Rebel,* 602 S.W.2d at 792–93 * * *. For each type of nuisance, different types of damages are recoverable, and the relevant statute of limitations is applied differently. For a permanent nuisance, there can be only one recovery for what is deemed to be a single tortious act, and the limitations period begins immediately upon the creation of the nuisance—such as when the structure is completed or installed—or once the tortious effect manifests itself. *See Schwartz,* 685 S.W.2d at 959 (citing *Rebel,* 602 S.W.2d at 792). But for a temporary nuisance, much like a continuing trespass, the continuance of the nuisance each day is considered a repetition of the original wrong, and successive actions accrue as to each injury:

> The period of limitations as to a temporary nuisance[ ] runs anew from the accrual of injury from every successive invasion of interest. The recovery is for the damage actually sustained to the commencement of suit, but not for prospective injury. . . . The right to a successive action for the continuance of a nuisance rests on the principle that the tort-feasor . . . is under [a] legal obligation to remove, change, or repair the structure or thing complained of, and thereby terminate the injury to his neighbor; and, failing so to do, each day's continuance of the nuisance is a repetition of the original wrong, and a new action will lie therefor. *Rebel,* 602 S.W.2d at 792–93 (quotation marks omitted). And, again similar to a continuing trespass theory, the plaintiffs' recovery for a temporary nuisance is limited to those damages that accrued within the relevant limitations period immediately preceding the lawsuit.

Claims of permanent nuisance are governed by the five-year statute of limitations in section 516.120. * * * Although the parties have failed to address whether this statute also applies to claims of temporary nuisance, Missouri courts have repeatedly held—often citing section 516.010—that a ten-year period of limitation applies to temporary nuisances.[6] *Moore v. Weeks,* 85 S.W.3d 709, 719 (Mo.App. W.D.2002); *Thomas,* 92 S.W.3d. at 100; *Shade,* 69 S.W.3d at 509–10; *Campbell v. Anderson,* 866 S.W.2d 139, 142 (Mo.App. W.D.1993); *Rebel,* 602 S.W.2d at 794 n. 7; *City of Fredericktown v. Osborn,* 429 S.W.2d 17, 24 (Mo.App.1968). * * * We find that the ten-year limitations period applies.

Here, the Cooks have alleged that DeSoto continues to unreasonably interfere with their use and enjoyment of their property by "releasing" chemicals onto it. They claim that the source of their injury is one or more of DeSoto's leaking USTs and that DeSoto knew or should have known about the releases. These allegations could constitute a nuisance resulting from either negligence or a continuing known invasion. *See Frank,* 687 S.W.2d at 881–82. Instead of alleging that an underground gasoline storage tank inherently causes injury to nearby property in the course of its usual and lawful operation, the Cooks assert that the leaking USTs that caused the contamination have become injurious because of DeSoto's negligence in operating its gas station. *See, e.g., Shelley,* 37 S.W.2d at 520 (leak in oil pipeline caused by the defendant's negligence was deemed a temporary nuisance). Therefore, the Cooks have adequately presented a temporary nuisance claim. *See Spain,* 484 S.W.2d at 504 ("a nuisance created by negligence is a temporary one"). If proven, they are allowed to recover those damages that accrued within the ten-year period preceding

---

6. Under section 516.010, "[n]o action for the recovery of any lands, tenements or hereditaments, or for the recovery of the possession thereof, shall be commenced, had or maintained by any person . . . unless it appear that the plaintiff, his ancestor, predecessor, grantor or other person under whom he claims was seized or possessed of the premises in question, within ten years before the commencement of such action."

this lawsuit, that is, since March 30, 1991, which appears to encompass all of their damages from the nuisance. * * *

C.   Summary and Disposition

In sum, DeSoto has failed to establish the facts necessary to support its affirmative defense that the Cooks' claims are barred by the statute of limitations. Therefore, summary judgment was inappropriate. * * * The Cooks may proceed with their claims to the following extent. Under the trespass count, the Cooks can no longer recover for damages resulting from the initial invasion of contaminants, but they are entitled to seek damages arising from any continued migration or seepage of contaminants onto their property within the five-year period preceding this lawsuit. Under the temporary nuisance count, the Cooks are entitled to seek damages arising from the continued unreasonable interference with their enjoyment of the property within the ten-year period preceding this lawsuit. We express no opinion as to whether the damages recoverable under these two counts are the same.

III.   CONCLUSION

The judgment is reversed, and the case is remanded for further proceedings consistent with this opinion.

CLIFFORD H. AHRENS, P.J. and NANNETTE A. BAKER, J. CONCURRING.

NOTE

On the topic of the statute of limitations, consider Dolph v. Mangus, 400 N.E.2d 189 (Ind.Ct.App.1980), in which the defendants had altered the natural flow of surface waters, causing flooding and erosion of plaintiff's crop land, since 1948:

> The [trial] court found that these actions constituted a trespass but that plaintiffs' complaint, which was not filed until July 24, 1974, was barred by the statute of limitations.

> The plaintiffs acknowledge that the six (6) year statute of limitations found in IC 34–1–2–1 applies to the claim before us. It is the plaintiffs' position on appeal, however, that while the statute would bar a "permanent" injury created in 1948, the injuries complained of were of the type referred to as "temporary" or "recurring." Thus, they argue that recovery should have been permitted for the damages incurred up to six years prior to commencement of the action. The defendants respond that in reality the court found the existence of a prescriptive easement since more than twenty (20) years had elapsed since the origin of the injury.

> We do not accept defendants' assertion that the court found a prescriptive easement. The essential difference between prescription and the operation of a statute of limitations is that the former is positive and creates rights while limitation is negative and destroys. To establish an easement by prescription the burden is upon the party asserting the easement to show actual, open, notorious, continuous, uninterrupted,

adverse use. Here the court repeatedly stated that it found plaintiffs' claim *barred* by the statute of limitations. Moreover, neither the defendants' answer nor the evidence adduced at trial were directed to prescription. Rather they merely asserted the claims were barred by the statute of limitations.

As the plaintiffs have pointed out, many jurisdictions dealing with this type of problem have drawn a distinction between injuries termed "original" or "permanent" on the one hand and those referred to as "temporary," "transient," "continuing" or "recurring" on the other. In the former category the courts have held that a plaintiff has but one claim for relief in which he may recover for all damages, past, present and prospective. In the latter category each new injury is treated as a new claim for relief and recovery is limited to that specific injury.

Thus, if the claim is of the permanent variety, the action must be commenced within the statutory period or it is barred. On the other hand, if the injury is of the temporary variety, each new injury starts the limitations statute running anew with the effect that at any given time the plaintiff can recover the actual damage incurred for the various temporary injuries which have occurred within the statutory period preceding the filing of the complaint.

We also agree that Indiana subscribes to this "dual rule" distinction. * * *

The problem that arises in any given case, of course, is to determine into which category the injury properly falls. The annotation in 5 A.L.R. 2d 302 collects the cases from the various jurisdictions and attempts to identify various factors the courts have deemed significant in particular cases involving waters overflowing the lands of another.[2] What is readily apparent is that no particular factor is controlling and that even within a single jurisdiction the cases are often irreconcilable. * * *

One additional observation may be made. Apart from its involvement with the statute of limitations, the underlying purpose in these distinctions is an effort to accurately assess the damages the plaintiff has suffered. Is the injury such that he should recover only for the damage experienced from a particular occurrence, or are the consequences sufficiently certain that a broader recovery should be permitted and required? In response to this concern it is reasonable that the courts have recognized that injuries of the "recurring" variety when continued over a protracted period of time may, through the regularity of their recurrence and the nature of the damage caused, become "permanent." In such cases, the statute of limitations should commence to run upon the permanent injury when its permanence is discernable. *See* City of Stillwater v. Robertson (1943), 192 Okl. 395, 136 P.2d 923 and cases cited in 5

---

2. These include (1) whether the structure causing the injury is necessarily injurious; (2) the extent to which the injurious result is certain and predictable; (3) whether the overflows are intermittent and caused only in conjunction with a supervening cause; (4) whether the structure causing the injury is permanent; (5) whether the structure was lawfully erected on property other than the plaintiff's; (6) whether the structure was negligently and improperly constructed, maintained or operated; (7) whether a nuisance created is abatable; (8) which theory the plaintiff used in bringing his action.

A.L.R.2d 320 n.12. *Compare* Hayes v. St. Louis & S.F.R. Co. (1913), 177 Mo.App. 201, 162 S.W. 266.

* * *

While the flooding of plaintiffs' cropland might be considered a recurring type of injury, the complaint appears to have alleged permanent injury. The evidence favoring the decision supports the determination that in the more than twenty-five years which occurred between the installation of the defendants' tile system and the bringing of the action the damages had become permanent. Plaintiff Robert Dolph described the overflow as continuous. There was evidence concerning the gullies that had quickly washed into the area in question. In addition much of plaintiffs' damage evidence described permanent damage and depreciated the value of 51 acres of plaintiffs' land by 50% as a result thereof.

Accordingly, we find that the evidence supports the conclusion that the injuries to plaintiffs' land had become permanent more than six years prior to commencement of the action and the court therefore correctly concluded the claim was barred by the statute of limitations.

Id. at 190–92.

DAN B. DOBBS, HANDBOOK ON THE LAW OF REMEDIES

335, 343–44 (1973).*

§ 5.4   The Permanent Nuisance and Prospective Damages

Repeated, Continuing and Permanent Invasions

In a number of cases courts have drawn a distinction between *damages* that are permanent and those that are temporary, allowing recovery of diminished market value where the injury was permanent and allowing cost of repairs where it was temporary or repairable at reasonable cost. In other situations courts have drawn a confusingly similar, but actually quite different distinction. This is the distinction between permanent *sources* of damages, such as nuisances or trespasses that cannot or will not be abated, and temporary sources of damage, such as nuisances or trespasses that will naturally terminate or those that will be terminated by court order. Courts sometimes overlook the distinction with resulting confusion. * * *

Permanent Invasions and the Statute of Limitations

Courts classify invasions as "permanent" for two purposes: one purpose is related to assessment of damages, and a distinct purpose is application of the statute of limitations. There is not much doubt that the classification as permanent is much influenced by the purpose for which the classification is made, so that what is permanent for damages purposes is not necessarily permanent for statute of limitations purposes. Put more

---

* Reprinted with permission of West Publishing Co.

bluntly, the classification as "permanent" is not a finding of fact nor a logical deduction; it is only a short-hand way of saying that certain policy decisions have been made.

In theory, if a nuisance is deemed permanent, there is only one unceasing invasion of the plaintiff's interests and only one cause of action. This necessarily arises when the invasion first began or was first manifest. The statute of limitations on the one cause of action must, then, begin running from the time the invasion began, or from the time it became manifest. In contrast, if the nuisance or trespass is "temporary," or "continuous," a new cause of action arises day by day or injury by injury, with the result that the plaintiff in such a case can always recover for such damages as have accrued within the statutory period immediately prior to suit. There is a hybrid situation in which a permanent nuisance or trespass is created, so that the statute of limitations begins to run from its inception, but in which the defendant later substantially increases the damaging character of the invasion, either by a new permanent nuisance or by a series of new damage-causing acts that are not permanent. In such cases, the statute begins to run from the inception of the original invasion, but a new cause of action or series of actions may be created with their own statutes of limitations when the substantial new damage appears. In deciding statute of limitations questions in these cases, courts are not always influenced by the same considerations involved in deciding the measure of damages, even though the word "permanent" may be used to explain conclusions in both kinds of cases. For instance, there is an Illinois decision in which a city raised a street grade, blocking access to the plaintiff's alley by vehicles. This could have been remedied by building a ramp, apparently at relatively small cost. Had the plaintiff brought an action within weeks or months after the grade was raised, * * * the nuisance would be called a temporary one and cost of repair rather than diminution in property value would be the measure of damages. However, in the actual case the plaintiff waited over 15 years to bring his action. The question before the court was not the measure of damages, but whether a five year statute of limitation had run, and the court, not surprisingly, held that it had and that the plaintiff was barred. It expressed this conclusion in part by treating the nuisance as "permanent." This might not be a very good solution if the issue were damages, but it was a very good solution indeed on the statute of limitations issue.

NOTE

If anything, the "permanent-temporary" distinction has created more difficulty in applying the statute of limitations in nuisance cases than in the trespass context. Consider, in this regard, the discussion of the distinction in Capogeannis v. Superior Court, 12 Cal.App. 4th 668, 15 Cal.Rptr.2d 796 (1993):

If a nuisance is *permanent,* then in the ordinary case the plaintiff must "bring one action for all past, present and future damage within

three years after the permanent nuisance is erected. [Citations.] ...
Damages are not dependent upon any subsequent use of the property but
are complete when the nuisance comes into existence. [Citation.]" (Baker
v. Burbank–Glendale–Pasadena Airport Authority (1985) 39 Cal.3d 862,
869, 218 Cal.Rptr. 293, 705 P.2d 866.) If, on the other hand, the nuisance
is *continuing*, then "[e]very repetition of [the] continuing nuisance is a
separate wrong," subject to a new and separate limitation period, "for
which the person injured may bring successive actions for damages until
the nuisance is abated, even though an action based on the original wrong
may be barred" (Phillips v. City of Pasadena (1945) 27 Cal.2d 104, 107–
108, 162 P.2d 625), but "[r]ecovery is limited * * * to actual injury
suffered [within the three years] prior to commencement of each action"
(Baker v. Burbank–Glendale–Pasadena Airport Authority, *supra*, 39
Cal.3d at p. 869, 218 Cal.Rptr. 293, 705 P.2d 866; *cf.* Mangini v. Aerojet–
General Corp., *supra*, 230 Cal.App.3d 1125, 1148, 281 Cal.Rptr. 827) and
"[p]rospective damages are unavailable." (Baker v. Burbank–Glendale–
Pasadena Airport Authority, *supra*, 39 Cal.3d at p. 869, 218 Cal.Rptr. 293,
705 P.2d 866.)

* * *

The great weight of California authority has articulated the basic
distinction between permanent and continuing nuisances in broad terms
of whether the nuisance can be discontinued, or abated, "at any time":
"[I]f the nuisance may be discontinued at any time it is considered
continuing in character." (Phillips v. City of Pasadena, *supra*, 27 Cal.2d
104, 107–108, 162 P.2d 625.) * * *

It should be apparent, however, that the discontinued-or-abated
rubric cannot be mechanically applied. It may be assumed that if it can
reasonably be foreseen that a nuisance *cannot* in any event be abated, the
nuisance must be regarded as permanent. But it would be a rare case in
which an alleged nuisance could *not* be abated were countervailing
considerations (such as expense, time, and legitimate competing interests)
disregarded.

Id. at 675–78, 15 Cal.Rptr.2d at 800–01.

What then should be the abatability standard for statute of limitations
purposes? Suppose, for example, defendant has caused hazardous waste contamination of plaintiff's land. According to the California Supreme Court, a
nuisance is "abatable" if it "can be remedied at a reasonable cost by
reasonable means." Mangini v. Aerojet–General Corp., 12 Cal.4th 1087, 912
P.2d 1220, 51 Cal.Rptr.2d 272 (1996) (lack of evidence that hazardous waste
contamination was "abatable" at reasonable cost barred nuisance action after
the expiration of three-year statute of limitations applicable to permanent
nuisance).

B. SPECIFIC RELIEF

1. Trespass

a. *Ejectment*

Ejectment is a legal remedy that affords a plaintiff specific relief after there has been a trial on the merits, as illustrated by the next cases. Ejectment is to be distinguished from the injunction, which is an equitable form of specific relief that is available both prior to a trial on the merits and at the end of a trial on the merits.

HEROUX v. KATT

Supreme Court of Rhode Island, 1949.
76 R.I. 122, 68 A.2d 25.

FLYNN, CHIEF JUSTICE.

This action in trespass and ejectment was brought by a lessee for years to obtain possession of a portion of the demised premises alleged to be occupied by the defendants and wrongfully detained by them from the plaintiff. In the superior court, at the conclusion of the evidence for the plaintiff, the defendants rested their case and each party then moved for a directed verdict. The trial justice granted the plaintiff's motion and denied that of the defendants. * * *

The following undisputed facts appear in the evidence. The land described in the writ and declaration is located at the corner of Broad and Babcock streets in the city of Providence and is owned in fee simple by George A. and Elizabeth Follett. By a lease in writing, said premises were demised by these owners to the plaintiff Joseph F. Heroux for a period of five years from April 27, 1948, the lease also containing a privilege of renewal for an additional period of five years on the same terms and conditions.

At the time this lease was executed the defendants were the owners of land adjoining the demised premises and were the occupants of a building located in part upon their own land and in part upon the land leased by the plaintiff. The portion of the building thus upon the leased land measures approximately 22.50 feet long by 20.05 feet wide.

The defendants were aware that such part of this building was located upon land that did not belong to them. Indeed, they had deliberately erected the building knowing that it encroached upon the land belonging to the Folletts. However, neither of the Folletts nor the plaintiff was aware at any time prior to entering into the lease that such building encroached upon the demised premises. Only after plaintiff had a survey of the premises made did it become known to him and the owners of the land that a portion of the defendants' building approximating 451 square feet in area was wrongfully located and maintained upon a part of the leased premises.

When the defendants refused to deliver possession of the land to the plaintiff the instant action was commenced in the district court by a writ of trespass and ejectment. * * *

* * * [The defendants] make several contentions which may be briefly summarized as follows. (1) Trespass and ejectment is not a proper action to remove encroachment by a building owned and occupied by defendants on the "locus in quo" because the only proper action was in equity to enjoin the continuing trespass or nuisance and because an execution to the sheriff would be ineffective to deliver possession in an action at law. (2) The plaintiff is not a proper party to bring trespass and ejectment because the ejector at the commencement of the action must possess the fee to the reversionary interest of the locus in quo. * * *

* * * In support of their first contention that the plaintiff was restricted to a suit in equity to enjoin them from a continuing trespass and that only a court of equity had jurisdiction to give relief in the circumstances of record the defendants have cited several cases from other jurisdictions and rely strongly on the case of Rasch v. Noth, 99 Wis. 285, 74 N.W. 820 [(1898)]. However, most, if not all, such cases relate generally to suits brought in equity where the respondents sought to defeat equity's jurisdiction by contending that there was an adequate remedy at law. The courts therein rightly held that equity jurisdiction can be justified where the remedy at law is found to be inadequate, as for example in a case of a continuing trespass or nuisance. But in our opinion none of those cases hold that equity is the *exclusive* forum where relief can be had in circumstances like those in the instant case. Undoubtedly equity could have taken and justified its jurisdiction and perhaps might have granted more effective and complete relief. Nevertheless it does not follow from that potentiality that the law court must be ousted of its ordinary jurisdiction if the plaintiff elected to pursue his legal remedy in trespass and ejectment. Such an election is a matter for plaintiff's consideration and not one of defense to the action in trespass and ejectment.

* * *

Even where it appears that the ability of a sheriff to deliver possession upon serving an execution is accepted as a test of whether the action of trespass and ejectment may properly be brought, it has been held that ejectment will lie because there is a disseisin measured by the size of the visible and tangible encroachment; and the sheriff can physically remove the structure and thereby restore the owner to possession. Butler v. Frontier Telephone Co., 186 N.Y. 486, 79 N.E. 716 [(1906)]. * * * The defendants' first contention is without merit.

Nor do we agree with his second contention to the effect that only the owner of the fee in reversion may maintain an action of trespass and ejectment against an admitted trespasser who is wrongfully detaining a portion of the premises from the possession of a lessee. * * * As plaintiff points out, a lessee for years in this state has a right to bring trespass and ejectment against such strangers under General Laws 1938, chapter 435, § 10, and G.L.1938, chap. 538, § 12.

* * *

Moreover, this statute seems to carry out the concepts of the old action of ejectment. In Tyler on Ejectment, at page 169, it is stated: "Clearly, a tenant for life, or for years, has the exclusive right of possession of the land, and his title, therefore, enables him to maintain the action of ejectment. * * * Indeed, the very object of the remedy by ejectment in its original conception was to enable one who had a lease for years, to repair the injury done him by dispossession, and enable him to recover his term." To a similar effect, see 2 Taylor's Landlord and Tenant, 9th Ed., 310, § 698; Tiedeman on Real Property, 3d Ed., 165, § 131.[80]

* * * Therefore, whether we consider the instant case under our statute or at common law, we think there is ample authority for a plaintiff lessee for years to bring an action of trespass and ejectment to vindicate his rights of entry and immediate possession against one who wrongfully detains from him possession of a portion of the leased premises.

* * *

The defendants' exceptions are overruled, and the case is remitted to the superior court for entry of judgment for the plaintiff on the verdict as directed.

NOTES

1. It has long been recognized that "[e]jectment is a proper remedy for the removal of an encroachment on the land of another, where a party is legally entitled to possession of the premises, the party has been wrongfully ousted from possession of the land in question, and possession of the realty has been wrongfully detained." Amkco, Ltd. v. Welborn, 127 N.M. 587, 593, 985 P.2d 757, 763 (N.M.Ct.App.1999). Even though ejectment is available in encroachment cases, it may, however, prove to be an inadequate remedy at law because of the impracticability of a sheriff executing a writ of possession. *Id.* As a result, a more commonly used remedy in this setting is a mandatory injunction directing the wrongdoer to remove the encroachment. *See* L.C. Warden, Annotation, *Mandatory Injunctions to Compel Removal of Encroachments by Adjoining Landowner*, 28 A.L.R.2d 679 (1953). The following excerpt from a Report by the New York Law Revision Commission, which recommends that a plaintiff should be able to enjoin an encroachment, explains why this is the case:

> In most American jurisdictions it is recognized that a mandatory injunction is a proper remedy to compel the removal of encroaching structures. This is an exception to the general rule that equity will not grant possession by injunction, made necessary by the insufficiency of the

---

80. For a fuller discussion of the historical development of ejectment, see Soffer v. Beech, 487 Pa. 255, 409 A.2d 337 (1979) (lessee who has not entered into possession may bring ejectment action against lessor and lessees in possession under allegedly expired lease).

legal remedy of ejectment. In ejectment actions the sheriff will usually return an execution unsatisfied and refuse to deliver possession by taking down the encroaching structure, because it would subject him to an unreasonable risk to do so. *Cf.* Baron v. Korn, 127 N.Y. 224, 228, 27 N.E. 804, 1891; Blake v. McCarthy, 115 N.Y.S. 1014, Sup.1909. In most states, therefore, the landowner has been held entitled to the remedy of injunction, which will place the risk and the cost of the removal of the encroachment on the shoulders of the wrongdoer. * * *

The long established rule permitting equitable relief was brought into question when the Court of Appeals, in City of Syracuse v. Hogan, 234 N.Y. 457, 138 N.E. 406, 1923, held that an action for an injunction against an encroachment was in essence an action to recover real property and therefore section 425 of the Civil Practice Act, requiring a jury trial, was applicable. In Johnson v. Purpura, 208 App.Div. 505, 203 N.Y.S. 581, 1924, this decision was held to preclude the granting of an injunction for the removal of encroaching structures. Consequently, a landowner is now without any effective remedy in such a case.

The Commission believes that the equitable remedy by injunction should not be withheld, for the reasons stated by Cardozo, in his dissenting opinion in Syracuse v. Hogan, *supra*:

> This is not an action of ejectment. It is an action in equity to enjoin the obstruction of a highway. Ejectment furnishes some remedy, but not one complete and adequate. In an action at law, execution must direct the sheriff to deliver the possession of the property to the party thereto entitled. "The sheriff might not regard it as his duty to deliver possession by taking down the wall, which would burden him with the risk of injury to other portions of defendant's buildings" (Baron v. Korn, 127 N.Y. 224, 228, 27 N.E. 804.). Even if he stood ready to assume the risk, he would expect the plaintiff to assume the cost. "In equity, the obligation to remove can be placed directly on the party who caused the wall to be erected" (Baron v. Korn, *supra*). An owner is entitled to the remedy that will place the risk and the cost upon the shoulders of the wrongdoer.

> Equitable remedies being necessary for the attainment of complete relief, there is no rule that a court of equity must wait until the suitor's title to the land has been first made out at law. Such a rule there may once have been. It may still prevail in other states. In this state it has long been abandoned * * *. We have left far in the distance the wasteful duplication of remedies and trials. We shall set the clock back many years if we return to it today.

The Commission further believes that the remedy by injunction should be expressly made available to the owners of any legal estate, so as to afford protection against impairment of the rights of holders of future interests.

The proposed remedy is designed to be supplemental to the action of ejectment, not to replace it. In its application, the court will still retain all its equitable powers, and in reaching a determination it may consider hardship on one side and a corresponding lack of benefit upon the other.

In a proper case, it may even withhold the injunction in whole or in part and compensate the plaintiff in damages.

Report, New York Law Revision Commission 73–74 (1942).

2. At common law, the plaintiff who obtained possession by means of an ejectment action could bring a second suit for "mesne profits." Under modern procedural rules, the two actions often are joined. Wilkerson v. Gibbs, 405 So.2d 1053 (Fla.Dist.Ct.App.1981). Mesne profits are typically "measured by the [rental] value of the land" during the period held by the defendant. Dan B. Dobbs, Law of Remedies 529 (2d ed. 1993). Although the measure of damages in actions for mesne profits and trespass are usually the same, the statute of limitations for mesne profits may be longer. *E.g.*, Dumas v. Ropp, 98 Idaho 61, 558 P.2d 632 (1977) (three-year statute of limitations for trespass; six-year statute of limitations for mesne profits).

3. An unlawful detainer action is another form of specific legal relief that can be used to protect a possessory interest in real property. It is most often invoked by landlords against tenants who refuse to leave upon the termination of the tenancy. The actions for ejectment and unlawful detainer are compared in Dan B. Dobbs, Handbook on the Law of Remedies 370–71 (1973).*

> [The unlawful detainer] remedy, affording both damages and possession as it does, bears resemblance to ejectment. But there are important differences. Aside from historical differences, the unlawful detainer action differs from ejectment in its summary character—trial, usually in a justice or some other inferior court, is summary at least in the sense that trial and eviction can be had within a few days after service of process. Because the procedure is summary and because the jurisdiction of inferior courts is usually invoked, statutes often provide that the decision in forcible entry or unlawful detainer suits is not binding as to title. Thus if title is in any serious issue, a second and more plenary suit in ejectment or possibly trespass is contemplated. Further than this the forcible entry or unlawful detainer suit is limited to cases in which the plaintiff's right to possession is probably very clear, since summary proceedings would hardly be justified under any other circumstances.

MICELI v. RILEY

New York Supreme Court, Appellate Division, 1981.
79 A.D.2d 165, 436 N.Y.S.2d 72.

MOLLEN, PRESIDING JUDGE.

This appeal presents us with a difficult and troubling issue. Both sides have important interests at stake. Both are entirely blameless and without responsibility for the controversy which has engulfed them and which we are now called upon to resolve. The determination we reach is not a happy one, but we can come to no other in view of the principles of law involved and the virtually unique circumstances surrounding the dispute.

---

* Reprinted with permission of West Publishing Co.

[The plaintiff claimed that she purchased a one-acre parcel of land (Miceli East) from the DeMares as unimproved land in 1951. She recorded her deed on March 31, 1955.]

Those defendants involved in the dispute over Miceli East predicate their claims to the parcel upon a deed from the same DeMares to the Selden Land Corporation. That deed was dated June 7, 1955, and was recorded in the office of the County Clerk on August 8, 1955. In 1969 and 1970, the property purchased by the Selden Land Corporation was improved by the construction of houses and was sold to the individual defendant homeowners. Plaintiff's claim is that the land and houses purchased by five of those defendants, and for which two of the defendant mortgagees hold mortgages, encroach upon Miceli East.

* * * [W]e agree with Trial Term that the plaintiff established her claim [of trespass].

* * *

Although Trial Term found that the plaintiff had established her cause of action, it declined to adhere strictly to section 601 of the Real Property Actions and Proceedings Law and refused to order ejectment and delivery of the property to the plaintiff. Instead, the court chose to invoke its equity powers in order to fashion a remedy which, in its view, would avoid hardship and an unjust result based upon "what can only fairly be called a mistake either of the surveyors or title examiners or both." Accordingly, the court ordered the plaintiff to elect between two options as a method of calculating her damages. She could either sell Miceli East to the defendants at a sum equal to twice the value of any one acre of undeveloped land in the immediate vicinity of the property or she could take possession of Miceli East upon payment to the defendants of the market value of the improvements made thereon together with reimbursement for all realty taxes paid by the defendants on the property for the preceding six years.

Both sides appealed and, following oral argument in this court, decision was withheld as the parties made serious efforts to settle the dispute. * * *

It is clear that Trial Term invoked its equity powers out of concern for the plight of the defendant homeowners. The record shows beyond question that they acted entirely in good faith and under color of title. They invested much in their homes, moved in with their possessions and established a good life for their families as welcome members of the community in which they had chosen to live. The plaintiff, on the other hand, had long shown little interest in the property, allowing it to remain unimproved for over 20 years. Yet it is equally clear that she did everything the law requires of a property owner. She properly recorded her deed in the office of the County Clerk, thereby giving notice to the world that she owned Miceli East, and she consistently paid taxes on the property from the time she acquired it. Moreover, we agree with Trial

Term that plaintiff did not lose any right to the property through adverse possession since the land was not cultivated, improved or enclosed by the defendants prior to 1969 (see [Real Property Actions and Proceedings Law, § 512], RPAPL, subds. 1, 2).

The crucial factor in the case, however, and the one which, in our view, must resolve the dispute, is the finding of the trial court that the plaintiff did not have knowledge of the encroachment upon her property until sometime *after* the construction of the homes. The record contains sufficient evidence to support the court's conclusion in that regard. However, it is that very conclusion that makes the court's resort to its equity powers inappropriate in the case at bar.

An action to recover real property pursuant to section 601 of the Real Property Actions and Proceedings Law, where plaintiff seeks ejectment of the defendant, is an action at law. Nevertheless, it has long been held that a defendant in such an action may raise equitable defenses. (*See, e.g.,* Crary v. Goodman, 12 N.Y. 266.) It appears, however, that in each case in which the court has chosen to fashion an equitable remedy rather than to award the plaintiff unconditional possession of the property, there has been a finding that the plaintiff himself had engaged in some inequitable conduct or had failed to act appropriately when he knew, or should have known, that something was amiss with respect to his property rights. * * *

* * * Hence, the question upon which this case must finally turn is whether equity will compel * * * a property owner—one who has complied with all notice requirements and who is entirely innocent of any inequitable conduct—to reach an accommodation with a trespasser simply because the trespasser himself has acted in good faith and in ignorance of the owner's rights and would suffer substantial loss if forced to surrender his wrongful possession of the land. We hold that a fee owner may not be so compelled for, plainly, were it otherwise, property rights and rights of title would be rendered uncertain.

Regardless, then, of the hardship that may befall the individual homeowner defendants here through no fault of their own, we are constrained to modify the judgment by granting unconditionally to the plaintiff's executrix the right of possession to the property known as Miceli East.

The final question concerns the plaintiff's claim for damages. Since the defendants acted wholly in good faith under color of title and in ignorance of the plaintiff's rights, they are entitled to offset the value of their improvements up to, but not beyond, the amount by which plaintiff has been damaged by the wrongful withholding of her property. (*See* Real Property Actions and Proceedings Law, § 601.) The record here supports Trial Term's finding that the defendants' improvements "are so substantial * * * as to render plaintiff's recovery of money damages impossible." Accordingly, although entitled to delivery of the land, plaintiff may not have money damages.

NOTES

1. Other than the homeowners, which other parties are losers in *Miceli*? What about the mortgage lenders who have mortgages on the defendants' property? What about title insurance companies, if any, who issued title policies on the property?

2. Note that *Miceli* succeeds in using ejectment as the legal equivalent of the neutron bomb—the houses remain, but those in possession must leave. Suppose, instead, that the homeowners had sought to remove the houses from Ms. Miceli's land. Would the court have prevented them from doing so? After all, under the accession principle, once the houses were constructed, they became part of her real estate. Consider how a subsequent decision by the New York Court of Appeals dealt with this question:

> Plaintiff builder constructed a home for defendants Brazauskas on a parcel of land belonging to defendant Kraft due to the Brazauskas' mistaken belief as to the true location of their land. Under these unique circumstances, [the trial court] properly exercised its equity jurisdiction in directing plaintiff, whom it found "blameless," to remove the construction, restore defendant Kraft's land to its preconstruction condition and reimburse him for any damages caused by the removal * * *. Strict application of the doctrine of accession, which would entitle the true landowner to retain the house * * *, would result in a windfall to defendant Kraft and is inappropriate here, where the proposed remedy of removal is feasible, can make the true owner whole * * *, and will avoid a forfeiture for plaintiff builder, who asserted no claim to title or right, but merely performed his contract with defendants Brazauskas.

DeAngelo v. Brazauskas, 86 N.Y.2d 746, 655 N.E.2d 165, 631 N.Y.S.2d 124 (1995).

b.   Injunction

DAN B. DOBBS, HANDBOOK ON THE LAW OF REMEDIES

348 (1973).

Historically, courts have shown some reluctance to enjoin trespasses. At least three separate strands of this reluctance can be identified, though at times they are inseparably woven together. First, there is the adequacy test: a trespass will not be enjoined if there is what is conceived to be an adequate remedy at law. Second, there is, or was, a rule that equity would not try title, and hence if title was in issue, would withhold any injunction until the law courts had decided title. Third, and somewhat less obvious in the decisions, there was a feeling if not a rule that equity should not transfer possession by injunction.

ATTORNEY GENERAL v. DIME SAVINGS
BANK OF NEW YORK

Supreme Judicial Court of Massachusetts, 1992.
413 Mass. 284, 596 N.E.2d 1013.

ABRAMS, JUSTICE.

The Attorney General brought this action for declaratory and injunctive relief against The Dime Savings Bank of New York, FSB (Dime). The dispute arises out of mortgage loans made by Dime in Massachusetts which have resulted in foreclosure. After foreclosing, Dime has brought actions in trespass against foreclosed mortgagors and tenants holding over after notice to quit and has sought and obtained injunctions to eject holdover mortgagors and tenants from the mortgaged properties. The Attorney General seeks a declaration that Dime's practice violates G.L. c. 184, § 18 (1990 ed.). The complaint also asks that we enjoin Dime from pursuing such a course in the future. * * *

1. *Background.* On April 7, 1992, the Attorney General began this action by filing a complaint in the Supreme Judicial Court for Suffolk County. The complaint invokes the court's equitable and supervisory powers under G.L. c. 214, § 1 (1990 ed.), and G.L. c. 211, § 3 (1990 ed.), respectively, as well as G.L. c. 231A (1990 ed.) (declaratory judgment). The case came before a single justice of the county court on a statement of agreed facts. The stipulations of fact concern a number of individual foreclosures and resulting dispossessions. After oral argument, the single justice reserved and reported the matter to this court.

The following is a summary of the statement of agreed facts. In each of the cases on which this controversy is founded, Dime held a mortgage of real property as security for an obligation. In each instance, the mortgagor defaulted on the obligation. After default, Dime recorded memoranda of entry, conducted foreclosure sales, and acquired perfected title to the properties by purchasing them at the foreclosure sales. Dime has neither sought nor accepted payments of rent from the occupants, and the Commonwealth stipulates that Dime has done nothing to create new, postforeclosure tenancies between itself and the occupants.

In each of the cases in question, the property was occupied at the time of foreclosure either by the mortgagor or a tenant of the mortgagor. * * * All such occupants initially entered the respective properties lawfully. In each of the cases in which the holdover occupants were tenants of the mortgagor, the creation of the tenancy postdated the grant of the mortgage.

After Dime foreclosed its mortgages, it sent notices to the occupants demanding immediate possession of the properties. In each case, the occupants refused to relinquish possession on receiving notice to do so. Dime responded by bringing actions for trespass against the occupants in Superior Court. In each of these actions, Dime sought preliminary and permanent injunctions ordering the occupants to vacate the mortgaged premises. In some cases, the prayer for preliminary relief was heard on a "short order[ ] of notice." In no case, however, have fewer than thirty days passed between the issuance of the demand and the commencement of legal proceedings. [The Court then concluded that the Attorney General had statutory authority to bring the action.]

* * *

3. G.L. c. 184, § 18. General Laws c. 184, § 18, provides, in pertinent part, that "[n]o person shall attempt to recover possession of land or tenements in any manner other than through an action brought pursuant to [G.L. c. 239] or such other proceedings authorized by law." Dime argues that a mortgagee's use of a trespass action to recover possession of mortgaged premises is "authorized by law." G.L. c. 184, § 18. Dime further maintains that a court's common law power to enjoin a continuing trespass justifies an injunction ordering holdover mortgagors or their tenants to vacate the premises. Because an action for trespass will not lie in the cases as stated, however, we conclude that the "other proceedings authorized by law" include neither a common law action for trespass nor an injunction based thereon.

It is well settled that "[a]n action of trespass, being a possessory action, cannot be maintained, unless the plaintiff had the actual or constructive possession of the property trespassed upon at the time of the trespass." Emerson v. Thompson, 2 Pick. 473, 484 (1824). * * * Neither party contends that Dime has actual possession of the properties in question. Indeed, the disputed issue in this case is the means by which Dime may gain such possession.

We have not addressed the question whether an owner out of possession has constructive possession sufficient to maintain an action of trespass where actual possession is in another. Courts that have considered the question, however, have concluded that, for the purposes of a trespass action, there can be no constructive possession by an owner of property actually possessed by another. See Frost v. Johnson, 256 Ala. 383, 54 So.2d 897 (1951); More v. Urbano, 151 Conn. 381, 198 A.2d 211 (1964); McCausland v. York, 133 Me. 115, 174 A. 383 (1934); Jaycox v. E.M. Harris Bldg. Co., 754 S.W.2d 931 (Mo.Ct.App.1988); Green v. Pettingill, 47 N.H. 375 (1867); Daniels v. Coleman, 253 S.C. 218, 169 S.E.2d 593 (1969). The "fiction of 'constructive possession' has no application when another is in actual possession." W. Prosser & W. Keeton, Torts § 13, at 77 n.99 (5th ed. 1984).

Dime argues that the label attached to its action is irrelevant. Dime suggests that it might have brought an action for writ of entry under G.L. c. 237, or a common law action in ejectment. The short answer to this argument is that Dime did not bring such actions. The propriety of such other actions therefore is not before us.

Moreover, Dime's argument is self-contradictory. Although it maintains that the trespass label is insignificant, Dime also contends that a court's traditional power to enjoin a continuing trespass justifies the injunctions it has obtained. However, each case cited by Dime for the proposition that a court will enjoin a continuing trespass involves an owner or owners of real property in actual or constructive possession. *See, e.g.,* Fenton v. Quaboag Country Club, Inc., 353 Mass. 534, 233 N.E.2d 216 (1968) (homeowners suffered injuries to person and property from golf balls which were hit from adjacent course); Anntco Corp. v. Shrewsbury Bank & Trust Co., 353 Mass. 250, 230 N.E.2d 795 (1967) (store owner and commercial landlord aggrieved by overburdening of easement for drainage); Chesarone v. Pinewood Builders, Inc., 345 Mass. 236, 186 N.E.2d 712 (1962) (owner of unoccupied land complained of flooding caused by drainage system constructed on neighboring land); Doody v. Spurr, 315 Mass. 129, 51 N.E.2d 981 (1943) (homeowner sought decree enjoining defendant from parking automobile on and driving over homeowner's property); Suburban Land Co. v. Billerica, 314 Mass. 184, 49 N.E.2d 1012 (1943) (land owner and water company complain of town's construction of water pipes across plaintiffs' property without taking by eminent domain); Ferrone v. Rossi, 311 Mass. 591, 42 N.E.2d 564 (1942) (owner of vacant land aggrieved by defendant's construction of wall that encroached on landowner's property); Franchi v. Boulger, 12 Mass.App.Ct. 376, 425 N.E.2d 372 (1981) (trustees of condominium trust object to improperly constructed retaining wall built partially on plaintiffs' property). In all but two of these cases, *Chesarone* and *Ferrone,* the plaintiff was in actual possession of the property in question. In both Chesarone v. Pinewood Builders, Inc., *supra,* and Ferrone v. Rossi, *supra,* the land in question was unoccupied. Thus, none of the cases cited by Dime supports its argument that, in these circumstances, it is entitled to an injunction for continuing trespass.

Dime argues that, even if it could not properly invoke the doctrine of continuing trespass, it could have brought actions in ejectment. Dime contends that it could then invoke the court's general equitable jurisdiction to obtain an injunction. Dime, however, could not get equitable relief at common law.[10] Dime next asks the courts to "fashion a remedy to fit [Dime's] right" to immediate possession of the properties on which it has

---

10. At common law, a bill in equity brought by an owner out of possession to recover possession of his estate would have been dismissed because summary process offers "a plain, adequate, and complete remedy at law." Weiss v. Levy, 166 Mass. 290, 293, 44 N.E. 225 (1896). *See* Glickman v. Kastel, 323 Mass. 148, 150, 80 N.E.2d 469 (1948) ("There is not, and has never been, any equity in the bill requesting an injunction to recover possession of land"), and cases cited. *Accord* Root v. Woolworth, 150 U.S. 401, 410, 14 S.Ct. 136, 138, 37 L.Ed. 1123 (1893) ("It is undoubtedly true that a court of equity will not ordinarily entertain a bill solely for the purpose of establishing the title of a party to real estate, or for the recovery of possession thereof, as these objects can generally be accomplished by an action of ejectment at law," citing Hipp v. Babin, 60 U.S. (19 How.) 271, 15 L.Ed. 633 [(1856)]); Rocky Mountain Fuel Co. v. New Standard Coal Mining Co., 89 F.2d 147 (10th Cir.1937); Perry v. Warnock, 246 Ala. 470, 20 So.2d 867 (1945); Welbrot v. Levenberg, 98 Conn. 217, 118 A. 911 (1922); Slaughter v. Land, 190 Ga. 491, 9 S.E.2d 754 (1940); Kertesz v. Falgiano, 140 W.Va. 469, 84 S.E.2d 744 (1954). "[P]laintiffs in such cases [were required to] resort to the ordinary remedies for the recovery of the possession of land." Glickman v. Kastel, *supra,* 323 Mass. at 150, 80 N.E.2d 469.

foreclosed. There is no need. The Legislature already has fashioned a remedy; it is the summary process statute. *See* Serreze v. YWCA of W. Mass., Inc., 30 Mass.App.Ct. 639, 644, 572 N.E.2d 581 (1991) ("[I]t is not a characteristic feature of summary process law that the landlord who seeks possession is without a speedy remedy").[12] *See also* Weiss v. Levy, 166 Mass. 290, 44 N.E. 225 (1896).

We remand this matter to the Supreme Judicial Court for the county of Suffolk for entry of a declaration that a mortgagee who forecloses on residential property by power of sale may not bring a trespass action against a holdover tenant or mortgagor in actual possession of the foreclosed premises.

NOTES

1. The *Dime Savings Bank* case stands for the proposition that an out-of-possession plaintiff normally may not use an injunction to regain possession of real estate. This is because ejectment or a summary proceeding usually provides an adequate remedy at law. In that sense, it is hardly an extraordinary case. On the other hand, Dime, the lender, clearly had a right to possession after having validly foreclosed on the real estate. Should it really matter which remedy is used to regain possession so long as the defendants receive adequate procedural protection? Does the court's result and reasoning illustrate a rigid adherence to form over substance? Does the intervention by the Massachusetts Attorney General suggest a political dimension to this case?

2. On the other hand, courts routinely grant injunctive relief to in-possession plaintiffs against recurring (continuing) trespasses. Here the theory is that an injunction will prevent a multiplicity of actions at law for damages. For example, in Cobai v. Young, 679 P.2d 121 (Colo.Ct.App.1984), the court issued a permanent injunction prohibiting the defendants from allowing snow to slide from their roof in such a manner as to strike the plaintiff's house:

> Defendants next argue that the trial court improperly granted the Cobais an injunction because a suit at law for damages is an adequate remedy. We disagree. Since defendants' trespass is continuous, the Cobais' only remedy at law would involve a multiplicity of suits for each recurrence of the trespass. As such, the remedy at law is inadequate. And, where further trespasses of the same kind are threatened, an injunction will lie.

* * *

> Citing Cass Company–Contractors v. Colton, 130 Colo. 593, 279 P.2d 415 (1955), defendants contend that the injunction should not stand

---

12. At oral argument, counsel for Dime stated:

"It certainly is true that in 98 percent of the summary process cases that are heard in the District Courts in the Commonwealth of Massachusetts ..., the demandant wins; there's a judgment for possession; there is no appeal; and [the cases] are over within 27.82 days, or whatever it said in that study [submitted by the amici]...."

because it is vague and uncertain. There, our Supreme Court reversed the trial court's injunction because it had ordered the parties to negotiate the blasting methods the defendant could use in its quarry operations so as to prevent damage to the plaintiff's homes. In contrast, the injunction here does not order the parties to negotiate how defendants may use their property; rather it provides that defendants:

> are enjoined and prohibited from allowing snow and related materials to slide or be propelled from their house in such a manner as to strike or otherwise impact upon the Plaintiffs' house with sufficient force to cause damage to the Plaintiffs' house. The solution devised by the Defendants to comply with this injunction shall not unreasonably interfere with the Plaintiffs' ability to remove snow from the roof of their house.

We find the order to be clear and unambiguous.

Id. at 124.

The principle that equity will enjoin recurring (continuing) trespasses is frequently employed by landowners to prevent multiple incursions on their land by defendants who are politically or ideologically motivated. We have already seen this use of injunctive relief in Chapter 2. For another excellent example of the use of injunctions for this purpose, see Franklin v. War Tax Resistors, 1993 WL 818588 (Mass.Super.Ct.1993).

FRANCHER v. FAGELLA

Supreme Court of Virginia, 2007.
274 Va. 549, 650 S.E.2d 519.

Present: HASSELL, C.J., and KEENAN, KOONTZ, KINSER, LEMONS, and AGEE, JJ., and RUSSELL, S.J.

Opinion by SENIOR JUSTICE CHARLES S. RUSSELL.

This is an interlocutory appeal taken * * * from an order denying injunctive relief. The dispositive question is whether an injunction may issue to compel an adjoining landowner to remove a tree, the roots of which intrude into, and cause significant, continuous and increasing structural damage to the plaintiff's property. The appeal requires us to revisit our holding in *Smith v. Holt,* 174 Va. 213, 5 S.E.2d 492 (1939).

FACTS AND PROCEEDINGS

The essential facts are not in dispute. Richard A. Fancher and Joseph B. Fagella are the owners of adjoining townhouses in the Cambridge Court subdivision in Fairfax County. Fagella's property is higher in elevation than Fancher's and a masonry retaining wall running along the property line behind the townhouses supports the grade separation. There is a sunken patio behind Fancher's townhouse, covered by masonry pavers.

Fancher brought this suit against Fagella, alleging that Fagella has on his property a large sweet gum tree that constitutes a noxious nuisance; the tree's invasive root system has damaged and displaced the retaining wall between the parties' properties, displaced the pavers on Fancher's patio, caused blockage of his sewer and water pipes and has impaired the foundation of his house. Fancher also complained that the tree's over-hanging branches grow onto his roof, depositing leaves and other debris onto his roof and rain gutters. He contended that he had attempted self-help, by trying to repair the damage to the retaining wall and the rear foundation of the house, as well as trying to cut back the overhanging branches, but that these steps were ineffectual because of the continuing expansion of the root system and branches. Fancher prayed for an injunction compelling Fagella to remove the tree and its invading root system entirely, and an award of damages to cover the cost of restoring the property to its former condition.

* * *. At the hearing, Fancher testified that the tree's trunk was on Fagella's property, about "two to three feet from the party/common wall." Fancher estimated the tree was about 60 feet high at the present time and two feet in trunk diameter at its base.

Fancher presented the testimony of an arborist who qualified as an expert witness and testified that the sweet gum is native to the area, that it grows to "incredible heights of 120 to 140 feet" at maturity and would eventually reach a trunk diameter of 4 to 6 feet. The arborist testified that the tree was deciduous, dropped "spiky gumballs," had a "heavy pollen load," an "extremely invasive root system" and a "high demand for water." His opinion was that the tree was presently "only at mid-maturity," that it would continue to grow, and that "[n]o amount of concrete would hold the root system back." The root system was, in his opinion, the cause of the damage to the retaining wall and the pavers and "in the same line as those cracks to the wall and the foundation." The arborist stated that the tree was "noxious" because of its location and that the only way to stop the continuing damage being done by the root system was to remove the tree entirely, because the roots, if cut, would grow back.

Fancher also presented the expert testimony of two engineers, who opined that the pressure of the tree's expanding root system was the cause of the structural damage to the retaining wall. At the conclusion of Fancher's case, Fagella moved to strike the prayer for injunctive relief. The court, relying on our decision in *Smith v. Holt,* granted the motion to strike and entered an order denying injunctive relief, retaining for further adjudication Fancher's claim for damages. We awarded Fancher an inter-locutory appeal.

ANALYSIS

A.   Right of action

The issues raised by vegetation encroaching across property lines have frequently confronted courts throughout the country, leading to results that are less than harmonious. The earlier decisions, including our own, were decided in times when the population was far less densely concentrated than at present, and more often engaged in agriculture. More recent cases have been concerned with problems arising in more urban settings. A thorough review and analysis of those cases was recently made by the Supreme Court of Tennessee in *Lane v. W.J. Curry & Sons,* 92 S.W.3d 355, 360–63 (Tenn.2002) * * *.

Suffice it to say that, as the Tennessee court explained in *Lane,* several rules have evolved. (1) The "Massachusetts Rule," holds that a landowner's right to protect his property from the encroaching boughs and roots of a neighbor's tree is limited to self-help, i.e., cutting off the branches and roots at the point they invade his property. That rule was based on *Michalson v. Nutting,* 275 Mass. 232, 175 N.E. 490 (1931), where the court observed that the "common law has recognized that it is wiser to leave the individual to protect himself, if harm results to him from this exercise of another's right to use his property in a reasonable way, than to subject that other to the annoyance, and the public to the burden, of actions at law, which would be likely to be innumerable and, in many instances, purely vexatious." *Id.* at 491. (2) The "Virginia Rule," holds that the intrusion of roots and branches from a neighbor's plantings which were "not noxious in [their] nature" and had caused no "sensible injury" were not actionable at law, the plaintiff being limited to his right of self-help. That rule was based on our holding in *Smith v. Holt,* 174 Va. 213, 5 S.E.2d 492 (1939), where we also said, "when it appears that a sensible injury has been inflicted by the protrusion of roots from a noxious tree or plant onto the land of another, he has, after notice, a right of action at law for the trespass committed." *Id.* at 219, 5 S.E.2d at 495. We affirmed the trial court's order sustaining a demurrer in that case, holding that neither equitable relief nor damages were warranted because the invading roots came from a privet hedge that was not "noxious" in nature and had caused no "sensible injury." *Id.* at 220, 5 S.E.2d at 495. (3) The "Restatement Rule," based on *Restatement (Second) of Torts* §§ 839, 840 (1979), imposes an obligation on a landowner to control vegetation that encroaches upon adjoining land if the vegetation is "artificial," i.e., planted or maintained by a person, but not if the encroaching vegetation is "natural." (4) The "Hawaii Rule," holds that living trees and plants are ordinarily not nuisances, but can become so when they cause actual harm or pose an imminent danger of actual harm to adjoining property. That rule is based upon *Whitesell v. Houlton,* 2 Haw.App. 365, 632 P.2d 1077 (1981), where the court said: "[W]hen overhanging branches or protruding roots actually cause, or there is imminent danger of them causing, [substantial] harm to property other than plant life, in ways other than by casting shade or dropping leaves, flowers, or fruit, the damaged or imminently endangered neighbor may require the owner of the tree to pay for the damages and to cut back the endangering branches or roots and, if such is not done within a reasonable time, the ... neighbor may cause the cut-back to be done at the tree owner's expense." *Id.* at 1079. The Tennessee court, in *Lane,* after considering the merits and weaknesses of the foregoing rules, decided to adopt the Hawaii approach, partially overruling an earlier Tennessee decision that had generally adhered to the "Massachusetts Rule." *Lane,* 92 S.W.3d at 363–64.

The "Massachusetts Rule" has been criticized on the ground that it is unsuited to modern urban and suburban life, although it may still be suited to many rural conditions. The "Restatement Rule" has been criticized on the grounds that it is often impossible to determine whether a plant has originated naturally or has been introduced or nurtured by human activity; further, that rule illogically imposes liability on a landowner who carefully maintains his property and spares one who neglects his land and permits his vegetation to "run wild."

Our "Virginia Rule" is subject to the just criticism that the classification of a plant as "noxious" depends upon the viewpoint of the beholder. "Noxious" has been defined as "Hurtful; offensive; offensive to the smell. The word 'noxious' includes the complex idea both of insalubrity and offensiveness. That which causes or tends to cause injury, especially to health or morals." Black's Law Dictionary 1065 (6th ed.1990). Many would agree that poison ivy meets that definition because of its proclivity to cause personal injury. Some would include kudzu because of its tendency toward rampant growth, smothering other vegetation. Few would include healthy shade trees, although they may cause more damage, and be more expensive to remove, than the others. We conclude that continued reliance on the distinction between plants that are "noxious," and those that are not, imposes an unworkable standard for determining the rights of neighboring landowners.

Accordingly, we now overrule *Smith v. Holt,* insofar as it conditions a right of action upon the "noxious" nature of a plant that sends forth invading roots or branches into a neighbor's property. We find the reasoning of the Tennessee court in *Lane* persuasive, and adopt the Hawaii approach as expressed in that case:

> Accordingly, we hold that encroaching trees and plants are not nuisances merely because they cast shade, drop leaves, flowers, or fruit, or just because they happen to encroach upon adjoining property either above or below the ground. However, encroaching trees and plants may be regarded as a nuisance when they cause actual harm or pose an imminent danger of actual harm to adjoining property. If so, the owner of the tree or plant may be held responsible for harm caused to [adjoining property], and may also be required to cut back the encroaching branches or roots, assuming the encroaching vegetation constitutes a nuisance. We do not, however, alter existing ... law that the adjoining landowner may, at his own expense, cut away the encroaching vegetation to the property line whether or not the encroaching vegetation constitutes a nuisance or is otherwise causing harm or possible harm to the adjoining property. Thus, the law of self-help remains intact....

Lane, 92 S.W.3d at 364. We also overrule *Smith v. Holt* insofar as its language may be read to imply that equitable relief is precluded even when a nuisance is found to exist.

B. Remedy

In a proper application of *stare decisis,* the circuit court followed *Smith v. Holt* in denying injunctive relief in the present case. Because of the rule we now adopt, it becomes necessary to consider the appropriate remedy. The facts pleaded, if proved by Fancher, would constitute a continuing trespass, resulting in actual harm to his property. Under traditional equitable principles, a chancellor may enjoin a continuing trespass, even when each increment of trespass is trivial or the damage is trifling, in order to avoid a multiplicity of actions at law. *Seventeen, Inc. v. Pilot Life Ins. Co.,* 215 Va. 74, 78, 205 S.E.2d 648, 653 (1974). Thus, on remand, the circuit court may properly consider injunctive relief in the present case.

Not every case of nuisance or continuing trespass, however, may be enjoined. The decision whether to grant an injunction always rests in the sound discretion of the chancellor, and depends on the relative benefit an injunction would confer upon the plaintiff in contrast to the injury it would impose on the defendant. Any burden imposed on the public should also be weighed. *Akers v. Mathieson Alkali Works,* 151 Va. 1, 8–9, 144 S.E. 492, 494 (1928).

In weighing the equities in a case of this kind, the chancellor must necessarily first consider whether the conditions existing on the adjoining lands are such that it is reasonable to impose a duty on the owner of a tree to protect a neighbor's land from damage caused by its intruding branches and roots. In the absence of such a duty, the traditional right of self-help is an adequate remedy. It would be clearly unreasonable to impose such a duty upon the owner of historically forested or agricultural land, but entirely appropriate to do so in the case of parties, like those in the present case, who dwell on adjoining residential lots.

Further, if such a duty is found to exist on the part of the tree owner, the chancellor must determine the extent of the remedy. Under the circumstances of the case, will self-help by cutting off the invading roots and branches, followed by an award of damages to compensate the plaintiff for his expenses, afford an adequate and permanent remedy, obviating the need for an injunction? If not, will complete removal of the defendant's tree be the appropriate remedy when the equities are balanced? An affirmative answer to the latter question will necessitate a mandatory injunction. As in all cases in which equitable relief is sought, the chancellor's decision must necessarily depend on the particular facts shown by the evidence, guided by traditional equitable principles.

CONCLUSION

Because the circuit court, following our decision in *Smith v. Holt,* did not consider equitable relief to be available, we will reverse the order appealed from and remand the case for further proceedings consistent with this opinion.

NOTE

If a neighbor delays too long in dealing with encroaching tree limbs or roots, does she run the risk of the creation of an easement by prescription against her real estate? Consider the language of the following recent case that probably represents the dominant view:

> Encroaching tree parts, by themselves, do not establish "open and notorious" use of the land. Neither roots below ground nor branches above ground fairly notify an owner of a claim for use at the surface. In the absence of additional circumstances, such as use of the ground for maintenance or collection of leaves or fruit, roots and branches alone do not alert an owner that his exclusive dominion of the ground is challenged.

Koresko v. Farley, 844 A.2d 607, 612 (Pa.Commw.Ct.2004). While the foregoing clearly makes sense with respect to underground root encroachments, is it similarly sound as to above-ground encroachments by tree limbs? According to one court, "[a]ny other result would cause landowners to seek self-help or to litigate each time a piece of vegetation starts to overhang their property for fear of losing the use or partial use of their property as the vegetation grows." Pierce v. Casady, 11 Kan.App.2d 23, 25, 711 P.2d 766, 768 (1985).

GOULDING v. COOK

Supreme Judicial Court of Massachusetts, 1996.
422 Mass. 276, 661 N.E.2d 1322.

Before: LIACOS, C.J., and ABRAMS, LYNCH, O'CONNOR and FRIED, JJ.

FRIED, JUSTICE.

The plaintiffs in this case (Gouldings) sought an injunction in the Land Court, enjoining the defendants (Cooks) to end a trespass on their property. The parties own neighboring residences in Scituate. When installation of another neighbor's swimming pool caused the Cooks's cesspool, which was partly under that neighbor's land, to malfunction, they were forced to find an alternative sewage disposal system. The town required a septic system, and the only suitable site for such a system was on a 2,998 square foot triangle of land that the Cooks claimed belonged to them but which the Gouldings claimed was part of their residential property. While the town was pressing them, the Cooks negotiated with the Gouldings to no avail. The matter came to litigation. The Gouldings sought a preliminary injunction against the Cooks's use of their land as well as a declaration that they were the fee simple owners of the land, free of any claims by the Cooks. The preliminary injunction was denied on August 8, 1991, and thereafter the Cooks entered on the land and installed the septic system. The Land Court entered a final judgment on October 7, 1992, finding ownership in the disputed triangle to be in the

Gouldings but granting an easement to the Cooks for the maintenance of their septic system "at a price to be negotiated by the parties and with provisions for maintenance, repair and replacement as counsel so agree." * * * [T]he Appeals Court affirmed. * * *

I

It is commonplace today that property rights are not absolute, and that the law may condition their use and enjoyment so that the interests of the public in general or of some smaller segment of the public, perhaps even just immediate neighbors, are not unduly prejudiced. Restrictions from architectural approvals to zoning regulations are accepted features of the legal landscape. *See* Euclid v. Ambler Realty Co., 272 U.S. 365, 395, 47 S.Ct. 114, 121, 71 L.Ed. 303 (1926); Harris v. Old King's Highway Regional Historic Dist. Comm'n, 421 Mass. 612, 658 N.E.2d 972 (1996). But, except in "exceptional" cases,[3] we draw the line at permanent physical occupations amounting to a transfer of a traditional estate in land. *See* Peters v. Archambault, 361 Mass. 91, 93, 278 N.E.2d 729 (1972), and cases cited therein. * * * And certainly that line, because the interests on either side of it are themselves conventional and the creatures of the law, is often hard to draw. *See* Lucas v. South Carolina Coastal Council, 505 U.S. 1003, 112 S.Ct. 2886, 120 L.Ed.2d 798 (1992); Lopes v. Peabody, 417 Mass. 299, 629 N.E.2d 1312 (1994). But we are committed to maintaining it, because the concept of private property represents a moral and political commitment that a pervasive disposition to balance away would utterly destroy. The commitment is enshrined in our Constitutions. Where the line is crossed and the commitment threatened, even in the interests of the general public, just compensation is required. *See* art. 10 of the Declaration of Rights of the Massachusetts Constitution; Fifth Amendment to the United States Constitution. And by implication, where the encroachment is not for a public use, the taking may not be justified at

---

3. *Compare* Keystone Bituminous Coal Ass'n v. DeBenedictis, 480 U.S. 470, 107 S.Ct. 1232, 94 L.Ed.2d 472 (1987); Penn Cent. Transp. Co. v. New York City, 438 U.S. 104, 98 S.Ct. 2646, 57 L.Ed.2d 631 (1978), *with* Nollan v. California Coastal Comm'n, 483 U.S. 825, 107 S.Ct. 3141, 97 L.Ed.2d 677 (1987); Loretto v. Teleprompter Manhattan CATV Corp., 458 U.S. 419, 102 S.Ct. 3164, 73 L.Ed.2d 868 (1982). *See also* Fragopoulos v. Rent Control Bd. of Cambridge, 408 Mass. 302, 309, 557 N.E.2d 1153 (1990). "In rare cases, referred to in our decisions as 'exceptional,' courts of equity have refused to grant a mandatory injunction and have left the plaintiff to his remedy of damages, 'where the unlawful encroachment has been made innocently, and the cost of removal by the defendant would be greatly disproportionate to the injury to the plaintiff from its continuation, or where the substantial rights of the owner may be protected without recourse to an injunction, or where an injunction would be oppressive and inequitable. But these are the exceptions.... What is just and equitable in cases of this sort depends very much on the particular facts and circumstances disclosed.'" (Citations omitted.) Peters v. Archambault, 361 Mass. 91, 93, 278 N.E.2d 729 (1972). *See* Franchi v. Boulger, 12 Mass.App.Ct. 376, 379, 425 N.E.2d 372 (1981). "Such cases have been based upon estoppel (*see* Malinoski v. D.S. McGrath, Inc., 283 Mass. 1, 10–11, 186 N.E. 225 [(1933)]; Ferrone v. Rossi, 311 Mass. 591, 594–595, 42 N.E.2d 564 [(1942)]); or on laches (see the Geragosian v. Union Realty Co. case, 289 Mass. 104, 109–110, 193 N.E. 726 [(1935)], where the earlier decisions are reviewed; *cf.* Westhampton Reservoir Recreation Corp. v. Hodder, 307 Mass. 288, 290–291, 29 N.E.2d 913 [(1940)]); or on the trivial nature of the encroachment or injury (*see* Tramonte v. Colarusso, 256 Mass. 299, 301, 152 N.E. 90 [(1926)]; *cf.* Goldstein v. Beal, 317 Mass. 750, 758, 59 N.E.2d 712 [(1945)]). *See* Lynch v. Union Inst. for Sav., 159 Mass. 306, 308–310, 34 N.E. 364 [(1893)]." Peters v. Archambault, *supra* at 93 n.2, 278 N.E.2d 729.

all. Although we deplore the disposition to turn every dispute into a Federal (constitutional) case and no constitutional claim was—or needed to be—made here, it is to these constitutional commitments that the dissent in the Appeals Court's decision referred when it observed that "[o]ur law simply does not sanction this type of private eminent domain," 38 Mass.App.Ct. 92, 99, 645 N.E.2d 54 (1995) (Armstrong, J., dissenting) * * *. For an analysis that comes to this same conclusion from another perspective, see Kaplow, *Property Rules Versus Liability Rules: An Economic Analysis*, 109 Harv. L. Rev. 713, 757–773 (1996).

No doubt the Cooks considered themselves in desperate straits, but theirs was not the kind of desperation that justifies self-help with financial adjustments thereafter. * * * *See generally* Keeton, *Conditional Fault in the Law of Torts*, 72 Harv.L.Rev. 401 (1959). It is not cynicism to suppose that some sum of money would suffice to assuage the Goulding's sense of having been imposed on and thus to suggest that one way of looking at this case is to ask who shall set that sum and where will the bargaining advantage lie. *See* Restatement (Second) of Torts § 941 comment c, at 583–584 (1979). The Cooks, threatened with possible destruction of their ability to use their home at all, might have been willing to pay a very large sum to be able to obtain this needed facility from the Gouldings. The Appeals Court's disposition may be seen as moved by its revulsion at the thought that the Gouldings should be able to extract so large a rent for so minor an accommodation. The power of eminent domain is granted just to prevent private property owners from extracting such strategic rents from the public. *See* Epstein, Takings: Private Property and the Power of Eminent Domain (1985). And because of the Gouldings's "lock hand," the Land Court, by denying the Gouldings an injunction, assigned to itself the authority to establish the price at which the easement, 2,998 square feet of the Gouldings's land, shall be transferred to the Cooks.

II

Like most propositions in the law the one we reaffirm now has some play at the margins. Accordingly, the Appeals Court is quite right that the courts will not enjoin truly minimal encroachments, especially when the burden on a defendant would be very great. The classic example is given in Restatement (Second) of Torts § 941 comment c, *supra* at 583:

> The defendant has recently completed a twenty-story office building on his lot. The work was done by reputable engineers and builders, and they and the defendant all acted in good faith and with reasonable care. It is, however, found that from the tenth floor upward the wall on the plaintiff's side bulges outward and extends over the line. The extent of the encroachment varies at different points, the maximum being four inches.

Such accommodation recognizes the necessarily approximate nature of all legal lines and principles. To extend the accommodation to this case where the defendants seek to install a potentially permanent, possibly malodorously malfunctioning septic system encroaching on a spatially significant portion of the plaintiffs' lot is not to accommodate the principle but to obliterate it in favor of a general power of equitable adjustment and enforced good neighborliness. That is particularly the case here, where the defendants' "good faith" consists at most in an honest belief supported by objective facts that they were the owners of the land. Although this claim was sharply disputed, they were told that they proceeded at their peril, and the matter was in litigation and awaiting disposition when they went ahead and acted. It changes nothing that what we have here is the Land Court's decision to deny injunctive relief, an equitable power which leaves much to the court's discretion, if that discretion was exercised on a legal criterion that we conclude is incorrect. To draw an analogy, it is the law in this Commonwealth that easements of necessity can only be granted in very limited circumstances of reasonable or absolute necessity. *See, e.g.,* Supraner v. Citizens Sav. Bank, 303 Mass. 460, 464, 22 N.E.2d 38 (1939), and cases cited therein; Mt. Holyoke Realty Corp. v. Holyoke Realty Corp., 284 Mass. 100, 105, 187 N.E. 227 (1933). If a court were to deny an injunction against trespass on the premise that some wider rule of easements of necessity obtains, we would not hesitate to overturn that exercise of discretion. The same holds here.

As such, we hold that the Cooks must remove the septic system and pay damages.

The decision of the Land Court is vacated and remanded for proceedings consistent with this opinion.

NOTES

1. Massachusetts courts have been especially unwilling to "balance the hardships" as the basis for denying injunctive relief and substituting permanent damages. The following language from that state's Supreme Judicial Court aptly illustrates this perspective:

> In Massachusetts a landowner is ordinarily entitled to mandatory equitable relief to compel removal of a structure significantly encroaching on his land, even though the encroachment was unintentional or negligent and the cost of removal is substantial in comparison to any injury suffered by the owner of the lot upon which the encroachment has taken place.

Peters v. Archambault, 361 Mass. 91, 92, 278 N.E.2d 729, 730 (1972). This approach is partially driven by the fact that a substantial portion of the land in Massachusetts is part of a "Torrens" or "Land Registration" system, a title system used in seven or eight other states, including Illinois and Minnesota. A Torrens title is issued by the state, much in the same way states issue certificates of title for motor vehicles. A Torrens title is considered more secure because of the government's role in issuing it. For example, one may not acquire title by adverse possession against Torrens real estate. However, even Massachusetts refuses injunctive relief against encroachments that are innocent and "trivial." *See, e.g.,* Capodilupo v. Vozzella, 46 Mass.App.Ct. 224,

704 N.E.2d 534 (1999) (injunction denied where innocent encroachment was 3–4 inches).

Most states are more inclined than Massachusetts to employ a "balancing the hardships" approach, which in some cases can result in a substitution of permanent damages for injunctive relief. Of course, courts uniformly refuse to follow this approach where the encroachment is intentional. To do so would allow the wrongdoer knowingly to exercise the power of eminent domain, a governmental prerogative. On the other hand, in the case of innocent encroachments, courts normally engage in such a balancing process. Consider how the Michigan Supreme Court has characterized this process:

> Fashioning an appropriate remedy where a structure encroaches on the land of another poses special problems and has resulted in special solutions. Dobbs, Remedies, § 5.6, p. 355. In such cases the approach is to balance several factors—the relative hardship to the parties and the equities between them—and to grant or deny the injunction as the balance may seem to indicate. *Id.*

> This Court has long recognized that "it will examine into all the circumstances of the case, and, if it is apparent that the relief sought is disproportionate to the nature and extent of the injury sustained, or likely to be, the court will not interfere but will leave the parties to seek some other remedy." Hall v. Rood, 40 Mich. 46, 49 (1879).

> The process is perhaps best described as "balancing all of the equities of the situation." 4 Restatement Torts, 2d, § 941, comment a, p. 581. In balancing the hardships and equities regarding encroachment, courts are guided by two central considerations: An interest in avoiding judicial approval of private eminent domain by the encroacher, and an interest in preventing extortion by the encroachee, who may use the injunction to "compromise" the claim. Dobbs, *supra.*

> Thus, unless the burden to the defendant of removing the encroachment is disproportionate to the hardship to the plaintiff in allowing the encroachment to remain, an injunction will issue. *Id.* at 356; *Hall, supra* at 49. However, the question is not resolved merely by determining what advantage the plaintiff will gain if an injunction issues; a just resolution of the question requires examining the hardship the plaintiff will suffer in the absence of an injunction. In other words, the inquiry is not merely

> > a nice measurment [sic] of relative advantages and a denial of the injunction if the scales tip in the defendant's favor. The law does not grant an injunction merely because of the advantage that the plaintiff might reap from it, and it does not refuse an injunction merely because of the convenience that the refusal might afford the defendant. 4 Restatement Torts, 2d, § 941, comment a, pp. 580–581.

> As the drafters of the Restatement recognized, the inquiry goes further. The court should also examine the "character of the conduct (including the respective motives) of the defendant and the plaintiff...." *Id.* at 581.

> Thus, the drafters of the Restatement expressly noted that a plaintiff may be partially responsible for the hardship a defendant would suffer

from the grant of an injunction and that a factor that would weigh against a plaintiff is the plaintiff's "knowledge of the existence of ... adverse affects [sic]" of the plaintiff's decision to move to an adversely affected area. *Id.*, comment b, p. 581.

While a court is not bound to engage in a balancing of the relative hardships and equities if the encroachment resulted from an intentional or wilful act, Dobbs, *supra* at 355, 357, we agree with the defendant's assertion that there is no evidentiary support that the encroachment was wilful or intentional, and that the trial court erred in issuing a mandatory injunction without balancing the relative hardships to the parties.

Kratze v. Independent Order of Oddfellows, 442 Mich. 136, 142–43, 500 N.W.2d 115, 119–21 (1993). *See* Szymczak v. LaFerrara, 280 N.J.Super. 223, 655 A.2d 76 (1995) (damages substituted for mandatory injunction where encroachment on plaintiff's lot was innocent, albeit substantial). What standard should be used to determined whether a particular encroachment is innocent? When should reliance on a surveyor suffice? *See* Urban Site Venture II Limited Partnership v. Levering Associates Limited Partnership, 340 Md. 223, 234, 665 A.2d 1062, 1067 (1995) ("[w]here an encroachment results from reasonable, good faith reliance on the mistaken work of competent surveyors, the encroachment is innocent.").

2. Suppose the defendant encroaches on an easement rather than on land owned by the plaintiff in fee simple absolute. Here there are fewer conceptual roadblocks to injunctive relief than there are in the fee simple context. Because an easement is not an estate in land, the holder has no "possessory" rights in it. Rather, she is deemed to have only an "incorporeal" right to "use" land. Thus, the traditional possessory legal remedies of trespass, ejectment and the summary proceeding are unavailable. *See* Nelson v. Russo, 844 A.2d 301 (Del.2004) (townhome owner sought ejectment against a neighbor who had erected a fence in what the documents of the development classified as a "common area"—ejectment held to be unavailable to recover use of an incorporeal hereditament). As a result, such remedies stand as no bar to injunctive relief. Consequently, injunctions are a commonly granted remedy in the easement encroachment setting. *See* Dan B. Dobbs, Law of Remedies § 5.10(3) (2d ed. 1993). Such injunctions "may issue to prevent obstructions or to restore access; injunctions may issue to require removal of substantial structures or to regulate the extent and nature of use." *Id*. To what extent will courts in easement encroachment cases "balance the equities" and substitute damages for injunctive relief? In this regard, consider the following case.

VOSSEN v. FORRESTER

Court of Appeals of Oregon, 1998.
155 Or.App. 323, 963 P.2d 157.

RIGGS, PRESIDING JUDGE.

* * *

Defendant Norman Forrester bought a beachfront lot in Yachats in November 1993, after making inquiries of the city planner about whether a house could be built on the lot and receiving an affirmative answer. A title report on the property disclosed the existence of an easement described only by reference to Book 128, Page 315, Deed Records of Lincoln County, as well as several other easements described with more particularity. A map attached to the title report did not disclose the location of the easement described at Book 128, Page 315, Deed Records of Lincoln County, and defendant's deed made no reference to that easement.

After defendant bought the property, a group called the "Friends of the 804 Trail" asserted that the lot was too small for a house and opposed the issuance of a building permit [and the latter group commenced litigation]. Ultimately, the permit was issued and, in July 1994, while appeals in the above-described litigation were still pending, defendant began excavation in preparation for building his house. At that time, defendant did not have actual knowledge that the easement described in Book 128, Page 315, Deed Records of Lincoln County ran over the north portion of his property in such a manner that the planned house encroached 2.08 feet onto the southern portion of that easement. Defendant believed that the easement described in the title report was an easement over another portion of his lot. The actual easement described in Book 128, Page 315, Deed Records of Lincoln County was not apparent based on a visual inspection of the property.

When defendant started construction in mid–1994, plaintiffs, who own the four properties benefitted by the easement, believed that the house might be encroaching on their easement. Several months before that time, they had observed that defendant had placed a number of other encroachments on the easement, including boulders and trees. They did not attempt to use the easement, however, and did not notify defendant either of the existence of the easement or of their belief that he was encroaching on it. Plaintiffs took no action because they believed that defendant would be ordered to tear down his house as a result of the "Friends of the 804 Trail" litigation.

In April 1995, when the house was substantially completed, plaintiffs filed this action seeking a mandatory injunction requiring defendant to remove the house and the various other obstructions from the easement, as well as a preliminary injunction to prevent defendant from occupying the house. Defendant attempted to settle this case by offering plaintiffs an easement over a different portion of the lot, slightly further to the north, but plaintiffs refused.

The trial court granted partial summary judgment in favor of plaintiffs concerning the existence of the easement, and the parties went to trial on whether laches barred plaintiffs' claim and whether the trial court should balance the relative hardships to the parties in determining an appropriate remedy. * * *

The trial court concluded that defendant "knew or should have known" of the location of the easement, and that the defense of laches therefore did not apply. The trial court further concluded that because defendant "knew or should have known" of the location of the easement, it was precluded from balancing the relative hardships of the parties in determining the appropriate relief. The trial court granted a mandatory injunction requiring defendant to remove the house, as well as the other encroachments, from the easement.

* * *

We turn first to the question of laches. Where a defendant raises a defense of laches, but the analogous statute of limitations for an action at law has not run, the defendant bears the burden of proving that laches applies. * * * In the present case, the parties agree that defendant bore the burden of proof. Defendant therefore was required to establish the three elements of laches: (1) that plaintiffs delayed in asserting their claim for an unreasonable length of time; (2) that plaintiffs had full knowledge of all of the relevant facts; and (3) that the delay resulted in such substantial prejudice to defendant that it would be inequitable to grant plaintiffs the relief requested. * * *

* * *

In order to determine whether plaintiffs delayed for an unreasonable length of time in bringing this action, we must first determine when plaintiffs had full knowledge of all of the relevant facts. Plaintiffs assert that they did not have full knowledge of all of the relevant facts until they were permitted to conduct a survey of defendant's property after this lawsuit was initiated. Defendant asserts that plaintiffs had full knowledge of all of the relevant facts by the summer of 1994, when they observed the foundation of the house being constructed and suspected that it encroached on their easement.

We agree with defendant that the date from which the laches defense should be measured is mid–1994. Before that time, plaintiffs had observed that defendant had obstructed the easement with boulders, shrubs, and various other items. Plaintiffs saw the location of the foundation of the house, and suspected that the house was on the easement. Plaintiffs did not attempt to survey the property to find out if the house actually was on the easement until April 1995, the same month this litigation was commenced. Plaintiffs chose not to take action until April 1995, not because they lacked knowledge of the relevant facts, but because they hoped that other litigation would force defendant to remove his house. We conclude that plaintiffs were chargeable with full knowledge of all of the relevant facts by mid–1994 at the latest. *See* Collins v. Rathbun, 43 Or.App. 857, 866, 604 P.2d 441 (1979), *rev. den.* 288 Or. 701 (1980) ("the period for the application of laches commences when a plaintiff could have, through the exercise of due diligence, become aware or actually did become aware of a threatened violation, whichever comes first") * * *.

We next turn to the question of whether plaintiffs delayed for an unreasonable time in bringing this action. Plaintiffs argue that delay to await resolution of other litigation is necessarily excusable * * *. Here, the "Friends of the 804 Trail" litigation concerned whether defendant could build a house on his lot. It did not concern whether defendant could place encroachments in plaintiffs' easement. Even if the "Friends of the 804 Trail" litigation had been successful, it would not have prevented defendant from encroaching on plaintiffs' easement. Awaiting the outcome of litigation that pertains to an entirely different legal issue and that would not supply plaintiffs with a remedy does not justify a delay in bringing an action.

Although we reject plaintiffs' arguments that the pendency of the "Friends of the 804 Trail" litigation excused their delay, that does not end our inquiry. The question remains whether plaintiffs' delay in bringing this action between July 1994, when they had full knowledge of all of the relevant facts, and April 1995, when they first acted on their knowledge, was unreasonable. A delay of nine months in bringing a claim of this sort does not seem unreasonable, particularly given that defendant most likely would have had to possess the easement adversely for a period of 10 years in order to extinguish plaintiffs' easement. *See generally* ORS 105.620. Although plaintiffs' delay in bringing this action until defendant had expended considerable time and money in substantially completing his residence is not to be commended, we are unable to conclude that plaintiffs delayed for such an unreasonable amount of time that laches bars their claim. The trial court did not err in rejecting defendant's laches defense.

The remaining question, then, is whether the remedy ordered by the trial court was appropriate. Plaintiffs did not rebut defendant's evidence that the encroaching 2.08 feet of the house could not be removed without harming the structural integrity of the house, and the parties appear to agree that the trial court's order means that defendant must tear down the house entirely. Given the unrebutted evidence, we accept that assumption as well. The question is whether such relief is appropriate in this case.

* * * In cases involving encroachments, "[u]nder the proper circumstances the court will consider the relative hardship of the parties and if the removal of the encroaching structure would cause damage to the defendant disproportionate to the injury which the encroachment causes plaintiff, an injunction will not issue." Tauscher v. Andruss, 240 Or. 304, 308–09, 401 P.2d 40 (1965). The trial court apparently concluded that the present case did not constitute "proper circumstances" for the application of that rule because defendant "knew or should have known" of the existence and location of plaintiffs' easement before he constructed his house. However, the trial court explicitly found: "Prior to the filing of this action, defendant did not know the exact location of the boundary lines of plaintiffs' easement." Thus, it would appear that the trial court's conclusion on this point was based on its belief that defendant "should have known," rather than that defendant "knew," that he was encroaching on the easement. Defendant argues on appeal that case law does not support the trial court's conclusion that whether a party "should have known" of

an encroachment determines whether a court should engage in balancing the hardships to the parties when crafting an equitable remedy.

Plaintiffs do not attempt to argue that the trial court's use of the "should have known" standard was correct but rather argue that the record supports their contention that defendant "knowingly" encroached on their easement. Plaintiffs contend that the court should apply the rule announced in Swaggerty v. Petersen, 280 Or. 739, 747–49, 572 P.2d 1309 (1977), that a court in equity should not balance the hardships to the parties where the defendant constructed the encroachment " 'with full notice of the other party's claim.' " Id. at 749, 572 P.2d 1309, quoting 5 Pomeroy's Equity Jurisprudence 4477 (2d ed 1919). See also Seagrove Owners Assn. v. Smith, 114 Or.App. 45, 49, 834 P.2d 469 (1992) (court would not engage in balancing of hardships where defendant built in knowing violation of restrictive covenants). But see Glover v. Santangelo, 70 Or.App. 689, 694, 690 P.2d 1083, rev. den. (1984) (even though defendant continued to construct house in violation of restrictive covenant after notice of plaintiff's claim, ordering house removed was inappropriate where modification of the structure could be undertaken in order to "balance the competing interests").

Plaintiffs argue that actual notice, constructive notice and inquiry notice all constitute sufficient notice to preclude balancing of hardships in cases such as this. We do not agree. Defendant had actual notice that the easement existed from his title report, and certainly was on inquiry notice as to its location, but simply held a mistaken belief about its location. That does not mean, as plaintiffs assert, that defendant had actual knowledge that he was encroaching on their easement. This case is more comparable to Seid v. Ross, 120 Or.App. 564, 853 P.2d 308 (1993), than to the cases cited by plaintiff where the defendants constructed a building with actual knowledge that it encroached on an easement or violated a restrictive covenant. In Seid, one of the defendants built a retaining wall between his and the plaintiff's property without first obtaining a survey. Subsequently, it was discovered that the wall encroached up to 18 inches onto the plaintiff's property. * * * It is unquestionable that the defendants such as those in Seid had at least constructive notice of the location of their property line. However, this court determined that a mandatory injunction requiring removal of the encroaching wall would not be equitable, given the minimal nature of the encroachment and the costs involved in removing the wall. * * *

* * *

[W]e conclude that, in the present case, a mandatory injunction requiring defendant to remove his house from plaintiff's easement is not a proper remedy. In reaching that conclusion, we take into consideration the following factors. First, the cost of removing the house from the easement would be very substantial, given the unrebutted evidence that it would destroy the structural integrity of the house, because of the unique construction features designed to protect the structure from tidal wave action. * * * Second, the encroachment of defendant's house onto the easement is minimal. Third, defendant did not know that he was encroaching on the easement when he built his house. *Swaggerty*, 280 Or. at 749, 572 P.2d 1309; *Seagrove*, 114 Or.App. at 49, 834 P.2d 469. Fourth, the hardship to defendant far outweighs any benefit to plaintiffs in this case, and, in fact, plaintiffs concede as much.[3] Finally, plaintiffs' conduct in this action is comparable in many ways to that of the plaintiff in Andrews, because they "expressly * * * permit[ted] defendant to proceed with construction" and delayed seeking a remedy for their own advantage.

We conclude that the trial court erred in issuing a mandatory injunction requiring removal of defendant's house from plaintiff's easement. We reverse and remand with instructions to relocate plaintiffs' easement to the north of defendant's house.

NOTES

1. Where a court finds that a defendant actually knows that he or she is building on a plaintiff's easement, it will almost invariably grant injunctive relief. Consider the language used by a Florida appellate court to reverse a trial court that denied an injunction to compel removal of a masonry retaining wall that encroached on the plaintiff's and other subdivision owners' 50–foot right of way easement for ingress and egress:

> The record in this case is not appropriate for denial of a mandatory injunction because of the "balancing of the equities" doctrine. In a proper case a mandatory injunction can be refused but some damages or costs must be assessed to compensate the dominant * * * tenement owners for any loss. * * * In this case no delay or laches were proved against * * * [the plaintiff]. * * *

> However, the most distinguishing factor in this case is that [the defendant] (through its agents) *intentionally* placed the wall in its present location with full knowledge of the exact location of the [easement line]. When necessary to save trees, the wall was jogged always south into the easement area and never north into the subdivision's landscape easement area. In places it jogged at least twenty feet—far more than necessary to preserve the largest of the trees.

> We, as well as authorities writing in this area of the law, acknowledge that the application of the "balancing the equities" or "comparative hardships" doctrine under some circumstances amounts to allowing the servient tenement owner to acquire the dominant tenement owner's easement interest by a form of private eminent domain. This raises serious constitutional problems. * * * That is no doubt why courts usually refuse to apply this balancing doctrine where the encroachment is done intentionally or willfully. * * *

---

3. As noted above, the easement in question, although created for roadway purposes, was not even visible when defendant purchased the property. Plaintiffs submitted evidence that they had used it on occasion to gain access to a nearby public trail and the beach. At oral argument, plaintiffs' counsel conceded that a balancing of hardships would weigh in defendant's favor.

Diefenderfer v. Forest Park Springs, 599 So.2d 1309, 1313–14 (Fla.Dist.Ct. App.1992). In *Diefenderfer*, the defendant, prior to building the wall, offered to pay each of the other affected easement owners $2500 for permission to build the wall in the easement. The other owners agreed and only plaintiff refused this offer. Do you think this should have influenced the court? For other similar cases where the court refused to permit a "balancing of equities" approach because the encroachment on the easement was intentional, see Friess v. Quest Cherokee, L.L.C., 209 P.3d 722 (Kan.App.2009); Carrier v. Lindquist, 37 P.3d 1112 (Utah 2001).

　　2. In *Vossen* the court balanced the hardships in defendant's favor. However, note that the result was not the substitution of damages in lieu of a mandatory injunction, but rather the court ordered that plaintiffs' easement be relocated on defendant's property. Is this good policy? Is it practical to employ this approach in most easement encroachment cases?

2. Violations of Restrictive Covenants

GLOVER v. SANTANGELO

Court of Appeals of Oregon, 1984.
70 Or.App. 689, 690 P.2d 1083.

ROSSMAN, JUDGE.

Defendant appeals the issuance of a mandatory injunction which ordered him to tear down his house because it obstructed plaintiffs' view in violation of a restrictive covenant. * * *

Plaintiffs and defendant are the owners of adjacent parcels of real property in Klamath Falls. Both lots are on a hillside overlooking Mt. Shasta, Lake Ewana and the downtown area. Defendant's lot is on the downhill side of plaintiffs' lot and is encumbered by a restrictive covenant which benefits plaintiffs' property.

At the time the covenant was executed, the house in which plaintiffs now live was completed or nearly completed, and defendant's property was bare land. The covenant was executed "so that the value of Lot 9 [plaintiffs' lot] as a 'view Lot would not be impaired by future erections on Lot 10 [defendant's lot]." It provides, in pertinent part:

　　* * * [N]o second story shall ever be erected on any building on said Lot 10 except in the area which is within 51 feet of the front lot line (bordering on Huron Street) and that any one-story dwelling erected anywhere on said Lot 10 other than in said 51 foot area shall have a roof pitch of not to exceed 2:12.[1] This covenant shall be appurtenant to and forever run with the land as a burden upon said Lot 10 for the benefit of said Lot 9.

In the fall of 1980, defendant began construction of a house on his property, a substantial portion of which lies outside the 51 foot area. The

---

　　1. A 2:12 pitch roof means that, for every two inches of vertical rise, there is a 12 inch horizontal run. Defendant's compliance with the roof pitch restrictions is not an issue in this appeal.

house consists of a main level and a daylight basement. As soon as it became apparent to plaintiffs that the house was going to ruin their view, they attempted to obtain a temporary injunction to halt construction. Although it was denied, the trial judge told defendant that any further construction was at his own peril. It is beyond dispute that defendant's house substantially impairs plaintiffs' western view. However, their southern view of Mt. Shasta and Lake Ewana, across another neighbor's property, remains unaffected.

After completion of defendant's house, plaintiffs' request for a permanent injunction was tried to the bench. The court concluded that defendant's house violated the covenant, because it was a two-story structure which he finished at his own risk with full knowledge of plaintiffs' complaint. The court based its conclusion on a finding that on the uphill side of the house, approximately one-third of the basement is constructed above what would have been the original grade of the property. It was also found that damages would be very difficult, if not impossible, to determine in regard to the loss of view. Accordingly, the court issued a mandatory injunction ordering removal of the encroaching structure.

Defendant raises a number of arguments on appeal, but they can be distilled down to three basic contentions. First, he argues that his house complies with the intent of the covenant. He contends that because the best view from plaintiffs' property is to the south, toward Mt. Shasta and Lake Ewana, the covenant must have been intended to protect the view in that direction. * * *

* * * It seems highly unlikely that the original parties to the covenant intended to protect plaintiffs' southern view by imposing height restrictions on a lot which lay directly west of their property. Rather, we conclude, protection of the western view was the object of the covenant.

Next defendant argues that his house complies with the express terms of the covenant. * * *

From the express language prohibiting a second story, it is apparent that the covenant in this case was designed to limit construction on defendant's lot to a one story structure. Defendant asserts that, because his house complies with the Uniform Building Code definition of a single story structure, it cannot violate the covenant. Whether it does or not is irrelevant, because the code definition to which he refers did not exist when the covenant was executed, so it could not have been contemplated as the proper standard for judging compliance.

There is other, more compelling evidence that clearly establishes a violation. After examining the evidence and reviewing the testimony, we note that defendant's house was built so that there are basement windows on its uphill side. To accommodate the windows, the main floor had to be raised off the ground several feet, necessitating a split entry design, where one enters at ground level but must climb either up or down a short flight of stairs to reach the main floor or the lower level. Clearly, defendant's house is higher than one story. * * *

For his last argument, defendant asserts that, under the circumstances of this case, an award of damages would be more equitable than demolition of his house. In a proper case, a mandatory injunction can be denied if the damages associated with removal of the encroaching structure are disproportionate to the injury which the encroachment causes. Tauscher v. Andruss, 240 Or. 304, 308–09, 401 P.2d 40 (1965). This is not such a case. A view is a unique asset for which a monetary value is very difficult to determine. Plaintiffs testified that the view was a crucial factor in their decision to buy the house. In fact, the view was one of the main reasons they were willing to negotiate the steep and occasionally icy streets leading to the house. Defendant's position is made weaker by the fact that he purchased with full knowledge of the covenant. He was, therefore, obligated to comply with it. * * * Furthermore, following the preliminary injunction hearing, he made no effort to modify the design of his house, even though he had been advised by the trial judge that he would finish construction at his peril. Accordingly, we hold that plaintiffs are entitled to have the illegally obstructed portion of their view restored.

Nevertheless, we do not believe that defendant should be required to tear down his house if the structure can be modified to comply with the covenant. There is nothing in the record regarding any feasible alternatives. Recognizing the equitable nature of these proceedings and our need to balance the competing interests, we remand this case for further proceedings to determine whether defendant's house can be modified to comply with the deed restrictions. We leave it to the trial court to specify what modification must be made by defendant if the court concludes that modification can bring defendant's house into compliance. We do not intend to preclude the trial court from again ordering that the house be torn down if the court determines that there is no alternative.

Affirmed and remanded for further proceedings.

NOTES

1.   The nature of restrictive covenants is discussed in United Properties, Inc. v. Walsmith, 312 N.W.2d 66 (Iowa Ct.App.1981):

> The law reflects a two-fold nature. Such covenants are promises respecting the use of the land which, on the one hand, create proprietary interests and, on the other hand, create contractual rights. Compiano v. Kuntz, 226 N.W.2d 245, 248 (Iowa 1975); Thodos v. Shirk, 248 Iowa 172, 179, 79 N.W.2d 733, 737 (1956). Historically, there has been no unanimity of opinion among the jurisdictions as to whether equity is enforcing the promise as a contract or as an incorporated property interest. *Id.* * * *
>
> * * * Promises respecting the use of land can be made in a variety of ways: a) by a single restricting instrument in which all lot owners join; b) by a landowner's series of deeds containing restrictions on lots in a tract; or c) by a landowner's restricting instrument on lots in a tract followed by deeds to these lots. * * *

Id. at 70–71.

2. Modern courts are often willing to presume that the legal remedy for a violation of a restrictive covenant is inadequate:

> Finally, respondents argue appellants are not entitled to an injunction because they have shown no irreparable harm and money damages are an adequate remedy. Generally, restrictive covenants may be enforced irrespective of the amount of damages which will result from a breach. * * * 7 Thompson on Real Property 187 § 3171.

Gladstone v. Gregory, 95 Nev. 474, 480, 596 P.2d 491, 495 (1979); *accord* Tubbs v. Brandon, 374 So.2d 1358, 1361 (Ala.1979); Crimmins v. Simonds, 636 P.2d 478, 480 (Utah 1981).

3. What would have been the measure of damages in *Glover?* In Drulard v. LeTourneau, 286 Or. 159, 593 P.2d 1118 (1979), the court refused to enjoin the alleged violation of building restrictions designed to protect the view from plaintiff's house and authorized damages in the following amount:

> [W]e believe that the proper measure of damages in such a case would be the difference between the value of plaintiffs' property with the nonconforming structure on defendants' lot (defendants' house, as built), and the value of plaintiffs' property with a structure that *conformed* to the restrictions on defendants' lot.

Id. at 169, 593 P.2d at 1123.

4. In *Glover,* why do you think the trial court denied the plaintiff's request for a "temporary" injunction?

5. The balance of hardships defense is discussed in the context of an action to enjoin the violation of a restrictive covenant in Crimmins v. Simonds, 636 P.2d 478, 480 (Utah 1981):

> [U]nder a "balance of injury" test * * *, an equity court may exercise its discretion not to grant injunctive relief when the plaintiff is not irreparably harmed by the violation, the violation was innocent, defendants' cost of removal would be disproportionate and oppressive compared to the benefits plaintiffs would derive from it, and plaintiffs can be compensated by damages. Papanikolas Bros. Ent. v. Sugarhouse Shopping Ctr. Ass'n, Utah, 535 P.2d 1256 (1975).

And, in Gladstone v. Gregory, 95 Nev. 474, 480, 596 P.2d 491, 495 (1979), the court said:

> The equitable principle of relative hardship is available only to innocent parties who proceed without knowledge or warning that they are acting contrary to others' vested property rights. * * * Respondents clearly assumed the risk of increased damages when they continued construction after notice of Gladstone's objections.

Did the *Glover* court apply a "balance of hardships" test? For a case where the Arkansas Supreme Court refused to balance the hardships and ordered the removal of a deck that violated a restrictive covenant side-yard building line, see Clifford Family Limited Liability Co. v. Cox, 334 Ark. 64, 971 S.W.2d 769 (1998). *See also,* Flying Diamond Airpark, L.L.C. v. Meienberg, 215 Ariz. 44, 156 P.3d 1149 (Ariz.Ct.App.2007) (refusal to balance hardships where violation of covenant was intentional).

TURPIN v. WATTS

Missouri Court of Appeals, 1980.
607 S.W.2d 895.

HOGAN, JUDGE.

This is an action for a mandatory injunction. Plaintiffs and defendants, to whom we shall refer in the singular, own adjoining lakefront lots situated on the Osage arm of the Lake of the Ozarks. Alleging that defendant had violated a restrictive covenant by constructing a residence lakewards of a setback or building line, thereby obstructing his view, plaintiff sought to compel defendant to move the residence to comply with the restrictive covenant. The cause was tried to the court sitting without a jury. * * * The trial court entered a general finding for the defendant. * * *

* * *

* * * Chimney View Estates is divided into 12 lots. Lots 1, 2, 3, 4 and half of Lot 5 abut the lake on the east. We are concerned with Lots 3 and 4. Plaintiff's property is Lot 3; defendant owns Lot 4, upon which the allegedly offending residence was constructed. The shoreline of Lot 4 meanders from southeast to northwest a distance of 90 feet more or less; the lake frontage of Lot 3, which adjoins Lot 4 on the south, is 75 feet more or less. The plat bears the following legend, among others:

> No building shall be erected between the 20 foot minimum building line and the 660 countour [sic] line of the Lake of the Ozarks.

The "building line" or setback is sketched along the perimeter of the subdivision. By warranty deed dated March 6, 1973, [prior owners] conveyed all of Lots 3 and 4 to defendant and his wife. The parcel conveyed is described as follows:

> All of Lots 3 and 4 in Chimney View Estates, a subdivision, filed for record in Book 14 at page 82 in the Camden County Recorder's Office, being a resurvey of Lots 51 and 51A in SHAWNEE BEND NO. 3, all as shown on the plat of said subdivision filed for record in Plat Book 4, page 27, Office of Recorder of Deeds, Camden County, Missouri. Subject to restrictions, reservations, conditions and easements of record. . . .

* * *

Two other factual aspects of the case must be considered. The course of dealing between the plaintiff and the defendant is of considerable importance. Plaintiff testified that he became interested in buying his lakeshore property—Lot 3 in Chimney View subdivision—about the middle of November 1975. Lot 3 had a residence on it; Lot 4 was unimproved. Plaintiff negotiated with defendant and on December 4, the parties entered into a contract for the sale and purchase of Lot 3 and some miscellaneous chattels. For the total sum of $52,000 plaintiff was to receive Lot 3, together with the improvements thereon; defendant was to provide a title insurance policy; the sale included a good deal of furniture, "major" appliances, a boat and a boat dock. At plaintiff's request, "closing" was deferred to April 3, 1976.

In March 1976, plaintiff observed stakes on Lot 4. Plaintiff testified he spoke to the defendant, telling defendant he was "entirely too close" to the setback. Defendant replied that he could not build "further back" because dynamiting would be required, and defendant was unable to obtain a permit to blast. Plaintiff rejoined: "... change your style of house."

On cross-examination, plaintiff was asked if, in March, defendant did not offer to rescind the whole transaction. Plaintiff's testimony was that defendant only offered to move plaintiff's furniture back to Kansas City; counsel went over the offer of rescission several times, but plaintiff denied that defendant ever offered to make full restitution. Plaintiff nevertheless signed the contract, watched the construction proceed, and finally commenced this action on July 16, 1976.

Defendant's testimony about his offer to rescind was considerably different. His testimony was that in March 1976, plaintiff was "very objectionable to the constructing on [defendant's] property." Plaintiff became irate, according to the defendant, and defendant "told [plaintiff] [defendant] would be happy to give [plaintiff] his money back and pay for the boat and pay for the shipping of his furniture back to Kansas City." Defendant "even offered to go to the house and make the telephone call to cancel the real estate contract that was made at that point." Defendant's evidence was that his construction was three-fourths complete when this action was commenced.

A final factual aspect of the case to be noted is the gross disproportion between the injury proved and the relief sought. Defendant's surveyor, as noted, produced a number of plats or surveys. Defendant's exhibit D was designed to show the "percent of view" defendant's residence blocked or shut off beyond the setback. The defendant's surveyor then testified as follows concerning his calculations which were incorporated into exhibit D: (our emphasis)

Q. With respect to the percentage of the loss of view on the side of [plaintiff's] house closest to the common lot lines between 3 and 4, what is that percentage? * * *

A. *It would be 3.9 percent.*

By comparison, there was evidence that the cost of razing and reconstructing defendant's residence, assuming salvaged materials were used, would be about $39,000.

* * *

The only conclusion permitted by the pleadings and the proof is that this is an action upon an express restrictive covenant. There is no claim of encroachment; the evidence completely negatives plaintiff's acquisition of a reciprocal negative easement or implied equitable servitude of the order discussed in Campbell v. Stout, 408 S.W.2d 585 (Mo.App.1966). The sole question before the court is whether plaintiff was entitled to a *mandatory* injunction; in all such cases, the chancellor has discretion, and should refuse relief if it would be inequitable to grant relief. * * *

The court is well aware that proof of damages is not essential to an award of mandatory injunctive relief to enforce restrictive covenants. * * * All the same, "In granting, or refusing to grant, a mandatory injunction to enforce a restrictive covenant ..., the courts apply the general principles of equity with some strictness, and the complainant may often find himself deprived of this remedy by his own conduct...." Annotation., 57 A.L.R. 336, 337 (1928). Two of the basic maxims of equity are that he who seeks equity must have done equity, and that equity aids the vigilant. Upon the record, the chancellor could have found that the defendant offered to rescind the contract and make full restitution before plaintiff ever became bound to purchase lot 3, and the offer was refused out of hand. Further, the chancellor could have found that the plaintiff, aware that his rights were being infringed, allowed the defendant to proceed, to defendant's injury. No temporary restraining order was sought; no legal redress of any order was sought until defendant's construction was almost complete. In addition, there was evidence that violation of the setback restriction was widespread in the Chimney View subdivision. Given these circumstances, the chancellor might well have found the plaintiff estopped to complain. *See,* as illustrative: Loud v. Pendergast, 206 Mass. 122, 92 N.E. 40 (1910); Meaney v. Stork, 80 N.J.Eq. 60, 83 A. 492 (1912), *aff'd* 81 N.J.Eq. 210, 86 A. 398 (1913).

More importantly, the relief sought is wholly disproportionate to the injury sustained. Whatever status one accords the testimony of defendant's surveyor, it is clear that the obstruction of plaintiff's "view" is minimal. To compel the defendant to raze and reconstruct his residence at a cost of nearly $39,000 so plaintiff might enjoy an unobstructed view of the lake would be manifestly inequitable. Relief was rightfully refused upon this ground, if no other. Forsee v. Jackson, 192 Mo.App. 408, 411–412, 182 S.W. 783, 785[4, 5] (1916). *See also,* Freed v. Miami Beach Pier Corporation, 93 Fla. 888, 112 So. 841, 52 A.L.R. 1177 (1927). As plaintiff neither prayed for nor proved any money damages, none could have been allowed.

For the reasons noted, the judgment is in all respects affirmed.

NOTES

1. The distinction between laches and estoppel is discussed in Tubbs v. Brandon, 374 So.2d 1358, 1360–61 (Ala.1979) (action to enjoin a violation of a "setback" restriction):

> Laches concerns a prior failure to enforce a restrictive covenant against this defendant rather than a prior failure to enforce a restrictive

covenant against other prior violators. Lapse of time alone is insufficient to establish laches. Prejudice to the party arguing laches, sufficient to make it inequitable to disregard the delay and its consequences, must be caused by plaintiff's delay in asserting his rights. 5 R. Powell, The Law of Real Property ¶ 683 at pp. 228.4–228.5 (rev. ed. 1979). Whether laches is established will vary from case to case depending on the operative facts therein. * * *

Estoppel, however, requires activity both by the plaintiff and by the defendant. The plaintiff must have acted so as to evidence an intent not to enforce his rights under the restrictive covenant and the defendant must have acted in reliance upon plaintiff's conduct so as to make it inequitable for the plaintiff to assert his rights. 5 R. Powell, *supra,* at p. 228.7. One will not be estopped from enforcing restrictive covenants just because he has previously allowed others to deviate in minor respects from the covenants. Abbott v. Arthur, 261 S.C. 31, 198 S.E.2d 261 (1973).

2. In Goodfarb v. Freedman, 76 A.D.2d 565, 431 N.Y.S.2d 573 (1980), the court rejected the defendant's assertion that the plaintiff's claim was barred by "post-summons" laches. The plaintiffs sought to enjoin the construction of a professional photographic studio as a violation of a "residential use" restriction. Prior to construction, the defendants had misrepresented that they were going to build a "small studio" for personal use. The defendants appealed from the trial court's grant of a mandatory injunction:

[O]n their appeal the Freedmans have turned much of their focus from their original emphasis on plaintiffs' laches in failing to take action earlier to plaintiffs' omission to make any effort to preserve the *status quo* once the action commenced. The Freedmans argue that plaintiffs' failure to move for a temporary injunction resulted in further expenditures for construction after the lawsuit began thus depriving the plaintiffs of the right to the remedy of demolition. * * *

* * *

The defendants' postulation of post-summons laches as a substitute for their failed contention of pre-action laches suffers from two serious ailments. * * * Successful invocation of the defense of laches requires proof of prejudice as well as lapse of time (Marcus v. Village of Mamaroneck, 283 N.Y. 325, 28 N.E.2d 856; Pomeroy, Equity Jurisprudence [5th ed.], § 419d). Unfortunately for the Freedmans, the record does not reflect how much money they spent on the construction once the lawsuit began. During the trial, both counsel stipulated that the amount expended by the Freedmans up to September 1, 1977, shortly before they were sued, was $26,454. * * * What the defendants have, then, is their statement that sums were expended on construction after September 1, 1977, but there is no indication as to how much, if any, was spent after October 24, 1977 when the legal action commenced. * * *

On this record, moreover, defendants' reliance on Finn v. Morgan Is. Estates, 283 App.Div. 1105, 132 N.Y.S.2d 46, *modfg.,* Sup., 124 N.Y.S.2d 645, and Forstmann v. Joray Holding Co., 244 N.Y. 22, 154 N.E. 652, is misplaced. In *Finn,* the laches of which the court spoke occurred before the action was commenced, for the structure was 70% completed by that time. Here, pre-action laches is not available to the defendants because of their own conduct in misleading their neighbors into inaction. *Finn* thus restates the familiar proposition that laches may bar a remedy but it does not advance the Freedman's cause. The *Forstmann* case is important but it does not redound in defendants' favor. *Forstmann* involved a business building constructed at Seventieth Street and Madison Avenue in New York City, a business zoned district, in which defendants' property was restricted to residential use by a covenant which still had five years to run. In striking down a mandatory injunction, the Court of Appeals indulged in a balancing of the equities, noting that the covenant would terminate in five years; the block had no special advantages for residence purposes; the value of defendants' property for residential purposes was small; and finally: "The destruction of defendants' building or the denial of their right to erect such a building would inflict a loss on defendants and would neither add to the value of plaintiffs' property nor make their building more desirable for residence purposes." Having undertaken this four-factor analysis which, in essence, struck down the restrictive covenant, the court noted that the defendants, "in what appears to be at worst an honest mistake of law as to the effect of the restrictive covenant," had spent a large sum of money and if they were fast to build the "plaintiffs were slow to invoke the process of the court to preserve the status quo." * * *

When the *Forstmann* criteria are applied to the instant facts, affirmance seems well warranted. Thus, the current restrictive covenants run with the land and are not limited by time; the Twenty–One Acres area has special advantages for residential use and constitutes an ideal residential setting; the defendants' property is residential in nature and clearly has significant value for such use; and while it is apparent that demolition will impose a financial loss upon the defendants, the eradication of their offending structure obviously will add to the value of their neighbors' property. Plaintiffs' real estate expert testified that the Goodfarbs' property was reduced in value by 20% and that of the other plaintiffs 10% as a result of the structure.

Id. at 569–72, 431 N.Y.S.2d at 576–78. *See generally* Jan M. Zitter, Annotation, *Laches or Delay in Bringing Suit as Affecting Right to Enforce Restrictive Covenant,* 25 A.L.R. 4th 233 (1994).

3. One way to avoid the defense of "pre-action" laches is to file a request for a declaratory judgment determining the application of a restrictive covenant to the defendant's proposed structure. *See, e.g.,* Ellis v. George Ryan Co., 424 N.E.2d 125 (Ind.Ct.App.1981).

4. Instead of requesting pre-trial injunctive relief, which usually requires the giving of security, the plaintiff may request a stay pending a final resolution of the case on the merits. *See* Zoning Board of Adjustment v. DeVilbiss, 729 P.2d 353 (Colo.1986) (holding that a request for a permanent injunction became moot upon completion of construction of the defendant's facility in the absence of a request by the plaintiff for either a preliminary injunction or a stay).

5. Another way of characterizing the outcome in *Turpin* might be to say that the plaintiff "came to the violation of the restrictive covenant." In Egan v. Catholic Bishop of Lincoln, 219 Neb. 365, 363 N.W.2d 380 (1985), the court recognized this defense. The plaintiff attempted to dissuade the court from recognizing the defense by analogizing the violation of a restrictive covenant to the maintenance of a nuisance:

> We have held that one's right to enjoin a nuisance is not defeated by the fact that he purchased his property after the nuisance came into existence. Seifert v. Dillon, 83 Neb. 322, 119 N.W. 686 (1909). The analogy, however, is inapposite. The law does not tolerate a nuisance, because it is essentially unlawful or wrongful in character. City of Omaha v. Flood, 57 Neb. 124, 77 N.W. 379 (1898). On the other hand, the law disfavors restrictions on the use of land. Knudtson v. Trainor, 216 Neb. 653, 345 N.W.2d 4 (1984). Thus, the law of nuisances bears no relationship to the question of when one has waived the right to enforce a restriction on the use of land.

Id. at 371, 363 N.W.2d at 384.

3. Violations of Zoning Ordinances

RADACH v. GUNDERSON

Court of Appeals of Washington, 1985.
39 Wash.App. 392, 695 P.2d 128.

WORSWICK, CHIEF JUDGE.

Ole and Barbara Gunderson decided to build a house on their ocean-front lot in the City of Ocean Shores. They contracted the job to David Bickmore. Bickmore mistakenly placed the house 10 feet closer to the ocean-front property line than permitted by the City's zoning code. Eugene and Adriana Radach, neighbors two lots away, complained to the City from almost the beginning, but the City did nothing and the house was completed. The Radachs brought action against the Gundersons and the City for injunctive relief. The Gundersons cross-claimed for indemnity against the City and Bickmore.

The trial court found a zoning code violation, but also found that the Gundersons were "completely innocent," and that the Radachs had suffered no substantial injury. It also found the City negligent, but concluded that it had no duty to the Radachs.[2] Therefore, having balanced the equities between the Radachs and Gundersons only, it concluded that no injunction or other relief was warranted.

On the Radachs' appeal, we reverse. We hold that the City had a duty to the Gundersons which, in the circumstances of this case, was sufficient to impose ultimate liability on the City, and that a balancing of the equities should have taken the egregious negligence of the City into account. We hold, on the undisputed facts in this record, that an injunc-

---

2. The claim against Bickmore fell by the wayside when Gundersons settled Bickmore's claim against them for the balance of the construction cost.

tion must issue compelling the Gundersons to move the house, and that the City must bear the entire expense.

The Radachs have owned their Ocean Shores vacation home since about 1971. The Gundersons owned the second lot to the south, separated by a 60 foot wide vacant lot. The City's zoning code specifies that structures on such lots be no nearer than 50 feet to the property line that parallels and is closest to the waterfront. City Ordinance § 17.50.080. The City building inspector is required to enforce the setback provisions. City Ordinance § 17.62.010.

In 1977, the Gundersons hired Bickmore to build their house and obtain all necessary permits. The Gundersons were not residents of the area; they left all the details to Bickmore. Unfortunately, he thought the setback was 40 feet. When he applied for the building permit, he submitted a plot plan showing the proposed house 40 feet from the ocean-front property line. A secretary for the City Building Department issued the permit without noticing that it violated the zoning code. A few days later, the building inspector checked the foundation forms on the ground and approved them because they were set as shown on the plot plan. He also failed to notice the violation.

The Radachs first saw the construction during the 1977 Thanksgiving vacation. Mr. Radach noticed that the foundation was too close to the ocean. He reported the violation to the Building Department the following Monday. There were no workmen on the site at the time, and Mr. Radach did not know how to contact the Gundersons. The complaint prompted the building inspector to check the Gundersons' plan against the code. Now realizing that he had approved an illegal building, he visited the site and attempted unsuccessfully to locate Bickmore. He made no attempt to contact the Gundersons. By now, the exterior walls and roof were nearly completed.

During December, the inspector tried, again unsuccessfully, to call Bickmore or to talk with him at the site. He left messages with workmen to have Bickmore call him, but never told them that the building violated the code. He decided not to contact the Gundersons, feeling that his first responsibility was to work something out with Bickmore. Meanwhile, at least two other residents complained to the inspector about the violation. Still, he did nothing more until January, and then only referred the problem to the city attorney's office.

On January 4, the City sent letters to the Gundersons and Bickmore urging them to review the situation with neighbors before continuing the construction. The letter intimated that the house violated restrictive covenants[3] but said nothing about the zoning code violation. It did not mention that construction could be stopped by the City. This was the first notice of a problem to be received by the Gundersons. They contacted Bickmore who suggested they ask for a zoning variance. They did so.

3. The area is also subject to restrictive covenants. However, no issue as to these covenants is before us on this appeal.

A hearing was conducted before the Board of Adjustment on February 2. The Radachs and several other property owners appeared and objected. The Board unanimously rejected a variance; the Gundersons thereupon stopped construction.

On February 7, the City notified the Gundersons that the building permit would not be revoked. On March 9, the City notified property owners in the area that it would allow the house to be completed. On March 10, it notified the Gundersons that it had no objections to their continuing construction. The Gundersons then completed the house. This action followed.

The Radachs make two basic assertions here. First, they argue that the City owed them a duty, for violation of which the City should be held liable. Second, they argue that they were absolutely entitled to an injunction, because the court was not permitted to balance the equities in view of a clear violation of the zoning code. We conclude that the Radachs should prevail, but for reasons other than those argued.

As to the City's duty, the questioned acts of the City here were entirely ministerial. It cannot assume the cloak of discretionary immunity. Miotke v. Spokane, 101 Wash.2d 307, 678 P.2d 803 (1984). The only remaining question is whether its acts and omissions violated a duty running not just to the general public, but to any interested individual; liability must be predicated on such a violation of a duty to an individual.
* * *

A City owes an actionable duty to an individual where a special relationship exists or has developed between that individual and the city's agents. Chambers–Castanes v. King Cy., 100 Wash.2d 275, 669 P.2d 451 (1983). Such a duty clearly ran from the City to the Gundersons. The Gundersons' liability runs to Radach and the City's duty runs to the Gundersons. The Gundersons have claimed indemnity from the City. For the reasons that follow, we conclude that a sufficient basis exists for imposing ultimate liability on the City regardless of whether the City owed a specific duty to the Radachs.

The posture of the case is this: the City was negligent; because of that negligence, the Gundersons innocently violated the zoning code; the Radachs are entitled to redress. Because the Radachs have been unable to show monetary damages, their remedy must be an injunction. Were this purely an action at law, there is no doubt at all that the Gundersons would be entitled to indemnity from the City for any relief granted against them. * * * We see no reason why the same principles should not apply in equity. We hold that they do.

There remains the question of balancing the equities. The Radachs essentially argue that this is appropriate only where the litigation concerns purely private interests. They are incorrect. The process of balancing the equities involves the recognition that, in certain instances, courts should refuse equitable remedies where legal rights have been violated. The factors to be considered are:

(a) the character of the interest to be protected, (b) the relative adequacy to the plaintiff of injunction in comparison with other remedies, (c) the delay, if any, in bringing suit, (d) the misconduct of the plaintiff, if any, (e) the relative hardship likely to result to the defendant if an injunction is granted and to the plaintiff if it is denied, (f) the interest of third persons and of the public, and (g) the practicability of framing and enforcing the order or judgment.

* * * The protection afforded by this process is not available to one who proceeds with knowledge that his actions encroach on the property rights of others. * * * The dispositive question in this case is whether the trial court balanced the conduct of the right parties. We hold it did not.

* * *

* * * The trial court balanced the equities between the Radachs and the Gundersons only, and found that the scale tipped in favor of the Gundersons. This was not tenable, as the actions of the City were completely excluded from the equation.

The posture of this case being what it was, the Radachs had the right to have their interest and injury balanced against the interest and actions of the City, which had a duty to—and therefore, as to ultimate liability, stands in the shoes of—the Gundersons. When the City's conduct is included in the balance, it becomes plain that equitable relief must be granted to the Radachs at the expense of the City. * * *

The Radachs sued to protect their view and to prevent the City from allowing encroaching buildings to destroy the legally enforceable setback line. Injunctions have often been used to protect such interests. * * * Although the trial court found that the injury did not devalue the Radachs' property, a demonstrable financial loss is not essential to support an injunctive remedy for a zoning violation. Welton v. 40 East Oak Street Building Corp., 70 F.2d 377 (7th Cir.1934). The improper setback creates a continuing condition which adversely affects the Radachs' enjoyment of their property. A continuing injury is remedied properly by injunction. In our view, the equities must be very compelling indeed to avoid an injunction to correct a clear violation of a zoning ordinance. Therefore, we generally agree that:

> [A]n action for injunctive relief is the appropriate remedy of an aggrieved property owner who seeks to bar the erection of a structure on adjoining or nearby premises in violation of express zoning regulations.

Lesron, Jr., Inc. v. Feinberg, 13 A.D.2d 90, 213 N.Y.S.2d 602, 607 (1961).

Coupled with the injury to Radachs' property interest is the public injury caused by the City's complete failure to enforce the setback ordinance. The public interest is properly considered in determining if a zoning violation should be enjoined. Welton v. 40 East Oak Street Building Corp., 70 F.2d at 383. "The enforcement of a zoning ordinance by injunction is essential if the amenities of the area sought to be protected are to be preserved." Mercer Island v. Steinmann, 9 Wash.App. 479, 486, 513 P.2d 80 (1973). The City's inaction served to defeat rather than preserve the public interest which it was charged with protecting.

The Radachs were not guilty of delay or misconduct, and the injunction can be practicably framed and enforced. The injunction will affect the City financially, but the City ignored its responsibility and allowed the Gundersons to expend a great deal of money constructing a house that was illegally situated. In so doing, it knowingly violated its duty to the Gundersons, apparently taking a calculated risk that the problem would disappear. It was or should have been aware of the serious exposure this created for the Gundersons. The City was egregiously negligent; its financial hardship will not now insulate it. * * *

* * *

Because it is clear to us that an injunction must issue, we see no need to burden the trial court with unnecessary further proceedings. This is an appropriate case for the application of RAP 12.2. Therefore, we reverse and remand with directions to issue an injunction requiring the Gundersons' house to be brought into compliance with zoning setback requirements and, after appropriate further proceedings, to enter judgment against the City for the expense thereof.

NOTES

1. The rather novel theory of "municipal liability" that the court recognized in the *Radach* case has been approved by some commentators. Shelly K. Speir, *The Public Duty Doctrine and Municipal Liability for Negligent Administration of Zoning Codes*, 20 Seattle U. L. Rev. 803 (1997). *But see* Anita R. Brown–Graham, *Local Governments and the Public Duty Doctrine After* Wood v. Guilford County, 81 N.C. L. Rev. 2291 (2003).

2. Note that, in most encroachment cases, the plaintiffs clearly have standing. Typically, an encroachment violates a plaintiff's ownership of a fee estate or of an easement, both of which are clearly defined property interests. Moreover, when the encroachment violates a restrictive covenant, the plaintiff is able to assert a violation of a contract right or of an incorporeal interest in land.

However, in cases like *Radach*, serious standing questions arise. When a plaintiff attempts to enforce a zoning ordinance, he or she is not asserting a private property right, but rather the public interest. Should the plaintiff be permitted to do so? Should enforcement rest solely with the government? In some jurisdictions, if the plaintiff establishes "special injury," he or she will be permitted to sue. Presumably, owning property in close proximity to the zoning violation suffices for this purpose because the plaintiff's injury is clearly different in kind and degree from that suffered by members of the general public. *See, e.g.,* Welton v. 40 East Oak St. Building Corp., 70 F.2d 377 (7th Cir.1934). Moreover, in many states, this standing issue has been addressed by legislation. As one commentator has noted, statutes "in a substantial number of states authorize a taxpayer or other private person to institute an action to enjoin a violation of zoning regulations." Kenneth H. Young, Anderson's American Law of Zoning § 29.01 (4th ed. 1997).

TOWN OF SHERBURNE v. CARPENTER

Supreme Court of Vermont, 1990.
155 Vt. 126, 582 A.2d 145.

Before PECK and DOOLEY, JJ., KATZ, SUPERIOR JUDGE, and CONNARN and SPRINGER, DISTRICT JUDGES (Ret.), Specially Assigned.

DOOLEY, JUSTICE.

* * *

Defendant owned a building on Route 4 in Sherburne and used it to operate his plumbing business. The zoning ordinance required structures in defendant's zone to be set back one hundred feet from Route 4. Defendant's building represented a nonconforming preexisting use that was set back only fifty-five feet from Route 4. In addition, the building had a preexisting porch that further reduced the set-back, although the actual depth of the porch (between eight and ten feet) is in dispute. In 1986, the Town granted defendant a zoning permit to enclose the porch without changing the amount of set-back from Route 4.

Defendant actually tore down the porch and built an enclosed structure in its place. During construction work, the Town zoning administrator viewed the property and determined that the new enclosure would be ten feet deep even though the plan submitted by defendant showed that the porch had been only eight feet deep and the new enclosure would retain this dimension. The zoning administrator sent defendant a letter stating that the new enclosure would be two feet closer to Route 4 than the former porch and, therefore, violated the zoning ordinance. The letter stated that unless defendant reduced the size of the enclosure the Town would sue to have the extra two feet removed from the building. Defendant completed the enclosure without reducing its size, and the Town brought suit for an injunction * * *.

Defendant responded to the Town's action by arguing that the dimensions on the plans he had submitted were erroneous and the enclosed building front was only two inches closer to Route 4 than the edge of the roof on the former porch. He also testified that the zoning administrator, when he issued the permit, had assured him that a couple of feet would not matter. The trial court rejected both of these defenses and found that the porch violated the set-back requirements of the zoning ordinance.

Without findings or reasons addressing the law of injunctive relief, the court determined, however, that it would not require the defendant to tear down the new enclosure. * * *

On appeal, the Town argues that it was entitled to an injunction as a matter of law * * *.

It is clear that 24 V.S.A. § 4445 authorizes the Town to bring an action to abate or correct a violation of the zoning ordinance. *See, e.g.,* Town of Brighton v. Griffin, 148 Vt. 264, 267, 532 A.2d 1292, 1293 (1987). The section does not specify the nature or extent of trial court discretion in acting on such a request. It is a command to the zoning administrator to bring an appropriate proceeding. It is silent on the court's power in acting on the administrator's action.

In Town of Bennington v. Hanson–Walbridge Funeral Home, 139 Vt. 288, 295–96, 427 A.2d 365, 369–71 (1981), this Court considered whether a trial court had discretion under § 4445 to refuse to enjoin the operation of a funeral home crematory being operated in violation of the town zoning ordinance. The Court discussed the concept of relative injury in deciding whether to issue an injunction but declined to rule whether this concept was consistent with § 4445, finding that on the facts of the case it would not apply in any event. It concluded that the town was entitled to an injunction as a matter of law and enjoined the defendant from using its premises for the cremation of human bodies.

The opinion in *Hanson-Walbridge Funeral Home* distinguished Thompson v. Smith, 119 Vt. 488, 509–10, 129 A.2d 638, 652–53 (1957), where the Court held that in an injunction action brought by a neighbor to remove a building constructed in violation of a zoning ordinance, a balancing test applies. The balancing test in *Thompson* requires the trial court to weigh the "relative convenience or inconvenience, the relative injury sought to be cured as compared with the hardship of injunctive relief." *Id.* at 509, 129 A.2d at 652. *Hanson-Walbridge Funeral Home* emphasized that *Thompson* dealt with private landowners where it was possible to compare the "respective hardships" and noted that the "harm upon development of the town as a whole ... cannot be weighed against the financial loss to the defendant." 139 Vt. at 295–96, 427 A.2d at 370.

The issue left open in *Hanson-Walbridge Funeral Home* is present here since the Town seeks a mandatory injunction to require defendant to tear down his enclosure or that part of the enclosure that reduces the set-back by two feet and the trial court refused to issue the injunction. The question is whether the trial court had such discretion.

There is a split of authority on which of the equitable requirements for injunctive relief must be shown if a governmental entity seeks to enjoin a violation of a statute or ordinance, and especially when a municipality seeks a mandatory injunction to require a property owner to remove a structure erected in violation of an ordinance. Generally, where a statute authorizes a municipality or public agency to seek an injunction in order to enforce compliance with a local ordinance or state statute, and is silent as to the injury caused, the municipality is not required to show irreparable harm or the unavailability of an adequate remedy at law before obtaining an injunction; rather, all that must be shown is a violation of the ordinance. *See, e.g.,* Johnson v. Murzyn, 1 Conn.App. 176,

180–81, 469 A.2d 1227, 1230 (1984).* The divergence of views comes on whether the state or municipality must also show that the balance of equities lies on the side of issuance of the injunction.

Some states hold that it is also inappropriate to allow the trial court to balance the equities in a statutory injunction case, reasoning that

> there is no need for judicial accommodation of the defendant's use to that of the plaintiff. For a court to do so would be to usurp the legislative function. Specifically, in the case now before us, if the defendants can continue the unlawful use of the property after complying with the relief granted on remand, the trial court's judgment would have worked to rezone the land with conditions notwithstanding the fact that the power to do so is reserved to the town board alone.

Little Joseph Realty, Inc. v. Town of Babylon, 41 N.Y.2d 738, 745, 363 N.E.2d 1163, 1168, 395 N.Y.S.2d 428, 433–34 (1977). *See also* Metropolitan Development Comm'n v. Douglas, 180 Ind.App. 567, 571, 390 N.E.2d 663, 666 (1979). In Ackerman v. Tri–City Geriatric & Health Care, Inc., 55 Ohio St.2d 51, 378 N.E.2d 145, 149 (1978), an action to enjoin the operation of an unlicensed nursing home, the Supreme Court of Ohio held that the Director of Health did not need to show irreparable injury or lack of an adequate legal remedy once he had shown the statutory violation, and that it would be inappropriate to balance the equities because statutory provisions "which authorize a governmental agent to sue to enjoin activities deemed harmful by the [legislature] are not designed primarily to do justice to the *parties* but to prevent harm to the general public." *Id.* at 57, 378 N.E.2d at 149 (emphasis in original); *see also* Plater, *Statutory Violations and Equitable Discretion,* 70 Calif.L.Rev. 524, 527 (1982) (when there is a continuing violation of statutory law, the court "has no discretion or authority to balance the equities so as to permit that violation to continue"). This reasoning is much the same as our discussion in *Hanson-Walbridge Funeral Home.*

Other states still retain the equitable requirement of balancing the equities. *See, e.g.,* Town of Shapleigh v. Shikles, 427 A.2d 460, 464–65 (Me.1981); City of East Providence v. Rhode Island Hosp. Trust Nat'l Bank, 505 A.2d 1143, 1145–46 (R.I.1986). In the *Shikles* and *Rhode Island Hospital Trust* cases, the Supreme Courts of Maine and Rhode Island emphasized that injunctive relief remains within the discretion of the trial court to be exercised under basic principles of equity and justice and that the statutory authorization for injunctive relief in zoning cases did not eliminate that discretion.

We are faced with two levels of difficulties with the trial court's action in this case. The trial court was silent on why it declined to grant the injunction. Since it refused to grant the injunction, it is fair to assume that it balanced the equities and found that they tipped in defendant's

---

* *Accord* Midland Enterprises, Inc. v. City of Elmhurst, 226 Ill.App.3d 494, 191 Ill.Dec. 725, 624 N.E.2d 913 (1993).

favor. We are left to speculate, however, on the grounds relied upon by the trial court in denying the injunction request. Even if we accept that it could balance the equities in this case, we cannot fairly review the trial court's action and must reverse and remand for an explicit statement of the balance struck. *See, e.g.,* McCormick v. McCormick, 150 Vt. 431, 438, 553 A.2d 1098, 1103 (1988).

The second level of difficulty is with the balancing of the equities in this case. For the guidance of the trial court on remand, we must answer the question left open by *Hanson-Walbridge*. We hold that the trial court has only limited discretion to refuse to issue a mandatory injunction in a case like this. *Hanson-Walbridge Funeral Home* teaches that trial courts cannot weigh the injury to the public of a property use in violation of the zoning ordinance against the cost of compliance to defendant. 139 Vt. at 296, 427 A.2d at 370. Normally, we must assume that the public injury outweighs the private cost.

In considering the issuance of an injunction on remand, the trial court's decision should focus on two areas of inquiry. The first is whether the violation of the zoning ordinance is substantial. While we recognize the difficulty in weighing public injury against private loss in the typical case, there comes a point where the violation is so insubstantial that it would be unjust and inequitable to require the removal of an offending structure through a mandatory injunction. *See* 4 A. & D. Rathkopf, The Law of Planning and Zoning § 45.07, at 45–78 (1981). We emphasize that once the court finds that a violation is substantial, further balancing of injury and cost is generally inappropriate.

The second area is whether the landowner's violation is innocent or, alternatively, involves conscious wrongdoing. *See, e.g.,* County of Kauai v. Pacific Standard Life Ins., 65 Haw. 318, 339 n.22, 653 P.2d 766, 781 n.22 (1982). Courts have generally found that a conscious decision to go forward, in the face of a direction not to from the regulatory body, outweighs factors pointing against the issuance of a mandatory injunction. *See, e.g.,* Planning & Zoning Comm'n v. Desrosier, 15 Conn.App. 550, 556, 545 A.2d 597, 601 (1988); Town of East Hampton v. Buffa, 157 A.D.2d 714, 716, 549 N.Y.S.2d 813, 815 (1990). An injunction may be an excessive remedy where the nonconforming use was constructed without knowledge that it violated the zoning ordinance. *See* Hargreaves v. Skrbina, 662 P.2d 1078, 1081 (Colo.1983) (no injunction can be issued against construction in violation of set-back requirement where permit allowing construction was given erroneously by city).

The record does not disclose whether the factors that would allow denial of the injunction were present in this case, because the trial court made no findings in those areas. Defendant testified and argued that he went forward with the construction because the enclosure encroached on the set-back only a few inches more than the former porch roof. An additional encroachment of a few inches might well not be substantial enough to warrant a mandatory injunction. Nor do we preclude the possibility that the trial court could find that a two-foot encroachment into the set-back was insubstantial in this case. Even if defendant's measurements were inaccurate, it is possible that defendant believed in good faith that he had not reduced the set-back more than a few inches. The question may, in turn, depend on whether the former porch roof overhang is counted in determining the set-back. We leave the resolution of these questions to the trial court on remand.

NOTES

1. Ultimately, whether a specific statutory authorization of injunctive relief bars a court from exercising its traditional equitable discretion is a matter of legislative intent. Presumably the legislature could simply say that a court *must* issue an injunction once it determines a zoning ordinance has been violated. In addition, it could use language specifically prohibiting a court from balancing the hardships or employing the other equitable defenses. Usually, however, legislative intent is at best ambiguous. For example, in Forest County v. Goode, 219 Wis.2d 654, 579 N.W.2d 715 (1998) (reversing the trial court's denial of the county's request for an injunction and remanding for a new hearing), the trial court had balanced the equities and refused to compel a homeowner to relocate his house that violated a county zoning ordinance requiring a 50–foot setback from a lake front. Under state legislation, "the [county zoning] ordinances shall be enforced by appropriate forfeitures [(fines)]. Compliance with such ordinances may also be enforced by injunctional order instituted at the suit of the county or an owner of real estate within the district affected by the regulation." Wis. Stat. § 59.69 (11) (2000). In interpreting this statute for the purpose of providing guidance to the trial court on remand, the Wisconsin Supreme Court held:

> In deciding whether to deny a request for an injunction based upon a shoreland zoning ordinance violation, the circuit court should take evidence and weigh any applicable equitable considerations including the substantial interest of the citizens of Wisconsin in the vigilant protection of the state's shorelands, the extent of the violation, the good faith of other parties, any available equitable defenses such as laches, estoppel or unclean hands, the degree of hardship compliance will create, and the role, if any, the government played in contributing to the violation. This list is not meant to be exhaustive but only to illustrate the importance of the circuit court's consideration of the substantial public interest in enforcing its shoreland zoning ordinances.

> Once a violation is established, a circuit court should grant the injunction except, in those rare cases, when it concludes, after examining the totality of the circumstances, there are compelling equitable reasons why the court should deny the request for an injunction.

Id. at 684, 579 N.W.2d at 729; *accord* Town of Delafield v. Winkelman, 269 Wis.2d 109, 675 N.W.2d 470 (2004).

2. Zoning ordinance setback cases frequently involve an allegation by the property owner that he or she acted in reliance on a representation by a government official that the encroachment would not be actionable and that

the government should therefore be estopped to enforce the ordinance. An estoppel argument, however, is difficult to sustain against the government, as illustrated by *In re* Letourneau, 168 Vt. 539, 726 A.2d 31 (1998):

> Phillip Letourneau (landowner) appeals from a decision of the environmental court imposing a civil fine and awarding injunctive relief in connection with an addition he placed on his home in Derby without a zoning permit and in violation of applicable setback requirements. Landowner [takes] the position that the town should be estopped from bringing this enforcement action * * *.

> Many of the trial court's findings are undisputed, and we summarize them here: The home in question is located on landowner's farm of approximately 184 acres * * * in an area * * * designated a "rural lands" district by the town's zoning ordinance. The building, and landowner's title to it, antedate the Derby zoning ordinance, enacted in 1977. The ordinance contains a 50–foot setback requirement for homes in this district. All but the rear four feet of the house are located within the setback zone from Holland Road. As of the time the zoning ordinance went into effect, the house included a roofed porch, six feet deep, along the front facing Holland Road and one side of the building. There was also a set of three steps leading to the porch.

> * * * [L]andowner decided in 1995 to expand the [living room] * * * in the direction of the porch, which by then had become dilapidated.

> A neighbor of landowner, Susan Judd, was in 1995 the chair of the Derby Planning Commission and had recently served as the town's zoning administrator. Prior to beginning construction on the living room expansion, landowner asked Judd if he needed a permit to tear down and rebuild his porch. He did not tell Judd that he intended to enlarge the enclosed living space of the house into the area occupied by the porch, nor did he tell her that his plan included expanding the building's footprint beyond that of the porch structure. According to the environmental court, Judd told landowner "that she did not anticipate a problem with his plans. She did not tell [landowner] that the project did or did not require a permit."

> Based upon this discussion, landowner commenced construction. Judd said nothing further to landowner when she drove by his home and noticed he was removing the porch. In place of the porch, landowner constructed an L-shaped addition, 12 feet deep, extending 24 feet along the front of the house and 21 feet along one side. The trial court determined that this "increased the degree of nonconformity of the porch [with the setback requirement] by an additional six feet to the front and to the side (or an additional three feet in the area formerly occupied by the front steps[)]."

> After landowner had made substantial progress on this addition, Judd stopped by the house, told landowner he needed a zoning permit, helped him fill out an application and told him to see the town's zoning administrator. The zoning administrator denied the application based on noncompliance with the 50–foot setback requirement and advised land-

owner to seek a variance. While the application process was ongoing, landowner completed work on the addition.

Following a public hearing, the town's zoning board of adjustment denied the variance request on December 15, 1995. * * * [T]he town in March 1996 filed an enforcement action in the environmental court seeking the imposition of * * * a permanent injunction requiring landowner to remove the addition to his home. * * *

* * * On August 22, 1997, the environmental court entered its final judgment * * * ordering landowner, or, if applicable, his heirs and assigns, to remove the addition and to restore the house to its previous footprint prior to any transfer of interest in the property.

On appeal, landowner [contends] * * * that * * * the town should be estopped from enforcing the zoning ordinance * * * because of the actions of * * * Susan Judd.

Under Vermont law, a party seeking to invoke the doctrine of equitable estoppel must establish four elements: (1) the party to be estopped must know the facts; (2) the party to be estopped must intend that its conduct shall be acted upon, or the conduct must be such that the party asserting estoppel has a right to believe it is intended to be acted upon; (3) the party asserting estoppel must be ignorant of the true facts; and (4) the party asserting estoppel must detrimentally rely on the conduct of the party to be estopped. Agency of Natural Resources v. Godnick, 162 Vt. 588, 652 A.2d 988, 991 (1994). Estoppel, which is "based upon the grounds of public policy, fair dealing, good faith, and justice," is rarely invoked against the government; that result is appropriate only when the injustice would ensue from a failure to find an estoppel sufficiently outweighs any effect upon public interest or policy that would result from estopping the government in a particular case. Id. at 592–93, 652 A.2d at 991. The trial court determined that * * * "[a] zoning permit is required for any structural alteration or enlargement of a building" regardless of any setback issues. We agree with landowner that this is a "fact" for purposes of the estoppel elements enumerated above. We can further assume arguendo that Judd knew this fact, that landowner was ignorant of it, and that [her] status as chair of the planning board was such that representations made by her would be sufficient to bind the town in these circumstances. * * *

We nevertheless agree with the trial court that this is not one of those rare situations in which it is appropriate to estop a governmental entity. * * * Landowner's failure to disclose to Judd that he intended to expand his house further into the setback zone did not merely contribute to the problem—it is the problem around which this case revolves. We do not assume that the town would simply have overlooked the possibly less significant zoning transgression of remodeling without a permit if it did not involve enlarging a noncomplying structure. Nevertheless, it would be inconsistent with the relevant considerations of public policy, good faith, fair dealing and justice to estop a government entity in connection with inferences drawn by one of its officials based on a disclosure to her that was lacking the critical facts to evaluate the proposed land development.

We conclude that landowner has failed to demonstrate the first element of the test and that the town is not estopped from enforcing the setback requirement against landowner.

Id. at 541–42, 547–48, 726 A.2d at 34, 37–38; *see generally* Douglas W. Kmiec, Zoning and Planning Deskbook § 7.49 (2d ed. 2004) (estoppel may sometimes be successfully asserted as a defense against the government).

4. Nuisance

a. *Private Nuisance*

PATE v. CITY OF MARTIN

Supreme Court of Tennessee, 1981.
614 S.W.2d 46.

COOPER, JUSTICE.

Appellants filed an action in the Chancery Court of Weakley County seeking the abatement of a nuisance and damages to real property resulting from the nuisance. The chancellor found that a sewage lagoon, owned and maintained by the City of Martin, was a permanent nuisance and awarded appellants $10,000.00 in damages. The chancellor also found that "an injunction would be too harsh a remedy and should be denied." The Court of Appeals concurred in the chancellor's finding that the lagoon, as maintained, is a nuisance; however, the court classed the nuisance as temporary rather than permanent, reversed the award of damages which was based on the before and after value of appellants' property, and dismissed appellants' action for failure to prove damages for impairment of the use and enjoyment of property, which is the basis for damages resulting from a temporary nuisance. * * *

In 1969, the City of Martin built a lagoon into which raw sewage is piped from the city's sewer system. Theoretically, in a properly constructed and maintained sewage lagoon, sewage sinks to the bottom of a lagoon, where it is decomposed through bacterial action. Little, if any, odor is attendant to this process.

The evidence establishes that objectionable odors did not emit from the lagoon for the first two or three years of its operation, indicating that the lagoon was properly constructed. However, since that time, more often than not the surface of the lagoon has had a thick scum of raw sewage floating on top of the water. The odor from the scum is so strong that it makes habitation of dwellings in the vicinity almost impossible. The evidence further shows that this condition can be remedied by the adding of additional enzymes to the sewage and by scattering or churning the surface scum so that it will settle to the bottom of the lagoon.

After receiving complaints of the unsightly condition of the lagoon and odors emanating therefrom, the City of Martin purchased a motor boat and used it in the lagoon to churn the scum. However, the city ceased this activity after a few months, and at a time the city should have known the odors would be magnified by seasonal heat and lack of wind and rain. There is no indication in the record that the City of Martin ever added more than a minimal amount of enzymes to the sewage.

A nuisance has been defined as anything which annoys or disturbs the free use of one's property, or which renders its ordinary use or physical occupation uncomfortable. In City of Nashville v. Nevin, 12 Tenn.App. 336, it was said that a nuisance extends to everything that endangers life or health, gives offense to the senses, violates the laws of decency, or obstructs the reasonable and comfortable use of property.

* * *

In this case, the description of the odors emanating from the sewage lagoon convinces us, as it did the chancellor and the Court of Appeals, that the lagoon as maintained is a nuisance in fact. We also are of the opinion, as was the Court of Appeals, that the nuisance can be corrected by the expenditure of labor and money on the part of the City of Martin.

A nuisance which can be corrected by the expenditure of labor or money is a temporary nuisance. Where the nuisance is temporary, damages to property affected by the nuisance are recurrent and may be recovered from time to time until the nuisance is abated. * * *

Further, being charged with the duty of protecting property rights against damage from a nuisance, a court of equity will on application of the person injured, enjoin the nuisance. * * * This is especially true where the nuisance is classed as "temporary." Seldom, if ever, will an award of damages, standing alone, be an adequate remedy where the nuisance gives every promise of continuing and is one that can be corrected by the expenditure of labor or money. However, in this case the chancellor denied plaintiffs' application for injunctive relief, giving as his reason "that an injunction would be too harsh a remedy." This conclusion was predicated on the chancellor's finding that the lagoon, as located and maintained, was a permanent nuisance—that is, one that the City of Martin could not correct by the expenditure of labor and money and that a consequent result of an injunction would be the denial to the City of Martin of a needed sewage lagoon. As heretofore noted, the nuisance that is the subject of this action, in fact, is one that can be corrected by the expenditure of time and labor. * * * In view of past inaction on the part of the City of Martin, we are of the opinion that an injunction should issue from the Chancery Court of Weakley County requiring the City of Martin to take all reasonable steps to terminate odors from the lagoon, including but not limited to the twice daily operation of a motorboat over the surface of the lagoon to churn and break up surface matter and the addition of enzymes in an amount sufficient to effect the speedy reduction of waste material without the presence of offensive odors.

Evidence of damage to appellants' real property from the nuisance was directed to proving the depreciation in its market value. This was in the mistaken belief that the nuisance was, as found by the chancellor, permanent in nature. The measure of damages for a temporary nuisance is the injury to the value of the use and enjoyment of the property, which is usually shown by evidence of the extent that the rental value of the property is diminished by the nuisance. The chancellor's award of damages, being predicated on the wrong measure, was improper and the Court of Appeals acted correctly in setting aside the award. The Court of Appeals also dismissed appellants' action, which we think was error. Appellants demonstrated that they are entitled to the aid of a court of equity in the abatement of a nuisance. They also showed that the nuisance interfered with the use and enjoyment of their property. They are entitled to damages for the loss of this use and enjoyment. * * *

* * *

The judgment of the Court of Appeals dismissing the action is reversed. The cause is remanded to the Chancery Court of Weakley County for the entry and enforcement of a mandatory injunction directed to the abatement of the nuisance, and for the taking of proof on the issue of damages. * * *

ESCOBAR v. CONTINENTAL BAKING CO.

Appeals Court of Massachusetts, 1992.
33 Mass.App.Ct. 104, 596 N.E.2d 394.

Dreben, Justice.

The plaintiffs purchased a three-decker house on Purchase Street in New Bedford adjacent to land on which the defendant operates a bakery distribution center. Bakery deliveries are made in trucks and tractor trailers, and, in order to insure the freshness of the product, some deliveries occur between the hours of midnight and 7:00 A.M. Contending that the noise from the trucks is a nuisance, the plaintiffs brought this action to enjoin the nighttime (early morning) deliveries to the site. A judge of the Superior Court denied injunctive relief, finding that the utility of the defendant's conduct far outweighs the harm to the plaintiffs. Instead, he awarded $36,000 in damages, not for the diminution in value of the plaintiffs property, as none was shown, but for the "nuisance which has affected their sleep." * * *

In this appeal by the defendant, we must consider whether, under circumstances where an injunction is too severe a remedy, damages may be awarded, and, if so, whether they may be recovered by the plaintiffs in this case. To be decided is whether it is reasonable to require that a cost—the harm to the plaintiffs—of the defendant's socially desirable activity be borne by the defendant. * * *

In contending that the judge's findings establish that its activities do not constitute a nuisance, the defendant recognizes that "[t]he law of nuisance affords no rigid rule to be applied in all instances. It is elastic. It undertakes to require only that which is fair and reasonable under all the circumstances." Stevens v. Rockport Granite Co., 216 Mass. 486, 488, 104

N.E. 371 (1914). What the defendant fails to acknowledge is that, under the current law of nuisance, the denial of an injunction is not always a precedent for the denial of damages. Even where the utility of the defendant's conduct outweighs the gravity of the harm, a court may conclude, in some circumstances, that "a cost of carrying on that activity should be borne by the defendant; therefore, the activity is a nuisance, justifying a tort action for damages." Prosser & Keeton, Torts § 88A, at 631 (5th ed. 1984). *See also id.* § 89, at 641. As stated in comment d, Restatement (Second) of Torts § 822 (1977), "It may be reasonable to continue an important activity if payment is made for the harm it is causing but unreasonable to initiate or continue it without paying." *See also id.* § 826 comment f; * * * Boomer v. Atlantic Cement Co., 26 N.Y.2d 219, 226, 309 N.Y.S.2d 312, 257 N.E.2d 870 (1970).

While there has been no explicit adoption of this concept by Massachusetts decisions, the focus in our cases on the balance of equities and what is reasonable under the circumstances, as well as the flexibility of relief afforded, leads us to conclude that the Supreme Judicial Court would concur in this approach. For example, in Pendoley v. Ferreira, 345 Mass. 309, 315, 187 N.E.2d 142 (1963), Justice Cutter, writing for the court, determined that, while the plaintiffs were entitled to have the offensive operation (a piggery) terminated, an injunction should be delayed to allow for a reasonable adjustment of the defendant's affairs. During the period of delay, additional payments were to be made to the plaintiffs for the harm caused. We see little difference in principle in allowing a defendant to continue its operations for a longer or more permanent time but with a concurrent obligation to pay a plaintiff for the loss.

Before recounting the facts found by the judge, we point out that we do not consider ourselves bound by his conclusion that it was unreasonable for the defendant to act as it did without paying for the harm that was inflicted on the plaintiffs. Whether a nuisance exists is factually based. * * * The finding of a nuisance, however, embraces not only factual determinations but is also "a ruling as to what facts are sufficient in law to constitute a nuisance under the circumstances disclosed." * * * It "is a sufficiently mixed question of law and fact to permit an appellate court to resolve the issue at least where [as here] the action below was tried to the court." * * *

We turn to the facts as found by the judge and occasionally quote from his findings. Continental Baking Company's facility and the plaintiffs' adjacent three-decker house are both located on Purchase Street, a major north-south traffic route in New Bedford. "The neighborhood surrounding the plaintiffs' property has been commercial, busy and fairly noisy for decades." Also abutting the plaintiffs' building are a parking lot and a large commercial laundry that causes noise and emits odors. Trains run on railroad tracks next to, and parallel with, Purchase Street. Within two blocks of the plaintiffs' building are a major six-lane highway (Route

195), a major east-west traffic route (Coggeshall Street), and an all-night Sunoco gasoline station.

The defendant's building has been used in connection with the baking industry since 1915. Acquired by the defendant in 1926, the building was operated until 1965 as both a bakery and a distribution facility. From 1965 on, the property was used as a site for distribution of bakery products, and, until 1980, it also housed a thrift store where the defendant conducted retail sales. After the termination of its baking and retail operations, the defendant's activities generated less nighttime noise than before.

The defendant's use of the building has always entailed nighttime activities. The nighttime schedule of deliveries between 12:00 midnight and 7:00 A.M. has been in effect since at least 1963. After 10:00 P.M. and before 11:30 A.M., deliveries to the New Bedford facility only take place once a night. The purpose of these deliveries is to maximize freshness, "the single most important attribute in the bakery business."

Products having a wholesale value of seven million dollars and a retail value of nearly nine million dollars are distributed annually from the New Bedford facility, where the defendant employs thirty-eight persons. Because freshness is important in order to be competitive, an injunction prohibiting nighttime deliveries would necessitate relocation of the defendant's plant. It would cost the defendant approximately $1.7 million to build a new distribution site.

The plaintiffs knew there was a bakery business next door when they bought their property for $35,900 in 1977.[2] The 1977 price reflected the property's location and the defendant's business activities.

Applying a balancing test of harm to the plaintiffs and hardship to the defendant, the judge found that injunctive relief was inappropriate because, as we indicated earlier, "the utility of the defendant's conduct far outweighs the harm done to the plaintiffs." *See* Restatement (Second) of Torts § 826. He found, however, that the sleep of the plaintiffs was affected and that the plaintiffs had suffered damage due to the unreasonable interference with their use and enjoyment of their property. As compensation, the judge awarded them $36,000 to cover all past, present, and future damages.

While our cases have not discussed the factors which determine whether the plaintiff or the defendant should bear the loss to the plaintiff from conduct which is sufficiently in the social interest that it should not be enjoined, we think the same (or similar) considerations which have traditionally informed our nuisance determinations should also be applicable in deciding whether the less severe remedy of damages should be awarded. This is consistent with what Prosser and Keeton suggest as some of the relevant factors:

---

2. Jose Escobar testified that at the time of trial their property was worth $155,000. He also testified that he conducts a siding business there with three trucks.

(1) the amount of the harm resulting from the interference;

(2) the relative capacity of the plaintiff and the defendant to bear the loss by way of shifting the loss to the consuming public at large as a cost of doing business or by other means such as some type of insurance;

(3) the nature of the plaintiff's use of his property;

(4) the nature of the defendant's use of his property;

(5) the nature of the locality;

(6) priority in time as to the respective activities of the plaintiff and the defendant in the area.

Prosser & Keeton, Torts § 88, at 630. We also find instructive the authors' examples:

Those who build residences in a rural area, and beyond the limits of a city and zoning regulations and the protection thus afforded, do so for many reasons, but they may justly and fairly be required to accept certain hazards of so doing. Moreover, if an industrial enterpriser first arrived in an area and plaintiff at a modest price purchased a tract for residential use, the fact that his use and enjoyment for such a purpose is substantially affected is not, generally speaking, a sufficient justification for relief.

Ibid.

Applying these or analogous considerations to the findings of the judge, we conclude that this is not a case where it is reasonable to impose upon the defendant the cost of the noise encountered by the plaintiffs. While the plaintiffs have suffered some physical discomforts, they have obtained considerable benefits by coming to the area. They purchased the property at a price that reflected its location and the defendant's adjacent business; the property has increased considerably in value, *see* note 2, *supra*, and has, as Jose Escobar testified, special value to him as he can store his materials and trucks on the property and can maintain his construction business from the site. When they purchased the property, the plaintiffs were aware of the bakery business and that the area was, in large measure, commercial.

In determining whether a nuisance exists, the "character of the locality is a circumstance of great importance." * * * Moreover, while coming to a nuisance in itself does not bar relief, it, too, is a significant factor in determining what is fair and reasonable. "No one can move into a quarter given over to foundries and boiler shops and demand the quiet of a farm." Stevens v. Rockport Granite Co., 216 Mass. at 488, 104 N.E. 371. There is here no suggestion that the neighborhood is changing or becoming less industrial, *see* * * * Pendoley v. Ferreira, 345 Mass. at 310, 187 N.E.2d 142, or that by withholding damages the court is preventing changes in the locale thereby "arrogat[ing to the defendant] a good deal of the value of the adjoining land." *Cf.* Richmond Bros., Inc. v. Hagemann,

359 Mass. 265, 268, 268 N.E.2d 680 (1971), quoting from a predecessor draft to Restatement (Second) of Torts, § 840D, comment b. Although the judge made no findings concerning the relative capacity of the plaintiffs and the defendant to reduce the effects of the noise, Escobar in testifying acknowledged that he did not use an air conditioner in the summer and also indicated that he did not think the defendant's offer to build a wall and a cover over its trucking activities would be helpful.

In sum, we conclude that there was error in the award of damages. The judgment for the plaintiffs is reversed and judgment is to enter for the defendant.

Notes

1. The *Escobar* court articulates the "majority view" regarding the "coming to the nuisance" doctrine, holding that it is just one factor to be considered in determining whether the defendant is liable in damages. The history of the "coming to the nuisance" concept is set forth in Weida v. Ferry, 493 A.2d 824 (R.I.1985) (holding that the defendant, a dairy farmer, could be held liable for nuisance and that the plaintiff's coming to the nuisance was simply one factor for the trial court to consider on remand when determining whether to hold the defendant liable in damages):

> The defense is called the doctrine of coming to the nuisance, and at common law it was defined thus:
>
>> If my neighbor makes a tan-yard so as to annoy and render less salubrious the air of my house or gardens, the law will furnish me with a remedy: but if he is first in possession of the air, and I fix my habitation near him, the nuisance is of my own seeking, and may continue.
>
> 2 Blackstone, Commentaries on the Laws of England 402 (17th ed. 1830).
>
> Thus, before the turn of the century, [the courts held]:
>
>> If one voluntarily moves into a town or neighborhood where smoke or noxious gases abound, it may be presumed that he does so for sufficient reasons, and he should not be permitted to come into a court of equity and restrain the prosecution of industries already established, and upon which the business interests and welfare of the community may depend.
>
> Tuttle v. Church, 53 F. 422, 426 (D.R.I. 1892).
>
> The doctrine has been modified so that one's coming to the nuisance no longer acts as an absolute bar to recovering damages in a nuisance action. This modification came from a recognition that an absolute bar to a finding of nuisance would, in effect, give the offending activity a perpetual servitude upon the land of its neighbors without the payment of any compensation. * * * We believe that one's coming to the nuisance is simply one factor that may be considered in determining whether or not a defendant's or a respondent's conduct was an unlawful interference with

a neighbor's real estate. Prosser and Keeton, The Law of Torts 635 (5th ed. 1984).

Id. at 827. The policy considerations behind the "minority view," which still recognizes the "coming to the nuisance" doctrine as an absolute bar to a cause of action for damages, are set forth in *Jerry Harmon Motors, Inc. v. Farmers Union Grain Terminal Ass'n*, 337 N.W.2d 427 (N.D.1983) (holding that the defendant, a feed plant that discharged dust into the atmosphere, was not liable in damages because the plaintiff had come to the nuisance):

> We cannot disregard the obvious fact that our state is not as densely populated as many of the states which comprise or follow the majority view. North Dakota has many open spaces available which many of the industrial eastern states do not enjoy. We must also consider what role the alleged nuisance activity has with the general business activities of the community and state, which are primarily farming and agricultural. * * * Grain elevators and feed-grinding businesses are needed and support the farming and agricultural activities of this state. * * *

>   * * *

> We therefore conclude that any individual or corporation or partnership that comes to an alleged nuisance has a heavy burden to establish liability.

Id. at 431–32. While Massachusetts has not adopted the "minority view," how important was the "coming to the nuisance" concept in the resolution of *Escobar?*

    2. Earlier in this chapter we saw that plaintiff-homeowners are often able to protect their scenic views by obtaining injunctive relief to enforce restrictive covenants limiting building height. Assuming the absence of such restrictive covenants, may a homeowner's view be protected by the private nuisance concept? Consider the language of *Kruger v. Shramek*, 5 Neb.App. 802, 565 N.W.2d 742 (1997) (denying an injunction to a plaintiff whose 180–degree view of a golf course was obscured by approximately 20 degrees due to the defendant's fence and landscaping):

> The general rule is that a lawful building or structure cannot be complained of as a private nuisance merely because it obstructs the view of neighboring property. *See* 44 Plaza Inc. v. Gray–Pac Land Co., 845 S.W.2d 576 (Mo.App.1992); Collinson v. John L. Scott, Inc., 55 Wash.App. 481, 778 P.2d 534 (1989); Mohr v. Midas Realty Corp., 431 N.W.2d 380 (Iowa 1988); Venuto v. Owens–Corning Fiberglas Corp., 22 Cal.App.3d 116, 99 Cal.Rptr. 350 (1971) * * *.

> The above rule finds its genesis in the repudiation of the traditional English doctrine of ancient lights. Under that doctrine, a landowner acquired an easement for light across an adjoining landowner's property and could prevent the adjoining landowner from obstructing the light once the easement was established by the passage of time. *See* * * * Prah v. Maretti, 108 Wis.2d 223, 321 N.W.2d 182 (1982) * * *. The ancient lights doctrine as applied to claims involving views has been repudiated by every state considering it. One basis for the doctrine's repudiation is that "it is not adapted to the conditions existing in the country and could

not be applied to rapidly growing communities without working mischievous consequences to property owners." * * * An additional basis for the doctrine's repudiation is that providing a landowner with what is essentially an unwritten negative prescriptive easement over a neighbor's property would frustrate the purpose of the recording statutes, one objective of which is to ensure that all property rights are recorded and discoverable by a diligent title search. * * *

Id. at 808, 565 N.W.2d at 747. On the other hand, the next case suggests that there may be an alternative approach to protecting a view in some jurisdictions.

DOWDELL v. BLOOMQUIST

Supreme Court of Rhode Island, 2004.
847 A.2d 827.

FLAHERTY, JUSTICE.

"Tree at my window, window tree, My sash is lowered when night comes on; But let there never be curtain drawn Between you and me."

—Robert Frost

In the matter before us, four western arborvitae trees are at the plaintiff's window. Sadly, however, the curtains between the neighboring parties have long since been drawn, forever dividing what was once an amicable relationship between them. The fate of the offending trees now hangs in the balance.

The plaintiff, Cheryl Dowdell, brought this action in Superior Court alleging that the defendant, Peter Bloomquist, planted four western arborvitae trees on his Charlestown property solely to exact revenge against her, to retaliate by blocking her view, and in violation of the spite fence statute, G.L.1956 § 34–10–20.[1] She sought legal and equitable relief. * * *

The parties' homes are on adjoining lots in a subdivision of Charlestown, each approximately one acre in size. Dowdell's home sits at a higher elevation than Bloomquist's and has a distant view of the ocean over the Bloomquist property. In June 2000, defendant acquired the home from his mother, Lorraine Bloomquist. Prior to that time, the Dowdell family had an amicable relationship with defendant's mother. Change was in the wind in the fall of 2000, however, when defendant petitioned for a zoning variance from the Charlestown zoning board seeking permission to build a second-story addition to his home. The plaintiff expressed concern about the petition, anxious that the addition would compromise her view of the

---

1. General Laws 1956 § 34–10–20 provides as follows:

Spite fences.—A fence or other structure in the nature of a fence which unnecessarily exceeds six feet (6') in height and is maliciously erected or maintained for the purpose of annoying the owners or occupants of adjoining property, shall be deemed a private nuisance, and any owner or occupant who is injured, either in the comfort or enjoyment of his or her estate thereby, may have an action to recover damages for the injury.

Atlantic Ocean. For six months the parties argued before the Charlestown Zoning Board of Review as to the merits of the addition. As a result, the relationship between the neighbors became less than friendly. In March 2001, defendant began clearing land and digging holes to plant the disputed trees in a row between their homes. In April, defendant's counsel sent a letter to plaintiff warning him against trespass onto the Bloomquist property. In May, one day after the zoning board closed its hearing on defendant's variance request defendant began planting the four western arborvitae trees that now stand in a row bordering the property line. Although the forty-foot-high trees enabled little light to pass into Dowdell's second-and third-story picture windows, testimony at trial evidenced that the vegetation was not a bar to the unkind words between the neighbors.

After the trial justice heard four days of testimony and viewed the property, he made a finding that the row of trees were a fence, based on the language of § 34–10–1.[6] He further found that the objective of privacy claimed by defendant was "no more than a subterfuge for his clear intent to spite his neighbors by erecting a fence of totally out of proportion trees." Hence, the trial justice found that the trees constituted a spite fence in violation of § 34–10–20. He noted testimony that plaintiff's real estate values had depreciated by as much as $100,000. Nonetheless, he found that money damages could not adequately compensate her and that equitable relief was more appropriate. Bloomquist was ordered "to cut the four Western Arborvitae to no more than 6' in height and keep them at that level or remove them entirely with no more Western Arborvitae to be planted."

* * * In his appeal, defendant asserts that the offending trees do not constitute a fence. Moreover, defendant contends that even if the trees were considered a fence, the trial justice erroneously granted relief in the face of testimony that the trees serve a useful purpose of privacy for defendant. To support that contention, defendant relies on Musumeci v. Leonardo, 77 R.I. 255, 259–60, 75 A.2d 175, 177–78 (1950), for the proposition that when a fence is erected for a useful purpose, despite spiteful motive, no relief may be granted. Moreover, defendant alleges that the trial justice lacked the authority to award injunctive relief based on the holding of *Musumeci* as well as the specific language of the spite fence statute, which states that one "may have an action to recover damages for the injury." Section 34–10–20. Additionally, defendant urges that the trial justice erred by granting relief that amounted to an easement for light or view where no such remedy exists at common law.

* * *

This is the first occasion this Court has had to address the issue of whether a row of trees may be considered a fence within the meaning of

---

6. Section 34–10–1 includes in its definition of lawful fences "[a] hedge" of specified proportions. The trial justice concluded that the four arborvitae trees may be considered a hedge based on expert testimony at trial and that, therefore, the trees constitute a fence.

the spite fence statute, § 34–10–20. We believe the trial justice properly referred to the definition of "lawful fences" found in § 34–10–1 to understand the simple meaning and legislative intent behind its use of the word "fence." Based upon the language of § 34–10–1, a fence clearly includes a hedge. And based upon the expert testimony relied on by the trial justice, a row of western arborvitae trees may constitute a hedge. However, even if the trees were not a hedge per se, the spite fence statute refers to "[a] fence or other structure in the nature of a fence." The trial justice considered the proximity of the four trees that touched one another, and the broad span of sixty feet across which they spread, and rationally interpreted that the trees were a fence. Although defendant argues that he presented expert testimony that the western arborvitae is not a hedge plant, we nonetheless believe that the trees, when taken as a whole, fall well within the statutory definition of a "structure in the nature of a fence." * * * We are not alone in this assessment. Recently, a California appellate court found a row of evergreen trees to be a fence within the meaning of the California spite fence statute.[8] Wilson v. Handley, 97 Cal.App.4th 1301, 119 Cal.Rptr.2d 263 (2002). That court stated,

> In light of this statutory purpose, a structure need not be built to prevent intrusion from without or straying from within to be a "fence or other structure in the nature of a fence" within the meaning of the spite fence statute. Instead, the structure need only be built to separate or mark the boundary between adjoining parcels—albeit, in an unnecessarily high and annoying manner.

Id. at 269.

We next consider defendant's contention that the trial justice erroneously discounted defendant's testimony that the trees were erected for the beneficial purpose of privacy. We recognize that some useful purpose for a fence may render the victim of one even maliciously erected without a remedy. In *Musumeci*, this Court determined that a fence served the useful purpose of preventing water from entering the premises of the first floor of the complainant's house. Hence, because the purpose of the fence was not wholly malicious, it was not enjoined as a private nuisance. *Musumeci*, 77 R.I. at 258–59, 75 A.2d at 177 (citing Burke v. Smith, 69 Mich. 380, 37 N.W. 838 (1888) (one of the first cases announcing the new American rule on spite fences, now considered to embody the prevailing modern view)). However, based on the turbulent history between the parties, the provocative statements made by defendant, the notice of trespass letter sent to plaintiff, and the size, timing, and placement of the trees, we cannot say that the trial justice was wrong to give defendant's

---

8. Section 841.4 of the California Civil Code, entitled "spite fences," provides as follows: "Any fence or other structure in the nature of a fence unnecessarily exceeding 10 feet in height maliciously erected or maintained for the purpose of annoying the owner or occupant of adjoining property is a private nuisance. Any owner or occupant of adjoining property injured either in his comfort or the enjoyment of his estate by such nuisance may enforce [certain code-prescribed] remedies * * *." Cal. Civil Code § 841.4 (West 1982).

testimony little weight and to find his claim that the fence was installed to enhance his privacy lacked credibility. * * *

[T]he final issue to be determined is whether injunctive relief was an appropriate remedy for the aggrieved plaintiff. The defendant relies on *Musumeci* for the proposition that plaintiff is not entitled to injunctive relief because the loss of light and view that she alleges is not a private nuisance that equity will enjoin. Moreover, he maintains that the spite fence statute provides only for a monetary damages remedy. However, upon careful review of the language of § 34–10–20, this Court's discussion in *Musumeci*, and the law of private nuisance, we believe that injunctive relief is an available remedy for a violation of the spite fence statute. * * *

* * * Although *Musumeci* confirms that there is no common law right to light and air, it does not preclude equitable relief for erection of a spite fence. When the spite fence statute is violated, which was not the case in *Musumeci*, the offending action is deemed a "private nuisance." *See* § 34–10–20. Under private nuisance law, equitable relief is an appropriate remedy. *See* Harris v. Town of Lincoln, 668 A.2d 321 (R.I.1995) (private nuisance of emission of noises, odors, and vibrations by sewer-processing facility pumping station onto neighboring residential property warranted injunctive relief, in addition to monetary damages); Weida v. Ferry, 493 A.2d 824 (R.I.1985) (noxious smells and flies emanating from dairy farm operations more suitably classified as a private nuisance rather than negligence action; case remanded for new trial with presumption that equitable relief would be an appropriate remedy had the farm not already ceased operations by this time); DeNucci v. Pezza, 114 R.I. 123, 329 A.2d 807 (1974) (injunctive relief properly granted upon trial justice's finding that noise from freight trucks hitching and unhitching in parking lot during early morning hours was unreasonable private nuisance interfering with the plaintiff's use and enjoyment of his residential property).

We look to the case of *Wilson* for additional support that a spite fence that blocks light, air, or view is properly considered an actionable private nuisance because the statute defines it as such. In *Wilson*, the court held that a row of trees blocking the plaintiff's view of Mt. Shasta may be considered a violation of the statute even though the fence interfered with nothing more than light and air. The court acknowledged that although interference with light and air was not considered a nuisance under the general definition of "nuisance," the spite fence statute never specified that the fence need interfere with more than light and air for it to be considered a nuisance. The court concluded that "we are not at liberty to read any such additional requirement into the statute." *Wilson*, 119 Cal.Rptr.2d at 270. We agree. What makes a spite fence a nuisance under § 34–10–20 is not merely that it blocks the passage of light and view, but that it does so "unnecessarily" for the malicious purpose of "annoyance." This is a notable distinction.

Finally, defendant correctly asserts that the statute specifically allows for "an action to recover damages." Specifically, the statute states that one who is injured by a spite fence *"may* have an action to recover damages for the injury." Section 34–10–20. (Emphasis added.) However, contrary to defendant's assertion, we believe this language merely sanctions the additional remedy of damages, but does not exclude injunctive relief, which is a remedy logically rooted in the nature and purpose of the statute. To support this holding, we look to the remedial practice in other states that recognize the erection of a spite fence as actionable. Connecticut, Idaho, Indiana, Massachusetts, Montana, New Hampshire, and South Dakota all allow injunctive relief for violations of spite fence law. Especially illustrative is the law as it stands in Massachusetts, whose statute is strikingly similar to § 34–10–20. The Massachusetts statute provides:

> A fence or other structure in the nature of a fence which unnecessarily exceeds six feet in height and is maliciously erected or maintained for the purpose of annoying the owners or occupants of adjoining property shall be deemed a private nuisance. Any such owner or occupant injured * * * may have an action of tort for damages * * *.

Mass. Gen. Laws Ann. ch. 49, § 21 (West 1994).

In interpreting this law, the Supreme Judicial Court of Massachusetts recognized that despite the lack of explicit language, the court had the authority to order a spite fence to be "abated," in addition to damages and costs. Rice v. Moorehouse, 150 Mass. 482, 23 N.E. 229 (1890) (trial justice properly ordered abatement of so much of a spite fence as exceeded six feet in height). The Court relied on the law of nuisance as the basis for its decision, just as we do today.

For the reasons set forth above, we affirm the judgment of the Superior Court. The record shall be remanded to the Superior Court.

JUSTICE GOLDBERG did not participate.

JUSTICE FLANDERS, concurring in part and dissenting in part. [Opinion omitted.]

NOTES

1. For a similar approach to *Dowdell,* see Alberino v. Balch, 185 Vt. 589, 969 A.2d 61 (2008).

2. A suit for a permanent injunction against what is alleged to be a private nuisance frequently entails a "double balancing" process. First, the factfinder must determine whether a nuisance exists. In determining whether defendant's activity unreasonably interferes with the use and enjoyment of plaintiff's land, the factfinder, as we have seen earlier, considers and balances numerous factors. If the first balancing process results in a nuisance determination, the judge must determine whether a permanent injunction should issue, and this latter determination also entails a balancing process. Sometimes the court will determine that the hardships on the defendant and the community are so substantial that it will simply deny a permanent injunction and substitute permanent damages as the sole remedy. This is what happened in Boomer v. Atlantic Cement Co., the case we next consider. At other times,

the court will refuse to enjoin defendant's operation completely, and instead will issue an injunction that purports to abate the nuisance while permitting defendant's activity to continue. Consider the language of McCombs v. Joplin 66 Fairgrounds, Inc., 925 S.W.2d 946 (Mo.Ct.App.1996), where plaintiff-residential landowners sought a permanent injunction against the continued operation of a dirt automobile race track, but the trial judge, after finding that a nuisance existed, entered a "tailored injunction" purporting to abate the nuisance by imposing noise restrictions while permitting defendant's activity to continue:

> Based on * * * [the] findings by the court, we believe the court-ordered noise restrictions properly balance the utility of the racetrack's operation against the gravity of plaintiffs' harm, especially with the "normal person" standard in mind.

> We reach this conclusion based on Racine v. Glendale Shooting Club, Inc., 755 S.W.2d 369 (Mo.App.1988), and Massey v. Long, 608 S.W.2d 547 (Mo.App.1980), where, in each case, a nuisance from noise was found and restrictions were imposed to control the noise. In *Massey*, plaintiffs' home was adjacent to defendants' six apartment air-conditioning units. The trial court found the operation of the air-conditioning units was a nuisance and enjoined defendants from operating the air-conditioning units between the hours of 10 p.m. to 7 a.m. The appellate court decided that substantial proof supported the injunction and said:

>> The trial court, rather than enjoining all use of the air conditioning units, sought, and this court believes achieved, a proper balancing of the equities between the parties. Enjoining [defendants'] use of the air conditioning units during certain fixed nighttime hours cannot be said to have subjected them (or their tenants) to a degree of discomfort unconscionably disproportionate to the disruptive annoyance experienced by the [plaintiffs] from the noise emitted by the air conditioning units.

> 608 S.W.2d at 550.

> In *Racine*, plaintiffs were adjoining landowners to the defendant's gun club. The trial court entered a limited injunction in plaintiffs' favor restricting the discharge of large caliber, high-powered firearms except under certain limited conditions such as the times of firing, the number of shooting matches, and the number of participants. On appeal the court noted that "[n]oise is not a nuisance per se but may be of such a character or so excessive as to become one, even though it arises from the operation of a lawful business." 755 S.W.2d at 372. In upholding the limited rather than a complete injunction, the court said, "The trial court's relief was an effort to restrict the club's activities to a level which did not constitute a substantial impairment of plaintiffs' peaceful enjoyment of their property." *Id.* at 373.

> As in *Racine*, the trial court in this case restricted the racetrack's operation to a level which did not constitute a substantial impairment of Plaintiffs' peaceful enjoyment of their property. The restrictions are based on substantial evidence to that effect. * * *

Id. at 951. For a similar approach, see Edmunds v. Sigma Chapter of Alpha Kappa Lambda Fraternity, 87 S.W.3d 21 (Mo.Ct.App.2002).

For another interesting example of a "tailored" injunction, see Eva Community Ass'n v. Buchanan, 1991 WL 241159 (Tenn.Ct.App.1991), where the court rejected a permanent injunction against defendant operating a mussel shell purchasing business in a residential area near a lake, but nevertheless approved a "modified" version of it:

> The defendants in the present case are operating a lawful business and have attempted to operate it in as unobtrusive a manner as possible. While the record indicates that the business does somewhat interfere with the neighbors' use and enjoyment of their property, the interference is not extreme and is limited to normal business hours. Therefore, we do not believe that the facts of this case warrant completely enjoining the defendants from operating their mussel shell purchasing business. We believe that a more appropriate remedy is to order the defendants to do everything possible to eliminate the offensive aspects of the operation of their business. This includes requiring the defendants to take any steps which will reduce the noise coming from their business. * * * [W]e believe that the defendants should continue to do everything possible to operate the business in a manner consistent with the local health codes and standards and to continue to do everything necessary to make sure that odors, insects and rodents do not become a problem. Since the institution of our decision may require court supervision for a limited period of time to oversee the defendants' compliance with the modified injunction, the trial court might find it beneficial to appoint a master to oversee the imposition of this order.

> We find that the trial court correctly held that the operation of the defendants' business constitutes a nuisance. We hold, however, that the circumstances surrounding this case do not support the Chancellor's decision permanently enjoining the defendants from operating their mussel shell purchasing business. Therefore, the Chancellor's order permanently enjoining the defendants from operating their mussel shell purchasing business is modified. The defendants are required to take any possible affirmative steps to reduce the noise produced by the operation of their business and to see that the mussel shell divers do not park their vehicles in a way which obstructs traffic in the area. Finally, the defendants are permitted to operate their business only during the daylight hours.

BOOMER v. ATLANTIC CEMENT CO.

New York Court of Appeals, 1970.
26 N.Y.2d 219, 309 N.Y.S.2d 312, 257 N.E.2d 870.

BERGAN, JUDGE.

Defendant operates a large cement plant near Albany. [The plant was built in 1962 at a cost of $40,000,000 and the defendant installed the most efficient devices available to prevent the discharge of dust.] These are actions for injunction and damages by [eight] neighboring land owners alleging injury to property from dirt, smoke and vibration emanating from the plant. A nuisance has been found after trial, temporary damages [in amounts ranging from $40.00 per moth to $150.00 per month for a period of 57 months] have been allowed; but an injunction has been denied.

The public concern with air pollution arising from many sources in industry and in transportation is currently accorded ever wider recognition accompanied by a growing sense of responsibility in State and Federal Governments to control it. Cement plants are obvious sources of air pollution in the neighborhoods where they operate.

But there is now before the court private litigation in which individual property owners have sought specific relief from a single plant operation. The threshold question raised by the division of view on this appeal is whether the court should resolve the litigation between the parties now before it as equitably as seems possible; or whether, seeking promotion of the general public welfare, it should channel private litigation into broad public objectives.

A court performs its essential function when it decides the rights of parties before it. Its decision of private controversies may sometimes greatly affect public issues. Large questions of law are often resolved by the manner in which private litigation is decided. But this is normally an incident to the court's main function to settle controversy. It is a rare exercise of judicial power to use a decision in private litigation as a purposeful mechanism to achieve direct public objectives greatly beyond the rights and interests before the court.

Effective control of air pollution is a problem presently far from solution even with the full public and financial powers of government. In large measure adequate technical procedures are yet to be developed and some that appear possible may be economically impracticable.

It seems apparent that the amelioration of air pollution will depend on technical research in great depth; on a carefully balanced consideration of the economic impact of close regulation; and of the actual effect on public health. It is likely to require massive public expenditure and to demand more than any local community can accomplish and to depend on regional and interstate controls.

* * *

The cement making operations of defendant have been found by the court at Special Term to have damaged the nearby properties of plaintiffs in these two actions. That court, as it has been noted, accordingly found defendant maintained a nuisance and this has been affirmed at the Appellate Division. The total damage to plaintiffs' properties is, however, relatively small in comparison with the value of defendant's operation and with the consequences of the injunction which plaintiffs seek.

The ground for the denial of injunction, notwithstanding the finding both that there is a nuisance and that plaintiffs have been damaged substantially, is the large disparity in economic consequences of the nuisance and of the injunction. This theory cannot, however, be sustained without overruling a doctrine which has been consistently reaffirmed in several leading cases in this court and which has never been disavowed here, namely that where a nuisance has been found and where there has been any substantial damage shown by the party complaining an injunction will be granted.

The rule in New York has been that such a nuisance will be enjoined although marked disparity be shown in economic consequence between the effect of the injunction and the effect of the nuisance.

The problem of disparity in economic consequence was sharply in focus in Whalen v. Union Bag & Paper Co., 208 N.Y. 1, 101 N.E. 805 [(1913)]. A pulp mill entailing an investment of more than a million dollars polluted a stream in which plaintiff, who owned a farm, was "a lower riparian owner". The economic loss to plaintiff from this pollution was small. The court, reversing the Appellate Division, reinstated the injunction granted by the Special Term against the argument of the mill owner that in view of "the slight advantage to plaintiff and the great loss that will be inflicted on defendant" an injunction should not be granted * * *. "Such a balancing of injuries cannot be justified by the circumstances of this case," Judge Werner noted * * *. He continued: "Although the damage to the plaintiff may be slight as compared with the defendant's expense of abating the condition, that is not a good reason for refusing an injunction" * * *.

Thus the unconditional injunction granted at Special Term was reinstated. The rule laid down in that case, then, is that whenever the damage resulting from a nuisance is found not "unsubstantial," viz., $100 a year, injunction would follow. This states a rule that had been followed in this court with marked consistency * * * (Campbell v. Seaman, 63 N.Y. 568 [(1876)]).

* * *

Although the court at Special Term and the Appellate Division held that injunction should be denied, it was found that plaintiffs had been damaged in various specific amounts up to the time of the trial and damages to the respective plaintiffs were awarded for those amounts. The effect of this was, injunction having been denied, plaintiffs could maintain successive actions at law for damages thereafter as further damage was incurred.

The court at Special Term also found the amount of permanent damage attributable to each plaintiff, for the guidance of the parties in the event both sides stipulated to the payment and acceptance of such permanent damage as a settlement of all the controversies among the parties. The total of permanent damages to all plaintiffs thus found was $185,000 [in amounts ranging from $11,000 to $70,000 for each of the eight plaintiffs]. This basis of adjustment has not resulted in any stipulation by the parties.

This result at Special Term and at the Appellate Division is a departure from a rule that has become settled; but to follow the rule literally in these cases would be to close down the plant at once. This court is fully agreed to avoid that immediately drastic remedy; the difference in view is how best to avoid it. One alternative is to grant the injunction but postpone its effect to a specified future date to give opportunity for technical advances to permit defendant to eliminate the nuisance; another is to grant the injunction conditioned on the payment of permanent damages to plaintiffs which would compensate them for the total economic loss to their property present and future caused by defendant's operations. For reasons which will be developed the court chooses the latter alternative.

If the injunction were to be granted unless within a short period— e.g., 18 months—the nuisance be abated by improved methods, there would be no assurance that any significant technical improvement would occur.

The parties could settle this private litigation at any time if defendant paid enough money and the imminent threat of closing the plant would build up the pressure on defendant. If there were no improved techniques found, there would inevitably be applications to the court at Special Term for extensions of time to perform on showing of good faith efforts to find such techniques.

Moreover, techniques to eliminate dust and other annoying by-products of cement making are unlikely to be developed by any research the defendant can undertake within any short period, but will depend on the total resources of the cement industry nationwide and throughout the world. The problem is universal wherever cement is made.

For obvious reasons the rate of the research is beyond control of defendant. If at the end of 18 months the whole industry has not found a technical solution a court would be hard put to close down this one cement plant if due regard be given to equitable principles.

On the other hand, to grant the injunction unless defendant pays plaintiffs such permanent damages as may be fixed by the court seems to do justice between the contending parties. All of the attributions of economic loss to the properties on which plaintiffs' complaints are based will have been redressed.

The nuisance complained of by these plaintiffs may have other public or private consequences, but these particular parties are the only ones who have sought remedies and the judgment proposed will fully redress them. The limitation of relief granted is a limitation only within the four corners of these actions and does not foreclose public health or other public agencies from seeking proper relief in a proper court.

It seems reasonable to think that the risk of being required to pay permanent damages to injured property owners by cement plant owners would itself be a reasonably effective spur to research for improved techniques to minimize nuisance.

The power of the court to condition on equitable grounds the continuance of an injunction on the payment of permanent damages seems undoubted. * * *

The damage base here suggested is consistent with the general rule in those nuisance cases where damages are allowed. * * *

* * *

Thus it seems fair to both sides to grant permanent damages to plaintiffs which will terminate this private litigation. The theory of damage is the "servitude on land" of plaintiffs imposed by defendant's nuisance. (*See* United States v. Causby, 328 U.S. 256, 261, 262, 267, 66 S.Ct. 1062, 90 L.Ed. 1206 [(1946)], where the term "servitude" addressed to the land was used by Justice Douglas relating to the effect of airplane noise on property near an airport.)

The judgment, by allowance of permanent damages imposing a servitude on land, which is the basis of the actions, would preclude future recovery by plaintiffs or their grantees. * * *

This should be placed beyond debate by a provision of the judgment that the payment by defendant and the acceptance by plaintiffs of permanent damages found by the court shall be in compensation for a servitude on the land.

Although the Trial Term has found permanent damages as a possible basis of settlement of the litigation, on remission the court should be entirely free to re-examine this subject. It may again find the permanent damage already found; or make new findings.

The orders should be reversed, without costs, and the cases remitted to Supreme Court, Albany County to grant an injunction which shall be vacated upon payment by defendant of such amounts of permanent damage to the respective plaintiffs as shall for this purpose be determined by the court.

JASEN, JUDGE (dissenting). I agree with the majority that a reversal is required here, but I do not subscribe to the newly enunciated doctrine of assessment of permanent damages, in lieu of an injunction, where substantial property rights have been impaired by the creation of a nuisance.

It has long been the rule in this State, as the majority acknowledges, that a nuisance which results in substantial continuing damage to neighbors must be enjoined. (Whalen v. Union Bag & Paper Co., 208 N.Y. 1, 101 N.E. 805 [(1913)]; Campbell v. Seaman, 63 N.Y. 568 [(1876)] * * *). To now change the rule to permit the cement company to continue polluting the air indefinitely upon the payment of permanent damages is, in my opinion, compounding the magnitude of a very serious problem in our State and Nation today.

* * *

The specific problem faced here is known as particulate contamination because of the fine dust particles emanating from defendant's cement plant. The particular type of nuisance is not new, having appeared in many cases for at least the past 60 years. (*See* Hulbert v. California Portland Cement Co., 161 Cal. 239, 118 P. 928 [(1911)]). It is interesting to note that cement production has recently been identified as a significant source of particulate contamination in the Hudson Valley. This type of pollution, wherein very small particles escape and stay in the atmosphere, has been denominated as the type of air pollution which produces the greatest hazard to human health. We have thus a nuisance which not only is damaging to the plaintiffs, but also is decidedly harmful to the general public.

I see grave dangers in overruling our long-established rule of granting an injunction where a nuisance results in substantial continuing damage. In permitting the injunction to become inoperative upon the payment of permanent damages, the majority is, in effect, licensing a continuing wrong. It is the same as saying to the cement company, you may continue to do harm to your neighbors so long as you pay a fee for it. Furthermore, once such permanent damages are assessed and paid, the incentive to alleviate the wrong would be eliminated, thereby continuing air pollution of an area without abatement.

* * *

This kind of inverse condemnation may not be invoked by a private person or corporation for private gain or advantage. Inverse condemnation should only be permitted when the public is primarily served in the taking or impairment of property. The promotion of the interests of the polluting cement company has, in my opinion, no public use or benefit. * * *

Nor is it constitutionally permissible to impose servitude on land, without consent of the owner, by payment of permanent damages where the continuing impairment of the land is for a private use. * * * This is made clear by the State Constitution (art. I, § 7, subd. [a]) which provides that "[p]rivate property shall not be taken for *public use* without just compensation" (emphasis added). It is, of course, significant that the section makes no mention of taking for a *private* use.

* * *

I would enjoin the defendant cement company from continuing the discharge of dust particles upon its neighbors' properties unless, within 18 months, the cement company abated this nuisance.

It is not my intention to cause the removal of the cement plant from the Albany area, but to recognize the urgency of the problem stemming from this stationary source of air pollution, and to allow the company a specified period of time to develop a means to alleviate this nuisance.

I am aware that the trial court found that the most modern dust control devices available have been installed in defendant's plant, but, I submit, this does not mean that *better* and more effective dust control devices could not be developed within the time allowed to abate the pollution.

Moreover, I believe it is incumbent upon the defendant to develop such devices, since the cement company, at the time the plant commenced production (1962), was well aware of the plaintiffs' presence in the area, as well as the probable consequences of its contemplated operation. Yet, it still chose to build and operate the plant at this site.

In a day when there is a growing concern for clean air, highly developed industry should not expect acquiescence by the courts but should instead plan its operations to eliminate contamination of our air and damage to its neighbors.

Accordingly, the orders of the Appellate Division, insofar as they denied the injunction, should be reversed, and the actions remitted to Supreme Court, Albany County to grant an injunction to take effect 18 months hence, unless the nuisance is abated by improved techniques prior to said date.

FULD, C.J., and BURKE and SCILEPPI, JJ., concur with BERGAN, J. BREITEL and GIBSON, JJ., taking no part.

NOTES

1. An excellent discussion of the development of American private nuisance law, the availability of injunctive relief, and the differing approaches of the First and Second Restatements of Torts appears in Carpenter v. Double R Cattle Co., 105 Idaho 320, 669 P.2d 643 (Idaho Ct.App.1983) (adopting Restatement (Second) of Torts), *rev'd*, 108 Idaho 602, 701 P.2d 222 (1985):

American tort law in the nineteenth and early twentieth centuries was founded upon the rock of "fault." As the notion of fault burrowed into the concept of nuisance, the strict liability which had attended nuisance in property law began to deteriorate. American courts stressed that liability for nuisance would arise only from "unreasonable" uses of property. * * *

However, American emphasis upon the element of reasonableness persisted. Our courts also underscored the distinction between conditions which are inherently nuisances (nuisances per se) and those conditions which may or may not constitute nuisances, depending upon the surrounding circumstances (nuisances per accidens). Of cases in the latter category, it became customary for the courts to say that whether an invasion of another's enjoyment of property was unreasonable would depend upon all circumstances in the case. These circumstances typically would include the location of the claimed nuisance, the character of the neighborhood, the nature of the offending activity, the frequency of the intrusion, and the effect upon the enjoyment of life, health and property.

Moreover, the American transformation resulted in diminished application of the principle—derived from property law—that where property

rights were substantially impaired by a nuisance, the complaining party
was entitled to an injunction. This principle, which had complemented
the property-based concept of strict liability, entitled a property owner to
block an offensive activity on neighboring property, regardless of disparate economic consequences. American courts apparently found this approach ill-suited to the demands of a developing nation.

There evolved two lines of American response to the problem of
injunctions. One response was to narrow the scope of cases in which
injunctions would be granted, while continuing to recognize an entitlement to damages for injury to property rights. * * *

* * *

The second line of American response to the injunction problem was
to narrow the scope of cases in which nuisances were found to exist. This
was achieved by incorporating the social value—the "utility"—of the
offending activity into the litany of circumstances to be weighed in
determining whether a particular use of property was "unreasonable."
Thus, the utility of an offending activity militated not merely against the
issuance of an injunction, but also against a determination that the
offending activity was a nuisance at all. This second line of response
found expression in the general ("black letter") principles set forth by the
Restatement of Torts (1932) (herein cited as the First Restatement).
Section 826 of the First Restatement declared that an invasion of another's enjoyment of property would be deemed unreasonable, and therefore
a nuisance, unless the utility of the actor's conduct outweighed the
gravity of the harm.

* * *

Dissatisfaction with the First Restatement also was expressed by the
courts. In Boomer v. Atlantic Cement Co., 26 N.Y.2d 219, 309 N.Y.S.2d
312, 257 N.E.2d 870 (1970), the New York Court of Appeals held that
parties adversely affected by dust from a cement plant would be entitled
to recover damages for the harm, although the value of the cement plant
to the community was so great that its operation would not be enjoined.
* * *

* * *

* * * [Ultimately, the American Law Institute adopted the Restatement (Second) of Torts in 1977.] The Second Restatement, like its
predecessor, divides nuisances into two groups: (a) "intentional and
unreasonable" invasions of another's interest in the use and enjoyment of
property, and (b) invasions which are "unintentional" but otherwise
actionable under general tort principles. Second Restatement at § 822.

The first category is broader than the term "intentional" at first
glance might suggest. Section 825 of the Second Restatement explains
that an invasion is "intentional" if the actor knows that the invasion is
resulting, or is substantially certain to result, from his activity. Thus, the
purpose of an activity, such as a feedlot, may not be to invade its
neighbors' interests in the use and enjoyment of their property; but the

invasion is "intentional" within the meaning of the Second Restatement if the proprietors of the activity know that such an invasion is resulting—or is substantially certain to result—from the intended operation of their business. * * *

The Second Restatement treats such an "intentional" invasion as a nuisance if it is "unreasonable." Section 826 of the Second Restatement now provides two sets of criteria for determining whether this type of nuisance exists:

An intentional invasion of another's interest in the use and enjoyment of land is unreasonable if

> (a) the gravity of the harm outweighs the utility of the actor's conduct, or

> (b) the harm caused by the conduct is serious and the financial burden of compensating for this and similar harm to others would not make the continuation of the conduct not feasible.

* * *

The Second Restatement clearly has rejected the notion that if an activity's utility exceeds the harm it creates, the activity is not a nuisance and therefore is free from all liability in damages or for injunctive relief. * * * It discards those earlier authorities which had responded to the problem of disparate economic consequences of injunctions by narrowing the concept of nuisance. * * *

* * *

* * * [The Second Restatement recognizes] that utility of the activity alleged to be a nuisance is a proper factor to consider in the context of injunctive relief; but that damages may be awarded regardless of utility. Evidence of utility does not constitute a defense against recovery of damages where the harm is serious and compensation is feasible. Were the law otherwise, a large enterprise, important to the local economy, would have a lesser duty to compensate its neighbors for invasion of their rights than would a smaller business deemed less essential to the community.

* * * [The Second Restatement also recognizes] the fundamental difference between making an activity compensate those whom it harms, and forcing the activity to discontinue or to modify its operations. The damage question goes to a person's basic right in tort law to recover for harm inflicted by another. The injunction question is broader; it brings into play the interest of other persons who may benefit from the activity. Comparative benefits and hardships must be weighed in determining whether injunctive relief is appropriate. * * *

* * * The Second Restatement deals effectively with the problem of "externalities" identified in the ALI proceedings. Where an enterprise externalizes some burdens upon its neighbors, without compensation, our market system does not reflect the true cost of products or services provided by that enterprise. Externalities distort the price signals essential to the proper functioning of the market.

This problem affects two fundamental objectives of the economic system. The first objective, commonly called "efficiency" in the economic theory, is to promote the greatest aggregate surplus of benefits over the costs of economic activity. The second objective, usually termed "equity" or "distributive justice," is to allocate these benefits and costs in accordance with prevailing societal values. The market system best serves the goal of efficiency when prices reflect true costs; and the goal of distributive justice is best achieved when benefits are explicitly identified to the correlative costs.

Although the problem of externalities affects both goals of efficiency and distributive justice, these objectives are conceptually different and may imply different solutions to a given problem. In theory, if there were no societal goal other than efficiency, and if there were no impediments to exchanges of property or property rights, individuals pursuing their economic self-interests might reach the most efficient allocation of costs and benefits by means of exchange, without direction by the courts. *See* Coase, *The Problem of Social Cost*, 3 J.L. & Econ. 1 (1960). However, the real world is not free from impediments to exchanges, and our economic system operates within the constraints of a society which is also concerned with distributive justice. Thus, the courts often are the battlegrounds upon which campaigns for efficiency and distributive justice are waged.

[The history of nuisance law] has reflected the differing emphases upon efficiency and distributive justice. As noted, the English system of property law placed a preeminent value upon property rights. It was thus primarily concerned with distributive justice in accord with those rights. For that reason the English system favored the injunction as a remedy for a nuisance, regardless of disparate economic consequences. However, when the concept of nuisance was incorporated into American law, it encountered a different value system. Respect for property rights came to be tempered by the tort-related concept of fault, and the demands of a developing nation placed greater emphasis upon the economic objective of efficiency relative to the objective of distributive justice. The injunction fell into disfavor. The reaction against the injunction, as embodied in the First Restatement, so narrowed the concept of nuisance itself that it rendered the courts impotent to deal with externalities generated by enterprises of great utility. This reaction was excessive; neither efficiency nor distributive justice has been well served.

In order to address the problem of externalities, the remedies of damages and injunctive relief must be carefully chosen to accommodate the often competing goals of efficiency and distributive justice. *See generally* Polinsky, *Resolving Nuisance Disputes: The Simple Economics of Injunctive and Damage Remedies*, 32 Stan. L. Rev. 1075 (1980); Ellickson, *Alternatives to Zoning: Covenants, Nuisance Rules, and Fines as Land Use Controls*, 40 U. Chi. L. Rev. 681 (1973). * * * Section 826(a) of the Second Restatement allows both injunctions and damages to be employed where the harm created by an economic activity exceeds its utility. Section 826(b) allows the more limited remedy of damages alone to be employed where it would not be appropriate to enjoin the activity but the activity is imposing harm upon its neighbors so substantial that they cannot reasonably be expected to bear it without compensation. *Id.* at 647–54.

2. Compare the balancing of the hardships in nuisance cases with the balancing test applied in trespass cases regarding encroachments. *See* Thomas W. Merrill, *Trespass, Nuisance, and the Costs of Determining Property Rights*, 14 J. Legal Stud. 13 (1985).

3. Professor Daniel Farber believes that it was proper to deny injunctive relief in *Boomer* but he maintains that "victims of an egregious nuisance should be entitled to injunctive relief except where such relief is infeasible. Essentially this means that only where the balance tilts very strongly against the plaintiffs will an injunction be denied." Daniel A. Farber, *Reassessing* Boomer: *Justice, Efficiency, and Nuisance Law, in* Property Law and Legal Education: Essays in Honor of John E. Cribbet 17 (1988). In these latter situations, he argues that "a generous measure of damages should be used, based on the market price of the right to the injunction against the nuisance. In essence we are arranging a 'forced sale' to the defendant of the plaintiff's right to an injunction, and we should measure compensation accordingly." *Id.* at 20. As an example of this approach to damages, he explains that "if the pollution caused a $200,000 decrease in the value of the land for its present use and a profit to the polluter of $500,000, the right to pollute would sell for something between $200,000 and $500,000." *Id.* at 18.

4. The *Boomer* result is far from inevitable. In several recent nuisance cases, courts have balanced the hardships at the remedy stage and granted precisely the injunctive relief requested by the plaintiff. *See, e.g.,* Tichenor v. Vore, 953 S.W.2d 171 (Mo.Ct.App.1997) (affirming permanent injunction against defendants' "operating, maintaining or having a dog kennel or otherwise keeping or maintaining more than two dogs" on their property). Similarly, consider the language of Penland v. Redwood Sanitary Sewer Service District, 156 Or.App. 311, 965 P.2d 433 (1998) (affirming the grant of a permanent injunction in favor of plaintiff-homeowners enjoining a sewer district from operating a composting operation in treating raw sewage):

> [W]e must compare the benefit to plaintiffs with the hardship to the District resulting from a permanent injunction. The benefit to plaintiffs is the ability to enjoy their property in a manner consistent with its rural character—to garden, and eat outside, and keep their windows open on summer evenings. For plaintiffs, an injunction would mean being able to use and enjoy their property as they did before the nuisance came to them—to live, and breathe, free from a pervasive, nauseating odor.
>
> The concomitant detriment to the District is essentially, but not completely, economic. If use of the existing composting facility is enjoined, the District has, at least, two arguably feasible alternatives: (1) move the composting activities to another site; or (2) return to its prior practice of trucking the sludge and applying it to acceptable agricultural sites. Either of those options, even if otherwise practicable, would involve substantial additional expense. In addition, a return to the District's prior practice of land application would result in loss of significant environmental benefits.

The District's plant manager, Robert Webber, and Steven Gilbert, an environmental engineer retained by the District, testified persuasively that composting was an environmentally superior alternative to land application of biosolids. Webber explained, in some detail, why returning to its previous practice of land application was no longer a feasible alternative for the District, notwithstanding the fact that many districts and nearby municipalities in southern Oregon, including the City of Grants Pass, continue that practice. The concerns that Webber identified include groundwater contamination monitoring, site constraints, land use restrictions, sludge runoff, and grazing restrictions.

In contrast, the District's objections to relocating the composting operation to an alternative, non-residential site appear to be purely financial. * * *

Assessing those alternatives, we conclude, as did the trial court, the hardship to the District from the issuance of an injunction does not "greatly outweigh" the benefit to plaintiffs. There is no question that relocating the composting operation will, in fact, be expensive. Nevertheless, two factors especially bear on our assessment of the equities.

First, although a precise apportionment is impossible, the District's relocation expenses have been exacerbated by actions and additional expenditures that the District undertook after becoming aware of the Penlands' initial complaints in 1991 and of other plaintiffs' complaints by late 1992. This was not merely a case of the nuisance coming to the homeowners, but of the District expanding its operations after plaintiffs protested. * * *

Second, although the additional cost to the District will be substantial, the impact will be ameliorated because it can be spread among the District's rate-payers—over 1,800 households. * * *

* * * If the District and those whom it serves are committed to the environmental values and benefits of composting, that may well be laudable. But the cost of that commitment should be commonly borne and not visited solely upon a handful of "involuntary contributors who happen to lie in the path of progress." We emphasize that this is not a case of simple-minded "NIMBY" parochialism—of narrow-minded refusal to assume burdens that are, reasonably and necessarily, part of living as a community. It is, rather, a clear and compelling case of living next to a * * * nuisance. The equities favor the issuance of an injunction.

Id. at 321–24, 965 P.2d at 439–40. How does *Penland* differ from *Boomer?*

5. For yet another perspective on *Boomer,* consider the following advocacy of a "pliability" approach:

Pliability, or pliable, rules are contingent rules that provide an entitlement owner with property rule or liability rule protection so long as some specified condition obtains: however, once the relevant condition changes, a different rule protects the entitlement—either liability or property, as the circumstances dictate. Pliability rules, in other words, are dynamic rules, while property and liability rules are static. This can be seen by revisiting [*Boomer*]. * * * Calabresi and Melamed [in Calebresi &

Melamed, *Property Rules, Liability Rules, and Inalienability: One View from the Cathedral*, 85 Harv. L. Rev. 1089 (1972)] viewed the case as presenting a choice between enforcing property rule protection, as the homeowners demanded, or liability rule protection, as the court eventually ruled. Calabresi and Melamed believed these to be the two basic options because they—like the theorists that followed them—focused on discrete moments of legal protection in isolation. In reality, though, the court could have chosen a pliability rule. For example, the court might have allowed Atlantic Cement to pay damages and continue operating for five years to avoid immediate and massive layoffs at the plant, but also could have decreed that at the end of the five years, the injunction would become absolute to enable homeowners' quiet and clean use of their realty. This pliable rule—a five-year liability rule, followed by indefinite property rule protection—would have permitted the court to combine the features of liability and property rules over the course of time.

Abraham Bell & Gideon Parchomovsky, *Pliability Rules*, 101 Mich. L. Rev. 1, 5–6 (2002); *see also* Abraham Bell & Gideon Parchomovsky, *Givings*, 111 Yale L.J. 547 (2000); Ezra M. Holzer, *Boomer Revisisted: Using Experimental and Partial Injunctions in Private Nuisance Actions*, 64 Def. Couns. J. 99 (1997); Henry E. Smith, *Exclusion and Property Rules in the Law of Nuisance*, 90 Va. L. Rev. 965 (2004).

SPUR INDUSTRIES, INC. v. DEL E. WEBB DEVELOPMENT CO.

Supreme Court of Arizona, 1972.
108 Ariz. 178, 494 P.2d 700.

CAMERON, VICE CHIEF JUSTICE.

From a judgment permanently enjoining the defendant, Spur Industries, Inc., from operating a cattle feedlot near the plaintiff Del E. Webb Development Company's Sun City, Spur appeals. * * * Although numerous issues are raised, we feel that it is necessary to answer only two questions. They are:

1. Where the operation of a business, such as a cattle feedlot, is lawful in the first instance, but becomes a nuisance by reason of a nearby residential area, may the feedlot operation be enjoined in an action brought by the developer of the residential area?

2. Assuming that the nuisance may be enjoined, may the developer of a completely new town or urban area in a previously agricultural area be required to indemnify the operator of the feedlot who must move or cease operation because of the presence of the residential area created by the developer?

* * *

It is clear that as to the citizens of Sun City, the operation of Spur's feedlot was both a public and a private nuisance. They could have successfully maintained an action to abate the nuisance. Del Webb, having shown a special injury in the loss of sales, had standing to bring suit to enjoin the nuisance. Engle v. Clark, 53 Ariz. 472, 90 P.2d 994 (1939). The judgment of the trial court permanently enjoining the operation of the feedlot is affirmed.

MUST DEL WEBB INDEMNIFY SPUR?

A suit to enjoin a nuisance sounds in equity and the courts have long recognized a special responsibility to the public when acting as a court of equity * * *.

In addition to protecting the public interest, however, courts of equity are concerned with protecting the operator of a lawfully, albeit noxious, business from the result of a knowing and willful encroachment by others near his business.

In the so-called "coming to the nuisance" cases, the courts have held that the residential landowner may not have relief if he knowingly came into a neighborhood reserved for industrial or agricultural endeavors and has been damaged thereby:

> Plaintiffs chose to live in an area uncontrolled by zoning laws or restrictive covenants and remote from urban development. In such an area plaintiffs cannot complain that legitimate agricultural pursuits are being carried on in the vicinity, nor can plaintiffs, having chosen to build in an agricultural area, complain that the agricultural pursuits carried on in the area depreciate the value of their homes. The area being *primarily agricultural,* any opinion reflecting the value of such property must take this factor into account. The standards affecting the value of residence property in an urban setting, subject to zoning controls and controlled planning techniques, cannot be the standards by which agricultural properties are judged. * * *

Dill v. Excel Packing Company, 183 Kan. 513, 525, 526, 331 P.2d 539, 548, 549 (1958). * * *

Were Webb the only party injured, we would feel justified in holding that the doctrine of "coming to the nuisance" would have been a bar to the relief asked by Webb, and, on the other hand, had Spur located the feedlot near the outskirts of a city and had the city grown toward the feedlot, Spur would have to suffer the cost of abating the nuisance as to those people locating within the growth pattern of the expanding city. * * *

We agree, however, with the Massachusetts court that:

> The law of nuisance affords no rigid rule to be applied in all instances. It is elastic. It undertakes to require only that which is fair and reasonable under all the circumstances. In a commonwealth like this, which depends for its material prosperity so largely on the continued growth and enlargement of manufacturing of diverse varieties, "extreme rights" cannot be enforced. * * *

Stevens v. Rockport Granite Co., 216 Mass. 486, 488, 104 N.E. 371, 373 (1914).

There was no indication in the instant case at the time Spur and its predecessors located in western Maricopa County that a new city would spring up, full-blown, alongside the feeding operation and that the developer of that city would ask the court to order Spur to move because of the new city. Spur is required to move not because of any wrongdoing on the part of Spur, but because of a proper and legitimate regard of the courts for the rights and interests of the public.

Del Webb, on the other hand, is entitled to the relief prayed for (a permanent injunction), not because Webb is blameless, but because of the damage to the people who have been encouraged to purchase homes in Sun City. It does not equitably or legally follow, however, that Webb, being entitled to the injunction, is then free of any liability to Spur if Webb has in fact been the cause of the damage Spur has sustained. It does not seem harsh to require a developer, who has taken advantage of the lesser land values in a rural area as well as the availability of large tracts of land on which to build and develop a new town or city in the area, to indemnify those who are forced to leave as a result.

Having brought people to the nuisance to the foreseeable detriment of Spur, Webb must indemnify Spur for a reasonable amount of the cost of moving or shutting down. It should be noted that this relief to Spur is limited to a case wherein a developer has, with foreseeability, brought into a previously agricultural or industrial area the population which makes necessary the granting of an injunction against a lawful business and for which the business has no adequate relief.

It is therefore the decision of this court that the matter be remanded to the trial court for a hearing upon the damages sustained by the defendant Spur as a reasonable and direct result of the granting of the permanent injunction. Since the result of the appeal may appear novel and both sides have obtained a measure of relief, it is ordered that each side will bear its own costs.

Affirmed in part, reversed in part, and remanded for further proceedings consistent with this opinion.

HAYS, C.J., STRUCKMEYER and LOCKWOOD, JJ., and UDALL, RETIRED JUSTICE.

NOTES

1. In a provocative article, Professor Rabin advocates a new approach to resolving private nuisance disputes that puts an increased emphasis on the use of conditional injunctions:

When the light from a racetrack owned by one person interferes with an outdoor movie theater owned by another, what is the proper resolution of the conflict? Traditionally, courts have assumed such a question to be a simple one. If the interference did not constitute a nuisance, the cinema owner would have no legal remedy. She would have to tolerate the interference or ameliorate its effects at her own expense, such as by shielding the cinema from the lights. If the interference constituted a "nuisance," a court would issue an injunction forcing the track owner to shade his lights or otherwise to protect the cinema at his own expense.

Professors Calabresi and Melamed have identified two additional alternatives in a * * * stimulating article.[3] First, a court could award the cinema owner damages for future harm, while denying an injunction against the track owner.[4] This article suggests that a court generally should enforce the right to damages by issuing an injunction against the track owner that would be dissolvable upon his payment of the damages. Such an injunction is one form of what may be called a conditional injunction. The measure of damages probably would be the cost to the cinema owner of erecting a shield against the light, as this would be required of her by the duty to avoid adverse consequences. Second, a court could issue an injunction requiring the track owner to shade his lights, conditional upon the cinema owner's paying the cost.[5] This remedy is another form of conditional injunction.

Four alternative dispositions, therefore, are available in a nuisance action. Which alternative should be used, and under what circumstances, are the subjects of this article. * * *

* * *

III

PROPOSED-SOLUTION

Courts too often confuse the question of "who should pay for it?" with the question of "what should be done?" The questions are distinct and require separate treatment. The question of who should pay can be answered only with reference to the criterion of fairness, involving an assessment of relative moral fault. In contrast, the second question should be resolved by the criterion of efficiency.

The procedure here proposed for resolving private nuisance cases involves two steps. The first step would be to determine who is morally more blameworthy for the existence of the conflict. That person should bear the expense of resolving the conflict. This should satisfy the fairness criterion. The second step in the proposed procedure would be to determine how the conflict can be resolved with least expense. This resolution of the conflict would satisfy the efficiency criterion. As a result, the person at fault would pay the cost of resolving the conflict caused by the

---

3. Calabresi & Melamed, *Property Rules, Liability Rules and Inalienability: One View of the Cathedral*, 85 Harv. L. Rev. 1089 (1972).

4. *E.g.*, State v. Board of Education, 116 N.J.Super. 305, 282 A.2d 71 (1971) (Board recovered cost of air conditioning and sound proofing to buffer the noise of adjacent highway). The leading modern case illustrating the trend toward awarding damages rather than an injunction in nuisance cases is Boomer v. Atlantic Cement Co., 26 N.Y.2d 219, 309 N.Y.S.2d 312, 257 N.E.2d 870 (1970). *See also* Harrison v. Indiana Auto Shredders Co., 528 F.2d 1107 (7th Cir.1975) * * *. Of course, damages for past interference would be appropriate whether or not an injunction is issued.

5. Apparently, the only case that has adopted this remedy is Spur Indus. Inc. v. Del E. Webb Dev. Co., 108 Ariz. 178, 494 P.2d 700 (1972).

nuisance in the most efficient manner. This result would be both fair and efficient.

The following chart summarizes the solutions that the proposed procedure would yield for variations of the hypothetical posed earlier.

RESOLVING LAND USE CONFLICTS TO OPTIMIZE FAIRNESS AND EFFICIENCY

		PARTY AT FAULT	
		Track Owner	**Cinema Owner**
MOST EFFICIENT SOLUTION		Court Order: Track owner enjoined from interfering with cinema unless he pays damages equal to least expensive solution.	Court Order: Track owner enjoined from interfering with cinema if cinema owner pays track owner the cost of compliance.*
Physical changes less expensive than abandoning either use.	Shading track lights cheaper.	*Track owner will shade lights at his expense, complying with the injunction.*	*Cinema owner will pay track owner cost of installing shades, and track owner will install them in compliance with injunction.*
	Shielding cinema cheaper.	*Track owner will pay damages to cinema owner, measured by cost of shielding cinema, thereby lifting the injunction.*	*Cinema owner will build a light shield at her own expense rather than enforce an injunction.**
Physical changes more expensive than abandoning *either use.*	Abandoning track cheaper.	*Track owner will abandon track.*	*Cinema owner will pay track owner cost of abandoning track, and injunction will be imposed.*
	Abandoning cinema cheaper.	*Track owner will pay damages to cinema owner, measured by profits lost because of abandonment of cinema. Injunction will be lifted and cinema abandoned.*	*Cinema owner will abandon cinema, and injunction will not be imposed.**

* Of course, where the cinema owner is at fault, and the efficient solution is either shielding or abandoning the cinema, the cinema owner will not attempt to enforce her right to an injunction conditional upon her payment of the track owner's cost of compliance.

The procedure suggested here departs from the traditional method of analysis used in nuisance cases. Under the traditional method the court simply determines whether the interference is a nuisance. If the court finds that it is, the remedy is an unconditional injunction. If the court finds that it is not, an injunction is refused. Occasionally, a court will award damages but refuse an injunction. Such cases are explainable by reference to the doctrine of comparative hardship. Only rarely does a plaintiff receive an injunction that is dissolvable if the defendant pays damages. And apparently in only one case has a plaintiff obtained an injunction conditional on her paying defendant the cost of his compliance. This article contends that these rarely used conditional injunctions should become the usual remedies, and the other remedies should become the rarities. Such conditional injunctions will promote economic efficiency more effectively without sacrificing fairness.

Edward Rabin, *Nuisance Law: Rethinking Fundamental Assumptions*, 63 Va. L. Rev. 1299, 1300, 1309–11 (1977).*

2.   Although the conditional decrees developed by the courts in *Boomer* and *Spur* have been favored by commentators who engage in economic analysis, Professor Polinsky has compared the damages and injunctive remedies and has concluded that neither is clearly superior:

> The resolution of nuisance disputes may, following Calabresi and Melamed[6] be viewed as involving two steps. First, a determination must be made as to who is entitled to prevail. The polluter can be granted the right to pollute, or the pollutee can be granted the right to be free from pollution. Then, in the language of Calabresi and Melamed, a decision must be made whether to protect the entitlement by a "property rule" or a "liability rule." The former grants the holder of the entitlement an injunction, while the latter awards him damages determined by some collective authority such as a court. Thus, in their framework, there are four possible types of solutions, depending on who is given the entitlement and how it is protected.[7]
>
> Most recent legal commentaries on nuisance law have strongly recommended the use of damages rather than injunctions.[8] Whether court decisions also favor the damage remedy is unclear, although many commentators perceive a trend in this direction.[9] Three arguments have been suggested for this preference; I will refer to these as the extortion, strategic behavior, and "bonus payment" arguments.
>
> The first argument against injunctive remedies is that they allow the plaintiff to "extort" the defendant. This possibility arises whenever the potential cost that enforcement of the injunction would impose on the defendant exceeds the loss borne by the plaintiff if the activity in question

---

* Reprinted with permission of the Virginia Law Review Association and Fred B. Rothman & Co.

6. Calabresi & Melamed, *Property Rules, Liability Rules, and Inalienability: One View of the Cathedral*, 85 Harv. L. Rev. 1089 (1972).

7. These solutions are a property rule with the entitlement held by the polluter; a property rule with the entitlement held by the pollutee; a liability rule with the entitlement held by the polluter; and a liability rule with the entitlement held by the pollutee.

8. *See, e.g.,* Ellickson, *Alternatives to Zoning: Covenants, Nuisance Rules, and Fines as Land Use Controls*, 40 U. Chi. L. Rev. 681, 738–48 (1973); Rabin, *Nuisance Law: Rethinking Fundamental Assumptions*, 63 Va. L. Rev. 1299, 1309–48 (1977); Comment, *Internalizing Externalities: Nuisance Law and Economic Efficiency*, 53 N.Y.U. L. Rev. 219, 228–40 (1978).

9. The leading modern American cases illustrating the use of damage remedies are Boomer v. Atlantic Cement Co., 26 N.Y.2d 219, 257 N.E.2d 870, 309 N.Y.S.2d 312 (1970), and Spur Indus., Inc. v. Del E. Webb Dev. Co., 108 Ariz. 178, 494 P.2d 700 (1972). English courts apparently favor injunctive relief relative to damages. Ogus & Richardson, *Economics and the Environment: A Study of Private Nuisance*, 36 Cambridge L.J. 284, 308–09 (1977). But recently there may have been "[s]ome easing in the judicial attitude" with regard to this preference. *Id.* at 310 (citing Miller v. Jackson and Another, [1977] 3 W.L.R. 20).

occurs. Suppose, for example, that operation of a plant injures a pollutee by $1,000 while the polluter would lose $10,000 in profits if the plant were shut down by an injunction. Because the defendant may be willing to pay up to his entire potential profit to prevent the shutdown, the plaintiff might be able to exact compensation well in excess of his actual damages. Under a damage remedy, however, the court dictates the plaintiff's compensation—presumably $1,000 in this example—leaving no scope for extortion.

Note that the extortion argument relates to the goal of distributional equity, not economic efficiency. In the previous example, it is efficient for the plant to continue to operate since the gains are $10,000 while the costs are only $1,000. If, because of the threat of an injunction, the polluter pays the pollutee $9,000 in order to continue operating, this may be inequitable, but it is not inefficient.

The second argument against injunctive remedies—the strategic behavior argument—concerns the consequences for economic efficiency of *unsuccessful* extortion. Strategic behavior consists of bargaining conduct in which a party, perhaps misperceiving his opponent's bargaining position, holds out for a settlement that is never reached (or that is reached after undue delay or negotiation cost). Under an injunctive remedy, strategic behavior may prevent the parties from reaching an efficient resolution of the dispute. In the previous example, the plaintiff might hold out for $8,000 while the defendant, also behaving strategically, might refuse to pay anything over $5,000. As a result, the plaintiff might enforce the injunction and shut down the defendant's plant (at least for some period). In contrast, a damage award seems to overcome strategic behavior problems because the defendant does not have to obtain the consent of the plaintiff. In the example, the defendant presumably would choose to pay any court-determined damage award under $10,000 and keep his plant in operation.

The third argument for damage remedies—the "bonus payment" argument—is offered less frequently than the other two arguments. Once it has been decided to use a damage remedy for either of the other reasons, it is possible to pursue additional distributional goals by making the defendant's liability more or less than the plaintiff's actual damages. In the example, suppose the plaintiff is poorer than the defendant and a more equal distribution of income is desired. The damage award could be augmented by a "bonus payment" to achieve the precise amount of redistribution preferred. If redistribution by other means—such as the income tax system—is costlier (in an efficiency sense), then using a damage remedy to achieve this end may be appropriate. Under the injunctive remedy, on the other hand, distributional outcomes are uncertain. For example, extortion may lead the defendant to pay the plaintiff any amount between $1,000 and $10,000. The actual sum will depend on the parties' relative bargaining strengths. Alternatively, strategic behavior may lead to enforcement of the injunction, forcing the defendant to shut down, with a loss of $10,000 to him and a gain of $1,000 in pollution damage avoided to the plaintiff.

These three arguments amount to the proposition that damage remedies are better able to achieve the efficient outcome (by avoiding strategic behavior) and to promote the desired distributional outcome (by avoiding extortion and allowing bonus payments). This article will demonstrate, however, that in realistic circumstances the preference for damage remedies is not always justified. In terms of achieving efficiency, it will be shown that damage remedies are just as susceptible to strategic behavior problems as injunctive remedies when, realistically, courts cannot correctly determine actual damages. And in terms of achieving distributional equity, it will be shown that damage remedies are not nearly as flexible distributionally as is usually presumed. Damage remedies are still preferable in some circumstances, but injunctive remedies are superior in other circumstances. By systematically exploring the relative merits of the remedies in different situations, I hope to provide a better understanding of when each should be used.

* * *

The basic conclusions of the article can be briefly stated as follows: In the best of all possible worlds—cooperative behavior, costless redistribution, and perfect information—injunctive and damage remedies are equally desirable. The presence of strategic behavior alone does not change this conclusion. However, if it is also costly to redistribute income, the remedies are no longer equivalent. When there are a small number of litigants in these circumstances, neither remedy is generally preferable. When there are a large number of litigants, however, the damage remedy is superior. Finally, and most realistically, if the courts also have imperfect information, neither remedy is generally preferable. Depending on what information is available, either the injunctive or the damage remedy may be more desirable in any specific instance. Given the presence of these complications, the view that damage remedies are generally superior is not supported.

A. Mitchell Polinsky, *Resolving Nuisance Disputes: The Simple Economics of Injunctive and Damage Remedies*, 32 Stan. L. Rev. 1075, 1076–80 (1980).*

3.   The famous Calabresi and Melamed article discussed in Notes 1 and 2 has spawned a substantial body of literature that focuses on property rights and liability rules to protect entitlements and uses nuisance cases to analyze them. In addition,

> [t]his literature builds on the insight that parties to lawsuits can, at least in principle, continue bargaining after judgment is rendered. If bargaining is not too costly, the rights at stake in a case inevitably will end up in the hands of the party willing to the pay the most for them.

Ward W. Farnsworth, *Do Parties to Nuisance Cases Bargain After Judgment? A Glimpse Inside the Cathedral*, 66 U. Chi. L. Rev. 373, 374 (1999). Interestingly, Professor Ward Farnsworth studied twenty nuisance cases and found no post-judgment bargaining in any of them. "Nor did the lawyers in these cases think there would have been bargaining if the litigation had ended with

---

* Reprinted with permission of the Stanford Law Review. Copyright 1982 by the Board of Trustees of the Leland Stanford Junior University.

a judgment in the opposite direction." *Id.* at 379. For example, in Tichenor v. Vore, 953 S.W.2d 171 (Mo.Ct.App.1997), the defendant was permanently enjoined from operating a dog kennel. After that decision, the injunction was enforced. There were no discussions of the possibility that the defendant purchase from the plaintiffs the right to operate the kennel. The plaintiffs' lawyer predicted that, if Vore had made such overtures, his clients would have said "not only 'No' but 'Hell, no: get your dogs out of there.'" Farnsworth, *supra*, at 387. But what if Vore had won the case—would the plaintiffs have paid him to get rid of the dogs? Both lawyers thought not. *Id.* According to Professor Farnsworth, in most of the cases, strong personal animosity, questions of "principle" and a variety of non-economic considerations stood in the way of post-judgment bargaining. Should we assume that every person has his or her price? Are there some issues about which we harbor such strong feelings that rational bargaining is simply unrealistic? What does this tell us, if anything, about the value of economic analysis in many of these landowner disputes?

As you read the next case, consider the impact of the "right to farm" statutes on the majority rule regarding the "coming to the nuisance" doctrine.

LINDSEY v. DeGROOT

Court of Appeals of Indiana, 2009
898 N.E.2d 1251.

BRADFORD, JUDGE.

* * *

In 1998, the Lindseys purchased approximately ten acres of undeveloped woods in rural Huntington County, located at 1491 South 900 West, Andrews, Indiana. After purchasing the property, the Lindseys constructed their 4000 square foot home, which included a veranda and an indoor swimming pool. At various times since purchasing the property, the Lindseys have had a number of animals living on their property, including four horses, three dogs, a bird, and a rabbit. The nature of the landscape surrounding the Lindseys' property was, at all times relevant to this appeal, agricultural, and a number of farmers in the immediate area own livestock.

In 2001, Johannes DeGroot, a Dutch national, purchased an operational hog farm from John and Joy Baker, located at 8373 West 200 South, Andrews, Indiana, for the purpose of opening a dairy, and relocated his family from the Netherlands to Andrews, Indiana. DeGroot contracted with Vreba–Hoff Dairy Development LLC for the construction of the new barns and equipment necessary to run the dairy operation. DeGroot Dairy raises approximately 1500 milking cows and 100 dry cows and dairy calves. DeGroot Dairy began its milking operations on June 24, 2002.

DeGroot Dairy is a regulated entity under the Indiana Department of Environmental Management's ("IDEM") Confined Feeding Operation ("CFO") regulations and operates under a CFO approval, approval number AW 5076. Throughout the course of the dairy's operation, IDEM has periodically alleged violations of CFO regulations. None of IDEM's past allegations against DeGroot Dairy has ever been substantiated.

DeGroot Dairy owns a farm field directly north of the Lindseys' property, consisting of approximately 68.09 acres, which is regularly used for planting corn, soybeans, and wheat. A grass strip runs along the boundary between the two properties. Following allegations by the Lindseys that an employee or agent of DeGroot Dairy had trespassed upon the grass strip, Johannes DeGroot hired Larry E. Manship, a licensed surveyor from Marion, Indiana, to survey the border between the Lindseys' property and the DeGroot Dairy cornfield. On August 24, 2004, Manship prepared a written survey of the properties in question. The Manship survey indicated that the Lindseys were mistaken about the ownership of the grass strip and that while the Lindseys own the southern half of the grass strip, DeGroot Dairy owns the northern half of the grass strip. Although the Lindseys claim that they do not agree with the Manship survey, they have never arranged for another survey to be conducted. Also in response to the Lindseys' allegations, Johannes DeGroot instructed employees to stay "well clear" of the Lindseys' property. * * *

On December 9, 2003, the Lindseys filed suit against DeGroot Dairy seeking to enjoin the dairy from further operation and for compensation for nuisance, negligence, trespass, criminal mischief, and intentional infliction of emotional distress. DeGroot Dairy filed a motion for summary judgment on September 17, 2007. A hearing was held on DeGroot Dairy's motion on February 25, 2008. On April 24, 2008, the court issued an order granting summary judgment to DeGroot Dairy. In its summary judgment order, the trial court determined that the Indiana Right to Farm Act was constitutional and applied to the instant action, barring the Lindseys' nuisance claims. The trial court also determined that no genuine issues of material fact existed regarding the Lindseys' trespass, criminal mischief, and intentional infliction of emotional distress claims. This appeal follows.

* * *

II. CONSTITUTIONALITY AND APPLICATION OF THE RIGHT TO FARM ACT

The Indiana Right to Farm Act (the "Act") was adopted by the General Assembly in an attempt to limit the circumstances under which agricultural operations could become subject to nuisance suits. The Act, codified at Indiana Code section 32–30–6–9 (2007), provides the following:

(a) This section does not apply if a nuisance results from the negligent operation of an agricultural or industrial operation or its appurtenances.

(b) The general assembly declares that it is the policy of the state to conserve, protect, and encourage the development and improvement of its agricultural land for the production of food and other agricultural products.... It is the purpose of this section to reduce the loss to the state of its agricultural resources by limiting the circumstances

under which agricultural operations may be deemed to be a nuisance.
* * *

(d) An agricultural or industrial operation or any of its appurtenances
is not and does not become a nuisance, private or public, by any
changed conditions in the vicinity of the locality after the agricultural
or industrial operation, as the case may be, has been in operation
continuously on the locality for more than one (1) year if the following
conditions exist:

(1) There is no significant change in the type of operation. A
significant change in the type of agricultural operation does not
include the following:

(A) The conversion from one type of agricultural operation to
another type of agricultural operation.

(B) A change in the ownership or the size of the agricultural
operation.

(C) The:

(i) enrollment; or

(ii) reduction or cessation of participation; of the agricultural operation in a government program.

(D) Adoption of new technology by the agricultural operation.

(2) The operation would not have been a nuisance at the time the
agricultural or industrial operation began on that locality.

The General Assembly defined an agricultural operation as "any
facility used for the production of crops, livestock, poultry, livestock
products, poultry products, or horticultural products or for growing timber." Ind.Code § 32–30–6–1 (2003). DeGroot Dairy, a farming operation
that produces milk as well as crops, is clearly an agricultural operation for
the purposes of the Indiana Right to Farm Act.

A.   Whether the Indiana Right to Farm Act is Constitutional

The Lindseys first contend that the Act is unconstitutional, arguing
that the Act amounts to an unconstitutional taking of their property
without just compensation because it essentially awards DeGroot Dairy an
easement over their property. "Article I, Section 21 of the Indiana
Constitution includes a prohibition against the taking of property without
just compensation." *Cheatham v. Pohle,* 789 N.E.2d 467, 472 (Ind.2003).
"The Fifth Amendment to the United States Constitution includes the
same proscription, and applies to the states through the Fourteenth
Amendment." *Id.* Therefore, both the federal and Indiana constitutions
provide that " 'no person's property shall be taken by law, without just
compensation.' " *Id.* at 473 (citing Ind. Const. art. I, s 21).

"Only 'property' is protected from taking under either clause." *Id.*
"To be a taking in the constitutional sense, the state action at issue must

be more than a consequential limitation on the use or enjoyment of property; a taking involves an actual interference with a property right." *Gorka v. Sullivan*, 671 N.E.2d 122, 132 (Ind.Ct.App.1996) * * *.

In support of their argument, the Lindseys rely upon the Iowa Supreme Court's decision in *Bormann v. Bd. of Supervisors in and for Kossuth County*, 584 N.W.2d 309 (Iowa 1998). In *Bormann*, a group of property owners challenged an action by the Board of Supervisors (the "Board") in creating an agricultural area near their property, arguing that the Board's action constituted a taking of their land without just compensation because Iowa's agricultural land preservation statute granted farms and farmers immunity from nuisance suits, effectively granting the farms and farmers the right to maintain a nuisance. *Bormann*, 584 N.W.2d at 313. The Iowa Supreme Court agreed and concluded that in light of Iowa's longstanding common law proposition, dating back to the Iowa Supreme Court's 1895 decision in *Churchill v. Burlington Water Co.*, 94 Iowa 89, 62 N.W. 646 (Iowa 1895), that the right to maintain a nuisance is an easement, as well as the proposition that easements are property interests subject to the just compensation requirements of both the federal and Iowa constitutions, the portion of Iowa's agricultural land preservation act granting a farm or a farm operation located in an agricultural area immunity from nuisance actions violated both the federal and the Iowa constitutions. *Id.* at 321.

In *Moon v. North Idaho Farmers Ass'n,* 140 Idaho 536, 96 P.3d 637 (2004), the plaintiffs challenged the constitutionality of the Idaho counterpart to our Right to Farm Act, claiming that under the Iowa Supreme Court's holding in *Bormann*, the immunity granted to the farmers under the Idaho act created an easement in favor of the farmers over their property, and therefore violated the Takings Clause of both the Idaho and federal constitutions. The Idaho Supreme Court, however, refused to apply the Iowa Supreme Court's holding in *Bormann* because the court found that there was no direct authority in Idaho holding that the right to maintain a nuisance is an easement. 96 P.3d at 644. The Idaho Supreme Court also expressly declined to hold that the nuisance immunity provision included in the Idaho counterpart to our Right to Farm Act created an easement in favor of the farmers. *Id.* at 645. The Idaho Supreme Court concluded that the provision of the Idaho counterpart to our Right to Farm Act granting immunity to the farmers "[did] not represent an unconstitutional taking under either the state or federal constitution." *Id.* at 646.

Likewise, in *Barrera v. Hondo Creek Cattle Co.*, 132 S.W.3d 544 (Tex.App.2004), the plaintiffs challenged the Texas counterpart to our Right to Farm Act claiming that the provision limiting the circumstances under which a nuisance claim could be brought against a farming operation violated both the Texas and federal constitutions because the limitation amounted to a "taking." The Texas Court of Appeals rejected plaintiff's claim and concluded that the plaintiffs had failed to establish the required elements of a taking. 132 S.W.2d at 549.

We note that like the Idaho and Texas courts, we have found nothing to suggest that Indiana has adopted the seemingly unique Iowa holding that the right to maintain a nuisance is an easement, and the Lindseys have failed to explain why we should. Therefore, we expressly decline the Lindseys' invitation to adopt Iowa's proposition that the right to maintain a nuisance contained in the Act creates an easement in favor of DeGroot Dairy. Having rejected the claim that the Act effectively grants an easement to DeGroot Dairy over the Lindseys' property, we turn our attention to the application of the Act to the instant matter.

B.   Whether the Indiana Right to Farm Act Bars the Lindseys' Nuisance Claim

The underlying basis of the Lindseys' nuisance claim against DeGroot Dairy is that the operation of DeGroot Dairy is a nuisance that interferes with the Lindseys' use and enjoyment of their property. Indiana law defines a nuisance as "[w]hatever is: (1) injurious to health; (2) indecent; (3) offensive to the senses; or (4) an obstruction to the free use of property; so as essentially to interfere with the comfortable enjoyment of life or property." Ind.Code § 32–30–6–6 (2003). When deciding whether or not the use of property amounts to a nuisance, it is necessary to balance the competing interests of the affected landowners, and in doing so, we must use a common sense approach. *Shatto v. McNulty,* 509 N.E.2d 897, 898–99 (Ind.Ct.App. 1987).

> While mere annoyances or inconveniences will not support an action on account of a nuisance, one may not use his property for his own profit so as to damage, confiscate, or destroy the property of his neighbor. Even a lawful business may be conducted in such a manner or be so situated as to become a nuisance. Whether the act complained of is in reality a nuisance, or not, is measured by ordinary sensibilities, tastes, and habits in light of the circumstances of each case.

Id. at 899.

Here, DeGroot Dairy began milking operations on June 24, 2002. Approximately eighteen months later, on December 9, 2003, the Lindseys filed suit alleging that the dairy was a nuisance. Because DeGroot Dairy had been in operation for more than one year when the Lindseys filed suit, the Act applies and bars the Lindseys' nuisance suit unless there has been a significant change in the type of operation, the operation would have been a nuisance at the time the operation began in its current locality, or the nuisance results from the negligent operation of the agricultural operation.

On appeal, the Lindseys assert that there has been a significant change in the type of operation. The record, however, establishes that the Lindseys did not allege that a significant change in the type of operation had occurred before the trial court. "Issues not raised before the trial court on summary judgment cannot be argued for the first time on appeal and are waived." *Dunaway v. Allstate Ins. Co.*, 813 N.E.2d 376, 387 (Ind.Ct.App.2004). In the instant matter, the Lindseys' response to De-Groot Dairy's motion for summary judgment stated that "[t]he Lindseys do not take issue with the 'type' of farm DeGroot operates, but rather, with its negligent operation." * * * The Lindseys' response further stated that "DeGroot Dairy has only itself to blame for operating in a negligent manner and abandoning the protection of the Right to Farm Act." * * * Because the Lindseys did not challenge the type of operation or allege any significant change in the type of operation before the trial court, the Lindseys have waived this claim on appeal. Likewise, the Lindseys failed to argue before the trial court, and have therefore waived their claim, that the Act should not apply because the dairy would have been a nuisance at the time the agricultural operation began in that locality. Therefore, we conclude that the Lindseys' nuisance claim is barred by the Act unless they can establish that the alleged nuisance resulted from the negligent operation of DeGroot Dairy.

C.   Whether Application of the Right to Farm Act was Improper Because the Claimed Nuisance Resulted from the Negligent Operation of DeGroot Dairy

The Lindseys next contend that the application of the Act was improper because their claimed nuisance resulted from the negligent operation of DeGroot Dairy. The Lindseys' claim of negligence is based exclusively on DeGroot Dairys alleged violations of IDEM's CFO regulations.

* * *

Having concluded that the Lindseys failed to designate any evidence establishing that their claimed injury was a foreseeable consequence of the alleged violations and that their claimed injury would not have occurred had the requirements of the statute been observed, we conclude that the Lindseys have failed to create a genuine issue of fact regarding whether DeGroot Dairy's alleged statutory violations were the proximate cause of the Lindseys' claimed injury. Furthermore, having concluded that De-Groot Dairy's statutory violations were not the proximate cause of the Lindseys' alleged injury, we conclude that DeGroot Dairy's alleged violation of a statute does not give rise to liability for the Lindseys' claimed injury, and because the Lindseys have alleged no general claims of negligence, they cannot establish that the claimed nuisance results from the negligent operation of DeGroot Dairy. Therefore, there is no issue of material fact as to whether the Indiana Right to Farm Act applies, and the trial court correctly awarded DeGroot Dairy summary judgment on the Lindseys' nuisance claim.

[The court then further held that the trial court properly granted summary judgment on the Lindseys' trespass, criminal mischief, and intentional inflictions of emotional distress claims.]

In sum, [we conclude] that the Lindseys have failed to designate any evidence contrary to the trial court's determination that the Indiana Right to Farm Act applied to the instant matter and barred the Lindseys' nuisance claim against DeGroot Dairy * * *.

The judgment of the trial court is affirmed.

FRIEDLANDER, J., and MAY, J., concur.

NOTES

1. Since 1978, right-to-farm statutes have been enacted in some form in all 50 states. Alexander A. Reinert, Note, *The Right to Farm: Hog–Tied and Nuisance–Bound*, 73 N.Y.U. L. Rev. 1694, 1695 (1998). Their purpose is to protect farmers and farming operations from nuisance liability. Although the language of the statutes varies, "most provide in essence that when the plaintiff has come to the nuisance, the defendant agricultural operation either is not, or is presumed not to be, a nuisance." Margaret R. Grossman & Thomas G. Fischer, *Protecting the Right to Farm: Statutory Limits on Nuisance Actions Against the Farmer*, 1983 Wis. L. Rev. 95, 117 (discussing the environmental and constitutional implications of the right-to-farm statutes). The authors also propose a model right-to-farm statute. *Id.* at 163–65.

2. How would the *Spur* case, *supra*, have been decided under Indiana's right-to-farm statute, which is similar to Arizona's right-to-farm statute? *See* Comment, *The Arizona Agricultural Nuisance Protection Act*, 1982 Ariz. St. L.J. 689, 721–22.

3. Right-to-farm statutes have become controversial because they are viewed as protecting large corporate cattle feedlots, hog feeder operations, and poultry farms, rather than small "traditional" or family farms. *See* Neil D. Hamilton, *Right–To–Farm–Laws Reconsidered: Ten Legislative Efforts to Resolve Agricultural Nuisances May be Ineffective*, 3 Drake J. Agric. L. 103 (1998); Alexander A. Reinert, Note, *The Right to Farm: Hog–Tied and Nuisance–Bound*, 73 N.Y.U. L. Rev. 1694 (1998). Some commentators advocate repeal or substantial alteration of existing statutes. *Id.* In the meantime, courts should "interpret the substantive provisions of the statutes as narrowly as possible," and refuse to "extend [their] protection * * * to industrial operations unless the law clearly supports this outcome." 73 N.Y.U. L. Rev. at 1737.

For a discussion and criticism of the *Bormann* case discussed in *Lindsey*, see Eric Pearson, *Immunities as Easements as Takings*: Bormann v. Board of Supervisors, 48 Drake L. Rev. 53 (1999).

HOBBS v. SMITH

Supreme Court of Colorado, 1972.
177 Colo. 299, 493 P.2d 1352.

HODGES, JUSTICE.

The Court of Appeals affirmed a trial court judgment which granted an injunction prohibiting the continuation of circumstances which constituted a private nuisance. The petitioner * * * [contends] that when legislative authorities, by zoning ordinances, permit an act or a particular use of land, a court has no authority to enjoin a public or private nuisance naturally resulting therefrom. * * *

The trial court found that the petitioner kept one to two horses in the backyard of her home, which was located in a residential section of Jefferson County. A Jefferson County Zoning Ordinance permitted the keeping of two horses on petitioner's property. The trial court found that petitioner was exercising all reasonable skill and care in maintaining the property where the animals were kept and that no health regulations were being violated. However, the trial court also found that flies were attracted to the general area by the horses and that noxious odors therefrom permeated the area. It was found that the respondents suffered a substantial interference with the use and enjoyment of their property which adjoined petitioner's property. The trial court ruled that while the keeping of horses did not violate the zoning ordinance, it did constitute a nuisance in fact (per accidens) and therefore, there was a proper basis for granting an injunction prohibiting the keeping of horses on the petitioner's property. * * *

In its opinion, affirming the trial court's judgment, the Court of Appeals held that even though zoning regulations permit an act to be done, and the act is being done with reasonable care and skill, the courts may grant relief where it is found that the acts complained of constitute a nuisance per accidens, and that to hold otherwise would be to state that the legislative body may license a nuisance.

* * *

Judgment affirmed.

PRINGLE, C.J., and DAY and KELLEY, JJ., dissent.

DAY, JUSTICE (dissenting):

I respectfully dissent.

I hasten to add my fears that the precedent of the majority decision could curtail the effective gains which have been made in creating legislative awareness of good long-range land use planning. When the legislative authority has validly declared that a given activity is lawfully permitted in a particular zone, and the activity is lawfully conducted, to permit the courts to enjoin the use provides a judicial veto of proper, valid legislative functions.

I submit the better reasoned position to take is that land use regulations are best conceived by the legislative branch under its constitutional exercise of police power whereby there is afforded broad application for the public good. The court should not act to set aside or prevent that which the legislative branch has determined to be permitted. This will seriously affect long-range land use planning.

Such planning has salutory two-fold aspects. One provides for orderly growth; the other provides for the possibility of citizens finding a place in which to live and enjoy their own particular tastes. * * * There have been conceived in many states equine country clubs for persons who enjoy horseback riding, jumping, polo, etc. In such developments citizens can build and live and indulge in their recreational hobby. People who do not have similar tastes should not and probably would not establish a home in such an environment. * * *

I would reverse the trial court injunction.

NOTES

1.   The impact of zoning on an action to enjoin a nuisance is described in Dan B. Dobbs, Handbook on the Law of Remedies 363 (1973).*

In a good many instances the activity of the defendant, which the plaintiff seeks to enjoin as a nuisance, is the kind of activity permitted by a zoning ordinance or license or special statute. Most courts faced with this situation hold that zoning ordinances do not protect a nuisance from injunction merely by authorizing the general kind of use. The zoning ordinance is, of course, relevant in such cases as indicating something of the present and probable future character of the neighborhood, but it does not prevent an injunction by its bare existence. These rules seem reasonable, because though zoning ordinances do legitimize the authorized businesses within the prescribed areas, they seem to legitimize general models, not particular methods of operation. Much the same attitude is taken where the defendant has procured a license to operate his plant, or shows he has complied with administrative regulations addressed to his business.

Several courts have followed the "minority view" to the effect that an injunction will not issue against a nuisance if the activity is one authorized by a zoning ordinance or statute.

For a recent example of the majority approach see Burch v. Nedpower Mount Storm, LLC, 647 S.E.2d 879 (W.Va.2009) (an injunction against a proposed wind power facility as a private nuisance may be available even though the facility had been granted a siting certificate by state agency).

2.   California has codified the zoning defense in section 731a of the Code of Civil Procedure:

§ 731a.   Injunction in Industrial or Commercial Zones or Airports

Whenever any city, city and county, or county shall have established zones or districts under authority of law wherein certain manufacturing or commercial or airport uses are expressly permitted, except in an action to abate a public nuisance brought in the name of the people of the State of California, no person or persons, firm or corporation shall be enjoined or restrained by the injunctive process from the reasonable and necessary operation in any such industrial or commercial zone or airport of any use

---

* Reprinted with permission of West Publishing Co.

expressly permitted therein, nor shall such use be deemed a nuisance without evidence of the employment of unnecessary and injurious methods of operation. Nothing in this act shall be deemed to apply to the regulation and working hours of canneries, fertilizing plants, refineries and other similar establishments whose operation produce offensive odors.

The California cases applying the statute to private nuisance actions for injunctive relief are discussed in Sierra Screw Products v. Azusa Greens, Inc., 88 Cal.App.3d 358, 151 Cal.Rptr. 799 (1979) (mandatory injunction granted requiring defendant to redesign two holes on properly zoned golf course so that golf balls would not fall on plaintiff's adjoining property).

Is the California statute applicable to actions for damages, or only to actions for injunctive relief? *See* Wilson v. Interlake Steel Co., 32 Cal.3d 229, 185 Cal.Rptr. 280, 649 P.2d 922 (1982).

How does the California statute compare with Vermont's right to farm statute, quoted in *Trickett, supra*? Does either statute apply to trespass actions? *See generally* Comment, *Remedies for Intangible Intrusions: The Distinction Between Trespass and Nuisance Actions Against Lawfully Zoned Businesses in California*, 17 U.C. Davis L. Rev. 389 (1983).

b. Public Nuisance and Statutory Remedies

VILLAGE OF WILSONVILLE v. SCA SERVICES, INC.

Supreme Court of Illinois, 1981.
86 Ill.2d 1, 55 Ill.Dec. 499, 426 N.E.2d 824.

CLARK, JUSTICE:

On April 18, 1977, the plaintiff village of Wilsonville (the village) filed a complaint seeking injunctive relief in the circuit court of Macoupin County. Plaintiffs Macoupin County and the Macoupin County Farm Bureau were granted leave to intervene on April 29, 1977, and May 9, 1977, respectively. They filed complaints substantially similar to the village's complaint. The gravamen of the complaints was that the operation of the defendant's chemical-waste-disposal site presents a public nuisance and a hazard to the health of the citizens of the village, the county, and the State. The Attorney General of Illinois filed a complaint on May 26, 1977, seeking an injunction pursuant to the Environmental Protection Act (Ill.Rev.Stat.1975, ch. 111½, pars. 1003(d), 1003(n), 1012(d), 1043). * * * Trial began on June 7, 1977, consumed 104 days, and resulted in judgment for the plaintiffs on August 28, 1978. The trial court's judgment order concluded that the site constitutes a nuisance and enjoined the defendant from operating its hazardous-chemical-waste land-fill in Wilsonville. It ordered the defendant to remove all toxic waste buried there, along with all contaminated soil found at the disposal site as a result of the operation of the landfill. Further, the court ordered the defendant to restore and reclaim the site.

* * * The Appellate Court for the Fourth District unanimously affirmed the trial court's judgment. (77 Ill.App.3d 618, 33 Ill.Dec. 163, 396 N.E.2d 552.) * * *

* * *

The defendant has operated a chemical-waste landfill since 1977. The site comprises approximately 130 acres, 90 of which are within the village limits of the plaintiff village. The remaining 40 acres are adjacent to the village. The defendant enters into agreements with generators of toxic chemical waste to haul the waste away from the generators' locations. The defendant then delivers it to the Wilsonville site, tests random samples of chemical waste, and then deposits the waste in trenches. There are seven trenches at the site. Each one is approximately 15 feet deep, 50 feet wide, and 250 to 350 feet long. Approximately 95% of the waste materials were buried in 55–gallon steel drums, and the remainder is contained in double-wall paper bags. After the materials are deposited in the trenches, uncompacted clay is placed between groups of containers and a minimum of one foot of clay is placed between the top drum and the top clay level of the trench.

The site is bordered on the east, west, and south by farmland and on the north by the village. The entire site, the village, and much of the surrounding area is located above the abandoned Superior Coal Mine No. 4, which operated from 1917 to 1954. The No. 6 seam of the mine was exploited in this area at a depth of 312 feet. The mining method used to extract coal was the room-and-panel method, whereby about 50% of the coal is left in pillars which provide some support for the earth above the mine. There was testimony at trial by Dr. Nolan Augenbaugh, chairman of the Department of Mining, Petroleum and Geological Engineering at the University of Missouri at Rolla, that pillar failure can occur in any mine where there is a readjustment of stress. * * *

* * *

On February 11, 1976, the defendant applied to the IEPA for a permit to develop and operate the hazardous-waste landfill. A developmental permit was issued by the IEPA on May 19, 1976. * * *

The materials deposited at the site include polychlorinated biphenyls (PCBs), a neurotoxic, possibly carcinogenic chemical which it has been illegal to produce in this country since 1979. Due to the extensive use of PCBs in electrical equipment such as transformers, capacitors, and heat-transfer systems, and in hydraulic systems, any PCBs that were produced legally now have to be disposed of when they are no longer in use. * * *

* * *

Finally, considerable testimony was adduced, much of it conflicting, as to dust, odors, and spills of chemical waste which have occurred in the village. * * *

* * *

We conclude that the evidence in this case sufficiently establishes by a preponderance of the evidence that the chemical-waste-disposal site is a nuisance both presently and prospectively. * * *

* * *

* * * Moreover, the General Assembly has, since the inception of this suit, passed a statute prohibiting the placement of a hazardous-waste-disposal site above [an active or inactive] shaft or tunneled mine. * * * (Ill.Rev.Stat.1979, ch. 111½, par. 1021(g).) * * *

The instant disposal site is above an inactive tunneled mine lying partly within the corporate limits of the village of Wilsonville. Without an express statutory provision stating an act is to have retroactive effect, it can only be applied prospectively. Thus, the defendant cannot be thought to be in violation of the * * * [statute]. The fact remains, however, that the instant site, which is intended to be permanent, is located above an inactive tunneled mine.

* * *

The trial court herein concluded that defendant's chemical-waste-disposal site constitutes both a private and a public nuisance. Professor Prosser has defined a private nuisance as "a civil wrong, based on a disturbance of rights in land" (Prosser, Torts sec. 86, at 572 (4th ed. 1971)), and a public nuisance as "an act or omission 'which obstructs or causes inconvenience or damage to the public in the exercise of rights common to all Her Majesty's subjects.' " (Prosser, Torts sec. 88, at 583 (4th ed. 1971)) * * *

The defendant herein argues that "[e]ven if some or all of plaintiffs' evidence is deemed believable, the findings of the courts below that [defendant's] conduct constitutes a prospective nuisance must be reversed for failure to * * * balance the reasonableness and utility of the defendant's conduct, the harm to the plaintiff, and the general societal policy toward risk-taking before [a court may] find an actionable nuisance present." The defendant continues that the law of Illinois requires that the circuit court engage in a balancing process before reaching a conclusion that the waste disposal site presents a prospective nuisance. * * *

* * *

[However], the trial court did engage in a balancing process, as is made clear by the following excerpt from the trial court's memorandum opinion.

It is the opinion of the Court that the state of the law is such that nuisance cannot be justified on the ground of necessity, pecuniary interest, convenience or economic advantage.

The Court understands as does counsel that there is a need for disposal of industrial hazardous wastes. However, where disposal of wastes create a nuisance said disposal site may be closed through legal action.

Substantial sums of money have been expended by the defendant in developing and operating the Earthline site at Wilsonville. Not only is the site convenient to nearby industries but it is a profit producer for the defendant. All of these elements are relevant to our economic system but notwithstanding the same it is the opinion of the Court that nuisances cannot be justified on such grounds when we have substantial injury to individual rights, community rights, substantial damage to human beings and other living things.

* * *

The importance of an industry to the wealth and prosperity of an area does not as a matter of law give to it rights superior to the primary or natural rights of citizens who live nearby. *However, such matters may be considered and have been in this case.*

* * *

* * * In this case the defendant established its chemical waste landfill near the area where persons of the Village had resided for many years. * * *

An industrial waste disposal site in and adjacent to a village means that the hazardous waste disposal operation is near or next to homes, families—children, youth, middle aged and old people—sick people, well people—sensitive persons and anxious and fearful persons. The location of a business has significance in reference to being a nuisance or not being a nuisance. (Emphasis added.)

We think the foregoing indicates that the trial court did carefully engage in a balancing process between the site's social utility and the plaintiffs' right to enjoy their property and not suffer deleterious effects from chemical wastes. Accordingly, the defendant's argument that the trial court did not balance the equities in this case is without merit.

The defendant's next contention is that the courts below were in error when they failed to require a showing of a substantial risk of certain and extreme future harm before enjoining operation of the defendant's site. We deem it necessary to explain that a *prospective* nuisance is a fit candidate for injunctive relief. Prosser states: "Both public and private nuisances require some substantial interference with the interest involved. Since nuisance is a common subject of equity jurisdiction, the damage against which an injunction is asked is often merely threatened or potential; but even in such cases, there must be at least a threat of a substantial invasion of the plaintiff's interests." (Prosser, Torts sec. 87, at 577 (4th ed. 1971).) The defendant does not dispute this proposition; it does, however, argue that the trial court did not follow the proper standard for determining when a prospective nuisance may be enjoined. The defendant argues that the proper standard to be used is that an injunction is proper only if there is a "dangerous probability" that the threatened or potential injury will occur. (*See* Restatement (Second) of Torts sec. 933(1), at 561, comment *b* (1979).) The defendant further argues that the appellate court looked only at the potential consequences of not enjoining the operation of the site as a nuisance and not at the likelihood of whether harm would occur. The defendant assigns error on this basis.

We agree with the defendant's statement of the law, but not with its urged application to the facts of this case. Again, Professor Prosser has offered a concise commentary. He has stated that "[o]ne distinguishing feature of equitable relief is that it may be granted upon the threat of harm which has not yet occurred. The defendant may be restrained from entering upon an activity where it is highly probable that it will lead to a nuisance, although if the possibility is merely uncertain or contingent he may be left to his remedy after the nuisance has occurred." (Prosser, Torts sec. 90, at 603 (4th ed. 1971).) This view is in accord with Illinois law. * * * In *Fink* the plaintiff sought to enjoin construction of a dam and also the discharge of sewage effluent in a watercourse which flowed past plaintiffs' property. Construction of the dam was not enjoined, but the discharge of effluent was prospectively enjoined. The court stated:

> While, as a general proposition, an injunction will be granted only to restrain an actual, existing nuisance, a court of equity may enjoin a threatened or anticipated nuisance, where it clearly appears that a nuisance will necessarily result from the contemplated act or thing which it is sought to enjoin. This is particularly true where the proof shows that the apprehension of material injury is well grounded upon a state of facts from which it appears that the danger is real and immediate. While care should be used in granting injunctions to avoid prospective injuries, there is no requirement that the court must wait until the injury occurs before granting relief. (71 Ill.App.2d 276, 281–82, 218 N.E.2d 240.)

We agree.

In this case there can be no doubt but that it is highly probable that the chemical-waste-disposal site will bring about a substantial injury. Without again reviewing the extensive evidence adduced at trial, we think it is sufficiently clear that it is highly probable that the instant site will constitute a public nuisance if, through either an explosive interaction, migration, subsidence, or the "bathtub effect," the highly toxic chemical wastes deposited at the site escape and contaminate the air, water, or ground around the site. That such an event will occur was positively attested to by several expert witnesses. A court does not have to wait for it to happen before it can enjoin such a result. Additionally, the fact is that the condition of a nuisance is already present at the site due to the location of the site and the manner in which it has been operated. Thus, it is only the damage which is prospective. Under these circumstances, if a court can prevent any damage from occurring, it should do so.

* * *

The next issue we consider is whether the trial court erroneously granted a permanent injunction. * * * The second argument raised is that the courts below did not balance the equities in deciding to enjoin the defendant from continuing to operate the waste-disposal site. Defendant cites Harrison v. Indiana Auto Shredders Co. (7th Cir.1975), 528 F.2d 1107, for the proposition that the court must balance the relative harm and benefit to the plaintiff and defendant before a court may enjoin a * * * nuisance.

* * *

The court concluded in *Harrison* that since the defendant was not in violation of any relevant zoning standards, and since the shredder did not pose an imminent hazard to the public health, the defendant should not be prevented from continuing to operate. The court then ordered that the defendant be permitted a reasonable time to "launder its objectionable features." 528 F.2d 1107, 1125.

This case is readily distinguishable for the reason that the gist of this case is that the defendant is engaged in an extremely hazardous undertaking at an unsuitable location, which seriously and imminently poses a threat to the public health. We are acutely aware that the service provided by the defendant is a valuable and necessary one. We also know that it is preferable to have chemical-waste-disposal sites than to have illegal dumping in rivers, streams, and deserted areas. But a site such as defendant's, if it is to do the job it is intended to do, must be located in a secure place, where it will pose no threat to health or life, now, or in the future. This site was intended to be a *permanent* disposal site for the deposit of extremely hazardous chemical-waste materials. Yet this site is located above an abandoned tunneled mine where subsidence is occurring several years ahead of when it was anticipated. Also, the permeability-coefficient samples taken by defendant's experts, though not conclusive alone, indicate that the soil is more permeable at the site than expected. Moreover, the spillage, odors, and dust caused by the presence of the disposal site indicate why it was inadvisable to locate the site so near the plaintiff village.

Therefore, we conclude that in fashioning relief in this case the trial court did balance relative hardship to be caused to the plaintiffs and defendant, and did fashion reasonable relief when it ordered the exhumation of all material from the site and the reclamation of the surrounding area. The instant site is akin to Mr. Justice Sutherland's observation that "Nuisance may be merely a right thing in a wrong place—like a pig in the parlor instead of the barnyard." Village of Euclid v. Ambler Realty Co. (1926), 272 U.S. 365, 388, 47 S.Ct. 114, 118, 71 L.Ed. 303, 311, quoted in 2 J. Dooley, Modern Tort Litigation, sec. 31.15, at 225 (1977).

* * *

Accordingly, for all the reasons stated, the judgments of the circuit and appellate courts are affirmed and the cause is remanded to the circuit court to enable it to retain jurisdiction to supervise the enforcement of its order. * * *

NOTES

1. When a governmental plaintiff brings a public nuisance action, as compared with a case in which a private citizen brings a private nuisance action, the courts do not have "quite the same freedom to balance the harm that will be done by an injunction against that of which the plaintiff complains * * *." Georgia v. Tennessee Copper Co., 206 U.S. 230, 27 S.Ct. 618, 51 L.Ed. 1038 (1907). Therefore, injunctions are more apt to be issued in public nuisance actions. *Id.* As one recent New York decision emphasizes,

> [w]hile economic consequences between the effect of the injunction and the effect of the nuisance may be appropriately considered in a private nuisance action [*see Boomer*], they are not to be considered in a public nuisance action * * *. In the context of a public nuisance lawsuit, the rule in New York is that the nuisance will be enjoined despite a marked disparity between the effect of the injunction and the effect of the nuisance * * *.

State v. Monoco Oil Co., 185 Misc.2d 742, 751, 713 N.Y.S.2d 440, 446 (N.Y.Sup.Ct.2000) (preliminary injunction issued against the operation of an asphalt storage facility that produced fumes which caused numerous people to experience headaches, stinging eyes, coughing, and asthma attacks); *accord,* Hoover v. Durkee, 212 A.D.2d 839, 842, 622 N.Y.S.2d 348, 351 (1995) ("We find the balancing of the interests detailed in [*Boomer*] inapplicable in the context of this public nuisance."). Some commentators have suggested that "under the *Boomer* facts the attorney general or other official representative might have been successful in obtaining an injunction under a public nuisance theory * * *." Robert Abrams & Val Washington, *The Misunderstood Law of Public Nuisance: A Comparison with Private Nuisance Twenty Years After Boomer*, 54 Alb. L. Rev. 359, 390 (1990).

2. The public nuisance concept has become an increasingly useful device in dealing with environmental problems and related matters. Consider, for example, the language of the United States Supreme Court in Illinois v. City of Milwaukee, 406 U.S. 91, 92 S.Ct. 1385, 31 L.Ed.2d 712 (1972), a case in which the state of Illinois sought to have Milwaukee's release of sewage into Lake Michigan enjoined as a public nuisance:

> The remedy sought by Illinois is not within the precise scope of remedies prescribed by Congress. Yet the remedies which Congress provides are not necessarily the only federal remedies available. "It is not uncommon for federal courts to fashion federal law where federal rights are concerned." Textile Workers v. Lincoln Mills, 353 U.S. 448, 457, 77 S.Ct. 912, 918, 1 L.Ed.2d 972. When we deal with air or water in their ambient or interstate aspects, there is a federal common law, as Texas v. Pankey, 10 Cir., 441 F.2d 236, recently held.

> The application of federal common law to abate a public nuisance in interstate or navigable waters is not inconsistent with the Water Pollution Control Act. Congress provided in § 10(b) of that Act that, save as a

court may decree otherwise in an enforcement action, "State and interstate action to abate pollution of interstate or navigable waters shall be encouraged and shall not * * * be displaced by Federal enforcement action."

* * *

When it comes to water pollution this Court has spoken in terms of "a public nuisance," New York v. New Jersey, 256 U.S. 296, 313, 41 S.Ct. 492, 497, 65 L.Ed. 937; New Jersey v. New York City, 283 U.S. 473, 481, 482, 51 S.Ct. 519, 521, 75 L.Ed. 1176. In Missouri v. Illinois, 200 U.S. 496, 520–521, 26 S.Ct. 268, 269–270, 50 L.Ed. 572, the Court said, "It may be imagined that a nuisance might be created by a State upon a navigable river like the Danube, which would amount to a casus belli for a State lower down, unless removed. If such a nuisance were created by a State upon the Mississippi the controversy would be resolved by the more peaceful means of a suit in this court."

It may happen that new federal laws and new federal regulations may in time pre-empt the field of federal common law of nuisance. But until that comes to pass, federal courts will be empowered to appraise the equities of the suits alleging creation of a public nuisance by water pollution. While federal law governs, consideration of state standards may be relevant. * * * Thus, a State with high water quality standards may well ask that its strict standards be honored and that it not be compelled to lower itself to the more degrading standards of a neighbor. There are no fixed rules that govern; these will be equity suits in which the informed judgment of the chancellor will largely govern.

Id. at 103–09, 92 S.Ct. at 1392–95, 31 L.Ed.2d 712.

State governments and their agencies have successfully utilized public nuisance theory to obtain injunctions against environmental problems whether or not other statutory criminal or civil penalties were applicable. *See, e.g.,* Commonwealth v. Barnes & Tucker Co., 455 Pa. 392, 319 A.2d 871 (1974) (even though statute regulating the area did not authorize injunction to require mine owner to treat acid mine drainage, injunction was available under public nuisance doctrine); *see also* State *ex rel.* New Mexico Water Quality Control Commission v. Molybdenum Corp. of America, 89 N.M. 552, 555 P.2d 375 (N.M.Ct.App.1976) (same; river pollution); *see generally* Karol Boudreaux & Bruce Yandle, *Public Bads and Public Nuisance: Common Law Remedies for Environmental Decline*, 14 Fordham Envtl. L.J. 55 (2002) (discussing public nuisance cases, including *Village of Wilsonville*).

3. In Illinois v. City of Milwaukee, 406 U.S. 91, 92 S.Ct. 1385, 31 L.Ed.2d 712 (1972), the court left open the question of whether the result was affected by the passage of the 1972 Amendments to the Water Pollution Control Act. On remand, the lower court concluded that the federal common law cause of action had survived the new statute and that injunctive relief was appropriate. 599 F.2d 151 (7th Cir.1979). On appeal, the Supreme Court reversed that decision, holding that the plaintiff's federal common law cause of action was displaced by the Federal Water Pollution Act Amendments of 1972. City of Milwaukee v. Illinois, 451 U.S. 304, 101 S.Ct. 1784, 68 L.Ed.2d

114 (1981). One commentator has observed that nothing in the 1972 Amendments expressly indicates an intention to preempt federal common law, and therefore the Court's holding "seems to have been based on the desire to avoid an independent policymaking role for the courts in an area where Congress had acted." Daniel A. Farber, *Equitable Discretion, Legal Duties, and Environmental Injunctions*, 45 U. Pitt. L. Rev. 513, 520 (1984). Another commentator has taken the position that, while the Supreme Court justifiably held that the federal antipollution statutes displaced federal common law, the Court's justification does not support the preemption of state nuisance law. Andrew Jackson Heimert, *Keeping Pigs Out of Parlors: Using Nuisance Law to Affect the Location of Pollution*, 27 Envtl. L. 403 (1997).

4. In a public nuisance action, zoning provisions and environmental regulations are less apt to bar injunctive relief than in a private nuisance action, as illustrated by California Code of Civil Procedure § 731a, *supra. See, e.g.*, State *ex rel.* Dresser Industries, Inc. v. Ruddy, 592 S.W.2d 789, 793 (Mo. 1980) ("Clean Water Law did not pre-empt the field of water pollution 'public nuisance' law in Missouri."). However, a state legislature may displace a common law public nuisance action if it chooses to do so. *See, e.g.*, People v. New Penn Mines, Inc., 212 Cal.App.2d 667, 28 Cal.Rptr. 337 (1963) (The Dickey Water Pollution Act displaced the Attorney General's power to abate a public nuisance because it was a specific statute which trumped California Code of Civil Procedure § 731a.) For a discussion of the effect of statutes on common law public nuisance actions, see William H. Rodgers, Jr., Environmental Law: Air and Water § 2.11 (2004).

5. Historically, the courts have been reluctant to recognize the defenses of laches and estoppel in public nuisance actions brought by a governmental agency on the ground that abating a public nuisance is an exercise of the police power of the State. More recently, however, both defenses have been recognized against governmental plaintiffs in the interest of fairness. For a discussion of this modern trend, see Randy L. Parcel, *Making the Government Fight Fairly: Estopping the United States*, 27 Rocky Mtn. Min. L. Inst. 41 (1982); Comment, *Emergence of an Equitable Doctrine of Estoppel Against the Government—The Oil Shale Cases*, 46 U. Colo. L. Rev. 433 (1975); Comment, *Equitable Estoppel of the Government*, 47 Brook. L. Rev. 423 (1981); Comment, *Equitable Estoppel of the Government*, 79 Colum. L. Rev. 551 (1979); Comment, *Estopping the State: Just and Equitable Considerations*, 34 Drake L. Rev. 197 (1984); Note, 22 Howard L.J. 513 (1979) (summarizing cases that have recognized laches as a bar to an action by the government).

6. The remedies available in public and private nuisance actions were compared in State *ex rel.* Dresser Industries v. Ruddy, 592 S.W.2d 789 (Mo.1980) (en banc) (public nuisance action brought by the State of Missouri for past pollution of waterways caused by rupture of "dam" of defendant's settling basin, which contained waste from barite mining operation; complaint sought $1,000,000 in actual damages and $2,000,000 in statutory penalties):

> Actual and punitive damages are permitted in conjunction with the maintenance of suits involving private nuisances. * * * Injunctions or abatements have been the traditional remedies where the state brings suit for a public nuisance, 66 C.J.S. Nuisances § 77 (1950), but the prayer

in Count II of the state's petition, admittedly based on the common law, seeks "damages" only. Neither party has cited any precedent in this state wherein it was declared that "damages," absent some statutory authority, were or were not recoverable by public authorities for a public nuisance. Argument is made that such a recovery should follow necessarily, based on the theory that a protectible interest of the state is recognized; that such an interest can be harmed; that a legitimate interest which can be harmed is entitled to a rejuvenating compensation to repair that interest, including past injuries wrongfully caused by a nuisance; that absent such recovery, those causing damage to a public interest suffer no penalty whatever if the "cause" has been corrected and no private individual can show a "special" damage; that abatement or injunctive relief in retrospect would be a moot issue and constitute no relief at all. Whether or not actual or punitive damages are appropriate, in any event, would depend on the facts of a particular case. Punitive damages usually follow gross negligence on the part of a defendant or willful or continual perpetration of tortious activity. Absent any relevant factual record, we leave it to the trial court in the first instance, to determine whether or not damages are appropriate or allowable under Count II.

Id. at 793. In some jurisdictions, the legislature has provided for the recovery of damages in public nuisance actions. *See, e.g.*, State v. Arellano, 599 S.E.2d 415 (N.C.Ct.App.2004).

7. Under the traditional approach, a private party may not bring a public nuisance action unless he or she has sustained "special injury" or one that is "different in kind" from that suffered by members of the public at large. *See, e.g.*, Koll–Irvine Center Property Owners Ass'n v. County of Orange, 24 Cal.App. 4th 1036, 29 Cal.Rptr.2d 664 (1994); *see also* Restatement (Second) of Torts § 821C(1) (1979); *see generally* William B. Johnson, Annotation, *What Constitutes Special Injury that Entitles Private Party to Maintain Action Based on Public Nuisance—Modern Cases*, 71 A.L.R.4th 13 (1989). Presumably, the purpose of this limitation is to preserve the meaningfulness of the public prosecutor's discretion and to protect defendants from a multiplicity of lawsuits. There is a recent trend to relax this limitation. For example, in Akau v. Olohana Corp., 65 Haw. 383, 652 P.2d 1130 (1982), the Hawaii Supreme Court held that

a member of the public has standing to sue to enforce the rights of the public [against a public nuisance] even though his injury is not different in kind from the public's generally, if he can show that he has suffered an injury in fact, and that the concerns of a multiplicity of suits are satisfied by any means, including a class action.

Id. at 1134; *see also* Restatement (Second) of Torts § 821C(2) (1979); *see generally* Denise E. Antolini, *Modernizing Public Nuisance: Solving the Paradox of the Special Injury Rule*, 28 Ecology L.Q. 755 (2001); Skotnicki, Note, *Private Actions for Damages Resulting from an Environmental Public Nuisance: Overcoming the Barrier to Standing Posed by the "Special Injury Rule,"* 16 Am. J. Trial Advoc. 591 (1992).

In jurisdictions that continue to require proof of an injury "different in kind" from that sustained by the general public, private parties may prove that they have standing when the act complained of is both a private nuisance and a public nuisance. *See, e.g.*, Birke v. Oakwood Worldwide, 87 Cal.Rptr.3d 602 (Cal.App.2009) (where second hand smoke in public areas of apartment complex could be characterized as both a public and private nuisance, resident asthmatic had standing to sue) Newhall Land & Farming Co. v. Superior Court, 19 Cal.App.4th 334, 23 Cal.Rptr.2d 377 (1993) (defendant's natural gas plant contaminated soil and groundwater). For example, a smoking factory may well constitute a private nuisance to an adjoining owner in that it unreasonably interferes with the use and enjoyment of his or her real estate and at the same time it may represent a public nuisance to the community at large. Similarly, if pollution of a river destroys fish, "such pollution would constitute a private nuisance where the river flowed through private property and a public nuisance in those areas where the public right to fish was interfered with." Patrick E. Murphy, *Environmental Law: New Legal Concepts in the Antipollution Fight*, 36 Mo. L. Rev. 78, 84 (1971).

A few jurisdictions by statute authorize private suits on behalf of the state to enjoin public nuisances even though the private plaintiffs are not specially injured. *See* Joseph L. Sax & Joseph F. DiMento, *Environmental Citizen Suits: Three Years' Experience Under the Michigan Environmental Protection Act*, 4 Ecology L.Q. 1 (1974) (Michigan statute allows "any person" to bring a public nuisance action to protect the environment). In addition, some legislation expressly authorizes non-injured private parties to bring injunction suits against certain special types of public nuisance. *See, e.g.*, Littleton v. Fritz, 65 Iowa 488, 22 N.W. 641 (1885) (illegal liquor establishments).

MARK v. STATE DEPARTMENT OF FISH & WILDLIFE

Court of Appeals of Oregon, 1999.
158 Or.App. 355, 974 P.2d 716.

Before WARREN, PRESIDING JUDGE, and EDMONDS and ARMSTRONG, JUDGES.

WARREN, P.J.

Plaintiffs have lived on Sauvie Island since June 1990. They bought their land, which is surrounded by the Sauvie Island Wildlife Area (wildlife area), in February 1990. The portion of the wildlife area near where they live is a popular location for public nudity to an extent that, plaintiffs assert, constitutes both a private and a public nuisance. Defendant Division of State Lands (State Lands) owns the wildlife area, which it leases to defendant Department of Fish and Wildlife (Fish and Wildlife). In this case, plaintiffs seek compensation for the effects of the nudity on their land and an injunction restraining defendants from allowing public nudity in the wildlife area. * * * On defendants' motions * * * the trial court determined that defendants are immune from liability under the Oregon Tort Claims Act because they were exercising a discretionary function * * *. It therefore dismissed both the original and amended complaints. We reverse on the injunction claims and otherwise affirm.

* * *

The activities of the nude users have created a situation where plaintiffs, other local residents, and visitors to the area are helpless to prevent "continuous and oftentimes daily exposure" to full adult nudity. Plaintiffs and their family, friends, and guests have been forced to witness adult nudity and "repeated acts of depravity, illegality and lewdness" because of their location adjacent to defendants' lands. Plaintiffs, other residents, and other members of the public have reported those facts to defendants and informed them of the harm that results from the public nudity and related activities.

According to plaintiffs, defendants have the authority, obligation, and duty to control the activities of the public in the wildlife area in a way reasonably calculated to prevent harm to the rights and safety of adjacent landowners and the public in general and to the value of surrounding private property. Defendants have knowingly and intentionally failed to exercise that control in a way calculated to prohibit or reasonably restrict public nudity, resulting in harm to plaintiffs and their property. The harm to plaintiffs is that their use of their property and their social life have been restricted by their reluctance to expose themselves, family, friends, and guests to public nudity and open sexual activity, that they are fearful for their safety due to their proximity to the nude beach activities, that they are embarrassed, offended and angered by coming in contact with nude adult behavior, that their right to go for a walk and enjoy the public beaches adjacent to their home has been restricted by harassment from nude sunbathers, and that those things have greatly diminished the value of their property.

In the first and second claims in their original complaint, plaintiff asserted that defendants' actions constituted both a private (first claim) and a public (second claim) nuisance. They sought damages and an injunction prohibiting defendants from allowing the use of the wildlife area for public nudity. In their third and fourth claims, they alleged that defendants' actions so reduced the value of their property that it constituted a taking for public use, thus entitling them to damages for inverse condemnation under the state (third claim) and federal (fourth claim) constitutions.

The trial court dismissed plaintiffs's original complaint in its entirety for failure to state a claim. * * *

The trial court dismissed the nuisance claims on the ground that defendants' actions came within the discretionary function exception to a public body's liability in tort. ORS 30.265(3)(c). After the trial court's decision, the Supreme Court held that that provision does not apply to an action for an injunction, because an injunction does not involve potential monetary liability. Penland v. Redwood Sanitary Sewer Service Dist., 327 Or. 1, 956 P.2d 964 (1998). At least as to the claims for an injunction, thus, the trial court decision was erroneous on the ground on which the trial court relied. However, the state also argued that the facts that plaintiffs alleged do not constitute a public or private nuisance. Because that argument, if correct, would support the trial court's decision dismissing those claims in their entirety, we begin with it.

The doctrines of public nuisance and private nuisance have different origins and protect different interests. However, many of the governing rules are the same, and we will therefore treat the claims together. A public nuisance is the invasion of a right that is common to all members of the public. Because the primary responsibility for preventing public nuisances is with the public authorities, a private action to enforce that right requires proof that the plaintiff suffered an injury distinct from the injury that the public as a whole suffered. A private nuisance is an unreasonable non-trespassory interference with another's private use and enjoyment of land. The right to recover is in the person whose land is harmed. *See* Smejkal v. Empire Lite–Rock, Inc., 274 Or. 571, 574, 547 P.2d 1363 (1976); Raymond v. Southern Pacific Co., 259 Or. 629, 634, 488 P.2d 460 (1971); Restatement (Second), Torts (1979) §§ 821A, 821B, 821D, and introductory note.

Undesired exposure to sexual activity, such as the presence of a neighboring house of prostitution, is one of the traditional grounds for finding either a public or a private nuisance. *See* Prosser and Keeton on the Law of Torts, 5th ed. (W. Page Keeton, ed.1984), § 87 at 620, § 90 at 644; 66 C.J.S. 796, Nuisances § 45. * * *

* * *

We have not found any Oregon case that indicates that nudity in itself, with no clear sexual component, constitutes a nuisance. On the one hand, public nudity is not illegal unless it occurs with the intent of arousing the sexual desire of either the actor or another person. *See* ORS 163.465. On the other hand, an activity that is otherwise legal may still constitute a nuisance. *See* Lunda v. Matthews, 46 Or.App. 701, 706–07, 613 P.2d 63 (1980). Otherwise, among other things, there would have been no need to provide that farming and forestry practices conducted on land zoned for farm or forestry use outside an urban growth boundary do not give rise to an action for nuisance. *See* ORS 30.930 through ORS 30.947 [(Oregon's right-to-farm statute)]. The allegations in plaintiffs' original complaint are not limited to mere nudity but would support proof of uncontrolled and intrusive nudity occurring on the area immediately around their property. Whether a particular activity is a nuisance is primarily a factual question that requires applying well-established criteria. *See* Penland v. Redwood Sanitary Sewer Service Dist., 156 Or.App. 311, 315, 965 P.2d 433 (1998). Although the question is the effect of the challenged activity on an ordinary person, and although the law does not protect the delicate, *see* Amphitheaters, Inc. v. Portland Meadows, 184 Or. 336, 349, 198 P.2d 847 (1948), plaintiff's allegations would allow finding that the nudity constituted a nuisance.

Plaintiffs also allege that they have been exposed not merely to nudity but also to a variety of sexual activity. A court could find that the routine use of defendants' land for public sexual activity was a public nuisance.

Plaintiffs' allegations would also allow proof that, because of the proximity of their land to the intrusive nudity and the sexual activity, those things have affected their property or their enjoyment of it. If so, plaintiffs' injury would be different in kind from that of the public at large, and they would be entitled to sue to enjoin the public nuisance. The same facts would support a finding that the intrusive nudity and sexual activity impair their use and enjoyment of their land; they would thus constitute a private nuisance for which they could seek damages or an injunction.

That these actions on defendants' land may constitute a nuisance does not, in itself, create a claim against defendants. As state agencies rather than natural persons, defendants are not capable of engaging in public nudity or sexual activity, at Sauvie Island or elsewhere. Plaintiffs do not allege that defendants' employees acting in the course of their employment participated in any of the activity about which they complain. Rather, plaintiffs' complaint is that defendants do not prevent third parties from engaging in public nudity and sexual activity on defendants' lands. That raises the question of whether a court can hold defendants responsible for the acts of third parties when those third parties' actions on defendants' land may constitute a nuisance.

The Restatement suggests that, in order to be liable for the acts of third parties that create a nuisance on their land, defendants must both (1) know that the activity is being carried on and will involve an unreasonable risk of causing the nuisance and (2) consent to the activity or fail to exercise reasonable care to prevent it. Restatement (Second), Torts § 838 (1979). * * *

Plaintiffs allege that defendants have the authority to exercise control over the behavior of the members of the public who congregate in the wildlife area and that defendants, either knowingly and intentionally, or with reckless disregard for the rights and safety of the public, failed to exercise control over nudity in the wildlife area. That is sufficient to allege that defendants are responsible for the actions of the public under the criteria of section 838.

* * *

In plaintiffs' second assignment of error they assert that the trial court erred when it granted defendants' motion to dismiss their amended complaint, which was limited to claims for private and public nuisance. The primary difference between the original complaint and the amended complaint is that, in the amended complaint, plaintiffs focussed on a management plan that defendants adopted in 1993 in order to regulate nudity in the wildlife area. Plaintiffs first attack the underlying decision to regulate and control public nudity rather than to attempt to eliminate it. That approach, they allege, conflicts with defendants' mission to permit only wildlife-related activities in the wildlife area. Plaintiffs then describe the plan as, among other things, distinguishing between "clothing optional" and "clothed" areas, providing for buffer areas between the clothing optional area and private lands, and prohibiting any use of those buffer areas during the warmer months. The plan also contains provisions concerning signs and other matters that were intended to discourage or eliminate public nudity outside of the designated nude beach area.

Plaintiffs next allege that defendants have failed to implement this policy adequately in a number of respects, with the result that "hundreds of members of the public traverse nude throughout the Sauvie Island Wildlife Area, including the beaches outside the designated 'clothing optional' beach, the roads, the woods and the lands surrounding plaintiffs' residence." Plaintiffs and other residents are helpless to prevent "continuous and oftentimes daily exposure" to nudity. They allege that defendants are negligent by failing to develop a plan that is adequate to control, discourage, or eliminate nudity, by failing adequately to implement the plan that they did adopt, and by failing to consider the effect that nude recreation would have on plaintiffs' interests in their private property, thus breaching a nondiscretionary duty to plaintiffs under ORS 496.138. Those things allegedly harmed plaintiffs in the ways described in the original complaint.

Whether plaintiffs' amended complaint states a claim for a public or private nuisance is a closer issue than is their original complaint. It is less clear from the amended complaint that plaintiffs' land has been affected by sexual activity rather than simple nudity, and it now appears that defendants are in fact attempting to reduce the impact of public nudity on plaintiffs. As plaintiffs describe the plan, if implemented it will eliminate the effect of intrusive nudity on their land, thus ending any private nuisance. It will similarly end the special injury to plaintiffs from any public nuisance.

Plaintiffs' continuing claims must be based on their allegation that defendants are failing to implement the plan adequately. Under section 838 of the Restatement, they must also show that defendants' failure to implement the plan is the result of their lack of reasonable care. A number of plaintiffs' concerns, such as embarrassment at coming in contact with public nudity or their fear for their safety because of their proximity to the nude beach, are things that they share in common with the public at large and thus cannot support a claim for a public nuisance. Those things are also not directly related to the use and enjoyment of plaintiffs' land and therefore do not support a claim for a private nuisance. Plaintiffs' reliance on ORS 496.138 to establish that defendants have a duty to them as property owners to prevent nudity and limit the use of the wildlife area to wildlife-related uses is unavailing. As we discuss below, the statute sets forth the general duty of the State Fish and Wildlife Commission to implement state policies for the management of wildlife. Nothing in the statement of the Commission's responsibilities creates any private rights. * * *

We conclude, despite these concerns, that the amended complaint states a claim for both a public and private nuisance, because its allegations could be read to include those things that we found sufficient in the original complaint and because it alleges that defendants have failed to implement the management plan. That conclusion means that plaintiffs are entitled to pursue their injunction claims. Whether they are entitled to pursue their claims for damages depends on whether defendants are immune under the OTCA.

The essence of plaintiffs' claim for damages is that defendants had a non-discretionary duty to exercise their authority over the wildlife area to reduce or eliminate nudity and its effects. They base that assertion on * * * ORS 496.138(1), which provides that the Commission "shall implement the policies and programs of this state for the management of wildlife," and ORS 496.138(2), which provides that it "shall adopt such rules and standards as it considers necessary and proper to implement the policy and objectives of ORS 496.012 * * *."

* * *

* * * Those statutes require the Commission to adopt rules of some sort on some subject, but they give the Commission discretion in deciding what subjects to cover and what rules to adopt. * * * The Commission, thus, has discretion about whether to regulate nude recreation in the wildlife area and, if so, how to regulate it. That is the essence of discretionary immunity under ORS 30.265(3)(c).

* * *

Finally, Fish and Wildlife did not create the nuisance, which would require it to take steps to eliminate it. Although the nuisance, if any, exists on land that it controls, the nuisance is the result of the independent actions of third parties, not of Fish and Wildlife. Even if Fish and Wildlife had created the nuisance, it would have discretion in deciding what steps to mitigate the effects of its actions and would be immune from liability for money damages if those steps were not fully effective. * * * The mere existence of a common law nuisance may be sufficient to support an injunction, because that does not involve a claim for monetary damages, but it does not in itself overcome discretionary immunity from such damages.

There is, thus, no basis for holding that Fish and Wildlife's alleged inaction before it adopted the policy described in the amended complaint violated any nondiscretionary duty to act. The trial court correctly dismissed plaintiffs' nuisance claims to the extent that they sought monetary damages rather than injunctive relief. * * *

* * *

Reversed and remanded on claims for injunctive relief for private and public nuisance; otherwise affirmed.

EDMONDS, J., dissenting.

The majority holds that plaintiffs have properly pled a claim for nuisance against the defendant agencies but that the agencies are immune from liability for damages under ORS 30.265(3)(c). * * *

* * *

Defendants are agencies of the State of Oregon that derive their authority and their exposure to liability from statutes. ORS 30.320 provides that an action may be maintained against the State of Oregon in the name of the appropriate state agency for liability in tort as provided in ORS 30.260 to 30.300. ORS 30.260 *et seq.* does not prohibit nuisance claims and expressly permits, under certain circumstances, claims for damages based on common-law tort theories. When those circumstances exist, the tort liability of an agency is no different from that of a private landowner under the common law. At common law, a civil division of a state that "in the exercise of its corporate powers, * * * create[d] or permit[ted] a nuisance by misfeasance or nonfeasance * * * [could be] liable in damages to any person suffering special injury therefrom" in the absence of a statute immunizing them from liability. * * * The import of that observation is not to suggest that the legislature in enacting ORS 30.265 intended to adopt the common-law criteria for public body liability for a nuisance but to emphasize that the concept of such liability is not an unprecedented notion. To the extent that ORS 30.265 waives the sovereign immunity of the State of Oregon for liability for common-law torts, the agencies are liable for damages resulting from any nuisance that they have permitted to affect plaintiffs' property.

The inaction of a public body to prevent harm is not always immune from liability under ORS 30.265(3)(c). For instance, in Miller v. Grants Pass Irrigation, 297 Or. 312, 686 P.2d 324 (1984), the issue was whether an irrigation district's failure to install a warning device for boaters regarding its dam on the Rogue River involved a discretionary function under the statute. The court indicated:

> If there is a legal duty to protect the public by warning of a danger or by taking prevent[ative] measures, or both, the choice of means may be discretionary, but the decision whether or not to do so at all is, by definition, not discretionary.

Id. at 320. It concluded:

> Because ORS 30.265(3)(c) provides immunity for failure to exercise a discretionary function or duty but not for failure to undertake a nondiscretionary function or duty, it follows that the district would not be immune for wholly disregarding and declining to consider whatever duty it had under tort law.

Id. at 321.

* * *

In my view, the duty of a state agency to exercise discretion to prevent harm to adjoining lands from activities on land under its control is nondiscretionary under the statute. It is like the duty of a public body to exercise discretion to prevent harm from a known dangerous condition such as the existence of a dam on a river typically used by boaters or the duty to exercise discretion to maintain traffic signals so that motorists will not be misled and injured when they use a public intersection. * * *

Although the agencies have discretion about how to regulate the activities on their lands so as to prevent a nuisance, they do not have discretion to disregard and to decline to consider their duty to regulate in the face of obvious harm. The latter is the gravamen of plaintiffs' pleadings.

* * *

For these reasons, I dissent.

NOTE

On remand, the trial court in *Mark* refused to find a "public nuisance," but issued a permanent injunction ordering the defendant to abate the "private nuisance." The appellate court affirmed because the plaintiffs had proven that, at least a dozen times a year, they had seen adults engaged in explicit sexual conduct on the defendant's property, and because the plaintiffs had not "come to the nuisance." 191 Or.App. 563, 84 P.3d 155 (2004). The injunction ordered the defendant to (1) "establish a buffer of sufficient length to avoid viewing of nude sunbathers on Collins Beach from plaintiffs' real property"; [and] (2) "adequately staff the area in and around plaintiffs' property to adequately police compliance with the nude beach boundaries and address incidents of public sexual behavior" * * *. *Id.* at 572, 84 P.3d at 161.

ENVIRONMENTAL DEFENSE FUND v. LAMPHIER

United States Court of Appeals, Fourth Circuit, 1983.
714 F.2d 331.

Before WINTER, CHIEF JUDGE, and MURNAGHAN and ERVIN, CIRCUIT JUDGES.

ERVIN, CIRCUIT JUDGE:

The cause of this appeal is a judgment by the district court holding that the defendants violated state and federal antipollution laws and committed a common law nuisance. * * *

I.

James and Janet Lamphier are co-owners of a farm in Culpepper County, Virginia. Since 1974 the farm has been headquarters for "Jim's Liquid Waste," a sole proprietorship belonging to James Lamphier and engaged in the business of industrial waste disposal.

In the fall of 1979, the Virginia State Water Control Board ("SWCB") and the State Department of Health ("SDH") learned that Lamphier was transporting various wastes to his farm and disposing of them by land application and lagooning of bulk liquids, and burial of drummed liquids. After visits to the farm, both state agencies ordered Lamphier to cease his disposal activities. On December 5, 1979, the SWCB issued an emergency order requiring Lamphier to contain all runoff from lagoons and land application areas and submit a list of wastes deposited at the facility. Subsequently, the SWCB ordered Lamphier to devise a land reclamation plan and to construct proper facilities for the disposal of septic wastes. In compliance with these orders, Lamphier halted dumping activities (although he continued to receive shipments of wastes through March, 1980) and, sometime after November 5, 1980, submitted a plan for waste containment and land reclamation to both the SWCB and the SDH. The SWCB subsequently approved the plan, but the SDH did not.

In March, 1980, an investigator for the SDH visited the Lamphier farm and found several 55–gallon drums containing solvents buried on the property. On April 11, 1980, the SDH investigator returned along with a special agent of the state police and, armed with a search warrant, collected samples of well waters and of wastes found in numerous barrels. Tests performed on these samples revealed a high degree of flammability, which under regulations of the Resource Conservation and Recovery Act of 1976 ("RCRA"), 42 U.S.C. §§ 6901 et seq., qualified the wastes as hazardous. See 40 C.F.R. § 261.21.

* * *

On June 16, 1980, federal officials intervened. Representatives from the Environmental Protection Agency ("EPA") visited the farm to ascertain whether the materials posed an "imminent hazard" warranting immediate action under § 7003 of RCRA, 42 U.S.C. § 6973. Samples taken revealed no imminent hazard, but in the report to the SWCB, Jack Brinkmann of the EPA left open the possibility that other RCRA violations might be present.

* * *

On November 19, 1980, major new RCRA provisions went into effect, requiring all hazardous waste treatment, storage and disposal facilities to register for permits or non-permit interim status and to comply with certain operating standards. Lamphier took no action to obtain an operator's permit.

* * *

The Environmental Defense Fund, Inc. ("EDF") and the Chesapeake Bay Foundation ("CBF"), two private environmental groups, joined the dispute on October 5, 1981, by filing a complaint against Lamphier under the "citizen suit" provision of RCRA, 42 U.S.C. § 6972, alleging violations of RCRA notification and permit requirements, 42 U.S.C. §§ 6930 and 6925. The Commonwealth of Virginia intervened on January 12, 1982, appending several state law charges to EDF and CBF's action. In addition to injunctive relief, the Commonwealth sought response costs under the Comprehensive Environmental Response, Compensation and Liability Act of 1980, 42 U.S.C. §§ 9601 et seq.

After a bench trial, the court found the defendants guilty of common law nuisance and of violations of RCRA and Virginia state law. As relief, the court issued an injunction ordering Lamphier henceforth to comply with applicable hazardous waste regulations. The court further ordered the Lamphiers to provide the plaintiffs and plaintiff-intervenors access to the farm for the purpose of monitoring wastes. Fees and costs were also awarded.

II.

* * *

[The court held that the defendant was in violation of federal law.]

III.

Originally, the EDF and CBF sought civil penalties against Lamphier of $25,000 for each day of violation under the citizen suit provision of RCRA, 42 U.S.C. § 6972. However, at trial, the plaintiffs voluntarily dismissed this claim, limiting the remedy sought to an injunction, plus costs and attorneys fees.

Lamphier maintains that once plaintiffs waived their original claim for civil penalties, no jurisdiction remained over claims for statutory and common law injunctive relief, since the citizen suit provision of RCRA, 42 U.S.C. § 6972, does not expressly authorize such relief. Lamphier cites Middlesex County Sewerage Authority v. National Sea Clammers Association, 453 U.S. 1, 14–15, 101 S.Ct. 2615, 2623–2624, 69 L.Ed.2d 435 (1981), for the proposition that "where a statute expressly provides a particular remedy or remedies, a court must be chary of reading others into it." In *Sea Clammers*, a private association brought a claim seeking damages and declaratory and injunctive relief under the citizen suit provision of the Federal Water Pollution Control Act ("FWPCA"), 33 U.S.C. § 1365(a), and federal common law. Section 1365(a) authorizes citizen suits against any person alleged to be in violation of an effluent standard or a government order under the Act and confers on the district court jurisdiction to enforce such standards or orders and to impose any appropriate civil penalties. The question before the Court was whether section 1365(a) additionally permitted suits for private relief—damages and an injunction—as opposed to "private attorneys general" actions to obtain enforcement of federal law through injunctive relief and civil penalties. The Court held that the plain language of the FWPCA did not authorize a private right of action for injunctive and monetary relief. Although 33 U.S.C. § 1365(a) enumerates only civil penalties, the Court presumed the statute authorized private persons to sue for civil injunctions to enforce the regulatory scheme, provided the private plaintiff complied with the notice requirements set out in section 1365(b). But the plaintiffs in *Sea Clammers* ignored these procedures and thus forfeited their claim for injunctive relief as well as losing their quest for a private award of damages.

Sea Clammers is readily distinguishable from the instant case. The private plaintiffs here did not seek an award of damages but rather acted as private attorneys general in seeking the assessment of civil penalties and an injunction against Lamphier. Under the citizen suit provision of RCRA, 42 U.S.C. § 6972, the district court is authorized to enforce RCRA regulations or orders, presumably to the full extent of its legal and equitable powers. 42 U.S.C. § 6972(a). Provided plaintiffs are genuinely acting as private attorneys general rather than pursuing a private remedy, nothing in RCRA, as in the FWPCA, bars injunctive relief. *See* 42 U.S.C. § 6928.[4]

* * *

IV.

Lamphier next attacks the award of injunctive relief requiring future compliance with the registration requirements of RCRA and directing that Lamphier open up his land to monitoring of wastes. He points out the hornbook rule that to obtain injunctive relief, a plaintiff must prove that legal remedies are inadequate, that risk of an irreparable injury exists, and that the balance of equities justifies an injunction. Since the plaintiffs here did not attempt to prove irreparable injury, Lamphier argues that the grant of injunctive relief was improper.

This argument fails on at least two counts. First, the law of injunctions differs with respect to governmental plaintiffs (or private attorneys general) as opposed to private individuals. Where the plaintiff is a sovereign and where the activity may endanger the public health, "injunctive relief is proper, without resort to balancing." Illinois v. Milwaukee, 599 F.2d 151, 166 (7th Cir.1979), *rev'd on other grounds*, 451 U.S. 304, 101 S.Ct. 1784, 68 L.Ed.2d 114 (1981). Second, in cases of public health legislation, the emphasis shifts from irreparable injury to concern for the general public interest:

> It is contended that the government has not shown irreparable injury and that it has an adequate remedy at law * * *. The United States, however, is not bound to conform with the requirements of private litigation when it seeks the aid of the courts to give effect to the policy of Congress as manifested in a statute. It is a familiar doctrine that an injunction is an appropriate means for the enforcement of an Act of Congress when it is in the public interest.

Shafer v. United States, 229 F.2d 124, 128 (4th Cir.1956). This rationale applies equally to state enforcement of federal and state health laws.

Furthermore, 42 U.S.C. § 6928, the enforcement provision of RCRA, explicitly calls for the judicial issuance of injunctions to coerce compliance with the Act's requirements. Where a statute authorizes injunctive relief for its enforcement, plaintiffs need not plead and prove irreparable injury. * * * The injunctive relief impliedly authorized under 42 U.S.C. § 6972(a) was amply warranted in this case.

---

4. From this analysis it follows that the citizen plaintiffs here are not specially entitled to the benefits of substantive relief. We discern a minor trespass on this proposition in the district court's final order, in which Lamphier is directed to provide ongoing access to his property both to the Commonwealth and to the private plaintiffs for the purpose of monitoring wastes. At oral argument, the EDF and CBF conceded that they are not entitled to personal access to Lamphier's property, and we so construe the district court's order. Access is to be granted to the Commonwealth only.

Lamphier further urges that the injunction issued by the district court was not sufficiently specific to pass legal muster.

* * *

In its Memorandum Opinion and Order filed May 14, 1982, the district court ordered that:

> Plaintiffs and Plaintiff–Intervenor and their agents are granted an injunction and they are expressly authorized to enter onto Defendant's property at reasonable times in order to take such samples and make such tests as the Commonwealth deems appropriate. No bond shall be required.

We find no fatal flaw in the terms of this injunction, which merely requires Lamphier to open up his property to state inspection at reasonable times. By the language of the order, Lamphier is fully apprised of what he must do in order to avoid contempt proceedings. The open-ended duration of the injunction is justified by Lamphier's prior lack of cooperation with authorities. Until such time as Lamphier demonstrates abiding compliance with hazardous waste laws, his farm should remain subject to monitoring by health officials.

* * *

For the foregoing reasons, the judgment of the district court is affirmed.

NOTES

1. Preliminary injunctions are frequently issued in public nuisance actions brought by a governmental entity to enforce a violation of a zoning statute or permit, as evidenced by IT Corp. v. County of Imperial, 35 Cal.3d 63, 69–72, 196 Cal.Rptr. 715, 719–21, 672 P.2d 121, 125–27 (1983) (action by county for preliminary injunction restraining IT from disposing of unauthorized wastes at its hazardous waste disposal facility):

> The principal question raised by this appeal concerns the proper standard for the issuance of a preliminary injunction when a governmental entity seeks to enjoin an alleged violation of a zoning ordinance which specifically provides for injunctive relief.

* * *

> This court has traditionally held that trial courts should evaluate two interrelated factors when deciding whether or not to issue a preliminary injunction. The first is the likelihood that the plaintiff will prevail on the merits at trial. The second is the interim harm that the plaintiff is likely to sustain if the injunction were denied as compared to the harm that the defendant is likely to suffer if the preliminary injunction were issued.
> * * *

> This court has not addressed the question as to whether this two-factor test is the proper rule to apply when a governmental entity seeks

to enjoin an alleged violation of a zoning ordinance which provides for injunctive relief.

IT contends that the injunction was erroneously issued because the trial court did not balance the relative hardships to the parties. * * *

* * * The County properly points out that once a trial court has determined that the governmental entity will probably succeed at trial in proving a statutory violation, the court is justified in presuming that public harm will result if an injunction is not issued. The reasoning underlying this argument is sound. Where a legislative body has enacted a statutory provision proscribing a certain activity, it has already determined that such activity is contrary to the public interest. Further, where the legislative body has specifically authorized injunctive relief against the violation of such a law, it has already determined (1) that significant public harm will result from the proscribed activity, and (2) that injunctive relief may be the most appropriate way to protect against that harm. * * *

* * *

* * * On the other hand, IT is correct that an important function of preliminary injunctions—that of preventing serious interlocutory harm to the ultimately successful party—would be thwarted if an irrebuttable presumption in favor of the governmental entity were created. A conclusive presumption would fail to protect those defendants who might suffer grave or irreparable immediate harm from the issuance of an injunction even where that harm far outweighs the harm the public might suffer if no injunction were issued. * * *

It is apparent from the case law and from the considerations underlying the parties' arguments that the purposes of a preliminary injunction are best served in the present circumstances by an adaptation of the traditional test which incorporates elements of both parties' positions. * * *

Accordingly, the propriety of an injunction must be judged by the following standard. Where a governmental entity seeking to enjoin the alleged violation of an ordinance which specifically provides for injunctive relief establishes that it is reasonably probable it will prevail on the merits, a rebuttable presumption arises that the potential harm to the public outweighs the potential harm to the defendant. If the defendant shows that it would suffer grave or irreparable harm from the issuance of the preliminary injunction, the court must then examine the relative actual harms to the parties.

A recent Illinois case involving similar facts is more emphatic in concluding that a government entity need not establish the traditional equitable conditions precedent in seeking a preliminary injunction specifically authorized by statute:

When seeking injunctive relief that is expressly provided for by statute, a plaintiff is not required to plead or prove irreparable harm and an inadequate remedy at law. * * * The State or agency need only show that the statute was violated and that the statute relied upon specifically allows injunctive relief. * * * The principle underlying the willingness of the courts to issue statutory injunctions to public bodies to restrain violations of a statute is that harm to the public at large can be presumed from the statutory violation alone.

Village of Riverdale v. Allied Waste Transportation, Inc., 334 Ill.App.3d 224, 228–29, 267 Ill.Dec. 881, 885, 777 N.E.2d 684, 688 (2002); *accord* State v. Monoco Oil Co., 185 Misc.2d 742, 713 N.Y.S.2d 440 (2000). For a discussion of nuisance law hazardous waste injuries, see Richard A. Epstein, *Standing in Law & Equity: A Defense of Citizen and Taxpayer Suits*, 6 Green Bag 2d 17 (2002); David R. Hodas, *Private Actions for Public Nuisance: Common Law Citizen Suits for Relief from Environmental Harm*, 16 Ecol. L.Q. 883 (1989); Kenneth M. Murchison, *Does NEPA Matter?—An Analysis of the Historical Development and Contemporary Significance of the National Environmental Policy Act*, 18 U. Rich. L. Rev. 557 (1984); Richard E. Schwartz & David P. Hackett, *Citizen Suits Against Private Industry Under the Clean Water Act*, 17 Nat. Resources Law. 327 (1984); Shay S. Scott, *Combining Environmental Citizen Suits & Other Private Theories of Recovery*, 8 J. Envtl. L. & Litig. 369 (1994).

2.　During the past several decades the federal government has been a major source of environmental legislation. Among the most significant of these statutes are the Clean Air Act, 42 U.S.C.A. § 7401 *et seq.*; Clean Water Act, 33 U.S.C.A. § 1251 *et seq.*; Safe Drinking Water Act, 42 U.S.C.A. § 300f *et seq.*; Resource Conservation and Recovery Act of 1976, 42 U.S.C.A. § 6901 *et seq.*; Comprehensive Environmental Response, Compensation, and Liability Act (CERCLA), 42 U.S.C.A. § 9601 *et seq.*; Surface Mining Control and Reclamation Act, 30 U.S.C.A. § 1201 *et seq.*; and National Environmental Policy Act, 42 U.S.C.A. § 4321 *et seq.*

As we have seen earlier, private parties can experience significant standing roadblocks in public nuisance litigation. With respect to much of the foregoing federal legislation, however, Congress has generally been receptive to citizen judicial enforcement. For example, the language of § 505 of the Clean Water Act provides: "[A]ny citizen may commence a civil action on his own behalf—(A) * * * against any person * * * who is alleged to be in violation of * * * an effluent standard or limitation under this chapter or * * * an order issued by the Administrator or state with respect to such a standard or limitation." 33 U.S.C.A. § 1365(a)(2). Moreover, at least a dozen other major federal environmental statutes contain similar grants of standing to private citizens. *See* Zygmunt J.B. Plater et al., Environmental Law and Policy: Nature, Law and Society 566 (1992); *see generally* James B. Brown & Glen C. Hansen, *Nuisance Law and Petroleum Underground Storage Tank Contamination: Plugging the Hole in the Statute*, 21 Ecol. L.Q. 643 (1994); Richard deC. Hinds, *Liability Under Federal Law for Hazardous Waste Injuries*, 6 Harv. Envtl. L. Rev. 1 (1982).

NATURAL RESOURCES DEFENSE COUNCIL, INC.
v. TEXACO REFINING & MARKETING, INC.

United States Court of Appeals, Third Circuit, 1990.
906 F.2d 934.

Before HIGGINBOTHAM, CHIEF JUDGE, COWEN and NYGAARD, CIRCUIT JUDGES.

COWEN, CIRCUIT JUDGE.

This appeal arises out of a citizen suit filed by the Natural Resources Defense Council, Inc. and the Delaware Audubon Society (collectively referred to hereafter as "the NRDC") under § 505 of the Clean Water Act ("the Act"), 33 U.S.C. § 1365 (1982 and Supp. III), alleging that Texaco Refining and Marketing, Inc. ("Texaco") illegally discharged effluent into the Delaware River at its Delaware City refinery. * * *

I.

In order "to restore and maintain the chemical, physical, and biological integrity of the Nation's waters," 33 U.S.C. § 1251(a), the Act makes unlawful the discharge of any pollutant into navigable waters except as authorized under specific sections of the Act. *See generally* Gwaltney of Smithfield v. Chesapeake Bay Found., Inc., 484 U.S. 49, 52–53, 108 S.Ct. 376, 379, 98 L.Ed.2d 306 (1987). One of these is § 402 which establishes the National Pollutant Discharge Elimination System ("NPDES"). 33 U.S.C. § 1342. Under § 402 either the Administrator of the Environmental Protection Agency ("EPA"), or a state which has established its own EPA-approved permit program, may issue a permit allowing effluent discharges in accordance with specified conditions. 33 U.S.C. § 1342(b), (c).

The holder of a state permit is subject to enforcement action by both the EPA and the state for failure to comply with the permit's conditions. 33 U.S.C. § 1319, 1342(b)(7). In addition, private citizens may bring civil actions against any person alleged to be in violation of a state permit if the federal or state agencies have not acted. 33 U.S.C. § 1365(a)(1). The Act allows the court in a citizen suit to order injunctive relief and/or impose monetary penalties. 33 U.S.C. § 1365(a).

The State of Delaware received its NPDES permit delegation from the EPA on April 1, 1974, and issued a permit to Texaco in 1977 allowing it to discharge limited quantities of 19 categories of industrial waste from its Delaware City refinery into the Delaware River. The permit imposes on Texaco both limitations on the amount of pollutants that can be discharged and monitoring requirements.

As required by the Act, the NRDC notified Texaco in March 1988 that they intended to file a citizen suit against the company for 342 permit violations occurring at the Delaware City refinery between January 1983 and October 1987. Subsequently, on May 17, 1988, the NRDC filed a complaint charging Texaco with 354 violations, including some violations that had occurred since October 1987. The NRDC later dropped 11 alleged violations apparently in response to a statute of limitations argument raised by Texaco.

On December 9, 1989, Texaco filed a motion for partial summary judgment based on several grounds * * *. One week later the NRDC filed their own motion for summary judgment on the issue of liability based on the reported parameter exceedances in Texaco's DMRs. In their motion, the NRDC sought declaratory and injunctive relief, and requested a hearing to determine the appropriate amount of damages. * * *

The district court denied Texaco's motion for partial summary judgment reasoning that even if some of the parameter violations alleged by the NRDC were wholly past violations, i.e., not ongoing or likely to recur, the fact that other parameter violations were ongoing at the time the complaint was filed gave the court jurisdiction over all permit violations. * * *

The district court granted the NRDC's motion for summary judgment based on the submitted DMRs. * * *

Having established that Texaco violated the Act, the court enjoined the company, its officers, agents, servants, employees, and those persons in active concert or participation with Texaco, and who receive actual notice of the court's order, from violating terms of the new permit which were either carried over from the old permit or were made stricter in the new version. * * *

Texaco now appeals the district court's order denying both its motion for summary judgment and its supplemental motion for summary judgment. In addition, Texaco appeals the district court's order granting the NRDC's motion for summary judgment and the issuance of a permanent injunction against the company. We have jurisdiction over that part of the district court's order granting injunctive relief pursuant to 28 U.S.C. § 1292(a)(1) (1982).

II.

Texaco argues on appeal that the district court erred by applying the wrong standard in determining whether to grant the NRDC's request for a permanent injunction. More specifically, Texaco argues that the court failed to apply traditional equitable principles in reaching its decision to enjoin the company, including placing the burden on the NRDC to prove that irreparable harm would ensue if the injunction was not granted. * * *

Although somewhat unclear, from our reading of the opinion it does appear that the district court presumed irreparable harm from the mere fact that the Act had been violated. * * *

We agree with Texaco that the district court abused its discretion in this case by presuming irreparable harm and not explicitly applying the traditional equitable standard in determining whether an injunction was appropriate for remedying Texaco's violations of the Act. We believe that the United States Supreme Court's decisions in Weinberger v. Romero–Barcelo, 456 U.S. 305, 102 S.Ct. 1798, 72 L.Ed.2d 91 (1982), and Amoco Prod. Co. v. Village of Gambell, 480 U.S. 531, 107 S.Ct. 1396, 94 L.Ed.2d 542 (1987), establish that equitable principles are not displaced by the Act. Furthermore, every circuit court that has interpreted *Romero-Barcelo* in this context is in accord with our view, as well as numerous district court opinions in this circuit and elsewhere. Finally, we find that the cases relied upon by the district court for its apparently contrary view that an injunction should automatically follow upon a finding of statutory violation are distinguishable from this case.

In *Romero-Barcelo*, the district court found that the Navy had violated the Act by discharging ordnance into the Atlantic Ocean during training operations without first obtaining an NPDES permit from the EPA. * * * The court declined to enjoin the training operations, however, and simply ordered the Navy to apply for a permit from the Administrator of the EPA. * * * Emphasizing in its opinion the broad discretion a court in equity possesses in deciding appropriate relief, the district court reasoned that the Navy's activities were not causing any appreciable harm to the environment, while injunctive relief would cause grievous, and perhaps irreparable, harm to the Navy and the general welfare. * * * The Court of Appeals for the First Circuit reversed and directed the district court to enjoin all Naval training activities until the Navy obtained a permit. The Court of Appeals held that the traditional equitable balancing of interests was inappropriate where there was an absolute statutory duty to refrain from any pollutant discharge until the permit procedure is followed. * * *

The Supreme Court reversed the Court of Appeals and remanded the case to the appellate court to review the district court's decision under an abuse of discretion standard. The Court noted that it had "repeatedly held that the basis for injunctive relief in the federal courts has always been irreparable injury and the inadequacy of legal remedies." * * * The court explained that in each case the court must balance the competing claims of injury and must consider the consequences to each party, and the public, of the granting or withholding of the requested relief. * * * Thus, "[t]he grant of jurisdiction to ensure compliance with a statute hardly suggests an absolute duty to do so under any and all circumstances, and a federal judge sitting as chancellor is not mechanically obligated to grant an injunction for every violation of law." * * *

The Court cautioned that:

> Of course, Congress may intervene and guide or control the exercise of the courts' discretion, but we do not lightly assume that Congress has intended to depart from established principles. As the Court said in Porter v. Warner Holding Co., 328 U.S. 395, 398, 66 S.Ct. 1086, 1089, 90 L.Ed. 1332 (1946):

> Moreover, the comprehensiveness of this equitable jurisdiction is
> not to be denied or limited in the absence of a clear and valid
> legislative command. Unless a statute in so many words, or by a
> necessary and inescapable inference, restricts the court's jurisdic-
> tion in equity, the full scope of that jurisdiction is to be recog-
> nized and applied.

Romero-Barcelo, 456 U.S. at 313, 102 S.Ct. at 1804 (citations omitted).[5]
However, the Court found nothing in the Clean Water Act's language,
structure or legislative history evidencing Congress' intent to deny courts
their traditional equitable discretion. * * * The Court of Appeals had
erroneously focused on the integrity of the permit process rather than on
the integrity of the Nation's water, the real purpose of the Act. * * *

Similarly in Amoco Prod. Co. v. Village of Gambell, 480 U.S. 531, 107
S.Ct. 1396, 94 L.Ed.2d 542 (1987), the Court of Appeals for the Ninth
Circuit found that the Secretary of the Interior had likely failed to comply
with provisions of the Alaska National Interest Lands Conservation Act
("ANILCA") and directed the district court to grant a preliminary injunction preventing certain oil and gas lease activity. * * * The Ninth Circuit
ruled that "injunctive relief is the appropriate remedy for a violation of an
environmental statute absent rare or unusual circumstances." * * *

The Supreme Court again reversed, "see[ing] nothing which distinguishes *Romero-Barcelo* from the instant case" and finding "no clear
indication in [ANILCA] that Congress intended to deny federal district
courts their traditional equitable discretion in enforcing the [statute]
* * *." *Amoco*, 480 U.S. at 544, 107 S.Ct. at 1403. The Court stated:

> Like the First Circuit in *Romero-Barcelo*, the Ninth Circuit errone-
> ously focused on the statutory procedure rather than on the underly-
> ing substantive policy the process was designed to effect—preserva-
> tion of subsistence resources. The District Court's refusal to issue a
> preliminary injunction against all exploration activities did not under-
> mine this policy. The District Court * * * expressly found that
> exploration activities would not significantly restrict subsistence uses.
> The Court of Appeals did not conclude that this factual finding was
> clearly erroneous * * *. Instead, the court stated that "irreparable

---

5. As an example of legislative intervention, the Court cited TVA v. Hill, 437 U.S. 153, 98
S.Ct. 2279, 57 L.Ed.2d 117 (1978). In that case, the Court held that Congress had foreclosed the
traditional discretion exercised by a court in equity:

The statute involved, the Endangered Species Act, 87 Stat. 884, 16 U.S.C. 1531 *et seq.*, required
the District Court to enjoin completion of the Tellico Dam in order to preserve the snail darter,
a species of perch. The purpose and language of the statute under consideration in *Hill*, not the
bare fact of a statutory violation, compelled that conclusion. Section 7 of the Act, 16 U.S.C.
§ 1536, requires federal agencies to "insure that actions authorized, funded, or carried out by
them do not jeopardize the continued existence of [any] endangered species * * * or result in
the destruction or modification of habitat of such species which is determined * * * to be
critical." The statute thus contains a flat ban on the destruction of critical habitats.

Weinberger v. Romero–Barcelo, 456 U.S. 305, 313–14, 102 S.Ct. 1798, 1804, 72 L.Ed.2d 91 (1982).
Since it was conceded that the Tellico Dam would destroy the snail darters' habitat, an injunction
had to be issued because "Congress, it appeared to us, had chosen the snail darter over the dam."
Id. at 314, 102 S.Ct. at 1804. Turning to the Clean Water Act, the Court noted: "That is not the
case here. An injunction is not the only means of ensuring compliance [with the Act]." *Id.*

damage is presumed when an agency fails to evaluate thoroughly the environmental impact of a proposed action." * * * This presumption is contrary to traditional equitable principles and has no basis in ANILCA. Moreover, the environment can be fully protected without this presumption.

Id. at 544–45, 107 S.Ct. at 1403–04.

Every Court of Appeals which has considered the question has interpreted *Romero-Barcelo* and *Amoco* to require a district court to apply the traditional equitable standard before granting an injunction in cases such as this. For example, the Court of Appeals for the Second Circuit, in Town of Huntington v. Marsh, 884 F.2d 648 (2d Cir.1989), *cert. denied*, 494 U.S. 1004, 110 S.Ct. 1296, 108 L.Ed.2d 473 (1990), found that the "teaching of these [Supreme Court] cases seems clear." *Id.* at 652. "[I]n the area of environmental statutes, the Supreme Court has explicitly rejected the notion that an injunction follows as a matter of course upon a finding of statutory violation." *Id.* at 651. * * * *See also* Northern Cheyenne Tribe v. Hodel, 851 F.2d 1152, 1155–56, 1157–58 (9th Cir.1988); National Wildlife Fed'n v. Burford, 835 F.2d 305, 318, 323–24 (D.C.Cir.1987); Commonwealth of Mass. v. Watt, 716 F.2d 946, 951–53 (1st Cir.1983). *Cf.* United States v. Lambert, 695 F.2d 536, 540 (11th Cir.1983) (without citing *Romero-Barcelo*, the court held that: "Environmental litigation is not exempt from [the] requirement" that the plaintiff must prove "irreparable harm is likely if an injunction is not granted [for a violation of the Act]"). Indeed, district courts both in this circuit, *see, e.g.*, Public Interest Research Group of N.J., Inc. v. CP Chemicals, Inc., 26 E.R.C. 2017 (D.N.J.1987), and in other circuits, *see, e.g.*, Natural Resources Defense Council, Inc. v. Outboard Marine Corp., 692 F.Supp. 801, 821–23 (N.D.Ill. 1988), have applied the traditional equitable standard in determining whether to grant preliminary and permanent injunctions for violations of the Act.

The two cases cited by the district court in support of its apparently contrary position are inapposite. In United States Postal Service v. Beamish, 466 F.2d 804 (3d Cir.1972), this Court affirmed an injunction by the district court even though the district court had not applied the traditional equitable standard. And, in Government of Virgin Islands, Dep't of Conservation and Cultural Affairs v. Virgin Islands Paving, Inc., 714 F.2d 283 (3d Cir.1983), the NRDC apparently contends—and the district court appears to assume—that this Court reversed the district court's denial of a preliminary injunction because the district court should not have applied the traditional equitable standard in deciding the question. However, both of these cases are distinguishable from the case sub judice because the statutes under which the injunctions were sought in *Beamish* and *Virgin Islands* clearly circumscribed the traditional equitable discretion courts possess in granting injunctive relief. In *Beamish*, the postal service provision in question provided that: "the United States district court * * * shall * * * upon a showing of probable cause to believe * * * [that 39 U.S.C. § 3005] is being violated, enter a temporary restraining order and preliminary injunction * * *." *Beamish*, 466 F.2d at 806 (quoting from 39 U.S.C. § 3007) (emphasis added). Likewise, in *Virgin Islands*, the statute in question, the Virgin Islands Coastal Zone Management Act of 1978, provided for preliminary injunctive relief upon a "prima facie showing of a violation." *Virgin Islands*, 714 F.2d at 284 (quoting from 12 V.I.C. § 913(b)(1)) (emphasis added). In both of these cases, the legislature had effectively intervened through the statute and guided or controlled the exercise of the courts' traditional discretion. Thus, both of these statutes are the type that the Supreme Court distinguished from the Clean Water Act in *Romero-Barcelo*. *See Romero–Barcelo*, 456 U.S. at 313–14, 102 S.Ct. at 1804–05.

Thus, it is clear to us that a district court may issue a permanent injunction under the Act only after a showing both of irreparable injury and inadequacy of legal remedies, and a balancing of competing claims of injury and the public interest. *Amoco*, 480 U.S. at 544–47, 107 S.Ct. at 1403–05. From our reading of the district court's opinion in this case it is far from certain that such issues were considered and decided upon by the court. Rather, the district court—especially in light of its finding that no violation of the new permit has occurred—appears to have erroneously presumed irreparable harm from the mere fact of statutory violation, thus improperly focusing on the integrity of the permit process rather than the integrity of the Nation's waters. We will remand the case to the district court, therefore, for a proper determination of whether an injunction should issue. However, we do recognize, and so advise the district court on remand, that in applying the traditional equitable standard: "Environmental injury, by its nature, can seldom be adequately remedied by money damages and is often permanent or at least of long duration, i.e., irreparable. If such injury is sufficiently likely, therefore, the balance of harms will usually favor the issuance of an injunction to protect the environment." *Amoco*, 480 U.S. at 545, 107 S.Ct. at 1404.

* * *

In summary, we find that the district court erred in issuing a permanent injunction against Texaco without first applying the traditional equitable standard as to when such an order is appropriate. Thus, we will vacate the portion of the district court's order enjoining Texaco not to violate its new NPDES permit and remand this case to the district court to apply the proper standard. Each party to bear its own costs.

NOTES

1. On remand, the trial court in the case above granted summary judgment for the NRDC and entered a permanent injunction against the defendant. The appellate court affirmed the finding of liability, but reversed and remanded the injunction, ordering the trial court to narrow the scope of the injunction. 2 F.3d 493 (3d Cir.1993).

2. Professor Plater has written a critique of *Romero-Barcelo*, suggesting that it is the first case in which the Court has exercised its equitable

discretion so as to "override the specific prohibitions of a statute." Zygmunt J.B. Plater, *Statutory Violations and Equitable Discretion*, 70 Cal. L. Rev. 524, 594 (1982); *see also* Richard J. Lazarus, *Restoring What's Environmental about Environmental Law Claims in the Supreme Court*, 47 UCLA L. Rev. 703 (2000). Another commentator, in an effort to restrict the impact of the *Romero-Barcelo* decision, distinguishes between four different types of statutory injunctions:

A typology of statutory injunctions, demonstrating the distinctive relations between different injunctive provisions and underlying legal duties, will serve to obviate some of the confusion. The critical factors in determining the nature of a statutory injunction are its relationship to a defendant's underlying legal duty and the nature of that duty. Based on this analysis, injunctions can be divided into four groups.

1. *The Enforcement Injunction.* This category involves direct enforcement of an absolute legal duty. In these cases, the defendant is under a legal duty, but refuses to carry out actions that a law-abiding citizen would perform voluntarily. The purpose of the injunction is to force the defendant to do that which the defendant ought to have done without legal compulsion. TVA v. Hill is a clear example of this type of injunction. Since the purpose of the injunction is simply to put the defendant in the same position as the law-abiding citizen, balancing the equities is inappropriate. Asking a court to balance the virtues of obedience to the law against the benefits of violating the law is wholly inappropriate.

2. *The Compliance Injunction.* This category involves cases like *Weinberger*, in which the defendant is in breach of a qualified duty. Once again, the purpose of the injunction is to force the defendant to act as law-abiding citizens voluntarily do, but here the duty does not amount to immediate compliance. Congress did not intend that citizens shut plants as a routine method of meeting permit deadlines. For the same reason, Congress did not expect courts to make this a routine remedy. As before, the remedy tracks the underlying legal duty. In this category, however, there is more room for consideration of burden in defining the underlying duty itself.

3. *The Ancillary Injunction.* In the preceding two categories, the hypothetical defendant was in breach of a legal duty that was the basis of the injunction. Often, however, the defendant is in breach of a procedural duty. Obviously, the court can order the defendant to apply for a permit, issue an environmental impact statement or comply with some other procedure. The question is the extent to which a court should also enjoin the activity to which the procedure relates. For example, Congress requires agencies engaging in major federal actions with substantial environmental impacts to issue environmental impact statements. The relevant statute does not, however, expressly create a legal duty to refrain from implementing a project until the impact statement is prepared. But it would be futile for a court simply to issue an order to prepare an impact statement while allowing the underlying federal action to proceed. In *Weinberger*, the Navy was not under a direct duty to refrain from

discharges while its permit application was pending. Nevertheless, if those discharges had been causing ecological harm, allowing the activity to continue until the permit proceeding had been completed would have undermined the function of the permit process.

* * *

4. *The Freestanding Injunction*. In each of the previous categories, the injunction was used as a means of enforcing, either directly or indirectly, an underlying statutory duty. Congress sometimes provides, however, for an injunctive proceeding without creating any separate statutory duties to be enforced in the proceeding, as in the emergency provision under the Clean Water Act. Three possible interpretations of such provisions are possible. First, Congress may simply intend that the provision create a federal forum in which state law will be applied. Second, Congress's aim might be that federal courts create a body of federal common law governing these disputes. Third, such provisions may signify that Congress intends injunctive relief to be mandatory once statutory threshold requirements are met. Environmental emergency provisions arguably are intended to trigger creation of a federal common law, but they actually seem to come closer to the mandatory injunction category. The discretion a court has in issuing emergency injunctions relates more to fashioning the most effective form of relief than to balancing the public health against hardship to the defendant.

One of the reasons for the considerable confusion in the area of statutory injunctions seems to have been a failure to distinguish clearly between these various varieties of statutory injunction. While the typology given here certainly will not resolve all disputes about statutory injunctions, it may provide a clearer framework for settling these disputes.

Daniel A. Farber, *Equitable Discretion, Legal Duties, and Environmental Injunctions*, 45 U. Pitt. L. Rev. 513, 538–42 (1984).*

3. The application of traditional equitable conditions precedent to injunctive relief will depend on numerous variables: the language and legislative history of the statute in question; whether the injunctive relief being sought is temporary or permanent; and, if an administrative proceeding is involved, its nature and setting. *Compare* Federal Trade Commission v. Simeon Management Corp., 532 F.2d 708 (9th Cir.1976) (independent judicial examination of the equities required as a condition precedent to granting a temporary injunction against deceptive trade practices under section 53 of the Federal Trade Commission Act), *with* Federal Trade Commission v. National Commission on Egg Nutrition, 517 F.2d 485 (7th Cir.1975) (Congress did not intend an independent judicial weighing of the equities under section 53 of the Act). For a thorough consideration of how state courts deal with these issues, see Town of Sherberne v. Carpenter, *supra* Chapter 6, Section 2.B.3.

---

* Reprinted with permission of the University of Pittsburgh Law Review.

C. RESTITUTION

1. Trespass and/or Improvements

RAVEN RED ASH COAL CO. v. BALL

Supreme Court of Virginia, 1946.
185 Va. 534, 39 S.E.2d 231.

HUDGINS, JUSTICE.

* * *

There is no substantial conflict in the evidence. Plaintiff proved that he is the present owner of approximately 100 acres of land lying in Russell county which was a part of a 265–acre tract formerly owned by Reuben Sparks, and that Reuben Sparks and his wife, by deed dated November 19, 1887, conveyed the coal and mineral rights on the 265–acre tract to Joseph I. Doran and William A. Dick. The deed conveying the mineral rights to Doran and Dick, their heirs and assigns, conveyed an easement expressed in the following language: "The right to pass through, over and upon said tract of land by railway or otherwise to reach any other lands belonging to the said Joseph I. Doran and Wm. A. Dick or those claiming such other lands by, through or under them, for the purpose of digging for, mining, or otherwise securing the coal and other things hereinbefore specified, and removing same from such other land."

It seems that on or about November 19, 1887, Doran and Dick owned approximately 3,000 acres of land lying in Russell and Tazewell counties, Virginia. [T]he Raven Red Ash Coal Company became the lessee of all the coal and mineral rights on and under this 3,000 acres. Probably 25 years ago the Raven Red Ash Coal Company, under the easement purchased of Reuben Sparks, built a tramway or railroad through and over the 265 acres formerly owned by Sparks, which right of way extends for approximately 2800 feet across the 100 acres of land now owned by plaintiff.

The Raven Red Ash Coal Company acquired coal and mineral rights on five tracts of land not originally owned by Doran and Dick. * * *

The testimony reveals that, during the past five years, defendant transported 49,016 tons of coal mined from the five small tracts over the tramway erected across plaintiff's land and transported 950,000 tons of coal mined from lands formerly owned by Doran and Dick. There remains to be mined approximately 8,000,000 tons of coal on the tracts formerly owned by Doran and Dick and 180,000 tons of coal on the other small tracts.

Defendant's * * * assignments of error present two questions: (1) whether the facts entitle plaintiff to maintain an action of trespass on the case in assumpsit; and (2) what test should be applied to determine the amount of damages to be allowed.

Ball concedes that defendant exercised its right in transporting across [Ball's] land the 950,000 tons of coal mined from tracts of land formerly owned by Doran and Dick, but contends that it violated the property rights of [Ball] in transporting the 49,016 tons of coal mined from the five small tracts described above across [Ball's] land to defendant's tipple. * * *

* * * [E]very use of an easement not necessarily included in the grant is a trespass to realty and renders the owner of the dominant tenement liable in a tort action to the owner of the servient tenement for all damages proven to have resulted therefrom, and, in the absence of proof of special damage, the owner of the servient tenement may recover nominal damages only.

Plaintiff did not prove any specific damage to the realty by the illegal use of the easement, and admitted that he suffered "no more damage other than the exclusion of use during that moment and that's the reason we have sued for use and occupancy."

It thus appears that plaintiff bases his sole ground of recovery on the right to maintain assumpsit for use and occupation. * * *

* * *

While plaintiff has not cited, and we have not found, any controlling Virginia authority on this phase of the case, a short review of the theory and modern development of the action of assumpsit will be helpful in deciding the question.

Assumpsit is classified as an action *ex contractu* as distinguished from an action *ex delicto*. Hence, in order to sustain the action, it is necessary for the plaintiff to establish an express contract or facts and circumstances from which the law will raise an implication of a promise to pay. In such a case, a plaintiff may waive the tort and institute his action in assumpsit for money had and received. * * *

The overwhelming majority of the decided cases holds that where a person has illegally seized another's personal property and converted it to his own use, the owner may bring trespass, trover, detinue or assumpsit. By bringing the action of assumpsit, the owner waives all claim from wrongful taking, detention and conversion. * * *

Where a naked trespass is committed, whether upon the person or property, assumpsit will not lie. If one commits an assault and battery upon another, it is absurd to imply a promise by the defendant to pay the victim a reasonable compensation. There is no basis for an implication of a contract where cattle inadvertently invade a neighbor's premises and trample down and destroy his crops. In each instance, a wrong and nothing more and nothing less has been committed. On the other hand, if a trespasser invades the premises of his neighbor, cuts and removes timber or severs minerals from the land and converts them to his own use, the owner may waive the tort and sue in assumpsit for the value of the materials converted. 1 Cooley on Torts, 4th Ed., sec. 61, p. 181. Such a person has depleted the value of the owner's property and materially enhanced his own possessions.

The same principle is stated in 4 Am. Jur., 503–04, as follows: "... in the absence of a contractual relationship, the general rule is that where one person derives a benefit from the commission of a tort against the property of another, the law will, at the election of the person injured, imply a contract on the part of the tort-feasor to pay to the person injured a just remuneration for the damages sustained as a consequence of the wrong, and on this contract implied by law general assumpsit lies. But a promise will be implied in such a case only because *it will be deemed that it was intended that it should be, or because natural justice requires it on consideration of some benefit received,* and where no benefit accrues, or is intended to accrue to the tort-feasor, the action of assumpsit cannot, as a general rule, be substituted for the proper form of action on the tort." (Italics supplied.) *See* 1 C.J.S., Actions, § 50, p. 1131.

* * *

The precise question has never been decided in this jurisdiction. If the rule in force in the majority of States is followed, the landowner will be placed in this position: If he maintains an action for tort, he will be limited to nominal damages only. He may obtain an injunction and restrain the defendant from the further unlawful use of the easement, and thus indirectly, perhaps, force him to agree to pay for future additional burdens imposed on the easement. Such proceedings would not give the owner compensation for past illegal use of his property, although the wrongdoer had received and retained substantial benefits by reason of his own wrongs.

* * *

* * * To hold that a trespasser who benefits himself by cutting and removing trees from another's land is liable on an implied contract, and that another trespasser who benefits himself by the illegal use of another's land is not liable on an implied contract is illogical. The only distinction is that in one case the benefit he received is the diminution of another's property. In the other case, he still receives the benefit but does not thereby diminish the value of the owner's property. In both cases, he has received substantial benefit by his own wrong. As the gist of the action is to prevent the unjust enrichment of a wrongdoer from the illegal use of another's property, such wrongdoer should be held on an implied promise in both cases.

The facts in Edwards v. Lee's Adm'r, 265 Ky. 418, 96 S.W.2d 1028, were that Edwards discovered a cave on the land belonging to himself and his wife, which he developed and advertised as the "Great Onyx Cave." Later, Lee, the owner of an adjoining tract, filed suit against Edwards and the heirs of his wife, claiming that a portion of the cave was under his land. He asked for an accounting of the profits which resulted from the operation of the cave and for an injunction prohibiting Edwards and his associates from further trespassing or using that part of the cave under his land. It was said that the action was based on repeated trespasses to land and that, although no damage or injury was shown to plaintiff's land, plaintiff was entitled to recover on the ground of an implied promise to pay. The measure of recovery was fixed at one-third of the net profits inasmuch as one-third of the cave was under plaintiff's land. It was contended that the use of the cave by the trespasser did not damage or diminish Lee's property, but the court held that the gist of the action was the unjust enrichment of the wrongdoer, which would support an implied promise to pay.

In the Notes on Restatement of Restitution by Warren A. Seavey and Austin W. Scott, commenting on this case at p. 194, this is said: "The decision (Edwards v. Lee's Adm'r) is a welcomed departure from the result in Phillips v. Homfray, 24 Ch.D. 439 (1883), where recovery was denied against a person who had used a passage-way under the plaintiff's land for the removal of coal."

The illegal transportation of the coal in question across plaintiff's land was intentional, deliberate and repeated from time to time for a period of years. Defendant had no moral or legal right to enrich itself by this illegal use of plaintiff's property. To limit plaintiff to the recovery of nominal damages for the repeated trespasses will enable defendant, as a trespasser, to obtain a more favorable position than a party contracting for the same right. Natural justice plainly requires the law to imply a promise to pay a fair value of the benefits received. Defendant's estate has been enhanced by just this much. Pomeroy's Remedies and Remedial Rights, 2d Ed., pp. 630–635.

* * *

While plaintiff offered no evidence to establish the value of the illegal use of the easement, we, as reasonable men, know that the transportation of 49,016 tons of coal over the tramroad across the plaintiff's land was a benefit to defendant. However, in the absence of proof of the value of the benefit, the court could enter no judgment for plaintiff. This proof is supplied by the testimony of the general manager on his cross-examination. The substance of his testimony on this point is that the prevailing rate of payment, or purchase of a right of way for transportation of coal across another's land, is one cent per ton, and that this purchase includes the right to construct and maintain a tramway for distances varying up to 2½ miles; but that, where the owner of the easement has already entered upon the land, and has constructed and is maintaining a tramroad for the transportation of coal from certain specified tracts, the purchase price should be much less—a small fraction of a cent per ton. The jury were instructed that they should fix the amount of damages, if any, at such as would fairly compensate plaintiff for the use and occupation of this strip of land in the hauling and transportation of 49,016 tons of coal over the same.

While the evidence on the value of the benefits retained by defendant is not as clear and full as it could be, and perhaps should have been, the jury had all the facts and circumstances before it and evidently concluded that the value of the benefit to the defendant for the illegal use of the easement should be computed at one cent per ton. Viewing the case as a whole, we find no reversible error, and the judgment of the trial court is affirmed.

NOTE

For a result similar to that in *Raven Red Ash* in a more recent case, see Monarch Accounting Supplies, Inc. v. Prezioso, 170 Conn. 659, 368 A.2d 6 (1976). The plaintiff in *Monarch Accounting* had leased a building from William Prezioso. Although Prezioso had not reserved the roof of that building for himself, he later leased it to Murphy, Inc., for Murphy to erect a large sign. The Supreme Court of Connecticut said:

The [trial] court found that the plaintiff was entitled to receive, on an equitable basis by way of reimbursement, one-half of the total rent received by the defendant from Murphy, Inc. The court also awarded one-half of the rent to be expected from Murphy, Inc., for the remainder of the plaintiff's term. The plaintiff claims the award can be sustained under the doctrine of unjust enrichment. The inquiry then, is whether the plaintiff is entitled to damages for the unjust enrichment of the defendant. The inquiry goes not only to the type of recovery but also to whether recovery of any type was allowable.

The doctrine of unjust enrichment "is based upon the principle that one should not be permitted unjustly to enrich himself at the expense of another but should be required to make restitution of or for property received, retained or appropriated.... It is not necessary, in order to create an obligation to make restitution, * * * that the party unjustly enriched should have been guilty of any tortious or fraudulent act. The question is: Did he, to the detriment of someone else, obtain something of value to which he was not entitled?" * * *

The defendant, under its agreement with Murphy, Inc., receives rental payments. That agreement overlooks the plaintiff's possessory interest in the roof, and, in that regard, it is to the detriment of the plaintiff. Although the plaintiff did not show any material physical damage to the premises, it has a right either to sublet or assign the roof with the defendant's permission. The defendant can hardly claim that permission would not be granted to sublet or assign the roof in view of his agreement with Murphy, Inc. Even if the circumstances of this case admitted of a conditional right in the plaintiff to assign or sublet, the defendant, by his actions, removed the plaintiff's ability to negotiate with the defendant for the use of the roof. The facts of the case, therefore, show the defendant's receipt of a benefit, to which he was not entitled, to the detriment of the plaintiff. * * * *See* Restatement, Restitution § 4(f).

The measure of recovery in this case focuses on the benefit to the defendant rather than on the loss to the plaintiff. The damages should be the benefit received. * * * The benefit was the rent that was received by the defendant less his expenses, if any, in dealing with Murphy, Inc. The court, therefore, was in error in awarding only one-half of the accrued rent.

The court also erred by awarding a portion of the rent from the date of judgment until the end of the plaintiff's term. That rent has been neither received nor retained by the defendant even though he has the right, under the agreement with Murphy, Inc., to receive it. A prospective award is not properly includable within the concept of damages in this case since the focus of damages in unjust enrichment is not on the damage proximately caused by an injury, but on the benefit unjustly received and retained by the defendant. *See* * * * Restatement, Restitution § 155. Whether the defendant will retain the rent from the sign for the period from February, 1975 to May, 1977, the unexpired term of the plaintiff's lease at the time of judgment, cannot be adjudged.

Further, the other item of damages awarded, one-half of the expense of the structural engineer, appears to have been part of an expenditure that was necessary for the proper support of the sign on the roof and as the defendant is not entitled to retain the benefit of the lease to Murphy, Inc., he would not be liable for such expenditures.

Id. at 665–67, 368 A.2d at 10–11. Is the court correct that "rent from the date of judgment until the end of the plaintiff's term" is not a benefit to the defendant? *See supra* Chapter 4, Section 6 for a discussion of the defendant's benefit. How would the concept of present value help the plaintiff? *See supra* Chapter 3, Section 4.B.3 for a discussion of that topic.

SOMERVILLE v. JACOBS

Supreme Court of Appeals, West Virginia, 1969.
153 W.Va. 613, 170 S.E.2d 805.

HAYMOND, PRESIDENT:

The plaintiffs, W.J. Somerville and Hazel M. Somerville, * * * the owners of Lots 44, 45 and 46 in the Homeland Addition to the city of Parkersburg, in Wood County, believing that they were erecting a warehouse building on Lot 46 which they owned, mistakenly constructed the building on Lot 47 owned by the defendants, William L. Jacobs and Marjorie S. Jacobs * * *. [The building was leased to the Parkersburg Coca–Cola Bottling Company.] Soon after the building was completed but not until then, the defendants learned that the building was on their property and claimed ownership of the building and its fixtures on the theory of annexation. The plaintiffs then instituted this proceeding for equitable relief in the Circuit Court of Wood County and in their complaint prayed, among other things, for judgment in favor of the Somervilles for $20,500.00 as the value of the improvements made on Lot 47, or, in the alternative, that the defendants be ordered to convey their interest in lot 47 to the Somervilles for a fair consideration. * * *

* * *

By final judgment rendered June 11, 1968, the circuit court required the defendants within 60 days to elect whether they would (1) retain the building and pay W.J. Somerville $17,500.00 or suffer judgment against themselves in his favor in that amount, or (2) convey title to Lot 47 of Homeland Addition to W.J. Somerville for the sum of $2,000.00 cash. * * *

* * *

* * * [T]he material facts, which are not disputed, were stipulated * * *.

The stipulation concerning the facts is in this form:

"1. The plaintiffs, W.J. Somerville and Hazel M. Somerville, in mistaken reliance upon a surveyor's report and plat, constructed the building described in the complaint upon Lot No. 47 of of Homeland Addition to the City of Parkersburg, in Wood County, West Virginia, believing that they were constructing the building upon Lot No. 46 of said addition."

* * *

In Voss v. Forque, 84 So.2d 563 [(Fla. 1956)], the court held that where a landowner mistakenly constructed a dwelling on a lot adjacent to one he owned and the two adjoining lots were substantially the same in value and the landowner was innocent of wrongdoing and the adjacent landowner was not shown to have been harmed, equity at the suit of the first landowner compelled both landowners to exchange deeds to their respective lots, upon payment by the first landowner of a certain sum and court costs. * * *

* * *

The undisputed facts, set forth in the agreed statement of counsel representing all parties, is that the plaintiff W.J. Somerville in placing the warehouse building upon Lot 47 entertained a reasonable belief based on the report of the surveyor that it was Lot 46, which he owned, and that the building was constructed by him because of a reasonable mistake of fact and in the good faith belief that he was constructing a building on his own property and he did not discover his mistake until after the building was completed. It is equally clear that the defendants who spent little if any time in the neighborhood were unaware of the construction of the building until after it was completed and were not at any time or in any way guilty of any fraud or inequitable conduct or of any act that would constitute an estoppel. In short, the narrow issue here is between two innocent parties and the solution of the question requires the application of principles of equity and fair dealing between them.

It is clear that the defendants claim the ownership of the building. Under the common law doctrine of annexation, the improvements passed to them as part of the land. * * * This is conceded by the plaintiffs but they assert that the defendants cannot keep and retain it without compensating them for the value of the improvements, and it is clear from the testimony of the defendant William L. Jacobs in his deposition that the defendants intend to keep and retain the improvements and refuse to compensate the plaintiffs for their value. The record does not disclose any express request by the plaintiffs for permission to remove the building from the premises if that could be done without its destruction, which is extremely doubtful as the building was constructed of solid concrete blocks on a concrete slab, and it is reasonably clear, from the claim of the defendants of their ownership of the building and their insistence that certain fixtures which have been removed from the building be replaced, that the defendants will not consent to the removal of the building even if that could be done.

In that situation if the defendants retain the building and refuse to pay any sum as compensation to the plaintiff W.J. Somerville they will be unjustly enriched in the amount of $17,500.00, the agreed value of the building, which is more than eight and one-half times the agreed $2,000.00 value of the lot of the defendants on which it is located, and by the retention of the building by the defendants the plaintiff W.J. Somerville will suffer a total loss of the amount of the value of the building. If, however, the defendants are unable or unwilling to pay for the building which they intend to keep but, in the alternative, would convey the lot upon which the building is constructed to the plaintiff W.J. Somerville upon payment of the sum of $2,000.00, the agreed value of the lot without the improvements, the plaintiffs would not lose the building and the defendants would suffer no financial loss because they would obtain payment for the agreed full value of the lot and the only hardship imposed upon the defendants, if this were required, would be to order them to do something which they are unwilling to do voluntarily. To compel the performance of such an act by litigants is not uncommon in litigation in which the rights of the parties are involved and are subject to determination by equitable principles. * * * Under the facts and circumstances of this case, if the defendants refuse and are not required to exercise their option either to pay W.J. Somerville the value of the improvements or to convey to him the lot on which they are located upon his payment of the agreed value, the defendants will be unduly and unjustly enriched at the expense of the plaintiff W.J. Somerville who will suffer the complete loss of the warehouse building which by bona fide mistake of the fact he constructed upon the land of the defendants. * * *

To prevent such unjust enrichment of the defendants, and to do equity between the parties, this Court holds that an improver of land owned by another, who through a reasonable mistake of fact and in good faith erects a building entirely upon the land of the owner, with reasonable belief that such land was owned by the improver, is entitled to recover the value of the improvements from the landowner and to a lien upon such property which may be sold to enforce the payment of such lien, or, in the alternative, to purchase the land so improved upon payment to the landowner of the value of the land less the improvements and such landowner, even though free from any inequitable conduct in connection with the construction of the building upon his land, who, however, retains but refuses to pay for the improvements, must, within a reasonable time either pay the improver the amount by which the value of his land has been improved or convey such land to the improver upon the payment by the improver to the landowner of the value of the land without the improvements.

* * *

In Cautley v. Morgan, 51 W.Va. 304, 41 S.E. 201 [(1902)], the defendants * * * and the plaintiff Cautley were owners of adjoining lots * * *. The plaintiff, being desirous of building a party wall between the lots for a business building on her lot, entered into an agreement with the defendants by which, among other things, she was given the right to construct the wall to the extent of ten inches upon the lot of the defendants. In constructing the wall the plaintiff, by mistake, built it six inches farther on the land of the defendants than the ten inches provided for in the contract. * * * [A]fter unsuccessful efforts were made to adjust the matter, the defendants instituted an action of ejectment against the plaintiff to recover the land on which the plaintiff had encroached in the construction of the wall. In a suit by the plaintiff to enjoin the prosecution of the action of ejectment, the court refused the injunction and dismissed the bill with costs. * * * [T]he plaintiff, in undertaking to build the wall and assuming the responsibility of fixing the location herself, had the duty to see that it was properly located and * * * she had sufficient data to enable her to avoid the mistake if she had used the data with proper care. In other words the plaintiff, by not making proper use of the available data, was guilty of careless or negligent conduct in making the mistake. She was limited by the contract to place the wall upon only ten inches of the defendants' property and in making an encroachment of more than ten inches she was also guilty of breach of the contract. Accordingly she was not entitled to equitable relief and the case is distinguishable from the case at bar for those reasons and for the additional reason that the loss of a portion of the wall of the width of only six inches would be a relatively insignificant hardship compared to the complete loss here involved of an entire building of the admitted value of $17,500.00.

* * *

The judgment of the Circuit Court of Wood County is affirmed.

CAPLAN, JUDGE, dissenting:

Respectfully, but firmly, I dissent from the decision of the majority in this case. Although the majority expresses a view which it says would result in equitable treatment for both parties, I am of the opinion that such view is clearly contrary to law and to the principles of equity and that such holding, if carried into effect, will establish a dangerous precedent.

Basically, I believe that the principles expressed in Cautley v. Morgan, 51 W.Va. 304, 41 S.E. 201, reflect my view of this matter and that that case cannot realistically be distinguished from the instant case, as was attempted in the majority opinion. In that opinion it was said that the plaintiff who encroached upon the defendant's property was guilty of "careless or negligent conduct in making the mistake." The opinion reasoned that the plaintiff had the duty to see that the wall was properly located and that she had sufficient data to enable her to avoid the mistake if she had used the data with proper care. Certainly, in the instant case the plaintiff, had he caused to be made a proper survey and had exercised proper care, would have constructed the subject building on his own property rather than on that of the defendant. It occurs to me that the failure to use proper care is more evident in this case than it was in *Cautley.*

* * *

I am aware of the apparent alarmist posture of my statements asserting that the adoption of the majority view will establish a dangerous precedent. Nonetheless, I believe just that and feel that my apprehension is justified. On the basis of unjust enrichment and equity, the majority has decided that the errant party who, without improper design, has encroached upon an innocent owner's property is entitled to equitable treatment. That is, that he should be made whole. How is this accomplished? It is accomplished by requiring the owner of the property to buy the building erroneously constructed on his property or by forcing (by court edict) such owner to sell his property for an amount to be determined by the court.

What of the property owner's right? The solution offered by the majority is designed to favor the plaintiff, the only party who had a duty to determine which lot was the proper one and who made a mistake. The defendants in this case, the owners of the property, had no duty to perform and were not parties to the mistake. Does equity protect only the errant and ignore the faultless? Certainly not.

It is not unusual for a property owner to have long range plans for his property. He should be permitted to feel secure in the ownership of such property by virtue of placing his deed therefor on record. He should be permitted to feel secure in his future plans for such property. * * *

In my opinion for the court to permit the plaintiff to force the defendants to sell their property contrary to their wishes is unthinkable and unpardonable. This is nothing less than condemnation of private property by private parties for private use. Condemnation of property (eminent domain) is reserved for government or such entities as may be designated by the legislature. * * *

I am aware of the doctrine that equity frowns on unjust enrichment. However, contrary to the view expressed by the majority, I am of the opinion that the circumstances of this case do not warrant the application of such doctrine. It clearly is the accepted law that as between two parties in the circumstances of this case he who made the mistake must suffer the hardship rather than he who was without fault. Cautley v. Morgan, *supra.*

I would reverse the judgment of the Circuit Court of Wood County and remand the case to that court with directions that the trial court give the defendant, Jacobs, the party without fault, the election of purchasing the building, of selling the property, *or* of requiring the plaintiff to remove the building from defendant's property.

I am authorized to say that Judge Berry concurs in the views expressed in this dissenting opinion.

NOTE

In Realmark Developments, Inc. v. Ranson, 214 W.Va. 161, 588 S.E.2d 150 (2003), the tenants, thinking they had an option to purchase the building, made improvements. They were unable to exercise their option due to the landlord's breach of an agreement to help with financing. The landlord had cited *Somerville* as holding that a plaintiff can recover only the increased value of defendant's property in a mistaken improver restitution action. The court in *Realmark* held, however, that "the measure of damages in an unjust enrichment claim is the greater of the enhanced market value of the property or the cost of the improvements to the property." *Id.* at 166, 588 S.E.2d at 155. The court said further that "[t]o the extent that * * * *Somerville* differs from this holding, it is hereby modified." *Id.* As a result, the court held that the plaintiffs could present evidence of both the increased value of the property due to their improvements and the cost of those improvements.

IN RE HOSKINS

United States Bankruptcy Court, Northern District of West Virginia, 2009.
405 B.R. 576.

PATRICK M. FLATLEY, BANKRUPTCY JUDGE.

Memorandum Opinion

In 1998, Mr. Kungle constructed, for himself, a cabin on 15 acres of real property belonging to Larry and Pamela Hoskins (the "Debtors"). In 2004, after a dispute regarding Mr. Kungle's use of their land, the Debtors prohibited Mr. Kungle from accessing the cabin. Mr. Kungle now claims that the Debtors owe him $98,348 for the cabin, and he filed an unsecured proof of claim in the Debtors' Chapter 13 bankruptcy case in that amount. The Debtors object to the proof of claim arguing that they owe Mr. Kungle nothing, or, in the alternative, that Mr. Kungle's claim should not exceed $13,679.

* * *

I. BACKGROUND

The Debtors own approximately 364 acres of rural land in Tyler County, West Virginia. On the property is a hovel, described by the parties as "the old red cabin." Over thirty years ago, Mr. Hoskins' father began allowing Mr. Kungle's family to use the old red cabin for hunting and recreation purposes. Although the amount of time Mr. Kungle spent at the old red cabin varied, he would generally be there about one month per year. He would also call the Debtors in advance to alert them of his coming, and inform them about any guests that he was bringing with him. The old red cabin has no electricity or gas; it consists of a single room, a wood stove, and six bunk beds. It has an attached outhouse.

In 1997 or 1998, Mr. Kungle approached Mr. Hoskins about building a new cabin on the Debtors' property. Mr. Kungle offered to buy the 15 acre parcel on which the new cabin was to sit, but the Debtors were adamant that no part of their land be sold. The Debtors were willing, however, to execute a long term lease, and, according to Mr. Kungle, he believed that they may have offered him a life estate in the 15 acres of land.

With no formal agreement, and with nothing more than a handshake over the notion that Mr. Kungle would be allowed to build a new cabin and use it for hunting and recreational purposes, Mr. Kungle began to construct the new cabin at his own expense. The Debtors provided some raw materials for the cabin's construction, and Mr. Hoskins actively assisted Mr. Kungle with labor and other services. It soon became apparent to Mr. Hoskins, however, that the new cabin was going to be much different than the old red cabin. Unlike the old red cabin, the new cabin has a full basement, two bedrooms on the ground floor, and a large loft. * * * Consistent with its purpose of being a hunting and recreation cabin, it is located about 0.9 miles from the county road and is not accessible year round.

* * *

* * * Mr. Kungle's use of the new cabin, however, became a source of tension with the Debtors:

> * * * [H]e got so with that [new] cabin that he would just show up. * * *

> [T]hey would run four-wheelers all hours of the day and night past the trailer. * * * [W]e had a problem with the number of people he was bringing. * * *

(Pamela Hoskins Depo. p. 68).

On September 7, 2004, the Debtors sent a letter to Mr. Kungle accusing him of taking advantage of their good nature and generosity * * *.

* * *

In an effort to settle the dispute, Mr. Kungle hired an attorney and * * * offered to purchase the 15 acre parcel of land on which the cabin sits for $15,000. * * * Mr. Hoskins stated that he "had no more use for him," and that Mr. Kungle could only come back to the new cabin with an appointment when he was ready to move it. Although Mr. Kungle investigated the possibility of moving the new cabin, he ultimately decided against it.

In the Debtors' bankruptcy case, which was filed on April 17, 2008, they propose a Chapter 13 plan that pays Mr. Kungle $16,752.24 as an unsecured creditor. The Debtors have substantial non-exempt equity in their real property. The Schedule A value of their 364 acres is $300,000, and the only claim secured by the value of that real property is for $50,325. Apart from Mr. Kungle, the Debtors only have one unsecured debt owed to the U.S. Department of Education in the amount of $1,346. Consequently, after deducting their applicable West Virginia bankruptcy exemptions, any Chapter 13 plan confirmed by the Debtors will have to pay Mr. Kungle 100% of his unsecured claim.

II. DISCUSSION

Under a theory of unjust enrichment, Mr. Kungle asserts that he is entitled to recover from the Debtors the value of the new cabin, which he contends is $68,000, and, adding pre-judgment interest from 2004, he asserts that the Debtors owe him $98,348 as of May 19, 2008.

The Debtors acknowledge that the new cabin adds value to their real property, but assert that the new cabin is not worth anything to them on the basis that they would rather have the cabin removed from their property. In their view, Mr. Kungle's unjust enrichment claim should fail on the grounds that he built the cabin on the Debtors' property knowing that he did not own or have identifiable rights to their real property. * * *

As stated by the Supreme Court of Appeals of West Virginia, "[t]he law of unjust enrichment indicates that if one person improves the land of another ... through the affixation of chattels to the land, that person is entitled to restitution for the improvements if certain other circumstances are present." *Realmark Devs. v. Ranson*, 208 W.Va. 717, 542 S.E.2d 880, 884 (W.Va. 2000) (citing *Restatement, 1st Restitution*, § 53 (1937)). As indicated by the Court, those "certain other circumstances" are the ones set forth in the *Restatement 1st of Restitution. Id*. In general, the *Restatement* imposes a duty of restitution on any person that has tortiously interfered with the property rights of another person. *See Restatement 1st of Restitution*, §§ 128–30 (1937). The term " '[t]ortiously' refers to such wrongful conduct as gives rise to a civil action either at law or at equity...." § 128 cmt. (a).

* * *

A. The Legal Relationship Between the Debtors and Mr. Kungle

Mr. Kungle asserts that he had a life estate in the new cabin, and on the 15–acre tract of land on which it sits. The Debtors state that Mr. Kungle never had more than an oral lease for the new cabin, for which no consideration was paid to the Debtors. Contrary to both positions, no estate in land was ever conveyed to Mr. Kungle, and no lease was ever agreed-on by the parties.

Mr. Kungle had a right to access the Debtors' real property that extended back at least 30 years, but he never had any possessory interest in the Debtors' property. A right to access property without a possessory interest is a license. As defined by *Black's Law Dictionary*, 938 (8th ed.

2004), a "license" is "[a] permission, usu. revocable, to commit some act that would otherwise be unlawful; esp., an agreement (not amounting to a lease or profit a prendere) that it is lawful for the licensee to enter the licensor's land to do some act that would otherwise be illegal, such as hunting game." A license does not grant any estate in land, it is not assignable, and it is based on personal confidence between the parties. * * *

While a "bare license" "may ordinarily be revoked, and the licensee deprived of any right to act thereunder," the "rule is not without its limitations." * * * As stated in one treatise, "[a] license may ... become irrevocable where the licensee makes great expenditures and permanent improvements in justifiable reliance on the licensor." * * *

Mr. Kungle had a license to access the Debtors' real property for purposes of hunting and recreation. In reliance on his license, and with the consent and active assistance of the Debtors, Mr. Kungle built the new cabin with considerable effort and expense. * * * Consequently, Mr. Kungle's license to access the Debtors' real property for purpose of hunting and recreation became irrevocable in 1998 when the cabin was constructed.

B.   Tortious Interference with Mr. Kungle's License Coupled With an Interest

Mr. Kungle maintains that the Debtors have prohibited him from entering their land so that he no longer has use of the new cabin.

* * *

* * * Although Mr. Kungle may have exceeded the scope of his license by having as many as 16 guests at the new cabin, neither that action—nor the unwanted ATV use—would give the Debtors the right to unilaterally terminate Mr. Kungle's license coupled with an interest. Indeed, after the Debtors sent Mr. Kungle their September 7, 2004 letter complaining of his excessive use of their property, Mr. Kungle stopped the offensive conduct. * * * See generally, Restatement, 3d of Property: Servitudes §§ 7.1–7.16 (2000) (setting forth the grounds on which a servitude may terminate).

* * *

Accordingly, the court finds that the Debtors tortiously interfered with Mr. Kungle's license coupled with an interest to use the Debtors' property, and the new cabin, for purposes of hunting and recreation. * * *

C.   Damages for Unjust Enrichment

Having been forbidden to reenter the Debtors' real property to make use of his license coupled with an interest, Mr. Kungle asserts that he is entitled to money damages under an unjust enrichment theory of recovery. The parties do not dispute that the value of the Debtors' real property increased as a result of Mr. Kungle's construction of the new cabin, even though the Debtors would rather not have it on their land.

In *Realmark Devs. v. Ranson*, 214 W.Va. 161, 588 S.E.2d 150, 155 (2003), the Supreme Court of Appeals of West Virginia summarized the proper measure for restitution damages under circumstances where a lessee improved the property of the lessor based on the lessor's representation that the lessor would agree to sell the building to the lessee at the end of the lease term. The Court stated that if " 'a sum of money is awarded to protect a party's restitution interest,' " the amount of the restitution award is measured, as justice requires:

> by either (a) the reasonable value to the other party of what he received in terms of what it would have cost him to obtain it from a person in the claimant's position, or (b) the extent to which the other party's property has been increased in value or his other interests advanced. The greater of the above two measures should be used in cases in which work has increased the value of the defendant's property, but there is some discrepancy between the reasonable value of that work and the amount of enhancement.

Id. at 155 (*quoting* 22 Am.Jur.2d *Damages* § 56 (1988)); *see also Restatement 1st of Restitution*, § 151 (1937) (noting that the proper measure of damages where a person has been dispossessed of rights under "consciously tortious conduct ... is the value of the property at the time of its improper acquisition, retention, or disposition...."); *Restatement 3d of Property: Servitudes* § 8.3 (2000) (including restitution as one of the proper measures for awarding damages in a suit to enforce a servitude).

In this case, neither party has elected to submit information regarding the actual costs of the cabin's construction; thus, the only issue is the extent to which the value of the Debtors' property has been increased. * * *

* * *

* * * On August 25, 2007, Mr. Kungle had the new cabin, and the 15 acres on which the new cabin sits, appraised by Larry McDaniel. * * *

* * * In his opinion, the total contributory value of the improvements to the Debtors' real property is $68,000.

In October 2008, the Debtors hired K. Reed Judy to view the new cabin and to evaluate the appraisal prepared by Mr. McDaniel. Mr. Judy generally agreed with Mr. McDaniel's report; however, he did have some concerns. Namely, the new cabin does not have its own water supply, and the cost of a new well would be about $2,500. Mold was found in the basement, and the estimated clean-up costs are $2,000. Finally, the new cabin is located about 0.9 miles from the county road. * * * Making allowances for these additional deductions, Mr. Judy believes a sale comparison approach would yield a contributory valuation of $41,060.

* * *

Based on the appraisal of Mr. McDaniel, as analyzed by Mr. Judy, the court believes that the value of the new cabin for purposes of awarding restitution is $45,461 as of August 25, 2007. The court credits Mr. Judy's report over that of Mr. McDaniel because the comparison sales used by Mr. McDaniel were suitable for daily use, whereas the new cabin is not due to its remote location. Also, no indication exists that Mr. McDaniel's comparison properties had a shared well like the new cabin, a factor that would also negatively impact its value in a market sale. The court does not believe it is appropriate to make a $2,000 deduction for mold remediation because there is no indication in the record that mold was present in the new cabin when the Debtor forbid Mr. Kungle further access on November 7, 2004. * * *

* * *

CONCLUSION

The court concludes that Mr. Kungle is entitled to an allowed unsecured claim against the Debtors' bankruptcy estate based on his claim for unjust enrichment. The applicable date for measuring Mr. Kungle's claim, and the contributory value of the new cabin, is November 7, 2004. * * * [T]he court has determined the value of the new cabin as of August 25, 2007, to be $45,461—based on the submission of the parties—in an effort to assist them in reaching a settlement of this issue without further resort to the court. * * *

The court will enter a separate order scheduling an evidentiary hearing as to the value of the new cabin on November 7, 2004. The parties may avoid the evidentiary hearing by submitting to the court an agreed order setting forth the value of the new cabin as of November 7, 2004 * * *.

JEFFS v. STUBBS

Supreme Court of Utah, 1998.
970 P.2d 1234.

ZIMMERMAN, JUSTICE:

This case involves a dispute over the occupancy of land between twenty-one individuals ("the claimants") and the United Effort Plan Trust ("the UEP"). The claimants built improvements on land located in Hildale, Utah, and Colorado City, Arizona, which they occupy but which is owned by the UEP. Claimants filed an action in Washington County, Utah, to determine their rights in the UEP land they occupy.

Claimants asserted ten causes of action: for relief under the Utah Occupying Claimants Act, and for breach of express contract, breach of implied contract, negligent misrepresentation, constructive fraud, estoppel, unjust enrichment, breach of fiduciary duty, accounting, and distribution of trust. * * * After trial, the court relied on an unjust enrichment theory to hold that the claimants were entitled to occupy the UEP land during their lifetimes or to receive compensation for the improvements they made. The court imposed a constructive trust in favor of the claimants. * * *

Each party appealed. * * *

Sometime in the late nineteenth century, some members of the Church of Jesus Christ of Latter–Day Saints organized a movement called the Priesthood Work ("The Work") to continue the practice of plural marriage outside that church. In the early part of this century, The Work's leadership—the Priesthood Council—decided to settle its membership in an isolated area to avoid interference with their religious practices. * * *

* * *

From its inception, the UEP invited members to build their homes on assigned lots on UEP land. Through this system, the UEP intended to localize control over all local real property and to have the religious leaders manage it. Members who built on the trust land were aware that they could not sell or mortgage the land and that they would forfeit their improvements if they left the land. However, the UEP did encourage its members to improve the lots assigned to them and represented to its members that they could live on the land permanently, by using such phrases as "forever" or "as long as you wanted." The leaders also told members that having a home on UEP land was better than having a deed because creditors could not foreclose upon the land for members' debts.

Sometime during the late 1960s or early 1970s, dissension over a doctrinal issue arose * * *. The dissension broke into the open in 1984 when adherents of The Work split into two groups: One group, led by Rulon T. Jeffs ("Jeffs"), acquired control of the UEP. A second group, led by J. Marion Hammon and Alma Timpson, includes most of the claimants in the present case.

In 1986, Jeffs declared that all those living on UEP land were tenants at will. Before this declaration, neither the UEP nor any of its representatives had told the claimants that they were tenants at will. * * *

* * *

The first question is whether the trial court correctly interpreted the Utah Occupying Claimants Act. Section 57–6–1 of the Act provided:

> Where an occupant of real estate has *color of title* thereto, and in *good faith* has made *valuable improvements* thereon, and is afterwards in proper action found not to be the owner, no execution shall issue to put the plaintiff in possession of the same after the filing of a complaint as hereinafter provided, until the provisions of this chapter have been complied with.

Utah Code Ann. § 57–6–1 (1994)* (emphasis added). * * * The district court found that the claimants had made valuable improvements. Howev-

---

* The Utah Occupying Claimants Act provides the following remedy once the court determines that an occupier has color of title and has made valuable improvements in good faith:

er, it did not determine whether claimants had color of title because it had first concluded that the claimants did not make the improvements in "good faith" as required by the statute.

* * *

* * * The facts found by the district court show that the UEP knew that all the claimants were improving the land and encouraged them to do so. In many cases, claimants obtained consent from The Work's leadership to improve the land. The claimants, therefore, have color of title [as required under section 57–6–1].

* * * The trial court concluded that the claimants did not make the improvements in good faith because they had "not even claimed that they actually own the land they occupy" and because "they were installed upon the property of the UEP, knowingly by those who were using the land by permission." We conclude that the trial court erred in its interpretation of "belief of ownership."

The trial court appears to have assumed that "ownership" means possession of a fee simple interest in land. But it is settled law that * * * "[t]he term owner is often used to characterize the possessor of an interest less than that of absolute ownership, such as ... a tenant for life." * * * We therefore conclude that a good faith belief in a life interest in land satisfies the good faith requirement of the Utah Occupying Claimants Act.

* * *

This does not end this matter, however. Those claimants occupying land in Arizona have no remedy under the Utah Occupying Claimants Act. * * * [I]f, on remand, the trial court determines that some or all of the Utah claimants did not have a good faith belief in a life estate, we must determine if the court properly granted these claimants an unjust enrichment equitable remedy under Utah law.

* * * [W]e will analyze the trial court's equity ruling under both Arizona and Utah law because the court's equitable remedy affects real property in both Arizona and Utah. *See* Restatement (Second) of Conflicts of Law § 235 (1971).[8] * * *

* * *

* * * Arizona recognizes the equitable remedy of unjust enrichment and generally provides that " '[a] person who has been unjustly enriched

---

The plaintiff in the main action may thereupon pay the appraised value of the improvements and take the property, but should he fail to do so after a reasonable time, to be fixed by the court, the defendant may take the property upon paying its value, exclusive of the improvements. If this is not done within a reasonable time, to be fixed by the court, the parties will be held to be tenants in common of all the real estate, including the improvements, each holding an interest proportionate to the values ascertained on the trial.

Utah Code Ann. § 57–6–3.

8. Although the Utah and Arizona laws of unjust enrichment are very similar, we apply each state's law in deference to the general rule that the law of the situs applies.

at the expense of another is required to make restitution to the other.' "
* * * A person is unjustly enriched if (i) he received a benefit, and (ii) his
retention of that benefit would be unjust. * * * We find that the trial
court correctly concluded that claimants proved both elements.

Regarding the first element, the trial court found: "There can be no
doubt from the evidence presented that [claimant] has conferred a benefit
on the UEP by improving the lot." Arizona law defines a benefit as "any
form of advantage." Artukovich & Sons, Inc. v. Reliance Truck Co., 126
Ariz. 246, 614 P.2d 327, 329 (1980) (en banc). In making its finding, the
court relied on evidence showing that the claimants spent a considerable
amount of money and time improving the UEP land, that these improvements increased the value of the land, and that the UEP will benefit from
the increased value. We agree that this evidence supports the finding that
UEP received some advantage, and, thus, a benefit.

The claimants must also show that the UEP's retention of these
benefits would be unjust. The UEP argues that because the claimants
knew that the UEP owned the land and because the claimants intended to
"donate" the improvements, they cannot recover. We disagree.

* * *

* * * [T]he claimants plainly did not confer the service officiously.
"Officiousness means interference in the affairs of another not justified by
the circumstances under which the interference takes place." Restatement
of Restitution § 2 cmt. a (1937). Thus, an officious person is one who
"thrust[s] benefits upon others." Id. Here, the claimants did not interfere
or thrust benefits on the UEP. To the contrary, the UEP encouraged the
claimants to improve the land. * * *

* * *

The Restatement of Restitution * * * provides:

A person who has rendered services to another ... is entitled to
restitution therefor if the services were rendered ... in the mistaken
belief, of which the other knew or had reason to know, that the
services would inure to the benefit of the one giving them....

Restatement of Restitution § 40 (1937). * * * Section 42 of that Restatement, which limits a party's right to recovery for improvements to land,
specifies that section 40 applies when the true owner, "having notice of
the error and of the work being done, stands by and does not use care to
prevent the error from continuing." Id. § 42 cmt. b. A comment to section
40 clarifies that an owner "cannot retain a benefit which knowingly he
has permitted another to confer upon him by mistake." Id. § 40 cmt. d.

* * *

* * * [W]e conclude that the trial court's disposition was adequately
supported by the evidence and was consistent with the Arizona substantive law. We therefore find that the trial court did not abuse its discretion

in requiring the UEP to allow claimants to live on the land for their lifetimes or to compensate them for the improvements.

We next consider the trial court's unjust enrichment ruling under Utah law, as that law governs the claims of any Utah residents who may not be covered by the Occupying Claimants Act or for whom an equitable remedy is more favorable. Utah law, like Arizona's, recognizes the remedy of unjust enrichment. A party may prevail on an unjust enrichment theory by proving three elements:

> (1) a benefit conferred on one person by another; (2) an appreciation or knowledge by the conferee of the benefit; and (3) the acceptance or retention by the conferee of the benefit under such circumstances as to make it inequitable for the conferee to retain the benefit without payment of its value.

American Towers Owners Ass'n, Inc. v. CCI Mechanical, Inc., 930 P.2d 1182, 1192 (Utah 1996) (citations omitted). Although these elements are phrased differently than Arizona's, we find the analysis to be much the same.

* * *

* * * [W]e uphold the trial court's equitable ruling allowing the claimants to remain on the land for their lifetimes or requiring UEP to compensate the claimants for the benefit it received if the UEP seeks to remove the claimants. However, we find that the trial court erred in its interpretation of the Utah Occupying Claimants Act and that the findings are insufficient for us to determine whether any or all of the claimants have life estates. * * * Therefore, we remand that issue to the trial court for further proceedings consistent with this opinion.

Howe, C.J., Durham, A.C.J., and Russon, J., concur in Justice Zimmerman's opinion.

Stewart, J., dissents. [Without opinion.]

Notes

1. The finding of an expectation of long-term residency was crucial to the claimants' recovery in *Jeffs* because the general rule is that improvements which are fixtures become part of the real estate and thus belong to and do not unjustly enrich the landlord. *See* Roger A. Cunningham et al., The Law of Property § 6.49 (2d ed. 1993); *see also* Chesney v. Stevens, 435 Pa.Super. 71, 78, 644 A.2d 1240, 1244 (1994) (Tenants could recover for improvements on the basis of unjust enrichment because, while they could not claim title, "they did make a reasoned claim of right to long-term (life estate) occupancy.").

2. The court in *Jeffs* held that the Utah Occupying Claim Act applied to the plaintiffs living in Utah. The Utah statute is one of several types of legislation which some states have enacted to try to balance the competing interests of improvers of land and landowners. For further discussion of Occupying Claim Acts and Betterment Statutes, see Dan B. Dobbs, Law of

Remedies § 5.8(3), at 797–800 (2d ed. 1993). Professor Dobbs also suggests a number of additional remedies that would be useful: "if it is financially feasible to remove the improvement the improver should be permitted to do so in spite of technical doctrines of accession, provided damage done in the removal is repaired by the improver"; and "instead of requiring a cash payment by the landowner, an equitable lien with postponed enforcement might be imposed upon the property to guarantee that the improver will be paid when the property is sold or transferred and the value of the improvement is realized." *Id.* at 798; *see also* 2 George E. Palmer, Law of Restitution § 10.9(b) (1978); Note, *The Rights and Remedies of One Who Improves the Land of Another Under the South Carolina Betterment Statute*, 17 S.C. L. Rev. 397 (1965). For a discussion of equitable liens see Section 5.B of Chapter 4.

2. Nuisance

CITY OF ST. LOUIS v. AMERICAN TOBACCO COMPANY, INC.

United States District Court, Eastern District of Missouri, 1999.
70 F.Supp.2d 1008.

WEBBER, DISTRICT J.

* * *

I. STATEMENT OF RELEVANT FACTS

* * * The plaintiffs in the action include one municipality and a number of hospitals and medical care entities. The defendants are cigarette manufacturers, distributors, and other similar entities. In this action, plaintiffs allege that defendants, through * * * the manufacture, advertising, sale and promotion of tobacco products in the state of Missouri, have caused damage to the plaintiffs. Plaintiffs also allege that other defendants, through * * * the sale, distribution, promotion and advertising of tobacco products in Missouri, have damaged the plaintiffs. This latter group of defendants (hereinafter referred to as the "Distributor Defendants"), are all citizens of the State of Missouri. Plaintiffs allege that they have suffered damage, because the defendants fraudulently and falsely promoted, advertised, and sold highly addictive tobacco products that cause lung cancer, throat cancer, emphysema, heart disease, and other diseases. Plaintiffs claim that in discharging their governmental public benefit functions, they were required to provide unreimbursed healthcare to Medicaid and medically indigent patients for these tobacco related illnesses caused by defendants' addictive tobacco products. For this reason, plaintiffs bring a variety of claims to recover these damages from the defendants, including a claim in Count VII for public nuisance, in Counts VIII and IX for products liability based upon strict liability, in Count X for products liability based upon negligence, and in Count XI a cause of action based upon the Restatement of Restitution § 115.

On December 17, 1998, defendants removed the plaintiffs' action to this Court, alleging that this Court has diversity jurisdiction pursuant to

28 U.S.C. § 1332. Defendants allege that diversity * * * jurisdiction exists in this case because plaintiffs have fraudulently joined the Distributor Defendants in this cause of action for the purpose of insuring state court's jurisdiction. On January 29, 1999, plaintiffs filed the instant motion to remand this action to the Missouri court system, contending that this Court lacks subject matter jurisdiction, because they have [shown that they will be able to establish] their causes of action against the Distributor Defendants [in state court].

II. DISCUSSION

* * *

A. *Applicable Legal Standards*

Pursuant to 28 U.S.C. § 1332, federal district courts have "original jurisdiction of all civil actions where the matter in controversy exceeds the sum or value of $75,000" and the matter is between "citizens of different States." 28 U.S.C. § 1332(a)(1). * * * [T]he removing party bears the burden of demonstrating fraudulent joinder. * * * In order to meet this burden, the removing party must show * * * there is no possibility that the plaintiff would be able to establish a cause of action against the in-state defendant in state court * * * Placing this heavy burden on the defendants is a necessary corollary of the "considerable deference" that federal courts generally give "to a plaintiff's choice of forum." * * *

B. *The Remoteness Doctrine Does Not Clearly Preclude Plaintiffs' Claims.*

Defendants first argue that plaintiffs' claims against the Distributor Defendants are barred by the remoteness doctrine. * * * [D]efendants note that plaintiffs are attempting to recover damages equivalent to the resources and funds expended by plaintiffs in treating individuals suffering from smoking-related illnesses. Defendants argue that this claim made by plaintiffs for indirect and derivative injuries runs counter to the "bedrock principle" that a plaintiff generally stands at too remote a distance to recover for harms against a third person.

Understanding this argument advanced by defendants, the Court does not find that plaintiffs' claims are clearly barred by the remoteness doctrine under Missouri law. The Court agrees with defendants that several courts have dismissed similar or identical claims like those advanced by the plaintiffs * * *. However, the Court does not find the opinions of the state Supreme Courts cited by defendants particularly persuasive when the Missouri state courts have not thoroughly considered a claim like the instant matter under Missouri law. * * * In addition, the Court does not find defendants' citation of other federal court decisions particularly helpful, because those courts are in some disharmony on the issue of whether the remoteness principle bars a plaintiff's common law claims. *See generally* Steamfitters Local Union 420 Welfare Fund v. Philip Morris, Inc., 171 F.3d 912 (3d Cir.1999) (rejecting union health and welfare fund suits against tobacco companies on remoteness grounds); Arkansas Blue Cross and Blue Shield v. Philip Morris, Inc., 47 F.Supp.2d 936 (N.D.Ill.1999) (finding that plaintiffs had stated a cause of action notwithstanding defendants' arguments that the claims were barred by the remoteness doctrine) * * *. [T]he Court is unable to conclude that there is no possibility that plaintiffs' Missouri state law claims would succeed due to the remoteness doctrine.

* * *

* * * Defendants have cited two Missouri cases [from 1901 and 1921] to support their position * * *. This Court, like the Eastern District of New York court in *Blue Cross and Blue Shield of New Jersey, Inc.*, believes that a substantial period of "radical change in society, its institutions, and tort and criminal law" has passed since the early years of this century when these two cases were decided. * * * In particular, the courts in those two cases did not address a claim brought pursuant to the Restatement of Restitution Section 115 * * *.

In this case, plaintiffs have alleged that defendants' conduct, intentionally engaging in a conspiracy to deceive the public and intentionally marketing their products to minorities and children, has caused foreseeable harm to plaintiffs in the form of costs to treat smoking victims. Because proximate cause and issues related to foreseeability are "somewhat an exercise in subjectivity," * * * and "usually a question for the jury," * * * the Court is unable to find controlling Missouri case law indicating that plaintiffs' causes of action, in particular plaintiffs' cause of action under the Restatement of Restitution Section 115, are too remote from defendants for plaintiffs to prevail. * * *

C. *Plaintiffs Have Stated a Cause of Action Against the Distributors Based Upon the Restatement of Restitution.*

Having decided that plaintiffs' claims are not clearly barred by a general theory of remoteness does not end the Court's inquiry, because defendants also allege that each of plaintiffs' individual Missouri claims fail to state causes of action against the Distributor Defendants. * * * [T]he Court concludes that a reasonable basis exists for plaintiffs' claims against the Distributor Defendants in Count XI. * * *

* * *

First, the Court does not believe that the fact that no Missouri court has recognized a right of recovery pursuant to Restatement of Restitution § 115 indicates that this Court should find that plaintiffs' claim must fail. To the contrary, the Court believes that this fact suggests that such a cause of action should first be presented to a Missouri state court as opposed to this federal court for resolution if possible. * * *

On the other hand, the Court understands that the rules related to fraudulent joinder could be easily circumvented if federal courts simply held that all novel theories of law must be presented to state courts if the state courts have yet to resolve an issue. * * * In this case, however, the Court believes that plaintiffs' theory of recovery may in fact be recognized for several reasons. First, courts in other states have adopted and recognized the Restatement of Restitution § 115. * * * Recognition by these courts of that theory of recovery indicates that plaintiffs' theory is not frivolous or lacking a reasonable basis, notwithstanding the fact that no Missouri court has recognized the theory.

Second, Missouri state courts have often relied upon and adopted other provisions contained in the Restatement of Restitution.[4] * * *

The Court not only finds that Missouri state courts would likely allow a claim pursuant to the Restatement of Restitution § 115, but also finds that plaintiffs have stated a cause of action pursuant to that section. The Restatement of Restitution § 115 provides as follows:

> A person who has performed the duty of another by supplying things or services, although acting without the other's knowledge and consent, is entitled to restitution from the other if
>
> (a) he acted unofficiously and with the intent to charge therefore, and
>
> (b) the things or services supplied were immediately necessary to satisfy the requirements of public decency, health or safety.

Restatement of Restitution § 115 (1937). Plaintiffs have attempted to allege each of the elements of this cause of action in their complaint as follows:

> 290.   Defendants, through their wrongful conduct, as described in all of the Counts of this Petition, have caused Plaintiffs in discharging their governmental public benefit functions to provide unreimbursed healthcare to Medicaid and medically indigent patients for their tobacco related illnesses.
>
> 291.   Plaintiffs acted unofficiously in providing such healthcare and in intending to charge for such services.
>
> 292.   The healthcare provided to Medicaid and medically indigent patients for tobacco related illnesses was immediately necessary to satisfy the requirements of public decency and health.
>
> 293.   Plaintiffs are entitled to restitution from Defendants for their unreimbursed costs for healthcare provided to Medicaid and medically indigent patients for their tobacco-related illnesses. In equity and fairness, the Defendants, and not Plaintiffs, should bear the cost of tobacco related diseases and have a duty to do so.

* * * Defendants argue that plaintiffs have not adequately alleged that defendants had a duty to provide health care to Medicaid and medically indigent patients. However, plaintiffs do allege that defendants

---

4. Missouri courts have not only relied upon the Restatement of Restitution in the past, but have also recognized restitution as a remedy for unjust enrichment. Blue Cross Health Services v. Sauer, 800 S.W.2d 72, 75 (Mo.Ct.App.1990) (quoting the Restatement of Restitution § 1). As plaintiffs note, section 115 is grounded on principles of unjust enrichment. Independent Sch. Dist. No. 197 v. W.R. Grace & Co., 752 F.Supp. 286, 303 (D.Minn.1990).

"have a duty" to "bear the cost of tobacco related diseases" and that they were required to discharge their public benefit functions due to defendants' wrongful conduct. * * *

* * *

In addition, the Court finds the reasoning quoted with approval by the court in *Independent School District No. 197* instructive on this issue. In that case, the court favorably cited a Minnesota district court for the proposition that a court considering the concept of duty under section 115 in a claim made by schools seeking the recovery of costs of removing hazards allegedly caused by asbestos should not ignore the following in regards to the concept of duty:

> the reality [is] that the defendants may be under a duty to answer in damages—to pay for the consequences of the harm done unless the harm were removed, avoided, or abated by them. . . . If the defendants are unwilling to remove the product (to restore the property to an "uninjured" nonhazardous condition) notwithstanding a duty to refrain from putting abroad in the marketplace a defective product, the plaintiffs may well find themselves confronted with an emergency (the impending exposure of an unaware public of users and occupants of the plaintiffs' facilities) to which the plaintiffs must respond. When, then, defendants have been given the opportunities to restore the properties and have refused to do so, all expenses to which the plaintiffs are put in the restoration confer on the defendants a dollar for dollar benefit for which they may be liable. * * *

The Court believes these same principles could apply to the defendants in this case, because plaintiffs allege that the "Tobacco Defendants" have fraudulently and falsely promoted, advertised, and sold a highly addictive product that causes lung cancer, throat cancer, emphysema, heart disease, and other diseases. * * * Plaintiff claims that the Distributor Defendants have assisted in distributing tobacco related advertisements and promotions to Medicaid recipients and the medically indigent and derive economic benefits from the distribution and sale of cigarettes and tobacco products notwithstanding the fact that they knew or should have known that their actions would lead tobacco consumers to require care and medical treatment, which was eventually provided by the plaintiffs. * * *

* * *

For the reasons set forth * * *, the Court finds that plaintiff's Motion to Remand should be granted.

NOTES

1. The approach that the plaintiffs took in *City of St. Louis* is analogous to the approach that public entities are taking to combat and rectify other public health problems. Much attention has been given to those situations in

which premises have been left in a condition that threatens the health of those in the area. This form of "environmental pollution" presents many problems for those who are anxious to restore the property in question to a condition which again permits its use in conventional ways. Identifying and locating those responsible may be a problem. The litigation which ensues is likely to be long, drawn out, and costly, while there may be a pressing need for early return of the premises to the use for which they were intended. This situation has prompted a number of local governments to proceed to remedy the situation themselves and then to sue the party allegedly responsible in quasi-contract. The court in *City of St. Louis* cited some of those cases, including Independent School Dist. No. 197 v. W.R. Grace & Co., 752 F.Supp. 286 (D.Minn.1990), from which it quoted, and Unified School District No. 500 v. United States Gypsum Co., 788 F.Supp. 1173 (D.Kan.1992). Both of those cases involved school districts that sued asbestos manufacturers for the costs the schools incurred in removing and replacing the materials containing asbestos. The plaintiff school districts had each brought suit under a number of claims, including one based on Restatement of Restitution § 115. In both cases the courts denied defendants' motions for summary judgment. The court in *Unified School District* described that action as follows:

> Under Kansas law, restitution is applied in two distinct senses. It sometimes means restoration. In this sense it connotes a general description of the relief afforded by a cause of action, rather than a cause of action itself. *See* Dobbs, Remedies 222 (1973). However, Kansas also recognizes that restitution may be substantive. In this sense, restitution may be a cause of action based on unjust enrichment or a theory of quasi-contract. * * *

> The substance of a cause of action for restitution or unjust enrichment resides in a "promise implied in law that one will restore to the person entitled thereto that which in equity and good conscience belongs to him." * * * The doctrine prevents one party from profiting unjustly at the expense of another, "but there must be some specific legal principle or situation which equity has established or recognized to bring a case within the scope of the doctrine." * * *

> * * *

> Plaintiff argues that because defendants put defective and unreasonably dangerous products into the stream of commerce, which products were installed in public buildings, defendants should be made, in equity and good conscience, to pay for the removal and replacement of those products.

> * * * The court is of the opinion, based on Kansas' view of restitution, that Kansas courts would, in equity, imply a promise on the part of these defendants to abate the asbestos contamination created by them. A decision to the contrary would unjustly enrich defendants.

Id. at 1175–76.

2. Lead paint and water pollution are other hazards that have caused public entities to bring suits in restitution. New York City and some of its agencies sued manufacturers of lead paint to recover money spent "in

inspecting, testing, monitoring and abating the hazards arising from the use of the lead paint, in testing children at risk of lead poisoning and in treating the child victims of such poisoning * * *." City of New York v. Lead Industries Ass'n, Inc., 222 A.D.2d 119, 122, 644 N.Y.S.2d 919, 920 (1996). *Lead Industries* was cited in *City of St. Louis.* In reversing the trial court's dismissal of the action, the Appellate Division in *Lead Industries* said, "in undertaking such expenditures plaintiffs discharged a duty which, although imposed upon plaintiffs by statute and regulation, should properly have been borne by defendants who were responsible for having created this danger to public health and safety," *id.* at 124, 644 N.Y.S.2d at 922, and said further that

> [t]o deny plaintiffs the right to seek recovery of the very substantial sums that they have been caused to expend, in remediating and inhibiting the potential for injury and damages due to defendant's unsafe project, would be to permit the alleged defendant wrongdoers to be "unjustly enriched" by insulating them, at plaintiffs' expense, from potential tort and indemnity liability that would otherwise have arisen.

Id. at 129, 644 N.Y.S.2d at 925. In United States v. P/B STCO 213, 756 F.2d 364 (5th Cir.1985), the Fifth Circuit held that a six-year statute of limitations, not a three-year one, governed the United States' action to recover clean up costs from water polluters under the Federal Water Pollution Control Act. The six-year statute was for "contracts express or implied in law or fact," while the three-year one was for torts. The court reasoned that, although pollution might be analogized to a tort, the action was in quasi-contract (contract implied in law) because "unjust enrichment may consist * * * of one's avoidance and consequent shifting to another of the cost of performing a duty that one is primarily obligated to perform." *Id.* at 371. The court had consolidated three district court cases. It reversed the two that had dismissed the claims as time barred and affirmed the one that had awarded the United States the full amount of the clean up costs.

3. Professor Doug Rendleman described and analyzed the case that led to a $206 billion settlement between tobacco companies and Mississippi and other states that had filed restitution actions against those companies. Doug Rendleman, *Common Law Restitution in the Mississippi Tobacco Settlement: Did the Smoke Get in Their Eyes?,* 33 Ga. L. Rev. 847 (1999).* He concluded that Mississippi's allegations would not state a cause of action for restitution.

Mississippi sought to recover for Medicaid claims that the State had paid for tobacco-related illnesses. The action was brought on the grounds of "restitution—unjust enrichment, indemnity, public nuisance, and injunction." *Id.* at 852. Professor Rendleman summarized and analyzed Mississippi's restitutionary argument as follows:

> Pursuant to its duty to assuage the plight of its infirm citizens, the State has established Medicaid to pay their medical costs, many of them caused by smoking. The tobacco companies created many of these medical costs by selling their addictive and harmful product to smokers. The costs "rightfully should have been borne by the tobacco companies."

---

* Reprinted with permission of the Georgia Law Review.

The State, in other words, asked the court to base restitution-indemnity on State Medicaid payments to Infirm Citizen [Medicaid recipient with tobacco-related illness] of an amount for which the tobacco companies have not been held liable to Infirm Citizen, but for which the tobacco companies ought to be liable to Infirm Citizen. The State may recover restitution from tobacco companies because the tobacco companies are unjustly enriched when the product they sell causes medical expenses that they are not paying. The amount [by which] the tobacco companies are unjustly enriched is the amount they "save" by not paying for the medical expenses tobacco causes. The amount the State should recover is the amount it pays to deal with the insalubrious consequences of tobacco.

Id. at 885.

The tobacco companies had argued that Mississippi sued in restitution to avoid stricter legal standards applied to tobacco products liability claims, including the often successful defense of smokers' assumption of the risk. Professor Rendleman summarized the companies' argument as follows:

Products liability * * * represents the struggle of courts and legislatures to balance the competing interests of consumers and manufacturers. The State's restitution characterization would absorb all of the balanced law of products liability. It would impose damages on the tobacco companies although they have consistently prevailed in products liability lawsuits. It would be extended to create similar liability for other risky but nondefective products.

Id. at 875.

Professor Rendleman explained that Mississippi's action is not for the type of restitution that is an alternative to tort because the tobacco companies are not liable in tort; therefore, the action is for the type of restitution that states a cause of action based on unjust enrichment. He refers to this type of restitution as freestanding restitution. Freestanding restitution began with Moses v. Macferlan, *supra*, Chapter 4, Section 2, and is articulated under the Restatement of Restitution § 1: "A person who has been unjustly enriched at the expense of another is required to make restitution to the other." Professor Rendleman discussed two views that scholars hold about freestanding restitution:

Imprecision in the pursuit of justice is, in [a broad view of restitution] a virtue. "Unjust enrichment," Professor Dobbs said "cannot be precisely defined, and for that very reason has potential for resolving new problems in striking ways." * * * If a court were to accept a broad, or section 1 [of the Restatement of Restitution], view of unjust enrichment and freestanding restitution and perhaps stretch it, then the State's Medicaid restitution might have prevailed.

Id. at 889–90. On the other hand Professor Rendleman said:

Broad restitution based on freestanding unjust enrichment as a default for courts to employ when other principles fail has both virtues and vices, for as then-Professor Sullivan reminded us, "The perception of what is just is by no means an objective vision and varies from generation to generation, from case to case, and from court to court." * * *

Id. at 889. *Compare* Timothy D. Lytton, *Should Government Be Allowed to Recover the Costs of Public Services from Tortfeasors?: Tort Subsidies, the Limits of Loss Spreading, and the Free Public Services Doctrine*, 76 Tul. L. Rev. 727 (2002) (arguing that those who create harm should include the cost of that harm in their activities).

4. Can private plaintiffs protecting their own interests recover in quasi-contract from a polluter? Consider the next case.

BRANCH v. MOBIL OIL CORP.

United States District Court, Western District of Oklahoma, 1991.
778 F.Supp. 35.

DAVID L. RUSSELL, DISTRICT JUDGE.

[Homer and Lois Branch brought suit against Mobil Oil Corporation and other oil corporations claiming that their oil wells and salt-water pits had polluted plaintiffs' surface and subsurface soil and water.]

* * *

Defendant Citation's motion to dismiss Plaintiffs' claims of unjust enrichment and public nuisance is denied. Unjust enrichment can occur when a defendant uses something belonging to the Plaintiff in such a way as to effectuate some kind of savings which results in or amounts to a business profit. *See* D. Dobbs, Handbook on the Law of Remedies § 4.5 (1973) at p. 278. *See also* Tilghman v. Proctor, 125 U.S. 136, 146, 8 S.Ct. 894, 899, 31 L.Ed. 664, 667 (1888); Olwell v. Nye & Nissen Co., 26 Wash.2d 282, 173 P.2d 652 (1946). Oklahoma recognizes a claim for negative unjust enrichment. *See* McBride v. Bridges, 202 Okla. 508, 215 P.2d 830, 832 (1950). *See also* Booker v. Sears Roebuck & Co., 785 P.2d 297, 303 (Okla.1989) (Summers, J., dissenting). The Court cannot say that Plaintiffs' Complaint does not state a claim for unjust enrichment on which relief can be granted based on a failure to allege a benefit conferred on Defendants. * * * It can be inferred from Plaintiffs' Amended Complaint that Defendants used Plaintiffs' property to dispose of pollutants and saved the expenses of otherwise collecting and disposing of same. Upon consideration of Okla.Stat. tit. 82, § 926.4, Okla.Stat. tit. 50, §§ 8 & 10, and Plaintiffs' First Amended Complaint, the Court cannot say that Plaintiffs have failed to state a claim for abatement of a public nuisance on which relief can be granted.

The motion of Defendant Citation Oil & Gas Corporation to dismiss Plaintiffs' claims of unjust enrichment and public nuisance is denied.

NOTES

1. Are the plaintiffs in *Branch* intermeddlers? Notice that they are not suing for their clean up costs, but are suing for defendant's benefit measured

by what the defendant saved in not having installed equipment that would have prevented the pollution. The court cites Olwell v. Nye & Nissen Co., *supra* Chapter 4, Section 6, and Tilghman v. Proctor, 125 U.S. 136, 146, 8 S.Ct. 894, 899, 31 L.Ed. 664, 667 (1888). The Court in *Tilghman* said: "If, for example, the unauthorized use by the defendant of a patented process produced a definite saving in the cost of manufacture, he must account to the patentee for the amount so saved." *Id. at* 145, 8 S.Ct. at 899, 31 L.Ed. at 667.

2. For a case in which a plaintiff recovers the costs of repairing environmental damage (dumped concrete) that awards plaintiff's clean-up costs, but does not discuss restitution, see Myers v. Arnold, *supra*, Chapter 6, Section 2.A.1. *See also* Robert A. Bass, *Florida's Troubled Inland Protection Trust Fund: Common Law Actions as Alternative Remedies for an Innocent Buyer of Contaminated Commercial Land*, 11 J. Land Use & Envtl. L. 139 (1995) (suggesting that buyers of contaminated property be able to bring an action in restitution to recover their cleanup costs from the polluting landowner); Allan Kanner, *Unjust Enrichment in Environmental Litigation*, 20 J. Envtl. L. & Litig. 111 (2005) (advocating greater use of restitution in pollution cases).

3. A number of environmental statutes pattern liability, at least in part, on restitutionary principles of unjust enrichment, as did the Branches in their common law claim. These principles can be applied when determining procedural issues, such as statutes of limitations, as seen in the next case.

UNITED STATES v. SUNOCO, INC.

United States District Court, Eastern District of Pennsylvania, 2007.
501 F. Supp. 2d 641.

ANITA B. BRODY, J.

I. INTRODUCTION

The United States has filed suit against defendants Sunoco et al. and Atlantic Richfield Company et al. ("AR") under the Pennsylvania Storage Tank and Spill Prevention Act, 35 Pa. C. S. § 6021.101, et seq., ("Tank Act"), the Pennsylvania Uniform Contribution Among Tortfeasors Act, 42 Pa. C. S. § 8324 ("UCATA"), the Clean Streams Act, 35 Pa. C. S. § 691.1, et seq., ("CSA") and the federal Declaratory Judgment Act, 28 U.S.C. § 2201(a). The suit alleges that the Point Breeze oil refinery, owned by the defendants at various points in time, caused underground petroleum pollution to an adjacent military supply depot called the Defense Supply Center Philadelphia ("DSCP property").[1] The United States has moved for a judgment on the applicable statute of limitations, * * * as well as for a determination of whether the claims are time barred. * * *

II. FACTS AND COMPLAINT

The complaint alleges that the DSCP, located in South Philadelphia and separated by a 550 foot wide corridor from the Point Breeze refinery, was contaminated by underground migration of petroleum products from

---

1. The federal hazardous waste statute, CERCLA, excludes petroleum contamination. 42 U.S.C. § 9601(14).

the refinery. ¶ 12. Although the military retains the surface and subsurface property rights, the air rights were transferred to the Philadelphia Authority for Industrial Development in 2001. The property is currently used as a civilian shopping mall called "Quartermaster Plaza." ¶ 16. According to the original complaint, the United States first detected contamination in 1987 from a fuel leak from a United States gas station located on the DSCP property itself. The Pennsylvania environmental agency notified the DSCP that it was in violation of state regulations. ¶ 17. When the United States further investigated the pollution (through studies by the Army Corps of Engineers and outside consultants), it found "widespread petroleum contamination" that could not have come from the DSCP gas station. ¶ 18–34. In 1995, one such study commissioned by the United States concluded that Point Breeze was the most likely source of the contamination. ¶ 29–30. The pollution is still continuing to migrate from Point Breeze to the United States property. ¶ 45, 47. To date, the United States has incurred $22,000,000 in cleanup costs. ¶ 75.

The United States sought cost recovery under the Tank Act * * * The Tank Act is a comprehensive regulatory scheme governing petroleum storage tanks in Pennsylvania. 35 Pa. St. Cons. § 6021.101, et seq. Violations of the Tank Act are "public nuisances," § 6021.1304, and are "abatable in the manner provided by law or equity for the abatement of public nuisances," § 6021.1305(a). The Tank Act allows "any person having an interest which is or may be affected" to file a suit to "compel compliance" with the Act. § 6021.1305(c). This express private right of action has been interpreted by the Pennsylvania Supreme Court to include the right to cost recovery and diminution of property value. * * *

* * *

III.   MOTIONS ON STATUTE OF LIMITATIONS

The United States has filed a Motion for Order on Applicability of Statutes of Limitations, seeking a ruling on only the legal question of which statute of limitations applies to its Tank Act and UCATA claims. * * *

IV.   SOVEREIGN STATUS

* * * When the United States is a plaintiff asserting state or federal law claims in its sovereign capacity, it is not subject to any statute of limitations unless Congress waives sovereign immunity and imposes a limit itself. * * * If "public policies are served and the public interest is advanced by the litigation," the government is acting in its sovereign capacity and is not subject to statutes of limitations. * * *

In this case, the United States seeks to facilitate environmental protection and restoration of public land by imposing liability on polluters through state law. * * * [I]t is clear that the United States is operating in its sovereign capacity * * *.

V.   GENERAL FEDERAL STATUTE OF LIMITATIONS: 28 U.S.C. § 2415

Although the United States acts here as a sovereign, it may have statutorily waived its immunity to statutes of limitation under 28 U.S.C. § 2415. Section 2415 statute provides that:

(a) . . . every action for money damages brought by the United States or an officer or agency thereof which is founded upon any contract express or implied in law or fact, shall be barred unless the complaint is filed within six years after the right of action accrues.

(b) . . . every action for money damages brought by the United States or an officer or agency thereof which is founded upon a tort shall be barred unless the complaint is filed within three years after the right of action first accrues.

28 U.S.C. § 2415. The United States argues that it is not subject to § 2415 because the statutes it sues under are not "torts" or "contracts" for "money damages." If the United States is correct, then it is subject to no statute of limitations at all.

* * *

VI.   TANK ACT CLAIMS

* * *

A.   Resemblance to Torts

The United States seeks both cost recovery and diminution of property value under the Tank Act. By the plain language of the statute, these Tank Act claims resemble torts. * * *

* * *

C.   Cost Recovery: Contract Implied In Law

The cost recovery claim is not as easily analyzed as the diminution of property value claim, despite its resemblance to a tort. Section 2415(a)'s six-year limitations period extends to contracts "implied in law," which may be triggered by a tort.

The CERCLA cost recovery cases provide important guidance for determining the nature of a pollution cost recovery claim. In *Hatco Corp. v. W.R. Grace & Co.*, 59 F.3d 400, 412 (3d Cir. 1995), the court determined that CERCLA cost recovery remedies are restitutionary, citing the Restatement (First) of Restitution § 115. *Id.* Restatement § 115 is entitled "Performance of Another's Duty to the Public."[10] Under § 115, when one person undertakes to perform another's pre-existing duty, he is entitled to restitution for the amount of money he expended. That duty may be triggered by a tort. This type of restitution, which is based on the concept

---

10. Under Restatement § 115

A person who has performed the duty of another by supplying things or services, although acting without the other's knowledge or consent, is entitled to restitution from the other if (a) he acted unofficiously and with intent to charge therefor, and (b) the things or services supplied were immediately necessary to satisfy the requirements of public decency, health, or safety.

of unjust enrichment, is also referred to as "quasi-contract" or "contract implied in law." Dan B. Dobbs, *Law of Remedies* § 4.2(3), at 385–86, and § 5.2(5), at 505–06 (2d ed. 1993) (Hornbook Series). * * *

* * *

The Fifth and Ninth Circuits and the Southern District of New York have found that, for statute of limitations purposes, cost recovery under the Clean Water Act is an "implied in law" contract under § 2415(a) because of its restitutionary nature. * * * Those courts reasoned that the Clean Water Act establishes the polluter's duty to clean up his pollution, and that a contract implied in law forms when the United States undertakes the polluter's duty. * * *

* * *

D. Cost Recovery: Money Damages

Even if the cost recovery claim is for a contract implied in law under § 2415(a), it must also be "for money damages" to fall under the statute's six-year limitation period. According to the United States, the term "money damages" refers to remedies at law rather than equitable remedies; and because cost recovery is equitable not legal, it is not covered by § 2415.[12] * * * The only possible interpretation is that "money damages" in § 2415(a) extends to monetary judgments sought under the guise of a contract implied in law, such as the United States's claim for cost recovery.[13] Otherwise, § 2415(a) could never encompass any contract implied in law——a result manifestly at odds with the plain language of the statute's command to impose a statute of limitations on contracts implied in law.

* * *

X. CONCLUSION

* * * The United States' Tank Act claim for diminution of property value is a tort claim for money damages under § 2415(b) and is subject to the three year statute of limitations. The Tank Act claims for cost recovery and the UCATA claim for contribution are contracts implied in law under § 2415(a) and are subject to the six year statute of limitations.

---

12. * * * But the United States's assumption that restitution is equitable may also be called into question * * * [T]he Supreme Court has since clarified that restitution may be both legal and equitable. *See Great–West Life & Annuity Ins. Co. v. Knudson*, 534 U.S. 204, 122 S.Ct. 708, 151 L. Ed. 2d 635 (2002). * * *

13. Section 2415(a) does contain some apparent contradictions. A contract implied in law provides a restitutional remedy. A restitutional remedy is measured by the defendant's gain rather than the plaintiff's loss. Damages, conversely, are measured by the plaintiff's loss rather than the defendant's gain. Thus, a "contract implied in law for money damages" is a contradiction in terms from a strictly academic point of view because it mixes up damages and restitution, which are (in theory) two different things. But Congress decided that § 2415(a) includes such a chimera. Therefore, it must exist. The most sensible interpretation is that § 2415(a) extends to money judgments for a contract implied in law. Any theoretical inconsistencies diminish in importance where, as here, the measure of restitution and damages would be identical: In paying to remediate the pollution, the United State's lost as much as the defendants gained by *not* paying to remediate.

The United States is time barred from asserting both of its Tank Act claims against AR. AR may refile its motion on the statute of limitations for the UCATA claims at a later date. Whether the Tank Act and UCATA claims against Sunoco are time barred is not reached in this opinion.

* * *

SECTION 3. INJUNCTION AND DAMAGES ACTIONS BY GOVERNMENT AGAINST PUBLIC NUISANCES AND OTHER WRONGS

GOOSE v. COMMONWEALTH *EX REL.* DUMMIT, ATTORNEY GENERAL

Court of Appeals of Kentucky, 1947.
305 Ky. 644, 205 S.W.2d 326.

STANLEY, COMMISSIONER.

For a number of years a gambling establishment and saloon, called the "Sycamore Cafe," was conducted at 238–240 Central Avenue, in Louisville. The premises are located in an industrial and residential district in the southern part of the city, and across the street from a Railroad Y.M.C.A.

The property is owned by Roscoe Goose. A saloon license was held by J.W. Goose, but it appears a renewal was lately denied. A soft drink and restaurant license was in the name of Luther Goose. They are brothers and were joint proprietors.

Numerous raids by police officers revealed extensive taking of bets on horse races and other forms of gambling with cards, dice and other devices. During the past five years, J. William Goose and Luther Goose were arrested a number of times on charges of suffering gaming on the premises, gambling, disorderly conduct, malicious assault and other offenses. The records show that all of these charges were "filed away" in court, although on a few occasions the defendants paid petty fines for disorderly conduct. Numerous others were arrested at the same place for the same offenses. Most of them were employees conducting the operations, or stooges to "take the rap." * * * It is a sordid record of wide open, flagrant violations of the laws of the state, both felonies and misdemeanors, particularly maintaining premises on which "persons assemble to wager money or anything of value on the result of any horse race." KRS 436.440. In short, there is portrayed a "common gambling house," conducted by common and professional gamblers.

These men confess a general course of criminality at this place. They have in some way been able to set the law at naught and to continue their criminal project. The processes of the criminal courts seem to have broken down in dealing with this place and these men. At least, they have failed to accomplish their primary purposes of protecting society, reforming the wayward and preventing future offenses of the same kind. As a consequence, the Commonwealth has invoked the processes of the court of equity and obtained an injunction against the named persons to abate their use of the property for the unlawful purposes.

* * *

Courts of equity will not ordinarily enjoin the commission of a crime. The statutes themselves are standing injunctions. But the mere fact that the act constituting a nuisance is also a crime does not hinder the use of the civil processes to procure its abatement where the use of property is a part. There may also be a remedy by indictment and upon conviction an abatement by order of the criminal court where the nuisance may be of a continuing character. This remedy is sometimes confused with the other. But there is a clear distinction between enjoining an individual from committing a crime and enjoining him from using his or another's property so as to make it a nuisance to others, and between a proceeding in equity to abate a nuisance and a criminal prosecution to punish the offender for maintaining it. * * *

It is an historic function of courts of equity to grant preventative as well as remedial relief. Irreparable injury to property rights is perhaps the most common of causes for injunctive relief. Surely irreparable injury to public morals and individual character is of as grave concern as mere loss of dollars and cents. The ground of the jurisdiction is the ability of the chancellor to give a more complete and perfect remedy by a perpetual injunction. It is a weapon from the arsenal of equity to be used to protect Society—to meet the social need that continuation of the offenses at a given place shall be repressed. This abatement by injunction, independent of the criminal prosecution, is supported by ancient precedents and modern instances.

Though aimed at the use of specific property, the injunction operates upon the person of those who shall so use it and may be executed by process of contempt. And no subterfuge will be tolerated.

The principal ground upon which the appellants rely for a reversal of the judgment is thus stated:

"In an action of this character, it is necessary for the Commonwealth to prove that gaming operations were conducted on the premises, but in addition thereto, before injunctive relief can be procured, it is necessary for the Commonwealth to establish other facts showing that the peace and quiet or morals of the community are injured as a result thereof; that dissolute or criminal characters frequent the premises; that residents are forced to come in contact with a lower strata of society or that the health or morals of the public generally are suffering by reason of the actions of appellants."

In short, the contention seems to be that so long as one operates a "den of iniquity," or other demoralizing business in a quiet, peaceful and gentle way he is beyond the pale of the law and should be let alone. This idea may have had its origin in the long ago when the common law of England did not regard ordinary gambling as an offense per se. 24 Am.Jur., Gaming and Prize Contests, secs. 11, 12, 38. It was once regarded in this state that buying of pools on horse races was not within the statute which fixed a penalty against suffering any game on premises at which money was bet. This is not the law now. In these later days all forms of gambling and the promotion thereof are condemned by the statutes (KRS 436.190 to 436.530) except betting through parimutuel machines at race courses under license by the state. KRS 436.480. But at common law a common gambling house was regarded as a common nuisance because of its tendencies to bring together disorderly persons, promote immorality and lead to breaches of the peace.

Stronger and stronger has become the disposition of the legislatures and the courts to extend the law of nuisances to every sort of gambling irrespective of its connection with other offenses, or of its potentiality of spawning them, or of other conditions which brought it within the classification of a nuisance in former days. It long ago ceased to be essential to injunctive redress that the gambling should be in view of the public or that the public be disturbed by noise therefrom. Nor is it requisite to show that dissolute or criminal characters frequent the premises or that respectable citizens have been "forced to come in contact with a lower strata of society," as appellants submit. * * *

Neither principle nor precedent supports the absolution claimed by these defendants. If the moral fiber of its manhood and womanhood is not a state concern, we may ask, what is? The court does not falter for an answer.

The argument of the appellants is not new. It was put to this court nearly forty years ago and deliberately and clearly answered. We did not then and do not now perceive that the arm of justice is too short to protect the people from a vicious enterprise of this sort—from anything which tends to corrupt or destroy their morals and character. * * *

* * *

We have given this case, and the companion cases, the careful consideration which the appellants request and regarded the consequences of affirmance which they suggest, namely, that "Courts of equity will become a cesspool for the trial of similar actions if appellees' contentions are upheld." Not "cesspools" but "filters."

The judgment is affirmed.

NOTES

1. The starting point of this section is the traditional maxim that equity will not enjoin the commission of a crime. This is because criminal prosecution usually is an adequate remedy at law. We seldom, if ever, hear of courts enjoining murder, rape, robbery, or arson. Long prison sentences suffice from

society's perspective. But sometimes prosecutors find the criminal sanction inadequate. This can be the case, for example, with criminal activity that is on the fringes of criminal law—where the conduct is criminal but society has not seen fit to impose substantial penalties on it. As a result, many courts today hold that equity will enjoin a crime if the criminal conduct is also a "public nuisance." While the content of this term is often malleable and imprecise, courts frequently define a public nuisance as the "doing of or the failure to do something that injuriously affects the safety, health, or morals of the public, or works some substantial annoyance, inconvenience or injury to the public generally." United States v. County Board of Arlington County, 487 F.Supp. 137, 143 (E.D.Va.1979). Some courts take the position that "where a statute is openly, publicly, repeatedly, continuously, persistently, and intentionally violated a public nuisance is created." State *ex rel.* Turner v. United Buckingham Freight Lines, Inc., 211 N.W.2d 288 (Iowa 1973) (enjoining defendant from future violations of statute regulating truck length and weight). Indeed, some jurisdictions take the position that courts have the inherent authority to define and abate activities as public nuisances. *See* State *ex rel.* Carlson v. Hatfield, 183 Neb. 157, 158 N.W.2d 612 (1968).

It would be a mistake, however, to view the "public nuisance" concept as an open-ended license to courts to sanction any activity that is capable of falling within the foregoing amorphous definition. Many states require varying degrees of legislative authorization for judicial action against such nuisances. As one Hawaii court stated, "absent a statute or valid ordinance declaring activities in violation of general concepts of public policy to be a nuisance or subject to abatement, equity courts generally are without jurisdiction to enjoin such activities unless they in fact constitute a nuisance." Marsland v. Pang, 5 Haw.App. 463, 701 P.2d 175, 177 (1985). Moreover, as much of the material in this section illustrates, the public nuisance injunction must not only satisfy a variety of equitable conditions precedent, but, in many instances, must surmount significant constitutional and public policy hurdles as well. For further analysis of these limitations on the public nuisance concept, see Note, 40 Mo. L. Rev. 145 (1975).

2. "Public nuisance" litigation has varied with the times. As *Goose* illustrates, gambling was a common focus of prosecutors during the middle of the past century. So too was the habitual practice of charging usurious interest rates to necessitous borrowers. *Compare* Larson v. State *ex rel.* Patterson, 266 Ala. 589, 97 So.2d 776 (1957) (injunction granted); State *ex rel.* Beck v. Basham, 146 Kan. 181, 70 P.2d 24 (1937) (same), *with* Nash v. State *ex rel.* Attorney General, 271 Ala. 173, 123 So.2d 24 (1960) (borrowers not necessitous; injunction improper). The public nuisance doctrine has been extended in one case to allow injunctive relief against usurious revolving charge accounts, notwithstanding the availability of severe criminal penalties or the apparent absence of necessitous borrowers. *See* State v. J.C. Penney Co., 48 Wis.2d 125, 179 N.W.2d 641 (1970).

The "public nuisance" concept also has been used to enjoin the unauthorized practice of a profession. *See* Arizona State Board of Dental Examiners v. Hyder, 114 Ariz. 544, 562 P.2d 717 (1977) (unauthorized practice of dentistry); The Florida Bar v. Borges–Caignet, 321 So.2d 550 (Fla.1975) (unauthorized practice of law); State Board of Medical Examiners v. Olson, 295 Minn.

379, 206 N.W.2d 12 (1973) (unauthorized practice of medicine); State *ex rel.* Meyer v. Weiner, 190 Neb. 30, 205 N.W.2d 649 (1973) (unlicensed real estate practices); People *ex rel.* Bennett v. Laman, 277 N.Y. 368, 14 N.E.2d 439 (1938) (practicing medicine without a license); Dempsey v. Chicago Title Insurance Co., 10 Ohio App.3d 281, 462 N.E.2d 184 (1983) (unlawful practice of surveying). For a rejection of the public nuisance doctrine in this setting, see Massachusetts Society of Optometrists v. Waddick, 340 Mass. 581, 165 N.E.2d 394, 90 A.L.R. 2d 1 (1960).

3. States have frequently used the public nuisance injunction as a weapon against obscenity. Consider the following analysis:

> Generally speaking, three kinds of nuisance statutes have been applied to obscenity cases. Two of them, the so-called Red Light laws and general public nuisance abatement statutes, do not explicitly refer to obscenity; hence, courts have had to interpret their language broadly to include obscenity within their strictures, and most courts have rejected attempts to apply such laws to pornography.
>
> The third kind of nuisance law, the modern moral nuisance abatement statute, is drafted with obscenity specifically in mind. In the last decade, several states have passed such laws or have amended their old nuisance laws to cover obscenity, thereby removing all doubts of legislative intent. These statutes have generally incorporated the *Miller* definition of obscenity. The blanket injunction and padlock provisions of these statutes, although aimed specifically at obscenity, are similar to the classic Red Light laws, under which certain establishments—mainly houses of prostitution or gambling—could be permanently banned or shut down for the good of the community.
>
> The padlock order is the most effective and arguably most suppressive sanction that can be authorized against an adult bookstore or theater. Once an establishment is found to have purveyed obscene material, an injunction may be issued closing down the entire premises for a specified period, usually a year. The closure order usually can be lifted if the owner posts a bond for the full value of the property and demonstrates that the nuisance will not recur. A padlock order declares that the store or theater itself, in addition to the obscene material, is a nuisance.

* * *

> Most courts that have considered moral nuisance abatement laws providing for padlock orders have either construed the padlock provision as inapplicable to sexually explicit material, thereby avoiding any constitutional issue, or have struck down the provision flatly on constitutional grounds. In so doing, these courts generally have assumed that padlock orders are prior restraints without engaging in substantial analysis under prior restraint doctrine.

Note, *Pornography, Padlocks and Prior Restraints, The Constitutional Limits of the Nuisance Power,* 58 N.Y.U. L. Rev. 1478, 1485–89 (1983) (analyzing padlock order and concluding that it "is too blunt an instrument to withstand

First Amendment scrutiny").* *See also* Doug Rendleman, *Civilizing Pornography: The Case for an Exclusive Obscenity Nuisance Statute,* 44 U. Chi. L. Rev. 509 (1977).

4.   To what extent may a bookstore be ordered closed based on past sexual conduct on the premises rather than on the content of what is being sold? In Arcara v. Cloud Books, Inc., 478 U.S. 697, 106 S.Ct. 3172, 92 L.Ed.2d 568 (1986), the United States Supreme Court, 6–3, upheld the use of an injunction to close an adult bookstore where illicit sexual activities were occurring. The injunction issued pursuant to a New York statute that defined places of "lewdness, assignation or prostitution" as "public health nuisances." According to the Court,

> [i]t is true that the closure order in this case would require respondents to move their bookselling business to another location. Yet we have not traditionally subjected every criminal and civil sanction imposed through legal process to "least restrictive means" scrutiny simply because each particular remedy will have some effect on the First Amendment activities of those subject to sanction. Rather, we have subjected such restrictions to scrutiny only where it was conduct with a significant expressive element that drew the legal remedy in the first place, * * * or where a statute based on a nonexpressive activity has the inevitable effect of singling out those engaged in expressive activity, * * *. This case involves neither situation, and we conclude the First Amendment is not implicated by the enforcement of a public health regulation of general application against the physical premises in which respondents happen to sell books.

Id. at 706–07, 106 S.Ct. at 3177, 92 L.Ed.2d 568.

State decisions after *Arcara* have reached similar results. *See, e.g.,* E.W.A.P., Inc. v. City of Los Angeles, 56 Cal.App.4th 310, 65 Cal.Rptr.2d 325 (1997); State *ex rel.* Rear Door Bookstore v. Tenth District Court of Appeal, 63 Ohio St.3d 354, 588 N.E.2d 116 (1992); State *ex rel.* Bowers v. Elida Road Video & Books, Inc. 120 Ohio App.3d 78, 696 N.E.2d 668 (1997); State *ex rel.* Roszmann v. Lions Den, 89 Ohio App.3d 775, 627 N.E.2d 629 (1993). *Contra* People *ex rel.* Arcara v. Cloud Books, Inc., 68 N.Y.2d 553, 510 N.Y.S.2d 844, 503 N.E.2d 492 (1986) (upon remand from Supreme Court in *Arcara*, the New York Court of Appeals held that closure of bookstore violated owner's rights of free expression under the New York constitution).

5.   The public nuisance concept has been used successfully in regulating motorcycle gang annual "swap meets," massage parlors, "health spas," live sexual entertainment, and related activities. Unlike the bookstore or motion picture theatre setting, these cases more clearly involve physical conduct and, consequently, the First Amendment is a somewhat less significant concern. The cases are numerous. *See, e.g.,* People *ex rel.* Hicks v. Sarong Gals, 27 Cal.App.3d 46, 103 Cal.Rptr. 414 (1972) (lewd unclothed dancing); City of Chicago v. Cecola, 75 Ill.2d 423, 27 Ill.Dec. 462, 389 N.E.2d 526 (1979) (masturbatory massage parlor); City of Chicago v. Geraci, 30 Ill.App.3d 699, 332 N.E.2d 487 (1975) ("masturbatory massage parlor"); Commissioner of the Department of Buildings of the City of New York v. Sidne Enterprises, Inc.,

* Reprinted with permission of New York University Law Review.

90 Misc.2d 386, 394 N.Y.S.2d 777 (N.Y.Sup.Ct.1977) (topless and bottomless dancing); State *ex rel.* Montgomery v. Pakrats Motorcycle Club, Inc., 118 Ohio App.3d 458, 693 N.E.2d 310 (1997) (motorcycle club's annual gathering enjoined as public nuisance because of pervasive sexual conduct associated with it). *Contra* City of Revere v. Aucella, 369 Mass. 138, 338 N.E.2d 816 (1975) (nude "go-go" dancing).

CITY OF MILWAUKEE v. BURNETTE

Court of Appeals of Wisconsin, 2001.
248 Wis.2d 820, 637 N.W.2d 447.

FINE, JUDGE.

Michelle Burnette, Yolanda Jenkins, Vivian Nicholson, Theresa Roth, and Patricia Wheeler appeal from a judgment permanently enjoining them from engaging in prostitution-related activities within certain specified areas in the City of Milwaukee; namely:

· Engaging in, beckoning to stop, or engaging male or female passers-by in conversation, or stopping or attempting to stop motor vehicle operators by hailing, waving of arms or any other bodily gesture, or yelling in a loud voice;

· Having or offering to have or requesting to have nonmarital sexual intercourse for anything of value; committing or offering to commit an act of sexual gratification, in public or private, involving the sex organ of one person and the mouth or anus of another for anything of value; masturbating a person or offering to masturbate a person for anything of value; and committing or offering to commit or requesting to commit an act of sexual contact for anything of value;

· Walking off public sidewalks into the City streets to meet occupied motor vehicles to discuss any activity listed [in the immediately preceding bulleted paragraph] or to direct the vehicle operator acting in concert with the [person subject to the injunction] to a destination other than the point of initial contact between the [person subject to the injunction] and the operator such as directing the vehicle off of a high volume traffic street to a more secluded street in which the [person subject to the injunction] walks to the vehicle and then enters the vehicle at the new vehicle location;

· Waiting at bus stops for more than one cycle of busses [*sic*] or waiting at bus stops with no money or bus transfers on their person or standing at pay phones for lengthy periods of time without making an actual telephone call;

· Loitering in doorways of businesses whether open or closed, sitting on the porch or standing anywhere on private residential property without the permission of the property owner or a legal resident of the property;

· Standing, sitting, walking, driving, gathering or appearing anywhere in public view within 25 (twenty-five) feet of any other [person subject to the injunction] engaged in any of the above listed activities.

The injunction was entered by the trial court on an amended complaint filed by the City alleging that the appellants were [over 100] prostitutes and that their prostitution activities in specified areas were a "public nuisance" under Wis. Stat. § 823.02. Section 823.02 authorizes a "city" to bring "[a]n action to enjoin a public nuisance."[1]

The case was decided on summary judgment. * * *

* * *

A.

Summary judgment is used to determine whether there are any disputed facts that require a trial, and, if not, whether a party is entitled to judgment as a matter of law. Wis. Stat. Rule 802.08(2); U.S. Oil Co. v. Midwest Auto Care Servs., Inc., 150 Wis.2d 80, 86, 440 N.W.2d 825, 827 (Ct.App.1989). * * *

Prostitution is illegal in Wisconsin. Wis. Stat. § 944.30. Loitering or soliciting for purposes of prostitution is also illegal. Wis. Stat. § 947.02(3) (declaring that a person is guilty of a Class C Misdemeanor if he or she is "[a] prostitute who loiters on the streets or in a place where intoxicating liquors are sold, or a person who, in public, solicits another to commit a crime against sexual morality"). Injury to the public "in its civil or property rights or privileges or in respect to public health to any degree" constitutes a "public nuisance." State v. H. Samuels Co., 60 Wis.2d 631, 638, 211 N.W.2d 417, 420. Although "equity will not enjoin a crime because it is a crime," the mere fact that acts that injure the public are criminal "does not bar injunctional relief." Id., 60 Wis.2d at 636, 211 N.W.2d at 419.

An injunction may be no more broad than is "equitably necessary." * * * This is similar to the test that is also applied when constitutional rights are implicated: that the injunction may not burden those rights any more "than necessary to accomplish its goal," rather than the "strict scrutiny" test the appellants propose. Madsen v. Women's Health Ctr., Inc., 512 U.S. 753, 764–768, 114 S.Ct. 2516, 129 L.Ed.2d 593 (1994) (speech).

B.

The initial issues presented by this appeal are whether, based on the City's evidentiary submissions that have not been controverted, prostitution activities in the areas encompassed by the permanent injunction sufficiently injure the public to constitute a nuisance, and, if so, whether injunctive relief entered by the trial court was reasonably related to

---

1. The original complaint named seventy-five persons, plus "Jane Doe(s) and John Doe(s)," but not the appellants as defendants.

abatement of the nuisance. If these initial hurdles are cleared, we have to assess whether the injunction entered by the trial court deprived the appellants of their constitutional rights.

As we have seen, there is no dispute in this case:

· that prostitutes frequent the areas encompassed by the permanent injunction;

· that persons living and working in those areas have complained to the police department about the prostitution-related activity, and are, in fact, harmed by that activity;

· that although it is illegal for a person to solicit or commit acts of prostitution, and to loiter on streets for purposes of prostitution, undercover law-enforcement officers face significant hazards in their efforts to gather evidence that persons whom they suspect of engaging in prostitution are, in fact, violating the anti-prostitution laws.

Further, we may take judicial notice of the harm that endemic prostitution activity has on a community. *See* State v. J.C. Penney Co., 48 Wis.2d 125, 155, 179 N.W.2d 641, 657 (1970) (appellate court may take judicial notice of the extent of practice that harms the public) ("widespread use of the revolving charge account and of the large number of Wisconsin citizens affected by these practices"); Wis. Stat. Rule 902.01(3) (court may take judicial notice "whether requested or not"); Wis. Stat. Rule 902.01(6) ("Judicial notice may be taken at any stage of the proceeding.").

Although it is true, as the appellants argue, that the infusion of prostitution in the affected areas can, on one level at least, be addressed by the enforcement of the laws making that and related activity illegal, the difficulties and dangers inherent in that route make injunctive relief appropriate because enforcement of the injunction can be done by police officers in uniform with adequate means of self-protection. Additionally, although the individual appellants are but a small part of the problem, the same is true of all the persons prostituting themselves in the affected areas. A rule that prohibited injunctive relief against a person acting independently but whose independent acts when combined with the independent acts of others created a public nuisance, merely because the person was acting independently, would render this type of public nuisance immune to effective redress. Accordingly, the trial court had the authority to issue an injunction to abate the appellants' role in what the undisputed evidentiary submissions prove is a public nuisance.

C.

We now turn to the appellants' argument that the permanent injunction violates their constitutional rights. They contend that specific parts of the injunction are unconstitutionally vague, that they violate their right of association, that they violate their rights to freedom of speech and assembly, and that they violate their right to freedom of movement in public places. * * *

906   Remedies—Tortious Wrongs   Ch. 6

1. *Vagueness.*

Appellants contend that the parts of the injunction that prohibit loitering in the doorways of the private property of others, that prohibit loitering at bus stops and pay phones, and that impose a twenty-five foot no-intrusion radius from any other person who may be violating any provisions of the injunction are unconstitutionally vague. We agree in part and disagree in part with their contentions.

We have discussed previously the standards that determine whether governmental regulation of conduct is impermissibly vague:

> A law regulating conduct must give adequate notice of what is prohibited, so as not to delegate "basic policy matters to policemen, judges, and juries for resolution on an *ad hoc* and subjective basis."

Grayned v. City of Rockford, 408 U.S. 104, 108–109 (1972). Thus, "a statute which either forbids or requires the doing of an act in terms so vague that men of common intelligence must necessarily guess at its meaning and differ as to its application violates the first essential of due process of law." Connally v. General Constr. Co., 269 U.S. 385, 391 (1926). Although the enactment must have "a reasonable degree of clarity," Roberts v. United States Jaycees, 468 U.S. 609, 629 (1984), exacting precision is not required, *Grayned,* 408 U.S. at 110, unless the enactment infringes rights that are specifically protected by the constitution, such as those of free speech and association protected by the First Amendment, Vill. of Hoffman Estates v. Flipside, Hoffman Estates, Inc., 455 U.S. 489, 499 (1982).

a. *Loitering in doorways.* Contrary to the appellants' contention, there is nothing vague about the injunction's prohibition against "[l]oitering in doorways of businesses whether open or closed, sitting on the porch or standing anywhere on private residential property without the permission of the property owner or a legal resident of the property." The prohibitions are clear and easy to obey. * * *

b. *Loitering at bus stops or pay phones.* Similarly, we reject appellants' argument that the injunction's prohibition against "[w]aiting at bus stops for more than one cycle of busses [*sic*] or waiting at bus stops with no money or bus transfers on their person or standing at pay phones for lengthy periods of time without making an actual telephone call" is impermissibly vague. Although appellants quibble about what "one cycle" of buses means, the prohibition in this portion of the injunction also gives fair notice and is easy to obey.

c. *Twenty-five foot restriction.* Appellants also challenge the provision of the injunction that prohibits them from "[s]tanding, sitting, walking, driving, gathering or appearing anywhere in public view within 25 (twenty-five) feet of any other [person subject to the injunction] engaged in any of the [activities proscribed by the injunction]." We agree that this provision does not give to the appellants fair warning of prohibited conduct. There is nothing in the record that indicates that any of the appellants are sufficiently familiar with all those subject to the injunction so that compliance with this provision would not be a haphazard, guessing adventure. Indeed, Jenkins's affidavit avers that she does "not know more than a few of the defendants to this action." The City does not dispute this. Similarly, Burnette's affidavit avers that she is "afraid of being arrested [for violating the injunction] by talking to someone who may, without my knowledge, be a prostitute." The City also does not dispute this. Burnette additionally avers that she is "also afraid of being arrested for purely legal social and personal conversation with friends who may or may not be defendants in this injunction action." The City does not dispute this either. Accordingly, on remand, the trial court should strike this prohibition from the permanent injunction.

2. *Alleged deprivation of specific constitutional rights.*

Appellants argue that portions of the injunction violate their specific rights to associate with family and friends, their rights to freedom of speech and assembly, and their right to freedom of movement in public places. * * *

a. *Right of association.* There is no doubt but that members of our society have a constitutional right to associate with family and friends without undue restriction. The right of association is generally broken down into two main elements: 1) the right of intimate association, which encompasses such family-type relationships as marriage, cohabitation, and procreation; and 2) the right of expressive association, which includes political-type activity. *Roberts*, 468 U.S. at 617–626, 104 S.Ct. 3244.

Appellants challenge that portion of the injunction that prohibits them from "[e]ngaging in, beckoning to stop, or engaging male or female passersby in conversation." They contend that this restriction would prohibit them from talking to their friends and relatives. We agree that this broad restriction, as phrased, is susceptible to this interpretation. As such, it is broader "than necessary to accomplish its goal" of suppressing prostitution-related activities. * * * Accordingly, on remand, the trial court should modify this aspect of the permanent injunction to ensure that it does not encompass appellants' relatives and friends (that is, persons with whom appellants had social relationships before the activity described by the restriction).

Appellants also challenge the restriction insofar as it applies to strangers as infringing on their right to expressive association. Appellants point to nothing in the record however, that indicates in any way that prohibiting them from approaching strangers on the street prevents them from doing anything other than soliciting for purposes of prostitution; there is *no* evidence in the record that appellants seek to approach and converse with strangers as part of any group effort to accomplish any of the goals protected by the right of expressive association—the "wide variety of political, social, economic, educational, religious, and cultural" activities in which groups engage. *See Roberts*, 468 U.S. at 622, 104 S.Ct. 3244. Thus, this aspect of appellants' challenge is without merit.

b. *Right of free speech.* Appellants challenge those parts of the injunction that prohibit them from "[e]ngaging in, beckoning to stop, or engaging male or female passersby in conversation" and from "stopping or attempting to stop motor vehicle operators by hailing, waving of arms or any other bodily gesture, or yelling in a loud voice" as violating their First Amendment right to free speech. These challenges are without merit. There is no evidence in the record that such actions—insofar as they are directed to strangers—have any purpose *other* than the solicitation for prostitution, which is specifically prohibited by Wis. Stat. §§ 947.02(3) (unlawful for a person to "in public, solicit another to commit a crime against sexual morality") and 944.30(5) (unlawful to either "offer" or "request" another person to commit various sex acts "for anything of value"). Carving away the unlawful speech of soliciting for purposes of prostitution, the prohibition against approaching and talking to strangers is *content neutral,* and, indeed, is not a restriction on speech *qua* speech but rather on *conduct. See* State v. Zwicker, 41 Wis.2d 497, 511–513, 164 N.W.2d 512, 519–520 (1969) (recognizing that conduct may be prohibited even though tinctured with elements of speech) * * *.

Prohibiting persons from attempting to stop cars by waiving and yelling (other than an attempt to get the attention of a taxicab driver—an argument that appellants do not make but, as seen in footnote four, we accommodate), is akin to the law against disorderly conduct, which prohibits "boisterous, unreasonably loud or otherwise disorderly conduct" in "public" places "under circumstances in which the conduct tends to cause or provoke a disturbance," Wis. Stat. § 947.01.[4] The disruptive nature of either stopping or trying to stop drivers (other than those driving taxicabs) "by hailing, waving of arms or any other bodily gesture, or yelling in a loud voice," and the concomitant right of government to prohibit that conduct, validates this aspect of the injunction, especially, as noted, when stripped of the unlawful speech of soliciting for purposes of prostitution, the prohibition is *content neutral. See* Ward v. Rock Against Racism, 491 U.S. 781, 796, 109 S.Ct. 2746, 105 L.Ed.2d 661 (1989) (government has " 'a substantial interest in protecting its citizens from unwelcome noise' ") (quoted source omitted); *Zwicker,* 41 Wis.2d at 512–513, 164 N.W.2d at 519–520; *cf.* Gresham v. Peterson, 225 F.3d 899, 904–906 (7th Cir.2000) (upholding ordinance limiting begging in public places and banning all "aggressive panhandling" despite the recognition that "[b]eggers at times may communicate important political or social messages in their appeals for money, explaining their conditions related to veteran status, homelessness, unemployment and disability, to name a few.") ("The city has a legitimate interest in promoting the safety and convenience of its citizens on public streets.").

---

4. Appellants have not asserted that this portion of the injunction interferes with their ability to hail taxicabs that may be cruising the streets looking for fares. We may, however, as noted in the main body of this opinion, take judicial notice "whether requested or not" of matters that are "generally known within the territorial jurisdiction of the trial court." Wis. Stat. Rule 902.01(2)(a), 902.01(3), & 902.01(6). On remand, the trial court should modify this portion of the injunction to permit the appellants to hail taxicabs licensed pursuant to the authority granted by Wis. Stat. § 349.24.

Subject to footnote four, the restrictions here are no more restrictive "than necessary to accomplish [their] goal" of suppressing prostitution-related activities. *See Madsen*, 512 U.S. at 764–768, 114 S.Ct. 2516.

c. *Right of travel.* Appellants also challenge the restrictions on: attempting to speak to strangers who are either on foot or in cars, being within twenty-five feet of other persons subject to the injunction, and loitering at pay phones or bus stops as abridging their right to travel. We have already indicated that the twenty-five-foot restriction is unconstitutionally vague; accordingly, we do not discuss appellants' alternative argument in connection with that aspect of the injunction. * * *

Orders and judgment and affirmed in part; reversed in part and cause remanded for further proceedings.

NOTE

An attempt by New York City to obtain an injunction against public solicitation by prostitutes met a hostile judicial reception. *See* City of New York v. Andrews, 186 Misc.2d 533, 719 N.Y.S.2d 442 (N.Y.Sup.Ct.2000) (even accepting that prostitution being openly conducted constituted a public nuisance, city was not entitled to an injunction that had the effect of banishing certain prostitutes and pimps from appearing in a certain neighborhood from 11:00 p.m until 7:00 a.m.; such an injunction burdened defendants' freedom to travel more than needed to serve city's interest in suppressing prostitution); *see also* City of St. Louis v. Varahi, Inc., 39 S.W.3d 531 (Mo.Ct.App. 2001) (insufficient evidence existed to show that hotel used by prostitutes was a public nuisance where there was no proof that prostitutes were agents of the hotel; evidence of three arrests inside the hotel over a five-year period and the hotel's reputation as a place frequented by prostitutes "did not support a reasonable inference that the hotel's three-hour rental policy set in motion a chain of events that caused prostitutes to solicit on the streets of the neighborhood.").

IN RE ENGLEBRECHT

California Court of Appeal, Fourth District, 1998.
67 Cal.App.4th 486, 79 Cal.Rptr.2d 89.

HALLER, ASSOCIATE JUSTICE.

In this proceeding, we are asked to decide the constitutionality of two provisions of a preliminary injunction, which prohibit:

—"Standing, sitting, walking, driving, bicycling, gathering or appearing anywhere in public view with any other defendant herein, or with any other known Posole [gang] member" and

—"Using or possessing pagers or beepers in any public place."

* * *

FACTUAL AND PROCEDURAL BACKGROUND

On November 24, 1997, the district attorney filed a complaint for a temporary restraining order and permanent injunction to abate a public nuisance. The complaint alleged that members of the street gang known as Varrio Posole Locos or Posole had created a public nuisance by engaging in illegal activity and terrorizing residents within the Target Area—roughly a one-square mile area in Oceanside commonly referred to as "Eastside." [FN1] The complaint named 28 individuals, including Englebrecht, and 50 Does as defendants.

In alleging the Posole gang members have created a public nuisance, the complaint stated gang members regularly commit violent crimes, such as murders, shootings, assaults and batteries, robberies, and also use and sell illegal drugs within the Target Area. Other nuisance activities include: the playing of loud music, which disturbs the peace and quiet of the Target Area; congregating in large groups, which blocks the free passage of persons and interferes with the free use of property; applying graffiti, which adds to the blight of the Target Area; and repeatedly and continually committing trespass upon private property to conduct their illegal and harassing activities. In short, the complaint alleged:

> Defendants regularly annoy, harass, intimidate, and confront the residents of the Target Area by their activities and cause the residents of the Target Area to fear for their property, their safety and their lives.

On December 11, 1997, the Superior Court issued a preliminary injunction against the defendants.

On February, 13, 1998, Detective Ruben Sandoval of the Oceanside Police Department gang unit saw Englebrecht and his young son standing with Mark Neenan in the front yard of 1408 Lemon Street, which is the residence of Englebrecht's grandmother. The trio walked down the street to Balderama Park.

Neenan is a documented Posole gang member, but was not named in the complaint for the preliminary injunction. Neenan, who was released on parole on February 3, 1998, had spent the past four years in prison.

Sandoval drove to the Balderama Park parking lot. As Englebrecht passed the detective's car, Sandoval warned Englebrecht that if he was with Neenan he was violating the injunction.

Later that afternoon, Detective Dwight Ayers, of the Oceanside Police Department's gang unit, observed Englebrecht, Neenan and Juan Banuelos standing in front of 1408 Lemon Street. Banuelos, a documented Posole 93 gang member, is a named defendant in the complaint for the preliminary injunction and had been served with the restraining order.

Ayers reported his viewing to Sandoval and other officers assembled by Sandoval nearby. The officers drove to Lemon Street, where Englebrecht, Neenan and Banuelos were walking away eastbound in single file. When the three men saw the officers, Neenan ran away, Englebrecht crossed the street toward Balderama Park and Banuelos continued to walk eastbound on Lemon Street. Ayers arrested Englebrecht in Balderama Park; the other two gang members also were arrested.

At the police station, officers found a pager in Englebrecht's possession.

On April 17, 1998, the trial court found Englebrecht in contempt of court for violating two provisions of the preliminary injunction: (1) associating with a known member of the Posole gang within the Target Area in violation of paragraph (a); and (2) possessing a pager within the Target Area in violation of paragraph (n). The trial court sentenced Englebrecht to concurrent five-day terms on each violation and fined him $1,000.

DISCUSSION

I. Use of Civil Injunctions to Enjoin Public Nuisance of Gangs

The use of civil injunctions to abate gang-related problems is a relatively new law enforcement approach that relies on the centuries-old public nuisance law. (People *ex rel.* Gallo v. Acuna (*Acuna*) 14 Cal.4th 1090, 1102–1103, 60 Cal.Rptr.2d 277, 929 P.2d 596; *see generally* Yoo, *The Constitutionality of Enjoining Criminal Street Gangs as Public Nuisances* (1994) 89 Nw.U.L.Rev. 212.) Public nuisance law originated from the ancient maxim " 'sic utere tuo ut alienum non laedes,' " which means "one must so use his rights as not to infringe on the rights of others." (CEEED v. California Coastal Zone Conservation Com. (1974) 43 Cal. App.3d 306, 318, 118 Cal.Rptr. 315.)

As early as 1872, California codified the common law definition of public nuisance in Penal Code section 370: "[a]nything which is injurious to health, or is indecent, or offensive to the senses, or an obstruction to the free use of property, so as to interfere with the comfortable enjoyment of life or property by an entire community or neighborhood...." Civil Code sections 3479 and 3480, also enacted in 1872, have virtually identical definitions. The remedies against a public nuisance are (1) indictment or information, (2) civil action, or (3) abatement. (Civ.Code,§ 3491.) Code of Civil Procedure section 731 authorizes district attorneys and city attorneys to seek enjoinment of public nuisances within their jurisdictions in the name of the people of the State of California.

Either criminal or noncriminal conduct may be abated, but the equitable remedy lies only "where the objectionable activity can be brought within the terms of the statutory definition of public nuisance." (People v. Lim (1941) 18 Cal.2d 872, 879, 118 P.2d 472.) A nuisance must be substantial and unreasonable to qualify as a public nuisance and be enjoinable. * * *

In *Acuna, supra,* the city attorney of San Jose sought a preliminary injunction directed against specific gang members and specific activities in a four-square-block neighborhood. The trial court issued the preliminary injunction enjoining 24 activities by gang members. The Court of Appeal modified the preliminary injunction, upholding only those provisions enjoining criminal conduct. The Supreme Court, at the request of the city attorney, granted review with respect to two of the provisions of the preliminary injunction.

Those provisions enjoined defendants from:

[(a)] "Standing, sitting, walking, driving, gathering or appearing anywhere in public view with any other defendant ... or with any other known 'VST' (Varrio Sureno Town or Varrio Sureno Treces) or 'VSL' (Varrio Sureno Locos) member";

[(k)] "[C]onfronting, intimidating, annoying, harassing, threatening, challenging, provoking, assaulting and/or battering any residents or patrons, or visitors to 'Rocksprings' ... known to have complained about gang activities." (*Acuna, supra,* 14 Cal.4th at pp. 1110, 1118, 60 Cal.Rptr.2d 277, 929 P.2d 596, italics deleted.)

The high court reversed, finding, among other things, the two provisions fell within the superior court's equitable power to abate a public nuisance and passed constitutional muster. (*Acuna, supra,* 14 Cal.4th at p. 1102, 60 Cal.Rptr.2d 277, 929 P.2d 596.)

II. *Non–Association Provision*

Englebrecht contends the non-association provision is unconstitutional because it infringes on the First Amendment right to peaceable assembly and is vague with respect to the use of "known" gang members. In *Acuna, supra,* 14 Cal.4th at pages 1110 to 1112 and 1115 to 1118, 60 Cal.Rptr.2d 277, 929 P.2d 596, our Supreme Court reviewed the same issues regarding the same non-association provision that is before us and concluded there was no constitutional infirmity.

With respect to association, the *Acuna* court noted there were two kinds of associations entitled to First Amendment protection—"those with an 'intrinsic' or 'intimate' value, and those that are 'instrumental' to forms of religious and political expressions and activity." (*Acuna, supra,* 14 Cal.4th at p. 1110, 60 Cal.Rptr.2d 277, 929 P.2d 596.) The *Acuna* court went on to find the street gang did not fit into either category:

It is evident that whatever else it may be in other contexts, the street gang's conduct in Rocksprings at issue in this case fails to qualify as either of the two protected forms of association. Manifestly, in its activities within the four-block area of Rocksprings, the gang is not an association of individuals formed *"for the purpose* of engaging in protected speech or religious activities." * * * Without minimizing the value of the gang to its members as a loosely structured, elective form of social association, that characteristic is in itself insufficient to command constitutional protection, at least within the circumscribed area of Rocksprings. As the court pointed out in Dallas v. Stanglin [1989] 490 U.S. [19] at page 25 [109 S.Ct. 1591, 104 L.Ed.2d 18], "[i]t is possible to find some kernel of expression in almost every activity a person undertakes—for example, walking down the street or meeting one's friends at a shopping mall—but such a kernel is not sufficient to bring the activity within the protection of the First Amendment."

Nor do the circumstances in this case implicate the other associational form worthy of First Amendment protection—personal affiliations whose characteristics include "relative smallness, a high degree of selectivity in decisions to begin and maintain the affiliation, and seclusion from others in critical aspects of the relationship." * * *

Freedom of association, in the sense protected by the First Amendment, "does not extend to joining with others for the purpose of depriving third parties of their lawful rights." * * * We do not, in short, believe that the activities of the gang and its members in Rocksprings at issue here are either "private" or "intimate" as constitutionally defined; the fact that defendants may "exercise *some* discrimination in choosing associates [by a] selective process of inclusion and exclusion" * * * does not mean that the association or its activities in Rocksprings is one that commands protection under the First Amendment. (*Acuna, supra,* 14 Cal.4th at pp. 1111–1112, 60 Cal.Rptr.2d 277, 929 P.2d 596.)

With respect to whether the use of "known" gang members in the non-association provision was impermissibly vague, the *Acuna* court pointed out that when facially vague language is read in context, it may acquire "constitutionally sufficient concreteness" and all that is required is " 'reasonable specificity' " or " '[r]easonable certainty.' " (*Acuna, supra,* 14 Cal.4th at pp.1116–1117, 60 Cal.Rptr.2d 277, 929 P.2d 596.)

Given these guiding principles, the *Acuna* court found, the use of "known" gang members was not void for vagueness * * *.

* * *

Englebrecht urges us to depart from *Acuna* because: (1) the two-square mile Target Area here is significantly greater than the four-block area in *Acuna*; and (2) none of the defendant gang members in *Acuna* lived in the Target Area whereas some of the defendant Posole gang members either live in the Target Area or have relatives who do.

No one disputes that the geographical area of the Target Area here is considerably larger than the Target Area in *Acuna*. However, relative size is not determinative. What matters is whether the Target Area in this case burdened "no more speech than necessary to serve a significant government interest." (Madsen v. Women's Health Center, Inc. (1994) 512 U.S. 753, 765, 114 S.Ct. 2516, 129 L.Ed.2d 593.) The Target Area encompasses "Eastside"—the turf of the Posole gang and the area that the gang has made a public nuisance. Despite its larger size, the Target Area is well defined by distinct boundaries—highways and major streets. The injunction specifically and narrowly describes the Target Area within legal requirements. There has been no showing that the Target Area is larger than it need be to abate the public nuisance. From this record, we can only conclude the size of the Target Area does not make the non-association provision of the preliminary injunction constitutionally infirm—even though it encompasses a much larger area than the Target Area in *Acuna*.

The fact that some of the defendants here live or have relatives in the Target Area is another distinction with *Acuna* that does not make a difference.

Englebrecht misreads the injunction. It does not enjoin him from being in the Target Area; he is free to visit his grandmother and other relatives who reside there. What the injunction prohibits is his association with other Posole gang members within the Target Area. Here, Englebrecht's contempt is based on his walking down the street with Neenan and later with Neenan and Banuelos—both Posole gang members—not relatives. The injunction does not violate Englebrecht's constitutional right of intimate family association.

Englebrecht also misreads the law. The *Acuna* court did indeed hold that the associational rights of the gang members did not merit constitutional protection because the gang activities were neither "intimate" nor "intrinsic." However, the fact that some Posole gang members live or have relatives who live in the Target Area does not transform their gang activities to "intimate" or "intrinsic" associational activities. The gang activities remain non-intimate activities. The familial nexus of some Posole gang members to the Target Area does not bestow constitutional protection on associational gang activity, which is often criminal or terrorizing or both. The familial nexus is not carte blanche for creating a public nuisance.

In sum, the non-association provision of the preliminary injunction is constitutional. *Acuna* is controlling. The factual distinctions between *Acuna* and this case are of no moment.

III. Pager and Beeper Provision

Englebrecht contends the provision enjoining the use and possession of pagers or beepers in the Target Area is unconstitutionally overbroad. We agree.

In today's world of instant and mobile communications, cellular telephones, pagers and beepers are almost becoming ubiquitous; they are important communication devices. In this regard, they are analogous to the telephone, which for much of the twentieth century has been an essential tool for disseminating speech. Regulation of such modes of communication must not run afoul of the First Amendment; any regulation must be narrowly tailored so that it does not proscribe a substantial amount of protected speech. * * *

* * *

The problem with paragraph (n) is that pagers and beepers are not only used for illicit reasons, but have countless lawful, legitimate and everyday uses, both in the personal sense and professionally. For example, pagers and beepers are used to contact workers in the field in numerous businesses and professions, and they enable parents or family members to be readily contacted if the need arises.

These modern communicative devices are, of course, subject to government regulation. However, as long as the devices are not used for illegal purposes, any such regulations must be narrowly tailored so as not to run afoul of the First Amendment.

Because constitutionally protected communications are swept within the ambit of paragraph (n), it is overbroad and infirm. Paragraph (n), as written, goes beyond what the state can properly proscribe. Such an all-encompassing ban on pagers and beepers poses a greater burden on the defendants' right to free speech than is necessary to serve the district attorney's legitimate interest in curtailing illegal gang activity and abating the public nuisance in the Target Area, which the Posole gang has created.

Having found paragraph (n) unconstitutional, we note there was no attempt made below to create a nexus between the use of pagers and beepers and the public nuisance, which the preliminary injunction is intended to abate. There was no attempt to narrow the provision so that it enjoins the use of these devices to abet criminal activities—e.g., to facilitate drug sales or to assist fellow gang members to elude police—the type of conduct that has contributed to the public nuisance.

The trial court is directed to vacate its finding that Englebrecht was in contempt of court for possessing a pager within the Target Area. In all other respects, the petition is denied.

WORK, ACTING P.J., and McINTYRE, J., concur.

NOTES

1. Law enforcement authorities increasingly use the public nuisance injunction as a means of controlling gang activity. As *Englebrecht* illustrates, this not only requires courts to deal with traditional public nuisance questions, but difficult constitutional issues as well. Some jurisdictions, instead, rely on special criminal statutes or ordinances to deal with the gang problem. Consider, in this regard, the following Chicago ordinance, which resulted in over 42,000 arrests during the three years it was in force:

(a) Whenever a police officer observes a person who he reasonably believes to be a criminal street gang member loitering in any public place with one or more other persons, he shall order all such persons to disperse and remove themselves from the area. Any person who does not promptly obey such an order is in violation of this section. * * *

(c)(1) "Loiter" means to remain in any one place with no apparent purpose.

(c)(2) "Criminal street gang" means any ongoing organization, association in fact or group of three or more persons, whether formal or informal, having as one of its substantial activities the commission of one or more of the criminal acts [enumerated elsewhere in the ordinance] and whose members individually or collectively engage in or have engaged in a pattern of criminal gang activity.

Chicago Municipal Code § 8–4–015. The United States Supreme Court, 6–3, struck down this ordinance in City of Chicago v. Morales, 527 U.S. 41, 119 S.Ct. 1849, 144 L.Ed.2d 67 (1999). In the view of a six-justice majority, the ordinance violated the due process clause of the Fourteenth Amendment because it failed to establish minimal guidelines to govern law enforcement:

> As the Illinois Supreme Court interprets that definition [of loitering], it provides "absolute discretion to police officers to determine what activities constitute loitering." * * * We have no authority to construe the language of a state statute more narrowly than the construction given by that State's highest court.

Id. at 61, 119 S.Ct. at 1861.

Moreover, in the opinion of a four-justice plurality, the ordinance was void for vagueness under the Due Process Clause because it failed "to give the ordinary citizen adequate notice of what is forbidden and what is permitted." *Id.*

Is the gang injunction in *Englebrecht* similarly constitutionally defective? Does it make a difference that the injunction is the product of a judicial proceeding? Is it relevant that the defendants in a gang injunction are often named parties who, at least at the preliminary and permanent injunction stages, have a right to an adversary hearing? Does the fact that a gang injunction usually covers a much smaller geographic area than the Chicago ordinance make it less constitutionally objectionable? Does the fact that the gang injunction does not refer to "loitering" make a difference?

2. Res judicata and collateral estoppel can be an issue when injunctive relief is sought by governmental authorities after a not guilty finding or other disposition favorable to the defendant has been entered in a criminal prosecution. As one court has stated, "the fact that a criminal prosecution fails does not mean that an injunction in the civil courts may not be applied for, even where the criminal charge is based on the same alleged violation as is the petition for injunction." City of New Orleans v. Lafon, 61 So.2d 270 (La.Ct. App.1952). This seems to represent the majority approach. For similar holdings, see Blackmon v. Richmond County, 224 Ga. 387, 162 S.E.2d 436 (1968); City of Girard v. Girard Egg Corp., 87 Ill.App.2d 74, 230 N.E.2d 294 (1967); Town of Natick v. Sostilio, 358 Mass. 342, 264 N.E.2d 664 (1970). Res judicata and collateral estoppel concepts normally are inapplicable because the burden of proof is usually heavier on the prosecution in a criminal case and, thus, it is difficult to identify what was decided in the criminal action. *See also* City of Chicago v. Provus, 115 Ill.App.2d 176, 253 N.E.2d 182 (1969) (estoppel by verdict held applicable to prevent a subsequent injunction action because the ordinance prosecution was considered civil and not criminal).

A related argument is that to permit the injunction action after a prior not guilty determination constitutes unconstitutional double jeopardy because, if a defendant violates the injunction, he or she could then be charged with contempt and be punished for the same offense that was the basis for the criminal acquittal. Normally this contention will fail because the criminal and the injunction proceedings are considered separate offenses. *See, e.g.,* City of New Orleans v. Lafon, 61 So.2d 270 (La.Ct.App.1952).

3. As the foregoing material indicates, the injunction has been the traditional government remedy against the public nuisance. During the past decade, however, government officials and agencies have increasingly sued to recoup the cost to government of remedying the externalities caused by harms that they have attempted to characterize as public nuisances. The following New Jersey Supreme Court is emblematic of this type of litigation

IN RE LEAD PAINT LITIGATION

Supreme Court of New Jersey, 2007.
191 N.J. 405, 924 A.2d 484.

JUSTICE HOENS delivered the opinion of the Court.

In these consolidated complaints, twenty-six municipalities and counties seek to recover, from manufacturers and distributors of lead paints, the costs of detecting and removing lead paint from homes and buildings, of providing medical care to residents affected with lead poisoning, and of developing programs to educate residents about the dangers of lead paint. Although the complaints initially sought recovery through a wide variety of legal theories, we are called upon to consider only whether these plaintiffs have stated a cognizable claim based on the common law tort of public nuisance. Because we conclude that plaintiffs cannot state a claim consistent with the well-recognized parameters of that tort, and because we further conclude that to find otherwise would be directly contrary to legislative pronouncements governing both lead paint abatement programs and products liability claims, we reverse the judgment of the Appellate Division and remand for dismissal of the complaints.

* * *

II.

* * *

A.

Lead is a naturally occurring metal. Centers for Disease Control and Prevention (CDC), *Third National Report on Human Exposure to Environmental Chemicals* 38 (2005). For many years, lead has been used for a wide variety of purposes and has found numerous applications, including use in batteries, paints, glassware, and plastics. *Ibid.*

Lead, however, has also been linked to serious health effects. The most recent annual report prepared by the New Jersey Department of Health and Senior Services (DHSS) describes lead paint and the risk it poses as follows:

When absorbed into the human body, lead affects the blood, kidneys and nervous system. Lead's effects on the nervous system are particularly serious and can cause learning disabilities, hyperactivity, decreased hearing, mental retardation and possible death. Lead is particularly hazardous to children between six months and six years of age because their neurological system and organs are still developing.

[*Childhood Lead Poisoning in New Jersey: Annual Report* 4 (2005) [hereinafter *Annual Report*].]

In addition, according to the United States Department of Health and Human Services, children tend to absorb lead more readily than do adults, because most lead ingested by adults is excreted, while children typically only excrete about one-third of the lead they ingest. *See* Agency for Toxic Substances & Disease Registry, *Draft Toxicological Profile for Lead* 8 (2005). * * *

B.

Congress first addressed the nationwide problem of lead paint exposure in 1971 through the passage of the Lead-based Paint Poisoning Prevention Act (LPPPA), Pub.L. No. 91–695, 84 Stat.2078 (1971) (formerly codified at 42 *U.S.C.A.* §§ 4801 to 4846 (1971)). Initially, the LPPPA authorized a series of grants to discover the extent of the effects of lead exposure in children. *See ibid.; see also Ashton v. Pierce,* 716 *F.*2d 56, 58 (D.C.Cir.1983). At the same time, Congress authorized the HUD Secretary to promulgate regulations to eliminate the harms of lead-based paint from federally-owned or-funded housing. *See Ashton, supra,* 716 *F.*2d at 58–59. Through amendments to the LPPPA, and through promulgating increasingly strict regulations, by the late 1970s, the federal government had effectively banned the general use or sale of paint containing lead and was moving "to eliminate as far as practicable" the existing hazards in federal housing. *Ibid.*

Thereafter, the LPPPA was further expanded and supplemented, including through the 1992 passage of the Residential Lead-based Paint Hazard Reduction Act (RLPHRA), Pub.L. No. 102–550, 106 Stat. 3897 (1992) (codified at 42 *U.S.C.A.* §§ 4851 to 4856 (1992)). That Act sought to address the continuing problem of deteriorating lead paint in residential units throughout the country. *See* 42 *U.S.C.A.* § 4851(6). As a part of its legislative findings, Congress recognized that federal assistance to create an appropriate infrastructure was still required. *See* 42 *U.S.C.A.* § 4851(8). The RLPHRA therefore created a system of grants for the purpose of educating the public, identifying housing with lead contamination, and remediating the hazard in certain target housing. *See* 42 *U.S.C.A.* § 4852(e). * * *

C.

New Jersey also responded to the problem posed by lead paint through the 1971 enactment of legislation known as the Lead Paint Act. *See L.* 1971, *c.* 366 (originally codified at *N.J.S.A.* 24:14A–1 to–12). The sponsor of the bill that eventually became the Lead Paint Act described the purposes of the Act and the concerns that motivated its passage as follows:

* * *

This bill is designed to set up a comprehensive program both at the State and local level to eliminate the causes of lead poisoning in New Jersey, to treat the incidents thereof, and to enable both State and local government units to take advantage of Federal funding for such programs.

[*Statement to Senate Bill No. 998,* at 3 (Dec. 10, 1970).]

As initially enacted, the Lead Paint Act prohibited anyone from "knowingly apply[ing] lead paint to toys, furniture, or the exposed interior surfaces of any dwelling ... or facility occupied ... by children." *L.* 1971, c. 366, § 1 (codified at *N.J.S.A.* 24:14A–1). The Act made violations a disorderly persons offense. *See id.* at § 3 (codified at *N.J.S.A.* 24:14A–3). In addition, the Act included a provision that declared the "presence of lead paint upon the interior of any dwelling causing a hazard to the occupant ... to be a public nuisance," *id.* at § 5 (codified at *N.J.S.A.* 24:14A–5), and vested "primary responsibility" for investigating and enforcing the Act in local boards of health, *id.* at § 6 (codified at *N.J.S.A.* 24:14A–6).

* * *

The statute was amended in 1976, essentially for the purpose of extending its reach to encompass "any facility occupied or used by children" by expanding the definition of "dwelling." *L.* 1976, c. 116, § 3 (codified at *N.J.S.A.* 24:14A–4d). This amendment was largely based on our Legislature's effort to ensure that lead paint in buildings being used as "nursery schools, day care centers and similar facilities" was included within the enforcement provisions of the Act. Senate Law, Public Safety and Defense Committee, *Statement to Senate Bill No. 152* (Apr. 23, 1976).

In 1985, the Legislature, through the Lead Poisoning Abatement and Control Act, amended the Lead Paint Act to expand the directives to the State Department of Health that were formerly included in Section 12. *See L.* 1985, c. 84, § 10. In short, the Legislature repealed the general directive relating to creation of a lead poisoning program and enacted a far more detailed program to be established by the Department of Health. *See L.* 1985, c. 84 (codified at *N.J.S.A.* 26:2–130 to–137). As part of this enactment, the Legislature appropriated funds to assist the Department of Health in fulfilling its mandate, *see id.* at § 9, and directed the Commissioner of Health to "prepare a comprehensive plan to control lead poisoning" no later than September 25, 1985, *see id.* at § 5 (codified at *N.J.S.A.* 26:2–134).* * *

In 1995, the Legislature again addressed the lead poisoning problem. Concluding that screening of pre-school children for lead poisoning was essential and that identifying the children at risk was necessary, the

Legislature created a "universal lead screening program." *L.* 1995, *c.* 328 (codified at *N.J.S.A.* 26:2–137.2 to–137.7). Although the program was to be implemented and overseen by the Department of Health, primary responsibility for testing was placed on physicians, registered professional nurses, and health care facilities, with a directive to the Department of Health to attempt to maximize available federal funding to defray the costs. * * *.

Finally, in 2003, the Legislature enacted the Lead Hazard Control Assistance Act (LHCAA), *L.* 2003, *c.* 311 (codified at *N.J.S.A.* 52:27D–437.1 to–437.15). The LHCAA provided for further assistance in lead paint remediation through the creation of the Lead Hazard Control Assistance Fund and the Emergency Lead Poisoning Relocation Fund. *See id.* at §§ 4, 9 (codified at *N.J.S.A.* 52:27D–437.4,–437.9). These low-cost loan and grant programs, together with the creation of a registry of lead-safe housing, *see id.* at § 7 (codified at *N.J.S.A.* 52:27D–437.7), not only provided homeowners and owners of certain multi-family dwellings with financial assistance for abatement of existing lead in those premises, but created a database from which lead-safe housing could be identified. At the same time, the LHCAA required that all dwellings subject to inspections pursuant to *N.J.S.A.* 55:13A–13—with the exception of dwellings constructed during or after 1978, seasonal rental units, and owner-occupied dwellings—be inspected for "lead hazard control work." *Id.* at §§ 10, 12 (codified at *N.J.S.A.* 52:27D–437.10,–437.12). It also required the fees charged for these inspections, as well as a portion of the taxes collected from sales of paint and similar materials, to be dedicated to the fund created by the LHCAA.* * *

As this explanation of the several statutes demonstrates, the Legislature separated the statutory scheme for the abatement of lead paint in buildings from the programs devoted to the health care aspects of lead exposure and lead poisoning. Funding sources for addressing the health concerns arising from lead exposure are now both many and varied. In addition to Department of Health grants to local health departments, our Legislature has enacted statutes requiring health maintenance organizations, hospital services corporations, and insurers to provide for, or to cover the costs of, blood lead screening and resulting medical evaluation and treatment for lead-related disorders. * * *

In contrast, under the Lead Paint Act, responsibility for the costs of abatement rests largely on the property owners. Indeed, that statute specifically empowers local boards of health to sue owners to recover abatement costs. Although the LHCAA, the most recent of these statutes, provides for grants and low-cost loans to certain property owners, eligibility is limited, with the result that owners still bear much of the cost burden. Notably, the Legislature specifically directed that these programs be funded through increased inspection fees paid by owners and by a portion of the sales taxes attributable to currently-available paint products.

It is only in light of this statutory framework that the arguments of the parties concerning the viability of a cause of action sounding in public nuisance can be evaluated. We turn, then, to an examination of the elements of that common law tort and to its relationship to this statutory framework.

III.

* * *

A.

The common law tort of public nuisance, which one commentator has described as being "vaguely defined" and "poorly understood," Donald G. Gifford, *Public Nuisance as a Mass Products Liability Tort*, 71 *U. Cin. L.Rev.* 741, 774 (2003), can be traced back for centuries, *see id.* at 790–806. By carefully examining the historical antecedents of public nuisance and by tracing its development through the centuries, clear and consistent parameters that define it as a cognizable theory of tort law become apparent. Through our use of this analytical methodology, however, we can only conclude that plaintiffs' loosely-articulated assertions here cannot find their basis in this tort. Rather, were we to permit these complaints to proceed, we would stretch the concept of public nuisance far beyond recognition and would create a new and entirely unbounded tort antithetical to the meaning and inherent theoretical limitations of the tort of public nuisance.

Even more notable, however, is the fact that, unlike plaintiffs' complaints, our Legislature's use of the term "public nuisance" in the Lead Paint Act is in keeping with the term's historical meaning and intent. As a consequence, were we to agree with the Appellate Division that there is a basis sounding in public nuisance for plaintiffs' assertions, we would be creating a remedy entirely at odds with the pronouncements of our Legislature.

B.

* * * Originally, public nuisance was created as a criminal offense, *see* William L. Prosser, *Private Actions for Public Nuisance*, 52 *Va. L.Rev.* 997, 999 (1966), which was used to allow public officials, acting in the place of the sovereign, to prosecute individuals or require abatement of activities considered to be harmful to the public, *see* Gifford, *supra*, 71 *U. Cin. L.Rev.* at 745–46. As the commentary to the *Restatement (Second) of Torts* notes, the historical focus of public nuisance prosecutions included attacking such behaviors as "keeping diseased animals or the maintenance of a pond breeding malarial mosquitoes [,] . . . storage of explosives[,] . . . [operating] houses of prostitution [,] . . . [causing] loud and disturbing noises[,] . . . disseminat[ing] bad odors, dust and smoke[,] . . . [and] obstruction of a public highway or a navigable stream." *Restatement (Second) of Torts* § 821B comment b (1979).

Essential to the concept of public nuisance, as illustrated by these historical examples, is the "interference with the interests of the community at large." *Ibid.* In modern times, the criminal prosecution for such activities has been subsumed within a wide variety of statutes, and we no longer recognize the existence of a common law crime of public nuisance. *See N.J.S.A.* 2C:1–5(a) (abolishing common law crimes in favor of statutory enactments); *see also Restatement (Second) of Torts* § 821B comment c (1979) (noting elimination of common law crimes). Nevertheless, a common law tort remedy to redress public nuisance has been recognized in light of the fact that these same activities might also give rise to tort-based recoveries. * * *

Notwithstanding that development, the essential elements of public nuisance as a theory of tort recovery find their genesis in this historical basis in crime and criminal prosecution. *See* Gifford, *supra,* 71 *U. Cin. L.Rev.* at 781. This is not to suggest that the existence of a common law tort remedy sounding in public nuisance is a particularly modern development. Indeed, in spite of the suggestion of at least one commentator that the first formalized appearance of the tort of public nuisance, distinct from its criminal concepts, is found in the *Restatement (Second) of Torts, see id.* at 807–08, it appears that the concept of a common law tort of public nuisance can also be traced back to English common law, albeit of somewhat more recent vintage, *see* Denise E. Antolini, *Modernizing Public Nuisance: Solving the Paradox of the Special Injury Rule,* 28 *Ecology L.Q.* 755, 796–800 (2001) (tracing English common law precedents of tort of public nuisance). Rather, our recognition of the nuisance concept's historical antecedents in criminal law gives us the context for our understanding of the meaning of the more modern tort principles.

Equally essential to the concept of a public nuisance tort, however, is the fact that it has historically been linked to the use of land by the one creating the nuisance. *See* Gifford, *supra,* 71 *U. Cin. L.Rev.* at 831–33. The link to land may arise either because the nuisance is on that person's land, as in a mosquito pond, or because an activity conducted on that land interferes with a right of the general public, as in a stream-polluting business. *See id.* at 832 (explaining that public nuisance claim may arise because of defendant's use of land or because "the defendant has interfered with the plaintiff's use and enjoyment of public land."). In either case, public nuisance has historically been tied to conduct on one's own land or property as it affects the rights of the general public. This is not to say that the focus for public nuisance, like private nuisance, involves an interference by defendant with a particular plaintiff's use and enjoyment of his own land. *See Restatement (Second) of Torts* § 821B comment h (1979). Rather, the nuisance, traditionally arising on the defendant's land, must instead involve an interference with a public right. *See id.* at § 821B comment g.

C.

Our modern concepts of public nuisance are set forth in the *Restatement (Second) of Torts.* There, public nuisance is defined, *see id.* at

§ 821B; the persons or entities permitted to recover for a public nuisance, either to collect damages or to prosecute an abatement action, are specifically indicated, *see id.* at § 821C; public nuisance is distinguished from private nuisance, *see id.* at § 821D; and those who may recover for private nuisance are identified, *see id.* at § 821E, separately from those who may sue, as private plaintiffs, for a public nuisance, *see id.* at § 821C. Because much of the debate in this matter arises from confusion about the essential elements of the tort of public nuisance, and the basis for any cause of action arising from public nuisance, we address these concepts as they have developed.

Scholars familiar with the development of the *Restatement (Second)*, and with the adoption of the sections relating to public nuisance in particular, point to the influence of individuals and entities seeking an avenue for redress of environmental pollution in the development of those sections, which were not found in the first *Restatement. See* Antolini, *supra*, 28 *Ecology L.Q.* at 829–49; Victor E. Schwartz & Phil Goldberg, *The Law of Public Nuisance: Maintaining Rational Boundaries on a Rational Tort*, 45 *Washburn L.J.* 541, 547–48 (2006). Although now largely subsumed in statutory pronouncements, environmental tort litigation had its origins in concepts of public nuisance, and its influence in the language adopted in the *Restatement (Second)* is in part a reflection of early environmentalists' hopes of creating means to ensure broad-based avenues for pollution control. * * *

While the influence of those concerned about tort-based grounds on which to pursue polluters played a role in the creation of the public nuisance sections of the *Restatement (Second)*, the definitional language nonetheless continues to adhere to the traditional notion that the tort of public nuisance fundamentally involves the vindication of a right common to the public. The *Restatement (Second)* defines a public nuisance as follows:

(1) A public nuisance is an unreasonable interference with a right common to the general public.

(2) Circumstances that may sustain a holding that an interference with a public right is unreasonable include the following:

(a) Whether the conduct involves a significant interference with the public health, the public safety, the public peace, the public comfort or the public convenience, or

(b) whether the conduct is proscribed by a statute, ordinance or administrative regulation, or

(c) whether the conduct is of a continuing nature or has produced a permanent or long-lasting effect, and, as the actor knows or has reason to know, has a significant effect upon the public right.

[*Restatement (Second) of Torts* § 821B (1979).]

Although it might appear that the tort is expressed in rather general terms, those terms are not without meaning. In particular, the right with which the actor has interfered must be a public right, in the sense of a right "common to all members of the general public," rather than a right merely enjoyed by a number, even a large number, of people. *Id.* at § 821B comment g.

In explaining the difference between an interference with a common right and an interference with a right merely enjoyed by a large number of people, the *Restatement (Second)* provides the following example:

> A public right is one common to all members of the general public. It is collective in nature and not like the individual right that everyone has not to be assaulted or defamed or defrauded or negligently injured. Thus the pollution of a stream that merely deprives fifty or a hundred lower riparian owners of the use of the water for purposes connected with their land does not for that reason alone become a public nuisance. If, however, the pollution prevents the use of a public bathing beach or kills the fish in a navigable stream and so deprives all members of the community of the right to fish, it becomes a public nuisance.

[*Ibid.*]

* * *

Second, however, and to some extent of more interest to the commentators, has been the distinction between public and private rights of action arising from public nuisance. These distinctions are explained in Section 821C of the *Restatement (Second)* as follows:

Who Can Recover for Public Nuisance

> (1) In order to recover damages in an individual action for a public nuisance, one must have suffered harm of a kind different from that suffered by other members of the public exercising the right common to the general public that was the subject of interference.

> (2) In order to maintain a proceeding to enjoin to abate a public nuisance, one must

>> a) have the right to recover damages, as indicated in Subsection (1), or

>> (b) have authority as a public official or public agency to represent the state or a political subdivision in the matter, or

>> (c) have standing to sue as a representative of the general public, as a citizen in a citizen's action or as a member of a class in a class action.

[*Id.* at § 821C.]

As this section illustrates, there is a distinction between suits for damages and proceedings for the injunctive remedy of abatement.* * *. The only basis for a money damage remedy arises in the context of a private action for public nuisance.

In considering who may sue to collect damages, by way of a private action for public nuisance, the focus of the scholars has been upon the *Restatement (Second)'s* continued adherence to the special injury rule. *See* Antolini, *supra,* 28 *Ecology L.Q.* at 844–54. Accordingly, a private plaintiff can sue for damages caused by the public nuisance only if the private plaintiff has "suffered harm of a kind different from that suffered by other members of the public." *Restatement (Second) of Torts* § 821C(1) (1979).

Although this Court has not considered the parameters of the tort of public nuisance in light of the *Restatement (Second)'s* formulation, we have previously adhered strictly to the requirement that a private plaintiff proceeding on a public nuisance theory demonstrate special injury. *See Poulos v. Dover Boiler & Plate Fabricators,* 5 *N.J.* 580, 587–89, 76 A.2d 808 (1950) (dismissing public nuisance complaint of property owner whose only claim was of greater inconvenience than that suffered by other members of the public). Similarly, in published decisions, our trial and appellate courts have followed this traditional interpretation. * * *

Under the *Restatement (Second)'s* formulation, if a private plaintiff has a right to sue for damages because of a harm different in kind, then that party may also pursue an action to abate the nuisance as it affects all members of the public. *See Restatement (Second) of Torts* § 821C(2)(a) (1979). Conversely, however, the public entity, as the modern representative of the sovereign in public nuisance litigation, has only the right to abate. *See id.* at § 821C(2)(b). Although historically that has included the right to visit upon the owner of the land from which the public nuisance emanates, the obligations, including the costs, of the abatement, * * * there is no right either historically, or through the *Restatement (Second)'s* formulation, for the public entity to seek to collect money damages in general, *see Restatement (Second) of Torts* § 821C(1) (1979). Rather, there is only a private plaintiff's right to recover damages through an action arising from a special injury. *See ibid.*

The significance, then, of the evolution of public nuisance law is threefold. First, a public nuisance, by definition, is related to conduct, performed in a location within the actor's control, which has an adverse effect on a common right. Second, a private party who has suffered special injury may seek to recover damages to the extent of the special injury and, by extension, may also seek to abate. Third, a public entity which proceeds against the one in control of the nuisance may only seek to abate, at the expense of the one in control of the nuisance. * * *

IV.

Before we can accurately decide whether these complaints state a claim sounding in public nuisance, we must consider the implication of the Legislature's use of that term in the Lead Paint Act. Plaintiffs suggest, and the appellate panel agreed, that the Legislature's inclusion of a declaration of public nuisance in that statute supports the conclusion that plaintiffs therefore have a right to proceed in tort on that theory. * * *

A.

We therefore consider what the Legislature intended when it declared in the Lead Paint Act that the presence of lead paint in buildings is a public nuisance. *See N.J.S.A.* 24:14A–5,–8. * * *. In light of the fact that public nuisance is itself a common law tort, we must decide whether the Legislature intended to refer to that tort or, as plaintiffs suggest, intended to use the term in some general, ill-defined, or colloquial meaning of the words "public nuisance."

We conclude that the Legislature's use of the term "public nuisance" can only have been intended in its strict historical sense. In general, technical terms, terms of art, and terms with existing legal meanings, "[i]n the absence of legislative intent to the contrary, or other overriding evidence of a different meaning" are understood to have been used in accordance with those meanings. 2A Norman J. Singer, *Sutherland Statutory Construction* §§ 47:29, 47:30 (6th ed.2000); *N.J.S.A.* 1:1–1 (declaring that "words having a special or accepted meaning in the law, shall be construed in accordance with [that] ... meaning."). The statute itself demonstrates faithfulness to the traditional meaning of public nuisance.

Central to our analysis of the Act in this regard are three fundamental aspects of the statute in terms of the common law meaning of public nuisance. First, the Legislature, in making the declaration of a public nuisance, attached to the activity so identified a criminal penalty, declaring that the use of lead paint would be a disorderly persons offense. *See N.J.S.A.* 24:14A–3. Second, the Legislature, in addressing the problem of lead paint, directed local boards of health to effect an abatement of the nuisance. *See N.J.S.A.* 24:14A–9. Finally, the Legislature, as a part of that remedy, directed that the owners of the premises where the public nuisance is found would be liable for the costs of the abatement. *See N.J.S.A.* 24:14A–7,–8,–9. In each of these respects, the Legislature addressed the lead paint problem in a manner completely in accord with our historical notions of public nuisance. By attaching a criminal penalty, by ordering an abatement through a public entity, and by maintaining a focus on the owner of premises as the actor responsible for the public nuisance itself, the Legislature's approach remained tethered to the historical bases that have defined public nuisance dating back centuries. * * *

Although our analysis of the Lead Paint Act and our Legislature's declaration of public nuisance does not suggest that the Legislature intended to create a public nuisance right of action more general than the one specified in the statute, we nonetheless must consider whether the appellate panel correctly concluded that these plaintiffs have stated a claim which was "complementary" and "parallel" to that legislative scheme. * * *

C.

[W]e find no ground for recognizing a public nuisance cause of action in plaintiffs' complaints. Assuming, based on the legislative declaration in the Lead Paint Act, that the continuing presence of lead paint in homes qualifies as an interference with a common right sufficient to constitute a public nuisance for tort purposes, plaintiffs' complaints fail nonetheless. Unlike the Legislature's adherence to traditional public nuisance motions, plaintiffs' complaints aim wide of the limits of that theory.

In examining the Lead Paint Act and its relationship to public nuisance generally, we find its focus on owners as the relevant actors to be instructive. The significance is that the presence of lead paint in buildings is only a hazard if it is deteriorating, flaking, or otherwise disturbed, and if it therefore can be ingested either directly or indirectly by being eaten, inhaled, or absorbed through the soil. Viewed in this light, we must conclude that the Legislature, consistent with traditional public nuisance concepts, recognized that the appropriate target of the abatement and enforcement scheme must be the premises owner whose conduct has, effectively, created the nuisance. In public nuisance terms, it is the premises owner who has engaged in the "conduct [that] involves a significant interference with the public health," *id.* at § 821B(2)(a), and therefore is subject to an abatement action. * * *

Contrary, however, to the Legislature's recognition of the required focus on conduct of the relevant actor, plaintiffs seek to base their complaints on conduct of another. * * * Although one might argue that the product, now in its deteriorated state, interferes with the public health, one cannot also argue persuasively that the conduct of defendants in distributing it, at the time when they did, bears the necessary link to the current health crisis. Absent that link, the claims of plaintiffs cannot sound in public nuisance. Indeed, the suggestion that plaintiffs can proceed against these defendants on a public nuisance theory would stretch the theory to the point of creating strict liability to be imposed on manufacturers of ordinary consumer products which, although legal when sold, and although sold no more recently than a quarter of a century ago, have become dangerous through deterioration and poor maintenance by the purchasers.

D.

Even were we to conclude that the distribution of lead-based paint products constituted actionable conduct for purposes of permitting a tort-based recovery, we would nonetheless reject plaintiffs' complaints. As our explanation of public nuisance has made plain, the remedies available traditionally vary as between public and private plaintiffs. A public entity proceeding in public nuisance vindicates the common right and thus pursues either criminal penalties or civil actions to abate the nuisance at the property owner's expense. *See Restatement (Second) of Torts* § 821C(2) comment a (1979). A private plaintiff, on the other hand, does not necessarily sue to vindicate a public right, but seeks recompense for damages to the extent of the special injury sustained, apart from the interference with the public right. *See id.* at § 821C(1). The damage award, however, is limited to the extent of the special injury sustained by the private plaintiff, and is not a remedy available to a public entity plaintiff to the extent that it acts in the place of the "sovereign." *See id.* at § 821C(2)(b).

Applying these time-honored principles to plaintiffs leads inevitably to the conclusion that these complaints do not state a claim in public nuisance. * * * [T]he complaints seek damages rather than remedies of abatement. As such, they fall outside the scope of remedies available to a public entity plaintiff. *See id.* at § 821C comment j. That being the case, these plaintiffs may only proceed in the manner of private plaintiffs. *See ibid.* Assuming that is permissible, they must, therefore, identify a special injury as to which an award of money damages may attach.

Plaintiffs, however, have not, and cannot, identify any special injury. Rather, all of the injuries plaintiffs have identified are general to the public at large. As we have seen, special injury has a specific and well-defined meaning in public nuisance jurisprudence. It must be an injury different in kind, rather than in degree. *See id.* at § 821C comment b; *Poulos, supra,* 5 *N.J.* at 586–87, 76 *A.*2d 808; *Baird, supra,* 110 *N.J. Eq.* at 605, 160 *A.* 537; *Mosig, supra,* 122 *N.J. Eq.* at 386, 194 *A.* 248. Because plaintiffs have confused private rights of action with public prosecutions, they have argued that they need not identify a special injury. At the same time, however, the only basis for damages that plaintiffs have identified are those directly arising from the common right. Those damages are inadequate to support a claim sounding in public nuisance.

V.

Our analysis of both traditional and modern concepts of the tort of public nuisance demonstrates that plaintiffs' complaints cannot be understood to state such a claim. Equally supportive of that conclusion, however, is the inescapable fact that carefully read, the claims asserted would instead be cognizable only as products liability claims. [The court then analyzed the New Jersey Product Liability Act (PLA)]. We conclude, therefore, that the claim here sounds in products liability * * *.

* * *

Indeed, were we to recognize plaintiffs' right to pursue these manufacturers, we would create a cause of action entirely inconsistent with the PLA's comprehensive legislative scheme.

VI.

Our Legislature, in recognizing the scope and seriousness of the adverse health effects caused by exposure to and ingestion of deteriorated lead paint, acted swiftly to address that public health crisis. Its careful and comprehensive scheme did so in conformity with traditional concepts of common law public nuisance. Nothing in its pronouncements suggests it intended to vest the public entities with a general tort-based remedy or that it meant to create an ill-defined claim that would essentially take the place of its own enforcement, abatement, and public health funding scheme. Even less support exists for the notion that the Legislature intended to permit these plaintiffs to supplant an ordinary product liability claim with a separate cause of action as to which there are apparently no bounds. We cannot help but agree with the observation that, were we to find a cause of action here, "nuisance law 'would become a monster that would devour in one gulp the entire law of tort.'" *Camden County Bd. of Chosen Freeholders v. Beretta, U.S.A. Corp.,* 273 F.3d 536, 540 (3d Cir.2001) (quoting *Tioga Pub. Sch. Dist. v. U.S. Gypsum Co.,* 984 F.2d 915, 921 (8th Cir.1993)). Although there may be room, in other circumstances, for an expanded definition of the tort of public nuisance, we find no basis in this record to conclude that these plaintiffs have stated such a claim. * * *

VII.

We reverse the judgment of the Appellate Division and remand this matter to the Law Division for entry of a judgment in favor of defendants.

[The dissenting opinion of CHIEF JUSTICE ZAZZALI, is omitted—Eds.]

NOTE

Public nuisance damage actions against lead paint manufacturers have also been rejected by appellate courts in Missouri and Rhode Island See City of St. Louis v. Benjamin Moore & Co., 226 S.W.3d 110 (Mo.2007); State v. Lead Indus. Ass'n, 951 A.2d 428 (R.I. 2008); City of Milwaukee v. NL Industries, 762 N.W.2d 757 (Wis.App.2008). For a thoughtful analysis of the foregoing cases as well as public nuisance litigation against asbestos and gun manufacturers, see Peter Tipps, *Controlling the Lead Paint Debate: Why Control is Not An Element of Public Nuisance,* 50 B.C.L.Rev. 605 (2009).

NOTE: DOES SPECIFIC STATUTORY AUTHORIZATION OF INJUNCTIVE RELIEF OPERATE TO BAR OTHER EQUITABLE REMEDIES?

Now let us shift our focus from public nuisance litigation to a related question. The past century has witnessed the creation of the regulatory state. Countless federal and state statutes specifically authorize courts to grant injunctions against a wide variety of wrongs. Where such authorization exists, but the statute is silent concerning other equitable remedies, did the legislature intend to preclude the grant of such other equitable relief? This issue frequently arises in the context of the federal Food, Drug and Cosmetic Act (FDCA) which, among other things, prohibits the sale of unapproved or misbranded new drugs. The FDCA provides only three remedies for violations: (1) injunctive relief; (2) criminal prosecution; and (3) seizure. *See* 21 U.S.C.A. §§ 332–334. The unresolved question is whether a court may order restitution (recall of the drug) or disgorgement of the defendant's profits. Consider how the United States Court of Appeals for the Sixth Circuit resolved this question:

> Restitution and disgorgement are part of courts' traditional equitable authority. * * *

Absent a clear command by Congress that a statute providing for equitable relief excludes certain forms of such relief, this court will presume the full scope of equitable powers may be exercised by the courts. In Porter v. Warner Holding Co., 328 U.S. 395, 66 S.Ct. 1086, 90 L.Ed. 1332 (1946) (in analyzing Emergency Price Control Act of 1942), the Supreme Court established that "[u]nless otherwise provided by statute, all the inherent equitable powers of the District Court are available for the proper and complete exercise of that jurisdiction." *Id.* at 398, 66 S.Ct. 1086. *Porter* held that restitution "is within the recognized power and within the highest tradition of a court of equity." *Id.* at 402, 66 S.Ct. 1086. * * *

* * *

A contrary standard upon which Appellants rely, that the statute must explicitly authorize restitution, was accepted by the Ninth Circuit in United States v. Parkinson, 240 F.2d 918 (9th Cir.1956). This approach, however, was rejected by the U.S. Supreme Court in Mitchell v. Robert DeMario Jewelry, Inc., 361 U.S. 288, 290–92, 80 S.Ct. 332, 4 L.Ed.2d 323 (1960) (interpreting Fair Labor Standards Act). *DeMario* held the following:

> The court below took as the touchstone for decision the principle that to be upheld the jurisdiction here contested "must be expressly conferred by an act of Congress or be necessarily implied from a congressional enactment." In this, the court was mistaken. The proper criterion is that laid down in Porter v. Warner Holding Co.... When Congress entrusts to an equity court the enforcement of prohibitions contained in a regulatory enactment, it must be taken to have acted cognizant of the historic power of equity to provide complete relief in light of statutory purposes.

DeMario, 361 U.S. at 290–92, 80 S.Ct. 332 (citation omitted).The citation in *DeMario* to *Porter*, as well as this circuit's acceptance of the *Porter* approach * * *, illustrates that Appellants' argument should be rejected. Notably, the *DeMario* Court also recognized that a district court's equitable powers are even broader and more flexible when the public interest is involved, as here. * * *

Appellants also rely on a number of district court cases that determine that recalls and disgorgement are unavailable under the FDCA. *See* United States v. C.E.B. Prods., Inc., 380 F.Supp. 664 (N.D.Ill.1974) (recalls); United States v. Superpharm Corp., 530 F.Supp. 408 (E.D.N.Y. 1981) (recalls) * * *. Portions of the legislative history relating to the FDCA indicates that Congress was concerned about the harshness and seriousness of the remedy of seizure. *See, e.g.,* 74 Cong. Rec. 150 (1935); 74 Cong. Rec. 4915 (1935); S.Rep. No. 74–361, at 11 (1935). Injunctive procedures, it is argued, "were viewed as a means to alleviate the hardships seizures might cause to manufacturers." *C.E.B. Prods.,* 380 F.Supp. at 668. *See also Superpharm* (following the reasoning of *C.E.B. Products*); *Ten Cartons,* 888 F.Supp. at 404–05 (following *Superpharm*). Based on that legislative history, the court in *C.E.B. Products* reasoned that a recall provision was probably not within the court's power because it would, in the court's opinion, make an injunction as harsh as a seizure, contrary to the intent of Congress. *See C.E.B. Prods.* 380 F.Supp. at 668. Other district courts, however, have rejected this line of reasoning. *See, e.g.,* United States v. Barr Laboratories, Inc., 812 F.Supp. 458, 489 (D.N.J.1993); United States v. K–N Enterprises, Inc., 461 F.Supp. 988, 991 (N.D.Ill.1978); * * * United States v. Lit Drug Co., 333 F.Supp. 990, 997–1000 (D.N.J.1971) (calling for, among other remedies, recall of adulterated and misbranded drugs); United States v. Lanpar Co., 293 F.Supp. 147, 155 (N.D.Tex.1968) (requiring defendant to recall and destroy illegal products and related literature).

We reject the holdings in the *Parkinson* and *C.E.B. Products* line of cases. First, the existence of the remedy of seizure exists alongside an explicit authorization for injunctive relief to cure violations of the FDCA. The express provision for general equitable relief without the enumeration of any exceptions makes it difficult for this court to find any legitimate means for implicitly carving out such exceptions as we see fit. Even if Congress expressed some concern that seizure should remain the harshest relief available, there is no convincing argument that, in all cases, restitution creates a more harsh result than seizure, procedurally or substantively. Moreover, even accepting the references to legislative concerns relied upon by the *Parkinson* and *C.E.B. Products* line, these concerns are far from a clear statement of Congress's intent to exclude restitution, recalls, disgorgement, or any other traditional form of equitable relief. Finally, as *DeMario* instructs, we must presume that Congress is cognizant of the scope of equity, knows what it is doing when it provides for general equitable relief in a regulatory statute, and can use that knowledge to clearly and explicitly limit the scope of a court's equitable powers under any particular regulatory structure in which such an authorization lies. * * *

Appellants have not established that the FDCA by "a necessary and inescapable inference, restricts the court's jurisdiction in equity." *DeMario*, 361 U.S. at 291, 80 S.Ct. 332. Nothing in the FDCA explicitly precludes a district court from ordering restitution. To find that restitution is unauthorized, this court "require[s] Congress to make plain its desire to limit the courts' inherent powers because 'the great principles of equity, securing complete justice, should not be yielded to light inferences or doubtful construction.' " *Hadix*, 144 F.3d at 937 (quoting *Porter*, 328 U.S. at 398, 66 S.Ct. 1086). Appellants have not demonstrated that the FDCA or its legislative history "compels a departure from the courts' inherent power to ... achieve equity." * * *

United States v. Universal Management Services, Inc., 191 F.3d 750, 760–62 (6th Cir.1999); *accord* United States v. Lane Labs–USA, Inc., 324 F.Supp.2d 547 (D.N.J.2004) (adopting *Universal* and holding that restitution is available under FDCA).

Consider the approach of the California Supreme Court in People v. Superior Court, 9 Cal.3d 283, 107 Cal.Rptr. 192, 507 P.2d 1400 (1973):

This is a civil action by the Attorney General against various sellers of encyclopedias and similar publications by door-to-door solicitation, charging false and misleading advertising (Bus. & Prof.Code, § 17500). The complaint prays, inter alia, that defendants be ordered to offer each customer who has been solicited by a fraudulent sales presentation the opportunity to rescind his contract, return the products, and obtain a refund. * * *

* * *

At the time the complaint was filed Business and Professions Code section 17535 provided that false or misleading advertising "may be enjoined" in an action by the Attorney General, but was silent as to the power of the trial court to order restitution in such a proceeding. On the other hand the statute did not restrict the court's general equity jurisdiction "in so many words, or by necessary and inescapable inference." (Porter v. Warner Co., 328 U.S. 395, 398, 66 S.Ct. 1086, 90 L.Ed. 1332, 1337 (1946).) In the absence of such a restriction a court of equity may exercise the full range of its inherent powers in order to accomplish complete justice between the parties, restoring if necessary the status quo ante as nearly as may be achieved. * * * In particular, in an action by the Attorney General under section 17535 a trial court has the inherent power to order, as a form of ancillary relief, that the defendants make or offer to make restitution to the customers found to have been defrauded. * * *

Id. at 285, 107 Cal.Rptr. at 194, 507 P.2d at 1402.

SECTION 4. INTERFERENCE WITH CONSTITUTIONAL RIGHTS

A. DAMAGES

MEMPHIS COMMUNITY SCHOOL DISTRICT v. STACHURA

Supreme Court of the United States, 1986.
477 U.S. 299, 106 S.Ct. 2537, 91 L.Ed.2d 249.

JUSTICE POWELL delivered the opinion of the Court.

This case requires us to decide whether 42 U.S.C. § 1983 authorizes an award of compensatory damages based on the factfinder's assessment of the value or importance of a substantive constitutional right.

I

Respondent Edward Stachura is a tenured teacher in the Memphis, Michigan, public schools. When the events that led to this case occurred, respondent taught seventh-grade life science, using a textbook that had been approved by the School Board. The textbook included a chapter on human reproduction. During the 1978–1979 school year, respondent spent six weeks on this chapter. As part of their instruction, students were shown pictures of respondent's wife during her pregnancy. Respondent also showed the students two films concerning human growth and sexuality. These films were provided by the County Health Department, and the Principal of respondent's school had approved their use. Both films had been shown in past school years without incident.

After the showing of the pictures and the films, a number of parents complained to school officials about respondent's teaching methods. These complaints, which appear to have been based largely on inaccurate rumors about the allegedly sexually explicit nature of the pictures and films, were discussed at an open School Board meeting held on April 23, 1979. Following the advice of the School Superintendent, respondent did not attend the meeting, during which a number of parents expressed the view that respondent should not be allowed to teach in the Memphis school system.[1] The day after the meeting, respondent was suspended with pay. The School Board later confirmed the suspension, and notified respondent that an "administration evaluation" of his teaching methods was underway. No such evaluation was ever made. Respondent was reinstated the next fall, after filing this lawsuit.

Respondent sued the School District, the Board of Education, various Board members and school administrators, and two parents who had participated in the April 23 School Board meeting. The complaint alleged that respondent's suspension deprived him of both liberty and property without due process of law and violated his First Amendment right to academic freedom. Respondent sought compensatory and punitive damages under 42 U.S.C. § 1983 for these constitutional violations.

At the close of trial on these claims, the District Court instructed the jury as to the law governing the asserted bases for liability. Turning to damages, the court instructed the jury that on finding liability it should award a sufficient amount to compensate respondent for the injury caused by petitioners' unlawful actions:

> You should consider in this regard any lost earnings; loss of earning capacity; out-of-pocket expenses; and any mental anguish or emotional distress that you find the Plaintiff to have suffered as a result of conduct by the Defendants depriving him of his civil rights. App. 94.

In addition to this instruction on the standard elements of compensatory damages, the court explained that punitive damages could be awarded, and described the standards governing punitive awards. Finally, at respondent's request and over petitioners' objection, the court charged that damages also could be awarded based on the value or importance of the constitutional rights that were violated:

---

1. One member of the School Board described the meeting as follows:

"At this time, the public was in a total uproar and completely out of control.... People were hollering and shouting and the statement was made from the public that if Mr. Stachura was allowed to return in the morning, they would be there to picket the school.

"At this point of total panic, [the School Superintendent] stated in order to maintain peace in our school district, we would suspend Mr. Stachura with full pay and get this mess straightened out." * * *

If you find that the Plaintiff has been deprived of a Constitutional right, you may award damages to compensate him for the deprivation. Damages for this type of injury are more difficult to measure than damages for a physical injury or injury to one's property. There are no medical bills or other expenses by which you can judge how much compensation is appropriate. In one sense, no monetary value we place upon Constitutional rights can measure their importance in our society or compensate a citizen adequately for their deprivation. However, just because these rights are not capable of precise evaluation does not mean that an appropriate monetary amount should not be awarded.

The precise value you place upon any Constitutional right which you find was denied to Plaintiff is within your discretion. You may wish to consider the importance of the right in our system of government, the role which this right has played in the history of our republic, [and] the significance of the right in the context of the activities which the Plaintiff was engaged in at the time of the violation of the right. *Id.*, at 96.

The jury found petitioners liable, and awarded a total of $275,000 in compensatory damages and $46,000 in punitive damages.[4] * * *

In an opinion devoted primarily to liability issues, the Court of Appeals for the Sixth Circuit affirmed, holding that respondent's suspension had violated both procedural due process and the First Amendment. Stachura v. Truszkowski, 763 F.2d 211 (C.A.6 1985). Responding to petitioners' contention that the District Court improperly authorized damages based solely on the value of constitutional rights, the court noted only that "there was ample proof of actual injury to plaintiff Stachura both in his effective discharge ... and by the damage to his reputation and to his professional career as a teacher. Contrary to the situation in Carey v. Piphus, 435 U.S. 247, 98 S.Ct. 1042, 55 L.Ed.2d 252 (1978) ..., there was proof from which the jury could have found, as it did, actual and important damages." *Id.*, at 214.

We granted certiorari limited to the question whether the Court of Appeals erred in affirming the damages award in the light of the District Court's instructions that authorized not only compensatory and punitive damages, but also damages for the deprivation of "any constitutional right."[5] 474 U.S. 918, 106 S.Ct. 245, 88 L.Ed.2d 254 (1985). * * *

---

4. The bulk of the award was against the School Board, which was assessed $233,750 in compensatory damages. Three of the individual defendants were each assessed $8,250, while six others were each charged $2,750. Nine individual defendants were assessed punitive damages, ranging from $1,000 to $15,000.

5. Since our decision in Carey v. Piphus, 435 U.S. 247, 98 S.Ct. 1042, 55 L.E.2d 252 (1978), several of the Courts of Appeals have concluded that damages awards based on the abstract value of constitutional rights are proper, at least as long as the right in question is substantive. *E.g.,* Bell v. Little Axe Independent School Dist. No. 70, 766 F.2d 1391 (C.A.10 1985); Herrera v. Valentine, 653 F.2d 1220, 1227–1229 (C.A.8 1981); * * *. *See also* Love, *Damages: A Remedy for the Violation of Constitutional Rights*, 67 Calif.L.Rev. 1242 (1979). Other courts have determined that our reasoning in *Carey* forecloses such awards. *E.g.,* Hobson v. Wilson, 237 U.S.App.D.C. 219,

II

Petitioners challenge the jury instructions authorizing damages for violation of constitutional rights on the ground that those instructions permitted the jury to award damages based on its own unguided estimation of the value of such rights. Respondent disagrees with this characterization of the jury instructions, contending that the compensatory damages instructions taken as a whole focused solely on respondent's injury and not on the abstract value of the rights he asserted.

We believe petitioners more accurately characterize the instructions. The damages instructions were divided into three distinct segments: (i) compensatory damages for harm to respondent, (ii) punitive damages, and (iii) additional "compensat[ory]" damages for violations of constitutional rights. No sensible juror could read the third of these segments to modify the first. On the contrary, the damages instructions plainly authorized—in addition to punitive damages—two distinct types of "compensatory" damages: one based on respondent's actual injury according to ordinary tort law standards, and another based on the "value" of certain rights. We therefore consider whether the latter category of damages was properly before the jury.

III

A

We have repeatedly noted that 42 U.S.C. § 1983[8] creates " 'a species of tort liability' in favor of persons who are deprived of 'rights, privileges, or immunities secured' to them by the Constitution." Carey v. Piphus, 435 U.S. 247, 253, 98 S.Ct. 1042, 1047, 55 L.Ed.2d 252 (1978), quoting Imbler v. Pachtman, 424 U.S. 409, 417, 96 S.Ct. 984, 988, 47 L.Ed.2d 128 (1976). * * * Accordingly, when § 1983 plaintiffs seek damages for violations of constitutional rights, the level of damages is ordinarily determined according to principles derived from the common law of torts. * * *

Punitive damages aside,[9] damages in tort cases are designed to provide "compensation for the injury caused to plaintiff by defendant's breach of duty." 2 F. Harper, F. James, & O. Gray, Law of Torts § 25.1, p. 490 (2d ed. 1986) (emphasis in original), quoted in Carey v. Piphus, *supra*,

---

278–279, 737 F.2d 1, 60–61 (1984), *cert. denied*, 470 U.S. 1084, 105 S.Ct. 1843, 85 L.Ed.2d 142 (1985); Familias Unidas v. Briscoe, 619 F.2d 391, 402 (C.A.5 1980) * * *.

8. Section 1983 reads:

"Every person who, under color of any statute, ordinance, regulation, custom, or usage, of any State or Territory or the District of Columbia, subjects, or causes to be subjected, any citizen of the United States or other person within the jurisdiction thereof to the deprivation of any rights, privileges, or immunities secured by the Constitution and laws, shall be liable to the party injured in an action at law, suit in equity, or other proper proceeding for redress."

9. The purpose of punitive damages is to punish the defendant for his willful or malicious conduct and to deter others from similar behavior. * * * In Smith v. Wade, 461 U.S. 30, 103 S.Ct. 1625, 75 L.Ed.2d 632 (1983), the Court held that punitive damages may be available in a proper § 1983 case. As the punitive damages instructions used in this case explained, however, such damages are available only on a showing of the requisite intent. App. 94–95 (authorizing punitive damages for acts "maliciously, or wantonly, or oppressively done"); Smith v. Wade, *supra*, at 51, 103 S.Ct., at 1637.

435 U.S., at 255, 98 S.Ct., at 1047. * * * To that end, compensatory damages may include not only out-of-pocket loss and other monetary harms, but also such injuries as "impairment of reputation ..., personal humiliation, and mental anguish and suffering." Gertz v. Robert Welch, Inc., 418 U.S. 323, 350, 94 S.Ct. 2997, 3012, 41 L.Ed.2d 789 (1974). *See also* Carey v. Piphus, *supra*, 435 U.S., at 264, 98 S.Ct., at 1052 (mental and emotional distress constitute compensable injury in § 1983 cases). Deterrence is also an important purpose of this system, but it operates through the mechanism of damages that are *compensatory*—damages grounded in determinations of plaintiffs' actual losses. * * * Congress adopted this common-law system of recovery when it established liability for "constitutional torts." Consequently, "the basic purpose" of § 1983 damages is *"to compensate persons for injuries* that are caused by the deprivation of constitutional rights." Carey v. Piphus, 435 U.S., at 254, 98 S.Ct., at 1047 (emphasis added). * * *

Carey v. Piphus represents a straightforward application of these principles. *Carey* involved a suit by a high school student suspended for smoking marijuana; the student claimed that he was denied procedural due process because he was suspended without an opportunity to respond to the charges against him. The Court of Appeals for the Seventh Circuit held that even if the suspension was justified, the student could recover substantial compensatory damages simply because of the insufficient procedures used to suspend him from school. We reversed, and held that the student could recover compensatory damages only if he proved actual injury caused by the denial of his constitutional rights. * * * We noted: "Rights, constitutional and otherwise, do not exist in a vacuum. Their purpose is to protect persons from injuries to particular interests...." *Id.*, at 254, 98 S.Ct., at 1047. Where no injury was present, no "compensatory" damages could be awarded.

The instructions at issue here cannot be squared with *Carey*, or with the principles of tort damages on which *Carey* and § 1983 are grounded. The jurors in this case were told that, in determining how much was necessary to "compensate [respondent] for the deprivation" of his constitutional rights, they should place a money value on the "rights" themselves by considering such factors as the particular right's "importance ... in our system of government," its role in American history, and its "significance ... in the context of the activities" in which respondent was engaged. App. 96. These factors focus, not on compensation for provable injury, but on the jury's subjective perception of the importance of constitutional rights as an abstract matter. *Carey* establishes that such an approach is impermissible. The constitutional right transgressed in *Carey*—the right to due process of law—is central to our system of ordered liberty. * * * We nevertheless held that no compensatory damages could be awarded for violation of that right absent proof of actual injury. * * *

Carey thus makes clear that the abstract value of a constitutional right may not form the basis for § 1983 damages.[11]

Respondent nevertheless argues that *Carey* does not control here, because in this case a substantive constitutional right—respondent's First Amendment right to academic freedom—was infringed. The argument misperceives our analysis in *Carey*. That case does not establish a two-tiered system of constitutional rights, with substantive rights afforded greater protection than "mere" procedural safeguards. We did acknowledge in *Carey* that "the elements and prerequisites for recovery of damages" might vary depending on the interests protected by the constitutional right at issue. * * * But we emphasized that, whatever the constitutional basis for § 1983 liability, such damages must always be designed "to compensate injuries caused by the [constitutional] deprivation." *Id.*, at 265, 98 S.Ct., at 1053 (emphasis added).[13] * * * That conclusion simply leaves no room for non-compensatory damages measured by the jury's perception of the abstract "importance" of a constitutional right.

Nor do we find such damages necessary to vindicate the constitutional rights that § 1983 protects. *See* n.11, *supra*. Section 1983 presupposes that damages that compensate for actual harm ordinarily suffice to deter constitutional violations. *Carey*, *supra*, 435 U.S., at 256–257, 98 S.Ct., at 1043 ("To the extent that Congress intended that awards under § 1983 should deter the deprivation of constitutional rights, there is no evidence that it meant to establish a deterrent more formidable than that inherent in the award of compensatory damages"). Moreover, damages based on the "value" of constitutional rights are an unwieldy tool for ensuring compliance with the Constitution. History and tradition do not afford any sound guidance concerning the precise value that juries should place on constitutional protections. Accordingly, were such damages available, juries would

---

11. We did approve an award of nominal damages for the deprivation of due process in *Carey*. 435 U.S., at 266, 98 S.Ct., at 1053. Our discussion of that issue makes clear that nominal damages, and not damages based on some undefinable "value" of infringed rights, are the appropriate means of "vindicating" rights whose deprivation has not caused actual, provable injury:

Common-law courts traditionally have vindicated deprivations of certain 'absolute' rights that are not shown to have caused actual injury through the award of a nominal sum of money. By making the deprivation of such rights actionable for nominal damages without proof of actual injury, the law recognizes the importance to organized society that those rights be scrupulously observed; but at the same time, it remains true to the principle that substantial damages should be awarded only to compensate actual injury or, in the case of exemplary or punitive damages, to deter or punish malicious deprivations of rights.

Ibid. (footnote omitted).

13. *Carey* recognized that "the task . . . of adapting common-law rules of damages to provide fair compensation for injuries caused by the deprivation of a constitutional right" is one "of some delicacy." * * * We also noted that "the elements and prerequisites for recovery of damages appropriate to compensate injuries caused by the deprivation of one constitutional right are not necessarily appropriate to compensate injuries caused by the deprivation of another." *Id.*, at 264–265, 98 S.Ct., at 1053. *See also* Hobson v. Wilson, 237 U.S.App.D.C., at 279–281, 737 F.2d, at 61–63. This "delicate" task need not be undertaken here. None of the parties challenges the portion of the jury instructions that permitted recovery for actual harm to respondent, and the instructions that are challenged simply do not authorize compensation for injury. We therefore hold only that damages based on the "value" or "importance" of constitutional rights are not authorized by § 1983, because they are not truly compensatory.

be free to award arbitrary amounts without any evidentiary basis, or to use their unbounded discretion to punish unpopular defendants. *Cf. Gertz*, 418 U.S., at 350, 94 S.Ct., at 3012. Such damages would be too uncertain to be of any great value to plaintiffs, and would inject caprice into determinations of damages in § 1983 cases. We therefore hold that damages based on the abstract "value" or "importance" of constitutional rights are not a permissible element of compensatory damages in such cases.

B

Respondent further argues that the challenged instructions authorized a form of "presumed" damages—a remedy that is both compensatory in nature and traditionally part of the range of tort law remedies. Alternatively, respondent argues that the erroneous instructions were at worst harmless error.

Neither argument has merit. Presumed damages are a substitute for ordinary compensatory damages, not a supplement for an award that fully compensates the alleged injury. When a plaintiff seeks compensation for an injury that is likely to have occurred but difficult to establish, some form of presumed damages may possibly be appropriate. *See Carey*, 435 U.S., at 262, 98 S.Ct., at 1051; *cf.* Dun & Bradstreet, Inc. v. Greenmoss Builders, 472 U.S. 749, 760–761, 105 S.Ct. 2939, 2946, 86 L.Ed.2d 593 (1985) (opinion of POWELL, J.); Gertz v. Robert Welch, Inc., *supra*, 418 U.S., at 349, 94 S.Ct., at 3011. In those circumstances, presumed damages may roughly approximate the harm that the plaintiff suffered and thereby compensate for harms that may be impossible to measure. As we earlier explained, the instructions at issue in this case did not serve this purpose, but instead called on the jury to measure damages based on a subjective evaluation of the importance of particular constitutional values. Since such damages are wholly divorced from any compensatory purpose, they cannot be justified as presumed damages.[14] Moreover, no rough substitute

---

14. For the same reason, Nixon v. Herndon, 273 U.S. 536, 47 S.Ct. 446, 71 L.Ed. 759 (1927), and similar cases do not support the challenged instructions. In *Nixon*, the Court held that a plaintiff who was illegally prevented from voting in a state primary election suffered compensable injury. *Accord*, Lane v. Wilson, 307 U.S. 268, 59 S.Ct. 872, 83 L.Ed. 1281 (1939). This holding did not rest on the "value" of the right to vote as an abstract matter; rather, the Court recognized that the plaintiff had suffered a particular injury—his inability to vote in a particular election— that might be compensated through substantial money damages. *See* 273 U.S., at 540, 47 S.Ct., at 446 ("the petition . . . seeks to recover for private damage").

Nixon followed a long line of cases, going back to Lord Holt's decision in Ashby v. White, 2 Ld.Raym. 938, 92 Eng.Rep. 126 (1703), authorizing substantial money damages as compensation for persons deprived of their right to vote in particular elections. *E.g.*, Wiley v. Sinkler, 179 U.S. 58, 65, 21 S.Ct. 17, 20, 45 L.Ed. 84 (1900); Wayne v. Venable, 260 F. 64, 66 (C.A.8 1919). Although these decisions sometimes speak of damages for the value of the right to vote, their analysis shows that they involve nothing more than an award of presumed damages for a nonmonetary harm that cannot easily be quantified:

> In the eyes of the law th[e] right [to vote] is so valuable that damages are presumed from the wrongful deprivation of it without evidence of actual loss of money, property, or any other valuable thing, and the amount of the damages is a question peculiarly appropriate for the determination of the jury, because each member of the jury has personal knowledge of the value of the right.

Ibid.

for compensatory damages was required in this case, since the jury was fully authorized to compensate respondent for both monetary and non-monetary harms caused by petitioners' conduct.

Nor can we find that the erroneous instructions were harmless. * * * Although the verdict specified an amount for punitive damages, it did not specify how much of the remaining damages was designed to compensate respondent for his injury and how much reflected the jury's estimation of the value of the constitutional rights that were infringed. The effect of the erroneous instruction is therefore unknowable, although probably significant: the jury awarded respondent a very substantial amount of damages, none of which could have derived from any monetary loss.[15] It is likely, although not certain, that a major part of these damages was intended to "compensate" respondent for the abstract "value" of his due process and First Amendment rights. For these reasons, the case must be remanded for a new trial on compensatory damages.

IV

The judgment of the Court of Appeals is reversed, and the case is remanded for further proceedings consistent with this opinion.

JUSTICE BRENNAN and JUSTICE STEVENS join the opinion of the Court and also join JUSTICE MARSHALL's opinion concurring in the judgment.

JUSTICE MARSHALL, with whom JUSTICE BRENNAN, JUSTICE BLACKMUN, and JUSTICE STEVENS join, concurring in the judgment.

I agree with the Court that this case must be remanded for a new trial on damages. Certain portions of the Court's opinion, however, can be read to suggest that damages in § 1983 cases are necessarily limited to "out-of-pocket loss," "other monetary harms," and "such injuries as 'impairment of reputation ..., personal humiliation, and mental anguish and suffering.'" See ante, at 2542. I do not understand the Court so to hold, and I write separately to emphasize that the violation of a constitutional right, in proper cases, may itself constitute a compensable injury.

The appropriate starting point of any analysis in this area is this Court's opinion in Carey v. Piphus, 435 U.S. 247, 98 S.Ct. 1042, 55 L.Ed.2d 252 (1978). In Carey, we recognized that "the basic purpose of a § 1983 damages award should be to compensate persons for injuries caused by the deprivation of constitutional rights." Id., at 254, 98 S.Ct., at 1047; see ante, at 2542–2543. We explained, however, that application of that principle to concrete cases was not a simple matter. 435 U.S., at 257,

---

See also Ashby v. White, supra, at 955, 92 Eng.Rep., at 137 (HOLT, C.J.) ("As in an action for slanderous words, though a man does not lose a penny by reason of the speaking [of] them, yet he shall have an action"). The "value of the right" in the context of these decisions is the money value of the particular loss that the plaintiff suffered—a loss of which "each member of the jury has personal knowledge." It is not the value of the right to vote as a general, abstract matter, based on its role in our history or system of government. Thus, whatever the wisdom of these decisions in the context of the changing scope of compensatory damages over the course of this century, they do not support awards of noncompensatory damages such as those authorized in this case.

15. Throughout his suspension, respondent continued to receive his teacher's salary.

98 S.Ct., at 1048. "It is not clear," we stated, "that common-law tort rules of damages will provide a complete solution to the damages issue in every § 1983 case." *Id.*, at 258, 98 S.Ct., at 1049. Rather, "the rules governing compensation for injuries caused by the deprivation of constitutional rights should be tailored to the interests protected by the particular right in question—just as the common-law rules of damages themselves were defined by the interests protected in various branches of tort law." *Id.*, at 259, 98 S.Ct., at 1050.

Applying those principles, we held in *Carey* that substantial damages should not be awarded where a plaintiff has been denied procedural due process but has made no further showing of compensable damage. We repeated, however, that "the elements and prerequisites for recovery of damages appropriate to compensate injuries caused by the deprivation of one constitutional right are not necessarily appropriate to compensate injuries caused by the deprivation of another." *Id.*, at 264–265, 98 S.Ct., at 1053. We referred to cases that support the award of substantial damages simply upon a showing that a plaintiff was wrongfully deprived of the right to vote, without requiring any further demonstration of damages. *Id.*, at 264–265, n. 22, 98 S.Ct., at 1052–1053, n.22.

Following *Carey*, the Courts of Appeals have recognized that invasions of constitutional rights sometimes cause injuries that cannot be redressed by a wooden application of common-law damages rules. In Hobson v. Wilson, 237 U.S.App.D.C. 219, 275–281, 737 F.2d 1, 57–63 (1984), *cert. denied*, 470 U.S. 1084, 105 S.Ct. 1843, 85 L.Ed.2d 142 (1985), which the Court cites, *ante*, at 2544, and n. 13, plaintiffs claimed that defendant Federal Bureau of Investigation agents had invaded their First Amendment rights to assemble for peaceable political protest, to associate with others to engage in political expression, and to speak on public issues free of unreasonable government interference. The District Court found that the defendants had succeeded in diverting plaintiffs from, and impeding them in, their protest activities. The Court of Appeals for the District of Columbia Circuit held that that injury to a First Amendment-protected interest could itself constitute compensable injury wholly apart from any "emotional distress, humiliation and personal indignity, emotional pain, embarrassment, fear, anxiety and anguish" suffered by plaintiffs. 237 U.S.App.D.C., at 280, 737 F.2d, at 62 (footnotes omitted). The court warned, however, that that injury could be compensated with substantial damages only to the extent that it was "reasonably quantifiable"; damages should not be based on "the so-called inherent value of the rights violated." *Ibid.*

I believe that the *Hobson* court correctly stated the law. When a plaintiff is deprived, for example, of the opportunity to engage in a demonstration to express his political views, "[i]t is facile to suggest that no damage is done." Dellums v. Powell, 184 U.S.App.D.C. 275, 303, 566 F.2d 167, 195 (1977). Loss of such an opportunity constitutes loss of First Amendment rights " 'in their most pristine and classic form.' " *Ibid.*, quoting Edwards v. South Carolina, 372 U.S. 229, 235, 83 S.Ct. 680, 683, 9

L.Ed.2d 697 (1963). There is no reason why such an injury should not be compensable in damages. At the same time, however, the award must be proportional to the actual loss sustained.

The instructions given the jury in this case were improper because they did not require the jury to focus on the loss actually sustained by respondent. Rather, they invited the jury to base its award on speculation about "the importance of the right in our system of government" and "the role which this right has played in the history of our republic," guided only by the admonition that "[i]n one sense, no monetary value we place on Constitutional rights can measure their importance in our society or compensate a citizen adequately for their deprivation." App. 96. These instructions invited the jury to speculate on matters wholly detached from the real injury occasioned respondent by the deprivation of the right. Further, the instructions might have led the jury to grant respondent damages based on the "abstract value" of the right to procedural due process—a course directly barred by our decision in *Carey*.

The Court therefore properly remands for a new trial on damages. I do not understand the Court, however, to hold that deprivations of constitutional rights can never themselves constitute compensable injuries. Such a rule would be inconsistent with the logic of *Carey*, and would defeat the purpose of § 1983 by denying compensation for genuine injuries caused by the deprivation of constitutional rights.

NOTES

1. In cases in which the plaintiff's damages are solely attributable to a denial of procedural due process (i.e., cases in which the plaintiff would have lost at a "due process" hearing if one had been held), the courts have allowed the recovery of substantial proven emotional distress damages. *E.g.*, Laje v. R.E. Thomason General Hospital, 665 F.2d 724 (5th Cir.1982) (affirming $20,000 jury verdict awarded to discharged doctor for emotional distress caused by failure to afford timely hearing). But none of these emotional distress awards has been as high as the compensatory damages award in *Stachura*, which may help to explain why Justice Powell said: "The effect of the erroneous instruction is therefore unknowable, although probably significant * * *."

2. In a post-*Stachura* case brought by an assistant fire chief who was forced to retire in violation of his First Amendment rights, the plaintiff was allowed to recover $25,000 for his proven emotional distress in addition to $368,445 for loss of pay. Meyers v. City of Cincinnati, 14 F.3d 1115 (6th Cir.1994). *See generally* Daniel A. Klein, Annotation, *Excessiveness or Adequacy of Awards of Compensatory Damages in Civil Actions for Deprivation of Rights Under 42 U.S.C.A. § 1983—Modern Cases*, 99 A.L.R. Fed. 501 (1990).

3. Proof of "actual injury" does not require proof of "such things as medical expenses, missed work, and lost income"; rather, "compensatory damages may be awarded based on physical pain and suffering." Slicker v. Jackson, 215 F.3d 1225, 1230 (11th Cir.2000). When plaintiffs bring constitu-

tional tort claims for emotional distress damages, they do not need to establish the elements of a common law tort claim for emotional distress, nor do they need to prove that they have experienced "severe emotional distress." *See, e.g.*, Chatman v. Slagle, 107 F.3d 380 (6th Cir.1997) (citing cases from other circuits). Furthermore, they do not need to introduce expert testimony to corroborate a claim for emotional distress. *See, e.g.*, Bolden v. Southeastern Pennsylvania Transportation Authority, 21 F.3d 29 (3d Cir.1994) (citing cases from other circuits).

4. In what types of cases might the courts allow the recovery of presumed damages after *Stachura*? Justice Powell suggested that presumed damages might be available in voting rights cases, and lower courts have upheld awards of presumed damages in cases alleging violations of free speech rights where the plaintiffs were protesters and strikers. *E.g.*, Walje v. City of Winchester, 827 F.2d 10 (6th Cir.1987) (affirming district court's award of $5,000 to striking fireman for "general damages"); *see also* Hessel v. O'Hearn, 977 F.2d 299, 301 (7th Cir.1992) (approving presumed general damages for violations of the First Amendment and the Fourth Amendment in dictum); Baumgardner v. Secretary, 960 F.2d 572 (6th Cir.1992) (approving the concept of presumed general damages when a plaintiff is unable to prove actual injury, but refusing to award such damages in the sex discrimination case before the court because the plaintiff had proven $1500 in actual damages for "emotional distress" and "inconvenience" in an action against his landlord for housing discrimination); Clarkson v. Town of Florence, 198 F.Supp.2d 997, 1016 (E.D.Wis.2002). *See generally* Jean C. Love, *Presumed General Compensatory Damages in Constitutional Tort Litigation: A Corrective Justice Perspective*, 49 Wash. & Lee L. Rev. 67 (1992); Michael L. Wells, *Section 1983, the First Amendment, and Public Employee Speech: Shaping the Right to Fit the Remedy (and Vice–Versa)*, 35 Ga. L. Rev. 939 (2001). *But see* Hershell Gill Consulting Engineers, Inc. v. Miami–Dade County, 333 F.Supp.2d 1305 (S.D.Fla.2004) (refusing to award presumed general compensatory damages to corporate plaintiffs in a reverse discrimination cause of action under § 1983 where the plaintiffs had alleged a violation of the Equal Protection Clause of the Fourteenth Amendment; assessing nominal damages at $100 for each corporate plaintiff).

5. Some lower courts are uncomfortable with the notion of awarding "presumed damages," but are willing to allow the recovery of emotional distress damages that are "inferred from the circumstances" of a violation of the plaintiff's constitutional rights. *See, e.g.*, Berger v. Iron Workers Reinforced Rodmen, 170 F.3d 1111 (D.C.Cir.1999) (upholding compensatory damages awards for race discrimination ranging from $2,500 to $25,000 that were awarded to 18 African–American ironworkers who had to enroll in an unnecessary training program for two years before they were allowed to take the union entrance exam); *see also* Dan B. Dobbs, Law of Remedies § 7.1(2) (2d ed. 1993).

6. The United States Supreme Court has ruled that, in § 1983 cases brought for a denial of equal protection, a plaintiff may sue for injunctive relief upon proof of "inability to compete on an equal footing," but may be denied damages upon proof that the defendant "would have made the same decision absent the alleged discrimination." Texas v. Lesage, 528 U.S. 18, 120

S.Ct. 467, 145 L.Ed.2d 347 (1999). For essays on Texas v. Lesage, see Ashutosh Bhagwhat, *Injury Without Harm:* Texas v. Lesage *and the Strange World of Article III Injuries*, 28 Hastings Const. L.Q. 445 (2001); Sheldon Nahmod, Mt. Healthy *and Causation-in-Fact: The Court Still Does Not Get It!*, 51 Mercer L. Rev. 603 (2000); Christina B. Whitman, *An Essay on* Texas v. Lesage, 51 Mercer L. Rev. 621 (2000).

7. Even if a plaintiff fails to prove actual or presumed general compensatory damages, the plaintiff may still recover nominal damages upon proof of liability in most constitutional tort actions. Schneider v. County of San Diego, 285 F.3d 784 (9th Cir.2002) (procedural due process case); Slicker v. Jackson, 215 F.3d 1225 (11th Cir.2000) (excessive force case). *See generally* Mark T. Morrell, Comment, *Who Wants Nominal Damages Anyway? The Impact of an Automatic Entitlement to Nominal Damages Under § 1983*, 13 Regent U. L. Rev. 225 (2000) (nominal damages may provide prevailing party status, may justify attorney's fees, and may rescue a case from dismissal and mootness). For a case that awarded attorney's fees based upon a nominal damages award, see Phelps v. Hamilton, 120 F.3d 1126 (10th Cir.1997) (First Amendment free speech case). *See generally* Joseph Bean, Note, *Felling the Farrar Forest: Determining Whether Federal Courts Will Award § 1988 Attorney's Fees to Prevailing Civil Rights Plaintiff Who Only Recovers Nominal Damages*, 33 U. Mem. L. Rev. 573 (2003).

The availability of both nominal damages and compensatory damages for violations of constitutional rights has made it much easier for plaintiffs to establish that they have standing to sue in federal courts. *See, e.g.,* Utah Animal Rights Coalition v. Salt Lake City Corp., 371 F.3d 1248 (10th Cir. 2004) (action for denial of free speech rights by organization whose application to conduct protest at Olympics had been processed slowly; held that organization had standing and its claim was not moot because it could claim nominal damages); Irish Lesbian & Gay Organization v. Giuliani, 143 F.3d 638 (2d Cir.1998) (action for denial of free speech rights brought by organization whose application to conduct parade before annual St. Patrick's Day parade had been denied by the City of New York; held that organization had standing because it could claim nominal damages plus compensatory damages for the "loss of the opportunity to express its views").

8. In a case decided after *Carey*, the Supreme Court explicitly authorized the recovery of punitive damages in constitutional tort litigation "when the defendant's conduct is motivated by evil motive or intent, or when it involves reckless or callous indifference to the federally protected rights of others." Smith v. Wade, 461 U.S. 30, 56, 103 S.Ct. 1625, 1640, 75 L.Ed.2d 632 (1983).

9. Congress did not provide for a federal survival or wrongful death cause of action when the victim of a constitutional tort is killed, and therefore the federal courts usually "borrow" state law in such cases, leading to a lack of uniform remedies. For a discussion of this problem, see Michael D. Moberly, *For Whom Bell Tolls: A Decedent's Right to § 1983 Pain and Suffering Damages in the Ninth Circuit*, 40 Santa Clara L. Rev. 409 (2000); Martin A. Schwartz et al., *Wrongful Death Actions Under Section 1983*, 19 Touro L. Rev. 707 (2003); Michael LeBoff, Comment, *A Need for Uniformity: Survivorship Under 42 U.S.C. § 1983*, 32 Loyola L.A. L. Rev. 221 (1998);

Felix Shafir, Comment, *Flawed Assumptions: A Critique of* Garcia v. Superior Court of Los Angeles, 93 Nw. U. L. Rev. 301 (1998).

10. The effectiveness of damages as a remedy for the violation of constitutional rights is severely impaired by the immunities accorded to public officials and governmental entities. Professor Whitman, in a thought-provoking article, has suggested that, instead of regarding damages as the "ordinary" form of relief for constitutional torts, the courts should regard injunctions as the preferred remedy. Christina B. Whitman, *Constitutional Torts*, 79 Mich. L. Rev. 5 (1980).

KERMAN v. CITY OF NEW YORK

United States Court of Appeals, Second Circuit, 2004.
374 F.3d 93.

Before: FEINBERG, KEARSE, and RAGGI, CIRCUIT JUDGES.

KEARSE, CIRCUIT JUDGE.

This case returns to us after proceedings on remand following an appeal in which we, *inter alia,* reversed district judges' dismissals as a matter of law, on the ground of qualified immunity, of certain claims brought by plaintiff Robert Kerman under 42 U.S.C. § 1983 against defendant William Crossan * * *, a New York City police officer, in connection with Crossan's order that Kerman be detained and taken to a hospital for psychiatric observation, *see* Kerman v. City of New York, 261 F.3d 229 (2d Cir.2001) ("*Kerman II*"), *aff'g in part and rev'g in part* Kerman v. City of New York, No. 96 Civ. 7865(LMM), 1999 WL 509527 (S.D.N.Y. July 19, 1999) ("*Kerman I*"). Kerman now appeals (a) from so much of the final judgment entered in the United States District Court for the Southern District of New York, following a retrial * * *, as dismissed his Fourth Amendment unlawful seizure claim against Crossan, as well as his parallel state-law false imprisonment claims against Crossan and defendant City of New York ("City"), for unlawful detention and involuntary hospitalization; and (b) from a postjudgment order (i) denying, on the ground that Crossan is entitled to qualified immunity as a matter of law, Kerman's motion to correct the judgment in light of the jury's finding that Crossan had ordered Kerman's detention and involuntary hospitalization without probable cause, and (ii) denying Kerman's motion for a new trial as to damages for that deprivation of his liberty. On appeal, Kerman contends principally that the district court erred in ruling that Crossan was entitled to qualified immunity as a matter of law * * *. Kerman also contends that the court abused its discretion in denying his motion for a new trial as to damages on his unlawful seizure and false imprisonment claims, given the jury's refusal to award more than nominal damages despite its finding that he had been deprived of his liberty without probable cause. * * *

I. BACKGROUND

* * *

[The plaintiff, who had a history of depression and borderline personality disorder, was handcuffed in his home after his girlfriend had called 911. She stated that he had threatened to buy a gun, kill his psychiatrist, and then commit suicide. No gun was found in his home. The plaintiff was then placed in a "restraint bag" and taken to Bellevue Hospital, where he was held overnight for observation. He was released the next day.]

II. DISCUSSION

A. Crossan's Qualified Immunity and Privilege Defenses

[The court held that the defendant could not successfully claim a qualified immunity because the plaintiff had a clearly established right not to be involuntarily hospitalized by an officer who had not determined that he was dangerous.]

B. Kerman's Entitlement to Correction of the Judgment

The April 23, 2002 judgment entered by the district court after the jury returned its verdict dismissed all of Kerman's claims. The court ruled in *Kerman III* that Kerman's Rule 60 motion, seeking correction of the judgment to reflect that he prevailed on his Fourth Amendment claim for unlawful seizure and his state-law claims for false imprisonment, had merit despite a possible inconsistency in the jury's answers to the interrogatories. We agree.

With respect to those claims, the jury had been instructed that it should not find Crossan liable for Kerman's injuries unless it found that Crossan acted without probable cause and proximately caused the injuries to which Kerman testified. The jury found that Crossan had detained Kerman and ordered him taken to the hospital without probable cause but that Kerman had not proven that that unlawful conduct was the proximate cause of his claimed injuries. The jury nonetheless concluded that Kerman should be awarded nominal damages. Because the jury had been instructed that it should not reach the issue of damages unless it found that Kerman had established Crossan's liability, there appeared to be some tension between its finding that Kerman had not shown proximate cause and its finding that he was entitled to nominal damages. Where there appears to be an inconsistency between the jury's interrogatory answers, "[i]t is the duty of the district court to reconcile the jury's general verdict and its interrogatory responses if reasonable reconciliation is possible." 9A Charles Alan Wright & Arthur R. Miller, Federal Practice and Procedure, § 2513, at 229 (2d ed.1995). * * *

Applying this principle, the district court properly reconciled any apparent inconsistency between the jury's finding that Kerman was entitled to nominal damages and its finding that Crossan's conduct did not proximately cause Kerman injury. The court had instructed the jury on the need to find proximate cause only in the context of the court's discussion of compensatory damages * * *, and in that category of damages the court had referred only to "medical expenses," "physical pain and suffering," and "emotional and mental anguish." * * * As to nominal damages, in contrast, the court instructed that the jury could make such an award if it found that, other than the deprivation of a legal right, Kerman had "suffered no actual damages," * * * presumably referring to the medical expenses, pain and suffering, and emotional distress for which the court had instructed that Kerman might recover compensatory damages.

In reconciling the jury's answers, the court reasoned that the jury had found a violation of Kerman's rights but simply had "found that ... Plaintiff had suffered no actual damages"; and, citing Carey v. Piphus, 435 U.S. 247, 266, 98 S.Ct. 1042, 55 L.Ed.2d 252 (1978), the court concluded that Kerman was entitled to an award of nominal damages because he had established that Crossan's conduct violated his constitutional rights. * * * In light of the instructions, the district court properly ruled that the jury's interrogatory answers were consistent. And in light of an individual's right to be free of official physical restraint in the absence of probable cause, the district court correctly concluded that, on the basis of the jury's findings, Kerman had prevailed on his Fourth Amendment claim for unlawful seizure and his state-law claims for false imprisonment.

C. Kerman's Entitlement to a New Trial on Damages

In his posttrial Rule 59 motion, Kerman contended that in light of the fact that he had prevailed on the unlawful seizure and false imprisonment claims, he was entitled to an award of more than nominal damages. He moved for a new trial on damages, contending that the jury's verdict was against the weight of the evidence. He also argued that given the undisputed evidence that he had been held in custody for some 24 hours, he was entitled to at least compensatory damages as a matter of law because "[t]he right involved here—to be free from unlawful seizures—is the right to liberty.... The jury in this case found that defendant Crossan violated Kerman's right to liberty." * * *

The district court denied Kerman's Rule 59 motion on various grounds. The court stated that the jury found that Kerman had not suffered actual damage as a result of Crossan's actions, * * * and that that finding was supported by the record * * *.

On appeal, Kerman contends * * * that the court misapplied the pertinent legal principles. * * *

* * *

1. Kerman's Claims of Physical, Mental, and Emotional Injury

A finding that the plaintiff has been deprived of a constitutional right does not automatically entitle him to a substantial award of damages. "The cardinal principle of damages in Anglo–American law," which applies to actions brought under § 1983, "is that of *compensation* for the injury caused to plaintiff by defendant's breach of duty." Carey v. Piphus,

435 U.S. at 254–55, 98 S.Ct. 1042 (emphasis in original). For example, when a defendant has deprived the plaintiff of liberty or property without affording him a hearing as required by the Due Process Clause, but the defendant proves that the adverse action would have been taken even if a proper and timely hearing had been held, the plaintiff has not proved compensable injury and is entitled only to nominal damages. *See id.* at 260–63, 98 S.Ct. 1042. * * *

Similarly, when a jury has found that the plaintiff proved a defendant used excessive force against him in violation of his rights under the Fourth or Fifth Amendment, a verdict that the plaintiff is not entitled to compensatory damages is not necessarily impermissible. A jury could reasonably find that only nominal damages are appropriate where, for example, a plaintiff's testimony as to his injuries lacks objective support or credibility, or where both justified force and unjustified force were used, either of which could have caused his injuries, or where some of the plaintiff's injuries could have been caused by a codefendant who was not found to have used excessive force. * * *

In light of these principles, we cannot conclude that Kerman is entitled to a new trial on damages for most of his claimed injuries. The injuries to which he testified were relatively minor physical injuries (pain from being transported with his hands cuffed under him and subsequent soreness in his back and neck) and emotional or psychological injuries. Taking the evidence in the light most favorable to Crossan, as the party against whom a new trial is sought, we see no valid reason why the jury could not have rejected these claims of injury. The jury could, for example, have found that any physical pain Kerman suffered was de minimis in light of both the hospital record that described him as arriving at Bellevue "in no apparent physical distress" * * * and Kerman's own trial testimony that, after leaving Bellevue, he did not seek medical treatment for any physical injuries * * *.

* * *

Accordingly, we cannot conclude that Kerman was entitled as a matter of law to compensatory damages on the basis of his claims of physical pain, medical expenses, emotional suffering, and psychological injuries.

2. *Kerman's Claim of Loss of Liberty*

In contrast, where the jury has found a constitutional violation and there is no genuine dispute that the violation resulted in some injury to the plaintiff, the plaintiff is entitled to an award of compensatory damages as a matter of law. *See, e.g.*, Atkins v. City of New York, 143 F.3d 100, 103 (2d Cir.1998); * * * Raysor v. Port Authority of New York and New Jersey, 768 F.2d 34, 39 (2d Cir.1985), *cert. denied,* 475 U.S. 1027, 106 S.Ct. 1227, 89 L.Ed.2d 337 (1986); Wheatley v. Beetar, 637 F.2d 863, 867 (2d Cir. 1980). In *Wheatley,* for example, a bifurcated trial was held on the plaintiff's claim that he had been beaten by county police officers. In the first phase of the trial, the jury found the defendants liable for use of excessive force in violation of the plaintiff's constitutional rights; in the second phase, the jury awarded damages of just $1. The plaintiff moved unsuccessfully for a new trial on the issue of damages. On appeal, we reversed. We noted that although the jury could reasonably have rejected some of the plaintiff's evidence of injury, other injury claims were well substantiated and uncontradicted. Since the jury's verdict that excessive force had been used plainly accepted the plaintiff's testimony that he had been beaten, we concluded that the plaintiff was entitled as a matter of law to some compensation. *See* 637 F.2d at 865. Thus, we held that in the second phase of the trial, "[i]t was error to charge the jury that an award of nominal damages was permissible and an abuse of discretion not to set [such an award] aside." *Id.*

Similarly, where the plaintiff was indisputably deprived of his liberty, and the conduct of the defendant responsible for the deprivation was found to be unlawful, we have held that the plaintiff is entitled to compensatory, not merely nominal, damages. *See* Raysor v. Port Authority of New York and New Jersey, 768 F.2d at 38–39 ("*Raysor*"). In *Raysor*, the plaintiff, [a law school drop-out,] while attempting to return approximately $16 worth of pills to a store, was arrested and was detained for several hours. Following his exoneration, he brought suit under § 1983 and state law for false arrest and malicious prosecution. The jury found against him on the constitutional claims but found one defendant liable on the state-law claims; it awarded the plaintiff compensatory damages of $16. We held that this award was inadequate to compensate the plaintiff for, *inter alia*, "the loss of time . . . involved in a case of false arrest." 768 F.2d at 39 (internal quotation marks omitted). We noted that

> New York cases uphold awards of up to $10,000 for eve[n] short periods of confinement without proof of actual damages. *See, e.g.,* Hallenbeck v. City of Albany, 99 A.D.2d 639, 472 N.Y.S.2d 187 (1984) ($10,000 for three hours); Woodard v. City of Albany, 81 A.D.2d 947, 439 N.Y.S.2d 701 (1981) ($7,500 for five hours); Guion v. Associated Dry Goods Corp., 56 A.D.2d 798, 393 N.Y.S.2d 8 (1977) ($10,000 for three hours), *aff'd,* 43 N.Y.2d 876, 403 N.Y.S.2d 465, 374 N.E.2d 364 (1978).

Raysor, 768 F.2d at 39. We inferred that the inadequate verdict was likely the product of a jury charge that did not inform the jury that the plaintiff was entitled to recover for the loss of intangible rights:

> The admonition not to award "speculative damages" was, of course, correct, as was the court's instruction that Raysor had "the burden of proof with respect to the nature and extent of his injuries, and with respect to his resulting losses." *But the court should have made it clear to the jury that it could award monetary damages—the amount necessarily arbitrary and unprovable—for the intangibles which we have referred to above.*

Id. (emphasis added).

Raysor is consistent with traditional common-law principles governing entitlement to damages for the tort of false imprisonment. That tort "is complete with even a brief restraint of the plaintiff's freedom"; "it is not necessary that any damage result from it other than the confinement itself." Prosser & Keeton, The Law of Torts § 11, at 48 (5th ed. 1984) (*"Prosser & Keeton"*). The compensatory damages that may be awarded for false imprisonment fall into two categories: general damages and special damages. *See, e.g.,* McCormick, Handbook on the Law of Damages § 107, at 375–77 (1935) (*"McCormick on Damages"*). General damage is a "harm of a sort inseparable from [the unlawful] restraint." *Id.* at 375. For "false imprisonment, upon pleading and proving merely the unlawful interference with his liberty, the plaintiff is entitled to 'general' damages for loss of time and humiliation or mental suffering." *Id.* * * * Items of "special damage" commonly include "physical discomfort, shock, or injury to health," "loss of ... employment," and "injury to the plaintiff's reputation or credit," and must be specifically pleaded and proven. *McCormick on Damages* at 376. In contrast, " '[g]eneral' damage ... need not be specifically proved—it may be inferred from the circumstances of the arrest or imprisonment" and "would include at least the value of the time lost by the plaintiff during the period of detention." *Id.*

The damages recoverable for loss of liberty for the period spent in a wrongful confinement are separable from damages recoverable for such injuries as physical harm, embarrassment, or emotional suffering; even absent such other injuries, an award of several thousand dollars may be appropriate simply for several hours' loss of liberty. * * * Thus, a verdict that a plaintiff should not receive more than nominal damages for physical injury, economic loss, or mental suffering does not foreclose a more substantial award for his loss of liberty.

In the present case, the facts with regard to Kerman's actual loss of liberty were largely uncontroverted. There was no dispute that Kerman was kept in handcuffs after the officers completed their search for a gun and that he was taken to Bellevue Hospital where he remained overnight; * * * and there was no dispute that Kerman did not go to the hospital willingly.

The jury, however, was not instructed that Kerman was entitled to compensatory damages for his loss of liberty. This may have been attributable in part to the district court's view, stated in its posttrial discussion of the jury's failure to return a verdict for more than nominal damages, that Crossan could not be held responsible for any loss of liberty after Kerman's arrival at Bellevue. The court stated, *inter alia,* that Kerman's detention in the hospital was not attributable to Crossan but rather was based on the independent decision of the Bellevue doctors. * * * That view, however, is contrary to the principle that "tort defendants, including those sued under § 1983, are 'responsible for the natural consequences of [their] actions,' " Warner v. Orange County Department of Probation, 115 F.3d 1068, 1071 (2d Cir.1997) (quoting Malley v. Briggs, 475 U.S. 335, 344 n.7, 106 S.Ct. 1092, 89 L.Ed.2d 271 (1986)) (other internal quotation marks omitted). * * *

Although foreseeability is normally an issue of fact, * * * it is unquestionable here that Kerman's detention in the hospital for some period of time was a foreseeable consequence of Crossan's sending him there. Crossan has contended throughout that he ordered Kerman taken to the hospital on the premise that Kerman, if left at large, was a danger to himself or others * * *. No rational factfinder could fail to find that it was foreseeable to Crossan that his sending Kerman to the hospital for evaluation as whether he was suicidal or homicidal would result in Kerman's detention in the hospital for some period of time. Accordingly, we reject the district court's view that Crossan could not be held responsible for any of the period during which Kerman was detained at Bellevue.

* * *

* * * The court's instructions gave no indication that if the jury found that Crossan detained Kerman and sent him to the hospital without probable cause, which necessarily curtailed Kerman's liberty, Kerman was, independently of his claims of physical, mental, emotional, or economic injury, entitled to be compensated for that loss of liberty. The jury should have been so instructed.

Although Kerman argued after trial that he was entitled to compensatory damages for his loss of liberty, we see in the record no indication that he objected at trial to the court's failure to give the jury such an instruction. Absent an objection prior to the submission of the case to the jury, a claimed error in instructions is not preserved for normal appellate review, *see* Fed.R.Civ.P. 51, and, in a civil case, is reviewable only for fundamental error. * * *

* * *

In the present case, where there was no dispute that Crossan caused the postsearch curtailment of Kerman's liberty, and where that loss of liberty indisputably lasted at least 10 hours without any evidence of Kerman's consent, the trial court should have informed the jury that if it found Crossan acted without probable cause it should award Kerman compensation for the loss of his liberty. Given that a loss of liberty is inherent in an unlawful confinement, the failure to give that instruction deprived the jury of the legal guidance needed for a rational decision and thus constituted fundamental error.

The dissent disagrees with our view that it was fundamental error for the trial court to fail to instruct the jury that, upon finding that Crossan unlawfully deprived Kerman of his liberty, the jury could award Kerman compensatory damages for that loss of liberty. The dissent suggests principally that Kerman's failure to request such an instruction was strategic * * *, that there can be no compensatory damages for a loss of liberty unless that injury is reflected in emotional or economic harm * * *, and that the district court's "failure to instruct the jury that it could award [Kerman] compensatory damages for a *loss of liberty in the abstract,* without regard to any injury compensable at common law" was not error (*id.* at 137 (citing Memphis Community School District v. Stachura, 477 U.S. 299, 106 S.Ct. 2537, 91 L.Ed.2d 249 (1986)) (emphasis ours)). Taking these points in reverse order, we remain unpersuaded for the reasons that follow.

We see no parallel between Kerman's claims in the present case and the abstract concepts that were at issue in *Stachura.* In *Stachura,* the Court dealt with claims for violations of the plaintiff's rights to procedural due process and academic freedom, and the trial court had instructed the jury that it could award damages for "the abstract 'value' or 'importance' of constitutional rights." * * * There is no question in the present case of any attempt to vindicate the liberty rights of society at large.

Further, the Supreme Court in *Stachura,* in disapproving the instructions that would have allowed an award based on the abstract societal value of constitutional protections, expressly distinguished that impermissible abstraction from the theory that is pertinent here, to wit, the traditionally permissible concept of "presumed damages." The Court noted, citing Carey v. Piphus, 435 U.S. at 262, 98 S.Ct. 1042, 55 L.Ed.2d 252, that "[w]hen a plaintiff seeks compensation for an injury that is likely to have occurred but difficult to establish, some form of presumed damages may possibly be appropriate," *Stachura,* 477 U.S. at 310–11, 106 S.Ct. 2537, 91 L.Ed.2d 249, and that "presumed damages may roughly approximate the harm that the plaintiff suffered and thereby compensate for harms that may be impossible to measure," *id.* at 311, 106 S.Ct. 2537. In *Carey,* which involved a denial of procedural due process before suspensions from school, the Court noted that the doctrine of presumed damages in the common law of defamation *per se* deals with harms that are "virtually certain" to be caused by such defamation. 435 U.S. at 262, 98 S.Ct. 1042.

The present case does not involve either procedural due process or an attempt to vindicate an abstract societal interest. Rather, it involves an anything-but-abstract physical detention. And although a given person's loss of time may be difficult to evaluate in terms of dollars, his loss of liberty is not just "virtually certain" to occur; it is inseparable from the detention itself.

Accordingly, the availability of compensatory damages for time lost as a result of an unlawful detention was recognized at common law. We disagree with the dissent's view that the common-law concept of loss of time encompasses only loss of economic opportunity * * *. A loss of time, in the sense of loss of freedom, is inherent in any unlawful detention and is compensable as "general damages" for unlawful imprisonment without the need for pleading or proof. *See, e.g.,* McCormick on Damages § 107, at 375 ("For ... false imprisonment, upon pleading and proving merely the unlawful interference with his liberty, the plaintiff is entitled to *'general' damages for loss of time....*" (emphasis added)). The loss of time, an injury distinct from mental suffering or humiliation, may, but need not, have economic consequences; if recovery for an economic loss is sought, the common law treats that loss as an item of special damage that must be pleaded and proven. *See, e.g., id.* at 376, ("'*General*' damages [for false imprisonment] would *include* at least *the value of the time lost* by the plaintiff during the period of detention *and* any mental suffering or humiliation sustained in consequence of the arrest or restraint.... [I]tems of *special* damages ... [include] *the interruption of business, or the loss of a particular business opportunity or employment....*" (emphases added)).

* * *

* * * [T]he dissent states that "[a] loss of liberty, by itself, does not warrant a compensatory damages award any more than any other constitutional violation," * * * and that "to recover compensatory damages for a loss of liberty in a § 1983 action, a plaintiff must show that he suffered an injury compensable under the common law of torts." * * * [T]he New York and hornbook authorities reveal that the loss of liberty inherent in an unlawful detention is an injury compensable under the common law of torts.

* * *

Finally, we note that the damage done by the court's failure to instruct the jury that it could award Kerman compensatory damages for the loss of liberty inherent in an unlawful detention may well have been compounded by the court's erroneous instruction on nominal damages. The court instructed that "when the plaintiff has been deprived of a right.... as a result of any of the defendant's conduct," but no "actual" damages have been suffered, "[n]ominal damages *may* be awarded," and "if you find ... the deprivation of a legal right" but no other injury, "you *may* award, *if you so choose,* nominal damages not to exceed $1." (Tr. 761 (emphases added).) It is established, however, that "[i]f a jury finds that a constitutional violation has been proven but that the plaintiff has not shown injury sufficient to warrant an award of compensatory damages,.... it is plain error to instruct the jury merely that, having found a violation, it 'may' [rather than must] award nominal damages." * * * The jury here did in fact find that Kerman should receive nominal damages, making the court's use of "may" rather than "must," inconsequential insofar as nominal damages were concerned. But we have no confidence that the jury would not have awarded compensatory damages for the deprivation that it found unlawful if the court had instructed it that, upon such a finding, the jury "must" award Kerman at least nominal damages and could award him compensatory damages. Unquestionably the law authorizes the vindication of constitutional violations resulting in nonserious injury through awards of nominal damages. But it is the province of the jury to determine whether the plaintiff's injury resulting from a demonstrated loss of liberty was serious or nonserious and, if serious, to determine what compensation should be awarded. The jury here was not given instructions that provided it with guidance adequate to carry out that function.

* * * [W]e conclude that the failure in this case to give the jury any indication that it could consider awarding compensatory damages for an injury that was inherent in a confinement found to be unlawful was a fundamental error. Kerman remains entitled to have a jury assess the compensation he should be awarded on his Fourth Amendment claim against Crossan and his state-law claims against Crossan and the City for his loss of liberty for the time spent in the postsearch confinement without his consent.

3. The Scope of the New Trial

* * *

* * * We conclude that the liability issues were fairly tried and resolved. Accordingly, in light of the jury's finding that Crossan acted without probable cause, Kerman was entitled as a matter of law to an award of compensatory damages for so much of his postsearch loss of liberty as was attributable to Crossan, and it is appropriate to limit the new trial—the third trial in this case—to the amount of compensatory damages that Kerman should receive for his loss of liberty.

* * *

CONCLUSION

We have considered all of Crossan's contentions on this appeal and have found them to be without merit. The order of the district court granting judgment as a matter of law to Crossan is reversed. The April 23, 2002 judgment dismissing the complaint is vacated to the extent that it dismissed Kerman's Fourth Amendment claim against Crossan and the false imprisonment claims against Crossan and the City following the officers' completion of their search for a gun. The matter is remanded for a new trial on the issue of the amount of compensatory damages to be awarded to Kerman for loss of liberty.

RAGGI, CIRCUIT JUDGE, concurring in part and dissenting in part.

I concur in the majority opinion to the extent it reverses the grant of judgment as a matter of law to Crossan. I respectfully dissent, however, from Part III.C.2, which concludes that the district court committed fundamental error in failing to charge the jury that it could award Kerman compensatory damages for lost liberty based on the loss of his time while he was unlawfully confined. * * *

* * *

CALHOUN v. DETELLA

United States Court of Appeals, Seventh Circuit, 2003.
319 F.3d 936.

Before RIPPLE, ROVNER, and EVANS, CIRCUIT JUDGES.

ILANA DIAMOND ROVNER, CIRCUIT JUDGE.

Illinois prisoner Tyrone Calhoun sued under 42 U.S.C. § 1983, alleging in relevant part that prison employees at the Stateville Correctional Center conducted a deliberately harassing strip search in front of female guards that constituted cruel and unusual punishment under the Eighth Amendment. Relying on 28 U.S.C. § 1915A, the district court *sua sponte* dismissed Calhoun's complaint prior to service for failure to state a claim upon which relief may be granted. * * *

According to his amended complaint, prison guards removed Calhoun from his cell and escorted him from the prison's segregation unit to an open telephone area of the day room to conduct a strip search. When they reached the day room, Calhoun pleaded for the guards to take him to a more private area, but the guards ordered him to strip directly in front of several female guards who had no official role in conducting the search. Calhoun contends that he was forced to remove his clothing even after informing the guards that such a search, absent emergency circumstances, would violate the federal constitution, state law, and prison regulations. Further, he alleges that during the search the male and female officers laughed at him, made "sexual ribald comments," forced him to perform "provocative acts," and "pointed their sticks towards his anal area" while he bent over and spread his buttocks to permit visual inspection for contraband. Moreover, Calhoun contends, then-warden George DeTella and an assistant warden observed the search but took no corrective action. Finally, Calhoun alleges that the search constituted "sexual harassment," and that after his "traumatic experience" he sought psychological treatment, but did not receive the help he needed. He requested compensatory and punitive damages and injunctive and declaratory relief, as well as "such other relief as it may appear plaintiff is entitled."

In screening and dismissing the amended complaint under 28 U.S.C. § 1915A, the district court reasoned that Calhoun's suit was precluded by 42 U.S.C. § 1997e(e) [of the Prison Reform Litigation Act (PLRA)] because he alleges only psychological, and not physical injury. Calhoun timely moved to alter or amend the judgment, pointing out that § 1997e(e) does not foreclose injunctive and declaratory relief. *See* Zehner v. Trigg, 133 F.3d 459, 462–63 (7th Cir.1997); Davis v. Dist. of Columbia, 158 F.3d 1342, 1346 (D.C.Cir.1998). The district court denied the motion, concluding that the amended complaint did not allege grounds for either injunctive or declaratory relief. Calhoun appealed, and we appointed counsel to represent him.

In his amended complaint Calhoun asserts that the strip search violated * * * the Eighth Amendment * * *. He argues that the allegations in his amended complaint state a viable Eighth Amendment claim, and that even absent physical injury § 1997e(e) does not preclude him from recovering nominal and punitive damages for the constitutional violation. He concedes, however, that § 1997e(e) bars his recovery of compensatory damages for mental and emotional harm, and that his claims for declaratory and injunctive relief are now moot because he was transferred from Stateville to the Pontiac Correctional Facility during the pendency of this appeal. * * *

We review dismissals under § 1915A for failure to state a claim *de novo,* viewing all allegations in the complaint as true and in the light most favorable to the plaintiff. * * * With this standard in mind, we must first determine whether Calhoun's allegations, that prison guards purposefully demeaned and sexually harassed him while strip searching him in front of female officers, are sufficient to state a claim of cruel and unusual punishment under the Eighth Amendment.

There is no question that strip searches may be unpleasant, humiliating, and embarrassing to prisoners, but not every psychological discomfort a prisoner endures amounts to a constitutional violation. For example, the strip search of a male prisoner in front of female officers, if conducted for a legitimate penological purpose, would fail to rise to the level of an Eighth Amendment violation. *See* Johnson v. Phelan, 69 F.3d 144, 150–51 (7th Cir.1995). Instead, the Eighth Amendment prohibits unnecessary and wanton infliction of pain, thus forbidding punishment that is "so totally without penological justification that it results in the gratuitous infliction of suffering." Gregg v. Georgia, 428 U.S. 153, 173, 183, 96 S.Ct. 2909, 49 L.Ed.2d 859 (1976). Such gratuitous infliction of pain always violates contemporary standards of decency and need not produce serious injury in order to violate the Eighth Amendment. *See* Hudson v. McMillian, 503 U.S. 1, 9, 112 S.Ct. 995, 117 L.Ed.2d 156 (1992). Moreover, physical injury need not result for the punishment to state a cause of action, for the wanton infliction of psychological pain is also prohibited. *See id.* at 16, 112 S.Ct. 995 (Blackmun, J., concurring) * * *. Accordingly, to state an Eighth Amendment claim Calhoun must show that the strip search in question was not merely a legitimate search conducted in the presence of female correctional officers, but instead a search conducted in a harassing manner intended to humiliate and inflict psychological pain. * * *

* * * Calhoun alleges that the officers sexually harassed him through behavior unrelated to legitimate prison needs. In particular, he alleges that the guards made "ribald comments" and sexually explicit gestures during the search, and that they forced him to perform sexually provocative acts. Furthermore, he alleges that the female guards present during the search were neither mere passersby nor performing the legitimate penological function of conducting or monitoring the search; they were instead invited spectators. These allegations, if true, can only lead to the conclusion that the prison guards conducted the strip search in a manner designed to demean and humiliate Calhoun, and we therefore conclude that he sufficiently states a claim under the Eighth Amendment. * * *

Because Calhoun does not claim to have suffered a physical injury, we must next consider whether § 1997e(e) [of the PLRA] precludes his suit altogether by barring him from seeking recovery of nominal and punitive damages for the alleged Eighth Amendment violation. Section 1997e(e) provides that "[n]o Federal civil action may be brought by a prisoner ... for mental or emotional injury suffered while in custody without a prior showing of physical injury." 42 U.S.C. § 1997e(e). The Attorney General argues that a plain reading of § 1997e(e) bars Calhoun's suit entirely, reasoning that the statute makes a showing of physical injury a filing prerequisite for every civil rights lawsuit involving mental or emotional injury. We cannot agree. This contention if taken to its logical extreme would give prison officials free reign to maliciously and sadistically inflict psychological torture on prisoners, so long as they take care not to inflict any physical injury in the process.

Clearly this argument sweeps too broadly, and there is no longer room for the position the Attorney General espouses. As we have observed before and reemphasize here, "[i]t would be a serious mistake to interpret section 1997e(e) to require a showing of physical injury in all prisoner civil rights suits." Robinson v. Page, 170 F.3d 747, 748 (7th Cir.1999). On several occasions we have explained that § 1997e(e) may limit the relief available to prisoners who cannot allege a physical injury, but it does not bar their lawsuits altogether. See Cassidy v. Ind. Dep't of Corr., 199 F.3d 374, 376–77 (7th Cir.2000) (damages for mental and emotional injuries barred, but prisoner may pursue all other claims for damages); Zehner, 133 F.3d at 462 (injunctive relief available). As its title suggests, § 1997e(e) is a "limitation on recovery." Accordingly, physical injury is merely a predicate for an award of damages for mental or emotional injury, not a filing prerequisite for the federal civil action itself. See Robinson, 170 F.3d at 749.

We agree that, absent a showing of physical injury, § 1997e(e) would bar a prisoner's recovery of compensatory damages for mental and emotional injury. See Cassidy, 199 F.3d at 376. But if that same prisoner alleges some other type of non-physical injury, the statute would not foreclose recovery, assuming that the damages sought were not "for" any mental or emotional injuries suffered. See id.; Robinson, 170 F.3d at 749. This view is not novel. Indeed, in the context of First Amendment claims, we have held explicitly that prisoners need not allege a physical injury to recover damages because the deprivation of the constitutional right is itself a cognizable injury, regardless of any resulting mental or emotional injury. Rowe v. Shake, 196 F.3d 778, 781–82 (7th Cir.1999); see also Searles v. Van Bebber, 251 F.3d 869, 879–81 (10th Cir.2001) (nominal and punitive damages for First Amendment violation not barred); Allah v. Al–Hafeez, 226 F.3d 247, 252 (3d Cir.2000) (same); Canell v. Lightner, 143 F.3d 1210, 1213 (9th Cir.1998) (any form of relief for First Amendment violations available, if not for mental or emotional injury). Using a similar rationale, several of our sister circuits have concluded that § 1997e(e) does not bar all recovery for violations of due process or the right to privacy. *See* Thompson v. Carter, 284 F.3d 411, 418 (2d Cir.2002) (nominal and punitive damages available for deprivation-of-property claim); Oliver v. Keller, 289 F.3d 623, 630 (9th Cir.2002) (compensatory, nominal, or punitive damages available if premised on alleged unconstitutional conditions of pretrial confinement, and not emotional or mental distress suffered); Doe v. Delie, 257 F.3d 309, 314 n.3 & 323 (3d Cir.2001) (nominal and punitive damages available for violation of inmates' newly recognized right to medical privacy); *but cf.* Harris v. Garner, 190 F.3d 1279, 1282, 1287–88 & n.9 (§ 1997e(e) precludes compensatory and punitive damages for alleged violations of Fourth, Eighth, and Fourteenth Amendments, but expressing no view on nominal damages), *vacated & reh'g en banc granted*, 197 F.3d 1059 (11th Cir.1999), *reinstated in pertinent part*, 216 F.3d 970 (11th Cir.2000); *Davis*, 158 F.3d at 1348–49 (compensatory and punitive damages for violations of constitutional right to privacy barred, but expressing no view on nominal damages). These decisions reflect an emerging view that § 1997e(e), as the plain language of the statute would suggest, limits recovery "for mental and emotional injury," but leaves unaffected claims for nominal and punitive damages, which seek to remedy a different type of injury. *See Robinson*, 170 F.3d at 748.

We believe that the same reasoning effectively answers the question posed here, namely, whether § 1997e(e) forecloses an action for nominal or punitive damages for an Eighth Amendment violation involving no physical injury. Just as a "deprivation of First Amendment rights standing alone is a cognizable injury," *Rowe*, 196 F.3d at 781, so too is the violation of a person's right to be free from cruel and unusual punishment, *see* Harper v. Showers, 174 F.3d 716, 719 (5th Cir.1999) (claim of Eighth Amendment violation "is distinct from" any claim to entitlement for compensation for resulting mental or emotional damages). Although § 1997e(e) would bar recovery of compensatory damages "for" mental and emotional injuries suffered, the statute is inapplicable to awards of nominal or punitive damages for the Eighth Amendment violation itself.

This conclusion readily follows from the fact that nominal damages "are not compensation for loss or injury, but rather recognition of a violation of rights." Redding v. Fairman, 717 F.2d 1105, 1119 (7th Cir.1983); *see* Sahagian v. Dickey, 827 F.2d 90, 100 (7th Cir.1987). The Attorney General * * * argues that an award of nominal damages for Eighth Amendment violations would be inappropriate because the constitutional guarantee against cruel and unusual punishment, unlike the right to procedural due process, is not an "absolute" right. *Cf.* Carey v. Piphus, 435 U.S. 247, 266, 98 S.Ct. 1042, 55 L.Ed.2d 252 (1978) (because right to procedural due process is "absolute," nominal damages are available for denial of right even absent actual injury). * * * [W]e long ago decided that, at a minimum, a plaintiff who proves a constitutional violation is entitled to nominal damages. *See* Hessel v. O'Hearn, 977 F.2d 299, 302 (7th Cir.1992); Ustrak v. Fairman, 781 F.2d 573, 578 (7th Cir.1986). In particular, we have approved the award of nominal damages for Eighth

Amendment violations when prisoners could not establish actual compensable harm. *See* Madison County Jail Inmates v. Thompson, 773 F.2d 834, 844 (7th Cir.1985); *see also* Briggs v. Marshall, 93 F.3d 355, 360 (7th Cir.1996) (nominal damages available to remedy Fourth Amendment excessive force claim). Moreover, we note that several of our sister circuits have expressed similar approval of nominal damage awards for Eighth Amendment claims. *See, e.g.*, Gibeau v. Nellis, 18 F.3d 107, 110–11 (2d Cir.1994); Butler v. Dowd, 979 F.2d 661, 672 (8th Cir.1992) (en banc); Beyah v. Coughlin, 789 F.2d 986, 989 (2d Cir.1986); Green v. McKaskle, 788 F.2d 1116, 1124 (5th Cir.1986); Lancaster v. Rodriguez, 701 F.2d 864, 866 (10th Cir.1983); Doe v. Dist. of Columbia, 697 F.2d 1115, 1122–23 (D.C.Cir.1983); *see also* Slicker v. Jackson, 215 F.3d 1225, 1231 (11th Cir.2000) (approving of nominal damage award in excessive force case). Because nominal damages are awarded to vindicate rights, not to compensate for resulting injuries, we hold that § 1997e(e) does not bar a suit seeking nominal damages to vindicate Eighth Amendment rights. *See Thompson*, 284 F.3d at 418 (holding that § 1997e(e) does not limit availability of nominal damages for Eighth Amendment violations) * * *.

For similar reasons we believe that § 1997e(e) does not preclude claims for punitive damages for violations of the Eighth Amendment. *See Thompson*, 284 F.3d at 418 (punitive damages for Eighth Amendment violations not barred); *see also Benefield*, 241 F.3d at 1272 n.3 (suggesting without deciding that punitive damages for Eighth Amendment claims not barred); *Oliver*, 289 F.3d at 630 (punitive damages for constitutional violation not barred); *Doe*, 257 F.3d at 314 n.3 (same); *Searles*, 251 F.3d at 881 (same); *Allah*, 226 F.3d at 251–52 (same); *but see Harris*, 190 F.3d at 1286–87 (punitive damages barred); *Davis*, 158 F.3d at 1348 (same). Punitive damages are awarded to punish and deter reprehensible conduct. *See* Memphis Cmty. Sch. Dist. v. Stachura, 477 U.S. 299, 306 n.9, 106 S.Ct. 2537, 91 L.Ed.2d 249 (1986) * * *. And in Smith v. Wade, itself an Eighth Amendment case, the Supreme Court established that punitive damages may be awarded under § 1983 upon a showing of "evil motive or intent, or ... reckless or callous indifference to the federally protected rights of others." 461 U.S. 30, 56, 103 S.Ct. 1625, 75 L.Ed.2d 632 (1983) * * *. Moreover, nothing prevents an award of punitive damages for constitutional violations when compensatory damages are not available. *See* Erwin v. Manitowoc County, 872 F.2d 1292, 1299 (7th Cir.1989); *Sahagian*, 827 F.2d at 100. Because punitive damages are designed to punish and deter wrongdoers for deprivations of constitutional rights, they are not compensation "for" emotional and mental injury. *See Stachura*, 477 U.S. at 306, 106 S.Ct. 2537. We therefore conclude that Calhoun may pursue his claims for punitive damages as well.

* * *

For the foregoing reasons, we vacate the dismissal of Calhoun's amended complaint insofar as it alleges an Eighth Amendment violation, and remand for further proceedings on that claim. * * *

NOTE

The Prison Litigation Reform Act was enacted to keep frivolous suits out of the federal court system. For commentary on the Prison Litigation Reform Act, see Elizabeth J. Norman & Jacob E. Daly, *Statutory Civil Rights*, 53 Mercer L. Rev. 1499 (2002); James E. Robertson, *A Saving Construction: How to Read the Physical Injury Rule of the Prison Litigation Reform Act*, 26 S. Ill. U. L.J. 1 (2001); James E. Robertson, *Psychological Injury and the Prison Litigation Reform Act: A "Not Exactly" Equal Protection Analysis*, 37 Harv. J. on Legis. 105 (2000); Ashby F. Richbourg, Comment, *Civil Rights—Allah v. Al–Hafeez: Section 1997e(e) of the Prison Litigation Reform Act: A Recovery Limitation on Frivolous or Legitimate Claims?*, 32 U. Mem. L. Rev. 1031 (2002); Mary R. Schimmels, Comment, *First Amendment Suits and the Prison Litigation Reform Act's "Physical Requirement": The Availability of Damage Awards for Inmate Claimants*, 51 U. Kan. L. Rev. 935 (2003).

DISORBO v. HOY

United States Court of Appeals, Second Circuit, 2003.
343 F.3d 172.

Before: WALKER, CHIEF JUDGE, LEVAL, KATZMANN, CIRCUIT JUDGES.

KATZMANN, CIRCUIT JUDGE.

This case involves disturbing allegations of police brutality. In the early morning hours of December 27, 1998, while at the Union Inn Bar in Schenectady, New York, plaintiff-appellee-cross-appellant Rebecca DiSorbo was arrested by defendant-appellant-cross-appellee Ronald Pedersen, a Schenectady police officer. Rebecca DiSorbo claims she was arrested only because she rejected his personal advances. Rebecca DiSorbo's sister, plaintiff-cross-appellant Jessica DiSorbo, was arrested shortly thereafter, and both sisters were transported to the police station where they allegedly were victims of heinous acts of police aggression committed by Pedersen and two of his colleagues, defendants-cross-appellees officers Matthew Hoy and Kenneth Hill. Rebecca DiSorbo alleges that she was choked, slammed against the wall, thrown to the ground, and struck while defenseless on the floor. Jessica DiSorbo contends that she was slammed into a door and was forcibly dragged through the station.

After three jury trials, judgment was entered by the United States District Court for the Northern District of New York * * *. Rebecca DiSorbo prevailed in her excessive force, battery, and abuse of process claims against Pedersen, and the jury awarded compensatory [($400,000)] and punitive damages [($1.275 million)] totaling $1.675 million, for which the court ordered defendant-appellant-cross-appellee City of Schenectady to indemnify Pedersen. The jury also found municipal liability for the City under Monell v. Department of Social Services, 436 U.S. 658, 690–91, 98 S.Ct. 2018, 56 L.Ed.2d 611 (1978), upon concluding that Rebecca DiSorbo's constitutional rights were violated as a result of a City practice or custom.

In an order also filed this date, we uphold Pedersen's liability for excessive force, battery, and abuse of process, as well as the City's liability under *Monell*. Because we conclude that Pedersen and the City should be liable for the brutal attack suffered by Rebecca DiSorbo, we now address the District Court's rulings regarding damages.

This opinion considers whether the District Court improperly required the City to indemnify Pedersen and whether the punitive and compensatory damages awards were excessive. We conclude that a state court decision affirming the City's refusal to indemnify Pedersen for compensatory and punitive damages collaterally estops Pedersen from seeking indemnification here and therefore vacate the District Court's indemnification order. We note, however, that because the City is liable under *Monell*, the City is jointly and severally liable for the compensatory damages award, regardless of whether the City had an independent duty to indemnify Pedersen. With respect to the size of the damages awards, while we fully appreciate the gravity of the harm suffered by Rebecca DiSorbo and the justification for substantial compensatory and punitive damages in the face of such repulsive police misconduct, we are bound by precedent to compare the awards in this case with the awards in analogous cases. In so doing, we find that they were excessive. A new trial on damages therefore is necessary unless Rebecca DiSorbo chooses to accept a reduced damages award, a process referred to as remittitur. Accordingly, we remand for a new trial on damages, unless the plaintiff agrees to remit, resulting in $250,000 in compensatory damages and $75,000 in punitive damages.

* * *

III. EXCESSIVENESS OF PUNITIVE DAMAGES AWARD

The jury awarded Rebecca DiSorbo a total of $1.275 million in punitive damages against Pedersen, including $625,000 for the excessive force claim and $650,000 for the federal and state abuse of process claims. Pedersen and the City argue that this award was excessive under the factors set forth by the Supreme Court in BMW of North America v. Gore, 517 U.S. 559, 574–75, 116 S.Ct. 1589, 134 L.Ed.2d 809 (1996).

A jury may "assess punitive damages in an action under § 1983 when the defendant's conduct is shown to be motivated by evil motive or intent, or when it involves reckless or callous indifference to the federally protected rights of others." Smith v. Wade, 461 U.S. 30, 56, 103 S.Ct. 1625, 75 L.Ed.2d 632 (1983). As with compensatory damages, the standard for appellate review of punitive damages awarded under § 1983 considers "whether the award is so high as to shock the judicial conscience and constitute a denial of justice." * * * The Supreme Court in *Gore* identified three "guideposts" for determining whether a punitive damages award is excessive: 1) the degree of reprehensibility; 2) the disparity between the harm or potential harm and the punitive damages award; and 3) the difference between the remedy and the civil penalties authorized or imposed in comparable cases. *Gore*, 517 U.S. at 574–75, 116 S.Ct. 1589. We review a trial court's application of the *Gore* guideposts to a jury award *de novo*. Cooper Indus., Inc. v. Leatherman Tool Group, Inc., 532 U.S. 424, 443, 121 S.Ct. 1678, 149 L.Ed.2d 674 (2001). Guided by these standards, we consider each of the *Gore* factors in turn.

A. Degree of Reprehensibility

"Perhaps the most important indicium of the reasonableness of a punitive damages award is the degree of reprehensibility of the defendant's conduct." *Gore*, 517 U.S. at 575, 116 S.Ct. 1589. Reprehensibility in this context entails more than merely asking whether the conduct was unacceptable. Lee v. Edwards, 101 F.3d 805, 809 (2d Cir.1996). The fact that conduct is sufficiently reprehensible so as to trigger tort liability and damages "does not establish the high degree of culpability that warrants a substantial punitive damages award." *Gore*, 517 U.S. at 580, 116 S.Ct. 1589. The Court in *Gore* identified certain aggravating factors to be considered when assessing the degree of reprehensibility: 1) whether a defendant's conduct was violent or presented a threat of violence; 2) whether a defendant acted with malice as opposed to mere negligence; and 3) whether a defendant has engaged in repeated instances of misconduct. *Id.* at 576, 116 S.Ct. 1589.

Crediting Rebecca DiSorbo's version of the events at the police station, Pedersen engaged in highly reprehensible conduct that, to some extent, satisfy each of *Gore's* aggravating factors. Rebecca DiSorbo alleges that Pedersen violently slammed her against the wall, choked her to the point where she began to lose vision, pushed her to the ground, and struck her while she was on the ground. The deliberate nature of these attacks demonstrate that Pedersen was not merely negligent, but was acting with malice toward Rebecca DiSorbo. Further, Rebecca DiSorbo alleges that Pedersen engaged in repeated acts of violence against her at the station. Accordingly, Pedersen's actions were sufficiently reprehensible under *Gore* to justify punitive damages.

B. Disparity Between Harm and Punitive Damages Award

To assess the appropriateness of the ratio of the punitive damages award to the harm, "the proper inquiry is whether there is a reasonable relationship between the punitive damages award and the harm likely to result from the defendant's conduct as well as the harm that actually has occurred." *Gore*, 517 U.S. at 581, 116 S.Ct. 1589 (quotation marks and emphasis omitted). This consideration requires courts to "ensure that the measure of punishment is both reasonable and proportionate to the amount of harm to the plaintiff and to the general damages recovered." State Farm Mut. Auto. Ins. Co. v. Campbell, 538 U.S. 408, 123 S.Ct. 1513, 1524, 155 L.Ed.2d 585 (2003). Our reasonableness determination does not entail a "simple mathematical formula," as there may be cases where "a particularly egregious act has resulted in only a small amount of economic damages." *Gore*, 517 U.S. at 582, 116 S.Ct. 1589; *see Lee*, 101 F.3d at 810–

11 (refusing to rely on a mathematical multiplier to assess the reasonableness of the award where the compensatory award was nominal).

Consideration of the disparity between the punitive damages award and the harm provides minimal assistance in the instant case. For example, if we assume that Rebecca DiSorbo remits to yield a $250,000 compensatory damages award for the excessive force claim, the ratio between compensatory and punitive damages would be 2.5–to –1, which would not appear to be an unreasonable ratio. If we look at the abuse of process claim, however, the jury awarded only nominal compensatory damages, yielding a staggering 650,000–to –1 ratio of punitive damages to compensatory damages. We therefore conclude that "the use of a multiplier to assess punitive damages is not the best tool here." *Lee*, 101 F.3d at 811.

C. Difference Between Remedy and Civil Penalties in Comparable Cases

The final *Gore* factor compares the punitive damages award with the civil and criminal penalties for comparable misconduct. *Gore*, 517 U.S. at 583, 116 S.Ct. 1589. The rationale for this consideration is that, if the penalties for comparable misconduct are much less than a punitive damages award, the tortfeasor lacked fair notice that the wrongful conduct could entail a sizable punitive damages award. *Lee*, 101 F.3d at 811.

The most relevant crime in New York would likely be assault in the third degree, which is a class A misdemeanor. N.Y. Pen. L. § 120.00 ("A person is guilty of assault in the third degree when: 1. With intent to cause physical injury to another person, he causes such injury to such person.... Assault in the third degree is a class A misdemeanor."). A class A misdemeanor carries a maximum sentence of one year, *id.* at § 70.15[1], and a maximum penalty of one thousand dollars, *id.* at § 80.05[1]. While a year's imprisonment is undoubtedly a substantial punishment, a maximum fine of $1,000 gives little warning that the action could result in a $1.275 million punitive damages award. *See Lee,* 101 F.3d at 811.

As we noted in *Lee*, however, criminal penalties understate the notice when the misconduct is committed by a police officer. *Lee*, 101 F.3d at 811. We assumed in *Lee* "that [the defendant officer's] training as a police officer gave him notice as to the gravity of misconduct under color of his official authority, as well as notice that such misconduct could hinder his career." *Id*. Still, in *Lee* the court concluded that this guidepost weighed in favor of finding the $200,000 punitive damages award to be excessive. The court explained that, notwithstanding the officer's notice as to the gravity of his actions, "nothing could conceivably have prepared him for a punitive damage award amounting to the sacrifice of the better part of a policeman's after-tax pay for a decade." *Id*.

D. Totality of Gore Factors

Police brutality cannot be tolerated in our society, and punitive damages awards serve a critical role in deterring such misconduct. *See*

State Farm Mut. Auto. Ins. Co., 538 U.S. at 416, 123 S.Ct. at 1519 ("By contrast [with compensatory damages], punitive damages serve a broader function; they are aimed at deterrence and retribution."). Pedersen abused a position of respect and authority to commit malicious and repeated acts of violence against a vastly weaker and helpless victim. We are thoroughly convinced that this conduct was sufficiently reprehensible to justify some degree of punitive damages. There must, however, be an upper limit to that award, and after carefully evaluating the *Gore* factors, and taking into consideration the sizable compensatory damages award Rebecca DiSorbo would receive if she remits, we are compelled to conclude that the $1.275 million punitive damages award exceeded that limit. *See id.* at 1526.

To determine the appropriate level of punitive damages, we assess such awards in other police misconduct cases. *See Lee*, 101 F.3d at 812. The defendant officer in *Lee* struck the plaintiff, who was handcuffed, eight or nine times in the head with his police baton, to the point where the plaintiff was knocked unconscious and had to be hospitalized. *Id.* at 807–08. Although similar to the instant case, the brutality of these strikes seems to have been more severe than those inflicted by Pedersen on Rebecca DiSorbo, as Pedersen did not use a weapon and did not beat her to the point of unconsciousness. After weighing the *Gore* factors, we determined in *Lee* that the jury's $200,000 punitive damages award was excessive, and ordered a new trial unless the plaintiff agreed to remit $125,000, and accepted a $75,000 punitive damages award. *Id.* at 813.

In Ismail v. Cohen, 899 F.2d 183 (2d Cir.1990), we upheld a $150,000 punitive damages verdict. * * * [T]he defendant officer in *Ismail* struck the plaintiff in the side of the head without warning, causing him to lose consciousness, pressed his gun against the plaintiff's head, implanted his knee into the plaintiff's back, and threatened to kill the plaintiff. * * * The officer's conduct in *Ismail* appears to have been even more reprehensible than the conduct in our case. While Rebecca DiSorbo suffered a heinous attack at the hands of Pedersen, Pedersen did not beat Rebecca DiSorbo to the point of losing consciousness, never brandished a firearm, and never threatened her life.

We find further guidance from O'Neill v. Krzeminski, 839 F.2d 9 (2d Cir.1988), where we upheld a $185,000 punitive damages award for the brutal beating by several police officers of a defenseless plaintiff at a police station. The plaintiff, while handcuffed and unable to defend himself, was struck repeatedly in the face and head, with at least one blow struck by using a blackjack. * * * An officer "then dragged [the plaintiff] by the throat across the detention area, castigating him for 'bleeding all over my floor.' " *Id.* Pedersen's use of excessive force was of a different order than the beating inflicted by the officers in *O'Neill*. Moreover, the jury in the case before us only found liability based on a single officer's misconduct, rather than several officers as was the situation in *O'Neill*.

Upon careful review of misconduct in these cases, we are compelled to conclude that a punitive damages award of $75,000 more accurately reflects the severity of Pedersen's acts under the *Gore* guideposts. We therefore remand for a new trial on punitive damages, unless Rebecca DiSorbo agrees to remit $1.2 million, yielding a $75,000 punitive damages award, which is comparable to the upper limits of the punitive damages awarded in similar police brutality cases.[9]

* * * Unless Rebecca DiSorbo agrees to accept $250,000 in compensatory damages and $75,000 in punitive damages, which would entail remitting $150,000 of the compensatory damages award and $1.2 million of the punitive damages award, we order a new trial on damages.

NOTE

For a § 1983 case awarding nominal damages plus $100,000 in punitive damages to the victim of a procedural due process violation, see Caban–Wheeler v. Elsea, 71 F.3d 837 (11th Cir.1996). Usually, when a plaintiff recovers nominal damages without compensatory damages under § 1983, the amount of the punitive damages award does not exceed $15,000. Williams v. Kaufman County, 352 F.3d 994, 1016 n.78 (5th Cir.2003) (surveying federal court cases). For scholarly commentary on punitive damages in Section 1983 actions, see Michael Wells, *Punitive Damages for Constitutional Torts*, 56 La. L. Rev. 841 (1996); John R. Williams, *Punitive Damages in Section 1983 Cases*, 17 Touro L. Rev. 575 (2001).

B. INJUNCTIVE RELIEF

1. School Desegregation and the Structural Injunction

BROWN v. BOARD OF EDUCATION (BROWN II)

Supreme Court of the United States, 1955.
349 U.S. 294, 75 S.Ct. 753, 99 L.Ed. 1083.

Before WARREN, CHIEF JUSTICE, BLACK, REED, FRANKFURTER, DOUGLAS, BURTON, CLARK, MINTON, HARLAN, JUSTICES.

MR. CHIEF JUSTICE WARREN delivered the opinion of the Court.

These cases were decided on May 17, 1954. The opinions of that date,[1] declaring the fundamental principle that racial discrimination in public education is unconstitutional, are incorporated herein by reference. All

---

9. If there is a new trial on punitive damages, and in light of our earlier holding that the District Court erred in requiring the City to indemnify Pedersen for punitive damages, we note that the District Court should admit evidence of Pedersen's financial situation. "[O]ne purpose of punitive damages is deterrence, and that deterrence is directly related to what people can afford to pay." *Lee*, 101 F.3d at 813 (citing Vasbinder v. Scott, 976 F.2d 118, 121 (2d Cir.1992)); *see* City of Newport v. Fact Concerts, Inc., 453 U.S. 247, 270, 101 S.Ct. 2748, 69 L.Ed.2d 616 (1981) (noting that "evidence of a tortfeasor's wealth is traditionally admissible as a measure of the amount of punitive damages that should be awarded").

1. 347 U.S. 483; 347 U.S. 497.

provisions of federal, state, or local law requiring or permitting such discrimination must yield to this principle. There remains for consideration the manner in which relief is to be accorded.

Because these cases arose under different local conditions and their disposition will involve a variety of local problems, we requested further argument on the question of relief.[2] In view of the nationwide importance of the decision, we invited the Attorney General of the United States and the Attorneys General of all states requiring or permitting racial discrimination in public education to present their views on that question. * * *

* * *

Full implementation of these constitutional principles may require solution of varied local school problems. School authorities have the primary responsibility for elucidating, assessing, and solving these problems; courts will have to consider whether the action of school authorities constitutes good faith implementation of the governing constitutional principles. Because of their proximity to local conditions and the possible need for further hearings, the courts which originally heard these cases can best perform this judicial appraisal. Accordingly, we believe it appropriate to remand the cases to those courts.

In fashioning and effectuating the decrees, the courts will be guided by equitable principles. Traditionally, equity has been characterized by a practical flexibility in shaping its remedies and by a facility for adjusting and reconciling public and private needs. These cases call for the exercise of these traditional attributes of equity power. At stake is the personal interest of the plaintiffs in admission to public schools as soon as practicable on a nondiscriminatory basis. To effectuate this interest may call for elimination of a variety of obstacles in making the transition to school systems operated in accordance with the constitutional principles set forth in our May 17, 1954, decision. Courts of equity may properly take into

2. Further argument was requested on the following questions, 347 U.S. 483, 495–496, n.13, previously propounded by the Court:

4. Assuming it is decided that segregation in public schools violates the Fourteenth Amendment

(*a*) would a decree necessarily follow providing that, within the limits set by normal geographic school districting, Negro children should forthwith be admitted to schools of their choice, or

(*b*) may this Court, in the exercise of its equity powers, permit an effective gradual adjustment to be brought about from existing segregated systems to a system not based on color distinctions?

5. On the assumption on which questions 4 (*a*) and (*b*) are based, and assuming further that this Court will exercise its equity powers to the end described in question 4 (*b*),

(*a*) should this Court formulate detailed decrees in these cases;

(*b*) if so, what specific issues should the decrees reach;

(*c*) should this Court appoint a special master to hear evidence with a view to recommending specific terms for such decrees;

(*d*) should this Court remand to the courts of first instance with directions to frame decrees in these cases, and if so what general directions should the decrees of this Court include and what procedures should the courts of first instance follow in arriving at the specific terms of more detailed decrees?

account the public interest in the elimination of such obstacles in a systematic and effective manner. But it should go without saying that the vitality of these constitutional principles cannot be allowed to yield simply because of disagreement with them.

While giving weight to these public and private considerations, the courts will require that the defendants make a prompt and reasonable start toward full compliance with our May 17, 1954, ruling. Once such a start has been made, the courts may find that additional time is necessary to carry out the ruling in an effective manner. The burden rests upon the defendants to establish that such time is necessary in the public interest and is consistent with good faith compliance at the earliest practicable date. To that end, the courts may consider problems related to administration, arising from the physical condition of the school plant, the school transportation system, personnel, revision of school districts and attendance areas into compact units to achieve a system of determining admission to the public schools on a nonracial basis, and revision of local laws and regulations which may be necessary in solving the foregoing problems. They will also consider the adequacy of any plans the defendants may propose to meet these problems and to effectuate a transition to a racially nondiscriminatory school system. During this period of transition, the courts will retain jurisdiction of these cases.

The judgments below * * * are accordingly reversed and the cases are remanded to the District Courts to take such proceedings and enter such orders and decrees consistent with this opinion as are necessary and proper to admit to public schools on a racially nondiscriminatory basis with all deliberate speed the parties to these cases. * * *

NOTES

1. The previous case referred to in *Brown II* was, of course, *Brown I*, which held that separate but equal can never be equal. Chief Justice Earl Warren said, for a unanimous Court:

> To separate [children] from others of similar age and qualifications solely because of their race generates a feeling of inferiority as to their status in the community that may affect their hearts and minds in a way unlikely ever to be undone. * * *

> * * *

> We conclude that in the field of public education the doctrine of "separate but equal" has no place. Separate educational facilities are inherently unequal. Therefore, we hold that the plaintiffs and others similarly situated for whom the actions have been brought are, by reason of the segregation complained of, deprived of the equal protection of the laws guaranteed by the Fourteenth Amendment.

Brown v. Board of Education, 347 U.S. 483, 494–95, 74 S. Ct. 686, 691–92, 98 L.Ed. 873, 881(1954) (*Brown I*).

2. Before *Brown I*, segregation had been a way of life in many states since the Civil War, and was legitimated more than fifty years before *Brown* by Plessy v. Ferguson, 163 U.S. 537, 16 S.Ct. 1138, 41 L.Ed. 256 (1896). *Plessy*, which was overruled by *Brown I*, had held, in the context of seating on public railway carriages, that separate but equal facilities for blacks and whites were not unconstitutional. As a result, desegregating schools in a segregated world could not involve simple equitable orders to someone to do or not do something. As the Court in *Brown II* anticipated, courts were going to need to change institutions. Court orders to change, or "restructure," institutions became known as "structural injunctions." *See* Owen M. Fiss, The Civil Rights Injunction (1978).

3. Many commentators over the years have criticized the Court's phrase "all deliberate speed" in *Brown II* as a retreat from the requirements of *Brown I*. Given the lack of resources of the all-black schools, however, simply equalizing enrollments between the black and white schools was not going to be possible. In addition, there was great hostility towards integration, hostility that often led to defiance of court orders and violence. As Professor Kovacic–Fleischer has stated:

> While there were many talented and dedicated black teachers, the schools were seriously underfunded and lacked facilities and supplies. Because schools were unequal, large numbers of students could not immediately be integrated. With only a few black students initially transferred to white schools, whites had safety in numbers while a few black students had to bear the brunt of taunts and threats. * * *

* * *

* * * [A] case that reached the Supreme Court a decade after *Brown* illustrates how far school officials would go to avoid desegregation. In Griffin v. County School Board of Prince Edward County, [377 U.S. 218, 84 S.Ct. 1226, 12 L.Ed.2d 256 (1964)], school officials closed public schools rather than integrate them. The Supreme Court upheld the trial judge's order to the officials to open the schools and levy taxes.

Candace Saari Kovacic–Fleischer, *Comparing Remedies for School Desegregation and Employment Discrimination: Can Employers Now Help Schools?* 41 San Diego L. Rev. 1695, 1699–1704 (2004). Many judges were also hostile and reluctant to issue meaningful orders. Some southern federal judges, however, with great courage and at personal risk, did enforce desegregation. *See, e.g.*, Jack Bass, Unlikely Heroes (1990). The case that follows is an example of an equally courageous judge attempting to "restructure" a segregated school district in the North, where the problems were no less difficult than in the South.

MORGAN v. McDONOUGH

United States Court of Appeals, First Circuit, 1976.
540 F.2d 527.

Before COFFIN, CHIEF JUDGE, MCENTEE and CAMPBELL, CIRCUIT JUDGES.

LEVIN H. CAMPBELL, CIRCUIT JUDGE.

This appeal was filed on December 10, 1975, by the Boston School Committee (the Committee) from orders of the district court designating a temporary receiver for South Boston High School and ordering the transfer, without reduction in pay, of certain of its staff. The question before us is whether under the extraordinarily difficult and troubled circumstances confronting the School in the fall and early winter of 1975, the district court exceeded its powers in entering such orders. The instant appeal does not deal with how long such a receivership may properly last.

First integrated by court order in 1974 ("Phase I"), the South Boston High School was serving a racially mixed enrollment in 1975–76 under Phase II, a city wide desegregation plan formulated by the district court and upheld on appeal to this court. * * * In November, 1975, the plaintiffs, representing a class of all black Boston public school students and parents, moved to close the School, alleging that black students there were being denied a peaceful, integrated and nondiscriminatory education. Following a lengthy hearing and several visits to the School, the district court found plaintiffs' basic allegations to be correct, but declined to close the School, ordering instead that it be placed in the temporary receivership of the court, effective December 10, 1975. The court first named as receiver a senior official of the Boston School Department, who was, in fact, the assistant superintendent for the district within which the School was located, but on January 9, 1976, after this appeal was filed, the court appointed Boston's Superintendent of Schools, Marion J. Fahey, as temporary receiver in place of the previous receiver. The stated purpose of the receivership was to effectuate as soon as possible "such changes in the administration and operation of South Boston High School as are necessary to bring the School into compliance with the student desegregation plan dated May 10, 1975 [Phase II], and all other remedial orders entered by the court in these proceedings, e.g., desegregation of faculty and staff." The court directed the receiver to (1) arrange for the transfer of the School's headmaster, full-time academic administrators, and football coach, without reduction in compensation, benefits, or seniority; (2) evaluate the qualifications of all faculty and educational personnel and arrange the transfer and replacement of whomever he sees fit for the purposes of desegregation, without reduction in compensation, benefits, or seniority; (3) file a plan with the court for the renovation of the School; (4) try to enroll non-attending students and establish catch-up classes; and (5) make recommendations to the court relative to certain provisions of the plan. It is the receivership order and the foregoing directions, including especially those for transfer of staff, which are the subject of this appeal.

As the district court's primary orders requiring South Boston High School and other Boston schools to be desegregated have been reviewed and sustained, * * * the time is no longer ripe to consider arguments against Phase II itself. The questions now before us are simply whether the lower court properly determined that plaintiff's rights under the desegregation plan were being violated at South Boston High School, and if so, whether the temporary remedies ordered were reasonable and lawful. We answer these questions in the affirmative. Given the lawfulness of the court's desegregation decrees, there is little question that it had the power to take reasonable steps to ensure compliance therewith and to protect the students attending the city's desegregated schools. The evidence here does not show that the court went beyond what might reasonably be considered necessary to cope with a grave threat to the desegregation plan and to the safety and rights of the black students at South Boston High School.

* * *

The district court's central impression was that the services provided at South Boston High were "primarily custodial and only incidentally educational." The court characterized the atmosphere as not so much filled with racial tension, or even any tension, as with a "pervasive lassitude and emptiness." * * *

* * *

The district court's findings indicate that, as the court concluded, black students attending the School were not receiving a "peaceful, desegregated education". Rather they were subject to insult, intimidation and continued segregation. * * * Doubtless the difficulty stemmed in no small measure from intentional conduct by private organizations and individuals in the South Boston community. But difficult as was the position of school officials, there was reason to believe that conditions could have been, and still could be, ameliorated by them, and that their active and passive conduct contributed to the grave situation so clearly at odds with the court's prior decrees. * * *

The question thus boils down to the propriety of the relief that was ordered. A district court's power to fashion and effectuate desegregation decrees is broad and flexible, and the remedies may be "administratively awkward, inconvenient, and even bizarre". Swann v. Charlotte–Mecklenburg Board of Education, 402 U.S. 1, 15–16, 28, 91 S.Ct. 1267, 1282, 28 L.Ed.2d 554 (1971). Remedial devices should be effective and relief prompt. * * * While a receivership has been instituted only once in a reported desegregation case, Turner v. Goolsby, 255 F.Supp. 724 (S.D.Ga. 1965), receiverships are and have for years been a familiar equitable mechanism. See Fed.R.Civ.P. 66; 4 Pomeroy, Equity Jurisprudence § 1330 et seq. (Symons ed.1941). They are commonly a vehicle for court supervision of distressed businesses, but have not been limited to that role. The Supreme Court indicated many years ago that a receiver might take charge of a company to enforce compliance with the antitrust laws. * * * Receiverships and court-appointed officials with some of the same functions as the receiver here have been approved in other contexts. See, e.g., Inmates of Attica Correctional Facility v. Rockefeller, 453 F.2d 12, 25 (2d Cir.1971). * * * Masters have been used extensively to formulate plans and recommendations, one of the present receiver's chief functions. * * *

Finally, there is precedent for a district court having desegregation responsibilities to order personnel shifts. * * *

We thus find nothing impermissible *per se* about any of the actions the court took. The test is one of reasonableness under the circumstances. To be sure, direct judicial intervention in the operation of a school system is not to be welcomed, and it should not be continued longer than necessary. But if in extraordinary circumstances it is the only reasonable alternative to noncompliance with a court's plan of desegregation, it may, with appropriate restraint, be ordered. * * *

The receivership here was a means to enlist without delay top Boston School Department leadership to work in conjunction with the court on the troubles of the School. The court utilized the device to ensure priority attention by senior administrators, under court supervision, to South Boston High's unique problems. The more usual remedies—contempt proceedings and further injunctions—were plainly not very promising, as they invited further confrontation and delay; and when the usual remedies are inadequate, a court of equity is justified, particularly in aid of an outstanding injunction, in turning to less common ones, such as a receivership, to get the job done. * * *

Had the School Committee then in office been cooperative, a voluntary approach might have summoned similar resources without need for a formal receivership. However, the then School Committee had continuously resisted desegregation, and its leaders had advised the court on more than one occasion that they would obey nothing but direct orders. The court had reasonable cause, therefore, to discount the likelihood of effective cooperation. It also had reason to fear that even direct orders to that Committee would, as in the past, be met by resistance, subterfuge, or, at very least, delay. * * * Finally, it bears emphasizing that the principal alternative being suggested to the receivership order was to order that South Boston High be closed. That alternative would not only have involved the abandonment of a large and useful facility but would have necessitated the planning, expense, and inconvenience of finding places for some 2000 students. Without expressing any opinion on the propriety of ordering the School closed, it can be said that the district court demonstrated both restraint and wisdom in selecting the receivership option. For all of the foregoing reasons, therefore, we see the district court's action not as excessive but as reasonably tailored to carrying out the court's responsibilities.

Nor do we find unreasonable the transfer of the headmaster, coach and other staff. Apart from finding overt resistance to the segregation plan by the coach, the court also noted adverse faculty attitudes and a lack of leadership by the School administration in implementing the plan. Given the situation that had developed at the School under existing leadership, the court was entitled to conclude that a change in command was indicated. The change tied into the appointment of the receiver, giving the latter, in conjunction with the court, the opportunity, after study, to bring in administrators and perhaps faculty that seemed best able to cope with the extraordinary difficulties and pressures at the School.

It is true that the court's actions, while not reaching beyond the professional School Department, supplanted the supervisory authority of the elected Committee in this area. However, judicial desegregation necessarily involves some displacement of decision-making powers, as we have already witnessed in other aspects of this case, *e.g.*, drawing of district lines, teacher hiring, and so on. * * * The extent of the court's power is limited to what is required to ensure students their right to a non-segregated education, but within that parameter it may do what reasonably it must. * * *

Here, contrary to the Committee's assertions, we find no evidence of any intrusion by the district court upon the School Committee's right to determine "educational philosophy" except as that philosophy might impermissibly encourage a racially separate school system. The "limited, general purpose of said receivership", as the lower court stated, is only to bring the School into compliance with the desegregation plan and orders. As the receiver is the Superintendent of Schools, we can see little danger that the receivership will introduce educational policies contrary to those prevailing in the system as a whole. * * *

We would, however, add a *caveat*. Obviously the substitution of a court's authority for that of elected and appointed officials is an extraordinary step warranted only by the most compelling circumstances. Those circumstances here were the failure of local officials to give effect to the court's desegregation orders in a meaningful manner. The receivership should last no longer than the conditions which justify it make necessary, and the court's utilization of the receivership must not go beyond the constitutional purposes which the device is designed to promote. We have no doubt that the district court will exercise appropriate restraint in this respect and, in particular, will give thought to appropriate conditions under which the receivership can be terminated at the earliest opportunity consistent with the rights of children and parents to a peaceful non-segregated education.

Affirmed.

NOTES

1. Swann v. Charlotte–Mecklenburg Board of Education, 402 U.S. 1, 91 S.Ct. 1267, 28 L.Ed.2d 554 (1971), cited in *Morgan*, involved one school district in a county in North Carolina that had maintained two separate school systems on the basis of race. The Court authorized a wide range of remedies to desegregate the two school systems, including an interim use of gerrymandered school districts and busing of students. The Court said: "Once a right and a violation have been shown, the scope of a district court's equitable powers to remedy past wrongs is broad, for breadth and flexibility

are inherent in equitable remedies." *Id.* at 15, 91 S.Ct. at 1276, 28 L.Ed.2d at 566. The same year that *Swann* was decided, the Federal District Court of the Eastern District of Michigan found that state and local officials in Detroit had created segregated public schools by, among other things, gerrymandering school districts and using busing to ensure racially homogeneous schools. Bradley v. Milliken, 338 F.Supp. 582 (E.D.Mich.1971). The district court found that desegregation in Detroit would not work because of the white flight to the suburbs and therefore issued an interdistrict remedy, affirmed by the Sixth Circuit, that would have distributed school attendance across political boundaries in Detroit and its suburbs. 484 F.2d 215 (6th Cir.1973). The Supreme Court, by a vote of five to four, reversed the interdistrict injunction. Milliken v. Bradley, 418 U.S. 717, 94 S.Ct. 3112, 41 L.Ed.2d 1069 (1974) (*Milliken I*). Chief Justice Burger, who had also authored the opinion in *Swann*, wrote for the majority and expressed concern that an interdistrict remedy would require the district court judge to "become first, a *de facto* 'legislative authority' to resolve these complex questions, and then the 'school superintendent' for the entire area." *Id.* at 743–44, 94 S.Ct. at 3126–27, 41 L.Ed.2d at 1090. The majority then said:

> The controlling principle consistently expounded in our holdings is that the scope of the remedy is determined by the nature and extent of the constitutional violation. * * * Thus an interdistrict remedy might be in order where the racially discriminatory acts of one or more school districts caused racial segregation in an adjacent district, or where district lines have been deliberately drawn on the basis of race. * * *

> The record before us, voluminous as it is, contains evidence of *de jure* segregated conditions only in the Detroit schools.

Id. at 744–45, 94 S.Ct. at 3127, 41 L.Ed.2d at 1091.

Justice White, in his dissenting opinion, disagreed, saying:

> The Michigan Supreme Court has observed that "[t]he school district is a State agency." * * *

> I cannot understand, nor does the majority satisfactorily explain, why a federal court may not order an appropriate inter-district remedy, if this is necessary or more effective to accomplish this constitutionally mandated task.

Id. at 772, 94 S.Ct. at 3140, 41 L.Ed.2d at 1106–07.

Justice Marshall, in his dissenting opinion, also disagreed with the majority, saying:

> The State must * * * bear part of the blame for the White flight to the suburbs * * *. Having created a system where whites and Negroes were intentionally kept apart so that they could not become accustomed to learning together, the State is responsible for the fact that many whites will react to the dismantling of that segregated system by attempting to flee to the suburbs. Indeed, by limiting the District Court to a Detroit-only remedy * * *, the Court today allows the State * * * to perpetuate for years to come the separation of the races it achieved in the past by purposeful state action.

Id. at 806, 94 S.Ct. at 3157, 41 L.Ed.2d at 1126.

The majority answered the dissenters, saying:

Our assumption * * * that state agencies did participate in the maintenance of the Detroit system, should make it clear that it is not on this point that we part company. The difference between us arises instead from established doctrine laid down by our cases. * * * [T]he remedy is necessarily designed, as all remedies are, to restore the victims of discriminatory conduct to the position they would have occupied in the absence of such conduct. Disparate treatment of white and Negro students occurred within the Detroit school system, and not elsewhere, and on this record the remedy must be limited to that system.

Id. at 746, 94 S.Ct. at 3128, 41 L.Ed.2d at 1092.

2. If interdistrict remedies cannot be used to desegregate the schools despite "white flight," what remedies are available? In *Milliken II*, the district court ordered, among other things, remedial training for students and teacher training, to be paid for by both the school district and the State. The Supreme Court rejected the State's argument that these remedies exceeded the scope of the constitutional violation and provided a three-part test for remedial orders: first, the remedy must relate to the violation; second, it must "restore the victims of discriminatory conduct to the position they would have occupied in the absence of such conduct," as far as practicable; and, third, it "must take into account the interest of state and local authorities in managing their own affairs." Milliken v. Bradley, 433 U.S. 267, 280–81, 97 S.Ct. 2749, 2757, 53 L.Ed.2d 745, 756 (1977) (*Milliken II*).

3. In Jenkins v. Missouri, 639 F.Supp. 19 (W.D.Mo.1985), to counteract the effects of white flight, the District Court ordered that each school in Kansas City be made both academically and structurally as good or better than the suburban schools. Because the changes ordered would be expensive, the school officials wanted to raise taxes, but they were constrained by a state statute that prohibited them from raising property taxes without voter approval. When four school district referenda did not pass, the school district officials asked the district court for an injunction. The court issued an order raising property taxes on residents and income taxes on nonresidents who worked in Kansas City. 672 F.Supp. 400 (W.D.Mo.1987). The Eighth Circuit reversed any increase in the income tax, but reversed the increase in the property tax only on the ground that the trial court should have ordered the local officials to set the tax rate, rather than setting the rate itself. Jenkins v. Missouri, 855 F.2d 1295 (8th Cir.1988). The Supreme Court granted the writ of certiorari only on the issue of taxing, not on the propriety of the scope of the remedy, and unanimously agreed that the Eighth Circuit's reversal was correct, but, again by a vote of five to four, for different reasons. Justice White, writing for the majority, said: "It is * * * clear that a local government with taxing authority may be ordered to levy taxes in excess of the limit set by state statute when there is reason based in the Constitution for not observing the statutory limitation." 495 U.S. 33, 57, 110 S.Ct. 1651, 1666, 109 L.Ed.2d 31, 58 (1990) (*Jenkins II*). (Missouri v. Jenkins, 491 U.S. 274, 109 S.Ct. 2463, 105 L.Ed.2d 229 (1989) (*Jenkins I*) was a case that had involved attorney's fees.) However, Justice Kennedy, in his concurrence, stated: "Our

cases throughout the years leave no doubt that taxation is not a judicial function." 495 U.S. at 65, 110 S.Ct. at 1670, 109 L.Ed.2d at 63 (Kennedy, J., concurring). With whom do you agree?

4. In *Morgan*, Judge Garrity was fortunate to be able to appoint Boston's Superintendent of Schools as the temporary receiver, having found that "direct orders" to the School Committee were "not very promising." In contrast to *Morgan*, the local officials in *Jenkins* wanted to raise the property taxes. When local officials are not cooperative, does a court intrude less in the operation of local government by appointing a receiver to comply with the order, or by holding the local jurisdiction and officials in contempt? In *Morgan*, what would have happened if no state educational employee had been willing to effectuate Judge Garrity's orders? *Cf.* Spallone v. United States, 493 U.S. 265, 272, 110 S.Ct. 625, 107 L.Ed.2d 644 (1990) (overturning coercive contempt fines imposed by district court against individual council members for violating consent decree in which they had agreed to take council action to correct constitutional violations in housing; holding that, because a court must use the "least possible power adequate to the end proposed," such fines should be used only if the fines imposed on the city had failed). *See generally* Candace S. Kovacic–Fleischer, *The Remedial Problems of* Spallone v. United States *and* Jenkins v. Missouri, 24 Urb. Law. 621, 628 (1992). For a discussion of contempt, see *supra* Chapter 2, Section 9.C. The use of masters and receivers in civil rights litigation, and the degree of their discretion, are described in Debra Dobray, *The Role of Masters in Court Ordered Institutional Reform*, 34 Baylor L. Rev. 581 (1982); D. Bruce La Pierre, *Voluntary Interdistrict School Desegregation in St. Louis: The Special Master's Tale*, 1987 Wis. L. Rev. 971; David I. Levine, *The Authority of Remedial Special Masters in Federal Institutional Reform Litigation: The History Reconsidered*, 17 U.C. Davis L. Rev. 753 (1984); James S. DeGraw, Note, *Rule 53, Inherent Powers, and Institutional Reform: The Lack of Limits on Special Masters*, 66 N.Y.U. L. Rev. 800 (1991); Comment, *The Wyatt Case: Implementation of a Judicial Decree Ordering Institutional Change*, 84 Yale L.J. 1338, 1340–1347 (1975).

5. Five years after *Jenkins II*, the Supreme Court again reviewed orders in the still on-going case, Missouri v. Jenkins, 515 U.S. 70, 115 S.Ct. 2038, 132 L.Ed.2d 63 (1995) (*Jenkins III*). Again, in a five to four opinion, the Court held that the remedy of creating magnet schools to attract suburban students to Kansas City schools was an interdistrict remedy that, like the remedy in *Milliken I*, exceeded the scope of the violation. The Court remanded, instructing the district court to "bear in mind that its end purpose is not only 'to remedy the violation' to the extent practicable, but also 'to restore state and local authorities to the control of a school system that is operating in compliance with the Constitution.' " *Id.* at 102, 115 S.Ct. at 2056, 132 L.Ed.2d at 89. Justice Souter, writing for the dissenters said:

> [T]he District Court has consistently treated salary increases as an important element in remedying the systemwide reduction in student achievement resulting from segregation in the [school district]. * * * [T]he Court does not question this remedial goal, which we expressly approved in *Milliken II*. * * * The only issue, then, is whether the salary

increases ordered by the District Court have been reasonably related to achieving that goal.

Id. at 121, 115 S.Ct. at 2081, 132 L.Ed.2d at 154–55. For a discussion of *Jenkins III, see* Chelsey Parkman, Note, *Missouri v. Jenkins: The Beginning of the End for Desegregation*, 27 Loy. U. Chi. L.J. 715 (1996). The following two articles reflect opposing views about the role of the courts and school desegregation. *Compare* Drew S. Days III, *School Desegregation Law in the 1980s: Why Isn't Anybody Laughing?*, 95 Yale L.J. 1737 (1986) (reviewing Paul Dimond, Beyond Busing: Inside the Challenge to Urban Segregation (1985)), *with* Neal Devins, *Interest Balancing and Other Limits to Judicially Managed Equal Educational Opportunity*, 45 Mercer L. Rev. 1017 (1994) (replying to Erwin Chemerinsky, *Lost Opportunity: The Burger Court and the Failure to Achieve Equal Educational Opportunity*, 45 Mercer L. Rev. 999 (1994)). *See also* Wendy Parker, *The Supreme Court and Public Law Remedies: A Tale of Two Cities*, 50 Hastings L.J. 475 (1999).

6.   When does a court know that the unconstitutional school segregation has been remedied? In Board of Education v. Dowell, 498 U.S. 237, 111 S.Ct. 630, 112 L.Ed.2d 715 (1991), *supra* Chapter 2, Section 8, a district court dissolved the desegregation injunction against the school district of Oklahoma City on the grounds that, although demographic changes were creating segregated schools, "the school district had bused students for more than a decade in good-faith compliance with the court's orders * * * [and] present residential segregation was the result of private decisionmaking and economics, and * * * it was too attenuated to be a vestige of former school segregation." *Id.* at 243, 111 S.Ct. at 634–35, 112 L.Ed.2d at 725. The Tenth Circuit reversed, holding that the district court had not applied the standard for modifying injunctions set forth in United States v. Swift & Co., 286 U.S. 106, 52 S.Ct. 460, 76 L.Ed. 999 (1932). (*Swift* held that a decree remains in force until the defendant can show "grievous wrong evoked by new and unforeseen conditions" and "dramatic" unforeseen changes.) The Supreme Court in *Dowell* reversed, holding that desegregation decrees are meant to be transitional, unlike the decree in *Swift*, which had enjoined an antitrust violation. The Court said:

> [A] finding by the District Court that the Oklahoma City School District was being operated in compliance with the commands of the Equal Protection Clause of the Fourteenth Amendment, and that it was unlikely that the Board would return to its former ways, would be a finding that the purposes of the desegregation litigation had been fully achieved.

Dowell, 498 U.S. at 247, 111 S. Ct. at 636–37, 112 L.Ed.2d at 728. The Court remanded with an admonishment that the District Court "look * * * to every facet of school operations" to determine that "the vestiges of *de jure* segregation had been eliminated as far as practicable." *Id.* at 250, 111 S.Ct. at 638, 112 L.Ed.2d at 730. Justice Marshall, dissenting, said that "the inquiry [the majority] commends to the District Court fails to recognize explicitly the threatened reemergence of one-race schools as a relevant 'vestige' of *de jure* segregation." *Id.* at 251, 111 S.Ct. at 639, 112 L.Ed.2d at 731.

7.   More recently, a number of school districts have found that the effects of past *de jure* discrimination have been eliminated, even if *de facto*

housing segregation patterns have developed, and the courts have modified or dismissed injunctions designed to remedy *de jure* discrimination. In Robinson v. Shelby County Bd. of Ed., 566 F.3d 642, 646, 651 (6th Cir. 2009) (the Sixth Circuit reversed the district court's denial of the motion of all parties "to dissolve all outstanding orders, declare the school district a unitary school system and terminate the litigation" as to "student assignment, faculty integration, and extracurricular activities" because in weighing competing interests of not letting parties undercut desegregation and of favoring settlement, district court did not give "sufficient weight" to parties' settlement and facts they cited to justify it. *See also* Morgan v. Nucci, 831 F.2d 313 (1st Cir.1987) (Boston) (subsequent motion in the case previously named Morgan v. McDonough, *supra* this section); Riddick v. School Board of the City of Norfolk, 784 F.2d 521 (4th Cir.1986); Reed v. Rhodes, 179 F.3d 453 (6th Cir.1999) (Cleveland); Capacchione v. Charlotte–Mecklenburg Schools, 57 F.Supp.2d 228 (W.D.N.C.1999) (subsequent motion in the case previously named Swann v. Charlotte–Mecklenburg Board of Education); *see generally* Erwin Chemerinsky, *The Segregation and Resegregation of American Public Education: The Courts' Role,* 81 N.C. L. Rev. 1597, 1605–10 (2003). A number of scholars and other commentators view cases such as these as a signal that the commitment to achieving *Brown's* goals has been waning. *See, e.g.,* Wendy Parker, *The Decline of Judicial Decisionmaking: School Desegregation and District Court Judges,* 81 N.C. L. Rev. 1623 (2003) (describing two Alabama judges actively overseeing desegregation orders, but noting that they are the exception, not the rule). Many have written that *Brown's* goal has not been achieved. *See, e.g.,* Derrick Bell, Silent Covenants: Brown v. Board of Education and the Unfulfilled Hopes for Racial Reform (2004); Charles J. Ogletree, Jr., All Deliberate Speed: Reflections on the First Half Century of Brown v. Board of Education (2004); Jerome M. Culp, Jr., *Black People in White Face: Assimilation, Culture, and the* Brown *Case,* 36 Wm. & Mary L. Rev. 665 (1995); Davison M. Douglas, *Introduction: The Promise of* Brown *Forty Years Later,* 36 Wm. & Mary L. Rev. 337, 339 (1995); Paul Gewirtz, *Remedies and Resistance,* 92 Yale L.J. 585, 588 (1983); Cheryl Brown Henderson, *The Legacy of* Brown *Forty-Six Years Later,* 40 Washburn L.J. 70, 76 (2000); Candace Saari Kovacic–Fleischer, *Comparing Remedies for School Desegregation and Employment Discrimination: Can Employers Now Help Schools?* 41 San Diego L. Rev. 1695, 1696 (2004); Mark Tushnet, *The Significance of* Brown v. Board of Education, 80 Va. L. Rev. 173, 175 (1994). *Cf.* Richard A. Epstein, *The Remote Causes of Affirmative Action, or School Desegregation in Kansas City, Missouri,* 84 Cal. L. Rev. 1101 (1996) (questioning whether the wrongs of 1954 should be guiding the allocation of educational resources so many years later)).

8.   In Parents Involved in Community Schools v. Seattle School District No. 1, 551 U.S. 701, 127 S.Ct. 2738, 168 L.Ed.2d 508 (2007) the Supreme Court held, in a 5–4 decision, that the race-based student assignment plans that had been adopted by school boards in Seattle and Louisville were not narrowly tailored to withstand constitutional scrutiny. Professor James E. Ryan said that with *Parents Involved* "the Supreme Court wrote the latest chapter on school desegregation." James E. Ryan, The Supreme Court, 2006 Term: Comment, *The Supreme Court and Voluntary Integration,* 121 Harv. L.

Rev. 131, 131 (2007). Professor Ryan introduced his analysis of *Parents Involved* by asking the question, "is this decision important and, if so, why?" He responds:

> My answer is mixed. On the one hand, this decision does not change much on the ground. The truth is that racial integration is not on the agenda of most school districts and has not been for over twenty years. Modern education reform efforts might still share the goal of equalizing educational opportunities for minority students, which the Court in *Brown* embraced. But integration is not generally the means of choice to achieve that goal, nor is the Supreme Court the key arena. Advocates and reformers have turned their attention elsewhere, and today battles are waged in legislatures and in state courts over school funding, school choice, standards and testing, and access to preschool. * * *

> * * * [The Court] has failed, throughout the entire half-century of desegregation cases, to confront the primary contemporary cause of single-race schools: residential segregation. Partly as a result of the Court's decisions and partly as a result of its evasions, most school districts today could not integrate, even if they wanted to, because their students are primarily if not exclusively of one race or ethnicity.

* * *

> * * * The Court certainly has not done all it could to encourage integration in practice, but in the past it seemed to support the goal of integration. At the very least, it was not hostile. In *Parents Involved*, however, the Court seems to have changed its mind. Instead of encouraging the pursuit of a worthwhile goal, four Justices make the goal itself seem dastardly, while Justice Kennedy accepts the goal but voices intense distaste over the most straightforward means of achieving it.

> To be sure, the Court's decision does not take away much that is tangible, as it will not affect many current student assignment plans. But it takes away some hope. Hope that the Court would stand firmly on the side of school integration. Hope that, despite past disappointments, new ways could be found to integrate schools, ways that were acceptable to local citizens of every color and ethnicity. Hope that schools would be places where students go not just to improve their test scores but also to become better citizens and better people. Hope that integrated schools would lead, slowly but finally, to an integrated society. So, yes, the decision is in one sense not terribly significant. But it is no small thing to dash hope.

Id. at 132–33. The UNC Center for Civil Rights, the UCLA Civil Rights Project, and the University of Georgia Education Policy and Evaluation Center organized a conference that seemed designed to reestablish hope. *See, e.g.,* Chinh Q. Le, Looking to the Future: Legal and Policy Options for Racially Integrated Education in the South and the Nation: Article, *Racially Integrated Education and the Role of the Federal Government*, 88 N.C. L. Rev. 725 (2010); Kimberly Jenkins Robinson, Looking to the Future: Legal and Policy Options for Racially Integrated Education in the South and the Nation: Article, *Resurrecting the Promise of* Brown: *Under-*

standing and Remedying How the Supreme Court Reconstitutionalized Segregated Schools, 88 N.C. L. Rev. 787 (2010). *See also*, Wendy Parker, *Desegregating Teachers*, 86 Wash. U. L. Rev. 1, 8 (2008)(noting continuing segregation, arguing that the "approach" of *Parents United* "is wrong" and saying what is needed is a "call for integration from the public itself.")

2. Use of Writs of Mandamus, Stays and Injunctions

    a. For Judicial Administration of Televising Proceedings

28 U.S.C. § 1651. Writs

(a) The Supreme Court and all courts established by Act of Congress may issue all writs necessary or appropriate in aid of their respective jurisdictions and agreeable to the usages and principles of law.

Rules of the Supreme Court of the United States, 2010

Rule 10. Considerations Governing Review on Certiorari

Review on a writ of certiorari is not a matter of right, but of judicial discretion. A petition for a writ of certiorari will be granted only for compelling reasons. The following * * * indicate the character of the reasons the Court considers:

(a) a United States court of appeals has entered a decision in conflict with the decision of another United States court of appeals on the same important matter; has decided an important federal question in a way that conflicts with a decision by a state court of last resort; or has so far departed from the accepted and usual course of judicial proceedings, or sanctioned such a departure by a lower court, as to call for an exercise of this Court's supervisory power;

(b) a state court of last resort has decided an important federal question in a way that conflicts with the decision of another state court of last resort or of a United States court of appeals;

(c) a state court or a United States court of appeals has decided an important question of federal law that has not been, but should be, settled by this Court, or has decided an important federal question in a way that conflicts with relevant decisions of this Court.

* * *

Rule 20. Procedure on a Petition for an Extraordinary Writ

Issuance by the Court of an extraordinary writ authorized by 28 U. S. C. § 1651(a) is not a matter of right, but of discretion sparingly exercised. To justify the granting of any such writ, the petition must show that the writ will be in aid of the Court's appellate jurisdiction, that exceptional circumstances warrant the exercise of the Court's discretionary powers, and that adequate relief cannot be obtained in any other form or from any other court.

NOTES

1. A writ of mandamus is issued by a court to a public official or by an appellate court to a lower court. The Supreme Court described the propriety of an appellate court issuing a writ of mandamus pursuant to the All Writs Act, quoted above, in Will v. United States, 389 U.S. 90, 95–96, 88 S. Ct. 269, 273–74, 19 L. Ed. 2d 305, 310–311 (1967):

> The peremptory writ of mandamus has traditionally been used in the federal courts only "to confine an inferior court to a lawful exercise of its prescribed jurisdiction or to compel it to exercise its authority when it is its duty to do so." Roche v. Evaporated Milk Assn., 319 U.S. 21, 26 (1943).* * * "[I]t is clear that only exceptional circumstances amounting to a judicial "usurpation of power" will justify the invocation of this extraordinary remedy." De Beers Consol. Mines, Ltd. v. United States, 325 U.S. 212, 217 (1945). Thus the writ has been invoked where unwarranted judicial action threatened "to embarrass the executive arm of the Government in conducting foreign relations," Ex Parte Republic of Peru, 318 U.S. 578, 588 (1943), where it was the only means of forestalling intrusion by the federal judiciary on a delicate area of federal-state relations, Maryland v. Soper, 270 U.S. 9 (1926), where it was necessary to confine a lower court to the terms of an appellate tribunal's mandate, United States v. United States Dist. Court, 334 U.S. 258 (1948), and where a district judge displayed a persistent disregard of the Rules of Civil Procedure promulgated by this Court, La Buy v. Howes Leather Co., 352 U.S. 249 (1957) * * *.

Cf., Cheney v. United States District Court for the District of Columbia, 542 U.S. 367, 380–381, 124 S. Ct. 2576, 2586–2587, 159 L. Ed. 2d 459, 477–478 (2004).

2. To facilitate ease of reading, voluminous references to the record in the next case have been deleted without indication.

HOLLINGSWORTH v. PERRY

Supreme Court of the United States, 2010.
130 S.Ct. 705.

PER CURIAM.

We are asked to stay the broadcast of a federal trial. We resolve that question without expressing any view on whether such trials should be broadcast. We instead determine that the broadcast in this case should be stayed because it appears the courts below did not follow the appropriate procedures set forth in federal law before changing their rules to allow such broadcasting. Courts enforce the requirement of procedural regularity on others, and must follow those requirements themselves.

* * *

I

Proposition 8 was passed by California voters in November 2008. It was a ballot proposition designed to overturn a ruling by the California

Supreme Court that had given same-sex couples a right to marry. Proposition 8 was and is the subject of public debate throughout the State and, indeed, nationwide. Its advocates claim that they have been subject to harassment as a result of public disclosure of their support. See, *e.g.*, Reply Brief for Appellant 28–29 in *Citizens United v. Federal Election Comm'n,* No. 08–205, now pending before this Court. * * *.

Respondents filed suit in the United States District Court for the Northern District of California, seeking to invalidate Proposition 8. They contend that the amendment to the State's Constitution violates the Equal Protection and Due Process Clauses of the Fourteenth Amendment of the United States Constitution. The State of California declined to defend Proposition 8, and the defendant-intervenors (who are the applicants here) entered the suit to defend its constitutionality. A bench trial began on Monday, January 11, 2010, before the Chief Judge of the District Court, the Honorable Vaughn R. Walker.

On September 25, 2009, the District Court informed the parties at a hearing that there was interest in the possibility that the trial would be broadcast. Respondents indicated their support for the idea, while applicants opposed it. * * *

One month later, Chief Judge Kozinski of the United States Court of Appeals for the Ninth Circuit appointed a three-judge committee to evaluate the possibility of adopting a Ninth Circuit Rule regarding the recording and transmission of district court proceedings. * * *

On December 17, the Ninth Circuit Judicial Council issued a news release indicating that it had approved a pilot program for "the limited use of cameras in federal district courts within the circuit." * * * The release explained that the Council's decision "amend[ed] a 1996 Ninth Circuit policy" that had banned the photographing, as well as radio and television coverage, of court proceedings. * * *

On December 21, a coalition of media companies requested permission from the District Court to televise the trial challenging Proposition 8. Two days later, the court indicated on its Web site that it had amended Civil Local Rule 77–3, which had previously banned the recording or broadcast of court proceedings. * * * Applicants objected to the revision, arguing that any change to Ninth Circuit or local rules would require a sufficient notice and comment period.

On December 31, the District Court revised its Web site * * * indicating a "proposed revision of Civil Local Rule 77–3" * * * had been "approved for public comment" * * * by Friday, January 8, 2010.

On January 4, 2010, the District Court again revised its Web site. * * * This third version stated that the revised Rule was "effective December 22, 2009," and that "[t]he revised rule was adopted pursuant to the 'immediate need' provision of Title 28 Section 2071(e)." * * *

On January 6, 2010, the District Court held a hearing regarding the recording and broadcasting of the upcoming trial. The court announced that an audio and video feed of trial proceedings would be streamed live to certain courthouses in other cities. It also announced that, pending approval of the Chief Judge of the Ninth Circuit, the trial would be recorded and then broadcast on the Internet. * * *

On January 7, 2010, the District Court filed an order formally requesting that Chief Judge Kozinski approve "inclusion of the trial in the pilot project * * *." Applicants filed a petition for a writ of mandamus in the Court of Appeals, seeking to prohibit or stay the District Court from enforcing its order. The following day, a three-judge panel of the Court of Appeals denied the petition.

On January 8, 2010, Chief Judge Kozinski issued an order approving the District Court's decision to allow real-time streaming of the trial to certain federal courthouses listed in a simultaneously issued press release. Five locations had been selected: federal courthouses in San Francisco, Pasadena, Seattle, Portland, and Brooklyn. * * *

Chief Judge Kozinski's January 8 order noted that the request to broadcast the trial on the Internet was "still pending" before him. * * *

On January 9, 2010, applicants filed in this Court an application for a stay of the District Court's order. Their petition seeks a stay pending resolution of forthcoming petitions for the writs of certiorari and mandamus.

II

* * *

To obtain a stay pending the filing and disposition of a petition for a writ of certiorari, an applicant must show (1) a reasonable probability that four Justices will consider the issue sufficiently meritorious to grant certiorari; (2) a fair prospect that a majority of the Court will vote to reverse the judgment below; and (3) a likelihood that irreparable harm will result from the denial of a stay. In close cases the Circuit Justice or the Court will balance the equities and weigh the relative harms to the applicant and to the respondent. * * * To obtain a stay pending the filing and disposition of a petition for a writ of mandamus, an applicant must show a fair prospect that a majority of the Court will vote to grant mandamus and a likelihood that irreparable harm will result from the denial of a stay. Before a writ of mandamus may issue, a party must establish that (1) "no other adequate means [exist] to attain the relief he desires," (2) the party's "right to issuance of the writ is 'clear and indisputable,'" and (3) "the writ is appropriate under the circumstances." * * * This Court will issue the writ of mandamus directly to a federal district court "only where a question of public importance is involved, or where the question is of such a nature that it is peculiarly appropriate that such action by this court should be taken." *Ex parte United States,* 287 U. S. 241, 248–249, 53 S. Ct. 129, 77 L. Ed. 283 (1932). These familiar standards are followed here, where applicants claim that the District Court's order was based on a local rule adopted in violation of federal law.

* * *

A district court has discretion to adopt local rules. * * * Federal law, however, requires a district court to follow certain procedures to adopt or amend a local rule. Local rules typically may not be amended unless the district court "giv[es] appropriate public notice and an opportunity for comment." 28 U. S. C. § 2071(b); see also Fed. Rule Civ. Proc. 83(a). A limited exception permits dispensing with this notice-and-comment requirement only where "there is an immediate need for a rule." § 2071(e). Even where a rule is amended based on immediate need, however, the issuing court must "promptly thereafter afford ... notice and opportunity for comment."

* * *

The amended version of Rule 77–3 appears to be invalid. In amending this rule, it appears that the District Court failed to "giv[e] appropriate public notice and an opportunity for comment," as required by federal law. 28 U. S. C. § 2071(b). * * *

* * *

The need for a meaningful comment period was particularly acute in this case. Both courts and legislatures have proceeded with appropriate caution in addressing this question. In 1996, the Judicial Conference of the United States adopted a policy opposing the public broadcast of court proceedings. This policy was adopted after a multi-year study of the issue by the Federal Judicial Center which drew on data from six district and two appellate courts, as well as state-court data. In light of the study's findings, the Judicial Conference concluded that "the intimidating effect of cameras on some witnesses and jurors [is] cause for concern." * * *

* * *

Applicants also have shown that irreparable harm will likely result from the denial of the stay. Without a stay, the District Court will broadcast the trial. It would be difficult—if not impossible—to reverse the harm from those broadcasts. The trial will involve various witnesses, including members of same-sex couples; academics, who apparently will discuss gender issues and gender equality, as well as family structures; and those who participated in the campaign leading to the adoption of Proposition 8. This Court has recognized that witness testimony may be chilled if broadcast. * * * Some of applicants' witnesses have already said that they will not testify if the trial is broadcast, and they have substantiated their concerns by citing incidents of past harassment. * * * These concerns are not diminished by the fact that some of applicants' witnesses are compensated expert witnesses. There are qualitative differences between making public appearances regarding an issue and having one's testimony broadcast throughout the country. Applicants may not be able to obtain adequate relief through an appeal. The trial will have already been broadcast. It is difficult to demonstrate or analyze whether a witness would have testified differently if his or her testimony had not been broadcast. And witnesses subject to harassment as a result of broadcast of their testimony might be less likely to cooperate in any future proceedings.

The balance of equities favors applicants. While applicants have demonstrated the threat of harm they face if the trial is broadcast, respondents have not alleged any harm if the trial is not broadcast. The issue, moreover, must be resolved at this stage, for the injury likely cannot be undone once the broadcast takes place.

This Court also has a significant interest in supervising the administration of the judicial system. * * * The Court may use its supervisory authority to invalidate local rules that were promulgated in violation of an Act of Congress. * * * The Court's interest in ensuring compliance with proper rules of judicial administration is particularly acute when those rules relate to the integrity of judicial processes. The District Court here attempted to revise its rules in haste, * * * to allow broadcasting of this high-profile trial without any considered standards or guidelines in place. * * *

By insisting that courts comply with the law, parties vindicate not only the rights they assert but also the law's own insistence on neutrality and fidelity to principle. Those systematic interests are all the more evident here, where the lack of a regular rule with proper standards to determine the guidelines for broadcasting could compromise the orderly, decorous, rational traditions that courts rely upon to ensure the integrity of their own judgments. These considerations, too, are part of the reasons leading to the decision to grant extraordinary relief.

In addressing a discrete instance authorizing a closed-circuit broadcast of a trial, Congress has illustrated the need for careful guidelines and standards. The trial of the two defendants in the Oklahoma City bombing case had been transferred to the United States District Court for the District of Colorado, so it was set to take place in Denver. * * * Congress passed a statute that allowed victims' families to watch the trial on closed-circuit television. 42 U. S. C. § 10608. The statute was drawn with care to provide precise and detailed guidance * * *. In the present case, by contrast, over a span of three weeks the District Court and Ninth Circuit Judicial Council issued, retracted, and reissued a series of Web site postings and news releases. These purport to amend rules and policies at the heart of an ongoing consideration of broadcasting federal trials. And they have done so to make sure that one particular trial may be broadcast. * * *

If Local Rule 77–3 had been validly revised, questions would still remain about the District Court's decision to allow broadcasting of this particular trial * * *.

III

* * * The Court grants the application for a stay of the District Court's order of January 7, 2010, pending the timely filing and disposition of a petition for a writ of certiorari or the filing and disposition of a petition for a writ of mandamus.

It is so ordered.

JUSTICE BREYER, with whom JUSTICE STEVENS, JUSTICE GINSBURG and JUSTICE SOTOMAYOR join, dissenting.

The Court today issues an order that will prevent the transmission of proceedings in a nonjury civil case of great public interest to five other federal courthouses * * *. I must dissent.

First, consider the merits of the legal issue: The United States Code, in a chapter entitled "Rules of Courts," states that "[a]ny rule ... shall be prescribed only after giving appropriate public notice and an opportunity for comment." 28 U. S. C. § 2071(b). The question here is whether the District Court accompanied the modification of its anti-video rule with "appropriate public notice and an opportunity for comment."

Certainly the parties themselves had more than adequate notice and opportunity to comment before the Rule was changed. On September 25, 2009, the trial judge, Chief Judge Vaughn Walker, discussed the possibility of broadcasting trial proceedings both within the courthouse and beyond, and asked for the parties' views. No party objected to the presence of cameras in the courtroom for transmissions within the courthouse * * * and both sides made written submissions to the court regarding their views on other transmissions. * * *

Nor, in practice, did other members of the Judiciary lack information about the issue. In May 1996 the Circuit Council adopted a policy permitting video in connection with appellate proceedings, but prohibiting its use in the district court. Subsequently, appellate court panels have frequently permitted electronic coverage. * * * In 2007 the lawyers and judges present at the Ninth Circuit Judicial Conference considered a resolution that favored the use of cameras in district court civil nonjury proceedings. And, voting separately, both lawyers and judges "approved the resolution by resounding margins." * * * Subsequently, a committee of judges was created to study the matter. And on December 17, 2009, the Circuit Council voted to authorize a pilot program permitting the use of video in nonjury civil cases * * *.

In this context the United States District Court for the Northern District of California amended its local rules on December 22, 2009 to bring them into conformity with Ninth Circuit policy. * * * [O]n December 31, the Court revised its public notice to ask for comments directly. By January 8, 2010, the Court had received 138,574 comments, all but 32 of which favored transmitting the proceedings.

Viewed in light of this history, the Court satisfied the statute's insistence that "notice" be "appropriate." *Cf.* 28 U. S. C. §§ 2071(b), (e).

* * * And the rule change itself is simply a change that conforms local rule to Circuit policy—a conformity that the law may well require. * * *

* * *

Second, this legal question is not the kind of legal question that this Court would normally grant certiorari to consider. There is no conflict among the state or federal courts regarding the procedures by which a district court changes its local rules. *Cf.* this Court's Rules 10(a)-(b). The technical validity of the procedures followed below does not implicate an open "important question of federal law." *Cf.* Rule 10(c). Nor do the procedures below clearly conflict with any precedent from this Court. *Cf. ibid.*

[I]n a word, this Court micromanages district court administrative procedures in the most detailed way. * * *

* * *

I recognize that the Court may see this matter not as one of promulgating and applying a local rule but, rather, as presenting the larger question of the place of cameras in the courtroom. But the wisdom of a camera policy is primarily a matter for the proper administrative bodies to determine. See 28 U. S. C. § 332. * * * The relevant question of law here concerns the procedure for amending local rules. And the only relevant legal principles that allow us here to take account of the immediate subject matter of that local rule, namely cameras, are those legal principles that permit us—indeed require us—to look to the nature of the harm at issue and to balance equities, including the public interest. I consequently turn to those two matters.

Third, consider the harm: I can find no basis for the Court's conclusion that, were the transmissions to other courtrooms to take place, the applicants would suffer irreparable harm. Certainly there is no evidence that such harm could arise in this nonjury civil case from the simple fact of transmission itself. By my count, 42 States and two Federal District Courts currently give judges the discretion to broadcast civil nonjury trials. * * *

The applicants also claim that the transmission will irreparably harm the witnesses themselves, presumably by increasing the public's awareness of who those witnesses are. And they claim that some members of the public might harass those witnesses. But the witnesses, although capable of doing so, have not asked this Court to set aside the District Court's order. * * * And that is not surprising. All of the witnesses supporting the applicants are already publicly identified with their cause. They are all experts or advocates who have either already appeared on television or Internet broadcasts, already toured the State advocating a "yes" vote on Proposition 8, or already engaged in extensive public commentary far more likely to make them well known than a closed-circuit broadcast to another federal courthouse.

The likelihood of any "irreparable" harm is further diminished by the fact that the court order before us would simply increase the trial's viewing audience from the occupants of one courtroom in one courthouse to the occupants of five other courtrooms in five other courthouses (in all of which taking pictures or retransmissions have been forbidden). By way of comparison literally hundreds of national and international newspapers are already covering this trial and reporting in detail the names and testimony of all of the witnesses. * * * Moreover, if in respect to any particular witness this transmission threatens harm, the District Court can prevent that harm. Chief Judge Walker has already said that he would keep the broadcast "completely under the Court's control, to permit the Court to stop it if [it] proves to be a problem, if it proves to be a distraction, [or] if it proves to create problems with witnesses." * * *

Fourth, no fair balancing of the equities (including harm to the public interest) could support issuance of the stay. See *Times-Picayune Publishing Corp. v. Schulingkamp,* 419 U. S. 1301, 1305, 95 S. Ct. 1, 42 L. Ed. 2d 17 (1974) (Powell, J. in Chambers) (recognizing "significant public and private interests balanced on both sides" when "present[ed with] a fundamental confrontation between the competing values of free press and fair trial"). As I have just explained, the applicants' equities consist of potential harm to witnesses—harm that is either nonexistent or that can be cured through protective measures by the District Court as the circumstances warrant. The competing equities consist of not only respondents' interest in obtaining the courthouse-to-courthouse transmission that they desire, but also the public's interest in observing trial proceedings to learn about this case and about how courts work. See *Nebraska Press Ass'n v. Stuart,* 427 U. S. 539, 587, 96 S. Ct. 2791, 49 L. Ed. 2d 683 (1976) (Brennan, J., concurring in judgment); see also Exh. 2, at 42, App. to Pet. (statement of Chief Judge Walker) ("[I]f the public could see how the judicial process works, they would take a somewhat different view of it." "I think the only time that you're going to draw sufficient interest in the legal process is when you have an issue such as the issues here, that people think about, talk about, debate about and consider"). With these considerations in the balance, the scales tip heavily against, not in favor, of issuing the stay.

* * *

I respectfully dissent.

NOTES

1. Since the proceedings in the case challenging Proposition 8, Perry v. Schwarzenegger, could not be televised, filmmakers John Ireland and John Ainsworth used actors to recreate the trial by reading from the publicly available transcript. "That means that a portrayal of the entire trial is available online through their video channel." http://tech.blorge.com/Structure:%20/2010/06/18/youtube-recreation-gets-round-prop–8–trial-tv-ban /(June 18, 2010).

2. Closing arguments ended on June 18, 2010. Less than a month later, on August 4, Chief Judge Vaughn Walker permanently enjoined state officials from enforcing Proposition 8, holding that it violated the due process and equal protection clauses of the Fourteenth Amendment. Perry v. Schwarzenegger, 2010 WL 1691193 (N.D. Cal. 2010). He stayed the order "until the motion to stay pending appeal * * * has been decided." *Id.* On August 16, the Ninth Circuit stayed the order pending appeal and expedited the appeal. Perry v. Schwarzenegger, 2010 WL 3212786 No. 10–16696 (9th Cir.2010).

---

b.   During the 2000 presidential election

"*The only disagreement is as to remedy.*" Bush v. Gore, 531 U.S. 98, 111, 121 S. Ct. 525, 533, 148 L. Ed. 2d 388 (2000). The 2000 presidential election between then Governor George W. Bush and Vice President Albert Gore was close. After the votes had been counted in all of the states, neither candidate had a majority of electoral votes. One state's outcome was in doubt. The election in Florida was close. After the first count George Bush was ahead by 1,784 votes, less than one half of one percent. That slim margin triggered Florida's statutory recount procedures. The first of those procedures involved an automatic recount from the voting machines. That recount resulted in an even closer race, triggering discretionary manual recounts. The Democrats were entitled to request manual recounts from the county canvassing boards and asked for manual recounts from several boards. Those boards granted the requests. The Florida Secretary of State, Katherine Harris, declared that she would not accept the results of manual recounts beyond the statutory one week deadline for certifying an election, November 14.

Litigation ensued. The Republicans filed suit on November 11, in the United States District Court for the Southern District of Florida, seeking a Temporary Restraining Order and Preliminary Injunction to stop the manual recounts. On November 13 one of the canvassing boards filed suit in the Florida Circuit Court of the Second Judicial Circuit in Leon County seeking declaratory and injunctive relief to order the Secretary to accept votes counted after November 14. A procedural ruling by the Circuit Court enabled the Secretary to announce on November 15 that she would reject those votes. On November 16, the Democrats filed suit in the Leon County Court, seeking a injunction to require the Secretary to accept the votes.

Of particular concern to both the Republicans and the Democrats was the group of ballots that had not been able to be counted by the voting machines. The Democrats were concerned that those ballots had not been counted and argued that the Circuit Court had been mistaken in its interpretation of the Florida statutes when it held that the Secretary could reject tallies of manually counted votes after the one week deadline. The Republicans were concerned that those ballots could not be reliably counted. They argued that one of the problems was in the election districts that used punch cards, which required a voter to punch out a "chad" next to the name of the preferred candidate. Some of the ballots did not have completely detached chads. Some chads were left hanging, with varying degrees of attachment. Some were indented but not detached.

In their November 11 suit, the Republicans argued that the manual recount violated the equal protection and due process clauses of the federal constitution because the "intent of the voter" was too vague a standard for determining how much of a "chad" needed to be detached or whether an indented chad was enough to indicate that intent. The Republicans also objected that the Florida statutes did not require manual recounts in all voting districts, and that the Democrats were asking for recounts only in selected districts. The case was argued in the District Court on November 13. The court denied the motions on November 14, and the plaintiffs filed a notice of appeal the same day.

On November 17, the Supreme Court of Florida "accepted jurisdiction [of the consolidated state cases filed between November 11 and 16 by the Democrats], set an expedited briefing schedule, and enjoined the Secretary and the Elections Canvassing Commission (Commission) from certifying the results of the presidential election until further order of this Court." Palm Beach County Canvassing Board v. Harris, 772 So.2d 1220 (Fla. 2000). On November 21, after a lengthy discussion of the Florida election statutes, the Court held:

> The text of our Florida Constitution begins with a Declaration of Rights, a series of rights so basic that the founders accorded them a place of special privilege. The court long ago noted the venerable role the Declaration plays in our tripartite system of government in Florida * * *.

> The right of suffrage is the preeminent right contained in the Declaration of Rights, for without this basic freedom all others would be diminished * * *.

> To the extent that the Legislature may enact laws regulating the electoral process, those laws are valid only if they impose no "unreasonable or unnecessary" restraints on the right of suffrage * * *. Because election laws are intended to facilitate the right of suffrage, such laws must be liberally construed in favor of the citizen's right to vote:

>> Generally, the courts, in constructing statutes relating to elections, hold that the same should receive a liberal construction in favor of the citizen whose right to vote they tend to restrict and in so doing to prevent disenfranchisement of legal voters, and the intention of the voters should prevail when counting ballots . . . . . It is the intention of the law to obtain an honest expression of the will or desire of the voter.

State *ex rel.* Carpenter v. Barber, 144 Fla. 159, 198 So. 49, 51 (Fla. 1940).

Based on the foregoing, we conclude that the authority of the Florida Secretary of State to ignore amended returns submitted by a County Canvassing Board may be lawfully exercised only under limited circumstances as we set forth in this opinion. The clear import of the penalty provision of section 102.112 is to deter Boards from engaging in dilatory conduct contrary to statutory authority that results in the late certification of a county's returns. This deterrent purpose is achieved by the fines in section 102.112, which are substantial and personal and levied on each member of the Board. The alternative penalty, i.e., ignoring the county's returns, punishes not the Board members themselves but rather the county's electors, for it in effect disenfranchises them.

* * *

Because the right to vote is the pre-eminent right of the Declaration of rights of the Florida Constitution, the circumstances under which the Secretary may exercise her authority to ignore a county's returns filed after the initial statutory date are limited. * * *

* * * [T]he Florida election Code must be construed as a whole. * * * [S]ection 102.111, which provides that the Secretary "shall" ignore late returns, conflicts with section 102.112 which provides that the Secretary "may" ignore late returns, In the present case, we have used traditional rules of statutory construction to resolve these ambiguities to the extent necessary to address the issues presented here. We decline to rule more expansively, for to do so would result in this Court substantially rewriting the Code. We leave that matter to the sound discretion of the body best equipped to address it, the Legislature.

Because of the unique circumstances and extraordinary importance of the present case, * * * we conclude that we must invoke the equitable powers of this Court to fashion a remedy that will allow a fair and expeditious resolution of the questions presented here.

Accordingly, in order to allow maximum time for contests pursuant to section 102.168, amended certifications must be filed with the Elections Canvassing Commission by 5 p.m. on Sunday, November 26, 2000, and the Secretary of State and the Elections Canvassing Commission shall accept any such amended certifications * * *. The stay order entered on November 17, 2000, by this Court shall remain in effect until the expiration of the time for accepting amended certifications set forth in this opinon.

Id. at 1236–40.

Bush petitioned the Supreme Court of the United States for a writ of certiorari from the Supreme Court of Florida's order of November 21, and the Court granted the petition on November 24. The Court directed the parties to file briefs on November 28 and heard oral argument on December 1. The Court's opinion, which is set forth below, was delivered three days later.

BUSH v. PALM BEACH COUNTY CANVASSING BOARD

Supreme Court of the United States, December 4, 2000.
531 U.S. 70, 121 S.Ct. 471, 148 L.Ed.2d 366.

PER CURIAM

* * *

As a general rule, this Court defers to a state court's interpretation of a state statute. But in the case of a law enacted by a state legislature applicable not only to elections to state offices, but also to the election of Presidential electors, the legislature is not acting solely under the authority given it by the people of the State, but by virtue of a direct grant of authority made under Art. II, § 1, cl. 2, of the United States Constitution. That provision reads:

> Each State shall appoint, in such Manner as the Legislature thereof may direct, a Number of Electors, equal to the whole Number of Senators and Representatives to which the State may be entitled in the Congress. . . .

* * *

There are expressions in the opinion of the Supreme Court of Florida that may be read to indicate that it construed the Florida Election Code without regard to the extent to which the Florida Constitution could, consistent with Art. II, § 1, cl. 2, "circumscribe the legislative power." The opinion states, for example, that "[to] the extent that the Legislature may enact laws regulating the electoral process, those laws are valid only if they impose no 'unreasonable or unnecessary' restraints on the right of suffrage" guaranteed by the state constitution. * * * The opinion also states that "[b]ecause election laws are intended to facilitate the right of suffrage, such laws must be liberally construed in favor of the citizens' right to vote. . . ." * * *.

In addition, 3 U.S.C. § 5 provides in pertinent part:

> If any State shall have provided, by laws enacted prior to the day fixed for the appointment of the electors, for its final determination of any controversy or contest concerning the appointment of all or any of the electors of such State, by judicial or other methods or procedures, and such determination shall have been made at least six days before the time fixed for the meeting of the electors, such determination * * * shall be conclusive, and shall govern in the counting of the electoral votes * * * so far as the ascertainment of the electors appointed by such State is concerned.

The parties before us agree that whatever else may be the effect of this section, it creates a "safe harbor" for a State insofar as congressional consideration of its electoral votes is concerned. * * * The Florida Supreme Court cited 3 U.S.C. §§ 1–10 in a footnote of its opinion, * * * but did not discuss § 5. Since § 5 contains a principle of federal law that would assure finality of the State's determination if made pursuant to a state law in effect before the election, a legislative wish to take advantage of the "safe harbor" would counsel against any construction of the Election Code that Congress might deem to be a change in the law.

After reviewing the opinion of the Florida Supreme Court, we find "that there is a considerable uncertainty as to the precise grounds for the decision." Minnesota v. National Tea Co., 309 U.S. 551, 555, 60 S.Ct. 676, 84 L.Ed. 920 (1940). This is sufficient reason for us to decline at this time to review the federal questions asserted to be present. * * *

> It is fundamental that state courts be left free and unfettered by us in interpreting their state constitutions. But it is equally important that ambiguous or obscure adjudications by state courts do not stand as barriers to a determination by this Court of the validity under the federal constitution of state action. Intelligent exercise of our appellate powers compels us to ask for the elimination of the obscurities and ambiguities from the opinions in such cases. *Id.*, at 557.

Specifically, we are unclear as to the extent to which the Florida Supreme Court saw the Florida Constitution as circumscribing the legislature's authority under Art. II, § 1, cl. 2. We are also unclear as to the consideration the Florida Supreme Court accorded to 3 U.S.C. § 5. The judgment of the Supreme Court of Florida is therefore vacated, and the case is remanded for further proceedings not inconsistent with this opinion.

NOTE

While the state litigation was proceeding, so too was the federal litigation. It was resolved on December 6.

SIEGEL v. LePORE

United States Court of Appeals, Eleventh Circuit, *en banc*, December 6, 2000.
234 F.3d 1163.

PER CURIAM

This is an appeal from the denial of a preliminary injunction.

* * *

On November 11, 2000, registered voters * * * along with the Republican candidates for President and Vice-President, George W. Bush and Richard Cheney (collectively "Plaintiffs"), filed a Complaint and a Motion for a Temporary Restraining Order and Preliminary Injunction in the district court for the Southern District of Florida. Plaintiffs sued members of the county canvassing boards of Volusia, Palm Beach, Broward, and Miami–Dade Counties. Plaintiffs' Complaint alleged that the manual recounts violate the Fourteenth Amendment's guarantees of due process and equal protection, and deny and burden the First Amendment's protection of votes and political speech.

* * *

The Motion for a Temporary Restraining Order and Preliminary Injunction which Plaintiffs filed with their Complaint asked, *inter alia*, that the district court prohibit the county canvassing boards from proceeding with manual recounts of the November 7th election results. * * *

The district court heard oral argument on the motion on November 13, 2000, and Plaintiffs' request for a preliminary injunction was denied. On November 14, 2000, Plaintiffs filed a notice of appeal.

During the pendency of this appeal, several Florida cases were appealed to the Florida Supreme Court. In these cases, some plaintiffs challenged Florida Secretary of State Katherine Harris's decision to refuse to accept the results of manual recounts submitted by county canvassing boards after the statutory deadline of 5:00 p.m. on November 14, 2000. On November 21, 2000, in the consolidated cases of Palm Beach County Canvassing Bd. v. Harris, Volusia County Canvassing Bd. v. Harris, and Florida Democratic Party v. Harris, the Supreme Court of Florida decided that Florida Secretary of State Harris must accept the late-reported results of manual recounts from these counties submitted by the evening of November 26, 2000. The Florida Supreme Court expressly stated that neither party had raised as an issue on appeal the constitutionality of Florida's election laws, and it did not address federal constitutional issues in its opinion.

On appeal, Plaintiffs filed an Emergency Motion for an Injunction Pending Appeal, asking this Court to prohibit the county canvassing board Defendants from proceeding with manual ballot recounts. This motion was denied without prejudice on November 17, 2000. Among other things, we then said:

> Both the Constitution of the United States and 3 U.S.C. § 5 indicate that states have the primary authority to determine the manner of appointing Presidential Electors and to resolve most controversies concerning the appointment of Electors. The case law is to the same effect, although, of course, federal courts may act to preserve and decide claims of violations of the Constitution of the United States in certain circumstances, especially where a state remedy is inadequate. In this case, the State of Florida has enacted detailed election dispute procedures. These procedures have been invoked, and are in the process of being implemented, both in the form of administrative actions by state officials and in the form of actions in state courts, including the Supreme Court of Florida. It has been represented to us that the state courts will address and resolve any necessary federal constitutional issues presented to them, including the issues raised by Plaintiffs in this case. If so, then state procedures are not in any way inadequate to preserve for ultimate review in the United States Supreme Court any federal questions arising out of such orders.

Order Denying Plaintiffs' Emergency Motion for Injunction Pending Appeal, Touchston v. McDermott, 234 F.3d 1130 (11th Cir.2000) (citations omitted).

Plaintiffs moved this Court to expedite the underlying appeal, which motion we granted. * * * Plaintiffs ask this Court either to reverse the district court's decision, enjoin the canvassing board Defendants from conducting manual recounts or certifying election results that include manual recounts, or order the deletion and/or non-inclusion of final vote tabulations that reflect the results of manual recounts.[4]

This Court has carefully considered Plaintiffs' appeal, as well as the other documents filed, and has conferred *en banc* on numerous occasions. We heard oral argument on December 5, 2000. Recognizing the importance of a resolution to this case, a prompt decision on the appeal is required.

* * *

We first consider whether *Rooker-Feldman* bars our exercise of subject matter jurisdiction over Plaintiffs' claims.

The *Rooker-Feldman* doctrine provides that federal courts, other than the United States Supreme Court, have no authority to review the final judgments of state courts. * * *

In light of the United States Supreme Court's decision [on December 4, 2000] vacating the Florida Supreme Court's November 21, 2000, decision, it is unclear at the moment that any final judgments giving rise to *Rooker-Feldman* concerns now exist. * * * Thus, we conclude that *Rooker-Feldman* does not bar Plaintiffs from bringing these particular constitutional challenges to the implementation of Florida's manual recount provision.

* * *

Defendants argue that we should abstain from hearing this case under Burford v. Sun Oil Co., 319 U.S. 315, 63 S.Ct. 1098, 87 L.Ed. 1424 (1943), or under Railroad Comm'n of Tex. v. Pullman Co., 312 U.S. 496, 61 S.Ct. 643, 85 L.Ed. 971 (1941). * * *

The *Burford* abstention doctrine allows a federal court to dismiss a case only if it presents difficult questions of state law bearing on policy problems of substantial public import whose importance transcends the

---

4. Plaintiffs' request on appeal is thus broader than their request for an injunction pending appeal, which asked only that we halt manual recounts then underway. * * * [W]e must decline to convert this appeal of a denial of a preliminary injunction into a final hearing on the merits of Plaintiffs' claims. Our review of such a case is normally limited to whether the district court abused its discretion; however, we recognize that an appellate court under some circumstances may decide the merits of a case in connection with its review of a denial of a preliminary injunction. *See* Thornburgh v. American College of Obstetricians & Gynecologists, 476 U.S. 747, 755–56, 106 S.Ct. 2169, 2176, 90 L.Ed.2d 779 (1986).

In *Thornburgh*, the Supreme Court said that "if a district court's ruling rests solely on a premise as to the applicable rule of law, and the facts are established or of no controlling relevance, that ruling may be reviewed even though the appeal is from the entry of a preliminary injunction." * * *

This case * * * represents the very situation in which the Supreme Court held that appellate review was not appropriate. The answer to the constitutional questions is anything but clear. And, in stark contrast to *Thornburgh*, we have before us a factual record that is largely incomplete and vigorously disputed. * * *

result in the case then at bar, or if its adjudication in a federal forum would disrupt state efforts to establish a coherent policy with respect to a matter of substantial public concern. * * * The case before us does not threaten to undermine Florida's uniform approach to manual recounts; indeed, the crux of Plaintiffs' complaint is the absence of strict and uniform standards for initiating or conducting such recounts. Finally, we note that *Burford* abstention represents an "extraordinary and narrow exception to the duty of a District Court to adjudicate a controversy properly before it." * * * We do not believe that the concerns raised by Defendants in this case justify our abstention under this narrow doctrine.

Perhaps the most persuasive justification for abstention advanced by Defendants is based on *Pullman*. * * * Under the *Pullman* abstention doctrine, a federal court will defer to "state court resolution of underlying issues of state law." * * * Two elements must be met for *Pullman* abstention to apply: (1) the case must present an unsettled question of state law, and (2) the question of state law must be dispositive of the case or would materially alter the constitutional question presented. * * * The purpose of *Pullman* abstention is to "avoid unnecessary friction in federal-state functions, interference with important state functions, tentative decisions on questions of state law, and premature constitutional adjudication." * * *

Plaintiffs claim that Florida's manual recount provision is unconstitutional because the statute does not provide sufficient standards. * * * There has been no suggestion by Defendants that the statute is appropriately subject to a more limited construction than the statute itself indicates.

Our conclusion that abstention is inappropriate is strengthened by the fact that Plaintiffs allege a constitutional violation of their voting rights. In considering abstention, we must take into account the nature of the controversy and the importance of the right allegedly impaired. *See* Edwards v. Sammons, 437 F.2d 1240, 1243 (5th Cir. 1971) (citing, as examples of cases where the Supreme Court referred to the nature of the right involved in upholding a refusal to abstain, Harman v. Forssenius, 380 U.S. 528, 537, 85 S.Ct. 1177, 1183, 14 L.Ed.2d 50 (1965) (voting rights); Griffin v. County Sch. Bd. of Prince Edward County, 377 U.S. 218, 84 S.Ct. 1226, 12 L.Ed.2d 256 (1964) (school desegregation); Baggett v. Bullitt, 377 U.S. 360, 84 S.Ct. 1316, 12 L.Ed.2d 377 (1964) (First Amendment rights)). * * * In light of this precedent, the importance of the rights asserted by Plaintiffs counsels against our abstention in this case; although, as discussed below, we are mindful of the limited role of the federal courts in assessing a state's electoral process.

* * *

* * * Plaintiffs state two main claims. First, Plaintiffs argue that Florida's manual recount scheme * * * is unconstitutional because it contains no standards for when a ballot not read by the machine may be counted. * * *

Second, Plaintiffs assert that they are denied due process and equal protection because * * * ballots in one county may be manually recounted while ballots in another county are not. * * *

* * *

The district court, weighing the parties' arguments, determined that Plaintiffs had failed to show a substantial likelihood of success on the merits. We have reviewed the competing arguments. To some extent, our consideration of these arguments is shaped by the practical difficulties of marshaling an adequate record when ongoing and unexpected events continually alter the key facts. In this case, only limited affidavits and a few documents were introduced into the record before the district court. No formal discovery has been undertaken, and, as yet, no evidentiary hearing has been held in this case. Many highly material allegations of facts are vigorously contested. Preliminary injunction motions are often, by necessity, litigated on an undeveloped record. But an undeveloped record not only makes it harder for a plaintiff to meet his burden of proof, it also cautions against an appellate court setting aside the district court's exercise of its discretion.

However, we need not decide the merits of the case to resolve this appeal, and therefore, do not decide them at this time. The district court rejected Plaintiffs' preliminary injunction motion not only because it found no likelihood of success on the merits, but also on the separate and independent ground that Plaintiffs had failed to show that irreparable injury would result if no injunction were issued. We may reverse the district court's order only if there was a *clear* abuse of discretion. * * *

A district court may grant injunctive relief only if the moving party shows that: (1) it has a substantial likelihood of success on the merits; (2) irreparable injury will be suffered unless the injunction issues; (3) the threatened injury to the movant outweighs whatever damage the proposed injunction may cause the opposing party; and (4) if issued, the injunction would not be adverse to the public interest. * * * In this Circuit, "[a] preliminary injunction is an extraordinary and drastic remedy not to be granted unless the movant clearly established the 'burden of persuasion'" as to each of the four prerequisites. * * *

* * *

At this time, Plaintiffs cannot demonstrate a threat of continuing irreparable harm. At the moment, the candidate Plaintiffs (Governor Bush and Secretary Cheney) are suffering no serious harm, let alone irreparable harm, because they have been certified as the winners of Florida's electoral votes notwithstanding the inclusion of manually recounted ballots. Moreover, even if manual recounts were to resume pursuant to a state court order, it is wholly speculative as to whether the results of those recounts may eventually place Vice President Gore ahead. * * * At the moment it also remains speculative whether such an order may be forthcoming. * * * Moreover, as noted earlier, the United States Supreme

Court has now vacated the Florida Supreme Court's decision, raising still further doubt about the likelihood of any substantial injury.

* * * No voter Plaintiff claims that in this election he was prevented from registering to vote, prevented from voting or prevented from voting for the candidate of his choice. Nor does any voter claim that his vote was rejected or not counted. * * *

Plaintiffs' other allegations of irreparable injuries to justify a preliminary injunction are unconvincing. The candidate Plaintiffs contend that if the manual recounts are allowed to proceed, simply rejecting the results of those recounts after the conclusion of this case will not repair the damage to the legitimacy of the Bush Presidency caused by "broadcasting" the flawed results of a recount that put Vice President Gore ahead. But the pertinent manual recounts have already been concluded, and the results from those recounts widely publicized. Moreover, we reject the contention that merely counting ballots gives rise to cognizable injury.

Plaintiffs also contend that a violation of constitutional rights always constitutes irreparable harm. Our case law has not gone that far, however. *See, e.g.*, Ass'n. of General Contractors v. City of Jacksonville, 896 F.2d 1283, 1285 (11th Cir.1990) ("No authority from the Supreme Court or the Eleventh Circuit has been cited to us for the proposition that the irreparable injury needed for a preliminary injunction can properly be presumed from a substantially likely equal protection violation."); Cunningham v. Adams, 808 F.2d 815, 821–22 (11th Cir.1987) (affirming denial of preliminary injunction in action alleging Fourteenth Amendment violations, and finding no abuse of discretion in district court's rejection of the plaintiff's argument that "irreparable injury will be presumed where there has been a violation of substantive constitutional rights"); *see also* Hohe v. Casey, 868 F.2d 69, 73 (3d Cir.1989) ("Constitutional harm is not necessarily synonymous with the irreparable harm necessary for issuance of a preliminary injunction."). The only areas of constitutional jurisprudence where we have said that an on-going violation may be presumed to cause irreparable injury involve the right of privacy and certain First Amendment claims establishing an imminent likelihood that pure speech will be chilled or prevented altogether. *See City of Jacksonville*, 896 F.2d at 1285 * * *; *see also Hohe*, 868 F.2d at 72–73 ("The assertion of First Amendment rights does not automatically require a finding of irreparable injury, thus entitling a plaintiff to a preliminary injunction if he shows a likelihood of success on the merits. Rather, ... it is the 'direct penalization, as opposed to incidental inhibition, of First Amendment rights [which] constitutes irreparable injury.' ") * * * This is plainly not such a case. * * *

* * *

Accordingly, we cannot say that the district court abused its broad discretion in finding that Plaintiffs did not meet their burden of showing at least a substantial likelihood of irreparable injury. Because proof of irreparable injury is an indispensable prerequisite to a preliminary injunction, Plaintiffs are not entitled to a preliminary injunction at this time; and the district court's order must be affirmed. * * * The Court does not at this time decide the merits of Plaintiffs' constitutional arguments.

Affirmed.

CARNES, CIRCUIT JUDGE, dissenting,

* * * I disagree * * * with the Court's conclusion that irreparable injury has not been shown in these two cases. * * * Because the existence and nature of the constitutional violation is inextricably linked to the question of irreparable injury, I turn first to a discussion of the selective manual recounts * * *.

* * *

The record in this case is not replete with factual detail, but there are sufficient undisputed facts to establish a constitutional violation based upon the selective manual recounts that were undertaken in only a few punch card counties and the resulting discriminatory treatment or weighting of the votes of similarly situated voters. For present purposes, I accept as fact everything represented as fact in the affidavits filed by the Democratic Party. * * * Proceeding in that manner makes it appropriate to decide the merits and whether permanent relief should be granted in these two appeals from the denials of preliminary injunctions. * * * The *Thornburgh* decision establishes that a court of appeals may decide the final merits of a case in an appeal from the grant or denial of a preliminary injunction if "the facts are established or of no controlling relevance * * *." The facts that are established or undisputed in these two cases entitle the plaintiffs to relief for reasons I will explain, and thus all disputed or undeveloped facts are of "no controlling relevance."[3]

* * *

The standard for a permanent injunction is essentially the same as for a preliminary injunction except that the plaintiff must show actual success on the merits instead of a likelihood of success. Amoco Prod. Co. v. Village of Gambell, 480 U.S. 531, 546 n.12, 107 S.Ct. 1396, 1404 n.12, 94 L.Ed.2d 542 (1987). In addition to succeeding on the merits, a plaintiff must "demonstrate the presence of two elements: continuing irreparable injury if the injunction does not issue, and the lack of an adequate remedy at law." * * * Explaining the distinction between "irreparable injury" and "adequate remedy at law," our predecessor circuit said:

> [T]he essential prerequisite to a permanent injunction is the unavailability of an adequate remedy at law. Irreparable injury is, however, one basis, and probably the major one, for showing the inadequacy of any legal remedy.... Often times the concepts of "irreparable injury" and "no adequate remedy at law" are indistinguishable.... "[T]he irreparable injury rubric is intended to describe the quality or severity

---

3. When a court of appeals decides the final legal merits of a case on an appeal from the denial of a preliminary injunction, it does not review merely for an abuse of discretion. Instead, its scope of review is plenary.

of the harm necessary to trigger equitable intervention. In contrast, the inadequate remedy test looks to the possibilities of alternative modes of relief, however serious the initial injury."

Lewis v. S.S. Baune, 534 F.2d 1115, 1124 (5th Cir.1976) (citations omitted).

Here, I believe that the plaintiffs in these two cases have succeeded on the merits by establishing that the disparate treatment of similarly situated voters violates the Equal Protection Clause. That constitutional injury to their right to vote is irreparable, since it "cannot be undone through monetary remedies." Cunningham v. Adams, 808 F.2d 815, 821 (11th Cir.1987), both because of the unquantifiable nature of the right to vote as well as its fundamental importance in our system of representative democracy. *See* Reynolds v. Sims, 377 U.S. 533, 562, 84 S.Ct. 1362, 1381, 12 L.Ed.2d 506(1964). * * *

Not surprisingly, there is no suggestion by the defendants that there is an adequate remedy at law to address the voting-rights injury presented in this case. *See* Dillard v. Crenshaw County, 640 F.Supp. 1347, 1363 (M.D.Ala.1986) ("Given the fundamental nature of the right to vote, monetary remedies would obviously be inadequate in this case; it is simply not possible to pay someone for having been denied a right of this importance."). There is an irreparable injury to the right to vote for which there is no adequate remedy at law. Accordingly, granting the requested injunctive relief is the only appropriate remedy.

NOTES

1. In *Siegel*, the *per curiam* opinion and the dissenting opinion by Justice Carnes appear to debate whether irreparable injury can be presumed from the existence of a constitutional violation. How does the discussion of presumed general compensatory damages in Memphis Community School District v. Stachura, *supra* Chapter 6, Section 4.A, relate to the issue debated in *Siegel*? For a discussion of presumed general compensatory damages in the context of defamation, see *infra* Chapter 6, Section 5.A.

2. For what purpose did the *per curiam* opinion in *Siegel* refer to the the Supreme Court's order of December 4 in Bush v. Palm Beach County Canvassing Board, *supra*?

3. On December 11, 2000, the Florida Supreme Court reissued a "Corrected Opinion" in *Palm Beach County Canvassing Board* stating that its order of November 21 had been based on Florida statutory law enacted prior to the election. Palm Beach County Canvassing Board v. Harris, 772 So.2d 1273 (Fla.2000).

4. The previous cases involved the "protest phase" of Florida's election statutes, which covered the time between the election and its certification. The case that follows, Gore v. Harris, later titled Bush v. Gore, was filed pursuant to Florida's "contest phase" statutes, which cover challenges brought after certification. Since the two phases are governed by different

statutes, any case filed during the contest phase is procedurally unrelated to cases filed during the protest phase.

GORE v. HARRIS

Supreme Court of Florida, December 8, 2000.
772 So.2d 1243.

PER CURIAM

* * *

On November 26, 2000, the Florida Election Canvassing Commission (Canvassing Commission) certified the results of the election and declared Governor George W. Bush and Richard Cheney, the Republican candidates for President and Vice President, the winner of Florida's electoral votes. The November 26, 2000, certified results showed a 537–vote margin in favor of Bush.

On November 27, pursuant to the legislatively enacted "contest" provisions, Gore filed a complaint in Leon County Circuit Court contesting the certification on the grounds that the results certified by the Canvassing Commission included "a number of illegal votes" and failed to include "a number of legal votes sufficient to change or place in doubt the result of the election."

Pursuant to the legislative scheme providing for an "immediate hearing" in a contest action, the trial court held a two-day evidentiary hearing on December 2 and 3, 2000, and on December 4, 2000, made an oral statement in open court denying all relief * * *.

* * *

Through no fault of appellants, a lawfully commenced manual recount in Dade County was never completed and recounts that were completed were not counted. * * * On this record there can be no question that there are legal votes within the 9,000 uncounted votes sufficient to place the results of this election in doubt. * * *

Although in all elections the Legislature and the courts have recognized that the voter's intent is paramount, in close elections the necessity for counting all legal votes becomes critical. However, the need for accuracy must be weighed against the need for finality. The need for prompt resolution and finality is especially critical in presidential elections where there is an outside deadline established by federal law. Notwithstanding, consistent with the legislative mandate and our precedent, although the time constraints are limited, we must do everything required by law to ensure that legal votes that have not been counted are included in the final election results. * * *

* * *

In addition to the relief requested by appellants to count the Miami–Dade undervote, claims have been made by the various appellees and intervenors that because this is a statewide election, statewide remedies would be called for. As we discussed in this opinion, we agree. While we recognize that time is desperately short, we cannot in good faith ignore both the appellant's right to relief as to their claims concerning the uncounted votes in Miami–Dade County nor can we ignore the correctness of the assertions that any analysis and ultimate remedy should be made on a statewide basis.

We note that the contest statutes vest broad discretion in the circuit court to "provide any relief appropriate under the circumstances." * * * [T]he circuit court has jurisdiction * * * to order the Supervisor of Elections and the Canvassing Boards, as well as the necessary public officials, in all counties that have not conducted a manual recount or tabulation of the undervotes in this election to do so forthwith, said tabulation to take place in the individual counties where the ballots are located.[22]

* * * [W]e reverse the final judgment of the trial court * * * and remand this cause for the circuit court to immediately tabulate by hand the approximate 9000 Miami–Dade [undervote] ballots * * *. The circuit court is ordered to enter such orders as are necessary to add any legal votes to the total statewide certifications and * * * to ensure the inclusion of the additional legal votes for Gore in Palm Beach County * * *.

* * *

In tabulating the ballots and in making a determination of what is a "legal" vote, the standard to be employed is that established by the Legislature in our Election Code which is that the vote shall be counted as a "legal" vote if there is "clear indication of the intent of the voter." Section 101.5614(5), Florida Statutes (2000).

ANSTEAD, PARIENTE, LEWIS, and QUINCE, JJ., concur.

HARDING, J., dissents, with an opinion, in which SHAW, J., concurs. [Opinion omitted.]

WELLS, C.J., dissenting.

* * *

I want to make it clear at the outset of my separate opinion that I do not question the good faith or honorable intentions of my colleagues in the majority. However, I could not more strongly disagree with their decision to reverse the trial court and prolong this judicial process. I also believe that the majority's decision cannot withstand the scrutiny which will certainly immediately follow under the United States Constitution.

---

22. We are mindful of the fact that due to the time constraints, the count of the undervotes places demands on the public servants throughout the State to work over this week-end. However, we are confident that with the cooperation of the officials in all the counties, the remaining undervotes in these counties can be accomplished within the required time frame. * * *

My succinct conclusion is that the majority's decision to return this case to the circuit court for a count of the under-votes from either Miami–Dade County or all counties has no foundation in the law of Florida as it existed on November 7, 2000, or at any time until the issuance of this opinion. The majority returns the case to the circuit court for this partial recount of under-votes on the basis of unknown or, at best, ambiguous standards with authority to obtain help from others, the credentials, qualifications, and objectivity of whom are totally unknown. That is but a first glance at the imponderable problems the majority creates.

Importantly to me, I have a deep and abiding concern that the prolonging of judicial process in this counting contest propels this country and this state into an unprecedented and unnecessary constitutional crisis. I have to conclude that there is a real and present likelihood that this constitutional crisis will do substantial damage to our country, our state, and to this Court as an institution.

* * *

I would affirm * * * [the circuit court].

NOTES

1. Pursuant to the Florida Supreme Court's order of December 8, on Saturday, December 9, the Circuit Judge of Leon County began to supervise a massive statewide recounting of all of the undervote ballots.

2. On December 8, the day that the Florida Supreme Court had issued its order in Gore v. Harris, Bush filed a petition in the Florida Supreme Court "For a Stay of the Court's Order Pending Review of Petition For Writ of Certiorari in the United States Supreme Court," but the court dismissed it. Later that day, Bush filed an "Emergency Application for a Stay of Enforcement of the Judgment Below Pending the Filing and Disposition of a Petition for a Writ of Certiorari to the Supreme Court of Florida."

BUSH v. GORE
Supreme Court of the United States, December 9, 2000.
531 U.S. 1046, 121 S.Ct. 512, 148 L.Ed.2d 553.

The application for stay presented to Justice Kennedy and by him referred to the Court is granted, and it is ordered that the mandate of the Supreme Court of Florida * * * is hereby stayed pending further order of the Court. In addition, the application for stay is treated as a petition for a writ of certiorari, and petition for writ of certiorari granted. The briefs of the parties, not to exceed 50 pages, are to be filed with the Clerk and served upon opposing counsel on or before 4 p.m. Sunday, December 10, 2000. * * * The case is set for oral argument on Monday, December 11, 2000, at 11 a.m., and a total of 1 1/2 hours is allotted for oral argument.

JUSTICE SCALIA, concurring.

Though it is not customary for the Court to issue an opinion in connection with its grant of a stay, I believe a brief response is necessary to Justice Stevens' dissent. I will not address the merits of the case, since they will shortly be before us in the petition for certiorari that we have granted. It suffices to say that the issuance of the stay suggests that a majority of the Court, while not deciding the issues presented, believe that petitioners have a substantial probability of success.

On the question of irreparable harm, however, a few words are appropriate. The issue is not, as the dissent puts it, whether "[c]ounting every legally cast vote ca[n] constitute irreparable harm." One of the principal issues in the appeal we have accepted is precisely whether the votes that have been ordered to be counted are, under a reasonable interpretation of Florida law, "legally cast vote[s]." The counting of votes that are of questionable legality does in my view threaten irreparable harm to petitioner Bush, and to the country, by casting a cloud upon what he claims to be the legitimacy of his election. Count first, and rule upon legality afterwards, is not a recipe for producing election results that have the public acceptance democratic stability requires. Another issue in the case, moreover, is the propriety, indeed the constitutionality, of letting the standard for determination of voters' intent—dimpled chads, hanging chads, etc.—vary from county to county, as the Florida Supreme Court opinion, as interpreted by the Circuit Court, permits. If petitioners are correct that counting in this fashion is unlawful, permitting the count to proceed on that erroneous basis will prevent an accurate recount from being conducted on a proper basis later, since it is generally agreed that each manual recount produces a degradation of the ballots, which renders a subsequent recount inaccurate.

For these reasons I have joined the Court's issuance of a stay, with a highly accelerated timetable for resolving this case on the merits.

JUSTICE STEVENS, with whom JUSTICE SOUTER, JUSTICE GINSBURG, and JUSTICE BREYER join, dissenting.

To stop the counting of legal votes, the majority today departs from three venerable rules of judicial restraint that have guided the Court throughout its history. On questions of state law, we have consistently respected the opinions of the highest courts of the States. On questions whose resolution is committed at least in large measure to another branch of the Federal Government, we have construed our own jurisdiction narrowly and exercised it cautiously. On federal constitutional questions that were not fairly presented to the court whose judgment is being reviewed, we have prudently declined to express an opinion. The majority has acted unwisely.

Time does not permit a full discussion of the merits. It is clear, however, that a stay should not be granted unless an applicant makes a substantial showing of a likelihood of irreparable harm. In this case, petitioners have failed to carry that heavy burden. Counting every legally cast vote cannot constitute irreparable harm. On the other hand, there is a danger that a stay may cause irreparable harm to respondents—and, more importantly, the public at large—because of the risk that "the entry of the stay would be tantamount to a decision on the merits in favor of the applicants." National Socialist Party of America v. Skokie, 434 U.S. 1327, 1328, 98 S.Ct. 14, 54 L.Ed.2d 38 (1977) (STEVENS, J., in chambers). Preventing the recount from being completed will inevitably cast a cloud on the legitimacy of the election.

It is certainly not clear that the Florida decision violated federal law. The Florida Code provides elaborate procedures for ensuring that every eligible voter has a full and fair opportunity to cast a ballot and that every ballot so cast is counted. * * * In fact, the statutory provision relating to damaged and defective ballots states that "[n]o vote shall be declared invalid or void if there is a clear indication of the intent of the voter as determined by the canvassing board." * * * In its opinion, the Florida Supreme Court gave weight to that legislative command. * * * As a more fundamental matter, the Florida court's ruling reflects the basic principle, inherent in our Constitution and our democracy, that every legal vote should be counted. See Reynolds v. Sims, 377 U.S. 533, 544–555, 84 S.Ct. 1362, 12 L.Ed.2d 506 (1964) * * *.

Accordingly, I respectfully dissent.

NOTES

1. After the stay was announced on Saturday, December 9, at about 2:00 p.m., all of the recounting that had begun the day before halted. The Supreme Court issued its opinion on the merits on the following Tuesday.

2. The texts of the constitutional provision and the statute cited in Bush v. Gore, below, can be found earlier in this subsection in the U.S. Supreme Court's December 4 decision in Bush v. Palm Beach County Canvassing Board.

BUSH v. GORE

Supreme Court of the United States, December 12, 2000.
531 U.S. 98, 121 S.Ct. 525, 148 L.Ed.2d 388.

PER CURIAM

On December 8, 2000, the Supreme Court of Florida ordered that the Circuit Court of Leon County tabulate by hand 9,000 ballots in Miami–Dade County. * * * The court further held that relief would require manual recounts in all Florida counties where so-called "undervotes" had not been subject to manual tabulation. The court ordered all manual recounts to begin at once. Governor Bush and Richard Cheney, Republican candidates for President and Vice President, filed an emergency application for a stay of this mandate. On December 9, we granted the application, treated the application as a petition for a writ of certiorari, and granted certiorari. * * *

* * * On November 8, 2000, the day following the Presidential election, the Florida Division of Elections reported * * * a margin of 1,784 for Governor Bush. * * *

On November 26, the Florida Elections Canvassing Commission certified the results of the election and declared Governor Bush the winner of
Florida's 25 electoral votes. On November 27, Vice President Gore, pursuant to Florida's contest provisions, filed a complaint in Leon County
Circuit Court contesting the certification. * * *

* * *

The Supreme Court held that Vice President Gore had satisfied his
burden of proof. * * * The court therefore ordered a hand recount of the
9,000 ballots in Miami–Dade County. * * * [T]he Supreme Court further
held that the Circuit Court could order "the Supervisor of Elections and
the Canvassing Boards, as well as the necessary public officials, in all
counties that have not conducted a manual recount or tabulation of the
undervotes ... to do so forthwith, said tabulation to take place in the
individual counties where the ballots are located." * * *

* * *

The petition presents the following questions: whether the Florida
Supreme Court established new standards for resolving Presidential election contests, thereby violating Art. II, § 1, cl. 2, of the United States
Constitution and failing to comply with 3 U.S.C. § 5, and whether the use
of standardless manual recounts violates the Equal Protection and Due
Process Clauses. With respect to the equal protection question, we find a
violation of the Equal Protection Clause.

* * *

Seven Justices of the Court [(including JUSTICES SOUTER and BREYER,
dissenting)] agree that there are constitutional [equal protection] problems with the recount ordered by the Florida Supreme Court that demand
a remedy. * * * The only disagreement is as to the remedy. Because the
Florida Supreme Court has said that the Florida Legislature intended to
obtain the safe-harbor benefits of 3 U.S.C. § 5, JUSTICE BREYER'S proposed
remedy—remanding to the Florida Supreme Court for its ordering of a
constitutionally proper contest until December 18—contemplates action in
violation of the Florida Election Code [, which requires that any contest be
completed by December 12,] and hence could not be part of an "appropriate" order authorized by Fla. Stat. Ann. § 102.168(8) (Supp.2000).

* * *

None are more conscious of the vital limits on judicial authority than
are the Members of this Court, and none stand more in admiration of the
Constitution's design to leave the selection of the President to the people,
through their legislatures, and to the political sphere. When contending
parties invoke the process of the courts, however, it becomes our unsought
responsibility to resolve the federal and constitutional issues the judicial
system has been forced to confront.

The judgment of the Supreme Court of Florida is reversed, and the case is remanded for further proceedings not inconsistent with this opinion.

CHIEF JUSTICE REHNQUIST, with whom JUSTICE SCALIA and JUSTICE THOMAS join, concurring.

We join the *per curiam* opinion. We write separately because we believe there are additional grounds that require us to reverse the Florida Supreme Court decision.

* * *

* * * Though we generally defer to state courts on the interpretation of state law * * *, there are of course areas in which the Constitution requires this Court to undertake an independent, if still deferential, analysis of state law.

* * *

* * * [W]e decided Bouie v. City of Columbia, 378 U.S. 347, 84 S.Ct. 1697, 12 L.Ed.2d 894 (1964), in which the state court had held, contrary to precedent, that the state trespass law applied to black sit-in demonstrators who had consent to enter private property but were then asked to leave. * * * [W]e concluded that the South Carolina Supreme Court's interpretation of a state penal statute had impermissibly broadened the scope of that statute beyond what a fair reading provided, in violation of due process. * * * What we would do in the present case is precisely parallel: hold that the Florida Supreme Court's interpretation of the Florida election laws impermissibly distorted them beyond what a fair reading required, in violation of Article II.

* * *

For these reasons, in addition to those given in the *per curiam* opinion, we would reverse.

JUSTICE STEVENS, with whom JUSTICE GINSBURG and JUSTICE BREYER join, dissenting.

* * *

Even assuming that aspects of the remedial scheme might ultimately be found to violate the Equal Protection Clause, I could not subscribe to the majority's disposition of the case. * * * [T]he appropriate course of action would be to remand to allow more specific procedures for implementing the legislature's uniform general standard to be established.

In the interest of finality, however, the majority effectively orders the disenfranchisement of an unknown number of voters whose ballots reveal their intent—and are therefore legal votes under state law—but were for some reason rejected by ballot-counting machines. It does so on the basis of the deadlines set forth in Title 3 of the United States Code. * * * [T]hose provisions merely provide rules of decision for Congress to follow when selecting among conflicting slates of electors. * * * Indeed, in 1960,

Hawaii appointed two slates of electors and Congress chose to count the one appointed on January 4, 1961, well after the Title 3 deadlines. * * *

* * *

* * * Although we may never know with complete certainty the identity of the winner of this year's Presidential election, the identity of the loser is perfectly clear. It is the Nation's confidence in the judge as an impartial guardian of the rule of law.

I respectfully dissent.

JUSTICE SOUTER, with whom JUSTICE BREYER joins, and with whom JUSTICE STEVENS and JUSTICE GINSBURG join as to all but Part III, dissenting.

The Court should not have reviewed either Bush v. Palm Beach County Canvassing Bd. * * * or this case, and should not have stopped Florida's attempt to recount all undervote ballots * * * by issuing a stay of the Florida Supreme Court's orders during the period of this review * * *. If this Court had allowed the State to follow the course indicated by the opinions of its own Supreme Court, it is entirely possible that there would ultimately have been no issue requiring our review, and political tension could have worked itself out in the Congress following the procedure provided in 3 U.S.C. § 15. The case being before us, however, its resolution by the majority is another erroneous decision.

As will be clear, I am in substantial agreement with the dissenting opinions of JUSTICE STEVENS, JUSTICE GINSBURG, and JUSTICE BREYER. I write separately only to say how straight-forward the issues before us really are.

There are three issues: whether the State Supreme Court's interpretation of the statute providing for a contest of the state election results somehow violates 3 U.S.C. § 5; whether that court's construction of the state statutory provisions governing contests impermissibly changes a state law from what the State's legislature has provided, in violation of Article II, § 1, cl. 2, of the national Constitution; and whether the manner of interpreting markings on disputed ballots failing to cause machines to register votes for President (the undervote ballots) violates the equal protection or due process guaranteed by the Fourteenth Amendment. None of these issues is difficult to describe or to resolve.

I

The 3 U.S.C. § 5 issue is not serious. That provision sets certain conditions for treating a State's certification of Presidential electors as conclusive in the event that a dispute over recognizing those electors must be resolved in the Congress under 3 U.S.C. § 15. * * * But no State is required to conform to § 5 if it cannot do that (for whatever reason); the sanction for failing to satisfy the conditions of § 5 is simply loss of what has been called its "safe harbor." And even that determination is to be made, if made anywhere, in the Congress.

II

* * * [T]here is no question here about the state court's interpretation of the related provisions dealing with the antecedent process of "protesting" particular vote counts. * * * The issue is whether the judgment of the state supreme court has displaced the state legislature's provisions for election contests: * * * statutes require interpretation, which does not without more affect the legislative character of a statute within the meaning of the Constitution. * * *

* * *

III

Petitioners have raised an equal protection claim * * * in the charge that unjustifiably disparate standards are applied in different electoral jurisdictions to otherwise identical facts. It is true that the Equal Protection Clause does not forbid the use of a variety of voting mechanisms within a jurisdiction, even though different mechanisms will have different levels of effectiveness in recording voter's intentions; local variety can be justified by concerns about cost, the potential value of innovation, and so on. But evidence in the record here suggests that a different order of disparity obtains under rules for determining a voter's intent that have been applied * * * to identical types of ballots used in identical brands of machines and exhibiting identical physical characteristics (such as "hanging" or "dimpled" chads). * * * The differences appear wholly arbitrary.

In deciding what to do about this, we should take account of the fact that electoral votes are due to be cast in six days. I would therefore remand the case to the courts of Florida with instructions to establish uniform standards for evaluating the several types of ballots that have prompted differing treatments, to be applied within and among counties when passing on such identical ballots in any further recounting (or successive recounting) that the courts might order.

Unlike the majority, I see no warrant for this Court to assume that Florida could not possibly comply with this requirement before the date set for the meeting of electors, December 18. * * * There is no justification for denying the State the opportunity to try to count all disputed ballots now.

I respectfully dissent.

JUSTICE GINSBURG, with whom JUSTICE STEVENS joins, and with whom JUSTICE SOUTER and JUSTICE BREYER join as to Part I, dissenting.

I

* * *

Rarely has this Court rejected outright an interpretation of state law by a state high court. * * * *Bouie,* stemming from a lunch counter "sit-in" at the height of the civil rights movement, held that the South Carolina Supreme Court's construction of its trespass laws—criminalizing conduct not covered by the text of an otherwise clear statute—was "unforeseeable" and thus violated due process when applied retroactively to the petitioners. * * *

* * * The Florida Supreme Court concluded that counting every legal vote was the overriding concern of the Florida Legislature when it enacted the State's Election Code. The court surely should not be bracketed with state high courts of the Jim Crow South.

* * *

The extraordinary setting of this case has obscured the ordinary principle that dictates its proper resolution: Federal courts defer to a state high court's interpretations of the State's own law. * * *

II

I agree with JUSTICE STEVENS that petitioners have not presented a substantial equal protection claim. * * *

Even if there were an equal protection violation, I would agree with JUSTICE STEVENS, JUSTICE SOUTER, and JUSTICE BREYER that the Court's concern about "the December 12 deadline" * * * is misplaced. Time is short in part because of the Court's entry of a stay on December 9, several hours after an able circuit judge in Leon County had begun to superintend the recount process. More fundamentally, the Court's reluctance to let the recount go forward—despite its suggestion that "[t]he search for intent can be confined by specific rules designed to ensure uniform treatment," * * *—ultimately turns on its own judgment about the practical realities of implementing a recount, not the judgment of those much closer to the process.

* * *

I dissent.

JUSTICE BREYER, with whom JUSTICE STEVENS and JUSTICE GINSBURG join except as to Part I–A–1, and with whom JUSTICE SOUTER joins as to Part I, dissenting.

The Court was wrong to take this case. It was wrong to grant a stay. It should now vacate that stay and permit the Florida Supreme Court to decide whether the recount should resume.

I.

The political implications of this case for the country are momentous. But the federal legal questions presented, with one exception, are insubstantial.

* * *

II.

* * *

* * * [T]here is no reason to believe that federal law either foresees or requires resolution of such a political issue by this Court. Nor, for that matter, is there any reason to think that the Constitution's Framers would have reached a different conclusion. Madison, at least, believed that allowing the judiciary to choose the Presidential electors "was out of the question." Madison, July 25, 1787 (reprinted in 5 Elliot's Debates on the Federal Constitution 363 (2d ed. 1876)).

The decision by both the Constitution's Framers and the 1886 Congress to minimize this Court's role in resolving close federal Presidential elections is as wise as it is clear. * * *

Moreover, Congress was fully aware of the danger that would arise should it ask judges, unarmed with appropriate legal standards, to resolve a hotly contested Presidential election contest. Just after the 1876 Presidential election, Florida, South Carolina, and Louisiana each sent two slates of electors to Washington. Without these States, Tilden, the Democrat, had 184 electoral votes, one short of the number required to win the Presidency. With those States, Hayes, his Republican opponent, would have had 185. In order to choose between the two slates of electors, Congress decided to appoint an electoral commission composed of five Senators, five Representatives, and five Supreme Court Justices. Initially the Commission was to be evenly divided between Republicans and Democrats with Justice David Davis, an Independent, to possess the decisive vote. However, when at the last minute the Illinois Legislature elected Justice Davis to the United States Senate, the final position on the Commission was filled by Supreme Court Justice Joseph P. Bradley.

The Commission divided along partisan lines, and the responsibility to cast the deciding vote fell to Justice Bradley. He decided to accept the votes by the Republican electors, and thereby awarded the Presidency to Hayes.

Justice Bradley immediately became the subject of vociferous attack. Bradley was accused of accepting bribes * * * and of an eleventh-hour change in position after a night in which his house "was surrounded by carriages" of Republican partisans * * *. Many years later, Professor Bickel concluded that Bradley was honest and impartial. He thought that "the great question" for Bradley was, in fact, whether Congress was entitled to go behind election returns or had to accept them as certified by state authorities * * *. Nonetheless, Bickel points out, the legal question upon which Justice Bradley's decision turned was not very important in the contemporaneous political context. He says that "in the circumstances the issue of principle was trivial, it was overwhelmed by all that hung in the balance, and it should not have been decisive." * * *

* * *

* * * [A]bove all, in this highly politicized matter, the appearance of a split decision runs the risk of undermining the public's confidence in the Court itself. That confidence is a public treasure. It has been built slowly over many years, some of which were marked by a Civil War and the tragedy of segregation. It is a vitally necessary ingredient of any successful effort to protect basic liberty and, indeed, the rule of law itself. * * *

I fear that in order to bring this agonizingly long election process to a definitive conclusion, we have not adequately attended to that necessary "check upon our own exercise of power" * * *.

* * * What it does today, the Court should have left undone. I would repair the damage done as best we now can, by permitting the Florida recount to continue under uniform standards.

I respectfully dissent.

NOTES

1. If you had been one of the Justices on either the Florida Supreme Court or the United States Supreme Court, how would you have decided these cases? For scholarly commentary on the remedial aspects of Bush v. Gore, see Nelson Lund, *The Unbearable Rightness of* Bush v. Gore, 23 Cardozo L. Rev. 1219 (2002) ("Bush v. Gore was a straightforward and legally correct decision"); Michael W. McConnell, *Two-and-a-Half Cheers for* Bush v. Gore, 68 U. Chi. L. Rev. 657 (2001) (the Court "forfeited" the "half cheer * * * by failing to produce a bipartisan consensus on the remand issue"); Tracy A. Thomas, *The Prophylactic Remedy: Normative Principles and Definitional Parameters of Broad Injunctive Relief*, 52 Buff. L. Rev. 301 (2004) ("the [Court's] * * * quick and dramatic default to prophylactic relief raised universal criticism").

2. The federal courts that decided the presidential election cases discussed the relationship between state and federal courts. On that issue, is *Siegel* consistent with Bush v. Gore, or are the cases distinguishable? Is Bush v. Gore consistent with the abstention doctrines that have been adopted by the federal judiciary? See *infra* Chapter 6, Section 4.B.4.

3. *Griffin*, the case in which the Supreme Court ordered a county to open its schools after they had been closed to avoid desegregation, is cited in *Siegel* as a case in which it would have been inappropriate for a federal court to abstain. For further discussion of *Griffin*, see *supra* Chapter 6, Section 4.B.1.

4. Some of the presidential election cases discuss the relationship between the federal courts and the state courts. Many of the school desegregation cases that limit the remedies do so on the grounds of federalism and comity. The cases below continue to explore these themes.

3. State Court Injunctions Against Pending Criminal Proceedings

NORCISA v. BOARD OF SELECTMEN
OF PROVINCETOWN

Supreme Judicial Court of Massachusetts, 1975.
368 Mass. 161, 330 N.E.2d 830.

QUIRICO, JUSTICE.

This is an appeal by the defendants, the board of selectmen of Provincetown (selectmen) and their agent, from a decree entered by the judge of the Probate Court for Barnstable County, apparently acting under G.L. c. 231A, §§ 1, 2, and under G.L. c. 215, § 6, as appearing in St.1963, c. 820, § 1, declaring that the plaintiff and her retail clothing business in the town of Provincetown (town) are not within the scope of G.L. c. 101, §§ 1–12, the Transient Vendor Statute, and ordering that the town and its agents, servants, and employees "are hereby restrained and permanently enjoined from enforcing * * * any of the provisions of Mass.G.L. c. 101, §§ 1–12, against the Petitioner or the retail business she operates." This appeal was first entered in the Appeals Court and we then transferred it to this court, acting on our own motion. G.L. c. 211A, § 10(A), inserted by St.1972, c. 740, § 1. Prior to the commencement of this suit in equity, a criminal complaint had issued in the Second District Court of Barnstable County charging the plaintiff with violating G.L. c. 101, §§ 6, 8. This criminal complaint was still pending when the decree appealed from issued. The obvious purpose and effect of the decree was to enjoin the pending criminal prosecution. We reverse.

The facts apparently relied on by the judge in issuing the final decree were contained in a document signed by attorneys for both the plaintiff and the defendants, entitled "Agreed Statement of Facts." It appears from this document that sometime late in 1973 the plaintiff, who was a resident of Provincetown, opened a retail clothing business in that town under the name of The Town Crier Wearhouse. At the time she opened her business, the plaintiff was informed by the agent for the selectmen "that she would not be able to open and operate her business unless she paid to Provincetown a license fee of two hundred dollars ($200.00), furnished a bond of five hundred dollars ($500.00), to the Commonwealth, and applied for both a state and town Transient Vendor's License, all of the above pursuant to and authorized by G.L. c. 101, § 3."

General Laws c. 101, § 3, requires that anyone "before commencing business in the commonwealth as a transient vendor" shall apply for a State license, good for one year, to do business as a transient vendor, subject to local rules and regulations. * * * A "transient vendor" is defined as "any person, either principal or agent, who engages in a temporary or transient business in the commonwealth selling goods, wares or merchandise, either in one locality or in traveling from place to place." G.L. c. 101, § 1. "Temporary or transient business" is further defined as "any exhibition and sale of goods, wares or merchandise which is carried on in any tent, booth, building or other structure, unless such place is open for business during usual business hours for a period of at least twelve consecutive months." G.L. c. 101, § 1.

The plaintiff's position as stated in the "Agreed Statement of Facts" is that she was not a transient vendor at the time the selectmen sought to categorize her as one, that she had not been a transient vendor in the past, and that she would not be a transient vendor in the future. * * * The defendants' position, in the court below as well as in their brief here, has been "that under the terms of the statute petitioner is required to take out a transient vendor's license unless she has been 'open for business during usual business hours *for a period of at least twelve consecutive months*' " (emphasis added).

* * *

At one time, it was common for courts to express the view that an equity court had no "jurisdiction" to enjoin a criminal prosecution. * * *

In this Commonwealth, however, it was early established that courts with general equity powers have the power to restrain criminal prosecutions. * * * Shuman v. Gilbert, 229 Mass. 225, 118 N.E. 254 (1918). * * *

As pointed out in the *Shuman* case, the occasions when an equity court may properly enjoin a criminal prosecution remain the exception to the "general rule" of nonintervention. Some of the basic policy reasons underlying the rule of nonintervention were well-expressed by the Supreme Court of Hawaii: "Courts of equity are not constituted to deal with crimes and criminal proceedings. They have no power to punish admitted offenders of a challenged penal statute after holding it to be valid, or to compensate those injured by the violations thereof while the hands of the officers of the law have been stayed by injunction. To that extent such courts are incapable of affording a complete remedy. Equity, therefore, takes no part in the administration of the criminal law. It neither aids, restrains, nor obstructs criminal courts in the exercise of their jurisdiction. Ordinarily a court of equity deals only with civil cases involving property rights where it can afford a complete remedy by injunctive relief. Hence it does not interfere in the enforcement of penal statutes even though invalid unless there be exceptional circumstances and a clear showing that an injunction is urgently necessary to afford adequate protection to rights of property so as to circumvent great and irreparable injury until the validity of the particular penal statute is sustained." Liu v. Farr, 39 Haw. 23, 35–36 (1950).

Both the *Shuman* and *Liu* cases quoted above indicated that equity would act only to protect "property rights" from irreparable damage by criminal prosecution. In the leading case of Kenyon v. Chicopee, 320 Mass. 528, 70 N.E.2d 241 (1946), however, we largely rejected the personal rights-property rights distinction as a factor in considering whether an injunction should issue. * * *

The plaintiff variously claims that G.L. c. 101, §§ 1–12, is either unconstitutional on its face or as applied, or that the statute, properly construed, does not apply to her at all. In accordance with these claims, she asserts that she cannot be prosecuted for failure to comply with the statute. If we assume, again without deciding the question, that the plaintiff indeed cannot properly be prosecuted under this statute, the issue resolves itself simply to whether the available defenses to the District Court criminal complaint amount to an adequate remedy at law. In the circumstances of this case, we think they plainly do.

In both the *Shuman* and *Kenyon* cases, the question was considered whether, in the circumstances of those cases, the defense to the criminal prosecution provided an adequate remedy at law. Since the injunction was denied in the former case and granted in the latter, it is instructive to compare them.

In the *Shuman* case, six merchants alleged that the defendant chief of police of Northampton threatened to prosecute them for conducting a business without a license, which they claimed they were not obligated to obtain. The plaintiffs' bill sought to make out a case of irreparable damage and inadequacy of legal remedy by alleging, inter alia, that it would take several months to obtain a decision on the case from an appellate court and that in the intervening period the loss of profits and advantageous business relations would cause the plaintiffs great and irreparable damage. To these averments, a demurrer was sustained. This court upheld the sustaining of the demurrer. After noting that in the event of multiple, oppressive, and wrongful prosecutions, an injunction might properly issue, we said: "A possibility that complaints may be lodged against six persons is not enough under these circumstances to make out a case of multiplicity. The allegations as to repeated complaints are not sufficient to warrant the inference that the courts of this commonwealth will countenance continued and oppressive prosecutions when once a genuine test case open to fair question has been presented and is on its way to final decision." 229 Mass. at 229, 118 N.E. at 256 (1918). We further rejected any notion that our courts of criminal jurisdiction could not protect the rights in question: "[The bill] assumes that one innocent of any infraction of the law will be found guilty by the district court and by the superior court, a presumption which as a matter of law cannot be indulged, at least upon such general allegations. The allegations as to property damage are nothing more than the ordinary averments which might be made by anybody engaged in business, undertaking a branch of commercial adventure believed by the officers charged with enforcing the law to be in contravention of some penal statute confessedly valid in itself. Simply that one is in business, and may be injured in respect of his business by prosecution for an alleged crime, is no sufficient reason for asking a court of equity to ascertain in advance whether the business as conducted is in violation of a penal statute." 229 Mass. at 230, 118 N.E. at 256 (1918).

In the *Kenyon* case, by contrast, we reversed interlocutory decrees sustaining demurrers where the bill alleged that members of Jehovah's

Witnesses had been repeatedly, on different dates, arrested, prosecuted, and convicted under an unconstitutional ordinance. * * * We observed: "The plaintiffs' rights are of the most fundamental character. According to the bill they have been violated repeatedly. It is plain that the legal remedies, by defending against repeated complaints and bringing successive actions for malicious prosecution or false arrest, are not adequate." 320 Mass. at 534, 70 N.E.2d at 245 (1946).

In the present case, the plaintiff is the subject of a complaint charging a single violation of the statute. She avers that the statute is either unconstitutional on its face or as applied, or that, properly construed, it is inapplicable to her. These averments, of course, would, if established, each constitute a complete defense to the violation charged. We repeat here a passage from a United States Supreme Court case which applies equally to the matter before us: "It is a familiar rule that courts of equity do not ordinarily restrain criminal prosecutions. No person is immune from prosecution in good faith for his alleged criminal acts. Its imminence, even though alleged to be in violation of constitutional guarantees, is not a ground for equity relief since the lawfulness or constitutionality of the statute or ordinance on which the prosecution is based may be determined as readily in the criminal case as in a suit for injunction. * * * It does not appear from the record that petitioners have been threatened with any injury other than that incidental to every criminal proceeding brought lawfully and in good faith, or that a * * * court of equity by withdrawing the determination of guilt from the * * * [criminal] courts could rightly afford petitioners any protection which they could not secure by prompt trial and appeal pursued to this Court." Douglas v. Jeannette, 319 U.S. 157, 163–164, 63 S.Ct. 877, 881, 87 L.Ed. 1324 (1943).

In general, we believe the Federal policy of ordinarily refusing to enjoin pending State criminal prosecutions is sound. This policy, based partly on principles of Federal–State comity and partly on the general equitable principles we have summarized in this opinion, * * * prohibits equitable interference with criminal prosecutions absent "very special circumstances." Younger v. Harris, 401 U.S. 37, 45, 91 S.Ct. 746, 27 L.Ed.2d 669 (1971). "Very special circumstances" may be merely a shorthand way of requiring a stricter application of general equitable principles, for example, that no injunction will issue unless the plaintiff will suffer irreparable and immediate injury without it. But however the concept is phrased, the necessity of defending a single criminal prosecution rarely, if ever, justifies issuance of the injunction.

* * *

[The court also concluded that declaratory relief was unavailable. For further consideration of declaratory relief in this context, see *supra* Chapter 5.]

For the reasons given above, the injunction and declaratory relief should not have been granted. The final decree is reversed and a new judgment is to be entered dismissing the bill.

NOTES

1. The principal case is representative of a strong judicial sentiment against enjoining criminal prosecution, at least in the absence of exceptional circumstances, such as prosecutorial harassment and bad faith. Professor Dobbs has articulated succinctly the reasons behind this rule:

> If the injunction-seeker has a good defense, he can usually present it in the criminal proceeding itself, perhaps even obtain a dismissal in an early probable cause hearing. While an injunction may be a preferable remedy for any number of reasons, the normal rules of criminal procedure may be thought to require that courts keep hands off the criminal process. If the court hears all the evidence in the injunction suit and decides the prosecution can proceed, then all the evidence will be produced again before another judge in the criminal suit. If the evidence is not heard in the injunction suit, the question may be abstract and not suitable for a final determination. Either way, it seems better to use the criminal process unless its use can be shown to be a wrong and also one that threatens important rights of the plaintiff.

Dan B. Dobbs, Law of Remedies 176 (2d ed. 1993); *accord* State v. Morales, 869 S.W.2d 941, 944–46 (Tex.1994).

2. Where a person is confronted by a threatened prosecution, it is arguable that injunction suits should receive somewhat more favorable treatment. In such a situation, the injunction suit does not duplicate an already commenced criminal action. Moreover, a person whose actions may be inhibited by a statute may wish to challenge its constitutionality:

> If he has already violated it, he can [challenge its constitutionality] in the criminal prosecution that ensues. However, he should not be forced to violate a statute in order to discover whether it can validly limit his activities. * * * If the plaintiff is in real need of determining his rights so that his full freedom of action can be assured on the one hand and his freedom from prosecution can be assured on the other, there is no very obvious reason why the courts of the state should not determine the constitutionality of the statute in an equity suit to enjoin its prosecution.

Dan B. Dobbs, Handbook on the Law of Remedies 114 (1973). Nevertheless, courts continue to require a showing of irreparable injury and, in some instances, that property or commercial interests are threatened. *See, e.g.,* S.S. Kresge Co. v. Davis, 277 N.C. 654, 178 S.E.2d 382 (1971); State v. Logue, 376 S.W.2d 567 (Tex.1964). The standard is relaxed a bit when the plaintiff claims a violation of the First Amendment, as discussed in Spartacus Youth League v. Board of Trustees of Illinois Industrial University, 502 F.Supp. 789 (N.D.Ill. 1980) (action by youth organization challenging university regulations governing sale and distribution of literature at student union) (preliminary injunction granted):

> The standard for justiciability determinations is "... whether the facts alleged ... show that there is a substantial controversy, between parties having adverse legal interests, of sufficient immediacy and reality to warrant ... judicial review." Maryland Casualty Co. v. Pacific Coal &

Oil Co., 312 U.S. 270, 273, 61 S.Ct. 510, 512, 85 L.Ed. 826 (1941). The test is an imprecise one, with only the opposite poles of the factual continuum providing clear guidance. A plaintiff need not invariably wait until he has been directly subjected to a law or policy before he brings a judicial challenge, but he cannot go to court simply by showing that a regulation exists and that he believes it will be enforced against him. National Student Association v. Hershey, 412 F.2d 1103, 1110 (D.C.Cir. 1969). Between these principles fall the majority of the cases, where the probability of several contingencies must be evaluated on a case-by-case basis: "... the likelihood that the complainant will disobey the law, the certainty that such disobedience will take a particular form, any present injury occasioned by the threat of prosecution, and the likelihood that a prosecution will actually ensue." Regional Rail Reorganization Act Cases, 419 U.S. 102, 143 n.29, 95 S.Ct. 335, 358 n.29, 42 L.Ed.2d 320 (1974).

In the First Amendment area, however, a somewhat relaxed standard of uncertainty is applicable. Injury to First Amendment rights may result from the threat of enforcement itself, since it may chill the plaintiff's ardor and eliminate his desire to engage in protected expression. Dombrowski v. Pfister, 380 U.S. 479, 85 S.Ct. 1116, 14 L.Ed.2d 22 (1965); 13 Wright, Miller & Cooper, Federal Practice & Procedure § 3532, at 245 n. 29 (1975). "The threat of sanctions may deter their [First Amendment rights'] exercise almost as potently as the actual application of sanctions." Dombrowski v. Pfister, *supra*; NAACP v. Button, 371 U.S. 415, 433, 83 S.Ct. 328, 338, 9 L.Ed.2d 405 (1963). Although not every chill will create a justiciable controversy, it may be enough that the plaintiff raises "a credible threat of enforcement and plausible allegations of intent or desire to engage in the threatened activities...." *Hershey, supra*, 412 F.2d at 1111–12.

Id. at 796–97.

3.   Suppose the suit to enjoin the pending proceeding is filed in federal court. The plaintiff then must confront the federal anti-injunction statute, which provides that a federal court "may not grant an injunction to stay proceedings in a State court except as expressly authorized by Act of Congress, or where necessary in aid of its jurisdiction, or to protect or effectuate its judgments." 28 U.S.C.A. § 2283. Section 1983 has been construed as a Congressional authorization of injunctive relief under the first exception to the anti-injunction statute, Mitchum v. Foster, 407 U.S. 225, 92 S.Ct. 2151, 32 L.Ed.2d 705 (1972), but such a federal suit often will be barred by "Our Federalism," an important abstention doctrine enunciated by the Supreme Court in Younger v. Harris, 401 U.S. 37, 91 S.Ct. 746, 27 L.Ed.2d 669 (1971).

4.   Federal Court Injunctions Against Pending Proceedings

YOUNGER v. HARRIS

Supreme Court of the United States, 1971.
401 U.S. 37, 91 S.Ct. 746, 27 L.Ed.2d 669.

MR. JUSTICE BLACK delivered the opinion of the Court.

Appellee, John Harris, Jr., was indicted in a California state court, charged with violation of the California Penal Code §§ 11400 and 11401, known as the California Criminal Syndicalism Act, set out below.[1] He then filed a complaint in the Federal District Court, asking that court to enjoin the appellant, Younger, the District Attorney of Los Angeles County, from prosecuting him, and alleging that the prosecution and even the presence of the Act inhibited him in the exercise of his rights of free speech and press, rights guaranteed him by the First and Fourteenth Amendments. * * *

The case is before us on appeal by the State's District Attorney Younger, pursuant to 28 U.S.C. § 1253. In his notice of appeal and his jurisdictional statement appellant presented two questions: (1) whether the decision of this Court in Whitney v. California, 274 U.S. 357, 47 S.Ct. 641, 71 L.Ed. 1095, holding California's law constitutional in 1927, was binding on the District Court and (2) whether the State's law is constitutional on its face. In this Court the brief for the State of California, filed at our request, also argues that * * * issuance of the injunction was a violation of a longstanding judicial policy and of 28 U.S.C.§ 2283, which provides:

> A court of the United States may not grant an injunction to stay proceedings in a State court except as expressly authorized by Act of Congress, or where necessary in aid of its jurisdiction, or to protect or effectuate its judgments.

See, e.g., Atlantic Coast Line R. Co. v. Engineers, 398 U.S. 281, 285–286, 90 S.Ct. 1739, 1742–1743, 26 L.Ed.2d 234 (1970). Without regard to the questions raised about Whitney v. California, supra, since overruled by Brandenburg v. Ohio, 395 U.S. 444, 89 S.Ct. 1827, 23 L.Ed.2d 430 (1969), or the constitutionality of the state law, we have concluded that the judgment of the District Court, enjoining appellant Younger from prosecuting under these California statutes, must be reversed as a violation of the national policy forbidding federal courts to stay or enjoin pending state court proceedings except under special circumstances.[3] We express no view about the circumstances under which federal courts may act when

---

1. § 11400. Definition

"Criminal syndicalism as used in this article means any doctrine or precept advocating, teaching or aiding and abetting the commission of crime, sabotage (which word is hereby defined as meaning wilful and malicious physical damage or injury to physical property), or unlawful acts of force and violence or unlawful methods of terrorism as a means of accomplishing a change in industrial ownership or control, or effecting any political change."

§ 11401. Offense; punishment

"Any person who: 1. By spoken or written words or personal conduct advocates, teaches or aids and abets criminal syndicalism * * * is guilty of a felony and punishable by imprisonment in the state prison not less than one nor more than 14 years."

3. Appellees did not explicitly ask for a declaratory judgment in their complaint. They did, however, ask the District Court to grant "such other and further relief as to the Court may seem just and proper," and the District Court in fact granted a declaratory judgment. For the reasons stated in our opinion today in Samuels v. Mackell, 401 U.S. 66, 91 S.Ct. 764, 27 L.Ed.2d 688 [(1971)], we hold that declaratory relief is also improper when a prosecution involving the challenged statute is pending in state court at the time the federal suit is initiated.

there is no prosecution pending in state courts at the time the federal proceeding is begun.

* * *

II

Since the beginning of this country's history Congress has, subject to few exceptions, manifested a desire to permit state courts to try state cases free from interference by federal courts. In 1793 an Act unconditionally provided: "[N]or shall a writ of injunction be granted to stay proceedings in any court of a state * * *." 1 Stat. 335, c. 22,§ 5. A comparison of the 1793 Act with 28 U.S.C.§ 2283, its present-day successor, graphically illustrates how few and minor have been the exceptions granted from the flat, prohibitory language of the old Act. During all this lapse of years from 1793 to 1970 the statutory exceptions to the 1793 congressional enactment have been only three; (1) "except as expressly authorized by Act of Congress"; (2) "where necessary in aid of its jurisdiction"; and (3) "to protect or effectuate its judgments." In addition, a judicial exception to the longstanding policy evidenced by the statute has been made where a person about to be prosecuted in a state court can show that he will, if the proceeding in the state court is not enjoined, suffer irreparable damages. See *Ex parte* Young, 209 U.S. 123, 28 S.Ct. 441, 52 L.Ed. 714 (1908).[4]

The precise reasons for this longstanding public policy against federal court interference with state court proceedings have never been specifically identified but the primary sources of the policy are plain. One is the basic doctrine of equity jurisprudence that courts of equity should not act, and particularly should not act to restrain a criminal prosecution, when the moving party has an adequate remedy at law and will not suffer irreparable injury if denied equitable relief. The doctrine may originally have grown out of circumstances peculiar to the English judicial system and not applicable in this country, but its fundamental purpose of restraining equity jurisdiction within narrow limits is equally important under our Constitution, in order to prevent erosion of the role of the jury and avoid a duplication of legal proceedings and legal sanctions where a single suit would be adequate to protect the rights asserted. This underlying reason for restraining courts of equity from interfering with criminal prosecutions is reinforced by an even more vital consideration, the notion of "comity," that is, a proper respect for state functions, a recognition of the fact that the entire country is made up of a Union of separate state governments, and a continuance of the belief that the National Government will fare best if the States and their institutions are left free to perform their separate functions in their separate ways. This, perhaps for lack of a better and clearer way to describe it, is referred to by many as "Our Federalism," and one familiar with the profound debates that ushered our Federal Constitution into existence is bound to respect those

---

4. For an interesting discussion of the history of this congressional policy up to 1941, see Toucey v. New York Life Ins. Co., 314 U.S. 118, 62 S.Ct. 139, 86 L.Ed. 100 (1941).

who remain loyal to the ideals and dreams of "Our Federalism." The concept does not mean blind deference to "States' Rights" any more than it means centralization of control over every important issue in our National Government and its courts. The Framers rejected both these courses. What the concept does represent is a system in which there is sensitivity to the legitimate interests of both State and National Governments, and in which the National Government, anxious though it may be to vindicate and protect federal rights and federal interests, always endeavors to do so in ways that will not unduly interfere with the legitimate activities of the States. It should never be forgotten that this slogan, "Our Federalism," born in the early struggling days of our Union of States, occupies a highly important place in our Nation's history and its future. * * *

It is against the background of these principles that we must judge the propriety of an injunction under the circumstances of the present case. Here a proceeding was already pending in the state court, affording Harris an opportunity to raise his constitutional claims. There is no suggestion that this single prosecution against Harris is brought in bad faith or is only one of a series of repeated prosecutions to which he will be subjected. * * *

The District Court, however, thought that the *Dombrowski* decision substantially broadened the availability of injunctions against state criminal prosecutions and that under that decision the federal courts may give equitable relief, without regard to any showing of bad faith or harassment, whenever a state statute is found "on its face" to be vague or overly broad, in violation of the First Amendment. * * *

* * * Procedures for testing the constitutionality of a statute "on its face" in the manner apparently contemplated by *Dombrowski* * * * are fundamentally at odds with the function of the federal courts in our constitutional plan. The power and duty of the judiciary to declare laws unconstitutional is in the final analysis derived from its responsibility for resolving concrete disputes brought before the courts for decision; a statute apparently governing a dispute cannot be applied by judges, consistently with their obligations under the Supremacy Clause, when such an application of the statute would conflict with the Constitution. Marbury v. Madison, 5 U.S. (1 Cranch) 137, 2 L.Ed. 60 (1803). But this vital responsibility, broad as it is, does not amount to an unlimited power to survey the statute books and pass judgment on laws before the courts are called upon to enforce them. Ever since the Constitutional Convention rejected a proposal for having members of the Supreme Court render advice concerning pending legislation it has been clear that, even when suits of this kind involve a "case or controversy" sufficient to satisfy the requirements of Article III of the Constitution, the task of analyzing a proposed statute, pinpointing its deficiencies, and requiring correction of these deficiencies before the statute is put into effect, is rarely if ever an appropriate task for the judiciary. * * *

For these reasons, fundamental not only to our federal system but also to the basic functions of the Judicial Branch of the National Government under our Constitution, we hold that the Dombrowski decision should not be regarded as having upset the settled doctrines that have always confined very narrowly the availability of injunctive relief against state criminal prosecutions. We do not think that opinion stands for the proposition that a federal court can properly enjoin enforcement of a statute solely on the basis of a showing that the statute "on its face" abridges First Amendment rights. There may, of course, be extraordinary circumstances in which the necessary irreparable injury can be shown even in the absence of the usual prerequisites of bad faith and harassment. For example, as long ago as Watson v. Buck, 313 U.S. 387, 61 S.Ct. 962, 85 L.Ed. 1416 (1941), we indicated:

> It is of course conceivable that a statute might be flagrantly and patently violative of express constitutional prohibitions in every clause, sentence and paragraph, and in whatever manner and against whomever an effort might be made to apply it. 313 U.S., at 402, 61 S.Ct., at 967.

Other unusual situations calling for federal intervention might also arise, but there is no point in our attempting now to specify what they might be. It is sufficient for purposes of the present case to hold, as we do, that the possible unconstitutionality of a statute "on its face" does not in itself justify an injunction against good-faith attempts to enforce it, and that appellee Harris has failed to make any showing of bad faith, harassment, or any other unusual circumstance that would call for equitable relief. * * *

The judgment of the District Court is reversed, and the case is remanded for further proceedings not inconsistent with this opinion.

MR. JUSTICE BRENNAN with whom MR. JUSTICE WHITE and MR. JUSTICE MARSHALL join, concurring in the result.

NOTES

1. The anti-injunction statute addresses the question of whether a federal court may enjoin state court proceedings. To what extent may state courts enjoin federal judicial proceedings? In Donovan v. City of Dallas, 377 U.S. 408, 84 S.Ct. 1579, 12 L.Ed.2d 409 (1964), and General Atomic Co. v. Felter, 434 U.S. 12, 98 S.Ct. 76, 54 L.Ed.2d 199 (1977), the Court held that a state court may not enjoin either pending or prospective in personam actions in federal courts because states cannot limit the jurisdiction of federal courts. There is disagreement, however, as to whether this rule prevents a state court from enjoining a federal court action in order to protect the state court's jurisdiction over property brought under its control by proceedings in rem or quasi in rem. *Compare* Meridian Investing & Development Corp. v. Suncoast Highland Corp., 628 F.2d 370 (5th Cir.1980), *with* Moody v. State *ex rel.* Payne, 351 So.2d 552 (Ala.1977).

2.   The "Our Federalism" doctrine is a bar to a federal court injunction only when a state proceeding is pending. *See* Zablocki v. Redhail, 434 U.S. 374, 379 n. 5, 98 S.Ct. 673, 677 n. 5, 54 L.Ed.2d 618 (1978). A prosecutor can avoid the *Younger* problem in the threatened prosecution setting, however, simply by filing the state prosecution after the initiation of the federal injunction suit, but before "any proceedings of substance on the merits have taken place in federal court." Hicks v. Miranda, 422 U.S. 332, 95 S.Ct. 2281, 45 L.Ed.2d 223 (1975). As to when the federal action becomes a "proceeding of substance," consider the following Supreme Court explanation:

> Whether issuance of [a] temporary restraining order [is] a substantial federal court action or not, issuance of [a] preliminary injunction certainly [is]. *See* Doran v. Salem Inn, Inc., 422 U.S. 922, 929–931, 95 S.Ct. 2561, 2566–2567, 45 L.Ed.2d 648 (1975). A federal court action in which a preliminary injunction is granted has proceeded well beyond the "embryonic stage," *id.*, at 929, 95 S.Ct., at 2566, and considerations of economy, equity, and federalism counsel against *Younger*-abstention at that point.

Hawaii Housing Authority v. Midkiff, 467 U.S. 229, 238, 104 S.Ct. 2321, 2328, 81 L.Ed.2d 186 (1984).

It is important to emphasize that, while the absence of a pending state proceeding avoids a *Younger* problem, a party seeking injunctive relief against state enforcement needs to be able to establish at least some likelihood or threat of enforcement by state authorities in order to avoid having the suit dismissed for want of a "case or controversy" under Article III of the United States Constitution. There is no "case or controversy" in the following circumstances: "When plaintiffs do not claim that they have ever been threatened with prosecution, that a prosecution is remotely possible, they do not allege a dispute susceptible to resolution by a federal court." Babbitt v. United Farm Workers National Union, 442 U.S. 289, 298, 99 S.Ct. 2301, 2309, 60 L.Ed.2d 895 (1979).

3.   To what extent does *Younger* apply to civil suits generally? Doubts in the lower courts as to whether *Younger* ever applied in a civil action solely between private parties (*see* Diaz v. Stathis, 576 F.2d 9 (1st Cir.1978)) were settled by Pennzoil Co. v. Texaco, Inc., 481 U.S. 1, 107 S.Ct. 1519, 95 L.E.2d 1 (1987), which held that the federal courts should not have entertained an injunction suit challenging the constitutionality of a Texas appeal bond statute in an on-going case between private litigants in the Texas courts. The Supreme Court reasoned that the state's interest in the enforceability of the judgments of its courts was comparable to its interest in the enforceability of judicial orders by civil contempt proceedings, which had been held to be subject to the *Younger* abstention doctrine in Juidice v. Vail, 430 U.S. 327, 97 S.Ct. 1211, 51 L.Ed.2d 376 (1977). The majority opinion, however, disclaimed any rule that "*Younger* abstention is always appropriate whenever a civil proceeding is pending in a state court." 481 U.S. at 14 n.12, 107 S.Ct. at 1527 n.12, 95 L.Ed.2d 1. In concurring in the judgment, Justice Brennan stated that the merits should have been decided, and the statute should have been upheld on the merits. He adhered to his oft-stated view "that *Younger* is, in general, inapplicable to civil proceedings, especially when the plaintiff brings a

§ 1983 action alleging a violation of federal constitutional rights" and he argued that the "State's interest in this case is negligible." 481 U.S. at 19, 107 S.Ct. at 1530, 95 L.Ed.2d 1.

On the other hand, two years later, in New Orleans Public Service, Inc. v. Council of the City of New Orleans, 491 U.S. 350, 109 S.Ct. 2506, 105 L.Ed.2d 298 (1989) the Court stressed that not all civil proceedings are subject to the *Younger* abstention doctrine. That case held that *Younger* did not bar a federal injunction and declaratory judgment action by a utility against a city rate-making proceeding. The Court stated:

> Although our concern for comity and federalism has led us to expand the protection of *Younger* beyond state criminal proceedings, * * * and even to civil proceedings involving certain orders that are uniquely in further-ance of the state courts' ability to perform their judicial functions, * * * [see *Juidice* and *Pennzoil*], it has never been suggested that *Younger* requires abstention in deference to a state judicial proceeding reviewing legislative or executive action. * * *
>
> * * *
>
> * * * While we have expanded *Younger* beyond criminal proceedings, and even beyond proceedings in courts, we have never extended it to proceedings that are not "judicial in nature." *See* Middlesex County Ethics Comm. v. Garden State Bar Ass'n, 457 U.S. 423, 432, 102 S.Ct. 2515, 2521, 73 L.Ed.2d 116 (1982) ("It is clear beyond doubt that the New Jersey Supreme Court considers its bar disciplinary proceedings as 'judicial in nature.' As such, the proceedings are of a character to warrant federal-court deference."). *See also* Ohio Civil Rights Comm'n v. Dayton Christian Schools, Inc., 477 U.S. 619, 106 S.Ct. 2718, 91 L.Ed.2d 512 (1986) ("Because we found that the administrative proceedings in *Mid-dlesex* were 'judicial in nature' from the outset, . . . it was not essential to the decision that they had progressed to state-court review by the time we heard the federal injunction case."). The Council's proceedings in the present case were not judicial in nature.

491 U.S. at 367–370, 109 S.Ct. at 2517–19, 105 L.Ed.2d 298.

For further examination of the *Younger* doctrine, see George S. King, *Federal Injunctive Relief Against Pending State Civil Proceedings:* Younger *Days Are Here Again*, 44 La. L. Rev. 967 (1984); Martin H. Redish, *The Doctrine of* Younger v. Harris: *Deference in Search of a Rationale*, 63 Cornell L. Rev. 463 (1978); Avaim Soifer & H.C. Macgill, *The* Younger *Doctrine: Reconstructing Reconstruction*, 55 Tex. L. Rev. 1141 (1971); Brian Stagner, *Avoiding Abstention: The* Younger *Exceptions*, 29 Tex. Tech. L. Rev. 137 (1998); Howard B. Stravitz, Younger *Abstention Reaches a Civil Maturity*, 57 Fordham L. Rev. 997 (1989); Louise Weinberg, *The New Judicial Federalism*, 29 Stan. L. Rev. 1191 (1977); Donald H. Ziegler, *A Reassessment of the* Younger *Doctrine in Light of the Legislative History of Reconstruction*, 1983 Duke L.J. 987.

4.   To what extent does the *Younger* doctrine bar federal declaratory judgment actions as well as injunctive relief? *See supra* Chapter 5.

5. In addition to the *Younger* abstention doctrine, the federal courts also recognize the *Burford* and the *Pullman* abstention doctrines, which are discussed in Siegel v. LePore, *supra* Chapter 6.4.B.2.

6. Sometimes courts will issue injunctions to enjoin the relitigation of issues that have already been judicially resolved. In Eddy *ex rel.* Pfeifer v. Christian Science Board of Directors, 62 Ill.App.3d 918, 19 Ill.Dec. 781, 379 N.E.2d 653 (1978), the plaintiff's pro se complaint alleged that Ralph W. Cessna did not teach a primary class in accordance with the church manual bylaw requiring that the class be taught from the chapter entitled "Recapitulation" in the book "Science and Health with Key to the Scriptures" by Mary Baker Eddy. The circuit court dismissed the complaint and enjoined the plaintiff from pursuing related litigation in both the Illinois and federal courts. The appellate court voided the injunction against litigating in the federal courts, citing *Donovan* and *General Atomic Co.*, *supra* Note 1. The court then addressed the other issue:

> The injunction restraining plaintiff from instituting or proceeding with related actions in the State courts stands on a different footing. We believe it is clear that the court had the power to enter such an order under appropriate circumstances. * * *

> It is well settled that Illinois courts may restrain the maintenance of vexatious and harassing litigation. (Bowman v. Lake County Public Building Commission, 31 Ill.2d 575, 203 N.E.2d 129 (1964)). * * * Although plaintiff may be sincere in his feeling that a wrong has been committed, it is apparent that unless enjoined he may continually attempt to evade the clear mandate of this court. Furthermore, because his actions are filed pro se and consist of lengthy documents whose language is often hard to follow, his litigation becomes even more burdensome to the court and opposing litigants. Therefore, we find that the court did not abuse its discretion by issuing an injunction.

Id. at 920, 379 N.E.2d at 655.

Federal courts are also empowered to enjoin relitigation of an issue. For an excellent discussion of the justifications for occasionally issuing an injunction, rather than relying exclusively on res judicata and collateral estoppel to protect the prevailing party, see Michigan v. City of Allen Park, 573 F.Supp. 1481, 1488 (E.D.Mich.1983) ("The interests of repose, finality of judgments, protection of defendants from unwarranted harassment, and concern for maintaining order in the court's dockets have been deemed sufficient * * * to warrant such a prohibition against relitigation claims.").

The *Eddy* case represents a traditional use of the equitable bill of peace to restrain numerous actions at law when they are being used to harass or vex the plaintiff or when such actions are pending in inferior courts where complete relief cannot be obtained. *See* Henry L. McClintock, Equity § 179 (2d ed. 1948); *see also* Rudnicki v. McCormack, 210 F.Supp. 905 (D.R.I.1962) (plaintiff enjoined from further litigation against state or federal judges and their employees unless permission of court is obtained); Muka v. New York State Bar Ass'n, 120 Misc.2d 897, 466 N.Y.S.2d 891 (1983) (non-lawyer law school graduate who had previously filed "hundreds of actions" against defendant and countless other state and federal judges and other officials enjoined from filing further civil actions against defendant unless represented by counsel). *Cf.* Hill v. Estelle, 423 F.Supp. 690 (S.D.Tex.1976) (injunction against prisoners to prevent repetitious frivolous suits). *But see In re* Davis' Custody, 248 N.C. 423, 103 S.E.2d 503 (1958) (bill of peace not available to husband to enjoin former spouse from challenging prior child custody agreement). For an example of a legislative attempt to deal with the problem, see Cal.Civ.Proc.Code §§ 391–391.6, which authorizes a court on motion to require that a plaintiff who is designated as a "vexatious litigant" provide security as a condition for suit. *See In re* Shieh, 17 Cal.App.4th 1154, 21 Cal.Rptr.2d 886 (Cal.App.1993) (attorney who was determined to be a "vexatious litigant" under foregoing statute enjoined from filing new litigation without leave of court). *But see* Standard Management v. Kekona, 98 Haw. 95, 43 P.3d 232 (Haw.Ct.App.2001) (refusing to enjoin an attorney).

7. A state court that has acquired jurisdiction over the parties may enjoin them from proceeding with another action in a different state. Huff v. Huff, 69 N.C.App. 447, 317 S.E.2d 65 (1984) (divorce proceeding). Similarly, one federal district court has the power to enjoin a litigant before it from proceeding in another federal district court. Barclaysamerican/Commercial, Inc. v. Consumer Industries, Inc., 585 F.Supp. 1340 (W.D.N.C.1984). However,

> the situation could arise in which one court entered an injunction restraining the litigant from proceeding in the other forum and the other forum issued a counter-injunction enjoining the litigant from seeking enforcement of the prior injunction. The result of the injunctions would only serve to undermine the integrity of two United States District Courts if they engaged in this unseeming battle. The time, therefore, to dispose of this unsavory spectacle of judicial disorder is when it begins. As Justice Holmes succinctly stated, "[u]niversal distrust creates universal incompetence." Graham v. United States, 231 U.S. 474, 480, 34 S.Ct. 148, 151, 58 L.Ed. 319 (1913).

Id. at 1342. For reasons of necessity as well as comity, then, courts of coordinate jurisdiction rarely issue injunctions designed to restrict the exercise of the other's jurisdiction. Ordinarily the forum court will require the plaintiff to show that the defendant's conduct in bringing the foreign action constitutes fraud, gross wrong or oppression. *See* Crawley v. Bauchens, 57 Ill.2d 360, 312 N.E.2d 236 (1974).

SECTION 5.   INTERFERENCE WITH DIGNITY INTERESTS

A.   DAMAGES

DAN B. DOBBS, LAW OF REMEDIES
623 (2d ed. 1993).*

§ 7.1 Dignitary Invasions Generally

* * *

The injuries considered in this chapter can be called dignitary injuries or injuries to the personality. This means that, though economic or

---

* Reprinted with permission of West Publishing Co.

physical loss may be associated with the injury in some cases, the primary or usual concern is not economic at all, but vindication of an intangible right.

Many dignitary claims are recognized torts that involve some confrontation with the plaintiff in person or some indirect affront to the plaintiff's personality—assault, battery, false imprisonment, malicious prosecution, intentional infliction of mental distress, libel and slander, invasion of privacy, and alienation of affections are all in this category. In addition, these torts have their statutory and constitutional analogues so that essentially the same sort of interests may be protected under a variety of statutes, including federal or state civil rights statutes. Dignitary interests may also be vindicated incidentally, in the course of protecting some other interest, as where mental distress damages are awarded incident to some other tort.

All these dignitary harms may cause economic harm as well as affront to personality. If so, economic damages may be recovered. However, in a great many of the cases, the only harm is the affront to the plaintiff's dignity as a human being, the damage to his self image, and the resulting mental distress.

ANGUS v. VENTURA

Court of Appeals of Ohio, 1999.
1999 WL 33287 (unpublished opinion).

DICKINSON.

Defendant Jim Ventura has appealed from a jury verdict in the Medina County Common Pleas Court that awarded plaintiff James Angus $1,000 in damages on a breach of contract claim, $20,000 in damages on emotional distress and battery claims, and $5,000 in punitive damages. Defendant has argued that: (1) the $20,000 damages award for emotional distress and battery was against the manifest weight of the evidence * * *.

* * *

Plaintiff is a contractor who does home improvement work. This lawsuit concerns a house defendant built in Hinckley, Ohio, during 1994. During February, April, and May of that year, defendant and plaintiff entered into three contracts for roofing and siding work at defendant's house. Plaintiff completed the work around October 11, 1994. Defendant had made down payments on the contracts and paid some of the balance while the work progressed. According to plaintiff, however, when the work was finished, defendant still owed $1,000. Defendant admitted that he owed the money, but claimed that, due to defects in the work performed by plaintiff, he was not obligated to pay.

On October 12, 1994, plaintiff arrived at defendant's house to ask for the amount still owed. Plaintiff claimed that defendant grew angry and complained that several shingles on the roof were damaged. Plaintiff offered to fix them. Defendant then said that he would not pay the rest of the money owed.

Plaintiff turned to leave, but defendant followed him and threatened him. Plaintiff entered his truck. Defendant knocked on the window of the truck, and plaintiff rolled down the window. According to plaintiff, defendant then spit in his face. Plaintiff immediately reported the incident to police, but no charges were filed against defendant.

Plaintiff apparently grew depressed over the incident and visited a psychologist for treatment. According to that psychologist, plaintiff experienced significant anxiety and depression, lost his ability to concentrate, could not sleep, and, generally, exhibited signs of "labile affect." Plaintiff's condition improved quickly, however, and, after five sessions, he no longer needed to see the psychologist.

* * *

Defendant's first assignment of error is that the jury's award of $20,000 damages on plaintiff's emotional distress and battery claims was against the manifest weight of the evidence. He has argued that plaintiff suffered neither serious emotional distress nor bodily harm and that the jury's award was merely a "manifestation of passion and prejudice."

* * *

Defendant has claimed that plaintiff suffered neither serious emotional distress nor bodily harm. For example, he has asserted that plaintiff continued to work after the alleged spitting incident, which, he has claimed, demonstrated that plaintiff was functioning normally. Plaintiff's damages, defendant has argued, were not $20,000.

A plaintiff states a claim for battery when he demonstrates that the defendant acted "intending to cause a harmful or offensive contact, and when a harmful [or offensive] contact results." Retterer v. Whirlpool Corp. (1996), 111 Ohio App.3d 847, 854, 677 N.E.2d 417, quoting Love v. Port Clinton (1988), 37 Ohio St.3d 98, 99, 524 N.E.2d 166. In this case, defendant's act of spitting on plaintiff's face constituted a battery, notwithstanding his argument that that act was merely a "simple assault." *See* Leichtman v. WLW Jacor Communications, Inc. (1994), 92 Ohio App.3d 232, 235, 634 N.E.2d 697 (blowing cigar smoke in plaintiff's face constituted a battery). Plaintiff testified that defendant spit on him. A friend of both defendant and plaintiff testified that defendant called him the week after the incident allegedly occurred and bragged that he had, in fact, spit on plaintiff. The jury's finding that the spitting occurred was not against the manifest weight of the evidence. Its award of $10,000 for that battery was also not against the manifest weight of the evidence. In a battery action, "the wrong is said to be damages in and of itself." Stokes v. Meimaris (1996), 111 Ohio App.3d 176, 187, 675 N.E.2d 1289. This

Court cannot conclude that $10,000 was an unreasonable amount for the jury to award in this case.

A plaintiff states a claim for the intentional infliction of serious emotional distress when he demonstrates that the defendant engaged "intentionally or recklessly in extreme or outrageous conduct causing the plaintiff to suffer serious emotional distress." * * * Plaintiff testified that he was upset following the incident. His psychologist diagnosed him as suffering "significant anxiety and depression." Plaintiff suffered crying spells and severe mood swings and required psychological treatment. The jury could reasonably have found that defendant did spit on plaintiff and that the damages caused by that act, consisting not only of the psychologist's fee, but also of plaintiff's anxiety and depression, amounted to $10,000. Defendant failed to introduce evidence that overwhelmingly rebutted plaintiff's version of the incident or that demonstrated plaintiff's damages to be significantly less than the amount awarded. Consequently, the jury did not lose its way and create such a manifest miscarriage of justice that its verdict must be reversed.

* * *

Defendant's assignments of error are overruled. The judgment of the trial court is affirmed.

NOTES

1. Was the jury allowed to presume general compensatory damages in the battery action? *See generally* Dan B. Dobbs, Law of Remedies § 7.3(2) (2d ed. 1993).

2. Was the plaintiff required to prove emotional distress in the action for intentional infliction of emotional distress? If so, what type of proof did the court find persuasive? *See generally* Dan B. Dobbs, Law of Remedies § 7.2(6) (2d ed. 1993).

3. Presumed general compensatory damages were a common remedy in traditional defamation cases, but, as the next three cases demonstrate, they are not always available in the United States today. Defamation laws vary from state to state and may be governed either by common law or by statutory law. Judge Flaum of the Seventh Circuit summarized the defamation law of Illinois, which is representative of the defamation laws of many states, in Republic Tobacco Co. v. North Atlantic Trading Co., 381 F.3d 717 (7th Cir.2004):

> A defamatory statement is one that "tends to cause such harm to the reputation of another that it lowers that person in the eyes of the community or deters third persons from associating with him." * * * To make out a defamation claim under Illinois law, the plaintiff must show "that the defendant made a false statement concerning him, [and] that there was an unprivileged publication to a third party with fault by the defendant, which caused damage to the plaintiff." * * *

Defamatory statements may be actionable *per se* or actionable *per quod.* * * * If a statement qualifies as defamatory *per se,* * * * it is unnecessary for a plaintiff to demonstrate actual damage to reputation. Rather, statements that fall within these *per se* categories are thought to be so obviously and materially harmful to the plaintiff that injury to its reputation may be presumed. * * * In contrast, with a *per quod* action, in order to recover, the plaintiff must plead and prove that it sustained actual damage of a pecuniary nature ("special damages"). * * * [E]ven a statement that falls into one of the limited *per se* categories will not be found defamatory *per se* if it is "reasonably capable of an innocent construction." * * *

A number of common law privileges and defenses exist that may shield a defendant from liability for making an otherwise defamatory statement. First, a statement that does not contain any verifiable facts (as some call, "an opinion") is not actionable under Illinois law. * * * Second, substantial truth is a complete defense to an allegation of defamation. * * * Third, under Illinois law, publication of defamatory matters in a report of an official proceeding that deals with a matter of public concern is privileged as long as the report is accurate and complete. * * * Fourth, Illinois law confers a privilege upon "statements made within a legitimate business context." * * * Under this rule, "[a] statement is conditionally privileged when the defendant makes it (1) in good faith; (2) with an interest or duty to be upheld; (3) limited in scope to that purpose; (4) on a proper occasion; and (5) published in a proper manner only to proper parties."

Id. at 726–27.

TACKET v. DELCO REMY DIVISION OF GENERAL MOTORS CORP.

United States Court of Appeals, Seventh Circuit, 1991.
937 F.2d 1201.

Before BAUER, CHIEF JUDGE, CUDAHY, and COFFEY, CIRCUIT JUDGES.

BAUER, CHIEF JUDGE.

According to the age-old children's rhyme, "Sticks and stones may break your bones, but names can never hurt you." Plaintiff-appellee Thomas Tacket and the law of defamation, however, argue otherwise. According to Tacket, another mellifluous rhyme, one that read "TACKET TACKET WHAT A RACKET," when painted on the inside wall of General Motors', Anderson, Indiana, assembly plant and allowed to remain there for seven or eight months, defamed him and irreparably damaged his reputation.

In this appeal, we revisit a case that we remanded to the district court in 1987. In the instant appeal, we are asked to review the district court's decision that the jury properly could award Tacket $100,000 for the damages he suffered due to the display of the five-word rhyme. Applying settled law from both the state of Indiana and this circuit, we find that

Tacket failed to prove the requisite "special damages," and therefore, his award must be reversed.

* * *

Tacket filed this defamation claim in 1985 against his former employer, General Motors, in an Indiana court. General Motors removed it to federal court based on diversity jurisdiction. Tacket alleged that his reputation was irreparably damaged by the sign described above, which was written and displayed by managerial employees of General Motors. * * *

* * * The evidence revealed the following: Thomas Tacket was an employee at Delco Remy Division of General Motors ("Delco") in Anderson, Indiana. Tacket was first employed by Delco in 1971, and rose to the level of night superintendent in 1983. In February 1985, Delco's Anderson facility was working on a generator production contract entitled the "9–S1 Project." A problem arose concerning the attainment of wooden shipping crates. Ed Spearman, one of Tacket's subordinates, suggested that "S & T Specialties" provide the needed crates. Tacket received requisition forms for the crates and processed them during off-duty hours. Both he and Spearman signed the forms.

Some time later, the union representing Delco's workers discovered that Delco was buying the crates from an outside supplier and protested the "out-sourcing" of work that Delco's own staff could have performed. The union also discovered that Spearman was the "S", and suspected that Tacket was the "T", of "S & T Specialties". (The crates were being constructed in Spearman's garage.) Delco promptly suspended both Spearman and Tacket pending an investigation. Delco ultimately fired Spearman, but concluded that it had insufficient evidence to discharge Tacket. He returned to work on April 9, 1985, but his relationship with the workers had soured. Delco thereafter transferred him to a "quality assurance team" with the same rank and salary but with fewer subordinates.

Upon learning of the out-sourcing, the workers spread rumors about Spearman and Tacket. At some point, a sign approximately 3' x 30' appeared inside the plant proclaiming the infamous rhyme "TACKET TACKET WHAT A RACKET." This sign stayed up for two to three days during Tacket's suspension. A second, smaller sign approximately 1' x 4' proclaiming the same message was stenciled on the inside wall of the plant * * * and remained there for at least seven months.

On the issue of damages, Tacket offered the testimony of Frank Connolly, a psychologist, who diagnosed Tacket to have suffered a psychiatric illness know as depressive neurosis. Connolly testified that Tacket was alienated, dysfunctional, and lacked energy. Connolly linked Tacket's condition to the small sign and noted that it affected his job performance. Tacket's job performance prior to the incident was better than after the incident, as reflected by the poor job performance ratings he received.

At the close of the evidence, the district court instructed the jurors that Tacket could prove damage from the sign in two ways: 1) if the sign were found to impute a crime or to prejudice him in his profession, then injury to his reputation would be established; or, 2) if the sign did not impute such things, then the jury was instructed that the plaintiff could recover only if "special damages" were proven. Special damages were defined as the loss of something having economic or pecuniary value, or the loss of a benefit that has an indirect financial value to the plaintiff. Special interrogatories were given to the jury to aid their deliberations.

The jury returned a verdict for the plaintiff in the amount of $100,000. The jury indicated on its special verdict form that the sign did not tend to damage the plaintiff's reputation without regard to extrinsic circumstances, but that it did defame the plaintiff when considered with other facts. The jury further found that Delco intentionally and unreasonably failed to remove that sign (thereby "publishing" it), and that plaintiff exercised proper care for the protection of his own interests.

Delco then moved to set aside the verdict, arguing that the jury's finding that the sign did not defame Tacket without consideration of extrinsic facts, coupled with Tacket's alleged failure to plead and prove "special damages," mandated entry of judgment in its favor. In its Order of July 6, 1989, the district court determined that Indiana libel law allowed recovery of proven psychological injuries as part of special damages, and permitted Tacket to amend his pleadings to conform them to the evidence. Thus, on the basis of the amended pleadings and the jury's verdict, the district court found that Tacket had indeed pleaded and proved special damages. The district court denied Delco's motion and allowed the verdict to stand. Delco then filed a motion to alter or amend the judgment, arguing that Tacket's cause of action fell within the exclusive remedy provisions of the Indiana Worker's Compensation Act, Ind.Code § 22–3–6. The district court, by Order dated October 13, 1989, held that, though the defense presented by the motion was meritorious, it was not raised before the conclusion of the trial and, therefore, was not timely. Delco appealed.

* * *

Though Delco presents several claims on appeal, only one issue concerns us today: whether Tacket, under Indiana law, adequately proved special damages. In order to resolve this dispute, we need first consider the broader outlines of defamation law in Indiana. As the district court appropriately noted, defamation, defined as holding a person up to ridicule, scorn or contempt, *see* Black's Law Dictionary at 417 (6th ed. 1990), is comprised of two related torts: libel and slander. Libel generally is concerned with defamatory communications of a permanent sort, such as printed matter, films, and art work. Slander, on the other hand, involves transitory, ephemeral communications, such as speech, gestures, and sign language. *See generally* Prosser and Keeton, The Law of Torts 785–97 (5th ed. 1984) ("[L]ibel is that which is communicated by the sense of sight, or perhaps also by touch or smell, while slander is that which is communicated by the sense of hearing.'').

In addition to these related torts, the law of defamation includes certain categories and labels. In its July 6, 1989 Order, the district court ably reviewed the history of defamation law and discussed the meaning of the labels "per se" and "per quod." For our purposes, suffice it to say that defamation per se involves words (whether slanderous or libelous) which, by themselves and without reference to extrinsic circumstances, injure the reputation of the person to whom they are applied, whereas defamation per quod requires an allegation of facts and circumstances, aside from the words contained in the publication, to show how the words damage the plaintiff. Black's Law Dictionary at 417. It generally is agreed that words, whether they be in the form of libel or slander, and which are defamatory per se or per quod, are actionable without allegation and proof of any special harm if they: a) impute to another the commission of a crime; b) impute to another a loathsome disease; c) impute unchastity to a woman; or d) tend to injure another in his trade or profession. Gibson v. Kincaid, 140 Ind.App. 186, 221 N.E.2d 834, 843 (1966) (Faulconer, J., concurring).

In libel actions, it was well-established by the beginning of the nineteenth century that any libel was actionable per se, meaning that it was actionable without the necessity of pleading and proving that the plaintiff suffered any harm from the defamatory writing. Prosser and Keeton, *supra*, at 795. As time passed, however, a sharp disagreement developed about the need to prove special damages in libel per quod cases—that is, in cases where the publication became defamatory only to those who were aware of defamatory facts extrinsic to the matter published. *Id.* Because the jury's special verdict made clear that they found the small, painted sign defamatory only when extrinsic circumstances were taken into account, it is undisputed that libel per quod is implicated in this case. Thus, the crucial questions are whether libel per quod requires pleading and proof of special damages under Indiana law, and, if so, whether Tacket accomplished these tasks in this case. We will consider each question in turn.

Given that special damages are required to be pleaded and proved in Indiana libel per quod cases, we turn to the next question: whether Tacket has done so in this case. To resolve this issue, we must determine what constitutes "special damages." As noted above, the district court instructed the jury that special damages mean that Tacket must show some economic or pecuniary loss, or the loss of a benefit that places on Tacket an indirect financial burden. Yet, in its July 6 Order, the district court interpreted Indiana law "to allow recovery of any damage, pecuniary or otherwise, that is specially pleaded and proved to be a proximate result of the complained of circumstances in a defamation case." The district court determined that, because Tacket showed a specific, psychiatric injury resulting from the sign, he need not demonstrate any pecuniary loss.

We disagree with the district court's interpretation of Indiana law.
* * * Tacket's evidence of psychological injury simply does not fall within
the class of special damages.

* * *

Tacket's burden was to show damages that are "pecuniary in nature"
and that "have been actually incurred as a natural and proximate consequence of the wrongful act." Stanley v. Kelley, 422 N.E.2d 663, 668
(Ind.App.1981). *Accord*, C. McCormick, Damages § 114 (1935) ("The 'special damage' required in defamation cases must be some material or
pecuniary injury. Injury to reputation without more, humiliation, mental
anguish, physical sickness—these do not suffice."). In the instant case,
Tacket presented no evidence of any pecuniary loss.[2] Instead, he demonstrated that he suffered emotional distress and psychological injury. But
such maladies, however painful to Tacket, are only general damages—the
kind that routinely follow a defamation. Injury to the plaintiff's reputation
and standing in the community, personal humiliation, and mental anguish
and suffering are the sort of damages that the law presumes to be the
natural result of the publication; they are not special damages. * * *

Though we may imagine the rare case, not before this court, where a
plaintiff in a defamation per quod case might satisfy the "special damages" requirement with evidence that did not directly involve economic
loss, the customary and inevitable psychological injuries following a defamation—all that Tacket proved at trial—surely cannot suffice. *See* Elliott
v. Roach, 409 N.E.2d 661, 683 (Ind.App.1980) ("Special damages, as
opposed to such generally 'presumed' damages, are not assumed to be
necessary or inevitable results of the defamation, and must be shown by
allegation and proof. They generally are of a pecuniary nature."). By
finding that Tacket's psychological injuries were sufficient, the district
court has, in effect, dismissed the "special damages" requirement from
Indiana law for libel per quod cases.

* * *

For the foregoing reasons, we find Tacket's evidence of psychological
injury insufficient to demonstrate the special damages necessary to uphold
the jury's award. With this conclusion, we need not examine Delco's other
claims on appeal. The order of the district court denying Delco's motion
for judgment notwithstanding the verdict is, therefore, reversed. We

---

2. In his brief, Tacket argues that there was, in fact, evidence of pecuniary loss. He suggests
that, though it was not reflected in his salary or benefits, his psychological distress nonetheless
interfered with his job performance and ultimately caused his termination from Delco. Thus,
Tacket maintains that his "ability to make a living was diminished by the defamation published
by Delco." * * * It is unnecessary to consider whether proving loss of employment would have
been sufficient to establish special damages. No such proof is before this court. In a pretrial
motion in limine, the court granted Delco's motion to exclude any evidence relating to the
termination of Tacket's employment by Delco. Therefore, we find Tacket's claims regarding
economic injury without sufficient support in the record properly to be considered pecuniary loss.
* * *

vacate the judgment on the verdict, and remand this case to the district court to enter judgment for Delco, each party to bear its own costs.

CUDAHY, CIRCUIT JUDGE, dissenting.

It is, to say the least, disheartening—and perhaps even productive of a depressive neurosis—to see the scholarly efforts of a district court judge to make sense of Indiana libel law set at naught. I agree with Judge McKinney that "[t]here is no precedential or jurisprudential reason to allow a libel plaintiff to call witnesses to specially prove his business losses, but to disallow expert and other testimony to prove his psychological injuries."

The majority seems to be mired in the jurisdictional conflicts between the ecclesiastical and the common law courts of the sixteenth century. The ecclesiastical courts regarded defamation as a sin and punished it with a penance. For a considerable period of time, therefore, the common law courts held that, unless "temporal" damage could be proved, defamation was a "spiritual" matter to be left to the Church. *See* Prosser, The Law of Torts 772; *see also* Veeder, *The History and Theory of the Law of Defamation*, 3 Colum.L.Rev. 546 (1903). Perhaps the majority, too, views a psychological diagnosis as in the "spiritual" realm and thus beyond our competence.

In fact, psychologists may not have really added much to what in another day would have been perceived as a problem of the spirit, best left to ecclesiastical attention. But, given modern postulates and perspectives, I see no reason to equate what purports to be a scientific diagnosis threatening adverse economic consequences (through lowered job performance) with a mere presumption of mental anguish and emotional distress. This is the equation, however, that the majority makes. Despite the scientific trappings of expert testimony, the majority is unwilling to factor these matters of the "spirit" into its calculations.

* * *

By seeking to interpret Indiana law as congruent with modern concepts of psychology as a science, the district court has hit upon a perfectly acceptable basis for abandoning jurisdictional distinctions of the sixteenth century that have, as far as I can see, no current utility. The majority, on the other hand, adopts a view which might regard proof even of irreversible psychosis as a mere restatement of mental anguish and emotional distress. For a psychosis, too, is a thing of the spirit (albeit an evil one).

I therefore respectfully dissent.

NOTES

1. If Tacket had introduced proof of pecuniary loss, then he would have been able to establish a prima facie case of libel *per quod*, which in turn would have entitled him to recover presumed general compensatory damages for the harm to his reputation. Dan B. Dobbs, Law of Remedies § 7.2(3) (2d ed. 1993).

2.   The entire saga of Tacket's litigation against General Motors is told in Tacket v. General Motors Corp., Delco Remy Division, 93 F.3d 332 (7th Cir.1996). It all began in 1985, of course, when someone painted the now infamous sign on the wall. Tacket's defamation action was first tried to a jury in 1987, but the trial court judge directed a verdict in favor of the defendant. Two weeks later, Tacket was terminated. He appealed the directed verdict, and the Seventh Circuit reversed and remanded for a jury trial, which resulted in a $100,000 verdict for the plaintiff. That verdict was reversed in 1991, and upon remand, the trial court entered judgment for General Motors. Meanwhile, however, Tacket had filed a wrongful discharge claim against General Motors in 1987. The trial court judge had granted summary judgment for General Motors, but was reversed on appeal in 1992. Upon remand, Tacket amended his complaint to state a claim for intentional infliction of emotional distress, and General Motors moved for summary judgment on the ground that the Indiana Worker's Compensation Act preempted his claim for emotional distress. The trial court judge granted the motion in 1994. Tacket appealed to the Seventh Circuit, which reversed and remanded the case in 1996 on the ground that claims for emotional distress may not be filed under Indiana's Worker's Compensation Act, and therefore the Act's exclusive remedy clause does not bar tort actions for intentional infliction of emotional distress. General Motors objected that, throughout the defamation litigation, Tacket had argued that his emotional distress had caused physical pain in his wrists and arms that had interfered with his job performance, ultimately leading to his termination, and thereby causing him to suffer pecuniary loss. Judge Bauer responded: "This may well be true, but the testimony that General Motors cites pertains solely to Tacket's original defamation action. Tacket has not alleged any physical injury resulting from his discharge, and as long as he does not, his action may proceed." *Id.* at 335. The parties must have finally settled, as no further litigation was reported.

3.   When the content of speech is at issue in the courts, so too is the federal Constitution. The First Amendment became prominent in defamation law with the Supreme Court's decision in New York Times v. Sullivan, 376 U.S. 254, 84 S.Ct. 710, 11 L.Ed.2d 686 (1964), which imposed constitutional limitations on defamation actions brought by public officials or public figures, as summarized by the Supreme Court in Dun & Bradstreet, Inc. v. Greenmoss Builders, Inc., below. Later, in Gertz v. Robert Welch, Inc., 418 U.S. 323, 94 S.Ct. 2997, 41 L.Ed.2d 789 (1974), the Supreme Court also imposed constitutional limitations on the remedies recoverable in defamation actions brought by private individuals when the defamatory statement addressed an issue of public concern:

> Our accommodation of the competing values at stake in defamation suits by private individuals allows the States to impose liability on the publisher or broadcaster of defamatory falsehood on a less demanding showing than that required by *New York Times*. This conclusion is not based on a belief that the considerations which prompted the adoption of the *New York Times* privilege for defamation of public officials and its extension to public figures are wholly inapplicable to the context of private individuals. Rather, we endorse this approach in recognition of the strong and legitimate state interest in compensating private individu-

als for injury to reputation. But this countervailing state interest extends no further than compensation for actual injury. For the reasons stated below, we hold that the States may not permit recovery of presumed or punitive damages, at least when liability is not based on a showing of knowledge of falsity or reckless disregard for the truth.

The common law of defamation is an oddity of tort law, for it allows recovery of purportedly compensatory damages without evidence of actual loss. Under the traditional rules pertaining to actions for libel, the existence of injury is presumed from the fact of publication. Juries may award substantial sums as compensation for supposed damage to reputation without any proof that such harm actually occurred. The largely uncontrolled discretion of juries to award damages where there is no loss unnecessarily compounds the potential of any system of liability for defamatory falsehood to inhibit the vigorous exercise of First Amendment freedoms. Additionally, the doctrine of presumed damages invites juries to punish unpopular opinion rather than to compensate individuals for injury sustained by the publication of a false fact. More to the point, the States have no substantial interest in securing for plaintiffs such as this petitioner gratuitous awards of money damages far in excess of any actual injury.

* * * We need not define "actual injury," as trial courts have wide experience in framing appropriate jury instructions in tort actions. Suffice it to say that actual injury is not limited to out-of-pocket loss. Indeed, the more customary types of actual harm inflicted by defamatory falsehood include impairment of reputation and standing in the community, personal humiliation, and mental anguish and suffering. Of course, juries must be limited by appropriate instructions, and all awards must be supported by competent evidence concerning the injury, although there need be no evidence which assigns an actual dollar value to the injury.

* * * Like the doctrine of presumed damages, jury discretion to award punitive damages unnecessarily exacerbates the danger of media self-censorship* * *. In short, the private defamation plaintiff who establishes liability under a less demanding standard than that stated by *New York Times* may recover only such damages as are sufficient to compensate him for actual injury.

Id. at 348–50, 94 S.Ct. at 3011–12, 41 L.Ed.2d at 810–11. Does depriving juries of the ability to award presumed damages while allowing them to award damages for "mental anguish and suffering" diminish "the potential of any system of liability for defamatory falsehood to inhibit the vigorous exercise of First Amendment freedoms"? For a discussion of pain and suffering damages, see *supra* Chapter 3, Section 7.A.1.b.

4.   For an interesting discussion of the relationship between tort law and First Amendment law, see David A. Anderson, *First Amendment Limitations on Tort Law*, 69 Brook. L. Rev. 755 (2004). Professor Anderson contrasts tort law's reliance on juries with the First Amendment's distrust of juries and recommends that the Supreme Court take an approach which would involve less preemption of state law in the area of "speech" torts. As you read the

next case, consider how the Supreme Court's rulings intersect with the state law governing remedies.

DUN & BRADSTREET, INC. v. GREENMOSS BUILDERS, INC.

Supreme Court of the United States, 1985.
472 U.S. 749, 105 S.Ct. 2939, 86 L.Ed.2d 593.

JUSTICE POWELL announced the judgment of the Court and delivered an opinion, in which JUSTICE REHNQUIST and JUSTICE O'CONNOR joined.

In Gertz v. Robert Welch, Inc., 418 U.S. 323, 94 S.Ct. 2997, 41 L.Ed.2d 789 (1974), we held that the First Amendment restricted the damages that a private individual could obtain from a publisher for a libel that involved a matter of public concern. More specifically, we held that in these circumstances the First Amendment prohibited awards of presumed and punitive damages for false and defamatory statements unless the plaintiff shows "actual malice," that is, knowledge of falsity or reckless disregard for the truth. The question presented in this case is whether this rule of *Gertz* applies when the false and defamatory statements do not involve matters of public concern.

I.

Petitioner Dun & Bradstreet, a credit reporting agency, provides subscribers with financial and related information about businesses. All the information is confidential; under the terms of the subscription agreement the subscribers may not reveal it to anyone else. On July 26, 1976, petitioner sent a report to five subscribers indicating that respondent, a construction contractor, had filed a voluntary petition for bankruptcy. This report was false and grossly misrepresented respondent's assets and liabilities. That same day, while discussing the possibility of future financing with its bank, respondent's president was told that the bank had received the defamatory report. He immediately called petitioner's regional office, explained the error, and asked for a correction. In addition, he requested the names of the firms that had received the false report in order to assure them that the company was solvent. Petitioner promised to look into the matter but refused to divulge the names of those who had received the report.

After determining that its report was indeed false, petitioner issued a corrective notice on or about August 3, 1976, to the five subscribers who had received the initial report. The notice stated that one of respondent's former employees, not respondent itself, had filed for bankruptcy and that respondent "continued in business as usual." Respondent told petitioner that it was dissatisfied with the notice, and it again asked for a list of subscribers who had seen the initial report. Again petitioner refused to divulge their names.

Respondent then brought this defamation action in Vermont state court. It alleged that the false report had injured its reputation and sought both compensatory and punitive damages. The trial established that the error in petitioner's report had been caused when one of its employees, a 17–year-old high school student paid to review Vermont bankruptcy pleadings, had inadvertently attributed to respondent a bankruptcy petition filed by one of respondent's former employees. Although petitioner's representative testified that it was routine practice to check the accuracy of such reports with the businesses themselves, it did not try to verify the information about respondent before reporting it.

After trial, the jury returned a verdict in favor of respondent and awarded $50,000 in compensatory or presumed damages and $300,000 in punitive damages. Petitioner moved for a new trial. * * * The trial court indicated some doubt as to whether *Gertz* applied to "non-media cases," but granted a new trial "because of . . . dissatisfaction with its charge and . . . conviction that the interests of justice required" it. * * *

The Vermont Supreme Court reversed. * * * Although recognizing that "in certain instances the distinction between media and nonmedia defendants may be difficult to draw," the court stated that "no such difficulty is presented with credit reporting agencies, which are in the business of selling financial information to a limited number of subscribers who have paid substantial fees for their services." * * * [T]he court concluded that such firms are not "the type of media worthy of First Amendment protection as contemplated by New York Times Co. v. Sullivan, 376 U.S. 254, 84 S.Ct. 710, 11 L.Ed.2d 686 (1964), and its progeny." * * * Accordingly, the court held "that as a matter of federal constitutional law, the media protections outlined in *Gertz* are inapplicable to nonmedia defamation plaintiffs." * * *

III.

In New York Times Co. v. Sullivan, *supra*, the Court for the first time held that the First Amendment limits the reach of state defamation laws. That case concerned a public official's recovery of damages for the publication of an advertisement criticizing police conduct in a civil rights demonstration. As the Court noted, the advertisement concerned "one of the major public issues of our time." * * * Noting that "freedom of expression upon public questions is secured by the First Amendment" * * * and that "debate on public issues should be uninhibited, robust, and wide-open," * * * the Court held that a public official cannot recover damages for defamatory falsehood unless he proves that the false statement was made with " 'actual malice'—that is, with knowledge that it was false or with reckless disregard of whether it was false or not." * * * In later cases, all involving public issues, the Court extended this same constitutional protection to libels of public figures, *e.g.*, Curtis Publishing Co. v. Butts, 388 U.S. 130, 87 S.Ct. 1975, 18 L.Ed.2d 1094 (1967), and in one case suggested in a plurality opinion that this constitutional rule should extend to libels of any individual so long as the defamatory statements involved a "matter of public or general interest," Rosenbloom v. Metromedia, Inc., 403 U.S. 29, 44, 91 S.Ct. 1811, 1820, 29 L.Ed.2d 296 (1971) (opinion of BRENNAN, J.).

In Gertz v. Robert Welch, Inc., 418 U.S. 323, 94 S.Ct. 2997, 41 L.Ed.2d 789 (1974), we held that the protections of *New York Times* did not extend as far as *Rosenbloom* suggested. *Gertz* concerned a libelous article appearing in a magazine called American Opinion, the monthly outlet of the John Birch Society. The article in question discussed whether the prosecution of a policeman in Chicago was part of a Communist campaign to discredit local law enforcement agencies. The plaintiff, *Gertz*, neither a public official nor a public figure, was a lawyer tangentially involved in the prosecution. The magazine alleged that he was the chief architect of the "frame-up" of the police officer and linked him to Communist activity. Like every other case in which this Court has found constitutional limits to state defamation laws, Gertz involved expression on a matter of undoubted public concern.

In *Gertz*, we held that the fact that expression concerned a public issue did not by itself entitle the libel defendant to the constitutional protections of *New York Times*. These protections, we found, were not "justified solely by reference to the interest of the press and broadcast media in immunity from liability." * * * Rather, they represented "an accommodation between [First Amendment] concern[s] and the limited state interest present in the context of libel actions brought by public persons." * * * In libel actions brought by private persons we found the competing interests different. Largely because private persons have not voluntarily exposed themselves to increased risk of injury from defamatory statements and because they generally lack effective opportunities for rebutting such statements, * * * we found that the State possessed a "strong and legitimate . . . interest in compensating private individuals for injury to reputation." * * * Balancing this stronger state interest against the same First Amendment interest at stake in *New York Times*, we held that a State could not allow recovery of presumed and punitive damages absent a showing of "actual malice." Nothing in our opinion, however, indicated that this same balance would be struck regardless of the type of speech involved.

* * *

IV.

We have never considered whether the *Gertz* balance obtains when the defamatory statements involve no issue of public concern. To make this determination, we must employ the approach approved in *Gertz* and balance the State's interest in compensating private individuals for injury to their reputation against the First Amendment interest in protecting this type of expression. This state interest is identical to the one weighed in *Gertz*. * * * A State should not lightly be required to abandon it,

> for, as Mr. Justice Stewart has reminded us, the individual's right to the protection of his own good name reflects no more than our basic concept of the essential dignity and worth of every human being—a concept at the root of any decent system of ordered liberty. The

protection of private personality, like the protection of life itself, is left primarily to the individual States under the Ninth and Tenth Amendments.

The First Amendment interest, on the other hand, is less important than the one weighed in *Gertz*. * * *

* * * [S]peech on matters of purely private concern is of less First Amendment concern. * * *

While such speech is not totally unprotected by the First Amendment, * * * its protections are less stringent. In *Gertz*, we found that the state interest in awarding presumed and punitive damages was not "substantial" in view of their effect on speech at the core of First Amendment concern. * * * This interest, however, is "substantial" relative to the incidental effect these remedies may have on speech of significantly less constitutional interest. The rationale of the common-law rules has been the experience and judgment of history that "proof of actual damage will be impossible in a great many cases where, from the character of the defamatory words and the circumstances of publication, it is all but certain that serious harm has resulted in fact." W. Prosser, Law of Torts § 112, p. 765 (4th ed. 1971) * * * As a result, courts for centuries have allowed juries to presume that some damage occurred from many defamatory utterances and publications. Restatement of Torts § 568, Comment b, p. 162 (1938) (* * * damages were to be presumed for libel as early as 1670). This rule furthers the state interest in providing remedies for defamation by ensuring that those remedies are effective. In light of the reduced constitutional value of speech involving no matters of public concern, we hold that the state interest adequately supports awards of presumed and punitive damages—even absent a showing of "actual malice."[7]

V.

The only remaining issue is whether petitioner's credit report involved a matter of public concern. * * * It was speech solely in the individual interest of the speaker and its specific business audience. * * * This particular interest warrants no special protection when—as in this case—the speech is wholly false and clearly damaging to the victim's business reputation. * * * Moreover, since the credit report was made available to only five subscribers, who, under the terms of the subscription agreement, could not disseminate it further, it cannot be said that the report involves any "strong interest in the free flow of commercial information." * * *

In addition, the speech here, like advertising, is hardy and unlikely to be deterred by incidental state regulation. * * * It is solely motivated by the desire for profit. * * * Arguably, the reporting here was also more

---

7. The dissent, purporting to apply the same balancing test that we do today, concludes that speech on purely private matters is entitled to the protection of *Gertz*. * * * The dissent would, in effect, constitutionalize the entire common law of libel.

objectively verifiable than speech deserving of greater protection. * * * In any case, the market provides a powerful incentive to a credit reporting agency to be accurate, since false credit reporting is of no use to creditors. Thus, any incremental "chilling" effect of libel suits would be of decreased significance.

VI.

We conclude that permitting recovery of presumed and punitive damages in defamation cases absent a showing of "actual malice" does not violate the First Amendment when the defamatory statements do not involve matters of public concern. Accordingly, we affirm the judgment of the Vermont Supreme Court.

* * *

CHIEF JUSTICE BURGER, concurring in the judgment.

* * *

* * * I agree that *Gertz* is limited to circumstances in which the alleged defamatory expression concerns a matter of general public importance, and that the expression in question here relates to a matter of essentially private concern. I therefore agree with the plurality opinion to the extent that it holds that *Gertz* is inapplicable in this case * * *.

I continue to believe, however, that *Gertz* was ill-conceived, and therefore agree with JUSTICE WHITE that *Gertz* should be overruled. * * *

* * *

JUSTICE WHITE, concurring in the judgment.

Until New York Times Co. v. Sullivan, * * * the law of defamation was almost exclusively the business of state courts and legislatures. Under the then prevailing state libel law, the defamed individual had only to prove a false written publication that subjected him to hatred, contempt, or ridicule. Truth was a defense; but given a defamatory false circulation, general injury to reputation was presumed; special damages, such as pecuniary loss and emotional distress, could be recovered; and punitive damages were available if common-law malice were shown. General damages for injury to reputation were presumed and awarded because the judgment of history was that "in many cases the effect of defamatory statements is so subtle and indirect that it is impossible directly to trace the effects thereof in loss to the person defamed." Restatement of Torts § 621, Comment a, p. 314 (1938). The defendant was permitted to show that there was no reputational injury; but at the very least, the prevailing rule was that at least nominal damages were to be awarded for any defamatory publication actionable per se. This rule performed

> a vindicatory function by enabling the plaintiff publicly to brand the defamatory publication as false. The salutary social value of this rule is preventive in character since it often permits a defamed person to expose the groundless character of a defamatory rumor before harm

to the reputation has resulted therefrom. *Id.* § 569, Comment b, p. 166.

Similar rules applied to slanderous statements that were actionable per se.[1]

New York Times Co. v. Sullivan was the first major step in what proved to be a seemingly irreversible process of constitutionalizing the entire law of libel and slander. Under the rule announced in that case, a public official suing for libel * * * could not establish liability and recover any damages, whether presumed or actually proved, unless he proved "malice," which was defined as knowing falsehood or a reckless disregard for the truth. Given that proof, however, the usual damages were available, including presumed and punitive damages. * * *

* * *

I joined the judgment and opinion in *New York Times*. I also joined later decisions extending the *New York Times* standard to other situations. But I came to have increasing doubts about the soundness of the Court's approach and about some of the assumptions underlying it. * * * I dissented in *Gertz*, asserting that the common-law remedies should be retained for private plaintiffs. I remain convinced that *Gertz* was erroneously decided. I have also become convinced that the Court struck an improvident balance in the *New York Times* case between the public's interest in being fully informed about public officials and public affairs and the competing interest of those who have been defamed in vindicating their reputation.

In a country like ours, where the people purport to be able to govern themselves through their elected representatives, adequate information about their government is of transcendent importance. That flow of intelligence deserves full First Amendment protection. Criticism and assessment of the performance of public officials and of government in general are not subject to penalties imposed by law. But these First Amendment values are not at all served by circulating false statements of fact about public officials. On the contrary, erroneous information frustrates these values. * * * Yet in *New York Times* cases, the public official's complaint will be dismissed unless he alleges and makes out a jury case of a knowing or reckless falsehood. Absent such proof, there will be no jury verdict or judgment of any kind in his favor, even if the challenged publication is admittedly false. * * * The public is left to conclude that the challenged statement was true after all. Their only chance of being accurately informed is measured by the public official's ability himself to counter the lie, unaided by the courts. That is a

---

1. At the common law, slander, unlike libel, was actionable per se only when it dealt with a narrow range of statements: those imputing a criminal offense, a venereal or loathsome and communicable disease, improper conduct of a lawful business, or unchastity of a woman. Restatement of Torts § 570 (1938). To be actionable, all other slanderous statements required additional proof of special damages other than an injury to reputation or emotional distress. The special damages most often took the form of material or pecuniary loss. *Id.* § 575 and Comment b, pp. 185–187.

decidedly weak reed to depend on for the vindication of First Amendment interests—"it is the rare case where the denial overtakes the original charge." * * *

* * * The upshot is that the public official must suffer the injury, often cannot get a judgment identifying the lie for what it is, and has very little, if any, chance of countering that lie in the public press.

The *New York Times* rule thus countenances two evils: first, the stream of information about public officials and public affairs is polluted and often remains polluted by false information; and second, the reputation and professional life of the defeated plaintiff may be destroyed by falsehoods that might have been avoided with a reasonable effort to investigate the facts. In terms of the First Amendment and reputational interests at stake, these seem grossly perverse results.

* * *

In *New York Times*, instead of escalating the plaintiff's burden of proof to an almost impossible level, we could have achieved our stated goal by limiting the recoverable damages to a level that would not unduly threaten the press. Punitive damages might have been scrutinized as Justice Harlan suggested in *Rosenbloom*, * * * perhaps even entirely forbidden. Presumed damages to reputation might have been prohibited, or limited, as in *Gertz*. Had that course been taken and the common-law standard of liability been retained, the defamed public official, upon proving falsity, could at least have had a judgment to that effect. His reputation would then be vindicated; and to the extent possible, the misinformation circulated would have been countered. He might have also recovered a modest amount, enough perhaps to pay his litigation expenses. At the very least, the public official should not have been required to satisfy the actual malice standard where he sought no damages but only to clear his name. In this way, both First Amendment and reputational interests would have been far better served.

* * *

JUSTICE BRENNAN, with whom JUSTICE MARSHALL, JUSTICE BLACKMUN, and JUSTICE STEVENS join, dissenting.

The four who join this opinion would reverse the judgment of the Vermont Supreme Court. We believe that, although protection of the type of expression at issue is admittedly not the "central meaning of the First Amendment," * * * *Gertz* makes clear that the First Amendment nonetheless requires restraints on presumed and punitive damages awards for this expression. * * *

* * *

Relying on the analysis of the Vermont Supreme Court, respondent urged that * * * [we restrict] the applicability of *Gertz* to cases in which the defendant is a "media" entity. Such a distinction is irreconcilable with the fundamental First Amendment principle that "[t]he inherent worth of

... speech in terms of its capacity for informing the public does not depend upon the identity of its source, whether corporation, association, union, or individual." * * *

* * *

Eschewing the media/nonmedia distinction, the opinions of both JUSTICE WHITE and JUSTICE POWELL focus primarily on the content of the credit report as a reason for restricting the applicability of *Gertz*. Arguing that at most *Gertz* should protect speech that "deals with a matter of public or general importance," * * * [they] decide that the credit report at issue here falls outside this protected category. * * *

* * *

In professing allegiance to *Gertz*, the plurality opinion protests too much. * * * Even accepting the notion that a distinction can and should be drawn between matters of public concern and matters of purely private concern, * * * the analyses presented by both JUSTICE POWELL and JUSTICE WHITE fail on their own terms. Both, by virtue of what they hold in this case, propose an impoverished definition of "matters of public concern" that is irreconcilable with First Amendment principles. The credit reporting at issue here surely involves a subject matter of sufficient public concern to require the comprehensive protections of *Gertz*. Were this speech appropriately characterized as a matter of only private concern, moreover, the elimination of the *Gertz* restrictions on presumed and punitive damages would still violate basic First Amendment requirements.

* * *

Speech about commercial or economic matters, even if not directly implicating "the central meaning of the First Amendment," * * * is an important part of our public discourse. * * *

* * *

Given that the subject matter of credit reporting directly implicates matters of public concern, the balancing analysis the Court today employs should properly lead to the conclusion that the type of expression here at issue should receive First Amendment protection from the chilling potential of unrestrained presumed and punitive damages in defamation actions.

* * *

Accordingly, Greenmoss Builders should be permitted to recover for any actual damage it can show resulting from Dun & Bradstreet's negligently false credit report, but should be required to show actual malice to receive presumed or punitive damages. Because the jury was not instructed in accordance with these principles, we would reverse and remand for proceedings not inconsistent with this opinion.

NOTES

1. Judge Flaum summarizes the relationship between state and federal law with respect to defamation, saying:

> Federal constitutional law adds another layer of limitations on the kind of defamatory statements for which a defendant may be found liable. At common law defamation was a strict liability tort, but constitutional doctrine has imposed culpability, or fault, requirements in most cases. * * * The level of culpability is determined by whether the statement was of public concern and whether the plaintiff is a public or private figure. Moreover, overlapping with the common law rule, the First Amendment protects statements on matters of public concern that are not provably false. *See* Milkovich v. Lorain Journal Co., 497 U.S. 1, 20, 111 L. Ed. 2d 1, 110 S. Ct. 2695 (1990). For further discussion of various First Amendment limitations to defamation actions, see Ronald D. Rotunda & John E. Nowak, Treatise on Constitutional Law: Substance and Procedure §§ 20.33–20.35 (2d ed.1992).

Republic Tobacco Co. v. North Atlantic Trading Co., 381 F.3d 717, 727–28 (7th Cir.2004). For a critique of the public/private distinction in *Dun & Bradstreet*, see Nat Stern, *Private Concerns of Private Plaintiffs: Revisiting a Problematic Defamation Category*, 65 Mo. L. Rev. 597 (2000). For a suggestion that punitive damages ought to be abolished in defamation actions against public officials and public figures, see Charles Rothfeld, *The Surprising Case Against Punitive Damages in Libel Suits Against Public Figures*, 19 Yale L. & Pol'y Rev. 165 (2000).

2. Although Justice Brennan's position—that presumed damages in defamation actions are *per se* unconstitutional because they violate the First Amendment—has not been adopted by a majority of the Court, some state courts have abolished the right to recover presumed damages as a matter of common law. *See, e.g.*, United Insurance Co. v. Murphy, 331 Ark. 364, 961 S.W.2d 752 (1998) (holding that presumed damages in defamation would be abolished prospectively; defendant defamed plaintiff by falsely stating that she stole premiums while working as an insurance agent; jury awarded $3,000,000 in compensatory damages, remitted to $600,000, and $2,000,000 in punitives; plaintiff had introduced proof of actual damages).

3. Constitutional challenges continue to be raised by defendants. For example, in Sleem v. Yale University, 843 F.Supp. 57 (M.D.N.C.1993), the plaintiff alleged that the defendant had published a reunion directory containing the following entry, which the plaintiff had not submitted, and which was false: "I have come to terms with my homosexuality and the reality of AIDS in my life. I am at peace." *Id.* at 59. Yale pressed the "novel argument" that presumed general damages are unconstitutional in violation of the Due Process Clause of the United States Constitution because they are "inherently speculative and irrational" and because they "offend our fundamental notions of fairness." *Id.* at 66. The court rejected Yale's contentions:

> The court concedes that, as a policy matter, reasons exist to disfavor presumed damages. See Francis D. Murnaghan, *From Figment To Fiction*

To Philosophy—The Requirement of Proof Of Damages in Libel Actions, 22 Cath. U.L. Rev. 1 (1972); David A. Anderson, *Reputation, Compensation and Proof*, 25 Wm. & Mary L. Rev. 747, 749–56 (1984). However, there are also policy concerns which justify the allowance of presumed damages, including the perceived need to compensate victims of defamation whose reputation may be harmed even though specific proof of actual damages may be difficult. Yale overlooks that the defamatory language itself may be evidence upon which a reasonable jury could find damages. W. Page Keeton et al., Prosser and Keeton on the Law of Torts, § 166A, at 843 (5th ed. 1984). As a result, while there may be room for debate concerning the wisdom of presumed damages, this court concludes that presumed damages do not violate our fundamental notions of fairness.

In addition, this court notes that the United States Supreme Court has had ample opportunity to strike down presumed damages and has not done so. * * * It is true that in these cases presumed damages were considered in the context of the First Amendment rather than Due Process, but the point remains that the Supreme Court has upheld presumed damages in some contexts. Perhaps the Supreme Court will one day decide to find presumed damages unconstitutional, but obviously that has not yet occurred.

Id. at 66–67 (denying Yale's motion for a partial summary judgment with respect to the plaintiff's claim for presumed damages in the plaintiff's cause of action for libel *per se*).

4. The value to the defamation plaintiff of the right to recover presumed damages is illustrated by Owens v. Schoenberger, 681 N.E.2d 760 (Ind.Ct.App. 1997). The plaintiff was a freshman at Ball State University, and after she refused to marry the defendant, he falsely accused her of transmitting "an STD" to him and to members of his fraternity. His accusations became nearly universal knowledge on campus. Her case went to trial, and the jury returned a verdict for the plaintiff with presumed compensatory damages in the amount of "$0" and with punitive damages in the amount of $2,700. The judge, with the permission of the lawyers, reformed the verdict to make it $1.00 in compensatory damages. The plaintiff's lawyer then challenged the amount of the reformed verdict, claiming that the compensatory damages were "inadequate." The trial court increased the amount of the presumed damages award to $5,400. The appellate court upheld the modification, ruling that "an award of $1 in compensatory damages is not within the range of the evidence, and therefore the trial court did not abuse its discretion in granting additur." *Id.* at 767.

5. In an effort to break the deadlock between the proponents and the opponents of presumed damages in defamation actions, several commentators have suggested that the declaratory judgment remedy should be developed as an alternative remedy to damages. *See* Dan B. Dobbs, Law of Remedies § 7.2(14) (2d ed. 1993). For further discussion of declaratory judgments, see *supra* Chapter 5.

HAYES v. SMITH

Colorado Court of Appeals, 1991.
832 P.2d 1022.

Opinion by JUDGE DUBOFSKY.

In this action for defamation, defendants, Roger Smith and Samantha Smith, appeal the judgment entered on a jury verdict awarding damages to plaintiff, Kathleen Hayes. * * *

Plaintiff and defendants were active participants in a conservative Christian community. Plaintiff is a high school teacher, lecturer, and writer. She and Samantha Smith jointly created a corporation to further business ideas related to their common religious outlook. Over time, the relationship between the plaintiff and defendants deteriorated resulting in harassment and verbal accusations.

In May 1986, defendants met with plaintiff's school superintendent with the ostensible purpose of obtaining the superintendent's help in stopping plaintiff from harassing them. Plaintiff alleged that, during the meeting between defendants and the superintendent, defendants defamed her by, inter alia, stating that: (1) plaintiff had tried to establish a homosexual relationship with Samantha Smith; (2) plaintiff had "proposed marriage" to Samantha Smith; and (3) plaintiff had in the past been discharged from a teaching position.

Thereafter, based primarily on these statements to the superintendent, plaintiff filed this defamation action. The jury returned a verdict in favor of the plaintiff and awarded $1,000 in actual damages and $26,000 in special damages.

I.

Defendants argue that the trial court erred in determining that the statements accusing plaintiff of homosexual conduct were slanderous per se and in, therefore, instructing the jury on that basis. We agree.

Cases in various jurisdictions have reached different conclusions in deciding whether statements which falsely accuse a person of being a homosexual or engaging in homosexual activity constitute slander per se. *Compare* Moricoli v. Schwartz, 46 Ill.App.3d 481, 5 Ill.Dec. 74, 361 N.E.2d 74 (1977) (statements referring to a singer as a "fag" held to be slander per quod, and not slander per se), *and* Boehm v. American Bankers Insurance Group, 557 So.2d 91 (Fla.Dist.Ct.App.1990) ("The modern view considering the issue, has not found statements regarding sexual preference to constitute slander per se let alone intrinsic evidence of express malice."), *with* Manale v. New Orleans, 673 F.2d 122 (5th Cir.1982) (police roll call statement referring to plaintiff as "ya little fruit" held to be slanderous per se), *and* Mazart v. State, 109 Misc.2d 1092, 441 N.Y.S.2d 600 (1981) (inasmuch as certain homosexual activity was still a crime in New York, reference to plaintiffs as being "members of a gay community" was slanderous per se). Our analysis of the present state of the law leads us to conclude that the per se classification is inappropriate for the statements at issue here.

Historically, defamation was actionable per se only if the defamatory remark imputed a criminal offense; a venereal or loathsome and communicable disease; improper conduct of a lawful business; or unchastity by a woman. *See* Restatement (First) of Torts § 569 (1938) and Gertz v. Robert Welch, Inc., 418 U.S. 323, 94 S.Ct. 2997, 41 L.Ed.2d 789 (1974).

However, the Restatement (Second) of Torts reflects a trend toward limiting the per se category of slander to those instances in which the defamatory remark is apparent from the publication itself without reference to extrinsic facts. *See* Restatement (Second) of Torts §§ 571–574 (1977); *Gertz, supra* (White, J., dissenting). As to the specific matter at issue here, the Restatement (Second) of Torts expressly left open the issue whether an accusation of homosexuality fell into the per se category.

The primary advantage to a plaintiff claiming slander per se is that certain damages are presumed if the statement is so categorized, e.g., loss of reputation, and therefore, need not be proved. This presumption has been considered desirable because injuries such as loss of reputation can be difficult to prove since the recipients of the information may be reluctant to testify that the publication affected their relationship with the plaintiff and because the words may affect the recipients' view of the relationship in subtle ways of which the recipient is not necessarily aware. *See Gertz, supra* (White, J., dissenting).

Another advantage to a per se classification is that the plaintiff need not prove the statements were defamatory within the context in which they were made. In *Gertz*, the court was also concerned that per se classifications inhibit and punish freedom of speech by making it too easy to prove defamation and damages.

In *Gertz, supra*, the majority indicated that per se classifications and presumed damages, even where constitutional, are not favored. Indeed, the *Gertz* court held that, as to a public official or public figure, a presumed damage award without proof of reckless or malicious conduct violates the First Amendment rights of the publisher of the false statement.

Thus, the right to presumed damages no longer depends entirely on the nature of the accusation; rather, it also depends on whether the statements were made about a public official or public figure with malice or recklessness as defined in New York Times v. Sullivan, 376 U.S. 254, 84 S.Ct. 710, 11 L.Ed.2d 686 (1964).

Furthermore, here, the trial court determined, without objection, that plaintiff was a public official. * * * Moreover, defamatory statements to the superintendent may have been of a public concern. * * *

In *Gertz*, however, the court emphasized that, even though presumed damages may be unavailable, plaintiff can recover for any actual injuries caused by the defamation. The *Gertz* court stated:

> Suffice it to say that actual injury is not limited to out-of-pocket loss. Indeed the more customary types of actual harm inflicted by defamatory falsehood include impairment of reputation and standing in the community, personal humiliation, and mental anguish and suffering.

These non-economic and non-reputation damages can be awarded without an initial or predicate determination awarding damages because of either harm to reputation or economic loss. Time v. Firestone, 424 U.S. 448, 96 S.Ct. 958, 47 L.Ed.2d 154 (1976); Walker v. Colorado Springs Sun, Inc., 188 Colo. 86, 538 P.2d 450 (1975).

In many instances, it is easier for a person injured by defamatory comments to prove personal humiliation and mental anguish and suffering than to prove economic loss or reputation damage. Since these non-economic damages do not require predicate or initial proof of reputation or economic loss, a person who has been slandered will be compensated even if there is a failure of proof as to the reputation or economic loss claims. Time v. Firestone, *supra*.

Furthermore, this approach brings the damages in libel and slander cases more in line with the damages provided for other types of tort actions. *See Gertz, supra.*

Moreover, in this modern era, new methods exist for proving economic and reputational damages in a defamation case, including testimony by economists, psychologists, and other expert witnesses. These factors lessen the need for per se classifications before plaintiffs can recover damages.

We, therefore, interpret the import of *Gertz*, *Firestone*, and *Walker* as furthering an earlier trend to limit and not expand the use of per se characterizations and presumed damages in defamation cases.

There are also several other factors which bear on our decision to conclude that accusations of homosexuality are not slanderous per se.

First, the fact that sexual activities between consenting adults of the same sex are no longer illegal in Colorado tends to indicate that an accusation of being a homosexual is not of such a character as to be slanderous per se. See Colo.Sess.Laws 1975, ch. 171, § 18–3–405 at 630.

Second, if a person is falsely accused of belonging in a category of persons considered deserving of social approbation, i.e., thief, murderer, prostitute, etc., it is generally the court's determination as to whether such accusation is considered slander per se so that damages are presumed. * * * A court should not classify homosexuals with those miscreants who have engaged in actions that deserve the reprobation and scorn which is implicitly a part of the slander/libel per se classifications. *See* Shelley v. Kraemer, 334 U.S. 1, 68 S.Ct. 836, 92 L.Ed. 1161 (1948).

For a characterization of a person to warrant a per se classification, it should, without equivocation, expose the plaintiff to public hatred or contempt. * * * However, there is no empirical evidence in this record demonstrating that homosexuals are held by society in such poor esteem. Indeed, it appears that the community view toward homosexuals is mixed. *See* Denver Revised Municipal Code 28–91, *et seq.* (1990); Boulder Revised Code 12–1–2, *et seq.* (1981); Colorado Executive Order In Regard to Human Rights (Colo. Dec. 10, 1990).

* * *

Although we agree that, in light of the plaintiff's showing of malicious or reckless conduct by defendants, there is no constitutional prohibition against these false accusations of homosexuality being treated as slander per se, we, nevertheless, are unwilling to do so. We reach this conclusion because of the *Gertz* hostility to expanding the scope of defamation per se and because there are serious doubts whether homosexuality meets the criteria for such a classification. We, therefore, reverse the trial court on this issue.

II.

* * *

Plaintiff implicitly argues that, even if the statements made here would not be slanderous per se outside her employment context, since they were made to her supervisor in an employment context, they did injure her in her profession as a teacher and on that basis, are slanderous per se. We do not agree.

We recognize that teachers' reputations are very vulnerable to injury when they are the subject of false accusations. *See* Wertz v. Lawrence, 66 Colo. 55, 179 P. 813 (1919). We conclude, however, for the reasons stated above, that false statements concerning homosexuality are not slander per se even though they arise in an employment context and are directed at plaintiff's business reputation.

In this regard, we further note the availability of proven actual damages to compensate an injured plaintiff in this setting. Plaintiff is entitled to receive compensation not only for economic damages and loss of reputation, but also for other proven damages, i.e., humiliation, mental suffering. *See Gertz, supra* * * *. Thus, even though the statements are not accorded slander per se status, plaintiff, on retrial, may receive compensation for those damages proven to have resulted from the statements.

III.

Although the plaintiff did not request and thus did not receive a presumed damage instruction, we conclude that the slander per se instruction here was error nonetheless. The improper advantage plaintiff received by the slander per se instruction was that she did not have to prove as part of her claim that in the context in which the statements were made, they were defamatory and caused damage to her. *See* CJI–Civ. 22:9 (1989). On retrial, plaintiff must prove that the statements, in the context in which they were made, were defamatory and that they in turn caused her injury. *See* CJI–Civ. 22:9, 22:11, and 22:12 (1989).

The judgment is reversed, and the cause is remanded for a new trial.

NOTES

1. A few other courts have refused to classify a false imputation of homosexuality as defamation per se. *E.g.*, Donovan v. Fiumara, 114 N.C.App. 524, 442 S.E.2d 572 (1994)(collecting cases). For further commentary on the issue, see Randy M. Fogle, *Is Calling Someone "Gay" Defamatory?: The Meaning of Reputation, Community Mores, Gay Rights, and Free Speech*, 3 Law & Sexuality 165 (1993). For a critique of defamation law's concern with women's chastity, see Lisa R. Pruitt, *Her Own Good Name: Two Centuries of Talk About Chastity*, 63 Md. L. Rev. 401 (2004).

2. Note that the court in *Hayes* identified two cities in Colorado that had passed ordinances prohibiting discrimination on the basis of sexual orientation. After *Hayes* was decided, the United States Supreme Court ruled that Colorado's Amendment 2, which would have repealed those gay rights ordinances, violated the Equal Protection Clause. Romer v. Evans, 517 U.S. 620, 116 S.Ct. 1620, 134 L.Ed.2d 855 (1996). The Supreme Court also ruled that a Texas same-sex sodomy statute violated the Due Process Clause. Lawrence v. Texas, 539 U.S. 558, 123 S.Ct. 2472, 156 L.Ed.2d 508 (2003). As a result of *Lawrence*, an accusation of homosexuality no longer imputes criminality in the United States. Since *Hayes*, a number of state supreme courts have also struck down laws forbidding same-sex marriage. *See, e.g.*, Goodridge v. Department of Pub. Health, 440 Mass. 309, 798 N.E.2d 941 (2003). Should these legal developments have any impact on a judge who is deciding whether or not it is defamatory to falsely identify another person as a gay man or a lesbian? Courts are split on this question.

In Callahan v. First Congregational Church of Haverhill, 441 Mass. 699, 808 N.E.2d 301 (2004), the Massachusetts Supreme Judicial Court held that "[a] false accusation of homosexuality may be actionable." *See id.* at 717 n.19. The court relied upon a pre-*Lawrence* New Jersey case that came to this conclusion after reviewing the law of jurisdictions throughout the country, including the *Hayes* decision. *See* Gray v. Press Communications, LLC, 342 N.J. Super. 1, 775 A.2d 678 (App. Div. 2001). Recently, however, a federal district court applying New Jersey Law has called *Gray* into question in light of developments in that state according all of the rights and benefits of marriage to same-sex couples. *See* Murphy v. Millennium Radio Group, LLC, 2010 WL 1372408, at *7 (D.N.J. 2010).

Note that none of these cases answers the question of whether imputation of homosexuality can ever be defamatory *per se*. On that question, the answer in Massachusetts after *Lawrence* and *Goodridge* appears to be no. *See* Albright v. Morton, 321 F. Supp. 2d 130, 137 (D. Mass. 2004)(rejecting "the implication of plaintiffs' argument that, even without the implicit accusation of a crime, portions of the community 'feel homosexuals are less reputable than heterosexuals' "). In other jurisdictions, the answer is not always so clear. For example, a court applying New York law has held that imputation of homosexuality is defamatory *per se*. Gallo v. Alitalia–Linee Aeree Italiane–Societa per Azioni, 585 F. Supp. 2d 520, 549–50 (S.D.N.Y. 2008)(McMahon, J.) ("[T]his decision is based on the fact that the prejudice gays and lesbians experience is real and sufficiently widespread so that it would be premature to declare victory. If the degree of this widespread prejudice disappears, this Court welcomes the red flag that will attach to this decision."). However, in Stern v. Cosby, 645 F. Supp. 2d 258 (S.D.N.Y. 2009)(Chin, J.), the same court came to a different conclusion. There, Judge Chin reasoned:

> While I certainly agree that gays and lesbians continue to face prejudice, I respectfully disagree that the existence of this continued prejudice leads to the conclusion that there is a widespread view of gays and lesbians as contemptible and disgraceful. Moreover, the fact of such prejudice on the part of some does not warrant a judicial holding that gays and lesbians, merely because of their sexual orientation, belong in the same class as criminals.

Id. at 275. Significantly, in *Stern*, Lambda Legal Defense and Education Fund, one the country's largest gay and lesbian advocacy organizations, argued in an *amicus curiae* brief that imputation of homosexuality is not defamatory *per se* because being identified as gay or lesbian is "neither shameful nor disgraceful." *Id.* at n.10.

Should the question of whether imputation of homosexuality can ever be defamatory, either *per se* or *per accidens*, depend upon an individual's occupation? For example, under a federal statute known as "Don't Ask Don't Tell," members of the military may be discharged if they are believed to be lesbian or gay. *See* 10 U.S.C. § 654. According to the court in *Albright*, "if an individual was in a business that forbade participation by homosexual individuals, such as the military or the clergy, such an allegation could immediately affect their livelihood." *See* 321 F. Supp. 2d at 139 n.12. The court left open the possibility of finding defamation under those circumstances.

B. INJUNCTIVE RELIEF

KRAMER v. THOMPSON

United States Court of Appeals, Third Circuit, 1991.
947 F.2d 666.

Before BECKER, NYGAARD and ALITO, CIRCUIT JUDGES.

BECKER, CIRCUIT JUDGE.

These appeals, from various injunctive orders and a damages judgment of the district court for the Eastern District of Pennsylvania in a bizarre libel case founded upon our diversity jurisdiction, present the interesting question under Pennsylvania law of the ability of a judge to enjoin future libels and to compel the retraction of past libels. * * *

I. FACTS AND PROCEDURAL HISTORY

The parties' relationship began in July 1982, when Thompson retained Kramer to bring a securities fraud claim against Thompson's former broker, Prudential–Bache, Inc. No question was raised by Thompson concerning Kramer's stewardship for the next three years. Indeed, during this time, Thompson wrote on several occasions praising Kramer's performance.[1] Then, in the fall of 1985, Kramer was contacted by an F.B.I. agent to whom Thompson previously had complained about his investment losses at Prudential–Bache. The agent asked Kramer whether the stocks at issue were completely worthless. Kramer responded that Thompson had purchased the stocks for roughly $120,000 and later had sold them for approximately $15,000. Thus, while informing the agent that Thompson had suffered a very substantial loss, Kramer also informed the agent that technically the stocks were not worthless. When Thompson learned of this conversation, however, he became enraged, and accused Kramer of deliberately dissuading the F.B.I. from investigating the matter. The parties' relationship deteriorated rapidly thereafter and, in October 1985, Thompson discharged Kramer as his counsel.

Seeking to ensure that he ultimately would be compensated for his services, Kramer refused to return the case files to Thompson until the latter agreed to deposit the proceeds of any future judgment or settlement with the court pending resolution of the attorney's fees issue. Thompson would not agree, and Kramer secured an order from the district court which provided that any funds recovered would be placed in escrow, and that the fee dispute would be arbitrated. Kramer then made the case files available to Thompson and his new counsel.

On February 4, 1986, Thompson wrote to the Disciplinary Board of the Pennsylvania Supreme Court (the "Disciplinary Board") alleging that Kramer had failed to represent him effectively in the Prudential–Bache action[2] At about the same time, Thompson began writing a series of critical and accusatory letters about Kramer to various private attorneys, federal judges, F.B.I. agents, federal and state prosecutors, newspapers, and television stations in the Philadelphia area.[3] With varying degrees of repetition, these letters alleged that Kramer: (1) had "thrown" Thompson's case; (2) had deliberately destroyed certain documents related to the case; (3) had used drugs and was a member of the highly publicized "Yuppie Drug Ring" organized by Philadelphia dentist Lawrence Lavin;[4] (4) was connected to organized crime; and (5) had committed arson on his own car. Kramer demanded a retraction, but Thompson refused.

---

1. Thompson is a self-employed exporter of pumps and other equipment and a self-styled consumer activist, who writes frequently under the letterhead of the "Thompson–American Antifraud League."

2. On April 8, 1986, the Disciplinary Board dismissed Thompson's complaint.

3. Thompson sent a total of at least 160 separate letters to 60 different individuals or entities.

4. Thompson's apparent basis for this accusation was Kramer's representation of several minority shareholders of WMOT Enterprises, Inc., a company which had been infiltrated and bilked of funds by one of Lavin's co-conspirators.

Kramer thereupon brought a libel action against Thompson in the Court of Common Pleas of Philadelphia County. Undaunted by Kramer's suit, Thompson continued his letter-writing campaign. The court eventually entered a default judgment on the issue of liability against Thompson for failure to comply with discovery.

After the default judgment was entered against him, Thompson ceased to write critically about Kramer for approximately two years. In early 1989, however, Thompson became aware of a suit filed by Kramer in federal district court against Mano Arco, a garage that had performed repair work on Kramer's car. Kramer's suit alleged that Mano Arco's negligent workmanship had been responsible for the fire that engulfed his car while it was travelling on the New Jersey Turnpike. Thompson took it upon himself to contact, first by phone and then by letter, the lawyer for Mano Arco. After informing the lawyer of his view that Kramer had committed arson on his own car, Thompson resumed his accusations that Kramer had thrown Thompson's securities fraud case, and that he was involved in the Yuppie Drug Ring and the underworld. Thompson's letter to Mano Arco's attorney purported to be copied to the state Disciplinary Board, the federal judge hearing the case, The *Philadelphia Inquirer*, the United States Justice Department, and Kramer.

Kramer then filed the instant libel action in the United States District Court for the Eastern District of Pennsylvania, alleging diversity of citizenship. Thompson filed an answer, naming thirteen third-party defendants and asserting counterclaims for libel and slander, legal malpractice, obstruction of justice, malicious prosecution, and civil RICO violations. The district court later dismissed the third-party defendants and the counterclaims, and imposed sanctions on Thompson with respect to one of the third-party defendants.

Trial commenced on April 2, 1990. Having determined that Thompson's statements were *per se* libelous in that they were false and made in reckless disregard of their truth or falsity, the court directed a verdict for Kramer at the close of Kramer's case—i.e., without hearing Thompson's defense on the issue of liability. The court restricted the scope of Thompson's case to evidence relevant to the calculation of compensatory and punitive damages. * * *

* * *

The jury ultimately awarded Kramer $100,000 in compensatory and $38,000 in punitive damages, and the district court entered judgment accordingly on April 10, 1990. The court simultaneously entered a permanent injunction, prohibiting Thompson from making further statements about Kramer of the type adjudged libelous, and ordering him to write letters of retraction to all persons who had received prior libelous communications. Thompson's post-trial motions for judgment n.o.v. and for a new trial were denied. * * *

After learning that Thompson had failed to send all the retraction letters required by the court's permanent injunction, Kramer moved to hold Thompson in contempt of court. Although declining to hold Thompson in civil contempt, the district court, *inter alia,* again ordered him to make the appropriate retractions.

Shortly thereafter, Thompson submitted a petition, which he later amended, seeking leave to appear as *amicus curiae* in the case of Matthews v. Freedman, Appeal No. 89–2112, then pending before this court. *Matthews* involved an appeal by Kramer of sanctions imposed on him by a district court in a matter unrelated to his litigation with Thompson. Thompson's petition contained renewed accusations that Kramer had "thrown" his case, was associated with the Yuppie Drug Ring, and generally was guilty of perjury, forgery, fraud, and extortion. In the petition, Thompson also repudiated the prior retraction letter that the district court had "forced" him to write. Thompson sent copies of his petition to the Disciplinary Board, U.S. Attorney's Office, F.B.I., I.R.S., and lawyers associated with the *Matthews* case.

Kramer filed a second motion to hold Thompson in contempt. This time, the district court declared Thompson in civil contempt of the permanent injunction, and ordered that he be confined and fined $500 per day until he purged himself of contempt by withdrawing all statements and court filings related to the *Matthews* case. Thompson then drafted, and the court edited and approved, the required letter of withdrawal. The court also ordered Thompson to advise the Clerk of this court, in regard to the instant appeal, that he had "admitted under oath in the trial of this matter that he defamed Steven Kramer and promised the jury, before verdict, that he apologized and would not in the future make such statements as were accused as defamatory by plaintiff."

On August 24, 1990, the district court entered an expanded injunction prohibiting Thompson from contacting any person with whom Kramer conducts his business. Thompson filed a second notice of appeal * * *, which was consolidated with Thompson's pending appeal. We granted expedited argument, but refused Thompson's motion to stay enforcement of the injunction pending disposition of his appeal. After hearing argument, however, we stayed enforcement of the injunction, pending that disposition.

II. DISCUSSION

Thompson appeals from a variety of orders of the district court, raising numerous allegations of error. * * * We will limit our inquiry in this opinion to the challenges to the permanent injunction entered by the district court against Thompson after trial and to that injunction's subsequent enforcement and expansion.

As discussed above, this injunction essentially provided Kramer with two forms of equitable relief, in addition to the $138,000 in damages awarded by the jury. First, the court, threatening civil contempt, enjoined

Thompson initially from issuing new statements of the type found libelous, and ultimately from contacting anyone with whom Kramer does
business. Second, the injunction required Thompson to retract or withdraw various previously issued libelous statements and court filings.
Thompson argues that the permanent injunction thus had the effect of
"prohibiting and mandating" speech in violation of the First Amendment
to the United States Constitution and Article I, section 7 of the Pennsylvania Constitution. We will consider separately Thompson's challenges to
the prohibitory injunction and to the retraction order.

A. *Injunction Against Further Defamatory Statements*

It is axiomatic in this diversity case that the injunction cannot stand
if it contravenes *either* the United States or Pennsylvania Constitutions.
Because Thompson presses his claim principally by reference to the
Pennsylvania Constitution, we will begin our analysis there. * * *

Thompson relies primarily upon Willing v. Mazzocone, 482 Pa. 377,
393 A.2d 1155 (1978), which he argues is on all fours with the instant
dispute, and which stands for the proposition that the Pennsylvania
Constitution does not tolerate an injunction against libelous speech. * * *

In 1968, defendant Helen Willing retained plaintiffs Carl Mazzocone
and Charles Quinn, who practiced law together, to represent her in a
worker's compensation claim. The two lawyers successfully obtained a
settlement for Willing, from which she collected disability benefits for
several years. In addition to their fee, Mazzocone and Quinn deducted
$150 from the settlement as costs of the case. They claimed, and their
records verified, that the money had been paid to one Dr. Robert DeSilverio, a psychiatrist who had been retained to testify on Willing's behalf.

At some point, for an unknown reason (and contrary to all available
evidence), Willing came to believe that Mazzocone and Quinn had diverted
for their own benefit $25 of the $150 allegedly paid to Dr. DeSilverio. For
two days in 1975, Willing marched in protest in an area adjacent to the
court buildings at City Hall in Philadelphia where the Court of Common
Pleas, before which Mazzocone and Quinn practiced, was located. While
marching, Willing wore a "sandwich-board" sign around her neck and on
which she had written:

LAWFIRM
of
QUINN–MAZZOCONE
Stole money from me—and
Sold-me-out-to-the
INSURANCE COMPANY

To attract attention while marching, Willing pushed a shopping cart
bearing an American flag, continuously rang a cow bell, and blew on a
whistle.

Mazzocone and Quinn attempted unsuccessfully to discourage Willing from further public protest. The two then filed a complaint in equity in the Court of Common Pleas * * * seeking an injunction against further demonstration. The court found that there was no factual basis for Willing's defamatory protest, but noted that "either by reason of eccentricity or an even more serious mental instability," Willing could not be convinced that she had not been defrauded. * * * The court enjoined Willing from further demonstration or picketing and from "carrying placards which contain defamatory and libelous statements and or uttering, publishing and declaring defamatory statements against [Mazzocone and Quinn]." * * *

On appeal, the Superior Court of Pennsylvania affirmed the injunction, although narrowing it somewhat so as to prohibit Willing only from "uttering or publishing statements to the effect that Mazzocone and Quinn, Attorneys-at-Law stole money from her and sold her out to the insurance company." *Mazzocone v. Willing*, 246 Pa.Super. 98, 369 A.2d 829, 834 (1976). In affirming the injunction, the Superior Court openly rejected the "traditional view that equity does not have the power to enjoin the publication of defamatory matter." *Id.*, 369 A.2d at 831 (citations omitted).[12] The court noted that four reasons traditionally have been offered to justify equity's refusal to enjoin defamation:

> (1) equity will afford protection only to property rights; (2) an injunction would deprive the defendant of his right to a jury trial on the issue of the truth of the publication; (3) the plaintiff has an adequate remedy at law; and (4) an injunction would be unconstitutional as a prior restraint on freedom of expression.

Id. The court then went on to state that "the logic and soundness of these reasons have been severely criticized by numerous commentators,"[13] and

---

12. The origin of this common-law precept is generally traced to Lord Eldon's *dicta* in Gee v. Pritchard, 2 Swans. 402, 36 Eng.Rep. 670 (1818), as adopted in the United States in Brandreth v. Lance, 8 Paige 24 (N.Y.Ch.1839). These decisions reflected a distrust of equitable jurisdiction over libel, traceable, in part, to the Star Chamber which "once exercised the power of cutting off the ears, branding the foreheads, and slitting the noses of the libellers of important personages . . . and [which] was [also] . . . in the habit of restraining the publication of such libels by injunction." *Brandreth*, 8 Paige at 26. *See generally* Kwass v. Kersey, 139 W.Va. 497, 81 S.E.2d 237, 242 (1954) (reviewing rationale for evolution of common-law rule). As an out-growth of *Gee* and *Brandreth*, libel plaintiffs in the United States generally have been limited to legal relief in the form of money damages.

13. The first assault on the common law's refusal to enjoin a defamation was led by Dean Roscoe Pound, *see* Pound, *Equitable Relief Against Defamation and Injuries to Personality*, 29 Harv.L.Rev. 640 (1916), who apparently became so convinced of the wisdom and inevitability of abandoning the rule that he and Professor Chafee published a casebook detailing the emerging trend, *see* R. Pound and Z. Chafee, Cases on Equitable Relief Against Defamation and Injuries to Personality (1930). Pound's work has spawned a considerable body of literature over the years which has criticized the common-law rule, lamented the inadequacy of money damages as a remedy for defamation, and advocated a variety of alternative equitable remedies including declaratory judgment, right of reply, voluntary or mandatory retraction, injunction, and arbitration. *See generally* Long, *Equitable Jurisdiction to Protect Personal Rights*, 33 Yale L.J. 115 (1923); Chafee, *Possible New Remedies for Errors in the Press*, 60 Harv.L.Rev. 1 (1946); Donnelly, *The Right of Reply: An Alternative to an Action for Libel*, 34 Va.L.Rev. 867 (1948); Leflar, *Legal Remedies for Defamation*, 6 Ark.L.Rev. & B. Ass'n J. 423 (1952); Note, *Developments in the Law of Defamation*, 69 Harv.L.Rev. 875 (1956) [hereinafter Note, *Developments in Defamation*]; Note,

that "[o]ur own analysis compels us to conclude that blind application of the majority view to the instant case would be antithetical to equity's historic function of maintaining flexibility and accomplishing total justice whenever possible." *Id.* The court then reviewed each of the four traditional justifications.

First, the court noted that the Pennsylvania Supreme Court had expressly repudiated the maxim that equity will protect property rights but not personal rights. *Id.* (citing Everett v. Harron, 380 Pa. 123, 110 A.2d 383 (1955)).[14] Pennsylvania apparently is now in line with the Restatement and the vast majority of other jurisdictions in this regard. *See* Kenyon v. City of Chicopee, 320 Mass. 528, 70 N.E.2d 241, 244 (1946); *see generally* Restatement (Second) of Torts § 937 comment (a) (1969); Gold, *supra* note 13, at 236–37; Note, *Developments in Injunctions, supra* note 13, at 998–1000. *But see* Murphy v. Daytona Beach Humane Society, 176 So.2d 922, 924 (Fla.App.1965) (denying injunction against defamation based on traditional view that equity will not protect rights of personality).

Second, the Superior Court reasoned that the argument that a defendant has a right to a jury determination as to the truth of a publication[15]

Developments in the Law of Injunctions, 78 Harv.L.Rev. 994 (1965) [hereinafter Note, *Developments in Injunctions*]; Note, *Vindication of the Reputation of a Public Official,* 80 Harv.L.Rev. 1730 (1967); Bertelsman, *Injunctions Against Speech and Writing: A Re–Evaluation,* 59 Ky.L.J. 319 (1970); Note, *Corporate Defamation and Product Disparagement: Narrowing the Analogy to Personal Defamation,* 75 Colum.L.Rev. 963 (1975); Hulme, *Vindicating Reputation: An Alternative to Damages As a Remedy for Defamation,* 30 Am.U.L.Rev. 375 (1981); Gold, *Does Equity Still Lack Jurisdiction to Enjoin a Libel or Slander?,* 48 Brook.L.Rev. 231 (1982); Barron, *The Search for Media Accountability,* 19 Suffolk U.L.Rev. 789 (1985); Franklin, *A Declaratory Judgment Alternative to Current Libel Law,* 74 Cal.L.Rev. 809 (1986); Leval, *The No–Money, No–Fault Libel Suit: Keeping Sullivan in its Proper Place,* 101 Harv.L.Rev. 1287 (1988); Wissler, Bezanson, Cranberg & Soloski, *Why Current Libel Law Doesn't Work and What Judges Can Do About It,* 27 Judges' J. 29 (1988); and Dienes, *Libel Reform: An Appraisal,* 23 U.Mich.J.L.Ref. 1 (1989).

14. The differential protection provided in equity for property and personal rights was a particular source of annoyance for Dean Pound:

If a threatened tort involves injury to property for which the legal remedy is inadequate ... preventive relief is normally available. But if an injury to personality is threatened, wholly destructive of plaintiff's dearest interest, we are told that his only recourse is the legal remedy of damages although no pecuniary measure can possibly be applied to the interest and no pecuniary standard to the wrong. May we give any reasons other than purely historical for a doctrine which at first blush is so arbitrary and unjust? Do the rules which our books still announce upon this subject rest upon any basis more legitimate than unintelligent adherence to the *dicta* of a great judge in the pioneer case? May we put this corner of the law in the order of reason by making the rules thereof conform to the general principle of concurrent jurisdiction where the legal remedy for a legal right is inadequate or by showing sound reason why, in this one spot, that general principle should not obtain?

Pound, *supra* note 13 at 640–41. * * *

15. The notion of the right to a jury determination as to the libelous nature of speech apparently originated with Fox's Libel Act, 32 Geo. II, c. 60, § 1 (1792), which stated:

On every such trial the jury sworn to try the issue may give a general verdict of guilty or not guilty upon the whole matter put in issue ... and shall not be required or directed by the Court or judge ... to find the defendant ... guilty merely on the proof of publication by such defendant ... of the paper charged to be a libel....

Prior to Fox's Act, English judges had determined whether a particular statement was libelous; the jury merely determined whether there had been publication of the statement. *See* Leflar, *supra* note 13, at 434 n.37. Fox's Act thus expanded the jury's role, a development which was transplanted to America when many of the states subsequently patterned their respective

"loses all persuasion . . . in those situations where the plaintiff has clearly established before a judicial tribunal that the matter sought to be enjoined is both defamatory and false." 369 A.2d at 831. Because there was no doubt that Willing's sign was both false and malicious, the Superior Court reasoned that "[t]o refuse injunctive relief under the circumstances of this case on the grounds that defendant would be denied a jury trial is to elevate form over substance." *Id.* 369 A.2d at 832.

Third, the Superior Court challenged the precept that plaintiffs do not need equitable relief because they have an adequate remedy at law for damages[16] In particular, the Superior Court reasoned that Mazzocone and Quinn did *not* have an adequate remedy at law because: (1) the value of their professional and personal reputations, and the diminution in that value resulting from Willing's libel, were difficult to prove and measure; (2) given Willing's apparent mental instability, it was reasonable to assume that she would continue to libel the plaintiffs, necessitating a multiplicity of damage actions on their behalf; and (3) Willing was indigent, rendering any action for damages a "pointless gesture" in any event.[17] 369 A.2d at 832. In light of these factors, the Superior Court concluded that Mazzocone and Quinn did not have an adequate remedy at law.

Fourth, although the Superior Court acknowledged that the argument that an injunction against defamation is an unconstitutional prior restraint on free expression "is by far the most cogent of all the reasons offered in support of the traditional view,[19] it reasoned that not all

---

constitutional and statutory provisions governing libel upon the Act, *see* Note, *Developments in Defamation*, *supra* note 13, at 944. Since this time, numerous courts have referred to the right to a jury trial in denying injunctions against defamation, generally reasoning that the jury provides a safeguard against judicial censorship of speech. *See* Schmoldt v. Oakley, 390 P.2d 882, 886 (Okl.1964). *See generally* Annotation, *Injunction as Remedy Against Defamation of Person*, 47 A.L.R.2d 715, 727–28 [§ 5b] (1956) (citing cases).

16. This precept is also of considerable vintage:

The adequate remedy rule well reflected Chancery's subordinate position as it developed in medieval England against the background of the established courts of law. Equity was a "gloss" on the law; its sole justification for assuming jurisdiction was that traditional legal remedies and procedures could not offer the plaintiff satisfactory relief.

Note, *Developments in Injunctions*, *supra* note 13, at 997 (citations omitted). Although law and equity have been merged in most jurisdictions, the adequate remedy rule continues to be cited frequently as a ground for denying injunctive relief against defamation. *See* Alberti v. Cruise, 383 F.2d 268 (4th Cir.1967); Annotation, *Injunction as Remedy Against Defamation of Person*, 47 A.L.R.2d 715, 724–25 [§ 4a] (1956) (and cases cited therein).

17. The adequate remedy at law rationale for denying injunctions against defamations has been rejected or criticized in numerous reported decisions and in the literature. *See generally* Dino DeLaurentiis Cinematografica, S.p.A. v. D–150, Inc., 366 F.2d 373, 375–76 (2d Cir.1966); Menard v. Houle, 298 Mass. 546, 11 N.E.2d 436, 437 (1937); *Murphy*, 176 So.2d at 927 (Wigginton, J. specially concurring); Note, *Developments in Injunctions*, *supra* note 13, at 1000–04; Bertelsman, *supra* note 13, at 320; Gold, *supra* note 13, at 262. These cases and articles generally adopt the modern view, reflected in the Restatement (Second) of Torts § 936 (1969), that the availability of legal remedies is merely one of the factors to be considered in determining the appropriateness of an injunction against a threatened tort.

19. *See* Konigsberg v. Time, Inc., 288 F.Supp. 989 (S.D.N.Y.1968) ("To enjoin any publication, no matter how libelous, would be repugnant to the First Amendment to the Constitution."); Krebiozen Research Foundation v. Beacon Press, Inc., 334 Mass. 86, 93, 134 N.E.2d 1, 6 (1956) ("[T]he constitutional protection of free speech and public interest in the discussion of many

restrictions on speech constitute prior restraints." 369 A.2d at 832. Invoking Justice Frankfurter's opinion in Kingsley Books, Inc. v. Brown, 354 U.S. 436, 441–42, 77 S.Ct. 1325, 1327–28, 1 L.Ed.2d 1469 (1957), the court maintained instead that "a pragmatic and modern rather than a theoretical and historical approach" should be employed in determining what constitutes a prior restraint. 369 A.2d at 832–33. As explicated by the Superior Court, this pragmatic approach should attempt to weigh, on a case-by-case basis, the likelihood that the alleged defamatory statements were true, the magnitude of the harm done to the plaintiff if the speech is not restrained, the adequacy of legal remedies, and, most importantly, whether the public interest will be disserved by suppressing the speech. 369 A.2d at 833–34 (citations omitted). Under this pragmatic approach, the court concluded, the injunction against Willing should not be considered an unconstitutional prior restraint.

The Supreme Court of Pennsylvania reversed, essentially refuting the reasoning of the Superior Court on two grounds. 482 Pa. 377, 393 A.2d 1155 (1978). First, invoking Blackstone and referencing the pernicious English Licensing Acts, * * * the Supreme Court noted that the Commonwealth of Pennsylvania long has rejected any prior restraint on the exercise of speech as reflected in Article I, section 7 of the Pennsylvania Constitution and in the Court's own decision in Goldman Theatres v. Dana, 405 Pa. 83, 173 A.2d 59, *cert. denied,* 368 U.S. 897, 82 S.Ct. 174, 7 L.Ed.2d 93 (1961).

Second, the Supreme Court addressed the Superior Court's argument that Mazzocone and Quinn did not have an adequate remedy at law because Willing was indigent and unable to satisfy a damages action. In unequivocal terms, the Supreme Court stated that Willing's constitutional rights should not be contingent upon her financial status.

The Supreme Court added that, as a matter of common-law precedent, the Superior Court had been wrong in assuming that Willing's indigency in any way was relevant to determining whether Mazzocone and Quinn had an adequate remedy at law.

* * *

Given the similarities between *Willing* and the instant dispute, and the Pennsylvania Supreme Court's flat rejection of the Superior Court's avoidance of the traditional rule against enjoining defamation, it arguably

issues greatly limit the areas in which the power to grant injunctive relief may or should be exercised in defamatory cases."); Northwestern Pac. R. Co. v. Lumber & Sawmill Workers' Union, 31 Cal.2d 441, 189 P.2d 277, 282 (1948) ("[Equity] will not restrain the commission of a libel or slander, for that is prior censorship—a basic evil denounced by the constitutions of the United States and California in protecting freedom of speech and press."). *See generally* Annotation, *Injunction as Remedy Against Defamation of Person,* 47 A.L.R.2d 715, 726–27 (1956) ("The most formidable obstacle to the grant of injunctive relief against personal defamation in this country has been the feeling of the courts that to allow such relief would infringe the constitutionally guaranteed freedoms of speech and of the press by setting up what would be, at least potentially, a system of judicial censorship."); *Bertelsman, supra* note 13 at 323 ("[T]he constitutional problem of prior restraint ... has proved to be the most formidable obstacle to the granting of injunctive relief in cases involving speech or writing.").

would be appropriate to overturn the district court's injunction against Thompson without further elaboration. We believe, however, contrary to Thompson's assertions, that there is a material difference between the two cases that makes further analysis unavoidable.

As noted previously, *Willing* originated when Mazzocone and Quinn filed a suit in equity in the Court of Common Pleas of Philadelphia seeking to enjoin Willing's defamatory protest. The two lawyers never sought damages, nor did a jury ever pass upon the veracity of Willing's statements. The Common Pleas judge, satisfied that the statements obviously lacked foundation and that Willing was mentally imbalanced, issued the injunction based entirely upon his view of the situation and his equitable powers. Thompson, by contrast, was enjoined from further defamatory speech as an adjunct to Kramer's successful action at law for damages. Because the district court directed a verdict in Kramer's favor on the issue of liability, leaving to the jury only the issue of damages, we recognize that it is not entirely accurate to state that Thompson was afforded a jury determination as to the veracity of his statements. However, since the directed verdict is functionally equivalent to a jury award, at least in theory Thompson's comments were found to be libelous after a full and fair jury trial.

The existence of a jury trial is a potentially crucial distinction between *Willing* and this case. Two of the three traditional reasons for barring equity from enjoining a defamation, as described by the Pennsylvania Supreme Court in *Willing,* are obviated once a jury has determined that the enjoined statements are indeed libelous. First, it obviously cannot be said that a defendant has been denied the right to a jury determination of the veracity of his statements if a judge issues an injunction against further statements *after* a jury has determined that the same statements are untrue and libelous. Second, not all injunctions against speech constitute prior restraints. The United States Supreme Court has held repeatedly that an injunction against speech generally will not be considered an unconstitutional prior restraint if it is issued after a jury has determined that the speech is not constitutionally protected. *See, e.g.,* Pittsburgh Press Co. v. Pittsburgh Comm'n on Human Rel., 413 U.S. 376, 390, 93 S.Ct. 2553, 2561, 37 L.Ed.2d 669 (1973) ("The special vice of a prior restraint is that communication will be suppressed, either directly or by inducing excessive caution in the speaker, before an adequate determination that it is unprotected by the First Amendment."). The Pennsylvania cases appear to be in accord. Because libelous speech is not protected by either the United States or the Pennsylvania Constitutions, * * * it follows that, once a jury has determined that a certain statement is libelous, it is not a prior restraint for the court to enjoin the defendant from repeating that statement.

Mindful of our responsibility to predict how the Pennsylvania Supreme Court would decide this case under its laws and Constitution, the case appears to be reducible to the following question: Would the Pennsylvania Supreme Court have upheld the injunction against Willing if

Mazzocone and Quinn had first obtained a jury determination that her statements were libelous? Stated more broadly, would the Pennsylvania Supreme Court be willing to permit an exception to the rule that equity will not enjoin a defamation in cases where there already has been a jury determination that the defendant's statements were libelous?

Although this is apparently a question of first impression under Pennsylvania law, it has been considered in other jurisdictions. To begin with, our research reveals four Missouri cases that suggest in *dicta* that an injunction can issue against further publication of defamatory statements once the plaintiff had secured a jury verdict. *See* Flint v. Hutchinson Smoke Burner Co., 110 Mo. 492, 19 S.W. 804, 806 (1892); Wolf v. Harris, 267 Mo. 405, 184 S.W. 1139, 1141–42 (1916); Ryan v. Warrensburg, 342 Mo. 761, 117 S.W.2d 303, 308 (1938); Downey v. United Weatherproofing Inc., 363 Mo. 852, 253 S.W.2d 976, 983 (1953). * * *

* * *

In 1975, the Supreme Courts of Ohio and Georgia became the first courts clearly to adopt this exception to the general rule that equity will not enjoin a defamation. *See* O'Brien v. University Community Tenants Union, 42 Ohio St.2d 242, 327 N.E.2d 753 (1975); Retail Credit Co. v. Russell, 234 Ga. 765, 218 S.E.2d 54 (1975). *O'Brien* was instituted by a landlord who claimed that he was being defamed and blacklisted by a tenants' group. The landlord secured a jury determination that certain statements were libelous and then sought and obtained an injunction against further libel. The Supreme Court of Ohio affirmed the injunction stating:

> Once speech has judicially been found libelous, if all the requirements for injunctive relief are met, an injunction for restraint of continued publication of that same speech may be proper. The judicial determination that specific speech is defamatory must be made prior to any restraint.

327 N.E.2d at 756.

In *Retail Credit*, the plaintiff, the subject of a credit report containing statements adjudged libelous by a jury, obtained a permanent injunction prohibiting the defendant from republishing the libelous statements. * * *

Nearly a decade later, the Minnesota Supreme Court followed suit in Advanced Training Systems v. Caswell Equipment Co., 352 N.W.2d 1 (Minn.1984). * * *

We find the reasoning and policies undergirding these cases quite persuasive. But that is not dispositive here. Our function is to look, as best we can, into the minds of the members of the Pennsylvania Supreme Court, and to ascertain their likely disposition of this case. Although the prediction is difficult, the available evidence leads us to the conclusion that the Pennsylvania Supreme Court would overturn the injunction against prospective libel issued by the district court against Thompson. In reaching this conclusion, we are persuaded by five factors.

First, the maxim that equity will not enjoin a libel has enjoyed nearly two centuries of widespread acceptance at common law. The welter of academic and judicial criticism of the last seventy years has, in truth, done little more than chip away at its edges. In any event, as evidenced by the Pennsylvania Supreme Court's unqualified rejection of the Superior Court's "modern" view in *Willing,* Pennsylvania would appear firmly bound to the traditional rule. * * *

Second, although an exception to the general rule has been recognized in several cases where there has been a jury determination of the libelous nature of specific statements, we would do well not to overstate the degree of acceptance that has been accorded to this exception. For the better part of this century, this exception existed, as best we can determine, only in Missouri, and there based entirely on a single line of *dicta*. That three state supreme courts have affirmatively adopted the exception in the last two decades may represent the trickle that presages the collapse of the common-law dam. But, for now, it remains a trickle. And as far as we can tell, the Pennsylvania Supreme Court is more likely to plug the holes in the dam than to contribute to its destruction.

Third, even if we thought that the Pennsylvania Supreme Court might be inclined to adopt the jury determination exception, we doubt that this is the case in which it would do so. The district court in this case took the decidedly unusual step of directing a verdict on the issue of liability against Thompson before he put on a defense, finding that the statements were so patently libelous that no justification or defense could possibly exist. In theory, of course, a directed verdict at law is tantamount to a jury verdict. From the defendant's perspective, however, a directed verdict is indistinguishable from the decree of a court sitting in equity. Given the fear of judicial censorship that has pervaded this area of jurisprudence, and the almost talismanic significance that the case law attaches to the decisions of juries, we think it likely that, even if the Pennsylvania Supreme Court were willing to adopt this exception, it would do so only when there *actually* has been a jury determination regarding the libelous nature of the defendant's statements.

Fourth, and perhaps most importantly, we believe that the Pennsylvania Supreme Court would not adopt the jury determination exception if confronted with this case because, as *Willing* pointedly suggests, that Court continues to place great emphasis on the adequate remedy doctrine as a bar to equitable relief. * * *

Whether or not that court would have felt less passionately about the adequate remedy rule had it been satisfied that the rights to trial by jury and free speech were not also implicated is difficult to discern. In the end, we can do no more than take the *Willing* court's words at face value. * * *

Fifth and finally, we note that this case presents a stronger case than *Willing* for denying equitable relief. Unlike Willing, there has been no showing that Thompson is indigent (the record suggests that he is moderately affluent), or that the threat of future damages is inadequate to deter him or to compensate Kramer. * * *

For the foregoing reasons, we will reverse those portions of the district court's orders that enjoined Thompson from repeating the statements deemed libelous and from communicating with anyone doing business with Kramer.

B. Mandatory Retraction and Withdrawal of Prior Statements and Court Filings

We need not tarry very long over those portions of the district court's orders that sought to force Thompson to write letters of retraction to recipients of prior libelous statements and to withdraw libelous court filings. We have reviewed the available literature and reported decisions. Although the notion of *compelled* retraction occasionally has been advanced in the literature, we have not found a single case in which such a remedy has been awarded.

* * *

To our knowledge, the only two cases that even remotely come close to addressing mandatory retraction are Miami Herald Publishing Co. v. Tornillo, 418 U.S. 241, 94 S.Ct. 2831, 41 L.Ed.2d 730 (1974), and Coughlin v. Westinghouse Broadcasting and Cable, Inc., 689 F.Supp. 483 (E.D.Pa. 1988). In *Miami Herald*, the Supreme Court was called upon to assess the constitutionality of a Florida statute that provided a so-called "right of reply" to political candidates whose personal or official records were assailed by the media. Under the statute, newspapers were required to print, free of cost to the candidate, and subject to punishment if they refused, any reply that a candidate wished to make to the newspapers' charges. The Court declared the statute unconstitutional stating:

> [T]he Court has expressed sensitivity as to whether a restriction or requirement constituted the compulsion exerted by government on a newspaper to print that which it would not otherwise print. The clear implication has been that any such compulsion to publish that which " 'reason' tells them should not be published" is unconstitutional. A responsible press is an undoubtedly desirable goal, but press responsibility is not mandated by the Constitution and like many other virtues cannot be legislated.

Miami Herald, 418 U.S. at 256, 94 S.Ct. at 2838–39 (citations omitted).

A "right of reply" differs from a mandatory retraction in that the former merely requires the defamer to provide space for a reply, whereas the latter requires the defamer to mouth or pen the words the plaintiff would have him say. As such, the unconstitutionality of compelled retraction would seem to follow *a fortiori* from the Court's declaration that Florida's "right of reply" statute is unconstitutional. * * *

Coughlin is also somewhat related to our inquiry. There, a policeman, who claimed that he had been defamed by a television station, wrote the management of the station demanding retraction, but was rebuffed. Apparently unable to prove that the statements had been made with sufficient recklessness to support a typical damages action for libel, the policeman sought damages invoking the novel theory that the station had breached a common-law duty under Pennsylvania law to retract what it later knew to be false. * * *

Judge Pollak reviewed the authorities speaking to the constitutionality of mandatory retraction, focusing on *Miami Herald* * * *. He concluded, in *dicta*, that "[m]y view of the matter is that a carefully crafted retraction statute could well be constitutional." *Id.* at 489. Judge Pollak denied the plaintiff's claim, however, concluding that even if mandatory retraction would survive constitutional scrutiny, such a cause of action properly should originate with the Pennsylvania legislature, not the courts. * * * We agree.

In sum, we find no support for the various retractions and withdrawals forced upon Thompson by the district court. Consequently, those orders of the district court compelling such retractions and withdrawals, and the associated contempt citations, must be reversed.

III. CONCLUSION

For the foregoing reasons, we will reverse those portions of the orders of the district court, * * * that permanently enjoined defendant from uttering libelous statements, mandated the retraction or withdrawal of past libelous statements, held defendant in civil contempt, and awarded plaintiff attorney's fees arising out of contempt proceedings. * * *

NOTE

Consider the following facts in Balboa Island Village Inn, Inc. v. Lemen, 40 Cal.4th 1141, 57 Cal.Rptr.3d 320, 156 P.3d 339 (2007):

In 1989, defendant Anne Lemen purchased the "Island Cottage," which lies across an alley from the Village Inn. She lives there part of the time and rents the cottage as a vacation home part of the time. Lemen is a vocal critic of the Village Inn and has contacted the authorities numerous times to complain of excessive noise and the behavior of inebriated customers leaving the bar. In an effort to document these abuses, Lemen videotaped the Inn approximately 50 times. According to Lemen, she made these videotapes while on her own property, although she acknowledged that, on one occasion, she parked her Volkswagen bus across from the Inn and videotaped from there.

The Village Inn introduced evidence that Lemen's actions were far more intrusive. For more than two years, Lemen parked across from the Inn at least one day each weekend and made videotapes for hours at a time. Customers often asked Lemen not to videotape them as they entered or left the building. Numerous times, she followed customers to or from their cars while videotaping them. She took many flash photographs through the windows of the Inn a couple of days each week for a year, upsetting the customers. She called customers "drunks" and "whores." She told customers entering the Inn, "I don't know why you would be going in there. The food is shitty." She approached potential customers outside the Inn more than 100 times, causing many to turn away. One time, she stopped her vehicle in front of the Village Inn and sounded her horn for five seconds.

Lemen had several encounters with employees of the Village Inn. She told bartender Ewa Cook that Cook "worked for Satan," was "Satan's wife," and was "going to have Satan's children." She asked musician Arturo Perez if he had a "green card" and asked whether he knew there were illegal aliens working at the Inn. Lemen referred to Theresa Toll, the owner's wife, as "Madam Whore" and said, in the presence of her tenant, Larry Wilson: "Everyone on the island knows you're a whore." Three times, Lemen took photographs of cook Felipe Anaya and other employees while they were changing clothes in the kitchen.

Lemen collected 100 signatures on a petition opposing the Village Inn. As she did so, she told neighbors that there was child pornography and prostitution going on in the Inn, and that the Village Inn was selling drugs and was selling alcohol to minors. She said that sex videos were being filmed inside the Village Inn, that it was involved with the Mafia, that it encouraged lesbian activity, and that the Inn stayed open until 6:00 a.m. When defendant began collecting signatures door to door and making these statements, the Village Inn's sales dropped more than 20 percent.

Id. at 156 P.3d 341–342.

The Village Inn then sought a permanent injunction against Lemen. After the trial court determined that Lemen's communications were defamatory, it entered a permanent injunction. Ultimately, while the California Supreme Court determined that parts of the trial court's injunction were overbroad, it nevertheless held that "following a trial at which it is determined that the defendant defamed the plaintiff, the court may issue an injunction prohibiting the defendant from repeating the statements determined to be defamatory." *Id.* at 156 P.3d 331. As a result, a modified permanent injunction against Lemen was upheld. Should the fact that the *trial court* and not *a jury* made the defamation finding represent a less compelling case for injunctive relief?

BINGHAM v. STRUVE

New York Supreme Court, Appellate Division, 1992.
184 A.D.2d 85, 591 N.Y.S.2d 156.

Before SULLIVAN, J.P., and WALLACH, KUPFERMAN and KASSAL, JJ.

PER CURIAM.

Plaintiffs, A. Walker Bingham III and his wife, Nicolette P. Bingham, commenced this action on or about February 7, 1991, seeking a permanent injunction and money damages for alleged libel and intentional infliction of emotional distress. * * *

This litigation arose from the repeated oral and written communications of defendant, Catherine T.A. Struve, to plaintiffs' family members, business associates, neighbors, and former colleagues, which charge, *inter alia,* that plaintiff-husband raped her in 1953, when she was a 19–year-old librarian, and he a 24–year-old first-year law student, at Harvard Law School. The allegedly libelous communications, which started in or about December 1989 with letters and telephone calls, took a new form in August 1991, when defendant began to picket in front of plaintiffs' apartment building in Manhattan. The hand-lettered sandwich board which she wore on these almost daily occasions proclaimed as follows:

ATTENTION
RESIDENTS
OF
19 EAST 72ND ST.
A. WALKER BINGHAM 3
RAPED ME
AND IS NOW
SUING ME FOR
LIBEL

It is undisputed that plaintiff-husband and defendant had a youthful affair, which commenced in 1953 and ended in 1955, and that for the next 30 years they lived separate lives. Defendant married in 1965, had two children, and was divorced in 1984. Plaintiff-husband was also married, first in the 1950's, which marriage ended in divorce, and then to plaintiff-wife in 1967. He has three children.

After a chance encounter between plaintiff-husband and defendant in 1983, a second affair began and lasted until 1989 when, defendant contends, the memory of the alleged rape, which she had repressed for 36 years, was unlocked. Defendant states that she then realized that this was why she had been depressed and dysfunctional for years, and that it accounted for her inability to pursue a career and succeed in her marriage. It is defendant's further claim that, by publicizing her charges against plaintiff-husband, she will be able to come to terms with the traumatic event and heal emotionally, a process that requires an admission of guilt and expression of remorse from plaintiff-husband.

The law is well-established that a party seeking preliminary injunctive relief must demonstrate a likelihood of ultimate success on the merits, irreparable harm in the absence of injunctive relief, and a weighing of equities in his favor * * *. A judicial determination regarding likelihood of success on the merits does not * * * amount to a pre-determination of the issues. Rather, "the showing of a *likelihood* of success ... must not be equated with the showing of a *certainty* of success" on the merits * * *.

Here, the undisputed evidence was sufficient to demonstrate a likelihood of plaintiffs' ultimate success. Plaintiffs established a prima facie case of libel on the merits, since the offending statements injure plaintiff-husband's reputation and good name, and otherwise expose him to "public contempt, scorn, obloquy, ridicule, shame or disgrace", and "induce an evil opinion of him in the minds of right-thinking persons" (Lawlor v. Gallagher Presidents' Report, Inc., 394 F.Supp. 721, 726 (S.D.N.Y.1975), *remanded*, 538 F.2d 311 (2d Cir.1976); Privitera v. Town of Phelps, 79 A.D.2d 1, 3, 435 N.Y.S.2d 402). In contrast, defendant's charge of a 38–year-old rape is unsupported by any objective evidence or corroborating testimony, as is, necessarily, its accompanying claim of repressed memory. Indeed, the allegation of rape is seriously challenged by the *undisputed* fact that the 1953 affair continued for two years after its occurrence, and that defendant had a second, six-year affair with plaintiff-husband 30 years later.

Further, defendant's credibility is likely to be hampered by the shocking and, again, unsupported accusations of a sexual nature with which she has impugned the morals of plaintiff-husband's 89–year-old mother and plaintiff-wife, and by the various contradictions contained in documents authored by defendant, including a claim that she bore plaintiff-husband's child in the 1950's, and a subsequent denial that she had ever made such a claim.

Defendant's attempt to continue her offending communications as protected free speech under the First Amendment and its New York State Constitution analogue, Article One, Section Eight, must fail. Constitutional free speech protections are intended to encourage "debate on public issues [that is] uninhibited, robust, and wide-open" (New York Times Co. v. Sullivan, 376 U.S. 254, 270, 84 S.Ct. 710, 721, 11 L.Ed.2d 686). Distinctions are drawn where, as here, the defamatory speech does not advance such societal interests and, indeed, concerns a private individual (Gertz v. Robert Welch, Inc., 418 U.S. 323, 344, 94 S.Ct. 2997, 3009, 41 L.Ed.2d 789). Moreover, these protections are not absolute (Nebraska Press Association v. Stuart, 427 U.S. 539, 570, 96 S.Ct. 2791, 2808, 49 L.Ed.2d 683). As noted in Gitlow v. State of New York, 268 U.S. 652, 666, 45 S.Ct. 625, 630, 69 L.Ed. 1138, "the freedom of speech ... secured by the Constitution, does not confer an absolute right to speak or publish, without responsibility, whatever one may choose * * *."

In assessing plaintiffs' entitlement to a preliminary injunction, we have further concluded that the potential harm caused by defendant's continued communications and the picketing of plaintiffs' home is irreparable, as it is capable of injuring plaintiff-husband's standing and reputation in all aspects of his personal and professional life, and of inflicting serious psychological and emotional damage to both plaintiffs, as well as to their family members. Such harm is not readily compensable in damages.

We have also weighed the relative hardship that may be suffered by defendant if the preliminary injunction is granted, and conclude that the degree of harm to be caused to plaintiffs if the conduct continues unabated far exceeds any which may be caused to defendant if her picketing and other communications are enjoined pending the trial.

With respect to the production of defendant's sealed divorce records, it is our conclusion that defendant's allegations that plaintiff-husband deprived her of "any chance for a happy marriage" and so traumatized her that she lost the "possibility of intimacy and friendships with either sex", render these records potentially relevant to the instant proceeding. We are cognizant, however, that the interests of defendant's former husband may be affected, and it is, accordingly, the directive of this Court that the records be examined *in camera* for materiality and relevance to this litigation, and that discovery rulings be tailored to meet any reasonable objections raised by defendant's former spouse.

Finally, it is the view of this Court that plaintiffs have failed to put forth a sufficiently compelling reason to overcome the strong public policy of favoring open judicial proceedings (Judiciary Law § 4 * * *).

Accordingly, the order, * * * which denied plaintiffs' motion for a preliminary injunction and for closure of all proceedings and a sealing of the record, should be modified, on the law and in the exercise of discretion, to grant plaintiffs' motion for a preliminary injunction, and otherwise affirmed, without costs; and the order of said court, entered July 23, 1991, which, *inter alia,* granted defendant's motion for a protective order, and denied plaintiffs' cross-motion to compel production of sealed records pertaining to defendant's 1985 divorce, should be modified, on the law and in the exercise of discretion, to grant plaintiffs' cross-motion, to the extent that said records will be produced for *in camera* inspection, with notice and opportunity to be heard accorded to defendant's former spouse before any discovery determinations are made, and otherwise affirmed, without costs.

* * *

All concur.

NOTES

1. While the property right/personal right distinction is usually no longer a bar to injunctive relief, courts may nevertheless refuse relief because of a variety of other considerations. Sometimes the denials may be based on traditional equitable concepts, such as adequacy of the legal remedy. Oftentimes, a refusal to grant an injunction may be couched in traditional equitable maxims that tend to mask the underlying constitutional or policy concerns. A good example of this is Sixty–Seventh Minnesota State Senate v. Beens, 406 U.S. 187, 92 S.Ct. 1477, 32 L.Ed.2d 1 (1972), where the Supreme Court, in reversing a lower court order reducing the size of the Minnesota state legislature, seemed to emphasize limits on the remedial powers of equity as well as expressing its constitutional and federalism concerns. At other times, courts will rely overtly on such non-equitable considerations. Much of the defamation and privacy material in this section exemplifies this approach.

The material in this section also emphasizes the practicability concerns that sometimes preclude the issuance of injunctive relief. These are not unique to injunctions and are treated extensively in the chapter on specific performance of contracts. *See infra* Chapter 7. Practicability concerns include (1) a court's reluctance or inability to supervise or become significantly involved in the policing of the injunction; and (2) the futility of utilizing an injunction to force unwilling parties to continue a strained personal relationship. While the property right/personal right distinction will not normally bar injunctive relief, the more a case involves personal or societal concerns, as opposed to tangible property interests, the more practicability becomes a potential obstacle to the injunctive remedy.

2. Are *Kramer* and *Bingham* reconcilable? Should it make a difference that *Kramer* involves permanent injunctive relief while the *Bingham* plaintiff seeks only a preliminary injunction? Or does that fact make the cases even more difficult to reconcile? Is it relevant that *Bingham* more than *Kramer* involves sensitive matters of personal privacy?

3. Traditionally, injunctive relief has been more available in the trade libel area than in personal reputation defamation cases. For example, in perhaps the most graphic business defamation cases, courts have enjoined dissatisfied car owners from painting lemons or white elephants on automobiles so as to identify them as having been sold by the plaintiffs. *See, e.g.,* Carter v. Knapp Motor Co., 243 Ala. 600, 11 So.2d 383 (1943); Menard v. Houle, 298 Mass. 546, 11 N.E.2d 436 (1937). *But cf.* Schmoldt v. Oakley, 390 P.2d 882 (Okl.1964). This greater willingness to enjoin trade libel

> reflects a recognition by the courts that, apart from the inadequacy of the damage remedy to protect the plaintiff's needs, the defendant's claim to jury trial and to protection against prior restraint on speech is not compelling. The facts are often undisputed, and jury trial is not necessary to protect free speech, since judges are not likely to be prejudiced against communication of this sort.

Developments in the Law—Injunctions, 78 Harv. L. Rev. 994, 1010 (1965).

This distinction may have been diminished by recent constitutional developments in the "commercial speech" area. In an early case, Valentine v. Chrestensen, 316 U.S. 52, 62 S.Ct. 920, 86 L.Ed. 1262 (1942), the United States Supreme Court stated that the First Amendment imposes no restraint on government with respect to regulating "purely commercial advertising." From this statement, the theory developed that expression "tainted by some commercial element was second class speech, undeserving of First Amendment protection." Comment, *Prior Restraints and Restrictions on Advertising After* Virginia Pharmacy Board: *The Commercial Speech Doctrine Reformulated,* 43 Mo. L. Rev. 64 (1978). However, more recently, the United States Supreme Court has rejected the theory and made it clear that commercial speech, like other speech and expression, is protected by the First Amendment. *See, e.g.,* Virginia State Bd. of Pharmacy v. Virginia Citizens Consumer Council, Inc., 425 U.S. 748, 96 S.Ct. 1817, 48 L.Ed.2d 346 (1976).

Nevertheless, the degree of First Amendment protection for commercial speech (speech that advertises a product or proposes a commercial transaction) is not as substantial as that afforded other types of speech activity. Indeed, false or misleading commercial speech remains largely unprotected. This arguably may provide some support for sanctioning injunctive relief against trade libel, even though the First Amendment prohibits other types of defamation from being similarly enjoined. Nevertheless, in contrast to the earlier cases involving disgruntled automobile purchasers, more recent commercial defamation decisions rely heavily on the prior restraint concept to deny injunctive relief. *See, e.g.,* Paradise Hills Associates v. Procel, 235 Cal.App.3d 1528, 1 Cal.Rptr.2d 514 (1991) (preliminary injunction against home purchasers denied on prior restraint grounds at least where developer did not allege that purchasers' statements were false); Degroen v. Mark Toyota–Volvo, Inc., 811 P.2d 443 (Colo.Ct.App.1991) (attempt to enjoin picketing of auto dealership by disgruntled father of purchaser constituted an invalid prior restraint under First Amendment); Pittman v. Cohn Communities, Inc., 240 Ga. 106, 239 S.E.2d 526 (1977) (injunctive relief denied on First Amendment grounds against home purchasers who placed signs in their yards stating, "BEFORE YOU BUY IN SUNWOOD TALK TO THIS DISSATISFIED OWNER"); Sid Dillon Chevrolet–Oldsmobile–Pontiac, Inc. v. Sullivan, 251 Neb. 722, 559 N.W.2d 740 (1997) ("absent a prior adversarial determination that the complained of publication is false or a misleading representation of fact, equity will not issue to enjoin a libel or slander, unless [it] is published (1) in violation of a trust or contract or (2) in aid of another tort or unlawful act, or injunctive relief is essential for the preservation of a property right"; request for injunction by auto dealer against disgruntled customer denied); Franklin Chalfont Associates v. Kalikow, 392 Pa.Super. 452, 573 A.2d 550 (1990) (attempt by developer to enjoin use of signs and peaceful picketing by home purchasers that disparaged developer and its product held to be unconstitutional prior restraint).

Should comments by a consumer about a seller's product be treated as "advertising" and thus be afforded a lower degree of First Amendment protection or should such consumer speech be given full First Amendment protection? After all, isn't it only sellers who advertise? Should a court be more suspicious of an action to enjoin the speech of a disgruntled consumer than it is of an attempt to regulate or suppress such speech by a product seller? On the other hand, shouldn't a court be concerned about activities that are aimed at "blackmailing" or otherwise coercing a seller into compliance with a consumer's unwarranted demand?

GALELLA v. ONASSIS

United States Court of Appeals, Second Circuit, 1973.
487 F.2d 986.

Before SMITH, HAYS and TIMBERS, CIRCUIT JUDGES.

J. JOSEPH SMITH, CIRCUIT JUDGE:

Donald Galella, a free-lance photographer, appeals from a summary judgment dismissing his complaint against three Secret Service agents for false arrest, malicious prosecution and interference with trade (S.D.N.Y., Edward C. McLean, Judge), the dismissal after trial of his identical complaint against Jacqueline Onassis and the grant of injunctive relief to defendant Onassis on her counterclaim. * * * Galella raises the First Amendment as an absolute shield against liability to any sanctions. The judgments dismissing the complaints are affirmed; the grant of injunctive relief is affirmed as herein modified. * * *

Galella is a free-lance photographer specializing in the making and sale of photographs of well-known persons. Defendant Onassis is the widow of the late President, John F. Kennedy, mother of the two Kennedy children, John and Caroline, and is the wife of Aristotle Onassis, widely known shipping figure and reputed multimillionaire. John Walsh, James Kalafatis and John Connelly are U.S. Secret Service agents assigned to the duty of protecting the Kennedy children under 18 U.S.C.A. § 3056, which provides for protection of the children of deceased presidents up to the age of 16.

Galella fancies himself as a "paparazzo" (literally a kind of annoying insect, perhaps roughly equivalent to the English "gadfly.") Paparazzi make themselves as visible to the public and obnoxious to their photographic subjects as possible to aid in the advertisement and wide sale of their works.

Some examples of Galella's conduct brought out at trial are illustrative. Galella took pictures of John Kennedy riding his bicycle in Central Park across the way from his home. He jumped out into the boy's path, causing the agents concern for John's safety. The agents' reaction and interrogation of Galella led to Galella's arrest and his action against the agents; Galella on other occasions interrupted Caroline at tennis, and invaded the children's private schools. At one time he came uncomfortably close in a power boat to Mrs. Onassis swimming. He often jumped and postured around while taking pictures of her party notably at a theater opening but also on numerous other occasions. He followed a practice of bribing apartment house, restaurant and nightclub doormen as well as romancing a family servant to keep him advised of the movements of the family.

After detention and arrest following complaint by the Secret Service agents protecting Mrs. Onassis' son and his acquittal in the state court, Galella filed suit in state court against the agents and Mrs. Onassis. Galella claimed that under orders from Mrs. Onassis, the three agents had falsely arrested and maliciously prosecuted him, and that this incident in addition to several others described in the complaint constituted an unlawful interference with his trade.

Mrs. Onassis answered denying any role in the arrest or any part in the claimed interference with his attempts to photograph her, and counterclaimed for damages and injunctive relief, charging that Galella had invaded her privacy, assaulted and battered her, intentionally inflicted emotional distress and engaged in a campaign of harassment.

* * *

Certain incidents of photographic coverage by Galella, subsequent to an agreement among the parties for Galella not to so engage, resulted in the issuance of a temporary restraining order to prevent further harassment of Mrs. Onassis and the children. Galella was enjoined from "harassing, alarming, startling, tormenting, touching the person of the defendant . . . or her children . . . and from blocking their movements in the public places and thoroughfares, invading their immediate zone of privacy by means of physical movements, gestures or with photographic equipment and from performing any act reasonably calculated to place the lives and safety of the defendant . . . and her children in jeopardy." Within two months, Galella was charged with violation of the temporary restraining order; a new order was signed which required that the photographer keep 100 yards from the Onassis apartment and 50 yards from the person of the defendant and her children. Surveillance was also prohibited.

* * *

After a six-week trial the court dismissed Galella's claim and granted relief to both the defendant and the intervenor. Galella was enjoined from (1) keeping the defendant and her children under surveillance or following any of them; (2) approaching within 100 yards of the home of defendant or her children, or within 100 yards of either child's school or within 75 yards of either child or 50 yards of defendant; (3) using the name, portrait or picture of defendant or her children for advertising; (4) attempting to communicate with defendant or her children except through her attorney.

* * *

[The court then concluded that the dismissal of Galella's claim against the Secret Service agents had been proper because they were entitled to official immunity.]

* * *

Discrediting all of Galella's testimony the court found the photographer guilty of harassment, intentional infliction of emotional distress, assault and battery, commercial exploitation of defendant's personality, and invasion of privacy. Fully crediting defendant's testimony, the court found no liability on Galella's claim. Evidence offered by the defense showed that Galella had on occasion intentionally physically touched Mrs. Onassis and her daughter, caused fear of physical contact in his frenzied attempts to get their pictures, followed defendant and her children too closely in an automobile, endangered the safety of the children while they were swimming, water skiing and horseback riding. Galella cannot successfully challenge the court's finding of tortious conduct.

Finding that Galella had "insinuated himself into the very fabric of Mrs. Onassis' life . . .," the court framed its relief in part on the need to prevent further invasion of the defendant's privacy. Whether or not this accords with present New York law, there is no doubt that it is sustainable under New York's proscription of harassment.

Of course legitimate countervailing social needs may warrant some intrusion despite an individual's reasonable expectation of privacy and freedom from harassment. However the interference allowed may be no greater than that necessary to protect the overriding public interest. Mrs. Onassis was properly found to be a public figure and thus subject to news coverage. *See* Sidis v. F–R Publishing Corp., 113 F.2d 806 (2d Cir.), *cert. denied,* 311 U.S. 711, 61 S.Ct. 393, 85 L.Ed. 462 (1940). Nonetheless, Galella's action went far beyond the reasonable bounds of news gathering. When weighed against the *de minimis* public importance of the daily activities of the defendant, Galella's constant surveillance, his obtrusive and intruding presence, was unwarranted and unreasonable. If there were any doubt in our minds, Galella's inexcusable conduct toward defendant's minor children would resolve it.

Galella does not seriously dispute the court's finding of tortious conduct. Rather, he sets up the First Amendment as a wall of immunity protecting newsmen from any liability for their conduct while gathering news. There is no such scope to the First Amendment right. Crimes and torts committed in news gathering are not protected. * * * There is no threat to a free press in requiring its agents to act within the law.

* * *

Injunctive relief is appropriate. Galella has stated his intention to continue his coverage of defendant so long as she is newsworthy. * * *

The injunction, however, is broader than is required to protect the defendant. Relief must be tailored to protect Mrs. Onassis from the "paparazzo" attack which distinguishes Galella's behavior from that of other photographers; it should not unnecessarily infringe on reasonable efforts to "cover" defendant. Therefore, we modify the court's order to prohibit only (1) any approach within twenty-five (25) feet of defendant or any touching of the person of the defendant Jacqueline Onassis; (2) any blocking of her movement in public places and thoroughfares; (3) any act foreseeably or reasonably calculated to place the life and safety of defendant in jeopardy; and (4) any conduct which would reasonably be foreseen to harass, alarm or frighten the defendant.

NOTES

1. The common law right of privacy being enforced in *Galella* has been described by one court as follows:

> The tort of invasion of privacy was originally conceptualized by Samuel D. Warren and Louis D. Brandeis in their seminal law review article entitled "The Right to Privacy", 4 Harv.L.Rev. 193 (1890). Warren and Brandeis characterized the right of privacy as "the right to be let alone", and they advanced two major threats to privacy. * * * One threat was the press, which they viewed as "overstepping in every direction the obvious bounds of propriety and of decency." * * * The second threat was the advent of "numerous mechanical devices" which "threaten[ed] to make good the prediction that" what is whispered in the closet shall be proclaimed from the house-tops. *Id.* at 195.

> The next major advancement in the development of the tort of invasion of privacy occurred seventy years later when William L. Prosser

published his law review article "Privacy." 48 Cal.L.Rev. 383 (1960). Prosser asserted that privacy was comprised of four distinct torts: (1) intrusion upon seclusion or solitude; (2) public disclosure of private facts; (3) publicity which places the plaintiff in a false light; and (4) appropriation of name or likeness. *Id.* at 389. These four torts were later adopted by the Restatement (Second) of Torts in sections 652B–652E. * * *

* * *

An actionable intrusion upon seclusion consists of "an intentional interference with [a person's] interest in solitude or seclusion, either as to his person or his private affairs or concerns...." Restatement (Second) of Torts § 652B, comment a. As stated in comment b of § 652B, the interference may be

> by physical intrusion into a place in which the plaintiff has secluded himself, as when the defendant forces his way into the plaintiff's room in a hotel or insists over the plaintiff's objection in entering his home. It may also be by the use of the defendant's sense, with or without mechanical aids, to oversee or overhear the plaintiff's private affairs, as by looking into his upstairs windows with binoculars or tapping his telephone wires.

This tort generally does not apply to matters which occur in a public place or a place otherwise open to the public eye. * * *

* * *

Conduct that amounts to a persistent course of hounding, harassment and unreasonable surveillance, even if conducted in a public or semi-public place, may nevertheless rise to the level of invasion of privacy based on intrusion upon seclusion. *See, e.g., Galella.* The Restatement recognizes that conduct that is repeated with such persistence and frequency as to amount to a "course of hounding the plaintiff, [and] becomes a substantial burden to his existence" may constitute an invasion of privacy. § 652 B, comment d. * * *

Wolfson v. Lewis, 924 F.Supp. 1413, 1418–20 (E.D.Pa.1996).

Courts have generally been willing to issue injunctive relief against intrusive privacy violations. *See, e.g., Wolfson, supra* (injunction granted against "harassing, hounding, following, intruding, frightening or terrorizing plaintiffs" where defendant made use of shotgun mikes, cameras and sound equipment); Goosen v. Walker, 714 So.2d 1149 (Fla.Dist.Ct.App.1998) (injunction granted enjoining neighbor from photographing or videotaping plaintiffs or pretending to do so); *see* Ethan E. Litwin, *The Investigative Reporter's Freedom & Responsibility: Reconciling Freedom of Press with Privacy Rights,* 86 Geo. L.J. 1093 (1998).

2. An injunction was also issued against intrusive conduct in Kramer v. Downey, 680 S.W.2d 524 (Tex.App.1984). The plaintiff, a married man, had had an extramarital affair with the defendant. After he ended the brief affair, she "began a pattern of conduct to thrust herself into his presence and otherwise to disrupt his domestic and professional life." *Id.* at 525. The plaintiff was granted an injunction analogous to that used in domestic

relations cases to minimize friction between estranged couples. In addition, the plaintiff was awarded $1,000 in actual damages and $25,000 in exemplary damages, of which $13,500 were remitted. For a discussion of the damages recoverable in actions for invasion of privacy, see Dorsey D. Ellis, *Damages and the Privacy Tort: Sketching a "Legal Profile,"* 64 Iowa L. Rev. 1111 (1979).

MICHAELS v. INTERNET ENTERTAINMENT GROUP, INC.

United States District Court, Central District of California, 1998.
5 F.Supp.2d 823.

PREGERSON, DISTRICT JUDGE.

This matter comes before the Court on the motions of the plaintiff, Bret Michaels ("Michaels"), and the intervenor, Pamela Anderson Lee ("Lee") (collectively, the "plaintiffs"), for a preliminary injunction to prevent dissemination of a videotape ("the Tape") * * *. Dissemination of the Tape by defendant Internet Entertainment Group, Inc. ("IEG") is currently prohibited by this Court's Temporary Restraining Order ("TRO"), issued February 27, 1998. IEG has consented to several extensions of the TRO.

* * *

A. FACTUAL AND PROCEDURAL BACKGROUND

Michaels is a musician, best known as the lead singer of the rock band "Poison." Michaels asserts that he is now engaged in a second career as a feature film director. * * * Lee is a well-known television and film actor. * * *

Defendant IEG is a corporation involved in the distribution of adult entertainment material through a subscription service on the Internet.

On or about October 31, 1994, Michaels and Lee recorded the Tape, which depicts them having sex.

On December 31, 1997, Michaels received a letter from IEG claiming that IEG had acquired the Tape and all rights necessary to publish the Tape. * * *

On January 12, 1998, Michaels wrote to IEG through counsel to advise IEG that Michaels had not authorized any distribution of the Tape, and notifying IEG that any publication of the Tape would violate Michaels's copyright therein, as well as his common law and statutory rights to privacy and publicity involving his name and likeness. * * * The letter denied that any third party had the right to convey Michaels's interest in the Tape. The letter included a demand that IEG cease and desist from attempts to disseminate or exploit the Tape.

On January 22, 1998, Michaels registered the Tape with the Register of Copyrights as an audiovisual work entitled "Private Home Tape" and authored by Michaels. * * *

Michaels filed this action on January 23, 1998, alleging five claims: (1) copyright infringement against IEG; (2) false designation of origin under the Lanham Act against IEG; (3) state-law invasion of privacy based on publicity of the Tape over Westwood One's radio affiliates against all defendants; (4) violation of the California common law right of publicity against all defendants; and (5) violation of the California statutory right of publicity under California Civil Code section 3344 against all defendants. In addition, Michaels's complaint includes a sixth cause of action which is a prayer for injunctive relief on all claims.

Also on January 23, 1998, Michaels applied ex parte for a temporary restraining order to prohibit the defendants from duplicating, publishing, promoting, marketing or advertising the Tape. The application alleged that IEG announced that it would publish the Tape on its Internet subscription service, "ClubLove," on Monday, January 26, 1998. The Court issued the TRO on January 23, 1998. The Court required that Michaels post a $50,000 bond. The Court scheduled a preliminary injunction hearing for February 2, 1998.

* * *

[The Court then concluded that the plaintiffs were entitled to a preliminary injunction prohibiting acts that would violate their exclusive rights in the Tape under the Copyright Act.]

C.   RIGHT TO PUBLICITY

Under California law, the plaintiffs own the right to exploit their names and likenesses for commercial gain. The common law of California recognizes this right of publicity in a person's name, likeness and identity. *See* Midler v. Ford Motor Company, 849 F.2d 460, 462 (9th Cir.1988). The California legislature has created a statutory right of publicity in a person's "name, voice, signature, photograph, or likeness." Cal. Civ.Code § 3344(a). The statutory right complements, rather than codifies, the common law right. This distinction is important because the common law right protects a broader range of interests against a broader range of infringing conduct than does the statutory right. *See* White v. Samsung Electronics America, Inc., 971 F.2d 1395, 1397–99 (9th Cir.1992); Eastwood v. Superior Court (National Enquirer), 149 Cal.App.3d 409, 198 Cal.Rptr. 342, 346 n.6 (1983).

Under California law, the plaintiffs may seek to protect their rights of publicity through an action for damages. The plaintiffs may also seek to enjoin others from exploiting their names or likenesses at all. *See* Lugosi v. Universal Pictures, 25 Cal.3d 813, 160 Cal.Rptr. 323, 328, 603 P.2d 425 (Cal.1979); *Eastwood*, 198 Cal.Rptr. at 348.

* * *

[The Court then concluded that plaintiffs' claim for violation of the right to publicity was not preempted by the Copyright Act.]

The elements of a common law right to publicity claim are "(1) the defendant's use of the plaintiff's identity; (2) the appropriation of plaintiff's name or likeness to defendant's advantage, commercial or otherwise; (3) lack of consent; and (4) resulting injury." *Eastwood*, 198 Cal.Rptr. at 347. The statutory cause of action under section 3344 requires two additional elements: knowing use of the plaintiff's name, photograph or likeness for purposes of advertising or solicitation of purchases, and a "direct connection" between the use and the commercial purpose. *Id*.

The first element, use of the plaintiffs' names and identities, is satisfied by evidence that IEG used the plaintiffs' names and bodily descriptions to promote the tape on television and radio. * * *

The second element, commercial advantage, is satisfied by IEG's statements regarding the nature of its business. IEG is a subscription service with approximately 100,000 members, each of whom pay $14.95 per month. * * * IEG's president estimated that up to one-third of its paying members would cancel their subscriptions if IEG did not deliver the Tape. * * *

The third element, lack of consent, is not seriously contested. IEG's assertion that Michaels or Lee secretly licensed it to distribute the Tape is not supported by any evidence and is controverted by Michaels's and Lee's declarations and deposition testimony. If IEG had come forward with evidence of consent, this element might require an evidentiary hearing in order for the Court to weigh the credibility of conflicting testimony. Under these circumstances, however, the evidence of lack of consent is uncontroverted.

The fourth element, injury, is satisfied by two showings. First, if IEG's membership revenue has increased due to its use of the plaintiffs' names and likenesses, IEG has deprived the plaintiffs of money they could have made by exploiting their right to publicity on their own or through licensees. Second, the plaintiffs have presented evidence that publicity in association with pornography has damaged their attempts to establish and maintain careers in mainstream entertainment. * * *

Lee has submitted a declaration by entertainment lawyer Henry Holmes, who states that in his opinion, Lee's prospects as an actor and endorser of products will be damaged by publicity in association with pornography. * * *

The Court also finds that the statutory elements are satisfied. IEG knew that it was using the plaintiffs' names and likeness in connection with promotion of the Tape. The use of their names and likenesses was directly connected with promotion of the Tape.

In light of the foregoing, the Court concludes that the plaintiffs have demonstrated a likelihood of success on the merits of their claim for violation of the California common law and statutory right to publicity.

Several courts have held that a celebrity's property interest in his name and likeness is unique, and cannot be adequately compensated by money damages. *See* Ali v. Playgirl, Inc., 447 F.Supp. 723, 729 (S.D.N.Y. 1978); Uhlaender v. Henricksen, 316 F.Supp. 1277, 1283 (D.Minn.1970); *see generally* 1 J. Thomas McCarthy, Rights of Publicity & Privacy § 11.6[B] (1997).

The plaintiffs have submitted evidence that they have invested years of effort in establishing their public personae, and that their ability to exploit their investments will be irreparably harmed by exploitation of their names and likeness in connection with the marketing of the Tape. * * * The Court concludes based on this evidence that the plaintiffs have made the requisite showing of irreparable injury.

While the plaintiffs have an exclusive right to exploit their names and likenesses for commercial purposes, they do not have an exclusive right to the use of their names and likenesses in the publication of matters of public interest. California's publicity statute specifically exempts "use of a name, voice, signature, photograph, or likeness in connection with any news, public affairs, or sports broadcast or account, or any political campaign." Cal. Civ.Code § 3344(d). Courts applying the common law right of publicity have recognized that the First Amendment requires a similar exemption for uses in connection with matters of public interest. *See Eastwood*, 198 Cal.Rptr. at 349; Cher v. Forum Int'l, Ltd., 692 F.2d 634, 639 (9th Cir.1982).

The plaintiffs are entitled to an injunction against uses of their names or likenesses to sell the Tape. The injunction may not reach the use of their names or likenesses to report or comment on matters of public interest. Nor may it reach the use of their names or likenesses to attract attention to IEG as a news medium. *See Cher*, 692 F.2d at 639 (holding that use of a person's name or likeness to advertise a magazine is not actionable provided that advertisement does not falsely claim endorsement); Montana v. San Jose Mercury News, 34 Cal.App.4th 790, 40 Cal.Rptr.2d 639, 642 (1995).

Crafting an injunction to prevent irreparable injury arising from violation of the plaintiffs' rights to publicity requires "a weighing of the private interest of the right of publicity against matters of public interest calling for constitutional protection, and a consideration of the character of these competing interests." * * * Where the relief sought is damages, the plaintiff's property rights can be protected at minimal risk to free expression. *See* Zacchini v. Scripps–Howard Broadcasting Co., 433 U.S. 562, 97 S.Ct. 2849, 53 L.Ed.2d 965 (1977). Where, as here, the plaintiffs ask the Court to impose a prior restraint, the risk to free expression is at its highest. *See* Nebraska Press Ass'n v. Stuart, 427 U.S. 539, 559, 96 S.Ct. 2791, 2803, 49 L.Ed.2d 683 (1976); Matter of Providence Journal Co., 820 F.2d 1342, 1350 (1st Cir.1986).

The words "promotion, marketing, and advertising" in this preliminary injunction therefore apply only to the use of the plaintiffs' names, likenesses or identities to sell the Tape. This limitation is required to prevent the imposition of a prior restraint on IEG's ability to comment on matters of public interest.

"Promotion, marketing, and advertising" are to be understood as a form of commercial speech, that is speech which "proposes a commercial transaction." Board of Trustees of the State University of New York v. Fox, 492 U.S. 469, 482, 109 S.Ct. 3028, 3036, 106 L.Ed.2d 388 (1989). This distinction between speech that proposes a commercial transaction, and speech that comments on matters of public interest has been applied regularly to distinguish protected speech from actionable misuse of a person's name or likeness for commercial gain. The Ninth Circuit recognized this distinction in an action for damages resulting from the use of a famous basketball player's name to sell cars: "While Lew Alcindor's basketball record may be said to be 'newsworthy,' its use is not automatically privileged. GMC used the information in the context of an automobile advertisement, not in a news or sports account." Abdul–Jabbar v. General Motors Corp., 85 F.3d 407, 416 (9th Cir.1996); *see also, Midler,* 849 F.2d at 462. Other courts have recognized this distinction in enjoining commercial uses of a person's name, likeness or identity. *See* Onassis v. Christian Dior–New York, Inc., 122 Misc.2d 603, 614, 472 N.Y.S.2d 254, 262 (N.Y.Sup.Ct.1984); *Ali,* 447 F.Supp. 723; Rosemont Enterprises, Inc. v. Urban Systems, Inc., 72 Misc.2d 788, 340 N.Y.S.2d 144 (N.Y.Sup.Ct. 1973), *as modified,* 42 A.D.2d 544, 345 N.Y.S.2d 17 (1973); *see also,* Shamsky v. Garan, Inc., 167 Misc.2d 149, 632 N.Y.S.2d 930 (N.Y.Sup.Ct. 1995).

D. RIGHT TO PRIVACY

California recognizes a tort cause of action for violation of the right to privacy. *See* Diaz v. Oakland Tribune, Inc., 139 Cal.App.3d 118, 188 Cal.Rptr. 762 (1983). Four distinct torts are included under the rubric of right to privacy: (1) public disclosure of private facts; (2) intrusion upon the plaintiff's solitude or into his private affairs; (3) false light publicity; and (4) appropriation of the plaintiff's name and likeness. *Id.* at 767. The fourth branch of the tort is analyzed extensively above under the right to publicity claim. Michaels and Lee have also asserted the first and second branches of the privacy tort, public disclosure of private facts and intrusion into private affairs.

The elements of the tort of public disclosure of private facts are (1) public disclosure (2) of a private fact (3) which would be offensive and objectionable to the reasonable person and (4) which is not of legitimate public concern. *Id.* at 768. The elements of the tort of intrusion into private affairs are similar. The intrusion into private affairs need not be physical, and in order to be actionable must be offensive to a reasonable person. *See* Aisenson v. American Broadcasting Co., Inc., 220 Cal.App.3d 146, 269 Cal.Rptr. 379, 387 (1990).

Both the public disclosure and intrusion torts are subject to a newsworthy privilege, which protects the First Amendment freedom to report on matters of public concern. * * * Newsworthiness is defined broadly to include not only matters of public policy, but any matter of public concern, including the accomplishments, everyday lives, and romantic involvements of famous people. *See Eastwood*, 198 Cal.Rptr. at 350.

The privilege to report newsworthy information is not without limit. "Where the publicity is so offensive as to constitute a morbid and sensational prying into private lives for its own sake, it serves no legitimate public interest and is not deserving of protection." *Diaz*, 188 Cal.Rptr. at 767 (internal quotation marks omitted); Virgil v. Time, Inc., 527 F.2d 1122, 1129 (9th Cir.1975); Restatement 2d Torts 652D cmt. h.

Here, distribution of the Tape on the Internet would constitute public disclosure. The content of the Tape—Michaels and Lee engaged in sexual relations—constitutes a set of private facts whose disclosure would be objectionable to a reasonable person.

IEG makes three related contentions based on Lee's status as a "sex symbol." First, IEG contends that matters regarding sex should not be considered private with regard to Lee because her acting career is in part based on sex. Second, IEG contends that because a foreign Internet source has already released part of the Tape, the facts it contains are no longer private. Third, IEG contends that Lee's status as a sex symbol, and Michaels's status as a rock star make the sex acts depicted on the Tape newsworthy.

IEG contends that because Lee has appeared nude in magazines, movies and publicly distributed videotapes, the facts contained on the Tape depicting her having sex are no longer private. IEG's contention unreasonably blurs the line between fiction and reality. Lee is a professional actor. She has played roles involving sex and sexual appeal. The fact that she has performed a role involving sex does not, however, make her real sex life open to the public. * * *

IEG contends that the wide distribution of a different videotape, one depicting sexual relations between Lee and her husband Tommy Lee, negates any privacy interest that Lee might have in the Tape depicting sexual relations with Michaels. The facts depicted on the Tommy Lee tape, however, are different from the facts depicted on the Michaels Tape. Sexual relations are among the most personal and intimate of acts. The Court is not prepared to conclude that public exposure of one sexual encounter forever removes a person's privacy interest in all subsequent and previous sexual encounters.

It is also clear that Michaels has a privacy interest in his sex life. While Michaels's voluntary assumption of fame as a rock star throws open his private life to some extent, even people who voluntarily enter the public sphere retain a privacy interest in the most intimate details of their lives. * * *

The Court notes that the private matter at issue here is not the fact that Lee and Michaels were romantically involved. Because they sought fame, Lee and Michaels must tolerate some public exposure of the fact of their involvement. *See Eastwood*, 198 Cal.Rptr. at 351. The fact recorded on the Tape, however, is not that Lee and Michaels were romantically involved, but rather the visual and aural details of their sexual relations, facts which are ordinarily considered private even for celebrities. For this reason, IEG's reliance on Carlisle v. Fawcett Publications, Inc., 201 Cal.App.2d 733, 20 Cal.Rptr. 405 (1962), is misplaced. *Carlisle*, like *Eastwood*, involved publicity about the fact of a famous person's romantic involvement, as well as some of the details of that involvement. Neither case, however, involved graphic depictions of the most intimate aspects of the relationships.

In short, the Court concludes that the private facts depicted on the Michaels Tape have not become public either by virtue of Lee's professional appearances as an actor, or by dissemination of the Tommy Lee videotape.

IEG presents evidence that a 148–second clip from the Tape was posted on the Internet on or about April 16, 1998. * * * IEG contends that the publication of this clip converts the intimate activities depicted on the Tape to matters of public knowledge, and that, therefore, the plaintiffs no longer have a privacy interest to assert in the Tape. *See* Lee v. Penthouse Int'l Ltd., 1997 WL 33384309, 25 Med. L. Rptr. 1651, 1656 (C.D.Cal.1997) (granting defendant's motion for summary judgment on claim for disclosure of private facts because photographs at issue had already been published); Sipple v. Chronicle Publ'g Co., 154 Cal.App.3d 1040, 201 Cal.Rptr. 665 (1984) (holding that plaintiff's sexual orientation was no longer a private fact because it had previously been published).

In *Sipple* and *Lee*, however, all of the matters in which the plaintiffs asserted privacy were already well-known before the defendants re-published the information. Here, however, exposure of a small portion of the Tape began to occur ten days ago. The Court cannot conclude from this recent publication that the contents of the 148–second clip are now matters of public knowledge. Additionally, in *Sipple* and *Lee* the previously published information corresponded exactly to the information in which the plaintiffs asserted a privacy interest. *Sipple*, 201 Cal.Rptr. at 669; *Lee*, 25 Med. L. Rptr. at 1652. Here, the plaintiffs assert a privacy interest in all of the intimate activity depicted on the Tape. The plaintiffs' privacy interest in the unreleased portions of the Tape is undiminished.

The Court also notes that the ability of the plaintiffs to assert a privacy interest in the 148–second segment of the Tape does not affect the preliminary injunctive relief to which the plaintiffs are entitled. While the plaintiffs' privacy interest in the 148–second clip might be diminished, the plaintiffs' copyright in this portion of the Tape is unaffected. * * *

In order to determine whether the contents of the Tape are covered by the privilege for reporting private but newsworthy information, the Court must balance (1) the social value of the facts published; (2) the depth of the intrusion into ostensibly private affairs; and (3) the extent to which the party voluntarily acceded to a position of public notoriety. * * *

The first factor, the social value of the facts published, weighs against a finding of newsworthiness. It is difficult if not impossible to articulate a social value that will be advanced by dissemination of the Tape.

The second factor, depth of intrusion, also weighs against a finding of newsworthiness. This factor is to be applied with an eye toward community mores as to the depth of intrusion. *See Virgil*, 527 F.2d at 1131. At trial, it will be for the finder of fact to determine the state of community mores regarding the depth of intrusion. *Id.* For purposes of this motion, the Court determines that the plaintiffs are likely to convince the finder of fact that sexual relations are among the most private of private affairs, and that a video recording of two individuals engaged in such relations represents the deepest possible intrusion into such affairs.

The third factor, voluntary accession to fame, weighs in favor of a finding of newsworthiness. Michaels and Lee declare that they have cultivated fame throughout their careers. * * * In Lee's case, her fame arises in part from television and movie roles based on sex and sexual appeal.

The first two factors weigh heavily against a finding of newsworthiness for the contents of the Tape. The third factor weighs somewhat in favor of a finding of newsworthiness for the contents of the Tape. Weighing the factors together, the Court concludes that the plaintiffs have demonstrated a likelihood of success in meeting their burden to show that the contents of the Tape are not covered by the newsworthiness privilege.

The Court notes, however, a critical distinction which IEG has attempted to blur in its papers. The fact that the Tape exists and that it is the focus of this dispute is newsworthy. While the fact of the Tape's existence is somewhat intrusive into the plaintiffs' privacy, this intrusion is outweighed by the strong public interest in litigation concerning individuals' right to privacy. Although this preliminary injunction prohibits IEG from violating the plaintiffs' right to privacy by disseminating the contents of the Tape, the injunction does not restrict IEG's ability to participate in public discussion about the Tape or this litigation. * * *

By definition, an actionable disclosure of private facts must be highly offensive to a reasonable person. The injury inflicted is therefore to the plaintiffs' "human dignity and peace of mind." Although monetary damages are available for such injuries, they are difficult to quantify, and such injuries are to some extent irreparable. Furthermore, the privacy of the acts depicted on the Tape cannot be restored by monetary damages after the Tape becomes public. The nature of the Internet aggravates the irreparable nature of the injury. Once the Tape is posted on IEG's web site, it will be available for instant copying and further dissemination by IEG's subscribers.

In light of the foregoing, the Court concludes that the plaintiffs are entitled to a preliminary injunction prohibiting the dissemination of the

Tape in order to prevent a violation of the plaintiffs' state law right of privacy in the contents of the Tape.

* * *

IT IS HEREBY ORDERED that, pending final judgment or dismissal of this action, defendant IEG and its agents, officers, employees, attorneys, and those acting in concert with them are temporarily restrained from:

    1. Selling, attempting to sell, causing to be sold, permitting any other individual or entity to sell, copying, reproducing, preparing derivative works, publishing, disseminating, distributing, circulating, promoting, marketing, and advertising of the Michaels/Lee videotape (the "Tape");

    2. Selling, attempting to sell, causing to be sold, permitting any other individual or entity to sell, copying, reproducing, preparing derivative works, publishing, disseminating, distributing, circulating, promoting, marketing, and advertising of still photographs from the Tape, captured images from the Tape displayed on the Internet, and/or any downloaded hard copies of images from the Tape;

    3. Selling, attempting to sell, causing to be sold, permitting any other individual or entity to sell, copying, reproducing, preparing derivative works, publishing, disseminating, distributing, circulating, promoting, marketing, and advertising of all advertising, promotional material, or packaging referring to the Tape;

    4. Taking orders for copies of the Tape through the Internet or any other means;

    5. Shipping copies of the Tape to those purchasers who already have placed orders for copies of the Tape, or to anyone else; and

    6. Using Michaels's or Lee's name, likeness or identity in any manner, on or in products, merchandise, or goods, or for purposes of advertising or selling, or soliciting purchases of, products, merchandise, goods or services.

A bond in the amount of $50,000 shall be deemed adequate security for the payment of such costs and damages that may be incurred by the defendants if the relief herein is found to have been improvidently granted. Lee is directed to provide security for one-half of the $50,000 bond.

NOTES

    1. Another federal court has relied on *Michaels* to hold that a television news anchor, who was videotaped in various states of undress while taking part in a nightclub "wet t-shirt contest," was entitled to a preliminary injunction to restrain the commercial use of her videotaped images to promote the sale of sexually-related videos, website memberships, and other related goods. *See* Bosley v. Wildwett.com, 310 F.Supp.2d 914 (N.D.Ohio 2004).

2.   The foregoing material deals with each of the privacy torts except the "false light" category. Under the Restatement, publicity "that places [another] before the public in a false light is subject to liability * * * if (a) the false light in which the other is placed would be highly offensive to a reasonable person, and (b) the actor had knowledge of or acted in reckless disregard as to the falsity of the publicized matter and the false light in which the other would be placed." Restatement (Second) of Torts § 652E (1977). Note that while "false light" cases often involve defamation, this need not be the case. "It is enough that [plaintiff] is given unreasonable and highly objectionable publicity that attributes to him characteristics, conducts or beliefs that are false, and so is placed before the public in a false position." *Id.* cmt. b. Consider the following Restatement illustration:

> A is a war hero, distinguished for bravery in a famous battle. B makes and exhibits a motion picture concerning A's life, in which he inserts a detailed narrative of a fictitious private life attributed to A, including a nonexistent romance with a girl. B knows this matter to be false. Although A is not defamed by the motion picture, B is subject to liability to him for invasion of privacy.

Id. illus. 5.* Subsection (b) of the Restatement takes into account Time Inc. v. Hill, 385 U.S. 374 (1967), dealing with a magazine's pictorial treatment of a play based on a real episode which suggested that certain fictitious events in the play actually took place with respect to the real life parties. The Supreme Court in *Time, Inc.* held that the New York Times v. Sullivan standard was applicable to false light privacy cases. Why do you suppose injunctions are more difficult to obtain in false light cases than in other privacy invasions? Can the harm in other types of privacy cases be cured by more speech? What about in false light privacy cases? *See* Note, *Right of Privacy—Availability of Injunctive Relief for Invasions of Privacy*, 39 Mo. L. Rev. 647 (1974). For cases suggesting that injunctive relief may be available in false light privacy situations, see Leavy v. Cooney, 214 Cal.App.2d 496, 29 Cal.Rptr. 580 (1963); Commonwealth v. Wiseman, 356 Mass. 251, 249 N.E.2d 610 (1969). For an example of a refusal to permit injunctive relief in an arguable "false light" setting, see Doe v. Roe, 638 So.2d 826 (Ala.1994).

BORRA v. BORRA

Superior Court of New Jersey, Chancery Division, 2000.
333 N.J.Super. 607, 756 A.2d 647.

TORACK, J.S.C.

The issue presented is one of first impression: whether or not a Family Court can enjoin an ex-husband from contesting an ex-wife's application for membership in a country club in which the parties were members during the marriage. * * *

The parties were married on June 25, 1978. Two children were born of the marriage, William age eighteen, and Erik age eleven. The complaint

---

* Copyright 1977 by the American Law Institute. Reprinted with permission of the American Law Institute.

for divorce was filed by plaintiff, William E. Borra, III, (hereinafter "the husband"), on October 20, 1998. The parties entered into a property settlement agreement on March 7, 2000 resolving the majority of issues surrounding the divorce litigation. The parties provided in the property settlement agreement that the country club issue would be submitted to the court for determination. On March 15, 2000 the parties appeared before this court to be heard. The Final Judgment of Divorce was subsequently entered on March 29, 2000.

The parties joined the Tuxedo Country Club (hereinafter "the Club") in 1984. The initial bond for membership was paid from joint marital funds, as were the monthly membership fees. Under Club regulations the membership was acquired in the husband's name. The defendant, Jill Borra (hereinafter "the wife"), was extensively involved in Club activities, chairing various functions at the Club, hosting dinner parties for members, arranging golf tournaments with other country clubs, assisting in fundraising for tournaments, and attending various business meetings. The children regularly participate in golf lessons, children's tournaments, activities at the swimming pool, and other events at the Club. Since the parties' separation in April 1999, both parties have continued to regularly use and enjoy the Club facilities. During that time, they encountered each other only once at the Club. No words were exchanged.

As part of equitable distribution, the club membership and its value went to the husband. Once divorced, the wife will be allowed to use the facilities only as a "guest," limiting her access to the golf course, tennis courts, the pool, etc., to once every thirty days. The children are allowed to regularly use the facilities and to participate in the various activities and events offered by the Club. * * *

The wife has applied for membership in her own name, at her own expense. Upon filing the wife's name will be posted at the Club for ten days, during which time any member can object. After expiration of the ten-day period, the governing body makes the final determination on the application.

The husband intends to object to the wife's application. His reason for objection is that he did not want to encounter the wife while he is at the Club either alone or with another woman. The husband testified that he would feel uncomfortable and embarrassed if the wife were present while he is at the Club with his female companion. The wife's concern is that the husband's formal objection will preclude her from membership in the Club.

* * *

* * * In the best interests of the parties and the children, the husband was restrained from formally objecting to the wife's application.

I.

The husband has now filed a Notice of Motion for Reconsideration raising state and federal constitutional issues, seeking to dissolve the restraint imposed upon him. The husband's position is that the court, by enjoining him from objecting to the wife's application for membership into the Club, has violated his freedom of speech rights under the New Jersey Constitution. Article I, Section 6 of the New Jersey Constitution provides:

> Every person may freely speak, write and publish his sentiments on all subjects, being responsible for the abuse of that right. No law shall be passed to restrain or abridge the liberty of speech or of the press. [N.J. Const. art I, § 6.]

Based upon this provision, the husband argues that the judicial restraint imposed upon him effectively serves as a "prior restraint" and is therefore unconstitutional.

In support of his position, the husband cites *In re* Marriage of Candiotti, 34 Cal.App.4th 718, 40 Cal.Rptr.2d 299 (1995). In *Candiotti* the California trial court issued an injunction prohibiting the publication of certain comments by the ex-wife relating to the ex-husband's new wife. The trial court justified the restriction based upon its concerns with the ex-wife's motivation for disseminating the information and the derivative harm that might befall the children of the prior marriage. * * * The California Court of Appeals reversed the trial court and dissolved the injunction finding that it was a "prior restraint" in violation of the California Constitution, which is virtually identical to the New Jersey Constitution. * * * The California Court of Appeals acknowledged that it had the power to "issue orders bearing upon parties' relationship with their children and with each other." *Id.* at 725, 40 Cal.Rptr.2d 299. However, the court went on to hold that the order went further because it actually impinged on a person's right to speak about another adult, outside the presence of the children, and therefore, the court found no basis to continue the restraint. * * * The California Court of Appeals held that the comments by the ex-wife were too attenuated from conduct directly affecting the children to support a prior restraint on the ex-wife's constitutional right to utter them. *Ibid*; *but see In re* Tiffany G., 29 Cal.App.4th 443, 35 Cal.Rptr.2d 8 (1994) (order prohibiting stepfather from disseminating confidential documents generated during dependency proceeding was not invalid prior restraint or violation of stepfather's First Amendment speech rights).

* * * The *Candiotti* case dealt with the dissemination of information regarding a step-mother and the possible indirect effects such comments may have on the children. In the present matter the court is faced with the direct and harmful effects likely to be suffered by the children as a result of their father openly seeking to exclude their mother from the Club. This situation differs substantially from the "attenuated" circumstances found in *Candiotti*. There exists a far greater likelihood that the husband's objection to the wife's application for membership will have a direct and harmful affect [sic] upon the children.

II.

The court rests its decision upon its inherent parens patriae authority. The exercise of parens patriae jurisdiction is always foremost, such that when presented with a choice between parent's rights and children's rights, children's welfare and best interests will always be paramount. * * * In this context, despite the husband's argument that the Court has infringed upon his rights of freedom of speech, the court's first and primary concern must be the welfare of the children.

Decisional law supports the position that injunctive relief is proper where the welfare of minor children is involved. In Dickson v. Dickson, 12 Wash.App. 183, 529 P.2d 476 (1974), *cert. denied*, 423 U.S. 832, 96 S.Ct. 53, 46 L.Ed.2d 49 (1975), a Washington court enjoined an ex-husband from making defamatory comments about the ex-wife due to the present threat of emotional harm to the ex-wife, and the clear threat of detrimental emotional effect on the children. In the *Dickson* case, the ex-husband asserted similar arguments, specifically that the injunction denied him rights of free speech. The *Dickson* court found that First Amendment rights are not absolute. *Id.* at 186, 529 P.2d 476. This finding has ample support in New Jersey case law as well. New Jersey courts have consistently recognized that the "best interests" of the children can be made paramount to other fundamental rights. * * *

In *Dickson* the Court of Appeals of Washington found that "in addition to the indirect effect this will have on the children because their mother will be upset, there will be a direct effect on them through damage to the reputation of their family and to their feelings about their mother." *Ibid.* Therefore, in balancing the equities, the *Dickson* Court held that the interference with the ex-wife's privacy and the children's well being outweighed the ex-husband's absolute exercise of his First Amendment rights. * * *

Most relevant to the present case is the *Dickson* Court's finding that the conduct of the ex-husband interfered with the welfare of the minor children. * * *

This court is faced with a similar situation. It is without doubt that a substantial part of the wife's life is invested in the Club. The children are significantly involved in Club activities in which the wife has always taken part. If the wife's membership is declined, surely she would be emotionally harmed and, in turn, the children would feel this harm as well. If the husband is permitted to file a formal objection to the wife's application and she is subsequently denied membership, then the husband and the wife are likely to be the target of blame and resentment from each other and from the children as well, depending upon each parent's influence on the children. This result would occur even if the husband's formal objection is not the deciding factor in the wife's application. The court cannot predict the outcome of the wife's application, but the court is all too aware of the harmful effects upon children caught in parental conflicts. The husband's objection to the wife's application can only work to the detriment of the children and their relationship with the parties, regardless of the final determination by the Club's governing body.

III.

Further support for the injunction is in the limited context in which the injunction was issued. The husband is enjoined only from formally objecting to the wife's application for membership. The husband did not contend that his objection is based upon some misconduct or wrongdoing by the wife at the Club. Rather, the husband's reasons for objecting are found to emanate from bad faith. In Schutz v. Schutz, 581 So.2d 1290 (Fla.1991), the Florida court found that an order directing the mother to "create in the minds of the children a loving and caring feeling toward the father" could be sustained against a First Amendment challenge if it "furthers an important or substantial government interest ... and if the incidental restriction on alleged First Amendment freedoms is no greater than is essential to the furtherance of that interest." *Id.* at 1292 * * *.

The restraint in the present matter is very limited in form and is incidental to the important governmental interest in protecting and promoting the welfare of children. Further, this restraint is the least restrictive means to protect the children's best interests under these circumstances. * * *

* * * In determining whether or not a restriction is in fact a "prior restraint" one of the factors a court considers is whether the restraint prevents the expression of a message. The husband is not completely restrained from expressing his feelings or his "message." He is restricted only from voicing his objection to the governing body of the Club. The injunction is not a complete preclusion. The injunction serves to enjoin only that act which will interfere with the welfare of the children, as well as the wife's parity of social and recreational movement. * * *

IV.

In conclusion, the wife is permitted to seek continuation of her membership free from bad faith interference of the husband. It is clear that the husband wishes to continue the combat of the divorce litigation post-judgment and to exercise control over the wife's social life.

The incidental, minor restriction upon the husband's right to make a formal objection to the governing body of the Club is not constitutionally prohibited in light of the paramount parens patriae interest in the welfare of the children, as well as the wife's right of parity of movement and social independence. The court does not deny that the husband has a First Amendment right to speak his mind freely. However, counterbalancing the restriction on his First Amendment rights is the State's interest in preserving and fostering a healthy relationship between parents and their children. * * * Therefore, plaintiff's Motion for Reconsideration is hereby denied. The injunction issued upon the husband shall remain.

NOTES

1. What practicability problems do you see with the order issued in *Borra*? Do you think that the governing body of the club does not know the former husband's views on the membership question?

2. Note that *Borra* relies substantially on Schutz v. Schutz, 581 So.2d 1290 (Fla.1991), a Florida Supreme Court decision. However, the quotation from *Schutz* is somewhat misleading. In fact, in affirming the trial court order in *Schutz*, the Florida Supreme Court construed that order much more narrowly than the *Borra* language would indicate. Indeed, the Florida Supreme Court interpreted the order

> to require nothing more of the mother than a good faith effort to take those measures necessary to restore and promote the frequent and continuing positive interaction (e.g., visitation, phone calls, letters) between the children and their father and to refrain from doing or saying anything likely to defeat that end. There is no requirement that [the mother] express opinions that she does not hold, a practice disallowed by the first amendment.

Id. at 1292. To what extent does the "narrower" order approved by the Florida Supreme Court obviate those problems? Are you bothered by an order against the mother that prohibits "saying anything" that will defeat the end "of frequent and positive interaction between the children and the father"? For the view that the Florida Supreme Court in *Schutz* "misconstrued the requirements [imposed by the trial court's order] and incorrectly applied constitutional scrutiny," see David L. Ferguson, Schutz v. Schutz: *More Than a Mere "Incidental" Burden on First Amendment Rights*, 16 Nova L. Rev. 937, 951 (1992).

In California, a standard court form "Child Custody and Visitation Order" provides that "neither parent shall make any disparaging remarks about the other parent in the presence of minor children." Judicial Council Form No. 1296.31A. Is this order constitutional? Are there practicability problems with it? Is such an order futile? On the other hand, is any harm done by issuing it?

2. Injunctive relief is frequently sought in disputes between former spouses concerning the surname of the children of the marriage. The maxim that equity will protect property, but not personal, rights has been virtually abandoned in the name-change context. Moreover, the universal standard guiding courts in this area is the best interests of the child. *See, e.g., In re* Grimes, 530 Pa. 388, 609 A.2d 158 (1992), and authorities cited therein. *See generally* Annotation, 92 A.L.R.3d 1091 (1979). The more controversial issue, however, is whether the father has a special or presumptive interest in the child's use of his surname. Consider, in this regard, the language of the Oklahoma Supreme Court in Tubbs v. Harrison, 620 P.2d 384 (Okla.1980):

> It is generally recognized that a father has a protectible claim in the continued use by the child of the paternal surname in accordance with the usual custom, even though the mother may be the custodial parent. The paternal interest has been alluded to by various terms—a natural

right, a fundamental right, a primary or time-honored right, a common-law right, a protectible interest and even a legal right. It has been protected by a variety of procedural devices. While the authorities appear somewhat divided, the better view is that a non-custodial father whose paternal bond remains unsevered has a recognized interest in the child's continued use of his surname.

Various courts have taken the position that to deprive a child of his father's surname is a serious and far-reaching action. This is so because a name, in addition to furnishing a means of identifying a person, signifies a particular relationship. The paternal surname is said to have a tendency to identify the relationship between a father and his children whether it is bestowed as a matter of law or centuries-old custom. It has been recognized that change of a child's paternal surname may foster an unnatural barrier between the father and the child and erode a relationship that should be nurtured. Some authorities believe that whenever the parents of a child are divorced and the custody is in the mother, the remaining bond between the father and child is at best tenuous and may be further weakened, if not utterly destroyed, by a change of the minor's surname. Rights in a parental bond have been variously classified as "essential rights" "basic civil rights", "fundamental rights" and "personal rights" more precious than those of property. The interest comprised within the parental bond is the subject of constitutional protection under both the Due Process and Equal Protection Clauses.

Id. at 386–87. Compare the approach to the foregoing problem adopted by the Supreme Court of California in *In re* Marriage of Schiffman, 28 Cal.3d 640, 169 Cal.Rptr. 918, 620 P.2d 579 (1980):

Surnames have been used at least since the Norman Conquest. In early days they were derived from individual reputations, characteristics, occupations, or places of birth and residence and were not passed from generation to generation. The custom of patrilineal succession seems to have been a response to England's medieval social and legal system, which came to vest all rights of ownership and management of marital property in the husband. "[T]he inheritance of property was often contingent upon an heir's retention of the surname associated with that property." (Note, *The Controversy Over Children's Surnames: Familial Autonomy, Equal Protection and the Child's Best Interests*, 1979 Utah L.Rev. 303, 305). * * *

At common law a married woman had little legal identity apart from her husband's. After marriage, custom dictated that the wife give up her surname and assume the husband's. She could no longer contract or litigate in her own name; nor could she manage property or earn money. (Babcock, Freedman, Norton & Ross, Sex Discrimination and the Law (1975) pp. 561–563.) Allowing the husband to determine the surname of their offspring was part of that system, wherein he was sole legal representative of the marriage, its property, and its children.

Today those bases for patrimonial control of surnames have virtually disappeared. * * *

* * *

It is argued that rules preferring the paternal surname are justified because they formalize long-standing custom, provide a convenient and certain surname system, make official record-keeping simpler, and minimize confusion and difficulty with public and private bureaucracies. (Utah Note, at pp. 307–308.) Moreover, courts and commentators have pointed out that identification with the paternal surname may give the child a healthy sense of family as well as ethnic and religious identity and also maintain her or his rightful link with an absent or noncustodial father. (*Id.*, at pp. 321–325.)

None of those concerns mandates retention of the father's preference. Surnames now may be changed in many situations, and the patrilineal rule has hardly been absolute. Our record-keeping and genealogical systems cope well with the truly significant number of individuals and families that already deviate from the biological-patrilineal norm. We see no reason why these systems cannot accommodate to a fairer standard for resolving disputes between biological parents.

Further, the changing family patterns that are recognized and encouraged by the Uniform Parentage Act support the conclusion that once-accepted assumptions about "family identity" and "noncustodial fathers" are losing force. To the extent that understandable concerns do arise in particular cases, cannot they be fully considered in the context of the "child's best interest" test?

* * *

We conclude that the rule giving the father, as against the mother, a primary right to have his child bear his surname should be abolished. Henceforth, as in parental custody disputes, the sole consideration when parents contest a surname should be the child's best interest. * * *

Under the test thus revised the length of time that the child has used a surname is to be considered. * * * If, as here, the time is negligible because the child is very young, other facts may be controlling. For instance, the effect of a name change on preservation of the father-child relationship, the strength of the mother-child relationship, and the identification of the child as part of a family unit are all pertinent. The symbolic role that a surname other than the natural father's may play in easing relations with a new family should be balanced against the importance of maintaining the biological father-child relationship. "[T]he embarrassment or discomfort that a child may experience when he bears a surname different from the rest of his family" should be evaluated.

Id. at 643–47, 169 Cal.Rptr. at 925, 620 P.2d at 581–84.

For the view that the "paternal surname is neither a fundamental right nor a law of nature" and espousing a "dual naming system [which] would protect for each parent the symbolic value of the child's surname," see Comment, *Like Father, Like Child: The Rights of Parents In Their Childrens' Names*, 70 Va. L. Rev. 1313, 1354 (1984). For a comprehensive discussion of the issues raised in *Tubbs* and *Schiffman*, see MacDougall, *The Right of Women to Name Their Children*, 3 Law & Ineq. 91, 131–59 (1985). *See also* Merle H. Weiner, *"We Are Family": Valuing Associationalism in Disputes*

Over Children's Surnames, 75 N.C. L. Rev. 1625 (1997). Courts continue to be active in this area. *See, e.g.,* Acevedo v. Burley, 994 P.2d 389 (Alaska 1999) (mother was enjoined from changing child's surname without following statutory change of name standards); *In re* Matter of Stratton, 90 P.3d 566 (Okla.Ct.App.2004) (trial court erred in granting mother's petition to change the surname of ex-husband's biological children to that of mother's new husband).

BREKKE v. WILLS

California Court of Appeals, Third District, 2005
125 Cal.App.4th 1400, 23 Cal.Rptr.3d 609.

SCOTLAND, P.J.

This case is a parent's nightmare come true. Plaintiff's 16–year-old daughter, Danielle, started acting out after she became the girlfriend of a 15–year-old boy, defendant, whom she met at school. In addition to her behavioral problems at home, Danielle began skipping school, her grades declined, and she failed three classes. Fearing that her daughter might be using drugs, plaintiff openly searched Danielle's room and found some disturbing letters written by defendant, instructing Danielle how to retaliate against plaintiff for the restrictions that she had imposed on Danielle. Believing that defendant was a cause of Danielle's behavior problems, plaintiff told them they could no longer see each other.

Defendant became angry and wrote three vile and vitriolic letters to Danielle, anticipating that plaintiff would discover and read them. One letter—repeatedly demonstrating that defendant's favorite word is "fuck"—relates his plan to deliberately provoke plaintiff or Danielle's father into physically attacking defendant, whereupon he would sue them and, "[w]hen we're eighteen then we can use the money to be together." Another letter, with the salutation, "Dear Bev [plaintiff]," warns that her efforts to stop Danielle from seeing defendant are for naught, "Fuck you in the ass. You won't win," and states "just fucking give up and let us live our own damn lives." Saying, he " 'oughta' " date your " 'daughter,' " because " 'I like the way she tastes,' " defendant tells plaintiff to "[j]ust get away from my ass and rape yourself you psychotic fucking whore." Yet another letter contemplates defendant and Danielle killing plaintiff and her husband, after which there "will be no trace of your parents. Then we'll go hang out."

Alarmed that defendant became angry when plaintiff told Danielle she could no longer see him, that he wrote letters "instructing/coaching my daughter to create disharmony in my home," and that he even contemplated killing plaintiff and her husband, plaintiff sought "a temporary restraining order and an injunction prohibiting harassment" by defendant. (Code Civ. Proc., § 527.6.)

Apparently coddled rather than castigated by his parents, the 15–year-old defendant showed up in court with an attorney to defend what appears to be indefensible. Wrapping himself with the "[f]reedom of speech, freedom of association, [and] right of privacy," defendant declared he did "nothing to Plaintiff or any member of her family that would merit an injunction." According to defendant, his letters were "not a threat to anyone," but were "a joke" designed to prove that plaintiff was searching Danielle's room since "we knew she would say something if she found it." In defendant's view, the letters would not have caused a reasonable person in plaintiff's position to suffer substantial emotional harm because "any parent should expect some emotional distress when they do not like their children's choice of friends." Defendant denied that he had ever manipulated Danielle or coached her to create disharmony in plaintiff's home, and he blamed plaintiff for Danielle's problems in school.

[At the hearing, plaintiff testified that defendant's actions toward plaintiff and her family were "disturbing." After testifying that the threat to kill "kind of came off like a joke," plaintiff nonetheless stated she took it "very seriously." In her words, "I have to say that when you deal with an imbalanced [sic] person or seemingly imbalanced [sic] person, irrational person, there is no way of telling what that person is capable of doing." Plaintiff also testified that she felt harassed and annoyed by defendant's conduct. As for Danielle, plaintiff testified that her daughter was "doing much better" in terms of school and behavior at home "since there has been the no contact."

[Defendant's mother, Donna Wills, testified that during their conversations, plaintiff never expressed any fear of defendant. Mrs. Wills asked plaintiff to drop the case against defendant "[b]ecause in your bringing this to the court, that put him in a precarious situation that I was not willing to just leave him dangling." Instead, Mrs. Wills wanted plaintiff to "work together with me and my husband to work with our children."

[Defendant's father, Daniel Wills, testified that his son's letters were "not ones that made me very happy," but that plaintiff expressed no fear because, in Mr. Wills's words, the letters "were not believable." Rather than a no-contact order, he wanted to "minimize the contact between the two but don't force them apart otherwise it would end up like a Romeo and Juliet situation." Mr. Wills acknowledged seeing defendant "so upset that it was very hard for him to control himself." However, he opined that defendant was not a threat—"He may punch a wall but no he walks away. He will not hurt somebody." Mr. Wills opposed an injunction because, in his words, "I think it would actually antagonize things and make things worse. And put [defendant] closer to an edge we don't want him [to be] near. That at any given time somebody might do something that could push him over the edge of the restraining order and cause him further legal problems."]

Unmoved by defendant's pronouncement that he and Danielle "would like our parents to accept the fact that we love each other, and that we would never hurt each other or each other's families, either," the trial court enjoined defendant from contacting Danielle and members of her family, and ordered him to stay at least 100 yards away from them, except at school where he must stay at least 20 feet away.

On appeal, defendant contends the order must be reversed because (1) there was no evidence of a credible threat of violence or a knowing and willful course of conduct by defendant that would seriously alarm, annoy, or harass a person, (2) the injunction violates his rights of freedom of expression and association, and his right to privacy, and (3) the order is void because it contains no expiration date.

* * *

I

* * *

A

The United States Supreme Court has "long recognized that not all speech is of equal First Amendment importance. It is speech on ' "matters of public concern" ' that is 'at the heart of the First Amendment's protection.' [Citations.]" (*Dun & Bradstreet v. Greenmoss Builders* (1985) 472 U.S. 749, 758–759, 105 S.Ct. 2939, 2944–45, 86 L.Ed.2d 593, 602, The " 'special concern [for speech on public issues] is no mystery:' [¶] 'The First Amendment "was fashioned to assure unfettered interchange of ideas for the bringing about of political and social changes desired by the people." [Citations.] "[S]peech concerning public affairs is more than self-expression; it is the essence of self-government." [Citation.] . . . .' " (*Id.* at p. 759, 105 S.Ct. at 2945 86 L.Ed.2d at pp. 602–603.) "In contrast, speech on matters of purely private concern"—while "not totally unprotected"—"is of less First Amendment concern." (*Id.* at pp. 759, 760, 105 S.Ct. at pp. 2945–46, 86 L.Ed.2d at p. 603.) When such speech-for example, as in defamation or the intentional infliction of emotional distress—causes damage, civil sanctions may be imposed because " '[t]here is no threat to the free and robust debate of public issues; there is no potential interference with a meaningful dialogue of ideas concerning self-government; and there is no threat of liability causing a reaction of self-censorship by the press. . . .' [Citation.]" (*Id.* at pp. 760, 761, 105 S.Ct. at 2945–46, 86 L.Ed.2d at pp. 603, 604.)

Here, defendant's speech was between purely private parties, about purely private parties, on matters of purely private interest. Thus, this case is " 'wholly without the First Amendment concerns with which the Supreme Court of the United States has been struggling.' [Citation.]" (*Dun & Bradstreet v. Greenmoss Builders, supra,* 472 U.S. at p. 760, 105 S.Ct. at 2945–46, 86 L.Ed.2d at p. 603); and the trial court properly considered defendant's speech in determining whether to issue injunctive relief pursuant to Code of Civil Procedure section 527.6.

Nevertheless, defendant argues the court erred in considering, as evidence of harassment, the lyrics that defendant quoted in his "Dear Bev" letter. This is so, he argues, because song lyrics are entertainment protected by the First Amendment. (See *McCollum v. CBS, Inc.* (1988) 202 Cal.App.3d 989, 999, 249 Cal.Rptr. 187 ["First Amendment guaranties of freedom of speech and expression extend to all artistic and literary expression, whether in music, concerts, plays, pictures or books"].)

However, as expressed in words of the song "Fair Warning," by Todd Rundgren, "You know, wishing won't make it so." By including the lyric in his "Dear Bev" letter, defendant was not singing or otherwise attempting to entertain. He used the lyric to ridicule and annoy plaintiff. They were not constitutionally protected in this context.

B

Defendant's assertion that the no-contact order violates his right to freedom of association reflects a juvenile view of the First Amendment.

We categorically reject the absurd suggestion that defendant's freedom of association trumps a parent's right to direct and control the activities of a minor child, including with whom the child may associate. (*Troxel v. Granville* (2000) 530 U.S. 57, 65–66, 72, 120 S.Ct. 2054, 2059–60, 2063–64, 147 L.Ed.2d 49, 56–57, 60; *Gibson v. Gibson* (1971) 3 Cal.3d 914, 921, 92 Cal.Rptr. 288, 479 P.2d 648; *Emery v. Emery* (1955) 45 Cal.2d 421, 429–430, 289 P.2d 218; *Burge v. City & County of San Francisco* (1953) 41 Cal.2d 608, 617, 262 P.2d 6.) "The liberty interest . . . of parents in the care, custody, and control of their children . . . is perhaps the oldest of the fundamental liberty interests recognized by [the United States Supreme Court]." (*Troxel v. Granville, supra,* 530 U.S. at p. 65, 120 S.Ct. at p. 2059–60, 147 L.Ed.2d at p. 56.) Whether a child likes it or not, parents have broad authority over their minor children. (*Id.* at p. 66, 120 S.Ct. at p. 2060, 147 L.Ed.2d at p. 57.) The "fundamental right of parents to make child rearing decisions" includes deciding who may spend time with a minor child. (*Id.* at pp. 72–73, 120 S.Ct. at 2063–64, 147 L.Ed.2d at p. 61.)

Not only do parents have a constitutional right to exercise lawful control over the activities of their minor children, the law *requires* parents to do so. (*Williams v. Garcetti* (1993) 5 Cal.4th 561, 570–575, 20 Cal. Rptr.2d 341, 853 P.2d 507; Pen.Code, § 272, subd. (a)(1), (a)(2) [parents of a child under the age of 18 years shall have the duty to exercise reasonable care, supervision, protection, and control over their minor child so as not to encourage or cause the child to become or to remain a person within the provisions of Section 300 [juvenile dependency], 601 [habitually disobedient or truant], or 602 [juvenile delinquency] of the Welfare and Institutions Code and are subject to criminal punishment for a violation of that duty]; Ed.Code, §§ 48260.5, subds. (b), (c); 48293 [parents who fail to compel their child's attendance at school are subject to criminal prosecution]; see also Civ.Code, § 1714.1 [parents may be liable for the torts of their minor child]; Gov.Code, § 38772, subd. (b) [parents are jointly and severally liable with their minor child for the child's defacement of property by graffiti]; Ed.Code, § 48904, subd. (a) [parents are liable for damages caused by the willful misconduct of their minor child in injuring or killing a pupil or school employee or volunteer, or in damaging property belonging to a school or school employee]; Pen.Code, § 490.5, subd. (b) [parents may be liable for petty theft committed by a minor child under their custody and control].)

By imposing upon parents a duty to exercise reasonable care, supervision, protection, and control over their minor child, Penal Code section 272 is intended to "safeguard children from those influences which would tend to cause them to become delinquent." (*People v. Calkins* (1941) 48 Cal.App.2d 33, 36, 119 P.2d 142; Pen.Code, § 272, subd. (b)(5).) Ample evidence in this case showed that defendant was such a negative influence on Danielle.

In sum, defendant had no right to associate with plaintiff's minor child, Danielle, or to otherwise interfere with her parents' exercise of their right to control Danielle's activities.

C

Also without merit is defendant's claim that his letters cannot support the injunction because they were "private letters ... within the right of privacy protected by the constitutions of the United States and the State of California."

First, his premise is wrong. Substantial evidence supports the trial court's finding that this was not private correspondence to Danielle; defendant intended that plaintiff would read and be annoyed by them. In any event, defendant had no reasonable expectation of privacy in letters he wrote to a minor girlfriend who was subject to the supervision and control of parents entitled to search her room and possessions in hopes of finding out why she was misbehaving. Second, as we have explained, defendant had no right to communicate, privately or publicly, with Danielle against her parents' wishes.

II

In another attack on the injunction, defendant contends there is no clear and convincing evidence to support it. He is wrong.

A

Code of Civil Procedure section 527.6, subdivision (a) states: "A person who has suffered harassment as defined in subdivision (b) may seek a temporary restraining order and an injunction prohibiting harassment as provided in this section." * * *

Subdivision (b) of section 527.6 states: "For the purposes of this section, 'harassment' is unlawful violence, a credible threat of violence, or a knowing and willful course of conduct directed at a specific person that seriously alarms, annoys, or harasses the person, and that serves no legitimate purpose. The course of conduct must be such as would cause a reasonable person to suffer substantial emotional distress, and must actually cause substantial emotional distress to the plaintiff."

A "credible threat of violence" is defined as "a knowing and willful statement or course of conduct that would place a reasonable person in fear for his or her safety, or the safety of his or her immediate family, and that serves no legitimate purpose." (§ 527.6, subd. (b)(2).)

A "course of conduct" that seriously alarms, annoys, or harasses a person and serves no legitimate purpose is defined as "a pattern of conduct composed of a series of acts over a period of time, however short, evidencing a continuity of purpose, including following or stalking an individual, making harassing telephone calls to an individual, or sending harassing correspondence to an individual by any means, including, but not limited to, the use of public or private mails, interoffice mail, fax, or computer e-mail. Constitutionally protected activity is not included within the meaning of 'course of conduct.' " (§ 527.6, subd. (b)(3).)

Section 527.6 was enacted "to protect the individual's right to pursue safety, happiness and privacy as guaranteed by the California Constitution." (Stats.1978, ch. 1307, § 1, p. 4294; *Schraer v. Berkeley Property Owners' Assn.* (1989) 207 Cal.App.3d 719, 729–730, 255 Cal.Rptr. 453.) It does so by providing expedited injunctive relief to victims of harassment.
* * *

B

In defendant's view, there was "simply no evidence" that he made a "credible threat of violence" against plaintiff and her husband. He points to plaintiff's testimony that the threat to kill "came off like a joke." But he ignores that plaintiff also said she took the threat "very seriously." She explained: "I have to say that when you deal with [a] ... seemingly imbalanced [*sic*] person, irrational person, there is no way of telling what that person is capable of doing."

We recognize that writings, such as defendant's, may use "symbolism, exaggeration, and make-believe" to shock or express anger. (*In re Ryan D.* (2002) 100 Cal.App.4th 854, 857, 123 Cal.Rptr.2d 193; see also *In re George T.* (2004) 33 Cal.4th 620, 637, 16 Cal.Rptr.3d 61, 93 P.3d 1007.) However, as the trial court pointed out, in our post-Columbine High School world, fantastical threats that once were taken lightly as fancies of immature youth now cause reasonable persons to pause and even to become fearful. Such concern is particularly understandable where, as here, defendant's father testified that he has seen defendant "so upset that it was very hard for him to control himself." * * *

We need not decide this question since defendant's letters and actions were "harassment" within the meaning of the injunction statute because they constituted a knowing and willful course of conduct directed at plaintiff that seriously alarmed, annoyed, or harassed her, that served no legitimate purpose, and that would cause a reasonable person to suffer substantial emotional distress. (§ 527.6, subd. (b)(3).)

C

Defendant raises a two-fold argument that the evidence fails to establish a course of conduct within the meaning of the anti-harassment statute.

First, he contends that three letters, written to Danielle not plaintiff, are insufficient to constitute a course of conduct, and that there was no evidence he would write more such letters. We disagree. As we have noted, the evidence shows that defendant wrote the letters with the intention that they would be discovered and read by plaintiff. And his actions were not limited to the three vile and vitriolic letters. Earlier, he had written letters to Danielle instructing her on retaliatory measures she could take against her parents for their restrictions on her. He also taunted plaintiff during his telephone conversation with her. It is readily apparent from the tone and content of his letters and telephone call that defendant had no intention of ceasing his behavior toward plaintiff. Thus, we have no trouble concluding that all of his actions constituted a course of conduct, i.e., "a series of acts over a period of time, however short, evidencing a continuity of purpose. . . ." (§ 527.6, subd. (b)(3); * * *.)

Therefore, we turn to defendant's claim that his conduct did not constitute harassment within the meaning of the statute. This is so because, he says, his conduct would not have seriously alarmed, annoyed, or harassed a reasonable person. Quoting out of context language from *Schild v. Rubin* (1991) 232 Cal.App.3d 755, 763, 283 Cal.Rptr. 533, he argues a reasonable " 'person must realize that complete emotional tranquility is seldom attainable, and some degree of transitory emotional distress is the natural consequence' " of parenting a teenage child. * * *

Defendant truly is living in a fantasy world in claiming that no reasonable parent of a teenage daughter would have been seriously alarmed, annoyed, or harassed by his letters and conduct. Even his trial attorney-now appellate attorney-admitted while defending this case in the trial court: "I'd be enraged if I got a letter like that, really angry."

Without doubt, defendant's socially unacceptable course of conduct would have seriously alarmed, annoyed, or harassed a reasonable person, and would have caused a reasonable person to suffer substantial emotional distress. (§ 527.6, subd. (b); *Schild v. Rubin, supra,* 232 Cal.App.3d at pp. 762–763, 283 Cal.Rptr. 533.)

Equally without merit is defendant's claim that the evidence is insufficient to find plaintiff actually suffered substantial emotional distress.

Defendant repeatedly undermined plaintiff's efforts to deal with her daughter's behavioral problems that began after Danielle became defendant's girlfriend. Among other things, defendant told plaintiff that if she persisted in exercising parental authority to stop her daughter from skipping school and receiving failing grades, he would cause Danielle to skip more classes. Defendant laughed at plaintiff, ridiculed her intelligence and expressions of concern for Danielle, and described plaintiff in abhorrent terms, including calling her a " 'psychotic fucking whore' " who should "keep fucking yourself in the ass." He made a sexual innuendo about plaintiff's daughter, saying, "I like the way she tastes," and concocted a scenario in which he would provoke plaintiff to hurt him, then sue her and use the money to marry Danielle. Defendant even urged Danielle to contemplate killing her parents with him. And he sought to make it clear that Danielle was under his influence, rather than plaintiff's control, and that he intended to keep it that way. Defendant even taunted plaintiff by saying that he had a "good lawyer" and plaintiff could not get a restraining order because the "judge will laugh at her."

Well, the trial court did not laugh, nor do we. Plaintiff's statements and demeanor in court demonstrate that defendant caused her substantial emotional distress, and that the injunction was appropriate and necessary.

III

In his last challenge to the injunction, defendant asserts that it is void because it does not contain an expiration date. * * * [W]e conclude that the expiration date of the order must be modified to expire on June 14, 2005, when Danielle turns 18 years of age and becomes an adult. She will then have the right and responsibility to make her own decisions; her parents' role will become one of influence and persuasion, rather than direction and control. Of course, Danielle could seek to renew the injunction for a period beyond her 18th birthday. (§ 527.6, subd. (d).) But that would be a matter of her choice, not of her parents' choosing.

We concur: HULL and ROBIE, JJ.

NOTES

1. Suppose Danielle had secured her own counsel (through legal aid or another source) and had opposed her mother's request for injunctive relief. Would the court have granted the injunction? Would the parents' right and obligation to exercise control over minor children have trumped Danielle's privacy right? In any event, would practicability issues have been much more substantial? Would an injunction have been futile? Would the court have been concerned about supervision?

2. Do you see some irony in this case? The court approves a parental petition for injunctive relief that prevents Danielle from having any physical contact with the defendant. On the other hand, had the relationship resulted in a pregnancy, the ultimate decision as to an abortion would have been the minor child's and not the parents.

3. How would you liked to have been the attorney representing the defendant? The courts hearing the case were overwhelmingly hostile to the defendant. Indeed, the defendant lost the appeal even though the plaintiff never entered an appearance before the appellate court.

4. Should injunctive relief be available against alienation of affections? "Equitable relief by way of injunction against the defendants for interference

with marital relations is not often sought and is probably impractical. * * * [Most] courts have generally denied such injunctions as a serious infringement of personal freedom of the other spouse and beyond the appropriate reach of equity." W. Page Keeton, Dan B. Dobbs, Robert F. Keeton, David G. Owen, Prosser & Keeton on the Law of Torts 923–24 (5th ed. 1984).

5.   Thirty-five states by statute have abolished or limited the cause of action for alienation of affections and five have done so by judicial decision. Jennifer E. McDougal, *Legislating Morality: The Actions for Alienation of Affections and Criminal Conversation in North Carolina*, 33 Wake Forest L. Rev. 163, 172–73 (1998).

On the other hand, a few state courts have refused to abolish this cause of action. *See* Bland v. Hill, 735 So.2d 414 (Miss.1999); Cannon v. Miller, 313 N.C. 324, 327 S.E.2d 888 (1985); Norton v. Macfarlane, 818 P.2d 8 (Utah 1991). Indeed, in North Carolina the tort seems increasingly popular, and large punitive damages awards are not unusual. *See, e.g.*, Oddo v. Presser, 358 N.C. 128, 592 S.E.2d 195 (2004).

MARKEY v. JONATHAN CLUB

California Court of Appeal, Second District, 2002.
2002 WL 1904416 (unpublished opinion).

RUBIN, J.

* * *

FACTS AND PROCEDURAL HISTORY

Christian E. Markey III (Markey) was a member of the Jonathan Club (the Club), which is organized for social and recreational purposes as a California nonprofit mutual benefit corporation. (Corp.Code, § 7110, *et seq.*) In December 1997, an incident between Markey and three underage girls took place at the Club's Santa Monica beach facility, leading to the filing of criminal charges against Markey. In December 1998, Markey pleaded no contest to three misdemeanor counts of annoying or molesting a child under the age of 18 (Pen.Code, § 647.6, subd. (a)) and was placed on probation for three years. As part of the sentence, he had to pay a fine and make restitution to his victims, was ordered to have no contact with the girls, and was required to undergo psychological testing.

In April 1999, the Club's board of directors (the board) considered the status of Markey's membership and in a May 21, 1999, letter notified Markey that it had decided to expel him from the Club. In making its decision, the board "considered, among other things, the proceedings [in Markey's criminal prosecution], the facts and circumstances surrounding that matter, the location of the incident and the ultimate disposition." Based on that, the board terminated Markey's membership under Club bylaw 8.1, which authorized the expulsion of a member for conduct that was "prejudicial to the best interests, welfare, character and reputation of the Club. . . ." The letter advised Markey that the Club's bylaws gave him the right to a hearing no less than five days before his termination took effect.

After various delays, the hearing took place before the committee [composed of three members of the board] on August 9, 1999. Markey was represented by two lawyers, one of whom was a Club member and former member of the board. In anticipation of the hearing, Markey sent each board member a 25–page letter giving his reasons against the proposed termination of his membership. After the hearing, when the committee told Markey he could supplement his showing, Markey sent the board another letter stating his contentions. The committee later recommended that the board expel Markey. On August 31, 1999, the board voted unanimously to terminate Markey's membership, effective September 3, 1999.

Markey then sued the Club and filed a pleading styled as a "PETITION FOR WRIT OF MANDATE" seeking to compel the Club to reinstate his membership.[2] Markey alleged that the Club violated its own bylaws because it did not provide him a hearing before the full board. He also alleged that the hearing before the committee instead of the entire board violated Corporations Code section 7341, which sets forth the procedural protections that should be used when a nonprofit mutual benefit corporation such as the Club decides to expel or suspend a member. * * *

* * *

When the parties appeared for the April 20, 2001, hearing, the court issued a written tentative decision denying Markey's petition. * * * Finding that the Club's procedure complied with Corporations Code section 7341, the court ruled that Markey had received a fair hearing. The tentative decision next considered the Club's use of Markey's no contest plea as the basis for its decision, noting that Corporations Code section 7341 applied to only the procedural issues and not the substantive merits of the board's actions. The court's tentative decision said that the Club's use of the no contest plea might have been improper had this been an action for administrative mandate or had Markey's Club membership conferred on him sufficient property and economic rights. Because this was not so, the tentative decision said the court would not interfere with the Club's actions.

When the hearing began, the court's tentative decision touched off a heated exchange over whether Markey's Club membership conveyed sufficient property rights to preclude the Club's use of the no contest plea. Markey's counsel asked for a continuance and a chance to amend the petition or present evidence on that issue. The Club objected that Markey had his chance to put on his case, that he had no property rights in his membership and that, in any event, the board's use of the no contest plea was outside the scope of the pleadings. The court denied the motions and,

---

2. Markey, who is a lawyer, represented himself when the petition was filed. At all other relevant times, however, he was represented by counsel.

in conformity with its written tentative decision, ordered the Club to submit a proposed judgment within 10 days, which it would then hold for another 10 days before signing and filing it. The Club's proposed judgment included part of the court's tentative decision, but omitted any mention of the no contest plea issue. The court signed the judgment but added a notation that it had deleted the Club's proposed findings because portions of the tentative decision had been omitted. As a result, the judgment contained no findings and simply stated that the petition had been denied.

Markey next moved for a new trial * * *. The trial court denied the motion * * *.

DISCUSSION
* * *

2. Markey's Petition And The Right of Fair Procedure

Markey's petition was brought under Corporations Code section 7341 (section 7341), which governs the procedure for expelling members of nonprofit mutual benefit corporations. The statute creates a "safe harbor" provision by which an expulsion procedure is deemed fair and reasonable when: it is set forth in the bylaws or articles; gives 15 days' notice before the expulsion; and provides the member an opportunity to be heard, orally or in writing, no less than five days before his expulsion "by a person or body authorized to decide that the proposed expulsion ... not take place." (§ 7341, subds.(a), (b), (c); see Leg. Com. com., Deering's Ann. Corp.Code, (1994 ed.) foll. § 7341, p. 269.) When the full circumstances of the expulsion are considered, however, other procedures may also be found both fair and reasonable. (§ 7341, subd. (b).) The statute is procedural only and an expulsion based on substantive grounds that violate a member's contractual or other rights is not made valid by compliance with this statute. (§ 7341, subd. (f).)

* * * Section 7341 was part of the nonprofit corporation laws passed by the Legislature in 1979 and was designed to codify existing case law concerning the procedural due process required for suspending or expelling members. (Ferry v. San Diego Museum of Art (1986) 180 Cal.App.3d 35, 42, fn. 4, 45, 225 Cal.Rptr. 258 [interpreting identical companion provisions of Corp.Code, § 5341]; see Leg. Com. com., Deering's Ann. Corp.Code, (1994 ed.) foll. § 7341, p. 269.) Our courts early on established a common law right of fair procedure that applied to members of private associations. Over the years, that right was expanded and applied to members of labor unions, professional trade associations, and the medical staff of private hospitals. (See Potvin v. Metropolitan Life Ins. Co. (2000) 22 Cal.4th 1060, 1066–1071, 95 Cal.Rptr.2d 496, 997 P.2d 1153, and cases cited therein.) The right has been applied to expulsions from the Boy Scouts (Curran v. Mount Diablo Council of the Boy Scouts (1983) 147 Cal.App.3d 712, 195 Cal.Rptr. 325 (*Curran*)) as well as private country clubs. (Warfield v. Peninsula Golf & Country Club (1989) 214 Cal.App.3d 646, 658–659, 262 Cal.Rptr. 890 (*Warfield*); Youngblood v. Wilcox (1989)

207 Cal.App.3d 1368, 1373–1374, 255 Cal.Rptr. 527 (*Youngblood*).) Because members of such private organizations stand to lose the privileges associated with membership, their right of fair procedure does not depend on the existence of any specific, vested property right. * * *

A member's expulsion is arbitrary and in violation of the common law right of fair procedure when it is substantively unreasonable, contrary to the association's own rules, or is procedurally unfair. Procedural fairness requires adequate notice of the charges and a reasonable opportunity to respond. An expulsion is substantively unreasonable when it rests on a rule that is substantively capricious or contrary to public policy. (*Curran, supra*, 147 Cal.App.3d at p. 720, 195 Cal.Rptr. 325.)

Although some courts have equated the right of fair procedure with constitutional due process requirements (*see* Hackethal v. California Medical Assn. (1982) 138 Cal.App.3d 435, 442, 187 Cal.Rptr. 811), the common law right of fair procedure is different from and lesser than due process rights. (Pinsker v. Pacific Coast Society of Orthodontists (1974) 12 Cal.3d 541, 550, 116 Cal.Rptr. 245, 526 P.2d 253, fn. 7 (*Pinsker*) [disapproving prior use of the term "due process," a concept that is "applicable only in its broadest, nonconstitutional connotation."]) "The common law requirement of a fair procedure does not compel formal proceedings with all the embellishments of a court trial * * *, nor adherence to a single mode of process. It may be satisfied by any one of a variety of procedures which afford a fair opportunity for an applicant [or member] to present his position. As such, this court should not attempt to fix a rigid procedure that must invariably be observed. Instead, the associations themselves should retain the initial and primary responsibility for devising a method which provides ... notice of the 'charges' ... and a reasonable opportunity to respond. In drafting such procedure, and determining, for example, whether [one] is to be given an opportunity to respond in writing or by personal appearance, the organization should consider the nature of the tendered issue and should fashion its procedure to insure a *fair* opportunity ... to present [one's] position. Although the association retains discretion in formalizing such procedures, the courts remain available to afford relief in the event of the abuse of such discretion." (*Pinsker, supra*, 12 Cal.3d at pp. 555–556, 116 Cal.Rptr. 245, 526 P.2d 253, fn. omitted, original italics.)

Finally, the plaintiff claiming a denial of his fair procedure rights must show he was actually prejudiced as a result. * * *

3. *Markey Received a Fair Hearing*

The hearing on Markey's expulsion was held before the committee, which was comprised of three board members. The committee made its recommendation to the full board, which had the power to accept or reject the committee's report. * * *

The Club's interrogatory responses show that Markey provided written statements of his contentions to each of the board members both before and after the committee hearing in August 1999. The committee presented a report to the board about three weeks later, recommending Markey's expulsion from the Club. Each board member had complete access to the record, including all documents supplied by Markey. After discussing the matter thoroughly and deliberating, the board voted to expel Markey. Markey has never acknowledged the existence of this evidence.[9] He has offered neither discussion nor citation to authority to show that the procedure used was not otherwise reasonable or fair under section 7341, subdivision (b) or that he was somehow prejudiced by its use. * * * Because we must imply that the trial court found for the Club on this ground, we hold that Markey has waived the issue by failing to address it. * * *

Markey also contends that in response to his request for a hearing before the entire board, a Club official said the board was too busy to hear from him. According to Markey, this violated Club bylaw 8.1(ii), which required that the expulsion hearing be held by the full board. There is, however, substantial evidence in the record to support an implied contrary finding.

First, the bylaw Markey cites is not so clear on this issue. It says that before a member may be expelled, he "shall have the opportunity to be heard, orally or in writing, not less than five days before the effective date of the expulsion, suspension or termination by the Board." Markey apparently contends that the ending phrase "by the Board" relates back to the initial phrase "opportunity to be heard." Had that been the Club's intent, however, it could just as easily have drafted the provision to read that the affected member "shall have the opportunity to be heard by the Board ... not less than five days before the effective date of the ... termination." By placing the phrase "by the Board" where it did, the bylaws could be interpreted to provide for a hearing by some unspecified person or group selected by the Board as part of the Board's decisionmaking process.

Next, contrary to fundamental tenets of appellate practice, Markey fails to mention certain unfavorable evidence which supports such an interpretation. * * * This includes the Club's interrogatory response where it denied making any statement to the effect that it was too busy to afford Markey a hearing before the entire board. It also includes the declaration of Club director Lyon, who said that the procedure used was the same available to every club member being considered for termination and was in conformity with Club bylaw 8.21.1, which permitted the committee to act for the board. While the courts are not bound by the Club's construction of its bylaws, we will follow any practical construction placed on them by the corporation that is not unreasonable or contrary to public policy. * * * Because Markey fails to address this issue, and

---

9. Markey instead relies solely on his own favorable version of events, as set forth in his declaration and that of Robert Wrede, the lawyer and former Club director who appeared with Markey at the committee's expulsion hearing.

because he has failed to set forth and discuss all the applicable evidence, we deem it waived. * * *

The Club's initial letter notifying Markey of his imminent expulsion said that the board had considered the criminal proceedings brought against Markey, "the facts and circumstances surrounding that matter, the location of the incident and the ultimate disposition." The decision to terminate was based on Club bylaw 8.1, because Markey's conduct was "prejudicial to the best interests, welfare, character and reputation of the Club...." Despite Markey's repeated requests, the board declined to provide any more information about the charges. As a result, Markey contends he did not receive adequate notice of the charges against him or their factual basis. * * *

In its May 21, 1999, letter to Markey, the Club wrote that he was being expelled on account of the criminal proceedings against him and the facts and circumstances of the case. The case name and caption number were also provided. In a June 1, 1999, letter to Markey, the Club wrote, "As you have been aware for some time, the Board's action took into account the incident in which you were involved . . . at the Beach facility on December 7, 1997," along with the resultant criminal proceedings and the disposition of the case.

We start with the obvious: in December 1998 Markey pleaded no contest to three counts of molesting a minor based on a December 7, 1997, incident at the Club's beach facility.[10] This fact alone raises a reasonable inference that Markey knew enough about the incident, his accusers and the evidence against him to enter such a plea. Markey not only fails to acknowledge or discuss those inferences, he also omits any mention of statements in his own letters to the Club that show his knowledge of both the charges and their factual circumstances. In a June 25, 1999, letter, Markey wrote, "The Board should already know that the three girls involved were demonstrably and repeatedly untruthful to Club staff, management and others in an obvious attempt to avoid being held responsible for their transgressions at the Club, including an extensive pattern of inappropriate conduct and significant, impermissible abuse of someone else's membership number. [¶] With perspicacity of hindsight, what I thought was simple hospitality, and a willingness as a Beach Committee member to help others, was misconstrued." In a July 7, 1999, letter, he said that because the board had failed to specify the factual bases for its decision, he assumed the board relied upon only a certain December 7, 1997, report. When combined with his presumed knowledge of the facts from his participation in the criminal proceedings, we conclude there is substantial evidence to support an implied finding that Markey received adequate notice of the charges against him and their factual basis. * * *

---

10. Markey contends, by way of his lawyer's declaration, that in December 2000 two of the three girls recanted their accusations and dropped lawsuits against the Club and Markey.

Markey contends that the Club violated his fair procedure rights because it presented no evidence or witnesses, thus preventing him from confronting and cross examining his accusers. * * *

Although some cases state that the ability to confront and cross examine witnesses is an essential part of the fair procedure right (Cason v. Glass Bottle Blowers Assn. (1951) 37 Cal.2d 134, 144, 231 P.2d 6; Hackethal v. California Medical Assn., *supra*, 138 Cal.App.3d at p. 442, 187 Cal.Rptr. 811), others do not mention it, referring instead to the need for flexible procedures whose basic ingredients include notice and a hearing. (Delta Dental Plan v. Banasky (1994) 27 Cal.App.4th 1598, 1608, 33 Cal.Rptr.2d 381; Rhee v. El Camino Hospital Dist. (1988) 201 Cal. App.3d 477, 497, 247 Cal.Rptr. 244.) * * *

As also noted earlier, the *Pinsker* court was careful to distinguish the lesser common law right of fair procedure from the more rigorous requirements of constitutional due process. (*Pinsker, supra,* 12 Cal.3d at p. 550, fn. 7, 116 Cal.Rptr. 245, 526 P.2d 253.) In line with this, the Supreme Court later held that the right to counsel was not a required part of the " 'minimal due process' which is applicable in proceedings of this kind * * *." (*Anton, supra,* 19 Cal.3d at p. 827, 140 Cal.Rptr. 442, 567 P.2d 1162.) Under section 7341, subdivision (b) we look to all the circumstances when determining whether a corporation's expulsion procedure was fair. We believe the circumstances of this case support an implied finding that the Club did not violate Markey's fair procedure rights by failing to introduce any evidence or put on any witnesses at the hearing.

In response to an interrogatory by Markey asking the Club to describe any evidence presented to Markey before the hearing, the Club pointed to its letters to Markey that identified his criminal prosecution and the facts and circumstances surrounding that matter as the basis for the board's actions. In response to another interrogatory asking the Club to justify its denial of a request for admission that the Club knew there was no basis for terminating Markey's membership, the Club identified several documents: the superior court files and records from Markey's criminal prosecution; two different police reports; and three letters from the Club to Markey. We take this to mean that the Club contends its decision was based primarily on the records and proceedings from Markey's criminal prosecution and that by so advising Markey, it was effectively presenting the evidence against him.

This might not have been the ideal procedure, but we conclude it was fair and reasonable under the circumstances. As with the related notice issue discussed earlier, it is reasonable to infer that Markey knew all the evidence associated with the charges against him before deciding to enter his no contest plea, including the identity of his three accusers. His letters to the board also show his knowledge of the evidence against him, including matters related to the credibility of the three girls involved in the incident. Markey never acknowledges this inference. Nor does he suggest how the Club might have put on evidence gleaned from court files and police reports, produced three underage girls for questioning and cross examination by their acknowledged molester, or otherwise litigated a criminal case that was settled by a no contest plea and therefore never went to trial. In recognition of the "practical limitations" that prevented a "full airing of disputed factual issues" (Ezekial v. Winkley, *supra*, 20 Cal.3d at p. 278, 142 Cal.Rptr. 418, 572 P.2d 32), we hold that under the unique circumstances of this case, the Club did not abuse its discretion by the procedure used (*Pinsker*, *supra*, 12 Cal.3d at pp. 555–556, 116 Cal. Rptr. 245, 526 P.2d 253) and that Markey received the "minimal due process" applicable to proceedings of this kind. * * *

* * *

4. Use of the No Contest Plea

Although a no contest plea to a felony charge is treated the same as a guilty plea for all purposes, no contest pleas to misdemeanor charges "may not be used against the defendant as an admission in any civil suit based upon or growing out of the act upon which the criminal prosecution is based." (Pen.Code, § 1016, subd. (3).) With certain statutory exceptions, evidence of such a plea is not admissible in administrative disciplinary hearings because a no contest plea is not a reliable indicator of actual guilt and instead reflects a compromise between the prosecution and the accused. * * * Markey contends the Club violated this rule by relying on his no contest plea when deciding to terminate his membership. He is once more defeated by his failure to discuss the applicable law or accurately describe the facts.

First, Markey contends that John Shiner, the Club's general counsel, told him the board's decision was based solely on the plea. Markey fails to mention that Shiner denied making any such statement, however, contending instead that he offered Markey the same reasons set forth in the Club's correspondence. Markey also ignores the Club's response to an interrogatory asking for details about its use of the no contest plea, where the Club stated that the board "was aware of" the criminal proceedings, the facts and circumstances of the incident, and Markey's no contest plea. In other interrogatory responses, the Club detailed its investigation into the matter, which included: communicating with the victims, speaking to Markey and his lawyers, interviewing Club employees, reviewing police reports, communicating with the prosecutors, and monitoring both the criminal prosecution and certain State Bar disciplinary proceedings. We also note that Markey was sentenced in February 1999 and the Club evaluated the status of Markey's membership two months later.

It appears from this evidence that the Club was keeping track of the criminal proceedings and did not consider action against Markey until those proceedings were concluded by Markey's no contest plea. Because the Club said it had been "aware" of the plea, it is inferable that its "use" of the plea was limited to no more than determining that the criminal proceedings were at an end, thus allowing it to consider whether Markey's expulsion was warranted. Because Markey has failed to acknowledge this evidence or discuss it in light of the applicable authorities, we deem the issue waived. * * *

We alternatively hold that this evidence supports an implied finding that the Club did not impermissibly rely on Markey's no contest plea because it also shows that the Club independently examined the facts to determine whether Markey committed the charged offenses. * * *

* * *

For the reasons set forth above, the judgment is affirmed. * * *

We concur: COOPER, P.J., and BOLAND, J.

NOTES

1. Traditionally, equity courts have been reluctant to intervene in membership disputes of private associations, clubs, professional and religious organizations and honorary societies. *See, e.g.* Williams v. Black Rock Yacht Club, Inc., 877 A.2d 849, 854 (Conn.App.2005). What practicability concerns are reflected in this reluctance? Today, judicial intervention in this area is increasing substantially. There are several reasons for this. First, to the extent that the private organization is significantly involved with the government, it may be treated as the "state" for Fourteenth Amendment purposes and its membership practices thus may become subject to constitutional scrutiny. *See, e.g.*, Indiana High School Athletic Ass'n, Inc. v. Carlberg, 694 N.E.2d 222 (Ind.1997) (decisions of Indiana High School Athletic Association concerning student transfers constitute "state action" for purposes of the Fourteenth Amendment). Second, contemporary state and local public accommodations legislation prohibits many private associations from engaging in a wide variety of discriminatory practices. *See, e.g.*, Brounstein v. American Cat Fanciers Ass'n, 839 F.Supp. 1100 (D.N.J.1993) (member of cat fancier association whose "cat judge" license was revoked, she alleged, because she was Jewish, stated valid claim for intervention because association was a "public accommodation" under New Jersey's antidiscrimination law); Warfield v. Peninsula Golf & Country Club, 10 Cal.4th 594, 42 Cal.Rptr.2d 50, 896 P.2d 776 (1995) (gender discrimination by country club impermissible because country club deemed to be a "business establishment" under Unruh Civil Rights Act); Beynon v. St. George–Dixie Lodge No. 1743, Benevolent & Protective Order of Elks, 854 P.2d 513 (Utah 1993) (prohibition on female Elks barred by state statute on "regulation of enterprises"). *But see* Curran v. Mount Diablo Council of the Boy Scouts of America, 17 Cal.4th 670, 72 Cal.Rptr.2d 410, 952 P.2d 218 (1998) (Boy Scouts are not a "business establishment" under the Unruh Civil Rights Act.). Finally, irrespective of such legislation, equity courts are much more inclined to intervene in the affairs of a private association where admission practices affect the excluded person's ability to earn a livelihood. A succinct statement to this effect is in Falcone v. Middlesex County Medical Society, 34 N.J. 582, 596, 170 A.2d 791, 799 (1961), where the court said:

When courts originally declined to scrutinize admission practices of membership associations they were dealing with social clubs, religious organizations and fraternal associations. Here the policies against judicial intervention were strong and there were no significant countervailing policies. When the courts were later called upon to deal with trade and professional associations exercising virtually monopolistic control, different factors were involved. The intimate personal relationships which pervaded the social, religious and fraternal organizations were hardly in evidence and the individual's opportunity of earning a livelihood and serving society in his chosen trade or profession appeared as the controlling policy consideration.

See, e.g., DeGregorio v. American Board of Internal Medicine, 1993 WL 719564 (D.N.J.1993) (physician-plaintiff who challenged Board's new practice of issuing time-limited membership certificates stated valid claim for intervention).

2.   It is also much more common for a court to intervene where there has been an expulsion from membership, as opposed to a refusal to admit. This is largely because the expelled member can assert certain rights that are unavailable to his or her counterpart seeking admission. For example, the expelled member may claim: (1) the deprivation of some property interest of the member; (2) the breach of a contractual relationship; or (3) tortious interference with the member's relationship with the organization. *See* Zechariah Chafee, Jr., *The Internal Affairs of Associations Not for Profit,* 43 Harv. L. Rev. 991, 999–1010 (1930).

While courts frequently intervene in expulsion situations to compel a private association to follow its own rules, this is not invariably the case. Consider, for example, the language of the New Jersey Supreme Court in reversing a lower court order reinstating a member of a masonic order who had been expelled from his lodge for alleged misappropriation of lodge funds:

> In determining whether an organization is bound by its established procedures, we would again balance the organization's interest in autonomy and its reasons for straying from its rules against the magnitude of interference with the member's interest in the organization and the likelihood that the established procedure would safeguard that interest.

Rutledge v. Gulian, 93 N.J. 113, 123, 459 A.2d 680, 685 (1983).

3.   Consider the implications of Zelenka v. Benevolent & Protective Order of the Elks, 129 N.J.Super. 379, 324 A.2d 35 (1974). In that case a New Jersey appellate court ruled that it was error for the Chancery Court to have refused to order reinstatement of an expelled member who, without the prior authorization of the Grand Exalted Ruler, had published a letter to the editor calling for an end to the organization's "white male" membership requirement. The court stated:

> We can take judicial notice that the Elks order, comprising about 1 1/2 million members, is one of the most widely located fraternal organizations in the country and that membership in it is highly prized in many communities. There is justification for inferring deep interest in his membership by the present plaintiff, a former head of his lodge. The

personal value to plaintiff of his membership in the order thus calls for an evaluation of his relational interests, weighed against the assertion by the order of a constitutional right of selectivity in the private associations of its members. * * *

* * *

The most searching recent analysis of the general subject, "Developments in the Law—Judicial Control of Actions of Private Associations," 76 Harv.L.Rev. 983 *et seq.* (1963) persuasively observes:

> * * * a court can most confidently adjudicate cases where the group imposes sanctions to enforce a rule or policy which prohibits or inhibits the performance by the individual of a duty or function for the performance of which the state normally relies on individual initiative. The role of the member as a responsible citizen—voter, witness, petitioner to the legislature—is protected. *Id.* at 1006.

The parties are in agreement that the issue here is not whether defendants were justified in expelling plaintiff for urging a change in the order's membership criteria. It is agreed that that was not the basis for the action, but rather plaintiff's expressing any opinion publicly on the matter at all, whether for or against the membership rule, without complying with the lodge regulation requiring approval of the expression by the Grand Exalted Ruler. Defendants urge that their policy against "public washing of private organizational linen" is a justified one and that plaintiff voluntarily sacrificed his right of unqualified freedom of speech to that extent when he joined the order. It may be observed, however, that the pertinent statute of the order does not preclude public expression by a member concerning a fraternal matter if one man—the Grand Exalted Ruler—approves, and such approval is left to that official's absolute discretion.

There is probably no right more fundamental to the liberties of the people and to the successful functioning of the democratic system than that of individual freedom of expression. Undoubtedly that right is qualified in numerous respects by our public laws, and it is similarly qualified in respect of its exercise in the course of one's participation in the activities of private associations. A member of a Republican club, for example, could not expect to be allowed by the courts to campaign for a Democratic candidate and nevertheless remain immune to expulsion from the club for cause.

In the present case, however, defendants profess not to be concerned over plaintiff's espousal of reform of their membership policies. Moreover, nothing in the order's basic purposes and objects, as we read them expressed in the preamble of its constitution, appears to be offended by a member's public plea for support by fellow members on an issue of the significance of racial qualifications for membership in the order without obtaining advance approval by the national head of the order. Nor do defendants contend to the contrary.

The question devolves, then, to one of offense to general public policy in a regulation of the character under consideration. We are not here faced with a regulation enjoining secrecy as to lodge ritual, or imposing restrictions on public discussion by members of matters of peculiar concern to the lodge or order, such as the amount of initiation or other fees or the times and places of meetings, etc., with respect to which there is no general public interest or concern. On the other hand, the matter of racial qualifications for membership in an organization as large, as widespread and as socially significant as the Elks, albeit a private voluntary organization, is a subject conspicuously touching what interests and concerns the general public. *See, e.g.*, Brunson v. Rutherford Lodge, 128 N.J.Super. 66, 319 A.2d 80 (Law Div.1974).

The public policy undergirding the principle of free discussion of issues of such broad public interest as that mentioned, entirely independently of its constitutional sanction in respect of state abridgement, appears to us to far outweigh the private interest of defendants in restricting public discussion of such an issue by their members to those instances in which advance approval is vouchsafed by a single official at national headquarters.

Id. at 382–87, 324 A.2d at 37–39.

4. Suppose a local branch of the NAACP expels a member because she is a Republican or refuses to admit a person because of her race. Or suppose the Knights of Columbus expels a member because he advocates a "pro-choice" position on abortion. Or, alternatively, suppose the National Organization of Women removes a national officer because she decides to advocate the abolition of abortion rights. May a court intervene in any of the foregoing situations? Would judicial intervention in such cases violate the organization's right to association under the First Amendment? Consider Hurley v. Irish–American Gay, Lesbian & Bisexual Group of Boston, 515 U.S. 557, 115 S.Ct. 2338, 132 L.Ed.2d 487 (1995). In that case the City of Boston authorized the South Boston Allied War Veterans Council to conduct the St. Patrick's Day–Evacuation parade (commemorating the evacuation of British forces from Boston in 1776). After the Veterans Council refused to permit a group of gay, lesbian and bisexual veterans to march in the parade, Massachusetts courts ruled that this refusal was impermissible discrimination under a public accommodations law. The United States Supreme Court reversed, holding that, under the First Amendment, a state public accommodation law may not be applied to require "private citizens who organize a parade to include among the marchers a group imparting a message the organizers do not wish to convey." *Id.* Consider also the following analysis:

Perhaps it is best to think of associational rights as proceeding on a continuum from the least protected form of association in commercial activities to the most protected forms of association to engage in political or religious speech or for highly personal reasons, such as family relationships. The association of persons for law practice may thus be regulated to prohibit discrimination on the basis of sex or race. Regulations of law practice that relate to the ability of persons to associate for the advancement of social goals, however, may be protected to a greater extent from governmental regulation.

A boycott for political purposes may receive significant First Amendment protection, although a similar boycott for purposes of maintaining a preferred economic position for one's business or union may receive very little protection. A prohibition of race or sex discrimination in the employment practices of commercial enterprises or in the admissions practices of schools open to a wide segment of the public should not present significant freedom of association problems. A similar restriction on the membership practices of a religious organization that was highly selective in its membership and dedicated to goals totally inconsistent with the acceptance of members of a particular race or sex might present a more significant freedom of association problem even if the Court were to find the goal of ending that form of discrimination would override associational rights.

John E. Nowak & Ronald D. Rotunda, Constitutional Law 1296 (7th ed. 2004).

For an example of the constitutional right of association trumping a state public accommodations statute, see Boy Scouts of America v. Dale, 530 U.S. 640, 120 S.Ct. 2446, 147 L.Ed.2d 554 (2000) (ruling, 5–4, that the Boy Scouts' First Amendment right of expressive association barred the application of a New Jersey public accommodations statute which would have required the Boy Scouts to admit a publicly declared homosexual as a scoutmaster).

5. To what extent should principles governing private associations be applicable to expulsion of students by private colleges and universities? Consider in this regard the language of Harvey v. Palmer College of Chiropractic, 363 N.W.2d 443 (Iowa Ct.App.1984):

Although the due process clause of the fourteenth amendment is applicable only to state action, * * * "[t]he requirements imposed by the common law on private universities parallel those imposed by the due process clause on public universities." Abbariao v. Hamline University School of Law, 258 N.W.2d 108, 113 (Minn.1977). Courts have analyzed the relationship between a student and a private university under several legal theories, including the law of contracts and the law of associations. * * * Neither theory fits perfectly and, therefore, should not be rigidly applied. * * * It is clear, however, that a private university may not expel a student arbitrarily, unreasonably, or in bad faith. * * *

Courts are reluctant to intervene in cases involving dismissal for academic deficiencies since such decisions are within the expertise of the school; but dismissals for disciplinary reasons are more closely scrutinized by the courts. * * *

In Tedeschi v. Wagner College, 49 N.Y.2d 652, 661, 404 N.E.2d 1302, 1306, 427 N.Y.S.2d 760, 765 (1980), a student had been suspended for both academic and nonacademic reasons. However, she was not accorded a hearing before the Student–Faculty Hearing Board as required by the published college guidelines for student suspensions and dismissals. The

New York Court of Appeals found it unnecessary to belabor the legal theory most applicable to the student-college relationship. The court held:

> Whether by analogy to the law of associations, on the basis of a supposed contract between university and student, or simply as a matter of essential fairness in the somewhat one-sided relationship between the institution and the individual, we hold that when a university has adopted a rule or guideline establishing the procedure to be followed in relation to suspension or expulsion that procedure must be substantially observed.

Id. at 660, 404 N.E.2d at 1306, 427 N.Y.S.2d at 764. The court reinstated the plaintiff as a student unless prior to the opening of the fall term she had been disciplined in accordance with established procedures. * * *

A similar result was reached by a federal district court applying New Jersey law in Clayton v. Trustees of Princeton University, 519 F.Supp. 802 (D.N.J.1981). In that case the plaintiff was accused of changing a test answer during a lab practical. He was convicted by the Princeton Honor Committee and suspended from school for one year. *Id.* at 803. After analyzing the New Jersey law of associations the court concluded:

> Certainly the proposition that once an organization has established rules for itself it must follow them is not a radical proposition. Princeton voluntarily promulgated the procedures that Mr. Clayton claims it violated in suspending him. It is not unreasonable to hold Princeton to the requirement of substantial compliance with these procedures.

Id. at 806. The court found there was a material dispute of fact over whether plaintiff had been accorded the procedural protections to which he was entitled under school regulations and, therefore, denied the cross-motions for summary judgment. * * *

Id. at 444–45.

Courts nevertheless apply the above principles with substantial deference to the internal procedures of private colleges and universities. *See, e.g.,* Rollins v. Cardinal Stritch University, 626 N.W.2d 464 (Minn.Ct.App.2001) (holding that school's disciplinary action was not arbitrary and rejecting the argument that a student handbook was a contract between school and student); Schaer v. Brandeis University, 432 Mass. 474, 735 N.E.2d 373 (2000) (the hearing process by which a student was suspended for an alleged rape did not violate fundamental fairness). If anything, courts are more deferential to private high schools in this context. *See* Hernandez v. Don Bosco Preparatory High, 322 N.J.Super. 1, 730 A.2d 365 (1999) (affirming expulsion of student and holding that "a private high school, when expelling a student for misconduct, must follow a two-prong process. First, the private high school must adhere to its own established procedures for dismissal. Second, in executing the dismissal, the school must follow a procedure this is fundamentally fair.").

C. RESTITUTION

NOSSEN v. HOY

United States District Court, Eastern District of Virginia, 1990.
750 F.Supp. 740.

MERHIGE, DISTRICT JUDGE.

* * *

This is an action for the unlawful appropriation of Plaintiff Richard Nossen's name, reputation and work, for conversion of Nossen's property, and for quasi-contract. Nossen, a Virginia citizen, is former Assistant Director of the Internal Revenue Service's Criminal Investigation Division. He is an expert in the field of detection and investigation of financial crimes. He has authored two works in his field: *The Seventh Basic Investigative Technique* and *Determination of Undisclosed Financial Interest*. These books, according to Defendant's pleadings, were published for and by the United States Government, which holds the rights to them.

Defendant Michael Hoy, a citizen of the State of Washington and sole proprietor of Loompanics Unlimited, is a self-described publisher of "controversial and unusual books." He engages in mail order sales of the books he publishes; some of these sales occur in Virginia. Among the books advertised for sale in the 1990 Loompanics catalogue is a publication entitled *Advanced Investigative Techniques for Private Financial Records*, by Richard A. Nossen. This book is a combined reprinting of Nossen's two works. In the book, authorship is specifically attributed to Nossen, whose brief biography appears on the publication's second page. A full page advertisement for the book appears on page three of the catalogue and Hoy has advertised the book in numerous other catalogues. Hoy's advertisement of the book, and its consequent sale for profit, all occurred without Nossen's knowledge, consent or permission.

Nossen alleges that Hoy promotes his publications to those who may wish to engage in criminal activity. He further alleges that Hoy intentionally distorted the characterization of Nossen's works attempting to make sales to his clientele. Nossen alleges that Hoy's activity has led the public to believe that Nossen approves of Hoy's publications and alleges that, as a result of Hoy's appropriation of his name and reputation, Nossen has suffered embarrassment, mental distress and damage to his professional reputation. Nossen alleges that Hoy's actions have and will continue absent intervention from this Court.

Based on these allegations, Nossen has filed suit against Hoy for the unauthorized use of his name pursuant to Virginia Code § 8.01–40, for the unlawful conversion of Nossen's property (his name, reputation and work), and for quasi-contract for the alleged unjust enrichment achieved by Hoy with the use of Nossen's property.

* * *

II. MOTIONS TO DISMISS

Defendant Hoy has submitted a Motion to Dismiss both the conversion claim and the quasi-contract claim. * * *

A. The Conversion Count

Defendant Hoy has moved to dismiss Nossen's action for conversion, which allegedly was due to the wrongful appropriation and use of "the good name, reputation and work of Nossen." * * * [C]onversion occurs where one uses another's personal property as his own and exercises dominion over it without the consent of the owner. * * *

Hoy first contends that Nossen does not state a claim for conversion, arguing that one does not hold a personal property interest in one's name and reputation. Virginia precedent clearly establishes that an individual may hold a property interest in his or her name and likeness. * * * In addition, an individual holds a similar property interest in his or her reputation, which represents the individual's personal identity in the community and which is the thing of value in the individual's name. To attempt to splice an individual's reputation from his or her name, in this context, would countenance disingenuous and unproductive indulgence in semantics. The Court thus concludes that because Nossen alleges that Hoy exercised dominion over his name and reputation—allegedly exploiting both for his financial benefit—Nossen states a claim for conversion of his property interests in his name and reputation * * *.

* * *

* * * Nossen does not allege that he holds a copyright in his work, nor even that the work is copyrighted at all.* * *

B. The Quasi–Contract Contract

Defendant Hoy moves to dismiss Nossen's action for quasi-contract for failure to state a claim. Hoy argues that courts may imply a contract-in-fact only where one person has enriched himself at the expense of another and that, in this case, Nossen has not alleged the loss of a benefit. In addition, Hoy asserts that an action for quasi-contract can succeed only based on joint dealings of the parties and that where, as here, the parties have not dealt with each other, no such action can stand. Hoy confuses the concepts of implied-in-fact contract and quasi-contract.

The implied-in-fact contract is a true contract, containing all of the elements that construct an enforceable agreement. It differs from an actual contract in that the parties have not reduced it to a writing or to an oral agreement; rather, the court infers the implied-in-fact agreement from the course of conduct of the parties. In contrast, a quasi-contract is not a contract at all but rather an equitable remedy thrust upon the recipient of a benefit under conditions where that receipt amounts to unjust enrichment. *See* Marine Dev. Corp. v. Rodak, 225 Va. 137, 300 S.E.2d 763, 766 (1983); C. Kaufman, Corbin on Contracts, § 19, at 50

(Supp.1989) (discussing distinction between implied-in-fact agreement and quasi-contract). At issue here is only the latter concept.

The quasi-contract is a plaintiff's remedy at law when the facts establish that a defendant has been unjustly enriched at the expense of the plaintiff, but where the facts fail to establish that the parties established any form of agreement. To establish a quasi-contract a plaintiff generally must show three elements: (1) A benefit conferred on the defendant by the plaintiff; (2) Knowledge on the part of the defendant of the conferring of the benefit; and (3) Acceptance or retention of the benefit by the defendant in circumstances that render it inequitable for the defendant to retain the benefit without paying for its value. *See* Corbin on Contracts, § 19, at 50 * * *. Both Virginia and Washington recognize the quasi-contract action to recover unjust enrichment. * * *

The facts alleged by Nossen are sufficient to state a claim for quasi-contract. Nossen alleges that Hoy has received a benefit from the use of Nossen's property: his name and reputation. Hoy therefore, allegedly has received a benefit from Nossen without having paid fair consideration and therefore—allegedly—has been unjustly enriched. In addition, Nossen has alleged that Hoy had knowledge of the benefit and has accepted and retained the benefit under circumstances that would make it unfair for him to not pay fair value for its use. To the extent Nossen alleges that Hoy used his name and reputation absent permission and knowingly received a benefit from that use, Nossen states a claim for quasi-contract under both Virginia and Washington law.

* * *

For the foregoing reasons, this Court * * * will deny Defendant's Motion to Dismiss the Conversion Count and the Quasi–Contract Count, insofar as they pertain to Defendant's alleged use of Plaintiff's name and reputation * * *.

NOTES

1. Nossen and Hoy apparently settled their dispute as no further court decisions are reported. Are there any problems with measuring the unjust enrichment recovery? In Hart v. E.P. Dutton & Co., 197 Misc. 274, 93 N.Y.S.2d 871 (1949), *aff'd*, 277 App.Div. 935, 98 N.Y.S.2d 773, *reconsideration denied*, 277 App.Div. 962, 99 N.Y.S.2d 1014 (1950), the plaintiff, Merwin Hart, sued the publisher of a 1943 book entitled "Under Cover" in 1949 on the ground that it had libelously referred to him as a traitor to the United States during World War II. Rather than seeking damages for defamation, which had a one-year statute of limitations, Hart sought to recover the defendant's profits in a quasi-contract action with a six-year statute of limitations. The Court said:

"A quasi or constructive contract rests upon the equitable principle that a person shall not be allowed to enrich himself unjustly at the expense of another" and is created when "because [of] the acts of the parties" a person is possessed of money or property which in equity or good conscience he should not retain. The application of this rule requires inquiry, not only into the acts of the defendant, but also the acts of the plaintiff. One who publishes a libel, especially if done maliciously, as charged in this complaint, is guilty of conduct which makes him liable for damages. An action for damages affords the plaintiff full compensation for any injuries which he has suffered. In addition to compensatory damages he may recover punitive damages if proper foundation is established by the proof. The law requires that a plaintiff must bring his action to recover such damages within one year. It would seem that it is not equitable and just to permit a person, who has been the subject of a libellous article published in a book, to acquiesce in or permit the sale and distribution of such book to continue for a period of nearly six years without taking any steps whatsoever to protest or stop the sale and distribution of the book and then to maintain an action for the profits derived from the sale and distribution of the book. The publication of a book entails great expense and effort on the part of the publisher and the profits derived therefrom are due in large measure to elements outside of the printed matter contained therein. To permit such an action as the plaintiff has brought, under the circumstances alleged in the complaint, would have the effect of making the publisher, for a period of years, the servant of the plaintiff, who, despite his failure to avail himself of a complete legal remedy, may now assert a right to the fruits of the defendant's labor and investment even beyond that which may flow from the alleged libel. Such a situation would be inequitable and would result in the unjust enrichment of the plaintiff. Under such circumstances no contract should be "implied in law" requiring the defendant to account to the plaintiff for profits derived from the publication of the book.

Id. at 280, 93 N.Y.S.2d at 877. With respect to a plaintiff recovering the defendant's gain from the defendant's publication of a book that violated a person's privacy, Professor Palmer has observed that "there would be a virtually insurmountable difficulty in ascertaining the portion of the profits attributable to the parts of the book which constituted an invasion of privacy." 1 George E. Palmer, Law of Restitution, § 2.9, at 129 (1978). With respect to a violation of a person's right of publicity, however, he has said: "The substantive question is whether the defendant is unjustly enriched when he profits through the wrongful use of the plaintiff's name and likeness. If he is, the profit should be recoverable." *Id.* at 46 n.30a (1990 Supp.). *Cf.* Ventura v. Titan Sports, Inc., 65 F.3d 725 (8th Cir. 1995) (plaintiff was allowed to recover royalties in unjust enrichment based on defendant's violation of his right of publicity when defendant showed tapes of plaintiff's live commentary).

2. In Greenspan v. Osheroff, 232 Va. 388, 351 S.E.2d 28 (1986), the defendant, Dr. Greenspan, attempted to take over the medical practice of his partner, Dr. Osheroff, by defaming him to the hospital where he had privileges, and to his patients. Dr. Osheroff sued for a constructive trust upon Dr. Greenspan's profits. The trial court imposed a constructive trust on half of the profits on the ground that Dr. Greenspan had violated his fiduciary duty to Dr. Osheroff. The Virginia Supreme Court held that the award "renders

moot any further consideration of the arguments on appeal relating to defamation and tortious interference with contractual relationships." *Id.* at 399, 351 S.E.2d at 36. Although the Virginia Supreme Court did not find it necessary to rule on the finding of the trial court that the plaintiff had also proven a right to damages at law based upon defamation (because they were cumulative of other damages), is it possible that the profits to which the constructive trust applied could have been awarded as damages in an action for defamation? For further discussion of constructive trusts, see *supra* Chapter 4, Section 3.B.

3. For a discussion of difficulties with using unjust enrichment for interference with reputation or privacy, see Daniel Friedmann, *Restitution of Benefits Obtained Through the Appropriation of Property or the Commission of a Wrong*, 80 Colum. L. Rev. 504 (1980). *See also* Kenneth York, *Extension of Restitutional Remedies*, 4 UCLA L. Rev. 499, 539 (1957).

4. The Supreme Court has held that the First and Fourteenth Amendments do not prevent a state from protecting plaintiff's right of publicity and "the rationale for [protecting that right] is the straightforward one of preventing unjust enrichment." Zacchini v. Scripps–Howard Broadcasting Co., 433 U.S. 562, 576, 97 S.Ct. 2849, 53 L.Ed.2d 965 (1977). What happens when the state wants to *limit* someone's right of publicity? Consider the next case.

SIMON & SCHUSTER, INC. v. MEMBERS OF THE NEW YORK STATE CRIME VICTIMS BOARD

Supreme Court of the United States, 1991.
502 U.S. 105, 112 S.Ct. 501, 116 L.Ed.2d 476.

JUSTICE O'CONNOR delivered the opinion of the Court.

New York's "Son of Sam" law requires that an accused or convicted criminal's income from works describing his crime be deposited in an escrow account. These funds are then made available to the victims of the crime and the criminal's other creditors. We consider whether this statute is consistent with the First Amendment.

* * *

This case began in 1986, when the Board first became aware of the contract between petitioner Simon & Schuster and admitted organized crime figure Henry Hill.

B

Looking back from the safety of the Federal Witness Protection Program, Henry Hill recalled: "At the age of twelve my ambition was to be a gangster. To be a wiseguy. To me being a wiseguy was better than being president of the United States." N. Pileggi, Wiseguy: Life in a Mafia Family 19 (1985) (hereinafter *Wiseguy*). Whatever one might think of Hill, at the very least it can be said that he realized his dreams. After a career spanning 25 years, Hill admitted engineering some of the most daring crimes of his day, including the 1978–1979 Boston College basketball point-shaving scandal, and the theft of $6 million from Lufthansa Airlines in 1978, the largest successful cash robbery in American history. *Wiseguy* 9. Most of Hill's crimes were more banausic: He committed extortion, he imported and distributed narcotics, and he organized numerous robberies.

Hill was arrested in 1980. In exchange for immunity from prosecution, he testified against many of his former colleagues. Since his arrest, he has lived under an assumed name in an unknown part of the country.

In August 1981, Hill entered into a contract with author Nicholas Pileggi for the production of a book about Hill's life. The following month, Hill and Pileggi signed a publishing agreement with Simon & Schuster. Under the agreement, Simon & Schuster agreed to make payments to both Hill and Pileggi. * * *

The result of Hill and Pileggi's collaboration was *Wiseguy*, which was published in January 1986. The book depicts, in colorful detail, the day-to-day existence of organized crime, primarily in Hill's first-person narrative. Throughout *Wiseguy*, Hill frankly admits to having participated in an astonishing variety of crimes. * * *

Wiseguy was reviewed favorably. * * *

From Henry Hill's perspective, however, the publicity generated by the book's success proved less desirable. The Crime Victims Board learned of *Wiseguy* in January 1986, soon after it was published.

C

On January 31, the Board notified Simon & Schuster: "It has come to our attention that you may have contracted with a person accused or convicted of a crime for the payment of monies to such person." * * *

The Board reviewed the book and the contract, and on May 21, 1987, issued a Proposed Determination and Order. The Board determined that *Wiseguy* was covered by § 632–a of the Executive Law, that Simon & Schuster had violated the law by failing to turn over its contract with Hill to the Board and by making payments to Hill, and that all money owed to Hill under the contract had to be turned over to the Board to be held in escrow for the victims of Hill's crimes. The Board ordered Hill to turn over the payments he had already received, and ordered Simon & Schuster to turn over all money payable to Hill at that time or in the future.

Simon & Schuster brought suit in August 1987, under 42 U.S.C. § 1983, seeking a declaration that the Son of Sam law violates the First Amendment and an injunction barring the statute's enforcement. After the parties filed cross-motions for summary judgment, the District Court found the statute consistent with the First Amendment. 724 F.Supp. 170 (S.D.N.Y. 1989). A divided Court of Appeals affirmed. Simon & Schuster, Inc. v. Fischetti, 916 F.2d 777 (C.A.2d 1990).

Because the Federal Government and most of the States have enacted statutes with similar objectives, *see* 18 U.S.C. § 3681; Note, Simon & Schuster, Inc. v. Fischetti: *Can New York's Son of Sam Law Survive First*

Amendment Challenge?, 66 Notre Dame L. Rev. 1075, 1075, n.6 (1991) (listing state statutes), the issue is significant and likely to recur. * * *

* * *

A statute is presumptively inconsistent with the First Amendment if it imposes a financial burden on speakers because of the content of their speech. * * *

* * *

The Son of Sam law is such a content-based statute. It singles out income derived from expressive activity for a burden the State places on no other income, and it is directed only at works with a specified content. Whether the First Amendment "speaker" is considered to be Henry Hill, whose income the statute places in escrow because of the story he has told, or Simon & Schuster, which can publish books about crime with the assistance of only those criminals willing to forgo remuneration for at least five years, the statute plainly imposes a financial disincentive only on speech of a particular content.

* * *

The Son of Sam law establishes a financial disincentive to create or publish works with a particular content. In order to justify such differential treatment, "the State must show that its regulation is necessary to serve a compelling state interest and is narrowly drawn to achieve that end." Arkansas Writers' Project, Inc. v. Ragland, 481 U.S. 221, 231, 107 S.Ct. 1722, 1728 (1987).

* * *

The Board disclaims, as it must, any state interest in suppressing descriptions of crime out of solicitude for the sensibilities of readers. * * * As we have often had occasion to repeat, " '[T]he fact that society may find speech offensive is not a sufficient reason for suppressing it. Indeed, if it is the speaker's opinion that gives offense, that consequence is a reason for according it constitutional protection.' " Hustler Magazine, Inc. v. Falwell, 485 U.S. 46, 55, 99 L.Ed.2d 41, 108 S.Ct. 876 (1988). * * * The Board thus does not assert any interest in limiting whatever anguish Henry Hill's victims may suffer from reliving their victimization.

There can be little doubt, on the other hand, that the State has a compelling interest in ensuring that victims of crime are compensated by those who harm them. * * *

The State likewise has an undisputed compelling interest in ensuring that criminals do not profit from their crimes. Like most if not all States, New York has long recognized the "fundamental equitable principle," Children of Bedford v. Petromelis, 77 N.Y.2d, at 727, 570 N.Y.S.2d, at 460, 573 N.E.2d, at 548, that "[n]o one shall be permitted to profit by his own fraud, or to take advantage of his own wrong, or to found any claim upon his own iniquity, or to acquire property by his own crime." Riggs v.

Palmer, 115 N.Y. 506, 511–512, 22 N.E. 188, 190 (1889). The force of this interest is evidenced by the State's statutory provisions for the forfeiture of the proceeds and instrumentalities of crime. *See* N.Y.Civ.Prac.Law §§ 1310–1352 (McKinney Supp.1991).

The parties debate whether book royalties can properly be termed the profits of crime, but that is a question we need not address here. For the purposes of this case, we can assume without deciding that the income escrowed by the Son of Sam law represents the fruits of crime. We need only conclude that the State has a compelling interest in depriving criminals of the profits of their crimes, and in using these funds to compensate victims.

* * *

As a means of ensuring that victims are compensated from the proceeds of crime, the Son of Sam law is significantly overinclusive. As counsel for the Board conceded at oral argument, the statute applies to works on *any* subject, provided that they express the author's thoughts or recollections about his crime, however tangentially or incidentally. * * * In addition, the statute's broad definition of "person convicted of a crime" enables the Board to escrow the income of any author who admits in his work to having committed a crime, whether or not the author was ever actually accused or convicted. § 632–a(10)(b).

These two provisions combine to encompass a potentially very large number of works. Had the Son of Sam law been in effect at the time and place of publication, it would have escrowed payment for such works as The Autobiography of Malcolm X, which describes crimes committed by the civil rights leader before he became a public figure; Civil Disobedience, in which Thoreau acknowledges his refusal to pay taxes and recalls his experience in jail; and even the Confessions of Saint Augustine, in which the author laments "my past foulness and the carnal corruptions of my soul," one instance of which involved the theft of pears from a neighboring vineyard. *See* A. Haley & Malcolm X, The Autobiography of Malcolm X 108–125 (1964); H. Thoreau, Civil Disobedience 18–22 (1849, reprinted 1969); The Confessions of Saint Augustine 31, 36–37 (Franklin Library ed. 1980). Amicus Association of American Publishers, Inc., has submitted a sobering bibliography listing hundreds of works by American prisoners and ex-prisoners,including works by such authors as Emma Goldman and Martin Luther King, Jr. A list of prominent figures whose autobiographies would be subject to the statute if written is not difficult to construct: The list could include Sir Walter Raleigh, who was convicted of treason after a dubiously conducted 1603 trial; Jesse Jackson, who was arrested in 1963 for trespass and resisting arrest after attempting to be served at a lunch counter in North Carolina; and Bertrand Russell, who was jailed for seven days at the age of 89 for participating in a sit-down protest against nuclear weapons. The argument that a statute like the Son of Sam law would prevent publication of *all* of these works is hyperbole—some would have been written without compensation—but the Son of Sam law clearly reaches a wide range of literature that does not enable a criminal to profit from his crime while a victim remains uncompensated.

* * *

The Federal Government and many of the States have enacted statutes designed to serve purposes similar to that served by the Son of Sam law. Some of these statutes may be quite different from New York's, and we have no occasion to determine the constitutionality of these other laws. We conclude simply that in the Son of Sam law, New York has singled out speech on a particular subject for a financial burden that it places on no other speech and no other income. The State's interest in compensating victims from the fruits of crime is a compelling one, but the Son of Sam law is not narrowly tailored to advance that objective. As a result, the statute is inconsistent with the First Amendment.

The judgment of the Court of Appeals is accordingly reversed.

JUSTICE BLACKMUN, concurring in the judgment.

I am in general agreement with what the Court says in its opinion. I think, however, that the New York statute is underinclusive as well as overinclusive and that we should say so. Most other States have similar legislation and deserve from this Court all the guidance it can render in this very sensitive area.

JUSTICE KENNEDY, concurring in the judgment.

The New York statute we now consider imposes severe restrictions on authors and publishers, using as its sole criterion the content of what is written. The regulated content has the full protection of the First Amendment and this, I submit, is itself a full and sufficient reason for holding the statute unconstitutional. In my view it is both unnecessary and incorrect to ask whether the State can show that the statute " 'is necessary to serve a compelling state interest and is narrowly drawn to achieve that end.' "

NOTES

1. After *Simon & Schuster* was decided, the New York legislature amended the "Son of Sam" law to "avoid[ ] the prior law's first amendment infirmities by targeting all profits of a crime rather than solely specified speech. In 2001, the statute was amended to include not only profits from the crime, but money received by the imprisoned criminal from any source. The current statute has thus far survived constitutional challenges." Thompson v. 76 Corp., 233 N.Y.L.J. 67 (Sup. Ct. 2005). The statute continues to be applied. *See* New York State Crime Victim's Board *ex rel.* Organick v. Harris, 891 N.Y.S.2d 175 (App. Div. 2009) (affirming preliminary injunction pursuant to "Son of Sam" statute ordering funds from guardianship account about to be released to inmate held until claims of victims of inmate could be resolved).

2. For a federal judge's personal opinion as to how Congress should legislate so that federal criminals do not profit from their crime, with a review

of some of the "Son of Sam" statutes that have and have not survived constitutional challenge, see Paul G. Cassell, *Crime Shouldn't Pay: A Proposal to Create an Effective and Constitutional Federal Anti–Profiting Statute*, 19 Fed. Sent. R. 119 (2006).

3.   Is the New York Son of Sam statute restitutionary? *See* Gareth Jones, *Restitution and Unjust Enrichment: Stripping a Criminal of the Profits of Crime*, 1 Theoretical Inquiries L. 59 (2000) (asserting that the purpose of restitution is to prevent a criminal from benefitting from a crime, not to compensate the victim).

4.   Is Snepp v. United States, 444 U.S. 507, 100 S.Ct. 763, 62 L.Ed.2d 704 (1980) reconcilable with *Simon & Schuster*? In *Snepp* a former CIA employee published a book entitled "Decent Interval" about CIA activities in Vietnam without obtaining prepublication clearance from the CIA, as required by his contracts with the Agency. The Supreme Court upheld a constructive trust on Snepp's proceeds from the book, discussing the First Amendment arguments in a footnote:

> The Court of Appeals and the District Court rejected each of Snepp's defenses to the enforcement of his contract. * * * In his petition for certiorari, Snepp relies primarily on the claim that his agreement is unenforceable as a prior restraint on protected speech.

> When Snepp accepted employment with the CIA, he voluntarily signed the agreement that expressly obligated him to submit any proposed publication for prior review. He does not claim that he executed this agreement under duress. Indeed, he voluntarily reaffirmed his obligation when he left the Agency. We agree with the Court of Appeals that Snepp's agreement is an "entirely appropriate" exercise of the CIA Director's statutory mandate to "protec[t] intelligence sources and methods from unauthorized disclosure," 50 U.S.C. § 403(d)(3). 595 F.2d at 932. Moreover, this Court's cases make clear that—even in the absence of an express agreement—the CIA could have acted to protect substantial government interests by imposing reasonable restrictions on employee activities that in other contexts might be protected by the First Amendment. The Government has a compelling interest in protecting both the secrecy of information important to our national security and the appearance of confidentiality so essential to the effective operation of our foreign intelligence service. * * * The agreement that Snepp signed is a reasonable means for protecting this vital interest.

Id. at 510 n.3, 100 S.Ct. at 765 n.3, 621 L.Ed.2d 404. Can First Amendment rights be relinquished by contract, but not by murder? Are national security interests *sui generis*? For a comparison of *Simon & Schuster* and *Snepp*, see Garrett Epps, *Wising Up: "Son of Sam" Laws and the Speech and Press Clauses*, 70 N.C. L. Rev. 493 (1992). *See also* Andrew Kull, *Private Law, Punishment, and Disgorgement: Restitution's Outlaws*, 78 Chi.-Kent L. Rev. 17 (2003) (expressing concern that the government did not make allowance for the value of Snepp's efforts when it imposed a constructive trust on all of the proceeds from the unapproved book).

5.   Can a prohibition against profiting in any way from a crime be imposed as part of a criminal sentence? *See* Commonwealth v. Power, 420

Mass. 410, 650 N.E.2d 87 (1995). Katherine Ann Power was an anti-Vietnam War protester who was involved in the killing of a policeman. She turned herself in to police after having hidden for 23 years. As part of her plea bargain, in which she was sentenced to eight to twelve years in jail and twenty years' probation, she agreed not to engage in any "profit or benefit generating activity relating to the publication of facts or circumstances pertaining to [her] involvement in the criminal acts for which [she was] convicted." The Supreme Court of Massachusetts upheld the plea agreement against a First Amendment challenge, and distinguished *Simon & Schuster* on the ground that she was allowed to speak: the only restriction was "profiting" and furthermore *"Simon & Schuster* * * * involved a statute of general applicability * * *. The defendant in the case at bar is a convicted felon and the special condition is part of her probationary sentence." *Id.* at 414–16, 650 N.E.2d at 90–91; *see also* Shaun B. Spencer, Note, *Does Crime Pay—Can Probation Stop Katherine Ann Power from Selling Her Story?*, 35 B.C. L. Rev. 1203 (1994) (arguing that Power's probationary restriction was unnecessary and unconstitutional); Shana Weiss, Note, *A Penny for Your Thoughts: Revisiting* Commonwealth v. Power, 17 Loy. L.A. Ent. L. Rev. 201 (1996) (arguing that *Power's* restriction would be unconstitutional if judged under an intermediate scrutiny test).

CHAPTER 7

REMEDIES FOR BREACH OF CONTRACT AND FRAUD

■ ■ ■

After reviewing basic principles of damages for breach of contract, this Chapter focuses on considerations involved in choosing between damages and rescission for both breach of contract and fraudulently induced contracts. It then focuses on remedies for breaches of contracts for different subject matters: goods, real property and services. Because of the differences among these three types of transactions, each has some remedies that are not transferable to the other. Next this Chapter considers complications when parties have agreed to resolve their differences through arbitration. The last section of the Chapter covers the rare occasions when parties may be able to obtain an equitable court order reforming a contract.

SECTION 1. BASIC PRINCIPLES

Besides discussing different contractual interests that can be protected by different remedies, this first case also cautions students about the importance of understanding remedial theory.

FREUND v. WASHINGTON SQUARE PRESS, INC.

Court of Appeals of New York, 1974.
34 N.Y.2d 379, 357 N.Y.S.2d 857, 314 N.E.2d 419.

SAMUEL RABIN, JUDGE.

In this action for breach of a publishing contract, we must decide what damages are recoverable for defendant's failure to publish plaintiff's manuscript. In 1965, plaintiff, an author and a college teacher, and defendant, Washington Square Press, Inc., entered into a written agreement which, in relevant part, provided as follows. Plaintiff ("author") granted defendant ("publisher") exclusive rights to publish and sell in book form plaintiff's work on modern drama. Upon plaintiff's delivery of the manuscript, defendant agreed to complete payment of a nonreturnable $2,000 "advance". Thereafter, if defendant deemed the manuscript not

1125

"suitable for publication," it had the right to terminate the agreement by written notice within 60 days of delivery. Unless so terminated, defendant agreed to publish the work in hardbound edition within 18 months and afterwards in paperbound edition. The contract further provided that defendant would pay royalties to plaintiff, based upon specified percentages of sales. (For example, plaintiff was to receive 10% of the retail price of the first 10,000 copies sold in the continental United States.) If defendant failed to publish within 18 months, the contract provided that "this agreement shall terminate and the rights herein granted to the Publisher shall revert to the Author. In such event all payments theretofore made to the Author shall belong to the Author without prejudice to any other remedies which the Author may have." * * *

Plaintiff performed by delivering his manuscript to defendant and was paid his $2,000 advance. Defendant thereafter merged with another publisher and ceased publishing in hardbound. Although defendant did not exercise its 60–day right to terminate, it has refused to publish the manuscript in any form.

Plaintiff commenced the instant action * * * and initially sought specific performance of the contract. The Trial Term Justice denied specific performance but, finding a valid contract and a breach by defendant, set the matter down for trial on the issue of monetary damages, if any, sustained by the plaintiff. At trial, plaintiff sought to prove: (1) delay of his academic promotion; (2) loss of royalties which would have been earned; and (3) the cost of publication if plaintiff had made his own arrangements to publish. The trial court found that plaintiff had been promoted despite defendant's failure to publish, and that there was no evidence that the breach had caused any delay. Recovery of lost royalties was denied without discussion. The court found, however, that the cost of hardcover publication to plaintiff was the natural and probable consequence of the breach and, based upon expert testimony, awarded $10,000 to cover this cost. It denied recovery of the expenses of paperbound publication on the ground that plaintiff's proof was conjectural.

The Appellate Division (3 to 2) affirmed, finding that the cost of publication was the proper measure of damages. In support of its conclusion, the majority analogized to the construction contract situation where the cost of completion may be the proper measure of damages for a builder's failure to complete a house or for use of wrong materials. The dissent concluded that the cost of publication is not an appropriate measure of damages and consequently, that plaintiff may recover nominal damages only.[1] We agree with the dissent. In so concluding, we look to the basic purpose of damage recovery and the nature and effect of the parties' contract.

It is axiomatic that, except where punitive damages are allowable, the law awards damages for breach of contract to compensate for injury

---

1. Plaintiff does not challenge the trial court's denial of damages for delay in promotion or for anticipated royalties.

caused by the breach—injury which was foreseeable, i.e., reasonably within the contemplation of the parties, at the time the contract was entered into. * * * Money damages are substitutional relief designed in theory "to put the injured party in as good a position as he would have been put by full performance of the contract, at the least cost to the defendant and without charging him with harms that he had no sufficient reason to foresee when he made the contract." (5 Corbin, Contracts, § 1002, pp. 31–32; 11 Williston, Contracts [3d ed.], § 1338, p. 198.) In other words, so far as possible, the law attempts to secure to the injured party the benefit of his bargain, subject to the limitations that the injury—whether it be losses suffered or gains prevented—was foreseeable, and that the amount of damages claimed be measurable with a reasonable degree of certainty and, of course, adequately proven. (*See, generally,* Dobbs, Law of Remedies, p. 148; *see, also,* Farnsworth, *Legal Remedies for Breach of Contract*, 70 Col.L.Rev. 1145, 1159.) But it is equally fundamental that the injured party should not recover more from the breach than he would have gained had the contract been fully performed. (* * * Dobbs, Law of Remedies, p. 810.)

Measurement of damages in this case according to the cost of publication to the plaintiff would confer greater advantage than performance of the contract would have entailed to plaintiff and would place him in a far better position than he would have occupied had the defendant fully performed. Such measurement bears no relation to compensation for plaintiff's actual loss or anticipated profit. Far beyond compensating plaintiff for the interests he had in the defendant's performance of the contract—whether restitution, reliance or expectation (*see* Fuller & Perdue, *Reliance Interest in Contract Damages*, 46 Yale L.J. 52, 53–56) an award of the cost of publication would enrich plaintiff at defendant's expense.

Pursuant to the contract, plaintiff delivered his manuscript to the defendant. In doing so, he conferred a value on the defendant which, upon defendant's breach, was required to be restored to him. Special Term, in addition to ordering a trial on the issue of damages, ordered defendant to return the manuscript to plaintiff and plaintiff's restitution interest in the contract was thereby protected. (*Cf.* 5 Corbin, Contracts, § 996, p. 15.)

At the trial on the issue of damages, plaintiff alleged no reliance losses suffered in performing the contract or in making necessary preparations to perform. Had such losses, if foreseeable and ascertainable, been incurred, plaintiff would have been entitled to compensation for them. * * *

As for plaintiff's expectation interest in the contract, it was basically twofold—the "advance" and the royalties. (To be sure, plaintiff may have expected to enjoy whatever notoriety, prestige or other benefits that might have attended publication, but even if these expectations were compensable, plaintiff did not attempt at trial to place a monetary value on them.) There is no dispute that plaintiff's expectancy in the "advance" was fulfilled—he has received his $2,000. His expectancy interest in the royalties—the profit he stood to gain from sale of the published book—while theoretically compensable, was speculative. Although this work is not plaintiff's first, at trial he provided no stable foundation for a reasonable estimate of royalties he would have earned had defendant not breached its promise to publish. In these circumstances, his claim for royalties falls for uncertainty. * * *

Since the damages which would have compensated plaintiff for anticipated royalties were not proved with the required certainty, we agree with the dissent in the Appellate Division that nominal damages alone are recoverable. * * * Though these are damages in name only and not at all compensatory, they are nevertheless awarded as a formal vindication of plaintiff's legal right to compensation which has not been given a sufficiently certain monetary valuation. * * *

In our view, the analogy by the majority in the Appellate Division to the construction contract situation was inapposite. In the typical construction contract, the owner agrees to pay money or other consideration to a builder and expects, under the contract, to receive a completed building in return. The value of the promised performance to the owner is the properly constructed building. In this case, unlike the typical construction contract, the value to plaintiff of the promised performance—publication—was a percentage of sales of the books published and not the books themselves. Had the plaintiff contracted for the printing, binding and delivery of a number of hardbound copies of his manuscript, to be sold or disposed of as he wished, then perhaps the construction analogy, and measurement of damages by the cost of replacement or completion, would have some application.

Here, however, the specific value to plaintiff of the promised publication was the royalties he stood to receive from defendant's sales of the published book. Essentially, publication represented what it would have cost the defendant to confer that value upon the plaintiff, and, by its breach, defendant saved that cost. The error by the courts below was in measuring damages not by the value to plaintiff of the promised performance but by the cost of that performance to defendant. Damages are not measured, however, by what the defaulting party saved by the breach, but by the natural and probable consequences of the breach *to the plaintiff.* In this case, the consequence to plaintiff of defendant's failure to publish is that he is prevented from realizing the gains promised by the contract—the royalties. But, as we have stated, the amount of royalties plaintiff would have realized was not ascertained with adequate certainty and, as a consequence, plaintiff may recover nominal damages only.

Accordingly, the order of the Appellate Division should be modified to the extent of reducing the damage award of $10,000 for the cost of publication to six cents * * *.

Order modified, with costs and disbursements to plaintiff respondent * * * and as so modified, affirmed.

NOTES

1. The Restatement (Second) of Contracts defines the purposes of contractual remedies as follows:

Judicial remedies under the rules stated in this Restatement serve to protect one or more of the following interests of a promisee:

(a) his "expectation interest," which is his interest in having the benefit of his bargain by being put in as good a position as he would have been in had the contract been performed,

(b) his "reliance interest," which is his interest in being reimbursed for loss caused by reliance on the contract by being put in as good a position as he would have been in had the contract not been made, or

(c) his "restitution interest," which is his interest in having restored to him any benefit that he has conferred on the other party.

Restatement (Second) of Contracts § 344 (1981).* For a discussion of the restitution interest in contract see Section 4.B of Chapter 4.

2. Plaintiff's expectation interest can be met with either equitable or legal relief. Professor Freund originally asked for specific performance, which is the label for equitable relief for breach of contract. Why do you think the trial judge in Freund denied the professor's request for specific performance?

3. Each of the three types of transactions covered in Sections 3–5 of this Chapter—the sale of goods, real property, and services—has a section on specific performance. While the basic underpinnings of specific performance are the same for each type of transaction, there are also substantially different rules that reflect the tangible differences between goods, real property and services.

4. Legal expectation damages are composed of three different measurements. Direct damages measure the value of the breached promise by comparing the contract price with the fair market or mitigated value of the goods, real property or services, as will be seen in Sections 3–5. Whether the contract price is subtracted from the comparative value or vice verse depends on whether the seller or buyer is in breach. Incidental damages measure the cost of acquiring mitigation, if mitigation is available. Consequential damages measure certain other losses caused by the breach, but not part of the promised performance of the breaching party. As discussed in Section 3.B of Chapter 3, a nonbreaching party can recover consequential damages only if that party can prove that those damages were contemplated by the parties at the time of contracting. Since direct and incidental damages measure the value of the stated promise that was breached, and its mitigation if available, the formula used to measure those damages will always be contemplated by the parties at the time of contracting, even if the amount of the comparative values will not.

---

* Reprinted with permission of The American Law Institute.

5. The court in *Freund* listed reliance as one of the interests protected by one of the types of contractual remedies. When does a plaintiff in a breach of contract action seek reliance damages instead of expectation damages? *See* C.C. Hauff Hardware, Inc. v. Long Manufacturing Co., 260 Iowa 30, 148 N.W.2d 425 (1967). In *C.C. Hauff Hardware*, the plaintiff was wrongfully terminated as an exclusive dealer of defendant's farm machinery. The plaintiff was unable to prove the amount of his lost profits for the remainder of his contract, but had incurred promotional and other costs. The appellate court affirmed an award for plaintiff, saying:

> Being a new enterprise with considerable promotional expense plaintiff's profit from 13 months operation was only $3299.44. The trial court subtracted the profit from the total expenses and found defendant liable to plaintiff for promotional expenses of $2436.68.

> The fact that profits in the future are too uncertain for recovery does not prevent a judgment for the amount of plaintiff's expenditures. Expenditures in preparation and part performance are recoverable as an alternative measure of gains prevented especially when other measures fail. * * * 22 Am.Jur.2d, Damages, section 159, pages 227, 228, states: "A party who has entered into a contract may incur certain expenses in reliance on that contract being performed. Where the other party to the contract defaults on his promise, those reliance expenses may be valueless to the nondefaulting party. * * * In this type of situation—where expenses were incurred in reliance on the contract and are valueless to the nondefaulting party—courts award reliance expenses if those expenses were foreseeable by the defaulting party at the time the contract was entered into."

Id. at 34–35, 148 N.W.2d at 428. Would the recovery have been different if the plaintiff were operating at a loss? *See* Wartzman v. Hightower Productions, Ltd., 53 Md. App. 656, 662, 456 A.2d 82, 86 (1983) ("If it can be shown that full performance would have resulted in a net loss, the plaintiff cannot escape the consequences of a bad bargain by falling back on his reliance interest.").

6. Can a plaintiff seek reliance damages if they would yield a better recovery than would expectation damages? Can a plaintiff recover both reliance and expectation damages? *See* Beefy Trail, Inc. v. Beefy King International, Inc., 267 So.2d 853 (Fla.Dist.Ct.App.1972), in which the court said:

> Had the defaulting party performed, the plaintiff would have had the opportunity of realizing profits which, however, cannot be recovered as damages because of the rule against allowing speculative damages. Since the reliance expenses are not speculative, there is no reason to deny their recovery if they were foreseeable at the time the contract was entered into. Of course, if profits from the collateral transactions are recovered and if they are computed so as to cover the reliance expenses, then awarding these expenses as a further item of damages would amount to double recovery and should not be allowed.

Id. at 856.

7. *Freund* identified expectation as one type of recovery for breach of contract, but rejected the method plaintiff used to measure those damages. If

you had represented Professor Freund, how would you have sought to prove his expectation damages?

SECTION 2.   RESCISSION OR DAMAGES

A.   RESCISSION

PETRUCELLI v. PALMER

United States District Court for the District of Connecticut, 2009.
596 F. Supp. 2d 347.

CHARLES S. HAIGHT, JR., SENIOR UNITED STATES DISTRICT JUDGE.

* * *

This is a case of mistake in a real estate transaction. Plaintiffs Michael and Margaret Petrucelli mistakenly believed that a weekend home they were buying from defendant Jeannine Palmer was fully contained within the boundaries of its plot, and that there were no problems with encroachment onto adjacent properties.

The mistake may or may not have been mutual: defendant Palmer claims she did not know that the property had any such problems, but plaintiffs question her credibility. The mistake also might or might not have been caused by Palmer's representations on a schedule attached to the contract for sale—the Petrucellis say they relied on this form, but Palmer disputes that claim. But these disputes, while important, are not dispositive.

It is undisputed that within weeks of the closing, a survey revealed to the Petrucellis, for the first time, that a corner of the house itself as well as most or all of the septic system are located beyond the rear boundary of the property, on the strip of shoreline that surrounds the lake and is controlled by a power company.

Once this fact was revealed, it imposed considerable restraints on what the Petrucellis could do with their newly acquired property. They promptly demanded a rescission of the transaction. Defendant refused, and this lawsuit followed. * * *

* * * [T]he parties have cross-moved for summary judgment. The Petrucellis ask the Court to rescind the transaction entirely.[2] Palmer seeks a judgment that any recovery is barred because the mistake was more the fault of the Petrucellis than her own.

In the final analysis, whether Palmer had absolutely no knowledge of the problems or whether she knew everything and lied is not material. Similarly, there is no genuine issue as to whether or not the Petrucellis relied on her representations. For the reasons that follow, the Court

---

2. Plaintiffs also assert, as part of the equitable remedy of rescission, monetary claims in amounts sufficient to place themselves in the position they were in prior to the transaction, while still arguing that the motion "exclusively requests the remedy of rescission." Pls.'s Reply Mem. [doc. #33] at 2. * * *

concludes that this case is tailor-made for application of the equitable remedy of rescission.

* * *

The property that changed hands * * * is a small plot of land measuring 0.109 acres. It backs up against the shoreline of Candlewood Lake. The location of that rear boundary was originally determined based on a fixed elevation of 440 feet above sea level.[4] The parties' submissions refer to this line as the "440' contour line." I will do so in this opinion.

* * *

The uncontroverted testimony is that Margaret Petrucelli knew, prior to the closing, that the 440' contour line determined the rear boundary of her property. But crucially, she did not know what that line was, or where precisely on the property it was located. The Petrucellis allege, and Palmer admits, that "[u]pon receipt and review of the Property Survey ... the plaintiffs were shocked to learn that a portion of the house at the Premises and almost all of the rear yard, including the area where the septic tank and leaching fields are located, are beyond the rear boundary line of the Premises." * * *

Less clear from the record is how much Palmer knew about the location of the 440' contour line or the encroachment problems posed by the rear corner of the house and the septic system. In her statement of material facts as to which she contends there is no dispute, Palmer alleges:

> 7. At no time during her period of ownership was Palmer aware of any issues regarding the location of the septic system or how the house was situated on the lot.

* * *

> 13. Palmer's husband had taken care of issues relating to the property.

Def.'s Local Rule 56(a)(1) Statement [doc. #25] at 2–3.

The Petrucellis contest these assertions. They acknowledge that Palmer "testified during her deposition on May 29, 2008, that she was not aware of any issues regarding the encroachments at the premises," but seek to discredit this testimony by pointing to other perceived inconsistencies between what Palmer has said and written with respect to her knowledge of the boundaries at the Premises. * * *

---

4. The reason for determining the boundary based on a fixed elevation apparently relates to the fact that the water level on Candlewood Lake fluctuates based on the usage of a hydroelectric dam currently operated by licensee FirstLight. In order to permit the operator of that dam to control the water level, the Federal Energy Regulatory Commission was given title to all the shoreline up to that certain elevation. * * *

This dispute may be genuine, but it is not material under the governing law. The result is the same, whether Palmer was telling the truth in her deposition or not.

* * *

C. Written Representations

I begin with the transaction documents. The Petrucellis argue that they contain unambiguous representations that are demonstrably inaccurate.

The most salient of these representations appear in Schedule B to the contract of sale. Schedule B's prefatory paragraph reads: "Seller has no reasonable cause to doubt the accuracy of *and hereby represents, in order to induce Buyer to enter into this Contract, that* ... *the following statements are accurate:....*" * * * Paragraph D provides in part: "Any buildings, appurtenances, systems and driveways servicing said Premises are entirely within the boundary lines of said Premises." Paragraph K provides in part: "The *Seller represents* that the Premises are serviced by a septic tank and leaching fields located entirely within the lot lines of the Premises, [and] that the tank and fields serve no other Premises." * * * (emphasis added).

Palmer concedes that the statements in paragraphs D and K of Schedule B were inaccurate. Given the post-sale survey, she must do so. * * *

* * *

E. Liability in Contract

The plaintiffs' first cause of action is for breach of contract. * * * Since it uncontested that the Premises that Palmer delivered did not comport with those representations, I conclude without difficulty that there is no genuine issue of material fact on Count One. Palmer breached the Contract.

As to the relief requested, Connecticut law clearly allows and even encourages rescission as a remedy for complaint that sounds in "breach of contract." Connecticut's Appellate Court has said that "rescission and restitution is an alternative to damages in an action for breach of contract.... [Rescission] places the parties, as nearly as possible, in the same situation as existed just prior to the execution of the contract." * * *

In a complaint that sounds in breach of contract, the elements of a successful claim for rescission are that "there has been a *material misrepresentation* of fact upon which a party *relied* and which *caused* it to enter the contract. The material misrepresentation, when made in connection with the sale of land, may be an innocent misrepresentation." * * *

Because the misrepresentation may be innocent, Palmer's state of mind when making the misrepresentation is irrelevant to the claim for breach of contract, and thus with respect to the claim for breach of contract, any issue of fact with respect to Palmer's knowledge of the boundary is not material.

* * *

Another "condition precedent to rescission is the offer to restore the other party to its former condition as nearly as possible." * * * Here, there is no dispute that the plaintiffs made such an offer, and that the defendant refused. * * *

Finally, if rescission is chosen as a remedy, it usually operates as a waiver of the right to sue for damages. * * * Usually, a judgment cannot stand if both damages and rescission are awarded. * * * Since the Petrucellis have expressly disavowed any claim for damages at the summary judgment stage, they are entitled to seek rescission.[10]

Another contract theory which supports the rescission of the Contract in this case is the concept of mistake, whereby a contract is voidable when one or both parties to the contract are suffering under a misconception as to the actual state of the world. * * * Indeed, it is blackletter law that a contract is voidable on grounds of "mistake, fraud, or unconscionability."

According to the Restatement (Second) of Contracts, a mutual mistake by all parties to the contract renders the agreement voidable, see Restatement (Second) of Contracts § 152 (1981), and a mistake by one party renders the contract voidable at that party's election if enforcement would be unconscionable or if "the other party had reason to know of the mistake or his fault caused the mistake." * * * Thus, if both the Petrucellis and Palmer were mistaken as to the location of the rear boundary at the Premises, then the contract is voidable by the Petrucellis, who are the "adversely affected party." * * * In any event, the Petrucellis are entitled to rescind the contract because "[Palmer's] fault caused the mistake," since (even accepting Palmer's denial of knowledge of the boundary) she affirmatively represented in Schedule B something she did not know to be true, and the Petrucellis relied on that misrepresentation.

Because I hold that the Petrucellis are entitled to rescission on a purely contractual theory, there is no need to decide the remainder of their claims, which sound in tort and equity. However, in the interests of a full and complete resolution of this matter, I nevertheless consider all those claims in the alternative.

* * *

---

10. The Petrucellis do make a claim for *consequential* damages as part of the equitable remedy of rescission, since that remedy seeks to return the parties as nearly as possible to the *status quo ante*. That is not the same as a pure claim for damages, which would operate to preclude a claim for rescission. * * *

F. Liability in Tort

The Petrucellis have alleged three counts that sound in tort: fraud in the sale of property (Count Two), negligent misrepresentation (Count Three), and innocent misrepresentation (Count Four).

1. Count Two: Fraud in the Sale of Property

In order for the plaintiffs to succeed on a claim of fraud, they must prove by clear and convincing evidence that "(1) a false representation was made as a statement of fact; (2) it was untrue and known to be untrue by the party making it; (3) it was made to induce the other party to act upon it; and (4) the other party did so act upon that false representation to his injury." * * *

The Petrucellis' claim of fraud is weakest on the question of whether Palmer actually knew that the representations she made in Schedule B were untrue. But under an a series of earlier Connecticut Supreme Court cases, a claim for fraud can also succeed if a defendant "asserts that he knows what he does not know." * * * Under this line of cases, Palmer is liable for fraud whether she knew her misrepresentations in Schedule B to be false or not. * * *

* * *

* * * [T]here is a higher standard of proof required to succeed in a claim for fraudulent misrepresentation. That standard is clear and convincing evidence, as opposed to a preponderance of the evidence in negligent and innocent misrepresentation theories. * * *

* * *

While the *per se* fraud liability rule announced in * * * older cases may still be viable, it seems more likely to me that such strict-liability claims like the one the Petrucellis assert are better raised today under the caption of negligent or innocent misrepresentation. * * * I cannot conclude on this record that a reasonable jury would be forced to conclude, by clear and convincing evidence, that Palmer's misrepresentations were made with the intentionality or "recklessness" that a successful claim for fraudulent misrepresentation appears to require.

2. Count Three: Negligent Misrepresentation

The elements of a claim for negligent misrepresentation are set forth in the Restatement of Torts: "One who ... supplies false information for the guidance of others in their business transactions, is subject to liability for pecuniary loss caused to them by their justifiable reliance upon the information, if he fails to exercise reasonable care or competence in obtaining or communicating the information." Citino v. Redev. Agency of the City of Hartford, 721 A.2d at 1206, 51 Conn. App. at 273–274 (quoting Restatement (Second) of Torts § 552 (1979); collecting Connecticut cases). * * *

* * *

I conclude that no reasonable jury could find other than that Palmer is liable for her misstatements under a theory of negligent misrepresentation. * * * Thus, the plaintiffs are entitled to their requested remedy on this count.

3. Count Four: Innocent Misrepresentation

Of all of the counts alleged by the Petrucellis, the claim of innocent misrepresentation comes the closest to a "strict liability" tort * * * which "is predicated on principles of warranty." * * *

The elements of a claim for innocent misrepresentation are simpler than those for fraudulent or negligent misrepresentation.

> The elements of innocent misrepresentation are (1) a representation of material fact (2) made for the purpose of inducing the purchase, (3) the representation is untrue, and (4) there is justifiable reliance by the plaintiff on the representation by the defendant and (5) damages.

* * * [A]ll the elements of a claim for innocent representation are clearly established in the record, and no reasonable jury could find otherwise. Since the plaintiffs have elected to forego the traditional remedy of damages, rescission is appropriate.

* * *

G. Plaintiffs' Equitable Claim for Rescission

For their fifth and final cause of action, the Petrucellis simply plead "rescission." In seeking this equitable remedy, the plaintiffs cite Connecticut case law which allows rescission to be pled as a separate claim for relief. * * *

Balancing the equities "is a matter for the discretion of the trial court." *Wallenta v. Moscowitz*, 839 A.2d at 660, 81 Conn. App. at 241. "[T]he decision to award a remedy for rescission for breach of contract always depends upon a showing of what justice requires in the particular circumstances, and thus necessarily rests in the discretion of the trial court." * * *

Palmer contends that this transaction should not be disturbed, and the plaintiffs' claims should be denied, because "there is a workable solution" to allow for a new septic system to be installed, and "a license can be obtained for the encroachment of the house." Def.'s Mem. in Opp'n [doc. #30] at 10. Without placing any particular reliance on possibly inadmissible expert testimony, I would simply note that the Petrucellis allege, and Palmer admits, that a representative of FirstLight advised Mrs. Petrucelli that "it would not issue a license or grant other permission to maintain the septic system encroachment," but might allow the house encroachment to remain in place. * * *

But more importantly, the Petrucellis did not intend to purchase, nor does it appear that Palmer intended to sell, a piece of property that was legally and physically constrained in the way the Premises now appear to be. I am guided in particular by the Connecticut Appellate Court's reasoning in Kavarco:

> The equitable remedy of rescission is not barred because of the fact that the defrauded party suffered no pecuniary loss. The purchase of real estate for a residence happens infrequently in the lifetime of the average family. The very fact that the land did not have the fundamental characteristics which were attributed to it by the seller is sufficient in and of itself to show that the buyer suffered damage or irreparable harm. If damages would be inadequate for justice in a particular case, rescission and restitution is the proper remedy.[16]

Kavarco [v. T.J.E., Inc., 2 Conn.App. 294, 299–300, 478 A.2d 257, 261 (1984), *overruled on burden of proof issue by* Kaczynski v. Kaczynski, 294 Conn. 121, 981 A.2d 1068 (2009)]. I find that here, damages would indeed be "inadequate for justice," and therefore rescission is the only proper remedy.

* * *

In addition to a complete unmaking of the contract, the Petrucellis have also sought to be compensated, in equity, for the expenses they incurred as a result of the voidable contract to buy the Premises. Those claimed expenses total $90,323.69. They are itemized in an affidavit executed by Margaret Petrucelli. The principal items are legal fees and costs the plaintiffs incurred in this action, totaling $37,319.92, and mortgage payments paid by plaintiffs after the closing, totaling $23,982.00. The other items are for closing costs, taxes, surveys, minor repairs to the house, and similar expenses.

"Rescission, simply stated, is the unmaking of a contract. It is a renouncement of the contract and any property obtained pursuant to the contract and places the parties, as nearly as possible, in the same situation as existed *just prior to the execution of the contract.*" * * *

For the non-legal expenses itemized in Margaret Petrucelli's affidavit, Palmer's liability for them turns upon principles of equity. That question is not free from doubt. There is no compelling basis upon which to conclude that Palmer knew the representations she made in Schedule B with respect to the Premises' boundaries were not true, and that she made them with the specific intent to mislead the Petrucellis. The inference I

---

16. Although the Appellate Court refers to both "rescission and restitution" as though they were part of the same remedy (singular), I note that these are more appropriately considered as two separate concepts. See Black's Law Dictionary, "Restitution" (8th ed. 2004) (defining restitution primarily as a kind of compensation for "unjust enrichment," and the set of associated remedies "in which the measure of recovery is usu[ally] based not on the plaintiff's loss, but on the defendant's gain"). As the Appellate Court considered in Wallenta v. Moscowitz, principles of restitution, in a case of rescission, will address the question of how to credit each side for the benefits they have derived from the property that changed hands, during the time between the execution of the contract and its later rescission. See 839 A.2d at 660–62. Neither party in this case has alleged that the Court should setoff any recovery to account for such unjust enrichment.

draw from the record is that Palmer relied upon her late husband for the administration of the second home they enjoyed together, and did not know that a corner of the house and the septic system were outside the boundaries of the plot of land she owned. She is liable to the Petrucellis only because Connecticut law takes that harsh view with respect to those who represent that something is true when they do not know if it is. Nor, I imagine, was Palmer sufficiently schooled in the law to understand the meaning, effect, and potential consequences of the representations made in her name in Schedule B. For that understanding, she relied upon the attorney she retained to protect her interests; and *quaere* whether counsel should have agreed to Schedule B as drafted by the Petrucellis' attorney without first making sure that the representations by Palmer contained therein were accurate.

While these factors might incline a court of equity to regard Palmer with sympathy, the equitable case for the Petrucellis is stronger. They did not make the false representations. Mrs. Palmer did so—even if, as I will assume, unwittingly—and the Petrucellis relied upon those representations to their cost. The Petrucellis paid taxes on the Premises because they were listed on the tax rolls as owners of the property: a status they would not have had if Palmer's false representations had not induced them to purchase it. The case is the same with respect to the other expenses itemized in Margaret Petrucelli's affidavit. Someone must bear these expenses. It is more equitable that Palmer bear them, since if she does not, the Petrucellis are out of pocket through no fault of their own and are not returned to the economic position they were in immediately prior to the closing.

Furthermore, most of the Petrucellis' non-legal expenses, such as taxes and reasonable charges for utilities, insurance, and other upkeep, would have been incurred by Palmer if she had retained title to the property. Those expenditures were effectively an investment in the property itself. Upon rescission of the contract, Palmer will inherit the benefit of those expenses, and it is only fair that she must pay for that benefit.

* * *

Finally, the limited monetary compensation I award here is not foreclosed by the rule that a party may seek a remedy of rescission or damages, but not both.* * * That rule prohibits a party from seeking both the *legal* remedy of damages and the *equitable* remedy of rescission. But it does not prohibit parties from seeking to be made whole, in equity, simply because that remedy would demand more than a mere reversal of the properties exchanged in the contract. * * *

* * *

Because they have elected to rescind their contract, the Petrucellis are not entitled under the Contract to recover "all costs of said litigation including reasonable attorney's fees," even though that relief is provided by the plain language of the Contract, in paragraph R of Schedule B. That is because "[h]e who elects to rescind a contract can claim nothing under it. * * *"

Courts in Connecticut have equitably shifted the burden of legal fees in some cases, such as where the defendant committed a fraud that rises to a greater level of culpable deception. * * * But as I have already discussed, the plaintiffs in this case have not demonstrated at this stage that Palmer's misrepresentations were made with such intent or recklessness as to require compensation for their attorneys' fees.

Furthermore, the Supreme Court has permitted exceptions to the "American Rule" that each party bears its own legal costs only in very limited circumstances: "This default rule can, of course, be overcome by statute. It can also be overcome by an 'enforceable contract' allocating attorney's fees." *Travelers Cas. & Sur. Co. of America v. Pacific Gas & Elec. Co.* 549 U.S. 443, 127 S.Ct. 1199, 1203, 167 L. Ed. 2d 178 (2007) (internal quotation marks and citations omitted). Neither circumstance applies here.

* * *

Plaintiffs are entitled to an Order and Judgment of rescission with respect to title to the Premises and the return by defendant to the plaintiffs of the purchase price.

Plaintiffs are also entitled to a Judgment for the monetary amounts they claim, with the exception of attorneys' fees and legal expenses incurred in connection with the filing and litigation of this action.

NOTES

1. After having said that Connecticut law "allows and even encourages rescission as a remedy" for breach of contract, the court in *Petrucelli* said "another 'condition precedent to rescission is the offer to restore the other party to its former condition as nearly as possible.'" In some situations there will be practical problems making it difficult or impossible for the party seeking rescission to restore the status quo ante. For example, in Carey v. Wallner, 223 Mont. 260, 725 P.2d 557 (1986), *aff'd after remand on damages*, 229 Mont. 57, 744 P.2d 881 (1987), the Careys had made a down payment and monthly payments to the sellers, the Wallners, pursuant to a contract to buy an elder care facility that housed five to ten residents, the license for which the Wallners had let lapse. Both parties and at least one state official had thought, erroneously, that the facility did not need a license. The error was not discovered until after the Careys had converted a carport into an office

and had built a separate garage. After the error was discovered, the Careys were no longer able to use the property as an elder care home and were unable to obtain a license because the prior license had been grandfathered and could not be reissued. The trial court granted rescission to the Careys. The Wallers had opposed on the ground, *inter alia*, that they could not be restored to the *status quo*. The appellate court affirmed the rescission, saying:

> Absolute and literal restoration is not required, it being sufficient if the restoration be such as is reasonably possible or as may be demanded by equity. The Careys contracted for real estate and an ongoing business, but in return received real estate and an illegal business.

Id. at 266–67, 725 P.2d at 561. For a discussion of the manner in which the courts have dealt with a variety of situations where restoration "in a strict literal sense" was not possible, see Dan B. Dobbs, Law of Remedies § 4.8 (2d ed. 1993); 1 George E. Palmer, Law of Restitution § 3.11 (1978).

2.   Besides the prerequisites to rescission discussed in the note above, another prerequisite is that the party seeking rescission give the other prompt notice of that decision. In *Petrucelli*, the court noted that the Petrucellis "promptly demanded a rescission." What is the reason for the prerequisites to rescission? *See* Gannett Co., Inc. v. Register Publishing Co., 428 F. Supp. 818, 824 (D. Conn. 1977)("If the injured party neglects to notify the other party promptly of his intention to rescind, or if he accepts benefits under the contract and thereby affirms it, he loses his right to rescind.") What is the purpose of these requirements? In *Gannett*, the Register Publishing Co. wanted to rescind its purchase of Gannett's newspaper. The court denied rescission and scheduled a trial on damages because Register, after discovering the fraud, did not act as a bailee in its operation of the paper to maintain its value. Rather, Register made major business decisions, including making a large financial investment to change from cold type to hot metal, raising the price of the paper, changing the geographic circulation area, and changing its editorial policy. The court held that "the pattern of the changes indicates the Register's intention to treat the *Times* as its own." *Id.* at 839–840. The court in *Gannett* cited Caruso v. Moy, 164 Neb. 68, 81 N.W. 2d 826 (1957) in which rescission was denied, saying:

> * * * [T]he plaintiff bought a prosperous Chinese–American restaurant, changed the bill of fare to Italian–American, and tried to rescind the contract of sale on the ground of fraud when business fell off. The court found that he had continued to operate the business for too long a period of time after learning of the fraud before seeking rescission and that he had thereby made the business his own. He changed the restaurant substantially so that business fell off to less than half what it had been previously, possibly due in part to his own mismanagement. On these facts, he was not entitled to rescission.

Gannett, 428 F. Supp. at 827.

BLOOR v. FRITZ

Court of Appeals of Washington, Division Two, 2008.
143 Wash. App. 718, 180 P.3d 805.

ARMSTRONG, J.

Eddie and Eva Bloor purchased a home from Robert and Charmaine Fritz through Lance Miller, an agent at LC Realty, Inc. After learning that the home was contaminated by a methamphetamine lab, the Bloors sued the Fritzes, Miller, LAM Management, Inc., LC Realty, and Cowlitz County. * * *

FACTS

Robert Fritz owned a home and approximately five acres of land on Spirit Lake Highway in Cowlitz County. He and his wife, Charmaine, moved from the home in 2001 and hired LAM Management, Inc. (LAM) to manage the property as a rental. Lance Miller and Jayson Brudvik are co-owners and operators of LAM. Miller and Brudvik are also licensed real estate agents for LC Realty.

In January 2004, [tenants] occupied the Spirit Lake property under a rental agreement through LAM. On January 30, the Cowlitz–Wahkiakum Joint Narcotics Task Force executed a search warrant at the property. Task force members discovered a marijuana growing operation in the house's basement and implements of methamphetamine manufacturing on and under the house's rear deck and in a hot tub on the deck. Although the task force processed the site as a methamphetamine lab, no one from the task force or any other law enforcement agency notified the Cowlitz County Health Department, the Washington State Department of Health, or any other state agency of the methamphetamine lab. * * *

LAM initiated eviction proceedings against the Waddington tenants, and they left the property in February or March 2004. LAM subsequently re-rented the property for a short period of time but evicted those tenants in May 2004. The Fritzes then decided to sell the property.

In preparation for the sale, the Fritzes cleaned the house, painted it, and changed the floor coverings. * * *

Eddie and Eva Bloor moved to Cowlitz County from Missouri in 2004 and began looking for a home to purchase. Brudvik showed them the Spirit Lake property. The Bloors decided to make an offer to buy the property. Miller represented both the Fritzes and the Bloors in the transaction.

Robert completed a seller's disclosure statement in which he represented that the property had never been used as an illegal drug manufacturing site. Miller reviewed the disclosure statement with the Bloors, but he did not disclose that the drug task force had discovered a marijuana grow operation or methamphetamine lab on the property. The Fritzes accepted the Bloors' offer and the transaction closed in August 2004. The Bloors moved into the home shortly thereafter.

In September, the Bloors' son heard from a member of the community that the property was known as a "drug house." Clerk's Papers (CP) at 20. The Bloors began investigating and found an on-line version of the February 1 *Daily News* article. Eva contacted the task force, where Sergeant Kevin Tate confirmed that the task force had confiscated a methamphetamine lab at the property. She then contacted the Cowlitz County Health Department, where Audrey Shaver confirmed that nobody had reported the lab to the health department and that it would investigate the matter to determine what action it would take.

On October 22, Shaver told the Bloors that the health department had determined that the property was contaminated by the methamphetamine manufacturing and was not fit for occupancy. She told the Bloors that they could not remove their personal property from the house because of the risk of cross-contamination. The Bloors left the residence as instructed, leaving nearly all their personal belongings in the house and garage.

The health department posted an order prohibiting use of the property. The order stated that the Bloors were financially responsible for the cost of remediation, that a certified decontamination contractor would have to perform the remediation, and that use of the property was subject to criminal charges. Occupancy of buildings contaminated by methamphetamine manufacturing is dangerous to the health and safety of occupants.

The Bloors stayed with relatives until they could secure a place to live, eventually moving to Spokane. They had to repurchase clothing, bedding, furniture, and other necessities. They were unable to both support themselves and make their monthly mortgage payments. The Bloors experienced emotional distress and anxiety due to the loss of their home, personal effects, and keepsakes.

The Bloors sued the Fritzes, Miller, LAM Management, LC Realty, and Cowlitz County. After a bench trial, the trial court ruled for the Bloors, awarding them damages jointly and severally against all the defendants for emotional distress, loss of personal property, loss of income, loss of use of the property, and damage to the Bloors' credit. It also awarded the Bloors $10,000.00 as punitive damages and $13,907.30 for attorney fees against Miller and LC Realty under the Act. It ordered the contract between the Bloors and the Fritzes rescinded, requiring the Fritzes to pay the Bloors' lender the purchase price, accrued interest, late charges, and foreclosure fees, and the Bloors to return the property to the Fritzes. Finally, the trial court awarded the Bloors $18,975.55 in expenses against the Fritzes and, applying a 1.2 multiplier, $125,335.25 in attorney fees against the Fritzes, Miller, and LC Realty; it awarded the Bloors their statutory costs against all defendants.

Miller and LC Realty (collectively Miller) principally argue that (1) insufficient evidence supports the trial court's findings that Miller knew about the methamphetamine lab, (2) the trial court erred in finding that he violated the Act, and (3) the trial court erred in awarding attorney fees with a multiplier and all the Bloors' litigation expenses. In addition to joining Miller in several claimed errors, the Fritzes principally argue that (1) the economic loss rule precludes the Bloors from seeking damages for the tort of negligent misrepresentation, (2) the trial court erred in rescinding the contract rather than awarding damages, and (3) the trial court erred in awarding damages for emotional distress, income loss, and injury to the Bloors' credit ratings. We hold that the trial court erred only in awarding the Bloors damages beyond those necessary to restore them to their precontract position.

ANALYSIS

Miller and LC Realty's Appeal

* * *

III.　Negligent Misrepresentation

Miller contends that the trial court erred in concluding that his failure to disclose the history of illegal drug manufacturing on the property was a negligent misrepresentation.

A plaintiff claiming negligent misrepresentation must prove by clear, cogent, and convincing evidence that (1) the defendant supplied information for the guidance of others in their business transactions that was false, (2) the defendant knew or should have known that the information was supplied to guide the plaintiff in his business transactions, (3) the defendant was negligent in obtaining or communicating the false information, (4) the plaintiff relied on the false information, (5) the plaintiff's reliance was reasonable, and (6) the false information proximately caused the plaintiff damages. * * *

* * *

* * * [B]ecause substantial evidence supports the trial court's finding that Miller knew of the illegal drug manufacturing on the property, and Miller does not claim that he disclosed the drug problem to the Bloors, Miller's argument fails.

* * *

The Fritzes' Appeal

I.　Negligent Misrepresentation

* * *

The Fritzes argue that the trial court erred in denying their motion to dismiss the Bloors' negligent misrepresentation claim, asserting that no claim exists for economic loss resulting from the sale of a residence. They assert that the Washington Supreme Court's recent decision in Alejandre v. Bull, 159 Wash.2d 674, 153 P.3d 864 (2007), reversed the Court of Appeals decision that the Bloors relied on below to argue to the contrary and decided this "precise issue." * * *

* * *

The economic loss rule bars recovery for an alleged breach of tort duties where a contractual relationship exists and the losses are economic. *Alejandre*, 159 Wash.2d at 683. Economic losses are those losses arising directly from the defect, such as repair costs for defective construction. * * * But the economic loss rule does not bar recovery for personal injury or damage to property other than the defective property. *Alejandre*, 159 Wash.2d at 684.

* * *

II. Rescission

The Fritzes next argue that the trial court erred in rescinding the real estate purchase and sale agreement. * * *

Contract rescission is an equitable remedy in which the court attempts to restore the parties to the positions they would have occupied had they not entered into the contract. * * * We review a trial court's decision to rescind a contract for an abuse of discretion. * * * A court sitting in equity has broad discretion to shape relief. * * *

In their closing argument, the Bloors stated that they preferred rescission of the contract over contractual damages, and the trial court ordered rescission in its oral decision. When the parties expressed confusion as to how rescission would work, the court directed the parties to work out the details and to advise the court if they could not. The Bloors later told the trial court that the parties had concluded that rescission was not feasible because the Fritzes would be unable to return the purchase price to the Bloors. Accordingly, the Bloors requested damages for the cost of decontamination and restoration of the property instead. The Fritzes agreed with the change. Yet at the next hearing, the Fritzes told the court that they preferred rescission over contractual damages and that they were "willing and able" to go forward with rescission. * * * The trial court continued the hearing to allow the Bloors to consider whether they were willing to accept rescission as their remedy. The Bloors elected to return to the rescission remedy.

Given the trial court's broad discretion in shaping an equitable remedy, we cannot say that the trial court abused its discretion in ordering rescission. The Fritzes requested rescission after the Bloors had agreed to accept contractual damages, also at the Fritzes' request. Although the Bloors' attorney expressed frustration with the Fritzes' shifting position, the Bloors agreed to return to the rescission remedy. A party cannot set up an error below and then complain of it on appeal. * * * Moreover, the Fritzes did not argue before the trial court that there was not a complete failure of consideration or that the cost to remediate the property was not high enough to justify rescission. Rescinding the contract put the Bloors as close as possible to the position they would have been in had they never purchased the property. The trial court did not err * * *.

The Fritzes argue in the alternative that the trial court erred in awarding the Bloors interest on the total purchase price of $149,000 and lender fees as part of the rescission remedy because to do so goes beyond restoring the parties to their original positions. * * *

* * *

Upon completing the contract, the Fritzes received the full purchase price from the Bloors' lender and the Bloors became indebted to the lender for that amount. But the Bloors did not lose the use of $149,000 by financing the purchase. * * * To restore the Bloors to their precontract position, the Fritzes must pay the $149,000 debt together with the unpaid interest that has actually accrued, penalties, and foreclosure costs the lender assessed against the Bloors. The Bloors are not entitled to any excess funds. After the Fritzes demonstrate that they have paid all these obligations, they are entitled to an order quieting title to the property.

III. Damages

A. *Loss of Income and Damage to Credit Rating*

The Fritzes next argue that insufficient evidence supports the trial court's award of damages for loss of income and damage to the Bloors' credit rating.

* * *

Ed Bloor testified that in the weeks after he moved into the house, he obtained a business license in order to start a siding business and was in the process of obtaining a bond for it. He owned all the tools necessary for siding and stored them in the garage at the Spirit Lake property. While he prepared to start his business, he performed remodeling work, earning a couple thousand dollars. But because the garage where he stored his tools was contaminated, he had to abandon his tools when he left the house and was unable to start a siding business or continue the remodeling work. * * *

In addition to leaving behind Ed Bloor's siding tools, the Bloors were unable to remove their clothing, bedding, furniture, cooking utensils, or personal items from the home. They had to replace all these items. Ed Bloor testified that they used the funds they had at the time to "try to get [their] life back to where [they] could live." RP at 370. This evidence, along with the evidence about Ed Bloor's loss of income, supports the finding that the Bloors were unable to make the mortgage payments because of the property contamination.

The Fritzes do not dispute that the Bloors' credit ratings dropped by about 100 points each from the time they bought the house to the time of trial, but the Fritzes attribute that drop to the Bloors' history of poor financial management rather than the loss of the house. Yet the Fritzes do not explain how the Bloors' past financial mismanagement would cause a current drop in their credit ratings. The Bloors' expert testified that a 100–point drop in credit rating would cause a buyer to incur about $10,000 more in interest costs over the first seven years of a loan. * * *

B. Emotional Distress

The Fritzes contend that the trial court erred in awarding the Bloors damages for emotional distress, arguing that emotional distress damages are not available for rescission of a contract or breach of a contract and repeating their argument that the economic loss rule bars damages for negligent misrepresentation.

But the trial court specified that it awarded emotional distress damages as a consequence of the negligent misrepresentation, not under a contract theory. * * *

The Fritzes do not challenge the trial court's findings of fact in support of emotional distress damages. These include that the Bloors suffered from anxiety and discomfort as a result of the loss of their home, personal effects, and keepsakes. * * *

C. Litigation Expenses

The Fritzes argue that the trial court erred in awarding the Bloors their litigation expenses beyond the statutory costs allowed in RCW 4.84.010. * * *

Under RCW 4.84.010, "there shall be allowed to the prevailing party upon the judgment certain sums by way of indemnity for the prevailing party's expenses in the action, which allowances are termed costs * * *." And in an action on a contract that specifically provides for the award of attorney fees and costs to the prevailing party, the prevailing party is "entitled to reasonable attorney's fees in addition to costs and necessary disbursements." RCW 4.84.330.

Here, the real estate purchase and sale agreement provided, "If Buyer or Seller institutes suit against the other concerning this Agreement, the prevailing party is entitled to reasonable attorney's fees and expenses." * * *

* * *

Attorney Fees

* * *

In Washington, a party may recover attorney fees only when a statute, contract, or recognized ground of equity permits recovery. * * * Whether a party is entitled to an award of attorney fees is a question of law that we review de novo. * * * Whether the fee award is reasonable is a matter of discretion for the trial court, which we will alter only if we find an abuse of discretion. * * *

* * *

Also contrary to the Fritzes' assertions, the trial court excluded hours that it found to be duplicative or unnecessary, including 13 hours of the time it took to draft the complaint and the hours that a second attorney spent attending depositions.

II. Lodestar Multiplier

Finally, Miller contends that the trial court erred in applying a 1.2 multiplier to its award of attorney fees against Miller and the Fritzes, arguing that the evidence does not support the trial court's findings in support of enhancing the attorney fee award.

* * *

Under the lodestar method of calculating an award of attorney fees, the court must first determine that counsel expended a reasonable number of hours in securing a successful recovery for the client and that the hourly rate counsel billed the client was reasonable. * * * The court must exclude any wasteful or duplicative hours. * * * The lodestar fee is the reasonable number of hours incurred in obtaining the successful result multiplied by the reasonable hourly rate. * * *

* * * The court presumes that the lodestar amount is a reasonable fee.* * * But in rare instances, the court may, in its discretion, adjust the lodestar amount up or down to adjust for factors that the lodestar calculation has not already taken into account.* * *

Here, the Bloors requested a 1.5 multiplier on the attorney fee award. The trial court found that the complexity of the case, the fact that it presented novel issues, the contingent nature of success, the high quality of representation, and the loss of other work made an enhancement appropriate. But because several of these factors were not relevant to the claims on which it awarded fees, it concluded that a 1.2 multiplier was appropriate.

* * *

The trial court considered appropriate factors in considering whether to adjust the lodestar amount, and it did not abuse its discretion in deciding to apply a 1.2 multiplier.

III. Attorney Fees on Appeal

The Bloors request their attorney fees on appeal under RAP 18.1. Where a statute or contract allows an award of attorney fees at trial, an appellate court has authority to award fees on appeal. * * * The trial court awarded the Bloors their attorney fees under the real estate purchase and sale agreement and the Act. Because they have prevailed on appeal, we award the Bloors their attorney fees under RAP 18.1 in an amount to be set by a commissioner of this court.

We affirm but vacate the damage award and remand for the trial court to enter new judgment for the Bloors consistent with this opinion.

NOTES

1. The court in *Bloor* itemized damages that the Bloors could recover to restore them to the position they were in before having contracted to buy the house that turned out to be contaminated. The court in *Petrucelli* referred to those damages that restore the *status quo ante* after a rescission as "consequential" and distinguished them from the damage recovery a plaintiff would receive if the plaintiff affirmed the contract. Unfortunately, the term "consequential damages" is also used to refer to a type of expectation damages that are caused by a breach of contract. For a discussion of the circumstances under which a plaintiff who has affirmed a contract can recover consequential damages, also known as special damages, for breach see Section 3 of Chapter 3.

2. Compare the result on attorney's fees in *Bloor* with the result in *Petrucelli*. Which result to you think is correct? What about the opposite situation? If a plaintiff seeks damages for fraud, not breach of contract, by affirming the contract, is the plaintiff also affirming a clause limiting damages? In Mike Finnin Ford, Inc. v. Automatic Data Processing, Inc., 220 F. Supp. 2d 970 (D. Iowa 2001), the court said no. It explained:

> * * * [T]he right to elect a remedy is fundamentally a benefit to the plaintiff. It permits the plaintiff to assess his situation upon discovery of the fraud and then decide whether rescission or affirmation is better for him. There are many reasons why a plaintiff may opt for the latter—e.g., obligations to third parties which flow from the initial contract, the object of the contract is unavailable elsewhere, etc.—and it does not follow that an affirming plaintiff waives his right to any claim for tort damages merely because he agrees to be bound by the contract regarding contractual matters. He retains the right to be placed in the same financial position as if the fraudulent representations had in fact been true. Otherwise, a defendant could evade application of Iowa's tort remedies by including a limited damages clause in a contract even though, absent the tort, no contract would have been executed.

Id. at 978.

HUTCHISON v. PYBURN

Court of Appeals of Tennessee, 1977.
567 S.W.2d 762.

DROWOTA, JUDGE.

This is a case involving fraud in the sale of realty in which plaintiffs-vendees were awarded both rescission of the deed and punitive damages by the Chancery Court of Davidson County.

In January of 1973, plaintiffs William and Jo Lynn Hutchison purchased a house and lot from defendants Robert and Carol Pyburn for $24,000.00. * * * Defendant Jack Williams built the house and sold the property to the Pyburns, and his brother defendant John Williams, was real estate agent for the Pyburns in the sale of the property to plaintiffs. In July of 1973, plaintiffs noticed seepage from their sewage disposal system, investigated, and discovered that their property had not been approved as a home site by the Metropolitan Board of Health because it lacked the requisite topsoil to sustain the septic tank and overflow field needed for sewage disposal. Further, the Metropolitan Department of Codes Administration had been informed of the problem, and had issued a building permit to defendant Jack Williams only by mistake. Evidently defendant Pyburn had become aware of the sewage problem after purchasing the property from Williams and had prevailed on Williams to release him from his obligation to purchase it, whereupon Pyburn and Williams negotiated the sale to plaintiffs.

Plaintiffs brought suit, alleging that the defendants Pyburn and Williams knew of the property's condition and that there was no practical means of correcting it at the time of the sale. * * * The Chancellor dismissed the case against defendant John Williams, but entered a decree in favor of plaintiffs against the Pyburns and Jack Williams. The decree allowed plaintiffs rescission of the contract, incidental damages in the form of expenses incurred in connection with the property, moving costs, and attorney's fees, from all of which was deducted the reasonable rental value of the property for the period of plaintiffs occupancy. In addition to the sum due the plaintiffs in incidental damages, the Chancellor assessed $5,000.00 in punitive damages against the defendants and made a specific finding that defendants' misrepresentation was fraudulent. * * *

* * *

Defendants * * * assert that the trial court erred in awarding punitive damages for misrepresentations incident to a contract when rescission of the contract and deed was also decreed. * * *

Punitive or exemplary damages are awarded to punish a defendant for his wrongful conduct and to deter others from similar conduct in the future. * * * They are awarded in cases of fraud, malice, gross negligence, or oppression, or in similar cases involving wilful misconduct. * * * Such damages relate to the nature of the defendant's actions in inflicting or causing the injury rather than to the extent of the injury that results. * * *

In Tennessee it is established that courts of equity are empowered to award punitive damages. * * * Kneeland v. Bruce, 47 Tenn.App. 136, 336 S.W.2d 319 (1960). *Kneeland* was an injunction action by a plaintiff who had been fraudulently induced to sign two mortgage notes and trust deeds and had consequently lost her property to a *bona fide* purchaser. Both compensatory and punitive damages were awarded. The court upheld the latter award with the statement that Chancery Courts have jurisdiction to give punitive damages "in proper cases." * * *

One objection raised to the award of punitive damages in this case is that it is inconsistent with rescission of the deed under the doctrine of election of remedies. That doctrine estops a plaintiff who has clearly chosen to pursue one of two inconsistent and irreconcilable remedies from later resorting to the other. * * * The "essential element" here is "that the remedies be inconsistent." * * * There is no such inconsistency, however, between the remedy of rescission and an award of punitive damages. The latter, as we have already noted, is designed to penalize and deter, and results from the nature of defendant's conduct rather than from the harm it causes. The character of punitive damages, then, is in no wise inconsistent with rescission and its concomitant remedies of restitution and incidental damages. The latter are all aimed at *redressing* the harm done the plaintiff and, while this means they may be considered inconsistent with a remedy such as compensatory damages, which also aims at redress but by a different method, they may not be so considered with respect to the *deterrent* sanction of punitive damages and [that remedy] does not estop them from making that request.

* * *

Finally, defendants point to a proposition which we agree is the general rule in Tennessee and elsewhere: punitive damages may not be recovered in an action for breach of contract. * * * This case, however, is not one for breach of contract, for plaintiffs asked that the contract be made a nullity by rescission. Further, the pleadings and memorandum of the trial court indicate that the main thrust of the action is a claim of fraud and misrepresentation against all the defendants, although an additional claim of breach of warranty was asserted against the Pyburns, with whom plaintiffs were in privity. Thus, regardless of any overtones of contract that may appear in this suit, there also clearly exists here a cause of action against all defendants for the sort of tortious misconduct required as a basis for recovery of punitive damages. * * *

* * *

Affirmed.

NOTE

For further discussion of the principles governing punitive damages, see Section 5 of Chapter 3.

B. DAMAGES

LIGHTNING LITHO v. DANKA INDUSTRIES

Court of Appeals of Indiana, 2002.
776 N.E.2d 1238.

VAIDIK, JUDGE.

* * *

Thomas Haab is the owner of Litho, a small company in South Bend, Indiana that specializes in printing. Danka Industries, Inc. (Danka) supplies office equipment manufactured by other parties to various businesses throughout the United States. Danka also services and provides supplies for the equipment. During the summer of 1996, Scott Linn, a salesperson at Danka's South Bend office, approached Haab at Litho on numerous occasions about leasing a high-volume copier, which produces 500,000 to 1,000,000 copies per month. Because Litho only had a need for 5000 to 20,000 copies per month and already had an adequate copier for that volume, Haab continually turned down Linn's offer.

In the fall of 1996, Linn approached Haab again and told him that he had an account for him that would warrant leasing a high-volume copier. When Haab asked who the account was, Linn responded that he would not tell him until the lease was signed. However, Linn told Haab that the account would generate six million copies and $50,000 in profit a year. When Haab expressed doubt about the account, Linn responded, "No, it's a done deal. The account is in my back pocket, it goes with the machine." * * * The very next day, Linn returned to Litho with John Leiter, a manager for Danka. When Haab told Leiter that he wanted everything put in writing, Leiter replied, "We can't do that, we checked with corporate, they won't allow us to do that. If Scott Linn says the account goes with the machine, the account goes with the machine." * * * Convinced that the account accompanied the copier, Haab signed a lease with American Business Credit Corporation for a Kodak 3100 copier on November 14, 1996. The terms of the lease were $755 per month for sixty months. Haab also signed an Equipment Maintenance and Supply Annual Agreement with Danka.

Shortly after the copier was delivered to Litho, Linn told Haab that the account was Commercial Driver's Institute (CDI). When Linn and Haab visited CDI, it quickly became apparent that there was no account. Furthermore, Linn was never able to secure a replacement account for Litho. Nevertheless, Litho continued to make lease payments on the copier for nearly two years before finally defaulting.

On April 27, 1999, Litho filed a complaint against Danka, which it amended on June 18, 1999. In its Amended Complaint, Litho alleged, among other things, fraud in the inducement and requested "rescission of the Contract Documents and a return of the parties to the status quo ante." * * * It also requested a jury trial. On January 15, 2001, Danka filed a Motion to Strike Jury Demand, asserting that Litho was not entitled to a jury trial because rescission is an equitable remedy that must be tried to the court. The trial court granted the motion. On August 23, 2001, Litho filed a Motion for Leave of Court to File a Second Amended Complaint and Jury Request, which the trial court granted. In its Second Amended Complaint, Litho abandoned its request for rescission of the contract and instead requested "an award of contract and tort damages" in order to obtain a jury trial. * * *

This matter proceeded to jury trial on March 19, 2002. At the close of Litho's case-in-chief, Danka moved for judgment on the evidence on Litho's fraudulent inducement claim pursuant to Indiana Trial Rule 50. Specifically, Danka alleged that Litho had failed to present any evidence to support its request for damages. The trial court granted the motion. * * *

* * *

Fraudulent inducement occurs when a party is induced through fraudulent misrepresentations to enter into a contract. * * * Generally, a party bringing an action for fraud in the inducement must elect between two remedies. A.J.'s Auto. Sales, Inc. v. Freet, 725 N.E.2d 955, 969 (Ind.Ct.App.2000). * * * One alternative is to rescind the contract, return any benefits received, and be returned to the status quo. * * * The other alternative is to affirm the contract, retain the benefits, and seek damages. * * *

Here, Litho abandoned its rescission claim when it filed its Second Amended Complaint and has therefore affirmed the contract. When a party elects to affirm a contract induced by fraudulent misrepresentations, the party may only seek tort damages. 7 Corbin on Contracts, Avoidance and Reformation § 28.23 (2002); 37 Am.Jur.2d, Fraud and Deceit § 279 (2002). In the majority of jurisdictions, these damages are measured using the "benefit of the bargain" rule. 48 Am.Jur. Proof of Facts 3d, Fraudulent Inducement § 17 (1998). This rule compels the party guilty of fraud to make good his or her representations, and under its operation, the parties are placed in the same position as if the contract and representations had been fully performed. 37 Am.Jur.2d, *supra,* § 416; *see also* 48 Am.Jur. Proof of Facts 3d, *supra,* § 17 (providing that this form of relief seeks to give the aggrieved party the benefit of the bargain as if the fraudulent misrepresentations of the other party were true). Although the benefit of the bargain rule is traditionally used to measure damages in breach of contract cases, it is also used to measure damages in fraudulent inducement cases because fraudulent inducement is a "hybrid" of tort and contract. * * *

Despite the fact that the majority of jurisdictions use the benefit of the bargain rule when measuring damages in fraudulent inducement or fraudulent misrepresentation cases, there are Indiana cases providing that "[a] buyer's desire to enjoy the benefit of his bargain is not an interest that tort law traditionally protects." * * * However, these cases are inapposite to the present one because the theory of recovery was negligence, not fraudulent inducement, which is a "hybrid" of tort and contract. Moreover, there are other Indiana cases recognizing that the "measure of damages for fraud in the sale or exchange of property is the difference between the value of the property received by the party alleged to have been defrauded and the value of such property at the time, had it been as represented to be by the vender." Stoll v. Grimm, 681 N.E.2d 749, 758 (Ind.Ct.App.1997); see also Johnson v. Naugle, 557 N.E.2d 1339, 1343 (Ind.Ct.App.1990); Loer v. Neal, 127 Ind.App. 246, 137 N.E.2d 728, 737 (1956). Although the courts in these cases do not call this the benefit of the bargain rule, that is essentially what it is. See 48 Am.Jur. Proof of Facts 3d, supra, § 17 ("Generally, the benefit of the bargain measure of damages is measured as the difference between the value of the property, as represented, and the actual value of the property.") (quotation omitted). Therefore, we join those jurisdictions that measure damages in fraudulent inducement and fraudulent misrepresentation cases by the benefit of the bargain rule.

When asked at trial what damages Litho was seeking, Haab testified, "there's no way I could be brought back to zero like it never happened. That could never happen, because of the law, but I would like my lease payments back...." * * * Haab also testified that he wanted Danka to take the copier back. Counsel for Litho then introduced Exhibit 5, which showed the total amount of damages requested as $31,929.07. * * * Besides $575, which was the cost to install the copier and sound panels, the remainder of this figure represented what Litho had already paid under the lease and what it still had left to pay under the lease. In support of its motion for judgment on the evidence, Danka argued that Litho failed to present "evidence showing that it incurred any damages" because the damages it was seeking were rescission-type damages, not tort damages. * * * The trial court agreed and granted Danka's motion. The trial court reasoned as follows:

> Clearly, the plaintiff has made the election to "affirm the contract." Unfortunately, the lease payments—past and future—are the plaintiff's obligation to pay under the very contract the plaintiff has affirmed. Damages cannot be premised upon the cost of compliance with a legal duty arising out of that contract.

Appellant's App. p. 14.

* * *

We agree with the trial court that a reimbursement of lease payments and a return of the copier are not proper damages in this case because this is the remedy that Litho would have been entitled to had it followed through on its claim for rescission of the contract. * * * However, Haab testified at trial that Linn promised him that the account, which came with the copier, would generate six million copies and $50,000 in profit per year. * * * This is a proper measure of benefit of the bargain damages, [and it would] place the parties in the same position as if the contract and representations had been fully performed. Considering the evidence in a light most favorable to Litho, we conclude that the trial court abused its discretion in granting Danka's motion for judgment on the evidence because there is evidence in the record to support an award of benefit of the bargain damages.

Reversed and remanded.

NOTES

1. On remand, if the case did not settle, would the plaintiff have been entitled to $50,000 per year for the number of years it had the machine? Note that the court in *Lightning Litho* defined benefit of the bargain damages as "the difference between the value of the property, as represented, and the actual value of the property."

2. Why did the court in *Lightning Litho* say that "Litho abandoned its rescission claim when it filed its Second Amended Complaint and has therefore affirmed the contract"? The court in *Petrucelli* referred to the same concept when it said that "[t]he Petrucellis do make a claim for *consequential* damages as part of the equitable remedy of rescission, since that remedy seeks to return the parties as nearly as possible to the *status quo ante*. That is not the same as a pure claim for damages which would operate to preclude a claim for rescission." Both courts were referring to a concept called "election of remedies." Since rescission involves disaffirming a contract, while seeking expectation damages involves affirming the contract, some courts view that as requiring an "election" that precludes pleading them in the alternative.

In Walraven v. Martin, 123 Mich.App. 342, 333 N.W.2d 569 (1983), the court explained:

> This case requires us to consider the continued viability of the common law doctrine of election of remedies.[1] It has long been stated that a party who elects to proceed on one theory of recovery is *thereafter* barred from asserting any inconsistent remedy. * * * Generally, the doctrine applies only where two or more inconsistent remedies were available and the party has actually chosen and pursued the one to the exclusion of the other. * * * That situation is in contrast to the instant case where the aggrieved party has not yet chosen one remedy to the exclusion of the other. The inconsistency in the present case stems from plaintiff's request for rescission of the contract, and plaintiff's request for damages resulting from fraud committed on him, which involves affirmance of the contract.
>
> Plaintiff herein, by seeking inconsistent remedies simultaneously, has not "elected" a remedy. Nevertheless, several cases from other jurisdictions support defendants' claim that the trial court may compel an

---

1. Numerous articles have been written about the election doctrine; none are favorable. *See,* Fraser, *Election of Remedies: An Anachronism,* 29 Okla.L.Rev. 1 (1976); Patterson, *Improvements in the Law of Restitution,* 40 Cornell L.Q. 667 (1955); Yerkes, *Election of Remedies in Cases of Fraudulent Misrepresentation,* 26 S.Cal.L.Rev. 157 (1953); Note, *Election of Remedies: A Delusion?,* 38 Colum.L.Rev. 292 (1938); Hine, *Election of Remedies, A Criticism,* 26 Harv.L.Rev. 707 (1913); Dobbs, Remedies, § 1.5 p. 13; 1 G. Palmer, Law of Restitution (1978) § 3.10, p. 283.

election between inconsistent remedies at any stage of the proceedings. * * *

Modern rules of civil procedure, * * * current legal periodicals, and the Supreme Court's decision in Gruskin v. Fisher, 405 Mich.51, 273 N.W.2d 893 (1979), lead us to conclude that plaintiff may simultaneously pursue all of his remedies against the sellers and other defendants herein regardless of legal consistency, *so long as plaintiff is not awarded double recovery*. While defendants emphasize the basic repugnance of allowing plaintiff to "blow hot and cold" at the same time, the inconsistency only involves legal theories of recovery. Under rescission plaintiff would be required to restore all benefits received and would be entitled to the purchase price of the restaurant and consequential damages,* * * whereas his actual damages * * * consist of plaintiff's loss of the bargain measured by the difference between the actual value of the property and its value if it had been as represented. * * * There is no inconsistency in the factual basis plaintiff relies upon in support of each theory. * * * We also note that defendants are adequately protected from the plaintiff's changing course in midstream by our doctrines of equitable estoppel, waiver, accord and satisfaction and res judicata.

Several other jurisdictions have rejected the election prior to trial doctrine by caselaw, or by statute.[2] Our rejection of election prior to trial is consistent with Michigan's rules of civil procedure. * * *

Id. at 346–49, 333 N.W.2d at 572–73.

3. Did the plaintiff in *Lightning Litho* need to drop its request for rescission when it amended its complaint for damages? The court in Rahemtulla v. Hassam, 2008 WL 2247195 (M.D. Pa. 2008) said:

Pennsylvania courts have established that a plaintiff "may not maintain at the same time in separate counts of one action, or in two different suits claims for rescission of a contract and restitution on the one hand and for damages for breach of the same contract together with expectation interest, on the other hand." * * * The doctrine of "election of remedies" stems from the principle that rescission and damages are fundamentally inconsistent remedies. Rescission is an annulment or unmaking of a contract and a restoration of the status quo whereas damages, a legal remedy, involves an affirmance of the contract. * * *

* * * In light of the foregoing, the defendants' motion will be granted to the extent that the plaintiffs will be required to make an election of remedies.

Where the court disagrees with the defendants is with respect to the timing of the election. * * *

---

2. N.Y. CPLR § 3002(e) (McKinney) states that in any case based on fraud, claims for rescission or for damages shall not be deemed inconsistent and the aggrieved party shall be allowed to obtain complete relief in one action, but such complete relief shall not include duplication of benefits. Ga.Code § 3–114 states that a plaintiff may pursue any number of consistent or inconsistent remedies against the same person or different persons until he shall obtain a satisfaction from some of them. *See also,* UCC § 2–703, which eliminates the election doctrine in sale-of-goods cases.

Generally, a party must make an election of remedies after the case is submitted to the jury and the verdict is entered, but prior to the entry of judgment. * * * However, an earlier election may be required where the evidence concerning the inconsistent remedies would be confusing to the jury or the remedies are so fundamentally inconsistent that only an earlier election will suffice. * * * Substantial prejudice to the defendant is also a factor to be considered. * * *

In this case, while the court finds that the plaintiffs' alternative remedies are fundamentally inconsistent, there is no indication that allowing the legal claims to go to the jury prior to an election would be unduly confusing to the jury such that an earlier election will be necessary. Further, there has been no showing of substantial prejudice to the defendants in allowing the plaintiffs to defer their election of remedies until after the jury has been presented with the facts on the legal claims and a determination of liability has been made. The court finds no distinction in the facts which will be presented in support of the legal claims, as opposed to the potential equitable claims. As such, there is no indication that the jury will hear evidence which will be irrelevant to any jury question. There is also no indication that the defendants' preparation for trial would be unnecessarily complicated without an earlier election. Therefore, the defendants' motion will be denied to the extent that they request that the court require the plaintiffs to make an election of remedies prior to trial.

But see Merritt v. Craig, 130 Md. App. 350, 746 A.2d 923 (2000)(recognizing that a case in equity can be tried before a jury if it has "at least some legal claim," but holding that, because rescission is a "purely equitable remedy," plaintiffs must elect before trial whether to affirm or disaffirm a contract. *Id.* at 362–63, 746 A.2d at 929.)

4. For a discussion of pleading in the alternative see Chapter 3, Section 3.

5. Most suits for rescission are brought in equity to have a court order that the contract be undone. However, if one of the parties rescinds the contract before suit by returning the property and then brings suit to recover the purchase price, that action is at law. For example in Kracl v. Loseke, 236 Neb. 290, 461 N.W.2d 67 (1990), the sellers who had intentionally hidden signs of termite damage to their house from the buyers tried to oppose the buyers' suit to rescind the contract on the ground that the buyers had not tendered the house to them before suit. The court rejected the defense saying,

[A] plaintiff's restitution or tender of property is unnecessary before commencement of an action in equity to rescind a contract or conveyance. * * * As further observed in D. Dobbs, Handbook on the Law of Remedies, Principles of Restitution § 4.8 at 294 (1973):

In equity the suit is not on rescission, but for rescission; it is not a suit based upon rescission already accomplished by the plaintiff, but a suit to have the court decree a rescission.... Since rescission is not accomplished "in equity" until the court so decrees, the plaintiff has no obligation before suit to make restitution of goods or money he received from the defendant....

This does not mean that the plaintiff is entitled to get back what he gave and keep what he got, too. It means only that he need not make formal tender before suit.

Id. at 299, 461 N.W.2d at 73. *See also* Commercial Recycling Center, Ltd. v. Hobbs Industries, Inc., 228 P.3d 93, 98–99 (Alaska 2010) (stating " '[r]escission at law is a suit based upon rescission already accomplished . . . [in which] the court has nothing to do with the rescission itself.' Rescission at law occurs where at least one of the parties to a contract rescinds the contract and then turns to a court for enforcement of that rescission and an award of damages. * * * Unlike rescission at law, rescission in equity occurs only upon a court's decree.")

6. *Lightning Litho* distinguished Indiana cases that held that benefit of the bargain damages are not appropriate in negligence cases. Why would the remedy vary depending upon the defendant's state of mind? Consider the next case.

BDO SEIDMAN, LLP v. MINDIS ACQUISITION CORP.

Supreme Court of Georgia, 2003.
276 Ga. 311, 578 S.E.2d 400.

FLETCHER, CHIEF JUSTICE.

We granted certiorari in this case to consider the proper measure of damages in a negligent misrepresentation case. * * *

Mindis Acquisition Corporation (MAC) was formed to purchase Mindis Corporation. After the purchase was complete, MAC discovered that the inventory value of Mindis was less than what appeared on Mindis's financial statements. MAC then sued Mindis's accountants, BDO Seidman, LLP, for negligent misrepresentation, contending that BDO was negligent in its audit of Mindis's financial statements. The trial court instructed the jury that damages were to be determined by the standard used in fraud and deceit cases, a benefit-of-the-bargain standard.[1] The jury found in favor of MAC and awarded $44 million. The Court of Appeals rejected BDO's contention that the jury was charged on an improper fraud standard of damages and affirmed the jury's verdict.

* * * In Robert & Co. v. Rhodes–Haverty Partnership, 250 Ga. 680, 300 S.E.2d 503 (1983), this Court first recognized a claim for negligent misrepresentation and adopted the liability standard set forth in section 552 of the Restatement (Second) of Torts. This Court again considered negligent misrepresentation in Hardaway Co. v. Parsons, Brinckerhoff, Quade & Douglas, Inc., 267 Ga. 424, 479 S.E.2d 727 (1997), and agreed with the Court of Appeals that the proper statute of limitations for a negligent misrepresentation case must be determined by applying principles of negligence law. Consistent with our prior cases treating this cause

---

1. See McCrary v. Pritchard, 119 Ga. 876, 883, 47 S.E. 341 (1904); Kunzler Enterprises v. Rowe, 211 Ga.App. 4, 5, 438 S.E.2d 365 (1993) (damages for fraudulent misrepresentation are difference between the value of the thing sold at the time of delivery and what would have been its value if the representations made by the defendants had been true).

of action as one sounding in negligence, we now conclude that the damages standard for a negligent misrepresentation claim is the traditional negligence standard, which is also set forth in the Restatement (Second) § 552. Under Restatement (Second) of Torts § 552B, the amount of damages awarded for negligent misrepresentation is measured by an "out-of-pocket" standard:

> The damages recoverable for a negligent misrepresentation are those necessary to compensate the plaintiff for the pecuniary loss to him of which the misrepresentation is a legal cause, including (a) The difference between the value of what he has received in the transaction and its purchase price or other value given for it; and (b) Pecuniary loss suffered otherwise as a consequence of the plaintiff's reliance upon the representation.

The out-of-pocket measure of damages [(i.e., the difference between the actual value of the scrap metal inventory and the amount that MAC paid for Mindis)] is consistent with Georgia's general measure of damages in negligence cases, which seeks to place the injured party in the same place it would have been had there been no injury or breach of duty.[5] It is also consistent with our prior decision in *Robert & Co.*, in which we recognized that the important distinction between cases of intentional misrepresentation and cases of negligent misrepresentation is the culpability of the defendant. As noted in the commentary to section 552B, an out-of-pocket measure of damages is commensurate with the culpability of the tortfeasor, who acted negligently, rather than intentionally or maliciously. Furthermore, utilizing the out-of-pocket standard for negligent misrepresentation and the benefit-of-the-bargain standard for fraudulent misrepresentation is a middle position that is consistent with our * * * adoption of section 552 * * *.[9] Finally, a majority of jurisdictions favor the Restatement position.

In adopting the benefit-of-the-bargain standard, the Court of Appeals failed to recognize how this standard is related to the culpability of the defendant. A benefit-of-the-bargain standard gives the wronged party the benefit of the contract he made, but it also ensures that the fraudfeasor does not enjoy any fruits of his misdeeds.[11] The dual purposes of this

---

5. *See, e.g.,* * * * Southeast Consultants v. O'Pry, 199 Ga.App. 125, 126–127, 404 S.E.2d 299 (1991) (measure of damages for negligent misrepresentation by engineers who performed erroneous percolation tests for new house is the difference in the current value of the house and the value as it should have been built); Perma Ad Ideas v. Mayville, 158 Ga.App. 707, 707–708, 282 S.E.2d 128 (1981) (measure of damages for injuries to a motor vehicle caused by negligence is the difference between the value of the vehicle before and after the negligence). * * *

9. * * * A few states may permit benefit-of-the-bargain damages for negligent misrepresentation. See Forsberg v. Burningham & Kimball, 892 P.2d 23, 27 (Utah Ct.App.1995) (relying on § 552B, but stating standard associated with benefit-of-the-bargain); Ryan v. Kanne, 170 N.W.2d 395, 406–407 (Iowa 1969); *but see* Sain v. Cedar Rapids Community Sch. Dist., 626 N.W.2d 115 (Iowa 2001) (citing § 552B with approval). Six states do not permit benefit-of-the-bargain damages even for fraudulent misrepresentation. See Restatement (Second) of Torts § 549, reporter's note (1977).

11. *McCrary,* 119 Ga. at 883, 47 S.E. 341; *but see* Brooks v. Dime Sav. Bank of New York, FSB, 217 Ga.App. 441, 457 S.E.2d 706 (1995) (measure of damages for fraudulent misrepresenta-

standard have no application in a negligence misrepresentation case where there was no privity because the defendant was not a party to the transaction and thus, has not been unjustly enriched.

* * * [A] new trial utilizing the proper measure of damages is required.

Judgment reversed. All the Justices concur.

NOTES

1. *BDO Seidman* cites the Restatement (Second) of Torts § 552B, which states that, in addition to out-of-pocket damages, a plaintiff can recover consequential damages for negligent misrepresentation. The same is true in a fraud action, whether the general damages for the misrepresented transaction are measured by the benefit-of-the-bargain or out-of-pocket theory. Consequential damages measure other losses proximately caused by the tort.

2. The two methods for measuring damages for fraud that are referred to in *BDO Seidman* sound like reliance and expectation damages. Fraud, however, is a tort, but it often occurs during the formation of a contract. What are the two different ways of stating the goal of tort damages in a cause of action for fraud, and how do those relate to the two different measurements of damages? For a discussion of remedial goals see Chapter 3, Section 2.

3. Many jurisdictions require an action for misrepresentation to be intentional. Some, as described in *BDO Seidman*, allow an action for negligent misrepresentation, but usually restrict plaintiffs to the out-of-pocket measure of recovery. *See, e.g.*, Lack Industries, Inc. v. Ralston Purina Co., 327 F.2d 266, 279 (8th Cir. 1964) (feed company negligently advised poultry business to expand; court held that poultry businesses' recovery of operating losses was equivalent to the out-of-pocket measure of damages allowed under Minnesota law); Goodrich & Pennington Mortgage Fund, Inc. v. J.R. Woolard, Inc., 120 Nev. 777, 101 P.3d 792 (2004)(holding out-of-pocket, not benefit-of-the-bargain, damages appropriate for negligent misrepresentation, relying on *BDO Seidman).* For an interesting discussion of the development of the tort of negligent misrepresentation and its application to investment advice, see Seth E. Lipner and Lisa A. Catalano, *The Tort of Giving Negligent Investment Advice*, 39 U. Mem. L. Rev. 663 (2009).

4. Some jurisdictions specify by statute whether a plaintiff may recover benefit-of-the-bargain or out-of-pocket damages in a fraud action. *See, e.g.*, Fragale v. Faulkner, 110 Cal. App.4th 229, 1 Cal. Rptr.3d 616 (2003) (holding that California statutes provide that damages for fraud are measured by the out-of-pocket rule, but damages for fraud by a fiduciary are measured by the benefit-of-the-bargain rule in the case of an intentional misrepresentation).

5. In a fraud action, a plaintiff may have the option of choosing between a tort action for damages or an action for restitution. *See* Williams Electronics Games, Inc. v. Garrity, 366 F.3d 569 (7th Cir. 2004). In *Williams*, Judge Posner described bribery as a "garden variety fraud" and said:

---

tion in artificially inflating price of home is difference between what plaintiffs paid for their properties and what those properties were worth at the time of purchase).

Commercial bribery is a deliberate tort, and one way to deter it is to make it worthless to the tortfeasor by stripping away all his gain, since if his gain exceeded the victim's loss a damages remedy would leave the tortfeasor with a profit from his act. * * * The amount of the bribe paid is of course not a profit to the briber, but an expense, and it should not enter into the net profit calculation sketched above. It can be used as a minimum estimate of damages, however, on the theory that no one would pay a bribe who didn't anticipate garnering net additional revenue at least equal to the amount of the bribe; and that additional revenue is, at least as a first approximation, an additional expense to the person whose agent was bribed. * * *

Restitution is available in any intentional-tort case in which the tortfeasor has made a profit that exceeds the victim's damages (if the damages exceed the profit, the plaintiff will prefer to seek damages instead), whether or not the tort involved a breach of fiduciary duty * * *.

Id. at 576. For further discussion of restitution see Chapter 4.

SECTION 3. CONTRACTS RELATING TO PERSONAL PROPERTY (SALE OF GOODS)

Most of the cases in this section were decided under Article 2 of the Uniform Commercial Code (UCC), which governs transactions in goods. Article 2 was first drafted in 1952 by an Editorial Board chaired by United States Circuit Judge Herbert F. Goodrich. Karl N. Llewellyn was the Chief Reporter and Soia Mentschikoff, Associate Chief Reporter.

The National Conference of Commissioners on Uniform State Laws and the American Law Institute proposed amendments to Article 2 that were approved by those bodies in 2003. As of June, 2010, the amendments had not been adopted by any state although they had been introduced as a bill in the Oklahoma House Judiciary Committee. *See* the National Conference of Commissioners on Uniform State Laws, http://www.nccusl.org/nccusl/uniformact_factsheets/uniformacts-fs-ucc22A03.asp. For a detailed analysis of the drafting process of the amendments to Article 2, the support and opposition to the amendments and his conclusion that they should be adopted see Fred H. Miller, *Uniform Commercial Code Article 2 On Sales of Goods and the Uniform Law Process: A True Story of Good v. ?*, 11 Duq. Bus. L.J. 143 (2009).

This Section is designed to show students how remedies are determined when movable objects are involved; it is not designed to teach the intricacies of Article 2 remedies. For the most part, the provisions of Article 2 covered in this Section mirror the common law. Detailed analysis of Article 2 is left to a course on it or the UCC in general. Citations to Article 2 in this Section are to the original version.

A. DAMAGES

1. Action by Buyer

a. *Goods Not Received or Accepted*

AZTEC CORP. v. TUBULAR STEEL, INC.

Court of Appeals of Texas, 14th District, 1988.
758 S.W.2d 793.

MURPHY, JUSTICE.

The dispute underlying this appeal concerned a sale of goods. * * * Tubular is a Missouri corporation specializing in the wholesale distribution of steel tubular goods, including pipe used in oil field operations. In November 1981 Tubular received an order from its customer, Peabody World Trade, to supply 22,060 feet of 7–inch outside diameter, 29–pound pipe with long thread and couple. The pipe was to be accompanied by mill papers, certifying the physical and chemical composition of the pipe. The end finish on the pipe was critical in order that its segments could be screwed together for use in the oil field.

In attempting to fill the Peabody order according to its specifications, Tubular salesmen called several sources, including Aztec, a Louisiana corporation specializing in the purchase and sale of pipe. Mr. Ken Chalaire, Aztec's operations manager, quoted Tubular a price of $29.23 per foot to supply the pipe to which Tubular orally agreed. A written purchase order was then mailed to Aztec, reciting the quantity, price and specifications and other requisites, such as mill papers and thread protectors. * * * Time was critical to Tubular's customer, Peabody, because the pipe was to be shipped out of the country from the port of Houston on a given date. In order to meet the deadline imposed by Peabody, Aztec instructed Tubular to wire payment directly to the account of LaBouve Drilling at a Houston bank. The funds were transferred, but the pipe that arrived at the port of Houston did not meet the specifications of the purchase order and was rejected by Peabody. Fortunately, Tubular was able to find pipe that conformed to Peabody's specifications for $29.79 per foot, or $67,325. When Tubular was unable to obtain a refund from Aztec or LaBouve of $64,739 paid for the nonconforming goods, it sued for its cost of cover and incidental expenses incurred in disposing of the pipe.

In response to special issues, the jury found * * * that $35,000 would compensate Tubular for its damage.

* * *

* * * Aztec's contentions are based upon the duty of an injured party to mitigate damages. Tubular, Aztec argues, could have and should have had the pipe ends rethreaded in a machine shop for approximately $5,000. Aztec's argument ignores the fact that the pipe would still have lacked the

mill certificates essential to the contract; it ignores the fact that there were tight time constraints of which Aztec was aware; and it ignores the fact that unrefuted evidence showed that Tubular had tried to mitigate damages by selling the pipe but was unsuccessful. It further ignores applicable law regarding buyers' remedies upon rightful rejection of non-conforming goods.

Applicable sections of the Texas Business and Commerce Code (Texas UCC) provide that where there is support in the evidence, aggrieved buyers are entitled to the following remedies:

§ 2.711 Buyer's Remedies in General; Buyer's Security Interest in Rejected Goods

(a) Where ... the buyer rightfully rejects ... with respect to any goods involved, ... the buyer may cancel and ... in addition to recovering so much of the price as has been paid

(1) "cover" and have damages under the next section [Section 2.712] as to all the goods affected whether or not they have been identified to the contract.

* * *

(c) On rightful rejection or justifiable revocation of acceptance a buyer has a security interest in goods in his possession or control for any payments made on their price and any expenses reasonably incurred in their inspection, receipt, transportation, care and custody and may [hold] such goods and resell them in like manner as an aggrieved seller (Section 2.706).

§ 2.712 "Cover"; Buyer's Procurement of Substitute Goods

(a) After a breach within the preceding section the buyer may "cover" by making in good faith and without unreasonable delay any reasonable purchase of or contract to purchase goods in substitution for those due from the seller.

(b) The buyer may recover from the seller as damages the difference between the cost of cover and the contract price together with an[y] incidental or consequential damages as hereinafter defined (Section 2.715) but less expenses saved in consequence of the seller's breach.

§ 2.715 Buyer's Incidental and Consequential Damages

(a) Incidental damages resulting from the seller's breach include expenses reasonably incurred in inspection, receipt, transportation and care and custody of goods rightfully rejected, any commercially reasonable charges, ... and any other reasonable expenses incident to the delay or other breach.

Tex.Bus. & Com.Code Ann. §§ 2.711, 2.712, 2.715 (Tex.UCC) (Vernon 1968).

Under section 2.711(a), upon a finding of liability, an aggrieved buyer is entitled to recover as much of the contract price as he has paid. Section 2.711 *et seq.* establish the exclusive means for modifying the amount of recovery sought under the Texas UCC. Damages may exceed the price paid upon findings by the jury of cost of cover exceeding contract price (§§ 2.711 and 2.712) and by findings of incidental or consequential damages (§§ 2.712 and 2.715). Conversely, damages must be reduced by the amount of profit derived from the buyer's resale of the goods. Section 2.711(c) gives the aggrieved buyer a security interest in the goods and a right to possession pending their sale or seller's repayment of contract price paid. Any sale must be made in good faith and conducted in a commercially reasonable manner. Tex.Bus. & Com.Code Ann. §§ 2.706 and 2.711 (Tex.UCC) (Vernon 1968). In addition to challenging buyer's evidence on the amount he was paid, a defendant seller could attack the buyer's good faith, the commercial reasonableness of the sale, or the amount derived from sale. An aggrieved buyer may retain the goods for collateral and offer them for sale. In the event that the buyer (now a section 2.711 secured party) is unsuccessful in finding a purchaser for the collateral, the Texas UCC does not permit that he be charged with the value of the collateral as a set off to his recovery. Therefore, in determining damages a jury may not consider the fact that the buyer retained possession of the goods. Nonconforming goods are by definition goods other than those ordered; those that do not sell are more likely a liability to the secured party than an asset. Furthermore, there is no Texas UCC provision requiring that a buyer of nonconforming goods rework or refabricate the goods to make them conform to the original contract between the parties.

At trial Tubular presented evidence to show its damages under the applicable Texas UCC provisions as follows:

Recovery of price paid under contract § 2.711	$64,739.00
Cost of cover minus contract price ($67,325.40 − 64,739.00) § 2.712	2,586.40
Incidental expenses §§ 2.712 and 2.715	3,400.00
TOTAL	$70,725.40

* * *

These amounts were uncontroverted.

Evidence documenting the cost of cover came in during the testimony of a disinterested witness, a former employee, now a competitor of Tubular. An interested witness, Tubular's president, James Morgan, testified as to the incidental expenses of transportation and storage. Although the evidence was uncontroverted, the jury could have disbelieved the documentary evidence and testimony on cost of cover and incidental expenses. By awarding Tubular less than the uncontroverted amount paid under the contract, the jury determined the amount of each to be nothing.

The trier of fact is the sole judge of the credibility of the witnesses. * * * A jury may or may not believe a witness's testimony in whole or in part. We cannot substitute our judgment for that of the jury and order additur with respect to these two elements of recovery. * * * Although the evidence would have supported the award of damages for cost of cover and incidental expenses, the award of unliquidated damages could be corrected only by granting a new trial. Such has not been prayed for by Tubular.

A different situation exists with respect to the amount paid under the contract. That amount was conclusively established. * * * The jury findings that a contract existed, that Aztec failed to deliver goods conforming to that contract, and that such failure was a proximate cause of damages establish as a matter of law that Tubular was entitled to recovery as an aggrieved buyer under the applicable provisions of the Texas UCC. As described above, the starting point for determining the amount of this recovery was the uncontroverted amount paid by Tubular under the contract. * * * The finding of $35,000 by the jury can only indicate that it believed that some amount was paid on the contract, but the dollar amount found has no support in the evidence. A jury shall not substitute a finding of its own creation for a fact conclusively established under the evidence. * * *

The sole evidence presented as to the amount paid under the contract was $64,739. Aztec's defense to the suit was two-fold: it denied liability and testified that Tubular could have remade and used the nonconforming goods. It did not contest the amount paid. The only evidence which a jury might properly consider to reduce the recovery of the full amount paid on the contract would be evidence that a sale of the goods resulted in a set off or evidence that the unsuccessful sale was not conducted in good faith and in a commercially reasonable manner so as to realize the full and proven value of the nonconforming goods. No such evidence was presented. Testimony that Tubular could have had the pipe ends rethreaded was not competent evidence to reduce the buyer's recovery under section 2.711.

We hold that Tubular's damages in the amount of $64,739 were established as a matter of law. Judgment n.o.v. is authorized under Rule 301 of the Texas Rules of Civil Procedure when a directed verdict would have been proper. After the jury determined liability, a directed verdict would have been proper as to the amount paid under the contract to be recovered, leaving to the jury only the issues of cost of cover and incidental damages. * * * Tubular's cross point is sustained with respect to recovery of the full amount paid on the contract; it is denied with respect to cost of cover and incidental expenses.

The judgment of the trial court is affirmed as modified.

NOTES

1. Damages should put plaintiff Tubular in what position? See Uniform Commercial Code (U.C.C.) § 1–106(1), which provides:

The remedies provided by this Act shall be liberally administered to the end that the aggrieved party may be put in as good a position as if the other party had fully performed but neither consequential or special nor penal damages may be had except as specifically provided in this Act or by other rule of law.

How does this section of the U.C.C. compare with the common law principles discussed in the first section of this Chapter?

2. Notice that the sections of Article II of the U.C.C. providing for a buyer's remedies codify the basic common-law principles of direct, incidental and consequential damages. What were the direct and incidental damages in *Aztec*? What would the consequential damages have been and why didn't Tubular seek them?

3. When the court increased the jury's award for one type of damages but not others, was the court's reasoning internally inconsistent? Does it affect your answer that Tubular did not seek consequential damages?

4. U.C.C. § 2–712(1) provides that "the buyer may 'cover' by making in good faith and without unreasonable delay any reasonable purchase of or contract to purchase goods in substitution for those due from the seller." May a purchaser cover by producing internally the goods that the seller did not deliver? If so, may that buyer recover the costs of production as well as the profits it would have made had it produced goods for sale to others? *See* Dura–Wood Treating Co. v. Century Forest Industries, 675 F.2d 745 (5th Cir.1982), *cert. denied*, 459 U.S. 865, 103 S.Ct. 144, 74 L.Ed.2d 122, *appeal after remand*, 694 F.2d 112 (5th Cir.1982) (buyer may cover by producing goods internally but cannot collect costs of production and foregone profits if those are greater than the cost of purchasing goods from an outside source).

KOENEN v. ROYAL BUICK CO.

Court of Appeals of Arizona, 1989.
162 Ariz. 376, 783 P.2d 822.

ROLL, JUDGE.

* * *

In September 1986, Thomas Koenen learned from automobile literature that General Motors planned to manufacture 500 special editions of the Buick Regal Grand National automobile. The vehicle, dubbed the Grand National Experimental (GNX) was the quickest limited production car in the United States at that time. The GNX, like the Grand National, was available only in black and had a 3.8 turbo-charged fuel-injected hand-built motor. The GNX, however, had additional features including an intercooled turbo-charged V–6 engine with special body, special tires and suspension, and special wheels. The GNX was featured on the cover of *Autoweek* and *Popular Mechanics*.[1]

Several months before Royal Buick, a Tucson-based automobile dealership, received official notification that it would receive one of the 500

---

1. Mandel, "Speedway Born," *Autoweek*, Feb. 16, 1987, at 63; Allen, "Speed Thrills," *Popular Mechanics*, March 1987, at 63.

GNX autos, Koenen contacted salesperson William Yalen at Royal Buick. Koenan, along with his father and brother, collected cars under the name of Koenen Classic Cars. Their collection was stored in an air-conditioned California warehouse. Koenen had previously conducted transactions with Royal Buick and Yalen. In March 1986, Koenen purchased a 1986 Grand National from Royal Buick for cash. Yalen was the salesperson. In August 1986, Koenen purchased a 1987 Grand National through Yalen from Royal Buick for cash.

In November 1986, Koenen went to Yalen and told him that he wished to buy a GNX. Koenen showed Yalen current literature regarding Buick's plan to offer a limited number of this special edition. During discussions with Yalen and new car sales manager Robert Sagar, Koenen agreed to pay the window sticker price for the vehicle, that is, the price placed on the car at the factory.

In December 1986, Royal Buick General Manager Tom Bird orally agreed to sell the GNX to Gary Gerovac. No purchase order was completed, however. On January 5, 1987, Jeff Buchner signed a purchase order agreement to purchase a GNX from Royal Buick. Although Buchner offered to give Royal Buick a $1000 deposit in connection with the purchase order, he was told that a $100 deposit was satisfactory. At that time, sales manager Sagar assured Buchner that he was "first in line."

On February 16, 1987, a purchase order form was signed by Koenen, Yalen, and Sagar regarding the GNX. * * * Koenen was listed on the form as the purchaser. Koenen told Sagar and Yalen that he was willing to pay up to $30,000 if that was the sticker price. Sagar and Yalen told Koenen that no one else had made a deposit and that Koenen was number one to receive a GNX. Koenen gave Yalen a check for $500 as a deposit for the GNX but asked that the check not be cashed. On February 17, 1987, Royal Buick filled out a purchase order form for David Woon and accepted a $500 deposit from him for purchase of the GNX. On February 20, 1987, Koenen replaced the February 16, 1987 check with a $500 check from his father.

In a letter dated April 21, 1987, General Motors notified Royal Buick that it would receive one GNX. The window sticker price for the vehicle was $29,290. Royal Buick General Manager Tom Bird placed a market value of $44,900 on the vehicle. Yalen contacted Koenen to see if Koenen wanted to bid on the vehicle.

On May 8, 1987, Royal Buick returned the deposits to Koenen, Buchner, and Woon. When Buchner received the letter, he contacted Sagar to protest. Sagar asked Buchner if he would be interested in bidding on the vehicle. Royal Buick received the GNX in September 1987. Royal Buick placed a price of $44,900 on the vehicle. Bird testified as to the process by which he arrived at the $44,900 figure:

Q. Who came up with the price?

A. I did.

Q. And how did you come up with that price?

A. In doing a little search as to what the cars were bringing around the country, that that [sic] seemed to be somewhat of a mean figure.

Q. About $45,000?

A. Right. We wanted to be a little cheaper than anybody else, so we cut it down a hundred dollars.

Q. Four hundred?

A. Forty-four nine.

Q. Forty-four nine?

A. I was being facetious in that last comment, but it was forty-four nine.

In April 1988, Royal Buick sold the vehicle for $39,750 to an Oklahoma physician.

* * *

Koenen received Royal Buick's May 8, 1987 letter informing him that he would not be able to purchase the GNX. The letter included a check in the amount of Koenen's $500 deposit, but Koenen declined to cash the check. Koenen proceeded to file a civil complaint alleging breach of contract on the part of Royal Buick. As part of the complaint, Koenen sought a temporary restraining order preventing Royal Buick from selling the GNX. By stipulation of the parties, Royal Buick agreed not to sell the vehicle. On November 30, 1987, a preliminary injunction was denied and Royal Buick was permitted to sell the GNX.

Koenen's complaint against Royal Buick was joined with a complaint filed by Buchner, who also sought damages based upon Royal Buick's refusal to sell the GNX to him.

The matter was tried to the court without a jury. The trial court awarded Koenen and Buchner $15,610 each, representing the difference between the manufacturer's suggested retail price ($29,290) and the fair market value of the automobile ($44,900).

* * *

[Royal Buick raised numerous defenses to enforceability of the contract: arguing that no contract had been formed; that the purchase order did not satisfy the statute of frauds; that parol evidence should not have been admissible to contradict the terms of the purchase order. None of these were successful.]

Royal Buick next argues that the contract for the sale of the car was void because Koenen planned on transporting the vehicle to California in violation of California Health and Safety Code § 43151(a).

* * *

However, simply because Koenen, with his father and brother, stores vehicles in a warehouse located in California does not establish that Koenen operates an established place of business in California. In addition, the record indicates that Koenen would not have driven the vehicle but merely placed it in storage. * * * Even assuming that the California statute could operate so as to negate an Arizona contract for the sale of a car, no evidence was presented that Koenen intended to use, register, or sell the vehicle in California. In addition, there was no evidence that the car did not comply with California standards. We find the contract was valid.

* * *

Finally, Royal Buick argues that the trial court should have computed damages as the difference between the cost to cover the loss and the contract price, and that Koenen failed to prove the cost of cover.

The UCC permits a buyer to elect the remedy when damaged by the actions of the seller. A.R.S. § 47–2711. Here, Koenen elected the difference between the fair market value and the contract price. A.R.S. § 47–2713.

Koenen's father purchased a GNX for the family collection from another source. No evidence was introduced as to the purchase price of that particular vehicle. Royal Buick argues that because Koenen's father succeeded in obtaining a GNX from a different source, Koenen suffered no damages or, alternatively, that Koenen was required to introduce evidence as to the purchase price for the other GNX so that the court would be able to determine the fair market value of the GNX which Koenen was unable to purchase from Royal Buick.

We disagree. First, the fact that Koenen's father purchased a substitute vehicle is not dispositive. If the father's purchase was proven to be a reasonable substitute for the contracted car then the measure of damages would be the difference between the cost of cover and the contract price. No evidence shows that the vehicle was purchased specifically to substitute for the lost bargain under the Royal Buick contract. The car was purchased in April or May 1988, some 11 or 12 months after Royal Buick repudiated the contract. Also, Koenen testified that even after acquiring the GNX, he was still possibly in the market for another one.

"The burden of proof as to mitigation of damages is on the party asserting the requirement." * * * Royal Buick failed to introduce any evidence that the father's purchase substituted for the Royal Buick contract or that the purchase of that car in any way mitigated the damages under the contract. Therefore, Royal Buick cannot claim that the buyer elected the remedy of cover. * * *

Royal Buick also argues that Koenen was required to introduce evidence as to the purchase price for the other GNX so the court could determine the fair market value of the contracted GNX. We disagree. A.R.S. § 47–2713 requires that market price be determined at the time the buyer learned of the breach. Royal Buick breached its contract with Koenen on May 8, 1987. Evidence of the purchase price of a GNX one year later is not dispositive of the fair market value of the vehicle in 1987. Significantly, when the Royal Buick general manager testified regarding the fair market value of the GNX which Royal Buick was selling, he testified that he surveyed Buick dealerships and determined that $45,000 was a fair market value for the GNX. This concession by Royal Buick could certainly be considered by the trial court.

The trial court correctly computed damages as the difference between the fair market value and the contract price. Sufficient evidence was presented to support the trial court's conclusion that $44,900 was the market value of the vehicle.

We affirm.

ATTORNEYS' FEES

A.R.S. § 12–341.01 authorizes an award to the successful party in any contested action arising out of contract. Section 12–341.01 applies to appeals as well as trials. * * * Appellee Koenen is awarded attorneys' fees incurred in the defense of this appeal.

NOTES

1. The difference between the market price and the contract price is sometimes called "hypothetical cover." Egerer v. CSR West, LLC, 116 Wash. App. 645, 649, 67 P.3d 1128, 1131 (2003).

2. Dealers of unique cars should be careful. See Hessler v. Crystal Lake Chrysler–Plymouth, Inc., 338 Ill. App.3d 1010, 788 N.E.2d 405 (2003). In *Hessler*, the plaintiff contracted with the defendant to buy a new promotional vehicle, the Plymouth Prowler, should it be manufactured, for $5,000 over the $39,000 list price. When the dealer received the Prowler, it sold the car to someone else for $10,000 over list. When the plaintiff sued, the dealer claimed that the market value of the Prowler was $10,000 over list, making the damages $5,000. Plaintiff, however, had contacted 38 dealers to buy the Prowler and had to pay $77,706 for it. The court held that plaintiff could recover the difference between the cover price and the contract price.

3. If a buyer does not cover and a seller's breach was anticipatory, that is, it occurred before performance was due, may the buyer wait until performance is due to measure the difference between the market price and the contract price? What if the market price for the undelivered goods is rising during that time? See Cosden Oil & Chemical Co. v. Karl O. Helm Aktiengesellschaft, 736 F.2d 1064, 1072 (5th Cir.1984) (Buyer of polystyrene who chose not to cover after anticipatory breach during rising market must measure the market "at the time he could have covered—a reasonable time after repudiation.").

4. Can a plaintiff recover incidental and consequential damages without attempting to cover? Consider the next case.

JEWELL–RUNG AGENCY, INC. v. THE HADDAD ORGANIZATION, LTD.

United States District Court, Southern District of New York, 1993.
814 F.Supp. 337.

ROBERT P. PATTERSON, JR., DISTRICT JUDGE.

Plaintiff Jewell–Rung Agency, Inc. ("Jewell–Rung"), seeks damages in excess of $350,000 for the defendant's alleged breach of contract. Defendant The Haddad Organization, Ltd. ("Haddad"), moves for summary judgment on the issue of damages * * *.

* * *

Jewell–Rung is a Canadian corporation engaged in the business of importing and selling men's clothing at wholesale. Haddad is a New York corporation that manufactures men's outerwear sold under the "Lakeland" label.

In 1990, Jewell–Rung ordered samples of Lakeland men's outerwear from Haddad so that it might seek orders for this clothing from Canadian retailers. Haddad supplied Jewell–Rung with the ordered samples, which Jewell–Rung used to obtain orders from customers in Canada.

In January of 1991, Jewell–Rung placed an initial purchase order with Haddad for 2,325 garments of Lakeland men's outerwear, having a total listed price of approximately $250,000 in American currency, for the Fall 1991 season. By February 1991, Plaintiff had taken orders for 372 of these garments at a wholesale price of $107,506 in Canadian currency.

According to Jewell–Rung's Complaint, Haddad accepted its purchase order in January 1991 with the understanding that Jewell–Rung would obtain an exclusive distributorship of Lakeland outerwear in Canada, but Haddad, after accepting the order, granted a third party, Olympic Pant and Sportswear Co. ("Olympic"), the exclusive right to sell, manufacture, and market Lakeland outerwear throughout Canada. Plaintiff alleges that Haddad's acceptance of its January 1991 purchase order created a binding contract, which Haddad subsequently breached by failing to fill the purchase order and entering into its exclusive distributorship agreement with Olympic. Plaintiff further alleges that because it did not learn of Haddad's alleged breach until February of 1991, it was unable to fill its customers' orders for Lakeland goods for the Fall 1991 season or to obtain a substitute line of men's outerwear and, as a result, sustained over $350,000 in damages.

For the purposes of this summary judgment motion only, Defendant Haddad concedes that its acceptance of Jewell–Rung's January 1991 purchase order created a binding contract and that Haddad's agreement with Olympic constituted a breach of that contract. The defendant seeks summary judgment with respect to damages on three grounds: (1) Plaintiff's failure to mitigate damages bars any recovery; (2) Plaintiff's refusal to cover prohibits recovery of consequential damages; and (3) alternatively, any recovery by Plaintiff of lost profits must be limited to the profits derived from the orders already placed by Plaintiff's customers at the time of Defendant's breach of contract.

DISCUSSION

* * *

Motion for Summary Judgment

A. *The availability of damages in general*

New York's Uniform Commercial Code provides that a buyer may recover damages for a seller's breach of a contract of sale by either of two methods. N.Y.U.C.C. § 2–711(1). The buyer may either "cover" and obtain damages under N.Y.U.C.C. § 2–712, or recover damages for non-delivery as provided under N.Y.U.C.C. § 2–713.

It is undisputed that Jewell–Rung, the buyer in this case, did not "cover" and may seek damages under section 2–713 only. This section provides that "the measure of damages for non-delivery or repudiation by the seller is the difference between the market price at the time when the buyer learned of the breach and the contract price together with any incidental and consequential damages ..., but less expenses saved in consequence of the seller's breach."

Haddad asserts that at the time when Jewell–Rung learned of the alleged breach of contract, Olympic offered to sell Jewell–Rung Lakeland outerwear to fill all of its orders at the contract price to which Jewell–Rung and Haddad had agreed. According to Haddad, the market price of the goods at the time when the buyer learned of the breach was therefore equivalent to the contract price, and the buyer is deemed to have suffered no damage under section 2–713.

Plaintiff has, however, demonstrated the existence of a genuine issue of fact as to whether Olympic actually offered to supply Jewell–Rung with the same goods at the same price agreed upon by Haddad. * * *

* * * The submission by each party of competent but conflicting accounts as to the nature of any offers made by Olympic to Jewell–Rung presents a genuine issue of material fact as to the available market price for the Lakeland goods at the time of Defendant's alleged breach of contract.

Haddad further contends that the existence of this genuine issue of fact as to price is immaterial to Plaintiff's claim for damages because Plaintiff concedes that it would have rejected Olympic's offer to sell it substitute goods at any price. Plaintiff maintains that purchasing and selling Lakeland goods manufactured by Olympic would have operated to the detriment of its own sales of competing lines of outerwear in the future. Haddad asserts that Plaintiff's refusal to buy from Olympic constitutes a breach of its duty to mitigate damages and therefore bars recovery in this action.

Haddad's argument boils down to an assertion that Plaintiff's failure to effect cover bars recovery of damages under section 2–713. However, the Uniform Commercial Code makes clear that "cover" is an alternative to the relief authorized under section 2–713, *see* N.Y.U.C.C. § 2–711(1), and that failure of a buyer to effect cover "does not bar him from any other remedy." *Id.* at § 2–712(3). "Recovery of damages based on market price fluctuation under Section 2–713 is not ... contingent upon the buyer's attempting to cover." * * * Accordingly, Plaintiff's failure to purchase substitute goods from Olympic or any other seller does not preclude recovery of damages for Haddad's alleged breach of contract.

B.   *The availability of consequential damages*

Haddad maintains that Jewell–Rung's failure to effect cover bars it from recovering consequential damages. Although N.Y.U.C.C. § 2–712(3) explicitly states that "[f]ailure of the buyer to effect cover * * * does not bar him from any other remedy," the Official Comment to this section of the Uniform Commercial Code cautions that it must be read in conjunction with section 2–715(2)(a). *See* N.Y.U.C.C. § 2–712 Official Comment at 645 (McKinney 1964). Section 2–715(2)(a) limits consequential damages to losses "which could not reasonably be prevented by cover or otherwise."

As previously stated, Jewell–Rung does not dispute that it did not attempt to effect cover. However, a genuine issue of material fact exists as to whether Jewell–Rung's failure to seek cover was reasonable under the circumstances.

Jewell–Rung provides several reasons why it did not seek cover. In explaining why it did not buy goods from Olympic, Jewell–Rung states that it had the following concerns: that its customers would not be satisfied with the quality of Lakeland goods manufactured by Olympic, which specializes in the production of lower-priced clothing for discounters and department stores, * * * that supplying its customers with outerwear manufactured by Olympic for the Fall 1991 season would provide Olympic with an entree to those customers for all of the next season's goods,* * * and that purchasing goods from Olympic would place it at the complete mercy of a competitor for the timely supply of goods * * *.

Jewell–Rung further points out that it had no source other than Olympic for Lakeland goods, which were not fungible but were "branded goods, manufactured from specific patterns and specific styles." * * * In addition, Jewell–Rung alleges that substitutions for Lakeland goods were not available that late in the purchasing cycle, and that it was in fact unable to find a replacement line for two seasons. * * *

Based upon the reasons put forth by Jewell–Rung for its failure to cover, this Court cannot say at this time that such failure to cover was unreasonable as a matter of law. The cases cited by Defendant, Happy Dack Trading Co. v. Agro–Industries, Inc., 602 F.Supp. 986 (S.D.N.Y.

1984), and Hilord Chem. Corp. v. Ricoh Elecs., Inc., 875 F.2d 32 (2d Cir.1989), are factually distinguishable. In *Happy Dack*, the Court denied recovery of lost profits because the plaintiffs failed to effect cover as to a fungible good, i.e. resin, that was available on the open market. *Happy Dack*, 602 F.Supp. at 994. Specific brands and styles of clothing, such as the Lakeland goods at issue here, are not so fungible. * * * In *Hilord Chem. Corp.*, the Court did not actually decide that the plaintiff had unreasonably failed to cover; it held only that the trial court should have instructed the jury on the issue of cover in light of testimony that specific sources of substitute goods were available to the plaintiff. *Hilord Chem. Corp.*, 875 F.2d at 38.

Accordingly, the defendant's motion for summary judgment is also denied insofar as it seeks to bar recovery for consequential damages.

C. Limitation on recovery of lost profits

In the alternative, Haddad asserts that any lost profits awarded to Jewell–Rung should be limited to those derived from confirmed orders placed by Jewell–Rung's customers at the time of the alleged breach.

Under New York law, recovery of lost profits has three prerequisites. First, the party seeking lost profits must demonstrate "with certainty that such damages have been caused by the breach and, second, the alleged loss must be capable of proof with reasonable certainty." Kenford Co. v. County of Erie, 67 N.Y.2d 257, 502 N.Y.S.2d 131, 132, 493 N.E.2d 234, 235 (1986). Third, "there must be a showing that the particular damages were fairly within the contemplation of the parties to the contract at the time it was made." *Id.* * * *

Before any evidence of lost profits is presented in this matter, Haddad asks the Court to rule as a matter of law that lost profits, with the exception of anticipated payments for garments already ordered by retailers at the time of breach, are incapable of proof with reasonable certainty. Haddad makes two arguments in support of this position.

First, Haddad cites *Texpor Traders*, 720 F.Supp. at 1114, Wullschleger & Co. v. Jenny Fashions, Inc., 618 F.Supp. 373, 378 (S.D.N.Y.1985), and Harbor Hill Lithographing Corp. v. Dittler Bros., Inc., 76 Misc.2d 145, 348 N.Y.S.2d 920, 924 (S.Ct.Nassau Cty.1973), for the proposition that in the case of a wholesaler, lost profits are restricted to those pertaining to confirmed orders of resale. None of these cases comes close to establishing such a per se rule. Each case merely limits recovery of lost profits after the plaintiff has presented evidence and failed to demonstrate a reasonable basis for calculating lost profits other than those derived from confirmed orders that were in place at the time of breach.

Second, Haddad maintains that lost profits are rarely appropriate where the injured party is a new business because such damages are by nature highly speculative. When a "new business" seeks to recover lost profits, "a stricter standard" of proof is required "for the obvious reason that there does not exist a reasonable basis of experience upon which to estimate lost profits with the requisite degree of reasonable certainty." *Kenford Co.*, 502 N.Y.S.2d at 132, 493 N.E.2d at 235 * * *. This heightened standard of proof for new businesses indicates that new ventures will have difficulty demonstrating lost profits; it does not mean that new businesses should be denied an opportunity to present their evidence of such damages at trial.

Whether Jewell–Rung is in fact a "new business" within the meaning of *Kenford Co.* is itself unclear. It is new to the business of selling Lakeland products in Canada, but its experience as a wholesaler of men's clothing in Canada is evidence of its viability as an enterprise and could, for example, yield evidence as to previous patterns of profit on resale of similar lines of clothing.

* * *

* * * Defendant's motion for summary judgment is denied.

NOTES

1. How would you try to settle this case at this point? What arguments for settlement would you make for both parties?

2. Why was the plaintiff in *Jewell-Rung Agency* seeking only consequential, but not direct or incidental damages? *See* R.B. Matthews, Inc. v. Transamerica Transportation Services, Inc., 945 F.2d 269, 275–76 (9th Cir.1991) (case remanded to see if buyer of drop frame trailers had opportunity to cover after seller breached contract; if not, consequential damages improper).

3. The court in *Jewell-Rung Agency* identified three requirements that must be met before consequential damages may be recovered by the plaintiff. The defendant only addressed two of those requirements. What was the requirement that was not addressed, and why do you think it was not discussed? U.C.C. § 2–715(2) provides:

> Consequential damages resulting from the seller's breach include (a) any loss resulting from general or particular requirements and needs of which the seller at the time of contracting had reason to know and which could not reasonably be prevented by cover or otherwise; and (b) injury to person or property proximately resulting from any breach of warranty.

Compare *Jewell–Rung Agency* with Gerwin v. Southeastern California Ass'n of Seventh Day Adventists, 14 Cal.App.3d 209, 92 Cal.Rptr. 111 (1971) (holding lost profits for new business disallowed because plaintiff attempted to conceal identity from defendant at time of contracting, thereby depriving defendant of reason to know of the extent of lost profits with reasonable certainty), *and* Bockman Printing & Services, Inc. v. Baldwin–Gregg, Inc., 213 Ill.App.3d 516, 157 Ill.Dec. 630, 572 N.E.2d 1094, 1101 (1991) (defendants had no reason to know that plaintiff would contract for more business based on contract with defendants to design and manufacture a machine to fold papers since past two attempts to build such a machine had failed). For further discussion of the foreseeability requirement for consequential damages in contract law and how it differs from the foreseeability requirement for damages in tort law see Section 3 of Chapter 3.

b. Goods Accepted, But Defective

RAZOR v. HYUNDAI MOTOR AMERICA

Appellate Court of Illinois, First District, Third Division, 2004.
349 Ill.App.3d 651, 813 N.E.2d 247.

Before: KARNEZIS, J. HOFFMAN, P.J., and HALL, J.

JUSTICE KARNEZIS delivered the opinion of the court.

Plaintiff Shante Razor brought an action pursuant to the Magnuson–Moss Warranty—Federal Trade Commission Improvement Act (15 U.S.C. § 2301 et seq. (1994)) (Magnuson–Moss Act) and the Illinois New Vehicle Buyer Protection Act (815 ILCS 380/1 et seq. (West 2002)). * * *

* * *

On August 4, 2001, plaintiff purchased and took delivery of a new 2001 Hyundai Sonata GLS. She purchased the car from Gartner Buick, Inc. (Gartner), in Aurora, Illinois. It was manufactured and distributed by defendant. Defendant's new vehicle limited warranty covered the car for 60 months or 60,000 miles, whichever came sooner.

* * * On January 7, 2002, plaintiff * * * asserted claims for (I) breach of written warranty under the Magnuson–Moss Act; (II) breach of implied warranty under the Magnuson–Moss Act; (III) revocation of acceptance under the Magnuson–Moss Act; and (IV) violation of the Illinois New Vehicle Buyer Protection Act. * * *

Plaintiff testified at trial that the Sonata was her first new car and that she bought it because she had heard good things about the car, she needed dependable transportation to get to and from work and "every place else" and the price was reasonable. * * *

Plaintiff took her new car home on August 4, 2001. * * *

On September 26, 2001, when plaintiff attempted to start the car with her key, the car did not crank. She checked multiple things to make sure that she was not the cause of the failure to start, such as whether the gear shift was engaged, but could find no reason for the problem. She called roadside assistance and had the car towed to Gartner. The odometer on the car read 3,518 miles. Gartner's work order shows that when Gartner service technicians checked the car it started every time and they found no problems with the battery, cables and connections. Plaintiff received the car back that afternoon but missed a day of work as a result of having to take the car for repair.

On October 6, 2001, plaintiff brought the car into Gartner again, complaining that the car would not start when cold. The odometer on the car read 3,931 miles. Gartner checked the car and it started. Technicians found the starter was intermittently open and replaced it. They also performed an oil change free of charge. Gartner provided plaintiff with a loaner car during the two days her car was being serviced.

On October 16, 2001, plaintiff had the car towed to Gartner again, complaining that the car would "not crank sometimes." The repair order shows that technicians replaced a shorted "ECU power relay" but does not state that it was the cause of the problem. Gartner had the car for three days.

On October 25, 2001, plaintiff again brought the car in complaining that it would not start. * * *

* * *

When plaintiff got the car back in November 2001 after having been without it for two weeks, she thought it was fixed. When she turned the key in the ignition on November 21 and nothing happened again, she "just broke down" and a Gartner service manager's statement to her that it must be something plaintiff was doing to cause the no-start problem "just aggravated the whole situation." Plaintiff stated that besides the aggravation, she was inconvenienced as a result of the car's problems because she missed work, was late for work, had to depend on other people when she did not have a loaner car, and had to wait for tows.

Plaintiff was the sole witness in her case. * * *

* * *

At the close of evidence, the court denied defendant's motion for a directed verdict. The jury found in favor of plaintiff on the breach of written warranty and breach of implied warranty of merchantability counts, and awarded plaintiff $5,000 as breach of warranty damages, $3,000 for aggravation and inconvenience and $500 for loss of use. * * *

* * * The court granted plaintiff's petition for fees and costs, awarding her $12,277 in addition to the $8,500 damage award. Defendant timely appeals.

* * *

FAILURE TO PROVE DAMAGES

Defendant first argues that the judgment must be reversed because plaintiff failed to prove damages, an essential element of her *prima facie* case for breach of warranty. Plaintiff filed her action for breach of warranties pursuant to the Magnuson–Moss Act, which provides that "a consumer who is damaged by the failure of a supplier, warrantor, or service contractor to comply with any obligation under this chapter, or under a written warranty, implied warranty, or service contract, may bring suit for damages and other legal and equitable relief." 15 U.S.C. § 2310(d)(1) (1994). By implication, because the Magnuson–Moss Act does not address damages for breach of limited and implied warranties, the Uniform Commercial Code (UCC) (810 ILCS 5/1 *et seq.* (West 2002)) is used for such determinations. * * *

Section 2–714 of the UCC provides that "the measure of damages for breach of warranty is the difference at the time and place of acceptance between the value of the goods accepted and the value they would have had if they had been as warranted, unless special circumstances show proximate damages of a different amount." 810 ILCS 5/2–714(2) (West 2000). The UCC also provides for incidental and consequential damages in proper cases. 810 ILCS 5/2–714(3) (West 2000). The special circumstances exception to section 2–714(2) must be read in conjunction with section 1–106 of the UCC (810 ILCS 5/1–106(1) (West 2000)), which provides that remedies found in the UCC "shall be liberally administered to the end that the aggrieved party may be put in as good a position as if the other party had fully performed." * * *

Plaintiff presented evidence of the purchase price of the car, the car's chronic failure to start, the number of times the car was taken for repair and the amount of time she was without the car. She testified that the value of the car she received (a vehicle that intermittently failed to start) was less than the value of the car she thought she was buying (a new car with no such problems, *i.e.,* a car that was capable of starting and being driven on demand). She testified that, if she had known at the time of purchase what she knew at trial, she would not have bought the car and would certainly not have paid the price she paid for a "new car with used problems." She testified that she missed work and that she and her family suffered inconvenience and aggravation as a result of the car's failure to start. The jury found for plaintiff and awarded her damages for breach of the limited and implied warranties, loss of use and for aggravation and inconvenience damages.

Mathematical precision is not required in proof of loss, especially in the determination of consequential damages. * * * Rather, the amount of damages is determined by the trier of fact in the exercise of sound discretion and in any manner reasonable under the circumstances, as long as the award is not punitive. * * * "Where the right to recovery exists[,] the defendant cannot escape liability because the damages are difficult to prove." * * * Based on its own experience and plaintiff's testimony, the jury could reasonably determine the difference between the value of the car as promised (a problem-free, reliable car capable of being driven at will) and the value of the car as plaintiff actually received it (an unreliable car, prone to not starting and, on such occasions, incapable of being driven), as well as incidental and consequential damages. We do not find "a total failure or lack of evidence to prove" the damages element necessary to the plaintiff's case such that judgment NOV was warranted.

LACK OF PRIVITY

Defendant argues that plaintiff cannot state a claim for breach of implied warranty under the Magnuson–Moss Act because there is no privity between plaintiff and defendant. We recently considered and rejected this argument in Mekertichian v. Mercedes–Benz U.S.A., L.L.C.,

(2004), 347 Ill. App.3d 828, 807 N.E.2d 1165, 283 Ill. Dec. 324, and can summarily dispose of this issue.

* * * Pursuant to the UCC, a buyer of goods seeking purely economic damages for a breach of implied warranty has " 'a potential cause of action only against his immediate seller.' " * * * Therefore, pursuant to the UCC, plaintiff would only have a cause of action against Gartner and not against defendant.

However, in actions where (1) a consumer filed against a manufacturer pursuant to the Magnuson–Moss Act and (2) the manufacturer had expressly warranted a product to the consumer, the privity requirement has been relaxed. *Mekertichian*, citing *Szajna*, 115 Ill.2d at 315–16, 503 N.E.2d at 769, and *Rothe*, 119 Ill. 2d at 294–95, 518 N.E.2d at 1030. In such cases, "vertical privity will be deemed to exist with respect to that consumer, enabling him to file an action for breach of implied warranty [against the manufacturer] as well." *Mekertichian* (manufacturer held in vertical privity with consumer where manufacturer provided limited written warranty with new automobile; pursuant to doctrine of *stare decisis*, Illinois Supreme Court decisions regarding state privity requirements under the Magnuson–Moss Act are binding on all Illinois courts where United States Supreme Court has not addressed the issue) * * *. Accordingly, because defendant provided a written limited warranty with the Sonata, it is deemed to be in vertical privity with plaintiff * * *.

BREACH OF LIMITED WARRANTY

Defendant argues that plaintiff failed to prove that defendant breached its limited warranty to repair and replace defective parts. * * *

Pursuant to section 2–719(2) of the UCC, " 'where circumstances cause an exclusive or limited remedy [such as repair or replacement] to fail of its essential purpose, remedy may be had as provided in this Act.' " * * * "A manufacturer does not have an unlimited time or an unlimited number of attempts to repair an automobile." * * *

* * *

It is clear that a defect existed in the car given that the ordinary purpose for which a car would be used, i.e., as a mode of transportation, would necessarily entail being able to start the car so that it can be driven. * * *

* * *

CONSEQUENTIAL DAMAGES

Defendant lastly argues that the court erred in entering judgment on the jury award of consequential damages because the limited warranty specifically excluded recovery for incidental and consequential damages. However, where a contract limits a remedy to repair and/or replacement of defective parts or goods and the remedy failed in its essential purpose, a provision excluding incidental and consequential damages will have no effect and those damages will be available to the plaintiff pursuant to the UCC. * * * The court did not err in entering judgment on the jury's award of such damages.

ATTORNEYS' FEES AND COSTS

The trial court awarded attorneys' fees and costs to plaintiff as the prevailing party. Pursuant to Section 2310(d)(2) of the Magnuson–Moss Act, such an award is within the trial court's discretion and will not be disturbed on review absent an abuse of that discretion. * * *

Affirmed.

NOTES

1. *Mekertichian*, cited in *Razor*, discusses the conflicting authorities on whether privity can be relaxed under the Magnuson–Moss Act. Because the Magnuson–Moss Act incorporates state law, unless there should be a definitive ruling that Congress intended that the privity requirement be uniform, it would not be unusual for different states to come to different conclusions.

2. In Kim v. Mercedes–Benz, U.S.A., Inc., 353 Ill.App.3d 444, 288 Ill.Dec. 778, 818 N.E.2d 713 (2004), the plaintiff sued Mercedes–Benz for breach of warranty because of problems with the fuel gauge, windows, and other parts of the car. Because the plaintiff did not disclose any expert witnesses prior to trial, the court ruled that he could not call any. The trial court granted defendant's motion for a directed verdict on the ground that the plaintiff had failed to prove damages. The plaintiff relied on *Razor* to argue that he was competent to testify about the value of the car. The court of appeals quoted the plaintiff's testimony: "I purchased a new vehicle expecting there would not be any problems, and I paid a lot of money to buy a good car. If I had known there would be so much problems, I would have bought a cheap car." *Id.* at 725. The court then said,

> This testimony is simply not the same as Razor's testimony that "[s]he would not pay the price she paid because the problems she had with the new Sonata were akin to those she had with her previous car which had been used and from which she had expected some problems. Plaintiff testified that 'I would not pay that for a new car, with used problems as it were.' " * * *

* * *

> The *Razor* opinion did not discuss in any manner or form the foundational requirements which must be considered when determining the admissibility of a vehicle owner's testimony relating to diminished value. Unlike the court in *Razor*, we were asked by the parties in this case to address this issue and nothing in our reading of *Razor* changes our analysis.

Id. at 725–26. Is the court in *Kim* implying that the *Razor* court erred in admitting the vehicle owner's testimony relating to diminished value, or are *Kim* and *Razor* distinguishable?

3.   If a wholesaler who buys defective goods has to reduce the resale price of those goods to the buyer who had contracted to purchase the goods, is that reduction the "difference at the time and place of acceptance between the value of the goods accepted and the value they would have had if they had been warranted" under Section 2-714(2) of the Uniform Commercial Code? Carbontek Trading Co. v. Phibro Energy, Inc., 910 F.2d 302 (5th Cir.1990) says it is. Do you agree? How does *Carbontek* compare with Transoil (Jersey) Ltd. v. Belcher Oil Co., 950 F.2d 1115 (5th Cir.1992) (buyer of oil with higher vanadium content than provided in contract cannot use price at which it sold the nonconforming oil as evidence of the value of the oil received because that price may have reflected a collapse of the market for oil), *cert. denied*, 506 U.S. 829, 113 S.Ct. 90, 121 L.Ed.2d 53 (1992)?

2.   Action by Seller

SPRAGUE v. SUMITOMO FORESTRY CO.

Supreme Court of Washington, *en banc*, 1985.
104 Wash.2d 751, 709 P.2d 1200.

DORE, JUSTICE.

This action involves a claim by Clyde Sprague against Sumitomo Forestry Company, Ltd. for breach of contract arising from Sumitomo's unconditional cancellation of a log purchase contract. * * *

* * *

Via a special verdict form, the jury found (1) that there was no mutual rescission; (2) that there was a breach and no waiver; (3) that the contract price was $197,204 and the resale price was $144,924 with net contractual damages of $52,280; (4) that Sprague sustained incidental damages of $216,498 for the following items: (a) cost of refinancing, $39,674; (b) extra transportation cost, $5,612; (c) loss of revenue on Flip Blowdown not covered by contract, $9,121; (d) loss of logging time, 11 weeks, $171,200; and (e) cost of moving tower, $2,115.

The major thrust of Sumitomo's appellate argument here is that Sprague did not give the requisite notice of intention to resell the canceled goods as required by RCW 62A.2–706(3) and, therefore, Sprague is not entitled to recover the difference between the contract price and the resale price.

RESALE PRICE DIFFERENTIAL

The catalogue of a seller's remedies in a breach of contract case governed by the sale of goods provisions of the Uniform Commercial Code is found in RCW 62A.2–703. In the present case, the catalogue of available remedies can quickly be reduced to two; these are:

(1) resale and recovery under RCW 62A.2–706, or

(2) recovery of the difference between the contract price and the market price under RCW 62A.2–708(1).

At trial Sprague apparently proceeded, pursuant to RCW 62A.2–706, to recover as damages the difference between the resale price and contract price. RCW 62A.2–706(1) provides that if the seller acts in good faith and in a commercially reasonable manner, he may recover the difference between the resale price and the contract price, together with any incidental damages allowed under RCW 62A.2–710, less expenses saved.

RCW 62A.2–706(2) goes on to permit resale at public or private sale. Of critical importance here is the requirement of RCW 62A.2–706(3) which provides that where an aggrieved seller resells goods which are the subject of a breach at a private sale, he must give the buyer "reasonable notification of his intention to resell."

* * *

* * * [C]an the notice requirement be satisfied by the fact that the buyer knew or should have known that the seller intended to resell? From the plain language of RCW 62A.2–706, the giving by the seller of notice of intention to resell is a specific requirement to entitle seller to claim as damages the difference between resale price and the contract price. The words of subsection (3) are precise: "the seller *must* give the buyer reasonable notification of his intention to resell." (Italics ours.) RCW 62A.2–706(3).

* * *

MARKET PRICE DIFFERENTIAL

It is a general rule of appellate practice that the judgment of the trial court will not be reversed when it can be sustained on any theory, although different from that indicated in the decision of the trial judge. * * * Although the jury verdict cannot be upheld under the resale method of determining damages, we find that the record supports the verdict under the alternate method of establishing damages, computed by measuring the difference between the market price and the contract price as provided in RCW 62A.2–708. This provision states:

(1) Subject to subsection (2) and to the provisions of this Article with respect to proof of market price (RCW 62A.2–723), the measure of damages for non-acceptance or repudiation by the buyer is the difference between the market price at the time and place for tender and the unpaid contract price together with any incidental damages provided in this Article (RCW 62A.2–710), but less expenses saved in consequence of the buyer's breach.

(2) If the measure of damages provided in subsection (1) is inadequate to put the seller in as good a position as performance would have done then the measure of damages is the profit (including reasonable overhead) which the seller would have made from full performance by the buyer, together with any incidental damages provided in this Article (RCW 62A.2–710), due allowance for costs reasonably incurred and due credit for payments or proceeds of resale.

It is fundamental under RCW 62A.2–703 and the sections that follow that an aggrieved seller is not required to elect between damages under RCW 62A.2–706 and 62A.2–708. RCW 62A.2–703 cumulatively sets forth the remedies available to a seller upon the buyer's breach. The pertinent commentary thereto indicates specifically that the remedies provided are cumulative and not exclusive and that as a fundamental policy Article 2 of the U.C.C. rejects any doctrine of election of remedy.

The seller has the burden of proof with respect to market price or market value. A seller cannot avail himself of the benefit of RCW 62A.2–708 when he has not presented evidence of market price or market value. However, the resale price of goods may be considered as appropriate evidence of the market value at the time of tender in determining damages pursuant to RCW 62A.2–708. * * *

While, admittedly, Sprague's resale came after the time for tender, it can still be utilized as a market price. * * * RCW 62A.2–723(2) states:

> (2) If evidence of a price prevailing at the times or places described in this Article is not readily available the price prevailing within any reasonable time before *or after* the time described or at any other place which in commercial judgment or under usage of trade would serve as a reasonable substitute for the one described may be used * * *.

(Italics ours.)

The court is granted a "reasonable leeway" (Official Comments to RCWA 62A.2–723) in measuring market price. During the trial of this action, not only was there testimony to the effect that in an effort to mitigate damages, respondent Sprague sold the Flip Blowdown logs to five purchasers at private sales in 1981 and 1982, there was also testimony that the market price remained at the same level as at the time and place of tender in late 1980.

The net contractual damages of $52,280 ($197,204 contract price [minus] $144,924 resale price) which was awarded respondent under the jury verdict thus equaled the measure of damages available under RCW 62A.2–708(1). We affirm this award.

INCIDENTAL DAMAGES

Sprague is entitled also to incidental damages. RCW 62A.2–708 provides that the seller is entitled to the difference between the market price and contract price "together with any incidental damages provided in this Article (RCW 62A.2–710), but less expenses saved in consequence of the buyer's breach." Incidental damages are defined in RCW 62A.2–710 as follows:

> Incidental damages to an aggrieved seller include any commercially reasonable charges, expenses or commissions incurred in stopping delivery, in the transportation, care and custody of goods after

the buyer's breach, in connection with return or resale of the goods or otherwise resulting from the breach.

At trial, the jury found that respondent sustained incidental damages of $216,498 for the following items: (a) cost of refinancing, $39,674; (b) extra transportation cost, $5,612; (c) loss of revenue on Flip Blowdown not covered by contract, $9,121; (d) loss of logging time, 11 weeks, $171,200; and (e) cost of moving tower, $2,115.

Sumitomo contends that some of these items are not incidental damages but more properly classified as consequential. Consequential damages are *not* allowed except as specifically provided in RCW Title 62A or by other rule of law. RCW 62A.1–106. Washington Comment to section 2–710 indicates that consequential damages are denied to sellers under the Uniform Commercial Code. RCWA 62A.2–710.

The distinction between consequential and incidental damages was made in Petroleo Brasileiro, S.A. Petrobras v. Ameropan Oil Corp., 372 F.Supp. 503, 508 (E.D.N.Y.1974):

> While the distinction between the two is not an obvious one, the Code makes plain that incidental damages are normally incurred when a buyer (or seller) repudiates the contract or wrongfully rejects the goods, causing the other to incur such expenses as transporting, storing, or reselling the goods. On the other hand, *consequential damages* do not arise within the scope of the immediate buyer-seller transaction, but rather *stem from losses incurred by the non-breaching party in its dealings, often with third parties,* which were a proximate result of the breach, and which were reasonably foreseeable by the breaching party at the time of contracting.

(Citations omitted. Italics ours.)

We find that the loss of logging time is an inappropriate item of incidental damages. Sprague's damage claim for loss of logging time is essentially a claim for lost profits on a contract with Mt. Baker Plywood. * * * Sprague's loss clearly did not arise within the scope of his contract with Sumitomo; instead, Sprague incurred this loss as a consequence of his delay in performing his contract with Mt. Baker Plywood, a third party. The fact that Sumitomo's conduct proximately caused Sprague's loss is irrelevant to this analysis. The focus is upon losses arising within the scope of the immediate contract. Accordingly, Sprague's loss can only be characterized as consequential. Therefore, the judgment awarded Sprague is reduced by $171,200.

The remaining costs are not seriously contested by appellant and appear to be appropriate items of incidental damages. * * *

* * *

The judgment is reduced by $171,200 to eliminate an improper element of damages. As modified, the judgment is affirmed.

NOTES

1. The revision of the U.C.C. was finalized in 2003, but as noted in the introduction to this section, has not been adopted by the states. One of the changes was to the language of § 2–710, as reflected in the change to its title. Presently it says "Seller's Incidental and Consequential Damages." Previously it had said "Seller's Incidental Damages." It is now symmetric with U.C.C. § 2–715 ("Buyer's Incidental and Consequential Damages") and with rules for common law contract remedies. The other provisions relating to seller's remedies have also added the phrase "consequential damages" where necessary to make it clear that the seller is entitled to those damages. Had these revisions been effective and enacted by the Washington legislature before *Sprague* was decided, the court would have had to consider whether the lost weeks of logging had been contemplated by the parties. Do you think they were? For further discussion of consequential damages in contract actions, see *supra* Chapter 3, Section 3. Why do you think the U.C.C. did not permit sellers to recover consequential damages? Why do you think the rule was changed?

2. Section 2–706, discussed in *Sprague*, is the counterpart to the buyer's remedy of cover. As the court in *Sprague* noted, the resale in § 2–706 must be made in good faith and be commercially reasonable. This requirement has prohibited a plaintiff corporation from collecting damages based on the resale price of iron scrap to its sister corporation at a noticed public sale when a previously held private sale of scrap that had been identified to the breached contract had yielded a higher resale price. *See* Afram Export Corp. v. Metallurgiki Halyps, S.A., 592 F.Supp. 446 (E.D.Wis.1984), *aff'd in part, rev'd in part,* 772 F.2d 1358 (7th Cir.1985); *see also* Apex Oil Co. v. Belcher Co. of New York, Inc., 855 F.2d 997 (2d Cir.1988). In *Apex,* heating oil on a ship destined for the defendant was sold shortly after the defendant's breach, but the plaintiff claimed resale damages for oil sold later, at a lower price. The Second Circuit said "at least with respect to fungible goods, identification for the purposes of a resale transaction does not necessarily require that the resold goods be the exact goods that were rejected or repudiated." *Id.* at 1002. But it also cautioned that:

> The rule that a "resale should be made as soon as practicable after * * * breach" * * * should be stringently applied where, as here, the resold goods are not those originally identified to the contract. In such circumstances, of course, there is a significant risk that the seller, who may perhaps have already disposed of the original goods without suffering any loss, has identified new goods for resale in order to minimize the resale price and thus to maximize damages.

Id. at 1007.

P.F.I., INC. v. KULIS

Superior Court of New Jersey, Appellate Division, 2003.
363 N.J.Super. 292, 832 A.2d 931.

Before JUDGES KESTIN, AXELRAD, and WINKELSTEIN.

AXELRAD, J.T.C. (temporarily assigned).

* * *

Defendant and her late husband operated a gasoline station and automobile repair shop. Plaintiff is a gasoline wholesaler that negotiates contracts with service stations and supplies stations with Texaco gasoline. On October 1, 1991, the parties executed a product sales agreement and rider by which plaintiff would supply gasoline to defendant for a five-year period, with defendant required to purchase a minimum of 2,000,000 gallons "in substantially equal monthly quantities" during that period, or thereafter until the minimum purchase was attained. * * *

Defendant's husband died in 1994, and she closed the automobile repair part of the service station. As a result, gasoline sales declined. Defendant could no longer purchase the quantities of gasoline she was obligated to receive under the sales agreement, and * * * plaintiff ceased delivery and demanded full payment of the outstanding account balance.

On August 30, 2000, plaintiff filed suit for unpaid invoices, * * * and also sought lost profits. Following a bench trial, * * * judgment was entered in favor of plaintiff * * * for unpaid gasoline invoices * * * [and] $30,415.95 for lost profits. * * *

The court relied on Van Ness Motors, Inc. v. Vikram, 221 N.J.Super. 543, 535 A.2d 510 (App.Div. 1987), and found that plaintiff was a lost volume seller and entitled to an anticipated lost profit of five cents per gallon on 608,319 gallons, the outstanding minimum purchase obligation under the contract, in addition to the outstanding contractual balance. * * *

* * *

The record does not support plaintiff's entitlement to lost profits based on defendant's inability to make the minimum purchase of 2,000,-000 gallons under the contract. This element of damages is not provided for in the contract and, based on the parties' relationship, did not appear to be contemplated by the parties. Moreover, plaintiff failed to demonstrate it was a lost volume seller and that normative contract damages were inadequate to put it in as good a position as performance would have done. Additionally, the testimony presented by plaintiff is insufficient to support the calculation of damages based on an anticipated profit margin of five cents per gallon.

The trial court's reliance upon Van Ness, supra, for its lost profit award to plaintiff, is misplaced. In Van Ness, an automobile dealership brought suit for breach of contract damages against a customer who refused to accept delivery of a truck after the parties had entered into a written contract. * * * The trial court dismissed the complaint at the conclusion of the dealership's case, holding there were no lost profit damages because the truck was sold to another purchaser for approximately the same price. * * * We discussed the concept of lost volume status, i.e., that a dealer-seller of standardized goods in unlimited supply, would have made two sales instead of one if the breaching buyer had performed. * * * We also recognized that the seller must sustain the burden of establishing that he is a lost volume seller. * * * We reversed and remanded to allow plaintiff to demonstrate it was a lost volume seller and entitled to lost profit damages under U.C.C. § 2–708(2) (1989), N.J.S.A. 12A:2–708(2), and for the customer to present a defense to the contract and damage claim. *Id.* at 546.

As our Supreme Court recognized * * * " 'in order to recover for lost profits under [section 2–708(2)], the plaintiffs must prove the amount of damages with a reasonable degree of certainty, that the wrongful acts of the defendant caused the loss of profit, and that the profits were reasonably within the contemplation of the parties at the time the contract was entered into' * * *."

In the case before us, lost profits were not anticipated by the contract. The parties' contract * * * made no mention of profit, let alone a guarantee of profit. Where the terms of an agreement are clear, we ordinarily will not make a better deal for a party than that party voluntarily made for itself, particularly in a commercial, arms-length setting. * * *

Additionally, lost profits are available under U.C.C. § 2–708 (1989), N.J.S.A. 12A:2–708(2), only if the normative contract remedy would not place the seller in as good a position as performance would have done. Contrary to plaintiff's and the trial court's interpretation, subsection (2) is not an automatic remedy for the buyer's non-acceptance or repudiation of the goods. N.J.S.A. 12A:2–708(2) provides:

> If the measure of damages provided in subsection (1) [difference between the market price at the time and place for tender and the unpaid contract price together with any incidental damages ..., but less expenses saved in consequence of the buyer's breach] is inadequate to put the seller in as good a position as performance would have done then the measure of damages is the profit (including reasonable overhead) which the seller would have made from full performance by the buyer, together with any incidental damages provided in this Chapter (12A:2–710), due allowance for costs reasonably incurred and due credit for payments or proceeds of resale.

Plaintiff failed to sustain its burden to demonstrate its status as a lost volume seller, the inadequacy of damages under N.J.S.A. 12A:2–708(1), and its actual lost profits. The record is devoid of any testimony by plaintiff's representatives that it had an unlimited supply of gasoline, an unlimited market, and had defendant purchased the minimum gallons of fuel required under the product sales agreement, it would have made two sales instead of one. * * * Nor was there any testimony as to the inadequacy of N.J.S.A. 12A:2–708(1) damages. Moreover, the trial judge made no finding as to any of these essential elements of lost profit damages.

Even if plaintiff had demonstrated a basis for entitlement to lost profit damages, its evidence was insufficient to prove the amount with reasonable certainty. * * * [Charles E. Fears, one of plaintiff's salesmen], testified that in negotiating the contract, he anticipated a profit of approximately five cents a gallon, calculated as follows:

> I took a typical, an average gross margin, defined as my sale price to the customer minus my cost of goods sold, goods sold * * * [at] approximately 12 and a half cents a gallon. I allocated two cents a gallon, two cents a gallon of freight, five and a half cents a gallon marketing and administrative expenses * * * Twelve and a half minus seven and a half equals five cents per gallon.

Plaintiff produced no testimony or documentary evidence to support its claim of actual lost profits on the 608,319 gallons remaining unpurchased by defendant under the product sales agreement. Anticipated profits that are too speculative or uncertain can not be recovered.

Affirmed in part; reversed in part; judgment is modified in accordance with this opinion.

NOTES

1. One method of calculating "lost profits (including reasonable overhead)" under Section 2–708(2) is to deduct from the contract price the "direct costs" that are attributed to contract performance. Under this formula, because recoverable damages include lost profits and reasonable overhead, it is important for the plaintiff to distinguish direct costs from overhead. How can one tell the difference? See Neumiller Farms, Inc. v. Cornett, 368 So.2d 272 (Ala.1979):

> The total amount expended in performance of a contract is composed of "fixed costs" and "variable costs." The "fixed costs," sometimes called "overhead," are those relatively stable expenses which are essential to performance and which continue even if the performance of a specific contract is temporarily halted. Recovery of overhead, to the extent that it is reasonably incurred, is specifically allowed as part of the award for profit by subsection (2). * * *

> The "variable costs" are those expenses, incurred in reliance on the contract, which may be identified to a specific contract and which, if the contract were not to be performed, could be avoided. This element usually includes such items as the costs of material and labor which go directly to the production of the contract goods. If the breach occurs at a time when the aggrieved seller has already incurred variable costs, recovery for these damages is allowable as part of "costs reasonably incurred" under subsection (2).

Id. at 276.

2. The Seventh Circuit has a three-part test for identifying a lost volume seller. See R.E. Davis Chemical Corp. v. Diasonics, Inc., 924 F.2d 709 (7th Cir.1991):

[I]n order to qualify as a lost volume seller, a plaintiff must establish the following three factors:

(1) that it possessed the capacity to make an additional sale,

(2) that it would have been profitable for it to make an additional sale, and

(3) that it probably would have made an additional sale absent the buyer's breach.

Id at 711; *see also* Gianetti v. Norwalk Hosp., 266 Conn. 544, 554, 833 A.2d 891 (2003).

3. The defendant in *Kulis* was a merchant. Would the remedy imposed have been equally appropriate if the defendant had been a consumer? Consider the following hypothetical:

Buyer, a law school student, contracts with Seller, a local stereo dealer, to purchase a stereo set, to be delivered one month later, for $750. Before the factory has begun to fill Buyer's order, Buyer repudiates the contract. Seller's factory cost for the stereo set ordered by Buyer is $450. Seller may purchase as many stereo sets from the manufacturer as it can sell.

Although an application of the "lost volume seller" rule would permit Seller to recover "lost profits (including reasonable overhead)" from Buyer, few retailers in fact attempt to recover such damages from breaching consumers. Melvin A. Eisenberg, *The Bargain Principle and Its Limits*, 95 Harv. L. Rev. 741, 797–98 (1982). Both Professors Eisenberg and Goldberg suggest that a cancellation charge would be a preferable remedy under these circumstances. *Id.*; Victor P. Goldberg, *An Economic Analysis of the Lost–Volume Retail Seller*, 57 S. Cal. L. Rev. 283 (1984)

4. Courts generally will not let parties use Section 2–708(2) to recover windfalls. For example, in Tesoro Petroleum Corp. v. Holborn Oil Co., 145 Misc.2d 715, 547 N.Y.S.2d 1012, 1016 (N.Y.Sup.Ct.1989), the plaintiff had contracted to sell gasoline at $1.30 per gallon, sold it a few days after defendant's breach for $1.10 per gallon, but sought damages measured by the difference between the contract price and the market price at the time of the breach of $.80 per gallon. The court said "granting [plaintiff] the $3,000,000 additional recovery that it seeks would result in a windfall which cannot be said to have been in the contemplation of the parties at the time of their negotiations, and would be inconsistent with the policy of the Code".

5. Professor Eisenberg has suggested that a seller who resells under § 2–706 should be precluded from recovering contract-market differential damages when the market price is lower than the resale price, just as a buyer who covers is limited to cover damages when the market price is higher than the cover price. Melvin A. Eisenberg, *The Responsive Model of Contract Law*, 36 Stan. L. Rev. 1107, 1141–44 (1984). Other commentators on seller's remedies under the Uniform Commercial Code have concluded that the Code as construed by the courts provides appropriate remedies. *See, e.g.,* William L. Schlosser, *Damages for the Lost–Volume Seller: Does an Efficient Formula Already Exist?*, 17 UCC L.J. 238 (1985). For a discussion of cases decided under Section 2–708(2) of the Uniform Commercial Code, see John A. Sebert,

Jr., *Remedies Under Article Two of the Uniform Commercial Code*, 130 U. Pa. L. Rev. 360, 383–407 (1981). For a discussion of the intent and legislative history behind Section 2–708(2), see Note, *Seller's Recovery of Lost Profits for Breach of a Sales Contract: Uniform Commercial Code Section 2–708(2)*, 11 Wm. Mitchell L. Rev. 227, 238–41 (1985). For a debate about measuring damages under Section 2–708, see John M. Breen, *The Lost Volume Seller and Lost Profits Under U.C.C. 2–708(2): A Conceptual and Linguistic Critique*, 50 U. Miami L. Rev. 779 (1996), and Daniel W. Matthews, Comment: *Should The Doctrine of Lost Volume Seller Be Retained? A Response to Professor Breen*, 51 U. Miami L. Rev. 1195 (1997).

B. RESCISSION

Section 2–721 of Article 2 of the UCC is designed to explicitly eliminate the misuse of the "election of remedies" concept described in Section 2.B of this Chapter. As quoted in Melms v. Mitchell, 266 Or. 208, 219, 512 P.2d 1336, 1342 (1973), it provides:

> Remedies for material misrepresentation or fraud include all remedies available under ORS 72.1010 to 72.7250 for nonfraudulent breach. Neither rescission or a claim for rescission of the contract for sale nor rejection or return of the goods shall bar or be deemed inconsistent with a claim for damages or other remedy. ORS 72.7210

C. SPECIFIC PERFORMANCE

1. Action by Buyer

CURRAN v. BAREFOOT

Court of Appeals of North Carolina, 2007.
183 N.C. App. 331, 645 S.E.2d 187.

Tyson, Judge.

* * *

Defendant owns a house ("the lake house") on Lake Tillery in Mt. Gilead, North Carolina. On 19 November 2003, plaintiffs and defendant executed an Offer to Purchase and Contract ("the contract"). Defendant agreed to convey the lake house to plaintiffs. An addendum accompanying the contract listed certain items of personal property defendant agreed to convey with the lake house: (1) "[a]ll furniture, linens, window treatments, appliances, pictures, towels, flatware, dishes, and all other items currently in the [lake] house" except "clothes and personal items;" (2) "[o]ne antique wardrobe located in an upstairs bedroom;" (3) "[o]ne small table located in [the] downstairs hallway;" and (4) "[a]ll watercraft and accessories." Defendant refused to tender and convey on the scheduled closing date.

On 29 January 2004, plaintiffs filed suit against defendant seeking specific performance of the contract. After a bench trial, the trial court found and concluded as a matter of law: (1) an enforceable contract existed between plaintiffs and defendant; * * * (3) defendant repudiated the contract in late December 2003, refused to close the transaction, and breached the contract; (4) the subject real property is unique such that money damages are not an adequate remedy; and (5) plaintiffs are entitled to specific performance of their contract with defendant for conveyance of the subject real property and the associated personal property listed in the addendum, including watercraft. The trial court entered judgment on 30 December 2005.

On 9 January 2006, defendant moved for relief from the trial court's 30 December 2005 judgment, or alternatively for a new trial. The trial court denied defendant's motions * * *

* * *

Defendant argues the trial court erred by granting plaintiffs specific performance of all terms of the contract. Defendant asserts specific performance is not an appropriate remedy for contracts involving personal property. We disagree.

1. Personal Property Included in the Contract

The trial court concluded plaintiffs were entitled to specific performance of the entire contract which included: (1) the lake house; (2) the listed fixtures under paragraph two of the contract; (3) "[a]ll furniture, linens, window treatments, appliances, pictures, towels, flatware, dishes, and all other items currently in the [lake] house" except "clothes and personal items;" (4) "[o]ne antique wardrobe located in an upstairs bedroom;" (5) "[o]ne small table located in [the] downstairs hallway;" and (6) "[a]ll watercraft and accessories."

* * *

"As a general rule, the remedy for a breach of contract for the sale of personal property is an action at law, where damages are awarded." * * * However, our Supreme Court has stated "there are recognized exceptions." *Trust Co. v. Webb*, 206 N.C. 247, 250, 173 S.E. 598, 600 (1934). "Jurisdiction to enforce specific performance rests, not on the distinction between real and personal property, but on the ground that damages at law will not afford a complete remedy." * * *

Here, the plain language of the contract, defendant's admissions, and other competent evidence in the record clearly proves defendant intended to convey to plaintiffs a furnished lake house with three watercraft for $550,000.00. The trial court's judgment ordering specific performance of both the real and personal property provides "a complete remedy" to plaintiffs. * * * The trial court did not err as a matter of law by awarding plaintiffs specific performance of a sales contract for the purchase of the real property, that included incidental personal property, as a consideration for and part of the conveyance.

2. Other Jurisdictions

Other state jurisdictions have held specific performance may be granted for breach of a contract to sell real property that includes personal property. "Where part of an entire contract relates to ordinary personal property and the rest to a subject matter, such as land, over which equity jurisdiction is commonly exercised, specific performance may be had of the whole contract, including the part that relates to personal property." *Taylor v. Highland Park Corp.*, 210 S.C. 254, 261, 42 S.E.2d 335, 338 (S.C. 1947) (internal citations omitted) * * *.

The Supreme Court of Georgia considered a case concerning specific performance of a contract involving both real and personal property in *Gabrell v. Byers*, 178 Ga. 16, 172 S.E. 227 (Ga. 1933). A property owner had contracted to sell her farmland, along with all personal property located thereon, for a lump sum. *Id.* at 16–17, 172 S.E. at 228. The contract specifically listed all the personal property including livestock, six mules, farm equipment, and vehicles. *Id.* at 17, 172 S.E. at 228. When the purchaser failed to make the first payment, the seller sued and sought specific performance. *Id.* at 17–18, 172 S.E. at 228. The court stated:

> As a general rule, the remedy of a decree for specific performance relates only to real estate, and is not applicable to personalty. So the cardinal rules which apply to the remedy of specific performance are applied with greater strictness where personalty is concerned than where realty is involved. *In the case at bar the contract, including both real estate and various species of personal property, is entire and indivisible, so far as the remedy by decree for specific performance is concerned.*

Id. at 18, 172 S.E. at 228–29 (emphasis supplied).

* * *

* * * A party can prove inadequate relief at law by showing: (1) irreparable damages will result without specific performance; (2) damages will be uncertain or difficult to ascertain; (3) the property "has some intrinsic or special value, such as ... an heirloom, having a special and peculiar value to its owner over and above any market value that can be placed in accordance with strict legal rules;" or (4) the property is unique and not easily reproduced, as with works of art. *Id.* at 21, 172 S.E. at 230.

* * *

The value of a unitary vacation home to a buyer is the furnished lake house and accessories. This value is similar to the value to a buyer of a working farm including the farmland, livestock, and implements. Just as the farmland in the case above would be much less desirable if the items of livestock and implements were not conveyed, a barren lake house without the personal property listed in the contract would not provide plaintiffs a "complete remedy." * * *

The trial court did not err as a matter of law by awarding plaintiffs specific performance of a contract involving real property and incidental personal property to be conveyed part and parcel therewith as a unit. * * *

IV. RULE 60(b) MOTION

* * *

After the trial and entry of the judgment, defendant moved for relief from the judgment solely on the basis it was, and is, not the record owner of the watercraft ordered to be conveyed to plaintiffs. In support of its motion, defendant relied upon the Affidavit of Quint Barefoot ("Quint"), the trustee's son, in which Quint states the three watercraft are not owned by defendant. Defendant also submitted purchase agreements and a registration card as evidence that it does not own the three watercraft. This evidence was not presented during the bench trial from which the trial court's judgment was entered.

"The test for whether a judgment, order or proceeding should be modified or set aside under Rule 60(b)(6) is two pronged: (1) extraordinary circumstances must exist, and (2) there must be a showing that justice demands that relief be granted." * * *

Here, "extraordinary circumstances exist" and "justice demands" the judgment be modified. * * * The trial court ordered defendant to convey personal property it did not own. "Specific performance may not be granted where the performance of the contract is impossible" and "specific performance will not be decreed against a defendant who is unable to comply with the contract even though the inability to perform is caused by the defendant's own act." * * *

The trial court erred by denying defendant's motion for relief from the judgment in part. The matter is remanded to the trial court to award plaintiffs money damages for the fair market value of the three watercraft or other appropriate relief, if defendant does not or cannot deliver clear and unencumbered title of the watercraft to plaintiffs at closing.

* * *

CUMBEST v. HARRIS
Supreme Court of Mississippi, 1978.
363 So.2d 294.

WALKER, JUSTICE, for the Court:

This is an appeal from an order of the Chancery Court of Jackson County, Mississippi, dismissing appellant Cumbest's bill of complaint.

The sole question presented is whether the personal property, which was the subject of the controversy, is of such peculiar, sentimental or unique value as to come within the exception to the general rule that a chancery court will not ordinarily decree specific performance of a contract involving personal property.

Cumbest's bill of complaint and exhibits attached thereto aver, among other things, that on May 19, 1976, Donald Ronnie Cumbest and Bedford Harris, respectively, contracted for the sale and purchase of certain hi-fi equipment via a bill of sale. An option agreement was also signed on the same date allowing Cumbest to repurchase the audio equipment on or before 5:00 p.m., Monday, June 7, 1976. The language of these two instruments is clear and unambiguous and both were signed and notarized.

The complainant averred that the transaction was intended to be a loan, in substance, and that the audio equipment was to serve as collateral. It also states that from early morning on Monday, June 7, 1976, until late that evening every effort humanly possible was made to pay the required amount of money to the defendant. The defendant purposely avoided meeting with him at various places during the day, thereby fraudulently and deliberately evading the receipt of the money as contracted for in The Option to Repurchase Agreement. In desperation the complainant deposited the required amount of money with the defendant's landlord on the evening of June 7, 1976, and approximately a week later initiated this lawsuit seeking equitable relief. * * *

The amended complaint further averred that the complete assemblage of the audio equipment took several years for the appellant to acquire and because of the unique nature and irreplaceability of much of the equipment the court should assert jurisdiction of the case and grant such equitable relief as it deems appropriate. Finally, the complainant prays for the defendant to be enjoined against the disposition, sale or removal of the property and for the court to mandate specific performance of the contract to reconvey.

The chancellor allowed a hearing solely on the question of whether the property was of such sentimental value or so unique as to come within the exception to the general rule that the chancery court will not ordinarily decree specific performance of a contract involving personal property.

Cumbest was the only witness to testify at the proceeding. The property involved was a stereo system allegedly valued at $10,000. The system consisted of twenty separate parts accumulated over a period of fifteen years. There was testimony that Cumbest had acquired experience in stereophonic and recording equipment over the years by working in hi-fi stores in Oxford and Gulfport. He also did some recording of a professional nature. According to him, the items involved were a part of a recording studio which consisted of carefully matched parts, rather than a mere stereo set as contended by the defendant. The parts involved could not function alone, and could not be matched to just any standard stereo system. Cumbest testified that many of the integral parts of the system could no longer be replaced, e.g., the main reel to reel recorder; a stereo quadraphonic four channel logic decoder which, according to Cumbest, was originally on order for two years; a stereo three channel crossover preamplifier with base boost and turn over frequency control; some speaker components, and the particular diamond needle in the turntable system. Other equipment was personally designed and built by Cumbest himself. He testified that he purchased the parts and assembled the speakers to accommodate his particular system, and that the cabinets were designed and handmade by him after extensive study and research to meet the needs of his particular system.

* * *

In other testimony he pointed out that even those items which are still available are of the type which require special order purchases and that in obtaining them originally there were six months to two years waiting periods. As to sentimental value, Cumbest testified:

> As far as the snetimental [sic] value of the equipment, it is very great, blood, sweat and tears have gone into it, I spent 15 years acquiring it piece by piece and I would never seel [sic] it at any price.

Defendant put on no witnesses to contradict Cumbest's testimony.

As the chancellor recited in his order, the general rule is that, ordinarily, specific performance will not be decreed if the subject matter of the contract sought to be enforced is personalty. However, this general principle is subject to several well recognized exceptions, such as: (1) Where there is no adequate remedy at law; (2) Where the specific articles or property are of peculiar, sentimental or unique value; and (3) Where due to scarcity the chattel is not readily obtainable. 81 C.J.S. Specific Performance §§ 81–83 (1977). These exceptions are partly founded on the principle of the inadequacy of a remedy at law and the remedy may, in a proper case, be allowed where damages are not readily ascertainable.

* * *

Such equitable relief is justified by the fact that the legal remedy of replevin is subject to defects of procedure which prevent the successful plaintiff from invariably recovering possession of the chattel. There is also considerable authority, old and new, showing liberality in the granting of an equitable remedy. 11 Williston Contracts § 1419 (3d ed. 1968); Miss. Code Ann. § 75–2–716 (1972).

In the present case, there was uncontradicted testimony that some components of the system were irreplaceable. Other components were replaceable but only with difficulty and long waiting periods. Additionally, Cumbest testified that the system was acquired over a fifteen-year span and that he personally designed and built parts of it specifically to match that particular system. Based on that testimony, we must conclude the property had both a unique value and falls into the category of property which is not readily obtainable due to scarcity.

For the above reasons, we hold that the chancellor erred in not finding that the property was sufficiently unique to justify the equitable jurisdiction of a chancery court. The cause will be remanded for a hearing on the merits.

NOTES

1. Section 2–716 of the Uniform Commercial Code, which is cited by the *Cumbest* court, gives the buyer of goods an action for specific performance "where the goods are unique or in other proper circumstances" and gives the buyer "a right of replevin for goods identified to the contract." Comment 1 to that section indicates that it is intended "to further a more liberal attitude than some courts have shown in connection with the specific performance of contracts of sale."

2. For the drafting history of Section 2–716 and summaries of the cases decided under the Uniform Commercial Code, see Elliot Axelrod, *Specific Performance of Contracts for Sales of Goods: Expansion or Retrenchment in the 1980s,* 7 Vt. L. Rev. 249 (1982).

3. In *Curren* and *Cumbest,* the courts held that the plaintiff was entitled to specific performance because the nature of the goods was unique. *See also* Ruddock v. First National Bank, 201 Ill.App.3d 907, 147 Ill.Dec. 310, 559 N.E.2d 483 (1990) (astronomical clock unique). The U.C.C. may authorize specific performance when the goods are unique only in light of the buyer's individual or subjective preferences. *Compare* Schweber v. Rallye Motors, Inc., 12 U.C.C.Rep.Serv. 1154 (N.Y.Sup.Ct.1973) (Rolls Royce Corniche of the desired style and color; specific performance appropriate, preliminary injunction restraining the defendant from selling or transferring the automobile pending the trial of the case granted), *with* Paloukos v. Intermountain Chevrolet Co., 99 Idaho 740, 588 P.2d 939 (1978) (specific performance of a Chevrolet pickup truck in short supply denied).

4. Although the Uniform Commercial Code does not explicitly state that adequacy of the legal remedy precludes specific performance, "such a position is implicit in the Code's emphasis on cover as its principal buyer's remedy." Harold Greenberg, *Specific Performance Under Section 2–716 of the Uniform Commercial Code: "A More Liberal Attitude" in the "Grand Style,"* 17 New Eng. L. Rev. 321, 352 (1982). Section 2–716 (3) also conditions a buyer's right of replevin on the inability to effect cover. *See, e.g.,* T & T Air Charter, Inc. v. Duncan Aircraft Sales, 566 So.2d 361 (Fla.Dist.Ct.App.1990) (writ of replevin erroneously issued by trial judge because buyer did not show reasonable efforts to cover or that efforts would be unavailing). Nevertheless, buyers occasionally request replevin. *See, e.g.,* Big Knob Volunteer Fire Co. v. Lowe & Moyer Garage, Inc., 338 Pa.Super. 257, 487 A.2d 953 (1985) (buyer replevied goods identified to the contract from seller's creditor).

2. Action by Seller

ROYAL JONES & ASSOCIATES, INC. v.
FIRST THERMAL SYSTEMS, INC.

District Court of Appeal of Florida, 1990.
566 So.2d 853.

ZEHMER, JUDGE.

Royal Jones & Associates, Inc., appeals from a final judgment of the lower court finding that it breached a contract with First Thermal Systems, Inc., and awarding damages to First Thermal Systems, Inc., in the amount of the contract price pursuant to section 672.709, Florida Statutes (1987). Because the goods under the contract were specially manufactured for Royal Jones, were not suitable for sale to others in the ordinary course of First Thermal's business, and it appeared that any efforts on behalf of First Thermal to resell the goods would have been unavailing, we affirm.

On October 4, 1988, Royal Jones ordered three steel rendering tanks from First Thermal for use in its business of constructing rendering plants. Under the terms of the contract, First Thermal would manufacture the tanks according to Royal Jones's specifications for a price of $64,350. Royal Jones was to receive the tanks at First Thermal's place of manufacture in Chattanooga, Tennessee. Royal Jones failed to appear at First Thermal's plant to take delivery of the tanks, refused to accept shipment of the tanks, and refused to pay the contract price. As of the date of the trial, the tanks were still being held for Royal Jones at First Thermal's plant.

The lower court found that Royal Jones had breached the contract, and that the only testimony before it was that the goods were specially manufactured for Royal Jones and were not suitable for sale in the ordinary course of First Thermal's business. Concluding that mitigation of damages was not a viable defense, the court entered judgment for First Thermal, pursuant to section 672.709, awarding First Thermal the contract price of $64,350, interest to the date of trial in the amount of $8,630.56, and attorney's fees and costs in the amount of $3,528.07.

Section 672.709(1)(b) provides that when the buyer fails to pay the price for goods as it becomes due, the seller may recover, together with incidental damages, the price "[o]f goods identified to the contract if the seller is unable after reasonable effort to resell them at a reasonable price or the circumstances reasonably indicate that such effort will be unavailing." Royal Jones contends that the lower court erred in awarding First Thermal the full contract price as damages for the tanks pursuant to section 672.709, because there was no evidence presented at trial that either First Thermal was unable to resell the tanks after making a reasonable effort to do so, or that the circumstances reasonably indicated that such effort would be unavailing. In reply, First Thermal contends that there was uncontroverted testimony at trial that the tanks were specially manufactured for Royal Jones and that any efforts at resale would have been unavailing.

While there are no Florida appellate decisions interpreting section 672.709 that would be applicable to these circumstances, cases from other jurisdictions support the lower court's decision to award First Thermal the full contract price. Thus, in FMI, Inc. v. RMAX, Inc., 286 S.C. 343, 333 S.E.2d 360 (1985), the court held that where there was evidence that the seller specially manufactured goods for the buyer, the buyer failed to pay for those goods, and the seller had no other customer to which to sell the goods, such evidence was sufficient to warrant submitting to the jury the issue of whether any effort to resell the goods would be unavailing. 333 S.E.2d at 362. * * *

* * * [W]e hold that the trial court did not err in awarding First Thermal the full contract price as damages, because the evidence presented at trial by First Thermal was sufficient to meet its burden of proving that the circumstances reasonably indicated that any effort to resell the tanks would have been unavailing. There was testimony at trial that First Thermal specially manufactured the tanks for Royal Jones according to drawings supplied by Royal Jones and that First Thermal had not taken any steps to resell the tanks because it did not know how to market or resell rendering tanks. First Thermal proved that any effort at resale would have been unavailing because these were the only rendering tanks First Thermal ever made, the tanks were manufactured according to Royal Jones's specifications, First Thermal had no other customers to which it could resell the tanks, and it was unaware how the tanks could have been marketed for resale. Also, the tanks were built without needed internal components and to a special size in accordance with Royal Jones's specifications and could not be used as rendering tanks without special engineering to which First Thermal had no access. Finally, there was testimony that the tanks had only scrap value to First Thermal of about $700 if they were processed for a scrap dealer. This evidence was sufficient to shift the burden to Royal Jones to show that any effort at resale would not have been unavailing, or that the tanks had some potential market value beyond the salvage value claimed by First Thermal. * * * However, Royal Jones presented no evidence to the contrary at trial, and the lower court did not err in awarding First Thermal the full contract price pursuant to section 672.709.

Royal Jones next contends that allowing First Thermal to recover the contract price, while allowing it to keep the rendering tanks, amounts to an impermissible double recovery on the part of First Thermal, citing Page Avjet v. Cosgrove Aircraft Svc., 546 So.2d 16 (Fla. 3d DCA 1989). In Page Avjet, the Third District Court of Appeal held that the trial court erred in permitting the seller to recover the purchase price of a turbine and to retain the turbine that the buyer had returned to the seller without considering the buyer's defenses of set-off and return of the turbine. 546 So.2d at 17–18. The court stated that "to permit [the seller] to retain both the turbine and the purchase price would constitute an impermissible double recovery." 546 So.2d at 17–18.

First Thermal contends that section 672.709(2) permits it to hold the tanks prior to collecting on the judgment. Section 672.709(2) provides that:

> [w]here the seller sues for the price he must hold for the buyer any goods which have been identified to the contract and are still in his control except that if resale becomes possible he may resell them at any time prior to collection of the judgment. The net proceeds of any such resale must be credited to the buyer and payment of the judgment entitles him to any goods not resold.

Section 672.709(2) permits First Thermal to hold the tanks for Royal Jones's credit prior to collection of the judgment and requires First Thermal to credit Royal Jones with the net proceeds of any resale of the tanks made prior to collection on the judgment or to turn over any tanks not resold upon Royal Jones's payment of the judgment. First Thermal has reaffirmed its willingness to turn the tanks over to Royal Jones upon payment. Consequently, there is no impermissible double recovery. The *Page Avjet* decision is not applicable to these circumstances.

Finding no error in the trial court's ruling, the judgment is affirmed.

Note

Professor Eisenberg described Section 2–709(1) as the seller's "counterpart to the buyer's remedies of specific performance and replevin." Melvin A. Eisenberg, *The Responsive Model of Contract Law*, 36 Stan. L. Rev. 1107, 1136 (1984).

SECTION 4. CONTRACTS RELATING TO REAL PROPERTY

A. DAMAGES

The two most common remedies for breaches of real estate sale contracts are damages and specific performance. An award of damages usually contemplates that the vendor will keep the property, or will sell it to someone else. An order of specific performance, on the other hand, is predicated on the vendor conveying it to the buyer, who will pay the contract price. In general, either buyer or seller may seek either remedy if the other party breaches.

Loss of bargain damages are traditionally measured as the difference between the contract price and the market value of the land on the date of breach. Under this measure, the vendor can obtain nothing if the property's value is higher than the contract price, while the purchaser can recover nothing if the property is worth less than the contract amount. But the "pure" loss of bargain computation may be only one of many items in the total claim for damages, as the following case illustrates.

DONOVAN v. BACHSTADT

Supreme Court of New Jersey, 1982.
91 N.J. 434, 453 A.2d 160.

[Defendant Bachstadt contracted to sell real estate to plaintiffs Donovans for $58,900. The contract provided that Bachstadt would finance $44,000 by way of a purchase money mortgage, thus helping the Donovans avoid the necessity of bank financing, which at the time was available only at very high interest rates. Under applicable usury statutes, the purchase money mortgage could not have borne an interest rate exceeding 10.5%. It developed that Bachstadt did not have and could not obtain good title to the property.]

When defendant could not obtain marketable title, the Donovans commenced this suit for compensatory and punitive damages. * * * [T]he trial court granted plaintiffs' motion for summary judgment. It was indisputable that the defendant had breached the agreement. The only issue was damages. The trial court held that plaintiffs were entitled under N.J.S.A. 2A:29–1 to recovery of their costs for the title search and survey. Plaintiffs had apparently in the interim purchased a home in Middlesex County and obtained a mortgage loan bearing interest at the rate of 13¼% per annum. Plaintiffs sought the difference between 10½% and 13¼% as compensatory damages, representing their loss of the benefit of the bargain. The trial court denied recovery because the contract was for the sale of the property and the financing "was only incidental to the basic concept."

The Appellate Division reversed. 181 N.J.Super. 367, 437 A.2d 728 (1981). It held that N.J.S.A. 2A:29–1 was declarative of the general common law right to recover consequential damages for breach of a contract and that the statute modified the preexisting law, which limited a realty purchaser to recovery of his deposit upon a seller's breach due to a defective title. The court concluded the statute intended that the general law of damages for breach of a contract applies and stated that the difference in interest rates could be the basis for a measure of damages depending on whether the plaintiffs "have entered into a comparable transaction for another home ... or are likely to do so in the near future...." *Id.* at 376, 437 A.2d 728. The Appellate Division cautioned that any award of future damages should represent the true life of the mortgage and be reduced to present value. Further, the plaintiffs should be held to a duty to mitigate. Lastly, if the proofs should demonstrate that plaintiffs have not purchased and are not likely to purchase a home in the near future, their damages would be remote and speculative. The cause was remanded for a plenary hearing.

I

The initial inquiry is whether plaintiffs are entitled to compensatory damages. We had occasion recently to discuss the measure of damages available when a seller breaches an executory contract for the sale of real property. St. Pius X House of Retreats v. Diocese of Camden, 88 N.J. 571, 582–87, 443 A.2d 1052 (1982). We noted that New Jersey follows the English rule, which generally limits a buyer's recovery to the return of his deposit unless the seller wilfully refuses to convey or is guilty of fraud or deceit. * * * In *St. Pius* we found no need to reexamine the English rule, though we raised the question whether the American rule that permits a buyer to obtain benefit of the bargain damages irrespective of the nature of the reasons for the seller's default might not be more desirable.

* * *

We are satisfied that the American rule is preferable. The English principle developed because of the uncertainties of title due to the complexity of the rules governing title to land during the eighteenth and nineteenth centuries. Oakley, *Pecuniary Compensation for Failure to Complete a Contract for the Sale of Land*, 39 Cambridge L.J. 58, 69 (1980). At that time the only evidence of title was contained in deeds which were in a phrase attributed to Lord Westbury, "difficult to read, disgusting to touch, and impossible to understand." The reason for the English principle that creates an exception to the law governing damages for breaches of executory contracts for the sale of property is no longer valid, and the exception should be eliminated. *Cessante ratione legis, cessat et ipsa lex* (the reason for a law ceasing, the law itself ceases). *See* Fox v. Snow, 6 N.J. 12, 14, 22–23, 76 A.2d 877 (1950) (Vanderbilt, C.J., dissenting). Indeed in England the rule has been modified by placing the burden of proof on the vendor to establish that he has done everything within his power to carry out the contract. Malhotra v. Choudhury, [1978] 3 W.L.R. 825; [1979] 1 All E.R. 186 (C.A.).

Whether titles are clear may be ascertained by record searches. *See* N.J.S.A. 46:21–1; Jones, *The New Jersey Recording Act—A Study of its Policy*, 12 Rutgers L.Rev. 328, 329–30 (1957). Moreover, limitation periods may be applicable. See N.J.S.A. 2A:14–30; 13A N.J. Practice (Lieberman, Abstracts and Titles) § 1643 at 140 (3d ed. 1966). Thus, it is standard practice for title examiners to search the back title for 60 years and until a warranty deed is found in the chain of title. Palamarg Realty Co. v. Rehac & Piatkowski, 80 N.J. 446, 460, 404 A.2d 21 (1979). Further the parties may insert appropriate provisions in their agreements protecting them from title defects so that to a very large extent sellers may control the measure of redress.

There is no sound basis why benefit of the bargain damages should not be awarded whether the subject matter of the contract is realty or personalty. Serious losses should not be borne by the vendee of real estate to the benefit of the defaulting vendor. This is particularly so when an installment purchase contract is involved that extends over a period of years during which the vendee makes substantial payments upon the principal, as well as extensive improvements to the property.

The innocent purchaser should be permitted to recover benefit of the bargain damages irrespective of the good or bad faith of the seller. Contract culpability depends on the breach of the contractual promise. 4A Corbin, Contracts §§ 943–44, at 806–08 (1951). Where, as here, the seller agreed that title would be marketable, the seller's liability should depend upon his breach of that promise. * * *

The English rule is consistent with the limitation on recovery in suits on a covenant for breach of warranty [in a deed]. The damages for a buyer, who has taken title and is ousted because the title is defective, are limited to the consideration paid and interest thereon. Gerbert v. Congregation, 59 N.J.L. 160, 180, 35 A. 1121 (E.&A.1896). There appears to be no real difference between that situation and one where the vendor who does not have good title refuses to convey. In both cases the buyer loses the property because of a defect in the title. The fact that one sues for breach of a warranty covenant does not justify depriving a buyer of compensatory damages to which he is justly entitled when the seller breaches the contract of sale. Professor Corbin has suggested that any inconsistency in this respect should be resolved by awarding full compensatory damages when the action is for breach of warranty. 5A Corbin, *supra*, § 1098, at 533. Moreover, an anomaly already exists, for our courts have acknowledged that a buyer may recover such damages upon a showing of the seller's bad faith. *See* Ganger v. Moffett, 8 N.J. 73, 83 A.2d 769 (1951).

We are satisfied that a buyer should be permitted to recover benefit of the bargain damages when the seller breaches an executory contract to convey real property. * * * The next question is how to compute those compensatory damages.

II

Judicial remedies upon breach of contract fall into three general categories: restitution, compensatory damages and performance. Separate concepts undergird each of these remedial provisions. The rationale for restitution is to return the innocent party to his status before the contract was executed. Compensatory damages are intended to recompense the injured claimant for losses due to the breach, that is, give the innocent party the benefit of the bargain. Performance is to effect a result, essentially other than in terms of monetary reparation, so that the innocent party is placed in the position of having had the contract performed. We have now adopted the American rule providing for compensatory damages upon the seller's breach of an executory contract to sell realty and we must examine the appropriate elements that should properly be included in an award.

"Compensatory damages are designed 'to put the injured party in as good a position as he would have had if performance had been rendered as promised.' 5 Corbin, Contracts § 992, p. 5 (1951)." 525 Main Street Corp. v. Eagle Roofing Co., 34 N.J. 251, 254, 168 A.2d 33 (1961). * * * What that position is depends upon what the parties reasonably expected. It follows that the defendant is not chargeable for loss that he did not have reason to foresee as a probable result of the breach when the contract was made. Hadley v. Baxendale, 9 Exch. 341, 5 Eng.Rul.Case 502 (1854); *accord* Crater v. Binninger, 33 N.J.L. 513 (E. & A.1869). * * * *See* Restatement (Second) of Contracts § 351 (1981). * * * Further the loss must be a reasonably certain consequence of the breach although the exact amount of the loss need not be certain. * * *

The specific elements to be applied in any given case of a seller's breach of an executory agreement to sell realty may vary in order to achieve the broad purposes of reparations; some items, however, will almost invariably exist. Thus the purchaser will usually be entitled to the return of the amount paid on the purchase price with interest thereon. Costs and expenses incurred in connection with the proposed acquisition, such as for the title search and survey, would fall in the same category. The traditional test is the difference between the market price of the property at the time of the breach and the contract price. * * * Under this standard the buyer who had taken possession before title passed would be entitled to recover for improvements he made that increased the value of the property. Sabaugh v. Schrieber, 87 Ind.App. 588, 162 N.E. 248 (1928).

The difference between market and contract price may not be suitable in all situations. Thus where a buyer had in turn contracted to sell the realty, it is reasonable to measure his damages in terms of the actual lost profit. *See* Bonhard v. Gindin, 104 N.J.L. 599, 142 A. 52 (E.&A.1928) (awarding the consideration paid, search fees, taxes and assessments paid, and lost profits from a sale to a third person); *see also* Giumarra v. Harrington Heights, 33 N.J.Super. 178, 109 A.2d 695 (App.Div.1954) (awarding contract buyer of realty lost profits in action against contract buyer's assignee). What the proper elements of damage are depend upon the particular circumstances surrounding the transaction, especially the terms, conditions and nature of the agreement.

The plaintiffs here assert that their damages are equivalent to the difference in interest costs incurred by them in purchasing a different home at another location. This claim assumes that the financial provision of the contract concerning the purchase money mortgage that the defendant agreed to accept was independent and divisible from the purchase of the land and house. The defendant contends that he did not agree to loan these funds in connection with the purchase of some other property, but that this provision was incidental to the sale of the house. Neither position is entirely sound. This financing was an integral part of the transaction. It can be neither ignored nor viewed as an isolated element.

The relationship of the financing to the purchase of a home has changed in recent years. As interest rates rose and the availability of first mortgage funds was sharply reduced, potential homeowners, though desirous of purchasing homes, found financing difficult to obtain. The seller's acceptance of a purchase money mortgage became an important factor in effecting a sale. *See* Rand, *Home Resale Market: Pattern Shift*, N.Y. Times,

March 22, 1981, § 11, at 18, col. 3. In evaluating a contract such a financial arrangement could play an important part in determining price. The rise in interest rates, the expense of mortgage credit and the availability of funds has rendered traditional methods of financing acquisition of homes impractical. Walleser, *The Changing Complexion of Home Mortgage Financing in America*, 31 Drake L.Rev. 1, 2 (1981). Favorable vendor financing could lead to increased market value. Only then might a buyer be able to purchase. Iezman, *Alternative Mortgage Instruments: Their Effect on Residential Financing*, Real Est.L.J. 3, 4 (1981). The importance of a seller's purchase money mortgage to the overall agreement to convey property was recognized in King v. Ruckman, 24 N.J.Eq. 298 (Ch.), *aff'd*, 24 N.J.Eq. 556 (E.&A.1873). The seller agreed to convey certain property and to accept as part of the purchase price a purchase money mortgage with 6% interest payable in five annual installments. The seller refused to convey. The buyer obtained a final decree for specific performance including the purchase money mortgage. The Chancery Court's view of the mortgage confirmed by the Court of Errors and Appeals on review was:

> The benefit accruing to the purchaser from having time for the payment of the bulk of the principal, and of the rate agreed on for interest, is apparent. It is a material ingredient of the bargain, as much so in reality, though not in degree, as the price, and cannot be withheld from the purchaser in this case by the willful misconduct of the vendor, for the sole benefit of the vendor himself. 24 N.J.Eq. at 303.

The interest rate is not sufficiently discrete to calculate damages in terms of it alone under these circumstances.

In some circumstances interest rate differentials are an appropriate measure of damages. Where the buyer has obtained specific performance, but because of the delay has incurred higher mortgage rates, then his loss clearly should include the higher financing cost. Godwin v. Lindbert, 101 Mich.App. 754, 300 N.W.2d 514 (1980), is illustrative. The buyers lost their commitment for a mortgage with an interest rate of 8¾% when the seller refused to convey. The buyers succeeded in obtaining specific performance but were compelled to borrow funds at 11½%. They were awarded the difference reduced to present value. * * * Moreover, we are not unmindful of the possibility that a buyer might demonstrate that a lending institution's commitment to advance the funds initially at a certain interest rate was due to the buyer's financial condition. The particular realty might well be a secondary and incidental consideration for the loan. Therefore an interest differential occasioned by the seller's default might be a proper factor in fixing damages where the buyer shortly thereafter purchased another property financed at a higher interest rate.

This is not such a situation. The defendant's motive was to sell a house and not to lend money. In measuring the plaintiffs' loss there should be a determination of the fair market value of the property and house that could be acquired with a purchase money mortgage in the principal amount of $44,000 at an interest rate of 10½% (no appeal was taken from the judgment of reformation) for a 30–year term. The valuation should be at the time the defendant failed to comply with the judgment of specific performance. The plaintiffs would be entitled to the difference between $58,900 and that fair market value. If the fair market value was not more than the contract price, the plaintiffs would not have established any damage ascribable to the loss of the bargain. They are also entitled to their expenditures for the survey, search, and counsel fees for services rendered in preparation of the aborted closing. The plaintiffs have hitherto received the return of the deposit.

NOTES

1. The English rule, discussed in *Donovan*, limiting the purchaser to restitutionary recovery when the seller's title is defective but the seller has acted in good faith, is followed in about half of the American jurisdictions. However, it does not apply if the vendor breaches the contract, even in good faith, for reasons unrelated to his title. See Beard v. S/E Joint Venture, 321 Md. 126, 581 A.2d 1275 (1990), for a thorough discussion of this issue.

Suppose the contract itself restricts the buyer's remedy to restitution. If the seller acted in bad faith, can the buyer still get loss-of-bargain damages? The court so held in Wolofsky v. Waldron, 526 So.2d 945 (Fla.Dist.Ct.App. 1988).

2. How is "fair market value" determined for purposes of the "loss of bargain" rule? With single family dwellings, the primary approach is to utilize recent sales of comparable properties in the geographical area. Suppose, however, we are dealing with commercial or residential rental real estate. How is fair market value determined? Consider the following analysis:

Fair market value of the property is the price at which the property would change hands between a willing buyer and seller, neither being under any compulsion to consummate the sale. Ohio Casualty Insurance Co. v. Ramsey (1982), Ind.App., 439 N.E.2d 1162, 1167, *trans. denied.* In *Ohio Casualty,* we set out three well recognized methods of determining a property's fair market value taken by eminent domain:

(1) the current *cost of reproducing* the property less depreciation from all sources; (2) the "*market data*" approach or value indicated by recent sales of comparable properties in the market, and (3) the "*income-approach,*" or the value which the property's net earning power will support based upon the capitalization of net income. This three-approach means of reaching market value is usually combined. It is stated in American Institute of Real Estate Appraisers. "The Appraisal of Real Estates" (3d ed.) at page 66: " * * * In the majority of his assignments, the appraiser utilizes all three approaches. *On occasion he may believe the value indication from one approach will be more significant than from the other two,* yet he will use all three as a check against each to test his own judgment. All three methods have been judicially approved."

Annon II, Inc. v. Rill, 597 N.E.2d 320, 326–27 (Ind.Ct.App.1992).

3. In addition to the traditional loss-of-bargain damages, available to a buyer only if the property's value is higher than the contract price, what other elements of damage ("incidental" or "consequential") might an innocent buyer attempt to recover?

(a) Expenditures for title examination, survey, and attorneys' fees in preparation for the closing? *See Donovan, supra.*

(b) Airfare for travel to negotiate and execute the contract which the seller subsequently breached? *See* Fountain v. Mojo, 687 P.2d 496 (Colo. Ct.App.1984).

(c) Additional rent, taxes, mortgage interest, and other carrying costs at the buyer's present location while the buyer locates and purchases substitute property?

(d) Loss of particularly favorable financing from a bank or savings association, no longer available as a result of interest rate changes? *See* Wall v. Pate, 104 N.M. 1, 715 P.2d 449 (1986).

(e) The cost of leasing temporary quarters elsewhere, including rent, advertising for a place to lease, and the expense of moving to the leased premises? *See* Gorzelsky v. Leckey, 402 Pa.Super. 246, 586 A.2d 952 (1991).

If any of these items are recoverable as damages, should any such items be offset by the fact that the purchaser still has the purchase money, and may have earned interest on it (if it was to have been paid in cash) or has saved the interest which would have been paid on it (if the buyer had intended to borrow it)? *See* ULTA § 2–514. Should these items be offset by general declines in property values, on the theory that the purchaser can subsequently obtain similar property at a lower cost?

4. Consider the general compensatory damages recoverable by the seller when the buyer breaches. The traditional measure of loss-of-bargain damages measures the property's market value as of the date of the breach. *See* Jones v. Lee, 126 N.M. 467, 971 P.2d 858 (N.M.Ct.App.1998). Is this a fair or relevant date? Frequently the seller will be forced to put the property back on the market and may wait for months or even years before another buyer is found. In a declining market, the ultimate sale price may be much lower than the value on the date of the breach. Assuming that the seller has continued to make a diligent effort to resell, shouldn't the actual resale price be the relevant value for purposes of computing damages? The court so held in Kuhn v. Spatial Design, Inc., 245 N.J.Super. 378, 385–86, 585 A.2d 967, 971 (1991), following the rule for sales of goods found in U.C.C. §§ 2–706, 2–708 and in ULTA §§ 504–507.

Under the traditional approach, however, where an actual resale occurs, what do you think should be used as evidence of fair market value as of the time of breach? *See* Crabby's Inc. v. Hamilton, 244 S.W.3d 209 (Mo.App.2008) ("An essential element of the seller's case is proof of market value, and if he does resell within a reasonable time after the breach, the price obtained is some evidence of market value."—sale within eleven and a half months after breach deemed to be a reasonable time). *See generally* Gerald Korngold,

Seller's Damages from a Defaulting Buyer of Realty: The Influence of the Uniform Land Transactions Act on the Courts, 20 Nova L. Rev. 1069 (1996).

5. A further reason the courts may prefer to rely on the actual reselling price as the pertinent measure of value is that otherwise they must act on the basis of appraisal testimony, which is notoriously imprecise. For example, in Askari v. R & R Land Co., 179 Cal.App.3d 1101, 225 Cal.Rptr. 285 (1986), the appraisers for the two parties were $400,000 apart in their estimates of value as of the trial date—an amount which was 32% of the original contract price of $1.25 million. Such variations in appraisals are not unusual, and scarcely build one's confidence in the measurement of damages.

6. Consider the "incidental" and "consequential" damages recoverable by a seller. Should they include the following?

(a) Carrying costs of the property until it is resold (assuming continuing reasonable efforts to resell)? Such costs might include property taxes, insurance, utilities, and maintenance. *See* Allen v. Enomoto, 228 Cal.App.2d 798, 803–804, 39 Cal.Rptr. 815 (1964) (approving these items); Mueller v. Johnson, 60 Wash.App. 683, 806 P.2d 256 (1991). *But see* Quigley v. Jones, 255 Ga. 33, 334 S.E.2d 664 (1985) (refusing to allow the vendor damages (during the period of time he attempted to remarket the property) for taxes, insurance, utilities, repairs, or loss of use of the sales proceeds).

(b) Interest on existing mortgage loans on the property until it is resold?

(c) Interest income the seller expected to earn on the purchase price, or on purchase-money mortgage financing he was obligated under the contract to provide to the purchaser? *Compare* Van Moorlehem v. Brown Realty Co., 747 F.2d 992 (10th Cir.1984) (denying recovery for interest seller expected to earn on cash purchase price), *with* Askari v. R & R Land Co., 179 Cal.App.3d 1101, 225 Cal.Rptr. 285 (1986) (approving recovery of lost interest on purchase-money financing).

(d) The cost of a second real estate broker's commission on the resale, if the seller was obliged to pay a commission on the first sale even though it did not close? *Compare* Mueller v. Johnson, 60 Wash.App. 683, 806 P.2d 256 (1991) (approving this item), *with* Johnston v. Curtis, 70 Ark.App. 195, 16 S.W.3d 283 (2000) (rejecting it). Other resale expenses (e.g., advertising) would presumably be treated similarly.

(e) Increased tax liability as a result of changes in the tax laws occurring between the scheduled closing under the original contract and the date of a later resale? *See* Morgan v. Tzung, 278 Cal.Rptr. 221 (Cal.Ct.App.1991) (denying recovery) (ordered not published, Rule 976, Cal. Rules of Ct.).

See generally ULTA § 2–507; William B. Stoebuck & Dale A. Whitman, Property § 10.3 (3d ed. 2000). Should these items be recoverable for the entire time period to the date of resale (again, assuming reasonable efforts to resell), or merely to the date of breach? Should it matter whether the seller's land was tied up in litigation with the buyer (perhaps with a *lis pendens* filed) so that, as a practical matter, the property could not be resold until the litigation was concluded? *See* Morgan v. Tzung, *supra*.

Suppose the value of the property rises during the period the seller is attempting to remarket it, and he sells it for more than the original contract price. Should this increase offset his recovery of incidental or consequential damages? *See* Lawson v. Menefee, 132 S.W.3d 890, 895 (Ky.Ct.App.2004) ("To allow the [sellers] to retain the entire gain on the resale of the property, and to recover the consequential damages, would represent a windfall to them and would not place them in the same position as if the contract had not been breached."). *But see* Turner v. Benson, 672 S.W.2d 752 (Tenn.1984).

What about the use value of the property during the period the seller is attempting to resell? If the seller in fact lets the property to a tenant during the interim, it seems obvious that the rent collected should offset the seller's claim for incidental and consequential damages. Should a similar result follow, with an offset for fair rental value, if the seller continues to use the land himself? Or suppose the seller does not in fact use the property, but it remains available and adaptable to the seller's use?

7. Even if the contract is eventually performed, either under a decree of specific performance or voluntarily (but after an unjustified delay), should the non-breaching party also be permitted to recover some or all of the elements mentioned in the above notes as damages? *See* Shelter Corp. of Canada, Ltd. v. Bozin, 468 So.2d 1094 (Fla.Dist.Ct.App.1985) (where vendor breached and was ordered to specifically perform, purchaser failed to prove damages); Dato v. Mascarello, 197 Ill.App.3d 847, 145 Ill.Dec. 411, 557 N.E.2d 181 (1989) (where purchaser breached and was ordered to specifically perform, vendor could also recover damages for interest on purchase money mortgage purchaser should have been paying, and for vendor's carrying costs of the property, during the period of delay); III Lounge, Inc. v. Gaines, 227 Neb. 585, 419 N.W.2d 143 (1988) (same); H.C. Lind, Annotation, *Measure of Vendee's Recovery in Action for Damages for Vendor's Delay in Conveying Real Property*, 74 A.L.R.2d 578 (1960); *cf.* McCoy v. Alsup, 94 N.M. 255, 609 P.2d 337 (N.M.Ct.App.1980).

B. RESCISSION AND RESTITUTION

HARPER v. ADAMETZ

Supreme Court of Errors of Connecticut, 1955.
142 Conn. 218, 113 A.2d 136.

BALDWIN, ASSOCIATE JUSTICE.

This action, based upon fraud, was brought by the plaintiff against the named defendant and his son Walter Adametz. The court rendered judgment for the defendants and the plaintiff has appealed.

* * * Joseph B. Tesar was conservator of the estate of his father, William Tesar, an incompetent, who owned eighty acres of land and the buildings thereon in the town of Haddam. The defendant Jere Adametz, a real estate agent, hereinafter referred to as Jere, was acting as agent for

the sale of Tesar's property. Jere advertised a portion of it, consisting of five acres and an old colonial house, for $6200, and the advertisement, in a New Haven newspaper, came to the attention of the plaintiff. On December 6, 1948, the plaintiff wrote to Jere expressing an interest in the property * * *. On December 12, Jere showed the plaintiff the eighty-acre farm and told him that the seller was asking $8500 for it but that the buildings and a smaller acreage could be bought for less. The plaintiff made no offer but showed an interest in purchasing the smaller acreage. On the following day, December 13, Jere wrote to Joseph Tesar, the conservator, stating that he had a client who had offered $6500 cash for the farm (meaning eighty acres) and asked for an immediate reply. On December 15, the attorney for Tesar wrote to Jere stating that Tesar would accept the offer for the entire farm subject to the approval of the Probate Court and asking that a written offer with at least a 10 per cent deposit be sent to him.

The plaintiff visited the property on December 19 and 26, and on one of those dates he made an offer to Jere of $7000 for the entire farm. Jere promised to convey this offer to Tesar, but he did not do so. Instead, he sent his own check for $500 to Tesar on December 29 as a deposit on the purported offer of $6500. Jere told Fred Mazanek, a relative of the Tesars, that the plaintiff wanted to purchase only a small portion of the acreage and that he, Jere, would like to obtain the rest for his son but that he did not want to lose his commission. He prevailed upon Mazanek and John Hibbard, a friend of the family, to act as a medium for the passing of title to the farm. On or about January 2, 1949, Jere told the plaintiff that his offer had been rejected because Tesar desired to keep a major portion of the farm in the family and that certain relatives of the Tesars wished to buy most of the acreage, but that he Jere, could arrange for the plaintiff to buy the buildings and part of the land. The plaintiff then made an offer of $6000 for seventeen acres, including the buildings, and Jere accepted the offer. The plaintiff was satisfied with his purchase.

On January 4 Joseph Tesar signed a contract to sell the entire farm of eighty acres to Mazanek and Hibbard for $6500. The sale was approved by the Probate Court, and a conservator's deed dated January 26, was delivered on February 8 to Mazanek and Hibbard. At the same time, on February 8, they executed and delivered a deed for seventeen acres, including the buildings, to the plaintiff, who paid $6000. On March 11, Mazanek and Hibbard conveyed sixty-three acres, the balance of the farm, to the defendant Walter Adametz, Jere's son. Mazanek and Hibbard were mere "go betweens" who paid nothing when they "bought" the farm and received nothing when they "sold" it to the plaintiff and Walter. Walter paid nothing for the sixty-three acres he acquired. Tesar did not know of the plaintiff's offer of $7000 for the entire farm, and the plaintiff did not know that this offer had not been transmitted to Tesar. The representation by Jere to Tesar on December 13 that he had a $6500 offer for the farm was false. At the time he sent his own check for $500 to Tesar on the purported offer of $6500, the only offer he had was the plaintiff's offer of

$7000. Jere engineered the transactions herein related to obtain sixty-three acres of the farm for himself and Walter at the price of $500 and at the same time collect a commission of $325 for the sale.

On these facts, the court concluded that Jere was the agent for Tesar and not for the plaintiff, that there was no contract between Tesar and the plaintiff for the purchase of any property other than the buildings and seventeen acres of land, that the plaintiff sustained no loss by reason of any misrepresentation made by Jere, and that therefore the plaintiff had failed to prove actionable fraud.

It is the general rule that in an action at law for fraud the plaintiff, to recover, must prove that he has been injured. * * * In the ordinary case, this means that the plaintiff must sustain a substantial pecuniary loss. *See* Prosser, Torts, p. 768; Harper, Torts, p. 470. The plaintiff in this action did receive what he paid for. * * * He did not, however, because of Jere's fraud, obtain what he was seeking. While acting as an agent for Tesar but with the intent of making a secret profit for himself, Jere told his principal that he had a cash offer of $6500 for the entire farm. This statement was false, and in making it Jere violated his trust. His conduct was a fraud upon Tesar. * * *

Jere was not the agent of the plaintiff. Nevertheless, he could not deliberately deceive him. It was Jere's advertisement in the newspaper which had aroused the interest of the plaintiff in the property. * * * It can be claimed that when the plaintiff made his $7000 offer Tesar had already signified his willingness to accept the purported offer of $6500 made by Jere in behalf of a fictitious client and that the plaintiff's offer came too late. But the $6500 offer was a fraud and Tesar was not bound to accept it. He could have revoked Jere's authority. * * * Thereafter, he could have sold the property to the plaintiff. Jere's false statements, his concealment of the facts, his promise to submit the plaintiff's offer to Tesar when everything indicates that he had no intention of doing so, worked a fraud upon the plaintiff. * * * As a result, the plaintiff has been denied the right to have his bona fide offer of $7000 submitted to Tesar. In short, the plaintiff has been deprived of his bargain. Jere and Walter, by their fraud, have acquired sixty-three acres of land for $175.

This is an action in equity as well as at law. Equity is a system of positive jurisprudence founded upon established principles which can be adapted to new circumstances where a court of law is powerless to give relief. 1 Pomeroy, Equity Jurisprudence (5th Ed.) p. 78. In equity, as in law, misrepresentation, to constitute fraud, must be material. 3 *Id.*, § 876; Bogert, 3 Trusts & Trustees, § 473. That is to say, the representation must prejudice the party relying upon it. He must suffer some injury or pecuniary loss. Some courts have held that the pecuniary loss need be only slight. * * * Others have held that mere lack of pecuniary injury or loss does not prevent the granting of relief by way of rescission and restitution. * * *

The plaintiff had a clear right to have his offer for the farm transmitted to Tesar. Having been invited by Jere's advertisement to bid for the property, he had a right to assume that Jere would deal honestly with him and be faithful to his principal. Instead, Jere withheld the offer, later lied to the plaintiff about it and, by using the plaintiff's willingness to accept seventeen acres, acquired the farm for himself for less than the plaintiff had offered for it. He induced the plaintiff to make an offer and then used that offer, and the plaintiff's money, to make a secret profit. By his fraudulent misrepresentations, he deprived the plaintiff of his bargain and obtained for himself some of the land which the plaintiff had offered to buy. "If one acquires property by means of a fraudulent misrepresentation of a material fact, equity will assist the defrauded person by fastening a constructive trust on the property."* Bogert, 3 Trusts & Trustees, p. 20; 3 Scott, Trusts, § 462.2; Restatement Restitution, § 133, comment a, §§ 160, 169; 4 Pomeroy, Equity Jurisprudence (5th Ed.) § 1044 * * *. It is true that this rule is most often applied in situations where the relationship between the plaintiff and the defendant is one which equity clearly recognizes as fiduciary. But equity has carefully refrained from defining a fiduciary relationship in precise detail and in such a manner as to exclude new situations. It has left the bars down for situations in which there is a justifiable trust confided on one side and a resulting superiority and influence on the other. 3 Pomeroy, *op. cit.*, § 956a.

Equity will not permit these defendants to keep a benefit which came to them by reason of Jere's fraudulent conduct. It is true that Tesar has not acted to right the wrong done to him. Had he done so, it is probable that the plaintiff could have had the farm. This should not prevent the plaintiff, in his own right, from having a remedy for the wrong done to him. The plaintiff has proffered $1000, which represents the balance of the amount of his original offer over and above the purchase price he paid for the seventeen acres. Upon the payment of this sum into court, to await further order, an order should enter directing the defendant Walter to convey the sixty-three acres to the plaintiff.

There is error, the judgment is set aside and the case is remanded to the Superior Court for proceedings in accordance with this opinion.

O'SULLIVAN, ASSOCIATE JUSTICE, filed a dissenting opinion. [Opinion omitted].

NOTES

1. In *Harper* the court emphasized that the defendant's conduct arguably might not constitute tortious misrepresentation because the plaintiff had received what he had paid for. If the trade were induced by a misrepresentation, it was necessarily an "immaterial" one. A somewhat similar situation was presented in Hunter v. Shell Oil Co., of Section 3.B in Chapter 4. *See also* Moore & Co. v. T–A–L–L, Inc., 792 P.2d 794 (Colo.1990) (holding that a real

---

* *See* John P. Dawson, Unjust Enrichment: A Comparative Analysis 26–33 (1951).

estate broker who violated fiduciary duty owed to client by failing to disclose relevant information may be liable in quasi-contract for the commission received even where the violation has resulted in no actual monetary loss to the client); Ward v. Taggart, 51 Cal.2d 736, 336 P.2d 534 (1959) (holding that agent who profited by secretly selling less land to buyer than principal had agreed to sell for buyer's price, and who kept extra land for himself, was required to disgorge extra land to buyer).

2. Professor Palmer described the *Harper* case as one involving restitution to protect unrealized contract expectations. 1 George E. Palmer, Law of Restitution § 3.18 (1978).

C. SPECIFIC PERFORMANCE

1. Suits by Buyer or Seller

CENTEX HOMES CORP. v. BOAG

Superior Court of New Jersey, Chancery Division, 1974.
128 N.J.Super. 385, 320 A.2d 194.

[Centex constructed a condominium project in New Jersey which, when completed, would include six 31–story buildings containing more than 3600 units. The Boags signed a contract to purchase a condominium unit for $73,700, but shortly thereafter Mr. Boag was transferred by his employer to Chicago. The Boags stopped payment on the check they had given as earnest money, and refused to complete the purchase. Centex then brought this action for specific performance, or in the alternative, for liquidated damages in the amount of the earnest money.]

* * *

* * * [U]nder a condominium housing scheme each condominium apartment unit constitutes a separate parcel of real property which may be dealt with in the same manner as any real estate. Upon closing of title the apartment unit owner receives a recordable deed which confers upon him the same rights and subjects him to the same obligations as in the case of traditional forms of real estate ownership, the only difference being that the condominium owner receives in addition an undivided interest in the common elements associated with the building and assigned to each unit. See the Condominium Act, N.J.S.A. 46:8B–1 *et seq.*; 15 Am.Jur.2d, Condominiums and Cooperative Apartments, at 977 *et seq.*; Note, 77 Harv.L.Rev. 777 (1964).

Centex urges that since the subject matter of the contract is the transfer of a fee interest in real estate, the remedy of specific performance is available to enforce the agreement under principles of equity which are well-settled in this state. * * *

The principle underlying the specific performance remedy is equity's jurisdiction to grant relief where the damage remedy at law is inadequate. The text writers generally agree that at the time this branch of equity

jurisdiction was evolving in England, the presumed uniqueness of land as well as its importance to the social order of that era led to the conclusion that damages at law could never be adequate to compensate for the breach of a contract to transfer an interest in land. Hence specific performance became a fixed remedy in this class of transactions. *See* 11 Williston on Contracts (3d ed. 1968) § 1418A; 5A Corbin on Contracts § 1143 (1964).
* * *

While the inadequacy of the damage remedy suffices to explain the origin of the vendee's right to obtain specific performance in equity, it does not provide a *rationale* for the availability of the remedy at the instance of the vendor of real estate. Except upon a showing of unusual circumstances or a change in the vendor's position, such as where the vendee has entered into possession, the vendor's damages are usually measurable, his remedy at law is adequate and there is no jurisdictional basis for equitable relief. *But see* Restatement, Contracts § 360, comment c.[2] The early English precedents suggest that the availability of the remedy in a suit by a vendor was an outgrowth of the equitable concept of mutuality, i.e., that equity would not specifically enforce an agreement unless the remedy was available to both parties. See the discussion in Stoutenburgh v. Tompkins, 9 N.J.Eq. 332, 342–346 (Ch.1853); 4 Pomeroy, Equity Jurisprudence (5th ed. 1941), § 1405; Annotation, 65 A.L.R. 7, 40 (1930); Jones v. Newhall, 115 Mass. 244, 15 Am.Rep. 97, 103 (Sup.Jud.Ct. 1874); Comment, 10 Villanova L.Rev. 557, 568–569 (1965).

So far as can be determined from our decisional law, the mutuality of remedy concept has been the prop which has supported equitable jurisdiction to grant specific performance in actions by vendors of real estate.
* * *

Our present Supreme Court has squarely held, however, that mutuality of remedy is not an appropriate basis for granting or denying specific performance. Fleischer v. James Drug Stores, 1 N.J. 138, 62 A.2d 383 (1948); *see also,* Restatement, Contracts § 372; 11 Williston, Contracts (3d ed. 1968), § 1433. The test is whether the obligations of the contract are mutual and not whether each is entitled to precisely the same remedy in the event of a breach. In *Fleischer* plaintiff sought specific performance against a cooperative buying and selling association although his membership contract was terminable by him on 60 days' notice. Justice Heher said:

---

2. The Restatement's reasoning, as expressed in § 360, comment c, amounts to the inconsistent propositions that (1) because the vendor may not have sustained any damage which is actionable at law, specific performance should be granted, and (2) he would otherwise sustain damage equal to the loss of interest on the proceeds of the sale. Yet loss of interest is readily measurable and can be recovered in an action at law, and to the extent that the vendor has sustained no economic injury, there is no compelling reason for equity to grant to him the otherwise extraordinary remedy of specific performance. At the end of the comment, the author suggests that the vendor is entitled to specific performance because that remedy should be mutual, a concept which is substantially rejected as a decisional basis in §§ 372 and 373 of the Restatement.

And the requisite mutuality is not wanting. The contention contra rests upon the premise that, although the corporation "can terminate the contract only in certain restricted and unusual circumstances, any 'member' may withdraw at any time by merely giving notice."

Clearly, there is mutuality of obligation, for until his withdrawal complainant is under a continuing obligation of performance in the event of performance by the corporation. It is not essential that the remedy of specific performance be mutual. * * * The modern view is that the rule of mutuality of remedy is satisfied if the decree of specific performance operates effectively against both parties and gives to each the benefit of a mutual obligation. * * *

The fact that the remedy of specific enforcement is available to one party to a contract is not in itself a sufficient reason for making the remedy available to the other; but it may be decisive when the adequacy of damages is difficult to determine and there is no other reason for refusing specific enforcement. Restatement, Contracts (1932), sections 372, 373. It is not necessary, to serve the ends of equal justice, that the parties shall have identical remedies in case of breach.

The disappearance of the mutuality of remedy doctrine from our law dictates the conclusion that specific performance relief should no longer be automatically available to a vendor of real estate, but should be confined to those special instances where a vendor will otherwise suffer an economic injury for which his damage remedy at law will not be adequate, or where other equitable considerations require that the relief be granted. *Cf.* Dover Shopping Center, Inc. v. Cushman's Sons, Inc., 63 N.J.Super. 384, 394, 164 A.2d 785 (App.Div.1960). As Chancellor Vroom noted in King v. Morford, 1 N.J.Eq. 274, 281–282 (Ch.Div.1831), whether a contract should be specifically enforced is always a matter resting in the sound discretion of the court and * * * considerable caution should be used in decreeing the specific performance of agreements, and * * * the court is bound to see that it really does the complete justice which it aims at, and which is the ground of its jurisdiction.

Here the subject matter of the real estate transaction—a condominium apartment unit—has no unique quality but is one of hundreds of virtually identical units being offered by a developer for sale to the public. The units are sold by means of sample, in this case model apartments, in much the same manner as items of personal property are sold in the market place. The sales prices for the units are fixed in accordance with [a] schedule filed by Centex as part of its offering plan, and the only variance as between apartments having the same floor plan (of which six plans are available) is the floor level or the building location within the project. In actuality, the condominium apartment units, regardless of their realty label, share the same characteristics as personal property.

From the foregoing one must conclude that the damages sustained by a condominium sponsor resulting from the breach of the sales agreement are readily measurable and the damage remedy at law is wholly adequate. No compelling reasons have been shown by Centex for the granting of specific performance relief and its complaint is therefore dismissed as to the first count.

NOTES

1. The court in *Centex* makes a good deal of the fact that the condominium units were numerous and very similar. What relevance does this fact have to the *vendor's* right to specific performance? *See* Note, 48 Temp. L.Q. 847 (1975); Note, 43 U. Cin. L. Rev. 935 (1974). See ULTA § 2–506, which would often produce a result similar to *Centex*. Recall our earlier discussion about the difficulty of measuring loss of bargain damages on the basis of the testimony of appraisers. If Centex Homes had sought damages instead of specific performance, would it have had this difficulty? Given the fact that it had an ongoing sales program and a clearly-defined price schedule for its condominium units, would it not have been able to establish their current market value easily and reliably? Moreover, would not its success (or lack of success) in that sales program make it quite easy to estimate how long it would take Centex to remarket the unit the Boags refused to buy, and for that matter, what the cost of remarketing it would be? Do you suppose these factors influenced the court in reaching its conclusion that specific performance was unnecessary?

2. Other cases casting doubt on the usual assumption that a vendor may have specific performance as a matter of course include Perron v. Hale, 108 Idaho 578, 701 P.2d 198 (1985); Seabaugh v. Keele, 775 S.W.2d 205 (Mo.Ct. App.1989); and Wolf v. Anderson, 334 N.W.2d 212 (N.D.1983).

3. Should the holding of *Centex* apply to a specific performance action by a *purchaser*? Assume the unit is one of hundreds of virtually identical units in a large condominium project. Is the lack of uniqueness enough to deny the purchaser's claim? At least two cases have refused to apply the reasoning of *Centex* to purchasers, and have granted them specific performance. *See* Giannini v. First National Bank of Des Plaines, 136 Ill.App.3d 971, 91 Ill.Dec. 438, 483 N.E.2d 924 (1985); Pruitt v. Graziano, 215 N.J.Super. 330, 521 A.2d 1313 (1987). Why are purchasers different from sellers in this respect?

In *Giannini*, the successor in interest of a developer of a large condominium project decided to refrain from filing a condominium declaration on certain of the buildings, and to place them in rental service instead. However, Giannini had signed a contract to purchase a unit in one of these buildings, and sued for specific performance. The defendant claimed that specific performance was impossible because the "property" did not exist (since the building had not officially been converted to condominium status). The court rejected this argument and ordered specific performance. It also noted that Giannini's legal remedies were literally "inadequate" because the original developer of the project had become insolvent and had been dissolved, and the real estate had been transferred to the lending institution which had held the mortgage on it.

More recently, an Illinois appellate court affirmed a decree of specific performance in favor of the purchasers of a condominium unit, albeit with somewhat equivocal language:

> On one side is the argument that condominium units are real estate, *per se* unique and thus entitled to a remedy in equity. *See Giannini* * * *. On the other side is the argument that a condominium unit is but one of thousands with the same layout, typically in the same building, and therefore * * * only entitled to remedies at law. *See Centex* * * *. However, using either argument, there is no question that the condominium unit in this case is unique. * * * The condominium unit was not sold as a sample; it was substantially upgraded to [purchasers'] specifications. Furthermore, [purchasers] themselves have made improvements to the condominium unit. Lastly, and most importantly, the condominium unit in this case has been [purchasers'] home for the past two years. The uniqueness of this condominium unit to the [purchasers] makes it an unquestionably proper subject for specific performance and makes the remedy at law inadequate.

Schwinder v. Austin Bank of Chicago, 809 N.E.2d 180, 196 (Ill.App.Ct.2004).

4. As can be seen in *Centex* and the notes, at times, courts have struggled with whether they can order specific performance for a nonbreaching party if, had the tables been turned, the breaching party would not have been entitled to specific performance. Many years ago a "negative" mutuality doctrine was articulated by John Norton Pomeroy, following a similar articulation by Sir Edmond Fry. Sir Fry said:

> A contract to be specifically enforced by the Court must be mutual, that is to say, such that it might, at the time it was entered into, have been enforced by either of the parties against the other of them. When, therefore, whether from personal incapacity to contract, or the nature of the contract, or any other cause, the contract is incapable of being enforced against one party, that party is generally incapable of enforcing it against the other, though its execution in the latter way might in itself be free from the difficulty attending its execution in the former.

Sir Edmond Fry, Special Performance § 286 (1858). Professor Pomeroy, assuming that Sir Fry meant "specifically enforce" every time he said "enforce" stated:

> If at the time of the filing of the bill in equity, the contract being yet executory on both sides, the defendant, himself free from fraud or other personal bar, could not have the remedy of specific performance against the plaintiff, then the contract is so lacking in mutuality that equity will not compel the defendant to perform but will leave the plaintiff to his remedy at law.

Janet Leach Richards, *Mutuality of Remedy—A Call for Reform*, 13 Mem. St. U. L. Rev. 1, 15 (1982) (*quoting* 2 Pomeroy, A Treatise on Equitable Remedies § 769, at 1291–92 (1905)).

Courts began following Professor Pomeroy's rule, denying specific performance to the plaintiff if the defendant would not have been entitled to it. Now, however, most courts, have rejected the doctrine, as has the Restatement (Second) of Contracts. See if you can interpret Sir Fry's statement to be consistent with Chief Judge Rose Bird's opinion in Bleecher v. Conte, 29 Cal.3d 345, 213 Cal.Rptr. 852, 698 P.2d 1154 (Cal. 1981):

> The only real issue before this court is whether the presence of the liquidated damages clause affected the *remedy* to which the buyers were entitled. Thus, the court must decide whether the buyers were prevented from obtaining specific performance because the liquidated damages clause stated that the seller waived that remedy if the buyers failed to perform their duties.

> For many years this view was adopted by the courts. One party to a contract could not obtain specific performance if that remedy was unavailable to the other party. * * * However, the Restatement of Contracts rejected this rule. "The fact that the remedy of specific enforcement is not available to one party is not a sufficient reason for refusing it to the other party." (Rest., Contracts, § 372, subd. (1). *See also* 7 Witkin, Summary of Cal.Law (8th ed. 1974) pp. 5274–5276.)

> The comment to section 372 is instructive. "The substantial purpose of all attempted rules requiring mutuality of remedy is to make sure that the defendant will not be compelled to perform specifically without good security that he will receive specifically the agreed equivalent in exchange." (Rest., Contracts, § 372, com. a on subd. (1), at p. 678.) Section 373 of the Restatement recognized that "[s]pecific enforcement may properly be refused if a substantial part of the agreed exchange for the performance to be compelled is as yet unperformed and its concurrent or future performance is not well secured to the satisfaction of the court."

> In 1969, the California Legislature discarded the rigid and outdated requirement of mutuality of remedy with respect to specific performance. Civil Code section 3386 was amended to provide that "[n]otwithstanding that the agreed counterperformance is not or would not have been specifically enforceable, specific performance may be compelled if: [¶] (a) Specific performance would otherwise be an appropriate remedy; and [¶] (b) The agreed counterperformance has been substantially performed or its concurrent or future performance is assured or, if the court deems necessary, can be secured to the satisfaction of the court." (*See* Stats.1969, ch. 156, § 1, p. 410.)

Id. at 352–53, 213 Cal.Rptr. at 856, 698 P.2d at 1158.

Another reason the "mutuality of remedy" doctrine has been disfavored is because, not only has it been used to *deny* a plaintiff specific performance, but also it has been used to *permit* specific performance to a plaintiff who might otherwise not be entitled to it.

5. Earlier, we considered the enforceability of liquidated damages provisions in the context of contracts for the sale of chattels. Here, however, the focus is on the extent to which such clauses limit the availability of equitable relief. More specifically, to what extent does the presence of a liquidated damages provision prohibit the granting of specific performance? Consider the analysis of this issue by Professor Dobbs:

> If the liquidated damage clause by its terms specifies a deposit or a stipulated sum as the sole remedy for the plaintiff, or declares that its payment terminates the obligations of the parties, then of course the plaintiff cannot have specific performance any more than he could have actual damages; the remedy would be limited to the stipulated damages. But if the liquidated damages clause is not the sole remedy and not intended to give the defendant the option of buying out of the contract at the price specified, specific performance remains an option for the plaintiff. A liquidated damages or forfeiture clause that limits the liability of one party does not necessarily limit the liability of the other. The land buyer whose only liability upon default is to lose his earnest money deposit may still have specific performance against the seller unless the seller's liability is also limited by the agreement.
>
> But even if, as a matter of contract interpretation, the liquidated damages clause did not foreclose specific performance, courts at one time worried that provision for liquidated damages might be inconsistent with the underlying premises of specific performance. If a land buyer or seller provides for liquidated damages, it may seem that the contract only signifies money, not a unique thing, hence that specific performance should be or could be denied. This view attaches too much significance both to the liquidated damages clause and to specific adequacy rules. Some courts have avoided the impact of this view by finding that the clause was not a true liquidated damages clause. But such a ruling is distortive. The easy answer is that even if the adequacy test is still dominant, the option to use liquidated damages might be a prudent provision to have at the time the contract is made and one not at all inconsistent with a genuine desire to enforce the contract for its unique qualities. So the presence of a non-exclusive liquidated damages clause does not in itself preclude specific performance. The liquidated damages clause precludes specific performance only if the clause was intended to be an exclusive remedy.

Dan B. Dobbs, Law of Remedies 268–69 (2d ed. 1993).*

6. Sometimes a court will deny specific performance because the contract is insufficiently certain. This issue was discussed at length in Barry M. Dechtman, Inc. v. Sidpaul Corp., 89 N.J. 547, 446 A.2d 518 (1982):

* Reprinted with permission of West Publishing Co.

The oft-stated rule is that the terms of the contract must be definite and certain so that the court may decree with some precision what the defendant must do. 11 Williston, Contracts (3 ed. Jaeger), § 1414 at 810; 5A Corbin, Contracts (2 ed. 1964), § 1174 at 278. Whether the contract meets the test need not depend upon a literal reading. The court must also examine the situation of the parties and the accompanying circumstances to ascertain the meaning of the agreement. * * * Seeming difficulties of enforcement due to uncertainties attributable to language may vanish in the light of practicalities and a full understanding of the parties' intent. Reasonable certainty of the terms is sufficient. The two leading authorities on contracts have cautioned against refusal to order specific performance because of an apparent uncertainty in the terms of the contract. Professor Williston states:

> It seems probable that the difficulty regarding uncertainty has been overemphasized; certainly, it should not be allowed to hamper or restrict equitable relief further than necessity requires. 11 Williston, *supra*, § 1424 at 819.

Professor Corbin agrees:

> There are cases in which the court has made a mountain out of a molehill and refused a decree that might well have been granted. Apparent difficulties of enforcement that arise out of uncertainties in expression often disappear in the light of courageous common sense and reasonable implications of fact. 5A Corbin, *supra*, at 283.

Id. at 552–53, 446 A.2d at 521.

Some courts require a greater degree of certainty when the plaintiff is seeking specific performance than when the plaintiff sues for damages. *E.g.*, Homart Development Co. v. Sigman, 868 F.2d 1556 (11th Cir.1989); Fox v. Sails at Laguna Club Development Corp., 403 So.2d 456 (Fla.Dist.Ct.App. 1981) (denying claim for specific performance and remanding for consideration of cause of action for damages).

7. There are a variety of situations where specific performance may be denied and the plaintiff left to other remedies. These include the following types of cases:

(a) If the vendor has resold the land to a purchaser who had no notice of the prior contract, the court will not force the innocent purchaser to give up the land in order to award specific performance to the original buyer. *See* Krantz v. Donner, 285 So.2d 699 (Fla.Dist.Ct.App. 1973). On the other hand, where a subsequent purchaser takes with notice of the prior contract, she will lose the land if the original purchaser insists on specific performance. Frankel v. Northeast Land Co., 391 Pa.Super. 226, 570 A.2d 1065 (1990).

(b) Both specific performance and other remedies may be denied if there are precedent or concurrent conditions which have not been satisfied or if the plaintiff is in substantial breach.

(c) If the purchaser was buying the land for the purpose of immediate resale at a profit, its supposed uniqueness arguably is of little importance to him and damages is sometimes considered an adequate remedy. *See* Watkins v. Paul, 95 Idaho 499, 511 P.2d 781 (1973); *cf.* Chan v. Smider, 31 Wash.App. 730, 644 P.2d 727 (1982); Henry L. McClintock, *Equity* § 60 (2d ed. 1948); Paul J. Brenner, *Specific Performance of Contracts for the Sale of Land Purchased for Resale or Investment*, 24 McGill L.J. 513 (1978). However, where the purchaser has already entered into a resale contract, is there a sound policy argument for granting specific performance of the original contract?

8.   In 1984, the California legislature amended Civil Code § 3387 to provide that damages are conclusively presumed inadequate to compensate a purchaser of a single-family dwelling who intends to occupy it, while in other cases of a breach of contract by vendors, damages are merely presumed to be inadequate. The latter rebuttable presumption has nevertheless proven difficult for a vendor to overcome in contracts involving commercial real estate. In reversing a trial court's denial of specific performance to a purchaser of a mobile home park, a recent California decision stated:

> The fact that other mobilehome parks had sold within a recent period does not mean that damages would be adequate to compensate [purchaser] for the loss of *this* property and accompanying investment opportunity. As one commentator has pointed out, to disprove the presumption, "a seller must show not only abstract replaceability but concrete availability of reasonably interchangeable property at terms within the buyer's means." (Bird, *Toward Understanding California's Rebuttable Presumption that Land is Unique,* 1 Cal.Real Property Journal No. 3 (Summer 1983).) There was no information in the appraiser's testimony or his report showing that [purchaser] could purchase one of these indentified mobilehome park properties on similar terms, or whether [purchaser] would be in a similarly situated investment position if it did complete a purchase. Because land is unique, different locations are not necessarily interchangeable, without evidence showing this to be the case.

Real Estate Analytics, LLC v. Vallas, 160 Cal.App.4th 463, 475, 72 Cal.Rptr.3d 835, 843 (2008).

9.   Even when specific performance is ordered, a court may give a judgment for past damages as well to compensate the innocent party for the delay or for other harms which have ensued since the date the contract should have been performed. *See, e.g.*, Woliansky v. Miller, 146 Ariz. 170, 704 P.2d 811 (Ariz.Ct.App.1985) (damages for deterioration to improvements on the land during five-year delay); Bravo v. Buelow, 168 Cal.App.3d 208, 214 Cal.Rptr. 65 (1985) (damages resulting from rise in cost to purchaser of constructing a house on the land). Numerous cases have awarded damages for the higher cost of mortgage financing which the purchaser must pay because interest rates have risen during the period of delay. *See, e.g.*, Hutton v. Gliksberg, 128 Cal.App.3d 240, 180 Cal.Rptr. 141 (1982); Appollo v. Reynolds, 364 N.W.2d 422 (Minn.Ct.App.1985); *see* William B. Stoebuck & Dale A. Whitman, Property § 10.5 nn.20–22 (3d ed. 2000); William E. Garland, *Purchaser's Interest Rate Increase: Caveat Venditor*, 27 N.Y.L. Sch. L. Rev. 745 (1982); Note, 12 Seton Hall L. Rev. 916 (1982).

10.   If the seller does not own all of the property covered by the contract, the purchaser may request, and can generally obtain, specific performance

with an abatement of the price to reflect the shortage in the land. *See, e.g.,* Burk v. Hefley, 32 Ark.App. 133, 798 S.W.2d 109 (1990); Ewing v. Bissell, 105 Nev. 488, 777 P.2d 1320 (1989). The same principle is applied if the seller owns only a fractional undivided interest in the property that he or she contracted to sell. *See* Chastain v. Schomburg, 258 Ga. 218, 367 S.E.2d 230 (1988).

11.   If the vendor breaches but refuses to return the purchaser's earnest money, some states give the purchaser a "vendee's lien" on the property to secure its recovery. *See* Sparks v. Charles Wayne Group, 568 So.2d 512 (Fla.Dist.Ct.App.1990) (purchaser may file a notice of lis pendens in support of the vendee's lien). Unless the contract is recorded (which is unlikely), a conveyance by the vendor to a good faith purchaser without notice of the contract will free the land of the lien. *See* State Savings & Loan Ass'n v. Kauaian Development Co., 50 Haw. 540, 445 P.2d 109 (1968); *cf. In re* Pearl, 40 B.R. 860 (Bankr.D.N.J.1984). See ULTA § 2–512, which provides for recordation of a "notice of lien" by the purchaser.

12.   Suppose the vendor not only agrees to sell Blackacre, but also to finance part of the purchase price by taking back from the purchaser a promissory note and a purchase money mortgage. In essence, the vendor is agreeing to make a loan to the purchaser for part of the purchase price. Will a court grant specific performance of this promise? Traditionally, many courts have been unwilling to grant borrowers specific performance of agreements to lend money on the theory that breaches of such contracts can always be fully compensated in damages. *See, e.g.,* Rogers v. Challis, 27 Beav. 175, 54 Eng.Rep. 68 (Ch.1859); City Centre One Associates v. Teachers Insurance & Annuity Ass'n of America, 656 F.Supp. 658 (D.Utah 1987); Bechtold Paving, Inc. v. City of Kenmare, 446 N.W.2d 19 (N.D.1989). However, this rule is not followed uniformly. Consider the language of Bregman v. Meehan, 125 Misc.2d 332, 479 N.Y.S.2d 422 (N.Y.Sup.Ct.1984), where the court granted the purchaser's request for specific performance of a purchase money mortgage:

> A review of the facts and analysis set forth, *supra,* reflects there is considerable difficulty in fairly evaluating the real extent of the plaintiffs' harm in this case. An accurate calculation of damages in cases concerned with mortgage lending now involves complexities not foreseen 100 years ago. D.C. Draper, *The Broken Commitment: A Modern View of the Mortgage Lender's Remedy,* 59 Cornell L.Rev. 418, 429 (Nov.–Mar. 1973– 1974). It is not the same as in 1859, when Roger v. Challis was decided, and the court could say with equanimity: "There is a mere matter of calculation, and a jury would easily assess the amount of damages which the Plaintiff has sustained."

> * * * [A] money judgment on the purchase money mortgage in this case would be substantially unfair to either plaintiff or defendant, depending upon the method of calculation employed, as compared to requiring specific performance of that mortgage obligation. The problem arises primarily because interest rates in recent years have been subject to unusual fluctuations, and rate trends are not predictable even with reasonable probability. This fact is demonstrated by the varying discount rates employed by courts over even a brief period of years. *Compare* Reis

v. Sparks (547 F.2d 236 [(4th Cir.1976)]) using 5%, *with* Hutton v. Gliksberg (128 Cal.App.3d 240, 180 Cal.Rptr. 141 [(2d Dist.1982)]) applying 14%. These are problems beyond this Court's control.

Thus, in recent years, there has been a noticeable erosion of the rule that a borrower cannot obtain specific performance on an agreement to lend money. Rather, specific performance has been granted, particularly when the loan relates to the sale of real property. * * *

* * * As one authority has stated, a purchase money mortgage such as this, given by a seller at lower than commercially available rates, is usually for the purpose of encouraging a sale. It generally indicates that a buyer has agreed either to pay a higher price than he would otherwise have paid, or a price he could not otherwise afford absent the purchase money mortgage. In return, as here, the buyer has the benefit of relatively lower mortgage payments and a much smaller down payment than could be achieved with more traditional financing. (Ominsky, *Creative Mortgaging: PMMS, Wraps and Various Participations*, 14 Real Estate Rev. 74, 75) [(Spring 1984)].

* * * [I]t is highly unlikely these plaintiffs will find another lender willing to give them a $60,000 second mortgage at 12% with a 15 year term, prepayment rights and a balloon payment. The principal amount, the term, and the prepayment right may all be different, making the substitute performance too costly or otherwise unacceptable. One authority has stated that "specific performance is the only realistic protection available for the borrower's expectation interest, since only specific performance can protect against all the intangible and immeasurable losses occasioned by a broken commitment." M.J. Mehr and L.A. Kilgore, *Enforcement of the Real Estate Loan Commitment: The Improvement of the Borrower's Remedies*, 24 Wayne L.Rev. 1011, 1034. That is true in this case.

Id. at 346–48, 479 N.Y.S.2d at 432–33. *See generally* L. Travis Brannon, Jr., *Enforceability of Mortgage Loan Commitments*, 18 Real Prop. Prob. & Tr. J. 724 (1983); Annotation, 82 A.L.R.3d 1116 (1978).

RESTATEMENT (SECOND) OF CONTRACTS

§ 364 (1981).*

§ 364. Effect of Unfairness

(1) Specific performance or an injunction will be refused if such relief would be unfair because

(a) the contract was induced by mistake or by unfair practices,

(b) the relief would cause unreasonable hardship or loss to the party in breach or to third persons, or

(c) the exchange is grossly inadequate or the terms of the contract are otherwise unfair. * * *

Comment:

    a. Types of unfairness. Courts have traditionally refused equitable relief on grounds of unfairness or mistake in situations where they would not necessarily refuse to award damages. Some of these situations involve elements of mistake (§§ 152, 153), misrepresentation (§ 164), duress (§ 175) or undue influence (§ 177) that fall short of what is required for avoidance under those doctrines. Others involve elements of impracticability of performance or frustration of purpose that fall short of what is required for relief under those doctrines. Still others involve elements of substantive unfairness in the exchange itself or in its terms that fall short of what is required for unenforceability on grounds of unconscionability (§ 208). The gradual expansion of these doctrines to afford relief in an increasing number of cases has resulted in a contraction of the area in which this traditional distinction is made between the availability of equitable and legal relief. Nevertheless, the discretionary nature of equitable relief permits its denial when a variety of factors combine to make enforcement of a promise unfair, even though no single legal doctrine alone would make the promise unenforceable. Such general equitable doctrines as those of laches and "unclean hands" supplement the rule stated in this Section.

HILTON v. NELSEN

Supreme Court of Minnesota, 1979.
283 N.W.2d 877.

Bruce C. Stone, Justice.

    This is an appeal from the order of the district court awarding plaintiff specific performance of a contract for the sale of farmland and damages. * * *

    In September 1974, defendants Dale and Geraldine Nelsen entered into negotiations for the sale of their 720-acre farm to plaintiff, Irvin Hilton, a Missouri real estate investor who had come to defendants' real estate agency, Phelps Farm Sales, looking for farm situations and investment opportunities in northwestern Minnesota. The rather lengthy and complex contract that was eventually entered into was drafted by Hilton's attorney, although some of the provisions were suggested by the Nelsens after several hours of discussion between the parties. The Nelsens were not represented by an attorney until after they had signed the contract.

    The contract, dated October 4, 1974, provided generally for the sale of the property to Hilton for $180,000. * * *

    * * * Although the Nelsens thought they had signed a contract for deed, the agreement provided for title and possession to pass at closing.

    Because the purchaser's performance was contingent on his ability to obtain an owner's title insurance policy without exceptions, Nelsen saw an attorney in March 1975 to help him clear certain title defects. After being advised by his attorney that the agreement was not a contract for deed,

Nelsen instructed his attorney to tell Hilton that he would not close unless he had a contract for deed. On March 28, Nelsen's attorney sent Hilton's attorney a letter to this effect; the latter replied that if the Nelsens refused to close, Hilton would sue for specific performance as provided by the remedies clause of the contract.[1] Nelsen's attorney then advised Nelsen to attempt to close. * * *

The Nelsens were able to clear the defects in title, except for a real estate mortgage, a reservation of mineral rights by the State of Minnesota, and easements for existing public roads and underground telephone cables. At the end of April 1975, the Nelsens bought and moved to a farm in Nebraska. On May 7 or 8, 1975, Nelsen called Hilton from Nebraska and advised him that he was ready to close.

The evidence was in dispute as to this telephone conversation; the Nelsens claimed that Hilton demanded a reduction of $16,000 to close, and Hilton claimed that he could not recall such a conversation. * * * Nelsen, believing that Hilton had defaulted, returned to Minnesota and made no further attempt to close. Nelsen farmed the land in 1975 but lost the crop.

In February 1976, Hilton's attorney wrote to notify Nelsen that Hilton would be ready to close on May 1, 1976, the last closing date on the contract. * * * The next day, Nelsen's attorney wrote to Hilton's attorney informing him that Nelsen had decided not to sell the farm. Hilton then instructed his attorney to bring this action, which was filed on May 17, 1976.

Meanwhile, some time in April 1976, Phelps told Hilton that Nelsen's mortgage was about to be foreclosed. Hilton * * * successfully bid $67,-000—the amount of the unpaid balance on the mortgage—and purchased it subject to the 1–year right of redemption. Nelsen continued to occupy and work the land throughout 1976.

On May 23, 1977, pursuant to a conversation with a law partner of Nelsen's attorney, defendant Lyle Mandt agreed to purchase the Nelsen farm by redeeming the mortgage. * * * The Nelsens gave a quitclaim deed to Mandt and Mandt gave Nelsen an option to repurchase the property by January 1, 1978, for $121,074.05. Nelsen farmed the property in 1977.

The trial court sitting without a jury found that the Nelsens had breached the contract, ordered specific performance for the plaintiff against both the Nelsens and Mandt, and ordered that plaintiff be allowed to deduct from the downpayment in the original agreement the sum of $39,600, representing the fair and reasonable rental value of the property during the years 1976 and 1977.

* * *

---

1. The contract provided that "all * * * parties who have signed said contract agree that in the event should [sic] any said party refuse to close said contract, that Purchaser shall have available to him the remedy of specific performance or damages at law, at Purchaser's option."

2. SPECIFIC PERFORMANCE

Because the trial court's factual findings are reasonably supported by the evidence, they are not clearly erroneous and must be affirmed. Rule 52.01, Rules of Civil Procedure. Thus, we affirm the findings that the sellers materially breached the contract by their repudiation by letter on April 28, 1976, and their failure to close on May 1, 1976. However, it does not automatically follow that Hilton is entitled to specific performance of the contract, as ordered by the trial court. * * * In this case, a combination of the following factors convinces us that ordering specific performance is not an appropriate exercise of the court's equitable discretion:

(a) Purchaser Hilton did not intend to farm or homestead on the land, but rather intended to rent the property to a tenant farmer. Because any equivalent parcel of Minnesota farmland would serve these investment purposes, the uniqueness of the land is less weighty here as a factor calling for specific performance, especially if damages at law are an adequate remedy for the sellers' breach. In this case, the plaintiff has not detrimentally changed his position in reliance upon the sellers' performance to such an extent that specific performance is necessary or a damages remedy inadequate. The plaintiff may easily be compensated in damages for losses occasioned by this contractual relationship.

(b) There were elements of unfairness, or at least overreaching, in the contract itself. * * *

First, the contract lacked mutuality of remedy. Although that alone will not render specific performance inequitable, mutuality is one element which may be considered in determining whether to award specific performance. * * *

Here, according to the contractual provisions, the sellers' only remedy in the event of default by the purchaser would be the retention of $2,500 earnest money as liquidated damages. If the sellers defaulted, however, the purchaser could elect either specific performance or damages as a remedy. * * *

Second, the contract was subject to unilateral termination by the purchaser for a variety of reasons * * *.

Third, the payment terms evidenced overreaching by the purchaser. Of a total contract price of $180,000, the purchaser need only pay $2,500 into escrow as an earnest deposit and $49,700 cash upon closing—a total of $52,200 paid when the title transferred. The remaining $127,800 was to be financed by a part-purchase money note secured by a 10-year mortgage or deed of trust to the sellers. Prior to the end of the 10th year, the sellers' only return would be interest on the unpaid amount at 7 percent annually plus $2,000 a year in the 6th through 9th year of the contract. Thus, apart from interest, the sellers would receive during 9 years and 11 months only $60,200 toward property worth $180,000, while the purchaser would be receiving rental income on the land which, the trial court found, had a median rental value of approximately $20,000 per year. * * *

(c) The testimony in evidence indicated that the basic terms of the contract were misunderstood by the defendants. Significantly, the defendant-sellers were not represented by an attorney in negotiations with plaintiff-purchaser. The contract, which was lengthy and complex, was drafted and explained to the Nelsens by the plaintiff's attorney. * * * Only when the Nelsens consulted an attorney for assistance in clearing the title did they learn that the contract was not a contract for deed, as they had thought it was. The Nelsens erroneously understood that May 1, 1975, was the *only* closing date under the contract. They also thought, incorrectly, that Hilton's initial payment would pay off their mortgage. * * *

(d) Circumstances have arisen since the formation of the contract which further undermine the fairness of specific performance. * * * Third-party interests have intervened by way of Mandt's redemption of the property. Mandt now has legal and equitable title to the property. There was no finding that Mandt had personal knowledge of Hilton's rights under the October 4, 1974, contract. The contract for sale was not recorded, and Mandt testified that he had no knowledge of the contract. If he did not, specific performance of the contract would necessarily be subject to Mandt's property rights.

In light of the totality of the circumstances discussed above, we conclude that, as a matter of law, this contract is not one which the court in its equitable discretion may specifically enforce. Plaintiff must seek his remedy at law. We do not mean to suggest that any one of the factors discussed above is necessarily sufficient to render specific performance inequitable. Considering them together, however, we feel compelled to the decision we have reached, which is necessarily limited to the narrow facts presented here.

3. DAMAGES

Having concluded that the contract is not specifically enforceable and that plaintiff's remedy is at law, we need not reach the question of whether an allowance for lost rents was properly awarded by the trial court, which sat in equity rather than at law. Accordingly, we reverse the judgment and, because the first trial was in equity, remand this case for a new trial at law on the question of damages.[5] The parties, of course, may demand a jury trial on this issue.[6]

Affirmed in part, reversed in part, and remanded.

---

5. The measure of damages was not argued before the trial court or on appeal. However, without so holding, we observe that the measure of damages appears to be the difference between the market value of the land on May 1, 1976, and the contract price of $180,000, plus such additional expenses as the purchaser may reasonably have incurred to that date in a bona fide attempt to comply with the contract.

6. The record is not clear as to whether jury trial was waived on all issues below. Regardless, our decision that the contract is not specifically enforceable requires a new opportunity to elect a jury trial.

NOTES

1. Plaintiffs-purchasers and defendants-vendors, husband and wife, enter into an otherwise enforceable contract for the sale of a house. Between the date of the contract and the closing date, the medical condition of defendant wife—spinal muscular atrophy (SMA)—worsens. Defendants then argue that the wife's deteriorating medical condition should excuse specific performance of the contract. In refusing specific performance, the court stated:

> This court finds that defendants will suffer great hardship if the contract is enforced because [wife's] health is rapidly deteriorating and the further physical and mental exhaustion of the move may exacerbate her condition. Although specific performance is the usual remedy for a breach of a land sale contract where both parties' conduct has been fair and just, it is not the appropriate remedy in this case. * * * Since the contract was signed, defendant-wife has gotten weaker and frequently falls. The court finds the factual circumstance * * * compelling. She spends her time in a wheelchair when not in bed. He left arm is completely paralyzed and her right arm is so weak that she can no longer take care of her basic daily living activities, such as dressing and bathing. * * * This court finds that these drastic changes to her health require relief from the obligations under the contract so that she may remain in familiar surroundings and avoid the additional stress of a move that could exacerbate her deterioration.

> This court also finds that plaintiffs are entitled to reimbursement for costs associated with the breach of contract. Compensatory damages are intended to recompense the injured claimant for losses due to the breach. In other words, the innocent party should receive the benefit of the bargain. * * * If the buyer subsequently purchased another property financed at a higher interest rate, [the interest rate differential] might be a proper factor in fixing damages. Accordingly, this court will consider documentation of interest rates on their subsequent mortgage, as well as out of pocket expenses and attorney's fees associated with the breach, so that this court can award costs accordingly.

Kilarjian v. Vastola, 379 N.J.Super. 277, 285–86, 877 A.2d 372, 377 (2004).

2. For scholarly commentary on specific performance and damages as alternative remedies for the breach of a real estate contract, see Melvin Aaron Eisenberg, *The Bargain Principle and Its Limits*, 95 Harv. L. Rev. 741, 748–85 (1982); Daniel A. Farber, *Contract Law and Modern Economic Theory*, 78 Nw. U. L. Rev. 303 (1983); Robert Kratovil, *The Restatement (Second) of Contracts and the UCC: A Real Property Law Perspective*, 16 J. Marshall L. Rev. 287, 290–99 (1983) (discussing section 2–302 of the Uniform Commercial Code); Alan Schwartz, *The Case for Specific Performance*, 89 Yale L.J. 271, 273, 298–303, 306 (1979) ("defenses to requests for specific performance that rest on unfairness of contract terms or prices and that differ from the defenses in actions at law should be eliminated"); Peter J. Shedd, *Real Estate Transactions and the Principles of Unconscionability*, 13 Real Est. L.J. 334 (1985).

LAZY M RANCH, LTD. v. TXI OPERATIONS, LP

Court of Appeals of Texas, Austin, 1998.
978 S.W.2d 678.

POWERS, JUSTICE.

* * *

TXI wished to explore a portion of the Lazy M land for sand, gravel, and other construction materials and to obtain an option right to mine the materials if prospects proved favorable. In September 1995 the company began negotiations with Dr. George Morris, Jr., the owner of Lazy M.

In February 1996 Dr. Morris informed TXI of the creation of Lazy M Ranch, Ltd., ("Lazy M"), a limited partnership. Dr. Morris was president of Lazy M's sole general partner, Lazy M Management, L.L.C. Ownership of the ranch had been transferred to the partnership. At this time, Dr. Morris was suffering from a serious illness but continued to negotiate the lease on behalf of Lazy M.

On April 1, 1996, TXI and Dr. Morris (representing Lazy M) executed a written contract. The contract required TXI to pay Lazy M $2,000 for the right to explore by conducting subsurface tests on a part of Lazy M land—1,669 acres specifically described in the contract by metes and bounds. For the same consideration, the contract gave TXI an exclusive and irrevocable option to lease 300 of the 1,669 acres to mine subsurface materials. To exercise the option right, the contract required TXI to (1) give Lazy M written notice of its election within six months of the April 1 contract and (2) tender $98,000 to Lazy M. TXI paid the required $2,000 and began exploration under the contract.

Dr. Morris died in August 1996. On September 27, 1996, TXI attempted to exercise its option by delivering the required written notice accompanied by a $98,000 bank check. Dr. Morris's son, George Morris, III, who had succeeded his father as president of Lazy M Management, L.L.C., refused to lease any of the land to TXI. He returned TXI's check with a letter explaining that Lazy M would not lease the land as promised because TXI had breached the contract by entering upon and testing Lazy M's land outside the 1,669 acres specified in the contract. Morris further stated he believed TXI had unfairly procured the agreement by taking advantage of the ailing Dr. Morris.

TXI sued Lazy M for specific performance of its obligation to give a lease. The trial court granted TXI's summary-judgment motion and awarded TXI specific performance. Lazy M brings [three] points of error: (1) there exists a genuine issue of material fact as to whether Dr. Morris had the mental capacity to enter into a binding contract at the time the contract was executed; (2) TXI materially breached the contract before attempting to exercise the option, thereby excusing Lazy M from performance; [and] (3) TXI is not entitled in equity to specific performance because TXI had "unclean hands" in the transaction * * *.

* * *

MATERIAL BREACH EXCUSING LAZY M FROM PERFORMANCE

The parties do not dispute that TXI gave timely notice of its election to lease the property described in the contract; they do not dispute that TXI tendered the required $98,000. In its second point of error Lazy M contends the summary judgment is nevertheless erroneous because the record contained genuine issues of material fact. These pertain to Lazy M's affirmative defense that TXI materially breached the contract while Lazy M's obligation to deliver a lease remained executory. * * *

* * *

It is generally said that breach of a "dependent" covenant of the contract may give the non-breaching party an election to terminate the contract while breach of an "independent" covenant will not; in the latter case, the non-breaching party may only recover for the breach in a separate cause of action. *See, e.g.,* Investors' Utility Corp. v. Challacombe, 39 S.W.2d 175, 178 (Tex.Civ.App.—Waco 1931, no writ). It is also said that whether a covenant is dependent or independent depends on the parties' intention at the time the contract is made. *See, e.g.,* John R. Ray & Sons, Inc. v. Stroman, 923 S.W.2d 80, 86 (Tex.App.—Houston [14th Dist.] 1996, writ denied). The parties' intention is, however, not always discernable from the contract language and the parties often neglect entirely to consider whether they intend a particular covenant to be dependent or independent. For that reason, "it is better to drop any talk about the intention of the parties when they express none and rest doctrines of [constructive dependence] solely on their fairness—a quite sufficient basis." 6 Williston on Contracts § 825 (3d ed.1962).

In the present case, the parties' contract expressly limits the ranch area that TXI would be permitted to explore. By agreeing to this restriction, TXI impliedly covenanted not to explore outside the restricted area. [The court found that the facts showed "prima facie a material breach" of that covenant.] Nothing in the contract language expressly indicates, however, whether the parties intended the implied covenant to be dependent or independent. We turn then to the question of fairness as suggested by Williston.

* * *

The following factors * * * suggest that it would be unreasonable, inequitable, and oppressive to regard the breach as pertaining merely to an independent covenant * * *.

The Morris affidavit shows prima facie that TXI's trespasses were intentional and repeated over several protests by Lazy M. In addition to injuries to the surface of land outside the restricted area, TXI obtained information about the geology of the subsurface of that land—information that belonged to Lazy M and information that TXI acquired in violation of the contract and without any right whatever. This is distinctly unlike a simple case of surface trespass and the repair of any surface injury for which reasonable compensation may be calculated and paid. The record does not show that TXI made any reasonable assurances regarding a cure for its wrongs or the injuries it inflicted on Lazy M, including compensation for any non-tangible injuries resulting from the sub-surface information it obtained. The factor of good faith and fair dealing weighs most heavily against TXI in light of its repeated testing of areas outside the area specified in the contract over Lazy M's repeated objections. Nothing in the record refutes Morris's affidavit declaration that "[i]n the sand and gravel business, the data from testing and coring is valuable" and that TXI "stole valuable information about the subsurface potential of the ranch." In light of these factors, we believe it would be inequitable, unreasonable, and oppressive to construe as an independent covenant TXI's implied covenant not to explore outside the area delimited in the contract.

* * *

For the foregoing reasons, we sustain Lazy M's second point of error.

SPECIFIC PERFORMANCE

* * *

Lazy M argues that even if its failure to honor the option agreement entitled TXI to some relief, perhaps damages, TXI is not entitled to the equitable remedy of specific performance because it comes to the court with "unclean hands." Under the doctrine of unclean hands, a court may refuse to grant equitable relief to a plaintiff who has been guilty of unlawful or inequitable conduct regarding the issue in dispute. See Right to Life Advocates, Inc. v. Aaron Women's Clinic, 737 S.W.2d 564, 571 (Tex.App.—Houston [14th Dist.] 1987, writ denied).

TXI contends that the doctrine of "unclean hands" cannot apply in the present circumstances. According to TXI, even if it breached the lease by trespassing outside the restricted area, its inequitable conduct was unrelated to the issue in dispute. See Axelson v. McIlhany, 798 S.W.2d 550, 556 (Tex.1990) (doctrine of unclean hands held inapplicable where inequitable conduct unrelated to relief sought by petitioners).

We do not believe TXI's trespass was unrelated to TXI's attempt to enforce the contract. We agree the doctrine of unclean hands does not apply when a party is guilty of inequitable conduct with regard to a transaction separate from the one in dispute. 1st Coppell Bank v. Smith, 742 S.W.2d 454, 464 (Tex.App.—Dallas 1987, no writ). But in this case, the issue in dispute is whether TXI is entitled to enforce rights embodied in the very contract that TXI allegedly violated.

> The equitable maxim as to clean hands "is confined to misconduct in regard to, or at all events connected with, the matter in litigation, so that it has in some measure affected the equitable relations subsisting between the two parties, and arising out of the transaction; it does not extend to any misconduct, however gross,

which is unconnected with the matter in litigation, and with which the opposite party has no concern."

* * *

The rule does not go so far as to prohibit a court of equity from giving its aid to a bad or faithless man or a criminal. The dirt upon his hands must be his bad conduct in the transaction complained of. If he is not guilty of inequitable conduct toward the defendant in that transaction, his hands are as clean as the court can require.

2 Pomeroy's Equity Jurisprudence § 399 at 95–96 (5th ed.1941) * * *. It may not reasonably be contended that TXI's alleged misconduct did not grow out of or is unconnected to the lease-option transaction, or that it is a matter with which Lazy M has no concern. We hold accordingly.

The points of error discussed above are dispositive of the appeal.

We reverse the summary judgment and remand the cause to the trial court.

NOTES

1. The defense of unclean hands is an equitable defense, suggesting that the plaintiff who is not entitled to equitable relief might nevertheless be able to obtain legal relief. Consider, for example, the following passage from Finnerty v. Reed, 2 Mass.App.Ct. 846, 312 N.E.2d 578 (1974) (action by seller of real estate for specific performance of a written agreement):

The evidence shows that the plaintiff's son, who acted as the plaintiff's agent for the sale, admitted that the defendant specifically asked him if there were restrictions on the lot, that at that time he knew of the restriction in the deed to the plaintiff's predecessor in title which barred issuance of a building permit until the lot had been "approved for an individual sewerage disposal system by the Board of Health," and that he did not disclose the existence of that restriction in response to the defendant's inquiry. The unsuitability of the lot in this respect could and did in fact thwart what the plaintiff's son knew to be the defendant's sole purpose in purchasing the lot. The evidence falls short of showing misrepresentation of a material fact; but even if we assume that the contract is good at law, it does not follow that it will be specifically enforced in equity. It is a universally recognized principle, that a court of equity will not decree specific performance of a contract when it would be inequitable to do so. Specific performance may be refused when a contract is "hard and unreasonable, so that enforcement of it would be oppressive to the defendant, or where there has been [a] misrepresentation by the plaintiff on a material point, or other unfair conduct, although it may not be sufficient to invalidate the contract...." Chute v. Quincy, 156 Mass. 189, 191, 30 N.E. 550, 551 (1892). See also Shikes v. Gabelnick, 273 Mass. 201, 206–207, 173 N.E. 495 (1930); Freedman v. Walsh, 331 Mass. 401, 406, 119 N.E.2d 419 (1954). As the plaintiff has not, in our opinion, shown himself to be entitled to specific performance, the judge was not in error in dismissing the bill. * * *.

Id. at 847, 312 N.E.2d at 579; *accord* Carmen v. Fox Film Corp., 269 F. 928 (2d Cir.1920); Stachnik v. Winkel, 394 Mich. 375, 230 N.W.2d 529 (1975).

Compare John P. Frank & John Endicott, *Defenses in Equity and "Legal Rights,"* 14 La. L. Rev. 380 (1954).*

> The books are full of expressions to the effect that the law will do dirty work which a "court of conscience" is too refined to touch. Here are typical examples: * * * "Even though the plaintiff's conduct has not been such as to cause a court to refuse him a judgment for damages, * * * it may be such as to disentitle him to the remedy of specific performance." * * *

> The precise question for analysis here is whether the distinction in law implicit in these quotations is also a distinction in fact. The rule of law obviously contemplates that there may be a legal remedy which survives a rejection of the equitable claim. Does such a remedy actually exist?

> To find out the practical value of that remedy at law, we have examined 350 reported cases in which the defenses of clean hands, inadequacy of consideration, hardship and misrepresentation have been raised in the past ten years. * * *

> Of the 350 "pure conscience" cases, 150 most clearly turned on clean hands, inadequacy of consideration, hardship or misrepresentation. Letters were sent to counsel of record inquiring as to the subsequent history of these 150 cases. Fifty-six responses were received. While the sample is too small to permit of firm conclusions, the results are sufficiently suggestive to be worth reporting as a possible starting point for analysis by others.

> The fifty-six surviving cases were utterly diverse, involving specific performance and injunction, tort and contract. Yet in one respect they were uniform: In every instance, an equitable defeat was a total defeat. In no instance did the defeated claimant gain anything by virtue of any reserved legal rights; in only two instances did he so much as try.

Id. at 380–81.

2. A few courts have applied the unclean hands doctrine in actions for damages. Three arguments support these decisions: "(1) the merger of law and equity; (2) equitable and legal remedies are many times equally harsh; and (3) conduct not warranting an equitable remedy does not warrant a legal remedy either." Note, *The Application of the Clean Hands Doctrine in Damages Actions*, 57 Notre Dame L. Rev. 673 (1982).

3. To what extent do you believe the court in *Lazy M Ranch* was influenced by the claim that Dr. Morris lacked mental capacity, even though the court never evaluated it?

FITZGERALD v. O'CONNELL

Supreme Court of Rhode Island, 1978.
120 R.I. 240, 386 A.2d 1384.

KELLEHER, JUSTICE.

This is an appeal from the denial by a Superior Court justice, after a hearing, of the plaintiffs' complaint seeking specific performance of a

---

* Reprinted with permission of Louisiana Law Review.

contract to sell real estate. The trial justice based his denial on his findings that the plaintiffs were guilty of laches by not acting with reasonable diligence to secure their rights and dismissed their complaint.

In an undated, sealed agreement the Fitzgeralds agreed to purchase, and Gertrude S. O'Connell to sell, a parcel of unimproved real estate on Binney Street in Newport, Rhode Island. The parcel abuts other real estate owned by the Fitzgeralds, who wished to enlarge their own property. Under the terms of the purchase and sales agreement, the purchase price was $500. The Fitzgeralds paid $250 upon execution of the agreement and were to pay the balance upon delivery of the deed at the closing, which was to take place on October 24, 1963.

Gertrude O'Connell died on July 19, 1963, and by will devised an undivided two-thirds interest in the property to her son, Jay K. O'Connell, and his wife, defendant Cathleen D. O'Connell, as joint tenants. The remaining one-third interest was devised to her two granddaughters, defendants Linda O'Connell and Anne O'Connell.

Sometime in September 1963, the Fitzgeralds forwarded a check for $250, representing the balance of the purchase price, to Jay O'Connell who, along with his wife Cathleen, was acting as co-executor of his mother's estate. This check was never cashed. Mr. O'Connell later advised the Fitzgeralds that he was going to rip up the check as a gift to their newly born twins.

Approximately a year later the Fitzgeralds asked Mr. O'Connell when the conveyance could be completed. Mr. O'Connell replied that his mother's estate was "a little mixed up" and that he would let them know when the transfer could be taken care of. The Fitzgeralds' attorney inquired of the attorney representing the estate of Gertrude O'Connell as to when the estate would be in a position to carry out the purchase and sales agreement and was advised that the conveyance would have to wait until the probate proceedings were completed. Two years later, in October 1966, Mr. O'Connell died, and his wife Cathleen, as joint tenant, acquired his interest in the real estate. After waiting a "respectful" period of time, the Fitzgeralds contacted Cathleen O'Connell, advised her of the purchase and sales agreement, and asked to be notified when the estate was settled. According to the Fitzgeralds, Mrs. O'Connell did not dispute the agreement in any way.

The first and final account for the estate of Gertrude S. O'Connell was allowed on July 9, 1970. The lien on the property of the State of Rhode Island for inheritance taxes due from the estate of Jay K. O'Connell was not discharged until February 21, 1972.

Sometime later the Fitzgeralds learned from Cathleen O'Connell that she planned to sell the real estate to a third party. In July 1972, the

Fitzgeralds filed a copy of the purchase and sales agreement in the Newport Land Evidence Records. This litigation was commenced in October 1973.

There is no dispute that, but for the O'Connells' defense of laches, the Fitzgeralds would be entitled to a decree ordering the O'Connells to specifically perform the contract of sale. * * *

In their answer the O'Connells asserted that the claim was barred by both the statute of limitations and by the doctrine of laches. In his introductory remarks at the beginning of the trial, the trial justice stated that the defense of laches was really the only issue. In his view the defense of the statute of limitations did not apply "because this is an instrument under seal." Presumably, he meant to say that the general 6–year statute of limitations contained in G.L.1956 (1969 Reenactment) § 9–1–13 did not apply and that the 20–year period applicable to instruments under seal would not bar this claim. * * *

We must first resolve the issue of whether the doctrine of laches may be applied at all. Since 1912 an unquestioned (and perhaps ignored) rule of Rhode Island law has been that suits in equity to compel the conveyance of property are diligently brought if they are brought within the period of limitation fixed by statute. Knowles v. Knowles, 33 R.I. 491, 494, 82 A. 257, 258 (1912). There we held that the defense of laches was "not open" since the suit was brought within the period of limitation. Since the purchase and sales agreement involved here is one under seal, the *Knowles* doctrine would indicate that the Fitzgeralds' claim could never be barred by laches before 1983—regardless of the prejudice to the O'Connells. Not only is this result contrary to what was the majority view at common law prior to the merger of law and equity[4] but insofar as we have been able to discover, it is not followed by any jurisdiction today, save our own. * * *

Having in mind the mid–1960 adoption of the Superior Court Rules of Civil Procedure with its accompanying merger of law and equity and the abolition of the forms of action, whatever may have been the validity or wisdom of the *Knowles* principle, we believe it should no longer be followed. Today in this jurisdiction there is but one form of action, a "civil action," Super.R.Civ.P. 2, and "all civil actions" now have an applicable statute of limitation. Section 9–1–13. Thus, were we to continue to apply the *Knowles* rule, the doctrine of laches could never be invoked: the defense would be unavailable if the statute had not run and unnecessary if it had. Accordingly, we overrule *Knowles* and hold that the defense of laches may be asserted in civil actions seeking equitable relief notwithstanding the fact that the period fixed by the applicable statute of limitations has not expired.

---

4. 2 Lawrence, Equity Jurisprudence § 1038 at 1123 (1929); 2 Pomeroy, Equity Jurisprudence § 419(b) at 175 (5th ed. 1941); Pomeroy, Specific Performance of Contracts § 403 at 855–56, note (e) (3d ed. 1926); Re, Cases and Materials on Equity and Equitable Remedies 765 (5th ed. 1975).

Whether the Fitzgeralds were guilty of laches in prosecuting this cause of action is a question of fact and, in the first instance, one which is committed to the sound discretion of the trial justice. But such discretion is not unlimited and will be reviewed by this court for an abuse thereof. As we have noted many times, mere lapse of time does not constitute laches. It is only where unexplained and inexcusable delay has the effect of visiting prejudice on the other party that the defense may be successfully invoked. This principle was best stated in Chase v. Chase, 20 R.I. 202, 203–04, 37 A. 804, 805 (1897):

> Laches, in legal significance, is not mere delay, but delay that works a disadvantage to another. So long as parties are in the same condition, it matters little whether one presses a right promptly or slowly, within limits allowed by law; but when, knowing his rights, he takes no steps to enforce them until the condition of the other party has, in good faith, become so changed that he cannot be restored to his former state, if the right be then enforced, delay becomes inequitable and operates as an estoppel against the assertion of the right. The disadvantage may come from loss of evidence, change of title, intervention of equities and other causes, but when a court sees negligence on one side and injury therefrom on the other, it is a ground for denial of relief.

In order to bar the Fitzgeralds' claim because of its staleness, the burden was on the O'Connells to show that the claim was " 'first asserted after an unexplained delay of such great length as to render it difficult or impossible for the court to ascertain the truth of the matters in controversy and do justice between the parties, or as to create a presumption against the existence or validity of the claim, or a presumption that it has been abandoned or satisfied.' " Lombardi v. Lombardi, 90 R.I. at 210, 156 A.2d at 913. While the Fitzgeralds' delay in this case was certainly lengthy (10 years), it was not without explanation. The trial justice, in his decision, implied that the Fitzgeralds had adequately explained the reason why they had not brought suit on the contract from October 1963 to July 1970, the date Gertrude O'Connell's estate was closed. Throughout this period the Fitzgeralds and their attorney made repeated requests of the O'Connells to complete performance of the agreement. Each time they were assured that performance would be forthcoming and were asked to wait until the estate of Gertrude O'Connell was settled. A delay is excusable where it is induced or caused by the adverse party, as by acknowledging the justness of the claim and promising to make good thereon. * * *

The trial justice was of the opinion that the Fitzgeralds should have acted to protect their rights once Gertrude O'Connell's estate was closed in July 1970, even though he acknowledged that the inheritance tax lien of Jay O'Connell's estate remained a cloud on the title until February 1972. Once the inheritance tax lien was cleared in February 1972, the Fitzgeralds waited almost a year and a half (October 1973) before instituting this action. The trial justice apparently felt this year-and-a-half delay to be both unexplained and prejudicial.

We need not decide whether the Fitzgeralds' delay in bringing suit was unexplained and inexcusable, for we believe the O'Connells have failed to show how they have been prejudiced by this delay. The trial justice found that the O'Connells had been prejudiced by two factors: by the payment of $728.48 in property taxes since 1963 and by the increase in the value of the property.[6] The trial justice's reliance on the payment of taxes as sufficient evidence of prejudice is most curious, since the Fitzgeralds offered to reimburse the O'Connells for any taxes paid on the property prior to the commencement of the suit. In short, the Fitzgeralds stood willing to alleviate this prejudicial element, and the trial justice could well have conditioned the grant of specific performance on this fact. * * *

In addition to the taxes which had been paid, the trial justice noted that "there might even be some prejudice going to the present value of the property." Since the Fitzgeralds' delay in asserting their rights from 1963 to 1970 was induced, at least in part, by Jay O'Connell's assurances that performance would be forthcoming as soon as his mother's estate was settled, only the rise in value from 1970 to 1973 could be considered in assessing prejudice. As noted above, no evidence was presented indicating the fair market value of the property prior to 1972. Even assuming the property appreciated from 1970 to 1973, or even from 1963 to 1973, it is hard to see how the O'Connells have been prejudiced thereby. The mere fact that the value of the property contracted for has increased in value will not warrant a refusal to carry out its terms in the absence of circumstances indicating fraud or bad faith. Humble Oil & Refining Co. v. Lennon, 94 R.I. 509, 517, 182 A.2d 306, 311 (1962).

In the past, typical examples of prejudice that have supported the defense of laches have been the loss of evidence, a change of title, or the death of a key witness. * * * Lister v. Lister, 47 R.I. 366, 133 A. 437 (1926). Evidence that a defendant expended sums of money in constructing improvements has also been held to be sufficient prejudice to support a finding of laches. Motta v. Gouveia, 84 R.I. 149, 122 A.2d 159. Where the subject matter is speculative and subject to rapid fluctuation in value, such as oil and mining properties, the doctrine of "speculative delay" may bar a claim to ownership if the claimant asserts his interest only after the risk has passed and the value of the property has become apparent. West Los Angeles Institute for Cancer Research v. Mayer, 366 F.2d 220, 228 (9th Cir.1966); McIver v. Norman, 187 Or. 516, 546–47, 213 P.2d 144, 153 (1949).

While there is no hard and fast rule for determining what constitutes sufficient prejudice to invoke the doctrine of laches, we believe the trial

---

6. A real estate agent in Newport, Rhode Island, testified that, in his opinion, the $2,820 assessed value of the property also represented the fair market value of the property. No evidence was presented regarding the fair market value of the parcel in 1963. The $2,820 figure was established in 1972, when the entire city was reevaluated.

justice erred in the instant case. The O'Connells have neither suffered the loss of material evidence nor constructed improvements upon the property. No rights of third parties have been called into question. Nothing in the record suggests that the Fitzgeralds awaited the rise in value of the property before asserting their claim. To the contrary, the Fitzgeralds have, since 1963, stood ready, willing, and able to perform their part of the bargain in order to extend the boundaries of their homestead. In short, the fact that the value of the property has appreciated does not in and of itself convert delay into laches. * * *

The plaintiffs' appeal is sustained, the judgment appealed from is reversed, and the case is remanded to the Superior Court with direction to enter judgment for the plaintiffs.

NOTES

1. For a case that is in accord with *Fitzgerald*, see Thirty–Four Corp. v. Sixty–Seven Corp., 15 Ohio St.3d 350, 474 N.E.2d 295 (1984). On the other hand, there are a significant number of cases in which laches has defeated specific performance. *See* Wagner v. Estate of Fox, 717 N.E.2d 195, 204 (Ind.Ct.App.1999) ("[T]he [purchasers] were aware of the legal problems surrounding the Fox farm. Rather than intervening in [this litigation], they chose to sit on the sidelines [for seven years] while the seller made significant improvements to the farm. Because the land has significantly increased [by at least 100%] in value, the sellers * * * would be prejudiced under the purchase agreements. Thus, the trial court did not err in applying the doctrine of laches."); Gaglione v. Cardi, 120 R.I. 534, 388 A.2d 361 (1978) (property rose in value from $20,000 in 1966 to $100,000 in 1972; "plaintiff's unexplained delay in bringing this suit, coupled with the dramatic rise in the value of the parcel, makes this case a proper one for invoking the doctrine of laches").

2. When the plaintiff seeks specific performance of an option to purchase real estate, the courts are more apt to invoke the defense of laches and deny equitable relief, as illustrated by Schroeder v. Schlueter, 85 Ill.App.3d 574, 41 Ill.Dec. 12, 407 N.E.2d 204 (1980):

> The parties entered into an agreement dated March 31, 1969 which granted to the plaintiff and his former wife, the exclusive right to purchase approximately 200 acres of farmland for the sum of $70,000, conditioned upon the delivery of a notice of election to purchase by "12 noon on December 30, 1969." The evidence was in conflict as to whether this deadline had been met or missed, and it appears no further action was ever taken to exercise the option. * * * The complaint which initiated this action was filed on March 2, 1978, and at no time prior to that date did the plaintiff assert his rights under the contract * * *.

> * * *

> The limiting doctrine known as laches has been defined repeatedly in this state as such neglect or omission to assert a right, taken in conjunction with a lapse of time of greater or lesser duration and other circum-

stances causing prejudice to an adverse party, as will operate to bar relief in equity. * * *

* * *

* * * [A] marked appreciation or depreciation in the value of the property which is the object of controversy, such that the granting of relief would itself work an inequity, is evidence of injury or prejudice justifying the invocation of laches. * * * We believe the rule to be especially applicable where an option contract is concerned because time is a material element of the consideration running to the optionee. * * * In regard to the right at equity to have specific performance of a contract of sale, unreasonable delay coupled with a material advance in value is fatal for equity will not allow a purchaser to remain in the wings gambling on the future rise in price. * * *

In the case at bar, * * * appellees made significant improvements to the land by clearing wooded areas, improving and monitoring soil conditions and drainage characteristics, all in the interest of their farming operations. Appellant was well aware of these actions since he occupied a portion of the acreage concerned. * * * Meanwhile, its total worth increased from the purchase price of $70,000 to $500,000. * * * It has been held that a party is guilty of laches, which ordinarily will defeat whatever rights he may have, when he remains passive while another party "incurs risk, enters into obligations, or makes expenditures for improvements or taxes." The present facts are an excellent illustration of the rule. * * *

Id. at 575–77, 41 Ill.Dec. at 13–14, 407 N.E.2d at 205–07.

3. Laches is also more likely to be a successful defense to an action for specific performance based upon a contract that expressly declares time to be of the essence. *E.g.*, Wagner v. Estate of Fox, 717 N.E.2d 195 (Ind.Ct.App. 1999); Boyd v. Mercantile–Safe Deposit & Trust Co., 28 Md.App. 18, 344 A.2d 148 (1975).

4. It is often stated that statutes of limitations bar legal relief only unless otherwise expressly provided, and that only laches would operate to bar equitable relief, even though analogous legal relief would be barred by the statute. *See* Blankenship v. Boyle, 329 F.Supp. 1089 (D.D.C.1971); William Q. DeFuniak, Handbook of Modern Equity § 24 (1956). As a practical matter, however, many states have made their statutes of limitation applicable to equity suits, either by express statutory language or by judicial construction. *See, e.g.*, Ludwig v. Scott, 65 S.W.2d 1034 (Mo.1933).

The relationship between the legal defense of the statute of limitations and the equitable defense of laches is discussed in Shell v. Strong, 151 F.2d 909, 911 (10th Cir.1945):

Lapse of time alone does not constitute laches. Delay will not bar relief where it has not worked injury, prejudice, or disadvantage to the defendant or others adversely interested.

Since laches is an equitable defense, its application is controlled by equitable considerations. It cannot be invoked to defeat justice, and it will be applied only where the enforcement of the right asserted will work injustice.

> A court of equity is not bound by the statute of limitations, but, in the absence of extraordinary circumstances, it will usually grant or withhold relief in analogy to the statute of limitations relating to actions at law of like character. Under ordinary circumstances, a suit in equity will not be stayed for laches before, and will be stayed after, the time fixed by the analogous statute, but if unusual conditions or extraordinary circumstances make it inequitable to allow the prosecution of a suit after a briefer, or to forbid its maintenance after a longer, period than that fixed by the analogous statute, a court of equity will not be bound by the statute, but will determine the extraordinary case in accordance with the equities which condition it. When a suit is brought within the time fixed by the analogous statute, the burden is on the defendant to show, either from the face of the complaint or by his answer, that extraordinary circumstances exist which require the application of the doctrine of laches. On the other hand, when the suit is brought after the statutory time has elapsed, the burden is on the complainant to aver and prove circumstances making it inequitable to apply laches to his case.

See also Goodman v. McDonnell Douglas Corp., 606 F.2d 800, 804–05 (8th Cir.1979), *cert. denied*, 446 U.S. 913, 100 S.Ct. 1844, 64 L.Ed.2d 267 (1980).

2. The Equitable Conversion Concept

WILLIAM B. STOEBUCK & DALE A. WHITMAN, THE LAW OF PROPERTY
786–87 (3d ed. 2000).*

During the period between formation and performance of a land sale contract, a variety of events may occur which raise questions about the contract's significance. Some of them have their principal effect on only one of the parties: the death of a party, a judgment obtained against him, or the like. Such events may trigger the operation of legal rules, such as an intestate succession statute or a judgment lien act, which depend on *characterization* of the party's interest as real or personal property. In most American jurisdictions, this characterization is based on the theory of equitable conversion, which holds that once the parties have entered into a contract which equity would specifically enforce, the buyer's interest in the contract is converted into real estate and the seller's interest into personal property. This result is said to follow from the view that equity regards as having been done that which ought to be done, and which equity would order done—namely, the conveyance of the title to the buyer and payment of the price to the seller.[8]

* Reprinted with permission of West Publishing Co.

8. The doctrine's modern form originated with Lord Eldon's opinion in Seaton v. Slade, 7 Ves.Jun. 265 (1802); *see* John L. Davis, *The Origin of the Doctrine of Equitable Conversion by Contract*, 25 Ky.L.Rev. 58 (1936). *See generally* 3 Am.L.Prop. §§ 11.22–.35 (1952); 3A Corbin,

NOTE

The equitable conversion doctrine, if applied literally and consistently, would have a substantial impact on diverse fact situations that have as a common element a contract for the sale of land. How will the doctrine affect the interests of such parties as heirs, devisees and personal representatives when either the vendor or vendee dies prior to the consummation of the contract? How does the doctrine affect creditors of the vendor or vendee? What consequences follow from recognizing the doctrine when there has been a casualty loss prior to contract consummation? Although the equitable conversion principle is relevant to other aspects of land sale contracts (such as dower, condemnation, claims regarding rents and profits, and taxation), space considerations dictate that the following material focus on an examination of equitable conversion in the context of the basic questions posed above.

It should be stressed that courts frequently employ the equitable conversion concept indiscriminately to two distinctly different types of land contracts—the earnest money contract (also known as a "binder" or "marketing contract") and the installment land contract (also known as a "contract for deed" or a "long term land contract"). The earnest money contract, which is the one most frequently encountered in this casebook, is used primarily to establish the parties' rights and liabilities during the period of approximately one or two months between the date of the bargain and the date of closing. On the latter date, title passes to the purchaser, and security agreements, if any, are consummated. The installment land contract is a substitute for the purchase money mortgage. Both instruments enable the seller to finance the unpaid portion of the real estate purchase price. Under an installment land contract, the purchaser normally takes possession and makes monthly installment payments of principal and interest until the principal balance is paid off. The seller retains legal title until the final payment is made, at which time full title is conveyed to the purchaser. Such contracts may be amortized over time periods as short as a year or as long as twenty years or more. In studying the following material, consider whether the equitable conversion concept, assuming its application is appropriate at all, should be employed in both types of land contract settings.

COE v. HAYS

Court of Appeals of Maryland, 1992.
328 Md. 350, 614 A.2d 576.

ROBERT M. BELL, JUDGE.

* * *

In 1979, the decedent Gail A. Lewis ("Lewis") executed his Last Will and Testament. It provided, in pertinent part:

SECOND: Unto Fannie C. Hays, I give *all of my personal property, including but not limited to all furniture and fixtures in my residen-*

Contracts § 667 (1960); Sidney P. Simpson, *Legislative Changes in the Law of Equitable Conversion by Contract: I*, 44 Yale L.J. 559 (1935).

tial home, any motor vehicles which I may own and any monies which I may have at the time of my death. Also, unto the said Fannie C. Hays, I give and devise a life estate in and for the term of her life, in and to a parcel of real estate located in the Hauver's Election District of Frederick County, Maryland, improved with a residential home, containing 8 acres, more or less, and being all and the same parcel of real estate shown and described as parcel #1 in a deed dated December 6th, 1952 from Roscoe G. Wolfe, et al., unto Gail A. Lewis and wife, said deed being recorded in Liber 518, folio 538, among the Land Records of Frederick County, Maryland. * * *

THIRD: All the rest, residue and remainder of my estate, I give unto my children equally. (Emphasis added).

More than eight years after the will was executed, Lewis entered into a contract to sell certain real property he owned for $100,000.00. By his will, the respondent, Ms. Hays, was granted a life estate in that property and, because it was not otherwise bequeathed, the remainder would have passed under the residuary clause. The buyers having paid $1000.00 down, settlement was scheduled on or before June 1, 1988, when the balance was to be paid. The contract required Lewis to convey good and marketable title * * *.

Prior to settlement, Lewis and the buyers executed an addendum to the contract. It stated, "[b]ecause a title problem has arisen and a complete survey is necessary, we hereby extend this contract until a good and marketable title can be transferred." Lewis died on June 19, 1988, before the sale was finalized.

On November 16, 1988, Ms. Hays settled on the property in accordance with her powers as the appointed personal representative. Subsequently, she filed the estate's First and Final Administration Account, which showed the proceeds from the real estate sale being distributed to her as personalty under the doctrine of equitable conversion. Petitioners, the decedent's [four]children and residuary legatees, ("the children"), filed exceptions to the account.

On August 11, 1989, the children filed a Complaint For Construction of Will in the Circuit Court for Washington County. They alleged that the proceeds of the real estate sale should be treated as realty, rather than as personalty, and distributed to them. * * *

In an oral opinion, the trial court found the doctrine of equitable conversion inapplicable. Finding, by virtue of the residuary clause, that Lewis intended his children to receive his real property, it concluded that applying the doctrine would produce a result inconsistent with that intent. Alternatively, the court opined that equitable conversion did not occur "because of the cloud [on the title] that existed at that time." It ordered the proceeds treated as realty, to which, pursuant to the residuary clause, the children were entitled.

Ms. Hays appealed to the Court of Special Appeals * * *.

Reversing, the intermediate appellate court concluded that Lewis' bequest to Ms. Hays encompassed both tangible and intangible personal property. Hays v. Coe, 88 Md.App. 491, 498–99, 595 A.2d 484, 487–88 (1991). Next, being unpersuaded by the trial court's rationale, the court held that, because the contract was executed before Lewis' death, although not settled until afterward, the doctrine of equitable conversion did apply to pass the proceeds of the sale to Ms. Hays. *Id.* at 503, 595 A.2d at 490. * * *

Under the doctrine of equitable conversion, "real estate is considered for certain purposes as personal property and personal property as real estate." Harrison v. Prentice, 183 Md. 474, 479, 38 A.2d 101, 104 (1944). * * *

* * *

Equitable conversion by contract rests on similar, though not identical, underpinnings [as in the case of direction in a will]. In *Himmighoefer,* we explained:

> The legal cliche, that equity treats that as being done which should be done, is the basis of the theory of equitable conversion. Hence, when the vendee contracts to buy and the vendor to sell, though legal title has not yet passed, in equity the vendee becomes the owner of the land, the vendor of the purchase money. In equity the vendee has a real interest and the vendor a personal interest. Equity treats the executory contract as a conversion, whereby an equitable interest in the land is secured to the purchaser for whom the vendor holds the legal title in trust. This is the doctrine of equitable conversion. (citation omitted).

Id., 302 Md. at 278, 487 A.2d at 286 (quoting 8A Thompson, Real Property, § 4447 at 273–74 (Grimes Repl.Vol.1963)). The determination whether real property, the subject of a contract of sale at the testator's death, is realty or personalty depends upon the intent of the testator as well as whether the contract of sale was "valid and binding, free from equitable imperfections, and such as a court of equity will specifically enforce against an unwilling purchaser." Birckner v. Tilch, 179 Md. 314, 323, 18 A.2d 222, 226, *cert. denied,* 314 U.S. 635, 62 S.Ct. 68, 86 L.Ed. 509 (1941). Ordinarily, the conversion occurs when the contract is executed, assuming that the contract of sale is "bona fide made for a valuable consideration," Hampson v. Edelen, 2 H. & J. 64, 66 (1806), and, at that time, is specifically enforceable. Watson v. Watson, 304 Md. at 61, 497 A.2d at 800; *Birckner,* 179 Md. at 323, 18 A.2d at 226. It can not occur later than the seller's death, however; if the contract is not specifically enforceable at that time, no conversion can occur.

Equitable conversion, then, is a theoretical change of property from realty to personalty, or vice versa, in order that the intention of the parties, in the case of a contract of sale, or the directions of the testator, in the case of directions in a will, may be given effect. Harrison, 183 Md. at

479, 38 A.2d at 104–105; Cunningham, The Law of Property § 10.13 at 698–705.

In the case *sub judice*, real property which would pass under the testator's will was also the subject of an executory contract of sale at the time of the testator's death. The will contained no direction for the sale of that real property. *See Cronise,* 47 Md. 433. Nor, but for the executory contract, would there be any question presented concerning how that property would pass under the will. Therefore, if a conversion occurred it was a conversion by contract, and not by will. Its effect, nevertheless, was to determine to whom the proceeds of that sale ought to pass under the will. *Birckner,* 179 Md. at 323, 18 A.2d at 226.

To be specifically enforceable, a contract within the Statute of Frauds ordinarily must be signed by the party to be charged, or by his or her authorized agent and, with reasonable certainty, identify the parties to the contract, the subject matter of the contract, and "the terms and conditions of all the promises constituting the contract and by whom and to whom the promises are made." Forsyth v. Brillhart, 216 Md. 437, 440, 140 A.2d 904, 906–907 (1958). * * *

Moreover, a contract for the sale of real estate is not specifically enforceable against an unwilling purchaser unless the seller of the real estate is able to convey "good and marketable" title. Berlin v. Caplan, 211 Md. 333, 343, 127 A.2d 512, 518 (1956) * * *. When the contract does not prescribe a specific time in which clear title must be delivered, a reasonable time will be presumed to have been meant. Caplan v. Buckner, 123 Md. 590, 601–602, 91 A. 481, 485 (1914). This does not mean, however, that specific performance can be ordered at a time when the required performance could not have been tendered. In *Caplan*, the Court made clear that although the plaintiff could not have delivered the good title for which the purchaser contracted when the contract was executed, "at the time appointed for the settlement, he was ready and able to comply with [his] agreement." *Caplan*, 123 Md. at 601, 91 A. at 485. We quoted Miller's Equity Proc., § 686:

> When the agreement shows that the vendor has not, at the time, a clear and unencumbered title, but is to acquire it, and then convey, if he is able to give a clear title at the time when by the equities of the particular case he is required to execute the conveyance in order to entitle himself to the consideration, there will be no obstacle to a specific enforcement by the vendor. * * *

Review of the contract demonstrates that, not only did the parties intend to contract, but that the terms of the contract, including the duties of the parties, were clear. Were that the complete contract, we could conclude that, as executed, it was specifically enforceable. In the case *sub judice*, however, the addendum to the contract also relates to its specific enforceability; the addendum was made necessary "because a title problem has arisen," which required the extension "until a good and marketable title can be transferred."

* * *

The record is silent as to the status, on June 19, 1988, of the title to the real property. The record did not reveal the nature of the title problem acknowledged in the addendum and whether it had been resolved at that time so that good and marketable title could then have been delivered. Unless, however, good and marketable title could have been conveyed when Lewis died, specific performance of the sale contract could not have been ordered and, consequently, equitable conversion could not have occurred.

* * *

The trial court did not state what cloud it found to exist on the property's title. Nor did it explain why that cloud foreclosed the occurrence of equitable conversion. Since the nature of the cloud on title is critical to the determination of whether equitable conversion occurred, we shall remand to the circuit court for a further explanation of its alternative holdings. The court should identify the cloud on title to which it referred and provide the reasons for its conclusion that the property did not equitably convert upon Lewis' death. * * *

ELDRIDGE, J., concurs in the vacation of the judgment of the Court of Special Appeals.

NOTES

1. Upon remand, the trial court determined that while there was a title defect, it was almost 90 years old and therefore was not serious enough to render the title unmarketable. As a result, equitable conversion occurred to convert the home and eight acres to personalty in favor of Ms. Hays. After yet another appeal, the intermediate appellate court affirmed. *See* Coe v. Hays, 105 Md.App. 778, 661 A.2d 220 (1995). Consequently, after all of this complex and protracted litigation over a $100,000 piece of real estate, the testator's children were losers. They were "done in" by the doctrine of equitable conversion.

2. Suppose a testator executes a will leaving "Blackacre to my son John, the rest, residue and remainder of my estate to my daughter Rebekah." Later, the testator signs an earnest money contract to sell Blackacre. Then, the testator dies before the contract is closed. Courts apply the equitable conversion principle so that the devisee, John, receives no beneficial interest in the real estate. Sometimes courts reach the same result by holding that a devise is revoked or adeemed by a subsequent contract to sell the land. Consider how the following case resolved this issue using both an ademption and an equitable conversion analysis:

[U]nder principles of ademption, it can be said * * * that, had the sale actually closed prior to [the testatrix'] death, the [specific devisee] would have no claim against the proceeds derived from the sale, even in the circumstance where they remained a separate asset of the testatrix, readily identifiable as being the fruits of the transaction.

The issue to be determined is whether the unanticipated death of [the testatrix], coming after execution of a binding contract of sale but before the contract was finally carried out, produces the same result. The chancellor relied on the doctrine of equitable conversion to conclude that the execution of a binding contract of sale transformed [the testatrix'] title to the real estate into personalty consisting essentially of the right to receive the contracted-for price, while the purchaser under the contract became, on equitable considerations, the owner of the property. Thus, insofar as [the testatrix] was concerned, upon the execution of the contract, she no longer owned the exact item devised in the will, which was the real property itself, the result being that the devise was adeemed. This resulted in an ademption of the previous devise of the real property.

In re Estate of Pickett, 879 So.2d 467, 472–73 (Miss.Ct.App.2004). *Accord* Garneski v. Hack, 2004 WL 326951 (Del.Ct.Com.Pl.2004).

Suppose, instead, in the prior hypothetical, the will devising Blackacre to John comes after the testator enters into a contract to sell it, but the testator dies prior to the closing. Does it make sense to apply equitable conversion to John's detriment? Surely the testator must have intended that John get something vis-à-vis Blackacre.

3. Now suppose that the testator is the vendee under a land contract. Here the application of equitable conversion also involves the principle of exoneration. If the vendee has devised land, whether before or after entering into the contract to purchase, and then dies, the devisee under the will receives the vendee-testator's equitable title and the purchase price is paid by the residuary personal estate against which there is a right of exoneration. The result is that the devisee benefits at the expense of the residuary legatees. *See generally* William B. Stoebuck & Dale A. Whitman, The Law of Property § 10.13 (3d ed. 2000).

The results reached by the application of the equitable conversion doctrine in the testate succession situations have been reversed or modified in a number of jurisdictions by statute. Consider how Section 474.440 of the Missouri Revised Statutes (1969) would affect the application of equitable conversion principles:

474.440. *Bond to convey does not revoke devise.*—A bond, covenant or agreement made for a valuable consideration, by a testator, to convey any property devised or bequeathed in any last will previously made, does not constitute a revocation of the previous devise or bequest, either in law or equity; but the property passes by the devise or bequest, subject to the same remedies on the bond, covenant or agreement, for specific performance or otherwise, against the devisees or legatees, as might be had by law against the heirs of the testator, or his next of kin, if the same had descended to them.

4. Now suppose the vendor or vendee dies without a will. "In most states [equitable conversion] is unimportant when the vendor dies intestate, since the heirs and the next-of-kin are typically the same persons taking the

same shares in the property; whether it is seen as realty or personalty is irrelevant." William B. Stoebuck & Dale A. Whitman, The Law of Property 788 (3d ed. 2000). Nevertheless, in a few states, the realty-personalty distinction continues to be important under intestate succession statutes. For example, the Texas statute provides that, where the intestate dies without children, but with a surviving spouse, the latter "shall be entitled to all of the personal estate, and to one-half of the lands of the intestate." Tex. Prob. Code Ann. § 38(b)(2) (Vernon 1980). For an excellent analysis of the equitable conversion concept in the context of the latter statute, see Parson v. Wolfe, 676 S.W.2d 689 (Tex.App.1984).

5. Now we shift our focus from death situations to the rights of creditors of either the vendee or vendor under installment land contracts (most creditor cases involve installment land contracts rather than earnest money contracts). In almost all states, a judgment creates a lien on the real property, but usually not on the personal property, of the judgment debtor. *See* David G. Epstein, Debtor–Creditor Law 46, 52–53 (2d ed. 1980). While the mechanics of obtaining the lien and its effective date vary somewhat, typically the lien applies to all real estate of the judgment debtor in the county in which the judgment is docketed (entered by a court clerk in an appropriate docket book). The time of docketing usually determines lien priority. Consequently, when the judgment debtor is either a purchaser or a vendor under either type of land contract described earlier, the characterization of the judgment debtor's interest as real or personal property can be crucial in determining the rights of the judgment creditor.

First, suppose that a creditor obtains a judgment against an installment land contract vendor. A slight majority of the cases, the equitable conversion concept notwithstanding, treat the vendor's interest as real estate for judgment lien purposes. Under the reasoning of several of these cases, the judgment lien "extends to all of the vendor's interest remaining in the land and binds the land to the extent of the unpaid purchase price." First Security Bank of Idaho v. Rogers, 91 Idaho 654, 429 P.2d 386 (1967). Under this approach, the vendor has a real estate interest because she retains legal title to the land until the contract is fully performed and a deed is delivered to the purchaser. Note, 47 Mo. L. Rev. 328, 331 (1982). A growing minority of courts, however, apply equitable conversion or other theories to treat the vendor's interest as personalty. In order to understand the practical impact of the majority and minority approaches, the following example should be helpful:

> Suppose that an installment contract vendor was entitled to collect $50,000 over the next four years. X then docketed a $20,000 judgment against vendor in a county where the contract land was located. Y then docketed a $40,000 judgment against vendor in the same county. Y holds an execution sale on the judgment and he purchases at the sale for $40,000. Y clearly paid too much. Under the majority rule the vendor's interest is real estate and thus both judgments were liens on that interest. Their relative priority is determined by the date each judgment was docketed. Accordingly, since Y's judgment was docketed later than X's, Y purchased the vendor's interest subject to X's unpaid $20,000 lien. On the other hand, if the foregoing fact situation occurs in a minority jurisdiction, Y is much better off. In such states the vendor's interest is

personalty. As such, a judgment creditor can obtain no interest in it until it is levied upon by the sheriff pursuant to the issuance of a writ of execution. The date of judgment docketing establishes no priority; rather, the first execution sale passes title to the personalty free and clear of any other judgment no matter when it was docketed. Thus, in our example, even though Y's judgment was obtained after X's, Y purchased at the execution sale a title free and clear of any lien in favor of X.

1 Grant S. Nelson & Dale A. Whitman, Real Estate Finance Law 169–70 (5th ed. 2007).

The vendee's situation vis-à-vis his or her judgment creditor is less ambiguous. Almost all states hold that the vendee's interest is real estate for purposes of judgment lien legislation and that a creditor who holds a judgment against the vendee thus obtains a valid lien on the vendee's contract interest. *See* 1 Grant S. Nelson & Dale A. Whitman, Real Estate Finance Law 167 (5th ed. 2007). Courts reach this result either by employing equitable conversion or legislative intent:

> The practical implications of this rule can be illustrated by the following hypothetical: Suppose that a vendee has paid off $40,000 of an installment land contract price of $100,000. The land then has a fair market value free and clear of liens of $100,000. Vendee's creditor then dockets a $15,000 judgment against vendee in a county where the contract land is located. Vendee then borrows $30,000 from mortgagee and gives it a mortgage on the contract land, which mortgage mortgagee promptly records. Vendee then defaults on the mortgage and mortgagee forecloses. Because the judgment against the vendee is a valid lien on the vendee's interest and because it was docketed prior to the execution and recordation of the mortgage, the purchaser at the foreclosure sale will buy the vendee's interest subject to the judgment lien.

* * *

Under the equitable conversion theory, from the time an earnest money or installment land contract is executed, the vendee's interest is considered in equity to be real estate while the vendor's retention of legal title and the right to receive the balance of the purchase price is deemed primarily to be personalty.[4] Other courts eschew the equitable conversion approach and simply hold that the legislature intended that the vendee's interest be treated as real estate for purposes of judgment lien legislation.[5] This statutory construction approach is preferred by these courts because of a concern over the uncertainty of the equitable conversion concept and the implications its application would create for other areas such as devolution at death, wills and trusts.[6]

---

4. Hume, *Real Estate Contracts and the Doctrine of Equitable Conversion in Washington: Dispelling the* Ashford *Cloud*, 7 U.P.S.L.Rev. 233, 240 (1984); * * * Bank of Santa Fe v. Garcia, 102 N.M. 588, 698 P.2d 458 (App.1985); Mutual Building & Loan Association v. Collins, 85 N.M. 706, 516 P.2d 677 (1973); Bartz v. Paff, 95 Wis. 95, 69 N.W. 297 (1896); *cf.*, Westfair Corp. v. Kuelz, 90 Wis.2d 631, 280 N.W.2d 364 (App.1979).

5. Cascade Security Bank v. Butler, 88 Wash.2d 777, 567 P.2d 631 (1977); Joseph v. Donovan, 114 Conn. 79, 157 A. 638 (1931); Hoffman v. Semet, 316 So.2d 649 (Fla.App.1975); Butler v. Wilkinson, 740 P.2d 1244 (Utah 1987); Note, 47 Mo.L.Rev. 328, 321 (1982).

6. *See e.g.*, Cascade Security Bank v. Butler, 88 Wash.2d 777, 567 P.2d 631 (1977).

Id. at 135–36.

6.   Finally, we focus on how equitable conversion can affect the rights of the parties in the casualty loss setting. Suppose that during the executory period of an earnest money contract, a casualty loss occurs that is the fault of neither party. As a result, the property's value or usefulness is diminished. Which of the parties must absorb the risk or sustain the loss? Stated more specifically, must the buyer complete the purchase despite the loss, or may she rescind or at least insist on a reduction of the price? Here, assuming the contract is silent as to this issue, equitable conversion plays an important role in many states. Because the buyer is deemed to own "real estate" from the time of execution of the contract, the loss is imposed on the buyer. She is subject to a decree of specific performance, even though the real estate has been devalued by the loss. Which party had possession at the time of the loss is said to be irrelevant.

BRUSH GROCERY KART, INC. v. SURE FINE MARKET, INC.

Supreme Court of Colorado, en banc, 2002.
47 P.3d 680.

JUSTICE COATS delivered the Opinion of the Court.

* * *

In October 1992 Brush Grocery Kart, Inc. and Sure Fine Market, Inc. entered into a five-year "Lease with Renewal Provisions and Option to Purchase" for real property, including a building to be operated by Brush as a grocery store. Under the contract's purchase option provision, any time during the last six months of the lease, Brush could elect to purchase the property at a price equal to the average of the appraisals of an expert designated by each party.

Shortly before expiration of the lease, Brush notified Sure Fine of its desire to purchase the property and begin the process of determining a sale price. Although each party offered an appraisal, the parties were unable to agree on a final price by the time the lease expired. Brush then vacated the premises, returned all keys to Sure Fine, and advised Sure Fine that it would discontinue its casualty insurance covering the property during the lease. Brush also filed suit, alleging that Sure Fine failed to negotiate the price term in good faith and asking for the appointment of a special master to determine the purchase price. Sure Fine agreed to the appointment of a special master and counterclaimed, alleging that Brush negotiated the price term in bad faith and was therefore the breaching party.

During litigation over the price term, the property was substantially damaged during a hail storm. With neither party carrying casualty insurance, each asserted that the other was liable for the damage. The issue was added to the litigation at a stipulated amount of $60,000. The court appointed a special master pursuant to C.R.C.P. 53 and accepted his appraised value of $375,000. The court then found that under the doctrine of equitable conversion, Brush was the equitable owner of the property and bore the risk of loss. It therefore declined to abate the purchase price or award damages to Brush for the loss.

Brush appealed the loss allocation, and the court of appeals affirmed on similar grounds. * * * Noting that allocation of the risk of loss in circumstances where the vendee is not in possession had not previously been addressed by an appellate court in this jurisdiction, the court of appeals went on to conclude that a "bright line rule" allocating the risk of loss to the vendee, without regard to possession, would best inform the parties of their rights and obligations under a contract for the sale of land. * * *

* * *

The legislature has simply failed to assign the risk of casualty loss during the executory period of a contract for the sale of real property in this or apparently any other statute. Where no statute controls, interests in real property must be determined by reference to the common law. * * *

* * *

The assignment of the risk of casualty loss in the executory period of contracts for the sale of real property varies greatly throughout the jurisdictions of this country. What appears to yet be a slim majority of states, see Randy R. Koenders, Annotation, *Risk of Loss by Casualty Pending Contract for Conveyance of Real Property Modern Cases*, 85 A.L.R.4th 233 (2001), places the risk of loss on the vendee from the moment of contracting, on the rationale that once an equitable conversion takes place, the vendee must be treated as owner for all purposes. *See* Skelly Oil v. Ashmore, 365 S.W.2d 582, 588 (Mo.1963) (criticizing this approach). Once the vendee becomes the equitable owner, he therefore becomes responsible for the condition of the property, despite not having a present right of occupancy or control. In sharp contrast, a handful of other states reject the allocation of casualty loss risk as a consequence of the theory of equitable conversion and follow the equally rigid "Massachusetts Rule," under which the seller continues to bear the risk until actual transfer of the title, absent an express agreement to the contrary. *See, e.g.,* *Skelly Oil*, 365 S.W.2d at 588–89. A substantial and growing number of jurisdictions, however, base the legal consequences of no-fault casualty loss on the right to possession of the property at the time the loss occurs. *Koenders, supra.* This view has found expression in the Uniform Vendor and Purchaser Risk Act and while a number of states have adopted some variation of the Uniform Act, others have arrived at a similar position through the interpretations of their courts. *See, e.g.,* Lucenti v. Cayuga Apartments, 48 N.Y.2d 530, 423 N.Y.S.2d 886, 399 N.E.2d 918, 923–24 (1979) * * *.

* * *

Those jurisdictions that indiscriminately include the risk of casualty loss among the incidents or "attributes" of equitable ownership do so largely in reliance on ancient authority or by considering it necessary for consistent application of the theory of equitable conversion. *See Skelly Oil*, 365 S.W.2d at 592 (Stockman, J. dissenting) (quoting 4 Williston, Contracts, § 929, at 2607: "Only the hoary age and frequent repetition of the maxim prevents a general recognition of its absurdity."); *see also* Paine v. Meller, (1801) 6 Ves. Jr. 349, 31 Eng. Reprint 1088. Under virtually any accepted understanding of the theory, however, equitable conversion is not viewed as entitling the purchaser to every significant right of ownership, and particularly not the right of possession. As a matter of both logic and equity, the obligation to maintain property in its physical condition follows the right to have actual possession and control rather than a legal right to force conveyance of the property through specific performance at some future date. * * *

The equitable conversion theory is literally stood on its head by imposing on a vendee, solely because of his right to specific performance, the risk that the vendor will be unable to specifically perform when the time comes because of an accidental casualty loss. It is counterintuitive, at the very least, that merely contracting for the sale of real property should not only relieve the vendor of his responsibility to maintain the property until execution but also impose a duty on the vendee to perform despite the intervention of a material, no-fault casualty loss preventing him from ever receiving the benefit of his bargain. Such an extension of the theory of equitable conversion to casualty loss has never been recognized by this jurisdiction, and it is neither necessary nor justified solely for the sake of consistency.

By contrast, there is substantial justification, both as a matter of law and policy, for not relieving a vendee who is entitled to possession before transfer of title * * * of his duty to pay the full contract price, notwithstanding an accidental loss. In addition to having control over the property and being entitled to the benefits of its use, an equitable owner who also has the right of possession has already acquired virtually all of the rights of ownership and almost invariably will have already paid at least some portion of the contract price to exercise those rights. By expressly including in the contract for sale the right of possession, which otherwise generally accompanies transfer of title, *see, e.g.*, § 38–30–120, 10 C.R.S. (2001)("Conveyance carries right of possession"), the vendor has for all practical purposes already transferred the property as promised, and the parties have in effect expressed their joint intention that the vendee pay the purchase price as promised. *Williston, supra,* § 50:46 at 454–55. * * *

* * *

Furthermore, where a vendee is entitled to rescind as a result of casualty loss, the vendee should generally also be entitled to partial specific performance of the contract with an abatement in the purchase price reflecting the loss. Where the damage is ascertainable, permitting partial specific performance with a price abatement allows courts as nearly as possible to fulfill the expectations of the parties expressed in the contract, while leaving each in a position that is equitable relative to the other. * * * Partial specific performance with a price abatement has long been recognized in this jurisdiction as an alternative to rescission in the analogous situation in which a vendor of real property is unable to convey marketable title to all of the land described in the contract. *See* Murdock v. Pope, 156 Colo. 7, 396 P.2d 841 (1964) (collecting cases into the nineteenth century) * * *.

Where Brush was not an equitable owner in possession at the time of the casualty loss, it was entitled to rescind its contract with Sure Fine. At least under the circumstances of this case, where Brush chose to go forward with the contract under a stipulation as to loss from the hail damage, it was also entitled to specific performance with an abatement of the purchase price equal to the casualty loss. The judgment of the court of appeals is therefore reversed and the case is remanded for further proceedings consistent with this opinion.

NOTES

1. While the losses which equitable conversion imposes on the purchaser are usually the result of fire or other physical hazards, the risk of changes in the property's legal status is sometimes allocated to the purchaser in the same way. The following cases are illustrative:

    (a) Zoning change: Mohave County v. Mohave–Kingman Estates, Inc., 120 Ariz. 417, 586 P.2d 978 (1978); J.C. Penney Co. v. Koff, 345 So.2d 732 (Fla.Dist.Ct.App.1977); *cf.* Clay v. Landreth, 187 Va. 169, 45 S.E.2d 875 (1948) (contract will not be enforced if zoning change has made property unusable for purchaser's intended purpose).

    (b) Building code change: Cox v. Supreme Savings & Loan Ass'n, 126 Ill.App.2d 293, 262 N.E.2d 74 (1970).

    (c) Eminent domain action: Arko Enterprises, Inc. v. Wood, 185 So.2d 734 (Fla.Dist.Ct.App.1966); Annotation, 27 A.L.R.3d 572 (1969).

2. In the vast majority of risk of loss situations, the property is covered by casualty insurance. To what extent should such coverage alter traditional analysis in this area?

    The legal rules governing risk of loss are complicated when the loss is covered by a casualty insurance policy. If there is only one policy and it insures the party on whom the law or the contract imposes the risk of loss, the problems are minimal. But all too often the logic of equitable conversion puts the risk on the buyer when the seller is the only party insured. If the seller recovers the full price for the land and also collects from his insurer, he seems to receive an unwarranted stroke of good fortune. The seller may argue that there is no reason to give the buyer any benefit from the insurance, which is, after all a personal contract of indemnity between insurer and insured. But the seller's windfall has been too much for most modern courts to swallow, and the cases generally permit him to enforce the contract only if he is willing to abate the price to the extent of his insurance recovery. This result, which is often explained as the imposition of a constructive trust on the insurance funds in favor of the purchaser, greatly mitigates the original unfairness of equitable conversion.

William B. Stoebuck & Dale A. Whitman, The Law of Property 796 (3d ed. 2000).* *See* Hillard v. Franklin, 41 S.W.3d 106 (Tenn.Ct.App.2000) (where purchasers bear the risk of loss as a result of equitable conversion, they are entitled to have the purchase price reduced by the amount of the insurance proceeds received by the vendor).

SECTION 5. CONTRACTS RELATING TO SERVICES

A. DAMAGES

1. Action by Buyer

When an employer sues an employee for breaching a personal services contract, the employer's recovery is measured by the difference between the contract price and the cost of obtaining substitute services. The latter cost may be proven by establishing the cost of cover or, if no substitute is available, by looking to the higher wages that the former employee is earning from a new employer. *See, e.g.*, Roth v. Speck, 126 A.2d 153 (D.C.1956); *see generally* 3 Dan B. Dobbs, Law of Remedies § 12.22(1) (2d ed. 1993). Note that if the services are defective, the usual remedy is termination of the employee, rather than damages for the difference between the value of the services actually rendered and the contract price. Incidental and consequential damages are recoverable by a buyer of services, but consequential damages for lost profits are often very difficult to prove. *Id.* A common method of protecting an employer against breach by a key employee is a clause providing that the employee will not compete with the employer during the term of the contract. *Id.* at § 12.22(2).

The next case involves the breach of a construction contract in a case where the services were defective.

SMITH v. MARK COLEMAN CONSTRUCTION, INC.

District Court of Appeal of Florida, 1992.
594 So.2d 812.

PARKER, JUDGE.

John H. and Sharon A. Smith appeal a final judgment entered in their favor, arguing the award of damages was inadequate. * * *

The Smiths contracted with appellee, Mark Coleman Construction, Inc., to build a house at a construction price of $266,614. The house,

---

* Reprinted with permission of West Publishing Co.

completed in about June 1987, contained numerous defects. On October 28, 1988, the Smiths filed a breach of contract action against Coleman Construction. After a nonjury trial, the trial judge awarded damages for approximately nine items of repairs. This appeal involves only the damages awarded for a hump in the floor of two second-story bedrooms.

Neither party or any witness disputes that prominent humps exist which are obvious to the naked eye. The hump is in the center of the two bedrooms and remains a hump across the floor to the wall in these bedrooms. There is approximately a one and three-eighths inch rise between the height of the floor at the bedroom doorways and the level of the floor at the hump. Apparently the trusses were not sealed properly and the humps appeared when tiles were placed on the roof, causing the trusses to become unaligned. The Smiths discovered the humps three or four months before the completion of the house and brought this to the attention of Coleman Construction. Coleman Construction installed a series of lag bolts to prevent further deterioration of the alignment. The repair, however, did nothing to eliminate the hump, yet Coleman Construction continued construction on the house to completion.

The Smiths attempted to present evidence to support two alternative theories of recovery. The Smiths tried to present the testimony of a real estate appraiser as to the market value of the home with the hump to support their claim that they were entitled to receive an award of the diminution of the market value between a house like theirs with no hump and their house as it existed with a hump in two bedrooms. The trial court disallowed this testimony, ruling that such an award was not the proper measure of damages in this case. The Smiths presented the testimony of a general contractor to support their alternative theory of damages which was the cost of removing the hump. Coleman Construction presented the testimony of a general contractor who testified to the cost of disguising the hump effect.

Based upon the trial judge's comments about the amount he would permit the Smiths to recover as to each repair and the total amount awarded in the final judgment, it is clear that the judge awarded $3,640 for a cosmetic masking of the floor defect. We find that award, based upon all the evidence, to be inadequate.

The supreme court, in Grossman Holdings Ltd. v. Hourihan, 414 So.2d 1037 (Fla.1982), adopted section 346(1)(a) of the Restatement (First) on Contracts (1932) as the measure of damages for a breach of a construction contract * * *:

(a) For defective or unfinished construction * * * [the contracting party] can get judgment [from the builder] for either

(i) the reasonable cost of construction and completion in accordance with the contract, if this is possible and does not involve unreasonable economic waste; or

(ii) the difference between the value that the product contracted for would have had and the value of the performance that has been received by the plaintiff, if construction and completion in accordance with the contract would involve unreasonable economic waste.

Hourihan, 414 So.2d at 1039 (quoting Restatement (First) of Contracts § 346(1)(a) (1932)). The supreme court also cited the following comment to subsection 346(1)(a):

The purpose of money damages is to put the injured party in as good a position as that in which full performance would have put him; but this does not mean he is to be put in the same specific physical position. Satisfaction for his harm is made either by giving him a sum of money sufficient to produce the physical product contracted for or by giving him the exchange value that that product would have had if it had been constructed * * *. Sometimes defects in a complete structure cannot be physically remedied without tearing down and rebuilding, at a cost that would be imprudent and unreasonable. The law does not require damages to be measured by a method requiring such economic waste. If no such waste is involved, the cost of remedying the defect is the amount awarded as compensation for failure to render the promised performance.

Id. (quoting Restatement (First) of Contracts § 346(1)(a) comment (1932)). In short, a party is entitled to recover the cost of repairing a defect so that it is in compliance with the contract or, if that would result in economic waste, the diminution of value between a house built in accordance with the contract and the one actually built. * * *

Applying the *Hourihan* holding to the instant case, we conclude that the trial court erred in precluding the testimony relating to diminution of value. The Smiths presented the testimony of an engineer who testified that he had no suggestion as to a practical method of eliminating the hump. Such a repair would include removing the subflooring, flooring, and ceiling and tracking the exterior end of the truss in order to lower the interior end to the girder. The engineer cautioned that shaving or cutting the truss would be detrimental to the structural integrity of the house.

The Smiths' general contractor expert estimated that the removal of the hump by jacking up the trusses and leveling the floor would cost between $10,000 and $15,000, not including the incidental repairs that such a procedure would necessitate such as repairing the cracks in the interior and exterior walls and fixing the bedroom cabinets. * * *

The trial judge apparently relied upon the general contractor's testimony in ruling that no economic waste would occur in repairing the hump. Based on the testimony of the engineer and the general contractor, this ruling was in error. The engineer was the only witness competent to testify to the feasibility of such a repair on the structural integrity of the house, and he knew of no way of practically eliminating the hump. Even though the general contractor estimated that he might be able to remove the hump for between $10,000 and $15,000, he did not know the effect of such repair on the structural integrity of the house. Upon initial consideration, it may seem that the Smiths should have presented experts who could testify definitively regarding whether such a repair could be effected and the exact cost for doing so. The Smiths, however, were in a difficult situation because no person could testify competently on this matter unless the person tore up the floor and examined the structure. This court is hesitant to require such a drastic and expensive course of action when Coleman Construction had the opportunity to eliminate the hump months before the house was completed.

Even if this court would find that diminution of value was not a proper measure of damages in this case, there is no substantial, competent evidence to support the amount which the trial judge awarded. Coleman Construction's expert did not testify to any method to eliminate the hump. His recommended methods of repair involved masking the hump to make it less noticeable. His first suggestion was to utilize wood leveling cant strips tapered away from the hump. This method would create a noticeable "step-up" at each bedroom doorway. His alternative suggestion was to utilize multiple coats of a laminate base material and to feather the material out into the hallway to eliminate the "step-up" at the bedroom doorways. The expert testified that the maximum cost to make the repair would be $2,800 plus a thirty percent profit margin. This totals $3,640, the amount the trial court awarded.

We find that the Smiths should not have to accept a final judgment that awards only a cosmetic fix to a noticeable construction defect. The only evidence in the record as to the cost of removing the hump was a minimum of $10,000. Thus, we conclude that the trial court erred in awarding only $3,640 for the removal of the hump. Accordingly, we reverse the final judgment and remand for a new trial on the amount of damages relating to the hump. At a new trial, the Smiths should be awarded either (1) the reasonable cost of removing the hump if it does not involve unreasonable economic waste or (2) if the floor cannot be repaired without creating economic waste, the difference in value of their house with the hump in the floor and the value of a house built in accordance with the contract.

Reversed and remanded for new trial.

RYDER, A.C.J., and LEHAN, J., concur.

RESTATEMENT (SECOND) OF CONTRACTS

§ 348 (1981).*

§ 348. Alternatives to Loss in Value of Performance

* * *

---

(2) If a breach results in defective or unfinished construction and the loss in value to the injured party is not proved with sufficient certainty, he [or she] may recover damages based on

(a) the diminution in the market price of the property caused by the breach, or

(b) the reasonable cost of completing performance or of remedying the defects if that cost is not clearly disproportionate to the probable loss in value to him [or her].

* * *

Comment:

* * *

c. Incomplete or defective performance. If the contract is one for construction, including repair or similar performance affecting the condition of property, and the work is not finished, the injured party will usually find it easier to prove what it would cost to have the work completed by another contractor than to prove the difference between the values to him [or her] of the finished and the unfinished performance. Since the cost to complete is usually less than the loss in value to him [or her], * * * [the injured party] is limited by the rule on avoidability to damages based on cost to complete. * * * If * * * [the injured party] has actually had the work completed, damages will be based on his [or her] expenditures * * *.

Sometimes, especially if the performance is defective as distinguished from incomplete, it may not be possible to prove the loss in value to the injured party with reasonable certainty. In that case he [or she] can usually recover damages based on the cost to remedy the defects. Even if this gives * * * [the injured party] a recovery somewhat in excess of the loss in value to him [or her], it is better that he [or she] receive a small windfall than that he [or she] be undercompensated by being limited to the resulting diminution in the market price of his [or her] property.

Sometimes, however, such a large part of the cost to remedy the defects consists of the cost to undo what has been improperly done that the cost to remedy the defects will be clearly disproportionate to the probable loss in value to the injured party. Damages based on the cost to remedy the defects would then give the injured party a recovery greatly in excess of the loss in value to him [or her] and result in a substantial windfall. Such an award will not be made. It is sometimes said that the award would involve "economic waste," but this is a misleading expression since an injured party will not, even if awarded an excessive amount of damages, usually pay to have the defects remedied if to do so will cost him [or her] more than the resulting increase in value to him [or her]. If an award based on the cost to remedy the defects would clearly be excessive and the injured party does not prove the actual loss in value to him [or her], damages will be based instead on the difference between the market price that the property would have had without the defects and the market price of the property with the defects.

NOTES

1. In *Hourihan*, the major case relied upon in *Smith*, a purchaser entered into a contract with a builder for a house to be built on particular lot according to specific plans and specifications. Prior to construction, the purchaser discovered that the builder intended to build the house as a "mirror image" of the house specified in the plans. The purchaser protested but the builder erected the mirror image house nonetheless. The purchaser took possession and title to the house and sued for damages. Should the purchaser be able recover damages sufficient to reconstruct the house as called for in the original plans and specifications? Or should the purchaser be able to obtain diminution in value damages only? Should it be relevant that the purchaser could now sell the house at a profit? According to the Florida Supreme Court in *Hourihan*,

> damages for a breach of contract should be measured as of the date of the breach. * * * Fluctuations in value after the breach do not affect the nonbreaching party's recovery. Here, it may be possible to demonstrate a difference in value as of the date of delivery between the house the [purchaser] contracted for and the house that [the builder] built.

414 So.2d at 1040.

2. The measure of general compensatory damages in an action by a purchaser of services against a breaching provider is discussed in Melvin A. Eisenberg, *The Responsive Model of Contract Law*, 36 Stan. L. Rev. 1107, 1155–65 (1984).*

> Suppose now that a contract for the provision of services is breached by the service-provider. As in a breach by a seller of goods, the expectation principle might appear to entitle the injured party to either specific performance or damages measured by the difference between the contract price and the value that he subjectively places on the services. However, specific performance will usually be either impracticable or unavailable for reasons of policy, and direct judicial measurement of the injured party's subjective value presents obvious problems of administration. Nevertheless, the courts usually can protect the injured party's actual expectation by applying an objective but individualized measure, based on the cost required to put the subject matter of the contract into its promised state—a measure generally known as cost of completion. At least where the injured party has actually had the work completed, cost of completion is analogous to cover. Like cover, cost of completion is both objective, since it does not depend on direct measurement of subjective valuation, and individualized, since it depends on the circumstances of the individual case. Moreover, cost of completion, like cover, should normally put the plaintiff in the same position as performance would have done.

---

* Reprinted with permission of the Stanford Law Review.

An alternative measure of damages for nonperformance of services is generally known as diminished value. Under this measure, the plaintiff recovers the difference between the market value of the contract's subject matter as it stands, and its market value had the seller performed as promised. Although this measure is essentially standardized, in a market with perfect information, cost-of-completion and diminished-value damages would usually be approximately equal, since the difference between the market value of the subject matter in its actual and promised states should usually equal the cost of transforming the subject matter from one state to the other. * * *

In certain circumstances, however, the two measures will differ. In some such cases, the courts have limited the recovery to diminished-value damages, over the injured party's objection. * * *

* * *

[T]he cases applying this principle have spelled out its rationale poorly at best, and the competing rules that have been advanced for imposing the limit are generally unsatisfactory. One rule, reflected in Section 346(1)(a)(i) of Restatement (First), is that the court should not award cost of completion if that measure would involve unreasonable economic waste. An award of damages, however, merely redistributes wealth between the parties, and therefore cannot in itself involve waste. While a plaintiff may use the proceeds of a damage recovery to engage in activity the court would regard as wasteful, that has never been a criterion for selecting among damage measures.

A second rule * * * is that courts should not award cost of completion if damages so measured would be "grossly and unfairly out of proportion" to the "result," "good," or "end" to be attained. * * * Disparity between cost of completion and diminution in market value, however, should not in itself present a ground for refusing cost-of-completion damages. * * *

A third rule, reflected in some of the commentary, is that the courts should not award cost of completion if that measure would create a windfall. This rule, however, provides no guidance for determining when a windfall would result. If completion is required to satisfy the plaintiff's expectation, it is hard to see why its cost would constitute a windfall. Indeed, limiting the plaintiff's damages to diminution in value may give the defendant a windfall.[149]

---

149. Many other rules have also been proposed by the commentators. *See, e.g.,* D. Dobbs, *supra* note 58, at 902 (where an owner is interested only in economic value to begin with, the difference between cost of completion and diminished value should be split between the parties); Farnsworth, *Legal Remedies for Breach of Contract*, 70 Colum.L.Rev. 1145, 1175 (1970) (where there is uncertainty concerning the difference between the value to the owner of the promised and the rendered performance, and cost of completion varies widely from diminished value, the trier of fact should have discretion to fix any figure, not unreasonable under the circumstances, so long as it lies within those two limits); Harris, Ogus & Phillips, *supra* note 62, at 601–10 (courts should award the injured party the value he places on the promised performance); Marschall, *Willfulness: A Crucial Factor in Choosing Remedies for Breach of Contract*, 24 Ariz.L.Rev. 733 (1982) (the choice between cost of completion and diminished value should turn on whether the breach was willful); Muris, *supra* note 148, at 395–96 (cost of completion should be awarded when (i) the original purchase price exceeds the fair market value at the time of purchase and the cost

The underlying problem with all three rules is that they attempt to solve an essentially subjective problem with objective tests. The guiding rationale is very simple. The purpose of expectation damages is to put the injured party where he would have been had the contract been performed. Since cost-of-completion damages usually accomplish that objective, this measure should usually be utilized. It need not be utilized, however, where the factfinder is convinced it would not accomplish that objective because both the market and the plaintiff value the difference between the existing and promised states of the contract's subject matter at less than the cost of completion, and the plaintiff therefore would not use a recovery measured by that cost to achieve completion.

* * *

While the ultimate issue is therefore subjective, the courts should normally determine that issue by looking to objective indicators, particularly whether the subject matter of the contract involved personal rather than strictly commercial interests, or whether strategic considerations, such as location, would lead the plaintiff to assign a value to the subject matter in its promised state higher than would the market.

* * *

In short, in cases where cost of completion substantially exceeds diminution in value, the analysis should proceed in three steps. First, if the plaintiff has actually paid a third party to have the work completed, damages should always be measured by cost of completion, since we know that cost of completion does not exceed the plaintiff's valuation of the differential between the existing and promised states of the subject matter of the contract. Second, if the plaintiff has not had the work completed, damages should be measured by cost of completion unless the defendant convincingly demonstrates that the plaintiff's valuation of the differential is significantly less than the cost of completion, and that the plaintiff therefore probably does not intend to complete. Third, if such a demonstration is made, damages should normally be measured by the

---

figure reflects the original cost of production; (ii) cost of completion is less than or equal to diminution in value; (iii) diminution in value is too difficult to calculate with reasonable certainty; or (iv) subjective value is relevant and cost of completion does not grossly exceed the likely subjective value); Yorio, *In Defense of Money Damages for Breach of Contract*, 82 Colum.L.Rev. 1365, 1388–1423 (1982) (cost of completion should be awarded in all cases, unless the breach was inadvertent or due to changed circumstances; in those cases the innocent party should receive (i) half the difference between cost of completion and diminished value, (ii) half the gain that resulted to the contractor by virtue of the breach, or (iii) at least where the owner has derived no benefit, restitution of amounts paid to the contractor). Most of these rules turn in whole or in part on objective tests, or at least on an attempt to avoid determining subjective intent, and are therefore subject to the same problems as the rules advanced by the courts. Marschall's rule appears to turn on a subjective test—the willfulness of the breach—but as regards nonwillful breaches, Marschall suggests a balancing of the conventional objective factors, such as waste and disproportionality.

Professor Farnsworth has written a second article recommending that when a provider of services has rendered "a defective performance that leaves the injured party with no opportunity to use that party's return performance to obtain a reasonable substitute," the injured party may invoke a restitutionary remedy to disgorge any gain resulting from the breach. E. Allan Farnsworth, *Your Loss or My Gain? The Dilemma of the Disgorgement Principle in Breach of Contract*, 94 Yale L.J. 1339 (1985).

greater of (i) diminution in value or (ii) the plaintiff's valuation of the differential * * *.

3. Consequential damages for lost profits caused by a delay in the completion of construction are often very difficult to prove. 3 Dan B. Dobbs, Law of Remedies §§ 12.19(1) (2d ed. 1993). One way to solve this problem is through the use of liquidated damages clauses, and they are widely used and approved by the courts in construction contracts. *Id.*

4. The next case considers whether a buyer of services may sue for consequential emotional distress damages when there has been a breach of services contract.

LANE v. KINDERCARE LEARNING CENTERS, INC.

Court of Appeals of Michigan, 1998.
231 Mich.App. 689, 588 N.W.2d 715.

Before GRIBBS, P.J., and SAWYER and DOCTOROFF, JJ.

PER CURIAM.

Plaintiff enrolled her eighteen-month-old daughter in day care with defendant. On December 9, 1992, plaintiff dropped off her daughter at defendant's facility at lunch time. Plaintiff's daughter had been prescribed medication, and plaintiff filled out an authorization form granting defendant's employees permission to administer the medication to her daughter that day. Just after 5:00 p.m. on December 9, 1992, one of defendant's employee's placed the child, who had fallen asleep, in a crib in the infant room. At approximately 6:00 p.m., defendant's employees locked the doors of the facility and went home for the day, apparently unaware that plaintiff's daughter was still sleeping in the crib. Shortly thereafter, plaintiff returned to the facility to pick up her daughter and found the facility locked and unlit. Plaintiff called 911. A police officer who responded to the call looked through a window of the facility, with the aid of a flashlight, and saw the child sleeping in the crib. Another officer then broke a window and retrieved the child from the building. The child was upset after the incident, but was not physically harmed. When plaintiff went into the facility to retrieve her daughter's belongings, she apparently found the medication authorization form and observed that it had not been initialed to indicate that the child had been given the medication. Plaintiff alleged that she suffered emotional distress as a result of the incident.

Plaintiff filed a complaint against defendant, alleging breach of contract * * *. After a hearing, the trial court granted summary disposition of plaintiff's claim * * *.

Plaintiff first argues that the trial court erred in granting summary disposition of her breach of contract claim * * * on the ground that plaintiff failed to allege compensable emotional distress. * * *

The recovery of damages for the breach of a contract is limited to those damages that are a natural result of the breach or those that are contemplated by the parties at the time the contract was made. Kewin v. Massachusetts Mut. Life Ins. Co., 409 Mich. 401, 414, 295 N.W.2d 50 (1980); Hadley v. Baxendale, 9 Exch 341, 156 Eng Rep 145 (1854). Therefore, it is generally held that damages for emotional distress cannot be recovered for the breach of a commercial contract. *Kewin, supra* at 414, 295 N.W.2d 50. However, our Supreme Court has recognized that damages for emotional distress may be recovered for the breach of a contract in cases that do not involve commercial or pecuniary contracts, but involve contracts of a personal nature. Stewart v. Rudner, 349 Mich. 459, 469, 84 N.W.2d 816 (1957). Our Supreme Court explained:

> When we have a contract concerned not with trade and commerce but with life and death, not with profit but with elements of personality, not with pecuniary aggrandizement but with matters of mental concern and solicitude, then a breach of duty with respect to such contracts will inevitably and necessarily result in mental anguish, pain and suffering. In such cases the parties may reasonably be said to have contracted with reference to the payment of damages therefor in event of breach. Far from being outside the contemplation of the parties they are an integral and inseparable part of it. *Id.* at 471, 84 N.W.2d 816.

Examples of personal contracts include a contract to perform a cesarean section, *Stewart, supra*; a contract for the care and burial of a dead body, Allinger v. Kell, 102 Mich.App. 798, 812, 302 N.W.2d 576 (1981) (Allen, J.), *rev'd in part on other grounds* 411 Mich. 1053, 309 N.W.2d 547 (1981); a contract to care for the plaintiff's elderly mother and to notify the plaintiff in the event of the mother's illness, Avery v. Arnold Home, Inc., 17 Mich.App. 240, 243, 169 N.W.2d 135 (1969); and a promise to marry, Vanderpool v. Richardson, 52 Mich. 336, 17 N.W. 936 (1883).[1]

We believe that a contract to care for one's child is a matter of "mental concern and solicitude," rather than "pecuniary aggrandizement." *Stewart, supra* at 471, 84 N.W.2d 816. Therefore, like the contract to care for the plaintiff's elderly mother in *Avery, supra*, the contract involved in the instant case was personal in nature, rather than commercial. At the time the contract was executed, it was foreseeable that a breach of the contract would result in mental distress damages to plaintiff, which would extend beyond the mere "annoyance and vexation" that normally accompanies the breach of a contract. *Kewin, supra* at 417, 295 N.W.2d 50. Such damages are clearly within the contemplation of the parties to such a contract. * * *

We therefore conclude that the trial court erred in granting summary disposition of plaintiff's breach of contract claim * * *.

---

1. Contracts that have been held to be commercial, rather than personal, include a no-fault automobile insurance contract, Butler v. DAIIE, 121 Mich.App. 727, 735, 329 N.W.2d 781 (1982); a disability insurance contract, *Kewin, supra* at 419, 295 N.W.2d 50; a hospitalization insurance contract, Shikany v. Blue Cross & Blue Shield of Michigan, 134 Mich.App. 603, 609–610, 350 N.W.2d 910 (1984); and a contract for the construction of a house, Jankowski v. Mazzotta, 7 Mich.App. 483, 487, 152 N.W.2d 49 (1967).

2. Action by Seller

3 DAN B. DOBBS, LAW OF REMEDIES

§ 12.21(2) (2d ed. 1993).*

An employee wrongfully discharged in violation of contract may recover damages measured by the contract price, less replacement income under the avoidable consequences rules, plus recoverable consequential damages. The recoverable contract price includes both direct wages and other employment benefits. It may, for example, include deferred compensation for past services, such as commissions payable in the future or a future share in the business. It also includes an employer's payments to a retirement benefit fund, at least if the payments would result in benefits to the plaintiff.

In most states the recovery is based on the full price due for the unexpired term of the contract, subject to the rules for minimizing damages. Where the employee is only guaranteed a specified time period to work after notice, the unexpired term for which compensation is due is the notice period. Where the employee is guaranteed [permanent employment], unless there is good cause for discharge, the effect may be that the employee can recover wages [over] the remainder of her working life, subject only to deductions for avoidable consequences and reductions to present value. An older way of proceeding was to require separate suits for installments as due, and some states still use this rule. Past due installments may still be the only sums due if the contract term has expired when suit is brought or the employee has been reinstated.

The first and second rules of avoidable consequences. The avoidable consequences rules place two limitations on the plaintiff's recovery. Under the first rule the defendant is entitled to a credit for any income the plaintiff actually earns in lieu of the employment income. This rule credits the defendant with realized income even if it was realized in a job that would not count as a substitute.

* * *

"Reasonable diligence". Courts sometimes speak of the second rule by saying that the plaintiff is expected to use "reasonable diligence" to find suitable substitute employment. The reasonable diligence statement can be misleading, however. If the plaintiff does exercise reasonable diligence but finds no comparable employment, that fact strongly supports the view that no comparable employment exists and tends to rebut any evidence the defendant may offer to the contrary. The plaintiff's lack of diligence might also corroborate the defendant's evidence that comparable employment existed. But the second rule does not dismiss the plaintiff for lack of diligence. If the defendant fails to prove that comparable employment was available, the plaintiff's lack of diligence does not defeat or reduce [his or] her claim. The claim is reduced under the second rule only if suitable

---

substitute employment was available and to the extent that it would have or did provide replacement income.

* * *

Suitable, comparable, or substitute employment. A suitable substitute job must be one that the plaintiff could have obtained with reasonable effort or expense; it must not be "inferior" work and it must provide the plaintiff with a similar rank or status. In the case of artists or professionals, similar professional experience and exposure is also important in judging suitability of the proposed substitute job. In many instances a similar job in a distant locality will not count as a substitute, although where mobility is a common attribute of particular employment the locality feature might be unimportant. Or what is considered the same locality might be different depending on whether the employee is a high level executive or a school teacher. When the employee can minimize damages only by accepting otherwise suitable re-employment with the defendant, he [or she] is usually expected to do so; his [or her] damages are reduced if the defendant makes a re-employment offer in good faith.

Note

Professor Eisenberg compares the measure of damages recoverable by a seller of goods, a seller of services under a construction contract, and a seller of personal services in Melvin A. Eisenberg, *The Responsive Model of Contract Law*, 36 Stan. L. Rev. 1107, 1147–55 (1984).*

The obligation of a buyer of services, like that of a buyer of goods, is normally limited to the payment of money. As in the case of goods, therefore, if the buyer breaches, the seller's actual expectation can normally be satisfied without taking his [or her] subjective value into account, provided the seller's remedies are individualized.

The established formula for measuring damages for breach by a buyer of services is based on the difference between the contract price and the seller's out-of-pocket cost of completion at the time of breach. This formula mirrors the net-proceeds measure afforded a seller of goods under section 2–708(2) of the Uniform Commercial Code. There is, however, an important difference between the rules governing goods cases and services cases. In goods cases, both the formula and its application are individualized, since the section 2–708(2) net-proceeds measure is available only where the breach does not enable the seller to make a replacement sale that he [or she] could not otherwise have made. In contrast, in most types of services cases courts have applied the net-proceeds measure in a highly standardized fashion, without regard to the presence of a replacement sale.

Take, for example, the following hypothetical:

Busy Plumber. Plumber engages in the business of upgrading plumbing in old commercial buildings; he operates at full capacity,

---

* Reprinted with permission of the Stanford Law Review.

and must often turn down jobs. On January 1, Plumber enters into a contract to do a plumbing job for Owner 1 for $6000, the work to begin on February 1 and to be completed in two weeks. On January 30, Owner 1 repudiates the contract. On January 31, Plumber enters into a contract to do a plumbing job for Owner 2 for $7600, the work to begin on February 1 and to be completed in two weeks. Plumber could not have accepted the job with Owner 2 but for the breach by Owner 1. Plumber's out-of-pocket costs for performing his contract with Owner 1 would have been $3400. His out-of-pocket costs for performing his contract with Owner 2 are $2900. Plumber now sues Owner 1.

In assessing Plumber's recovery, the expectation principle would require the contract with Owner 2 to be taken as an offset, lest damages place him in a better position than performance would have done. In the past, however, the courts have usually not permitted such an offset. * * *

In striking contrast, in cases where "personal services" *are* involved—that is, in contracts of employment—if the buyer (employer) breaches, the law reduces the damages of the seller (employee) not only by any replacement wages he [or she] actually earns, but by any wages he [or she] would have earned had he [or she] used reasonable efforts to find a replacement job. This difference between the employment and nonemployment cases is highly anomalous. For one thing, an employment contract is only a special case of a contract for the provision of services. For another, if the law must treat employment contracts differently than other services contracts, one would expect it to be more tenderhearted to employees than to business organizations.

Two kinds of arguments have been made in support of the traditional no-offset rule applied in nonemployment cases. One follows from a concept of business economics, and the other from a concept of reciprocity. The business-economics argument, advanced by Professor Patterson, is that, "As an enterpriser, [a] builder may take on an indefinite number of contracts and make a profit on all of them."[115] This argument is empirically wrong. Factors such as managerial resources, working capital, and bonding limits constrain the number of jobs a contractor can take on. Of course, a contractor often can expand capacity within limits. In most cases, therefore, a buyer's breach may not enable a contractor to make a replacement contract he [or she] could not otherwise have made. * * * That is no reason, however, to prohibit the buyer from establishing that, in his [or her] case, the breach enabled the seller to take on a replacement job that he [or she] could not otherwise have performed.

The reciprocity argument * * * is that "[i]t would not be just to give the defendant the benefit of a good contract and not charge him [or her] with the loss of a bad one when plaintiff had honestly used his [or her] skill, time, and capital."[117] This argument rests on the tacit assumption that the defendant is not liable for the loss on a bad replacement

---

115. Patterson, *Builder's Measure of Recovery for Breach of Contract*, 31 Colum.L.Rev. 1286, 1306 (1931).

117. Grinnell Co. v. Voorhees, 1 F.2d 693 (3d Cir.1924).

contract. That assumption might be questioned: By way of analogy, if the employer breaks an employment contract and the employee incurs expenses in seeking a replacement job, those expenses are added to the employee's damages even if the search is unsuccessful. In any event, both the seller's damages and the offset should be measured by net proceeds—that is, by the difference between out-of-pocket expenses and the contract price—not by net profits. Many service contracts result in negative net profits, but few will be likely to result in negative net proceeds. It is therefore letting the tail wag the dog to deny an offset for a replacement contract that yields positive net proceeds, on the theory that a defendant should not bear the burden of (an extremely unlikely) replacement contract that yields negative net proceeds. Furthermore, negative-net-proceeds contracts might be distinguished from positive-net-proceeds contracts on the grounds that they are not reasonably foreseeable (because so unlikely), and that they probably result from the seller's lack of skill, which the defendant should not have to subsidize.

Finally, the reciprocity argument does not square with the courts' treatment of employment contracts in cases where the employee starts his [or her] own business during the unexpired term of the breached contract. The general rule is that the employee's recovery is reduced by what he [or she] has earned and can reasonably expect to earn in his [or her] new business during the unexpired term of the broken agreement. If the reciprocity argument were correct, it would apply to this case as well.

In short, the rule traditionally applied to nonemployment services contracts is triply anomalous: It is inconsistent with the expectation principle, with the rules governing contracts for the sale of goods, and with the rules governing a kindred class of contracts for the sale of services. Therefore, it is not surprising that the rule seems to be eroding. For example, in M & R Contractors & Builders v. Michael[121] the court said that if a contractor "could *not* have worked on another job or project unless [it] had been discharged from the performance of the defendant's contract, then the gains from the other employment or undertaking must be deducted from [its] damages."[122] Similarly, the comment to section 347 of Restatement (Second) of Contracts adopts the rule that if an injured party makes substitute arrangements for the use of resources he [or she] would have needed to perform the original contract, the net profit from the substitute arrangements reduces his [or her] damages. The comment continues:

> *f. Lost volume.* ... Since entrepreneurs try to operate at optimum capacity ... it is possible that an additional transaction would not have been profitable and that the injured party would not have chosen to expand his [or her] business by undertaking it had there been no breach. It is sometimes assumed that he [or she] would have done so, but the question is one of fact to be resolved according to the circumstances of each case....

---

121. 215 Md. 340, 138 A.2d 350 (1958).

122. *Id.* at 355, 138 A.2d at 358 (emphasis in original); *see also* Kearsarge Computer, Inc. v. Acme Staple Co., 116 N.H. 705, 709–10, 366 A.2d 467, 471 (1976); McCullen v. Wel–Mil Corp., 23 N.C.App. 736, 209 S.E.2d 507 (1974); 5 A. Corbin, *supra* note 52, §§ 1041, 1094 (1964).

[Illustration] 16. *A* contracts to pave *B's* parking lot for $10,000. *B* repudiates the contract and *A* subsequently makes a contract to pave a similar parking lot for $10,000. *A's* business could have been expanded to do both jobs. *Unless it is proved that he would not have undertaken both,* *A's* damages are based on the net profit he would have made on the contract with *B,* without regard to the subsequent transaction.[123]

Suppose now that a seller of services could have obtained a replacement job but did not. This problem has not been worked out in the context of nonemployment contracts, because under the traditional rule replacement jobs were irrelevant in that context. In the context of employment contracts, however, the well-established rule is that the employee has a duty to mitigate, so that wages he [or she] could have earned on a replacement job, but did not, will be offset against his [or her] recovery. This duty complements the rule that wages the employee actually does earn on a replacement job offset his [or her] recovery. Under the latter rule, an employee who takes a replacement job in effect works for the breaching employer * * *. Unless a duty to take such a job existed, therefore, the offset rule might encourage employees to stand idle. For this reason, the same duty should apply to other sellers of services.

But what rule determines whether the duty to mitigate has been satisfied? The traditional statement of the duty frames the issue in objective and even standardized terms: The plaintiff has a duty to take a replacement job if it involves "similar employment, with similar conditions of employment and rank and in the same locality." However, a job that is objectively comparable, on an abstract level, to the job originally contracted for, may not satisfy the plaintiff for perfectly good reasons, ranging from quality of management to degree of risk. In such a case, a rule that in effect forces the plaintiff to take the replacement job violates the expectation principle because it places him [or her] in a worse position than he [or she] would have occupied had the defendant performed the original contract, which presumably involved a satisfactory job. A preferable approach, therefore, would be to treat an employee or other seller of services in the same manner as a covering buyer of goods, so that the search for a replacement is tested by a standard of reasonableness, but the substantive decision is tested by a standard of good faith. * * *

The leading case of Parker v. Twentieth Century–Fox Film Corp[129] supports this bifurcated approach to search and decision. Shirley MacLaine had contracted with Fox to play the female lead in *Bloomer Girl* at a minimum compensation of $750,000. Before production started, Fox decided not to produce the picture and offered MacLaine the lead in *Big Country, Big Man* for identical compensation. *Big Country* was to be filmed at the time scheduled for *Bloomer Girl,* but *Bloomer Girl* would have been a musical while *Big Country* would be a dramatic western, and

123. Restatement (Second) of Contracts § 347 comment f (1981) (emphasis added).
129. 3 Cal.3d 176, 474 P.2d 689, 89 Cal.Rptr. 737 (1970).

Bloomer Girl would have been filmed in California while *Big Country* would be filmed in Australia. Also, the *Bloomer Girl* contract gave MacLaine the power of director and screenplay approval, but the *Big Country* contract provided only that Fox would consult with MacLaine on these issues. MacLaine rejected *Big Country* and brought suit for breach of contract. Fox pleaded that MacLaine, by refusing to accept *Big Country,* had failed to mitigate damages.

The California Supreme Court affirmed a summary judgment for MacLaine. The court made obeisance to the traditional statement of the mitigation rule by finding that the two roles were not equivalent, and that the changed contract provisions made *Big Country* "an offer of inferior employment." The thrust of the opinion, however, went considerably further. First, the court seemed to eviscerate the traditional, standardized test by indicating that any distinction between two jobs would render them different in kind as a matter of law. Second, the court properly drew a sharp distinction between search and decision:

> In the present case defendant has raised no issue of *reasonableness of efforts* by plaintiff to obtain other employment.... Despite defendant's arguments to the contrary, no case ... holds or suggests that reasonableness is an element of a wrongfully discharged employee's option to reject, or fail to seek, different or inferior employment.... [132]

* * *

In summary, if a buyer of services breaches, the seller should recover under an individualized net-proceeds measure of damages. If the seller accepts a replacement job, his [or her] net proceeds on that job should offset his [or her] recovery against the buyer. The seller should make reasonable efforts to search for such a job, but his [or her] decision to reject a replacement job that he [or she] finds should be judged by the subjective standard of good faith.

MONGE v. BEEBE RUBBER CO.
Supreme Court of New Hampshire, 1974.
114 N.H. 130, 316 A.2d 549.

LAMPRON, JUSTICE.

Action of assumpsit to recover damages for an alleged breach of an oral contract of employment. Plaintiff was hired in September 1968 at wages of $1.84 per hour to work on a conversion machine in defendant's factory and was allegedly told that if she worked well she would get better jobs with better pay. Plaintiff claims that she was harassed by her foreman because she refused to go out with him and that his hostility, condoned if not shared by defendant's personnel manager, ultimately resulted in her being fired. Trial by jury resulted in a verdict for the plaintiff in the amount of $2,500. * * *

* * *

---

132. *Id.* at 182 n.5, 474 P.2d at 693 n.5, 89 Cal.Rptr. at 741 n.5 (emphasis in original).

Plaintiff sued for breach of an employment contract for an indefinite period of time. The employer has long ruled the workplace with an iron hand by reason of the prevailing common-law rule that such a hiring is presumed to be at will and terminable at any time by either party. * * *

The law governing the relations between employer and employee has evolved over the years to reflect changing legal, social and economic conditions. 3A A. Corbin, Contracts § 674 at 205, 206 (1960). In this area "[w]e are in the midst of a period in which the pot boils the hardest and in the process of change the fastest." Although many of these changes have resulted from the activity and influence of labor unions, the courts cannot ignore the new climate prevailing generally in the relationship of employer and employee.

* * * We hold that a termination by the employer of a contract of employment at will which is motivated by bad faith or malice or based on retaliation is not in the best interest of the economic system or the public good and constitutes a breach of the employment contract. Such a rule affords the employee a certain stability of employment and does not interfere with the employer's normal exercise of * * * [the] right to discharge * * *.

The sole question on appeal is whether there was sufficient evidence to support the jury's finding that defendant, through its agents, acted maliciously in terminating plaintiff's employment. * * *

The jury could draw the not-so-subtle inference from the evidence before it that the hostility of defendant's foreman and connivance of the personnel manager resulted in * * * [her] discharge. The foreman's overtures and the capricious firing at 2:00 a.m., the seeming manipulation of job assignments, and the apparent connivance of the personnel manager in this course of events all support the jury's conclusion that the dismissal was maliciously motivated.

In our opinion, however, the verdict included elements of damage not properly recoverable. The plaintiff lost 20 weeks employment at an average pay of $70.81 per week. This would account for $1,416.20 of the verdict, leaving $1,083.80 attributable to mental suffering. Such damages are not generally recoverable in a contract action. They could not be found in this case to have resulted from the discharge. Plaintiff had been having difficulty with her husband and had been receiving annoying telephone calls which upset her. She presented no medical testimony. Although she alleged that her discharge caused her mental suffering, her difficulties all preceded the discharge. We therefore remand the case for a new trial unless the plaintiff consents to a reduction of the verdict by the amount of $1,083.80.

Remanded.

NOTES

1. In *Monge*, the court held that a wrongfully discharged at-will employee may not recover damages for mental distress. The same rule normally applies even when a contract provides for job security. *See, e.g.*, Valentine v. General American Credit, Inc., 420 Mich. 256, 261–63, 362 N.W.2d 628, 630–31 (1984) ("[B]ecause an employment contract is not entered into primarily to secure the protection of personal interests and pecuniary damages can be estimated with reasonable certainty, * * * a person discharged in breach of an employment contract may not recover mental distress damages.").

2. For further consideration of what satisfies the "public policy" exception to the at-will doctrine, see Green v. Ralee Engineering Co., 19 Cal.4th 66, 78 Cal.Rptr.2d 16, 960 P.2d 1046 (1998) (employee's allegation that his termination was caused by complaints to government regulators about employer's defective manufacture of aircraft parts stated valid claim under "public policy" exception); Hummer v. Evans, 129 Idaho 274, 923 P.2d 981 (1996) (termination on the ground that employee testified as a witness in a criminal case was a violation of public policy). *But see* Winters v. Houston Chronicle Publishing Co., 795 S.W.2d 723 (Tex.1990) (private at-will employee who was discharged for reporting illegal activities of fellow employees to upper-level management failed to state a cause of action because he did not come within any of the statutory or common law exceptions). For a good discussion of the at-will doctrine and the developing public policy exception, see W. Dudley McCarter, *Wrongful Discharge Cause of Action in Violation of Public Policy*, 66 J.Mo.Bar 62 (2010) (Missouri Law); Stewart J. Schwab, *Wrongful Discharge Law and the Search for Third Party Effects*, 74 Tex. L. Rev. 1943 (1996); *see also* Cynthia Estlund, *How Wrong Are Employees About Their Rights, and Why Does it Matter?*, 77 N.Y.U. L. Rev. 6 (2002); Cynthia Estlund, *Wrongful Discharge Protections in an At–Will World*, 74 Tex. L. Rev. 1655 (1996); Cass Sunstein, *Human Behavior and the Law of Work*, 87 Va. L. Rev. 205 (2001); Sandra S. Park, Note, *Working Towards Freedom from Abuse: Recognizing a "Public Policy" Exception to Employment–At–Will for Domestic Violence Victims*, 59 N.Y.U. Ann. Surv. Am. L. 121 (2003).

3. Many courts allow a tort action for a wrongful or retaliatory discharge. As one California court recently described this action,

> [O]ur Supreme Court held that employees may bring an action in tort when their discharge contravenes the dictates of fundamental public policy. As the tort is predicated on public policy, rather than the terms and conditions of the employment relationship, an employee may assert it whether his employment is "at-will" or is based on an employment contract for a specific term. * * * Courts have recognized this tort in cases where the employee was terminated for (1) refusing to violate a statute, (2) performing a statutory obligation, (3) exercising a constitutional or statutory right, or (4) reporting a statutory violation for the public benefit.

Houck v. Calabasas Motorcards, Inc., 2009 WL 2553025 (Cal.App.2009). *See, e.g.*, Green v. Ralee Engineering Co., 19 Cal.4th 66, 78 Cal.Rptr.2d 16,

960 P.2d 1046 (1998); Adams v. George W. Cochran & Co., 597 A.2d 28 (D.C.1991). A few courts recognize a contract action instead of a tort action. Brockmeyer v. Dun & Bradstreet, 113 Wis.2d 561, 335 N.W.2d 834 (1983). The differences between tort and contract actions are discussed in *Brockmeyer*:

> Whether the cause of action for wrongful discharge should be maintained in tort or contract or both needs to be resolved. Those cases implying a contractual term of good faith dealing sounded in contract. Most, though not all of the public policy exception cases from other states were tort actions. The most significant distinction in our view between the two causes of action in wrongful discharge suits is in the damages that may be recovered. In tort actions, the only limitations are those of "proximate cause" or public policy considerations. Punitive damages are also allowed. In contract actions, damages are limited by the concepts of foreseeability and mitigation. The remedies established by the majority of Wisconsin wrongful discharge statutes are limited to reinstatement and backpay, contractual remedy concepts. We believe that reinstatement and backpay are the most appropriate remedies for public policy exception wrongful discharges since the primary concern in these actions is to make the wronged employee "whole." Therefore, we conclude that a contract action is most appropriate for wrongful discharges.

Id. at 574–75, 335 N.W.2d at 841; *see also* Strozinsky v. School District of Brown Deer, 237 Wis.2d 19, 614 N.W.2d 443 (2000).

Note that even in jurisdictions following the Wisconsin approach, courts sometimes allow the recovery of tort damages in the wrongful discharge setting where the employer's conduct is so egregious as to constitute the torts of "outrage" or "fraud." Consider the language of Sterling Drug, Inc. v. Oxford, 294 Ark. 239, 743 S.W.2d 380 (1988):

> One is subject to liability for outrage if he or she willfully or wantonly causes severe emotional distress to another by extreme and outrageous conduct. M.B.M. Co., Inc. v. Counce, 268 Ark. 269, 596 S.W.2d 681 (1980). In *Counce* we stated, "By extreme and outrageous conduct, we mean conduct that is so outrageous in character, and so extreme in degree, as to go beyond all possible bounds of decency, and to be regarded as atrocious, and utterly intolerable in civilized society." The employer in *Counce* discharged an employee supposedly because her services were no longer needed. After her termination, the employer told the employee that she would have to take a polygraph test in connection with a money shortage at the store before the company would release her last paycheck. Even though she passed the test, the employer deducted $36.00 from her paycheck as her share of the missing money. We found that there was a material issue of fact as to whether the employer's conduct was extreme and outrageous.

> In Tandy Corp. v. Bone, 283 Ark. 399, 678 S.W.2d 312 (1984), an employer interrogated an employee, whom it suspected of theft, at thirty minute intervals for most of a day, denied him valium when he was under obvious stress, and threatened him with arrest. In holding there was substantial evidence to support the jury verdict for outrage, we placed

special emphasis on the fact that even though the employer knew of the employee's lower than normal emotional stamina, it refused to permit him to take his medication during the interrogation.

In Hess v. Treece, 286 Ark. 434, 693 S.W.2d 792 (1985), *cert. denied*, 475 U.S. 1036, 106 S.Ct. 1245, 89 L.Ed.2d 354 (1986), Treece, a police officer, sued Hess, the Little Rock City Director, for outrage. Hess, who was angry with Treece over a personal matter, conducted surveillance of Treece, communicated to other individuals that he would have Treece fired at any cost, and apparently made false reports concerning Treece's employment conduct. Basing our decision in part on the fact that Hess' actions continued over a two year time span, we found there was substantial evidence to support the jury verdict for outrage.

Id. at 243–44, 743 S.W.2d at 382. *But see* Mackenzie v. Miller Brewing Co., 241 Wis.2d 700, 623 N.W.2d 739 (2001) (refusing to permit an at-will employee to sue for fraudulent inducement of the employment contract).

DAN B. DOBBS, LAW OF REMEDIES

618 (2d ed. 1993).*

About the same time that exceptions were developing to the "at will" rule, courts began dealing with important statutory provisions against retaliatory[4] and discriminatory discharges as well as with provisions against other forms of employment discrimination.[5] A patchwork of some complexity has resulted. Common law job rights, federal statutory rights and state statutory rights[6] must all be made to work with each other[7] and also with preexisting systems such as workers' compensation[8] and union-management grievance and arbitration procedures.[9] Because statutes protect against several forms of job discrimination and not merely against discharge[10] they are broader in scope than the present section, which considers discharge and closely analogous actions, such as discriminatory refusal to hire or promote.

Many strategy issues lurk in these materials, because remedies may be quite different depending on the claim asserted. For example, the

---

* Reprinted with permission of West Publishing Co.

4. *E.g.*, 42 U.S.C.A. § 7622; 42 U.S.C.A. § 5851; N.Y.—McKinney's Labor Law § 740. * * *

5. *E.g.*, 42 U.S.C.A. 2000e *et seq.* (Title VII of the 1964 Civil Rights Act). * * *

6. *E.g.*, Iowa Code Ann. § 601A.6.

7. *See* Froyd v. Cook, 681 F.Supp. 669 (E.D.Cal.1988) (state Fair Employment Housing Act did not preempt or displace state common law wrongful discharge action); Chrisman v. Philips Industries, Inc., 242 Kan. 772, 751 P.2d 140 (1988) (plaintiff contended he was discharged in part because he refused to approve the employer's defective products to be used in nuclear industry, claim held preempted by a federal anti-retaliatory statute dealing with nuclear industry); Lally v. Copygraphics, 85 N.J. 668, 428 A.2d 1317 (1981) (administrative remedy for retaliatory firing attributable to employee's workers' compensation claim does not bar tort suit).

8. *See* Note, *Workers' Compensation Exclusivity and Wrongful Termination Tort Damages: An Injurious Tug of War?*, 39 Hast.L.J. 1229 (1988).

9. *See* Korn, *Collective Rights and Individual Remedies: Rebalancing the Balance after Lingle v. Norge Division of Magic Chef, Inc.*, 41 Hastings L.J. 1149 (1990).

10. Wage and hour legislation, labor-management relations legislation for example. * * *

common law claims usually do not carry with them any award of attorney fees to the prevailing plaintiff, but the statutory claims routinely provide for such awards. On the other hand, some of the statutory claims did not traditionally permit punitive damages or mental distress damages or even consequential damages, while such damages are recoverable in some common law cases and under other statutes.[13]

NOTE

Probably the most important federal legislation dealing with discriminatory discharges and other forms of employment discrimination is Title VII of the Civil Rights Act of 1964. *See* 42 U.S.C.A. § 2000e *et seq.* Important amendments to Title VII contained in the Civil Rights Act of 1991 significantly expanded the remedies available to an aggrieved employee. This is especially the case with emotional distress and punitive damages. These remedial changes to Title VII have been described as follows:

Previously, under Title VII a prevailing plaintiff was entitled to injunctive relief, including reinstatement, backpay, lost benefits, attorneys' fees, certain litigation costs, and interest.[55] Under the Civil Rights Act of 1991, a prevailing plaintiff in a claim for intentional discrimination under Title VII also may be entitled to: (1) compensatory damages, including those for emotional pain, suffering, inconvenience, mental anguish, and loss of enjoyment of life; and (2) punitive damages if the plaintiff demonstrates that the employer engaged in discriminatory conduct with malice or with reckless indifference to the employee's federally protected rights.[56] For each complaining party, the amount of compensatory and punitive damages must not exceed:

—$50,000 for employers with more than 14 and fewer than 101 employees;[57]

—$100,000 for employers with more than 100 and fewer than 201 employees;

—$200,000 for employers with more than 200 and fewer than 501 employees; and

—$300,000 for employers with more than 500 employees.[58]

Significantly, the Act provides that a plaintiff who seeks compensatory or punitive damages may demand a jury trial.[59] A plaintiff may also be granted expert fees as part of an attorney's fee award.[60]

Under the Act, a defendant will be liable for declaratory and certain injunctive relief and a plaintiff's attorney's fees and costs if a plaintiff

---

13. Under 42 U.S.C.A. §§ 1981 and 1983 in particular.

55. 42 U.S.C.A. § 2000e–5 (1988).

56. 42 U.S.C.A. § 1981a (Supp.III 1992).

57. The employer must have the stated number of employees in each of 20 or more calendar weeks in the current or preceding year. These caps may be removed in the future.

58. 42 U.S.C.A. § 1981a(b) (Supp.III 1992).

59. *Id.* § 1981a(c).

60. *Id.* § 1988(b).

proves that race, color, religion, sex, or national origin was a "motivating factor" for any employment decision, even though other factors also motivated the employment decision, and where the defendant demonstrates that it would have taken the same action absent the impermissible motivation.[61] In those situations, however, a plaintiff is not allowed admission, reinstatement, hiring, promotion, backpay, or compensatory or punitive damages.[62]

The potential under the Act for the receipt of greater monetary rewards by plaintiffs and their attorneys undoubtedly will cause an increase in the number of discrimination charges and lawsuits filed against employers. In particular, the Act now provides a monetary remedy for sexual harassment victims not dependent on lost compensation. Previously, a sexually harassed employee could receive compensation only for economic losses under Title VII. Since loss of pay often does not accompany harassment, little or no monetary relief was provided for such claims. The possibility of greater financial rewards for plaintiffs and their counsel necessarily results in a substantial increase in employers' financial expo sure and makes settlement more difficult.

Now that plaintiffs can recover for emotional distress, mental anguish, pain and suffering, and may also recoup expert witness fees, plaintiffs are expected increasingly to use experts at trial. This will require employers seriously to consider utilizing experts on their own behalf which will result in more expensive litigation. It also makes trials more complex and more difficult for employers to win.

Marian C. Haney, *Litigation of a Sexual Harassment Case After the Civil Rights Act of 1991*, 68 Notre Dame L. Rev. 1037, 1044–45 (1993)*; *see also* Joanna Stromberg, *Sexual Harrassment: Discrimination or Tort?*, 12 UCLA Women's L.J. 317 (2003).

B.   RESTITUTION

In Chapter 4 we saw cases in which wives or female cohabitants were disadvantaged when seeking to recover a share of the household's assets because of laws and presumptions relating to property, marriage, divorce and cohabitation. In 2002, in *In re Estate* of Bunde, in Section 4.A of that Chapter, a woman who worked with her companion in his bakery until his death was denied, because of an erroneous application of the "express contract preclusion" rule, the opportunity to claim under unjust enrichment that she was entitled to recover from his estate based on promises he made. There was a dissent.

Much earlier, in 1959, in Verity v. Verity, in Section 5.B, Mrs. Verity sought a constructive trust over land, titled only in her husband's name, that she and her husband had purchased with money from farming where "she helped her husband." While the court awarded her an equitable lien

---

61. *Id.* §§ 2000e–2(m), 2000e–5(g)(2)(B).

62. *Id.* § 2000e–5(g)(2)(B).

* Reprinted with permission of the Notre Dame Law Review.

on the property for the amount of money she had spent managing the property, it denied the constructive trust. Even earlier, in 1948, in Dusenka v. Dusenka, *see* Section 7.B, a widow was denied a share from the business in which she had helped her husband because he had transferred it, unbeknownst to her, to his son from a prior marriage before his death and, according to the court, she had no expectation of compensation for her services.

Lest one think that the holdings in *Verity* and *Dusenka* are relegated to the pre-women's movement era, in 1993, in Kuder v. Schroeder, in Section 7.B, a wife who, at personal sacrifice, supported her husband through many years of education was unable to recover anything after he left her immediately upon finding a job. The judge writing for the majority of the court explained that "there is a personal duty of each spouse to support the other." The concurring judge thought it was unfortunate that there were no assets to distribute under the state's divorce laws. There was a dissent in this case as well as in *In re* Estate of Bunde.

In these cases from Chapter 4, the disadvantaged plaintiffs were women. Plaintiffs in this category of suit usually are women because they are more likely than men to provide more services than income to the household, and more likely than men not to acquire legal title to property or businesses in which they think they are a partner. *But see* Mitchell v. Moore, 1999 PA Super. 77, 729 A.2d 1200 (holding that the presumption that services were gratuitous was not rebutted in a case involving the dissolution of a relationship between two men). *Cf.*, Richards v. Brown, 2009 UT App 315, 222 P.3d 69 (awarding male cohabitant the value of his contributions to female cohabitant's house during the 10 years they lived together because otherwise the female would be unjustly enriched).

This section will look at some cases in which plaintiffs have been somewhat successful. For cases involving services in the commercial context, and a discussion of the dual use of the term *quantum meruit* to mean either contract implied in fact or, inconsistently, contract implied in law, see Section 2 of Chapter 4.

WATTS v. WATTS

Court of Appeals of Wisconsin, 1989.
152 Wis.2d 370, 448 N.W.2d 292.

FINE, JUDGE.

Sue Ann Watts (Bischoff) and James E. Watts lived together from May, 1969, to December, 1981, and represented themselves as being married to one another, though they were not. They purchased property together, and filed tax returns as husband and wife. Additionally, Bischoff and the two children of their relationship assumed the Watts surname with Watts' consent. Bischoff also helped Watts in his landscaping business, and maintained their cohabitational household.

In March, 1982, some three months after the relationship ended, Bischoff sued Watts seeking a share of the wealth accumulated by Watts during their twelve years of cohabitation. In 1987, the Wisconsin Supreme Court ruled that Bischoff could maintain an action against Watts under * * * express contract, implied-in-fact contract, unjust enrichment (implied-in-law contract or quasi-contract), and partition [*Watts I*]. On remand * * *, the case was tried to a jury, and these appeals follow.

* * *

* * * On the second issue, the jury found that Watts was unjustly enriched by Bischoff, and awarded her $113,090.08.

* * *

Watts raises two issues in connection with Bischoff's claim for unjust enrichment. First, he contends that there was no evidence from which the jury could have awarded $113,090.08. * * *

* * *

The basis for an unjust enrichment claim in a cohabitation case was framed by the Supreme Court in *Watts I*:

> Many courts have held, and we now so hold, that unmarried cohabitants may raise claims based upon unjust enrichment following the termination of their relationships where one of the parties attempts to retain an unreasonable amount of the property acquired through the efforts of both.

* * * There was extensive evidence concerning the services that Bischoff performed for Watts, in the upkeep of their home as well as in the service of his business, from which the jury could have determined that Bischoff's efforts fertilized the increased value of Watts' property, not only by helping him in the business but also by freeing him from many nonbusiness tasks. The jury also had ample information from which it could determine the increased value of that property during the time Watts and Bischoff lived and worked together as husband and wife. Financial statements for both Watts and his business for every year from 1970 through 1981 were in evidence, and Bischoff's expert indicated that Watts' net worth had increased by $1,113,900.88, from $382,756.12 in May of 1970 to $1,496,657 in 1981. The jury also knew that in 1972 Watts executed a will that would have given Bischoff ten per cent of his property, excluding personal property "directly used in connection with the operation" of his business, and excluding a parcel of real estate used in the business. The jury could have inferred that this was the value Watts placed on Bischoff's services in 1972, and, although the will excluded much business-related property, it was not unreasonable for the jury to use the ten per cent figure as a guide to determine an appropriate award to Bischoff for unjust enrichment for the 12 year relationship.[7]

Although neither party presented expert testimony on the value of the specific services performed by Bischoff for Watts, such expert testimony

---

7. Ten per cent of the increase in Watts' net worth given by Bischoff's expert ($1,113,900.88) is $111,390.08. The jury awarded Bischoff $113,090.08.

was not necessary. *See* Redepenning v. Dore, 56 Wis. 2d 129, 135–136, 201 N.W.2d 580, 584 (1972). *Cf.* Kujawski v. Arbor View Health Care Center, 139 Wis. 2d 455, 463, 407 N.W.2d 249, 252–253 (1987) (expert testimony not required when "determination involves matters within the common knowledge" or "within the realm of the ordinary experience of mankind.").

We agree with the trial court that there was sufficient evidence to support the jury's finding that Watts was unjustly enriched by Bischoff's efforts by $113,090.08, which is a little less than $12,000 a year.

* * *

MAGLICA v. MAGLICA

Court of Appeal, Fourth District, California, 1998.
66 Cal.App.4th 442, 78 Cal.Rptr.2d 101.

Sills, Presiding Justice.

I. Introduction

This case forces us to confront the legal doctrine known as *"quantum meruit"* in the context of a case about an unmarried couple who lived together and worked in a business solely owned by one of them. *Quantum meruit* is a Latin phrase, meaning "as much as he deserves," and is based on the idea that someone should get paid for beneficial goods or services which he or she bestows on another.

The trial judge instructed the jury that the reasonable value of the plaintiff's services was either the value of what it would have cost the defendant to obtain those services from someone else or the "value by which" he had "benefitted [sic] as a result" of those services. The instruction allowed the jury to reach a whopping number in favor of the plaintiff—$84 million—because of the tremendous growth in the value of the business over the years.

As we explain later, the finding that the couple had no contract in the first place is itself somewhat suspect because certain jury instructions did not accurately convey the law concerning implied-in-fact contracts. However, assuming that there was indeed no contract, the *quantum meruit* award cannot stand. The legal test for recovery in *quantum meruit* is not the value of the benefit, but value of the services (assuming, of course, that the services were beneficial to the recipient in the first place). In this case the failure to appreciate that fine distinction meant a big difference. People who work for businesses for a period of years and then walk away with $84 million do so because they have acquired some *equity* in the business, not because $84 million dollars is the going rate for the services of even the most workaholic manager. In substance, the court was allowing the jury to value the plaintiff's services as if she had made a sweetheart stock option deal—yet such a deal was precisely what the jury found she did not make. So the $84 million judgment cannot stand.

On the other hand, plaintiff was hindered in her ability to prove the existence of an implied-in-fact contract by a series of jury instructions which may have misled the jury about certain of the factors which bear on such contracts. The instructions were insufficiently qualified. They told the jury flat out that such facts as a couple's living together or holding themselves out as husband and wife or sharing a common surname did not mean that they had any agreement to share assets. That is not exactly correct. Such factors can, indeed, when taken together with other facts and in context, show the existence of an implied-in-fact contract. At most the jury instructions should have said that such factors do not *by themselves necessarily* show an implied-in-fact contract. Accordingly, when the case is retried, the plaintiff will have another chance to prove that she indeed had a deal for a share of equity in the defendant's business.

II. FACTS

The important facts in this case may be briefly stated. Anthony Maglica, a Croatian immigrant, founded his own machine shop business, Mag Instrument, in 1955. He got divorced in 1971 and kept the business. That year he met Claire Halasz, an interior designer. They got on famously, and lived together, holding themselves out as man and wife—hence Claire began using the name Claire Maglica—but never actually got married. And, while they worked side by side building the business, Anthony never agreed—or at least the jury found Anthony never agreed—to give Claire a share of the business. When the business was incorporated in 1974 all shares went into Anthony's name. Anthony was the president and Claire was the secretary. They were paid equal salaries from the business after incorporation. In 1978 the business began manufacturing flashlights, and, thanks in part to some great ideas and hard work on Claire's part (for example, coming out with a purse-sized flashlight in colors), the business boomed. Mag Instrument is now worth hundreds of millions of dollars.

In 1992 Claire discovered that Anthony was trying to transfer stock to his children but not her, and the couple split up in October. In June 1993 Claire sued Anthony for, among other things, breach of contract, breach of partnership agreement, fraud, breach of fiduciary duty and *quantum meruit*. The case came to trial in the spring of 1994. The jury awarded $84 million for the breach of fiduciary duty and *quantum meruit* causes of action, finding that $84 million was the reasonable value of Claire's services.

III. DISCUSSION

A. *The Jury's Finding That There Was No Agreement to Hold Property for One Another Meant There Was No Breach of Fiduciary Duty*

* * *

* * * A variety of statutes impose rights and obligations on married people. One set * * * establish[es] a fiduciary duty between spouses with regard to the management and control of community assets * * * and provide[es] for remedies for a breach of that duty. * * *

It would be contrary * * * to the evident policy of the law to promote formal (as distinct from common law) marriage to impose fiduciary duties based on a common law marriage. * * *

* * *

B.   Quantum Meruit Allows Recovery for the Value of Beneficial Services, Not the Value by Which Someone Benefits From Those Services

The absence of a contract between Claire and Anthony, however, would not preclude her recovery in *quantum meruit*: As every first year law student knows or should know, recovery in *quantum meruit* does not require a contract. * * *

The classic formulation concerning the measure of recovery in *quantum meruit* is found in Palmer v. Gregg, *supra*, 65 Cal.2d 657, 56 Cal.Rptr. 97, 422 P.2d 985. Justice Mosk, writing for the court, said: "The measure of recovery in *quantum meruit* is the reasonable value of the services rendered provided they were of direct benefit to the defendant." * * *

The underlying idea behind *quantum meruit* is the law's distaste for unjust enrichment. If one has received a benefit which one may not justly retain, one should "restore the aggrieved party to his [or her] former position by return of the *thing* or its *equivalent* in money." * * *

* * * [C]ourts have always required that the plaintiff have bestowed some benefit on the defendant as a prerequisite to recovery.

But the threshold requirement that there be a benefit from the services can lead to confusion, as it did in the case before us. It is one thing to require that the defendant be benefited by services, it is quite another to *measure* the reasonable value of those services by the value by which the defendant was "benefited" as a *result* of them. Contract price and the reasonable value of services rendered are two separate things; sometimes the reasonable value of services exceeds a contract price. * * * And sometimes it does not.

At root, allowing *quantum meruit* recovery based on "resulting benefit" of services rather than the reasonable value of beneficial services affords the plaintiff the best of both contractual and quasi-contractual recovery. Resulting benefit is an open-ended standard, which, as we have mentioned earlier, can result in the plaintiff obtaining recovery amounting to de facto ownership in a business all out of reasonable relation to the value of services rendered. After all, a particular service timely rendered can have, as Androcles was once pleasantly surprised to discover in the case of a particular lion, disproportionate value to what it would cost on the open market.

The facts in this court's decision in Passante v. McWilliam (1997) 53 Cal.App.4th 1240, 62 Cal.Rptr.2d 298, illustrate the point nicely. In

Passante, the attorney for a fledgling baseball card company gratuitously arranged a needed loan for $100,000 at a crucial point in the company's history; because the loan was made the company survived and a grateful board promised the attorney a three percent equity interest in the company. The company eventually became worth more than a quarter of a billion dollars, resulting in the attorney claiming *$33 million* for his efforts in arranging but a single loan. This court would later conclude, because of the attorney's duty to the company as an attorney, that the promise was unenforceable. * * * Interestingly enough, however, the one cause of action the plaintiff in *Passante* did not sue on was *quantum meruit*; while this court opined that the attorney should certainly get paid "something" for his efforts, a *$33 million* recovery in *quantum meruit* would have been too much. Had the services been bargained for, the going price would likely have been simply a reasonable finder's fee. * * *

The jury instruction given here allows the value of services to depend on their impact on a defendant's business rather than their reasonable value. True, the services must be of benefit if there is to be any recovery at all; even so, the benefit is not necessarily related to the reasonable value of a particular set of services. Sometimes luck, sometimes the impact of others makes the difference. Some enterprises are successful; others less so. Allowing recovery based on resulting benefit would mean the law imposes an exchange of equity for services, and that can result in a windfall—as in the present case—or a serious shortfall in others. Equity-for-service compensation packages are extraordinary in the labor market, and always the result of specific bargaining. To impose such a measure of recovery would make a deal for the parties that they did not make themselves. If courts cannot use *quantum meruit* to change the terms of a contract which the parties did make * * *, it follows that neither can they use *quantum meruit* to impose a highly generous and extraordinary contract that the parties did not make.

* * *

Telling the jury that it could measure the value of Claire's services by "[t]he value by which Defendant has benefited as a result of [her] services" was error. It allowed the jury to value Claire's services as having bought her a de facto ownership interest in a business whose owner never agreed to give her an interest. On remand, that part of the jury instruction must be dropped.

* * *

D. Certain Jury Instructions May Have Misled the Jury Into Finding There Was No Implied Contract When In Fact There Was One

As we have shown, the *quantum meruit* damage award cannot stand in the wake of the jury's finding that Claire and Anthony had no agreement to share the equity in Anthony's business. But the validity of that very finding itself is challenged in Claire's protective cross-appeal, where she attacks a series of * * * jury instructions, specially drafted and proffered by Anthony. * * *

The problem with the three instructions is this: They isolate three uncontested facts about the case: (1) living together, (2) holding themselves out to others as husband and wife, (3) providing services "such as" being a constant companion and confidant—and, seriatim, tell the jury that these facts definitely do not mean there was an implied contract. True, none of these facts by *themselves* and *alone* necessarily *compels* the conclusion that there was an implied contract. But that does not mean that these facts cannot, in conjunction with all the facts and circumstances of the case, establish an implied contract. In point of fact, they can.

Unlike the "quasi-contractual" *quantum meruit* theory which operates *without* an actual agreement of the parties, an implied-in-fact contract entails an actual contract, but one manifested in conduct rather than expressed in words. * * *

We certainly do not say that living together, holding themselves out as husband and wife, and being companions and confidants, even taken together, are *sufficient in and of themselves* to show an implied agreement to divide the equity in a business owned by one of the couple. However, * * * such facts, together with others bearing more directly on the business and the way the parties treated the equity and proceeds of the business, *can* be part of a series of facts which do show such an agreement. The vice of the three instructions here is that they affirmatively suggested that living together, holding themselves out, and companionship could not, as a matter of law, even be *part* of the support for a finding of an implied agreement. That meant the jury could have completely omitted these facts when considering the other factors which might also have borne on whether there was an implied contract.

On remand, the three instructions should not be given. The jury should be told, rather, that while the facts that a couple live together, hold themselves out as married, and act as companions and confidants toward each other do not, by themselves, show an implied agreement to share property, those facts, when taken together and in conjunction with other facts bearing more directly on the alleged arrangement to share property, can show an implied agreement to share property.

DISPOSITION

The judgment is reversed. The case is remanded for a new trial. At the new trial, the jury instructions identified in this opinion as erroneous shall not be given.

NOTES

1. Would you try to settle *Watts* or *Maglica* after these opinions had been handed down? What leverage does each party have?

2. In *Watts*, what might the result have been had the defendant not put Bischoff (Sue Ann Watts) in his will. Would you recommend that the plaintiff receive a proportionate share of the wealth? *See generally* Carol S. Bruch, *Property Rights of De Facto Spouses Including Thoughts on the Value of Homemakers' Services*, 10 Fam. L.Q. 101 (1976). Or would you award the reasonable value of her services, as in *Maglica*, unless the jury on remand were to find a contract implied-in-fact? Which approach is consistent with the goals of restitution? Restitution is covered in detail in Chapter 4.

3. Plaintiffs in cohabitation cases have been barred by the rules that (1) disallow recovery to someone who was in a "meretricious relationship," and (2) disallow payment for services within a household on the presumption that such services are gratuitous. Professor Peter Linzer has said, "One thing that should be apparent, but isn't to many people, is that both these rules are heavily loaded against women: women usually provide services within a household, and the 'meretricious relationship' ban will almost always leave a man with happy memories and a woman with nothing." Peter Linzer, *Rough Justice: A Theory of Restitution and Reliance, Contracts and Torts*, 2001 Wis. L. Rev. 695, 705 (2001). Do the rules articulated in either *Watts* or *Maglica* continue to be "heavily loaded against women"? *See also* Jill Elaine Hasday, *Intimacy and Economic Exchange*, 119 Harv. L. Rev. 491 (2005) ("efforts to denote the sanctity of intimate relationships through the regulation of economic exchange appear to systematically perpetuate and exacerbate distributive inequality for women and the poor").

4. Marvin v. Marvin, 18 Cal.3d 660, 134 Cal.Rptr. 815, 557 P.2d 106 (1976), was one of the leading cohabitation cases holding that a claim for recovery was not invalid because of the unmarried status of the plaintiff and the defendant. It involved a claim by a female plaintiff who had given up her professional career and cohabitated for six years with the defendant, a successful actor. At the end of this period, the defendant asked the plaintiff to leave his premises. The plaintiff alleged that she had given up a lucrative career as an entertainer and singer in order to "devote her full time to defendant ... as a companion, homemaker, housekeeper and cook" after the defendant agreed that they would share, equally, the property accumulated "as a result of their efforts whether individual or combined" and would hold themselves out to the public as husband and wife. She sought a declaratory judgment as to her contract and property rights, and a constructive trust of one-half of the property acquired during the course of the relationship. The trial court had dismissed her suit. In remanding, the Supreme Court of California stated:

> The courts may inquire into the conduct of the parties to determine whether that conduct demonstrates an implied contract or implied agreement of partnership or joint venture * * * or some other tacit understanding between the parties. The courts may, when appropriate, employ principles of constructive trust * * * or resulting trust * * *. Finally, a nonmarital partner may recover in *quantum meruit* for the reasonable value of household services rendered less the reasonable value of support received if he can show that he rendered services with the expectation of monetary reward. * * *

Since we have determined that plaintiff's complaint * * * can be amended to state a cause of action independent of allegations of express contract, we must conclude that the trial court erred in granting defendant a judgment on the pleadings.

Id. at 684–85, 134 Cal.Rptr. at 831–32, 557 P.2d at 122–23.

On remand, the trial court, without a jury, found that the defendant had made no agreement with the plaintiff for sharing income or to provide for her financial needs, that she had benefitted "economically and socially" from the cohabitation, and that there was no "fiduciary relationship" and no unjust enrichment as a result of the relationship. However, the court awarded the plaintiff $104,000 to be used for her "economic rehabilitation," because it was doubtful that she could return to the career she enjoyed before the relationship began and she, therefore, "was in need of rehabilitation—i.e., to learn new employable skills." The defendant appealed.

The Court of Appeals set the award aside. While the record showed the plaintiff's need and defendant's ability to respond to the need, the court stated: "The award, being nonconsensual in nature, must be supported by some recognized underlying obligation in law or in equity. A court of equity admittedly has broad powers, but it may not create totally new substantive rights under the guise of doing equity." Marvin v. Marvin, 122 Cal.App.3d 871, 876, 176 Cal.Rptr. 555, 559 (1981).

5. In 2000, the American Law Institute approved the Principles of the Law of Family Dissolution, which includes a chapter governing the dissolution of cohabitants' relationships. *See* Grace Ganz Blumberg, *Unmarried Partners and the Legacy of* Marvin v. Marvin*: The Regularization of Nonmarital Cohabitation: Rights and Responsibilities in the American Welfare State*, 76 Notre Dame L. Rev. 1265 (2001). In addition, Tentative Draft No. 3 (2003) of the Restatement (Third) of Restitution and Unjust Enrichment has added a section to permit one cohabitant to sue the other for unjust enrichment. Both of these apply to opposite-sex and same-sex relationships. As the ALI recognizes, attitudes towards the rights of unmarried cohabitants have been changing, but they are not changing universally or consistently. *See* Ann Laquer Estin, *Ordinary Cohabitation*, 76 Notre Dame L. Rev. 1381 (2001). For a review of the variety of approaches that states use either to refuse or to permit recovery to a cohabitant, see D. Kelly Weisberg & Susan Frelich Appleton, *Unmarried Couples' Rights* Inter Se, *in* Modern Family Law: Cases and Materials 416–45 (1998). Will the changing attitudes reflected in the American Law Institute's works recognizing the rights of cohabitants make it easier for plaintiffs in the twenty-first century to recover when their relationships have come to an end than it was previously? How important is the role of restitution?

C. SPECIFIC PERFORMANCE
AND INJUNCTIVE RELIEF

FRANKLIN POINT, INC. v. HARRIS
TRUST & SAVINGS BANK

Appellate Court of Illinois, First District, 1995.
277 Ill.App.3d 491, 214 Ill.Dec. 13, 660 N.E.2d 204.

JUSTICE McNULTY delivered the opinion of the court:

* * *

On July 30, 1990, [Franklin Point, Inc.] FPI and Harris Bank entered into a written contract pursuant to which Harris Bank agreed to build and occupy an office building at an eight-acre, multi-use commercial real estate development located near Chicago's downtown, called Franklin Point. Harris Bank agreed to purchase a certain parcel of land in the development for approximately $11,500,000. Harris Bank agreed that by July 30, 1993, it would commence construction on that land of a high-rise office building containing not more than 1,200,000 square feet and not less than 800,000 square feet. The contract stressed the importance of Harris Bank's building as an anchor of the Franklin Point development.

Harris Bank paid FPI approximately $11,500,000 for the sale of the property, but Harris Bank failed to begin construction of the high-rise office building by July 30, 1993. No other part of Franklin Point was developed. FPI brought suit against Harris Bank for specific performance and damages. The trial court dismissed FPI's claim for specific performance on the basis that "Illinois law is well-settled that specific performance of construction projects is forbidden as a matter of law." The trial court also denied with prejudice FPI's request for leave to file an amended complaint.

FPI appeals, contending that specific performance is not forbidden in all construction contracts and is appropriate in this particular case since: (1) the parties contractually agreed to a dispute resolution mechanism regarding approval of construction plans and designs that would avoid judicial supervision of the building process; (2) Harris Bank was bound contractually to follow a set of detailed development guidelines when building its office building; and (3) Harris Bank expressly agreed in the contract that specific performance is an appropriate remedy.

* * *

Since Klingbeil [v. Becklenberg, 249 Ill.App. 39 (1928)], Illinois courts of review have upheld trial court decisions refusing to grant specific performance of contracts to construct a building in several cases. These courts denied specific performance not simply on the basis that a construction contract was involved, but rather after making a determination that the courts would have to become involved with prolonged and continuous oversight of the construction process. * * *

In Bezin v. Ginsburg (1980), 91 Ill.App.3d 555, 47 Ill.Dec. 284, 415 N.E.2d 9, the plaintiff sought to have rebuilt a building defendant had torn down. The court denied plaintiff's request for specific performance on the basis that ordering the rebuilding of the building would force the court to become an expert in the methods and skills of the construction industry and involve the court in constant and prolonged supervision over the construction process through supplementary proceedings designed to assure that the order was being carried out by a party who obviously had no desire to carry it out. * * *

As other courts have recognized, specific performance of a construction contract should not be denied simply because it involves the construction of a building. In Grayson–Robinson Stores, Inc. v. Iris Construction Corp. (1960), 8 N.Y.2d 133, 137, 202 N.Y.S.2d 303, 305, 168 N.E.2d 377, 378, the majority found specific performance appropriate where the plans and specifications for the building were completed or practically complete. The majority explained that "[t]here is no hard and fast rule against applying the remedy of specific performance to [building construction] contracts, especially when the parties have by agreement provided for just that remedy." 8 N.Y.2d at 137, 202 N.Y.S.2d at 305, 168 N.E.2d at 378.

In City Stores Co. v. Ammerman (D.C.Cir.1967), 266 F.Supp. 766, aff'd (1968), 394 F.2d 950, the court found specific performance appropriate and enforced an option that required a party to construct a building. The court found that the standards to be followed in construction of the store were set out in the leases with specific particularity, making design and approval of the store a fairly simple matter if the parties dealt with each other in good faith. The court noted that specific performance should not be denied merely on the generic subject matter of the contract, but should instead involve a weighing of the need for ongoing judicial supervision with the importance of enforcement to the plaintiff.

Thus we view the critical inquiry in the instant case to be not simply whether FPI is seeking specific performance of a construction contract, but rather, whether if specific performance is granted, the court will be required to become involved in prolonged supervision of the building's construction if disputes arise. * * *

* * *

FPI's complaint alleges that under the terms of FPI and Harris Bank's agreement, there would be no need for the trial court to become involved in Harris Bank's construction of the building. FPI claims that its contract with Harris Bank granted Harris Bank the sole discretion in the design and construction of the interior of the building. According to FPI, this eliminates the need for any judicial supervision as to the building's interior. Furthermore, the parties contractually agreed that an architectural review board (the ARB) would be appointed and that Harris Bank would need to obtain the ARB's approval on all other construction plans. FPI claims that the ARB's role in preapproval of all construction plans and designs would remove the potential for disputes and obviate the need for judicial oversight in the construction process.

* * *

Harris Bank, on the other hand, contends that because FPI has the authority to appoint the majority of the members of the ARB, the ARB will never approve Harris Bank's construction plans. Harris Bank also claims that it will likely challenge any decision made by the ARB. We must assume, however, that the parties will deal with each other in good faith. Also, because FPI is the party seeking the construction of the building, it is unlikely that the members of the ARB will unreasonably disapprove of construction plans so as to hinder the construction process. Nonetheless, we are not convinced, based on FPI's allegations in its current complaint for specific performance, that the ARB will completely eliminate the need for prolonged and constant judicial supervision of the building's construction.

FPI maintains that given the opportunity to amend its complaint, it will be able to demonstrate that the ARB will eliminate any need for continuous and prolonged judicial supervision of the building's construction. The establishment of the ARB under the contract in the case at bar presents us with a factual situation unlike those previously addressed by Illinois courts. * * *

* * *

In the case at bar, we are not ordering the trial court to grant specific performance. We are merely directing the trial court to permit FPI one opportunity to amend its complaint to attempt to show that the ARB will [be able to perform its functions so that] a decree of specific performance would not embroil the court in the ongoing supervision of the construction contract disputes. Therefore, since we are not ordering the trial court to grant specific performance in this case, the fact that * * * no [Illinois] court of review has found that the trial court's refusal to decree specific performance in a building construction case was an abuse of discretion does not require us to conclude that specific performance is unavailable in a building construction case as a matter of law.

We do not suggest that the parties can require a court to recognize the remedy of specific performance merely by contractually agreeing to it should there be a breach. A court has the independent duty to determine whether the contract can be specifically performed without inordinate monitoring or supervision of performance by the court, notwithstanding the fact the parties agreed to the appropriateness of the remedy. Therefore, we believe that FPI should have at least one opportunity to amend its complaint in order to allege additional facts more clearly demonstrating how the ARB will operate and why the presence of the ARB would obviate the necessity of judicial oversight of the building's construction. * * *

* * *

Accordingly, for the reasons set forth above, the trial court's order denying FPI an opportunity to amend count I of its complaint requesting specific performance is reversed and this case is remanded for further proceedings.

* * *

THOMAS J. O'BRIEN, J., concurs.

JUSTICE COUSINS, dissenting:

* * *

Finding no Illinois case to support its opinion, the majority seeks to rely upon the New York case of Grayson–Robinson Stores, Inc. v. Iris Construction Corp. * * * *Grayson-Robinson* is an arbitration award case. There, the court found specific performance appropriate where the plans and specifications for the building were completed or practically completed. However, the *Grayson-Robinson* decision, where the plans were completed or practically completed, was expressly rejected in Yonan v. Oak Park Federal Savings & Loan Association (1975), 75 Ill.App.3d 967, 975, 326 N.E.2d 773, where the court wrote: "However, it is our opinion that the traditional and well-established principal that specific performance of building and construction contracts will be denied is the better reasoned rule of law. We espouse the view that the trial courts are not particularly well suited to supervise building construction and that denial of specific performance of such contracts promotes the goal of all litigation, finality." * * *

Regarding the futility of specific performance in the case sub judice, see also New Park Forest Associates II v. Rogers Enterprises, Inc. (1990), 195 Ill.App.3d 757, 765, 142 Ill.Dec. 474, 552 N.E.2d 1215, wherein the court, in denying injunctive relief, wrote: "It is possible that, during the life of a mandatory injunction, the court would never have to enforce any of those terms or judge 'better quality.' Problems may never arise. If problems did arise, however, the court would find itself in the business of managing a shopping center." * * *

NOTE

For a discussion of the law governing specific performance of construction contracts, see Fran Realty, Inc. v. Thomas, 30 Md.App. 362, 354 A.2d 196 (1976); Eliot L. Axelrod, *Judicial Attitudes Toward Specific Performance of Construction Contracts*, 7 U. Dayton L. Rev. 33 (1981); Edward F. Barnicle, Jr., *Expediting Construction by Enjoining Performance*, 21 Prac. Law. 59 (July, 1975); Comment, *Specific Performance of Construction Contracts— Archaic Principles Preclude Necessary Reform*, 47 Notre Dame L. Rev. 1025 (1972). *See generally* M.T. Van Hecke, *Changing Emphases in Specific Performance*, 40 N.C. L. Rev. 1, 13–14 (1961); Annotation, 38 A.L.R.3d 1052 (1971). For an excellent discussion of the use of special masters in specific performance litigation, see Alan Schwartz, *The Case for Specific Performance*,

89 Yale L.J. 271, 292–96 (1979) (recommending that breaching party bear costs of special master).

M. LEO STORCH LIMITED PARTNERSHIP
v. EROL'S, INC.

Court of Special Appeals of Maryland, 1993.
95 Md.App. 253, 620 A.2d 408.

BISHOP, JUDGE.

* * *

Storch is the owner of Hilltop Plaza Shopping Center located in Bowie, Maryland. The rentable area of Hilltop Plaza is 116,075 square feet. On August 7, 1984, Hannah Storch, Storch's predecessor, and Erol's entered into an agreement for the lease of a 5,400 square foot portion (4.6522%) of the shopping center. Erol's planned to use the leased premises ("Hilltop Erol's") to sell and rent televisions, video cameras, video tape recorders, videotapes, movies, and accessories. The initial term of the lease was five years, beginning October 1, 1984. Erol's exercised its option to renew the lease for an additional five year term, ending September 30, 1994. Erol's rent obligation was fixed—the monthly rent did not fluctuate with Hilltop Erol's monthly gross sales.

Starting in August 1990, Hilltop Erol's averaged 3,000 customers per month. In order to turn a profit, however, Hilltop Erol's was required to average over 5,000 customers per month. Accordingly, Hilltop Erol's operated at a loss; the store projected that it would continue to operate at a loss in 1992. The entire Erol's chain experienced similar difficulties.

* * *

After learning of Erol's intention to close Hilltop Erol's, Storch filed the action *sub judice*. In Count III of the complaint, Storch averred:

Defendants are bound to operate the leased premises "during the entire term of this Lease with due diligence and efficiency" and to "carry at all times in said premises a stock of merchandise of such size, character and quality as shall be reasonably designed to produce the maximum return to Landlord and Tenant." Defendants are breaching this covenant by closing the Hilltop Plaza store. Plaintiffs are being irreparably injured and will continue to be irreparably injured by defendants' breach.

Wherefore plaintiffs pray that the Court issue a temporary and permanent injunction enjoining defendants closing of the Hilltop Plaza store.

Storch relied on, in part, the "continuous operation clause" found in paragraph nine of the agreement which provides:

Tenant shall operate all of the leased premises during the entire term of this Lease with due diligence and efficiency so as to produce all of the gross sales which may be produced by such manner of operation, unless prevented from doing so by causes beyond Tenant's control. Subject to inability by reason of strikes or labor disputes, Tenant shall carry at all times in said premises a stock of merchandise of such size, character and quality as shall be reasonably designed to produce the maximum return to Landlord and Tenant.

On February 3, 1992, the trial court denied Storch's motion for ex parte injunctive relief, and, instead, issued a show cause order. Three days later, Hilltop Erol's closed. At the time of the hearing on the show cause order (i.e., the hearing on the motion for interlocutory injunctive relief), Hilltop Erol's had been closed for over six weeks; two years, five months remained until Erol's obligation under the lease agreement would terminate.

Pamela Handy ("Handy"), Erol's district manager, testified that each Erol's store requires a manager, assistant manager, two part-time managers and two part-time associates. Erol's managers must be able to control inventory and "shrinkage," review profit and loss reports, work within budgets, and handle payroll, hiring and firing. Erol's employees undergo a ninety-day training class when they are first hired. According to Handy, in order to be successful within the video industry:

> you really need to have some type of movie knowledge; being able to select and help purchase tapes that [Erol's] will select for certain stores. You have to know your customers, what titles are going to rent in a particular store, how many copies you need to buy for that. You need to be able to supply customers with that knowledge; to be able to put a movie in their hands and let them rent.

Handy testified that, in order to reopen Hilltop Erol's, Erol's would have to interview, hire, and train new employees, and would have to purchase five to eight thousand movie titles.

* * *

* * * We hold that the trial court did not abuse its discretion when it denied interlocutory injunctive relief because Storch did not prove a "likelihood of success on the merits."

* * *

Storch is seeking injunctive relief to enforce the continuous operation clause of the lease agreement. Maryland courts have allowed "[i]njunctive relief * * * as the functional equivalent of specific performance." *SECI, Inc.*, 63 Md.App. at 726, 493 A.2d 1100. However, " '[a] suit for an injunction which seeks to accomplish all the purposes of a decree for specific performance is subject to the principles which apply to an application for the latter remedy * * *.' " *Id.* (quoting Smith v. Meyers, 130 Md. 64, 67, 99 A. 938 (1917)) (alteration in original).

It is well-settled that

where [a] contract is, in its nature and circumstances, unobjectiona-
ble—or, as it is sometimes stated, fair, reasonable and certain in all its
terms—it is as much a matter of course for a court of equity to decree
specific performance of it as it is for a court of law to award damages
for its breach.

Gross v. J & L Camping & Sports Ctr., Inc., 270 Md. 539, 543–44, 312
A.2d 270 (1973) (quoting Glendale Corp. v. Crawford, 207 Md. 148, 154,
114 A.2d 33 (1955)). * * * It is equally settled, however,

that specific performance will not [ordinarily] be decreed if the
performance is of such a character as to make effective enforcement
unreasonably difficult or to require such long-continued supervision
by the court as is disproportionate to the advantages to be gained
from such a decree and to the harm to be suffered in case it is denied.

Edison Realty Co. v. Bauernschub, 191 Md. 451, 460, 62 A.2d 354 (1948)
* * *. Although the trial court *may* award injunctive relief notwithstanding the difficulty of enforcement, the failure to grant an injunction under
such circumstances does not constitute an abuse of the court's discretion.
See Bauernschub, 191 Md. at 460, 62 A.2d 354.

* * *

Storch cites * * * Dover Shopping Ctr., Inc. v. Cushman's Sons, Inc.,
63 N.J.Super. 384, 164 A.2d 785 (App.Div.1960), and Lincoln Tower Corp.
v. Richter's Jewelry Co., 152 Fla. 542, 12 So.2d 452 (1943), to demonstrate
that courts have specifically enforced continuous operation clauses of
shopping center leases. These cases, however, "are both old * * * and
against the weight of authority." *CBL & Assocs., Inc.,* 761 F.Supp. at 812.
See generally John A. Glenn, Annotation, *Lease of Store as Requiring
Active Operation of Store,* 40 A.L.R.3d 971 (1971 & Supp.1992). Several
courts have recently rejected *Dover Shopping Ctr., Inc.* and *Lincoln Tower
Corp.* and have followed the established principle of equity that

* * * "[C]ontracts which by their terms stipulate for a succession of
acts, whose performance cannot be consummated by one transaction,
but will be continuous, and require protracted supervision and direction, with the exercise of special knowledge, skill, or judgment in
such oversight, * * * are not, as a rule, specifically enforced." Pomeroy on Specific Performance of Contracts, § 312, and cases cited in
note 5; Waterman on Specific Performance of Contracts, § 49; Electric Co. v. Mobile, *supra* [109 Ala. 190, 195, 19 So. 721] * * *.

Lorch, Inc. v. Bessemer Mall Shopping Ctr., Inc., 294 Ala. 17, 310 So.2d
872, 875 (1975) (quoting Tombigbee Valley R.R. v. Fairford Lumber Co.,
155 Ala. 575, 47 So. 88 (1908)).

For example, in New Park Forest Assocs. II v. Rogers Enters., Inc.,
195 Ill.App.3d 757, 142 Ill.Dec. 474, 552 N.E.2d 1215, *cert. denied,* 133
Ill.2d 559, 149 Ill.Dec. 324, 561 N.E.2d 694 (1990), the plaintiff shopping
center brought an action against one of its tenants, seeking a temporary
injunction, an order of specific performance, and a permanent injunction

to prevent the defendant from closing its store in violation of a continuous operation clause. The lease required defendant to "operat[e] [the] store for the 'sale and repair of better quality jewelry' " and prohibited defendant from " 'vacat[ing] or abandon[ing] the Premises at any time during the Term.' " *Id.* 142 Ill.Dec. at 475, 552 N.E.2d at 1216. The Appellate Court of Illinois held that the plaintiff did not have a likelihood of success on the merits:

> In this case, success on the merits means that the court would order specific performance of the long term lease.

> * * *

> Generally, Illinois courts have refused to enter mandatory injunctions to enforce contracts "which by their terms call for a succession of acts whose performance can not be consummated by one transaction, and which require protracted supervision and direction. * * * A court of equity will not assume what it can not practically accomplish."

Id. 142 Ill.Dec. at 477, 552 N.E.2d at 1218 (quoting Grape Creek Coal Co. v. Spellman, 39 Ill.App. 630, 632 (1891)).

> The contract in this case calls for [defendant's] continuous occupancy and use of the leased space until approximately December 31, 1997, nine years after [plaintiff] first requested an injunction and specific performance. The lease contains numerous detailed provisions for hours, signs, displays, painting, common areas and other operational requirements. Even the very purpose of the lease, the operation of a premises for the "sale and repair of better quality jewelry," raises enforcement problems for a court which could be placed in the position of deciding what constitutes "better quality." It is possible, that during the life of a mandatory injunction, the court would never have to enforce any of those terms or judge "better quality." Problems may never arise. If problems did arise, however, the court would find itself in the business of managing a shopping center.

Id. 142 Ill.Dec. at 478–79, 552 N.E.2d at 1219–20.

Similarly, the New York Supreme Court, Appellate Division, held that the plaintiff shopping plaza was not entitled to an order of specific performance in Grossman v. Wegman's Food Mkts., Inc., 43 A.D.2d 813, 350 N.Y.S.2d 484 (N.Y.App.Div.1973). The Court recognized

> that a food store will draw people to a shopping center who will also patronize the other stores and that while the food store is closed the business of the other stores will be diminished. There might well be damage to the other tenants while the food store remains vacant, and, if the vacancy extends over a long period of time, it is possible that a tenant might also vacate its premises with resulting damage to plaintiffs.

Id. 350 N.Y.S.2d at 485. The Court, however, followed an earlier case, Price v. Herman, 81 N.Y.S.2d 361 (N.Y.Sup.Ct.1948), *aff'd,* 275 App.Div.

675, 87 N.Y.S.2d 221 (N.Y.App.Div.1949), where it was held that a court would not grant an injunction or order specific performance to enforce a continuous operation clause of a lease " 'requir[ing] the performance of varied and continuous acts, or the exercise of special skill, taste, and judgment, * * * because the execution of the decree would require such constant superintendence as to make judicial control a matter of extreme difficulty.' " *Id.* 81 N.Y.S.2d at 362 * * *.

We conclude "that the decisions denying injunctive relief reflect the modern trend and the majority rule." 8600 Assocs., Ltd. v. Wearguard Corp., 737 F.Supp. 44, 46 (E.D.Mich.1990); *see also CBL & Assocs., Inc.,* 761 F.Supp. at 812; *Lorch, Inc.,* 310 So.2d at 876; Madison Plaza, Inc. v. Shapira Corp., 180 Ind.App. 141, 387 N.E.2d 483, 487 (1979). An interlocutory injunction that requires Erol's to reopen its Hilltop store would be of the "mandatory" variety—Erol's would have to interview, hire, train, and oversee management and employees. Handy's testimony makes clear that the day-to-day operations of the store would necessarily include varied and continuous acts that require the exercise of special skill, taste, and judgment. *See Lorch, Inc.,* 310 So.2d at 875; Grossman v. Wegman's Food Mkts., Inc., 350 N.Y.S.2d at 485–86.

Although it is quite possible that, during the life of a mandatory injunction, the court would never have to enforce any of the terms of the continuous operation clause, if problems did arise, the court would find itself in the business of managing a retail video operation. * * * We do not hold that injunctive relief may never be ordered to enforce a continuous operation clause under compelling circumstances. That decision lies within the sound discretion of the trial court. We hold only that the trial court did not abuse its discretion in the case *sub judice* because the injunction could require the continuous supervision of the court over an extended period of time and, therefore, would make "effective enforcement unreasonably difficult." * * *

NOTES

1. As the principal case illustrates, many courts are reluctant to grant specific performance of continuous operation provisions because of a perceived supervision problem. As one recent commentator emphasizes:

> Courts do not want to involve themselves in the business of operating a shopping center. The knowledge needed to operate a store in a shopping center may exceed the expertise of the court. Specialized "knowledge, skill and judgment is necessarily involved in selecting and investing in inventory, selecting, training and compensating adequate personnel and innumerable other day-to-day business decisions." 8600 Assoc. v. Wearguard Corp., 737 F.Supp. 44, 46 (E.D.Mich.1990). Courts and their personnel normally do not possess the specialized knowledge that is necessary for the proper operation of the business.

Austin Hood, *Continuous Operation Clauses and Going Dark*, 36 Real Prop. Prob. & Tr. J. 365, 387 (2001). Is supervision a genuine concern? Most national lessees have good will to protect. If ordered to operate, are such lessees likely to do a less than adequate job? In any event, can't a lessee who is "compelled to operate" negotiate with the landlord for the "purchase" of the injunction?

What type of fact situation provides the strongest case for overcoming the supervision objection to specific performance? Consider the following language by a federal court interpreting Ohio law:

> [T]he court further finds that the circumstances presented in this case would justify an order requiring specific performance of a continuous operation obligation, if Hills [the tenant] had committed to such an obligation. Specifically, (1) Hills is the sole anchor tenant at the [shopping enter], occupying over 45% of the leased space, (2) the obligations of other tenants turn, at least in part, on Hills' presence in the shopping center, (3) Hills is a well-established entity whose concern with its business reputation would relieve the Court of the need to continuously supervise its operations if ordered to continue and (4) likely damage to [landlord's] real property interests from Hills' decision to vacate the leased premises are not readily quantifiable, making money damages an insufficient remedy.

Hamilton West Development, Ltd. v. Hills Stores Co., 959 F.Supp. 434, 441 (N.D.Ohio 1997).

2. Note that the landlord's likelihood of obtaining injunctive relief will be enhanced if equitable relief is sought promptly. In many instances, the landlord is aware that the lessee is planning to cease operations and vacate the premises. In such circumstances, the landlord should immediately seek a temporary restraining order and/or a preliminary injunction to prevent this from occurring. If equitable relief is sought after the lessee vacates and "goes dark," the costs of reopening may then be so substantial for the lessee that a court will be much less likely to grant it. This observation is reinforced by the language of the Pennsylvania Supreme Court:

> [Landlord] contends * * * that it was inappropriate for the trial court to consider [Lessee's] reopening costs because such expenses were caused solely by [Lessee's] "wrongful" departure from [the shopping center]. * * * We, however, reject the notion that the trial court was not permitted to consider [Lessee's] reopening costs, as [Landlord] was notified * * * of [Lessee's] imminent departure, yet did not promptly seek an order to prevent its occurrence. Rather, [Landlord] waited until over six weeks had elapsed and [Lessee] had long departed to file its petition for a preliminary injunction. Thus, as [Landlord] failed to take swift action in an attempt to prevent [Lessee's] departure, it cannot now complain that the natural consequences of that departure were considered in the trial court's equity calculus. * * * [W]e are also troubled by the [appellate court's] failure to even acknowledge that its reversal of the trial court order was the equivalent of granting a mandatory preliminary injunction, an extraordinary remedy that should be utilized only in the rarest of cases.

Summit Towne Centre, Inc. v. Shoe Show of Rocky Mount, Inc., 573 Pa. 637, 652–53, 828 A.2d 995, 1004–05 (2003). What do you think of the Pennsylvania

Supreme Court's last sentence? Suppose Landlord had acted promptly and sought a preliminary injunction "enjoining Lessee from vacating and ceasing operation" of the leased premises. To what extent would such an injunction, if granted, not be mandatory?

PINGLEY v. BRUNSON

Supreme Court of South Carolina, 1979.
272 S.C. 421, 252 S.E.2d 560.

RHODES, JUSTICE:

This appeal is from an order compelling appellant, Carl Brunson, to fulfill his contract to provide entertainment at respondent's restaurant, and further enjoining him from playing musical instruments for any other establishment during times that would conflict with performance of his contract. We reverse, concluding that neither specific performance nor injunctive relief was a proper remedy for enforcement of appellant's contract for personal services.

During the past several years the appellant, who is an automobile repairman by trade, has been playing the organ as part time employment for various establishments in the Mullins area.

On December 6, 1977, appellant entered into a contract to play the organ for respondent's restaurant for a period of three years. By terms of the contract, appellant agreed to play in respondent's place of business for three designated nights each week and an additional night during certain specified months. For his services, respondent agreed to pay Brunson $50.00 per night. The contract further set out: (1) that the respondent was purchasing musical instruments at the price of $4,262.96 for use by the appellant at his restaurant; and (2) that monthly installments on the cost of the instruments were to be provided by deduction from appellant's pay checks. After payment in full, the instruments were to become the property of the appellant. The contract further provided that any breach by appellant would result in his forfeiting any claim to the instruments.

The appellant commenced performing for respondent on the night of December 6, 1977 and played for nine evenings thereafter. On December 27, appellant did not appear for his performance and has failed and refused to perform in accordance with his contract since that time.

Courts of equity will not ordinarily decree specific performance of a contract for personal services, particularly where the performance of the services contracted for would be continuous over a long period of time. 81 C.J.S. Specific Performance § 96 (1977). This rule has been applied to various personal service contracts including, but not limited to, performance as an actor, a singer, a sales agent, and a ball player. Restatement of Contracts § 379 (1932). On the other hand, where services have a unique and peculiar value, specific performance has been awarded under limited circumstances. 81 C.J.S. Specific Performance, *supra*.

Assuming that a valid contract was effected between the parties, the personal services required of appellant were to be performed on a sustained basis over a three year period. The idea of compelling a close personal association over a protracted period of time after disputes have arisen and loyalty and confidence dissipated has been repugnant to courts facing the situation. 11 S. Williston, Contracts § 1423 (3d ed. W. Jaegar 1968).

The exception allowing specific performance of a personal service contract is confined to instances where the performer possesses unique and exceptional skill or ability in his area of expertise. Even though respondent's witnesses asserted appellant's exceptional talent as a major attraction to an area establishment, the further evidence revealed that five other organists of comparable ability were available for hire in the Mullins area. In this regard, we find the general rule to be that if the subject matter of a contract is such that its substantial equivalent is readily obtainable from others rather than defendant in an exchange for a money payment, this factor will be sufficient to deny specific performance. 5 A. Corbin, Contracts § 1142 (1960). Under the circumstances of the case at bar, we cannot conclude from the evidence that appellant's musical talent is of such a unique quality as to warrant an award of specific performance; instead, the availability of other local organ players persuades us that respondent's remedy was at law and not in equity.

For the foregoing reasons, we conclude that the trial court erred in granting a decree of specific performance, compelling the appellant to comply with terms of his contract for personal services. Likewise in error was the lower court's injunctive relief prohibiting the acceptance by respondent of other employment during specified periods. The contract between appellant and respondent did not contain a covenant not to compete or to perform elsewhere. In the absence of an express negative covenant as a basis for injunctive relief, the general rule is as follows:

> In a number of cases the question has arisen as to whether injunction may issue against the breach of an employment contract by an employee and the furnishing of his services to another, where there is no covenant in the contract to the effect that he is not to enter the employment of another during the term of the contract. As a rule, the court does not award injunction in the absence of an express negative covenant in the contract.

42 Am.Jur.2d, Injunctions, § 104 (1969).

Reversed.

LEWIS, C.J., and LITTLEJOHN, NESS and GREGORY, JJ., concur.

NOTE

The decision in *Pingley* is in accord with the general approach in other jurisdictions. Consider how the New York Court of Appeals analyzes the issues raised in *Pingley:*

Courts of equity historically have refused to order an individual to perform a contract for personal services. * * * Originally this rule evolved because of the inherent difficulties courts would encounter in supervising the performance of uniquely personal efforts. * * * During the Civil War era, there emerged a more compelling reason for not directing the performance of personal services: the Thirteenth Amendment's prohibition of involuntary servitude. It has been strongly suggested that judicial compulsion of services would violate the express command of that amendment (Arthur v. Oakes, 63 F. 310, 317; Stevens, *Involuntary Servitude by Injunction*, 6 Corn.L.Q. 235; Calamari & Perillo, The Law of Contracts [2d ed.], § 16–5). For practical, policy and constitutional reasons, therefore, courts continue to decline to affirmatively enforce employment contracts.

Over the years, however, in certain narrowly tailored situations, the law fashioned other remedies for failure to perform an employment agreement. Thus, where an employee refuses to render services to an employer in violation of an existing contract, and the services are unique or extraordinary, an injunction may issue to prevent the employee from furnishing those services to another person for the duration of the contract. Such "negative enforcement" was initially available only when the employee had expressly stipulated not to compete with the employer for the term of the engagement. Later cases permitted injunctive relief where the circumstances justified implication of a negative covenant. In these situations, an injunction is warranted because the employee either expressly or by clear implication agreed not to work elsewhere for the period of his contract. And, since the services must be unique before negative enforcement will be granted, irreparable harm will befall the employer should the employee be permitted to labor for a competitor.

American Broadcasting Companies, Inc. v. Wolf, 52 N.Y.2d 394, 401–03, 438 N.Y.S.2d 482, 485–86, 420 N.E.2d 363, 366–67 (1981).

The latter situation deals with what is sometimes referred to as the "coextensive covenant not to compete" and its enforcement by injunction is occasionally characterized as "negative specific performance." The enforcement of an implied negative covenant is aimed, in part, at coercing the breaching employee to perform for his or her original employer. The next case focuses on a different problem—the so-called "post-termination covenant not to compete." Again, the language of the New York Court of Appeals is helpful:

After a personal service contract terminates, the availability of equitable relief against the former employee diminishes appreciably. Since the period of service has expired, it is impossible to decree affirmative or negative specific performance. Only if the employee has expressly agreed not to compete with the employer following the term of the contract, or is threatening to disclose trade secrets or commit another tortious act, is injunctive relief generally available at the behest of the employer * * *. Even where there is an express anticompetitive covenant, however, it will be rigorously examined and specifically enforced only if it satisfies certain established requirements * * *.

Id. The following material focuses on these "established requirements" in New York and in other jurisdictions.

TICOR TITLE INSURANCE CO. v. COHEN

United States Court of Appeals, Second Circuit, 1999.
173 F.3d 63.

Before: NEWMAN, CARDAMONE, and PARKER, CIRCUIT JUDGES.

CARDAMONE, CIRCUIT JUDGE:

* * *

Plaintiffs are affiliated companies that sell title insurance nationwide. Title insurance insures the buyer of real property, or a lender secured by real property, against defects in the legal title to the property, and guarantees that, in the event a defect in title surfaces, the insurer will reimburse the insured for losses associated with the defect, or will take steps necessary to correct it. This kind of insurance is almost always purchased when real estate is conveyed. Ticor has been, and remains today, the leading title insurance company in New York State. It focuses primarily on multi-million dollar transactions that are handled by real estate lawyers. * * *

Defendant Cohen was employed by Ticor as a title insurance salesman. Title insurance salespeople contact real estate attorneys, handle title searches for them, and sell them policies; those salespeople from different title insurance companies compete to insure the same real estate transaction, seeking their business from the same group of widely-known attorneys. Due to the nature of the business, those attorneys commonly have relationships with more than one title insurance company.

Cohen began working for Ticor in 1981, shortly after graduating from college, as a sales account manager and within six years was a senior vice president in charge of several major accounts. Thus, he has been a title insurance salesman for Ticor for nearly all of his professional career. His clients have consisted almost exclusively of real estate attorneys in large New York law firms. As his supervisor testified, Cohen obtains his business due to his knowledge of the business, his professionalism, his ability to work through problems, and his ability to get things done.

Ticor and Cohen, both represented by counsel, entered into an Employment Contract on October 1, 1995. There were extensive negotiations over its terms, including the covenant not to compete, which is at issue on this appeal. The contract's stated term is until December 31, 1999, although Cohen—but not Ticor—could terminate it without cause on 30 days' notice.

The non-compete provision, enforced by the district court, stated that during his employment with Ticor and "for a period ending on the earlier of ... June 30, 2000 or ... 180 days following [his] termination of employment," Cohen would not:

for himself, or on behalf of any other person, or in conjunction with any other person, firm, partnership, corporation or other entity, engage in the business of Title Insurance ... in the State of New York.

[The Employment Contract] also contains the following express representation regarding the material nature of the covenant not to compete:

> [Ticor] is willing to enter into this Contract only on condition that [Cohen] accept certain post-employment restrictions with respect to subsequent reemployment set forth herein and [Cohen] is prepared to accept such condition.

* * *

In consideration for Cohen's agreeing to the recited post-employment restrictions, he was made one of the highest paid Ticor sales representatives, being guaranteed during the term of the Employment Contract annual compensation of $600,000, consisting of a base salary of $200,000 plus commissions. His total compensation in 1997 exceeded $1.1 million.

* * *

On April 20, 1998 TitleServ, a direct competitor of Ticor, offered to employ Cohen. As part of that offer, TitleServ agreed to indemnify Cohen by paying him a salary during the six-month period (i.e., the 180 days hiatus from employment) in the event that the covenant not to compete was enforced. Defendant sent plaintiff a letter on April 21, 1998 notifying it of his resignation effective May 21, 1998 and agreed to begin working for TitleServ on May 27, 1998.

Appellant commenced employment with his new employer on that date. His employment contract there guarantees him a minimum salary of $750,000 and a signing bonus of $2 million dollars, regardless of the outcome of this litigation. Cohen has received this signing bonus and has begun receiving salary payments, as scheduled. * * *

Ticor commenced this action on June 5, 1998 and applied that day for a temporary restraining order and preliminary injunction. After receiving Cohen's opposition papers and hearing argument, the district court entered a temporary restraining order. The parties conducted expedited discovery and briefed the relevant issues over the ensuing ten days. On June 19, 1998 the district court heard further argument and extended the temporary restraining order for an additional ten days. It scheduled an evidentiary hearing, held on June 29, 1998, at the close of which the parties consented to consolidate the hearing with a trial on the merits of Ticor's cause of action seeking a permanent injunction.

On July 1, 1998 the district court issued its opinion and order permanently enjoining Cohen from working in the title insurance business and from appropriating Ticor's corporate opportunities with its current or prospective customers for a period of six months. * * *

* * *

I. INJUNCTIVE RELIEF

* * *

An injunction should be granted when the intervention of a court of equity is essential to protect a party's property rights against injuries that would otherwise be irremediable. * * * The basic requirements to obtain injunctive relief have always been a showing of irreparable injury and the inadequacy of legal remedies. * * *

[W]e think for several reasons irreparable harm was shown to be present in this case. Initially, it would be very difficult to calculate monetary damages that would successfully redress the loss of a relationship with a client that would produce an indeterminate amount of business in years to come. In fact, the employment contract sought to be enforced concedes that in the event of Cohen's breach of the post-employment competition provision, Ticor shall be entitled to injunctive relief, because it would cause irreparable injury. Such, we think, might arguably be viewed as an admission by Cohen that plaintiff will suffer irreparable harm were he to breach the contract's non-compete provision. Further, the district court thought as a matter of law, as stated in a footnote to its written decision, that New York cases in the covenant-not-to-compete context apparently assume an irreparable injury to plaintiff. We agree with the district court that irreparable injury exists in this case.

II. COVENANT NOT TO COMPETE

* * *

The issue of whether a restrictive covenant not to compete is enforceable by way of an injunction depends in the first place upon whether the covenant is reasonable in time and geographic area. *See* Reed, Roberts Assocs. v. Strauman, 40 N.Y.2d 303, 307, 386 N.Y.S.2d 677, 353 N.E.2d 590 (1976). In this equation, courts must weigh the need to protect the employer's legitimate business interests against the employee's concern regarding the possible loss of livelihood, a result strongly disfavored by public policy in New York. *See id.*

A scholarly commentator described the tension between these competing concerns, which we face in the case at hand, in this fashion: An employer will sometimes believe its clientele is a form of property that belongs to it and any new business a salesperson drums up is for its benefit because this is what the salesperson was hired and paid to do. The employee believes, to the contrary, that the duty to preserve customer relationships ceases when employment ends and the employee's freedom to use contacts he or she developed may not be impaired by restraints that inhibit competition and an employee's ability to earn a living. The always present potential problem is whether a customer will come to value the salesperson more than the employer's product. When the product is not that much different from those available from competitors, such a customer is ripe to abandon the employer and follow the employee should he go to work for a competitor. *See* Harlan M. Blake, *Employee Agreements Not To Compete*, 73 Harv. L.Rev. 625, 654 (1960).

That scenario fits the circumstances revealed by the present record. The way to deal with these conflicting interests is by contract, which is what the parties before us purported to do, only now appellant insists * * * that the non-compete provision is void as a contract in restraint of trade and therefore violates public policy.

* * * Because of strong public policy militating against the sanctioning of a person's loss of the ability to earn a livelihood, New York law subjects a non-compete covenant by an employee to "an overriding limitation of reasonableness" which hinges on the facts of each case. Karpinski v. Ingrasci, 28 N.Y.2d 45, 49, 320 N.Y.S.2d 1, 268 N.E.2d 751 (1971). Assuming a covenant by an employee not to compete surmounts its first hurdle, that is, that it is reasonable in time and geographic scope, enforcement will be granted to the extent necessary (1) to prevent an employee's solicitation or disclosure of trade secrets, (2) to prevent an employee's release of confidential information regarding the employer's customers, or (3) in those cases where the employee's services to the employer are deemed special or unique. * * * In the case at hand we are satisfied that the reasonableness test was met because the duration of the covenant was relatively short (six months) and the scope was not geographically overbroad. In any event, appellant does not argue that the covenant is unreasonable in time and scope. Rather, he argues that the services he provided to Ticor were not sufficiently unique to justify injunctive relief.

* * *

Unique services have been found in various categories of employment where the services are dependent on an employee's special talents; such categories include musicians, professional athletes, actors and the like. In those kinds of cases injunctive relief has been available to prevent the breach of an employment contract where the individual performer has such ability and reputation that his or her place may not easily be filled. * * * We recognized this category of uniqueness in the case of the services of an acrobat who, in his performance, with one hand lifted his co-performer, a grown man, from a full length position on the floor, an act described as "the most marvelous thing that has ever been [done] before." Shubert Theatrical Co. v. Rath, 271 F. 827, 829–30 (2d Cir.1921). We later said that where services are unique the issuance of an injunction "is not an open question in this court," and commented that this "principle is equally well settled in the courts of New York." Associated Newspapers v. Phillips, 294 F. 845, 850 (2d Cir.1923) (employee writer of feature articles for the daily press provided unique services).

It has always been the rule, however, that to fall within this category of employees against whom equity will enforce a negative covenant, it is not necessary that the employee should be the only "star" of his employer, or that the business will grind to a halt if the employee leaves. *See* Comstock v. Lopokowa, 190 F. 599, 601 (C.C.S.D.N.Y.1911). * * *

* * *

The trial court found Cohen's relationships with clients were "special" and qualified as unique services. It deemed these relationships unique for several reasons. First, since the costs and terms of title insurance in New York are fixed by law, competition for business relies more heavily on personal relationships. Second, since potential clients— New York law firms with real estate practices—are limited and well known throughout the industry, maintaining current clients from this established group is crucial. Third, the trial court noted that * * * Cohen had negotiated his employment contract and the non-compete clause with the assistance of counsel and not from an inferior bargaining position.

Here, the non-compete period is six months, and quite plainly Cohen is not disabled from reviving his relationships with clients after the six months' absence, which would allow a new Ticor salesman sufficient opportunity to establish a fledgling relationship with Cohen's clients at Ticor.

* * *

We recognize that New York decisions reveal many situations where a particular employee was found not to be "special, unique or extraordinary." *See Columbia Ribbon*, 42 N.Y.2d at 500, 398 N.Y.S.2d 1004, 369 N.E.2d 4 (salesmen here provide standard services and are therefore not unique); Clark Paper & Mfg. Co. v. Stenacher, 236 N.Y. 312, 140 N.E. 708 (1923) (same); Kaumagraph Co. v. Stampagraph Co., 235 N.Y. 1, 138 N.E. 485 (1923) (printers of fabric designs not unique); Frederick Bros. Artists Corp. v. Yates, 271 A.D. 69, 62 N.Y.S.2d 714 (1st Dep't 1946), *aff'd without opinion*, 296 N.Y. 820, 72 N.E.2d 13 (1947) (theatrical booking agent); Corpin v. Wheatley, 227 A.D. 212, 237 N.Y.S. 205 (4th Dep't 1929) (beauty parlor employee); Magid v. Tannenbaum, 164 A.D. 142, 149 N.Y.S. 445 (1st Dep't 1914) (traveling representative for tailors); Small v. Kronstat, 175 Misc. 626, 24 N.Y.S.2d 535 (Sup.Ct.1940) (skilled watch artisan).

Yet, it still remains true that where the employee's services are "special, unique or extraordinary," then injunctive relief is available to enforce a covenant not to compete, if the covenant is reasonable, and even though competition does not involve disclosure of trade secrets or confidential lists. *See Purchasing Assocs.*, 13 N.Y.2d at 273, 246 N.Y.S.2d 600, 196 N.E.2d 245. In a similar vein, we ruled in Bradford v. New York Times Co., 501 F.2d 51 (2d Cir.1974), that an employee can be unique. Bradford, an employee of the New York Times, left the publisher where he had been serving as general manager, vice-president and director, to go to work for a competitor, Scripps–Howard Newspapers, where he took the post of assistant general manager. As part of an incentive compensation plan with his former employer he had signed a non-compete contract and upon seeking the plan's benefits was told he had breached the non-compete clause and thus had been terminated from the plan. His suit against the New York Times was dismissed by the district court. We affirmed, holding that since Bradford was a unique employee the non-compete clause was enforceable.

As stated in Service Sys. Corp. v. Harris, 41 A.D.2d 20, 23–24, 341 N.Y.S.2d 702 (4th Dep't 1973), "[a]n employer has sufficient interest in retaining present customers to support an employee covenant where the employee's relationship with the customers is such that there is a substantial risk that the employee may be able to divert all or part of the business." In the present case this risk is clearly evidenced by the fact that in 1997 another employee left Ticor for TitleServ and took 75 percent of his clients with him. And, this is further demonstrated by appellant's successful solicitation of a law firm to follow him to TitleServ. Moreover, one appellate court in New York affirmed the grant of an injunction in favor of an employer in a restrictive employment covenant case where the employee was held to be a "star" salesman. Uniform Rental Div., Inc. v. Moreno, 83 A.D.2d 629, 441 N.Y.S.2d 538 (2d Dep't 1981). Thus, we do not think our holding contravenes established law in New York.

* * *

For the reasons stated, therefore, the judgment entered in district court enjoining defendant under the non-competition contract is affirmed.

NOTES

1. For a recent decision applying the New York approach to grant injunctive relief in the high-tech context, see International Business Machines Corp. v. Papermaster, 2008 WL 4974508 (S.D.N.Y.2008). Unlike New York, some jurisdictions focus mainly on the reasonableness of the time and area requirements in employee post-termination covenants—there is no requirement that the employee also be unique. *See, e.g.*, Professional Business Services, Co. v. Rosno, 256 Neb. 217, 589 N.W.2d 826 (1999) ("[A] court must determine whether a restriction is reasonable in the sense that it is not injurious to the public, that it is not greater than is reasonably necessary to protect the employer in some legitimate interest, and that it is not unduly harsh and oppressive on the employee."). For a further discussion of covenants not to compete, see Harlan N. Blake, *Employee Agreements Not to Compete*, 73 Harv. L. Rev. 625 (1960); Phillip J. Closius & Henry M. Schaffer, *Involuntary Nonservitude: The Current Judicial Enforcement of Employee Covenants Not to Compete—A Proposal for Reform*, 57 S. Cal. L. Rev. 531 (1984); Milton Handler & Daniel E. Lazaroff, *Restraint of Trade and the Restatement (Second) of Contracts*, 57 N.Y.U. L. Rev. 669 (1982); Stephen E. Kalish, *Covenants Not to Compete and the Legal Profession*, 29 St. Louis U. L.J. 423 (1985); Gary P. Kreider, *Trends in the Enforcement of Restrictive Employment Contracts*, 35 U. Cin. L. Rev. 16 (1966); Jeffrey L. Liddle & William F. Gray, Jr., *Proof of Damages for Breach of a Restrictive Covenant or Noncompetition Agreement*, 9 Empl. Rel. L.J. 455 (1984); Kathryn L. Powers, *Drafting Non–Compete Covenants: Statutory and Common Law Constraints,*

13 Colo. Law. 757 (1984); Paul H. Rubin & Peter Shedd, *Human Capital and Covenants Not to Compete*, 10 J. Legal Stud. 93 (1981) (economic analysis).

As to reasonableness of time and area limitations in post-employment covenants, see the annotations in 41 A.L.R.2d 15 (1955) and 43 A.L.R.2d 94 (1955), respectively. There are four basic approaches to overly broad restrictive covenants:

1. Deny enforcement of the entire covenant;

2. Adopt the blue pencil approach, in which a court will grant enforcement of the covenant if it can blue pencil or strike out objectionable language without changing the impact of the clause;

3. Grant reformation of an overly broad restraint without regard to the severability of contract language; and

4. Regulate by statute.

Note, *Post Employment Restraints: An Analysis of Theories of Enforcement, and a Suggested Supplement to the Covenant Not to Compete*, 17 Tulsa L.J. 155, 156 (1981) (analyzing cases in all fifty states). For an example of a refusal to reform an unreasonable covenant, see Whitten v. Malcolm, 249 Neb. 48, 541 N.W.2d 45 (1995) ("It is not the function of courts to reform unreasonable covenants for the purpose of making them enforceable."). The New York Court of Appeals subscribes to "the prevailing, modern view":

> The prevailing, modern view rejects a per se rule that invalidates entirely any overbroad employee agreement not to compete. Instead, when, as here, the unenforceable portion is not an essential part of the agreed exchange, a court should conduct a case specific analysis, focusing on the conduct of the employer in imposing the terms of the agreement * * *. Under this approach, if the employer demonstrates an absence of overreaching, coercive use of dominant bargaining power, or other anticompetitive misconduct, but has in good faith sought to protect a legitimate business interest, consistent with reasonable standards of fair dealing, partial enforcement may be justified.

BDO Seidman v. Hirshberg, 93 N.Y.2d 382, 393, 690 N.Y.S.2d 854, 860, 712 N.E.2d 1220, 1225 (1999).

In any event, the blue-pencil or reformation approach will not be applied if the employer is guilty of bad faith or where the covenant suggests that the employer clearly intended to apply oppressive burdens on the employee. Where this is the case, the covenant will not be modified and, instead, will be treated as void. *See, e.g.*, Ellis v. James V. Hurson Associates, 565 A.2d 615 (D.C.1989); Dryvit System, Inc. v. Rushing, 132 Ill.App.3d 9, 87 Ill.Dec. 434, 477 N.E.2d 35 (1985); Durapin, Inc. v. American Products, Inc., 559 A.2d 1051 (R.I.1989).

2. It is important to distinguish two types of covenants not to compete. One is a covenant specifying that the seller of a business will not compete with the buyer ("covenant ancillary to the sale of a business"). The other, as in *Ticor*, specifies that an employee, upon termination of employment, will not compete with his or her former employer. The former covenant has received

much more favorable treatment from the courts than the latter. As an Illinois appellate court stated:

> If the covenant is ancillary to the sale of a business by the covenantor to the covenantee, then all the covenantee must show is that the restriction is reasonable as to time, geographical area and scope of prohibited business activity. If, however, the covenant is ancillary only to an employment agreement, the covenantee must show additional special circumstances, such as a near-permanent relationship with his employer's customers and that, but for his association with the employer, the former employee would not have had contact with the customers, * * * or the existence of customer lists, trade secrets or other confidential information.

Hamer Holding Group, Inc. v. Elmore, 202 Ill.App.3d 994, 1007, 148 Ill.Dec. 310, 318–19, 560 N.E.2d 907, 915–16 (1990). On the other hand, even covenants ancillary to the sale of a business are sometimes held to be unreasonably restrictive. *See, e.g.,* Presto–X–Co. v. Beller, 253 Neb. 55, 568 N.W.2d 235 (1997).

Interestingly, California courts use a state statute as the basis for rejecting the rule of reason in the employment covenant context and for refusing all enforcement of a covenant that completely bars the employee from engaging in a business, trade, or profession. Cal. Bus. & Prof. Code § 16600 (West 1997); *see, e.g.,* Whyte v. Schlage Lock Co., 101 Cal.App.4th 1443, 125 Cal.Rptr.2d 277 (2002); Bosley Medical Group v. Abramson, 161 Cal.App.3d 284, 207 Cal.Rptr. 477 (1984). Only certain partial limitations on the employee are upheld. *See, e.g.,* Campbell v. Board of Trustees of Leland Stanford Junior University, 817 F.2d 499, 503 (9th Cir.1987) (if employee's profession were characterized as a "psychologist," a covenant not to use psychological tests would not prevent completely his professional activity; if his profession were characterized as a "psychological tester," the covenant would be void as a complete prohibition on the practice of his profession). On the other hand, another California statute validates reasonable restrictions with respect to the sale of a business or partnership. Cal. Bus. & Prof. Code §§ 16601–16602 (West 1997).

Professor Gillian Lester describes why some legal scholars view the California approach as optimal:

> Some legal scholars have recently argued that the success of Silicon Valley compared with other high-technology industrial districts may be attributable in significant measure to California's weak restrictions on postemployment competition. The argument is that "high-velocity" labor markets, in which employees move fluidly between firms taking ideas and innovations with them, permit the rapid diffusion of information, creating joint technological gains that would be unattainable in a regime favoring strong enforcement of intellectual property rights.

Gillian Lester, *Restrictive Covenants, Employee Training, and the Limits of Transaction Cost Analysis*, 76 Ind. L.J. 1, 74 (2001). While she finds the foregoing analysis "at least partially persuasive," she suspects:

[T]here is a nontrivial subclass of situations where employers would inefficiently underinvest in their employees absent some form of protection. If this conjecture were borne out empirically, I would share with a handful of other commentators some optimism about a hybrid approach in which restrictive covenants are deemed unenforceable by statute, with an explicit exception made for discrete repayment contracts. Colorado statutory law permits employers to enforce contracts requiring employees of less than two years' tenure to repay education and training expenses. A statute of this sort could also contain a provision allowing contractual arrangements specifying the discrete terms of access to clients, again, with limitations on duration.

Id. at 75–76. Do you agree?

Why do courts and legislatures enforce covenants ancillary to the sale of a business more readily than covenants in employment contracts? Who is likely to have more bargaining strength, the seller of a business or an employee?

ENDRESS v. BROOKDALE COMMUNITY COLLEGE

Superior Court of New Jersey, Appellate Division, 1976.
144 N.J.Super. 109, 364 A.2d 1080.

Before JUDGES FRITZ, SEIDMAN and MILMED.

The opinion of the court was delivered by

SEIDMAN, J.A.D.

These consolidated appeals are from a judgment in favor of plaintiff reinstating her as a member of the faculty of defendant college with back pay and other benefits, and awarding her damages, both compensatory and punitive, plus counsel fees and costs.

On June 27, 1974 plaintiff Patricia H. Endress, an Assistant Professor of Journalism at Brookdale Community College, a public institution of higher learning located in Lincroft, Monmouth County, was discharged from her employment and her contract for the next academic year was rescinded by resolution adopted by the college board of trustees upon the recommendation of the president, [Donald Smith].

The controversy which led to Professor Endress' dismissal and this litigation had its origin in an editorial written by her which appeared in the April 26, 1974 edition of *The Stall,* the student newspaper of which she was the faculty advisor. In substance, it accused the chairman of the board of trustees of a conflict of interest in allegedly making "a deal" whereby his nephew's company received a contract from the college for the furnishing of audio-visual equipment. * * *

In recommending the dismissal to the board of trustees the president of the college asserted as the alleged causes for such action plaintiff's violation of "both the tradition established under Board policy, and the philosophical platform and goals of the College as the same pertain to freedom of the press and student responsibility for the college newspapers," and of the "editorial prerogatives of the student editor and the student staff," in ordering and directing the editor of the newspaper "to publish certain material without his approval," and in causing the publication of "libelous matter contrary to accepted journalistic standards."

Professor Endress thereupon filed a multi-count complaint * * * [alleging] that her employment had been wrongfully terminated, * * * and that she was discharged solely by reason of her exercise of her constitutional right of "freedom of the press, association and speech."

Defendants contended generally that the discharge of Professor Endress and the rescission of her new contract were (we quote from the oral decision of the trial judge) "all due and proper actions incumbent upon them in the exercise of their duties in their respective capacities, were in no way arbitrary, capricious or conspiratorial, and that the action did not breach any of their respective contractual obligations [with plaintiff]." * * *

At the conclusion of the trial, the judge below, sitting without a jury, entered [a judgment for the plaintiff awarding her $14,121.00 as back pay for the period from July 1, 1974 through June 30, 1975; ordering specific performance of a new employment contract from July 1, 1975 through June 30, 1976; and awarding $10,000 compensatory damages and $70,000 punitive damages for the violation of her constitutional rights].

* * *

We discern no sound basis for disturbing the holding below that just cause did not exist for dismissing plaintiff from her employment or for rescinding the 1974–1975 contract.

It is evident that at the time of plaintiff's dismissal only three days remained before the existing contract would have expired. Consequently, the substantial relief adjudged below was that plaintiff was entitled to specific performance of the new contract. Additionally, since plaintiff would thereby have acquired tenure, the trial judge also ordered the college to give plaintiff a contract for the year July 1, 1975 to June 30, 1976, with any concomitant salary increment. * * *

The college contends that as the employment contract was one which called for the rendering of personal services by plaintiff, specific performance could not be adjudged. It is settled law, of course, as the trial judge here readily acknowledged, that personal service contracts are generally not specifically enforceable affirmatively. * * *

But we held in Katz v. Gloucester Cty. College Bd. of Trustees, 125 N.J.Super. 248, 250, 310 A.2d 490 (App.Div.1973), that it was no longer open to question that a public agency may neither dismiss from employment nor withhold renewal of a contract from a nontenured public employee for a reason or reasons founded upon the exercise of a constitutionally protected right. See Perry v. Sindermann, 408 U.S. 593, 92 S.Ct. 2694, 33 L.Ed.2d 570 (1972); Board of Regents v. Roth, 408 U.S. 564, 92 S.Ct. 2701, 33 L.Ed.2d 548 (1972). * * * Although not clearly articulated below by the trial judge on the dismissal and reinstatement issue, it is thoroughly clear from a reading of the entire opinion that he was of the view, with support in the record, that plaintiff's employment was terminated improperly because of her exercise of First Amendment rights of free speech and press. In such case, the remedy of specific performance is appropriate. In American Ass'n of Univ. Prof. v. Bloomfield College, 136 N.J.Super. 442, 346 A.2d 615 (App.Div.1975), in which we affirmed the trial court's determination that financial exigency was not the bona fide cause for the decision to terminate tenured faculty members, appellants asserted, as they had below, that the remedy of specific performance ran counter to the line of legal precedents denying such relief in cases involving personal service contracts. We found no merit in the argument:

> We agree with the trial judge that the general rule is not inflexible and that the power of a court of equity to grant such a remedy depends upon the factual situation involved and the need for that type of remedy in a particular case. A lack of precedent, or mere novelty, is no obstacle to equitable relief which may be appropriate in a particular fact complex. In view of the uncertainty in admeasuring damages because of the indefinite duration of the contract and the importance of the status of plaintiffs in the milieu of the college teaching profession, it is evident that the remedy of damages at law would not be complete or adequate. * * * The relief granted herein is appropriate to achieve equity and justice. 136 N.J.Super. at 448, 346 A.2d at 618.

We are entirely satisfied that the trial judge here correctly accorded plaintiff [back pay and specific performance]. * * *

* * *

That portion of paragraph 5 of the judgment which awards compensatory damages to plaintiff is modified by reducing the amount to $2500; as modified, it is affirmed.

So much of paragraph 5 of the judgment as awards [$60,000] punitive damages against the individually named trustees is reversed. The award of $10,000 punitive damages against defendant Donald H. Smith is reduced to $2500, and, as modified, that portion of the judgment is affirmed.

The matter is remanded solely for the entry of an amended judgment * * *.

NOTES

1. Under the traditional rule, specific performance is unavailable against an employer who breaches an employment contract. *See* Redgrave v. Boston Symphony Orchestra, Inc., 557 F.Supp. 230 (D.Mass.1983); Barndt v. County of Los Angeles, 211 Cal.App.3d 397, 259 Cal.Rptr. 372 (1989). In the latter case, the plaintiff cardiologist sought specific performance of a settlement agreement that entitled plaintiff to be reinstated in the cardiology department of a county hospital. The court rejected the plaintiff's request, noting that the position required "a marked degree of cooperation and goodwill among the parties which an equitable decree cannot regulate." According to the court:

It has long been established that a contract to perform personal services cannot be specifically enforced, regardless of which party seeks enforcement. (Poultry Producers etc. v. Barlow (1922) 189 Cal. 278, 288, 208 P. 93; 5A Corbin, Contracts, § 1204, p. 398; Dobbs, Remedies, § 12.25, pp. 929–931.) The rule evolved because of the inherent difficulties courts would encounter in supervising the performance of uniquely personal efforts. "A fundamental reason why courts will not order specific performance of personal services contracts is because such an order would impose on the courts a difficult job of enforcement and of passing judgment upon the quality of performance. [Citations.] As Corbin observes in his treatise, 'An artist does not work well under compulsion, and the court might find it difficult to pass judgment upon the performance rendered.' (5A Corbin, *supra*, § 1204, p. 400.)" (Motown Record Corp. v. Brockert (1984) 160 Cal.App.3d 123, 137, 207 Cal.Rptr. 574.) During the Civil War era, there emerged a more compelling reason for not directing the performance of personal services: the Thirteenth Amendment's prohibition of involuntary servitude. (Beverly Glen Music, Inc. v. Warner Communications, Inc. (1986) 178 Cal.App.3d 1142, 1144, 224 Cal.Rptr. 260.) More importantly, however, the common law disfavored specific performance to avoid the friction and social costs that often result when employer and employee are reunited in a relationship that has already failed. (*See* Poultry Producers etc. v. Barlow, *supra*, 189 Cal. at p. 288, 208 P. 93; Rest.2d, Contracts, § 367 comm. (a) at p. 192.) This rationale is particularly applicable where the services to be rendered require mutual confidence among the parties and involve the exercise of discretionary authority. (*See* Rautenberg v. Westland (1964) 227 Cal. App.2d 566, 573, 38 Cal.Rptr. 797.)

* * *

Whatever remedy the plaintiff in our case may have for recovery of damages for the claimed breach of contract by the county, we think it clear that the settlement agreement contemplates the rendition of personal services which cannot be enforced by an action for specific performance. The public policy against compelling an employer to retain the services of an employee after disputes have arisen and loyalty and confidence have been eroded is particularly applicable here. * * * In light of the personality conflict which plaintiff concedes exists between himself and the chief of the cardiology section, the remedy of specific performance is simply not available to enforce the terms of the settlement agreement.

Id. at 403–04, 259 Cal.Rptr. at 376–77. Is the Thirteenth Amendment relevant when an *employee* is seeking specific performance? Is involuntary servitude imposed on the employer by awarding such relief?

2.   As *Endress* illustrates, when an employer violates a statute or the constitution, courts often reinstate the wrongfully discharged employee and, in the process, award the substantial equivalent of specific performance. Indeed, as one federal circuit court emphasized, "we, as well as other circuits have repeatedly emphasized the importance of equitable relief [reinstatement] in Title VII cases." Reiter v. MTA, 457 F.3d 224, 230 (2d Cir.2006). *See, e.g.,* Brown v. Trustees of Boston University, 891 F.2d 337 (1st Cir.1989) (in

reinstating a professor and ordering the grant of tenure, the court noted that "once a university has been found to have impermissively discriminated [because of gender] in making a tenure decision, as here, the University's prerogative to make tenure decisions must be subordinated to the goals embodied in Title VII."); Allen v. Autauga County Board of Education, 685 F.2d 1302 (11th Cir.1982) (employee's First Amendment rights violated); Jeffreys v. My Friend's Place, Inc., 719 F.Supp. 639 (M.D.Tenn.1989) (employee discharged after reporting for jury duty). If reinstatement is increasingly common in the statutory or constitutional context, why not grant specific performance against all employers who breach an employment contract?

3. Two commentators who have engaged in economic analysis have reached the conclusion that specific performance should be more readily available as a remedy for breach of contract. Professor Schwartz recommends that the "inadequacy of legal remedy" doctrine be abolished:

> The compensation goal of contract law can be achieved by requiring the promisor to pay damages or by requiring the promisor to render the promised performance. Under current law, a promisee is entitled to a damage award as of right but the court retains discretion to decide whether specific performance should be granted. Because specific performance is a superior method for achieving the compensation goal, promisees should be able to obtain specific performance on request. An expanded specific performance remedy would not generate greater transaction costs than the damage remedy involves, nor would its increased use interfere unduly with the liberty interests of promisors. Making specific performance freely available also would eliminate the uncertainty costs of planning and litigation created by the difficulty of predicting whether the remedy will be available. In addition, this reform would reduce the negotiation costs incurred by parties in attempting to create forms of contractual specific performance such as liquidated damage clauses.[96] Further, defenses to requests for specific performance that rest on unfairness of contract terms or prices and that differ from the defenses in actions at law should be eliminated; the grounds for denial of specific performance should be the same as those that now will bar a damage suit. Finally, the defense based on difficulty of supervision should

---

96. This conclusion is similar to the conclusion Professor Fiss reached with regard to injunctions:

> I will urge that the traditional view give way to a nonhierarchical conception of remedies, where there is no presumptive remedy, but rather a context-specific evaluation of the advantages and disadvantages of each form of relief. It should not be necessary to establish the inadequacy of alternative remedies before the injunction becomes available; at the same time, the superiority of the injunction should not be presumed, but rather dependent on an analysis of its technical advantages and the system of power allocation that it implies.

> My plea is not confined to the civil rights injunction, but should extend to all types of injunctions.

O. Fiss, The Civil Rights Injunction 6 (1978). Contract remedies also should be "nonhierarchical," so that promisees need not "establish the inadequacy of alternative remedies before" specific performance is available. Id. This Article's argument goes further toward authorizing equitable relief than does Professor Fiss's analysis, both because of the clear superiority of specific performance over damages in achieving the compensation goal and because "a context-specific evaluation of the advantages and disadvantages of each form of relief," id., shows that this superiority can usually be purchased at relatively slight, if any, net cost.

be greatly restricted. If the law is committed to putting disappointed promisees in as good a position as they would have been had their promisors performed, specific performance should be available as a matter of course to those promisees who request it.

Alan Schwartz, *The Case for Specific Performance*, 89 Yale L.J. 271, 305–06 (1979).* Professor Ulen contends that specific performance should be the routine remedy for breach of contract:

> The reasons for this conclusion may be briefly summarized here. First, if contractual parties are on notice that valid promises will be specifically enforced, they will more efficiently exchange reciprocal promises at formation time. In particular, they will have a stronger incentive than currently exists under the dominant legal remedy to allocate efficiently the risks of loss from breach rather than leaving that task, in whole or in part, to the court or to post-breach negotiations conducted under the threat of a potentially inefficient legal remedy. Second, and perhaps most importantly, specific performance offers the most efficient mechanism for protecting subjective values attached to performance. Thus, it promotes contract breach only if it is efficient, that is, if someone will be better off and no one will be worse off because of the breach. In this regard, specific performance and an expansive enforcement of stipulated remedies constitute integral and inseparable parts of a unified theory of efficient contract remedies. Third, if specific performance were the routine remedy, the post-breach costs of adjusting a contract in order to move the promise to the highest-valuing user would be lower than under the most efficient legal remedy. The central reason for this is that under specific performance the costs of determining various parties' valuation of performance are borne by those parties in voluntary negotiations. This means that the costs of determining willingness-to-pay are borne by those most efficiently placed to determine that amount. Finally, because the costs of ascertaining any subjective values of the innocent party through evidence presented to a court are so high and because, therefore, the possibility of undercompensating the innocent party through a damage remedy is high, specific performance is far less likely to be undercompensatory and far more likely to protect the breachee's subjective valuation than is any other judicially imposed contract remedy.

Thomas S. Ulen, *The Efficiency of Specific Performance: Toward A Unified Theory of Contract Remedies*, 83 Mich. L. Rev. 341, 365–66 (1984).

R.R. v. M.H.
Supreme Judicial Court of Massachusetts, 1998.
426 Mass. 501, 689 N.E.2d 790.

Before WILKINS, C.J., and ABRAMS, LYNCH, GREANEY, MARSHALL and IRELAND, JJ.

WILKINS, CHIEF JUSTICE.

On a report by a judge in the Probate and Family Court, we are concerned with the validity of a surrogacy parenting agreement between

---

* Reprinted by permission of The Yale Law Journal Company and Fred B. Rothman & Company.

the plaintiff (father) and the defendant (mother). Both the mother and the father are married but not to each other. A child was conceived through artificial insemination of the mother with the father's sperm, after the mother and father had executed the surrogate parenting agreement. The agreement provided that the father would have custody of the child. During the sixth month of her pregnancy and after she had received funds from the father pursuant to the surrogacy agreement, the mother changed her mind and decided that she wanted to keep the child.

The father thereupon brought this action and obtained a preliminary order awarding him temporary custody of the child. The mother's appeal from that order is moot because the parties have since agreed on custody and visitation and the judge has approved that agreement. We, therefore, do not discuss the circumstances of the temporary custody order, and nothing we say in this opinion should be understood to suggest that the subjects of custody or visitation need be reconsidered. The judge's order granting the preliminary injunction is before us on her report of the propriety of that order which was based in part on her conclusion that the father was likely to prevail on his assertion that the surrogacy agreement is enforceable. On our own motion, we transferred here the appeal and the report, which a single justice of the Appeals Court had consolidated. The question of the enforceability of the surrogacy agreement is before us and, although we could defer any ruling until there is a final judgment entered, the issue is one on which we elect to comment because it is fully briefed and is of importance to more than the parties. This court has not previously dealt with the enforceability of a surrogacy agreement.

* * *

The agreement provided for compensation to the mother in the amount of $10,000 "for services rendered in conceiving, carrying and giving birth to the Child." Payment of the $10,000 was to be made as follows: $500 on verification of the pregnancy; $2,500 at the end of the third month; $3,500 at the end of the sixth month; and $3,500 at the time of birth "and when delivery of child occurs." The agreement stated that no payment was made in connection with adoption of the child, the termination of parental rights, or consent to surrender the child for adoption. The father acknowledged the mother's right to determine whether to carry the pregnancy to term, but the mother agreed to refund all payments if, without the father's consent, she had an abortion that was not necessary for her physical health. The father assumed various expenses of the pregnancy, including tests, and had the right to name the child. The mother would be obliged, however, to repay all expenses and fees for services if tests showed that the father was not the biological father of the child, or if the mother refused to permit the father to take the child home from the hospital. The agreement also provided that the mother would maintain some contact with the child after the birth.

The judge found that the mother entered into the agreement on her own volition after consulting legal counsel. There was no evidence of undue influence, coercion, or duress. The mother fully understood that she was contracting to give custody of the baby to the father. She sought to inseminate herself on November 30 and December 1, 1996. The attempt at conception was successful.

The lawyer for the father sent the mother a check for $500 in December, 1996, and another for $2,500 in February. In May, the father's lawyer sent the mother a check for $3,500. She told the lawyer that she had changed her mind and wanted to keep the child. She returned the check uncashed in the middle of June. The mother has made no attempt to refund the amounts that the father paid her, including $550 that he paid for pregnancy-related expenses.

* * *

Approximately two weeks after the mother changed her mind and returned the check for $3,500, and before the child was born, the father commenced this action against the mother seeking to establish his paternity, alleging breach of contract, and requesting a declaration of his rights under the surrogacy agreement. Subsequently, the wife's husband was added as a defendant. The judge appointed a guardian ad litem to represent the interests of the unborn child. * * *

* * *

A significant minority of States have legislation addressing surrogacy agreements. Some simply deny enforcement of all such agreements. *See* Ariz.Rev.Stat. Ann. § 25–218(A) (West 1991); D.C.Code Ann. § 16–402(a) (1997); Ind.Code Ann. §§ 31–20–1–1, 31–20–1–2 (Michie 1997); Mich. Comp. Laws Ann. § 722.855 (West 1993); N.Y. Dom. Rel. Law § 122 (McKinney Supp.1997)[4]; N.D. Cent.Code § 14–18–05 (1991); Utah Code Ann. § 76–7–204 (1995). Others expressly deny enforcement only if the surrogate is to be compensated. *See* Ky.Rev.Stat. Ann. § 199.590(4) (Michie 1995): La.Rev.Stat. Ann. § 9:2713 (West 1991); Neb.Rev.Stat. § 25–21,200 (1995); Wash. Rev.Code §§ 26.26.230, 26.26.240 (1996). Some States have simply exempted surrogacy agreements from provisions making it a crime to sell babies. *See* Ala.Code § 26–10A–34 (1992); Iowa Code § 710.11 (1997); W. Va.Code § 48–4–16(e)(3) (1996). A few States have explicitly made unpaid surrogacy agreements lawful. *See* Fla. Stat. ch. 742.15 (1995); Nev.Rev.Stat. § 126.045 (1995); N.H.Rev.Stat. Ann. § 168–B:16 (1994 & Supp.1996); Va.Code Ann. §§ 20–159, 20–160(B)(4) (Michie 1995). Florida, New Hampshire, and Virginia require that the intended mother be infertile. *See* Fla. Stat. ch. 742.15(2)(a); N.H.Rev.Stat. Ann. § 168–B:17(II) (1994); Va.Code Ann. § 20–160(B)(8). New Hampshire and Virginia place restrictions on who may act as a surrogate and require

---

4. This statute changed the law established in Adoption of Baby Girl L.J., 132 Misc.2d 972, 505 N.Y.S.2d 813 (N.Y.Sur.Ct.1986), in which the court approved the terms of a surrogate parenting agreement which required the payment of compensation to the surrogate and delivery of the child to the natural father and his wife for adoption. See Adoption of Paul, 146 Misc.2d 379, 385, 550 N.Y.S.2d 815 (N.Y.Fam.Ct.1990), voiding a surrogacy agreement and approving adoption of the child only if the surrogate agreed not to accept compensation from the intended parents.

advance judicial approval of the agreement. *See* N.H.Rev.Stat. Ann. §§ 168–B:16(I)(b), 168–B:17; Va.Code Ann. §§ 20–159(B), 20–160(B)(6).[6] Last, Arkansas raises a presumption that a child born to a surrogate mother is the child of the intended parents and not the surrogate. Ark.Code Ann. § 9–10–201(b), (c) (Michie 1993).

There are few appellate court opinions on the enforceability of traditional surrogacy agreements. The Kentucky Legislature * * * has provided that a compensated surrogacy agreement is unenforceable (Ky.Rev. Stat.Ann. § 199.590[4]), thus changing the rule that the Supreme Court of Kentucky announced in Surrogate Parenting Assocs., Inc. v. Commonwealth *ex rel.* Armstrong, 704 S.W.2d 209 (Ky.1986). In *In re* Marriage of Moschetta, 25 Cal.App.4th 1218, 30 Cal.Rptr.2d 893 (1994), the court declined to enforce a traditional surrogacy agreement because it was incompatible with California parentage and adoption statutes. * * * The surrogate, who was to be paid $10,000, had agreed that (a) the father could obtain sole custody of any resulting child, (b) she would agree to terminate her parental rights, and (c) she would aid the father's wife in adopting the child. * * * The court sent the case back to the trial court for a determination whether the father should be awarded primary physical custody. * * *

The best known opinion is that of the Supreme Court of New Jersey in Matter of Baby M., 109 N.J. 396, 537 A.2d 1227 (1988), where the court invalidated a compensated surrogacy contract because it conflicted with the law and public policy of the State. * * * The Baby M surrogacy agreement involved broader concessions from the mother than the agreement before us because it provided that the mother would surrender her parental rights and would allow the father's wife to adopt the child. * * * The agreement, therefore, directly conflicted with a statute prohibiting the payment of money to obtain an adoption and a statute barring enforcement of an agreement to adoption made prior to the birth of the child. The court acknowledged that an award of custody to the father was in the best interests of the child, but struck down orders terminating the mother's parental rights and authorizing the adoption of the child by the husband's wife. * * * The court added that it found no "legal prohibition against surrogacy when the surrogate mother volunteers, without any payment, to act as a surrogate and is given the right to change her mind and to assert her parental rights." *Id.* at 469, 537 A.2d 1227.

DISCUSSION

1. The governing law. * * * The child was conceived and born in Massachusetts, and the mother is a Massachusetts resident, all as contemplated in the surrogacy arrangement. The significance, if any, of the

---

6. New Hampshire permits the surrogate to opt out of the agreement to surrender custody at any time up to seventy-two hours after birth. N.H.Rev.Stat. Ann. § 168–B:25(IV) (1994). Virginia allows a surrogate who is the child's genetic mother to terminate the agreement within 180 days of the last assisted conception. Va.Code Ann. § 20–161(B) (Michie 1995).

surrogacy agreement on the relationship of the parties and on the child is appropriately determined by Massachusetts law.

2. General Laws c. 46, § 4B. The case before us concerns traditional surrogacy, in which the fertile member of an infertile couple is one of the child's biological parents. Surrogate fatherhood, the insemination of the fertile wife with sperm of a donor, often an anonymous donor, is a recognized and accepted procedure. If the mother's husband consents to the procedure, the resulting child is considered the legitimate child of the mother and her husband. G.L. c. 46, § 4B. Section 4B does not comment on the rights and obligations, if any, of the biological father, although inferentially he has none. In the case before us, the infertile spouse is the wife. No statute decrees the consequences of the artificial insemination of a surrogate with the sperm of a fertile husband. This situation presents different considerations from surrogate fatherhood because surrogate motherhood is never anonymous and her commitment and contribution is unavoidably much greater than that of a sperm donor.[10]

We must face the possible application of G.L. c. 46, § 4B, to this case. Section 4B tells us that a husband who consents to the artificial insemination of his wife with the sperm of another is considered to be the father of any resulting child. In the case before us, the birth mother was married at the time of her artificial insemination. Despite what he told the psychologist, her husband was not supportive of her desire to become a surrogate parent but acknowledged that it was her decision and her body. The husband, who filed a complaint for divorce on August 8, 1997, may have simply been indifferent because he knew that the marriage was falling apart. The judge found that he was not the biological father of the child. His interest might have been vastly greater if he had been informed that § 4B literally says that any child produced by the artificial insemination of his wife with his consent would be his legitimate child whom he would have a duty to support. It is doubtful, however, that the Legislature intended § 4B to apply to the child of a married surrogate mother. Section 4B seems to concern the status of a child born to a fertile mother whose husband, presumably infertile, consented to her artificial insemination with the sperm of another man so that the couple could have a child biologically related to the mother.

3. Adoption statutes. Policies underlying our adoption legislation suggest that a surrogate parenting agreement should be given no effect if the mother's agreement was obtained prior to a reasonable time after the child's birth or if her agreement was induced by the payment of money. Adoption legislation is, of course, not applicable to child custody, but it

---

10. A situation which involves considerations different from those in the case before us arises when the birth mother has had transferred to her uterus an embryo formed through in vitro fertilization of the intended parents' sperm and egg. This latter process in which the birth mother is not genetically related to the child (except coincidentally if an intended parent is a relative) has been called gestational surrogacy. In Johnson v. Calvert, 5 Cal.4th 84, 96, 19 Cal.Rptr.2d 494, 851 P.2d 776, *cert. denied*, 510 U.S. 874, 114 S.Ct. 206, 126 L.Ed.2d 163, *and cert. dismissed sub nom.* Baby Boy J. v. Johnson, 510 U.S. 938, 114 S.Ct. 374, 126 L.Ed.2d 324 (1993), the Supreme Court of California gave effect to a contract that provided that the mother of a child born as a result of a gestational surrogacy would be the egg donor and not the surrogate. *Id.*

does provide us with some guidance. Although the agreement makes no reference to adoption and does not concern the termination of parental rights or the adoption of the child by the father's wife, the normal expectation in the case of a surrogacy agreement seems to be that the father's wife will adopt the child with the consent of the mother (and the father). Under G.L. c. 210, § 2, adoption requires the written consent of the father and the mother but, in these circumstances, not the mother's husband. Any such consent, written, witnessed, and notarized, is not to be executed "sooner than the fourth calendar day after the date of birth of the child to be adopted." *Id.* That statutory standard should be interpreted as providing that no mother may effectively agree to surrender her child for adoption earlier than the fourth day after its birth, by which time she better knows the strength of her bond with her child. Although a consent to surrender custody has less permanency than a consent to adoption, the legislative judgment that a mother should have time after a child's birth to reflect on her wishes concerning the child weighs heavily in our consideration whether to give effect to a prenatal custody agreement. No private agreement concerning adoption or custody can be conclusive in any event because a judge, passing on custody of a child, must decide what is in the best interests of the child.

Adoptive parents may pay expenses of a birth parent but may make no direct payment to her. *See* G.L. c. 210, § 11A; 102 Code Mass. Regs. § 5.09 (1997). Even though the agreement seeks to attribute that payment of $10,000, not to custody or adoption, but solely to the mother's services in carrying the child, the father ostensibly was promised more than those services because, as a practical matter, the mother agreed to surrender custody of the child. She could assert custody rights, according to the agreement, only if she repaid the father all amounts that she had received and also reimbursed him for all expenses he had incurred. The statutory prohibition of payment for receiving a child through adoption suggests that, as a matter of policy, a mother's agreement to surrender custody in exchange for money (beyond pregnancy-related expenses) should be given no effect in deciding the custody of the child.

4. Conclusion. The mother's purported consent to custody in the agreement is ineffective because no such consent should be recognized unless given on or after the fourth day following the child's birth. In reaching this conclusion, we apply to consent to custody the same principle which underlies the statutory restriction on when a mother's consent to adoption may be effectively given. Moreover, the payment of money to influence the mother's custody decision makes the agreement as to custody void. Eliminating any financial reward to a surrogate mother is the only way to assure that no economic pressure will cause a woman, who may well be a member of an economically vulnerable class, to act as a surrogate. It is true that a surrogate enters into the agreement before she becomes pregnant and thus is not presented with the desperation that a poor unwed pregnant woman may confront. However, compensated surrogacy arrangements raise the concern that, under financial pressure, a woman will permit her body to be used and her child to be given away.

There is no doubt that compensation was a factor in inducing the mother to enter into the surrogacy agreement and to cede custody to the father. If the payment of $10,000 was really only compensation for the mother's services in carrying the child and giving birth and was unrelated to custody of the child, the agreement would not have provided that the mother must refund all compensation paid (and expenses paid) if she should challenge the father's right to custody. Nor would the agreement have provided that final payment be made only when the child is delivered to the father. We simply decline, on public policy grounds, to apply to a surrogacy agreement of the type involved here the general principle that an agreement between informed, mature adults should be enforced absent proof of duress, fraud, or undue influence.

We recognize that there is nothing inherently unlawful in an arrangement by which an informed woman agrees to attempt to conceive artificially and give birth to a child whose father would be the husband of an infertile wife. We suspect that many such arrangements are made and carried out without disagreement.

If no compensation is paid beyond pregnancy-related expenses and if the mother is not bound by her consent to the father's custody of the child unless she consents after a suitable period has passed following the child's birth, the objections we have identified in this opinion to the enforceability of a surrogate's consent to custody would be overcome. Other conditions might be important in deciding the enforceability of a surrogacy agreement, such as a requirement that (a) the mother's husband give his informed consent to the agreement in advance; (b) the mother be an adult and have had at least one successful pregnancy; (c) the mother, her husband, and the intended parents have been evaluated for the soundness of their judgment and for their capacity to carry out the agreement; (d) the father's wife be incapable of bearing a child without endangering her health; (e) the intended parents be suitable persons to assume custody of the child; and (f) all parties have the advice of counsel. The mother and father may not, however, make a binding best-interests-of-the-child determination by private agreement. Any custody agreement is subject to a judicial determination of custody based on the best interests of the child.

The conditions that we describe are not likely to be satisfactory to an intended father because, following the birth of the child, the mother can refuse to consent to the father's custody even though the father has incurred substantial pregnancy-related expenses. A surrogacy agreement judicially approved before conception may be a better procedure, as is permitted by statutes in Virginia and New Hampshire. A Massachusetts statute concerning surrogacy agreements, pro or con, would provide guidance to judges, lawyers, infertile couples interested in surrogate parenthood, and prospective surrogate mothers.[12]

* * *

---

12.   The National Conference of Commissioners on Uniform State Laws has approved alternative proposals concerning surrogacy agreements. One alternative simply states that "[a]n agree-

A declaration shall be entered that the surrogacy agreement is not enforceable. Such further orders as may be appropriate, consistent with this opinion, may be entered in the Probate and Family Court.

* * *

NOTE

Suppose a court holds that surrogacy contracts do not violate public policy. Does this mean that a court must specifically enforce such contracts? Suppose the contract is silent about abortion. Or suppose that it gives the adoptive couple a right to veto any abortion decision made by the surrogate. Would a court issue an injunction against an abortion? Or suppose that the contract provides that the surrogate will undergo an abortion in the event genetic testing indicates an abnormal fetus and the fetus in fact has significant abnormalities, but the surrogate refuses to have an abortion. Would a court compel her to have one?

SECTION 6. ARBITRATION

Arbitration is a private method of adjudication whereby parties voluntarily submit disputes to a neutral third person for a final determination based on evidence and arguments presented in a hearing before the arbitrator. *See* Martin M. Domke, Commercial Arbitration § 1:01 (rev. ed. 1997). There are normally two types of arbitration agreements: (1) an agreement to arbitrate future disputes; and (2) an agreement to arbitrate an existing dispute, or a submission agreement.

The arbitrator may be selected by several methods. Often the parties agree in advance on a single arbitrator or, at least agree to allow some independent group, such as the American Arbitration Association, to select the arbitrator. This frequently results in the arbitrator being an expert in the subject matter of the dispute. Under a second selection method, each party selects one arbitrator and the two so selected then appoint a third, if necessary.

Arbitration is often preferred to judicial proceedings for a number of reasons. Speed is probably the main advantage of arbitration. This can be especially important in complex commercial arrangements, such as construction contracts. A prompt decision may also very well reduce the turmoil and bitterness that frequently are associated with protracted judicial proceedings. This is especially important when the parties value a future commercial relationship. Arbitration proceedings are private, which can be advantageous when confidential matters are involved. Further, the

---

ment in which a woman agrees to become a surrogate or to relinquish her rights and duties as parent of a child thereafter conceived through assisted conception is void." Uniform Status of Children of Assisted Conception Act, Alternative B, § 5, 9B U.L.A. 208 (Master ed. Supp.1997). The other alternative provides for judicial approval of an agreement before conception if various conditions are met and allows the payment of compensation. *Id.* at 201–207, Alternative A, §§ 5, 6, 9(a). * * *

arbitration process permits greater remedial flexibility than adjudication. As Professor Dobbs has pointed out,

> law courts tend to grant all-or-nothing remedies at least in theory. They tend to make broad rules to cover many cases and to worry very little about particular cases. Arbitration tends, on the contrary, to ignore rules in many situations and to concentrate on working out a pragmatic solution, though of course the arbitrator may be bound by contractual terms or procedures provided by the parties.

Dan B. Dobbs, Handbook on the Law of Remedies 936 (1973).

On the other hand, there may be substantial disadvantages in the arbitration process. Consumers and the plaintiff's bar often view arbitration as a device to deprive them of a jury trial, and they view juries as generally more sympathetic to their claims. Moreover, the flexibility referred to above may result in an undesirable lack of predictability. Because arbitration opinions often are not published, there is no precedent to guide the decision-maker. Consequently, when substantial sums of money or important legal issues are at stake, the parties sometimes prefer what they perceive to be the greater certainty of the judicial process.*

The United States Arbitration Act has made a major impact on modern arbitration. The Act, which was originally enacted in 1925 and revised as the Federal Arbitration Act in 1947, 9 U.S.C. §§ 1–14, mandates that a contract to arbitrate future or existing disputes is deemed irrevocable and specifically enforceable under federal law if the contract relates to a maritime transaction or to a "transaction involving" interstate commerce. The Act excludes certain "contracts of employment." It was enacted as a response to the common law's general hostility to the arbitration process, as the following excerpt from a California decision makes clear:

> The purpose of the act "was to reverse the longstanding judicial hostility to arbitration agreements that had existed at English common law and had been adopted by American courts." (Domke on Commercial Arbitration (rev. ed. 1997) Ch. 4, Statutory Arbitration Law, § 4.04, p. 6 * * *). A 1924 Senate Report described the "old law": "But it is very old law that the performance of a written agreement to arbitrate would not be enforced in equity, and that if an action at law were brought on the contract containing the agreement to arbitrate, such agreement could not be pleaded in bar of the action; nor would such an agreement be ground for a stay of the proceedings until arbitration was had. Further, the agreement was subject to

---

* For further consideration of the law of commercial arbitration, see Martin Domke, The Law and Practice of Commercial Arbitration (3rd ed.2003); Thomas H. Oehmke, Oehmke Commercial Arbitration (3rd ed.2003). Discussion of and proposals for amending federal arbitration law can be found at *Symposium—Rethinking the Federal Arbitration Act: An Examination of Whether and How the Statute Should be Amended*, 8 Nev.L.J. 1 (2007). For a criticism of binding pre-dispute arbitration agreements as unfair, *see* David S. Schwartz, *Mandatory Arbitration and Fairness*, 84 Notre Dame L.Rev. 1247 (2009). A comprehensive review of alternative methods of dispute resolution is available at Stephen J. Ware, Principles of Alternative Dispute Resolution (2nd ed.2007).

revocation by either of the parties at any time before the award. With this as the state of the law, such agreements were in large part ineffectual, and the party aggrieved by the refusal of the other party to carry out the arbitration agreement was without adequate remedy. Until recently in England, and up to the present time in nearly, if not quite all, the States of the Union, such has been the law in regard to arbitration agreements. The Federal courts have in the main been governed by the same rules and, as a consequence, have denied relief to the parties seeking to compel the performance of executory agreements to settle and determine disputes by arbitration." (Sen.Rep. No. 536, 68th Cong., 1st Sess., p. 2 (1924).) A 1924 House Report explained the effect of the legislation as follows: "Arbitration agreements are purely matters of contract, and the effect of the bill is simply to make the contracting party live up to his agreement. He can no longer refuse to perform his contract when it becomes disadvantageous to him. An arbitration agreement is placed upon the same footing as other contracts, where it belongs." (H.R.Rep. No. 96, 68th Cong., 1st Sess., p. 1 (1924).)

Blue Cross of California v. Superior Court of Los Angeles County, 67 Cal.App.4th 42, 48–49, 78 Cal.Rptr.2d 779, 783 (1998).

Most states also have enacted "modern" arbitration legislation. Such legislation is so designated if it provides for the enforcement of agreements to arbitrate future, as well as existing, disputes. Normally such legislation also authorizes both direct and indirect means of specific enforcement of the arbitration agreement. Direct specific performance is a court order compelling a party to arbitrate. Indirect specific performance can consist of the following: (1) an order staying any court action instituted in violation of the arbitration agreement; or (2) a court order appointing arbitrators with the power to act. Many states have adopted the Uniform Arbitration Act, originally promulgated in 1956. The Act, which was adopted by approximately 27 states, applies to both existing and future disputes and provides for both direct and indirect enforcement.* A newer version of the Act, promulgated in 2000, has been adopted by almost a dozen states.

Labor arbitration has largely developed as a special area. Not only do some states provide special legislation for dealing with labor disputes, but labor arbitration has largely been subsumed by federal labor law. In this connection, agreements to arbitrate disputes arising out of labor-management contracts are specifically enforceable under a judicial interpretation of section 301 of the Taft–Hartley Act, 29 U.S.C. § 185. *See* 14 Penn Plaza LLC v. Pyett, 129 S.Ct. 1456 (2009); Textile Workers Union v. Lincoln Mills, 353 U.S. 448, 77 S.Ct. 912, 1 L.Ed.2d 972 (1957).

Finally, it is important to distinguish between arbitration and appraisal. Unlike arbitration, "appraisal simply involves valuation of proper-

---

* For a discussion of the Act, see Unif. Arbit. Act 1956, 7 U.L.A. 99 (2009); Maynard E. Pirsig, *Some Comments on Arbitration Legislation and the Uniform Act*, 10 Vand. L. Rev. 685 (1957).

ty, which may be regarded as something referable to independent standards, more a matter of pricing items than of adjudicating disputes." Dan B. Dobbs, Handbook on the Law of Remedies 937 (1973). Traditionally, many courts that have denied direct or indirect specific enforcement of arbitration agreements have been more inclined to grant at least the indirect equivalent of such equitable relief in cases involving agreements for appraisal. *See, e.g.*, School District No. 1 of Silver Bow County v. Globe & Republic Insurance Co. of America, 146 Mont. 208, 404 P.2d 889 (1965). Some courts, for example, have granted indirect specific performance of appraisal agreements in insurance policies by making consent to appraisal a condition precedent to a suit by an insured to collect on the policy. *See, e.g.*, Dworkin v. Caledonian Insurance Co., 285 Mo. 342, 226 S.W. 846 (1920). One of the reasons for this difference in approach is based on a judicial belief that arbitrators "act like judges" in making "legal" determinations, whereas the process of appraisal is simply a means of determining the value of property or services. Moreover, some courts emphasize that arbitration awards are reducible to judgment and thus "oust" a court of jurisdiction, while an appraisal determination simply results in evidence and does not result in an independent cause of action. *See* Gerald D. McBeth, *Commercial Arbitration: The Need for Reform*, 36 Mo. L. Rev. 343, 346 (1971).

3 DAN B. DOBBS, LAW OF REMEDIES
510–13 (2d ed. 1993).*

The Arbitrator's Remedies

Compensatory damages. What remedies may arbitrators award? The power to award remedies is like the other powers of the arbitrator; it is determined by the parties' agreement. In the absence of restriction, the arbitrator usually has a free hand so long as the remedies do not violate the court's conception of public policy.[54] The arbitrator certainly may award money compensation, including unliquidated sums.[55]

Equitable or non-monetary relief. Reinstatement in a job or to job status or privileges is a common kind of award when employment is in issue.[56] At least some courts have held that arbitrators may exercise what might be called equity powers and have approved arbitration awards of specific performance[57] and injunctive orders.[58] One court upheld an award by an arbitration panel which required the defendant to post a substan-

---

* Reprinted with permission of West Publishing Co.

54. *See* Garrity v. Lyle Stuart, Inc., 40 N.Y.2d 354, 386 N.Y.S.2d 831, 353 N.E.2d 793, 83 A.L.R.3d 1024 (1976) (stating the rule, but insisting that the award of punitive damages by an arbitrator violated public policy).

55. *E.g.*, Bankers & Shippers Ins. Co. v. Gonzalez, 234 So.2d 693 (Fla.App.1970) (uninsured motorist arbitration, award of $7300).

56. *E.g.*, Local Union 560, I.B.T. v. Eazor Express Inc., 95 N.J.Super. 219, 230 A.2d 521 (1967).

57. Staklinski v. Pyramid Elec. Co., 6 N.Y.2d 159, 188 N.Y.S.2d 541, 160 N.E.2d 78 (1959).

58. Ruppert v. Egelhofer, 3 N.Y.2d 576, 170 N.Y.S.2d 785, 148 N.E.2d 129, 70 A.L.R.2d 1048 (1958) (injunction against slowdown as part of arbitrator's award was proper, though the contract did not mention remedies at all).

tial bond to secure future arbitration orders against the defendant.[59] Michigan, however, has taken a narrower view, holding that if an arbitrator is to have equity powers, the parties must explicitly confer them.[60]

Relief courts would refuse. Can the arbitrator award equitable remedies which the courts themselves would refuse? Some important cases have said so. In Staklinski v. Pyramid Elec. Co.,[61] an arbitrator ordered reinstatement of an employee as a production manager for a utility company at a large salary and percentage of the profits. Personal services contracts are not traditionally enforced, so the court's approval of the award suggests that arbitrators can go further than courts. It is possible that the case merely signals increasing doubt about the personal services rule where an employee seeks to retain a job.[62] But other cases in other areas also approve arbitral relief that courts have traditionally denied.[63] In addition, the Uniform Act specifically provides that the arbitrator's award is not to be vacated merely because it affords relief not available in law or equity.[64]

NOTE

The past decade has witnessed an explosive expansion in the use of arbitration. This has especially been the case in three contexts: (1) employment termination controversies (other than in the collective bargaining setting); (2) consumer product disputes; and (3) complaints against the conduct of brokers in handling investment accounts. Employers, merchants and brokerage institutions, wishing to avoid adjudication, have aggressively sought specific performance of agreements to arbitrate.

This increasing reliance on the arbitration remedy has been controversial, to say the least. Employees and consumers have asserted that the arbitration process is "stacked against them." In their view, they are being unfairly deprived of their day in court based on agreements to arbitrate that, they claim, violate public policy or are unconscionable. On the other hand, a strong presumption in favor of enforcement of such agreements, as we noted earlier, has been the hallmark of a modern arbitration system. The following case explores these issues.

NYULASSY v. LOCKHEED MARTIN CORP.

Court of Appeal of California, Sixth District, 2004.
120 Cal.App.4th 1267, 16 Cal.Rptr.3d 296.

WALSH, J.*

Our Supreme Court has upheld employment agreements that require the employee to arbitrate disputes, so long as the arbitration clause does

---

59. Compania Chilena De Navegacion Interoceanica, S.A. v. Norton, Lilly & Co., Inc., 652 F.Supp. 1512, 1516–1517 (S.D.N.Y.1987).

60. Carr v. Kalamazoo Vegetable Parchment Co., 354 Mich. 327, 92 N.W.2d 295 (1958) ("The arbitrator is not a chancellor. He possesses no equitable power excepting as the submission may expressly grant such.").

61. Staklinski v. Pyramid Elec. Co., 6 N.Y.2d 159, 188 N.Y.S.2d 541, 160 N.E.2d 78 (1959).

62. *See* § 12.20(3) above.

63. Matter of Grayson–Robinson Stores, Inc. v. Iris Const. Corp., 8 N.Y.2d 133, 202 N.Y.S.2d 303, 168 N.E.2d 377 (1960) (building contract, award of specific performance).

64. Uniform Arbitration Act § 12(a).

not impair the employee's statutory rights and is not unconscionable. (*See Armendariz v. Foundation Health Psychcare Services, Inc.* (2000) 24 Cal.4th 83, 99 Cal.Rptr.2d 745, 6 P.3d 669 (*Armendariz*).) We are called upon here to examine whether a mandatory employment arbitration agreement—executed by the employee in connection with the settlement of a previous dispute with the employer's predecessor after advice from the employee's attorney—is unconscionable or otherwise unenforceable.

* * *

FACTS

I. Prior Dispute

Plaintiff was employed for approximately 20 years by Western Development Labsand/or Loral Aerospace Corporation, company/companies subsequently acquired by defendant (collectively, defendant's predecessor). In December 1994, defendant's predecessor terminated plaintiff.

As a result of his termination, plaintiff brought an action in Santa Clara Superior Court, * * * asserting, inter alia, a claim for age discrimination. Plaintiff was represented in that prior case by Randall Widmann, his attorney in the present action. The parties to the prior case settled their dispute in November 1997 and signed the agreements that are central to the issue of the arbitrability of the present dispute. The terms of the settlement included a payment to plaintiff and an agreement that defendant would hire plaintiff as an employee.

II. Settlement Agreement

In or about November 1997, the parties to the prior case—plaintiff and defendant's predecessor—entered into a written agreement (settlement agreement) entitled, "Confidential Settlement Agreement And Release Of Claims." * * * The settlement agreement was signed by plaintiff; it was also signed by attorney Widmann, as plaintiff's counsel, below the block lettering, "APPROVED AS TO FORM."

Paragraph 18 of the settlement agreement provided in part: "The parties stipulate that any action involving the validity, interpretation or enforcement of the Agreement, or for any claim for breach of this Agreement, shall be subject to the arbitration provision in Exhibit 'C.' " The document referenced as "Exhibit C" was the employment agreement * * * entered into by the parties at the time of the settlement. * * *

III. Employment Agreement

At or about the time the settlement agreement was signed, plaintiff and defendant signed an employment agreement. That agreement was a

---

* Judge of the Santa Clara County Superior Court * * *.

standard form document; it was modified or supplemented, however, in several respects by the settlement agreement. One notable change made plaintiff's employment relationship terminable only for good cause for a period of three years after the date of his employment, notwithstanding the "at-will" provision in the form employment agreement. The settlement agreement also contained supplemental terms of plaintiff's employment, including starting salary, the identity of plaintiff's supervisor, and other specifics.

The employment agreement provided that all disputes or controversies that plaintiff had concerning his employment would be subject to binding arbitration conducted under the employment dispute resolution rules of the American Arbitration Association. Under this arbitration agreement, plaintiff waived all rights to pursue any claims against defendant through judicial proceedings. Plaintiff—as a precondition to arbitration—was also required to attempt to resolve any employment disputes by engaging in discussions with various levels of management. The employment agreement provided further that plaintiff waived his arbitration remedy if he did not exercise it (a) within 180 days of his employment termination (if a termination claim), or, alternatively, (b) within 180 days after such other dispute or controversy arose.

* * *

PROCEDURAL HISTORY

Plaintiff filed his complaint on May 15, 2003. The complaint alleged four causes of action arising out of plaintiff's employment relationship with defendant, namely, (1) wrongful demotion in violation of public policy (claimed under, inter alia, Lab.Code, § 6310), (2) violation of statute (Lab.Code, § 6310), (3) breach of employment contract; and (4) breach of implied good faith covenant.

The complaint alleged that, as of March 2001, plaintiff managed defendant's QA department in Santa Clara County, and at that time, he was given additional responsibility for the management of the QA department in the "RSAIIA project," located in Santa Maria. Plaintiff alleged that he made complaints to management both about his employer's abusive treatment of his subordinates in Santa Maria, and regarding its insistence that defendant deliver a product to the United States government that the company knew was defective. The complaint alleged further that, sometime after receiving extremely favorable reviews in January 2002 and June 2002, plaintiff was "abruptly" given an "[u]nsatisfactory" interim performance review, removed from his management position, and was told that he should retire. He claimed that defendant took this adverse employment action as a result of his protected activities of complaining "about the treatment of ... employees and his complaining about and resisting [defendant's] efforts to sell defective products to the government."

Defendant filed its motion on August 1, 2003, requesting that the court issue an order compelling arbitration and staying the action until the matter was resolved through binding arbitration. It asserted that the written employment contract and settlement agreement between the parties expressly mandated that the controversy alleged in the complaint be resolved through binding arbitration.

In his opposition to the motion, plaintiff contended, inter alia, that the mandatory employment arbitration agreement was unenforceable because (1) it was unconscionable, and (2) it was against public policy in that it failed to meet the minimum requirements enunciated in *Armendariz, supra* * * *.

* * *

In its order entered on October 24, 2003, the court denied the motion. The court stated: " * * * The agreement is unenforceable because it is unconscionable. * * * "

* * *

DISCUSSION

* * *

I. Standard Of Review

* * * Where * * * there is no disputed extrinsic evidence considered by the trial court, we will review its arbitrability decision de novo. (Abramson v. Juniper Networks, Inc. (2004) 115 Cal.App.4th 638, 650, 9 Cal.Rptr.3d 422 (*Abramson*).)

II. Issues On Appeal

Defendant contends that the trial court erred in concluding that the arbitration clause in the employment agreement was unconscionable. It asserts that the court's ruling disregarded the public policy favoring arbitration. Defendant claims that the court ignored the critical distinction between the "postdispute" circumstances surrounding the execution of the employment agreement here, and the typical "predispute" situation proscribed by *Aremendariz* in which a mandatory arbitration agreement is imposed upon the employee by the employer. Defendant argues further that, because plaintiff executed the employment agreement as part of an overall settlement of a prior dispute with defendant and defendant's predecessor, plaintiff's claims that the arbitration clause in unconscionable and against public policy necessarily fail.

Our analysis of defendant's contentions requires a brief overview of general law concerning arbitration agreements, unconscionable contracts, and the Supreme Court's holdings in *Armendariz, supra* 24 Cal.4th 83, 99 Cal.Rptr.2d 745, 6 P.3d 669, and in Little v. Auto Stiegler, Inc. (2003) 29 Cal.4th 1064, 130 Cal.Rptr.2d 892, 63 P.3d 979 (*Little*).

III. Applicable Law

A. *Arbitration agreements*

Code of Civil Procedure section 1281 provides: "A written agreement to submit to arbitration an existing controversy or a controversy thereafter arising is valid, enforceable and irrevocable, save upon such grounds as exist for the revocation of any contract." The California statute corresponds with federal law (i.e., the Federal Arbitration Act), which states that arbitration agreements are "valid, irrevocable, and enforceable, save upon such grounds as exist at law or in equity for the revocation of any contract." (9 U.S.C. § 2.)

California courts have uniformly acknowledged that "[t]here is a strong public policy in favor of arbitration agreements." (Blake v. Ecker (2001) 93 Cal.App.4th 728, 741, 113 Cal.Rptr.2d 422 * * *).

"Despite the strong policy favoring arbitration, there are circumstances in which California courts may invalidate or limit agreements to arbitrate. Employing 'general contract law principles,' courts will refuse to enforce arbitration provisions that are 'unconscionable or contrary to public policy.' * * * " (*Abramson, supra,* 115 Cal.App.4th at p. 651, 9 Cal.Rptr.3d 422, quoting *Armendariz, supra,* 24 Cal.4th at p. 99, 99 Cal.Rptr.2d 745, 6 P.3d 669.)

B. *Public policy considerations* * * *

Four years ago, in *Armendariz,* the Supreme Court considered a challenge to a mandatory arbitration clause contained in the employment agreements of two employees. * * * The employees claimed that, as a matter of law, they could not be compelled to arbitrate their statutory discrimination claims under the Fair Employment and Housing Act, Government Code section 12900 et seq. (FEHA). * * * The court rejected the blanket view that such mandatory employment arbitration agreements are per se invalid with respect to the assertion of FEHA claims. * * * Instead, it "conclude[d] that such claims are in fact arbitrable if the arbitration permits an employee to vindicate his or her statutory rights." (*Id.* at p. 90, 99 Cal.Rptr.2d 745, 6 P.3d 669.)

Such vindication of statutory rights meant that the arbitration agreement perforce needed to "meet certain minimum requirements." (*Armendariz, supra,* 24 Cal.4th at p. 91, 99 Cal.Rptr.2d 745, 6 P.3d 669.) Adopting the standards described by the District of Columbia Circuit in Cole v. Burns Intern. Security Services (D.C.Cir.1997) 105 F.3d 1465 (*Cole*), the court in *Armendariz* held that "[s]uch an arbitration agreement is lawful if it '(1) provides for neutral arbitrators, (2) provides for more than minimal discovery, (3) requires a written award, (4) provides for all of the types of relief that would otherwise be available in court, and (5) does not require employees to pay either unreasonable costs or any arbitrators' fees or expenses as a condition of access to the arbitration forum.' " (*Armendariz, supra,* 24 Cal.4th at p. 102, 99 Cal.Rptr.2d 745, 6 P.3d 669 * * *).

Last year, the Supreme Court extended its holding in *Armendariz* to certain employee claims other than FEHA discrimination claims. (*Little, supra*, 29 Cal.4th 1064, 130 Cal.Rptr.2d 892, 63 P.3d 979.) The employee in *Little* asserted that he was wrongfully demoted and then terminated in retaliation for his reporting of warranty fraud. (*Id.* at p. 1069, 130 Cal.Rptr.2d 892, 63 P.3d 979.) He therefore alleged, inter alia, a *Tameny* claim[10] for wrongful termination in violation of public policy. (*Ibid.*) Plaintiff urged that, as was the case with FEHA claims, a mandatory arbitration agreement relating to an employee claim for wrongful termination in violation of public policy was subject to the same "minimum requirements" enunciated in *Armendariz*. *Id.* at p. 1076, 130 Cal.Rptr.2d 892, 63 P.3d 979.

The Supreme Court agreed. It held that "a legitimate *Tameny* claim is designed to protect a public interest and therefore ' "cannot be contravened by private agreement." ' (*Armendariz, supra*, 24 Cal.4th at p. 100, 99 Cal.Rptr.2d 745, 6 P.3d 669.) In other words, an employment agreement that required employees to waive claims that they were terminated in violation of public policy would itself be contrary to public policy. Accordingly, because an employer cannot ask the employee to waive *Tameny* claims, it also cannot impose on the arbitration of these claims such burdens or procedural shortcomings as to preclude their vindication. Thus, the *Armendariz* requirements are as appropriate to the arbitration of *Tameny* claims as to unwaivable statutory claims." *Little, supra*, 29 Cal.4th at p. 1077, 130 Cal.Rptr.2d 892, 63 P.3d 979. The court reasoned that "[t]he *Armendariz* requirements are therefore applications of general state law contract principles regarding the unwaivability of public rights to the unique context of arbitration, ... and ... there is no reason under *Armendariz*'s logic to distinguish between unwaivable statutory rights and unwaivable rights derived from common law." (*Id.* at p. 1079, 130 Cal. Rptr.2d 892, 63 P.3d 979).

As noted, Plaintiff argues that the mandatory employment arbitration agreement is both unconscionable and fails to meet the five *Cole* requirements as enunciated in *Armendariz*. As we discuss *post*, we agree that the arbitration agreement is unconscionable; thus, the trial court's decision to deny the motion to compel arbitration on that basis was proper. Therefore, we need not address whether the trial court could have also denied enforcement of the arbitration agreement because it violates public policy, in that it fails to meet the five minimum requirements for lawful arbitration agreements enunciated in *Armendariz, supra*, 24 Cal.4th 83, 99 Cal.Rptr.2d 745, 6 P.3d 669. * * *

* * *

C. *Unconscionable Contracts*

An arbitration agreement—in order to be enforceable, and irrespective of whether public or only private rights are implicated—must also

---

10. Tameny v. Atlantic Richfield Co. (1980) 27 Cal.3d 167, 178, 164 Cal.Rptr. 839, 610 P.2d 1330.

satisfy traditional contract standards of conscionability. As we have recently held: "[I]n addition to satisfying the *Armendariz* requirements, an agreement to arbitrate public rights necessarily must be conscionable as well. That conclusion inevitably follows from the great deference accorded unwaivable public rights by both the Legislature and the California Supreme Court. * * * If agreements to arbitrate claims arising from ordinary private rights must meet conscionability standards, then certainly those that affect revered public values warrant the same consideration." (*Abramson, supra,* 115 Cal.App.4th at p. 655, 9 Cal.Rptr.3d 422.)

In *Little*, the Supreme Court succinctly described the applicable law: "To briefly recapitulate the principles of unconscionability, the doctrine has 'both a " 'procedural' and a 'substantive' element," the former focusing on " 'oppression' or 'surprise' " due to unequal bargaining power, the latter on " 'overly harsh' or 'one-sided' " results." (*Armendariz, supra,* 24 Cal.4th at p. 114, 99 Cal.Rptr.2d 745, 6 P.3d 669.) The procedural element of an unconscionable contract generally takes the form of a contract of adhesion, ' "which, imposed and drafted by the party of superior bargaining strength, relegates to the subscribing party only the opportunity to adhere to the contract or reject it." ' * * * " (*Little, supra,* 29 Cal.4th at p. 1071, 130 Cal.Rptr.2d 892, 63 P.3d 979, quoting *Armendariz, supra,* 24 Cal.4th at p. 113, 99 Cal.Rptr.2d 745, 6 P.3d 669).

" 'Substantive unconscionability' focuses on the terms of the agreement" and whether those terms are "so one-sided as to 'shock the conscience.' " * * * (Kinney v. United HealthCare Services, Inc. (1999) 70 Cal.App.4th 1322, 1330, 83 Cal.Rptr.2d 348 * * *.) A contractual provision that is substantively unconscionable "may take various forms, but may generally be described as unfairly one-sided." (*Little, supra,* 29 Cal.4th at p. 1071, 130 Cal.Rptr.2d 892, 63 P.3d 979.) "[T]he paramount consideration in assessing [substantive] conscionability is mutuality." (*Abramson, supra,* 115 Cal.App.4th at p. 657, 9 Cal.Rptr.3d 422.)

We have recently identified on a nonexclusive basis certain types of provisions in mandatory employment arbitration contracts that have been held substantively unconscionable. (*See Abramson, supra,* 115 Cal.App.4th at pp. 656–657, 9 Cal.Rptr.3d 422.) Those cases include: (1) where the agreement unfairly favored the employer by allowing for appeal of arbitration awards in excess of $50,000 (*Little, supra,* 29 Cal.4th at pp. 1072–1074, 130 Cal.Rptr.2d 892, 63 P.3d 979); (2) where the employer imposed forum costs on the employee (McManus v. CIBC World Markets Corp. (2003) 109 Cal.App.4th 76, 93, 134 Cal.Rptr.2d 446); (3) where the employee's damage remedy was limited, the employee was required to pay all costs, and the required hearing location was Oakland (Pinedo v. Premium Tobacco Stores, Inc. (2000) 85 Cal.App.4th 774, 781, 102 Cal. Rptr.2d 435); and (4) where the contract provided that, pending the arbitration hearing, the employee lost his job, salary, and benefits. (Stirlen v. Supercuts, Inc. (1997) 51 Cal.App.4th 1519, 1542, 60 Cal.Rptr.2d 138.)

" 'Procedural unconscionability' concerns the manner in which the contract was negotiated and the circumstances of the parties at that time. * * * It focuses on factors of oppression and surprise. * * * The oppression component arises from an inequality of bargaining power of the parties to the contract and an absence of real negotiation or a meaningful choice on the part of the weaker party. * * * " (Kinney v. United HealthCare Services, Inc., *supra*, 70 Cal.App.4th at p. 1329, 83 Cal.Rptr.2d 348.) "The component of surprise arises when the challenged terms are 'hidden in a prolix printed form drafted by the party seeking to enforce them. * * * ' (Kinney v. United HealthCare Services, Inc., *supra*, 70 Cal.App.4th at p. 1329, 83 Cal.Rptr.2d 348.) Where an adhesive contract is oppressive, surprise need not be shown." (*Abramson*, *supra*, 115 Cal. App.4th at p. 656, 9 Cal.Rptr.3d 422.)

In evaluating a claim of unconscionability, courts are mindful of the interplay between "procedural" and "substantive" unconscionability: " 'The prevailing view is that [procedural and substantive unconscionability] must both be present in order for a court to exercise its discretion to refuse to enforce a contract or clause under the doctrine of unconscionability.' (Stirlen v. Supercuts, Inc., *supra*, 51 Cal.App.4th at p. 1533 * * *). But they need not be present in the same degree. * * * "

IV. The Arbitration Agreement Is Unconscionable

* * *

A. Substantive unconscionability

The employment agreement requires plaintiff only to arbitrate any and all of his employment claims. The arbitration clause plainly contains only a unilateral agreement to arbitrate; any claims that defendant may have that arise out of plaintiff's employment are not subject to the arbitration clause. Defendant's argument to the contrary notwithstanding, the parties' agreement to arbitrate disputes concerning "the validity, interpretation, or enforcement" of the settlement agreement does not infuse an element of bilaterality into the employment agreement. It is true that the settlement agreement contains a bilateral agreement to arbitrate settlement-related disputes; that agreement, however, does not extend to all disputes arising after plaintiff and defendant's predecessor settled the prior case and plaintiff commenced employment with defendant. A dispute arising out of plaintiff's employment, occurring many years after the settlement—such as the present dispute—would not invoke the arbitration provision of the settlement agreement.

The employment agreement—in addition to compelling plaintiff to arbitrate all of his disputes with defendant—requires him to submit to discussions with his supervisors in advance of, and as a condition precedent to, having his dispute resolved through binding arbitration. While on its face, this provision may present a laudable mechanism for resolving employment disputes informally, it connotes a less benign goal. Given the unilateral nature of the arbitration agreement, requiring plaintiff to submit to an employer-controlled dispute resolution mechanism (i.e., one without a neutral mediator) suggests that defendant would receive a "free peek" at plaintiff's case, thereby obtaining an advantage if and when plaintiff were to later demand arbitration.

Moreover, the unilateral arbitration clause places time limitations upon plaintiff's assertion of any claims against defendant. In limiting the time to assert a claim to a maximum of 180 days of the date of his employment termination or "after such other dispute or controversy first arose," plaintiff's time for bringing a claim [for breach of his employment agreement] is shortened, * * * by a period of *more than three and one-half years*. Of course, the employment agreement limits none of the employer's rights against the employee (including the statutory time for bringing suit against him).

We have little trouble concluding that, taken together, these three aspects of the mandatory employment arbitration agreement render it substantively unconscionable. * * *

B. *Procedural unconscionability*

The evidence is less dominant on the question of whether the mandatory arbitration clause in the employment agreement is procedurally unconscionable. We first summarily dispose of any claim that the employment agreement is procedurally unconscionable due to "surprise."

Plaintiff did not submit evidence that he was "surprised" by the arbitration clause. The subject agreement is less than two pages, and the arbitration clause is in all capital letters, thereby alerting the reader that it might contain matters of particular importance. Further, plaintiff was represented by an attorney at the time he executed the settlement agreement and employment agreement. That attorney—the same attorney representing plaintiff in the present case—presumably explained the terms of the documents to his client. * * *

Turning then to "oppression," the employment agreement was a standard form utilized by defendant at the time for the hiring of its employees. It was undisputed that plaintiff—as part of the process of being hired by defendant in connection with the settlement of the prior case—was required to sign the employment agreement. Likewise, the undisputed evidence was that the terms of the agreement (other than the "at-will" provision) were nonnegotiable.

Defendant attempts to distinguish this case from others in which courts have held mandatory employment arbitration agreements unconscionable; here, the parties agreed to certain changes and additions to the employment agreement that were confirmed in the settlement agreement. Of the greatest significance in this respect, the parties agreed that plaintiff could be terminated only for good cause for a period of three years after his employment commenced. Defendant also urges that the arbitration agreement is not unconscionable because it was entered into as part of the settlement of a prior dispute. * * *

We reject defendant's contention—as a general proposition—that the discussion of unconscionability contained in *Armendariz expressly excepted* the circumstance where an employer and employee entered into a binding arbitration agreement after a dispute had arisen. * * * We do not read *Armendariz* to hold that mandatory employment arbitration agreements are *necessarily conscionable* because they are entered into by the parties "postdispute."

Moreover, we do not agree that the mandatory employment arbitration agreement here is a "postdispute" agreement. We acknowledge that the parties' settlement agreement (including the arbitration provisions therein) is a "postdispute" agreement; any action to enforce or interpret that agreement, in our view, would relate back to the prior dispute between plaintiff and defendant's predecessor. The employment agreement, however, contemplated that the parties were starting a new employer-employee relationship with specific terms. Unlike an action concerning the settlement agreement, a dispute arising out of the new employment relationship between the parties—which dispute might occur many years after the 1997 settlement of the prior case—would not be one that related to the prior dispute.

Further, we cannot agree that the facts emphasized by defendant *negate a finding* of procedural unconscionability. Plaintiff had been unemployed for nearly three years while the prior case was pending and he needed the job from defendant to support his family. The fact that plaintiff was able to negotiate a three year "good cause" provision in the employment agreement did not, of itself, place him on equal footing with defendant in the negotiation process. We recently—in *Abramson, supra*—rejected a similar argument by the employer: "Plaintiff's ability to negotiate other aspects of his employment with [his employer] has no bearing on the question of whether he had power to negotiate the *arbitration* provision." (*Abramson, supra*, 115 Cal.App.4th at p. 662, 9 Cal.Rptr.3d 422 * * *.)

Defendant urges that the agreement here was not unconscionable because plaintiff was represented by an attorney at the time it was executed. We agree that this fact has significance—particularly in the context of any claim that the agreement was procedurally unconscionable because of "surprise." The uncontroverted evidence, however, from plaintiff and his counsel was that the mandatory arbitration provision in the employment agreement was nonnegotiable. Thus, on the facts presented here, we are not prepared to say that the mere fact that plaintiff was represented by counsel in the negotiation and execution of the employment agreement prevents him from later asserting that the agreement is unconscionable

Admittedly, plaintiff's negotiating position in this case is not at the far end of the spectrum customarily seen in cases where the employee has an absence of any bargaining power. There was nonetheless—based upon the evidence presented, including the absence of negotiation of the standard form arbitration clause and plaintiff's need for employment—a degree of "inequality of bargaining power of the parties to the contract and an absence of real negotiation or a meaningful choice on the part of the weaker party." (Kinney v. United HealthCare Services, Inc., *supra*, 70 Cal.App.4th at p. 1329, 83 Cal.Rptr.2d 348.)

In short, we conclude that there is oppression presented in the parties' mandatory employment arbitration agreement. The facts presented here—including the significant degree of substantive unconscionability discussed above, and the absence of evidence that the arbitration clause was the subject of specific bargaining by the parties—warrant such a finding. We therefore conclude that the employment agreement is procedurally unconscionable.

C. *Interplay between procedural and substantive unconscionability*

Having found that the mandatory employment arbitration agreement is both substantively and procedurally unconscionable, we next evaluate the interplay between these two findings upon the ultimate determination of whether the agreement is unconscionable. In doing so, we apply a "sliding scale" described in *Armendariz*; we compare the extent of regularity in the procedural process by which the contract was entered into with the degree of harshness or unreasonableness of the substantive terms of the contract. (*Armendariz*, *supra*, 24 Cal.4th at p. 114, 99 Cal.Rptr.2d 745, 6 P.3d 669).

As we have noted, the mandatory arbitration clause in the employment agreement has at least three features that make it substantively unconscionable. Of the greatest overall significance is the fact that it imposes on the employee only a unilateral obligation to arbitrate: "In assessing substantive unconscionability, the paramount consideration is mutuality." (*Abramson*, *supra*, 115 Cal.App.4th at p. 664, 9 Cal.Rptr.3d 422.) Given the high degree of substantive unconscionability therefore, we readily hold that this fact—coupled with the lower quantum of procedural unconscionability discussed *ante*—warrants the conclusion that the mandatory arbitration agreement is unconscionable.

* * *

DISPOSITION

Our de novo review of the record leads us to conclude that the arbitration clause in the employment agreement is unconscionable. Therefore, we affirm the trial court's order denying defendant's motion to compel arbitration.

We Concur: RUSHING, P.J., and PREMO, J.

NOTES

1. Was the *Nyulassy* court correct in concluding that the agreement to arbitrate was unconscionable? Shouldn't the fact that the employee was

represented by counsel go a long way toward obviating the unconscionability claim, whether substantive or procedural?

2.   Another essential attribute of a modern arbitration regime is "finality." For example, while a trial court judgment may be reversed based on "legal error," this is not the case with respect to an arbitration award. On the other hand, such awards clearly do not enjoy complete immunity from judicial review and reversal. The next case explores the extent to which courts may upset arbitration awards.

SANDS v. MENARD, INC.

Supreme Court of Wisconsin, 2010.
787 N.W.2d 384.

MICHAEL J. GABLEMAN, J.

I. BACKGROUND

Dawn Sands is a 1993 graduate of the William Mitchell College of Law. In 1998, John Menard, founder and president of Menard, approached Sands, the sister of his then-girlfriend Debra Sands, about working for Menard's legal department. John Menard told Sands he was dissatisfied with the performance of the legal department in general, and of David Coriden, Vice President and General Counsel, specifically.

* * *

A.   Sands' Tenure at Menard

On June 1, 1999, Sands began working in a newly-created position at the corporate legal office of Menard. John Menard asked Sands to assess and oversee the in-house legal department, including Coriden, and to create a title that reflected this oversight. Sands adopted the title of Executive General Counsel. In addition to her legal duties, Sands operated as the spokesperson for Menard, handling inquiries from the media and generally acting as a public representative for the company.

* * *

On August 17, 1999, just months after Sands began working at Menard, Coriden was terminated following a disagreement with John Menard. Sands then assumed all of Coriden's duties while continuing to oversee Menard's in-house legal department. At the time of his termination, Coriden was paid a yearly salary of $104,999.96, plus a bonus. Shortly after Coriden's termination, John Menard told Sands, "[I]f you are here in a year, wouldn't you like to be making over a hundred thousand? If you are you will be."

* * *

In June 2001, after working for Menard for two years without any pay increases, Sands made verbal and written requests to John Menard to raise her salary to $70,000 per year. Menard responded by increasing her wage to $30.92 per hour (a $4.00 per hour raise), or $64,313.60 per year without overtime, effective July 29, 2001.

Over the next several years, Sands made repeated requests to John Menard for a pay raise. * * *

B. Sands' Termination

On January 11, 2006, Sands received an e-mail from Jessica Bierman of the corporate human resources office advising that Charlie Menard [Chief Operating Officer of Menards] wanted a job description to include with a new compensation agreement. Several e-mails were exchanged between Sands, Charlie Menard, and Bierman, including an e-mail from Sands to Charlie Menard dated January 20, 2006, which stated, "Not only do I WANT to get paid more, but, in point of fact, I MUST be paid more (in both cash as well as bonus) if you intend to avoid a lawsuit."

* * *

A little over six weeks later, on Monday, March 6, 2006, Charlie Menard entered Sands' office with a proposed employment contract. The contract included a wage of $30.92 per hour and an unspecified bonus to be paid in March and July of 2007. Sands told Charlie Menard that this was the same wage she had received for approximately five years. Charlie Menard then wrote "$50,029.98" on a Post-it note and affixed it to the second page of the contract, stating that this was the bonus she would receive if she continued to work for Menard for another year. Sands responded, "I've been sitting here working my butt off and I get nothing. I just get all these promises. . . . [W]hat is that, just a big lie to make me keep working?" Charlie Menard shrugged and said, "Worked, didn't it?" Sands replied that as a 43–year-old woman with no one else to rely on, she needed to be concerned about her retirement. Charlie Menard responded, "[W]hy don't you get married like every other girl?" Sands countered, "Charlie, you understand there is a law called the Equal Pay Act?" Charlie Menard then told Sands that she would be unsuccessful at Menard if she continued to threaten the company with lawsuits, and asked if she was planning to sign the contract. Sands replied that she did not know and was going to think about it.

On Thursday and Friday of that week (March 9 and 10, 2006), Sands went to Chicago on business for Menard. The following Monday, March 13, 2006, Sands returned to the office and found a memo from Charlie Menard dated Thursday, March 9, 2006, in her in-box. In the memo, Charlie Menard communicated his belief that Sands was not likely to accept the proposed contract, that an agreement on compensation might not be possible, and that she should suggest some ways to professionally dissolve their relationship. Sands viewed this as a threat to her job and did not immediately respond. Later that evening, Charlie Menard sent a follow-up e-mail to Sands, requesting that she respond to the memo. Sands replied that she would work on his request and get back to him.

* * * [O]n the evening of Tuesday, March 14, 2006, Sands was preparing for a meeting in her office when John Menard stepped in. "This isn't working, is it," he said. "I'm sick to death of your not getting back to Charlie and you don't respond and your threats." John Menard then instructed Sands to work out an agreement with Charlie Menard by the end of business the next day or she would be "all done." Then he left her office.

Moments later, John Menard returned and declared, "[Y]ou know what, you're all done right now. Pick your shit up; I want your ass out of here. You've got five minutes." Sands asked if he was firing her. John Menard stated that he was placing her on administrative leave. Sands asked for a clarification and stated that Menard did not have an administrative leave policy. John Menard repeated that Sands was on administrative leave, that she had better get moving, and that she now had only four minutes. "[D]o you understand what you're doing right now is unlawful?" Sands asked. "I don't care," John Menard replied. "I want your ass out of here."

At some point during this encounter, Sands turned to her computer in an attempt to log off. John Menard saw this, approached her from the other side of her desk with his hand in a fist, and ordered her to get away from the computer. He then continued to tell Sands to get "[her] ass out of there" and that he wanted "[her] ass gone." Sands collected a few personal items, and left with John Menard following her out of the building.

Sands later testified that during this incident, she felt "intimidat[ed]" by John Menard, who seemed "out of control"; she further testified that she was "scared," "humiliated," and "so embarrassed" by these events. The following day, John Menard had Sands' office door secured with a chain and padlock, which was removed a few days later when the lock was changed. * * *

C.   Arbitration and Award

After her termination, Sands maintained that she had been defamed by Menard and was the victim of gender-based discrimination and then retaliation for claiming discrimination. Sands and Menard initially attempted to settle their dispute independently. Among their efforts was a private meeting between Sands and John Menard in May 2006 that ultimately proved unsuccessful. On October 23, 2006, Sands and Menard mutually agreed to enter into binding arbitration.

The arbitration agreement bound both parties to resolve "all disputes" arising from Sands' employment with Menard. The agreement further provided "that both state and federal laws may apply and that Sands may be entitled to remedies under both." The agreement also required Sands to identify "the nature of relief sought." * * *

On October 19, 2007, the arbitration panel came back with its written award. While it rejected Sands' defamation and Title VII pay discrimination claims, the panel found that Sands (1) was the victim of pay discrimination under the Equal Pay Act ("EPA") due to Menard's failure to compensate her on par with Coriden; and (2) was discharged in retaliation for her assertion of her statutory rights to be free from pay discrimination in violation of the EPA, Title VII, and the Wisconsin Fair Employment Act.

Because of these violations, the panel awarded Sands various monetary damages. She was awarded $267,108 in back wages and an equal amount in liquidated damages for disparate pay and willful violation of the EPA; $114,944.71 in back pay and bonus for lost wages due to termination, as allowed by the EPA and Title VII; $100,000 in compensatory damages for emotional distress; and $900,000 in punitive damages. Menard also was required to pay Sands' attorneys' fees, which totaled $129,120.25. In sum, Menard's obligations totaled $1,778,280.96.

In addition to these monetary damages, the panel ordered that Sands be reinstated to the position of Vice President and Executive General Counsel within 30 days of the date of the award. Sands' reinstatement was to come with a salary of $166,250, to be increased to $175,000 effective January 1, 2008. The panel also ordered Menard to pay her a profit sharing bonus of 15% of her 2007 earnings.

As justification for the reinstatement award, the panel noted that reinstatement is one of the remedies available for violation of the EPA and Title VII. See 29 U.S.C. s 215(a)(3); 42 U.S.C. s 2000e–5(g)(1). It also noted that front pay may be ordered in lieu of reinstatement when reinstatement is inappropriate, citing *Williams v. Pharmacia, Inc.*, 137 F.3d 944, 951–52 (7th Cir.1998). * * *

After the arbitration award was handed down, Menard prepared a check for the full amount of the panel's monetary award. In a letter to Sands, Menard indicated that the check was available to pick up, but that Menard would not reinstate Sands. Despite many additional communications between the parties, Menard continued to refuse to reinstate Sands.

D.   The Case Goes to Court

On December 20, 2007, Sands filed suit in the Circuit Court for Eau Claire County, Paul J. Lenz, Judge, seeking to clarify the arbitration award and subsequently confirm it. In addition to other claims, Sands sought to compel Menard to abide by the terms of the reinstatement award. Menard filed a motion to vacate the award in full or in part, maintaining that the attorney-client relationship is vital to a company, as is the right to choose counsel, and that because of their broken relationship, Sands could no longer represent Menard, Inc., the Menards brothers, or their interests. Sands responded that she could represent Menard, and that she would accept reinstatement if she could be assured of her personal safety. Judge Lenz confirmed the arbitration award in its entirety and denied all motions to modify, correct, or vacate the award.

Menard appealed, again arguing that the arbitration panel disregarded the law by requiring reinstatement. The court of appeals affirmed. It concluded that reinstatement is a statutory remedy under the EPA and Title VII, and that neither provides an exception for in-house attorneys. *Sands v. Menard*, 2009 WI App 70, ¶ 10, 318 Wis.2d 206, 767 N.W.2d 332. The court of appeals held that the panel's reinstatement order rested on substantial authority, and that the panel did not manifestly disregard the law. *Id.*, ¶¶ 10–11. Additionally, the court found that awarding front pay in lieu of reinstatement is discretionary, and courts do not review arbitration awards for erroneous exercise of discretion. *Id.*, ¶ 12. To choose one over the other is not a manifest disregard of the law, the court reasoned. *Id.*

Menard then petitioned this court for review * * *.

II. DISCUSSION

The question before us is whether the arbitration panel exceeded its authority in ordering Sands' reinstatement. * * *

A. Reinstatement and Front Pay Generally

We first turn to a general overview of the remedial framework for Title VII violations, with a specific focus on the remedy of reinstatement.

Under Title VII, courts may "order such affirmative action as may be appropriate, which may include, but is not limited to, reinstatement or hiring of employees, with or without back pay . . ., or any other equitable relief as the court deems appropriate." 42 U.S.C. s 2000e–5(g)(1). Reinstatement is the preferred remedy for violations because this accords with making the victim of discrimination whole. *Equal Employment Opportunity Commission v. Kallir, Philips, Ross, Inc.*, 420 F.Supp. 919, 926 (S.D.N.Y.1976).

However, reinstatement is not appropriate or even possible in all cases. Numerous courts, including the Seventh Circuit, have held that front pay-compensation for projected future earnings-may be awarded in Title VII cases where reinstatement is unavailable or inappropriate. *Williams*, 137 F.3d at 951–52.

Reinstatement may be inappropriate for a number of reasons. * * *

The most common situation where reinstatement is inappropriate is when the employer-employee relationship is "pervaded by hostility." Id. at 952 (citing *McNeil v. Econ. Lab., Inc.*, 800 F.2d 111, 118 (7th Cir.1986)). This unacceptably high level of hostility, however, cannot simply constitute employer-generated frustration over the lawsuit. *McKnight v. Gen. Motors Corp.*, 908 F.2d 104, 116 (7th Cir.1990). Refusing reinstatement because of the natural frustration an employer would feel when an employee files suit "would arm the employer to defeat the court's remedial order." Id. But courts have routinely recognized that granting reinstatement is not appropriate when animosity and hostility are so extreme that "a productive and amicable working relationship would be impossible."

Sasser v. Averitt Express, Inc., 839 S.W.2d 422, 433 (Tenn.Ct.App.1992).
* * *

* * *

A second situation where reinstatement may be inappropriate is when the employee served in a managerial or unusually high-level role, as a representative to the public, or other such sensitive position. Dickerson v. Deluxe Check Printers, Inc., 703 F.2d 276, 280 (8th Cir.1983) ("Those cases in which courts have declined to reinstate injured plaintiffs have frequently involved high level, unique or unusually sensitive positions in defendant's organization."). Success in these positions of trust is difficult or impossible when trust has been broken. Whether the position is such that reinstatement would be unworkable due to the break in the relationship again depends upon the facts of each case.

* * *

These principles emerge from this analysis: While reinstatement is the preferred remedy under Title VII, it is an equitable remedy that may or may not be appropriate depending upon the facts of each case. Where the level of hostility is unusually high, or where the position is a sensitive one requiring a high degree of trust and cooperation between management and the employee, reinstatement is generally not appropriate.

B. The Panel Exceeded Its Authority

Menard challenges the reinstatement portion of the arbitration award on multiple grounds. First, it alleges that the Wisconsin Constitution guarantees Menard its choice of counsel. Second, Menard argues that reinstatement was not feasible and appropriate under governing case law and employment law. Third, it maintains that the arbitrators lacked the authority under the arbitration agreement to order reinstatement. Finally, Menard argues that the panel exceeded its authority by ignoring the Rules of Professional Conduct for attorneys.

Our review of arbitration awards is limited. *Lukowski v. Dankert,* 184 Wis.2d 142, 149, 515 N.W.2d 883 (1994). Our task is to ensure that the parties receive what they bargained for-the adjudication of their dispute via the arbitration process. *Id.* Though limited, a court's role is not a mere formality; a court must overturn an arbitrator's award when the panel exceeds its powers. Wis. Stat. § 788.10(1)(d). An arbitration panel exceeds its powers when it engages in perverse misconstruction or positive misconduct, when the panel manifestly disregards the law, or where the award itself is illegal or violates strong public policy. *Racine County v. Int'l Ass'n of Machinists & Aerospace Workers,* 2008 WI 70, ¶ 11, 310 Wis.2d 508, 751 N.W.2d 312. Whether the panel's decision meets any of these standards is a question of law we review de novo. *Id.*

We conclude that an attorney's ethical obligations, particularly an attorney's duty of loyalty to her clients under our cases and the Rules of Professional Conduct, embody the strong public policy of the State of

Wisconsin. Therefore, an arbitration panel exceeds its powers when it orders the reinstatement of an attorney where reinstatement would clearly lead to a violation of that attorney's ethical obligations. Moreover, we are persuaded that the panel exceeded its authority here because reinstatement of Sands would cause her to violate her ethical obligations as an attorney.

It is a rare occasion for this court to overturn an arbitration award on public policy grounds. The public policy exception to the general rule of judicial deference should be narrowly construed and limited to situations where the public policy "is well defined and dominant, and is to be ascertained by reference to the laws and legal precedents and not from general considerations of supposed public interests." *State v. New England Health Care Employees Union*, 271 Conn. 127, 855 A.2d 964, 970 (Conn.2004). A public policy violation must be clear, and the burden of proving such a violation rests with the party seeking to overturn the award. *Id.*

We stand on firm ground in this case, however, because this court has supervisory authority over the practice of law in Wisconsin. Wis. Const. art. VII, § 3(1); *State v. Cadden*, 56 Wis.2d 320, 324, 201 N.W.2d 773 (1972). The legal profession is unique in that it is mostly self-regulating with ultimate authority vested largely in the courts. SCR ch. 20 Preamble (10). As part of our oversight, we have adopted Rules of Professional Conduct to guide attorney conduct. *See* SCR ch. 20.

While the Rules vary in emphasis and importance, some rules are so deeply established as to embody the strong public policy of the State of Wisconsin. For example, we could not countenance an arbitration award that ordered an individual to engage in the unauthorized practice of law, or one that ordered an attorney to use funds from the attorney's trust account in a fashion prohibited by the Rules of Professional Conduct. Similarly, we cannot countenance an award that forces an attorney to represent a client when it is clear that the complete disintegration of mutual goodwill, trust, and loyalty renders ethical representation by that attorney impossible.

Attorneys owe a fiduciary duty of loyalty to their clients. Berner Cheese Corp. v. Krug, 2008 WI 95, ¶ 41, 312 Wis.2d 251, 752 N.W.2d 800. This obligation of absolute loyalty means that attorneys are required to act solely for the benefit of their clients. *Zastrow v. Journal Commc'ns, Inc.*, 2006 WI 72, ¶ 31, 291 Wis.2d 426, 718 N.W.2d 51. * * *

* * *

In this case, it is clear that Sands cannot in good faith represent Menard without violating her ethical obligations as an attorney.

Leading up to and throughout the arbitration process, all parties agreed that the relationship was irretrievably broken. Sands understood this and unequivocally testified against reinstatement before the arbitration panel, even going so far as to state that "no reasonable person would entertain reinstatement as a possibility." She further made clear her view of the prospective employment conditions at Menard, stating, "[I]t would be impossible to return to such a hostile environment." Understanding that reinstatement was not feasible or available here, Sands sought two years of front pay instead.

Sands also made clear her views of Menard's leadership—her clients if reinstatement were upheld. In her briefing before the arbitration panel, Sands stated that John Menard's conduct was "so monstrous and reprehensible that it shocks the conscience"; that he is a "reckless, callous actor who care[s] nothing about anyone else's rights or reputation"; that he "is a man with no parameters, no limits, no respect for the law and obviously, no self-discipline to control or limit his own behavior-nor does he see any need to"; that his honesty and integrity are "completely illusory"; and that his "dishonesty is serious and overwhelming."

Let there be no mistake—the mutual animosity and distrust between Sands and the executive leadership of Menard, the very people to whom her absolute loyalty would be owed, continued throughout the arbitration hearing and shows no signs of abating today. Sands was right. No reasonable person would consider reinstatement a possibility in this situation. * * *

If the level of hostility alone was not enough, Sands performed an unusually high-level and sensitive role at Menard. She was the Executive General Counsel, heading up the in-house legal operations and supervising the legal work for all of Menard. She also served as Menard's spokesperson and was a public representative to the community. More than most attorneys, her position required a high degree of confidence and trust and a close relationship with Menard's executive leadership. In order to perform her role, Sands had to represent the company's best interests with outside partners, attorneys, and the media. Sands' unique and significant role at Menard required the highest level of good faith, loyalty, and mutual trust.

* * *

In its written award, the panel discussed the difficulty that hostility posed to reinstatement. It recognized both John Menard's hostile behavior toward Sands, and that Sands believed reinstatement would be inappropriate as a result of the hostile relationship. In the end, the panel chose reinstatement because front pay, it felt, would "reward the company for its mistreatment" and "would tend to send the wrong message to company employees who otherwise might be inclined to make meritorious complaints about unlawful conduct occurring within the company."

Though the panel's decision was otherwise thorough, nowhere did the panel consider the applicability of Sands' ethical obligations as an attorney. It never examined whether Sands could ethically perform her role if it awarded reinstatement. If it had, it would have reached the same conclusion Sands had: no reasonable person would entertain reinstatement as a possibility.

The panel was right in seeking to make Sands whole. Even though it seemed to understand the complete breakdown in the relationship, the panel went forward anyway in order to send a message. While a message surely needed to be sent—and it was, to the tune of more than $1.6 million, including $900,000 in punitive damages—we conclude that reinstatement of Sands in this situation would cause her to violate her ethical obligations as an attorney. We further hold that an arbitration award requiring an attorney to violate her ethical obligations is void as a matter of strong public policy. The panel therefore exceeded its powers under Wis. Stat. § 788.10(1)(d). *Racine County*, 310 Wis.2d 508, ¶ 11, 751 N.W.2d 312.

We do not conclude that reinstatement is always inappropriate for in-house lawyers or general counsels, or that reinstatement is always inappropriate when the relationship is acrimonious or the employee served in a high-level role. The specific circumstances of each case must be considered. * * *

C. Remedying the Panel's Error

Because the panel exceeded its powers, the reinstatement award cannot stand. Under Wis. Stat. § 788.10(1)(d), an award may be vacated "[w]here the arbitrators exceeded their powers." As we have already explained, arbitrators exceed their powers when their award is in violation of strong public policy.

Both parties agree that the court may vacate the reinstatement portion of the award while leaving the rest intact. Menard urges us to vacate the reinstatement award and thus end the dispute. Sands argues that if we find reinstatement improper, we should remand for an award of front pay to effectuate the panel's clear intention to make the successful plaintiff whole.

We agree with Sands. Reinstatement is intended to put the employee in the position he or she would have been in before the adverse employment action. But courts have recognized that where reinstatement is inappropriate, "an award of front pay as a substitute for reinstatement ... [i]s a necessary part of the 'make whole'" purposes of Title VII. *Pollard v. E.I. du Pont de Nemours & Co.*, 532 U.S. 843, 850, 121 S.Ct. 1946, 150 L.Ed.2d 62 (2001). Like reinstatement, front pay is an equitable remedy. *Williams*, 137 F.3d at 951. It "is the functional equivalent of reinstatement because it is a substitute remedy that affords the plaintiff the same benefit (or as close an approximation as possible) as the plaintiff would have received had she been reinstated." *Id.* at 952.

The panel made clear that it was going to award either front pay or reinstatement ("Whether to award reinstatement or front pay to Sands is a difficult decision."). In order to make Sands whole in accord with the intentions of the arbitration panel, we vacate the award of reinstatement and remand to the circuit court for a determination on the equities of an appropriate front pay award.

III. CONCLUSION

In sum, we agree with Menard that the panel exceeded its authority. An arbitration panel exceeds its authority when its award violates strong public policy. An attorney owes a fiduciary duty of loyalty to her clients, a duty so replete in our cases and in the Rules of Professional Conduct as to be axiomatic. Such a duty is deeply rooted in our laws and embodies the strong public policy of the State of Wisconsin. In this case, we conclude that by accepting reinstatement, Sands would be forced to violate her ethical obligations as an attorney. Thus, we vacate the panel's award of reinstatement on the grounds that it is void as a violation of strong public policy. Under the applicable employment discrimination laws, front pay is a substitute for reinstatement. Accordingly, we vacate the panel's award of reinstatement and remand to the circuit court to determine an appropriate award of front pay.

The decision of the court of appeals is reversed and remanded.

SHIRLEY S. ABRAHAMSON, C.J. (DISSENTING).

I do not join the majority opinion because I conclude that the majority has "exceeded its powers" by "manifestly disregarding the law" in its decision to vacate the arbitration panel's award of reinstatement.

I agree with the circuit court and court of appeals, both of which denied Menard's motion to vacate the arbitration award for reinstatement of Dawn Sands. These courts reached the right result, largely because they correctly understood the very limited role courts play in reviewing arbitration awards.

* * *

Now, after Menard, who initially submitted to arbitration, has challenged the outcome of that arbitration through three courts, the majority does just what the court of appeals recognized that courts could not and should not do: The majority recognizes for the first time a "clear strong public policy" and concludes, as the panel did not, that the arbitration award would clearly lead to a violation of Sands' ethical obligations as an attorney and thereby violate public policy. On the basis of its newly announced public policy, and its own conclusion that the panel award would necessarily violate that policy, the majority vacates the arbitration award in the very case where it first sets forth the policy. Yet the ordinary standard of review is that "[i]f the correctness of the award, including its resolution of the public-policy question, is reasonably debatable, judicial intervention is unwarranted."

The majority's result undermines the goals and practice of arbitration in Wisconsin and defeats the intent of the parties who entered this arbitration in particular. How will parties in the future who voluntarily submit to arbitration be confident that the efficient and final resolution that arbitration promises will not be set aside by this court? What other "strong public policies" may be lurking, not-previously articulated, that this court could use to vacate an arbitration award that one party seeks to escape and with which four members of this court simply disagree?

It may well be that in some cases a direct conflict will arise between the mostly state laws governing the attorney-client relationship and the mostly-federal statutes and case law governing employment discrimination, including the provisions for reinstatement. As nearly as I can tell, this touches on a question of first impression, whether in some circumstances, employment reinstatement ordered under the federal employment law may violate a state's attorney-client law, and if so, how to resolve the two? But the place to resolve novel and emerging questions of law is not in a court's review of a private arbitration award. Parties submit disputes to arbitration to reach swift resolution and specifically to avoid the lengthy appeals in which courts can definitively resolve every question of law and in the process create precedent. Review of an arbitration to which parties voluntarily submitted is not the appropriate vehicle for this court to announce new rules of law or to hold forth about generalized public policy.

* * *

Although the majority's conclusions about a public policy are indeterminate, there is no doubt that attorneys have fiduciary and ethical duties and obligations of professional conduct. Other employees also have fiduciary and ethical obligations to their employers.

The problem is that the majority is unable to pin down a particular rule, duty, or obligation or offer more than its own repeated assertions that if the award stands, a violation of ethical obligations would be the necessary result. The majority claims that because the panel did not affirmatively discuss Sands' ethical duties as an attorney, this necessarily implies that the panel "never examined whether Sands could ethically perform her role if it awarded reinstatement." Majority op., ¶ 63. The majority parlays this supposition into the conclusion that the award of reinstatement "would have the practical effect of forcing Sands to violate her ethical obligations." Majority op., ¶ 65. Both the claim and the observation are at best speculative and moreover are belied by the record.

There is no reason to believe, much less to affirmatively conclude as the majority has done, that the arbitration panel did not consider the applicability of Sands' ethical obligations as an attorney. It is no secret that Sands is an attorney. Through its 49–page factual review, legal analysis, and ultimate findings, the panel was amply aware of Sands' professional role and her responsibilities toward the Menard corporation, its officers, and the individuals representing the corporation. The panel explicitly acknowledged the "difficult[y]" of the "hostile" relationship between the parties. In doing so they necessarily assessed the dynamic between attorney and client and the issues inherent therein. Even if there were uncertainty as to what law the panel did or did not consider, the majority oversteps its bounds in review of an arbitration award when it construes ambivalence or silence in the record to justify overturning a result it disfavors. As the majority recognizes, the party seeking to overturn the panel award bears the burden of proof.

Significantly, Sands and Menard explicitly stipulated that each member of the panel would be an attorney. Each of the arbitrators was an experienced and successful attorney, themselves bound by the Rules of Professional Conduct and bound to be versed in those rules, which the majority opinion invokes to justify its result in the present case.

It strains credulity when the majority assumes these three attorneys failed to consider the rules of their profession or the nature of the attorney-client relationship when they assessed whether a reinstatement award would be feasible on the facts before them. The majority considerably exceeds the supervisory role of a court in review of an arbitration award when it construes the record to presume that a capable arbitration panel somehow ignored the obvious.

The majority declares that in order to vacate an arbitrator's award on the grounds of public policy, "[a] public policy violation must be clear, and the burden of proving such a violation rests with the party seeking to overturn the award." Majority op., ¶ 50. The majority does not, however, apply this standard to the instant case.

Rather, the majority attempts to persuade us that every one of the three arbitrators, along with the circuit court judge, the three judges on the court of appeals panel, and Sands herself, all lawyers, all overlooked a "clear violation of a strong public policy" and that all the lawyers involved in the present case overlooked the majority's own determination that "Sands cannot in good faith represent Menard without violating her ethical obligations." Majority op., ¶ 56.

* * *

The majority cites SCR 20:1.7(a)(2), which states that "a lawyer shall not represent a client if the representation involves a concurrent conflict of interest. A concurrent conflict of interest exists if ... there is a significant risk that the representation of one or more clients will be materially limited by ... a personal interest of the lawyer" (emphasis added).

The majority goes on to hold that it is "clear that Sands can not in good faith represent Menard without violating her ethical obligations as an attorney." Majority op., ¶ 56. The majority's opinion is unpersuasive. It is far from clear that if the reinstatement award stands, Sands will necessarily violate this ethical obligation.

First, the commentary to this section of the Rules, SCR 20:1.7(a)(2) indicates that the phrase "personal interest" refers not to one's own emotive state or stake, but rather to substantive, material conflicts of interest. Notably, the comments identify business-related examples, such as "when a lawyer has discussions concerning possible employment with an opponent of the lawyer's client," and further direct the reader to "Rule

1.8 for specific Rules pertaining to a number of personal interest conflicts, including business transactions with clients." No such objective, material business conflict has been identified here as a conflicting "personal interest" of Sands. * * *

Second even assuming that "feelings" are within the scope of SCR 20:1.7(a)(2), this case still does not provide sufficient support for the majority's contention that Sands would "clearly" violate her ethical obligations by that "personal interest." * * * Her statements do not establish that an ethics violation either had or would occur if the reinstatement award were to stand. Of all the quotes reported by the majority in sensationalist fashion, none refers at all to Sands' opinion or that of the panel or any other party as to her own future conduct or ethical obligations with respect to Menard.

* * *

Third, the majority's holding that letting the reinstatement award stand would "force" or "require" Sands to violate her ethical obligations is not supported by the record and defies logic. The majority assumes that only a single course of conduct can result from Sands' reinstatement-namely, Sands' professional misconduct following a return to employment at Menard.

Suppose, faced with reinstatement, both parties accede to Sands' return. It is neither impossible nor unreasonable to think that as the resolution gleaned from arbitration took hold, hurt feelings would fade and be overtaken by the professional nature and interests of both parties. It is entirely possible that Sands could resume her representation with no ethical violation whatsoever. More importantly, the award of reinstatement gives Sands the opportunity to make that assessment for herself. Sands would be the most capable person to do so. Oddly, the majority seems to find itself better positioned than the lawyer involved. The majority without hesitation reports "it is clear that Sands cannot in good faith represent Menard without violating her ethical obligations as an attorney."

* * *

There is another potential outcome that the majority does not acknowledge. If the reinstatement award stands, and if the parties truly view reinstatement as untenable and mutually undesirable, then rather than enter a situation where, in the majority's view, an ethical violation is likely to occur, the parties could simply negotiate a settlement that avoids Sands' actual return to Menard. Courts and commentators alike have recognized that parties are free to reach a more efficient or desirable result by negotiating an alternative solution to a court-imposed remedy. * * * In other words, if the parties could not live with reinstatement, they were free to negotiate for another result.

Under such circumstances, the normal and well-established rules of deference to the arbitral process must prevail.

* * *

In the end, the only thing that is "clear" from the majority's treatment of the present case is that the majority does not like the reinstatement award and has substituted its discretion for that of the arbitrators, in violation of the limitations on the court's standard of review.

Because no clear violation of a strong public policy is present here, and no other grounds exist for vacating the arbitration panel's award as exceeding its powers, the majority's analysis becomes little more than a strained analytical effort to overturn an arbitration award with which four members of this court disagree. The majority has improperly extended the authority of this court, at the cost of the well-established and highly deferential standard of review a court gives to arbitration awards.

For the reasons set forth, I write separately in dissent.

I am authorized to state that JUSTICES ANN WALSH BRADLEY and N. PATRICK CROOKS join this opinion.

NOTES

1. Assuming Sands had prevailed in the Wisconsin Supreme Court on the reinstatement issue, do you think it likely that she would have resumed employment in her former position with Menard? Given the bad blood between the parties, would this have been a realistic expectation? As a practical matter, wouldn't her employer "purchase" the reinstatement order from her for an amount that will reflect her strong bargaining position?

2. There has been substantial debate about whether "manifest disregard of the law" is a valid basis for vacating an arbitration award under the Federal Arbitration Act and the impact of Hall Street Associates, L.L.C. v. Mattel, Inc., 552 U.S. 576, 128 S.Ct. 1396, 170 L.Ed.2d 254 (2008). Consider in this regard the following recent language of the United States Court of Appeals for the 5th Circuit:

Congress embraced this notion that arbitration awards should generally be upheld barring some sort of procedural injustice, and §§ 10 and 11 of the FAA enumerate the circumstances under which an award may be vacated, modified, or corrected when the action is one brought under the Act. Under § 10, courts are permitted to vacate an arbitration award.

(1) where the award was procured by corruption, fraud or undue means;

(2) where there was evident partiality or corruption in the arbitrators, or either of them;

(3) where the arbitrators were guilty of misconduct in refusing to postpone the hearing, upon sufficient cause shown, or in refusing to hear evidence pertinent and material to the controversy; or of any

other misbehavior by which the rights of any party have been prejudiced; or

(4) where the arbitrators exceeded their powers, or so imperfectly executed them that a mutual, final, and definite award upon the subject matter submitted was not made.

9 U.S.C. § 10(a).

As we have earlier noted, the Supreme Court in *Hall Street* has recently addressed the extent to which courts may vacate or modify the work of arbitrators on grounds beyond those found in §§ 10 and 11. In their agreement to arbitrate, the *Hall Street* parties agreed contractually to give the district court the authority to vacate or modify the award on grounds that were not provided in §§ 10 and 11. The agreement was negotiated during the litigation of the case and was entered as an order by the district court. It required the district court to "vacate, modify or correct any award: (i) where the arbitrator's findings of facts are not supported by substantial evidence, or (ii) where the arbitrator's conclusions of law are erroneous." *Hall Street*, 128 S.Ct. at 1400–01. After arbitration, the district court vacated the award for legal error. Ultimately, the Ninth Circuit held that the terms controlling judicial review were unenforceable and ordered the arbitration award reinstated. The Supreme Court then "granted certiorari to decide whether the grounds for vacatur and modification provided by §§ 10 and 11 of the FAA are exclusive." *Id.* at 1401. The petitioner argued that the agreement to expand the court's review beyond the specific provisions of the statute should be respected because "arbitration is a creature of contract, and the FAA is motivated, first and foremost, by a congressional desire to enforce agreements into which parties ha[ve] entered." *Id.* at 1404 * * *. The Court rejected this argument.

The Supreme Court observed that § 9 of the FAA, which states that upon the application for an order confirming an arbitration award the court "must grant such an order unless the award is vacated, modified, or corrected as prescribed in sections 10 and 11 ...," suggests that the judicial review is constrained by the statute. There "is nothing malleable about 'must grant,' which unequivocally tells courts to grant confirmation in all cases, except when one of the 'prescribed' exceptions applies." *Id.* at 1405.

Hall Street also found that the Act's legislative history indicated that Congress intended the statutory grounds for vacatur and modification to be the exclusive means for setting aside or changing an arbitration award challenged under the FAA. In a brief submitted to the House and Senate Subcommittees of the Committees on the Judiciary, one of the primary drafters of the Act said, "The grounds for vacating, modifying, or correcting an award are limited. If the award [meets a condition of § 10], then and then only the award may be vacated.... If there was [an error under § 11], then and then only it may be modified or corrected...." *Id.* at 1406 n. 7 (citing Arbitration of Interstate Commercial Disputes, Joint Hearings before the Subcommittees of the Committees on the Judiciary on S. 1005 and H.R. 646, 68th Cong., 1st Sess., 34 (1924)) (additions and omissions in *Hall Street*).

Based both on the text and on the legislative history, *Hall Street* concluded that §§ 10 and 11 provide the exclusive regimes for review under the FAA. The Court reiterated this holding several times: "We hold that the statutory grounds are exclusive"; "We agree with the Ninth Circuit that they are [exclusive] ..."; "We now hold that * * * §§ 10 and 11 provide exclusive regimes for the review provided by the statute...." *Hall Street* 128 S.Ct. at 1400, 1401, 1403, 1406. This rule, *Hall Street* determined, is consistent with the "national policy favoring arbitration with just the limited review needed to maintain arbitration's essential virtue of resolving disputes straightway." *Id.* at 1405. * * *

Before we leave *Hall Street,* we must point out that the petitioner, citing Wilko v. Swan, 346 U.S. 427, 436—47, 74 S.Ct. 182, 98 L.Ed. 168 (1953), argued that the widespread judicial recognition of manifest disregard of the law as a nonstatutory ground for vacatur suggests that §§ 10 and 11 are not exclusive. *Hall Street,* 128 S.Ct. at 1403. They argued that if this judicial expansion is permissible, then the instant contractual expansion similarly should be accepted. The Supreme Court, however, questioned whether *Wilko* should even be read as creating an independent ground for vacatur. *Id.* at 1404. That issue, *Hall Street* observed, was not before the Court in *Wilko,* and *Wilko*'s language, upon which the circuit courts have based the standard, is vague. The *Hall Street* Court speculated and concluded:

> Maybe the term "manifest disregard" was meant to name a new ground for review, but maybe it merely referred to the § 10 grounds collectively, rather than adding to them. Or, as some courts have thought, "manifest disregard" may have been shorthand for § 10(a)(3) or § 10(a)(4), the subsections authorizing vacatur when the arbitrators were "guilty of misconduct" or "exceeded their powers." We, when speaking as a Court, have merely taken the *Wilko* language as we found it, without embellishment, and now that its meaning is implicated, *we see no reason to accord it the significance that [the petitioner] urges.*

Id. (citations omitted) (emphasis added). In short, *Hall Street* rejected manifest disregard as an independent ground for vacatur, and stood by its clearly and repeatedly stated holding, as noted in the earlier paragraph, that §§ 10 and 11 provide the exclusive bases for vacatur and modification of an arbitration award under the FAA.

Citigroup Global Markets, Inc. v. Bacon, 562 F.3d 349, 351–353 (5th Cir. 2009). *But see* Stolt–Nielsen S.A. v. AnimalFeeds International Corp., 130 S.Ct. 1758, 1768 n.3 (2010) (refusing to decide whether "manifest disregard" survives *Hall Street*); Rent-A-Center, West, Inc. v. Jackson, 130 S.Ct. 2772 (2010) (refusing to consider the scope of *Hall Street*). For further analysis of *Hall Street, see* Thomas J. Stipanowich, *Arbitration and Choice: Taking Charge of the "New Litigation,"* 7 De Paul Bus. & Com. L.J. 383, 428–29 (2009).

3. The past decade has witnessed substantial controversy over the fairness of enforcing predispute arbitration agreements against consumers, investors, employees and franchisees. Proposed legislation dealing with this issue has frequently been introduced in Congress over the past several sessions. Most recently, the Arbitration Fairness Act of 2009, introduced in the House of Representatives, would amend the FAA to provide that: "No predispute arbitration agreement shall be valid or enforceable if it requires arbitration of—(1) an employment, consumer, or franchise dispute; or (2) a dispute arising under any statute intended to protect civil rights or to regulate contracts or transactions between parties of unequal bargaining power." H.R. 1020, 11th Cong. § 4 (2009). For an analysis of such proposed legislation and the fairness issue, *see* David S. Schwartz, *Mandatory Arbitration and Fairness,* 84 Notre Dame L.Rev. 1247 (2009); Thomas E. Carbonneau, *"Arbitracide": The Story of Anti-Arbitration Sentiment in the U.S. Congress,* 18 Am.Rev. Int'l Arb. 233 (2007).

4. Considerable controversy has also risen over the use of class actions in arbitration. In *Stolt–Nielsen,* the United States Supreme Court held, 5–3, that "a party may not be compelled under the FAA to submit to class arbitration unless there is a contractual basis for concluding that the party *agreed* to do so." *Id.* at 1763. Prior to *Stolt–Nielsen,* controversy had arisen over the use of class action waivers. The opposing positions are described by the United States Circuit Court of Appeals for the Second Circuit as follows:

> One commentator has recently contended that "[t]he outright banning of class action in mandatory arbitration clauses has become a standard of policy for many corporations that transact with consumers." Bryan Allen Rice, "Comment: *Enforceable or Not?: Class Action Waivers in Mandatory Arbitration Clauses and the Need for a Judicial Standard,*" 45 Hous.L.Rev. 215, 224 (2008).[2] We acknowledge at the outset, as have other courts that have considered questions arising from the enforcement of class action waivers, in both consumer and commercial contracts, that the wisdom and utility of these provisions have become the subject of intense debate. *See* Skirchak v. Dynamics Research Corp., 508 F.3d 49, 63 (1st Cir.2007) ("We recognize that there is a policy debate about whether class action waivers essentially act as exculpatory clauses, allowing for violations of laws where individual cases involve low dollar amounts and so will not adequately address or prevent illegality."). The opposing positions in this frequently impassioned debate have been dispassionately described as follows:

>> Companies' use of class action waivers is motivated by the view that plaintiffs exploit the class action procedure in order to wrest large and unfair settlements from defendants.... Class action waivers are viewed by these companies as a way to defend themselves from consumers who are ganging up on companies through the leverage

2. Two commentators have suggested that this is particularly so in the credit card industry: "Credit card companies have shown themselves to be even less enthusiastic about classwide arbitration than about class action litigation. The 'devil you know' phenomenon is compounded by the uncertainty of judicial review of class certification in arbitration and the concomitant fear of a 'renegade arbitrator' certifying a class and exposing a company to massive liability." Samuel Issacharoff & Erin F. Delaney, *"Credit Card Accountability,"* 73 U.Chi.L.Rev. 157, 179 (2006).

inherent in the aggregation of large numbers of claims. In further support of these waivers, corporations argue that the many (perceived) advantages of arbitration to a plaintiff make up for any disadvantages or inconveniences that the plaintiff may incur by sacrificing the ability to be part of a class action.

... Opponents of class action waivers contend that the ability to aggregate claims is crucial to protect the rights of those individuals ... who do not have the resources to litigate individual claims. Further, many individual claims are only viable if brought on a class-wide basis. Indeed, by prohibiting class actions in ... lawsuits[ ] where the expected recovery is dwarfed by the cost of litigating or arbitrating the claim, individuals are effectively prevented from pursuing their claims. As a result, businesses are able to engage in unchecked market misbehavior....

J. Maria Glover, *"Beyond Unconscionability: Class Action Waivers and Mandatory Arbitration Agreements,"* 59 Vand. L. Rev. 1735, 1746–47 (2006) (footnotes and internal quotation marks omitted). * * *

* * *

We note that two standard treatises on the conduct of class action litigation appear to take opposing positions as well. *Compare* 1 Joseph M. McLaughlin, *McLaughlin on Class Actions: Law and Practice,* § 2:14 (3d ed. 2006) ("As the potential availability of class-wide arbitration threatens to multiply exponentially the exposure on what is facially a single-consumer issue, companies should strongly consider including in their standard arbitration agreements an express provision barring class action litigation or arbitration.") *with* 3 Alba Conte & Herbert B. Newberg, *Newberg on Class Actions,* § 9:67 n.2 (4th ed. 2008) ("The bar on class arbitration threatens the premise that arbitration can be a fair and adequate mechanism for enforcing statutory rights.").

In re American Express Merchants' Litigation, 554 F.3d 300, 303–04 (2d Cir. 2009), *vacated and remanded for further consideration in light of* Stolt–Nielsen, S.A. v. AnimalFeeds Int'l Corp., 130 S.Ct. 1758 (2010). Has the "class action waiver" issue been resolved by *Stolt–Nielsen*?

5. Suppose in an employment discrimination case under the FAA, an agreement to arbitrate contains a specific provision that the arbitrator will determine the enforceability of the arbitration agreement. According to the Supreme Court, by a 5–4 holding, if a party challenges the arbitration agreement itself as unconscionable, that challenge is for the arbitrator, but if the challenge is to the specific agreement delegating the enforceability question to the arbitrator, that issue must be decided by the district court. *See* Rent–A–Center, West, Inc., v. Jackson, ___ U.S. ___, 130 S.Ct. 2772 (2010).

SECTION 7. REFORMATION

HAUG v. CARTER

Court of Appeals of Texas, Austin, 2004.
2004 WL 1685619 (unpublished opinion).

Before CHIEF JUSTICE LAW, JUSTICES PATTERSON and PURYEAR.

W. KENNETH LAW, CHIEF JUSTICE.

* * *

In the early 1990's, Thomas Trotter, acting through the Trotter Trust, developed Thurman Bend Estates, a twenty-seven lot residential subdivision on the south shore of Lake Travis. * * * Trotter relied on Southwest Properties, a real estate company, to act as his sales agent in marketing subdivision lots. Trial evidence showed that both Trotter and Southwest Properties represented both orally and in written advertising materials that the subdivision lot owners would have the use of a one-acre homeowner's park on Lake Travis. These statements represented to lot purchasers that the homeowner's park on Lake Travis would allow recreational activities such as "picnicking, swimming, sunbathing, fishing, and similar recreational activities, including the launching of water craft and associated automobile and watercraft trailer parking." The Declaration of Covenants, Conditions and Restrictions for the subdivision provided that the developer would convey a "lake side park area easement and an access easement for the usage by all Owners" to the Thurman Bend Property Owners Association ("Owners Association"). From the inception of the development, the represented location of the one-acre park was on the portion of the subdivision that became platted as Lot 18.

Haug was a licensed real estate agent working at Southwest Properties. * * * Haug sold at least one lot in the subdivision. In 1996, Haug purchased Lot 18 from Trotter. According to the trial court, Haug had actual knowledge that the one-acre park was located on Lot 18 and that recreational activities would be allowed at the park. * * *

In 1996, Haug and Trotter entered into an earnest money contract for the purchase of Lot 18. In that agreement, a handwritten provision "reserve[d] the right to retain a 1 acre recreational easement (Dimensions 100' x 400') along the east boundary line of this lot for the benefit of the property owners association. Said easement shall have access across Lot 18 to Thurman Bluff Rd. and be recorded by separate instrument after the subdivision plat is approved and recorded." * * *

Before the final sale of Lot 18, and contrary to the earnest money contract, Haug requested that Trotter's attorney, Tom Davies, change the language of the proposed park easement on Lot 18 from a "lake side park easement" to "boat launch easement." Trial testimony from Davies indicated that he agreed to this change because including the term "boat launch" in the easement description would offer a more accurate description of the easement without changing Trotter's intention,* * * [and] that Trotter instructed him to reject an attempt by Haug to change the language of the easement so that it prohibited recreational activities formerly advertised to lot owners.

At trial, Davies testified that two surveyors produced the Grant of Easements document. One surveyor, James Garon, performed field work and wrote notes concerning the property in 1995. The other, Roy Smith, later used those notes to draw up the Grant of Easements. Although Davies would normally have one surveyor do this work, he had scheduling and communication problems with Garon, so he turned to Smith to complete the work. According to Smith, he produced the final grant document solely based on Garon's notes and a freehand sketch faxed to him by Davies. He did not speak with Garon, Davies, or Trotter concerning the dimensions they intended for the easement. Smith did not receive a copy of the earnest money contract, which detailed the intended dimensions of the easement.

On February 26, 1996, a Grant of Easements—referring to a "Right-of-Way Easement" and to a "Boat Launch Easement"—was executed on Lot 18, and this document was supposed to implement, according to Davies, the formal creation of the homeowner's lakeside park as described by the Declaration. However, the land area comprised in the metes and bounds description for the Boat Launch Easement was of 10,934 square feet (approximately 92 feet by 110 feet), rather than the approximately 40,000 square feet described in the earnest money contract. The Grant of Easements also referred to an easement strip twenty feet in width, abutting the high water line of Lake Travis for the purpose of passage and use by the public for public sports and amusements, that was contained in the original deed that Trotter acquired with the property. The Right-of-Way easement describes a pedestrian and vehicle ingress and egress easement across Lot 18 to the easement along the lakeside. * * *

In a letter dated April 2000, Haug notified his fellow lot owners that the boat launch easement on his property was "provided for the immediate loading and unloading of watercraft, but does not provide for a park or picnic area." He further wrote that the boat launch easement included a "limitations of use" section that prohibited "parking, fishing, picnicking, loitering, camping, including fires, [and] swimming." Haug indicated that unattended vehicles would be towed at the owner's expense and that "all pedestrian traffic should be limited to boat launching only."

In July 2000, Thurman Bend Estates lot owners filed suit against Haug and other defendants seeking, among other things, the reformation of the easement across Lot 18 into a "lake side park area easement" and payment of attorney's fees; the intervening Owners Association joined the case in November 2001. In response, Haug filed a counterclaim, seeking a declaration to enforce the Grant of Easements as written and attorney's fees. After a three-day bench trial in November 2002, the court found that the Grant of Easements failed to set forth the actual and full intention of the developer to provide for the grant of an easement on Lot 18 for a one-acre homeowner's park to be used for recreational activities. * * *

The trial court also found that the Grant of Easements failed to attach a correct legal description of the area on Lot 18 subject to the lakeside park area easement. The court said that this failure arose from a lack of coordination or clear communication between the attorney who prepared the Grant of Easement and Smith, the surveyor who prepared the legal description. It concluded that the legal description of the easement on Lot 18 is a mistaken description that is not consistent with the agreement, understanding, and intent of the parties at the time Haug purchased Lot 18.

The trial court then reformed the legal description of the easement to conform to the intent of the parties by modifying the term "Boat Launch Easement" to read "Lake Side Park Area Easement." The court also said that activities such as "picnicking, swimming, sunbathing, fishing" and launching of watercraft were allowed on the easement. In addition, the court voided the Grant of Easement's prohibition on "activities of extended duration" within the former twenty-foot easement strip along Lake Travis. The court also reformed the Official Real Property Records in Travis County and the Grant of Easements to reflect the reformation of the easement into a "Lake Side Park Area Easement."

* * *

* * * Haug argues that the district court erred in reforming the "Boat Launch Easement" located in the Grant of Easements into a "Lake Side Park Easement" as described in representations to Thurman Bend Estates lot owners.

In reforming a written instrument, there must be evidence of the true intention of the parties, and the reformation must conform to that agreement and not create an agreement that never existed. * * * By implication, then, reformation requires two elements: (1) an original agreement and (2) a mutual mistake, made after the original agreement, in reducing the original agreement to writing. * * * Unilateral mistake by one party, and knowledge of that mistake by the other party, is equivalent to mutual mistake. * * *

* * *

In this case, the trial court concluded that the failure of the Grant of Easements to set forth the actual and full agreements and understandings of the parties and to attach a correct legal description of the access easement and the one-acre lakeside park area easement was the result of mutual mistake by all parties, including Haug, and the surveyor's error. The court held in the alternative that the failure of the Grant of Easements to set forth actual and full agreements and understandings of the parties and to attach a correct legal description of the lakeside park area easement was the result of a unilateral mistake by Thomas Trotter, the Trotter Trust, and the Owners Association. It also held that Haug's actions constituted inequitable and fraudulent conduct by misrepresenting his contemporaneous agreement and understanding of the effect of the Grant of Easements at the time of its execution and his purchase of Lot 18, knowing that he would later assert an inconsistent legal position regarding the effect of the Grant of Easements.

* * *

In response, Haug argues that the trial court should have followed Wal–Mart Stores, Inc. v. Sturges and treated his fraudulent conduct as a mere savvy business deal. *See* 52 S.W.3d 711 (Tex.2001). In *Sturges,* the supreme court held that a real estate investor could not recover against Wal–Mart for tortious interference in a prospective business deal. *Id.* at 727. That case, however, involved two competing business deals from a sophisticated corporation and a real estate investor that stood to reap economic gain from a property deal. This case does not involve economic gain or a prospective business deal; rather, it involves lot owners seeking to reform an easement that was changed without their knowledge. * * *

* * *

Finally, Haug argues that previous agreements describing a lakeside park area—such as the Earnest Money Contract and the Declaration—are not enforceable because this term merged into the Grant of Easements as the final written agreement between the parties. It is a rule of general application that in the absence of fraud, accident, or mistake, all prior agreements entered into between the parties are considered merged in the deed. Commercial Bank, Unincorporated, of Mason v. Satterwhite, 413 S.W.2d 905, 909 (Tex.1967). However, the underlying objective of reformation is to correct a mutual mistake made in preparing a written instrument, so that the instrument truly reflects the original agreement of the parties. Cherokee Water Co. v. Forderhause, 741 S.W.2d 377, 379 (Tex. 1987).

We reject Haug's argument that the merger doctrine should limit our analysis to the language of the Grant of Easements. We have determined that unilateral mistake and fraud occurred in this case. These elements are the legal equivalent of mutual mistake in the case of an easement. *Davis,* 750 S.W.2d at 768. Therefore, there is evidence both of fraud and mistake in this case, and the merger doctrine does not apply. * * *

* * *

Because we overrule all of Haug's issues on appeal, we affirm the judgment of the district court reforming the easement into a lakeside park easement * * *.

NOTES

1. The court in Kish v. Kustura, 190 Or.App. 458, 79 P.3d 337 (2003) stated succinctly the elements for reformation:

> To obtain reformation of a contract, a party must prove by clear and convincing evidence

(1) that there was an antecedent agreement to which the contract can be reformed; (2) that there was a mutual mistake or a unilateral mistake on the part of the party seeking reformation and inequitable conduct on the part of the other party; and that the party seeking reformation was not guilty of gross negligence.

Id. at 462, 79 P.3d at 339.

2. Reformation actions may, and often do, become mere "swearing matches," Sims v. Wilson, 255 Ark. 465, 468, 501 S.W.2d 214, 216–17 (1973) (Harris, C.J., dissenting); therefore, as the preceding note indicates, courts uniformly require a burden of proof higher than that which is customary in civil actions. *See, e.g.,* Aetna Insurance Co. v. Paddock, 301 F.2d 807 (5th Cir.1962) (clear and convincing evidence); Elton v. Davis, 123 S.W.3d 205 (Mo. Ct.App.2003) (clear, cogent, and convincing evidence); Murray v. Laugsand, 179 Or.App. 291, 39 P.3d 241 (2002) (clear and convincing evidence); Basin Paving, Inc. v. Port of Moses Lake, 48 Wash.App. 180, 737 P.2d 1312 (1987) (substantial evidence). *Compare* Frierson v. Sheppard, 201 Miss. 603, 29 So.2d 726 (1947) (proof beyond a reasonable doubt), criticized in Note, 19 Miss. L.J. 363 (1948). An elevated level of proof reflects a judicial awareness that the reformation remedy, while designed to prevent a party from enjoying the benefits of fraud or mistake in integration, may be resorted to in an effort to avoid performance where the writing correctly states the actual contract. One party's word against that of the other ordinarily fails to satisfy the burden of proof for reformation and corroborative evidence supporting the assertions of the party seeking reformation is necessary. *See, e.g.,* Ingram v. Forrer, 563 P.2d 181 (Utah 1977); Rolph v. McGowan, 20 Wash.App. 251, 579 P.2d 1011 (1978).

3. An example of the type of mistake for which courts will not reform a contract is Reynolds v. Wood, 219 N.C. 626, 14 S.E.2d 642 (1941). In that case, the purchaser brought suit to recover the price paid for Lot No. 198, to which the vendor had no title. The vendor counterclaimed for reformation of the deed to convey Lot No. 196, which the vendor did own, alleging a mutual mistake in the description and that plaintiff intended to purchase and defendant intended to convey Lot No. 196. The Municipal Court overruled plaintiff's motion to dismiss the counterclaim, and ordered the deed reformed as prayed. The Superior Court reversed and the Supreme Court affirmed, saying:

> We do not think there was evidence to support the finding [in the Municipal Court] that there was a mutual mistake in the description of the lot conveyed so as to entitle the defendant to the equity of reformation. All the evidence is to the effect that the plaintiff wished to purchase Lot No. 198 and not Lot No. 196, and that she had no intention of purchasing Lot No. 196. There is no evidence that the parties had gone upon the premises, or that they had mistakenly inserted a different description of the lot intended to be conveyed. At the time plaintiff offered to purchase Lot No. 198 it was erroneously supposed that defendant owned that lot. There was no meeting of the minds of the parties as to the purchase of Lot No. 196, and plaintiff did not agree to purchase that lot, and does not wish to do so. The court cannot, under the guise of

reformation, enforce a contract which the parties themselves have not made.

Id. at 626–27, 14 S.E.2d at 642–43; *see also* Denaxas v. Sandstone Court of Bellevue, L.L.C., 148 Wash.2d 654, 667, 63 P.3d 125, 131 (2003) ("Purchaser had ample opportunity to read the survey, title reports, and closing documents. Had purchaser exercised reasonable care, it could have known their contents.").

4.   It is often said that a reformation decree "relates back" to the date of the execution of the writing in question. While this is the usual effect, reformation will not be allowed to impair the rights of innocent purchasers who have bought between the date of the mistake in integration and that of the reformation order. *See* 3 George E. Palmer, The Law of Restitution § 13.1 (1978).

5.   Because reformation is an equitable remedy, equitable defenses such as laches and estoppel are available. *See* Wehner v. Schroeder, 354 N.W.2d 674 (N.D.1984). For a discussion of equitable defenses, see *supra* Chapter 2, Section 5.

6.   Professor Williston explained how reformation and the parol evidence rule can coexist:

> The right of reformation, wherever allowed, is necessarily an invasion or limitation of the parol evidence rule, since when equity reforms a writing, it enforces an oral agreement at variance with the writing which the parties had agreed upon as a memorial of their bargain.
>
> This limitation is necessary to work justice, and there seems no more reason to object to it in case of reformation than in case of rescission for fraud or for mistake. It is understood that to warrant reformation or rescission, the court must be persuaded by the clearest kind of evidence that a mistake has been made by both parties, or in some cases by one, or that some other basis exists upon which relief should be granted.
>
> In either case, unless the mistake precludes the existence of a contract at law, it should not be denied that the writing correctly states the actual contract or conveyance which has been made, but since it is inequitable to allow the enforcement of it, and, since justice requires the substitution of another in its place, equity gives relief, where reformation is appropriate, and to that end, generally and necessarily admits any relevant parol or other extrinsic evidence.

13 Samuel Williston, Contracts § 1552 (3d ed. 1970)*; *see also* Restatement (Second) of Contracts § 155 (1981); George E. Palmer, *Reformation and the Parol Evidence Rule*, 65 Mich. L. Rev. 833 (1967).

7.   Scholarly commentary on reformation includes Restatement (Second) of Contracts § 155 (1981); 3 George E. Palmer, Law of Restitution §§ 13.1–13.19 (1978); Howard W. Brill, *Reformation in Arkansas*, 1998 Ark. L. Notes 1; Joseph W. deFuria, Jr., *Mistakes in Will Resulting From Scriveners' Error: The Argument for Reformation*, 40 Cath. U. L. Rev. 1 (1990); Ralph A. Newman, *Relief for Mistake in Contracting*, 54 Cornell L. Rev. 232 (1969);

---

* Reprinted with permission of The Lawyers Co-operative Publishing Co.

George E. Palmer, *The Effect of Misunderstanding on Contract Formation and Reformation Under the Restatement of Contracts Second*, 65 Mich. L. Rev. 33 (1966); Edward H. Rabin, *A Proposed Black–Letter Rule Concerning Mistaken Assumptions in Bargain Transactions*, 45 Tex. L. Rev. 1273 (1967).

8. There are situations where, due to the special circumstances in question, the court gives what it calls "reformation" relief to avoid an inequitable result that would result from an award of a conventional form of relief (usually rescission) and, in some instances, to avoid unjust enrichment. These cases do not fit into the traditional pattern of reformation cases because the court is not simply conforming the writing to an earlier oral agreement. *See, e.g.*, Wright v. Heizer Corp., 503 F.Supp. 802 (N.D.Ill.1980) (notes evidencing a loan by a corporate controller to the corporation he controlled had been obtained as part of certain conduct in violation of the controller's duty to the corporation; the notes in question were "reformed," by alteration of their terms, in the course of unraveling the several transactions involved in a manner that would protect the corporation's current interests); Thomas v. Satfield Co., 363 Mich. 111, 108 N.W.2d 907 (1961) (lease between two corporations with interlocking directors in contravention of directors' fiduciary duties not cancelled, but "reformed" by reducing the amount of the rent).

9. In some instances, reformation has been considered appropriate where the writing in the form executed by the parties was illegal or unenforceable, or had an undesired effect upon the rights of third parties. For example, some courts have shown a willingness to "reform" ("blue-pencil") and order specific performance of a restrictive covenant which was found to be unreasonable, contrary to public policy, and therefore unenforceable as written. *See* Justin Belt Co. v. Yost, 502 S.W.2d 681 (Tex.1973). *See also* Stoltz, Wagner & Brown v. Duncan, 417 F.Supp. 552 (W.D.Okla.1976) (provision violated the rule against perpetuities until reformed pursuant to Oklahoma statute that allowed reformation where appropriate "to give effect to general intent" of the creator of the interest); Turney v. Roberts, 255 Ark. 503, 501 S.W.2d 601 (1973) (interest provision provided a rate which was usurious until reformed); McPherson v. First & Citizens National Bank, 240 N.C. 1, 81 S.E.2d 386 (1954) (the court indicated a willingness, if unborn children could be effectively represented, to reform an irrevocable *inter vivos* trust so as to eliminate a violation of the rule against remoteness of vesting); Dickey v. Barnes, 268 Or. 226, 519 P.2d 1252 (1974) (instrument violated the statute regulating condominiums until reformed).

CHAPTER 8

LAW AND EQUITY MERGER: JURY TRIAL AND RELATED PROBLEMS

■ ■ ■

The Seventh Amendment to the United States Constitution guarantees the right to jury trial in the federal courts "in suits at common law, where the value in controversy shall exceed twenty dollars." Although the Seventh Amendment is not now binding on the states (*see, e.g.*, Hammons v. Ehney, 924 S.W.2d 843, 848 (Mo.1996)), there are similar state constitutional and statutory provisions. Courts often interpret these provisions by using the "historical" approach. In other words, the right to jury trial as to a particular claim depends upon how that claim was tried at the time of the enactment of the constitutional or statutory provision in effect in the jurisdiction in question.

Based on the foregoing, it is generally accurate, if somewhat oversimplified, to state that traditionally designated common-law actions carry a right to jury trial, whereas suits where equity would have taken jurisdiction do not. The procedural merger of law and equity has, for the most part, not significantly altered this situation. As to pure suits in equity, such as a simple suit for specific performance of a contract, there is no jury trial even though it will be tried in the same court as any other action. On the other hand, a tort action for damages, as an action of common-law origin, will entail the right to a jury trial.

Nevertheless, this area is not without difficulty. The state courts' adherence to and application of the historical approach, even to simple traditionally equitable claims, is not without problems and is, at best, in a confusing state of flux. Moreover, state courts often have serious conceptual and analytical problems in this area. Consequently, it is necessary to give significant coverage to jury trial problems in actions where any form of equitable relief is sought.

The most troublesome jury trial questions, however, arise when, as a result of the procedural merger of law and equity, legal and equitable claims are present in the same action. Some of these questions include the following: How should the factual issues be tried in a case where the plaintiff joins legal and equitable claims? What effect should the interjection of a legal or equitable defense or counterclaim have on the right to jury trial? How do res judicata concepts complicate such problems? The following material places substantial emphasis on these problems.

NOTE

The literature on the right to jury trial is voluminous. *See generally* Harold Chesnin & Geoffrey C. Hazard, Jr., *Chancery Procedure and the Seventh Amendment: Jury Trial of Issues in Equity Cases Before 1791*, 83 Yale L.J. 900 (1974); James Fleming, *Right to a Jury Trial in Civil Actions*, 72 Yale L.J. 646 (1963); Paul F. Kirgis, *The Right to a Jury Decision on Questions of Fact under the Seventh Amendment*, 64 Ohio St. L.J. 1125 (2003); John H. Langbein, *Fact Finding in the English Court of Chancery: A Rebuttal*, 83 Yale L.J. 1620 (1974); A. Leo Levin, *Equitable Clean-up and the Jury: A Suggested Orientation*, 100 U. Pa. L. Rev. 320 (1951); Margaret L. Moses, *What the Jury Must Hear: The Supreme Court's Evolving Seventh Amendment Jurisprudence*, 68 Geo. Wash. L. Rev. 183 (2000); Lars Noah, *Civil Jury Nullification*, 86 Iowa L. Rev. 1601 (2001); R.J. Simeone, *Right to a Jury Trial—Existence of Equitable Claims When Both Equitable and Legal Claims are Presented in a Suit*, 36 Rutgers L.J. 1551 (2005); Ellen E. Sward, *The Seventh Amendment and the Alchemy of Fact and Law*, 33 Seton Hall L. Rev. 573 (2003); Ann Woolhandler & Michael G. Collins, *The Article III Jury*, 87 Va. L. Rev. 587 (2001).

For an analysis of the federal right to jury trial, see Thomas M. Jorde, *The Seventh Amendment Right to Jury Trial of Antitrust Issues*, 69 Cal. L. Rev. 1 (1981); Mary K. Kane, *Civil Jury Trial: The Case for Reasoned Iconoclasm*, 28 Hastings L.J. 1 (1976); John C. McCoid II, *Procedural Reform and the Right to Jury Trial: A Study of* Beacon Theatres, Inc. v. Westover, 116 U. Pa. L. Rev. 1281 (1978); John C. McCoid II, *Right to Jury Trial in the Federal Courts*, 45 Iowa L. Rev. 726 (1960); Martin H. Redish, *Seventh Amendment Right to Jury Trial: A Study in the Irrationality of Rational Decision Making*, 70 Nw. U. L. Rev. 486 (1975); Gary M. Ropski, *The Federal Trademark Jury Trial—Awakening of a Dormant Constitutional Right*, 70 Trademark Rep. 177 (1980); Note, *The Right to Jury Trial in Complex Civil Litigation*, 92 Harv. L. Rev. 898 (1979); Comment, Ross v. Bernhard: *The Uncertain Future of the Seventh Amendment*, 81 Yale L.J. 112 (1971).

For an analysis of the right to jury trial in state courts, see Richard W. Bourne & John A. Lynch, Jr., *Merger of Law and Equity Under the Revised Maryland Rules: Does It Threaten Trial by Jury?*, 14 U. Balt. L. Rev. 1 (1984); Ronan E. Degnan, *Right to Civil Jury Trial in Utah: Constitution and Statute*, 8 Utah L. Rev. 97 (1962); Edward E. Erickson, *The Right to a Jury Trial in Equitable Cases*, 69 N.D. L. Rev. 559 (1993); Carlton W. Mayhall, Jr., *A Note on Recent Cases Discussing Jury Trials in Cases Combining Legal and Equitable Relief*, 38 Ala. Law. 216 (1977).

SECTION 1.   THE FEDERAL APPROACH: A PREFERENCE FOR JURIES

ROSS v. BERNHARD

Supreme Court of the United States, 1970.
396 U.S. 531, 90 S.Ct. 733, 24 L.Ed.2d 729.

MR. JUSTICE WHITE, delivered the opinion of the Court.

The Seventh Amendment to the Constitution provides that in "[s]uits at common law, where the value in controversy shall exceed twenty dollars, the right of trial by jury shall be preserved." Whether the Amendment guarantees the right to a jury trial in stockholders' derivative actions is the issue now before us.

Petitioners brought this derivative suit in federal court against the directors of their closed-end investment company, the Lehman corporation and the corporation's brokers, Lehman Brothers. They contended that Lehman Brothers controlled the corporation through an illegally large representation on the corporation's board of directors, in violation of the Investment Company Act of 1940, 54 Stat. 789, 15 U.S.C.A. § 80a–1 *et seq.*, and used this control to extract excessive brokerage fees from the corporation. * * * Petitioners requested that the defendants "account for and pay to the Corporation for their profits and gains and its losses." Petitioners also demanded a jury trial on the corporation's claims.

On motion to strike petitioners' jury trial demand, the District Court held that a shareholder's right to a jury on his corporation's cause of action was to be judged as if the corporation were itself the plaintiff. Only the shareholder's initial claim to speak for the corporation had to be tried to the judge. 275 F.Supp. 569. Convinced that "there are substantial grounds for difference of opinion as to this question and * * * an immediate appeal would materially advance the ultimate termination of this litigation," the District Court permitted an interlocutory appeal. 28 U.S.C.A. § 1292(b). The Court of Appeals reversed, holding that a derivative action was entirely equitable in nature, and no jury was available to try any part of it. 403 F.2d 909. It specifically disagreed with DePinto v. Provident Security Life Ins. Co., 323 F.2d 826 (C.A. 9th Cir.1963), *cert. denied*, 376 U.S. 950, 84 S.Ct. 965, 11 L.Ed.2d 969 (1964), on which the District Court had relied. Because of this conflict, we granted certiorari 394 U.S. 917, 89 S.Ct. 1190, 22 L.Ed.2d 450 (1969).

We reverse the holding of the Court of Appeals that in no event does the right to a jury trial preserved by the Seventh Amendment extend to derivative actions brought by the stockholders of a corporation. We hold that the right to jury trial attaches to those issues in derivative actions as to which the corporation, if it had been suing in its own right, would have been entitled to a jury.

* * *

However difficult it may have been to define with precision the line between actions at law dealing with legal rights and suits in equity dealing with equitable matters, Whitehead v. Shattuck, 138 U.S. 146, 151, 11 S.Ct. 276, 277, 34 L.Ed. 873 (1891), some proceedings were unmistakably actions at law triable to a jury. The Seventh Amendment, for example, entitled the parties to a jury trial in actions for damages to a person or property, for libel and slander, for recovery of land, and for conversion of personal property. Just as clearly, a corporation, although an artificial being, was commonly entitled to sue and be sued in the usual forms of action, at least in its own State. *See* Paul v. Virginia, 8 Wall. 168, 19 L.Ed. 357 (1869). Whether the corporation was viewed as an entity separate from its stockholders or as a device permitting its stockholders to carry on their business and to sue and be sued, a corporation's suit to enforce a legal right was an action at common law carrying the right to jury trial at the time the Seventh Amendment was adopted.

The common law refused, however, to permit stockholders to call corporate managers to account in actions at law. The possibilities for abuse, thus presented, were not ignored by corporate officers and directors. Early in the 19th century, equity provided relief both in this country and in England. * * * The remedy made available in equity was the derivative suit, viewed in this country as a suit to enforce a *corporate* cause of action against officers, directors, and third parties. As elaborated in the cases, one precondition for the suit was a valid claim on which the corporation could have sued; another was that the corporation itself had refused to proceed after suitable demand, unless excused by extraordinary conditions. Thus the dual nature of the stockholder's action: first, the plaintiff's right to sue on behalf of the corporation and, second, the merits of the corporation claim itself.

Derivative suits posed no Seventh Amendment problems where the action against the directors and third parties would have been by a bill in equity had the corporation brought the suit. Our concern is with cases based upon a legal claim of the corporation against directors or third parties. Does the trial of such claims at the suit of a stockholder and without a jury violate the Seventh Amendment?

The question arose in this Court in the context of a derivative suit for treble damages under the antitrust laws. Fleitmann v. Welsbach Street Lighting Co., 240 U.S. 27, 36 S.Ct. 233, 60 L.Ed. 505 (1916). Noting that the bill in equity set up a claim of the corporation alone, Mr. Justice Holmes observed that if the corporation were the plaintiff, "no one can doubt that its only remedy would be at law," and inquired "why the defendants' right to a jury trial should be taken away because the present plaintiff cannot persuade the only party having a cause of action to sue,— how the liability which is the principal matter can be converted into an incident of the plaintiff's domestic difficulties with the company that has been wronged"? *Id.*, at 28, 36 S.Ct., at 234. His answer was that the bill did not state a good cause of action in equity. Agreeing that there were "cases in which the nature of the right asserted for the company, or the failure of the defendants concerned to insist upon their rights, or a different state system, has led to the whole matter being disposed of in equity," he concluded that when the penalty of triple damages is sought, the antitrust statute plainly anticipated a jury trial and should not be read as "attempting to authorize liability to be enforced otherwise than through the verdict of a jury in a court of common law." *Id.,* at 28–29, 36 S.Ct., at 234. Although the decision had obvious Seventh Amendment overtones, its ultimate rationale was grounded in the antitrust laws.

Where penal damages were not involved, however, there was no authoritative parallel to *Fleitmann* in the federal system squarely passing on the applicability of the Seventh Amendment to the trial of a legal claim presented in a premerger derivative suit. What can be gleaned from this Court's opinions is not inconsistent with the general understanding, reflected by the state court decisions and secondary sources, that equity could properly resolve corporate claims of any kind without a jury when properly pleaded in derivative suits complying with the equity rules.

Such was the prevailing opinion when the Federal Rules of Civil Procedure were adopted in 1938. It continued until 1963 when the Court of Appeals for the Ninth Circuit, relying on the Federal Rules as construed and applied in Beacon Theatres Inc. v. Westover, 359 U.S. 500, 79 S.Ct. 948, 3 L.Ed.2d 988 (1959), and Dairy Queen Inc. v. Wood, 369 U.S. 469, 82 S.Ct. 894, 8 L.Ed.2d 44 (1962), required the legal issues in a derivative suit to be tried to a jury. DePinto v. Provident Security Life Ins. Co., 323 F.2d 826. It was this decision that the District Court followed in the case before us and that the Court of Appeals rejected.

Beacon and *Dairy Queen* presaged *DePinto*. Under those cases, where equitable and legal claims are joined in the same action, there is a right to jury trial on the legal claims which must not be infringed either by trying the legal issues as incidental to the equitable ones or by a court trial of a common issue existing between the claims. The Seventh Amendment question depends on the nature of the issue to be tried rather than the character of the overall action.[2] *See* Simler v. Conner, 372 U.S. 221, 83 S.Ct. 609, 9 L.Ed.2d 691 (1963). The principle of these cases bears heavily on derivative actions.

We have noted that the derivative suit has dual aspects: first, the stockholder's right to sue on behalf of the corporation, historically an equitable matter; second, the claim of the corporation against directors or third parties on which, if the corporation had sued and the claim presented legal issues, the company could demand a jury trial. * * * The corporation is a necessary party to the action; without it the case cannot proceed. Although named a defendant, it is the real party in interest, the stockholder being at best the nominal plaintiff. The proceeds of the action

---

2. As our cases indicate, the "legal" nature of an issue is determined by considering, first, the pre-merger custom with reference to such questions; second, the remedy sought; and, third, the practical abilities and limitations of juries. Of these factors, the first, requiring extensive and possibly abstruse historical inquiry, is obviously the most difficult to apply. *See* James, *Right to a Jury Trial in Civil Actions*, 72 Yale L.J. 655 (1963).

belong to the corporation and it is bound by the result of the suit. The heart of the action is the corporate claim. If it presents a legal issue, one entitling the corporation to a jury trial under the Seventh Amendment, the right to a jury is not forfeited merely because the stockholder's right to sue must first be adjudicated as an equitable issue triable to the court. *Beacon* and *Dairy Queen* require no less.

If under older procedures, now discarded, a court of equity could properly try the legal claims of the corporation presented in a derivative suit, it was because irreparable injury was threatened and no remedy at law existed as long as the stockholder was without standing to sue and the corporation itself refused to pursue its own remedies. Indeed, from 1789 until 1938, the judicial code expressly forbade courts of equity from entertaining any suit for which there was an adequate remedy at law. This provision served "to guard the right of trial by jury preserved by the Seventh Amendment and to that end it should be liberally construed." Schoenthal v. Irving Trust Co., 287 U.S. 92, 94, 53 S.Ct. 50, 51, 77 L.Ed. 185 (1932). If, before 1938, the law had borrowed from equity, as it borrowed other things, the idea that stockholders could litigate for their recalcitrant corporation, the corporate claim, if legal, would undoubtedly have been tried to a jury.

Of course, this did not occur, but the Federal Rules had a similar impact. Actions are no longer brought as actions at law or suits in equity. Under the Rules there is only one action—a "civil action"—in which all claims may be joined and all remedies are available. Purely procedural impediments to the presentation of any issue by any party, based on the difference between law and equity, were destroyed. In a civil action presenting a stockholder's derivative claim, the court after passing upon the plaintiff's right to sue on behalf of the corporation is now able to try the corporate claim for damages with the aid of a jury. Separable claims may be tried separately, Fed.Rule Civ.Proc. 42(b), or legal and equitable issues may be handled in the same trial. Fanchon & Marco, Inc. v. Paramount Pictures, Inc., 202 F.2d 731 (C.A.2d Cir.1953). The historical rule preventing a court of law from entertaining a shareholder's suit on behalf of the corporation is obsolete; it is no longer tenable for a district court, administering both law and equity in the same action, to deny legal remedies to a corporation, merely because the corporation's spokesmen are its shareholders rather than its directors. Under the rules, law and equity are procedurally combined; nothing turns now upon the form of the action or the procedural devices by which the parties happen to come before the court. The "expansion of adequate legal remedies provided by * * * the Federal Rules necessarily affects the scope of equity." Beacon Theatres, Inc. v. Westover, 359 U.S., at 509, 79 S.Ct., at 956.

Thus, for example, before-merger class actions were largely a device of equity, and there was no right to a jury even on issues that might, under other circumstances, have been tried to a jury. 5 J. Moore, Federal Practice ¶ 38.38[2] (2d ed. 1969); 3B id., ¶ 23.02[1]. Although at least one post-merger court held that the device was not available to try legal issues, it now seems settled in the lower federal courts that class action plaintiffs may obtain a jury trial on any legal issues they present. Montgomery Ward & Co. v. Langer, 168 F.2d 182 (C.A. 8th Cir.1948); * * * 2 W. Barron & A. Holtzoff, Federal Practice and Procedure § 571 (Wright ed. 1961).

Derivative suits have been described as one kind of "true" class action. *Id.,* § 562.1. We are inclined to agree with the description, at least to the extent it recognizes that the derivative suit and the class action were both ways of allowing parties to be heard in equity who could not speak at law. 3B J. Moore, Federal Practice ¶ ¶ 23.02[1], 23.1.16[1] (2d ed. 1969). After adoption of the rules there is no longer any procedural obstacle to the assertion of legal rights before juries, however the party may have acquired standing to assert those rights. Given the availability in a derivative action of both legal and equitable remedies, we think the Seventh Amendment preserves to the parties in a stockholder's suit the same right to a jury trial that historically belonged to the corporation and to those against whom the corporation pressed its legal claims.

In the instant case we have no doubt that the corporation's claim is, at least in part, a legal one. The relief sought is money damages. There are allegations in the complaint of a breach of fiduciary duty, but there are also allegations of ordinary breach of contract and gross negligence. The corporation, had it sued on its own behalf, would have been entitled to a jury's determination, at a minimum, of its damages against its broker under the brokerage contract and of its rights against its own directors because of their negligence. Under these circumstances it is unnecessary to decide whether the corporation's other claims are also properly triable to a jury. Dairy Queen, Inc. v. Wood, 369 U.S. 469, 82 S.Ct. 894, 8 L.Ed.2d 44 (1962). The decision of the Court of Appeals is reversed.

MR. JUSTICE STEWART, with whom THE CHIEF JUSTICE and MR. JUSTICE HARLAN join, dissenting. [Dissenting opinion omitted. The dissenting opinion is discussed by the Iowa Supreme Court in Weltzin v. Nails, *infra* Chapter 8, Section 2.]

NOTES

1. *Ross* was given an especially expansive interpretation in Chauffeurs, Teamsters & Helpers, Local 391 v. Terry, 494 U.S. 558, 110 S.Ct. 1339, 108 L.Ed.2d 519 (1990). In that case, Justice Marshall, writing for a plurality of the Court, concluded that employees seeking back pay from their union for the latter's breach of its duty of fair representation were entitled to a jury trial. He stressed that the nature of the issues, rather than the action as a whole, determined whether a jury was required. Even though he conceded that the action resembled a traditional equity suit by a beneficiary against a trustee, he examined the underlying issues and determined that they were more closely similar to a legal action for breach of contract. Moreover, his conclusion was buttressed by the fact that the employees sought a monetary remedy, damages, which typically are characterized as "legal." According to

the three judge dissent, however, "[a]lthough we have divided self-standing legal claims from equitable, declaratory, accounting, and derivative procedures, we have never parsed legal elements out of equitable claims absent specific justifications." *Id.* at 590, 110 S.Ct. at 1358, 108 L.Ed.2d 519.

2. Footnote 2 in *Ross* suggests that the "practical ability and limitations of juries" is a relevant factor in determining the "legal" nature of an issue and thus, whether the Seventh Amendment mandates a jury trial. The foregoing language has provided ammunition for the argument that a jury trial is not constitutionally required in a variety of sophisticated and complex civil cases. Consider the following analysis of this argument:

> The last fifty years have seen a tremendous liberalization of civil procedure and an unprecedented proliferation of new causes of action, which together make it possible for civil litigation to reach a level of complexity exceeding anything imaginable in the common law courts of 1791. Modern securities and antitrust cases, for example, can involve an enormous number of parties and claims, highly technical factual inquiries, tremendous volumes of documentary evidence, and trials lasting several years. Even when confronted with exceedingly complex litigation, some courts have refused to foreclose a jury trial, holding that complexity is not a constitutionally appropriate ground for denying a jury.[10] Yet other federal courts have denied demands for a jury trial in complex cases, generally resting their decisions on one of two grounds: first, that a trial of such a case to an uncomprehending jury would constitute a denial of due process[11] and second, that such cases are inherently beyond the understanding of a jury, so that trying them to a jury would constitute an inadequate remedy at law. * * *

> * * *

> * * * Insofar as analogies based on complexity are appropriate, complex modern litigation bears much closer resemblance to equitable actions in 1791, heard without a jury, than to common law actions. Nonetheless, it would probably also be incorrect to conclude from this fact alone that modern complex litigation, such as one finds in actions brought under the securities or antitrust laws, falls outside the protection afforded the civil jury right by the seventh amendment.

> The defect in the existing analysis of the seventh amendment is that it pays too little attention to the enormous differences between civil litigation in 1791 and civil litigation today. The framers, schooled in the traditions of the British legal system, were undoubtedly aware of the restricted scope of actions at common law, as well as the limited role of the jury. It seems likely that they were also aware of the reasons for the narrow ambit of the common law jury system. By "preserving" the distinctions between law and equity, they tacitly acknowledged that the right to a jury trial should not extend to those situations where the jury would be an inappropriate fact-finding body. Their conception of a

---

10. *See, e.g., In re* U.S. Fin. Sec. Litig., 609 F.2d 411 (9th Cir.1979), *cert. denied*, 446 U.S. 929, 100 S.Ct. 1866, 64 L.Ed.2d 281 (1980).

11. *See, e.g.,* Zenith Radio Corp. v. Matsushita Elec. Indus. Co. (*In re* Japanese Elec. Prods. Antitrust Litig.), 631 F.2d 1069 (3d Cir.1980).

"Suit[ ] at common law" must have embodied these notions as much as it embodied notions about the types of rights cognizable and remedies available in the common law courts. Under modern rules of pleading and procedure, a case may be brought that bears so little resemblance to anything that could ever have occurred in the common law courts in 1791 that the difference between them is more aptly called a difference in kind, rather than in degree. Submission of such a case to a jury represents a repudiation, rather than an application, of a historical test. One might as easily assert that a jury is appropriate because the litigation is conducted in a courtroom that was in use in 1791.

In most cases, the current doctrine's focus on the "substantive" aspects of the case, the remedies and rights, may be appropriate. It is, however, futile to assume that an unwavering line can be drawn between substance and procedure. More importantly, it flies in the face of a claimed reliance on history to conclude that, in an action involving, for example, over 100 parties contesting eighteen consolidated class actions, with cross claims so numerous as to require a five-page chart merely to list them and a trial expected to last two years and involve about 500 witnesses and 24,000 documents, a jury is constitutionally required simply because the plaintiffs seek money damages, a remedy traditionally granted at law. When one considers that the modern rules on class actions, discovery, and joinder of parties and claims are all derived primarily from equity, it is an abandonment, rather than an application, of a historical view of the seventh amendment to call such an action a "Suit[ ] at common law." Stated differently, even if one accepts the Court's current focus on substantive rights and remedies, there comes a point at which the changes in procedure have been so extensive that there has been a change in the *substantive* character of the action as well. When such a point is reached, an effort to distinguish cases on the basis of the rights asserted and the remedies sought seeks to preserve the right to a jury trial in what can no longer in any realistic sense be called a suit at common law.

The ultimate question is determining when that point has been reached. As with other constitutional standards, a determination as to the availability of a jury trial should depend on a consideration of the totality of circumstances in light of a number of relevant factors. These include not only the nature of the rights and remedies, but also the number of parties, the relations they bear to one another, the complexity of the legal and factual issues, the number of claims, and the amount and complexity of the evidence that will be adduced to establish those claims. If the case is so complex because of the combination of flexible procedure and intricate substantive inquiries that, except for the remedy sought, it bears no resemblance whatsoever to suits heard in the English common law system, it is simply not an action for which the jury right can be said to be "preserved."

Douglas King, Comment, *Complex Civil Litigation and the Seventh Amendment Right to a Jury Trial*, 51 U. Chi. L. Rev. 581, 581–82, 611–13 (1984).*

---

* Reprinted with permission of the University of Chicago Law Review.

The foregoing perspective is to some extent reflected in Markman v. Westview Instruments, Inc., 517 U.S. 370, 116 S.Ct. 1384, 134 L.Ed.2d 577 (1996). There the Court confronted a patent infringement case in which the dispute centered on whether the word "inventory" should properly have been determined by a jury rather than the court. The Court held that the patent holder's Seventh Amendment right to a jury trial was not violated when the trial court substituted its construction of the disputed term for that which the jury presumably had given it. In reaching this conclusion, the Court stated that it not only should consult existing precedent, but also "consider both the relative interpretive skills of judges and juries." *Id.* at 384, 116 S.Ct. at 1393, 134 L.Ed.2d 577. Moreover, it reasoned that:

> Where history and precedent provide no clear answers, functional considerations also play their part in the choice between judge and jury to define terms of art. We [have] said * * * that when an issue falls somewhere between a pristine legal standard and a simple historical fact, the fact/law distinction at times has turned on a determination that, as a matter of the sound administration of justice, one judicial actor is better positioned than another to decide the issue in question. So it turns out here, for judges, not juries, are the better suited to find the acquired meaning of patent terms.

Id. at 388, 116 S.Ct. at 1395, 134 L.Ed.2d 577. According to one leading commentary, while

> it would be wrong to assume that this one decision marks a retreat by the Court from its general preference for jury trials * * *, [*Markman*] does indicate * * * the continued vitality of an inquiry into the practical ability of a jury to act as a decisionmaker as the basis for making a Seventh Amendment analysis, at least when history provides no clear guidance.

Jack H. Friedenthal et al., Civil Procedure 517 (3d ed. 1999). *See also* Margaret L. Moses, *What the Jury Must Hear: The Supreme Court's Evolving Seventh Amendment Jurisprudence*, 68 Geo. Wash. L. Rev. 183 (2000) ("More recent Supreme Court decisions * * * suggest that *Markman's* impact may be quite limited."); *see generally* Morris S. Arnold, *An Historical Inquiry into the Right to Trial by Jury in Complex Civil Litigation*, 128 U. Pa. L. Rev. 829 (1980); James S. Campbell & Nicholas LePoidevin, *Complex Cases and Jury Trials: A Reply to Professor Arnold*, 128 U. Pa. L. Rev. 986 (1980); Morris S. Arnold, *A Modest Replication to a Lengthy Discourse*, 128 U. Pa. L. Rev. 986 (1980); Comment, *The Constitutionality of a Complexity Exception to the Seventh Amendment*, 73 Chi.-Kent L. Rev. 865 (1998).

3. When Congress legislates new causes of action, it sometimes mandates a right to jury trial. Usually, however, the legislation says nothing about the right to jury trial. In this situation, the Supreme Court often looks for historical analogues to the statutory cause of action in existence at the time of the Seventh Amendment's adoption. *See* Feltner v. Columbia Pictures Television, Inc., 523 U.S. 340, 118 S.Ct. 1279, 140 L.Ed.2d 438 (1998) (because copyright suits for damages were triable to juries at the time the Seventh Amendment was adopted, there is a constitutional right to jury trial in statutory damages actions for copyright infringement). For examples of how

lower federal courts have dealt with this issue, *see* Pichler v. UNITE, 542 F.3d 380 (3d Cir.2008) (employees have right to jury trial on their punitive damages claim under the Driver's Privacy Protection Act); Lutz v. Glendale Union High School, 403 F.3d 1061 (9th Cir. 2005) (employee has no right to jury trial under Americans with Disabilities Act on issue of back pay); Schmidt v. Levi Strauss & Co., 621 F.Supp.2d 796 (N.D.Cal.2008) (former employees terminated in violation of Sarbanes–Oxley Act were not entitled to jury trial).

Jury trial questions have been especially common in the context of civil rights legislation. Consider the following discussion of this issue by the United States Supreme Court in Curtis v. Loether, 415 U.S. 189, 94 S.Ct. 1005, 39 L.Ed.2d 260 (1974), an action for compensatory and punitive damages under Title VIII by a black woman (petitioner) who claimed that the white defendants had refused to rent an apartment to her because of her race:

> Title VIII * * * provides that "[t]he court may grant as relief, as it deems appropriate, any permanent or temporary injunction, temporary restraining order, or other order, and may award to the plaintiff actual damages and not more than $1,000 punitive damages, together with court costs and reasonable attorney fees * * *."

* * *

The legislative history on the jury trial question is sparse, and what little is available is ambiguous. There seems to be some indication that supporters of Title VIII were concerned that the possibility of racial prejudice on juries might reduce the effectiveness of civil rights damages actions. On the other hand, one bit of testimony during committee hearings indicates an awareness that jury trials would have to be afforded in damages actions under Title VIII. Both petitioner and respondents have presented plausible arguments from the wording and construction of § 812. We see no point to giving extended consideration to these arguments, however, for we think it is clear that the Seventh Amendment entitles either party to demand a jury trial in an action for damages in the federal courts under § 812.

The Seventh Amendment provides that "[i]n suits at common law, where the value in controversy shall exceed twenty dollars, the right of trial by jury shall be preserved." Although the thrust of the Amendment was to preserve the right to jury trial as it existed in 1791, it has long been settled that the right extends beyond the common-law forms of action recognized at that time. * * *

Petitioner nevertheless argues that the Amendment is inapplicable to new causes of action created by congressional enactment. As the Court of Appeals observed, however, we have considered the applicability of the constitutional right to jury trial in actions enforcing statutory rights "as a matter too obvious to be doubted." 467 F.2d, at 1114. Although the Court has apparently never discussed the issue at any length, we have often found the Seventh Amendment applicable to causes of action based on statutes. *See, e.g.,* Dairy Queen, Inc. v. Wood, 369 U.S. 469, 477, 82 S.Ct. 894, 899, 8 L.Ed.2d 44 (1962) (trademark laws); Hepner v. United

States, 213 U.S. 103, 115, 29 S.Ct. 474, 479, 53 L.Ed. 720 (1909) (immigration laws); *cf.* Fleitmann v. Welsbach Street Lighting Co., 240 U.S. 27, 36 S.Ct. 233, 60 L.Ed. 505 (1916) (antitrust laws), and the discussion of *Fleitmann* in Ross v. Bernhard, 396 U.S. 531, 535–536, 90 S.Ct. 733, 736–737, 24 L.Ed.2d 729 (1970). Whatever doubt may have existed should now be dispelled. The Seventh Amendment does apply to actions enforcing statutory rights, and requires a jury trial upon demand, if the statute creates legal rights and remedies, enforceable in an action for damages in the ordinary courts of law.

NLRB v. Jones & Laughlin Steel Corp., 301 U.S. 1, 57 S.Ct. 615, 81 L.Ed. 893 (1937), relied on by petitioner, lends no support to her statutory-rights argument. The Court there upheld the award of back pay without jury trial in an NLRB unfair labor practice proceeding, rejecting a Seventh Amendment claim on the ground that the case involved a "statutory proceeding" and "not a suit at common law or in the nature of such a suit." *Id.,* at 48, 57 S.Ct. at 629. *Jones & Laughlin* merely stands for the proposition that the Seventh Amendment is generally inapplicable in administrative proceedings, where jury trials would be incompatible with the whole concept of administrative adjudication and would substantially interfere with the NLRB's role in the statutory scheme. * * * These cases uphold congressional power to entrust enforcement of statutory rights to an administrative process or specialized court of equity free from the strictures of the Seventh Amendment. But when Congress provides for enforcement of statutory rights in an ordinary civil action in the district courts, where there is obviously no functional justification for denying the jury trial right, a jury trial must be available if the action involves rights and remedies of the sort typically enforced in an action at law.

We think it is clear that a damages action under § 812 is an action to enforce "legal rights" within the meaning of our Seventh Amendment decisions. * * * A damages action under the statute sounds basically in tort—the statute merely defines a new legal duty, and authorizes the courts to compensate a plaintiff for the injury caused by the defendant's wrongful breach. As the Court of Appeals noted, this cause of action is analogous to a number of tort actions recognized at common law. More important, the relief sought here—actual and punitive damages—is the traditional form of relief offered in the courts of law.

* * *

We need not, and do not, go so far as to say that any award of monetary relief must necessarily be "legal" relief. *See, e.g.,* Mitchell v. Robert DeMario Jewelry, Inc., 361 U.S. 288, 80 S.Ct. 332, 4 L.Ed.2d 323 (1960); Porter v. Warner Holding Co., 328 U.S. 395, 60 S.Ct. 1086, 90 L.Ed. 1332 (1946). A comparison of Title VIII with Title VII of the Civil Rights Act of 1964, where the courts of appeals have held that jury trial is not required in an action for reinstatement and back pay, is instructive, although we of course express no view on the jury trial issue in that context. In Title VII cases the courts of appeals have characterized back pay as an integral part of an equitable remedy, a form of restitution. But the statutory language on which this characterization is based—

> [T]he court may enjoin the respondent from engaging in such unlawful employment practice, and order such affirmative action as may be appropriate, which may include, but is not limited to, reinstatement or hiring of employees, with or without back pay * * *, or any other equitable relief as the court deems appropriate, 42 U.S.C.A. § 2000e–5(g) (1970 ed., Supp. II)—

contrasts sharply with § 812's simple authorization of an action for actual and punitive damages. In Title VII cases, also, the courts have relied on the fact that the decision whether to award back pay is committed to the discretion of the trial judge. There is no comparable discretion here: if a plaintiff proves unlawful discrimination and actual damages, he is entitled to judgment for that amount. Nor is there any sense in which the award here can be viewed as requiring the defendant to disgorge funds wrongfully withheld from the plaintiff. Whatever may be the merit of the "equitable" characterization in Title VII cases, there is surely no basis for characterizing the award of compensatory and punitive damages here as equitable relief.

We are not oblivious to the force of petitioner's policy arguments. Jury trials may delay to some extent the disposition of Title VIII damages actions. But Title VIII actions seeking only equitable relief will be unaffected, and preliminary injunctive relief remains available without a jury trial even in damages actions. Dairy Queen, Inc. v. Wood, 369 U.S., at 479 n.20, 82 S.Ct., at 901. Moreover, the statutory requirement of expedition of § 812 actions, 42 U.S.C.A. § 3614 (1970), applies equally to jury and nonjury trials. We recognize, too, the possibility that jury prejudice may deprive a victim of discrimination of the verdict to which he or she is entitled. Of course, the trial judge's power to direct a verdict, to grant judgment notwithstanding the verdict, or to grant a new trial provides substantial protection against this risk, and respondents' suggestion that jury trials will expose a broader segment of the populace to the example of the federal civil rights laws in operation has some force. More fundamentally, however, these considerations are insufficient to overcome the clear command of the Seventh Amendment. The decision of the Court of Appeals must be affirmed.

Id. at 189–98, 94 S.Ct. at 1006–10, 39 L.Ed.2d 260.

4. The Civil Rights Act of 1991 significantly expanded the remedies available to a Title VII employee. *See supra* Chapter 7, Section 5. While previously the major remedies under Title VII were back pay and reinstatement, the Act expanded the relief available to include compensatory and punitive damages. *Id.* The Act also specifically provides for a right to jury trial: "If a complaining party seeks compensatory or punitive damages * * *, any party may demand a trial by jury * * *." 42 U.S.C.A. § 1981a.

Even though the Americans with Disabilities Act (ADA) incorporates the remedies available under Title VII, the United States Court of Appeals for the Ninth Circuit has held that "there is no right to have a jury determine the appropriate amount of back pay under Title VII, and thus the ADA, even after the Civil Rights Act of 1991. Instead, back pay remains an equitable remedy to be awarded by the district court in its discretion." Lutz v. Glendale Union High School, District No. 205, 403 F.3d 1061 (9th Cir.2005).

By contrast, 42 U.S.C. § 1983 is silent on the question of whether there is a right to jury trial in constitutional tort actions. Consider the next case.

SANTIAGO–NEGRON v. CASTRO–DAVILA

United States Court of Appeals, First Circuit, 1989.
865 F.2d 431.

Before BOWNES, TORRUELLA and SELYA, CIRCUIT JUDGES.

BOWNES, CIRCUIT JUDGE.

The lawsuit giving rise to this appeal was an aftermath of the November 1984 elections in Puerto Rico. Prior to that election, the Mayor of the Municipality of Las Piedras and the majority of its Municipal Assembly were members of the New Progressive Party (NPP). As a result of the election, political control of Las Piedras shifted to the Popular Democratic Party (PDP); the newly-elected Mayor and a majority of the Municipal Assembly belonged to the PDP. Animated by the venerable political and military maxim that "to the victor belongs the spoils," the new Mayor and his administration proceeded to replace Municipal employees belonging to the NPP with those whose allegiance was to the PDP.
* * *

* * * Hence a 42 U.S.C. § 1983 civil rights action was brought against the Mayor of Las Piedras, its Personnel Officer, and the Director of Public Works, the President of the Municipal Assembly, the Municipality itself, and the Commonwealth of Puerto Rico. All of the city officials were sued individually and in their official capacity. The complaint alleged that the defendants violated the plaintiffs' constitutional rights to due process and freedom of speech either by firing them or by transferring, demoting, and discriminating against them because of their political affiliation.

* * *

After a jury trial, all the defendants, except the Municipality were found liable to some or all of the plaintiffs; compensatory damages were assessed against the defendants separately on each claim and three of the plaintiffs were awarded punitive damages. The district court incorporated into the judgment a reinstatement and back pay order for each plaintiff. * * * [The defendants] raise [the] issue [of] the district court's back pay and reinstatement orders * * *.

* * *

* * * We now turn to the more difficult question of whether it should be the judge or jury who awards back pay in a section 1983 case based upon an alleged unconstitutional political discharge where a jury will

determine liability and compensatory damages. This is a question of first impression in this circuit.

Most of the courts of appeals that have grappled with the problem have focused on the nature of the relief sought: equitable or legal. The Sixth Circuit formulated the classic test in Hildebrand v. Board of Trustees of Michigan State University, 607 F.2d 705 (6th Cir.1979) (citation and footnote omitted):

> The above-cited authorities mandate that the chief focus to be made when determining whether a jury trial right exists is the nature of the relief sought. If the remedy sought is injunctive relief and/or back pay, no jury trial right attaches. In the ordinary case, if the relief sought includes compensatory and/or punitive damages, then there does exist a right to trial by jury.

Id. at 708.

This reasoning was carried to its logical conclusion in Moore v. Sun Oil Company of Pennsylvania, 636 F.2d 154 (6th Cir.1980), in which it was held in a 42 U.S.C. § 1981 action that even though reinstatement was not sought, back pay was equitable relief and the parties were not entitled to a jury trial on that issue. The court then went on to hold that since compensatory and punitive damages were legal relief, plaintiff had a right to a jury trial on those claims.

The rule in the Eleventh Circuit also is grounded on the nature of the remedy sought.

> The district court was correct in holding that appellant's claims were equitable and therefore not the proper subject of a jury trial. Appellant seeks reinstatement, backpay and reimbursement for "other lost professional benefits," all of which are equitable whether sought under Title VII or section 1983. Harkless v. Sweeny Independent School District, 427 F.2d 319, 323–24 (5th Cir.1970), *cert. denied*, 400 U.S. 991, 91 S.Ct. 451, 27 L.Ed.2d 439 (1971); Johnson v. Georgia Highway Express, Inc., 417 F.2d 1122, 1125 (5th Cir.1969).

Sullivan v. School Board of Pinellas County, 773 F.2d 1182, 1187 (11th Cir.1985) (footnote omitted).

The Ninth Circuit in a combination Title VII and 42 U.S.C. § 1981 case held that section 1981 provides both legal and equitable remedies, and that the legal remedies include compensatory and punitive damages which carry with them the right to a jury trial. Back pay is characterized as "either equitable or as a legal remedy incidental to an equitable cause of action, and accordingly not sufficient to create a right to a jury trial." Williams v. Owens–Illinois, Inc., 665 F.2d 918, 929 (9th Cir.) (footnote omitted), *cert. denied*, 459 U.S. 971, 103 S.Ct. 302, 74 L.Ed.2d 283 (1982).

In Bertot v. School District No. 1, Albany County, 613 F.2d 245, 250 (10th Cir.1979), the Tenth Circuit held that back pay was an element of equitable relief and was not precluded by a good faith defense. *But cf.* Skinner v. Total Petroleum, Inc., 859 F.2d 1439 (10th Cir.1988) (Where trial is both to jury and court due to presence of both equitable and legal issues, seventh amendment requires that essential factual issues central to both must first be tried to the jury. In a combination Title VII and § 1981 case, jury determination of back pay award in the § 1981 case must be accepted by court in the Title VII case, if supported by the evidence.).

In a political affiliation-discharge case, the Third Circuit held that a "party seeking compensation or other legal relief under 42 U.S.C. § 1983 has a right to a jury trial * * *, although the request for back pay under section 1983 seeks only equitable relief." Laskaris v. Thornburgh, 733 F.2d 260, 263 (3d Cir.), *cert. denied,* 469 U.S. 886, 105 S.Ct. 260, 83 L.Ed.2d 196 (1984).

The only circuit, as far as we can determine, that has explicitly found back pay to be legal damages is the Eighth. Setser v. Novack Investment Co., 638 F.2d 1137 (8th Cir.), *cert. denied,* 454 U.S. 1064, 102 S.Ct. 615, 70 L.Ed.2d 601 (1981) was a section 1981 case in which the plaintiff sought back pay, other compensatory damages, and punitive damages. Reinstatement was not sought. The issue was whether plaintiff was entitled to a jury trial on the claim of back pay. After a review of the case law, the court held that back pay determinations "are inherently in the nature of legal damages and require a jury trial." *Id.* at 1142.

In contrast to the other circuits, the Seventh Circuit has blithely ignored the problem or decided that none existed. In that circuit, back pay is routinely submitted to the jury in § 1983 cases. And, at least in the cases we have read, there is no discussion of equitable versus legal relief. *See* Webb v. City of Chester, Ill., 813 F.2d 824, 836 (7th Cir.1987) * * *.

Although the Supreme Court has not squarely addressed the question, we find its opinions in the general area instructive. * * * [The Court's analysis of *Dairy Queen, Beacon Theatres,* and *Ross* is omitted.]

* * *

The most recent case in this area is Tull v. United States, 481 U.S. 412, 107 S.Ct. 1831, 95 L.Ed.2d 365 (1987).[9] The question was,

> whether the Seventh Amendment guaranteed petitioner a right to a jury trial on both liability and amount of penalty in an action instituted by the Federal Government seeking civil penalties and injunctive relief under Clean Water Act, 62 Stat. Ch. 758, as amended, 33 U.S.C. § 1251, *et seq.*

---

9. We are aware that in Bowen v. Massachusetts, 487 U.S. 879, 108 S.Ct. 2722, 2731–32, 101 L.Ed.2d 749 (1988), the Court restated the longstanding principle that an equitable action for specific relief may include an order for reinstatement with back pay. The issue in *Bowen* was whether a district court had jurisdiction to review a final order of the Secretary of Health and Human Services refusing to reimburse a state for a category of expenditures under its Medicaid program. The Court's statement was made as part of its explanation of why there could be judicial review of the Secretary's disallowance decision. The Court pointed out that the complaint sought declaratory and injunctive relief, not money damages. Because of the nature of the action, there could be no jury trial. We do not think that the statement is relevant to the issue before us.

Id. 107 S.Ct. at 1833. The Court examined "both the nature of the action and the remedy sought." *Id.* at 1835. In the course of determining the nature of the action the Court stated:

> We need not rest our conclusion on what has been called an "abstruse historical" search for the nearest 18th-century analogue. *See* Ross v. Bernhard, 396 U.S., at 538, n.10, 90 S.Ct., at 738, n.10. We reiterate our previously expressed view that characterizing the relief sought is "[m]ore important" than finding a precisely analogous common law cause of action in determining whether the Seventh Amendment guarantees a jury trial. Curtis v. Loether, 415 U.S. 189, at 196, 94 S.Ct. 1005, at 1009, 39 L.Ed.2d 260 (1974).

Id. at 1837 (footnote omitted). The Court found that the assessment of civil penalties did not "involve the 'substance of a common-law right to trial by jury', nor a 'fundamental element of a jury trial.' " *Id.* at 1840. In holding that the jury determines liability and the trial court assesses the penalty, the Court noted: "In this case, highly discretionary calculations that take into account multiple factors are necessary in order to set civil penalties under the Clean Water Act. These are the kinds of calculations traditionally performed by judges." *Id.* at 1840 (citation omitted).

Following the teachings of the Court, we look to the nature of the action and the relief sought. There can be no doubt that § 1983 actions create tort liability with damages determined under the common law of torts.

> We have repeatedly noted that 42 U.S.C. § 1983 creates " 'a species of tort liability' in favor of persons who are deprived of 'rights, privileges, or immunities secured' to them by the Constitution." Carey v. Piphus, 435 U.S. 247, 253, 98 S.Ct. 1042, 1047, 55 L.Ed.2d 252 (1978), quoting Imbler v. Pachtman, 424 U.S. 409, 417, 96 S.Ct. 984, 988, 47 L.Ed.2d 128 (1976). *See also* Smith v. Wade, 461 U.S. 30, 34, 103 S.Ct. 1625, 1628, 75 L.Ed.2d 632 (1983); Newport v. Fact Concerts, Inc., 453 U.S. 247, 258–259, 101 S.Ct. 2748, 2755–2756, 69 L.Ed.2d 616 (1981). Accordingly, when § 1983 plaintiffs seek damages for violations of constitutional rights, the level of damages is ordinarily determined according to principles derived from the common law of torts. *See* Smith v. Wade, *supra*, 461 U.S. at 34, 103 S.Ct. at 1628; Carey v. Piphus, *supra*, 435 U.S. at 257–258, 98 S.Ct. at 1049; *cf.* Monroe v. Pape, 365 U.S. 167, 196, and n.5, 81 S.Ct. 473, 488, and n.5, 5 L.Ed.2d 492 (1961) (Harlan, J., concurring).

Memphis Community School District v. Stachura, 477 U.S. 299, 305–06, 106 S.Ct. 2537, 2542, 91 L.Ed 2d 249 (1986).

In tort actions for personal injury tried to a jury, lost wages are invariably treated as being part of compensatory damages. Unlike the calculations required to assess the civil penalty in *Tull,* the computation of back pay normally requires only the addition (or multiplication) of a fixed sum. To paraphrase *Tull,* these are the kinds of calculations traditionally performed by juries. *See* 107 S.Ct. at 1840. Our analysis leads us to conclude that the determination of back pay as a factor of compensatory damages involves the substance of a common-law right to a trial by jury. *See Tull*, 107 S.Ct. at 1840.

In addition to the seventh amendment implication, there is also a sound practical reason for having the jury factor in back pay when determining compensatory damages. Submission of the issue of back pay to the jury as a factor to be considered in its award of compensatory damages eliminates the inevitable overlap between compensatory damages and back pay. In most cases of an alleged unconstitutional firing, there will be evidence of the employee's pay. To expect a jury to ignore this is unrealistic, especially where it may constitute the major item of compensatory damages. This case illustrates the point * * *.

Applying the analysis mandated by the Supreme Court, we hold that in a § 1983 case based upon an alleged unconstitutional political firing where the issues of liability and compensatory damages will be determined by a jury, back pay shall be considered by the jury as one of the items of compensatory damages. We are constrained to add that we are not dissolving the traditional legal-equitable dichotomy. Where only reinstatement and back pay are requested, or if they are the only issues, in addition to liability, remaining in the case, then both reinstatement and back pay shall be for the court. Since this rule is contrary to the procedure followed by some district courts in this circuit, it shall be given prospective effect only. We, therefore, affirm the procedure followed in this case. * * * [But] we agree with appellants that the court's instructions on compensatory damages could well have resulted in duplicative damages. * * *

Affirmed in Part. Reversed in Part. Remanded [for a new trial on the issue of damages and "back pay must, of course, be determined by the jury"].

NOTES

1. After *Santiago-Negron* was handed down, the Supreme Court confronted the jury trial issue in a different type of § 1983 case. In City of Monterey v. Del Monte Dunes at Monterey, Ltd., 526 U.S. 687, 119 S.Ct. 1624, 143 L.Ed.2d 882 (1999), a real estate developer, whose plans were rejected five times, brought a damages action against the city under § 1983 on the theory that a regulatory taking had occurred. In a 5–4 decision, the Court determined that, for Seventh Amendment purposes, the action sounded in tort and was "an action at law for damages." *Id.* at 706, 712, 119 S.Ct. at 1637, 1640, 143 L.Ed.2d 882. The Court held that "the issue of whether a landowner has been deprived of all economically viable use of his property is a predominately factual question" that "is for the jury." *Id.* at 717, 119 S.Ct. at 1643, 143 L.Ed.2d 882.

2. In Atlas Roofing Co. v. Occupational Safety & Health Review Commission, 430 U.S. 442, 97 S.Ct. 1261, 51 L.Ed.2d 464 (1977) the Supreme Court considered a Seventh Amendment challenge to the Occupational Safety and Health Act ("OSHA") enforcement procedure, which is relatively unique.

Under most regulatory legislation the government can obtain a court judgment to enforce an administrative penalty only after a de novo civil action is conducted in a federal court. Under the OSHA procedure, however, the judicial action is not de novo and relitigation of the facts of the violation in federal court is not required.

The *Atlas* petitioners argued that the OSHA procedure violated the Seventh Amendment because it used the federal courts to enforce the administrative imposition of a penalty without also making provision for a right to trial by jury. The Supreme Court sustained the procedure and held that the Seventh Amendment did not invalidate the OSHA procedure because of a newly recognized "public rights" exception to the Seventh Amendment involving "cases in which the Government sues in its sovereign capacity to enforce public rights created by statutes within the power of Congress to enact." 430 U.S. at 450, 97 S.Ct. at 1266, 51 L.Ed.2d 464. * * * For an excellent analysis of *Atlas*, see Roger W. Kirst, *Administrative Penalties and the Civil Jury: The Supreme Court's Assault on the Seventh Amendment*, 126 U. Pa. L. Rev. 1281 (1978). *See also* Paul K. Sun Jr., Note, *Congressional Delegation of Adjudication Power to Federal Agencies and the Right to Trial by Jury*, 1988 Duke L.J. 539.

3.   The "equitable clean-up doctrine," which has been repudiated by the United States Supreme Court, has been described as follows:

> Historically, when a case had both legal and equitable aspects, the chancery courts employed the so-called "clean-up doctrine." This meant that once it was determined that equitable jurisdiction over an action existed, the chancellor would decide all aspects of the controversy, both legal and equitable, thereby obviating the need for two proceedings. But the doctrine would be applied only when the legal aspects of the case were subordinate to the equitable issues. Thus, prior to *Beacon Theatres*, the Seventh Amendment inquiry had focused largely on ascertaining the "basic nature of the case" to determine whether a sufficiently important legal claim had been presented giving rise to a right to jury trial.

> Judge Kalodner in Fraser v. Geis[11] succinctly stated the problem: "Where the complaint states one cause of action giving rise to alternative remedies in law or in equity, and where the complainant similarly prays for relief in the alternative, what is the rule as respects the right of trial by jury?" His answer illustrates the typical pre-*Beacon* analysis. "The decision as to whether or not the plaintiff is entitled to jury trial 'as of right' must rest upon a prior determination as to whether the action, in its essence, is one at law or in equity." Under this approach, when an action was classified as "essentially equitable," the federal court could dispose of any incidental legal claims without a jury. *Beacon Theatres* expressly overruled this interpretation of the Seventh Amendment and held that no test utilizing traditional equity procedure could interfere with the right to have a jury determine all the factual issues associated with a legal claim.

---

11.   1 F.R.D. 267 (E.D.Pa.1940).

Jack H. Friedenthal et al., Civil Procedure 509 (3d ed. 1999).* While the equitable clean-up doctrine retains continued vitality in a significant number of states, as will be seen in Chapter 8, Section 2, the extent of its federal demise should be considered in the context of the following principal case.

AMOCO OIL CO. v. TORCOMIAN

United States Court of Appeals, Third Circuit, 1983.
722 F.2d 1099.

Before ALDISERT, BECKER, CIRCUIT JUDGES and COHILL, DISTRICT JUDGE.

BECKER, CIRCUIT JUDGE.

The question presented by this appeal is whether the district court erred in refusing to afford defendants John Torcomian and Albert Torcomian a jury trial with respect to both the complaint of plaintiff Amoco and the Torcomians' compulsory counterclaim. The basis of the denial was that the claims, which arose out of the parties' dealings concerning an Amoco service station, were equitable in nature. The district court, following a bench trial, found for Amoco on all issues, and the Torcomians appeal. * * *

* * *

Amoco originally sought extensive relief including: (1) ejectment of the defendants from the service station; (2) a permanent injunction restraining defendants from continued use, enjoyment and possession of Parkside Amoco; (3) a permanent injunction restraining defendants from use of the Amoco logo, tradename, service mark or trademark; (4) judgment in the amount of $46,675 for profits lost as a result of defendants' wrongful possession and fraudulent misrepresentations; (5) judgment for $12,000 for defendants' mesne profits and wrongful use of the Amoco logo, tradename, service mark or trademark; and (6) attorneys' fees. At the beginning of trial, however, Amoco attempted to orally amend its complaint to delete, as we understand it, portions of its complaint that sought money damages other than for mesne profits so as to eliminate any claims that might be construed as legal and to thereby foreclose the defendants' right to a jury trial. * * *

* * * [T]he defendants sought "(1) [an] injunction enjoining plaintiff to comply with its franchise agreement with John Torcomian; (2) [a] judgment against plaintiff in an amount in excess of $100,000.00 for profits lost by John Torcomian as a result of plaintiff's failure to comply with its franchise agreement and for plaintiff's fraudulent misrepresentations; [and] (3) [a] judgment against plaintiff in the amount of defendants reasonable attorneys' fee [sic] and other costs involved in defending this action."

In its bench opinion on the merits, rendered after a two-day trial, the district court concluded that defendants were at most tenants at will, and

_____

* Reprinted with permission of West Publishing Co.

that there had never been a valid written or oral lease between Amoco and either or both of the defendants that would authorize them to occupy the property. It further concluded that no representative of Amoco having power to do so had ever told John Torcomian he was a dealer, and that John Torcomian, by failing to go to Dealer Development School * * *, had failed to fulfill a condition of his becoming an official dealer. The district court expressly resolved all questions of credibility in favor of Amoco and stated that it disbelieved testimony of John and Albert Torcomian. * * * Accordingly, it ordered the defendants to vacate Parkside Amoco and awarded Amoco $30,000 because it had been prevented from deriving a profit in that amount as a result of defendants' wrongful occupancy of Parkside Amoco.

II.   WERE THE COMPONENTS OF AMOCO'S CLAIM LEGAL OR EQUITABLE?

It has long been settled law that neither joinder of an equitable claim with a legal claim nor joinder of a prayer for equitable relief with a claim for legal relief as to a legal claim can defeat an otherwise valid seventh amendment right to a jury trial. See Beacon Theatres, Inc. v. Westover, 359 U.S. 500, 79 S.Ct. 948, 3 L.Ed.2d 988 (1959); Dairy Queen, Inc. v. Wood, 369 U.S. 469, 82 S.Ct. 894, 8 L.Ed.2d 44 (1962). Thus, in order to assess the district court's denial of the defendants' demand for a jury trial as to the main claim, we must consider whether it comprised any legal claims seeking legal relief. If we find such claims, we must vacate the judgment, at least as to those claims, unless we are persuaded that Amoco was entitled to a directed verdict on those claims. * * *

At the outset, we note that on its surface Amoco's complaint appears to present a number of essentially legal claims. The complaint sought ejectment, a form of action long regarded as legal. * * * It also sought damages, a form of relief usually treated as legal. Plaintiff offers several theories, however, to counter this surface interpretation.

To rebut the normal rule that ejectment is an action at law, plaintiff cites two Pennsylvania cases. Williams v. Bridy, 391 Pa. 1, 8, 136 A.2d 832, 836 (1957); and Fisher v. Knelly, 68 Sch.L.R. 117, 119 (Schuylkill C.P.1972). These cases purportedly hold that, where actual title to property is not in doubt, an action for injunction against defendant's continued possession of property leased to plaintiff is equitable. While our preliminary reading of the cited cases suggests that Amoco's interpretation and conclusions are dubious, there is a more telling problem with its argument: Pennsylvania's characterization of ejectment is irrelevant. See Simler v. Conner, 372 U.S. 221, 222, 83 S.Ct. 609, 610, 9 L.Ed.2d 691 (1963) (per curiam). As the Supreme Court there held, "[i]n diversity cases, of course, the substantive dimension of the claim asserted finds its source in state law ... but the characterization of that state-created claim as legal or equitable for purposes of whether a right to jury trial is indicated must be made by recourse to federal law." And federal law, as we have indicated, unequivocally holds actions seeking ejectment to be legal, not equitable.[8]

While apparently conceding that damages for profits lost by dint of the defendants' wrongful occupancy * * * constitute legal relief, Amoco argues that it abandoned that claim in the oral amendment to its complaint and that the remaining remedy of restitution—which we presume refers to the disgorgement of mesne profits—was equitable. While we do not quibble with this characterization, we regard it too as irrelevant. For while restitution may have been what Amoco wanted, restitution is not what Amoco got. The district court was presented with little evidence on the subject during trial, made no factual findings on the matter, and ordered no accounting. More importantly, the district court explicitly said it was awarding damages because "[a]s a result of defendants' occupancy against the will of the plaintiff, plaintiff has been prevented from deriving a profit from the property in the amount of $30,000." Thus, Amoco apparently never effectively retracted its original demand for legal relief.

III.   WERE THE COMPONENTS OF THE DEFENDANTS' COUNTERCLAIM EQUITABLE OR LEGAL?

It is settled law in this Circuit and elsewhere, *see* Eldredge v. Gourley, 505 F.2d 769, 770 (3d Cir.1974) (per curiam); Thermo–Stitch, Inc. v. Chemi–Cord Processing Corp., 294 F.2d 486, 488 (5th Cir.1961), that even an equitable main claim cannot preclude a jury trial on a legal counterclaim, at least when the counterclaim is compulsory. A rule to the contrary would enable the preemptive filing of a complaint by the holder of an equitable claim, coupled with the doctrine of res judicata, to deprive the holder of a legal claim of his seventh amendment right to a jury trial. * * *

Although the defendants did ask for equitable relief in their counterclaim (i.e., fulfillment of Amoco's obligation under the alleged franchise agreement), defendants also sought damages for the past breach of that agreement. A routine claim such as that presented here for damages stemming from breach of contract is legal. *See* Rogers v. Exxon Research & Engineering Co., 550 F.2d 834, 838 (3d Cir.1977). As we have noted in Part II of this opinion, the fact that equitable relief is sought in addition to substantial legal relief does not eliminate a right to a jury trial.

* * *

We have concluded that Amoco's main claim and the defendant's counterclaim contained a number of legal components as to which the defendant's were entitled to a jury trial under the Seventh Amendment. Accordingly, the judgment of the district court will be vacated and the case remanded for a new trial.

---

8. Our ruling here is in consonance with the old common law rule that "a claimant out of possession who has open to him the remedy of ejectment cannot escape a jury trial of the question of fact on which his claim depends by presenting that issue in some form of equitable action." * * *

NOTES

1. In Parklane Hosiery Co. v. Shore, 439 U.S. 322, 99 S.Ct. 645, 58 L.Ed.2d 552 (1979), the Supreme Court confronted the question "whether a party who has had issues of fact adjudicated adversely to it in an equitable action may be collaterally estopped from relitigating the same issues before a jury in a subsequent legal action brought against it by a new party." In concluding that the Seventh Amendment did not preclude the use of collateral estoppel in such a setting, the Court stated:

"[T]he thrust of the [Seventh] Amendment was to preserve the right to jury trial as it existed in 1791." Curtis v. Loether, 415 U.S. 189, 193, 94 S.Ct. 1005, 1007, 39 L.Ed.2d 260. At common law, a litigant was not entitled to have a jury determine issues that had been previously adjudicated by a chancellor in equity. * * *

Recognition that an equitable determination could have collateral-estoppel effect in a subsequent legal action was the major premise of this Court's decision in Beacon Theatres v. Westover, 359 U.S. 500, 79 S.Ct. 948, 3 L.Ed.2d 988. In that case the plaintiff sought a declaratory judgment that certain arrangements between it and the defendant were not in violation of the antitrust laws, and asked for an injunction to prevent the defendant from instituting an antitrust action to challenge the arrangements. The defendant denied the allegations and counterclaimed for treble damages under the antitrust laws, requesting a trial by jury of the issues common to both the legal and equitable claims. The Court of Appeals upheld denial of the request, but this Court reversed, stating:

[T]he effect of the action of the District Court could be, as the Court of Appeals believed, "to limit the petitioner's opportunity fully to try to a jury every issue which has a bearing upon its treble damage suit," for determination of the issue of clearances by the judge might "operate either by way of res judicata or collateral estoppel so as to conclude both parties with respect thereto at the subsequent trial of the treble damage claim." 359 U.S., at 504, 79 S.Ct., at 953.

It is thus clear that the Court in the *Beacon Theatres* case thought that if an issue common to both legal and equitable claims was first determined by a judge, relitigation of the issue before a jury might be foreclosed by res judicata or collateral estoppel. To avoid this result, the Court held that when legal and equitable claims are joined in the same action, the trial judge has only limited discretion in determining the sequence of trial and "that discretion ... must, wherever possible, be exercised to preserve jury trial." * * *

Both the premise of *Beacon Theatres,* and the fact that it enunciated no more than a general prudential rule were confirmed by this Court's decision in Katchen v. Landy, 382 U.S. 323, 86 S.Ct. 467, 15 L.Ed.2d 391. In that case the Court held that a bankruptcy court, sitting as a statutory court of equity, is empowered to adjudicate equitable claims prior to legal claims, even though the factual issues decided in the equity action would have been triable by a jury under the Seventh Amendment if the legal claims had been adjudicated first. The Court stated:

> Both *Beacon Theatres* and *Dairy Queen* recognized that there might be situations in which the Court would proceed to resolve the equitable claim first even though the results might be dispositive of the issues involved in the legal claim. 382 U.S., at 339, 86 S.Ct., at 478.

> Thus the Court in Katchen v. Landy recognized that an equitable determination can have collateral estoppel effect in a subsequent legal action, and that this estoppel does not violate the Seventh Amendment.

Id. at 333–35, 99 S.Ct. at 652–53, 58 L.Ed.2d 552. Note, however, that the Supreme Court declined

> to extend *Parklane Hosiery Co.* * * * and to accord collateral-estoppel effect to a district court's determinations of issues common to equitable and legal claims where the court resolved the equitable claims first solely because it erroneously dismissed the legal claims. To hold otherwise would seriously undermine a plaintiff's right to a jury trial under the Seventh Amendment.

Lytle v. Household Manufacturing, Inc., 494 U.S. 545, 553–56, 110 S.Ct. 1331, 1338, 108 L.Ed.2d 504 (1990).

2. In Katchen v. Landy, 382 U.S. 323, 86 S.Ct. 467, 15 L.Ed.2d 391 (1966), petitioner claimed that when a creditor who has received an alleged preference files a claim in bankruptcy and the trustee not only objects to its allowance, but in addition demands the surrender of the preference, the Federal Bankruptcy Act does not give the bankruptcy court summary jurisdiction to order the surrender of the preference. To permit such a result, the petitioner argued, would violate the Seventh Amendment jury trial protection. The Supreme Court held that the summary jurisdiction is conferred by the Act and, as to the jury trial argument, stated:

> [A]lthough petitioner might be entitled to a jury trial on the issue of preference if he presented no claim in the bankruptcy proceeding and awaited a federal plenary action by the trustee, * * * when the same issue arises as part of the process of allowance and disallowance of claims, it is triable in equity. The Bankruptcy Act, passed pursuant to the power given to Congress by Art. I, § 8, of the Constitution to establish uniform laws on the subject of bankruptcy, converts the creditor's legal claim into an equitable claim to a pro rata share of the res, * * * a share which can neither be determined nor allowed until the creditor disgorges the alleged voidable preference he has already received. * * * As bankruptcy courts have summary jurisdiction to adjudicate controversies relating to property over which they have actual or constructive possession, * * * and as the proceedings of bankruptcy courts are inherently proceedings in equity, * * * there is no Seventh Amendment right to a jury trial for determination of objections to claims.

Id. at 336–37, 86 S.Ct. at 476–77, 15 L.Ed.2d 391.

Post-*Katchen* case law has been slightly more friendly to the right to jury trial in the bankruptcy context. Consider the language of Matter of Hallahan, 936 F.2d 1496 (7th Cir.1991):

> By placing emphasis on the forum in which the claim arose, *Katchen* seemed to give bankruptcy courts broad discretion to deny jury trials for claims related to the administration or division of the estate. In 1978, the Bankruptcy Reform Act was enacted, eliminating the old summary/plenary distinction and creating "core" and "non-core" matters. Though "core proceedings" were defined significantly more broadly than summary jurisdiction, some courts read the 1978 Bankruptcy Reform Act and *Katchen* together to conclude that there was no right to a jury trial in all "core" proceedings. *See, e.g., In re* Chase & Sanborn Corp., 835 F.2d 1341, 1349 (11th Cir.1988), *certiorari granted sub nom.* Granfinanciera, S.A. v. Nordberg, 486 U.S. 1054, 108 S.Ct. 2818, 100 L.Ed.2d 920, *reversed*, 492 U.S. 33, 109 S.Ct. 2782, 106 L.Ed.2d 26 * * *.

> Granfinanciera, S.A. v. Nordberg, 492 U.S. 33, 109 S.Ct. 2782, dramatically revived the rights of some creditors in bankruptcy court to demand a jury trial. *Granfinanciera* involved a trustee's attempt to recover an allegedly fraudulent conveyance from the bank Granfinanciera. The bank, for its part, denied receiving any funds before bankruptcy. As an initial matter, the Court criticized the notion that the core/non-core distinction created by Congress was determinative of a party's jury trial rights.

> > Congress cannot eliminate a party's Seventh Amendment right to a jury trial merely by relabeling the cause of action to which it attaches and placing exclusive jurisdiction in an administrative agency or a specialized court of equity.

> 492 U.S. at 61, 109 S.Ct. at 2800. The inquiry must focus on the legal or equitable nature of the cause of action, and not Congress' "taxonomic change[s]." *Id.* A proper determination of whether the Seventh Amendment confers a right to jury trial for a claim heard in bankruptcy court entails a two-part inquiry:

> > First, we compare the statutory action to 18th-century actions brought in the courts of England prior to the merger of the courts of law and equity. Second, we examine the remedy sought and determine whether it is legal or equitable in nature.

> 492 U.S. at 42, 109 S.Ct. at 2790, citing Tull v. United States, 481 U.S. 412, 417–418, 107 S.Ct. 1831, 1835, 95 L.Ed.2d 365. Applying the test, the Court held that Granfinanciera could obtain a jury trial in spite of the fact that fraudulent conveyance actions are "core" proceedings under the Act. The Court discussed at some length the fact that actions to recover preferential or fraudulent transfers were brought at law in 18th-century England. It also held that the nature of the relief sought in a fraudulent conveyance action is legal rather than equitable. Because the claim was legal in nature and Congress was without power to change that characterization, Granfinanciera was entitled to a jury under the Seventh Amendment.

Granfinanciera did not overrule *Katchen*. Instead the Court distinguished *Katchen* in a manner relevant to this case. *Granfinanciera* restated the notion set forth in *Katchen* that a bankruptcy court having actual or constructive possession of the bankruptcy estate could adjudicate objections by the trustee and claims against the estate. However, the Court held that in *Katchen* it was the creditor's submission of a claim to the bankruptcy court which triggered the process of "the allowance and disallowance of claims" and subjected the creditor's otherwise legal claim to the bankruptcy court's equitable power. In *Granfinanciera,* the party seeking the jury trial (Granfinanciera) had never filed a claim against the estate, and thus the trustee had been forced to initiate what amounted to a legal action against the bank to recover a monetary transfer. In these circumstances, the Court held, defendant is entitled to a jury trial. *Granfinanciera,* 492 U.S. at 57–58, 109 S.Ct. at 2798. The proposition which emerges from a reading of *Katchen* and *Granfinanciera* together, that a creditor's right to a jury trial on a bankruptcy trustee's preference claim depends upon whether the creditor has submitted a claim against the estate, was reaffirmed by the Court last Term in Langenkamp v. Culp, 498 U.S. 42, 111 S.Ct. 330, 112 L.Ed.2d 343.

Id. at 1503–05.

In Langenkamp v. Culp, 498 U.S. 42, 111 S.Ct. 330, 112 L.Ed.2d 343 (1990), the creditors had submitted a claim against a bankruptcy estate, and the trustee in bankruptcy then had instituted proceedings against the creditors to recover allegedly preferential monetary transfers. The Court held:

> "[A] creditor's right to a jury trial on a bankruptcy trustee's preference claim depends upon whether the creditor has submitted a claim against the estate." *Granfianciera,* 492 U.S. at 58, 109 S.Ct. at 2799. Respondents filed claims against the bankruptcy estate, thereby bringing themselves within the equitable jurisdiction of the Bankruptcy Court. Consequently, they were not entitled to a jury trial on the trustee's preference action.
> * * *

Id. at 45, 111 S.Ct. at 331–32, 112 L.Ed.2d 343. Thus, *Langenkamp* announces a "bright line" rule that a creditor who has filed a proof of claim has voluntarily submitted to the bankruptcy court's equitable jurisdiction, and is no longer entitled to a jury trial on either the creditor's claim or the trustee's counterclaim. Billing v. Ravin, Greenberg & Zackin, P.A., 22 F.3d 1242, 1248–49 (3d Cir. 1994). *See generally* E. Scott Fruehwald, *Jury Trials in Bankruptcy Court After* Granfianciera, 24 Cumb. L. Rev. 79 (1994).

For recent right to jury trial decisions in the bankruptcy context, *compare* Braunstein v. McCabe, 571 F.3d 108 (1st Cir.2009) (individual debtors had no right to jury trial in statutory cause of action by Chapter 7 trustee against debtors to compel turnover of insurance proceeds) *with* Pereira v. Farace, 413 F.3d 330 (2d Cir.2005) (defendants ex-CEO, officers and directors of debtor-corporation had right to jury trial in action by Chapter 7 trustee for monetary relief in the nature of "compensatory damages," rather than as "restitution.").

3. Although many courts, such as the *Amoco* court, talk about restitution as an equitable action, restitutionary remedies may be either equitable or legal. See *supra* Chapter 4.

SECTION 2. THE STATE APPROACH: CONFLICTING CROSS–CURRENTS

WELTZIN v. NAIL

Supreme Court of Iowa, 2000.
618 N.W.2d 293.

SNELL, JUSTICE.

This is an interlocutory appeal from the Black Hawk County District Court. The appellant shareholders contend that their demand for a jury trial in their derivative suit was improperly stricken. * * *

I. BACKGROUND FACTS AND PROCEEDINGS

The plaintiffs/appellants in this case are shareholders of LaPorte City Cooperative Elevators. On behalf of the company, they brought a shareholder's derivative lawsuit against its directors and officers. A derivative lawsuit is unique in that the shareholders allege the company's directors have directly harmed it by their acts and omissions such that the company has suffered a loss. The shareholders indirectly assert their rights through the rights of the company.

In the present suit, the shareholders assert that the company's former directors and officers committed multiple breaches. Specifically, the shareholders allege former manager Michael Nail committed a negligent breach of his fiduciary duties and made fraudulent misrepresentations. They seek compensatory and punitive damages from Nail for his actions. The shareholders also contend that several former directors and the company's loan officer committed negligence in the performance of their duties. For these actions, the shareholders seek money damages. Although in equity, the shareholders filed a demand for jury trial with their petition.

In response to the petition, Nail answered with the affirmative defense of comparative fault, including a failure to mitigate damages, and asserted he was immune from liability for actions taken in performance of his duties. *See* Iowa Code § 499.59 (1997). Similarly, the other defendants asserted their immunity under section 499.59. All defendants joined in a motion to strike the jury demand made by the shareholders.

It is from this backdrop that the issue of the present appeal stems. The district court sustained the defendants' motion to strike the plaintiffs' demand for a jury trial. The court explained that a shareholder's derivative lawsuit could only be brought in equity and, therefore, no jury was warranted. While the court recognized that several claims and defenses were legal ones, because "the underlying essential character of the action [was] equitable in nature ... plaintiffs [were] not entitled to a jury trial."

* * * The shareholders argue that because their suit raises legal issues and remedies they are entitled to a jury determination. Specifically, the issue is: Under Iowa law, do shareholders in a derivative lawsuit have the right to a jury, when several claims are legal in nature, all affirmative defenses are legal, and Iowa recognizes the general inviolate right to a jury trial, but the overall nature of the action is equitable?

* * *

III. ISSUE ON APPEAL

Whether the plaintiff in a shareholder's derivative suit is entitled to a jury is a fairly unsettled question across the country. *Compare* Nelson v. Anderson, 72 Cal.App.4th 111, 84 Cal.Rptr.2d 753, 760 (1999) ("A minority shareholder's action for damages for the breach of fiduciary duties of the majority shareholder is one in equity, with no right to a jury trial."), *with* Rocha Toussier y Asociados, S.C. v. Rivero, 201 A.D.2d 282, 607 N.Y.S.2d 282, 282 (1994) (holding that the plaintiff in a shareholder's derivative suit was entitled to a jury where demand for relief was legal in nature although it also contained equitable demands).

While never addressing the derivative suit issue, we have recognized that there is no right to a jury trial generally in cases brought in equity. Moser v. Thorp Sales Corp., 312 N.W.2d 881, 896 (Iowa 1981). * * * Other legal sources have reached a similar conclusion specifically regarding shareholder's derivative suits. * * *

A. Iowa Jurisprudence

Iowa has previously addressed the issue of jury trials in an equity case involving a trust. Carstens v. Cent. Nat'l Bank & Trust Co., 461 N.W.2d 331 (Iowa 1990). * * * [T]he trust case was originally brought at law. *Id.* We held that because the trust beneficiaries' rights had not yet vested, the suit could only be brought in equity * * *.

* * * [We held] that no jury was warranted because the action was actually one in equity. * * * The court * * * stated: "We look at the *essential nature* of the cause of action, rather than solely at the remedy, to determine if a party is entitled to a jury trial." *Id.* at 333 (emphasis added); *see Moser,* 312 N.W.2d at 895 (finding that the fact the remedy is legal in nature does not automatically take the case out of the purview of the equity court). This suggests that the remedy sought is of minimal importance—it is the nature of the cause of action * * *.

It should be noted that in *Carstens* there was a dispute about what type of action the trust claim was, legal or equitable. * * * Here, it is clear that the nature of a shareholder's derivative suit is equitable only. * * * Likewise, there is no common law counter-part to a derivative suit available to shareholders. The derivative suit exists only in equity. * * *

1. The Effect of Legal Remedies Sought on the Equitable Claim

In their brief, the shareholders urge us to accept the proposition that "[t]he essential character of a cause of action to determine whether the right to jury trial exists is the *relief* it seeks." In support of this statement, the shareholders cite *Carstens*. This is a misstatement of the court's holding in that case. As noted earlier, the court explained that it was the *nature* of the case itself rather than solely the remedy that tips the balance in favor of or against providing a jury. * * * The court found that even though the trust beneficiaries were seeking money damages, a *legal* remedy, because the case could only be founded in equity, there was no right to a jury. * * *

2. The Effect of Legal Defenses Asserted on the Equitable Claim

The shareholders also assert that a jury should hear legal defenses raised. Regarding legal defenses in equity, several Iowa cases have held:

> We have recognized that a defendant has no right to a trial by jury of law issues raised in the answer to an action properly brought in equity. Once equity has obtained jurisdiction of a controversy the court will determine all questions material or necessary to accomplish full and complete justice between the parties, even though in doing so the court may be required to pass upon certain matters ordinarily cognizable at law.

In re Marriage of Stogdill, 428 N.W.2d 667, 670 (Iowa 1988) * * *.

Similarly, if an action was brought at law, and an equitable defense raised, that would not invoke equity jurisdiction automatically. * * *

3. The Effect of a Counterclaim on the Equitable Claim

Iowa does provide the right to a jury trial for defendants who assert a legal counterclaim in an equity action. *See* Conrad v. Dorweiler, 189 N.W.2d 537, 538–39 (Iowa 1971) (holding that this is true where the counterclaim raises severable issues); *see also* 27A Am.Jur.2d Equity § 235 ("A defendant also may have a right to jury trial if he or she is required compulsorily to assert his or her legal counterclaim. . . ."). While Iowa courts have recognized that not all equity cases can proceed without a jury on every issue, we choose not to extend this holding to the plaintiffs in a shareholder's derivative suit.

B.   Federal Jurisprudence

The United States Supreme Court has oppositely ruled on this issue and held that a plaintiff in a shareholder's derivative suit, although in equity, is entitled to a jury under the Seventh Amendment. Ross v. Bernhard, 396 U.S. 531, 532–37, 542, 90 S.Ct. 733, 735–38, 740, 24 L.Ed.2d 729, 733–36, 738 (1970). However, the persuasion of this case is hindered by the fact that the Seventh Amendment has never been made applicable to the states. * * *

1. Comparison Between Federal and Iowa Jury Provisions

The Seventh Amendment states in part that "the right of trial by jury shall be preserved. . . ." U.S. Const. amend. VII * * *. Similarly, the Iowa Constitution proclaims: "The right of trial by jury shall remain inviolate. . . ." Iowa Const. art. I, § 9. While not identical, both federal and state provisions appear to provide the same general preference for jury trials. Iowa has not made this mandate limitless, however, evidenced by its own civil rules. "Issues for which a jury is demanded shall be tried to a jury *unless* the court finds that there is *no* right thereto. . . ." Iowa R. Civ. P. 178 (emphasis added). This rule recognizes that in some cases, there is simply no right to a jury.

* * * [A] derivative suit can only be brought in equity because "[t]he common law refused . . . to permit stockholders to call corporate managers to account in actions at law" where a jury would be available. *Ross*, 396 U.S. at 534, 90 S.Ct. at 736, 24 L.Ed.2d at 733–34. Nonetheless, the Supreme Court found this right did exist in an equitable derivative action where "the corporation, if it had been suing in its own right, would have been entitled to a jury." *Id.* at 532–33, 90 S.Ct. at 735, 24 L.Ed.2d at 733.

2. Ross's Usefulness Under Our Circumstances

* * *

Similar to our facts, in *Ross,* the shareholders of Lehman Corporation brought a derivative suit on behalf of the corporation alleging breach of fiduciary duties and negligence and requesting money damages. * * * Generally, a fiduciary duty claim is one reserved for equity. However, tort claims such as negligence, breach of contract (asserted in *Ross*), and fraudulent misrepresentation (asserted in the present case) are direct wrongs against the corporation itself where the corporation could sue at law to obtain relief. The Supreme Court questioned why, when these legal claims were raised by shareholders instead, the " 'right to a jury trial should be taken away because the present plaintiff [could not] persuade the only party having a cause of action to sue . . .'?" *Id.* at 535, 90 S.Ct. at 736, 24 L.Ed.2d at 734 (quoting Fleitmann v. Welsbach St. Lighting Co. of Am., 240 U.S. 27, 28, 36 S.Ct. 233, 234, 60 L.Ed. 505, 506 (1916)). Accordingly, it held that the legal claims must be heard by a jury under the Seventh Amendment. * * *

3. Determining Which Issues Are Legal

If we adopt the holding in *Ross,* it would then be necessary to determine which of the shareholders' claims in the present case are legal such that they should be heard by a jury. Fraudulent misrepresentation is a legal claim. * * * Negligence is a legal claim. * * * Breach of fiduciary duty is an equitable claim. * * *

Confusion would be triggered when negligence or fraud were the actions that caused the alleged equitable breach. A breach of fiduciary duty claim is not an individual tort in its own right at common law. * * *

It is usually brought at law, bootstrapped by a tort like negligence or fraudulent misrepresentation. * * * However, it is a recognized individual claim in equity under a derivative suit. Rowen v. LeMars Mut. Ins. Co., 282 N.W.2d 639, 651–52 (Iowa 1979) * * *.

The question here becomes, if this court were to adopt the *Ross* reasoning, would the negligence and fraud claims be severable from the breach of duty claim such that a jury should hear them? Were we to adopt *Ross*, this would create quite a quandary for the lower courts to distinguish between the claims. For this reason, as well as those stated throughout the opinion, we choose not to extend the Supreme Court's holding in relation to the Seventh Amendment to shareholder's derivative suits brought in Iowa.

The *Ross* minority similarly recognized this classification problem created by the majority. *See Ross*, 396 U.S. at 550, 90 S.Ct. at 744, 24 L.Ed.2d at 743 (Stewart, J., dissenting). Justice Stewart stated:

> The fact is, of course, that there are, for the most part, no such things as inherently "legal issues" or inherently "equitable issues." There are only factual issues, and like chameleons [they] take their color from surrounding circumstances. Thus, the Court's "nature of the issue" approach is hardly meaningful.

Id. (Stewart, J., dissenting) (quotations and footnote omitted).

The issue of money damages makes it no clearer. "[A]n action seeking recovery of monetary damages will generally give rise to a right to trial by jury...." 19 Am.Jur.2d *Corporations* § 2465 * * *. However, just because shareholders are seeking money damages in a derivative suit does not mean a jury is warranted because the derivative suit itself is founded in equity. * * * The Minnesota Supreme Court has addressed the issue of money damages in an equity case and held: "[A] right to a jury trial is not guaranteed merely because plaintiffs only seek monetary damages." Uselman v. Uselman, 464 N.W.2d 130, 137 (Minn.1990). A request for reimbursement/restitution disguised as money damages is properly heard in equity. *See id.*

In the present case, the shareholders seek money damages for the actions of the officers and directors that led to LaPorte City Cooperative Elevators losing a substantial amount of money by, *e.g.,* failing to collect on accounts receivable, failing to comply with the company's credit policy, and failing to maintain awareness about the company's financial situation. Through the defendant's actions, the shareholders are alleging the company lost money. Thus, they are actually seeking restitution, styled as money damages. * * *

Money damages to remedy the corporation are not uncommon in derivative suits—yet the case remains in equity. *See generally Rowen*, 282 N.W.2d at 656 ("[A] money award in a derivative suit is more appropriately referred to as a judgment for restitution rather than as one for damages.... [W]e use the terms interchangeably."). Similarly, punitive damages, like the kind asked for in the present case, are also within the purview of the equity court. Holden v. Constr. Mach. Co., 202 N.W.2d 348, 359 (Iowa 1972) (holding this is true even where no actual damages can be shown); Charles v. Epperson & Co., 258 Iowa 409, 432, 137 N.W.2d 605, 617–618 (1965) (finding exemplary damages appropriate for defendant's fraudulent conduct). *But see Fleitmann*, 240 U.S. at 28–29, 36 S.Ct. at 234, 60 L.Ed. at 506–07 (declaring claims for treble damages should be heard by a jury).

4. The National Treatment of Ross Regarding Derivative Suits

It should be noted there was a strong dissent in *Ross* claiming the majority opinion was ill-conceived and biased in favor of more juries. * * * Specifically, the dissent argued the Seventh Amendment only preserved the right to a jury trial to suits cognizable at common law. * * * A shareholder's derivative suit does not exist under common law and is solely a case in equity regardless that legal issues are raised. * * *

Many states have taken the same approach and not afforded the right to a jury in derivative suits because of their equitable nature. *See, e.g.*, Hames v. Cravens, 332 Ark. 437, 966 S.W.2d 244, 246–48 (1998); *Rankin*, 121 Cal.Rptr. at 358–59; Lanman Lithotech, Inc. v. Gurwitz, 478 So.2d 425, 426–27 (Fla.Dist.Ct.App.1985) * * *.

Alabama, New York, and Wyoming have parted with the trend and extended the right to a jury to legal issues raised in derivative suits. Finance, Inv. & Rediscount Co. v. Wells, 409 So.2d 1341, 1344 (Ala.1981); *Rivero*, 607 N.Y.S.2d at 282; Hyatt v. Hyatt, 769 P.2d 329, 333–34 (Wyo.1989). For a detailed discussion of the national treatment of this issue, see Jean E. Maess, Annotation, *Right to Jury Trial in Stockholder's Derivative Action*, 32 A.L.R.4th 1111 (1984 & Supp.1999).

The national trend appears to agree with the *Ross* dissent. Among the handful of states that allow a jury to hear legal issues stemming from equitable suits, many only provide advisory juries. *See, e.g.*, * * * Bowers v. Westvaco Corp., 244 Va. 139, 419 S.E.2d 661, 666 (1992). * * * The plaintiff is able to present his case to a jury, but the court is not bound by the jury's recommendation. We have never recognized the usefulness of this process, nor do we do so today.

C. Complexity of the Derivative Suit and Its Effect on Due Process

Lastly, this court recognizes that in a shareholder's derivative suit a judge is simply better equipped to hear the complicated corporation and duty claims. *See* Alsea Veneer, Inc. v. State, 318 Or. 33, 862 P.2d 95, 100 (1993) ("An equity court is better able to decide questions relating to the exercise of corporate discretion than is a jury."). The *Ross* dissent addressed the complexity problem: "[W]here the issues in the case are complex—as they are likely to be in a derivative suit—much can be said for allowing court discretion to try the case itself." *Ross*, 396 U.S. at 545 n. 5, 90 S.Ct. at 741 n.5, 24 L.Ed.2d at 740 n.5 (Stewart, J., dissenting).

For this reason, Justice Stewart boldly concluded that the majority's opinion had "a questionable basis in policy and no basis whatsoever in the Constitution." *Id.* (Stewart, J., dissenting).

To adopt a similar public policy argument today does not offend any constitutional right to a jury because generally this right does not exist in equity. * * * Moreover, allowing this type of complex case to be adjudicated by a jury may actually *offend* Iowa's constitutional mandate of due process under article I, section 9. Not only does our constitution declare that the right to a jury trial is inviolate, it also provides: "[N]o person shall be deprived of life, liberty, or property, without due process of law." Iowa Const. art. I, § 9. This is significant because several courts have denied "the parties a jury trial, reasoning that because a competent jury cannot be impaneled to decide such cases, the due process right to a fair trial is violated if the jury resolves the dispute." Keith Broyles, Note, *Taking the Courtroom into the Classroom: A Proposal for Educating the Lay Juror in Complex Litigation Cases*, 64 Geo. Wash. L. Rev. 714, 716 (1996).

The Supreme Court in *Ross* listed juror competence as one of the considerations to be used when determining if a jury is warranted. * * * It recognized that "the practical abilities and limitations of juries" could be an important factor in complex derivative suits. * * * Several courts following *Ross* have concluded that case complexity may indeed trump the right to a jury in order to satisfy due process requirements. *See, e.g.*, In re Japanese Elec. Prods. Antitrust Litig., 631 F.2d 1069, 1084–89 (3d Cir. 1980) * * *. Factors used to consider complexity are the amount of discovery, length of trial, difficulty of case concepts, intricacy of expert testimony, etc. * * *

Certainly case complexity is present in almost every shareholder's derivative suit because the jury is asked to pass judgment on the intricate workings of a corporation. Often concepts like the business judgment rule and breach of fiduciary duty are difficult to understand. * * * Similarly, derivative suits usually involve voluminous amounts of discovery and records to trace the actions of the corporation's officers and directors. With massive discovery comes increased length of trial. Moreover, there may be several plaintiffs and multiple defendants each being represented by different counsel. The present case is no exception. The shareholders are alleging negligence occurred over an extended period of time and was committed by multiple officers, directors, and contractors. Such a make-up is a recipe for complexity. Because juror competence would be challenged in almost every derivative suit, the court is further persuaded not to provide a jury.

* * * Our jurisprudence has never provided an absolute right to a jury trial in every case. One modern jurist recognized: "Of course, in a very considerable number of cases, no right to trial by jury exists because of historically determined fortuities.... Were jury trial as beneficent as its ardent devotees proclaim, such differences would be indefensibly irra-

tional." Skidmore v. Baltimore & O.R. Co., 167 F.2d 54, 57 n.6 (2d Cir.1948). This court agrees that equity does not require trial by jury in a derivative suit.

IV. CONCLUSION

We deny the shareholders the right to a jury trial in this case because their right to bring a derivative suit exists only in equity where there is no general preference for a jury trial. To provide an avenue for shareholders to have a jury for their legal claims would prove inefficient and overly burdensome on the lower courts as well as untrained juries. To hold otherwise would further complicate already complex cases and force the court to determine which issues are legal and which are purely equitable prior to hearing an issue or submitting it to a jury.

Decision of the district court affirmed; case remanded for further proceedings.

All justices concur except TERNUS, J., who takes no part.

NOTES

1. *Accord* Caira v. Offner, 126 Cal.App.4th 12, 24 Cal.Rptr.3d 233 (2005) (there is no right to jury trial in shareholder derivative actions even where punitive damages are sought). Where either the underlying cause of action or the remedy sought is traditionally looked upon as equitable, many state courts continue to interpret their state constitutions so as to deny a jury trial. *See, e.g.,* Walton III v. Walton, 31 Cal.App.4th 277, 36 Cal.Rptr.2d 901 (1995) (specific performance of oral contract to make a will); Strauss v. Summerhays, 157 Cal.App.3d 806, 204 Cal.Rptr. 227 (1984) (quiet title action); Robair v. Dahl, 80 Mich.App. 458, 264 N.W.2d 27 (1978) (constructive trust); State Bank of Lehi v. Woolsey, 565 P.2d 413 (Utah 1977) (mortgage foreclosure). Moreover, the language of a New Jersey case is instructive:

> In short, the remedies provided in the statute are injunction, restitution and appointment of a receiver, all clearly equitable in nature. No constitutional right exists to a jury trial in equity actions for injunctive relief. If [the] relief provided is equitable rather than legal in nature, the right to jury trial does not attach, even if financial restitution is part of the equitable relief available.

Kugler v. Banner Pontiac–Buick, Opel, Inc., 120 N.J.Super. 572, 581, 295 A.2d 385, 389 (1972) (action by attorney general for consumer fraud; a state statute authorized the restoration of money wrongfully acquired).

In Karnes Enterprises, Inc. v. Quan, 221 Kan. 596, 561 P.2d 825 (1977), the Kansas Supreme Court stated:

> Some of the specific types of actions held to be equitable in nature are the following: quiet title actions, actions for specific performance, cancellation of a lease, creation of a resulting trust with an accounting, actions to determine the priority of mortgages and other liens, for an accounting, and to impress liens on real estate.

Id. at 601–02, 561 P.2d at 830.

2.   Consider the following analysis by a California appellate court concerning whether a cause of action for damages for breach of fiduciary duty brought by a minority shareholder (IMA) against majority shareholders and directors of a corporation triggers a right to jury trial under either California or Delaware law:

Under both Delaware law and California law, entitlement to jury trial depends on whether an action is legal or equitable. (Park Oil, Inc. v. Getty Refining & Marketing (Del.Supr.1979) 407 A.2d 533, 535; Southern Pac. Transportation Co. v. Superior Court (1976) 58 Cal.App.3d 433, 435, 129 Cal.Rptr. 912.) In Delaware, the equity jurisdiction of the Court of Chancery as it existed prior to the separation of the colonies determines whether an action is legal or equitable. (Du Pont v. Du Pont (Del.Supr. 1951) 85 A.2d 724, 727.) In California, the right to a jury trial is coextensive with that right as it existed in 1850 under English common law. (C & K Engineering Contractors v. Amber Steel Co. (1978) 23 Cal.3d 1, 8, 151 Cal.Rptr. 323, 587 P.2d 1136.)

To ascertain whether IMA is entitled to a jury trial we must first classify its action—a claim for breach of fiduciary duty brought under Delaware law in which the plaintiff seeks damages—as legal or equitable. * * *

Under Delaware law, a board of directors of a corporation owes its shareholders duties of good faith, loyalty, and due care. * * * Those duties are derived from "[a] public policy, existing through the years [which] has established a rule that demands of a corporate officer or director, peremptorily and inexorably, the most scrupulous observance of his duty, not only affirmatively to protect the interests of the corporation committed to his charge, but also to refrain from doing anything that would work injury to the corporation...."(Weinberger v. UOP, Inc. (Del.Supr.1983) 457 A.2d 701, 710.) Violation of one of those tripartite duties constitutes grounds for an action for breach of fiduciary duty. * * *

The parties agree that in Delaware, analysis of a breach of fiduciary duty claim involves application of the "entire fairness test." * * *

"[T]he determination that a board has failed to demonstrate entire fairness will be the basis for a finding of substantive liability. The Court of Chancery must identify the breach or breaches of fiduciary duty upon which that liability will be predicated...." * * * If the court finds a breach, the appropriate relief becomes an issue, but "only after a transaction is determined not to be entirely fair." * * * In this case, the trier of fact will be required to determine whether the majority stockholders and directors followed the requisite "entire fairness" in merging [the prior corporation into the new corporation]. * * *

Determining which state's law applies would be critical if the choice of Delaware or California law were dispositive of the parties' underlying contention—whether IMA is entitled to a jury trial. But it is not. As we explain, this action is equitable under both Delaware and California law. Applying either law, a party is not entitled to a jury trial in an equitable action.

Delaware law characterizes " 'fairness' suits for alleged fraud and breach of fiduciary duty" as equitable claims, not cognizable at law. (Harman v. Masoneilan Intern., Inc. (Del.Supr.1982) 442 A.2d 487, 498–499.) The right to a trial by jury is not available in Delaware for a claim brought in equity. * * *

The more difficult question is the classification of Delaware's breach of fiduciary duty action under California law. That classification depends on the "gist of the action." * * * IMA argues that the gist of this action is legal because the remedy of damages is adequate and is all that is sought. For support, IMA relies on Mortimer v. Loynes (1946) 74 Cal. App.2d 160, 168 P.2d 481, Ripling v. Superior Court (1952) 112 Cal. App.2d 399, 247 P.2d 117, and Paularena v. Superior Court (1965) 231 Cal.App.2d 906, 42 Cal.Rptr. 366.

* * *

Relying in part on *Mortimer* and *Ripling*, the court in *Paularena* emphasized the relief sought in characterizing an action as between law and equity. (Paularena v. Superior Court, *supra*, 231 Cal.App.2d at p. 912, 42 Cal.Rptr. 366.) "The fact that equitable principles are applied in the action does not necessarily identify the resultant relief as equitable. * * * Equitable principles are a guide to courts of law as well as of equity. * * * Furthermore, the incidental adoption of equitable sounding measures to effect the application of equitable principles in an action at law, such as for damages, does not change the character of that action. * * *" (*Ibid.*)

Without specifically overruling those cases, our Supreme Court has determined: "A jury trial must be granted where the gist of the action is legal, where the action is in reality cognizable at law.... On the other hand, if the action is essentially one in equity and the relief sought depends upon the application of equitable doctrines, the parties are not entitled to a jury trial.... Although we have said that the legal or equitable nature of a cause of action ordinarily is determined by the mode of relief to be afforded ... the prayer for relief in a particular case is not conclusive.... Thus, the fact that damages is one of a full range of possible remedies does not guarantee ... the right to a jury...." (C & K Engineering Contractors v. Amber Steel Co., *supra*, 23 Cal.3d at p. 9, 151 Cal.Rptr. 323, 587 P.2d 1136, citations and internal quotation marks omitted.)

In *C & K Engineering*, the court found that the parties were not entitled to a jury trial even though the plaintiff's suit was for damages. The action was entirely based on the equitable doctrine of promissory estoppel. * * * The fact that "[b]oth historically and functionally, the task of weighing such equitable considerations is to be performed by the trial court, not the jury" was critical to the court's rationale. (Id. at p. 11, 151 Cal.Rptr. 323, 587 P.2d 1136.)

Based on *C & K Engineering*, a claim of breach of fiduciary duty by trust beneficiaries concerning the management of a trust was found equitable because it was based on an equitable right. (Van de Kamp v.

Bank of America (1988) 204 Cal.App.3d 819, 865, 251 Cal.Rptr. 530.) The fact that the plaintiff sought damages did not alter the court's conclusion since "[a]n action is one in equity where the only manner in which the legal remedy of damages is available is by application of equitable principles." (*Ibid.*)

As in *C & K Engineering* and *Van de Kamp*, IMA's cause of action is based on equitable principles. The fiduciary duty of a controlling shareholder or director to a minority shareholder is based on "powers in trust." (Jones v. H.F. Ahmanson & Co. (1969) 1 Cal.3d 93, 107, 81 Cal.Rptr. 592, 460 P.2d 464.) " 'For that power is at all times subject to the equitable limitation that it may not be exercised for the aggrandizement, preference, or advantage of the fiduciary. . . . Where there is a violation of these principles, equity will undo the wrong or intervene to prevent its consummation.' " (*Id.* at p. 109, 81 Cal.Rptr. 592, 460 P.2d 464 * * *).

Trust relationships are premised on equitable principles. * * * In addition, "entire fairness" is about adjusting equities. * * * The test requires weighing various considerations in order to reach a just result. * * * That standard illustrates a court's equitable power to weigh various considerations in order to reach a just result. The sole method of obtaining damages in this case is by application of equitable principles. It follows that this action, under California law, is properly classified as an equitable action.

Under California law, a party is not entitled to a jury trial in an equitable action. (Southern Pac. Transportation Co. v. Superior Court, *supra*, 58 Cal.App.3d 433, 435, 129 Cal.Rptr. 912.) Accordingly, IMA is not entitled to a jury trial in the present action under California law. * * * Application of Delaware or California law to the question of whether IMA is entitled to a jury trial results in the same conclusion: the action is equitable and as such IMA is not entitled to a jury trial.

Interactive Multimedia Artists v. Superior Court of Los Angeles County, 62 Cal.App.4th 1546, 1550–1556, 73 Cal.Rptr.2d 462, 465–470 (1998).

3.   Declaratory judgment actions have presented difficult jury trial questions. *See generally* Annotation, Jean E. Maess, *Right to Jury Trial in Action for Declaratory Relief in State Court*, 33 A.L.R.4th 146 (1984). In large measure this is attributable to the fact that the remedy did not exist at common law. Consequently,

> courts have had to determine whether the remedy was sought as a substitute for a remedy traditionally available only in an action at law or bill in equity. The decision whether to honor a jury trial demand hinges upon this prior determination.

Precisely how the determination is made varies. Opinions of several federal courts of appeals, after Beacon Theatres, Inc. v. Westover,[19] are instructive of the federal view. These cases hold that a declaratory judgment will be characterized as legal if, but only if, it appears from the facts that legal type relief would be possible at the time of the lawsuit.

---

19.   359 U.S. 500, 79 S.Ct. 948, 3 L.Ed.2d 988 (1959).

Thus, in a school desegregation case, the inclusion of a request for a declaratory remedy does not authorize a jury trial. Similarly, in a suit for a declaratory judgment construing an oil and gas lease, followed by a counterclaim for possession of the property on account of breach of the lease constituting termination, the court treated the action as a reverse equitable bill for cancellation, not as a reverse claim for ejectment. Because the lease itself provided no automatic provisions for termination, the defendant had no immediate right to possession until the court cancelled the lease. Therefore, no jury trial was authorized. * * *

* * *

There is language in Beacon Theatres, Inc. v. Westover which suggests that courts must go much further in order to protect trial by jury. *Beacon's* holding—that factual issues common to the claim and counterclaim regarding the reasonableness of the operator's practices should be triable of right to a jury—is itself not radical. But two of the Court's rationales were radical. First, the Court found that the declaratory judgment act provided a *legal* remedy which "necessarily affects the scope of equity".[20] Second, it suggested that the fact that the jury trial right is constitutional warrants a requirement that judicial discretion, "wherever possible, be exercised to preserve jury trial."[21]

Few decisions since *Beacon* have followed either of these lines of thought. In Alabama, the courts have held that where the underlying facts indicate that a legal remedy may become available to one of the parties, jury trial as of right is available;[22] but these courts have declined to extend the right to cases where the only conceivable alternative relief would be equitable.[23] In Florida, the supreme court has indicated that doubtful questions regarding the distinction between law and equity should be resolved in favor of jury trial because of the fundamental guaranty of the state constitution;[24] but this court has declined to characterize all declaratory judgment actions as inherently legal.[25]

A few courts are more restrictive than are the federal courts. In Lazarus v. Village of Northbrook,[26] the Supreme Court of Illinois was confronted with an action for declaration of invalidity of a zoning ordinance as applied to plaintiff's property. The complaint contained a prayer for injunctive relief but indicated that it was filed at law. The defendant

---

20. *Beacon Theatres*, 359 U.S. at 509. As James and Hazard have pointed out, the logic of this part of *Beacon* would make all declaratory judgment actions triable by jury. F. James & G. Hazard, Civil Procedure § 8.10, at 385–86 (2d ed. 1977).

21. *Beacon Theatres*, 359 U.S. at 510.

22. *See* Sherer v. Burton, 393 So.2d 991, 991–92 (Ala.1981). *But cf.* Shubin v. United States Dist. Court, 313 F.2d 250 (9th Cir.1963) (where the federal court declined to treat as legal a future claim as to which no damages had been inflicted or suffered).

23. *See, e.g.,* Burnham v. City of Mobile, 277 Ala. 659, 174 So.2d 301 (1965).

24. Hollywood, Inc. v. City of Hollywood, 321 So.2d 65, 71 (Fla.1975).

25. *See id.* at 73. In *Hollywood*, the court characterized as legal the tax assessor's bill for declaratory and equitable relief against alternative claimants to land. The court explained that the suit sounded in ejectment because it would likely lead to ouster of a party in possession of property. *Id.* at 71–72.

26. 31 Ill.2d 146, 199 N.E.2d 797 (1964).

asked for a jury trial. The court stated that, when a declaration alone is sought,

> the right to trial by jury must be determined by an examination of the disputed issues and an appraisal of their predominant characteristics as indicating the appropriateness of legal or equitable relief. But when, as is ordinarily the case, relief in addition to the naked declaration of rights is sought, the nature of that relief determines the right to a trial by jury.

The court therefore denied jury trial. Ohio's courts show a marked willingness to subordinate parallel claims for legal relief to those for equitable relief and thus to deny jury trial rights as to all claims.[27] Ohio refuses to treat defensive actions for declaratory relief of nonliability of an insurance policy as legal unless that claimant has reduced his claim to judgment and is actively seeking payment.[28] Both the Illinois and Ohio approaches risk the loss of jury rights in many actions in which, but for the statute, the right would probably be available.

Richard W. Bourne & John A. Lynch, Jr., *Merger of Law and Equity Under the Revised Maryland Rules: Does It Threaten Trial By Jury?*, 14 U. Balt. L. Rev. 1, 47–50 (1984).* *See, e.g.*, Kann v. Kann, 344 Md. 689, 690 A.2d 509 (1997) (declaratory judgment action to determine rights and obligations of parties under trust does not require a jury trial because this use of declaratory judgment was analogous historically to equity jurisdiction over administration of trusts); *In re* Environmental Insurance Declaratory Judgment Actions, 149 N.J. 278, 693 A.2d 844 (1997) (declaratory judgment actions by insureds against insurers to compel indemnification for future environmental cleanup costs were essentially actions for specific performance to which the right to jury trial did not attach); Arrow Communication Laboratories, Inc. v. Pico Products, Inc., 219 A.D.2d 859, 632 N.Y.S.2d 903 (1995) (fact that plaintiff sought a declaratory judgment did not defeat its demand for jury trial where primary relief sought was money judgment for legal restitution).

4.   Like their federal counterparts, state courts also must determine the extent to which state constitutional jury trial provisions mandate a right to jury trial in statutory causes of action. Consider, in this regard, the language of the Vermont Supreme Court when it decided whether to grant the plaintiff's request for a jury trial in a Fair Employment Practices Act (FEPA) case for back pay only:

> Defendant argues that the right to a jury under the Vermont Constitution does not apply to statutory actions but only to common-law causes of action. It maintains that because FEPA does not grant a right to jury trial, there is no such right in actions under the Act. The petitioner in *Curtis* advanced the same argument, but the Court held that "[t]he Seventh Amendment does apply to actions enforcing statutory rights, and

27. *See, e.g.*, Miles v. N.J. Motors, Inc., 44 Ohio App.2d 351, 338 N.E.2d 784 (1975) (court discharged debtors from a series of cognovit notes and subordinated debtors' requests for declaratory relief to their claim for injunctive relief to compel defendant to comply with debtors' rights and sell repossessed vehicles at public sales).

28. *See, e.g.*, Republic Indem. Co. v. Durell, 105 Ohio App. 153, 151 N.E.2d 687 (1957).

* Reprinted with permission of University of Baltimore Law Review.

requires a jury trial upon demand, if the statute creates legal rights and remedies, enforceable in an action for damages in the ordinary courts of law." 415 U.S. at 194, 94 S.Ct. at 1008. Similarly, this Court has found that "[t]he [Vermont] [C]onstitution was intended to provide for the future as well as the past, to protect the rights of the people * * * whether those rights then existed by the rules of the common law, or *might from time to time arise out of subsequent legislation.*" Plimpton, 33 Vt. at 291 (emphasis added). Thus, we conclude that the right to trial by jury under the Vermont Constitution is not limited to causes of action recognized at common law in 1793.

Defendant also argues that we should adopt the federal rule, under which there was no right to trial by jury in a Title VII action, because FEPA is patterned on Title VII of the Civil Rights Act of 1964, 42 U.S.C. §§ 2000e–2000e–17. *See* Graff v. Eaton, 157 Vt. 321, 323 n.2, 598 A.2d 1383, 1384 n.2 (1991) ("The consensus has been that there is no right to trial by jury under Title VII because the remedy it provides—reinstatement and award of back pay—is essentially equitable."). The decisions denying trial by jury under the federal employment discrimination law, however, were based on the remedy provided under Title VII prior to its amendment in 1991. *See id.*; *Curtis*, 415 U.S. at 197, 94 S.Ct. at 1010. Unlike FEPA, Title VII relief was essentially equitable in nature until 1991, when Congress amended Title VII, extending the relief available to include compensatory and punitive damages. *See* Civil Rights Act of 1991, Pub.L. No. 102–166, § 102, 105 Stat. 1071, 1072 (1991) (codified at 42 U.S.C. § 1981a). In 1981, the Vermont Legislature extended FEPA remedies to include "damages" by an amendment in which it provided for private actions under the Act. *See* 21 V.S.A. § 495b(b). Thus, we are not inclined to follow pre–1991 Title VII case law on the jury trial issue. Accordingly, to the extent that factual issues are in dispute, the parties to an action under FEPA are entitled to trial by jury when the plaintiff requests legal damages.

Hodgdon v. Mt. Mansfield Co. 160 Vt. 150, 624 A.2d 1122, 1126 (1992) (holding, however, that plaintiff was not entitled to a jury trial because her complaint sought no legal relief). *Accord:* State v. Irving Oil Corp., 183 A.2d 1098 (2008) (no right to jury trial under Waste Management Act where relief sought was essentially equitable in nature). For a similar holding in the context of a state statute prohibiting disability discrimination, see FUD's, Inc. v. State, 727 A.2d 692 (R.I.1999). *See also* Crespo v. Crespo, 972 A.2d 1169 (N.J.Super.2009) (no right to jury trial under Prevention of Domestic Violence Act).

LEONARDI v. SHERRY

Supreme Court of Missouri, En Banc, 2004.
137 S.W.3d 462.

WILLIAM RAY PRICE, JR., JUDGE.

* * *

II.

Pharmaceutical companies contracted with Radiant Research, Inc., to oversee human clinical trials testing new drugs. Radiant and Leonardi, a medical doctor, entered into several clinical trial consulting agreements whereby Leonardi agreed to conduct some of those trials for Radiant. The agreements included restrictive covenants that prohibited Leonardi from conducting further trials for the pharmaceutical companies for one year following the termination of the consulting agreements unless Radiant served as the intermediary.

After notifying Radiant approximately two weeks in advance, Leonardi terminated their relationship in November 2001. Radiant filed a six-count petition against Leonardi in February 2002 seeking injunctive relief and damages on every count. Radiant's claims included breach of contract, anticipatory repudiation, tortious interference with contracts, and civil conspiracy. In its requests for injunctive relief, Radiant sought to enforce restrictive covenants in the consulting agreements.

In response to Radiant's petition, Leonardi filed a four-count counter-claim and asserted multiple affirmative defenses, including laches, estoppel, and unclean hands. He included actions for breach of contract and breach of the implied covenant of good faith and fair dealing. He also requested a declaratory judgment.

Following a hearing in January 2003, the trial court denied Radiant's request for a preliminary injunction * * * because it would "not have the necessary effect of reinstating Radiant as the site manager." * * * The trial court entered an order later that month setting the case for trial during a certified jury week.

In February 2003, Leonardi voluntarily dismissed his action for a declaratory judgment. He then filed a motion for a ruling on the merits of Radiant's equitable claims. In early March 2003, the trial court heard arguments and received briefs from Radiant and Leonardi discussing the availability of a jury trial and the applicability of the equitable cleanup doctrine.

The trial court issued an order on March 21, 2003, stating that its denial of Radiant's request for a preliminary injunction did not dispose of Radiant's request for a permanent injunction and that Radiant's requests for equitable relief and damages were still before it. The trial court concluded that Leonardi was not entitled to a jury trial because it retained jurisdiction over Radiant's claims pursuant to the equitable cleanup doctrine in that "a court of equity may retain jurisdiction to award damages where equity requires this form of relief in the circumstances."

Following the trial court's denial of a jury trial, Leonardi filed his request for a writ in prohibition. A preliminary order in prohibition was issued instructing the trial court to refrain from all action in the case until further notice. Leonardi argues that the equitable cleanup doctrine is inapplicable under the circumstances and that the trial court violated his constitutional right to a jury.

III.

The problem of determining whether a jury trial should occur in cases involving claims for both damages and equitable relief is not new, nor is it simple, in Missouri or elsewhere. * * * In its present state, the law in Missouri is inconsistent and confusing. Throughout the precedent, different principles have been repeatedly cited.

Some cases state that "once having acquired jurisdiction equity will retain it, under a prayer for general relief ... to administer full and complete justice, within the scope of pleadings and evidence, between the parties." State *ex rel.* Drey v. Hoester, 608 S.W.2d 401, 404 (Mo. banc 1980) * * *. Similarly phrased is the rule that "when a court of equity once acquires jurisdiction of a cause it will not relax its grasp upon the *res* until it shall have avoided a multiplicity of suits by doing full, adequate and complete justice between the parties." Real Estate Saving Inst. v. Collonious, 63 Mo. 290, 295 (1876). * * * Similarly, Rockhill Tennis Club of Kansas City v. Volker noted that "a court of equity when unable to grant specific performance of a contract will not dismiss the bill, but will retain jurisdiction and award damages in place of such performance." 331 Mo. 947, 56 S.W.2d 9, 20 (1932).

Another line of cases, however, states that "a court of equity does not have jurisdiction to render a judgment for a plaintiff on legal issues in the absence of a finding that some equitable right of the plaintiff has also been violated," Krummenacher v. Western Auto Supply Co., 358 Mo. 757, 217 S.W.2d 473, 475 (1949), and "where a case for relief in equity fails a court of equity is without jurisdiction to award other relief by way of disposing of the entire controversy; unless, indeed, it appears that the remedy at law will be inadequate." Jaycox v. Brune, 434 S.W.2d 539, 543 (Mo.1968). Or, "when the [f]acts relied on to sustain the equity jurisdiction fail of establishment" a case will not proceed in equity "because a court of equity does not have jurisdiction to render a judgment for a plaintiff on legal issues in the absence of a finding that some equitable right of the plaintiff has also been violated." State *ex rel.* Willman v. Sloan, 574 S.W.2d 421, 422–23 (Mo. banc 1978). * * *.

In Krummenacher v. Western Auto Supply Company, the plaintiffs filed a one-count petition seeking equitable relief, namely abatement of a nuisance, and damages from that nuisance. 217 S.W.2d at 473. Both types of relief thus relied on the same factual pleadings and proof. The trial court denied the equitable relief but found, without a jury, that the plaintiffs sustained damages and awarded them $500. * * * The plaintiffs did not appeal the denial of equitable relief, but the defendants appealed the judgment. * * * This Court reversed and remanded for a jury to determine damages, holding that "a court of equity does not have jurisdiction to render a judgment for a plaintiff on [claims at law] in the absence of a finding that some equitable right of the plaintiff has been violated."

Id. at 475. Thus, two trials were necessary to resolve the plaintiffs' claims: the first without a jury and the second with a jury.

In Burnett v. Johnson, the plaintiffs asserted a claim for damages to which the defendant responded with equitable affirmative defenses and counterclaims in equity and at law. 349 S.W.2d 19, 20 (Mo.1961). The trial court ruled that the counterclaims converted the case from one at law to one in equity. * * * Despite agreeing with the trial court that "equitable rights must be both averred and proved before purely legal rights will be determined by a court of equity," this Court reversed. *Id.* at 23. The Court noted that if the equitable claims and defenses were unsuccessful, the claims at law should have been tried before a jury. * * * But, because the plaintiffs introduced evidence and submitted their claims at law to the trial court alone, they waived any right to a jury trial of those claims. * * * Again, had the plaintiffs preserved their claim of error as to their right to a jury trial, two trials would have been required to resolve the parties' claims in this case.

In Jaycox v. Brune, the plaintiff sued the administrator of an estate to enforce an oral contract to make a will in his favor and, in the alternative, for the recovery of money for services the plaintiff had rendered to the deceased. 434 S.W.2d at 541. The trial court granted the defendants' motion to dismiss the equitable claim to enforce the oral contract and found in favor of the administrator on the action to recover money. * * * This * * * Court * * * held that the dismissal of the plaintiff's first count, for which he was not entitled to a jury, caused the trial court to lose its equitable jurisdiction and the plaintiff's request for a jury trial subsequently should have been granted. * * * The plaintiff was therefore entitled to a second trial wherein a jury would determine his claims. * * *

In Willman v. Beheler, a medical doctor violated the restrictive covenant in his contract. 499 S.W.2d 770, 777 (Mo.1973) (hereinafter *"Willman I"*). The doctor's former partner, Willman, sued to enforce the covenant and to enjoin the defendant, Beheler, from practicing in violation of the restrictive covenant. * * * By the time the case worked its way to this Court, the five-year restriction on the defendant's practice had nearly expired. * * * The Court concluded that, even though the passage of time had rendered the equitable remedy—a permanent injunction—ineffectual, because "[e]quity will not suffer a wrong to be without a remedy," the "conditions and exigencies of the case" permitted the trial court to proceed in equity despite the knowledge that it would award a "mere money judgment." * * * It remanded the case to allow the parties to present evidence as to the damages incurred by the plaintiff as a result of the defendant's violation of the covenant. * * *

The case later returned to the Court in an action for a writ of prohibition in State *ex rel.* Willman v. Sloan, 574 S.W.2d 421 (Mo. banc 1978) (hereinafter *"Willman II"*). On remand following *Willman I*, the trial court granted the defendant's request for a jury to determine the plaintiff's damages, and the plaintiff sought a writ in prohibition to prevent the trial court from impaneling a jury for that purpose. * * * The Court reiterated the rule that "[a]lthough damages are usually a legal remedy, a court of equity may decree them where they are the relief necessary in order to do equity." *Id.* (citing *Willman I,* 499 S.W.2d at 778). The Court issued a writ in prohibition to prevent the trial court from impaneling a jury to determine damages in the underlying suit because *Willman I* found that "there was merit to [the plaintiff's] claim, and that he was entitled to enforce the covenant in equity" even though the equitable remedy no longer remained viable because of the passage of time.

These cases are difficult, if not impossible, to reconcile. *Jaycox, Burnett,* and *Krummenacher* concluded that if equitable relief was not granted, a second and separate proceeding at law with a jury was required to award money damages. * * *. In *Rockhill Tennis Club, Willman I,* and *Willman II,* the proof of an equitable right appears to have been severed from the granting of equitable relief. The courts in these cases, sitting in equity, were allowed to grant monetary relief although the traditional forms of equitable relief were not justified. One might wonder, then, whether equitable "jurisdiction" is "established" by facts pleaded, defenses asserted, relief requested, facts proved, relief granted, or some ever changing combination of the above. One might also wonder when a remedy at law would not be adequate and complete after it has been determined that an equitable remedy will not be granted.

This procedural quagmire, however, is not necessary. It does not take into account the consolidation of equitable and legal jurisdiction in our circuit courts. It also fails to give appropriate consideration to the historical preference for trial by jury expressed in Article I, section 22(a) of the Constitution of the State of Missouri.

IV.

The dichotomy of separate jurisdiction for courts of law and courts of equity evolved in old England. 27A Am.Jur.2d Equity sec. 3 (1996); Ellen E. Sward, *A History of the Civil Trial in the United States,* 51 U. Kan. L. Rev. 347, 348–50 (2003). The King's courts, or court's of law * * * were restricted to following the "unbending application of common-law rules and statutes." * * * Courts of law were criticized because they "were slow to develop new types of actions or grant new forms of relief, and were inflexible and technical in pleading and practice...." Note, *The Right to a Nonjury Trial,* 74 Harv. L. Rev. 1176, 1179 (1961). As a result, the courts of law could not always provide litigants with justice, and the king's subjects continued to petition him to prevent injustice that was without remedy in the courts of law. * * * Another body of law developed in the late 13th or early 14th century to overcome the "shortcomings" of the courts of law. * * *

This supplemental body of jurisprudence was called equity, and the responsible tribunal was called the High Court of Chancery. * * * Equity refers to "a system of rules and principles" that originated "as an alternative to the harsh rules of common law ... based on what was fair in a particular situation." Black's Law Dictionary 540 (6th ed.1990). * * *

This system was very inefficient, however, as the two courts were often at odds with each other. For example, courts of equity would enjoin claimants at law from prosecuting their actions when the chancellor decided that permitting the suit to proceed at law would cause inequity because an equitable defense existed that the court of law would not recognize. Fleming James, Jr. & Geoffrey C. Hazard, Jr., Civil Procedure sec. 1.5, at 14 (3d ed.1985); Note, *The Right to a Nonjury Trial*, 74 Harv. L. Rev. 1176, 1181–82 (1961). Additionally, claims at law often were dismissed because the proper remedy was in equity, and parties in an action at law were precluded from establishing equitable claims or defenses relating to the issue being tried at law. Fleming James, Jr. & Geoffrey C. Hazard, Jr., Civil Procedure sec. 1.5, at 16 (3d ed.1985). "In many situations two or more suits had to be brought to adjust properly the rights and remedies of the same parties growing out of a single transaction." *Id.* at 17. * * *

Under the doctrine known as equitable cleanup, courts of equity would occasionally grant, in addition to equitable remedies, relief obtainable at law when it was incidental to a request for equitable relief. *Id.;* Note, *The Right to a Nonjury Trial*, 74 Harv. L. Rev. 1176, 1181–82 (1961). When a court of equity invoked its power of equitable cleanup, a jury trial was precluded, thereby eliminating the multiplicity of actions that would otherwise occur if equity dismissed the suit and required the remainder of the litigation to be resolved through an action at law. Note, *The Right to a Nonjury Trial*, 74 Harv. L. Rev. 1176, 1181–82 (1961). When litigants propounded claims and defenses containing overlapping issues in equity and at law, the employment of equitable cleanup eliminated the retrying of lawsuits. Thus, the equitable cleanup doctrine developed as a means to attain a more practical and efficient resolution of disputes with both claims at law and in equity. * * *

V.

Similar to the dual courts of equity and law in England, Missouri's original constitution established a judiciary with equitable powers vested in a body distinct from the legal tribunals. * * *

However, Missouri almost immediately abandoned this dichotomy of its courts. Before the office of chancellor could take root in the state's legal culture, the general assembly proposed two articles of amendments abolishing the office and vesting equity jurisdiction in this Court and the circuit courts. *See* Mo. Const. amds. 1, 2 at RSMo 1825, vol. 1, at 65. The following proposed articles of amendment were approved by the voters and took effect in 1823:

Section 1. The office of chancellor is hereby abolished, and the supreme court and circuit courts shall exercise chancery jurisdiction, in such manner and under such restriction as shall be prescribed by law.

Section 2. The judicial power, as to matters of law and equity, shall be vested in a supreme court, in circuit courts, and in such inferior tribunals as the general assembly may, from time to time, ordain and establish; provided, the general assembly may establish a court or courts of chancery, and from time to time prescribe the jurisdiction, powers and duties thereof.

Id. Furthering the trend, the state's second constitution, in 1865, omitted entirely any reference to chancery: "Section I. The judicial power, as to matters of law and equity, shall be vested in a supreme court, in district courts, in circuit courts, and in such inferior tribunals as the general assembly may, from time to time, establish." Mo. Const. art. VI, sec. I (1865).

VI.

Even though the Missouri constitution merged the jurisdiction of equity and law in 1823 and generally vested their combined jurisdiction in the courts, the terms "legal jurisdiction" and "equitable jurisdiction" continue to be used. *See, e.g.*, Ryan v. Spiegelhalter, 64 S.W.3d 302, 306 (Mo. banc 2002) ("By virtue of its equitable jurisdiction, the probate division is not limited to questions of legal title."); Deutsch v. Wolff, 994 S.W.2d 561, 567 (Mo. banc 1999) ("[O]nce equity acquires jurisdiction, it will retain it so as to afford complete justice between the parties."). Using these terms to discuss litigation in modern courts is a misnomer insofar as the constitution eliminated any separate legal or equitable jurisdiction. As stated above, the current version of the constitution refers only to the "judicial power" of the state being "vested in a supreme court, a court of appeals . . ., and circuit courts" and does not distinguish or mention any dual system of law and equity. Mo. Const. art. V, sec. 1.

* * *

The idea of equitable cleanup jurisdiction is also a misnomer. Any circuit court with jurisdiction over the parties and a controversy can render whatever relief is required, be it equitable or a request for damages. There is never a need to have two separate proceedings, one in equity and one at law. The difficulties that arise when claims and defenses at law and in equity are joined in a single lawsuit are not jurisdictional, but practical: What issues should be tried to the court or to the jury, in what order, and how will the order of the trial affect issue preclusion and the practical efficiency in the trial process?

VII.

The practice of trial by jury also dates back to old England. Jury trials began evolving after the Norman Conquest of 1066. Ellen E. Sward, *A History of the Civil Trial in the United States*, 51 U. Kan. L. Rev. 347, 353 (2003). The first juries were remnants of the Norman inquest, a method by which the king obtained information through summoning people and requiring them to provide him, under oath, with the information he desired. * * * Inquest jurors, then, were summoned to swear under oath as to the truth in the matter disputed at trial. * * * If they did not know the truth, the jurors made inquiries until they learned the truth to a degree of certainty such that they would swear to it. * * *

The evolution of the jury from witnesses to impartial fact finders continued over the next several centuries. * * * By the time the United States of America was founded, the English common law civil trial included a presentation of evidence to a jury of 12 qualified men— property owners who had no personal knowledge of the matter before them—to determine issues of fact in the common law courts. * * * The jury heard the evidence and rendered its decision accordingly. * * *

The right to a trial by jury has become a fundamental element of our judicial system, expressing the faith of our people in the common wisdom of ordinary people to ferret out the truth from conflicting evidence. This right is guaranteed in the Seventh Amendment of the U.S. Constitution and in Article I, section 22(a) of the Missouri Constitution.[11]

Missouri's constitutional guarantee to a jury trial has never been applied to claims seeking equitable relief. *See* State *ex rel*. Diehl v. O'Malley, 95 S.W.3d 82, 85 (Mo. banc 2003). Early Missouri cases appear to have followed the doctrine of equitable cleanup jurisdiction in mixed claims. * * * However, Article I, section 22(a) of the Missouri Constitution nonetheless reflects the general historical preference for trial by jury in our state. To allow the doctrine of equitable cleanup as a blanket rule to supplant a litigant's ability otherwise to have a jury trial of his or her claims at law demonstrates inadequate respect for this preference.

VIII.

Missouri trial courts have jurisdiction to try cases involving requests for equitable relief and damages in one proceeding. The trial court has discretion to try such cases in the most practical and efficient manner possible, consistent with Missouri's historical preference for a litigant's ability to have a jury trial of claims at law. Unless circumstances clearly demand otherwise, trials should be conducted to allow claims at law to be tried to a jury, with the court reserving for its own determination only equitable claims and defenses, which it should decide consistently with the factual findings made by the jury. As the United States Supreme Court noted in Beacon Theatres, Inc. v. Westover, 359 U.S. 500, 510, 79 S.Ct. 948, 3 L.Ed.2d 988 (1959):

> If there should be cases where the availability of declaratory judgment or joinder in one suit of legal and equitable causes would not in all respects protect the plaintiff seeking equitable relief from irreparable harm while affording a jury trial in the legal cause, the trial court will

---

11. Article I, section 22(a) declares that "the right of trial by jury as heretofore enjoyed shall remain inviolate...."

necessarily have to use its discretion in deciding whether the legal or equitable cause should be tried first. Since the right to jury trial is a constitutional one, however, while no similar requirement protects trials by the court, that discretion is very narrowly limited and must, whenever possible, be exercised to preserve jury trial.

(footnote omitted). If necessary, special interrogatories to the jury may be used.

In some situations, the practical and efficient trial of a case may require limited incidental claims at law to be tried to the court in connection with equitable matters. Trying incidental claims at law to the court, however, should be the exception and not the rule. Care should be taken to guard against attempts to characterize claims requesting damages as "incidental" in a strategic effort to avoid a jury trial. Dairy Queen, Inc. v. Wood, 369 U.S. 469, 470, 82 S.Ct. 894, 8 L.Ed.2d 44 (1962); *see Krummenacher*, 217 S.W.2d at 475; Dan B. Dobbs, Law of Remedies § 2.6(4), at 119 (2d ed.1993).

This procedure preserves the trial court's flexibility to try cases in the most practical and efficient manner possible. It also preserves and maintains the distinction between equitable relief and damages while respecting the historical preference for trial by jury. Furthermore, it escapes the inconsistent application of outdated historical theories inherent in our existing case law. It does not, however, enlarge or expand the right to a jury trial in this state. Equitable issues that traditionally have been tried to the court shall still be tried to the court.

IX.

In this case, Leonardi seeks damages in three counts of his counterclaim, titled: Breach of Contract, Breach of Implied Covenant of Good Faith and Fair Dealing (Contract Claim), and Breach of Implied Covenant of Good Faith and Fair Dealing (Tort Claim). The trial court denied his request for a jury trial for all of these claims.

The existence of Radiant's equitable claims cannot alone justify a wholesale denial of Leonardi's request for a jury trial of his counterclaims. * * * The preliminary order in prohibition is made absolute as modified.

WOLFF, STITH, and TEITELMAN, JJ., and HOLLIGER, SP.J., concur.

BENTON, J., dissents in separate opinion filed.

LIMBAUGH, J., concurs in opinion of BENTON, J.

WHITE, C.J., not participating.

DUANE BENTON, JUDGE, dissenting.

Missouri has a clear rule: equity retains jurisdiction once acquired, until the facts that sustain equity jurisdiction "fail of establishment." State *ex rel*. Willman v. Sloan, 574 S.W.2d 421, 422–23 (Mo. banc 1978) (unanimous court) * * *.

The facts "fail of establishment" when: 1) legal relief alone is sought, or 2) plaintiff's equitable claims are dismissed or terminated adversely. *Willman*, 574 S.W.2d at 423. The judge retains jurisdiction until he or she "decides all of the issues adequately and fairly between the parties." Custom Muffler and Shocks, Inc. v. Gordon Partnership, 3 S.W.3d 811, 817 (Mo.App.1999). "It is a well-established rule that where a court of equity once acquires jurisdiction of a cause it will retain it to do full and complete justice." Seested v. Dickey, 318 Mo. 192, 300 S.W. 1088, 1101–02 (1927). This rule has been consistently followed for over 100 years. * * *

The majority labels the established law "inconsistent and confusing." The cases cited by the majority are not inconsistent. There is (1) the general rule, and (2) the "fail of establishment" exception. The doctrine is clear, but the results differ, depending on the facts.

All the cases cited by both opinions follow the general proposition that once equity attaches, the court retains jurisdiction. *Krummenacher, Burnett,* and *Jaycox* all apply the "fail of establishment" exception, and therefore require a jury trial. The *Rockhill* and the *Willman* decisions, on the other hand, do not reach the "fail of establishment" exception to the general rule.

The majority opinion suggests that *Rockhill* and *Willman* are inconsistent with the others. To the contrary, the cases are wholly consistent based on the type of *claim* (the final form of relief—money—does not matter.) In both *Rockhill* and *Willman* the court awarded money damages for the equitable claim, and a legal claim was never raised. "Although damages are usually a legal remedy, a court of equity may decree them where they are the relief necessary in order to do equity." *Willman*, 574 S.W.2d at 422 * * *.

In *Krummenacher, Burnett,* and *Jaycox,* both legal and equitable claims were raised. These cases apply the "fail of establishment" exception. The equitable claims were dismissed or terminated adversely— leaving only legal claims—and therefore, a jury trial was required.

In this case, the facts did not fail of establishment. Legal relief was not the sole remedy sought. Further, Plaintiff's claim for injunction was not dismissed or terminated adversely. The trial judge expressly reserved the claim for a permanent injunction for the bench trial, and legal relief wholly depended on the claim for a permanent injunction. The trial judge thus retained jurisdiction over all claims.

The rule has been followed for over a century because it is fair and efficient. It spurs early resolution of equitable claims, because (1) if the judge grants temporary relief, full relief can follow promptly, or (2) if the judge denies all equitable relief, legal claims still go to the jury. The Missouri rule brings prompter disposition of most cases, avoiding a waste of judicial time and resources, and unnecessary litigation expenses. * * * There is no reason to abandon settled law, as reflected in the long line of cases in the appendix. I dissent.

NOTES

1. Like Missouri, a significant number of state courts are following the federal approach in deciding jury trial questions in cases involving mixed legal and equitable elements. For examples of cases in which jury trial was required on "legal" counterclaims to equitable causes of action, see Construction Systems & Engineering, Inc. v. Jennings Construction Corp., 413 So.2d 1236 (Fla.Dist.Ct.App.1982); Higgins v. Barnes, 310 Md. 532, 530 A.2d 724 (1987).

2. On the other hand, equitable clean-up continues to flourish in numerous states. See, e.g., Farmers Bank & Trust Co. v. Ross, 401 N.E.2d 74, 76 (Ind.Ct.App.1980) ("[O]nce equity has the case, even a counterclaim sounding in law must be tried under the umbrella of equity; in short, there is no right to trial by jury as to the counterclaim."). Consider the following language of the Nebraska Supreme Court in Kuhlman v. Cargile, 200 Neb. 150, 262 N.W.2d 454 (1978):

> The rule is that when a cause of action for equitable relief is stated, and when the plaintiff prays for equitable relief, a jury trial cannot be demanded as a matter of right by the defendant. * * * Even if the defendant pleads legal defenses or a counterclaim for damages, he is not entitled to a jury trial, as when a court of equity acquires jurisdiction over a cause * * * for any purpose it may retain the cause for all purposes and proceed to a final determination on all matters put in issue in the case. * * * It is the general rule that if a court of equity has properly acquired jurisdiction in a suit for equitable relief, it may make complete adjudication of all matters properly presented and involved in the case and grant relief, legal or equitable, as may be required and thus avoid unnecessary litigation.

Id. at 156, 262 N.W.2d at 458.

3. Courts often experience difficulty in determining whether cases involving mixed equitable and legal elements are "primarily equitable or legal." Consider the approach suggested by the Court of Appeals of Washington in State v. State Credit Association, Inc., 33 Wash.App. 617, 657 P.2d 327 (1983):

> In such cases trial courts are accorded wide discretion in determining whether the case is primarily equitable or legal, thus meriting a bench or a jury trial. Brown v. Safeway Stores, Inc., 94 Wash.2d 359, 617 P.2d 704 (1980). This judicial discretion should be exercised with reference to the following factors:
>
> > (1) who seeks the equitable relief; (2) is the person seeking the equitable relief also demanding trial of the issues to the jury; (3) are the main issues primarily legal or equitable in their nature; (4) do the equitable issues present complexities in the trial which will affect the orderly determination of such issues by a jury; (5) are the equitable and legal issues easily separable; (6) in the exercise of such discretion, great weight should be given to the constitutional right of trial by jury and if the nature of the action is doubtful, a jury trial should be allowed; (7) the trial court should go beyond the pleadings to ascertain the real issues in dispute before making the determination

as to whether or not a jury trial should be granted on all or part of such issues.

Brown, at 368, 617 P.2d 704.

Id. at 622, 657 P.2d at 331.

INDEX

References are to Pages

†